WORKMAN
PUBLISHING C<u>O</u>

708 BROADWAY
N·E·W Y·O·R·K
N·Y 10003-9555

☎ 212·254·5900
FAX: 212·254·8098
www.workman.com

D0841798

February 23, 2004

Dear Bookseller,

Just in time for the opening of training camp, BASEBALL PROSPECTUS; a book that has been hailed as "the standard by which all scouting guides should be measured" by Oakland A's general manager, Billy Beane.

No other book provides the in-depth analysis that BASEBALL PROSPECTUS does, which is why, for many, the book is, "The clear successor to Bill James's Baseball Abstract."—Bob Neyer, espn.com

The book has been put together by a team of experts on baseball talent, and through the years the book has become the essential guide for the 3.4 million serious fantasy baseball players and the perfect game-side companion for millions more seamheads who want to understand the inside game.

Members of the Baseball Prospectus Team of Experts will be touring throughout the Spring and Summer: NYC, Boston, Atlanta, Baltimore/Washington, Miami, Philadelphia, Chicago, Detroit, Minneapolis, St. Louis, Denver, Dallas, San Francisco, Los Angeles, and San Diego.

Also, the book will be promoted through *Baseball Prospectus Radio* which reaches 1,000s of baseball fans coast-to-coast. The Baseball Prospectus Team of Experts are frequent contributors to espn.com and their own website, baseballprospectus.com receives over <u>4-million hits a month</u>.

Simply, no fan of baseball can do without BASEBALL PROSPECTUS.

Enjoy!

Susan Shaw

Baseball Prospectus 2004

Mark Armour • David Cameron • Will Carroll

Clay Davenport • Gary Huckabay • Rany Jazayerli

Chris Kahrl • Jonah Keri • Doug Pappas • Dave Pease

Dayn Perry • Joe Sheehan • Nate Silver • Ryan Wilkins

Michael Wolverton • Keith Woolner • Derek Zumsteg

WORKMAN PUBLISHING • NEW YORK

Copyright © 2004 by Prospectus Entertainment Ventures LLC

All rights reserved. No portion of this book may be reproduced—
mechanically, electronically, or by any other means, including
photocopying—without written permission of the publisher.
Published simultaneously in Canada by Thomas Allen & Son,
Limited.

Library of Congress Cataloging-in-Publication Data is available.

ISBN 0-7611-3402-6

Workman books are available at special discounts when
purchased in bulk for premiums and sales promotions as well
as for fund-raising or educational use. Special editions or book
excerpts can also be created to specification. For details,
contact the Special Sales Director at the address below.

Design by Barbara Balch
Cover design by Paul Gamarello

Workman Publishing Company, Inc.
708 Broadway
New York, NY 10003-9555
www.workman.com

Printed in the U.S.A.
First printing January 2004

10 9 8 7 6 5 4 3 2 1

Contents

Foreword

by Gary Huckabay

Welcome, and thank you for purchasing *Baseball Prospectus 2004.* We know how hard you work for your money, and we know how valuable your time is, so we're all grateful that you've chosen to spend a little of each on this book. We've worked very hard to put it together, and we'll try not to let you down.

If you're not familiar with *Baseball Prospectus,* here's what we're all about: understanding the game better, and innovating in order to do it. That's it. Nothing more or less than simply that. Everyone at BP loves the game of baseball with a passion that most people just don't understand. We feel that this greatest of games is so compelling that we want to know everything about it. We always want to improve our understanding of the game—each player, each play, each pitch, each throw, each hit—what does it really mean? Those arguments that take place in bars about the relative merits of different players? We really want to know the definitive answer to those questions. But we don't want to kill the joy of the game while we're looking.

There's basically one core goal we have when it comes to using numbers: We want to be able to compare players on an apples-to-apples level. Most every baseball fan understands, at least on some level, that it's easier to hit .300 in Coors Field than Network Associates Coliseum. We calculate how much easier it is, and allow you to see the players' performances without the distortion of park and league effects. It's not a very complicated idea, but it can be kind of daunting at first, so please, bear with us a little bit, and make sure you actually read the explanation section. You don't have to read it first—this book is best used by immediately turning to your favorite two or three players and checking out their comments, reading the capsule essay for your favorite club, then moving around from there.

One result of the kind of analysis that's the core of this book is increased appreciation of the talent of a large number of minor league players. More and more, teams are beginning to understand that there is no bright dividing line between a minor leaguer and a major leaguer. As a result, teams are slowly coming to realize that they have more options than they think when it comes to putting together their major league roster. Over the next few years, you can reasonably expect to see greater salary stratification among major leaguers, with fewer stars making more money at the very top, a slow deterioration of the "middle class" of ballplayers, and more and more players earning salaries not far from the league minimum. It's part of the accelerated evolution of the business taking place in MLB front offices, as a result of better understanding of what's going on between the lines.

To a great extent, Major League Baseball has been insulated from many of the competitive pressures that other businesses face every day. Aside from the paper benefits of an anti-trust exemption, baseball's also enjoyed a hallowed place in the American psyche, held onto the moniker of "America's Pastime," and maintained a depth and breadth of mythology and sepia-toned backstory not enjoyed by any other business. In part because of that, modern management techniques have been slow to arrive in MLB front offices. The intense pressure that drove millions of businesses to invest and focus on improvement was simply absent, or at least barely noticeable in the office of the general manager.

Not anymore.

Innovation is in. Club presidents, GMs, and owners know that they have to move forward in order to keep pace. At its core, the contract between a free agent and a club is a venture capital deal. And where once, that contract would be executed based heavily on gut feel, subjective perception, and an eye towards a short-term budget, today, the process is more involved. Just as a venture capital firm like Cardinal Ventures, Draper Fisher Jurvetson, or Kleiner Perkins has a "due diligence" process they go through before committing to an investment, MLB clubs are finally following suit. Some were surprised, even offended, to learn that front offices actually place a hard number on the value of a player.

But, when you think about it, isn't it foolish to either sign a contract or trade a player without carefully calculating that value?

The information revolution has finally arrived in baseball. It's not going to spread evenly, and there's going to be some untoward moments and unfortunate casualties, but there's no stopping it, much to the chagrin of some who know only that they're comfortable with the status quo. Subjectivity and intuition will always have their place, but they're going to have to exist within a frightening new reality—a level of accountability that's higher than ever before, and only headed upward from here.

Is this going to damage the game? Will its poetry be lost amidst a blizzard of derived numbers? Not in the slightest. The game is going to be better than ever before. Because better players will be playing. As we measure defense more and more effectively, teams will value it more highly, and you'll see better defense on the field. Everything fits together, in a kind of hyper-Darwinian maelstrom, spitting out great plays and memorable moments for the next generation of fans to burn into their memories. The difference is that the players our kids watch will be better than the ones we watched.

And that's the way it should be. Life's supposed to get better, not worse. Despite what your mom or dad probably told you, the average player today is stronger, faster, better trained, better fed, and knows more about how to play the game than his predecessors. This isn't some semi-pro game with artificial constraints on who can play it because of skin color, geography, or upbringing. It really is the big leagues now; the typical list of names on a club would fit in better with the United Nations than your grandfather's version of MLB, and those guys from other countries didn't get here by accident. Stan Musial no longer gets to dodge Satchel Paige. Today, Hee Seop Choi pounds the fastball of a California boy, Ichiro Suzuki guns down that Kid From the Bronx at third base, and Barry Bonds destroys the will to live of pitchers of all stripes from around the world.

BP 2004 is your guide through this new world of baseball. Inside, you'll find the obscure Australians likely to become stars, the flame-throwing Dominicans who'll be contending for a Cy Young, and the kid from Eastern Kentucky who'll make opposing pitchers call in sick. Of course, you'll also find the info on all the familiar players, and an assessment of what's going on (and why) in each front office. You're part of the accountability process, which is really your job as a fan. You're part of the enforcement process, ensuring that baseball makes progress, rather than just changing randomly. There's really no better job to have. So dig in, put your hard hat on, and above all else, have fun with this book. We have fun writing it, albeit in an exasperating, frenetic, meth-fiend carny kind of way, and everyone understands that it's all about the game on the field, and how we can do our part to make it better.

I'm very pleased to say that the future of *Baseball Prospectus* is brighter than our past. Over the past 24 months, it's been our great privilege to have a number of exceptional and terrifyingly young people join BP. Where in the past, you might see material written and researched by a team of perhaps 10 people, with the bulk of the work being done by a familiar group, there's now a new generation of exceptionally dedicated and talented young people working to provide you with a focused look at baseball.

Over the next few years, you'll likely become acquainted with people like Ryan Wilkins, Chaim Bloom, Zack Wolf, Jason Grady, James Click, Sean Passanisi, Susan Graham, Austin Johnson, Adam Katz, Cliff Roscow, Jason Karegeannes, and Steve Lin, all of whom are working to make BP better than it's been. We're lucky to have all of them, and they not only do great work in their own right, they keep the elder group on their respective toes. Our thanks to all of them for their efforts.

It'd be easy to fill this entire foreword with a list of people to whom we owe a tremendous debt of gratitude, and when you make a list of people to thank, you invariably forget one or two. So with apologies to the inevitable unintentional omissions, our heartfelt thanks go out to Peter Gammons, Jayson Stark, Allen Barra, Alan Schwarz, Sam Stoloff, Sydelle Kramer, Richard Rosen, Stacey Alper, Ben Cherington, Michael Lewis, Fay Vincent, Sandy Alderson, Billy Beane, David Forst, Betty Shinoda, Paul DePodesta, Bill Stoneman, Ken Forsch, Jim Hendry, Keith Law, J.P. Ricciardi, Debbie Gallas, Jim Young, Sherri Nichols, Jeff Erickson, John Sickels, Jeri Sickels, Paul Mahler, Jim Greenwald, Peter Workman, Rob Neyer, Theron Skyles, Dan Young, Chris Goddu, Jeff Barton, Tom Tippett, Dave Barton, Mark Wolfson, Ray Fosse, Mike Woodsworth, Tim Marchman, Zach Manprin, Scott McCauley, Louie Belina, Ryen Russillo, Brian Sabean, Ned Colletti, Maria Jacinto, David Schoenfield, Matt Szefc, Tyler Pope, Scott Boras, Ron Antinoja, John Strubel, Dave Coaklin, Travis Rodgers, Jim Rome, Mike Sorce, Eddie Epstein, Ted Turner, Jamey Newberg, Dan Feinstein, Stan Conte, Chris Antonetti, Mark Shapiro, Grady Fuson, Mike Flanagan, Jon Sciambi, Josh Paley, Marianne Fogle, Greg Fogle, Amory Foreman, Alan Plutzik, Chris Schofield, Don Rodgers, Eric Chavez, Don Fehr, Gene Orza, Billy McMillon, Andy Marte, Allard Baird, Brian Cashman, Gene Michael, Rick Peterson, John Henry, Josh Lewin, Ivan Santucci, Kim Ng, Kevin Towers, Rickey Henderson, Dan Levitt, Dave Van Horne, Paul Dickson, Kevin Youkilis, Matt Tagliaferri, Geoff Silver, Zach Day, Roger Angell, Craig Counsell, Mark Verstegen, Brad Kullman, the wonderful Mairede, Scott Davis, Dick Dorf, Randy Hood, Jeff Smith, Dan Birkhaeuser, Rob Bramson, Jennifer Rosenberg, Mark McClusky, Mike Curto, David Cameron, Mat Olkin, Steven Goldman, Boyd Nation, Keith Scherer, Gary Gillette, Jeff Bower, Stu Shea, John Blake, Bert Bradley, Sheila Eldred, Tim Ireland, Fred Stanley, Peter Spomer, Mike Schmidt, Tom Verducci, John Dowd, Tim Purpura, Stephanie Myles, Brent Strom, Tommy John, Mike Berardino, Michael Levesque, Bill King, David Koppett, and Jon Miller.

Most importantly, thank you for taking a chance on us and buying *BP 2004*. We hope you'll enjoy it as much as we enjoy bringing it to you.

Gary Huckabay
Clayton, CA
January 5, 2004

Your Handy, Dandy Guide to Baseball Prospectus Stats

by Keith Woolner, Clay Davenport, and Nate Silver

With this year's edition of Baseball Prospectus, we continue a tradition of presenting the most advanced statistical view of a player available. We use a variety of techniques unique to *Baseball Prospectus,* and so this section will serve as a brief introduction to those methods for the first-time reader, as well as a refresher for our loyal long-time customers.

For each player in the book, we use his stats from every significant stint in the majors, minors, or prominent international league (Japanese and Mexican) between 2001 and 2003. An example is provided in table 1.

The first row of the entry contains the player's name and some basic biographical information—batting and throwing hand, birth date, primary position, and "baseball" age (his age as of July 1, 2004). Following that are the player's statistical lines over the course of the previous three seasons, arranged in chronological order. The first few columns of data show time and assignment data— what year, team, and league the player played for, and how old the player was at the time. You'll find a complete key to the team abbreviations in the ballpark index in the back of the book. For "age" we always use the player's effective "baseball age"—that is, age as of July 1 of that year, for the entire season.

The next few columns are your standard back of the baseball card info. The first block (AB, H, 2B, 3B, HR, BB, SO, SB, CS) shows the actual statistical totals the player compiled during this playing stint in at-bats, hits, doubles, triples, home runs, walks, strikeouts, stolen bases, and times caught stealing. The next three columns (AVG, OBP, SLG) show the three most commonly used rate statistics— batting average, on-base percentage, and slugging average— again in raw, unadjusted form.

Baseball Prospectus's unique take on player evaluation is concentrated in the remaining columns. The three columns EQBA, EQOBP, EQSLG are the "translated" rate statistics. Baseball Prospectus's Davenport Translations convert a player's statistics to a common baseline, adjusting for the player's home park, the offensive environment of the league he plays, and, perhaps most important, the difficulty of the competition. Batting .380 against Florida State League competition, as Blalock did in 2001, is not the same as batting .380 in the majors. The pitchers in the FSL are simply not of the same quality, and thus it's easier to hit against them. Similarly, most of the batters in the FSL aren't major league-quality, so good pitchers will be able to post better ERAs and strikeout numbers than they would if they played in the majors.

Most fans intuitively understand this concept. The translation process makes adjustments for the lesser quality of opposition explicit and quantitative, and converts what the player did against the competition he faced to an "equivalent" (hence, the EQ- prefix) major league performance. EQBA, EQOBP, and EQSLG for one player can be directly compared against other players regardless of which league the raw stats were posted in. Note that the

TABLE 1. HITTER STATISTICS EXAMPLE

HANK BLALOCK   3B   Bats: L   Throws: L   Born: 21-Nov-80   Age: 23

YEAR	TM	LG	AGE	AB	H	2B	3B	HR	BB	SO	SB	CS	AVG	OBP	SLG	MLVR	EQBA	EQOBP	EQSLG	EQMLVR	VORP	DEFENSE	
2001	PCH	FLA	20	237	90	19	1	7	26	31	7	4	.380	.437	.557	.517	.300	.352	.457	.072	19.6	62-3B	8
2001	PEO	AFL	20	122	42	8	2	11	19	20	5	2	.344	.437	.713	.626	.269	.348	.563	.184	41.3		
2001	TUL	TEX	20	272	89	18	4	11	39	38	3	3	.327	.413	.544	.372	.264	.340	.444	.001	15.7	66-3B	-1
2002	OKL	PCL	21	387	119	32	1	8	34	61	2	1	.307	.363	.457	.149	.279	.333	.418	-.036	15.8	89-3B	-11
2002	TEX	AL	21	147	31	8	0	3	20	43	0	0	.211	.306	.327	-.214	.224	.325	.347	-.188	-0.3	39-3B	-3
2003	TEX	AL	22	567	170	33	3	29	44	97	2	3	.300	.350	.522	.147	.312	.365	.545	.233	43.2	131-3B	0
2004	*TEX*	*AL*	*23*	*516*	*150*	*33*	*2*	*23*	*48*	*84*	*4*	*2*	*.291*	*.352*	*.499*	*.139*	*.284*	*.349*	*.487*	*.089*	*37.4*	*135-3B*	*-2*

Breakout: 19%   *Improve: 61%*   *Collapse: 14%*

equivalent stats are set up such that an average player posts an EQBA of .270, and EQOBP of .340, and an EQSLG of .440.

The next step in understanding the player lines is to focus on the MLVR and EQMLVR columns, which represent Marginal Lineup Value rates of production. With Marginal Lineup Value, we estimate the value of a player by computing the change in expected run scoring between an average team, and a team with eight average players and the batter in question. If we were to swap one of the nine average players for the 2003 version of Barry Bonds, we would, naturally, expect them to score more runs. Similarly, if you replaced one such player with Brad Ausmus, expected run scoring would decrease:

	Team A	Team B	Team C
1	Joe Average	Joe Average	Joe Average
2	Joe Average	Joe Average	Joe Average
3	Joe Average	Joe Average	Joe Average
4	Joe Average	Joe Average	Joe Average
5	Joe Average	BARRY BONDS	BRAD AUSMUS
6	Joe Average	Joe Average	Joe Average
7	Joe Average	Joe Average	Joe Average
8	Joe Average	Joe Average	Joe Average
9	Joe Average	Joe Average	Joe Average
Expected runs/game	4.641	5.472	4.381
Difference in runs/game versus Team A	0	+0.832	−0.260

Since the difference in expected run scoring between Team A and Team B is entirely due to having Barry Bonds in the lineup, we call this difference his Marginal Lineup Value Rate (MLVR). As you can see in the case of Brad Ausmus, who was a below-average hitter in 2003, negative MLVR is certainly possible, and actually quite common. A player who was exactly league average would have a MLVR of zero, and anyone below league average would have a negative MLVR.

There is a cumulative version of MLVR, simply called Marginal Lineup Value (MLV), that takes into account playing time. If Barry Bonds plays 120 games during the year, then the total impact on his team's lineup can be estimated by taking his MLVR (0.832) and multiplying it by his games played (120).

$$MLV = 0.832 \times 120 = 99.8 \text{ runs}$$

This means that an average team would have scored about 100 more runs with Bonds in the lineup for 120 games than they would have with a league-average player. What if he played all 162 games?

$$MLV = 0.832 \times 162 = 134.8 \text{ runs}$$

MLVR is a rate of production (how well he did on a per-game basis). MLV measures total hitting contribution by including how often he played. MLV itself is not printed in the book, but forms the basis for VORP, which is discussed below, and MLV can be found on the statistical reports on the BP Web site.

What, then, is the difference between MLVR and EQMLVR? The answer is simple, but subtle:

MLVR is based on the player's untranslated statistics; it compares a player to the average of the league he played in, after adjusting for a player's home park. It does not translate a player's production to major league level.

EQMLVR is based on a player's translated statistics; it puts the player on an equal footing with players from other leagues (major and minor).

Minor league players will typically have much better MLVR (which compares them to their league competition) than EQMLVR (which compares them to major league-quality competition). Major league players will have less of a gap between MLVR and EQMLVR. Why would there be any gap at all? Well, the translation process converts all leagues, major and minor, across the years, to a single standard. As even the major leagues vary in difficulty and quality over time, there will be slight variations between the "reference league" of the translations and the 2003 National League, for example. The translation process also has some adjustments for differences in rules across league, most notably that some leagues use the designated hitter, and others do not. The translation process tries to even out all of these factors to compare players on as equal and undistorted a basis as possible.

The second-to-last column in Blalock's lines above is VORP, which stands for Value Over Replacement-level Player.

VORP is an estimate of total player value, which builds on MLVR and incorporates what position the player plays, how many games he played, and what "replacement level" is for his position. Replacement level is a concept discussed in great detail in "Understanding and Measuring Replacement Level," an article by Keith Woolner found in the 2002 edition of *Baseball Prospectus,* so we will only briefly restate it here.

Metrics, such as MLVR, that compare a player to league-average offense are incomplete by themselves, since they do not properly account for the value of having a player healthy and in the lineup. Losing a starting player typically results in more starts given to a bench player who is significantly below average. By comparing a player's production to the level of a typical bench player or Quadruple-A journeyman (which we dub replacement level), we recognize the value of a player's durability. As defined in *BP2002,* replacement level is "the expected level of performance a major league team can receive from one or more of the best available players who substitute for a suddenly unavailable starting player at the same position and who can be (or were) obtained with minimal expenditure of team resources." Though we have been discussing it in terms of position players, the concept of VORP equally applies to pitchers.

VORP has been available on the BP Web site for several years, and is updated daily during the season. A couple of minor points about how VORP is presented here in *BP2004* are worth noting:

- Minor league players are rated at their most frequently played position, rather than a weighted average across all positions they appeared at, as is done with major league players. That is, if a minor league player plays 100 games at second base and 20 at shortstop, he would be considered to be purely a second baseman in calculating his VORP. If a major league player played 100 games at second, and 20 at shortstop, we would his compute his weighted positional average, with second base having five times the weight of shortstop (100 G@2B / 20 G@SS = 5).

- Most minor leagues typically have shorter seasons than the majors do, and as a result, even excellent translated rates of production may not produce as high a VORP as a player with the benefit of a 162-game schedule.

Although VORP looks at a player's position, it does not directly consider how well he fields that position. Thus we turn to the final column in the batter's lines—Defense—which shows the position, number of games, and fielding rating for the player at one or more positions. Thus "150-SS 3" means that the player played in 150 games at shortstop, with a defensive performance three runs prevented above average for shortstops.

"Games" in this case is not actual games played, but an estimate of innings played (for major league players, innings are known) divided by nine; someone who appeared in 80 games as a defensive replacement may only be credited with 20 games played. The fielding ratings in this year's Prospectus are slightly different from those shown

in last year's book, especially for outfielders. The basic procedure remains the same: the entire team is rated as a unit, separating the team's total defense into pitching and fielding components. The team's fielding is then broken down into catching, infield, and outfield components, after which each of those is broken into individual positions, and then each position is split amongst the individuals who played it. The process for splitting the team into infield and outfield components—essentially, identifying the groundball/flyball tendencies of the pitching staff—has been radically changed, and the average error on estimated ground/fly ratios (known for the major leagues, but not the minors) has been cut by more than half. In addition, the outfielders are now rated as three separate positions, so that center fielders are compared against other center fielders, not against a generic outfielder; this has the effect of taking 5–10 runs away from center and adding 3–5 runs to the corners, compared to last year's ratings. It also results in better estimates of playing time at each position.

The 2004 line is the PECOTA projection for the player in the upcoming season. Note that the player is projected into the league and park context as indicated by his team abbreviation; Miguel Tejada is now in Baltimore, and so forth. The three numbers beneath the player's 2004 line—Breakout, Improve, and Collapse—are also a part of PECOTA, and estimate the likelihood of changes in performance relative to a player's previously-established level of production. As you might expect, high Breakout scores and Improve scores are a good thing, while high Collapse scores are a bad thing; Nate Silver will have more to say about all things PECOTA in his projections essay, which follows this one.

Now, let's take a look at a pitcher's entry in table 2.

The first line and the YEAR, TM, LG, and AGE columns are the same as in the hitter's example above, and should be self-explanatory. The next set of columns—G, GS, IP, H, BB, SO, HR—are the actual, unadjusted totals compiled by the pitcher during this stint, his games, games started, innings pitched, hits and walks allowed, strikeouts, and home runs given up. The ERA column is the pitcher's actual, unadjusted earned run average.

The next five columns, all starting with "EQ", are the pitcher's rates of production (hits allowed per nine innings,

TABLE 2. PITCHER STATISTICS EXAMPLE

MARK PRIOR　　　　　　　　　　**Bats: R**　　**Throws: R**　　　　　　**Born: 07-Sep-80**　　**Age: 23**

YEAR	TM	LG	AGE	G	GS	IP	H	BB	SO	HR	ERA	EQERA	EQH9	EQBB9	EQSO9	EQHR9	PERA	VORP	STF
2002	CHC	NL	21	19	19	116.7	98	38	147	14	3.32	3.50	7.9	2.5	9.8	1.1	3.90	26.4	65
2002	IOW	PCL	21	3	3	16.3	13	8	24	1	1.66	4.60	6.9	5.2	11.5	0.6	3.64	1.7	71
2002	WTN	SOU	21	6	6	34.7	26	10	55	0	2.59	4.26	8.8	2.8	10.8	0.3	3.57	4.7	75
2003	CHC	NL	22	30	30	211.3	183	50	245	15	2.43	2.97	8.1	1.9	9.3	0.6	3.33	63.8	67
2004	CHC	NL	23	25	25	198.7	168	46	203	18	2.79	2.97	7.6	1.8	8.3	0.8	3.09	57.6	32

Breakout: 29%　　　Improve: 42%　　　Collapse: 17%

strikeouts per nine innings, etc.) based on his "translated" statistics. As with the hitter example above, a pitcher's raw statistics are adjusted and converted to a neutral-park major league equivalent performance. We present the translated (or equivalent) ERA (EQERA), as well as the per-nine inning rates of hits allowed (EQH9), walks issued (EQBB9), strikeouts recorded (EQSO9), and home runs surrendered (EQHR9). The equivalent league is set up such that an average pitcher allows nine hits, three walks, and one home run per nine innings, while recording six strikeouts.

The next column is Peripheral ERA, abbreviated as PERA. PERA is the EqERA a pitcher would be expected to have given his EqH9, EqBB9, EqSO9, and EqHR9. A PERA lower than his actual EqERA may indicate that he was somewhat unlucky, and could be expected to improve his EqERA next season even without substantial change in peripheral rates of production

VORP (Value Over Replacement-level Player) is based on the translated statistics: A pitcher's VORP is the number of extra runs that a replacement-level pitcher would have allowed to score if he pitched the same number of innings as this pitcher.

The final column is Stuff rating (STF). Stuff is a short-hand rating of a pitcher's demonstrated skills, relative to his age and level; its primary use is to evaluate prospects, not established major league pitchers. An average major league starter, or a pitcher who has shown the talent to eventually become an average major league starter, will score a 10. Pitchers who score above 20 are excellent prospects; those above 30 belong to the truly elite. The largest single component of STUFF is strikeout rate, but walk rate, home run rate, hit rate, ERA, innings pitched per game, age, and age relative to league all figure in to the final STUFF rating.

In most cases, the pitcher will also have a 2004 PECOTA line available. (The exceptions are pitchers who are so young, or whose performance has been so poor, that we cannot get the system to run a meaningful projection for them.) As with the hitters, the pitchers have a Breakout/Improve/Collapse line, indicating the likelihood of change relative to their previously established levels of performance.

With that, you should be able to dissect any player in the book. As always, we're happy to answer in-depth questions about what we do, so feel free to get in touch with us through www.baseballprospectus.com.

PECOTA 2004: A Look Back and a Look Ahead

by Nate Silver

For four weeks each November, I quit returning phone calls. Bills go unpaid. The Red Bull piles up on my coffee table. When I can manage a few hours of sleep, I dream about regression equations. November, you see, is PECOTA time.

There's a ton of work that goes into PECOTA, *Baseball Prospectus'* exclusive projection system, now in its sophomore season. PECOTA is the only system that explicitly identifies comparable players—say, Albert Pujols and Hank Aaron, or Ray Durham and Lou Whitaker—and uses them to make its projections. It's the only system that models a forecast range rather than a single set of numbers, predicting the likelihood of breakout seasons and their opposites. It's the only system that dares to project performance more than one year into future, something that we've taken advantage of in determining our Top 50 Prospects list.

All of this requires a tremendous attention to detail, and a tremendous amount of labor. And while PECOTA takes advantage of the contributions of the entire BP brain trust—it employs minor league translations provided by Clay Davenport, replacement level research conducted by Keith Woolner, the principals of the Vladimir projection model developed by Gary Huckabay—much of that work, invariably, falls on my shoulders.

I bring this up not because I expect any sympathy, but because I want to emphasize how different PECOTA is from other projection models. PECOTA takes into account more information than any other system, and uses it in a larger variety of ways. It is possible to create a perfectly reasonable projection simply by taking a weighted average of a player's performance in his previous three seasons. But we're perfectly *un*reasonable people, that's not good enough for us. Baseball is a game won and lost at the margins, and we want the most accurate projection system possible.

A lengthy explanation of how PECOTA works was included in last year's book, so I'll provide only a Cliff's Notes version this time around. Those of you who are already familiar with the system can feel free to skip ahead, where we'll look at how PECOTA made out for itself 2003, and what improvements we've made to the system this time around.

PECOTA in 1500 Words or Less

There are three essential steps required to create a PECOTA forecast:

1. Generation of a player's Baseline;
2. Identification of comparable players;
3. Creation of a forecast range based on comparable player performances.

Step 1: Generation of the Baseline

The first step involved in creating a PECOTA does not differ that greatly from the techniques employed by most other forecasting models. A Baseline performance is developed based on the player's previous three seasons of performance. Both major league and minor league performances are considered.

A player's past statistics are weighted based on playing time, as well as how recently the season occurred—his 2003 performance will have more impact on the forecast than his 2001 performance. These weightings also differ based on the particular statistical category; our research indicates, for example, that it is correct to place heavier emphasis on the most recent year of performance when predicting walk rate as opposed to batting average.

The Baseline is also structured such that the interactions between various statistical categories are considered. Doubles, for example, are helpful in predicting home runs, while stolen bases are helpful in predicting triples.[1] Finally, the Baseline accounts for some degree of regression to the mean, which is important when projecting a highly volatile

---

[1] There are, in fact, a slew of such permutations, which PECOTA takes advantage of by means of a technique called seemingly unrelated regression.

category like a hitter's batting average, or a pitcher's home runs allowed rate. The idea is to remove the impact of luck from a player's forecast line, and to focus on isolating his core set of skills.

Step 2: Identification of Comparable Players

The identification of comparable players is the heart of the PECOTA system. While analysts have attempted for years to quantify player similarity, the PECOTA comparability scores take into account more factors than any other system, and were designed for maximum predictive value going forward. That is, those factors that receive the highest weight in the PECOTA similarity store are those that have the most influence on the course of a player's future development.[2]

PECOTA compares each pitcher against a historical database of more than 10,000 major league seasons since World War II, and each offensive player against a database of more than 20,000 major and minor league seasons since World War II. Players are compared only against others of the same age. The system takes into account the factors shown in tables 1 and 2 in determining its similarity scores, arranged in descending order of influence.[3]

It's no coincidence that the most influential factors in the similarity scores—batting average, walk rate, and iso-

TABLE 1. SIMILARITY FACTORS FOR POSITION PLAYERS

1. Isolated power
2. Walk rate
3. Batting average
4. Historical playing time (plate appearances)
5. Defensive position
6. Speed score[1]
7. Length of major league career
8. Weight in pounds
9. Strikeout rate
10. Handedness
11. Height in inches
12. Defensive rating

[1] The speed score is a variation of the original formulation developed by Bill James, and considers five sub-factors: stolen bases, stolen base percentage, triples, grounded into double plays, and runs scored as a percentage of times on base. PECOTA weights some of these categories more heavily than others.

TABLE 2. SIMILARITY FACTORS FOR PITCHERS

1. Strikeout rate
2. Walk rate
3. Home runs allowed rate
4. Batters faced per game[1]
5. Length of major league career
6. Hits allowed rate
7. Change in strikeout rate[2]
8. Groundball-to-flyball ratio
9. Total batters faced
10. Change in batters faced
11. Height in inches
12. Handedness
13. Weight in pounds

[1] This factor is used to distinguish starting pitchers from relievers.

[2] Our research suggests that single-year changes in strikeout rate and batters faced have a statistically significant impact in projecting the performance of pitchers. This analogous result does not appear to hold for position players.

lated power for hitters, strikeout rate, walk rate, and home run rate for pitchers—are also the most influential factors in the creation and prevention of runs. At the same time, a number of other categories, such as body type, handedness, and defensive position also have an impact on player development, and PECOTA takes these into account.

The upshot of all of this is a list such as shown in table 3.

Cabrera's comparables list consists of other players who demonstrated an ability to hit major league pitching at a very young age. Most of the comparables, like Cabrera, were outfielders or third basemen, and all had good isolated power scores.

Needless to say, Cabrera's is a very favorable list; six of his top 10 comparables have either been elected to the Hall of Fame, or eventually should be (I'm pulling for you, Ronnie). At the same time, the list provides a reminder that no player is invulnerable. Curt Flood and Lloyd Moseby were good players, but never stars, while Adrian Beltre and Ed Kirkpatrick did not develop into the great players that they were expected to be.

Which leads us to Step Three...

Step 3: Creation of the Forecast Range

The final step involved in creating a PECOTA is really a combination of the previous two: PECOTA evaluates how

[2] This distinction is important to consider when evaluating a factor such as a hitter's speed. While speed has only a marginal impact on a player's value in the present day—the stolen base is a highly overrated weapon—it has a relatively significant impact on his future development; players who display good speed tend to age much more favorably.

[3] Analysis of variance (ANOVA) was used in order to determine the relative weights of the similarity factors.

TABLE 3. MOST SIMILAR PLAYERS TO MIGUEL CABRERA[1]

1. Ron Santo
2. Gary Sheffield
3. Hank Aaron
4. Sammy Sosa
5. Curt Flood
6. Willie Mays
7. Adrian Beltre
8. Ed Kirkpatrick
9. Brooks Robinson
10. Lloyd Moseby

[1] For the sake of brevity, we have included only Cabrera's top 10 comparables here; PECOTA uses as many as 100 comparables in generating its forecasts.

the comparable players performed relative to *their* Baselines in order to estimate how the player it is projecting will perform relative to *his* Baseline. Santo, for example, might have improved upon his Baseline by 10% in his age-21 season. PECOTA applies a series of algorithms to figure what Cabrera's statistics would look like if he also improved upon his Baseline by 10%, and uses the result as one point in his forecast range.

By performing a similar exercise for each of Cabrera's comparables, it is possible to produce a probability distribution for Cabrera's expected performance—a range of all the potential outcomes that he could achieve. That looks something like figure 1.

Note that the probability distribution provided in the graph is somewhat asymmetrical. While most of Cabrera's

comparables performed well in their age 21-seasons, around 20% of them had disappointing seasons, significantly underperforming their Baselines. By considering player performance in this fashion, PECOTA is able to assess the risk associated with each player. Some players—say, Adam Dunn, who has a variety of good and bad things going for him—are riskier than others—like, say, Magglio Ordonez—and PECOTA takes this into account.

I Stopped Having Acne Years Ago. What Is This Breakout Thing?

The premium portion of www.baseballprospectus.com includes a series of graphs and comparables lists, similar to the examples provided for Cabrera, for each player who receives a PECOTA. It is not possible to account for this level of detail in the book. Instead, we provide a single line that we refer to as a player's weighted mean forecast—essentially, the average of all the outcomes contained on the graph—as well as a series of three metrics, called Breakout, Improve, and Collapse, that assess the likelihood of change from the player's previously established level of performance. In particular:

- Breakout is the percent chance that a given hitter's productivity, as measured by Equivalent Runs per Game (EqR/G), will improve by at least 20% above his Baseline level of performance. For pitchers, it is the percent chance that his ERA will improve by at least 20% relative to its baseline. High Breakout scores are an indicator of upside risk.

- Collapse is the mirror image of Breakout, and represents downside risk. For hitters, Collapse is the percent chance that his EqR/G will decline by at least 20%, and for pitchers, the chance that his ERA will increase by at least 25%.[4]

- Improve is the percent chance that a given hitter's EqR/G, or a given pitcher's ERA, will improve at all relative to his baseline. It measures, quite simply, how likely a player is to be better than he has been in the past. A player who is expected to perform just the same as he has in the past will have an Improve rating equal to 50%.

Thus, for each player, a Breakout/Improve/Collapse ("BIC") triplet is presented. A player with substantial downside risk might have a BIC triplet on the order of 5%/35%/25%. This indicates that he has a 35% chance to improve upon his Baseline—and therefore a 65% chance to decline. Moreover, his Collapse score of 25% indicates that there is a one-in-four chance that his performance will decline *substantially*.

FIGURE 1. EQUIVALENT AVERAGE (EQA) OUTCOMES FOR MIGUEL CABRERA

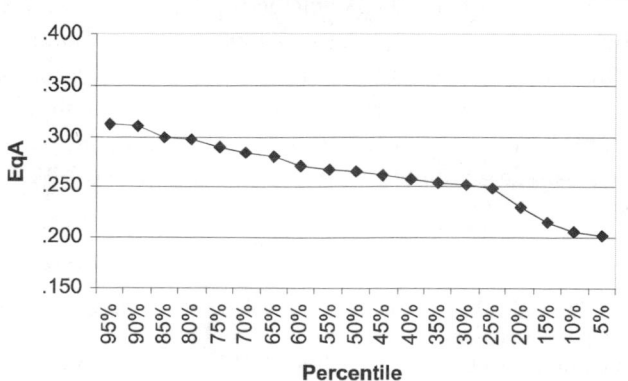

---

[4] 25% is used instead of 20% because of the non-linearity of ERA. Even with this adjustment, most pitchers have a Collapse rate that exceeds their Breakout rate.

When evaluating a player's BIC triplet, keep in mind that they measure change *relative to a player's previously established level of performance.* A poor player with a lot of room for improvement might have a high Breakout rate, but even if he had a breakout season, he would not be somebody you'd want on your roster. Derek Zumsteg and I have dubbed this the Ugueto Effect in honor of the light-hitting Mariner shortstop.

Playing Time Forecasts

PECOTA differs from other projection systems in that it seeks to predict playing time from a player's performance history, rather than impose playing time based on a guess at how the player's team will use its resources. There are advantages and disadvantages to this approach. A veteran player whom PECOTA projects to receive substantially less playing time than he has in the past may be an injury risk, something that a system with preordained playing time limits would not pick up upon. At the same time, the playing time forecast should not override common sense in the presence of other factors, such as a trade or free agent signing.

Results

As interesting as all this theory might be, we wouldn't use PECOTA if it didn't do its job well. Lots of people publish projections; we rounded up seven of the usual suspects and checked the systems for accuracy. The forecasters that we evaluated were:

The Contenders

- BBHQ   Ron Shandler's Baseball HQ (www.baseballhq.com).

- DMB   Diamond Mind Baseball forecasts created by Tom Tippett.[5]

- PECOTA   Web version.[6]

- Primer   Baseball Primer / ZiPS Projections, available in a series of articles at www.baseballprimer.com.

- RotoTimes www.rototimes.com.

- RotoWire   www.rotowire.com.

TABLE 4. COMPARISON OF PREDICTED VERSUS ACTUAL OPS, 360 COMMON PLAYERS

	Correlation	Rank	Mean Error	Rank	RMSE	Rank
BBHQ	.691	(4)	.068	(3)	.086	(4)
DMB	.696	(3)	.066	(2)	.085	(1)
PECOTA	.700	(2)	.065	(1)	.085	(1)
Primer	.685	(5)	.070	(5)	.090	(6)
RotoTimes	.674	(6)	.069	(4)	.089	(5)
RotoWire	.649	(7)	.076	(6)	.098	(7)
Warren	.709	(1)	.066	(2)	.085	(1)

- Warren   Ken Warren's projections, available for free at http://www.attheplate.com /2003/03_warren_hit.htm.[7]

There were a total of 360 position players who achieved the rookie minimum of at least 130 PA in 2003, and who had a projection supplied for by each of the seven systems. In table 4 we've compared the OPS projections provided by each system against the actual OPS put up by each player, evaluating the systems according to three metrics: correlation coefficient, mean error, and root mean square error (RMSE).

PECOTA acquitted itself well, finishing second in correlation coefficient, first in mean error, and tied for first in RMSE (in spite of Javy Lopez's Herculean efforts to the contrary; we thought he'd have a horrible year). While the differences between the best and the worst systems are relatively small, they are nevertheless important to a general manager looking to refine his roster, or to a fantasy player looking to win a Yoo-hoo shower.

We performed the same exercise for the 285 pitchers common to each system that recorded at least 50 IP in 2003. The models were compared in terms of their ability to predict ERA. (See table 5.)

In this case, PECOTA emerged as a clear winner, predicting, among other things, a fine debut by Dontrelle Willis, a breakout year by Kerry Wood, and a tough season for Tom Glavine. Nevertheless, it's the curse of ambitious people never to be satisfied with their own success, so we've made a number of improvements to PECOTA for 2004.

---

[5] These projections are not available in raw form, but instead were included in DMB's 2003 projection disk. DMB, available for purchase at www.diamond-mind.com, is a tremendously accurate simulation game and a favorite of many BP authors.

[6] For each set of projections, we attempted to use the most recent version of the predictions available. The Web version of the PECOTAs, available at www.baseballprospectus.com, differed somewhat from the version provided in last year's book in order to reflect team changes, as well as slight refinements to the projection model.

[7] Ken Warren is a long-time Scoresheet Baseball player who creates excellent projections specifically geared toward Scoresheet.

TABLE 5. COMPARISON OF PREDICTED VERSUS ACTUAL ERA, 285 COMMON PITCHERS

	Correlation	Rank	Mean Error	Rank	RMSE	Rank
BBHQ	.430	(4)	.88	(2)	1.14	(2)
DMB	.441	(2)	.89	(3)	1.16	(4)
PECOTA	.479	(1)	.85	(1)	1.11	(1)
Primer	.395	(6)	.90	(4)	1.14	(2)
RotoTimes	.428	(5)	.90	(4)	1.16	(4)
RotoWire	.341	(7)	.90	(7)	1.18	(7)
Warren	.431	(3)	.96	(4)	1.24	(6)

Improvements

Groundball-to-Flyball Ratio

First, we have introduced groundball-to-flyball ratio ("GB%") as a means to evaluate pitchers. GB% is used both as a factor in identifying comparable pitchers, and in generating the forecasts themselves. Thanks to the good people at Retrosheet (www.retrosheet.org), data on GB% is available for all major league pitchers going back to 1972—about two-thirds of the pitchers in our database.[8]

GB%, it turns out, is a tremendously robust metric: With rare exception, pitchers who are once groundball pitchers are always groundball pitchers, and vice versa. In table 6 I've provided the year-over-year correlations for a selection of performance metrics for all pitchers since 1975 with at least 50 IP in consecutive seasons.

GB%, more than any other pitching metric, remains constant from season to season. It is close to being a fun-

TABLE 6. YEAR-OVER-YEAR CORRELATIONS, SELECTED METRICS, MAJOR LEAGUE PITCHERS

GB%	.79
K/BFP[1]	.77
BB/BFP	.60
Hits/BFP	.44
HBP/BFP	.39
HR/BFP	.38

[1] BFP designates batters faced, so K/BFP is the percentage of hitters that the pitcher strikes out, BB/BFP the percentage of hitters that he walks, and so forth.

damental descriptive characteristic of a pitcher in the way that, say, handedness is.

GB% also has significant predictive power. Specifically,

1. Pitchers with a high GB% allow significantly fewer home runs going forward. In fact, GB% is a better predictor of future home run rate than HR/BFP itself.

2. Pitchers with a high GB% allow significantly more base hits going forward as a percentage of balls in play.

These two categories—HR rate and hit rate on balls in play—are notoriously difficult to project. So, while you won't see GB% included in the statistical lines in the book, it provides for a substantially more accurate ERA projection. Its inclusion is particularly important when evaluating a pitcher like Carlos Zambrano or Greg Maddux, whose ability to induce groundballs is a fundamental part of his game.

Defensive projections

For the first time, we are attempting to project a position player's defensive performance in addition to his offensive statistics. These projections operate according to the same principles applied to a player's offensive PECOTA line. First, using Clay Davenport's defensive runs, we create a Baseline forecast by evaluating a player's defensive performance during the previous three seasons. We then adjust the projection accordingly based on the performances of his comparable players. We have found that, in general, a player's defensive value declines somewhat as he ages.

To be sure, defensive performance is harder to quantify than offensive performance, and the defensive projection model is considerably more simple-minded. But defense is an essential factor to consider when evaluating a position player's value, and we think that PECOTA does a good enough job of projecting it to merit its inclusion.

The defensive ratings are also used as a factor in determining the comparability scores for position players. Last season, PECOTA considered Bobby Bonilla and Scott Rolen to be highly comparable—they play the same position, and have a similar set of offensive skills. But while Rolen is a defensive wizard at the hot corner, Bonilla's approach to third base involved standing a few feet to the left of the bag and hoping that nothing hit him in the jaw. With the introduction of defense into the equation, the similarity score between Rolen and Bonilla would be reduced.

---

[8] We create a proxy for GB% where it is not available by looking at a pitcher's HR rate, the distribution of putouts by his team, and other relevant factors.

This is not to suggest that PECOTA considers defense to be of overwhelming importance; it receives, in fact, the least weight of any of the 12 factors used to identify similar position players. But it does have some predictive value, particularly in evaluating the progress of minor league players, whose defensive ratings can vary significantly.

Backend Improvements

Some of the improvements we have made to PECOTA will not be highly transparent. These involve refining the algorithms used in establishing a player's Baseline, and in extrapolating the performances of his comparables to determine his forecast range—Steps One and Three as we described them above. The goal of these refinements was to create a system that is more aggressive about predicting breakout and collapse seasons, without compromising accuracy.

We have, necessarily, left a lot of ground uncovered. If you've got other questions that you'd like to have answered, feel free to browse the PECOTA glossary on our Web site, or e-mail me at nsilver@baseballprospectus.com. In the meantime, I need to get some rest, and find a good treatment center for caffeine addiction. Enjoy.

Arizona Diamondbacks

When you're a win-now team armed with older talent and a sense that tomorrow's promise isn't quite so rosy as today's possibilities, you get judged by some pretty cruel standards. After all, you're supposed to win now, and if you don't, it raises questions about what you're here for. It also means that, as an organization, you've taken on a responsibility to take that opportunity seriously, even if it means risking the future.

On both levels, Arizona failed. A year after losing in the playoffs, and two years removed from their World Series win, the Snakes didn't even reach the playoffs. What's particularly galling is that they could have and probably should have given the possibilities. As this year's playoffs demonstrated, nobody was guaranteed anything.

The loss is even more exasperating because it reflects a failure to treat their present as seriously as you must when you're in a win-now mode. As old as the team's core talent is, you have to carefully consider every move, every gamble, because there aren't a lot of tomorrows likely for players like Curt Schilling, Randy Johnson, or Luis Gonzalez. The problem has been a failure to take the right risks to maximize their shot at October glory. We pointed out last year that the Snakes were a team with plenty of good things going on, but one that is flawed by its habit of acting impulsively. In 2003, that particular flaw generated especially bitter rewards. Having won in the past on the merits of the Big Two at the front of the rotation, they attempted to anticipate an injury to either Johnson or Schilling. This was pretty sensible, considering that Johnson and Schilling are both in their late 30s and couldn't be counted on for 35 starts year after year.

Unfortunately, the Snakes didn't give the matter nearly enough thought. Joe Garagiola Jr. impulsively dove into the trade that brought them Elmer Dessens instead of a quality starter. What was supposed to give them a third wheel to support the Big Two instead left them doubly hobbled. Their participation in the four-team swap got Billy Beane his white whale (Erubiel Durazo), while sticking Arizona with an easily-tuckered out fifth starter. Dessens had posted a low ERA in the midst of what was an otherwise normal season for him; the Snakes decided that represented a development that would persist, essentially because they hoped so.

DIAMONDBACKS PROSPECTUS

2003 record: 84–78; Third place, NL West

Pythagenport record: 84–78

Runs scored per game: 4.4 (10th in NL)

Runs allowed per game: 4.2 (3rd in NL)

Team EqA: .252 (12th in NL)

2003 Batters Age: 31.3 (4th oldest in NL)

2003 Pitchers Age: 29.8 (5th oldest in NL)

Ballpark: Bank One Ballpark; Severe hitter's park; Park Factor of 1.060

2003: The season looks more successful when considering the big two only combined for 42 starts.

2004: The last hurrah for a team heavily relying on some old position players and Randy Johnson in the rotation.

But it was a little more unfortunate than that. Dealing Durazo left them having to rely on either Mark Grace or Lyle Overbay in a key offensive role. At its root, the decision reflected a failure to understand what they had and what they could expect. Grace was coming off of a year that showed he was done, while Overbay was arriving with a minor league track record that suggested he wasn't going to provide the sort of power the team needed. With hitting numbers inflated by one affiliate's bandbox after another, Overbay could be mistaken for a Keith Hernandez or Grace type, when he was unfortunately closer to Hal Morris territory.

Limiting their choices to Grace or Overbay reflected just one aspect of what's been a comprehensive failure to understand what sort of offensive talent they had on hand. Garagiola went into 2003 feeling he had a strong lineup, but that was based on a series of superficial judgments. Rather than recognizing Junior Spivey's 2002 as a peak season, they wishcasted that into the expectation of an All-Star career. This despite Spivey being oldish for a prospect, with a solidly mediocre track record in the minors. They continued to think they could get use out of Matt Williams, despite the three previous years that should have taught them otherwise. They also went into the year figuring they'd get by in right field again, meaning that at three key power positions—first and third bases and an outfield corner—they foolishly felt they were in good shape. They continued to pretend that Tony Womack fulfilled some useful purpose to boot. These were all problems they'd been able to turn a blind eye to when they had examples like Johnson, Schilling, and Luis Gonzalez suggesting the organization had a golden touch with graying talent.

The season opened with a series of quick reminders of how poorly the Diamondbacks had evaluated themselves. In the first two months, they struggled to score more than four runs per game, with the top of the order struggling to get on base. Johnson broke down quickly, and Schilling would follow by June. Pressed into the limelight, Dessens flopped, failing to give the team a single quality start in May. The front office got frustrated, blaming the Byung-Hyun Kim experiment as a starter and shipping him to Boston to add Shea Hillenbrand to the lineup. At that point, robbing the rotation to patch the lineup was defensible, because Brandon Webb had arrived on the scene and Miguel Batista had once again risen to the role he'd been pressed into. But by dealing Kim, they were effectively replacing him with Dessens while having downgraded from Durazo to Hillenbrand.

Still, a 20–6 June run—while Schilling was on the DL no less—helped place the D-Backs at 52–42. They were a game behind the Phillies (and 3.5 games ahead of the Marlins), in good position to fight for the Wild Card. The June run was fueled by Webb and Batista in the rotation, and Jose Valverde in the pen. The offense finally scored, averaging 5.7 runs per game during the month. Beyond standbys like Gonzalez and Steve Finley, they were scoring because of the contributions of farmhands like Robby Hammock, Matt Kata, and Alex Cintron, all of whom had come up to replace banged-up veterans. Unfortunately, the June run had also been produced by something beyond their own merits as a team: They'd caught a soft part of the schedule, facing teams from both Central Divisions. What looked like a breakout was followed by a season-long reversion to form; June was the only month where the Snakes were above .500 (see table 1).

That's the profile of a .500 team that had a good month, not a powerhouse. Admittedly, one good month and five months of .500 ball can propel you into the play-offs. But this was mid-season, and the Snakes' mediocrity brought them back to the pack while the Marlins rocketed off to destiny. Although Schilling and Johnson were back in the rotation after the All-Star break, the team's fortunes didn't take a turn for the better. Stretch moves like hauling in overrated mediocrity Raul Mondesi didn't significantly improve an offense that needed help.

So what did the organization learn from this? One of the hardest things, for a baseball team or you and me, is to look in the mirror and see yourself. The Snakes took a look

TABLE 1. DIAMONDBACKS' 2003 PERFORMANCE BY MONTH

Month	Record	Runs Scored	Runs Allowed	Pythagenport
March/April	12–16	108	117	13–15
May	13–14	127	124	14–13
June	20–6	149	99	18–8
July	11–16	99	103	13–14
August	14–14	110	107	14–14
September	14–12	123	133	12–14

at themselves this off-season and still saw a contender. They decided to re-fix the first base problem they've had from the moment they invested $10 million in Travis Lee by trading for Richie Sexson. While the package of goodies shipped off to the Brewers for Sexson adds up to just big league-ready depth, the expectation that Sexson's acquisition represents is that this team still holds a win-now mentality.

In that context, dealing Schilling to the Red Sox might seem strange. That decision was driven by the previous choice to make Gonzalez an eight-figure-salary player, as well as a general expectation that they're going to work their way down from spending almost $100 million on salary in 2003 to closer to $55 million in 2005. All of which makes it clear the organization feels the win-now window closes after 2004, which is about as pragmatic as the Snakes have ever been. But if they stumble through a first half similar to what they put up five out of the six months of the '03 season, there's the danger that they'll let some of the well-aged meat on the roster turn to rancid jerky before they can peddle it.

As much as an impulsive desire to hold onto 2001's halo might define the goings-on at the big league level, organizationally Arizona is starting to embody a sturdier mindset. The Snakes used to follow their same free-spending ways on the free agent market with a few pricey high-stakes investments in amateur talent. In particular, they paid top dollar to haul in Lee and John Patterson, neither of whom justified the investment any more than Jay Bell or Matt Williams did at the big league level. But beyond those noisily splashy disappointments, the Snakes have built up an underrated player development program that bodes well for the future. Their expansion cousins in Tampa might get more headlines for their current crop of minor league talent, but the Snakes seem to have a comprehensive approach to player development, with all the hallmarks of a well-run operation. They've got several players ready or nearly ready to contribute in the big leagues, and talented pitching at every level. Young pitchers are generally given workloads that they can handle. In scouting for amateur talent, the Diamondbacks have been almost singularly aggressive in Mexico, but they're as global as any organization when it comes to hunting for the next crop of Snakelings.

That's not to say they don't have their share of developmental problems. There's an odd double standard in play here, which helped produce the high expectations for somebody like Lyle Overbay while letting Brandon Webb slip into the big leagues almost unheralded by prospect mavens. This points to a more fundamental problem with interpretation. The Snakes' three top affiliates—Tucson, El Paso, and Lancaster—are all extreme hitter's parks. Those affiliations help mask that they've got a lot of good young pitching in the organization. But those same affiliates produce the lens through which the Snakes looked at Overbay and decided they had a good offensive prospect on their hands; that remains the perspective through which they view their young hitters.

That said, the Snakes have people who will hit in the big leagues. Chad Tracy and Scott Hairston will hit, and further down, kids like Conor Jackson and Sergio Santos could become productive hitters if they reach their potential. The problem is that the Snakes' young bats aren't quite as good as the team thinks they are, and only Tracy

is going to wind up at the position he's currently playing. Jackson, Santos, and Hairston all seem likely to drift into the outfield corners or first base. Long-term, that's a problem, though not the worst problem to have.

Which leaves Arizona in an interesting point of time. They have enough promise in the minors that they should be able field a strong team relying on homegrown talent inside of three years. They have a 2004 season to look forward to that will still rely upon some vestiges of the 2001 talent core, but both Luis Gonzalez and Randy Johnson are showing significant signs of wear. Happily, the last veterans will be supported by a farm system that will shore up the pitching staff and eventually the lineup. Since nobody in the division looks like they're going to rattle off 100 wins, the Snakes can afford the luxury of considering themselves every bit as competitive going into 2004 as they saw themselves in '03.

But this is still just a team in that fuzzy 75- to 85-win range. If things go right and they're at the high end of that range, their usual brand of in-season upgrades likely wouldn't be enough to push them over the top. As last hurrahs go, this one looks meek, but the future holds enough promise that the organization won't need to tear itself down.

HITTERS

CRAIG ANSMAN   C   Bats: R   Throws: R   Born: 10-Mar-78   Age: 26

YEAR	TM	LG	AGE	AB	H	2B	3B	HR	BB	SO	SB	CS	AVG	OBP	SLG	MLVR	EQBA	EQOBP	EQSLG	EQMLVR	VORP	DEFENSE	
2001	SBN	MID	23	345	114	30	4	21	29	85	4	1	.330	.402	.623	.494	.248	.304	.473	-.037	14.9	66-C	8
2002	LNC	CAL	24	374	114	21	7	18	34	113	3	3	.305	.385	.543	.258	.224	.284	.402	-.192	-2.1	68-C	-2
2002	ELP	TEX	24	53	12	3	0	3	6	7	0	0	.226	.311	.453	.000	.189	.265	.377	-.286	-2.7		
2003	ELP	TEX	25	213	69	17	1	15	31	58	5	3	.324	.421	.624	.438	.246	.336	.483	.032	13.7	46-C	-8
2004	ARI	NL	26	190	49	12	1	9	18	51	1	1	.259	.334	.476	.041	.250	.323	.462	-.016	12.1	54-C	-6

Breakout: 29%   *Improve: 55%*   *Collapse: 24%*

You might see some people refer to Ansman as a prospect, but you should check your enthusiasm. For starters, although he has a strong arm, he's got Mackey Sasser-type issues with actually handling the catching part of his catching responsibilities. He's also been old for his leagues, and the Snakes much prefer Chris Snyder. Ansman's hitting looks impressive, and it was enough to make him a Texas League All-Star, but playing in the Diamondbacks' chain gives hitters the benefit of one bandbox after another. He might turn out okay as somebody's DH someday.

CARLOS BAERGA   PH/IF   Bats: B   Throws: R   Born: 04-Nov-68   Age: 35

YEAR	TM	LG	AGE	AB	H	2B	3B	HR	BB	SO	SB	CS	AVG	OBP	SLG	MLVR	EQBA	EQOBP	EQSLG	EQMLVR	VORP	DEFENSE			
2001	LGI	ATL	32	203	64	9	3	9	19	24	3	0	.315	.388	.522	.292	.259	.314	.434	-.065	4.7				
2002	BOS	AL	33	182	52	11	0	2	7	20	6	0	.286	.316	.379	-.068	.306	.341	.404	-.019	6.9	13-2B	-2		
2003	ARI	NL	34	207	71	13	0	4	18	20	1	1	.343	.396	.464	.193	.337	.394	.457	.181	17.3	14-1B	0	13-2B	1
2004	ARI	NL	35	193	57	12	1	3	16	23	3	1	.294	.351	.417	.019	.283	.340	.404	-.037	8.0	54-2B	-10		

Breakout: 8%   *Improve: 32%*   *Collapse: 40%*

Formerly dead, a Baerga life cycle rotates from one-time stardom to abject waste of space to a Julio Franco-style renaissance as a useful pinch-hitter and spot starter. He's more useful than Franco because he'll stand around at second or third when asked, but anything more than a part-time role would be a mistake. He looks much better because of the BOB, but the ability to make hard contact off the bench is handy in anybody's park.

ROD BARAJAS C Bats: R Throws: R Born: 05-Sep-75 Age: 28

YEAR	TM	LG	AGE	AB	H	2B	3B	HR	BB	SO	SB	CS	AVG	OBP	SLG	MLVR	EQBA	EQOBP	EQSLG	EQMLVR	VORP	DEFENSE			
2001	TUC	PCL	25	162	52	13	0	9	9	23	3	1	.321	.366	.568	.231	.277	.319	.484	.031	5.6	20-1B	0	17-C	-2
2001	ARI	NL	25	106	17	3	0	3	4	26	0	0	.160	.191	.274	-.581	.160	.191	.274	-.590	-11.4	24-C	-5		
2002	TUC	PCL	26	16	7	1	0	1	1	2	0	0	.438	.471	.688	.737	.375	.375	.625	.454	2.7				
2002	ARI	NL	26	154	36	10	0	3	10	25	1	0	.234	.288	.357	-.166	.239	.296	.361	-.216	-1.7	38-C	-3		
2003	ARI	NL	27	220	48	15	0	3	14	43	0	0	.218	.265	.327	-.298	.217	.263	.326	-.344	-9.5	67-C	4		
2004	*TEX*	*AL*	*28*	*195*	*49*	*11*	*0*	*6*	*10*	*33*	*1*	*0*	*.249*	*.290*	*.400*	*-.127*	*.243*	*.287*	*.390*	*-.179*	*-0.1*	*53-C*	*-3*		

Breakout: 39%   Improve: 58%   Collapse: 27%

Let's not insult the memory of Mark Parent here. As backup catchers go, Barajas is as low as you can be on the totem pole without being on your company softball team. He doesn't hit and doesn't get on base. His career line (.210/.257/.325) is low enough that Mike Matheny (.237/.293/.334) can confidently kick sand in his face. Barajas can shut down a running game well, so if he was on a team with a great hitter behind the plate, he might make an adequate caddy. On this team, he played often enough to be a handicap. Signed to a deal with Texas.

BRIAN BARDEN 3B Bats: R Throws: R Born: 02-Apr-81 Age: 23

YEAR	TM	LG	AGE	AB	H	2B	3B	HR	BB	SO	SB	CS	AVG	OBP	SLG	MLVR	EQBA	EQOBP	EQSLG	EQMLVR	VORP	DEFENSE	
2002	LNC	CAL	21	269	90	19	1	8	16	63	3	1	.335	.370	.502	.212	.253	.284	.389	-.189	-0.7	55-3B	6
2002	YAK	NWN	21	15	5	1	0	0	1	1	0	0	.333	.412	.400	.254	.312	.328	.312	-.176	-0.4		
2003	ELP	TEX	22	383	110	24	5	3	29	78	10	4	.287	.348	.399	.009	.230	.286	.331	-.283	-11.6	100-3B	-6
2004	*ARI*	*NL*	*23*	*234*	*59*	*13*	*2*	*4*	*17*	*51*	*4*	*2*	*.253*	*.312*	*.382*	*-.124*	*.244*	*.302*	*.371*	*-.177*	*5.0*	*64-3B*	*-5*

Breakout: 36%   Improve: 57%   Collapse: 21%

A 2002 draft choice out of Oregon State, Barden was pushed up to Double-A in his second professional season, with adequate results. Is he a prospect? He's young enough and can handle third well enough. But let's keep in mind that although Barden didn't fall on his face in his first year at Double-A, he didn't slug .400 in El Paso, and 29 walks in 426 plate appearances adds up to a pretty inoffensive third baseman. He needs to improve before he's going to graduate to trade bait, because with Hillenbrand and Tracy ahead of him, that's his future in purple, copper, and teal.

DANNY BAUTISTA OF Bats: R Throws: R Born: 24-May-72 Age: 32

YEAR	TM	LG	AGE	AB	H	2B	3B	HR	BB	SO	SB	CS	AVG	OBP	SLG	MLVR	EQBA	EQOBP	EQSLG	EQMLVR	VORP	DEFENSE			
2001	ARI	NL	29	219	66	11	2	5	14	30	3	2	.301	.346	.438	.035	.299	.343	.434	.022	5.1	24-RF	1	22-CF	2
2002	ARI	NL	30	154	50	5	2	6	11	21	4	2	.325	.367	.500	.226	.321	.361	.500	.171	9.3	31-RF	-3		
2003	ARI	NL	31	284	78	16	3	4	21	50	3	2	.275	.330	.394	-.061	.270	.327	.389	-.096	-1.5	53-RF	-5	15-CF	-1
2004	*ARI*	*NL*	*32*	*252*	*70*	*13*	*2*	*6*	*20*	*40*	*3*	*2*	*.277*	*.332*	*.416*	*-.028*	*.267*	*.321*	*.404*	*-.084*	*0.9*	*68-RF*	*-1*		

Breakout: 18%   Improve: 32%   Collapse: 39%

Right-handed hitting outfielders that throw well and make contact and cover an alley are handy, but the legend of their usefulness can overshadow their ready availability. There are always guys like Bautista or Tito Landrum or Henry Cotto hanging around. Some, like Bautista, get noticed for being in the right place at the right time. Because of the team's budget cuts, he might end up starting in right. Even at his best, he's not a significant asset in the lineup, forcing the Snakes to find runs elsewhere if they want to field a really potent offense.

ALEX CINTRON SS Bats: B Throws: R Born: 17-Dec-78 Age: 25

YEAR	TM	LG	AGE	AB	H	2B	3B	HR	BB	SO	SB	CS	AVG	OBP	SLG	MLVR	EQBA	EQOBP	EQSLG	EQMLVR	VORP	DEFENSE			
2001	TUC	PCL	22	425	124	24	3	3	15	48	9	6	.292	.315	.384	-.149	.249	.278	.331	-.287	-10.6	92-SS	-17	13-2B	-1
2002	TUC	PCL	23	351	113	22	3	4	11	33	9	5	.322	.345	.436	.045	.284	.308	.386	-.125	7.8	47-SS	-4	34-2B	-5
2002	ARI	NL	23	75	16	6	0	0	12	13	0	0	.213	.322	.293	-.199	.224	.322	.303	-.253	-1.6	12-2B	2		
2003	TUC	PCL	24	107	42	11	2	2	8	6	1	0	.393	.435	.589	.481	.327	.375	.510	.216	13.1	23-SS	0		
2003	ARI	NL	24	448	142	26	6	13	29	33	2	3	.317	.359	.489	.147	.311	.354	.482	.123	33.3	88-SS	-6	14-3B	-3
2004	*ARI*	*NL*	*25*	*475*	*137*	*29*	*4*	*9*	*35*	*45*	*6*	*3*	*.289*	*.339*	*.423*	*.004*	*.278*	*.328*	*.411*	*-.053*	*19.7*	*123-SS*	*-6*		

Breakout: 11%   Improve: 36%   Collapse: 27%

Cintron came into 2003 looking like a man whose time may never come. The Snakes seemed happy with Tony Womack—no accounting for taste—and the organization has a gaggle of young shortstops on the way up through the system. A convenient combination of injuries and ineptitude among the big league regulars garnered Cintron another look, and he hit well enough to stick. He's not an asset in the field, but he is competent. More importantly, as a hitter, he's not just a BOB illusion, having slugged around .450 on the road in his brief big league career. Middle infielders that do that have value. Cintron will be an effective regular and could slip into an All-Star game at some point during the next four years.

CRAIG COUNSELL   IF   Bats: L   Throws: R   Born: 21-Aug-70   Age: 33

YEAR	TM	LG	AGE	AB	H	2B	3B	HR	BB	SO	SB	CS	AVG	OBP	SLG	MLVR	EQBA	EQOBP	EQSLG	EQMLVR	VORP	DEFENSE			
2001	ARI	NL	30	458	126	22	3	4	61	76	6	8	.275	.359	.362	-.067	.272	.358	.356	-.081	15.7	46-SS	-1	49-2B	7
2002	ARI	NL	31	436	123	22	1	2	45	52	7	5	.282	.348	.351	-.041	.283	.347	.356	-.095	9.8	94-3B	8	16-SS	-1
2003	ARI	NL	32	303	71	6	3	3	41	32	11	4	.234	.328	.304	-.207	.230	.322	.302	-.251	-4.9	48-3B	6	21-SS	1
2004	MIL	NL	33	256	63	11	1	2	30	35	6	3	.248	.329	.331	-.165	.249	.329	.331	-.177	3.0	71-3B	+2		

Breakout: 19%   Improve: 40%   Collapse: 35%

Doomed to be mistaken for a pre-teen for several years to come, Counsell's days of being valuable are almost over. He's not a great shortstop, but after David Eckstein's 15 minutes on national television, teams might be more willing to forgive an arm that doesn't smoke those throws from the hole. Offensively, Counsell used to be an on-base source, but he took a major dive last year, and always wears down as the season progresses. In Milwaukee, he'll be more popular locally than Royce Clayton, but he's nothing more than a temp, keeping the seat warm for J. J. Hardy.

BRAD CRESSE   C   Bats: R   Throws: R   Born: 31-Jul-78   Age: 25

YEAR	TM	LG	AGE	AB	H	2B	3B	HR	BB	SO	SB	CS	AVG	OBP	SLG	MLVR	EQBA	EQOBP	EQSLG	EQMLVR	VORP	DEFENSE	
2001	ELP	TEX	22	429	124	39	1	14	44	116	0	1	.289	.373	.483	.146	.232	.303	.391	-.166	1.0	92-C	-13
2002	TUC	PCL	23	126	34	10	0	2	4	38	0	0	.270	.306	.397	-.120	.234	.268	.355	-.282	-3.9	33-C	1
2002	ELP	TEX	23	240	55	15	0	3	16	74	1	0	.229	.282	.329	-.202	.192	.238	.287	-.461	-20.7	42-C	3
2003	TUC	PCL	24	306	70	21	1	10	18	89	0	0	.229	.282	.402	-.167	.195	.248	.351	-.351	-15.7	78-C	0
2004	ARI	NL	25	158	36	9	0	5	12	46	0	0	.228	.290	.388	-.171	.220	.281	.377	-.223	-1.8	45-C	-5

Breakout: 45%   Improve: 65%   Collapse: 20%

Despite shoulder problems that plagued him as the season progressed, the former LSU star continued to flash improved glovework behind the plate. Unfortunately, now that he hasn't hit in two years, he's reduced to hoping he can push Rod Barajas aside someday, except that the organization seems wildly enthusiastic about Chris Snyder. It would be interesting to see what happens with Cresse in another organization, because he's rotting away as a Snake.

DOUG DEVORE   OF   Bats: L   Throws: L   Born: 14-Dec-77   Age: 26

YEAR	TM	LG	AGE	AB	H	2B	3B	HR	BB	SO	SB	CS	AVG	OBP	SLG	MLVR	EQBA	EQOBP	EQSLG	EQMLVR	VORP	DEFENSE			
2001	ELP	TEX	23	476	140	32	11	15	46	118	11	3	.294	.358	.502	.154	.233	.291	.402	-.173	-15.7	120-RF	-8		
2002	TUC	PCL	24	436	114	20	6	14	27	103	9	6	.261	.311	.431	-.071	.225	.272	.374	-.254	-24.2	104-RF	-1		
2003	TUC	PCL	25	462	135	29	7	14	44	95	5	7	.292	.357	.476	.105	.246	.308	.412	-.117	-8.6	64-LF	-3	54-RF	-4
2004	ARI	NL	26	186	47	11	2	6	17	44	2	1	.254	.321	.435	-.037	.245	.311	.422	-.093	1.8	53-RF	-3		

Breakout: 41%   Improve: 61%   Collapse: 25%

Devolving from lesser prospectdom to the stale existence of an organizational soldier, Devore's listed because the Snakes will have openings for outfield reserves, Danny Bautista has a history of crumpling now and again, and anybody can catch a break with a nice camp. It worked for Dustan Mohr, and a nice month can get you a career. Devore did slug .516 against right-handed pitching, so he has his uses.

STEVE FINLEY   CF   Bats: L   Throws: L   Born: 12-Mar-65   Age: 39

YEAR	TM	LG	AGE	AB	H	2B	3B	HR	BB	SO	SB	CS	AVG	OBP	SLG	MLVR	EQBA	EQOBP	EQSLG	EQMLVR	VORP	DEFENSE	
2001	ARI	NL	36	495	136	27	4	14	47	67	11	7	.275	.337	.430	-.015	.272	.334	.424	-.032	15.6	127-CF	3
2002	ARI	NL	37	505	145	24	4	25	65	73	16	4	.287	.370	.499	.192	.284	.364	.501	.140	38.8	128-CF	5
2003	ARI	NL	38	516	148	24	10	22	57	94	15	8	.287	.363	.500	.140	.279	.355	.489	.103	33.6	128-CF	-3
2004	ARI	NL	39	342	94	18	4	11	41	59	6	3	.274	.354	.446	.048	.264	.343	.433	-.009	9.5	93-CF	-3

Breakout: 17%   Improve: 44%   Collapse: 21%

(continued next page)

Steve Finley *(continued)*

It's easy to pick on Finley's faults: He's gotten a nice boost from hitting in the BOB, he's old, and he's not a great hitter at the top of the order. But that's all old news. Finley's not generally asked to lead off these days, having moved down in the order where his ability to drive the ball is handy. He can still play a solid center. In the wake of the Schilling deal and what it portends for the team's competitiveness in 2004, and with the prices being bid on free agent center fielders this winter, Finley would make a great win-now pickup for a contender if the Snakes drift out of contention early.

JASON GARTHWAITE   OF   Bats: R   Throws: R   Born: 26-Nov-80   Age: 23

YEAR	TM	LG	AGE	AB	H	2B	3B	HR	BB	SO	SB	CS	AVG	OBP	SLG	MLVR	EQBA	EQOBP	EQSLG	EQMLVR	VORP	DEFENSE		
2002	YAK	NWN	21	51	9	5	0	1	3	12	0	0	.176	.236	.333	-.168	.154	.191	.288	-.574	-14.7	10-RF	-1	
2002	SBN	MID	21	162	40	10	2	2	11	62	2	2	.247	.301	.370	-.019	.199	.240	.313	-.418	-13.5	32-CF	-5	
2003	LNC	CAL	22	437	130	33	2	22	30	97	3	5	.297	.351	.533	.178	.214	.260	.394	-.256	-23.9	41-RF	0	38-CF -1
2004	*ARI*	*NL*	*23*	*240*	*54*	*14*	*1*	*8*	*16*	*67*	*1*	*1*	*.224*	*.278*	*.391*	*-.192*	*.216*	*.269*	*.379*	*-.244*	*-8.7*	*65-CF -11*		

Breakout: 34%   Improve: 59%   Collapse: 22%

A rangy product of the University of Washington, Garthwaite was drafted in 2002. Reflecting the ambition that animates so many of the organization's assignments, he was sensibly sent to high A-ball in his first full year. How many Division I players first go to low A-ball in their first year after being drafted? That invariably seems like a waste. Garthwaite may not have the range for center (his college position), reducing him to the fragile possibilities of tweenerdom, but he's young enough to have a career.

LUIS GONZALEZ   LF?   Bats: L   Throws: R   Born: 03-Sep-67   Age: 36

YEAR	TM	LG	AGE	AB	H	2B	3B	HR	BB	SO	SB	CS	AVG	OBP	SLG	MLVR	EQBA	EQOBP	EQSLG	EQMLVR	VORP	DEFENSE	
2001	ARI	NL	33	609	198	36	7	57	100	83	1	1	.325	.429	.688	.533	.321	.424	.677	.518	101.2	152-LF	5
2002	ARI	NL	34	524	151	19	3	28	97	76	9	2	.288	.400	.496	.234	.285	.397	.494	.188	35.6	137-LF	-2
2003	ARI	NL	35	579	176	46	4	26	94	67	5	3	.304	.402	.532	.257	.295	.393	.521	.227	43.1	153-LF	13
2004	*ARI*	*NL*	*36*	*488*	*145*	*30*	*3*	*26*	*80*	*68*	*4*	*2*	*.297*	*.398*	*.529*	*.245*	*.287*	*.385*	*.513*	*.184*	*33.3*	*135-LF*	*0*

Breakout: 24%   Improve: 58%   Collapse: 14%

While 2001 is still the outlier, Gonzo has been a remarkably consistent player, with his other four years as a Snake all grouped around the same productive level of offensive contribution. His five-year run in Arizona is remarkable when you compare it to his lack of productivity as a Cub, Astro, and Tiger. It's a five-year stretch as a Hall of Fame hitter tacked onto the back end of a mediocre career, although his power spike started with his single season in Detroit. He's much more of an upper-cut hitter than he was in his old Astrodome days, reflecting a player who learns, thereby challenging population-wide assumptions about how players should perform as they age. If he chooses to, it might be interesting to see what sort of hitting coach he'd make, since he's changed his approach at the plate so completely, and it wasn't like he was awful at the start. He might have been underpaid before, and while paying even more money after money well-spent reflects well on Colangelo's largesse, the real questions are whether the Snakes can compete despite the expense of Gonzalez's three-year, $30 million deal, and whether or not he'll be able to play left now that his elbow is scragged. He might be better off moving to first, but that's not really an option after the Sexson trade.

ANDY GREEN   2B   Bats: R   Throws: R   Born: 07-Jul-77   Age: 26

YEAR	TM	LG	AGE	AB	H	2B	3B	HR	BB	SO	SB	CS	AVG	OBP	SLG	MLVR	EQBA	EQOBP	EQSLG	EQMLVR	VORP	DEFENSE		
2001	SBN	MID	24	477	143	18	6	5	59	50	51	15	.300	.379	.394	.132	.230	.295	.310	-.295	-18.8	124-2B	-7	
2002	LNC	CAL	25	401	124	36	4	6	60	59	15	10	.309	.401	.464	.183	.219	.296	.332	-.269	-11.7	95-2B	4	
2002	TUC	PCL	25	99	22	8	0	1	9	17	2	1	.222	.294	.333	-.259	.184	.249	.276	-.458	-8.5	23-2B	-2	
2003	ELP	TEX	26	490	148	38	2	2	38	51	17	9	.302	.366	.400	.049	.246	.301	.337	-.236	-8.8	59-2B	2	39-SS -5
2004	*ARI*	*NL*	*26*	*186*	*48*	*11*	*1*	*3*	*16*	*25*	*4*	*2*	*.256*	*.323*	*.368*	*-.121*	*.246*	*.313*	*.357*	*-.173*	*1.9*	*53-2B*	*-2*	

Breakout: 37%   Improve: 54%   Collapse: 28%

Gifted with Glenn Hubbardly goodness, Green isn't going to be listed as anybody's prospect, but he could nevertheless wind up as somebody's starting second baseman for a stretch. He has some sock, fine bat control skills, runs well, draws a walk now and again, and he's considered a strong second baseman.

SCOTT HAIRSTON

2B?   **Bats: R**   **Throws: R**   Born: 25-May-80   Age: 24

YEAR	TM	LG	AGE	AB	H	2B	3B	HR	BB	SO	SB	CS	AVG	OBP	SLG	MLVR	EQBA	EQOBP	EQSLG	EQMLVR	VORP	DEFENSE			
2001	MSO	PIO	21	291	101	16	6	14	38	50	2	2	.347	.432	.588	.475	.217	.277	.372	-.252	-12.4	62-2B	-9		
2002	SBN	MID	22	394	131	35	4	16	58	74	9	3	.332	.426	.563	.460	.243	.319	.423	-.084	11.9	95-2B	-12	10-3B	-2
2002	LNC	CAL	22	79	32	11	1	6	6	16	1	0	.405	.442	.797	.805	.299	.333	.571	.205	7.6				
2003	ELP	TEX	23	337	93	21	7	10	30	80	6	2	.276	.345	.469	.088	.219	.280	.383	-.230	-5.5	74-2B	-5		
2004	*ARI*	*NL*	*24*	*208*	*54*	*13*	*2*	*8*	*20*	*46*	*2*	*1*	*.258*	*.327*	*.443*	*-.014*	*.249*	*.316*	*.430*	*-.070*	*9.0*	*58-2B*	*-6*		

Breakout: 35%   Improve: 58%   Collapse: 17%

Hairston is a great prospect, but how great? A back injury at the end of May sidelined him for a good chunk of the season. After rest and rehab, he returned to the form that makes him one of the best young hitters anywhere. The real question is how much his tough intro to Double-A can be explained away by the injury; he was hitting in El Paso, after all. Beyond those concerns, his defensive work might be charitably described as "improving." There are expectations that he'll get a shot at the job in camp, but it looks like he could use some further work on his defense and a month or two of consolidation in the minors before really being ready. From there on out, he should be an offensive terror, similar to Marcus Giles.

VICTOR HALL

OF   **Bats: L**   **Throws: L**   Born: 16-Sep-80   Age: 23

YEAR	TM	LG	AGE	AB	H	2B	3B	HR	BB	SO	SB	CS	AVG	OBP	SLG	MLVR	EQBA	EQOBP	EQSLG	EQMLVR	VORP	DEFENSE			
2001	SBN	MID	20	415	114	13	12	0	52	71	60	15	.275	.362	.364	.049	.215	.284	.290	-.352	-28.1	108-CF	-12		
2002	LNC	CAL	21	352	98	10	8	3	47	72	26	15	.278	.373	.378	.007	.198	.271	.275	-.408	-28.0	65-CF	-6	23-LF	-1
2002	ELP	TEX	21	161	46	4	5	0	6	23	7	4	.286	.322	.373	-.048	.244	.269	.325	-.317	-12.3	30-LF	-5		
2003	ELP	TEX	22	490	147	13	12	0	51	88	23	19	.300	.370	.376	.021	.237	.302	.301	-.289	-21.1	91-CF	-8	27-LF	-4
2004	*ARI*	*NL*	*23*	*240*	*56*	*10*	*3*	*2*	*21*	*45*	*7*	*3*	*.234*	*.303*	*.318*	*-.236*	*.226*	*.293*	*.309*	*-.286*	*-10.7*	*66-CF*	*-11*		

Breakout: 27%   Improve: 49%   Collapse: 27%

At the least, Hall is aspiring to a career as a spare set of legs. He has the speed to be an outstanding flycatcher, but his lack of experience as a baseball player (he didn't start playing until his senior year of high school) shows. He gets compared to Juan Pierre, but has a lot to learn in terms of reading pitchers and picking his spots to run. It's that lack of experience and his youth that makes him all the more promising, although again, you have to wonder how much a minor league career played in hitter's parks is going to contribute to some bad habits at the plate.

ROBERT HAMMOCK

C/UT   **Bats: R**   **Throws: R**   Born: 13-May-77   Age: 27

YEAR	TM	LG	AGE	AB	H	2B	3B	HR	BB	SO	SB	CS	AVG	OBP	SLG	MLVR	EQBA	EQOBP	EQSLG	EQMLVR	VORP	DEFENSE			
2001	SBN	MID	24	125	31	3	2	2	14	21	5	6	.248	.324	.352	-.044	.180	.239	.266	-.494	-13.1	17-C	-1	13-LF	0
2001	LNC	CAL	24	190	59	11	3	4	16	42	3	2	.311	.378	.463	.151	.229	.286	.346	-.263	-11.5	30-LF	0	14-C	-3
2001	ELP	TEX	24	74	12	5	0	0	7	18	2	2	.162	.235	.230	-.488	.122	.188	.176	-.743	-14.0				
2002	ELP	TEX	25	441	128	28	4	11	43	68	5	4	.290	.358	.447	.109	.236	.295	.374	-.202	-3.9	53-C	-2	37-LF	-3
2003	TUC	PCL	26	116	31	6	2	2	11	24	1	0	.267	.321	.405	-.070	.226	.288	.348	-.258	-2.9	20-C	-3		
2003	ARI	NL	26	195	55	10	2	8	17	44	3	2	.282	.343	.477	.075	.276	.338	.464	.035	9.0	31-C	-1	16-3B	4
2004	*ARI*	*NL*	*27*	*222*	*56*	*12*	*2*	*7*	*21*	*45*	*2*	*1*	*.251*	*.322*	*.410*	*-.072*	*.242*	*.311*	*.398*	*-.126*	*4.0*	*62-C*	*-8*		

Breakout: 35%   Improve: 55%   Collapse: 25%

It used to be that you'd see a lot of teams use catchers at other positions instead of limiting them to catching. Usually, it was a right-handed hitter who could mash lefties and do an acceptable job in the infield or outfield corners. You'd have guys ranging from Bob Brenly to Mike Heath to Johnny Wockenfuss to Floyd Rayford chipping in offensively and doing more than just catch. Hammock is cut from that mold: He may not be an everyday catcher, but he's versatile and has some pop. It's to Brenly's credit that he used Hammock similarly to how he was used during his own mid-80s heyday as a player with the "Hum Baby" Giants. Hammock will be the better half of a job-sharing arrangement with Brent Mayne.

SHEA HILLENBRAND

3B/1B   **Bats: R**   **Throws: R**   Born: 27-Jul-75   Age: 28

YEAR	TM	LG	AGE	AB	H	2B	3B	HR	BB	SO	SB	CS	AVG	OBP	SLG	MLVR	EQBA	EQOBP	EQSLG	EQMLVR	VORP	DEFENSE			
2001	BOS	AL	25	468	123	20	2	12	13	61	3	4	.263	.291	.391	-.130	.280	.310	.419	-.076	12.0	120-3B	-4		
2002	BOS	AL	26	634	186	43	4	18	25	95	4	2	.293	.330	.459	.073	.313	.351	.492	.134	48.9	150-3B	3		
2003	BOS	AL	27	185	56	17	0	3	7	26	1	0	.303	.335	.443	.048	.319	.358	.470	.120	7.5	26-3B	-3	21-1B	0
2003	ARI	NL	27	330	88	18	1	17	17	44	0	0	.267	.302	.482	.004	.263	.302	.477	-.022	6.7	48-1B	1	27-3B	-2
2004	*ARI*	*NL*	*28*	*466*	*133*	*29*	*2*	*15*	*25*	*66*	*2*	*1*	*.285*	*.329*	*.452*	*.024*	*.275*	*.319*	*.438*	*-.034*	*14.5*	*119-3B*	*-3*		

Breakout: 13%   Improve: 40%   Collapse: 26%

(continued next page)

Shea Hillenbrand *(continued)*

Hillenbrand isn't a star, but he liked hitting in the BOB, and as the fourth wheel in the new lineup featuring Richie Sexson, he'll probably set a career-high in RBI in 2004. He's still a mediocrity, and he's a defensive liability in an infield that doesn't have any glove men. He'll be useful, and he'll build up a Vinny Castilla sort of reputation as a "run producer" that might make him a wildly overpaid Tiger someday.

CONOR JACKSON   **OF**   **Bats: R**   **Throws: R**   Born: 07-May-82   Age: 22

YEAR	TM	LG	AGE	AB	H	2B	3B	HR	BB	SO	SB	CS	AVG	OBP	SLG	MLVR	EQBA	EQOBP	EQSLG	EQMLVR	VORP	DEFENSE		
2003	YAK	NWN	21	257	82	35	1	6	36	41	3	0	.319	.410	.533	.393	.222	.288	.383	-.212	-21.8	20-RF -1		
2004	ARI	NL	22	250	58	16	1	7	22	52	1	1	.231	.298	.386	-.158	.222	.289	.374	-.211	-6.3	69-DH -3		

Breakout: 18%   Improve: 44%   Collapse: 28%

The club's top choice in the 2003 draft, Jackson is a disciplined college hitter with more power potential than even his pro debut allows for—he was playing with a bad shoulder. The organization likes to push its more advanced prospects up the ladder, so Jackson should get an opportunity to put up some scary-looking numbers in the hitter's haven of Lancaster next summer. Assuming he makes the jump to Double-A by the end of the season, he'll get some press clippings in spring training '05, at which point he'll drift into the big league picture. He's as promising as they come.

MATT KATA   **2B/3B**   **Bats: B**   **Throws: R**   Born: 14-Mar-78   Age: 26

YEAR	TM	LG	AGE	AB	H	2B	3B	HR	BB	SO	SB	CS	AVG	OBP	SLG	MLVR	EQBA	EQOBP	EQSLG	EQMLVR	VORP	DEFENSE		
2001	LNC	CAL	23	494	146	19	6	10	41	79	30	8	.296	.355	.419	.046	.224	.270	.320	-.334	-22.8	111-2B -7		
2002	ELP	TEX	24	578	172	33	9	11	37	79	12	7	.298	.341	.443	.085	.247	.286	.383	-.199	-4.1	122-2B -1		
2003	TUC	PCL	25	201	58	13	5	3	9	29	2	3	.289	.327	.448	.015	.253	.288	.399	-.168	0.4	39-2B -5		
2003	ARI	NL	25	288	74	16	5	7	25	53	3	2	.257	.315	.420	-.064	.249	.311	.415	-.105	5.1	48-2B -4	19-3B	2
2004	ARI	NL	26	378	99	20	4	8	27	59	5	3	.262	.314	.400	-.091	.252	.304	.388	-.145	4.9	99-2B -4		

Breakout: 31%   Improve: 53%   Collapse: 28%

A worthy demonstration of the sort of value you can find in a farm system beyond the blue chippers. After the rash of injuries in the infield, they had to bring somebody up, and Kata did a great job of illustrating that a concept like "replacement value" can be set far too low. There's a limit to how far you should take this sort of feel-good vibe, though: Kata isn't young, he's only modestly useful at the plate, and utility infielders who can't play short end up being a source of concern when it comes to roster design. As a temporary solution until Hairston's ready to play second full-time, Kata will do.

JOSH KROEGER   **OF**   **Bats: L**   **Throws: L**   Born: 31-Aug-82   Age: 21

YEAR	TM	LG	AGE	AB	H	2B	3B	HR	BB	SO	SB	CS	AVG	OBP	SLG	MLVR	EQBA	EQOBP	EQSLG	EQMLVR	VORP	DEFENSE		
2001	SBN	MID	18	292	80	15	1	3	18	49	4	4	.274	.324	.363	-.013	.216	.256	.294	-.403	-31.7	46-LF -6	22-RF	-4
2002	LNC	CAL	19	497	117	20	7	7	23	136	2	4	.235	.274	.346	-.225	.178	.207	.265	-.562	-69.7	85-RF -6	34-LF	0
2003	LNC	CAL	20	305	104	30	6	5	35	58	6	6	.341	.409	.528	.298	.237	.300	.378	-.186	-11.0	58-RF -4	12-CF	0
2003	ELP	TEX	20	208	57	9	2	3	10	54	3	5	.274	.315	.380	-.078	.220	.258	.317	-.364	-13.0	27-CF -1	26-RF	-2
2004	ARI	NL	21	297	65	16	2	5	20	67	3	2	.220	.275	.340	-.267	.212	.266	.330	-.317	-17.8	79-RF -6		

Breakout: 32%   Improve: 57%   Collapse: 19%

Kroeger's big first half at Lancaster (.344/.415/.546) can be explained away as an example of repeating a level in a hitter's park, but he also deserves credit for doing a better job of not getting behind early in his at-bats. Also, he was the youngest regular in the California League in 2002. This year, he should be able to consolidate his gains in El Paso's offensive pleasure pen, but the real question is whether or not he'll add more power as he matures, because he's still very young. If he does, he's a solid outfield prospect.

QUINTON McCRACKEN   **OF**   **Bats: B**   **Throws: R**   Born: 16-Mar-70   Age: 34

YEAR	TM	LG	AGE	AB	H	2B	3B	HR	BB	SO	SB	CS	AVG	OBP	SLG	MLVR	EQBA	EQOBP	EQSLG	EQMLVR	VORP	DEFENSE		
2001	EDM	PCL	31	361	122	27	4	4	21	54	8	10	.338	.374	.468	.159	.296	.334	.411	-.030	12.1	48-CF -2	20-LF	-1
2001	MIN	AL	31	64	14	2	2	0	5	13	0	1	.219	.275	.313	-.297	.234	.290	.344	-.255	-2.2			
2002	ARI	NL	32	349	108	27	8	3	32	68	5	4	.309	.367	.458	.154	.306	.363	.462	.104	15.3	61-RF -2	26-CF	1
2003	ARI	NL	33	203	46	5	2	0	15	34	5	1	.227	.276	.271	-.348	.225	.275	.270	-.393	-13.3	20-RF -2	10-CF	0
2004	SEA	AL	34	172	45	9	2	2	12	31	4	2	.259	.310	.366	-.131	.262	.317	.377	-.130	0.4	49-RF -1		

Breakout: 29%   Improve: 52%   Collapse: 30%

What is it about this guy? Contenders or near-contenders take him seriously as a bench weapon. As a pinch-runner and fifth outfielder, there are a few worse options than McCracken, if you turn a blind eye to the expense. If you don't, he's on the short list for one of the worst uses of a spot on a 25-man roster anywhere in the big leagues. He's a great addition to the Mariners' "lose now" debuilding project.

CHAD MOELLER   C   **Bats: R**   **Throws: R**   Born: 18-Feb-75   Age: 29

YEAR	TM	LG	AGE	AB	H	2B	3B	HR	BB	SO	SB	CS	AVG	OBP	SLG	MLVR	EQBA	EQOBP	EQSLG	EQMLVR	VORP	DEFENSE
2001	TUC	PCL	26	274	75	20	0	8	25	54	1	4	.274	.337	.434	-.051	.226	.290	.363	-.234	-5.1	65-C -13
2001	ARI	NL	26	56	13	0	1	1	6	12	0	0	.232	.306	.321	-.250	.232	.306	.321	-.256	-1.3	14-C -2
2002	TUC	PCL	27	211	67	8	2	10	29	46	1	0	.318	.401	.517	.243	.263	.347	.435	-.000	11.5	59-C -1
2002	ARI	NL	27	105	30	11	1	2	17	23	0	1	.286	.385	.467	.173	.283	.382	.462	.117	8.4	35-C -2
2003	ARI	NL	28	239	64	17	1	7	23	59	1	2	.268	.335	.435	-.005	.262	.331	.429	-.038	7.3	64-C -8
2004	MIL	NL	29	264	65	14	1	9	27	62	1	1	.247	.320	.407	-.082	.248	.320	.407	-.094	6.7	73-C -2

Breakout: 22%   Improve: 44%   Collapse: 35%

A cheesehead returning to the land of milk and milk products, Moeller was run out of Arizona a bit early after falling out of favor. He's not a bad catcher, and although he struggled to control the running game, an injured throwing hand was partially to blame. He has a reasonable amount of sock, so he should be the Brewers' starting catcher. He might actually turn in a nice little career similar to that of the man he almost replaced, Damian Miller.

RAUL MONDESI   RF   **Bats: R**   **Throws: R**   Born: 12-Mar-71   Age: 33

YEAR	TM	LG	AGE	AB	H	2B	3B	HR	BB	SO	SB	CS	AVG	OBP	SLG	MLVR	EQBA	EQOBP	EQSLG	EQMLVR	VORP	DEFENSE	
2001	TOR	AL	30	572	144	26	4	27	73	128	30	11	.252	.342	.453	.030	.265	.355	.482	.080	22.4	144-RF 7	
2002	TOR	AL	31	299	67	16	1	15	31	57	9	2	.224	.301	.435	-.070	.237	.315	.467	-.035	2.4	59-RF -1	
2002	NYY	AL	31	270	65	18	0	11	28	46	6	4	.241	.315	.430	-.029	.265	.339	.474	.041	7.4	53-RF -2	11-CF -1
2003	NYY	AL	32	361	93	23	3	16	38	66	17	7	.258	.330	.471	.063	.278	.354	.512	.132	10.8	97-RF 1	
2003	ARI	NL	32	162	49	8	1	8	18	31	5	4	.302	.372	.512	.185	.288	.362	.497	.135	9.1	42-RF -2	
2004	ARI	NL	33	455	124	26	3	22	53	88	13	5	.273	.352	.489	.097	.263	.340	.474	.039	15.7	122-RF -2	

Breakout: 26%   Improve: 60%   Collapse: 13%

Although his reputation as a clubhouse knee-biter, drama queen, and all-around nuisance seems to be getting more elaborate with age, Mondesi actually put together what might have been his best year since '99. While there are questions about his age and attitude, for the right price, he might be useful as the right fielder on a team in a win-now situation that can afford to have him in a secondary offensive role. To make it work, it will probably require a mature Latin manager or player already in place with his new employer, because nobody's managed to get Mondesi to act his age; at least one team got rid of him because of the bad influence they felt he exerted on younger Latin players. And then there's the potential for ill will that might come of his getting what he's worth, instead of what he's been overpaid. Basically, he's a risk, and not an especially good one.

TIM OLSON   SS/UT   **Bats: R**   **Throws: R**   Born: 01-Aug-78   Age: 25

YEAR	TM	LG	AGE	AB	H	2B	3B	HR	BB	SO	SB	CS	AVG	OBP	SLG	MLVR	EQBA	EQOBP	EQSLG	EQMLVR	VORP	DEFENSE	
2001	LNC	CAL	22	239	69	12	4	6	14	49	13	9	.289	.336	.448	.049	.215	.251	.342	-.346	-9.7	33-SS -2	28-3B -1
2001	ELP	TEX	22	167	53	13	0	2	11	36	4	4	.317	.378	.431	.109	.261	.310	.358	-.179	1.2	46-SS -10	
2002	ELP	TEX	23	433	118	24	2	10	27	91	9	11	.273	.337	.406	.012	.227	.278	.352	-.272	-8.9	98-SS -3	11-CF -1
2003	ELP	TEX	24	56	11	2	0	2	5	19	0	2	.196	.258	.339	-.270	.143	.200	.268	-.587	-6.4	12-SS -2	
2003	TUC	PCL	24	397	104	22	0	6	31	77	11	2	.262	.323	.363	-.125	.224	.285	.314	-.312	-12.8	96-SS -15	
2004	ARI	NL	25	164	41	8	1	4	12	35	3	1	.249	.310	.380	-.135	.240	.300	.368	-.188	3.2	46-SS -8	

Breakout: 44%   Improve: 63%   Collapse: 22%

Olson is standing at the head of the organization's long line of maybes at "shortstop of the future?," ahead of Sergio Santos and Jerry Gil. Olson has modest power, speed, and a strong arm. That might make him a nice competitor on American Gladiators, but he's not much of a prospect. Since he can play second or third or the outfield, he might make it as a utility man, except that his erratic play at short makes him a poor roster choice to back up Cintron, who needs a defensive replacement.

LYLE OVERBAY 1B Bats: L Throws: L Born: 28-Jan-77 Age: 27

YEAR	TM	LG	AGE	AB	H	2B	3B	HR	BB	SO	SB	CS	AVG	OBP	SLG	MLVR	EQBA	EQOBP	EQSLG	EQMLVR	VORP	DEFENSE		
2001	ELP	TEX	24	532	187	49	3	13	67	92	5	4	.352	.423	.528	.338	.271	.341	.417	-.029	9.0	106-1B -2	22-LF	-6
2002	TUC	PCL	25	525	180	40	0	19	42	86	0	0	.343	.396	.528	.277	.292	.344	.455	.048	20.6	123-1B -4		
2003	ARI	NL	26	254	70	20	0	4	35	67	1	0	.276	.365	.402	.008	.271	.362	.396	-.020	3.9	71-1B 10		
2003	TUC	PCL	26	119	34	11	0	4	28	19	0	0	.286	.419	.479	.201	.227	.357	.387	-.072	0.5	33-1B 0		
2004	*MIL*	*NL*	*27*	*306*	*79*	*17*	*1*	*10*	*36*	*64*	*2*	*1*	*.259*	*.340*	*.420*	*-.021*	*.261*	*.340*	*.421*	*-.032*	*7.5*	*84-1B 2*		

Breakout: 18%   Improve: 42%   Collapse: 28%

The Snakes gave up on Overbay pretty quickly, but it's not hard to understand why. They wanted power from a power position, and power isn't Overbay's strong suit. Indeed, it's worth wondering why they ever felt it would be otherwise. He's already 27, so while he might be handy for a team hard-up for somebody to get on base, he's basically looking for a couple of years as a regular before he enters that period where he could be in Japan making money, or getting by as somebody's top pinch-hitter. Consider it the Steve Cox career path. A multi-year banishment to Milwaukee should do the trick.

SERGIO SANTOS SS? Bats: R Throws: R Born: 04-Jul-83 Age: 20

YEAR	TM	LG	AGE	AB	H	2B	3B	HR	BB	SO	SB	CS	AVG	OBP	SLG	MLVR	EQBA	EQOBP	EQSLG	EQMLVR	VORP	DEFENSE
2002	MSO	PIO	19	202	55	19	2	9	29	49	6	3	.272	.367	.520	.220	.171	.234	.332	-.419	-25.2	50-SS -11
2003	LNC	CAL	20	341	98	13	2	8	41	64	5	4	.287	.368	.408	.026	.201	.268	.293	-.388	-19.0	84-SS -10
2003	ELP	TEX	20	137	35	7	1	2	8	25	0	0	.255	.293	.365	-.146	.207	.246	.304	-.414	-8.4	35-SS -4
2004	*ARI*	*NL*	*20*	*267*	*56*	*13*	*1*	*6*	*21*	*58*	*2*	*1*	*.211*	*.271*	*.332*	*-.288*	*.204*	*.263*	*.322*	*-.337*	*-10.0*	*72-SS -11*

Breakout: 37%   Improve: 59%   Collapse: 27%

It's hard to get a read on Santos in terms of what he might become. Young, talented, rushed up to Double-A only a year after being drafted in the first round, his meteoric rise has been aided by the launching pads the Snakes favor for their affiliates. Strong-armed and big for a shortstop, he's been terrible afield, committing more than 60 errors in 184 professional games. He did reasonably well at the plate in the high-A California League, impressive for a high school hitter less than a year removed from being drafted, but he wasn't ready for Double-A. The D-Backs' aggressiveness in promotions with younger prospects could really hurt them in some cases. Santos is clearly talented, and just as clearly flawed. He could get screwed up in a hurry, and the likelihood that he's going to be moved off of short should make his young life that much more complicated. He could be a prospect, or he could be the next Jeff Kunkel.

CHRIS SNYDER C Bats: R Throws: R Born: 12-Feb-81 Age: 23

YEAR	TM	LG	AGE	AB	H	2B	3B	HR	BB	SO	SB	CS	AVG	OBP	SLG	MLVR	EQBA	EQOBP	EQSLG	EQMLVR	VORP	DEFENSE
2002	LNC	CAL	21	217	56	16	0	9	25	54	0	0	.258	.337	.456	.036	.184	.251	.332	-.378	-13.4	43-C 4
2003	LNC	CAL	22	245	77	16	2	10	35	43	0	1	.314	.414	.518	.266	.219	.301	.364	-.215	-3.2	56-C -4
2003	ELP	TEX	22	188	38	14	0	4	19	29	0	0	.202	.286	.340	-.218	.160	.230	.282	-.500	-18.6	47-C -2
2004	*ARI*	*NL*	*23*	*254*	*53*	*13*	*1*	*7*	*24*	*53*	*0*	*0*	*.210*	*.286*	*.349*	*-.240*	*.203*	*.277*	*.338*	*-.290*	*-7.9*	*70-C -7*

Breakout: 36%   Improve: 55%   Collapse: 25%

The Snakes have high hopes for Snyder after picking him in the second round of the 2002 draft out of the University of Houston. A big first half at Lancaster (.323/.425/.530) helped draw even more attention to him, but his prospect status relies just as much on his catching skills. After a rude introduction to Double-A, he'll have to regroup at that level, but a solid season could get him a September call-up, at which point he'll be in the picture for 2005.

JUNIOR SPIVEY 2B Bats: R Throws: R Born: 28-Jan-75 Age: 29

YEAR	TM	LG	AGE	AB	H	2B	3B	HR	BB	SO	SB	CS	AVG	OBP	SLG	MLVR	EQBA	EQOBP	EQSLG	EQMLVR	VORP	DEFENSE
2001	TUC	PCL	26	194	45	6	0	6	27	32	9	6	.232	.326	.356	-.206	.181	.272	.280	-.407	-14.6	50-2B 4
2001	ARI	NL	26	163	42	6	3	5	23	47	3	0	.258	.354	.423	-.006	.261	.353	.424	-.006	7.9	43-2B 0
2002	ARI	NL	27	538	162	34	6	16	65	100	11	6	.301	.389	.476	.203	.298	.384	.478	.156	47.3	139-2B 0
2003	ARI	NL	28	365	93	22	2	13	33	95	4	3	.255	.326	.433	-.032	.251	.320	.428	-.069	9.4	90-2B -3
2004	*MIL*	*NL*	*29*	*331*	*85*	*17*	*2*	*12*	*37*	*75*	*5*	*3*	*.256*	*.341*	*.428*	*-.011*	*.258*	*.341*	*.429*	*-.022*	*17.7*	*91-2B -2*

Breakout: 24%   Improve: 52%   Collapse: 21%

After an injury-marred 2003, Spivey is about to become an even greater disappointment. The problem is that he hasn't hit well outside of the BOB, and he really only thumps lefties. The park hid his limitations, to the point that Garagiola seemed certain of his continued success after an appropriately timed "Age 27" career year in 2002. Wisely, Spivey was dealt while he still had value. As a Brewer, Spivey will fit right in: He's superficially valuable-looking, actually fairly limited, and already expensive for what he provides.

LUIS TERRERO   OF   Bats: R   Throws: R   Born: 18-May-80   Age: 24

YEAR	TM	LG	AGE	AB	H	2B	3B	HR	BB	SO	SB	CS	AVG	OBP	SLG	MLVR	EQBA	EQOBP	EQSLG	EQMLVR	VORP	DEFENSE	
2001	LNC	CAL	21	71	32	9	1	4	1	14	5	0	.451	.466	.775	.874	.348	.352	.609	.355	9.7	14-CF	-2
2001	ELP	TEX	21	147	44	13	3	3	4	45	9	2	.299	.331	.490	.101	.248	.271	.421	-.171	-1.0	34-CF	-3
2002	ELP	TEX	22	360	103	20	6	8	23	89	18	22	.286	.342	.442	.075	.228	.271	.368	-.262	-12.3	99-CF	2
2003	TUC	PCL	23	467	134	20	15	3	31	103	23	19	.287	.345	.413	-.003	.243	.299	.359	-.211	-8.6	111-CF	-3
2004	*ARI*	*NL*	*24*	*244*	*63*	*14*	*3*	*6*	*15*	*60*	*7*	*3*	*.256*	*.310*	*.407*	*-.093*	*.247*	*.300*	*.395*	*-.147*	*-1.0*	*66-CF*	*-2*

Breakout: 36%   Improve: 60%   Collapse: 21%

Terrero might make a better outfield reserve than Quinton McCracken right now, although it might stunt the development of a still very raw player. He has the tools that make people pay attention, plus more power than you'd expect from a speed guy, improving patience, and unfortunately too many ill-considered basestealing attempts. He also has the arm and range to be a plus center fielder. That all makes for a useful reserve, but the question is whether Terrero might mature into something more valuable than that. The Snakes may not be the right organization to take the time to find out, and since they have speedy outfielders coming out of their ears, he could be an interesting bit of trade bait.

CHAD TRACY   3B   Bats: L   Throws: R   Born: 22-May-80   Age: 24

YEAR	TM	LG	AGE	AB	H	2B	3B	HR	BB	SO	SB	CS	AVG	OBP	SLG	MLVR	EQBA	EQOBP	EQSLG	EQMLVR	VORP	DEFENSE	
2001	SBN	MID	21	215	73	11	0	4	19	19	3	0	.340	.393	.447	.255	.260	.307	.347	-.201	-1.4	52-3B	-4
2002	ELP	TEX	22	514	177	39	5	8	38	51	2	3	.344	.389	.486	.252	.284	.327	.412	-.052	19.9	112-3B	-6
2003	TUC	PCL	23	522	169	31	4	10	41	52	0	2	.324	.372	.456	.128	.277	.329	.396	-.077	15.9	125-3B	7
2004	*ARI*	*NL*	*24*	*261*	*70*	*16*	*1*	*6*	*23*	*32*	*1*	*1*	*.269*	*.331*	*.401*	*-.055*	*.259*	*.321*	*.389*	*-.109*	*6.7*	*71-3B*	*0*

Breakout: 22%   Improve: 45%   Collapse: 40%

Tracy is casually termed a Boggs type, but that's not the right fit, not when a guy draws all of 38 walks on his own in 576 plate appearances. Of course, nobody compares prospects to Rance Mulliniks. A bit of Magadan name-dropping would fall even wider off the mark, since Tracy was named the best defender at the hot corner in the PCL by *Baseball America*'s tools poll. Bringing up Scott Cooper could be taken entirely the wrong way. Tracy had a big platoon split last year, flailing against lefties, so if he does get a look in the majors as Hillenbrand's caddy and defensive replacement, he'll need to be spotted. But for all that, it's easy to find right-handed hitters to platoon with Tracy, and he's about as big league-ready as a prospect can get. Hopefully, the Snakes won't get frustrated with his relative lack of power as quickly as they did with Overbay.

DAN UGGLA   IF   Bats: R   Throws: R   Born: 11-Mar-80   Age: 24

YEAR	TM	LG	AGE	AB	H	2B	3B	HR	BB	SO	SB	CS	AVG	OBP	SLG	MLVR	EQBA	EQOBP	EQSLG	EQMLVR	VORP	DEFENSE			
2001	YAK	NWN	21	278	77	21	0	5	20	52	8	4	.277	.341	.406	.098	.211	.259	.320	-.363	-29.6	69-2B	-7		
2002	SBN	MID	22	171	34	5	1	2	23	34	0	2	.199	.291	.275	-.180	.157	.227	.219	-.592	-23.0	46-3B	0		
2002	LNC	CAL	22	184	42	7	2	3	21	51	3	2	.228	.311	.337	-.178	.162	.229	.243	-.553	-20.9	30-2B	-4	15-3B	-4
2003	LNC	CAL	23	534	155	31	7	23	46	105	24	9	.290	.355	.504	.137	.211	.265	.373	-.278	-15.1	94-3B	6	40-2B	-2
2004	*ARI*	*NL*	*24*	*235*	*55*	*13*	*1*	*6*	*20*	*51*	*4*	*2*	*.234*	*.300*	*.376*	*-.166*	*.226*	*.290*	*.365*	*-.218*	*-0.3*	*65-3B*	*-1*		

Breakout: 58%   Improve: 70%   Collapse: 15%

Infielders with 60 or more extra-base hits have a way of drawing your attention, but Uggla was old for the level and repeating it, and he was in one of the Cal League's best hitter's parks. If you want a comp, think Tim Unroe or Matt Mieske. That's Uggla's upside.

MARLAND WILLIAMS   **CF**   **Bats: R**   **Throws: R**   Born: 22-Jun-81   Age: 23

YEAR	TM	LG	AGE	AB	H	2B	3B	HR	BB	SO	SB	CS	AVG	OBP	SLG	MLVR	EQBA	EQOBP	EQSLG	EQMLVR	VORP	DEFENSE
2002	YAK	NWN	21	280	69	4	8	3	27	86	51	7	.246	.311	.350	-.003	.196	.243	.285	-.452	-50.1	66-CF -13
2003	LNC	CAL	22	425	122	15	1	4	31	99	57	7	.287	.340	.355	-.092	.215	.260	.270	-.429	-34.4	89-CF -2
2004	ARI	NL	23	260	56	9	3	2	17	69	15	4	.215	.265	.298	-.342	.207	.257	.289	-.390	-16.5	69-CF -9

Breakout: 24%   Improve: 48%   Collapse: 31%

The latest model in the organization's attempt to hoard outfield speed guys. Williams missed nearly a month with a wrist injury, but when he returned, he was plugged into the leadoff slot and center, the two roles he's being groomed for. He's still got a lot to do if he's going to turn into a prospect; 20 extra-base hits in a season in Lancaster is pathetic. He's still very young, but he needs to be.

PITCHERS

GREG AQUINO   **Bats: R**   **Throws: R**   Born: 11-Jan-78   Age: 26

YEAR	TM	LG	AGE	G	GS	IP	H	BB	SO	HR	ERA	EQERA	EQH9	EQBB9	EQSO9	EQHR9	PERA	VORP	STF
2001	YAK	NWN	23	8	8	46.3	39	14	39	2	3.30	5.05	9.9	4.0	4.0	1.1	5.32	2.5	-13
2001	LNC	CAL	23	25	4	42.0	59	24	39	7	8.14	9.00	14.4	6.6	4.7	2.8	10.08	-14.4	-88
2002	YAK	NWN	24	6	6	35.0	26	17	34	0	2.06	3.86	9.5	6.2	4.7	0.3	4.91	5.9	6
2002	LNC	CAL	24	8	8	49.0	50	18	50	3	3.67	4.43	10.9	4.0	5.2	1.0	5.67	5.8	0
2003	ELP	TEX	25	20	20	106.7	115	38	91	5	3.46	4.06	10.1	4.0	5.5	0.8	5.09	17.1	0
2004	ARI	NL	25	21	13	75.3	84	38	51	9	5.30	5.07	9.7	3.9	5.6	1.0	5.13	5.0	-3

Breakout: 26%   Improve: 59%   Collapse: 20%

A converted shortstop, Aquino showed that, if nothing else, he had the arm for the position, regularly touching the high 90s. He struggled with some shoulder soreness that shut him down for nearly two months, and he does not have a consistent second pitch yet. He could be something very special, or Felix Rodriguez, or he could wind up like Tris Jerue, a converted position player who blows out his arm in the minors, never to be heard from again. The Snakes provide good coaching and seem to manage their young arms sensibly, so his chances are good.

MIGUEL BATISTA   **Bats: R**   **Throws: R**   Born: 19-Feb-71   Age: 33

YEAR	TM	LG	AGE	G	GS	IP	H	BB	SO	HR	ERA	EQERA	EQH9	EQBB9	EQSO9	EQHR9	PERA	VORP	STF
2001	ARI	NL	30	48	18	139.3	113	60	90	13	3.36	3.65	7.6	3.6	4.9	0.7	3.80	28.8	1
2002	ARI	NL	31	36	29	184.7	172	70	112	12	4.29	4.15	8.4	3.0	4.8	0.6	3.81	28.7	11
2003	ARI	NL	32	36	29	193.3	197	60	142	13	3.54	3.70	9.1	2.5	5.9	0.6	3.96	41.0	21
2004	TOR	NL	33	29	23	140.3	143	50	95	12	4.19	4.20	9.1	2.8	5.5	0.7	4.10	20.7	7

Breakout: 19%   Improve: 49%   Collapse: 21%

The self-described "utility pitcher" made it clear how little that title suits him anymore. He's become a nifty power-groundball pitcher with age, and although the Snakes were one of the worst defensive infields around, he was strong enough to put up one of the top seasons in the league. You can overstate his indestructibility, considering that he set a career high for innings pitched and still didn't make 30 starts or reach 200 IP, but at his age, he should be fine. As a Blue Jay, he's going to get better support offensively and defensively, so if he can handle 30+ starts, he's going to have a significantly better year than that projection suggests.

BRIAN BRUNEY   **Bats: R**   **Throws: R**   Born: 17-Feb-82   Age: 22

YEAR	TM	LG	AGE	G	GS	IP	H	BB	SO	HR	ERA	EQERA	EQH9	EQBB9	EQSO9	EQHR9	PERA	VORP	STF
2001	YAK	NWN	19	15	0	21.0	19	11	28	2	5.14	7.64	11.7	7.1	6.6	2.5	8.59	-4.0	-28
2001	SBN	MID	19	26	0	32.7	24	19	40	1	4.13	5.97	8.5	7.5	7.2	0.6	5.10	-1.2	16
2002	SBN	MID	20	37	0	48.3	37	17	54	1	1.68	3.95	8.7	4.4	6.2	0.4	4.16	7.9	19
2002	ELP	TEX	20	10	0	12.3	11	4	14	1	2.93	3.86	8.5	3.1	8.5	1.5	4.82	2.3	26
2003	ELP	TEX	21	28	0	31.3	29	13	28	1	2.59	4.20	7.8	4.5	6.0	0.6	3.97	4.7	14
2003	TUC	PCL	21	32	0	32.0	24	18	32	0	2.81	3.19	5.8	5.8	8.7	0.3	3.13	8.3	43
2004	ARI	NL	22	25	1	31.0	30	22	30	3	5.10	4.87	8.3	5.4	8.0	0.8	4.89	4.4	0

Breakout: 17%   Improve: 46%   Collapse: 23%

With heat in the mid-90s and a hard slider, you can understand why people think Bruney's going to be an effective big league reliever. But it wasn't automatic. Coaching improved his mechanics, giving him consistency and command, and coaching tweaked the slider to make it an excellent alternative to his heat. He was named the Texas League's best reliever in *Baseball America*'s tools poll, but suffered the indignity of being the man on the spot in Team USA's elimination from the Olympics. He'll get a look in camp and will pitch in the BOB at some point this summer, perhaps stepping into Valverde's setup role after Mantei breaks down again.

CHRIS CAPUANO   Bats: L   Throws: L   Born: 19-Aug-78   Age: 25

YEAR	TM	LG	AGE	G	GS	IP	H	BB	SO	HR	ERA	EQERA	EQH9	EQBB9	EQSO9	EQHR9	PERA	VORP	STF
2001	ELP	TEX	22	28	28	159.3	184	75	167	13	5.31	5.48	10.6	5.0	6.5	1.1	5.92	2.0	9
2002	TUC	PCL	23	6	6	36.3	30	11	29	1	2.73	3.12	7.3	3.1	5.7	0.3	3.02	9.6	36
2003	TUC	PCL	24	23	23	142.7	133	43	108	9	3.34	3.72	8.3	3.2	5.8	0.8	4.03	28.3	17
2003	ARI	NL	24	9	5	33.0	27	11	23	3	4.64	3.66	7.3	2.8	5.6	0.8	3.51	2.8	16
2004	*MIL*	*NL*	*25*	*22*	*15*	*89.3*	*90*	*39*	*67*	*11*	*4.64*	*4.76*	*9.1*	*3.4*	*6.1*	*0.9*	*4.70*	*8.4*	*3*

Breakout: 15%   Improve: 46%   Collapse: 28%

Wow, within months, Garagiola traded both David Dellucci and Capuano? What's a paesan to do, if he can't trust his own people? Capuano's another example of the changing timetables for medically altered careers: He made a quick recovery from last year's Tommy John surgery, throwing in spring training only nine months after his operation. For a guy who was supposed to go through the usual struggle of getting reacquainted with his arm, Capuano didn't have much trouble with his command. Although there's been speculation that he'll wind up in a relief role—lefties who don't crack 90 usually get mentioned this way—he doesn't sport a big platoon split, and the Brewers could do a lot worse than putting Cappy into their rotation. The real key will be to see if his improved post-surgery control sticks, because if it does, he will.

ELMER DESSENS   Bats: R   Throws: R   Born: 13-Jan-72   Age: 32

YEAR	TM	LG	AGE	G	GS	IP	H	BB	SO	HR	ERA	EQERA	EQH9	EQBB9	EQSO9	EQHR9	PERA	VORP	STF
2001	CIN	NL	29	34	34	205.0	221	56	128	32	4.48	4.44	9.4	2.3	4.7	1.2	4.73	25.6	-1
2002	CIN	NL	30	30	30	178.0	173	49	93	24	3.03	3.89	8.7	2.2	4.1	1.2	4.41	32.5	-2
2003	ARI	NL	31	34	30	175.7	212	57	113	22	5.07	5.06	10.7	2.6	5.1	1.1	5.27	9.2	-2
2004	*ARI*	*NL*	*32*	*28*	*24*	*143.7*	*163*	*45*	*84*	*20*	*4.69*	*4.48*	*9.9*	*2.4*	*4.9*	*1.1*	*4.66*	*18.2*	*2*

Breakout: 16%   Improve: 45%   Collapse: 22%

There are bold strokes that are bold for their own sake, but the Snakes pretty much have to regret their participation in the four-team swap that got Billy Beane Erubiel Durazo while sticking Arizona with a five-inning fifth starter. It doesn't take too long a look at these numbers to notice that the one anomaly was Dessens's ERA in 2002. The Snakes and Dessens claim they're going to work on his conditioning in the off-season, to help with his problems by the time he's gone through a lineup twice. But conditioning won't alter a basic problem: He doesn't fool people. Dessens is simply a pretty good fifth starter, if that isn't an oxymoron.

JARED DOYLE   Bats: L   Throws: L   Born: 30-Jan-81   Age: 23

YEAR	TM	LG	AGE	G	GS	IP	H	BB	SO	HR	ERA	EQERA	EQH9	EQBB9	EQSO9	EQHR9	PERA	VORP	STF
2002	YAK	NWN	21	16	8	62.7	44	29	70	1	2.87	4.58	8.7	5.7	5.4	0.5	4.60	6.2	9
2003	SBN	MID	22	27	26	148.7	124	65	93	6	2.78	5.75	10.1	5.7	3.9	1.2	6.00	-2.1	-18
2004	*ARI*	*NL*	*23*	*15*	*11*	*55.0*	*71*	*42*	*25*	*10*	*7.65*	*7.31*	*11.2*	*6.0*	*3.8*	*1.4*	*7.20*	*-1.4*	*-28*

Breakout: 28%   Improve: 65%   Collapse: 21%

No, he's not Jared the Subway guy, he's a lefty with heat that's routinely in the low 90s, and there's nothing more Pavlovian than the speed with which a lefty with velocity goes straight onto almost anybody's prospect radar. He's a long, long way off from the majors, but he had a solid first full season, avoided major injury, and did we mention he's a lefty who throws hard?

EDGAR GONZALEZ Bats: R Throws: R Born: 23-Feb-83 Age: 21

YEAR	TM	LG	AGE	G	GS	IP	H	BB	SO	HR	ERA	EQERA	EQH9	EQBB9	EQSO9	EQHR9	PERA	VORP	STF
2002	SBN	MID	19	23	23	151.3	141	34	110	4	2.91	4.91	9.0	2.6	4.0	0.6	3.99	10.8	22
2002	LNC	CAL	19	4	4	23.0	24	3	21	1	0.78	3.63	9.3	1.2	4.8	0.4	3.51	4.9	37
2003	ELP	TEX	20	6	6	36.0	40	11	30	1	3.50	4.33	8.7	3.3	5.9	0.5	3.93	5.0	37
2003	TUC	PCL	20	20	19	129.7	126	28	69	4	3.75	3.72	7.2	2.2	4.5	0.3	2.74	26.8	37
2003	ARI	NL	20	9	2	18.3	28	7	14	3	4.92	5.50	13.5	3.0	6.0	1.5	7.14	2.1	11
2004	ARI	NL	21	19	16	95.3	98	33	59	8	3.94	3.77	8.9	2.7	5.1	0.6	3.91	19.2	6

Breakout: 27%   Improve: 65%   Collapse: 2%

Sure, there's no such thing as a pitching prospect, but . . . if there were such things as pitching prospects, Gonzalez would be somewhere around the top of the short list. He's got exceptional command, avoids extra-base hits like a Bush dodges broccoli, keeps the ball on the ground, and has fine mechanics. Other than last year's cup of coffee, he has yet to struggle at any level, which as a young pitcher in Arizona's collection of bandboxed affiliates, is no easy feat. His June stint in the big league rotation was the product of injuries, but he'll get every opportunity to win that spot back in spring training. His low K rates remain his only flaw: With low-90s velocity and four pitches he can throw for strikes, Gonzalez is on the cusp of putting it all together.

ANDREW GOOD Bats: R Throws: R Born: 19-Sep-79 Age: 24

YEAR	TM	LG	AGE	G	GS	IP	H	BB	SO	HR	ERA	EQERA	EQH9	EQBB9	EQSO9	EQHR9	PERA	VORP	STF
2001	LNC	CAL	21	19	18	101.3	108	27	104	12	4.80	5.36	10.6	3.1	5.2	1.8	6.23	2.5	-5
2001	ELP	TEX	21	10	9	56.7	79	20	46	2	5.87	6.11	11.2	3.5	5.1	0.5	5.14	-3.2	19
2002	ELP	TEX	22	28	27	178.0	170	26	127	21	3.54	4.66	9.8	1.5	4.8	2.0	5.64	17.1	-5
2003	TUC	PCL	23	11	11	63.0	78	13	45	12	5.00	5.37	10.9	2.1	5.7	2.2	6.58	1.5	-13
2003	ARI	NL	23	16	10	66.3	74	16	42	15	5.29	5.18	9.8	2.0	5.0	2.0	5.68	2.0	-8
2004	ARI	NL	24	23	16	93.3	102	27	62	15	4.95	4.73	9.5	2.3	5.6	1.3	4.54	10.6	2

Breakout: 16%   Improve: 52%   Collapse: 25%

Good has made a decent recovery from his elbow surgery in 2000. He put on a solid big league debut, making five quality starts in 10 outings. However, right-handed junkballers have to catch every break, and compared to guys like Webb or Villareal, he wasn't particularly inspiring. Given the organization's wealth of young pitching talent, Good is in a tough place. After struggling following his demotion in July, he was left in the minors, not even meriting a September cuppajoe. He'll get consideration for a spot in the rotation in camp, but more likely, he'll be one of the Snakes' first alternates out of Tucson.

MIKE GOSLING Bats: L Throws: L Born: 23-Sep-80 Age: 23

YEAR	TM	LG	AGE	G	GS	IP	H	BB	SO	HR	ERA	EQERA	EQH9	EQBB9	EQSO9	EQHR9	PERA	VORP	STF
2002	ELP	TEX	21	27	27	166.7	149	62	115	7	3.13	4.06	8.1	3.8	4.7	0.6	3.96	26.9	22
2003	TUC	PCL	22	26	26	136.3	190	56	89	13	5.61	6.65	11.1	4.2	5.3	1.0	5.83	-15.6	3
2004	ARI	NL	23	15	12	67.0	78	36	42	10	5.90	5.64	10.1	4.2	5.2	1.2	5.62	3.3	-7

Breakout: 17%   Improve: 43%   Collapse: 28%

Gosling came into 2003 needing to show that he could repeat a full season in the minors. He did that—sort of—but was unfortunately mauled by the PCL before finally being diagnosed with a labrum tear that was fixed after the season. As a result, he's only exacerbated concerns that he might be a lot more hype than hope. The organization talks him up, which you'd expect when it comes to somebody who has terms like "Stanford," "Boras," "lefty," and "90+ heat" knocking around on his resume. But after a merely decent debut in 2002, and a 2003 where he struggled to get right-handed hitters out before going under the knife, he'll enter 2004 rehabbing, and may not be ready to mount a challenge for a big league job until after the All-Star break. Even then, he's going to have pitch better to earn that consideration.

RANDY JOHNSON Bats: R Throws: L Born: 10-Sep-63 Age: 40

YEAR	TM	LG	AGE	G	GS	IP	H	BB	SO	HR	ERA	EQERA	EQH9	EQBB9	EQSO9	EQHR9	PERA	VORP	STF
2001	ARI	NL	37	35	34	249.7	181	71	372	19	2.49	2.68	7.3	2.4	11.5	0.6	3.08	77.2	63
2002	ARI	NL	38	35	35	260.0	197	71	334	26	2.32	2.77	7.2	2.2	10.1	0.9	3.27	78.6	48
2003	ARI	NL	39	18	18	114.0	125	27	125	16	4.26	4.39	9.9	1.9	8.7	1.2	4.78	13.9	24
2004	ARI	NL	40	22	20	133.3	118	41	141	14	3.51	3.35	7.7	2.4	8.8	0.8	3.26	33.3	33

Breakout: 7%   Improve: 20%   Collapse: 33%

All those years, we worried that his arm would burn out, but Johnson's freakish build and his relentless conditioning meant that we were worried about the wrong joints. It isn't his arm that's breaking down, but his knees. Watch him carefully in camp, because there's real concern that he'll never be the workhorse he once was. It would be a shame to see him reduced to Sunday starter or a John Tudor/in-season trump role, but he may not be capable of more.

Not that he's a bad guy, but how does a pitcher with his command yet almost 150 hit batsmen on his career not get a headhunter rep? While a lot of it was in his wild, early days as a Mariner, he tied his single-season career high (18) in 2001. Johnson's at 146 on his career; the top five since the Deadball Era are Charlie Hough (174), Senator Jim Bunning (160), Nolan Ryan (158), Bert Blyleven (155), and Don Drysdale (154). If you're curious, Roger Clemens retired with 141, while Pedro's next victim will be his 100th. Some people just make better stories than others, apparently. Anyway, as a knuckleballer, Hough can be forgiven, although it's interesting to note Phil Niekro isn't on this list. But the other four were known to have mean/"competitive" streaks, and Johnson deserves similar regard.

MIKE KOPLOVE

Bats: R   Throws: R   Born: 30-Aug-76   Age: 27

YEAR	TM	LG	AGE	G	GS	IP	H	BB	SO	HR	ERA	EQERA	EQH9	EQBB9	EQSO9	EQHR9	PERA	VORP	STF
2001	ELP	TEX	24	34	0	44.0	44	19	43	3	2.66	3.67	9.3	4.5	6.0	0.9	4.92	8.9	-6
2001	TUC	PCL	24	17	0	22.3	17	10	22	1	2.83	2.57	6.9	4.7	6.4	0.4	3.44	7.1	15
2001	ARI	NL	24	9	0	10.0	8	9	14	1	3.60	5.59	8.4	7.4	10.2	0.9	5.28	0.0	16
2002	TUC	PCL	25	23	0	30.7	21	4	31	1	1.17	1.88	6.6	1.3	6.9	0.3	2.24	11.9	32
2002	ARI	NL	25	55	0	61.7	47	23	46	2	3.35	3.03	7.0	2.9	5.9	0.3	2.87	16.9	20
2003	ARI	NL	26	31	0	37.7	31	10	27	3	2.15	2.72	7.4	2.2	5.7	0.7	3.29	13.2	9
2004	ARI	NL	27	43	2	60.0	57	22	45	5	3.75	3.58	8.3	2.9	6.2	0.7	3.66	13.2	2

Breakout: 23%   Improve: 57%   Collapse: 19%

He doesn't garner the same attention as Mantei, but some feel Koplove is beginning to look equally fragile after a season that seemed lost to perpetual throwing sessions and indeterminate shoulder soreness. Still, Koplove's September shoulder surgery didn't reveal any major damage, and he's supposed to be good to go for spring training. If he is and Mantei's dealt, he'll be Valverde's primary setup man, perhaps nabbing a save opportunity here and there if the kid has a bad weekend or it's Coors Field or something.

SERGIO LIZARRAGA

Bats: R   Throws: R   Born: 23-Jul-81   Age: 22

YEAR	TM	LG	AGE	G	GS	IP	H	BB	SO	HR	ERA	EQERA	EQH9	EQBB9	EQSO9	EQHR9	PERA	VORP	STF
2001	MSO	PIO	19	15	15	81.3	104	23	57	10	5.09	9.29	14.6	3.8	3.4	2.6	9.30	29.4	-42
2002	YAK	NWN	20	16	13	91.0	90	19	86	6	4.05	6.16	11.9	2.6	4.7	1.8	6.67	-5.0	-6
2003	SBN	MID	21	42	9	96.0	71	29	85	6	1.78	3.90	9.5	3.9	5.5	1.8	5.96	15.7	-13
2004	ARI	NL	22	15	6	35.7	45	16	23	7	6.61	6.32	10.8	3.6	5.3	1.7	6.28	-0.9	-15

Breakout: 12%   Improve: 49%   Collapse: 23%

Lizarraga started the year as one of the organization's Mexican flyers, a spare arm with a prayer, but basically getting innings where he could. The maddening nature of pegging pitchers with futures being what it is, he finished the year as South Bend's ace starter down the stretch. While he can throw four pitches for strikes, he's crafty, and his breakthrough was courtesy of an improved changeup. He's got a lot to prove going forward, but he put himself on the map and bears watching.

MATT MANTEI

Bats: R   Throws: R   Born: 07-Jul-73   Age: 30

YEAR	TM	LG	AGE	G	GS	IP	H	BB	SO	HR	ERA	EQERA	EQH9	EQBB9	EQSO9	EQHR9	PERA	VORP	STF
2001	ARI	NL	28	8	0	7.0	6	4	12	2	2.57	4.05	8.1	5.4	13.5	2.7	6.50	1.2	-7
2002	ARI	NL	29	31	0	26.7	28	12	26	3	4.72	4.85	9.7	3.5	7.6	1.0	4.96	2.2	0
2003	ARI	NL	30	50	0	55.0	37	18	68	6	2.62	2.53	6.2	2.7	9.8	0.8	2.93	18.4	33
2004	ARI	NL	30	48	3	69.7	60	26	74	9	3.61	3.45	7.5	2.9	8.9	1.0	3.56	18.3	16

Breakout: 31%   Improve: 48%   Collapse: 20%

To paraphrase our own injury guru, Will Carroll, Mantei's natural state is injured. But Mantei had his '99, as did Rudy Seanez, and Chad Fox had his 2001, and people will keep hoping that these types can keep doing that sort of thing. They won't, but for the right price—like the Marlins nabbing Fox on waivers—a quality reliever with nasty movement and a little problem with being able to pitch on demand can be useful. The problem is that nobody should count on such a pitcher, and with his reputation and expense, Mantei is considered far more valuable than he'll ever actually be. If they're lucky, the Snakes won't be the only team that overrates and overpays in Mantei's case.

BRANDON MEDDERS   Bats: R   Throws: R   Born: 26-Jan-80   Age: 24

YEAR	TM	LG	AGE	G	GS	IP	H	BB	SO	HR	ERA	EQERA	EQH9	EQBB9	EQSO9	EQHR9	PERA	VORP	STF
2001	LNC	CAL	21	31	0	41.0	26	15	53	1	1.32	1.91	6.7	4.3	6.5	0.5	3.30	15.5	25
2002	LNC	CAL	22	43	12	98.7	111	36	104	9	5.38	6.58	11.8	4.1	5.4	1.4	6.52	-9.8	-20
2003	ELP	TEX	23	56	0	69.3	65	26	72	3	4.42	4.27	8.5	4.1	6.7	0.7	4.27	9.6	8
2004	*ARI*	*NL*	*24*	*15*	*7*	*40.7*	*42*	*20*	*33*	*5*	*4.69*	*4.49*	*8.9*	*3.8*	*6.7*	*0.9*	*4.63*	*5.7*	*2*

Breakout: 25%   Improve: 52%   Collapse: 22%

It doesn't look like much of a career so far, but there are a couple of mitigating circumstances. First, he was a flop as a starter in the Cal League in '02, posting an ERA of 7.85. As a reliever, he averaged more than 12 strikeouts per nine innings, and had an ERA of 1.96. Second, going up to Double-A in El Paso is tough, and he still managed to mow people down pretty well. Finally, the unexpected appearance of a nifty curve in the AFL got Medders onto the 40-man roster. He's already got good heat out of a tight, short-armed delivery, and while he ranks behind guys like Valverde or Bruney, he's not too far from earning a shot as a big league setup man.

MIKE MYERS   Bats: L   Throws: L   Born: 26-Jun-69   Age: 35

YEAR	TM	LG	AGE	G	GS	IP	H	BB	SO	HR	ERA	EQERA	EQH9	EQBB9	EQSO9	EQHR9	PERA	VORP	STF
2001	COL	NL	32	73	0	40.0	32	24	36	2	3.60	3.26	7.4	4.9	6.8	0.5	3.78	10.1	9
2002	ARI	NL	33	69	0	37.0	39	17	31	2	4.38	4.25	9.8	3.5	6.5	0.5	4.45	5.4	5
2003	ARI	NL	34	64	0	36.3	38	21	21	4	5.70	5.05	9.1	4.5	4.5	1.0	5.01	1.1	-24
2004	*ARI*	*NL*	*35*	*36*	*1*	*43.0*	*45*	*24*	*29*	*4*	*4.89*	*4.68*	*9.0*	*4.4*	*5.6*	*0.8*	*4.93*	*4.4*	*-11*

Breakout: 28%   Improve: 42%   Collapse: 27%

A traditional Joe Garagiola Jr.-oriented consumer item: aged reliever carpaccio, with uncertain reliability but for just enough expense that it makes you think "quality." At his age, after faltering in the primary LOOGY role, Myers will be lucky to get more than a NRI to spring training, but like Jesse Orosco, he'll be a near-lock to make the team. The real question is if he's worth the roster space; Orosco hasn't been for a while, and Myers isn't demonstrably more useful than an organizational soldier like Stephen Randolph.

DUSTIN NIPPERT   Bats: R   Throws: R   Born: 06-May-81   Age: 23

YEAR	TM	LG	AGE	G	GS	IP	H	BB	SO	HR	ERA	EQERA	EQH9	EQBB9	EQSO9	EQHR9	PERA	VORP	STF
2002	MSO	PIO	21	17	11	54.7	42	9	77	2	1.65	2.64	10.4	2.1	6.6	0.9	4.80	15.7	19
2003	SBN	MID	22	17	17	95.7	66	32	96	4	2.82	4.35	9.1	4.4	6.2	1.2	5.16	11.5	7
2004	*ARI*	*NL*	*23*	*21*	*15*	*85.0*	*91*	*38*	*68*	*11*	*5.19*	*4.97*	*9.3*	*3.5*	*6.7*	*1.1*	*4.82*	*7.7*	*5*

Breakout: 9%   Improve: 44%   Collapse: 23%

Nippert is the sort of prospect that scouts have to wear bibs around. At 6′7″ with a power arm that delivers a nasty curve as well, can you blame them? In another credit to the organization's minor league instruction, a few mechanical tweaks after he was drafted added velocity, so that he's now a mid-90s flamethrower. He missed time early on in 2003 after having a benign tumor removed from his shoulder, but quickly reminded everyone he might be the organization's prize with a great stint in the AFL. The Snakes aren't afraid to push kids up the ladder, and Nippert is far more breakout consideration-worthy than PECOTA seems to allow.

EDDIE OROPESA   Bats: L   Throws: L   Born: 23-Nov-71   Age: 32

YEAR	TM	LG	AGE	G	GS	IP	H	BB	SO	HR	ERA	EQERA	EQH9	EQBB9	EQSO9	EQHR9	PERA	VORP	STF
2001	SWB	INT	29	14	1	15.3	14	4	11	1	2.35	4.50	9.6	2.6	5.1	0.6	4.31	1.7	-6
2001	PHI	NL	29	30	0	19.0	16	17	15	1	4.74	4.91	7.9	7.4	5.9	0.5	4.67	1.4	-11
2002	TUC	PCL	30	29	0	25.7	23	13	26	2	3.85	4.18	9.1	5.3	6.8	0.8	4.94	3.7	-10
2002	ARI	NL	30	32	0	25.3	39	15	18	6	10.32	9.49	13.9	4.7	5.5	2.2	8.57	-10.7	-68
2003	TUC	PCL	31	15	0	15.3	14	4	9	0	2.35	2.51	8.2	2.5	4.4	0.0	3.03	4.9	13
2003	ARI	NL	31	47	0	38.7	38	27	39	3	5.81	5.21	9.0	5.4	7.8	0.7	4.84	-1.2	0
2004	*SDP*	*NL*	*32*	*35*	*0*	*42.3*	*43*	*25*	*35*	*4*	*4.90*	*5.37*	*9.3*	*4.7*	*6.6*	*0.7*	*5.29*	*1.3*	*-7*

Breakout: 28%   Improve: 47%   Collapse: 27%

Mike Myers's struggles, combined with the problems in the rotation created a deepening sense of desperation, convinced Brenly to get even more managerial as the season progressed. As a result, he needed extra situational lefties, and that meant Oropesa getting the biggest break he's ever going to get. If you're wildly optimistic, you might recall that Tony Fossas didn't get to stick in the bigs until he was 31, but the difference is that Fossas could pitch. Oropesa's wild without being dominant, consistently blowing situations with runners on. Now a Pad person.

JOHN PATTERSON Bats: R Throws: R Born: 30-Jan-78 Age: 26

YEAR	TM	LG	AGE	G	GS	IP	H	BB	SO	HR	ERA	EQERA	EQH9	EQBB9	EQSO9	EQHR9	PERA	VORP	STF
2001	ELP	TEX	23	5	5	25.3	30	9	19	2	4.27	4.81	10.4	3.7	4.4	1.1	5.48	2.1	-6
2001	TUC	PCL	23	13	12	67.7	82	31	40	9	5.85	5.86	9.7	4.6	4.0	1.2	5.57	-1.9	-14
2002	TUC	PCL	24	19	18	112.7	117	45	104	14	4.23	5.04	10.0	4.1	6.3	1.4	5.66	6.6	-1
2002	ARI	NL	24	7	5	30.7	27	7	31	7	3.22	3.68	8.3	1.8	8.0	2.1	5.05	6.3	8
2003	TUC	PCL	25	18	18	109.3	100	43	74	6	2.63	3.65	8.0	4.2	5.1	0.7	4.07	22.5	8
2003	ARI	NL	25	16	8	55.0	61	30	43	7	6.05	5.53	9.9	4.4	6.2	1.0	5.29	-2.3	-3
2004	ARI	NL	26	23	15	86.7	91	43	63	13	5.32	5.08	9.1	3.9	6.0	1.1	5.00	6.1	-2

Breakout: 21%   Improve: 47%   Collapse: 20%

Patterson was handed all sorts of opportunities to finally realize his long-awaited potential last year, and consistently blew every one of them. Although he's well beyond the expected recovery period from Tommy John surgery, mechanically, he's still not right; he still puts too much pressure on his elbow, and he still doesn't have the control you'd like to see. His curve is still a thing of beauty, but with the horde of talented Snakelings pushing for pitching jobs, Patterson is about to be superseded en masse. He should earn a crack at the rotation for Opening Day, but from there, it's up to him to fend off notions of making him a reliever.

BELTRAN PEREZ Bats: R Throws: R Born: 24-Oct-81 Age: 22

YEAR	TM	LG	AGE	G	GS	IP	H	BB	SO	HR	ERA	EQERA	EQH9	EQBB9	EQSO9	EQHR9	PERA	VORP	STF
2001	SBN	MID	19	27	27	160.0	142	35	157	10	2.81	4.72	9.7	2.7	5.6	1.2	4.97	14.2	24
2002	ELP	TEX	20	20	19	97.0	114	33	77	10	5.47	6.73	10.6	3.4	5.7	1.5	5.89	-11.6	8
2002	LNC	CAL	20	5	5	32.3	31	3	30	1	2.51	3.23	9.1	0.9	4.7	0.3	3.24	8.1	38
2003	ELP	TEX	21	29	20	147.7	180	54	88	13	5.30	5.73	9.9	4.0	4.0	1.3	5.61	-2.1	-5
2004	ARI	NL	22	15	10	57.7	67	25	33	9	5.67	5.42	10.1	3.4	4.8	1.2	5.28	3.5	-8

Breakout: 7%   Improve: 50%   Collapse: 33%

For all the success that the D-Backs have had finding talent in Mexico, it needs to be remembered that they're chasing down Dominicans too. Perez is still a wisp of a pitcher struggling to make that huge leap to Double-A at an early age and through one of the least pitching-friendly venues at the level. He's not a power pitcher, but more of a command type that they're hoping fills out and picks up velocity. The best you can say is that he endured in his trial by fire as a Diablo, and he's still standing.

STEPHEN RANDOLPH Bats: L Throws: L Born: 01-May-74 Age: 30

YEAR	TM	LG	AGE	G	GS	IP	H	BB	SO	HR	ERA	EQERA	EQH9	EQBB9	EQSO9	EQHR9	PERA	VORP	STF
2001	ELP	TEX	27	18	14	75.0	69	53	66	11	5.16	5.48	9.0	7.7	5.5	2.2	7.16	0.9	-67
2001	TUC	PCL	27	18	0	21.3	24	19	16	2	6.34	5.85	9.9	9.4	4.9	0.9	6.52	-0.6	-48
2002	TUC	PCL	28	28	27	163.3	151	81	129	15	3.47	4.33	9.0	5.1	5.4	1.1	5.18	21.4	-11
2003	ARI	NL	29	50	0	60.0	50	43	50	7	4.05	4.12	7.5	5.6	6.6	0.9	4.45	11.2	-6
2004	ARI	NL	30	28	3	39.7	44	28	29	7	6.16	5.89	9.6	5.6	6.2	1.4	6.19	-0.4	-16

Breakout: 14%   Improve: 41%   Collapse: 29%

Randolph is not a situational type, instead making a solid long reliever and emergency starter. If you're left-handed, you don't have to pitch for food—people will take the time to wait on you to see what you might do. Although Randolph lost most of '99 and 2000 to injury, and didn't help himself in 2001, a big year in the Sidewinders' rotation in 2002 arguably saved his career. While he didn't get much opportunity in 2003, he was also a pretty good hitter (15 for 45) in 2002. In a move many a Strat-O-Matic manager (or Ned Yost with Brooks Kieschnick) might recognize, it might make sense for the Snakes to let Randolph hit for himself now and again.

ADRIANO ROSARIO   Bats: R   Throws: R   Born: 16-May-85   Age: 19

YEAR	TM	LG	AGE	G	GS	IP	H	BB	SO	HR	ERA	EQERA	EQH9	EQBB9	EQSO9	EQHR9	PERA	VORP	STF
2002	MSO	PIO	17	4	4	20.0	26	3	14	0	6.30	7.11	11.8	1.9	3.3	0.5	4.99	-3.2	11
2003	SBN	MID	18	27	27	160.3	149	30	119	3	2.86	5.44	9.5	2.3	4.8	0.4	3.95	2.6	33

A Dominican as green as grass but already throwing consistently in the mid-90s, Rosario bears watching because of his talent and success despite much experience. He was signed in 2002, so that's the sum of his career, and while older Latin players struggle to adapt to life in the States upon being imported, Rosario started off well and only seems to be improving. As with anybody this young and this raw, he could flame out faster than you'll remember him, but the Snakes have so much pitching talent that somebody's going to make it.

CURT SCHILLING   Bats: R   Throws: R   Born: 14-Nov-66   Age: 37

YEAR	TM	LG	AGE	G	GS	IP	H	BB	SO	HR	ERA	EQERA	EQH9	EQBB9	EQSO9	EQHR9	PERA	VORP	STF
2001	ARI	NL	34	35	35	256.7	237	39	293	37	2.98	3.36	8.9	1.3	8.8	1.1	4.04	60.7	33
2002	ARI	NL	35	36	35	259.3	218	33	316	29	3.23	3.05	7.9	1.0	9.6	1.0	3.38	70.3	45
2003	ARI	NL	36	24	24	168.0	144	32	194	17	2.95	2.88	7.8	1.6	9.3	0.9	3.35	50.6	45
2004	BOS	AL	37	29	28	186.3	175	38	177	23	3.35	3.19	7.9	1.7	8.5	1.0	3.28	55.8	32

Breakout: 15%   Improve: 45%   Collapse: 34%

Now that the Rocket's name is permanently blackened in Beantown by his happy ending in pinstripes, is there anyone better equipped to be the equally beefy doppelganger in Boston's emotional landscape? We know he's great when healthy, and you ought to worry that, reunited with Terry Francona, he'll get to dictate how long he stays in the game again. Schilling is at an age where he may not be good for 30 starts, multiplying the Pedro problem by two. But even so, Schilling is moving out of a bandbox that tacked a half-run onto his ERA, and away from a weak defensive club. He's going to a more neutral park and playing for a team built to score runs anywhere, anytime. Sure, he'll have to face DHs, but he won't have to face the Red Sox. It isn't hard to envision an ERA under 3.00 in 20–25 starts, and if the self-management issue doesn't get out of hand, one of those insanely high winning percentage seasons you saw from David Cone and still get from Pedro.

PHIL STOCKMAN   Bats: R   Throws: R   Born: 25-Jan-80   Age: 24

YEAR	TM	LG	AGE	G	GS	IP	H	BB	SO	HR	ERA	EQERA	EQH9	EQBB9	EQSO9	EQHR9	PERA	VORP	STF
2001	LNC	CAL	21	8	0	17.7	11	9	18	2	5.08	4.50	6.8	6.2	5.1	1.7	5.12	2.0	-17
2001	YAK	NWN	21	15	14	76.0	81	22	48	5	4.26	6.82	11.1	3.8	2.9	1.7	6.59	-9.3	-31
2002	LNC	CAL	22	20	20	108.3	91	58	108	10	4.40	5.02	8.8	6.0	5.1	1.5	5.79	6.4	-11
2003	ELP	TEX	23	26	26	147.7	137	64	146	9	3.96	4.34	8.4	4.8	6.4	1.0	4.70	19.5	12
2003	TUC	PCL	23	2	1	9.0	8	4	5	0	1.00	2.08	7.3	4.2	4.2	0.0	3.10	3.4	26
2004	ARI	NL	24	19	13	69.7	77	43	52	11	5.98	5.71	9.6	4.8	6.2	1.2	5.69	2.7	-6

Breakout: 20%   Improve: 51%   Collapse: 19%

A big (6′ 7″) Australian project with a good delivery, Stockman was signed by the Snakes in 1997, and is only now rounding into something. A torn labrum cost him a couple of years, so his career didn't really start until 2000, but 2003 was a huge step forward. His problem is consistency. His fastball can flirt with the low 90s, but usually dips under. He basically needs mound experience; last year represents almost 40% of his career total of professional innings pitched.

JOSE VALVERDE   Bats: R   Throws: R   Born: 24-Jul-79   Age: 24

YEAR	TM	LG	AGE	G	GS	IP	H	BB	SO	HR	ERA	EQERA	EQH9	EQBB9	EQSO9	EQHR9	PERA	VORP	STF
2001	ELP	TEX	21	39	0	41.3	36	27	72	1	3.92	3.96	8.6	7.0	11.4	0.2	4.54	7.1	53
2002	TUC	PCL	22	49	0	47.7	45	23	65	8	5.85	5.76	8.7	4.8	10.1	1.6	5.42	-0.8	17
2003	TUC	PCL	23	22	0	29.0	26	14	26	1	3.10	3.58	7.5	4.9	7.2	0.3	3.65	6.2	22
2003	ARI	NL	23	54	0	50.3	24	26	71	4	2.15	2.39	4.6	4.2	11.2	0.7	2.53	16.5	56
2004	ARI	NL	24	45	8	79.3	64	42	98	9	3.98	3.80	7.0	4.1	10.3	0.9	3.76	15.6	22

Breakout: 24%   Improve: 41%   Collapse: 9%

If he hasn't already, Valverde is about to leap to the head of the class in terms of closers who fill the part as if straight out of central casting. Nearly impossible to hit, triple-digit velocity, and, distinctly from somebody like Scott Garrelts, who could do those things too, Valverde looks ornery enough to close in the eyes of baseball professionals. Advice from

Jose Mercedes produced a slower delivery, which makes for a better contrast to the blazing heat that comes out of that delivery. The nagging concerns are all too predictable: Does he have a second pitch, and can he stay healthy? He wasn't able to say "yes" to either question until last year, and he still needs a second pitch, even if only for show. Brenly pushed his limits early on, using him in seven of eight days shortly after his promotion, and getting five saves. It didn't matter; once Mantei was in one of his unusual healthy stretches, Valverde was back in a supporting role. Going forward, that shouldn't last. Mantei is ridiculously unreliable, so there's no reason to fret about Valverde's relative inexperience.

OSCAR VILLARREAL   Bats: L   Throws: R   Born: 22-Nov-81   Age: 22

YEAR	TM	LG	AGE	G	GS	IP	H	BB	SO	HR	ERA	EQERA	EQH9	EQBB9	EQSO9	EQHR9	PERA	VORP	STF
2001	ELP	TEX	19	27	27	140.7	154	63	108	10	4.41	5.13	8.0	4.6	5.3	0.8	4.27	7.3	25
2002	ELP	TEX	20	14	12	84.3	73	26	85	2	3.74	3.92	7.8	3.1	7.2	0.3	3.33	15.0	52
2002	TUC	PCL	20	10	10	64.0	68	22	40	8	4.36	5.03	8.3	3.3	4.7	1.1	4.46	4.0	19
2003	ARI	NL	21	86	1	98.0	80	46	80	6	2.57	3.30	7.4	3.8	6.5	0.5	3.44	23.7	32
2004	ARI	NL	22	42	9	76.3	77	37	61	9	4.73	4.52	8.7	3.8	6.6	0.9	4.49	9.8	-1

Breakout: 10%   Improve: 35%   Collapse: 32%

While not exactly deserving to be consigned to fate as the third wheel among the Snakes' trio of outstanding rookie pitchers, Villareal didn't rate with Webb and Valverde because he wasn't in the high-profile roles of either starting or closing. Instead, he was pitching in high-leverage middle innings, tackling long relief, and basically plugging every hole dug by a banged-up rotation. It'll be interesting to see what they do with him from here on out. He could be an asset as a starter, and an improvement on Dessens if you set your expectations low, or he could be the middle relief anchor this team will need as the rotation gets retooled. If he's really 22, another year or two relieving older rookies isn't such a bad idea.

BRANDON WEBB   Bats: R   Throws: R   Born: 09-May-79   Age: 25

YEAR	TM	LG	AGE	G	GS	IP	H	BB	SO	HR	ERA	EQERA	EQH9	EQBB9	EQSO9	EQHR9	PERA	VORP	STF
2001	LNC	CAL	22	29	28	162.3	174	44	158	9	3.99	4.83	10.2	3.1	4.8	0.9	4.97	13.1	7
2002	ELP	TEX	23	26	25	152.0	141	59	122	4	3.14	4.32	9.0	4.0	5.3	0.4	4.20	20.2	19
2003	TUC	PCL	24	3	3	18.0	18	9	17	0	6.00	5.82	9.0	5.3	7.4	0.0	4.11	-0.4	32
2003	ARI	NL	24	29	28	180.7	140	68	172	12	2.84	2.93	7.0	3.0	7.6	0.6	3.15	51.9	44
2004	ARI	NL	25	26	25	158.7	153	64	131	9	3.79	3.62	8.4	3.2	6.9	0.5	3.61	32.6	20

Breakout: 23%   Improve: 49%   Collapse: 20%

As a sinkerballer of absurd ability, did we underrate him coming into 2003? Minor league infields and minor league infielders can be a nuisance, without doubt, but we clearly sold him short after a brilliant 2002 in El Paso. If it wasn't for two bad outings to finish what had become a meaningless year (he gave up almost a quarter of his season's total of runs allowed), he'd have wound up looking even more dominant on the year. Although PECOTA might seem pretty frosty on him, keep in mind it also says that he's got a 50–50 shot at improving on that rookie season. He's added velocity as he's progressed, has tremendous movement on his breaking pitches as well as his sinker, throws four pitches for strikes, and owns a groundball-flyball ratio of nearly 3.5 to 1. The leaky infield the D-Backs will be playing in 2004 won't help him, but if you're a Snake on the mound, you don't like things in the air. Webb will build on his first season.

Atlanta Braves

R umors of the Braves' death were greatly exaggerated. A year ago, many a preseason prognosticator felt safe in proclaiming that the end of the Braves' dynasty had come. Our humble publication was no exception—the opening words of the Atlanta essay in *BP 2003* were: "It's over." Between the absence of Tom Glavine and Kevin Millwood, and the presence of an aging offensive core, it seemed like a safe enough bet.

But Southerners are famous for their strength in old age, and like a wrinkled Georgia grandma with a twinkle in her eye, the Braves came roaring back, winning 101 games and wrapping up the NL East title by the All-Star break. It was a remarkable year—highlighted by a quartet of remarkable seasons from Marcus Giles, Gary Sheffield, Javy Lopez, and Rafael Furcal, and it extended a remarkable dynasty. The 13 seasons since Terry Pendleton and Steve Avery first lifted the Braves to national prominence are among the most impressive stretches of sustained success in baseball history, equaled only by the Yankee dynasties of the 20s and 30s, and the Yankee and Dodger runs of the 50s. Only the Braves, of course, have managed such a feat in the free agency era, John Schuerholz masterfully turning the roster over one bit at a time as the dynasty's lineage extended into its second and third generations.

Given that success, surely we wouldn't make the same mistake of prematurely predicting the Braves' demise a second time around. This is a franchise that deserves our respect, after all, and our better judgment.

Well, guess what folks. It's over. Not the era of good Braves teams—this is a well-run organization that isn't about to morph into the Devil Rays or the Falcons—but the Schuerholz dynasty, for all intents and purposes, is over, and 2003 was its last hurrah. As of our publication deadline, the Braves had added J. D. Drew, Eli Marrero, John Thomson, and Gary Matthews Jr., but subtracted Greg Maddux, Gary Sheffield, Javy Lopez, Vinny Castilla, Jason Marquis, and Ray King. It doesn't take General Sherman to figure out that the organization's talent base has eroded significantly. Schuerholz is sure to do some tweaking before the season begins, but the NL East is going to be a dogfight.

In a grander sense, the dynasty is over not because of the loss of any particular set of players, but because the Braves' economic situation is deteriorating. Major league executives are eager to use financial distress as an excuse

BRAVES PROSPECTUS

2003 record: 101–61; First place, NL East; Lost to Cubs in Division Series

Pythagenport record: 96–66

Runs scored per game: 5.6 (1st in NL)

Runs allowed per game: 4.6 (9th in NL)

Team EqA: .283 (1st in NL)

2003 Batters Age: 30.6 (5th oldest in NL)

2003 Pitchers Age: 31.1 (4th oldest in NL)

Ballpark: Turner Field; Slight pitcher's park; Park Factor of 0.986

2003: A surprising, league-best offense propelled the Braves to their 12th consecutive division title.

2004: With budgetary constraints and an exodus of talent, this may finally be the year the Braves fall short of the postseason.

for disappointing performances, and usually, those claims deserve to be taken about as seriously as Bud Selig's hairpiece. But in Atlanta's case, there is real reason to believe Schuerholz's claims that the franchise cannot maintain the luxuries that it once did.

Using data scavenged from Doug Pappas' Business of Baseball Web page, and *Forbes Magazine*'s survey of major league baseball finances, it is possible to come up with a financial statement for the Braves that bears some basis in reality. The largest single source of revenue for most clubs, the Braves being no exception, are gate receipts, which can be estimated from publicly-available data on attendance and average ticket prices. Payroll figures are also disclosed publicly; for consistency's sake, we have used Atlanta's Opening Day payrolls as reported by the Associated Press.

There are other things, of course, that affect a team's bottom line, including television and media revenue, licensing and concession money, and entitlements provided by Major League Baseball. Besides payroll expenses, teams also pay significant costs for maintaining player development operations, performing stadium maintenance, conducting advertising, and operating their front offices. It is here where the math can become fuzzy, especially for a team with a related-party media monolith like Time Warner, and it is here where we turn to *Forbes* for

TABLE 1. BRAVES INCOME STATEMENT

	1999	2000	2001	2002	2003
Attendance	3.3m	3.2m	2.8m	2.6m	2.4m
Average Ticket Price	$19.21	$19.78	$22.05	$21.86	$18.59
Gate Receipts	$63.4m	$63.3m	$61.7m	$56.8m	$44.6m
Payroll	($73.6m)	($84.5m)	($91.9m)	($93.5m)	($104.6m)
Other Income, Net	$28.5m	$289m	$39.7m	$46.2m	$50.0m
Operating Income	$18.3m	$7.7m	$9.5m	$9.5m	($10.0m)

assistance. By taking the difference between operating income as estimated by *Forbes* (as opposed to MLB's questionable numbers), and the income and costs we can determine directly, we come up with a catch-all category entitled "other income, net", which is used to make the financial statement stay in balance (see table 1).

Forbes provides operating income data up through 2002; the 2003 figure is estimated. Last season, in spite of having lowered ticket prices, the Braves drew just 2.4 million fans to Turner Field, their lowest figure since 1991. We estimate that this resulted in a $12 million decrease in gate receipts. At the same time, Atlanta's payroll increased by $11 million as a result of Greg Maddux's hefty arbitration payday and the ballooning figures associated with some of their long-term contracts. Even providing for a modest increase in "other income," it is evident that the Braves lost money last season; we place the hit in the neighborhood of $10 million. For most businesses, it's easier to reduce expenses than to increase revenue, and so it is little surprise that the Braves' tried this winter to trim their payroll. An enlightened management team might be willing to accept short-term losses for the sake of long-term profits if it felt those were likely to come down the road, but sadly, there is little reason to believe that the Braves' financial picture will brighten.

For one thing, the Braves' cachet as "America's Team" is fading. The Braves' national prominence had come about, in large part, because of their presence on WTBS; there was a time in ancient prehistory, before ESPN began to televise games, that a fan's only viewing options were the Braves, the Cubs, and, where one existed, the local team. Millions of kids grew up Braves fans because that was the only team that they'd be to watch on a regular basis. Nowadays, with the proliferation of games on ESPN and other cable outlets, and the introduction of such alternatives as *MLB Extra Innings,* fans can pick and choose their baseball viewing options almost at will. It's a great deal for everyone involved—except for the Braves, who have substantially reduced the number of games that they broadcast on their flagship network (now TNT). All of this has had a notable effect on the team's eminence: Based on

surveys conducted by Harris Interactive, the number of adults who consider the Braves to be their favorite team has slipped from a league-high 18% in 1994, to 11% in 2003—this after the Braves had averaged 98 wins per season and brought home eight consecutive division titles in the intervening years.

Closer to home, Atlanta is proving to be a problematic baseball market. It is natural to attribute the decline in attendance to a sort of fatigue effect—the Braves have been so good for so long, the theory goes, that they've become boring, victimized by their own success. But there are also scores of demographic and geographic factors working against the franchise. While Atlanta and its surrounding areas continue to grow rapidly, this growth is occurring around the town's perimeter, rather than in the city center. With few natural boundaries to contain its sprawl, Atlanta has come to resemble a southeastern version of L.A. Atlanta's transit situation also mirrors that of Los Angeles, with intolerable commute times into and out of town; a two-hour round-trip to see a Braves game is a lot to ask, even of a die-hard fan. The public transit system is better than L.A.'s, but that's not saying much. Moreover, many people who move into the area come from the North, with no ingrown loyalty to the Braves.

Implicit in all of this is the issue of race. The faces in the Turner Field crowd are overwhelmingly white, and affluent. The Braves differ little from other major league teams in this respect, save perhaps for the Yankees. But the city of Atlanta is not very white—and, indeed, the closer one moves toward the city center where the ballpark is located, the less white it becomes. Among those Atlantans living within the city limits proper, 39% are white, according to Census Bureau figures. Among those within Fulton and DeKalb counties—the two counties that buffer the ballpark—but outside the city itself, 45% are white. Among those living within the other, peripheral counties that make up Atlanta's metropolitan area, 72% are white; these are precisely the fans that face the most daunting travel times in reaching Turner Field. The socioeconomic and cultural factors that have produced the race gap in attendance at professional sporting events are complex, and well outside of the Braves' control. But the fact remains that it is going to be difficult for the team to improve or even maintain its existing attendance levels without a substantial increase in the percentage of black fans that attend Braves games.

And so it is apparent that the Braves are going to have to stop behaving like a big-market club, and begin behaving like a middle-market club. The initial stages of the transition may be painful. Without further improvements to the roster, the Braves project to win in the neighborhood of 85 games, a figure that is sure to send attendance slumping, and Furman Bisher ranting. But with proper management, the Braves can continue to make regular playoff appearances over the course of the next decade.

What does behaving like a middle-market club entail? The single most important thing that a middle-market team can do to is to develop cheap talent from within. Fortunately, this is an area in which the Braves excel. The team boasts one of the most extensive scouting networks in the game, and both the position player and pitcher talent ranks among the best in baseball, highlighted by Andy Marte, Jeff Francoeur, and a host of promising arms. Certainly, the Braves do not espouse the amateur scouting philosophy that we have come to preach at *BP*, which emphasizes college players above preps, and manifest skills above raw athleticism. But it should be kept in mind that this strategy is intended a means to success, not an end unto itself. If a team's comparative advantage lies in scouting high school players, or in developing tools-laden prospects into valuable major leaguers, then it may well be in its best interest to continue to draft accordingly.

In fact, the Braves do employ a systematic process in evaluating their amateurs. They focus heavily—almost exclusively—on prep players from the South. Since 2000, the Braves have selected 35 high school players in the first 10 rounds of the June draft. Of those, 10 hailed from Georgia, five apiece from Florida and North Carolina, three from Texas, two from Alabama, and one from Virginia. It seems, at first, like an archaic strategy that would be more befitting of former Georgia Bulldog coach Vince Dooley. But scouting is an inexact science, and the process of preparing for the amateur draft, with literally thousands of players available for the choosing, is practically overwhelming. By focusing on Southern talent, the Braves go for depth rather than breadth, gaining a comparative advantage by getting to know a particular subset of players extraordinarily well. Their strategy, in a bizarro way, is not dissimilar from the Oakland model, which emphasizes college hitters with good walk rates, and college pitchers with good strikeout rates: Both serve, among other things, to narrow the range of players under consideration. What's

more, every one of the Braves' minor league affiliates is located in the South, neatly resolving the difficulties inherent in having a bunch of impressionable teenagers getting their baseball feet wet while stationed thousands of miles from home.

A middle-market team also needs to pick and choose its spots for bringing in players from outside the organization. A contract like the one given two winters ago to Vinny Castilla goes from being a wanton indulgence to a crippling death blow, as an organization operating on a tight budget must spend money in areas that provide for larger marginal improvements. Taken in this light, the Braves' strategy this winter has not been poor: They let Javy Lopez go, but have Johnny Estrada, who should be a league-average backstop, ready to replace him. Mark DeRosa should be a competent third baseman until Andy Marte is ready. The merits of the probable first-base platoon—Adam LaRoche and Julio Franco—are more debatable, but at the very least, it will be cheap.

The catch in all of this is that the team can afford nothing less than All-Star caliber performance from the players that it does sign to big contracts. Chipper and Andruw Jones are inked through 2006 and 2007, respectively (Chipper's deal may be vested through 2008 if he meets certain performance requirements). Both deals looked like reasonable ones at the time they were signed; Andruw's contract, in fact, was widely regarded as a heist. But Chipper has already begun to show some signs of slippage, and Andruw appears as though he may never achieve the superstardom that so many had envisioned for him. That brings us to another concept that middle-market clubs must become acquainted with—that of sunk costs. If Chipper and Andruw are not providing the Braves with enough firepower to lead a playoff-caliber offense, the franchise will need to accept that these players are overpaid, and replace their production elsewhere on the diamond, even if it means going a little bit above the optimal budget dreamed up by Time Warner.

Finally, while it might require some creativity, the Braves need not resign themselves to a passive position with respect to the difficult demographics of the Atlanta market. In particular, the Braves have more to gain than any other club from minority-outreach efforts. Subsidizing baseball programs in Atlanta's inner city, sponsoring community and church group ballpark outings in black neighborhoods, enhancing public-transit alternatives to and from Turner Field, and increasing the presence of minorities in the team's front offices are not surefire solutions, but they may lay the foundation for a better relationship between the Braves and Atlanta's black population.

It is difficult to accept when we are no longer capable of doing the things that we one were; this is the gist of the unfortunate phenomenon we call aging. The Braves are a mature franchise now, no longer able to run with the A-list crowd by virtue of youthful exuberance alone. Instead, they will have to conserve their energy, pick their battles, and use the wisdom they have acquired to their advantage. John Schuerholz and his management team have long been among the best in baseball, but they will need to change the way that they do their business in order to conform to the team's new economic reality. Schuerholz and company have surprised us before, and it will not surprise us if they surprise us again.

HITTERS

WILSON BETEMIT — 3B — Bats: B — Throws: R — Born: 02-Nov-81 — Age: 22

YEAR	TM	LG	AGE	AB	H	2B	3B	HR	BB	SO	SB	CS	AVG	OBP	SLG	MLVR	EQBA	EQOBP	EQSLG	EQMLVR	VORP	DEFENSE	
2001	MYR	CAR	19	318	88	20	1	7	23	71	8	5	.277	.324	.412	.134	.237	.281	.372	-.231	-2.9	83-SS	-1
2001	GRN	SOU	19	183	65	14	0	5	12	36	6	2	.355	.394	.514	.326	.308	.342	.449	.051	14.9	46-SS	-2
2002	RIC	INT	20	343	84	17	1	8	34	82	8	5	.245	.312	.370	-.078	.228	.294	.352	-.240	-4.0	87-SS	-16
2003	RIC	INT	21	478	125	23	13	8	38	115	8	5	.262	.315	.414	.007	.244	.301	.400	-.149	4.7	98-3B	-18
2004	ATL	NL	22	271	66	14	2	7	24	61	4	2	.244	.307	.390	-.128	.247	.309	.404	-.119	8.3	73-3B	-7

Breakout: 29%   Improve: 45%   Collapse: 25%

It isn't happening for him. Betemit spent his second year at Richmond, and made only cosmetic improvements, failing to display either the power or the plate discipline that you'd associate with a big league third baseman. The Braves are also asking questions about his weight and his defense, and with Andy Marte in the system, they might be inclined to trade him if he gets off to a hot start. Betemit still has youth on his side, and a move to another organization might provide him with the wake-up call that he needs.

GREGOR BLANCO — OF — Bats: L — Throws: L — Born: 12-Dec-83 — Age: 20

YEAR	TM	LG	AGE	AB	H	2B	3B	HR	BB	SO	SB	CS	AVG	OBP	SLG	MLVR	EQBA	EQOBP	EQSLG	EQMLVR	VORP	DEFENSE			
2002	MCN	SAL	18	468	127	14	9	7	85	120	40	16	.271	.392	.385	.137	.198	.287	.291	-.353	-48.2	63-LF	-12	43-RF	-6
2003	MYR	CAR	19	461	125	19	7	5	54	114	34	16	.271	.357	.375	.091	.228	.292	.328	-.277	-19.9	110-CF	-20	11-RF	-1
2004	ATL	NL	20	280	58	12	3	4	25	73	10	4	.207	.281	.313	-.298	.210	.282	.325	-.295	-13.8	76-CF	-17		

Breakout: 18%   Improve: 41%   Collapse: 29%

Blanco's best attribute is his good walk rate, but those walks appear to have been the result of sheer stubbornness rather than an uncanny batting eye. Blanco doesn't have enough power to be worthy of pitching around, and his strikeout totals were high. Simply taking a lot of pitches doesn't work as well as you move up levels and the pitchers are better able to hit their spots and make adjustments of their own, and most players of Blanco's profile don't develop well. Blanco is fast, but demonstrated poor instincts when the Braves tried him in center field. The odds are against him.

HENRY BLANCO — C — Bats: R — Throws: R — Born: 29-Aug-71 — Age: 32

YEAR	TM	LG	AGE	AB	H	2B	3B	HR	BB	SO	SB	CS	AVG	OBP	SLG	MLVR	EQBA	EQOBP	EQSLG	EQMLVR	VORP	DEFENSE	
2001	MIL	NL	29	314	66	18	3	6	34	72	3	1	.210	.290	.344	-.256	.214	.291	.352	-.254	-7.3	96-C	8
2002	ATL	NL	30	221	45	9	1	6	20	51	0	2	.204	.267	.335	-.235	.214	.278	.357	-.273	-5.8	61-C	2
2003	ATL	NL	31	151	30	8	0	1	10	21	0	0	.199	.252	.272	-.371	.211	.263	.283	-.407	-9.1	40-C	0
2004	MIN	AL	32	147	33	6	1	3	12	26	0	0	.224	.287	.330	-.237	.223	.290	.336	-.257	-2.6	42-C	1

Breakout: 50%   Improve: 63%   Collapse: 24%

Whatever psychic benefit Blanco might have provided to Greg Maddux, could it possibly have been worth the difference between having his bat and Javy Lopez's in the lineup? The Braves were correct to begin pairing Maddux with Lopez in September, and correct to release Blanco in October. He had a bad year behind the plate to boot, throwing out just 25% of opposing basestealers; beware the sample size, but defensive skills can decline with age, too. Signed on with the Twins as a catch-and-throw backup, the last full measure of his value.

DARREN BRAGG
OF   **Bats: L**   **Throws: R**   Born: 07-Sep-69   Age: 34

YEAR	TM	LG	AGE	AB	H	2B	3B	HR	BB	SO	SB	CS	AVG	OBP	SLG	MLVR	EQBA	EQOBP	EQSLG	EQMLVR	VORP	DEFENSE			
2001	NYM	NL	31	57	15	6	0	0	4	23	3	2	.263	.323	.368	-.109	.276	.331	.379	-.098	0.4				
2001	NOR	INT	31	99	33	4	0	4	23	22	5	2	.333	.468	.495	.410	.298	.422	.452	.187	11.0				
2001	COH	INT	31	199	58	11	2	7	27	51	3	2	.291	.379	.472	.202	.270	.351	.441	.021	4.8	20-LF	0		
2002	ATL	NL	32	212	57	15	2	3	24	52	5	2	.269	.347	.401	.033	.278	.352	.421	.002	3.8	27-RF	-2	13-CF	1
2002	RIC	INT	32	75	22	5	0	1	20	15	4	2	.293	.442	.400	.209	.256	.396	.359	-.014	1.4	16-RF	0		
2003	ATL	NL	33	162	39	5	1	0	13	38	2	1	.241	.305	.284	-.232	.250	.311	.293	-.275	-7.2	15-RF	-1	18-LF	-1
2004	*ATL*	*NL*	*34*	*131*	*33*	*7*	*1*	*2*	*15*	*31*	*3*	*1*	*.254*	*.337*	*.370*	*-.097*	*.257*	*.338*	*.383*	*-.088*	*2.5*	*40-RF*	*-3*		

Breakout: 35%   *Improve: 53%*   *Collapse: 29%*

The skills that once made Bragg one of the league's best fourth outfielders are in decline. He had just six extra-base hits last year, stole just two bases, and posted the lowest walk rate of his career. He's stretched in center field, though that's always been true. The Braves have brought in Little Sarge to replace him.

VINNY CASTILLA
3B   **Bats: R**   **Throws: R**   Born: 04-Jul-67   Age: 36

YEAR	TM	LG	AGE	AB	H	2B	3B	HR	BB	SO	SB	CS	AVG	OBP	SLG	MLVR	EQBA	EQOBP	EQSLG	EQMLVR	VORP	DEFENSE	
2001	TBY	AL	34	93	20	6	0	2	3	22	0	0	.215	.247	.344	-.301	.226	.263	.376	-.267	-2.0	24-3B	0
2001	HOU	NL	34	445	120	28	1	23	32	86	1	4	.270	.320	.492	.031	.266	.318	.484	.019	24.0	121-3B	3
2002	ATL	NL	35	543	126	23	2	12	22	69	4	1	.232	.268	.348	-.199	.242	.276	.367	-.244	-8.7	136-3B	0
2003	ATL	NL	36	542	150	28	3	22	26	86	1	2	.277	.310	.461	.048	.282	.316	.477	.021	23.7	141-3B	3
2004	*COL*	*NL*	*36*	*384*	*100*	*21*	*1*	*15*	*23*	*62*	*1*	*1*	*.261*	*.306*	*.437*	*-.054*	*.252*	*.297*	*.418*	*-.118*	*9.0*	*99-3B*	*-2*

Breakout: 26%   *Improve: 56%*   *Collapse: 17%*

All things considered, Castilla had a pretty good season. Though his walk totals don't reflect it, Castilla took more pitches (3.27/PA vs. 3.12 in 2002), and drove the ball instead of hitting a lot of 275-foot flies. Castilla might make a fine platoon partner and defensive caddy, but somebody will overpay and overplay him . . . like, for instance, the Rockies.

RAMON CASTRO
IF   **Bats: R**   **Throws: R**   Born: 23-Oct-79   Age: 24

YEAR	TM	LG	AGE	AB	H	2B	3B	HR	BB	SO	SB	CS	AVG	OBP	SLG	MLVR	EQBA	EQOBP	EQSLG	EQMLVR	VORP	DEFENSE			
2001	GRN	SOU	21	261	80	19	5	6	25	56	5	8	.307	.383	.487	.224	.257	.318	.411	-.091	9.6	58-SS	-1		
2001	RIC	INT	21	135	30	8	2	1	7	30	1	2	.222	.266	.333	-.217	.213	.255	.331	-.355	-6.2	28-SS	1		
2002	GRN	SOU	22	210	68	17	2	5	39	44	14	8	.324	.446	.495	.368	.259	.360	.412	-.011	14.0	42-SS	-1		
2002	RIC	INT	22	121	28	7	1	6	14	22	4	3	.231	.340	.455	.067	.211	.309	.431	-.115	2.3	18-2B	0	16-SS	-1
2003	RIC	INT	23	84	13	2	0	0	10	22	0	0	.155	.242	.179	-.477	.153	.242	.188	-.602	-10.8	11-SS	3		
2003	GRN	SOU	23	204	59	9	1	5	27	39	4	5	.289	.376	.417	.155	.248	.320	.367	-.156	1.7	34-3B	0	11-SS	-1
2004	*OAK*	*AL*	*24*	*207*	*51*	*11*	*1*	*5*	*21*	*41*	*4*	*2*	*.245*	*.323*	*.390*	*-.085*	*.253*	*.335*	*.407*	*-.064*	*11.0*	*59-SS*	*-5*		

Breakout: 45%   *Improve: 68%*   *Collapse: 19%*

For the third straight season, Castro started out well at Greenville, hit a wall when he was moved up to Richmond, and was sent back down. Sure, he didn't hit well at the higher level, but that also gives you some idea of what the organization thinks about him—this year's experiment lasted for fewer than 100 PA. Castro has flashed both reasonable power and outstanding plate discipline, and has a future ahead of him as a utility guy for another organization, one that focuses on performance rather than tools. Perhaps thinking just that, he signed with Oakland.

MARK DeROSA
IF   **Bats: R**   **Throws: R**   Born: 02-Feb-75   Age: 29

YEAR	TM	LG	AGE	AB	H	2B	3B	HR	BB	SO	SB	CS	AVG	OBP	SLG	MLVR	EQBA	EQOBP	EQSLG	EQMLVR	VORP	DEFENSE			
2001	RIC	INT	26	186	55	18	0	2	17	22	7	3	.296	.351	.425	.098	.275	.337	.402	-.055	8.7	24-SS	0	17-3B	0
2001	ATL	NL	26	164	47	8	0	3	12	19	2	1	.287	.350	.390	-.019	.293	.355	.401	-.009	8.8	38-SS	2		
2002	RIC	INT	27	55	14	3	0	0	5	2	2	0	.255	.339	.309	-.106	.250	.317	.304	-.248	-2.1				
2002	ATL	NL	27	212	63	9	2	5	12	24	2	3	.297	.339	.429	.080	.306	.347	.449	.057	12.5	28-2B	1	16-SS	2
2003	ATL	NL	28	266	70	14	0	6	16	49	1	0	.263	.316	.383	-.062	.271	.322	.394	-.097	5.1	24-2B	1	20-3B	-1
2004	*ATL*	*NL*	*29*	*206*	*53*	*11*	*1*	*4*	*16*	*32*	*2*	*1*	*.256*	*.321*	*.370*	*-.123*	*.259*	*.323*	*.383*	*-.114*	*6.0*	*57-2B*	*-3*		

Breakout: 14%   *Improve: 38%*   *Collapse: 32%*

DeRosa's got some weird trends lurking beneath those dreary statistical lines. His strikeout totals and pitches seen have increased markedly over the course of the past two seasons, while he's cut his GB/FB ratio in half. That could be a sign of either burgeoning power or a slowing bat, or maybe a sort of identity crisis: Who really wants to be associated with the Denny Hockings of the world? He's Atlanta's cheapest option at third base entering the season, and he can handle the position defensively, so he might keep the position warm for Andy Marte for a year or so. DeRosa's a big enough guy with enough skill to hit for some power, so let's go out on a limb and predict 20 homers for him, PECOTA be damned.

CARLOS DURAN   OF   Bats: L   Throws: L   Born: 27-Dec-82   Age: 21

YEAR	TM	LG	AGE	AB	H	2B	3B	HR	BB	SO	SB	CS	AVG	OBP	SLG	MLVR	EQBA	EQOBP	EQSLG	EQMLVR	VORP	DEFENSE	
2002	MCN	SAL	19	534	144	22	10	7	29	80	23	17	.270	.312	.388	.025	.215	.246	.322	-.384	-38.9	123-CF	-15
2003	MYR	CAR	20	415	93	20	6	3	17	60	11	10	.224	.257	.323	-.162	.201	.227	.303	-.457	-50.5	79-RF 2	20-LF -1
2004	ATL	NL	21	262	56	12	3	3	12	46	4	3	.214	.253	.311	-.349	.217	.254	.322	-.347	-17.6	69-RF -3	

Breakout: 40%   Improve: 62%   Collapse: 15%

Can't hit for power, can't take a called strike.
Can't play the field, can't shun a green light.
There are many things that Carlos can't do.
But his 40 time is just four-point-two!

JOHNNY ESTRADA   C   Bats: B   Throws: R   Born: 27-Jun-76   Age: 28

YEAR	TM	LG	AGE	AB	H	2B	3B	HR	BB	SO	SB	CS	AVG	OBP	SLG	MLVR	EQBA	EQOBP	EQSLG	EQMLVR	VORP	DEFENSE
2001	PHI	NL	25	298	68	15	0	8	16	32	0	0	.228	.273	.359	-.247	.238	.284	.371	-.226	-4.2	80-C 1
2001	SWB	INT	25	131	38	13	0	0	5	6	0	0	.290	.319	.389	-.006	.280	.315	.379	-.125	1.8	30-C 3
2002	SWB	INT	26	434	121	27	0	11	26	53	1	0	.279	.322	.417	.025	.263	.311	.403	-.111	7.7	112-C 4
2003	RIC	INT	27	354	116	29	0	10	30	30	0	0	.328	.393	.494	.293	.304	.372	.471	.131	33.5	81-C -4
2003	ATL	NL	27	36	11	0	0	0	0	3	0	0	.306	.359	.306	-.066	.333	.375	.333	-.038	0.7	
2004	ATL	NL	28	216	54	11	0	6	18	26	0	0	.251	.317	.384	-.114	.254	.319	.398	-.105	6.0	60-C -4

Breakout: 14%   Improve: 30%   Collapse: 43%

Estrada has a rap as a Quadruple-A hitter, and while we're on record as denying the existence of such beasts, one should be wary of those gaudy numbers at Richmond—you don't learn to hit at age 27. Still, Estrada is capable defensively, and has good enough bat speed to take advantage of the pitcher's mistakes. He'll be average, and cheap, which is a nice combination for Atlanta, even if it wasn't worth Kevin Millwood.

ROBERT FICK   1B   Bats: L   Throws: R   Born: 15-Mar-74   Age: 30

YEAR	TM	LG	AGE	AB	H	2B	3B	HR	BB	SO	SB	CS	AVG	OBP	SLG	MLVR	EQBA	EQOBP	EQSLG	EQMLVR	VORP	DEFENSE	
2001	DET	AL	27	401	109	21	2	19	39	62	0	3	.272	.339	.476	.097	.294	.363	.516	.169	36.7	74-C -11	19-1B -2
2002	DET	AL	28	556	150	36	2	17	46	90	0	1	.270	.331	.433	.035	.295	.356	.478	.104	25.8	135-RF 2	
2003	ATL	NL	29	409	110	26	1	11	42	47	1	0	.269	.335	.418	.022	.275	.342	.431	-.005	7.0	101-1B -16	
2004	TBY	AL	30	364	97	22	1	12	34	54	1	1	.266	.332	.434	.001	.269	.339	.454	.016	13.0	97-1B -3	

Breakout: 13%   Improve: 41%   Collapse: 22%

Cub fans were screaming a minor variation of his surname when Fick attempted to clothesline Eric Karros during Game 4 of the Division Series. Not that baseball players should be toting copies of *How to Win Friends and Influence People* in their gym bags, but when you're an aging free-agent first baseman with catcher's knees and an average bat, having a reputation as a Class-A Jerk isn't going to help you in your job hunt. Pinch hitting and roller derby are his most likely career paths going forward, and where else but Tampa can you combine the two?

JULIO FRANCO   Old   Bats: R   Throws: R   Born: 23-Aug-58   Age: 45

YEAR	TM	LG	AGE	AB	H	2B	3B	HR	BB	SO	SB	CS	AVG	OBP	SLG	MLVR	EQBA	EQOBP	EQSLG	EQMLVR	VORP	DEFENSE
2001	MCT	MEX	42	407	178	34	5	18	50	56	15	6	.437	.504	.678	.746	.323	.383	.519	.237	54.6	
2001	ATL	NL	42	90	27	4	0	3	10	20	0	0	.300	.376	.444	.116	.304	.377	.457	.120	5.2	22-1B -1
2002	ATL	NL	43	338	96	13	1	6	39	75	5	1	.284	.357	.382	.034	.294	.365	.395	.002	7.8	81-1B -6
2003	ATL	NL	44	197	58	12	2	5	25	43	0	1	.294	.372	.452	.151	.300	.378	.460	.122	11.2	45-1B 0
2004	ATL	NL	45	227	66	14	1	7	32	60	2	1	.248	.329	.381	-.110	.251	.330	.394	-.090	-3.4	74-1B -1

Breakout: 0%   Improve: 0%   Collapse: 100%

Back in the days of leopard prints and Huxtables, how many kids in Lorain and Shaker Heights messed up their baseball careers by attempting to imitate Franco's tornado of a swing? A generation later, those kids are accountants and

(continued next page)

Julio Franco *(continued)*

lawyers and gas station attendants, and Franco is still making a living playing major league ball. He was hitting right up to the end of the year, including a three-hit day in the Division Series against Chicago. If age alone were going to stop him, wouldn't it have done so a long time ago?

MATT FRANCO — 1B — Bats: L — Throws: R — Born: 19-Aug-69 — Age: 34

YEAR	TM	LG	AGE	AB	H	2B	3B	HR	BB	SO	SB	CS	AVG	OBP	SLG	MLVR	EQBA	EQOBP	EQSLG	EQMLVR	VORP	DEFENSE			
2001	NOR	INT	31	433	106	25	1	8	52	72	5	2	.245	.325	.363	-.054	.235	.313	.352	-.198	-2.5	78-3B	-5	34-1B	2
2002	RIC	INT	32	173	50	11	0	6	14	19	1	0	.289	.349	.457	.129	.269	.327	.440	-.024	3.1	32-1B	-1		
2002	ATL	NL	32	205	65	15	4	6	27	31	1	0	.317	.395	.517	.304	.321	.398	.531	.277	20.1	40-1B	-5		
2003	ATL	NL	33	134	33	5	0	3	11	26	0	1	.246	.299	.351	-.149	.257	.308	.368	-.171	-0.2	13-1B	-3		
2004	*ATL*	*NL*	*34*	*99*	*25*	*5*	*0*	*2*	*11*	*18*	*0*	*0*	*.249*	*.329*	*.381*	*-.100*	*.253*	*.330*	*.394*	*-.090*	*1.6*	*31-1B*	*0*		

Breakout: 32%   Improve: 47%   Collapse: 33%

El otro Franco did not have a good season, going just 15-for-78 as a pinch-hitter. He's got little of his positional versatility intact, having made just one start at a position other than first base since coming to Atlanta. At some point you begin to prefer the unknown quantity.

JEFFREY FRANCOEUR — CF — Bats: R — Throws: R — Born: 08-Jan-84 — Age: 20

YEAR	TM	LG	AGE	AB	H	2B	3B	HR	BB	SO	SB	CS	AVG	OBP	SLG	MLVR	EQBA	EQOBP	EQSLG	EQMLVR	VORP	DEFENSE	
2002	DNV	APP	18	147	48	12	1	8	15	34	8	5	.327	.395	.585	.424	.216	.262	.385	-.264	-11.0	36-CF	6
2003	ROM	SAL	19	524	147	26	9	14	30	68	14	6	.281	.325	.445	.155	.233	.263	.383	-.253	-17.3	125-CF	-15
2004	*ATL*	*NL*	*20*	*312*	*71*	*16*	*2*	*7*	*17*	*55*	*4*	*2*	*.227*	*.270*	*.364*	*-.239*	*.230*	*.271*	*.377*	*-.234*	*-8.9*	*81-CF*	*-8*

Breakout: 25%   Improve: 49%   Collapse: 36%

Francoeur didn't overwhelm the league in his full-season debut at Rome, but for a guy who played mostly football in high school, it was an impressive start. His power and wheels are for real, and the scouting reports on his defense are better than the DTs would suggest. He'll need to learn how to handle breaking pitches, and improve his approach at the plate in general, but he's got time. According to David Cameron, who studies these things extensively, Francoeur also has the hottest girlfriend in the entire minor leagues.

RAFAEL FURCAL — SS — Bats: B — Throws: R — Born: 24-Oct-77 — Age: 26

YEAR	TM	LG	AGE	AB	H	2B	3B	HR	BB	SO	SB	CS	AVG	OBP	SLG	MLVR	EQBA	EQOBP	EQSLG	EQMLVR	VORP	DEFENSE	
2001	ATL	NL	23	324	89	19	0	4	24	56	22	6	.275	.321	.370	-.110	.280	.330	.377	-.100	9.2	78-SS	4
2002	ATL	NL	24	636	175	31	8	8	43	114	27	15	.275	.323	.387	-.022	.283	.327	.402	-.067	22.2	143-SS	6
2003	ATL	NL	25	664	194	35	10	15	60	76	25	2	.292	.352	.443	.103	.295	.354	.453	.065	47.6	149-SS	-11
2004	*ATL*	*NL*	*26*	*596*	*171*	*32*	*6*	*11*	*52*	*82*	*23*	*7*	*.287*	*.345*	*.416*	*.001*	*.290*	*.346*	*.430*	*.014*	*34.8*	*154-SS*	*-4*

Breakout: 10%   Improve: 38%   Collapse: 16%

An exciting step forward. Furcal refined his approach at the plate—getting back to the more patient style that made him a budding star in 2000—stayed healthy, and leveraged improved strength into solid power numbers. His arm is every bit as good as billed, and if he cuts back on the mental miscues, he'll be one of the better defenders in the game. His career path looks something like Alan Trammell's, and Trammell continued to develop power as he aged.

JESSE GARCIA — IF — Bats: R — Throws: R — Born: 24-Sep-73 — Age: 30

YEAR	TM	LG	AGE	AB	H	2B	3B	HR	BB	SO	SB	CS	AVG	OBP	SLG	MLVR	EQBA	EQOBP	EQSLG	EQMLVR	VORP	DEFENSE			
2001	RIC	INT	27	375	100	22	3	2	22	54	18	6	.267	.313	.357	-.076	.256	.301	.346	-.216	-1.6	84-SS	-6	13-2B	0
2002	RIC	INT	28	230	69	12	1	6	16	32	9	5	.300	.349	.439	.115	.280	.331	.414	-.045	9.1	40-2B	-1	11-SS	-3
2002	ATL	NL	28	61	12	1	0	0	0	14	0	1	.197	.197	.213	-.531	.213	.213	.230	-.584	-6.0	13-2B	2		
2003	RIC	INT	29	425	130	17	3	2	12	50	29	9	.306	.329	.374	.009	.293	.322	.365	-.122	10.1	86-SS	1		
2004	*ATL*	*NL*	*30*	*184*	*48*	*9*	*1*	*2*	*11*	*27*	*6*	*3*	*.260*	*.306*	*.357*	*-.164*	*.264*	*.307*	*.370*	*-.156*	*3.7*	*51-SS*	*-4*		

Breakout: 22%   Improve: 41%   Collapse: 35%

Fringe player with reasonable defense and some empty batting averages at Triple-A. As likely to see 200 big league plate appearances as Marilyn Quayle is to see *Urinetown, The Musical!*

MARCUS GILES   2B   Bats: R   Throws: R   Born: 18-May-78   Age: 26

YEAR	TM	LG	AGE	AB	H	2B	3B	HR	BB	SO	SB	CS	AVG	OBP	SLG	MLVR	EQBA	EQOBP	EQSLG	EQMLVR	VORP	DEFENSE	
2001	RIC	INT	23	252	84	19	1	6	22	48	13	5	.333	.387	.488	.273	.307	.363	.459	.101	21.8	61-2B -4	
2001	ATL	NL	23	244	64	10	2	9	28	37	2	5	.262	.338	.430	-.004	.266	.341	.435	-.008	11.6	57-2B 2	
2002	ATL	NL	24	213	49	10	1	8	25	41	1	1	.230	.315	.399	-.051	.240	.317	.419	-.095	4.6	48-2B -2	
2002	RIC	INT	24	115	37	6	0	3	13	15	3	0	.322	.385	.452	.207	.299	.364	.419	.038	7.8	13-2B -1	13-3B 2
2003	ATL	NL	25	551	174	49	2	21	59	80	14	4	.316	.390	.526	.302	.320	.393	.538	.277	63.4	137-2B -1	
2004	*ATL*	*NL*	*26*	*462*	*129*	*28*	*3*	*16*	*51*	*73*	*9*	*4*	*.280*	*.358*	*.457*	*.072*	*.284*	*.359*	*.473*	*.088*	*36.5*	*125-2B -2*	

Breakout: 6%   *Improve: 35%*   *Collapse: 25%*

Giles's breakout was one of the nicest stories of the season, as he overcame both the personal demons that haunted him a year ago and a nasty July collision with Mark Prior to put together the sort of year that his strong minor league numbers have always portended. His defense improved too, both according to casual observation and the usual assortment of range metrics. Though it is unusual, especially these days, to see such power output from a player who's just 5′ 8″, Giles uses his size to his advantage by maintaining a small strike zone and a compact swing. The pessimistic PECOTA reflects the fact that second basemen tend to peak early, but Giles doesn't have the skill set of a typical second baseman. He should be one of the league's better players once again in 2004.

KELLY JOHNSON   SS   Bats: L   Throws: R   Born: 22-Feb-82   Age: 22

YEAR	TM	LG	AGE	AB	H	2B	3B	HR	BB	SO	SB	CS	AVG	OBP	SLG	MLVR	EQBA	EQOBP	EQSLG	EQMLVR	VORP	DEFENSE
2001	MCN	SAL	19	415	120	22	1	23	71	111	25	6	.289	.404	.513	.340	.212	.301	.381	-.197	0.8	109-SS -27
2002	MYR	CAR	20	482	123	21	5	12	51	105	12	15	.255	.325	.394	.058	.208	.268	.335	-.326	-19.3	118-SS -4
2003	GRN	SOU	21	334	92	22	5	6	35	81	10	3	.275	.340	.425	.104	.240	.295	.386	-.182	2.2	85-SS -1
2004	*ATL*	*NL*	*22*	*255*	*58*	*14*	*1*	*7*	*25*	*60*	*4*	*2*	*.227*	*.298*	*.374*	*-.177*	*.230*	*.300*	*.387*	*-.170*	*1.9*	*70-SS -8*

Breakout: 31%   *Improve: 48%*   *Collapse: 25%*

He's not really a shortstop—his body's too big, and his feet too slow for the position—but Johnson might hit enough to make it at a corner. The raw numbers were down a bit at Greenville, but Johnson finished the year strongly after spending July on the shelf with a tired elbow, and followed it up with a solid AFL campaign. Not a blue-chipper, especially in this system, but he's got a good chance to be B. J. Surhoff.

ANDRUW JONES   CF   Bats: R   Throws: R   Born: 23-Apr-77   Age: 27

YEAR	TM	LG	AGE	AB	H	2B	3B	HR	BB	SO	SB	CS	AVG	OBP	SLG	MLVR	EQBA	EQOBP	EQSLG	EQMLVR	VORP	DEFENSE
2001	ATL	NL	24	625	157	25	2	34	56	142	11	4	.251	.312	.461	-.020	.257	.320	.472	-.002	25.4	161-CF 18
2002	ATL	NL	25	560	148	34	0	35	83	135	8	3	.264	.366	.512	.204	.270	.368	.529	.171	49.4	149-CF 18
2003	ATL	NL	26	595	165	28	2	36	53	125	4	3	.277	.338	.513	.165	.282	.344	.524	.136	40.5	152-CF 14
2004	*ATL*	*NL*	*27*	*532*	*142*	*29*	*2*	*29*	*59*	*116*	*5*	*2*	*.268*	*.344*	*.492*	*.086*	*.271*	*.346*	*.510*	*.102*	*26.4*	*141-CF 7*

Breakout: 22%   *Improve: 46%*   *Collapse: 16%*

Have we seen the best of it? In spite of the attention paid to the magical age of 27, every player ages differently. Plenty of players peak early, and there are signs that Jones may be one of them. His speed metrics were way down for the second year in a row, and his inconsistency reveals a player who, like Jose Cruz Jr. or Aramis Ramirez, lets go of one skill as soon he picks up another. Particularly frustrating is his inability to sustain gains in his walk rate—Andruw's plate discipline collapsed in the second half and he managed just a .314 OBP after the break. We may need to settle for Jones being merely a very good player.

CHIPPER JONES   LF   Bats: B   Throws: R   Born: 24-Apr-72   Age: 32

YEAR	TM	LG	AGE	AB	H	2B	3B	HR	BB	SO	SB	CS	AVG	OBP	SLG	MLVR	EQBA	EQOBP	EQSLG	EQMLVR	VORP	DEFENSE
2001	ATL	NL	29	572	189	33	5	38	98	82	9	10	.330	.427	.605	.451	.331	.428	.606	.439	106.6	142-3B -15
2002	ATL	NL	30	548	179	35	1	26	107	89	8	2	.327	.435	.536	.396	.331	.438	.550	.377	68.1	144-LF 9
2003	ATL	NL	31	555	169	33	2	27	94	83	2	2	.305	.402	.517	.296	.309	.407	.530	.277	46.7	140-LF -8
2004	*ATL*	*NL*	*32*	*511*	*152*	*32*	*2*	*23*	*83*	*79*	*4*	*2*	*.298*	*.394*	*.505*	*.208*	*.302*	*.396*	*.523*	*.228*	*42.6*	*141-LF 0*

Breakout: 7%   *Improve: 38%*   *Collapse: 21%*

A fine player, but showing signs of age. Jones doesn't steal bases anymore, doesn't hit quite as many line drives, and has become an equal-opportunity defensive liability. Those hitters who maintain their value into their 30s do so by compensating for these weaknesses with improved power output, but Jones' isolated power has now sunk to 30% off its 1999 peak. He should be OK in the near term, but could be an albatross by the time he rakes in $17 million in '06.

RYAN LANGERHANS   OF   Bats: L   Throws: L   Born: 20-Feb-80   Age: 24

YEAR	TM	LG	AGE	AB	H	2B	3B	HR	BB	SO	SB	CS	AVG	OBP	SLG	MLVR	EQBA	EQOBP	EQSLG	EQMLVR	VORP	DEFENSE			
2001	MYR	CAR	21	450	129	30	3	7	55	104	22	13	.287	.374	.413	.211	.240	.311	.359	-.189	-18.5	104-RF	1	18-CF	0
2002	GRN	SOU	22	391	98	23	2	9	68	83	10	5	.251	.366	.389	.064	.213	.305	.345	-.237	-12.0	107-CF	-1		
2003	GRN	SOU	23	336	85	23	2	6	46	85	10	10	.253	.348	.387	.050	.217	.294	.344	-.257	-12.3	87-CF	-3		
2003	RIC	INT	23	132	37	10	2	4	11	29	2	1	.280	.338	.477	.143	.261	.320	.455	-.023	1.7	32-RF	-2		
2004	*ATL*	*NL*	*24*	*225*	*54*	*13*	*2*	*6*	*24*	*52*	*4*	*2*	*.241*	*.317*	*.390*	*-.113*	*.244*	*.318*	*.404*	*-.103*	*1.8*	*63-CF*	*-4*		

Breakout: 36%   *Improve: 59%*   *Collapse: 26%*

Toolsy player who has also posted some solid walk rates as he's moved through the system. Like Gregor Blanco, his walks have resulted partly from his inability to make contact with breaking pitches, which places him into a lot of deep counts—call it Jeremy Giambi syndrome. There's a chance that he turns into Kevin McReynolds, but otherwise, he might want to invest in a Starbucks card, because he projects to get a lot of cups of coffee.

ADAM LaROCHE   1B   Bats: L   Throws: L   Born: 06-Nov-79   Age: 24

YEAR	TM	LG	AGE	AB	H	2B	3B	HR	BB	SO	SB	CS	AVG	OBP	SLG	MLVR	EQBA	EQOBP	EQSLG	EQMLVR	VORP	DEFENSE	
2001	MYR	CAR	21	471	118	31	0	7	30	108	10	8	.251	.305	.361	.025	.222	.267	.335	-.320	-35.2	119-1B	-5
2002	MYR	CAR	22	250	84	17	0	9	27	37	0	2	.336	.406	.512	.397	.273	.332	.431	-.025	4.7	64-1B	-8
2002	GRN	SOU	22	173	50	9	0	4	19	38	1	1	.289	.363	.410	.115	.250	.307	.369	-.176	-5.2	45-1B	2
2003	GRN	SOU	23	219	62	12	1	12	34	53	1	2	.283	.381	.511	.278	.235	.321	.438	-.066	1.3	60-1B	0
2003	RIC	INT	23	264	78	21	0	8	27	58	1	2	.295	.360	.466	.175	.272	.344	.444	.014	8.1	71-1B	4
2004	*ATL*	*NL*	*24*	*219*	*54*	*12*	*1*	*7*	*22*	*46*	*2*	*1*	*.249*	*.322*	*.412*	*-.071*	*.252*	*.323*	*.427*	*-.060*	*4.9*	*61-1B*	*2*

Breakout: 32%   *Improve: 47%*   *Collapse: 33%*

The junior college product hits loads of line drives, has a semblance of the strike zone, and plays a great defensive first base—all the skills of Doug Mientkiewicz, but without all those pesky consonants. This is the sort of player for whom "gritty" and "gamer" come up a lot in the scouting reports, and thus the sort that an organization can overrate, causing problems down the road.

JAVY LOPEZ   C   Bats: R   Throws: R   Born: 05-Nov-70   Age: 33

YEAR	TM	LG	AGE	AB	H	2B	3B	HR	BB	SO	SB	CS	AVG	OBP	SLG	MLVR	EQBA	EQOBP	EQSLG	EQMLVR	VORP	DEFENSE	
2001	ATL	NL	30	438	117	16	1	17	28	82	1	0	.267	.322	.425	-.038	.275	.329	.435	-.023	18.0	116-C	-4
2002	ATL	NL	31	347	81	15	0	11	26	63	0	1	.233	.299	.372	-.113	.244	.305	.392	-.152	1.9	94-C	4
2003	ATL	NL	32	457	150	29	3	43	33	90	0	1	.328	.378	.687	.526	.332	.380	.698	.504	74.7	114-C	1
2004	*BAL*	*AL*	*33*	*368*	*99*	*19*	*1*	*18*	*25*	*70*	*0*	*1*	*.269*	*.323*	*.472*	*.037*	*.278*	*.335*	*.495*	*.071*	*26.3*	*96-C*	*-3*

Breakout: 1%   *Improve: 27%*   *Collapse: 32%*

Because he had achieved semi-star status early in his career, Lopez's big season didn't have people dropping the f-word as liberally as they did in response to, say, Brady Anderson's 1996 or Davey Johnson's 1973. But in many respects, Lopez's year was just as surprising. Here was an injury-prone, 32-year-old catcher, whose slugging percentage had declined four years running. PECOTA thought there was less than a 5% chance that Lopez would match even his career averages. Instead, he had one of the best offensive seasons by a catcher in baseball history.

We've provided a forecast for him above; it says he's going to be better than he was in 2002, and worse than he was in 2003. What? You could have told us that? The truth is that nobody knows why Lopez had the season he did, and so nobody knows how much of the bounce he'll retain. The organization that knows him best thought he wouldn't be worth what he'd make in arbitration. It might be worth summoning up a memory of Earl Williams, another Brave turned Oriole.

ANDY MARTE   3B   Bats: R   Throws: R   Born: 21-Oct-83   Age: 20

YEAR	TM	LG	AGE	AB	H	2B	3B	HR	BB	SO	SB	CS	AVG	OBP	SLG	MLVR	EQBA	EQOBP	EQSLG	EQMLVR	VORP	DEFENSE	
2001	DNV	APP	17	125	25	6	0	1	20	45	3	0	.200	.306	.272	-.152	.135	.207	.188	-.682	-43.6	37-3B	3
2002	MCN	SAL	18	488	137	32	4	21	41	114	2	1	.281	.339	.492	.210	.216	.263	.389	-.256	-11.6	121-3B	-2
2003	MYR	CAR	19	463	132	35	1	16	67	109	5	2	.285	.372	.469	.246	.229	.303	.390	-.169	1.8	117-3B	-18
2004	*ATL*	*NL*	*20*	*301*	*65*	*15*	*1*	*8*	*28*	*76*	*2*	*1*	*.215*	*.283*	*.354*	*-.236*	*.217*	*.284*	*.367*	*-.231*	*-3.0*	*81-3B*	*-10*

Breakout: 22%   *Improve: 45%*   *Collapse: 35%*

There's a school of thought that the science of prospecting isn't so much about identifying strengths as it is about recognizing limitations. Reggie Abercrombie, for all the five-tool talent he has, is never going to develop the batting eye to become a good major league player; Bobby Jenks may never have the brain for it.

With Marte, there are no such limitations, and that's why he's regarded as among the best prospects in baseball. Marte has a short swing that projects to generate a lot of power as he fills out, a precocious idea of the strike zone, and an organization that should mentor him well. Perhaps most importantly, he's able to make adjustments midstream. This season, Marte got off to a subpar start at the plate, flirting with the Mendoza line, before learning the adaptations necessary to allow him to master the level; he hit well above .300 from May 1 on. The Braves are high on him, and while an April 2005 timetable sounds aggressive, Marte has met every challenge thus far.

BRIAN McCANN   C   Bats: L   Throws: R   Born: 20-Feb-84   Age: 20

YEAR	TM	LG	AGE	AB	H	2B	3B	HR	BB	SO	SB	CS	AVG	OBP	SLG	MLVR	EQBA	EQOBP	EQSLG	EQMLVR	VORP	DEFENSE
2003	ROM	SAL	19	424	123	31	3	12	24	73	7	4	.290	.329	.462	.193	.238	.266	.394	-.227	-7.2	63-C 3
2004	ATL	NL	20	293	64	15	1	6	15	58	3	1	.219	.257	.342	-.296	.222	.259	.354	-.292	-10.6	76-C -11
Breakout: 16%			Improve: 33%				Collapse: 51%															

McCann's upside is Matt LeCroy—a big-bootied guy with a big swing who can hit the ball a long way, and man the back-stop position just well enough to don the tools of ignorance. PECOTA likes him in 2008, but not in 2004, which is perhaps a pretty fair indication of how catchers tend to develop.

DONZELL McDONALD   OF   Bats: B   Throws: R   Born: 20-Feb-75   Age: 29

YEAR	TM	LG	AGE	AB	H	2B	3B	HR	BB	SO	SB	CS	AVG	OBP	SLG	MLVR	EQBA	EQOBP	EQSLG	EQMLVR	VORP	DEFENSE	
2001	COH	INT	26	374	96	11	9	8	42	79	20	4	.257	.342	.398	.021	.244	.323	.383	-.130	1.9	101-CF -14	
2002	OMA	PCL	27	452	118	15	15	7	56	102	30	6	.261	.346	.407	-.006	.233	.312	.367	-.181	-4.6	56-CF 0	52-RF -2
2003	RIC	INT	28	464	118	18	9	2	62	113	31	10	.254	.345	.345	-.037	.239	.327	.332	-.196	-7.3	106-CF -11	14-LF 0
2004	ATL	NL	29	195	48	9	3	3	22	43	8	3	.244	.326	.365	-.129	.247	.327	.378	-.121	1.5	56-CF -5	
Breakout: 33%			Improve: 51%				Collapse: 29%																

McDonald is a perennial six-year free agent and failed tools prospect at this point of his career. He'd improved his walk rate just enough that he'd make a capable fifth outfielder somewhere.

JARROD SALTALAMACCHIA   C   Bats: B   Throws: R   Born: 25-May-85   Age: 19

Regarded as a defensive catcher first, Saltalamacchia, the Braves' first-round pick in '03, took a bunch of walks in his first exposure to pro ball, and smacked 15 extra-base hits in 46 games on his way to being named the Gulf Coast League's third-best prospect. He's a huge guy, a switch-hitter, comes from a good high school program, and will be a nice prospect if he starts to make contact consistently.

GARY SHEFFIELD   RF   Bats: R   Throws: R   Born: 18-Nov-68   Age: 35

YEAR	TM	LG	AGE	AB	H	2B	3B	HR	BB	SO	SB	CS	AVG	OBP	SLG	MLVR	EQBA	EQOBP	EQSLG	EQMLVR	VORP	DEFENSE
2001	LAD	NL	32	515	160	28	2	36	94	67	10	4	.311	.417	.583	.405	.321	.427	.600	.417	73.8	120-LF 1
2002	ATL	NL	33	492	151	26	0	25	72	53	12	2	.307	.404	.512	.301	.312	.406	.529	.277	46.5	117-RF 1
2003	ATL	NL	34	576	190	37	2	39	86	55	18	4	.330	.419	.604	.465	.333	.423	.616	.448	77.3	143-RF 3
2004	NYY	AL	35	507	151	30	2	25	71	57	12	3	.297	.387	.515	.218	.303	.397	.535	.245	44.2	138-RF 0
Breakout: 6%			Improve: 30%				Collapse: 22%															

Compare him to Dick Allen all you want, make prickly asides about his performance in contract years, but Gary Sheffield is going to have one heck of a Hall of Fame case when it's all said and done. Last season was the sixth in which Sheff could be comfortably classified among the best players in his league. The key to everything is his amazingly strong wrists, which allow him to generate tremendous power and bat speed while only rarely striking out. Sheff's defense leaves much to be desired—he takes inefficient routes to the ball, moving laterally and not charging as many balls as he could. That aside, he's one of the best players in baseball, and should outperform the PECOTA forecast. Just don't ask him to negotiate your next contract.

SCOTT THORMAN

1B   Bats: L   Throws: R   Born: 06-Jan-82   Age: 22

YEAR	TM	LG	AGE	AB	H	2B	3B	HR	BB	SO	SB	CS	AVG	OBP	SLG	MLVR	EQBA	EQOBP	EQSLG	EQMLVR	VORP	DEFENSE
2002	MCN	SAL	20	470	138	38	3	16	51	83	2	2	.294	.367	.489	.253	.221	.277	.378	-.241	-24.0	121-1B -23
2003	MYR	CAR	21	445	108	26	2	12	42	79	0	0	.243	.311	.391	.024	.205	.258	.344	-.335	-36.7	116-1B -9
2004	ATL	NL	22	251	54	13	1	6	19	53	0	0	.214	.272	.349	-.263	.216	.273	.362	-.259	-11.1	68-1B -9

Breakout: 29%   Improve: 51%   Collapse: 20%

Thorman has the size and big swing to project as a power hitter, but he took a step backward last year, his numbers suffering as he attempted to pull everything. He'll be old for his level, and doesn't have much in the way of athletic skills, so he'll need to show improvement this year to remain on the radar screen. Thorman has just enough of an idea of what he's doing at the plate to turn into Brian Daubach, but that's not the sort of player that you build your organization around.

PITCHERS

JUNG BONG

Bats: L   Throws: L   Born: 15-Jul-80   Age: 23

YEAR	TM	LG	AGE	G	GS	IP	H	BB	SO	HR	ERA	EQERA	EQH9	EQBB9	EQSO9	EQHR9	PERA	VORP	STF
2001	MYR	CAR	20	28	28	168.0	151	47	145	7	3.00	5.82	9.8	3.6	4.9	0.9	4.97	-3.7	15
2002	GRN	SOU	21	27	17	122.0	136	45	107	6	3.25	5.75	11.4	3.5	5.9	0.9	5.62	-1.9	14
2003	ATL	NL	22	44	0	57.0	56	31	47	8	5.05	5.24	9.2	4.4	6.5	1.3	5.30	3.3	6
2003	RIC	INT	22	3	3	11.3	11	3	15	1	5.58	5.06	9.3	2.5	10.1	0.8	4.25	0.6	49
2004	ATL	NL	23	31	11	74.7	74	33	60	7	4.23	4.59	9.0	3.5	6.5	0.9	4.68	9.4	1

Breakout: 23%   Improve: 52%   Collapse: 23%

Bong may need a couple of years to hit his stride, but he's young, and his progress is all the more impressive given that when he left Korea, he was an outfielder. Bong had some command problems last year, and he's still trying to perfect a curveball that the Braves believe he'll need to master before returning to the starting rotation. He doesn't profile like a typical reliever either, however, as his best pitch is the change, and Keith Foulke types are rare. The best thing for Bong, especially given his relative lack of experience, will be to get him 25 starts somewhere, be that in Atlanta or Richmond. Too bad the ERA projection doesn't read 4.20.

PAUL BYRD

Bats: R   Throws: R   Born: 03-Dec-70   Age: 33

YEAR	TM	LG	AGE	G	GS	IP	H	BB	SO	HR	ERA	EQERA	EQH9	EQBB9	EQSO9	EQHR9	PERA	VORP	STF
2001	CLR	FLA	30	4	4	23.7	24	5	17	1	3.42	5.14	12.0	2.1	4.3	0.9	5.53	1.1	-10
2001	SWB	INT	30	5	5	37.0	34	7	35	4	3.65	5.08	10.2	2.1	6.7	1.3	5.15	1.9	0
2001	PHI	NL	30	3	1	10.0	10	4	3	1	8.10	6.52	9.3	3.7	1.9	0.9	4.86	-1.0	-33
2001	KCR	AL	30	16	15	93.3	110	22	49	11	4.05	4.28	10.4	2.0	4.4	0.9	4.77	13.2	4
2002	KCR	AL	31	33	33	228.3	224	38	129	36	3.90	3.72	8.3	1.4	4.9	1.3	3.97	46.5	6
2004	ATL	AL	33	38	15	98.3	113	21	48	15	4.88	5.00	10.0	1.8	4.3	1.3	4.88	12.9	-10

Breakout: 31%   Improve: 51%   Collapse: 36%

In the aftermath of serious injury, it is often a pitcher's command, not his velocity, that is last to recover. If that's the case here, then Byrd could be in some serious trouble; Paul Byrd without his command is a batting practice pitcher. The off-season reports on his health were not promising, pegging his return for mid-season at the earliest.

WILL CUNNANE

Bats: R   Throws: R   Born: 24-Apr-74   Age: 30

YEAR	TM	LG	AGE	G	GS	IP	H	BB	SO	HR	ERA	EQERA	EQH9	EQBB9	EQSO9	EQHR9	PERA	VORP	STF
2001	IND	INT	27	7	3	23.3	25	6	25	2	3.86	4.57	10.8	2.9	7.5	1.2	5.54	2.5	-4
2001	MIL	NL	27	31	1	51.7	66	22	37	6	5.40	6.16	11.8	3.6	5.4	0.9	5.85	-3.1	-16
2002	IOW	PCL	28	43	0	73.7	67	23	69	3	2.20	3.41	8.9	3.1	6.4	0.5	4.00	16.7	7
2002	CHC	NL	28	16	0	26.3	27	13	30	5	5.48	5.26	9.5	3.9	8.8	1.8	5.73	1.0	-11
2003	IOW	PCL	29	12	0	16.3	17	8	16	0	2.21	4.20	10.2	5.4	7.8	0.0	4.64	2.3	15
2003	RIC	INT	29	15	0	21.0	11	2	19	0	0.00	1.37	5.0	0.9	6.4	0.0	1.29	9.3	42
2003	ATL	NL	29	20	0	20.0	14	6	20	2	2.70	2.84	6.6	2.4	8.1	0.9	3.13	6.5	19
2004	ATL	NL	30	37	2	52.3	49	20	45	4	3.47	3.76	8.5	3.0	6.9	0.7	4.04	10.8	5

Breakout: 25%   Improve: 56%   Collapse: 18%

The Cubs had seen this before—Cunnane putting up good numbers in Des Moines. They didn't think it made him a big league pitcher, so they released him in May. The Braves picked him up, stashed him at Richmond, and Cunnane proceeded to reel off 21 consecutive scoreless innings, with the fine peripheral numbers to match, then followed that up with six solid weeks in Atlanta. Cunnane's strikeout rates have always been good. He won't overwhelm anyone with his hittable, low-90s fastball, but he's improved his command to the point that he should be an asset for a few years.

KYLE DAVIES   Bats: R   Throws: R   Born: 09-Sep-83   Age: 20

YEAR	TM	LG	AGE	G	GS	IP	H	BB	SO	HR	ERA	EQERA	EQH9	EQBB9	EQSO9	EQHR9	PERA	VORP	STF
2002	DNV	APP	18	14	14	69.3	73	23	62	2	3.51	6.75	12.0	4.1	4.3	0.6	5.77	-7.8	9
2003	ROM	SAL	19	27	27	146.3	128	53	148	9	2.89	5.65	10.3	4.4	5.9	1.5	5.98	-0.7	13
2004	ATL	NL	20	18	16	99.3	93	37	77	11	3.94	4.27	8.5	3.0	6.2	1.0	4.27	14.3	11

Breakout: 33%   Improve: 73%   Collapse: 0%

The small towns of America's Southeast were as teeming with Braves pitching prospects as they were with kudzu. Davies was one of the more verdant strains, leveraging a refined delivery into considerably improved velocity and a higher strikeout rate. That PECOTA looks a bit unrealistic, but 19-year-olds who strike out more than a batter per inning are impressive, and Davies should move through the system fast.

BRETT EVERT   Bats: L   Throws: R   Born: 23-Oct-80   Age: 23

YEAR	TM	LG	AGE	G	GS	IP	H	BB	SO	HR	ERA	EQERA	EQH9	EQBB9	EQSO9	EQHR9	PERA	VORP	STF
2001	MCN	SAL	20	6	6	36.3	25	3	34	0	0.74	2.51	8.4	1.1	4.7	0.3	2.96	11.1	40
2001	MYR	CAR	20	13	13	72.3	63	15	75	4	2.24	5.32	10.1	2.7	6.0	1.3	5.18	2.0	20
2002	MYR	CAR	21	10	10	57.7	53	21	51	3	3.74	6.57	10.7	4.6	5.7	1.2	5.98	-5.5	3
2002	GRN	SOU	21	16	15	93.7	94	35	84	15	4.90	6.72	11.3	3.6	6.2	2.8	7.86	-10.5	-16
2003	GRN	SOU	22	33	15	116.3	126	44	103	12	4.02	6.32	12.1	4.1	5.6	2.1	7.49	-8.3	-24
2004	ATL	NL	23	14	10	55.7	61	25	39	8	5.12	5.56	9.9	3.6	5.6	1.3	5.73	1.4	-4

Breakout: 21%   Improve: 59%   Collapse: 11%

Evert has regressed since a fine 2001 campaign, struggling to hit his spots with an average arsenal. Equally troubling is his high home runs allowed rate. If Evert can't fool hitters in Greenville, it is unlikely he'll have much more success down the road in Atlanta.

KEVIN GRYBOSKI   Bats: R   Throws: R   Born: 15-Nov-73   Age: 30

YEAR	TM	LG	AGE	G	GS	IP	H	BB	SO	HR	ERA	EQERA	EQH9	EQBB9	EQSO9	EQHR9	PERA	VORP	STF
2001	TAC	PCL	27	58	0	60.0	64	19	50	8	3.90	5.56	11.0	3.4	5.6	1.5	6.07	0.2	-36
2002	ATL	NL	28	57	0	51.7	50	37	33	6	3.48	4.93	9.7	5.7	5.1	1.1	5.66	3.7	-26
2003	ATL	NL	29	64	0	44.3	44	23	32	3	3.86	4.64	9.3	4.2	5.7	0.6	4.59	6.5	-5
2004	ATL	NL	30	48	0	47.7	48	25	36	4	4.07	4.41	9.0	4.1	6.1	0.7	4.87	6.5	-7

Breakout: 28%   Improve: 54%   Collapse: 26%

Most people are sexier with their clothes on; that way, you can imagine what's underneath, instead of seeing the naked, flaccid truth. In the same way, an injury can obscure a history of uninspired performance, as has happened in Gryboski's case. Gryboski's command has always been subpar, and at best, he'll fill out the back end of a bullpen. He was pitching again for the Braves just six weeks after having been diagnosed with a partial labrum tear, which tells you more about the organization's regard for him than about any magical recuperative powers he might have.

MIKE HAMPTON   Bats: R   Throws: L   Born: 09-Sep-72   Age: 31

YEAR	TM	LG	AGE	G	GS	IP	H	BB	SO	HR	ERA	EQERA	EQH9	EQBB9	EQSO9	EQHR9	PERA	VORP	STF
2001	COL	NL	28	32	32	203.0	236	85	122	31	5.41	5.30	10.2	3.5	4.5	1.1	5.39	6.6	-9
2002	COL	NL	29	30	30	178.7	228	91	74	24	6.14	6.16	11.3	4.0	3.2	1.1	6.06	-10.8	-24
2003	ATL	NL	30	31	31	190.0	186	78	110	14	3.84	4.35	9.1	3.4	4.6	0.6	4.30	26.8	8
2004	ATL	NL	31	27	25	155.7	165	63	88	14	4.37	4.74	9.6	3.2	4.5	0.8	4.85	13.4	0

Breakout: 19%   Improve: 63%   Collapse: 14%

(continued next page)

Mike Hampton (*continued*)

In the second half, Hampton got back to throwing his sinker as frequently as two-thirds of the time, and finally, after two terrible seasons in Colorado, looked like the Hampton of old. His strikeout rate wasn't that high, but the same was true in his Met and Astro days, when he was one of the league's best pitchers. If he continues to keep the ball down, he'll succeed by taking advantage of the defense behind him and avoiding the long ball. If you feel the need to say nice things about Leo Mazzone, go right ahead.

BUDDY HERNANDEZ Bats: R   Throws: R Born: 03-Mar-79   Age: 25

YEAR	TM	LG	AGE	G	GS	IP	H	BB	SO	HR	ERA	EQERA	EQH9	EQBB9	EQSO9	EQHR9	PERA	VORP	STF
2001	MCN	SAL	22	7	0	14.0	13	1	29	1	3.21	6.17	14.7	0.8	10.8	1.5	7.01	-0.7	18
2001	MYR	CAR	22	34	0	53.7	28	18	77	1	1.17	2.70	7.3	4.4	8.1	0.4	3.50	15.0	32
2002	GRN	SOU	23	40	0	59.0	36	23	81	0	1.22	2.70	7.6	3.7	8.9	0.2	3.20	17.2	42
2003	RIC	INT	24	53	0	71.0	65	31	82	2	3.42	4.39	9.0	4.8	8.4	0.4	4.37	8.8	20
2004	*ATL*	*NL*	*25*	*21*	*4*	*36.0*	*32*	*18*	*35*	*3*	*3.71*	*4.02*	*8.0*	*4.0*	*7.7*	*0.6*	*4.21*	*6.0*	*7*

Breakout: 33%   *Improve: 58%*   *Collapse: 19%*

The Atlanta organization doesn't like Hernandez, who has neither the height nor the fastball to suit their idea of a pitching prospect, and left him exposed in last year's Rule 5 draft. The A's snapped him up, gave him a long look in spring training, but ultimately repatriated him. Hernandez is phenomenally good at avoiding the long ball, and has some fantastic minor league strikeout rates, but he's going to need to find another analytically-minded team to get his chance, because from eyeballing him, you'd never know how he gets anybody out.

ROBERTO HERNANDEZ Bats: R   Throws: R Born: 11-Nov-64   Age: 39

YEAR	TM	LG	AGE	G	GS	IP	H	BB	SO	HR	ERA	EQERA	EQH9	EQBB9	EQSO9	EQHR9	PERA	VORP	STF
2001	KCR	AL	36	63	0	67.7	69	26	46	7	4.12	4.11	9.0	3.2	5.8	0.8	4.38	10.9	-1
2002	KCR	AL	37	53	0	52.0	62	12	39	6	4.33	4.41	10.2	1.9	6.4	0.9	4.64	6.7	2
2003	ATL	NL	38	66	0	60.0	61	43	45	10	4.35	5.86	9.6	5.7	6.0	1.4	5.93	1.1	-31
2004	*PHI*	*NL*	*39*	*48*	*0*	*29.7*	*33*	*21*	*26*	*4*	*6.07*	*6.38*	*9.9*	*5.7*	*7.1*	*1.0*	*6.33*	*-0.4*	*-13*

Breakout: 20%   *Improve: 58%*   *Collapse: 24%*

Then again, some reclamation projects fail. Hernandez still throws hard, but he couldn't find the strike zone in '03, and spent time on the DL with abdominal and hamstring injuries. His 4.35 ERA wasn't good to begin with, and far overstates his effectiveness. Now 39, and three years removed from his last good season, he's going to have to settle for a minor league contract. On second thought, the Phillies needed a new Jose Mesa.

TREY HODGES Bats: R   Throws: R Born: 29-Jun-78   Age: 26

YEAR	TM	LG	AGE	G	GS	IP	H	BB	SO	HR	ERA	EQERA	EQH9	EQBB9	EQSO9	EQHR9	PERA	VORP	STF
2001	MYR	CAR	23	26	26	173.0	156	18	139	13	2.76	5.42	11.1	1.4	4.4	1.8	6.06	3.0	-17
2002	RIC	INT	24	28	28	172.3	158	56	116	9	3.19	4.18	8.6	3.5	5.1	0.7	4.12	25.4	14
2003	ATL	NL	25	52	1	65.7	69	31	66	11	4.66	5.40	9.9	3.8	8.1	1.4	5.59	2.6	-5
2004	*ATL*	*NL*	*26*	*36*	*10*	*77.3*	*74*	*28*	*62*	*9*	*4.08*	*4.43*	*8.7*	*2.9*	*6.5*	*1.0*	*4.43*	*9.7*	*2*

Breakout: 27%   *Improve: 54%*   *Collapse: 16%*

Hodges's press clippings and minor league numbers suggested a command-and-control guy, but working out of the bullpen for the first time, he took better advantage of his sinker and struck out more than a batter per inning, trading off a few free passes in the process. Bobby Cox has compared him to John Burkett, which seems about right, and PECOTA thinks that he has a good chance to consolidate his skills set and put together a good year.

DARREN HOLMES Bats: R   Throws: R Born: 25-Apr-66   Age: 38

YEAR	TM	LG	AGE	G	GS	IP	H	BB	SO	HR	ERA	EQERA	EQH9	EQBB9	EQSO9	EQHR9	PERA	VORP	STF
2002	ATL	NL	36	55	0	54.7	41	12	47	3	1.81	2.63	7.7	1.8	6.8	0.5	3.06	16.9	23
2003	ATL	NL	37	48	0	42.0	47	11	46	5	4.29	4.91	10.5	2.2	8.9	1.1	5.03	4.0	9
2004	*ATL*	*NL*	*38*	*51*	*0*	*49.3*	*46*	*14*	*43*	*5*	*3.51*	*3.81*	*8.5*	*2.3*	*7.1*	*1.0*	*3.96*	*9.6*	*5*

Breakout: 22%   *Improve: 46%*   *Collapse: 48%*

Proponents of DIPS theory—the idea that the pitcher has little effect on whether batted balls in play turn into hits—have a good case on their hand in Holmes. Darren saw his hit rate on balls in play rate jump from 24.2% to 35.6%, and his ERA more than doubled as a result. His strikeout and walk numbers remained very good, and he'd be a reasonable gamble for a team with a good training staff.

RAY KING Bats: L Throws: L Born: 15-Jan-74 Age: 30

YEAR	TM	LG	AGE	G	GS	IP	H	BB	SO	HR	ERA	EQERA	EQH9	EQBB9	EQSO9	EQHR9	PERA	VORP	STF
2001	MIL	NL	27	82	0	55.0	49	25	49	5	3.60	3.93	8.4	3.8	6.8	0.7	4.09	9.8	5
2002	MIL	NL	28	76	0	65.0	61	24	50	5	3.05	3.73	8.6	2.9	6.0	0.7	3.99	13.0	4
2003	ATL	NL	29	80	0	59.0	46	27	43	3	3.51	3.97	7.3	3.7	5.9	0.5	3.39	5.5	6
2004	*STL*	*NL*	*30*	*64*	*0*	*52.7*	*49*	*25*	*41*	*3*	*3.55*	*3.87*	*8.4*	*3.6*	*6.3*	*0.6*	*4.16*	*9.5*	*-2*

Breakout: 37% Improve: 62% Collapse: 13%

King did pretty much the same thing he's always done, appearing in 80 games, posting an ERA in the mid-threes, and scamming enough lefties into chasing his big slider to remain effective. Traded to St. Louis, where he'll help to fulfill Tony La Russa's orgiastic fantasy involving a tag team of LOOGYs.

ANTHONY LEREW Bats: L Throws: R Born: 28-Oct-82 Age: 21

YEAR	TM	LG	AGE	G	GS	IP	H	BB	SO	HR	ERA	EQERA	EQH9	EQBB9	EQSO9	EQHR9	PERA	VORP	STF
2002	DNV	APP	19	14	14	83.0	60	25	75	2	1.73	3.65	8.5	3.6	4.3	0.5	3.97	16.0	24
2003	ROM	SAL	20	25	25	143.7	112	43	127	7	2.38	4.83	9.4	3.6	4.9	1.3	5.18	10.8	9
2004	*ATL*	*NL*	*21*	*20*	*15*	*92.0*	*92*	*42*	*58*	*10*	*4.36*	*4.72*	*9.0*	*3.6*	*5.1*	*0.9*	*4.84*	*9.2*	*-2*

Breakout: 18% Improve: 57% Collapse: 13%

Lerew hails from Pennsylvania—not exactly a baseball hotbed—so it's impressive that he's been a good professional right out of the gate; his 2.38 ERA at Rome was the best in the system. Lerew's fastball and change are both plus pitches, and he's already effective at varying speeds. Reports on his mechanics are mixed, however; he tends to push forward with his arm, placing undue strain upon it, and he needs to refine his breaking stuff. The Braves can afford to take it slowly with Lerew. Make sure to adjust for pitcher-friendly Myrtle Beach when we revisit him a year from now.

GREG MADDUX Bats: R Throws: R Born: 14-Apr-66 Age: 38

YEAR	TM	LG	AGE	G	GS	IP	H	BB	SO	HR	ERA	EQERA	EQH9	EQBB9	EQSO9	EQHR9	PERA	VORP	STF
2001	ATL	NL	35	34	34	233.0	220	27	173	20	3.05	3.55	8.9	1.0	5.8	0.7	3.57	50.2	26
2002	ATL	NL	36	34	34	199.3	194	45	118	14	2.62	3.91	9.7	1.8	4.8	0.7	4.17	35.0	14
2003	ATL	NL	37	36	36	218.3	225	33	124	24	3.96	4.38	9.6	1.3	4.6	1.0	4.28	23.3	6
2004	*ATL*	*NL*	*38*	*31*	*29*	*187.7*	*194*	*37*	*104*	*17*	*3.56*	*3.86*	*9.3*	*1.5*	*4.5*	*0.8*	*3.93*	*33.8*	*8*

Breakout: 22% Improve: 46% Collapse: 7%

Even chess players show their age after a while. While his control is still impeccable, and while his fastball is no slower than it's ever been, Maddux's strikeout rate declined for the third consecutive season. Hitters were also able to loft the ball against him more frequently, leading to a big jump in his home run rate. It is evident that the movement on his pitches isn't quite what it used to be. It is blasphemous to suggest, but Maddux might be more effective if he were willing to waste a few more pitches; opposing batters hit .367 and slugged .597 when they put the first ball in play against him. A reasonable risk at one year and about $6 million, especially when you consider what he might be able to teach to young pitchers, but the Braves were wise to resist the temptation to offer him more than that out of sentimentality.

JASON MARQUIS Bats: L Throws: R Born: 21-Aug-78 Age: 25

YEAR	TM	LG	AGE	G	GS	IP	H	BB	SO	HR	ERA	EQERA	EQH9	EQBB9	EQSO9	EQHR9	PERA	VORP	STF
2001	ATL	NL	22	38	16	129.3	113	59	98	14	3.48	4.44	8.3	3.8	5.8	0.9	4.27	15.9	19
2002	ATL	NL	23	22	22	114.3	127	49	84	19	5.04	6.08	11.1	3.5	5.9	1.6	6.26	-5.8	0
2003	ATL	NL	24	21	2	40.7	43	18	19	3	5.53	5.31	9.7	3.7	3.7	0.7	4.73	-1.9	-9
2003	RIC	INT	24	15	15	94.0	93	34	75	5	3.35	4.62	9.3	4.0	5.7	0.7	4.65	9.5	13
2004	*STL*	*NL*	*25*	*58*	*11*	*101.3*	*103*	*43*	*69*	*10*	*4.37*	*4.77*	*9.1*	*3.3*	*5.5*	*0.9*	*4.78*	*8.3*	*-7*

Breakout: 23% Improve: 55% Collapse: 21%

(continued next page)

Jason Marquis (*continued*)

The good news is that Marquis is not nearly as uncoachable as Bruce Chen. But the Braves didn't appreciate his boo-hooing about his demotion, and that, combined with a history of inconsistent performances, was enough to transform him into a Cardinal. Marquis looks like a pitcher out there, and he throws hard enough, but his pitches are so lacking in movement that he tops out as a #4. He'll fight with Haren, Simontacchi, and Carpenter for one of the last two slots in St. Louis.

MACAY McBRIDE

Bats: L   **Throws: L**   Born: 24-Oct-82   Age: 21

YEAR	TM	LG	AGE	G	GS	IP	H	BB	SO	HR	ERA	EQERA	EQH9	EQBB9	EQSO9	EQHR9	PERA	VORP	STF
2002	MCN	SAL	19	25	25	157.3	119	48	138	6	2.12	4.18	8.7	3.7	4.9	0.8	4.41	22.1	24
2003	MYR	CAR	20	27	27	164.7	164	49	139	5	2.95	5.33	10.2	3.4	5.5	0.7	4.80	4.5	25
2004	ATL	NL	21	20	16	93.0	95	39	61	9	4.32	4.68	9.2	3.3	5.3	0.9	4.79	9.4	1

Breakout: 7%   Improve: 57%   Collapse: 11%

McBride has a lot going for him, including a devastating slider, a mean streak against left-handed opponents, and a propensity for avoiding the long ball. There's some speculation that he'll wind up as a reliever if he fails to develop another pitch, but then again, we're talking about a 20-year-old pitcher in A-ball. It's a bit like the seven-year-old prodigy down the block whose daddy talks non-stop about the relative merits of Harvard and Yale. You've gotta master long division first, kiddo, then we can talk.

KENT MERCKER

Bats: L   **Throws: L**   Born: 01-Feb-68   Age: 36

YEAR	TM	LG	AGE	G	GS	IP	H	BB	SO	HR	ERA	EQERA	EQH9	EQBB9	EQSO9	EQHR9	PERA	VORP	STF
2002	COL	NL	34	58	0	44.0	55	22	37	12	6.14	6.49	11.3	4.0	6.5	2.3	7.34	-4.3	-48
2003	CIN	NL	35	49	0	38.3	31	25	41	5	2.35	3.58	7.4	5.3	8.4	1.2	4.57	11.0	0
2003	ATL	NL	35	18	0	17.0	15	7	7	1	1.06	2.76	8.3	3.3	3.3	0.6	3.84	7.6	-7
2004	CHC	NL	36	28	7	57.0	54	27	48	7	3.99	4.25	8.5	3.8	6.8	1.1	4.75	9.3	0

Breakout: 33%   Improve: 60%   Collapse: 20%

Check out that walk rate. Mercker's peripherals would normally be associated with an ERA in the mid-fours. With few exceptions, differences between PERA and ERA tend to converge over time, so Mercker is at considerably more risk of a relapse into mediocrity than his superficially solid season lets on. Teams looking for a free-agent lefty need to proceed cautiously. You've been warned, Cubbies.

DAN MEYER

Bats: R   **Throws: L**   Born: 03-Jul-81   Age: 22

YEAR	TM	LG	AGE	G	GS	IP	H	BB	SO	HR	ERA	EQERA	EQH9	EQBB9	EQSO9	EQHR9	PERA	VORP	STF
2002	DNV	APP	21	13	13	65.7	47	18	77	4	2.74	4.13	9.8	3.5	5.6	1.4	5.51	9.3	6
2003	ROM	SAL	22	15	15	81.7	76	15	95	6	2.86	5.99	12.0	2.3	6.6	1.9	6.72	-3.1	0
2003	MYR	CAR	22	13	13	78.3	69	17	63	7	2.87	4.93	10.3	2.6	5.2	2.2	6.39	5.2	-7
2004	ATL	NL	22	16	11	64.7	68	24	47	10	5.02	5.44	9.5	3.0	5.8	1.4	5.27	1.9	-1

Breakout: 6%   Improve: 36%   Collapse: 32%

The college product has a tremendous changeup and plus command. The trouble is that he's been hittable, especially for distance, and his high HR rates suggest that he'll need to develop a complementary pitch to sustain his success at higher levels—the Braves have him working on a curveball.

BUBBA NELSON

Bats: R   **Throws: R**   Born: 26-Aug-81   Age: 22

YEAR	TM	LG	AGE	G	GS	IP	H	BB	SO	HR	ERA	EQERA	EQH9	EQBB9	EQSO9	EQHR9	PERA	VORP	STF
2001	MCN	SAL	19	25	24	151.0	144	57	154	16	3.93	6.82	11.8	5.2	5.6	2.2	7.80	-17.5	-6
2002	MYR	CAR	20	23	23	135.7	98	44	105	4	1.72	4.19	7.7	4.0	5.0	0.7	3.87	19.2	25
2003	GRN	SOU	21	23	20	119.0	106	45	77	7	3.18	4.92	8.9	3.9	4.2	1.1	4.81	8.3	4
2003	RIC	INT	21	11	0	14.3	10	5	7	1	1.89	2.63	5.3	4.0	4.0	0.7	2.77	4.5	9
2004	ATL	NL	22	13	9	51.7	55	29	31	7	5.56	6.03	9.6	4.4	4.8	1.2	5.87	0.3	-12

Breakout: 9%   Improve: 47%   Collapse: 28%

This is what you get when you draft a lot of rural kids: Bubbas are supposed to be big, huge guys—but this one is barely above six feet, and a few pounds shy of his listed 200. Bubba was named after his dad. Nelson relies mostly on his slider, throwing it more than half the time. His translated strikeout rates have declined at each level, but that's the predictable, troubling result of relying too heavily on a breaking pitch. Nelson's delivery of his slider also places a lot of torque on his elbow, and his innings pitched total was down last year. As pitching prospects go, he's on the overrated side, though he might work out nicely as a reliever in the Scott Williamson mold.

RUSS ORTIZ   Bats: R   Throws: R   Born: 05-Jun-74   Age: 30

YEAR	TM	LG	AGE	G	GS	IP	H	BB	SO	HR	ERA	EQERA	EQH9	EQBB9	EQSO9	EQHR9	PERA	VORP	STF
2001	SFG	NL	27	33	33	218.7	187	91	169	13	3.29	3.73	7.9	3.5	5.9	0.5	3.61	43.6	23
2002	SFG	NL	28	33	33	214.3	191	94	137	15	3.61	4.36	8.5	3.5	5.1	0.7	4.11	28.1	10
2003	ATL	NL	29	34	34	212.3	177	102	149	17	3.82	4.10	7.8	3.9	5.6	0.7	3.92	30.7	13
2004	ATL	NL	30	28	28	175.7	171	78	120	18	4.27	4.63	8.8	3.5	5.5	1.0	4.71	18.6	5

Breakout: 10%   Improve: 48%   Collapse: 14%

Ortiz is sort of the anti-Maddux. His fastball-curve combo is plenty good, but he gets tentative on the mound, and throws far more pitches than he really needs to. His hits allowed were lower than they should have been based on his strikeout rate, his walk totals routinely push the century mark, and he's got a lot of mileage on that arm, so he's a good candidate to regress this year. Schuerholz deserves credit for disposing of Damian Moss when his value was at its highest, but if Ortiz is the Opening Day starter, the Braves could be in for a long season.

ANDY PRATT   Bats: L   Throws: L   Born: 27-Aug-79   Age: 24

YEAR	TM	LG	AGE	G	GS	IP	H	BB	SO	HR	ERA	EQERA	EQH9	EQBB9	EQSO9	EQHR9	PERA	VORP	STF
2001	TUL	TEX	21	27	26	168.0	175	57	132	18	4.61	6.04	10.1	3.7	5.2	1.5	5.79	-7.6	3
2002	GRN	SOU	22	20	18	93.0	92	44	67	5	4.26	6.08	10.7	4.6	4.7	1.0	5.69	-4.5	-3
2002	RIC	INT	22	6	6	40.7	35	9	36	2	3.10	3.69	7.4	2.3	7.2	0.5	3.01	8.3	48
2003	RIC	INT	23	28	27	156.0	146	77	161	10	3.40	4.99	8.7	5.4	7.7	0.9	4.86	9.9	22
2004	ATL	NL	24	17	12	70.0	67	39	60	7	4.68	5.07	8.7	4.4	7.0	1.0	5.08	6.0	5

Breakout: 24%   Improve: 49%   Collapse: 28%

Pratt is lacking in command and oomph alike, and might not be thought of as a prospect at all he wasn't left-handed. His strikeout rates, however, have held up well as he's climbed the ladder, thanks in large part to a deceptive arm slot that hides the ball well as it leaves his hand. He'll need to reduce his walks by 20% to have a real shot.

HORACIO RAMIREZ   Bats: L   Throws: L   Born: 24-Nov-79   Age: 24

YEAR	TM	LG	AGE	G	GS	IP	H	BB	SO	HR	ERA	EQERA	EQH9	EQBB9	EQSO9	EQHR9	PERA	VORP	STF
2002	GRN	SOU	22	16	16	92.0	85	32	64	5	3.03	4.95	9.9	3.3	4.5	1.0	5.01	6.0	6
2003	ATL	NL	23	29	29	182.3	181	72	100	21	4.00	4.64	9.2	3.2	4.4	1.0	4.74	22.0	9
2004	ATL	NL	24	25	23	140.0	148	60	85	16	4.70	5.10	9.5	3.4	4.9	1.0	5.11	7.8	-1

Breakout: 11%   Improve: 44%   Collapse: 26%

A fringe prospect at the start of the year, Ramirez emerged as the surprise winner of the fourth-starter derby in spring training, then pitched effectively throughout the season. He lived and died by the double play: According to Keith Woolner's statistics, Ramirez was the most effective pitcher in the NL at inducing DPs given his opportunities. Since Ramirez neither throws a splitter nor had a tremendously lopsided GB:FB ratio, it's doubtful that result is sustainable, and without it, his ERA will likely go north.

One piece of insight into what the Braves think about him: As a result of some post-season roster shenanigans, Ramirez became eligible for Team USA, and the organization sent him to Latin America to be the team's nominal ace. Fortunately for Ramirez's labrum, Team USA's attempt to reach the Olympics proved to be abortive. I'm sure John Schuerholz is a patriotic guy and everything, but that's pushing it.

SHANE REYNOLDS

Bats: R   Throws: R   Born: 26-Mar-68   Age: 36

YEAR	TM	LG	AGE	G	GS	IP	H	BB	SO	HR	ERA	EQERA	EQH9	EQBB9	EQSO9	EQHR9	PERA	VORP	STF
2001	HOU	NL	33	28	28	182.7	208	36	102	24	4.33	4.57	10.2	1.6	4.3	1.0	4.72	20.1	0
2002	HOU	NL	34	13	13	74.0	80	26	47	13	4.86	5.12	9.5	2.8	4.9	1.5	5.24	3.8	-12
2003	ATL	NL	35	30	29	167.3	191	59	94	20	5.43	5.50	10.6	2.9	4.5	1.1	5.28	-0.6	-7
2004	ARI	NL	36	26	22	133.7	157	44	73	17	4.90	4.69	10.2	2.6	4.5	1.0	4.80	13.5	-1

Breakout: 9%   Improve: 47%   Collapse: 15%

While he remained mostly healthy, Reynolds hasn't had the same command since his back problems finally caught up with him a year ago. Without said command, his eminently hittable mix of junk doesn't stand much of a chance. That PECOTA is on the optimistic side. Reynolds's lifetime strikeout-to-walk ratio is 3.4-to-1; he's had easily the worst career of any long-career pitcher with a figure in that territory. Sometimes, the peripheral numbers don't tell the whole story.

JOHN SMOLTZ

Bats: R   Throws: R   Born: 15-May-67   Age: 37

YEAR	TM	LG	AGE	G	GS	IP	H	BB	SO	HR	ERA	EQERA	EQH9	EQBB9	EQSO9	EQHR9	PERA	VORP	STF
2001	ATL	NL	34	36	5	59.0	53	10	57	7	3.36	3.70	8.5	1.4	7.4	1.0	3.76	11.8	14
2002	ATL	NL	35	75	0	80.3	59	24	85	4	3.25	3.45	7.6	2.4	8.4	0.5	3.12	18.1	30
2003	ATL	NL	36	62	0	64.3	48	8	73	2	1.12	1.76	7.2	1.0	9.2	0.3	2.38	31.2	50
2004	ATL	NL	37	46	5	75.7	65	16	73	6	2.70	2.92	7.8	1.7	7.8	0.7	3.00	22.6	17

Breakout: 28%   Improve: 42%   Collapse: 40%

Sure, the Dennis Eckersley parallels can be overdone, but who's a better comp? Few pitchers have achieved the level of dominance that Smoltz has in the closer role, and fewer still have done it after such a successful run as a starter. One more year like the last, and the only question will be whether he'll be wearing that same old '80s sitcom dad beard on his Hall of Fame plaque.

Smoltz was running on fumes in September and October after returning from the DL. Though his velocity was still in the mid-90s, his command was wavering, and he was reluctant to throw his breaking pitches. There's not believed to be anything structurally wrong with his arm, but his struggles call into question just how bright of an idea it would be to use him as a starter, in spite of his noble intimations to the contrary. Smoltzie is widely acknowledged by himself to be the best backgammon player in baseball.

BILLY SYLVESTER

Bats: R   Throws: R   Born: 01-Oct-76   Age: 27

YEAR	TM	LG	AGE	G	GS	IP	H	BB	SO	HR	ERA	EQERA	EQH9	EQBB9	EQSO9	EQHR9	PERA	VORP	STF
2001	GRN	SOU	24	26	0	30.3	18	24	41	3	2.38	3.67	7.7	8.7	8.3	1.7	6.11	5.8	-25
2001	RIC	INT	24	36	0	37.0	28	27	41	2	5.11	5.29	7.9	7.7	7.9	0.8	5.06	1.2	-3
2002	GRN	SOU	25	51	0	49.3	31	32	48	6	3.47	4.78	8.5	6.4	6.4	2.5	6.92	3.9	-65
2003	RIC	INT	26	12	1	18.7	11	19	27	1	3.85	4.86	6.5	11.9	10.8	0.5	5.20	1.4	-3
2003	GRN	SOU	26	41	0	41.7	22	25	55	0	1.51	2.68	7.1	6.6	8.3	0.2	3.83	12.0	11
2004	ATL	NL	27	31	0	33.0	34	29	35	4	5.85	6.34	9.3	7.0	8.6	1.0	6.77	0.6	-7

Breakout: 36%   Improve: 49%   Collapse: 40%

Split closer duties with Carl Tweedy at Greenville. Sylvester's got a 97-MPH fastball with plus movement, a fine slider, a good pitcher's body—and no earthly idea of how to find the strike zone. The teams that can afford to search for miracle cures aren't those in the midst of contention.

ADAM WAINWRIGHT

Bats: R   Throws: R   Born: 30-Aug-81   Age: 22

YEAR	TM	LG	AGE	G	GS	IP	H	BB	SO	HR	ERA	EQERA	EQH9	EQBB9	EQSO9	EQHR9	PERA	VORP	STF
2001	MCN	SAL	19	28	28	164.7	144	48	184	9	3.77	6.20	10.6	3.9	6.0	1.1	5.63	-9.6	20
2002	MYR	CAR	20	28	28	163.3	149	66	167	7	3.31	5.94	10.1	5.0	6.7	0.9	5.47	-5.5	24
2003	GRN	SOU	21	27	27	149.7	133	37	128	9	3.37	4.64	9.2	2.5	5.5	1.1	4.60	14.7	18
2004	STL	NL	22	18	13	79.3	81	32	58	9	4.54	4.95	9.2	3.2	5.9	1.0	4.83	6.9	3

Breakout: 10%   Improve: 47%   Collapse: 29%

Wainwright's control made a quantum leap forward last season, as he halved his walk rate while advancing levels. He may be ready for the big leagues as soon as this spring. Tall (6′6″) and rail thin, Wainwright has a good curveball, a good change, and a clean, repeatable delivery. Whether can add some zip to his 88–90 MPH fastball as he fills out will determine whether he can be Aaron Sele, or something better than that. Traded to St. Louis, where his stock goes down a bit.

JARET WRIGHT

Bats: R   **Throws: R**   Born: 29-Dec-75   Age: 28

YEAR	TM	LG	AGE	G	GS	IP	H	BB	SO	HR	ERA	EQERA	EQH9	EQBB9	EQSO9	EQHR9	PERA	VORP	STF
2001	CLE	AL	25	7	7	29.0	36	22	18	2	6.52	5.83	9.8	6.1	4.9	0.6	5.35	-0.7	-7
2001	BUF	INT	25	7	7	28.7	25	13	28	3	4.70	5.81	8.9	4.8	6.8	1.4	5.33	-0.6	-14
2002	CLE	AL	26	8	6	18.3	40	19	12	3	15.74	13.02	18.3	8.2	5.3	1.4	10.19	-15.4	-73
2002	BUF	INT	26	10	10	55.7	57	24	43	5	3.88	5.68	10.7	4.8	5.9	1.2	6.03	-0.5	-18
2003	SDP	NL	27	39	0	47.3	69	28	41	9	8.37	8.41	13.3	4.7	6.8	1.8	7.75	-18.3	-43
2003	POR	PCL	27	12	1	19.0	16	7	21	0	1.42	3.57	8.7	4.1	8.7	0.0	3.61	4.0	30
2003	ATL	NL	27	11	0	9.0	7	3	9	0	2.00	2.08	7.3	3.1	8.3	0.0	2.76	3.6	41
2004	*ATL*	*NL*	*28*	*28*	*7*	*54.0*	*60*	*30*	*41*	*8*	*5.88*	*6.38*	*10.0*	*4.4*	*6.1*	*1.4*	*6.19*	*0.5*	*-12*

Breakout: 26%   Improve: 55%   Collapse: 21%

Wright's fastball still pops off his arm and registers in the high-90s. He was as bad as a pitcher could be in San Diego—the worst reliever in the league, according to Michael Wolverton's RRE numbers. But once Leo Mazzone got hold of him, and impressed upon Wright the importance of keeping the ball down, he reeled off a series of effective September innings in Atlanta. Given the bruising that his statistical record has taken, it's no surprise that the projection is poor, but Wright has sleeper potential as a Brave.

ALEC ZUMWALT

Bats: R   **Throws: R**   Born: 20-Jan-81   Age: 23

YEAR	TM	LG	AGE	G	GS	IP	H	BB	SO	HR	ERA	EQERA	EQH9	EQBB9	EQSO9	EQHR9	PERA	VORP	STF
2002	MCN	SAL	21	24	0	39.7	39	16	34	2	4.31	7.08	11.8	5.0	4.7	1.3	6.69	-5.6	-25
2002	MYR	CAR	21	21	0	24.0	33	13	21	2	8.63	12.19	15.7	7.0	5.7	2.2	9.79	-15.2	-57
2003	MYR	CAR	22	30	0	44.7	29	16	43	2	2.21	3.63	7.7	4.3	6.1	1.1	4.42	8.7	0
2003	GRN	SOU	22	11	0	19.0	13	12	19	0	1.42	3.12	7.8	6.7	6.2	0.5	4.50	4.8	10
2004	*TBA*	*AL*	*23*	*18*	*5*	*34.7*	*38*	*23*	*24*	*5*	*6.06*	*6.38*	*9.7*	*5.2*	*5.7*	*1.3*	*6.29*	*-0.1*	*-17*

Breakout: 23%   Improve: 58%   Collapse: 21%

Minor league relievers are the flavor du jour in the Rule 5 draft. Their parent organizations generally won't bother protecting them, but the best ones can provide cheap bullpen help to teams that are short on internal options. Zumwalt, selected by Tampa Bay in the Rule 5 draft, doesn't really fit the bill. A converted infielder, he's posted some shiny ERAs, but is still learning the finer points of pitching, and has yet to display the control that would make him well-suited for Triple-A, let alone the major leagues. He needs another year of development in the minors, and that's exactly what his selection by the Devil Rays ensures that he won't get.

Chicago Cubs

ive more outs. The frenzy of blame that swirled like a twister of crushed leaves around Steve Bartman, Alex Gonzalez, and Dusty Baker was little more than a forlorn act of displacement—Chicago isn't the sort of city where you want to be seen crying in your beer. But make no mistake: This one hurt. It hurt because when you're the Cubs, these chances don't come along very often.

After all, ever since the days of Tinker, Evers, and Chance, Cubbie ambles in the post-season forest have been proceeded by long and solitary stints in the basement. As Bill James' Plexiglass Principle suggests, most playoff teams benefit from some serendipity. The best expectation, in the absence of other information, is that such teams' luck will run out and they'll regress back to the pack. But the Cubs' hangovers have been particularly severe: In the seasons following their previous three playoff appearances, the Cubs won 77, 77 and 67 games, respectively. Narratives of the Chicago Cubs tend to begin and end with ghost stories, and while we do not intend to repeat those here, the recent past provides some important lessons for this year's club.

1984

The 1984 team, which finished with the best record in the league, but lost the pivotal game of the NLCS in predictably heartbreaking fashion, had an emerging superstar in Ryne Sandberg and a good second fiddle in Leon Durham. But the duo was surrounded by a core of players who looked more potent than they really were. Ron Cey and Gary Matthews were 36 and 33, respectively, when the season ended. Rick Sutcliffe was a good pitcher, but not the ace that his gaudy 16–1 record suggested. Dennis Eckersley was years away from being reincarnated as a closer. Steve Trout and Scott Sanderson pitched well, but both were career years.

Prior to 1984, with much the same assemblage of talent, the Cubs had not had a winning record in a dozen seasons. That should have told them something. But then-GM Dallas Green brought back an almost identical roster: Among the starting positions, only shortstop Larry Bowa, who was eased into his wheelchair in mid-season by Shawon Dunston, and the fifth starter, Dick Ruthven, whose performance had been truly execrable, were turned over. The following year exposed the Cubs for what they had—one great player in Sandberg, a handful of average

CUBS PROSPECTUS

2003 record: 88–74; First place, NL Central; Lost to Marlins in Championship Series

Pythagenport record: 85–77

Runs scored per game: 4.5 (9th in NL)

Runs allowed per game: 4.2 (3rd in NL)

Team EqA: .258 (10th in NL)

2003 Batters Age: 29.7 (6th youngest in NL)

2003 Pitchers Age: 28.2 (8th youngest in NL)

Ballpark: Wrigley Field; Slight pitcher's park; Park Factor of 0.976

2003: Rode a young, fearsome front three and a little of Dusty's trademark magic one game short of the Series.

2004: A solid, short-term-oriented off-season makes the Cubs the team to beat in the division.

players, and a bunch of stiffs. BP wasn't writing books back then, but the demise of the team might very well have been predicted.

1989

The 1989 pennant was a youth-driven effort. Accounting for both pitchers and hitters, the Cubs had the second-youngest group of starters in the league. When young teams win titles, it's usually a sign of great things ahead.

But when the career paths of Jerome Walton—a toolsy player whose fine 1989 campaign had been driven almost entirely by batting average—and Dwight Smith—a collegian who was already 25 at the time of his debut—began to deteriorate prematurely, the Cubs were ill prepared to make up for the loss in run production. The pitching staff suffered when Mitch Williams fell off the tightrope, and Mike Harkey and Shawn Boskie, two homegrown players with first-round pedigrees, failed to develop as expected, Harkey's career undermined by a stream of injuries. The Cubs, emboldened by their unexpected success, did not hedge their bets by bringing in players from outside the organization. Among the starting rotation and position players, not one was acquired from another club. The Cubs danced around the .500 mark for four seasons before Sandberg retired for the first time and the bottom fell out.

1998

The 1998 group was the least talented of the bunch, edging the Giants for the Wild Card in a one-game playoff following breakout campaigns from Sammy Sosa and Kerry Wood, and uncharacteristically good seasons from a cast of veterans like Henry Rodriguez and Mickey Morandini. The motley scraps of players associated with a rebuilding period had been transformed, the Cubs believed, into the foundation of a contending club, and the team responded by retaining the services of a 33-year-old Morandini, a 35-year-old Lance Johnson, and a 40-year-old Gary Gaetti. The only significant players brought in from outside the organization were Benito Santiago, whose value had bottomed out after two difficult years in Toronto, and Jon Lieber, acquired in trade for Brant Brown.

The punch line this time around was a pair of career-threatening injuries to Wood and Jeremi Gonzalez, which coupled with the predictable decline of the aging offensive core, sent the Cubs into their customary downward spiral.

Each time the Cubs have tasted the post-season lager, they have overrated their holdings, keeping as much of the roster intact as possible, extending veterans for another year and failing to address areas of deficiency. Each time, that formula has failed.

This behavior has sometimes been attributed to a folk economic theory that might be called the Curse of the Bleachers; the idea being that the Cubs don't have much incentive to improve, since the bums will come out and taunt the opposing right fielder and drink Old Style, win, lose, rain or shine. To the extent that the Cubs resolve to pick and choose their players, the theory goes, they are more inclined to trot out familiar names, whatever their inadequacies, than replace them with less heralded or more expensive players.

Ignoring for a moment that the empirical results don't really bear the theory out—the Cubs set an attendance record this year in large part because their strong season kept walk-up sales strong through the traditionally sluggish months of May and September—that line of thinking obscures another characteristic that has been perhaps a more important influence on the team's behavior. Namely, the Cubs are, and have always been, a conservative organization. Though they were one of the first teams to be associated with corporate ownership—first the Wrigleys, now Tribune Corp.—they have always been run more along the lines of a family business, with a small front office staff consisting mostly of people who have been associated with the organization for years. The franchise, in large part because of its ballpark, has long been the symbolic guardian of baseball tradition and history. Tribune Corp. itself is a conservative organization, heavily invested in

Chicago's institutions, but lining up far to the right of the city in its political leanings.

The Cubs have resisted change at every turn, taking their sporadic successes as evidence that, well, they've really been doing things right all along, and their long periods of failure are attributable to billy goats or black cats or a thousand other things they are conveniently powerless to correct. When following the Cubs, one is frequently reminded of Bertrand Russell's inductive chicken: The bird has found that every day of its life, it walks up to the farmer and the farmer gives him feed. It is quite confident that this pattern will continue on indefinitely. Then, one day, the farmer wants something meaty on the table...

But past ineptitude is no guarantee of future failure. The Cubs' management team—both the baseball operations executives, and, importantly, Tribune Corp.—has been presented with a window of opportunity. Not since the Ron Santo/Billy Williams clubs of the late 60s have the Cubs had such an array of talent on hand, and never has the franchise had such strong brand equity and revenue-generating potential. At the same time, many of the team's most important assets have a sell-by date. Sammy Sosa is 35, and has already exhibited some signs of decline. The young pitchers are young pitchers, and they've been worked hard. The farm system is deep at the lower levels, but sparse at the upper ones, with few players who can be expected to make a big league contribution in the next two years. The team has dipped into the reservoir of goodwill that has carried the franchise through its rough stretches by raising ticket prices and pressing an indifferent mayor's office for improvements to the ballpark and its surrounding territory.

The team's behavior this off-season reflects, if nothing else, a recognition of this moment. Though one can debate their prices, Derrek Lee and LaTroy Hawkins are players who should substantially improve the team in 2004. Off the field, the act of raising ticket prices demonstrates recognition of the team's increasing popularity. Similarly, the club's secondary approaches to increasing revenue—its proposals to add rows of premium seating along the dugouts, expand the bleachers, increase the number of night games, and, yes, its attempt to capture bubbles in real-time demand by establishing an in-house scalping operation—reflect an ownership that is treating the Cubs more like a real business and less like a cuddly stuffed animal.

The Cubs also boast a capable public relations staff that can help to minimize the backlash stemming from these initiatives. Tellingly, the ticket price increases were announced in the immediate aftermath of the Lee and Hawkins acquisitions, and generated relatively little public outcry. The team has even established a statistical analyst position, and even if its invention reflects more a titular change than a philosophical one—Chuck Wasserstrom, the man appointed to the job, will carry out many of the same duties he held as the team's PR assistant—the move represents a tentative first step toward incorporating analytical modes of thought into the team's course of business.

But intent is one thing, and execution is another. The price paid for Lee was Hee Seop Choi, a cheap and promising player whose fall from grace within the organization reflects some of the team's worst and most long-standing biases in talent evaluation. Though the market for infielders tightened up more quickly than Jim Hendry had anticipated, the team was quick to settle for Mark Grudzielanek, a 34-year-old player with a career OBP of .329, but subsequently successfully seduced Todd Walker into the fold; he'll be 31, and he's coming off a year with a .333 OBP. The Cubs, as a rule, still give the power components of offensive output too much emphasis, the on-base components too little, and weight major league service time more highly than they should.

The disconnect between the team's income stream and its payroll shows no signs of abating. Given the team's dominant position in the third-largest media market in the country, its record-setting attendance, and its national exposure through WGN, it is reasonable to assume that the Cubs will take in the third- or fourth-largest revenue in baseball, behind only the AL East nuclear powers, and perhaps the Dodgers. Yet Chicago's Opening Day payroll has been pegged at a relatively modest $85 million, about $7 million higher than it was at the start of last season. Spending more money on players, of course, is no guarantee of success, but with the roster as it stood when Hendry checked out of the New Orleans Marriott in mid-December, there was the sinking feeling that the Cubs would come up just a little bit short. It is here that the Curse of the Bleachers would rear its ugly head: Tribune Corp. might think it worthwhile to upgrade from a poor Cubs team to a good one, but perhaps not from a good team to a great one.

That line of thinking would be a mistake. The additional money required to acquire Javy Lopez or Ivan Rodriguez or Greg Maddux would not only improve the Cubs' performance on the field; it might also increase their expected profit. Hendry is a highly competent executive, but not necessarily a creative one. He works as best as he can within a budget, but he's not likely to turn straw into gold, or Ricardo Rincon into Brian Giles. To transform the Cubs into an organization that is not merely competitive, but one of the premier franchises in baseball, he will need his ownership's support.

The stumbling block in all of this is Dusty Baker. We have deliberately avoided mention of Baker thus far, and with good reason. The popular history of the Cubs' 2003 season is sure to make Dusty the protagonist, but it is fair to say that he was neither as important a factor in their success as the pundits would have him be, nor as much of an impediment to it as some other analysts would suggest. Lesser tactics such as inefficient sacrifice bunting strategy, or bias in the choice of utility players, are not likely to make or break a team's season. Overuse of starting pitchers might, but those concerns are longer-term.

More to the point, we have subordinated the discussion of Baker to that of the Cubs' executives because that's how the chain of command should follow. If Dusty puts Mark Prior's arm through the grinder, the responsibility for that lies, ultimately, with Jim Hendry. The same thing holds if he refuses to play the players who, in the organization's judgment, will give it the best chance to maximize its win total over the course of the season.

Certainly, every professional relationship requires some give-and-take, and the uneasy situation that existed between Billy Beane and Art Howe in Oakland will not be sustainable in most instances. But if the team's chief executive feels the need to defer to the manager in matters as important as protecting the health of the club's prized young pitchers, then either the manager or the executive is the wrong man for the job. The irony is that, with the exception of in-game strategy, Baker excels at the very elements of his job—relating to his players, presenting a public face of the team to the media—that are more or less solely the responsibility of the manager.

The Cubs will enter 2004 on a wave of optimism, just as they entered 1985, 1990, and 1999. The organization seems poised to avoid the mistakes that made it a one-hit wonder in the past. Management believes that it has put a playoff club on the field, and if everything goes according to plan, the fans will forget about Game Six soon enough. One can faintly imagine a repentant Steve Bartman being invited to throw out the first pitch when the World Series comes to Wrigleyville, and the Cubs, lesson learned, taking the proactive course in exorcising the latest manifestation of their curse.

But the Cubs' margin over the Astros and the Cardinals is slim. The lineup is shallow and overwhelmingly right-handed. Chicago can reasonably expect to get better production out of first base, third base, and the fifth starter's position, but declines are probable at second, and possible throughout the outfield, and that's before accounting for the Armageddon scenario in which one or more of the young starters gets hurt. There's merit in not making the same mistakes thrice, but baseball teams are limitless in their capacity to invent new ways to fail, and the events of the off-season suggest that the Cubs may have identified a few.

HITTERS

MOISES ALOU   LF   **Bats: R**   **Throws: R**   Born: 03-Jul-66   Age: 37

YEAR	TM	LG	AGE	AB	H	2B	3B	HR	BB	SO	SB	CS	AVG	OBP	SLG	MLVR	EQBA	EQOBP	EQSLG	EQMLVR	VORP	DEFENSE
2001	HOU	NL	35	513	170	31	1	27	57	57	5	1	.331	.396	.554	.305	.326	.395	.544	.296	51.9	104-RF 3
2002	CHC	NL	36	484	133	23	1	15	47	61	8	0	.275	.337	.419	.053	.285	.345	.441	.023	9.9	109-LF 3
2003	CHC	NL	37	565	158	35	1	22	63	67	3	1	.280	.357	.462	.135	.285	.360	.477	.100	23.0	136-LF -5
2004	CHC	NL	37	392	106	21	1	11	40	51	3	1	.270	.338	.418	-.020	.272	.339	.430	-.013	6.5	104-LF -2

Breakout: 6%   Improve: 33%   Collapse: 33%

Alou had a better season in his second turn as a Cub, staying mostly healthy and mashing lefties, but he slumped badly in parts of August and September, not a good sign for a player his age. PECOTA thinks the end could come sooner rather than later, and the Cubs brought in Todd Hollandsworth to hedge against an Alou collapse. Spending $9.5 million for an injury-prone left fielder who should hit at about the league average isn't a particularly good use of resources, but the Cubs should have realized that before tossing Alou three years, $27 million at age 35.

As for the best way to use Alou, the Cubs should consider a different route—remaking him as a leadoff hitter. His on-base percentage projects to be better than that of Corey Patterson or Mark Grudzielanek, and because he's always had good bat control, it's possible that Alou could improve it further by focusing on working deeper into the count. It isn't going to happen on a team managed by Dusty Baker, who apparently banished his experimental demons in the 60s, but in an era when *bona fide* leadoff hitters are about as common as leisure suits at a Phish concert, teams need to explore all alternatives.

PAUL BAKO   C   **Bats: L**   **Throws: R**   Born: 20-Jun-72   Age: 32

YEAR	TM	LG	AGE	AB	H	2B	3B	HR	BB	SO	SB	CS	AVG	OBP	SLG	MLVR	EQBA	EQOBP	EQSLG	EQMLVR	VORP	DEFENSE
2001	ATL	NL	29	137	29	10	1	2	20	34	1	0	.212	.312	.343	-.206	.216	.314	.353	-.207	-1.3	44-C 0
2002	MIL	NL	30	234	55	8	1	4	20	46	0	2	.235	.295	.329	-.177	.245	.301	.346	-.224	-3.1	65-C -5
2003	CHC	NL	31	188	43	13	3	0	22	47	0	1	.229	.311	.330	-.160	.241	.319	.351	-.184	-1.9	53-C -4
2004	CHC	NL	32	150	35	8	1	3	16	34	1	1	.231	.307	.356	-.180	.233	.308	.367	-.178	0.4	44-C -2

Breakout: 34%   Improve: 56%   Collapse: 30%

Ladies and gentlemen, your prototypical backup catcher. Bako's caught-stealing numbers were down a bit this year (30%), but he's a solid defensive player and had a couple of fun catcher pickoffs. He also can't hit very much. Handedness aside, Bako and Damian Miller are redundant players, and it would be wise for the Cubs to retain one and replace the other with an offense-first, Bobby-Estalella type backstop for those days when the Shawn Estes proxy is pitching. They settled for flipping Miller to the A's for Michael Barrett, part of a December non-tender merry-go-round.

HEE CHOI   1B   **Bats: L**   **Throws: L**   Born: 16-Mar-79   Age: 25

YEAR	TM	LG	AGE	AB	H	2B	3B	HR	BB	SO	SB	CS	AVG	OBP	SLG	MLVR	EQBA	EQOBP	EQSLG	EQMLVR	VORP	DEFENSE
2001	IOW	PCL	22	266	61	11	0	13	34	67	5	1	.229	.313	.417	-.110	.201	.282	.369	-.257	-15.1	68-1B 3
2002	IOW	PCL	23	478	137	24	3	26	95	119	3	2	.287	.406	.513	.262	.247	.360	.440	.018	15.8	127-1B -12
2002	CHC	NL	23	50	9	1	0	2	7	15	0	0	.180	.281	.320	-.235	.196	.293	.353	-.260	-2.4	14-1B 0
2003	CHC	NL	24	202	44	17	0	8	37	71	1	1	.218	.350	.421	.020	.224	.352	.439	-.016	3.8	60-1B 0
2003	IOW	PCL	24	66	17	4	1	6	9	19	0	1	.258	.351	.621	.299	.224	.313	.537	.045	2.7	16-1B 2
2004	FLA	NL	25	346	87	20	1	17	50	90	2	2	.252	.353	.465	.053	.259	.359	.495	.094	21.0	97-1B -2

Breakout: 50%   Improve: 85%   Collapse: 7%

Choi started the year with a bang—posting a .241/.431/.556 line in April—and ended it with one—a scary, June 17 collision with Kerry Wood that left him concussive and unconscious. It didn't have to be that way; Choi came back from the injury, and hit pretty well at Iowa when he was playing every day. But the injury provided management with an excuse to dispose of a player whose approach they never really appreciated in the first place, and by the time Randall Simon had been brought in, Choi's career as a Cub was effectively over. Certainly, Choi had some rough at-bats in Wrigley in July and August, but it's tough to hit well when you're only getting a few times up a week and your organization has lost confidence in you.

Not that he is without his faults: Choi's approach at the plate can be too passive even by *BP* standards, and he can struggle with pitches that break in toward him. He's never going to be a huge batting average hitter. But Choi has abundant power, plays surprisingly good defense, and could be the second- or third-best hitter in a good lineup. The big ballpark and lack of good Korean BBQ joints aside, Florida is an excellent place for him. If you're willing to resign yourself to the Cubs' judgment that Choi is never going to break out as a hitter, then Derrek Lee makes for a pretty good replacement, but it didn't have to be this way.

BRIAN DOPIRAK   **1B**   **Bats: R**   **Throws: R**   Born: 20-Dec-83   Age: 20

YEAR	TM	LG	AGE	AB	H	2B	3B	HR	BB	SO	SB	CS	AVG	OBP	SLG	MLVR	EQBA	EQOBP	EQSLG	EQMLVR	VORP	DEFENSE			
2003	BOI	NWN	19	192	46	4	0	13	24	58	0	2	.240	.330	.464	.116	.167	.224	.333	-.439	-41.4	41-1B	3		
2003	LNS	MID	19	78	21	3	0	2	2	22	0	0	.269	.305	.385	.028	.228	.246	.342	-.348	-6.3	13-1B	-1		
2004	CHC	NL	20	242	43	10	0	7	16	82	0	1	.178	.232	.310	-.407	.180	.232	.319	-.411	-20.7	65-1B	-9		

Breakout: 33%   Improve: 52%   Collapse: 33%

A year ago, Dopirak was tabbed by *Baseball America* as having the best power in the draft, which is a backhanded compliment if there ever was one. He's big, he's strong...and he can't hit. The power numbers in Boise look good, but it's a wiffle ball park.

JASON DuBOIS   **RF**   **Bats: R**   **Throws: R**   Born: 26-Mar-79   Age: 25

YEAR	TM	LG	AGE	AB	H	2B	3B	HR	BB	SO	SB	CS	AVG	OBP	SLG	MLVR	EQBA	EQOBP	EQSLG	EQMLVR	VORP	DEFENSE			
2001	LNS	MID	22	443	131	28	9	24	46	120	1	2	.296	.377	.562	.325	.216	.278	.413	-.194	-17.9	59-RF	-8	28-LF	-3
2002	DAY	FLA	23	361	116	25	1	20	57	95	6	2	.321	.422	.562	.431	.245	.328	.443	-.038	3.2	86-RF	-11		
2003	WTN	SOU	24	443	119	31	4	15	57	118	2	4	.269	.367	.458	.190	.236	.317	.413	-.106	-6.1	104-RF	-11	13-1B	-3
2004	CHC	NL	25	252	64	15	1	11	26	64	1	1	.253	.333	.458	.011	.256	.334	.471	.019	9.9	70-RF	-5		

Breakout: 41%   Improve: 72%   Collapse: 18%

Dubois was selected by the Blue Jays in the Rule 5 draft last year and subsequently returned, which illustrates the difficulty here: If an analytically-oriented team like the Jays doesn't think he has enough value to be worthy of a roster slot, what is a scouty team like the Cubs going to think? Dubois is a good athlete who has shown flashes of power in the minors, and he put together an impressive campaign in the Arizona Fall League. But even if he learns to hit fastballs up in the zone and manages that breakout that PECOTA is predicting, he's really just a fourth outfielder, because while his arm strong, his range is a liability in either corner. Every now and then, a guy like this works his butt off and becomes Jody Gerut. But 24-year-old corner players who put up .240 EqAs have attrition rates that make the Maginot Line look like the Great Wall of China.

DOUG GLANVILLE   **CF**   **Bats: R**   **Throws: R**   Born: 25-Aug-70   Age: 33

YEAR	TM	LG	AGE	AB	H	2B	3B	HR	BB	SO	SB	CS	AVG	OBP	SLG	MLVR	EQBA	EQOBP	EQSLG	EQMLVR	VORP	DEFENSE	
2001	PHI	NL	30	634	166	24	3	14	19	91	28	6	.262	.285	.375	-.179	.271	.295	.388	-.156	-1.5	148-CF	7
2002	PHI	NL	31	422	105	16	3	6	25	57	19	2	.249	.292	.344	-.144	.263	.303	.365	-.181	-3.5	99-CF	0
2003	TEX	AL	32	195	53	5	0	4	6	25	4	0	.272	.294	.359	-.195	.284	.308	.376	-.140	-2.5	44-CF	-1
2003	CHC	NL	32	51	12	0	0	1	2	4	0	1	.235	.259	.294	-.375	.250	.278	.308	-.320	-3.5	13-CF	1
2004	PHI	NL	33	221	56	9	1	3	11	27	5	2	.255	.292	.352	-.200	.256	.291	.360	-.203	-5.0	59-CF	-3

Breakout: 34%   Improve: 55%   Collapse: 27%

It isn't exactly clear why the Cubs brought in Glanville, a likeable, intelligent guy who has had exactly one major league season in which he provided his team with much value. OK, so Kenny Lofton's defense isn't much good anymore, and Tom Goodwin was on the shelf for a couple of weeks around the trade deadline. Do you really trade anyone for a defensive replacement whose best game is *EverQuest?* Ed Wade seems to be a glutton for punishment.

ALEX GONZALEZ   **Goat**   **Bats: R**   **Throws: R**   Born: 08-Apr-73   Age: 31

YEAR	TM	LG	AGE	AB	H	2B	3B	HR	BB	SO	SB	CS	AVG	OBP	SLG	MLVR	EQBA	EQOBP	EQSLG	EQMLVR	VORP	DEFENSE	
2001	TOR	AL	28	636	161	25	5	17	43	149	18	11	.253	.303	.388	-.122	.266	.320	.412	-.079	20.0	152-SS	18
2002	CHC	NL	29	513	127	27	5	18	46	136	5	3	.248	.312	.425	-.002	.258	.319	.449	-.035	22.4	140-SS	-8
2003	CHC	NL	30	536	122	37	0	20	47	123	3	3	.228	.295	.409	-.084	.236	.301	.427	-.117	9.9	137-SS	7
2004	CHC	NL	31	403	101	21	2	13	35	92	4	2	.250	.313	.406	-.094	.252	.313	.418	-.089	13.0	107-SS	-2

Breakout: 25%   Improve: 56%   Collapse: 18%

Good range, good hands, durability, and some power. I'll take "Damning With Faint Praise" for $200, Alex. The second-most-famous misplay in Game Six notwithstanding, Gonzalez cut his error total by more than half after having struggled some with the adjustment to a natural grass field in 2002, and is one of the better defenders in the game. Gonzo has one more relatively expensive year on his contract, and that means he'll be back out there.

TOM GOODWIN CF Bats: L Throws: R Born: 27-Jul-68 Age: 35

YEAR	TM	LG	AGE	AB	H	2B	3B	HR	BB	SO	SB	CS	AVG	OBP	SLG	MLVR	EQBA	EQOBP	EQSLG	EQMLVR	VORP	DEFENSE			
2001	LAD	NL	32	286	66	8	5	4	23	58	22	8	.231	.286	.336	-.241	.244	.299	.354	-.217	-5.5	65-CF -5			
2002	FRE	PCL	33	62	14	3	1	0	8	8	3	2	.226	.314	.306	-.240	.194	.275	.258	-.424	-5.6	16-CF 0			
2002	SFG	NL	33	154	40	5	2	1	14	25	16	2	.260	.321	.338	-.087	.285	.339	.367	-.093	-1.5	20-LF 0	15-CF 1	
2003	CHC	NL	34	171	49	10	0	1	11	33	19	5	.287	.328	.363	-.047	.293	.332	.374	-.090	3.8	16-CF 0	11-LF 0	
2004	CHC	NL	35	130	33	6	1	2	10	23	8	2	.253	.307	.347	-.179	.255	.308	.358	-.177	-1.4	38-CF -5			

Breakout: 15%   Improve: 28%   Collapse: 40%

He had a good year. We're fond of mentioning Jazayerli's Law of Catcher Defense, which suggests that every season, a few backup catchers will have their day in a monkeys-typing-Shakespeare sort of way. Can the same be said about scrappy outfielders? Goodwin is a legitimately outstanding basestealer, now placed in the top 100 all-time in career swipes, just ahead of Gary Pettis, Fielder Jones, and the Hamburglar. He's been brought back for another year.

MARK GRUDZIELANEK 2B Bats: R Throws: R Born: 30-Jun-70 Age: 34

YEAR	TM	LG	AGE	AB	H	2B	3B	HR	BB	SO	SB	CS	AVG	OBP	SLG	MLVR	EQBA	EQOBP	EQSLG	EQMLVR	VORP	DEFENSE
2001	LAD	NL	31	539	146	21	3	13	28	83	4	4	.271	.317	.393	-.071	.284	.329	.413	-.047	18.7	131-2B -7
2002	LAD	NL	32	536	145	23	0	9	22	89	4	1	.271	.301	.364	-.074	.291	.318	.395	-.087	11.9	133-2B -7
2003	CHC	NL	33	481	151	38	1	3	30	64	6	2	.314	.366	.416	.116	.323	.372	.429	.088	31.0	119-2B -8
2004	CHC	NL	34	410	112	21	2	6	24	59	4	2	.273	.321	.379	-.100	.275	.322	.390	-.095	12.2	106-2B -5

Breakout: 11%   Improve: 24%   Collapse: 40%

Teams pay certain financial and strategic costs for hiring Dusty Baker; is this their reward? At age 33, Grudz posted the second-highest EqA of his career, and was especially impressive during the stretch run, flashing a .377 OBP after returning from a broken hand. The performances of Grudzielanek and Kenny Lofton were important factors in facilitating the Cubs' division title, won by the slimmest of margins in a second half when Moises Alou and Sammy Sosa were slumping.

Trouble is, the performance looks every bit like a fluke. Grudzielanek's solid season was driven mostly by a high batting average—his plate discipline was as marginal as ever. He hit a bunch of doubles, but it's doubtful they're a precursor of a late-career power surge: Grudzielanek's GB:FB ratio was 1.87, the largest figure since his rookie season. The trouble with bringing him back isn't so much that the 2004 Grudzielanek is going to be worse than the 2004 Fernando Vina or the 2004 Roberto Alomar, but that the 2004 Grudzielanek is likely going to be a lot worse than the 2003 Grudzielanek. If the Cubs don't account for that, they're going to be stuck watching Sammy Sosa come to the plate a lot with two outs and the bases empty.

BRENDAN HARRIS 3B/2B Bats: R Throws: R Born: 26-Aug-80 Age: 23

YEAR	TM	LG	AGE	AB	H	2B	3B	HR	BB	SO	SB	CS	AVG	OBP	SLG	MLVR	EQBA	EQOBP	EQSLG	EQMLVR	VORP	DEFENSE	
2001	LNS	MID	20	113	31	5	1	4	17	26	5	1	.274	.370	.442	.145	.198	.278	.328	-.322	-5.4	11-2B 4	
2002	DAY	FLA	21	425	140	35	6	13	43	57	16	4	.329	.395	.532	.368	.263	.315	.437	-.055	16.7	59-3B 5	54-2B -2
2002	WTN	SOU	21	53	17	4	1	2	2	5	1	1	.321	.345	.547	.330	.296	.309	.500	.057	2.8		
2003	WTN	SOU	22	435	122	34	7	5	51	72	6	7	.280	.364	.425	.153	.245	.314	.385	-.144	5.2	94-3B -13	15-2B -1
2004	CHC	NL	23	254	66	16	2	6	23	45	4	2	.258	.325	.414	-.056	.260	.326	.426	-.051	12.8	70-3B -3	

Breakout: 27%   Improve: 56%   Collapse: 17%

OK, so he's not going to be Albert Pujols, and Harris's line drive swing doesn't generate enough loft to project for big power numbers. He has neither the range you'd really want in a second baseman, nor the instincts you'd want in a third baseman, which makes him a perfect candidate to play shortstop for the Yankees, but otherwise a bit of a tweener. But this is a good hitter who can help a major league club as a cheap solution at second base for a few years. His solid finish in the AFL presages what should be a happier season ahead. Harris might be the next Jay Bell, and that's not a bad thing.

RYAN HARVEY OF Bats: R Throws: R Born: 30-Aug-84 Age: 19

Harvey comes out of high school with a reputation for a huge power bat, but he profiles more as a bigger, stronger version of Corey Patterson than as the next Mark McGwire. For that reason, the knee tear he suffered at the end of his junior year is a real concern; speed and plus defense in center field were two of Harvey's assets, and neither were at full strength during his brief debut in Arizona. There's no doubt that his upside is high, particularly in terms of power, and he should improve over the course of the season as he shakes the rust off, but Delmon Young or Rickie Weeks he isn't.

PHIL HIATT   1B   Bats: R   Throws: R   Born: 01-May-69   Age: 35

YEAR	TM	LG	AGE	AB	H	2B	3B	HR	BB	SO	SB	CS	AVG	OBP	SLG	MLVR	EQBA	EQOBP	EQSLG	EQMLVR	VORP	DEFENSE			
2001	LVG	PCL	32	436	144	29	5	44	52	109	6	4	.330	.406	.722	.535	.274	.348	.592	.230	56.5	85-3B	-1	15-1B	-2
2001	LAD	NL	32	50	12	3	0	2	3	19	0	0	.240	.283	.420	-.122	.255	.296	.431	-.105	0.3				
2002	LVG	PCL	33	355	108	14	2	23	42	88	1	2	.304	.375	.549	.244	.258	.328	.470	.010	6.8	35-LF	-3	33-1B	-1
2003	IOW	PCL	34	478	130	35	1	25	45	110	10	2	.272	.335	.506	.135	.242	.305	.457	-.063	3.0	84-1B	7	13-RF	0
2004	HOU	NL	35	107	25	6	0	5	12	29	1	1	.234	.316	.442	-.052	.232	.312	.440	-.078	2.6	33-1B	-1		

Breakout: 22%   Improve: 41%   Collapse: 41%

Then there is Phil Hiatt, hitting 30 home runs every year in Des Moines, or Indy, or Buffalo, or maybe Hanshin. There aren't many Crash Davises out there any more. Are there still Baseball Annies?

NIC JACKSON   OF   Bats: L   Throws: R   Born: 25-Sep-79   Age: 24

YEAR	TM	LG	AGE	AB	H	2B	3B	HR	BB	SO	SB	CS	AVG	OBP	SLG	MLVR	EQBA	EQOBP	EQSLG	EQMLVR	VORP	DEFENSE			
2001	DAY	FLA	21	503	149	30	6	19	39	96	24	10	.296	.355	.493	.237	.246	.288	.423	-.139	1.4	77-CF	-4	52-RF	-5
2002	WTN	SOU	22	131	38	9	1	3	6	23	8	2	.290	.329	.443	.127	.263	.291	.421	-.122	1.0	27-CF	-6		
2003	IOW	PCL	23	458	116	19	4	11	35	102	17	9	.253	.315	.384	-.081	.229	.288	.356	-.245	-13.6	109-CF	-1		
2004	CHC	NL	24	229	59	14	2	7	17	49	6	2	.256	.313	.420	-.070	.259	.313	.432	-.065	6.5	62-CF	-1		

Breakout: 40%   Improve: 64%   Collapse: 18%

Like rain on your wedding day. Like Nic Jackson's name, without that first K.

Jackson's utter lack of plate discipline is going to prevent him from being a major leaguer, and he doesn't have the bat speed to compensate. He's got an injury history to boot. Both the stats and the scouts have soured on him.

ERIC KARROS   1B   Bats: R   Throws: R   Born: 04-Nov-67   Age: 36

YEAR	TM	LG	AGE	AB	H	2B	3B	HR	BB	SO	SB	CS	AVG	OBP	SLG	MLVR	EQBA	EQOBP	EQSLG	EQMLVR	VORP	DEFENSE	
2001	LAD	NL	33	438	103	22	0	15	41	101	3	1	.235	.303	.388	-.132	.248	.315	.407	-.110	-3.2	111-1B	8
2002	LAD	NL	34	524	142	26	1	13	37	74	4	2	.271	.323	.399	.013	.289	.338	.430	-.002	11.2	131-1B	16
2003	CHC	NL	35	336	96	16	1	12	28	46	1	1	.286	.340	.446	.090	.290	.344	.457	.049	12.3	78-1B	2
2004	CHC	NL	36	268	69	14	1	8	24	42	1	1	.259	.321	.411	-.066	.261	.322	.423	-.061	4.9	72-1B	0

Breakout: 17%   Improve: 40%   Collapse: 35%

This was a pyrrhic victory of sorts. Taking on Karros and Mark Grudzielanek allowed the Cubs to get out from under Todd Hundley's contract, and Karros crushed left-handed pitching, just as he always has. But Karros is a considerable liability against righties, played poorly in the season's final two months, and his presence may have permanently hampered the development of Hee Seop Choi. After the season, Karros took out a full-page ad in the *Tribune* to thank the fans and the organization for their support. Depending on whom you ask, it was either the classiest farewell since Lou Gehrig's, or a tremendously shrewd PR move in the flagship paper of a franchise that is notorious for getting the warm fuzzies for its veterans. It didn't work; Karros won't be back with the Cubs next year, but wherever he lands, he'll entertain with his bizarre pre-game stretching routine, in which he looks like a drunken, constipated Teenage Mutant Ninja Turtle attempting to perform the Macarena.

DAVE KELTON   LF/RF   Bats: R   Throws: R   Born: 17-Dec-79   Age: 24

YEAR	TM	LG	AGE	AB	H	2B	3B	HR	BB	SO	SB	CS	AVG	OBP	SLG	MLVR	EQBA	EQOBP	EQSLG	EQMLVR	VORP	DEFENSE			
2001	WTN	SOU	21	224	70	9	4	12	24	55	1	3	.313	.378	.549	.343	.264	.321	.472	.006	13.7	50-3B	-9		
2002	WTN	SOU	22	498	130	28	6	20	52	129	12	6	.261	.332	.462	.132	.231	.284	.421	-.161	-12.0	120-1B	-9		
2003	IOW	PCL	23	442	119	24	3	16	46	115	8	2	.269	.338	.446	.055	.241	.307	.408	-.128	-8.6	35-RF	-2	29-3B	-10
2004	CHC	NL	24	235	60	14	2	9	23	60	3	1	.255	.322	.449	-.017	.258	.322	.462	-.010	9.5				

Breakout: 44%   Improve: 66%   Collapse: 18%

From time to time, we all have to do things we don't particularly like in order to further our career paths. Kelton's mental block against playing third base may have cost him his shot at a meaningful major league career. The Cubs didn't have him at the hot corner because they thought he'd be Scott Rolen, but because he's a good enough athlete that he had the chance to achieve adequacy over there, while hitting enough to become a respectable major league player. At an outfield corner, the offensive standards are much higher. Kelton has some of the secondary attributes you'd associate with a good hitter, including a relatively quick bat and good plate coverage, but he's not that young anymore, and fundamentally, he swings too much. There's a non-zero chance that he'll have a breakout year and position himself to replace Moises Alou in 2005, but if he doesn't, he's not likely to get many favors.

KENNY LOFTON   CF   Bats: L   Throws: L   Born: 31-May-67   Age: 37

YEAR	TM	LG	AGE	AB	H	2B	3B	HR	BB	SO	SB	CS	AVG	OBP	SLG	MLVR	EQBA	EQOBP	EQSLG	EQMLVR	VORP	DEFENSE	
2001	CLE	AL	34	517	135	21	4	14	47	69	16	8	.261	.322	.398	-.062	.277	.342	.428	-.007	18.7	127-CF	-11
2002	CWS	AL	35	352	91	20	6	8	49	51	22	8	.259	.348	.418	.015	.274	.365	.449	.061	20.1	91-CF	-1
2002	SFG	NL	35	180	48	10	3	3	23	22	7	3	.267	.353	.406	.064	.286	.365	.438	.056	9.8	42-CF	4
2003	PIT	NL	36	339	94	19	4	9	28	29	18	5	.277	.333	.437	.036	.277	.333	.443	-.002	13.4	79-CF	3
2003	CHC	NL	36	208	68	13	4	3	18	22	12	4	.327	.381	.471	.230	.330	.387	.481	.197	19.1	54-CF	0
2004	*NYY*	*NL*	*37*	*449*	*123*	*24*	*4*	*9*	*43*	*56*	*19*	*7*	*.275*	*.339*	*.407*	*-.016*	*.280*	*.348*	*.423*	*-.002*	*13.8*	*119-CF*	*0*

Breakout: 8%   Improve: 41%   Collapse: 17%

Lofton has made a nice career for himself, and did exactly what management was hoping for when it acquired him, getting on base at a .381 clip whilst wearing Cubbie blue, and swiping a dozen bags. Still, there are warning signs aplenty: Lofton no longer maintains the walk rate he did during his Cleveland days, and 36-year-olds, even quick ones, aren't likely to thrive on batting average alone. Though Wrigley's small center field minimized the impact, he's lost a step or five on defense. All of this makes Lofton a problematic player, too good to rot on the bench, but not quite valuable enough to start for a contending team, and certainly not at a corner position. Chicago would make more sense than most places if he were willing to accept a reserve role, but he'll bump Bernie Williams out of center as a Yankee instead.

RAMON MARTINEZ   IF   Bats: R   Throws: R   Born: 10-Oct-72   Age: 31

YEAR	TM	LG	AGE	AB	H	2B	3B	HR	BB	SO	SB	CS	AVG	OBP	SLG	MLVR	EQBA	EQOBP	EQSLG	EQMLVR	VORP	DEFENSE			
2001	SFG	NL	28	391	99	18	3	5	38	52	1	2	.253	.323	.353	-.133	.266	.336	.368	-.111	7.4	64-3B	-3	30-2B	4
2002	SFG	NL	29	181	49	10	2	4	14	26	2	0	.271	.335	.414	.049	.286	.345	.443	.027	10.7	32-SS	-3		
2003	CHC	NL	30	293	83	16	1	3	24	50	0	1	.283	.333	.375	-.022	.292	.346	.389	-.043	8.5	30-2B	-2	26-3B	-2
2004	*CHC*	*NL*	*31*	*221*	*56*	*11*	*1*	*3*	*20*	*35*	*1*	*1*	*.254*	*.320*	*.362*	*-.137*	*.257*	*.320*	*.373*	*-.133*	*6.0*	*62-2B*	*-5*		

Breakout: 10%   Improve: 27%   Collapse: 53%

Martinez sometimes gets mistaken for a member of the Dusty Baker Kiddie Corps, but unlike Shawn Estes or Shawon Dunston, he's always been a valuable and versatile player. He has better defensive instincts at short and second than at third base, but his arm hasn't been the same since Tommy Lasorda mangled it.

JACKSON MELIAN   OF   Bats: R   Throws: R   Born: 07-Jan-80   Age: 24

YEAR	TM	LG	AGE	AB	H	2B	3B	HR	BB	SO	SB	CS	AVG	OBP	SLG	MLVR	EQBA	EQOBP	EQSLG	EQMLVR	VORP	DEFENSE			
2001	CHT	SOU	21	426	101	22	0	16	36	95	10	7	.237	.311	.401	-.040	.207	.264	.359	-.302	-32.6	54-RF	-7	38-LF	-3
2002	HUN	SOU	22	184	41	6	1	6	35	63	10	3	.223	.362	.364	.016	.194	.303	.330	-.271	-13.1	41-RF	-2	13-CF	0
2002	WTN	SOU	22	234	72	17	0	4	17	62	10	6	.308	.375	.432	.192	.280	.328	.406	-.062	0.2	26-RF	-1	28-LF	0
2003	IOW	PCL	23	129	23	4	0	3	8	27	4	0	.178	.226	.279	-.430	.163	.212	.264	-.560	-19.0	33-RF	-1		
2003	WTN	SOU	23	252	65	8	3	7	20	47	8	7	.258	.318	.397	.031	.233	.278	.368	-.245	-15.4	42-LF	-4	15-RF	-2
2004	*CHC*	*NL*	*24*	*216*	*51*	*11*	*1*	*7*	*17*	*50*	*4*	*2*	*.236*	*.303*	*.386*	*-.146*	*.238*	*.303*	*.398*	*-.143*	*-1.5*	*60-RF*	*-3*		

Breakout: 48%   Improve: 64%   Collapse: 17%

Melian has Ruben Rivera disease: Every time he learns one part of the game, he forgets another. He's a little bit undersized to be a power hitter, and his home run totals have regressed. Now a six-year free agent; some misguided scouting director will take a chance on him.

DAMIAN MILLER   C   Bats: R   Throws: R   Born: 13-Oct-69   Age: 34

YEAR	TM	LG	AGE	AB	H	2B	3B	HR	BB	SO	SB	CS	AVG	OBP	SLG	MLVR	EQBA	EQOBP	EQSLG	EQMLVR	VORP	DEFENSE	
2001	ARI	NL	31	380	103	19	0	13	35	80	0	1	.271	.337	.424	-.027	.269	.335	.423	-.034	14.4	117-C	3
2002	ARI	NL	32	297	74	22	0	11	38	88	0	0	.249	.340	.434	.031	.250	.335	.443	-.021	12.1	89-C	1
2003	CHC	NL	33	352	82	19	1	9	39	91	1	0	.233	.310	.369	-.106	.241	.317	.384	-.143	2.0	108-C	5
2004	*OAK*	*AL*	*34*	*217*	*50*	*9*	*0*	*8*	*22*	*57*	*1*	*0*	*.228*	*.302*	*.376*	*-.150*	*.235*	*.313*	*.393*	*-.134*	*5.0*	*61-C*	*0*

Breakout: 25%   Improve: 42%   Collapse: 38%

Miller's season disappointed a lot of people, but 33-year-old catchers can expect to lose about 10% of their offensive output, and his numbers were only a hair below his PECOTA projection. To his credit, he provides some value with his defense—Miller threw out 38% of opposing base-stealers last year, blocks the plate well, and was a favorite target of Kerry Wood—but the Cubs don't have the offensive firepower to afford the luxury of a defensive specialist. Jim Hendry found a creative way to get out from under his contract, trading him to Oakland for Michael Barrett.

LUIS MONTANEZ   2B   **Bats: R**   **Throws: R**   Born: 15-Dec-81   Age: 22

YEAR	TM	LG	AGE	AB	H	2B	3B	HR	BB	SO	SB	CS	AVG	OBP	SLG	MLVR	EQBA	EQOBP	EQSLG	EQMLVR	VORP	DEFENSE			
2001	LNS	MID	19	499	127	33	6	5	34	121	20	7	.255	.316	.375	-.038	.198	.243	.300	-.430	-34.4	112-SS -16			
2002	DAY	FLA	20	487	129	21	5	4	44	89	14	8	.265	.333	.353	.000	.222	.275	.303	-.349	-22.1	98-SS -24		21-2B	-2
2003	DAY	FLA	21	486	123	18	3	5	33	89	11	4	.253	.305	.333	-.043	.221	.263	.304	-.372	-29.8	82-SS -11		32-SS	-7
2004	*CHC*	*NL*	*22*	*244*	*52*	*12*	*1*	*3*	*17*	*52*	*4*	*2*	*.214*	*.272*	*.311*	*-.313*	*.216*	*.272*	*.321*	*-.315*	*-6.7*	*66-2B -12*			

Breakout: 33%   *Improve: 48%*   *Collapse: 28%*

Save for a brilliant debut in the Arizona League three years ago, Montanez hasn't shown any indication that he's a prospect. He's easy to pitch to, and is particularly vulnerable to anything on the inside part of the plate. In spite of his reasonable range, the Cubs have moved him to second base following consistently high error totals at shortstop, which gives him even less chance at having a major league career.

TROY O'LEARY   OF   **Bats: L**   **Throws: L**   Born: 04-Aug-69   Age: 34

YEAR	TM	LG	AGE	AB	H	2B	3B	HR	BB	SO	SB	CS	AVG	OBP	SLG	MLVR	EQBA	EQOBP	EQSLG	EQMLVR	VORP	DEFENSE			
2001	BOS	AL	31	341	82	16	6	13	25	73	1	3	.240	.298	.437	-.072	.255	.317	.469	-.014	3.6	49-LF 3		38-RF	1
2002	MON	NL	32	273	78	12	2	3	34	47	1	2	.286	.371	.377	.047	.295	.373	.388	.008	4.6	65-LF -1			
2002	OTT	INT	32	86	29	6	0	3	7	15	0	1	.337	.387	.512	.317	.310	.362	.483	.137	5.1	20-LF 0			
2003	CHC	NL	33	174	38	9	0	5	14	31	3	0	.218	.275	.356	-.197	.227	.287	.369	-.230	-5.5	13-LF -1		24-RF	1
2004	*CHC*	*NL*	*34*	*107*	*27*	*6*	*0*	*3*	*11*	*21*	*1*	*1*	*.249*	*.323*	*.383*	*-.106*	*.251*	*.324*	*.395*	*-.101*	*0.0*	*33-LF -1*			

Breakout: 35%   *Improve: 51%*   *Collapse: 28%*

When Sammy Sosa went on the DL with a toe problem early in the year, O'Leary replaced him not just in right field, but also in the #4 slot in the batting order. He would have been roughly as suited to be a replacement for Roy Horn after the tiger mauling, but the *Mirage* didn't try Siegfried and Troy, now did they? O'Leary also had a brutal year as a pinch hitter (5-for-39).

AUGIE OJEDA   IF   **Bats: B**   **Throws: R**   Born: 20-Dec-74   Age: 29

YEAR	TM	LG	AGE	AB	H	2B	3B	HR	BB	SO	SB	CS	AVG	OBP	SLG	MLVR	EQBA	EQOBP	EQSLG	EQMLVR	VORP	DEFENSE			
2001	CHC	NL	26	144	29	5	1	1	12	20	1	0	.201	.269	.271	-.396	.212	.279	.281	-.376	-7.9	19-3B 0		23-SS	-1
2002	CHC	NL	27	70	13	4	0	0	5	5	1	0	.186	.247	.243	-.395	.197	.258	.268	-.444	-4.3	13-SS 1			
2002	IOW	PCL	27	291	67	20	4	1	31	30	5	3	.230	.318	.337	-.170	.208	.289	.307	-.323	-10.5	68-SS 1			
2003	IOW	PCL	28	283	71	10	3	2	34	25	4	0	.251	.351	.329	-.092	.228	.316	.305	-.260	-5.1	50-SS 7		25-2B	0
2004	*MIN*	*AL*	*29*	*178*	*43*	*9*	*2*	*2*	*15*	*21*	*2*	*1*	*.242*	*.317*	*.336*	*-.167*	*.241*	*.321*	*.342*	*-.183*	*2.0*	*51-SS -2*			

Breakout: 51%   *Improve: 67%*   *Collapse: 19%*

In spite of excelling at all the little things that you'd think Dusty Baker would love—defense, hustle, bunting—Ojeda was stationed at Triple-A for all but a couple of weeks to make room for such undistinguished gentlemen as Lenny Harris and Tony Womack. While he seemed destined to be an Iowa Cubbie for life, he's no longer young, and his best career move was to move on to another organization. If he's 5'8", as he's listed officially, then Gary Huckabay is the king of France, and Arnold Schwarzenegger is the governor of California.

COREY PATTERSON   CF   **Bats: L**   **Throws: R**   Born: 13-Aug-79   Age: 24

YEAR	TM	LG	AGE	AB	H	2B	3B	HR	BB	SO	SB	CS	AVG	OBP	SLG	MLVR	EQBA	EQOBP	EQSLG	EQMLVR	VORP	DEFENSE
2001	IOW	PCL	21	367	93	22	3	7	29	65	19	8	.253	.308	.387	-.144	.226	.280	.343	-.281	-15.3	86-CF -9
2001	CHC	NL	21	131	29	3	0	4	6	33	4	0	.221	.266	.336	-.302	.227	.274	.348	-.285	-4.9	32-CF -4
2002	CHC	NL	22	592	150	30	5	14	19	142	18	3	.253	.284	.392	-.090	.266	.293	.417	-.122	3.7	139-CF -13
2003	CHC	NL	23	329	98	17	7	13	15	77	16	5	.298	.329	.511	.176	.302	.332	.524	.138	24.2	76-CF -2
2004	*CHC*	*NL*	*24*	*411*	*112*	*23*	*4*	*13*	*27*	*86*	*16*	*5*	*.272*	*.321*	*.441*	*-.016*	*.274*	*.322*	*.454*	*-.008*	*13.9*	*106-CF -3*

Breakout: 16%   *Improve: 44%*   *Collapse: 22%*

Patterson injured himself on a play that typified the hustle that Cubs fans had come to appreciate. Stretching to beat out a slow-roller down the right-field line, Patterson landed awkwardly on the first base bag, then fell to the ground in pain. Though the injury did not look serious at first—Patterson was up and walking just a few moments afterward—he'd torn his ACL, and missed the last three months of the season. That was a shame, because Patterson was in the midst of a breakout year of sorts.

His batting average and power numbers had improved, but his walk rate hadn't, leaving open the question of just how well his numbers would have held up had he finished out the season—Alfonso Soriano and Rocco Baldelli, after all, suffered major second-half declines. The subjective impression is that Patterson was trying to take more pitches, but he wasn't taking the right ones, and that doesn't constitute good plate discipline. Even without a marked improvement in his approach at the plate, Patterson can still be a worthwhile player in the Devon White mold. The exception is if the injury has any lingering effect on his speed. Patterson relies on infield singles to prop up his batting average, and his wheels are an essential part of his defense. The plan is to have him back for spring training, but the early reports about the pace of his rehab are mixed.

JOSH PAUL C Bats: R Throws: R Born: 19-May-75 Age: 29

YEAR	TM	LG	AGE	AB	H	2B	3B	HR	BB	SO	SB	CS	AVG	OBP	SLG	MLVR	EQBA	EQOBP	EQSLG	EQMLVR	VORP	DEFENSE
2001	CHR	INT	26	75	21	4	0	4	7	18	0	0	.280	.337	.493	.144	.250	.313	.461	-.036	3.1	18-C -2
2001	CWS	AL	26	139	37	11	0	3	13	25	6	2	.266	.327	.410	-.037	.281	.346	.432	.009	6.8	45-C -5
2002	CHR	INT	27	231	63	15	2	0	17	45	10	4	.273	.323	.355	-.066	.254	.307	.336	-.220	-3.3	59-C 2
2002	CWS	AL	27	104	25	4	0	0	9	22	2	0	.240	.302	.279	-.261	.260	.329	.298	-.226	-1.4	31-C -3
2003	CHR	INT	28	64	12	0	1	2	5	14	1	1	.188	.243	.313	-.293	.185	.243	.308	-.426	-5.0	16-C 0
2003	CWS	AL	28	17	6	0	0	0	3	3	0	0	.353	.450	.353	.157	.353	.450	.353	.148	1.5	
2003	IOW	PCL	28	146	37	4	0	2	8	30	0	2	.253	.297	.322	-.199	.233	.271	.301	-.354	-7.8	22-C 4
2004	*ANA*	*AL*	*29*	*130*	*31*	*6*	*1*	*2*	*9*	*27*	*2*	*1*	*.237*	*.286*	*.342*	*-.218*	*.246*	*.297*	*.368*	*-.189*	*0.2*	*37-C -3*
Breakout: 43%			*Improve: 56%*			*Collapse: 26%*																

Paul brings a replacement-level bat and an exaggerated defensive reputation over from the cross-town rivals. Entertainingly, Paul, a lifelong Sox fan, was furious about being picked up by the Cubs, so much so that he cursed out the Northsiders on drive time radio. The Cubs are short on catching depth, so he might have had to sell his soul to the devil and spend some time at Wrigley this year. With those stakes, the Angels swooped in, stranding him in the PCL behind Los Dos Molinas.

FELIX PIE CF Bats: L Throws: L Born: 08-Feb-85 Age: 19

YEAR	TM	LG	AGE	AB	H	2B	3B	HR	BB	SO	SB	CS	AVG	OBP	SLG	MLVR	EQBA	EQOBP	EQSLG	EQMLVR	VORP	DEFENSE
2002	BOI	NWN	17	8	1	1	0	0	1	1	0	0	.125	.222	.250	-.320	.125	.222	.125	-.735	-2.8	
2003	LNS	MID	18	505	144	22	9	4	41	98	19	13	.285	.346	.388	.100	.226	.272	.321	-.327	-29.4	120-CF -10
2004	*CHC*	*NL*	*19*	*308*	*64*	*14*	*3*	*2*	*22*	*70*	*7*	*3*	*.209*	*.265*	*.298*	*-.346*	*.211*	*.265*	*.307*	*-.349*	*-18.3*	*82-CF -10*
Breakout: 26%			*Improve: 43%*			*Collapse: 27%*																

When a guy is playing pro ball at age 17, it's easy to dream quixotic dreams for him, and while Pie posted reasonable numbers in his full-season debut at Lansing, he has a long road to traverse toward a destination whose significance is uncertain. He's listed at 6′2″, 175, but plays smaller than that, maintaining a slap-hitting style and going the other way with everything. Pie has legitimately outstanding speed, and was voted the best defensive outfielder in the Midwest League. His best chance to become a good big leaguer involves continuing to improve his plate discipline, perhaps resembling a Juan Pierre with doubles power.

ARAMIS RAMIREZ 3B Bats: R Throws: R Born: 25-Jun-78 Age: 26

YEAR	TM	LG	AGE	AB	H	2B	3B	HR	BB	SO	SB	CS	AVG	OBP	SLG	MLVR	EQBA	EQOBP	EQSLG	EQMLVR	VORP	DEFENSE
2001	PIT	NL	23	603	181	40	0	34	40	100	5	4	.300	.350	.536	.184	.300	.350	.534	.180	60.7	154-3B -4
2002	PIT	NL	24	522	122	26	0	18	29	95	2	0	.234	.279	.387	-.133	.241	.286	.403	-.175	0.8	118-3B -2
2003	PIT	NL	25	375	105	25	1	12	25	68	1	1	.280	.330	.448	.048	.282	.334	.459	.027	17.5	94-3B -12
2003	CHC	NL	25	232	60	7	1	15	17	31	1	1	.259	.314	.491	.086	.264	.320	.506	.052	13.2	62-3B -1
2004	*CHC*	*NL*	*26*	*525*	*145*	*30*	*1*	*25*	*41*	*85*	*2*	*2*	*.276*	*.334*	*.481*	*.062*	*.278*	*.335*	*.495*	*.071*	*35.2*	*136-3B -3*
Breakout: 38%			*Improve: 68%*			*Collapse: 9%*																

Ramirez is not a superstar, and likely will never be, but average players have their value, especially when the alternatives are dim; Ramirez's acquisition was in fact one of Jim Hendry's best moves. The rap on his defense is that he makes the tough plays but muffs the easy ones, and his 33 errors did nothing to disprove that. He showed flashes of plate discipline while in the minor leagues, and PECOTA seems to think that a breakout is in store. That Ramirez cut down on his strikeouts after becoming a Cub is a good sign.

RANDALL SIMON   1B   Bats: L   Throws: L   Born: 26-May-75   Age: 29

YEAR	TM	LG	AGE	AB	H	2B	3B	HR	BB	SO	SB	CS	AVG	OBP	SLG	MLVR	EQBA	EQOBP	EQSLG	EQMLVR	VORP	DEFENSE
2001	TOL	INT	26	222	75	13	0	10	21	21	0	3	.338	.400	.532	.350	.310	.369	.491	.160	15.9	50-1B -6
2001	DET	AL	26	256	78	14	2	6	15	28	0	1	.305	.341	.445	.086	.326	.367	.477	.153	15.6	38-1B 1
2002	DET	AL	27	482	145	17	1	19	13	30	0	1	.301	.320	.459	.079	.326	.349	.500	.157	30.0	58-1B -6
2003	PIT	NL	28	307	84	14	0	10	12	30	0	0	.274	.305	.417	-.041	.277	.306	.426	-.076	0.6	70-1B -4
2003	CHC	NL	28	103	29	3	0	6	4	7	0	0	.282	.318	.485	.107	.288	.325	.500	.076	4.0	23-1B 0
2004	*CHC*	*NL*	*29*	*373*	*104*	*19*	*1*	*13*	*22*	*36*	*0*	*1*	*.280*	*.323*	*.439*	*-.009*	*.283*	*.324*	*.452*	*-.001*	*10.4*	*96-1B -4*

Breakout: 7%   Improve: 32%   Collapse: 34%

C'mon, you laughed too. Simon ranks high on entertainment value, and low on most qualities that matter to a big league club. His ability to make contact with anything thrown at him is truly phenomenal, and it'd be a fascinating experiment in weird science to pair him with, say, Walt Hriniak. Absent such a drastic solution, Simon's approach at the plate is unsustainable, and he's about to enter his decline phase. The Brewers, ironically, are said to be among his suitors.

SAMMY SOSA   RF   Bats: R   Throws: R   Born: 12-Nov-68   Age: 35

YEAR	TM	LG	AGE	AB	H	2B	3B	HR	BB	SO	SB	CS	AVG	OBP	SLG	MLVR	EQBA	EQOBP	EQSLG	EQMLVR	VORP	DEFENSE
2001	CHC	NL	32	577	189	34	5	64	116	153	0	2	.328	.437	.737	.638	.329	.443	.738	.636	125.4	152-RF 3
2002	CHC	NL	33	556	160	19	2	49	103	144	2	0	.288	.399	.594	.390	.296	.404	.616	.375	69.5	139-RF -6
2003	CHC	NL	34	517	144	22	0	40	62	143	0	1	.279	.358	.553	.260	.283	.362	.567	.227	39.3	128-RF -4
2004	*CHC*	*NL*	*35*	*448*	*124*	*23*	*2*	*32*	*69*	*116*	*1*	*1*	*.276*	*.374*	*.549*	*.214*	*.279*	*.375*	*.565*	*.227*	*38.1*	*124-RF -5*

Breakout: 15%   Improve: 46%   Collapse: 20%

Lost amidst the corked bat controversy, the beaning, and the toe injury was a profound decline in Sosa's productivity. Sammy managed a line of just .245/.305/.529 in the second half, numbers that look suspiciously like those that he used to post before 1998, when he was one of the most overrated players in baseball. Is the magic gone? The decrease in Sosa's plate discipline coincided in large part with the beaning, suggesting that root of his problems may have been psychological. Sammy was still seeing plenty of pitches—more than four per plate appearance—but he struggled tremendously once behind in the count, often bailing out with two strikes on him. In the post-season, Sosa had some of his swagger back, and his results were much improved. His PECOTA suggests some typical, age-related decline, but nothing that would wreck the Cubs' chances.

As for the corked bat, the issue is a non-starter. There's little evidence that corking helps a batter, and Sosa still hit the ball plenty far once he made good contact with it. The problem is that Sosa had defaulted to an approach that caused him to make good contact a bit less often.

TONY WOMACK   SS/2B   Bats: L   Throws: R   Born: 25-Sep-69   Age: 34

YEAR	TM	LG	AGE	AB	H	2B	3B	HR	BB	SO	SB	CS	AVG	OBP	SLG	MLVR	EQBA	EQOBP	EQSLG	EQMLVR	VORP	DEFENSE
2001	ARI	NL	31	481	128	19	5	3	23	54	28	7	.266	.307	.345	-.195	.264	.304	.341	-.212	-1.2	113-SS -7
2002	ARI	NL	32	590	160	23	5	5	46	80	29	12	.271	.325	.353	-.086	.270	.323	.356	-.150	7.9	139-SS -13
2003	ARI	NL	33	219	52	10	3	2	8	27	8	3	.237	.270	.338	-.265	.236	.265	.336	-.314	-5.4	49-SS -5
2003	COL	NL	33	79	15	2	0	0	0	9	3	1	.190	.200	.215	-.600	.177	.185	.203	-.695	-8.2	10-SS -1
2003	CHC	NL	33	51	12	2	1	0	1	11	2	1	.235	.250	.314	-.291	.250	.250	.346	-.319	-1.8	
2004	*CHC*	*NL*	*34*	*276*	*68*	*12*	*2*	*2*	*15*	*40*	*9*	*4*	*.246*	*.291*	*.325*	*-.243*	*.248*	*.291*	*.334*	*-.243*	*-0.6*	*73-SS -9*

Breakout: 35%   Improve: 59%   Collapse: 25%

Womack's offensive skills have eroded to the point that he's best used as a 25th man, if at all. Even then, he's of limited usefulness because his defense is sub-par. His awful season put his job prospects in doubt, and he'll have even bigger problems finding work after undergoing Tommy John surgery in October.

PITCHERS

ANTONIO ALFONSECA   Bats: R   Throws: R   Born: 16-Apr-72   Age: 32

YEAR	TM	LG	AGE	G	GS	IP	H	BB	SO	HR	ERA	EQERA	EQH9	EQBB9	EQSO9	EQHR9	PERA	VORP	STF
2001	FLA	NL	29	58	0	61.7	68	15	40	6	3.06	4.12	10.1	2.0	5.0	0.8	4.47	9.7	-2
2002	CHC	NL	30	66	0	74.3	73	36	61	5	4.00	4.11	8.8	3.9	6.3	0.6	4.27	12.0	3
2003	CHC	NL	31	60	0	66.3	76	27	51	7	5.84	5.32	10.4	3.2	6.2	1.0	5.16	-2.5	-9
2004	ATL	NL	32	46	3	63.3	64	23	45	4	3.79	4.10	9.1	2.9	5.8	0.6	4.22	9.5	-2

Breakout: 24%   Improve: 50%   Collapse: 19%

El Pulpo's reputation as a top-tier reliever was built on the mythology of the save and a history of ERAs that were better than his peripheral numbers. This year, his good fortune reversed itself: Alfonseca never got the Fire Chief title back from Joe Borowski after missing the first month with a hamstring pull, and opponents hit .404/.482/.660 against him with runners in scoring position, sending his ERA skyrocketing. While he should not emerge as a closer again, he's not as bad a pitcher as the bleacher bums make him out to be, effective in spurts with his heavy sinker.

FRANCIS BELTRAN   Bats: R   Throws: R   Born: 29-Nov-79   Age: 24

YEAR	TM	LG	AGE	G	GS	IP	H	BB	SO	HR	ERA	EQERA	EQH9	EQBB9	EQSO9	EQHR9	PERA	VORP	STF
2001	DAY	FLA	21	21	18	95.3	93	40	72	10	5.01	6.75	11.0	4.5	4.5	2.3	7.41	-10.9	-30
2002	WTN	SOU	22	39	0	41.7	28	19	43	2	2.59	3.82	7.9	4.5	6.7	1.0	4.37	7.5	7
2002	CHC	NL	22	11	0	12.0	14	16	11	2	7.50	8.25	10.5	10.5	6.8	1.5	7.61	-3.5	-20
2003	IOW	PCL	23	31	2	48.7	46	19	33	2	2.96	3.88	8.4	4.1	5.4	0.6	4.09	8.8	7
2004	CHC	NL	24	20	6	43.7	45	24	33	6	5.22	5.56	9.3	4.4	6.2	1.2	5.52	1.7	-8

Breakout: 19%   Improve: 54%   Collapse: 21%

Beltran was shut down in July with bicep tendinitis, and never returned. He hasn't pitched in winter ball this season, as he had in the past, so there's a question as to what his status will be to start the season. Beltran complements mid-90s heat with a good slider. The Cubs hope he can become Octavio Dotel Lite, but his command has never been big league caliber, and his strikeout rate was down at Iowa, perhaps presaging the injury.

CHADD BLASKO   Bats: R   Throws: R   Born: 09-Mar-81   Age: 23

YEAR	TM	LG	AGE	G	GS	IP	H	BB	SO	HR	ERA	EQERA	EQH9	EQBB9	EQSO9	EQHR9	PERA	VORP	STF
2003	LNS	MID	22	2	2	11.0	10	5	6	0	1.64	4.66	10.2	5.6	3.7	0.0	4.78	1.0	9
2003	DAY	FLA	22	24	24	136.3	100	43	131	3	1.98	3.45	8.3	3.7	6.0	0.7	4.01	29.3	25
2004	CHC	NL	23	22	15	89.0	88	40	69	9	4.56	4.86	8.9	3.5	6.3	0.9	4.68	8.4	4

Breakout: 12%   Improve: 38%   Collapse: 29%

Blasko is a classic power arm, standing a thick 6′7″, and throwing lots of fastballs. He's still developing a breaking ball, but given the leverage that his height provides, his curve could be a good one when it comes. He's not likely to post another sub-2.00 ERA as he moves up to West Tennessee, but Blasko has an intriguing arm, and provides more proof that it pays to have a good working relationship with Scott Boras. When he leaves one out over the plate, I guess you can call that a hanging cha . . . hey, folks, it's an election year. All we can promise is that we'll be funnier than the Capitol Steps.

JOE BOROWSKI   Bats: R   Throws: R   Born: 04-May-71   Age: 33

YEAR	TM	LG	AGE	G	GS	IP	H	BB	SO	HR	ERA	EQERA	EQH9	EQBB9	EQSO9	EQHR9	PERA	VORP	STF
2001	IOW	PCL	30	39	12	110.0	87	26	131	10	2.62	3.38	8.4	2.6	7.8	1.0	4.06	25.0	11
2002	CHC	NL	31	73	0	95.7	84	29	97	10	2.73	3.22	8.1	2.4	7.9	1.0	3.85	24.4	15
2003	CHC	NL	32	68	0	68.3	53	19	66	5	2.64	2.88	7.1	2.3	7.8	0.7	3.10	19.3	23
2004	CHC	NL	33	46	4	70.7	65	23	63	7	3.40	3.62	8.2	2.6	7.2	0.9	3.84	15.1	8

Breakout: 27%   Improve: 51%   Collapse: 26%

Case #9716 in proving that closers are made, not born. There's nothing particularly tricky about Borowski, whose fastball/slider/change-up combo is run-of-the-mill stuff. But he knows which pitches to throw and where to throw them, and he gets the job done. Whether or not he continues in the closer role, there's no reason to expect a marked decline in his performance. Borowski is well-liked in Chicago, but shouldn't a dude like this have a cheering section the size of Little Warsaw?

BOBBY BROWNLIE Bats: R Throws: R Born: 05-Oct-80 Age: 23

YEAR	TM	LG	AGE	G	GS	IP	H	BB	SO	HR	ERA	EQERA	EQH9	EQBB9	EQSO9	EQHR9	PERA	VORP	STF
2003	DAY	FLA	22	13	13	66.0	48	24	59	2	3.00	4.42	8.2	4.3	5.6	0.9	4.43	7.7	11
2004	CHC	NL	23	21	13	78.0	78	38	56	9	4.66	4.96	8.9	3.9	5.8	1.0	4.99	6.8	-2

Breakout: 19%   Improve: 49%   Collapse: 20%

That Brownlie was talked about as a potential #1 pick in 2002 is more an indication of the weakness of that draft than the strength of his status as a prospect. That said, Brownlie is a smart pitcher who was having a solid year in Daytona until the Cubs shut him down with a tired arm. He gets hitters out by mixing three average pitches and locating well. Brownlie gave up just two home runs last year, a good sign for a pitcher with this profile. The Cubs have taken a lot of heat for their abuse of the Big Three, and deservedly so, but kudos to them for proceeding more carefully with their minor league arms.

BEN CHRISTENSEN Bats: R Throws: R Born: 07-Feb-78 Age: 26

YEAR	TM	LG	AGE	G	GS	IP	H	BB	SO	HR	ERA	EQERA	EQH9	EQBB9	EQSO9	EQHR9	PERA	VORP	STF
2001	WTN	SOU	23	3	3	16.7	20	9	9	2	6.47	8.22	11.7	5.9	3.5	1.8	7.45	-4.5	-44
2002	WTN	SOU	24	12	12	64.0	73	35	36	6	6.33	8.16	12.7	5.3	3.6	1.9	7.89	-16.3	-54
2003	DAY	FLA	25	14	3	27.3	32	11	21	3	5.27	7.94	15.9	5.2	5.2	3.6	11.33	-5.9	-122
2004	CHC	NL	26	9	5	30.7	36	15	19	4	5.77	6.15	10.5	3.9	5.1	1.3	6.12	0.1	-12

Breakout: 35%   Improve: 75%   Collapse: 6%

Christensen isn't likely to get much sympathy from anyone who remembers his unconscionably idiotic beaning of Anthony Molina while in college, but he's had a rough go of it as a pro, losing the better part of the past three years due to shoulder problems. He displayed flashes of his good stuff during a brief FSL stint, but he'll be 26 next year. The clock is ticking—and it's not the one inside his head.

MATT CLEMENT Bats: R Throws: R Born: 12-Aug-74 Age: 29

YEAR	TM	LG	AGE	G	GS	IP	H	BB	SO	HR	ERA	EQERA	EQH9	EQBB9	EQSO9	EQHR9	PERA	VORP	STF
2001	FLA	NL	26	31	31	169.3	172	85	134	15	5.05	5.18	9.4	4.2	6.0	0.7	4.70	7.6	7
2002	CHC	NL	27	32	32	205.0	162	85	215	18	3.60	3.48	7.3	3.3	8.2	0.8	3.55	46.9	32
2003	CHC	NL	28	32	32	201.7	169	79	171	22	4.11	3.98	7.7	3.2	6.8	1.0	3.89	23.9	17
2004	CHC	NL	29	28	27	175.0	160	73	148	15	3.85	4.10	8.2	3.3	6.8	0.8	4.07	27.6	16

Breakout: 11%   Improve: 51%   Collapse: 20%

Clement is better on days when he has a big strike zone to work with, and his four-seamer isn't an effective pitch, coming in at 95 but without movement, and either missing the strike zone or getting hit. But as a fourth starter, he's durable and outstanding. Clement had some rough outings in May, but after he and Larry Rothschild worked out some mechanical kinks, all signs were go for the rest of the year. He's a safe bet to have another strong year, and the rare and deceptive example of a player with untapped potential who turns the corner and realizes it.

JUAN CRUZ Bats: R Throws: R Born: 15-Oct-78 Age: 25

YEAR	TM	LG	AGE	G	GS	IP	H	BB	SO	HR	ERA	EQERA	EQH9	EQBB9	EQSO9	EQHR9	PERA	VORP	STF
2001	WTN	SOU	22	23	23	121.3	107	60	137	6	4.01	5.11	9.4	5.2	6.9	0.7	4.99	6.0	20
2001	CHC	NL	22	8	8	44.7	40	17	39	4	3.22	3.35	8.2	3.1	6.7	0.6	3.76	10.8	41
2002	CHC	NL	23	45	9	97.3	84	59	81	11	3.98	4.74	7.9	4.7	6.4	1.0	4.51	9.1	8
2003	IOW	PCL	24	9	9	50.7	37	11	47	1	1.95	2.45	7.0	2.3	7.2	0.2	2.58	16.7	48
2003	CHC	NL	24	25	6	61.0	66	28	65	7	6.05	5.61	10.0	3.6	8.5	1.1	5.16	-6.8	16
2004	CHC	NL	25	24	16	96.0	91	42	82	9	4.22	4.50	8.5	3.4	6.9	0.9	4.42	11.2	9

Breakout: 21%   Improve: 43%   Collapse: 23%

You know that the prospect sheen has worn off when you lose your job to Shawn Estes. Cruz is a bit of a square peg. While his fastball/sinker combo can be impressive, his command isn't what you'd like for a high-leverage reliever, and with his slight frame and high pitch counts, he doesn't really have the capacity for long outings as a starter. Though he'll come into spring training with a shot to win the fifth starters' job, Cruz's best chance for stardom may be in the bullpen. He has the profile of someone who will struggle off and on for a couple years, and then click and become a dominant closer in 2006 or so, bringing a thousand *YooHoo!* showers to a thousand roto players across the country.

SHAWN ESTES

Bats: R **Throws: L** Born: 18-Feb-73 Age: 31

YEAR	TM	LG	AGE	G	GS	IP	H	BB	SO	HR	ERA	EQERA	EQH9	EQBB9	EQSO9	EQHR9	PERA	VORP	STF
2001	SFG	NL	28	27	27	159.0	151	77	109	11	4.02	4.47	8.7	4.0	5.2	0.6	4.24	19.2	10
2002	NYM	NL	29	23	23	132.7	133	66	92	12	4.54	4.99	9.3	3.9	5.4	0.8	4.74	8.7	3
2002	CIN	NL	29	6	6	28.0	38	17	17	1	7.71	6.91	12.2	4.6	4.6	0.3	5.69	-4.0	-5
2003	CHC	NL	30	29	28	152.3	182	83	103	20	5.73	6.20	10.8	4.4	5.4	1.2	5.90	-20.3	-14
2004	*CHC*	*NL*	*31*	*24*	*20*	*116.0*	*133*	*68*	*73*	*12*	*5.55*	*5.91*	*10.3*	*4.6*	*5.1*	*0.9*	*5.92*	*1.8*	*-7*

Breakout: 16%   *Improve: 46%*   *Collapse: 21%*

Estes is to Cubs fans what Chan Ho Park is to Ranger fans, or Kenny G to jazz enthusiasts. What success he'd had in the past was driven by pitching in big ballparks: between 2000 and 2002, Estes gave up just eight gopherballs per 500 plate appearances, including exactly zero in 15 starts at Pac Bell in 2001. At Wrigley Field, Estes had no such luxury, and the rising home run rate combined with his shoddy control and unimpressive fastball produced a rank season. Dusty Baker stuck with him for far too long, and the Cubs were fortunate that this act of loyalty didn't cost them the pennant. Mercifully, he was non-tendered.

KYLE FARNSWORTH

Bats: R **Throws: R** Born: 14-Apr-76 Age: 28

YEAR	TM	LG	AGE	G	GS	IP	H	BB	SO	HR	ERA	EQERA	EQH9	EQBB9	EQSO9	EQHR9	PERA	VORP	STF
2001	CHC	NL	25	76	0	82.0	65	29	107	8	2.74	3.08	7.5	3.0	9.9	0.8	3.53	22.1	33
2002	CHC	NL	26	45	0	46.7	53	24	46	9	7.32	7.29	10.2	3.9	7.7	1.8	6.17	-8.6	-28
2003	CHC	NL	27	77	0	76.3	53	36	92	6	3.30	3.28	6.6	3.8	9.6	0.7	3.28	16.1	27
2004	*CHC*	*NL*	*28*	*51*	*1*	*65.3*	*59*	*35*	*67*	*7*	*4.35*	*4.63*	*8.1*	*4.2*	*8.3*	*0.9*	*4.48*	*9.6*	*6*

Breakout: 26%   *Improve: 50%*   *Collapse: 29%*

The timbre of the cheers when Farnsworth's name is announced over the Wrigley Field loudspeaker is distinct: less a hearty rah-rah than a high-pitched, distinctly female shriek. There's always a Cub that plays this role, the sentimental favorite of the Lincoln Park Trixies, and with Mark Grace having moved along to dustier pastures, Farnsworth is the team's new it-boy.

The working assumption around Wrigleyville has long been that whenever Farnsworth runs into trouble, it's because of some off-the-field shenanigan involving booze, women, or both. While it's not our position to either confirm or deny such rumors, they obscure the fact that any big fastball pitcher with stiff mechanics and middling command is going to be subject to a great deal of inconsistency. He should be better than the projection above, but a run of seasons similar to 2001 is a long shot.

MARK GUTHRIE

Bats: R **Throws: L** Born: 22-Sep-65 Age: 38

YEAR	TM	LG	AGE	G	GS	IP	H	BB	SO	HR	ERA	EQERA	EQH9	EQBB9	EQSO9	EQHR9	PERA	VORP	STF
2001	OAK	AL	35	54	0	52.3	49	20	52	7	4.47	4.62	8.5	3.2	8.3	1.1	4.36	5.5	7
2002	NYM	NL	36	68	0	48.0	35	19	44	3	2.44	2.93	6.8	3.1	7.2	0.6	3.12	13.6	18
2003	CHC	NL	37	65	0	42.7	40	22	24	6	2.74	3.70	8.5	4.1	4.6	1.3	4.95	12.4	-24
2004	*CHC*	*NL*	*38*	*73*	*0*	*31.3*	*31*	*15*	*23*	*3*	*4.20*	*4.48*	*8.9*	*3.9*	*5.8*	*0.9*	*4.77*	*4.2*	*-10*

Breakout: 26%   *Improve: 48%*   *Collapse: 31%*

The ERA looks good, but Guthrie's strikeout rate declined by nearly half, and he spent three months on the shelf with elbow tendinitis. He wasn't at all effective against lefties, and he doesn't really have the stamina to face more than two or three hitters. The Cubs have a club option on him for 2004; Jim Hendry should treat him to a nice meal at *Tru* or *Trotter's,* then send him packing.

ANGEL GUZMAN

Bats: R **Throws: R** Born: 14-Dec-81 Age: 22

YEAR	TM	LG	AGE	G	GS	IP	H	BB	SO	HR	ERA	EQERA	EQH9	EQBB9	EQSO9	EQHR9	PERA	VORP	STF
2001	BOI	NWN	19	14	14	76.7	68	19	63	2	2.23	5.11	10.1	3.3	3.9	0.7	4.76	3.7	14
2002	LNS	MID	20	9	9	62.0	42	16	49	3	1.89	4.14	8.6	3.1	4.5	1.2	4.56	8.8	13
2002	DAY	FLA	20	16	15	94.0	99	33	74	2	2.39	4.55	9.7	3.7	5.0	0.4	4.43	10.4	27
2003	WTN	SOU	21	15	15	89.7	83	26	87	8	2.81	4.45	9.3	3.0	6.2	1.6	5.35	10.6	14
2004	*CHC*	*NL*	*22*	*20*	*15*	*88.0*	*94*	*37*	*59*	*12*	*4.91*	*5.23*	*9.6*	*3.3*	*5.4*	*1.2*	*5.22*	*5.2*	*-2*

Breakout: 7%   *Improve: 38%*   *Collapse: 35%*

(continued next page)

Angel Guzman *(continued)*

The torn labrum that ended Guzman's season apparently resulted neither from overuse nor from his mechanics, which by all reports were good. That, and the fact that the tear was small, are the silver linings here. But a tear is still a tear, and shoulders are dodgier bets to heal completely than elbows. There's no doubt that the upside is there—Guzman has three plus pitches, keeps the ball down, and has good command—but to expect him to make a contribution at the major league level next year, as the Cubs have intimated, is folly. Guzman is young, and his arbitration clock has yet to start running. A year of careful handling and limited action will put him in the best position to join Prior and company in 2005.

LUKE HAGERTY Bats: R   Throws: L   Born: 1-Apr-81   Age: 23

YEAR	TM	LG	AGE	G	GS	IP	H	BB	SO	HR	ERA	EQERA	EQH9	EQBB9	EQSO9	EQHR9	PERA	VORP	STF
2002	BOI	NWN	21	10	10	48.0	32	15	50	2	1.13	4.36	9.4	3.9	5.2	1.1	4.79	5.7	-2
2004	CHC	NL	23	8	5	30.0	31	13	23	4	4.71	5.01	9.4	3.4	6.1	1.1	5.07	3.0	0

Breakout: 17%   Improve: 52%   Collapse: 27%

Hagerty got his Tommy John surgery out of the way good and early, missing the year after tearing his ulnar collateral ligament in spring training. He'd done nothing but impress since turning pro, twirling a fine debut campaign at Boise, and displaying improved consistency with both his slider and fastball in the spring. But the injury sets his timetable back by at least two years. Six-foot-seven lefties who throw in the mid-90s don't come along every day, so he'll be given every chance.

JUSTIN JONES Bats: L   Throws: L   Born: 25-Sep-84   Age: 19

YEAR	TM	LG	AGE	G	GS	IP	H	BB	SO	HR	ERA	EQERA	EQH9	EQBB9	EQSO9	EQHR9	PERA	VORP	STF
2003	LNS	MID	18	16	16	71.0	56	32	87	1	2.28	4.92	8.6	5.6	8.2	0.3	4.27	4.8	52

If you're the type to get excited about teenaged pitchers, then Jones is a good one to get excited about. He's young, nine months younger than Cole Hamels. He's so young, in fact, that we can't get PECOTA to run a reasonable projection for him. You couldn't tell it from the way he pitched, though, as Jones mixed together a fastball, curve and change to put up an outstanding half-season and a tremendous strikeout rate at Lansing. He's tough to loft the ball against, and especially hard on lefties. The key to his medium-term development will be adding arm strength. Jones was shut down twice with a tired arm and was done pitching after the first week of August. Even if a club does everything right—and the Cubs have done everything right with Jones so far—the attrition rates for 19-year-old pitchers are extremely high.

SERGIO MITRE Bats: R   Throws: R   Born: 16-Feb-81   Age: 23

YEAR	TM	LG	AGE	G	GS	IP	H	BB	SO	HR	ERA	EQERA	EQH9	EQBB9	EQSO9	EQHR9	PERA	VORP	STF
2001	BOI	NWN	20	15	15	91.0	85	18	71	2	3.07	5.60	10.4	2.6	3.6	0.5	4.62	0.0	11
2002	LNS	MID	21	27	27	168.7	166	27	96	7	2.83	5.97	11.5	2.0	3.2	1.0	5.44	-6.1	-3
2003	WTN	SOU	22	25	24	145.7	162	41	128	6	3.34	5.79	11.0	2.9	5.3	0.8	5.20	-2.9	13
2003	CHC	NL	22	3	2	8.7	15	4	3	1	8.28	8.64	15.1	3.2	3.2	1.1	7.50	-2.8	-22
2004	CHC	NL	23	20	15	85.7	96	30	47	9	4.71	5.01	10.1	2.7	4.5	0.9	4.96	6.1	-5

Breakout: 12%   Improve: 47%   Collapse: 20%

When you're out on a date, and the girl you're wining and dining isn't as pretty as she seemed that night you got her digits at the bar, what to do when it comes time to pick the *vino?* You select the second-cheapest wine. When your ace is on the shelf for a turn or two, and you don't want to taint the psyche or the arbitration status of one of your best pitching prospects, what do you do? You call up Sergio Mitre. Mitre has a deceptive motion and goes great with *coq au vin*, but tops out as a #5 starter.

MARK PRIOR Bats: R   Throws: R   Born: 07-Sep-80   Age: 23

YEAR	TM	LG	AGE	G	GS	IP	H	BB	SO	HR	ERA	EQERA	EQH9	EQBB9	EQSO9	EQHR9	PERA	VORP	STF
2002	WTN	SOU	21	6	6	34.7	26	10	55	0	2.59	4.26	8.8	2.8	10.8	0.3	3.57	4.7	75
2002	IOW	PCL	21	3	3	16.3	13	8	24	1	1.66	4.60	6.9	5.2	11.5	0.6	3.64	1.7	71
2002	CHC	NL	21	19	19	116.7	98	38	147	14	3.32	3.50	7.9	2.5	9.8	1.1	3.90	26.4	65
2003	CHC	NL	22	30	30	211.3	183	50	245	15	2.43	2.97	8.1	1.9	9.3	0.6	3.33	63.8	67
2004	CHC	NL	23	25	25	198.7	168	46	203	18	2.79	2.97	7.6	1.8	8.3	0.8	3.09	57.6	32

Breakout: 29%   Improve: 42%   Collapse: 17%

Ten minutes before game time, Mark Prior can be seen practicing the Tom House towel drill in the bullpen along the left-field line. The drill consists of the pitcher going through his ordinary motion with a towel, rather than a baseball in his hand, and attempting to hit the outstretched glove of a catcher standing a specified distance away. While the drill looks unusual, it is a successful tool in ensuring that a pitcher's release point, foot placement, and extension remain consistent. Prior hits the glove on the nose every time.

That image captures the essence of Prior better than any other. Everything else—all the success he's had and will continue to have—is secondary to his uncannily consistent mechanics. Those mechanics allow him to place the ball essentially where he wants it, and while Prior has yet to develop Greg Maddux's aptitude for pitching psychology, he has the same great command and far better stuff. It's entirely possible that he'll improve his pitch sequencing after more experience against big league hitters, especially if he can refine his changeup. If that happens, a run of two or three years of sub-2.00 ERAs could follow. Do Prior's mechanics insulate him from risks associated with a heavy workload? To some extent, they reduce it. But the Cubs aren't working Prior hard because he has great mechanics; they're working him hard because, well, that's what they do with their pitchers. Carlos Zambrano and Kerry Wood have average mechanics, and they're getting worked hard too.

JAE-KUK RYU Bats: R Throws: R Born: 30-May-83 Age: 21

YEAR	TM	LG	AGE	G	GS	IP	H	BB	SO	HR	ERA	EQERA	EQH9	EQBB9	EQSO9	EQHR9	PERA	VORP	STF
2002	BOI	NWN	19	10	10	53.0	45	25	56	1	3.57	6.70	10.8	5.9	5.3	0.6	5.70	-5.6	14
2002	LNS	MID	19	5	4	19.0	26	8	21	1	7.11	10.80	15.7	5.4	6.5	1.1	8.13	-9.6	0
2003	LNS	MID	20	11	11	72.0	59	19	57	2	1.75	3.78	9.2	3.4	4.8	0.7	4.42	13.0	23
2003	DAY	FLA	20	4	4	20.7	14	11	22	1	3.04	5.89	7.9	6.4	6.9	1.5	5.41	-0.6	12
2003	WTN	SOU	20	11	11	58.0	63	25	45	3	5.43	6.67	9.6	4.4	5.0	0.8	4.99	-6.6	14
2004	CHC	NL	21	20	17	102.0	106	48	65	10	4.66	4.96	9.3	3.7	5.2	0.8	4.95	6.2	0

Breakout: 13% Improve: 65% Collapse: 4%

Ryu is best known for an incident in April that will forever have him branded, along with Dave Winfield, as among the world's most famous bird killers. We don't condone his behavior, of course, but part of the reason that Ryu may have been behaving like a stupid teenager is because he was, in fact, a teenager—just 19 at the time of the incident. The first couple of years of minor league ball can be difficult enough for a Georgia boy playing in Yakima, or a California kid playing in Batavia. They're not any easier for a Korean kid, who doesn't speak the language, playing in Daytona. Major league teams invest all sorts of effort in attempting to identify players with good "makeup" through a combination of interviews and psychological testing, but they vary in the extent to which they provide counseling and support services for their minor leaguers. After a series of ugly off-the-field incidents, the NFL has placed much time and effort into developing "life skills" programs for its rookies. The situation is not as simple in baseball, with its disaggregated minor leagues, but the potential rewards may be the same.

Between the lines, Ryu was and remains an interesting prospect, with three pitches that already approach major league quality. He also throws a sinker that has received mixed reviews, and he may be best off dropping the pitch entirely. Ryu's stamina and command need a bit of growth, but, as we've mentioned, the kid is young.

ANDY SISCO Bats: L Throws: L Born: 13-Jan-83 Age: 21

YEAR	TM	LG	AGE	G	GS	IP	H	BB	SO	HR	ERA	EQERA	EQH9	EQBB9	EQSO9	EQHR9	PERA	VORP	STF
2002	BOI	NWN	19	14	14	77.7	51	39	101	3	2.43	4.52	9.6	6.6	6.7	1.1	5.84	7.9	22
2003	LNS	MID	20	19	19	94.0	76	31	99	3	3.54	5.12	9.7	4.2	6.4	0.9	5.02	4.4	22
2004	CHC	NL	21	22	17	100.3	98	52	78	9	4.38	4.66	8.8	4.1	6.3	0.7	4.74	9.2	5

Breakout: 23% Improve: 65% Collapse: 0%

There's been a rash of Really Tall Dudes attempting to make it as pitchers in recent years, and Sisco might be the most imposing physical specimen yet. At 6'9" and around 265 pounds, Sisco looks like the result of some bizarre genetic foible involving Randy Johnson and David Wells (or, more fairly, David Wells with a recessive gene that motivates him to hit the gym twice a week). We've had point guards, quarterbacks, goalies, and tight ends that went on to be big league baseball players, but Sisco was recruited as a defensive lineman.

Sisco's fastball-curve combo is good and should continue to get better, as should his command. He's well ahead of where Randy Johnson was at the same age. The concern is his delivery. Sisco has an odd ⅝ths arm slot, and a habit of leaning forward with his body that leaves him off-kilter as he releases the ball. Although the injury that sidelined him for part of the summer did not occur while he was on the mound—Sisco broke his hand, reportedly as a result of punching a clubhouse wall—refining his mechanics is critical given the big frame he's carrying.

STEVE SMYTH   Bats: L   Throws: L   Born: 03-Jun-78   Age: 26

YEAR	TM	LG	AGE	G	GS	IP	H	BB	SO	HR	ERA	EQERA	EQH9	EQBB9	EQSO9	EQHR9	PERA	VORP	STF
2001	WTN	SOU	23	18	18	120.3	110	40	93	9	2.54	4.22	9.2	3.5	4.6	1.1	4.92	17.0	1
2002	WTN	SOU	24	11	11	73.0	62	18	74	7	3.58	5.01	10.3	2.5	6.7	1.9	6.03	4.2	-10
2002	IOW	PCL	24	6	6	31.0	35	10	25	4	5.81	6.21	10.9	3.4	5.6	1.6	6.11	-2.0	-15
2002	CHC	NL	24	8	7	26.0	34	10	16	9	9.35	8.53	11.7	2.8	4.6	3.2	8.47	-8.2	-61
2003	IOW	PCL	25	25	24	130.7	143	72	98	16	5.23	6.47	10.6	6.0	5.9	1.6	6.73	-11.7	-33
2004	*CHC*	*NL*	*26*	*17*	*10*	*58.0*	*62*	*31*	*44*	*9*	*5.62*	*5.99*	*9.6*	*4.2*	*6.1*	*1.3*	*5.83*	*0.5*	*-6*

Breakout: 25%   *Improve: 53%*   *Collapse: 15%*

Pronounced Smythe, as in the old-school NHL division. A big league pitcher is to Smyth as the Edmonton Oilers were to the Winnipeg Jets.

JASON SZUMINSKI   Bats: R   Throws: R   Born: 11-Dec-78   Age: 25

YEAR	TM	LG	AGE	G	GS	IP	H	BB	SO	HR	ERA	EQERA	EQH9	EQBB9	EQSO9	EQHR9	PERA	VORP	STF
2001	LNS	MID	22	14	4	36.3	56	17	22	2	6.45	8.64	14.9	5.7	3.2	1.1	7.95	-11.2	-44
2002	DAY	FLA	23	39	7	91.3	95	41	53	7	5.13	6.59	10.7	5.0	3.6	1.6	6.58	-9.2	-45
2003	DAY	FLA	24	13	0	24.7	29	9	23	0	3.64	6.23	13.7	4.2	5.8	0.4	6.29	-1.5	-9
2003	WTN	SOU	24	29	3	59.7	51	19	45	1	2.26	3.90	8.5	3.3	4.6	0.3	3.67	10.4	4
2003	IOW	PCL	24	3	2	12.7	11	1	5	0	3.54	3.00	7.5	0.8	3.0	0.0	2.26	3.5	24
2004	*SDP*	*NL*	*25*	*13*	*6*	*37.0*	*42*	*16*	*22*	*4*	*5.03*	*5.51*	*10.3*	*3.5*	*4.9*	*0.9*	*4.42*	*1.5*	*-10*

Breakout: 22%   *Improve: 49%*   *Collapse: 25%*

Talk about your interesting backstories. Szuminski graduated from MIT on an ROTC scholarship. As a result of that, he has a commitment to the Air Force, and needs to petition the USAF every year to continue to play baseball. The Padres acquired him in December in a pre-arranged trade with the Royals, who had picked him up in the Rule 5 draft, and the Friars appear to be serious about keeping him on the major league roster for the entire season. There's some speculation that the assurance of a big league roster spot will make Szuminski's obligation to the Air Force a moot point. Given his background, it's entirely understandable that Szuminski would be a late bloomer, and he had his best professional season in 2003, using his heavy, sinking fastball to keep the ball in the yard and his ERA down. If that approach translates to the major leagues, he has a good chance to be a league-average reliever, or better, and doing Keith Woolner proud.

DAVE VERES   Bats: R   Throws: R   Born: 19-Oct-66   Age: 37

YEAR	TM	LG	AGE	G	GS	IP	H	BB	SO	HR	ERA	EQERA	EQH9	EQBB9	EQSO9	EQHR9	PERA	VORP	STF
2001	STL	NL	34	71	0	65.7	57	28	61	12	3.70	4.60	8.3	3.6	7.2	1.4	4.80	7.0	-10
2002	STL	NL	35	71	0	82.7	67	39	68	12	3.48	4.35	8.0	3.8	6.5	1.4	4.65	10.9	-12
2003	CHC	NL	36	31	0	32.7	36	5	26	4	4.68	4.31	10.1	1.1	6.3	1.1	4.61	3.1	-1
2004	*CHC*	*NL*	*37*	*83*	*0*	*40.3*	*40*	*12*	*29*	*4*	*3.69*	*3.93*	*9.0*	*2.4*	*5.7*	*1.0*	*4.29*	*7.6*	*-5*

Breakout: 37%   *Improve: 54%*   *Collapse: 25%*

Veres spent substantial time on the disabled list due to shoulder tendinitis, but pitched better than his ERA suggests when he was available, walking just five hitters in 32.2 innings. Veres's trademark pitch is his sinker, which acts more like a breaking pitch than a power sinker like Kevin Brown's or Carlos Zambrano's. Veres intends to have off-season shoulder surgery, and he's a 37-year-old free agent, so this might be it for him.

TODD WELLEMEYER   Bats: R   Throws: R   Born: 30-Aug-78   Age: 25

YEAR	TM	LG	AGE	G	GS	IP	H	BB	SO	HR	ERA	EQERA	EQH9	EQBB9	EQSO9	EQHR9	PERA	VORP	STF
2001	LNS	MID	22	27	27	147.0	165	74	167	14	4.16	6.68	12.6	6.5	6.3	2.0	8.19	-15.5	-28
2002	DAY	FLA	23	14	14	73.7	63	19	87	7	3.79	4.64	10.2	2.9	7.4	2.0	6.19	7.0	-6
2002	WTN	SOU	23	8	8	46.0	33	18	37	2	4.70	4.93	7.9	3.9	5.1	0.9	4.12	3.1	8
2003	WTN	SOU	24	4	4	21.3	19	10	34	1	5.49	5.68	10.9	5.2	9.9	0.9	5.82	-0.2	19
2003	IOW	PCL	24	13	12	66.0	68	33	56	7	5.18	5.87	10.0	5.3	6.6	1.5	6.08	-1.8	-11
2003	CHC	NL	24	15	0	27.7	25	19	30	5	6.50	6.00	8.3	5.7	8.7	1.7	5.61	-5.2	-2
2004	*CHC*	*NL*	*25*	*15*	*11*	*62.0*	*64*	*34*	*52*	*8*	*5.40*	*5.75*	*9.3*	*4.3*	*6.8*	*1.2*	*5.54*	*-0.7*	*2*

Breakout: 15%   *Improve: 42%*   *Collapse: 25%*

Wellemeyer's debut was impressive. After five big league outings, his line read like something you'd see from Curt Schilling: 7.2 IP, 2 H, 0 ER, 0 BB, 13 K. He began to run into command problems shortly thereafter, though, and soon found himself doing time in Iowa. That pattern is typical of Wellemeyer's professional career: He can throw his big fastball by people, and his slider is a good pitch, but he doesn't hit his spots with enough consistency to be a top-flight pitcher. It's easy to envision great things if he can cut down his walk totals, but you can say that sort of thing about almost anyone. He should get a long look in spring training, and might be traded if he doesn't make the club. Because his changeup has been alternately nonexistent and ineffective, his future is probably in the bullpen.

KERRY WOOD

Bats: **Throws:**   Born: 16-Jun-77   Age: 27

YEAR	TM	LG	AGE	G	GS	IP	H	BB	SO	HR	ERA	EQERA	EQH9	EQBB9	EQSO9	EQHR9	PERA	VORP	STF
2001	CHC	NL	24	28	28	174.3	127	92	217	16	3.36	3.46	6.9	4.4	9.4	0.7	3.60	40.2	47
2002	CHC	NL	25	33	33	213.7	169	97	217	22	3.66	3.68	7.3	3.6	7.9	1.0	3.78	44.3	28
2003	CHC	NL	26	32	32	211.0	152	100	266	24	3.20	3.30	6.9	3.8	10.0	1.0	3.69	53.4	38
2004	CHC	NL	27	29	29	212.0	164	87	244	19	3.38	3.60	7.0	3.2	9.3	0.8	3.40	46.3	33

Breakout: 17%   Improve: 40%   Collapse: 14%

When he's on his game, Wood can be even more impressive than Mark Prior, mixing high heat with a sharp slider, and a changeup that's faster than a Jamey Moyer fastball. He's a power pitcher in the image of Nolan Ryan and Don Drysdale, dangerously wild, and unafraid to throw inside—he led the majors with 21 hit batsmen. He isn't likely to get much better than he was last season, but where he's at is plenty good. But like Ryan and Drysdale, Wood can require a lot of pitches to get his three outs. Partly as a result of that, and mostly as a result of Dusty Baker, Wood racked up the second-highest Pitcher Abuse Points total in the league. He encountered some back problems down the stretch, and was visibly fatigued in the post-season. His surgically repaired elbow has held up fine, thus far, but that's not really the point. Running a guy out there for 15 pitches too many doesn't guarantee that he'll be hurt. It makes him more *likely* to get hurt. We don't advocate that managers be more cognizant of pitch counts out of some benevolent concern for pitchers' health, but rather because it's winning baseball. Given how important Wood, Prior, and Zambrano are to the organization's future, the Cubs spent last season on the wrong side of the risk-reward nexus.

CARLOS ZAMBRANO

Bats: S   **Throws: R**   Born: 01-Jun-81   Age: 23

YEAR	TM	LG	AGE	G	GS	IP	H	BB	SO	HR	ERA	EQERA	EQH9	EQBB9	EQSO9	EQHR9	PERA	VORP	STF
2001	IOW	PCL	20	26	25	150.7	124	68	155	9	3.88	4.49	7.0	4.7	7.6	0.5	3.53	17.8	50
2001	CHC	NL	20	6	1	7.7	11	8	4	2	15.19	11.74	12.9	8.2	3.5	2.3	9.20	-5.3	-47
2002	IOW	PCL	21	3	3	9.0	2	6	11	0	0.00	0.00	2.2	6.5	9.7	0.0	1.62	5.2	71
2002	CHC	NL	21	32	16	108.3	94	63	93	9	3.66	4.26	7.8	4.5	6.6	0.8	4.14	15.7	31
2003	CHC	NL	22	32	32	214.0	188	94	168	9	3.11	3.57	8.0	3.6	6.3	0.4	3.61	44.0	42
2004	CHC	NL	23	25	24	158.0	143	70	134	10	3.77	4.01	8.1	3.5	6.9	0.6	3.88	26.6	18

Breakout: 29%   Improve: 47%   Collapse: 17%

The heavy workload is even more of a concern for Zambrano than it is for Prior or Wood. Carlos struggled notably down the stretch, and he relies on a pitch, the power sinker, that is tougher on a pitcher's mechanics than the usual assortment of fastballs and curves. Zambrano's ERA was a bit lower last year than you'd posit from his peripheral numbers, but that's a pattern common to extreme groundball pitchers; he saved himself from big innings by inducing 27 double plays last year. Power groundballers are a rare breed, and Zambrano—a big, goofy-looking guy who is fiery and animated on the mound—is a fun pitcher to watch. But in the near-term, he's a good candidate for a down season.

Cincinnati Reds

If there was a team that collapsed not despite of but *because of* the combined value of its merits—and even justifiable confidence in those merits—it was the 2003 Reds.

While expectations weren't all that high that the Reds would win the NL Central, nobody was expected to run away with the division, and the Reds were generally counted with the Astros, Cubs, and Cardinals as going concerns. The Great American Ballpark was opening its doors, and this was a club with Ken Griffey Jr., not to mention some guy an annual publication had put on its cover. It had a strong bullpen, young offensive talent, identifiable stars, and a long-standing fan favorite or two. It had smart guys in the front office, a general manager with a creative wheeler-dealer reputation, and a pitching coach on the short list for the game's best. With a new park for America's oldest baseball franchise, it was supposed to be a feel-good sort of year.

It wasn't. Instead, you've got a Reds franchise that seems to be racing for the title of divisional and national disgrace.

While the failure of the team's potentially potent outfield was the most visceral disappointment, Adam Dunn's struggles at the plate and the breakdowns of Griffey and Austin Kearns weren't what guaranteed the Reds' failure in 2003. Although a reserve outfield spot had to be spent on Wily Mo Pena—and another was wasted on Reggie Taylor—Ruben Mateo, Jose Guillen, Russell Branyan, and Dernell Stenson offered plausible alternatives. Pena and Taylor bring up another point; as much as we've picked on him in the past, it wasn't Bob Boone's tactical indiscretions or his fascination with speed that cost the Reds their season. It wasn't Barry Larkin's continuing decline into near-lifelike animatronic play at short, or Felipe Lopez's failure to develop. It's easy to exaggerate the importance of these issues, because while Boone's just an unhappy memory, the injuries in the outfield and the absence of a great choice at shortstop remain problems going into 2004. Lingering concerns can easily blow up into legendary ulcers, like the Cubs and third base, while failing to identify a more significant, enduring problem.

No, the fundamental source of the Reds' failure as an organization was their failure to assemble a big league rotation. What the Reds got out of their rotation in 2003 was historically awful in the era of divisional play.

REDS PROSPECTUS

2003 record: 69–93; Fifth place, NL Central

Pythagenport record: 62–100

Runs scored per game: 4.3 (13th in NL)

Runs allowed per game: 5.5 (15th in NL)

Team EqA: .250 (13th in NL)

2003 Batters Age: 31.8 (2nd oldest in NL)

2003 Pitchers Age: 27.5 (4th youngest in NL)

Ballpark: Great American Ballpark; Neutral park; Park Factor of 0.998

2003: Deep-sixed Jim Bowden and conducted the year's most celebrated fire sale, but didn't do much on the field.

2004: They've got a few good players to build on, but this team is going to give up a ton of runs.

Equally important was what that failure tells us about Jim Bowden's tenure as GM, and how the game has changed from a time when taking risks on retreads was more likely to reap rewards.

A thumbnail sketch of the worst rotations in terms of VORP since 1969 is shown in table 1.

Again, this is just a suggestive thumbnail, and perhaps not a definitive list. If you care to dig them up, you might be surprised that the '72 Rangers made the cut, but their staff ERA of 3.53 was the worst in the American League's final season without the Designated Hitter, during a strong pitcher's era. Anyway, the point of the chart is to reflect how ugly the Reds were in the starting pitcher department. And whereas the Brewers and Tigers entered 2003 with appropriately modest ambitions for completing their schedules, and the Rangers problems to put together a staff border on comic, the Reds were able to convince themselves that they weren't going to wind up in this sort of company (see table 2).

Think about that: The Reds got an actual quality start of six innings and three runs allowed—not earned runs, but runs—in only a third of their schedule. (Let the record reflect that does not count the seven quality starts that the starter lost in the seventh inning or later, but that begs the question, why would Bob Boone have anybody in this rotation on a long leash?) That's only a third of the sched-

TABLE 1: THE WORST ROTATIONS, 1969–2003*

Team	VORP	Notable Contributors
1. Florida, 1998	−49.1	Livan Hernandez, Brian Meadows, Jesus Sanchez, Andy Larkin
2. San Francisco, 1984	−48.8	Bill Laskey, Mike Krukow, Jeff Robinson, Mark Davis
3. Seattle Pilots, 1969	−48.1	Gene Brabender, Marty Pattin, Steve Barber, Fred Talbott
4. Seattle Mariners, 1978	−43.0	Paul Mitchell, Glenn Abbott, Rick Honeycutt, Jim Colborn
5. Texas, 2003	−42.8	John Thomson, Colby Lewis, Ismael Valdes, Joaquin Benoit
6. Texas, 2001	−36.2	Rick Helling, Doug Davis, Darren Oliver, Kenny Rogers
7. Detroit, 2003	−35.2	Mike Maroth, Nate Cornejo, Jeremy Bonderman, Gary Knotts
8. Texas, 1972	−33.7	Dick Bosman, Rich Hand, Pete Broberg, Bill Gogolewski
9. Baltimore, 1991	−30.6	Bob Milacki, Jose Mesa, Jeff Ballard, Ben McDonald
10. Cincinnati, 2003	−30.2	Paul Wilson, Danny Graves, Ryan Dempster, Jimmy Haynes
11. Milwaukee, 2003	−28.5	Ben Sheets, Wayne Franklin, Matt Kinney, Glendon Rusch

* Pitching VORP contributed by pitchers starting at least half of the games they appeared in; a pitcher with 20 appearances would have to have had at least 10 starts to be considered.

TABLE 2. THE REALLY BAD ROTATIONS OF 2003

TEAM	GS	QS	IP	H	R	ER	BB	SO	HR	W	L	BFP	TB	2B	3B	HBP	AVG/ NP	STRK %	G/F	RA	ERA	WHIP	AVG	OBP	SLG
CIN	162	54	883.0	1046	613	566	342	490	139	33	72	3975	1745	232	25	32	89.0	.616	1.10	6.25	5.77	1.61	.290	.357	.485
DET	162	59	885.7	1059	604	561	318	422	127	29	94	3958	1715	201	37	31	88.6	.608	1.13	6.14	5.70	1.59	.293	.356	.475
MIL	162	64	930.0	1061	613	566	370	620	144	39	73	4178	1759	200	33	37	95.3	.626	0.89	5.93	5.48	1.58	.281	.351	.466
TEX	162	51	832.0	976	610	575	344	533	147	47	65	3736	1667	196	27	35	87.8	.616	1.11	6.60	6.22	1.63	.291	.363	.497

ule where Reds starters did the bare minimum of putting their team in a position to win. In retrospect, it seems remarkable that they dodged 100 losses, considering everything else that went wrong.

But more basically, who was it that the Reds were counting on? Going into the season, they had a rotation of Paul Wilson, Ryan Dempster, Danny Graves, Jimmy Haynes, and Jimmy Anderson. Combined, they entered the year with a 187–222 record and a 5.02 ERA, which is better than it sounds, considering that Graves had spent the bulk of his career in the bullpen. Wilson was promising, especially since he'd managed to escape Tampa Bay without getting re-injured, but he had yet to really reward anybody's confidence. Dempster had been worked like a galley slave by Jeff Torborg before coming over, a mechanical mess doomed to the surgeon's table. Haynes was a fifth starter who'd been successful when handed tons of run support. Graves was an uncertain conversion project. Anderson had never posted an ERA under five as a rotation regular for three years in Pittsburgh, and was the hittable sort of guy that has no upside to anyone but the most wildly optimistic.

But the Reds had that kind of optimism, and not just because of the bullpen they felt would help them ice opposing lineups as early as the sixth inning. They had a foolhardiness born of experience, because they'd been spoiled by two people intimately associated with the team's fortunes. First, they had their association with Don Gullett, generally considered one of the game's great pitching coaches. Gullett's reputation as a retreader *par excellence* has a few success stories: Pete Schourek in '94, Kent Mercker and Mike Remlinger in '97, Pete Harnisch and Steve Parris in '98, Elmer Dessens in 2000, and arguably Jimmy Haynes in 2002. But you'll also notice that the miracles haven't been quite so frequent these days, and Dessens and Haynes only went from worthless to useful fourth or fifth starters. More recently, you see temporary flashes of promise that don't wind up working out, stints like those of Jason Bere in '98, Ron Villone and Steve Avery in '99, Ozzie Fernandez in 2000, and Joey Hamilton in 2002.

You shouldn't consider that an indictment of Gullett, however. A pitching coach can only do so much, and in an environment where teams are more aware of medical and performance risks and rewards than ever before, the market on retreads isn't quite so cheap, or as loaded with easy pickings, as it used to be. As a result, Gullett has been given dicier propositions to work with, like the rotations of 2002, 2003, and now probably 2004 as well.

But that brings us to the other man the Reds had come to rely upon for a bottomless hat filled with an endless supply of rabbits—Jim Bowden himself. With apologies to John Schuerholz or Pat Gillick, there isn't a general manager in the game that holds an important symbolic or historic place in the game today. There's no Branch Rickey in today's game, and no Whitey Herzog. It's a sign of the times; today's game also lacks "living history" archetypes like Gussie Busch or Connie Mack. It isn't the age for it. But more basically, in today's complicated economic environment, there certainly isn't room for the frenetics of the next "Trader" Frank Lane. Today's general managers may as well be descendants of either George Weiss (of Yankees dynasty fame) or Sal Bando (from the annals of Seligian sidekickdom), either builders with a killer instinct and a sense of the bottom line, or organizational apparatchiks who persist in the game's lingering semi-feudal management culture. The best of the current generation of GMs or GMs-to-be have generally come up together in player development, and have had similar interactions with modern notions of what you can do to save a buck and build a better ballclub.

In that cost-conscious environment, Bowden found it harder to wheel and deal. Already handicapped financially by Lindner's fiats to retain Barry Larkin or Sean Casey at any cost, he couldn't haul in a quality starter to stick at the front of the rotation after Pete Harnisch broke down again. With more teams picking through the bargain bin, looking for six-figure bargains poised to become surprise stories, Bowden couldn't work any particular magic on that front, which left him with his Frank Lane impulses, and little outlet for them. Worse yet, Bowden wound up being an outsider among his peers, as a generation of GMs who were more comfortable dealing with each other replaced the generation that Bowden had grown up around professionally. Bowden was the transactions junkie, addicted to making deals for dealing's sake, but left with few potential playmates who didn't take the game with a more deadly seriousness.

So what of a previous generation of fair-haired boys, now gone gray? Unfortunately, Bowden belongs to a time and place where he was the kid on the block, where he could curry favor with people like Tommy Lasorda or Fred Claire, or rub shoulders with peers like Dave Dombrowski or Randy Smith. As time went on, Bowden became that unhappiest contemporary phenomenon, the middle-aged anachronism. A career path that starts off at wunderkind and winds up in 40-something obsolescence might be old hat in the tech sector, but in baseball, it's a bit of a recent development.

As much as it's politically correct to say that life is not a popularity contest, in some respects, life is a popularity contest. Bowden had an endless faith in his own ability, and managed to annoy general managers with less tenure. The real question for someone like Bowden, or Dan Duquette, is whether or not he can survive a reputation for recent failure. As Duquette found out, personal skills matter, and matter more than building a winner in some cases. There are a few people in the industry who just aren't going to take a shine to Bowden, whatever his successes. By way of contrast, Bill Bavasi got retreaded in no time, and it would be hard to find anyone inside the industry who would say an ill word in public about Bavasi, Spiezio/McCracken fetishes or not.

After Bowden's in-season departure, the Reds went into something of a Bowden memorial phase of frenzied transactions, tearing down a non-winner to repair a farm system that had been given short shrift through Carl Lindner's budgetary diktats. Players and fans screamed about betrayal, as if they hadn't been betrayed by years of false expectations generated by an owner, an organization, and a ballpark all the way up to that point. If anything, last summer's trading frenzy was an overdue acknowledgment of the limitations of the present, and the need to build a future that wasn't dependent on executive tap-dancing and whatever booty the waiver wire had to offer. In this, the organization was doing what it had to do.

Unfortunately, in doing so, they made bright Assistant GM Brad Kullman appear the hatchet man, probably hurting his chances at being named the team's general manager. Naming a new GM would define the team's future, and perhaps in the least surprising development of the winter, rather than hire one of the new generation, Lindner brought over baseball lifer Dan O'Brien from the Rangers, where he'd been effectively sloughed over by the Hart/Fuson regime. O'Brien is a cipher, and his selection tells us nothing about where the Reds see themselves, and that in itself tells us something. O'Brien brought in another gray man, former Brewers GM Dean Taylor, to be his Assistant GM. It could work out just fine, but it isn't promising. If anything, the selections smack of Lindner's apparent aspirations to be the Rhineland's Steinbrenner, minus the distractions and expense of winning. As reprehensible as Marge Schott's legacy looks, at least she had something resembling a commitment to winning a few ballgames.

Hauling in Taylor seems especially appropriate considering the disappointment that the Great American Ballpark represents. Between the complaints about its antiseptic qualities, or the way it seems likely to boost homerun totals, or the cockamamie canyon that supposedly lets Lindner see home plate from the office, it rivals Miller Park as a contemporary architectural disappointment. Attendance was only moderately boosted by the new park novelty effect; the Reds seem to draw right around 1.8 million every year, with two exceptions, last year's 2.3 million, and 2000's 2.5 million. That's right, the new park didn't outdraw the team that followed 1999's run at the playoffs, which isn't anything surprising. Outside of Wrigleyville or Fenway, Americans like winning ballclubs more than they like ballparks.

Rather than act on that knowledge, the Reds instead seem to be indulging semi-secret fantasies about what a Pete Rose reinstatement might do for them, with pretty open speculation that having Rose in the dugout would work wonders at the turnstiles. If legit, such thinking would only confirm how hopelessly damned this franchise is to the caprices of Carl Lindner, which would be a shame. The Reds have some interesting young arms, a strong bullpen, two excellent building blocks in Kearns and Dunn, and a few intriguing prospects. If leveraged correctly, this team still has the makings of a decent future. But it's hard to feel optimistic about that future until the flailings at the top of the pyramid cease.

HITTERS

WILLIAM BERGOLLA   2B   Bats: R   Throws: R   Born: 04-Feb-83   Age: 21

YEAR	TM	LG	AGE	AB	H	2B	3B	HR	BB	SO	SB	CS	AVG	OBP	SLG	MLVR	EQBA	EQOBP	EQSLG	EQMLVR	VORP	DEFENSE			
2001	BIL	PIO	18	232	75	5	3	4	24	21	22	7	.323	.387	.422	.150	.212	.259	.277	-.423	-31.9	41-2B	-3	15-SS	-5
2002	BIL	PIO	19	210	74	9	1	3	24	26	16	5	.352	.408	.448	.263	.230	.278	.297	-.347	-20.4	50-2B	-10		
2002	DYT	MID	19	274	68	13	1	3	16	36	13	2	.248	.291	.336	-.086	.204	.236	.283	-.465	-23.9	47-2B	-4	14-SS	-1
2003	POT	CAR	20	523	142	25	3	2	29	59	52	18	.272	.309	.342	-.065	.228	.258	.297	-.388	-35.1	127-2B	-11		
2004	*CIN*	*NL*	*21*	*281*	*63*	*12*	*2*	*2*	*16*	*39*	*10*	*4*	*.224*	*.268*	*.302*	*-.326*	*.223*	*.266*	*.301*	*-.349*	*-12.0*	*74-2B*	*-10*		
Breakout: 22%			*Improve: 57%*				*Collapse: 20%*																	

Bergolla led the organization in stolen bases despite a .309 OBP, which gives you an idea of how much he was running. He's a slap hitter who puts the ball in play, and the Reds haven't yet tried to emphasize plate discipline with him. He has had problems later in the year, losing a lot of weight and strength in-season, in part because of some nutritional issues. His speed will give him opportunities, but his career will depend on him reaching base more.

LUIS BOLIVAR   SS   Bats: B   Throws: R   Born: 15-Feb-81   Age: 23

YEAR	TM	LG	AGE	AB	H	2B	3B	HR	BB	SO	SB	CS	AVG	OBP	SLG	MLVR	EQBA	EQOBP	EQSLG	EQMLVR	VORP	DEFENSE			
2003	DYT	MID	22	183	42	8	1	2	17	42	6	6	.230	.304	.317	-.090	.101	.235	.261	-.509	-17.8	24-SS	-1	19-3B	-4
2003	BIL	PIO	22	235	82	20	3	9	17	32	12	6	.349	.405	.574	.435	.237	.278	.397	-.201	0.2	37-SS	-8	10-2B	2
2004	*CIN*	*NL*	*23*	*231*	*52*	*12*	*2*	*4*	*16*	*51*	*4*	*3*	*.224*	*.281*	*.343*	*-.249*	*.223*	*.278*	*.342*	*-.273*	*-5.2*	*63-SS*	*-12*		
Breakout: 37%			*Improve: 59%*				*Collapse: 20%*																	

The Billings Mustangs won the Pioneer League title after a 41–35 season, and it's not hard to see why. Bolivar spent the first part of the season at Dayton and didn't hit before dropping down to the short-season circuit. He and Habelito Hernandez (né Juan Diaz, an AgeGate case) formed the league's best double-play combination before Hernandez (.377/.392/.673) was promoted (and subsequently separated his shoulder). Joey Votto and Miguel Perez also made big contributions. The position-player talent at the lower levels of this organization is highly encouraging for a team that has to develop its own talent to survive.

RUSS BRANYAN   3B/LF   Bats: L   Throws: R   Born: 19-Dec-75   Age: 28

YEAR	TM	LG	AGE	AB	H	2B	3B	HR	BB	SO	SB	CS	AVG	OBP	SLG	MLVR	EQBA	EQOBP	EQSLG	EQMLVR	VORP	DEFENSE			
2001	CLE	AL	25	315	73	16	2	20	38	132	1	1	.232	.316	.486	.020	.247	.334	.522	.082	21.9	61-3B	-6	21-LF	-3
2002	CLE	AL	26	161	33	4	0	8	17	65	1	2	.205	.278	.379	-.189	.222	.300	.420	-.139	-3.7	35-LF	0		
2002	CIN	NL	26	217	53	9	1	16	34	86	3	1	.244	.349	.516	.148	.245	.346	.523	.102	9.5	20-LF	-1	18-1B	1
2003	CIN	NL	27	176	38	12	0	9	27	69	0	0	.216	.322	.438	-.022	.219	.325	.449	-.056	3.2	20-3B	3	13-LF	0
2004	*ATL*	*NL*	*28*	*152*	*34*	*8*	*1*	*8*	*24*	*57*	*1*	*1*	*.226*	*.332*	*.448*	*-.023*	*.229*	*.334*	*.464*	*-.011*	*8.3*	*46-LF*	*1*		
Breakout: 34%			*Improve: 49%*				*Collapse: 29%*																	

Off-season surgery to repair a torn labrum caused Branyan to start the season late and occasionally affected his throwing throughout the year. He is never going to be a star, but his ridiculous power can help a team able to sacrifice some defense and contact at third base. The Reds, with great power in the outfield and lousy infield defense, aren't necessarily that team, and Branyan became a free agent after Cincy non-tendered him.

SEAN CASEY 1B Bats: L Throws: R Born: 02-Jul-74 Age: 29

YEAR	TM	LG	AGE	AB	H	2B	3B	HR	BB	SO	SB	CS	AVG	OBP	SLG	MLVR	EQBA	EQOBP	EQSLG	EQMLVR	VORP	DEFENSE	
2001	CIN	NL	27	533	165	40	0	13	43	63	3	1	.310	.369	.458	.112	.310	.368	.458	.111	28.3	124-1B	1
2002	CIN	NL	28	425	111	25	0	6	43	47	2	1	.261	.334	.362	-.061	.265	.334	.372	-.110	-3.0	103-1B	-5
2003	CIN	NL	29	573	167	19	3	14	51	58	4	0	.291	.350	.408	.043	.296	.353	.417	.013	13.3	141-1B	-6
2004	CIN	NL	29	458	129	27	2	10	45	53	3	2	.282	.349	.417	.007	.280	.346	.415	-.015	9.6	121-1B	-3

Breakout: 13%   Improve: 45%   Collapse: 15%

One of the most popular players in baseball, Casey doesn't do nearly enough on the field to separate himself from the pack of average first basemen who have been flooding the free-agent market the past couple of years. His 10.7 RARP (Runs Above Replacement Player) ranked ahead of just six first basemen with at least 400 plate appearances. In a winter when all the focus was on the game's bad contracts, little was made of Casey's three-year, $20.4-million deal. He's due $6.8 million in 2004 and $7.8 million in 2005, making him a millstone on the Reds' payroll.

JUAN CASTRO IF Bats: R Throws: R Born: 20-Jun-72 Age: 32

YEAR	TM	LG	AGE	AB	H	2B	3B	HR	BB	SO	SB	CS	AVG	OBP	SLG	MLVR	EQBA	EQOBP	EQSLG	EQMLVR	VORP	DEFENSE			
2001	CIN	NL	29	242	54	10	0	3	13	50	0	0	.223	.261	.302	-.371	.225	.262	.307	-.368	-10.6	27-SS	-3	20-2B	1
2002	CIN	NL	30	82	18	3	0	2	7	18	0	0	.220	.278	.329	-.227	.229	.281	.349	-.269	-1.4	12-SS	-1		
2003	CIN	NL	31	320	81	14	1	9	18	58	2	3	.253	.290	.388	-.128	.257	.296	.396	-.154	0.2	48-2B	6	19-3B	3
2004	CIN	NL	32	211	50	9	1	5	14	40	1	1	.236	.283	.352	-.226	.235	.280	.350	-.250	-2.9	57-2B	-1		

Breakout: 26%   Improve: 41%   Collapse: 40%

The nine home runs scream "fluke" for a guy who'd hit 11 in eight seasons prior to 2003. Castro is a very good defender, however, and worth the roster spot on a team carrying infielders being played for their bats. Castro has more value if D'Angelo Jimenez and Tim Hummel have starting jobs, as opposed to Rainer Olmedo.

ADAM DUNN LF/1B Bats: L Throws: R Born: 09-Nov-79 Age: 24

YEAR	TM	LG	AGE	AB	H	2B	3B	HR	BB	SO	SB	CS	AVG	OBP	SLG	MLVR	EQBA	EQOBP	EQSLG	EQMLVR	VORP	DEFENSE			
2001	CHT	SOU	21	140	48	9	0	12	24	31	6	3	.343	.449	.664	.596	.276	.366	.531	.177	11.3	21-LF	-1	12-RF	-1
2001	LOU	INT	21	210	69	13	0	20	38	51	5	1	.329	.441	.676	.572	.292	.398	.602	.342	27.1	51-LF	1		
2001	CIN	NL	21	244	64	18	1	19	38	74	4	2	.262	.371	.578	.231	.259	.365	.567	.207	19.4	36-RF	0	28-LF	0
2002	CIN	NL	22	535	133	28	2	26	128	170	19	9	.249	.400	.454	.155	.245	.392	.453	.091	23.3	90-LF	-3	40-1B	-6
2003	CIN	NL	23	381	82	12	1	27	74	126	8	2	.215	.354	.465	.066	.220	.355	.478	.037	10.4	93-LF	-5	10-1B	-1
2004	CIN	NL	24	453	126	26	2	32	86	124	11	4	.278	.401	.560	.270	.276	.397	.557	.249	40.9	130-LF	-4		

Breakout: 59%   Improve: 84%   Collapse: 5%

The idea that Dunn is being exposed each time around the league has merit. His strikeout rate has been increasing with time, and his four worst monthly rates all came in 2003. It's hard to be a productive hitter striking out in close to 40% of his at-bats, and that's the level Dunn reached last year.

Another problem Dunn faces is that his best five monthly batting averages on balls in play came in five of his first six months in the majors. It may just be that he was hitting in good luck, and that he's not really a .300 hitter, but one whose level is closer to .270. Adam Dunn hitting .270 is still a great player because of his secondary skills, but he's not going to be able to hit even .270 unless he gets his strikeouts under control. Dunn is one of the five most interesting players to watch this coming season, and PECOTA's optimistic.

EDWIN ENCARNACION 3B Bats: R Throws: R Born: 07-Jan-83 Age: 21

YEAR	TM	LG	AGE	AB	H	2B	3B	HR	BB	SO	SB	CS	AVG	OBP	SLG	MLVR	EQBA	EQOBP	EQSLG	EQMLVR	VORP	DEFENSE			
2001	SAV	SAL	18	170	52	9	2	4	12	34	3	3	.306	.355	.453	.228	.243	.287	.373	-.214	-1.8	44-3B	-10		
2001	BIL	PIO	18	211	55	8	2	5	15	29	8	1	.261	.307	.389	-.085	.180	.214	.275	-.533	-40.0	51-3B	-6		
2001	DYT	MID	18	37	6	2	0	1	1	5	0	1	.162	.184	.297	-.398	.135	.158	.216	-.748	-6.8				
2002	DYT	MID	19	518	146	32	4	17	40	108	25	7	.282	.338	.458	.160	.219	.264	.369	-.280	-15.8	116-3B	-11	15-SS	-4
2003	POT	CAR	20	215	69	15	1	6	24	32	7	1	.321	.387	.484	.267	.243	.302	.385	-.168	0.9	56-3B	-12		
2003	CHT	SOU	20	254	69	13	1	5	22	44	8	3	.272	.331	.390	.040	.239	.291	.359	-.229	-3.8	62-3B	-8		
2004	CIN	NL	21	305	71	15	1	9	22	57	4	2	.233	.287	.376	-.189	.232	.284	.374	-.213	-1.2	81-3B	-11		

Breakout: 23%   Improve: 53%   Collapse: 23%

Don't be disappointed by that Double-A line. Encarnacion opened 2003 as a 20-year-old in Chattanooga and hit .220/.279/.294 before being sent back to Potomac. Promoted again in July, he hit .310/.363/.462 over his last 145 at-bats. He may be the least-known good prospect in the game, and even if left at third base—which appears to be the plan after a dalliance with shortstop—is a building block kind of player for the Reds. He'll make an appearance in Cincinnati this September, and might never leave.

RYAN FREEL UT   Bats: R   Throws: R   Born: 08-Mar-76   Age: 28

YEAR	TM	LG	AGE	AB	H	2B	3B	HR	BB	SO	SB	CS	AVG	OBP	SLG	MLVR	EQBA	EQOBP	EQSLG	EQMLVR	VORP	DEFENSE		DEFENSE	
2001	SYR	INT	25	319	83	21	3	5	42	42	22	9	.260	.357	.392	.026	.238	.328	.364	-.151	-9.4	47-LF	2		
2001	TOR	AL	25	22	6	1	0	0	1	4	2	1	.273	.333	.318	-.148	.318	.368	.364	-.018	0.6				
2002	DUR	INT	26	448	117	27	4	8	38	51	37	10	.261	.337	.393	.002	.243	.315	.376	-.156	2.5	55-2B	-6	23-RF	0
2003	LOU	INT	27	215	59	11	1	3	21	32	25	6	.274	.336	.377	-.003	.257	.319	.362	-.158	1.1	36-2B	5		
2003	CIN	NL	27	137	39	6	1	4	9	13	9	4	.285	.344	.431	.060	.288	.341	.439	.016	6.0	19-CF	0		
2004	CIN	NL	28	319	84	19	3	6	32	43	19	7	.264	.341	.400	-.043	.262	.337	.398	-.065	10.1	87-2B	-6		

Breakout: 29%   Improve: 52%   Collapse: 25%

Freel, a shortstop prospect for the Blue Jays in the late 1990s, finally reached the majors having recast himself as a utility man. His playing time had more to with the Reds' injuries than his ability, but as a guy who can run a little and play five or six positions, he has value. Dave Miley, who had him at Louisville, should be able to help Freel from the manager's seat.

KEN GRIFFEY CF   Bats: L   Throws: L   Born: 21-Nov-69   Age: 34

YEAR	TM	LG	AGE	AB	H	2B	3B	HR	BB	SO	SB	CS	AVG	OBP	SLG	MLVR	EQBA	EQOBP	EQSLG	EQMLVR	VORP	DEFENSE	
2001	CIN	NL	31	364	104	20	2	22	44	72	2	0	.286	.365	.533	.186	.283	.364	.530	.179	33.7	79-CF	-8
2002	CIN	NL	32	197	52	8	0	8	28	39	1	2	.264	.358	.426	.063	.261	.357	.432	.013	8.7	41-CF	-4
2003	CIN	NL	33	166	41	12	1	13	27	44	1	0	.247	.370	.566	.245	.250	.369	.577	.217	16.8	36-CF	-3
2004	CIN	NL	34	218	58	11	1	13	30	50	1	1	.265	.361	.502	.124	.264	.358	.499	.102	15.3	63-CF	-5

Breakout: 26%   Improve: 56%   Collapse: 24%

There are differing schools of thought on Griffey remaining a center fielder. While some argue his legs can't take it, Griffey's injuries have been sudden, severe, and caused by awkward movements, not the kind of setbacks caused by the wear and tear of roaming the wide expanses of center. Still, Griffey's deteriorating defense gives the Reds added impetus to move him to an outfield corner and leave him there. With the obvious caveat of "if healthy," Griffey could be a championship-caliber hitter in a corner. Even fighting injuries, he was on pace to hit 40 home runs last year, and only in 2002 was his rate of production below par. He can still turn on a fastball, still walk 70 times and still hit .280–.300. Griffey hasn't become a bad player; he's just become a fragile one.

TIM HUMMEL IF   Bats: R   Throws: R   Born: 18-Nov-78   Age: 25

YEAR	TM	LG	AGE	AB	H	2B	3B	HR	BB	SO	SB	CS	AVG	OBP	SLG	MLVR	EQBA	EQOBP	EQSLG	EQMLVR	VORP	DEFENSE		DEFENSE	
2001	BIR	SOU	22	524	152	33	6	7	62	69	14	3	.290	.364	.416	.122	.255	.320	.373	-.142	5.3	91-2B	-13	35-SS	-7
2002	CHR	INT	23	523	136	33	0	4	51	95	6	5	.260	.332	.346	-.070	.242	.315	.328	-.223	-3.3	78-SS	1	53-2B	-3
2003	CHR	INT	24	476	135	25	3	15	46	83	9	3	.284	.350	.443	.121	.265	.333	.427	-.035	21.7	95-3B	-4	26-SS	-7
2003	CIN	NL	24	84	19	5	0	2	8	13	0	0	.226	.290	.357	-.176	.235	.301	.365	-.204	-0.8	14-3B	-2		
2004	CIN	NL	25	271	69	14	1	7	24	44	3	1	.255	.323	.393	-.090	.253	.320	.390	-.112	8.7	74-3B	-2		

Breakout: 27%   Improve: 47%   Collapse: 33%

Started last year stuck behind D'Angelo Jimenez, ended the year stuck behind D'Angelo Jimenez. Plus ça change... Hummel has been moved from shortstop to second base to third as a professional, and while his best position is second, the Reds would do worse than to play him at shortstop, take the defensive hit, and try and score 850 runs. He's a better player than David Eckstein, and a lot better than Rainer Olmedo.

D'ANGELO JIMENEZ 2B Bats: B Throws: R Born: 21-Dec-77 Age: 26

YEAR	TM	LG	AGE	AB	H	2B	3B	HR	BB	SO	SB	CS	AVG	OBP	SLG	MLVR	EQBA	EQOBP	EQSLG	EQMLVR	VORP	DEFENSE			
2001	COH	INT	23	214	56	11	1	5	24	31	5	6	.262	.333	.393	.003	.243	.317	.367	-.165	0.7	30-2B	-3	14-SS	2
2001	SDP	NL	23	308	85	19	0	3	39	68	2	3	.276	.355	.367	-.031	.288	.366	.383	-.017	16.1	85-SS	-2		
2002	SDP	NL	24	321	77	11	4	3	34	63	4	2	.240	.311	.327	-.126	.258	.326	.356	-.153	1.9	53-2B	0	31-3B	1
2002	CHR	INT	24	157	44	11	1	6	24	14	6	2	.280	.372	.478	.180	.256	.346	.438	-.003	10.2	42-SS	-6		
2002	CWS	AL	24	108	31	4	3	1	16	10	2	1	.287	.384	.407	.085	.303	.396	.440	.129	9.1	16-2B	3		
2003	CWS	AL	25	271	69	11	5	7	32	46	4	3	.255	.332	.410	-.048	.269	.351	.435	.012	7.3	64-2B	-4		
2003	CIN	NL	25	290	84	13	2	7	34	43	7	4	.290	.365	.421	.084	.293	.369	.425	.051	16.7	71-2B	7		
2004	*CIN*	*NL*	*26*	*487*	*132*	*25*	*4*	*10*	*59*	*75*	*8*	*5*	*.271*	*.349*	*.404*	*-.020*	*.269*	*.346*	*.401*	*-.041*	*18.0*	*130-2B*	*-1*		

Breakout: 8%   Improve: 34%   Collapse: 22%

Let's see if the pattern continues. Jimenez made the Padres happy in the second half of 2001, and was a White Sock by mid-2002. The Sox liked his play enough to make him the starting second baseman in 2003, then dumped him in July. Now the Reds, for whom Jimenez hit well down the stretch, will have the chance to grow tired of him. He doesn't play good defense and is often perceived as lazy; his career may depend on shedding those labels in 2004.

AUSTIN KEARNS RF Bats: R Throws: R Born: 20-May-80 Age: 24

YEAR	TM	LG	AGE	AB	H	2B	3B	HR	BB	SO	SB	CS	AVG	OBP	SLG	MLVR	EQBA	EQOBP	EQSLG	EQMLVR	VORP	DEFENSE			
2001	CHT	SOU	21	205	55	11	2	6	26	43	7	5	.268	.364	.429	.103	.229	.308	.367	-.191	-8.7	36-RF	-5	12-LF	-1
2002	CIN	NL	22	372	117	24	3	13	54	81	6	3	.315	.407	.500	.277	.313	.404	.501	.236	30.9	83-RF	3	12-LF	0
2003	CIN	NL	23	292	77	11	0	15	41	68	5	2	.264	.364	.455	.108	.267	.364	.463	.072	13.7	42-RF	2	40-CF	-2
2004	*CIN*	*NL*	*24*	*369*	*103*	*21*	*2*	*17*	*48*	*78*	*7*	*3*	*.278*	*.369*	*.484*	*.123*	*.276*	*.365*	*.481*	*.102*	*21.4*	*102-RF*	*3*		

Breakout: 14%   Improve: 49%   Collapse: 19%

Kearns missed the last three months of the season with a sore right rotator cuff that eventually required surgery. Before injuring the wing in a play at the plate on May 21, Kearns was hitting .309/.417/.599. After that, he hit just .208/.290/.277, playing his last game on July 8. His plate discipline was intact; he just couldn't hit the ball with any authority. Find someone who forgot about the injury and trade for Kearns, because he'll return to stud level in 2004 and handily beat that projection.

BARRY LARKIN SS Bats: R Throws: R Born: 28-Apr-64 Age: 40

YEAR	TM	LG	AGE	AB	H	2B	3B	HR	BB	SO	SB	CS	AVG	OBP	SLG	MLVR	EQBA	EQOBP	EQSLG	EQMLVR	VORP	DEFENSE	
2001	CIN	NL	37	156	40	12	0	2	27	25	3	2	.256	.373	.372	-.038	.253	.368	.367	-.060	6.6	39-SS	-7
2002	CIN	NL	38	507	124	37	2	7	44	57	13	4	.245	.305	.367	-.116	.246	.306	.375	-.173	4.0	122-SS	3
2003	CIN	NL	39	241	68	16	1	2	22	32	2	0	.282	.345	.382	-.009	.287	.348	.389	-.043	9.7	53-SS	-3
2004	*CIN*	*NL*	*40*	*201*	*50*	*13*	*1*	*3*	*21*	*27*	*2*	*1*	*.247*	*.321*	*.368*	*-.132*	*.246*	*.318*	*.366*	*-.154*	*5.4*	*56-SS*	*-5*

Breakout: 8%   Improve: 35%   Collapse: 48%

Jim Bowden took the fall in part because Larkin didn't come close to being worth the three-year, $27-million extension that Carl Lindner and John Allen dropped on him in 2000. Over the three years, Larkin played in just 260 games and hit .257/.326/.372. He's back on a one-year, $700,000 deal in 2004, which doesn't make sense from a baseball standpoint—Freel and Hummel are both more valuable players—and couldn't possibly provide that much goodwill. Larkin and the Reds would be better off without each other.

BRANDON LARSON 3B Bats: R Throws: R Born: 24-May-76 Age: 28

YEAR	TM	LG	AGE	AB	H	2B	3B	HR	BB	SO	SB	CS	AVG	OBP	SLG	MLVR	EQBA	EQOBP	EQSLG	EQMLVR	VORP	DEFENSE	
2001	LOU	INT	25	424	108	22	2	14	24	123	5	6	.255	.312	.415	-.019	.239	.292	.398	-.172	1.1	109-3B	14
2001	CIN	NL	25	33	4	2	0	0	2	10	0	0	.121	.171	.182	-.755	.121	.171	.182	-.771	-5.7		
2002	LOU	INT	26	297	101	20	1	25	24	70	1	1	.340	.393	.667	.518	.308	.363	.612	.322	43.2	64-3B	-4
2002	CIN	NL	26	51	14	2	0	4	6	10	1	0	.275	.362	.549	.237	.269	.343	.558	.169	4.0		
2003	CIN	NL	27	89	9	1	0	1	13	31	2	2	.101	.212	.146	-.647	.111	.223	.156	-.695	-13.2	22-3B	1
2003	LOU	INT	27	282	91	19	2	20	28	70	3	0	.323	.384	.617	.433	.294	.359	.570	.239	36.2	70-3B	6
2004	*CIN*	*NL*	*28*	*265*	*68*	*15*	*1*	*14*	*25*	*67*	*3*	*1*	*.257*	*.325*	*.474*	*.021*	*.256*	*.322*	*.471*	*-.002*	*16.5*	*72-3B*	*0*

Breakout: 19%   Improve: 41%   Collapse: 35%

Terribly overrated as a potential Rookie of the Year candidate coming into 2003—the Reds moved Aaron Boone to second base to clear space for him—Larson fell on his face, unable to make contact or drive the ball when he did. He was demoted April 19 and mashed the ball at Louisville, earning a recall in July, but a torn labrum that required surgery ended his season in August. Allowed to be part of a very interesting platoon with Branyan, Larson could contribute to the Reds. Those two could combine to go .250/.330/.520 with 35 homers and 190 strikeouts.

JASON LaRUE C Bats: R Throws: R Born: 19-Mar-74 Age: 30

YEAR	TM	LG	AGE	AB	H	2B	3B	HR	BB	SO	SB	CS	AVG	OBP	SLG	MLVR	EQBA	EQOBP	EQSLG	EQMLVR	VORP	DEFENSE
2001	CIN	NL	27	364	86	21	2	12	27	106	3	3	.236	.303	.404	-.140	.237	.302	.403	-.148	2.5	94-C 16
2002	CIN	NL	28	353	88	17	1	12	27	117	1	2	.249	.324	.405	-.030	.255	.324	.417	-.074	9.1	99-C 4
2003	CIN	NL	29	379	87	23	1	16	33	111	3	3	.230	.321	.422	-.034	.238	.323	.439	-.058	9.2	107-C -2
2004	CIN	NL	30	285	69	15	1	10	25	82	2	1	.243	.324	.412	-.072	.241	.321	.409	-.095	7.7	78-C -1

Breakout: 28%   Improve: 51%   Collapse: 27%

Michael Wolverton's evaluations place LaRue atop the league leaders in gunning down baserunners year-in and year-out. That plus 15 home runs and 15 HBPs a year make him a decent starting catcher. He's about to get expensive, though, and a good arm behind the plate is a luxury the Reds may decide to do without. LaRue continues to show a persistent backwards platoon split, a trend that's held up the past three years.

FELIPE LOPEZ SS Bats: B Throws: R Born: 12-May-80 Age: 24

YEAR	TM	LG	AGE	AB	H	2B	3B	HR	BB	SO	SB	CS	AVG	OBP	SLG	MLVR	EQBA	EQOBP	EQSLG	EQMLVR	VORP	DEFENSE		
2001	TEN	SOU	21	72	16	2	1	2	9	23	4	4	.222	.309	.361	-.117	.176	.247	.297	-.437	-5.3	11-SS -2		
2001	SYR	INT	21	358	100	19	7	16	30	94	13	5	.279	.337	.506	.155	.254	.313	.470	-.020	19.2	60-SS -8	18-2B	3
2001	TOR	AL	21	177	46	5	4	5	12	39	4	3	.260	.304	.418	-.076	.271	.321	.441	-.032	6.7	44-3B 1		
2002	SYR	INT	22	173	55	11	2	3	29	37	13	0	.318	.419	.457	.247	.284	.378	.415	.046	13.6	43-SS -2		
2002	TOR	AL	22	282	64	15	3	8	23	90	5	4	.227	.287	.387	-.156	.244	.305	.417	-.117	6.2	72-SS -1		
2003	CIN	NL	23	197	42	7	2	2	28	59	8	5	.213	.313	.299	-.218	.216	.315	.302	-.273	-3.8	45-SS -10		
2003	LOU	INT	23	143	40	11	0	2	12	38	2	5	.280	.333	.399	.025	.255	.312	.372	-.159	1.9	25-SS -5		
2004	CIN	NL	24	303	78	16	3	10	34	74	8	4	.259	.334	.430	-.019	.257	.331	.428	-.041	17.5	83-SS -7		

Breakout: 34%   Improve: 55%   Collapse: 13%

Lopez started the year as the Reds' shortstop, then was demoted in June amidst a hail of strikeouts (59, or one every 3.4 at-bats) and errors (15 at shortstop, for a .928 fielding percentage). An ugly dislocated ankle while at Louisville ended his season in July and required surgery. He is still very capable of being a Jose Valentin-type shortstop, with visible flaws marring a highly productive package, but the immediate question is whether he's recovered from the injury. His 2004 season may start late.

RUBEN MATEO OF Bats: R Throws: R Born: 10-Feb-78 Age: 26

YEAR	TM	LG	AGE	AB	H	2B	3B	HR	BB	SO	SB	CS	AVG	OBP	SLG	MLVR	EQBA	EQOBP	EQSLG	EQMLVR	VORP	DEFENSE		
2001	TEX	AL	23	129	32	5	2	1	9	28	1	0	.248	.322	.341	-.159	.264	.333	.364	-.124	-1.9	32-RF -1		
2001	LOU	INT	23	251	63	16	4	2	13	45	2	0	.251	.307	.371	-.089	.238	.292	.357	-.230	-12.0	59-RF -6		
2002	LOU	INT	24	209	63	14	0	9	11	40	6	2	.301	.342	.498	.176	.278	.323	.469	.018	4.9	28-RF -4	15-CF	-3
2002	CIN	NL	24	86	22	6	0	2	6	20	0	0	.256	.319	.395	-.047	.264	.317	.414	-.084	-0.4	14-RF 0		
2003	CIN	NL	25	207	50	9	0	3	12	53	0	0	.242	.290	.329	-.211	.249	.297	.340	-.237	-8.6	33-RF 0	11-CF	0
2003	LOU	INT	25	217	71	15	1	9	26	34	3	1	.327	.408	.530	.354	.299	.379	.493	.169	15.9	52-RF -5		
2004	CIN	NL	26	217	56	12	2	6	19	45	2	1	.257	.327	.414	-.052	.256	.324	.412	-.075	2.5	60-RF -2		

Breakout: 22%   Improve: 41%   Collapse: 41%

The flip side of Jose Guillen, Mateo started 2003 as a 25-year-old toolsy outfielder who had never lived up to expectations, and ended it as a 25-year-old toolsy outfielder who had never lived up to expectations. He did hit well at Triple-A again, but until he brings his patience with him upon a promotion (25 unintentional walks in 217 Triple-A at-bats last year, as opposed to 39 unintentional walks in 750 career major-league at-bats), he'll never hold a job.

CORKY MILLER   **C**   **Bats: R**   **Throws: R**   Born: 18-Mar-76   Age: 28

YEAR	TM	LG	AGE	AB	H	2B	3B	HR	BB	SO	SB	CS	AVG	OBP	SLG	MLVR	EQBA	EQOBP	EQSLG	EQMLVR	VORP	DEFENSE	
2001	CHT	SOU	25	170	47	12	0	9	25	32	1	2	.276	.425	.506	.296	.234	.347	.434	-.024	8.7	54-C	9
2001	LOU	INT	25	144	50	11	0	7	10	19	2	0	.347	.431	.569	.445	.322	.396	.534	.279	19.2	41-C	11
2001	CIN	NL	25	49	9	2	0	3	4	16	1	0	.184	.263	.408	-.246	.184	.267	.408	-.244	-1.0	16-C	3
2002	LOU	INT	26	134	31	5	0	6	16	21	1	2	.231	.340	.403	-.007	.207	.311	.378	-.185	-0.5	38-C	-1
2002	CIN	NL	26	114	29	10	0	3	9	20	0	0	.254	.328	.421	.001	.261	.333	.426	-.040	4.0	34-C	4
2003	LOU	INT	27	354	88	28	0	11	35	58	0	0	.249	.326	.421	.019	.232	.307	.405	-.139	3.7	97-C	-4
2003	CIN	NL	27	30	8	0	0	0	5	7	0	0	.267	.395	.267	-.079	.267	.399	.267	-.121	0.5		
2004	*CIN*	*NL*	*28*	*161*	*39*	*9*	*0*	*6*	*17*	*31*	*0*	*0*	*.242*	*.334*	*.418*	*-.047*	*.241*	*.331*	*.416*	*-.069*	*8.7*	*47-C*	*-4*

Breakout: 30%   Improve: 50%   Collapse: 32%

But for an utterly ridiculous contract extension granted to Kelly Stinnett, Miller would have spent all of 2003 in Cincinnati as LaRue's backup. There's virtually no difference between the two as players, although Miller has a stronger defensive reputation than Stinnett does. With Stinnett gone, Miller claims the backup job and is first in line if and when LaRue is traded to save some money.

RAINER OLMEDO   **SS**   **Bats: B**   **Throws: R**   Born: 31-May-81   Age: 23

YEAR	TM	LG	AGE	AB	H	2B	3B	HR	BB	SO	SB	CS	AVG	OBP	SLG	MLVR	EQBA	EQOBP	EQSLG	EQMLVR	VORP	DEFENSE			
2001	MUD	CAL	20	536	131	23	4	0	24	121	38	17	.244	.285	.302	-.200	.212	.243	.266	-.471	-42.0	126-SS	-7		
2002	CHT	SOU	21	478	118	21	1	3	53	86	15	16	.247	.331	.314	-.088	.217	.277	.282	-.377	-25.9	107-SS	-4	21-2B	1
2003	CHT	SOU	22	160	47	11	0	2	14	29	3	3	.294	.349	.400	.095	.258	.305	.362	-.185	0.9	43-SS	0		
2003	LOU	INT	22	25	6	1	0	1	2	6	0	0	.240	.296	.400	-.062	.240	.296	.360	-.217	-0.7				
2003	CIN	NL	22	230	55	6	1	0	13	46	1	1	.239	.280	.274	-.301	.246	.286	.280	-.346	-8.5	42-SS	-10	14-2B	0
2004	*CIN*	*NL*	*23*	*294*	*68*	*12*	*1*	*3*	*22*	*56*	*5*	*3*	*.231*	*.287*	*.316*	*-.270*	*.229*	*.285*	*.314*	*-.293*	*-5.9*	*79-SS*	*-6*		

Breakout: 31%   Improve: 51%   Collapse: 25%

Like a handful of other guys, Olmedo reached Cincinnati last year by virtue of staying ambulatory when others couldn't. He's a young shortstop prospect who had never hit before, and really didn't hit last year save for some extra singles falling in at Chattanooga. He's one of the worst basestealers in the game to boot (87-for-142 as a professional), so what he needs is to be ignored and given two years in Triple-A before he ever gets considered for another major league job.

WILY MO PENA   **CF**   **Bats: R**   **Throws: R**   Born: 23-Jan-82   Age: 22

YEAR	TM	LG	AGE	AB	H	2B	3B	HR	BB	SO	SB	CS	AVG	OBP	SLG	MLVR	EQBA	EQOBP	EQSLG	EQMLVR	VORP	DEFENSE			
2001	DYT	MID	19	511	135	25	5	26	33	177	26	10	.264	.327	.485	.133	.205	.250	.384	-.295	-23.2	102-CF	-1	26-RF	-2
2002	CHT	SOU	20	388	99	23	1	11	36	126	8	0	.255	.330	.405	.037	.227	.282	.374	-.233	-21.2	42-LF	-5	30-CF	-3
2002	CIN	NL	20	18	4	0	0	1	0	11	0	0	.222	.222	.389	-.242	.222	.222	.389	-.330	-0.9				
2003	CIN	NL	21	165	36	6	1	5	12	53	3	2	.218	.283	.358	-.193	.228	.285	.371	-.231	-4.6	22-CF	0		
2003	LOU	INT	21	51	19	3	0	4	5	13	0	0	.373	.450	.667	.643	.346	.424	.615	.465	9.6	11-CF	-3		
2004	*CIN*	*NL*	*22*	*309*	*84*	*17*	*2*	*18*	*26*	*85*	*5*	*2*	*.271*	*.340*	*.509*	*.104*	*.269*	*.337*	*.506*	*.081*	*26.7*	*84-CF*	*-6*		

Breakout: 61%   Improve: 77%   Collapse: 13%

It's been well documented that the only reason Pena was in the major leagues last season was his major league contract. Being out of options, he couldn't be demoted without going through waivers, and the Reds were terrified of losing him. Now, it's possible that Pena will help a team someday, but that day is at least 1,000 at-bats and two years away, and barring a trip through the Sosatron, he is never going to be a star. Given that they have no room to play him, the Reds should send Pena through waivers and let him get on with his career, even if it means he does so somewhere else. If Pena hits his 2004 PECOTA target, it'd be a shock.

MIGUEL PEREZ   **C**   **Bats: R**   **Throws: R**   Born: 25-Sep-83   Age: 20

YEAR	TM	LG	AGE	AB	H	2B	3B	HR	BB	SO	SB	CS	AVG	OBP	SLG	MLVR	EQBA	EQOBP	EQSLG	EQMLVR	VORP	DEFENSE	
2003	DYT	MID	19	58	10	0	0	0	4	19	1	0	.172	.273	.172	-.336	.169	.232	.169	-.644	-8.5	18-C	-1
2003	BIL	PIO	19	227	77	11	2	1	18	27	1	1	.339	.410	.419	.204	.231	.280	.293	-.348	-21.5	58-C	-1
2004	*CIN*	*NL*	*20*	*250*	*51*	*9*	*1*	*2*	*15*	*51*	*1*	*1*	*.206*	*.264*	*.271*	*-.384*	*.204*	*.262*	*.270*	*-.407*	*-14.7*	*68-C*	*-6*

Breakout: 21%   Improve: 42%   Collapse: 38%

Another young upside guy, Perez is the reason Dane Sardinha's prospect days are numbered. Perez gets good marks for his defense and puts runs on the board. Like Bolivar, he opened the season in the Midwest League but left for the Pioneer in June. The Reds don't have much in the way of international development; Perez is the best foreign prospect in the system.

CALVIN PICKERING   **1B**   **Bats: L**   **Throws: L**   Born: 29-Sep-76   Age: 27

YEAR	TM	LG	AGE	AB	H	2B	3B	HR	BB	SO	SB	CS	AVG	OBP	SLG	MLVR	EQBA	EQOBP	EQSLG	EQMLVR	VORP	DEFENSE	
2001	ROC	INT	24	461	130	25	0	21	64	149	0	1	.282	.379	.473	.191	.259	.351	.442	.014	14.0	67-1B	-6
2001	BOS	AL	24	50	14	1	0	3	8	13	0	0	.280	.379	.480	.157	.300	.397	.520	.237	4.4	11-1B	1
2003	VAQ	MEX	26	291	94	13	0	25	75	84	1	0	.323	.465	.625	.451	.211	.334	.421	-.082	5.5		
2003	LOU	INT	26	81	23	3	0	4	17	31	0	0	.284	.422	.469	.258	.262	.387	.440	.079	4.4	12-1B	-2
2004	KCR	AL	27	186	46	10	0	10	26	62	1	0	.248	.348	.464	.051	.237	.340	.449	-.014	4.7		

Breakout: 28%   Improve: 49%   Collapse: 23%

Pickering was supposed to be the next Cecil Fielder, but ate and whiffed his way almost completely out of baseball, missing the 2002 season after surgery on his right quad. He found his way into the Mexican League and promptly hit 25 homers in half a season. The Reds picked him up and let him help Louisville to an International League playoff spot. Now, he goes to camp with the Royals with a real chance to win their first-base job. He's a better hitter than Ken Harvey, and isn't that much worse than Harvey defensively. This could be one of the best stories of 2004.

DANE SARDINHA   **C**   **Bats: R**   **Throws: R**   Born: 08-Apr-79   Age: 25

YEAR	TM	LG	AGE	AB	H	2B	3B	HR	BB	SO	SB	CS	AVG	OBP	SLG	MLVR	EQBA	EQOBP	EQSLG	EQMLVR	VORP	DEFENSE	
2001	MUD	CAL	22	422	99	24	2	9	12	97	0	1	.235	.259	.365	-.165	.200	.219	.318	-.452	-33.8	109-C	13
2002	CHT	SOU	23	394	81	20	0	4	14	114	0	2	.206	.234	.287	-.301	.195	.209	.282	-.526	-40.4	100-C	5
2003	CHT	SOU	24	246	63	15	0	3	22	61	5	3	.256	.313	.354	-.046	.227	.278	.327	-.307	-10.2	69-C	5
2004	CIN	NL	25	175	38	8	0	4	9	44	1	1	.215	.258	.328	-.316	.213	.255	.327	-.340	-8.8	48-C	-3

Breakout: 39%   Improve: 53%   Collapse: 25%

Sardinha can catch with the best of them, but he just can't hit. (His .346 with power in the Arizona Fall League came in 52 at-bats; he struck out 13 times and walked once. Don't take it seriously.) He's exactly the wrong guy to be backing up LaRue, a player of similar strengths and weaknesses. Sardinha is likely in the early stages of a Mike Matheny career, where no number of .210 EqAs overrides his defensive reputation or his playing time. He's passed through waivers twice without being claimed.

MARK SCHRAMEK   **3B**   **Bats: L**   **Throws: R**   Born: 02-Jun-80   Age: 24

YEAR	TM	LG	AGE	AB	H	2B	3B	HR	BB	SO	SB	CS	AVG	OBP	SLG	MLVR	EQBA	EQOBP	EQSLG	EQMLVR	VORP	DEFENSE	
2003	DYT	MID	23	206	61	18	2	3	19	58	2	1	.296	.368	.447	.206	.227	.283	.360	-.251	-4.6	56-3B	0
2003	CHT	SOU	23	141	25	9	0	0	8	55	2	1	.177	.242	.241	-.344	.175	.221	.245	-.562	-16.3	40-3B	-2
2003	POT	CAR	23	128	26	4	0	2	6	42	0	0	.203	.261	.281	-.254	.171	.208	.248	-.587	-16.2	37-3B	-2
2004	CIN	NL	24	226	43	11	1	4	14	82	1	1	.192	.252	.300	-.376	.190	.249	.299	-.400	-12.9	62-3B	-5

Breakout: 26%   Improve: 51%   Collapse: 30%

The 40th pick in the 2002 draft finally signed and opened his professional career at Dayton, but like Encarnacion, struggled in his initial exposure to Double-A. Schramek is 24 years old and not as good as the younger player at the same position one level ahead of him. If there's a worse situation for a prospect, I'm not sure what it is.

STEVE SMITHERMAN   **LF**   **Bats: R**   **Throws: R**   Born: 01-Sep-78   Age: 25

YEAR	TM	LG	AGE	AB	H	2B	3B	HR	BB	SO	SB	CS	AVG	OBP	SLG	MLVR	EQBA	EQOBP	EQSLG	EQMLVR	VORP	DEFENSE			
2001	DYT	MID	22	497	139	45	2	20	43	113	16	7	.280	.348	.499	.192	.210	.262	.383	-.270	-33.5	118-LF	-12	12-RF	-1
2002	STO	CAL	23	482	151	36	1	19	39	126	17	2	.313	.362	.510	.280	.256	.300	.425	-.106	-7.4	112-LF	-2		
2003	CHT	SOU	24	365	113	21	2	19	54	95	11	3	.310	.402	.534	.357	.257	.337	.456	.006	7.2	92-LF	-4		
2003	LOU	INT	24	63	8	0	0	0	4	19	0	0	.127	.188	.127	-.654	.143	.202	.143	-.751	-13.0	15-LF	0		
2003	CIN	NL	24	44	7	2	0	1	3	9	1	0	.159	.213	.273	-.447	.159	.213	.295	-.517	-4.2				
2004	CIN	NL	25	240	60	14	1	10	22	59	4	2	.251	.319	.443	-.034	.249	.316	.441	-.057	4.4	66-LF	-2		

Breakout: 38%   Improve: 63%   Collapse: 17%

(continued next page)

Steve Smitherman *(continued)*

Smitherman has done nothing but hit since being drafted in 2000, yet can't seem to move up more than a level each year. He didn't perform in short stints at Cincinnati and Louisville in 2003, and the Reds not only have three starting outfielders but Pena's contract to deal with, so Smitherman will likely be back at Louisville to start the season, waiting for at least one trade. The improvement in his plate discipline is encouraging—he could be Geronimo Berroa, and at worst should be Shane Spencer.

DERNELL STENSON 1B/LF Bats: L Throws: L Born: 17-Jun-78 Age: 26

YEAR	TM	LG	AGE	AB	H	2B	3B	HR	BB	SO	SB	CS	AVG	OBP	SLG	MLVR	EQBA	EQOBP	EQSLG	EQMLVR	VORP	DEFENSE			
2001	PAW	INT	23	464	110	18	1	16	43	116	0	0	.237	.302	.384	-.080	.225	.289	.369	-.228	-24.5	118-LF	-18		
2002	PAW	INT	24	368	92	20	1	9	37	96	4	3	.250	.321	.383	-.037	.233	.303	.370	-.194	-15.6	98-LF	-12		
2003	CHT	SOU	25	356	109	28	0	14	39	74	4	5	.306	.371	.503	.274	.258	.316	.441	-.052	3.5	64-1B	-7	26-RF	-6
2003	LOU	INT	25	59	14	3	0	5	5	10	0	0	.237	.292	.542	.115	.217	.277	.517	-.052	0.2	14-RF	-3		
2003	CIN	NL	25	81	20	5	0	3	11	24	0	0	.247	.333	.420	-.003	.244	.333	.427	-.052	0.9	15-LF	-1		

Stenson was killed in Scottsdale, Arizona, November 5, the victim of what appeared to be a robbery but, as the winter dragged on, took on the sheen of something more sinister. Regardless, the game mourned the loss of one of its own, a player who had just started fulfill his potential in 2003.

REGGIE TAYLOR CF Bats: L Throws: R Born: 12-Jan-77 Age: 27

YEAR	TM	LG	AGE	AB	H	2B	3B	HR	BB	SO	SB	CS	AVG	OBP	SLG	MLVR	EQBA	EQOBP	EQSLG	EQMLVR	VORP	DEFENSE			
2001	SWB	INT	24	464	122	20	9	7	24	94	31	15	.263	.301	.390	-.054	.248	.289	.374	-.205	-7.7	105-CF	0		
2002	CIN	NL	25	287	73	15	4	9	14	79	11	8	.254	.291	.429	-.050	.255	.289	.431	-.118	2.1	50-CF	-4	23-LF	-1
2003	CIN	NL	26	180	39	5	2	5	11	68	7	0	.217	.266	.350	-.236	.220	.264	.363	-.288	-4.1	33-CF	-3		
2004	*CIN*	*NL*	*27*	*188*	*48*	*9*	*2*	*6*	*13*	*51*	*7*	*2*	*.254*	*.307*	*.412*	*-.092*	*.252*	*.304*	*.410*	*-.116*	*1.5*	*52-CF*	*-2*		

Breakout: 38%   Improve: 59%   Collapse: 28%

Taylor's 2003 season ended when he dove for a ball against the Astros in August, suffering a torn left labrum that required surgery. If you're counting, that's four torn labrums in this chapter, and you haven't seen a pitcher's name yet. Taylor is a useful fifth outfielder whose left-handed bat and raw speed make him a better bench player than many failed tools prospects, such as Mateo. On a team like the Reds that lacks a true center fielder, he can make a contribution. He didn't hurt his throwing arm and he didn't have a ton of power anyway, so he should be pretty much the same player he was before the injury.

JOEY VOTTO 1B Bats: L Throws: R Born: 10-Sep-83 Age: 20

YEAR	TM	LG	AGE	AB	H	2B	3B	HR	BB	SO	SB	CS	AVG	OBP	SLG	MLVR	EQBA	EQOBP	EQSLG	EQMLVR	VORP	DEFENSE	
2003	DYT	MID	19	195	45	8	0	1	34	64	2	5	.231	.348	.287	-.060	.172	.262	.216	-.516	-28.8	48-1B	-4
2003	BIL	PIO	19	240	76	17	3	6	56	80	4	0	.317	.452	.487	.343	.178	.278	.275	-.402	-47.5	61-1B	-10
2004	*CIN*	*NL*	*20*	*267*	*48*	*11*	*1*	*5*	*29*	*102*	*2*	*1*	*.178*	*.262*	*.283*	*-.386*	*.177*	*.259*	*.281*	*-.410*	*-23.1*	*74-1B*	*-11*

Breakout: 32%   Improve: 53%   Collapse: 32%

Votto was considered a catcher and a signability pick when the Reds took him in the second round of the 2002 draft. Just 19 last April, he was pushed to the Midwest League to start the year, didn't hit and dropped back with Bolivar and Perez to pound the Pioneer League. He played first base exclusively last year and will continue to do so, so he'll have to make hay with his bat. Votto gets a second crack at the Midwest League this year, and has a good shot at making our Top 50 list a year from now.

PITCHERS

JOSE ACEVEDO

Bats: R   **Throws: R**   Born: 18-Dec-77   Age: 26

YEAR	TM	LG	AGE	G	GS	IP	H	BB	SO	HR	ERA	EQERA	EQH9	EQBB9	EQSO9	EQHR9	PERA	VORP	STF
2001	CHT	SOU	23	16	11	78.0	68	25	82	6	3.69	4.52	9.2	3.4	6.4	1.1	4.82	8.6	9
2001	CIN	NL	23	18	18	96.0	101	34	68	17	5.44	5.11	9.2	2.9	5.3	1.3	4.94	5.1	7
2002	CIN	NL	24	6	5	23.7	28	12	14	8	7.22	7.43	10.6	3.9	4.7	3.1	8.10	-4.7	-56
2002	LOU	INT	24	23	23	154.7	146	34	128	16	3.20	4.14	8.9	2.3	6.2	1.3	4.58	23.6	10
2003	LOU	INT	25	29	3	60.3	56	20	57	5	3.43	4.47	8.8	3.7	6.7	1.1	4.70	7.1	-6
2003	CIN	NL	25	5	4	27.0	17	6	23	3	2.67	2.42	5.5	1.7	6.9	1.0	2.55	8.9	30
2004	*CIN*	*NL*	*26*	*19*	*11*	*70.0*	*66*	*25*	*59*	*10*	*4.29*	*4.50*	*8.7*	*2.9*	*6.8*	*1.1*	*4.42*	*9.0*	*8*

Breakout: 26%   *Improve: 49%*   *Collapse: 18%*

One of the ideas you've seen in BP over the years is that there is a class of pitchers who need to lop off one walk per nine innings to become major leaguers. Acevedo has done just that over the past two seasons, for which the organization credits his learning to control his emotions on the mound. He should have been in the Reds' Opening Day rotation, and you'd be more familiar with him if, when he finally did get the call, he hadn't slipped in the Dodger dugout and suffered an ankle injury that eventually required surgery. Acevedo is someone to watch in 2004.

CARLOS ALMANZAR

Bats: R   **Throws: R**   Born: 06-Nov-73   Age: 30

YEAR	TM	LG	AGE	G	GS	IP	H	BB	SO	HR	ERA	EQERA	EQH9	EQBB9	EQSO9	EQHR9	PERA	VORP	STF
2001	COH	INT	27	35	0	33.3	36	6	26	2	2.43	3.45	10.1	2.0	5.5	0.9	4.57	7.5	-5
2001	NYY	AL	27	10	0	10.7	14	2	6	2	3.36	4.35	11.3	1.7	4.4	1.7	6.12	1.4	-31
2002	LOU	INT	28	21	0	23.0	21	5	19	0	2.74	3.32	8.7	2.5	6.2	0.4	3.63	5.5	11
2002	CIN	NL	28	8	1	11.7	6	5	7	0	2.31	2.38	4.8	3.2	4.8	0.0	1.79	4.0	22
2003	LOU	INT	29	42	0	46.3	47	3	54	2	3.50	3.95	10.0	0.6	8.3	0.6	3.82	7.9	23
2004	*CIN*	*NL*	*30*	*24*	*0*	*31.7*	*31*	*7*	*26*	*3*	*3.27*	*3.43*	*8.9*	*1.6*	*6.7*	*0.8*	*3.61*	*7.7*	*8*

Breakout: 36%   *Improve: 54%*   *Collapse: 24%*

Almanzar was at the head of a controversy in July. He and Josias Manzanillo walked away from the Louisville Bats in protest after a number of teammates were promoted while they were overlooked. While you can understand Almanzar's frustration—he was in the middle of a good year at Triple-A, featuring an obscene 54:3 K:BB ratio, and the Reds had promoted pitchers who weren't doing nearly as well—that's exactly the kind of move that gets a player branded a malcontent, which is death in baseball. He was signed by the Rangers as a minor league free agent, and will be in the mix to set up Francisco Cordero. If his improved command is for real, he'll help them a lot.

JIMMY ANDERSON

Bats: L   **Throws: L**   Born: 22-Jan-76   Age: 28

YEAR	TM	LG	AGE	G	GS	IP	H	BB	SO	HR	ERA	EQERA	EQH9	EQBB9	EQSO9	EQHR9	PERA	VORP	STF
2001	PIT	NL	25	34	34	206.3	232	83	89	15	5.10	4.74	9.9	3.3	3.3	0.6	4.64	19.0	0
2002	PIT	NL	26	28	25	140.7	167	63	47	20	5.44	6.05	10.8	3.5	2.6	1.3	5.84	-6.8	-31
2003	CIN	NL	27	8	7	38.7	60	14	13	8	8.84	8.12	13.6	2.9	2.6	1.9	7.76	-14.8	-55
2003	LOU	INT	27	9	9	60.7	61	14	30	2	3.11	4.24	8.9	2.5	3.5	0.5	3.84	8.7	5
2003	FRE	PCL	27	8	8	43.3	65	15	17	3	6.44	7.24	13.4	3.7	2.9	0.9	6.64	-7.5	-32
2004	*CIN*	*NL*	*28*	*40*	*17*	*102.7*	*126*	*43*	*38*	*11*	*5.17*	*5.44*	*11.2*	*3.3*	*2.9*	*0.8*	*5.65*	*1.9*	*-21*

Breakout: 20%   *Improve: 52%*   *Collapse: 20%*

It's a real shock this didn't work out. Anderson was never very good, had been going backward ever since coming into the league, doesn't have great stuff, keeps himself in lousy shape and, by many accounts, has an inflated opinion of his abilities. All things considered, eight appearances with an 8.85 ERA might have been the optimistic expectation. Anderson floated into the Giants' organization after the Reds cut him loose, and will likely end up in Triple-A this year.

JOHN BALE

Bats: L   Throws: L   Born: 22-May-74   Age: 30

YEAR	TM	LG	AGE	G	GS	IP	H	BB	SO	HR	ERA	EQERA	EQH9	EQBB9	EQSO9	EQHR9	PERA	VORP	STF
2001	ROC	INT	27	9	7	30.7	31	5	41	1	2.05	3.14	10.4	1.6	9.1	0.3	3.95	7.8	41
2001	BAL	AL	27	14	0	26.7	18	17	21	2	3.03	3.81	5.9	5.2	6.6	0.7	3.40	5.2	6
2002	NOR	INT	28	12	2	28.0	22	7	27	2	3.54	3.76	7.5	2.7	7.2	1.0	3.74	5.4	4
2003	NOR	INT	29	8	0	13.7	11	3	15	0	3.28	3.55	8.5	2.1	7.8	0.0	3.03	2.9	35
2003	LOU	INT	29	26	2	43.7	36	13	43	1	3.30	3.73	7.7	3.3	7.0	0.2	3.20	8.5	20
2003	CIN	NL	29	10	9	46.3	50	12	37	7	4.47	4.60	9.6	2.0	6.4	1.4	4.92	5.0	0
2004	*CIN*	*NL*	*30*	*31*	*13*	*85.0*	*81*	*32*	*74*	*9*	*3.73*	*3.92*	*8.7*	*2.9*	*7.0*	*0.8*	*4.22*	*16.2*	*8*

Breakout: 25%   Improve: 56%   Collapse: 16%

Over the last two seasons, Bale has struck out 112 men and walked 35 in 131 ⅓ innings, most of those at Triple-A. Now, you can't judge a pitcher, especially a 29-year-old one who doesn't throw all that hard, just by that information, but it's certainly enough to get him into a book that has room for people like Reggie Abercrombie. Bale has been throwing strikes with his change-up for a while. After being released by the Mets in May of 2003, he ended last year in the Reds' rotation. However, Bale elected to go to Japan for 2004 rather than risk another season at Triple-A.

BOBBY BASHAM

Bats: R   Throws: R   Born: 07-Mar-80   Age: 24

YEAR	TM	LG	AGE	G	GS	IP	H	BB	SO	HR	ERA	EQERA	EQH9	EQBB9	EQSO9	EQHR9	PERA	VORP	STF
2001	BIL	PIO	21	6	6	29.7	36	17	37	2	4.85	9.25	15.9	8.1	6.3	1.5	9.27	-9.9	-30
2002	DYT	MID	22	13	13	87.7	64	9	97	4	1.64	3.48	9.4	1.3	6.1	1.2	4.34	18.3	22
2003	CHT	SOU	23	17	17	94.0	133	24	56	16	5.17	8.51	14.5	2.6	3.7	3.4	9.98	-27.7	-72
2003	POT	CAR	23	1	1	6.7	5	1	1	0	2.69	4.26	7.1	1.4	1.4	0.0	2.30	0.9	14
2004	*CIN*	*NL*	*24*	*18*	*10*	*61.3*	*71*	*22*	*33*	*11*	*5.45*	*5.73*	*10.6*	*2.8*	*4.3*	*1.3*	*5.69*	*-0.1*	*-12*

Breakout: 14%   Improve: 50%   Collapse: 15%

Basham regressed badly after an impressive 2002 that ended with a strong Arizona Fall League stint. While nothing has been diagnosed, Basham complained of arm discomfort and showed significant velocity loss this year. He was demoted to the Carolina League and then shut down in early August. Until he has some kind of extended success, be skeptical.

MATT BELISLE

Bats: B   Throws: R   Born: 06-Jun-80   Age: 24

YEAR	TM	LG	AGE	G	GS	IP	H	BB	SO	HR	ERA	EQERA	EQH9	EQBB9	EQSO9	EQHR9	PERA	VORP	STF
2002	GRN	SOU	22	26	26	159.3	162	39	123	18	4.35	6.01	11.5	2.4	5.1	2.1	6.87	-6.5	-14
2003	GRN	SOU	23	21	21	125.3	128	42	94	5	3.52	5.59	10.7	3.5	4.6	0.8	5.24	0.1	3
2003	RIC	INT	23	3	3	20.0	17	0	10	1	2.25	2.89	7.2	0.5	3.9	0.5	2.47	5.6	29
2003	LOU	INT	23	4	4	26.0	31	5	15	2	3.81	5.76	10.1	2.2	4.3	1.1	4.88	-0.4	2
2004	*CIN*	*NL*	*24*	*19*	*12*	*72.3*	*82*	*27*	*44*	*11*	*5.08*	*5.33*	*10.4*	*2.9*	*4.9*	*1.2*	*5.40*	*4.4*	*-6*

Breakout: 13%   Improve: 49%   Collapse: 23%

Getting something for nothing is always a good trade policy. The Reds got Belisle for the $550,000 they committed to Kent Mercker and the last six weeks of the veteran's season, which is pretty damn close to nothing. Belisle has worked his way back from back surgery in 2001, making 47 Double-A starts the past two years before finally getting promoted just before the trade. Still just 24, he throws strikes and keeps the ball in the park, two traits the Reds will be happy to see. He's a better bet for 2005 than 2004 due to a lack of experience above Double-A.

JUAN CERROS

Bats: R   Throws: R   Born: 25-Sep-76   Age: 27

YEAR	TM	LG	AGE	G	GS	IP	H	BB	SO	HR	ERA	EQERA	EQH9	EQBB9	EQSO9	EQHR9	PERA	VORP	STF
2001	BIN	EAS	24	13	0	18.3	24	7	14	2	4.92	6.48	13.0	4.9	4.9	1.6	7.53	-1.6	-46
2001	NOR	INT	24	38	1	57.0	65	22	32	5	3.95	6.45	11.0	4.1	3.9	1.0	5.80	-5.0	-28
2002	NOR	INT	25	25	3	37.7	40	11	23	2	3.34	5.30	9.6	3.0	4.5	0.8	4.55	1.2	-13
2003	MTR	MEX	26	50	0	48.0	44	14	24	2	2.44	3.83	8.7	2.8	4.4	0.6	3.91	8.8	-11
2003	CIN	NL	26	11	0	13.0	11	5	9	1	4.85	4.26	7.1	2.8	5.7	0.7	3.29	1.1	3
2004	*CIN*	*NL*	*27*	*26*	*2*	*36.3*	*39*	*14*	*21*	*5*	*4.75*	*4.99*	*9.9*	*3.1*	*4.6*	*1.0*	*5.14*	*3.8*	*-14*

Breakout: 25%   Improve: 63%   Collapse: 15%

Cerros was taken from the Mets in the minor league phase of the 2002 Rule 5 draft. He'd been languishing in the Mets' system since being signed out of the Mexican League in 1999, and while he doesn't light up the radar gun or opposing hitters, he has shown an ability to keep the ball in park. Since coming to the American minor leagues in 2000, he's allowed just 21 home runs in 215 ⅔ innings.

BRANDON CLAUSSEN   Bats: L   Throws: L   Born: 01-May-79   Age: 25

YEAR	TM	LG	AGE	G	GS	IP	H	BB	SO	HR	ERA	EQERA	EQH9	EQBB9	EQSO9	EQHR9	PERA	VORP	STF
2001	TAM	FLA	22	8	8	56.0	47	13	69	2	2.73	4.26	9.6	2.5	7.3	0.9	4.48	7.5	31
2001	NRW	EAS	22	21	21	131.0	101	55	151	6	2.13	3.99	8.6	5.1	7.2	0.7	4.57	21.0	30
2002	COH	INT	23	15	15	93.3	85	46	73	4	3.28	4.08	7.3	5.1	6.0	0.5	3.80	15.3	25
2003	TAM	FLA	24	4	4	22.0	16	3	26	0	1.64	3.26	9.3	1.4	7.4	0.5	3.61	5.0	37
2003	COH	INT	24	11	11	68.7	53	18	39	4	2.75	3.66	7.2	3.0	4.1	0.8	3.51	13.8	8
2003	LOU	INT	24	3	3	15.7	17	6	16	3	7.45	7.53	10.7	4.4	7.5	2.5	7.38	-3.1	-30
2004	*CIN*	*NL*	*25*	*19*	*16*	*97.7*	*97*	*43*	*73*	*12*	*4.47*	*4.70*	*9.1*	*3.5*	*6.0*	*1.0*	*4.81*	*10.2*	*5*

Breakout: 17%   *Improve: 54%*   *Collapse: 25%*

Claussen made a historic comeback from Tommy John surgery, pitching in the minor leagues less than one year after the operation. Acquired from the Yankees for Aaron Boone, he was shut down by the Reds not long after the trade. Speculation that he was injured was just that; Claussen's elbow is fine, and he goes into spring training as one of the top candidates for the rotation. He's going to be a good third starter.

RYAN DEMPSTER   Bats: R   Throws: R   Born: 03-May-77   Age: 27

YEAR	TM	LG	AGE	G	GS	IP	H	BB	SO	HR	ERA	EQERA	EQH9	EQBB9	EQSO9	EQHR9	PERA	VORP	STF
2001	FLA	NL	24	34	34	211.3	218	112	171	21	4.94	5.21	9.5	4.4	6.1	0.8	4.92	8.8	15
2002	FLA	NL	25	18	18	120.3	126	55	87	12	4.79	5.01	9.5	3.6	5.6	0.9	4.83	7.7	6
2002	CIN	NL	25	15	15	88.7	102	38	66	16	6.19	5.97	10.5	3.3	5.8	1.6	5.92	-3.5	-10
2003	CIN	NL	26	22	20	115.7	134	70	84	14	6.53	6.27	10.3	4.8	5.7	1.0	5.66	-16.7	-10
2003	LOU	INT	26	2	2	13.7	13	3	9	1	3.28	4.26	9.2	2.1	5.0	0.7	4.07	1.9	9
2004	*CHC*	*NL*	*27*	*22*	*19*	*112.3*	*122*	*60*	*80*	*13*	*5.29*	*5.63*	*9.8*	*4.2*	*5.7*	*1.0*	*5.59*	*0.8*	*-1*

Breakout: 12%   *Improve: 41%*   *Collapse: 33%*

Credit the Marlins with trading Dempster, who threw a ton of pitches in 2000 and 2001, at the right time. Dempster was about to get expensive and they had better pitchers coming. Juan Encarnacion has been a league-average right fielder for them, while Dempster gave the Reds 35 starts with an ERA of 6.39 before Tommy John surgery ended his time in Cincinnati. He's been released, and is unlikely to pitch in the majors in 2004. Moving Dempster is just one of many good moves Larry Beinfest made on his way to a championship.

PHILLIP DUMATRAIT   Bats: R   Throws: L   Born: 12-Jul-81   Age: 22

YEAR	TM	LG	AGE	G	GS	IP	H	BB	SO	HR	ERA	EQERA	EQH9	EQBB9	EQSO9	EQHR9	PERA	VORP	STF
2002	AUG	SAL	20	22	22	120.3	109	47	108	5	2.77	5.33	10.2	4.8	4.8	1.0	5.62	3.2	6
2002	SAR	FLA	20	4	4	14.0	10	15	16	0	3.86	6.57	8.0	12.4	8.0	0.0	5.49	-1.3	23
2003	SAR	FLA	21	21	20	104.3	74	59	74	4	3.02	5.07	8.1	6.6	4.5	1.1	5.21	5.4	-3
2003	POT	CAR	21	7	7	37.7	36	14	32	2	3.34	5.03	10.1	4.2	5.3	1.1	5.41	2.2	8
2004	*CIN*	*NL*	*22*	*14*	*10*	*46.0*	*64*	*46*	*17*	*10*	*9.38*	*9.85*	*12.8*	*7.9*	*3.0*	*1.7*	*9.69*	*-9.0*	*-48*

Breakout: 15%   *Improve: 54%*   *Collapse: 30%*

Dumatrait was acquired from the Red Sox for Scott Williamson and added to the 40-man roster over the winter. He's a curveball specialist, with a fastball that touches 90. He doesn't always have command of the two pitches—his walk rates have been high as a pro—and he doesn't use his change-up enough, so he has work to do. Dumatrait probably has the highest upside of the pitchers the Reds acquired in 2003, although he might reach it as a reliever.

Also picked up in that trade was Tyler Pelland. He's a 20-year-old left-hander taken in the 2002 draft. As someone the Reds like a lot, he's worth mentioning, even though he's a long way from the majors. Pelland had a strong instructional league, and is expected to be part of a good Dayton rotation in 2004.

DANNY GRAVES
Bats: R   **Throws: R**   Born: 07-Aug-73   Age: 30

YEAR	TM	LG	AGE	G	GS	IP	H	BB	SO	HR	ERA	EQERA	EQH9	EQBB9	EQSO9	EQHR9	PERA	VORP	STF
2001	CIN	NL	27	66	0	80.3	83	18	49	7	4.15	4.06	9.0	1.9	4.6	0.7	3.89	13.3	0
2002	CIN	NL	28	68	4	98.7	99	25	58	7	3.19	3.61	9.0	2.0	4.7	0.7	3.90	20.9	1
2003	CIN	NL	29	30	26	169.0	204	41	60	30	5.33	5.50	10.5	2.0	2.9	1.5	5.59	-2.3	-26
2004	CIN	NL	30	28	19	112.3	133	38	46	17	5.16	5.42	10.9	2.6	3.3	1.2	5.57	4.6	-15

Breakout: 9%   *Improve: 44%*   *Collapse: 31%*

Graves was awful as a starter, allowing nearly as many home runs in 169 innings as he had in the previous four years and 381.1 frames. The Reds are calling him their closer for 2004, which makes sense if it means that John Riedling and Ryan Wagner are going to be used in multiple-inning, high-leverage situations. It does waste Graves's ability to throw 100 relief innings, toss three innings at a time and get called in for double-play situations. A nice compromise would be to use all three relievers as situations warrant, with no labels. Jack McKeon already has a job, however.

CHRIS GRULER
Bats: R   **Throws: R**   Born: 11-Sep-83   Age: 20

YEAR	TM	LG	AGE	G	GS	IP	H	BB	SO	HR	ERA	EQERA	EQH9	EQBB9	EQSO9	EQHR9	PERA	VORP	STF
2002	BIL	PIO	18	4	4	16.7	11	6	11	1	1.08	3.00	7.8	4.2	3.0	1.8	5.23	4.3	-8
2002	DYT	MID	18	7	7	27.3	23	16	31	2	5.60	7.50	9.8	7.1	7.1	1.5	6.48	-5.1	14
2003	DYT	MID	19	3	3	5.7	10	12	6	0	26.84	27.00	19.3	28.9	7.7	0.0	11.90	-11.2	-69

The Reds' #1 draft pick from 2002 had shoulder surgery in April and missed the rest of the year. He might eventually work out, but right now he looks like a waste of $2.5 million. Given that they could have had Scott Kazmir for a few dollars more, the decision to take Gruler seems penny-wise and pound-foolish. The Reds also threw away their 2001 #1 pick on Jeremy Sowers, a pitcher they had no intention of signing. In 2000 they took David Espinosa, who has already been traded to the Tigers and is unlikely to have a career. If you really are a small-market team, you can't keep blowing first-round picks like this.

JOSH HALL
Bats: R   **Throws: R**   Born: 16-Dec-80   Age: 23

YEAR	TM	LG	AGE	G	GS	IP	H	BB	SO	HR	ERA	EQERA	EQH9	EQBB9	EQSO9	EQHR9	PERA	VORP	STF
2001	DYT	MID	20	22	22	132.3	117	39	122	4	2.65	4.72	9.4	3.7	5.0	0.6	4.50	11.7	23
2002	STO	CAL	21	7	7	43.7	31	13	51	1	2.27	3.92	8.8	3.5	6.2	0.5	3.97	7.3	35
2002	CHT	SOU	21	22	22	132.0	140	50	116	7	3.75	5.62	9.9	3.5	5.8	0.9	4.94	-0.3	20
2003	CHT	SOU	22	26	25	153.0	152	53	114	9	3.47	5.20	9.7	3.5	4.6	1.1	5.16	6.3	2
2003	CIN	NL	22	6	5	24.7	33	15	18	4	6.56	7.40	11.8	4.8	5.5	1.5	6.84	-6.6	-4
2004	CIN	NL	23	19	14	79.7	89	39	49	12	5.50	5.78	10.2	3.8	5.0	1.1	5.69	3.2	-8

Breakout: 17%   *Improve: 48%*   *Collapse: 23%*

A fastball/curveball right-hander who gets his outs with the big deuce, Hall is going to miss at least the first half of the season following shoulder surgery in August. Just 23, he still needs innings and a third pitch, and while the Reds have a lot of arms they can give innings to, they don't have a ton of guys with Hall's potential. Check back in 2005.

AARON HARANG
Bats: R   **Throws: R**   Born: 09-May-78   Age: 26

YEAR	TM	LG	AGE	G	GS	IP	H	BB	SO	HR	ERA	EQERA	EQH9	EQBB9	EQSO9	EQHR9	PERA	VORP	STF
2001	MID	TEX	23	27	27	150.0	173	37	112	9	4.14	5.39	10.7	2.6	4.6	0.8	5.02	3.3	4
2002	MID	TEX	24	3	3	16.7	12	7	21	0	1.08	2.35	7.6	4.7	8.2	0.0	3.35	5.5	48
2002	SAC	PCL	24	8	8	38.7	41	9	39	1	3.26	3.86	9.4	2.4	6.8	0.2	3.73	7.2	34
2002	OAK	AL	24	16	15	78.3	78	45	64	7	4.83	4.97	9.1	4.7	7.1	0.7	4.72	5.3	21
2003	SAC	PCL	25	12	12	69.7	62	17	60	5	2.71	3.74	8.7	2.6	6.6	1.0	4.22	13.4	14
2003	OAK	AL	25	7	6	30.3	41	9	16	5	5.35	5.90	12.4	2.5	4.7	1.2	6.24	1.0	-13
2003	CIN	NL	25	9	9	46.0	48	10	26	6	5.28	4.67	9.1	1.8	4.5	1.2	4.48	0.8	-2
2004	CIN	NL	26	23	17	102.3	110	39	75	13	4.69	4.93	9.8	3.0	5.9	1.0	4.94	10.0	4

Breakout: 13%   *Improve: 49%*   *Collapse: 20%*

A fourth starter picked up from the A's for Jose Guillen, Harang doesn't throw that hard for a big guy. He works up in the zone, which got him into trouble last year with long balls, something that's not likely to go away. Harang needs a big outfield patrolled by gazelles; he'll have neither in Cincinnati, so his success will depend on his walking almost no one.

JIMMY HAYNES   Bats: R   Throws: R   Born: 05-Sep-72   Age: 31

YEAR	TM	LG	AGE	G	GS	IP	H	BB	SO	HR	ERA	EQERA	EQH9	EQBB9	EQSO9	EQHR9	PERA	VORP	STF
2001	MIL	NL	28	31	29	172.7	182	78	112	20	4.85	5.15	9.7	3.7	4.9	0.9	4.95	8.3	-2
2002	CIN	NL	29	34	34	196.7	210	81	126	21	4.12	4.64	9.7	3.3	5.0	0.9	4.87	20.3	1
2003	CIN	NL	30	18	18	94.3	118	57	49	14	6.30	6.63	11.0	4.9	4.1	1.3	6.28	-15.0	-28
2004	CIN	NL	31	20	16	87.0	108	58	51	12	6.54	6.87	11.4	5.3	4.7	1.1	6.95	-5.2	-16

Breakout: 16%   Improve: 41%   Collapse: 27%

If you decide to evaluate pitchers based on wins, this is what you get: two years, $5 million for Jimmy Haynes, all because he was credited with 15 of them in 2002. He averaged less than six innings a start, had a 1.6/1 strikeout-to-walk ratio and an ERA of 4.12, but hey, the Reds scored a bunch of runs when he pitched, so make him a multi-millionaire. Haynes missed the second half of 2003 with a bulging disc; the Reds will give him his job back in the hopes that he can make himself tradable and save the team some money.

TY HOWINGTON   Bats: B   Throws: L   Born: 04-Nov-80   Age: 23

YEAR	TM	LG	AGE	G	GS	IP	H	BB	SO	HR	ERA	EQERA	EQH9	EQBB9	EQSO9	EQHR9	PERA	VORP	STF
2001	DYT	MID	20	6	6	39.0	15	9	47	0	1.15	1.80	5.1	2.8	6.7	0.3	2.03	14.8	56
2001	MUD	CAL	20	7	7	37.0	33	20	44	2	2.43	6.21	9.7	6.5	6.5	0.8	5.56	-2.3	18
2001	CHT	SOU	20	7	7	41.3	36	24	38	3	3.27	5.08	8.1	6.0	6.0	0.9	4.84	2.3	23
2002	CHT	SOU	21	15	15	65.0	65	33	51	5	5.12	6.02	9.4	4.7	5.1	1.3	5.52	-2.9	-1
2003	CHT	SOU	22	4	4	14.3	15	20	16	1	6.92	9.69	11.1	14.5	6.9	1.4	8.56	-5.9	-40
2003	POT	CAR	22	19	19	99.3	103	34	86	4	3.53	5.12	10.9	4.0	5.4	0.9	5.58	4.8	5
2004	CIN	NL	23	17	11	65.3	68	37	50	9	5.28	5.55	9.5	4.4	6.1	1.0	5.51	2.3	-3

Breakout: 21%   Improve: 51%   Collapse: 25%

The Reds' #1 pick in the 1999 draft struggled at the start of the season, then came on strong to earn a second crack at the Southern League. His command issues there contributed to the Reds' decision to leave him off their 40-man roster. The gamble paid off, as he wasn't selected in the Rule 5 draft. Howington is still just 23, and has had a reasonable workload, so keep an eye on him.

LUKE HUDSON   Bats: R   Throws: R   Born: 02-May-77   Age: 27

YEAR	TM	LG	AGE	G	GS	IP	H	BB	SO	HR	ERA	EQERA	EQH9	EQBB9	EQSO9	EQHR9	PERA	VORP	STF
2001	CAR	SOU	24	29	28	165.0	159	68	145	19	4.20	5.82	10.3	4.3	5.3	1.8	6.37	-3.7	-26
2002	CIN	NL	25	3	0	6.0	5	6	7	1	4.50	6.00	7.5	7.5	9.0	1.5	5.53	-0.3	-11
2002	LOU	INT	25	30	17	117.7	102	57	129	6	4.51	4.83	8.3	5.2	8.3	0.7	4.41	9.4	14
2004	CIN	NL	27	12	5	29.7	29	16	25	4	4.89	5.14	9.0	4.4	6.9	1.1	5.20	2.8	-1

Breakout: 28%   Improve: 47%   Collapse: 31%

Because he missed all of 2003 after surgery to repair a torn labrum, the Reds get another option on Hudson. One front-office member liked him enough to invoke Mark Prior's name, for Hudson's size and fastball/curveball repertoire. Like Prior, Hudson has a change-up that he doesn't use much. He'll start the 2004 season at Triple-A, getting reps in after his lost season, and might still end up as a reliever. If healthy—a big if—he'll be very good.

CHARLIE MANNING   Bats: L   Throws: L   Born: 31-Mar-79   Age: 25

YEAR	TM	LG	AGE	G	GS	IP	H	BB	SO	HR	ERA	EQERA	EQH9	EQBB9	EQSO9	EQHR9	PERA	VORP	STF
2001	STA	NYP	22	14	14	80.0	73	21	87	4	3.49	6.27	13.4	3.7	5.7	1.8	7.58	-4.9	-19
2002	TAM	FLA	23	17	16	100.0	82	31	85	4	3.24	5.08	9.3	3.5	5.3	0.9	4.67	5.2	6
2002	NRW	EAS	23	11	11	63.0	55	26	61	1	3.57	4.32	8.8	4.3	6.5	0.3	4.07	8.3	29
2003	TRN	EAS	24	23	6	46.0	53	35	34	1	6.26	6.85	10.2	8.1	5.2	0.4	5.79	-6.0	-22
2003	TAM	FLA	24	6	6	31.3	27	15	25	2	3.45	5.74	11.1	5.7	5.1	2.0	7.42	-0.4	-45
2003	POT	CAR	24	6	6	37.7	24	11	31	1	1.19	2.38	7.1	3.4	5.0	0.5	3.32	12.2	20
2004	CIN	NL	25	13	9	49.0	55	30	35	6	5.81	6.10	10.3	4.9	5.7	1.0	6.10	-1.4	-8

Breakout: 24%   Improve: 53%   Collapse: 24%

Like Claussen, Manning was acquired from the Yankees in the Aaron Boone deal. He doesn't have the story that Claussen does, and doesn't have Claussen's success at the upper levels. In fact, he was pounded badly enough at Trenton to lose his rotation spot early in the year. While he pitched very well for Potomac after the trade, that isn't that impressive for a 24-year-old. He'll need to be pushed to have a career.

DUSTIN MOSELEY   Bats: R   Throws: R   Born: 26-Dec-81   Age: 22

YEAR	TM	LG	AGE	G	GS	IP	H	BB	SO	HR	ERA	EQERA	EQH9	EQBB9	EQSO9	EQHR9	PERA	VORP	STF
2001	DYT	MID	19	25	25	148.0	158	42	108	10	4.20	6.60	10.6	3.5	4.1	1.3	5.69	-15.1	4
2002	STO	CAL	20	14	14	88.7	60	21	80	3	2.74	3.89	7.6	2.7	4.9	0.6	3.31	15.4	31
2002	CHT	SOU	20	13	13	80.7	91	37	52	5	4.13	6.12	9.7	4.2	4.4	0.9	5.09	-4.5	11
2003	CHT	SOU	21	18	18	112.7	116	28	73	10	3.83	5.35	9.6	2.5	4.1	1.6	5.37	2.9	-1
2003	LOU	INT	21	8	8	50.0	46	14	27	5	2.70	4.07	7.0	3.0	4.3	1.1	3.71	8.3	16
2004	CIN	NL	22	18	13	78.3	87	32	41	13	5.37	5.65	10.2	3.3	4.2	1.3	5.60	1.6	-10

Breakout: 3%   Improve: 36%   Collapse: 37%

What makes Moseley stand out in this organization is that, unlike the Reds' other investments in amateur pitching, he has stayed healthy. He doesn't light up the radar gun, topping out in the low 90s while mixing in a very good curve and change-up. His strikeout rate of 5.6 per nine innings since reaching Double-A is not encouraging, so keep expectations low. *Baseball America* compared Moseley to Rick Reed and Bob Tewksbury, neither of whom had much of a career until their 30s.

BRIAN REITH   Bats: R   Throws: R   Born: 28-Feb-78   Age: 26

YEAR	TM	LG	AGE	G	GS	IP	H	BB	SO	HR	ERA	EQERA	EQH9	EQBB9	EQSO9	EQHR9	PERA	VORP	STF
2001	CHT	SOU	23	18	18	104.3	103	42	89	10	3.97	6.00	10.0	4.2	5.2	1.4	5.78	-4.3	-10
2001	CIN	NL	23	9	8	40.3	56	16	22	13	7.82	7.71	11.8	3.2	4.1	2.5	7.68	-9.3	-37
2002	LOU	INT	24	23	22	132.7	137	46	99	15	4.75	5.50	9.7	3.7	5.6	1.4	5.52	1.4	-6
2002	SWB	INT	24	4	4	18.0	26	11	13	1	7.00	9.92	14.3	6.6	5.5	0.6	7.29	-7.8	-20
2003	LOU	INT	25	16	0	23.0	12	9	28	1	1.96	2.95	5.1	4.2	8.9	0.4	2.49	6.3	30
2003	CIN	NL	25	42	1	61.3	61	36	39	8	4.11	4.80	8.9	4.7	4.9	1.2	5.13	6.4	-20
2004	CIN	NL	26	32	8	62.3	64	31	48	9	4.95	5.20	9.3	3.9	6.1	1.1	5.28	3.6	-6

Breakout: 25%   Improve: 55%   Collapse: 17%

Still just 26, Reith has packed a lot of career into the past few seasons. He is only now getting it back together after his premature promotion in 2001, when the Reds wanted to show something from the Drew Henson trade and yanked Reith from Double-A to the majors. He has no star potential, but is a notch above the Jimmy Haynes class of Reds' starter candidates, and would be a decent innings muncher if given the chance.

CHRIS REITSMA   Bats: R   Throws: R   Born: 31-Dec-77   Age: 26

YEAR	TM	LG	AGE	G	GS	IP	H	BB	SO	HR	ERA	EQERA	EQH9	EQBB9	EQSO9	EQHR9	PERA	VORP	STF
2001	CIN	NL	23	36	29	182.0	209	49	96	23	5.29	5.16	10.0	2.2	4.0	1.0	4.73	8.6	5
2002	CIN	NL	24	32	21	138.3	144	45	84	17	3.64	4.66	9.4	2.6	4.8	1.1	4.66	13.9	2
2002	LOU	INT	24	3	3	21.0	17	8	13	2	3.86	4.58	7.3	4.1	4.6	1.4	4.46	2.2	-7
2003	LOU	INT	25	4	4	18.0	22	5	11	1	4.00	5.82	11.1	3.2	4.2	0.5	5.05	-0.4	-4
2003	CIN	NL	25	57	3	84.0	92	19	53	14	4.29	4.54	9.6	1.9	5.1	1.4	4.97	11.6	-14
2004	CIN	NL	26	32	13	85.0	95	27	51	11	4.68	4.92	10.2	2.5	4.9	1.0	4.92	7.5	-6

Breakout: 18%   Improve: 45%   Collapse: 21%

Despite his apparent settling into the closer role in 2003, Reitsma has both the arsenal and the stamina to be a starting pitcher. He doesn't miss enough bats to be a closer. Add in the presence of Ryan Wagner and several other hard-throwing relievers, the commitment to Graves as the closer, and the considerable rotation questions, and the path for Reitsma seems clear. Whether Dave Miley chooses the right one remains to be seen.

JOHN RIEDLING   Bats: R   Throws: R   Born: 29-Aug-75   Age: 28

YEAR	TM	LG	AGE	G	GS	IP	H	BB	SO	HR	ERA	EQERA	EQH9	EQBB9	EQSO9	EQHR9	PERA	VORP	STF
2001	CIN	NL	25	29	0	33.7	22	14	23	1	2.40	2.20	5.8	3.3	5.2	0.3	2.46	12.4	18
2002	CIN	NL	26	33	0	46.7	39	26	30	2	2.70	3.38	7.5	4.4	5.0	0.4	3.64	11.2	3
2003	CIN	NL	27	55	8	101.0	107	47	65	7	4.90	4.85	9.4	3.8	5.1	0.6	4.55	2.2	-4
2004	CIN	NL	28	34	12	81.3	83	37	53	7	4.37	4.60	9.4	3.6	5.2	0.7	4.65	8.2	-6

Breakout: 22%   Improve: 42%   Collapse: 27%

Bob Boone is so freaking annoying. Coming into 2003, Riedling had a career ERA of 2.54, compiled entirely in relief. He hadn't started a game since 1999. One month into the season, Riedling had an ERA of 5.09 in 13 appearances, so Boone thrust him into his rotation. Is it any wonder this team was done by the middle of May? Brought back to relieve in July, Riedling had an ERA of 3.02 the rest of the way, with 39 strikeouts and 16 walks in 47 ⅔ innings. He'll be effective in a set-up role in 2003, part of what should be an excellent Reds bullpen.

BRIAN SHACKELFORD — Bats: L — Throws: L — Born: 30-Aug-76 — Age: 27

YEAR	TM	LG	AGE	G	GS	IP	H	BB	SO	HR	ERA	EQERA	EQH9	EQBB9	EQSO9	EQHR9	PERA	VORP	STF
2002	WIC	TEX	25	22	0	25.7	23	26	15	1	3.50	6.75	10.3	11.1	4.0	0.8	6.99	-2.9	-62
2003	POT	CAR	26	18	0	27.3	17	8	20	1	1.98	2.59	7.0	3.3	4.4	0.7	3.45	8.1	-11
2003	CHT	SOU	26	13	1	20.0	26	14	19	3	6.30	9.87	15.1	7.8	6.2	3.1	10.84	-8.2	-121
2003	LOU	INT	26	12	0	15.7	15	7	10	0	2.29	3.68	8.6	4.9	4.3	0.0	3.88	3.1	0
2004	CIN	NL	27	17	1	18.7	26	22	11	6	10.63	11.17	12.9	9.1	4.6	2.7	11.42	-4.3	-58

Breakout: 23%   Improve: 42%   Collapse: 43%

Shackelford was a two-way player in college (Oklahoma), so with his career as an outfielder in the Royals system going nowhere, he moved to the mound in 2002. He's 27, but he has less than 100 innings of pitching experience. The Reds liked him enough to trade for him before the season, and they moved him through the system quickly, getting him to Triple-A in August. He should make his major league debut by mid-season as a lefty specialist.

JOE VALENTINE — Bats: R — Throws: R — Born: 24-Dec-79 — Age: 24

YEAR	TM	LG	AGE	G	GS	IP	H	BB	SO	HR	ERA	EQERA	EQH9	EQBB9	EQSO9	EQHR9	PERA	VORP	STF
2001	KAN	SAL	21	30	0	30.7	21	10	33	0	2.93	4.39	8.8	4.4	5.4	0.3	4.12	3.6	8
2001	WNS	CAR	21	27	0	44.7	18	27	50	0	1.01	2.79	5.1	8.1	6.3	0.2	3.47	12.1	17
2002	BIR	SOU	22	55	0	59.3	36	30	63	1	1.97	3.50	7.2	4.8	6.8	0.3	3.51	12.6	22
2003	SAC	PCL	23	40	0	52.3	44	37	53	5	4.82	5.92	8.0	7.6	8.3	1.3	5.55	-1.7	-5
2003	LOU	INT	23	9	0	11.3	5	3	8	0	0.80	1.69	3.4	2.5	5.1	0.0	1.11	4.6	33
2004	CIN	NL	24	17	0	18.7	17	14	17	2	5.17	5.43	8.5	5.9	7.3	0.8	5.44	0.4	-7

Breakout: 16%   Improve: 26%   Collapse: 32%

Valentine is a hard thrower who was picked up as part of the Jose Guillen deal. He throws a fastball, slider and splitter, with the fastball described as too "hittable," despite its velocity. Many people like him as a closer, but if he makes the Reds this year, it will be in a low-leverage role. He'll probably start the year at Louisville.

TODD VAN POPPEL — Bats: R — Throws: R — Born: 09-Dec-71 — Age: 32

YEAR	TM	LG	AGE	G	GS	IP	H	BB	SO	HR	ERA	EQERA	EQH9	EQBB9	EQSO9	EQHR9	PERA	VORP	STF
2001	CHC	NL	29	59	0	75.0	63	38	90	9	2.52	3.22	7.8	4.2	9.0	1.0	4.23	19.2	15
2002	TEX	AL	30	50	0	72.7	80	29	85	14	5.45	5.00	9.5	3.2	9.9	1.5	5.26	4.8	6
2003	TEX	AL	31	7	1	12.7	20	9	9	1	8.50	7.82	12.8	5.7	6.4	0.7	6.58	-5.0	-18
2003	LOU	INT	31	20	5	54.0	49	11	45	4	3.17	4.11	8.6	2.3	5.9	1.1	4.19	8.3	-4
2003	CIN	NL	31	9	4	35.7	31	6	25	7	4.54	3.93	7.6	1.3	5.5	1.8	4.24	4.3	-10
2004	CIN	NL	32	29	8	63.0	60	24	53	8	4.10	4.31	8.7	3.0	6.8	1.0	4.44	9.0	4

Breakout: 26%   Improve: 52%   Collapse: 22%

Life Is Not a Meritocracy, Exhibit 1,437: Van Poppel is going to be paid $3 million in 2004 in the last year of a three-year deal he signed with the Rangers in the winter of 2001. The right-hander happened to string together the only two good years of his career just before heading out to free agency. We mention this as a warning to general managers who might decide to pursue Van Poppel should he have the third good year of his career in 2004. The next frontier in applying performance analysis to the real world is convincing GMs that a free agent isn't going to keep performing at the career-best level he just reached the season prior. There's billions to be saved.

RYAN WAGNER   Bats: R   Throws: R   Born: 15-Jul-82   Age: 21

YEAR	TM	LG	AGE	G	GS	IP	H	BB	SO	HR	ERA	EQERA	EQH9	EQBB9	EQSO9	EQHR9	PERA	VORP	STF
2003	CHT	SOU	20	5	0	5.0	2	2	6	0	0.00	1.93	3.9	3.9	7.7	0.0	1.60	1.9	52
2003	LOU	INT	20	4	0	4.0	5	0	4	0	4.50	4.50	9.0	0.0	6.8	0.0	2.64	0.5	45
2003	CIN	NL	20	17	0	21.7	13	12	25	2	1.66	2.14	5.6	4.3	9.0	0.9	3.12	9.6	55
2004	CIN	NL	21	36	7	66.0	53	32	71	5	3.17	3.33	7.3	3.9	8.7	0.6	3.66	17.3	16

Breakout: 27%   Improve: 47%   Collapse: 24%

The Reds' #1 pick in the 2003 draft threw nine minor league innings and was in the majors on July 19. He's your basic college closer: two pitches, throws hard and harder, and is pretty much as good as he's ever going to be right now, which is pretty damn good. That's valuable, especially for a team trying to sort through a dozen pitchers who look alike. Talk that Wagner will be moved to the rotation is silly—he doesn't have the repertoire for it and his motion elicits concern that he is an injury risk. The Reds have enough injured pitchers; they should give themselves a shot at the first part of Gregg Olson's career.

PAUL WILSON   Bats: R   Throws: R   Born: 28-Mar-73   Age: 31

YEAR	TM	LG	AGE	G	GS	IP	H	BB	SO	HR	ERA	EQERA	EQH9	EQBB9	EQSO9	EQHR9	PERA	VORP	STF
2001	TBY	AL	28	37	24	151.3	165	52	119	21	4.88	4.74	9.4	2.9	6.6	1.1	4.74	14.1	4
2002	TBY	AL	29	30	30	193.7	219	67	111	29	4.83	4.90	9.7	2.9	4.9	1.2	5.08	14.7	-4
2003	CIN	NL	30	28	28	166.7	190	50	93	24	4.64	5.07	10.0	2.4	4.5	1.3	5.14	7.3	-8
2004	CIN	NL	31	25	23	142.0	155	47	85	20	4.78	5.02	10.0	2.6	4.8	1.1	5.02	10.2	1

Breakout: 11%   Improve: 43%   Collapse: 19%

It's time to stop thinking of Wilson as a potential top-tier starter and start looking at him as the innings guy he almost is. His performance record is a mystery, with a sharp drop-off in strikeouts and walks and an increase in groundball/flyball ratio even as he began allowing more extra-base hits in 2002. At a salary of $3.5 million in 2004, there's very little chance that Wilson will finish the season with the Reds. The shoulder pain that ended his 2003 season is expected to be gone in 2004.

Colorado Rockies

Now that their expansion twin has won its second World Series, it's as good a time as any to ask whether or not the Rockies have achieved anything in the full course of their existence.

Sure, having them in the league generates the kind of revenue that the Devil Rays or Expos will never reach the way they're going. Challenged only by the Nuggets, the Avalanche, and professional rodeo as potential sources of distraction from the spring minicamps of the Broncos and Buffaloes, the Rockies have a favorable place in Denver's sports culture. Did we mention that they introduced purple to baseball's uniform palette? Or the contributions of team owner Jerry McMorris as a hardcore management mouthpiece? Let's face it, the Rockies are more summer fun than either the Denver Gold or Joey Meyer's mashing exploits could ever hope to achieve.

Of course, beyond these bannerless exploits, you're still left having to ask, what are the Rockies for? Rather than address the organization's failure to build a really good ballclub in 11 years of existence, the team has coughed up a concoction of spin-doctoring worthy of the '90s at their worst, combining an old accusation with an old excuse in a new blend of how the whole thing is somehow somebody else's fault.

The latest is playing up the anxieties about Denver's market size that was such a source of concern before the Rockies' existence was a sure thing. The club's cash-cow status has been steadily losing ground as Rockies' attendance has gone through a seven-year slide. In the last three years, they've gone from 5th to 8th to 15th in average attendance, which translates into over 800,000 fewer fannies in Coors Field in 2003 than in 2001. Predictably, the Rockies are now claiming that they're a small-market team, while conveniently ignoring their initial seven-year run when they led all of baseball in attendance. By trying to place the onus on some overarching success-sucking force that transcends their feeble powers to build a winning ballclub, questions of responsibility get overshadowed. It's all part of the art of creating appropriately modest expectations after years of smug confidence that this was a franchise going places.

There were worthwhile reasons for that confidence, of course. Although the Marlins have won twice, they have been nothing if not unpredictable. Their relationship with their host city is uncomfortable at best, having gone

ROCKIES PROSPECTUS

2003 record: 74–88; Fourth place, NL West

Pythagenport record: 77–85

Runs scored per game: 5.3 (3rd in NL)

Runs allowed per game: 5.5 (15th in NL)

Team EqA: .258 (10th in NL)

2003 Batters Age: 27.6 (Youngest in NL)

2003 Pitchers Age: 27.0 (2nd youngest in NL)

Ballpark: Coors Field; Severe hitter's park; Park Factor of 1.126

2003: The Hampton trade acquisitions helped key a strong start, but a second-half slump kept the Rox under .500.

2004: The team is young, but it isn't good, and youth for youth's sake never won anything in baseball.

from the outstanding organization Dave Dombrowski put together to the franchise-wide meltdown after 1997 to being handed over to the Loria gang with all the formality of an industry-wide game of spin-the-bottle.

By contrast, the Rockies have been nothing if not brilliant in crafting and then executing an outstanding business plan, building and exploiting a cozy relationship with local government, and creating a great venue to catch a ballgame. Everywhere but on the diamond, the Rockies have been one of the best-run operations within the industry. It is that confidence in every aspect of the organization outside of baseball operations that, up until now, has retarded any realization that the rules that generally apply to everybody in the industry, also apply to the Rockies. Let's call it the triumph of actual results over modern business culture. Rockies Vice Chairman Charlie Monfort can brag about the team's organizational strength and cohesiveness, and nevertheless wonder why it doesn't lead to better results in terms of wins and losses.

But it is the attendance decline that describes the special power a losing team always has, the power to drive people into finding other ways to spend their leisure time. That's an inescapable source of concern for the business types who suddenly recognize they may have a hollow business model, all glitz and no product. It's also a reflection of a fan base appropriately tired of the team's perpetual excuse, the now insistent special pleading about their own very special problem, which is building a ballclub to win at altitude. The subject of their special problem has been a source of so much statistical rainbow-chasing that it drowns out the point we made last year: The Rockies need to get into the business of fielding a competitive baseball team, and stop reinventing the propeller beanie.

Set aside the location issue for a moment, and instead think about this team in terms of what it had after 2002, what it did to address its problems, how effectively those problems were solved, and what that leaves going into 2004. After 2002, the Rockies had a rotation that could boast its two big free agent flops, Mike Hampton and Denny Neagle, a nice pair of homegrown starters in Shawn Chacon in Jason Jennings, and Denny Stark, part of the swag from the deal that made Jeff Cirillo Seattle's problem. Although they had enjoyed some success in assembling bullpens in the past, their '02 pen was short of any reliable lefty help. The lineup was short of right-handed sock, with nothing set at second or behind the plate. Juan Pierre and Juan Uribe hadn't gotten better, they'd regressed. Todd Zeile had been barely effective as a placeholder at third while costing more than $6 million.

As is his wont, and to his credit, Dan O'Dowd acted. He dumped Pierre and Hampton, which brought him some right-handed power in Preston Wilson and Charles Johnson, and plugged the hole at catcher. The deal also brought in Pablo Ozuna, considered a plausible solution to the problem at second; to increase their options there, they brought in Ron Belliard. The deal also gave them veteran lefty Vic Darensbourg to help in the pen. To replace Zeile, O'Dowd signed Jose Hernandez, giving the team a third right-handed power hitter that winter. As a none-too-subtle message to Uribe, they brought in Chris Stynes, meaning they had an alternative at third base in case they decided to play Hernandez at short. To help plug the rotation, O'Dowd had Aaron Cook coming up from the minor leagues, with his rookie status for 2004 self-consciously preserved to follow in Jason Jennings's footsteps. He also had Scott Elarton coming back from his surgery, and journeymen Darren Oliver and Nelson Cruz were hauled in as experienced alternatives if something didn't work out. To fix up the pen, he brought back righty specialist Steve Reed, picked up promising lefty Javier Lopez from the Red Sox, and had another part of the Cirillo deal, Brian Fuentes, also coming up to give them alternatives in picking lefties for their '03 pen. He also hauled in journeymen Danny Miceli, Rich Garces, Chris Michalak, and Brad Clontz.

In short, the Rockies did a thorough job of bringing in alternatives that made sense individually. O'Dowd had achieved the miraculous feat of getting the team out from under more than $80 million owed to Hampton, re-used the money to afford Wilson and Johnson, and brought in everybody else on the cheap.

The problem is whether those moves could add up to an improvement on the 2002 Rockies. In a sense, yes: With a straight face, Monfort could point to their one-game improvement to 74 wins as a development worth mentioning. Offensively, they improved by 65 runs, helping to erase the memory of the franchise's worst run-scoring team since their inaugural '93 edition. The pitching staff gave up an almost identical number of runs.

Consider how many of these moves "worked": Preston Wilson had the sort of year he should have had. Jay Payton did even better than that, far outperforming anybody's expectations. Darren Oliver was wildly more effective than they could have hoped. Shawn Chacon gave them four great months in the rotation. The pen was much-improved, with Reed, Fuentes, and Lopez being three of the primary reasons; as a unit, they finished fifth in Adjusted Runs Prevented (one of Michael Wolverton's reliever evaluation tools you'll find at www.baseball prospectus .com). They found an effective temp at second base in Ron Belliard, or at least it worked for the first four months of the season. The setbacks? Charles Johnson, Jose Hernandez and Chris Stynes all played like they were over-the-hill, surprising few. In retrospect, Hernandez was coming from another good hitter's park, exacerbating a set of exaggerated expectations, Johnson was coming off of an injury-marred 2002, and Chris Stynes was Chris Stynes. Juan Uribe broke down with a stress fracture in his foot in camp, and managed to annoy them again upon his return. Cook didn't work out, and Stark got hurt, then struggled. Jose Jimenez and Todd Jones both pitched their way out of town. All in all, normal sorts of setbacks to normal sorts of players.

Which brings us to the issue of the ballpark, because along with the declining attendance, it's being used as an explanation for how hard it is for the organization to field a better team. It's offered as an excuse for why it's hard to attract people to pitch in Coors or do anything differently in terms of pitching staff management. And although only four National League teams had better home records than the Rockies (the playoff-bound Giants, Braves, and Marlins, plus the Expos), they posted a league-low and franchise history-worst 25 road wins. Again, as we said last year, the problem isn't Coors, it's in the talent they've put together. Now matter how clever the roster reshuffling gets, it isn't delivering a better product, just more of the same.

When you come down to it, that's the basis of the problem. What was this team's hoped-for upside, 75, perhaps even 80 wins? It isn't easy to make a team significantly better overnight, and no matter how intricate, involved, or comprehensive O'Dowd's solutions to his roster problems appear to be, they don't actually deliver much in the way of substantive improvement. From among the improvements of 2003, what's supposed to stick? Fuentes and

Lopez give them as good a pair of lefties in the pen as any in baseball, and Preston Wilson should be able to do his thing again. That's about the extent of the positive achievements on the big league roster. At some point, all of the motion can be easily mistaken for progress, instead of being appreciated as an elaborate series of finger-in-the-dyke solutions, with only so many fingers to go around. Although the organization sent the message that they were confident in O'Dowd's stewardship—extending his contract after 2003—there's the underlying popular sentiment that this team seems awfully busy for one stuck in place.

Part of the problem is the club's crippling financial inflexibility. Although liberated from their commitment to Hampton, they still have significant stumbling blocks in terms of payroll. Although he's declining steadily, Larry Walker is owed $25 million in 2004–05, plus a perhaps inevitable $1 million buyout of his option year in 2006; he also has an ironclad no-trade clause. Preston Wilson is locked in through 2005 for $21 million. They owe Charles Johnson $18 million through '05, and can't deal him until after '04. And then there's Helton's rapacious monster of a contract, bumping up to $11.6 million in 2004, $12.6 million in 2005, $16.6 million per annum through 2010, $19.1 million in 2011, and *then* they get to an option year.

Helton's even more of a stumbling block because he forces the organization's hand at one of its deepest positions, first base. Piled up behind Helton are Brad Hawpe and Ryan Shealy—out of desperation, they're trying to project Hawpe to an outfield corner. They may also try to deal from strength. The problem is that the Rockies have to be a little more ambitious in what they try to acquire in deals using Hawpe or Shealy; in discarding power-hitting prospect Jack Cust, they settled for broken-down bench fodder Chris Richard. A team trying to accumulate a strong talent base can't afford to keep repeating such giveaways.

The Cust deal does raise the question of how effectively the team's shell game is being conducted. Vinny Castilla looks like a marketing ploy. Acquiring Aaron Miles as a potential fix to the team's leadoff problem isn't encouraging—the guy's 27 and drew all of 38 walks on his own in over 600 plate appearances. Getting Miles cost them Juan Uribe, leaving them looking for a shortstop. You tell me: Would signing Deivi Cruz represent progress? Nontendering Jay Payton after failing to offer him arbitration earned the Rockies nothing for his nifty '03, making you wonder why they didn't deal him in July. Replacing Payton with Jeromy Burnitz should be ugly, as Burnitz has lost a lot as a hitter in recent years. Larry Walker and Todd Helton won't get any younger or any better, and the Rockies look no closer to building a lineup that will score enough runs anywhere.

A Burnitz-Wilson-Walker outfield could be defensively crippling for some clubs, but it does bring up something the team has been working on. The Rockies have been going out of their way to acquire or develop pitchers with pronounced groundball tendencies. Beyond that, they've got a crop of homegrown pitchers that represents the team's real source of hope, however fragile. Although Shawn Chacon's elbow is forcing him to the pen, they have as good a group of near-ready pitchers as any team in baseball. Beyond Jason Jennings, they should be able to break in Chin-Hui Tsao (if healthy) and Aaron Young in 2004, to be followed by Jeff Francis and perhaps Cory Vance. Freeing Joe Kennedy from Tampa might seem dicey, but Kennedy still has considerable promise. They have a gaggle of good homegrown right-handed relievers to join last year's new lefty duo. Generally, the Rockies don't blink when it comes to the expense of player development. Ching-Lung Lo follows Tsao in the organization's Taiwanese vein, and they're active in the Dominican and the Pacific Rim.

As promising as all that is, however, the team has to do a better job of assembling a genuinely strong lineup. Helton is one of the game's great hitters, but he's being surrounded by another assembly of merely adequate or mediocre hitters. Building on pitching might be the closest thing to a strategic vision as the club has at the moment, and it isn't a bad thing to do. It's always been easier to put together a quality lineup than procure a pitching staff. But to survive, O'Dowd is effectively betting on young pitching, while having to prove that he can break his habit of creating and plugging holes in the lineup willy-nilly. If you have your doubts about those two things working, you're not alone, but that's what they're selling.

HITTERS

GARRETT ATKINS   3B   Bats: R   Throws: R   Born: 12-Dec-79   Age: 24

YEAR	TM	LG	AGE	AB	H	2B	3B	HR	BB	SO	SB	CS	AVG	OBP	SLG	MLVR	EQBA	EQOBP	EQSLG	EQMLVR	VORP	DEFENSE
2001	SLM	CAR	21	465	151	43	5	5	74	98	6	4	.325	.421	.471	.341	.255	.338	.386	-.090	-1.1	125-1B -6
2002	CAR	SOU	22	510	138	27	3	12	59	77	6	6	.271	.345	.406	.069	.234	.293	.365	-.220	-6.2	119-3B -2
2003	CSP	PCL	23	439	140	30	1	13	45	52	2	4	.319	.382	.481	.167	.265	.330	.408	-.067	15.2	110-3B -1
2003	COL	NL	23	69	11	2	0	0	3	14	0	0	.159	.205	.188	-.632	.145	.190	.174	-.735	-8.3	14-3B -5
2004	COL	NL	24	274	73	18	1	8	28	44	2	1	.267	.339	.433	-.001	.258	.328	.414	-.063	11.2	75-3B -3

Breakout: 37%   Improve: 59%   Collapse: 18%

Between a solid season in the PCL and Chris Stynes's inescapable Styne-liness, Atkins earned an August call-up, but didn't get a whole lot of opportunity to actually make something of it after kicking a few balls. His defensive rep isn't great, but his shortcomings are overstated. It's worth debating who the better prospect might be between Atkins and the Snakes' Chad Tracy. Tracy has the better glove and hits lefty, while Atkins doesn't need to be platooned. Neither are blue-chip prospects in any case, which helps explain why both parent clubs are considering them fallbacks in 2004. Atkins seems strangely underrated, even by his parent organization; he'll make a solid four-year investment for somebody at third base.

JEFF BAKER   3B   Bats: R   Throws: R   Born: 21-Jun-81   Age: 23

YEAR	TM	LG	AGE	AB	H	2B	3B	HR	BB	SO	SB	CS	AVG	OBP	SLG	MLVR	EQBA	EQOBP	EQSLG	EQMLVR	VORP	DEFENSE
2003	ASH	SAL	22	263	76	17	0	11	30	79	4	2	.289	.377	.479	.206	.206	.271	.352	-.298	-9.6	61-3B-10
2004	COL	NL	23	236	50	11	1	9	20	77	2	1	.213	.286	.373	-.208	.205	.277	.357	-.265	-5.3	65-3B -7

Breakout: 30%   Improve: 57%   Collapse: 18%

Although the organization drafted Ian Stewart, Baker is the better third baseman, creating one of those nice organizational problems. A college shortstop, Baker is a good enough athlete that he could be a defensive asset in the outfield corners, and with the bat to carry him there, Baker should be in one of the team's infield or outfield corners by 2006. The problem is that Baker has required surgery on his left wrist three times, and twice in the last year. If he's healthy, between his Clemson pedigree and his having the right sort of work ethic, he could move up quickly, with his reaching Double-A at some point in 2004 being the minimum expectation. He has considerable promise, relative to what you see here.

CLINT BARMES   SS   Bats: R   Throws: R   Born: 06-Mar-79   Age: 25

YEAR	TM	LG	AGE	AB	H	2B	3B	HR	BB	SO	SB	CS	AVG	OBP	SLG	MLVR	EQBA	EQOBP	EQSLG	EQMLVR	VORP	DEFENSE
2001	ASH	SAL	22	285	74	14	1	5	17	37	21	7	.260	.314	.368	-.014	.201	.242	.294	-.439	-20.7	74-SS 10
2001	SLM	CAR	22	121	30	3	3	0	15	20	4	1	.248	.350	.322	.016	.213	.289	.283	-.353	-6.0	36-SS -3
2002	CAR	SOU	23	438	119	23	2	15	31	72	15	11	.272	.329	.436	.088	.240	.281	.402	-.186	2.2	101-SS-17
2003	CSP	PCL	24	493	136	35	1	7	22	63	12	7	.276	.316	.394	-.094	.238	.279	.345	-.272	-10.0	122-SS-11
2003	COL	NL	24	25	8	2	0	0	0	10	0	0	.320	.357	.400	-.017	.320	.361	.400	.023	0.9	
2004	COL	NL	25	229	59	11	1	5	14	36	4	2	.258	.312	.391	-.108	.249	.302	.374	-.168	4.8	62-SS -7

Breakout: 39%   Improve: 60%   Collapse: 20%

Barmes hits well enough, but only if you're using the Neifi scale to measure offensive skill; he's not someone to take seriously as a Rockies' shortstop of the future. The fact that the organization had Barmes playing short every day at Colorado Springs sort of helps explain why they signed Benji Gil. Barmes could win the Rockies' starting job in '04, but his defense isn't top-grade and he won't hit. If he doesn't win the job, he'll get consideration for a spot as the team's utility infielder.

MARK BELLHORN   IF   Bats: B   Throws: R   Born: 23-Aug-74   Age: 29

YEAR	TM	LG	AGE	AB	H	2B	3B	HR	BB	SO	SB	CS	AVG	OBP	SLG	MLVR	EQBA	EQOBP	EQSLG	EQMLVR	VORP	DEFENSE	
2001	SAC	PCL	26	156	42	6	0	12	22	60	3	0	.269	.370	.538	.191	.236	.332	.465	-.008	7.9	16-2B 4	
2001	OAK	AL	26	74	10	1	2	1	7	37	0	0	.135	.210	.243	-.543	.149	.222	.284	-.518	-7.5		
2002	CHC	NL	27	445	115	24	4	27	76	144	7	5	.258	.374	.512	.220	.270	.378	.539	.202	47.0	63-2B 1	24-3B -3
2003	CHC	NL	28	139	29	7	1	2	29	46	3	3	.209	.341	.317	-.133	.218	.350	.331	-.163	-0.6	38-3B -3	
2003	COL	NL	28	110	26	3	0	0	21	32	2	3	.236	.368	.264	-.214	.218	.346	.245	-.283	-2.7	15-2B -3	
2003	CSP	PCL	28	54	21	5	1	4	11	10	2	0	.389	.485	.741	.732	.302	.403	.585	.338	9.4	12-3B 1	
2004	BOS	AL	29	238	59	12	2	9	36	65	4	2	.248	.350	.427	.009	.243	.349	.429	-.018	13.3	69-3B -2	

Breakout: 22%   Improve: 42%   Collapse: 33%

While it would have been unreasonable to expect Bellhorn to flirt with another 30-homer season, the way he was run down and then out by Dusty Baker defies explanation, especially considering the Cubs' lack of alternatives. He's got a long stroke, so he'll have cold spells. He'll also keep on getting on base. But Dusty got cranky, Bellhorn was banished to Denver, got hurt, and it all added up to Bellhorn's second lost season in three. He's a stronger hitter against right-handed pitching, which should make him a nifty alternative to Pokey Reese in the Red Sox's second-base situation. As long as Reese only specifically draws the assignment for all of Derek Lowe's starts, and Bellhorn gets 300–400 plate appearances to chip in at second and third, it looks like Theo Epstein got another piece for his answer to "How do we score a thousand runs, anyway?"

RON BELLIARD — 2B — Bats: R — Throws: R — Born: 07-Apr-75 — Age: 29

YEAR	TM	LG	AGE	AB	H	2B	3B	HR	BB	SO	SB	CS	AVG	OBP	SLG	MLVR	EQBA	EQOBP	EQSLG	EQMLVR	VORP	DEFENSE			
2001	MIL	NL	26	364	96	30	3	11	35	65	5	2	.264	.335	.453	.015	.268	.337	.461	.022	20.3	94-2B	8		
2002	MIL	NL	27	289	61	13	0	3	18	46	2	3	.211	.257	.287	-.314	.225	.267	.307	-.358	-13.8	40-2B	-3	28-3B	-5
2003	COL	NL	28	447	124	31	2	8	49	71	7	2	.277	.351	.409	-.044	.265	.337	.395	-.072	10.5	104-2B	-10		
2004	CLE	AL	29	364	90	20	2	7	33	59	4	2	.248	.313	.368	-.130	.258	.325	.399	-.089	10.9	97-2B	-6		

Breakout: 29%   Improve: 56%   Collapse: 21%

In the end, the scouts were right: he's not the sort of guy who was physically built to last. Belliard started and finished hot, but he wilted in the summer heat, struggling badly in July and August. Still, Belliard can really hurt lefties, and he's every bit as valuable as Fernando Vina, without the expense. He'll give the Indians a nice placeholder until either Brandon Phillips gets his act together, or they conjure up another long-term alternative.

BRENT BUTLER — IF — Bats: R — Throws: R — Born: 11-Feb-78 — Age: 26

YEAR	TM	LG	AGE	AB	H	2B	3B	HR	BB	SO	SB	CS	AVG	OBP	SLG	MLVR	EQBA	EQOBP	EQSLG	EQMLVR	VORP	DEFENSE	
2001	CSP	PCL	23	272	91	20	3	7	15	26	4	2	.335	.375	.507	.168	.283	.328	.434	-.019	12.6	51-2B	-5
2001	COL	NL	23	119	29	7	1	1	7	7	1	1	.244	.287	.345	-.283	.227	.269	.328	-.323	-4.6	19-2B	-3
2002	CSP	PCL	24	105	35	9	1	2	6	12	0	0	.333	.375	.495	.177	.291	.328	.427	-.022	5.5	16-SS	1
2002	COL	NL	24	344	89	18	4	9	10	40	2	6	.259	.287	.413	-.106	.247	.273	.401	-.197	-1.9	62-2B	1
2003	COL	NL	25	90	19	3	1	1	7	13	1	0	.211	.276	.300	-.347	.200	.264	.289	-.402	-4.6	16-2B	0
2003	CSP	PCL	25	205	68	19	1	6	19	20	0	1	.332	.399	.522	.261	.274	.338	.448	.011	11.6	39-2B	-1
2004	STL	NL	26	236	60	13	2	4	18	29	1	1	.253	.315	.376	-.127	.258	.317	.395	-.108	9.0	64-2B	-3

Breakout: 25%   Improve: 47%   Collapse: 39%

It might seem harsh to call a guy who's just turning 26 a "neverwuzz," but let's face it, he never developed as a hitter, losing his patience in Double-A and never really developing the power he'd hinted at a few years ago. He'll get a shot at replacing Miguel Cairo as the Cardinals' utility infielder. He wasn't supposed to just be Mike Mordecai when he grew up, but that's what has happened.

J. D. CLOSSER — C — Bats: B — Throws: R — Born: 15-Jan-80 — Age: 24

YEAR	TM	LG	AGE	AB	H	2B	3B	HR	BB	SO	SB	CS	AVG	OBP	SLG	MLVR	EQBA	EQOBP	EQSLG	EQMLVR	VORP	DEFENSE	
2001	LNC	CAL	21	468	136	26	6	21	65	106	6	7	.291	.377	.506	.188	.205	.277	.360	-.276	-14.7	92-C	-3
2002	CAR	SOU	22	315	89	27	1	13	44	69	9	3	.283	.369	.498	.236	.238	.307	.430	-.100	7.4	64-C	-7
2003	TUL	TEX	23	410	116	28	5	13	47	79	3	2	.283	.359	.471	.166	.236	.304	.407	-.139	4.5	94-C	3
2004	COL	NL	24	216	54	12	1	8	21	43	2	1	.251	.319	.432	-.047	.242	.309	.414	-.109	3.2	60-C	-4

Breakout: 27%   Improve: 55%   Collapse: 25%

The organization's best catcher, Closser is a decent receiver making slow adjustments to his footwork to improve his throwing. If he masters it, he'll quickly become a premium catching prospect. Despite that wrinkle, he looks like a great bet to wind up catching in Denver before the summer's out. He hits with much more authority against right-handed pitching, which means he could be the playing time-heavy half of a platoon or job-sharing arrangement.

JAVIER COLINA IF Bats: R Throws: R Born: 15-Feb-79 Age: 25

YEAR	TM	LG	AGE	AB	H	2B	3B	HR	BB	SO	SB	CS	AVG	OBP	SLG	MLVR	EQBA	EQOBP	EQSLG	EQMLVR	VORP	DEFENSE			
2001	SLM	CAR	22	439	125	33	7	9	22	61	9	4	.285	.324	.453	.165	.242	.279	.401	-.190	-2.0	113-2B	-7		
2002	CAR	SOU	23	136	37	6	1	1	7	21	4	3	.272	.310	.353	-.053	.254	.278	.333	-.281	-4.3	32-2B	2		
2002	CSP	PCL	23	322	79	23	3	4	22	53	0	2	.245	.295	.373	-.198	.204	.255	.314	-.384	-19.6	64-2B	-6	22-3B	-1
2003	TUL	TEX	24	388	108	26	2	17	13	59	7	0	.278	.303	.487	.101	.243	.272	.439	-.148	3.1	71-2B	0	27-3B	-1
2004	*COL*	*NL*	*25*	*243*	*64*	*14*	*2*	*7*	*14*	*39*	*3*	*1*	*.262*	*.307*	*.420*	*-.076*	*.253*	*.297*	*.402*	*-.138*	*5.7*	*65-2B*	*-2*		

Breakout: 36%   Improve: 62%   Collapse: 19%

One of the team's project players out of Venezuela, the Rockies have been hoping he'd turn into a prospect after he hit .302/.339/.421 in the Sally League in 1999. They rushed him to Double-A in 2000, so this was his third season spending time at the level, spaced around his requiring a jump-start in A-ball in 2001 and a rough introduction to Triple-A in 2002. At this rate, they have to merely hope that Colina turns into a useful utility infielder. Scouts don't like his range at second, but he can handle the position as well as third. With his aversion to walking, it's his bat that won't keep him in a lineup.

BOBBY ESTALELLA C Bats: R Throws: R Born: 23-Aug-74 Age: 29

YEAR	TM	LG	AGE	AB	H	2B	3B	HR	BB	SO	SB	CS	AVG	OBP	SLG	MLVR	EQBA	EQOBP	EQSLG	EQMLVR	VORP	DEFENSE	
2001	SFG	NL	26	93	19	5	1	3	11	28	0	0	.204	.295	.376	-.187	.221	.307	.400	-.154	0.5	27-C	2
2001	COH	INT	26	171	44	10	1	10	21	45	0	2	.257	.340	.503	.153	.240	.319	.474	-.016	8.4	35-C	-4
2002	CSP	PCL	27	79	23	9	0	6	11	20	0	0	.291	.374	.633	.317	.231	.318	.526	.045	5.4	20-C	7
2002	COL	NL	27	112	23	8	0	8	14	33	0	1	.205	.285	.491	-.047	.196	.280	.473	-.124	1.5	34-C	-3
2003	COL	NL	28	140	28	7	0	7	19	55	2	0	.200	.294	.400	-.197	.193	.288	.379	-.237	-2.2	44-C	-1
2004	*DET*	*AL*	*29*	*219*	*45*	*10*	*0*	*9*	*26*	*68*	*2*	*1*	*.204*	*.295*	*.378*	*-.175*	*.212*	*.308*	*.407*	*-.141*	*4.2*	*62-C*	*1*

Breakout: 31%   Improve: 54%   Collapse: 23%

After requiring elbow surgery in September, he's supposed to be healthy for 2004, and there are plenty of teams looking for catching help. Estalella remains a useful option if you're not bidding for Pudge Rodriguez and need to get by for a year or two with a couple of temps. But after having surgery on almost all of the joints in his arms, it doesn't look like he'll ever be durable enough to be any more than that.

CHOO FREEMAN OF Bats: R Throws: R Born: 20-Oct-79 Age: 24

YEAR	TM	LG	AGE	AB	H	2B	3B	HR	BB	SO	SB	CS	AVG	OBP	SLG	MLVR	EQBA	EQOBP	EQSLG	EQMLVR	VORP	DEFENSE			
2001	SLM	CAR	21	517	124	16	5	8	31	108	19	7	.240	.292	.337	-.055	.209	.254	.304	-.397	-40.4	115-CF	-8		
2002	CAR	SOU	22	430	125	18	6	12	64	101	15	13	.291	.400	.444	.213	.245	.328	.388	-.113	4.7	116-CF	-7		
2003	CSP	PCL	23	327	83	9	4	7	23	71	2	8	.254	.315	.370	-.142	.211	.271	.317	-.344	-19.1	64-CF	-5	19-LF	-2
2004	*COL*	*NL*	*24*	*210*	*53*	*10*	*2*	*6*	*18*	*47*	*3*	*2*	*.253*	*.322*	*.406*	*-.075*	*.244*	*.312*	*.389*	*-.136*	*-0.6*	*59-CF*	*-3*		

Breakout: 51%   Improve: 69%   Collapse: 16%

After taking a big step forward in 2002, last season was a lost year for Freeman. He missed almost six weeks to an injury and a family tragedy, which didn't help his development. Despite tremendous footspeed, he still hasn't learned how to steal bases, his grasp of the strike zone still looks tenuous, and his power isn't going to get him a job if he can't stick in center. He's going to need a regrouping year in 2004, putting up consistent good work for the first three or four months in the PCL before he'll deserve any consideration for an outfield spot at the big league level.

GARRETT GENTRY C Bats: L Throws: R Born: 27-Jun-81 Age: 23

YEAR	TM	LG	AGE	AB	H	2B	3B	HR	BB	SO	SB	CS	AVG	OBP	SLG	MLVR	EQBA	EQOBP	EQSLG	EQMLVR	VORP	DEFENSE	
2001	MIC	MID	20	358	107	18	3	24	39	45	5	0	.299	.376	.567	.338	.219	.281	.416	-.182	-1.0	66-C	-7
2003	ASH	SAL	22	175	57	8	4	7	13	18	3	2	.326	.381	.537	.314	.239	.278	.409	-.183	-0.5	12-C	-2
2004	*COL*	*NL*	*23*	*250*	*64*	*14*	*1*	*10*	*18*	*34*	*2*	*1*	*.255*	*.312*	*.437*	*-.049*	*.246*	*.303*	*.418*	*-.111*	*4.4*		

Breakout: 33%   Improve: 54%   Collapse: 16%

Nobody doubts that Gentry can hit, but he's scragged his shoulder twice in the last three years, creating concern that he won't be a catcher for much longer. Catcher is a significant problem in the organization, since there's basically only Closser in the system, so Gentry will keep getting chances.

BRAD HAWPE — 1B/OF — Bats: L — Throws: L — Born: 22-Jun-79 — Age: 25

YEAR	TM	LG	AGE	AB	H	2B	3B	HR	BB	SO	SB	CS	AVG	OBP	SLG	MLVR	EQBA	EQOBP	EQSLG	EQMLVR	VORP	DEFENSE			
2001	ASH	SAL	22	393	105	22	3	22	59	113	7	4	.267	.363	.506	.219	.184	.266	.353	-.320	-33.3	49-RF	-10	52-1B	0
2002	SLM	CAR	23	450	156	38	2	22	81	84	1	1	.347	.447	.587	.522	.256	.343	.446	.002	12.7	120-1B	5		
2003	TUL	TEX	24	346	96	27	0	17	31	84	1	3	.277	.338	.503	.174	.232	.286	.433	-.139	-8.0	48-RF	-5	17-1B	-3
2004	COL	NL	25	236	62	14	1	12	26	55	1	1	.264	.338	.487	.066	.254	.328	.466	.001	6.8	66-1B	-2		

Breakout: 46%   Improve: 71%   Collapse: 16%

Hawpe's more than a little overrated, but that's in part because of his 2002, and in part because he can hit and he's in the Rockies' chain, exciting rotoheads everywhere. Because of Helton's contract, the Rox keep saying he's projected as a right fielder, but it's somewhere closer to Jack Cust than Ryan Klesko as outfield conversions go. That .447 OBP in Salem looks tasty, but keep in mind he was a top hitter from LSU playing in A-ball against younger competition; he was walked intentionally 23 times. His promotion to Double-A didn't work out entirely well: A separated shoulder kept Hawpe from playing a full season, and was still bothering him in the Arizona Fall League. He also struggled terribly in Tulsa.

TODD HELTON — 1B — Bats: L — Throws: L — Born: 20-Aug-73 — Age: 30

YEAR	TM	LG	AGE	AB	H	2B	3B	HR	BB	SO	SB	CS	AVG	OBP	SLG	MLVR	EQBA	EQOBP	EQSLG	EQMLVR	VORP	DEFENSE	
2001	COL	NL	27	587	197	54	2	49	98	104	7	5	.336	.432	.685	.492	.314	.413	.642	.445	90.1	153-1B	13
2002	COL	NL	28	553	182	39	4	30	99	91	5	1	.329	.429	.577	.380	.310	.415	.552	.321	63.9	153-1B	13
2003	COL	NL	29	583	209	49	5	33	111	72	0	4	.358	.458	.630	.464	.340	.445	.602	.469	81.7	155-1B	26
2004	COL	NL	30	541	174	39	3	33	94	83	3	2	.321	.422	.587	.378	.310	.408	.562	.306	58.5	151-1B	9

Breakout: 11%   Improve: 47%   Collapse: 15%

This was a relief. Rather than continue the slide from his '02 campaign, Helton was about as valuable as he'd been in 2001. He's still hitting well enough on the road to be a no-brainer All-Star first baseman, and he's as good a defensive first baseman as the game can boast of. Any stathead metric you care to name or use is going to put him in the National League's top 10 hitters. That said, his power is slipping, possibly because the back problems that plagued him in '02 may be lingering a bit. The Rockies need him at full strength, because the offense is in big trouble if he's anything less.

MATT HOLLIDAY — OF — Bats: R — Throws: R — Born: 10-Jan-80 — Age: 24

YEAR	TM	LG	AGE	AB	H	2B	3B	HR	BB	SO	SB	CS	AVG	OBP	SLG	MLVR	EQBA	EQOBP	EQSLG	EQMLVR	VORP	DEFENSE	
2001	SLM	CAR	21	255	70	16	1	11	33	42	11	3	.275	.350	.475	.227	.220	.294	.388	-.195	-12.0	24-LF	-1
2002	CAR	SOU	22	463	128	19	2	10	67	102	16	2	.276	.375	.391	.098	.240	.315	.352	-.191	-20.3	113-LF	-6
2003	TUL	TEX	23	522	132	28	5	12	43	74	15	9	.253	.313	.395	-.032	.217	.271	.350	-.294	-38.7	121-LF	-8
2004	COL	NL	24	272	69	15	2	9	26	50	5	2	.253	.323	.417	-.059	.244	.313	.399	-.120	-1.6	74-LF	-4

Breakout: 44%   Improve: 71%   Collapse: 11%

The upper levels of the organization are still pretty thin in terms of prospects, so Holliday still gets mentioned. Outfield corners who can't slug .400 should get to be non-prospects pretty quickly, but a nice AFL gave people a continuing excuse to call Holliday a talent. As much as you like to see people move up to Double-A early on in their careers, Holliday hasn't made progress since leaving A-ball, or since blowing out his elbow in 2001. A third weak year at the plate should get him booted from the 40-man roster.

CHARLES JOHNSON — C — Bats: R — Throws: R — Born: 20-Jul-71 — Age: 32

YEAR	TM	LG	AGE	AB	H	2B	3B	HR	BB	SO	SB	CS	AVG	OBP	SLG	MLVR	EQBA	EQOBP	EQSLG	EQMLVR	VORP	DEFENSE	
2001	FLA	NL	29	451	117	32	0	18	38	133	0	0	.259	.321	.450	-.002	.268	.328	.466	.013	23.3	120-C	3
2002	FLA	NL	30	244	53	19	0	6	31	61	0	0	.217	.301	.369	-.114	.229	.312	.394	-.147	1.7	69-C	5
2003	COL	NL	31	356	82	20	0	20	49	84	1	3	.230	.320	.455	-.069	.217	.312	.434	-.101	4.6	101-C	1
2004	COL	NL	32	277	69	16	0	13	34	67	1	1	.250	.334	.449	-.001	.242	.323	.430	-.064	10.2	77-C	-2

Breakout: 34%   Improve: 63%   Collapse: 21%

Another data point in the "Planet Coors Ruins Hitters' Timing" theory: Johnson hit .153/.242/.318 on the road last year. For that reason alone, it isn't hard to see him having a better 2004, if only because you'd like to think he'll adapt. Among Johnson's closest comps at this point of his career (Gus Triandos, Mike Macfarlane, and Lance Parrish), only Parrish had much gas left in the tank. Because Johnson's no-trade clause runs through 2004, the Rockies' best-case scenarios involve Johnson having a big bounceback season, or Closser being ready as soon as possible.

JAYSON NIX **2B** **Bats: R** **Throws: R** Born: 26-Aug-82 Age: 21

YEAR	TM	LG	AGE	AB	H	2B	3B	HR	BB	SO	SB	CS	AVG	OBP	SLG	MLVR	EQBA	EQOBP	EQSLG	EQMLVR	VORP	DEFENSE	
2001	CAS	PIO	18	153	45	10	1	5	21	43	1	5	.294	.385	.471	.162	.176	.241	.288	-.462	-22.7	39-SS	-4
2002	ASH	SAL	19	487	120	29	2	14	62	105	14	5	.246	.340	.400	.023	.172	.243	.287	-.461	-44.2	128-2B	-25
2003	VIS	CAL	20	562	158	46	0	21	54	131	24	8	.281	.351	.475	.123	.212	.270	.367	-.276	-17.3	135-2B	7
2004	COL	NL	21	286	62	15	1	8	24	70	5	2	.217	.284	.365	-.221	.209	.275	.349	-.277	-8.4	77-2B	-9

Breakout: 35% Improve: 58% Collapse: 23%

Laynce's younger brother had a breakthrough season of his own, tying Josh Barfield for the minor league-lead in doubles. Nix was also judged the best defensive second baseman in the Cal League, something supported by his performance statistically. In particular, he's got a strong arm and the lateral range to be a plus defender from here on out, and he hangs tough on the deuce. He's a lot more interesting as a prospect than that projection suggests.

GREG NORTON **PH** **Bats: B** **Throws: R** Born: 06-Jul-72 Age: 31

YEAR	TM	LG	AGE	AB	H	2B	3B	HR	BB	SO	SB	CS	AVG	OBP	SLG	MLVR	EQBA	EQOBP	EQSLG	EQMLVR	VORP	DEFENSE	
2001	COL	NL	29	225	60	13	2	13	19	65	1	0	.267	.321	.516	.024	.250	.306	.487	-.012	10.2	14-3B	-2
2002	COL	NL	30	168	37	8	1	7	24	52	2	3	.220	.314	.405	-.096	.208	.304	.387	-.186	-0.2	18-3B	-5
2003	COL	NL	31	179	47	15	0	6	16	47	2	1	.263	.325	.447	-.048	.251	.312	.430	-.081	5.4	27-3B	-6
2004	DET	AL	31	80	18	4	0	3	8	21	1	0	.224	.299	.385	-.148	.233	.312	.414	-.111	2.2	26-3B	-6

Breakout: 34% Improve: 48% Collapse: 40%

Norton had a particularly effective season as a pinch-hitter in 2003, going .324/.385/.606. As far as these things go, he had a good year in 2001, and a bad year in 2002 as a pinch-hitter, which means nothing besides pinch-hitting being a tough job, and it's hard to deliver consistently in the role. I wouldn't bet on Norton's success or failure one way or another, but he's a switch-hitter with pop who can handle both infield corners. He has his uses.

PABLO OZUNA **IF** **Bats: R** **Throws: R** Born: 25-Aug-74 Age: 29

YEAR	TM	LG	AGE	AB	H	2B	3B	HR	BB	SO	SB	CS	AVG	OBP	SLG	MLVR	EQBA	EQOBP	EQSLG	EQMLVR	VORP	DEFENSE			
2002	CLG	PCL	27	261	85	16	1	7	17	37	16	3	.326	.371	.475	.126	.278	.323	.412	-.064	8.9	39-2B	-5	12-RF	-2
2002	FLA	NL	27	47	13	2	2	0	1	3	1	1	.277	.300	.404	-.026	.292	.318	.417	-.054	0.8				
2003	COL	NL	28	40	8	1	0	0	2	6	3	0	.200	.273	.225	-.450	.200	.266	.200	-.519	-2.7				
2003	CSP	PCL	28	219	59	13	7	1	9	23	12	6	.269	.300	.406	-.108	.233	.266	.358	-.282	-6.8	17-2B	0	17-CF	-1
2003	TUL	TEX	28	59	15	3	0	0	2	5	4	2	.254	.279	.305	-.213	.220	.246	.271	-.454	-5.7				
2004	DET	AL	29	191	47	9	2	2	10	27	8	3	.248	.288	.354	-.191	.258	.301	.380	-.157	1.8	52-2B	-7		

Breakout: 35% Improve: 53% Collapse: 33%

Jose Ortiz may be one of the best-known AgeGate flops, but Ozuna isn't far behind. He did make our list as one of the game's top prospects once upon a time, after all. He can still make an adequate utility infielder, with enough speed to pinch-run and enough bat control to be a ball-in-play type of pinch-hitter. That's a lot less than anybody cares to remember.

JAY PAYTON **OF** **Bats: R** **Throws: R** Born: 22-Nov-72 Age: 31

YEAR	TM	LG	AGE	AB	H	2B	3B	HR	BB	SO	SB	CS	AVG	OBP	SLG	MLVR	EQBA	EQOBP	EQSLG	EQMLVR	VORP	DEFENSE			
2001	NYM	NL	28	361	92	16	1	8	18	52	4	3	.255	.298	.371	-.158	.264	.306	.387	-.143	0.5	93-CF	3		
2002	NYM	NL	29	275	78	6	3	8	21	34	4	1	.284	.336	.415	.057	.299	.347	.438	.035	13.2	67-CF	0		
2002	COL	NL	29	170	57	14	4	8	8	20	3	3	.335	.376	.606	.356	.318	.354	.582	.277	14.3	26-LF	1	13-CF	1
2003	COL	NL	30	600	181	32	5	28	43	77	6	4	.302	.354	.512	.111	.288	.340	.492	.090	19.7	142-LF	12		
2004	SDP	NL	31	434	121	23	3	12	31	59	5	3	.278	.330	.431	-.010	.285	.335	.453	.021	11.6	112-LF	6		

Breakout: 13% Improve: 36% Colapse: 32%

Upon being dealt by the Mets, Payton became a sort of anti-Hammonds. Not only did he have a good year in Coors, he had a plain old good year, hitting .281/.330/.483 on the road. As a result, after being non-tendered, he was one of the winter's better short-term fixes in center field. In a market where Randy Winn gets stupendously overpaid, it isn't a bad time to be on your own. The problem is whether everyone still remembers Hammonds or Jeff Cirillo or Fonzie Bichette for their squalid post-Coors careers, or if anyone remembers that Andres Galarraga, Eric Young, and even Vinny Castilla managed to be useful big league ballplayers after leaving Coors. The Pads signed him cheaply to fill their chasm in center; he'll be handy.

JORGE PIEDRA   **OF**   **Bats: L**   **Throws: L**   Born: 17-Apr-79   Age: 25

YEAR	TM	LG	AGE	AB	H	2B	3B	HR	BB	SO	SB	CS	AVG	OBP	SLG	MLVR	EQBA	EQOBP	EQSLG	EQMLVR	VORP	DEFENSE			
2001	WTN	SOU	22	441	108	26	6	8	37	80	12	5	.245	.310	.385	-.041	.221	.275	.354	-.278	-31.7	57-LF	-6	33-RF	-2
2002	WTN	SOU	23	60	10	3	1	0	3	11	2	0	.167	.219	.250	-.384	.164	.198	.262	-.591	-9.5	14-LF	0		
2002	SLM	CAR	23	392	118	37	12	13	37	55	10	2	.301	.366	.556	.341	.237	.294	.451	-.096	-5.0	58-LF	-2	41-RF	-3
2003	TUL	TEX	24	357	98	17	7	18	31	50	5	2	.275	.342	.513	.190	.231	.291	.444	-.116	-5.6	62-RF	0	14-LF	0
2004	COL	NL	25	232	62	14	2	9	19	37	3	1	.267	.330	.471	.035	.258	.319	.451	-.031	6.0	64-RF	-1		

Breakout: 41%   Improve: 59%   Collapse: 20%

Piedra has flirted with prospect status for years, showing promise in the Dodgers' organization before scuffling with the Cubs. Claimed on waivers by the Rockies, 2003 was a make-or-break year, and Piedra responded by finally proving he could handle Double-A. Prospect-wise, he doesn't get talked up in nearly the way that the guy in the next player comment has been, but he's shown more power and better command of the strike zone at each level at the same age that Reyes has. That may be damning with faint praise, but Piedra has some actual promise.

RENE REYES   **OF**   **Bats: B**   **Throws: R**   Born: 21-Feb-78   Age: 26

YEAR	TM	LG	AGE	AB	H	2B	3B	HR	BB	SO	SB	CS	AVG	OBP	SLG	MLVR	EQBA	EQOBP	EQSLG	EQMLVR	VORP	DEFENSE			
2001	ASH	SAL	23	484	156	27	2	11	28	80	53	12	.322	.371	.455	.209	.246	.286	.354	-.241	-26.0	59-RF	-7	57-1B	1
2002	CAR	SOU	24	455	133	33	4	14	29	69	10	11	.292	.339	.475	.172	.256	.290	.430	-.117	-7.0	46-RF	-6	37-1B	1
2003	CSP	PCL	25	370	127	23	3	6	22	56	12	8	.343	.380	.470	.173	.296	.335	.412	-.027	3.0	33-LF	-1	27-RF	-1
2003	COL	NL	25	116	30	7	1	2	5	19	2	1	.259	.287	.388	-.190	.250	.281	.371	-.223	-3.7	21-RF	-1		
2004	COL	NL	26	276	75	17	2	8	19	47	6	3	.272	.323	.431	-.026	.262	.313	.413	-.089	2.3	74-RF	-3		

Breakout: 32%   Improve: 55%   Collapse: 29%

Almost laughably overrated. Although Reyes has a good arm for right field, he doesn't have nearly enough of a bat to be a regular in an outfield corner, and he's not young enough to come up with it. For whatever reason, spray hitters in Coors just don't seem to derive a major benefit from the park, so there's not a lot of reason to think Reyes is about to break out. More power from the left side of the plate makes him a decent option as a fourth outfielder. Even Marvell Wynne had his moments, and that's the sort of ambition that should be nurtured for Reyes.

CHRIS RICHARD   **Bad Idea**   **Bats: L**   **Throws: L**   Born: 07-Jun-74   Age: 30

YEAR	TM	LG	AGE	AB	H	2B	3B	HR	BB	SO	SB	CS	AVG	OBP	SLG	MLVR	EQBA	EQOBP	EQSLG	EQMLVR	VORP	DEFENSE			
2001	BAL	AL	27	483	128	31	3	15	45	100	11	9	.265	.335	.435	.028	.290	.361	.478	.108	22.4	65-RF	1	34-CF	0
2002	BAL	AL	28	155	36	11	0	4	12	30	0	3	.232	.292	.381	-.129	.261	.320	.433	-.054	3.0				
2003	COL	NL	29	27	6	1	1	1	3	6	0	1	.222	.300	.444	-.119	.222	.300	.407	-.157	-0.3				
2004	COL	NL	30	217	58	13	2	9	25	46	2	2	.265	.348	.470	.061	.256	.337	.449	-.004	8.9	61-DH	3		

Breakout: 33%   Improve: 47%   Collapse: 33%

Richard will be lucky to get to 200 plate appearances, as he re-injured his shoulder in October. It wasn't a good idea to acquire him in the first place, let alone part with Jack Cust to get him. Now that he's a free agent with a bum wing, he may be done.

JEFF SALAZAR   **CF**   **Bats: L**   **Throws: L**   Born: 24-Nov-80   Age: 23

YEAR	TM	LG	AGE	AB	H	2B	3B	HR	BB	SO	SB	CS	AVG	OBP	SLG	MLVR	EQBA	EQOBP	EQSLG	EQMLVR	VORP	DEFENSE	
2002	TRI	NWN	21	268	63	5	4	4	47	43	10	6	.235	.351	.328	.046	.180	.261	.260	-.457	-50.7	71-CF	-5
2003	ASH	SAL	22	486	138	23	4	29	77	74	28	14	.284	.387	.527	.271	.192	.271	.363	-.292	-22.7	126-CF	0
2004	COL	NL	23	228	49	10	2	6	24	43	4	2	.215	.293	.353	-.219	.207	.284	.338	-.275	-12.0	64-CF	-5

Breakout: 45%   Improve: 65%   Collapse: 24%

Drafted out of Oklahoma State in 2002 as a contact hitter and defensive virtuoso, Salazar looks like more of a power prospect because of Asheville's short porch in right than he looks likely to become. He totaled 20 home runs at the juco and college levels. He led the entire minors in runs scored, and the Sally League in homers. He's going to have to move up the chain quickly to earn consideration as a worthwhile prospect, but he's surprised people so far.

RYAN SHEALY 1B   Bats: R   Throws: R   Born: 29-Aug-79   Age: 24

YEAR	TM	LG	AGE	AB	H	2B	3B	HR	BB	SO	SB	CS	AVG	OBP	SLG	MLVR	EQBA	EQOBP	EQSLG	EQMLVR	VORP	DEFENSE	
2002	CAS	PIO	22	231	85	21	1	19	50	52	0	0	.368	.497	.714	.730	.204	.304	.400	-.171	-12.3	65-1B	0
2003	VIS	CAL	23	341	102	31	1	14	42	72	0	0	.299	.391	.519	.261	.222	.299	.389	-.183	-10.6	76-1B	-7
2004	COL	NL	24	245	60	15	1	11	26	62	0	1	.242	.329	.448	-.018	.234	.318	.428	-.080	1.5	69-1B	-4

Breakout: 45%   Improve: 64%   Collapse: 14%

An understated variation on the problem confronting Hawpe. Shealy is a college hitter moving up slowly, but he's an even more dubious proposition at any position other than first than Hawpe is. Between the unlikelihood that he's going to get a shot at the big league job at first, and his need to progress quickly, Shealy is going to have to make an easy ascent into Double-A to really make himself a trade-worthy commodity. An injured knee slowed him up last year, and he can't afford those sorts of things if he wants a shot at a solid career.

IAN STEWART 3B   Bats: L   Throws: R   Born: 05-Apr-85   Age: 19

YEAR	TM	LG	AGE	AB	H	2B	3B	HR	BB	SO	SB	CS	AVG	OBP	SLG	MLVR	EQBA	EQOBP	EQSLG	EQMLVR	VORP	DEFENSE	
2003	CAS	PIO	18	224	71	14	5	10	29	54	4	1	.317	.401	.558	.327	.189	.253	.342	-.357	-22.5	51-3B	-7
2004	COL	NL	19	268	56	14	3	7	23	76	2	1	.209	.274	.362	-.246	.202	.266	.346	-.302	-7.9	72-3B	-10

Breakout: 37%   Improve: 64%   Collapse: 17%

The Rockies' first-rounder from the 2003 draft signed for nearly $2 million, after which he showed off his jaw-dropping power in the Pioneer League. Defensive expectations for him are modest, but there is confidence that Stewart can stick at third. He lacks Jeff Baker's athleticism, and neither player can go to first base with Todd Helton under contract through 2011. So long-term, Stewart will probably get third by default, while Baker moves to the outfield or perhaps second. Stewart is expected to move through the system quickly; a dominant hitter in California high schools can make quick progress.

CHRIS STYNES UT   Bats: R   Throws: R   Born: 19-Jan-73   Age: 31

YEAR	TM	LG	AGE	AB	H	2B	3B	HR	BB	SO	SB	CS	AVG	OBP	SLG	MLVR	EQBA	EQOBP	EQSLG	EQMLVR	VORP	DEFENSE			
2001	BOS	AL	28	361	101	19	2	8	20	56	4	5	.280	.322	.410	-.035	.296	.338	.439	.018	18.0	40-3B	-3	40-2B	0
2002	CHC	NL	29	195	47	9	1	5	21	29	1	1	.241	.314	.374	-.071	.256	.327	.402	-.088	4.8	28-3B	-4	12-2B	2
2003	COL	NL	30	443	113	31	3	11	48	76	3	1	.255	.335	.413	-.080	.242	.322	.398	-.113	6.1	109-3B	0		
2004	PIT	NL	31	301	76	17	2	6	27	50	2	2	.251	.319	.379	-.118	.254	.319	.393	-.110	8.7	81-3B	-3		

Breakout: 18%   Improve: 43%   Collapse: 31%

It's strange for a player to not actually play all that well, expressing some hostility to the fourth estate, and still get talked up as the sort of guy teams want, but the game's funny in its injustices. Now that he's a Pirate, he should be locked in as their Opening Day third baseman. Everyone who covets Stynes sees a gamer who hit .334 as a near-regular in 2000, and everyone who gets him finds a tweener who can't play second as well as they'd like or hit well enough to handle third on any regular basis. As a utility man, he has value, but everyone keeps expecting more and getting less.

CORY SULLIVAN CF   Bats: L   Throws: L   Born: 20-Aug-79   Age: 24

YEAR	TM	LG	AGE	AB	H	2B	3B	HR	BB	SO	SB	CS	AVG	OBP	SLG	MLVR	EQBA	EQOBP	EQSLG	EQMLVR	VORP	DEFENSE			
2001	ASH	SAL	21	258	71	12	1	5	25	56	13	9	.275	.344	.388	.059	.201	.257	.288	-.417	-22.1	45-CF	-4	24-LF	0
2002	SLM	CAR	22	560	161	42	6	12	36	70	26	5	.287	.340	.448	.151	.239	.282	.390	-.202	-9.2	79-CF	-6	36-RF	-1
2003	TUL	TEX	23	557	167	34	8	5	39	83	17	13	.300	.347	.417	.089	.256	.301	.369	-.184	-6.2	132-CF	-6		
2004	COL	NL	24	239	63	14	2	6	18	40	5	2	.263	.317	.410	-.072	.254	.307	.392	-.133	-0.3	65-CF	-6		

Breakout: 37%   Improve: 54%   Collapse: 23%

Sullivan has an outside shot at a big league job in 2004, primarily because of his defensive reputation and strong arm in center. As a hitter, he'll have his moments, but he didn't do much against lefties, and he doesn't get on base enough to make a great regular. But he does do the things that can catch an eye in camp: a couple of good defensive plays, a hard-hit liner or two, and he could stick. He's not especially young, so he'll need to make that sort of impression.

MARK SWEENEY   **PH**   **Bats: L**   **Throws: L**   Born: 26-Oct-69   Age: 34

YEAR	TM	LG	AGE	AB	H	2B	3B	HR	BB	SO	SB	CS	AVG	OBP	SLG	MLVR	EQBA	EQOBP	EQSLG	EQMLVR	VORP	DEFENSE	
2001	IND	INT	31	404	116	34	1	6	56	71	3	1	.287	.373	.421	.114	.266	.350	.395	-.047	0.9	44-LF	-1
2001	MIL	NL	31	89	23	3	1	3	12	23	2	1	.258	.347	.416	-.019	.256	.343	.422	-.031	0.6	13-LF	0
2002	SDP	NL	32	65	11	3	0	1	4	19	0	0	.169	.217	.262	-.423	.185	.232	.308	-.448	-5.4		
2003	CSP	PCL	33	165	49	10	1	5	34	32	1	4	.297	.407	.461	.161	.238	.352	.372	-.094	-1.6	23-RF	0
2003	COL	NL	33	97	25	9	0	2	9	27	0	1	.258	.321	.412	-.102	.247	.305	.392	-.150	-0.1		
2004	*COL*	*NL*	*34*	*106*	*26*	*6*	*0*	*3*	*14*	*26*	*0*	*0*	*.247*	*.338*	*.390*	*-.072*	*.238*	*.328*	*.373*	*-.131*	*0.4*	*33-RF*	*-4*

Breakout: 36%   *Improve: 45%*   *Collapse: 33%*

Even Greg Gross ran out of steam after a while. Sweeney's heyday as one of the game's best pinch-hitters was during the last presidential administration. He can drift into fifth-outfielder jobs for another year or two, but a career as a hitting coach awaits.

JUAN URIBE   **SS**   **Bats: R**   **Throws: R**   Born: 22-Jul-79   Age: 24

YEAR	TM	LG	AGE	AB	H	2B	3B	HR	BB	SO	SB	CS	AVG	OBP	SLG	MLVR	EQBA	EQOBP	EQSLG	EQMLVR	VORP	DEFENSE			
2001	CSP	PCL	21	281	87	27	7	7	12	43	11	8	.310	.340	.530	.115	.258	.292	.447	-.087	9.6	73-SS	2		
2001	COL	NL	21	273	82	14	11	8	8	55	3	0	.300	.325	.520	.069	.284	.309	.491	.031	16.4	67-SS	0		
2002	COL	NL	22	566	136	25	7	6	34	120	9	2	.240	.286	.341	-.212	.231	.277	.332	-.299	-14.0	150-SS	20		
2003	COL	NL	23	316	80	19	3	10	17	60	7	2	.253	.297	.427	-.126	.241	.285	.410	-.167	2.7	73-SS	8	11-2B	2
2004	*CWS*	*AL*	*24*	*423*	*110*	*22*	*3*	*12*	*22*	*74*	*10*	*3*	*.259*	*.300*	*.415*	*-.084*	*.264*	*.307*	*.417*	*-.092*	*13.9*	*108-SS*	*4*		

Breakout: 28%   *Improve: 56%*   *Collapse: 19%*

The organization kept getting annoyed with Uribe for what he was not. He failed to improve much after his debut, and despite repeated trials, he was never going to be useful at the top of the order. As good as he is defensively, he was stiff after missing the first two months with a stress fracture in his foot, making a few more errors than they considered acceptable. Still, the Rockies overreacted. Although he's offensively Neifi-riffic, Uribe is still young enough to be useful, and he plays an outstanding short. Between his glovework and the fact that he can bunt better than his new manager ever could, he could wind up getting a good chunk of playing time at Joe Crede's expense if Crede doesn't improve. Jose Valentin would slip over to third in that case. At the very least, Uribe makes for a nice bit of insurance and a good utility infielder for a team in win-now mode.

LARRY WALKER   **RF**   **Bats:**   **Throws:**   Born: 01-Dec-66   Age: 37

YEAR	TM	LG	AGE	AB	H	2B	3B	HR	BB	SO	SB	CS	AVG	OBP	SLG	MLVR	EQBA	EQOBP	EQSLG	EQMLVR	VORP	DEFENSE	
2001	COL	NL	34	497	174	35	3	38	82	103	14	5	.350	.449	.662	.504	.329	.433	.623	.467	76.7	122-RF	4
2002	COL	NL	35	477	161	40	4	26	65	73	6	5	.338	.421	.602	.411	.320	.405	.575	.348	54.4	116-RF	9
2003	COL	NL	36	454	129	25	7	16	98	87	7	4	.284	.422	.476	.156	.267	.404	.453	.130	24.1	122-RF	-5
2004	*COL*	*NL*	*37*	*378*	*112*	*22*	*2*	*19*	*60*	*70*	*6*	*3*	*.296*	*.398*	*.517*	*.228*	*.286*	*.385*	*.495*	*.160*	*25.5*	*106-RF*	*-1*

Breakout: 12%   *Improve: 48%*   *Collapse: 27%*

It's hard to separate out what value may be left in Walker's career, between the injuries and the park effect. His spiking walk rate isn't automatically a positive sign, since it can just as easily be interpreted as another indicator of slowing reflexes. He's not the glove he used to be, or the baserunner. This past season, he was playing with a bad knee and shoulder, sapping his power; he had both fixed in the off-season. Even if he wasn't already a relatively fragile player, he's at the age where something is always going to be wrong. He makes a nice supporting cast member on a team that wants to win now, as in right now, but he's nearly untradable. Walker has been a hell of a player, but he's close to the end.

PRESTON WILSON   **CF**   **Bats: R**   **Throws: R**   Born: 19-Jul-74   Age: 29

YEAR	TM	LG	AGE	AB	H	2B	3B	HR	BB	SO	SB	CS	AVG	OBP	SLG	MLVR	EQBA	EQOBP	EQSLG	EQMLVR	VORP	DEFENSE	
2001	FLA	NL	26	468	128	30	2	23	36	107	20	8	.274	.331	.494	.091	.281	.338	.509	.104	32.4	121-CF	5
2002	FLA	NL	27	510	124	22	2	23	58	140	20	11	.243	.329	.429	.031	.255	.335	.457	.002	20.3	128-CF	-13
2003	COL	NL	28	600	169	43	1	36	54	139	14	7	.282	.343	.537	.111	.266	.329	.512	.078	33.2	151-CF	-12
2004	*COL*	*NL*	*29*	*508*	*142*	*31*	*2*	*30*	*53*	*122*	*12*	*4*	*.279*	*.351*	*.529*	*.157*	*.270*	*.340*	*.506*	*.088*	*25.1*	*134-CF*	*-6*

Breakout: 32%   *Improve: 58%*   *Collapse: 11%*

Sure enough, Wilson got to Coors, his strikeout rate went down, his rate stats went up, and his power got a proportionate spike. A weak finish undermined the overall look of his year, but Wilson was an unholy terror early on. Beyond all

(continued next page)

Preston Wilson *(continued)*

of that, though, keep in mind, he's still Preston Wilson, the guy who hit .260/.316/.479 on the road. He's not without value, but he's losing his ability to handle center. He can also be something of a horse's ass on the subject of coming out of the lineup if he's dinged up, which is only going to get worse if somebody doesn't address the issue.

GREGG ZAUN

GREGG ZAUN — C — Bats: B — Throws: R — Born: 14-Apr-71 — Age: 33

YEAR	TM	LG	AGE	AB	H	2B	3B	HR	BB	SO	SB	CS	AVG	OBP	SLG	MLVR	EQBA	EQOBP	EQSLG	EQMLVR	VORP	DEFENSE
2001	KCR	AL	30	125	40	9	0	6	12	16	1	2	.320	.377	.536	.245	.323	.387	.540	.274	14.8	32-C -2
2002	HOU	NL	31	185	41	7	1	3	12	36	1	0	.222	.275	.319	-.246	.225	.274	.332	-.309	-6.4	41-C -10
2003	HOU	NL	32	120	26	7	0	1	14	14	1	0	.217	.299	.300	-.261	.215	.300	.306	-.298	-3.2	24-C -5
2003	COL	NL	32	46	12	1	0	3	5	7	0	1	.261	.333	.478	.004	.239	.314	.457	-.049	1.3	12-C -2
2004	MON	NL	33	150	41	8	1	4	16	22	1	1	.271	.344	.417	-.010	.255	.326	.385	-.107	3.2	44-C 4

Breakout: 44%   Improve: 67%   Collapse: 23%

At this point, Zaun is getting to the point that he's outlasted the legend of his usefulness, even among stathead circles. He's not a great catcher, he seems to have a way with annoying his teams, and he's a couple of years removed from what you might consider his "Junior Ortiz year" in 2001. He'll back up Brian Schneider, and try not to annoy Frank Robinson.

PITCHERS

ADAM BERNERO

ADAM BERNERO — Bats: R — Throws: R — Born: 28-Nov-76 — Age: 27

YEAR	TM	LG	AGE	G	GS	IP	H	BB	SO	HR	ERA	EQERA	EQH9	EQBB9	EQSO9	EQHR9	PERA	VORP	STF
2001	TOL	INT	24	26	25	140.3	172	54	99	13	5.13	6.31	11.3	4.0	4.9	1.1	5.93	-10.5	-10
2001	DET	AL	24	5	0	12.3	13	4	8	4	7.32	7.30	8.8	2.9	5.1	2.9	6.64	-2.3	-46
2002	TOL	INT	25	9	9	57.0	46	13	49	2	1.58	2.87	7.8	2.4	6.4	0.5	3.24	16.2	31
2002	DET	AL	25	28	11	101.7	128	31	69	17	6.19	5.65	10.6	2.5	5.7	1.3	5.49	-0.6	-7
2003	DET	AL	26	18	17	100.7	104	41	54	14	6.08	5.03	8.8	3.5	4.8	1.1	4.67	-4.1	-4
2003	COL	NL	26	31	0	32.7	33	13	26	5	5.23	4.78	8.7	3.1	6.2	1.1	4.52	0.9	-8
2004	COL	NL	27	29	13	79.7	92	34	52	13	5.75	5.44	10.1	3.3	5.4	1.2	5.29	3.6	-7

Breakout: 20%   Improve: 45%   Collapse: 29%

Acquired by the Rockies for Ben Petrick in an exchange of sources of disgust, Bernero was deposited in the Rockies pen for lack of any other idea of what to do with him. He flirted with usefulness early on, but then the league caught up to his assortment of junk, and there's little reason to expect him to be anything more than a (f)utility pitcher—apologies to Jay Jaffe—especially now that Nelson Cruz is out of the way.

KIP BOUKNIGHT

KIP BOUKNIGHT — Bats: R — Throws: R — Born: 16-Nov-78 — Age: 25

YEAR	TM	LG	AGE	G	GS	IP	H	BB	SO	HR	ERA	EQERA	EQH9	EQBB9	EQSO9	EQHR9	PERA	VORP	STF
2001	TRI	NWN	22	15	15	81.0	69	19	86	3	2.78	5.14	11.2	3.2	5.1	1.0	5.62	3.6	0
2002	SLM	CAR	23	27	27	166.7	156	48	120	13	3.35	5.72	10.8	3.6	4.5	1.8	6.45	-2.0	-24
2003	TUL	TEX	24	26	26	158.3	153	57	101	16	4.04	5.75	10.3	4.2	4.3	1.9	6.49	-2.4	-33
2004	COL	NL	25	15	11	58.0	72	29	34	11	6.57	6.22	11.0	3.9	4.9	1.4	6.17	-0.2	-12

Breakout: 24%   Improve: 53%   Collapse: 24%

As much as it's easy to like a savvy college pitcher with storied amateur accomplishments, solid command, and no appreciable platoon split, let's be clear: Bouknight is no more of a prospect than Kennie Steenstra was. Solid rotation regulars for your minor league affiliates have value to an organization, and Bouknight might either sneak up and stick as a reliever, or fill in on some injury-riddled big league staff someday. At this point, there's no reason to get wild about his future.

SHAWN CHACON

SHAWN CHACON — Bats: R — Throws: R — Born: 23-Dec-77 — Age: 26

YEAR	TM	LG	AGE	G	GS	IP	H	BB	SO	HR	ERA	EQERA	EQH9	EQBB9	EQSO9	EQHR9	PERA	VORP	STF
2001	CSP	PCL	23	4	4	24.0	18	7	28	3	2.25	2.35	6.3	3.1	7.8	1.2	3.41	8.3	35
2001	COL	NL	23	27	27	160.0	157	87	134	26	5.06	4.74	8.8	4.5	6.3	1.2	5.04	14.9	15
2002	CSP	PCL	24	4	4	20.7	23	10	15	3	4.78	4.50	9.0	4.9	4.9	1.4	5.45	2.4	-12
2002	COL	NL	24	21	21	119.3	122	60	67	25	5.73	5.59	9.1	4.0	4.3	1.8	5.72	0.1	-17
2003	COL	NL	25	23	23	137.0	124	58	93	12	4.60	3.88	7.6	3.3	5.3	0.7	3.70	21.0	16
2004	COL	NL	26	25	21	126.7	130	56	87	19	5.14	4.87	9.0	3.5	5.7	1.1	4.73	12.4	3

Breakout: 17%   Improve: 44%   Collapse: 20%

Chacon's elbow is enough of a source of concern that you have to wonder if the move to the pen will be enough to preserve him. Although O'Dowd would probably consider the virtues of trading his pets every six months, it says a lot that they were entertaining offers in November, right up to the winter meetings. Perhaps it's just as well; using Michael Wolverton's Support-Neutral stats, Chacon's performance earned him the rating as the majors' flakiest starter, and he got a good amount of help from the Rockies' pen. Chacon has the talent to be a major asset as a reliever, and he seems enthusiastic about it. Hopefully, he'll be able to sustain a multi-inning role, allowing the Rox to turn to the bullpen earlier in games, which could help them break in some of their young starters.

AARON COOK

Bats: R   **Throws: R**   Born: 08-Feb-79   Age: 25

YEAR	TM	LG	AGE	G	GS	IP	H	BB	SO	HR	ERA	EQERA	EQH9	EQBB9	EQSO9	EQHR9	PERA	VORP	STF
2001	SLM	CAR	22	27	27	155.0	157	38	122	4	3.08	5.80	10.7	3.2	4.3	0.6	4.91	-3.1	7
2002	CAR	SOU	23	14	14	95.0	73	19	58	4	1.42	2.77	7.8	2.0	3.9	0.7	3.39	27.6	17
2002	CSP	PCL	23	10	10	64.3	67	18	32	6	3.78	3.94	7.6	2.7	3.4	0.8	3.64	11.8	7
2002	COL	NL	23	9	5	35.7	41	13	14	4	4.54	4.46	10.2	2.9	3.1	1.0	5.15	4.3	-6
2003	COL	NL	24	43	16	124.0	160	57	43	8	6.02	5.52	10.8	3.7	2.7	0.5	5.07	-1.3	-11
2003	CSP	PCL	24	2	2	16.0	10	4	12	2	2.25	2.40	5.4	2.4	6.0	1.8	3.44	5.3	6
2004	*COL*	*NL*	*25*	*27*	*16*	*91.3*	*108*	*39*	*43*	*10*	*5.18*	*4.91*	*10.3*	*3.4*	*3.9*	*0.8*	*5.00*	*6.8*	*-12*

Breakout: 20%   *Improve: 50%*   *Collapse: 20%*

After all of the talk about how much Cook had learned command in 2002 during his work with Bob McClure in Triple-A, it didn't translate into anything resembling big league success in 2003. He had trouble with his sinker not sinking in the majors, which left him struggling with the question that has always plagued him: What good is a flat fastball, even if it is in the high 90s? He can overpower the occasional right-handed hitter with it, and still generates a lot of groundball outs, but he doesn't fool anybody, as last year's road ERA of 5.57 made clear. Whether he's ever going to be ironed out is anybody's guess, but it doesn't look good.

BEN CROCKETT

Bats: R   **Throws: R**   Born: 19-Dec-79   Age: 24

YEAR	TM	LG	AGE	G	GS	IP	H	BB	SO	HR	ERA	EQERA	EQH9	EQBB9	EQSO9	EQHR9	PERA	VORP	STF
2002	ASH	SAL	22	6	6	29.3	51	6	18	4	7.37	10.04	18.7	2.4	3.1	3.1	11.44	-12.8	-80
2002	TRI	NWN	22	7	6	25.0	26	3	21	2	2.88	6.00	14.6	1.7	4.3	2.6	8.71	-0.9	-48
2003	ASH	SAL	23	23	23	151.7	152	32	117	11	2.49	5.22	12.5	2.6	4.3	1.9	7.06	5.5	-27
2003	VIS	CAL	23	5	5	32.0	35	7	26	5	4.50	6.59	12.2	2.8	4.7	3.1	8.64	-3.2	-57
2004	*COL*	*NL*	*24*	*19*	*12*	*68.0*	*93*	*26*	*39*	*19*	*7.40*	*7.01*	*12.0*	*3.0*	*4.7*	*2.0*	*6.87*	*-4.9*	*-16*

Breakout: 13%   *Improve: 44%*   *Collapse: 18%*

You can't blame us if we say this is our sort of guy. Crockett throws in the low 90s, but came out of Harvard (better known as the University of Chicago of the East) with an economics degree. He's articulate and particularly forthright about trying to manage his workload in-game, having already earned a reputation for durability. He's not quite old enough to have that rep for keeps, but he's survived so far.

NELSON CRUZ

Bats: R   **Throws: R**   Born: 13-Sep-72   Age: 31

YEAR	TM	LG	AGE	G	GS	IP	H	BB	SO	HR	ERA	EQERA	EQH9	EQBB9	EQSO9	EQHR9	PERA	VORP	STF
2001	HOU	NL	28	66	0	82.3	72	24	75	11	4.16	3.99	8.0	2.4	6.9	1.0	3.85	14.1	5
2002	HOU	NL	29	43	5	78.3	90	29	61	12	4.48	5.19	10.1	2.9	6.0	1.3	5.34	3.5	-14
2003	COL	NL	30	20	7	53.7	65	11	38	15	7.21	5.98	10.3	1.7	5.6	2.2	6.14	-4.6	-34
2003	CSP	PCL	30	4	4	15.0	24	3	10	3	7.20	9.00	15.4	1.9	5.1	2.6	9.12	-5.3	-71
2004	*COL*	*NL*	*31*	*26*	*11*	*70.3*	*75*	*20*	*49*	*12*	*4.88*	*4.62*	*9.4*	*2.2*	*5.8*	*1.2*	*4.48*	*8.4*	*0*

Breakout: 16%   *Improve: 45%*   *Collapse: 28%*

People with a certain amount of big league playing time have to get comments, but Cruz is just an 11th pitcher holding onto the dream of becoming a 10th pitcher, with the concomitant job security that might bring. It's a little like wishing you had the choice spot in the trailer park, non-optional delusions of grandeur included. Cut in early September after ditching his rehab assignment, he now has a rep as a crank to overcome as well, so he might need a stint in the Atlantic League to get somebody interested.

SCOTT DOHMANN   Bats: R   Throws: R   Born: 13-Feb-78   Age: 26

YEAR	TM	LG	AGE	G	GS	IP	H	BB	SO	HR	ERA	EQERA	EQH9	EQBB9	EQSO9	EQHR9	PERA	VORP	STF
2001	ASH	SAL	23	28	28	173.0	165	33	154	27	4.32	5.98	12.9	2.7	4.6	3.6	9.51	-6.2	-70
2002	SLM	CAR	24	28	28	170.3	149	53	131	22	4.23	6.13	11.3	4.0	4.9	3.2	8.49	-8.6	-68
2003	TUL	TEX	25	50	4	93.7	94	29	102	11	4.13	5.68	11.9	3.7	7.4	2.3	7.52	-0.7	-48
2004	COL	NL	26	10	6	36.0	40	15	29	7	5.45	5.16	9.7	3.2	6.7	1.3	5.12	2.3	3

Breakout: 34%   Improve: 66%   Collapse: 19%

Dohmann has struggled as a starting pitcher since being drafted out of college, and didn't exactly have the sort of stuff that made you think he'd work it out: He's a big-time flyball pitcher, relying heavily on an occasionally effective slider, and that was sort of it. The Rockies finally came to terms with that, moving him to the pen in Tulsa, where he thrived, striking out 88 hitters in 74 IP. He also picked up a couple of ticks on the gun.

SCOTT ELARTON   Bats: R   Throws: R   Born: 23-Feb-76   Age: 28

YEAR	TM	LG	AGE	G	GS	IP	H	BB	SO	HR	ERA	EQERA	EQH9	EQBB9	EQSO9	EQHR9	PERA	VORP	STF
2001	HOU	NL	25	20	20	109.7	126	49	76	26	7.14	6.52	10.2	3.7	5.2	1.9	6.27	-10.9	-25
2001	COL	NL	25	4	4	23.0	20	10	11	8	6.65	5.64	7.3	3.6	3.6	2.4	5.50	-0.1	-40
2001	CSP	PCL	25	2	2	7.7	14	0	8	2	7.01	7.36	16.0	1.2	6.1	2.5	9.01	-1.4	-49
2003	CSP	PCL	27	20	20	118.7	146	39	92	15	5.31	5.66	11.6	3.5	5.9	1.6	6.52	-0.7	-23
2003	COL	NL	27	11	10	51.7	73	20	20	13	6.27	7.06	11.8	3.0	3.0	2.1	7.20	-8.5	-53
2004	COL	NL	28	19	15	86.0	108	38	47	19	6.51	6.16	11.0	3.4	4.6	1.6	6.23	-0.7	-12

Breakout: 20%   Improve: 39%   Collapse: 32%

One of hundreds of potential poster children for the prospect maven's mantra of TINSTAAPP: There Is No Such Thing As A Pitching Prospect. Like any bit of reductionism, you can take that seriously to an absurd degree, but Elarton was somebody everybody was high on, and one scragged shoulder later, he's as memorable as David Nied. Non-tendered but weighing a choice to re-sign with the Rockies on a minor league contract, he'd be better off taking his chances trying to land in somebody else's bullpen.

MICHAEL ESPOSITO   Bats: R   Throws: R   Born: 27-Sep-81   Age: 22

YEAR	TM	LG	AGE	G	GS	IP	H	BB	SO	HR	ERA	EQERA	EQH9	EQBB9	EQSO9	EQHR9	PERA	VORP	STF
2003	VIS	CAL	21	27	27	161.0	173	55	116	14	3.75	6.07	10.9	4.2	4.2	1.6	6.40	-7.7	-11
2004	COL	NL	22	16	11	62.3	79	32	36	14	7.02	6.65	11.2	4.0	4.7	1.6	6.56	-1.5	-16

Breakout: 14%   Improve: 53%   Collapse: 24%

A short sinkerball pitcher picked out of Arizona State in 2002, Esposito thrives on command and changing speeds. He had his elbow Tommy John'd in college and had some soreness before being drafted, which got him dropped him to the 12th round. The Rockies tweaked his delivery, and the expectation is that he'll be mechanically sound from here on out. He won't show up in 2004, but if he makes the jump to Double-A, he'll force his way onto the 40-man for '05, at which point anything could happen.

RANDY FLORES   Bats: L   Throws: L   Born: 31-Jul-75   Age: 28

YEAR	TM	LG	AGE	G	GS	IP	H	BB	SO	HR	ERA	EQERA	EQH9	EQBB9	EQSO9	EQHR9	PERA	VORP	STF
2001	NRW	EAS	25	25	25	158.7	156	63	115	13	2.78	5.12	10.9	4.9	4.5	1.3	6.23	7.5	-25
2002	OKL	PCL	26	15	0	20.3	22	5	16	1	5.76	5.12	9.8	2.3	5.1	0.5	4.13	1.0	-2
2002	TEX	AL	26	20	0	12.0	11	8	7	2	4.50	4.50	7.5	5.2	5.2	1.5	5.00	1.5	-29
2002	CSP	PCL	26	7	7	35.7	36	18	27	1	3.28	3.37	8.3	4.9	4.9	0.3	4.00	8.6	10
2002	COL	NL	26	8	2	17.0	29	8	7	5	9.53	9.18	15.1	3.8	3.2	2.7	9.64	-6.6	-88
2003	CSP	PCL	27	28	24	142.7	156	67	116	16	4.98	5.20	10.3	5.0	6.2	1.4	6.09	5.9	-22
2004	STL	NL	28	16	9	50.7	53	31	38	6	5.44	5.94	9.4	4.9	6.0	1.2	5.97	0.5	-9

Breakout: 27%   Improve: 50%   Collapse: 31%

Although it's been a long road for the former USC star, Flores is useful. To be sure, he's a journeyman, but he's pretty good at keeping the ball on the ground, posting better than a 2–1 groundball/flyball out ratio last year, and he's good against lefties. He could be a situational lefty and spot starter against teams reliant on lefties in their lineup. Of course, if the Rockies are hauling in people like Bernero or Cruz, who isn't potentially useful to them? Now a Cardinal, he could be the man who gets Lance Painter out of their system.

JEFF FRANCIS Bats: L Throws: L Born: 08-Jan-81 Age: 23

YEAR	TM	LG	AGE	G	GS	IP	H	BB	SO	HR	ERA	EQERA	EQH9	EQBB9	EQSO9	EQHR9	PERA	VORP	STF
2002	TRI	NWN	21	4	3	10.7	5	4	16	0	0.00	1.00	8.0	5.0	8.0	0.0	3.59	4.6	46
2002	ASH	SAL	21	4	4	20.0	16	4	23	2	1.80	3.57	9.7	2.5	6.1	2.0	5.86	4.0	0
2003	VIS	CAL	22	27	27	160.7	135	45	153	8	3.47	4.35	8.7	3.4	5.6	0.9	4.40	20.4	15
2004	COL	NL	23	18	14	83.7	88	36	65	12	4.99	4.73	9.2	3.3	6.4	1.0	4.66	9.5	7

Breakout: 18%   Improve: 44%   Collapse: 25%

The touted Stanford product struggled initially in his first full season, but Francis was red-hot in the second half, tearing up the Cal League with a 1.91 ERA over his last 15 starts. Although there's some fretting about his stamina, he has good velocity for a lefty, sound mechanics, changes speeds effortlessly, and possesses outstanding command. If any of the young guns in the organization don't thrive in their spots in the big league rotation—and let's face it, they're pitching in Coors, so some won't—Francis should make his big league debut no later than August.

BRIAN FUENTES Bats: L Throws: L Born: 09-Aug-75 Age: 28

YEAR	TM	LG	AGE	G	GS	IP	H	BB	SO	HR	ERA	EQERA	EQH9	EQBB9	EQSO9	EQHR9	PERA	VORP	STF
2001	TAC	PCL	25	35	0	52.0	35	25	70	4	2.94	3.80	7.4	5.3	9.1	1.0	4.32	9.5	7
2001	SEA	AL	25	10	0	11.7	6	8	10	2	4.62	4.09	5.7	5.7	7.4	1.6	4.41	1.8	-11
2002	CSP	PCL	26	41	0	48.7	44	32	61	0	3.70	3.72	8.4	6.7	8.4	0.2	4.39	9.6	11
2002	COL	NL	26	31	0	26.7	25	13	38	4	4.72	4.50	9.0	3.8	11.1	1.4	5.03	3.2	13
2003	COL	NL	27	75	0	75.3	64	34	82	7	2.75	2.92	7.4	3.6	8.5	0.7	3.64	25.9	21
2004	COL	NL	28	49	8	82.0	71	42	85	9	3.85	3.65	7.7	4.0	8.7	0.8	3.91	17.9	13

Breakout: 29%   Improve: 51%   Collapse: 27%

As if dumping Jeff Cirillo wasn't reward enough, Fuentes has proven to be the major prize of the trade. Maybe it's because memory stretches back only so far, but Fuentes followed the path that Kelly Wunsch followed, learning to throw sidearm and suddenly having a career. That's not entirely fair to Fuentes or Wunsch, in that both threw over 90, and lefties who do that usually see the majors at some point. But both have been valuable instead of merely making it. Fuentes is tough on everybody, as well as with men on, so no mere situational creature be he.

CHRIS GISSELL Bats: R Throws: R Born: 04-Jan-78 Age: 26

YEAR	TM	LG	AGE	G	GS	IP	H	BB	SO	HR	ERA	EQERA	EQH9	EQBB9	EQSO9	EQHR9	PERA	VORP	STF
2001	WTN	SOU	23	28	27	159.7	159	63	136	13	4.51	6.01	10.2	4.1	5.2	1.2	5.63	-6.7	-6
2002	IOW	PCL	24	28	27	154.3	177	61	133	19	6.12	6.47	10.9	4.0	5.9	1.4	6.17	-14.0	-12
2003	CSP	PCL	25	38	10	109.0	96	35	82	8	3.55	3.66	7.8	3.4	5.7	0.9	3.95	22.3	0
2004	COL	NL	26	13	8	47.7	50	21	36	6	5.00	4.73	9.3	3.5	6.2	1.0	4.70	4.6	2

Breakout: 24%   Improve: 51%   Collapse: 13%

Gissell is exactly the sort of guy who was crying out for a conversion to relief after years of laboring as a disappointing young starter. He throws hard and he's very tough on right-handed hitters, but he works high in the strike zone, so if he wasn't already dreaming of intentionally walking Barry Bonds, he can at least look forward to it.

JUSTIN HUISMAN Bats: R Throws: R Born: 16-Apr-79 Age: 25

YEAR	TM	LG	AGE	G	GS	IP	H	BB	SO	HR	ERA	EQERA	EQH9	EQBB9	EQSO9	EQHR9	PERA	VORP	STF
2001	ASH	SAL	22	55	0	58.3	35	14	53	1	1.70	3.31	7.1	3.1	4.5	0.3	3.07	13.2	7
2002	SLM	CAR	23	41	0	51.7	47	14	24	0	1.57	3.66	9.4	3.3	2.9	0.2	4.02	10.1	-5
2002	CAR	SOU	23	18	0	24.3	30	12	10	4	6.67	8.59	13.1	4.9	2.9	2.9	9.22	-7.3	-87
2003	TUL	TEX	24	57	0	61.7	55	7	46	1	1.75	3.79	9.0	1.3	4.9	0.3	3.32	11.5	11
2004	COL	NL	25	18	5	36.3	41	11	20	5	4.78	4.53	9.9	2.4	4.6	1.0	4.62	5.4	-9

Breakout: 19%   Improve: 43%   Collapse: 24%

Every once in a while, there's an exception that proves the rule. A closer at Ole Miss before moving into the same role as a pro, Huisman might be that rare minor league reliever who actually makes it to the majors. He gets twice as many groundball outs as flyouts, and is about as stingy at allowing extra-base hits as anybody at any level.

JASON JENNINGS   Bats: L   Throws: R   Born: 17-Jul-78   Age: 25

YEAR	TM	LG	AGE	G	GS	IP	H	BB	SO	HR	ERA	EQERA	EQH9	EQBB9	EQSO9	EQHR9	PERA	VORP	STF
2001	CAR	SOU	22	4	4	25.0	25	8	24	1	2.88	4.24	10.0	3.5	5.8	0.8	4.87	3.5	21
2001	CSP	PCL	22	22	22	131.7	145	41	110	9	4.72	4.32	8.2	3.1	5.6	0.5	3.71	18.7	29
2001	COL	NL	22	7	7	39.3	42	19	26	2	4.58	4.26	9.7	4.0	5.0	0.5	4.58	5.7	24
2002	COL	NL	23	32	32	185.3	201	70	127	26	4.52	4.66	9.7	3.0	5.4	1.2	5.05	18.8	12
2003	COL	NL	24	32	32	181.3	212	88	119	20	5.11	5.07	9.9	3.8	5.1	0.9	5.05	11.5	7
2004	*COL*	*NL*	*25*	*26*	*24*	*143.0*	*158*	*64*	*98*	*18*	*4.99*	*4.72*	*9.7*	*3.5*	*5.7*	*0.9*	*4.85*	*14.9*	*5*

Breakout: 12%   Improve: 47%   Collapse: 21%

Jennings did slightly better in terms of limiting the home runs allowed, but his command seemed to suffer for it, and he often had trouble with his off-speed pitches against lefties. As another one of the Rockies' near assembly line of sinkerball pitchers, he's a battler more than an overpowering young gun. But between his consistent, sound delivery and his ability to hit, he's the sort of the guy the Rockies are right to try and accumulate. They've been careful with him, and he should be an effective starter for as long as they can keep him.

JOSE JIMENEZ   Bats: R   Throws: R   Born: 07-Jul-73   Age: 30

YEAR	TM	LG	AGE	G	GS	IP	H	BB	SO	HR	ERA	EQERA	EQH9	EQBB9	EQSO9	EQHR9	PERA	VORP	STF
2001	COL	NL	28	56	0	55.0	56	22	37	6	4.09	4.05	9.1	3.4	5.1	0.8	4.51	9.2	-8
2002	COL	NL	29	74	0	73.3	76	11	47	7	3.56	3.71	9.3	1.2	5.0	0.8	3.89	14.8	2
2003	COL	NL	30	63	7	101.7	137	32	45	7	5.22	5.04	11.3	2.5	3.5	0.5	5.00	8.7	-11
2004	*CLE*	*AL*	*30*	*55*	*2*	*69.7*	*77*	*24*	*37*	*6*	*4.14*	*4.41*	*9.8*	*3.0*	*4.7*	*0.8*	*4.80*	*10.4*	*-11*

Breakout: 36%   Improve: 60%   Collapse: 20%

Early on, Jimenez appeared to have lost the touch on his sinker, but having an infield of Stynes, Hernandez, and Belliard while Juan Uribe was on the DL probably didn't help much. Since his sinker is the only thing that got him to and keeps him in the big leagues, he's that rare ace reliever who allows enough balls in play that he needs a team's best defensive alignment. It probably isn't coincidence that after July 1—once Uribe was playing short everyday—Jimenez's ERA was 4.10, including a seven-start stretch replacing Chacon in the rotation. On the right team, or more appropriately, with the right infield, Jimenez can be a significant asset.

UBALDO JIMENEZ   Bats: R   Throws: R   Born: 22-Jan-84   Age: 20

YEAR	TM	LG	AGE	G	GS	IP	H	BB	SO	HR	ERA	EQERA	EQH9	EQBB9	EQSO9	EQHR9	PERA	VORP	STF
2002	CAS	PIO	18	14	14	62.0	72	29	65	6	6.53	8.50	13.7	6.0	5.0	2.5	9.18	-17.4	-25
2003	ASH	SAL	19	27	27	153.7	129	67	138	11	3.45	5.31	9.6	5.3	5.2	1.6	6.10	4.4	6
2003	VIS	CAL	19	1	0	5.0	3	1	7	0	0.00	1.93	5.8	1.9	9.6	0.0	1.81	1.9	85

The latest bounty of the organization's Dominican program, the other Jimenez is already cited as one of the Rockies' best power arms, and he adds an outstanding curve to his mid-90s heat. The hope is that he'll add a changeup—consider that a good sign. Learning a changeup is a lot easier than learning to throw 95 mph. His ceiling is tremendous, but the usual caveats about surviving long enough to get anywhere apply.

JAVIER LOPEZ   Bats: L   Throws: L   Born: 11-Jul-77   Age: 26

YEAR	TM	LG	AGE	G	GS	IP	H	BB	SO	HR	ERA	EQERA	EQH9	EQBB9	EQSO9	EQHR9	PERA	VORP	STF
2001	ELP	TEX	23	22	1	40.0	64	14	21	6	7.42	8.15	13.7	3.7	3.3	2.1	8.23	-11.0	-61
2001	LNC	CAL	23	17	0	24.0	30	5	18	2	2.63	4.37	11.9	2.4	3.6	1.2	5.95	3.1	-25
2002	ELP	TEX	24	61	0	46.3	34	16	47	3	2.72	3.40	7.9	3.6	6.8	1.1	4.20	10.3	-2
2003	COL	NL	25	75	0	58.3	58	12	40	5	3.70	3.32	8.4	1.6	5.4	0.6	3.43	14.4	10
2004	*COL*	*NL*	*26*	*40*	*4*	*58.0*	*63*	*19*	*39*	*7*	*4.36*	*4.13*	*9.5*	*2.5*	*5.5*	*0.8*	*4.23*	*9.8*	*-3*

Breakout: 27%   Improve: 41%   Collapse: 28%

Acquired from the Red Sox in spring training after Boston snagged him from the Snakes in the 2002 Rule 5 draft, Lopez gave the Rockies a second sidearming lefty who kept the ball on the ground while laying lefties low at the plate. He doesn't throw hard, but between the arm action and passable off-speed stuff, he didn't get smacked around by righties either. As a result, the Rox have a good second lefty instead of a one-year use of a roster spot on a Rule 5 guy or a mere situational luxury.

MATT MILLER   Bats: R   Throws: R   Born: 23-Nov-71   Age: 32

YEAR	TM	LG	AGE	G	GS	IP	H	BB	SO	HR	ERA	EQERA	EQH9	EQBB9	EQSO9	EQHR9	PERA	VORP	STF
2001	POR	PCL	29	44	0	44.7	44	14	43	1	3.62	4.57	10.0	3.3	6.3	0.2	4.23	4.7	7
2002	SAC	PCL	30	54	0	71.0	81	28	63	5	4.31	5.05	10.4	4.0	5.9	0.8	5.19	4.1	-15
2003	COL	NL	28	4	0	4.3	5	2	5	0	2.09	2.08	10.4	4.2	8.3	0.0	4.38	1.8	34
2003	CSP	PCL	31	61	0	63.3	46	23	83	0	2.13	2.28	7.1	3.8	10.0	0.2	3.00	21.9	40
2004	*CLE*	*AL*	*32*	*26*	*4*	*43.0*	*40*	*18*	*40*	*3*	*3.65*	*3.89*	*8.1*	*3.7*	*8.1*	*0.7*	*4.13*	*9.2*	*10*

Breakout: 28%   Improve: 55%   Collapse: 22%

Ready to step into a Steve Reed sort of role as a right-handed relief specialist, after consistently showing a big platoon split. The Tribe's pen is pretty crowded, but he might yet stick.

DENNY NEAGLE   Bats: L   Throws: L   Born: 13-Sep-68   Age: 35

YEAR	TM	LG	AGE	G	GS	IP	H	BB	SO	HR	ERA	EQERA	EQH9	EQBB9	EQSO9	EQHR9	PERA	VORP	STF
2001	COL	NL	32	30	30	170.7	192	60	139	29	5.38	4.95	10.0	2.9	6.2	1.3	5.21	11.9	0
2002	COL	NL	33	35	28	164.3	170	63	111	26	5.26	4.86	9.3	3.0	5.3	1.4	5.02	13.1	-9
2003	COL	NL	34	7	7	35.3	47	12	21	12	7.90	6.94	11.1	2.6	4.6	2.8	7.58	-5.4	-56

Neagle is here as a reminder that he's on the 40-man roster. Although he's talking about being available to pitch in relief after the All-Star break, he almost certainly won't pitch in 2004 after having his elbow rebuilt, so his value is limited to whatever the Rox get in contract insurance.

DARREN OLIVER   Bats: R   Throws: L   Born: 06-Oct-70   Age: 33

YEAR	TM	LG	AGE	G	GS	IP	H	BB	SO	HR	ERA	EQERA	EQH9	EQBB9	EQSO9	EQHR9	PERA	VORP	STF
2001	TEX	AL	30	28	28	154.0	189	65	104	23	6.02	5.46	10.0	3.5	5.5	1.2	5.28	2.4	-4
2002	BOS	AL	31	14	9	58.0	70	27	32	7	4.66	4.98	10.9	3.9	4.8	1.0	5.61	3.9	-9
2002	MEM	PCL	31	5	5	16.0	17	17	9	1	7.88	9.82	10.4	11.0	3.7	0.6	6.84	-6.9	-62
2003	COL	NL	32	33	32	180.3	201	61	88	21	5.04	4.62	9.3	2.7	3.9	1.0	4.55	17.1	-4
2004	*COL*	*NL*	*33*	*26*	*21*	*122.3*	*144*	*46*	*65*	*19*	*5.33*	*5.04*	*10.3*	*2.9*	*4.4*	*1.1*	*5.18*	*7.9*	*-6*

Breakout: 11%   Improve: 46%   Collapse: 16%

Reduced to pitching for food after a long, ugly meltdown in Texas and then Boston—to the point that he wasn't brought up to help the desperate Cardinals down the stretch in 2002—Oliver drifted into Colorado. There he could, at best, hope for service time. He did a wee bit better than that, and now that he's departing through free agency, PECOTA doesn't think Oliver will have a year as good as his last. After years of disappointing his employers, neither should you. To tantalize, he did have 10 quality starts in 18 road outings, but that favorable breakdown doesn't entirely explain his outstanding year, because despite those ratios (10/18 road starts, versus 5/14 home starts), his ERA was almost a full run lower in Coors than on the road (4.50 vs. 5.45). In short, it was a fun year, but not the sort of thing that should convince you he's worth more than a low salary and a look-see.

ZACH PARKER   Bats: R   Throws: L   Born: 19-Aug-81   Age: 22

YEAR	TM	LG	AGE	G	GS	IP	H	BB	SO	HR	ERA	EQERA	EQH9	EQBB9	EQSO9	EQHR9	PERA	VORP	STF
2001	CAS	PIO	19	8	8	26.3	42	12	19	2	7.53	10.36	15.2	5.9	3.3	1.5	8.60	-12.9	-39
2002	ASH	SAL	20	28	28	168.3	174	64	119	11	4.01	5.90	10.4	4.6	3.7	1.4	6.12	-5.1	-7
2003	VIS	CAL	21	16	16	90.3	85	27	52	10	3.69	5.12	9.4	3.7	3.4	2.1	6.15	4.4	-22
2004	*COL*	*NL*	*22*	*13*	*11*	*60.3*	*75*	*34*	*35*	*13*	*7.02*	*6.65*	*10.9*	*4.3*	*4.8*	*1.6*	*6.55*	*-2.4*	*-15*

Breakout: 13%   Improve: 49%   Collapse: 27%

Parker is hard to get a read on, because he's been hard-pressed to stay on the mound. He finally had surgery to clean bone spurs out of his elbow last year, ending his season early. Parker lacks the mound time you'd want from a guy looking at making the jump to Double-A, but lefties who throw 90 don't grow on trees. The Rockies would be well-served to be cautious with him at this stage, but unfortunately they're already touting him, which helps create the sort of organizational inertia that can produce a bad decision.

STEVE REED   Bats: R   Throws: R   Born: 11-Mar-66   Age: 38

YEAR	TM	LG	AGE	G	GS	IP	H	BB	SO	HR	ERA	EQERA	EQH9	EQBB9	EQSO9	EQHR9	PERA	VORP	STF
2001	ATL	NL	35	39	0	31.0	30	13	25	3	3.48	4.55	9.1	3.6	6.1	0.9	4.63	3.5	-6
2001	CLE	AL	35	32	0	27.3	22	10	21	3	3.63	3.00	6.3	3.0	6.3	1.0	3.26	7.8	4
2002	NYM	NL	36	24	0	26.0	23	4	14	0	2.08	2.55	8.4	1.1	4.4	0.4	3.05	8.4	13
2002	SDP	NL	36	40	0	41.0	33	10	36	2	1.98	2.47	7.0	1.8	6.8	0.4	2.68	13.9	25
2003	COL	NL	37	67	0	63.3	59	26	39	9	3.27	3.47	7.8	3.3	4.8	1.2	4.22	18.4	-14
2004	COL	NL	38	45	0	44.7	45	19	29	5	3.99	3.78	8.9	3.2	5.5	0.8	4.34	9.2	-7

Breakout: 27%   Improve: 47%   Collapse: 30%

Today's shallower benches and the currently orthodox reluctance to use them makes life easier for a situational right-hander. Whereas situational lefties barely get to work or have to make their living getting mauled by Barry Bonds, and rarely get to see as many left-handed hitters as might justify their existence on big league rosters, life is better for Steve Reed and his ilk. There are more right-handed hitters in the first place, and situational righties rarely force opposing managers to think about pulling an adequate righty hitter. So guys who are far more consistent when it comes to mowing down their platoon victims get to roll along as consistently useful bit parts, while teams throw bigger money at whatever lefty is considered today's Ken Dayley. Reed won't cost nearly as much, and seems far better suited to pitch forever than Jesse Orosco.

JUSTIN SPEIER   Bats: R   Throws: R   Born: 06-Nov-73   Age: 30

YEAR	TM	LG	AGE	G	GS	IP	H	BB	SO	HR	ERA	EQERA	EQH9	EQBB9	EQSO9	EQHR9	PERA	VORP	STF
2001	CLE	AL	27	12	0	20.7	24	8	15	5	6.96	5.66	9.1	3.0	6.1	1.7	5.40	-0.1	-24
2001	CSP	PCL	27	11	0	12.3	10	7	16	0	1.46	1.54	7.7	6.2	8.5	0.0	3.78	5.3	27
2001	COL	NL	27	42	0	56.0	47	12	47	8	3.70	3.17	7.5	1.8	6.3	1.0	3.45	14.6	7
2002	CSP	PCL	28	12	0	14.0	20	3	14	2	3.86	4.61	12.5	2.0	6.6	1.3	6.19	1.5	-18
2002	COL	NL	28	63	0	62.3	51	19	47	9	4.33	3.75	7.3	2.4	5.8	1.2	3.76	12.3	-4
2003	COL	NL	29	72	0	73.3	73	23	66	11	4.05	4.00	8.5	2.5	7.1	1.2	4.36	13.1	0
2004	TOR	AL	30	54	0	60.7	63	18	46	10	4.67	4.43	8.9	2.5	6.8	1.3	4.42	11.3	0

Breakout: 24%   Improve: 41%   Collapse: 23%

Speier topped his breakthrough in 2002 with an even better year, solidifying his reputation as an underrated relief asset. Swapped to Toronto, he should shine now that he's far removed from high-altitude nightmares that make *Ravenous* seem like cartoon fun. (I mean, c'mon, Guy Pearce eating people? There's some attempted suspension of disbelief there that's beyond most of us, especially since Pearce doesn't look like he could scare carrots.) Anyway, Speier can freeze lefties with a good splitter and righties with his gas, and he's effective from the stretch. He could wind up an All-Star pitching for a Blue Jays team that should generate leads.

DENNY STARK   Bats: R   Throws: R   Born: 27-Oct-74   Age: 29

YEAR	TM	LG	AGE	G	GS	IP	H	BB	SO	HR	ERA	EQERA	EQH9	EQBB9	EQSO9	EQHR9	PERA	VORP	STF
2001	TAC	PCL	26	24	24	151.7	124	41	130	12	2.37	3.75	8.5	2.9	5.6	0.9	4.13	28.6	7
2001	SEA	AL	26	4	3	14.7	21	4	12	5	9.18	9.00	13.5	2.6	7.1	2.6	8.33	-5.3	-46
2002	CSP	PCL	27	7	7	37.7	35	14	38	4	3.82	3.72	8.2	3.7	6.7	1.2	4.56	7.6	0
2002	COL	NL	27	32	20	128.3	108	64	64	25	4.00	4.40	7.4	3.9	3.9	1.7	4.78	16.6	-27
2003	COL	NL	28	17	13	78.7	98	33	30	12	5.83	5.68	10.3	3.4	3.0	1.3	5.58	-1.3	-27
2004	COL	NL	29	20	14	82.3	92	36	44	13	5.44	5.15	9.9	3.4	4.4	1.2	5.14	6.3	-9

Breakout: 28%   Improve: 55%   Collapse: 23%

The Rockies thought they had an asset on their hands, but surprising few outside of the organization, they were wrong. For starters, Stark wasn't too likely to repeat his 2002 Coors ERA of 3.21. Although he's a battling righty junker who could be handy as a fifth starter on some teams, between his mechanics and his mediocrity, he's not a great bet to last. Think Steve Parris, and you wouldn't be far off.

CHIN-HUI TSAO

Bats: R **Throws: R** Born: 02-Jun-81 Age: 23

YEAR	TM	LG	AGE	G	GS	IP	H	BB	SO	HR	ERA	EQERA	EQH9	EQBB9	EQSO9	EQHR9	PERA	VORP	STF
2001	SLM	CAR	20	4	4	17.3	23	5	18	1	4.68	8.04	13.8	3.4	5.7	1.1	6.97	-4.3	2
2002	SLM	CAR	21	9	9	47.3	34	12	45	3	2.09	3.86	8.6	3.2	6.0	1.5	4.90	8.1	12
2003	TUL	TEX	22	18	18	113.3	88	26	125	7	2.46	3.48	8.4	2.6	7.4	1.1	4.24	24.3	32
2003	COL	NL	22	9	8	43.3	48	20	29	11	6.03	5.65	9.2	3.6	5.2	2.1	6.01	0.5	-5
2004	COL	NL	23	21	17	99.3	106	39	80	15	4.91	4.65	9.3	3.1	6.7	1.1	4.67	11.7	9

Breakout: 10% Improve: 43% Collapse: 25%

The prospect that Cook wasn't, easily the Texas League's best pitcher, and one of the game's best big league-ready pitching prospects, Tsao came back from his 2001 Tommy John surgery with a vengeance. His slider had bite and is especially tough on lefties, and his velocity was back in the low 90s. There's just about nothing he doesn't do well, and he takes his fielding, hitting, and baserunning seriously. A hamstring injury after his call-up cut into his big league debut, keeping him rookie-eligible. The tragedy, such as it is, is that he's coming to Coors, which over the next five years or so might make him the most unappreciated big league starter since Pedro Astacio.

CORY VANCE

Bats: L **Throws: L** Born: 20-Jun-79 Age: 25

YEAR	TM	LG	AGE	G	GS	IP	H	BB	SO	HR	ERA	EQERA	EQH9	EQBB9	EQSO9	EQHR9	PERA	VORP	STF
2001	SLM	CAR	22	26	26	154.0	129	65	142	9	3.10	5.48	9.6	5.6	5.1	1.3	5.90	1.8	-7
2002	CAR	SOU	23	25	25	150.3	142	76	114	8	3.77	4.96	9.8	4.8	4.9	1.0	5.40	9.8	0
2003	CSP	PCL	24	24	24	157.3	179	50	96	18	4.63	4.82	10.1	3.3	4.6	1.4	5.57	12.9	-9
2003	COL	NL	24	9	3	27.3	31	10	12	6	5.60	5.33	9.3	3.0	3.3	1.7	5.46	0.3	-26
2004	COL	NL	25	19	12	68.0	81	38	43	12	6.25	5.92	10.4	4.4	5.3	1.3	5.95	1.4	-11

Breakout: 20% Improve: 54% Collapse: 28%

Vance was a Georgia Tech lefty picked a year after fellow Yellow Jacket lefty Chuck Crowder had joined the Rockies. Crowder got early touts, then flamed out, whereas Vance got fewer plugs, but survived. Like a lot of lefties, he doesn't throw hard, instead getting by with a curve and a change. He's not the sort of guy you see making it as a rotation regular in Coors, not when the altitude flattens junk, making it easier for every right-handed hitter to merdilate it, extra biscuit for breakfast or not. A future as a lefty swingman beckons.

JASON YOUNG

Bats: R **Throws: R** Born: 28-Sep-79 Age: 24

YEAR	TM	LG	AGE	G	GS	IP	H	BB	SO	HR	ERA	EQERA	EQH9	EQBB9	EQSO9	EQHR9	PERA	VORP	STF
2001	SLM	CAR	21	17	17	104.7	104	28	91	8	3.44	5.95	11.3	3.5	4.8	1.8	6.60	-3.6	-8
2002	CAR	SOU	22	14	14	88.7	71	30	76	1	2.64	3.40	8.2	3.2	5.5	0.2	3.43	20.0	35
2002	CSP	PCL	22	13	13	79.7	87	38	74	10	4.97	4.76	8.2	4.5	6.6	1.1	4.68	7.4	20
2003	CSP	PCL	23	23	21	116.3	128	37	99	10	3.95	4.50	9.4	3.3	6.7	1.0	4.72	13.7	18
2003	COL	NL	23	8	3	21.3	34	9	18	8	8.45	8.44	13.5	3.4	6.3	3.0	9.05	-6.2	-39
2004	COL	NL	24	20	14	83.0	88	35	68	11	4.82	4.56	9.3	3.3	6.8	0.9	4.56	10.8	9

Breakout: 22% Improve: 54% Collapse: 24%

Although his big league stints were ugly, it was a year where he saw the elephant, prepping him for a shot at a big league job in 2004. He didn't struggle with lefties, freezing them with a slider and change-up, while consistently throwing his heat in the low 90s. He had some back troubles during the season, but it wasn't anything anyone expects to be chronic. Young might be headed for the pen, where he'll get to work in long relief, but with Chacon moving into the closer's role, anybody could wind up doing anything. A year in the pen wouldn't be a bad role for him to start off with, because he's done with the minors.

Florida Marlins

They were lucky.

There's no other way to say it, nor any shame in admitting it: The Marlins, a team few picked to contend and many picked to finish near the bottom of the league, won the 2003 World Series largely because of luck.

That's not to say this team wasn't talented, hard-working, and opportunistic. The Marlins were all of those things. It's also true that any team that survives a grueling 162-game regular season and three rounds of playoffs, no matter how talented, needs a modicum of luck to get through the rough spots.

But this wasn't just your garden-variety brand of luck. We're talking three-hour run at the craps table, Jessica Alba just called and would *love* to have dinner with you Friday night good fortune. Consider this chain of events:

- Flash back to the trade deadline, 2002. The Cubs wanted Matt Clement and Antonio Alfonseca from Florida. The Marlins ran through a list of pitching prospects in the Cubs' system. After being turned down again and again, they settled for a pitcher considered the third- or fourth-best lefty in the system, let alone anywhere near the best prospect. After the trade was consummated, all the Marlins talked about was payroll flexibility. They barely even mentioned Dontrelle Willis.

- Willis may have never gotten a chance in 2003 if not for A. J. Burnett's elbow injury. Burnett's subsequent Tommy John surgery opened the door for Willis, who didn't disappoint. Armed with a deceiving high leg kick, a winning smile, and a humble attitude, Willis plowed his way to the top of the Marlins' rotation, packing normally moribund Pro Player Stadium and picking up the NL Rookie of the Year award for his troubles.

- The Marlins began the 2002–03 off-season targeting Mike Hampton. When they acquired him in the three-way trade with the Rockies and Braves, the Fish tried to convince him to stay. When Hampton refused, he was shipped to Atlanta, and the Marlins were forced to pay part of his freight.

  With Hampton gone, the Marlins pursued Bartolo Colon, hoping to find a veteran ace to

MARLINS PROSPECTUS

2003 record: 91–71; Second place, NL East; Beat Yankees in World Series, 4–2

Pythagenport record: 87–75

Runs scored per game: 4.6 (7th in NL)

Runs allowed per game: 4.3 (6th in NL)

Team EqA: .267 (5th in NL)

2003 Batters Age: 28.1 (2nd youngest in NL)

2003 Pitchers Age: 26.6 (Youngest in NL)

Ballpark: Pro Player Stadium; Severe pitcher's park; Park Factor of 0.955

2003: Midseason managerial hire Jack McKeon and his balanced squad of Fighting Fish won it all.

2004: Defending their title won't be easy, especially since the Marlins aren't even the best team in their division.

lead their staff of young guns. The brouhaha over Brad Penny's phantom MRI and frayed shoulder scared the Expos away from dealing with the Marlins and instead into a Biddles and Bits deal with the White Sox.

Plan C was Pudge Rodriguez. Even then, there were fears that another team would outbid the Fish, until Rodriguez's back problems and salary demands scared away other suitors. Rodriguez responded by putting up a huge year, finishing second in the National League in Value Over Replacement Player (VORP) and almost single-handedly knocking the Giants out of the NLDS, with an all-time collision at the plate to end it.

- Looking to bolster the back of the bullpen, the Marlins' planned to acquire a closer with their first move of the summer. Their initial target: Armando Benitez. The Fish offered Adrian Gonzalez, Will Smith, and Ryan Snare to the Mets for Benitez. When New York wouldn't pick up enough of Benitez's salary, Florida settled for Ugueth Urbina from the Rangers. A good reliever his whole career, Urbina was nothing short of great down the stretch for the Marlins, lopping nearly three runs off his Texas ERA, and bumping Braden Looper out of the ace reliever role.

- With the end of July and the trade deadline approaching, the Marlins had their sights set on Rondell White or Reggie Sanders to claim the left field job. Though Miguel Cabrera had done a decent if erratic job replacing Todd Hollandsworth in left, Florida planned to send Cabrera back to the minors if they acquired White or Sanders. The 20-year-old phenom caught fire just as the trade rumors heated up, prompting the Marlins to stick with Cabrera. Rather than just hold his own, Cabrera played well down the stretch, then charged through the playoffs with a performance reminiscent of Andruw Jones' coming out party as a 19-year-old in the '96 World Series.

- Before the Marlins considered White and Sanders, they went hard after the man dubbed Mr. Marlin, Jeff Conine. The absurd notion that Conine would somehow attract scores of warm-and-fuzzy-feeling fans longing for the team's expansion days aside, Conine would have added little to the lineup, and like White or Sanders, would likely have shut Cabrera out of the stretch run. Worse yet, the Marlins planned to trade Derrek Lee, one of the best all-around first basemen in baseball, for Conine's mediocrity.

  After the initial Lee/Conine deal fell through, the Marlins chugged along for several weeks, rapidly gaining ground in the Wild Card race. When Mike Lowell went down to a broken left hand at the end of August though, Florida, needing just an average player to play a corner outfield spot until Lowell returned, called the Orioles back and again asked for Conine. This time the price was a two-player package, one of the two being Don Levinski, an arm who would have long before gone to the Expos in trade had the Colon-Penny worked out.

- After nabbing Urbina, the Marlins still had several bullpen holes to fill. With Vladimir Nunez bombing and Tim Spooneybarger going down to elbow surgery, the Marlins cycled through a laundry list of relievers. They tried to get Antonio Alfonseca back from the Cubs. They pursued Mike DeJean. Seeking a situational lefty, they went after Scott Sauerbeck. Finally, the Marlins settled on Chad Fox off of waivers. An injury-prone tin man who'd yielded a fugly 17 walks and 19 hits in 18 innings with the Red Sox to earn an unceremonious dumping, Fox was little more than speculative grist for Jack McKeon's bullpen mill. Amazingly, the move worked like a charm. Fox rewarded them with a 2.13 ERA over 25.1 innings of solid pitching. Rick Helling was also rescued from the scrap heap after a lousy first few months in the AL, and yielded less than a baserunner and inning and just one run over 16.1 frames down the stretch.

There were plenty of other improbable moments that hinted at the Marlins' good fortune—Mike Mordecai hitting only two homers all year, but both being extra-inning game-winners, for one. But let's not sell the Fish short. As Branch Rickey often said: "Luck is the residue of design."

The hiring of Jack McKeon and Wayne Rosenthal and firing of Jeff Torborg and Brad Arnsberg set the tone. Though McKeon made his share of blunders with the pitching staff—treating Mark Redman like a rag doll at times and calling Tim Spooneybarger out for dogging it just before he went under the knife chief among them—he and Rosenthal did a better of handling Marlin arms than the T-n'-A combo. McKeon's strategic moves paid off handsomely. He successfully rode his young core of everyday players hard given the lack of a solid bench. In the playoffs, McKeon's eschewing of set roles for his pitchers worked like a charm, capped by stellar relief work by his starters and Josh Beckett's dazzling Game 6 shutout on three days rest to win the World Series.

The Marlins started the year with a solid nucleus. Derrek Lee, Luis Castillo, and Alex Gonzalez came up through the system on similar schedules to form the infield's core. Lee and Castillo had already blossomed into solid players, and Gonzalez finally put together an effective season, after going four years since his solid rookie campaign. Mike Lowell proved a great grab from the Yankees before the '99 season, rounding out the infield. Refusing to give him away for three quarters on the dollar, the Marlins opted not to trade Lowell to the Cubs or Dodgers in June, a non-move that later paid dividends.

Even more widely panned was the off-season deal that brought Juan Pierre and Tim Spooneybarger to Florida. The Marlins ditched power-hitting center fielder Preston Wilson and veteran catcher Charles Johnson in the trade, leading many to tab it a salary dump. Indeed, the key player in the deal, Pierre, was coming off a dreadful season in Colorado. The Marlins made noise about emulating the speed and aggressiveness that brought a title to Anaheim. But while Pierre brought plenty of both, skeptics wondered how he'd steal first, given Pierre's struggles combined with a shift to a pitcher's haven at Pro Player. Worse, the team was lambasted for picking up the last three years of Mike Hampton's contract as part of the three-way deal, paying $38 million to a player who'd never wear Marlin teal.

Chucking Wilson and Johnson's huge contracts still provided a tidy net gain, paving the way for a major Marlin signing, which became Ivan Rodriguez. Meanwhile Pierre enjoyed a strong season, putting up a career high in walks, swiping a league-high 65 bases with a solid success rate, and playing a sound center field.

The pitching staff came together through a similar convergence of homegrown talent and clever moves. A. J. Burnett, Brad Penny, and Josh Beckett formed a top of the rotation that ranked with any in baseball for potential. Though Burnett was lost for the season and Beckett for several weeks due to injury, Beckett and Penny still threw plenty of big innings in 2003. Mark Redman and Carl Pavano rounded out the staff with gusto: Redman enjoyed a career year despite an erratic second half, after being acquired from Detroit for middling pitching prospects. Pavano, acquired from Montreal in the 2002 Cliff Floyd trade, overcame years of injuries to finally fulfill his potential.

The farm system provided the last, crucial push. When Miguel Cabrera went up for bid more than four years ago, the Marlins didn't flinch, paying a record $1.8 million signing bonus for a 16-year-old Venezuelan player. Cabrera developed quickly in the Marlins system, and beat most timetables with his impressive arrival. Dontrelle Willis had the same dynamic effect on the pitching staff, only for a bigger chunk of the year. Though perhaps over-looked, the Marlins' collection of other quality prospects, including Denny Bautista, Don Levinski, Will Smith, Ryan Snare, Adrian Gonzalez, and others, made key late-season deals possible.

Before Jeb Bush gives the Jeffrey Loria/David Samson/ Larry Beinfest combo a key to the Everglades or Epcot or even that Cracker Barrel off I-95 north of West Palm Beach, we should note that most of the above moves happened in the Dave Dombrowski era. Give the new regime credit for making some good tweaks, but throw some love Motown's way, even if Dombrowski is now struggling to revive the Tigers.

So where does all this leave the 2004 defending World Champion Florida Marlins? Loria and company made a lot of noise about avoiding the fate of the 1997 Mar-lins, stripped for parts by former owner Wayne Huizenga after their first World Series title. But complacency is no better, and can often hurt a team even more—just ask the Angels. Failing to address weaknesses in the name of vague feelings of supposed good will toward the fans won't win games. Neither will overpaying several players for the sake of keeping them around. While Florida should get a nice year-after boost in ticket sales and other revenue, the honeymoon will end quickly if the team tanks on the field.

For all the talk of standing pat though, management turned over a number of roster spots. The Marlins wisely jettisoned Juan Encarnacion, flipping him to the Dodgers for a PTBNL, then watching L.A. overpay him at two years and $8 million. They smartly let Ugueth Urbina leave via free agency and non-tendered Braden Looper.

Several bigger names also departed. When Pudge Rod-riguez refused to budge from his hefty contract demands, the Marlins dropped out of the bidding. The catching situation remained unsettled at press time, with Ramon Castro fully capable of producing above-average offense at the position but facing rape charges, and Mike Redmond not a viable solution.

The trade of Derrek Lee to the Cubs for young Korean slugger Hee Seop Choi was a challenge trade that could become pure gold for the Fish, though probably not right away. While scouts have moaned about the holes in Choi's swing, he showed power and patience in the minors, and could provide six years of big production, the first three at rock-bottom prices. While Lee ranked as one of the best all-around first basemen in baseball, he was also one year away from walking, so credit Beinfest and company for a sweet deal, even if Lee outperforms Choi in the first year after the trade.

While Dave Dombrowski is mostly responsible for the 2003 Marlins, the new regime will deserve a huge chunk of the credit or blame for what happens next. In addition to making changes behind the plate, at first, and in the bullpen, the front office looked at the incumbent second and third basemen, and liked what they saw.

Signing Luis Castillo to a three-year, $16 million deal could backfire, however. Lacking any semblance of power, Castillo's value rests almost entirely on his speed and agil-ity. A lingering hip injury has put that speed and agility in jeopardy, resulting in a brutal stolen base success rate and problems with lateral movement afield in 2003. Throw in the threat of reaching base less often on dink hits, and the Marlins could be staring at a slightly better version of David Eckstein through 2006, 2007 if Castillo's option year vests.

It's Mike Lowell's four-year, $32 million deal that most clearly plants the new guard's stamp on the Marlins. The agreement stipulates that the contract kick in for years two through four only if the Marlins get a new stadium deal approved. If the stadium deal doesn't happen, the contract becomes a one-year affair, with the decision to stay longer solely in Lowell's hands. The Marlins have thus put the onus squarely on taxpayers' heads: If they don't give Loria a new ballpark, then the voters obviously don't care about their team or regional pride.

There's more. Lowell's agents knocked their clients' asking price down to $8 million a year instead of $10 mil-lion in exchange for taking an out clause away from the Marlins. But if a new ballpark doesn't happen in '04 and they overvalue their client's worth, the Marlins could get off paying Lowell for what'll likely be his most productive season, with decline as he plods deeper into his 30s the best bet thereafter.

Thus, if Lowell bolts, Loria wins. If the stadium gets built, Loria wins big. The only downside would be Lowell staying and collecting the other $24 million—even in a tight market for third basemen, that's a bad tail end of a contract waiting to happen.

Add it all up and you get a team that could go either way. The starting rotation looks set, with Beckett, Penny, Willis, and Pavano in place and Burnett due back in June. The team's fate will rest on the Marlins' ability to intelligently spend the added payroll they freed with various deals and departures, after accounting for re-ups and raises.

If they get Castro's services for the year or sign an above-average catcher, the offense could hold up, with a full season of Cabrera instead of Encarnacion offsetting a temporary downgrade from Lee to Choi—with the hope that Choi enters his peak by years two and three of his Marlin tenure. The bullpen could use another power arm or two.

As they were last year, the Phillies are again the best team in the NL East on paper, while the Braves remain a perennial threat despite a weakened roster. If the Marlins shop well, they could compete again for the Wild Card. The smart money, however, rests on a return to .500. The Marlins had their luck—the run at the craps table ends now.

HITTERS

CHRIS AGUILA   OF   Bats: R   Throws: R   Born: 23-Feb-79   Age: 25

YEAR	TM	LG	AGE	AB	H	2B	3B	HR	BB	SO	SB	CS	AVG	OBP	SLG	MLVR	EQBA	EQOBP	EQSLG	EQMLVR	VORP	DEFENSE			
2001	BRV	FLA	22	272	75	15	3	10	21	54	8	4	.276	.328	.463	.167	.236	.274	.414	-.185	-3.3	72-CF	-3		
2001	PME	EAS	22	241	62	16	1	4	18	50	5	7	.257	.312	.382	-.046	.217	.273	.328	-.321	-19.0	50-RF	-3		
2002	PME	EAS	23	429	126	28	4	6	48	101	14	8	.294	.369	.420	.103	.247	.310	.359	-.187	-18.6	64-LF	-3	49-CF	-2
2003	CAR	SOU	24	337	108	21	3	11	36	67	6	2	.320	.384	.499	.299	.272	.329	.438	-.021	3.6	43-LF	-2	25-RF	1
2004	FLA	NL	25	221	55	12	1	6	18	46	3	1	.250	.311	.395	-.112	.256	.315	.421	-.079	2.2	61-LF	1		

Breakout: 28%   Improve: 56%   Collapse: 27%

Bubba Trammell Dos? A stocky right-handed hitter, Aguila showed decent power in Double-A. That it was his third visit to the level, and at age 24 no less, dampens enthusiasm for his outlook considerably. The Marlins thought enough of Aguila to send him to the Arizona Fall League, where he showed more of his power and middling patience against sub-par pitching. He's a viable bench option for a team that lacked right-handed juice off the pine while somehow finding a roster spot for Lenny Harris.

CHAD ALLEN   LF   Bats: R   Throws: R   Born: 06-Feb-75   Age: 29

YEAR	TM	LG	AGE	AB	H	2B	3B	HR	BB	SO	SB	CS	AVG	OBP	SLG	MLVR	EQBA	EQOBP	EQSLG	EQMLVR	VORP	DEFENSE			
2001	MIN	AL	26	175	46	13	2	4	19	37	1	2	.263	.333	.429	-.008	.274	.349	.451	.035	4.2	14-LF	-2	13-RF	0
2002	BUF	INT	27	279	84	20	1	10	15	34	0	1	.301	.340	.487	.168	.281	.321	.466	.013	5.5	35-LF	1		
2003	ABQ	PCL	28	337	109	30	2	8	18	48	11	10	.323	.364	.496	.149	.271	.315	.424	-.067	-1.2	55-LF	-4	13-CF	1
2003	FLA	NL	28	24	5	1	1	0	0	5	0	0	.208	.240	.333	-.287	.208	.234	.375	-.337	-1.4				
2004	TEX	AL	29	213	58	13	1	6	15	36	3	2	.272	.324	.434	-.008	.265	.321	.424	-.059	3.3	58-LF	-1		

Breakout: 30%   Improve: 57%   Collapse: 31%

We're now five years removed from Allen's sub-par '99 season, when he somehow wrung out 477 at-bats from a Twins team in the early building stages. He brings nothing useful to the table at this point. Signed to a minor league contract by the Rangers; even odds he becomes a Devil Ray before he hangs 'em up, 5–1 he finds 200 at-bats when he does. Come on, Chuck LaMar, papa needs a new pair of shoes!

CHIP AMBRES   CF   Bats: R   Throws: R   Born: 19-Dec-79   Age: 24

YEAR	TM	LG	AGE	AB	H	2B	3B	HR	BB	SO	SB	CS	AVG	OBP	SLG	MLVR	EQBA	EQOBP	EQSLG	EQMLVR	VORP	DEFENSE	
2001	KNE	MID	21	377	100	26	8	5	53	81	19	15	.265	.369	.416	.127	.197	.276	.315	-.344	-23.3	87-CF	-8
2002	JUP	FLA	22	509	120	25	7	9	57	98	23	8	.236	.323	.365	.004	.204	.268	.325	-.342	-31.1	122-CF	-12
2003	CAR	SOU	23	380	98	23	8	10	72	81	9	6	.258	.376	.439	.160	.215	.314	.377	-.175	-3.6	106-CF	-10
2004	FLA	NL	24	244	57	13	2	6	26	52	4	2	.236	.316	.376	-.137	.242	.320	.401	-.106	2.6	68-CF	-4

Breakout: 51%   Improve: 67%   Collapse: 19%

The flashes he showed in the AFL in 2002 (.256/.356/.444) earned him a promotion to Double-A, since his performance at Jupiter certainly didn't warrant it. Ambres struggled again this year, especially with making contact. He showed some decent power, rapping an extra-base hit nearly every 10 at-bats, but otherwise remains an offensive sieve with a spotty glove in center. The raw athleticism makes you consider sticking with him. The lack of results makes you wise up.

BRIAN BANKS   LF/PH   Bats: S   Throws: R   Born: 28-Sep-70   Age: 33

YEAR	TM	LG	AGE	AB	H	2B	3B	HR	BB	SO	SB	CS	AVG	OBP	SLG	MLVR	EQBA	EQOBP	EQSLG	EQMLVR	VORP	DEFENSE			
2001	CLG	PCL	30	357	104	27	4	23	32	97	5	4	.291	.352	.583	.180	.240	.302	.474	-.047	4.1	72-1B	4		
2002	CLG	PCL	31	439	136	38	3	19	73	77	10	5	.310	.410	.540	.259	.252	.350	.439	.002	12.6	67-1B	-2	31-LF	2
2002	FLA	NL	31	28	9	1	0	1	1	6	0	0	.321	.345	.464	.171	.345	.345	.517	.198	2.2				
2003	FLA	NL	32	149	35	6	2	4	25	38	2	1	.235	.348	.383	-.006	.243	.356	.401	-.044	3.3	15-LF	0		
2004	FLA	NL	33	141	34	8	1	4	19	33	2	1	.242	.337	.394	-.073	.249	.342	.420	-.040	3.6	43-1B	-3		

Breakout: 30%   Improve: 48%   Collapse: 33%

One of the best bats on a lousy bench; credit Jack McKeon with recognizing that weakness and using his regulars more than most. Banks hit righties well enough and took enough walks to be a useful pinch-hitter. Though he was nominally kept around for his ability to catch, he never got a chance on a team that rode Pudge hard and had two capable backups in Redmond and Castro. His best shot at sticking around is the Dave Hansen/Mark Sweeney career path.

MIGUEL CABRERA   3B/LF/RF   Bats: R   Throws: R   Born: 18-Apr-83   Age: 21

YEAR	TM	LG	AGE	AB	H	2B	3B	HR	BB	SO	SB	CS	AVG	OBP	SLG	MLVR	EQBA	EQOBP	EQSLG	EQMLVR	VORP	DEFENSE			
2001	KNE	MID	18	422	113	19	4	7	37	76	3	0	.268	.328	.382	.020	.208	.256	.303	-.395	-24.3	87-SS	-10		
2002	JUP	FLA	19	489	134	43	1	9	38	85	10	1	.274	.333	.421	.118	.238	.282	.380	-.217	-5.4	87-3B	-4		
2003	CAR	SOU	20	266	97	29	3	10	31	49	9	4	.365	.429	.609	.550	.304	.363	.527	.195	32.0	64-3B	12		
2003	FLA	NL	20	314	84	21	3	12	25	84	0	2	.268	.325	.468	.095	.276	.332	.483	.052	11.5	54-LF	-1	27-3B	1
2004	FLA	NL	21	457	121	29	3	15	38	90	5	2	.264	.323	.439	-.021	.271	.328	.467	.017	22.9	120-3B	1		

Breakout: 30%   Improve: 50%   Collapse: 19%

Already a franchise cornerstone and playoff hero, Cabrera won't reach legal drinking age until April. Read that sentence again. Cabrera uses a strong lower body and solid swing mechanics to crush the ball to all fields. It's scary to think what he might do once he strengthens his upper body. The last step is refining his plate discipline. If the Marlins plan to make Cabrera into an everyday corner outfielder, they'll need him to do a lot better than three strikeouts for every walk. He's got the three biggest ingredients needed to make that happen and become a star: a whole lot of time, a good head, and talent to burn. Three years from now those mentioning Willis and Cabrera in the same breath will be laughed at.

LUIS CASTILLO   2B   Bats: S   Throws: R   Born: 12-Sep-75   Age: 28

YEAR	TM	LG	AGE	AB	H	2B	3B	HR	BB	SO	SB	CS	AVG	OBP	SLG	MLVR	EQBA	EQOBP	EQSLG	EQMLVR	VORP	DEFENSE	
2001	FLA	NL	25	534	140	16	10	2	66	90	33	16	.262	.343	.341	-.110	.270	.349	.350	-.108	10.2	132-2B	-5
2002	FLA	NL	26	606	185	18	5	2	55	76	48	15	.305	.364	.361	.044	.319	.375	.381	.021	31.0	140-2B	-8
2003	FLA	NL	27	595	187	19	6	6	63	60	21	19	.314	.381	.397	.130	.321	.386	.406	.079	38.6	150-2B	-3
2004	FLA	NL	28	539	154	24	5	4	60	64	23	9	.285	.357	.369	-.043	.292	.362	.393	-.008	28.2	143-2B	-4

Breakout: 15%   Improve: 38%   Collapse: 20%

Lacking power, and only a fair base-on-balls threat, Castillo's offense relies on his cobbling together enough dribblers, bleeders, and bunt hits to bat well over .300. The odds are against him: With a hip injury that turned him into a bases-stealing liability rather than an asset last year an enduring concern, plus a history of other nagging injuries and a march toward his 30s, an offensive regression similar to his '01/'02 decline is the smart bet; a decline in his lateral movement could hurt his already overrated defense. A limited supply of quality free agent second basemen and a World Series glow helped trigger the three-year, $16 million contract Castillo signed to stay with the Marlins. That doesn't mean they didn't overpay.

RAMON CASTRO   C   Bats: R   Throws: R   Born: 01-Mar-76   Age: 28

YEAR	TM	LG	AGE	AB	H	2B	3B	HR	BB	SO	SB	CS	AVG	OBP	SLG	MLVR	EQBA	EQOBP	EQSLG	EQMLVR	VORP	DEFENSE	
2001	CLG	PCL	25	390	131	33	0	27	38	74	1	1	.336	.393	.628	.357	.273	.334	.512	.093	32.6	84-C	-2
2002	FLA	NL	26	101	24	4	0	6	14	24	0	0	.238	.322	.455	.049	.243	.333	.476	.014	5.2	23-C	-3
2003	FLA	NL	27	53	15	2	0	5	4	11	0	0	.283	.333	.604	.317	.296	.345	.611	.278	6.8		
2004	FLA	NL	28	195	48	10	0	10	21	42	0	0	.245	.319	.453	-.026	.251	.323	.482	.012	11.7	55-C	-5

Breakout: 8%   Improve: 19%   Collapse: 51%

Though the Free Erubiel Durazo! Campaign has ended, the Free Ramon Castro! train rolls on. Too bad it's pitch black, the conductor's getting drowsy, and there's a possum on the tracks. Castro still has the bat to be an above-average starting major league catcher. But the winter's *other* professional athlete rape proceedings cast his future into doubt. If acquitted and allowed to play, he'll beat that projection.

JEFF CONINE   LF/1B   Bats: R   Throws: R   Born: 27-Jun-66   Age: 38

YEAR	TM	LG	AGE	AB	H	2B	3B	HR	BB	SO	SB	CS	AVG	OBP	SLG	MLVR	EQBA	EQOBP	EQSLG	EQMLVR	VORP	DEFENSE		
2001	BAL	AL	35	524	163	23	2	14	64	75	12	8	.311	.386	.443	.166	.341	.418	.490	.273	51.1	78-1B	-4	22-LF 0
2002	BAL	AL	36	451	123	26	4	15	25	66	8	0	.273	.307	.448	.020	.298	.338	.492	.097	21.0	103-1B	-8	
2003	BAL	AL	37	493	143	33	3	15	37	60	5	0	.290	.338	.460	.105	.313	.369	.502	.179	22.4	118-1B	2	
2003	FLA	NL	37	84	20	3	0	5	13	10	0	0	.238	.337	.452	.068	.244	.343	.477	.034	1.9	24-LF	2	
2004	*FLA*	*NL*	*38*	*409*	*107*	*22*	*2*	*11*	*41*	*56*	*3*	*2*	*.263*	*.331*	*.407*	*-.053*	*.270*	*.335*	*.433*	*-.017*	*9.1*	*108-1B*	*-2*	

Breakout: 7%   *Improve: 34%*   *Collapse: 31%*

The two-year contract extension at $3 million a year he signed when the Fish dealt for him late last season was a reach. Letting Conine's peachy keen counting stats and his rep as Mr. Marlin (has Billy signed off on that?) convince the Fish to install the soon-to-be 38-year-old as the team's starting left fielder was a clear-cut mistake. Conine is a useful player in the right platoon, and a liability when playing every day. The Marlins may yet hit a run of great luck similar to the one that helped them win it all last year. But every bad decision like this one means another fortunate bounce needed for a repeat.

JUAN ENCARNACION   OF   Bats: R   Throws: R   Born: 08-Mar-76   Age: 28

YEAR	TM	LG	AGE	AB	H	2B	3B	HR	BB	SO	SB	CS	AVG	OBP	SLG	MLVR	EQBA	EQOBP	EQSLG	EQMLVR	VORP	DEFENSE			
2001	DET	AL	25	417	101	19	7	12	25	93	9	5	.242	.292	.408	-.104	.265	.318	.449	-.031	3.7	60-RF	-4	53-CF	-4
2002	CIN	NL	26	321	89	11	2	16	26	63	9	4	.277	.330	.474	.092	.277	.328	.477	.037	15.4	59-CF	0	28-RF	0
2002	FLA	NL	26	263	69	11	3	8	20	50	12	5	.262	.317	.418	.010	.276	.330	.444	-.007	3.9	51-RF	-3	11-CF	0
2003	FLA	NL	27	601	162	37	6	19	37	82	19	8	.270	.313	.446	.047	.280	.323	.466	.015	11.5	151-RF	-2		
2004	*LAD*	*NL*	*28*	*506*	*133*	*25*	*4*	*20*	*38*	*87*	*12*	*5*	*.263*	*.318*	*.447*	*-.020*	*.274*	*.326*	*.462*	*.007*	*12.0*	*131-RF*	*0*		

Breakout: 20%   *Improve: 53%*   *Collapse: 19%*

Already a problem at a corner outfield spot with sub-par power and poor on-base skills, a nagging shoulder injury he kept under wraps further hurt Encarnacion's production. He's expected to be recovered in time for Opening Day, and will man left field for the Dodgers after the Marlins flipped him to L.A. for a player to be named later rather than get nothing after a non-tender. If that's what passes for a Dodger offensive upgrade—at two years, $8 million, no less—expect more punchless flailing at Chavez Ravine.

MATT ERICKSON   2B/3B   Bats: L   Throws: R   Born: 30-Jul-75   Age: 28

YEAR	TM	LG	AGE	AB	H	2B	3B	HR	BB	SO	SB	CS	AVG	OBP	SLG	MLVR	EQBA	EQOBP	EQSLG	EQMLVR	VORP	DEFENSE			
2001	CLG	PCL	25	413	128	21	1	2	39	69	11	4	.310	.386	.380	-.020	.255	.326	.314	-.213	-1.3	52-SS	-2	56-2B	-2
2002	CLG	PCL	26	379	109	30	2	1	31	63	15	4	.288	.359	.385	-.047	.244	.306	.330	-.237	-7.3	57-2B	4	29-3B	4
2003	ABQ	PCL	27	298	102	22	4	2	43	42	14	9	.342	.442	.463	.241	.278	.372	.385	-.011	15.8	41-3B	0	31-2B	-5
2004	*FLA*	*NL*	*28*	*177*	*44*	*10*	*1*	*2*	*18*	*30*	*4*	*2*	*.251*	*.334*	*.347*	*-.133*	*.257*	*.339*	*.369*	*-.104*	*7.7*	*51-2B*	*-3*		

Breakout: 25%   *Improve: 42%*   *Collapse: 33%*

All hail David Eckstein, patron saint of scrubs. Erickson's got a few inches and a couple dozen pounds on Eckstein, but his game looks similar. A natural second baseman who lacks the arm to play short, Erickson could have value to a team as a no-power on-base threat and utility infielder. He's a six-year free agent facing long odds: St. Eck got his shot three years ago, and Erickson shares the same 1975 in his date of birth column.

ANDY FOX   UT   Bats: L   Throws: R   Born: 12-Jan-71   Age: 33

YEAR	TM	LG	AGE	AB	H	2B	3B	HR	BB	SO	SB	CS	AVG	OBP	SLG	MLVR	EQBA	EQOBP	EQSLG	EQMLVR	VORP	DEFENSE	
2001	FLA	NL	30	81	15	0	1	3	15	17	1	0	.185	.327	.321	-.212	.193	.327	.349	-.199	0.1	11-SS	-2
2002	FLA	NL	31	435	109	14	5	4	49	94	31	7	.251	.338	.333	-.075	.268	.350	.360	-.094	12.6	104-SS	-6
2003	FLA	NL	32	108	21	5	1	0	7	29	1	2	.194	.269	.259	-.341	.211	.279	.284	-.373	-5.8		
2004	*MON*	*NL*	*33*	*165*	*43*	*8*	*2*	*3*	*19*	*35*	*5*	*2*	*.258*	*.341*	*.382*	*-.070*	*.242*	*.324*	*.353*	*-.162*	*2.0*	*48-SS*	*-8*

Breakout: 32%   *Improve: 52%*   *Collapse: 32%*

After a season filling in for the injured Alex Gonzalez that delighted rotoheads, Fox returned to his utility infielder's role, where he flat out stunk, small sample size or not. It's possible he could recapture whatever marginal magic he found in 2002. But at age 33, teams are better off promoting from within to see if a quasi-prospect can turn a utility role into something more down the road. He was signed by Texas as a minor league free agent and later plucked by the Expos in the Rule 5 draft, where he'll fill a utility infielder slot.

ALEX GONZALEZ   SS   Bats: R   Throws: R   Born: 15-Feb-77   Age: 27

YEAR	TM	LG	AGE	AB	H	2B	3B	HR	BB	SO	SB	CS	AVG	OBP	SLG	MLVR	EQBA	EQOBP	EQSLG	EQMLVR	VORP	DEFENSE	
2001	FLA	NL	24	518	130	36	1	9	31	107	2	2	.251	.304	.376	-.143	.262	.313	.392	-.124	11.1	141-SS	-19
2002	FLA	NL	25	151	34	7	1	2	12	32	3	1	.225	.296	.325	-.177	.240	.306	.351	-.210	-0.3	40-SS	2
2003	FLA	NL	26	528	135	33	6	18	33	106	0	4	.256	.313	.443	.030	.267	.322	.468	.005	24.4	149-SS	6
2004	*FLA*	*NL*	*27*	*417*	*107*	*24*	*3*	*11*	*29*	*82*	*2*	*2*	*.256*	*.315*	*.403*	*-.090*	*.262*	*.319*	*.430*	*-.056*	*16.4*	*109-SS*	*2*

Breakout: 18%   Improve: 43%   Collapse: 21%

SeaBass started the year with his best ARod impression, bashing .352/.404/.670 in April and .310/.340/.563 in May. Reality struck, and struck hard, as Gonzalez hit only .208/.285/.344 after the break. A career's worth of popgunnery says his second half was much closer to the real deal. Staring at an arbitration award of about $3 million, the Marlins blinked, giving him the money while hoping the second half slumbers won't reappear. Gonzalez remains one of the least patient players in the league. His defense will hold some value for now, but the Fish need to find a young replacement in the vein of the Willis and Choi deals. Quickly.

LENNY HARRIS   Zimmer   Bats: L   Throws: R   Born: 28-Oct-64   Age: 39

YEAR	TM	LG	AGE	AB	H	2B	3B	HR	BB	SO	SB	CS	AVG	OBP	SLG	MLVR	EQBA	EQOBP	EQSLG	EQMLVR	VORP	DEFENSE	
2001	NYM	NL	36	135	30	5	1	0	8	9	3	2	.222	.266	.274	-.379	.234	.276	.292	-.356	-8.5		
2002	MIL	NL	37	197	60	8	2	3	14	17	4	1	.305	.355	.411	.084	.310	.357	.425	.044	5.1	13-LF	0
2003	CHC	NL	38	131	24	3	0	1	13	20	1	0	.183	.255	.229	-.423	.195	.262	.248	-.464	-9.1	24-3B	-1
2003	FLA	NL	38	14	4	0	0	0	3	1	0	0	.286	.412	.286	.015	.286	.412	.286	-.060	0.6		
2004	*FLA*	*NL*	*39*	*85*	*20*	*3*	*0*	*1*	*9*	*11*	*1*	*0*	*.230*	*.305*	*.298*	*-.260*	*.236*	*.309*	*.318*	*-.238*	*-2.9*	*27-3B*	*-7*

Breakout: 11%   Improve: 45%   Collapse: 45%

Veteran leadership and a likeable nature are all he has left to offer, because his bat is dead and buried. Never possessing any power, Harris' bat speed has slowed to where a bloop single is a huge chore. You can't call him a professional pinch-hitter anymore either, not after going 8 for 40 with no extra-base hits in the role last year. Harris signed a minor league deal to return to the Marlins. It'd be a shock if Dusty doesn't make him his bench coach someday.

JEREMY HERMIDA   RF   Bats: L   Throws: R   Born: 30-Jan-84   Age: 20

YEAR	TM	LG	AGE	AB	H	2B	3B	HR	BB	SO	SB	CS	AVG	OBP	SLG	MLVR	EQBA	EQOBP	EQSLG	EQMLVR	VORP	DEFENSE
2002	JAM	NYP	18	47	15	2	1	0	7	10	1	3	.319	.407	.404	.223	.204	.278	.265	-.404	-9.4	10-RF -2
2003	GRB	SAL	19	468	133	23	5	6	80	100	28	2	.284	.387	.393	.155	.211	.290	.301	-.327	-43.3	123-RF -15
2004	*FLA*	*NL*	*20*	*296*	*61*	*14*	*2*	*3*	*28*	*71*	*6*	*2*	*.205*	*.276*	*.300*	*-.325*	*.211*	*.280*	*.320*	*-.305*	*-17.0*	*80-RF -10*

Breakout: 32%   Improve: 55%   Collapse: 22%

The best hitting prospect in the system by a mile, the Marlins' '02 first-round pick put up a precocious season for a 19-year-old. Scouts love his projectable 6'4", 200 frame, but Hermida's no raw tools freak. Eighty walks and 28 steals in 30 tries from a player with average speed point to some finely developed baseball instincts well beyond Hermida's years. Several Sally League parks played as more pitcher-friendly than usual last year, depressing Hermida's power numbers somewhat. Though it won't get any easier in the Florida State or Southern leagues, watch for a season of further development, complete with plenty of doubles, and walks. If he acquits himself at the next two levels, you can start to imagine the future Marlins outfield, with Cabrera and Hermida punishing NL staffs from '06–'09.

TODD HOLLANDSWORTH   OF   Bats: L   Throws: L   Born: 20-Apr-73   Age: 31

YEAR	TM	LG	AGE	AB	H	2B	3B	HR	BB	SO	SB	CS	AVG	OBP	SLG	MLVR	EQBA	EQOBP	EQSLG	EQMLVR	VORP	DEFENSE			
2001	COL	NL	28	117	43	15	1	6	8	20	5	0	.368	.408	.667	.479	.336	.379	.621	.396	14.0	15-LF	0		
2002	COL	NL	29	298	88	21	1	11	26	71	7	8	.295	.352	.483	.118	.279	.337	.461	.032	6.8	57-LF	-1	15-RF	0
2002	TEX	AL	29	132	34	6	0	5	14	27	1	0	.258	.327	.417	-.033	.273	.347	.439	.014	2.4	17-LF	-1	10-CF	1
2003	FLA	NL	30	228	58	23	3	3	22	55	2	3	.254	.317	.421	.006	.263	.327	.440	-.029	2.0	57-LF	0		
2004	*CHC*	*NL*	*31*	*262*	*71*	*17*	*2*	*8*	*25*	*58*	*4*	*2*	*.273*	*.336*	*.449*	*.020*	*.275*	*.337*	*.462*	*.028*	*9.3*	*71-LF*	*-1*		

Breakout: 24%   Improve: 49%   Collapse: 30%

The Marlins messed up when they let Kevin Millar walk and replaced him with the brittle, power-challenged Hollandsworth. Given $1.5 million to fill the hole in left field, Hollandsworth flopped, not hitting nearly enough to justify an everyday job, or even hitting righties well enough to be worth platooning. Miguel Cabrera's lighting-quick rise to the majors papered over a bad move, yet another chapter in the Marlins' string of amazing luck. Not worth more than a pinch-hitter's job at this stage, he might be a token lefty bat on the Cubs' bench.

KEVIN HOOPER   2B/SS   Bats: R   Throws: R   Born: 07-Dec-76   Age: 27

YEAR	TM	LG	AGE	AB	H	2B	3B	HR	BB	SO	SB	CS	AVG	OBP	SLG	MLVR	EQBA	EQOBP	EQSLG	EQMLVR	VORP	DEFENSE			
2001	KNE	MID	24	65	19	2	0	0	11	13	3	1	.292	.390	.323	.058	.221	.303	.250	-.365	-4.0	17-2B	-1		
2001	PME	EAS	24	468	144	19	6	2	59	78	24	12	.308	.392	.387	.123	.262	.338	.331	-.161	2.1	114-2B	-2		
2002	CLG	PCL	25	452	130	21	3	2	34	51	17	10	.288	.341	.361	-.111	.241	.293	.302	-.304	-14.2	72-SS	1	42-2B	3
2003	ABQ	PCL	26	493	131	9	4	1	35	62	25	9	.266	.325	.306	-.213	.225	.282	.260	-.393	-31.5	77-2B	-2	48-SS	7
2004	*FLA*	*NL*	*27*	*166*	*39*	*7*	*1*	*1*	*14*	*25*	*5*	*2*	*.235*	*.303*	*.304*	*-.253*	*.241*	*.308*	*.324*	*-.230*	*0.7*	*48-2B*	*1*		

Breakout: 40%   Improve: 51%   Collapse: 35%

With Andy Fox and Matt Erickson gone and Hooper clinging to the 40-man, we could be looking at Mike Mordecai's utility wingman for 2004. Hooper followed a mediocre 2002 in Calgary with an awful '03 in Albuquerque; it takes a special kind of suckiness to manage 14 extra-base hits and 35 walks in 130 games. Unless the Fish make some great talent snags during spring training, expect another lousy bench and more of McKeon pushing his starting lineup to the limit.

RYAN JORGENSEN   C   Bats: R   Throws: R   Born: 04-May-79   Age: 25

YEAR	TM	LG	AGE	AB	H	2B	3B	HR	BB	SO	SB	CS	AVG	OBP	SLG	MLVR	EQBA	EQOBP	EQSLG	EQMLVR	VORP	DEFENSE	
2001	DAY	FLA	22	188	53	12	1	8	23	39	1	3	.282	.366	.484	.226	.228	.290	.399	-.182	-0.6	40-C	9
2001	WTN	SOU	22	109	13	4	0	2	11	38	0	0	.119	.195	.211	-.531	.125	.183	.214	-.702	-18.8	29-C	-3
2002	JUP	FLA	23	223	58	16	0	3	24	38	4	1	.260	.335	.372	.046	.224	.278	.332	-.301	-8.9	55-C	4
2002	PME	EAS	23	144	32	4	0	2	12	33	3	1	.222	.287	.292	-.247	.193	.248	.255	-.485	-14.3	41-C	4
2003	CAR	SOU	24	211	51	16	0	6	30	53	1	0	.242	.337	.403	.046	.211	.290	.362	-.244	-4.9	62-C	3
2004	*FLA*	*NL*	*25*	*176*	*38*	*8*	*1*	*4*	*16*	*42*	*1*	*1*	*.217*	*.287*	*.339*	*-.246*	*.223*	*.292*	*.361*	*-.222*	*-2.6*	*50-C*	*-2*

Breakout: 42%   Improve: 58%   Collapse: 18%

Once thought the key to the Alfonseca/Clement deal, Dontrelle Willis's emergence and injuries have dented Jorgensen's prospect status. As he had in prior years, he struggled with injuries all season. The Marlins like his power and love his catch-and-throw ability, but fear that neither skill will develop if he keeps hitting the DL. Approaching 25, with the Marlins' catching situation a mystery, Jorgensen needs a strong, injury-free season in the minors to give him a shot at the everyday job in '05.

DERREK LEE   1B   Bats: Throws: Born: 06-Sep-75   Age: 28

YEAR	TM	LG	AGE	AB	H	2B	3B	HR	BB	SO	SB	CS	AVG	OBP	SLG	MLVR	EQBA	EQOBP	EQSLG	EQMLVR	VORP	DEFENSE	
2001	FLA	NL	25	561	158	37	4	21	50	126	4	2	.282	.346	.474	.096	.290	.354	.488	.110	30.2	147-1B	10
2002	FLA	NL	26	581	157	35	7	27	98	164	19	9	.270	.378	.494	.215	.282	.385	.520	.199	45.9	160-1B	1
2003	FLA	NL	27	539	146	31	2	31	88	131	21	8	.271	.379	.508	.241	.279	.387	.528	.211	44.4	151-1B	5
2004	*CHC*	*NL*	*28*	*504*	*140*	*30*	*4*	*29*	*74*	*117*	*14*	*6*	*.279*	*.375*	*.522*	*.183*	*.281*	*.376*	*.537*	*.195*	*40.8*	*138-1B*	*1*

Breakout: 16%   Improve: 45%   Collapse: 14%

One of the most underrated players in the game, Lee offers the rare combination of power, patience, defense, and even speed for a first baseman. His trade to the Cubs for Hee Seop Choi and a PTBNL sparked plenty of debate in BP circles. Some see Choi as a player six years from free agency who'll mash at rock-bottom prices through '06, while Lee's a year from free agency and already expensive. But Lee's already one of the best first baseman in baseball, and his skill set suggests he'll age well. Meanwhile PECOTA offers a mixed bag of comparables for Choi, and every prospect comes with some question marks. Given the Cubs are staring at a window of two to three years with Sosa aging and Dusty cracking the whip on the pitching staff, the trade could work out great for both teams. Flags fly forever, as the Marlins can attest.

MIKE LOWELL   3B   Bats: R   Throws: R   Born: 24-Feb-74   Age: 30

YEAR	TM	LG	AGE	AB	H	2B	3B	HR	BB	SO	SB	CS	AVG	OBP	SLG	MLVR	EQBA	EQOBP	EQSLG	EQMLVR	VORP	DEFENSE	
2001	FLA	NL	27	551	156	37	0	18	43	79	1	2	.283	.340	.448	.052	.294	.352	.463	.075	38.8	142-3B	15
2002	FLA	NL	28	597	165	44	0	24	65	92	4	3	.276	.346	.471	.139	.287	.357	.493	.120	47.6	154-3B	10
2003	FLA	NL	29	492	136	27	1	32	56	78	3	1	.276	.350	.530	.231	.285	.358	.550	.199	48.3	127-3B	7
2004	*FLA*	*NL*	*30*	*488*	*135*	*30*	*1*	*22*	*53*	*80*	*2*	*2*	*.276*	*.351*	*.476*	*.083*	*.284*	*.356*	*.508*	*.127*	*40.5*	*130-3B*	*2*

Breakout: 13%   Improve: 46%   Collapse: 20%

Give Jeffrey Loria and company credit in one sense. Tying Lowell's new four-year, $32 million contract to construction of a new ballpark by offering Lowell an escape clause should the new park not get built is a great way to deflect blame

(continued next page)

Mike Lowell (*continued*)

to the insensitive masses, who obviously don't care enough about the team and South Florida's identity if they're not willing to hand a multi-millionaire $300 million for no good reason. Funny thing is, the Marlins would catch a break if Lowell leaves before the contract blows up in the team's face. Though it's uncomfortable to bring up, Lowell's lingering mid-season groin injury required several tests to determine if he'd suffered a recurrence of the testicular cancer that forced him into surgery in 1999, which raises a red flag. Paying what's now top-of-the-market money for four years of a player whose comparable player list hardly drips with Hall of Famers, and who turns 30 in February, is a bad decision. At best we'd project Lowell to hold steady for the next two or three years. He's a much better bet to decline than improve, starting this season.

JESUS MEDRANO   2B   Bats: R   Throws: R   Born: 11-Sep-78   Age: 25

YEAR	TM	LG	AGE	AB	H	2B	3B	HR	BB	SO	SB	CS	AVG	OBP	SLG	MLVR	EQBA	EQOBP	EQSLG	EQMLVR	VORP	DEFENSE		
2001	BRV	FLA	22	454	114	15	2	1	51	81	61	8	.251	.331	.300	-.064	.223	.282	.272	-.377	-29.9	98-2B -12	18-SS	1
2002	PME	EAS	23	414	123	27	6	3	79	82	39	18	.297	.411	.413	.163	.239	.340	.336	-.164	1.5	114-2B -9		
2003	ABQ	PCL	24	114	26	3	1	1	14	26	7	2	.228	.310	.298	-.268	.186	.264	.248	-.464	-10.1	28-2B 0		
2003	CAR	SOU	24	251	63	15	2	2	41	48	18	6	.251	.356	.351	.014	.219	.308	.312	-.272	-8.1	68-2B -9		
2004	*FLA*	*NL*	*25*	*182*	*42*	*9*	*1*	*2*	*19*	*37*	*8*	*2*	*.230*	*.309*	*.322*	*-.222*	*.236*	*.314*	*.343*	*-.197*	*1.6*	*52-2B -4*		

Breakout: 33%   Improve: 58%   Collapse: 23%

After a great 2002 season that looked terribly out of place, Medrano took a huge step backwards, watching his OBP implode in the process. Lacking power or the ability to play a decent shortstop, he's a limited player if he can't hit .280 with a ton of walks. The tools-obsessed Marlins like his speed though, and may yet give him a chance. Castillo re-upping for three-plus years further lengthens those odds.

MIKE MORDECAI   UT   Bats: R   Throws: R   Born: 13-Dec-67   Age: 36

YEAR	TM	LG	AGE	AB	H	2B	3B	HR	BB	SO	SB	CS	AVG	OBP	SLG	MLVR	EQBA	EQOBP	EQSLG	EQMLVR	VORP	DEFENSE		
2001	MON	NL	33	254	71	17	2	3	19	53	2	2	.280	.330	.398	-.064	.280	.332	.397	-.067	8.1	32-3B -3	24-2B	-2
2002	MON	NL	34	74	15	4	0	0	8	14	1	1	.203	.289	.257	-.300	.213	.297	.267	-.358	-3.5	11-3B -1		
2002	FLA	NL	34	77	22	4	0	0	5	13	1	1	.286	.337	.338	-.049	.304	.344	.367	-.069	2.6	17-SS 2		
2003	FLA	NL	35	89	19	4	0	2	8	21	3	0	.213	.276	.326	-.228	.222	.286	.344	-.270	-1.1			
2004	*FLA*	*NL*	*36*	*90*	*20*	*4*	*0*	*1*	*8*	*20*	*2*	*1*	*.227*	*.292*	*.316*	*-.263*	*.233*	*.296*	*.337*	*-.239*	*0.9*	*29-3B -3*		

Breakout: 26%   Improve: 42%   Collapse: 37%

With more staying power than Sting on Viagra, Mordecai's parlayed a hustling attitude and occasional flashes of decent play into a shockingly long career. He'll probably hang around a few more seasons on guile and spunk. Led the majors with a perfect game-winning home run ratio of 1.000, as both his homers won the game for the Marlins. OK, that's a pretty useless stat, but it's still more useful than Elias's Productive Outs.

ABRAHAM NUNEZ   CF/RF   Bats: B   Throws: R   Born: 05-Feb-77   Age: 27

YEAR	TM	LG	AGE	AB	H	2B	3B	HR	BB	SO	SB	CS	AVG	OBP	SLG	MLVR	EQBA	EQOBP	EQSLG	EQMLVR	VORP	DEFENSE		
2001	PME	EAS	24	467	112	14	9	17	83	155	26	19	.240	.357	.418	.059	.192	.296	.339	-.275	-20.1	134-CF 1		
2002	CLG	PCL	25	428	107	24	5	21	51	112	31	6	.250	.329	.477	-.007	.206	.283	.392	-.221	-10.1	118-CF 3		
2003	ABQ	PCL	26	212	66	13	2	11	32	56	9	4	.311	.398	.547	.257	.250	.339	.447	-.009	3.8	32-RF -1	27-CF	0
2004	*FLA*	*NL*	*27*	*171*	*38*	*9*	*1*	*6*	*22*	*50*	*5*	*2*	*.222*	*.310*	*.389*	*-.138*	*.228*	*.315*	*.414*	*-.108*	*1.9*	*50-CF -2*		

Breakout: 40%   Improve: 58%   Collapse: 29%

Nunez tacked on two years during AgeGate and has endured endless injuries—including a serious hamstring problem last season—wiping away much of his prospectdom. There's room for him at the ranch as a backup outfielder and bench upgrade. It wouldn't be a shock if he outperformed Jeff Conine, come to think of it.

JUAN PIERRE   CF   Bats: L   Throws: L   Born: 14-Aug-77   Age: 26

YEAR	TM	LG	AGE	AB	H	2B	3B	HR	BB	SO	SB	CS	AVG	OBP	SLG	MLVR	EQBA	EQOBP	EQSLG	EQMLVR	VORP	DEFENSE
2001	COL	NL	23	617	202	26	11	2	41	29	46	17	.327	.378	.415	.037	.307	.357	.388	-.012	22.1	145-CF 5
2002	COL	NL	24	592	170	20	5	1	31	52	47	12	.287	.332	.343	-.104	.276	.317	.332	-.192	-6.8	137-CF 2
2003	FLA	NL	25	668	204	28	7	1	55	35	65	20	.305	.361	.373	.055	.313	.368	.385	.009	32.0	160-CF -6
2004	*FLA*	*NL*	*26*	*607*	*182*	*30*	*7*	*2*	*47*	*39*	*46*	*13*	*.299*	*.355*	*.380*	*-.021*	*.307*	*.360*	*.405*	*.016*	*25.5*	*157-CF -2*

Breakout: 24%   Improve: 54%   Collapse: 12%

In the category of line of the year, few topped this gem: "Florida's Juan Pierre gets $200,000 for finishing 10th" in the National League MVP voting. It's hard to say which was nuttier: a position player who slugged .373 finishing 10th in the MVP voting, or an agent prescient enough to so accurately peg voters' stupidity. Pierre ranked seventh in Value Over Replacement Player . . . on his own team. He needs to continue hitting above .300 to be a valuable player, given he doesn't walk enough for a leadoff hitter, his defense is nothing special, and a Pierre homer is cause for a national holiday. He's not far removed from a terrible '02 season to boot. A nice little player signed to an affordable contract for the next two years, the Marlins can't afford to fall in love with Pierre's bunt-tastic ways and sign him to a huge extension.

MIKE REDMOND

C   **Bats: R**   **Throws: R**   Born: 05-May-71   Age: 33

YEAR	TM	LG	AGE	AB	H	2B	3B	HR	BB	SO	SB	CS	AVG	OBP	SLG	MLVR	EQBA	EQOBP	EQSLG	EQMLVR	VORP	DEFENSE
2001	FLA	NL	30	141	44	4	0	4	13	13	0	0	.312	.376	.426	.109	.319	.382	.438	.115	11.4	41-C 2
2002	FLA	NL	31	256	78	15	0	2	21	34	0	2	.305	.372	.387	.091	.317	.381	.408	.069	16.1	70-C 7
2003	FLA	NL	32	125	30	7	1	0	7	16	0	0	.240	.302	.312	-.182	.252	.312	.331	-.219	-1.3	27-C -5
2004	FLA	NL	33	118	31	6	0	1	9	16	0	0	.262	.329	.346	-.137	.269	.333	.369	-.107	3.7	36-C -2

Breakout: 15%   Improve: 34%   Collapse: 42%

However the Fish decide to handle their catching situation, hopefully they've figured out that Redmond isn't the answer. A decent backup if leveraged against lefties, he'd be a good fit alongside one of the few lefty-hitting catchers out there . . . Brian Schneider? Brent Mayne? Terry Kennedy? Pudge's departure, the Marlins' pointless three-catcher fetish, and Ramon Castro's legal trouble make a change of address unlikely.

ERIC REED

CF   **Bats: L**   **Throws: L**   Born: 02-Dec-80   Age: 23

YEAR	TM	LG	AGE	AB	H	2B	3B	HR	BB	SO	SB	CS	AVG	OBP	SLG	MLVR	EQBA	EQOBP	EQSLG	EQMLVR	VORP	DEFENSE
2002	JAM	NYP	21	250	77	5	1	0	17	30	19	10	.308	.348	.336	.050	.235	.270	.263	-.409	-35.8	60-CF -2
2002	KNE	MID	21	50	18	1	0	0	3	11	7	1	.360	.396	.380	.222	.308	.333	.327	-.146	0.0	11-CF -1
2003	JUP	FLA	22	514	154	15	8	0	52	83	53	18	.300	.367	.360	.122	.260	.312	.321	-.228	-13.7	125-CF 1
2004	FLA	NL	23	252	60	10	2	1	18	44	10	4	.237	.289	.303	-.280	.243	.293	.323	-.257	-7.6	68-CF -4

Breakout: 21%   Improve: 44%   Collapse: 27%

Reed is a 5'10", 170-pound slap hitter with no pop, modest plate discipline, and decent center field defense. He's also really, really fast, swiping 53 bases in his first year of full-season ball. The Marlins love him, so much so that they named him minor league hitter of the year. Let that thought float around in your mind for a minute, then go back and look at Reed's 2003 stat line. That tells you all you need to know about the organization.

IVAN RODRIGUEZ

C   **Bats: R**   **Throws: R**   Born: 30-Nov-71   Age: 32

YEAR	TM	LG	AGE	AB	H	2B	3B	HR	BB	SO	SB	CS	AVG	OBP	SLG	MLVR	EQBA	EQOBP	EQSLG	EQMLVR	VORP	DEFENSE
2001	TEX	AL	29	442	136	24	2	25	23	73	10	3	.308	.347	.541	.201	.320	.360	.567	.267	48.0	103-C 17
2002	TEX	AL	30	408	128	32	2	19	25	71	5	4	.314	.353	.542	.228	.330	.372	.572	.305	49.0	97-C 4
2003	FLA	NL	31	511	152	36	3	16	55	92	10	6	.297	.369	.474	.203	.308	.379	.494	.179	45.7	127-C 2
2004	FLA	NL	32	454	129	27	2	17	41	81	8	3	.285	.347	.465	.069	.292	.352	.495	.112	35.4	119-C -2

Breakout: 9%   Improve: 41%   Collapse: 26%

Amazing what five games can do. Pudge went from being pegged for occasional surliness, a cranky back, and a rep for poorly handling pitchers to team leader and Clutch Playoff God. He did it not through contrived yelling and screaming, but by example. Rodriguez's performance in the Marlins' dramatic NLDS victory over San Francisco had everything: timely hitting, terrific defense, and a jaw-dropping, series-ending collision at home plate, with Pudge hanging onto the ball and holding it aloft for the world to see. That performance will earn him a few dollars on the free agent market, though the heavy mileage on his odometer and past injuries still dampen his price and raise questions about his future performance. Rodriguez will likely never top his '03 season, but he's still a valuable player who can help most teams. He'll always have his ring, and the memories.

JASON STOKES
1B   Bats: R   Throws: R   Born: 23-Jan-82   Age: 22

YEAR	TM	LG	AGE	AB	H	2B	3B	HR	BB	SO	SB	CS	AVG	OBP	SLG	MLVR	EQBA	EQOBP	EQSLG	EQMLVR	VORP	DEFENSE	
2001	UTI	NYP	19	130	30	2	1	6	11	48	0	0	.231	.299	.400	.015	.172	.217	.313	-.478	-27.3		
2002	KNE	MID	20	349	119	25	0	27	47	96	1	1	.341	.421	.645	.587	.251	.319	.484	.007	10.3	86-1B	-2
2003	JUP	FLA	21	462	119	31	3	17	36	135	6	4	.258	.312	.448	.134	.222	.267	.403	-.225	-21.2	100-1B	-8
2004	*FLA*	*NL*	*22*	*276*	*60*	*13*	*1*	*11*	*23*	*88*	*2*	*1*	*.216*	*.278*	*.390*	*-.197*	*.221*	*.282*	*.416*	*-.169*	*-3.8*	*74-1B*	*-7*

Breakout: 20%   *Improve: 50%*   *Collapse: 28%*

A terrible first half and better second half added up to a disappointing season for Stokes. Though the leap in opponents' quality and ballpark effects are huge between the Midwest and Florida State leagues, it's hard to feel good about the Marlins' best 2003 hitting prospect putting up a .312 OBP. Stokes's walks plunged and his massive strikeout totals didn't as he struggled to put together good at-bats. While we don't usually make a big deal about hitters' strikeouts, a lumbering player with no speed, insufficient walks and a ton of strikeouts raises concerns about how he'll get on base in the show. A defensive liability whether he plays first or a corner outfield slot, Stokes is also now a health risk, having incurred some of the same wrist problems that made the Marlins sour on their last former first base phenom, Adrian Gonzalez. Stokes's best hope is a promotion to Double-A and 15 warning track outs evolving into homers in the more generous Southern League. It's easy to overstate the importance of a prospect's most recent season, but we're a lot more worried now than we were a year ago.

ROB STRATTON
RF   Bats: R   Throws: R   Born: 07-Oct-77   Age: 26

YEAR	TM	LG	AGE	AB	H	2B	3B	HR	BB	SO	SB	CS	AVG	OBP	SLG	MLVR	EQBA	EQOBP	EQSLG	EQMLVR	VORP	DEFENSE			
2001	BIN	EAS	23	483	120	30	1	29	53	201	9	5	.248	.332	.495	.112	.207	.282	.415	-.190	-19.6	63-RF	0	44-LF	-1
2002	CSP	PCL	24	80	17	2	1	7	6	42	0	1	.212	.308	.525	-.002	.177	.261	.443	-.214	-3.5	18-RF	0		
2002	NOR	INT	24	256	63	8	0	20	18	84	6	3	.246	.305	.512	.108	.232	.291	.494	-.045	1.5	56-RF	1	14-LF	1
2003	ABQ	PCL	25	372	79	12	2	32	36	175	6	4	.212	.283	.513	-.050	.174	.245	.424	-.271	-23.0	85-RF	-3		
2004	*SFG*	*NL*	*26*	*192*	*42*	*9*	*1*	*11*	*21*	*82*	*2*	*1*	*.216*	*.300*	*.447*	*-.086*	*.216*	*.299*	*.460*	*-.087*	*0.3*	*55-RF*	*-2*		

Breakout: 50%   *Improve: 67%*   *Collapse: 15%*

A mountain of a man, Stratton spent another year in the minors swinging from the heels, coming up empty nearly half the time. Had he stayed in the lineup every day, he'd have smashed his own mark of 201 strikeouts, a trick he turned in Binghamton in '01. Stratton possesses immense power, but no other discernable skills. Comparisons to Rob Deer are unfair: Deer had several useful major league seasons, Stratton won't have any. Signed to a minor league deal by the Giants—we'd pay big money to see him chase liners into the right-center triangle at Pac Bell, even if the odds of such a spectacle happening are slim and none.

WILSON VALDEZ
SS/2B   Bats: R   Throws: R   Born: 20-May-78   Age: 26

YEAR	TM	LG	AGE	AB	H	2B	3B	HR	BB	SO	SB	CS	AVG	OBP	SLG	MLVR	EQBA	EQOBP	EQSLG	EQMLVR	VORP	DEFENSE	
2001	CLN	MID	23	214	54	8	1	0	9	22	6	7	.252	.286	.299	-.182	.200	.228	.242	-.541	-21.6	58-SS	14
2001	JUP	FLA	23	233	58	13	2	2	10	33	7	3	.249	.286	.348	-.072	.223	.245	.324	-.378	-12.4	63-SS	3
2002	PME	EAS	24	375	98	19	5	1	15	47	18	6	.261	.294	.347	-.139	.231	.259	.314	-.360	-18.1	107-SS	-8
2003	ABQ	PCL	25	338	97	12	4	0	19	37	33	9	.287	.326	.346	-.145	.248	.288	.299	-.314	-10.9	79-SS	0
2003	CAR	SOU	25	144	45	6	2	0	15	17	16	5	.313	.373	.382	.120	.277	.327	.351	-.145	1.4	32-2B	-3
2004	*FLA*	*NL*	*26*	*208*	*48*	*9*	*2*	*1*	*12*	*27*	*8*	*3*	*.231*	*.274*	*.309*	*-.303*	*.237*	*.278*	*.329*	*-.281*	*-1.8*	*56-SS*	*-5*

Breakout: 32%   *Improve: 52%*   *Collapse: 32%*

Another in the organization's long line of punchless middle infielders, the Marlins still like him for . . . what else, his speed. Valdez's 49 steals and decent glove at short keep him on the radar for a future big league job. The next time he slugs .400 as a professional ballplayer will be the first.

JOSH WILLINGHAM
C/UT   Bats: R   Throws: R   Born: 17-Feb-79   Age: 25

YEAR	TM	LG	AGE	AB	H	2B	3B	HR	BB	SO	SB	CS	AVG	OBP	SLG	MLVR	EQBA	EQOBP	EQSLG	EQMLVR	VORP	DEFENSE			
2001	KNE	MID	22	320	83	20	2	7	53	85	24	2	.259	.382	.400	.122	.195	.287	.305	-.336	-16.0	80-3B	8		
2002	JUP	FLA	23	376	103	21	4	17	63	88	18	5	.274	.394	.487	.285	.222	.314	.407	-.130	-5.8	30-1B	-3	20-3B	-2
2003	JUP	FLA	24	193	51	17	1	12	46	42	9	2	.264	.422	.549	.397	.198	.324	.425	-.104	5.0	35-C	-7		
2003	CAR	SOU	24	67	20	2	1	5	13	20	0	0	.299	.434	.582	.444	.243	.352	.486	.061	4.3				
2004	*FLA*	*NL*	*25*	*251*	*60*	*14*	*1*	*9*	*32*	*63*	*5*	*2*	*.239*	*.338*	*.420*	*-.040*	*.246*	*.343*	*.448*	*-.004*	*12.5*	*72-DH*	*4*		

Breakout: 44%   *Improve: 69%*   *Collapse: 13%*

In his first extended exposure to catching since high school, Willingham didn't embarrass himself. A good athlete who played short in college and then third for much of his minor league career, Willingham has worked hard to hone his footwork, throwing and game-calling skills. He's also hit the weights in an effort to better handle the rigors of regular catching—he had his right knee scoped to repair a torn meniscus last year. His hitting certainly didn't suffer, as he cranked out 17 homers and 38 extra-base hits in 260 at-bats between Jupiter and Carolina. Willingham needs a full year in Double-A to keep pounding the ball while rounding his catching into shape. Age could soon start to work against him, but for now, given the scarcity of catchers who can hit, he's a prospect.

JOSH WILSON   SS   Bats: R   Throws: R   Born: 26-Mar-81   Age: 23

YEAR	TM	LG	AGE	AB	H	2B	3B	HR	BB	SO	SB	CS	AVG	OBP	SLG	MLVR	EQBA	EQOBP	EQSLG	EQMLVR	VORP	DEFENSE			
2001	KNE	MID	20	506	144	28	5	4	28	60	17	11	.285	.325	.383	.030	.228	.262	.314	-.356	-26.6	63-2B	-2	49-SS	-6
2002	JUP	FLA	21	398	102	17	1	11	28	67	7	10	.256	.318	.387	.039	.222	.266	.349	-.302	-11.9	103-SS	3		
2002	PME	EAS	21	41	14	3	0	2	2	6	0	1	.341	.372	.561	.349	.293	.326	.463	.029	2.9	12-SS	1		
2003	CAR	SOU	22	434	110	30	6	3	27	70	6	5	.253	.294	.371	-.052	.227	.264	.345	-.309	-14.0	110-SS	-8		
2004	FLA	NL	23	253	60	13	1	4	15	42	3	2	.236	.286	.344	-.233	.242	.290	.366	-.207	1.9	68-SS	-7		

Breakout: 42%   Improve: 65%   Collapse: 15%

A third-round pick in the 1999 draft, Wilson looked like a find when he hit 11 homers in Jupiter in 2002, no mean feat in a brutal park for long balls. His homers turned to doubles in '03, and Wilson's production fell sharply. A passable glove at short, Wilson is young enough to have a future. He needs to strengthen his 6'0", 165-pound frame and most importantly improve his plate discipline to get anywhere, or even to be the best JoshWil in the system.

PITCHERS

PHIL AKENS   Bats: R   Throws: R   Born: 09-Aug-82   Age: 21

YEAR	TM	LG	AGE	G	GS	IP	H	BB	SO	HR	ERA	EQERA	EQH9	EQBB9	EQSO9	EQHR9	PERA	VORP	STF
2001	UTI	NYP	18	9	9	50.0	40	22	34	3	3.24	6.12	9.9	6.1	3.8	1.9	6.84	-2.5	-11
2002	KNE	MID	19	28	26	160.0	180	47	109	14	4.89	7.71	12.5	3.6	4.0	2.1	7.59	-33.4	-15
2003	GRB	SAL	20	16	16	100.0	89	28	70	4	3.15	5.01	10.4	3.4	3.9	1.0	5.34	5.8	5
2003	JUP	FLA	20	11	11	65.7	67	14	45	0	2.88	5.34	10.1	2.4	4.5	0.3	4.12	1.8	26
2004	FLA	NL	21	17	14	84.3	90	38	50	9	4.79	5.36	9.6	3.6	4.8	1.1	5.42	2.7	-6

Breakout: 16%   Improve: 54%   Collapse: 12%

All things being equal, we give pitchers with strong minor league K/BB rates better odds of future success than those with weaker rates. Dayn Perry's research at baseballprospectus.com looked at samples of successful major league pitchers, and found low home run rates to also be a key predictor of future success, possibly the most important one. The 6'6", 200-pound Akens yielded just four homers in 27 starts last season, including a goose egg in 11 starts at Jupiter. Granting how it often takes a grenade launcher to get a ball out at Jupiter, that's still impressive for a pitcher who turned 21 the final week of the Florida State League season. The Marlins' 13th-round choice out of a Maryland high school, Akens isn't overpowering for his size, but the Marlins like his learning curve. He could reach Double-A by year's end, where he'll be tested.

ARMANDO ALMANZA   Bats: L   Throws: L   Born: 26-Oct-72   Age: 31

YEAR	TM	LG	AGE	G	GS	IP	H	BB	SO	HR	ERA	EQERA	EQH9	EQBB9	EQSO9	EQHR9	PERA	VORP	STF
2001	FLA	NL	28	52	0	41.0	34	26	45	8	4.83	5.22	7.7	5.2	8.4	1.6	5.12	1.7	-14
2002	FLA	NL	29	51	0	45.7	36	23	57	8	4.33	4.47	7.5	3.9	9.7	1.6	4.64	5.6	1
2003	FLA	NL	30	51	0	50.3	59	25	49	10	6.08	6.57	10.6	4.0	7.7	1.8	6.40	-7.2	-28
2004	ATL	NL	31	34	4	53.7	54	27	49	9	5.15	5.59	9.0	4.0	7.4	1.5	5.49	3.2	-3

Breakout: 26%   Improve: 45%   Collapse: 33%

After getting lefties out in 2001, then faring better against righties in 2002, Almanza got lit up by everyone last year—rumor has it Jack McKeon was hitting 450-foot rockets off him in BP. Almanza ended his forgetful season in August with surgery to remove a bone chip from his left pitching elbow. Thirty-one-year-old lefties coming off a lousy year and surgery and eligible for arbitration shouldn't count on job security. Non-tendered by the Marlins, he'll show just how replaceable Ray King is among second lefties.

JOSH BECKETT   **Bats: R**   **Throws: R**   Born: 15-May-80   Age: 24

YEAR	TM	LG	AGE	G	GS	IP	H	BB	SO	HR	ERA	EQERA	EQH9	EQBB9	EQSO9	EQHR9	PERA	VORP	STF
2001	BRV	FLA	21	13	12	65.7	32	15	101	0	1.23	2.45	6.9	2.5	9.4	0.3	2.67	20.5	67
2001	FLA	NL	21	4	4	24.0	14	11	24	3	1.50	3.13	5.5	3.9	7.8	1.2	3.28	6.3	48
2001	PME	EAS	21	13	13	74.3	50	19	102	8	1.82	3.29	8.6	3.2	9.2	1.4	4.70	16.9	45
2002	FLA	NL	22	23	21	107.7	93	44	113	13	4.09	4.40	8.0	3.2	8.2	1.1	4.18	13.9	39
2003	FLA	NL	23	24	23	142.0	132	56	152	9	3.04	3.72	8.5	3.2	8.5	0.6	3.85	32.5	51
2004	*FLA*	*NL*	*24*	*23*	*22*	*143.0*	*127*	*51*	*140*	*13*	*3.52*	*3.94*	*8.0*	*2.8*	*7.9*	*0.9*	*3.93*	*26.9*	*24*

Breakout: 23%   *Improve: 42%*   *Collapse: 23%*

Grew up more than any player in baseball last year. Beckett's maturation started after A. J. Burnett had to undergo Tommy John surgery. Beckett, who'd been hiding elbow stiffness for three weeks, wisely told the Marlins he may need to sit a while. While on the DL, Dontrelle Willis mania took hold. Once considered the phenom, Beckett watched Willis get all the accolades, and he wasn't happy about it. After the All-Star break, he caught fire, putting up an ERA a 2.55 ERA and striking out 93 in 88.1 second-half innings. Called on to relieve Mark Redman in Game 7 of the NLCS, Beckett's four innings of one-hit ball pushed the Fish into the World Series. When Jack McKeon tapped him to pitch Game 6 of the World Series at Yankee Stadium on three days rest, the debate raged over whether he'd succeed, or if his young arm could even take the burden. Beckett threw gas by Yankee hitters all night, throwing a five-hit shutout to win the Series and a shoulder ride around the mound by delirious teammates.

With Torborg's butcherly inclinations gone and Beckett's blister problems apparently behind him, and with a wiser head on his shoulders, the Marlins just have to hope the added load on October has no long-term effect on Beckett's golden right arm. If it doesn't, the sky's the limit.

DONNIE BRIDGES   **Bats: R**   **Throws: R**   Born: 10-Dec-78   Age: 25

YEAR	TM	LG	AGE	G	GS	IP	H	BB	SO	HR	ERA	EQERA	EQH9	EQBB9	EQSO9	EQHR9	PERA	VORP	STF
2001	HAR	EAS	22	3	3	16.7	14	13	14	2	3.23	6.75	9.2	9.8	5.5	1.8	7.33	-1.9	-28
2001	OTT	INT	22	13	13	55.3	60	43	49	11	7.49	8.54	10.1	8.2	6.8	2.1	7.58	-16.9	-23
2002	HAR	EAS	23	14	13	63.0	63	42	49	7	6.14	7.58	10.6	7.1	5.4	1.7	7.16	-12.5	-35
2002	PME	EAS	23	6	3	15.7	29	18	6	1	13.18	15.43	18.6	12.2	2.6	1.3	10.89	-15.3	-97
2003	CAR	SOU	24	31	19	134.7	85	70	109	6	2.81	4.19	7.4	5.5	5.1	0.9	4.40	18.8	-6
2004	*FLA*	*NL*	*25*	*15*	*10*	*50.3*	*63*	*43*	*32*	*5*	*7.23*	*8.08*	*11.3*	*6.8*	*5.0*	*0.9*	*7.83*	*-4.9*	*-24*

Breakout: 19%   *Improve: 50%*   *Collapse: 25%*

With nowhere to go but up after a horrific 2002, Bridges shaved almost five runs off his ERA. The same bugaboos still haunt him: off-field emotional baggage and a galling lack of control. That the Marlins were somewhat encouraged by Bridges's 109/70 K/BB rate in 134.2 innings last year tells you how bad it had gotten. A six-year free agent, Bridges is still young enough, and pitching scarce enough, that someone will get the former #1 draft choice a shot.

NATE BUMP   **Bats: R**   **Throws: R**   Born: 24-Jul-76   Age: 27

YEAR	TM	LG	AGE	G	GS	IP	H	BB	SO	HR	ERA	EQERA	EQH9	EQBB9	EQSO9	EQHR9	PERA	VORP	STF
2001	PME	EAS	24	11	8	54.7	55	10	41	10	5.27	7.80	12.5	2.3	4.8	2.7	8.00	-11.6	-54
2002	PME	EAS	25	20	20	127.7	110	29	81	5	3.38	4.06	9.4	2.4	4.2	0.6	4.18	19.7	6
2003	ABQ	PCL	26	15	15	85.3	89	24	52	4	4.43	4.13	9.4	3.0	4.6	0.6	4.24	13.2	6
2003	FLA	NL	26	32	0	36.3	34	20	17	3	4.71	4.84	8.2	4.3	3.8	0.8	4.29	0.8	-18
2004	*FLA*	*NL*	*27*	*20*	*10*	*62.0*	*67*	*25*	*35*	*6*	*4.64*	*5.19*	*9.7*	*3.2*	*4.5*	*1.0*	*5.18*	*3.4*	*-10*

Breakout: 17%   *Improve: 46%*   *Collapse: 25%*

Known as a control artist his last couple of years in the minors, Bump lost the plate after his late-June callup, walking more batters than he struck out by season's end. Remember when Jason Grilli and Bump were back-to-back first-round Giants picks in '97 and '98? File two more under TINSTAAPP. In *BP 1999,* we said: "Look out for this guy." What we really meant was 'look out, because an errant slider might bean you in the side of the head if you're not careful.'

A. J. BURNETT   Bats: R   Throws: R   Born: 03-Jan-77   Age: 27

YEAR	TM	LG	AGE	G	GS	IP	H	BB	SO	HR	ERA	EQERA	EQH9	EQBB9	EQSO9	EQHR9	PERA	VORP	STF
2001	FLA	NL	24	27	27	173.3	145	83	128	20	4.05	4.20	7.7	4.0	5.6	0.9	4.08	26.0	15
2002	FLA	NL	25	31	29	204.3	153	90	203	12	3.30	3.50	7.0	3.5	7.7	0.5	3.22	46.2	37
2003	FLA	NL	26	4	4	23.0	18	18	21	2	4.70	4.76	7.1	6.4	7.1	0.8	4.37	0.8	9
2004	FLA	NL	27	37	22	130.0	117	69	112	12	4.37	4.88	8.1	4.2	6.9	0.9	4.75	10.0	4

Breakout: 9%   Improve: 44%   Collapse: 24%

With the recovery timetable from Tommy John surgery shaved down to as little as twelve months, there's some hope that Burnett could return by May. Though Burnett's on the same aggressive timetable that got Brandon Claussen back in about that time, don't count on a lightning-quick recovery. Burnett had been one of the most abused young arms in the game long before the last Torborgian straw snapped his ulnar collateral ligament. The Marlins hope the time off allows Burnett to reflect and cut down on some of his self-destructive off-field behavior. He's got a world of talent, and could slot in nicely in one of baseball's best rotations if he makes it back to full strength by the home stretch.

CHAD FOX   Bats: R   Throws: R   Born: 03-Sep-70   Age: 33

YEAR	TM	LG	AGE	G	GS	IP	H	BB	SO	HR	ERA	EQERA	EQH9	EQBB9	EQSO9	EQHR9	PERA	VORP	STF
2001	MIL	NL	30	65	0	66.7	44	36	80	6	1.89	2.67	6.5	4.5	9.1	0.7	3.43	20.8	24
2003	BOS	AL	32	17	0	18.0	19	17	19	2	4.50	5.00	9.0	8.0	9.0	1.0	5.79	1.9	-6
2003	FLA	NL	32	21	0	25.3	16	14	27	1	2.13	2.55	5.8	4.4	8.4	0.4	2.82	9.6	30
2004	FLA	NL	33	45	0	48.0	42	29	48	4	3.81	4.26	7.9	4.8	8.0	0.7	4.73	7.6	3

Breakout: 16%   Improve: 49%   Collapse: 22%

It may a weird genetic thing, or the result of his two Tommy John surgeries, but Fox's arm would ache last season after too much downtime. In fact, the book on him became to have him throw nearly every day, then have him toss as many as 50 warmup pitches before coming into a game. It's the same principle as sinkerballers getting better as they get more tired, except Fox isn't a sinkerballer, so chalk it to the same kind of weirdness as that night in Abilene involving Nate Silver, that Wal-Mart greeter, a mechanical bull, and a sixer of Coors. Fox's August move to Florida and subsequent strong performance after washing out in Boston earned him several off-season suitors, so he'll have a steady job in a major league pen waiting for him come spring.

FRANK GRACESQUI   Bats: B   Throws: L   Born: 20-Aug-79   Age: 24

YEAR	TM	LG	AGE	G	GS	IP	H	BB	SO	HR	ERA	EQERA	EQH9	EQBB9	EQSO9	EQHR9	PERA	VORP	STF
2001	CWV	SAL	21	35	2	65.3	60	34	66	1	3.17	6.55	10.5	7.2	5.3	0.3	5.62	-5.9	-5
2002	DUN	FLA	22	10	0	21.7	15	11	25	1	2.49	4.19	8.4	5.6	7.4	0.9	4.84	3.0	9
2002	TEN	SOU	22	41	0	42.7	40	34	48	3	4.64	6.69	10.4	7.6	7.4	1.4	6.74	-4.7	-15
2003	CAR	SOU	23	44	0	58.0	44	43	75	0	2.48	4.53	9.1	8.0	8.2	0.3	5.17	6.1	10
2004	FLA	NL	24	17	1	20.0	22	20	10	2	6.50	7.26	10.0	7.7	3.8	0.9	7.44	-1.4	-39

Breakout: 23%   Improve: 30%   Collapse: 26%

A 21st-round high school pick by the Blue Jays in '98, Gracesqui never could find the strike zone, eventually forcing the Jays to give up on him. While he didn't improve his control last year, a huge, 6′5″ lefty with 75 strikeouts, 44 hits and zero homers allowed in 58 Double-A innings isn't chopped liver. Well, it is if it's my bubby's delicious chopped liver, but you get the idea. With no above-average lefty relievers on last year's roster, Gracesqui could get a shot at the show at some point in '04.

RICK HELLING   Bats: R   Throws: R   Born: 15-Dec-70   Age: 33

YEAR	TM	LG	AGE	G	GS	IP	H	BB	SO	HR	ERA	EQERA	EQH9	EQBB9	EQSO9	EQHR9	PERA	VORP	STF
2001	TEX	AL	30	34	34	215.7	256	63	154	38	5.17	4.91	9.7	2.4	5.9	1.3	5.01	16.4	1
2002	ARI	NL	31	30	30	175.7	180	48	120	31	4.51	4.63	9.3	2.2	5.4	1.6	5.08	18.2	-7
2003	BAL	AL	32	24	24	138.7	156	40	86	30	5.71	5.55	9.4	2.4	5.4	1.8	5.43	-2.6	-15
2003	FLA	NL	32	11	0	16.3	11	5	12	1	0.55	1.15	5.7	2.3	5.7	0.6	2.41	9.2	21
2004	MIN	AL	33	27	21	124.3	136	36	77	22	4.96	4.84	9.5	2.5	5.5	1.4	4.85	14.7	1

Breakout: 20%   Improve: 47%   Collapse: 28%

(continued next page)

Rick Helling (continued)

Few teams in recent memory have scored more gains from trade deadline snags then the Marlins did last year. Chad Fox went from tin man to anchor, Uggy Urbina from good pitcher to great, Helling from "Lara Flynn Boyle could take this guy deep" to lights-out. Allowing for the small sample size of 16 innings and the drastically improved pitcher's environment of Pro Player, it's worth asking if Helling may be better suited to relief in the future. As a starter, he's been a tateriffic innings-eater his whole career, with future above-average seasons unlikely at age 33. Always a good control guy, Helling's ability to prevent the base on balls mixed with prudent usage could produce a nifty 80-inning-a-year righty neutralizer for peanuts.

LINCOLN HOLDZKOM Bats: R Throws: R Born: 23-Mar-82 Age: 22

YEAR	TM	LG	AGE	G	GS	IP	H	BB	SO	HR	ERA	EQERA	EQH9	EQBB9	EQSO9	EQHR9	PERA	VORP	STF
2002	KNE	MID	20	30	0	32.0	21	29	42	0	2.53	5.00	8.7	11.7	7.7	0.3	5.90	1.8	8
2003	GRB	SAL	21	43	0	57.0	36	27	74	0	2.84	4.56	8.6	5.8	7.3	0.4	4.42	5.7	17
2003	JUP	FLA	21	13	0	14.7	9	7	20	0	3.06	4.85	7.6	5.5	8.3	0.0	3.57	1.1	35
2004	FLA	NL	22	25	2	32.7	30	25	32	2	4.81	5.38	8.2	6.1	7.8	0.7	5.53	3.3	-4

Breakout: 28%   Improve: 70%   Collapse: 19%

A strikeout rate of nearly a dozen per nine innings pitched will get anyone's attention, even if it was in A-ball. Like Gracesqui, Holdzkom is an enormous guy who can bring it. A 7th-round pick out of an Arizona community college in 2001, Holdzkom's also two and a half years younger than Gracesqui, and not as wild. That's not to say that there aren't rough edges to smooth over; 11 wild pitches in 57 Sally League innings mean he's still raw. It'll be interesting to see how Holdzkom develops as he gets a full year of Florida State League ball under his belt and later challenges Double-A. He may lack the repertoire to be a starter, but it's worthwhile to wait and see what happens. The zero homers allowed in 71.2 innings—park effects and all—make him a prospect either way.

TREVOR HUTCHINSON Bats: R Throws: R Born: 08-Oct-79 Age: 24

YEAR	TM	LG	AGE	G	GS	IP	H	BB	SO	HR	ERA	EQERA	EQH9	EQBB9	EQSO9	EQHR9	PERA	VORP	STF
2003	CAR	SOU	23	8	6	35.0	32	13	18	1	3.86	6.19	9.6	3.9	3.1	0.6	4.62	-2.1	-9
2003	JUP	FLA	23	14	13	84.3	77	16	58	3	2.78	5.02	10.4	2.2	4.3	1.1	5.02	4.9	0
2004	FLA	NL	24	20	13	77.0	85	28	43	8	4.73	5.28	10.0	2.9	4.5	1.1	5.33	3.9	-8

Breakout: 16%   Improve: 46%   Collapse: 29%

The younger brother of former Cardinals farmhand-turned-quarterback Chad Hutchinson, Trevor logged 19 starts between Jupiter and Carolina and did a good job of keeping runners off base. He pitched well under pressure too, earning MVP honors in the Southern League Championship series by yielding just one earned run over 11.2 innings. The all-time leader in strikeouts for the Cal Golden Bears needs to make more batters miss in pro ball if he's to build on his success and reach the pot of gold at the end of the rainbow.

ALLEN LEVRAULT Bats: R Throws: R Born: 15-Aug-77 Age: 26

YEAR	TM	LG	AGE	G	GS	IP	H	BB	SO	HR	ERA	EQERA	EQH9	EQBB9	EQSO9	EQHR9	PERA	VORP	STF
2001	IND	INT	23	5	5	30.7	22	8	30	1	2.64	2.79	6.5	2.8	7.1	0.3	2.63	9.1	48
2001	MIL	NL	23	32	20	130.7	146	59	80	27	6.06	6.29	10.1	3.7	4.6	1.6	5.98	-9.7	-13
2002	SAC	PCL	24	24	23	111.3	145	45	81	15	6.39	6.90	11.4	4.0	4.9	1.5	6.48	-15.5	-25
2003	ABQ	PCL	25	21	0	25.7	12	9	18	2	1.40	1.48	4.1	3.7	5.2	1.1	2.56	11.1	-3
2003	FLA	NL	25	19	0	28.0	38	15	21	3	3.86	5.27	12.2	4.3	5.9	1.0	6.29	5.0	-13
2004	STL	NL	26	22	10	62	62	27	43	7	4.34	4.73	8.9	3.5	5.6	1.0	4.88	6.2	-4

Breakout: 32%   Improve: 52%   Collapse: 21%

Past the point where his youth excites you, Levrault looks like your garden-variety crappy pitcher at this point. Either his stuff isn't major league caliber or he can't disguise his pitches, because he remains incredibly hittable every year. You'd hope he could keep the ball in the park or maybe put good enough strikeout numbers to make him intriguing, but no luck there either. He's strictly NRI material at this point. The Cardinals showed how barren their system was, announcing THIRTY-SEVEN(!) minor league free agent signees on November 20, with Levrault being one of the better ones.

BRADEN LOOPER   Bats: R   Throws: R   Born: 28-Oct-74   Age: 29

YEAR	TM	LG	AGE	G	GS	IP	H	BB	SO	HR	ERA	EQERA	EQH9	EQBB9	EQSO9	EQHR9	PERA	VORP	STF
2001	FLA	NL	26	71	0	71.0	63	30	52	8	3.55	3.95	8.2	3.6	5.5	0.9	4.20	12.5	-6
2002	FLA	NL	27	78	0	86.0	73	28	55	8	3.14	3.47	7.6	2.6	5.0	0.9	3.61	19.6	-2
2003	FLA	NL	28	74	0	80.7	82	29	56	4	3.68	4.02	9.1	2.9	5.5	0.5	3.95	15.0	6
2004	FLA	NL	29	54	0	63.7	64	24	43	5	3.66	4.09	9.0	3.0	5.4	0.8	4.49	10.5	-6

Breakout: 30%   Improve: 58%   Collapse: 18%

The Marlins can carp all they want about Looper's makeup, personality, or the gravitational pull of Saturn making him a bad choice as a closer. The reason's much simpler than that: he's a ROOGY. In the last three years, Looper's held righties to a meager .225/.301/.309; meanwhile, lefties have hit .271/.326/.434 against him. While that's not Carlos Delgado against a gassed Dave Burba bad, it's still less comfort than you'd want from an ace reliever, whatever inning he may pitch. The three-year, $2.6 million plus bonuses contract he signed in 2001 expired, Looper was non-tendered, a good idea for a team that could use the $2 million in savings. Better still, he signed up with the Mets to be their closer, soaking up some of their revenues.

BLAINE NEAL   Bats: L   Throws: R   Born: 06-Apr-78   Age: 26

YEAR	TM	LG	AGE	G	GS	IP	H	BB	SO	HR	ERA	EQERA	EQH9	EQBB9	EQSO9	EQHR9	PERA	VORP	STF
2001	PME	EAS	23	54	0	53.3	43	21	45	1	2.36	4.40	9.4	5.0	5.4	0.2	4.41	6.3	4
2002	CLG	PCL	24	29	0	31.0	27	15	26	2	2.90	3.41	8.1	5.0	5.9	0.6	4.24	7.1	1
2002	FLA	NL	24	32	0	33.0	32	14	33	1	2.73	3.66	9.0	3.4	7.9	0.3	3.84	6.9	31
2003	ABQ	PCL	25	40	0	46.3	55	16	32	1	2.33	4.26	10.4	3.7	5.3	0.2	4.49	6.6	2
2003	FLA	NL	25	18	0	21.0	38	9	10	2	8.14	8.71	15.7	3.5	3.9	0.9	7.53	-7.8	-36
2004	FLA	NL	26	22	4	37.7	40	17	25	3	4.33	4.84	9.7	3.6	5.4	0.7	5.13	3.5	-8

Breakout: 26%   Improve: 54%   Collapse: 27%

A hard thrower with little idea how to pitch, Neal's raw enough to make you think he's still a raw prospect, but he turns 26 just after Opening Day. The supposed closer of the future every year since he saved 21 games at Brevard County and made his big league debut in 2001, the Marlins are still waiting for him to even settle in as a mop-up man. Neal's still cheap, so there's no harm in bringing him to camp every year to see if he finally sees the light.

VLADIMIR NUNEZ   Bats: R   Throws: R   Born: 15-Mar-75   Age: 29

YEAR	TM	LG	AGE	G	GS	IP	H	BB	SO	HR	ERA	EQERA	EQH9	EQBB9	EQSO9	EQHR9	PERA	VORP	STF
2001	FLA	NL	26	52	3	92.0	79	30	64	9	2.74	3.48	7.9	2.8	5.3	0.8	3.73	20.7	2
2002	FLA	NL	27	77	0	97.7	80	37	73	8	3.41	3.63	7.4	3.0	5.8	0.8	3.53	20.6	4
2003	ABQ	PCL	28	46	3	68.0	67	20	54	13	4.76	4.41	9.5	3.1	6.1	2.4	6.41	8.4	-50
2003	FLA	NL	28	14	0	10.7	21	7	10	7	15.98	16.03	17.7	5.1	7.6	5.9	15.27	-15.3	-175
2004	FLA	NL	29	67	0	59.3	56	21	46	7	4.03	4.51	8.6	2.8	6.3	1.2	4.49	7.4	-4

Breakout: 26%   Improve: 62%   Collapse: 14%

Michael Wolverton's Relievers Report at baseballprospectus.com tells the tale: Nunez put up a line of -17.5 Adjusted Runs Prevented in just 10.2 innings major league innings. He didn't fare well in Triple-A either, allowing 13 homers and five runs a game over 68 innings, lousy even in Albuquerque. Compare that to his 2001 and 2002 campaigns, when he tossed 190 combined innings of effective ball. So what happened? You can't blame increased workload, given Nunez was a workhorse the previous two years. The Marlins blamed his struggles on poor mechanics, and Nunez was designated for assignment in September. Given his mechanics were potentially dangerous long before last season, whichever team snags him would do well to check for injury before throwing him back to the wolves in '04.

KEVIN OLSEN   Bats: R   Throws: R   Born: 26-Jul-76   Age: 27

YEAR	TM	LG	AGE	G	GS	IP	H	BB	SO	HR	ERA	EQERA	EQH9	EQBB9	EQSO9	EQHR9	PERA	VORP	STF
2001	FLA	NL	24	4	2	15.0	11	2	13	0	1.20	1.88	6.9	1.3	6.9	0.0	2.11	5.9	53
2001	PME	EAS	24	26	26	154.7	123	21	144	11	2.68	4.30	10.0	1.7	5.9	1.1	4.66	19.6	11
2002	CLG	PCL	25	8	8	49.0	45	14	25	6	3.86	3.88	8.2	2.9	3.5	1.4	4.51	8.8	-14
2002	FLA	NL	25	17	8	55.7	57	31	38	5	4.52	5.13	9.3	4.3	5.3	0.8	4.83	2.8	-3
2003	ABQ	PCL	26	7	7	38.3	36	7	28	1	2.11	2.72	8.4	2.0	5.4	0.2	3.20	11.6	29
2003	FLA	NL	26	7	0	12.0	25	4	12	2	12.75	11.57	18.5	2.3	7.7	1.5	9.15	-11.3	-37
2004	FLA	NL	27	19	11	68.7	70	22	47	7	4.08	4.56	9.2	2.5	5.5	1.0	4.67	8.5	0

Breakout: 25%   Improve: 54%   Collapse: 23%

(continued next page)

Kevin Olsen *(continued)*

A misalignment in four vertebrae that affected his velocity and control was fixed after the '02 season, so the Marlins hoped to get good swingman production out of Olsen. After just missing the Opening Day roster, Olsen shined in seven Triple-A starts and was called up to replace Vlad Nunez in June. A line drive off Todd Walker's bat knocked Olsen out with a concussion, ruining what looked like a promising season. A soft-tosser who's never quite stuck, Olsen will always face an uphill climb.

SCOTT OLSEN Bats: L Throws: L Born: 12-Jan-84 Age: 20

YEAR	TM	LG	AGE	G	GS	IP	H	BB	SO	HR	ERA	EQERA	EQH9	EQBB9	EQSO9	EQHR9	PERA	VORP	STF
2003	GRB	SAL	19	25	24	128.3	101	59	129	4	2.81	5.10	9.2	5.6	5.9	0.7	5.03	6.3	23
2004	FLA	NL	20	15	13	62.7	127	14	32	-28	5.61	6.27	18.3	1.7	4.1	0.0	6.29	-3.1	-2

Breakout: 25% Improve: 64% Collapse: 11%

He went 7–8 in 2003, so he likely doesn't have much of a future . . . okay, just making sure you're paying attention. A sixth-round pick out of an Illinois high school in 2002, Olsen turned in a strong first pro campaign, fanning a batter an inning in the Sally League. You could see his progression as the year went on. More a thrower than a pitcher in the first half, Olsen began spotting his 90–92-mph fastball better as the year went on, using his curve and change more as he gained confidence in both pitches. He'll need to develop a pitch to neutralize lefties to take the next step, but he's got plenty of time.

CARL PAVANO Bats: R Throws: R Born: 08-Jan-76 Age: 28

YEAR	TM	LG	AGE	G	GS	IP	H	BB	SO	HR	ERA	EQERA	EQH9	EQBB9	EQSO9	EQHR9	PERA	VORP	STF
2001	MON	NL	25	8	8	42.7	59	16	36	7	6.32	6.48	12.1	3.0	6.3	1.3	6.26	-4.1	-5
2002	MON	NL	26	15	14	74.3	98	31	51	14	6.30	6.72	11.8	3.2	5.4	1.7	6.74	-9.0	-28
2002	OTT	INT	26	3	3	20.3	23	2	9	2	3.10	4.91	12.3	1.0	3.4	1.5	6.06	1.4	-21
2002	FLA	NL	26	22	8	61.7	76	14	41	5	3.79	5.01	11.1	1.8	5.2	0.8	4.88	3.9	0
2003	FLA	NL	27	33	32	201.0	204	49	133	19	4.30	4.31	9.0	2.0	5.3	0.8	4.04	22.3	13
2004	FLA	NL	28	26	23	142.0	149	38	95	15	4.13	4.62	9.5	2.1	5.4	1.0	4.58	15.2	7

Breakout: 11% Improve: 42% Collapse: 16%

Pavano looked like he'd forever be a once-great prospect who could never stay healthy. Then he went out and led the Marlins in regular season innings pitched and was the team's second-best starter in the playoffs behind Josh Beckett. Pavano credited off-season bikram yoga sessions for improving his focus, conditioning, and flexibility. The classes, held at room temperatures of 105 degrees and 60% humidity, are designed to strengthen bones and improve joint mobility and range of motion by working against gravity. We may never know if that or/and other factors turned Pavano around, but it's heartening to see players trying new and different methods to improve performance. This isn't your father's (or grandfather's) MLB, and that's a good thing.

BRAD PENNY Bats: R Throws: R Born: 24-May-78 Age: 26

YEAR	TM	LG	AGE	G	GS	IP	H	BB	SO	HR	ERA	EQERA	EQH9	EQBB9	EQSO9	EQHR9	PERA	VORP	STF
2001	FLA	NL	23	31	31	205.0	183	54	154	15	3.69	3.77	8.2	2.2	5.7	0.6	3.50	39.9	33
2002	FLA	NL	24	24	24	129.3	148	50	93	18	4.66	5.53	10.3	3.0	5.6	1.3	5.46	1.0	2
2003	FLA	NL	25	32	32	196.3	195	56	138	21	4.13	4.31	8.8	2.3	5.6	0.9	4.16	22.5	14
2004	FLA	NL	26	29	27	173.3	176	53	120	17	4.01	4.48	9.2	2.4	5.6	1.0	4.45	22.3	9

Breakout: 12% Improve: 49% Collapse: 13%

Speculation ran rampant last off-season that Penny had serious arm problems, leading to a possible three-way deal that would have sent Penny to Cincinnati getting nixed. His only official 2002 injury was a month on the DL due to biceps tendinitis, though an MRI later showed a frayed rotator cuff. With shoulder surgery still a crap shoot, more pitchers have opted for rest and strengthening exercises instead. Penny went that route, and turned in a strong '03 season, helping the push to a championship. He'll be an asset even at $3 million next year, though the Marlins have discussed trading from their pitching depth to fill other needs.

TOMMY PHELPS   Bats: L   Throws: L   Born: 04-Mar-74   Age: 30

YEAR	TM	LG	AGE	G	GS	IP	H	BB	SO	HR	ERA	EQERA	EQH9	EQBB9	EQSO9	EQHR9	PERA	VORP	STF
2001	ERI	EAS	27	15	2	32.7	33	8	31	1	3.58	4.97	11.5	3.1	5.9	0.3	4.93	2.0	1
2001	TOL	INT	27	29	0	59.7	74	19	53	4	3.62	5.50	12.0	3.4	6.1	0.8	5.75	0.6	-11
2002	CLG	PCL	28	51	0	74.3	76	21	62	8	3.15	3.76	9.9	2.9	5.7	1.2	5.05	14.2	-15
2003	FLA	NL	29	27	7	63.0	70	23	43	3	4.00	4.55	9.8	2.9	5.4	0.4	4.29	6.0	7
2004	FLA	NL	30	31	11	74.3	78	28	55	7	4.30	4.81	9.6	3.0	5.9	1.0	5.03	7.5	-2

Breakout: 30%   Improve: 56%   Collapse: 21%

With Burnett and Beckett out, Phelps was considered a candidate to keep a rotation spot for a while. But the Marlins found better options, and Phelps returned to the pen to serve as an effective lefty specialist, a role he could reprise in '04. Elbow, shoulder, leg, and neck problems cropped up during the second half, and he was forced to watch the Marlins' playoff run from the dugout. That ring looks real shiny either way.

MARK REDMAN   Bats: L   Throws: L   Born: 05-Jan-74   Age: 30

YEAR	TM	LG	AGE	G	GS	IP	H	BB	SO	HR	ERA	EQERA	EQH9	EQBB9	EQSO9	EQHR9	PERA	VORP	STF
2001	MIN	AL	27	9	9	49.0	57	19	29	6	4.22	4.91	10.4	3.2	4.9	0.9	5.16	3.7	-1
2001	DET	AL	27	2	2	9.0	11	4	4	1	6.00	6.00	10.0	4.0	4.0	1.0	5.28	-0.4	-17
2002	DET	AL	28	30	30	203.0	211	51	109	15	4.21	3.88	8.7	2.1	4.6	0.6	3.72	38.1	15
2003	FLA	NL	29	29	29	190.7	172	61	151	16	3.59	3.80	8.0	2.6	6.3	0.7	3.65	33.6	23
2004	OAK	AL	30	28	27	175.7	180	52	110	23	4.37	4.62	9.2	2.5	5.4	1.1	4.50	21.9	7

Breakout: 6%   Improve: 45%   Collapse: 14%

While A. J. Burnett's injury got most of the ink, Mark Redman went from a terrific first half to a fading second half to a punching bag by playoff time, thanks to repeated bouts of overuse. Redman finished fourth on BP's Pitcher Abuse Points list, with three starts over 130 pitches, including 138- and 140-pitch jaw-droppers under supposed lighter touch Jack McKeon. Raw pitch counts should be treated as merely one element of a larger data set when evaluating pitcher workload. But the repeated high-stress innings placed on Redman, with no regard for his prior injury history, was galling. Dealt to the A's for reliever Mike Neu, who signed him to a three-year deal for far too much.

TIM SPOONEYBARGER   Bats: R   Throws: R   Born: 21-Oct-79   Age: 24

YEAR	TM	LG	AGE	G	GS	IP	H	BB	SO	HR	ERA	EQERA	EQH9	EQBB9	EQSO9	EQHR9	PERA	VORP	STF
2001	GRN	SOU	21	15	0	21.0	20	4	24	1	5.14	5.12	9.8	1.9	7.4	0.5	3.95	1.0	31
2001	RIC	INT	21	42	0	50.7	33	21	58	1	0.71	1.88	6.0	4.3	9.2	0.2	2.71	19.8	57
2002	ATL	NL	22	51	0	51.3	38	26	33	4	2.63	3.70	7.4	4.1	5.2	0.7	3.82	10.3	11
2002	RIC	INT	22	18	0	20.0	13	8	21	1	0.90	1.89	5.7	4.3	8.5	0.5	2.82	7.8	42
2003	FLA	NL	23	33	0	42.0	27	11	32	1	4.07	3.12	5.8	2.2	6.0	0.2	2.11	4.3	33
2004	FLA	NL	24	51	4	76.7	68	29	64	5	3.49	3.91	8.0	3.0	6.7	0.7	3.83	13.8	4

Breakout: 21%   Improve: 50%   Collapse: 24%

Another member of the injured reliever brigade, Spooneybarger had turned in his best year to date despite a ballooning ERA, allowing less than a baserunner an inning and just one homer in 42 frames before complaining of tingling in his elbow. Though he wasn't nearly the butcher that the Torborg/Arnsberg combo had been, Jack McKeon's questioning Spooneybarger's toughness was a low point in Trader Jack's season. After Tommy John surgery in September, Spooneybarger won't be back until 2005. He'll be a great sleeper when he returns.

MIKE TEJERA   Bats: L   Throws: L   Born: 18-Oct-76   Age: 27

YEAR	TM	LG	AGE	G	GS	IP	H	BB	SO	HR	ERA	EQERA	EQH9	EQBB9	EQSO9	EQHR9	PERA	VORP	STF
2001	PME	EAS	24	25	25	141.0	143	41	131	17	3.57	5.84	12.6	3.7	6.0	1.8	7.26	-3.2	-22
2002	FLA	NL	25	47	18	139.7	144	60	95	17	4.45	4.85	9.3	3.4	5.3	1.1	4.91	11.3	-7
2003	FLA	NL	26	50	6	81.0	82	36	58	6	4.67	4.69	9.0	3.5	5.7	0.7	4.35	4.7	0
2004	FLA	NL	27	32	8	65.3	68	28	46	7	4.52	5.05	9.4	3.4	5.7	1.0	5.12	4.8	-7

Breakout: 24%   Improve: 46%   Collapse: 22%

Looking at his splits for the season, it's puzzling to look back and see "Throws: L" in his profile. Swingmen who throw 80 innings are prone to small sample-size flukes, but .224/.298/.329 vs. righties, and .392/.442/.595 vs. lefties? That's

(continued next page)

Mike Tejera *(continued)*

enough to give even Tony Womack hope. Tejera continues to muddle along with underwhelming stuff and peripherals, making the staff on his ability to spot-start and the Marlins' lack of good lefty choices. He's got one more year left before arbitration, so he'll likely provide another year of league-average pitching, plus Tommy John recovery tips for Spooney.

UGUETH URBINA Bats: R Throws: R Born: 15-Feb-74 Age: 30

YEAR	TM	LG	AGE	G	GS	IP	H	BB	SO	HR	ERA	EQERA	EQH9	EQBB9	EQSO9	EQHR9	PERA	VORP	STF
2001	MON	NL	27	45	0	46.7	42	21	57	8	4.24	4.34	8.1	3.7	9.1	1.4	4.63	6.4	3
2001	BOS	AL	27	19	0	20.0	16	3	32	1	2.25	2.29	7.3	1.4	13.3	0.5	2.63	7.2	70
2002	BOS	AL	28	61	0	60.0	44	20	71	8	3.00	2.93	6.8	2.8	10.2	1.1	3.42	17.3	28
2003	TEX	AL	29	39	0	38.7	33	18	41	6	4.19	3.72	6.8	4.0	9.1	1.2	3.85	7.4	12
2003	FLA	NL	29	33	0	38.3	23	13	37	2	1.41	1.95	5.4	2.7	7.8	0.5	2.25	17.7	32
2004	*FLA*	*NL*	*30*	*52*	*0*	*68.0*	*54*	*26*	*75*	*6*	*3.21*	*3.59*	*7.2*	*3.1*	*8.8*	*0.9*	*3.58*	*15.1*	*16*

Breakout: 22%   Improve: 57%   Collapse: 18%

No amount of park or league adjustments can explain Urbina lopping nearly three runs off his ERA from Texas to Florida; the Fish simply caught lightning in a bottle with every reliever they acquired last year. Uggy still has that same violent delivery that makes Will Carroll squirm and James Andrews prep an operating table, but he looks like he's put injuries behind him, with no serious owies since 2000. A half-notch below the Billy Wagner/Keith Foulke class first targeted in the off-season, he attracted plenty of second-tier shoppers in the free agent market, though he remained unsigned at press time.

JUSTIN WAYNE Bats: R Throws: R Born: 16-Apr-79 Age: 25

YEAR	TM	LG	AGE	G	GS	IP	H	BB	SO	HR	ERA	EQERA	EQH9	EQBB9	EQSO9	EQHR9	PERA	VORP	STF
2001	JUP	FLA	22	8	7	41.7	31	9	35	0	3.02	4.30	8.6	2.4	5.0	0.2	3.39	5.4	27
2001	HAR	EAS	22	14	14	92.7	87	34	70	4	2.62	4.18	9.6	4.4	4.7	0.6	4.83	13.3	14
2002	HAR	EAS	23	17	17	98.7	74	32	47	7	2.37	4.27	7.5	3.4	3.2	1.1	4.08	13.4	-5
2002	PME	EAS	23	7	7	42.7	43	13	30	3	4.85	5.54	10.6	3.2	4.8	1.2	5.51	0.3	-1
2002	FLA	NL	23	5	5	23.7	22	13	16	3	5.32	5.48	8.6	4.3	5.1	1.2	4.89	0.3	2
2003	ABQ	PCL	24	23	23	136.0	138	40	82	10	4.24	4.38	8.9	3.1	4.6	0.9	4.40	17.5	5
2003	FLA	NL	24	2	2	5.3	9	5	1	1	11.89	11.81	15.2	6.8	1.7	1.7	9.09	-4.0	-77
2004	*FLA*	*NL*	*25*	*18*	*13*	*75.7*	*82*	*32*	*46*	*9*	*5.00*	*5.59*	*9.8*	*3.4*	*4.9*	*1.2*	*5.45*	*2.4*	*-7*

Breakout: 19%   Improve: 49%   Collapse: 29%

Comparing Wayne to Mike Mussina because both are big righties out of Stanford is like comparing Barbara Walters to Charlize Theron because they both have blondish hair. Jeffrey Loria pushed hard to get Wayne included in the Cliff Floyd deal with the Expos in 2002 so he'd feel like he'd recouped the big signing bonus he gave the pitcher after the 2000 draft. He certainly wasn't getting much of a pitcher: Wayne's a run-of-the-mill righty with no out pitch to overwhelm hitters, and the lousy strikeout rates to prove it. The Marlins may as well as shop him; there are enough tools-obsessed organizations out there that may get excited simply because Wayne's 6'3" and ambulatory.

DONTRELLE WILLIS Bats: L Throws: L Born: 12-Jan-82 Age: 22

YEAR	TM	LG	AGE	G	GS	IP	H	BB	SO	HR	ERA	EQERA	EQH9	EQBB9	EQSO9	EQHR9	PERA	VORP	STF
2001	BOI	NWN	19	15	15	93.7	76	19	77	1	2.98	4.89	9.0	2.7	3.8	0.2	3.66	6.7	25
2002	KNE	MID	20	19	19	127.7	91	21	101	3	1.83	3.20	8.1	2.0	4.3	0.6	3.43	30.7	27
2002	JUP	FLA	20	5	5	30.0	24	3	27	2	1.80	3.62	8.9	1.0	5.9	1.3	4.19	6.0	30
2003	CAR	SOU	21	6	6	36.3	24	9	32	2	1.49	2.73	7.4	2.7	5.7	1.1	3.76	10.5	29
2003	FLA	NL	21	27	27	160.7	148	58	142	13	3.30	3.69	8.3	2.9	7.0	0.7	3.81	36.8	48
2004	*FLA*	*NL*	*22*	*26*	*24*	*155.7*	*153*	*56*	*120*	*15*	*3.89*	*4.35*	*8.9*	*2.9*	*6.2*	*0.9*	*4.51*	*21.9*	*12*

Breakout: 12%   Improve: 42%   Collapse: 25%

Not since Nomomania has a high-kicking rookie so captivated fans' imagination and handcuffed opposing hitters. Willis not only gave the Marlins a huge shot in the arm by replacing A. J. Burnett's productive innings, he also made Marlins baseball cool. Blessed with a solid fastball and curve that both hit the strike zone and a can't-say-no-to-anyone demeanor, he was everyone's darling, beating out Brandon Webb's superior season for Rookie of the Year honors. Expect some changes next year: Willis tired late in the season, largely from the effort needed to bring his leg above his head 100 times a game every five days. The Marlins had him working out of the stretch in the playoffs, and they're pushing him to scrap the huge leg kick for next season. Willis also puts on weight easily, especially in the lower body, something the Fish will monitor closely. PECOTA expects a drop-off in '04, and so do we.

Houston Astros

A year ago, we noted the list of problems the Astros face to remain a contender in the NL Central. One of those problems was a farm system that looked to be drying up after years of churning out great young talent:

"...The Astros don't have any clear grade-A prospects in the minors for the first time in recent memory. That could change quickly, though, as John Buck, Rodrigo Rosario, Tommy Whiteman, and Fernando Nieve are one breakout season away from ascending to that level."

Nieve had a strong season. Nearly every other prospect of note stunk. As a result, the Astros have sunk into an even deeper hole. It could soon become a chasm.

A dry farm system doesn't always condemn a team to failure. After a strong run that produced core players like Posada, Jeter, Williams, Pettitte, Rivera, and Soriano, the Yankees' well has almost run dry, yet they remain a perennial World Series threat. The Giants haven't developed a legitimate hitter from within since Rich Aurilia. But a strong veteran nucleus and a series of shrewd in-season trades and off-season signings by Brian Sabean and company have yielded four playoff berths in the last seven years, and seven straight NL West finishes of second place or better.

The Astros don't have the means to paper over a Sterling Hitchcock blunder here, a Rondell White there the way the Yankees do. While they feature one of the league's better players, Lance Berkman can't carry a team the way Barry Bonds can for the Giants. Thus the Astros find themselves in limbo—a team with a decent core a half-notch below championship level, lacking the minor league strength needed to bolster the team through promotion or trade, and the funds needed to spend their way out of trouble.

By taking a look at some of the lousy seasons turned in by various Astro farmhands, we can move closer to finding out what's gone wrong. Let's start with the names cited above:

- John Buck was considered the best of the Astros' prospects a year ago. Strong seasons in the Low-A Midwest and Sally leagues in 2000 and 2001 had forged his reputation as a power-hitting catcher with the goods to take over the big league job in a few years' time. Buck's plate discipline started

ASTROS PROSPECTUS

2003 record: 87–75; Second place, NL Central

Pythagenport record: 94–68

Runs scored per game: 5.0 (4th in NL)

Runs allowed per game: 4.2 (3rd in NL)

Team EqA: .261 (7th in NL)

2003 Batters Age: 31.7 (3rd oldest in NL)

2003 Pitchers Age: 27.9 (6th youngest in NL)

Ballpark: Minute Maid Park; Moderate hitter's park; Park Factor of 1.038

2003: The pitching staff couldn't stay healthy, and the Astros came up just short in the Central.

2004: With a rebuilt rotation and some top-shelf hitting talent, Houston should be a factor in the Central race, bad contracts and all.

to erode in 2001, then got worse in '02, as the Astros jumped him all the way to Double-A Round Rock. Of course they didn't have much of a choice; until 2003, the Astros remained the only MLB organization without a team in High-A ball. Having failed to master Double-A, the Astros promoted Buck to Triple-A anyway, where he fell apart. The promising walk rate he'd flashed in 2000 had entirely disappeared. More distressingly, Buck's power evaporated, even after adjusting for New Orleans' tough hitting environment. The Astros hope last year's regression was simply the result of a broken hand that caused Buck to miss two months. But troubling performance trends have cast Buck's future into doubt. His falling star pushed the Astros into a major mistake at the big league level to boot (more on that later).

- Rodrigo Rosario offered that rare combination of great stuff and minor league results to excite scouts and performance analysts alike. His ability to keep the ball down and in the ballpark looked especially promising for a future in Minute Maid Park. The arm pain he'd complained about in 2002? Tests turned up clean, and Rosario looked to be in the clear after 15 strong starts at Triple-A. Called up to bolster an injury-plagued rotation, he yielded just two runs and four hits in six-plus innings in his MLB debut...and then broke down in the second inning of his second start. Surgery to repair a rotator cuff tear and torn biceps tendon sealed his fate with management, and he was released at season's end. Rosario's breakdown was one of several injury- and performance-related meltdowns by Astros pitching prospects in 2003.

- While you'd never confuse 97 at-bats with a tell-all sample size, Tommy Whiteman's impressive showing in the Arizona Fall League following a solid '02 campaign in the Sally League seemed to portend a future force at shortstop. The Astros should have noted another small sample—the 56 ABs Whiteman racked up at Double-A Round Rock just before heading to Arizona, in which he hit a paltry .179/.246/.250. Starting the '03 season back at Round Rock, Whiteman struggled mightily, striking out three times as often as he walked, and regressing in the field. As with Buck, Whiteman looked overwhelmed by the jump to Double-A, having missed out on High-A development time.

Run through other Astro prospects and the same themes repeat themselves: hitters failing to develop, pitchers either breaking down due to injury, or pitching so poorly you had to wonder if they might be hurt. The regression by several prospects after skipping High-A ball may sort itself out over time. With a team installed in Salem of the Carolina League, recent draftees will get the same full allotment of development stops that other organizations offer. Hitters like Buck and Whiteman remain young enough to bounce back, though it may take at least a couple years to relearn some of the skills you'd hope they'd have already honed.

More troubling was the spate of pitching disappointments suffered last year, Rosario being the worst. The Astros also had high hopes for Jimmy Barrett, after the 1999 third-round pick fanned a batter an inning at Lexington in 2002. His velocity and performance both crashed last year at Salem, and observers insisted he was hiding an injury. Already a question mark after a rough 2002, an elbow injury and Tommy John surgery ended Tony Pluta's season after just three starts. Of the other pitching prospects above rookie ball, few progressed last year, and fewer still look like significant future MLB contributors.

It's tempting to point to BP's mantra, "There Is No Such Thing As A Pitching Prospect (TINSTAAPP)," and write the system's pitching woes off to the unpredictability of young arms. But the Astros would do better to continue scrutinizing their player development methods. Are there common factors involved in the numerous injuries suffered by young pitchers at various levels, from A-ball all the way to the majors? If so, what steps can be taken to prevent them?

The Astros' brain trust has shown itself to be well-equipped to handle similar questions in the past. Led by sharp talent like Assistant GM Tim Purpura, Houston has found success in the past by looking to roads less traveled by other teams. Their scouting efforts in Venezuela yielded players like Bobby Abreu and Freddy Garcia. Their willingness to go the draft-and-follow route produced Billy Wagner. Their focus on college talent—often talent unloved by scouts—led them to Kirk Saarloos. Their eschewing of traditional scouting principles has triggered their pursuit of talented, small pitchers, including Wagner, Roy Oswalt, and Carlos Hernandez.

But teams have started catching on to these previously untapped methods. The Astros still hold a lead in Venezuela, but that lead is shrinking. The swing toward college talent has intensified so rapidly, two teams scanned the big board last year and drafted college *relievers* in the first round, including an Expos franchise that had spent years chasing toolsy high school talent to little avail. Though fawning over the big, strapping righty with the blazing fastball remains alive and well in many parts, more teams are learning that sound mechanics and a great delivery do more for a pitcher's performance and health than a big frame can. Meanwhile, Drayton McLane's reluctance to spend has limited the Astros' player development budget. All those factors have played a role in leaving Houston with one of baseball's shallowest minor league talent pools.

To get the system pointed in the right direction, the team will have to continue zagging while others zig. That may mean taking a closer look at high school talent, if it becomes undervalued with the rush toward college players by other teams. The Braves have fared well by focusing on players from the South, especially Georgia boys. If the Astros could develop their own niche as the dominant player in scouting Texas amateurs, that could help rejuvenate the system. Not known for scouting efforts abroad, Houston can do some cost/benefit analysis to decide if increased European and Asian scouting would be worthwhile. Management has argued that the decline in the system's talent base is largely just a down cycle, spawned by major league promotions for star talent such as Berkman, Oswalt, and Wade Miller all in a short period of time. While those graduations certainly played a role, the bottom line is a combined 117–176 record for the Double-A and Triple-A teams last year, meaning help likely won't be coming any time soon.

The pitching injury problems that haunted the minor leagues made their way to Houston as well. BP's Will

Carroll flagged Oswalt as a significant injury risk heading into the 2003 season. While Oswalt's injury turned out to be a torn sheath around his groin muscle rather than elbow or shoulder distress, the damage done to the Astros' rotation was no less severe. After trying the rehab route for a year and a half following a shoulder injury suffered while diving into second base, Hernandez had surgery in February 2003 to repair tears in his rotator cuff and labrum. While the Astros have talked optimistically about a spring training return, the attrition rates on such injuries are high enough to paint Hernandez as a long shot for a healthy 2004, let alone an effective one. The Astros can manage fine without Hernandez in the rotation. But if Oswalt doesn't make a full recovery, the team could be in trouble, even with a pair of Yankees in the fold.

Meanwhile, bad contracts remain, limiting the team's flexibility. Granting that it was a different market for player contracts, the five-year, $85 million contract the Astros handed Jeff Bagwell after the 2000 season was a case of overpaying for a player going on 33 years old at the easiest position to fill on the diamond, with his most recent batting line inflated by a jump to a great hitter's park from a terrible one. Richard Hidalgo could make as much as $14 million after bonuses this season; while his contract was more a case of misjudging a young player's career arc, it's still a huge drain on the team's payroll.

Rather than shrug their shoulders and meekly accept their fate, the Astros shopped Hidalgo and Billy Wagner hard in the off-season. While they found no takers for Hidalgo, they quickly found one in Philadelphia for Wagner. Though the loss of one of the game's best relievers weakens the bullpen and puts added strain on talented pitchers Octavio Dotel and Brad Lidge, the Astros cleared $8 million off the 2004 payroll, plus the $9 million club option or $3 million buyout due in '05. This was no mere salary dump either. In Brandon Duckworth, Taylor Buchholz, and Ezequiel Astacio, the Astros obtained three promising righties, all of whom will come cheap for the next several years and offer much-needed depth and upside to the team's supply of young pitchers.

Wagner's departure freed up some of Drayton McLane's cash, despite the owner's constant kvetching over alleged losses. When Andy Pettitte made noise about coming home to Texas to pitch, Houston seized on the opportunity, inking him to a heavily backloaded, three-year, $31.5 million contract that pays just $5.5 million in 2004. When Roger Clemens re-thought his retirement, McLane again went to the well. These signings are a huge shot in the arm, even if Oswalt pitches 200 strong innings. If Oswalt misses any significant amount of time, they become absolutely essential.

Though the Astros deserve credit for those moves at the high end of the scale, they deserve equal reprimand for a pair of much smaller deals. Signing Brad Ausmus to a two-year, $4 million contract and re-upping Jose Vizcaino at one year, $1.2 million shows an appalling misunderstanding of the free agent market and the league's supply of readily available talent. While Ausmus remains one of the better defensive catchers in the game, even at age 35, he's also degenerated into one of the biggest offensive cancers in the game. John Buck may not be ready for prime time, but the team could have found better catching talent elsewhere, instead of flushing $4 million down the toilet in the name of misplaced loyalty to an Astro veteran. The same goes for Jose Vizcaino, who projects as an offensive and defensive liability in 2004. That superior options at both catcher and utility infielder could have been found while still saving enough dough to bolster the bullpen or add an effective bat for the bench only makes matters worse.

While it may seem excessive to come down so hard on the Astros for their moves at the margins, it's precisely this type of team that can't afford to make such errors. A mid-market club with both real and self-imposed limits on revenue and spending, one wonders if McLane will open his checkbook at the trade deadline if the Astros are in the race in July, or stand pat as he did in 2003, the Bagwell and Hidalgo contracts, but also the Ausmus and Vizcaino deals, tying up the team's disposable income. In a division where the Cubs and Cards will offer stiff, but far from unbeatable competition, it'd be a shame to see those last couple of games in the standings get needlessly frittered away.

HITTERS

JASON ALFARO   3B   Bats: R   Throws: R   Born: 29-Nov-77   Age: 26

YEAR	TM	LG	AGE	AB	H	2B	3B	HR	BB	SO	SB	CS	AVG	OBP	SLG	MLVR	EQBA	EQOBP	EQSLG	EQMLVR	VORP	DEFENSE			
2001	ROU	TEX	23	284	69	16	2	2	7	40	2	1	.243	.264	.335	-.223	.218	.240	.303	-.421	-20.3	27-2B	1	14-SS	-2
2002	ROU	TEX	24	455	143	36	2	16	50	75	11	9	.314	.393	.508	.311	.265	.331	.444	-.015	23.5	113-3B	5		
2003	ROU	TEX	25	81	12	3	0	0	5	20	0	1	.148	.198	.185	-.567	.136	.186	.173	-.747	-13.8	21-3B	-3		
2003	NWO	PCL	25	361	107	20	4	9	30	53	2	3	.296	.354	.449	.151	.278	.333	.433	-.016	17.9	40-3B	1	43-SS	-4
2004	HOU	NL	26	173	43	9	1	4	14	31	1	1	.246	.307	.380	-.141	.244	.303	.378	-.166	1.4	49-3B	-1		

Breakout: 22%   Improve: 40%   Collapse: 39%

(continued next page)

Jason Alfaro *(continued)*

Alfaro's stats appeared to nosedive after his big 2002 season in Round Rock. But don't let the PCL environment fool you: New Orleans is one of the best pitcher's parks in the league. Alfaro has enough on-base ability and doubles power to be an effective utility player in the majors, starting right now. Given some of the dreck masquerading as starting MLB third basemen, he could be more than that for a couple years, though he lacks the arm you'd like to see at the position. A six-year minor league free agent, the Astros re-signed him, a smart move given the team's thin system.

BRAD AUSMUS   C   Bats: R   Throws: R   Born: 14-Apr-69   Age: 35

YEAR	TM	LG	AGE	AB	H	2B	3B	HR	BB	SO	SB	CS	AVG	OBP	SLG	MLVR	EQBA	EQOBP	EQSLG	EQMLVR	VORP	DEFENSE
2001	HOU	NL	32	422	98	23	4	5	30	64	4	1	.232	.284	.341	-.272	.229	.281	.337	-.285	-12.8	118-C 14
2002	HOU	NL	33	447	115	19	3	6	38	71	2	3	.257	.322	.353	-.098	.259	.321	.361	-.154	2.2	120-C 7
2003	HOU	NL	34	450	103	12	2	4	46	66	5	3	.229	.303	.291	-.260	.230	.304	.294	-.299	-15.5	131-C 12
2004	HOU	NL	35	259	62	11	1	3	24	44	2	1	.238	.305	.330	-.215	.235	.301	.328	-.240	-4.1	71-C 1

Breakout: 27%   Improve: 46%   Collapse: 30%

The Astros can bitch and moan all they want about a tight budget. But while the Hidalgo and Bagwell contracts lock up a ton of money, Houston has made some of the worst moves at the margins of any team in baseball. Re-upping Ausmus for two years, $4 million?! Why? Are they going for the HACKING MASS championship? Ausmus slugged two-freaking-ninety-one last year in the hitter's haven of Juicy Juice Park. Abe Vigoda on Demerol could beat that. There are some smart people working in the Astros' front office. Unfortunately, they don't always get heard when contract time rolls around for the supposed good clubhouse guys.

JEFF BAGWELL   1B   Bats: R   Throws: R   Born: 27-May-68   Age: 36

YEAR	TM	LG	AGE	AB	H	2B	3B	HR	BB	SO	SB	CS	AVG	OBP	SLG	MLVR	EQBA	EQOBP	EQSLG	EQMLVR	VORP	DEFENSE
2001	HOU	NL	33	600	173	43	4	39	106	135	11	3	.288	.397	.568	.280	.282	.392	.554	.257	60.5	158-1B 15
2002	HOU	NL	34	571	166	33	2	31	101	130	7	3	.291	.401	.518	.268	.287	.398	.517	.222	49.1	151-1B 7
2003	HOU	NL	35	605	168	28	2	39	88	119	11	4	.278	.373	.524	.195	.273	.367	.520	.160	39.2	154-1B 3
2004	HOU	NL	36	492	135	28	3	27	79	104	8	3	.273	.377	.505	.158	.270	.372	.502	.134	31.1	136-1B 1

Breakout: 22%   Improve: 60%   Collapse: 17%

We've harped on Bagwell's awful contract before, but it looks worse than ever now, with the Astros still armed with a solid core but lacking—they claim anyway—the resources to add the last few pieces to push the team over the top. Bagwell had come off a 2000 season that looked better than it was given the leap to the new ballpark from the Astrodome. At the end of the day he was a great first baseman, but one going on 33 years old, playing the easiest position to fill in baseball. Giving him a five-year, $85 million contract was a terrible idea, even adjusting for the rapidly escalating salaries of that period. (Lest you think hindsight is 20/20, go back and read BP's Transaction Analysis, Jan. 4, 2001. We'll wait . . .) The deal will haunt the Astros for several more years, with Bagwell set to make $13, $15, and $17 million in the next three seasons, plus deferred payments, plus a $7 million buyout for 2007. The shoulder problems that have slowly sapped his power only makes things more painful. It's a crummy legacy to leave behind for a player who will see Cooperstown by 2013.

LANCE BERKMAN   LF   Bats: B   Throws: L   Born: 10-Feb-76   Age: 28

YEAR	TM	LG	AGE	AB	H	2B	3B	HR	BB	SO	SB	CS	AVG	OBP	SLG	MLVR	EQBA	EQOBP	EQSLG	EQMLVR	VORP	DEFENSE		
2001	HOU	NL	25	577	191	55	5	34	92	121	7	9	.331	.430	.620	.447	.321	.421	.602	.411	78.5	113-LF -2	38-CF	-2
2002	HOU	NL	26	578	169	35	2	42	107	118	8	4	.292	.405	.578	.350	.287	.398	.574	.299	73.1	96-CF -11	50-LF	0
2003	HOU	NL	27	538	155	35	6	25	107	108	5	3	.288	.412	.515	.253	.283	.406	.511	.224	40.6	148-LF 1		
2004	HOU	NL	28	497	149	33	3	31	91	96	5	3	.300	.412	.566	.316	.297	.407	.563	.291	51.5	140-LF 1		

Breakout: 23%   Improve: 55%   Collapse: 13%

With Bagwell, Biggio, and Kent well into their declines, the Astros need to squeeze every drop of production they can out of Berkman; dropping the switch-hitter act seems one of the easiest ways to do so. Berkman bounced back to post a decent line as a right-handed batter in '03 at 283/.403/.444, though he still slugged nearly 100 points higher left-handed. He hit .240/.351/.364 as a righty in '02, .308/.400/.467 in '01. Even if 2002 was the outlier, Berkman's one of the best hitters in the league as a lefty, a strong on-base/middling power guy in his best years as a righty. At age 28, a power spike from one or both sides is still quite possible, but the odds of a dramatic transformation dim with each passing season. Ditching his righty swinging could also allow Berkman to find a second gear from the left side and return to 40-homer seasons like '02. On a team that needs a dominant hitter, especially a lefty, it's the right thing to do.

CRAIG BIGGIO

CF Bats: R Throws: R Born: 14-Dec-65 Age: 38

YEAR	TM	LG	AGE	AB	H	2B	3B	HR	BB	SO	SB	CS	AVG	OBP	SLG	MLVR	EQBA	EQOBP	EQSLG	EQMLVR	VORP	DEFENSE	
2001	HOU	NL	35	617	180	35	3	20	66	100	7	4	.292	.382	.455	.108	.289	.377	.450	.096	46.7	149-2B	-9
2002	HOU	NL	36	577	146	36	3	15	50	111	16	2	.253	.330	.404	-.022	.256	.327	.413	-.073	15.3	139-2B	-5
2003	HOU	NL	37	628	166	44	2	15	57	116	8	4	.264	.350	.412	.002	.265	.345	.417	-.027	17.6	150-CF	-9
2004	HOU	NL	38	495	131	27	2	13	47	87	8	3	.264	.344	.404	-.034	.261	.339	.402	-.058	7.2	133-CF	-8

Breakout: 21% Improve: 45% Collapse: 27%

At age 37, Biggio enjoyed a mild bounceback season, with better health helping the cause. The drop in GIDP from 15 to 4 suggested a newfound spring in Biggio's step, but other speed indicators—batting average and steals chief among them—have dropped precipitously from his prime. The switch to center field was a product of the team's lack of alternatives, because Biggio's a defensive liability at the position. He'll make $3 million in '04; if the Astros are smart, they'll ditch sentimentality, toss Biggio a bundtcake and his $1 million buyout, and get cracking on finding a true center fielder for the next five years.

GEOFF BLUM

3B Bats: B Throws: R Born: 26-Apr-73 Age: 31

YEAR	TM	LG	AGE	AB	H	2B	3B	HR	BB	SO	SB	CS	AVG	OBP	SLG	MLVR	EQBA	EQOBP	EQSLG	EQMLVR	VORP	DEFENSE			
2001	MON	NL	28	453	107	25	0	9	43	94	9	5	.236	.313	.351	-.189	.238	.313	.354	-.194	-1.7	73-3B	-4	27-LF	0
2002	HOU	NL	29	368	104	20	4	10	49	70	2	0	.283	.367	.440	.108	.282	.364	.446	.062	24.2	93-3B	12		
2003	HOU	NL	30	420	110	19	0	10	20	50	0	0	.262	.295	.379	-.138	.262	.297	.381	-.170	-0.5	64-3B	11	15-2B	-1
2004	TBY	AL	31	272	67	14	1	6	20	44	1	1	.247	.302	.367	-.150	.250	.308	.384	-.145	5.2	73-3B	1		

Breakout: 17% Improve: 35% Collapse: 42%

Jimy Williams's decision-making reached a fever pitch of ridiculousness over the third-base situation. Blum's 2002 performance screamed career year, given the Truby-esque numbers he'd put up the rest of his career (it's no coincidence he'd actually been acquired for Truby himself). If reading a printout hurt the manager's eyes, all he needed to do was watch Blum flail away at the plate as the everyday 3B, while watching Morgan Ensberg crush the ball on the rare occasions he got into the lineup. Jeff Kent's mid-season injury gave Ensberg his shot at a regular job, but it worked out fine for Jimy, with Blum taking his hollow bat to 2B. Blum totaled 420 anemic ABs last year; given the Astros lost the division title by one game, it's no stretch to say that alone cost them their shot at the big dance. Dealt for pedestrian reliever Brandon Backe to Tampa Bay, where Blum's mediocrity will be better appreciated.

ERIC BRUNTLETT

SS Bats: R Throws: R Born: 29-Mar-78 Age: 26

YEAR	TM	LG	AGE	AB	H	2B	3B	HR	BB	SO	SB	CS	AVG	OBP	SLG	MLVR	EQBA	EQOBP	EQSLG	EQMLVR	VORP	DEFENSE			
2001	ROU	TEX	23	503	134	23	3	3	50	76	23	7	.266	.340	.342	-.063	.231	.294	.300	-.310	-16.8	111-SS	3		
2002	ROU	TEX	24	464	123	21	2	2	56	61	35	12	.265	.351	.332	-.026	.236	.308	.301	-.278	-10.9	83-SS	-1	33-2B	0
2002	NWO	PCL	24	68	14	3	0	0	10	10	1	1	.206	.308	.250	-.293	.200	.282	.243	-.427	-4.8	16-SS	1		
2003	NWO	PCL	25	324	84	10	0	2	35	51	9	4	.259	.332	.309	-.114	.248	.319	.300	-.250	-4.7	47-SS	0	26-2B	2
2003	HOU	NL	25	54	14	3	0	1	0	10	0	0	.259	.255	.370	-.221	.259	.259	.370	-.260	-1.0				
2004	HOU	NL	26	171	41	7	1	2	15	29	4	1	.242	.313	.326	-.203	.240	.309	.325	-.228	0.1	49-SS	-5		

Breakout: 38% Improve: 50% Collapse: 29%

Shouldn't be on a big league roster. Bruntlett is a punchless hitter with nowhere near Adam Everett's glove, and won't improve enough to earn a steady gig. He'd be best served taking up medicine or law or accounting or whatever it is mom keeps saying cousin Phil's doing these days.

JOHN BUCK

C Bats: R Throws: R Born: 07-Jul-80 Age: 23

YEAR	TM	LG	AGE	AB	H	2B	3B	HR	BB	SO	SB	CS	AVG	OBP	SLG	MLVR	EQBA	EQOBP	EQSLG	EQMLVR	VORP	DEFENSE	
2001	LEX	SAL	20	443	122	24	1	22	37	84	4	9	.275	.345	.483	.212	.211	.264	.379	-.271	-13.1	112-C	10
2002	ROU	TEX	21	448	118	29	3	12	31	93	2	3	.263	.314	.422	.034	.233	.278	.385	-.221	-6.4	99-C	-2
2003	NWO	PCL	22	274	70	18	2	2	14	53	1	0	.255	.301	.358	-.105	.249	.289	.357	-.229	-4.4	68-C	-2
2004	HOU	NL	23	219	52	13	1	6	15	45	1	1	.238	.295	.390	-.154	.235	.291	.389	-.180	2.0	60-C	-5

Breakout: 25% Improve: 49% Collapse: 31%

The best prospect in the organization a year ago, Buck's star dimmed considerably last season. Injuries were the biggest culprit, as he missed two months with a broken hand, never having time to get untracked. A big kid with a solid swing,

(continued next page)

John Buck *(continued)*

Buck was touted as a future perennial 20-homer guy, especially after cracking 22 bombs in the Sally League as a 20-year-old. But his plate discipline still needs a ton of work if he's to put it all together. Buck's slow throw times to second and big frame raise doubts about his future behind the dish as well. The worst part for the Astros? Buck's regression and Gerry Hunsicker's lack of creativity prompted Houston to re-up Brad Ausmus for two more years, another glaring example of how the weak farm system severely hurts the Astros.

CHRIS BURKE   **2B**   **Bats: R**   **Throws: R**   Born: 11-Mar-80   Age: 24

YEAR	TM	LG	AGE	AB	H	2B	3B	HR	BB	SO	SB	CS	AVG	OBP	SLG	MLVR	EQBA	EQOBP	EQSLG	EQMLVR	VORP	DEFENSE			
2001	MIC	MID	21	233	70	11	6	3	26	31	21	8	.300	.376	.438	.173	.227	.285	.336	-.280	-5.7	55-SS -7			
2002	ROU	TEX	22	481	127	19	8	3	39	61	16	15	.264	.330	.356	-.030	.233	.285	.321	-.298	-17.9	94-2B 5		42-SS -7	
2003	ROU	TEX	23	549	165	23	8	3	57	57	34	10	.301	.379	.388	.102	.260	.328	.343	-.165	1.6	93-2B 4		42-SS -9	
2004	HOU	NL	24	256	64	13	2	3	23	33	8	3	.250	.323	.352	-.146	.247	.319	.351	-.171	4.9	71-2B -1			

Breakout: 27%   Improve: 50%   Collapse: 24%

After a rough 2002, Burke fared well in a repeat season at Double-A. Though you'd normally discount gains made when a player repeats a level, the Astros' lack of a high-A team until last year may have contributed to Burke's struggles in '02, a year he'd ordinarily have been playing in the Carolina League if the Salem team existed at the time. Burke's skills include an ability to hit for average, a decent batting eye, and an excellent glove at second base following a successful conversion from short. He'll need a strong Triple-A season to keep his future on track. A future double play combo of Burke and Everett would be a joy to watch in the field. Given the duo's lack of power, it would also give bleacher bums a favorite moment to safely run to the beer stand—they wouldn't miss much.

RAUL CHAVEZ   **C**   **Bats: R**   **Throws: R**   Born: 18-Mar-73   Age: 31

YEAR	TM	LG	AGE	AB	H	2B	3B	HR	BB	SO	SB	CS	AVG	OBP	SLG	MLVR	EQBA	EQOBP	EQSLG	EQMLVR	VORP	DEFENSE			
2001	NWO	PCL	28	278	84	17	0	8	19	34	1	1	.302	.361	.450	.118	.282	.338	.421	-.020	13.7	75-C 13			
2002	NWO	PCL	29	373	85	10	0	3	21	50	3	4	.228	.278	.279	-.303	.225	.270	.276	-.395	-24.0	105-C 13			
2003	NWO	PCL	30	355	97	28	1	6	13	43	0	2	.273	.315	.408	.007	.265	.305	.405	-.118	5.7	55-C 3		38-3B 2
2003	HOU	NL	30	37	10	1	1	1	1	6	0	0	.270	.289	.432	-.067	.270	.289	.432	-.104	0.3				
2004	HOU	NL	31	156	39	8	0	3	10	23	0	1	.248	.307	.365	-.160	.246	.303	.363	-.185	-0.1	44-C -1			

Breakout: 26%   Improve: 44%   Collapse: 33%

The Astros love good catch-and-throw guys behind the dish, and Raul Chavez looks like Brad Ausmus v2.0 waiting to happen. A poor hitter with middling doubles power and contempt for the base on balls, Chavez's defense has nonetheless solidified his popularity with management. Gregg Zaun's release late last season makes Chavez the #2 catcher. That'd be a scary thought, but for the #1 guy being even worse.

BROOKS CONRAD   **2B**   **Bats: B**   **Throws: R**   Born: 16-Jan-80   Age: 24

YEAR	TM	LG	AGE	AB	H	2B	3B	HR	BB	SO	SB	CS	AVG	OBP	SLG	MLVR	EQBA	EQOBP	EQSLG	EQMLVR	VORP	DEFENSE
2001	PTS	NYP	21	232	65	16	5	4	26	52	14	2	.280	.375	.444	.230	.214	.283	.350	-.273	-13.2	59-2B -11
2002	MIC	MID	22	499	143	25	14	14	62	102	18	8	.287	.368	.477	.234	.217	.282	.371	-.244	-11.0	118-2B -8
2003	LEX	SAL	23	140	26	5	2	3	17	25	7	1	.186	.287	.314	-.140	.152	.223	.255	-.554	-17.4	38-2B 3
2003	SLM	CAR	23	345	98	24	3	11	42	60	4	2	.284	.369	.467	.216	.225	.293	.383	-.201	-2.9	95-2B -7
2004	HOU	NL	24	231	56	12	2	6	21	48	3	1	.243	.315	.398	-.105	.240	.311	.397	-.130	5.9	64-2B -5

Breakout: 50%   Improve: 75%   Collapse: 15%

The flip side to Chris Burke, Conrad is a stopgap at second defensively, but an intriguing hitter with extra-base power. He's not a big guy, but he may have the kind of short, powerful swing that allows his bat to carry third base. A graduate of Arizona State—Barry Bonds once called an ASU education the equivalent of spending four years in a Coppertone commercial—Conrad's clock is ticking. He needs a good showing at Round Rock and another bump in his power numbers to emerge as a viable candidate for a starting corner job.

MORGAN ENSBERG   3B   Bats: R   Throws: R   Born: 26-Aug-75   Age: 28

YEAR	TM	LG	AGE	AB	H	2B	3B	HR	BB	SO	SB	CS	AVG	OBP	SLG	MLVR	EQBA	EQOBP	EQSLG	EQMLVR	VORP	DEFENSE	
2001	EST	DWL	25	164	45	7	2	10	33	31	2	0	.274	.396	.524	.290	.235	.343	.459	.003	20.4		
2001	NWO	PCL	25	316	98	20	0	23	45	60	6	3	.310	.397	.592	.393	.276	.362	.525	.162	37.1	77-3B	5
2002	NWO	PCL	26	292	84	12	3	7	50	56	9	5	.288	.401	.421	.169	.266	.367	.389	-.023	14.8	77-3B	-8
2002	HOU	NL	26	132	32	7	2	3	18	25	2	0	.242	.346	.394	-.013	.241	.342	.398	-.076	3.7	38-3B	-2
2003	HOU	NL	27	385	112	15	1	25	48	60	7	2	.291	.377	.530	.221	.286	.372	.526	.190	37.2	98-3B	5
2004	*HOU*	*NL*	*28*	*346*	*95*	*19*	*2*	*16*	*46*	*61*	*6*	*2*	*.276*	*.368*	*.480*	*.115*	*.273*	*.363*	*.478*	*.091*	*29.2*	*96-3B*	*-1*

Breakout: 20%   *Improve: 47%*   *Collapse: 17%*

Now that the Astros have sent Geoff Blum to the purgatory of Tampa, Ensberg must be wondering if Jimy Williams plans to unveil Jose Offerman as the team's 2004 starting 3B. Williams screwed the pooch by sticking with Blum way too long, while stapling Ensberg's productive bat to the bench. The Astros' offense consists of Berkman, Hidalgo, several effective but quickly declining veterans, and too many pop-gun hitters. When he gets in the lineup, Ensberg brings the power and patience the team sorely needs and a player still young and cheap enough to be counted on for the next three seasons. If a healthy Ensberg doesn't see 550 plate appearances in 2004, a grand jury needs to intervene.

ADAM EVERETT   SS   Bats: R   Throws: R   Born: 05-Feb-77   Age: 27

YEAR	TM	LG	AGE	AB	H	2B	3B	HR	BB	SO	SB	CS	AVG	OBP	SLG	MLVR	EQBA	EQOBP	EQSLG	EQMLVR	VORP	DEFENSE	
2001	NWO	PCL	24	441	110	20	8	5	39	74	24	5	.249	.330	.365	-.107	.235	.308	.343	-.220	-2.5	113-SS	-12
2002	NWO	PCL	25	345	95	16	7	2	24	59	12	3	.275	.331	.380	-.027	.266	.316	.366	-.152	5.1	84-SS	13
2002	HOU	NL	25	88	17	3	0	0	12	19	3	0	.193	.297	.227	-.335	.202	.296	.236	-.406	-4.9	30-SS	0
2003	NWO	PCL	26	100	25	6	1	1	7	16	3	1	.250	.306	.360	-.098	.238	.291	.356	-.234	-0.9	21-SS	-2
2003	HOU	NL	26	387	99	18	3	8	28	66	8	1	.256	.320	.380	-.098	.256	.316	.385	-.132	6.9	116-SS	2
2004	*HOU*	*NL*	*27*	*364*	*93*	*19*	*3*	*5*	*29*	*60*	*8*	*3*	*.255*	*.321*	*.370*	*-.124*	*.253*	*.316*	*.368*	*-.149*	*7.9*	*98-SS*	*1*

Breakout: 18%   *Improve: 48%*   *Collapse: 25%*

Though the numbers above don't show it, Everett's one of the best glove men at short in the game. His range to his left is particularly impressive, as he gets good jumps on grounders, liners, and bloopers up the middle, making plays most other shortstops can't. Minor off-season surgery to repair a torn meniscus in his right knee shouldn't impact his defense.

Of course the big question remains: Can his glove carry his bat? Though he improved on his 2002 numbers, Everett remains a low-average hitter who doesn't walk enough or hit for power. To his credit, he's worked hard to improve the strength in his hands and wrists, and isn't as overwhelmed by inside heat as he once was. Astros management likes to say how the team can carry a great D/poor O player like Everett, with the big bats picking up his slack. Houston's problem is that their offense is likely to get worse, not better, over the next couple of years, and there's no thunder waiting in the minors to fill the breach. Everett would be best used as a vacuum cleaner at short for a big-hitting, poor-fielding team like the Yankees. Back in non-hypothetical land, even PECOTA's 90th percentile sees just a decent-average, no-power player—.283/.354/.411. Everett's best hope is to become a late bloomer and the next Mike Bordick.

HECTOR GIMENEZ   C   Bats: B   Throws: R   Born: 28-Sep-82   Age: 21

YEAR	TM	LG	AGE	AB	H	2B	3B	HR	BB	SO	SB	CS	AVG	OBP	SLG	MLVR	EQBA	EQOBP	EQSLG	EQMLVR	VORP	DEFENSE	
2002	LEX	SAL	19	297	78	16	1	11	25	78	2	3	.263	.320	.434	.088	.198	.243	.343	-.371	-17.7	81-C	0
2003	SLM	CAR	20	381	94	17	1	7	29	75	2	0	.247	.304	.352	-.055	.206	.253	.307	-.396	-26.9	99-C	5
2004	*HOU*	*NL*	*21*	*249*	*50*	*11*	*1*	*6*	*17*	*57*	*1*	*1*	*.202*	*.256*	*.321*	*-.335*	*.200*	*.253*	*.319*	*-.361*	*-12.7*	*67-C*	*-4*

Breakout: 29%   *Improve: 49%*   *Collapse: 28%*

John Buck's washout season and Gimenez's defensive ability have elevated Gimenez to a higher prospect status among some members of Houston's brain trust. That assessment isn't yet warranted. After posting some promising power numbers in his Sally League debut at age 19, Gimenez struggled with the lumber at High-A Salem. The Astros preach working the count to their farmhands, but Gimenez has been a slow learner in that regard. His arm is a legit cannon though, and it's got a lot of people excited, even people outside the organization. Legend has it an opposing manager who used to work in the Astros system put steal signs on one game against Gimenez, just to watch him throw.

RICHARD HIDALGO

RICHARD HIDALGO   **RF**   **Bats: R**   **Throws: R**   Born: 02-Jul-75   Age: 28

YEAR	TM	LG	AGE	AB	H	2B	3B	HR	BB	SO	SB	CS	AVG	OBP	SLG	MLVR	EQBA	EQOBP	EQSLG	EQMLVR	VORP	DEFENSE		
2001	HOU	NL	26	512	141	29	3	19	54	107	3	5	.275	.356	.455	.048	.271	.354	.450	.040	26.7	110-CF -1	28-RF	1
2002	HOU	NL	27	388	91	17	4	15	43	85	6	2	.235	.319	.415	-.038	.235	.315	.423	-.097	-3.3	103-RF 6		
2003	HOU	NL	28	514	159	43	4	28	58	104	9	7	.309	.385	.572	.307	.303	.378	.565	.272	44.4	135-RF 15		
2004	HOU	NL	28	460	128	28	3	23	52	91	7	3	.278	.358	.498	.124	.275	.353	.495	.099	22.1	123-RF 5		

Breakout: 13%   *Improve: 48%*   *Collapse: 16%*

Finally, a happy medium. Hidalgo's monster 2000 season earned him a four-year, $32 million contract and a spot on the cover of *BP 2001*. His next two seasons featured an assortment of mishaps and a regression that spiraled so far down that Hidalgo was rendered Orlando Merced's platoon partner for several weeks in 2002. Last season saw Hidalgo return to the realm of productive corner outfielders, as he regained his power stroke. Hidalgo can play an effective second fiddle to Lance Berkman's lead, were money not an issue. But with $12 million plus as much as $2 million more in bonuses coming in '04, the Astros were actively shopping him in the off-season, hoping to gain some payroll flexibility. Given the glacial signing pace for players of even Vlad Guerrero's caliber, a Hidalgo deal looked unlikely at press time, meaning he'll likely be back in '04 as an Astro. He'll beat that projection.

JEFF KENT

JEFF KENT   **2B**   **Bats: R**   **Throws: R**   Born: 07-Mar-68   Age: 36

YEAR	TM	LG	AGE	AB	H	2B	3B	HR	BB	SO	SB	CS	AVG	OBP	SLG	MLVR	EQBA	EQOBP	EQSLG	EQMLVR	VORP	DEFENSE		
2001	SFG	NL	33	607	181	49	6	22	65	96	7	6	.298	.369	.507	.206	.312	.385	.532	.247	70.3	130-2B 6	23-1B	-4
2002	SFG	NL	34	623	195	42	2	37	52	101	5	1	.313	.368	.565	.348	.325	.377	.595	.340	82.9	143-2B 2		
2003	HOU	NL	35	505	150	39	1	22	39	85	6	2	.297	.351	.509	.160	.295	.348	.507	.132	37.8	125-2B -3		
2004	HOU	NL	36	451	132	30	2	24	42	76	5	2	.292	.355	.523	.167	.289	.350	.521	.141	38.9	118-2B -4		

Breakout: 13%   *Improve: 40%*   *Collapse: 18%*

Perhaps having learned from past mistakes, Gerry Hunsicker's largesse was limited to a two-year deal for Kent after the 2002 season. Good thing, as the former all-world second baseman started showing chinks in his armor last season. Kent missed several weeks with left wrist tendinitis, and his 130 games played was his lowest total since 1995. More troubling, Kent's home run total plunged, despite moving to a far more tater-friendly park. Most puzzling is the nosedive in his walks column, given that older players often walk more as they age. Kent's drop from 90 to 39 walks in three years is a troubling, perplexing trend. He'll make $8.5 million in '04, after which the Astros need to decline his option and either chuck him or bring him back at a reduced rate if they want to get value.

Last year we gave Kent solid odds for making the Hall of Fame. If he leaves Minute Maid Park behind for a more neutral stadium after this season, the tail end of his career may start to look ugly quickly, and voters may hold that against him. Kent may want to consider Colorado as his next destination; we hear the schools are top-notch.

JASON LANE

JASON LANE   **OF**   **Bats: R**   **Throws: L**   Born: 22-Dec-76   Age: 27

YEAR	TM	LG	AGE	AB	H	2B	3B	HR	BB	SO	SB	CS	AVG	OBP	SLG	MLVR	EQBA	EQOBP	EQSLG	EQMLVR	VORP	DEFENSE		
2001	ROU	TEX	24	526	166	36	2	38	61	98	14	2	.316	.407	.608	.444	.262	.336	.509	.082	22.7	109-LF -3	29-RF	-1
2002	NWO	PCL	25	426	116	36	2	15	31	90	13	3	.272	.328	.472	.097	.259	.311	.449	-.049	12.3	84-CF -5		
2002	HOU	NL	25	69	20	3	1	4	10	12	1	1	.290	.375	.536	.252	.286	.367	.543	.205	5.1	17-RF 1		
2003	NWO	PCL	26	248	74	17	0	7	30	26	2	1	.298	.374	.452	.191	.280	.353	.433	.022	6.7	27-RF -4	15-CF	-3
2003	HOU	NL	26	27	8	2	0	4	0	2	0	0	.296	.296	.815	.513	.296	.296	.815	.511	3.9			
2004	HOU	NL	27	209	57	12	1	9	20	35	2	1	.272	.342	.474	.063	.269	.338	.472	.038	10.7	58-CF -9		

Breakout: 25%   *Improve: 46%*   *Collapse: 24%*

A sports hernia cut into Lane's season and sent him to the operating table at year's end. That's a shame, because the Astros still need to figure out if he has enough power to effectively man a corner outfield spot. Like Morgan Ensberg, Lane could put up a solid first full season at age 27, assuming he can find the playing time. Unlike Ensberg, the competition for playing time comes from two of the team's best players, and not Geoff Blum. A Hidalgo trade would have solved a lot of problems for him, but with Doggie still around, Lane looks like an overqualified bench warmer for another year.

DAVID MATRANGA   2B   Bats: R   Throws: R   Born: 08-Jan-77   Age: 27

YEAR	TM	LG	AGE	AB	H	2B	3B	HR	BB	SO	SB	CS	AVG	OBP	SLG	MLVR	EQBA	EQOBP	EQSLG	EQMLVR	VORP	DEFENSE			
2001	ROU	TEX	24	387	117	34	2	10	45	91	17	7	.302	.391	.478	.232	.254	.329	.412	-.072	12.6	97-2B	9		
2001	NWO	PCL	24	16	5	1	0	1	0	5	1	0	.313	.333	.563	.251	.312	.340	.500	.126	1.2				
2002	NWO	PCL	25	300	82	15	3	7	27	79	7	2	.273	.342	.413	.041	.259	.321	.393	-.110	5.9	53-2B	-1	14-SS	1
2003	NWO	PCL	26	315	76	16	4	3	21	71	3	3	.241	.296	.346	-.141	.232	.283	.342	-.273	-9.1	50-2B	-4	20-SS	-6
2003	HOU	NL	26	5	1	0	0	1	0	2	0	0	.200	.200	.800	.231	.200	.200	.800	.205	0.5				
2004	HOU	NL	27	186	47	11	1	5	16	44	2	1	.255	.322	.405	-.075	.252	.318	.403	-.101	8.2	52-2B	-3		

Breakout: 34%   Improve: 51%   Collapse: 32%

Matranga's been headed in the wrong direction since a strong 2001 season at Round Rock. Once a decent-looking middle infield candidate, he now looks like a fringe utility guy at best, only a mild step up from Eric Bruntlett. PECOTA seems to think the skills he flashed in '01 are waiting to come out though. Both man and software agree he's a better choice than Jose Vizcaino, let alone Vizcaino at four times the MLB minimum.

MITCH MELUSKEY   DH   Bats: B   Throws: R   Born: 18-Sep-73   Age: 30

YEAR	TM	LG	AGE	AB	H	2B	3B	HR	BB	SO	SB	CS	AVG	OBP	SLG	MLVR	EQBA	EQOBP	EQSLG	EQMLVR	VORP	DEFENSE	
2002	DET	AL	28	27	6	0	0	0	5	3	0	0	.222	.353	.222	-.224	.259	.408	.259	-.117	0.1		
2003	ROU	TEX	29	49	13	2	0	1	5	9	1	0	.265	.327	.367	-.037	.220	.278	.320	-.320	-3.0		
2003	HOU	NL	29	9	1	1	0	0	2	2	0	0	.111	.250	.222	-.490	.111	.273	.222	-.505	-0.7		
2004	HOU	NL	30	73	17	4	0	1	8	14	1	0	.234	.316	.338	-.186	.231	.312	.337	-.211	-1.0	24-DH	0

Breakout: 47%   Improve: 62%   Collapse: 25%

Oh, what might have been. Meluskey posted some gaudy minor league numbers in '97 and '98 and looked on his way to an All-Star career. A rookie season that saw him hit .300 with power and patience raised expectations another level. It's been one injury after another since then, with some choice clubhouse confrontations sprinkled in for bad measure. Meluskey's latest ailment is a disc problem in his back—the buzz was his combative nature made it difficult for medical staff to work with him, making it harder for him to recover. A six-year minor league free agent now on the wrong side of 30, it's hard to see Meluskey forging much of a career. Someone will take a flyer; the upside's a switch-hitting third catcher and part-time DH with pop.

ORLANDO MERCED   OF   Bats: L   Throws: R   Born: 02-Nov-66   Age: 37

YEAR	TM	LG	AGE	AB	H	2B	3B	HR	BB	SO	SB	CS	AVG	OBP	SLG	MLVR	EQBA	EQOBP	EQSLG	EQMLVR	VORP	DEFENSE			
2001	HOU	NL	34	137	36	6	1	6	14	32	5	1	.263	.333	.453	-.006	.261	.332	.442	-.019	1.8	13-RF	-1		
2002	HOU	NL	35	251	72	13	3	6	26	50	4	0	.287	.350	.434	.077	.287	.349	.441	.032	6.5	33-RF	1	16-LF	0
2003	HOU	NL	36	212	49	17	2	3	15	33	3	2	.231	.283	.373	-.188	.230	.283	.371	-.233	-4.8	15-RF	0		
2004	HOU	NL	37	99	25	5	1	2	9	19	1	1	.253	.317	.386	-.112	.250	.313	.384	-.137	-0.9	30-RF	-3		

Breakout: 26%   Improve: 44%   Collapse: 35%

Two solid seasons as the Astros' top utility outfielder turned to dust as Merced laid an egg in '03—turns out most 36-year-olds *don't* hit like Barry Bonds. Jason Lane will fill his role far more capably. Merced's unlikely to get anything more than a NRI after filing for free agency.

COLIN PORTER   CF   Bats: L   Throws: L   Born: 23-Nov-75   Age: 28

YEAR	TM	LG	AGE	AB	H	2B	3B	HR	BB	SO	SB	CS	AVG	OBP	SLG	MLVR	EQBA	EQOBP	EQSLG	EQMLVR	VORP	DEFENSE			
2001	ROU	TEX	25	100	32	5	5	2	5	25	1	3	.320	.358	.530	.273	.270	.308	.450	-.043	3.1	25-CF	-1		
2001	NWO	PCL	25	312	74	14	1	7	34	105	11	6	.237	.314	.356	-.160	.218	.292	.329	-.281	-13.9	58-CF	-5	20-RF	-2
2002	NWO	PCL	26	461	122	30	5	6	46	127	28	7	.265	.331	.390	-.020	.249	.311	.369	-.169	-14.5	103-RF	-2	13-CF	-2
2003	NWO	PCL	27	356	114	23	6	11	22	80	22	6	.320	.361	.511	.279	.302	.344	.493	.112	27.2	90-CF	3		
2003	HOU	NL	27	32	6	0	0	0	1	17	1	0	.188	.212	.188	-.585	.188	.212	.188	-.655	-3.6				
2004	HOU	NL	28	190	49	10	2	6	16	52	6	2	.258	.316	.433	-.047	.255	.312	.431	-.073	3.8	53-CF	-5		

Breakout: 22%   Improve: 44%   Collapse: 36%

An adequate center fielder with a touch of pop and plenty of speed, Porter should make a nifty lefty-swinging caddy for a player who'll surely need regular rest in Biggio. Porter's too old to be classified a prospect, but he's a much better option than Brian Hunter as a fifth outfielder, a reasonable plug-in if Biggio hits the DL, and a solid bet to earn his $300,000.

MIKE RODRIGUEZ   OF   Bats: L   Throws: L   Born: 15-Oct-80   Age: 23

YEAR	TM	LG	AGE	AB	H	2B	3B	HR	BB	SO	SB	CS	AVG	OBP	SLG	MLVR	EQBA	EQOBP	EQSLG	EQMLVR	VORP	DEFENSE		
2001	PTS	NYP	20	157	50	14	4	0	33	30	13	5	.318	.443	.459	.364	.212	.305	.318	-.274	-21.8	32-LF	-7	
2002	MIC	MID	21	499	126	23	4	4	65	85	35	11	.253	.338	.339	-.006	.197	.264	.270	-.429	-45.4	104-CF	-10	
2003	SLM	CAR	22	443	123	22	8	5	50	50	23	9	.278	.356	.397	.103	.226	.288	.336	-.275	-31.9	50-LF	-7	39-CF -6

A 2001 second-round pick out of the University of Miami, the erstwhile Hurricane has retained the same profile as he's slowly climbed the ladder: good speed, good batting eye, decent glove, a little pop. That's the nice version. The nasty take on Rodriguez would point to his lack of range negating his shot at handling center, his sub-par arm making right a tricky proposition, his mediocre bat making a career as a left fielder unlikely, and his thin 5'10" frame making a big breakout a long shot at best. Though he's still young, Rodriguez's upside looks like that of a fourth outfielder, which is pretty unexciting for a high draft choice.

HENRI STANLEY   LF   Bats: L   Throws: L   Born: 15-Dec-77   Age: 26

YEAR	TM	LG	AGE	AB	H	2B	3B	HR	BB	SO	SB	CS	AVG	OBP	SLG	MLVR	EQBA	EQOBP	EQSLG	EQMLVR	VORP	DEFENSE		
2001	MIC	MID	23	400	120	24	12	14	73	84	30	5	.300	.408	.525	.328	.205	.292	.364	-.242	-12.7	42-CF	0	19-LF -1
2002	ROU	TEX	24	456	143	36	10	16	72	85	14	9	.314	.408	.542	.375	.256	.339	.456	.009	9.4	57-LF	-4	35-CF -3
2003	NWO	PCL	25	506	148	28	8	11	60	93	15	7	.292	.368	.445	.166	.271	.342	.424	-.018	5.8	119-LF	5	
2004	*SDP*	*NL*	*26*	*217*	*53*	*12*	*3*	*6*	*24*	*46*	*4*	*2*	*.246*	*.323*	*.401*	*-.086*	*.252*	*.327*	*.422*	*-.060*	*5.5*	*61-LF*	*2*	

Breakout: 25%   *Improve: 45%*   *Collapse: 39%*

A feel-good success story, Stanley's advanced from undrafted free agent to the brink of a major league debut in four years. Unfortunately time, or more specifically age, is working against him. Stanley's put up good enough numbers in the minors to earn his first taste of the bigs, but at 26, with gap power and a good eye the best of his resume, his upside looks limited. What does it say about the Astros' system when losing Stanley to waivers wiped out one of their three best hitting prospects? The Padres found themselves a nice little upgrade to Gary Matthews Jr. among their outfield reserves.

JOSE VIZCAINO   2B/SS   Bats: B   Throws: R   Born: 26-Mar-68   Age: 36

YEAR	TM	LG	AGE	AB	H	2B	3B	HR	BB	SO	SB	CS	AVG	OBP	SLG	MLVR	EQBA	EQOBP	EQSLG	EQMLVR	VORP	DEFENSE		
2001	HOU	NL	33	256	71	8	3	1	15	33	3	2	.277	.322	.344	-.165	.275	.317	.341	-.180	1.6	37-SS	-3	11-2B -2
2002	HOU	NL	34	406	123	19	2	5	24	40	3	5	.303	.342	.397	.025	.305	.342	.400	-.024	18.4	47-SS	0	22-3B 2
2003	HOU	NL	35	189	47	7	3	3	8	22	0	1	.249	.281	.365	-.189	.247	.281	.368	-.230	-1.5	18-SS	-2	16-2B -1
2004	*HOU*	*NL*	*36*	*139*	*35*	*6*	*1*	*2*	*9*	*17*	*1*	*1*	*.254*	*.299*	*.344*	*-.196*	*.251*	*.295*	*.343*	*-.222*	*0.0*	*40-SS*	*-10*	

Breakout: 11%   *Improve: 28%*   *Collapse: 48%*

Said Gerry Hunsicker after signing Vizcaino to a one-year, $1.2 million deal at season's end: "He's a quality person and a tremendous influence on his team. He's a team player, he's a quality individual and a great role model. He's certainly the type of player we continue to look to bring into this organization." This is also the same organization whose owner bellyaches about rising player salaries every ten minutes, the same organization shackled with huge monetary commitments tied to a small core of untradable players. Making bad decisions at the tail end of the roster isn't something the Astros can afford to do. Vizcaino's a lousy hitter and lousy fielder who's a good bet to get even worse as he ages. Unless he's saving a couple of hundred fans' lives a night, his sparkling personality ain't worth the bucks.

TOM WHITEMAN   SS/3B   Bats: R   Throws: R   Born: 14-Jul-79   Age: 24

YEAR	TM	LG	AGE	AB	H	2B	3B	HR	BB	SO	SB	CS	AVG	OBP	SLG	MLVR	EQBA	EQOBP	EQSLG	EQMLVR	VORP	DEFENSE		
2001	LEX	SAL	21	389	124	26	8	18	34	106	17	13	.319	.380	.566	.397	.240	.290	.430	-.130	8.6	109-SS	-8	
2002	LEX	SAL	22	350	106	29	2	10	36	66	6	6	.303	.374	.483	.256	.223	.277	.368	-.254	-5.5	83-SS	0	
2002	ROU	TEX	22	56	10	2	1	0	4	17	1	1	.179	.246	.250	-.357	.175	.224	.246	-.554	-5.9	14-SS	-5	
2003	ROU	TEX	23	532	139	18	2	13	35	102	3	8	.261	.310	.376	-.056	.225	.270	.335	-.312	-17.6	98-SS	-18	33-3B -3
2004	*HOU*	*NL*	*24*	*228*	*57*	*12*	*1*	*7*	*17*	*49*	*2*	*1*	*.250*	*.306*	*.404*	*-.107*	*.248*	*.302*	*.402*	*-.133*	*5.9*	*62-SS*	*-9*	

Breakout: 57%   *Improve: 74%*   *Collapse: 9%*

After exciting management with a strong 2002 AFL campaign, Whiteman saw his first extended action at Double-A, and took a major step backward. None of his skills regressed as badly as his plate discipline, as Whiteman posted three strikeouts for every walk at Round Rock. Tall for a shortstop, with an athletic frame that suggests power potential, Whiteman has the tools that make for an intriguing prospect, but needs to achieve some results above Sally League ball to be taken seriously. The Astros' lack of a High-A affiliate was designed in part to challenge their better prospects. Whiteman could have used the time at that level, and few Astro farmhands have been hurt by the policy more than he has.

PITCHERS

JIMMY BARRETT — Bats: R — Throws: R — Born: 07-Jun-81 — Age: 23

YEAR	TM	LG	AGE	G	GS	IP	H	BB	SO	HR	ERA	EQERA	EQH9	EQBB9	EQSO9	EQHR9	PERA	VORP	STF
2001	MIC	MID	20	27	25	130.7	122	62	98	12	4.48	6.61	10.3	6.1	4.1	1.9	6.95	-13.0	-22
2002	LEX	SAL	21	27	22	134.3	112	40	131	13	2.81	5.84	11.3	3.9	5.5	2.4	7.42	-3.0	-22
2003	SLM	CAR	22	26	26	138.3	160	56	75	13	5.34	7.80	12.6	4.8	3.5	2.2	8.10	-29.9	-47
2004	HOU	NL	23	11	7	38.3	54	22	20	11	8.49	8.65	12.5	4.4	4.2	2.4	8.53	-5.0	-31

Breakout: 12%   Improve: 50%   Collapse: 25%

A year after putting together an impressive Sally League campaign, Barrett cratered on the jump to Salem. His velocity topped out at 90 after touching 94 in '02. Though he lasted the whole season, Barrett looked like he was hiding an injury. After getting burned by losing Johan Santana to the Rule 5 draft a few years ago, the Astros thought they were playing it safe by adding Barrett to the 40-man roster. Now it just looks like bad use of a roster spot. Such are the pitfalls of TINSTAAPP.

JUAN CAMPOS — Bats: R — Throws: R — Born: 28-Mar-80 — Age: 24

YEAR	TM	LG	AGE	G	GS	IP	H	BB	SO	HR	ERA	EQERA	EQH9	EQBB9	EQSO9	EQHR9	PERA	VORP	STF
2001	MIC	MID	21	13	13	78.3	90	10	69	8	4.60	7.04	12.9	1.7	4.9	2.0	7.23	-11.2	-14
2002	MIC	MID	22	36	0	58.3	50	8	63	1	2.01	4.56	10.9	1.8	6.0	0.5	4.51	5.9	12
2003	SLM	CAR	23	45	0	68.3	51	16	68	1	1.84	3.21	8.3	2.8	6.1	0.3	3.41	16.4	19
2003	ROU	TEX	23	9	0	12.7	19	3	17	1	8.50	8.49	15.4	2.3	9.3	1.5	7.78	-3.8	-7
2004	HOU	NL	24	19	8	51.3	56	16	39	6	4.38	4.46	9.7	2.5	6.2	0.9	4.50	7.7	3

Breakout: 16%   Improve: 43%   Collapse: 28%

You won't find too many A-ball relievers in this book, but in a system as thin as Houston's, with numbers like Campos put up last year, we'll make an exception. Author of a two-seam and four-seam fastball and nothing else of note, he totaled more strikeouts than baserunners allowed and yielded just one homer in 68.1 innings, easily disposing of Carolina League hitters. Relievers can find success for a short while without a useful breaking pitch, but Campos would do well to at least develop a show-me slider to complement his 93–94 MPH heat. Another product of Houston's extensive Venezuelan scouting efforts, PECOTA thinks Campos can be a league-average MLB reliever right now, but let's see what happens at Round Rock first.

OCTAVIO DOTEL — Bats: R — Throws: R — Born: 25-Nov-73 — Age: 30

YEAR	TM	LG	AGE	G	GS	IP	H	BB	SO	HR	ERA	EQERA	EQH9	EQBB9	EQSO9	EQHR9	PERA	VORP	STF
2001	HOU	NL	27	61	4	105.0	79	47	145	5	2.66	2.94	7.3	3.7	10.5	0.4	3.24	29.9	44
2002	HOU	NL	28	83	0	97.3	58	27	118	7	1.85	2.01	5.6	2.2	9.5	0.7	2.33	37.5	40
2003	HOU	NL	29	76	0	87.0	53	31	97	9	2.48	2.59	6.0	2.9	9.0	0.9	2.94	30.4	26
2004	HOU	NL	30	54	3	78.3	62	31	82	8	3.11	3.17	7.1	3.1	8.6	0.8	3.32	22.9	16

Breakout: 40%   Improve: 59%   Collapse: 13%

Jimy Williams's whip-cracking caught up to his bullpen in the season's dog days, as Dotel went through a brief slump due to fatigue. Meanwhile his end-of-season numbers were nearly as dominant as ever, with his K/BB rates dropping only slightly to "great" from its previous status of "superamazing." Wagner's departure makes him the closer and moves Brad Lidge into Dotel's previous eighth-inning role. The Astros need better work out of their new Pettitte-fied rotation and more trust in those starters from Williams, or they risk doing more serious damage to the weakened pen.

JARED FERNANDEZ — Bats: R — Throws: R — Born: 02-Feb-72 — Age: 32

YEAR	TM	LG	AGE	G	GS	IP	H	BB	SO	HR	ERA	EQERA	EQH9	EQBB9	EQSO9	EQHR9	PERA	VORP	STF
2001	LOU	INT	29	33	28	196.3	218	54	118	24	4.13	5.82	11.1	2.9	4.2	1.5	6.05	-4.4	-27
2001	CIN	NL	29	5	2	12.3	13	6	5	1	4.39	5.25	9.0	3.8	3.0	0.8	4.51	0.5	-19
2002	LOU	INT	30	26	18	128.3	151	31	80	14	3.93	5.32	11.2	2.5	4.7	1.4	5.93	3.7	-22
2002	CIN	NL	30	14	8	50.7	59	24	36	5	4.44	5.51	10.7	3.7	5.5	0.9	5.37	0.5	-7
2003	NWO	PCL	31	26	23	156.0	164	37	51	16	3.81	5.68	11.0	2.6	2.6	1.5	6.00	-1.3	-36
2003	HOU	NL	31	12	6	38.3	37	12	19	2	3.99	3.96	9.2	2.5	4.0	0.5	3.94	7.6	3
2004	HOU	NL	32	24	12	67.0	85	28	30	13	6.32	6.43	11.4	3.3	3.7	1.6	6.44	-2.6	-23

Breakout: 24%   Improve: 48%   Collapse: 25%

(continued next page)

Jared Fernandez *(continued)*

Called up in August to help patch the holes in the depleted rotation, Fernandez did what you'd expect, pitching well enough to win in half his six starts. He can be an effective spot starter for the Astros or any other team ballsy enough to use a knuckleballer.

Pulled the excellent 1989 Craig Wright/Tom House book *The Diamond Appraised* off the shelf the other day. In it, Wright laments the impending death of knuckleballers, with the fate of nations resting on Tom Candiotti's floater. Though a bewildering pitch when thrown properly and one that causes little strain on precious pitching arms, Wright argued that the knuckler wouldn't catch on under baseball's current structure, as scouts favor hard cheese and coaches shy away from teaching what they don't know. It'll take a creative, gutsy organization to revive the knuckler by signing and developing the few young pitchers out there trying it and implementing proper teaching methods in the minor leagues—the Diamondbacks have already taken a similar approach with sidearmers. Orthodoxy is nothing more than a cop-out; it squeezes the fun out of the game, and can hinder teams' ability to grab that handful of marginal wins that decide pennants every year.

CARLOS HERNANDEZ   Bats: B   Throws: L   Born: 22-Apr-80   Age: 24

YEAR	TM	LG	AGE	G	GS	IP	H	BB	SO	HR	ERA	EQERA	EQH9	EQBB9	EQSO9	EQHR9	PERA	VORP	STF
2001	ROU	TEX	21	24	23	139.0	115	69	167	11	3.69	5.13	9.0	5.5	8.1	1.1	5.32	6.6	29
2001	HOU	NL	21	3	3	17.7	11	7	17	1	1.02	1.59	5.8	3.2	7.4	0.5	2.63	7.6	60
2002	HOU	NL	22	23	21	111.0	112	61	93	11	4.38	4.64	9.0	4.3	6.5	0.8	4.69	11.6	26
2004	*HOU*	*NL*	*24*	*20*	*17*	*99.7*	*97*	*54*	*85*	*12*	*4.65*	*4.73*	*8.7*	*4.2*	*6.9*	*1.0*	*4.82*	*11.2*	*9*

Breakout: 11%   Improve: 43%   Collapse: 24%

One of the smarter tacks the Astros take in their player development program is to keep a weekly injury sheet on the other 29 clubs' upper-level prospects. A handy guide to have come trade time, it also offers a lot more data points to look at in projecting recovery rates for the team's own prospects. So the Astros could look at, say, Gil Meche's solid 2003 first half in his return from torn labrum surgery and gain hope for Hernandez's successful return. Of course Meche crashed in the second half, Hernandez's decent winter league performance should be taken with giant mouthfuls of salt given the circuit's level of play, and a torn labrum—even one suffered through a non-pitching activity like Hernandez's—remains as close to a death sentence as any injury around in this age of astounding medical technology. Houston hopes to get a healthy, effective Hernandez back in the rotation by Opening Day. Don't bet anything important on it.

JASON HIRSH   Bats: R   Throws: R   Born: 20-Feb-82   Age: 22

YEAR	TM	LG	AGE	G	GS	IP	H	BB	SO	HR	ERA	EQERA	EQH9	EQBB9	EQSO9	EQHR9	PERA	VORP	STF
2003	TCV	NYP	21	10	8	32.3	22	7	33	0	1.95	4.55	9.4	2.9	5.2	0.3	4.00	3.2	16

A 6'8", 250-pound specimen with the stuff to match his size, Hirsh brings the added effect of blocking out the sun as his 96 mph fastball zooms in on opposing hitters. With just a hard slider to complement the heat, some have suggested the Astros move Hirsh to the pen to become a closer. His impressive eight-start debut right out of Cal Lutheran University should shut down such talk for now. The second-round pick will work on developing a repeatable delivery for now and worry about the nuances of a change once he's faced hitters old enough to legally drink.

D. J. HOULTON   Bats: R   Throws: R   Born: 12-Aug-79   Age: 24

YEAR	TM	LG	AGE	G	GS	IP	H	BB	SO	HR	ERA	EQERA	EQH9	EQBB9	EQSO9	EQHR9	PERA	VORP	STF
2001	MAR	APP	21	13	13	72.0	67	7	71	7	2.50	6.18	13.9	1.5	4.1	2.7	8.53	-3.8	-40
2002	MIC	MID	22	35	16	140.7	120	30	138	12	3.13	5.62	11.6	2.7	5.6	2.3	7.21	-0.3	-27
2003	ROU	TEX	23	18	18	109.0	93	28	101	11	3.47	3.83	8.5	2.9	6.1	1.8	5.06	19.9	1
2003	NWO	PCL	23	11	11	61.7	70	19	48	12	5.40	7.31	11.6	3.3	6.4	2.7	7.82	-10.8	-29
2004	*HOU*	*NL*	*24*	*17*	*12*	*69.0*	*75*	*22*	*49*	*12*	*5.04*	*5.13*	*9.7*	*2.5*	*5.8*	*1.4*	*5.06*	*5.3*	*1*

Breakout: 17%   Improve: 54%   Collapse: 20%

Here's a rare recent case of an Astros prospect skipping High-A ball and not crashing. An 11th-round flyer out of University of the Pacific in 2001, Houlton jumped from the Midwest League to Double-A Round Rock last season and fared well, showing the same great control that hinted at a stealth prospect in '02. The Astros couldn't leave well enough alone though, pushing Houlton to Triple-A and watching him get smoked over his last 11 starts. His ability to throw strikes could make him a good back-of-the-rotation candidate by 2005, though he'll need to learn a bit more deception to keep the ball in the park.

BRAD LIDGE

Bats: R **Throws: R** Born: 23-Dec-76 Age: 27

YEAR	TM	LG	AGE	G	GS	IP	H	BB	SO	HR	ERA	EQERA	EQH9	EQBB9	EQSO9	EQHR9	PERA	VORP	STF
2001	ROU	TEX	24	5	5	26.0	21	7	42	1	1.73	3.09	10.0	3.1	10.4	0.8	4.66	6.5	43
2002	ROU	TEX	25	5	0	11.0	9	3	18	0	2.45	3.72	10.2	2.8	11.2	0.0	3.90	2.0	50
2002	NWO	PCL	25	24	19	111.7	83	47	110	9	3.38	4.63	8.4	4.5	7.0	1.0	4.59	10.9	3
2003	HOU	NL	26	78	0	85.0	60	42	97	6	3.60	3.53	6.9	4.1	9.1	0.7	3.48	18.6	24
2004	*HOU*	*NL*	*27*	*43*	*9*	*77.0*	*72*	*45*	*75*	*8*	*4.57*	*4.66*	*8.3*	*4.6*	*8.0*	*0.9*	*4.76*	*10.7*	*5*

Breakout: 26%   *Improve: 51%*   *Collapse: 30%*

Lidge will never be the top-of-the-rotation horse Houston envisioned when it used a first-round pick on him in 1998. But after repeated attempts to tiptoe around his proclivity for injuries, the Astros accepted their fate, put him in the bullpen for good, and watched him blossom into an excellent reliever. Lidge will remain a risk for the rest of his career: His rough mechanics put a lot of torque on his elbow, and he's vulnerable to the kind of fatigue that plagued him in stretches last year under Jimy Williams's demanding workload. But he now stands a great chance of providing three to four years of excellent relief for a low price, much to the Astros' credit.

RUDDY LUGO

Bats: R **Throws: R** Born: 22-May-80 Age: 24

YEAR	TM	LG	AGE	G	GS	IP	H	BB	SO	HR	ERA	EQERA	EQH9	EQBB9	EQSO9	EQHR9	PERA	VORP	STF
2001	BLT	MID	21	10	0	15.0	10	6	20	0	0.60	1.35	8.1	5.4	7.4	0.0	3.75	6.3	37
2001	WNC	SAL	21	16	0	31.0	29	13	23	2	3.77	7.71	12.3	6.0	3.9	1.4	7.27	-6.0	-38
2002	VRO	FLA	22	22	9	87.0	68	26	77	5	2.38	3.89	8.9	3.3	5.5	1.1	4.72	15.0	5
2002	JAX	SOU	22	11	2	33.3	34	13	23	3	4.05	6.44	12.0	4.0	4.6	1.8	7.14	-2.7	-28
2003	ROU	TEX	23	41	15	118.3	133	53	112	12	6.01	6.71	11.1	5.1	6.3	1.8	6.95	-13.4	-27
2004	*HOU*	*NL*	*24*	*12*	*5*	*31.0*	*35*	*17*	*23*	*5*	*5.75*	*5.86*	*10.0*	*4.4*	*6.0*	*1.4*	*5.96*	*1.3*	*-10*

Breakout: 27%   *Improve: 56%*   *Collapse: 18%*

Julio's little brother, Lugo can dial it up to 98, with no earthly idea of where the ball's going. His tanking at Round Rock came as a bit of a surprise, after his decent showing at A-ball in 2002. An extreme long shot at this point, all he cost in trade was noted cipher Daryle Ward. Remember when Daryle Ward and Lance Berkman were cited as twin building blocks of the next great Astros team? Was that prediction more or less apt than Carloses Febles and Beltran marching arm-in-arm to stardom? Discuss.

DAN MICELI

Bats: R **Throws: R** Born: 09-Sep-70 Age: 33

YEAR	TM	LG	AGE	G	GS	IP	H	BB	SO	HR	ERA	EQERA	EQH9	EQBB9	EQSO9	EQHR9	PERA	VORP	STF
2001	FLA	NL	30	29	0	24.7	29	11	31	5	6.92	7.12	10.9	3.8	9.4	1.5	6.05	-4.1	-10
2001	COL	NL	30	22	0	20.3	18	5	17	2	2.22	3.20	7.8	1.8	6.4	0.9	3.49	5.3	8
2002	TEX	AL	31	9	0	8.3	13	3	5	1	8.67	7.56	13.0	3.2	5.4	1.1	6.48	-1.8	-26
2003	COL	NL	32	14	0	20.7	24	9	18	7	5.65	5.75	9.7	3.5	6.6	2.7	6.92	1.4	-48
2003	CLE	AL	32	13	0	15.0	9	6	19	1	1.20	2.45	5.5	3.7	11.0	0.6	2.67	5.9	45
2003	NYY	AL	32	7	0	4.7	4	3	1	2	5.74	5.79	5.8	5.8	1.9	3.9	7.30	0.0	-112
2003	HOU	NL	32	23	0	30.0	22	7	20	3	2.10	2.54	7.0	1.9	5.4	1.0	3.20	12.1	5
2004	*HOU*	*NL*	*33*	*38*	*5*	*61.3*	*61*	*22*	*50*	*9*	*4.48*	*4.56*	*8.9*	*2.8*	*6.7*	*1.2*	*4.57*	*7.9*	*1*

Breakout: 22%   *Improve: 48%*   *Collapse: 23%*

Traded by the Yankees for a PTBNL in late July, The Alien That Took Over Dan Miceli's Body played a big role in keeping the Astros in it until the end, chipping in 30 innings of outstanding pitching that spanned slumps by both Dotel and Lidge. The Astros re-upped Miceli for one year at $600,000, hoping for another round of extraterrestrial intervention.

WADE MILLER

Bats: R **Throws: R** Born: 13-Sep-76 Age: 27

YEAR	TM	LG	AGE	G	GS	IP	H	BB	SO	HR	ERA	EQERA	EQH9	EQBB9	EQSO9	EQHR9	PERA	VORP	STF
2001	HOU	NL	24	32	32	212.0	183	76	183	31	3.40	3.79	7.9	3.0	6.6	1.1	4.12	41.1	21
2002	HOU	NL	25	26	26	164.7	151	62	144	14	3.28	3.59	8.2	3.0	6.8	0.7	3.83	35.8	27
2003	HOU	NL	26	33	33	187.3	168	77	161	17	4.13	4.32	8.6	3.4	6.9	0.8	4.19	24.9	18
2004	*HOU*	*NL*	*27*	*27*	*26*	*164.3*	*155*	*63*	*132*	*16*	*3.84*	*3.91*	*8.4*	*3.0*	*6.6*	*0.8*	*3.97*	*30.5*	*16*

Breakout: 18%   *Improve: 48%*   *Collapse: 19%*

(continued next page)

Wade Miller *(continued)*

Despite pitching with a sore elbow for much of the summer, Miller still put up his usual strong second half, finishing with another solid season. That Miller's ERA was nearly a run higher than in 2002 despite nearly identical peripherals is a function of last year's troubles with men on base:

None on: .219/.293/.346
Runners on: .278/.360/.422

Miller's mechanics started breaking down at the end of the year as he complained of dead-arm symptoms. An MRI revealed nothing more than tendinitis, and the Astros expect him to be fine for spring training. He'd better be, because from here on in he'll get expensive quickly.

BRIAN MOEHLER   Bats: R   Throws: R   Born: 31-Dec-71   Age: 32

YEAR	TM	LG	AGE	G	GS	IP	H	BB	SO	HR	ERA	EQERA	EQH9	EQBB9	EQSO9	EQHR9	PERA	VORP	STF
2002	DET	AL	30	3	3	19.7	17	2	13	3	2.28	2.33	7.0	0.9	5.6	1.4	3.34	7.0	15
2002	CIN	NL	30	10	9	43.3	61	11	18	8	6.03	6.91	12.7	1.9	3.2	1.7	6.87	-6.1	-40
2003	HOU	NL	31	3	3	13.7	22	6	5	4	7.88	8.31	15.2	3.5	2.8	2.8	9.73	-3.0	-82
2004	*HOU*	*NL*	*32*	*21*	*13*	*72.0*	*98*	*24*	*34*	*18*	*6.70*	*6.83*	*12.1*	*2.6*	*3.8*	*2.0*	*6.84*	*-3.6*	*-21*

Breakout: 14%   Improve: 40%   Collapse: 32%

Expected to fill in at the back of the rotation, Moehler lasted three starts before snapping his elbow and heading to the operating table. Tommy John surgery recovery time has grown shorter over the years, so Moehler could be recovered by the All-Star break. Given his mediocre stuff made him a marginal starter before he ever got hurt, he may not get much of a chance in '04 anyway. A free agent, Scuffy's waiting by the phone to take your call.

PETER MUNRO   Bats: R   Throws: R   Born: 14-Jun-75   Age: 29

YEAR	TM	LG	AGE	G	GS	IP	H	BB	SO	HR	ERA	EQERA	EQH9	EQBB9	EQSO9	EQHR9	PERA	VORP	STF
2001	OKL	PCL	26	33	8	88.7	89	43	73	12	4.67	5.64	10.1	5.3	5.4	1.5	6.25	-0.4	-40
2002	NWO	PCL	27	19	13	94.3	68	15	73	3	2.39	3.48	8.1	1.7	5.4	0.4	3.15	20.1	22
2002	HOU	NL	27	19	14	80.7	89	23	45	5	3.57	4.14	9.7	2.2	4.4	0.6	4.15	12.7	7
2003	HOU	NL	28	40	2	54.0	63	26	27	7	4.67	5.40	11.0	4.0	4.0	1.0	5.78	4.9	-28
2003	NWO	PCL	28	5	4	22.3	28	12	12	1	6.05	8.10	13.1	5.8	4.5	0.9	6.99	-5.6	-37
2004	*MIN*	*AL*	*29*	*28*	*12*	*71.3*	*81*	*31*	*38*	*8*	*4.81*	*4.69*	*9.8*	*3.7*	*4.7*	*0.9*	*5.03*	*8.4*	*-11*

Breakout: 27%   Improve: 56%   Collapse: 23%

A year after effectively filling the sixth starter/long reliever role, Munro lost the gains in command he'd garnered in 2002 and got hammered. How the Astros stuck with him for 54 innings of whack-a-mole is a mystery wrapped in a pulled barbecue sandwich. The Twins gave him a NRI, and Munro will try to land a job as Minnesota's 11th arm.

FERNANDO NIEVE   Bats: R   Throws: R   Born: 15-Jul-82   Age: 21

YEAR	TM	LG	AGE	G	GS	IP	H	BB	SO	HR	ERA	EQERA	EQH9	EQBB9	EQSO9	EQHR9	PERA	VORP	STF
2001	MAR	APP	18	12	8	38.0	27	21	49	2	3.79	7.34	10.9	8.5	5.6	1.5	7.30	-5.9	-10
2002	MAR	APP	19	13	13	67.7	46	27	60	5	2.39	4.55	8.3	4.9	4.2	1.7	5.49	6.9	-4
2003	LEX	SAL	20	28	28	150.3	133	65	144	10	3.65	6.26	11.6	5.4	5.5	1.7	7.13	-9.4	-6
2004	*HOU*	*NL*	*21*	*15*	*11*	*61.3*	*63*	*35*	*47*	*10*	*5.35*	*5.45*	*9.2*	*4.5*	*6.3*	*1.3*	*5.59*	*2.6*	*-3*

Breakout: 25%   Improve: 58%   Collapse: 9%

The most promising of the Astros' current crop of Venezuelan talent thanks to Carlos Hernandez's labrum tear, Nieve turned in a strong season in his first extended Sally League stint. Generously listed at 6'0", 170 with a screaming fastball that hits 99, he's the latest example of Houston's ability to find devastating arms in small packages. Nieve threw an overwhelming majority of fastballs last year, though that's in keeping with the Astros' development plan of A-ball pitchers establishing the pitch on both sides of the plate. When he's ready to diversify, Nieve's sharp overhand curve comes from a similar arm slot and befuddles hitters waiting for the heat. They've talked about being cautious with him, but Nieve may force his way to Round Rock in 2004 anyway. The Astros would do well to beef up their contingent of Spanish-speaking instructors, even hire some translators and English-language teachers, given their heavy emphasis on Latin talent. It's a blind spot for many teams, and when your best prospect speaks no English and plies his trade in the Deep South, that's the type of culture shock that needs to be softened.

ROY OSWALT

Bats: R   **Throws: R**   Born: 29-Aug-77   Age: 26

YEAR	TM	LG	AGE	G	GS	IP	H	BB	SO	HR	ERA	EQERA	EQH9	EQBB9	EQSO9	EQHR9	PERA	VORP	STF
2001	NWO	PCL	23	5	5	31.0	32	6	34	4	4.35	5.28	9.9	2.2	7.4	1.2	4.93	1.0	22
2001	HOU	NL	23	28	20	141.7	126	24	144	13	2.73	3.05	8.3	1.4	7.8	0.7	3.39	38.4	47
2002	HOU	NL	24	35	34	233.0	215	62	208	17	3.01	3.35	8.3	2.1	7.0	0.6	3.51	56.4	39
2003	HOU	NL	25	21	21	127.3	116	29	108	15	2.97	3.64	8.7	1.9	6.9	1.0	4.05	33.6	24
2004	HOU	NL	26	25	24	154.7	149	40	125	15	3.51	3.58	8.6	2.0	6.6	0.8	3.59	34.8	20

Breakout: 16%   Improve: 41%   Collapse: 25%

A pitcher's power starts with his lower body, and few prove that point better than Oswalt. Another "six-footer" (wink, wink) with a slight upper body, he generates tremendous heat on his nasty fastball through explosive leg drive. A torn sheath around his groin muscle caused him severe pain, forcing the Astros' medical staff to alternate between sitting him out and severely medicating him. The fear is that the injury will force Oswalt to alter his delivery, throwing his mechanics out of whack and raising the risk of arm problems. He still put up 21 solid starts last year, but the team needs its ace—Pettitte or no Pettitte, Oswalt's still the ace—healthy and productive over an entire season to get back to the playoffs. Watch the reports coming of spring training, as the Astros' season may hinge on them.

TONY PLUTA

Bats: R   **Throws: R**   Born: 28-Oct-82   Age: 21

YEAR	TM	LG	AGE	G	GS	IP	H	BB	SO	HR	ERA	EQERA	EQH9	EQBB9	EQSO9	EQHR9	PERA	VORP	STF
2001	LEX	SAL	18	26	26	132.3	107	86	138	7	3.20	6.61	9.5	9.0	6.0	1.0	6.35	-12.7	13
2002	MIC	MID	19	28	28	143.0	155	83	120	18	5.92	9.49	13.4	7.5	5.1	3.1	10.13	-52.4	-40
2003	SLM	CAR	20	3	3	12.3	13	8	14	1	5.85	8.18	11.5	7.4	7.4	1.6	7.43	-3.2	-1
2004	HOU	NL	21	15	13	69.7	82	63	56	14	7.98	8.12	10.5	7.1	6.5	1.7	7.98	-11.6	-16

Breakout: 46%   Improve: 57%   Collapse: 18%

Pluta has the arm to have a bright future, but his control is terrible, his approach to pitching as unrefined as you can get. Suggestions that he could pitch at 98–99 were the product of exaggeration, mixed with the Astros' continued use of the much faster JUGS gun despite most other teams junking that model for conventional radar guns. He blew out his elbow three starts into the season, adding Tommy John surgery to the long list of obstacles he'll need to overcome.

BRANDON PUFFER

Bats: R   **Throws: R**   Born: 05-Oct-75   Age: 28

YEAR	TM	LG	AGE	G	GS	IP	H	BB	SO	HR	ERA	EQERA	EQH9	EQBB9	EQSO9	EQHR9	PERA	VORP	STF
2001	ROU	TEX	25	56	0	82.7	52	35	91	4	2.07	3.16	7.7	4.7	7.1	0.9	4.21	20.1	-2
2002	NWO	PCL	26	11	0	15.0	8	4	13	1	1.80	2.63	6.6	2.6	5.9	0.7	2.95	4.5	8
2002	HOU	NL	26	55	0	69.0	67	38	48	3	4.43	4.52	8.5	4.3	5.3	0.4	4.03	8.1	0
2003	NWO	PCL	27	44	0	52.7	50	16	41	1	2.90	4.88	9.9	3.4	6.2	0.4	4.38	3.8	1
2003	HOU	NL	27	13	0	21.0	24	16	10	2	5.14	6.20	10.6	6.2	4.0	0.9	6.02	0.6	-33
2004	HOU	NL	28	30	5	52.0	52	25	38	5	4.46	4.54	9.0	3.8	5.9	0.7	4.59	6.2	-5

Breakout: 21%   Improve: 51%   Collapse: 24%

A trip for any batter looking for a hit last year, Puffer got lit up after his July promotion, stinking up the joint and earning his release after his command went to pot. A side-armer who makes hitters pound the ball into the grass when he's riding high, he'll hope to earn a spring training invite and smoke righties once more.

CHAD QUALLS

Bats: R   **Throws: R**   Born: 17-Aug-78   Age: 25

YEAR	TM	LG	AGE	G	GS	IP	H	BB	SO	HR	ERA	EQERA	EQH9	EQBB9	EQSO9	EQHR9	PERA	VORP	STF
2001	MIC	MID	22	26	26	162.0	149	31	125	8	3.72	5.10	10.1	2.4	4.2	1.0	4.92	8.1	1
2002	ROU	TEX	23	29	29	163.0	174	67	142	9	4.36	6.22	11.1	4.3	5.9	1.0	5.87	-10.3	0
2003	ROU	TEX	24	28	28	175.3	174	61	132	12	3.85	4.60	9.5	3.9	4.9	1.3	5.33	18.0	-8
2004	HOU	NL	25	20	13	77.3	83	34	51	9	4.99	5.08	9.6	3.4	5.4	1.0	5.01	4.6	-3

Breakout: 18%   Improve: 48%   Collapse: 26%

After a so-so Double-A season and a stint in the Arizona Fall League in '02, Qualls looked like he might return for a few more innings at Round Rock, then advance to New Orleans and maybe a cup of coffee in the bigs. Instead, the Astros held him back. A high-maintenance pitcher who needs his mechanics watched like a hawk, Qualls spent the year trying to mix in a change-up with his fastball and hard slider, knowing failure to do so could relegate him to a career of bullpen work. After failing to impress for most of the season, Qualls turned it on in the final third of the season, looking like the pitcher who blew through the Midwest League in 2001. He's back on track for a promotion in '04.

TIM REDDING

Bats: R   **Throws: R**   Born: 12-Feb-78   Age: 26

YEAR	TM	LG	AGE	G	GS	IP	H	BB	SO	HR	ERA	EQERA	EQH9	EQBB9	EQSO9	EQHR9	PERA	VORP	STF
2001	ROU	TEX	23	14	14	90.7	64	25	113	5	2.18	3.39	8.2	3.1	8.1	0.9	3.98	20.2	35
2001	NWO	PCL	23	6	6	37.7	22	19	42	4	4.54	4.41	6.0	5.5	7.8	1.0	3.82	4.6	24
2001	HOU	NL	23	13	9	55.7	62	24	55	11	5.49	5.83	10.2	3.5	7.5	1.5	5.70	-1.4	12
2002	NWO	PCL	24	11	7	38.0	32	13	50	6	5.21	5.82	10.1	3.7	9.5	2.1	6.37	-0.8	-6
2002	HOU	NL	24	18	14	73.3	78	35	63	10	5.40	5.53	9.4	3.8	6.7	1.3	5.17	0.6	4
2003	HOU	NL	25	33	32	176.0	179	65	116	16	3.68	4.50	9.6	3.0	5.4	0.8	4.60	28.4	9
2004	*HOU*	*NL*	*26*	*29*	*24*	*145.0*	*148*	*56*	*104*	*18*	*4.56*	*4.64*	*9.1*	*3.0*	*5.8*	*1.0*	*4.59*	*16.2*	*5*

Breakout: 12%   *Improve: 41%*   *Collapse: 23%*

Another promising arm with quirky mechanics, Redding spent much of the season searching for different arm slots and grips, trying to master his stuff. A full slate of 32 starts and a lowered home run rate were the good news, spotty command and struggles against lefties the bad. He hadn't previously shown that big a platoon split, so the Astros hope last year was just an aberration. Redding's a capable back-of-the-rotation starter who could be more if he can add an effective off-speed pitch.

JERIOME ROBERTSON

Bats: L   **Throws: L**   Born: 30-Mar-77   Age: 27

YEAR	TM	LG	AGE	G	GS	IP	H	BB	SO	HR	ERA	EQERA	EQH9	EQBB9	EQSO9	EQHR9	PERA	VORP	STF
2001	ROU	TEX	24	57	0	73.7	89	21	72	10	3.91	6.20	13.9	3.3	6.5	2.2	8.25	-4.4	-46
2002	NWO	PCL	25	27	27	180.0	160	45	114	13	2.55	4.34	9.5	2.6	4.5	0.9	4.54	22.9	1
2003	HOU	NL	26	32	31	160.7	180	64	99	23	5.10	5.52	10.6	3.3	5.0	1.2	5.58	6.3	-12
2004	*HOU*	*NL*	*27*	*26*	*20*	*116.3*	*132*	*43*	*73*	*17*	*5.05*	*5.14*	*10.1*	*2.9*	*5.1*	*1.2*	*5.22*	*6.7*	*-2*

Breakout: 17%   *Improve: 48%*   *Collapse: 26%*

Author of a 15–9 record despite allowing nearly 14 baserunners per nine innings, Robertson was rated the sixth-luckiest starter in the majors according to Michael Wolverton's Support-Neutral W/L Report at baseballprospectus.com, and such luck rarely lasts (new teammate Andy Pettitte was the luckiest—uh-oh). The Astros didn't expect much more than an ambulatory fill-in guy after shuttling in Robertson to replace the departed Shane Reynolds, and that's really all they got. Though thought of as a groundball pitcher, his GB/FB rate of 1.16 ranked him a shade below the median NL starter. If he's to keep his rotation spot as a finesse lefty, he'll need to induce more dribblers to take advantage of Adam Everett and keep the ball as far away from Biggio and company as possible.

RODRIGO ROSARIO

Bats: R   **Throws: R**   Born: 14-Mar-78   Age: 26

YEAR	TM	LG	AGE	G	GS	IP	H	BB	SO	HR	ERA	EQERA	EQH9	EQBB9	EQSO9	EQHR9	PERA	VORP	STF
2001	LEX	SAL	23	30	21	147.0	105	36	131	8	2.14	4.90	9.9	3.4	4.5	1.3	5.37	9.7	-13
2002	ROU	TEX	24	26	23	130.3	106	59	94	5	3.11	4.70	8.6	4.8	4.9	0.8	4.58	11.9	-2
2003	NWO	PCL	25	15	15	87.0	71	32	68	7	4.03	4.99	8.5	4.0	6.2	1.1	4.69	5.4	0
2003	HOU	NL	25	2	2	8.0	5	3	6	0	1.13	2.35	5.9	3.5	5.9	0.0	2.32	3.1	36
2004	*HOU*	*NL*	*26*	*20*	*12*	*71.3*	*72*	*35*	*50*	*9*	*4.83*	*4.92*	*9.1*	*3.8*	*5.7*	*1.0*	*4.92*	*5.2*	*-3*

Breakout: 19%   *Improve: 47%*   *Collapse: 17%*

After following a strong season at Double-A with 15 solid starts in New Orleans, Rosario made his greatly-anticipated major league debut. After a promising first start, he left his second outing in the second inning with right shoulder tightness. It all unraveled from there, as Rosario underwent surgery for a rotator cuff tear and torn biceps tendon. Once considered a top prospect in Houston's system, the lanky Dominican with great stuff and the results to back it up was unceremoniously released in November. Unless the Astros were simply the victims of an elaborate voodoo curse, the organization needs to address some serious issues regarding the attrition rates of its young arms.

KIRK SAARLOOS

Bats: R   **Throws: R**   Born: 23-May-79   Age: 25

YEAR	TM	LG	AGE	G	GS	IP	H	BB	SO	HR	ERA	EQERA	EQH9	EQBB9	EQSO9	EQHR9	PERA	VORP	STF
2001	LEX	SAL	22	22	0	30.7	18	7	40	1	1.17	3.12	9.0	3.1	6.9	0.7	4.19	7.2	15
2002	ROU	TEX	23	13	13	83.3	48	21	82	1	1.40	2.45	6.1	2.7	6.5	0.2	2.36	26.9	46
2002	NWO	PCL	23	4	2	16.0	12	2	19	1	2.25	3.07	8.0	1.2	8.6	0.6	3.08	4.1	48
2002	HOU	NL	23	17	17	85.3	100	27	54	12	6.01	5.64	10.3	2.5	4.9	1.2	5.20	-0.4	4
2003	NWO	PCL	24	13	7	61.3	54	11	34	4	3.08	4.31	8.9	1.9	4.3	1.0	4.15	8.1	2
2003	HOU	NL	24	36	4	49.3	55	17	43	4	4.93	5.17	10.7	2.9	7.1	0.8	4.98	1.1	12
2004	*HOU*	*NL*	*25*	*25*	*15*	*88.3*	*90*	*29*	*62*	*10*	*4.31*	*4.38*	*9.1*	*2.6*	*5.7*	*0.9*	*4.28*	*13.0*	*3*

Breakout: 16%   *Improve: 43%*   *Collapse: 31%*

The Astros need to stop jerking him around and give Saarloos a clean shot at making—and sticking in—the rotation. Jimy Williams's lack of faith in Saarloos's less-than-blazing fastball short-circuited any chance his young pitcher had of hitting a groove as a starter last year, even while his talents are best suited for befuddling lineups three times a game with his array of darting, speed-changing pitches. The obscenely low walk and home run rates Saarloos put up in the minors can translate into an effective 200-inning major league control artist if the Astros will get out of his way. Brandon Duckworth's arrival adds another name to the list of fifth-starter candidates, but the pen could use Duckworth's live arm, and Saarloos is a better choice as a starter than Robertson, Hernandez or—if they re-sign him—Ron Villone.

RICKY STONE   Bats: R   Throws: R   Born: 28-Feb-75   Age: 29

YEAR	TM	LG	AGE	G	GS	IP	H	BB	SO	HR	ERA	EQERA	EQH9	EQBB9	EQSO9	EQHR9	PERA	VORP	STF
2001	NWO	PCL	26	51	8	95.3	98	27	78	8	3.59	4.93	10.4	3.1	5.3	0.9	5.09	6.5	-15
2002	HOU	NL	27	78	0	77.3	78	34	63	9	3.61	4.42	9.0	3.5	6.3	1.1	4.69	9.9	-7
2003	HOU	NL	28	65	0	83.0	76	31	47	11	3.69	4.10	8.7	3.1	4.6	1.1	4.54	17.3	-16
2004	HOU	NL	29	38	6	63.7	66	25	40	7	4.15	4.23	9.3	3.1	5.2	0.9	4.56	9.9	-7

Breakout: 26%   Improve: 54%   Collapse: 24%

Could move up in the pecking order with Billy Wagner's departure, a potential danger for the Astros' bullpen. A righty-snuffer who induces a ton of ground balls, Stone needs to be leveraged as a righty specialist and in double play situations or risk being overwhelmed in key 7th-inning situations. If Astros starters stay healthy heading into Opening Day, the rotation's depth would allow Duckworth to slide into the Brad Lidge role, and Stone to keep filling the specific, structured role in which he can remain effective.

RON VILLONE   Bats: L   Throws: L   Born: 16-Jan-70   Age: 34

YEAR	TM	LG	AGE	G	GS	IP	H	BB	SO	HR	ERA	EQERA	EQH9	EQBB9	EQSO9	EQHR9	PERA	VORP	STF
2001	COL	NL	31	22	6	46.7	56	29	48	6	6.36	5.91	10.8	5.1	7.7	1.0	5.86	-1.6	-6
2001	HOU	NL	31	31	6	68.0	77	24	65	12	5.56	5.62	10.3	2.9	7.3	1.4	5.44	-0.1	-8
2002	PIT	NL	32	45	7	93.0	95	34	55	8	5.81	5.34	9.4	2.9	4.6	0.8	4.47	2.6	-9
2003	TUC	PCL	33	15	0	25.3	20	12	22	2	3.56	4.18	7.2	4.9	6.5	1.1	4.37	3.7	-16
2003	NWO	PCL	33	5	5	29.3	24	10	18	0	1.23	3.04	8.4	3.7	4.7	0.3	3.80	7.6	15
2003	HOU	NL	33	19	19	106.7	91	48	91	16	4.13	4.31	8.2	3.7	6.9	1.3	4.64	17.7	4
2004	HOU	NL	34	27	15	91.7	92	40	73	12	4.81	4.90	9.0	3.5	6.5	1.0	4.74	7.9	3

Breakout: 16%   Improve: 45%   Collapse: 17%

That low hit rate was a fluke, but he'll take it. Villone's .260 batting average allowed on balls in play helped make up for his high walk rate and scary home run total. The end result was a decent mid-season plug-in for a rotation that sorely needed one, but the Astros recognized Villone's limitations and cut him loose at season's end. With eight teams in the bank, Villone needs to stop going back to clubs he'd previously played for if he's to challenge the 12-team careers of the Mike Morgans of the world.

BILLY WAGNER   Bats: L   Throws: L   Born: 25-Jul-71   Age: 32

YEAR	TM	LG	AGE	G	GS	IP	H	BB	SO	HR	ERA	EQERA	EQH9	EQBB9	EQSO9	EQHR9	PERA	VORP	STF
2001	HOU	NL	29	64	0	62.7	44	20	79	5	2.73	2.55	6.8	2.7	9.6	0.6	2.93	20.3	36
2002	HOU	NL	30	70	0	75.0	51	22	88	7	2.52	2.60	6.2	2.4	9.2	0.9	2.84	24.2	29
2003	HOU	NL	31	78	0	86.0	52	23	105	8	1.78	2.20	6.0	2.2	9.9	0.8	2.62	36.6	38
2004	PHI	NL	32	59	0	76.0	57	23	86	6	2.48	2.60	6.8	2.4	9.2	0.7	2.73	24.6	23

Breakout: 25%   Improve: 54%   Collapse: 18%

The Phillies' new closer after being dealt for pitchers Brandon Duckworth, Taylor Buchholz, and Ezequiel Astacio, Wagner became expendable due to the $8 million he was due to make in 2004, plus the $9 million salary or $3 million buyout he had coming in '05. The Astros did well to get a nice array of booty for an $8 million closer, freeing up cash to sign Andy Pettitte to anchor the rotation in the process. But let's not sell the Phillies short here: They needed to upgrade their bullpen as the last step toward building a potential championship team, and Wagner's been as dominating as any reliever in baseball since 1996, the lone exception an injury-marred 2000 season. The classic good trade for both teams could put a shiny ring on Billy Wags's finger if a few things break right in Philly.

RICK WHITE   Bats: R   Throws: R   Born: 23-Dec-68   Age: 35

YEAR	TM	LG	AGE	G	GS	IP	H	BB	SO	HR	ERA	EQERA	EQH9	EQBB9	EQSO9	EQHR9	PERA	VORP	STF
2001	NYM	NL	32	55	0	69.7	71	17	51	7	3.87	4.59	9.3	2.0	5.5	0.8	4.17	7.5	0
2002	COL	NL	33	41	0	40.7	49	18	27	4	6.19	5.72	11.0	3.4	5.3	0.9	5.46	-0.5	-16
2002	STL	NL	33	20	0	22.0	13	3	14	0	0.82	1.74	6.1	1.3	5.2	0.0	1.81	8.9	32
2003	CWS	AL	34	34	0	47.7	56	13	37	11	6.60	6.26	10.6	2.3	6.8	2.0	6.12	-6.9	-26
2003	HOU	NL	34	15	0	19.3	18	8	17	2	3.73	4.34	8.7	3.4	7.2	1.0	4.40	3.4	3
2004	HOU	NL	35	42	1	55.0	59	19	40	7	4.81	4.90	9.5	2.8	5.9	1.0	4.64	5.1	-5

Breakout: 18%   Improve: 46%   Collapse: 30%

A year after stinking for much of the season with Colorado, then tossing 22 terrific innings down the stretch for the Cards, he pulled a similar trick in 2003, getting bombed while with the White Sox before logging 19.1 effective innings in the season's last seven weeks with Houston. White needs to string together six consecutive months of good pitching to find a sucker who'll give him one of those sweet multi-year reliever deals that's apparently squeezed through the cracks of the game's new economics.

Los Angeles Dodgers

Sometimes tradition is a good thing. At its best, tradition can provide a connection to the past that instills both a sense of pride and identity. It can bring individuals together, while letting them share in a unified sense of purpose.

But sometimes tradition can be a bad thing. At worst, it can be a stifling presence, one that hinders both progress and innovation. It can limit an individual's ability to test the boundaries of the status quo, punishing those who dare to think outside the box. Tradition can keep an individual in the past, at the expense of the future.

The Los Angeles Dodgers are an organization steeped in tradition, but for them, the bad outweighs the good. They're a franchise that experienced an extended period of success nearly 40 years ago, and have never quite gotten over it. It was then that the front office made up its mind on how a successful franchise should be built and run, and they've kept doing things that way because—by God—that's the way you do things. That's the Dodger Way.

The problem is that the Dodger Way hasn't been working. In fact, it hasn't worked since 1988, the last time the organization won a postseason game. From a drafting strategy that consistently puts more emphasis on tools than performance, to a front office that refuses to acknowledge that offense makes up just as much of the game as pitching and defense does, the Dodgers are clinging to ideas that the Flat Earth Society would find ridiculous.

Examples of this are everywhere, from the top of the organization down. Take General Manager Dan Evans. When Evans took over on October 3, 2001, many people envisioned that he would be the one to lead the Dodgers out of the darkness of the Kevin Malone Era and into the dawn. After all, Evans helped build one of the best organizations in baseball while with the White Sox. Both *USA Today* and *Baseball America* named the White Sox the Organization of the Year in 2000, honors that were earned in no small part due to Evans's contribution.

But Evans has struggled since taking the Dodger helm, unable to address the weaknesses of a team with clearly identifiable flaws. Take a look at table 1; when Evans assumed control of the organization from interim GM Dave Wallace, the Dodgers were eighth in the National League in offense despite fielding talent that was near or *below* replacement-level at four different positions—first base,

DODGERS PROSPECTUS

2003 record: 85–77; Second place, NL West

Pythagenport record: 83–79

Runs scored per game: 3.5 (16th in NL)

Runs allowed per game: 3.4 (1st in NL)

Team EqA: .244 (16th in NL)

2003 Batters Age: 30.3 (8th youngest in NL)

2003 Pitchers Age: 32.1 (2nd oldest in NL)

Ballpark: Dodger Stadium; Severe pitcher's park; Park Factor of 0.917

2003: Some brilliant pitching in Chavez Ravine, but the Bums could have used Tawny Kitaen's slugging.

2004: The solid rotation and bullpen could make this a dangerous team, but we're still waiting for Dan Evans to add offense.

second base, shortstop, and center field. Let's see how those four positions progressed during his tenure.

Any baseball executive worth his salt should have been able to look at the Dodgers' roster and immediately recognize its needs: league-average production up-the-middle and a .300 EqA at one of corners. Evans has done little to address this problem since taking charge. What he has done is replace mediocrities like Eric Karros, Mark Grudzielanek, and Marquis Grissom, but rarely has he *improved* upon them. As a result, the Dodgers have slipped from eighth to ninth to 16th in the league in runs scored under Evans's watch, missing the playoffs both years despite finishing among the top teams in the NL in run prevention.

Not all of this is Evans's fault. His predecessor, Kevin Malone, green-lighted a raft of contracts that looked bad even in the Manny-for-$160 million era. With a new, tighter market for talent taking hold, some of those deals now look downright ridiculous. We can only imagine Evans and company shaking their heads in disgust thinking about the $24 million they owe Darren Dreifort over the next two seasons.

Making matters worse, the Dodgers' methods of scouting and player development have failed over the last few years. Where organizations like Oakland and Cleveland

TABLE 1. OFFENSIVE HOLES

Position	Player	EqA	VORP
2001			
1B	Karros	.247	−9.3
2B	Grudzielanek	.253	16.6
SS	Cora	.213	−7.0
CF	Grissom	.226	−4.7
Total			−4.4
2002			
1B	Karros	.261	7.5
2B	Grudzielanek	.243	10.6
SS	Izturis	.204	−13.6
CF	Roberts	.276	19.4
Total			27.0
2003			
1B	McGriff	.266	6.5
2B	Cora	.225	−2.3
SS	Izturis	.216	−5.2
CF	Roberts	.248	1.0
Total			0.0

work to implement an "organizational philosophy"—emphasizing ideas like throwing strikes, working the count, and drawing walks—the Dodgers have been more than content to let their hitters hack away like kids on the schoolyard. Is it any wonder that the organization has developed just one elite hitter since the Reagan administration? Good thing the Dodgers saw fit to spend a 62nd round on Mike Piazza in 1988, out of nepotism no less.

One of the problems with evaluating a new front office regime is evaluating the progress of players drafted and developed early on in the process. That said, there's hope. Just as the White Sox produced one of the better minor league systems in all of baseball during Evans's tenure there, the Dodgers have used the draft over the past two seasons to collect such high-profile prospects as Edwin Jackson, Greg Miller, Joel Hanrahan, James Loney, and Delwyn Young. While acknowledging the BP mantra of "There is no such thing as a pitching prospect," few organizations can match the early returns of the Dodgers' best farm-hands. Evans and Director of Amateur Scouting Logan White deserve credit for starting to revamp a system that was barren when they arrived.

Despite the promise of those prospects, the organization still has room to improve its drafting strategy. Thanks to an approach that emphasizes tools over performance as well as a failure to differentiate between high school and college pitching, the Dodgers lack the depth of more pru-

dent organizations. Over the past two years, Evans and White have used the majority of their draft selections—including their first six picks in 2003—on kids fresh out of high school, particularly pitchers. Given the slew of studies that show much higher burnout rates for high school pitchers over any other class of draft choice, it's fair to say the Dodgers stack the odds against themselves every time they go to the well for another 18-year-old arm.

While we wait to see how Jackson, Miller, Loney, and the rest progress, the Dodgers show scant signs of improving at the big league level. While Kevin Malone surely dealt Evans a bad hand, the Dodgers were a competitive, high-revenue team in a division ripe for the taking when Evans arrived. With several obvious holes to address and enough financial flexibility—thanks to the Dodgers' large-market status and lucrative media deals—to overcome even Kevin Brown/Darren Dreifort-level contracts, Evans had a golden opportunity to bring several division titles to Chavez Ravine.

However, whether at the Winter Meetings or the trade deadline, Evans has repeatedly failed to provide his team with the talent it needed to make the playoffs. Yes, News Corp. has refused to let the team's payroll exceed the league's de facto salary cap, but it doesn't take much to improve upon Cesar Izturis at short, Alex Cora at second, and Dave Roberts in center. In fact, given the last two years' rock-bottom prices for baseball's middle class talent, one could dramatically upgrade each position for a few million all told. Evans hasn't been a Malone-style failure for the Dodgers, but he hasn't been a success, either—not by a long shot.

Which brings us to 2003, a year that exposed the weaknesses of Evans's ability as a GM and the Dodger Way for the world to see.

The '03 Dodgers might as well have been operating in the 1960s. Not since the era of Sandy Koufax, Free Love, and the Reserve Clause has a team leaned so far to the right on the run production/run prevention spectrum. Powered by a healthy Kevin Brown, a revitalized Hideo Nomo, and the best pitcher in the league during the second half, Wilson Alvarez, the pitching staff was a force to be reckoned with. Sadly, the offense was not. The Dodgers accounted for the largest difference between team pitching and hitting VORP—the number of runs produced and prevented above replacement-level talent—in major league history. (See table 2.)

It wasn't just the Dodger starters who exuded excellence. The bullpen was more dominant than a leather-clad Courtney Love locked in a room with David Gest. The 2003 Dodgers posted the highest Adjusted Runs Prevented (ARP) total in recorded history, with 96.4. In other words, their relievers prevented nearly 100 more runs from scoring than the average bullpen, even after adjusting for park effects, given the base/out situation in which they entered and left each game. From Eric Gagne (32.6 ARP), who had arguably the best season in history for any reliever in any era, to Guillermo Mota (23.2), to Paul Quantrill (22.3), to Tom Martin—who was among the best in the league at preventing inherited runners from scoring—the team's relief corps was a group that protected leads like none other.

The thing is, thanks to an offense that could charitably be described as "anemic," there weren't many big leads to protect. The Dodgers accumulated just 614 Equivalent Runs last season, the fewest in the National League by a country mile. This was thanks to a lineup made up of near- and below-replacement-level talent at *four* different positions—shortstop, second base, center field, and left field. We often talk about the negative effect of giving just *one* replacement-level hitter 500 plate-appearances over a full season; the Dodgers gave away four times that many in 2003.

The '03 Dodgers might as well have been operating in the past, and the following data further supports that idea. Last year's version of the Boys In Blue was the most run-averse team in major league history, scoring and allowing a combined 6.97 runs per game against a league average of 9.22 runs per game. (See table 3.)

This is an interesting list, in part because of the difference in quality of these teams. Where the 1927 Brooklyn Dodgers finished 28.5 games out of first place, the 1966 Dodgers won 95 games and the National League pennant. The 2003 Dodgers are more comparable to the 65-win 1927 version, as both teams finished last in the league in runs scored, while first in the league in runs allowed. (The '66 team's 3.74 RS, by comparison, was just 7% below the league average of 4.09).

TABLE 3. RUNS VS. LEAGUE AVERAGE

Year	Team	RS	RA	Total	League	% of League
2003	LAN	3.54	3.43	6.97	9.22	75.5%
1927	BRO	3.51	4.02	7.53	9.16	82.2%
1966	LAN	3.74	3.02	6.77	8.19	82.6%
1937	BSN	3.81	3.66	7.47	9.02	82.8%
1964	LAA	3.36	3.40	6.76	8.12	83.3%

To their credit, the Dodgers seem to be one of the few organizations that have a grasp on park effects. In fact, front office members have often spoken of shaping the roster to fit the extreme nature of Chavez Ravine. Said Evans in an interview with ESPN.com's Tim Kurkjian: "Dodger Stadium has been one of the greatest pitcher's parks for 42 years . . . We're going to tailor our team to it, with pitching and defense. You're not going to out-slug people in this park" (May 28, 2003).

The problem is, they don't seem to understand the above distinction: Yes, previous Dodger teams have been successful adhering to the orthodoxy of the Dodger Way (i.e., pitching and defense first), but that was in an era when run scoring was much lower across the board. As a result, they've taken the defensible approach of tailoring their roster to the extreme dimensions of Dodger Stadium, and dragged it past the logical extreme. Sure, scoring three-and-a-half runs per game might have been adequate in the 1960s, but it's unacceptable in the 2000s. An equal emphasis on run production as well as run prevention is what the team needs; the dimensions of Chavez Ravine can only give your team an advantage to a certain point, and the Dodgers passed that marker long ago.

The franchise will soon undergo some major changes. In November, real estate developer and multimillionaire Frank McCourt announced he'd be purchasing the team from Rupert Murdoch's News Corp. Since then, however, negotiations have stalled, with McCourt having trouble getting the proper financial backing together. As of this writing in early January, the team has yet to change ownership groups, and it seems more unlikely by the day that any meaningful alterations to the front office will occur for 2004, even if McCourt is to assume control of the franchise before Opening Day.

Evans and company have thus far apparently been stymied by ownership turmoil. (This despite clearing more than $20 million in salary between the departures of Brian Jordan and Andy Ashby, and the trade that sent Kevin Brown to the Yankees for Jeff Weaver.) What else could explain the organization's sideline-gazing while Miguel Tejada was signed away and Vladimir Guerrero remained

TABLE 2. PITCHING VORP VS. OVERALL TEAM VORP

Year	Team	Pitching VORP	Hitting VORP	Overall VORP	Difference
2003	LAN	315.8	62.9	378.7	252.9
1997	TOR	285.4	18.2	267.2	249.0
1941	CHA	243.9	14.4	229.5	215.2
1933	CLE	256.8	26.2	230.6	204.4
1936	BOS	404.2	100.6	303.7	203.1
1925	CIN	325.7	63.4	262.3	198.9
1998	TBA	269.1	36.4	232.7	196.4
1996	KCA	325.1	66.6	258.5	191.9
1983	TEX	310.6	60.5	250.1	189.6
1996	TOR	384.5	102.2	282.3	180.1

a free agent? We'll grant the Dodger front office the courtesy of recognizing that it's tough to do one's job when organizational structure is in question. But the minute you hold up *Juan Encarnacion* as the answer, you're asking the wrong question.

The best organizations in baseball, like the best businesses in the real world, are successful because they're always re-evaluating the way they do things, and remain open to new ideas. The Dodgers have done little of either for the past 30 years. Fortunately, they play in a division with many flaws, so the window of opportunity is still open. But it's going to take a change in their approach if they want to be successful now and down the road. This means honestly evaluating what they've done in the past, whether or not it's worked, and what they can do to improve upon it. Otherwise, Dodger fans may get another decade without so much as one playoff win.

HITTERS

REGGIE ABERCROMBIE — CF — Bats: R — Throws: R — Born: 15-Jul-80 — Age: 23

YEAR	TM	LG	AGE	AB	H	2B	3B	HR	BB	SO	SB	CS	AVG	OBP	SLG	MLVR	EQBA	EQOBP	EQSLG	EQMLVR	VORP	DEFENSE			
2001	WNC	SAL	20	486	110	17	3	10	19	154	44	11	.226	.272	.335	-.079	.204	.236	.312	-.424	-54.1	87-RF -12	29-CF	-3	
2002	VRO	FLA	21	526	145	23	13	10	27	158	41	17	.276	.321	.426	.073	.231	.263	.370	-.273	-35.0	90-RF -10	35-CF	-3	
2003	JAX	SOU	22	448	117	25	7	15	16	164	28	9	.261	.298	.449	.079	.243	.270	.432	-.162	-13.1	93-RF -8	22-CF	-2	
2004	LAD	NL	23	249	56	11	2	9	12	81	8	3	.225	.269	.391	-.206	.234	.275	.404	-.188	-5.5	66-RF -5			

Breakout: 32%   Improve: 50%   Collapse: 27%

Reggie Abercrombie is everything that's wrong with the Dodger player development system personified in one individual. He runs like the wind and throws like Jay Buhner, but draws only one walk for every 10 strikeouts. Prospects, errr... "prospects" with his M.O. simply do not develop into useful major league players. Abercrombie tore his ACL playing in the Arizona Fall League, and will miss the beginning of 2004. Normally, injuries of this nature will hurt a player's chances of moving through the system. In Abercrombie's case, it will simply give scouts another excuse for why he isn't producing when he returns in the summer.

ADRIAN BELTRE — 3B — Bats: R — Throws: R — Born: 07-Apr-79 — Age: 25

YEAR	TM	LG	AGE	AB	H	2B	3B	HR	BB	SO	SB	CS	AVG	OBP	SLG	MLVR	EQBA	EQOBP	EQSLG	EQMLVR	VORP	DEFENSE
2001	LAD	NL	22	475	126	22	4	13	28	82	13	4	.265	.310	.411	-.064	.281	.326	.436	-.022	20.5	123-3B 0
2002	LAD	NL	23	587	151	26	5	21	37	96	7	5	.257	.303	.426	.006	.273	.316	.459	-.013	25.4	151-3B -14
2003	LAD	NL	24	559	134	30	2	23	37	103	2	2	.240	.290	.424	-.022	.254	.303	.454	-.061	15.9	153-3B 9
2004	LAD	NL	25	504	130	26	3	21	36	86	5	2	.259	.312	.447	-.034	.269	.319	.461	-.008	22.7	130-3B 0

Breakout: 21%   Improve: 60%   Collapse: 11%

For all intents and purposes, Adrian Beltre should be a star by now. He was among the best hitters in the league at every level throughout the minors, and he was doing it when most boys his age were working to get to third base in that other, less wholesome way. So what happened? It's tough to tell. He doesn't appear to have any off-the-field issues. Despite reaching the majors at a young age, he wasn't rushed. Like Andruw Jones, Beltre will often look brilliant for weeks at a time, then regress for no apparent reason, leaving analysts scratching their heads. At 25, he still has some breakout potential left, but he's living proof that forecasting isn't an exact science.

JEROMY BURNITZ — OF — Bats: L — Throws: R — Born: 14-Apr-69 — Age: 35

YEAR	TM	LG	AGE	AB	H	2B	3B	HR	BB	SO	SB	CS	AVG	OBP	SLG	MLVR	EQBA	EQOBP	EQSLG	EQMLVR	VORP	DEFENSE			
2001	MIL	NL	32	562	141	32	4	34	80	150	0	4	.251	.347	.504	.093	.253	.349	.507	.093	26.2	148-RF 0			
2002	NYM	NL	33	479	103	15	0	19	58	135	10	7	.215	.311	.365	-.098	.231	.321	.399	-.122	-7.4	119-RF 2			
2003	LAD	NL	34	230	47	4	0	13	14	57	4	0	.204	.252	.391	-.164	.218	.262	.423	-.209	-7.4	50-LF -1			
2003	NYM	NL	34	234	64	18	0	18	21	55	1	4	.274	.344	.581	.293	.282	.348	.601	.251	20.1	38-RF -1	16-CF	1	
2004	COL	NL	35	333	85	16	1	20	38	83	3	2	.256	.337	.493	.066	.247	.327	.471	.001	9.0	91-RF -1			

Breakout: 45%   Improve: 67%   Collapse: 17%

Burnitz was the first of Dan Evans's feeble attempts to bolster the offense via trade in 2003. Instead of providing a needed boost in the outfield, he hit an Izturian .204/.252/.391, adding to the overall stench in a big way. At 35, Burnitz has become a liability in almost every facet of the game. His decline will be masked by the intoxicating aroma of Coors Field.

JOLBERT CABRERA   **UT**   **Bats: R**   **Throws: R**   Born: 08-Dec-72   Age: 31

YEAR	TM	LG	AGE	AB	H	2B	3B	HR	BB	SO	SB	CS	AVG	OBP	SLG	MLVR	EQBA	EQOBP	EQSLG	EQMLVR	VORP	DEFENSE			
2001	CLE	AL	28	287	75	16	3	1	16	41	10	4	.261	.312	.348	-.148	.281	.331	.378	-.096	-2.9	17-LF	-2	17-CF	-1
2002	CLE	AL	29	72	8	1	0	0	5	13	1	1	.111	.177	.125	-.744	.139	.203	.167	-.718	-11.1				
2002	LVG	PCL	29	102	35	8	1	2	14	18	2	3	.343	.417	.500	.282	.287	.366	.426	.042	3.0	16-LF	-1		
2002	LAD	NL	29	12	4	1	0	0	2	2	0	0	.333	.429	.417	.263	.333	.429	.500	.296	1.4				
2003	LAD	NL	30	347	98	32	2	6	17	62	6	4	.282	.332	.438	.107	.302	.349	.472	.091	18.7	36-2B	-4	23-CF	0
2004	*LAD*	*NL*	*31*	*254*	*64*	*14*	*2*	*4*	*19*	*44*	*4*	*3*	*.254*	*.317*	*.370*	*-.130*	*.264*	*.325*	*.382*	*-.108*	*3.3*	*69-2B*	*-9*		

Breakout: 15%   *Improve: 26%*   *Collapse: 41%*

A solid season for a normally generic infielder, Cabrera's production easily bested Dodger regulars like Alex Cora and Cesar Izturis. That isn't to he's the answer to anyone's problems in the middle infield, but Cabrera's pummeling of the incumbent starters performance-wise speaks volumes about the team's need to get some real upgrades. Cabrera will remain a useful utility man even if the Dodgers do make changes, especially if he keeps hitting lefties the way he did in '03 (.307/.336/.489 in 137 AB).

CHIN-FENG CHEN   **1B/OF**   **Bats: R**   **Throws: R**   Born: 28-Oct-77   Age: 26

YEAR	TM	LG	AGE	AB	H	2B	3B	HR	BB	SO	SB	CS	AVG	OBP	SLG	MLVR	EQBA	EQOBP	EQSLG	EQMLVR	VORP	DEFENSE			
2001	JAX	SOU	23	224	70	16	2	17	41	65	5	4	.313	.422	.629	.499	.252	.345	.513	.093	11.6	47-LF	-4		
2001	VRO	FLA	23	235	63	15	3	5	28	56	2	0	.268	.359	.421	.110	.213	.281	.350	-.277	-17.8	11-LF	2		
2002	LVG	PCL	24	511	145	26	4	26	58	160	1	0	.284	.352	.503	.125	.242	.309	.430	-.093	-1.5	94-1B	-6		
2003	LVG	PCL	25	474	133	30	5	26	59	106	6	4	.281	.360	.530	.188	.239	.318	.458	-.041	2.1	93-LF	-2	12-1B	-4
2004	*LAD*	*NL*	*26*	*205*	*50*	*10*	*1*	*10*	*23*	*55*	*2*	*1*	*.242*	*.318*	*.455*	*-.025*	*.252*	*.326*	*.470*	*.001*	*6.9*	*58-LF*	*-3*		

Breakout: 41%   *Improve: 60%*   *Collapse: 25%*

Normally, .281/.360/.530 looks pretty good. In Las Vegas in the Pacific Coast League, it's pretty mediocre, especially when coming from a 25-year-old who plays below-average defense. Chen isn't much of a prospect anymore, but could probably help the Dodgers as a bat off the bench.

RON COOMER   **1B**   **Bats: R**   **Throws: R**   Born: 18-Nov-66   Age: 37

YEAR	TM	LG	AGE	AB	H	2B	3B	HR	BB	SO	SB	CS	AVG	OBP	SLG	MLVR	EQBA	EQOBP	EQSLG	EQMLVR	VORP	DEFENSE			
2001	CHC	NL	34	349	91	19	1	8	29	70	0	0	.261	.316	.390	-.104	.266	.324	.398	-.092	8.7	63-3B	0	19-1B	2
2002	NYY	AL	35	148	39	7	0	3	6	23	0	0	.264	.290	.372	-.133	.282	.314	.403	-.090	3.2	18-3B	-3		
2003	LAD	NL	36	125	30	4	0	4	10	19	0	0	.240	.299	.368	-.085	.258	.311	.398	-.122	0.7	13-1B	0		
2004	*LAD*	*NL*	*37*	*79*	*18*	*3*	*0*	*2*	*6*	*15*	*0*	*0*	*.229*	*.287*	*.331*	*-.251*	*.238*	*.294*	*.342*	*-.234*	*-1.7*	*25-1B*	*-1*		

Breakout: 13%   *Improve: 21%*   *Collapse: 38%*

We were just as shocked to find out that Ron Coomer is still in baseball as you are right now.

ALEX CORA   **2B/SS**   **Bats: L**   **Throws: R**   Born: 18-Oct-75   Age: 28

YEAR	TM	LG	AGE	AB	H	2B	3B	HR	BB	SO	SB	CS	AVG	OBP	SLG	MLVR	EQBA	EQOBP	EQSLG	EQMLVR	VORP	DEFENSE			
2001	LAD	NL	25	405	88	18	3	4	31	58	0	2	.217	.285	.306	-.293	.235	.299	.333	-.252	-5.5	119-SS	-7		
2002	LAD	NL	26	258	75	14	4	5	26	38	7	2	.291	.371	.434	.158	.308	.381	.466	.143	23.9	50-SS	1	19-2B	-2
2003	LAD	NL	27	477	119	24	3	4	16	59	4	2	.249	.287	.338	-.144	.268	.303	.363	-.180	-1.3	125-2B	-4		
2004	*LAD*	*NL*	*28*	*362*	*91*	*17*	*2*	*6*	*24*	*50*	*3*	*2*	*.252*	*.311*	*.361*	*-.155*	*.262*	*.318*	*.373*	*-.133*	*7.3*	*96-2B*	*0*		

Breakout: 6%   *Improve: 29%*   *Collapse: 41%*

Following a season where he was an asset in limited time up the middle, Cora came crashing down to earth in 2003, reprising his role as a HACKING MASS All-Star. Like teammate Cesar Izturis, Cora is a useful ballplayer to have, assuming he's used in the correct role. The problem is, like Izturis, Cora was given far too many at-bats in 2003, further sinking that Titanic known as the Dodger offense. Barring a sudden leap in development from Joe Thurston (and you can hold your breath on that one) or a winter acquisition, Cora will continue to be misused in a full-time role. Boy, that's a high Collapse Rate for someone who's already scraping the bottom of the barrel.

SHAWN GREEN

RF   **Bats: L**   **Throws: L**   Born: 10-Nov-72   Age: 31

YEAR	TM	LG	AGE	AB	H	2B	3B	HR	BB	SO	SB	CS	AVG	OBP	SLG	MLVR	EQBA	EQOBP	EQSLG	EQMLVR	VORP	DEFENSE	
2001	LAD	NL	28	619	184	31	4	49	72	107	20	4	.297	.372	.598	.341	.308	.382	.618	.359	75.3	155-RF	-8
2002	LAD	NL	29	582	166	31	1	42	93	112	8	5	.285	.385	.558	.340	.298	.395	.592	.331	65.1	154-RF	5
2003	LAD	NL	30	611	171	49	2	19	68	112	6	2	.280	.355	.460	.174	.293	.367	.486	.133	33.8	156-RF	4
2004	LAD	NL	31	546	156	31	2	32	69	99	7	2	.286	.369	.529	.190	.297	.378	.546	.225	43.2	146-RF	2

Breakout: 23%   Improve: 54%   Collapse: 10%

Green struggled all season with a shoulder injury, which the Dodgers knew about but didn't want to treat aggressively. Green played through the pain, exceeding 150 games for the seventh consecutive season, but saw a significant drop in his power as well as his plate discipline—that is, until the beginning of August when hitting coach Jack Clark was scapegoated for the team's offensive woes. From that point on, Green doubled his walk rate, cut his strikeout rate, and upped his ISO by 40 points. We're not trying to blame Clark for Green's troubles, mind you, we just think it's interesting.

That said, the Dodgers' handling of Green's injury was both amateurish and short-sighted. At the beginning of September, the team was just two-and-a-half games behind the Wild Card leader. Had L.A. taken care of Green's injury when it first became a problem, it's not unreasonable to assume they could have been the front-runner down the stretch. Instead, they let their best hitter struggle through three months of .248/.304/.410 without more than a day's rest, ultimately resulting in an October filled with early tee times.

FRANKLIN GUTIERREZ

CF   **Bats: R**   **Throws: R**   Born: 21-Feb-83   Age: 21

YEAR	TM	LG	AGE	AB	H	2B	3B	HR	BB	SO	SB	CS	AVG	OBP	SLG	MLVR	EQBA	EQOBP	EQSLG	EQMLVR	VORP	DEFENSE			
2002	SGA	SAL	19	361	102	18	4	12	31	88	13	4	.283	.344	.454	.175	.221	.267	.372	-.269	-13.9	58-CF	-3	27-LF	-1
2003	VRO	FLA	20	425	120	28	5	20	39	111	17	5	.282	.345	.513	.243	.226	.277	.431	-.164	-2.4	102-CF	-2		
2003	JAX	SOU	20	67	21	3	2	4	7	20	3	3	.313	.387	.597	.446	.261	.325	.507	.059	4.5	15-CF	-3		
2004	LAD	NL	21	329	73	15	2	13	26	95	6	3	.222	.283	.403	-.168	.231	.290	.416	-.149	-2.0	87-CF	-7		

Breakout: 27%   Improve: 54%   Collapse: 20%

Gutierrez continued to show massive power as a 20-year-old, roping 44% of his hits for extra bases at Vero Beach, coupled with speed indicators that make for an intriguing combination. Like so many hitters in the Dodgers' farm system, however, Gutierrez lacks control of the strike zone. His long-term projection is strong, but we'd like to see him round out his game a little. He'll start next year in Jacksonville, hopefully fighting the organization's emphasis on aggressiveness at the plate. In a few years, he could very well be Juan Gonzalez.

JOEL GUZMAN

SS   **Bats: R**   **Throws: R**   Born: 24-Nov-84   Age: 19

YEAR	TM	LG	AGE	AB	H	2B	3B	HR	BB	SO	SB	CS	AVG	OBP	SLG	MLVR	EQBA	EQOBP	EQSLG	EQMLVR	VORP	DEFENSE	
2002	GRF	PIO	17	151	38	8	2	3	18	54	5	3	.252	.331	.391	-.018	.163	.220	.261	-.547	-29.6	42-SS	-2
2003	SGA	SAL	18	217	51	13	0	8	9	62	4	4	.235	.263	.406	-.022	.198	.216	.347	-.418	-14.4	57-SS	-4
2003	VRO	FLA	18	240	59	13	1	5	11	60	0	4	.246	.279	.371	-.049	.206	.231	.329	-.409	-16.1	57-SS	-11
2004	LAD	NL	19	288	55	13	1	8	15	87	3	2	.191	.230	.322	-.387	.198	.236	.333	-.377	-12.5	75-SS	-13

Breakout: 49%   Improve: 68%   Collapse: 21%

Guzman was a bonus baby, acquired for $2.25 million in July of 2001. Since then, he's been rushed, resulting in mediocre production across the board. Scouts love his athleticism, his speed, and his cannon for an arm—none of which have translated into useful defense thus far. At 19, he still has a long way to go.

RICKEY HENDERSON

Legend   **Bats: R**   **Throws: L**   Born: 25-Dec-58   Age: 45

YEAR	TM	LG	AGE	AB	H	2B	3B	HR	BB	SO	SB	CS	AVG	OBP	SLG	MLVR	EQBA	EQOBP	EQSLG	EQMLVR	VORP	DEFENSE	
2001	POR	PCL	42	40	11	3	0	0	1	9	1	0	.275	.293	.350	-.202	.250	.268	.325	-.315	-2.2		
2001	SDP	NL	42	379	86	17	3	8	81	84	25	7	.227	.366	.351	-.064	.244	.377	.374	-.039	1.8	83-LF	-4
2002	BOS	AL	43	179	40	6	1	5	38	47	8	2	.223	.369	.352	-.046	.243	.386	.387	-.006	2.5	44-LF	-4
2003	LAD	NL	44	72	15	1	0	2	11	16	3	0	.208	.321	.306	-.149	.230	.336	.338	-.175	-1.9	15-LF	-1
2004	LAD	NL	45	65	12	2	1	1	10	20	1	1	.178	.299	.262	-.341	.185	.306	.270	-.329	-6.1	23-LF	-26

Breakout: 0%   Improve: 0%   Collapse: 44%

One of the biggest complaints of fans in the post-free agent era is that with all the big money floating around, athletes don't play for the love of the game anymore. Rickey Henderson is proof that that's a lie. Despite being one of the greatest outfielders of the 20th century, Henderson spent half a season with the Newark Bears of the Independent League, riding on buses and playing for peanuts, all for the shot at being picked up by one of the big clubs. At 45(!), Henderson doesn't have a whole lot to give anymore, so it's possible that we've seen his last hurrah. If that's the case, let us just say that we'll miss you, Rickey—and we'll see you in Cooperstown in 2008.

KOYIE HILL

KOYIE HILL   **C**   **Bats: B**   **Throws: R**   Born: 09-Mar-79   Age: 25

YEAR	TM	LG	AGE	AB	H	2B	3B	HR	BB	SO	SB	CS	AVG	OBP	SLG	MLVR	EQBA	EQOBP	EQSLG	EQMLVR	VORP	DEFENSE
2001	WNC	SAL	22	498	150	20	2	8	49	82	21	12	.301	.368	.398	.187	.245	.299	.328	-.253	-13.0	91-C -3
2002	JAX	SOU	23	468	127	25	1	11	76	88	5	3	.271	.368	.400	.107	.233	.313	.357	-.193	-3.0	114-C -2
2003	JAX	SOU	24	101	23	7	0	0	6	19	2	1	.228	.271	.297	-.189	.214	.250	.291	-.420	-7.8	23-C 2
2003	LVG	PCL	24	312	98	18	0	3	15	39	5	0	.314	.345	.401	.018	.279	.314	.360	-.155	1.6	76-C -10
2004	LAD	NL	25	188	45	9	1	4	17	34	2	1	.241	.307	.359	-.171	.251	.315	.370	-.150	2.0	53-C -6

Breakout: 32%   Improve: 52%   Collapse: 22%

Hill's plate discipline deteriorated into nothing in 2003 (we suspect you're detecting a theme), and his status as a prospect is likely to follow if he doesn't get himself back on track. Hill hit an empty .314 in the hitter's haven of Las Vegas, with precious little power. A converted third baseman out of Wichita State, he has been known to show good opposite-field power, but it seems unlikely that his bat will be taking him to stardom anytime soon. The organization loves his defense, and will probably start using him as a backup by 2005.

TODD HUNDLEY

TODD HUNDLEY   **C**   **Bats: B**   **Throws: R**   Born: 27-May-69   Age: 35

YEAR	TM	LG	AGE	AB	H	2B	3B	HR	BB	SO	SB	CS	AVG	OBP	SLG	MLVR	EQBA	EQOBP	EQSLG	EQMLVR	VORP	DEFENSE
2001	CHC	NL	32	246	46	10	0	12	25	89	0	0	.187	.268	.374	-.267	.193	.273	.386	-.256	-5.8	65-C -11
2002	CHC	NL	33	266	56	8	0	16	32	80	0	0	.211	.301	.421	-.052	.221	.307	.446	-.092	5.8	74-C -8
2003	LAD	NL	34	33	6	1	0	2	8	13	0	1	.182	.341	.394	-.013	.206	.357	.412	-.053	1.2	
2004	LAD	NL	35	131	25	4	0	7	15	44	0	0	.189	.278	.376	-.233	.197	.285	.388	-.217	0.3	39-C -7

Breakout: 40%   Improve: 53%   Collapse: 39%

Hundley was a non-factor in 2003, out for most of the year with an injury to his back. His June surgery went well, though, and he recuperated more quickly than many people thought he would. Hundley will be paid $6.5 million next year to act as the whipping boy for fans and media members who thought trading Eric Karros and Mark Grudzielanek was a horrible idea.

CESAR IZTURIS

CESAR IZTURIS   **SS**   **Bats: B**   **Throws: R**   Born: 10-Feb-80   Age: 24

YEAR	TM	LG	AGE	AB	H	2B	3B	HR	BB	SO	SB	CS	AVG	OBP	SLG	MLVR	EQBA	EQOBP	EQSLG	EQMLVR	VORP	DEFENSE	
2001	SYR	INT	21	342	100	16	3	2	10	22	24	9	.292	.310	.374	-.053	.277	.301	.356	-.187	1.5	57-SS -2	24-2B 4
2001	TOR	AL	21	134	36	6	2	2	2	15	8	1	.269	.279	.388	-.154	.284	.299	.410	-.106	2.2	31-2B 3	
2002	LAD	NL	22	439	102	24	2	1	14	39	7	7	.232	.253	.303	-.269	.257	.276	.339	-.274	-7.9	110-SS -2	
2003	LAD	NL	23	558	140	21	6	1	25	70	10	5	.251	.282	.315	-.186	.271	.302	.343	-.209	-4.0	151-SS -1	
2004	LAD	NL	24	448	110	19	3	4	21	48	10	4	.247	.281	.328	-.256	.256	.287	.339	-.239	-3.2	113-SS 0	

Breakout: 5%   Improve: 37%   Collapse: 32%

Izturis has a flashy glove, which some people think makes up for his anemic bat. It doesn't. Even after you adjust for the negative effects of Dodger Stadium, Izturis still shows up as one of the worst hitters in all of baseball, a black hole the size of Marlon Brando in the Dodgers' lineup. This fact was only augmented by Jim Tracy's inexplicable decision to bat Izturis at the top of the lineup for a good portion of the year—something that hurt the offense even more. You know those "easily identifiable flaws" that we criticize Dan Evans for not correcting? He's one of them. (*Fun Fact:* Cesar Izturis is an anagram for "Crazier Suits.")

BRIAN JORDAN

BRIAN JORDAN   **OF**   **Bats: R**   **Throws: R**   Born: 29-Mar-67   Age: 37

YEAR	TM	LG	AGE	AB	H	2B	3B	HR	BB	SO	SB	CS	AVG	OBP	SLG	MLVR	EQBA	EQOBP	EQSLG	EQMLVR	VORP	DEFENSE	
2001	ATL	NL	34	560	165	32	3	25	31	88	3	2	.295	.334	.496	.110	.299	.341	.505	.122	28.4	141-RF 7	
2002	LAD	NL	35	471	134	27	3	18	34	86	2	2	.285	.338	.469	.147	.302	.352	.504	.142	24.2	115-LF 7	
2003	LAD	NL	36	224	67	9	0	6	23	30	1	1	.299	.372	.420	.163	.317	.387	.443	.129	12.0	44-LF 1	14-CF 1
2004	TEX	AL	37	259	73	15	1	8	21	40	1	1	.282	.340	.444	.039	.274	.337	.433	-.011	6.4	70-LF 0	

Breakout: 9%   Improve: 22%   Collapse: 34%

(continued next page)

Brian Jordan *(continued)*

Major League teams have been platooning players for decades, yet still have a problem identifying which individuals are best suited for that role. Brian Jordan is one of those individuals. A lefty killer of the highest order, Jordan's success as an every day player has always been dependent on how well he faired against northpaws. At the right price, he can still be an asset to a team. At $9.6 million—his salary for 2003—he's a waste, and another data point against John Schuerholz as a top-tier GM.

PAUL LO DUCA   C   Bats: R   Throws: R   Born: 12-Apr-72   Age: 32

YEAR	TM	LG	AGE	AB	H	2B	3B	HR	BB	SO	SB	CS	AVG	OBP	SLG	MLVR	EQBA	EQOBP	EQSLG	EQMLVR	VORP	DEFENSE			
2001	LAD	NL	29	460	147	28	0	25	39	30	2	4	.320	.374	.543	.292	.335	.393	.570	.341	65.9	86-C	4	23-1B	0
2002	LAD	NL	30	580	163	38	1	10	34	31	3	1	.281	.330	.402	.037	.301	.345	.434	.027	30.0	132-C	3		
2003	LAD	NL	31	568	155	34	2	7	44	54	0	2	.273	.335	.377	.017	.289	.348	.403	-.022	18.9	123-C	14	18-1B	0
2004	LAD	NL	32	463	125	25	1	11	38	41	1	1	.271	.331	.400	-.054	.281	.339	.413	-.028	15.9	121-C	1		

Breakout: 9%   *Improve: 30%*   *Collapse: 33%*

It's not uncommon for everyday players—especially those on the right end of the defensive spectrum—to see a decline in their production as the season wears on. A 162-game season, spending half your time avoiding someone's spikes on the double play or wearing the tools of ignorance is not particularly easy or comfortable. Cal Ripken Jr. often saw a noticeable decline in his production in the month of September; and who could forget Mike Piazza's limp to the finish line in 2000? That being said, it is really that much of a surprise that Lo Duca completely hit the wall in the second half? From the middle of July on, he batted a dismal .226/.282/.293 with just 14 extra-base hits. And it's not like this was new territory for the catcher; here are his first- and second-half splits over the past three seasons:

2001–2003	AB	AVG	OBP	SLG
Pre All-Star	899	.314	.373	.485
Post All-Star	883	.255	.308	.375

That's a 19% reduction in batting average and a 30% reduction in Isolated Slugging, for those of you scoring at home. Manager Jim Tracy did his best to give Lo Duca's knees a rest in the second half by playing him at first base, but it didn't seem to help much. An extra day off per week during the first half would probably go a long way toward helping Lo Duca stay productive during the dog days of summer.

JAMES LONEY   1B   Bats: L   Throws: L   Born: 07-May-84   Age: 20

YEAR	TM	LG	AGE	AB	H	2B	3B	HR	BB	SO	SB	CS	AVG	OBP	SLG	MLVR	EQBA	EQOBP	EQSLG	EQMLVR	VORP	DEFENSE	
2002	GRF	PIO	18	170	63	22	3	5	25	18	5	4	.371	.457	.624	.617	.228	.289	.398	-.186	-10.2	41-1B	-6
2002	VRO	FLA	18	67	20	6	0	0	6	10	0	0	.299	.356	.388	.089	.235	.288	.324	-.286	-4.5	12-1B	2
2003	VRO	FLA	19	468	129	31	3	7	43	80	9	4	.276	.337	.400	.085	.226	.275	.345	-.288	-32.5	106-1B	0
2004	LAD	NL	20	290	63	15	1	6	23	55	4	2	.218	.276	.346	-.257	.226	.283	.357	-.241	-9.6	77-1B	-6

Breakout: 25%   *Improve: 53%*   *Collapse: 25%*

Loney continued to show only moderate power at high-A Vero Beach, but youth (he's still only 19), a wrist fracture suffered in late 2002, and the tough Florida State League hitting environment will have that effect. Scouts love his picturesque swing, comparing him to a young Rafael Palmeiro, but think he'll need to put on some more weight before he starts converting those doubles into homers. He'll begin next season at Double-A Jacksonville as the most promising hitter in the organization. Expect him to take a big step forward.

FRED McGRIFF   1B   Bats: L   Throws: L   Born: 31-Oct-63   Age: 40

YEAR	TM	LG	AGE	AB	H	2B	3B	HR	BB	SO	SB	CS	AVG	OBP	SLG	MLVR	EQBA	EQOBP	EQSLG	EQMLVR	VORP	DEFENSE	
2001	TBY	AL	37	343	109	18	0	19	40	69	1	1	.318	.387	.536	.288	.336	.408	.571	.366	42.1	73-1B	-2
2001	CHC	NL	37	170	48	7	2	12	26	37	0	1	.282	.383	.559	.265	.289	.389	.566	.276	18.1	46-1B	-2
2002	CHC	NL	38	523	143	27	2	30	63	99	1	2	.273	.353	.505	.192	.282	.359	.527	.166	35.0	128-1B	-7
2003	LAD	NL	39	297	74	14	0	13	31	66	0	0	.249	.322	.428	.047	.263	.333	.454	.001	7.2	75-1B	-4
2004	LAD	NL	40	329	84	15	1	16	39	68	0	1	.256	.335	.457	.017	.267	.343	.472	.045	13.1	89-1B	-1

Breakout: 21%   *Improve: 55%*   *Collapse: 16%*

Will he be the first player with more than 500 home runs not to make the Hall of Fame? Possibly, assuming he gets there first. Unlike Rafael Palmeiro, McGriff hasn't fared well in MVP voting since the early '90s, and doesn't have the luster that most sluggers from his generation possess. Nevertheless, he's been at least Palmeiro's equal after you adjust for park effects, and he gets a slight bump depending on how you value his postseason success at the plate (.303/.391/.527 in 10 October series). Things won't stay that way for long, mind you, because Palmeiro is likely to wade through a couple years of post-decline ineffectiveness before he's forced out of the game—a time for him to pad his counting stats and make a lunge for 600 HR—while McGriff may not last much longer. There's little question that he's better than Tony Perez and a host of other Veterans Committee blunders, but that's damning with faint praise. He gets our vote, even if we are six years too early.

JASON REPKO   CF   Bats: R   Throws: R   Born: 27-Dec-80   Age: 23

YEAR	TM	LG	AGE	AB	H	2B	3B	HR	BB	SO	SB	CS	AVG	OBP	SLG	MLVR	EQBA	EQOBP	EQSLG	EQMLVR	VORP	DEFENSE			
2001	WNC	SAL	20	337	74	17	4	4	15	68	17	8	.220	.257	.329	-.113	.190	.222	.297	-.481	-29.2	77-SS	-15		
2002	VRO	FLA	21	470	128	29	5	9	25	92	29	13	.272	.319	.413	.050	.229	.263	.359	-.290	-21.5	88-CF	-6	30-LF	-1
2003	JAX	SOU	22	416	100	14	5	10	42	89	21	8	.240	.317	.370	-.013	.217	.279	.348	-.281	-30.5	70-LF	2	38-CF	-3
2004	LAD	NL	23	233	52	11	2	5	17	51	6	3	.222	.279	.353	-.240	.231	.286	.364	-.223	-8.2	63-LF	1		

Breakout: 38%   Improve: 60%   Collapse: 22%

At one time touted as a future star, Repko has fallen into the Guy Who Runs Really Fast But Does Little Else category. He works hard, so the Dodgers feel that he's a good player to have around the kids. The unfortunate thing is, it looks like he's destined to be surrounded by the kids for the rest of his career.

DAVE ROBERTS   CF   Bats: L   Throws: L   Born: 31-May-72   Age: 32

YEAR	TM	LG	AGE	AB	H	2B	3B	HR	BB	SO	SB	CS	AVG	OBP	SLG	MLVR	EQBA	EQOBP	EQSLG	EQMLVR	VORP	DEFENSE			
2001	BUF	INT	29	241	73	12	4	0	18	44	17	6	.303	.352	.386	.053	.287	.339	.365	-.095	-2.9	32-LF	0	24-CF	1
2002	LAD	NL	30	422	117	14	7	3	48	51	45	10	.277	.353	.365	.023	.300	.370	.396	.018	18.9	106-CF	1		
2003	LAD	NL	31	388	97	6	5	2	43	39	40	14	.250	.331	.307	-.105	.267	.344	.330	-.148	1.9	100-CF	2		
2004	LAD	NL	32	365	94	14	4	2	36	44	25	9	.257	.326	.334	-.162	.267	.333	.344	-.140	0.1	98-CF	-2		

Breakout: 12%   Improve: 34%   Collapse: 32%

One of Evans's few useful acquisitions, Roberts is still a middling outfielder on the wrong side of 30 with little offensive upside, and now with a nasty fallback season on his resume. At least he runs well, nabbing more than 40 bases in each of the last two seasons at above a 75% clip, augmenting his offensive value. Ideally the Dodgers will go hard after a Carlos Beltran-type replacement soon.

JASON ROMANO   UT   Bats: R   Throws: R   Born: 24-Jun-79   Age: 25

YEAR	TM	LG	AGE	AB	H	2B	3B	HR	BB	SO	SB	CS	AVG	OBP	SLG	MLVR	EQBA	EQOBP	EQSLG	EQMLVR	VORP	DEFENSE			
2001	OKL	PCL	22	149	47	6	1	4	20	28	3	4	.315	.394	.450	.169	.273	.351	.393	-.043	6.1	18-2B	-1	12-CF	-1
2001	TUL	TEX	22	186	45	9	1	1	16	31	8	3	.242	.304	.317	-.181	.213	.265	.277	-.410	-13.3	42-2B	-7		
2002	OKL	PCL	23	196	53	8	1	4	19	41	10	3	.270	.329	.383	-.050	.247	.307	.354	-.199	-2.9	23-CF	2	17-2B	-2
2002	TEX	AL	23	54	11	4	0	0	4	13	2	0	.204	.254	.278	-.377	.222	.276	.296	-.357	-3.2				
2002	CSP	PCL	23	129	40	7	2	0	6	27	8	3	.310	.338	.395	-.045	.268	.295	.346	-.220	-2.7	15-CF	-1		
2003	LVG	PCL	24	216	66	18	4	4	11	32	10	6	.306	.336	.481	.110	.268	.304	.432	-.078	4.3	24-CF	0		
2003	LAD	NL	24	36	3	0	0	0	1	8	2	0	.083	.108	.083	-.925	.111	.135	.111	-.947	-6.9				
2004	LAD	NL	25	217	54	11	1	4	16	42	7	2	.247	.302	.372	-.160	.257	.309	.384	-.139	-0.5	59-CF	-6		

Breakout: 31%   Improve: 53%   Collapse: 22%

Described by one scout as "Joe Thurston, but without the talent." A former first-round selection by the Rangers, Romano has evolved into a garden-variety utility player. In all likelihood, he'll never hit well enough to make it at the major league level. That's never really kept the Dodgers from giving Cesar Izturis at-bats, though, so it's possible you'll see him fill in down the road.

DAVE ROSS   C   Bats: R   Throws: R   Born: 19-Mar-77   Age: 27

YEAR	TM	LG	AGE	AB	H	2B	3B	HR	BB	SO	SB	CS	AVG	OBP	SLG	MLVR	EQBA	EQOBP	EQSLG	EQMLVR	VORP	DEFENSE		
2001	JAX	SOU	24	246	65	13	1	11	34	72	1	1	.264	.372	.459	.164	.228	.316	.402	-.129	3.7	69-C	2	
2002	LVG	PCL	25	293	87	16	2	15	35	86	1	1	.297	.384	.519	.210	.254	.337	.447	-.009	14.4	87-C	3	
2003	LVG	PCL	26	86	19	4	0	5	11	27	0	2	.221	.313	.442	-.052	.186	.276	.372	-.274	-2.7	24-C	3	
2003	LAD	NL	26	124	32	7	0	10	13	42	0	0	.258	.336	.556	.257	.268	.343	.591	.214	13.3	32-C	0	
2004	LAD	NL	27	267	64	13	1	15	32	81	1	1	.239	.330	.459	-.003	.248	.338	.474	.023	19.1	75-C	0	

Breakout: 37%   Improve: 59%   Collapse: 26%

Ross hit exceptionally well as a fill-in for Paul Lo Duca, displaying impressive power despite the effects of Dodger Stadium. At 27, it's possible that we've already seen the best 120 at-bats of his career, but that doesn't mean he's without value. If Jim Tracy begins to recognize that Paul Lo Duca might not be able to handle a full season behind the plate without seeing a precipitous decline in his production, Ross should be the person to fill in more often for Lo Duca during April, May, and June. Trading Lo Duca's contract and handing Ross the starter's job may not be a bad idea either, if the Dodgers use the savings to upgrade the offense elsewhere.

WILKIN RUAN   CF   Bats: R   Throws: R   Born: 18-Sep-78   Age: 25

YEAR	TM	LG	AGE	AB	H	2B	3B	HR	BB	SO	SB	CS	AVG	OBP	SLG	MLVR	EQBA	EQOBP	EQSLG	EQMLVR	VORP	DEFENSE			
2001	JUP	FLA	22	293	83	8	2	2	10	35	25	14	.283	.313	.345	-.013	.258	.273	.318	-.310	-14.4	66-CF	-4		
2001	HAR	EAS	22	117	29	7	0	0	3	18	6	0	.248	.279	.308	-.200	.222	.255	.282	-.419	-9.7	28-CF	2		
2002	JAX	SOU	23	324	82	16	6	3	17	33	23	3	.253	.306	.367	-.043	.239	.272	.361	-.263	-11.1	72-CF	-1		
2002	LVG	PCL	23	153	50	7	3	0	2	17	12	0	.327	.335	.412	.008	.291	.301	.371	-.155	-0.3	37-CF	-2		
2003	LVG	PCL	24	403	124	6	3	0	10	38	41	7	.308	.334	.337	-.096	.285	.312	.312	-.225	-8.9	83-CF	-1	11-RF	1
2003	LAD	NL	24	41	9	2	1	0	0	7	1	0	.220	.220	.317	-.321	.238	.238	.333	-.370	-1.9	11-CF	1		
2004	LAD	NL	25	238	57	10	2	1	9	30	10	3	.242	.275	.311	-.292	.251	.282	.321	-.276	-10.2	63-CF	-3		

Breakout: 11%   Improve: 31%   Collapse: 46%

Ruan would be an awfully good ballplayer if hitters were allowed to steal first base. Since they can't, he has little to contribute; he doesn't hit for average, doesn't hit for power, doesn't walk, and doesn't wear one of those humungous elbow guards like Craig Biggio that might allow him to reach base via the HBP all the time. He's a pinch-runner and defensive replacement on a team that has enough trouble scoring runs in the first place.

JOE THURSTON   2B   Bats: L   Throws: R   Born: 29-Sep-79   Age: 24

YEAR	TM	LG	AGE	AB	H	2B	3B	HR	BB	SO	SB	CS	AVG	OBP	SLG	MLVR	EQBA	EQOBP	EQSLG	EQMLVR	VORP	DEFENSE			
2001	JAX	SOU	21	544	145	25	7	7	48	65	20	18	.267	.338	.377	.003	.233	.290	.338	-.264	-15.6	121-2B	-12	12-SS	-2
2002	LVG	PCL	22	587	196	39	13	12	25	60	22	9	.334	.372	.506	.211	.295	.330	.451	.020	31.8	118-2B	6	17-SS	0
2003	LVG	PCL	23	538	156	27	6	7	31	48	1	12	.290	.345	.401	-.001	.254	.308	.359	-.186	-1.7	124-2B	4		
2004	LAD	NL	24	272	70	14	2	5	20	32	3	2	.259	.322	.385	-.099	.270	.330	.397	-.076	9.7	74-2B	1		

Breakout: 31%   Improve: 51%   Collapse: 22%

Thurston's development stalled in 2003, after entering spring training with plenty of buzz. According to the organization, Thurston spent last winter bulking up, hoping to add more power to his game; this resulted in a swing that was off-kilter for most of the season, and thus the disappointment. While that may be true, the fact remains Thurston drew just 56 walks in nearly 1,200 plate appearances in 2002–03. Thurston will likely get a shot to make the club in the spring, but projects as a scrappy backup who doesn't walk and hits for little power. Unfortunately, the Dodgers already have their share of those.

ROBIN VENTURA   1B/3B   Bats: L   Throws: R   Born: 14-Jul-67   Age: 36

YEAR	TM	LG	AGE	AB	H	2B	3B	HR	BB	SO	SB	CS	AVG	OBP	SLG	MLVR	EQBA	EQOBP	EQSLG	EQMLVR	VORP	DEFENSE	
2001	NYM	NL	33	456	108	20	0	21	88	101	2	5	.237	.359	.419	.009	.248	.368	.437	.029	29.3	131-3B	7
2002	NYY	AL	34	465	115	17	0	27	90	101	3	1	.247	.368	.458	.105	.272	.393	.505	.183	47.2	128-3B	3
2003	NYY	AL	35	283	71	13	0	9	40	62	0	0	.251	.344	.392	-.025	.270	.364	.428	.027	10.0	71-3B	8
2003	LAD	NL	35	109	24	5	1	5	18	25	0	0	.220	.331	.422	.031	.232	.338	.455	-.014	2.8	28-1B	-1
2004	LAD	NL	36	262	62	11	0	13	45	61	1	1	.237	.348	.426	-.017	.246	.356	.440	.009	15.6	75-3B	-2

Breakout: 30%   Improve: 53%   Collapse: 26%

"What do you mean you don't have Oreos? Fine, just give me some Hydrox and I'll be outta here." That's more or less the way the Dodgers acquired Ventura, who came from the Yankees at the trading deadline when the Yankees dealt for Aaron Boone. Dan Evans had his eye on a number of name-brand hitters toward the end of July, but by the deadline, all that was left were the old, store-brand leftovers. The Dodgers signed Ventura to a one-year, $1.2 million deal at the end of 2003; Dodger fans better hope there's a Plan B for the first-base job.

DARYLE WARD — 1B/LF — Bats: L — Throws: L — Born: 27-Jun-75 — Age: 29

YEAR	TM	LG	AGE	AB	H	2B	3B	HR	BB	SO	SB	CS	AVG	OBP	SLG	MLVR	EQBA	EQOBP	EQSLG	EQMLVR	VORP	DEFENSE			
2001	HOU	NL	26	213	56	15	0	9	19	48	0	0	.263	.323	.460	-.013	.260	.320	.460	-.017	2.2	23-LF	-1	12-RF	0
2002	HOU	NL	27	453	125	31	0	12	33	82	1	3	.276	.324	.424	.012	.277	.323	.432	-.036	2.1	84-LF	3		
2003	JAX	SOU	28	16	2	0	0	0	0	3	0	0	.125	.125	.125	-.702	.187	.187	.187	-.710	-2.7				
2003	LAD	NL	28	109	20	1	0	0	3	19	0	0	.183	.211	.193	-.536	.209	.236	.218	-.555	-12.8	12-1B	1		
2003	LVG	PCL	28	128	38	9	0	4	10	22	0	0	.297	.343	.461	.084	.260	.309	.409	-.109	-1.0	28-1B	3		
2004	PIT	NL	29	189	46	9	0	5	13	39	0	0	.243	.294	.377	-.169	.246	.295	.391	-.162	-4.2	52-LF	-1		

Breakout: 29%   Improve: 47%   Collapse: 36%

Daryle Ward had the unique accomplishment of earning zero Win Shares last season—something that's tough to do, given that the system virtually rewards players for things like "wearing a jock" and "being carbon-based." Yes, my friends, he was that bad. In completely unrelated news, the Pirates signed Ward in exchange for a sack of turnips just before the Winter Meetings. He's likely snacking on those turnips as you read this.

DELWYN YOUNG — 2B/OF? — Bats: B — Throws: R — Born: 30-Jun-82 — Age: 22

YEAR	TM	LG	AGE	AB	H	2B	3B	HR	BB	SO	SB	CS	AVG	OBP	SLG	MLVR	EQBA	EQOBP	EQSLG	EQMLVR	VORP	DEFENSE	
2002	GRF	PIO	20	240	72	18	1	10	27	60	4	2	.300	.380	.508	.267	.198	.249	.347	-.353	-24.2	42-2B	-7
2003	SGA	SAL	21	443	143	38	7	15	36	87	5	2	.323	.381	.542	.385	.251	.293	.437	-.106	9.9	110-2B	-15
2004	LAN	NL	22	293	64	15	1	9	21	72	1	1	.217	.273	.375	-.226	.225	.279	.386	-.209	-3.4	78-2B	-11

Breakout: 14%   Improve: 38%   Collapse: 29%

Young is an outfielder stuck playing second base, and he looks it. Nevertheless, he's shown impressive pop in the Pioneer League as well as the Sally League over the past two seasons, and his future looks bright. A switch to the outfield could allow Young to gain some defensive value, while removing him from a high-attrition rate position that's gobbled up far too many promising young hitters.

PITCHERS

WILSON ALVAREZ — Bats: L — Throws: L — Born: 24-Mar-70 — Age: 34

YEAR	TM	LG	AGE	G	GS	IP	H	BB	SO	HR	ERA	EQERA	EQH9	EQBB9	EQSO9	EQHR9	PERA	VORP	STF
2001	DUR	INT	31	4	4	18.0	20	6	16	2	3.00	5.51	12.1	3.9	6.1	1.7	6.91	0.2	-29
2001	ORL	SOU	31	5	5	20.3	24	6	18	2	4.43	6.00	13.5	3.0	5.5	1.5	7.15	-0.8	-35
2002	TBY	AL	32	23	10	75.0	80	36	56	13	5.28	5.25	9.3	3.9	6.4	1.5	5.39	2.9	-13
2003	LVG	PCL	33	8	8	47.0	36	6	33	1	1.34	2.03	6.9	1.4	5.3	0.2	2.34	17.6	37
2003	LAD	NL	33	21	12	95.0	80	23	82	5	2.37	3.10	8.2	2.0	7.0	0.5	3.32	30.1	32
2004	LAD	NL	34	24	17	102.7	97	32	83	14	3.83	4.29	8.9	2.5	6.4	1.0	4.45	15.2	9

Breakout: 26%   Improve: 48%   Collapse: 11%

Alvarez was arguably the best pitcher in the National League in the second half, posting an ERA of just 1.77 in more than 70 innings of work. All the caveats about overweight pitchers who have trouble staying healthy should apply to Alvarez, but at the right price and in the right home park he could be a decent back-of-the-rotation starter. The Dodgers re-upped him for one year, $1.5 million.

ANDY ASHBY — Bats: R — Throws: R — Born: 11-Jul-67 — Age: 36

YEAR	TM	LG	AGE	G	GS	IP	H	BB	SO	HR	ERA	EQERA	EQH9	EQBB9	EQSO9	EQHR9	PERA	VORP	STF
2001	LAD	NL	33	2	2	11.7	14	1	7	2	3.85	4.91	11.5	0.8	4.9	1.6	5.78	0.8	-10
2002	LAD	NL	34	30	30	181.7	179	65	107	20	3.91	5.06	9.8	2.9	4.7	1.1	4.93	10.2	-2
2003	LAD	NL	35	21	12	73.0	90	17	41	8	5.18	5.74	11.7	2.0	4.6	1.0	5.56	0.0	-12
2004	LAD	NL	36	24	14	83.7	94	25	44	11	4.47	5.01	10.6	2.4	4.1	1.0	5.33	5.9	-8

Breakout: 13%   Improve: 30%   Collapse: 20%

(continued next page)

Andy Ashby (*continued*)

Some people actually have to buy a ticket to win the lottery; others win by coming to the Dodgers in their early-30s, masquerading as a good investment. Ashby began the season in the bullpen, a decision he wasn't happy with. He didn't do much to improve Jim Tracy's confidence, however, though he was given starts when both Odalis Perez and Kazuhisa Ishii hit the sidelines with injuries. By the end of August, he was complaining of elbow soreness, a problem that resulted in him being shelved for the rest of the season. Ashby will miss all of 2004 upon undergoing Tommy John surgery.

TROY BROHAWN										Bats: L		Throws: L				Born: 14-Jan-73		Age: 31
YEAR	TM	LG	AGE	G	GS	IP	H	BB	SO	HR	ERA	EQERA	EQH9	EQBB9	EQSO9	EQHR9	PERA	VORP	STF
2001	ARI	NL	28	59	0	49.3	55	23	30	5	4.93	5.17	10.5	3.8	4.6	0.8	5.21	2.2	-17
2002	FRE	PCL	29	56	0	69.0	71	21	55	7	3.65	4.64	10.1	3.1	5.5	1.1	5.19	6.8	-21
2002	SFG	NL	29	11	0	5.7	5	1	3	1	6.32	5.06	8.4	1.7	5.1	1.7	4.61	0.3	-26
2003	LAD	NL	30	12	0	11.7	10	4	13	2	3.85	4.91	8.2	2.5	9.0	1.6	4.58	0.8	0
2003	LVG	PCL	30	1	0	4.0	3	0	1	1	4.50	4.91	7.4	0.0	2.5	2.5	4.48	0.3	-49
2004	LAD	NL	31	29	0	34.7	34	13	27	5	4.46	5.00	9.3	2.9	6.2	1.1	4.99	3.2	-5

Breakout: 18%   Improve: 42%   Collapse: 32%

An anonymous reliever who has spent the past few years on a yo-yo between Triple-A and the majors. A non-tender, he'll look for a spring training invite and another shot at LOOGYdom.

KEVIN BROWN										Bats: R		Throws: R				Born: 14-Mar-65		Age: 39
YEAR	TM	LG	AGE	G	GS	IP	H	BB	SO	HR	ERA	EQERA	EQH9	EQBB9	EQSO9	EQHR9	PERA	VORP	STF
2001	LAD	NL	36	20	19	115.7	94	38	104	8	2.64	3.34	7.7	2.8	6.9	0.6	3.41	27.7	31
2002	LAD	NL	37	17	10	63.7	68	23	58	9	4.80	5.85	10.8	2.8	7.3	1.4	5.65	-1.7	-3
2003	LAD	NL	38	32	32	211.0	184	56	185	11	2.39	3.42	8.5	2.2	7.2	0.5	3.51	59.2	35
2004	NYY	AL	39	30	27	175.3	175	46	128	12	3.58	3.69	8.8	2.2	6.4	0.6	3.61	38.9	19

Breakout: 17%   Improve: 48%   Collapse: 27%

Brown is still an outstanding pitcher and a borderline Hall of Famer. He combines a fastball that bores down-and-in on right-handed hitters with a splitter that's among the best in the game. He might not be worth the $15 million per year he's earning, but he's as good of an investment as a 39-year-old pitcher can be. Traded to the Yankees, it's likely that his ERA will jump by more than a run in 2004, given the tougher home park, plus the problem of his strengths (keeping the ball on the ground) lining up exactly with the Bombers' weaknesses (Jeter and Soriano's range).

JONATHAN BROXTON										Bats: R		Throws: R				Born: 16-Jun-84		Age: 20
YEAR	TM	LG	AGE	G	GS	IP	H	BB	SO	HR	ERA	EQERA	EQH9	EQBB9	EQSO9	EQHR9	PERA	VORP	STF
2002	GRF	PIO	18	11	6	29.3	22	16	33	0	2.76	4.56	9.1	7.0	5.3	0.4	4.99	3.0	14
2003	SGA	SAL	19	9	8	37.3	27	22	30	1	3.14	4.81	7.5	7.0	4.5	0.5	4.47	3.0	11

Looks like he just ate Jared from Subway. A power pitcher, Broxton's had a tough time developing because his mechanics are so hindered by his size (6'4", 250). He's a hard-thrower, in the 93–96 MPH range, but his command is awful. Like so many other pitchers in the minor leagues, he's a work in progress.

STEVE COLYER										Bats: L		Throws: L				Born: 22-Feb-79		Age: 25
YEAR	TM	LG	AGE	G	GS	IP	H	BB	SO	HR	ERA	EQERA	EQH9	EQBB9	EQSO9	EQHR9	PERA	VORP	STF
2001	VRO	FLA	22	24	24	120.3	101	77	118	16	3.97	6.58	10.9	7.2	6.1	3.0	8.87	-11.3	-49
2002	JAX	SOU	23	59	0	62.7	50	40	68	6	3.44	6.34	10.2	6.3	7.3	1.8	6.83	-4.5	-28
2003	LVG	PCL	24	44	0	47.7	44	22	50	1	3.21	3.80	8.6	4.8	8.0	0.2	3.98	9.0	23
2003	LAD	NL	24	13	0	19.7	22	9	16	0	2.74	3.86	11.1	3.9	6.8	0.0	4.63	5.8	26
2004	LAD	NL	25	19	5	39.0	38	22	34	5	4.76	5.34	9.3	4.5	6.9	0.9	5.42	1.4	-3

Breakout: 13%   Improve: 41%   Collapse: 27%

Colyer is a sinker/slider guy with some moderate control problems and decent K rates throughout the minors. He doesn't exactly have an out pitch, so it's unlikely that he'll pull a Brendan Donnelly and start dominating major league hitters. He'll compete for a job in spring training.

DARREN DREIFORT

Bats: R **Throws: R** Born: 03-May-72 Age: 32

YEAR	TM	LG	AGE	G	GS	IP	H	BB	SO	HR	ERA	EQERA	EQH9	EQBB9	EQSO9	EQHR9	PERA	VORP	STF
2001	LAD	NL	29	16	16	94.7	89	47	91	11	5.13	5.34	8.9	4.2	7.3	1.0	4.74	2.6	10
2003	LAD	NL	31	10	10	60.3	58	25	67	6	4.03	4.68	9.4	3.4	9.1	0.9	4.66	6.2	27
2004	LAD	NL	32	23	21	135.7	122	57	128	12	3.79	4.24	8.5	3.3	7.4	0.7	4.16	18.9	20
Breakout: 19%			Improve: 41%			Collapse: 28%													

Remember O. J. Simpson's character in the *Naked Gun* movies? How he'd spend most of his screen time in hospitals, thanks to some unlikely accident that could only happen to him? And remember how the other members of the police force just took it in stride? That's Darren Dreifort. He's always hurt, but it's become expected at this point. Sure, he can be a decent pitcher when healthy, but that happens about as often as a David Spade makes a film that doesn't make you bolt. Dreifort will be paid $24 million over the next two seasons, mostly to rehab.

JASON FRASOR

Bats: R **Throws: R** Born: 09-Aug-77 Age: 26

YEAR	TM	LG	AGE	G	GS	IP	H	BB	SO	HR	ERA	EQERA	EQH9	EQBB9	EQSO9	EQHR9	PERA	VORP	STF
2002	LAK	FLA	24	24	24	117.0	112	46	87	10	3.54	6.21	12.5	4.7	4.8	2.0	7.72	-6.8	-46
2003	VRO	FLA	25	15	0	24.3	16	4	36	0	1.85	3.00	9.4	2.1	9.4	0.4	3.80	6.1	30
2003	JAX	SOU	25	35	0	36.7	33	14	50	2	2.94	4.73	11.1	4.2	8.6	1.1	5.86	3.1	-9
2004	LAD	NL	26	11	6	34.0	33	15	33	4	4.31	4.83	9.3	3.4	7.6	1.0	4.95	3.6	9
Breakout: 23%			Improve: 52%			Collapse: 26%													

Frasor is a poor man's Billy Wagner—a pitcher who can bring the heat, but gets ignored because he's 5'10" at most. He's posted decent strikeout rates throughout the minors, and impressed a number of scouts in the Arizona Fall League, throwing in the mid-90s. Frasor showed a marked improvement in his command last season, cutting his Equivalent walk rate (EQBB9) by half. There's little reason to think he can't contribute at the major league level, though he'll be lucky to have half of Wagner's career.

JONATHAN FIGUEROA

Bats: L **Throws: L** Born: 15-Sep-83 Age: 20

YEAR	TM	LG	AGE	G	GS	IP	H	BB	SO	HR	ERA	EQERA	EQH9	EQBB9	EQSO9	EQHR9	PERA	VORP	STF
2002	GRF	PIO	18	7	7	31.7	16	19	48	0	1.42	3.00	7.7	8.0	7.3	0.3	4.58	7.8	41
2002	SGA	SAL	18	8	8	44.3	22	20	57	1	1.42	3.23	6.2	5.5	7.6	0.5	3.41	10.3	55
2003	SGA	SAL	19	17	17	78.3	79	42	74	4	4.94	7.71	10.8	6.4	5.4	1.2	6.43	-16.4	1
2004	LAN	NL	20	16	13	77	73	48	57	9	4.77	5.34	9.0	5.0	5.9	0.9	5.54	3.6	-2
Breakout: 22%			Improve: 62%			Collapse: 5%													

Figueroa was one of the Dodgers' most prized prospects in 2002. He showed up to camp 30 pounds overweight in '03, and his performance suffered for it. A big, hard-throwing lefty, Figueroa will get a chance to start again in 2004, where hopefully he'll rediscover the salad bar as well as his control. Only 20, he has time to turn things around and join Greg Miller, Edwin Jackson, and Joel Hanrahan as one of the best pitchers in the Dodgers' system.

ERIC "ICE COLD" GAGNE

Bats: R **Throws: R** Born: 07-Jan-76 Age: 28

YEAR	TM	LG	AGE	G	GS	IP	H	BB	SO	HR	ERA	EQERA	EQH9	EQBB9	EQSO9	EQHR9	PERA	VORP	STF
2001	LAD	NL	25	33	24	151.7	144	46	130	24	4.75	4.97	8.9	2.5	6.6	1.3	4.62	10.2	5
2002	LAD	NL	26	77	0	82.3	55	16	114	6	1.97	2.55	7.1	1.6	11.1	0.7	2.83	26.3	48
2003	LAD	NL	27	77	0	82.3	37	20	137	2	1.20	1.60	4.8	1.9	13.5	0.2	1.57	38.5	79
2004	LAD	NL	28	54	5	89.3	58	25	123	7	2.07	2.32	6.2	2.2	10.9	0.6	2.30	32.5	36
Breakout: 38%			Improve: 55%			Collapse: 31%													

Gagne had the greatest season in baseball history for a reliever, according to Clay Davenport's WARP numbers, holding the opposition to an ungodly .133/.196/.173 batting line in 82 innings of work. (To make a comparison, Cesar Izturis, arguably the worst everyday player in the major leagues last season, hit .251/.282/.315—massive compared to what Gagne allowed). There aren't many occasions when relief pitchers are objectively deserving of the Cy Young award, but this was one of those times, especially when you consider the high number of close, low-scoring games the Dodgers played in. Unlike Bobby Thigpen, Gagne's challenge of the single-season saves record was not a fluke, and he's likely to do it again, especially if the Dodgers are scrounging for runs in 2004. He'll fetch a mint once he hits the free agent market.

JOEL HANRAHAN

Bats: R   **Throws: R**   Born: 06-Oct-81   Age: 22

YEAR	TM	LG	AGE	G	GS	IP	H	BB	SO	HR	ERA	EQERA	EQH9	EQBB9	EQSO9	EQHR9	PERA	VORP	STF
2001	WNC	SAL	19	27	26	144.0	136	55	116	13	3.38	8.18	12.2	5.4	4.5	2.0	7.79	-34.7	-17
2002	VRO	FLA	20	25	25	143.7	129	51	139	11	4.20	5.52	9.9	3.9	6.3	1.5	5.66	1.2	16
2003	JAX	SOU	21	23	23	133.3	117	53	130	5	2.43	4.45	8.8	4.1	6.3	0.7	4.44	15.8	29
2003	LVG	PCL	21	5	5	25.0	36	20	13	2	10.08	9.49	10.9	8.0	4.4	0.7	6.44	-10.7	-10
2004	LAD	NL	22	19	12	67.3	73	40	48	11	5.99	6.71	10.3	4.7	5.7	1.3	6.54	-4.5	-11

Breakout: 2%   Improve: 49%   Collapse: 24%

Hanrahan succeeds with exceptional command of four solid pitches. Like Derek Lowe, he keeps the ball down, inducing a high number of ground balls to supplement his strong peripheral numbers. He's not as good as dominating as Edwin Jackson, or as young as Greg Miller, but he's in the same ballpark in terms of promise. Hanrahan finished the season in Triple-A Las Vegas, where he was beaten like a red-headed stepchild. We like his chances, but he'll need to cut down on the walks to get through Triple-A this time around. Credit the Dodgers with finding a gem in that noted hotbed of high school pitching, Norwalk, Iowa.

ERIC HULL

Bats: R   **Throws: R**   Born: 03-Dec-79   Age: 24

YEAR	TM	LG	AGE	G	GS	IP	H	BB	SO	HR	ERA	EQERA	EQH9	EQBB9	EQSO9	EQHR9	PERA	VORP	STF
2002	GRF	PIO	22	11	0	11.7	4	4	17	0	0.00	0.90	6.3	4.5	7.2	0.0	2.75	5.2	33
2002	SGA	SAL	22	13	0	22.0	22	6	13	1	2.05	4.66	11.6	3.3	3.3	0.9	5.77	2.0	-21
2003	VRO	FLA	23	31	14	110.7	82	40	105	9	2.68	4.47	10.1	4.4	6.2	2.5	7.09	11.9	-35
2004	LAD	NL	24	17	8	47.3	49	25	37	9	5.42	6.07	9.8	4.1	6.1	1.5	6.16	0.1	-9

Breakout: 27%   Improve: 65%   Collapse: 14%

Hull pitched well at Vero Beach, alternating between starts and relief appearances. His peripherals are strong, but he was a bit old for High-A at 23. He'll likely begin the year at Jacksonville as a reliever, and could get promoted quickly. Success against better competition will determine whether or not he'll be ready to contribute out of the bullpen in the near future.

KAZUHISA ISHII

Bats: L   **Throws: L**   Born: 09-Sep-73   Age: 30

YEAR	TM	LG	AGE	G	GS	IP	H	BB	SO	HR	ERA	EQERA	EQH9	EQBB9	EQSO9	EQHR9	PERA	VORP	STF
2001	YKL	JPC	27	27	27	175.0	135	82	173	18	0.00	4.67	8.7	4.5	7.5	1.2	4.94	16.3	2
2002	LAD	NL	28	28	28	154.0	137	106	143	20	4.27	5.62	9.0	5.5	7.3	1.2	5.42	-0.3	-2
2003	LAD	NL	29	27	27	147.0	129	101	140	16	3.86	5.03	8.6	5.6	7.6	1.0	5.03	13.6	6
2004	LAD	NL	30	21	18	103.3	98	68	97	15	5.17	5.79	9.0	5.2	7.4	1.1	5.91	4.9	4

Breakout: 22%   Improve: 53%   Collapse: 22%

Ishii is an above-average pitcher who survives because Dodger Stadium eats up most of the fly balls he allows. His K rate is strong, but he issues a ton of free passes—more than six (!) for every nine innings. At 30, it's unlikely that he's going to improve his peripherals any time soon. With a little bad luck, it wouldn't be all that shocking to see his ERA balloon into the 5.00s.

EDWIN JACKSON

Bats: R   **Throws: R**   Born: 09-Sep-83   Age: 20

YEAR	TM	LG	AGE	G	GS	IP	H	BB	SO	HR	ERA	EQERA	EQH9	EQBB9	EQSO9	EQHR9	PERA	VORP	STF
2002	SGA	SAL	18	19	19	104.7	79	33	85	2	1.98	4.36	7.9	3.8	4.7	0.4	3.60	13.1	32
2003	JAX	SOU	19	27	27	148.3	121	53	157	9	3.70	4.96	7.7	3.6	7.3	1.0	4.03	9.9	44
2003	LAD	NL	19	4	3	22.0	17	11	19	2	2.45	3.43	7.7	4.3	6.9	0.9	4.11	7.2	50
2004	LAD	NL	20	19	17	113.3	93	43	100	12	3.15	3.53	7.8	3.0	7.0	0.8	3.75	26.6	19

Breakout: 38%   Improve: 66%   Collapse: 4%

Some people consider Jackson to be the best pitcher under 21 in professional baseball. It's easy to understand why: After a full-season at Double-A Jacksonville at the age of 19 (where he struck out more than a batter per inning, and posted a K:BB ratio of three-to-one), Jackson debuted in Dodger Stadium on his 20th birthday, whereupon he beat Randy Johnson. Drafted out of out high school in 2001 as an outfielder, Jackson throws in the mid-90s with a good slider. He'll need to improve upon his other pitches before he can dominate major league hitters, but he's not far away. The fact that he'll spend his first six years in the spacious Dodger Stadium bodes well for his chances at developing into a top-tier pitcher.

TOM MARTIN   Bats: L   Throws: L   Born: 21-May-70   Age: 34

YEAR	TM	LG	AGE	G	GS	IP	H	BB	SO	HR	ERA	EQERA	EQH9	EQBB9	EQSO9	EQHR9	PERA	VORP	STF
2001	NOR	INT	31	23	0	23.0	31	10	24	4	6.26	8.27	14.4	4.8	7.4	2.2	8.73	-6.1	-62
2003	LAD	NL	33	80	0	51.0	36	24	51	6	3.53	3.88	7.0	3.9	8.1	1.1	3.92	9.1	5
2004	LAD	NL	34	44	0	50.0	49	23	47	7	4.73	5.30	9.3	3.6	7.5	1.1	5.15	3.1	0

Breakout: 29%   Improve: 56%   Collapse: 21%

Martin was the least-heralded member of the Dodger bullpen last season, with a mid-3.00s ERA that looked astronomical compared to his peers' numbers. Nevertheless, he was among the league's best at preventing inherited runners from scoring, as reflected in Michael Wolverton's Reliever Reports at www.baseballprospectus.com. A non-roster invitee at the beginning of 2003, the Dodger front office signed Martin to a two-year, $3 million deal at the end of the season. Even given his 2003 success, you'd think Martin's own humble beginnings would clue management into figuring out that others can be had for a similar low cost. Apparently not.

GREG MILLER   Bats: L   Throws: L   Born: 03-Nov-84   Age: 19

YEAR	TM	LG	AGE	G	GS	IP	H	BB	SO	HR	ERA	EQERA	EQH9	EQBB9	EQSO9	EQHR9	PERA	VORP	STF
2002	GRF	PIO	17	11	7	38.0	27	13	37	1	2.37	4.46	7.9	4.2	4.7	0.5	3.86	4.3	22
2003	VRO	FLA	18	21	21	115.7	103	41	111	5	2.49	4.82	9.1	4.0	6.8	1.0	4.80	9.2	39
2003	JAX	SOU	18	4	4	26.7	15	7	40	1	1.01	2.55	6.2	2.6	10.6	0.7	2.76	8.4	90
2004	LAD	NL	19	18	15	94	88	35	77	12	4.06	4.55	8.9	2.9	6.4	1.0	4.53	9.8	10

Breakout: 35%   Improve: 44%   Collapse: 21%

(There is no such thing as a pitching prospect.) Greg Miller hit the ground running at high-A Vero Beach, posting an ERA of 2.49 with strong peripherals as just an 18-year-old. (There is no such thing as a pitching prospect.) What really sets him apart, however, is the way he pitched upon being promoted to Double-A at the end of the season. (There is no such thing as a pitching prospect.) There, in 26.2 innings of work, Miller struck out 40 hitters while only walking seven—outstanding for anyone, but especially so for the youngest hurler in the league. (There is no such thing as a pitching prospect.) There's some concern about his reliance on breaking balls at this point, and some scouts think that will lead to arm trouble down the road. (There is no such thing as a pitching prospect.) Nevertheless, it's tough to ignore his performance thus far, especially against older competition. (There is no such thing as a pitching prospect.) Along with Cole Hamels of Philadelphia and Zack Greinke of Kansas City, he's a young one to watch.

GUILLERMO MOTA   Bats: R   Throws: R   Born: 25-Jul-73   Age: 30

YEAR	TM	LG	AGE	G	GS	IP	H	BB	SO	HR	ERA	EQERA	EQH9	EQBB9	EQSO9	EQHR9	PERA	VORP	STF
2001	MON	NL	27	53	0	49.7	51	18	31	9	5.25	4.84	8.8	3.0	4.7	1.5	4.94	4.1	-27
2002	LVG	PCL	28	20	0	36.7	34	8	38	1	2.94	3.34	8.5	2.3	6.9	0.3	3.31	8.8	22
2002	LAD	NL	28	43	0	60.7	45	27	49	4	4.15	4.40	7.5	3.6	6.4	0.6	3.62	7.6	7
2003	LAD	NL	29	76	0	105.0	78	26	99	7	1.97	2.62	7.3	2.1	7.7	0.6	3.06	40.7	26
2004	LAD	NL	30	53	4	80.3	71	25	68	8	3.30	3.70	8.3	2.5	6.7	0.8	3.78	17.1	6

Breakout: 33%   Improve: 55%   Collapse: 19%

In last year's book we said the following about Mota: "A converted shortstop, the Dodgers can always hope he's a late bloomer." Boy, did Mota bloom. He was among the best relievers in the National League in 2003, posting an ERA of 1.97 over 105 innings of work. Yes, this came virtually out of nowhere, but there are indicators to suggest that this wasn't a fluke: Mota's peripherals were outstanding, both at home and on the road, for instance. PECOTA thinks he'll take a bit of a step back, but we think the improvement is real. He's a taller, slightly older version of Octavio Dotel. Expect him to pitch that way going forward.

HIDEO NOMO   Bats: R   Throws: R   Born: 31-Aug-68   Age: 35

YEAR	TM	LG	AGE	G	GS	IP	H	BB	SO	HR	ERA	EQERA	EQH9	EQBB9	EQSO9	EQHR9	PERA	VORP	STF
2001	BOS	AL	32	33	33	198.0	171	96	220	26	4.50	3.92	7.4	4.0	9.2	1.1	4.07	36.4	29
2002	LAD	NL	33	34	34	220.3	189	101	193	26	3.39	4.62	8.7	3.7	7.0	1.1	4.68	22.7	9
2003	LAD	NL	34	33	33	218.3	175	98	177	24	3.09	3.94	7.8	3.7	6.6	1.0	4.18	47.4	12
2004	LAD	NL	35	29	28	177.3	163	79	148	23	4.13	4.63	8.7	3.5	6.6	1.0	4.77	20.2	11

Breakout: 19%   Improve: 47%   Collapse: 19%

(continued next page)

Hideo Nomo (continued)

Nomo again gave the Dodgers 220 exceptional innings, making his contract look like a bargain. And yet, he's 35, and his Equivalent Strikeout Rate has dropped by more than 25% over the last two seasons—variables that PECOTA thinks will contribute to a sizable bump in his ERA, as well as a decrease in his innings. It's hard to believe that Nomo's been in North America for nine seasons now, especially following those years in his early-30s when his velocity was down, and he was bouncing from team-to-team. All the while, however, his strikeout rate remained at a respectable level, thanks to a good splitter and a tornado-like motion that still seems to confuse hitters.

ODALIS PEREZ — Bats: L — Throws: L — Born: 11-Jun-77 — Age: 27

YEAR	TM	LG	AGE	G	GS	IP	H	BB	SO	HR	ERA	EQERA	EQH9	EQBB9	EQSO9	EQHR9	PERA	VORP	STF
2001	RIC	INT	24	5	5	23.0	23	2	22	1	2.74	3.38	10.1	0.8	6.8	0.4	3.78	5.3	36
2001	ATL	NL	24	24	16	95.3	108	39	71	7	4.91	5.34	10.7	3.5	5.7	0.6	4.97	2.6	12
2002	LAD	NL	25	32	32	222.3	182	38	155	21	3.00	3.64	8.2	1.4	5.6	0.9	3.58	45.2	21
2003	LAD	NL	26	30	30	185.3	191	46	141	28	4.52	5.12	9.9	2.0	6.2	1.4	5.08	9.3	1
2004	LAD	NL	27	27	25	168.3	164	43	121	19	3.60	4.03	9.2	2.0	5.7	0.8	4.12	29.3	13

Breakout: 24%   Improve: 56%   Collapse: 15%

Where in 2002 Perez was among the luckiest pitchers in MLB—allowing one of the league's lowest BABIP (Batting Average on Balls In Play) figures—last season he regressed to the mean, despite maintaining excellent walk and strikeout numbers. That gaudy home runs-allowed total played a big role in his regression. The Dodgers have been discussing dealing Perez for a mid-level bat all off-season. He could go either way in 2004: Perez does the important things well, like keeping runners off base, but that home run rate could be a killer. He could easily return to ace level in 2004, or put up numbers more befitting a fifth starter.

BRIAN PILKINGTON — Bats: R — Throws: R — Born: 17-Sep-82 — Age: 21

YEAR	TM	LG	AGE	G	GS	IP	H	BB	SO	HR	ERA	EQERA	EQH9	EQBB9	EQSO9	EQHR9	PERA	VORP	STF
2001	GRF	PIO	18	5	2	16.0	19	2	17	2	5.63	6.28	13.2	1.9	5.0	2.5	8.00	-1.1	-14
2002	SGA	SAL	19	20	18	112.3	129	13	78	8	3.45	6.97	12.6	1.4	3.9	1.6	6.50	-15.3	-2
2002	VRO	FLA	19	3	3	19.0	16	3	10	2	2.37	4.08	8.7	1.5	3.6	2.0	5.12	3.0	2
2003	VRO	FLA	20	21	21	125.3	136	16	74	9	3.88	5.85	11.9	1.4	3.9	1.9	6.57	-3.1	-6
2003	JAX	SOU	20	5	5	32.3	31	2	24	3	3.34	4.75	9.2	0.6	5.0	1.5	4.42	2.9	20
2004	LAD	NL	21	19	13	81.7	89	18	46	14	4.52	5.07	10.4	1.7	4.4	1.3	5.19	5.1	-4

Breakout: 13%   Improve: 48%   Collapse: 5%

Pilkington features outstanding control, but is inconsistent with his stuff. Scouts are divided on how to rate him; on some days he'll throw in the 88–92 MPH range, and on others he'll be as far down as 84–88. Either way, Pilkington hasn't dominated hitters like some of his fellow Dodger farmhands have, despite excellent K/BB ratios all throughout the minor leagues. He's a future reliever, most likely—even when his slider is on, he simply doesn't miss enough bats to take on major league hitters for six or seven innings at a time.

PAUL QUANTRILL — Bats: L — Throws: R — Born: 03-Nov-68 — Age: 35

YEAR	TM	LG	AGE	G	GS	IP	H	BB	SO	HR	ERA	EQERA	EQH9	EQBB9	EQSO9	EQHR9	PERA	VORP	STF
2001	TOR	AL	32	80	0	83.0	86	12	58	6	3.04	3.22	8.8	1.2	5.9	0.6	3.43	21.4	16
2002	LAD	NL	33	86	0	76.7	80	25	53	1	2.70	4.12	10.4	2.6	5.6	0.1	4.13	11.8	13
2003	LAD	NL	34	89	0	77.3	61	15	44	2	1.75	2.59	7.6	1.6	4.7	0.2	2.76	28.8	16
2004	NYY	AL	35	52	0	60.3	66	15	37	6	4.07	4.19	9.7	2.2	5.3	0.9	4.38	11.2	-5

Breakout: 21%   Improve: 45%   Collapse: 37%

A poor man's Chad Bradford, Quantrill keeps the ball on the ground and in the ballpark. Unfortunately, just like with Kevin Brown, keeping the ball on the ground isn't exactly an asset for the Yankees, and thus Quantrill will likely see a big jump in his number of hits allowed next season. He'll be roughly the same pitcher for the life of his new contract, no matter what his ERA (and his back account statement) looks like.

ORLANDO RODRIGUEZ   Bats: L   Throws: L   Born: 28-Nov-80   Age: 23

YEAR	TM	LG	AGE	G	GS	IP	H	BB	SO	HR	ERA	EQERA	EQH9	EQBB9	EQSO9	EQHR9	PERA	VORP	STF
2001	GRF	PIO	20	15	10	60.7	58	26	79	11	4.15	6.71	13.1	6.0	6.5	4.2	11.16	-6.3	-62
2002	SGA	SAL	21	20	0	28.3	12	10	42	0	0.00	0.37	6.7	4.4	8.1	0.4	3.20	14.1	41
2002	VRO	FLA	21	7	0	7.0	6	3	10	0	0.00	0.00	9.9	4.3	8.5	0.0	4.21	3.9	50
2003	JAX	SOU	22	11	0	12.0	10	7	14	1	3.75	5.06	10.1	5.9	7.6	1.7	6.53	0.6	-10

Rodriguez is another tiny flamethrower in the Dodgers' system—a lefty who dials it up into the mid-90s with a decent slider. He'll begin the year in Jacksonville with a chance at closing.

PAUL SHUEY   Bats: R   Throws: R   Born: 16-Sep-70   Age: 33

YEAR	TM	LG	AGE	G	GS	IP	H	BB	SO	HR	ERA	EQERA	EQH9	EQBB9	EQSO9	EQHR9	PERA	VORP	STF
2001	CLE	AL	30	47	0	54.3	53	26	70	1	2.82	3.50	8.2	3.8	10.5	0.2	3.46	12.6	45
2002	CLE	AL	31	39	0	37.3	31	10	39	1	2.41	2.43	6.8	2.2	8.8	0.2	2.51	13.0	42
2002	LAD	NL	31	28	0	30.7	25	21	24	2	4.40	5.52	8.3	5.5	6.1	0.6	4.48	0.3	-7
2003	LAD	NL	32	62	0	69.0	50	33	60	6	3.00	3.55	7.1	4.0	7.1	0.8	3.69	17.1	7
2004	LAD	NL	33	51	0	60.3	52	27	52	3	3.32	3.72	8.2	3.6	6.8	0.4	3.85	11.9	3

Breakout: 30%   Improve: 53%   Collapse: 36%

Despite improved peripherals, Shuey's ERA ballooned in the second half of last season, from 1.88 before the All-Star break to 4.40 after the break. The reason? A string of rough outings in the middle of July—two of which came at Coors Field—and a couple of one-inning beatings at the end of August. Otherwise, Shuey was an outstanding setup man for Jim Tracy, consistently taking the ball for more than an inning at a time before handing things off to Gagne. He'll remain in the same role for 2004.

Milwaukee Brewers

If constant success has left Yankees fans emotionally shallow, consider the fate of Brewers fans for the last dozen years. It's been a long, dim, squalid time in the history of Milwaukee baseball . . . so it's refreshing to finally report that the times are finally changing.

In part, a potential renaissance was expected with the firing of Sal Bando in 1999. It was a false spring; the timorous manner in which the Brewers embraced change was exemplified by their hiring a front office cipher, Dean Taylor, to be their new general manager. At least they'd hauled Taylor in from outside the Seligs' clutch of hometown cronies, but promoting Bud's daughter to an active role in the club's day-to-day affairs could hardly inspire confidence.

Less than three years later, Taylor was out, and the Brewers finally came to terms with the realization that they were awful. It was the acme of arrogance that they had taken this long to realize the obvious, but their priority for most of the '90s had been getting a new stadium, and to help them get it, they told the fashionable lie that a new ballpark would afford them better talent. As is often the case in situations like these—more often than cynics care to believe—the Brewers really thought they were getting better.

It's to their credit as an organization that they identified growing problems in terms of credibility and results with the management triumvirate of Wendy Selig-Prieb, Taylor, and Davey Lopes, and also to their credit that they made a clean sweep of all three in 2002. None of them had demonstrated any vision for improving the ballclub. Lopes had earned his shot to manage, and had subsequently earned his firing with his fascination with baserunning and deadball-era tactics. Taylor had spent money haphazardly, but had at least left behind some aspect of a promising legacy for having brought in Jack Zduriencik in a player development role, and acquiring Richie Sexson from the Indians in a package for Bob Wickman.

So the Brewers finally did the right thing, they turned the organization over to actual professionals. Not family members, empty suits, or famous ex-Brewers. Doug Melvin came in with a track record of success from his days in Texas. He'd inherited the disappointments of the Grieve era, and helped oversee the team's leap into contention. He brought with him Reid Nichols, a successful player development sidekick from Texas, and he retained Zduriencik,

BREWERS PROSPECTUS

2003 record: 68–94; Sixth place, NL Central

Pythagenport record: 65–97

Runs scored per game: 4.4 (10th in NL)

Runs allowed per game: 5.4 (14th in NL)

Team EqA: .261 (7th in NL)

2003 Batters Age: 30.3 (8th oldest in NL)

2003 Pitchers Age: 28.1 (7th youngest in NL)

Ballpark: Miller Park; Neutral park; Park Factor of 0.995

2003: Never a factor, the Brewers slide to their 11th straight losing season.

2004: The farm system's in good shape, but absurd self-imposed budget constraints will make it tough for this team to contend.

recognizing the virtue of having both on hand to help him rebuild the organization.

Coming into 2003, Melvin could have done what Taylor had, and spent some money splashily, generating false promise and perhaps exacerbating the local malaise. Instead, he was far more pragmatic. Beyond inherited talent, the 2003 Brewers were built on no-names assembled cheaply. Whether you want to call it an appreciation for freely-available talent, or good scouting, or singling out journeymen with nothing to lose, Melvin hauled in a big chunk of what would become a much-improved team, and he did it for less than $6 million all told.

His "big-ticket" free agents were Royce Clayton, Todd Ritchie, and John Vander Wal, and they barely added up to $3 million put together. He made deals, stealing Wes Helms for Ray King, and picking up Matt Kinney and Javier Valentin from the Twins. One of the advantages to inheriting a weak organization is that you get to treat the waiver wire as a personal cafeteria. The Brewers claimed Scott Podsednik and Brady Clark off waivers. In addition to acquiring Valentin, he grabbed two cheap veterans, Eddie Perez and Keith Osik, on non-roster-invites, spending less than a million bucks on the two of them; he also took a flyer on minor league vet Cody McKay. He committed a couple of roster spots to Rule 5 picks, holding onto lefty Matt Ford and infielder Enrique Cruz all year. He added minor league vets like Leo Estrella, Brooks Kieschnick,

Danny Kolb, Pasqual Coco, Scott Seabol, and Tim Crabtree. During the season, he would add more arms in minor dumps, unloading journeymen like Curtis Leskanic and Mike DeJean while adding Wes Obermueller and Mike Crudale, and also claiming Doug Davis on waivers.

When you're desperate, you learn that one man's garbage is another man's cuisine. A season's worth of dumpster diving didn't cost much, and it generated mixed results. Valentin flopped, and Ritchie got hurt. The catching situation was obviously a quick fix, not a solution; so too was Clayton at short. Kinney and the platoon in right field were merely adequate. But more importantly, none of the disappointments were crippling, not in the way a Hammonds deal is debilitating where the bottom line was concerned.

Better still, despite a ramshackle rotation (bested or worsted by only the Rangers for ineptitude) and a pen that was in transition all summer, this team improved, in large part thanks to the scrap heap gang. Helms and Podsednik and Kolb turned out to be the low-cost stars of the New Crew. They were the sorts of guys who hadn't caught a lot of breaks, and who are too old to be legitimate prospects. But they were also old enough and experienced enough to be ready, and instead of spending hand over fist to garner some marginal improvement, Yost and Melvin built a better team that had their stamp on it. No contrast was more stark than the one drawn by the early in-season switch in center field from one of Davey Lopes's pet projects, basepath commando Alex Sanchez, to Yost's plain old ballplayer, Podsednik.

Clearly, these types of gains are limited, and aren't the foundation of a much-improved franchise. What the big league team represented was mostly ceremonial cover for what Zduriencik has been working at for a couple of years, and what Nichols has joined him in helping fix: the organization's farm system. Five years ago, the Brewers were in the deepest hole of any player development program in baseball. That's no longer the case. Although Indianapolis, like Milwaukee, was stocked with temps, from Huntsville on down, the organization has put together a reasonable base of talent from which it can reasonably hope to build a better bunch of Brewers. The 2000–2003 drafts have brought the team a better collection of swag than the previous 15 years' efforts.

For starters, their blue-chip prospects are getting their due. Corey Hart, Prince Fielder, and Lou Palmisano all won their league's MVP awards in 2003. J. J. Hardy and Dave Krynzel were easy selections for the best defensive players at shortstop and center field (respectively) in the Southern League. Huntsville, High Desert, and Beloit all had promising arms on their pitching staffs, highlighted by Manny Parra, Dennis Sarfate, and Mike Jones.

The rush to congratulate the Brewers as an organization is still premature though, perhaps a testament to the success of baseball's campaign to intimidate and co-opt the fourth estate that has been merely one noisome aspect of the Selig regime. Getting off the short list for baseball's biggest laughingstock is progress, but the Brewers still have a long, long, long way to go.

For starters, despite the small core of top prospects, it still isn't a deep farm system. You can count the names with real promise in the system on your fingers. The Brewers have been aggressive about trying to create some esprit de corps within the organization's slender pickings, keeping the core of the Double-A Huntsville Stars together, and adding Brad Nelson to the group despite his bum wrist. Similarly, they had their top picks of 2003, Rickie Weeks and Tony Gwynn Jr., join Fielder in Beloit. Since Huntsville and Beloit were also bound for the playoffs, it's a good experience for all concerned.

If there's a problem, it's that the Brewers are too ambitious with their promotions. The sucking vacuum that seems to flow from the draft boards up through Indianapolis all the way to Milwaukee is endangering a few too many prospects. Ben Diggins was brought up way too soon in 2002, and was damaged by it; he won't be back from Tommy John surgery until 2005. Pitchers like Mike Jones and Parra and Ben Hendrickson need to be handled carefully, lest they break down as quickly as Diggins and Nick Neugebauer did. Among the hitters, Krynzel and Hardy and Nelson have all been pushed up the chain quickly, increasing the likelihood that one of them flames out early. Bill Hall arrived so soon and so raw that when he came up in 2002 people wondered whether he'd gotten any coaching on his defense at all. On that front, Reid Nichols has his work cut out for him, since assembling a quality minor league coaching cadre isn't the sort of thing you achieve overnight.

The Brewers have an even larger problem to combat, which is that of their credibility. If the 11 years since the firing of Harry Dalton have been a dark age for Milwaukee baseball, the problem with finally letting in a little light is that it suddenly reminds people that the recent past has been murky and miserable, highlighted by the hornswoggling of the entire southeastern corner of the state to finance a charmless mallpark with a moonroof. The relationship between the Seligs and their hirelings and the community they prey upon is a relationship akin to having the Cossacks sing "Do You Love Me?" before sacking the town in *Fiddler on the Roof*.

The relationship hit a new low this fall. Team president Ulice Payne had been brought in to inspire faith and hope, in part because he notionally represented a break from the team's traditional cronyism. He inspired that faith, right up to the point when he came clean about the team's consideration of a new round of payroll cuts. That uncomfortable bit of truth led to his resignation; the organization may have improved itself significantly, but honesty is still not the best policy in Beertown. Although the Brewers are claiming they'll open their books, they're being squirrelly on who sees them, asking for three of Bud's brethren from the business community, while the voters and politicians who built the Seligs Miller Park are asking for someone in state or local government to have a look. Beyond the broken promises of what the ballpark would provide, the memory of a few ugly graftastic aspects of the Miller Park project still linger. The situation reached took an interesting turn when the Seligs claimed they were going to sell; Carl Pohlad's been selling the Twins for a decade, so don't hold your breath.

It's unfortunate that the current baseball operations team gets tarred with the rest of the organization's past. It isn't likely that the size of the team's big league payroll is going to have much relationship to a lasting reconstruction. You would have thought that fans and the local media would not so quickly forget the pointless expense of players like Jeffrey Hammonds, Mark Loretta, Cal Eldred, Glendon Rusch, or Jamey Wright. Does anyone think another hefty millstone-like Burnitz contract is what this team needs? The Brewers have already bottomed out and should keep getting better. To lash out at the team because of ownership's incorrigible oiliness would be unfair, and more than a little self-spiting. If anything is hanging in the balance, it's the team's freedom of action to deal Geoff Jenkins. Setting aside whatever message fans might infer from a Jenkins deal, he's nearing free agency, already costs an oversized chunk of change, and he breaks down almost as easily as J. D. Drew. If that isn't a guy you want to deal when the right offer comes along, nobody is. Do the people of Milwaukee really win if they somehow acquire the power, real or moral, to force the Brewers to keep someone like Jenkins?

Minding his own business, Melvin is sticking with what worked last year. If there's a significant action item, it's fixing the pitching staff. On that front, the bullpen has real promise. They'll open the year with Kolb closing, with guys like Mike Crudale and Travis Phelps challenging for setup roles. Luis Vizcaino can't be anywhere near as bad as he was last year. This year's Rule 5 pick, Jeff Bennett, throws hard, naturally enough. A rotation of Ben Sheets, and some foursome from among Doug Davis, Matt Kinney, Wayne Franklin, Wes Obermueller, Dave Burba, Luis Martinez, and Chris Capuano isn't going to set the league on its ear. Nevertheless, there's hope; Sheets and Kinney could both keep improving, and Capuano is something of a sleeper.

Melvin also moved boldly in the one area he could: He dealt the last year he had Richie Sexson under contract for what he could get, bringing in a good lefty arm in Jorge De la Rosa, as well as another gaggle of serviceable temps to fill out the roster. Acquiring Chad Moeller, Junior Spivey, Craig Counsell, and Lyle Overbay isn't supposed to produce a team that will improve by another 12 games, but it will keep something resembling a big league team on the field until the prospects are ready. When players like Nelson and Weeks and Hardy and Corey Hart are ready to step in by 2005, the Brewers will have avoided any frivolous transitional commitments in the meantime.

That's when the good folks in Milwaukee will get a team they deserve, built by people with a sense of what they're doing. If Zduriencik keeps putting together sound drafts, and even unearths a superstar along the line, it isn't hard to envision a team built around his draft picks and Melvin's big league pickups contending by 2006. It helps being in a weak division, but better they keep building from the ground up.

HITTERS

BRADY CLARK   OF   Bats: R   Throws: R   Born: 18-Apr-73   Age: 31

YEAR	TM	LG	AGE	AB	H	2B	3B	HR	BB	SO	SB	CS	AVG	OBP	SLG	MLVR	EQBA	EQOBP	EQSLG	EQMLVR	VORP	DEFENSE	
2001	CIN	NL	28	129	34	3	0	6	22	16	4	1	.264	.373	.426	.037	.260	.365	.427	.020	2.8	13-LF -1	
2001	LOU	INT	28	167	44	5	1	2	18	17	6	2	.263	.354	.341	-.037	.249	.331	.325	-.191	-6.4	35-RF 1	
2002	CIN	NL	29	66	10	3	0	0	6	9	1	2	.152	.233	.197	-.507	.164	.232	.224	-.572	-7.7		
2002	LOU	INT	29	109	33	7	0	1	3	9	0	2	.303	.328	.394	.013	.284	.319	.376	-.119	-1.9	22-LF 1	
2003	IND	INT	30	34	9	3	0	0	2	6	1	0	.265	.306	.353	-.101	.235	.278	.353	-.265	-1.4		
2003	MIL	NL	30	315	86	21	1	6	21	40	13	2	.273	.330	.403	-.010	.282	.339	.417	-.024	4.7	56-RF -2	17-LF -2
2004	MIL	NL	31	214	55	11	1	4	18	29	5	2	.257	.324	.367	-.121	.259	.323	.367	-.133	-0.7	59-RF -2	

Breakout: 16%   Improve: 34%   Collapse: 42%

Clark finally got his long-deserved chance to stick in the bigs as a Brewer, serving as John Vander Wal's platoon partner in right, and handling a lot of the pinch-hitting duties. He'll handle the same role in right with Ben Grieve this year. Clark isn't a platoon monster, but he can make contact well enough and handle all three outfield positions. Why he wasn't somebody's fourth outfielder long before this defies explanation, but now that he's on the wrong side of 30, his career horizon is already running up on him.

DARYL CLARK

DARYL CLARK LF **Bats: L** **Throws: R** Born: 25-Sep-79 Age: 24

YEAR	TM	LG	AGE	AB	H	2B	3B	HR	BB	SO	SB	CS	AVG	OBP	SLG	MLVR	EQBA	EQOBP	EQSLG	EQMLVR	VORP	DEFENSE	
2001	BLT	MID	21	501	142	24	2	21	61	135	4	5	.283	.364	.465	.179	.207	.273	.345	-.303	-19.9	120-3B -30	
2002	HDS	CAL	22	340	83	18	2	19	58	117	4	5	.244	.352	.476	.075	.166	.257	.323	-.387	-22.5	50-3B -19	17-LF -3
2003	HDS	CAL	23	191	60	6	5	14	32	51	1	2	.314	.412	.618	.382	.206	.291	.413	-.177	-7.6	45-LF -5	
2003	HUN	SOU	23	202	47	11	1	2	40	62	6	1	.233	.363	.327	-.011	.204	.309	.294	-.301	-17.3	43-LF -5	
2004	*MIL*	*NL*	*24*	*230*	*50*	*11*	*1*	*9*	*28*	*68*	*2*	*1*	*.218*	*.305*	*.392*	*-.147*	*.219*	*.305*	*.392*	*-.160*	*-3.3*	*65-LF -5*	

Breakout: 45%   Improve: 68%   Collapse: 16%

Finally moved away from his hot corner follies, this Clark got to put in a full season in the outfield, and continued to do the things he does well, showing some modest power potential and taking a few pitches. He'll need to hit with more authority at Double-A to earn some sort of slender prospect status, but in the meantime he's a solid organizational soldier.

ROYCE CLAYTON

ROYCE CLAYTON SS **Bats: R** **Throws: R** Born: 02-Jan-70 Age: 34

YEAR	TM	LG	AGE	AB	H	2B	3B	HR	BB	SO	SB	CS	AVG	OBP	SLG	MLVR	EQBA	EQOBP	EQSLG	EQMLVR	VORP	DEFENSE
2001	CWS	AL	31	433	114	21	4	9	33	72	10	7	.263	.315	.393	-.084	.279	.336	.419	-.029	19.7	121-SS 11
2002	CWS	AL	32	342	86	14	2	7	20	67	5	1	.251	.295	.365	-.152	.268	.315	.394	-.113	7.8	99-SS 10
2003	MIL	NL	33	483	110	16	1	11	49	92	5	2	.228	.301	.333	-.186	.233	.305	.344	-.226	-3.5	136-SS 9
2004	*COL*	*NL*	*34*	*290*	*73*	*13*	*1*	*6*	*25*	*53*	*4*	*2*	*.253*	*.316*	*.371*	*-.133*	*.244*	*.306*	*.355*	*-.192*	*1.8*	*78-SS 2*

Breakout: 30%   Improve: 52%   Collapse: 30%

Clayton's hitting is bad enough that he's not even as much of a hoped-for intentional walk as you might want in the eighth slot; opposing pitchers and managers can generally take it for granted that they can knock the bat out of his hands at will. He isn't even hitting lefties with any authority any more. What he did do right was give the Brewers a regular while Bill Hall and J. J. Hardy got development time. He'll mark time with the Rockies, on the basis of his defensive skills, but the odds of Clayton being a useful regular on a good team are nil.

JASON CONTI

JASON CONTI OF **Bats: L** **Throws: R** Born: 27-Jan-75 Age: 29

YEAR	TM	LG	AGE	AB	H	2B	3B	HR	BB	SO	SB	CS	AVG	OBP	SLG	MLVR	EQBA	EQOBP	EQSLG	EQMLVR	VORP	DEFENSE	
2001	TUC	PCL	26	362	120	23	6	9	33	54	2	5	.331	.402	.503	.211	.279	.348	.423	-.002	16.4	82-CF -4	
2001	DUR	INT	26	157	48	12	0	5	9	31	3	1	.306	.347	.478	.169	.289	.330	.453	.017	7.6	30-CF -3	
2002	TBY	AL	27	222	57	15	2	3	18	55	4	2	.257	.315	.383	-.080	.281	.340	.420	-.019	2.7	26-RF -3	24-CF -2
2003	IND	INT	28	456	113	17	3	10	24	120	13	8	.248	.295	.364	-.115	.230	.281	.349	-.268	-16.5	115-CF 6	
2003	MIL	NL	28	48	11	2	0	2	2	18	0	1	.229	.255	.396	-.182	.229	.260	.396	-.243	-1.6	12-RF -2	
2004	*TEX*	*AL*	*29*	*210*	*54*	*10*	*2*	*6*	*16*	*47*	*4*	*2*	*.256*	*.319*	*.401*	*-.073*	*.249*	*.316*	*.391*	*-.123*	*1.3*	*58-CF -2*	

Breakout: 37%   Improve: 57%   Collapse: 30%

There was a moment when Conti looked like he'd win a job, but he got caught in the miseries of tweenerdom. At his best, he'd hit enough to have been an asset as a regular in center, but he's not quite a good center fielder. He has the arm for right, but he was never going to be enough of a hitter to stick in a corner. Now he's lost his peak years to near-misses. He can still help a team as a fifth outfielder if the starter in right is some immobile slugger, but the Cubs weren't interested. With the Rangers, he may stick as a reserve because of his shared roots in the D-Backs' organization with Buck Showalter.

ENRIQUE CRUZ

ENRIQUE CRUZ 3B/SS **Bats: R** **Throws: R** Born: 21-Nov-81 Age: 22

YEAR	TM	LG	AGE	AB	H	2B	3B	HR	BB	SO	SB	CS	AVG	OBP	SLG	MLVR	EQBA	EQOBP	EQSLG	EQMLVR	VORP	DEFENSE	
2001	CMB	SAL	19	438	110	20	2	9	59	106	33	7	.251	.346	.368	.063	.195	.268	.292	-.392	-31.3	102-3B -4	22-SS -5
2002	SLU	FLA	20	467	136	21	2	6	32	76	33	16	.291	.336	.383	.066	.247	.283	.335	-.273	-13.1	103-3B -7	21-SS -5
2003	MIL	NL	21	71	6	1	0	0	4	30	0	0	.085	.145	.099	-.845	.099	.156	.127	-.882	-11.8		
2004	*MIL*	*NL*	*22*	*173*	*39*	*8*	*1*	*4*	*14*	*40*	*5*	*1*	*.226*	*.287*	*.352*	*-.225*	*.228*	*.287*	*.352*	*-.239*	*2.7*	*49-3B -2*	

Breakout: 78%   Improve: 90%   Collapse: 8%

Well, there it was. Was Cruz worth a Rule 5 pick? The Brewers certainly had the roster space, he had hit well in the Florida State League at a young age, and even with a lost year on a big league bench, he'd be able to go back to Double-A in '04 with a lot of career ahead of him. Cruz might have the tools for short, but he desperately needs the playing time there if it's going to work out. If he's a third baseman, he'll have to do a whole lot of hitting, and the decision gets a little more iffy. The extent to which nobody knows what to expect is reflected in nobody claiming him when the Brewers outrighted him after the season.

PRINCE FIELDER   **1B/DH**   **Bats: L**   **Throws: R**   Born: 09-May-84   Age: 20

YEAR	TM	LG	AGE	AB	H	2B	3B	HR	BB	SO	SB	CS	AVG	OBP	SLG	MLVR	EQBA	EQOBP	EQSLG	EQMLVR	VORP	DEFENSE	
2002	OGD	PIO	18	146	57	12	0	10	37	27	3	4	.390	.531	.678	.749	.205	.310	.363	-.208	-11.6	35-1B	-9
2002	BLT	MID	18	112	27	7	0	3	10	27	0	0	.241	.320	.384	.015	.191	.246	.313	-.410	-11.5	30-1B	-8
2003	BLT	MID	19	502	157	22	2	27	71	80	2	1	.313	.409	.526	.369	.229	.305	.400	-.152	-11.4	125-1B	-15
2004	MIL	NL	20	312	67	14	1	12	32	65	1	1	.216	.298	.377	-.180	.217	.297	.378	-.194	-7.3	85-1B	-12

Breakout: 25%   *Improve: 57%*   *Collapse: 26%*

There's very little you shouldn't expect from Fielder at the plate for the next decade. He's patient, has power, and knows how to go with a pitch. Having learned to keep his weight back, Fielder has started to develop all-field power. Why not? With his natural heft, he gets more power into a late swing than any teenager on the planet. Given that there's considerable concern that his best position is going to be DH, he worked with Don Money on his glovework. The Brewers feel he improved as the season wore on. He's not the jellyroll you might remember from those high school video clips, but he's not Glenn Braggs yet either; he's making progress, and we'll just have to see how that turns out. He still needs to make the jump to Double-A, but that should happen at some point this year. The real question is at what point he'll get a shot at the big leagues, but don't get over-eager—it won't be this year.

KEITH GINTER   **UT**   **Bats: R**   **Throws: R**   Born: 05-May-76   Age: 28

YEAR	TM	LG	AGE	AB	H	2B	3B	HR	BB	SO	SB	CS	AVG	OBP	SLG	MLVR	EQBA	EQOBP	EQSLG	EQMLVR	VORP	DEFENSE			
2001	NWO	PCL	25	457	123	31	5	16	61	147	8	6	.269	.380	.464	.142	.247	.346	.426	-.027	23.1	86-2B	-6	30-LF	-2
2002	NWO	PCL	26	435	115	28	1	12	56	97	3	4	.264	.362	.416	.074	.247	.332	.393	-.098	10.4	56-2B	-9	53-3B	1
2002	MIL	NL	26	76	18	8	0	1	15	14	0	0	.237	.363	.382	.009	.247	.370	.390	-.030	3.4	20-3B	-3		
2003	MIL	NL	27	358	92	15	2	14	37	87	1	1	.257	.352	.427	.048	.264	.353	.441	.020	17.8	47-2B	-1	32-3B	-6
2004	MIL	NL	28	328	84	18	1	12	37	78	2	1	.257	.354	.431	.013	.258	.353	.432	.003	22.0	92-2B	-6		

Breakout: 30%   *Improve: 53%*   *Collapse: 18%*

Like a lot of second basemen who aren't great second basemen, Ginter isn't much of a third baseman either, but that's not what keeps him around. He'll give it his best shot at second or third or the outfield, and he'll hit in ways Lenny Harris only dreams of. As part of the cadre of tough-luck minor league vets getting a chance under the team's new management, Ginter earned his keep. He makes an effective temp, has the power you like to see in a Miller Park reserve, and he can change gears and produce as a pinch-hitter.

TONY GWYNN JR.   **CF**   **Bats: L**   **Throws: R**   Born: 04-Oct-82   Age: 21

YEAR	TM	LG	AGE	AB	H	2B	3B	HR	BB	SO	SB	CS	AVG	OBP	SLG	MLVR	EQBA	EQOBP	EQSLG	EQMLVR	VORP	DEFENSE	
2003	BLT	MID	20	236	66	8	0	1	32	31	14	2	.280	.364	.326	.035	.221	.291	.262	-.373	-17.6	61-CF	1
2004	MIL	NL	21	230	47	8	1	1	22	41	5	2	.207	.277	.266	-.365	.208	.277	.266	-.380	-16.9	63-CF	-6

Breakout: 14%   *Improve: 38%*   *Collapse: 27%*

Some people seem relieved that he's not with the Padres, who presumably would have picked the original Tony's son two picks after the Brewers did. Although it would be easy to glibly mention nepotism and lamentable memories of Chris Gwynn, Little Tony is instead a reminder of the young Tony Gwynn, quick and graceful in the field. As a college player, you might have expected him to thrive in Low-A, but he was nevertheless young for the level. He may move up quickly; the organization is ambitious in its promotion schedules, and Krynzel keeps throwing a piston every time it seems like his career is finally going to pick up steam.

BILL HALL   **2B/SS**   **Bats: R**   **Throws: R**   Born: 28-Dec-79   Age: 24

YEAR	TM	LG	AGE	AB	H	2B	3B	HR	BB	SO	SB	CS	AVG	OBP	SLG	MLVR	EQBA	EQOBP	EQSLG	EQMLVR	VORP	DEFENSE			
2001	HDS	CAL	21	346	105	21	6	15	22	78	18	9	.303	.348	.529	.185	.225	.263	.398	-.237	-3.4	89-SS	-9		
2001	HUN	SOU	21	160	41	8	1	3	5	46	5	3	.256	.279	.375	-.110	.235	.248	.346	-.333	-6.5	41-SS	-3		
2002	IND	INT	22	465	106	20	1	4	25	105	17	10	.228	.272	.301	-.258	.213	.259	.286	-.410	-28.8	125-SS	-23		
2002	MIL	NL	22	36	7	1	1	1	3	13	0	1	.194	.256	.361	-.227	.194	.256	.389	-.284	-1.5				
2003	IND	INT	23	354	100	25	2	5	27	79	10	11	.282	.335	.407	.031	.258	.312	.379	-.147	3.0	51-2B	-2	36-SS	-3
2003	MIL	NL	23	142	37	9	2	5	7	28	1	2	.261	.298	.458	.002	.266	.304	.462	-.037	5.1	18-SS	-1	18-2B	-3
2004	MIL	NL	24	293	72	16	2	8	23	64	6	3	.247	.305	.392	-.127	.248	.305	.393	-.140	6.5	78-SS	-8		

Breakout: 48%   *Improve: 67%*   *Collapse: 18%*

It's easy to latch onto everything that happened in 2002, or his premature promotion to Double-A in 2001, but Hall is actually turning out to be a useful player. No, he's not the star some tools-minded people had him out to be, but he isn't only a High Desert mirage, either. Cranking out Luis Aguayo Lite isn't going to win you accolades as a farm system, but utility infielders who can handle both middle positions while flashing more power than others of the breed have their uses. Hall will be a handy seatwarmer at short until Hardy's ready, and then he'll be a useful reserve.

J. J. HARDY SS Bats: R Throws: R Born: 19-Aug-82 Age: 21

YEAR	TM	LG	AGE	AB	H	2B	3B	HR	BB	SO	SB	CS	AVG	OBP	SLG	MLVR	EQBA	EQOBP	EQSLG	EQMLVR	VORP	DEFENSE	
2001	OGD	PIO	18	125	31	5	0	2	15	12	1	2	.248	.326	.336	-.153	.144	.207	.200	-.664	-33.4	35-SS	0
2002	HDS	CAL	19	335	98	19	1	6	19	38	9	3	.293	.327	.409	-.016	.226	.254	.316	-.370	-16.2	80-SS	17
2002	HUN	SOU	19	145	33	7	0	1	9	19	1	2	.228	.269	.297	-.216	.216	.242	.284	-.445	-10.8	37-SS	0
2003	HUN	SOU	20	416	116	26	0	12	58	54	6	4	.279	.368	.428	.152	.240	.316	.380	-.151	7.1	106-SS	9
2004	MIL	NL	21	280	63	13	1	6	24	37	2	1	.225	.288	.341	-.239	.226	.288	.342	-.253	-4.7	76-SS	-3

Breakout: 29%   Improve: 46%   Collapse: 28%

Even for the Brewers, they've been ambitious in terms of how they've pushed Hardy up the chain. It's easy to understand why though. Although a high school pick from 2001, he's unusually smooth at short, with a great arm and mobility that makes everything look easy. He missed three weeks with a hip injury, which some speculated cost him the Southern League MVP to Corey Hart. Comparisons to shortstops named Alex Gonzalez are being bandied about, but Hardy should turn out better than either one, as opposed to what everyone wishcast for them for a few years (ourselves being among the guilty). PECOTA doesn't like Hardy, but he's got a little bit of power, improving patience, and he might be the best defensive shortstop in the minors. He could win the job in camp, because the Brewers' infield of the future could be a menace in leather: Hart and Helms aren't good third basemen, and Weeks has much to prove at second. It's probably a better idea to let Hardy slip into the job by August.

COREY HART 3B Bats: R Throws: R Born: 24-Mar-82 Age: 22

YEAR	TM	LG	AGE	AB	H	2B	3B	HR	BB	SO	SB	CS	AVG	OBP	SLG	MLVR	EQBA	EQOBP	EQSLG	EQMLVR	VORP	DEFENSE			
2001	OGD	PIO	19	262	89	18	1	11	26	47	14	1	.340	.395	.542	.329	.217	.262	.357	-.302	-32.6	60-1B	-8		
2002	HDS	CAL	20	393	113	26	10	22	37	101	24	11	.288	.356	.573	.241	.210	.263	.414	-.225	-5.3	47-3B	-9	43-1B	0
2002	HUN	SOU	20	94	25	3	0	2	7	16	3	2	.266	.340	.362	.005	.250	.296	.344	-.233	-1.5	19-3B	-4		
2003	HUN	SOU	21	493	149	40	1	13	28	101	25	8	.302	.340	.467	.185	.269	.302	.434	-.078	15.4	114-3B	-13		
2004	MIL	NL	22	312	75	17	1	12	21	67	8	3	.242	.295	.416	-.117	.243	.294	.417	-.131	5.6	83-3B	-12		

Breakout: 26%   Improve: 52%   Collapse: 27%

If you remember Archi Cianfrocco clomping around the left side of an infield, you'll love Hart. At 6'6", he's Bunyanesque at the hot corner. It's also obvious that he's a converted first baseman. As a third baseman, there isn't a lot he does well: He doesn't know how to position himself to throw, and chucks a fair number of sailing floaters, keeping first base coaches on their toes. Given his youth and athleticism, he's almost as good an offensive player as you can be without having a lot of patience at the plate; his power projects to be top-notch, and he's quick on the bases. He might wind up in an outfield corner shortly, but it's worth giving the experiment at third another year.

WES HELMS 3B Bats: R Throws: R Born: 12-May-76 Age: 28

YEAR	TM	LG	AGE	AB	H	2B	3B	HR	BB	SO	SB	CS	AVG	OBP	SLG	MLVR	EQBA	EQOBP	EQSLG	EQMLVR	VORP	DEFENSE			
2001	ATL	NL	25	216	48	10	3	10	21	56	1	1	.222	.293	.435	-.113	.228	.298	.447	-.101	-1.1	51-1B	-4		
2002	ATL	NL	26	210	51	16	0	6	11	57	1	1	.243	.283	.405	-.090	.254	.295	.427	-.114	-1.6	32-1B	-1	14-3B	-2
2003	MIL	NL	27	476	124	21	0	23	43	131	0	1	.261	.330	.450	.044	.266	.335	.463	.020	22.1	129-3B	-11		
2004	MIL	NL	28	352	88	18	1	15	31	91	1	1	.250	.317	.441	-.040	.252	.317	.442	-.052	14.6	94-3B	-4		

Breakout: 25%   Improve: 48%   Collapse: 28%

One of Ned Yost's guys brought in because the boss was familiar with him from their time on the Braves, Helms justified the confidence placed in him. He's not a star and never will be, but he probably shares posterboy status with Scott Podsednik for the new Brewers. He had the sort of year he can, but he's too old to be someone you build around. A two-year deal signed in December should keep him locked in for a year, but then Hart should be pushing into the scene, making Helms trade bait or a first baseman for 2005. Which way that decision goes will depend a lot more on Prince Fielder's 2004 than Helms's.

GEOFF JENKINS LF Bats: L Throws: R Born: 21-Jul-74 Age: 29

YEAR	TM	LG	AGE	AB	H	2B	3B	HR	BB	SO	SB	CS	AVG	OBP	SLG	MLVR	EQBA	EQOBP	EQSLG	EQMLVR	VORP	DEFENSE
2001	MIL	NL	26	397	105	21	1	20	36	120	4	2	.264	.334	.474	.042	.269	.338	.480	.051	11.8	103-LF 12
2002	MIL	NL	27	243	59	17	1	10	22	60	1	2	.243	.320	.444	.022	.251	.320	.470	-.010	2.9	63-LF 4
2003	MIL	NL	28	487	144	30	2	28	58	120	0	0	.296	.375	.538	.252	.298	.377	.547	.240	34.6	122-LF 1
2004	MIL	NL	29	422	113	23	2	24	48	106	2	1	.267	.349	.500	.103	.269	.348	.501	.093	19.4	113-LF -1

Breakout: 16%   Improve: 46%   Collapse: 18%

For those counting, that's a pattern of good year, hurt year, hurt year, good year over the last four, although missing a month with a broken thumb is what you have to accept in a good Jenkins year. It doesn't have the cachet of Bret Saberhagen's even-odd year thing that he had going for most of his career, but it does illustrate the problem, which is that Jenkins actually is what people spent years accusing Paul Molitor of being: fragile enough to belong in somebody's nicknack cabinet. To be fair, Jenkins's problems aren't as chronic as J. D. Drew's, it's just that he's like the eight-year-old who always skins a knee, falls out of a tree, or takes a flying leap off his bike. As he gets older, you'd wish the kid would outgrow that stuff and learn he's mortal. Some don't. If he's dealt, it will hopefully be to a team with a great fourth outfielder.

BROOKS KIESCHNICK PH/11th Pitcher Bats: L Throws: R Born: 06-Jun-72 Age: 32

YEAR	TM	LG	AGE	AB	H	2B	3B	HR	BB	SO	SB	CS	AVG	OBP	SLG	MLVR	EQBA	EQOBP	EQSLG	EQMLVR	VORP	DEFENSE
2001	CSP	PCL	29	252	74	9	3	13	24	72	3	2	.294	.360	.508	.102	.246	.308	.423	-.102	-2.8	36-RF -3
2001	COL	NL	29	42	10	2	1	3	3	13	0	0	.238	.289	.548	-.012	.214	.267	.524	-.062	0.7	
2002	CHR	INT	30	189	52	11	0	13	14	46	0	0	.275	.320	.540	.179	.253	.304	.505	.012	7.9	
2003	MIL	NL	31	70	21	1	0	7	6	13	0	0	.300	.355	.614	.348	.296	.351	.620	.300	11.6	
2004	MIL	NL	32	134	34	6	0	8	14	33	0	0	.251	.322	.482	.023	.253	.322	.483	.011	5.4	

Breakout: 38%   Improve: 58%   Collapse: 24%

... and on the mound:

YEAR	TM	LG	AGE	G	GS	IP	H	BB	SO	HR	ERA	EQERA	EQH9	EQBB9	EQSO9	EQHR9	PERA	VORP	STF
2002	CHR	INT	30	25	0	31.3	30	10	30	1	2.59	3.72	9.6	3.4	7.1	0.3	4.17	6.1	14
2003	IND	INT	31	8	0	13.7	17	10	14	3	8.54	9.75	13.5	8.2	7.5	3.0	10.11	-5.5	-99
2003	MIL	NL	31	42	0	53.0	66	13	39	5	5.26	5.23	10.8	1.9	5.7	0.9	4.89	1.1	-4
2004	MIL	NL	32	35	7	64.0	72	23	46	6	4.67	4.79	10.3	2.8	5.9	0.7	4.81	5.7	-2

Breakout: 18%   Improve: 46%   Collapse: 26%

The game's lone legitimate multi-purpose player, Kieschnick gives the 25th spot on the roster real value, effectively extending the roster to 26 because of his dual roles. He finally avenged himself upon superscout Hugh Alexander's singling him out as a problem on the 1997 Cubs. True, he had to resume pitching to get there, but after years of speaking up in his defense, it's nice for all of us, fans and analysts alike, to finally see him out there. He's not a major asset on the mound, considering he's working with average heat and some adequate breaking junk, but it's more than good enough to let him mop up or handle low-leverage middle innings. He also hit significantly better when restricted to pitching or pinch-hitting assignments, and while it's not in a compelling sample size, it should help him keep his unique job.

DAVID KRYNZEL CF Bats: L Throws: L Born: 07-Nov-81 Age: 22

YEAR	TM	LG	AGE	AB	H	2B	3B	HR	BB	SO	SB	CS	AVG	OBP	SLG	MLVR	EQBA	EQOBP	EQSLG	EQMLVR	VORP	DEFENSE
2001	BLT	MID	19	141	43	1	1	1	9	28	11	5	.305	.364	.348	.040	.246	.290	.282	-.335	-8.1	34-CF -4
2001	HDS	CAL	19	383	106	19	5	5	27	122	34	17	.277	.329	.392	-.047	.205	.248	.297	-.421	-30.3	89-CF 0
2002	HDS	CAL	20	365	98	13	12	11	64	100	29	17	.268	.391	.460	.131	.184	.280	.314	-.344	-23.0	93-CF -4
2002	HUN	SOU	20	129	31	2	3	2	4	30	13	5	.240	.269	.349	-.138	.229	.244	.344	-.348	-7.7	30-CF -2
2003	HUN	SOU	21	457	122	13	11	2	60	119	43	21	.267	.357	.357	.037	.234	.308	.318	-.255	-16.1	115-CF -2
2004	MIL	NL	22	265	59	11	3	4	23	65	11	4	.224	.294	.336	-.235	.225	.293	.337	-.249	-9.7	72-CF -7

Breakout: 21%   Improve: 46%   Collapse: 23%

An outstanding baserunner and a fast one, as well as a well-regarded defender, Krynzel is typecast as a leadoff man. He's got a lot of work to do before he can earn that label; it's still an open question as to whether he's really making progress. He still strikes out a ton, and in consecutive seasons, he's flamed out in the second half, aerating infields at a pace that would make Rob Deer beam with pride. The Brewers keep seeing Johnny Damon, but it's a lot more likely they've got a NAFTA-generated, second-rate Rick Manning on their hands, and that's if he turns out OK. He's young enough to improve, and he has to.

CHRIS MORRIS   CF   Bats: B   Throws: R   Born: 01-Jul-79   Age: 25

YEAR	TM	LG	AGE	AB	H	2B	3B	HR	BB	SO	SB	CS	AVG	OBP	SLG	MLVR	EQBA	EQOBP	EQSLG	EQMLVR	VORP	DEFENSE
2001	PEO	MID	22	480	141	11	9	2	83	101	111	24	.294	.398	.367	.130	.231	.312	.291	-.286	-22.8	127-CF -10
2002	POT	CAR	23	422	105	17	2	0	58	92	55	19	.249	.348	.299	-.069	.201	.279	.245	-.430	-38.9	112-CF -7
2002	BLT	MID	23	14	5	2	0	0	1	3	1	0	.357	.400	.500	.366	.286	.333	.357	-.118	0.0	
2003	HDS	CAL	24	486	129	26	4	2	55	107	67	18	.265	.345	.348	-.114	.191	.257	.254	-.468	-48.3	121-CF -10
2004	*MIL*	*NL*	*24*	*199*	*43*	*8*	*2*	*1*	*20*	*46*	*11*	*4*	*.217*	*.295*	*.295*	*-.291*	*.218*	*.294*	*.295*	*-.305*	*-10.3*	*56-CF -5*

Breakout: 33%   *Improve: 58%*   *Collapse: 21%*

Faster than you can say Esix Snead (and say it quick, because Snead's fast enough to catch you before you finish), Morris has gone from a semi-prospecty vibe to downright pointlessness. Since his monster 111-steal year on Peoria's basepaths, Morris hasn't hit, not even in High Desert. You might pretend that's OK, since Juan Pierre wasn't the sort of guy anyone meant to play on Planet Coors, but Morris is old for his leagues and questionable afield. He's a better prospect than Chad Green right now, and nothing more.

BRAD NELSON   1B/LF?   Bats: L   Throws: R   Born: 23-Dec-82   Age: 21

YEAR	TM	LG	AGE	AB	H	2B	3B	HR	BB	SO	SB	CS	AVG	OBP	SLG	MLVR	EQBA	EQOBP	EQSLG	EQMLVR	VORP	DEFENSE
2001	OGD	PIO	18	42	11	4	0	0	3	9	0	0	.262	.298	.357	-.164	.190	.209	.238	-.591	-10.8	
2002	BLT	MID	19	417	124	38	2	17	34	86	4	1	.297	.353	.520	.277	.230	.274	.415	-.189	-13.7	103-1B -10
2002	HDS	CAL	19	102	26	11	0	3	12	28	0	0	.255	.333	.451	.022	.176	.243	.324	-.409	-10.1	26-1B 1
2003	HDS	CAL	20	167	52	9	1	1	12	22	2	2	.311	.363	.395	.009	.227	.271	.288	-.375	-14.5	30-1B -2
2003	HUN	SOU	20	143	30	12	0	1	11	34	2	2	.210	.274	.315	-.180	.192	.240	.301	-.438	-17.1	25-LF -3
2004	*MIL*	*NL*	*21*	*247*	*54*	*12*	*1*	*6*	*17*	*52*	*1*	*1*	*.218*	*.273*	*.350*	*-.258*	*.219*	*.272*	*.351*	*-.273*	*-11.7*	*67-1B -8*

Breakout: 34%   *Improve: 60%*   *Collapse: 20%*

The Brewers retain their faith in Nelson's being a prospect, and while 2003 didn't do much to help him with that, he did lose two months to a broken hamate. Credited with great work habits, he got a chance to show them during his recovery. Although he's always had a quick bat, once he returned he apparently settled for making contact as he played through healing up, and he was frank about being tentative when it came to taking full swings. Presumably, in 2004 he'll regain his stroke and get a full season of play in one of Huntsville's outfield corners, where he's projected to stay with Fielder coming up behind him. The concern is that he'll be no more of an effective left fielder than Kevin Reimer was.

KEITH OSIK   C   Bats: R   Throws: R   Born: 22-Oct-68   Age: 35

YEAR	TM	LG	AGE	AB	H	2B	3B	HR	BB	SO	SB	CS	AVG	OBP	SLG	MLVR	EQBA	EQOBP	EQSLG	EQMLVR	VORP	DEFENSE
2001	PIT	NL	32	120	25	4	0	2	13	24	1	0	.208	.299	.292	-.311	.215	.304	.298	-.301	-4.4	30-C 1
2002	PIT	NL	33	100	16	3	0	2	6	25	0	0	.160	.211	.250	-.473	.168	.214	.277	-.536	-9.5	20-C 0
2003	MIL	NL	34	241	60	12	0	2	31	44	0	1	.249	.342	.324	-.112	.254	.344	.332	-.153	0.8	71-C 4
2004	*BAL*	*AL*	*35*	*139*	*31*	*6*	*0*	*2*	*13*	*28*	*0*	*0*	*.220*	*.293*	*.312*	*-.253*	*.228*	*.304*	*.327*	*-.241*	*-2.4*	*41-C -1*

Breakout: 28%   *Improve: 46%*   *Collapse: 31%*

He still catches just well enough to hang on, and he'll stand around at positions other than catcher in emergencies, but he's in that stage where he's earned his journeyman card in the International Brotherhood of Backup Catchers, which he can redeem for a job invite with some suitably desperate outpost on the fringes of the big leagues. Because he was one of the replacements in 1994–95, he'll have more than usual trouble keeping teams interested, so he may not be far from moving into the coaching career track so many of his brethren are given as a reward.

LOU PALMISANO   C   Bats: R   Throws: R   Born: 16-Sep-82   Age: 21

YEAR	TM	LG	AGE	AB	H	2B	3B	HR	BB	SO	SB	CS	AVG	OBP	SLG	MLVR	EQBA	EQOBP	EQSLG	EQMLVR	VORP	DEFENSE
2003	HEL	PIO	20	174	68	13	2	6	18	29	13	2	.391	.458	.592	.591	.250	.308	.390	-.145	2.7	37-C -1
2004	*MIL*	*NL*	*21*	*257*	*58*	*13*	*2*	*6*	*20*	*56*	*7*	*3*	*.226*	*.294*	*.355*	*-.210*	*.227*	*.293*	*.356*	*-.223*	*-1.3*	*70-C -6*

Breakout: 11%   *Improve: 22%*   *Collapse: 43%*

A broken ankle suffered sliding into second ended his pro debut early. As an Italian-American, he immediately gets compared to Mike Piazza, which is about as unfair as you can get. Palmisano does have a quick bat, but has trouble laying off high heat. He's given good marks for his catching, showing nimble footwork and a good arm. If he gets pushed up to the California League for a full season, he should be the odds-on fave to win the Triple Crown. The hope is that he becomes everything B. J. Surhoff was not as a franchise catcher.

RICHARD PAZ   IF   Bats: R   Throws: R   Born: 30-Jul-77   Age: 26

YEAR	TM	LG	AGE	AB	H	2B	3B	HR	BB	SO	SB	CS	AVG	OBP	SLG	MLVR	EQBA	EQOBP	EQSLG	EQMLVR	VORP	DEFENSE			
2001	ALT	EAS	23	248	59	15	1	4	52	55	7	6	.238	.374	.355	.042	.202	.320	.304	-.267	-8.0	43-2B	0	28-3B	-7
2002	WIC	TEX	24	479	136	27	0	5	81	80	5	6	.284	.390	.372	.097	.241	.334	.323	-.193	-1.9	76-3B	-6	61-SS	0
2003	HUN	SOU	25	228	56	14	0	1	58	36	6	3	.246	.406	.320	.056	.204	.337	.271	-.274	-8.2	65-2B	-2		
2003	IND	INT	25	131	46	8	0	0	16	19	1	2	.351	.422	.412	.230	.323	.392	.376	.048	9.4	35-2B	-1		
2004	MIL	NL	26	137	32	6	1	2	18	25	2	1	.232	.327	.328	-.181	.233	.327	.328	-.193	0.0	41-2B	-4		

Breakout: 20%   Improve: 43%   Collapse: 40%

Anyone out there remember Charlie Montoyo? In the late '80s and early '90s, Montoyo was a walk-happy farmhand in the Brewers organization. In 1988, he drew 156 walks for Stockton with 18 extra-base hits; perhaps obviously, none of the walks were intentional. The next year, he drew 102 more walks. He did these things at 22 and 23, and I'm sure a lot of us seamheads would have been excited about him. He never really hit for a high average, even though he passed through El Paso and pre-Rockies Denver, and he really couldn't play anywhere but second. He made the show with the Expos for about eight seconds in 1993.

There's a point at which walks and nothing else make you a doubtful proposition against the best pitching on the planet. You can help an affiliate win some games by having this sort of guy around, but at the majors, more likely than not, a guy like this will wait for that fourth ball that isn't coming as often as he's used to, and then it's back down to the dogtowns. Paz is in that boat. He helped make Wichita and Huntsville winners, and he'll help somebody's affiliate right now, but odds are he'll never get to cross the Jordan with the prospects. With the right organization, one with a bunch of young infielders on the way up, he could stick. Somebody has to be their backup.

EDDIE PEREZ   C   Bats: R   Throws: R   Born: 04-May-68   Age: 36

YEAR	TM	LG	AGE	AB	H	2B	3B	HR	BB	SO	SB	CS	AVG	OBP	SLG	MLVR	EQBA	EQOBP	EQSLG	EQMLVR	VORP	DEFENSE
2002	CLE	AL	34	117	25	9	0	0	5	25	0	0	.214	.252	.291	-.348	.231	.273	.325	-.317	-4.3	35-C 1
2003	MIL	NL	35	350	95	17	1	11	17	47	0	1	.271	.304	.420	-.032	.277	.308	.432	-.063	8.2	91-C -7
2004	ATL	NL	36	243	60	12	1	6	12	40	0	1	.245	.283	.370	-.197	.248	.284	.383	-.190	0.1	65-C -4

Breakout: 21%   Improve: 39%   Collapse: 35%

Like more than a few guys, take him out of his element, and you suddenly see his true worth. Perez is no longer the defensive whiz he was when he first came up with the Braves, and he can't hit right-handed pitching. He has no business being a regular. Although he joined Helms as one of the Braves' bit players Yost brought in to help out initially, in Perez's case, they cut their losses pretty quickly, wishing him well in his return to his old team and old role.

SCOTT PODSEDNIK   CF   Bats: L   Throws: L   Born: 18-Mar-76   Age: 28

YEAR	TM	LG	AGE	AB	H	2B	3B	HR	BB	SO	SB	CS	AVG	OBP	SLG	MLVR	EQBA	EQOBP	EQSLG	EQMLVR	VORP	DEFENSE			
2001	TAC	PCL	25	269	78	15	4	3	13	46	12	5	.290	.327	.409	-.030	.268	.305	.375	-.159	-0.9	52-CF	-2	12-LF	0
2002	TAC	PCL	26	438	122	25	6	9	43	70	35	13	.279	.347	.425	.049	.253	.322	.389	-.118	4.1	91-CF	-7	30-LF	-1
2003	MIL	NL	27	558	175	29	8	9	56	91	43	10	.314	.379	.443	.153	.314	.378	.448	.118	41.0	120-CF	-7	13-RF	1
2004	MIL	NL	28	523	144	28	5	11	47	85	25	9	.276	.341	.410	-.022	.277	.340	.411	-.033	9.9	137-CF	-5		

Breakout: 6%   Improve: 30%   Collapse: 30%

The headliner for the new Brew, Podsednik swiped the job in center from the ridiculously overplayed Alex Sanchez in May. From there, it was a season of bliss, as he reminded the locals that there's a big difference between Sanchez's brand of flamboyantly brainless hustle and Podsednik's more stolid approach. Podsednik is no mere low-wattage Luis Castillo at the top of the order. Sure, he can run, and yes, he does a solid job of reaching base; he also puts a charge on the ball, making pitcher bunting that much more valuable, and making things tough on opposing pitchers. His 47-game on-base streak was second only to Bonds's 58-game run. The real question is whether somebody's supposed to wake up: Ned Yost, Podsednik, Brewer fans? They had no idea they finally had a starting center fielder on their hands when they signed him. Now that he's here, he affords them a year or three to sort out which kid in the minors has a future in center. If they sign him to a four-year deal instead, you'll know Doug Melvin's taken a big step backward.

RICHIE SEXSON   1B   Bats: R   Throws: R   Born: 29-Dec-74   Age: 29

YEAR	TM	LG	AGE	AB	H	2B	3B	HR	BB	SO	SB	CS	AVG	OBP	SLG	MLVR	EQBA	EQOBP	EQSLG	EQMLVR	VORP	DEFENSE	
2001	MIL	NL	26	598	162	24	3	45	60	178	2	4	.271	.342	.547	.162	.272	.343	.550	.161	41.4	155-1B	8
2002	MIL	NL	27	570	159	37	2	29	70	136	0	0	.279	.363	.504	.199	.284	.365	.519	.167	39.4	150-1B	15
2003	MIL	NL	28	606	165	28	2	45	98	151	2	3	.272	.379	.548	.262	.274	.379	.558	.233	50.3	162-1B	8
2004	ARI	NL	29	538	152	31	2	34	77	127	2	2	.282	.376	.537	.208	.272	.364	.521	.147	33.1	146-1B	4

Breakout: 22%   Improve: 47%   Collapse: 10%

How can you not love Richie Sexson? He doesn't have the legends that used to follow Babe Herman around, but he's got that towering Herman Munster thing going for him, and he's actually surprisingly graceful afield. He's got a relatively compact swing for a big man, providing tremendous power from bat speed more than mere brawn.

The Snakes only have him locked in place for a year, but they basically only gave up spare parts to get him. The real challenge for Arizona isn't enjoying having Sexson in 2004, it's deciding whether or not to re-sign him. He doesn't seem like the sort who's going to age well, but Sexson has exceeded expectations from the point he left Cleveland, and he's improved his plate discipline every step of the way (only seven of his 98 walks last year were intentional). The D-Backs need to weigh Sexson's skill vs. the abundance of first basemen in the world who can hit, rather than blindly tossing him a monster contract to justify the trade to themselves.

JOHN VANDER WAL   OF   Bats: L   Throws: L   Born: 29-Apr-66   Age: 38

YEAR	TM	LG	AGE	AB	H	2B	3B	HR	BB	SO	SB	CS	AVG	OBP	SLG	MLVR	EQBA	EQOBP	EQSLG	EQMLVR	VORP	DEFENSE			
2001	PIT	NL	35	313	87	22	3	11	42	84	7	4	.278	.361	.473	.095	.274	.361	.470	.083	13.8	42-RF	-2	15-LF	-2
2001	SFG	NL	35	139	35	6	1	3	26	38	1	2	.252	.370	.374	-.014	.266	.379	.392	.003	2.8	30-RF	2		
2002	NYY	AL	36	219	57	17	1	6	23	58	1	1	.260	.327	.429	.006	.281	.351	.466	.066	7.4	40-RF	-2		
2003	MIL	NL	37	327	84	25	1	14	46	104	1	2	.257	.350	.468	.098	.259	.349	.479	.060	11.2	69-RF	1		
2004	CIN	NL	38	152	37	8	1	5	21	44	1	0	.246	.337	.415	-.043	.245	.334	.413	-.065	2.5	45-RF	-2		

Breakout: 17%   Improve: 33%   Collapse: 38%

Vander Wal seems to have annoyed some people for being something less than they wished he was. When he went to the Giants down the stretch in '01, they wanted a slugger; they got a solid hitter instead. The Yankees signed him and crowed as if Oscar Gamble was back in town; he wasn't. Moving over to Milwaukee, he was simply what they needed, a useful lefty half of a platoon. He rejected an offer of arbitration from the Brewers, which is either a major misread of the money he'll get on the market, or a clear sign he wants to play for a winner before his career peters out. Becoming a Red means it was the former.

NOOCHIE VARNER   OF   Bats: R   Throws: R   Born: 07-Dec-80   Age: 23

YEAR	TM	LG	AGE	AB	H	2B	3B	HR	BB	SO	SB	CS	AVG	OBP	SLG	MLVR	EQBA	EQOBP	EQSLG	EQMLVR	VORP	DEFENSE			
2001	BIL	PIO	20	291	102	20	5	8	29	64	7	4	.351	.411	.536	.381	.226	.273	.354	-.279	-36.1	46-LF	-1	14-3B	-3
2002	DYT	MID	21	517	160	27	12	10	32	117	37	4	.309	.354	.466	.215	.245	.280	.386	-.207	-9.3	100-CF	-3	26-LF	0
2002	WMI	MID	21	17	3	1	1	0	0	4	0	0	.176	.176	.353	-.255	.176	.176	.294	-.585	-2.2				
2003	ERI	EAS	22	175	53	6	2	3	14	29	0	0	.303	.353	.411	.067	.257	.301	.360	-.196	-7.0	43-RF	0		
2003	HUN	SOU	22	293	79	12	2	6	14	52	7	3	.270	.304	.386	-.002	.245	.272	.366	-.251	-16.5	65-RF	-2		
2004	ARI	NL	23	247	63	14	2	6	16	52	4	2	.255	.303	.406	-.106	.246	.294	.394	-.160	-2.8	66-RF	-2		

Breakout: 26%   Improve: 56%   Collapse: 20%

The player named later sent to Arizona in the Sexson trade, Varner borders on being a prospect in the Snakes' chain. He's another tweener problem, in that he doesn't have the power for a corner, doesn't get on base often enough to make up for it, and doesn't play center. He can run, play the field, and make contact, which boils down to a lot of what teams look for in their fourth outfielders. If nothing else, he'll be an easy fan favorite, and with Danny Bautista's track record for breaking down, he'll surface in the majors.

RICKIE WEEKS   2B   Bats: R   Throws: R   Born: 13-Sep-82   Age: 21

YEAR	TM	LG	AGE	AB	H	2B	3B	HR	BB	SO	SB	CS	AVG	OBP	SLG	MLVR	EQBA	EQOBP	EQSLG	EQMLVR	VORP	DEFENSE	
2003	BLT	MID	20	63	22	8	1	1	15	9	2	0	.349	.494	.556	.531	.239	.360	.403	-.037	3.1	17-2B	-4
2003	MIL	NL	20	12	2	1	0	0	1	6	0	0	.167	.286	.250	-.351	.167	.275	.250	-.446	-0.7		
2004	MIL	NL	21	241	57	16	2	5	27	56	3	1	.234	.341	.385	-.081	.235	.341	.386	-.093	10.1	70-2B	-6

Breakout: 16%   Improve: 30%   Collapse: 39%

(continued next page)

Rickie Weeks (continued)

Quick hands and two Division-I batting titles for Southern got Weeks to the majors mere months after the Brewers tabbed him with their first-round pick, and he finished the year with a nifty little stint in the Arizona Fall League. The hype machine is already in full swing (in a flash of scouting excess, he's being compared to Joe Morgan), so let's touch on the negatives: Even the organization appreciates that he has room for improvement with the leather. He's bright and expected to be coachable. Steve Sax seems a better parallel, considering the questions about his scattershot throws, the uncertainty about how much power he'll have hitting with wood, and the relatively weak level of competition Weeks faced at Southern. Still, other people faced weak competition in college, and didn't set records; Weeks did. As much as you can say it about a guy with so little supporting data, he's a very good prospect. The parts acquired from the Sexson trade should put Weeks in the minors to open the season, but some hot hitting and an in-person introduction to Junior Spivey's limitations should help get Weeks up in short order.

PITCHERS

MIKE ADAMS
Bats: R Throws: R Born: 29-Jul-78 Age: 25

YEAR	TM	LG	AGE	G	GS	IP	H	BB	SO	HR	ERA	EQERA	EQH9	EQBB9	EQSO9	EQHR9	PERA	VORP	STF
2001	OGD	PIO	22	23	0	32.0	26	6	44	4	2.81	3.67	12.0	2.7	6.7	3.0	8.22	5.8	-47
2002	BLT	MID	23	11	0	15.3	13	2	21	1	2.94	4.05	11.5	1.4	7.4	2.0	6.34	2.3	-17
2002	HDS	CAL	23	10	0	14.0	9	7	23	2	2.57	3.75	9.0	6.0	9.0	2.2	6.67	2.5	-22
2002	HUN	SOU	23	13	0	18.7	14	12	17	3	3.37	6.48	9.2	6.5	5.9	3.2	8.20	-1.6	-69
2003	HUN	SOU	24	45	2	74.3	58	33	83	6	3.15	5.10	9.8	4.8	7.2	1.7	6.06	3.6	-23
2004	MIL	NL	25	13	3	25.0	26	13	22	5	5.51	5.65	9.5	4.0	7.1	1.5	5.64	0.1	-4

Breakout: 22%   Improve: 46%   Collapse: 21%

Because he's not considered a prospect, Adams needed a year of progress. That's mostly a question of his age, but he's got low-90s heat and a slider that Southern League lefties didn't hit. Although Huntsville was one of the stronger Double-A teams around, Adams was part of the reason why, instead of a reliever simply coasting on its coattails. He probably won't be on the A-list of options in the pen when camp breaks, instead losing out to some veteran with an NRI, but he has a great shot at earning a place on the team some time this summer.

GREG BRUSO
Bats: R Throws: R Born: 05-May-80 Age: 24

YEAR	TM	LG	AGE	G	GS	IP	H	BB	SO	HR	ERA	EQERA	EQH9	EQBB9	EQSO9	EQHR9	PERA	VORP	STF
2002	SLO	NWN	22	14	13	81.3	58	17	78	5	1.99	4.15	10.4	2.7	4.8	1.8	6.02	11.2	-12
2003	SJO	CAL	23	14	13	84.0	69	11	77	5	3.11	3.59	8.5	1.6	5.2	1.2	4.02	17.4	11
2003	NRW	EAS	23	11	11	76.3	72	11	45	6	3.42	4.04	9.0	1.5	4.2	1.4	4.50	12.4	0
2003	HUN	SOU	23	2	2	10.0	13	6	5	1	3.60	8.00	14.0	6.0	3.0	2.0	8.76	-2.4	-57
2004	MIL	NL	24	22	15	91.3	98	26	54	14	4.64	4.76	9.8	2.3	4.8	1.2	4.78	9.6	-2

Breakout: 13%   Improve: 52%   Collapse: 20%

A command and control right-hander out of UC Davis, Bruso was picked up from the Giants in the Eric Young deal. He isn't a great bet to have a career; guys who start off making a living on their changeup and slow heat are generally hard-pressed to become wildly successful. But this is the Brewers, and anybody can win almost any job. A good half season could get him into the rotation as easily as it once worked for Bill Wegman.

DAVE BURBA
Bats: R Throws: R Born: 07-Jul-66 Age: 37

YEAR	TM	LG	AGE	G	GS	IP	H	BB	SO	HR	ERA	EQERA	EQH9	EQBB9	EQSO9	EQHR9	PERA	VORP	STF
2001	CLE	AL	35	32	27	150.7	188	54	118	16	6.21	5.27	10.1	2.9	6.4	0.8	4.81	5.5	9
2002	TEX	AL	36	23	18	111.3	125	40	70	13	5.42	4.86	9.5	3.0	5.4	0.9	4.65	9.0	2
2002	CLE	AL	36	12	3	34.0	30	17	25	3	4.50	4.01	7.2	4.0	6.1	0.8	3.77	6.0	6
2003	BUF	INT	37	4	4	22.0	18	5	10	2	2.05	3.54	8.0	2.7	3.1	1.3	4.32	4.6	-17
2003	IND	INT	37	10	9	50.7	65	16	34	4	5.33	6.75	12.5	3.5	4.8	1.2	6.45	-6.0	-24
2003	MIL	NL	37	17	2	43.3	42	19	35	5	3.53	4.04	8.5	3.6	6.4	1.1	4.50	8.1	0
2004	MIL	NL	37	51	10	88.7	99	37	51	10	4.73	4.86	10.1	3.3	4.7	0.9	5.15	8.5	-12

Breakout: 21%   Improve: 54%   Collapse: 19%

Brought in as an elder statesman type to help out with the team's young group of moundsmen, Burba did a nifty job as a mop-up reliever and solid citizen, well enough to get guaranteed money in Milwaukee for 2004. It's the sort of work that should cinch a future job in player development for him, if he wants one.

MIKE CRUDALE   Bats: R   Throws: R   Born: 03-Jan-77   Age: 27

YEAR	TM	LG	AGE	G	GS	IP	H	BB	SO	HR	ERA	EQERA	EQH9	EQBB9	EQSO9	EQHR9	PERA	VORP	STF
2001	NHV	EAS	24	62	0	80.3	76	22	85	7	3.25	5.40	10.7	3.4	6.7	1.3	5.65	1.6	-14
2002	MEM	PCL	25	13	0	14.7	10	5	16	1	1.84	2.63	7.2	3.3	7.2	0.7	3.41	4.5	14
2002	STL	NL	25	49	1	52.7	43	14	47	3	1.88	2.72	8.2	2.2	7.1	0.5	3.39	15.9	24
2003	MEM	PCL	26	32	0	29.3	34	11	23	7	5.53	7.52	12.6	4.1	6.2	3.4	9.46	-5.6	-98
2003	STL	NL	26	13	0	11.3	11	12	6	1	2.39	4.91	9.0	8.2	4.1	0.8	5.75	2.0	-35
2003	MIL	NL	26	9	0	9.3	1	6	7	0	2.90	1.00	1.0	5.0	6.0	0.0	0.89	2.8	30
2004	MIL	NL	27	27	2	39.0	39	19	30	5	4.63	4.75	9.1	3.8	6.3	1.0	4.95	4.3	-6

Breakout: 25%   Improve: 52%   Collapse: 27%

Part of the swag brought in for Mike DeJean, Crudale delights in being a chuck-and-duck hurler, throwing hard, throwing straight, and generating Kodak moments. He managed to work his way off a team as desperate for pitching as the 2003 Cardinals, but a bad spring and a broken toe hindered him early on, and La Russa seemed annoyed with him on a couple of levels. The Brewers were sensible to recognize that he has more promise than his 2003 suggests. Although he'd be better off with any functioning change of pace in his assortment, a quickly gassed flamethrower can still contribute.

DOUG DAVIS   Bats: R   Throws: L   Born: 21-Sep-75   Age: 28

YEAR	TM	LG	AGE	G	GS	IP	H	BB	SO	HR	ERA	EQERA	EQH9	EQBB9	EQSO9	EQHR9	PERA	VORP	STF
2001	TEX	AL	25	30	30	186.0	220	69	115	14	4.45	4.39	9.6	3.0	5.1	0.6	4.39	24.8	15
2002	OKL	PCL	26	9	9	61.3	70	11	48	7	4.99	5.31	10.8	1.9	5.3	1.4	5.47	1.9	-12
2002	TEX	AL	26	10	10	59.7	67	22	28	7	4.97	4.76	9.5	3.1	4.0	0.9	4.71	5.5	-2
2003	OKL	PCL	27	4	4	27.7	29	1	18	3	3.25	4.15	10.0	0.3	4.8	1.4	4.66	4.2	-2
2003	TEX	AL	27	1	1	3.0	4	4	2	2	12.00	12.00	12.0	12.0	6.0	6.0	14.24	-1.8	-182
2003	TOR	AL	27	12	11	54.0	70	26	25	6	5.00	5.23	10.8	4.1	4.1	0.8	5.49	3.6	-11
2003	IND	INT	27	5	5	34.7	33	10	19	2	4.15	4.45	8.9	3.1	3.9	0.8	4.34	4.1	-4
2003	MIL	NL	27	8	8	52.3	49	21	35	8	2.58	3.71	8.1	3.2	5.3	1.4	4.59	14.7	-2
2004	MIL	NL	28	24	17	95.7	109	39	56	14	5.12	5.26	10.3	3.2	4.8	1.1	5.46	5.9	-7

Breakout: 15%   Improve: 40%   Collapse: 30%

A guy skips around this much, you might wonder what's going on. In this case, Davis appears to be unwilling to listen to his pitching coaches. When it was Oscar Acosta, you might have understood, but it moved beyond that last year. Given that he's less than dominant, you might find this monomaniacal conviction to use the Force surprising, but eventually he was going to get it his way, in that he could probably find some appropriately desperate team willing to take him, no questions asked. Certainly, six quick quality starts at season's end go a long way on this team. The real question is whether they'll tolerate him when he doesn't pitch well, because he is not going to keep doing that.

LEO ESTRELLA   Bats: R   Throws: R   Born: 20-Feb-75   Age: 29

YEAR	TM	LG	AGE	G	GS	IP	H	BB	SO	HR	ERA	EQERA	EQH9	EQBB9	EQSO9	EQHR9	PERA	VORP	STF
2001	CHT	SOU	26	3	3	14.7	13	4	14	0	3.67	4.05	9.4	2.7	5.4	0.0	3.62	2.3	23
2001	LOU	INT	26	34	5	62.7	67	27	37	8	4.88	6.24	10.6	4.5	4.1	1.6	6.34	-4.1	-50
2001	NOR	INT	26	8	1	17.3	23	8	10	1	3.12	6.19	12.9	5.1	3.9	0.6	6.39	-1.0	-28
2002	IOW	PCL	27	8	0	10.7	10	7	9	0	5.89	6.30	9.0	6.3	5.4	0.0	4.41	-0.8	-8
2002	WTN	SOU	27	10	3	24.7	23	8	18	0	3.28	5.32	10.6	3.3	4.9	0.4	4.72	0.7	-7
2002	NHV	EAS	27	14	5	39.3	46	20	23	4	4.81	7.97	12.9	5.7	3.9	1.8	7.92	-9.2	-74
2003	IND	INT	28	7	0	15.0	9	6	12	1	1.20	1.98	5.9	4.6	5.9	0.7	3.23	5.5	6
2003	MIL	NL	28	58	0	66.0	75	21	25	10	4.36	4.62	9.7	2.5	2.9	1.3	5.01	9.2	-30
2004	MIL	NL	29	30	9	62.7	71	27	32	8	4.85	4.98	10.3	3.3	4.2	1.0	5.32	5.6	-15

Breakout: 29%   Improve: 55%   Collapse: 26%

Estrella was once dealt to the Blue Jays from the Mets for Tony Phillips, and then peddled from the Jays to the Reds for Steve Parris. He'd since worked his way down to NRIs. He got a call-up late in April, and did the most with it that he could, rattling off two good months before the league started catching up to him. There isn't a lot to be optimistic about, although like many, he's not much of a fan of Miller Park, allowing nine of his 10 home runs at home. He gets a lot of groundball outs with a moderately effective sinker, but he doesn't fool people.

MATT FORD

										Bats: B			Throws: L					Born: 08-Apr-81		Age: 23

YEAR	TM	LG	AGE	G	GS	IP	H	BB	SO	HR	ERA	EQERA	EQH9	EQBB9	EQSO9	EQHR9	PERA	VORP	STF
2001	CWV	SAL	20	11	11	70.7	62	22	69	2	2.42	4.79	10.2	4.2	4.9	0.6	4.95	5.6	20
2001	DUN	FLA	20	13	12	60.0	67	37	48	8	5.85	8.00	12.2	6.7	5.0	2.7	8.89	-14.4	-34
2002	DUN	FLA	21	21	18	114.0	100	42	85	7	2.37	4.72	9.6	4.1	4.6	1.2	5.37	10.1	2
2003	MIL	NL	22	25	4	43.7	46	21	26	5	4.32	4.85	9.1	3.8	4.6	1.1	4.84	4.3	0
2004	*MIL*	*NL*	*23*	*16*	*9*	*47.7*	*55*	*28*	*30*	*10*	*6.59*	*6.76*	*10.5*	*4.6*	*5.0*	*1.6*	*6.73*	*0.0*	*-18*

Breakout: 25%   Improve: 46%   Collapse: 23%

Snagged via the Rule 5 draft away from the Blue Jays, Ford earned his keep in the little amount of time he was given in mop-up work early on. Then the Brewers got silly and plugged him into the rotation; he got drubbed by the Pirates twice and by the Rockies in Milwaukee, not the sorts of events that hint at readiness. Then he got shut down with elbow pain, which turned out to be bone chips that were removed in September; he should be ready come April. As a lefty with good velocity but uncertain off-speed offerings, he's not the type you condemn to lefty situational work, sort of similar to the problem Valerio de los Santos represented for so many years. Ford could be a solid middle reliever, but a year in the minors to get some secondary pitches working would be a better idea for his long-term future.

WAYNE FRANKLIN

										Bats: L			Throws: L					Born: 09-Mar-74		Age: 30

YEAR	TM	LG	AGE	G	GS	IP	H	BB	SO	HR	ERA	EQERA	EQH9	EQBB9	EQSO9	EQHR9	PERA	VORP	STF
2001	NWO	PCL	27	41	0	49.7	47	18	51	6	3.80	5.56	9.9	4.0	6.8	1.4	5.61	0.2	-27
2001	HOU	NL	27	11	0	12.0	17	9	9	4	6.75	7.71	12.3	6.2	5.4	2.3	8.40	-2.7	-68
2002	NWO	PCL	28	29	27	179.0	153	59	141	14	3.12	4.64	9.6	3.5	5.5	1.0	4.95	17.2	-3
2002	MIL	NL	28	4	4	24.0	16	17	17	1	2.63	3.47	6.2	5.4	5.4	0.4	3.31	5.5	17
2003	MIL	NL	29	36	34	194.7	201	94	116	36	5.50	5.56	8.9	3.9	4.7	1.6	5.37	-7.6	-22
2004	*MIL*	*NL*	*30*	*26*	*21*	*119.3*	*130*	*58*	*75*	*19*	*5.51*	*5.66*	*9.9*	*3.8*	*5.1*	*1.2*	*5.64*	*2.3*	*-6*

Breakout: 14%   Improve: 41%   Collapse: 26%

Left in the rotation because he was still standing at the end of May, Franklin did what any minor league vet would do in his situation: He took his turns, and blessed his good fortune. Sure, he got shellacked pretty frequently, and yes, he's only a fifth starter on most teams. The Brewers needed durability to help them get through to the end of the season, and Franklin gave them that. When he's out of the rotation, it'll be a sign of progress, but in the meantime, he's the willing spear carrier.

BEN HENDRICKSON

										Bats: R			Throws: R					Born: 04-Feb-81		Age: 23

YEAR	TM	LG	AGE	G	GS	IP	H	BB	SO	HR	ERA	EQERA	EQH9	EQBB9	EQSO9	EQHR9	PERA	VORP	STF
2001	BLT	MID	20	25	25	133.3	122	72	133	3	2.84	5.42	10.1	6.9	5.6	0.5	5.49	2.4	16
2002	HDS	CAL	21	14	14	81.3	61	41	70	3	2.55	3.46	7.4	5.5	4.3	0.6	4.10	17.9	14
2002	HUN	SOU	21	13	13	69.7	57	35	50	2	2.97	4.96	7.9	4.7	4.8	0.6	4.02	4.6	18
2003	HUN	SOU	22	17	16	78.3	82	28	56	6	3.45	6.01	11.5	3.8	4.5	1.5	6.53	-3.2	-15

Hendrickson missed time early with elbow inflammation, but when he returned, his curve still had bite. But the way he throws it puts even more pressure on the elbow, and he doesn't want to change how he throws it. Like Jones, the organization is insisting that Hendrickson will be fine for 2004, but his overreliance on Uncle Charlie has to be a concern. He's still mastering changing speeds, and he does throw in the low 90s, so he's not that far from becoming valuable. Much depends on how urgently the Brewers decide that they need him. If they let him learn when and how often to rely on his bender, he might work out. If they push, they could scrag him as quickly as they burned out Ben Diggins. Bears an uncanny resemblance to the lead singer of Midnight Oil.

MIKE JONES

										Bats: R			Throws: R					Born: 23-Apr-83		Age: 21

YEAR	TM	LG	AGE	G	GS	IP	H	BB	SO	HR	ERA	EQERA	EQH9	EQBB9	EQSO9	EQHR9	PERA	VORP	STF
2001	OGD	PIO	18	9	7	33.7	29	10	32	1	3.74	4.70	9.1	3.8	4.4	0.6	4.38	3.1	15
2002	BLT	MID	19	27	27	138.7	135	62	132	3	3.11	5.36	9.5	5.3	5.4	0.5	4.85	3.4	23
2003	HUN	SOU	20	17	17	97.7	87	47	63	4	2.40	5.06	8.5	5.0	4.4	0.7	4.56	5.4	15
2004	*MIL*	*NL*	*21*	*20*	*18*	*105.3*	*108*	*59*	*61*	*11*	*4.91*	*5.04*	*9.3*	*4.4*	*4.7*	*0.8*	*5.11*	*5.5*	*-5*

Breakout: 7%   Improve: 67%   Collapse: 2%

Clearly the system's best young pitcher coming into the year, beyond mid-90s heat, Jones won hearts and minds with a mature, coachable mindset, and a willingness to work on his off-speed stuff. Fears of an elbow injury cropped up after a brilliant first half, but it was diagnosed as a sprain that shut him down. The elbow was still tender in September, creating fear he might not have dodged the surgeon's table. There are some who fear he's going to wind up needing serious surgery, which would cost him a year or so and render him a candidate for the 2006 rotation at best. The Brewers need to be careful.

MATT KINNEY

Bats: R   Throws: R   Born: 16-Dec-76   Age: 27

YEAR	TM	LG	AGE	G	GS	IP	H	BB	SO	HR	ERA	EQERA	EQH9	EQBB9	EQSO9	EQHR9	PERA	VORP	STF
2001	EDM	PCL	24	29	29	161.7	178	74	146	25	5.06	5.83	9.6	4.8	5.8	1.6	5.93	-3.9	-15
2002	EDM	PCL	25	5	5	27.3	42	4	21	9	8.90	9.00	14.2	1.4	5.2	3.8	10.14	-9.8	-89
2002	MIN	AL	25	14	12	66.0	78	33	45	13	4.64	5.74	10.5	4.2	5.9	1.5	6.13	-1.0	-14
2003	MIL	NL	26	33	31	190.7	201	80	152	27	5.19	5.21	9.2	3.4	6.3	1.2	4.92	-2.1	1
2004	MIL	NL	27	24	21	123.0	130	52	92	20	5.15	5.29	9.6	3.4	6.1	1.2	5.23	6.0	3

Breakout: 11%   Improve: 39%   Collapse: 22%

Another member of the cobbled-together rotation, Kinney at least came in with some upside, having been nabbed from a Twins organization that needed space on its 40-man roster. Kinney's problems really seem to be ones of endurance, as his performance drops steadily from the first pitch, to the point that he's toast after 90 pitches. He also wore down at season's end, failing to post a quality start in his last five outings after being left in to blow one in the seventh inning on August 25. He presents the Brewers with an interesting problem: He's got the stuff to be a solid reliever, but if his envelope as a starter can be pushed to 110 pitches, he could still turn into a fine third starter. The Brewers need a bit of everything, but the risks for Kinney are clear. As a high-leverage reliever, he could move to wealth, health, and job security pretty quickly. As a starter, he could get even better compensation, but would have a greater chance of flaming out.

DANNY KOLB

Bats: R   Throws: R   Born: 29-Mar-75   Age: 29

YEAR	TM	LG	AGE	G	GS	IP	H	BB	SO	HR	ERA	EQERA	EQH9	EQBB9	EQSO9	EQHR9	PERA	VORP	STF
2001	PCH	FLA	26	7	3	18.7	21	2	16	1	3.85	5.62	14.6	1.1	5.1	1.1	6.75	0.0	-26
2001	OKL	PCL	26	12	0	19.0	13	4	21	1	1.42	2.04	7.1	2.0	7.1	0.5	2.86	7.0	23
2001	TEX	AL	26	17	0	15.3	15	10	15	2	4.71	4.11	8.2	5.3	8.2	1.2	4.92	2.5	-1
2002	TEX	AL	27	34	0	32.0	27	22	20	1	4.22	3.98	7.1	5.7	5.4	0.3	3.70	5.7	1
2003	IND	INT	28	26	0	39.3	26	13	46	1	1.37	2.72	6.7	3.7	8.4	0.2	2.90	11.6	30
2003	MIL	NL	28	37	0	41.3	34	19	39	2	1.96	2.68	7.4	3.8	7.4	0.4	3.41	15.9	21
2004	MIL	NL	29	37	5	57.7	54	27	50	3	3.68	3.78	8.5	3.7	7.1	0.4	3.91	11.5	6

Breakout: 32%   Improve: 53%   Collapse: 25%

Called up in June, Kolb did a great job over the final half of the season, and potentially gives the Brewers a truly effective closer, something they've lacked since Bob Wickman was traded. Kolb cooks with gas, and despite years of health woes, he's still up in the mid-90s. If he breaks down again, it isn't like it'll cost Milwaukee a shot at the World Series. If he doesn't, then the team has something of value which will produce a bit of a litmus test on Melvin and company: Will they do the sensible thing that Dean Taylor did with Wickman, dealing him for the good stuff this organization can't get enough of, or will they pay through the nose for saves?

DEREK LEE

Bats: L   Throws: L   Born: 20-Aug-74   Age: 29

YEAR	TM	LG	AGE	G	GS	IP	H	BB	SO	HR	ERA	EQERA	EQH9	EQBB9	EQSO9	EQHR9	PERA	VORP	STF
2001	HUN	SOU	26	28	28	162.3	173	39	109	10	3.38	5.55	11.7	2.6	4.1	1.0	5.64	0.8	-16
2002	HUN	SOU	27	34	16	127.3	138	45	104	6	3.04	5.73	12.0	3.5	5.3	0.9	5.96	-1.7	-20
2003	HUN	SOU	28	20	13	87.3	85	28	59	6	3.30	5.49	11.5	3.5	4.2	1.5	6.41	0.9	-39
2003	IND	INT	28	14	8	60.0	55	19	55	1	3.75	4.37	8.9	3.6	6.5	0.2	3.76	7.6	21
2004	MIL	NL	29	15	8	45.3	53	21	30	6	5.27	5.41	10.6	3.6	5.3	1.0	5.64	2.5	-8

Breakout: 24%   Improve: 48%   Collapse: 24%

This borders on a courtesy mention, since Lee has spent much of the last five years in Double-A, long enough to be nominated for the Huntsville Chamber of Commerce at any rate. He was a draft-and-follow the Brewers picked in '96 and signed in '97. He hasn't changed much over time, having been a crafty lefthander from the start. For more info, just wait for the action-packed Dolph Lundgren comeback vehicle, *Ultimate Organizational Soldier*. OK, it might not deserve to be made, especially with the creative license involved with letting him carry an M60 machine gun onto the mound, but at least it would be more true to life than Disney's retelling of the Jim Morris story.

PEDRO LIRIANO

				Bats: R			Throws: R						Born: 23-Oct-80			Age: 23		

YEAR	TM	LG	AGE	G	GS	IP	H	BB	SO	HR	ERA	EQERA	EQH9	EQBB9	EQSO9	EQHR9	PERA	VORP	STF
2001	PRO	PIO	20	15	14	77.7	80	31	76	3	2.78	6.07	11.0	5.3	4.7	0.8	5.81	-3.6	1
2002	RCU	CAL	21	28	28	167.3	129	74	176	14	3.60	4.51	8.6	5.0	5.4	1.4	5.35	18.4	4
2003	HUN	SOU	22	27	26	142.7	138	62	116	12	3.78	6.50	11.0	4.7	5.2	1.7	6.66	-12.7	-14
2004	MIL	NL	23	13	9	51.7	58	30	35	9	5.92	6.07	10.3	4.6	5.4	1.3	6.18	0.3	-10

Breakout: 30%   Improve: 57%   Collapse: 19%

It's pretty remarkable that they got something for Alex Ochoa, let alone something potentially useful, but Liriano has a frequently effective power slider that could give him a future. He still needs polish when it comes to changing speeds, but he hasn't been pushed too hard, and he survived his introduction to Double-A. You would think that would reflect the profile of someone with considerable promise, but a heap of unearned runs helped his ERA considerably, and his control issues don't seem to be getting much better. If he doesn't pick up better control, he could still be handy in the pen.

LUIS MARTINEZ

				Bats: L			Throws: L						Born: 20-Jan-80			Age: 24		

YEAR	TM	LG	AGE	G	GS	IP	H	BB	SO	HR	ERA	EQERA	EQH9	EQBB9	EQSO9	EQHR9	PERA	VORP	STF
2001	HDS	CAL	21	22	22	112.7	112	64	121	9	5.19	5.72	10.2	6.6	5.5	1.3	6.38	-1.4	-5
2001	HUN	SOU	21	7	0	9.3	13	9	13	0	6.77	9.35	14.5	10.4	8.3	0.0	7.54	-3.6	7
2002	HUN	SOU	22	29	18	109.0	114	65	106	6	5.20	7.11	11.2	5.7	6.3	1.0	6.18	-16.8	-2
2003	HUN	SOU	23	20	20	115.0	93	54	116	4	2.58	4.96	9.1*	5.0	6.4	0.7	4.79	7.3	15
2003	IND	INT	23	7	7	45.7	37	19	46	0	0.98	2.11	7.6	4.6	7.6	0.2	3.52	16.6	48
2003	MIL	NL	23	4	4	16.3	25	15	10	3	9.94	9.37	13.2	7.2	5.0	1.7	8.22	-7.9	-32
2004	MIL	NL	24	20	14	76.0	85	52	60	12	6.27	6.43	10.2	5.4	6.4	1.2	6.43	2.0	-7

Breakout: 29%   Improve: 57%   Collapse: 22%

There's been an ongoing temptation to make Martinez into a situational lefty, but finally left alone to sink or swim as a starter, he got his career in order, rocketing through the system. Unfortunately by the time he reached Milwaukee, he'd already pitched a career-high 160.2 IP, and seemed worn out. Although he's 6'6" and wild, he's only a flamethrower by portside standards, coming in around 90. Beyond the heat, he has a solid curve and change, so he's equipped with a broad enough arsenal to make it in a big league rotation. The question is whether the Brewers want their starters to be as workmanlike and pastable as last year's lot, because Martinez is sure to be initially frustrating with his wildness. They've been patient, and if they can afford to wait a little while longer, they could have something.

SHANE NANCE

				Bats: L			Throws: L						Born: 07-Sep-77			Age: 26		

YEAR	TM	LG	AGE	G	GS	IP	H	BB	SO	HR	ERA	EQERA	EQH9	EQBB9	EQSO9	EQHR9	PERA	VORP	STF
2001	VRO	FLA	23	21	0	48.0	28	21	63	3	2.63	3.64	8.1	4.9	7.9	1.5	5.15	9.1	-2
2001	JAX	SOU	23	28	0	45.3	31	17	44	4	1.59	3.79	8.3	4.0	6.0	1.3	4.81	8.1	-7
2002	LVG	PCL	24	37	0	58.3	58	26	53	5	4.17	4.85	8.7	4.5	6.1	1.0	4.77	4.6	-6
2002	IND	INT	24	9	0	16.7	12	6	10	0	0.00	0.00	7.0	4.1	4.7	0.0	2.99	9.5	25
2002	MIL	NL	24	4	0	6.3	4	4	5	1	4.29	4.50	6.0	4.5	6.0	1.5	4.06	0.7	-7
2003	IND	INT	25	35	1	52.3	34	13	53	4	1.38	2.40	6.5	2.8	7.2	1.1	3.35	17.3	8
2003	MIL	NL	25	26	0	24.3	34	10	25	5	4.81	6.38	12.4	3.4	7.9	1.9	7.12	-0.8	-22
2004	ARI	NL	26	34	5	57.0	55	24	48	7	4.07	3.89	8.4	3.3	7.1	0.9	4.14	11.1	4

Breakout: 27%   Improve: 56%   Collapse: 17%

While Richie Sexson was clearly the target in the deal, the question is whether or not Nance might wind up being the third-best player in the trade, behind Sexson and Jorge de la Rosa. For the Snakes, he has a shot at becoming the effective lefty reliever they lacked last year. He's got better velocity than your typical specialist, and reminds some of Greg Hibbard for his bulldog little lefty rep.

NICK NEUGEBAUER

				Bats: R			Throws: R						Born: 15-Jul-80			Age: 23		

YEAR	TM	LG	AGE	G	GS	IP	H	BB	SO	HR	ERA	EQERA	EQH9	EQBB9	EQSO9	EQHR9	PERA	VORP	STF
2001	HUN	SOU	20	21	21	106.7	94	52	149	6	3.46	5.11	9.1	5.0	9.3	0.7	4.77	5.4	51
2001	IND	INT	20	4	4	24.0	10	9	26	1	1.50	1.99	3.6	4.0	8.7	0.4	1.80	9.1	73
2001	MIL	NL	20	2	2	6.0	6	6	11	1	7.50	7.50	9.0	7.5	13.5	1.5	6.09	-1.3	69
2002	IND	INT	21	5	5	19.3	20	12	18	4	5.13	6.87	9.3	6.4	7.9	2.0	6.61	-2.6	4
2002	MIL	NL	21	12	12	55.3	56	44	47	10	4.72	6.00	9.5	6.2	6.5	1.7	6.33	-2.4	10
2004	MIL	NL	23	19	14	84.0	80	46	79	10	4.55	4.66	8.6	4.3	7.6	0.9	4.80	10.4	10

Breakout: 12%   Improve: 57%   Collapse: 25%

The Brewers are feigning confidence, but Neugebauer has required two shoulder surgeries in less than 18 months. He might be ready to pitch in the spring, but previous management helped rush him back early from his first surgery. The Melvin regime can't really be blamed for it; they inherited an ex-prospect with a bum shoulder, and if he gives them anything, it's a bonus.

WES OBERMUELLER

Bats: R **Throws: R** Born: 22-Dec-76 Age: 27

YEAR	TM	LG	AGE	G	GS	IP	H	BB	SO	HR	ERA	EQERA	EQH9	EQBB9	EQSO9	EQHR9	PERA	VORP	STF
2001	WIL	CAR	24	20	6	38.0	38	16	28	3	3.08	6.47	12.7	5.9	4.2	2.0	8.09	-3.1	-66
2002	WIL	CAR	25	8	4	45.7	38	14	44	1	2.76	4.54	10.4	3.9	5.9	0.5	4.82	4.7	8
2002	WIC	TEX	25	17	17	105.7	98	40	65	6	2.89	5.09	10.8	4.1	4.2	1.2	5.83	5.3	-20
2002	KCR	AL	25	2	2	7.7	14	2	5	3	11.69	9.39	15.3	2.3	5.9	3.5	10.40	-3.2	-74
2003	OMA	PCL	26	17	17	106.3	108	42	62	11	4.40	5.75	10.3	4.3	4.5	1.5	6.03	-1.6	-29
2003	IND	INT	26	3	3	15.3	18	6	11	1	4.71	5.79	11.6	4.5	5.1	0.6	5.71	-0.3	-8
2003	MIL	NL	26	12	11	65.7	81	25	34	10	5.07	5.60	10.6	3.1	4.1	1.3	5.61	1.0	-17
2004	*MIL*	*NL*	*27*	*20*	*13*	*70.7*	*88*	*36*	*40*	*13*	*6.29*	*6.46*	*11.2*	*4.0*	*4.6*	*1.4*	*6.57*	*-2.3*	*-16*

Breakout: 19%   *Improve: 44%*   *Collapse: 29%*

Obermueller came over from the Royals in exchange for Curtis Leskanic, and drifted into the Brewers' rotation almost immediately. You might see his ERAs, note that he gave them seven quality starts in the 11 he made, and think that they might have something here. But keep in mind that he missed most of the previous three seasons to shoulder surgery and soreness, three s's you don't want to hear together. Between the baserunners, his tateriffic tendencies, his mediocre assortment, and his list of hurts, he's all risk. The Brewers can afford a bit of risk, but Obermueller's a long-shot at best.

MANNY PARRA

Bats: L **Throws: L** Born: 30-Oct-82 Age: 21

YEAR	TM	LG	AGE	G	GS	IP	H	BB	SO	HR	ERA	EQERA	EQH9	EQBB9	EQSO9	EQHR9	PERA	VORP	STF
2002	OGD	PIO	19	11	10	47.7	59	10	51	3	3.21	6.80	13.0	2.5	4.9	1.4	6.73	-5.8	-2
2003	BLT	MID	20	23	23	138.7	127	24	117	9	2.73	4.50	10.5	2.2	5.1	1.7	5.80	15.2	6
2004	*MIL*	*NL*	*21*	*21*	*16*	*97.7*	*106*	*30*	*69*	*15*	*4.60*	*4.72*	*9.8*	*2.4*	*5.7*	*1.2*	*4.85*	*10.8*	*5*

Breakout: 21%   *Improve: 61%*   *Collapse: 8%*

A strained pectoral muscle shut Parra down early, but it doesn't diminish a tremendous season for the highly-touted 2001 draft-and-follow. He routinely gets into the low 90s, which sets up an effective curve and chango. Both off speed pitches need polish, but that should come with time. The only downside is that his stiff delivery conjures up nightmarish memories of Kyle Peterson's fate. A proud product of American River College, Parra will hopefully do it more pride than I remember it taking from the nifty philosophy course I took there one summer, or its use as a set for that classic Emilio Estevez brat-pack Bonnie and Clyde adventure, *Justice*. Check it out, folks, it's a must-miss. Anyway, Parra seems like he'll be on the fast track, just as well since the Cal League isn't a great stopover on a minor league career.

RUBEN QUEVEDO

Bats: R **Throws: R** Born: 05-Jan-79 Age: 25

YEAR	TM	LG	AGE	G	GS	IP	H	BB	SO	HR	ERA	EQERA	EQH9	EQBB9	EQSO9	EQHR9	PERA	VORP	STF
2001	IOW	PCL	22	22	22	141.7	124	48	150	13	2.99	4.08	7.9	3.5	7.5	0.9	3.98	22.7	37
2001	MIL	NL	22	10	10	56.7	56	30	60	9	4.60	5.10	9.2	4.4	8.1	1.3	5.30	3.0	31
2002	MIL	NL	23	26	25	139.0	159	68	93	28	5.76	6.50	10.5	3.9	5.2	1.8	6.39	-13.4	-10
2003	IND	INT	24	5	5	25.7	24	8	23	1	2.10	3.38	9.0	3.4	6.4	0.4	3.96	5.9	28
2003	MIL	NL	24	9	8	42.7	53	23	19	12	6.74	6.86	10.7	4.3	3.4	2.4	7.31	-5.4	-46
2004	*MIL*	*NL*	*25*	*52*	*13*	*99.3*	*116*	*48*	*65*	*19*	*6.09*	*6.25*	*10.6*	*3.8*	*5.3*	*1.5*	*6.28*	*-3.1*	*-16*

Breakout: 14%   *Improve: 43%*   *Collapse: 24%*

As Rod Stewart whined long ago, some guys really do get all the breaks. And then there are the other guys. Take Quevedo, apparently gifted with the ability to become easily loathed. Quevedo managed this despite giving the Brewers quality starts in five of his first six games (one was blown in the 7th when Yost left him hanging against the Cubs), leading a pitching-desperate team to get cranky and ship him off. Admittedly, it's doubtful Quevedo was ever going to thrive in Miller Park; he needs a homer-suppressing stadium to help keep some of his big flies in play. There are other concerns: His velocity has dropped into the mid-80s range, and he had a bout of shoulder tendinitis that shut him down for almost three months. With pitchers, youneverknow, but Quevedo needs to get healthy and pick his next organization carefully.

GLENDON RUSCH   **Bats: L**   **Throws: L**   Born: 07-Nov-74   Age: 29

YEAR	TM	LG	AGE	G	GS	IP	H	BB	SO	HR	ERA	EQERA	EQH9	EQBB9	EQSO9	EQHR9	PERA	VORP	STF
2001	NYM	NL	26	33	33	179.0	216	43	156	23	4.63	5.30	11.1	2.0	6.7	1.0	5.23	5.7	9
2002	MIL	NL	27	34	34	210.7	227	76	140	30	4.70	5.20	9.9	2.8	5.2	1.3	5.21	9.0	-5
2003	IND	INT	28	4	3	21.0	17	4	20	4	3.86	4.19	8.4	2.3	7.0	2.8	6.06	3.0	-35
2003	MIL	NL	28	32	19	123.3	171	45	93	11	6.42	6.32	12.1	2.9	6.0	0.7	5.63	-16.2	0
2004	*TEX*	*AL*	*29*	*27*	*20*	*116.7*	*145*	*38*	*73*	*17*	*5.45*	*4.92*	*10.4*	*2.7*	*5.7*	*1.1*	*4.96*	*11.8*	*2*

Breakout: 14%   Improve: 55%   Collapse: 24%

That year with the Mets gave everyone reason to think he might be something, and an awful lot of statheads noodled on what he'd become because of a nice K/BB ratio. But it wasn't a lot of strikeouts, and it was quite a few home runs for Shea. Transplanted to Lid-Poppin' Park's brand of tater generation, Rusch has been beaten with enough regularity that France awarded him the *Legion d'honneur*. It's one of those things that make you wonder what anybody was thinking, but like red pants, berets, and Nehru jackets, I guess these things go in cycles.

CHRIS SAENZ   **Bats: R**   **Throws: R**   Born: 14-Aug-81   Age: 22

YEAR	TM	LG	AGE	G	GS	IP	H	BB	SO	HR	ERA	EQERA	EQH9	EQBB9	EQSO9	EQHR9	PERA	VORP	STF
2001	OGD	PIO	19	21	4	46.7	43	14	48	5	4.24	5.66	10.7	3.9	5.0	2.2	6.92	-0.3	-21
2002	BLT	MID	20	37	0	74.3	59	32	99	5	3.51	4.85	9.8	5.4	7.5	1.7	6.24	5.4	3
2003	HDS	CAL	21	26	26	128.0	121	56	136	20	5.20	5.20	9.8	5.4	6.3	2.7	7.53	5.2	-22
2003	HUN	SOU	21	1	0	6.0	4	3	6	0	1.50	3.38	6.8	5.1	6.8	0.0	3.10	1.3	48
2004	*MIL*	*NL*	*22*	*14*	*9*	*48.0*	*53*	*29*	*38*	*10*	*6.49*	*6.66*	*10.0*	*4.8*	*6.3*	*1.5*	*6.54*	*-0.8*	*-9*

Breakout: 17%   Improve: 53%   Collapse: 19%

An unheralded 28th-round pick in the Brewers' celebrated 2001 draft, Saenz surprisingly was one of its first members to arrive on the 40-man roster. It helps that so many of the other guys were high school picks another year away from having to be added, so Saenz is on while people like Mike Jones or Brad Nelson or J. J. Hardy are not. Saenz is another pitcher possessed of the organization's assortment of choice (fastball, curve, change). He's a bit of a mechanical menace, but he and fellow Arizona juco product Dennis Sarfate have bragging rights for the time being.

DENNIS SARFATE   **Bats: R**   **Throws: R**   Born: 09-Apr-81   Age: 23

YEAR	TM	LG	AGE	G	GS	IP	H	BB	SO	HR	ERA	EQERA	EQH9	EQBB9	EQSO9	EQHR9	PERA	VORP	STF
2001	OGD	PIO	20	9	4	23.3	20	10	32	4	4.64	6.05	12.1	6.1	7.0	3.7	10.03	-1.0	-51
2003	BLT	MID	22	26	26	139.7	114	66	140	11	2.83	4.81	10.4	6.2	6.2	2.3	7.53	10.5	-27
2004	*MIL*	*NL*	*23*	*18*	*12*	*64.3*	*86*	*39*	*43*	*15*	*7.95*	*8.16*	*12.1*	*4.7*	*5.4*	*1.8*	*8.06*	*-8.7*	*-20*

Breakout: 24%   Improve: 61%   Collapse: 22%

Another 2001 pick out of an Arizona juco, Sarfate was a pure flamethrower when he first started out, jetting fastballs into the mid-90s. Then he lost 2002 to a blown elbow, so this was his first full season, and it came while having to deal with regaining his touch. He still had good velocity, and he made major progress in adding a curve and change. He was also hot down the stretch, helping push Beloit into the playoffs. He's a long way from making it, but those peripherals obviously look promising.

BEN SHEETS   **Bats: R**   **Throws: R**   Born: 18-Jul-78   Age: 25

YEAR	TM	LG	AGE	G	GS	IP	H	BB	SO	HR	ERA	EQERA	EQH9	EQBB9	EQSO9	EQHR9	PERA	VORP	STF
2001	MIL	NL	22	25	25	151.3	166	48	94	23	4.76	5.28	10.0	2.7	4.7	1.2	5.16	5.2	11
2002	MIL	NL	23	34	34	216.7	237	70	170	21	4.15	4.67	10.1	2.5	6.2	0.9	4.73	21.5	26
2003	MIL	NL	24	34	34	220.7	232	43	157	29	4.44	4.49	9.1	1.6	5.7	1.1	4.28	15.7	17
2004	*MIL*	*NL*	*25*	*30*	*30*	*199.7*	*210*	*52*	*137*	*24*	*4.08*	*4.19*	*9.5*	*2.0*	*5.6*	*0.9*	*4.26*	*31.4*	*11*

Breakout: 19%   Improve: 56%   Collapse: 13%

He's being touted as the pitcher the Brewers have been supposed to get since Cal Eldred's summers in Denver were news, which is unfair. Sheets remains short of that, but 2003 was a year of small, significant improvements. He started doing a better job of spotting his curve against lefties, and improved his command. He's been a workhorse, gives them a quality start half of the time out on the mound, and he's young enough to keep improving if he can endure the workload. Last year, we said he was on the cusp of becoming pretty special. He's not there yet, but he did get a little closer. His homers-allowed column will likely decide which side of a 4 ERA he finishes on.

LUIS VIZCAINO

Bats: R   **Throws: R**   Born: 06-Aug-74   Age: 29

YEAR	TM	LG	AGE	G	GS	IP	H	BB	SO	HR	ERA	EQERA	EQH9	EQBB9	EQSO9	EQHR9	PERA	VORP	STF
2001	SAC	PCL	26	27	0	42.0	35	10	56	5	2.14	3.00	8.8	2.5	8.8	1.4	4.61	11.3	2
2001	OAK	AL	26	36	0	36.7	38	12	31	8	4.66	4.84	9.4	2.8	7.1	1.8	5.48	3.0	-17
2002	MIL	NL	27	76	0	81.3	55	30	79	6	2.99	3.00	6.5	2.9	7.6	0.7	2.97	22.5	20
2003	MIL	NL	28	75	0	62.0	64	25	61	16	6.39	5.93	9.0	3.3	7.7	2.2	5.94	-6.4	-31
2004	MIL	NL	29	46	1	60.3	55	23	60	10	4.09	4.20	8.3	3.1	8.0	1.2	4.38	9.7	7

Breakout: 24%   Improve: 54%   Collapse: 14%

Vizcaino endured a year where everything went wrong, especially early on, allowing 11 home runs by the All-Star Break. He had a better season from there (4.28 ERA, with a baserunner and a strikeout per inning pitched), and he should be able to resume his place in the team's bullpen of the immediate future. There's always discussion about whether or not he's ever going to pick up a consistent second pitch, and that's a concern, considering he's going to turn 30. However, he's said to have come to the U.S. as one of the most poorly-educated players to have arrived from the Dominican in anyone's memory. If he hasn't learned by now, it might be because he isn't going to, or it could be that he's got a lot more to overcome than just learning to pitch. Either way, it's worth taking the time to keep him around and find out.

TOM WILHELMSEN

Bats: R   **Throws: R**   Born: 16-Dec-83   Age: 20

YEAR	TM	LG	AGE	G	GS	IP	H	BB	SO	HR	ERA	EQERA	EQH9	EQBB9	EQSO9	EQHR9	PERA	VORP	STF
2003	BLT	MID	19	15	15	88.0	78	27	63	6	2.76	4.88	9.4	3.9	4.5	1.7	5.75	6.3	4

A little league teammate of J. J. Hardy's, Wilhelmsen is a storky flamethrower snagged in last year's draft who broke down early on with elbow trouble. He's a hoped-for phenom in the A. J. Burnett mold, a free-spirited flamethrower, dialing up heat into the mid-90s, but generally closer to 90. He's not a great prospect, considering the arm trouble, his reputation for goofiness, and his lacking a breaking pitch or much movement, but if he only grew up to be Charlie Kerfeld, he'd still be a Wisconsin icon.

Montreal Expos

For years, Baseball Prospectus has pounded on teams to find soft spots in the talent market, and then take full advantage of them.

Start with a well-drafted, well-developed core of great young talent. Put those players to good use while they're in years 0–3 of their major league life span, when they're cheapest and most likely to improve. If an elite talent in his prime becomes available, spend the superstar money for the superstar player. Pass on bloated contracts to average players. Instead, wait for the market to come to you, and grab the useful players who've fallen through the cracks at bargain prices. Make shrewd trades for players who'll be underrated due to their unappreciated skills, be it their defense, plate discipline, or durability. Fill out your roster by searching under every rock, seeking out the six-year minor league free agents, independent league nobodies and Rule 5 forgottens that have shown a track record of performance, even if that track record was forged far from the majors.

Twenty-nine teams go into the every off-season able to follow each of these steps to build a winner. Is it harder to sign a superstar if you're the low-revenue Devil Rays? Sure. Is it tougher to make great trades if you have little good bait to offer, like the Tigers? Of course. But every team, given the right management people, has been free to use any or all of these methods to build a winner.

Except, that is, for the Expos.

Claiming that a team can't do something other teams can might seem odd coming from us. When Bud Selig and MLB's poor-mouthing owners complain every year that 10, 15, or 27 teams have no hope and faith heading into a given season, BP takes on those lame arguments, barrels blazing. But the Expos have been playing by a different set of rules for what seems like forever.

To understand the Expos' situation, try this date on for size: January 8, 1979. That date goes back further than 1981, the last time they made the playoffs, before putting together the longest current streak of any team in the four major North American team sports not to make it to post-season. It pre-dates the start of Rickey Henderson's big league career, Ronald Reagan's first term, MTV, and Paris Hilton's birth. It's the last time the Expos signed a legitimate free agent from another team.

In signing Elias Sosa, the Charles Bronfman-owned Expos grabbed a reliever who'd fared well in Oakland and

EXPOS PROSPECTUS

2003 record: 83–79; Fourth place, NL East

Pythagenport record: 80–82

Runs scored per game: 4.4 (10th in NL)

Runs allowed per game: 4.4 (8th in NL)

Team EqA: .247 (14th in NL)

2003 Batters Age: 28.2 (3rd youngest in NL)

2003 Pitchers Age: 27.0 (3rd youngest in NL)

Ballpark: Olympic Stadium/Hiram Bithorn Stadium; Severe hitter's park; Combined Park Factor of 1.067

2003: MLB's wards racked up the frequent flier miles, which along with Vlad's injury factored into second-half fade.

2004: Vazquez and Vlad are Expos no longer, but is rebuilding the right strategy with such an uncertain future?

Los Angeles, slamming the door in late-inning situations. The Expos finished second to the Pirates that year, falling just two games short. Sosa posted a stellar 1.96 ERA and 18 saves in nearly 100 innings that year, playing a big role in the team's success.

And that was it. When the Expos started the next decade billed as the Team of the 80s, they rode the contributions of homegrown stars like Gary Carter, Andre Dawson, and Tim Raines. They'd occasionally retain one of their own, as they did with Raines and Dennis Martinez in the mid-80s. But when shopping elsewhere, they never grabbed anyone who wasn't a reclamation project or a bust with nowhere else to sign. In the early 90s the Expos began building a core of good, young players, culminating in a near-miss in 1993 and the best record in 1994, before that season ended on a work stoppage. Not once did they sign even a decent major league regular coming off a productive season. Ditto the mid-90s, late 90s and the first few years of the aughts.

The Expos' incredible streak of non-signings has come to a head lately, with the price of solid, middle-class major league talent coming down to levels some lousy middle relievers would have sneered at just a few years ago. Players like Reggie Sanders, Jose Cruz Jr., and David Ortiz have started flooding the market the last couple years, with teams learning to exploit market inefficiencies and chucking arbitration-eligible and easily replaceable talent. The union's talk of collusion aside, teams have simply wised up to the increasing availability of middle-class talent and refused to pay much for it.

Montreal didn't take advantage of the new economics. Rather than snag Sanders or Kenny Lofton last off-season, they let Endy Chavez poison the lineup on an everyday basis. Frank Robinson's stubborn refusal to keep Chavez in the leadoff spot only made matters worse, short-circuiting scads of innings and making Chavez a HACKING MASS hero. Rather than pursue a Bill Mueller, they prayed that Fernando Tatis would fulfill even half his long-dormant potential or $6.5 million salary. Chavez and Tatis combined to finish 18.4 runs below replacement level. Given the Expos entered their late-August showdown with the Marlins tied for the Wild Card lead and finished with 83 wins, one wonders what might have been had the Expos fielded mere league-average players at those positions. Not all the blame can be placed on history: Omar Minaya made few creative moves to free up payroll and change the roster around, and the Expos' 29 co-owners weren't about to allow more than the bare minimum of payroll wiggle room, given they'd be funding a potential rival.

This year, things have finally started to change a bit. But the circumstances surrounding those changes still stink.

No event crystallized the Expos' plight as well as Vladimir Guerrero's departure to greener pastures. For starters, Vlad may have never left if the Commissioner's office hadn't put the kibosh on the team's contract offer to its star player. Well before Guerrero hit the free agent market, Minaya had floated the idea of a five-year, $75 million contract. Given that competitive bid, the ice-cold nature of this year's free agent market, and Vlad's comfort level in Montreal, the Expos would have had a good shot at keeping him. Of course, MLB wasn't about to let that happen. Not after the state in which the league had left the team— hanging in limbo, with no real ownership, no clear plan for staying put or relocation, and a travel schedule that barely stopped short of a three-game set with the Mets in Papua New Guinea. The notion that other teams were going to pay the Expos to keep the best free agent in-house and off the market was laughable.

Even the most loaded team in the game would take a hit if it lost a potential Hall of Famer in his prime. But smart teams adjust. Of course the Expos, until now, couldn't even sign second-tier free agents. Even the promise of playing time hadn't been enough to attract mid-level talent over the years. Only when a player finds nowhere else to play and has no alternative but to flip burgers does he reluctantly sign with the 'Spos.

Credit General Manager Omar Minaya with snapping that long-standing streak, even if the booty was relatively modest. In Carl Everett and Tony Batista, the Expos signed two established major league veterans. Both come with their share of warts: Everett struggles against lefties, has been injury-prone in the past, and has dealt with enough off-field controversy to scare away many other suitors. Still, Everett's a huge offensive upgrade over Endy Chavez or Ron Calloway, and the two-year, $7 million contract the Expos gave him didn't break the bank. Batista's a moderate power, low on-base hitter with a poor glove coming off the worst full season of his career. Considering the in-house alternative at 3B involved a Jamey Carroll/Scott Hodges/Nelson Muntz platoon though, the one-year, $1.5 million contract Minaya gave Batista, in an extremely weak year for available third base talent, at least adds a win or two for a low price.

The decision not to offer Vlad arbitration was more puzzling. After pulling the initial contract offer, the Expos made a last-ditch effort to re-sign Guerrero, offering a heavily backloaded five-year, $70 million contract just before the deadline to tender arbitration to free agents. When Vlad's camp turned it down, the Expos let him go. But why then, not offer arbitration? Minaya claimed the Expos would have been hosed had Guerrero accepted, as an arbitration award likely would have sucked up at least one-third of the team's allowed payroll of roughly $45 million. But Guerrero had already turned down $70 million, and his agents made it clear they were eyeing megabucks by demanding nine figures, even as press time in January rolled around. Bringing up the remote possibility of Vlad accepting arbitration was a convenient cop-out for a GM who'd repeatedly shown little regard for the team's on-field future; by non-tendering Guerrero the team couldn't even recoup the two compensation draft picks they'd have received once he signed elsewhere.

Watching Vlad leave reinforced two points: The Expos desperately needed to find some young offensive talent to help fill the void, and if possible trade players like Javier Vazquez and Jose Vidro before they bolt for free agent waters after the '04 season, leaving Montreal again holding the bag. While Vidro's still around, Minaya did find a taker for Vazquez. By trading the five-year veteran pitcher to the Yankees for Nick Johnson, Juan Rivera, and Randy Choate, Minaya found a potential impact first baseman, a corner outfielder with a Carlos Lee profile, and a decent back-of-the-bullpen lefty. Johnson's perennial hand and wrist injuries should be cause for concern among Expos fans used to watching talented young players like Fernando Tatis, Carl Pavano, and Tony Armas succumb to injuries, and Rivera and Choate have their limitations as well. But the trade improves the offense, and all three came cheap, allowing the Expos to parlay the savings into the Everett and Batista signings.

Though the team may no longer sport any gaping holes in the lineup, a lot of things will have to go right for the Expos to be better than it was with Vlad and Vazquez around. Along with shocker Livan Hernandez, Vazquez was one of the five most valuable players in the NL East last year as rated by Value Over Replacement Player (VORP). A Vaz-less rotation of out-of-nowhere ace Hernandez, fourth-starter-turned-#2 Tomo Ohka, plus Tony Armas, Zach Day, and Claudio Vargas—the last three having all suffered significant injuries last year—doesn't inspire much confidence.

Moreover, the team finished 12th in the NL last year with Vlad still an Expo, despite playing 22 games in the hitter's haven of San Juan. They went 64–53 with Guerrero in the lineup, 19–26 without. Vlad put up just under 50 runs above replacement value in 2003 while missing more than a quarter of the season, following lines of 71.3 and 57.1 the prior two years. It'll take healthy seasons from Johnson and Everett, along with a bounceback by Batista, just to match the combined output of Guerrero, Wil Cordero, and Jamey Carroll (which is to say, Guerrero and two place-holders). Add it all up and the team looks primed for another season around .500.

Of course, boiling down the 2003 Expos to a run-of-the-mill 83–79 team tells only a fraction of the story. Despite every off-effort to alienate the home fans, the faithful started showing up in spurts last season, as the Expos contended for much of the year. A May series with the Phillies featured more excitement than had been seen at the Big O in years; rowdy crowds made a comeback, including 33,236 who sounded like 100,000 for a Saturday night thriller ended by a Wil Cordero walk-off homer. Even trips to Puerto Rico snuffing fan momentum, combined with more dumping on Montreal by MLB all year, couldn't prevent several surprisingly large crowds at Pie-IX and Pierre-de-Coubertin.

Unfortunately, when the epitaph of the 2003 season gets written, it'll best be summed up by a series of events around Labor Day. The Expos reeled off five wins in a row to pull into a tie with Florida for the Wild Card lead. Facing the Marlins for a four-game set in Miami, the Fish swept the Expos out of town. The Marlins went on to win it all, while the Expos went on to improve their golf games.

As the Expos flailed away in that series and dropped out of the race over the next few days, they could point to their own lack of talent as the culprit. But save some blame for MLB, which wouldn't let the Expos so much as call up one player from Triple-A when rosters expanded, even with the team still in the race. Three players at one-sixth major league minimum salary, plus meal money, hotel, and miscellaneous costs might have run a couple hundred thousand bucks. Terrmel Sledge may not have

led the Expos to the pennant, but it'd have been nice to find out if the PCL MVP candidate could have injected some life into the Expo lineup.

MLB wasn't alone in nailing the '03 season shut—Minaya, despite his golden reputation in some circles, also misfired. The Livan Hernandez trade worked out to be one of the best deals in baseball in years. It didn't take a genius to trade three high-level prospects for Colon in '02, though we can applaud Minaya's desire to win there. After that, it gets ugly.

A shameless obsession with acquiring Latin players to the exclusion of others continued to dog him. Luis Ayala was a great snag. But when Juan Gonzalez vetoed a mid-season trade to Montreal, you had to wonder why Minaya didn't go after Everett—a comparable, highly available hitter without the injury issues—instead.

Minaya's lack of preparation continued to dog him as well. As mentioned in *BP 2003,* he went into the 2002 Winter Meetings knowing he had to make a trade, yet didn't properly research other teams' assets, dithered with several GMs, came away empty-handed, and eventually settled on Bartolo Colon for Rocky Biddle, El Duque's Medic Alert bracelet and the poor man's Fernando Seguignol. The Gonzalez snafu, and Minaya's lack of a Plan B in that case, further rammed the point home, and left fans who'd seen the team climb back into contention wondering what might have been with one more slugger batting behind Vlad.

To Minaya's credit, he's improved over time, soliciting help from others on the performance analysis side to augment his own scouting background. Everett could pay dividends, and a couple of well-placed moves at the margins, including an effective second catcher to replace the departed Michael Barrett and some pitching help, could give the Expos a legitimate shot at second place in the East, with the Phillies looking like the division's clear favorites on paper.

The real problem here is Minaya has to be Branch Rickey to make this work, and that's asking too much of any GM. Years of terrible drafting, development, trades, and cheapskatery by former regimes, as well as a deck stacked against the Expos by MLB, have combined to give Minaya one of the toughest jobs in sports. If everything breaks right, fans can talk about the Expos as contenders while sitting on Crescent St. terraces in the summer months. All things considered—a schedule that will feature 22 more "home" games in Puerto Rico, a team missing one of the best players in franchise history, continued status as MLB's wards, and the ever-present threats of relocation or contraction—that wouldn't be too bad.

HITTERS

MICHAEL BARRETT   C   **Bats: R**   **Throws: R**   Born: 22-Oct-76   Age: 27

YEAR	TM	LG	AGE	AB	H	2B	3B	HR	BB	SO	SB	CS	AVG	OBP	SLG	MLVR	EQBA	EQOBP	EQSLG	EQMLVR	VORP	DEFENSE
2001	MON	NL	24	472	118	33	2	6	25	54	2	1	.250	.289	.367	-.206	.252	.292	.370	-.202	-3.8	126-C -14
2002	MON	NL	25	376	99	20	1	12	40	65	6	3	.263	.332	.418	.019	.270	.337	.435	-.012	16.1	106-C -2
2003	MON	NL	26	226	47	9	2	10	21	37	0	0	.208	.280	.398	-.189	.207	.276	.396	-.228	-3.5	62-C -2
2004	CHC	NL	27	255	63	14	1	7	23	41	1	1	.247	.311	.393	-.115	.250	.312	.405	-.111	7.3	70-C -3

Breakout: 34%   *Improve: 55%*   *Collapse: 27%*

After watching Barrett flail to a line of .214/.278/.288 in 2000 while being jerked between catcher, third base, and the minors, you'd have thought nothing would ever approach that frustration. The 2003 season offered a sturdy challenge to that peak of suckitude. He started last season ice-cold, "hitting" .093/.109/.204 in April and .191/.250/.298 in June and losing time to Brian Schneider. Barrett finally heated up in July, but a severely strained hip flexor derailed his hot streak, knocking him onto the DL. Finally sent for a rehab assignment, Barrett broke his finger, missing another month and adding up to a lost season. We urged the Expos to trade Barrett and find a cheaper alternative after the '02 season, before he made $2.6 million last year. A slam-dunk non-tender, credit Omar Minaya with getting A's minor league pitcher Brett Price in the first of two trades that eventually landed Barrett with the Cubs. He'll bounce back somewhat, but keep your expectations reasonable.

PETER BERGERON   CF   **Bats: L**   **Throws: R**   Born: 09-Nov-77   Age: 26

YEAR	TM	LG	AGE	AB	H	2B	3B	HR	BB	SO	SB	CS	AVG	OBP	SLG	MLVR	EQBA	EQOBP	EQSLG	EQMLVR	VORP	DEFENSE	
2001	OTT	INT	23	206	49	5	3	0	20	42	15	7	.238	.307	.291	-.190	.225	.292	.282	-.342	-12.2	50-CF -3	
2001	MON	NL	23	375	79	11	4	3	28	87	10	7	.211	.275	.285	-.368	.212	.273	.288	-.379	-24.4	92-CF -2	
2002	MON	NL	24	123	23	3	2	0	22	44	10	3	.187	.310	.244	-.282	.200	.315	.256	-.341	-6.8	31-CF -2	
2002	OTT	INT	24	340	99	9	4	1	39	65	7	7	.291	.364	.350	.022	.272	.345	.329	-.144	-9.7	46-LF -1	43-CF -4
2003	EDM	PCL	25	388	117	19	7	1	37	64	12	3	.302	.360	.394	.057	.274	.334	.367	-.111	4.3	95-CF -5	
2004	MON	NL	26	231	60	11	3	3	22	45	5	3	.261	.331	.373	-.097	.246	.314	.344	-.188	-3.5	64-CF -4	

Breakout: 21%   *Improve: 38%*   *Collapse: 35%*

He's gone from a poor man's Brett Butler to a homeless man's Brett Butler. Bergeron's at least two years past due for a change of scenery, where he could probably help a few teams as a backup center fielder/24th man. That's a far cry from the player who showed a good blend of on-base ability, gap power, and solid defense in the Dodgers' organization last century and looked like a viable major league center fielder. Last year's modest spike was driven by a few extra points of batting average, with no progress in his plate approach and little power. Only the Expos' black hole of prospects kept Bergeron in this book.

LARRY BROADWAY   1B   **Bats: L**   **Throws: L**   Born: 17-Dec-80   Age: 23

YEAR	TM	LG	AGE	AB	H	2B	3B	HR	BB	SO	SB	CS	AVG	OBP	SLG	MLVR	EQBA	EQOBP	EQSLG	EQMLVR	VORP	DEFENSE
2002	VER	NYP	21	127	40	3	0	4	13	33	0	0	.315	.379	.433	.245	.227	.277	.333	-.300	-16.1	32-1B -1
2003	SAV	SAL	22	290	89	25	4	14	44	70	3	4	.307	.400	.566	.416	.223	.295	.420	-.148	-6.5	80-1B 4
2003	BRV	FLA	22	76	17	7	1	1	18	20	0	1	.224	.367	.382	.105	.183	.299	.317	-.302	-6.5	20-1B 2
2003	HAR	EAS	22	78	25	3	0	5	7	15	0	0	.321	.371	.551	.317	.269	.326	.462	.005	2.1	19-1B -1
2004	MON	NL	23	272	67	15	2	11	29	71	1	1	.246	.321	.435	-.044	.231	.305	.401	-.140	-1.9	75-1B -3

Breakout: 33%   *Improve: 58%*   *Collapse: 19%*

What's this? A hitting prospect? Yup, it's true. A third-round pick out of Duke in 2002, Broadway brings an honest-to-goodness blend of power and patience to an organization that's seen a similar approach from Brad Wilkerson and uh . . . how long ago was Larry Walker a prospect? Broadway's plate discipline has translated into decent walk totals—69 in just over 500 times up through three levels last year. But it's his improved ability to wait for a pitch to drive, then crush it when he gets one that has the Expos excited. After smoking the Sally League, Broadway zoomed all the way to Double-A, and looks primed to continue climbing in '04. Broadway's the most encouraging example of an Expos scouting and player development team that's started to favor polished, college-groomed players, rather than just tools freaks. For a team starved for legit bats in its system, this is a good thing.

ORLANDO CABRERA   SS   Bats: Throws: Born: 02-Nov-74   Age: 29

YEAR	TM	LG	AGE	AB	H	2B	3B	HR	BB	SO	SB	CS	AVG	OBP	SLG	MLVR	EQBA	EQOBP	EQSLG	EQMLVR	VORP	DEFENSE
2001	MON	NL	26	626	173	41	6	14	43	54	19	7	.276	.324	.428	-.035	.276	.325	.430	-.036	29.1	159-SS 29
2002	MON	NL	27	563	148	43	1	7	48	53	25	7	.263	.321	.380	-.049	.270	.325	.396	-.090	16.7	151-SS 0
2003	MON	NL	28	626	186	47	2	17	52	64	24	2	.297	.347	.460	.068	.290	.344	.452	.042	40.3	157-SS 3
2004	MON	NL	29	544	159	35	3	14	46	55	17	4	.291	.347	.443	.046	.274	.330	.409	-.056	20.2	141-SS -1

Breakout: 13%   Improve: 46%   Collapse: 23%

Cabrera's back injury, a bulging disk suffered in 2002, was worse than anyone let on. He lost some of his ability to drive the ball, with his '01 home run total getting sliced in half. More alarmingly, Cabrera went from a Gold Glove shortstop to an average one, losing range and flexibility. He worked all off-season to strengthen his back, losing weight and strengthening his abs in the process. The results were mixed. Cabrera enjoyed a career year with the bat; his defense improved from his '02 effort but still fell short of his 2001 Gold Glove standards. Perhaps most impressive were these figures: 24-2, his remarkable SB-CS totals, and 162, the number of games he played last season. Keep an eye on his back problems going forward—Cabrera woke up every morning last season in pain. His ability to stave off that pain will greatly influence his on-field performance, and will make a several-million dollar difference to his bank account as he enters his walk year.

RON CALLOWAY   OF   Bats: L   Throws: L   Born: 04-Sep-76   Age: 27

YEAR	TM	LG	AGE	AB	H	2B	3B	HR	BB	SO	SB	CS	AVG	OBP	SLG	MLVR	EQBA	EQOBP	EQSLG	EQMLVR	VORP	DEFENSE	
2001	OTT	INT	24	239	63	12	0	10	16	64	11	1	.264	.323	.439	.047	.252	.309	.426	-.091	4.0	31-CF -3	23-RF -3
2001	HAR	EAS	24	279	92	22	4	9	24	46	25	7	.330	.385	.534	.324	.277	.333	.456	.016	14.7	36-CF -5	16-RF -1
2002	OTT	INT	25	447	118	21	5	14	44	89	16	12	.264	.335	.427	.055	.244	.315	.407	-.113	-6.6	121-RF 3	
2003	MON	NL	26	340	81	17	1	9	20	80	9	2	.238	.282	.374	-.199	.235	.278	.370	-.241	-13.0	44-LF 3	35-RF -1
2004	MON	NL	27	281	75	16	2	11	25	60	8	3	.268	.332	.454	.016	.252	.315	.419	-.084	2.2	76-RF 2	

Breakout: 37%   Improve: 57%   Collapse: 21%

Like Endy Chavez, Calloway frequently went long stretches at a time doing nothing with the bat. Also like Chavez, just when it looked like he'd finally get buried on the bench, Calloway would come through with a big, timely hit. The numbers bear out Calloway's fortuitous timing: .185/.222./.274 with the bases empty, .291/.339/.471 with runners on. With enough studies out there disproving the existence of clutch hitters to choke a horse, it's wishful thinking to expect a similar split in the future. Which means Calloway will have to do a lot better than his awful overall line to be even a useful spare outfielder in the majors. A K:BB ratio considerably better than 4:1 would be a great place to start.

JAMEY CARROLL   3B   Bats: R   Throws: R   Born: 18-Feb-74   Age: 30

YEAR	TM	LG	AGE	AB	H	2B	3B	HR	BB	SO	SB	CS	AVG	OBP	SLG	MLVR	EQBA	EQOBP	EQSLG	EQMLVR	VORP	DEFENSE	
2001	OTT	INT	27	267	64	8	2	0	18	41	5	5	.240	.292	.285	-.225	.230	.281	.274	-.373	-15.6	27-2B -4	23-SS 1
2002	OTT	INT	28	421	118	19	2	8	37	39	6	10	.280	.342	.392	.033	.262	.323	.375	-.129	6.8	81-3B 15	27-2B 4
2002	MON	NL	28	71	22	5	3	1	4	12	1	0	.310	.347	.507	.205	.306	.342	.514	.144	5.9	13-3B -2	
2003	MON	NL	29	227	59	10	1	1	19	39	5	2	.260	.323	.326	-.178	.254	.316	.325	-.218	-2.2	55-3B 2	
2004	MON	NL	30	212	56	11	1	3	19	32	3	2	.263	.328	.373	-.101	.247	.312	.344	-.193	0.6	60-3B 1	

Breakout: 26%   Improve: 43%   Collapse: 34%

Thus endeth the excitement produced by small sample size. After an eye-catching September debut in '02, Carroll was exposed over a full season's work as the club's utility infielder. He doesn't flash enough glove or hit lefties well enough to make a usable platoon player anywhere in the infield either, even on an Expos team with no reliable third base solution since Tim Wallach circa 1990. The Expos have carried some stinky benches over the years. This one ranked among the ripest.

MATT CEPICKY   Bats: L   Throws: R   Born: 10-Nov-77   Age: 26

YEAR	TM	LG	AGE	AB	H	2B	3B	HR	BB	SO	SB	CS	AVG	OBP	SLG	MLVR	EQBA	EQOBP	EQSLG	EQMLVR	VORP	DEFENSE
2001	HAR	EAS	23	459	121	23	8	19	21	97	5	12	.264	.296	.473	.054	.225	.261	.408	-.227	-24.5	102-LF -1
2002	HAR	EAS	24	419	116	25	2	16	33	94	7	1	.277	.327	.461	.084	.237	.285	.400	-.184	-16.2	79-LF -4
2002	MON	NL	24	74	16	3	0	3	4	21	0	0	.216	.256	.378	-.193	.227	.266	.387	-.245	-3.6	11-LF 0
2003	EDM	PCL	25	442	133	23	4	7	31	82	7	2	.301	.349	.419	.070	.275	.324	.393	-.092	-4.9	89-LF -13
2003	MON	NL	25	8	2	1	0	0	0	2	0	0	.250	.250	.375	-.244	.250	.250	.375	-.277	-0.3	
2004	MON	NL	26	206	55	11	2	8	17	44	2	1	.268	.328	.454	.010	.252	.311	.419	-.091	0.8	57-LF -5

Breakout: 34%   Improve: 57%   Collapse: 26%

Cepicky upped his average over .300 and cut down a bit on his strikeouts, both somewhat encouraging signs. But he still doesn't walk, and his Plantier-like hacks generated only seven homers and 34 extra-base hits over a full season in Triple-A, when all he had going for him in the first place was his power potential. Given the Expos' perennial revenue crunch, they might consider charging two bits a head to see Cepicky take giant cuts in batting practice. If they ever gave him a regular big-league job, the team may have to pay the fans as penance.

ENDY CHAVEZ   OF   Bats: L   Throws: L   Born: 07-Feb-78   Age: 26

YEAR	TM	LG	AGE	AB	H	2B	3B	HR	BB	SO	SB	CS	AVG	OBP	SLG	MLVR	EQBA	EQOBP	EQSLG	EQMLVR	VORP	DEFENSE	
2001	WIC	TEX	23	168	50	6	1	1	16	13	11	6	.298	.353	.363	.003	.253	.306	.306	-.265	-6.2	38-CF	1
2001	OMA	PCL	23	104	35	6	0	0	0	13	4	3	.337	.333	.394	-.018	.301	.308	.359	-.152	-0.1	20-CF	-2
2001	KCR	AL	23	77	16	2	0	0	3	8	0	2	.208	.237	.234	-.489	.221	.250	.247	-.479	-8.2	15-LF	0
2002	OTT	INT	24	405	139	28	5	4	33	37	21	13	.343	.392	.467	.268	.316	.367	.438	.086	29.2	93-CF	6
2002	MON	NL	24	125	37	8	5	1	5	16	3	5	.296	.321	.464	.092	.299	.321	.472	.039	5.8	35-CF	3
2003	MON	NL	25	483	121	25	5	5	31	59	18	7	.251	.294	.354	-.197	.243	.287	.348	-.249	-10.4	119-CF	-2
2004	MON	NL	26	431	122	25	4	6	32	50	15	6	.283	.332	.403	-.040	.266	.315	.372	-.137	-2.6	112-CF	1

Breakout: 20%   *Improve: 41%*   *Collapse: 28%*

It's tough to overstate the damage Endy Chavez did to the Expos' playoff hopes last season. Unburdened by trivialities such as getting on base, Chavez put up numbers below replacement level, hacking at everything, hitting the ball hard about once a week, and short-circuiting gobs of potential rallies. The real blame goes to Frank Robinson here: Chavez spent more than four months polluting the lineup from the leadoff spot, where his out-tastic efforts hurt the most. The offense finally clicked (for a while, anyway) when Brad Wilkerson was promoted to leadoff and Chavez dropped to eighth. Chavez's defense could still make him a useful fourth outfielder if he can continue his modest improvement in pitches seen per plate appearance. He shouldn't be an option as a starter, and probably won't be with newly signed Carl Everett expected to push Brad Wilkerson to center.

CHAD CHOP   OF   Bats: L   Throws: L   Born: 21-Mar-80   Age: 24

YEAR	TM	LG	AGE	AB	H	2B	3B	HR	BB	SO	SB	CS	AVG	OBP	SLG	MLVR	EQBA	EQOBP	EQSLG	EQMLVR	VORP	DEFENSE			
2002	VER	NYP	22	272	69	18	0	5	19	50	3	2	.254	.308	.375	.031	.196	.237	.307	-.434	-58.6	61-LF	-10		
2003	SAV	SAL	23	485	156	26	5	11	32	75	10	8	.322	.368	.464	.261	.259	.292	.387	-.173	-18.6	77-LF	-12	39-1B	-4
2004	MON	NL	24	254	64	14	2	7	15	47	3	1	.252	.298	.407	-.115	.237	.283	.375	-.209	-8.1	68-LF	-7		

Breakout: 34%   *Improve: 49%*   *Collapse: 26%*

Just because you're one of the best hitting prospects in an organization doesn't mean you're actually good. He was drafted in the same class as Larry Broadway, but their vastly different plate approaches mean that's the only class they share. A 23-year-old corner outfield/first base prospect in the Sally League needs to show more power and patience than Chop did last year. By season's end, he was still in Savannah, while Broadway had marched all the way to Double-A Harrisburg. He'll need a breakthrough season to get on track for a useful major league career.

WIL CORDERO   1B   Bats: R   Throws: R   Born: 03-Oct-71   Age: 32

YEAR	TM	LG	AGE	AB	H	2B	3B	HR	BB	SO	SB	CS	AVG	OBP	SLG	MLVR	EQBA	EQOBP	EQSLG	EQMLVR	VORP	DEFENSE			
2001	CLE	AL	29	268	67	11	1	4	22	50	0	0	.250	.313	.343	-.160	.268	.332	.372	-.112	-3.9	30-LF	-3	20-1B	-2
2002	CLE	AL	30	18	4	0	0	0	0	3	0	0	.222	.222	.222	-.494	.278	.278	.278	-.348	-1.0				
2002	MON	NL	30	143	39	9	0	6	17	26	2	0	.273	.349	.462	.113	.276	.359	.476	.089	5.5	20-LF	-2		
2003	MON	NL	31	436	121	27	0	16	49	90	1	1	.278	.354	.450	.048	.272	.348	.445	.023	10.8	115-1B	1		
2004	MON	NL	32	268	69	13	1	8	26	52	1	1	.259	.327	.407	-.061	.244	.311	.376	-.156	-3.6	73-1B	-2		

Breakout: 18%   *Improve: 36%*   *Collapse: 35%*

With no major league-ready hitters, limited funds to spend, and a lack of creativity from Omar Minaya, the Expos were forced to lean on Cordero for more than platoon duty at first base. As he has his whole career, Cordero crushed lefties, tossing up a .324/.421/.528 line against them. What was a surprise was his ability to stay healthy and play decent defense in an everyday role, and not completely suck against righties. The net result was an adequate stopgap answer for $600,000 on a team that had much bigger problems elsewhere. The Expos found their everyday first baseman in Nick Johnson; if Cordero re-signs, it'll be as a lefty-masher off the bench.

VLADIMIR GUERRERO OF Bats: R Throws: R Born: 09-Feb-76 Age: 28

YEAR	TM	LG	AGE	AB	H	2B	3B	HR	BB	SO	SB	CS	AVG	OBP	SLG	MLVR	EQBA	EQOBP	EQSLG	EQMLVR	VORP	DEFENSE	
2001	MON	NL	25	599	184	45	4	34	60	88	37	16	.307	.377	.566	.279	.301	.370	.555	.243	53.2	149-RF	5
2002	MON	NL	26	614	206	37	2	39	84	70	40	20	.336	.417	.593	.450	.329	.410	.591	.389	76.4	153-RF	-4
2003	MON	NL	27	394	130	20	3	25	63	53	9	5	.330	.426	.586	.382	.318	.417	.571	.359	45.6	111-RF	-1
2004	ANA	AL	28	467	139	29	2	21	56	64	16	5	.297	.376	.504	.188	.307	.391	.542	.251	42.3	126-RF	-2

Breakout: 6%   Improve: 41%   Collapse: 21%

Add great work ethic to the list of Vlad superlatives. Guerrero often looked uncomfortable early last season, wincing after taking some of his patented violent swings and losing a step in the field. The Expos' fears were confirmed in early June when he was diagnosed with herniated disks in his back and placed on the DL. Rather than sulk or get discouraged, Vlad followed a grueling rehab schedule, working five, six hours a day and pushing himself beyond reasonable expectations. His legs took a while to come around after he returned, as he appeared flat-footed in the field and limped noticeably the first 10 days back. Even at half health, he showed his old magic, hitting one memorable homer in the Big O that hit the facing of the second deck over the bleachers in left, an impossible shot that made you thank heaven TiVo's instant replay function was invented. When he flew all the way around from first on a Cabrera game-winning double a few weeks after his return, you knew he was back.

As suitors mull the value of a uniquely talented player with all-time-great potential still in his prime, Vlad's health has become the $64 million question. He showed up to camp last year at 240 pounds, continuing his trend of adding 10 pounds every off-season and putting additional pressure on his back. A narrow spine canal he can do nothing about, a jaw-dropping swing he doesn't want to change, and years of pounding on the Big O's sadistic turf have raised further doubts. Now consider this: Ivan Rodriguez suffered the same injury in 2002, worked like crazy to get back, and became a team leader and playoff hero for the Marlins after other teams ran away from a perceived huge injury risk. Four years younger than Pudge, without the rigors of catching on his back, Vlad will be a steal for whichever team signs him, especially if his asking price is driven down by injury fears and a tighter market.

EDWARDS GUZMAN 3B Bats: L Throws: R Born: 11-Sep-76 Age: 27

YEAR	TM	LG	AGE	AB	H	2B	3B	HR	BB	SO	SB	CS	AVG	OBP	SLG	MLVR	EQBA	EQOBP	EQSLG	EQMLVR	VORP	DEFENSE			
2001	FRE	PCL	24	72	26	3	2	0	4	3	0	1	.361	.395	.458	.185	.310	.347	.408	.001	4.0	11-C	-3		
2001	SFG	NL	24	115	28	6	0	3	5	16	0	0	.243	.273	.374	-.207	.256	.287	.393	-.176	-0.1	14-C	1		
2002	FRE	PCL	25	390	116	22	0	5	16	26	1	3	.297	.324	.392	-.059	.264	.292	.352	-.220	-5.4	36-C	1	23-3B	1
2003	EDM	PCL	26	213	75	12	1	3	8	18	5	1	.352	.372	.460	.219	.321	.348	.429	.044	13.3	21-C	1	15-1B	-2
2003	MON	NL	26	146	35	5	0	1	5	17	0	0	.240	.263	.295	-.361	.233	.258	.295	-.388	-9.1	16-3B	1		
2004	TBY	AL	27	216	58	11	1	3	10	23	1	1	.267	.299	.374	-.134	.270	.305	.391	-.127	1.7	58-3B	-1		

Breakout: 33%   Improve: 44%   Collapse: 28%

The throw-in in the Livan Hernandez heist, Guzman hit an empty .300 with the big club for a couple weeks in June, then faded into punchless oblivion. A versatile player in the sense that he fields catcher, first and third base equally crappily, Guzman's unlikely to improve much at his advanced age, and doesn't stack up to dozens of other freely available players in the secondary talent market. The Devil Rays handed him a shot to lull Tampa's octogenarians to sleep in '04.

NOAH HALL OF Bats: R Throws: R Born: 09-Jun-77 Age: 27

YEAR	TM	LG	AGE	AB	H	2B	3B	HR	BB	SO	SB	CS	AVG	OBP	SLG	MLVR	EQBA	EQOBP	EQSLG	EQMLVR	VORP	DEFENSE			
2001	STP	NTH	24	352	110	19	4	8	45	45	37	6	.313	.398	.457	.825	.237	.313	.359	-.187	-10.5				
2002	CHT	SOU	25	42	7	1	0	0	2	5	2	0	.167	.213	.190	-.480	.186	.215	.209	-.620	-5.8	10-CF	-2		
2002	STO	CAL	25	90	25	5	1	3	17	16	6	5	.278	.409	.456	.240	.213	.311	.340	-.232	-2.5	22-CF	-3		
2003	HAR	EAS	26	449	138	23	4	10	91	67	33	9	.307	.434	.443	.250	.249	.362	.372	-.067	-1.9	74-LF	-3	40-RF	-3
2004	TOR	AL	27	193	49	10	1	5	23	35	7	3	.251	.343	.395	-.041	.248	.343	.392	-.072	3.3	56-LF	-1		

Breakout: 33%   Improve: 57%   Collapse: 31%

Them 91 walks sure is perrrty. Hall first reached the Double-A level in 2000. Since then he's bounced all over the place, including a stint with the independent St. Paul Saints in '01. When he returned to the Expos, via the Reds' system, Hall was a different player, showing better work habits and a better understanding of the game. He's another six-year free agent who'll face long odds to get his shot. The former 20th-round draft choice turns 27 in June; if he wants to make the big show as a Rich Becker clone, it's now or never. The Blue Jays, enamored with his plate discipline, inked him to a minor league deal.

SCOTT HODGES 3B Bats: L Throws: R Born: 26-Dec-78 Age: 25

YEAR	TM	LG	AGE	AB	H	2B	3B	HR	BB	SO	SB	CS	AVG	OBP	SLG	MLVR	EQBA	EQOBP	EQSLG	EQMLVR	VORP	DEFENSE	
2001	HAR	EAS	22	305	84	11	2	5	25	56	3	2	.275	.328	.374	-.015	.239	.291	.326	-.275	-9.3	73-3B	-4
2002	HAR	EAS	23	526	143	35	2	9	63	102	2	2	.272	.351	.397	.033	.228	.296	.339	-.254	-11.9	130-3B	-3
2003	EDM	PCL	24	482	139	21	3	12	29	93	5	2	.288	.327	.419	.024	.263	.306	.390	-.139	5.9	117-3B	3
2004	MON	NL	25	200	53	11	1	6	17	39	2	1	.266	.326	.416	-.044	.250	.310	.384	-.141	4.9	56-3B	-1

Breakout: 35%   Improve: 57%   Collapse: 25%

Physically, Hodges has made great strides, gaining back the weight he lost due to his 2001 bout with colitis and generally getting the disease as under control as can reasonably be expected. His prospect status looks a lot sicker. Hodges hasn't shown the power development the Expos expected out of him when he rapped 32 doubles and 14 homers as a 21-year-old in the hitter-killer Florida State League. Scouts still love his smooth, left-handed stroke, touting him as a potential .300/25-homer hitter. But if his ongoing health concerns don't make the odds for such success long enough, his poor strike zone judgment compounds the problem. With Tony Batista signed to play third in 2004, Hodges will likely get more minor league seasoning, then compete for the starter's job in '05.

JOHN LABANDEIRA SS Bats: R Throws: R Born: 25-Feb-79 Age: 25

YEAR	TM	LG	AGE	AB	H	2B	3B	HR	BB	SO	SB	CS	AVG	OBP	SLG	MLVR	EQBA	EQOBP	EQSLG	EQMLVR	VORP	DEFENSE	
2002	CLN	MID	23	493	141	27	3	8	45	73	15	12	.286	.350	.402	.111	.223	.276	.324	-.317	-18.2	127-SS	-10
2003	BRV	FLA	24	238	77	13	4	0	24	35	6	5	.324	.386	.412	.239	.270	.323	.359	-.146	4.7	55-SS	-9
2003	HAR	EAS	24	238	57	18	2	2	20	38	0	2	.239	.298	.357	-.132	.205	.256	.314	-.381	-12.9	60-SS	1

Like some kind of 21st-century F. P. Santangelo on speed, Labandeira's become the resident hustle and grit guy everyone loves. A 5'7" ball of energy, he runs to home plate when introduced and oozes energy with everything he does. His on-field results have been more modest. A sixth-round pick in 2001, he showed flashes of talent at Clinton, driving the ball to the gaps but not over the wall, showing good speed but not stealing bases effectively, making occasionally exciting plays at short but committing tons of errors. His '03 season went a little better, with Labandeira hitting for average but no power at Brevard County, ending the season at Harrisburg, then holding his own in the Arizona Fall League. Like Santangelo v1.0, it's not hard to imagine Labandeira making the majors on his go-getter attitude, then kicking around for a few years as a second utility man.

JOSE MACIAS UT Bats: B Throws: R Born: 25-Jan-72 Age: 32

YEAR	TM	LG	AGE	AB	H	2B	3B	HR	BB	SO	SB	CS	AVG	OBP	SLG	MLVR	EQBA	EQOBP	EQSLG	EQMLVR	VORP	DEFENSE			
2001	DET	AL	29	488	131	24	6	8	32	54	21	6	.268	.316	.391	-.064	.295	.343	.431	.014	24.7	82-3B	6	22-CF	1
2002	DET	AL	30	107	25	4	0	0	8	13	3	2	.234	.291	.271	-.280	.269	.324	.315	-.207	-0.9	16-2B	0		
2002	MON	NL	30	231	59	17	1	7	13	44	5	6	.255	.294	.429	-.034	.256	.295	.440	-.093	3.2	37-CF	-1	19-3B	-2
2003	MON	NL	31	272	65	15	2	4	11	45	4	3	.239	.273	.353	-.242	.234	.266	.352	-.290	-10.9	26-LF	0	16-3B	-1
2004	CHC	NL	32	177	42	8	1	2	11	29	3	2	.240	.289	.336	-.234	.242	.290	.346	-.233	-4.5	49-3B	-4		

Breakout: 25%   Improve: 38%   Collapse: 41%

Macias slugged 158 points higher in 2002 with the Expos than he did in a decrepit early-season stint that year in Detroit, sparking hope that Montreal had landed a useful utility player. The Detroit Virus struck him down in '03. The always hacktastic Macias mixed a disdain for reaching base with repeated ugly, costly defensive miscues to earn a special place on Expos fans' enemy lists. Not quite at the Rick Monday level, but easily in the Luis Rivera, five-wince category.

HENRY MATEO 2B Bats: B Throws: R Born: 14-Oct-76 Age: 27

YEAR	TM	LG	AGE	AB	H	2B	3B	HR	BB	SO	SB	CS	AVG	OBP	SLG	MLVR	EQBA	EQOBP	EQSLG	EQMLVR	VORP	DEFENSE			
2001	OTT	INT	24	500	134	14	12	5	33	89	47	14	.268	.322	.374	-.038	.257	.308	.362	-.179	-0.7	116-2B	-11		
2002	OTT	INT	25	285	73	10	6	5	18	53	15	6	.256	.306	.386	-.053	.244	.296	.373	-.196	-1.8	53-2B	3	22-SS	-5
2003	MON	NL	26	154	37	3	1	0	11	38	11	1	.240	.304	.273	-.292	.239	.295	.271	-.344	-4.3	28-2B	-2		
2004	MON	NL	27	214	54	9	3	3	17	43	12	3	.254	.316	.366	-.138	.239	.300	.338	-.228	0.8	59-2B	-2		

Breakout: 22%   Improve: 38%   Collapse: 38%

Actually got a few knocks to drop in early in the season, leading Frank Robinson to believe he was a viable pinch-hitter. It wasn't long before Mateo was revealed to be not a viable pinch-hitter or even an adequate bench jockey. He was actually Old Man Winters, from the amusement park. He would have gotten away with it too, if it wasn't for you meddling kids. Blow this bench up and bury the remains, Omar. You're scaring the children.

JOSH McKINLEY   **2B**   **Bats: B**   **Throws: R**   Born: 14-Sep-79   Age: 24

YEAR	TM	LG	AGE	AB	H	2B	3B	HR	BB	SO	SB	CS	AVG	OBP	SLG	MLVR	EQBA	EQOBP	EQSLG	EQMLVR	VORP	DEFENSE
2001	JUP	FLA	21	464	117	19	2	2	70	83	28	10	.252	.351	.315	-.015	.215	.292	.273	-.359	-28.6	127-2B -2
2002	HAR	EAS	22	325	76	17	0	7	42	81	2	4	.234	.321	.351	-.102	.196	.270	.299	-.378	-20.6	82-2B -11
2003	HAR	EAS	23	458	132	33	2	15	60	86	17	5	.288	.367	.467	.164	.238	.311	.400	-.134	5.9	118-2B -7
2004	MON	NL	24	242	62	14	1	8	28	49	5	2	.257	.336	.419	-.032	.242	.319	.386	-.128	6.7	68-2B -4

Breakout: 45%   Improve: 71%   Collapse: 14%

A first-round pick (11th overall) in the 1998 draft, McKinley washed out so badly he was barely considered for inclusion in last year's book. A repeat performance in Double-A yielded an impressive season of power, patience and bases-stealing, restoring some of McKinley's prospect sheen, to the point where he was a key part of the Juan Gonzalez deal that fell through at the deadline. Still just 24, McKinley could be in line for a starting major league job by 2005. It probably won't come at second base though, after the club sent him to the Arizona Fall League to work on catching. The early reports on McKinley behind the plate were OK hands, decent arm strength, and terrible footwork. You'd love to see the Expos send him to their instructional league, if, y'know, they still had one. Unfortunately, they haven't for a few years now, even given the small sum needed to run one. Let's all thank our lucky stars they still have enough money lying around to fly Tony Tavares home after every homestand though. What with all the whatever it is he does for the team, it's great to see him treated right.

VAL PASCUCCI   **OF/1B**   **Bats: R**   **Throws: R**   Born: 17-Nov-78   Age: 25

YEAR	TM	LG	AGE	AB	H	2B	3B	HR	BB	SO	SB	CS	AVG	OBP	SLG	MLVR	EQBA	EQOBP	EQSLG	EQMLVR	VORP	DEFENSE	
2001	HAR	EAS	22	476	116	17	1	21	65	114	8	8	.244	.344	.416	.042	.204	.295	.352	-.252	-30.1	112-RF -6	15-1B -2
2002	HAR	EAS	23	459	108	14	1	27	93	115	2	0	.235	.374	.447	.106	.191	.309	.364	-.217	-23.1	102-RF -6	17-1B -2
2003	EDM	PCL	24	459	129	29	1	15	101	132	3	2	.281	.419	.447	.208	.245	.371	.397	-.020	7.1	105-RF -2	27-1B -4
2004	MON	NL	25	247	62	12	1	13	38	65	1	1	.250	.359	.459	.054	.235	.341	.424	-.044	3.7	72-RF -5	

Breakout: 37%   Improve: 63%   Collapse: 21%

Wouldn't you know it? An Expo prospect who actually walks a lot, who's so patient he regularly watches fat pitches go by and strikes out with the bat on his shoulder. Pascucci needs to find that balance between making a pitcher work by waiting for his pitch and ripping it when he gets it, the same problem that's afflicted Brad Wilkerson in the past. Defensively, Pascucci's an interesting case. A former college pitcher, he's blessed with a great throwing arm to play right field, but looks awful chasing fly balls. He's adequate with the leather at first and may find his major league future there if he can tap into his power potential. Read those walk and strikeout totals again. You can buy two dogs, a poutine, and a Labatt's Blue, take your kids to pose with Youppi!, compose a 1,500-word hate letter to Bud Selig, and still make it back to see Pascucci waiting on another 3–2 pitch.

VINCE ROOI   **3B**   **Bats: R**   **Throws: R**   Born: 13-Dec-81   Age: 22

YEAR	TM	LG	AGE	AB	H	2B	3B	HR	BB	SO	SB	CS	AVG	OBP	SLG	MLVR	EQBA	EQOBP	EQSLG	EQMLVR	VORP	DEFENSE
2001	CLN	MID	19	422	107	22	0	9	61	94	5	4	.254	.349	.370	.011	.182	.258	.271	-.447	-36.8	115-3B -11
2002	BRV	FLA	20	367	71	11	1	4	52	86	7	5	.193	.295	.262	-.193	.167	.246	.230	-.533	-44.7	113-3B -9
2003	BRV	FLA	21	319	81	19	0	7	36	70	3	9	.254	.334	.379	.076	.213	.277	.339	-.300	-13.5	82-3B -6
2004	MON	NL	22	244	52	12	1	6	24	58	2	2	.213	.288	.341	-.247	.200	.273	.314	-.330	-8.4	68-3B -7

Breakout: 39%   Improve: 61%   Collapse: 23%

Signed as a 16-year-old non-drafted amateur free agent in '98, Rooi improved on his dreadful 2002 season in his repeat year at Brevard County. A stint on the Netherlands national team in the world championships offered him some big-game experience and added confidence. Rooi continued his extensive weight-lifting efforts, adding bulk to his growing frame but creating tension in his upper body and a stiff swing. Just 21 in high-A ball last year, he could become a factor if he can make that always-difficult leap to Double-A successfully and tap into the power potential expected of him while maintaining a serviceable glove. With only Scott Hodges around as a reasonable third base option in the minors, the opportunity's there for Rooi if he can seize it.

BRIAN SCHNEIDER C Bats: L Throws: R Born: 26-Nov-76 Age: 27

YEAR	TM	LG	AGE	AB	H	2B	3B	HR	BB	SO	SB	CS	AVG	OBP	SLG	MLVR	EQBA	EQOBP	EQSLG	EQMLVR	VORP	DEFENSE	
2001	OTT	INT	24	338	93	27	1	6	27	55	2	0	.275	.336	.414	.044	.259	.317	.399	-.109	6.5	89-C	11
2001	MON	NL	24	41	13	3	0	1	6	3	0	0	.317	.396	.463	.178	.310	.396	.476	.185	4.4	11-C	1
2002	MON	NL	25	207	57	19	2	5	21	41	1	2	.275	.339	.459	.096	.281	.343	.471	.059	12.7	56-C	6
2003	MON	NL	26	335	77	26	1	9	37	75	0	2	.230	.309	.394	-.132	.223	.303	.387	-.178	-0.8	97-C	12
2004	MON	NL	27	289	78	19	1	10	30	58	1	1	.269	.341	.450	.026	.253	.323	.415	-.075	9.9	79-C	2

Breakout: 30%   Improve: 47%   Collapse: 27%

Schneider teamed with Michael Barrett to post strong numbers in a 1/1a job-sharing situation in 2002. Barrett's slump and subsequent injury and the Expos' lack of another viable catching option shoved Schneider behind the plate on a near everyday basis for an extended period. The results weren't pretty: Already fighting to catch up conditioning-wise after spraining his ankle in spring training, Schneider wore down as the year went on, and his hitting suffered for it. The Expos need to secure a solid 250-AB catcher in the secondary talent market. Schneider's a good player to have around if used right, a liability if pushed too hard.

TERRMEL SLEDGE OF Bats: L Throws: L Born: 18-Mar-77 Age: 27

YEAR	TM	LG	AGE	AB	H	2B	3B	HR	BB	SO	SB	CS	AVG	OBP	SLG	MLVR	EQBA	EQOBP	EQSLG	EQMLVR	VORP	DEFENSE			
2001	HAR	EAS	24	448	124	22	6	9	51	72	30	8	.277	.359	.413	.084	.237	.312	.359	-.189	-15.7	117-1B	-10		
2002	HAR	EAS	25	396	119	18	6	8	55	70	11	8	.301	.401	.437	.185	.251	.335	.371	-.119	3.5	70-CF	2	16-LF	0
2002	OTT	INT	25	80	21	5	2	1	11	15	1	1	.263	.359	.412	.074	.244	.331	.390	-.106	-1.3	13-LF	-1		
2003	EDM	PCL	26	497	161	26	9	22	61	93	13	5	.324	.397	.545	.347	.287	.362	.493	.128	42.6	46-CF	-4	43-LF	-4
2004	MON	NL	27	203	56	11	2	8	23	39	4	2	.277	.359	.463	.080	.260	.341	.427	-.022	7.3	58-CF	-9		

Breakout: 20%   Improve: 42%   Collapse: 30%

Even after losing the first three games of a crucial series with the Marlins, the Expos stood just three games behind Florida for the Wild Card spot as the calendar hit September 1. A handful of callups could have helped the team's chances, especially with multiple holes in the lineup and several players wearing down from heavy use. The Expos didn't have many players likely to make a difference, but they did have Sledge, who'd crushed PCL pitching and more than earned his shot at the majors. Saying the team was over budget, MLB wouldn't allow even a handful of callups, preferring to watch the Expos twist in the wind in the name of a couple hundred thousand dollars, roughly the price of a Hyundai Accent for each of the Expos' 29 owners.

While Bud Selig tacked another pathetic episode onto his heinous record as commissioner, Expos fans wondered why Sledge hadn't gotten the call weeks earlier. He adjusted his stance and moved off the plate last season, gaining more leverage, pulling the ball with more authority, and hiking his power numbers enough to become a reasonable starting corner outfielder. Given Endy Chavez's strangling of the offense, it was worth trying Sledge in left and Wilkerson in center (or vice-versa), even at the expense of some outfield defense. With Vlad gone and Carl Everett in tow, Sledge will battle Juan Rivera for the third outfield slot. A platoon would yield cheap, tasty dividends.

FERNANDO TATIS 3B Bats: R Throws: R Born: 01-Jan-75 Age: 29

YEAR	TM	LG	AGE	AB	H	2B	3B	HR	BB	SO	SB	CS	AVG	OBP	SLG	MLVR	EQBA	EQOBP	EQSLG	EQMLVR	VORP	DEFENSE	
2001	MON	NL	26	145	37	9	0	2	16	43	0	0	.255	.339	.359	-.116	.259	.344	.361	-.110	3.0	34-3B	-9
2002	MON	NL	27	381	87	18	1	15	35	90	2	2	.228	.303	.399	-.078	.236	.307	.420	-.116	6.5	93-3B	-9
2003	MON	NL	28	175	34	6	0	2	18	40	2	1	.194	.281	.263	-.366	.193	.273	.261	-.425	-10.9	43-3B	1
2004	TBY	AL	29	202	46	10	1	4	19	46	2	1	.227	.305	.347	-.182	.230	.311	.363	-.179	0.5	57-3B	-3

Breakout: 44%   Improve: 62%   Collapse: 26%

Tatis's sad chapter in Expos history turned even sadder when word of his suffering from panic attacks surfaced late last season. Having turned into a shell of his 1999 phenom self through serious shoulder, groin, knee, chest and other injuries, you had to feel for Tatis. It was hard not to be frustrated too: Tatis's $6.5 million salary made him untradable, killing the Expos' chances of keeping Bartolo Colon after his monster 2002 season—leading to the infamous Biddles 'n Bits trade—and eating up a huge chunk of payroll Minaya could have used to upgrade the team. The Expos surprised no one by declining Tatis's option, making him a free agent. Considering how low he's sunk, it's hard to imagine him getting anything more than the NRI he received from the D-Rays; he'll contend with Geoff Blum and Jared Sandberg for a job.

JOSE VIDRO   2B   Bats: B   Throws: R   Born: 27-Aug-74   Age: 29

YEAR	TM	LG	AGE	AB	H	2B	3B	HR	BB	SO	SB	CS	AVG	OBP	SLG	MLVR	EQBA	EQOBP	EQSLG	EQMLVR	VORP	DEFENSE
2001	MON	NL	26	486	155	34	1	15	31	49	4	1	.319	.371	.486	.168	.321	.371	.488	.171	46.7	117-2B -7
2002	MON	NL	27	604	190	43	3	19	60	70	2	1	.315	.378	.490	.233	.318	.379	.502	.201	60.1	148-2B 3
2003	MON	NL	28	509	158	36	0	15	69	50	3	2	.310	.397	.470	.169	.303	.389	.463	.148	42.5	128-2B 2
2004	MON	NL	29	480	150	32	2	17	54	54	3	2	.313	.386	.492	.194	.295	.367	.454	.085	32.3	129-2B 0

Breakout: 16%   Improve: 35%   Collapse: 23%

The same patella tendinitis that signaled the end of Mark McGwire's career has put Vidro's future into question as well. Expected to go straight to surgery at the end of the season, October's silence led some to assume the worst. It later became clear that Vidro wanted to avoid surgery, given the mixed success rate linked to the procedure. He hired a trainer to work with him all winter on strengthening the knee and consulted the doctor who talked McGwire and Fernando Vina through their rehabs. The new turf at the Big O could help his recovery. Most shocking were Vidro's near-identical rate stats last season despite the knee problem and a nagging shoulder injury bothering him most of the year. Check out that walks column; Vidro's hugely improved plate discipline makes him a star even at less than full strength. Since he walks after the '04 season, the Expos may elect to trade him at the deadline if they're out of the race.

JOE VITIELLO   1B   Bats: R   Throws: R   Born: 11-Apr-70   Age: 34

YEAR	TM	LG	AGE	AB	H	2B	3B	HR	BB	SO	SB	CS	AVG	OBP	SLG	MLVR	EQBA	EQOBP	EQSLG	EQMLVR	VORP	DEFENSE
2001	ORX	JPP	31	407	112	21	0	22	36	125	0	0	.275	.334	.489	.079	.267	.314	.469	-.008	14.4	
2002	OTT	INT	32	431	142	34	0	16	39	58	1	0	.329	.390	.520	.324	.306	.368	.493	.157	32.3	100-1B -8
2003	FRE	PCL	33	75	16	5	0	0	8	9	0	0	.213	.289	.280	-.299	.187	.256	.253	-.473	-9.0	14-1B 0
2003	EDM	PCL	33	96	26	7	0	2	10	17	0	0	.271	.333	.406	.002	.247	.311	.371	-.168	-2.5	20-1B 1
2003	MON	NL	33	76	26	6	0	3	7	14	0	0	.342	.407	.539	.307	.329	.397	.539	.295	7.4	
2004	MON	NL	34	139	38	7	0	5	14	29	0	0	.271	.340	.441	.015	.255	.323	.407	-.085	2.7	41-1B -4

Breakout: 23%   Improve: 42%   Collapse: 48%

Your basic lefty-masher. Vitiello crushed the ball in limited playing time last year, offering much-needed relief to fans whose eyes had started bleeding from watching Ron Calloway hit like Cab Calloway against lefties. A free agent at 34, he'd still make a nifty get for a team like Oakland looking for a 1B/DH platoon partner or a pinch-hitter with pop.

BRANDON WATSON   OF   Bats: L   Throws: R   Born: 30-Sep-81   Age: 22

YEAR	TM	LG	AGE	AB	H	2B	3B	HR	BB	SO	SB	CS	AVG	OBP	SLG	MLVR	EQBA	EQOBP	EQSLG	EQMLVR	VORP	DEFENSE	
2001	CLN	MID	19	489	160	16	9	2	29	65	33	20	.327	.364	.409	.138	.256	.287	.325	-.274	-32.5	60-LF -6	46-CF -4
2002	BRV	FLA	20	424	113	16	2	0	27	53	22	13	.267	.314	.314	-.060	.239	.273	.284	-.371	-30.5	106-CF -1	
2003	HAR	EAS	21	565	180	17	6	1	38	60	18	17	.319	.362	.375	.055	.275	.314	.328	-.204	-9.7	138-CF -1	
2004	MON	NL	22	273	72	13	2	1	17	35	6	3	.265	.312	.345	-.165	.249	.296	.319	-.254	-10.4	73-CF -5	

Breakout: 23%   Improve: 42%   Collapse: 30%

Would you believe Endy Chavez Lite? Like Chavez in 2002, Watson hit over .300, deluding people into thinking he's a hitter. Yet while Chavez flopped as the Expos' starting CF last year, Watson showed equally awful plate discipline, even less power, and poorer baserunning instincts. Watson isn't a lost cause though. He finished last year on fire, will crack Triple-A at 22 in '04, has been timed at a blistering 3.7 running to first, and plays terrific center field defense, with great range and a good arm. That, plus actual hitting ability, and you've got something.

BRAD WILKERSON   OF   Bats: L   Throws: L   Born: 01-Jun-77   Age: 27

YEAR	TM	LG	AGE	AB	H	2B	3B	HR	BB	SO	SB	CS	AVG	OBP	SLG	MLVR	EQBA	EQOBP	EQSLG	EQMLVR	VORP	DEFENSE	
2001	OTT	INT	24	233	63	10	0	12	60	68	12	5	.270	.423	.468	.246	.239	.381	.416	.019	6.0	54-LF -2	
2001	MON	NL	24	117	24	7	2	1	17	41	2	1	.205	.304	.325	-.260	.203	.304	.331	-.263	-7.3	34-LF -1	
2002	MON	NL	25	507	135	27	8	20	81	161	7	8	.266	.370	.469	.151	.269	.370	.481	.109	36.3	56-CF -1	54-LF 0
2003	MON	NL	26	504	135	34	4	19	89	155	13	10	.268	.380	.464	.102	.258	.370	.452	.061	19.3	83-LF 6	30-CF -1
2004	MON	NL	27	419	115	24	3	22	72	118	10	5	.274	.384	.501	.166	.257	.365	.462	.060	17.2	118-LF 4	

Breakout: 25%   Improve: 61%   Collapse: 13%

An in-season chat with his hitting coach from the 2000 Olympics, Reggie Smith, helped him finish strong. Smith had Wilkerson move closer to the plate, allowing him to reach outside pitches and drive them to the opposite field. He maintained his batting eye, leading the majors in pitches seen per plate appearance. A stocky player at 6′0″, 205 with a bit of a rolling gait, he may not look like a leadoff man. But the Expos' offense took off once Wilkerson got bumped to the top of the lineup, as his on-base ability helped ease the horrible memory of Endy Chavez's outmaking prowess. Wilkerson's proven he can hit lefties too. The last step is a power breakout, as nagging knee and hip problems held him back last year. In this, his Age 27 season, we're calling it now.

TODD ZEILE

3B   **Bats: R**   **Throws: R**   Born: 09-Sep-65   Age: 38

YEAR	TM	LG	AGE	AB	H	2B	3B	HR	BB	SO	SB	CS	AVG	OBP	SLG	MLVR	EQBA	EQOBP	EQSLG	EQMLVR	VORP	DEFENSE	
2001	NYM	NL	35	531	141	25	1	10	73	102	1	0	.266	.359	.373	-.030	.276	.367	.389	-.016	10.4	143-1B 9	
2002	COL	NL	36	506	138	23	0	18	66	92	1	1	.273	.353	.425	.028	.259	.343	.412	-.042	19.2	134-3B -11	
2003	NYY	AL	37	186	39	8	0	6	24	36	0	0	.210	.294	.349	-.201	.230	.321	.385	-.141	-3.7	26-3B 0	21-1B 0
2003	MON	NL	37	113	29	2	2	5	10	18	1	0	.257	.331	.442	-.068	.248	.322	.442	-.048	2.2	32-3B -1	
2004	NYM	NL	38	183	43	8	1	4	22	34	1	1	.234	.317	.345	-.176	.237	.319	.361	-.165	-0.8	52-3B -5	

Breakout: 20%   *Improve: 40%*   *Collapse: 38%*

Claimed off the scrap heap with six weeks to play in the season, he was a huge upgrade over the dung heap that passed for third basemen the first three-quarters of the season. More importantly for the Expos, he galvanized the clubhouse in their battle with MLB, taking the union baton from Brian Schneider even as he faced free agency at season's end. Zeile emboldened the team to stand its ground in Bud Selig's latest efforts to strongarm players into a miserable travel schedule with limited payroll considerations for 2004, just as he had in '03. We tend to sneer at off-field contributions as unquantifiable and thus unimportant. But Zeile's influence helped the team get a few extra million to play with in exchange for allowing 22 games in San Juan. That makes him a leading candidate for the Expos' 2004 team MVP, even after he signed with the Mets.

PITCHERS

HECTOR ALMONTE

Bats: R   **Throws: R**   Born: 17-Oct-75   Age: 28

YEAR	TM	LG	AGE	G	GS	IP	H	BB	SO	HR	ERA	EQERA	EQH9	EQBB9	EQSO9	EQHR9	PERA	VORP	STF
2001	CLG	PCL	25	18	0	24.7	36	15	21	6	8.38	8.62	12.0	6.4	5.2	2.2	8.22	-8.1	-76
2002	YOM	JPC	26	27	1	24.0	18	7	18	2	0.00	2.91	7.5	3.7	5.0	0.8	3.85	6.5	-8
2003	PAW	INT	27	21	0	26.0	16	6	28	2	1.73	2.25	6.8	2.6	7.9	1.1	3.44	8.9	9
2003	BOS	AL	27	7	0	7.7	9	7	6	1	8.18	7.04	9.4	7.0	7.0	1.2	5.94	-1.9	-25
2003	MON	NL	27	28	0	29.0	34	17	26	4	6.83	6.35	10.8	4.8	7.0	1.3	6.08	-2.4	-21
2004	MON	NL	28	29	5	46.0	49	26	38	6	5.48	4.89	9.2	4.3	7.0	0.9	4.83	4.6	-2

Breakout: 28%   *Improve: 52%*   *Collapse: 23%*

As the bullpen wore down last year due to injuries and overuse of the few reliable options, the ugly result was high-leverage innings for stiffs like Almonte. It was tough to decide which was more irritating: seeing Frank Robinson repeatedly bring in Almonte with the game on the line, or watching Almonte's trademark blade of grass between his teeth just as he readied to serve up another meatball. When ne'er-do-well Expos fans die and go to hell, you've gotta figure they're subjected to repeated images of Almonte, Curt Schmidt, Drew Hall, and other awful Expo middle relievers, facing Barry Bonds in a tie game, ninth inning, bases loaded, two outs, full count. The horror! The horror!

TONY ARMAS

Bats: R   **Throws: R**   Born: 29-Apr-78   Age: 26

YEAR	TM	LG	AGE	G	GS	IP	H	BB	SO	HR	ERA	EQERA	EQH9	EQBB9	EQSO9	EQHR9	PERA	VORP	STF
2001	MON	NL	23	34	34	196.7	180	91	176	18	4.03	4.09	8.1	3.8	6.7	0.7	3.99	32.2	32
2002	MON	NL	24	29	29	164.3	149	78	131	22	4.44	4.62	8.2	3.7	6.2	1.2	4.54	17.4	12
2003	MON	NL	25	5	5	31.0	25	8	23	4	2.61	3.03	7.3	2.1	6.1	1.2	3.65	11.0	17
2004	MON	NL	26	37	21	125.7	131	51	97	19	4.93	4.40	9.0	3.1	6.5	1.1	4.43	18.8	5

Breakout: 22%   *Improve: 43%*   *Collapse: 28%*

(continued next page)

Tony Armas *(continued)*

Last year, we questioned Armas's ability to put it all together, citing his history of injuries. Sure enough, Armas tacked another disappointing season onto a career filled with disappointment. This time, the culprit was a series of small tears in Armas's labrum and rotator cuff and season-ending surgery in May. For all the talk of Armas maturing over the years, he's kept plenty of bad habits, including a tendency to recoil his arm violently, Uggy Urbina-style, adding unnecessary stress to his pitching motion. This despite close attention and instruction from pitching coach Randy St. Claire and the hopes of Expo Nation pinned on him since the day the team held him up as half of the future superstar duo they got for Pedro Martinez. Six years later, Carl Pavano's winning World Series games for Jeffrey Freaking Loria and Armas remains a heartbreaker. He's throwing again and is expected to be ready by spring training. The one blessing from his injury: Armas will come much cheaper than he would have had he tossed up an 18-win season. Yippee.

LUIS AYALA   Bats: R   Throws: R   Born: 12-Jan-78   Age: 26

YEAR	TM	LG	AGE	G	GS	IP	H	BB	SO	HR	ERA	EQERA	EQH9	EQBB9	EQSO9	EQHR9	PERA	VORP	STF
2001	SLM	CAR	23	13	0	13.3	19	5	10	0	4.06	9.26	15.4	4.6	3.9	0.0	6.73	-4.8	-24
2002	OTT	INT	24	6	0	7.7	7	4	6	1	3.51	5.14	10.3	5.1	6.4	1.3	5.98	0.4	-17
2003	MON	NL	25	65	0	71.0	65	13	46	8	2.92	3.44	8.2	1.5	5.3	0.9	3.61	19.2	4
2004	*MON*	*NL*	*26*	*45*	*5*	*69.0*	*76*	*20*	*45*	*8*	*4.21*	*3.76*	*9.5*	*2.2*	*5.5*	*0.7*	*3.96*	*14.0*	*-1*

Breakout: 25%   Improve: 47%   Collapse: 24%

Next to Livan Hernandez, the year's biggest pleasant surprise. Signed out of Mexico in 2002, lost to the Diamondbacks two months later, then reclaimed in the Rule 5 draft two months after that, Ayala emerged as the latest scrap heap project to put up a big year in relief, following the recent lead of Scott Stewart and Joey Eischen. Lacking a devastating fastball, Ayala uses a deceptive short-arm delivery to mess up hitters' vision. A low walk rate and a ton of routine grounders induced made Ayala the pen's anchor, especially after Rocky Biddle imploded. Ayala's skinny physique, concerns of overuse in Mexico, pre-existing shoulder problems, and a late-season DL stint due to shoulder inflammation raise red flags for 2004. Expect some injury time and an ERA a run higher this season.

CHAD BENTZ   Bats: R   Throws: L   Born: 05-May-80   Age: 24

YEAR	TM	LG	AGE	G	GS	IP	H	BB	SO	HR	ERA	EQERA	EQH9	EQBB9	EQSO9	EQHR9	PERA	VORP	STF
2001	VER	NYP	21	8	8	36.7	39	11	38	2	4.90	6.82	13.1	4.0	5.4	1.7	7.45	-4.3	-18
2002	BRV	FLA	22	23	0	29.7	30	14	34	1	3.64	6.15	12.0	5.5	7.2	0.7	6.13	-1.6	0
2003	HAR	EAS	23	52	0	84.7	72	39	56	4	2.55	4.31	8.6	5.0	4.8	0.8	4.72	11.1	-9
2004	*MON*	*NL*	*24*	*18*	*5*	*34.3*	*42*	*22*	*24*	*6*	*6.70*	*5.99*	*10.7*	*4.9*	*5.8*	*1.2*	*5.99*	*1.7*	*-14*

Breakout: 25%   Improve: 49%   Collapse: 27%

Born with a deformed right hand and raised in the noted baseball hotbed of Juneau, Alaska, you'd have a tough time finding a bigger long shot. But Bentz's combination of talent and work ethic have left him this close to the majors. Drafted in the 34th round out of high school by the Yankees, Bentz chose instead to attend Long Beach State. Eligible again for the draft in 2001, the Expos nabbed him with their seventh-round pick. He makes the book on more than his backstory. A good athlete at 6'2", 210 pounds with the same fielding prowess and bulldog approach as Jim Abbott, Bentz throws a solid fastball, curve, and cutter, and gets enough righties out to offer hope for more than a LOOGY's future. With his lukewarm K rates, he needs to cut back on his walks to win and keep a big league job.

ROCKY BIDDLE   Bats: R   Throws: R   Born: 21-May-76   Age: 28

YEAR	TM	LG	AGE	G	GS	IP	H	BB	SO	HR	ERA	EQERA	EQH9	EQBB9	EQSO9	EQHR9	PERA	VORP	STF
2001	CWS	AL	25	30	21	128.7	137	52	85	16	5.38	5.21	9.6	3.4	5.6	1.0	4.93	5.4	0
2002	CWS	AL	26	44	7	77.7	72	39	64	13	4.05	4.66	8.5	4.2	7.2	1.3	4.91	7.9	-7
2003	MON	NL	27	73	0	71.7	71	40	54	10	4.64	5.17	9.0	4.5	5.9	1.2	5.12	4.6	-18
2004	*MON*	*NL*	*28*	*36*	*5*	*56.0*	*61*	*26*	*41*	*8*	*5.11*	*4.57*	*9.4*	*3.6*	*6.2*	*1.0*	*4.67*	*6.9*	*-4*

Breakout: 25%   Improve: 44%   Collapse: 27%

A dogged competitor who helped the Expos stay in the hunt in the first half of last season, Biddle will nonetheless have a hard time being thought of as more than a symbol for as long as he's in Montreal. After El Duque's tattered arm ensured he wouldn't throw a pitch all year and Jeff Liefer flopped, Biddle became the lone hope for Omar Minaya's sad excuse for a Bartolo Colon trade. With those expectations, he wasn't going to make people happy even if he hadn't come apart in the second half due to fatigue and a knee injury that put stress on his delivery. The torn labrum and resulting surgery in 2001 remain a concern every time Biddle snaps off one of his sweeping curves, as does his knee. Minaya elected to tender an arbitration offer to Biddle. We *really* hope the next step is a trade.

ROY CORCORAN Bats: R Throws: R Born: 11-May-80 Age: 24

YEAR	TM	LG	AGE	G	GS	IP	H	BB	SO	HR	ERA	EQERA	EQH9	EQBB9	EQSO9	EQHR9	PERA	VORP	STF
2002	CLN	MID	22	48	1	80.0	82	24	106	5	4.16	6.62	13.0	3.8	7.5	1.7	7.27	-7.9	-17
2003	BRV	FLA	23	28	0	33.0	19	11	35	1	1.91	3.41	7.4	4.0	6.8	0.9	3.99	7.1	4
2003	HAR	EAS	23	14	0	23.7	14	7	26	0	0.38	2.08	6.6	3.3	7.9	0.4	2.92	8.5	35
2003	MON	NL	23	5	0	7.3	7	3	2	0	1.23	2.57	9.0	3.9	2.6	0.0	3.80	2.7	5
2004	MON	NL	24	20	6	41.3	42	20	33	6	4.79	4.28	8.8	3.7	6.7	1.0	4.47	6.7	1

Breakout: 25% Improve: 48% Collapse: 23%

A walk-on at LSU, Corcoran had to plead with the coaches in Baton Rouge to give him a shot. He did nothing for two years, then broke out in his junior year. After a solid senior year, he signed with the Expos as an undrafted free agent. Corcoran quickly climbed the ladder last season, zooming from A-ball all the way to the majors. Author of a sneaky, low-90s fastball, sharp breaking stuff and an ability to keep the ball in the park, he's as good a candidate as most to make the team out of spring training. With several members of last year's pen arbitration-eligible, he'd be a financially sensible choice too.

CHAD CORDERO Bats: R Throws: R Born: 18-Mar-82 Age: 22

YEAR	TM	LG	AGE	G	GS	IP	H	BB	SO	HR	ERA	EQERA	EQH9	EQBB9	EQSO9	EQHR9	PERA	VORP	STF
2003	BRV	FLA	21	19	0	26.3	17	10	17	1	2.05	4.24	7.3	4.6	4.2	1.2	4.39	3.5	-10
2003	MON	NL	21	12	0	11.0	4	3	12	1	1.64	1.69	3.4	2.5	8.4	0.8	1.67	5.0	52
2004	MON	NL	22	22	3	36.0	35	18	27	6	5.23	4.67	8.4	4.0	6.2	1.2	4.62	4.2	-6

Breakout: 12% Improve: 36% Collapse: 24%

The Expos tapped Cordero with the 20th overall pick in last year's amateur draft, looking for someone who'd make it to the show in a hurry. Draft watchers saw it as a signability pick and a reach. But what the heck, better than throwing a few million at a high school pitcher, wasting precious time and resources on him and watching him burn out from injuries, anyway. While spending a first-round pick on a reliever was a dubious move for a team so desperately in need of young hitters, Cordero at least looks like he's for real. He throws a fastball and slider from multiple arm angles, hitting the low 90s with the hard stuff and keeping hitters off stride. Having thrown in plenty of high-pressure situations for Cal State Fullerton, the Expos see him as a closer candidate, probably as soon as this season. A four-inning stint against Stanford last year was his longest since high school, so a conversion to starting is unlikely.

ZACH DAY Bats: R Throws: R Born: 15-Jun-78 Age: 26

YEAR	TM	LG	AGE	G	GS	IP	H	BB	SO	HR	ERA	EQERA	EQH9	EQBB9	EQSO9	EQHR9	PERA	VORP	STF
2001	AKR	EAS	23	22	22	136.7	123	45	94	8	3.09	4.95	9.4	4.0	4.3	0.8	4.78	8.9	2
2001	BUF	INT	23	1	1	6.0	3	1	4	0	1.50	1.59	4.8	1.6	4.8	0.0	1.37	2.5	48
2001	OTT	INT	23	6	5	26.7	38	8	15	2	7.42	8.17	13.1	3.2	3.9	0.7	6.17	-7.2	-11
2002	OTT	INT	24	17	16	90.0	77	32	68	5	3.50	4.72	9.1	3.8	5.8	0.8	4.55	8.0	10
2002	MON	NL	24	19	2	37.3	28	15	25	3	3.62	3.75	6.8	3.2	5.2	0.8	3.30	7.4	9
2003	MON	NL	25	23	23	131.3	132	59	61	8	4.18	4.32	9.0	3.6	3.7	0.5	4.20	22.3	5
2004	MON	NL	26	26	22	124.3	144	59	70	14	5.25	4.69	10.0	3.7	4.8	0.8	4.79	11.7	-3

Breakout: 12% Improve: 44% Collapse: 17%

Day made several people within the organization look smart for believing in him, starting the year on fire. Though his porous strikeout-to-walk ratio would seem to suggest failure, he ranked among the most extreme ground ball pitchers in the majors, keeping the ball in the park and giving himself a huge edge. A series of bizarre mishaps starting in mid-May sidetracked Day's breakthrough season. First, he was tossed from a game in Colorado for using a foreign substance on his finger, later revealed to be superglue for a blister. He was later hobbled by a cyst above his right knee cap, then suffered a mysterious tear in his rotator cuff, somehow caused by a collision with Wil Cordero at first base. Was it a coincidence that Day's season started unraveling after BP contacted him for a Q&A? Has the book cover jinx spread to inflict players featured at baseballprospectus.com? We're not taking any chances. This year's book cover comes player-free; those mentioned on the Web site will be forced to wear biohazard suits and bubble wrap for protection.

TIM DREW

				Bats: R			Throws: R					Born: 31-Aug-78			Age: 25	

YEAR	TM	LG	AGE	G	GS	IP	H	BB	SO	HR	ERA	EQERA	EQH9	EQBB9	EQSO9	EQHR9	PERA	VORP	STF
2001	BUF	INT	22	18	18	108.0	115	27	75	13	3.92	5.59	9.4	2.5	5.2	1.2	4.82	0.1	11
2001	CLE	AL	22	8	6	35.0	51	16	15	9	7.97	7.90	11.5	3.6	3.6	2.0	7.07	-9.0	-25
2002	BUF	INT	23	15	15	96.3	96	23	43	6	3.27	4.96	9.1	2.5	3.5	0.8	4.24	6.4	5
2002	OTT	INT	23	13	13	84.7	77	24	29	5	2.87	4.48	8.8	3.1	2.8	0.7	4.20	9.7	2
2002	MON	NL	23	7	1	16.0	12	2	10	1	2.81	3.52	6.5	1.2	4.7	0.6	2.41	3.5	21
2003	EDM	PCL	24	27	15	93.3	128	35	54	10	7.23	7.58	12.1	3.9	4.3	1.4	6.71	-19.6	-33
2003	MON	NL	24	6	1	8.7	12	8	3	3	12.41	10.38	12.5	7.3	3.1	3.1	9.78	-5.8	-96
2004	*ATL*	*NL*	*25*	*9*	*5*	*32.0*	*34*	*13*	*18*	*4*	*5.05*	*5.48*	*9.7*	*3.1*	*4.4*	*1.2*	*5.23*	*1.3*	*-10*

Breakout: 25%   Improve: 53%   Collapse: 23%

He's no Wilton, though his future contributions for the Expos may not amount to much more than that. J. D.'s little brother regressed badly from a decent if uninspiring 2002 season. His eminently hittable stuff was smoked across the PCL and his walk rate was just so-so for a finesse pitcher. Worse, Drew's home run rate nearly doubled, the result of struggles with command as much as tougher park and league effects. Stubborn at times, Drew didn't take well to instruction last year, especially after failing to make the big club out of spring training. He's a long way from the prospect who threw 93 with a biting slider in the Indians' system and a long shot to have much of a career.

JOEY EISCHEN

				Bats: L			Throws: L					Born: 25-May-70			Age: 34	

YEAR	TM	LG	AGE	G	GS	IP	H	BB	SO	HR	ERA	EQERA	EQH9	EQBB9	EQSO9	EQHR9	PERA	VORP	STF
2001	OTT	INT	31	34	1	52.3	42	11	54	6	2.24	3.40	8.9	2.3	7.4	1.5	4.75	11.7	-8
2001	MON	NL	31	24	0	29.7	29	16	19	4	4.85	4.66	8.4	4.3	4.7	0.9	4.55	3.0	-16
2002	OTT	INT	32	11	0	14.0	8	3	15	0	0.00	2.84	6.4	2.1	8.5	0.0	2.12	3.9	43
2002	MON	NL	32	59	0	53.7	43	18	51	1	1.34	2.42	7.3	2.6	7.4	0.2	2.78	18.4	33
2003	MON	NL	33	70	0	53.0	57	13	40	7	3.06	4.41	9.7	1.9	6.0	1.1	4.58	7.9	-4
2004	*MON*	*NL*	*34*	*47*	*1*	*60.0*	*63*	*19*	*46*	*6*	*3.91*	*3.49*	*9.0*	*2.5*	*6.5*	*0.7*	*3.75*	*14.0*	*4*

Breakout: 23%   Improve: 48%   Collapse: 26%

Raise your hand if you expected a repeat of his 1.34 ERA from 2002. Please put your hand down, Mrs. Eischen. A nagging elbow injury early in the year, deltoid aches late in the year and the law of averages all conspired to bring Eischen back to Earth. He still managed a functional—though erratic—season given his journeyman's background. Eischen's fine if he's the fourth or fifth option out of your pen. Injuries and ineffectiveness by other pen members forced him into a bigger role, and the Expos paid the price. The team still has holes to fill, and should look to trade Eischen rather than pay the $1.3 million he's due from his 2004 player option.

CLINT EVERTS

				Bats: R			Throws: R					Born: 10-Aug-84			Age: 19	

YEAR	TM	LG	AGE	G	GS	IP	H	BB	SO	HR	ERA	EQERA	EQH9	EQBB9	EQSO9	EQHR9	PERA	VORP	STF
2003	VER	NYP	18	10	10	54.0	49	35	50	4	4.17	6.50	11.8	9.3	5.3	2.8	9.51	-4.4	-24
2003	SAV	SAL	18	5	5	26.0	23	10	21	1	3.46	5.70	8.7	4.6	4.9	0.8	4.60	-0.3	21

The fifth overall pick in the 2002 draft, he's considered one of the gems of the farm system by the organization, along with Michael Hinckley. The good: sound delivery, solid change-up, fastball could get better as he fills out his skinny frame. Everts's curve earns the most praise; rather than slow his arm action like many pitchers do to get it over, he whips through it, creating a hard break that makes it tough to hit. The bad: struggles with his control, still has plenty of growing up to do. Everts's biggest shortcomings aren't his fault—the Expos chose to spit in the face of odds and draft a rail-thin high school pitcher despite a system void of good hitters and all but four players from that draft still available. So many things need to go right for such a decision to pan out, and the Expos have enough problems without taking on lousy risk/reward propositions.

LIVAN HERNANDEZ

				Bats: R .			Throws: R					Born: 20-Feb-75			Age: 29	

YEAR	TM	LG	AGE	G	GS	IP	H	BB	SO	HR	ERA	EQERA	EQH9	EQBB9	EQSO9	EQHR9	PERA	VORP	STF
2001	SFG	NL	26	34	34	226.7	266	85	138	24	5.24	5.61	10.7	3.1	4.6	0.9	5.19	-0.2	-2
2002	SFG	NL	27	33	33	216.0	233	71	134	19	4.38	5.27	10.3	2.6	5.0	0.8	4.85	7.5	3
2003	MON	NL	28	33	33	233.3	225	57	178	27	3.20	3.69	8.7	2.0	6.1	1.0	4.08	60.0	16
2004	*MON*	*NL*	*29*	*29*	*29*	*193.0*	*222*	*57*	*131*	*28*	*4.80*	*4.29*	*9.9*	*2.3*	*5.7*	*1.0*	*4.40*	*28.7*	*11*

Breakout: 15%   Improve: 52%   Collapse: 15%

Unfreakingbelievable. All Hernandez had going against him heading into 2003 were years of sled-dragging at the behest of Dusty Baker, an unimpressive track record brightened only by a confluence of good timing and Eric Greggery, a reputation as a clubhouse cancer in San Francisco, and a golf club v. elderly man confrontation in the off-season. When Omar Minaya offered Jim Brower and Matt Blank for Hernandez and Edwards Guzman, Brian Sabean jumped at the chance to dump Livan, paying his 2003 salary to boot. Hernandez looked like an adequate inning-eating replacement for half-brother Orlando early on, going deep into games and throwing strikes.

Then, an epiphany. Pitching against the Blue Jays in late June, his old manager Carlos Tosca suggested dropping down to throw some of his breaking pitches. Hernandez spent his next side session working with Randy St. Claire, and just like that, he'd mastered throwing all his pitches from the same three-quarter arm angle, completely befuddling hitters. From then on, he was a joy to watch, becoming the Expos' best player, pitching like a Cy Young candidate, and nearly carrying the team to the playoffs. His July and August numbers were filthy: 97 innings, 90 strikeouts, 21 walks, an 8–2 record, six complete games, and a 1.58 ERA. Hernandez led the NL in complete games with eight while appearing near the top of BP's Pitcher Abuse list for the umpteenth time. It may be time to admit that Livan's a freak of nature who can handle all the abuse you can pile on. He had more than enough in the tank to pitch 217 innings, hitting a pre-arranged target and triggering a $6 million salary for the 2004 season. If he repeats his 2003 performance, he'll be a steal at that price. PECOTA says no way, but we think he's got a shot to come close.

ORLANDO HERNANDEZ   Bats: R   Throws: R   Born: 11-Oct-69   Age: 34

YEAR	TM	LG	AGE	G	GS	IP	H	BB	SO	HR	ERA	EQERA	EQH9	EQBB9	EQSO9	EQHR9	PERA	VORP	STF
2001	NYY	AL	31	17	16	94.7	90	42	77	19	4.85	4.63	8.0	3.7	6.8	1.6	4.90	10.1	-3
2002	NYY	AL	32	24	22	146.0	131	36	113	17	3.64	3.47	7.7	2.0	6.6	0.9	3.54	33.8	24
2004	MON	NL	34	38	18	107.3	111	53	94	17	5.19	4.64	8.9	3.8	7.4	1.1	4.68	13.1	5

Breakout: 33%   Improve: 53%   Collapse: 19%

The only thing more fun than watching Livan pitch would have been seeing El Duque follow him in the rotation, especially after baby brother starting throwing Orlando's waycool eephus pitch. Unfortunately Duque became the latest damaged goods pitcher foisted on the Expos by those masters of efficient trash disposal, the Yankees. Expos trainers couldn't get a read on Hernandez from the Yankees' cryptic health report, yet Omar Minaya carried on with the disastrous Colon trade anyway. *Sacre bleu!* After a non-tender, Hernandez is a free agent who if healthy could be a solid swingman or high-leverage reliever for whoever gives him a shot.

SHAWN HILL   Bats: R   Throws: R   Born: 28-Apr-81   Age: 23

YEAR	TM	LG	AGE	G	GS	IP	H	BB	SO	HR	ERA	EQERA	EQH9	EQBB9	EQSO9	EQHR9	PERA	VORP	STF
2001	VER	NYP	20	7	7	35.7	22	8	23	0	2.27	3.03	6.3	2.8	3.0	0.3	2.57	9.3	20
2002	CLN	MID	21	25	25	146.7	149	35	99	7	3.44	5.66	10.6	2.8	3.6	1.1	5.39	-0.9	-3
2003	BRV	FLA	22	22	21	126.7	118	26	66	3	2.56	5.12	10.0	2.4	3.2	0.7	4.52	6.1	3
2003	HAR	EAS	22	4	4	20.3	23	11	12	0	3.55	6.27	11.1	5.8	4.3	0.5	5.68	-1.4	0
2004	MON	NL	23	20	15	83.7	102	32	37	13	5.73	5.12	10.6	3.0	3.7	1.1	5.07	6.6	-11

Breakout: 17%   Improve: 46%   Collapse: 25%

Granting that it takes a bazooka to launch a ball out of Brevard County's home park, Hill's three homers allowed in 25 starts last year got management's attention. Dayn Perry's research on low home run rates as a predictor of major league success offer further hope; while unlikely to go Brandon Webb on the NL at any point, Hill's ability to keep the ball down—along with command of a low-90s fastball, curve, and change—could produce a Zach Day Jr. by 2006. The Expos need to enforce the strict pitch count limits and general care they've exercised with all their minor league pitchers in recent years to keep Hill healthy and effective. A busy season that ended with four starts in Double-A and included an appearance in the Futures Game pushed the Ontario native to the limit, but not beyond, eh. With a low strikeout rate and the TINSTAAPP curse hanging over him, Hill will need to prove his mettle at Harrisburg to take that next step.

MICHAEL HINCKLEY   Bats: R   Throws: L   Born: 05-Oct-82   Age: 21

YEAR	TM	LG	AGE	G	GS	IP	H	BB	SO	HR	ERA	EQERA	EQH9	EQBB9	EQSO9	EQHR9	PERA	VORP	STF
2002	VER	NYP	19	16	16	91.7	60	30	66	4	1.37	3.32	8.5	4.6	3.8	1.5	5.28	19.9	2
2003	SAV	SAL	20	23	23	121.0	124	41	111	4	3.64	5.85	11.5	4.1	5.0	0.8	5.77	-3.0	10
2003	BRV	FLA	20	4	4	25.0	14	1	23	1	0.72	1.99	6.8	0.4	6.0	1.2	2.86	9.1	40
2004	MON	NL	21	17	13	73.7	88	36	43	12	5.71	5.10	10.3	3.8	4.9	1.1	5.35	5.3	-6

Breakout: 8%   Improve: 53%   Collapse: 15%

(continued next page)

Michael Hinckley *(continued)*

Started justifying the Expos' love last year, enjoying a solid season in the Sally League before closing the year with four lights-out starts at Brevard County. Hinckley throws a darting fastball at 91–92 and a curve that gets hitters out. A compact motion on the back side makes him look almost like a short-armer, adding deception to his repertoire. Injuries and trades made the Expos move some of their pitchers faster than they would have liked. If they're smart they'll give Hinckley at least a full year in the Florida State League rather than throwing him to the wolves in Double-A. At his tender age, with a history of elbow soreness in high school and in his first year as a pro, rushing your best pitching prospect makes no sense.

JOSH KARP
Bats: R **Throws: R** Born: 21-Sep-79 Age: 24

YEAR	TM	LG	AGE	G	GS	IP	H	BB	SO	HR	ERA	EQERA	EQH9	EQBB9	EQSO9	EQHR9	PERA	VORP	STF
2002	BRV	FLA	22	7	7	45.3	31	11	43	1	1.59	3.07	7.9	2.6	5.9	0.4	3.33	11.5	35
2002	HAR	EAS	22	16	16	86.7	83	34	69	6	3.84	5.47	10.0	4.2	5.4	1.0	5.35	1.1	6
2003	HAR	EAS	23	23	23	122.7	126	49	77	12	4.99	6.32	10.7	4.4	4.5	1.7	6.50	-8.9	-24
2004	MON	NL	24	18	13	70.7	87	40	47	15	6.80	6.07	10.6	4.4	5.6	1.4	6.03	0.6	-9

Breakout: 21%   Improve: 56%   Collapse: 22%

When Karp's UCLA Bruins and Mark Prior's USC Trojans went head-to-head in college, some insisted Karp was a good comp for Prior. The repercussions of those misguided . . . no, not misguided . . . let's say just insane comparisons have led both Karp and the Expos to a developmental cul-de-sac. The Expos reached for Karp in 2001, using the sixth overall pick in that year's draft on him. It's been a bumpy ride since. Karp didn't sign until late September that year, putting his instruction schedule on hold for several months. The nagging injuries he sustained at UCLA keep cropping up, with a DL stint for shoulder discomfort last year the latest setback. His second go-round at Double-A after half a season there in '02 yielded unimpressive results, as Karp struggled to put hitters away.

Highly touted his whole life, Karp has complained aloud, wondering why he's not in the majors yet, his pedestrian minor league results be damned. He has major league stuff, featuring a quality fastball and slurve and a nasty, low-80s circle change. But bad habit—including a dropping elbow that at times produces flat, mashable pitches—have combined with his sense of entitlement to cast doubt on his future. Barring major injury he'll still get his shot in the bigs late this year or in 2005. Just don't be surprised if he flops.

SUN-WOO KIM
Bats: R **Throws: R** Born: 04-Sep-77 Age: 26

YEAR	TM	LG	AGE	G	GS	IP	H	BB	SO	HR	ERA	EQERA	EQH9	EQBB9	EQSO9	EQHR9	PERA	VORP	STF
2001	PAW	INT	23	19	14	89.0	93	27	79	10	5.36	5.40	9.3	3.1	6.4	1.3	4.95	1.9	7
2001	BOS	AL	23	20	2	41.7	54	21	27	1	5.83	5.05	11.2	4.2	5.3	0.2	5.01	2.5	13
2002	PAW	INT	24	8	8	45.3	34	16	37	4	3.18	3.83	7.2	3.8	6.2	1.1	3.98	8.3	12
2002	BOS	AL	24	15	2	29.0	34	7	18	5	7.45	6.11	10.6	1.9	5.5	1.3	5.27	-1.6	-6
2002	OTT	INT	24	7	7	43.7	29	16	28	2	1.24	3.18	7.0	4.1	5.0	0.7	3.60	10.7	16
2002	MON	NL	24	4	3	20.3	18	7	11	0	0.89	1.83	7.8	2.7	4.1	0.0	2.93	8.3	32
2003	EDM	PCL	25	22	22	132.3	147	53	83	18	5.03	5.90	9.9	4.2	4.8	1.8	6.21	-4.2	-32
2003	MON	NL	25	4	3	14.0	24	8	5	6	8.36	9.22	15.1	4.6	2.6	3.3	10.64	-3.4	-100
2004	MON	NL	26	19	12	67.7	77	33	45	11	5.68	5.08	9.8	3.8	5.6	1.1	5.14	5.5	-4

Breakout: 23%   Improve: 45%   Collapse: 25%

Called up in June as a hoped-for solution to the team's rash of pitching injuries, Kim got rocked his first three starts. Asked after the third if he'd keep Kim in the rotation, Frank Robinson said: "Do I look like I am insane? Do I look like a man that wants to be tortured?" Way to build the kid's confidence, Frank. Though much was made of his broken spirit following Robinson's rip, Kim had put up lousy peripherals in Edmonton before his call-up, despite flashes of good command earlier in his career. Pegged as the club's likely fifth starter heading into Spring Training, his ugly season was one of the organization's biggest disappointments, especially after his progress in 2002 played a major role in Randy St. Claire's promotion to the Expos' pitching coach job. With several other options around, he's a long shot for a starter's job in '04.

LUKE LOCKWOOD
Bats: L **Throws: L** Born: 21-Jul-81 Age: 22

YEAR	TM	LG	AGE	G	GS	IP	H	BB	SO	HR	ERA	EQERA	EQH9	EQBB9	EQSO9	EQHR9	PERA	VORP	STF
2001	CLN	MID	19	26	26	163.3	152	49	114	8	2.70	5.67	9.9	3.8	4.0	0.9	5.07	-1.1	11
2002	BRV	FLA	20	26	26	147.0	155	38	86	13	3.37	6.35	11.3	2.9	3.8	1.8	6.56	-11.1	-10
2003	HAR	EAS	21	26	26	144.7	175	41	64	16	5.16	6.73	11.6	3.0	3.3	1.8	6.67	-16.8	-18
2004	MON	NL	22	11	9	52.0	69	24	27	11	6.86	6.13	11.4	3.6	4.4	1.4	6.12	0.4	-11

Breakout: 10%   Improve: 47%   Collapse: 39%

The Expos' rushing of several pitching prospects due to setbacks with others hurt Lockwood the most. The second-youngest pitcher in the Eastern League, he got pasted in Double-A. His long arm action was the culprit, as hitters saw the ball well off him and drilled it, again and again. Lockwood already lives on the margins, with a fastball around 86–87 and little trickery in his delivery. If his sinking fastball isn't working, he's toast. He finished the year with a 5–0 streak after working on his mechanics. A repeat season at Harrisburg could do him a lot of good, or push him closer to non-prospectdom.

JULIO MANON

Bats: L **Throws: R** Born: 10-Jun-73 Age: 31

YEAR	TM	LG	AGE	G	GS	IP	H	BB	SO	HR	ERA	EQERA	EQH9	EQBB9	EQSO9	EQHR9	PERA	VORP	STF
2001	OTT	INT	28	15	14	84.0	71	34	67	11	3.11	4.24	9.0	4.4	5.7	1.7	5.59	11.5	-21
2001	HAR	EAS	28	10	7	52.0	50	16	44	6	3.12	4.89	11.0	3.7	5.3	1.8	6.49	3.6	-35
2002	HAR	EAS	29	6	6	39.0	37	4	51	3	3.00	3.89	11.4	1.0	8.8	1.3	5.34	6.6	16
2002	OTT	INT	29	28	13	105.3	83	45	81	8	3.50	4.56	8.7	4.8	6.0	1.0	4.93	10.9	-11
2003	EDM	PCL	30	35	0	42.0	33	19	48	4	2.14	3.43	7.6	4.8	8.7	1.4	4.68	9.5	-7
2003	MON	NL	30	23	0	28.3	26	17	15	3	4.13	4.23	8.1	4.9	4.2	1.0	4.64	5.6	-21
2004	*MON*	*NL*	*31*	*14*	*6*	*35.0*	*38*	*19*	*30*	*6*	*5.61*	*5.01*	*9.3*	*4.1*	*7.1*	*1.2*	*5.06*	*3.4*	*0*

Breakout: 28%   Improve: 60%   Collapse: 21%

Manon shined early in the year as the closer in Edmonton, mixing a blazing fastball and diving splitter with aplomb. Called up in early June, he pitched four sparkling frames of extra-inning relief in his first major league appearance, earning Frank Robinson's confidence and thrusting him into a regular high-leverage role. Struggles with control proved his undoing, and Manon ended the year back in the minors. Recognizing the folly of operating with a scouting budget that ranks roughly 115th among MLB's 30 teams, Minaya sold Manon to the Kia Tigers of the Korean League, using the $200,000 from the transaction to bolster that weakness.

TOMOKAZU OHKA

Bats: R **Throws: R** Born: 18-Mar-76 Age: 28

YEAR	TM	LG	AGE	G	GS	IP	H	BB	SO	HR	ERA	EQERA	EQH9	EQBB9	EQSO9	EQHR9	PERA	VORP	STF
2001	PAW	INT	25	8	8	42.0	55	9	33	5	5.57	7.03	12.3	2.3	5.4	1.4	6.23	-6.3	-17
2001	BOS	AL	25	12	11	52.3	69	19	37	7	6.20	5.75	11.1	3.0	5.9	1.0	5.53	-0.9	0
2001	MON	NL	25	10	10	54.7	65	10	31	8	4.77	4.75	10.2	1.5	4.2	1.2	4.87	5.0	-2
2002	MON	NL	26	32	31	192.7	194	45	118	19	3.18	3.97	9.0	1.8	4.8	0.9	4.04	33.6	10
2003	MON	NL	27	34	34	199.0	233	45	118	24	4.16	4.79	10.5	1.8	4.7	1.0	4.93	25.4	1
2004	*MON*	*NL*	*28*	*29*	*25*	*152.0*	*184*	*43*	*90*	*23*	*5.22*	*4.66*	*10.5*	*2.2*	*5.0*	*1.1*	*4.70*	*16.9*	*3*

Breakout: 7%   Improve: 34%   Collapse: 24%

It's a game of inches, as Ohka showed all too clearly last year. Relying on command and smarts, he turned the fluky-cool trick of posting the exact same strikeout and walk totals—118 K, 45 BB—in two straight seasons. Over 200 innings, that leaves a lot of balls in play in question. In 2002, those balls in play often went for outs. Last year, they fell for hits, and Ohka's ERA rose a full run. Before we place too much of the blame on lucky bloop shots though, check out Ohka's extra-base hits allowed, 2002 vs. 2003:

Year	IP	2B	3B	HR
2002	192.2	36	7	19
2003	199.0	52	2	24

Hiram Bithorn's generous dimensions played a role here, but that's partially offset by Endy Chavez pushing Brad Wilkerson to left last year, bolstering the outfield defense; the guy just got whacked. Ohka's control will always keep him in ballgames, but he'll likely track closer to his 2003 performance than his 2002 line going forward.

DARRELL RASNER   Bats: R   Throws: R   Born: 13-Jan-81   Age: 23

YEAR	TM	LG	AGE	G	GS	IP	H	BB	SO	HR	ERA	EQERA	EQH9	EQBB9	EQSO9	EQHR9	PERA	VORP	STF
2002	VER	NYP	21	10	10	43.7	44	18	49	1	4.32	7.43	13.4	5.9	5.9	0.7	6.94	-7.4	-4
2003	SAV	SAL	22	22	22	105.3	106	36	90	8	4.19	6.41	12.2	4.2	4.7	2.0	7.47	-8.2	-32
2004	*MON*	*NL*	*23*	*18*	*11*	*61.7*	*81*	*34*	*38*	*11*	*6.85*	*6.12*	*11.3*	*4.2*	*5.2*	*1.3*	*6.19*	*0.6*	*-12*

Breakout: 26%   *Improve: 60%*   *Collapse: 22%*

The Expos' second-round pick out of the University of Nevada in 2002, and why not? It's not like the Expos could have used any quality hitters with their last half a decade of high picks. Rasner's your basic fastball/curve/change, good arm if he can harness his stuff and stay healthy prospect. He struggled with his consistency in the Sally League last year and didn't dominate the way many hoped. At 6'3", 210, he's got the big, strong, projectable body that makes scouts cuckoo for Cocoa Puffs. The Expos need to stop wasting their picks on those crummy toy plastic spaceships, Now In Every Box!

BRITT REAMES   Bats: R   Throws: R   Born: 19-Aug-73   Age: 30

YEAR	TM	LG	AGE	G	GS	IP	H	BB	SO	HR	ERA	EQERA	EQH9	EQBB9	EQSO9	EQHR9	PERA	VORP	STF
2001	OTT	INT	27	8	8	54.0	47	13	38	4	3.50	4.17	9.1	2.5	4.9	0.9	4.32	7.9	3
2001	MON	NL	27	41	13	95.0	101	48	86	16	5.59	5.61	9.3	4.2	6.8	1.4	5.33	-0.1	-14
2002	OTT	INT	28	7	7	42.0	31	14	26	3	2.79	4.26	8.1	3.6	4.7	0.9	4.19	5.7	-2
2002	MON	NL	28	42	6	68.0	70	38	76	8	5.03	5.43	9.5	4.3	8.7	1.1	5.14	1.3	2
2003	EDM	PCL	29	25	20	118.0	146	46	86	8	5.42	6.22	11.3	4.1	5.5	1.0	5.85	-7.7	-16
2004	*OAK*	*AL*	*30*	*43*	*10*	*79.3*	*86*	*45*	*58*	*11*	*5.52*	*5.84*	*9.8*	*4.8*	*6.3*	*1.1*	*5.79*	*4.6*	*-10*

Breakout: 25%   *Improve: 60%*   *Collapse: 24%*

Another who didn't make the big club out of Spring Training and stunk up the joint in the minors thereafter. Reames owns a sweet curveball and a fastball he tries to overthrow, usually with disastrous results. Between nagging shoulder problems, a scattershot approach, unimpressive stat lines dating back to last century, and a fast-approaching 30th birthday, he's flotsam at this point.

RICH RUNDLES   Bats: L   Throws: L   Born: 03-Jun-81   Age: 23

YEAR	TM	LG	AGE	G	GS	IP	H	BB	SO	HR	ERA	EQERA	EQH9	EQBB9	EQSO9	EQHR9	PERA	VORP	STF
2001	AUG	SAL	20	19	19	115.0	109	10	94	5	2.43	5.17	11.0	1.1	4.0	1.0	4.88	4.9	13
2001	CLN	MID	20	4	4	27.0	26	3	20	0	2.33	4.44	10.7	1.5	4.1	0.4	4.24	3.1	25
2002	BRV	FLA	21	12	11	57.3	66	16	31	5	4.08	7.41	12.9	3.2	3.4	1.9	7.51	-10.3	-30
2003	BRV	FLA	22	19	19	106.7	111	24	76	2	2.95	5.81	11.3	2.6	4.4	0.6	5.04	-2.2	9
2004	*MON*	*NL*	*23*	*19*	*15*	*82.0*	*108*	*32*	*33*	*15*	*6.37*	*5.69*	*11.4*	*3.0*	*3.4*	*1.2*	*5.62*	*4.6*	*-14*

Breakout: 13%   *Improve: 46%*   *Collapse: 31%*

For the second year in a row, Rundles was shut down early due to elbow concerns. Take that as a mixed blessing: The other player in the 2001 Urbina for Ohka trade may have to be watched closely for years to come, but the Expos have been cautious and proactive enough to pull Rundles off the mound and keep him away from James Andrews's operating table thus far. Despite his 6'5" frame, Rundles goes the finesse route, throwing a fastball in the high 80s, a quality change and a slow curve. He makes his bones controlling the outside corner, goading right-handed hitters into harmless grounders. Given how tough Brevard County is on righty hitters, we won't get a good read on Rundles until he gives Double-A a whirl, starting this year.

CHRIS SCHRODER   Bats: R   Throws: R   Born: 20-Aug-78   Age: 25

YEAR	TM	LG	AGE	G	GS	IP	H	BB	SO	HR	ERA	EQERA	EQH9	EQBB9	EQSO9	EQHR9	PERA	VORP	STF
2001	VER	NYP	22	11	0	12.0	8	5	18	1	1.50	2.79	11.2	6.5	8.4	2.8	8.46	3.0	-39
2001	JUP	FLA	22	10	0	15.7	12	4	20	1	2.29	4.61	9.9	2.6	7.9	1.3	5.11	1.5	9
2002	CLN	MID	23	22	0	27.3	15	14	42	1	1.65	3.09	8.1	6.6	8.9	1.2	5.19	6.5	0
2002	BRV	FLA	23	23	0	29.7	13	19	36	2	1.52	3.12	6.6	7.3	7.6	1.4	4.96	7.2	-10
2003	HAR	EAS	24	49	0	82.3	68	47	81	5	2.84	4.40	9.2	6.4	7.2	1.1	5.58	9.8	-12
2004	*MON*	*NL*	*25*	*14*	*4*	*28.0*	*31*	*21*	*24*	*5*	*6.47*	*5.78*	*9.6*	*5.7*	*7.3*	*1.1*	*5.75*	*0.3*	*-6*

Breakout: 10%   *Improve: 36%*   *Collapse: 34%*

A strikeout an inning, a homer every 16 innings and a swinging arm action that's tough on righties propelled Schroder onto the list of viable candidates who'd take the spots of the Biddles and Eischens of the pen should they get non-tendered and bolt. He still needs to stay on top of his slider to ensure the ball doesn't flatten out and get hammered, Strawberry off the ring of the Big O roof-style. The Expos sent him to the AFL to tighten his control, a must if he's to make the show come spring.

DAN SMITH

										Bats: R		Throws: R				Born: 15-Sep-75		Age: 28

YEAR	TM	LG	AGE	G	GS	IP	H	BB	SO	HR	ERA	EQERA	EQH9	EQBB9	EQSO9	EQHR9	PERA	VORP	STF
2001	BUF	INT	25	21	16	106.0	110	44	68	17	4.50	6.17	10.3	4.4	4.5	1.9	6.61	-6.2	-41
2002	OTT	INT	26	14	14	83.3	71	18	61	10	3.24	4.32	9.6	2.4	5.6	1.7	5.37	10.7	-13
2002	MON	NL	26	33	0	46.7	34	21	34	6	3.47	3.57	6.6	3.6	5.8	1.2	3.73	10.2	-6
2003	MON	NL	27	32	0	37.7	42	18	35	11	5.25	5.89	10.1	3.9	7.4	2.5	6.91	2.1	-42
2004	*MON*	*NL*	*28*	*22*	*7*	*46.3*	*51*	*21*	*38*	*9*	*5.17*	*4.62*	*9.4*	*3.5*	*6.9*	*1.3*	*4.98*	*5.8*	*0*

Breakout: 25%   Improve: 47%   Collapse: 17%

Smith failed to duplicate his surprise 2002 season after shoulder problems begat general crappiness, surgery, and an end to his season. If he's completely healthy by the spring, he could win back a spot as the bullpen's sixth arm. If not, there are dozens more Dan Smiths out there who'd be thrilled to make $300,000, stay in luxury hotels and eat well for six months a year.

SEUNG SONG

										Bats: R		Throws: R				Born: 29-Jun-80		Age: 24

YEAR	TM	LG	AGE	G	GS	IP	H	BB	SO	HR	ERA	EQERA	EQH9	EQBB9	EQSO9	EQHR9	PERA	VORP	STF
2001	AUG	SAL	21	14	14	75.0	56	18	79	3	2.04	4.25	9.3	3.3	5.3	1.0	4.70	9.9	14
2001	SAR	FLA	21	8	8	48.3	28	18	56	1	1.68	2.64	6.5	3.9	6.9	0.4	3.02	14.6	46
2002	TRN	EAS	22	21	21	108.7	106	37	116	11	4.39	5.17	9.8	3.6	7.1	1.5	5.57	4.8	11
2003	HAR	EAS	23	13	13	72.7	55	24	44	5	2.35	3.80	7.7	3.7	4.3	1.2	4.37	13.3	0
2003	EDM	PCL	23	13	13	73.7	69	33	40	6	3.79	4.46	7.6	4.6	4.3	1.0	4.38	9.0	1
2004	*MON*	*NL*	*24*	*20*	*13*	*76.3*	*83*	*37*	*51*	*13*	*5.39*	*4.82*	*9.4*	*3.7*	*5.6*	*1.1*	*4.91*	*7.5*	*-2*

Breakout: 23%   Improve: 54%   Collapse: 18%

One of the biggest challenges for the Expos' minor league instructors. Acquired in the Cliff Floyd trade with Boston in 2002, Song pitched one game at Harrisburg that year, got hurt and was shut down. He stayed healthy last year, putting up 26 starts. But after a decent stint at Double-A, Song struggled in Edmonton, barely managing a K:BB rate above 1:1 as more patient Triple-A hitters gave him problems. They think they can get Song to improve his command by speeding up his tempo. Better leg lift, they believe, will help him keep the ball down. A strong-willed pitcher, Song has been slow to embrace such instruction. That's too bad; the pitcher who struck out more than a batter an inning at Trenton in '02 could open some major league eyes if he can return to that form.

SCOTT STEWART

										Bats: R		Throws: L				Born: 14-Aug-75		Age: 28

YEAR	TM	LG	AGE	G	GS	IP	H	BB	SO	HR	ERA	EQERA	EQH9	EQBB9	EQSO9	EQHR9	PERA	VORP	STF
2001	MON	NL	25	62	0	47.7	43	13	39	5	3.77	3.50	7.8	2.3	6.2	0.8	3.50	10.8	9
2002	MON	NL	26	67	0	64.0	49	22	67	4	3.09	3.48	7.1	2.8	8.1	0.6	3.11	14.6	24
2003	MON	NL	27	51	0	43.0	52	13	29	5	3.98	4.75	10.8	2.4	5.4	1.1	5.26	6.3	-13
2004	*CLE*	*AL*	*28*	*43*	*0*	*47.3*	*48*	*14*	*32*	*4*	*3.70*	*3.95*	*9.0*	*2.6*	*5.9*	*0.8*	*4.16*	*10.1*	*-2*

Breakout: 31%   Improve: 56%   Collapse: 23%

Last year's missing ingredient in the bullpen. Stewart put up a terrific 2002 season until September bone chips cut that year short. He had surgery to clean out his elbow but never got back on track in '03. Stewart's ineffectiveness all year subtracted the team's top lefty reliever from late-inning situations and forced Biddle and Ayala to throw too many innings and wear down by season's end. A July appendectomy sealed the deal. The Expos needed Stewart back, healthy, and effective, plus reinforcements, if they want to improve what was one of the league's worst bullpens; instead, they dealt him to the Tribe for Ryan Church and Maicer Izturis.

T. J. TUCKER   Bats: R   Throws: R   Born: 20-Aug-78   Age: 25

YEAR	TM	LG	AGE	G	GS	IP	H	BB	SO	HR	ERA	EQERA	EQH9	EQBB9	EQSO9	EQHR9	PERA	VORP	STF
2001	OTT	INT	22	14	14	84.0	68	33	63	11	3.11	4.78	7.5	4.1	5.7	1.4	4.52	7.2	12
2001	HAR	EAS	22	13	13	82.0	77	37	57	10	3.73	5.62	9.8	5.5	4.4	1.7	6.38	-0.2	-16
2002	MON	NL	23	57	0	61.3	69	31	42	5	4.11	4.98	10.1	3.9	5.3	0.8	5.02	4.1	1
2003	EDM	PCL	24	3	3	16.3	16	7	6	2	2.76	4.11	8.2	4.7	2.9	1.8	5.53	2.5	-31
2003	MON	NL	24	45	7	80.0	90	20	47	8	4.72	4.91	10.2	2.0	4.7	0.8	4.58	4.2	0
2004	*MON*	*NL*	*25*	*33*	*11*	*75.3*	*84*	*30*	*47*	*9*	*4.94*	*4.41*	*9.7*	*3.0*	*5.2*	*0.9*	*4.44*	*10.1*	*-5*

Breakout: 19%   *Improve: 52%*   *Collapse: 22%*

A sandwich-round pick in 1997 as compensation for Mel Rojas, we can only assume Tucker's made his body an homage to Rojas's ample frame, or possibly to his own sandwich-related beginnings. Back problems remained an ongoing problem for Tucker, rendering him a liability in the bullpen. Bumped to the starting rotation to paper over injuries and salvage his season, Tucker showed flashes, mixing pitches well and showing the guile to battle out of jams before tiring, as you'd expect, around the fifth. Obscured by his weight is Tucker's athleticism—he's a good hitter who can also field his position. An off-season of work stretching him out could make Tucker a candidate for the back of the rotation as a decent six-inning-pitcher, especially if Armas's arm doesn't hold up.

CLAUDIO VARGAS   Bats: R   Throws: R   Born: 19-Jun-78   Age: 26

YEAR	TM	LG	AGE	G	GS	IP	H	BB	SO	HR	ERA	EQERA	EQH9	EQBB9	EQSO9	EQHR9	PERA	VORP	STF
2001	PME	EAS	23	27	27	159.0	122	67	151	25	4.19	5.75	9.7	5.3	6.1	2.3	6.92	-2.3	-25
2002	CLG	PCL	24	17	16	76.3	88	35	61	18	6.72	6.91	10.9	4.6	5.4	2.5	7.63	-10.4	-48
2002	HAR	EAS	24	8	8	33.0	38	9	34	2	4.64	5.76	12.7	3.0	7.0	0.9	6.10	-0.5	2
2003	HAR	EAS	25	2	2	12.0	7	3	13	0	0.75	1.64	6.5	2.5	7.4	0.0	2.29	4.8	53
2003	EDM	PCL	25	2	2	9.7	7	5	12	1	2.78	3.00	7.0	6.0	10.0	1.0	4.36	2.6	22
2003	MON	NL	25	23	20	114.0	111	41	62	16	4.34	4.50	8.7	2.9	4.3	1.2	4.61	16.2	-6
2004	*MON*	*NL*	*26*	*25*	*17*	*98*	*106*	*43*	*69*	*17*	*5.53*	*4.94*	*9.4*	*3.4*	*5.9*	*1.2*	*4.88*	*7.9*	*0*

Breakout: 22%   *Improve: 48%*   *Collapse: 17%*

Sometimes projects pay off. Acquired as a throw-in to the Expos' first Cliff Floyd trade of 2002, Vargas was billed as a hulking, flame-throwing righty with sub-par breaking stuff and poor control—he finished that season scuffling through Double-A. Side work in spring training revealed a quirk in his repertoire: a curve that broke like a slider, and a slider that didn't do anything. Vargas junked his old slider, called his curve his new slider, and finally tightened his delivery after repeated prior attempts. A fringe Rookie of the Year candidate for a while, he pounded hitters inside enough to overcome his lousy strikeout rate. A shoulder injury ostensibly wiped out the rest of his season. Vargas pitched all the way to the Caribbean World Series in '02, then tried to hide his fatigue and injury before going on the DL last year. The Expos hope he hasn't suffered any long-term damage, as they'll need him in '04.

JAVIER VAZQUEZ   Bats: R   Throws: R   Born: 25-Jul-76   Age: 27

YEAR	TM	LG	AGE	G	GS	IP	H	BB	SO	HR	ERA	EQERA	EQH9	EQBB9	EQSO9	EQHR9	PERA	VORP	STF
2001	MON	NL	24	32	32	223.7	197	44	208	24	3.42	3.29	7.8	1.6	7.0	0.8	3.34	55.5	37
2002	MON	NL	25	34	34	230.3	243	49	179	28	3.91	4.38	9.5	1.7	6.1	1.1	4.45	30.1	14
2003	MON	NL	26	34	34	230.7	198	57	241	28	3.24	3.44	7.9	2.0	8.4	1.0	3.69	57.4	32
2004	*NYY*	*AL*	*27*	*31*	*31*	*224.3*	*204*	*45*	*194*	*23*	*3.22*	*3.32*	*8.0*	*1.7*	*7.5*	*0.9*	*3.25*	*61.7*	*27*

Breakout: 33%   *Improve: 61%*   *Collapse: 9%*

Though he entered last season as the staff's ace, Vazquez integrated two pitches from newcomers into a lights-out second half. Livan Hernandez, who took on the unlikely role of staff mentor as the year went on, helped him refine a big, breaking curve. Luis Ayala, mature beyond his years or major league experience, showed Vazquez his grip on a two-seam fastball, a pitch Vazquez had tinkered with before but never used effectively for long until 2003. Vazquez continues to live near the top of BP's Pitcher Abuse Points list every year, and every year falls just short of the Pedro Jr. comparisons that have followed him forever. A better comp may be Andy Pettitte: a pitcher who's never completely healthy, dominant when he's close, effective but a little erratic when less so. One Pedro-like element you'd like to see more of: challenging hitters inside. Vazquez has enough command to nibble on the outside black, but too much great stuff to settle for a Glavine-only approach.

Traded to the Yankees for Nick Johnson, Juan Rivera, and Randy Choate, Vazquez should effectively replace Pettitte in the rotation, and New York should try to get his name on a long-term contract. It'll be interesting to see how fans in the Bronx respond to Vazquez's gopher problems. Though an elite pitcher, Vazquez's diving GB/FB rate means he's going to give up plenty of homers. If he keeps batters off base though, he'll yield a bunch of solo shots, Curt Schilling-style, adding another twist to the Boston-New York arms race featuring the two starters. Vazquez's superior health and youth make him the better bet for 2004 and beyond.

CHRIS YOUNG Bats: R   Throws: R   Born: 25-May-79   Age: 25

YEAR	TM	LG	AGE	G	GS	IP	H	BB	SO	HR	ERA	EQERA	EQH9	EQBB9	EQSO9	EQHR9	PERA	VORP	STF
2001	HIC	SAL	22	12	12	74.3	79	20	72	6	4.12	6.72	12.7	3.6	4.9	1.8	7.36	-8.0	-22
2002	HIC	SAL	23	26	26	144.7	127	34	136	11	3.11	5.40	11.7	3.0	5.2	2.0	6.89	2.7	-26
2003	BRV	FLA	24	8	8	50.0	26	5	39	3	1.62	2.68	7.2	1.2	4.9	1.9	4.06	14.2	-5
2003	HAR	EAS	24	15	15	83.0	83	22	64	9	4.01	5.21	11.0	2.9	5.6	1.9	6.50	3.2	-22
2004	MON	NL	25	19	13	76.0	96	27	54	18	6.69	5.97	10.9	2.8	6.0	1.6	5.73	0.0	-2

Breakout: 8%   Improve: 40%   Collapse: 33%

Learning to establish a good fastball should be the number-one goal for any young pitcher. Throwing it 43 times in a row, as Young did in one game this season, is overdoing it to the nth degree. If that's the echo of scouts' tut-tuting over Young's inability to go over 91 despite his 6' 10" frame, the Expos need to bring him in for reprogramming. Velocity is the product of arm speed, not height; thus Billy Wagner vs. . . . well, Chris Young. They're working on lengthening his stride and improving his slider. Young needs a better breaking ball to finish hitters off if he's to crack a major league pitching staff by 2005.

New York Mets

S teve Phillips got fired this season, after years and years of trying. Every off-season during his tenure the Mets spent everything they could, denying the increasingly desperate state of the team, until finally Phillips stood at the crater's edge. He looked over the smoking ruin of the franchise he'd brought to this sorry end, and as the first tear rolled down his cheek, Fred Wilpon came to his side, put a hand on Phillips' shoulder, and firmly pushed his GM off of the edge.

In the last decade, the Mets featured all the bad characteristics of the Yankees, but unencumbered by any of the winning. Instead, they've had petty politicking, public fights between the manager and the people who write the checks, and ownership problems so severe they required intervention by the commissioner. Much of this is old news, and now resolved: After the unpleasantness surrounding the ownership transfer, Fred Wilpon owns the team outright now. They have a new GM he's quite happy with, for now, and in turn they have a coaching staff that shouldn't get fired for... a while.

It's weird to write this about a team with such a large payroll, but the Mets should be looking a couple of years down the line, while still spending now.

It's something of a myth that teams should simply pour all their money into prospect acquisition if they're rebuilding. What's really to buy? The draft costs every team about the same. A club could try and draft signability risks, guys headed to college, and buy them out at a price above market value. Sometimes that works—Grady Sizemore turned out well, for instance—but in general, players who drop because teams are convinced they're going to college end up going to college. Other picks may be as talented or more so, with less risk involved.

You can open more baseball academies overseas, but that's not a spigot you get to turn on for a couple years after you start building it, and most teams already have worldwide organizations with their own areas of strength. A team can't simply decide to throw an extra $10 million into Dominican academies and be guaranteed a big, rapid return on that money.

You can augment your scouting budget. But unless you're the Expos, you've probably got a full roster of scouts employed already, and you run the risk of losing focus on key talent hotbeds if you spread your reach too far.

METS PROSPECTUS

2003 record: 66–95; Fifth place, NL East

Pythagenport record: 68–94

Runs scored per game: 4.0 (15th in NL)

Runs allowed per game: 4.7 (10th in NL)

Team EqA: .247 (14th in NL)

2003 Batters Age: 30.6 (6th oldest in NL)

2003 Pitchers Age: 34.2 (Oldest in NL)

Ballpark: Shea Stadium; Severe pitcher's park; Park Factor of 0.950

2003: Steve Phillips lost his job after assembling one old, expensive, bad Mets team too many.

2004: They'll need a miracle to contend, but finding suckers to take on the bad contracts might not be impossible.

So what to do with that cash if you've got it?

The Mets spend it, and spend it like it's going out of style. After 2002, they had a bad rotation and a terrible outfield, so they spent money on Tom Glavine and Cliff Floyd. Those weren't the finest choices: Unless you're close to contention, you'd do better to target younger, healthier players who offer more long-term upside. Rather than sign several middle-class free agents for inflated dollars, it makes more sense to target young, impact free agents like Vlad Guerrero—players who can help the team keep the fans coming to the park today and still be productive when you're ready to compete again. It's easy to forget the importance of fan retention while teams retool; over the course of several years, keeping a fan base interested and coming back to the park is a worthwhile goal, no matter the team's place in the standings.

The key is to spend wisely. Here, new GM Jim Duquette showed some chops. Faced with developing a pitching staff with no outfield behind it, he paid good money to bring in Mike Cameron, who was among the best defensive players in baseball last year. The new center fielder will help preserve Met arms, turning loads of potential hits into outs. The effects could also extend to the development of the Mets' younger pitchers: Freed to be aggressive in the zone knowing balls in play are more likely to become outs, pitchers can rely on their stuff and throw strikes early, rather than nibbling at the corners.

The three-year, $19.5 million contract given to Cameron was money well spent. But what about the three-year, $20 million deal New York gave Japanese import Kazuo Matsui? Jose Reyes is a blooming star for the Mets at shortstop, and looking at their projections, Matsui may not even noticeably outperform Reyes in 2004. Reyes could be a huge contributor with the bat and glove at short. At second base he is less valuable: His full talents afield have less of an impact, his skill at the plate relative to his position will be less pronounced, and given the high attrition rates of second basemen, the likelihood of injury goes up. Here the Mets used their money to set themselves back. They could have patched the second base hole with a minor signing, maybe retained Marcos Scutaro to challenge for the job, while keeping Reyes at short. The money saved could have been put toward a franchise player like Guerrero, a player who'd help on the field and off for the next half a decade.

The current CBA targets the Yankees specifically, and a rational Yankees organization would give in and get under the cap. Except it seems that George Steinbrenner cannot possibly avoid the escalating payroll taxes, and every year will pay more and more into the coffers of other teams. It's easy to imagine bad Yankee teams spending more than $200 million, trying each year to spend themselves into contention and causing more trouble in the long-term.

If by contrast the Mets keep their short-term, fan-friendly spending under control while maintaining a long-term plan, they could soon ascend to the title of best team in New York. Unlike the prospect-chucking Yankees, the Mets own the seeds of a tremendous core of young talent: hitters like Jose Reyes and David Wright, pitchers like Scott Kazmir and Aaron Heilman, players who are good bets to produce for the team while their salaries are still artificially depressed. And when this crop is ready, the Mets have the money to spend to surround it with quality free agent help. Suddenly, the doors swing wide: The Mets are one of two teams in the largest, richest market in the country. They'll even be free of their Cablevision contract in two years, sooner if Fred Wilpon decides to buy his way out of it.

The course the team sets will depend on Duquette. After taking over in-season following Phillips' firing, Duquette's moves to tear down and move on were something of a mixed bag (salaries are 2003 full-year figures):

- Second baseman Roberto Alomar, making $8 million, was dumped on the White Sox for nondescript relievers Royce Ring and Edwin Almonte, plus no-hit, old-for-the-Sally-League infielder Andrew Salvo. The Mets ate the money.

- Closer Armando Benitez, $6.9 million, was tossed over the fence to the Yankees for three right-handed pitchers: Jason Anderson, Ryan Bicondoa, and Anderson Garcia. Only Anderson looks interesting for the time being.

- Jeromy Burnitz, $12 million, traded to the Dodgers for second baseman Victor Diaz and righthanders Joselo Diaz and Kole Strayhorn. Diaz was the key, though with the Matsui/Reyes moves the team no longer has a slot for him. Reports say that the Dodgers paid only $2 million of Burnitz's remaining salary.

- Graeme Lloyd, $650,000, to the Royals for catcher-turned-pitcher Jeremy Hill.

- Rey Sanchez, $1.3 million, to the Mariners for tools goof/non-prospect Kenny Kelly.

The team shed a little salary, but didn't get much back, and the farm system is not in appreciably better shape for having purged the veterans. Perhaps we're spoiled by the amazing turns Mark Shapiro managed in Cleveland, but Duquette's moves in 2003 don't look like they'll amount to much beyond the absence of those excused.

For all the roster changes, the biggest acquisition the team made in '03 was new pitching coach Rick Peterson. Peterson is one of the smartest and most progressive pitching coaches in baseball today, willing to embrace concepts like pre-hab as a means toward avoiding injuries. It's certainly arguable whether Peterson flying the A's young arms to doctors to videotape and study their deliveries before anything went wrong did anything, given the capricious nature of sports injuries. But no one can look at the durability of that pitching staff and argue with a straight face that Peterson did harm, certainly not in the kind of way Dallas Green left a trail of bodies behind him.

In Oakland, Peterson embraced innovation and was supported by an organization willing to experiment if it might offer an advantage: Dual starters in the low minors? Why not. Not working out? Scrap it. The issue will be whether Peterson's truly free to innovate in New York, or if he'll find that with more money comes more problems, as Biggie Smalls warned us. Fortunately, Art Howe has already worked with Peterson, and isn't going to be running out the kids for 140 pitches a night, then waving off Peterson with a "he's a big strong kid, Rick, give it a rest." It will also be interesting to see how Peterson's magic works with older pitchers: Glavine is signed through 2005 with a mutual option for 2006, and Leiter through 2005.

Better still for the Mets, Peterson will oversee the development of the Mets' young pitchers, a group that will make or break the team's fortunes for the rest of the decade. He's already been through the development of a young starting rotation with the A's, and will now look to build around kids like Kazmir and Heilman. Duquette can look to target more young pitching in trades, knowing he's got a pitching coach and manager who'll foster a positive environment in which young arms can develop.

It's been a long, frustrating couple of years for the Mets, as they played out Steve Phillips's desperation-drive string. But the worst has now passed, and a healthy, competitive franchise should soon arrive.

HITTERS

RON ACUNA RF/CF Bats: R Throws: R Born: 30-Jun-79 Age: 25

YEAR	TM	LG	AGE	AB	H	2B	3B	HR	BB	SO	SB	CS	AVG	OBP	SLG	MLVR	EQBA	EQOBP	EQSLG	EQMLVR	VORP	DEFENSE			
2001	CMB	SAL	22	376	107	17	3	6	19	67	23	8	.285	.332	.394	.097	.238	.275	.336	-.293	-26.8	91-RF	-7		
2001	SLU	FLA	22	119	29	9	0	2	6	22	7	1	.244	.283	.370	-.060	.215	.243	.339	-.366	-11.5	15-LF	0	10-RF	-1
2002	SLU	FLA	23	443	132	18	5	2	38	74	36	12	.298	.365	.375	.102	.257	.307	.330	-.227	-22.0	112-RF	4		
2003	BIN	EAS	24	474	144	28	3	2	34	88	24	12	.304	.350	.388	.026	.257	.300	.333	-.236	-25.2	94-RF	3	33-CF	1
2004	NYM	NL	25	230	58	12	2	3	15	46	6	2	.251	.305	.354	-.175	.254	.306	.370	-.163	-3.4	62-RF	2		

Breakout: 33%   Improve: 55%   Collapse: 22%

Wheel! Of! Outfielders! Dun dun dun, da-dun-dun dun da dun. Spin the wheel, and ticka-a-ticka-ticka . . . it's a Mets outfield prospect who can't hit for power and is okay with the glove. Weird, it seems all the spots on the wheel are more alike than different. Can't get enough of these guys? This is your chapter. Stick around for Jeff Duncan and much, much more.

AARON BALDIRIS 3B Bats: R Throws: R Born: 05-Jan-83 Age: 21

YEAR	TM	LG	AGE	AB	H	2B	3B	HR	BB	SO	SB	CS	AVG	OBP	SLG	MLVR	EQBA	EQOBP	EQSLG	EQMLVR	VORP	DEFENSE			
2002	KNG	APP	19	217	71	9	1	3	14	24	9	5	.327	.390	.419	.168	.236	.268	.310	-.345	-22.5	55-3B	3		
2003	BRO	NYP	20	88	32	5	2	0	14	13	2	2	.364	.451	.466	.408	.247	.320	.323	-.217	-2.0	25-3B	-1		
2003	CMB	SAL	20	393	123	19	4	6	51	55	13	5	.313	.396	.427	.241	.238	.302	.333	-.244	-8.4	81-3B	-1	11-1B	-1
2004	NYM	NL	21	284	64	13	1	3	21	47	3	2	.225	.286	.311	-.281	.228	.287	.326	-.273	-6.7	76-3B	-6		

Breakout: 18%   Improve: 40%   Collapse: 23%

Baldiris has put up some impressive numbers, but he's been playing in hitter's parks. That shouldn't obscure the fact that he's young and can hit. Keep an eye on him as he enters High-A ball. He's talented, has a good idea of what he's doing at the plate, and may soon put on a clinic.

JAY BELL IF Bats: R Throws: R Born: 11-Dec-65 Age: 38

YEAR	TM	LG	AGE	AB	H	2B	3B	HR	BB	SO	SB	CS	AVG	OBP	SLG	MLVR	EQBA	EQOBP	EQSLG	EQMLVR	VORP	DEFENSE			
2001	ARI	NL	35	428	106	24	1	13	65	79	0	1	.248	.349	.400	-.054	.245	.348	.396	-.065	13.6	70-2B	2	32-3B	-1
2002	ARI	NL	36	49	8	1	0	2	5	9	0	0	.163	.250	.306	-.336	.163	.253	.327	-.392	-3.4				
2003	NYM	NL	37	116	21	1	0	0	22	38	0	0	.181	.319	.190	-.333	.203	.336	.212	-.352	-6.8				
2004	NYM	NL	38	70	15	4	0	1	12	18	0	0	.221	.332	.332	-.171	.224	.334	.348	-.161	-1.1	24-2B	-8		

Breakout: 53%   Improve: 72%   Collapse: 12%

Like many players at the end of their careers, Bell had become more of a mascot and coach than a player. Since he's retiring, let's look back on his career. (Pause.) That was okay, I guess. Bell was never a great player, but we should still tip our caps to him for a nice little career. He's considering getting into coaching after a break from baseball, so he might be the manager of your Arizona Diamondbacks come 2007 or so.

CRAIG BRAZELL 1B Bats: L Throws: R Born: 10-May-80 Age: 24

YEAR	TM	LG	AGE	AB	H	2B	3B	HR	BB	SO	SB	CS	AVG	OBP	SLG	MLVR	EQBA	EQOBP	EQSLG	EQMLVR	VORP	DEFENSE	
2001	CMB	SAL	21	331	102	25	5	19	15	74	0	3	.308	.343	.586	.379	.243	.273	.472	-.099	-1.6	56-1B	-5
2002	SLU	FLA	22	402	107	25	3	16	13	78	2	1	.266	.292	.463	.092	.230	.252	.414	-.231	-17.4	100-1B	-5
2002	BIN	EAS	22	130	40	8	0	6	1	28	0	2	.308	.343	.508	.186	.264	.287	.450	-.087	-0.1	28-1B	-5
2003	BIN	EAS	23	432	126	23	2	17	23	97	2	1	.292	.331	.472	.104	.247	.284	.413	-.160	-10.1	108-1B	-1
2003	NOR	INT	23	46	12	3	0	0	1	8	1	0	.261	.292	.326	-.144	.261	.302	.326	-.240	-2.1	12-1B	2
2004	NYM	NL	24	245	59	14	1	8	14	55	1	1	.241	.288	.406	-.143	.244	.289	.425	-.129	-1.6	65-1B	-4

Breakout: 29%   Improve: 51%   Collapse: 27%

Brazell was diagnosed with Bell's Palsy this year, a facial paralysis that results from damage to a cranial nerve. It's curable through medication, but set him back temporarily. Still, Brazell put up about the same sort of numbers while repeating a season at Double-A. He headed to the AFL to play the outfield, in part because he's been crowded off of first by the Piazza/Phillips situation. The problem is that Brazell isn't athletic enough to chase fly balls, and lacks arm strength in the outfield. The Mets hope his developing power will offset his other weaknesses and bolster an outfield that badly needs more bats.

ROGER CEDENO RF Bats: B Throws: R Born: 16-Aug-74 Age: 29

YEAR	TM	LG	AGE	AB	H	2B	3B	HR	BB	SO	SB	CS	AVG	OBP	SLG	MLVR	EQBA	EQOBP	EQSLG	EQMLVR	VORP	DEFENSE			
2001	DET	AL	26	523	153	14	11	6	36	83	55	15	.293	.337	.396	-.000	.316	.365	.432	.074	30.1	60-CF	-7	51-RF	-8
2002	NYM	NL	27	511	133	19	2	7	42	92	25	4	.260	.318	.346	-.084	.274	.328	.368	-.121	-8.9	114-LF	-9		
2003	NYM	NL	28	484	129	25	4	7	38	86	14	9	.267	.320	.378	-.036	.278	.329	.398	-.073	0.5	96-RF	-4	12-CF	2
2004	NYM	NL	29	368	97	18	4	5	31	63	13	5	.264	.322	.376	-.107	.267	.323	.394	-.093	0.6	97-RF	-3		

Breakout: 17%   Improve: 43%   Collapse: 20%

Well, he did hit a few more doubles. Cedeno hasn't hit for the kind of power you'd like to see from a corner outfielder since 1997, when he played in Albuquerque. He hasn't shown decent plate discipline since 2000, when in 74 games with the Astros he drew more walks than he has in his three seasons as a full-timer since then. He hasn't played good defense in the outfield . . . ever, really. He'll be paid $10 million over the next two seasons for that dazzling array of skills. No wonder they're going all out to trade him.

TONY CLARK 1B Bats: B Throws: R Born: 15-Jun-72 Age: 32

YEAR	TM	LG	AGE	AB	H	2B	3B	HR	BB	SO	SB	CS	AVG	OBP	SLG	MLVR	EQBA	EQOBP	EQSLG	EQMLVR	VORP	DEFENSE	
2001	DET	AL	29	428	123	29	3	16	62	108	0	1	.287	.374	.481	.176	.309	.401	.524	.259	40.8	69-1B	2
2002	BOS	AL	30	275	57	12	1	3	21	57	0	0	.207	.265	.291	-.327	.228	.287	.319	-.299	-15.1	74-1B	4
2003	NYM	NL	31	254	59	13	0	16	24	73	0	0	.232	.300	.472	.032	.240	.307	.492	-.013	7.2	55-1B	-6
2004	NYY	AL	32	163	39	9	0	7	17	38	0	0	.239	.311	.420	-.072	.244	.319	.436	-.061	3.4	47-1B	-3

Breakout: 29%   Improve: 54%   Collapse: 20%

All that's left of Clark's career is the lesser, right-swinging side of a first-base platoon, and Clark can't even match the Wil Corderos of the world in that department. Escalating back problems robbed him of the second half of a career, and Clark's now a free agent. He's been plugged into the Yankees' bench, presumably to mash lefties and do some spot glovework at first.

VICTOR DIAZ 2B Bats: R Throws: R Born: 10-Dec-81 Age: 22

YEAR	TM	LG	AGE	AB	H	2B	3B	HR	BB	SO	SB	CS	AVG	OBP	SLG	MLVR	EQBA	EQOBP	EQSLG	EQMLVR	VORP	DEFENSE			
2002	SGA	SAL	20	349	122	26	2	10	27	69	20	6	.350	.407	.521	.408	.268	.312	.419	-.082	10.7	62-3B	-10	11-2B	0
2002	JAX	SOU	20	152	32	7	0	4	7	42	7	5	.211	.258	.336	-.187	.200	.229	.329	-.417	-15.0	26-1B	-1		
2003	JAX	SOU	21	316	92	20	2	10	27	60	8	10	.291	.353	.462	.199	.255	.308	.422	-.096	7.9	77-2B	-8		
2003	BIN	EAS	21	175	62	11	0	6	8	32	7	5	.354	.382	.520	.306	.301	.326	.451	.019	10.3	43-2B	-8		
2004	NYM	NL	22	296	74	16	1	8	21	62	7	3	.250	.306	.392	-.124	.253	.307	.410	-.110	10.5	79-2B	-11		

Breakout: 31%   Improve: 47%   Collapse: 31%

Victor Diaz can hit. He's been young for every level he's played, his power numbers are rising, and only an improved batting eye may hold back from doing some serious damage to major league pitching. Diaz is shaky around the keystone, but on the plus side, a 6'0" and 200-pound frame may deter players from trying to take him out on the deuce. He's the most important piece the Mets got from the Burnitz trade, and may be the only player acquired in all of he dumps likely to amount to anything.

JEFF DUNCAN CF Bats: L Throws: L Born: 09-Dec-78 Age: 25

YEAR	TM	LG	AGE	AB	H	2B	3B	HR	BB	SO	SB	CS	AVG	OBP	SLG	MLVR	EQBA	EQOBP	EQSLG	EQMLVR	VORP	DEFENSE			
2001	CMB	SAL	22	318	69	16	8	3	46	97	41	3	.217	.320	.346	-.019	.176	.252	.283	-.446	-32.4	72-CF	-12	11-LF	-1
2002	CMB	SAL	23	150	59	13	3	4	18	34	15	3	.393	.468	.600	.625	.284	.340	.452	.029	7.4				
2002	SLU	FLA	23	102	35	5	0	2	24	15	10	1	.343	.472	.451	.378	.259	.367	.343	-.090	-1.3	20-LF	-2		
2003	BIN	EAS	24	278	80	11	5	4	36	59	24	10	.288	.376	.406	.080	.237	.312	.341	-.214	-6.1	58-CF	-4		
2003	NYM	NL	24	139	27	0	2	1	17	41	4	2	.194	.291	.245	-.314	.213	.305	.262	-.348	-8.0	46-CF	4		
2004	NYM	NL	25	267	65	13	2	5	30	64	11	4	.245	.326	.368	-.123	.248	.328	.385	-.109	3.2	75-CF	-3		

Breakout: 30%   Improve: 55%   Collapse: 23%

(continued next page)

Jeff Duncan *(continued)*

Whee! Another punchless outfielder? In fairness, at least with Duncan there are some indications he might not be abjectly bad forever. He's shown great speed, decent walk rates, and fair doubles and triples power thus far. Duncan is the one you want when the Mets' Wheel of Outfield Prospects comes to a stop.

CLIFF FLOYD   LF   Bats: L   Throws: R   Born: 05-Dec-72   Age: 31

YEAR	TM	LG	AGE	AB	H	2B	3B	HR	BB	SO	SB	CS	AVG	OBP	SLG	MLVR	EQBA	EQOBP	EQSLG	EQMLVR	VORP	DEFENSE		
2001	FLA	NL	28	555	176	44	4	31	59	101	18	3	.317	.390	.578	.353	.326	.397	.592	.367	66.2	136-LF	4	
2002	FLA	NL	29	296	85	20	0	18	58	68	10	5	.287	.414	.537	.340	.299	.420	.562	.330	33.5	60-RF	-3	20-LF 0
2002	MON	NL	29	53	11	2	0	3	3	10	1	0	.208	.263	.415	-.139	.222	.262	.444	-.176	-0.7			
2002	BOS	AL	29	171	54	21	0	7	15	28	4	0	.316	.374	.561	.305	.335	.394	.607	.396	19.7	18-LF	-1	
2003	NYM	NL	30	365	106	25	2	18	51	66	3	0	.290	.376	.518	.273	.299	.386	.540	.246	31.2	80-LF	-4	
2004	*NYM*	*NL*	*31*	*405*	*117*	*27*	*2*	*19*	*48*	*76*	*6*	*2*	*.288*	*.369*	*.507*	*.163*	*.292*	*.371*	*.530*	*.188*	*30.3*	*110-LF*	*-1*	

Breakout: 13%   *Improve: 47%*   *Collapse: 19%*

Along with Tom Glavine, Floyd is a fine example of how not to invest your free agent money if you're not desperate for a bat and in win-now mode. Sure, he hit well when he was healthy, but he's always a better bet to play 120 games than 150. It's clear he'll never be a good defensive outfielder again and has slowed down dramatically while fighting chronic knee problems. Floyd will remain a part-time asset, but it only gets worse from here.

DANIEL GARCIA   2B   Bats: R   Throws: R   Born: 12-Apr-80   Age: 24

YEAR	TM	LG	AGE	AB	H	2B	3B	HR	BB	SO	SB	CS	AVG	OBP	SLG	MLVR	EQBA	EQOBP	EQSLG	EQMLVR	VORP	DEFENSE		
2001	BRO	NYP	21	56	18	2	0	1	4	10	3	2	.321	.387	.411	.215	.259	.293	.328	-.256	-2.6	14-2B	-3	
2001	CMB	SAL	21	103	31	12	1	2	15	18	7	3	.301	.409	.495	.336	.229	.314	.376	-.167	0.3	30-2B	-7	
2002	SLU	FLA	22	432	118	34	5	4	53	77	13	6	.273	.369	.403	.126	.224	.296	.345	-.248	-10.0	105-2B	-17	17-SS -6
2003	BIN	EAS	23	117	39	12	1	3	10	20	2	2	.333	.391	.530	.310	.276	.331	.448	.000	6.4	28-2B	-8	
2003	NOR	INT	23	388	102	23	3	4	22	60	11	1	.263	.313	.369	-.049	.255	.308	.367	-.174	0.1	97-2B	-11	
2003	NYM	NL	23	56	12	2	0	2	2	11	0	0	.214	.274	.357	-.185	.228	.284	.386	-.212	-0.9	16-2B	-3	
2004	*NYM*	*NL*	*24*	*256*	*64*	*16*	*2*	*5*	*22*	*46*	*4*	*2*	*.250*	*.323*	*.383*	*-.107*	*.253*	*.324*	*.401*	*-.092*	*11.0*	*71-2B*	*-10*	

Breakout: 36%   *Improve: 56%*   *Collapse: 21%*

When Alomar or McEwing weren't playing second, the 2003 Mets featured the able Scutaro, team mascot Jay Bell, and Garcia. In September, owner Fred Wilpon came out and said Garcia was not the team's future at second base, which probably didn't do a lot for the guy's motivation. With Kaz Matsui pushing Reyes to the keystone, the most Garcia will vie for is a utility role.

RAUL GONZALEZ   OF   Bats: R   Throws: R   Born: 27-Dec-73   Age: 30

YEAR	TM	LG	AGE	AB	H	2B	3B	HR	BB	SO	SB	CS	AVG	OBP	SLG	MLVR	EQBA	EQOBP	EQSLG	EQMLVR	VORP	DEFENSE		
2001	LOU	INT	27	539	161	39	1	11	64	70	6	8	.299	.371	.436	.137	.274	.346	.403	-.037	18.3	128-CF	-5	
2002	LOU	INT	28	432	144	27	2	13	61	59	9	8	.333	.416	.495	.311	.298	.381	.456	.120	35.3	69-CF	-5	22-RF -2
2002	NYM	NL	28	81	21	2	0	3	4	17	2	2	.259	.291	.395	-.064	.277	.302	.434	-.071	1.1			
2003	NOR	INT	29	120	43	3	1	3	16	23	5	2	.358	.431	.475	.361	.331	.403	.452	.183	9.6	28-RF	1	
2003	NYM	NL	29	217	50	12	2	2	27	34	3	0	.230	.317	.332	-.130	.240	.325	.353	-.170	-3.5	26-LF	-1	18-RF 0
2004	*NYM*	*NL*	*30*	*240*	*61*	*13*	*1*	*5*	*28*	*40*	*3*	*2*	*.255*	*.336*	*.377*	*-.088*	*.258*	*.337*	*.395*	*-.073*	*3.8*	*67-RF*	*1*	

Breakout: 17%   *Improve: 38%*   *Collapse: 39%*

Spin the Wheel of Outfielders! Stop me if you've heard this before, but Gonzalez is an outfielder who doesn't hit well enough to be a regular—that line in Norfolk is as good as he's ever been—and he's an average fielder. But there are subtle distinctions: he's the oldest outfielder on the Wheel. See, they weren't cloned . . .

JUSTIN HUBER   C   Bats: R   Throws: R   Born: 01-Jul-82   Age: 22

YEAR	TM	LG	AGE	AB	H	2B	3B	HR	BB	SO	SB	CS	AVG	OBP	SLG	MLVR	EQBA	EQOBP	EQSLG	EQMLVR	VORP	DEFENSE
2001	KNG	APP	19	159	50	11	1	7	17	42	4	2	.314	.415	.528	.389	.212	.277	.364	-.266	-10.3	47-C -3
2002	CMB	SAL	20	330	96	22	2	11	45	81	1	2	.291	.408	.470	.282	.219	.300	.364	-.217	-4.7	69-C -4
2003	SLU	FLA	21	183	52	15	0	9	17	30	1	1	.284	.370	.514	.293	.234	.300	.441	-.101	4.3	34-C -5
2003	BIN	EAS	21	193	51	13	0	6	19	54	0	2	.264	.350	.425	.046	.218	.287	.363	-.245	-4.4	39-C -4
2004	*NYM*	*NL*	*21*	*263*	*57*	*14*	*1*	*8*	*22*	*66*	*1*	*1*	*.219*	*.296*	*.367*	*-.194*	*.221*	*.297*	*.384*	*-.183*	*0.4*	*72-C -11*

Breakout: 20%   *Improve: 39%*   *Collapse: 31%*

Huber made it up to Binghamton, tearing up the Florida State League to earn his promotion. He rapped 43 extra-base hits in 376 ABs between the two levels, and maintained a decent walk rate for a 21-year-old in his first exposure to Double-A. Huber's size and defensive issues—his throwing has been sub-par so far—may force him to move to first base. He needs to stay behind the plate and improve his pitch selection to maintain his status as a top prospect.

MIKE JACOBS   C   Bats: L   Throws: R   Born: 30-Oct-80   Age: 23

YEAR	TM	LG	AGE	AB	H	2B	3B	HR	BB	SO	SB	CS	AVG	OBP	SLG	MLVR	EQBA	EQOBP	EQSLG	EQMLVR	VORP	DEFENSE
2001	BRO	NYP	20	66	19	5	0	1	6	11	1	1	.288	.364	.409	.157	.221	.276	.324	-.318	-5.5	14-C 0
2001	CMB	SAL	20	180	50	13	0	2	13	46	0	1	.278	.328	.383	.075	.220	.265	.312	-.357	-10.6	36-C -6
2002	SLU	FLA	21	467	117	26	1	11	25	95	2	3	.251	.291	.381	-.029	.214	.246	.338	-.362	-26.3	56-C -5
2003	BIN	EAS	22	407	134	36	1	17	28	87	0	3	.329	.376	.548	.309	.275	.318	.470	.008	22.8	64-C -7
2004	NYM	NL	23	251	60	15	1	7	18	59	1	1	.238	.294	.386	-.161	.241	.295	.404	-.148	2.4	68-C -11

Breakout: 26%   Improve: 44%   Collapse: 27%

Like Huber, Jacobs can hit. Also like Huber, he may no longer be a catcher in a couple of years. Of the two, Jacobs is the lesser star, but with better pure power, at least for now. It's strange that the system aligned to put these two together, a promising catching tandem that may not produce a catcher between them.

KENNY KELLY   RF   Bats: R   Throws: R   Born: 26-Jan-79   Age: 25

YEAR	TM	LG	AGE	AB	H	2B	3B	HR	BB	SO	SB	CS	AVG	OBP	SLG	MLVR	EQBA	EQOBP	EQSLG	EQMLVR	VORP	DEFENSE	
2001	SAN	TEX	22	478	125	20	5	11	45	111	18	12	.262	.326	.393	-.001	.227	.284	.350	-.263	-17.0	118-CF -18	
2002	TAC	PCL	23	391	97	13	10	11	26	93	11	3	.248	.296	.417	-.079	.229	.275	.389	-.224	-19.3	68-RF -7	49-CF -3
2003	TAC	PCL	24	341	84	15	5	13	29	79	20	7	.246	.313	.434	-.002	.227	.291	.410	-.166	-10.4	82-RF 5	
2003	NOR	INT	24	92	24	6	2	4	6	25	5	0	.261	.306	.500	.115	.247	.293	.484	-.042	0.6	22-RF 0	
2004	NYM	NL	25	237	58	12	2	7	19	54	7	2	.244	.304	.400	-.121	.247	.305	.419	-.107	0.9	64-RF 1	

Breakout: 33%   Improve: 56%   Collapse: 22%

The Mets sent Rey Sanchez to the Mariners and got back a tools hound who looks good in uniform, can play passable defense in the corners, and has no idea what he's doing at the plate. Watching Kelly for a short period of time, you can become convinced he belongs in the Show—he looks so smooth, so confident. Your eyes deceive you. The Mets, having run through outfielder after outfielder like Kelly, unable to find one that could play at the major league level, just had to go out and get another one.

WAYNE LYDON   LF   Bats: B   Throws: R   Born: 17-Apr-81   Age: 23

YEAR	TM	LG	AGE	AB	H	2B	3B	HR	BB	SO	SB	CS	AVG	OBP	SLG	MLVR	EQBA	EQOBP	EQSLG	EQMLVR	VORP	DEFENSE	
2001	BRO	NYP	20	57	14	1	1	0	7	18	10	1	.246	.348	.298	-.027	.186	.259	.237	-.489	-11.6	12-CF -1	
2001	KNG	APP	20	98	18	7	0	0	11	35	15	1	.184	.266	.255	-.249	.137	.193	.186	-.714	-38.9	20-CF -1	
2002	CMB	SAL	21	473	139	9	5	0	54	104	87	13	.294	.368	.334	.055	.232	.289	.266	-.367	-46.8	78-LF -4	39-CF -3
2003	SLU	FLA	22	488	129	14	7	4	52	96	75	20	.264	.342	.346	.031	.228	.288	.313	-.306	-40.7	113-LF -8	18-CF -2
2004	NYM	NL	23	258	54	10	2	2	22	63	16	5	.211	.278	.287	-.335	.214	.279	.300	-.330	-15.0	70-LF -5	

Breakout: 15%   Improve: 41%   Collapse: 27%

Lydon's another fine Mets outfield prospect who struggles to get the ball past the infield and is no great shakes with the glove. His distinctions from the others are that he's started to switch-hit, and he's stolen 162 bases in the last two years. He may have a future as a pinch-runner if things break right for him.

KAZUO MATSUI   SS   Bats: B   Throws: R   Born: 23-Oct-75   Age: 28

YEAR	TM	LG	AGE	AB	H	2B	3B	HR	BB	SO	SB	CS	AVG	OBP	SLG	MLVR	EQBA	EQOBP	EQSLG	EQMLVR	VORP	DEFENSE
2001	SEI	JPP	25	552	170	28	2	24	46	83	26	0	.308	.361	.496	.173	.297	.336	.461	.047	28.9	
2002	SEI	JPP	26	582	193	46	6	36	53	112	33	0	.332	.391	.617	.453	.319	.370	.518	.210	60.3	
2003	SEI	JPP	27	587	179	36	4	33	55	124	13		.305	.368	.549	.221	.282	.336	.478	.057	32.7	
2004	NYM	NL	28	555	156	36	4	17	47	106	14	5	.281	.339	.456	.040	.285	.340	.477	.061	39.0	143-SS -1

Breakout: 13%   Improve: 43%   Collapse: 24%

(continued next page)

Kazuo Matsui *(continued)*

Given what's happened to the last couple of MLB Japanese imports, you have to question Matsui's power potential. But Matsui has been a true extra-base-hit machine in Japan, and at worst looks like he'll crank a ton of doubles in New York. While some view Matsui as a power-speed threat, we probably won't see him run much. Matsui's not Alex Rodriguez, but paying $7 million a year for a player expected to produce around the low end of Tejada's offensive range looks reasonable, and Matsui's young enough to hold his value for a few years. The only problem here is the Mets already had a star shortstop in the making, and derailing Jose Reyes's future may come back to bite them.

JOE McEWING						UT					Bats: R			Throws: R					Born: 19-Oct-72			Age: 31
YEAR	TM	LG	AGE	AB	H	2B	3B	HR	BB	SO	SB	CS	AVG	OBP	SLG	MLVR	EQBA	EQOBP	EQSLG	EQMLVR	VORP	DEFENSE
2001	NYM	NL	28	283	80	17	3	8	17	57	8	5	.283	.342	.449	.056	.295	.352	.469	.085	10.7	24-LF 0 16-3B 1
2002	NYM	NL	29	196	39	8	1	3	9	50	4	4	.199	.242	.296	-.325	.216	.256	.327	-.357	-14.6	16-RF 0 13-SS -2
2003	NYM	NL	30	278	67	11	0	1	25	57	3	0	.241	.309	.291	-.193	.254	.318	.307	-.239	-5.1	41-2B -1 30-SS 2
2004	NYM	NL	31	186	46	9	1	3	14	38	3	2	.249	.312	.357	-.160	.252	.313	.374	-.148	3.1	52-2B -4
Breakout: 35%			Improve: 48%				Collapse: 38%															

You have to wonder how the Mets could have given McEwing 278 at-bats with a line like that. The Mets tinkered with his stance in-season, which may or may not have led to his sizzling July (.296/.400/.426). Of course you're still left to explain his awful August (.207/.291/.259) and sorry September (.273/.310/.273). His Super Joe pixie dust must have landed him the guaranteed two-year, $1 million contract he signed in December, because he didn't earn it on the field. McEwing gives the Mets a running start toward a lousy bench.

LASTINGS MILLEDGE						OF					Bats: R			Throws: R					Born: 05-Apr-85			Age: 19
YEAR	TM	LG	AGE	AB	H	2B	3B	HR	BB	SO	SB	CS	AVG	OBP	SLG	MLVR	EQBA	EQOBP	EQSLG	EQMLVR	VORP	DEFENSE
2003	KNG	APP	18	26	6	2	0	0	3	4	5	1	.231	.323	.308	-.089	.185	.250	.222	-.529	-7.6	.

Milledge was a first-round draft pick last year, but negotiations stalled when the Mets learned that as an 18-year old, he'd gotten into trouble over a sexual relationship with a 15-year-old girl. The New York Daily News then reported that what got Milledge expelled from Northside Christian High in St. Petersburg, Fla. was consensual sexual contact with 12- and 13-year-old girls while he was 16. That got him investigated by the county sheriffs, and he avoided prosecution by completing a juvenile program that amounted to a small pile of beans. It was a pretty lousy year for an organization that also took a week to fire a front-office buffoon who mocked the ethnicity of an assistant GM in front of a room full of major league executives.

At any rate, Milledge has a quick bat, can handle center, and has as good a shot at a major league career as any first-round pick with his talent.

RODNEY NYE						3B					Bats: R			Throws: R					Born: 02-Dec-76			Age: 27
YEAR	TM	LG	AGE	AB	H	2B	3B	HR	BB	SO	SB	CS	AVG	OBP	SLG	MLVR	EQBA	EQOBP	EQSLG	EQMLVR	VORP	DEFENSE
2001	BIN	EAS	24	366	99	23	0	7	49	82	5	5	.270	.358	.391	.040	.224	.304	.328	-.255	-9.1	105-3B 3
2002	BIN	EAS	25	394	93	17	0	13	55	99	4	2	.236	.346	.378	-.035	.195	.286	.318	-.321	-17.9	95-3B 3
2003	BIN	EAS	26	474	148	41	5	10	58	72	3	5	.312	.387	.483	.219	.253	.322	.405	-.095	13.1	126-3B 4
2004	NYM	NL	27	165	39	9	1	4	19	36	1	1	.234	.317	.378	-.133	.237	.318	.395	-.120	7.1	48-3B 0
Breakout: 38%			Improve: 58%				Collapse: 33%															

A nice season at age 26 for Nye, but his upside is only that of a major league backup. There are worse fates within the organization—someone must have to Febreze Mr. Met's headpiece after every game, for example.

TIMO PEREZ						OF					Bats: L			Throws: L					Born: 08-Apr-75			Age: 29
YEAR	TM	LG	AGE	AB	H	2B	3B	HR	BB	SO	SB	CS	AVG	OBP	SLG	MLVR	EQBA	EQOBP	EQSLG	EQMLVR	VORP	DEFENSE
2001	NOR	INT	26	192	69	10	2	6	12	18	15	2	.359	.399	.526	.382	.342	.384	.510	.247	18.4	22-RF -3 17-CF -1
2001	NYM	NL	26	239	59	9	1	5	12	25	1	6	.247	.287	.356	-.206	.255	.295	.370	-.194	-8.3	51-RF 0
2002	NYM	NL	27	444	131	27	6	8	23	36	10	6	.295	.331	.437	.091	.311	.343	.467	.082	26.1	81-CF -2 20-LF 0
2003	NYM	NL	28	346	93	21	0	4	18	29	5	6	.269	.301	.364	-.088	.281	.317	.386	-.110	-3.2	32-LF -2 35-CF 3
2004	NYM	NL	29	301	83	17	2	5	20	29	5	3	.274	.321	.393	-.079	.278	.322	.411	-.063	4.2	80-CF -6
Breakout: 12%			Improve: 38%				Collapse: 39%															

Remember the good old days when people thought Timo Perez was going to amount to something? The year was 2000. Kenneth Lay started selling off Enron shares in November, and Perez was the future of the Mets outfield. Since then, Lay has been unmasked as one of the greatest corporate criminals in the history of capitalism, a ruthless liar and profiteer of the worst sort. Similarly exposed, Perez's subsequent major league career hasn't turned out much better After re-upping Perez for one year at $850,000, they'll keep him around as a spare outfielder.

JASON PHILLIPS 1B/C Bats: R Throws: R Born: 27-Sep-76 Age: 27

YEAR	TM	LG	AGE	AB	H	2B	3B	HR	BB	SO	SB	CS	AVG	OBP	SLG	MLVR	EQBA	EQOBP	EQSLG	EQMLVR	VORP	DEFENSE	
2001	BIN	EAS	24	317	93	21	0	11	31	25	0	1	.293	.362	.464	.155	.245	.311	.394	-.137	3.7	82-C -3	
2001	NOR	INT	24	66	20	2	0	2	7	8	0	0	.303	.365	.424	.136	.294	.351	.412	.001	3.7	15-C 1	
2002	NOR	INT	25	323	91	22	1	13	24	29	1	0	.282	.327	.477	.128	.266	.319	.459	-.014	15.5	80-C -4	
2003	NOR	INT	26	78	27	5	0	4	11	9	0	0	.346	.435	.564	.472	.312	.405	.537	.286	11.6	16-C 2	
2003	NYM	NL	26	403	120	25	0	11	39	50	0	1	.298	.373	.442	.169	.308	.378	.464	.135	25.6	79-1B -5	26-C -1
2004	NYM	NL	27	405	107	23	1	11	41	49	0	1	.265	.339	.408	-.034	.268	.341	.427	-.017	14.1	109-1B 6	

Breakout: 11%   Improve: 33%   Collapse: 33%

He's forcing the issue of whether Piazza should spend more time at first base. Phillips had a strong rookie season, and looks happy out there, like he should be whistling. And why not? He's 27 headed into 2004, he gets to wear cool glasses at first, he plays in the city that never sleeps, and he looks like a decent hitter. With Justin Huber's future as a catcher uncertain, it looks like Phillips can make a decent living as a two-position hybrid for a few years.

MIKE PIAZZA C Bats: R Throws: R Born: 04-Sep-68 Age: 35

YEAR	TM	LG	AGE	AB	H	2B	3B	HR	BB	SO	SB	CS	AVG	OBP	SLG	MLVR	EQBA	EQOBP	EQSLG	EQMLVR	VORP	DEFENSE
2001	NYM	NL	32	503	151	29	0	36	67	87	0	2	.300	.384	.573	.318	.308	.389	.587	.326	73.2	123-C -12
2002	NYM	NL	33	478	134	23	2	33	57	82	0	3	.280	.359	.544	.266	.290	.365	.571	.245	54.6	113-C -23
2003	NYM	NL	34	234	67	13	0	11	35	40	0	0	.286	.377	.483	.222	.296	.385	.504	.191	23.4	61-C -6
2004	NYM	NL	35	289	78	16	1	14	38	51	0	0	.269	.353	.470	.072	.272	.355	.491	.094	23.6	80-C -9

Breakout: 13%   Improve: 34%   Collapse: 34%

If Mike Piazza was a shortstop, an amazing hitter with a really bad glove, would he enjoy Derek Jeter's special aura of protection from criticism? It's baffling that Piazza has had to endure constant attacks for his poor play while wearing the tools of ignorance, a deficit he's certainly made up for with his historic offensive skill. That said, Piazza's hitting is regressing, and he needs to ease his catching workload to absorb the slide and prolong his career. Piazza and the Mets discussed trading him to another team, and an AL squad where he can DH once or twice a week would be an ideal fit. But if Piazza can play first competently, so that he's not frustrated or embarrassed out there, that may work just as well. Piazza may find the move helps his quest to set offensive records as a catcher, and then everyone's happy.

PRENTICE REDMAN OF Bats: R Throws: R Born: 23-Aug-79 Age: 24

YEAR	TM	LG	AGE	AB	H	2B	3B	HR	BB	SO	SB	CS	AVG	OBP	SLG	MLVR	EQBA	EQOBP	EQSLG	EQMLVR	VORP	DEFENSE	
2001	SLU	FLA	21	495	129	18	1	9	42	91	29	8	.261	.322	.356	-.011	.225	.271	.320	-.331	-44.1	92-LF 0	25-CF -1
2002	BIN	EAS	22	491	139	35	2	11	59	112	43	9	.283	.367	.430	.096	.238	.310	.368	-.180	-18.0	57-RF -7	38-LF -2
2003	NOR	INT	23	433	110	29	2	11	40	96	24	8	.254	.326	.406	.018	.241	.311	.395	-.139	-11.3	52-LF -1	50-RF -2
2004	NYM	NL	24	244	62	14	1	7	23	53	9	3	.255	.326	.405	-.069	.258	.327	.424	-.053	4.6	67-LF -1	

Breakout: 43%   Improve: 61%   Collapse: 18%

People sometimes ask us: Where do the Mets get these powerless outfielders? They scour the Earth looking for toolsy prospects who have trouble swatting away the mosquitoes in the Florida State League, or who can't defend themselves from horse flies in the Appalachian League. These kids are strictly prohibited from conditioning work and kept away from healthy foods that might help them grow into their bodies, and encouraged to develop extra-base power by slapping singles and running really, really fast. Unfortunately, while this long-running program is the most successful of any player development approach in turning out the template-stamped players it's intended to manufacture, the team never gave any thought to what it might do with an army of these guys, like one of Dr. Weird's plans-gone-awry.

JOSE REYES

SS **Bats: B** **Throws: R** Born: 11-Jun-83 Age: 21

YEAR	TM	LG	AGE	AB	H	2B	3B	HR	BB	SO	SB	CS	AVG	OBP	SLG	MLVR	EQBA	EQOBP	EQSLG	EQMLVR	VORP	DEFENSE	
2001	CMB	SAL	18	407	125	22	15	5	18	71	30	10	.307	.337	.472	.223	.251	.278	.396	-.192	1.3	108-SS	4
2002	SLU	FLA	19	288	83	10	11	6	30	35	31	13	.288	.353	.462	.191	.232	.286	.384	-.208	-0.5	69-SS	4
2002	BIN	EAS	19	275	79	16	8	2	16	42	27	11	.287	.331	.425	.038	.244	.280	.371	-.229	-2.2	63-SS	-9
2003	NOR	INT	20	160	43	6	4	0	15	25	26	5	.269	.333	.356	-.026	.258	.323	.350	-.167	1.8	37-SS	-2
2003	NYM	NL	20	274	84	12	4	5	13	36	13	3	.307	.334	.434	.103	.319	.349	.452	.078	18.5	67-SS	6
2004	*NYM*	*NL*	*21*	*494*	*135*	*27*	*6*	*9*	*34*	*68*	*27*	*8*	*.273*	*.320*	*.403*	*-.068*	*.276*	*.321*	*.422*	*-.052*	*23.2*	*127-SS*	*-2*

Breakout: 23%   *Improve: 49%*   *Collapse: 34%*

The Mets love him. They love him so much they were unable to see that Reyes was struggling in the International League, where he hit .269/.333/.356 and hadn't hit a home run all year. He was drawing some walks and keeping his strikeouts down, but Reyes could have used more at-bats and quality instruction to get used to recognizing the better pitches so he could walk and drive the ball more. Instead, he got promoted. He still held his own in the majors, with a .307/.334/.434 line. Of course the patience remains missing, and Reyes's development will depend in large part on learning to recognize good pitches to hit and laying off of junk.

It will be interesting to see if the Mets will continue to play Reyes at short when they can, possibly flipping him with Kaz Matsui if Matsui struggles. If they park Matsui at short for three years and never move him, Reyes's development will suffer for it, especially as his chance of getting seriously injured goes up.

MARCO SCUTARO

2B **Bats: R** **Throws: R** Born: 30-Oct-75 Age: 28

YEAR	TM	LG	AGE	AB	H	2B	3B	HR	BB	SO	SB	CS	AVG	OBP	SLG	MLVR	EQBA	EQOBP	EQSLG	EQMLVR	VORP	DEFENSE			
2001	IND	INT	25	495	146	29	3	11	62	83	11	11	.295	.382	.432	.150	.271	.354	.402	-.026	22.9	116-2B	-8		
2002	NOR	INT	26	354	113	22	6	7	30	61	7	8	.319	.375	.475	.233	.294	.351	.450	.055	24.8	48-2B	-6	25-SS	2
2003	NOR	INT	27	244	76	18	3	9	33	34	11	6	.311	.401	.520	.331	.287	.374	.490	.145	25.6	35-3B	-3	23-2B	-2
2003	NYM	NL	27	75	16	4	0	2	13	14	2	0	.213	.333	.347	-.090	.234	.343	.390	-.090	1.5	22-2B	-2		
2004	*OAK*	*AL*	*28*	*213*	*56*	*12*	*1*	*6*	*22*	*36*	*4*	*3*	*.262*	*.337*	*.412*	*-.023*	*.270*	*.349*	*.430*	*.002*	*13.9*	*60-2B*	*-5*		

Breakout: 18%   *Improve: 36%*   *Collapse: 43%*

These are the kind of players teams should be looking for to fill holes. Scutaro is too old to be a prospect, but he can hit a little, takes his walks, has some limited power, and plays passable defense up the middle, making him a useful piece as a spare or part-time player. Guys like this are all over the minors, so when your team instead plays Tony Womack every game, you should be really angry, because a guy you've never heard of like Scutaro is worth a game or two in the standings more than Womack over the course of a year. Claimed by Oakland, who should find a use for him.

TSUYOSHI SHINJO

CF **Bats: R** **Throws: R** Born: 28-Jan-72 Age: 32

YEAR	TM	LG	AGE	AB	H	2B	3B	HR	BB	SO	SB	CS	AVG	OBP	SLG	MLVR	EQBA	EQOBP	EQSLG	EQMLVR	VORP	DEFENSE			
2001	NYM	NL	29	400	107	23	1	10	25	70	4	5	.268	.320	.405	-.058	.280	.331	.423	-.032	12.6	44-CF	3	39-LF	1
2002	SFG	NL	30	362	86	15	3	9	24	46	5	0	.238	.294	.370	-.106	.255	.308	.401	-.126	2.0	96-CF	8		
2003	NYM	NL	31	114	22	3	0	1	6	12	0	1	.193	.238	.246	-.419	.209	.253	.270	-.446	-9.6	33-CF	2		
2003	NOR	INT	31	111	36	5	2	3	9	17	0	1	.324	.377	.486	.264	.301	.356	.469	.097	5.6	16-RF	-1		

When I was in high school, this girl I was deeply, madly, 18-year-oldly in love with gave me a hard time—she loved me, but she wasn't *in love* with me. She loved me, but more like a brother than a boyfriend. She loved me. Our relationship wasn't on-off so much as it was strobed.

One day, I was trying to get her to hang out with me, in the hopes that the switch would get flipped again. She'd offered to watch some musical with me a long time ago, during one of the "on" stretches, and I was trying to get her to honor that promise. She turned to me and said: "I want to tell you so you don't hear this from someone else. I'm seeing another guy." I blinked, and asked: "Can I still come over?"

When the Mets figure out their problems and are competitive again, fans will reminisce about Shinjo over drinks. "Boy, remember how excited we got over Timo Perez?" "Timo Perez, remember how much we loved Shinjo when he came over?" And everyone will have a good laugh, knowing we get irrationally attached to the strangest things. Shinjo signed with the Nippon Ham Fighters ("Bob Costas's Favorite Japanese Team") in the off-season.

MO VAUGHN — 1B — Bats: L — Throws: R — Born: 15-Dec-67 — Age: 36

YEAR	TM	LG	AGE	AB	H	2B	3B	HR	BB	SO	SB	CS	AVG	OBP	SLG	MLVR	EQBA	EQOBP	EQSLG	EQMLVR	VORP	DEFENSE
2002	NYM	NL	34	487	126	18	0	26	59	145	0	1	.259	.349	.456	.115	.273	.357	.485	.095	23.7	124-1B -15
2003	NYM	NL	35	79	15	2	0	3	14	22	0	0	.190	.323	.329	-.145	.200	.331	.350	-.186	-2.4	21-1B -5
2004	NYM	NL	36	154	37	7	0	6	23	41	0	0	.243	.350	.412	-.026	.246	.352	.431	-.009	9.4	46-1B -3

Breakout: 25%   Improve: 50%   Collapse: 43%

As you read this, Mo Vaughn is bicycling up a hill in the Adirondacks, the steel bike frame bending his bulk, looking for a reclusive hermit doctor he's heard rumors of who, if the good doctor's still jacked on quality hooch from the night before, might be willing to clear Vaughn to play again. Or he's working a dogsled team of valiant malamutes to the limits of their endurance across the frozen tundra of Alaska, on the hunt for an Eskimo woman who may be able to help his knee through the administration of a cream made from walrus ... parts.

Mo doesn't want to have surgery on his knee, instead wishing to do some rehab work and play next year hobbled. The Mets would prefer he do anything that allows them to collect insurance money. At press time, the two were heading for a Dykstra-like collision, where Vaughn goes into spring training insisting he can play and the team, for performance and collecting-the-insurance purposes, insisting that he can't.

MATT WATSON — LF — Bats: L — Throws: R — Born: 05-Sep-78 — Age: 25

YEAR	TM	LG	AGE	AB	H	2B	3B	HR	BB	SO	SB	CS	AVG	OBP	SLG	MLVR	EQBA	EQOBP	EQSLG	EQMLVR	VORP	DEFENSE		
2001	JUP	FLA	22	446	147	33	4	5	63	45	17	9	.330	.417	.455	.319	.269	.337	.385	-.083	-4.2	103-LF -7		
2002	BIN	EAS	23	437	122	26	2	10	39	52	12	8	.279	.339	.416	.031	.232	.285	.353	-.253	-26.9	72-LF 0	30-RF	-1
2003	NOR	INT	24	254	75	18	1	11	23	23	2	2	.295	.366	.504	.242	.278	.350	.483	.085	11.0	56-LF -3		
2004	OAK	AL	25	214	55	12	1	6	18	28	4	2	.256	.320	.403	-.067	.264	.332	.420	-.045	4.1	59-LF -1		

Breakout: 29%   Improve: 58%   Collapse: 24%

Another spot on the Wheel, Watson is notable for being the best of the hitters among Mets outfield prospects, though he's also no great shakes with the glove; after the season, the A's claimed him off of waivers. Well, it was a nice run there. We hope everyone enjoyed the Wheel of Outfielders. We'll be back next year with another great lineup.

TY WIGGINTON — 3B — Bats: R — Throws: R — Born: 11-Oct-77 — Age: 26

YEAR	TM	LG	AGE	AB	H	2B	3B	HR	BB	SO	SB	CS	AVG	OBP	SLG	MLVR	EQBA	EQOBP	EQSLG	EQMLVR	VORP	DEFENSE		
2001	NOR	INT	23	260	65	12	0	7	27	66	3	3	.250	.323	.377	-.036	.238	.309	.370	-.179	0.1	36-3B -13	20-2B	-2
2002	NOR	INT	24	383	115	26	3	6	43	50	5	3	.300	.366	.431	.143	.281	.351	.414	-.007	20.8	46-3B -11	31-2B	0
2002	NYM	NL	24	116	35	8	0	6	8	19	2	1	.302	.354	.526	.257	.319	.366	.563	.269	13.6	10-3B -1	12-2B	-1
2003	NYM	NL	25	573	146	36	6	11	46	124	12	2	.255	.318	.396	-.024	.266	.326	.417	-.061	18.2	151-3B -7		
2004	NYM	NL	26	495	129	28	3	13	46	97	9	3	.261	.328	.404	-.063	.264	.329	.422	-.046	19.0	130-3B -4		

Breakout: 19%   Improve: 45%   Collapse: 21%

Wigginton could be a good enough placeholder until David Wright arrives, as long as he hits closer to his 2003 first half (.267/.320/.414) than second half (.236/.315/.369). He's mobile around the hot corner, flashing some quick reflexes, though he's still inconsistent. He'd be well-matched with a platoon mate who can hit righties, but decent third basemen have become a rare commodity over the last few years.

DAVID WRIGHT — 3B — Bats: R — Throws: R — Born: 20-Dec-82 — Age: 21

YEAR	TM	LG	AGE	AB	H	2B	3B	HR	BB	SO	SB	CS	AVG	OBP	SLG	MLVR	EQBA	EQOBP	EQSLG	EQMLVR	VORP	DEFENSE
2001	KNG	APP	18	116	35	7	0	4	16	29	9	1	.302	.396	.466	.275	.197	.261	.311	-.379	-16.5	33-3B -1
2002	CMB	SAL	19	496	132	30	2	11	76	114	21	5	.266	.367	.401	.122	.197	.274	.308	-.357	-28.8	120-3B -7
2003	SLU	FLA	20	466	126	39	2	15	72	98	19	5	.270	.369	.459	.212	.216	.297	.385	-.197	-2.6	130-3B 1
2004	NYM	NL	21	280	60	15	1	6	28	65	4	2	.214	.289	.342	-.241	.217	.290	.358	-.232	-3.5	77-3B -7

Breakout: 22%   Improve: 46%   Collapse: 25%

A patient hitter with promising doubles power when we wrote him up last year, Wright's starting to crank those doubles over the walls in 2003. Combined with his control of the strike zone, he's clearly the best hitting prospect in the Mets system. His defense at third has upside as well: he owns a strong and accurate arm, moves well to either side and shows good reflexes. He could be ready by 2005.

PITCHERS

EDWIN ALMONTE   Bats: R   Throws: R   Born: 17-Dec-76   Age: 27

YEAR	TM	LG	AGE	G	GS	IP	H	BB	SO	HR	ERA	EQERA	EQH9	EQBB9	EQSO9	EQHR9	PERA	VORP	STF
2001	BIR	SOU	24	54	0	66.3	58	16	62	4	1.49	3.60	9.8	2.5	5.7	0.9	4.62	13.3	-2
2002	CHR	INT	25	50	0	60.3	52	12	56	6	2.24	3.36	8.5	2.1	7.0	1.3	4.25	14.0	0
2003	CHR	INT	26	30	0	34.0	45	14	24	6	6.88	8.22	13.8	4.7	5.3	2.6	9.11	-8.9	-86
2003	NOR	INT	26	16	0	17.7	16	6	14	0	2.54	3.31	8.8	3.9	5.5	0.0	3.67	4.1	12
2003	NYM	NL	26	12	0	11.3	21	5	7	3	11.15	11.45	16.4	3.3	4.9	2.5	9.69	-8.7	-81
2004	*NYM*	*NL*	*27*	*14*	*1*	*20.0*	*22*	*8*	*14*	*2*	*4.74*	*5.03*	*9.8*	*3.2*	*5.8*	*1.1*	*5.05*	*1.7*	*-8*

Breakout: 33%   *Improve: 55%*   *Collapse: 22%*

Almonte is better than that brief major league stint would lead you to believe, but he's still not particularly good, and he's old, even for a pitching prospect. Folks, if you loved the crop of barely distinguishable outfielders in the hitter half of this chapter, you are going to flip out over the glory of the second tier of the Mets' pitching talent.

JASON ANDERSON   Bats: L   Throws: R   Born: 09-Jun-79   Age: 25

YEAR	TM	LG	AGE	G	GS	IP	H	BB	SO	HR	ERA	EQERA	EQH9	EQBB9	EQSO9	EQHR9	PERA	VORP	STF
2001	STA	NYP	22	7	7	47.7	32	12	56	2	1.70	3.63	10.4	3.6	6.1	1.4	5.74	8.7	5
2001	GRB	SAL	22	23	19	124.3	127	40	101	9	3.77	7.26	12.4	4.5	4.1	1.7	7.29	-19.7	-31
2002	TAM	FLA	23	12	3	24.3	27	3	22	2	4.07	6.23	12.9	1.2	5.8	1.7	6.59	-1.5	-21
2002	NRW	EAS	23	16	0	19.3	14	5	21	1	0.93	2.04	7.6	2.5	7.1	1.0	3.73	7.0	16
2002	COH	INT	23	26	0	34.3	26	11	28	3	3.15	3.27	6.3	3.3	6.3	1.1	3.40	8.5	9
2003	NYY	AL	24	22	0	20.7	23	14	9	3	4.78	5.66	9.1	5.7	3.9	1.3	5.69	0.3	-30
2003	NOR	INT	24	10	5	23.3	18	7	9	3	2.70	3.74	7.1	3.3	2.9	1.7	4.45	4.5	-30
2003	NYM	NL	24	6	0	10.7	10	5	7	2	5.05	5.23	8.7	3.5	5.2	1.7	5.34	0.4	-19
2004	*NYM*	*NL*	*25*	*21*	*6*	*41.0*	*44*	*20*	*28*	*7*	*5.47*	*5.81*	*9.7*	*3.9*	*5.6*	*1.5*	*5.82*	*1.9*	*-13*

Breakout: 23%   *Improve: 53%*   *Collapse: 27%*

Acquired from the Yankees in the Armando Benitez deal, Anderson's your basic fringe pitching prospect who will come to camp every year and struggle trying to earn that sixth spot in the pen. We'll take the under on the six starts PECOTA's projected for him in '04.

PEDRO ASTACIO   Bats: R   Throws: R   Born: 28-Nov-69   Age: 34

YEAR	TM	LG	AGE	G	GS	IP	H	BB	SO	HR	ERA	EQERA	EQH9	EQBB9	EQSO9	EQHR9	PERA	VORP	STF
2001	COL	NL	31	22	22	141.0	151	50	125	21	5.49	4.81	9.6	2.9	6.7	1.1	4.87	12.0	9
2001	HOU	NL	31	4	4	28.7	30	4	19	1	3.14	3.29	9.5	1.3	4.9	0.3	3.60	7.0	28
2002	NYM	NL	32	31	31	191.7	192	63	152	32	4.79	5.15	9.4	2.6	6.3	1.6	5.17	9.2	-3
2003	NYM	NL	33	7	7	36.7	47	18	20	8	7.36	7.57	11.4	4.0	4.3	2.0	7.10	-8.6	-45
2004	*NYM*	*NL*	*34*	*46*	*17*	*108.3*	*122*	*42*	*74*	*16*	*5.21*	*5.53*	*10.0*	*3.0*	*5.5*	*1.4*	*5.55*	*4.6*	*-9*

Breakout: 13%   *Improve: 29%*   *Collapse: 41%*

A disastrous season. Astacio kept on throwing with a torn labrum, and Gil Meche has been about the only pitcher to come back from a torn labrum as some version of his former self. Some people will tell you that a torn labrum is not a professional death sentence, but we're still waiting to see more evidence to the contrary. A free agent at 34, Astacio's upside is 180 innings of 4.50 ERA pitching with average peripheral stats, so there should a few teams willing to throw him a deal to see if he can't be nursed back into a rotation regular.

MIKE BACSIK   Bats: L   Throws: L   Born: 11-Nov-77   Age: 26

YEAR	TM	LG	AGE	G	GS	IP	H	BB	SO	HR	ERA	EQERA	EQH9	EQBB9	EQSO9	EQHR9	PERA	VORP	STF
2001	AKR	EAS	23	4	4	27.3	21	3	19	2	1.98	3.24	8.3	1.4	4.3	1.1	3.82	6.6	12
2001	BUF	INT	23	21	20	121.3	115	25	81	13	3.26	4.50	8.9	2.1	4.9	1.2	4.43	13.9	9
2002	NOR	INT	24	25	14	108.3	134	25	75	13	3.74	5.54	11.4	2.5	5.2	1.6	6.16	0.7	-15
2002	NYM	NL	24	11	9	55.7	63	19	30	8	4.36	5.23	10.5	2.7	4.2	1.4	5.52	2.2	-8
2003	NOR	INT	25	22	21	117.7	129	34	62	13	4.97	6.07	10.3	3.2	3.8	1.6	5.82	-5.7	-30
2003	NYM	NL	25	5	3	17.7	28	8	12	5	10.17	9.87	14.0	3.6	5.2	2.6	8.91	-11.0	-63
2004	*TEX*	*AL*	*26*	*20*	*12*	*65.7*	*83*	*24*	*36*	*12*	*6.08*	*5.49*	*10.6*	*3.0*	*4.9*	*1.4*	*5.46*	*5.2*	*-9*

Breakout: 28%   *Improve: 52%*   *Collapse: 22%*

Bacsik has shown no evidence that he will, or can, be a successful major league pitcher. He should consider injecting himself with intelligent nanites that will give him super strength and control. After which, his kind will take over the planet.

HEATH BELL

Bats: R **Throws: R** Born: 29-Sep-77 Age: 26

YEAR	TM	LG	AGE	G	GS	IP	H	BB	SO	HR	ERA	EQERA	EQH9	EQBB9	EQSO9	EQHR9	PERA	VORP	STF
2001	BIN	EAS	23	43	0	61.3	82	19	55	13	6.02	7.88	13.5	3.7	5.5	2.9	9.07	-14.2	-63
2002	BIN	EAS	24	24	0	38.0	22	6	49	0	1.18	1.82	7.0	1.6	8.6	0.3	2.43	14.6	45
2002	NOR	INT	24	22	0	31.7	38	9	28	2	4.26	5.40	11.1	3.0	6.6	0.9	5.34	0.7	0
2003	NOR	INT	25	40	0	49.7	54	8	54	4	4.71	5.24	10.7	1.7	7.8	1.2	5.07	1.9	0
2004	NYM	NL	26	17	3	30.0	31	9	26	3	3.99	4.24	9.1	2.4	7.0	1.0	4.31	4.4	6

Breakout: 25%   Improve: 38%   Collapse: 24%

Unlike some of the other pitching prospects in this section, Heath Bell at least had a stretch where he pitched really well and convinced people that he could make a quality major league reliever. He's put up solid K/BB rates at every level and kept the ball in the park the last two years. PECOTA sees a decent back-of-the-pen righty for 2004.

P. J. BEVIS

Bats: R **Throws: R** Born: 28-Jul-80 Age: 23

YEAR	TM	LG	AGE	G	GS	IP	H	BB	SO	HR	ERA	EQERA	EQH9	EQBB9	EQSO9	EQHR9	PERA	VORP	STF
2001	YAK	NWN	20	12	0	14.0	9	7	22	0	0.64	2.25	9.0	6.8	7.5	0.0	4.49	4.5	31
2001	ELP	TEX	20	14	0	16.7	11	6	19	2	2.16	2.25	5.6	3.9	7.9	1.7	3.88	6.0	23
2002	ELP	TEX	21	49	0	63.7	50	29	62	3	2.83	3.64	7.6	4.7	6.8	0.8	4.07	12.9	19
2003	BIN	EAS	22	46	0	71.0	55	30	100	4	4.18	4.15	8.4	4.6	10.1	1.0	4.57	10.5	32
2004	NYM	NL	23	17	5	36.7	32	18	38	3	3.91	4.16	7.7	3.9	8.4	0.7	4.07	5.9	12

Breakout: 23%   Improve: 48%   Collapse: 37%

Bevis has major league pitches: his fastball is a notch above 90, and he's got a sweet big-breaking slow curve. He'd be the complete package with a good change, or a different breaking pitch, and a hair better control would help. Still, even if his development stopped today, those peripherals suggest he'd be a decent reliever if the team picked his spots well.

JAIME CERDA

Bats: L **Throws: L** Born: 26-Oct-78 Age: 25

YEAR	TM	LG	AGE	G	GS	IP	H	BB	SO	HR	ERA	EQERA	EQH9	EQBB9	EQSO9	EQHR9	PERA	VORP	STF
2001	SLU	FLA	22	28	0	55.7	40	12	56	3	0.97	2.52	8.6	2.3	6.1	1.3	4.41	17.1	7
2001	BIN	EAS	22	12	0	20.3	17	6	22	1	3.10	3.86	8.7	3.4	6.8	0.5	3.92	3.6	22
2002	BIN	EAS	23	14	0	31.7	21	10	33	0	2.27	2.48	7.1	3.4	7.1	0.3	3.08	10.1	32
2002	NOR	INT	23	12	0	21.0	10	7	17	0	0.43	1.35	4.1	3.6	6.3	0.0	1.61	9.4	39
2002	NYM	NL	23	32	0	25.7	22	14	21	0	2.45	3.28	8.4	4.4	6.6	0.4	3.96	6.4	23
2003	NYM	NL	24	27	0	32.3	32	20	19	4	5.85	5.68	8.8	4.8	4.5	1.1	5.11	-1.8	-19
2003	NOR	INT	24	22	0	32.3	29	10	35	3	1.67	3.30	9.0	3.3	7.8	1.2	4.76	7.7	8
2004	NYM	NL	25	33	5	52.3	52	24	41	5	4.37	4.64	8.8	3.6	6.3	0.9	4.71	5.7	-3

Breakout: 20%   Improve: 48%   Collapse: 25%

Cerda has a long track record of minor league success, and looked like a promising lefty reliever after his 2002 rookie season. Although he got shellacked in 2003, he's young enough and talented enough to lop a couple of runs off that ERA and bounce back.

JOSELO DIAZ (né Joselo Soriano né Jose Diaz)

Bats: R **Throws: R** Born: 13-Apr-80 Age: 24

YEAR	TM	LG	AGE	G	GS	IP	H	BB	SO	HR	ERA	EQERA	EQH9	EQBB9	EQSO9	EQHR9	PERA	VORP	STF
2002	SGA	SAL	22	19	0	25.7	14	25	33	1	4.20	6.00	8.1	12.9	7.3	0.9	6.50	-0.9	-25
2003	VRO	FLA	23	15	11	61.7	39	48	69	2	3.50	5.09	8.3	9.3	7.3	1.0	5.89	3.0	-9
2003	SLU	FLA	23	11	2	30.3	16	25	41	0	2.97	4.85	7.3	10.0	8.7	0.3	4.92	2.2	9
2004	NYM	NL	24	15	8	37.3	44	45	18	8	8.82	9.37	10.6	9.5	3.9	1.9	9.31	-11.3	-50

Breakout: 17%   Improve: 52%   Collapse: 21%

To clear up the confusion, this Joselo Diaz was Jose Diaz when he was a catcher. Then they found out he was actually Joselo Soriano and four years older. Now he's going by Joselo Diaz and he's a pitcher. Of the two players named Joselo Diaz he's the short and skinny one, where the other one . . . uhhh . . . isn't. Like a lot of converted catchers, Diaz has solid velocity, throwing well into the 90s, but the rest of his repertoire is pretty lousy for now. The Mets will give him a chance to add experience and see what shakes out.

LENNY DiNARDO   Bats: L   Throws: L   Born: 19-Sep-79   Age: 24

YEAR	TM	LG	AGE	G	GS	IP	H	BB	SO	HR	ERA	EQERA	EQH9	EQBB9	EQSO9	EQHR9	PERA	VORP	STF
2001	BRO	NYP	21	9	5	36.0	26	17	40	0	2.00	5.46	10.6	6.7	6.1	0.3	5.48	0.5	10
2002	CMB	SAL	22	24	19	101.3	106	56	103	3	4.35	7.39	12.2	7.0	5.5	0.7	6.68	-17.4	-12
2003	SLU	FLA	23	19	13	85.0	64	14	93	1	2.01	3.82	9.4	1.9	6.9	0.4	3.72	14.9	33
2003	BIN	EAS	23	7	7	40.0	35	13	36	3	3.60	4.17	8.8	3.4	6.4	1.2	4.78	5.8	11
2004	*NYM*	*NL*	*24*	*21*	*15*	*85.0*	*88*	*39*	*67*	*7*	*4.40*	*4.67*	*9.2*	*3.6*	*6.5*	*0.8*	*4.76*	*10.0*	*6*

Breakout: 23%   *Improve: 53%*   *Collapse: 26%*

DiNardo's a young version of Jamie Moyer without the control or the curve. Great changeup, though. It's hard to figure out how he's going to survive moving up the ladder without some good breaking stuff. If he really is a young Moyer, of course, he's got ten more years to figure it out.

PEDRO FELICIANO   Bats: L   Throws: L   Born: 25-Aug-76   Age: 27

YEAR	TM	LG	AGE	G	GS	IP	H	BB	SO	HR	ERA	EQERA	EQH9	EQBB9	EQSO9	EQHR9	PERA	VORP	STF
2001	JAX	SOU	24	54	0	60.3	41	11	55	3	1.94	3.19	8.4	2.0	5.7	0.8	3.76	14.4	3
2002	CHT	SOU	25	28	0	38.7	33	11	26	1	2.56	3.75	8.5	2.8	4.2	0.5	3.72	7.4	-4
2002	LOU	INT	25	20	0	26.7	35	4	19	3	3.03	4.97	12.1	1.4	5.3	1.4	5.98	1.8	-22
2003	NOR	INT	26	15	0	22.7	20	6	18	3	3.96	4.79	9.1	3.0	5.7	2.2	5.92	1.9	-45
2003	NYM	NL	26	23	0	48.3	52	21	43	5	3.35	4.60	9.8	3.4	7.1	1.0	4.91	8.2	2
2004	*NYM*	*NL*	*27*	*29*	*9*	*62.7*	*64*	*24*	*47*	*6*	*4.07*	*4.33*	*9.1*	*3.0*	*6.0*	*0.9*	*4.62*	*9.2*	*-1*

Breakout: 24%   *Improve: 52%*   *Collapse: 25%*

Feliciano's performance in 2003 was an aberration: You can see there that he owes a lot of that low ERA to luck after allowing 1.5 baserunners an inning. He needs to do something about that .407 OBP allowed vs. lefties last year, or he'll be out of the league right quick.

JOHN FRANCO   Bats: L   Throws: L   Born: 17-Sep-60   Age: 43

YEAR	TM	LG	AGE	G	GS	IP	H	BB	SO	HR	ERA	EQERA	EQH9	EQBB9	EQSO9	EQHR9	PERA	VORP	STF
2001	NYM	NL	40	58	0	53.3	55	19	50	8	4.05	4.56	9.5	3.0	7.2	1.2	4.93	5.9	-4
2003	NYM	NL	42	38	0	34.3	35	13	16	5	2.62	4.05	8.9	3.0	3.8	1.4	4.87	9.9	-27
2004	*NYM*	*NL*	*43*	*75*	*0*	*28.3*	*30*	*10*	*17*	*3*	*3.91*	*4.15*	*9.5*	*2.9*	*4.8*	*0.9*	*4.65*	*4.2*	*-13*

Breakout: 23%   *Improve: 49%*   *Collapse: 17%*

While it was nice to have him back to take a bow, it's also time to acknowledge that Franco doesn't have it anymore. The problem is that many players will keep going long past their expiry date as long as someone keeps giving them a shot, as the Mets did in re-upping Franco for one year, $1 million plus bonuses. The team can pretend all it wants, but Franco's not even an effective LOOGY, not after lefties slugged .467 against him last year.

TOM GLAVINE   Bats: L   Throws: L   Born: 25-Mar-66   Age: 38

YEAR	TM	LG	AGE	G	GS	IP	H	BB	SO	HR	ERA	EQERA	EQH9	EQBB9	EQSO9	EQHR9	PERA	VORP	STF
2001	ATL	NL	35	35	35	219.3	213	97	116	24	3.57	4.39	9.0	3.7	4.0	0.9	4.65	28.1	-3
2002	ATL	NL	36	36	36	224.7	210	78	127	21	2.96	4.27	9.3	2.8	4.6	0.9	4.52	31.2	3
2003	NYM	NL	37	32	32	183.3	205	66	82	21	4.52	5.07	9.9	2.9	3.5	1.0	4.94	16.0	-10
2004	*NYM*	*NL*	*38*	*26*	*22*	*130.0*	*150*	*52*	*59*	*15*	*4.69*	*4.99*	*10.3*	*3.2*	*3.7*	*1.0*	*5.45*	*9.1*	*-10*

Breakout: 16%   *Improve: 43%*   *Collapse: 19%*

It was a tough year for Glavine. For years he had triumphed over his foes through the use of a portable time-space distortion device he had invented; it produced an area in which perception was warped, The Tom Glavine Personal Strike Zone. Everything worked wonderfully for year, until villains from the planet Questec came down and laid a trap for him. Not only would the TGPSZ not work, but attempting to use it in some cases meant that things got even worse. Glavine's heroic composure cracked, and he began to whine. Without the benefit of an extended strike zone, Glavine's low strikeout rate is going to produce a ghastly ERA some time soon, maybe as soon as this season.

JEREMY GRIFFITHS

Bats: R   Throws: R   Born: 22-Mar-78   Age: 26

YEAR	TM	LG	AGE	G	GS	IP	H	BB	SO	HR	ERA	EQERA	EQH9	EQBB9	EQSO9	EQHR9	PERA	VORP	STF
2001	BIN	EAS	23	2	2	13.0	8	4	12	0	0.69	2.25	6.0	3.8	5.2	0.0	2.44	4.5	39
2001	SLU	FLA	23	23	20	132.0	126	35	95	9	3.75	5.51	11.0	2.9	4.4	1.6	6.14	1.2	-18
2002	BIN	EAS	24	27	26	152.7	157	54	126	12	3.89	5.20	11.1	3.8	5.6	1.2	5.86	6.1	-6
2003	NOR	INT	25	21	19	115.0	94	26	78	6	2.74	3.76	7.5	2.5	4.8	0.8	3.44	22.0	10
2003	NYM	NL	25	9	6	41.0	57	19	25	5	7.02	7.43	12.4	3.8	4.7	1.1	6.44	-10.1	-19
2004	*NYM*	*NL*	*26*	*23*	*15*	*86.3*	*96*	*35*	*57*	*10*	*5.02*	*5.33*	*9.9*	*3.2*	*5.3*	*1.1*	*5.28*	*6.0*	*-4*

Breakout: 17%   Improve: 52%   Collapse: 23%

Griffiths managed to drop his walk and home runs allowed rate some last year, but NL hitters lit him up with a .328 batting average against. A pedestrian pitcher with a fastball that's neither fast nor big on movement, the Mets' 2004 season's in big trouble if Griffiths gets those projected 15 starts.

AARON HEILMAN

Bats: R   Throws: R   Born: 12-Nov-78   Age: 25

YEAR	TM	LG	AGE	G	GS	IP	H	BB	SO	HR	ERA	EQERA	EQH9	EQBB9	EQSO9	EQHR9	PERA	VORP	STF
2001	SLU	FLA	22	7	7	38.3	26	13	39	0	2.35	3.37	7.8	3.6	6.0	0.3	3.39	8.6	34
2002	BIN	EAS	23	17	17	96.7	85	28	97	7	3.82	4.38	9.5	3.1	6.8	1.0	4.74	12.0	19
2002	NOR	INT	23	10	7	49.3	42	16	35	3	3.29	4.02	7.3	3.4	5.6	0.8	3.60	8.3	18
2003	NOR	INT	24	16	16	94.3	99	32	71	5	3.24	4.70	9.8	3.8	5.4	0.7	4.81	8.8	10
2003	NYM	NL	24	14	13	65.3	79	41	51	13	6.75	7.31	10.8	5.1	6.2	1.8	6.84	-14.8	-19
2004	*NYM*	*NL*	*25*	*22*	*18*	*109.0*	*112*	*50*	*81*	*11*	*4.75*	*5.05*	*9.2*	*3.6*	*6.0*	*0.9*	*4.92*	*6.1*	*4*

Breakout: 16%   Improve: 45%   Collapse: 30%

He wasn't ready, obviously. A first-round pick out of Notre Dame in 2001, the Mets sped him through the minors, thinking that Heilman was a polished product ready to handle major league hitters. Instead, he got hammered, with a home run allowed every five innings being the scariest part of the carnage. They need to be patient with him, especially with every lousy performance adding another tick to his service time clock. PECOTA sees a decent comeback, but expect some rough spots, including at least one demotion or trip to the pen before the year's out.

JEREMY HILL

Bats: R   Throws: R   Born: 08-Aug-77   Age: 26

YEAR	TM	LG	AGE	G	GS	IP	H	BB	SO	HR	ERA	EQERA	EQH9	EQBB9	EQSO9	EQHR9	PERA	VORP	STF
2001	BUR	MID	23	40	0	47.7	22	25	66	2	1.51	2.85	6.8	6.8	7.7	0.9	4.42	12.5	0
2002	WIC	TEX	24	56	0	76.3	61	32	80	4	2.36	4.50	9.5	4.5	7.1	1.1	5.20	8.3	-6
2003	OMA	PCL	25	26	1	40.3	42	42	41	5	7.82	8.92	10.7	11.4	8.2	1.7	8.09	-13.4	-63

He's old because he's a conversion project, which makes evaluating him a little more difficult: Do you give him credit for doing as well as he has on such a short timeframe, or does his age mean he has to be extraordinarily successful to have a chance at a big league career? Hill's big plus is a mid-90s fastball, but his other pitches aren't major league ready, and he needs to improve his command to progress. New York is blessed with a bunch of serviceable relief candidates, so they can afford to wait on Hill, get him some quality instruction (hello Rick Peterson), and see if he can't work out his issues.

SCOTT KAZMIR

Bats: L   Throws: L   Born: 24-Jan-84   Age: 20

YEAR	TM	LG	AGE	G	GS	IP	H	BB	SO	HR	ERA	EQERA	EQH9	EQBB9	EQSO9	EQHR9	PERA	VORP	STF
2002	BRO	NYP	18	5	5	18.0	5	7	34	0	0.50	1.76	5.3	5.3	10.6	0.0	2.50	6.5	81
2003	CMB	SAL	19	18	18	76.3	50	28	105	6	2.36	4.34	9.0	4.5	8.1	1.9	5.84	9.3	23
2003	SLU	FLA	19	7	7	33.0	29	16	40	0	3.27	5.76	9.7	5.5	8.5	0.3	4.73	-0.5	50
2004	*NYM*	*NL*	*20*	*14*	*12*	*73.3*	*66*	*33*	*74*	*6*	*3.78*	*4.02*	*8.0*	*3.6*	*8.2*	*0.8*	*4.16*	*13.9*	*22*

Breakout: 23%   Improve: 67%   Collapse: 11%

Kazmir gets all of the organization's minor league hype now that Reyes is in the majors, and he deserves every bit of it. His stuff is so good he could spread it on sandwiches. He could stand to drop his walk rate a bit, but Kazmir's overwhelmed minor league hitters so far, his gaudy strikeout totals portending future dominance.

Warning: This player comment contains future-looking information. Investing in any player, especially pitchers, involves an element of risk, and fans are encouraged to do their own research, as well as manage risk through a diversified portfolio of prospects to watch. Many pitchers suffer injuries that lower the rate of return or eliminate their worthiness as prospects entirely. These statements have not been evaluated by any oversight agency and may be entirely wrong.

(continued next page)

Scott Kazmir *(continued)*

All projections are based on the best information available to Baseball Prospectus at press time, but are limited by the accuracy of our statistical supplier and subject to change. Baseball Prospectus is not liable for damages, heartache, or money spent on player's minor league cards in the event that this or any other player fails to eventually realize all his talent.

BOB KEPPEL   Bats: R   Throws: R   Born: 11-Jun-82   Age: 22

YEAR	TM	LG	AGE	G	GS	IP	H	BB	SO	HR	ERA	EQERA	EQH9	EQBB9	EQSO9	EQHR9	PERA	VORP	STF
2001	CMB	SAL	19	26	20	124.3	118	25	87	6	3.11	5.70	9.6	2.6	3.6	1.0	4.65	-1.3	5
2002	SLU	FLA	20	27	26	152.0	162	43	109	13	4.32	6.15	11.1	3.1	4.7	1.7	6.33	-8.5	-1
2003	BIN	EAS	21	18	17	94.7	92	27	46	6	3.04	3.93	8.7	3.0	3.5	0.9	4.30	16.6	8
2004	NYM	NL	22	19	14	78.3	86	34	40	9	4.88	5.18	9.8	3.5	4.2	1.1	5.34	4.0	-10

Breakout: 7%   Improve: 51%   Collapse: 16%

Like Justin Huber, Keppel was 21 in Double-A this year, and did well against older, advanced competition. He needs to start missing more bats to have a shot at a successful career as a starter though. A forearm injury cost him some time this year, and shoulder stiffness kept him out of the Arizona Fall League. Be a little wary.

AL LEITER   Bats: L   Throws: L   Born: 23-Oct-65   Age: 38

YEAR	TM	LG	AGE	G	GS	IP	H	BB	SO	HR	ERA	EQERA	EQH9	EQBB9	EQSO9	EQHR9	PERA	VORP	STF
2001	NYM	NL	35	29	29	187.3	178	46	142	18	3.32	3.91	8.7	2.1	5.8	0.8	3.90	33.7	18
2002	NYM	NL	36	33	33	204.3	194	69	172	23	3.48	4.50	8.9	2.7	6.6	1.1	4.41	24.0	13
2003	NYM	NL	37	30	30	180.7	176	94	139	15	3.98	4.55	8.7	4.2	6.1	0.7	4.42	25.9	12
2004	NYM	NL	38	28	25	154.0	157	65	114	16	4.42	4.70	9.1	3.3	6.0	0.9	4.76	14.9	7

Breakout: 10%   Improve: 37%   Collapse: 18%

Leiter made Michael Wolverton's list of baseball's best 30 starters last year (as rated by Support-Neutral Wins Above Replacement level), but he's hardly ever mentioned among the elite anymore. Perhaps because he's faded a little every year, there's no story to be written ("Aging Ace Still Pretty Good"?). He'll need to regain better control in a hurry though, or risk a sudden collapse.

DAVID MATTOX   Bats: R   Throws: R   Born: 24-May-80   Age: 24

YEAR	TM	LG	AGE	G	GS	IP	H	BB	SO	HR	ERA	EQERA	EQH9	EQBB9	EQSO9	EQHR9	PERA	VORP	STF
2001	BRO	NYP	21	2	2	10.0	5	3	12	0	0.90	3.24	8.6	4.3	6.5	0.0	3.70	2.2	39
2001	KNG	APP	21	14	8	56.3	48	19	58	3	2.40	5.59	10.8	4.8	4.1	1.5	6.43	0.1	-25
2002	CMB	SAL	22	17	17	91.3	78	42	92	3	3.55	5.65	10.2	5.8	5.4	0.8	5.58	-0.4	0
2002	SLU	FLA	22	9	9	51.0	46	24	34	2	2.82	5.05	9.5	5.2	4.1	0.8	5.16	2.8	-1
2003	BIN	EAS	23	21	20	113.3	103	40	86	7	3.50	4.13	8.9	3.8	5.4	1.0	4.70	17.1	7
2004	NYM	NL	24	19	13	76.3	82	42	52	9	5.29	5.62	9.6	4.3	5.6	1.1	5.64	3.0	-6

Breakout: 24%   Improve: 52%   Collapse: 19%

It looks like he's putting it together, but the clock is ticking. Mattox throws a variety of pitches with movement, with concern about his maturity holding him back in the past. His walk rate is already improved, but he remains one of those prototypical "needs to drop another walk per game" pitchers if he's to find some kind of major league success.

JASON MIDDLEBROOK   Bats: R   Throws: R   Born: 26-Jun-75   Age: 29

YEAR	TM	LG	AGE	G	GS	IP	H	BB	SO	HR	ERA	EQERA	EQH9	EQBB9	EQSO9	EQHR9	PERA	VORP	STF
2001	MOB	SOU	26	10	9	52.7	36	9	51	1	1.20	2.47	8.2	1.9	5.9	0.4	3.19	16.4	27
2001	POR	PCL	26	15	15	90.3	86	23	66	5	3.29	4.09	9.4	2.7	4.7	0.6	4.23	14.0	7
2001	SDP	NL	26	4	3	19.3	18	10	10	6	5.13	5.79	8.2	4.3	3.9	2.4	6.16	-0.4	-50
2002	POR	PCL	27	10	7	36.7	42	13	32	6	5.64	7.44	12.9	3.9	6.3	2.2	7.95	-6.7	-54
2002	SDP	NL	27	12	2	35.3	31	15	28	1	5.10	4.15	7.5	3.4	6.2	0.3	3.20	5.6	21
2002	NOR	INT	27	5	5	23.7	13	1	22	1	2.66	2.42	5.2	0.4	6.9	0.4	1.51	7.9	43
2002	NYM	NL	27	3	3	16.0	13	7	14	1	3.94	4.11	7.6	3.5	7.0	0.6	3.59	2.5	24
2003	NOR	INT	28	23	23	118.3	121	33	91	21	4.49	5.83	10.5	3.2	5.6	2.7	7.23	-2.8	-53
2003	NYM	NL	28	5	0	7.0	13	4	3	0	10.29	9.45	17.6	4.1	4.1	0.0	7.47	-4.0	-22
2004	NYM	NL	29	17	11	66.3	68	24	47	8	4.46	4.74	9.1	2.9	5.8	1.1	4.65	6.3	2

Breakout: 21%   Improve: 55%   Collapse: 18%

Soft-tossing righties always live on the edge, and we may have seen Middlebrook at his best in his 2002 season. Injuries have cost him time, development, and opportunities, and now he's 29 and no longer a prospect. Barring a big turn-around, the Mets have better bullpen options.

ORBER MORENO   Bats: R   Throws: R   Born: 27-Apr-77   Age: 27

YEAR	TM	LG	AGE	G	GS	IP	H	BB	SO	HR	ERA	EQERA	EQH9	EQBB9	EQSO9	EQHR9	PERA	VORP	STF
2001	OMA	PCL	24	17	0	21.0	19	8	25	4	4.71	5.12	9.3	4.2	7.9	1.9	5.89	1.0	-17
2003	NOR	INT	26	38	0	52.0	36	17	58	1	1.90	2.62	6.9	3.6	8.1	0.4	3.08	15.9	24
2004	NYM	NL	27	23	4	41.3	38	17	38	4	3.90	4.14	8.3	3.2	7.4	0.9	4.19	6.8	7

Breakout: 25%   Improve: 49%   Collapse: 29%

Another refugee from the Royals system, it wasn't that long ago that some saw Moreno as a future elite closer. Going on 27, he's fallen off of most prospect lists, but his 2003 season shows his stuff is returning. Even after a long stretch of injuries, Moreno still throws hard, still strikes out more than a batter per inning, and does a good job of keeping the ball in the park. If healthy, he'll help, starting right now.

NEAL MUSSER   Bats: L   Throws: L   Born: 25-Aug-80   Age: 23

YEAR	TM	LG	AGE	G	GS	IP	H	BB	SO	HR	ERA	EQERA	EQH9	EQBB9	EQSO9	EQHR9	PERA	VORP	STF
2001	CMB	SAL	20	17	17	95.0	86	18	98	3	2.84	5.10	10.3	2.6	5.1	0.6	4.61	4.7	22
2001	SLU	FLA	20	9	9	45.7	45	19	40	2	3.54	6.05	10.4	4.5	5.4	0.9	5.42	-2.1	13
2003	SLU	FLA	22	7	6	34.7	41	9	16	5	4.67	7.76	15.5	3.1	3.1	4.3	11.97	-7.0	-95
2003	BIN	EAS	22	20	20	100.3	108	39	76	9	4.58	5.46	10.7	4.2	5.5	1.5	6.15	1.4	-4
2004	NYM	NL	23	17	12	66.0	78	32	39	11	5.84	6.20	10.6	3.9	4.8	1.5	6.28	1.4	-13

Breakout: 21%   Improve: 52%   Collapse: 21%

That jump to Double-A is often the toughest, and Musser didn't dazzle anyone in his attempt. The Mets hope he'll regain some of his former luster as he distances himself from a 2002 season lost to foot and arm injuries. He's spending the off-season in St. Lucie on a strength and conditioning program, hoping to add some durability.

WAYNE OUGH   Bats: R   Throws: R   Born: 27-Nov-78   Age: 25

YEAR	TM	LG	AGE	G	GS	IP	H	BB	SO	HR	ERA	EQERA	EQH9	EQBB9	EQSO9	EQHR9	PERA	VORP	STF
2001	BRO	NYP	22	7	3	16.7	11	17	19	1	6.47	9.95	11.4	15.6	6.4	2.1	9.71	-6.1	-04
2002	BRO	NYP	23	8	7	33.0	27	20	34	2	4.64	7.33	11.3	9.0	5.7	2.3	8.62	-5.2	-69
2002	CMB	SAL	23	19	10	77.3	69	42	58	5	3.61	6.11	10.7	6.9	4.1	1.6	7.08	-3.8	-46
2003	SLU	FLA	24	22	14	103.7	84	37	97	3	2.86	4.72	10.4	4.3	5.9	0.9	5.42	8.8	-3
2004	NYM	NL	25	15	11	57	65	41	39	5	6.09	6.47	10.1	5.7	5.6	0.8	6.31	-1.1	-11

Breakout: 22%   Improve: 54%   Collapse: 21%

Ough is like Stacie Orrico. You listen to a bouncy song, and you think: "Hey, she sounds kind of cool." So you investigate and bam! You find out she won some Christian Artist award at the age of 12 and is a rising, hot diva who combines Christian pop with an urban flare . . . bleeeaaaaghhhhhh. So it is with Ough. Too many people think that Ough had a good year when, on closer examination, he was old for A-ball and unlikely to amount to much . . . bleeaaaaccckkkkkkhhhhh.

MATT PETERSON   Bats: R   Throws: R   Born: 11-Feb-82   Age: 22

YEAR	TM	LG	AGE	G	GS	IP	H	BB	SO	HR	ERA	EQERA	EQH9	EQBB9	EQSO9	EQHR9	PERA	VORP	STF
2001	BRO	NYP	19	6	6	33.3	26	14	19	0	1.62	5.08	9.8	5.7	2.9	0.3	4.98	1.6	5
2001	CMB	SAL	19	18	14	79.3	87	29	72	9	4.99	7.75	12.3	4.9	4.8	2.3	8.10	-16.7	-21
2002	CMB	SAL	20	26	26	137.7	109	61	153	13	3.86	5.87	10.2	5.6	6.2	2.3	7.26	-3.5	-10
2003	SLU	FLA	21	15	15	84.0	65	24	73	2	1.71	3.98	9.2	3.4	5.5	0.7	4.40	13.4	24
2003	BIN	EAS	21	6	6	31.3	29	20	23	2	3.45	5.28	8.7	6.8	5.6	0.9	5.35	1.0	8
2004	NYM	NL	22	17	13	72.0	75	38	57	10	5.28	5.61	9.3	4.2	6.4	1.3	5.52	1.8	-1

Breakout: 13%   Improve: 52%   Collapse: 21%

Some sculptors say they acquire a block of stone and stare at it until the piece reveals itself. Then it's only a matter of chipping it down. Peterson made some positive strides last year, and is starting to look like the good pitcher he can become. He needs to get his change and curve over for strikes consistently. He's got a future if he can swing it.

ROYCE RING
Bats: L   Throws: L   Born: 21-Dec-80   Age: 23

YEAR	TM	LG	AGE	G	GS	IP	H	BB	SO	HR	ERA	EQERA	EQH9	EQBB9	EQSO9	EQHR9	PERA	VORP	STF
2002	WNS	CAR	21	21	0	23.0	20	11	22	2	3.91	5.85	10.4	5.8	6.3	1.8	6.79	-0.6	-20
2003	BIR	SOU	22	36	0	35.7	33	14	44	1	2.52	4.41	9.9	4.1	7.7	0.6	4.73	4.3	20
2003	BIN	EAS	22	18	0	21.7	13	11	18	2	1.66	2.29	6.4	5.5	5.9	1.4	4.41	7.2	-2
2004	NYM	NL	23	22	4	36.0	36	20	31	4	4.90	5.20	8.9	4.4	7.0	1.1	5.23	3.6	-3

Breakout: 24%   Improve: 57%   Collapse: 28%

Ring is left-handed and comes with a future closer label and some solid strikeout rates, so he'll make the major league team soon and provide some league-average relief. Still, you'd think the Mets could have done better for Robbie Alomar.

GRANT ROBERTS
Bats: R   Throws: R   Born: 13-Sep-77   Age: 26

YEAR	TM	LG	AGE	G	GS	IP	H	BB	SO	HR	ERA	EQERA	EQH9	EQBB9	EQSO9	EQHR9	PERA	VORP	STF
2001	NOR	INT	23	30	6	67.7	80	19	54	4	4.52	6.19	11.0	3.0	5.8	0.7	5.08	-4.2	3
2001	NYM	NL	23	16	0	26.0	24	8	29	2	3.81	3.96	8.6	2.5	8.6	0.7	3.86	4.6	37
2002	NYM	NL	24	34	0	45.0	43	16	31	3	2.20	3.32	8.7	2.9	5.4	0.6	3.97	11.0	11
2003	NYM	NL	25	18	0	19.0	19	3	10	0	3.79	4.00	9.0	1.5	4.5	0.0	3.10	2.4	17
2004	NYM	NL	26	30	3	43.3	46	16	26	3	3.94	4.19	9.5	2.9	4.9	0.7	4.49	7.1	-7

Breakout: 26%   Improve: 52%   Collapse: 23%

Roberts missed the first four months of the season with tendinitis in his pitching shoulder. He came back in August, looked good down the stretch, and should be a productive member of the 2004 pen. Now that Braden Looper is the closer, Roberts could stealth his way into a few saves if (or when) that doesn't work out so well.

There is no truth to the rumor that Mr. Roberts was an extra in Spicoli's van during the filming of *Fast Times at Ridgemont High*.

PHIL SEIBEL
Bats: L   Throws: L   Born: 28-Jan-79   Age: 25

YEAR	TM	LG	AGE	G	GS	IP	H	BB	SO	HR	ERA	EQERA	EQH9	EQBB9	EQSO9	EQHR9	PERA	VORP	STF
2001	JUP	FLA	22	29	21	134.3	144	28	88	12	3.95	6.85	12.6	2.3	4.0	2.1	7.38	-16.4	-32
2002	BIN	EAS	23	28	25	149.7	147	49	114	17	3.97	5.33	10.3	3.5	5.1	1.6	6.00	4.1	-12
2003	BIN	EAS	24	17	17	82.7	79	32	71	6	3.59	5.02	9.9	4.3	6.2	1.2	5.49	4.9	-5
2003	NOR	INT	24	11	5	34.3	38	17	25	5	6.03	7.39	10.8	5.4	5.4	2.0	7.12	-6.3	-42
2004	NYM	NL	25	12	8	43.7	51	22	30	7	5.89	6.26	10.4	4.0	5.6	1.5	6.26	0.0	-10

Breakout: 26%   Improve: 53%   Collapse: 25%

Another soft-tossing Moyer wannabe. Do the Mets clone their prospects, or is a total coincidence that they have so many of a few items in their organizational pantry? Seriously, if they are cloning these guys in some third-world country where that kind of research is legal, why are they using this technology on these guys and not picking off the DNA from Mark Prior's sunflower seeds?

JAE SEO
Bats: R   Throws: R   Born: 24-May-77   Age: 27

YEAR	TM	LG	AGE	G	GS	IP	H	BB	SO	HR	ERA	EQERA	EQH9	EQBB9	EQSO9	EQHR9	PERA	VORP	STF
2001	SLU	FLA	24	6	5	25.3	21	6	19	2	3.56	4.84	10.1	2.4	4.4	2.0	6.03	1.9	-35
2001	BIN	EAS	24	12	10	60.3	44	11	47	3	1.94	2.73	7.1	2.1	4.7	0.6	3.01	17.9	18
2001	NOR	INT	24	9	9	47.3	53	6	25	4	3.42	4.87	10.8	1.4	3.7	1.0	4.93	3.6	-3
2002	NOR	INT	25	26	24	128.7	145	22	87	14	3.99	5.40	10.4	1.8	5.0	1.4	5.29	2.7	-12
2003	NYM	NL	26	32	31	188.3	193	46	110	18	3.82	4.51	9.1	2.0	4.7	0.8	4.12	19.1	7
2004	NYM	NL	27	25	22	139.7	148	37	80	17	4.39	4.67	9.5	2.1	4.7	1.1	4.56	15.2	2

Breakout: 20%   Improve: 45%   Collapse: 21%

A fine season, but at 27, this may well be the height of his ability. After a strong first three months, Seo slumped badly in August (6.61 ERA) and September (5.34 ERA). Hitters started getting wise to his fastball/change-up combination, and he lost velocity for a while, too, which made matters worse. Watch the speed of his pitches early on, as continued velocity loss could indicate shoulder problems. Seo looks a lot like Tomo Ohka, right down to the big reverse split: .223/.285/.363 against lefties, .291/.320/.483 versus right-handers.

MIKE STANTON

Bats: L **Throws: L** Born: 02-Jun-67 Age: 37

YEAR	TM	LG	AGE	G	GS	IP	H	BB	SO	HR	ERA	EQERA	EQH9	EQBB9	EQSO9	EQHR9	PERA	VORP	STF
2001	NYY	AL	34	76	0	80.3	80	29	78	4	2.58	3.08	8.5	3.0	8.1	0.5	3.69	22.1	26
2002	NYY	AL	35	79	0	78.0	73	28	44	4	3.00	3.30	8.0	2.9	4.8	0.5	3.52	19.5	5
2003	NYM	NL	36	50	0	45.3	37	19	34	6	4.57	4.50	7.4	3.5	5.9	1.2	4.11	2.1	-11
2004	*NYM*	*NL*	*37*	*135*	*0*	*39.3*	*40*	*17*	*28*	*4*	*4.16*	*4.41*	*9.1*	*3.3*	*5.8*	*1.0*	*4.82*	*5.9*	*-10*

Breakout: 32%   *Improve: 56%*   *Collapse: 24%*

As the Yankees spent their way through bullpen troubles this year, much was written about how the loss of Stanton, combined with Jeff Nelson's earlier departure, had left a void in the bullpen that was impossible to fill. Lost in the discussion was the fact that Stanton had declined greatly in his last few years with the Yankees, the walks rising, the strikeouts down severely in his last year. Yankee writers could have looked across town and noticed that Stanton sucked in '03 too. Chris Hammond had a much better season as Stanton's replacement in pinstripes.

PAT STRANGE

Bats: R **Throws: R** Born: 23-Aug-80 Age: 23

YEAR	TM	LG	AGE	G	GS	IP	H	BB	SO	HR	ERA	EQERA	EQH9	EQBB9	EQSO9	EQHR9	PERA	VORP	STF
2001	BIN	EAS	20	26	24	153.3	171	52	106	18	4.87	6.33	9.5	3.9	4.5	1.4	5.38	-11.9	5
2002	NOR	INT	21	29	25	165.0	165	59	109	12	3.82	5.00	7.7	3.6	5.5	0.8	3.87	10.8	26
2003	NOR	INT	22	31	10	89.3	111	44	64	8	5.74	7.17	10.5	5.3	5.5	1.1	5.90	-14.9	-6
2003	NYM	NL	22	6	0	9.0	13	11	5	4	11.00	12.00	13.0	10.0	4.0	4.0	11.66	-5.9	-95
2004	*NYM*	*NL*	*23*	*10*	*7*	*39*	*42*	*21*	*27*	*5*	*5.17*	*5.49*	*9.7*	*4.2*	*5.6*	*1.2*	*5.64*	*2.7*	*-7*

Breakout: 18%   *Improve: 51%*   *Collapse: 23%*

Some people have said he's best suited for the pen, but Strange had his worst season ever when finally moved primarily to relief duty. It's possible he didn't make it all the way back from his 2002 off-season surgery to remove bone chips. Or maybe regular work suits him better, and working with Rick Peterson and his new staff will get him pointed in right direction. Still just 23, Strange has the talent and time to work it out.

SCOTT STRICKLAND

Bats: R **Throws: R** Born: 26-Apr-76 Age: 28

YEAR	TM	LG	AGE	G	GS	IP	H	BB	SO	HR	ERA	EQERA	EQH9	EQBB9	EQSO9	EQHR9	PERA	VORP	STF
2001	MON	NL	25	77	0	81.3	67	41	85	9	3.21	3.74	7.4	4.1	7.8	0.9	3.93	16.4	11
2002	NYM	NL	26	68	0	67.7	61	33	67	7	3.59	4.27	8.5	3.9	7.7	1.0	4.46	9.6	3
2003	NYM	NL	27	19	0	20.0	16	10	16	1	2.25	3.26	7.4	4.2	6.5	0.5	3.59	6.2	11
2004	*NYM*	*NL*	*28*	*54*	*0*	*41.3*	*38*	*20*	*34*	*5*	*4.20*	*4.46*	*8.2*	*3.9*	*6.8*	*1.1*	*4.67*	*5.7*	*-4*

Breakout: 23%   *Improve: 51%*   *Collapse: 25%*

A righty-eater who walks a few too many hitters, Strickland was doing his usual thing when he tore a ligament in his right elbow, forcing him to reconstructive surgery in June and 12–18 months of recovery. The Mets re-signed him for one year at $650,000, with bonuses that will be hard to reach considering he may not pitch at all this season.

STEVE TRACHSEL

Bats: R **Throws: R** Born: 31-Oct-70 Age: 33

YEAR	TM	LG	AGE	G	GS	IP	H	BB	SO	HR	ERA	EQERA	EQH9	EQBB9	EQSO9	EQHR9	PERA	VORP	STF
2001	NYM	NL	30	28	28	173.7	168	47	144	28	4.46	4.59	8.9	2.3	6.3	1.3	4.53	18.7	6
2002	NYM	NL	31	30	30	173.7	170	69	105	16	3.37	4.48	9.0	3.1	4.8	0.9	4.43	20.7	3
2003	NYM	NL	32	33	33	204.7	204	65	111	26	3.78	4.42	8.8	2.5	4.3	1.1	4.47	33.5	-2
2004	*NYM*	*NL*	*33*	*26*	*24*	*147.0*	*157*	*49*	*84*	*18*	*4.50*	*4.78*	*9.6*	*2.6*	*4.6*	*1.1*	*4.81*	*13.6*	*1*

Breakout: 13%   *Improve: 50%*   *Collapse: 17%*

Trachsel is fine as someone you can plug in and forget about. At the end of the season, he'll have eaten up a lot of innings, missed a couple of starts with something—aching back this year—and your team won't be much better or worse either way. That 2002 season was largely the product of an uncommonly low home run rate; Trachsel's a better bet to post ERAs in the fours than the threes from here on out.

DAVE WEATHERS Bats: R   Throws: R   Born: 25-Sep-69   Age: 34

YEAR	TM	LG	AGE	G	GS	IP	H	BB	SO	HR	ERA	EQERA	EQH9	EQBB9	EQSO9	EQHR9	PERA	VORP	STF
2001	MIL	NL	31	52	0	57.7	37	25	46	3	2.03	2.44	6.0	3.6	6.0	0.5	2.81	19.4	14
2001	CHC	NL	31	28	0	28.3	28	9	20	3	3.18	3.62	8.9	2.6	5.3	1.0	4.34	6.0	-6
2002	NYM	NL	32	71	0	77.3	69	36	61	6	2.91	3.98	8.3	3.7	6.1	0.7	4.11	13.4	1
2003	NYM	NL	33	77	0	87.7	87	40	75	6	3.08	4.11	9.0	3.7	6.8	0.6	4.28	20.2	6
2004	NYM	NL	34	46	3	64.7	63	29	52	5	3.73	3.97	8.7	3.5	6.5	0.7	4.35	11.7	0

Breakout: 32%   Improve: 48%   Collapse: 22%

Weathers can be a cheap, serviceable back-end piece of almost every team's bullpen, fill 70-something innings, and not embarrass himself. There's some value in that, but he'd be well-served to try and sneak onto a team with a bullpen in flux, steal 15–20 saves and then get someone to bite on him as a closer. Billy Beane would probably be willing to sign on for a cut of the proceeds from the subsequent free agent deal.

DAN WHEELER Bats: R   Throws: R   Born: 10-Dec-77   Age: 26

YEAR	TM	LG	AGE	G	GS	IP	H	BB	SO	HR	ERA	EQERA	EQH9	EQBB9	EQSO9	EQHR9	PERA	VORP	STF
2001	DUR	INT	23	18	10	65.3	72	11	39	11	5.24	7.23	10.6	1.8	4.4	1.9	6.00	-11.0	-25
2001	TBY	AL	23	13	0	17.7	30	5	12	3	8.64	7.79	14.5	2.6	5.7	1.6	7.58	-4.2	-16
2002	RIC	INT	24	27	25	155.0	163	42	110	23	4.65	5.80	10.2	2.9	5.4	1.9	6.11	-3.2	-18
2003	NOR	INT	25	22	5	45.7	48	16	44	4	3.94	5.10	10.2	3.8	7.0	1.3	5.57	2.4	-12
2003	NYM	NL	25	35	0	51.0	49	17	35	6	3.71	4.38	8.6	2.7	5.5	1.1	4.33	7.8	-5
2004	NYM	NL	26	30	8	61.3	64	23	45	8	4.61	4.90	9.4	3.0	6.0	1.2	4.90	6.0	-4

Breakout: 26%   Improve: 44%   Collapse: 17%

You'd think the Mets could help the rest of the league out by distributing some of these faceless, decent righty relievers, given the supposed shortage of arms some people keep whining about. Heath Bell, Grant Roberts, Dan Wheeler... after a while only their moms can tell them apart.

TYLER YATES Bats: R   Throws: R   Born: 07-Aug-77   Age: 26

YEAR	TM	LG	AGE	G	GS	IP	H	BB	SO	HR	ERA	EQERA	EQH9	EQBB9	EQSO9	EQHR9	PERA	VORP	STF
2001	MID	TEX	23	56	0	62.7	66	27	61	4	4.31	5.83	10.1	4.6	6.1	0.9	5.37	-1.5	-9
2002	NOR	INT	24	24	0	34.0	29	13	34	1	1.32	3.66	7.9	3.9	7.6	0.3	3.51	6.9	25
2003	SLU	FLA	25	14	11	48.0	41	24	49	5	4.31	6.92	13.2	6.5	6.9	3.7	10.53	-5.7	-108
2003	BIN	EAS	25	8	8	39.3	33	17	36	4	4.35	4.58	9.2	4.8	6.6	1.8	5.95	4.0	-25
2003	NOR	INT	25	4	4	20.0	22	9	15	1	4.05	5.30	10.1	4.8	5.3	0.5	4.99	0.6	1
2004	NYM	NL	26	16	9	51.3	55	29	34	7	5.55	5.89	9.6	4.5	5.4	1.2	5.79	1.0	-11

Breakout: 22%   Improve: 46%   Collapse: 26%

Yates broke his pinky finger punching out a water cooler, putting the poor thing in a splint for three weeks. The finger, that is. Tim Belcher used to beat up water coolers—had a pretty good career when you look back on it—but really knew how to pummel a water cooler. He was smart about it. You don't charge right at it. No, you want to come in from the sides, with more of a sweeping motion, meet the cooler with the palm of your hand, or backfist it—don't risk the digits that put the movement on the ball. Use equipment if you have to. Belcher would swing with his glove, his hat, bats, and on one famous August afternoon instead of doing his side work, Belcher used a shoulder-fired TOW missile to pick off a particularly insolent dugout cooler all the way from the bullpen. Take a lesson from Tim: There's no reason you can't abuse equipment in frustration for your own poor performances while protecting your health at the same time.

Philadelphia Phillies

It wasn't supposed to be like this.

With the opening of the brand new Citizen's Bank Ballpark scheduled for 2004, the Phillies decided it was time to open the wallet, spend some cash, and try to go into the new park on a winning note. They wrote out a large check to David Bell to take over at third base. They wrote an even bigger check to Jim Thome to play first. When the Braves were unable or unwilling to risk the $10 million that Kevin Millwood would get through arbitration, the Phillies decided they were both able and willing. Combined with an offense that would return players like Bobby Abreu and Pat Burrell, and a rotation that already had Randy Wolf and Vicente Padilla, they were widely picked to win the National League East.

Things did not go as planned. The Braves came out of the gate quickly, buoyed by a couple of nice surprises in Javy Lopez and Marcus Giles, while the Philly offense slumped at first. Jim Thome took a while to get adjusted to the National League, Bell was injured pretty much from the start, and Burrell started cold and stayed that way all year. While they struggled to find a reliable fifth starter, as virtually every team does, the front four of Wolf, Padilla, Millwood, and Brett Myers was as solid as any in baseball. Despite Burrell's Mendoza-line average and a 6+ ERA from nominal closer Jose Mesa, the Phillies found themselves with a 69–54 record on August 17, half a game ahead of the pesky Marlins in the Wild Card race.

After that, Philly wilted. A rigorous schedule (27 games in a row without a day off) was part of the problem. The release of Tyler Houston made the story of clubhouse dissension very public, and there was some sense that the players were either quitting or being beaten down by Larry Bowa's managerial style, depending on whose side of the story you were on. The Phils finished the season 17–22, and found themselves staring up at the Marlins from a five-game deficit. They went home; the Marlins went on to win the World Series.

From the wreckage of the blown season, three principal scapegoats emerged.

Scapegoat number one was Pat Burrell. Burrell was the young star of the team, a former first-round pick. In 2002, he'd hit 37 home runs and driven in 116, and was rewarded with a $50 million contract that runs through 2008. In 2003, he was supposed to fill the five-hole in the lineup, immediately behind Abreu and Thome, and hit

PHILLIES PROSPECTUS

2003 record: 86–76; Third place, NL East

Pythagenport record: 90–72

Runs scored per game: 4.9 (5th in NL)

Runs allowed per game: 4.3 (6th in NL)

Team EqA: .271 (3rd in NL)

2003 Batters Age: 28.7 (4th youngest in NL)

2003 Pitchers Age: 28.5 (7th oldest in NL)

Ballpark: Citizens Bank Park (New for 2004)

2003: The league's biggest free-agent spenders underachieved and missed the postseason.

2004: Larry Bowa might be able to keep them out of the postseason, but their division rivals probably can't.

another 30 homers, with plenty of run production. Not only did Burrell crap out in the power categories, but he also committed the completely unpardonable age-old sin of baseball: he hit under .200 for much of the season. He ramped up to .240 in September, his best month, to get to .209 at the end, but let's face it: However much batting average is an overrated statistic, it is almost impossible to be a valuable player when you hit .209.

It was ironic, then, that Burrell's most controversial moment came following a home run. At the end of August, Burrell homered against the Mets, and apparently walked past Bowa (standing at the near end of the dugout steps to congratulate him as he came in) to enter the far side of the dugout and clasp hands with teammates there. This was a Big Story in the next day's press, but went completely unnoticed by the TV announcers, radio announcers, and the MLB post-game recap. It was especially silly since Burrell, after entering the dugout, worked his way back down the dugout, glad-handing everyone along the way. In the minds of many, though, it confirmed that Burrell was part of an anti-Bowa cabal in the clubhouse . . . never mind that Burrell denied it, and subsequently agreed to spend part of the winter with Bowa to work on his swing. Still, Tyler Houston was released a couple of days after this happened, allegedly because he was a ringleader of the cabal, and everybody was pointing fingers at everybody else.

Whether it was pressure from Bowa, the weight of his contract, or some other life event that was bothering him, there was clearly something wrong with Burrell in 2003, and it wasn't due to any physical injury. The difference between the 2002 Burrell (when he had a VORP of 52.2) and 2003 (VORP 0.2) was approximately five games, the margin between the Phillies and Marlins in the standings.

Number two, and far more vilified in Philadelphia, was Jose Mesa. The really odd thing about Mesa's season was that he was actually a respectable 24 of 28 in save situations. So how much did Mesa *really* cost the Phillies in 2003? To figure that out, we need to consider just how good an "average closer" is. Table 1 lists all the pitchers who had at least 20 saves in 2003, the percentage of their appearances where they allowed a run (Pct), and their run average in games where they allowed a run (A-ERA):

The typical closer allowed a run in about 25% of his appearances, and averaged about 1.7 runs yielded in those games. Mesa not only was one of the worst in terms of how often he allowed runs—his .328 percentage means he allowed runs in five more games than an average closer—when he did allow runs, he allowed nearly three at a time, the worst RA in baseball. Even so, there were only seven games last season where Mesa entered the game either

TABLE 1. PITCHERS WHO HAD AT LEAST 20 SAVES IN 2003

Name	Games	Percent	A-ERA
Gagne	77	.091	14.73
Smoltz	62	.129	11.05
Wagner	78	.154	11.57
Percival	52	.192	18.56
Rivera	64	.203	10.38
Borowski	68	.206	15.14
Guardado	66	.227	14.14
Foulke	72	.236	8.10
Mantei	50	.240	10.43
MacDougal	68	.250	23.14
Baez	73	.274	16.87
Worrell	76	.276	14.54
Julio	64	.281	19.84
Looper	74	.284	13.91
Urbina	39	.308	13.15 (AL only)
Williams	68	.324	23.76
Mesa	61	.328	25.83
Biddle	73	.329	16.83
Carter	62	.387	10.03
Total	1247	.246	15.03

leading or tied which the Phillies eventually lost, seven times when you can legitimately say he cost them the game. The average closer had between four and five such games. Philly fans may have run him out of town on a rail, but you could argue he only cost them about 2.5 games compared to an average closer. Strange, but true.

And finally, there was Larry Bowa. Bowa is a divisive, polarizing manager; people divide into opposing camps around him, with very little middle ground. The buzzwords for Bowa depend on which of those camps the speaker belongs to: "fiery," "competitive," "wants to win" if they like him, "dictatorial," "oppressive," "a*****e" if they don't. There is clearly a role for such managers in baseball: for teams that have lost any sense of direction, teams that are undisciplined, teams that are more interested in the scene after the game than during it. The problem is that most players who have a choice don't want to play for a manager like Bowa, even though few will publicly admit it for fear of being portrayed as soft or undedicated to winning by an unsympathetic fourth estate. Privately, the players expressed that feeling by naming Bowa the game's worst manager in a *Sports Illustrated* poll last summer. The one thing that will get players to put up with a martinet is if he wins . . . and Bowa hasn't won.

Still, he has survived to manage another team, despite widespread speculation that he would be fired if the Phillies didn't make the playoffs. He even got his contract extended to 2007, if all the options are picked up. Contractual security isn't likely to save his job if he misses the playoffs again, though, because the Phillies look even more stacked entering 2004 than they did in 2003.

The only immediate problem the Phils faced after the '03 season was that most of their bullpen was headed for free agency. Since the pen was considered to be the source of their failure, this was an opportunity to improve. Jose Mesa, Mike Williams, Terry Adams, and Turk Wendell were cut loose, without regret. Dan Plesac couldn't be talked out of retirement one more time. They exercised their option on the suddenly dominant Rheal Cormier, one of the easiest decisions any team had to make this past off-season. They traded three young pitchers for Billy Wagner, getting an ace closer without giving up anyone they expected to provide significant value in 2004. They went into the free agent market and picked up Tim Worrell and Roberto Hernandez. Activity, though, doesn't equal quality, and Worrell and Hernandez (−10.8 combined Adjusted Runs Prevented) were considerably worse last year than Wendell and Adams (18.1 combined ARP). If Cormier comes back to Earth, the bullpen could actually be worse than it was in 2003, despite the huge improvement Wagner makes over Mesa.

The rotation only had one question mark after the season: Could they convince Millwood to stay? He did not get along with Larry Bowa, and supposedly couldn't wait to get out of town, but the team made a desperate effort to keep him. Just in case, they traded more spare parts to Minnesota for Eric Milton (again, not giving up anything really useful for 2004). At worst, Milton fills the fourth spot in the rotation and the Phillies would hold a spring casting call for the fifth spot—Amaury Telemaco, Josh Hancock, and Ryan Madson are the main internal options, maybe Bud Smith if his recovery goes well. In the best of all possible worlds, they wouldn't have to confront that choice, but would instead re-sign Millwood and have Eric Milton as their fifth starter. Happily, Millwood accepted the team's arbitration offer just before the deadline, so he'll be back and the rotation looks loaded.

The offense is the same as last year, with no noteworthy departures or arrivals. The Phillies are counting on a Burrell rebound, which is a reasonable assumption to make. They're also counting on a David Bell bounceback, a riskier bet, given his severe back problems. The biggest question mark in the Phillies' 2004 lineup is how to work Bell, Placido Polanco, and Chase Utley into two lineup spots. Beyond that, the Phillies had the third-best team Equivalent Average in the National League last year, and there is every reason to believe the same crew of hitters could meet or beat that mark in 2003.

Injuries, though, especially on offense, could kill the Phils. They have no depth. Their top two position prospects from a year ago, Utley and Marlon Byrd, both moved to the major leagues, and the positional cupboard is now bare at the farm's upper levels. Utley and Polanco probably give them enough flexibility to handle any infield injuries, but the best outfielder in the system will be whatever minor league free agents they sign in January. On the offensive side, they're truly operating in a "Win Now" setting.

The Phillies' pitching prospects, though, are among the best in the game. Cole Hamels is one of a handful of guys who could claim to be the best pitcher in the minors. Gavin Floyd has had scouts drooling for years, although he hasn't yet put all of his tools to use. Ryan Madson has been making steady progress, and could be the team's fifth starter this year. Another top arm, Taylor Buchholz, was used as bait to bring in Billy Wagner. While pitching prospects are as iffy as an Eric Gregg strike zone, there should be some talent taking to the Citizen's Bank mound in the next few years, while others can be used as further trade bait. That'll leave management free to concentrate on keeping the offense at a championship level.

Bottom line, this is a team that should have made the playoffs last year. Going into 2004, you can say that again.

HITTERS

BOB ABREU   RF   Bats: L   Throws: R   Born: 11-Mar-74   Age: 30

YEAR	TM	LG	AGE	AB	H	2B	3B	HR	BB	SO	SB	CS	AVG	OBP	SLG	MLVR	EQBA	EQOBP	EQSLG	EQMLVR	VORP	DEFENSE		
2001	PHI	NL	27	588	170	48	4	31	106	137	36	14	.289	.393	.543	.272	.291	.398	.545	.264	58.2	157-RF -10		
2002	PHI	NL	28	572	176	50	6	20	104	117	31	12	.308	.413	.521	.338	.317	.420	.543	.324	62.2	138-RF -4	17-CF	0
2003	PHI	NL	29	577	173	35	1	20	109	126	22	9	.300	.409	.468	.274	.313	.421	.492	.252	48.1	154-RF -1		
2004	PHI	NL	30	538	161	37	3	24	93	112	17	7	.299	.402	.513	.231	.300	.402	.525	.238	45.6	149-RF -1		
Breakout: 13%			Improve: 44%				Collapse: 8%																	

In 2003, Abreu displayed many of the signs of a player who is starting to slow down; while he still had good stolen base totals, they were off from previous seasons, and his double and triple rates were down sharply. He did have a leg injury late in the season, but he was already off before that. He's still a player you want on your team.

DAVID BELL   3B   Bats: R   Throws: R   Born: 14-Sep-72   Age: 31

YEAR	TM	LG	AGE	AB	H	2B	3B	HR	BB	SO	SB	CS	AVG	OBP	SLG	MLVR	EQBA	EQOBP	EQSLG	EQMLVR	VORP	DEFENSE		
2001	SEA	AL	28	470	122	28	0	15	28	59	2	1	.260	.303	.415	-.060	.281	.328	.450	.002	21.1	124-3B 12		
2002	SFG	NL	29	552	144	29	2	20	54	80	1	2	.261	.333	.429	.057	.276	.345	.458	.039	31.8	126-3B 5	11-2B	-2
2003	PHI	NL	30	297	58	14	0	4	41	40	0	0	.195	.296	.283	-.248	.209	.310	.305	-.282	-9.2	81-3B 6		
2004	PHI	NL	31	361	92	20	1	10	37	52	1	1	.256	.329	.398	-.073	.257	.328	.407	-.073	11.4	97-3B 0		
Breakout: 28%			Improve: 54%				Collapse: 18%																	

A league-average hitter with a good glove at third, Bell was heavily pursued in the off-season following the '02 season; the Giants, Yankees, D-Backs, and Mets were all interested. The Phillies finally won the sweepstakes by signing him to a four-year $17 million contract two months after his 30th birthday. It took less than a week before he started to miss games with back spasms. Between that and a sore hip, he managed to stay in the lineup until July, even though he couldn't follow through on his swing. And boy, did the results of that show up in his hitting. PECOTA sees a return to near respectability, but that barking back remains a big question mark.

JAKE BLALOCK   OF   **Bats: R**   **Throws: R**   Born: 06-Aug-83   Age: 20

YEAR	TM	LG	AGE	AB	H	2B	3B	HR	BB	SO	SB	CS	AVG	OBP	SLG	MLVR	EQBA	EQOBP	EQSLG	EQMLVR	VORP	DEFENSE			
2003	BAT	NYP	19	261	64	23	7	5	30	81	9	4	.245	.323	.444	.114	.177	.233	.325	-.427	-56.1	26-RF	-1	27-LF	-3
2004	PHI	NL	20	234	43	13	2	5	17	83	4	2	.186	.241	.315	-.379	.187	.241	.322	-.387	-18.6	63-LF	-9		

Breakout: 34%   Improve: 44%   Collapse: 38%

Hank's little brother isn't so little; at 6'4", 210, he towers over his older, 6'1" sibling. A fifth-round pick from the 2002 draft, Jake has massive power potential. He showed a little of it in 2003, even though he only hit 5 home runs. With 23 doubles and 7 triples, he led the New York-Penn League in extra-base hits, with more extra-base knocks than singles. The bad side effect of that "swing from the heels" mentality is that he very nearly led the league in strikeouts. He doesn't quite walk enough to be the next Rob Deer, but he's worth keeping an eye on.

PAT BURRELL   LF   **Bats: R**   **Throws: R**   Born: 10-Oct-76   Age: 27

YEAR	TM	LG	AGE	AB	H	2B	3B	HR	BB	SO	SB	CS	AVG	OBP	SLG	MLVR	EQBA	EQOBP	EQSLG	EQMLVR	VORP	DEFENSE	
2001	PHI	NL	24	539	139	29	2	27	70	162	2	1	.258	.346	.469	.063	.264	.352	.481	.073	19.8	133-LF	-6
2002	PHI	NL	25	586	165	39	2	37	89	153	1	0	.282	.376	.544	.288	.291	.383	.569	.272	52.2	149-LF	-5
2003	PHI	NL	26	522	109	31	4	21	72	142	0	0	.209	.309	.404	-.055	.220	.315	.429	-.100	-5.6	133-LF	-1
2004	PHI	NL	27	492	129	29	2	29	70	123	1	1	.263	.356	.506	.118	.265	.356	.517	.122	25.2	133-LF	0

Breakout: 33%   Improve: 64%   Collapse: 11%

Burrell's batting average dropped 73 points from 2002 to 2003, the 42nd-largest drop in history for a player with 500 at-bats in both seasons. That's bad enough, but there's only one other player above him who, like him, didn't hit .300 before plummeting. What happened? It wasn't strikeouts. He's always struck out a lot, no more in 2003 than in 2001 and 2002; the real problem was what happened when he didn't strike out:

STRIKEOUTS REMOVED		
Year	**BA**	**SLG**
2000	.394	.703
2001	.369	.671
2002	.381	.737
2003	.287	.555

Regardless of what head games Bowa may or may not have been playing, the final responsibility for his failure to hit comes down to Burrell.

MARLON BYRD   CF   **Bats: R**   **Throws: R**   Born: 30-Aug-77   Age: 26

YEAR	TM	LG	AGE	AB	H	2B	3B	HR	BB	SO	SB	CS	AVG	OBP	SLG	MLVR	EQBA	EQOBP	EQSLG	EQMLVR	VORP	DEFENSE			
2001	REA	EAS	23	510	161	22	8	28	52	93	32	5	.316	.386	.555	.348	.265	.333	.473	.029	28.8	109-CF	-6	18-LF	1
2002	SWB	INT	24	538	160	37	7	15	46	98	15	1	.297	.362	.476	.182	.276	.340	.450	.019	26.2	134-CF	-19		
2002	PHI	NL	24	35	8	2	0	1	1	8	0	2	.229	.250	.371	-.192	.250	.250	.417	-.215	-0.8				
2003	PHI	NL	25	495	150	28	4	7	44	94	11	1	.303	.366	.418	.138	.314	.376	.439	.102	32.5	129-CF	-4		
2004	PHI	NL	26	494	140	29	4	16	46	91	11	4	.283	.351	.454	.060	.285	.351	.464	.063	22.4	130-CF	-6		

Breakout: 19%   Improve: 49%   Collapse: 16%

Byrd was touted as a Rookie of the Year prospect coming into 2003, and if you could pretend his April and May didn't happen, he might have won it. He got off to a miserable start, spent some time on the DL, and dropped into a platoon role with Ricky Ledee. His season turned around after he reviewed tapes of himself the prior season (note to hitters: always, always get tapes of yourself when things are going well). He tweaked his stance, hit .325 with a .381 OBP after June 1, and took the leadoff spot away from Jimmy Rollins in July. If Byrd can keep progressing, he'll be a huge asset: You can count the number of center fielders who can hit and field on one hand, maybe a hand and a couple of fingers.

TRAVIS CHAPMAN 3B Bats: R Throws: R Born: 05-Jun-78 Age: 26

YEAR	TM	LG	AGE	AB	H	2B	3B	HR	BB	SO	SB	CS	AVG	OBP	SLG	MLVR	EQBA	EQOBP	EQSLG	EQMLVR	VORP	DEFENSE	
2001	CLR	FLA	23	329	101	22	0	4	44	39	3	1	.307	.400	.410	.192	.249	.321	.340	-.190	-1.1	88-3B	1
2002	REA	EAS	24	478	144	35	1	15	54	77	3	1	.301	.388	.473	.216	.254	.328	.409	-.078	15.4	105-3B	5
2003	SWB	INT	25	478	130	36	0	12	44	97	2	2	.272	.348	.423	.074	.255	.330	.406	-.078	15.1	130-3B	-8
2004	PHI	NL	26	176	43	9	1	5	17	33	1	1	.245	.328	.385	-.098	.247	.328	.393	-.099	8.8	51-3B	-3

Breakout: 28%   Improve: 42%   Collapse: 41%

Taken by the Indians in the Rule 5 draft and traded to Detroit, whose third base job was wide open, Chapman had a poor spring and was reclaimed by the Phillies. He retained the power stroke he found after spending the 2001–02 winter working out, although it appears his fielding may have suffered a bit. He'd be good insurance against further back problems for Bell if they kept him, but Philly non-tendered Chapman, and he was a free agent at press time.

McKAY CHRISTENSEN CF Bats: L Throws: L Born: 14-Aug-75 Age: 28

YEAR	TM	LG	AGE	AB	H	2B	3B	HR	BB	SO	SB	CS	AVG	OBP	SLG	MLVR	EQBA	EQOBP	EQSLG	EQMLVR	VORP	DEFENSE			
2001	CHR	INT	25	273	75	15	6	7	30	52	17	3	.275	.347	.451	.099	.256	.328	.426	-.053	7.9	64-CF	0		
2001	LVG	PCL	25	57	14	2	1	1	5	11	3	1	.246	.317	.368	-.186	.211	.270	.333	-.323	-3.1	14-CF	-2		
2001	LAD	NL	25	49	16	2	0	1	3	10	3	2	.327	.400	.429	.179	.340	.405	.440	.178	4.1				
2002	NOR	INT	26	377	107	23	6	5	26	72	20	13	.284	.341	.416	.071	.267	.322	.401	-.090	6.5	70-CF	-6	10-LF	0
2003	SWB	INT	27	181	43	10	1	4	14	48	7	1	.238	.294	.370	-.107	.220	.282	.352	-.268	-6.6	42-CF	1		
2004	PHI	NL	28	158	40	8	2	4	15	36	5	2	.254	.324	.404	-.073	.255	.324	.413	-.074	5.5	46-CF	-2		

Breakout: 36%   Improve: 54%   Collapse: 33%

Christensen is basically a sixth outfielder—the one who plays at Triple-A and gets called up when a regular outfielder is hurt, just to be a defensive replacement. He is a good center fielder, so long as hitting isn't part of the job requirement. Any chance of doing that for Philadelphia was lost when he fell victim to the dreaded SLAP lesion, a torn shoulder labrum.

KIEL FISHER 3B Bats: L Throws: R Born: 29-Sep-83 Age: 20

YEAR	TM	LG	AGE	AB	H	2B	3B	HR	BB	SO	SB	CS	AVG	OBP	SLG	MLVR	EQBA	EQOBP	EQSLG	EQMLVR	VORP	DEFENSE	
2003	BAT	NYP	19	97	33	4	2	1	13	26	3	1	.340	.420	.454	.315	.238	.302	.327	-.252	-4.2	23-3B	-1
2004	PHI	NL	20	225	46	9	2	3	20	71	2	2	.205	.272	.301	-.330	.206	.272	.308	-.337	-7.8	62-3B	-7

Breakout: 12%   Improve: 29%   Collapse: 52%

Fisher, a third-round pick in 2002, is a big, slick-fielding third baseman from southern California. He spent most of the season in the Gulf Coast League, hitting .323, and continued to play well after moving up to Batavia. Productive, lefty-hitting third basemen are a rare commodity, so keep an eye on him.

DANNY GONZALEZ SS Bats: B Throws: R Born: 20-Nov-81 Age: 22

YEAR	TM	LG	AGE	AB	H	2B	3B	HR	BB	SO	SB	CS	AVG	OBP	SLG	MLVR	EQBA	EQOBP	EQSLG	EQMLVR	VORP	DEFENSE	
2001	BAT	NYP	19	281	67	9	4	0	18	52	1	3	.238	.289	.299	-.125	.185	.221	.237	-.569	-57.2	73-SS	-4
2002	LWD	SAL	20	493	133	14	4	4	55	88	11	21	.270	.349	.339	.040	.211	.270	.269	-.412	-33.4	127-SS	5
2003	CLR	FLA	21	436	118	22	5	0	49	56	5	2	.271	.348	.344	.042	.228	.289	.299	-.323	-17.7	113-SS	8
2004	PHI	NL	22	258	56	11	1	2	21	44	2	2	.217	.280	.296	-.316	.218	.280	.303	-.322	-8.3	70-SS	-3

Breakout: 34%   Improve: 53%   Collapse: 26%

The Phillies have three shortstops in their system, Gonzalez, Machado, and Carlos Rodriguez, who project very similarly. They all look like mild-hitting shortstops with above-average gloves. Gonzalez is probably the weakest of the three as a hitter, but consider three things. One, he rates as the best fielder of the three by a fair margin—although the scouting reports differ. Two, he has been making steady improvement, unlike the other two. Three, he's been praised for his effort and attitude, while the other two have been criticized for lack of same.

TYLER HOUSTON   UT/Clubhouse Cancer?   Bats: L   Throws: R   Born: 17-Jan-71   Age: 33

YEAR	TM	LG	AGE	AB	H	2B	3B	HR	BB	SO	SB	CS	AVG	OBP	SLG	MLVR	EQBA	EQOBP	EQSLG	EQMLVR	VORP	DEFENSE
2001	MIL	NL	30	235	68	7	0	12	18	62	0	0	.289	.343	.472	.078	.290	.342	.475	.071	16.4	56-3B -4
2002	MIL	NL	31	255	77	15	2	7	14	41	1	0	.302	.347	.459	.134	.309	.350	.475	.104	18.8	60-3B -7
2002	LAD	NL	31	65	13	5	1	0	2	21	0	0	.200	.224	.308	-.334	.212	.235	.348	-.371	-4.7	11-1B -1
2003	PHI	NL	32	97	27	6	0	2	6	19	0	0	.278	.320	.402	.016	.293	.333	.424	-.016	4.2	17-3B -3
2004	*PHI*	*NL*	*33*	*163*	*42*	*9*	*1*	*4*	*12*	*34*	*0*	*0*	*.255*	*.308*	*.385*	*-.126*	*.256*	*.307*	*.394*	*-.128*	*5.2*	*46-3B -4*

Breakout: 20%   *Improve: 35%*   *Collapse: 41%*

When Houston was cut by the Phillies at the end of the August, he held back for about two days before laying into Larry Bowa and his managing style. Houston should know what he's talking about; having played for five organizations in five years, he's seen enough different styles to be able to form a credible opinion. On the other hand, he always seems to be having run-ins with his managers, which strongly suggests that the causality arrow follows the four fingers he's not pointing with. After the very public feud with Bowa, he may not find anyone else who is willing to overlook his character to acquire a mediocre, albeit versatile, player.

RYAN HOWARD   1B   Bats: L   Throws: L   Born: 19-Nov-79   Age: 24

YEAR	TM	LG	AGE	AB	H	2B	3B	HR	BB	SO	SB	CS	AVG	OBP	SLG	MLVR	EQBA	EQOBP	EQSLG	EQMLVR	VORP	DEFENSE
2001	BAT	NYP	21	169	46	7	3	6	30	55	0	0	.272	.384	.456	.221	.180	.266	.309	-.381	-30.9	41-1B -6
2002	LWD	SAL	22	493	138	20	6	19	66	145	5	4	.280	.367	.460	.231	.213	.280	.362	-.263	-29.2	118-1B -17
2003	CLR	FLA	23	490	149	32	1	23	50	151	0	0	.304	.374	.514	.320	.247	.304	.437	-.089	-0.9	114-1B -2
2004	*PHI*	*NL*	*24*	*267*	*61*	*14*	*1*	*11*	*26*	*85*	*1*	*1*	*.229*	*.301*	*.409*	*-.125*	*.230*	*.300*	*.418*	*-.127*	*-2.4*	*73-1B -5*

Breakout: 35%   *Improve: 52%*   *Collapse: 25%*

Howard fell 7 RBI short of winning the Triple Crown in the FSL last year and was named the league's MVP. That's the good news. The bad news is that, at 23, he was a year older than the league average and also led the league in strikeouts. Taken together, you've got someone who should hit like a lesser Preston Wilson, except that he's a slow first baseman and isn't getting an altitude boost to his numbers.

JEFF INGLIN   LF   Bats: R   Throws: R   Born: 08-Oct-75   Age: 28

YEAR	TM	LG	AGE	AB	H	2B	3B	HR	BB	SO	SB	CS	AVG	OBP	SLG	MLVR	EQBA	EQOBP	EQSLG	EQMLVR	VORP	DEFENSE	
2001	CHR	INT	25	481	131	25	6	24	43	103	3	4	.272	.338	.499	.145	.251	.314	.466	-.027	4.0	55-LF -1	
2002	CHR	INT	26	152	42	4	0	6	8	22	2	2	.276	.305	.421	-.004	.255	.292	.405	-.150	-4.3	30-LF -2	
2003	REA	EAS	27	539	153	27	1	24	45	58	7	3	.284	.346	.471	.137	.240	.296	.412	-.144	-14.7	96-LF 0	21-RF -3
2004	*DET*	*AL*	*28*	*164*	*39*	*7*	*1*	*5*	*11*	*28*	*2*	*1*	*.238*	*.293*	*.388*	*-.146*	*.248*	*.305*	*.416*	*-.108*	*0.3*	*46-LF -2*	

Breakout: 29%   *Improve: 45%*   *Collapse: 34%*

A former White Sox prospect, Inglin has never impressed the scouts, basically because he was too small and didn't run fast enough. He's certainly got enough power to be a useful bat off the bench, although the average has started to come down the last couple of years. Given that in the last two years he's had to go to Korea and then down to Double-A to keep playing, his career may be just about over.

RICKY LEDEE   OF   Bats: L   Throws: L   Born: 22-Nov-73   Age: 30

YEAR	TM	LG	AGE	AB	H	2B	3B	HR	BB	SO	SB	CS	AVG	OBP	SLG	MLVR	EQBA	EQOBP	EQSLG	EQMLVR	VORP	DEFENSE	
2001	TEX	AL	27	242	56	21	1	2	23	58	3	3	.231	.303	.351	-.192	.244	.318	.372	-.155	-5.6	49-RF -2	
2002	PHI	NL	28	203	46	13	1	8	35	50	1	2	.227	.342	.419	.026	.240	.349	.452	.008	8.8	33-CF -2	
2003	PHI	NL	29	255	63	15	2	13	34	59	0	0	.247	.334	.475	.114	.258	.344	.496	.074	14.0	30-CF 0	20-LF 0
2004	*PHI*	*NL*	*30*	*177*	*43*	*10*	*1*	*7*	*25*	*43*	*1*	*1*	*.244*	*.340*	*.428*	*-.023*	*.245*	*.340*	*.438*	*-.023*	*5.5*	*52-CF -7*	

Breakout: 20%   *Improve: 43%*   *Collapse: 28%*

Ledee, a former can't-miss prospect who did, served as the Phillies' top reserve outfielder last year, stepping in when the regular three were either too injured or too deep in Bowa's doghouse to play. For a brief time in May it looked like he might get into a platoon with Marlon Byrd, but that's about when Byrd broke out of his slump. He should remain a valuable part of the Phillies' bench.

JESSE LEVIS   C   Bats: L   Throws: R   Born: 14-Apr-68   Age: 36

YEAR	TM	LG	AGE	AB	H	2B	3B	HR	BB	SO	SB	CS	AVG	OBP	SLG	MLVR	EQBA	EQOBP	EQSLG	EQMLVR	VORP	DEFENSE	
2001	RIC	INT	33	192	57	6	0	1	24	15	2	0	.297	.381	.344	.041	.281	.360	.327	-.112	3.9	54-C	2
2002	LOU	INT	34	254	72	11	1	3	31	19	1	1	.283	.369	.370	.034	.261	.344	.346	-.129	3.4	55-C	-1
2003	SWB	INT	35	265	74	16	0	0	18	18	1	0	.279	.328	.340	-.064	.266	.318	.326	-.205	-2.5	75-C	0
2004	PHI	NL	36	66	16	3	0	0	5	6	0	0	.244	.303	.307	-.245	.246	.303	.314	-.249	-1.5	22-C	-6

Breakout: 23%   *Improve: 32%*   *Collapse: 32%*

An insurance policy in case something happened to Lieberthal or Pratt, Levis was so unimpressive at Scranton that the Phillies traded for Kelly Stinnett to be a backup in September, costing them Eric Valent. If he could hit for any power at all he might have had a nice career, but he's now an old catcher fading away.

MIKE LIEBERTHAL   C   Bats: R   Throws: R   Born: 18-Jan-72   Age: 32

YEAR	TM	LG	AGE	AB	H	2B	3B	HR	BB	SO	SB	CS	AVG	OBP	SLG	MLVR	EQBA	EQOBP	EQSLG	EQMLVR	VORP	DEFENSE	
2001	PHI	NL	29	121	28	8	0	2	12	21	0	0	.231	.316	.347	-.178	.244	.323	.366	-.154	0.7	33-C	2
2002	PHI	NL	30	476	133	29	2	15	38	58	0	1	.279	.349	.443	.111	.292	.356	.469	.089	31.9	123-C	2
2003	PHI	NL	31	508	159	30	1	13	38	59	0	0	.313	.373	.453	.207	.327	.383	.475	.178	43.7	128-C	-10
2004	PHI	NL	32	400	111	23	2	11	34	51	1	1	.278	.344	.423	.003	.280	.344	.432	.004	20.2	106-C	-6

Breakout: 6%   *Improve: 24%*   *Collapse: 39%*

Lieberthal got a lot of credit for his hitting last year, even though he didn't provide any more offense than he usually does—the only thing that was better about his hitting was his average. His defense was way off; he allowed 84 stolen bases, tops in the majors, and only threw out 19. He still has two years and $15 million to go on his contract, and if his defense drops any further he won't be a credible catcher. With Thome around, if he can't catch, he can't play.

ANDY MACHADO   SS   Bats: B   Throws: R   Born: 25-Jan-81   Age: 23

YEAR	TM	LG	AGE	AB	H	2B	3B	HR	BB	SO	SB	CS	AVG	OBP	SLG	MLVR	EQBA	EQOBP	EQSLG	EQMLVR	VORP	DEFENSE	
2001	CLR	FLA	20	272	71	5	8	5	31	66	23	9	.261	.342	.393	.056	.211	.274	.333	-.316	-10.1	82-SS	4
2001	REA	EAS	20	101	15	2	0	1	12	25	5	2	.149	.237	.198	-.445	.136	.219	.184	-.662	-15.0	30-SS	-1
2002	REA	EAS	21	450	113	24	3	12	72	118	40	11	.251	.353	.398	.026	.211	.299	.339	-.258	-8.1	122-SS	1
2003	REA	EAS	22	423	83	19	4	5	108	120	49	15	.196	.360	.296	-.123	.155	.292	.244	-.422	-32.8	121-SS	-10
2004	PHI	NL	23	244	50	11	2	4	34	67	13	4	.207	.307	.319	-.243	.208	.306	.326	-.248	-1.2	70-SS	-8

Breakout: 37%   *Improve: 63%*   *Collapse: 18%*

Regarded as the Phils' top shortstop prospect, he just spent his second full season at Reading, slugging an awful .296. He's well-regarded defensively, he's fast, and he knows how to take a walk; in fact, he led the league in walks and steals. The big "buts" here are hitting for average and striking out; the Phillies hope that retooling his stance will improve both of those problems, although that's what they were supposedly trying last year.

JASON MICHAELS   OF/PH   Bats: R   Throws: R   Born: 04-May-76   Age: 28

YEAR	TM	LG	AGE	AB	H	2B	3B	HR	BB	SO	SB	CS	AVG	OBP	SLG	MLVR	EQBA	EQOBP	EQSLG	EQMLVR	VORP	DEFENSE	
2001	SWB	INT	25	418	109	19	3	17	37	126	11	3	.261	.332	.443	.064	.248	.314	.425	-.086	-4.0	93-LF	-1
2002	PHI	NL	26	105	28	10	3	2	13	33	1	1	.267	.347	.476	.141	.280	.363	.495	.126	7.0		
2003	PHI	NL	27	109	36	11	0	5	15	22	0	0	.330	.416	.569	.456	.339	.421	.589	.415	15.9		
2004	PHI	NL	28	216	56	13	1	8	23	54	2	1	.260	.335	.446	.005	.262	.335	.456	.006	8.7	60-LF	-2

Breakout: 7%   *Improve: 26%*   *Collapse: 42%*

While you shouldn't expect him to hit .330 again, Michaels is an excellent backup outfielder and pinch-hitting option off of the bench. He can play all three spots in the outfield and hit with power, especially against lefties. Along with Ledee and the three starters, the Phillies may have the best outfield combination in baseball, one through five.

DAMON MINOR   **1B**   **Bats: L**   **Throws: L**   Born: 05-Jan-74   Age: 30

YEAR	TM	LG	AGE	AB	H	2B	3B	HR	BB	SO	SB	CS	AVG	OBP	SLG	MLVR	EQBA	EQOBP	EQSLG	EQMLVR	VORP	DEFENSE	
2001	FRE	PCL	27	406	125	22	3	24	44	83	1	1	.308	.380	.554	.241	.261	.333	.468	.019	13.8	100-1B	-7
2002	SFG	NL	28	173	41	6	0	10	24	34	0	0	.237	.333	.445	.060	.249	.344	.475	.037	5.7	37-1B	-4
2003	FRE	PCL	29	141	33	2	1	8	6	29	0	0	.234	.278	.433	-.101	.214	.257	.400	-.253	-7.0	20-1B	6
2003	SWB	INT	29	328	76	17	1	16	27	60	1	2	.232	.305	.436	-.008	.218	.289	.420	-.163	-7.9	39-1B	-2
2004	*PHI*	*NL*	*30*	*185*	*44*	*9*	*1*	*8*	*17*	*39*	*0*	*0*	*.240*	*.311*	*.420*	*-.084*	*.241*	*.311*	*.430*	*-.085*	*2.7*	*52-1B*	*-3*

Breakout: 19%   *Improve: 46%*   *Collapse: 35%*

Minor lost out to Andres Galarraga in a springtime fight for the Giants' backup first-base job, then made it through waivers. Maybe everybody knew something, because Minor didn't hit a lick in Fresno, and after a trade to the Phillies he couldn't hit in Scranton either. He'll probably bounce back a bit, while likely remaining a Triple-A vagabond.

JORGE PADILLA   **RF**   **Bats: R**   **Throws: R**   Born: 11-Aug-79   Age: 24

YEAR	TM	LG	AGE	AB	H	2B	3B	HR	BB	SO	SB	CS	AVG	OBP	SLG	MLVR	EQBA	EQOBP	EQSLG	EQMLVR	VORP	DEFENSE	
2001	CLR	FLA	21	358	93	13	2	16	40	73	23	6	.260	.343	.441	.119	.213	.274	.373	-.259	-22.7	87-RF	-4
2002	REA	EAS	22	484	124	30	2	7	40	77	32	11	.256	.322	.370	-.058	.225	.281	.329	-.299	-34.5	121-RF	-1
2003	REA	EAS	23	173	51	13	1	2	18	29	11	8	.295	.363	.416	.096	.241	.304	.356	-.206	-7.6	41-RF	-7
2004	*PHI*	*NL*	*24*	*210*	*53*	*12*	*1*	*6*	*18*	*40*	*7*	*2*	*.253*	*.319*	*.400*	*-.089*	*.254*	*.318*	*.409*	*-.090*	*1.1*	*58-RF*	*-1*

Breakout: 50%   *Improve: 72%*   *Collapse: 12%*

In his first three years as a pro, Padilla hit 38 home runs, one every 33 at-bats. Since reaching Reading in 2002, he's hit just 9, one every 73 at-bats, despite Reading and the Eastern League being a much better home run environment than his previous haunts. It is an unusual career path, and not a good one, which won't be helped any by the hand surgery that cut his 2003 season off in June.

TOMAS PEREZ   **UT**   **Bats: B**   **Throws: R**   Born: 29-Dec-73   Age: 30

YEAR	TM	LG	AGE	AB	H	2B	3B	HR	BB	SO	SB	CS	AVG	OBP	SLG	MLVR	EQBA	EQOBP	EQSLG	EQMLVR	VORP	DEFENSE			
2001	PHI	NL	27	135	41	7	1	3	7	22	0	1	.304	.347	.437	.060	.314	.354	.453	.083	9.4	18-2B	2		
2002	PHI	NL	28	212	53	13	1	5	21	40	1	0	.250	.319	.392	-.031	.264	.329	.417	-.057	6.5	31-2B	0	11-3B	-2
2003	PHI	NL	29	298	79	18	1	5	23	54	0	1	.265	.316	.383	-.031	.276	.325	.405	-.072	7.7	44-3B	1	20-2B	-2
2004	*PHI*	*NL*	*30*	*204*	*54*	*12*	*1*	*5*	*17*	*38*	*1*	*1*	*.263*	*.320*	*.399*	*-.080*	*.264*	*.320*	*.408*	*-.081*	*8.3*	*56-3B*	*-1*		

Breakout: 21%   *Improve: 40%*   *Collapse: 41%*

Perez is at his best as a utility man, able to get a spot start here and there. David Bell's injury meant that he had to play a lot more often that that, although Bowa spread him out by rotating him with Chase Utley and Tyler Houston, at least until Houston's release. He is signed through 2004.

PLACIDO POLANCO   **2B/3B**   **Bats: B**   **Throws: R**   Born: 10-Oct-75   Age: 28

YEAR	TM	LG	AGE	AB	H	2B	3B	HR	BB	SO	SB	CS	AVG	OBP	SLG	MLVR	EQBA	EQOBP	EQSLG	EQMLVR	VORP	DEFENSE			
2001	STL	NL	25	564	173	26	4	3	25	43	12	3	.307	.342	.383	-.030	.315	.349	.392	-.015	25.3	88-3B	17	34-SS	5
2002	STL	NL	26	342	97	19	1	5	12	27	3	1	.284	.316	.389	-.024	.296	.322	.408	-.057	10.6	66-3B	9	10-SS	0
2002	PHI	NL	26	206	61	13	1	4	14	14	2	2	.296	.353	.427	.109	.310	.363	.452	.094	14.3	53-3B	10		
2003	PHI	NL	27	492	142	30	3	14	42	38	14	2	.289	.352	.447	.142	.300	.361	.469	.105	36.4	96-2B	9	17-3B	2
2004	*PHI*	*NL*	*28*	*510*	*149*	*30*	*3*	*10*	*39*	*42*	*10*	*3*	*.293*	*.348*	*.419*	*.016*	*.294*	*.348*	*.429*	*.018*	*27.7*	*133-2B*	*2*		

Breakout: 10%   *Improve: 33%*   *Collapse: 29%*

If they would only leave him alone to play a full season at one position, be it second or third, he could legitimately win a Gold Glove. After spending most of the last two seasons at third, Polanco shifted to second base to let Bell play third; the failure of the Perez/Houston effort caused them to move Polanco back to third so they could call up Chase Utley. Through it all, he filled the #2 spot in the order impeccably and will be an asset again in '04.

TODD PRATT   C   Bats: R   Throws: R   Born: 09-Feb-67   Age: 37

YEAR	TM	LG	AGE	AB	H	2B	3B	HR	BB	SO	SB	CS	AVG	OBP	SLG	MLVR	EQBA	EQOBP	EQSLG	EQMLVR	VORP	DEFENSE
2001	NYM	NL	34	80	13	5	0	2	15	36	1	0	.163	.306	.300	-.290	.173	.314	.321	-.272	-2.4	21-C -3
2001	PHI	NL	34	93	19	3	0	2	19	25	0	0	.204	.345	.301	-.195	.211	.347	.316	-.192	-0.5	28-C -2
2002	PHI	NL	35	106	33	11	0	3	24	28	2	0	.311	.449	.500	.366	.321	.458	.523	.362	16.5	33-C -1
2003	PHI	NL	36	125	34	10	1	4	22	38	0	0	.272	.400	.464	.229	.281	.406	.492	.197	12.6	33-C -3
2004	PHI	NL	37	156	40	10	0	5	28	45	1	1	.259	.380	.425	.053	.260	.380	.435	.055	13.0	48-C -2

Breakout: 13%   Improve: 22%   Collapse: 41%

Between Pratt and Lieberthal, the Phillies didn't have to worry about low offensive production from their catchers. The two have an unusual day/night platoon arrangement. Lieberthal hates working day games, not so much because he caught the night before, but because they mess up his entire pre-game routine (which apparently takes all day). Meanwhile, Pratt has spent the last four years building up a .275/.412/.466 line in day games, against just .219/.349/.353 under the lights. Everybody wins, except the opposition.

NICK PUNTO   IF   Bats: B   Throws: R   Born: 08-Nov-77   Age: 26

YEAR	TM	LG	AGE	AB	H	2B	3B	HR	BB	SO	SB	CS	AVG	OBP	SLG	MLVR	EQBA	EQOBP	EQSLG	EQMLVR	VORP	DEFENSE
2001	SWB	INT	23	463	106	19	5	1	68	114	33	9	.229	.327	.298	-.149	.217	.309	.287	-.304	-14.8	120-SS 8
2002	SWB	INT	24	443	120	12	5	1	76	84	42	8	.271	.378	.327	-.003	.252	.354	.309	-.165	5.2	115-SS 10
2003	SWB	INT	25	111	35	7	1	0	7	13	7	1	.315	.353	.396	.080	.295	.336	.375	-.080	4.1	25-SS 7
2003	PHI	NL	25	92	20	2	0	1	7	22	2	1	.217	.273	.272	-.297	.237	.290	.290	-.329	-3.4	12-2B -2
2004	MIN	AL	26	188	46	8	2	2	19	35	9	2	.246	.317	.339	-.160	.246	.320	.345	-.176	4.0	53-SS -1

Breakout: 25%   Improve: 46%   Collapse: 34%

In the minors, Punto has been able to work pitchers for more than his fair share of walks, considering that he has no power whatsoever. In his first extended MLB audition last year, spread over three separate call-ups, he tried to work big league pitchers the same way, but they didn't give in to him, and he floundered. An excellent gloveman, Punto has a good shot at being Minnesota's primary backup infielder after being part of the package for Eric Milton.

JIMMY ROLLINS   SS   Bats: B   Throws: R   Born: 27-Nov-78   Age: 25

YEAR	TM	LG	AGE	AB	H	2B	3B	HR	BB	SO	SB	CS	AVG	OBP	SLG	MLVR	EQBA	EQOBP	EQSLG	EQMLVR	VORP	DEFENSE
2001	PHI	NL	22	656	180	29	12	14	48	108	46	8	.274	.323	.419	-.034	.282	.331	.432	-.017	33.3	155-SS 1
2002	PHI	NL	23	637	156	33	10	11	54	103	31	13	.245	.306	.380	-.073	.259	.316	.405	-.102	16.5	148-SS 1
2003	PHI	NL	24	628	165	42	6	8	54	113	20	12	.263	.320	.387	-.019	.275	.331	.408	-.057	21.5	153-SS 1
2004	PHI	NL	25	567	153	31	6	12	50	90	22	7	.270	.331	.411	-.042	.272	.330	.420	-.042	24.5	147-SS -1

Breakout: 16%   Improve: 51%   Collapse: 16%

Bowa has repeatedly stressed that he wants Rollins to be more of a slap hitter, to use his speed more and not try to drive the ball so much. We think that the extra-base power is what made Rollins so valuable in the first place, however unsuitable it may have seemed for a short guy; Rollins apparently agrees with us since he's strenuously resisted Bowa's efforts. In any event, his power and speed both appear to be dissipating, and without those he won't hold a starting job for long.

KELLY STINNETT   C   Bats: R   Throws: R   Born: 04-Feb-70   Age: 34

YEAR	TM	LG	AGE	AB	H	2B	3B	HR	BB	SO	SB	CS	AVG	OBP	SLG	MLVR	EQBA	EQOBP	EQSLG	EQMLVR	VORP	DEFENSE
2001	CIN	NL	31	187	48	11	0	9	17	61	2	2	.257	.333	.460	.006	.254	.329	.460	-.006	8.7	52-C -10
2002	CIN	NL	32	93	21	5	0	3	15	25	2	0	.226	.333	.376	-.066	.223	.330	.383	-.131	1.1	29-C -2
2002	LOU	INT	32	86	17	6	0	0	3	24	0	0	.198	.225	.267	-.400	.198	.225	.267	-.513	-8.1	22-C 0
2003	CIN	NL	33	179	41	13	0	3	13	51	0	0	.229	.294	.352	-.174	.238	.300	.365	-.204	-1.8	45-C 0
2003	PHI	NL	33	7	3	0	0	0	1	1	0	0	.429	.500	.429	.492	.429	.500	.429	.413	1.3	
2004	KCR	AL	34	152	40	8	0	4	15	37	1	0	.264	.337	.394	-.045	.252	.329	.382	-.109	3.9	44-C -3

Breakout: 16%   Improve: 35%   Collapse: 47%

Stinnett has been a thoroughly mediocre catcher for most of his career, but managed to pull things together in time to get multi-year contracts after 1999 and 2001. The Phillies have no actual need for him; he was acquired solely as an insurance policy, in case something bad happened to Lieberthal or Pratt down the stretch. When the policy expired at the end of the season, he turned into a free agent. He signed a one-year deal to be Benito Santiago's backup in Kansas City.

JIM THOME   **1B**   **Bats: L**   **Throws: R**   Born: 27-Aug-70   Age: 33

YEAR	TM	LG	AGE	AB	H	2B	3B	HR	BB	SO	SB	CS	AVG	OBP	SLG	MLVR	EQBA	EQOBP	EQSLG	EQMLVR	VORP	DEFENSE
2001	CLE	AL	30	526	153	26	1	49	111	185	0	1	.291	.416	.624	.413	.309	.434	.668	.503	88.5	142-1B -12
2002	CLE	AL	31	480	146	19	2	52	122	139	1	2	.304	.445	.677	.544	.328	.468	.736	.663	109.7	123-1B -7
2003	PHI	NL	32	578	154	30	3	47	111	182	0	3	.266	.385	.573	.344	.274	.391	.596	.303	61.4	152-1B -6
2004	PHI	NL	33	452	124	21	1	40	96	144	1	1	.273	.402	.592	.307	.275	.402	.605	.315	53.9	131-1B -5

Breakout: 15%   *Improve: 42%*   *Collapse: 10%*

While a lot of people were down on Thome last season, it simply wasn't reasonable to expect him to duplicate his career year of 2002. That is the danger with free agents: You pay for the outlier, but you get the regression to the mean. Still, he was far enough above the mean that even after regressing to it he cranked a league-leading 47 home runs and was one of the league's best hitters, so complaints that they didn't get what they paid for ring a little hollow, at least for now.

CHASE UTLEY   **2B**   **Bats: L**   **Throws: R**   Born: 17-Dec-78   Age: 25

YEAR	TM	LG	AGE	AB	H	2B	3B	HR	BB	SO	SB	CS	AVG	OBP	SLG	MLVR	EQBA	EQOBP	EQSLG	EQMLVR	VORP	DEFENSE
2001	CLR	FLA	22	467	120	25	2	16	37	88	19	8	.257	.324	.422	.065	.216	.264	.368	-.283	-16.1	114-2B -4
2002	SWB	INT	23	464	122	39	1	17	46	89	8	3	.263	.352	.461	.119	.245	.330	.437	-.043	19.0	123-3B -18
2003	SWB	INT	24	431	139	26	2	18	41	75	10	4	.323	.390	.517	.306	.297	.366	.490	.141	41.8	113-2B 1
2003	PHI	NL	24	134	32	10	1	2	11	22	2	0	.239	.322	.373	-.052	.257	.335	.397	-.079	3.2	32-2B 4
2004	PHI	NL	25	325	85	19	2	11	31	58	6	2	.262	.340	.429	-.008	.264	.339	.439	-.007	20.2	88-2B -3

Breakout: 18%   *Improve: 47%*   *Collapse: 22%*

The signing of David Bell by the Phillies was bad enough on its own, but it also blocked Utley, who had blossomed as a hitter at Scranton in 2002. That's how he found himself back in Triple-A in 2003, and at least he could go back to second base and stop pretending to play third. Utley proceeded to turn in an outstanding season in the International League, and was arguably the second-best hitter in the circuit after Fernando Seguignol. He didn't do quite as well in Philadelphia, though he still has a nice future ahead. But the biggest question for 2004 is again, where does he play?

PITCHERS

TERRY ADAMS   **Bats: R**   **Throws: R**   Born: 06-Mar-73   Age: 31

YEAR	TM	LG	AGE	G	GS	IP	H	BB	SO	HR	ERA	EQERA	EQH9	EQBB9	EQSO9	EQHR9	PERA	VORP	STF
2001	LAD	NL	28	43	22	166.3	172	54	141	9	4.33	4.42	9.8	2.7	6.5	0.5	4.19	20.8	19
2002	PHI	NL	29	46	19	136.7	132	58	96	9	4.35	4.82	9.2	3.4	5.6	0.6	4.29	11.3	3
2003	PHI	NL	30	66	0	68.0	68	23	51	1	2.65	3.60	9.4	2.8	6.1	0.1	3.75	19.2	18
2004	TOR	AL	31	43	5	64.3	74	26	41	6	4.67	4.43	9.9	3.4	5.7	0.7	4.60	10.1	-5

Breakout: 25%   *Improve: 47%*   *Collapse: 29%*

Adams was one of the three Phillie relief pitchers who were any good last year, and he managed to lead the team in appearances even though he only pitched once in the final month. The second half of 2003 was rough on Adams, involving one trip to the DL for a strained muscle, one surgery for bone chips in his elbow, and one guilty plea for disorderly conduct. He's gone to Toronto as one of several mercs stocking the Jays' refurbished pen.

TAYLOR BUCHHOLZ   **Bats: R**   **Throws: R**   Born: 13-Oct-81   Age: 22

YEAR	TM	LG	AGE	G	GS	IP	H	BB	SO	HR	ERA	EQERA	EQH9	EQBB9	EQSO9	EQHR9	PERA	VORP	STF
2001	LWD	SAL	19	28	26	176.7	165	57	136	8	3.36	6.63	10.6	4.4	4.1	1.0	5.67	-17.7	5
2002	CLR	FLA	20	23	23	158.7	140	51	129	11	3.29	5.11	9.6	3.6	5.3	1.4	5.36	7.9	12
2002	REA	EAS	20	4	4	23.0	29	6	17	5	7.43	8.86	12.7	2.5	5.5	3.0	8.48	-7.7	-19
2003	REA	EAS	21	25	24	144.7	136	33	114	14	3.55	4.56	9.2	2.5	5.9	1.5	5.03	15.5	15
2004	HOU	NL	22	19	15	90.7	97	35	62	14	5.04	5.13	9.6	3.0	5.6	1.2	5.03	6.2	1

Breakout: 6%   *Improve: 45%*   *Collapse: 27%*

Buchholz was part of the trade that brought Billy Wagner to Philadelphia—the Astros had demanded one of Buchholz, Gavin Floyd, or Cole Hamels as part of the package. He has an exceptional curve ball and a good fastball that's still prone to being left up in the zone to get hammered. He's working on a third pitch—a change—to go with them. Buchholz should look good working in an extreme pitcher's park like New Orleans, but it could get ugly in Houston.

DAVE COGGIN

Bats: R **Throws: R** Born: 30-Oct-76 Age: 27

YEAR	TM	LG	AGE	G	GS	IP	H	BB	SO	HR	ERA	EQERA	EQH9	EQBB9	EQSO9	EQHR9	PERA	VORP	STF
2001	PHI	NL	24	17	17	95.0	99	39	62	7	4.17	4.65	9.7	3.5	4.9	0.6	4.54	9.6	14
2001	SWB	INT	24	15	15	97.3	93	31	53	6	3.05	4.74	9.7	3.4	3.8	0.8	4.77	8.5	0
2002	PHI	NL	25	38	7	77.0	65	51	64	4	4.68	4.72	8.1	5.2	6.5	0.5	4.18	7.3	7
2004	PHI	NL	27	23	13	73.3	77	36	42	7	4.71	4.95	9.5	3.9	4.7	0.8	5.05	6.7	-10

Breakout: 27%   Improve: 49%   Collapse: 20%

Coggin had shoulder surgery in October 2002, and was supposed to have been ready to return sometime in the spring. He wasn't. He had one of those seasons where he was always a few weeks away, and the year ran out before that week ever arrived.

RHEAL CORMIER

Bats: L **Throws: L** Born: 23-Apr-67 Age: 37

YEAR	TM	LG	AGE	G	GS	IP	H	BB	SO	HR	ERA	EQERA	EQH9	EQBB9	EQSO9	EQHR9	PERA	VORP	STF
2001	PHI	NL	34	60	0	51.3	49	17	37	5	4.21	4.41	8.8	2.8	5.5	0.7	4.08	6.5	-1
2002	PHI	NL	35	54	0	60.0	61	32	49	6	5.25	5.62	9.7	4.2	6.4	0.9	5.07	-0.1	-10
2003	PHI	NL	36	65	0	84.7	54	25	67	4	1.70	2.33	6.0	2.4	6.4	0.4	2.44	33.9	24
2004	PHI	NL	37	42	2	58.7	55	22	45	5	3.36	3.53	8.4	3.0	6.2	0.7	3.95	13.6	1

Breakout: 37%   Improve: 64%   Collapse: 20%

Like Terry Adams, Cormier had a poor spring, allowing five home runs in 12 innings, and was nearly cut. He opened the season against the Marlins by giving up five runs in two innings of work. Once the team finally came north, he didn't allow another run for six weeks, then only allowed one run in June and July... combined. By Michael Wolverton's rankings at baseballprospectus.com, Cormier was the second-best reliever in baseball, trailing only Eric Gagne, and not by much. Don't expect a repeat: Cormier allowed 15 fewer hits than expected, four times what he's ever done in the past.

VALERIO DE LOS SANTOS

Bats: L **Throws: L** Born: 06-Oct-72 Age: 31

YEAR	TM	LG	AGE	G	GS	IP	H	BB	SO	HR	ERA	EQERA	EQH9	EQBB9	EQSO9	EQHR9	PERA	VORP	STF
2002	MIL	NL	29	51	0	57.7	42	26	38	4	3.12	3.40	6.6	3.6	5.2	0.6	3.24	13.6	2
2003	MIL	NL	30	45	0	48.0	38	22	35	8	4.13	4.21	6.9	3.6	5.7	1.5	4.27	6.0	-19
2003	PHI	NL	30	6	0	4.0	7	3	4	0	9.00	11.25	15.8	6.8	6.8	0.0	7.27	-4.9	-21
2004	TOR	AL	31	41	2	54.3	58	24	37	8	5.25	4.98	9.2	3.7	6.1	1.1	4.85	5.5	-1

Breakout: 24%   Improve: 48%   Collapse: 29%

It was hard to divine just what the Phillies were trying to do by getting de los Santos at the deadline, other than indulging Ed Wade's reliever fetish—they already had Plesac and Cormier working the left side out of the pen. The most reasonable explanation is that they were looking ahead to 2004, since Plesac decided to retire this time. Instead, the Blue Jays signed him to a one-year, $850,000 contract.

BRANDON DUCKWORTH

Bats: R **Throws: R** Born: 23-Jan-76 Age: 28

YEAR	TM	LG	AGE	G	GS	IP	H	BB	SO	HR	ERA	EQERA	EQH9	EQBB9	EQSO9	EQHR9	PERA	VORP	STF
2001	SWB	INT	25	22	20	147.0	122	36	150	14	2.63	4.02	9.0	2.6	7.2	1.2	4.60	23.6	12
2001	PHI	NL	25	11	11	69.0	57	29	40	2	3.52	3.68	7.6	3.5	4.5	0.3	3.34	14.1	21
2002	PHI	NL	26	30	29	163.0	167	69	167	26	5.41	5.70	9.9	3.3	8.1	1.5	5.51	-1.7	2
2003	PHI	NL	27	24	18	93.0	98	44	68	12	4.94	5.62	9.8	3.8	5.8	1.2	5.34	-3.5	-11
2003	SWB	INT	27	3	3	18.7	21	4	14	3	3.37	5.82	11.6	2.6	5.3	2.1	6.96	-0.4	-36
2004	HOU	NL	28	21	15	89.0	91	36	68	13	4.74	4.83	9.1	3.2	6.2	1.2	4.86	8.7	4

Breakout: 16%   Improve: 44%   Collapse: 28%

An Astro now, part of the Billy Wagner trade. There's little doubt that he needed to be dealt, since Bowa had clearly lost confidence in him, but Houston does not seem to be the ideal place for a pitcher with gopherball tendencies. The loss of Wagner, plus the Astros' improved rotation depth, may shunt Duckworth into a bullpen role.

GAVIN FLOYD Bats: R Throws: R Born: 27-Jan-83 Age: 21

YEAR	TM	LG	AGE	G	GS	IP	H	BB	SO	HR	ERA	EQERA	EQH9	EQBB9	EQSO9	EQHR9	PERA	VORP	STF
2002	LWD	SAL	19	27	27	166.0	119	64	140	13	2.77	5.51	9.0	4.9	4.9	1.9	6.05	1.4	0
2003	CLR	FLA	20	24	20	138.0	128	45	115	9	3.00	5.84	10.4	3.8	5.5	1.8	6.21	-3.3	3
2004	PHI	NL	21	17	15	94.3	94	45	68	13	4.85	5.09	9.0	3.8	5.8	1.1	5.04	4.9	4

Breakout: 25%   Improve: 51%   Collapse: 3%

Floyd was regarded as the jewel in the minor league system, before Hamels started blowing everybody away in Lakewood. Hamels' performance there stands in sharp contrast to Floyd, who is simply not getting results that are commensurate with his scouting reports; his 3.00 ERA hides another 15 unearned runs, and, numerically speaking, he doesn't rate as a high-level prospect. There is another story here, though, that he's doing this with one hand essentially tied behind his back. Phillie management won't let him use his best pitch, a curve, in order to force him to work on a changeup. It is a bizarre strategy, and we won't be able to evaluate it for some time.

GEOFF GEARY Bats: R Throws: R Born: 26-Aug-76 Age: 27

YEAR	TM	LG	AGE	G	GS	IP	H	BB	SO	HR	ERA	EQERA	EQH9	EQBB9	EQSO9	EQHR9	PERA	VORP	STF
2001	REA	EAS	24	29	13	112.3	101	21	88	14	3.61	5.01	10.1	2.3	4.8	1.8	5.74	6.6	-24
2001	SWB	INT	24	7	3	22.0	35	6	21	2	6.95	9.00	16.6	3.2	6.8	1.4	8.35	-7.6	-22
2002	SWB	INT	25	38	8	101.0	108	32	82	9	3.03	5.42	10.8	3.4	6.2	1.2	5.63	1.9	-13
2003	SWB	INT	26	46	3	87.7	73	13	80	3	2.16	3.00	8.4	1.7	6.6	0.4	3.29	23.4	20
2003	PHI	NL	26	5	0	6.0	8	3	3	0	4.50	4.76	12.7	4.8	4.8	0.0	5.60	0.6	-1
2004	PHI	NL	27	19	7	49.7	50	15	37	5	3.82	4.01	9.1	2.4	6.1	0.9	4.20	8.9	4

Breakout: 29%   Improve: 58%   Collapse: 17%

A short right-hander who was progressing through the Phillie system without really impressing anyone, Geary's switch to relief has revitalized his career. He actually got off to rough start last year, allowing 13 runs in his first nine games. That's the same number of runs he would ultimately allow in his next 37 games and 70 innings.

WAYNE GOMES Bats: R Throws: R Born: 15-Jan-73 Age: 31

YEAR	TM	LG	AGE	G	GS	IP	H	BB	SO	HR	ERA	EQERA	EQH9	EQBB9	EQSO9	EQHR9	PERA	VORP	STF
2001	PHI	NL	28	42	0	48.0	51	22	35	4	4.31	4.70	10.0	3.9	5.5	0.6	4.78	4.6	-4
2001	SFG	NL	28	13	0	15.0	21	7	17	3	8.40	7.98	12.9	3.7	8.6	1.8	7.36	-3.9	-28
2002	PAW	INT	29	42	0	71.7	61	28	54	8	2.64	4.34	8.4	4.2	5.7	1.5	5.11	9.3	-28
2002	BOS	AL	29	20	0	21.3	20	12	15	2	4.65	4.35	8.7	4.8	6.1	0.9	4.73	2.9	-7
2003	SWB	INT	30	46	0	48.7	31	24	43	1	2.59	3.22	6.4	5.4	6.4	0.2	3.26	11.8	9
2004	OAK	AL	31	22	3	34.7	34	20	26	4	4.77	5.05	8.8	4.9	6.5	0.9	5.09	2.8	-7

Breakout: 32%   Improve: 55%   Collapse: 26%

Gomes spent the spring pitching for Tampa Bay, got cut, and found a job with his old organization. He did a good job in Scranton, sporting a 1.69 ERA as late as June. Despite all the troubles the parent bullpen was having, though, it doesn't appear that Gomes was ever seriously considered for a call-up. By the time the situation became truly desperate in August, he'd hit the DL with biceps tendinitis. He can expect a Sacramento summer, helping the Rivercats try to repeat while giving Oakland some experienced insurance.

COLE HAMELS Bats: L Throws: L Born: 27-Dec-83 Age: 20

YEAR	TM	LG	AGE	G	GS	IP	H	BB	SO	HR	ERA	EQERA	EQH9	EQBB9	EQSO9	EQHR9	PERA	VORP	STF
2003	LWD	SAL	19	13	13	74.7	32	25	115	0	0.84	2.07	6.5	4.1	9.1	0.3	2.94	25.6	71
2003	CLR	FLA	19	5	5	26.3	29	14	32	0	2.74	5.62	11.2	6.0	8.2	0.4	5.61	-0.1	47
2004	PHI	NL	20	17	16	100.0	86	48	108	7	3.61	3.80	7.7	3.8	8.8	0.6	3.84	21.0	28

Breakout: 31%   Improve: 50%   Collapse: 19%

A rock 'n roll surfer dude from San Diego, Hamels was seen by many as the best pitcher available in the 2002 draft. Despite that, he was still available for the Phillies with the 17th pick, as a broken arm he'd suffered while pitching the year before apparently scared off other teams. He's no Tony Saunders (or Tom Browning), since it was apparently caused by stressing an injury he'd gotten from playing football. Hamels has a pretty good fastball and curveball, but his changeup was the pitch that ate Sally leaguers alive last year; it is a top-notch pitch that's made him one of the best pitching prospects around.

JOSH HANCOCK   Bats: R   Throws: R   Born: 11-Apr-78   Age: 26

YEAR	TM	LG	AGE	G	GS	IP	H	BB	SO	HR	ERA	EQERA	EQH9	EQBB9	EQSO9	EQHR9	PERA	VORP	STF
2001	TRN	EAS	23	24	24	130.7	138	37	119	8	3.65	4.80	10.0	3.3	5.5	0.8	4.84	10.8	10
2002	TRN	EAS	24	15	14	84.7	82	18	69	9	3.61	4.46	9.7	2.2	5.4	1.6	5.28	10.0	-7
2002	PAW	INT	24	8	8	44.3	39	26	29	2	3.45	4.79	8.1	6.3	5.0	0.7	4.66	3.7	1
2003	SWB	INT	25	28	27	165.7	147	46	122	14	3.86	4.35	8.7	3.1	5.3	1.2	4.60	21.3	-1
2003	PHI	NL	25	2	0	3.0	2	0	4	0	3.00	0.00	6.8	0.0	10.1	0.0	1.67	0.8	75
2004	PHI	NL	26	19	11	67.3	68	26	47	8	4.46	4.69	9.1	3.1	5.7	1.0	4.64	6.5	1

Breakout: 23%   Improve: 45%   Collapse: 19%

Hancock came to the Phillies from the Boston organization for Jeremy Giambi. He didn't really have a chance to make the team in spring, as he was still recuperating from off-season groin surgery. He made a dramatic improvement right across the board in the second half of the season:

'03 Season	W–L	IP	RA	H/9	BB/9	SO/9
First half:	4–7	75.1	5.14	9.6	3.1	5.7
Second half:	6–2	90.1	3.49	6.7	2.0	7.4

With the Phillies' 2004 rotation set, he's going to have to either wait for injuries or take a bullpen job if he wants to pitch in the majors this year.

ERIC JUNGE   Bats: R   Throws: R   Born: 05-Jan-77   Age: 27

YEAR	TM	LG	AGE	G	GS	IP	H	BB	SO	HR	ERA	EQERA	EQH9	EQBB9	EQSO9	EQHR9	PERA	VORP	STF
2001	JAX	SOU	24	27	27	164.0	143	56	116	19	3.46	5.72	10.4	3.7	4.4	1.9	6.37	-1.9	-30
2002	SWB	INT	25	29	29	180.7	170	67	126	16	3.54	5.04	9.5	4.0	5.4	1.1	5.20	10.3	-6
2002	PHI	NL	25	4	1	12.7	14	5	11	0	1.42	3.00	10.5	3.0	6.8	0.0	4.14	3.5	34
2003	SWB	INT	26	10	8	47.0	38	16	42	2	3.06	3.98	8.2	3.8	6.5	0.6	3.94	7.7	12
2003	PHI	NL	26	6	0	7.7	5	1	5	1	3.51	2.45	6.1	1.2	4.9	1.2	2.87	1.6	0
2004	PHI	NL	27	15	9	54.7	55	24	40	7	4.47	4.69	9.1	3.4	5.9	1.1	4.86	6.2	0

Breakout: 26%   Improve: 54%   Collapse: 26%

Junge didn't make the club out of spring training (he was optioned to Scranton in mid-March), but some early minor injuries to other pitchers caused the Phillies to call him up. And send him down. And call him up. And send him down. Junge was transferred between the Philadelphia and Scranton rosters seven times in two months, finally going to Scranton for good in mid-May. He might have bounced a few more times, but he hurt his shoulder in June and ultimately went under the knife. His future forecast calls for more yo-yoing ahead.

RYAN MADSON   Bats: L   Throws: R   Born: 28-Aug-80   Age: 23

YEAR	TM	LG	AGE	G	GS	IP	H	BB	SO	HR	ERA	EQERA	EQH9	EQBB9	EQSO9	EQHR9	PERA	VORP	STF
2001	CLR	FLA	20	22	21	117.7	137	49	101	4	3.90	7.12	11.7	4.4	5.3	0.7	5.75	-18.4	13
2002	REA	EAS	21	26	26	171.3	150	53	132	11	3.20	4.63	9.0	3.3	5.4	0.9	4.51	17.0	22
2003	SWB	INT	22	26	26	157.0	157	42	138	9	3.50	4.45	8.8	2.9	6.8	0.7	4.03	19.1	36
2004	PHI	NL	23	19	15	89.7	92	36	70	10	4.50	4.73	9.3	3.2	6.3	0.9	4.74	11.2	7

Breakout: 19%   Improve: 39%   Collapse: 30%

Madson was the model of consistency at Scranton last year: From May 7 until the end of the year, his ERA never left the threes. He's also been the model of development, improving his numbers every year but one since 1998. Madson came to Triple-A featuring a fastball/curve/changeup combination—the last is his best pitch—but the team had him junk the curve and develop a slider. After two big league innings at the end of '03, Madson should get another shot in '04, and projects as the first starter in should an injury occur.

HECTOR MERCADO

Bats: L   Throws: L   Born: 29-Apr-74   Age: 30

YEAR	TM	LG	AGE	G	GS	IP	H	BB	SO	HR	ERA	EQERA	EQH9	EQBB9	EQSO9	EQHR9	PERA	VORP	STF
2001	LOU	INT	27	12	0	13.3	12	6	13	0	1.35	2.92	9.5	5.1	6.6	0.0	4.28	3.7	13
2001	CIN	NL	27	56	0	53.0	55	30	59	6	4.08	4.70	9.4	4.7	8.4	0.9	4.98	5.2	4
2002	SWB	INT	28	26	0	33.3	22	12	43	2	1.62	2.67	7.4	3.9	9.8	0.9	3.84	9.9	19
2002	PHI	NL	28	31	3	39.0	32	25	40	2	4.62	4.54	8.1	5.0	8.1	0.5	4.10	4.4	14
2003	SWB	INT	29	14	2	32.0	34	11	20	2	1.41	4.30	10.4	4.0	4.6	0.9	5.38	4.2	-19
2003	PHI	NL	29	13	0	18.7	18	12	15	5	5.78	6.50	9.0	5.0	6.5	2.5	6.77	-1.1	-52
2004	*PHI*	*NL*	*30*	*27*	*1*	*34.3*	*34*	*19*	*27*	*4*	*4.73*	*4.97*	*9.0*	*4.3*	*6.3*	*1.0*	*5.17*	*2.9*	*-7*

Breakout: 23%   Improve: 48%   Collapse: 23%

Mercado was the team's supposed long reliever, but with four starters going strong he only made 13 appearances in two-and-a-half months on the active roster. At least in Scranton he got more regular work, which wasn't nearly as good as the 1.41 ERA makes it look—not many people can manage to allow more unearned runs (7) than earned runs (5).

JOSE MESA

Bats: R   Throws: R   Born: 22-May-66   Age: 38

YEAR	TM	LG	AGE	G	GS	IP	H	BB	SO	HR	ERA	EQERA	EQH9	EQBB9	EQSO9	EQHR9	PERA	VORP	STF
2001	PHI	NL	35	71	0	69.3	65	20	59	4	2.34	3.68	8.9	2.5	6.5	0.4	3.67	14.1	16
2002	PHI	NL	36	74	0	75.7	65	39	64	5	2.97	3.72	8.3	4.1	6.7	0.6	4.08	15.2	6
2003	PHI	NL	37	61	0	58.0	71	31	45	7	6.52	6.75	11.4	4.3	6.3	1.1	6.10	-10.5	-22
2004	*PHI*	*NL*	*38*	*48*	*0*	*41.3*	*43*	*19*	*29*	*4*	*4.26*	*4.48*	*9.4*	*3.5*	*5.7*	*0.8*	*4.84*	*5.6*	*-9*

Breakout: 31%   Improve: 56%   Collapse: 26%

Philadelphia's sacrificial goat. As his nightmare season progressed, a certain contract clause—specifying an automatic renewal for 2004 if he finished 55 games—precipitated panic in Pennsylvania. By losing the closer's job in September, he only wound up finishing 47, and was quickly (one would almost say rapturously) let go at the end of the season.

KEVIN MILLWOOD

Bats: R   Throws: R   Born: 24-Dec-74   Age: 29

YEAR	TM	LG	AGE	G	GS	IP	H	BB	SO	HR	ERA	EQERA	EQH9	EQBB9	EQSO9	EQHR9	PERA	VORP	STF
2001	ATL	NL	26	21	21	121.0	121	40	84	20	4.31	5.07	9.4	2.8	5.3	1.3	4.98	6.8	-5
2002	ATL	NL	27	35	34	217.0	186	65	178	16	3.24	3.93	8.6	2.4	6.6	0.7	3.86	37.9	24
2003	PHI	NL	28	35	35	222.0	210	68	169	19	4.01	4.24	8.9	2.5	6.1	0.8	4.04	29.5	18
2004	*PHI*	*NL*	*29*	*29*	*28*	*186.0*	*185*	*58*	*137*	*21*	*4.06*	*4.27*	*8.9*	*2.5*	*6.0*	*0.9*	*4.21*	*27.0*	*12*

Breakout: 10%   Improve: 49%   Collapse: 13%

When Greg Maddux fooled the Braves by accepting salary arbitration, Braves GM John Schuerholz decided he couldn't afford both Maddux and Millwood, and pulled the trigger on one of the silliest trades in history, acquiring middling catcher prospect Johnny Estrada in return. For the Phillies, Millwood was supposed to be the final key to the championship puzzle, and looked like he might fulfill his promise when he threw a no-hitter in April. In the end, though, he was just one more good, not great, pitcher in a strong rotation. He'll be back for 2004 after accepting the team's arbitration offer just before the deadline.

BRETT MYERS

Bats: R   Throws: R   Born: 17-Aug-80   Age: 23

YEAR	TM	LG	AGE	G	GS	IP	H	BB	SO	HR	ERA	EQERA	EQH9	EQBB9	EQSO9	EQHR9	PERA	VORP	STF
2001	REA	EAS	20	26	23	156.0	156	43	130	21	3.87	5.74	9.8	3.2	5.5	1.6	5.64	-2.2	12
2002	SWB	INT	21	19	19	128.0	121	20	97	9	3.59	4.52	8.1	1.6	6.4	0.7	3.39	14.8	41
2002	PHI	NL	21	12	12	72.0	73	29	34	11	4.25	5.11	9.6	3.3	3.8	1.4	5.38	3.7	5
2003	PHI	NL	22	32	32	193.0	205	76	143	20	4.43	4.95	9.9	3.2	6.0	0.9	4.89	15.5	26
2004	*PHI*	*NL*	*23*	*26*	*25*	*159.7*	*163*	*59*	*114*	*17*	*4.22*	*4.44*	*9.2*	*2.9*	*5.8*	*0.9*	*4.51*	*20.2*	*10*

Breakout: 11%   Improve: 47%   Collapse: 16%

Young, successful pitchers are a paradox: Their ability is needed, yet their use needs to be constrained, in part because they generally don't have the stamina to pitch well for a full season, and because of the injury risks that come from pitching while tired. Myers threw 200 innings at age 21, and was on pace to throw more than that last year. But he wore out in the second half, giving up a .398 average on balls hit in play the final three months in the process. The Phils will need to control Myers's workload to get the most out of him in '04 while still preserving his future.

AARON MYETTE   Bats: R   Throws: R   Born: 26-Sep-77   Age: 26

YEAR	TM	LG	AGE	G	GS	IP	H	BB	SO	HR	ERA	EQERA	EQH9	EQBB9	EQSO9	EQHR9	PERA	VORP	STF
2001	OKL	PCL	23	12	12	70.0	64	30	76	5	3.73	4.52	8.6	4.5	7.4	0.7	4.41	7.9	28
2001	TEX	AL	23	19	15	80.7	94	37	67	12	7.14	5.71	9.5	3.7	6.8	1.1	5.05	-1.0	16
2002	OKL	PCL	24	16	16	106.0	86	44	106	5	3.14	3.51	7.6	4.2	6.8	0.5	3.72	23.2	28
2002	TEX	AL	24	15	12	48.3	64	41	48	11	10.06	8.57	11.4	6.9	8.4	1.9	7.50	-15.9	-17
2003	BUF	INT	25	23	1	33.3	33	23	25	4	4.59	6.53	9.8	7.7	5.6	1.8	7.00	-3.1	-55
2003	SWB	INT	25	11	10	59.0	50	20	54	4	4.27	4.31	8.4	3.8	6.6	1.0	4.46	7.8	7
2004	CIN	NL	26	25	14	81.7	80	46	67	12	5.31	5.58	8.9	4.4	6.6	1.1	5.37	2.5	-2

Breakout: 25%   Improve: 49%   Collapse: 22%

Some of these players give you the idea that they are just waiting until they are written off completely, and that is when they'll pull it together and make you look like an idiot. Myette has the tools, primarily a sinking fastball, to do that, and continues to look pretty good in Triple-A, so we're not going to write him off yet. At least not completely; having signed with the Reds, he's proof some leopards don't change their spots, at least when it comes to retreads.

VICENTE PADILLA   Bats: R   Throws: R   Born: 27-Sep-77   Age: 26

YEAR	TM	LG	AGE	G	GS	IP	H	BB	SO	HR	ERA	EQERA	EQH9	EQBB9	EQSO9	EQHR9	PERA	VORP	STF
2001	SWB	INT	23	16	16	81.7	64	11	75	8	2.42	3.57	8.1	1.4	6.8	1.1	3.67	17.1	28
2001	PHI	NL	23	23	0	34.0	36	12	29	1	4.24	4.73	10.0	3.1	6.7	0.3	4.22	3.1	25
2002	PHI	NL	24	32	32	206.0	198	53	128	16	3.28	3.96	9.1	2.1	4.9	0.7	4.02	35.7	20
2003	PHI	NL	25	32	32	208.7	196	62	133	22	3.62	4.24	8.8	2.4	5.1	0.9	4.19	30.7	10
2004	PHI	NL	26	25	24	154.0	158	46	99	17	4.10	4.30	9.2	2.4	5.2	0.9	4.36	22.0	8

Breakout: 14%   Improve: 44%   Collapse: 20%

Padilla didn't pitch in the Mexican winter league last year, and it paid off, as he was able to stay strong through an entire major league season. How he handles the events of this past winter—Padilla walked away from a car accident in Nicaragua that killed his best friend—is pretty much uncharted territory for a baseball analyst, and more in the wheelhouse of another type of analyst.

DAN PLESAC   Bats: L   Throws: L   Born: 04-Feb-62   Age: 42

YEAR	TM	LG	AGE	G	GS	IP	H	BB	SO	HR	ERA	EQERA	EQH9	EQBB9	EQSO9	EQHR9	PERA	VORP	STF
2001	TOR	AL	39	62	0	45.3	34	24	68	4	3.58	3.22	6.6	4.4	12.5	0.6	3.34	11.8	46
2002	TOR	AL	40	19	0	13.3	11	6	14	1	3.38	3.46	6.9	3.5	9.0	0.7	3.32	3.1	24
2002	PHI	NL	40	41	0	23.0	16	12	27	5	4.70	4.50	7.0	4.1	9.4	2.0	4.92	2.7	-12
2003	PHI	NL	41	58	0	33.3	29	11	37	3	2.70	3.66	8.4	2.8	9.0	0.8	3.97	8.1	19

There was some talk about Plesac being done after 2002, but his shakiness proved to be a blip on the radar. Plesac was effective last year—against everybody, he's not just a lefty-killer—but he is so limited in the number of batters he can face that his value is minimal, simply because he has to quickly give way to someone else. He didn't have Jesse Orosco's staying power, choosing to retire this winter, although in fairness, even though he's much more valuable than Orosco.

ELIZARDO RAMIREZ   Bats: R   Throws: R   Born: 28-Jan-83   Age: 21

YEAR	TM	LG	AGE	G	GS	IP	H	BB	SO	HR	ERA	EQERA	EQH9	EQBB9	EQSO9	EQHR9	PERA	VORP	STF
2003	CLR	FLA	20	27	25	157.3	181	33	101	4	3.78	6.77	11.4	2.4	4.1	0.7	5.13	-18.9	11
2004	PHI	NL	21	18	13	80.0	89	24	43	7	4.33	4.55	10.0	2.3	4.4	0.8	4.56	8.5	-1

Breakout: 16%   Improve: 69%   Collapse: 2%

Ramirez spent what we in the States would think of as our high school years pitching for the Phillies in the Dominican Summer League. He graduated to the Gulf Coast League at 19, and skipped a few levels to reach Clearwater at 20. Last year was the first season he'd ever had an ERA over 2 (there tend to be a lot of errors in those low leagues, which help keep ERAs down) or walked more than 10 batters. Rail-thin, he has outstanding control, but gave up 19 more hits than expected; if that turns out to be a fluke rather than a trait, his numbers could take a big leap forward in '04.

CARLOS SILVA   Bats: R   Throws: R   Born: 23-Apr-79   Age: 25

YEAR	TM	LG	AGE	G	GS	IP	H	BB	SO	HR	ERA	EQERA	EQH9	EQBB9	EQSO9	EQHR9	PERA	VORP	STF
2001	REA	EAS	22	28	28	180.0	197	27	100	20	3.90	5.82	11.4	1.8	3.4	1.5	5.94	-4.0	-11
2002	PHI	NL	23	68	0	84.0	88	22	41	4	3.21	4.07	9.8	2.1	3.8	0.5	4.11	13.5	5
2003	PHI	NL	24	62	1	87.3	92	37	48	7	4.43	4.84	9.8	3.4	4.4	0.8	4.76	8.9	-5
2004	*MIN*	*AL*	*25*	*35*	*9*	*68.0*	*79*	*22*	*37*	*8*	*4.82*	*4.71*	*10.1*	*2.8*	*4.9*	*1.0*	*4.90*	*8.4*	*-9*

Breakout: 17%   Improve: 45%   Collapse: 23%

According to the BP reliever ratings, Silva was the worst pitcher in baseball last year at handling inherited runners. He let 19 of 31 runners in, costing the Phillies 10 extra runs that wound up on somebody else's ERA. For some strange reason he was anointed with the "closer in waiting" tag, despite a strikeout rate that is well below league average. Billy Wagner's acquisition certainly made that a dead letter, and shortly thereafter he was dealt to the Twins . . . who, coincidentally enough, have a closer vacancy.

BUD SMITH   Bats: L   Throws: L   Born: 23-Oct-79   Age: 24

YEAR	TM	LG	AGE	G	GS	IP	H	BB	SO	HR	ERA	EQERA	EQH9	EQBB9	EQSO9	EQHR9	PERA	VORP	STF
2001	MEM	PCL	21	17	17	108.0	114	28	78	6	2.75	4.08	8.2	2.6	5.2	0.5	3.56	17.9	33
2001	STL	NL	21	16	14	84.7	79	24	59	12	3.83	4.59	8.9	2.4	5.4	1.1	4.38	9.0	25
2002	MEM	PCL	22	6	6	38.0	33	13	34	1	2.13	3.75	7.8	3.5	6.8	0.2	3.32	7.4	44
2002	STL	NL	22	11	10	48.0	67	22	22	4	6.94	7.49	13.4	3.7	3.5	0.8	6.52	-9.6	-6
2002	SWB	INT	22	3	3	17.3	21	6	11	0	4.16	5.40	10.8	3.8	5.4	0.0	4.51	0.4	30
2003	REA	EAS	23	8	8	37.0	40	15	24	6	5.35	6.75	11.3	4.6	4.9	2.7	8.07	-4.3	-49
2004	*PHI*	*NL*	*24*	*27*	*17*	*98.7*	*108*	*45*	*62*	*14*	*5.25*	*5.51*	*9.8*	*3.6*	*5.1*	*1.2*	*5.49*	*4.3*	*-8*

Breakout: 17%   Improve: 50%   Collapse: 29%

The prized prospect from the Scott Rolen trade, Smith tore through the Cardinal minor league system and threw a no-hitter in his rookie year. But that was 2001. His shoulder started to hurt in spring 2002, but he tried to pitch through it anyway. He got traded, already hurt, and only made three starts before his shoulder gave out completely. He was well on the road to recovery, coming off three consecutive strong starts at Reading, when he suffered another torn labrum and had his second shoulder surgery in nine months. The odds of recovery from that . . . well, they ain't good.

AMAURY TELEMACO   Bats: R   Throws: R   Born: 19-Jan-74   Age: 30

YEAR	TM	LG	AGE	G	GS	IP	H	BB	SO	HR	ERA	EQERA	EQH9	EQBB9	EQSO9	EQHR9	PERA	VORP	STF
2001	SWB	INT	27	4	4	24.7	31	6	25	4	4.01	6.14	13.9	2.9	7.4	2.0	7.91	-1.3	-27
2001	PHI	NL	27	24	14	89.3	93	32	59	15	5.54	5.67	9.6	2.9	5.0	1.4	5.16	-0.7	-16
2003	SWB	INT	29	25	24	155.3	125	22	116	15	3.25	3.53	8.3	1.6	5.4	1.4	4.16	32.8	0
2003	PHI	NL	29	8	8	45.3	41	11	29	5	3.97	4.15	8.3	2.1	5.2	1.0	3.96	5.0	7
2004	*PHI*	*NL*	*30*	*24*	*12*	*73.0*	*77*	*20*	*49*	*10*	*4.40*	*4.62*	*9.4*	*2.2*	*5.5*	*1.1*	*4.52*	*8.5*	*0*

Breakout: 16%   Improve: 44%   Collapse: 28%

Shoulder surgery, or the year off (see Dave Coggin's 2003 for an idea of what Telemaco's 2002 was like), seems to have agreed with Telemaco, who hasn't had a season like this since . . . well, maybe Orlando in '95. Anyway, his control was outstanding, enabling him to get by with sub-standard raw stuff, and he finally gave the Phils a credible fifth starter, though too late to save the season. With Kevin Millwood accepting arbitration, Eric Milton acquired via trade, and Ryan Madson knocking on the door, Telemaco will need to take a number.

TURK WENDELL   Bats: L   Throws: R   Born: 19-May-67   Age: 37

YEAR	TM	LG	AGE	G	GS	IP	H	BB	SO	HR	ERA	EQERA	EQH9	EQBB9	EQSO9	EQHR9	PERA	VORP	STF
2001	NYM	NL	34	49	0	51.3	42	22	41	8	3.51	4.20	7.5	3.6	6.0	1.3	4.27	7.7	-11
2001	PHI	NL	34	21	0	15.7	21	12	15	4	7.45	8.22	12.3	6.5	7.0	1.8	7.74	-4.5	-47
2003	PHI	NL	36	56	0	64.0	54	28	27	6	3.38	3.82	7.8	3.5	3.4	0.9	4.01	14.6	-17
2004	*COL*	*NL*	*37*	*44*	*0*	*46.3*	*48*	*20*	*25*	*7*	*4.60*	*4.35*	*9.2*	*3.5*	*4.5*	*1.0*	*4.81*	*6.5*	*-15*

Breakout: 40%   Improve: 63%   Collapse: 13%

The Phillies finally managed to squeeze one productive year out of the three-year, $9.4 million mega-deal they committed to when they traded for Wendell. More accurately, they got an outstanding half-season (Wendell had an 0.67 ERA through the first three months) and a pedestrian half-season (5.35 in the last three months). Now that he's in Colorado, we hope he enjoys trying to add to his famed necklace of animal bits; it's only fair, since he'll get to spend his time on the mound as the hunted.

MIKE WILLIAMS										Bats: R		Throws: R					Born: 29-Jul-68		Age: 35
YEAR	TM	LG	AGE	G	GS	IP	H	BB	SO	HR	ERA	EQERA	EQH9	EQBB9	EQSO9	EQHR9	PERA	VORP	STF
2001	HOU	NL	32	25	0	22.3	21	14	16	3	4.04	4.57	8.3	5.0	5.4	1.2	5.02	2.5	-23
2001	PIT	NL	32	40	0	41.7	39	21	43	6	3.67	4.02	8.7	4.2	7.8	1.1	4.80	7.1	0
2002	PIT	NL	33	59	0	61.3	54	21	43	6	2.94	3.81	8.1	2.7	5.5	0.9	3.92	11.7	-2
2003	PIT	NL	34	40	0	37.3	42	22	20	5	6.27	5.94	10.2	4.7	4.2	1.2	5.81	-2.4	-36
2003	PHI	NL	34	28	0	25.7	24	19	19	0	5.95	5.47	9.1	6.2	5.8	0.4	4.79	-3.1	-7
2004	TBY	AL	35	48	0	41.0	44	21	25	5	5.12	5.10	9.3	4.3	5.5	1.0	5.03	3.7	-14

Breakout: 22%   Improve: 50%   Collapse: 31%

You have to wonder what Bizarro world the Phillies were playing in last season, when they apparently thought that acquiring the one closer in the league doing a worse job then Jose Mesa was a good idea. Williams is a one-pitch pitcher: If he can't throw his slider for strikes—and in 2003 he couldn't—then he's got about as much chance at outfoxing the opposition as Wile E. Coyote. Naturally, he makes an appropriate well-seasoned addition to Piniella's leathery-necks.

RANDY WOLF										Bats: L		Throws: L					Born: 22-Aug-76		Age: 27
YEAR	TM	LG	AGE	G	GS	IP	H	BB	SO	HR	ERA	EQERA	EQH9	EQBB9	EQSO9	EQHR9	PERA	VORP	STF
2001	PHI	NL	24	28	25	163.0	150	51	152	15	3.70	4.10	8.7	2.6	7.2	0.8	3.95	25.9	33
2002	PHI	NL	25	31	31	210.7	172	63	172	23	3.20	3.59	7.9	2.4	6.5	1.0	3.81	44.7	20
2003	PHI	NL	26	33	33	200.0	176	78	177	27	4.23	4.55	8.3	3.2	7.1	1.2	4.43	17.8	11
2004	PHI	NL	27	29	28	186.7	173	64	157	21	3.82	4.01	8.3	2.7	6.8	1.0	4.03	33.5	17

Breakout: 22%   Improve: 58%   Collapse: 16%

On July 23 last year, Wolf was staring at the possibility of a Cy Young award, sitting at 11–5 with a 3.07 ERA. He threw a four-hit shutout against the Cubs that day, striking out 13 while throwing 132 pitches—well above his 99 pitch per game average. In his next six starts, he allowed 33 runs in 30 innings; for the rest of the season, his ERA was 6.61. Was it worth the shutout?

Pittsburgh Pirates

There's a BP legend that has one of the group's members, upon being introduced to Dave Littlefield, commending him for his work with the "Superfund site" he inherited from Cam Bonifay.

Nearly three years into the cleanup of that site, it's an open question whether Littlefield is ever going to be able to construct anything of value on the land. While the Pirates are finally free of the most ridiculous elements of the Bonifay era, and play in the best of the 21st-century ballparks, the team in place still doesn't seem anywhere close to ready to contend in a division that is ripe for the taking.

The problems don't entirely stem from Littlefield's work, although as the GM, he bears ultimate responsibility. Pirates owner Kevin McClatchy has forced a raft of questionable decisions, including last summer's trade of Brian Giles and the selection of Bryan Bullington over B. J. Upton with the first pick of the 2002 draft. Littlefield's player-development staff lost almost an entire lineup to waivers and the Rule 5 draft over this past winter.

Littlefield has shown a knack for acquiring mid-level talent, both in trades and in the free-agent market. Two years ago, he brought in Pokey Reese to play second base, and was rewarded with one of Reese's best seasons. He's put together competitive bullpens from spare parts such as Mike Fetters, Mike Lincoln and Julian Tavarez. Last year, he assembled an entire starting outfield from low-demand free agents. Kenny Lofton, Reggie Sanders, and Matt Stairs combined to hit .284/.355/.525 with 66 home runs in 1,097 at-bats for the Pirates last year, while making less than $3 million.

Filling holes with inexpensive talent is an important skill for a GM. Every year, teams fall short of the postseason for lack of league-average performance at some positions. Littlefield deserves credit for mining the secondary talent markets for useful players, and in some cases, for flipping those veterans to contenders for prospects. Few GMs have done as well as Littlefield has in filling holes with good players.

The problem for Littlefield is that success in baseball is driven by superstar talent. Teams that lack guys capable of being worth seven to nine wins above replacement in a typical season need everything to go right, everyone to stay healthy, and few players to fall below replacement level. Now, this can happen—the championships won in recent years by the Angels and Marlins, two teams lacking high-

PIRATES PROSPECTUS

2003 record: 75–87; Fourth place, NL Central

Pythagenport record: 76–86

Runs scored per game: 4.6 (7th in NL)

Runs allowed per game: 4.9 (11th in NL)

Team EqA: .263 (6th in NL)

2003 Batters Age: 30.1 (7th youngest in NL)

2003 Pitchers Age: 28.4 (8th oldest in NL)

Ballpark: PNC Park; Neutral park; Park Factor of 1.009

2003: The Pirates got fine work from outfield temps, but traded keystone outfielder Brian Giles instead.

2004: The pitching staff is a mess, the position players are mediocre, and management can't be counted on.

profile superstars, argue in favor of it—but it's an unsure route to a title. Great teams tend to have a core of great players, with the long runs of the Yankees and Braves the best recent examples.

Littlefield certainly didn't inherit that kind of talent. The Pirates' farm system hasn't produced that kind of player since Jason Kendall made his debut in 1996. Kris Benson, the #1 overall pick in 1996 who carried the expectations of being this team's Mark Prior, has made just 106 career starts with an ERA of 4.27. Aramis Ramirez had one good year before being traded to the Cubs last summer. Brian Giles was the Pirates' superstar from 1999 until August of last year, when he was traded to the Padres.

The Pirates haven't traded for superstars, or prospects with that kind of potential. The guys Littlefield picked up in 2003—Freddy Sanchez, Bobby Hill, Ray Sadler, Jason Bay, Oliver Perez, Cory Stewart—are mostly older prospects with the potential to be above-average players. The additional revenue the Pirates generated in PNC Park hasn't been enough to convince them to compete for that kind of free agent.

More critically, the Pirates' approach in the draft hasn't lent itself to acquiring that caliber of player. The Pirates have spent their last five #1 picks on pitchers, the last three on college pitchers. While the last four choices rank among the top prospects in their system, and all will likely make the major leagues, only one of them has a superstar, #1 starter upside. Sean Burnett had the best '03 of the group, but his lack of a fastball and steadily declining strikeout rates raise serious questions about his ability to succeed at upper levels. Of the other three, John Van-Benschoten is the best, the one guy who might be a franchise pitcher. Paul Maholm and Bryan Bullington are mid-rotation guys, not staff aces, and they're the team's last two #1 picks.

The key moment of the last few seasons was the decision, heavily influenced by Kevin McClatchy, to select Ball State's Bullington with the first pick of the 2002 draft. Bullington wasn't a pure signability pick as much as he reflected a preference for risk avoidance, as opposed to Virginia high school shortstop B. J. Upton. The Devil Rays, drafting second, snatched Upton and now have one of the top prospects in baseball, a potential franchise player. Meanwhile, Bullington's unimpressive 2003 performance raised questions about his development and his eventual role in the majors. We've left him out of our Top 50 Prospects, a scathing indictment of a player who was the #1 pick just 20 months ago.

While the decision hasn't turned out well, that's not why it deserves criticism. With a rare chance to acquire a franchise player, to add high-upside talent to a system sorely lacking in just that, the Pirates elected the safe route. Perhaps the risk would be mitigated, but the chance that the team would find the best player on its next championship team was eliminated. That's bad baseball for a team that doesn't try to acquire great players in trade or as free agents, and pulls the sackcloth-and-ashes routine at nearly every opportunity.

How important is it to find superstars through the draft? Table 1 shows the Top 25 players in Value Over Replacement Player in 2003, more or less the top 25 players in baseball last year. As you can tell, you either need to have lots of money to spend, or be able to draft and develop these guys in-house. They don't often get traded.

The Pirates' inability to find great players in the draft keeps them from making the most of Littlefield's skill at filling holes with good players. It's one thing to emphasize short-to-the-majors college pitching when you're on the brink of contention and you have a lineup in place: Getting college starters who can reach the majors quickly is one of the most effective ways of adding a competitive pitching staff to a championship-caliber lineup, and it's a strategy you may see the Blue Jays implement this year—we already know about the success the A's had with their late-'90s drafts. It's the wrong strategy for Pittsburgh, given the team's lack of top-flight talent.

The Pirates' questionable draft practices may mean that Littlefield, despite showing some aptitude for the GM role, may have to wait until his next job to see the fruits of his work. Pittsburgh just doesn't have the star talent in the

TABLE 1. TOP 25 PLAYERS BY VORP, 2003

Player	Team	VORP	Acquired
Barry Bonds	Giants	114.6	Free agent
Albert Pujols	Cardinals	97.3	Drafted
Alex Rodriguez	Rangers	86.3	Free agent
Gary Sheffield	Braves	78.9	Acquired via trade
Javy Lopez	Braves	75.9	Amateur free agent
Bret Boone	Mariners	75.8	Free agent
Esteban Loaiza	White Sox	74.7	Free agent
Carlos Delgado	Blue Jays	72.2	Amateur free agent
Pedro Martinez	Red Sox	71.9	Acquired via trade
Tim Hudson	A's	69.5	Drafted
Jason Schmidt	Giants	69.3	Acquired via trade
Manny Ramirez	Red Sox	69.2	Free agent
Roy Halladay	Blue Jays	66.8	Drafted
Marcus Giles	Braves	64.7	Drafted
Mark Prior	Cubs	64.1	Drafted
Edgar Renteria	Cardinals	63.3	Acquired via trade
Todd Helton	Rockies	62.5	Drafted
Vernon Wells	Blue Jays	62.3	Drafted
Kevin Brown	Dodgers	60.2	Free agent
Bill Mueller	Red Sox	60.1	Free agent
Frank Thomas	White Sox	59.2	Drafted
Alfonso Soriano	Yankees	59.2	Signed from Japan
Edgar Martinez	Mariners	58.3	Amateur free agent
Nomar Garciaparra	Red Sox	58.3	Drafted
Dmitri Young	Tigers	58.3	Acquired via trade

organization that allows you to look ahead three years and see a champion. The Pirates of the next few years will be good enough to reach .500, maybe pass it and be in a Wild Card race. But the lack of a true superstar will limit their potential. Watching B. J. Upton become that player won't make the mediocrity any easier to swallow.

In the short term, the Pirates have another player-development problem: They were brutalized in December's Rule 5 draft. In fact, from the time 40-man rosters were set in November through the end of the draft, the Pirates lost nine members of their farm system, including five players among the first six selections in the Rule 5.

In some cases, this doesn't hurt all that much. Walter Young, lost on waivers to the Orioles, is a fun player to watch, but he's not likely to be another Cecil Fielder. Rich Thompson, the second pick in the Rule 5 draft, is a fast outfielder who looks more like Kerry Robinson than anything else. But the Pirates also lost A-ball masher Chris Shelton, who has a reasonable chance to become an offensive threat as a #2 catcher this year. Jose Bautista, a top prospect whose 2003 was lost to a self-inflicted broken hand, might well navigate the two-level jump to become the Orioles' third baseman. Frank Brooks, who the Pirates had acquired just months before in exchange for Mike Williams, is ready to be a swingman, although he will have trouble sticking with the A's and their revamped bullpen.

It would be one thing if the Pirates lost all these players because they had a surfeit of talent on their 40-man roster. They don't. Their roster as of December 15 included replaceable "talent" such as utility men Abraham Nunez and Rob Mackowiak and low-leverage relievers Joe Beimel and Mark Corey. That's terrible decision-making; guys like that have established themselves as minor contributors, players who can be replaced—especially by Littlefield—in the market. To give up on the upside of players like Shelton and Bautista in favor of Jason Boyd and Humberto Cota is inexplicable.

The most egregious example is Mike Lincoln. The 29-year-old right-hander with a career ERA of 5.16 was protected by the Pirates, then non-tendered less than one week later. That's a spot that could have been used on a Shelton or a Bautista, and was effectively used on air. That's a terrible waste.

In the aftermath of the draft, blame was spread among Littlefield and farm director Brian Graham, with much attention focused on the fact that the Pirates went into the draft with just 37 of the slots on their 40-man filled. To a certain extent, the loss of talent reflects a farm system that is deep in B and C prospects, which is a credit to Graham and the entire Pirates' player-development staff.

However, the decisions made in assembling a 40-man roster showed a lack of understanding of what is valuable in a baseball player to a team trying to build something. Upside matters. Potential matters. Certainty—especially the certainty of mediocre performance with little chance of growth—is something that can be sacrificed. Would the Pirates be worse off today with a roster that included Shelton and Bautista and Brooks, but lacked the waiver bait listed above? Of course not; sixth relievers and third catchers are available for the asking, and if there's any GM that has shown himself capable of adequately replacing the Carlos Riveras of the world, it's Littlefield.

By mid-summer, the fiasco that was the Rule 5 draft will probably be forgotten. The thought process behind it, however, the one that doesn't adequately balance risk and reward, will remain in place.

HITTERS

TONY ALVAREZ   OF   Bats: R   Throws: R   Born: 10-May-78   Age: 26

YEAR	TM	LG	AGE	AB	H	2B	3B	HR	BB	SO	SB	CS	AVG	OBP	SLG	MLVR	EQBA	EQOBP	EQSLG	EQMLVR	VORP	DEFENSE			
2001	LYN	CAR	23	93	32	4	0	2	7	11	7	3	.344	.390	.452	.280	.281	.324	.375	-.113	-1.7	18-LF	-5		
2001	ALT	EAS	23	254	81	16	1	6	9	30	17	11	.319	.359	.461	.214	.288	.325	.419	-.042	1.0	38-LF	-1	24-CF	-2
2002	ALT	EAS	24	507	161	37	1	15	27	71	29	18	.318	.361	.483	.229	.279	.315	.435	-.045	15.7	109-CF	-12	13-LF	-1
2002	PIT	NL	24	26	8	2	0	1	3	5	1	0	.308	.379	.500	.240	.308	.379	.500	.188	2.3				
2003	NAS	PCL	25	349	104	27	3	9	28	69	22	9	.298	.361	.470	.186	.278	.339	.448	.016	7.6	47-LF	1	25-CF	-1
2004	*PIT*	*NL*	*26*	*242*	*64*	*15*	*2*	*7*	*18*	*45*	*9*	*3*	*.264*	*.324*	*.422*	*-.043*	*.266*	*.325*	*.438*	*-.032*	*9.1*	*66-CF*	*-7*		

Breakout: 20%   *Improve: 52%*   *Collapse: 34%*

Alvarez didn't lose much in the jump to Triple-A. He was, however, probably the biggest loser in the Brian Giles trade, as the Pirates picked up a player superior in many ways in Jason Bay. With the improvement of J. J. Davis and Chris Duffy, his path to a job looks increasingly crowded. A one-week suspension in July for failing "to conform to the personal conduct standards" of his contract didn't help his cause. At this point, he's an extra outfielder on a team with better options all around, and needs a trade to have a career.

JOHN BARNES   LF   Bats: R   Throws: R   Born: 24-Apr-76   Age: 28

YEAR	TM	LG	AGE	AB	H	2B	3B	HR	BB	SO	SB	CS	AVG	OBP	SLG	MLVR	EQBA	EQOBP	EQSLG	EQMLVR	VORP	DEFENSE			
2001	EDM	PCL	25	311	91	21	2	8	27	28	3	2	.293	.368	.450	.078	.258	.328	.400	-.087	-2.0	35-RF	-2	28-LF	-3
2001	MIN	AL	25	21	1	0	0	0	1	3	0	0	.048	.130	.048	-.973	.095	.165	.095	-.905	-4.1				
2002	CSP	PCL	26	269	77	20	2	6	18	16	5	4	.286	.340	.442	.005	.242	.291	.377	-.201	-4.2	50-CF	-3		
2003	NAS	PCL	27	402	130	32	2	13	28	41	15	7	.323	.369	.510	.284	.300	.347	.484	.102	19.1	71-LF	-1		
2004	*PIT*	*NL*	*28*	*195*	*51*	*12*	*1*	*5*	*15*	*24*	*4*	*2*	*.264*	*.324*	*.414*	*-.053*	*.267*	*.325*	*.429*	*-.043*	*5.4*	*54-LF*	*0*		

Breakout: 22%   *Improve: 41%*   *Collapse: 37%*

Barnes reached Triple-A in 2000 and has a career line at that level of .323/.379/.501. Despite that, he has just 58 major-league at-bats, all with the Twins. Barnes doesn't walk a ton, and as a right-handed hitter, occupies the wrong side of a platoon. Regardless, he'd be a useful fourth outfielder for most teams in baseball, and could probably start for a few clubs. The Pirates, with their glut of outfielders, aren't one of them.

JOSE BAUTISTA   3B   Bats: R   Throws: R   Born: 19-Oct-80   Age: 23

YEAR	TM	LG	AGE	AB	H	2B	3B	HR	BB	SO	SB	CS	AVG	OBP	SLG	MLVR	EQBA	EQOBP	EQSLG	EQMLVR	VORP	DEFENSE
2001	WPT	NYP	20	220	63	10	3	5	21	41	8	1	.286	.364	.427	.192	.218	.271	.341	-.306	-16.5	56-3B -14
2002	HIC	SAL	21	438	132	26	3	14	67	104	3	2	.301	.402	.470	.263	.215	.292	.345	-.261	-11.6	118-3B -17
2003	LYN	CAR	22	165	40	14	2	4	27	48	1	5	.242	.359	.424	.096	.182	.274	.324	-.344	-9.5	44-3B 0
2004	*BAL*	*AL*	*23*	*193*	*42*	*10*	*1*	*5*	*18*	*50*	*1*	*1*	*.218*	*.292*	*.361*	*-.194*	*.226*	*.303*	*.378*	*-.177*	*2.4*	*55-3B -6*

Breakout: 44%   *Improve: 67%*   *Collapse: 18%*

We can project, predict, PECOTA and pronounce, but we can't know when a promising young man is going to lose his temper and a battle with a solid object. The one-round knockout by garbage can cost Bautista most of the year to a broken hand, kept him out of Double-A, and dropped him from prospect lists. He has excellent secondary skills for a player his age, good enough to move to an outfield corner—he messed around with it in winter ball—and still have a career. Another of the Pirates lost on Rule 5 Black Monday, Bautista will have an outside chance to win the Orioles' third-base job.

JASON BAY   OF   Bats: R   Throws: R   Born: 20-Sep-78   Age: 25

YEAR	TM	LG	AGE	AB	H	2B	3B	HR	BB	SO	SB	CS	AVG	OBP	SLG	MLVR	EQBA	EQOBP	EQSLG	EQMLVR	VORP	DEFENSE		
2001	CLN	MID	22	318	115	20	4	13	48	62	15	2	.362	.449	.572	.501	.255	.328	.411	-.074	-1.0	78-RF 10		
2001	JUP	FLA	22	123	24	4	1	1	18	26	10	3	.195	.306	.268	-.172	.172	.253	.242	-.501	-17.9	36-RF -1		
2002	SLU	FLA	23	261	71	12	2	9	34	54	22	2	.272	.363	.437	.159	.226	.297	.370	-.210	-13.0	45-LF -7	10-RF -2
2002	BIN	EAS	23	107	31	4	2	4	15	23	13	3	.290	.383	.477	.186	.241	.326	.398	-.106	-1.4	18-RF -2		
2002	MOB	SOU	23	81	25	5	2	4	13	22	4	2	.309	.411	.568	.404	.253	.337	.470	.022	3.9			
2003	POR	PCL	24	307	93	11	1	20	55	71	23	4	.303	.410	.541	.351	.271	.373	.490	.128	27.2	47-CF -2	37-RF -1
2003	PIT	NL	24	79	23	6	1	3	18	28	3	1	.291	.423	.506	.282	.287	.418	.500	.233	7.3	16-LF -1		
2004	*PIT*	*NL*	*25*	*298*	*77*	*16*	*2*	*12*	*37*	*69*	*10*	*3*	*.258*	*.348*	*.449*	*.028*	*.261*	*.349*	*.465*	*.040*	*13.7*	*83-RF -1*		

Breakout: 22%   *Improve: 53%*   *Collapse: 22%*

Comparisons to Brian Giles and other players who are much better than Bay are silly, but he's going to be a good one, comparable to Rusty Greer, or to Bobby Higginson's median years. Like those players, Bay can play center field but is an actual asset on a corner. He showed virtually no platoon split at Triple-A or in the majors, just another reason to like him. Shoulder surgery in November to repair a torn right labrum could delay the start of his 2004 season.

JOSH BONIFAY   LF   Bats: R   Throws: R   Born: 30-Jul-78   Age: 25

YEAR	TM	LG	AGE	AB	H	2B	3B	HR	BB	SO	SB	CS	AVG	OBP	SLG	MLVR	EQBA	EQOBP	EQSLG	EQMLVR	VORP	DEFENSE		
2001	HIC	SAL	22	65	21	4	0	2	5	15	2	3	.323	.380	.477	.282	.239	.286	.373	-.219	-1.9			
2001	LYN	CAR	22	323	96	14	1	13	26	87	5	4	.297	.355	.467	.217	.240	.290	.390	-.186	-13.6	51-LF -5	12-2B -4
2002	LYN	CAR	23	463	142	36	1	26	63	97	3	3	.307	.388	.557	.352	.228	.302	.425	-.124	7.5	75-2B -15	20-LF -1
2003	ALT	EAS	24	386	110	30	0	11	39	106	1	4	.285	.348	.448	.130	.245	.301	.401	-.146	-11.1	92-LF -6		
2004	*PIT*	*NL*	*25*	*159*	*38*	*8*	*1*	*7*	*14*	*44*	*1*	*1*	*.237*	*.301*	*.420*	*-.104*	*.239*	*.302*	*.435*	*-.096*	*2.1*	*45-LF -2*		

Breakout: 36%   *Improve: 55%*   *Collapse: 33%*

Bonifay, who graduated from nepotista to semi-prospect in 2002, didn't hold his gains in 2003 while making the jump to Double-A. It now appears that his performance in the Carolina League was more the result of his age (24) than his growth as a player. The attempt to make him a second baseman didn't take, leaving him an old outfield prospect in an organization with younger, better ones.

JOSE CASTILLO   SS/2B   Bats: R   Throws: R   Born: 19-Mar-81   Age: 23

YEAR	TM	LG	AGE	AB	H	2B	3B	HR	BB	SO	SB	CS	AVG	OBP	SLG	MLVR	EQBA	EQOBP	EQSLG	EQMLVR	VORP	DEFENSE	
2001	LYN	CAR	20	485	119	20	7	7	21	94	23	10	.245	.288	.359	-.042	.209	.245	.320	-.392	-28.4	117-SS -2	
2002	LYN	CAR	21	503	151	25	2	16	49	95	27	14	.300	.370	.453	.189	.233	.293	.367	-.218	-2.3	129-SS 9	
2003	ALT	EAS	22	498	143	24	6	5	40	81	19	10	.287	.339	.390	.035	.252	.301	.352	-.211	-5.4	71-2B -10	52-SS -1
2004	*PIT*	*NL*	*23*	*253*	*62*	*13*	*2*	*5*	*19*	*48*	*6*	*2*	*.244*	*.304*	*.367*	*-.164*	*.247*	*.305*	*.380*	*-.158*	*5.4*	*69-SS -7*	

Breakout: 37%   *Improve: 55%*   *Collapse: 21%*

After starting slowly, Castillo came on strong in the second half to at least approach the 2002 performance that launched him onto prospect lists. He also moved from shortstop to second base at mid-season, and may end up at third before reaching the major leagues. His bat may not support that move, and he's been adept enough defensively to not force a shift. The Pirates' loss of Bautista in the Rule 5 draft increases the chance that Castillo will slide across the diamond anyway.

J. J. DAVIS   RF   Bats: R   Throws: R   Born: 25-Oct-78   Age: 25

YEAR	TM	LG	AGE	AB	H	2B	3B	HR	BB	SO	SB	CS	AVG	OBP	SLG	MLVR	EQBA	EQOBP	EQSLG	EQMLVR	VORP	DEFENSE
2001	ALT	EAS	22	228	57	13	3	4	21	79	2	5	.250	.317	.386	-.006	.221	.283	.345	-.275	-15.2	60-RF -6
2002	ALT	EAS	23	348	100	17	3	20	33	101	7	4	.287	.351	.526	.244	.248	.302	.462	-.056	1.0	98-RF -8
2003	NAS	PCL	24	426	121	29	4	26	35	85	23	6	.284	.342	.554	.261	.262	.319	.520	.068	17.4	105-RF -5
2003	PIT	NL	24	35	7	0	0	1	3	13	0	1	.200	.263	.286	-.340	.200	.263	.286	-.408	-2.7	
2004	PIT	NL	25	272	68	16	2	12	24	69	7	3	.252	.315	.453	-.026	.254	.315	.470	-.015	8.0	73-RF -2

Breakout: 30%   Improve: 55%   Collapse: 20%

Having finally accepted the idea that he wasn't returning to the mound—he pitched successfully as an amateur—Davis had his best year as a pro. He's still more tools than anything else, but he applied those tools by stealing 23 bases while posting the best strikeout-to-walk ratio and power numbers of his career. He's the Pirates' outfield prospect with the highest upside, and a darkhorse pick for NL Rookie of the Year.

RYAN DOUMIT   C   Bats: B   Throws: R   Born: 03-Apr-81   Age: 23

YEAR	TM	LG	AGE	AB	H	2B	3B	HR	BB	SO	SB	CS	AVG	OBP	SLG	MLVR	EQBA	EQOBP	EQSLG	EQMLVR	VORP	DEFENSE
2001	HIC	SAL	20	148	40	6	0	2	10	32	2	1	.270	.333	.351	.025	.217	.264	.289	-.393	-10.2	22-C -3
2002	HIC	SAL	21	258	83	14	1	6	18	40	3	5	.322	.377	.453	.227	.249	.293	.364	-.211	-3.0	28-C -8
2003	LYN	CAR	22	458	126	38	1	11	45	79	4	0	.275	.351	.434	.122	.217	.279	.357	-.269	-14.5	82-C -10
2004	PIT	NL	23	245	55	12	1	5	19	50	2	1	.226	.292	.351	-.219	.228	.292	.364	-.214	-1.5	67-C -12

Breakout: 26%   Improve: 51%   Collapse: 22%

Finally free of the back problems that held him to a total of 114 games the previous two seasons, Doumit not only hit well but showed that he can hold up as a catcher. His defense still needs work, but there's no talk of moving him out from behind the plate—the Pirates are optimistic that he can learn to harness what is a very good arm. How he handles Double-A this year will tell us whether he's got a shot at a Jorge Posada career path.

CHRIS DUFFY   OF   Bats: L   Throws: L   Born: 20-Apr-80   Age: 24

YEAR	TM	LG	AGE	AB	H	2B	3B	HR	BB	SO	SB	CS	AVG	OBP	SLG	MLVR	EQBA	EQOBP	EQSLG	EQMLVR	VORP	DEFENSE
2001	WPT	NYP	21	221	70	12	4	1	33	33	30	5	.317	.440	.421	.305	.239	.323	.325	-.213	-9.1	55-CF -4
2002	LYN	CAR	22	539	162	27	5	10	33	101	22	7	.301	.353	.425	.129	.247	.288	.363	-.223	-12.2	126-CF -7
2003	ALT	EAS	23	494	135	23	6	1	44	78	34	12	.273	.355	.350	-.003	.246	.311	.322	-.237	-13.7	134-CF -7
2004	PIT	NL	24	239	60	12	2	3	19	44	8	3	.253	.319	.357	-.146	.255	.320	.370	-.139	-1.0	66-CF -5

Breakout: 33%   Improve: 57%   Collapse: 14%

Duffy was one of the most impressive players in the Arizona Fall League, hitting .348/.416/.438 and playing a good right field. Compared favorably to a young Lenny Dykstra, Duffy isn't likely to develop the power Dykstra eventually did. His plate discipline was much improved at Double-A, and while he showed less power, he turned on balls very well in the AFL. We'd still like to see higher walk totals over a full season, but Duffy could soon become a viable leadoff option for the Pirates.

JOSE HERNANDEZ   SS/3B   Bats: R   Throws: R   Born: 14-Jul-69   Age: 34

YEAR	TM	LG	AGE	AB	H	2B	3B	HR	BB	SO	SB	CS	AVG	OBP	SLG	MLVR	EQBA	EQOBP	EQSLG	EQMLVR	VORP	DEFENSE
2001	MIL	NL	31	542	135	26	2	25	39	185	5	4	.249	.300	.443	-.075	.252	.303	.447	-.072	19.5	143-SS 0
2002	MIL	NL	32	525	151	24	2	24	52	188	3	5	.288	.356	.478	.161	.292	.357	.494	.126	46.7	147-SS 15
2003	COL	NL	33	257	61	6	1	8	27	95	1	1	.237	.308	.362	-.201	.223	.297	.344	-.248	-3.2	62-SS 3
2003	CHC	NL	33	69	13	3	1	2	3	26	0	0	.188	.222	.348	-.323	.200	.233	.371	-.350	-3.1	12-3B 2
2003	PIT	NL	33	193	43	9	1	3	16	56	1	0	.223	.282	.326	-.240	.231	.288	.338	-.269	-5.1	54-3B 2
2004	PIT	NL	34	339	79	15	2	11	33	117	2	1	.233	.303	.381	-.155	.235	.304	.395	-.148	5.0	90-SS 0

Breakout: 26%   Improve: 40%   Collapse: 33%

One of the game's best bargains for the Brewers in 2002, Hernandez was a huge disappointment in 2003. His power was supposed to be a great fit for Coors Field, but he struck out 26 times in 69 at-bats as a Rockie, posting a 570 OPS. Traded first to the Cubs, then to the Pirates, he got a little better at each stop. Had the season been 14 months long, he might have had a killer final 150 at-bats in Madrid. A free agent nobody seems to covet, a status Hernandez is used to.

BOBBY HILL — 2B — Bats: B — Throws: R — Born: 03-Apr-78 — Age: 26

YEAR	TM	LG	AGE	AB	H	2B	3B	HR	BB	SO	SB	CS	AVG	OBP	SLG	MLVR	EQBA	EQOBP	EQSLG	EQMLVR	VORP	DEFENSE	
2001	WTN	SOU	23	209	63	8	1	3	32	39	20	8	.301	.396	.392	.147	.258	.340	.341	-.146	2.1	50-2B -1	
2002	IOW	PCL	24	354	99	23	3	8	49	66	29	5	.280	.382	.429	.106	.254	.343	.391	-.075	11.1	88-2B -2	
2002	CHC	NL	24	190	48	7	2	4	17	42	6	1	.253	.327	.374	-.041	.268	.335	.397	-.071	5.2	45-2B 0	
2003	IOW	PCL	25	361	104	23	4	6	37	65	8	7	.288	.365	.424	.086	.257	.330	.387	-.102	8.1	83-2B -10	
2003	NAS	PCL	25	66	11	2	1	1	8	8	1	2	.167	.257	.273	-.364	.164	.243	.269	-.489	-6.6	16-2B -2	
2004	PIT	NL	26	249	62	13	2	4	25	47	6	2	.248	.324	.368	-.126	.251	.324	.381	-.118	8.5	69-2B -4	

Breakout: 26%   Improve: 46%   Collapse: 33%

The PTBNL in the Aramis Ramirez/Kenny Lofton trade, Hill had his season ended by a back injury not long after being called up by the Pirates. He's been dogged by the kind of vague attitude questions that can ruin a career, and by not keeping the Cubs' second-base job last spring, crossed the line from prospect to suspect. This March, he'll battle Freddy Sanchez for the Pirates' second-base job, and while the two players would have comparable value over a full season, a direct comparison in the spring isn't likely to go well for Hill. Sanchez is the type of player who makes a better visual impression, hitting line drives and putting the ball in play. Hill's strength is plate discipline, and walks don't play as well as singles in a job fight.

J. R. HOUSE — C — Bats: R — Throws: R — Born: 11-Nov-79 — Age: 24

YEAR	TM	LG	AGE	AB	H	2B	3B	HR	BB	SO	SB	CS	AVG	OBP	SLG	MLVR	EQBA	EQOBP	EQSLG	EQMLVR	VORP	DEFENSE	
2001	ALT	EAS	21	426	110	25	1	11	37	103	1	1	.258	.323	.399	.027	.232	.292	.364	-.224	-6.9	88-C -10	11-1B -1
2002	ALT	EAS	22	91	24	6	0	2	13	21	0	0	.264	.349	.396	.044	.234	.308	.351	-.210	-1.1	20-C 0	
2003	ALT	EAS	23	63	21	6	0	2	5	11	0	0	.333	.382	.524	.336	.281	.324	.469	.022	2.9		
2004	PIT	NL	24	202	49	11	0	6	18	42	0	1	.241	.309	.387	-.132	.243	.309	.401	-.125	2.6	56-C -5	

Breakout: 18%   Improve: 36%   Collapse: 39%

House has fewer than 300 plate appearances over the past two years, the sad result of two abdominal surgeries and Tommy John surgery on his right elbow. Starting his 2003 season late, he hit fairly well at two levels and in the Arizona Fall League (.338/.386/.730). He's not regarded as anything special behind the plate, so he'll have to keep hitting well to avoid the fate of Craig Wilson. He's playing for his future in 2004.

ADAM HYZDU — OF — Bats: R — Throws: R — Born: 06-Dec-71 — Age: 32

YEAR	TM	LG	AGE	AB	H	2B	3B	HR	BB	SO	SB	CS	AVG	OBP	SLG	MLVR	EQBA	EQOBP	EQSLG	EQMLVR	VORP	DEFENSE	
2001	NAS	PCL	29	261	76	17	2	11	17	68	1	3	.291	.332	.498	.114	.263	.306	.454	-.047	1.4	34-RF 5	24-LF 2
2001	PIT	NL	29	72	15	1	0	5	4	18	0	1	.208	.260	.431	-.202	.219	.258	.438	-.194	-1.4		
2002	NAS	PCL	30	243	59	17	0	10	29	59	1	2	.243	.318	.436	-.009	.223	.294	.401	-.176	-8.4	49-RF -3	
2002	PIT	NL	30	155	36	6	0	11	21	44	0	0	.232	.324	.484	.067	.236	.325	.497	.022	7.4	27-CF -1	
2003	NAS	PCL	31	135	38	10	1	6	18	28	2	2	.281	.365	.504	.224	.254	.334	.471	.019	3.2	11-LF 0	
2003	PIT	NL	31	63	13	5	0	1	10	21	0	0	.206	.320	.333	-.171	.203	.318	.344	-.218	-0.9	12-CF 1	
2004	BOS	AL	32	165	41	9	0	7	17	39	1	1	.246	.317	.444	-.027	.242	.316	.446	-.055	3.6	47-CF -11	

Breakout: 39%   Improve: 56%   Collapse: 28%

The line between major leaguer and minor leaguer is so very thin for some players. Hyzdu will go into spring training trying to get Boston's fifth-outfielder spot, a job that will be much more accessible if the Sox go with 14 position players. Because Boston acquired Curt Schilling—giving them another workhorse starting pitcher—they are more likely to do just that. The biggest moves in the game affect pennant races and profit margins and fan bases, but they also impact 31-year-old guys just trying to get another chance to stick. Root for Hyzdu, because the line between us and our dreams is just as thin as the one that separates him from his.

JASON KENDALL — C — Bats: R — Throws: R — Born: 26-Jun-74 — Age: 30

YEAR	TM	LG	AGE	AB	H	2B	3B	HR	BB	SO	SB	CS	AVG	OBP	SLG	MLVR	EQBA	EQOBP	EQSLG	EQMLVR	VORP	DEFENSE	
2001	PIT	NL	27	606	161	22	2	10	44	48	13	14	.266	.335	.358	-.119	.266	.332	.358	-.133	6.9	125-C -5	18-LF -4
2002	PIT	NL	28	545	154	25	3	3	49	29	15	8	.283	.350	.356	-.020	.289	.352	.369	-.063	16.3	134-C -1	
2003	PIT	NL	29	587	191	29	3	6	49	40	8	7	.325	.399	.416	.155	.329	.398	.424	.133	43.3	143-C -10	
2004	PIT	NL	30	505	144	26	3	5	45	37	8	4	.284	.359	.376	-.030	.287	.359	.389	-.020	22.2	134-C -6	

Breakout: 9%   Improve: 41%   Collapse: 23%

(continued next page)

Jason Kendall *(continued)*

As with Alex Rodriguez and Manny Ramirez, Kendall's onerous contract, signed under the last Collective Bargaining Agreement, serves to obscure how good a player he is. His salary—Kendall is owed $42 million over the next four seasons—is a problem, but he is an excellent player, a durable catcher who posts high OBPs. Yes, he peaked early; stop comparing him to his best season and the money he got for it and judge him by how many wins he adds to the Pirates now.

ROB MACKOWIAK   UT   Bats: L   Throws: R   Born: 20-Jun-76   Age: 28

YEAR	TM	LG	AGE	AB	H	2B	3B	HR	BB	SO	SB	CS	AVG	OBP	SLG	MLVR	EQBA	EQOBP	EQSLG	EQMLVR	VORP	DEFENSE			
2001	NAS	PCL	25	118	31	5	0	4	7	39	1	1	.263	.302	.407	-.104	.237	.280	.373	-.231	-6.1	12-RF	0		
2001	PIT	NL	25	214	57	15	2	4	15	52	4	3	.266	.319	.411	-.074	.264	.319	.412	-.083	-1.0	30-RF	0	18-2B	-3
2002	PIT	NL	26	385	94	22	0	16	42	120	9	3	.244	.328	.426	.008	.251	.330	.441	-.032	3.5	47-RF	1	30-CF	-2
2003	NAS	PCL	27	217	50	11	1	2	18	51	7	3	.230	.286	.318	-.213	.219	.275	.311	-.339	-17.1	41-1B	-3	13-3B	-3
2003	PIT	NL	27	174	47	4	4	6	15	53	6	0	.270	.342	.443	.052	.273	.341	.455	.025	8.5	12-3B	-1		
2004	*PIT*	*NL*	*28*	*168*	*42*	*9*	*1*	*5*	*15*	*47*	*3*	*2*	*.251*	*.319*	*.408*	*-.080*	*.253*	*.320*	*.423*	*-.071*	*5.3*	*48-RF*	*-1*		

Breakout: 30%   Improve: 47%   Collapse: 31%

Mackowiak is a useful utility player who saw his playing time reduced, and rightly so, as the Pirates accumulated major league outfielders. As a left-handed hitter with some power, and a guy who has played five positions without embarrassing himself, he's worth the roster spot for as long as he'll work for six figures.

NATHAN McLOUTH   CF   Bats: L   Throws: R   Born: 28-Oct-81   Age: 22

YEAR	TM	LG	AGE	AB	H	2B	3B	HR	BB	SO	SB	CS	AVG	OBP	SLG	MLVR	EQBA	EQOBP	EQSLG	EQMLVR	VORP	DEFENSE			
2001	HIC	SAL	19	351	100	17	5	12	43	54	21	5	.285	.371	.464	.224	.213	.281	.354	-.272	-14.4	57-CF	-7	34-RF	-4
2002	LYN	CAR	20	393	96	23	4	9	41	48	20	7	.244	.324	.392	.006	.195	.259	.322	-.369	-38.4	62-LF	-7	27-RF	-1
2003	LYN	CAR	21	440	132	27	2	6	55	68	40	4	.300	.386	.411	.158	.236	.304	.334	-.240	-27.8	59-LF	-3	48-CF	-5
2004	*PIT*	*NL*	*22*	*265*	*62*	*14*	*2*	*5*	*24*	*44*	*8*	*3*	*.233*	*.302*	*.352*	*-.196*	*.235*	*.302*	*.365*	*-.191*	*-7.1*	*72-LF*	*-3*		

Breakout: 28%   Improve: 59%   Collapse: 15%

McLouth is another productive member of the 2000 draft for the Pirates, along with Bautista, Sean Burnett and Ian Oquendo. Left in Carolina for a second season, he improved across the board on the field and became adept at cross-stitching off of it. In an organization with many outfield prospects, he's one of the few legitimate center fielders, so he's got an edge on the group.

ABRAHAM NUNEZ   IF   Bats: B   Throws: R   Born: 16-Mar-76   Age: 28

YEAR	TM	LG	AGE	AB	H	2B	3B	HR	BB	SO	SB	CS	AVG	OBP	SLG	MLVR	EQBA	EQOBP	EQSLG	EQMLVR	VORP	DEFENSE			
2001	PIT	NL	25	301	79	11	4	1	28	53	8	2	.262	.326	.336	-.168	.263	.327	.336	-.175	2.4	37-SS	4	38-2B	-4
2002	PIT	NL	26	253	59	14	1	2	27	44	3	4	.233	.311	.320	-.166	.242	.316	.332	-.215	-2.8	39-2B	6	17-SS	-2
2003	PIT	NL	27	311	77	8	7	4	26	53	9	3	.248	.310	.357	-.134	.252	.314	.363	-.170	1.6	57-2B	3	16-SS	-2
2004	*PIT*	*NL*	*28*	*284*	*72*	*13*	*3*	*3*	*29*	*50*	*6*	*3*	*.252*	*.325*	*.356*	*-.136*	*.255*	*.326*	*.369*	*-.129*	*9.1*	*78-2B*	*0*		

Breakout: 32%   Improve: 57%   Collapse: 27%

For a bad team, the Pirates had a pretty good bench. Their worst players by RARP were starters like Kevin Young, Jose Hernandez, Pokey Reese and Randall Simon, who all performed below replacement level. Their bench had guys like Nunez, Mackowiak and Craig Wilson, all of whom were better than that. Nunez has been the fifth infielder for a while, and will be back in that role in 2004.

JEFF REBOULET   IF   Bats: R   Throws: R   Born: 30-Apr-64   Age: 40

YEAR	TM	LG	AGE	AB	H	2B	3B	HR	BB	SO	SB	CS	AVG	OBP	SLG	MLVR	EQBA	EQOBP	EQSLG	EQMLVR	VORP	DEFENSE			
2001	LAD	NL	37	214	57	15	2	3	33	48	0	1	.266	.367	.397	.025	.277	.374	.418	.037	15.2	41-SS	-6	13-2B	-1
2002	LVG	PCL	38	63	16	2	0	1	6	9	2	0	.254	.314	.333	-.194	.222	.279	.302	-.342	-3.1	10-2B	0		
2002	LAD	NL	38	48	10	3	0	0	6	13	0	0	.208	.291	.271	-.255	.224	.309	.306	-.275	-2.0				
2003	NAS	PCL	39	49	11	1	0	0	10	11	0	3	.224	.356	.245	-.177	.216	.322	.235	-.347	-3.7				
2003	PIT	NL	39	261	63	10	2	3	27	47	2	1	.241	.321	.330	-.155	.246	.321	.341	-.191	-1.2	62-2B	8		
2004	*PIT*	*NL*	*40*	*167*	*40*	*9*	*1*	*2*	*19*	*34*	*1*	*1*	*.236*	*.317*	*.346*	*-.173*	*.239*	*.318*	*.358*	*-.168*	*1.6*	*49-2B*	*-4*		

Breakout: 32%   Improve: 61%   Collapse: 20%

Once one the best utility infielders in the game, now Reboulet is just another guy. His early hot streak—he was at .300/.390/.400 through the end of June—and Pokey Reese's injury led to the highest at-bat total of his career. While that voids his warranty, it beats having Mike Benjamin signed to a three-year deal. Reboulet should return to anonymity in 2004.

TIKE REDMAN CF   Bats: L   Throws: L   Born: 10-Mar-77   Age: 27

YEAR	TM	LG	AGE	AB	H	2B	3B	HR	BB	SO	SB	CS	AVG	OBP	SLG	MLVR	EQBA	EQOBP	EQSLG	EQMLVR	VORP	DEFENSE	
2001	NAS	PCL	24	398	121	18	10	3	24	37	21	7	.304	.347	.422	.042	.278	.323	.388	-.099	6.0	78-CF	0
2001	PIT	NL	24	125	28	4	1	1	4	25	3	5	.224	.246	.296	-.404	.222	.246	.294	-.420	-9.2	28-CF	5
2002	NAS	PCL	25	311	84	9	4	2	21	24	16	7	.270	.315	.344	-.122	.252	.296	.325	-.259	-10.3	72-CF	-2
2003	NAS	PCL	26	360	106	12	7	4	36	32	42	9	.294	.357	.400	.077	.279	.338	.383	-.077	7.9	87-CF	-5
2003	PIT	NL	26	230	76	16	5	3	14	18	7	3	.330	.374	.483	.190	.330	.373	.485	.179	16.9	49-CF	-1
2004	*PIT*	*NL*	*27*	*407*	*110*	*20*	*5*	*4*	*32*	*41*	*18*	*6*	*.271*	*.326*	*.375*	*-.098*	*.273*	*.326*	*.389*	*-.089*	*5.5*	*107-CF*	*-2*

Breakout: 17%   *Improve: 40%*   *Collapse: 31%*

Thanks to hot two months at the right time, Redman looks like the starting center fielder. He's not a lot different from Adrian Brown, who was never healthy enough to hold the job. More a fourth outfielder than a solution, Redman does play defense well enough to allow Craig Wilson to lumber through right field. He'll lose the job to Alvarez or Sadler or someone by July.

POKEY REESE 2B   Bats: R   Throws: R   Born: 10-Jun-73   Age: 31

YEAR	TM	LG	AGE	AB	H	2B	3B	HR	BB	SO	SB	CS	AVG	OBP	SLG	MLVR	EQBA	EQOBP	EQSLG	EQMLVR	VORP	DEFENSE			
2001	CIN	NL	28	428	96	20	2	9	34	82	25	4	.224	.284	.343	-.268	.223	.283	.341	-.280	-9.0	74-SS	-4	48-2B	1
2002	PIT	NL	29	421	111	25	0	4	41	81	12	1	.264	.330	.352	-.073	.269	.334	.363	-.120	6.3	114-2B	5		
2003	PIT	NL	30	107	23	2	0	1	9	31	6	0	.215	.271	.262	-.350	.213	.274	.269	-.403	-5.2	33-2B	3		
2004	*BOS*	*AL*	*31*	*228*	*55*	*11*	*1*	*4*	*18*	*46*	*7*	*3*	*.242*	*.300*	*.349*	*-.181*	*.237*	*.299*	*.351*	*-.213*	*0.6*	*62-2B*	*0*		

Breakout: 23%   *Improve: 42%*   *Collapse: 35%*

It was a lost year for Reese, who opened the season in a slump before tearing ligaments in his left thumb while diving into second base on May 14. While recovery from surgery kept him out for the rest of the campaign, he's expected to be OK for 2004. At 31, Reese isn't going to make any great leaps forward, and will be a low-cost, league-average stopgap. Boston inked him to a one-year deal; if the Sox play Reese when groundball maestro Derek Lowe takes the mound and Mark Bellhorn most of the rest of the time, they could have the most interesting, best low-cost platoon in baseball.

CARLOS RIVERA 1B   Bats: L   Throws: L   Born: 10-Jun-78   Age: 26

YEAR	TM	LG	AGE	AB	H	2B	3B	HR	BB	SO	SB	CS	AVG	OBP	SLG	MLVR	EQBA	EQOBP	EQSLG	EQMLVR	VORP	DEFENSE	
2001	ALT	EAS	23	389	91	30	0	10	13	71	0	2	.234	.258	.388	-.112	.216	.246	.363	-.325	-28.4	95-1B	-3
2002	ALT	EAS	24	494	149	28	2	22	27	75	1	1	.302	.345	.500	.214	.268	.305	.452	-.048	5.3	112-1B	-3
2003	NAS	PCL	25	262	69	18	0	9	13	38	3	1	.263	.300	.435	.002	.250	.287	.420	-.142	-4.6	68-1B	4
2003	PIT	NL	25	95	21	5	0	3	8	28	0	0	.221	.283	.368	-.183	.229	.294	.375	-.207	-2.3	24-1B	-4
2004	*PIT*	*NL*	*26*	*235*	*58*	*13*	*1*	*8*	*15*	*43*	*1*	*1*	*.246*	*.294*	*.408*	*-.126*	*.248*	*.295*	*.423*	*-.118*	*-0.3*	*63-1B*	*-1*

Breakout: 31%   *Improve: 51%*   *Collapse: 24%*

Given the available options, the Pirates would be better off using Craig Wilson at first base and giving Alvarez or Davis the right-field job than playing Rivera. All three of those guys, and a bunch of the Pirates' outfield prospects, have more upside than he does. The Pirates kept Rivera on the 40-man roster instead of Walter Young and Chris Shelton. That's something. A weird something, but something.

RAY SADLER CF   Bats: R   Throws: R   Born: 19-Sep-80   Age: 23

YEAR	TM	LG	AGE	AB	H	2B	3B	HR	BB	SO	SB	CS	AVG	OBP	SLG	MLVR	EQBA	EQOBP	EQSLG	EQMLVR	VORP	DEFENSE			
2001	LNS	MID	20	378	129	27	3	10	22	58	18	7	.341	.378	.508	.301	.258	.290	.395	-.166	-12.6	61-LF	-9	16-CF	-2
2002	DAY	FLA	21	462	132	31	1	11	27	91	30	12	.286	.333	.429	.113	.242	.276	.376	-.231	-11.7	105-CF	-11		
2003	WTN	SOU	22	412	120	31	5	6	33	81	17	7	.291	.352	.434	.156	.261	.310	.405	-.112	4.7	102-CF	-8		
2003	ALT	EAS	22	53	14	5	0	1	3	16	0	0	.264	.310	.415	.007	.226	.275	.377	-.243	-1.9				
2004	*PIT*	*NL*	*23*	*265*	*68*	*15*	*2*	*7*	*18*	*55*	*7*	*3*	*.257*	*.311*	*.410*	*-.085*	*.260*	*.312*	*.425*	*-.076*	*4.5*	*71-CF*	*-7*		

Breakout: 34%   *Improve: 60%*   *Collapse: 16%*

(continued next page)

Ray Sadler *(continued)*

Acquired from the Cubs for Randall Simon, Donnie's cousin is a better ballplayer than he was, but because he doesn't have the one standout tool—speed—will have a harder time reaching the majors. Sadler isn't likely to pass Alvarez and Duffy or stay ahead of guys like McLouth, Vic Buttler or Chaz Lytle for very long, and projects as an organizational soldier. The Pirates have to find a way to convert some of these B-prospect outfielders into middle infielders and power hitters.

FREDDY SANCHEZ 2B/SS Bats: R Throws: R Born: 21-Dec-77 Age: 26

YEAR	TM	LG	AGE	AB	H	2B	3B	HR	BB	SO	SB	CS	AVG	OBP	SLG	MLVR	EQBA	EQOBP	EQSLG	EQMLVR	VORP	DEFENSE			
2001	SAR	FLA	23	280	95	19	4	1	22	30	5	3	.339	.388	.446	.260	.283	.321	.381	-.109	8.2	67-SS -2			
2001	TRN	EAS	23	178	58	20	0	2	9	21	3	1	.326	.363	.472	.223	.287	.329	.420	-.034	8.9	41-SS -4			
2002	TRN	EAS	24	311	102	23	1	3	37	45	19	3	.328	.403	.437	.224	.278	.346	.377	-.071	12.9	68-SS -11	11-2B	-1	
2002	PAW	INT	24	183	55	10	1	4	12	21	5	3	.301	.350	.432	.113	.286	.337	.416	-.026	9.5	35-SS -3	11-2B	0	
2003	PAW	INT	25	211	72	17	0	5	31	36	8	0	.341	.430	.493	.353	.310	.395	.458	.158	24.7	34-SS 2	20-2B	0	
2003	BOS	AL	25	34	8	2	0	0	0	8	0	0	.235	.235	.294	-.394	.265	.265	.324	-.313	-1.7				
2003	NAS	PCL	25	5	2	1	0	0	0	1	0	0	.400	.400	.600	.571	.400	.400	.600	.488	0.9				
2004	*PIT*	*NL*	*26*	*234*	*62*	*13*	*1*	*4*	*22*	*36*	*4*	*2*	*.263*	*.330*	*.374*	*-.096*	*.265*	*.331*	*.388*	*-.088*	*11.4*	*65-SS -4*			

Breakout: 12% *Improve: 29%* *Collapse:*

Sanchez is a pure average hitter who might hit .300 without a slugging average or OBP over .400. He's a better version of Mark Grudzielanek at the same age, capable of stealing 20 bases and playing an average shortstop or a good second base. He's likely to win the Pirates' second-base job and be a good, inexpensive solution for a few years. His batting average and steals will make him a great bet for NL Rookie of the Year.

REGGIE SANDERS RF Bats: R Throws: R Born: 01-Dec-67 Age: 36

YEAR	TM	LG	AGE	AB	H	2B	3B	HR	BB	SO	SB	CS	AVG	OBP	SLG	MLVR	EQBA	EQOBP	EQSLG	EQMLVR	VORP	DEFENSE		
2001	ARI	NL	33	441	116	21	3	33	46	126	14	10	.263	.337	.549	.136	.256	.331	.535	.103	20.5	112-RF 4		
2002	SFG	NL	34	505	126	23	6	23	47	121	18	6	.250	.324	.455	.069	.267	.337	.495	.069	17.7	127-RF 4		
2003	PIT	NL	35	453	129	27	4	31	38	110	15	5	.285	.345	.567	.240	.284	.343	.570	.202	32.5	77-RF -1	34-LF	0
2004	*STL*	*NL*	*36*	*382*	*102*	*21*	*3*	*19*	*36*	*93*	*9*	*4*	*.266*	*.335*	*.484*	*.059*	*.271*	*.337*	*.509*	*.087*	*16.5*	*101-RF -2*		

Breakout: 20% *Improve: 39%* *Collapse: 20%*

Another of the good spare parts Littlefield snagged in early 2003, Sanders will join his seventh team in seven years in 2004. With the exception of 2000 in Atlanta, Sanders has been above average for all of the teams he's left behind, and was downright great in 1999, 2001, and 2003. The fear of arbitration is what keeps Sanders's employers from re-signing him; he'd make a lot more through that process than he can on the market. There's nothing wrong with that; it's just led, in this case, to a strange career. He'll help the Cardinals as a handy replacement for J. D. Drew.

CHRIS SHELTON C/1B Bats: R Throws: R Born: 26-Jun-80 Age: 24

YEAR	TM	LG	AGE	AB	H	2B	3B	HR	BB	SO	SB	CS	AVG	OBP	SLG	MLVR	EQBA	EQOBP	EQSLG	EQMLVR	VORP	DEFENSE		
2001	WPT	NYP	21	174	53	11	0	2	33	31	4	1	.305	.415	.402	.241	.210	.296	.285	-.337	-18.5	40-C -3		
2002	HIC	SAL	22	332	113	27	2	17	47	74	0	0	.340	.425	.587	.477	.240	.309	.425	-.102	-2.0	51-1B -4	24-C	-6
2003	LYN	CAR	23	315	113	24	1	21	68	67	1	4	.359	.478	.641	.614	.248	.349	.454	.017	11.6	39-1B 0	28-C	-2
2003	ALT	EAS	23	122	34	10	1	0	8	23	0	1	.279	.331	.377	-.002	.252	.298	.341	-.232	-5.5	20-1B 1	10-C	-1
2004	*DET*	*AL*	*24*	*242*	*56*	*12*	*1*	*7*	*24*	*55*	*1*	*1*	*.230*	*.304*	*.380*	*-.141*	*.239*	*.317*	*.408*	*-.103*	*3.0*	*67-1B 0*		

Breakout: 19% *Improve: 37%* *Collapse: 35%*

Shelton was arguably the best hitter in the low minors the last two seasons, and can catch well enough to play the position twice a week. Hitting no homers in 122 Double-A at-bats made it easier for the Pirates to leave him off their 40-man roster, however, and they lost him in the Rule 5 draft to the Tigers. Shelton may not be ready to hit in the majors, but the Tigers can afford to carry him, giving him 200 plate appearances and letting him catch once a week. At worst, he should become a useful bench player.

MATT STAIRS   RF   Bats: L   Throws: R   Born: 27-Feb-68   Age: 36

YEAR	TM	LG	AGE	AB	H	2B	3B	HR	BB	SO	SB	CS	AVG	OBP	SLG	MLVR	EQBA	EQOBP	EQSLG	EQMLVR	VORP	DEFENSE				
2001	CHC	NL	33	340	85	21	0	17	52	76	2	3	.250	.358	.462	.063	.257	.363	.471	.073	15.7	68-1B	1	15-LF	2	
2002	MIL	NL	34	270	66	15	0	16	36	50	2	0	.244	.349	.478	.114	.252	.351	.493	.077	10.7	39-RF	-1	27-LF	1	
2003	PIT	NL	35	305	89	20	1	20	45	64	0	1	.292	.389	.561	.303	.291	.388	.563	.272	29.3	30-RF	0	22-1B	-4	
2004	KCR	AL	36	205	54	12	0	11	29	40	1	0	.264	.363	.485	.115	.252	.355	.470	.049	10.2	60-RF	-4			

Breakout: 12%   Improve: 32%   Collapse: 36%

The Pirates would have been well-served to trade Stairs, too, but there wasn't much of a market for hitters with limited defensive value at the trade deadline last July. Stairs still has the discipline and the bat speed to put up good numbers as half of a corner/DH platoon, and he'll do it for a million bucks. Unfortunately, Stairs is the type of player likely to be hurt by competing with younger, more complete players in a larger free-agent market. As good as Stairs is, if you can get Jose Cruz or Reggie Sanders for the same money, the choice is pretty clear. The Royals picked him up for one year at $1 million. In K.C., Stairs could easily outperform the departed, overrated Raul Ibanez.

RICH THOMPSON   OF   Bats: L   Throws: R   Born: 23-Apr-79   Age: 25

YEAR	TM	LG	AGE	AB	H	2B	3B	HR	BB	SO	SB	CS	AVG	OBP	SLG	MLVR	EQBA	EQOBP	EQSLG	EQMLVR	VORP	DEFENSE				
2001	DUN	FLA	22	454	141	14	6	1	44	72	39	11	.311	.380	.374	.111	.262	.313	.320	-.226	-22.8	56-RF	-3	53-CF	-4	
2001	SYR	INT	22	53	13	0	1	0	4	12	5	1	.245	.293	.283	-.233	.226	.281	.264	-.389	-5.2	15-LF	4			
2002	TEN	SOU	23	554	155	13	4	2	50	86	45	13	.280	.361	.329	-.017	.253	.309	.303	-.263	-34.3	95-LF	-8	29-CF	0	
2003	NHV	EAS	24	182	57	5	1	0	10	24	15	3	.313	.373	.352	.054	.290	.335	.333	-.146	-4.8	23-LF	-1			
2003	SYR	INT	24	112	33	2	1	0	9	10	11	1	.295	.373	.330	.007	.283	.354	.319	-.133	0.5	25-CF	2			
2003	NAS	PCL	24	109	28	3	2	0	9	21	22	3	.257	.333	.321	-.103	.255	.326	.327	-.195	-1.6	17-CF	0			
2004	KCR	AL	25	234	64	11	2	2	16	36	12	4	.272	.335	.359	-.089	.259	.327	.347	-.153	-1.4	65-CF	-10			

Breakout: 25%   Improve: 41%   Collapse: 34%

Thompson has started getting passed around like responsibility at a war-crimes trial. Drafted by the Blue Jays in 2000, he was traded to the Pirates at mid-season for John Wasdin, taken by the Padres in the Rule 5 draft, and immediately traded again to the Royals, who like him as a speedy extra outfielder. He played well enough in the Arizona Fall League to warrant the gamble, although it's hard to see that much difference between Thompson and Alexis Gomez. His upside is Orlando Palmeiro, with the last five years of Tom Goodwin's career a more likely outcome.

CRAIG WILSON   RF/1B/C   Bats: R   Throws: R   Born: 30-Nov-76   Age: 27

YEAR	TM	LG	AGE	AB	H	2B	3B	HR	BB	SO	SB	CS	AVG	OBP	SLG	MLVR	EQBA	EQOBP	EQSLG	EQMLVR	VORP	DEFENSE				
2001	PIT	NL	24	158	49	3	1	13	15	53	3	1	.310	.390	.589	.334	.312	.391	.587	.334	18.9	18-1B	1			
2002	PIT	NL	25	368	97	16	1	16	32	116	2	3	.264	.355	.443	.088	.271	.354	.461	.055	12.0	58-RF	0	29-1B	1	
2003	PIT	NL	26	309	81	15	4	18	35	89	3	1	.262	.360	.511	.166	.265	.357	.521	.137	19.3	37-RF	0	25-1B	-1	
2004	PIT	NL	27	300	79	16	2	15	31	83	3	2	.265	.355	.481	.087	.268	.356	.499	.102	20.4	83-RF	-1			

Breakout: 13%   Improve: 36%   Collapse: 21%

Is that all there is? It may be that Wilson, instead of being some '00s version of Chris Hoiles, is really just going to be a platoon outfielder/first baseman, crushing lefties and struggling mightily when exposed to righties. That has value, just not as much as a catcher with power and defensive problems would have. Even if the Pirates trade Kendall, the catching is more likely to fall to Cota and House than to Wilson.

JACK WILSON   SS   Bats: R   Throws: R   Born: 29-Dec-77   Age: 26

YEAR	TM	LG	AGE	AB	H	2B	3B	HR	BB	SO	SB	CS	AVG	OBP	SLG	MLVR	EQBA	EQOBP	EQSLG	EQMLVR	VORP	DEFENSE	
2001	PIT	NL	23	390	87	17	1	3	16	70	1	3	.223	.255	.295	-.388	.226	.258	.298	-.388	-19.7	98-SS	2
2002	PIT	NL	24	527	133	22	4	4	37	74	5	2	.252	.306	.332	-.148	.260	.309	.345	-.200	0.4	134-SS	5
2003	PIT	NL	25	558	143	21	3	9	36	74	5	5	.256	.303	.353	-.153	.259	.306	.361	-.183	-0.9	146-SS	0
2004	PIT	NL	26	465	119	22	3	6	32	64	5	3	.256	.308	.355	-.167	.258	.308	.367	-.160	6.5	121-SS	1

Breakout: 26%   Improve: 46%   Collapse: 20%

This Wilson didn't make any progress as a hitter in 2003, which was disappointing given that he'd shown some growth in '02. He remains a good defensive shortstop, and doesn't have to hit much better than this to help the Pirates. It would be surprising if he didn't get better, though . . . say, .275 with more doubles and walks. He can be a .250 EqA guy.

KEVIN YOUNG

1B **Bats: R** **Throws: R** Born: 16-Jun-69 Age: 35

YEAR	TM	LG	AGE	AB	H	2B	3B	HR	BB	SO	SB	CS	AVG	OBP	SLG	MLVR	EQBA	EQOBP	EQSLG	EQMLVR	VORP	DEFENSE	
2001	PIT	NL	32	449	104	33	0	14	42	119	15	11	.232	.310	.399	-.135	.230	.307	.397	-.151	-8.8	120-1B	7
2002	PIT	NL	33	468	115	26	1	16	50	101	4	6	.246	.322	.408	-.024	.251	.323	.423	-.070	1.7	130-1B	0
2003	PIT	NL	34	84	17	4	0	2	12	25	1	0	.202	.302	.321	-.221	.200	.299	.329	-.277	-3.4	22-1B	0
2004	*PIT*	*NL*	*35*	*191*	*44*	*10*	*1*	*6*	*23*	*51*	*2*	*1*	*.229*	*.319*	*.379*	*-.132*	*.231*	*.320*	*.392*	*-.125*	*-0.3*	*55-1B*	*-2*

Breakout: 41%   *Improve: 59%*   *Collapse: 27%*

WALTER YOUNG

1B **Bats: L** **Throws: R** Born: 18-Feb-80 Age: 24

YEAR	TM	LG	AGE	AB	H	2B	3B	HR	BB	SO	SB	CS	AVG	OBP	SLG	MLVR	EQBA	EQOBP	EQSLG	EQMLVR	VORP	DEFENSE	
2001	WPT	NYP	21	232	67	10	1	13	19	43	1	1	.289	.353	.509	.285	.217	.263	.392	-.251	-23.0	44-1B	-5
2002	HIC	SAL	22	492	164	34	2	25	36	102	2	6	.333	.390	.563	.400	.249	.293	.434	-.112	-4.3	75-1B	-13
2003	LYN	CAR	23	431	120	15	2	20	35	88	2	4	.278	.348	.462	.155	.222	.276	.383	-.235	-21.5	75-1B	-4
2004	*BAL*	*AL*	*24*	*271*	*62*	*12*	*0*	*11*	*17*	*61*	*1*	*1*	*.229*	*.283*	*.395*	*-.158*	*.237*	*.294*	*.415*	*-.139*	*-3.3*	*72-1B*	*-7*

Breakout: 32%   *Improve: 61%*   *Collapse: 13%*

Kind of a cross between Frank Thomas and a business park, Young will probably never make the major leagues. On the off chance you're in the same place as the Bowie Baysox this summer—Young was claimed on waivers by the Orioles—though, check out a game, because he's a lot of fun to watch. The spiritual successor to Juan (Large Human) Thomas.

PITCHERS

JONATHAN ALBALADEJO

Bats: R **Throws: R** Born: 30-Oct-82 Age: 21

YEAR	TM	LG	AGE	G	GS	IP	H	BB	SO	HR	ERA	EQERA	EQH9	EQBB9	EQSO9	EQHR9	PERA	VORP	STF
2003	HIC	SAL	20	29	20	139.0	114	19	110	14	3.11	4.96	10.9	1.7	4.5	2.6	6.93	8.5	-17

The 1,021st overall pick in the 2000 draft by the Giants out of a Puerto Rican high school, Albaladejo went to Miami-Dade Community College for a year before the Pirates grabbed him 457 spots higher in the '01 draft. An extreme control pitcher (5.5:1 strikeout-to-walk ratio), he's garnered attention by allowing less than a baserunner an inning in his first exposure to the Sally League. The home runs are a little high for a purported pitching prospect, and he'll need to keep honing his repertoire to neutralize lefty hitters.

JOE BEIMEL

Bats: L **Throws: L** Born: 19-Apr-77 Age: 27

YEAR	TM	LG	AGE	G	GS	IP	H	BB	SO	HR	ERA	EQERA	EQH9	EQBB9	EQSO9	EQHR9	PERA	VORP	STF
2001	PIT	NL	24	42	15	115.3	131	49	58	12	5.23	5.00	10.1	3.5	3.8	0.8	4.99	7.4	-8
2002	PIT	NL	25	53	8	85.3	88	45	53	9	4.64	5.25	9.5	4.2	4.9	1.0	5.07	3.2	-15
2003	PIT	NL	26	69	0	62.3	69	33	42	7	5.06	5.19	9.9	4.3	5.3	1.0	5.35	4.4	-19
2004	*PIT*	*NL*	*27*	*43*	*0*	*44.0*	*48*	*21*	*28*	*5*	*4.90*	*5.20*	*9.8*	*3.8*	*5.2*	*0.9*	*5.31*	*2.3*	*-14*

Breakout: 22%   *Improve: 42%*   *Collapse: 27%*

The Pirates were right to make Beimel a full-time reliever in 2003, but he failed to make much of an impact. He didn't get left-handers out (.311 BA) and he was completely unable to find the plate after May (25 walks in 39 innings). His inability to be a replacement for Scott Sauerbeck hurt the team in August, and makes it likely that he won't ever grow out of a low-leverage role. Beimel is the type of generic reliever who didn't need to be kept on the 40-man roster in favor of someone like Jose Bautista or Frank Brooks.

KRIS BENSON

Bats: R **Throws: R** Born: 07-Nov-74 Age: 29

YEAR	TM	LG	AGE	G	GS	IP	H	BB	SO	HR	ERA	EQERA	EQH9	EQBB9	EQSO9	EQHR9	PERA	VORP	STF
2002	PIT	NL	27	25	25	130.3	152	50	79	18	4.70	5.60	10.7	3.0	4.7	1.2	5.56	0.0	-12
2003	PIT	NL	28	18	18	105.0	127	36	68	14	4.97	5.58	10.8	2.7	5.1	1.2	5.45	-0.6	-5
2004	*PIT*	*NL*	*29*	*21*	*18*	*108.3*	*122*	*39*	*65*	*15*	*5.00*	*5.31*	*10.1*	*2.8*	*4.9*	*1.2*	*5.34*	*6.0*	*-2*

Breakout: 11%   *Improve: 42%*   *Collapse: 31%*

He's now 29, so it's fair to say that expectations have been lowered. What keeps going up is Benson's salary, a whopping $6.1 million in 2004 for a pitcher who's thrown 235 innings of replacement-level ball since 2000. Shoulder pain that did not require surgery ended his 2003 season, and early word is that he's back to 100% in the off-season. Believe it when you see it, because Benson is well past the point of deserving faith.

BRIAN BOEHRINGER

Bats: R **Throws: R** Born: 08-Jan-70 Age: 34

YEAR	TM	LG	AGE	G	GS	IP	H	BB	SO	HR	ERA	EQERA	EQH9	EQBB9	EQSO9	EQHR9	PERA	VORP	STF
2001	NYY	AL	31	22	0	34.7	35	12	33	3	3.11	3.71	8.7	2.9	7.9	0.8	4.10	7.1	17
2001	SFG	NL	31	29	0	34.3	32	17	27	4	4.20	4.91	8.7	4.1	6.0	1.1	4.78	2.5	-12
2002	PIT	NL	32	70	0	79.7	65	33	65	5	3.39	3.52	7.6	3.3	6.5	0.6	3.53	17.7	11
2003	PIT	NL	33	62	0	62.3	64	30	47	11	5.49	5.34	9.2	3.9	5.9	1.5	5.36	0.4	-24
2004	PIT	NL	34	48	0	52.0	51	23	40	7	4.51	4.78	8.9	3.5	6.3	1.1	4.94	5.7	-6

Breakout: 23%   Improve: 50%   Collapse: 23%

Generic right-handed reliever who was gifted with a two-year deal for $3.8 million after his effective 2001. Guys like this are a dime a dozen; your goal as a general manager is to not get attached to the one you have, while keeping an eye out for the next one coming down the pipe. Look, there's one on the next page!

BOBBY BRADLEY

Bats: R **Throws: R** Born: 15-Dec-80 Age: 23

YEAR	TM	LG	AGE	G	GS	IP	H	BB	SO	HR	ERA	EQERA	EQH9	EQBB9	EQSO9	EQHR9	PERA	VORP	STF
2001	LYN	CAR	20	9	9	49.0	44	20	46	3	3.12	5.82	9.8	5.4	5.4	1.2	5.80	-1.1	6
2003	LYN	CAR	22	12	12	50.3	43	28	36	1	3.40	4.96	8.7	6.6	4.6	0.4	4.77	3.2	1
2004	PIT	NL	23	17	11	53.0	67	48	25	7	7.61	8.08	11.3	7.1	3.9	1.2	7.98	-7.6	-34

Breakout: 28%   Improve: 56%   Collapse: 19%

In a perfect world, Bradley would be the first of many Pirates pitching prospects in this chapter ready to make an impact in black and gold. In the real world, the Pirates' #1 pick in 1999 sits apart from those who came after him, the victim of three arm surgeries in three years, including shoulder surgery that interrupted his 2003 campaign. He's two full, healthy seasons from the majors, and he may never get there. He'll be out of options soon, so the Pirates should push him to Double-A and find out what they have, if anything.

FRANK BROOKS

Bats: L **Throws: L** Born: 06-Sep-78 Age: 25

YEAR	TM	LG	AGE	G	GS	IP	H	BB	SO	HR	ERA	EQERA	EQH9	EQBB9	EQSO9	EQHR9	PERA	VORP	STF
2001	CLR	FLA	22	37	15	112.7	113	58	92	18	4.71	7.62	12.3	5.8	5.1	3.7	10.07	-22.0	-77
2002	CLR	FLA	23	35	0	39.0	34	27	33	2	3.46	6.03	10.2	7.9	5.2	1.0	6.42	-1.6	-33
2002	REA	EAS	23	17	1	29.0	29	12	23	1	3.10	5.13	10.6	4.4	5.5	0.7	5.30	1.4	-4
2003	REA	EAS	24	34	0	58.7	40	13	71	5	2.30	3.06	8.0	2.4	8.8	1.5	4.34	15.0	9
2003	NAS	PCL	24	16	0	28.3	22	11	22	2	2.54	3.76	7.5	4.1	6.2	1.0	4.15	5.4	-1
2004	OAK	AL	25	15	6	37.0	36	17	28	6	4.78	5.06	8.9	3.9	6.6	1.2	5.07	3.0	-2

Breakout: 23%   Improve: 45%   Collapse: 24%

The player extracted from the Phillies for Mike Williams didn't last long in the organization. Brooks was left off the 40-man roster, selected in the Rule 5 draft by the Mets and subsequently traded to the A's. Because they get so many good innings from their starters, the A's can afford to use a roster spot on a Rule 5 pick, as they did in 2003 with Michael Neu. If he makes the team, Brooks would be their fourth lefty reliever behind Arthur Rhodes, Ricky Rincon, and Chris Hammond. While he has a good minor league performance record, he isn't likely to have much of a role beyond mop-up in 2004.

BRYAN BULLINGTON

Bats: R **Throws: R** Born: 30-Sep-80 Age: 23

YEAR	TM	LG	AGE	G	GS	IP	H	BB	SO	HR	ERA	EQERA	EQH9	EQBB9	EQSO9	EQHR9	PERA	VORP	STF
2003	HIC	SAL	22	8	7	45.3	25	11	46	3	1.39	3.00	8.1	3.0	5.8	1.6	4.73	11.3	5
2003	LYN	CAR	22	17	17	97.3	101	27	67	5	3.05	5.03	11.0	3.2	4.3	1.1	5.65	5.6	-2
2004	PIT	NL	23	20	13	76.7	86	33	47	11	5.24	5.56	10.0	3.4	5.0	1.3	5.59	2.0	-8

Breakout: 15%   Improve: 46%   Collapse: 22%

(continued next page)

Bryan Bullington (continued)

The Pirates' #1 pick in 2002 progressed well in 2003, beating up the lower levels despite a considerable loss in velocity as compared to his junior year at Ball State. His size and track record argue that he'll return to the mid-90s form he flashed in college, which, along with his plus slider and developing curve and change-up, would make him one of the game's top pitching prospects. He could pass the next guy by the end of the year.

SEAN BURNETT
Bats: L **Throws: L** Born: 17-Sep-82 Age: 21

YEAR	TM	LG	AGE	G	GS	IP	H	BB	SO	HR	ERA	EQERA	EQH9	EQBB9	EQSO9	EQHR9	PERA	VORP	STF
2001	HIC	SAL	18	26	26	161.3	164	33	134	11	2.62	5.45	10.0	2.6	4.4	1.3	5.21	2.5	16
2002	LYN	CAR	19	26	26	155.3	118	33	96	4	1.80	3.70	7.3	2.5	4.1	0.5	3.12	30.3	30
2003	ALT	EAS	20	27	27	159.7	158	29	86	2	3.21	4.49	8.5	1.9	4.1	0.2	3.17	18.8	31
2004	PIT	NL	21	17	15	95.3	98	31	50	9	4.06	4.30	9.3	2.6	4.2	0.8	4.37	13.6	1

Breakout: 24%   Improve: 54%   Collapse: 7%

Another of the four #1 picks, Burnett presents a quandary for performance analysts. He's carved up the lower levels with a great assortment, including a plus sinker, but his inability to miss bats—look at the strikeout rate, and the direction it's heading—portends problems. He'll need a 4-to-1 G/F ratio to survive in the majors, something he actually might approach. He's allowed just 17 home runs in 506 pro innings. His great command keeps his pitch counts down, but his so-so fastball means that he's close to max effort a lot of the time.

What does it all mean? Burnett may find himself scuffling at Triple-A in 2004, and he's unlikely to make a major league impact until 2005, and probably later. While there are rare exceptions, it's usually just too hard to succeed with that low a strikeout rate.

MARK COREY
Bats: R **Throws: R** Born: 16-Nov-74 Age: 29

YEAR	TM	LG	AGE	G	GS	IP	H	BB	SO	HR	ERA	EQERA	EQH9	EQBB9	EQSO9	EQHR9	PERA	VORP	STF
2001	BIN	EAS	26	25	0	35.0	23	12	50	1	1.80	2.87	7.8	4.3	8.9	0.3	3.55	9.5	23
2001	NOR	INT	26	28	0	36.7	24	22	42	1	1.47	2.94	7.0	6.4	8.0	0.3	3.78	10.0	14
2002	NOR	INT	27	25	0	26.3	14	7	37	1	1.03	1.82	5.5	2.9	10.6	0.4	2.24	10.4	46
2002	NYM	NL	27	12	0	10.0	10	8	9	2	4.50	6.52	9.3	6.5	7.4	1.9	6.53	-1.0	-38
2002	COL	NL	27	14	0	12.0	22	8	12	7	12.00	11.25	16.5	5.2	7.5	4.5	12.78	-7.5	-123
2003	NAS	PCL	28	46	0	45.7	37	18	63	5	4.33	4.75	9.1	4.3	10.8	1.5	5.35	3.9	-4
2003	PIT	NL	28	22	0	30.3	29	11	27	2	5.35	4.60	8.6	3.1	7.1	0.6	3.91	0.0	11
2004	PIT	NL	29	35	3	50.0	44	24	52	5	4.03	4.27	7.9	3.8	8.4	1.0	4.34	7.5	9

Breakout: 24%   Improve: 47%   Collapse: 22%

The erstwhile Mets prospect, best known for a frightening seizure in the summer of 2002 (and the admission that he smoked marijuana before it), Corey set the Nashville Sounds record with 30 saves last year. He's struck out more than a batter an inning in the 21st century, so you figure he deserves a chance to keep a major league job. The main difference between him and Brian Boehringer is Boehringer's guaranteed contract.

JEFF D'AMICO
Bats: R **Throws: R** Born: 27-Dec-75 Age: 28

YEAR	TM	LG	AGE	G	GS	IP	H	BB	SO	HR	ERA	EQERA	EQH9	EQBB9	EQSO9	EQHR9	PERA	VORP	STF
2001	MIL	NL	25	10	10	47.3	60	16	32	11	6.09	7.29	11.4	2.8	5.1	1.8	6.47	-8.6	-26
2002	NYM	NL	26	29	22	145.7	152	37	101	20	4.94	5.10	9.7	2.0	5.5	1.3	4.86	7.7	-3
2003	PIT	NL	27	29	29	175.3	204	42	100	23	4.77	5.06	10.4	2.0	4.6	1.2	5.07	6.8	-3
2004	CLE	AL	28	26	24	157.3	167	37	115	26	4.70	5.02	9.3	2.0	6.4	1.5	4.82	14.2	11

Breakout: 15%   Improve: 53%   Collapse: 12%

Here's a scary thought: D'Amico's 175 ⅓ innings in 2003 were a career high. It's hard to sell yourself as an innings sponge when you don't pick up enough innings. D'Amico also posted a career-low strikeout rate, and fought the same battles with nagging injuries he does every season. The memory of 2000 (2.66 ERA in 162 ⅓ IP) will get him more opportunities, but he's basically Jeff Suppan without the durability. For the Tribe, he's this year's veteran stopgap until the kids are ready.

NELSON FIGUEROA   Bats: B   Throws: R   Born: 18-May-74   Age: 30

YEAR	TM	LG	AGE	G	GS	IP	H	BB	SO	HR	ERA	EQERA	EQH9	EQBB9	EQSO9	EQHR9	PERA	VORP	STF
2001	SWB	INT	27	13	12	87.3	74	18	74	6	2.47	4.31	9.3	2.3	6.0	0.9	4.33	11.4	10
2001	PHI	NL	27	19	13	89.0	95	37	61	8	3.94	4.64	9.9	3.5	5.3	0.7	4.79	9.1	3
2002	IND	INT	28	6	6	39.7	39	13	25	2	3.63	4.71	9.9	3.5	4.7	0.7	4.80	3.6	0
2002	MIL	NL	28	30	11	93.0	96	37	51	18	5.03	5.64	9.5	3.1	4.3	1.8	5.70	-0.4	-34
2003	NAS	PCL	29	23	23	151.3	144	37	121	11	2.97	4.14	9.7	2.7	6.2	1.0	4.76	22.5	5
2003	PIT	NL	29	12	3	35.3	28	13	23	8	3.31	3.67	7.1	2.9	5.2	1.8	4.47	9.3	-19
2004	*PIT*	*NL*	*30*	*36*	*12*	*85.0*	*88*	*31*	*59*	*11*	*4.39*	*4.66*	*9.3*	*2.8*	*5.6*	*1.1*	*4.81*	*10.3*	*-4*

Breakout: 23%   Improve: 46%   Collapse: 27%

His prospect status long since forgotten, Figueroa seems destined to be an injury replacement for bad teams. The skills that have made him successful in Triple-A—command and keeping the ball in the park—have deserted him in the majors, making it hard for him to establish himself. He'll be back in Nashville in 2004; the coming wave of Pirates pitchers will likely wash him out of the Sounds' rotation by the end of the summer.

JOSH FOGG   Bats: R   Throws: R   Born: 13-Dec-76   Age: 27

YEAR	TM	LG	AGE	G	GS	IP	H	BB	SO	HR	ERA	EQERA	EQH9	EQBB9	EQSO9	EQHR9	PERA	VORP	STF
2001	CHR	INT	24	40	16	114.7	129	30	89	19	4.79	6.22	11.4	2.8	5.5	2.0	6.69	-7.3	-30
2002	PIT	NL	25	33	33	194.3	199	69	113	28	4.35	4.97	9.4	2.8	4.6	1.3	4.99	13.1	-5
2003	PIT	NL	26	26	26	142.0	166	40	71	22	5.26	5.39	10.4	2.3	4.0	1.4	5.41	-0.2	-16
2004	*PIT*	*NL*	*27*	*21*	*18*	*107.3*	*120*	*34*	*59*	*15*	*4.77*	*5.07*	*10.0*	*2.5*	*4.5*	*1.2*	*5.16*	*7.2*	*-3*

Breakout: 14%   Improve: 44%   Collapse: 26%

Lose the change-up, lose the curve, lose the starting role, lose any outing in which you go past 45 pitches. Add the requisite 3–5 mph guys pick up when they move to the bullpen. Simmer.

Fogg lacks the stamina to be a starter, but would make a very good reliever. It's time. In two years, Fogg is going to have the scarlet "C" on his chest, along with all the requisite press nonsense about his fortitude and guts and bravery. No one talks about him having those things now, but that's because it never pops up until after a guy accumulates 35 saves.

MIKE GONZALEZ   Bats: R   Throws: L   Born: 23-May-78   Age: 26

YEAR	TM	LG	AGE	G	GS	IP	H	BB	SO	HR	ERA	EQERA	EQH9	EQBB9	EQSO9	EQHR9	PERA	VORP	STF
2001	LYN	CAR	23	14	2	30.7	28	7	32	3	2.93	5.47	11.6	3.1	5.8	2.4	7.39	0.4	-41
2001	ALT	EAS	23	14	14	87.3	81	36	66	5	3.71	5.35	9.5	5.0	4.7	0.8	5.08	2.2	0
2002	ALT	EAS	24	16	16	85.3	77	47	82	4	3.80	5.35	9.8	5.9	6.5	0.7	5.33	2.1	3
2003	LYN	CAR	25	5	0	7.0	7	5	9	0	5.14	9.00	12.0	9.0	7.5	0.0	6.28	-2.3	-24
2003	ALT	EAS	25	5	0	7.3	4	2	10	1	1.23	2.84	7.1	2.8	9.9	2.8	5.54	1.9	-27
2003	NAS	PCL	25	7	0	10.0	9	4	10	0	4.50	4.82	8.7	3.9	7.7	0.0	3.57	0.8	23
2003	PIT	NL	25	16	0	8.3	7	6	6	4	7.59	7.56	7.6	5.4	5.4	4.3	8.63	-1.7	-103
2004	*PIT*	*NL*	*26*	*13*	*7*	*38.7*	*40*	*23*	*32*	*5*	*5.38*	*5.71*	*9.2*	*4.7*	*6.8*	*1.1*	*5.64*	*0.5*	*-3*

Breakout: 18%   Improve: 41%   Collapse: 29%

Gonzalez went back and forth between the Pirates and Red Sox last summer as part of the twin trades for Jeff Suppan and Scott Sauerbeck. He'd be better known but for an assortment of injuries than have slowed his progress though the Pirates' system. Now healthy, he gets his fastball up over 95 and has a good slider. Command is a concern, but it'll come, either this year or next.

JOHN GRABOW   Bats: L   Throws: L   Born: 04-Nov-78   Age: 25

YEAR	TM	LG	AGE	G	GS	IP	H	BB	SO	HR	ERA	EQERA	EQH9	EQBB9	EQSO9	EQHR9	PERA	VORP	STF
2001	ALT	EAS	22	10	10	50.7	30	39	42	1	3.37	4.80	6.0	9.4	5.2	0.2	4.15	4.0	10
2001	LYN	CAR	22	7	7	36.7	42	26	35	3	6.38	9.58	13.4	9.6	5.5	1.7	8.88	-13.7	-43
2002	ALT	EAS	23	28	27	146.3	181	47	97	10	5.48	7.28	12.4	3.4	4.5	1.1	6.30	-25.1	-12
2003	ALT	EAS	24	24	9	83.0	87	19	73	9	3.36	5.33	11.6	2.5	6.4	1.9	6.66	2.2	-23
2003	NAS	PCL	24	17	0	24.7	31	7	26	0	4.74	6.26	12.5	3.1	8.2	0.4	5.43	-1.7	15
2004	*PIT*	*NL*	*25*	*10*	*6*	*33.7*	*36*	*15*	*26*	*4*	*4.82*	*5.11*	*9.6*	*3.4*	*6.3*	*1.0*	*5.08*	*1.9*	*1*

Breakout: 16%   Improve: 49%   Collapse: 26%

The Pirates third-round pick in 1997 finally squeaked into the majors in September. Grabow was rocketing through the system when, following minor elbow surgery in 2000, he lost his command. With that problem now under control, he projects as a low-leverage lefty reliever in the majors, someone who could replace Joe Beimel as soon as this year.

MIKE LINCOLN

Bats: R   **Throws: R**   Born: 10-Apr-75   Age: 29

YEAR	TM	LG	AGE	G	GS	IP	H	BB	SO	HR	ERA	EQERA	EQH9	EQBB9	EQSO9	EQHR9	PERA	VORP	STF
2001	NAS	PCL	26	18	13	91.7	90	25	71	10	3.44	4.61	10.2	3.0	5.1	1.3	5.38	9.2	-14
2001	PIT	NL	26	31	0	40.3	34	11	24	3	2.68	3.03	7.4	2.3	4.7	0.7	3.30	11.1	3
2002	NAS	PCL	27	10	0	14.7	14	2	15	0	1.22	1.98	9.9	1.3	7.2	0.0	3.39	5.5	37
2002	PIT	NL	27	55	0	72.3	80	27	50	7	3.11	4.39	10.2	3.0	5.4	0.9	4.96	9.4	-7
2003	NAS	PCL	28	8	0	12.7	8	4	9	1	0.71	2.31	6.2	3.1	5.4	0.8	3.01	4.3	2
2003	PIT	NL	28	36	0	36.3	38	13	28	5	5.21	5.09	9.4	2.8	6.1	1.3	4.93	1.0	-13
2004	STL	NL	29	31	4	51.3	51	17	37	4	3.49	3.81	8.9	2.6	5.8	0.8	4.19	10.2	-1

Breakout: 35%   Improve: 62%   Collapse: 17%

After missing the first half of the year rehabbing a right shoulder contusion, Lincoln was a disappointment for the Pirates. Really, he wasn't much different than he had been in 2001 and 2002, just with a couple of blow-up outings and not enough playing time to wash them away. Like Beimel, Lincoln occupied a roster spot in December that would have been better used on talent with upside. He'll probably stick with the Cards, but he'll be staff filler.

PAUL MAHOLM

Bats: L   **Throws: L**   Born: 25-Jun-82   Age: 22

YEAR	TM	LG	AGE	G	GS	IP	H	BB	SO	HR	ERA	EQERA	EQH9	EQBB9	EQSO9	EQHR9	PERA	VORP	STF
2003	WPT	NYP	21	8	8	34.3	25	10	32	1	1.84	5.97	10.7	4.1	5.0	1.3	5.88	-1.2	-8

The latest of the Pirates' first-round investments in pitching, Maholm dropped in competition from the SEC, where he pitched for Mississippi State, to the New York-Penn League. Predictably, he slapped the league around for eight starts. Like Burnett, he's more of a command guy than a stuff guy, which is why his upside comes in behind those of Bryan Bullington and John VanBenschoten.

BRIAN MEADOWS

Bats: R   **Throws: R**   Born: 21-Nov-75   Age: 28

YEAR	TM	LG	AGE	G	GS	IP	H	BB	SO	HR	ERA	EQERA	EQH9	EQBB9	EQSO9	EQHR9	PERA	VORP	STF
2001	KCR	AL	25	10	10	50.3	73	12	21	12	6.98	6.80	12.7	2.0	3.5	1.8	6.98	-6.5	-34
2001	OMA	PCL	25	18	18	105.0	143	20	74	21	6.17	7.30	12.9	2.0	4.6	2.1	7.36	-18.6	-41
2002	NAS	PCL	26	23	22	126.3	132	26	98	15	4.28	5.34	10.7	2.2	5.3	1.5	5.58	3.4	-16
2002	PIT	NL	26	11	11	62.7	62	14	31	7	3.88	4.22	9.1	1.8	3.9	1.1	4.28	9.2	0
2003	NAS	PCL	27	9	8	51.0	32	0	40	2	1.41	2.12	6.4	0.6	6.2	0.6	2.18	18.1	36
2003	PIT	NL	27	34	7	76.3	91	11	38	8	4.72	4.91	10.6	1.2	4.0	0.9	4.60	3.2	-7
2004	PIT	NL	28	28	13	84.0	92	17	48	10	4.09	4.34	9.8	1.6	4.7	1.0	4.41	12.0	-3

Breakout: 14%   Improve: 50%   Collapse: 20%

Meadows, by some accounts, is one of the good guys in the game. What he isn't is a very good pitcher. He has thrown 738 ⅓ innings in his career and has an ERA of 5.24. His "best" season was a 3.88 ERA for the Pirates in 2002. He doesn't strike guys out, doesn't eat a ton of innings, and has virtually no upside. At what point do you try and make him a scout, rather than give him $625,000 to pitch for you?

IAN OQUENDO

Bats: R   **Throws: R**   Born: 30-Oct-81   Age: 22

YEAR	TM	LG	AGE	G	GS	IP	H	BB	SO	HR	ERA	EQERA	EQH9	EQBB9	EQSO9	EQHR9	PERA	VORP	STF
2001	WPT	NYP	19	10	9	64.7	55	10	56	2	1.39	4.79	10.9	2.1	4.5	1.0	5.09	5.1	17
2002	HIC	SAL	20	24	22	139.7	127	45	149	8	2.71	5.28	11.3	4.1	5.9	1.3	6.24	4.3	11
2003	LYN	CAR	21	20	20	116.3	105	33	122	3	3.33	4.46	9.9	3.3	6.6	0.6	4.53	13.3	32
2003	ALT	EAS	21	6	6	36.7	36	10	23	2	1.96	4.76	9.3	2.9	4.8	0.8	4.40	3.2	19
2004	PIT	NL	22	20	13	77.0	82	31	58	8	4.74	5.03	9.5	3.2	6.1	1.0	4.91	6.4	3

Breakout: 12%   Improve: 47%   Collapse: 34%

Also known as Ian Snell, as well as "the really good Pirates' pitching prospect who wasn't a #1 pick," Oquendo is a small right-hander from a high school in Delaware. In other words, he's the polar opposite of Maholm. He's largely a two-pitch pitcher, with a fastball and a good curve. Between that and the physical resemblance, comparisons to Octavio Dotel and a similar role out of the bullpen in the future are apt.

OLIVER PEREZ

Bats: L **Throws: L** Born: 15-Aug-81 Age: 22

YEAR	TM	LG	AGE	G	GS	IP	H	BB	SO	HR	ERA	EQERA	EQH9	EQBB9	EQSO9	EQHR9	PERA	VORP	STF
2001	FTW	MID	19	19	19	101.3	84	43	98	9	3.46	5.14	9.0	5.3	5.5	1.8	6.03	4.7	5
2001	LEL	CAL	19	9	9	53.0	45	25	62	4	2.72	5.48	9.4	5.5	6.6	1.1	5.52	0.6	26
2002	LEL	CAL	20	9	8	48.7	36	24	66	0	1.85	3.48	8.6	5.5	7.4	0.2	4.19	10.4	46
2002	MOB	SOU	20	4	4	23.0	11	16	34	1	1.17	2.53	5.5	6.8	10.5	0.8	3.74	7.3	65
2002	SDP	NL	20	16	15	90.0	71	48	94	13	3.50	4.08	7.0	4.2	8.0	1.3	4.22	14.9	48
2003	SDP	NL	21	19	19	103.7	103	65	117	20	5.38	5.97	9.3	5.0	8.9	1.8	5.98	-5.8	33
2003	POR	PCL	21	8	8	47.7	44	12	48	6	3.02	4.30	7.8	2.5	8.8	1.4	4.15	6.6	45
2003	PIT	NL	21	5	5	23.0	26	12	24	2	5.87	5.64	10.5	4.0	8.5	0.8	5.20	-0.5	44
2004	*PIT*	*NL*	*22*	*20*	*18*	*112.3*	*101*	*60*	*110*	*14*	*4.28*	*4.54*	*8.1*	*4.2*	*8.0*	*1.1*	*4.69*	*14.6*	*16*

Breakout: 6%   *Improve: 56%*   *Collapse: 27%*

Perez throws a ton of pitches in a normal year, and elected to spend part of his winter throwing more in the Mexican League. Teams have less control over this than you would think; they can suggest that a player sit out winter ball, but they can't actually stop him from playing. Perez can deal, but the load on his arm to date makes him a candidate to get hurt in the next 18 months. He'll come back and be a star in his mid-20s.

DUANER SANCHEZ

Bats: R **Throws: R** Born: 14-Oct-79 Age: 24

YEAR	TM	LG	AGE	G	GS	IP	H	BB	SO	HR	ERA	EQERA	EQH9	EQBB9	EQSO9	EQHR9	PERA	VORP	STF
2001	LNC	CAL	21	10	10	59.0	65	18	49	7	4.58	6.18	10.4	3.4	4.1	1.8	6.21	-3.6	-14
2001	ELP	TEX	21	13	13	70.3	92	25	41	5	6.79	6.10	10.4	3.6	3.6	0.9	5.27	-3.9	0
2002	ELP	TEX	22	31	0	35.7	31	13	37	1	3.03	4.09	8.7	3.8	6.8	0.5	4.12	5.5	17
2002	NAS	PCL	22	20	0	22.7	23	11	20	2	4.76	5.40	9.1	5.0	6.6	0.8	4.93	0.5	6
2003	NAS	PCL	23	41	1	61.0	63	27	34	3	3.69	5.18	9.3	4.7	4.6	0.6	4.74	2.7	-7
2003	PIT	NL	23	6	0	6.0	15	1	3	2	16.50	15.00	21.0	1.5	4.5	3.0	12.00	-7.1	-78
2004	*PIT*	*NL*	*24*	*16*	*5*	*35.7*	*40*	*20*	*25*	*5*	*5.63*	*5.97*	*9.9*	*4.4*	*5.6*	*1.3*	*6.01*	*1.0*	*-13*

Breakout: 27%   *Improve: 56%*   *Collapse: 23%*

Sanchez is not always sure where his fastball is going, but he does get it there fast, dealing in the high 90s. He can't say the same about himself, however; Sanchez's June call-up was aborted when he arrived late for his first game. Waived in November, he landed in Los Angeles, where he could fill some of the innings left behind by free agent Paul Quantrill. He's out of options, so the Dodgers will have a reason to keep him around.

CORY STEWART

Bats: L **Throws: L** Born: 14-Nov-79 Age: 24

YEAR	TM	LG	AGE	G	GS	IP	H	BB	SO	HR	ERA	EQERA	EQH9	EQBB9	EQSO9	EQHR9	PERA	VORP	STF
2002	FTW	MID	22	17	11	64.0	46	18	86	4	2.39	4.23	9.9	3.6	7.6	1.8	5.94	8.4	0
2002	LEL	CAL	22	12	12	64.7	60	29	69	3	3.20	5.25	10.3	5.1	5.6	0.8	5.45	2.3	6
2003	MOB	SOU	23	24	24	125.7	104	50	133	10	3.72	4.89	9.7	4.2	6.7	1.6	5.82	8.9	-2
2004	*PIT*	*NL*	*24*	*20*	*12*	*70.3*	*70*	*35*	*60*	*9*	*4.83*	*5.13*	*9.0*	*4.0*	*6.9*	*1.1*	*5.10*	*5.4*	*3*

Breakout: 21%   *Improve: 52%*   *Collapse: 27%*

Acquired from the Padres in the Brian Giles deal, Stewart adds another chip to the Pirates' growing stack of pitching prospects. Unlike the #1 picks and 21-year-old phenoms, however, Stewart entered baseball through the back door, signing with the Padres out of the Texas-Louisiana League. He has a fair amount in common with Perez, the other pitcher in the trade, but Stewart is nearly two years older, which places him outside the injury nexus. He could reach Pittsburgh as a reliever this year, and is a better bet than Burnett or Maholm to have success in the short term.

JULIAN TAVAREZ

Bats: L **Throws: R** Born: 22-May-73 Age: 31

YEAR	TM	LG	AGE	G	GS	IP	H	BB	SO	HR	ERA	EQERA	EQH9	EQBB9	EQSO9	EQHR9	PERA	VORP	STF
2001	CHC	NL	28	34	28	161.3	172	69	107	13	4.52	4.89	9.5	3.5	5.0	0.6	4.51	12.3	4
2002	FLA	NL	29	29	27	153.7	188	74	67	9	5.39	5.85	10.9	3.8	3.4	0.5	5.16	-4.1	-8
2003	PIT	NL	30	64	0	83.7	75	27	39	1	3.66	3.46	7.9	2.6	3.7	0.1	3.05	15.8	8
2004	*STL*	*NL*	*31*	*37*	*12*	*81.7*	*89*	*40*	*43*	*5*	*4.34*	*4.73*	*9.8*	*3.9*	*4.3*	*0.6*	*5.16*	*8.8*	*-13*

Breakout: 37%   *Improve: 61%*   *Collapse: 18%*

(continued next page)

Julian Tavarez *(continued)*

Tavarez meandered into the closer role at the end of the season following the trade of Mike Williams. He's never been able to sustain success in any role, and his lousy strikeout rate and strikeout-to-walk ratio argue that 2004 won't be any different. Two things to keep in mind, however: Tavarez raised his G/F ratio to a huge 3.35:1, and not only did he not allow a stolen base last year, he didn't even allow an attempt. You can give up a lot of singles if you do that. He's now part of the cast of thousands the Cardinals brought in to fill up the back end of their pen, not to mention Memphis.

SALOMON TORRES Bats: R Throws: R Born: 11-Mar-72 Age: 32

YEAR	TM	LG	AGE	G	GS	IP	H	BB	SO	HR	ERA	EQERA	EQH9	EQBB9	EQSO9	EQHR9	PERA	VORP	STF
2002	NAS	PCL	30	26	24	162.3	169	39	136	12	3.83	4.86	10.6	2.5	5.8	0.9	4.98	12.3	3
2002	PIT	NL	30	5	5	30.0	28	13	12	2	2.70	3.72	8.4	3.4	3.1	0.6	3.99	6.1	1
2003	PIT	NL	31	41	16	121.0	128	42	84	19	4.76	4.85	9.5	2.8	5.5	1.4	5.10	11.4	-13
2004	PIT	NL	32	31	16	97.3	102	35	64	11	4.27	4.53	9.4	2.8	5.4	1.0	4.69	11.1	-2

Breakout: 19%   Improve: 40%   Collapse: 28%

Given his problems with left-handed batters last year, as well as his effectiveness as a reliever (3.20 ERA, strong peripherals), Torres seems best suited for a set-up role in which he can be paired with Grabow or Gonzalez to get through the seventh and eighth innings. If they choose wisely, the Pirates can have a deep, inexpensive, effective bullpen this year.

JOHN VanBENSCHOTEN Bats: R Throws: R Born: 14-Apr-80 Age: 24

YEAR	TM	LG	AGE	G	GS	IP	H	BB	SO	HR	ERA	EQERA	EQH9	EQBB9	EQSO9	EQHR9	PERA	VORP	STF
2001	WPT	NYP	21	9	9	25.7	23	10	19	0	3.50	6.95	11.0	5.3	3.7	0.4	5.48	-3.3	-13
2002	HIC	SAL	22	27	27	148.0	119	62	145	6	2.80	5.29	10.1	5.4	5.4	1.0	5.64	4.4	-1
2003	LYN	CAR	23	9	9	48.7	33	18	49	1	2.22	3.30	7.6	4.3	6.4	0.4	3.66	11.2	26
2003	ALT	EAS	23	17	17	90.3	95	34	78	5	3.69	5.90	10.8	4.2	6.2	1.0	5.63	-2.7	4
2004	PIT	NL	24	19	14	80.3	85	44	61	9	5.15	5.47	9.4	4.3	6.2	1.0	5.45	4.7	-1

Breakout: 19%   Improve: 51%   Collapse: 22%

While the decision to develop VanBenschoten as a pitcher and not a hitter was widely derided, and still could be considered a mistake, it has worked out well for both the player and the organization so far. VanBenschoten, a big guy who throws in the mid-90s, had a better year than the lines above indicate; he was great at Double-A before tiring at the end of the season. He hasn't been overworked, his secondary pitches (a slider and a change) are coming along, and he gets high marks from both scouts and statheads. Credit Mickey White for standing by a tough decision, and look for VanBenschoten to reach the majors for good in 2005.

RYAN VOGELSONG Bats: R Throws: R Born: 22-Jul-77 Age: 26

YEAR	TM	LG	AGE	G	GS	IP	H	BB	SO	HR	ERA	EQERA	EQH9	EQBB9	EQSO9	EQHR9	PERA	VORP	STF
2001	FRE	PCL	23	10	10	58.0	35	18	53	6	2.79	2.80	5.6	3.3	6.3	1.0	3.00	17.0	27
2001	SFG	NL	23	13	0	28.7	29	14	17	5	5.64	6.18	9.1	3.9	4.6	1.3	5.16	-1.8	-12
2001	NAS	PCL	23	6	6	31.7	26	15	33	2	3.97	4.60	8.0	5.2	7.4	0.6	4.24	3.3	26
2002	LYN	CAR	24	4	4	15.7	19	7	20	0	8.03	8.78	14.9	6.1	8.1	0.7	7.45	-4.7	-12
2002	ALT	EAS	24	8	8	43.7	47	10	35	5	5.56	6.64	11.7	2.5	5.5	1.8	6.58	-4.5	-23
2003	NAS	PCL	25	26	26	149.0	142	54	146	12	4.29	5.10	9.6	3.9	7.6	1.1	5.12	7.7	6
2003	PIT	NL	25	6	5	22.0	30	9	15	1	6.55	6.75	12.2	3.4	5.5	0.4	5.46	-5.0	2
2004	PIT	NL	26	19	13	75.3	75	34	64	9	4.81	5.10	9.0	3.5	6.9	1.1	4.87	5.0	6

Breakout: 20%   Improve: 46%   Collapse: 24%

Vogelsong pitched his first full season since being part of the Jason Schmidt trade in 2001. There wasn't a dime's worth of difference between his 2003 line and his last pre-injury performances, so he's one of the lucky ones. Without much in the way of expectations or competition, Vogelsong could settle in as a back-of-the-rotation guy while the Pirates wait for the recent draftees to reach the major leagues.

JOHN WASDIN   Bats: R   Throws: R   Born: 05-Aug-72   Age: 31

YEAR	TM	LG	AGE	G	GS	IP	H	BB	SO	HR	ERA	EQERA	EQH9	EQBB9	EQSO9	EQHR9	PERA	VORP	STF
2001	COL	NL	28	18	0	24.3	32	8	17	7	7.04	6.46	11.4	2.7	5.3	2.3	7.05	-2.3	-49
2001	ROC	INT	28	5	3	20.3	27	5	20	3	3.99	5.30	13.5	2.4	6.8	1.9	7.48	0.6	-29
2001	BAL	AL	28	26	0	49.7	54	16	47	4	4.16	4.28	9.7	2.6	8.0	0.7	4.39	7.1	18
2002	YOM	JPC	29	10	1	37.7	55	9	31	7	0.00	8.21	14.8	3.2	5.6	2.1	8.54	-9.9	-55
2003	NAS	PCL	30	18	18	112.3	101	24	116	4	3.05	3.99	9.3	2.3	8.0	0.5	3.91	18.6	32
2003	SYR	INT	30	10	1	20.7	28	1	21	1	5.22	5.59	13.5	0.5	7.0	0.5	5.26	0.0	12
2003	TOR	AL	30	3	2	5.0	16	4	5	2	23.40	19.80	27.0	7.2	9.0	3.6	15.39	-9.3	-129
2004	TEX	AL	31	22	12	69.0	81	21	50	10	5.13	4.64	9.9	2.5	6.5	1.1	4.60	9.6	6

Breakout: 21%   Improve: 51%   Collapse: 27%

After spending the 2002 season in Japan, Wasdin made a splashy return by tossing the first perfect game in Nashville Sounds history on April 6. While he continued to pitch well at Triple-A, his limited exposure to the big leagues with the Blue Jays was a disaster. Wasdin can be successful in the right circumstances—good outfield defense, good pitcher's park—but he's past the point where he gets many chances to succeed. The Rangers aren't a good fit for him, but he accepting their minor league contract offer anyway.

KIP WELLS   Bats: R   Throws: R   Born: 21-Apr-77   Age: 27

YEAR	TM	LG	AGE	G	GS	IP	H	BB	SO	HR	ERA	EQERA	EQH9	EQBB9	EQSO9	EQHR9	PERA	VORP	STF
2001	CHR	INT	24	4	4	25.3	26	8	24	2	3.56	5.01	10.4	3.5	6.6	0.8	5.02	1.5	16
2001	CWS	AL	24	40	20	133.3	145	61	99	14	4.79	5.02	9.9	3.8	6.3	0.8	4.97	8.3	10
2002	PIT	NL	25	33	33	198.3	197	71	134	21	3.59	4.44	9.2	2.8	5.3	0.9	4.48	24.6	9
2003	PIT	NL	26	31	31	197.3	171	76	147	24	3.28	3.68	7.8	3.1	5.9	1.0	4.00	47.4	11
2004	PIT	NL	27	28	26	161.7	159	63	116	15	4.07	4.32	8.8	3.1	5.8	0.8	4.36	21.3	10

Breakout: 12%   Improve: 45%   Collapse: 16%

Wells' won-loss record is deceptive. Support-Neutral metrics rated him as the ninth-best pitcher in the NL, and the same system had him as the second-most consistent pitcher in the league. The Pirate bullpen blew a number of games that Wells had left with a lead, something he could address by pitching a bit deeper into games in 2004. He has averaged just over six innings a start in two Pirate seasons, largely because of his high walk rate. With slightly better luck and slightly better control, he could have a 20-win season. Great fantasy pick.

St. Louis Cardinals

The 2003 St. Louis Cardinals were purveyors of one thing and one thing only: offense. The Cardinals boasted the second-best offense in the National League, but the team's true strengths were even more narrowly defined.

Half the of the Cardinals' starting position players contributed MVP-caliber seasons. Half. To put a finer point on it, Albert Pujols, Edgar Renteria, Scott Rolen, and Jim Edmonds were the best quartet fielded by any team in Major League Baseball; only the Braves came close.

Ultimately, 2003 turned out to be an echo of Mark McGwire's healthy years in St. Louis—historical achievements run to seed because of a sub-optimal supporting cast. Last season, St. Louis trotted out the best third baseman, center fielder and shortstop in the NL, and the second-best left fielder. In spite of this impressive core of talent, the Cardinals finished third in the middling NL Central.

This improbable failure was due to the front office's puzzling inability to flesh out the rest of the roster. Pujols, Renteria, Rolen, and Edmonds in 2003 posted an aggregate Value Over Replacement Player (VORP) of 272.7. In terms of VORP, only seven other teams since 1900 have assembled a four-pronged attack as potent as the Cardinals' in 2003 and still failed to make the post-season. Of those eight total clubs, last year's Cardinals finished with the lowest winning percentage (.525). Other than the Cloutin' Four and solid seasons from the top starters and a couple of relievers, the team failed in almost every other regard.

For sheer incompetence, the Cardinals' pen was outdone only by the Padres. Using Michael Wolverton's Adjusted Runs Prevented, Cardinal relievers as a group finished 55.3 runs below average. That's five games in the standings lost. As a whole, the bullpen posted a paltry 4.74 ERA, a lousy 1.52 K:BB ratio, and coughed up 68 homers in 484.1 innings. Tony LaRussa's noxious fidelity to Esteban Yan, Jeff Fassero, and Russ Springer was, well, noxious. Together, this self-immolating troika combined for 109 innings (almost a quarter of the total relief load), a 6.61 ERA and 27 (!) home runs allowed. When almost one-quarter of your bullpen innings are of this nature, you'll have trouble holding leads; remove them from the calculus, and the bullpen ERA becomes a more palatable 4.20.

One problem was that the Cardinals' two best relievers—Jason Isringhausen and Kiko Calero—both lost signifi-

CARDINALS PROSPECTUS

2003 record: 85–77; Third place, NL Central

Pythagenport record: 88–74

Runs scored per game: 5.4 (2nd in NL)

Runs allowed per game: 4.9 (11th in NL)

Team EqA: .279 (2nd in NL)

2003 Batters Age: 30.3 (7th oldest in NL)

2003 Pitchers Age: 31.7 (3rd oldest in NL)

Ballpark: Busch Stadium; Moderate pitchers' park; Park Factor of 0.974

2003: Albert Pujols and company wrecked many a pitcher's day but couldn't overcome an uneven pitching performance.

2004: As is becoming a custom in St. Louis, this squad will go as far as their pitching can take them.

cant time to injury. Calero didn't pitch beyond June because of a ruptured patellar tendon, and Isringhausen was sidelined until June 12 with an irritated shoulder capsule. These two injuries forced La Russa to depend upon the bullpen's lesser lights far more than he should have.

The rotation should also get its ample share of blame. Cardinal starters as a unit ranked 23rd in the league in Support-Neutral Value Added, "contributing" −3.3 wins to the cause. Matt Morris was solid for the most part, but, again according to Support-Neutral measures (found at www.baseballprospectus.com), was the fourth-least consistent starter in the majors. Morris was also troubled by a sore shoulder for much of the year, and missed more than a month due to a broken hand and sprained ankle.

Woody Williams led the staff in VORP, but that was mostly by dint of his innings advantage over Morris, who was more effective when healthy. After that, the rotation and staff as a whole struggled mightily. The St. Louis staff ranked 20th in the league in VORP, and Morris and Williams supplied 55% of that value. No team in the NL with at least 100 runs of pitching VORP had as high a percentage tied up in its top two starters. That lack of depth—and the Cards' inability to find strong reinforcements—was central to the Cardinals' failures in 2003.

The club's fourth and fifth starters for most of the year—Brett Tomko and Jason Simontacchi—combined for a VORP of 0.3, which means they were basically replacement-level pitchers who ate up 48 starts. That's only 12 fewer than Morris and Williams made. Throw in Dan Haren's 14 starts (2.0 VORP), and that's 62 starts frittered away on pitchers just a whisker above replacement level. In the NL, only the Pirates, Brewers, and Reds had a higher concentration of starts by pitchers at or below replacement level.

On the offensive side, the club did a poor job of surrounding its highly productive core hitters with adequate complementary pieces. Right fielder J. D. Drew was effective when healthy (20.9 VORP), but he logged fewer plate appearances than Orlando Palmeiro (−2.3 VORP), who, incidentally, was one of the few players offered salary arbitration by the Cardinals this past winter. Tino Martinez managed to post a vaguely tolerable EqA of .275 at first base, but he did see action in 60 games against left-handers, against whom he hit .235/.323/.346 and was as helpless as Jacques Derrida in an Amarillo bar fight. At catcher, Mike Matheny managed a VORP of only 1.5, even though he logged 490 plate appearances and benefited from positional scarcity. At second base, Fernando Vina and Bo Hart combined to finish just 7.6 runs above replacement.

Four players—the aforementioned Pujols, Renteria, Rolen, and Edmonds—supplied 60.4% of the team's total VORP of 451.4. This is at once bracing proof of the quartet's tremendous contributions and a stinging indictment of the front office's inability to find acceptable talent elsewhere on the diamond.

That the Cardinals didn't take steps to patch up the roster by mid-season is especially surprising, since deadline deals have been the Cards' house special under GM Walt Jocketty. Whereas most of Jocketty's endeavors on the free agent market can charitably be characterized as "friendly fire," he's shown a defter touch when it comes to making swaps. Since arriving just after the 1994 season, Jocketty has swung mostly one-sided deals for critical performers like McGwire, Renteria, Edmonds, Williams, Rolen, Will Clark, Chuck Finley, Darryl Kile, and others. In contrast, the summer of 2003 had to be especially disappointing for Cardinal fans when the deadline haul included only B-listers like Mike DeJean and Sterling Hitchcock. Deadline trades are generally overrated as a group, but it's exactly a team like the 2003 Cardinals, who were in the throes of a hotly fought race and burdened with actual (as opposed to perceived) pitching weaknesses, that should have been taking decisive steps to improve.

It may have been that they believed they simply didn't have the dispensable young talent to part with. After years of squandered draft picks and deadline, contender-style trades, the Cardinals' system is almost completely bereft of high-ceiling talents. Now that John Mozeliak is at the amateur-scouting switch, you can expect the organization to execute June drafts that will (mercifully) bear little

resemblance to the ones run by erstwhile scouting director-cum-unwitting saboteur Marty Maier. Mozeliak favors lower-risk selections (i.e., college talents) and will make a place at the table for serious quantitative analysis. However, it'll be a few years before Cardinal fans see the benefits of his enlightened approach. In the here and now, the farm system is arguably the worst in baseball.

But acquiring a high-profile talent in exchange for enough young bucks to shut down a Chelsea disco hasn't been any team's deadline M.O. since the Bartolo Colon trade of 2002. Since the institution of the last collective bargaining agreement, most teams have been eager to eschew large contracts or players on the cusp of their high-salary years. For contenders, both real and nominal, that means it no longer takes a king's ransom in prospects to land a deadline contributor, only a willingness to take on a contract. For whatever reason, the Cardinals—a "win now" team if ever there were such a beast—failed to leverage the new economic environment and didn't add the reliable arm they needed in the waning days of July.

The winter hasn't turned out much better for Cardinal Nation.

Heading into 2004, the offense could've been immediately improved by installing Eli Marrero as the starting catcher and confining the feckless Matheny to catch-and-throw backup status. However, Marrero was part of the winter meetings swap that also sent J. D. Drew to the Braves for Jason Marquis, Adam Wainwright, and Ray King. Trading Drew for pitching was an idea proposed in many circles; it also was unwise and uninspired. Drew's knee is problematic, but what really troubles him most is when he's forced to stop suddenly and change directions on the fly. These are things he'd do a lot less of in the position he'd like to return to—center field, where the foul-line walls aren't a concern. It sounds counterintuitive, but moving Drew to center might have been a serious boon to his health in 2004. Shifting Edmonds to right wouldn't play well with those who inaccurately see his defense in center as spectacular as opposed to solid (it's the latter that squares with statistical realities). But such a move should've happened irrespective of vox populi. A healthy and productive Drew could have turned the Cardinals' Quartet of Doom into a quintet, and would have ratcheted up their hopes in an imminently winnable NL Central. Instead, Drew's still-simmering potential will be the Braves' concern. If two potentially key contributors like Drew and Marrero were to be flipped for a big-league ready starter, it should've been someone a lot better than Marquis, whose reputation is mostly a function of the Braves' organizational hype rather than any sort of jaw-dropping record of performance (see also: Moss, Damian).

At least the organization wised up to Tino Martinez, jettisoning him and his dowry of intangibles to Tampa. Although the Cards were obliged to absorb most of

Martinez's 2004 salary, they did get Evan Rust in return, and he has the talent to be a bullpen contributor right away. Former D-Ray Steve Cox has been repatriated and may wind up as the club's starting first baseman. He'll be younger and cheaper than Tino, but might also be a little worse.

St. Louis did a good job landing Reggie Sanders to plug the right-field hole left by Drew. Although he's coming off his best offensive season since 1995, his production last year was out of step with recent history. He's a terror against lefties, but just adequate enough against righties to give the Cards 450 strong at-bats before being exposed to injury and fatigue risks.

The pitching side remained the most lacking, and the club didn't sign the front-of-the-rotation innings eater it badly needed. Morris' shoulder is a source of major concern for the upcoming season, and Williams also has a history of injuries. The team has signed Chris Carpenter in hopes that he'll be both fully recovered from labrum surgery and able to perform capably as a fourth or fifth starter. Haren has a strong minor league dossier, but there's no guarantee he's ready to contribute at the highest level on an extended basis. The club was positioned as a contender, and had the storied atmospherics to attract almost any free agent. That they didn't land or even heartily pursue a Kevin Millwood, Andy Pettitte, Bartolo Colon, or Javier Vazquez as of press time doesn't say much for the front office's off-season battle plans.

Having failed to make a superior addition to the rotation or bullpen via trade or Type-A free agency, they'll need to make sage use of their spring-training NRIs and carefully vet minor league free agents and the various and sundry non-tenders that are an indelible part of baseball under the "new economics."

The Rule 5 draft could have helped as well, as the Blue Jays, Expos, and Rockies proved last season with Aquilino Lopez, Luis Ayala, and Javier Lopez, respectively. It's possible to divine an effective major league reliever from Rule 5 picks. The Cardinals failed to take this approach at the winter meetings and thus squandered another opportunity to address a major shortcoming. Moreover, this past year's Rule 5 haul was notable for the abundance of bullpen-ready arms, namely Ray Aguilar of the Braves and Josh Stevens of the Red Sox. Not adding Jeremy Lambert, probably the best relief prospect in the system, to the 40-man roster and thus allowing him to leave as a minor league free agent was another misplay.

The Cardinals have two advantages heading into the upcoming season: clearly-defined and easily-filled voids in the roster and only a marginally competitive division. The organization needs to realize what a historical rarity they have in the quartet of Edmonds, Pujols, Renteria, and Rolen, and then they need to take the obvious steps needed to surround this core with at least league-average filler talent at all spots. If that's done, a post-season berth is all but inevitable. Then again, the failure to do just that was what scuttled their playoff hopes in 2003. Barring a bold 11th-hour move, it looks like they'll have learned nothing from their mistakes.

HITTERS

DARIC BARTON   C   Bats: L   Throws: R   Born: 16-Aug-85   Age: 18

YEAR	TM	LG	AGE	AB	H	2B	3B	HR	BB	SO	SB	CS	AVG	OBP	SLG	MLVR	EQBA	EQOBP	EQSLG	EQMLVR	VORP	DEFENSE
2003	JCY	APP	17	170	50	10	0	4	37	48	0	3	.294	.420	.424	.232	.168	.261	.246	-.480	-39.7	35-C -5
2004	STL	NL	18	249	43	10	0	5	26	81	0	1	.172	.256	.271	-.414	.175	.257	.285	-.408	-17.2	69-C -15

Breakout: 35%   *Improve: 57%*   *Collapse: 36%*

The Cards' top pick of the 2003 draft put up impressive numbers in 54 games in the Appalachian League. Of particular note was his impressive plate discipline, 37 walks in 214 plate appearances. The power was lacking, but that's to be expected in most players right out of high school. He didn't catch much as a prep, so taking that into account, the club was reasonably pleased with his defensive performance. He'll need to work on his defense, but it's promising.

SHAUN BOYD   CF/2B   Bats: R   Throws: R   Born: 15-Aug-81   Age: 22

YEAR	TM	LG	AGE	AB	H	2B	3B	HR	BB	SO	SB	CS	AVG	OBP	SLG	MLVR	EQBA	EQOBP	EQSLG	EQMLVR	VORP	DEFENSE	
2001	PEO	MID	19	277	78	12	2	5	33	42	20	3	.282	.357	.394	.093	.220	.282	.315	-.319	-13.1	79-2B 4	
2002	PEO	MID	20	520	163	36	5	12	54	78	32	7	.313	.379	.471	.278	.243	.295	.380	-.189	-2.2	127-2B -23	
2003	PMB	FLA	21	416	107	17	2	5	54	70	28	14	.257	.343	.344	.032	.215	.283	.303	-.337	-26.1	50-CF -1	42-2B -15
2003	TEN	SOU	21	88	24	6	0	0	4	12	2	2	.273	.305	.341	-.074	.247	.277	.315	-.314	-4.4	26-CF -1	
2004	STL	NL	22	245	58	13	1	4	21	44	7	3	.236	.299	.350	-.201	.240	.301	.368	-.186	-0.9	67-2B -12	

Breakout: 41%   *Improve: 62%*   *Collapse: 16%*

When the Cardinals drafted Boyd with the 13th overall pick in 2000, it was widely considered a fairly drastic overdraft. The critics were right. Boyd's produced at the plate in only one stop, and that was in the Midwest League in 2002, and then only after repeating the circuit. The experiment at second base is over, mostly the product of his having the hands of a stuffed alligator. The organization is holding out hopes that he can play center, but that's also probably a stretch. He hits the ball hard, but is easily fooled by breaking pitches, and has a slow bat with a hitch in his swing. That's to say, he'll never hit enough to be a corner outfielder at the major league level. The Cards probably should have packaged him for trade when his perceived value was at its highest, following the 2002 season.

MIGUEL CAIRO   UT   BATS: R   THROWS: R   Born: 04-May-74   Age: 30

YEAR	TM	LG	AGE	AB	H	2B	3B	HR	BB	SO	SB	CS	AVG	OBP	SLG	MLVR	EQBA	EQOBP	EQSLG	EQMLVR	VORP	DEFENSE		
2002	STL	NL	28	184	46	9	2	2	13	36	1	1	.250	.307	.353	-.111	.262	.316	.374	-.144	1.5	12-2B -1		
2003	STL	NL	29	261	64	15	2	5	13	30	4	1	.245	.289	.375	-.126	.254	.301	.390	-.155	-1.2	29-2B 2	14-LF	-1
2004	NYY	AL	30	225	59	13	2	5	15	31	3	2	.263	.315	.400	-.075	.268	.323	.415	-.064	6.1	62-2B -8		

Breakout: 32%   Improve: 61%   Collapse: 17%

Cairo's not completely without his uses. He runs well, plays credible defense at every position on the diamond except catcher, and even flashed a little power in St. Louis last year. Any team in a semblance of a pennant race that uses him as a regular role isn't serious about that pennant race.

J. D. DREW   RF   Bats: L   Throws: R   Born: 20-Nov-75   Age: 28

YEAR	TM	LG	AGE	AB	H	2B	3B	HR	BB	SO	SB	CS	AVG	OBP	SLG	MLVR	EQBA	EQOBP	EQSLG	EQMLVR	VORP	DEFENSE		
2001	STL	NL	25	375	121	18	5	27	57	75	13	3	.323	.414	.613	.431	.326	.418	.619	.436	56.1	90-RF -1	18-CF	1
2002	STL	NL	26	424	107	19	1	18	57	104	8	2	.252	.349	.429	.062	.262	.354	.449	.031	11.2	99-RF 0		
2003	STL	NL	27	287	83	13	3	15	36	48	2	2	.289	.374	.512	.241	.295	.377	.527	.209	22.6	43-RF 1	19-CF	1
2004	ATL	NL	28	312	85	16	2	15	45	59	4	2	.273	.369	.485	.120	.276	.370	.502	.137	23.7	88-RF 1		

Breakout: 12%   Improve: 40%   Collapse: 26%

Drew's chronic patellar tendinitis was and remains serious. It's the same injury that, in tandem with advanced age, ended Mark McGwire's career. In Drew's case, the condition was so advanced that surgeons had to remove a significant portion of dead tissue. He's as healed as he's ever going to be, and a nearly full season is possible, though something less than that is just about a historical imperative. In 2003, when he was able to play, he was effective. That's been the story almost his entire career. He'll replace Gary Sheffield in the Braves' lineup, forced to painfully chase more balls into the corners since Andruw Jones is a fixture in center.

JIM EDMONDS   CF   Bats: L   Throws: L   Born: 27-Jun-70   Age: 34

YEAR	TM	LG	AGE	AB	H	2B	3B	HR	BB	SO	SB	CS	AVG	OBP	SLG	MLVR	EQBA	EQOBP	EQSLG	EQMLVR	VORP	DEFENSE
2001	STL	NL	31	500	152	38	1	30	93	136	5	5	.304	.410	.564	.337	.307	.417	.568	.342	75.1	131-CF 3
2002	STL	NL	32	476	148	31	2	28	86	134	4	3	.311	.420	.561	.393	.320	.427	.582	.391	73.0	127-CF 10
2003	STL	NL	33	447	123	32	2	39	77	127	1	3	.275	.385	.617	.382	.281	.388	.632	.354	58.0	118-CF 5
2004	STL	NL	34	362	100	22	1	22	59	96	2	1	.275	.380	.524	.190	.279	.383	.552	.223	34.0	102-CF 0

Breakout: 13%   Improve: 34%   Collapse: 26%

According to VORP, Edmonds was easily the best center fielder in the National League last season. But are there reasons for concern? Edmonds posted his lowest AVG and OBP and played in his fewest games since becoming a Cardinal. Additionally, his numbers dropped notably after the All-Star break. On the upside, he posted the highest SLG and Isolated SLG of his career, and even with a normal decline, Edmonds should remain an excellent player if healthy.

JOHN GALL   1B   Bats: R   Throws: R   Born: 02-Apr-78   Age: 26

YEAR	TM	LG	AGE	AB	H	2B	3B	HR	BB	SO	SB	CS	AVG	OBP	SLG	MLVR	EQBA	EQOBP	EQSLG	EQMLVR	VORP	DEFENSE		
2001	PEO	MID	23	205	62	23	0	4	16	18	0	3	.302	.353	.473	.212	.234	.281	.373	-.232	-9.6	43-1B -5		
2001	POT	CAR	23	319	101	25	0	4	24	40	5	6	.317	.369	.433	.206	.258	.303	.365	-.184	-10.2	44-1B -3	28-3B	-4
2002	NHV	EAS	24	526	166	45	3	20	38	75	4	1	.316	.362	.527	.293	.277	.318	.469	.008	14.5	93-1B -10	17-3B	-5
2003	TEN	SOU	25	52	17	1	0	3	3	4	0	1	.327	.357	.519	.285	.283	.309	.472	.002	2.0			
2003	MEM	PCL	25	461	144	24	1	16	39	56	5	2	.312	.368	.473	.206	.288	.340	.444	.021	14.7	115-1B -12		
2004	STL	NL	26	231	59	13	1	6	19	34	2	1	.256	.315	.402	-.090	.261	.317	.423	-.069	4.5	63-1B -6		

Breakout: 21%   Improve: 42%   Collapse: 36%

(continued next page)

John Gall *(continued)*

A horrible April landed Gall back in Double-A, but there he showed more patience early in the count, earning a return to Memphis. In spite of an odd batting stance, he's been a fairly consistent hitter at most levels. The 45 doubles he smacked in the Eastern League in 2002 provide hope of developing power, but he still needs to improve his walk rates; he's also shown an annoying propensity for hitting into double plays in the high minors, something you'd like to see curbed. His footwork at first is improving, but he may be better suited to a corner outfield spot. To hear some tell it, Gall is the best position prospect in the system. To hear others tell it, well, someone has to be. Just like a Wings Hauser straight-to-video vehicle isn't worth your while, a farm system in which John Gall takes top billing probably isn't either.

REID GORECKI   OF   Bats: R   Throws: R   Born: 22-Dec-80   Age: 23

YEAR	TM	LG	AGE	AB	H	2B	3B	HR	BB	SO	SB	CS	AVG	OBP	SLG	MLVR	EQBA	EQOBP	EQSLG	EQMLVR	VORP	DEFENSE	
2002	NWJ	NYP	21	274	77	8	13	8	20	57	22	11	.281	.327	.493	.234	.212	.251	.385	-.287	-22.3	69-CF	0
2003	PEO	MID	22	480	128	19	8	15	51	90	23	11	.267	.338	.433	.144	.207	.264	.354	-.309	-25.3	127-CF	-11
2004	*STL*	*NL*	*23*	*238*	*52*	*11*	*3*	*5*	*18*	*56*	*6*	*3*	*.218*	*.277*	*.355*	*-.245*	*.221*	*.279*	*.373*	*-.231*	*-7.2*	*65-CF*	*-7*

Breakout: 38%   *Improve: 56%*   *Collapse: 22%*

The Cards selected Gorecki, a University of Delaware product, in the 13th round of the 2002 draft. In two seasons, he's shown some gap power, a .272 AVG and an improving—although still sub-par—walk rate. He's a college-trained talent who's been merely decent in the low minors, so it's hard to project much more than organizational soldier prospect status for him.

CODY HAERTHER   OF/3B   Bats: L   Throws: R   Born: 14-Jul-83   Age: 20

YEAR	TM	LG	AGE	AB	H	2B	3B	HR	BB	SO	SB	CS	AVG	OBP	SLG	MLVR	EQBA	EQOBP	EQSLG	EQMLVR	VORP	DEFENSE			
2003	JCY	APP	19	226	75	12	6	3	22	30	2	1	.332	.390	.478	.295	.222	.263	.335	-.328	-42.4	41-LF	-5	10-3B	-1
2004	*STL*	*NL*	*20*	*250*	*54*	*11*	*3*	*2*	*15*	*45*	*1*	*1*	*.216*	*.263*	*.314*	*-.324*	*.220*	*.265*	*.331*	*-.313*	*-12.9*	*67-LF*	*-5*		

Breakout: 22%   *Improve: 46%*   *Collapse: 36%*

Haerther hit for average in the Appy League and showed good gap power. He's a long way from the majors and could stand to improve his command of the strike zone, although it's not a glaring liability. He does have some raw offensive skills, and he's worth watching as he climbs through the system.

TRAVIS HANSON   3B   Bats: L   Throws: R   Born: 24-Jan-81   Age: 23

YEAR	TM	LG	AGE	AB	H	2B	3B	HR	BB	SO	SB	CS	AVG	OBP	SLG	MLVR	EQBA	EQOBP	EQSLG	EQMLVR	VORP	DEFENSE			
2002	NWJ	NYP	21	272	80	17	5	4	12	55	1	1	.294	.326	.438	.172	.233	.260	.366	-.283	-15.7	60-3B	2	11-SS	-2
2003	PEO	MID	22	527	146	31	5	9	35	104	3	4	.277	.325	.406	.098	.224	.263	.348	-.308	-21.2	134-3B	-6		
2004	*STL*	*NL*	*23*	*268*	*62*	*15*	*2*	*5*	*16*	*63*	*1*	*1*	*.233*	*.280*	*.359*	*-.225*	*.236*	*.282*	*.378*	*-.210*	*2.0*	*71-3B*	*-4*		

Breakout: 39%   *Improve: 58%*   *Collapse: 20%*

Hanson was drafted out of the University of Portland in the ninth round of the 2002 cattle call. After some early trials at shortstop, he's settled in as a well-regarded glove at third. His 31 doubles last season in the Midwest League offer some hope of projectable power, but there's little else to recommend him at this point. If he's going to be on the organization's radar as a corner defender, he must improve upon his .325 career OBP, lest he just wind up on the Stan Royer road to eminent forgettability.

BO HART   2B/SS   Bats: R   Throws: R   Born: 27-Sep-76   Age: 27

YEAR	TM	LG	AGE	AB	H	2B	3B	HR	BB	SO	SB	CS	AVG	OBP	SLG	MLVR	EQBA	EQOBP	EQSLG	EQMLVR	VORP	DEFENSE			
2001	POT	CAR	24	279	85	23	3	5	17	69	16	7	.305	.375	.462	.241	.255	.306	.402	-.128	4.1	72-2B	8		
2002	NHV	EAS	25	405	101	17	6	4	43	82	14	7	.249	.338	.351	-.041	.222	.293	.319	-.291	-14.6	98-2B	0		
2003	MEM	PCL	26	266	79	14	2	7	15	55	4	2	.297	.331	.444	.089	.276	.312	.425	-.067	8.5	39-2B	4	11-3B	0
2003	STL	NL	26	296	82	13	5	4	12	64	3	1	.277	.317	.395	-.025	.287	.325	.413	-.051	8.0	68-2B	-2		
2004	*STL*	*NL*	*27*	*370*	*94*	*20*	*3*	*7*	*25*	*78*	*5*	*3*	*.253*	*.310*	*.379*	*-.131*	*.257*	*.312*	*.399*	*-.112*	*9.6*	*97-2B*	*-2*		

Breakout: 28%   *Improve: 50%*   *Collapse: 27%*

Here's your winner of the Joe McEwing/Gordie Lockbaum Hustlin' Scrub Award. After being promoted to fill in for the injured Fernando Vina, Hart got off to a hot start, made a flurry of highlight-friendly plays afield and generally played hard. He thus endeared himself to local fans and media alike, because they like their hustle in St. Louis. But after a magma-hot June, Hart never again performed adequately at the plate. His minor league numbers don't forecast greatness, and his performance at the major league level doesn't, either. He won't be any better than decline-phase Fernando Vina, but at least he'll be cheaper.

DEE HAYNES   OF   Bats: R   Throws: R   Born: 22-Feb-78   Age: 26

YEAR	TM	LG	AGE	AB	H	2B	3B	HR	BB	SO	SB	CS	AVG	OBP	SLG	MLVR	EQBA	EQOBP	EQSLG	EQMLVR	VORP	DEFENSE	
2001	POT	CAR	23	417	121	24	3	13	14	82	5	1	.290	.329	.456	.163	.245	.277	.403	-.189	-15.7	77-RF	0
2002	NHV	EAS	24	504	157	29	4	21	25	67	3	2	.312	.355	.510	.256	.278	.313	.464	-.007	7.1	117-LF	-5
2003	MEM	PCL	25	441	111	24	3	18	15	50	3	1	.252	.279	.442	-.042	.238	.267	.425	-.181	-16.3	107-LF	-4
2004	STL	NL	26	231	58	13	1	7	13	35	1	1	.252	.297	.410	-.114	.256	.299	.432	-.093	0.1	62-LF	-2

Breakout: 32%   Improve: 55%   Collapse: 28%

Haynes is a streaky hitter with an alarming lack of patience at the plate. He suffered a leg injury and a death in the family in 2003, so those factors may explain the decline in his numbers at Memphis. The club believes he made decent progress with his defense in left, but until he improves his plate discipline and learns to adjust to breaking stuff he doesn't have much of a future at the highest level.

BUCKY JACOBSEN   1B/OF   Bats: R   Throws: R   Born: 30-Aug-75   Age: 28

YEAR	TM	LG	AGE	AB	H	2B	3B	HR	BB	SO	SB	CS	AVG	OBP	SLG	MLVR	EQBA	EQOBP	EQSLG	EQMLVR	VORP	DEFENSE	
2001	HUN	SOU	25	93	41	9	0	10	15	14	1	2	.441	.518	.860	1.082	.354	.429	.698	.601	22.3	22-1B	-3
2001	IND	INT	25	300	74	18	1	12	26	78	0	0	.247	.312	.433	.002	.230	.294	.414	-.153	-6.2	76-1B	-3
2002	HUN	SOU	26	198	50	9	2	11	22	41	2	2	.253	.336	.485	.153	.222	.283	.433	-.153	-4.4	44-1B	-3
2002	NHV	EAS	26	102	30	11	0	4	9	25	0	0	.294	.360	.520	.257	.260	.313	.462	-.026	1.8	13-1B	-1
2003	TEN	SOU	27	447	133	24	1	31	56	91	3	1	.298	.388	.564	.351	.247	.323	.479	.004	12.7	109-1B	-13
2004	STL	NL	28	174	41	9	1	7	17	42	1	1	.235	.310	.418	-.094	.239	.312	.440	-.073	2.6	50-1B	-5

Breakout: 19%   Improve: 41%   Collapse: 34%

In Jacobsen, we may have the next offshoot of the Billy McMillon/Morgan Burkhart/Jim Rushford neglected minor league hitter family tree. Jacobsen failed in his one crack at Triple-A back in 2001, but he's proved himself at Double-A and has strong numbers on the whole. He draws walks and hits for power, and in 2003 he put together his finest season to date. He's a minor league free agent, and in a just world someone will sign him and give him a chance to prove himself in the bigs. Or at least Triple-A.

ELI MARRERO   OF/C   Bats: R   Throws: R   Born: 17-Nov-73   Age: 30

YEAR	TM	LG	AGE	AB	H	2B	3B	HR	BB	SO	SB	CS	AVG	OBP	SLG	MLVR	EQBA	EQOBP	EQSLG	EQMLVR	VORP	DEFENSE			
2001	STL	NL	27	203	54	11	3	6	15	36	6	3	.266	.312	.438	-.039	.272	.321	.442	-.030	8.1	49-C	0		
2002	STL	NL	28	397	104	19	1	18	40	72	14	2	.262	.327	.451	.062	.272	.335	.473	.039	11.0	32-RF	1	25-C	-7
2003	STL	NL	29	107	24	4	2	2	7	18	0	1	.224	.267	.355	-.207	.231	.278	.370	-.244	-4.2	13-RF	-1		
2004	ATL	NL	30	217	55	11	2	7	20	37	3	1	.253	.316	.414	-.075	.257	.317	.429	-.064	3.8	60-RF	3		

Breakout: 24%   Improve: 44%   Collapse: 24%

It's a defensible position that Marrero's offensive numbers would decline were he to move behind the plate full-time, but even if that's the case he'd have been an upgrade over the banjo-hitting Matheny. For all the plaudits Matheny's defense garners, it's easy to forget that Marrero was a darn good defensive backstop when he played there regularly. Traded to Atlanta at the winter meetings, Marrero will battle for the Braves' starting catcher job.

TINO MARTINEZ   1B   Bats: L   Throws: R   Born: 07-Dec-67   Age: 36

YEAR	TM	LG	AGE	AB	H	2B	3B	HR	BB	SO	SB	CS	AVG	OBP	SLG	MLVR	EQBA	EQOBP	EQSLG	EQMLVR	VORP	DEFENSE	
2001	NYY	AL	33	589	165	24	2	34	42	89	1	2	.280	.329	.501	.118	.300	.351	.540	.190	41.4	143-1B	9
2002	STL	NL	34	511	134	25	1	21	58	71	3	2	.262	.337	.438	.063	.271	.342	.459	.031	15.7	136-1B	10
2003	STL	NL	35	476	130	25	2	15	53	71	1	1	.273	.352	.429	.077	.281	.359	.444	.049	14.7	118-1B	6
2004	TBY	AL	36	395	103	21	1	14	38	59	1	1	.261	.328	.424	-.023	.264	.335	.443	-.009	10.1	105-1B	1

Breakout: 16%   Improve: 37%   Collapse: 27%

(continued next page)

Tino Martinez *(continued)*

For two seasons, he's been the reigning contractual boondoggle in St. Louis. Tino's still a solid defender and managed a blip of adequacy against right-handed pitching last season, but he's comically overpaid and shouldn't be allowed in the ballpark when a lefty's starting for the opposition. Wisely, the team brass elected to eat his salary, filed him under "mistake and aura," and dealt him to the ever-pliant D-Rays for a handful of carbon-based trinkets.

MIKE MATHENY   C   Bats: R   Throws: R   Born: 22-Sep-70   Age: 33

YEAR	TM	LG	AGE	AB	H	2B	3B	HR	BB	SO	SB	CS	AVG	OBP	SLG	MLVR	EQBA	EQOBP	EQSLG	EQMLVR	VORP	DEFENSE	
2001	STL	NL	30	381	83	12	0	7	28	76	0	1	.218	.276	.304	-.327	.226	.284	.314	-.313	-14.8	112-C	12
2002	STL	NL	31	315	77	12	1	3	32	49	1	3	.244	.313	.317	-.152	.256	.325	.338	-.181	-0.6	88-C	6
2003	STL	NL	32	441	111	18	2	8	44	81	1	1	.252	.320	.356	-.093	.261	.328	.371	-.126	4.0	124-C	5
2004	STL	NL	33	258	63	12	1	4	25	47	1	1	.245	.314	.344	-.176	.249	.316	.362	-.160	0.9	71-C	0

Breakout: 25%   Improve: 47%   Collapse: 34%

His defense, most years, is genuinely good, but it doesn't compensate for his myriad offensive liabilities. He's a backup, plain and simple. The sooner the Cardinals realize that, the more runs they'll put on the board. At 33, it's only going to get worse from this point forward.

YADIER MOLINA   C   Bats: R   Throws: R   Born: 13-Jul-82   Age: 21

YEAR	TM	LG	AGE	AB	H	2B	3B	HR	BB	SO	SB	CS	AVG	OBP	SLG	MLVR	EQBA	EQOBP	EQSLG	EQMLVR	VORP	DEFENSE	
2001	JCY	APP	18	158	41	11	0	4	12	23	1	1	.259	.320	.405	.046	.185	.223	.290	-.491	-33.8	42-C	9
2002	PEO	MID	19	393	110	20	0	7	21	36	2	7	.280	.331	.384	.072	.231	.267	.328	-.324	-17.7	105-C	12
2003	TEN	SOU	20	364	100	13	1	2	25	45	0	1	.275	.327	.332	-.050	.247	.289	.304	-.305	-14.9	100-C	3
2004	STL	NL	21	246	54	11	0	3	15	32	0	1	.219	.269	.299	-.332	.223	.271	.314	-.321	-9.2	66-C	-2

Breakout: 26%   Improve: 44%   Collapse: 33%

Although Molina right now looks like classic Molina—all glove, no bat—the organization thinks he'll hit based upon his holding his own at Double-A this past season as a very young regular. That's certainly not to be discounted, but his complete lack of peripheral plate skills is a serious problem. He doesn't draw walks and had only 16 extra-base hits in almost 400 plate appearances this past season. But he is indeed young, and the Cards see him as their catcher of the future. If Mike Matheny is the unfortunate gold standard, they might be right.

JOHN NELSON   SS   Bats: R   Throws: R   Born: 03-Mar-79   Age: 25

YEAR	TM	LG	AGE	AB	H	2B	3B	HR	BB	SO	SB	CS	AVG	OBP	SLG	MLVR	EQBA	EQOBP	EQSLG	EQMLVR	VORP	DEFENSE			
2001	NWJ	NYP	22	252	60	16	3	8	35	76	14	3	.238	.332	.421	.107	.174	.245	.317	-.415	-39.1	40-CF	-6	19-RF	-3
2002	PEO	MID	23	481	132	28	5	16	54	123	16	3	.274	.349	.453	.182	.216	.273	.366	-.269	-10.0	129-SS	-6		
2003	TEN	SOU	24	506	120	22	1	5	44	117	10	5	.237	.301	.314	-.135	.212	.262	.287	-.403	-31.9	131-SS	4		
2004	STL	NL	25	182	41	9	1	4	15	45	3	1	.225	.287	.347	-.232	.229	.289	.365	-.218	0.4	51-SS	-3		

Breakout: 52%   Improve: 70%   Collapse: 21%

The good news is that he plays a key defensive position and . . . he plays a key defensive position. In fairness, Nelson, an eighth-rounder out of Kansas University in 2001, did have an All-Star season in the Midwest League in 2002. However, his solid work at Peoria is bookended by a weak showing in the NY-Penn League and a dreadful performance this past season in Double-A. He strikes out a great deal for someone with little power, and he's shown poor pitch-recognition skills in the high minors. He did skip a level, so there's probably some performance lag at work. But he's got a lot to prove in 2004.

JON NUNNALLY   OF   Bats: L   Throws: R   Born: 09-Nov-71   Age: 32

YEAR	TM	LG	AGE	AB	H	2B	3B	HR	BB	SO	SB	CS	AVG	OBP	SLG	MLVR	EQBA	EQOBP	EQSLG	EQMLVR	VORP	DEFENSE			
2001	OMA	PCL	29	316	66	9	0	18	54	109	11	3	.209	.329	.408	-.108	.181	.290	.353	-.274	-22.6	53-LF	-2	22-CF	-2
2002	OMA	PCL	30	58	14	5	0	3	8	19	1	3	.241	.343	.483	.074	.203	.294	.407	-.181	-1.0				
2002	MEM	PCL	30	302	73	14	1	14	34	82	13	1	.242	.322	.434	-.010	.222	.294	.402	-.175	-10.6	55-RF	3	20-CF	1
2003	MEM	PCL	31	428	115	20	5	25	98	126	19	11	.269	.408	.514	.284	.233	.361	.455	.028	26.1	54-CF	-4	52-RF	-1
2004	MIL	NL	32	141	33	7	1	8	22	45	3	1	.233	.340	.470	.021	.234	.339	.471	.010	8.3	43-RF	1		

Breakout: 42%   Improve: 59%   Collapse: 25%

Nunnally is at his best when he's not so pull-conscious and is willing to use the whole field. His uppercut swing makes him vulnerable to pitchers who work low in the zone, but his patience at the plate and raw power are both excellent. At 31, Nunnally needs a shot right now if he's going to cobble together any sort of extended stay in the majors. He deserves the chance, and could be a quality fourth or fifth outfielder in the majors for the next few years. Signed a minor league contract with the Brewers, where he might just get that chance.

ORLANDO PALMEIRO   OF   Bats: L   Throws: L   Born: 19-Jan-69   Age: 35

YEAR	TM	LG	AGE	AB	H	2B	3B	HR	BB	SO	SB	CS	AVG	OBP	SLG	MLVR	EQBA	EQOBP	EQSLG	EQMLVR	VORP	DEFENSE			
2001	ANA	AL	32	230	56	10	1	2	25	24	6	6	.243	.319	.322	-.177	.264	.344	.351	-.121	-3.4	20-RF	-1	18-LF	0
2002	ANA	AL	33	263	79	12	1	0	30	22	7	2	.300	.368	.354	.006	.323	.394	.380	.058	8.6	37-RF	0	25-LF	-1
2003	STL	NL	34	317	86	13	1	3	32	31	3	3	.271	.336	.347	-.064	.280	.348	.360	-.089	-0.5	38-RF	1	25-LF	0
2004	*HOU*	*NL*	*35*	*165*	*43*	*8*	*1*	*1*	*18*	*17*	*2*	*1*	*.263*	*.336*	*.341*	*-.130*	*.260*	*.331*	*.340*	*-.155*	*-2.7*	*48-RF*	*-2*		

Breakout: 15%   Improve: 29%   Collapse: 36%

Palmeiro has some on-base skills and can play all three outfield positions, so he's certainly not a liability as a fifth outfielder. However, something's amiss when he logs 357 plate appearances. He merits a place on the roster, but anything beyond spot starts and pinch-hitting indicates trouble in the outfield. He's not a walks machine, so when his ability to hit .280 or higher goes the way of Billy Ray Cyrus, so does most of his value. As an Astro, he'll replace Orlando Merced as the top pinch-hitter.

EDUARDO PEREZ   1B/3B/OF   Bats: R   Throws: R   Born: 11-Sep-69   Age: 34

YEAR	TM	LG	AGE	AB	H	2B	3B	HR	BB	SO	SB	CS	AVG	OBP	SLG	MLVR	EQBA	EQOBP	EQSLG	EQMLVR	VORP	DEFENSE	
2002	STL	NL	32	154	31	9	0	10	17	36	0	0	.201	.290	.455	-.041	.212	.300	.481	-.064	0.0	20-RF	0
2003	STL	NL	33	253	72	16	0	11	29	53	5	2	.285	.365	.478	.175	.292	.371	.494	.150	16.0	42-RF	-2
2004	*TBA*	*AL*	*34*	*199*	*49*	*11*	*0*	*8*	*21*	*43*	*3*	*1*	*.247*	*.324*	*.435*	*-.025*	*.250*	*.331*	*.455*	*-.012*	*8.7*	*56-RF*	*-2*

Breakout: 16%   Improve: 36%   Collapse: 43%

His skills, which boil down to torching lefties and standing on one of the diamond's corners, aren't too hard to find, but Perez fills his role quite well. He blistered southpaws to the tune of .353/.459/.667 last season and played four different positions. He's stretched as an everyday player, but every roster needs an Eduardo Perez. Bless him for his sense of charity, he's decided to become a D-Ray.

ALBERT PUJOLS   LF   Bats: R   Throws: R   Born: 16-Jan-80   Age: 24

YEAR	TM	LG	AGE	AB	H	2B	3B	HR	BB	SO	SB	CS	AVG	OBP	SLG	MLVR	EQBA	EQOBP	EQSLG	EQMLVR	VORP	DEFENSE			
2001	STL	NL	21	590	194	47	4	37	69	93	1	3	.329	.403	.610	.418	.334	.409	.618	.432	104.5	54-3B	4	33-1B	-3
2002	STL	NL	22	590	185	40	2	34	72	69	2	4	.314	.394	.561	.360	.322	.398	.584	.352	65.0	89-LF	-5	33-3B	0
2003	STL	NL	23	591	212	51	1	43	79	65	5	1	.359	.439	.667	.629	.362	.442	.679	.603	102.8	98-LF	-5	40-1B	2
2004	*STL*	*NL*	*24*	*572*	*185*	*41*	*2*	*36*	*83*	*73*	*5*	*2*	*.324*	*.413*	*.591*	*.375*	*.329*	*.416*	*.622*	*.417*	*75.0*	*156-LF*	*-4*		

Breakout: 9%   Improve: 39%   Collapse: 28%

He's no Barry Bonds, but no one else is Albert Pujols. Look for other players who've put together three initial seasons like Pujols, and you find only pantheon-dwellers: DiMaggio, Williams, Musial. And then the comparisons wither. It's still possible that he's older than advertised, but the signal-to-noise ratio on that front is dropping. He does it all: Power, average, walks. This is one hell of a hitter. Go see him play.

EDGAR RENTERIA   SS   Bats: R   Throws: R   Born: 07-Aug-75   Age: 28

YEAR	TM	LG	AGE	AB	H	2B	3B	HR	BB	SO	SB	CS	AVG	OBP	SLG	MLVR	EQBA	EQOBP	EQSLG	EQMLVR	VORP	DEFENSE	
2001	STL	NL	25	493	128	19	3	10	39	73	17	4	.260	.314	.371	-.135	.266	.322	.380	-.121	11.3	128-SS	0
2002	STL	NL	26	544	166	36	2	11	49	57	22	7	.305	.364	.439	.142	.315	.371	.459	.123	46.5	145-SS	-8
2003	STL	NL	27	587	194	47	1	13	65	54	34	7	.330	.394	.480	.269	.337	.402	.492	.245	67.7	153-SS	0
2004	*STL*	*NL*	*28*	*531*	*158*	*33*	*3*	*11*	*52*	*57*	*22*	*6*	*.297*	*.360*	*.432*	*.058*	*.302*	*.363*	*.455*	*.085*	*41.1*	*139-SS*	*-3*

Breakout: 9%   Improve: 30%   Collapse: 26%

At last, he's achieved undisputed excellence. Renteria was the best shortstop in the NL last season and the second-best player on the Cardinals. A .330/.394/.480 batting line, 47 doubles and Gold Glove defense at a critical position add up to an MVP candidate. At age 28, we may have just seen his best, but he'll still be an elite performer for the next two or three seasons. If there's a criticism, it's that he does most of his damage against lefties, but he still holds his own against right-handers.

KERRY ROBINSON OF Bats: L Throws: L Born: 03-Oct-73 Age: 30

YEAR	TM	LG	AGE	AB	H	2B	3B	HR	BB	SO	SB	CS	AVG	OBP	SLG	MLVR	EQBA	EQOBP	EQSLG	EQMLVR	VORP	DEFENSE			
2001	MEM	PCL	27	40	13	1	0	0	4	10	4	1	.325	.386	.350	.020	.275	.341	.300	-.191	-0.8				
2001	STL	NL	27	186	53	6	1	1	12	20	11	2	.285	.330	.344	-.125	.291	.339	.354	-.107	-2.7	25-LF	-1	13-CF	1
2002	STL	NL	28	181	47	7	4	1	11	29	7	4	.260	.301	.359	-.108	.272	.309	.375	-.148	-4.3	27-LF	-2		
2003	MEM	PCL	29	61	21	2	1	0	1	7	5	0	.344	.355	.410	.124	.328	.339	.393	-.020	2.2	15-CF	-1		
2003	STL	NL	29	208	52	6	3	1	8	27	6	1	.250	.281	.322	-.212	.257	.287	.333	-.262	-5.7	22-RF	0		
2004	STL	NL	30	143	37	6	2	1	8	20	4	2	.262	.304	.347	-.179	.267	.306	.365	-.162	-1.4	40-LF	2		

Breakout: 22%   Improve: 37%   Collapse: 39%

Robinson is a good defender and has speed on the bases, but he simply doesn't have the offensive skills to be on a major league roster, even in a limited role. He has no power and can't hit for average or draw walks. As a local product, he's popular among Cardinal fans, but he's a waste of roster space.

SCOTT ROLEN 3B Bats: R Throws: R Born: 04-Apr-75 Age: 29

YEAR	TM	LG	AGE	AB	H	2B	3B	HR	BB	SO	SB	CS	AVG	OBP	SLG	MLVR	EQBA	EQOBP	EQSLG	EQMLVR	VORP	DEFENSE	
2001	PHI	NL	26	554	160	39	1	25	74	127	16	5	.289	.378	.498	.186	.299	.389	.512	.212	62.9	148-3B	17
2002	PHI	NL	27	375	97	21	4	17	52	68	5	2	.259	.358	.472	.146	.271	.365	.497	.124	30.7	96-3B	5
2002	STL	NL	27	205	57	8	4	14	20	34	3	2	.278	.354	.561	.265	.287	.356	.584	.246	23.1	55-3B	11
2003	STL	NL	28	559	160	49	1	28	82	104	13	3	.286	.382	.528	.271	.295	.389	.546	.255	62.1	150-3B	-2
2004	STL	NL	29	528	148	34	3	27	71	99	10	4	.281	.373	.507	.162	.285	.375	.534	.194	54.7	144-3B	1

Breakout: 16%   Improve: 45%   Collapse: 12%

So maybe he's Ron Santo instead of Mike Schmidt. The Cardinals aren't complaining. Rolen's excellence in Philly was veiled only by the expectations he shouldered. He's a complete ballplayer and an elite performer. He'll have many more fine seasons like this past one. A bout of stiffness in his neck and shoulder before the All-Star break raised the specter of his back problems returning. Luckily for the Cards it was nothing serious, and his past problems appear—knock on wood—under control.

JOHN SANTOR 1B Bats: B Throws: R Born: 16-Nov-81 Age: 22

YEAR	TM	LG	AGE	AB	H	2B	3B	HR	BB	SO	SB	CS	AVG	OBP	SLG	MLVR	EQBA	EQOBP	EQSLG	EQMLVR	VORP	DEFENSE			
2001	NWJ	NYP	19	185	42	12	2	2	22	64	3	2	.227	.308	.346	-.027	.170	.226	.268	-.522	-46.2	20-1B	0	18-3B	-4
2002	NWJ	NYP	20	239	70	24	1	13	32	62	4	2	.293	.380	.565	.400	.202	.270	.405	-.230	-21.6	52-1B	-3		
2002	PEO	MID	20	4	0	0	0	0	0	1	0	0	.000	.000	.000	-1.038	.250	.250	.250	-.461	-0.4				
2003	PEO	MID	21	474	127	28	2	9	54	105	4	5	.268	.348	.392	.105	.209	.270	.321	-.341	-40.2	129-1B	-1		
2004	STL	NL	22	260	54	14	1	6	23	72	1	1	.209	.277	.346	-.261	.213	.279	.364	-.248	-9.9	71-1B	-5		

Breakout: 43%   Improve: 59%   Collapse: 14%

Santor began receiving attention as an upward-trending prospect after his excellent 2002 season in the NY-Penn League. However, the fact that he was repeating the circuit should've tempered expectations. His numbers dropped dramatically at Peoria this past season, and his power was wholly inadequate for a first baseman. He's solidly behind John Gall in the organizational queue, and Andy Schutzenhofer could soon pass him.

ANDY SCHUTZENHOFER 1B Bats: L Throws: L Born: 24-Jan-81 Age: 23

YEAR	TM	LG	AGE	AB	H	2B	3B	HR	BB	SO	SB	CS	AVG	OBP	SLG	MLVR	EQBA	EQOBP	EQSLG	EQMLVR	VORP	DEFENSE	
2003	JCY	APP	22	136	43	11	1	2	15	12	1	1	.316	.396	.456	.260	.209	.262	.309	-.374	-27.4	35-1B	1
2003	PMB	FLA	22	46	15	3	1	0	11	5	0	0	.326	.456	.435	.340	.245	.351	.347	-.124	-0.7	13-1B	0
2004	STL	NL	23	209	47	12	1	2	19	29	0	1	.227	.295	.325	-.246	.230	.297	.342	-.233	-6.2	58-1B	-3

Breakout: 30%   Improve: 57%   Collapse: 17%

The Cards signed Schutzenhofer last year as a non-drafted free agent, and so far it looks like an inspired decision. He split time between the Appy and Florida State leagues in '03, hitting for average, drawing walks and showing gap power at Johnson City and, despite skipping low-A altogether, did the same in the FSL. He has a quick, line-drive swing and an intelligent approach at the plate. Although he logged only 46 ABs for Palm Beach, he impressed the organization with his pitch-recognition skills. A strong season in '04 will place him on the fast track.

SCOTT SEABOL 1B/3B Bats: R Throws: R Born: 17-May-75 Age: 29

YEAR	TM	LG	AGE	AB	H	2B	3B	HR	BB	SO	SB	CS	AVG	OBP	SLG	MLVR	EQBA	EQOBP	EQSLG	EQMLVR	VORP	DEFENSE			
2001	NRW	EAS	26	128	32	7	0	4	5	30	1	1	.250	.290	.398	-.041	.231	.268	.377	-.253	-2.7	20-3B -3			
2001	COH	INT	26	282	75	19	1	10	14	56	3	4	.266	.308	.447	.036	.253	.294	.435	-.105	6.2	40-3B -9	11-LF	2	
2002	COH	INT	27	428	111	29	1	15	29	89	3	3	.259	.309	.437	.013	.244	.297	.418	-.131	-6.1	86-1B -4	12-SS	-4	
2003	IND	INT	28	81	19	1	2	0	4	18	0	1	.235	.264	.296	-.265	.222	.259	.284	-.408	-7.9	11-1B 0			
2003	MEM	PCL	28	307	92	22	1	16	32	64	2	0	.300	.376	.534	.292	.273	.346	.495	.090	25.8	78-3B -1			
2004	*STL*	*NL*	*29*	*172*	*42*	*9*	*1*	*5*	*14*	*40*	*1*	*1*	*.246*	*.307*	*.403*	*-.110*	*.250*	*.309*	*.424*	*-.090*	*5.2*	*48-3B -5*			

Breakout: 29%   Improve: 43%   Collapse: 37%

The former 88th-rounder mustered a career year at the plate in 2003 for Memphis, but only after earning his release from Indianapolis. The other bad news? His power faded as the season went on. He's also in a bit of a defensive quandary, since he lacks the footwork to adequately man third and lacks the bat to hold down a first-base job. His future looks dim as he turns 29.

SO TAGUCHI OF Bats: R Throws: R Born: 02-Jul-69 Age: 34

YEAR	TM	LG	AGE	AB	H	2B	3B	HR	BB	SO	SB	CS	AVG	OBP	SLG	MLVR	EQBA	EQOBP	EQSLG	EQMLVR	VORP	DEFENSE
2001	ORX	JPP	32	453	127	21	6	8	43	88	6	0	.280	.343	.406	-.017	.270	.321	.393	-.101	3.4	
2002	NHV	EAS	33	107	33	10	0	1	9	15	3	1	.308	.375	.430	.170	.275	.328	.394	-.083	2.1	26-CF 0
2002	MEM	PCL	33	304	75	17	0	5	13	44	6	3	.247	.286	.352	-.186	.233	.271	.334	-.307	-14.5	82-CF 0
2002	STL	NL	33	15	6	0	0	0	2	1	1	0	.400	.471	.400	.340	.400	.471	.400	.293	1.7	
2003	MEM	PCL	34	258	66	8	2	2	22	36	14	5	.256	.318	.326	-.134	.238	.299	.308	-.285	-10.9	60-CF -3
2003	STL	NL	34	54	14	3	1	3	4	11	0	0	.259	.310	.519	.120	.273	.322	.527	.094	3.0	
2004	*STL*	*NL*	*34*	*111*	*27*	*5*	*1*	*1*	*9*	*19*	*2*	*1*	*.243*	*.305*	*.341*	*-.197*	*.247*	*.307*	*.359*	*-.181*	*-2.2*	*33-CF -3*

Breakout: 33%   Improve: 45%   Collapse: 30%

Is Taguchi the poor man's Kerry Robinson? That the question can even be asked tells you all you need to know about his underwhelming potential. In any event, the Cardinals' first attempt to get in on the Asian invasion was more novelty act than earnest vetting of the talent pool in question. If he goes north with the big club, the Cards have a problem.

FERNANDO VINA 2B Bats: L Throws: R Born: 16-Apr-69 Age: 35

YEAR	TM	LG	AGE	AB	H	2B	3B	HR	BB	SO	SB	CS	AVG	OBP	SLG	MLVR	EQBA	EQOBP	EQSLG	EQMLVR	VORP	DEFENSE
2001	STL	NL	32	631	191	30	8	9	32	35	17	7	.303	.357	.418	.044	.311	.361	.428	.056	39.7	145-2B 8
2002	STL	NL	33	622	168	29	5	1	44	36	17	11	.270	.333	.338	-.074	.284	.343	.357	-.100	12.0	144-2B -1
2003	STL	NL	34	259	65	14	4	4	11	24	4	4	.251	.309	.382	-.078	.260	.312	.401	-.114	2.8	59-2B -4
2004	*DET*	*AL*	*35*	*339*	*90*	*17*	*3*	*4*	*19*	*31*	*6*	*3*	*.265*	*.318*	*.363*	*-.116*	*.276*	*.332*	*.390*	*-.076*	*12.4*	*89-2B -5*

Breakout: 26%   Improve: 57%   Collapse: 17%

Once a strong defender, Vina hasn't had a good year with the glove since 2001. What's more, he's been inadequate with the bat, even accounting for positional scarcity, for the past two seasons. Based on merit, he should be relegated to a utility role for the rest of his days, but that likely won't happen for another year or two. In any event, the Cardinals were wise to cut ties. Vina will now take his act to Detroit after signing an inexplicable two-year, $6 million deal. He'll play a key role in the Tigers' drive for 50 wins.

PITCHERS

RICK ANKIEL Bats: L Throws: L Born: 19-Jul-79 Age: 24

YEAR	TM	LG	AGE	G	GS	IP	H	BB	SO	HR	ERA	EQERA	EQH9	EQBB9	EQSO9	EQHR9	PERA	VORP	STF
2001	JCY	APP	21	14	14	87.7	42	18	158	1	1.33	2.33	8.8	3.1	7.4	0.2	3.66	26.6	48
2001	STL	NL	21	6	6	24.0	25	25	27	7	7.13	8.49	10.0	8.5	8.5	2.3	7.84	-7.5	2
2003	TEN	SOU	23	20	10	54.3	45	49	64	5	6.30	7.74	10.2	9.8	7.6	1.9	7.75	-11.3	-39
2004	*STL*	*NL*	*24*	*14*	*3*	*21.3*	*23*	*25*	*18*	*5*	*8.14*	*8.88*	*9.7*	*9.5*	*7.0*	*2.4*	*9.11*	*-2.7*	*-36*

Breakout: 22%   Improve: 35%   Collapse: 25%

(continued next page)

Rick Ankiel *(continued)*

There's no doubting his raw ability, but injuries and grievous control problems continue to conspire against him. He'll likely miss most of the 2004 season after undergoing Tommy John surgery in July. Since control problems often follow reconstructive elbow surgery, a meaningful evaluation of his progress in that regard can't be made until he's at least 12 months, and more likely 18–24 months out. Contrary to rumors, shifting him permanently to a hitting role isn't presently on the organizational radar.

KIKO CALERO   Bats: R   Throws: R   Born: 09-Jan-75   Age: 29

YEAR	TM	LG	AGE	G	GS	IP	H	BB	SO	HR	ERA	EQERA	EQH9	EQBB9	EQSO9	EQHR9	PERA	VORP	STF
2001	WIC	TEX	26	27	19	124.3	110	51	94	10	3.33	5.34	9.9	4.6	4.9	1.3	5.73	3.2	-30
2002	WIC	TEX	27	5	2	16.0	10	5	15	2	2.25	3.86	8.4	3.2	6.4	2.6	6.05	2.7	-48
2002	OMA	PCL	27	20	18	125.7	112	35	109	11	3.44	4.10	9.0	2.9	6.0	1.1	4.54	19.4	2
2003	STL	NL	28	26	1	38.3	29	20	51	5	2.82	3.62	7.2	4.1	10.6	1.2	4.12	11.7	20
2004	STL	NL	29	19	7	47.3	41	22	47	6	3.84	4.19	7.8	3.7	8.0	1.1	4.48	7.6	9

Breakout: 27%   Improve: 57%   Collapse: 14%

The Cardinals signed Calero as a minor league free agent coming off the best season of his career. It turned out to be a savvy pickup, because Calero was the club's second-best reliever for the season, at least until he injured his knee in late June and missed the rest of the year. He ruptured his patellar tendon, and by all accounts the injury was particularly nasty. The team is counting on him to be a part of the bullpen in 2004, but it remains to be seen how he'll fare post-injury.

CHRIS CARPENTER   Bats: R   Throws: R   Born: 27-Apr-75   Age: 29

YEAR	TM	LG	AGE	G	GS	IP	H	BB	SO	HR	ERA	EQERA	EQH9	EQBB9	EQSO9	EQHR9	PERA	VORP	STF
2001	TOR	AL	26	34	34	215.7	229	75	157	29	4.09	4.45	8.9	2.9	6.0	1.1	4.48	27.1	9
2002	TOR	AL	27	13	13	73.3	89	27	45	11	5.28	5.25	10.5	3.0	5.2	1.2	5.49	2.8	-6
2004	STL	AL	29	22	18	111.7	127	33	66	15	4.64	4.79	9.9	2.5	5.2	1.2	4.99	12.5	2

Breakout: 19%   Improve: 63%   Collapse: 15%

Carpenter is coming off labrum surgery, which makes him something of an unknown quantity for 2004. Still, it's a reasonable gamble for a team that's in need of rotation help. He'll never be anything better than a solid fourth starter, but then again his minor league numbers never really portended anything greater, despite the hype.

MIKE DeJEAN   Bats: R   Throws: R   Born: 28-Sep-70   Age: 33

YEAR	TM	LG	AGE	G	GS	IP	H	BB	SO	HR	ERA	EQERA	EQH9	EQBB9	EQSO9	EQHR9	PERA	VORP	STF
2001	MIL	NL	30	75	0	84.3	75	39	68	4	2.78	3.67	8.3	3.9	6.1	0.3	3.77	17.4	11
2002	MIL	NL	31	68	0	75.0	66	39	65	7	3.12	3.84	8.2	4.1	6.8	0.9	4.28	14.2	1
2003	MIL	NL	32	58	0	64.7	69	27	58	12	4.87	5.26	9.4	3.3	7.1	1.6	5.35	2.3	-16
2003	STL	NL	32	18	0	18.0	17	12	13	1	4.00	4.58	8.7	5.1	5.6	0.5	4.43	3.1	-4
2004	BAL	AL	33	50	0	61.3	62	26	44	7	4.35	4.53	9.1	3.7	6.2	0.9	4.71	9.0	-5

Breakout: 24%   Improve: 47%   Collapse: 30%

DeJean lucked into a closer's role and performed adequately in Milwaukee, thereby marking him as a Major League Reliever, and thereby immune to the indignity of scrambling for a job during spring training. He's not a particularly bad reliever, nor one a team should go out of its way to acquire. Although the Orioles rate him highly as a setup man, on a good team he would only be Third Righty Out Of The Pen.

CAL ELDRED   Bats: R   Throws: R   Born: 24-Nov-67   Age: 36

YEAR	TM	LG	AGE	G	GS	IP	H	BB	SO	HR	ERA	EQERA	EQH9	EQBB9	EQSO9	EQHR9	PERA	VORP	STF
2003	STL	NL	35	62	0	67.3	62	31	67	9	3.74	4.68	8.5	3.7	8.0	1.2	4.71	9.3	-1
2004	STL	NL	36	44	5	68.7	63	30	66	7	3.80	4.14	8.3	3.5	7.8	1.0	4.59	10.8	6

Breakout: 35%   Improve: 65%   Collapse: 13%

On the surface, Eldred was quite effective in 2003: 67.1 IP, 3.74 ERA, 67 strikeouts. However, according to Adjusted Runs Prevented, he was slightly below league average in terms of altering the base-out states he inherited. Most of this was due to his opponents' on-base percentages vaulting with runners on base, suggesting that Eldred has control problems when pitching from the stretch. Still, based on his peripheral indicators, he's not a bad bet to be reasonably successful as a reliever in 2004, assuming he keeps cheats the injury bug in consecutive seasons. It could happen.

JEFF FASSERO

Bats: L   **Throws: L**   Born: 05-Jan-63   Age: 41

YEAR	TM	LG	AGE	G	GS	IP	H	BB	SO	HR	ERA	EQERA	EQH9	EQBB9	EQSO9	EQHR9	PERA	VORP	STF
2001	CHC	NL	38	82	0	73.7	66	23	79	6	3.42	3.55	8.2	2.5	8.1	0.6	3.60	16.2	21
2002	CHC	NL	39	57	0	51.0	65	22	44	5	6.18	5.98	11.4	3.4	6.7	0.9	5.61	-2.1	-9
2002	STL	NL	39	16	0	18.0	16	5	12	4	3.00	4.24	8.5	2.1	5.3	2.1	5.25	2.6	-32
2003	STL	NL	40	62	6	77.7	93	34	55	17	5.68	6.45	10.9	3.6	5.6	1.9	6.58	-3.7	-41
2004	COL	NL	41	50	0	53.3	58	22	38	7	4.69	4.44	9.6	3.2	5.9	0.9	4.69	7.1	-6

Breakout: 20%   Improve: 66%   Collapse: 13%

There's no other way to put this: Fassero struck a semi-serious blow against the club's post-season hopes in 2003. On May 31, following a scoreless inning of work at home against the Pirates, Fassero's ERA, compiled solely in relief, stood at 5.71—a poor mark by even the most accommodating standards. Even so, whether by perceived necessity or preference, Tony LaRussa drastically ramped up Fassero's role for the balance of the season. Prior to June 1, Fassero averaged 2.9 batters faced per relief appearance; from June 1 onward, he would average 5.1 batters faced per relief outing, an increase of 55.9%. Fassero would end the season with a 6.52 ERA out of the bullpen. More was certainly not better. Although much less nefarious than Carson Daly, he's still overstayed his welcome beyond any reasonable sense of decorum.

DANNY HAREN

Bats: R   **Throws: R**   Born: 17-Sep-80   Age: 23

YEAR	TM	LG	AGE	G	GS	IP	H	BB	SO	HR	ERA	EQERA	EQH9	EQBB9	EQSO9	EQHR9	PERA	VORP	STF
2001	NWJ	NYP	20	12	8	52.3	47	8	57	6	3.10	6.39	13.2	2.1	5.8	3.9	9.95	-3.8	-45
2002	PEO	MID	21	14	14	101.7	89	12	89	6	1.95	4.94	10.9	1.5	4.9	1.5	5.55	6.5	4
2002	POT	CAR	21	14	14	92.0	90	19	82	8	3.62	5.27	11.0	2.5	5.6	1.9	6.29	3.0	0
2003	TEN	SOU	22	8	8	55.0	36	6	49	2	0.82	2.34	7.4	1.1	5.6	0.7	2.91	18.1	37
2003	MEM	PCL	22	8	8	45.7	50	8	35	6	4.92	6.02	10.0	1.9	6.4	1.7	5.35	-2.0	10
2003	STL	NL	22	14	14	72.7	84	22	43	9	5.08	5.66	10.4	2.4	4.8	1.2	5.20	0.4	10
2004	STL	NL	23	26	20	120.3	126	32	83	15	4.26	4.64	9.4	2.1	5.6	1.2	4.58	12.9	5

Breakout: 9%   Improve: 43%   Collapse: 8%

A second-rounder in 2001 out of Pepperdine, Haren has an exceptionally strong minor league profile (solid strikeout rate, 2.78 ERA, 5.9 K/BB), and that certainly augurs well for the coming seasons. Although he struggled to find much consistency in St. Louis this past season, his outstanding numbers on the farm earn him the benefit of the doubt. That he spent only 45 innings at the Triple-A level may have hampered his transition to the highest level. Better days lie ahead, starting with a solid sophomore season.

BLAKE HAWKSWORTH

Bats: R   **Throws: R**   Born: 01-Mar-83   Age: 21

YEAR	TM	LG	AGE	G	GS	IP	H	BB	SO	HR	ERA	EQERA	EQH9	EQBB9	EQSO9	EQHR9	PERA	VORP	STF
2002	JCY	APP	19	13	12	66.0	58	18	61	8	3.14	4.88	10.1	3.4	4.3	2.6	7.02	4.7	-20
2003	PEO	MID	20	10	10	54.7	37	12	57	0	2.30	3.70	8.1	2.8	6.3	0.4	3.40	10.3	41
2003	PMB	FLA	20	6	6	32.0	28	11	32	2	3.94	5.34	10.0	4.1	6.6	1.6	5.90	0.8	14
2004	STL	NL	21	21	17	106.7	101	42	83	11	3.91	4.27	8.5	3.1	6.3	1.0	4.37	15.6	9

Breakout: 23%   Improve: 64%   Collapse: 4%

His name calls to mind a Bond villain, pro wrestler or member of the House of Lords. Which is to say, it's a fairly cool name. His pitching isn't so bad, either. He's pitched as high as the FSL and has been strong at every stop. He has a plus fastball and change, but needs to refine his breaking stuff. His mechanics aren't the best, which certainly raises injury concerns for the future. But if there's a pitcher in the entire system that has front-of-the-rotation potential, it's Hawksworth. He'll likely start 2004 in Double-A.

STERLING HITCHCOCK

Bats: L   **Throws: L**   Born: 29-APR-71   Age: 33

YEAR	TM	LG	AGE	G	GS	IP	H	BB	SO	HR	ERA	EQERA	EQH9	EQBB9	EQSO9	EQHR9	PERA	VORP	STF
2001	SDP	NL	30	3	3	19.0	22	3	15	1	3.32	4.42	10.3	1.5	5.9	0.5	4.14	2.4	25
2001	NYY	AL	30	10	9	51.3	67	18	28	5	6.49	5.72	11.1	2.9	4.5	0.7	5.15	-0.7	-1
2002	NYY	AL	31	20	2	39.3	57	15	31	4	5.50	6.28	12.6	3.0	6.8	0.9	6.05	-2.9	-5
2003	NYY	AL	32	27	1	49.7	57	18	36	6	5.43	5.11	9.5	3.1	6.2	0.9	4.65	-1.1	-1
2003	STL	NL	32	8	6	38.0	34	14	32	8	3.79	4.66	8.1	2.9	6.6	2.0	5.11	6.4	-13
2004	SDP	NL	33	29	12	78.3	84	28	57	11	4.77	5.22	9.8	2.8	5.8	1.2	5.22	4.6	-3

Breakout: 22%   Improve: 48%   Collapse: 29%

(continued next page)

Sterling Hitchcock (*continued*)

Miraculously dealt by the Yankees, Hitchcock wasn't exactly a saviour for St. Louis as much as he was someone better than far too many of the alternatives. He managed to flip a few weeks of adequacy into a guaranteed contract. Previous claimants for "luckiest man in baseball" briefly included Darren Daulton, so it isn't really a title you want, but Hitchcock's on the short list.

JASON ISRINGHAUSEN   Bats: R   Throws: R   Born: 07-Sep-72   Age: 31

YEAR	TM	LG	AGE	G	GS	IP	H	BB	SO	HR	ERA	EQERA	EQH9	EQBB9	EQSO9	EQHR9	PERA	VORP	STF
2001	OAK	AL	28	65	0	71.3	54	23	74	5	2.65	3.01	7.1	2.8	8.8	0.5	3.04	19.8	32
2002	STL	NL	29	60	0	65.3	46	18	68	0	2.48	2.92	7.3	2.2	8.3	0.1	2.64	18.4	40
2003	STL	NL	30	40	0	42.0	31	18	41	2	2.36	3.32	6.9	3.5	7.7	0.4	3.11	12.0	23
2004	*STL*	*NL*	*31*	*59*	*0*	*45.7*	*39*	*17*	*42*	*3*	*3.18*	*3.47*	*7.7*	*2.9*	*7.4*	*0.6*	*3.47*	*10.5*	*7*

Breakout: 29%   *Improve: 54%*   *Collapse: 23%*

Of the high-profile injured closers in 2003 (Izzy, Robb Nen, Trevor Hoffman), Isringhausen was the only one to still make a significant contribution. Once he returned from his irritated shoulder capsule in June, he was, well, Jason Isringhausen. He's been an elite closer for the last three seasons, and considering he maintained his velocity and effectiveness after he returned last year, there's no reason to think he won't continue to thrive. He'll always be fragile, but he's no more of an injury risk than he has been at any point since Dallas Green had his way with him.

TYLER JOHNSON   Bats: B   Throws: L   Born: 07-Jun-81   Age: 23

YEAR	TM	LG	AGE	G	GS	IP	H	BB	SO	HR	ERA	EQERA	EQH9	EQBB9	EQSO9	EQHR9	PERA	VORP	STF
2001	JCY	APP	20	9	9	40.7	26	21	58	1	2.65	4.76	9.0	7.7	5.8	0.5	5.29	3.2	10
2001	PEO	MID	20	3	3	13.7	14	10	15	1	3.94	7.71	12.3	10.0	6.2	1.5	8.32	-2.7	-17
2002	PEO	MID	21	22	18	121.3	96	42	132	7	2.00	4.90	10.4	4.4	6.2	1.5	6.14	8.1	3
2003	PMB	FLA	22	22	10	79.0	79	38	81	2	3.08	5.37	11.1	5.6	6.5	0.8	5.91	1.8	4
2003	TEN	SOU	22	20	0	27.3	16	15	39	1	1.65	3.33	7.4	5.9	9.2	0.7	4.27	6.1	28
2004	*STL*	*NL*	*23*	*10*	*7*	*33.3*	*41*	*29*	*20*	*5*	*7.65*	*8.35*	*11.0*	*7.0*	*4.8*	*1.4*	*8.04*	*-3.5*	*-29*

Breakout: 16%   *Improve: 49%*   *Collapse: 31%*

Johnson throws an excellent curve, passable changeup and high-80s fastball. Think Neal Cotts with better mechanics and a bit less giddy-up. His occasional command struggles have led the Cardinals to move him to the bullpen on a permanent basis. Considering he wasn't far from developing a three-pitch repertoire, that may have been a bit hasty. In any event, relief work may serve to improve in his command. The organization doesn't think he has closer makeup, but they hope he can be an effective setup man in the bigs.

JIMMY JOURNELL   Bats: R   Throws: R   Born: 29-Dec-77   Age: 26

YEAR	TM	LG	AGE	G	GS	IP	H	BB	SO	HR	ERA	EQERA	EQH9	EQBB9	EQSO9	EQHR9	PERA	VORP	STF
2001	POT	CAR	23	26	26	151.0	121	42	156	8	2.50	4.73	10.5	3.8	5.8	1.3	5.69	12.5	0
2002	MEM	PCL	24	7	7	36.7	38	18	32	3	3.68	5.61	10.4	5.1	6.1	1.1	5.80	0.0	-3
2002	NHV	EAS	24	10	10	66.7	50	18	66	3	2.70	3.56	8.3	2.8	6.7	0.7	3.85	13.8	24
2003	MEM	PCL	25	40	7	78.0	80	32	70	3	3.92	5.50	10.2	4.4	7.0	0.5	4.90	0.8	1
2004	*STL*	*NL*	*26*	*15*	*9*	*52.3*	*53*	*27*	*42*	*4*	*4.54*	*4.95*	*9.1*	*4.0*	*6.5*	*0.8*	*5.00*	*3.4*	*2*

Breakout: 20%   *Improve: 48%*   *Collapse: 18%*

A shoulder injury after Tommy John surgery is a really big red flag among red flags, but the club believes he'll be mostly healthy for 2004. Journell doesn't want to start, and the organization doesn't think he has the mindset to close. So a career in middle relief probably lies ahead. The Cardinals believe he relies too much on his fastball, and until he develops more confidence in his slider he likely won't be a high-leverage reliever, even if healthy.

STEVE KLINE   Bats: B   Throws: L   Born: 22-Aug-72   Age: 31

YEAR	TM	LG	AGE	G	GS	IP	H	BB	SO	HR	ERA	EQERA	EQH9	EQBB9	EQSO9	EQHR9	PERA	VORP	STF
2001	STL	NL	28	89	0	75.0	53	29	54	3	1.80	2.54	6.8	3.3	5.6	0.4	3.00	24.1	13
2002	STL	NL	29	66	0	58.3	54	21	41	3	3.40	4.07	8.9	2.9	5.5	0.5	3.94	9.4	4
2003	STL	NL	30	78	0	63.7	56	30	31	5	3.81	4.26	7.9	3.8	4.0	0.7	4.00	10.1	-13
2004	*STL*	*NL*	*31*	*58*	*0*	*48.7*	*49*	*22*	*27*	*4*	*4.08*	*4.45*	*9.0*	*3.5*	*4.5*	*0.7*	*4.69*	*6.0*	*-15*

Breakout: 25%   *Improve: 47%*   *Collapse: 20%*

Kline's plunging strikeout rate and complete lack of command last season (31 strikeouts, 25 unintentional walks) bode ill for the future. He has name recognition and a strong profile among the less meaningful stats, so he's ripe to be over-valued. The one-year, $1.7 million contract he signed to stay with the Cards may come back to bite them in '04. Bet against a sub-four ERA.

JEREMY LAMBERT Bats: R Throws: R Born: 10-Jan-79 Age: 25

YEAR	TM	LG	AGE	G	GS	IP	H	BB	SO	HR	ERA	EQERA	EQH9	EQBB9	EQSO9	EQHR9	PERA	VORP	STF
2001	NHV	EAS	22	31	0	33.3	32	17	48	4	2.97	6.14	11.4	6.4	9.2	1.8	7.35	-1.8	-7
2001	MEM	PCL	22	28	0	30.7	23	8	39	7	3.22	4.34	7.1	2.8	9.0	2.2	4.77	4.1	9
2002	NHV	EAS	23	18	0	19.0	24	11	21	1	6.16	7.79	13.5	6.2	7.3	1.0	7.35	-4.2	-19
2003	TEN	SOU	24	33	0	41.3	31	15	56	5	2.18	4.25	10.2	4.0	8.8	2.5	7.03	5.4	-30
2003	MEM	PCL	24	12	0	11.7	11	5	9	1	3.85	5.06	9.3	5.1	5.9	0.8	5.04	0.6	-10
2004	*STL*	*NL*	*25*	*19*	*2*	*29.3*	*29*	*14*	*26*	*4*	*4.78*	*5.21*	*8.8*	*3.7*	*7.2*	*1.3*	*5.11*	*1.4*	*-1*

Breakout: 20%   *Improve: 42%*   *Collapse: 24%*

Considering the serious bullpen problems they had at the major league level, it might not have been wise to cut bait on their best relief prospect. But by choosing not to add Lambert to the 40-man roster, he was granted minor league free agency. Early in his career, Lambert was plagued by egregious control problems, but that hasn't been as much of a prob-lem since 1999. He's shown excellent strikeout rates since that point and has succeeded at every level. He could be a contributor if given a chance in 2004.

MATT MORRIS Bats: R Throws: R Born: 09-Aug-74 Age: 29

YEAR	TM	LG	AGE	G	GS	IP	H	BB	SO	HR	ERA	EQERA	EQH9	EQBB9	EQSO9	EQHR9	PERA	VORP	STF
2001	STL	NL	26	34	34	216.3	218	54	185	13	3.16	4.05	9.8	2.1	6.6	0.5	4.05	35.3	29
2002	STL	NL	27	32	32	210.3	210	64	171	16	3.42	4.29	9.8	2.4	6.5	0.7	4.38	29.0	20
2003	STL	NL	28	27	27	172.3	164	39	120	20	3.76	4.19	8.7	1.9	5.6	1.0	4.04	30.0	11
2004	*STL*	*NL*	*29*	*26*	*25*	*165.3*	*166*	*46*	*118*	*15*	*3.68*	*4.02*	*9.0*	*2.2*	*5.8*	*0.9*	*4.12*	*28.9*	*13*

Breakout: 11%   *Improve: 50%*   *Collapse: 20%*

When healthy, he was the Cardinals' most effective starter last season, but saying "when" is a major qualifier. Morris missed more than a month with a fractured hand and sprained ankle, but it was his sore shoulder that's more of a con-cern for the future. An MRI in July showed no structural problems, but he's a serious injury risk for 2004. His best hope is for a carefully-monitored workload, which could allow his rotator cuff to hold up as he soldiers through the season. The problem is the Cardinals desperately need him to make 30 starts and go deep into many of those to have a chance. It's worth noting that Morris's top PECOTA comps in the past have been non-luminaries like Dave Goltz, Shane Reynolds, Eric Hanson, Dock Ellis, and Mark Gubicza. Of those, none pitched effectively after the age of 33; Morris's slide could start earlier if his health deteriorates from here.

CHRIS NARVESON Bats: L Throws: L Born: 20-Dec-81 Age: 22

YEAR	TM	LG	AGE	G	GS	IP	H	BB	SO	HR	ERA	EQERA	EQH9	EQBB9	EQSO9	EQHR9	PERA	VORP	STF
2001	PEO	MID	19	8	8	50.0	32	11	53	3	1.98	2.98	7.3	2.8	6.0	1.2	3.86	13.2	33
2001	POT	CAR	19	11	11	66.7	52	13	53	4	2.56	4.35	8.6	2.5	4.8	1.2	4.39	8.3	22
2002	JCY	APP	20	6	6	18.3	23	6	16	2	4.92	7.71	13.8	3.9	3.9	2.2	8.40	-3.8	-44
2002	PEO	MID	20	9	9	42.3	49	8	36	5	4.47	8.25	15.0	2.5	5.0	3.2	9.98	-10.6	-40
2003	PMB	FLA	21	15	14	91.3	83	19	65	4	2.86	4.59	9.9	2.4	4.5	1.3	5.15	9.2	6
2003	TEN	SOU	21	10	10	57.0	56	26	34	6	3.00	5.40	10.3	4.9	3.8	1.9	6.71	1.1	-17
2004	*STL*	*NL*	*22*	*15*	*10*	*60.0*	*66*	*25*	*35*	*9*	*5.39*	*5.88*	*10.0*	*3.3*	*4.6*	*1.4*	*5.70*	*0.7*	*-10*

Breakout: 5%   *Improve: 41%*   *Collapse: 37%*

Stuff-wise, there's a lot to like about Narveson; injury-wise, there's very little to like. He already underwent Tommy John surgery in 2001, and last season battled shoulder tendinitis. When he's healthy, he can throw his fastball in the low 90s and also get his curve, slider, and change over for strikes. Although he struggled with his command at Double-A last season, the Cards have him slated to open 2004 in Memphis. Health and command concerns may eventually force him to the bullpen.

RHETT PARROTT

RHETT PARROTT   Bats: R   Throws: R   Born: 12-Nov-79   Age: 24

YEAR	TM	LG	AGE	G	GS	IP	H	BB	SO	HR	ERA	EQERA	EQH9	EQBB9	EQSO9	EQHR9	PERA	VORP	STF
2001	NWJ	NYP	21	11	11	45.7	45	28	58	3	4.92	8.76	14.1	9.0	6.8	2.4	9.83	-13.0	-47
2002	POT	CAR	22	19	19	113.0	91	41	82	6	2.71	4.34	8.5	4.4	4.5	1.2	4.86	14.2	0
2002	NHV	EAS	22	9	9	66.0	53	13	38	3	2.86	3.84	8.0	2.1	3.8	0.7	3.52	11.9	16
2003	TEN	SOU	23	21	21	124.0	122	40	112	11	3.27	5.37	11.2	3.4	5.7	1.7	6.46	2.8	-9
2003	MEM	PCL	23	7	7	40.7	39	19	25	2	3.54	4.97	8.8	5.0	5.0	0.7	4.66	2.7	8
2004	*STL*	*NL*	*24*	*18*	*13*	*71.3*	*81*	*42*	*51*	*12*	*6.13*	*6.69*	*10.2*	*4.7*	*5.8*	*1.6*	*6.60*	*-2.8*	*-12*

Breakout: 21%   *Improve: 51%*   *Collapse: 23%*

Parrott's numbers are solid, if unspectacular, and the Cardinals are high on his approach and makeup. He's poised on the mound, intelligent and unafraid to pitch inside. Parrott's at his best when he keeps his walks down, and the organization thinks he'll eventually be a fourth or fifth starter in the majors.

JOSH PEARCE

JOSH PEARCE   Bats: R   Throws: R   Born: 20-Aug-77   Age: 26

YEAR	TM	LG	AGE	G	GS	IP	H	BB	SO	HR	ERA	EQERA	EQH9	EQBB9	EQSO9	EQHR9	PERA	VORP	STF
2001	NHV	EAS	23	18	18	115.3	111	34	96	11	3.75	5.33	10.1	3.5	5.2	1.4	5.61	3.1	-4
2001	MEM	PCL	23	10	10	69.7	72	12	36	11	4.26	5.54	8.9	1.8	3.5	1.6	4.82	0.4	-11
2002	MEM	PCL	24	4	4	20.0	28	3	17	8	7.65	9.82	14.7	1.5	5.9	4.9	12.03	-8.6	-103
2002	STL	NL	24	3	3	13.0	20	8	1	1	7.62	8.76	14.6	5.1	0.7	0.7	7.38	-4.3	-44
2003	PMB	FLA	25	6	5	28.0	28	2	15	2	3.21	4.81	12.2	0.7	3.3	2.2	6.89	2.1	-49
2003	TEN	SOU	25	5	5	33.0	34	3	20	3	4.09	5.28	12.1	0.9	3.7	1.9	6.43	1.0	-31
2003	MEM	PCL	25	10	9	46.3	51	8	27	8	4.08	5.95	11.3	1.9	4.7	2.3	6.87	-1.6	-44
2004	*STL*	*NL*	*26*	*13*	*8*	*46.0*	*51*	*13*	*27*	*6*	*4.72*	*5.15*	*10.0*	*2.2*	*4.7*	*1.3*	*5.11*	*3.1*	*-6*

Breakout: 22%   *Improve: 47%*   *Collapse: 22%*

Pearce is a command specialist (3.1 career K/BB ratio) with a below-average collection of raw stuff. His strikeout rates have dropped in two separate stints at Triple-A. Additionally, he's always posted elevated hit rates and been a bit homer-prone. At age 26, a move to the bullpen is probably the best way for him to make it to the next level and stay there, though he projects as a low-impact guy even if he makes it through that door.

JASON SIMONTACCHI

JASON SIMONTACCHI   Bats: R   Throws: R   Born: 13-Nov-73   Age: 30

YEAR	TM	LG	AGE	G	GS	IP	H	BB	SO	HR	ERA	EQERA	EQH9	EQBB9	EQSO9	EQHR9	PERA	VORP	STF
2001	EDM	PCL	27	32	18	143.3	192	23	83	21	5.34	6.18	11.6	1.6	3.6	1.5	5.94	-8.9	-32
2002	MEM	PCL	28	6	6	42.3	44	5	28	2	2.34	3.92	10.6	1.2	4.6	0.7	4.42	7.3	10
2002	STL	NL	28	24	24	143.3	134	54	72	18	4.02	4.78	9.0	3.1	4.0	1.2	4.77	12.4	-9
2003	STL	NL	29	46	16	126.3	153	41	74	21	5.56	6.14	10.9	2.7	4.7	1.5	5.88	-5.0	-26
2004	*STL*	*NL*	*30*	*28*	*14*	*86.7*	*95*	*29*	*50*	*11*	*4.56*	*4.98*	*9.9*	*2.6*	*4.7*	*1.2*	*5.12*	*7.1*	*-8*

Breakout: 27%   *Improve: 48%*   *Collapse: 24%*

Simontacchi is an object lesson in just how much a pitcher's profile can be altered by defense and run support. In 2002, he earned cachet as a rotation stalwart by winning 11 games and posting a 4.02 ERA. In 2003, although his strikeout and walk rates improved, his ERA vaulted to 5.56, and he was exiled to long relief on more than one occasion. He pitched much better out of the bullpen (6.33 ERA in 85.1 innings as a starter, versus a 3.95 ERA in 41 relief innings), and that's probably the role to which he's best suited for the long-term.

GARRETT STEPHENSON

GARRETT STEPHENSON   Bats: R   Throws: R   Born: 02-Jan-72   Age: 32

YEAR	TM	LG	AGE	G	GS	IP	H	BB	SO	HR	ERA	EQERA	EQH9	EQBB9	EQSO9	EQHR9	PERA	VORP	STF
2002	MEM	PCL	30	3	3	12.7	12	2	12	0	3.54	3.86	10.0	1.5	6.2	0.0	3.54	2.3	32
2002	STL	NL	30	12	10	45.0	48	25	34	4	5.40	5.86	10.5	4.4	6.1	0.8	5.38	-1.2	-4
2003	STL	NL	31	32	27	174.3	167	60	91	30	4.60	5.05	8.6	2.8	4.2	1.6	4.91	12.8	-18
2004	*STL*	*NL*	*32*	*27*	*21*	*129.3*	*133*	*45*	*76*	*18*	*4.62*	*5.04*	*9.3*	*2.8*	*4.8*	*1.3*	*5.05*	*9.1*	*-3*

Breakout: 12%   *Improve: 37%*   *Collapse: 11%*

Other than Matt Morris and Woody Williams, Stephenson was the only Cardinal starter approaching adequacy in 2003. However, that's not to say he was much more than adequate. Low strikeout rates, frightening home run rates, and past injury concerns raise doubts about his value in 2004 and beyond. Looks like a better bet for a Lincolnesque fiver ERA-wise than something in the fours.

NICK STOCKS

Bats: R **Throws: R** Born: 27-Aug-78 Age: 25

YEAR	TM	LG	AGE	G	GS	IP	H	BB	SO	HR	ERA	EQERA	EQH9	EQBB9	EQSO9	EQHR9	PERA	VORP	STF
2001	NHV	EAS	22	16	15	82.0	89	33	63	10	5.16	6.96	11.4	4.9	4.8	1.7	6.93	-11.1	-20
2002	NWJ	NYP	23	7	7	22.0	28	13	24	0	5.73	10.59	19.1	9.0	6.4	0.5	9.55	-9.4	-42
2002	POT	CAR	23	3	3	15.7	18	6	11	3	5.73	8.78	14.2	4.7	4.7	4.7	12.18	-4.7	-113
2003	TEN	SOU	24	27	26	151.0	160	58	109	17	4.77	6.70	12.4	4.2	4.6	2.3	7.95	-16.3	-48
2004	STL		25	15	9	48.0	56	23	32	7	5.78	6.30	10.5	3.8	5.5	1.4	6.18	-0.4	-11

Breakout: 38%   Improve: 60%   Collapse: 17%

The Cardinals attribute Stocks's struggles last season to a couple of isolated disaster starts and maintain that he holds more promise than his numbers might indicate. But that simply doesn't square with the fact that he's 25 years old and yet to pitch well above low-A. Among so many other guys we're saying are not prospects, Stocks is so much more not a prospect.

JOSH TEEKEL

Bats: R **Throws: R** Born: 18-Sep-80 Age: 23

YEAR	TM	LG	AGE	G	GS	IP	H	BB	SO	HR	ERA	EQERA	EQH9	EQBB9	EQSO9	EQHR9	PERA	VORP	STF
2001	NWJ	NYP	20	15	0	36.0	23	15	31	1	1.75	3.73	7.8	5.7	4.3	0.9	4.59	6.5	-3
2002	NWJ	NYP	21	16	13	73.7	58	24	66	3	3.30	6.46	11.3	4.7	4.8	1.5	6.57	-5.9	-17
2003	PEO	MID	22	26	16	118.3	107	39	85	1	2.36	5.31	10.1	4.2	4.3	0.3	4.60	3.4	7
2004	STL	NL	23	17	10	58.7	65	32	33	6	5.36	5.85	9.9	4.3	4.5	1.0	5.76	-0.2	-14

Breakout: 15%   Improve: 38%   Collapse: 31%

Teekel got some attention last season for his 2.36 ERA at Peoria of the Midwest League. However, he was older than most of his peers, and his peripherals didn't justify the low ERA, which is to say he was a bit lucky. He's 23, yet to see action in the high minors and hasn't been terribly impressive to date. There's a lot that needs to happen before he becomes someone worth watching.

BRETT TOMKO

Bats: R **Throws: R** Born: 07-Apr-73 Age: 31

YEAR	TM	LG	AGE	G	GS	IP	H	BB	SO	HR	ERA	EQERA	EQH9	EQBB9	EQSO9	EQHR9	PERA	VORP	STF
2001	SEA	AL	28	11	4	34.7	42	15	22	9	5.19	6.89	11.8	3.9	5.5	2.2	7.47	-4.7	-45
2001	TAC	PCL	28	19	18	127.0	124	25	117	12	4.04	4.94	10.2	2.2	6.1	1.1	4.89	8.6	2
2002	SDP	NL	29	32	32	204.3	212	60	126	31	4.49	4.75	8.9	2.3	4.8	1.4	4.76	18.8	-7
2003	STL	NL	30	33	32	202.7	252	57	114	35	5.28	6.09	11.3	2.3	4.5	1.5	5.98	-2.3	-18
2004	SFG	NL	31	24	23	142.7	160	42	79	18	4.68	4.93	9.9	2.3	4.5	1.2	4.89	12.3	1

Breakout: 14%   Improve: 45%   Collapse: 24%

Coming out of 2002, there was reason to believe that Tomko could provide solid back-of-the-rotation help. Instead he burdened the Cardinals with more than 200 innings of barely above replacement-level pitching. He's always been prone to the long ball, and in 2003 lefties laid waste to him more than ever before. Opponents hit .305 against him, and the organization became frustrated with his mental approach as the season wore on. A free agent, Tomko's stock has fallen way down, and the list of interested suitors has shrunk with it.

WOODY WILLIAMS

Bats: R **Throws: R** Born: 19-Aug-66 Age: 37

YEAR	TM	LG	AGE	G	GS	IP	H	BB	SO	HR	ERA	EQERA	EQH9	EQBB9	EQSO9	EQHR9	PERA	VORP	STF
2001	SDP	NL	34	23	23	145.0	170	37	102	28	4.97	5.66	10.4	2.1	5.3	1.6	5.61	-0.9	-12
2001	STL	NL	34	11	11	75.0	54	19	52	7	2.28	3.04	7.0	2.2	5.3	0.8	3.09	20.2	21
2002	STL	NL	35	17	17	103.3	84	25	76	10	2.53	3.23	7.9	1.9	5.9	0.9	3.61	25.7	20
2003	STL	NL	36	34	33	220.7	220	55	153	20	3.87	4.33	9.1	2.0	5.6	0.8	4.06	34.6	15
2004	STL	NL	37	31	29	189.0	188	48	129	22	3.87	4.23	9.0	2.0	5.5	1.1	4.25	28.7	10

Breakout: 15%   Improve: 42%   Collapse: 17%

Since coming to St. Louis and adding some velocity to his cut fastball, Williams has been a different pitcher. He's also had injury problems, and La Russa rode him fairly hard in '03. That creates a modicum of concern going forward. His command has always been solid, and he's a good bet for another effective season, even if it doesn't approach his ludicrously superb 2002. He'll need to stay healthy for the Cards to have a strong chance in '04.

San Diego Padres

On April 8, the Padres will become the latest baseball team to occupy a brand-new ballpark. Of the 26 franchises that were in operation in 1991, 12 will open 2004 in buildings that didn't exist as the '90s dawned. That total includes the Padres, who move into Petco Park, and the Phillies, who christen Citizens Bank Ballpark on April 12.

For both franchises, the opening of a new park is being hailed as the dawn of a new era. The two teams have been building their rosters—and payrolls—for three years with an eye towards packed houses and higher prices for everything in their new playpens. That's the way it works these days; teams plan entire decades around the opening of a new, usually publicly-funded, ballpark, and use the construction of said park as an excuse for inferior baseball and a lack of investment in the team in the years leading up to its opening.

The recent spate of ballpark construction, from the Orioles in 1992 through the Reds in 2003, has three distinct phases. In each phase, the emphasis has shifted from looking at the new ballpark as a better place to watch a game than the flavorless stadium it is replacing, to making the new park the franchise's primary path to financial and on-field success. The problems with the latter should be evident, but as the most recent examples demonstrate, not everyone got that memo.

The first wave of new parks crested in 1992, when the O's opened Camden Yards. The Indians and Rangers christened Jacobs Field and The Ballpark in Arlington two years later. In all three cases, the teams entered the new parks on the rise, with a core of system-developed young talent that was maturing even in the final seasons before the move. While the teams all eagerly awaited the openings, in no case was the park seen as the franchise's savior.

Table 1 shows how each team did in the two years prior to, and first five years subsequent to, the new park's opening.

These three teams all had success in the new parks, which kept people coming back long after the new-park smell had worn off. It wasn't until long after the playoff appearances stopped that all three teams saw a loss in attendance, which illustrated, once again, that the key element isn't a new park, but success.

The ringing of the cash registers in Baltimore, Cleveland, and Arlington set off a wave of jealousy among the

PADRES PROSPECTUS

2003 record: 64–98; Fifth place, NL West

Pythagenport record: 65–97

Runs scored per game: 4.2 (14th in NL)

Runs allowed per game: 5.1 (13th in NL)

Team EqA: .261 (7th in NL)

2003 Batters Age: 28.9 (5th youngest in NL)

2003 Pitchers Age: 27.5 (5th youngest in NL)

Ballpark: Petco Field (New for 2004)

2003: The pitching staff took a dive, and an injury-plagued Padres squad flirted with .300.

2004: With the move into Petco Park and the division on the wane, there's plenty to like here.

teams playing elsewhere. Nine municipalities committed themselves to nine new ballparks before the decade was out, and a handful of others—Minneapolis-St. Paul, Montreal, Miami—resisted a series of entreaties and threats by local owners and the game's upper management. Before the 20th century ended, four more new parks opened. Table 2 shows how each team did in the two years prior to the opening, and how they've done since.

In three of these four cases, the teams moving into new parks were already good, or at least had the core of good clubs in place. In those three cases, the teams went on to have success in the new park that rivaled what they'd done previously.

The four parks were built under wildly differing circumstances. The Mariners positioned theirs as necessary to save the team. They won public financing only when the state legislature approved a plan, following the public's rejection of a similar referendum. The Giants financed theirs largely without public money, the only one of the recent parks to be built privately. The Tigers left Tiger Stadium in the face of considerable local opposition to the abandonment of what was a deteriorating, but popular, ballpark.

To a certain extent, all these parks were responses to the success of Camden Yards and the desire to cash in on that kind of revenue stream. However, only in the Mariners' case was the stadium positioned as the savior of the

TABLE 1. PERFORMANCE BY "FIRST WAVE" OF TEAMS WITH NEW PARKS

Team	Park −2	Park −1	Opening	Park 1	Park 2	Park 3	Park 4	Park 5
Orioles	76–85	67–95	89–73	85–77	63–49	71–73	88–74	97–64
Indians	76–86	76–86	66–47	100–44	99–62	86–75	89–73	97–65
Rangers	77–85	86–76	52–62	74–70	90–72	77–85	88–74	95–67

TABLE 2. PERFORMANCE BY "SECOND WAVE" OF TEAMS WITH NEW PARKS

Team	Park −2	Park −1	Opening	Park 1	Park 2	Park 3	Park 4
Mariners	90–72*	76–85	79–83	91–71	116–46	93–69	93–69
Astros	102–60	97–65	72–90	93–69	84–78	87–75	
Giants	89–74	86–76	97–65	90–72	95–66	100–61	
Tigers	65–97	69–92	79–83	66–96	55–106	43–119	

*The Mariners split 1999 between the Kingdome and Safeco Field

franchise, although the word "need" popped up in all four cities. "Need" would become the key word in the ballpark debates that followed, as teams blamed their facilities for their failures and insisted that a new home—paid for by taxpayers, of course—would enable the local nine to compete. The teams happily pointed to the successes of the Orioles, Rangers and Indians, but ignored the reality that those were good baseball teams at the time the new parks opened. After the initial glow, it wasn't the park that packed people in; but the baseball.

While the Tigers belong with the Mariners, Astros, and Giants chronologically, spiritually they belong in the next group. The 2000 Tigers became the first team to enter a new park with a bad team. Not a good team having an off-year, and not a young team a year away from success, a bad team. The Tigers were the first team to position the new park not as an enhancement to the product, but as the golden ticket that would make the baseball team a winner. The Brewers, Pirates, and Reds, all of whom gained financing in the "me, too" era, would also open parks near the start of the 21st century. Table 3 shows how that's gone.

These three teams, along with the Tigers, watched attendance fall through the floor soon after opening their new stadiums. All four are among the worst teams in baseball since the 1994 strike. Only the Reds have reached the postseason in that time. As you could see last summer, the new stadiums didn't hold people's attention for very long; the Brewers, Pirates and Tigers ranked 25th–27th in attendance in 2003, while the Reds ranked just 13th in their first year at Great American Ball Park, and played to just 69% of capacity.

It's not hard to see where the problem lies. The first wave of teams didn't make the new ballpark the center of their universe, in part because no one knew how powerful

TABLE 3. PERFORMANCE BY "THIRD WAVE" OF TEAMS WITH NEW PARKS

Team	Park −2	Park −1	Opening	Park 1	Park 2
Brewers	74–87	73–89	68–94	56–106	68–94
Pirates	78–83	69–93	62–100	72–89	75–87
Reds	66–96	78–84	69–93	—	—

a draw a new park would be. In the immediate aftermath of the three early-'90s openings, however, it is likely that we overrated the value of a new park to a team. In particular, we didn't do a good job of separating the importance of team success from the importance of the new park. The latter factor was much more important, but the argument that the park made the team successful was much more attractive to owners in other cities looking for large public subsidies, and there was no counterargument in place.

Because three of the next four teams that moved into new parks were also successful, the link between new parks and attendance was strengthened. When the Tigers couldn't keep pace with the other teams, they were seen as the exception, rather than the rule. The Tigers were just the first example of the problems with treating a new park as a franchise savior, and more important, they illustrate the main point: A new park will bring people out for a little while, but a winning team is what keeps them coming. The Brewers, Pirates, and Reds have had painfully short honeymoon periods in their new homes, as their on-field failures have turned people away.

What's truly scary, if you're a fan of one of those teams, is that there's no longer a fix on the horizon. After all, if the 1995–2000 period was spent hearing about how the ballpark would solve everything, and it didn't, what is the solution? Or more accurately, what does the organization see as the solution? Given the direction in which the payroll is going in Milwaukee, Cincinnati and Pittsburgh, it seems that the relationship between large taxpayer subsidies and expenditures on players is a tenuous one. In other words, the owners played the taxpayers for suckers.

What does all this mean for the Padres? Objectively, they do not measure up well. At 130–194 over the past two seasons, San Diego has the worst two-year record of any team opening a new park in the HOK era. The good news is that the Padres' talent base compares well with many of the newer-ballpark teams, and very well as compared to the more recent ones. The Padres should score runs thanks to veterans like Ryan Klesko, Brian Giles, and Phil Nevin. They have very good young players in Sean Burroughs, Jake Peavy, and Adam Eaton, and will open 2004 without any major holes on the roster. Although the Pads have been using the new park, and the delays in its construction, as an excuse for their mediocrity almost since the day they lost Game Four of the 1998 World Series, they have spent the last year ramping up in a way that should be encouraging for their fans.

The Padres seem certain to avoid the mistakes of the most recent movers. While they don't have the talent—or the soft competition—to be the late 1990s Indians, they should be able to compete with aging teams in San Francisco and Arizona that have led the division the past few years. Assuming they make good use of the increased revenue—something the Astros, for one, haven't really done—they should be set for a four- or five-year run in which they stay above .500 and make some playoff appearances.

Of the teams we've discussed, the best comp for the current Padres is probably the team that started all of this, the 1992 Orioles. The Orioles were under .500 in their last two seasons in Memorial Stadium, then played .500 or better baseball in five of the next six years, capping the run with back-to-back playoff appearances in 1996 and 1997. Like those Orioles, these Padres have a veteran-laden lineup with a strong, young pitching staff. They both feature a young right-hander with the potential to be a championship team's ace (Mike Mussina, Jake Peavy). They both even have a disappointing right fielder from a Pac-10 school (Jeffrey Hammonds, meet Xavier Nady).

Because they have been spending money and putting a core in place in the years leading up to opening Petco Park, the Padres are well-positioned to be successful in the short term. As the wonder of their new environs wears off, the excitement of a winning baseball team should take its place.

That's the best way to keep the new ballpark packed.

HITTERS

JOSH BARFIELD 2B Bats: R Throws: R Born: 17-Dec-82 Age: 21

YEAR	TM	LG	AGE	AB	H	2B	3B	HR	BB	SO	SB	CS	AVG	OBP	SLG	MLVR	EQBA	EQOBP	EQSLG	EQMLVR	VORP	DEFENSE		
2001	IDA	PIO	18	277	86	15	4	4	16	54	12	4	.310	.350	.437	.086	.212	.240	.304	-.423	-37.0	40-2B	2	23-SS -6
2002	FTW	MID	19	536	164	22	3	8	26	105	26	8	.306	.340	.403	.135	.260	.286	.353	-.233	-9.5	128-2B	-3	
2003	LEL	CAL	20	549	185	46	6	16	50	122	16	4	.337	.389	.530	.333	.255	.305	.412	-.116	9.6	130-2B	1	
2004	SDP	NL	21	332	79	17	2	7	21	73	6	2	.237	.284	.362	-.210	.243	.288	.381	-.189	1.1	87-2B	-5	

Breakout: 18%   Improve: 34%   Collapse: 26%

Bad news first: Barfield had surgery on his right wrist after last season. In addition, reading between the lines, you can already see his path to the outfield being smoothed, with questions being raised about his defense at second base and his eventual size. The good news is just about everything else, including his Cal League MVP season while playing most of the year with ligament damage in that wrist. Barfield improved most aspects of his game in 2003, in particular his plate discipline. The jump in power is what got people's attention, however, so know this: the Padres have had a bunch of guys go through Lake Elsinore and do much the same. Until Barfield does something at Mobile or Portland, be skeptical.

GARY BENNETT C Bats: R Throws: R Born: 17-Apr-72 Age: 32

YEAR	TM	LG	AGE	AB	H	2B	3B	HR	BB	SO	SB	CS	AVG	OBP	SLG	MLVR	EQBA	EQOBP	EQSLG	EQMLVR	VORP	DEFENSE	
2001	PHI	NL	29	75	16	3	1	1	9	19	0	0	.213	.294	.320	-.269	.227	.310	.333	-.235	-1.3	22-C	-1
2001	NOR	INT	29	67	20	5	0	2	4	12	0	0	.299	.342	.463	.148	.279	.326	.456	.005	3.7	14-C	1
2001	COL	NL	29	55	15	3	0	1	3	5	0	0	.273	.317	.382	-.159	.255	.303	.382	-.162	0.2	14-C	-2
2002	COL	NL	30	291	77	10	2	4	15	45	1	3	.265	.314	.354	-.134	.256	.299	.345	-.222	-3.6	79-C	-5
2003	SDP	NL	31	307	73	15	0	2	24	48	3	0	.238	.296	.306	-.182	.256	.312	.329	-.219	-3.5	77-C	-5
2004	MIL	NL	32	237	62	10	1	3	17	37	2	1	.260	.315	.353	-.154	.262	.314	.353	-.167	1.9	64-C	-4

Breakout: 16%   Improve: 37%   Collapse: 43%

Bennett is a backup catcher who played too much last year, as the Padres didn't have any better options. The acquisition of Ramon Hernandez pushes him out of a job, and he's too much like Hernandez to fit well as the backup. Outrighted to Triple-A after the season, relaminating his Society of Backup Catchers card and a quick refresher with the secret handshake got him a quick invitation to be a Brewer in 2004.

TAGG BOZIED — 1B — Bats: R — Throws: R — Born: 24-Jul-79 — Age: 24

YEAR	TM	LG	AGE	AB	H	2B	3B	HR	BB	SO	SB	CS	AVG	OBP	SLG	MLVR	EQBA	EQOBP	EQSLG	EQMLVR	VORP	DEFENSE	
2001	SXF	NTH	21	228	70	17	0	6	13	34	3	2	.307	.360	.461	.155	.239	.285	.372	-.222	-9.9		
2002	LEL	CAL	22	282	84	23	1	15	35	60	3	4	.298	.377	.546	.310	.226	.291	.420	-.153	-6.0	64-1B -7	
2002	MOB	SOU	22	234	50	14	0	9	16	43	1	0	.214	.268	.389	-.107	.193	.229	.366	-.369	-20.3	57-1B -5	
2003	POR	PCL	23	450	123	25	2	14	38	80	1	0	.273	.331	.431	.047	.251	.308	.405	-.123	-5.3	107-1B -3	
2004	SDP	NL	24	268	66	15	1	9	23	52	1	1	.248	.309	.417	-.087	.254	.313	.439	-.060	4.8	72-1B -2	

Breakout: 48%   Improve: 64%   Collapse: 18%

Bozied was hot at this time last season, but an unimpressive season at Triple-A has him sandwiched between a bunch of major leaguers ahead of him and Jon Knott coming up hard behind him. Bozied is one-dimensional and, like Xavier Nady, hasn't done anything above A-ball yet, calling into question whether he was overhyped based on a big year at Lake Elsinore. Now go back and read the Barfield comment again.

BRIAN BUCHANAN — RF/1B — Bats: R — Throws: R — Born: 21-Jul-73 — Age: 30

YEAR	TM	LG	AGE	AB	H	2B	3B	HR	BB	SO	SB	CS	AVG	OBP	SLG	MLVR	EQBA	EQOBP	EQSLG	EQMLVR	VORP	DEFENSE	
2001	MIN	AL	27	197	54	12	0	10	19	58	1	1	.274	.342	.487	.095	.289	.359	.518	.160	11.8	27-RF -1	
2002	MIN	AL	28	135	34	5	1	5	6	33	2	1	.252	.294	.415	-.088	.267	.311	.437	-.059	0.2	21-RF 0	
2002	SDP	NL	28	92	27	5	0	6	9	26	0	1	.293	.363	.543	.297	.316	.374	.589	.316	9.3	10-RF -2	
2003	SDP	NL	29	198	52	10	2	8	24	51	6	2	.263	.346	.455	.130	.281	.364	.488	.119	10.8	18-RF 0	16-1B 0
2004	SDP	NL	30	151	39	8	1	7	16	41	2	1	.262	.340	.458	.029	.269	.344	.482	.061	9.3	44-RF -4	

Breakout: 21%   Improve: 41%   Collapse: 38%

Buchanan is a useful platoon player, which means his value to the Padres is tied to Bruce Bochy's willingness to sit Ryan Klesko against lefties. Over the last three seasons, Klesko's peak against lefties, he's hit .252/.337/.422 against them. Buchanan's hit .270/.368/.528 against southpaws in that time, and isn't any worse than Klesko defensively in a corner. Sometimes, you have to let a player help you.

SEAN BURROUGHS — 3B — Bats: L — Throws: R — Born: 12-Sep-80 — Age: 23

YEAR	TM	LG	AGE	AB	H	2B	3B	HR	BB	SO	SB	CS	AVG	OBP	SLG	MLVR	EQBA	EQOBP	EQSLG	EQMLVR	VORP	DEFENSE	
2001	POR	PCL	20	394	127	28	1	9	37	54	9	2	.322	.386	.467	.188	.290	.350	.419	.005	23.2	96-3B 5	
2002	POR	PCL	21	179	54	16	2	2	21	16	1	0	.302	.380	.447	.162	.276	.351	.409	-.018	9.0	29-2B 1	14-3B -1
2002	SDP	NL	21	192	52	5	1	1	12	30	2	0	.271	.317	.323	-.102	.294	.335	.350	-.119	3.0	37-3B -5	
2003	SDP	NL	22	517	148	27	6	7	44	75	7	2	.286	.352	.402	.095	.304	.366	.428	.059	31.5	129-3B -3	
2004	SDP	NL	23	469	131	27	3	9	43	63	7	3	.280	.347	.408	-.011	.287	.351	.429	.019	27.7	124-3B -1	

Breakout: 14%   Improve: 41%   Collapse: 21%

His disappointing, injury-prone 2002 caused many people to forget that he was just 21 years old at the time. Healthy and left alone at third base in 2003, he hit pretty much as expected all year and showed a good glove. He's not going to be the player Hank Blalock is, but that shouldn't be the standard. Think Jeff Cirillo before Cirillo lost his talent in a bar bet.

BERNIE CASTRO — 2B — Bats: B — Throws: R — Born: 14-Jul-79 — Age: 24

YEAR	TM	LG	AGE	AB	H	2B	3B	HR	BB	SO	SB	CS	AVG	OBP	SLG	MLVR	EQBA	EQOBP	EQSLG	EQMLVR	VORP	DEFENSE	
2001	GRB	SAL	21	389	101	15	7	1	54	67	67	20	.260	.350	.342	.040	.207	.278	.276	-.388	-27.1	96-2B -14	
2001	STA	NYP	21	57	20	1	0	0	11	12	8	3	.351	.464	.368	.280	.233	.327	.250	-.310	-4.7	15-2B -2	
2002	MOB	SOU	22	419	109	13	3	0	52	67	53	20	.260	.345	.305	-.070	.233	.297	.280	-.331	-20.8	105-2B 4	
2003	POR	PCL	23	425	132	17	5	2	25	43	49	13	.311	.349	.388	.047	.293	.331	.372	-.095	9.8	94-2B -13	
2004	SDP	NL	24	213	52	9	2	1	19	32	12	4	.242	.307	.317	-.226	.248	.312	.333	-.206	2.2	59-2B -5	

Breakout: 24%   Improve: 39%   Collapse: 36%

(continued next page)

Bernie Castro *(continued)*

One of the Padres' better minor trades of the last few years was their acquisition of Castro, who they got from the Yankees in the spring of 2002 for non-prospect outfielder Kevin Reese. The slight speedster has established himself as at least a major-league utility infielder by stealing 180 bases at a 76% clip in four pro seasons. He's a slap hitter at the plate, making contact without driving the ball, a lesser version of Freddy Sanchez. Mark Loretta's contract doesn't make much sense when you look at Castro, who could be 85% of the player for 15% of the cost.

ALEX FERNANDEZ — RF — Bats: L — Throws: L — Born: 15-May-81 — Age: 23

YEAR	TM	LG	AGE	AB	H	2B	3B	HR	BB	SO	SB	CS	AVG	OBP	SLG	MLVR	EQBA	EQOBP	EQSLG	EQMLVR	VORP	DEFENSE			
2001	SBR	CAL	20	416	119	21	6	8	35	67	17	6	.286	.344	.423	.089	.232	.278	.348	-.274	-25.6	51-RF	-5	13-LF	0
2002	BIR	SOU	21	343	100	15	0	7	8	60	20	7	.292	.304	.397	.032	.275	.279	.387	-.185	-13.3	53-LF	-2	13-RF	-1
2002	MOB	SOU	21	66	18	4	0	1	3	8	6	1	.273	.296	.379	-.038	.254	.275	.358	-.251	-3.9	12-LF	2		
2002	POR	PCL	21	80	25	4	0	2	2	13	1	3	.313	.333	.438	.078	.287	.310	.425	-.061	0.1	19-RF	2		
2003	MOB	SOU	22	75	23	5	1	1	4	16	2	3	.307	.342	.440	.144	.263	.291	.395	-.160	-0.8				
2003	POR	PCL	22	379	115	23	2	10	13	53	16	6	.303	.327	.454	.099	.282	.309	.435	-.053	1.3	42-RF	-2	34-LF	0
2004	*SDP*	*NL*	*23*	*322*	*83*	*17*	*2*	*8*	*16*	*52*	*8*	*3*	*.259*	*.295*	*.393*	*-.136*	*.266*	*.299*	*.413*	*-.111*	*1.6*	*83-RF*	*-4*		

Breakout: 27%   Improve: 54%   Collapse: 25%

The general consensus is that he's older than 23, although he wasn't found out in either of the last two winters. If that was his biggest problem number in the 20s, he might still have a chance, but as long he's walking once every 21.5 at-bats, it's hard to see a future for him, no matter how much his power impresses scouts.

J. J. FURMANIAK — SS — Bats: R — Throws: R — Born: 31-Jul-79 — Age: 24

YEAR	TM	LG	AGE	AB	H	2B	3B	HR	BB	SO	SB	CS	AVG	OBP	SLG	MLVR	EQBA	EQOBP	EQSLG	EQMLVR	VORP	DEFENSE			
2001	FTW	MID	21	436	96	24	3	5	55	117	11	6	.220	.309	.323	-.114	.169	.237	.253	-.520	-45.4	116-SS	5		
2002	LEL	CAL	22	381	98	16	6	7	26	100	11	9	.257	.311	.386	-.047	.207	.248	.316	-.393	-23.5	69-3B	4	21-SS	-4
2003	LEL	CAL	23	309	97	22	8	9	36	55	10	4	.314	.397	.524	.310	.238	.306	.405	-.137	6.2	76-SS	-5		
2003	MOB	SOU	23	103	27	4	1	3	8	27	0	0	.262	.336	.408	.058	.229	.286	.381	-.214	-0.4	31-SS	-7		
2004	*SDP*	*NL*	*24*	*233*	*55*	*12*	*2*	*5*	*20*	*53*	*3*	*2*	*.236*	*.305*	*.370*	*-.163*	*.242*	*.309*	*.390*	*-.141*	*7.6*	*64-SS*	*-7*		

Breakout: 57%   Improve: 69%   Collapse: 20%

Another Lake Elsinore wonder, Furmaniak made the Cal League All-Star team in his second year at the level. Even if the Padres didn't have Castro and Khalil Greene ahead of him, he would still project as a utility infielder in the majors, albeit one with some pop. He was lousy in the Arizona Fall League.

JAKE GAUTREAU — 2B — Bats: L — Throws: R — Born: 14-Nov-79 — Age: 24

YEAR	TM	LG	AGE	AB	H	2B	3B	HR	BB	SO	SB	CS	AVG	OBP	SLG	MLVR	EQBA	EQOBP	EQSLG	EQMLVR	VORP	DEFENSE	
2001	EUG	NWN	21	178	55	19	0	6	22	47	1	1	.309	.389	.517	.328	.217	.282	.370	-.245	-6.7	44-3B	-1
2002	LEL	CAL	22	371	106	20	1	10	42	86	2	3	.286	.358	.426	.107	.224	.281	.338	-.287	-12.6	87-2B	-7
2003	MOB	SOU	23	438	106	24	0	14	50	131	1	4	.242	.324	.393	.007	.208	.275	.350	-.292	-16.4	109-2B	-13
2004	*SDP*	*NL*	*24*	*199*	*45*	*10*	*1*	*6*	*19*	*53*	*1*	*1*	*.224*	*.294*	*.367*	*-.194*	*.229*	*.298*	*.386*	*-.173*	*-0.1*	*56-2B*	*-7*

Breakout: 53%   Improve: 73%   Collapse: 18%

You want an argument against emphasizing college hitters, the Padres have it for you. Bozied hasn't hit above A-ball, Xavier Nady hasn't hit above A-ball, Gautreau hasn't hit above A-ball or taken to second base. You have to cut Gautreau some slack—colitis is tough to manage, and bit him hard again last year—but it doesn't change the fact that he, Bozied, and Nady, who were the future two years ago, now look like suspects.

BRIAN GILES — LF — Bats: L — Throws: L — Born: 20-Jan-71 — Age: 33

YEAR	TM	LG	AGE	AB	H	2B	3B	HR	BB	SO	SB	CS	AVG	OBP	SLG	MLVR	EQBA	EQOBP	EQSLG	EQMLVR	VORP	DEFENSE			
2001	PIT	NL	30	576	178	37	7	37	90	67	13	6	.309	.404	.590	.355	.304	.400	.583	.333	67.6	104-LF	-10	49-CF	-1
2002	PIT	NL	31	497	148	37	5	38	135	74	15	6	.298	.450	.622	.484	.293	.445	.622	.440	77.7	140-LF	1		
2003	PIT	NL	32	388	116	30	4	16	85	48	0	3	.299	.430	.521	.319	.299	.428	.522	.290	37.3	95-LF	2	16-CF	1
2003	SDP	NL	32	104	31	4	2	4	20	10	4	0	.298	.414	.490	.329	.315	.429	.519	.304	11.0	28-LF	-2		
2004	*SDP*	*NL*	*33*	*479*	*140*	*30*	*4*	*24*	*89*	*62*	*9*	*3*	*.294*	*.408*	*.524*	*.249*	*.301*	*.413*	*.551*	*.291*	*50.1*	*136-LF*	*1*		

Breakout: 6%   Improve: 47%   Collapse: 12%

The underrated superstar started 2003 late thanks to a small tear in his right MCL, his plant knee, and his power never really came around. It's impossible to know what Petco Park will do to his numbers, but it really doesn't matter; Giles can hit, and will be an offensive force as long as he's healthy and in the lineup. The bigger problem is that he may have to play center field after the Padres failed to land Mike Cameron or Kenny Lofton this off-season, despite strong overtures to both. Giles is 33 now—he wasn't a real good center fielder at 27.

WIKI GONZALEZ C Bats: R Throws: R Born: 17-May-74 Age: 30

YEAR	TM	LG	AGE	AB	H	2B	3B	HR	BB	SO	SB	CS	AVG	OBP	SLG	MLVR	EQBA	EQOBP	EQSLG	EQMLVR	VORP	DEFENSE
2001	SDP	NL	27	160	44	6	0	8	11	28	2	0	.275	.335	.463	.066	.288	.346	.485	.090	11.3	37-C -1
2002	LEL	CAL	28	53	18	8	0	1	12	3	0	0	.340	.486	.547	.502	.236	.352	.400	-.058	2.0	13-C -2
2002	SDP	NL	28	164	36	8	1	1	27	24	0	0	.220	.330	.299	-.139	.243	.347	.331	-.155	0.8	51-C 2
2003	POR	PCL	29	149	42	8	1	4	21	12	1	0	.282	.379	.430	.133	.252	.343	.397	-.068	4.9	41-C 0
2003	SDP	NL	29	65	13	5	0	0	5	13	0	0	.200	.264	.277	-.305	.212	.276	.303	-.352	-2.4	18-C -1
2004	SEA	AL	30	138	34	7	0	3	14	20	1	0	.244	.321	.371	-.115	.247	.328	.382	-.113	4.3	41-C -1

Breakout: 31%   Improve: 49%   Collapse: 30%

Gonzalez had one of the quickest releases in baseball a few years ago, but elbow surgery in 2002 took the bullets out of his gun, rendering him a generic backup. It gets very little attention, but the four-year, $4.5-million contract extension the Padres gave Gonzalez in 2001 has been quite the boondoggle.

KHALIL GREENE SS Bats: R Throws: R Born: 21-Oct-79 Age: 24

YEAR	TM	LG	AGE	AB	H	2B	3B	HR	BB	SO	SB	CS	AVG	OBP	SLG	MLVR	EQBA	EQOBP	EQSLG	EQMLVR	VORP	DEFENSE
2002	LEL	CAL	22	183	58	9	1	9	12	33	0	0	.317	.368	.525	.289	.259	.297	.432	-.099	5.5	37-SS -3
2003	MOB	SOU	23	229	63	17	2	3	16	55	2	3	.275	.327	.406	.052	.240	.281	.373	-.227	-1.7	47-SS -2
2003	POR	PCL	23	319	92	19	0	10	20	52	5	4	.288	.346	.442	.101	.268	.323	.421	-.059	13.3	76-SS -3
2003	SDP	NL	23	65	14	4	1	2	4	19	0	1	.215	.271	.400	-.109	.227	.280	.424	-.167	0.5	19-SS -2
2004	SDP	NL	24	280	70	15	2	8	19	57	2	2	.252	.308	.400	-.108	.258	.313	.421	-.082	12.0	75-SS -4

Breakout: 35%   Improve: 61%   Collapse: 23%

The Padres rushed Greene, who was just getting by at Double-A, through two levels last year and had him at Qualcomm just 15 months after draft day. A short, muscular player with decent power potential, Greene hasn't showed the plate discipline as a pro that helped him become the 13th pick in the 2000 draft. While he probably needs another half-season at Triple-A, or at least a job-share with Ramon Vazquez to start the year, the Pads look likely to hand him the keys right now; he'll start being a productive full-time shortstop in 2005. Think John Valentin if the walks come, Rich Aurilia if they don't, with similarly underrated work defensively.

FREDDY GUZMAN CF Bats: B Throws: R Born: 20-Jan-81 Age: 23

YEAR	TM	LG	AGE	AB	H	2B	3B	HR	BB	SO	SB	CS	AVG	OBP	SLG	MLVR	EQBA	EQOBP	EQSLG	EQMLVR	VORP	DEFENSE
2002	EUG	NWN	21	80	18	2	1	0	7	15	16	1	.225	.293	.275	-.135	.193	.236	.241	-.529	-17.3	18-CF -4
2002	FTW	MID	21	190	53	7	5	0	18	37	39	7	.279	.341	.368	.071	.234	.281	.320	-.306	-9.7	38-CF -3
2002	LEL	CAL	21	81	21	3	0	1	8	12	14	4	.259	.326	.333	-.092	.217	.261	.277	-.416	-8.7	11-LF -3
2003	LEL	CAL	22	281	80	12	3	2	40	60	49	10	.285	.375	.370	.038	.225	.298	.295	-.312	-14.3	48-CF -4
2003	MOB	SOU	22	177	48	5	2	1	26	34	38	7	.271	.368	.339	.023	.247	.324	.313	-.223	-4.4	45-CF -1
2004	SDP	NL	23	270	61	12	2	1	23	57	20	6	.225	.289	.300	-.290	.230	.293	.316	-.274	-8.4	73-CF -8

Breakout: 19%   Improve: 41%   Collapse: 29%

The Padres' most notable AgeGate case, Guzman picked up a new name (he was known as Pedro de los Santos) and two-plus years last winter. He was so flustered that he led the minors in steals with 90—swiping bags at an 82% clip—and showed enough patience to establish himself as the Padres' best leadoff prospect since Bip Roberts. He has frightfully little power, and still has to show that he can hit for a high enough average to be a viable regular, but his rapid ascent is encouraging for a team in dire need of a center fielder.

DAVE HANSEN PH **Bats: L** **Throws: R** Born: 24-Nov-68 Age: 35

YEAR	TM	LG	AGE	AB	H	2B	3B	HR	BB	SO	SB	CS	AVG	OBP	SLG	MLVR	EQBA	EQOBP	EQSLG	EQMLVR	VORP	DEFENSE			
2001	LAD	NL	32	140	33	10	0	2	32	29	0	1	.236	.371	.350	-.049	.250	.386	.375	-.017	2.9	20-1B	-2	16-3B	2
2002	LAD	NL	33	120	35	6	0	2	14	22	1	0	.292	.363	.392	.087	.315	.380	.419	.081	6.8				
2003	SDP	NL	34	135	33	4	1	2	23	25	1	0	.244	.358	.333	-.021	.259	.367	.360	-.067	4.7	13-1B	1		
2004	SEA	AL	35	77	19	3	0	1	10	14	0	0	.241	.332	.350	-.123	.244	.340	.360	-.122	0.8	26-1B	-1		

Breakout: 14%   Improve: 29%   Collapse: 44%

What more can you say about Dave Hansen? He could have had a long career as a regular third baseman but for a poor performance the one time he had a chance at a job. Since returning from Japan in 1999, he's been a useful pinch-hitter and spare left-handed bat at the infield corners. At 35, his bat his slowing just enough to make having him around a dicey proposition; he'll still draw his walks, but he may not be able to do much else.

KENNARD JONES CF **Bats: L** **Throws: L** Born: 08-Sep-81 Age: 22

YEAR	TM	LG	AGE	AB	H	2B	3B	HR	BB	SO	SB	CS	AVG	OBP	SLG	MLVR	EQBA	EQOBP	EQSLG	EQMLVR	VORP	DEFENSE	
2002	EUG	NWN	20	61	18	2	0	0	10	12	12	1	.295	.411	.328	.136	.231	.303	.262	-.344	-7.3	16-CF	-1
2002	FTW	MID	20	77	22	4	0	0	11	21	3	4	.286	.382	.338	.094	.210	.285	.259	-.395	-6.4	17-CF	-2
2003	FTW	MID	21	306	94	13	4	1	50	52	20	19	.307	.407	.386	.210	.229	.307	.297	-.289	-14.9	78-CF	-10
2003	LEL	CAL	21	76	19	3	2	0	4	11	3	2	.250	.287	.342	-.180	.197	.228	.276	-.495	-7.5	17-CF	-3
2004	SDP	NL	22	242	53	10	2	1	22	51	7	4	.218	.288	.295	-.303	.223	.292	.310	-.288	-11.7	67-CF	-8

Breakout: 30%   Improve: 62%   Collapse: 16%

Jones gets scouts' attention with his raw speed and statheads' affection with his OBP and ability to draw walks. A third-round pick out of Indiana in 2002, he made the Midwest League All-Star team on just a half-season's performance. A broken left hand curtailed his time in the Cal League, a stint that wasn't going real well anyway. Jones hasn't yet figured out how to apply his speed to a baseball game; he's a career 59% base stealer, and a poor center fielder. He needs time, something the presence of Guzman allows the Padres to give him.

RYAN KLESKO 1B/LF **Bats: L** **Throws: L** Born: 12-Jun-71 Age: 33

YEAR	TM	LG	AGE	AB	H	2B	3B	HR	BB	SO	SB	CS	AVG	OBP	SLG	MLVR	EQBA	EQOBP	EQSLG	EQMLVR	VORP	DEFENSE			
2001	SDP	NL	30	538	154	34	6	30	88	89	23	4	.286	.384	.539	.267	.298	.397	.558	.287	58.2	138-1B	-10		
2002	SDP	NL	31	540	162	39	1	29	76	86	6	2	.300	.388	.537	.332	.315	.400	.572	.330	61.3	109-1B	-9	21-RF	-3
2003	SDP	NL	32	397	100	18	0	21	65	83	2	5	.252	.354	.456	.142	.267	.371	.490	.121	20.0	102-1B	-1		
2004	SDP	NL	33	382	104	21	1	19	58	72	5	2	.271	.368	.480	.111	.278	.373	.505	.146	26.8	106-1B	-3		

Breakout: 6%   Improve: 40%   Collapse: 19%

Hitter who is a better left fielder—and a worse first baseman—than people think. Klesko's inability to handle throws, something no defensive metric picks up, is a hidden cost of playing him there. For a big guy, he moves fairly well and plays left field adequately. After years of insisting he could hit lefties, it's time to concede that he can't and give those 150 at-bats to Buchanan. The Padres need one more big season out of him if they're going to contend. PECOTA sees more missed time and declining production ahead.

JON KNOTT RF/1B **Bats: R** **Throws: R** Born: 04-Aug-78 Age: 25

YEAR	TM	LG	AGE	AB	H	2B	3B	HR	BB	SO	SB	CS	AVG	OBP	SLG	MLVR	EQBA	EQOBP	EQSLG	EQMLVR	VORP	DEFENSE			
2002	FTW	MID	23	126	42	12	3	3	17	33	2	1	.333	.411	.548	.443	.250	.315	.424	-.084	-0.8	19-RF	-3		
2002	LEL	CAL	23	367	125	33	8	8	46	68	5	4	.341	.414	.540	.400	.259	.322	.414	-.078	0.6	43-1B	-5	41-RF	-2
2003	MOB	SOU	24	432	109	32	0	27	82	117	5	3	.252	.387	.514	.254	.208	.320	.431	-.097	-4.7	65-RF	-6	50-1B	-3
2003	POR	PCL	24	26	9	1	0	1	4	3	0	0	.346	.433	.500	.377	.308	.400	.462	.170	2.4				
2004	SDP	NL	25	221	54	13	1	8	26	53	2	1	.244	.334	.427	-.035	.251	.338	.449	-.006	9.2	63-RF	-5		

Breakout: 36%   Improve: 62%   Collapse: 20%

Knott had the kind of transition to Double-A that other Padre hitters haven't, roping 59 extra-base hits and picking up 82 walks. He's 26 in May, though, and he struck out in 27% of his at-bats, opening up concern that he'll be exposed at higher levels. He's marginal in right field, which limits his options in the major leagues. So as impressive as the line is, Knott really isn't an answer to the Padres' problems getting prospects through the system either. Michael Johnson, the team's #2 pick in 2002 who signed just before the 2003 draft and hit fairly well at Lake Elsinore, is the best long-term option at first base.

MARK KOTSAY   CF   Bats: L   Throws: L   Born: 02-Dec-75   Age: 28

YEAR	TM	LG	AGE	AB	H	2B	3B	HR	BB	SO	SB	CS	AVG	OBP	SLG	MLVR	EQBA	EQOBP	EQSLG	EQMLVR	VORP	DEFENSE
2001	SDP	NL	25	406	118	29	1	10	48	58	13	5	.291	.366	.441	.105	.307	.381	.465	.141	32.8	104-CF -3
2002	SDP	NL	26	578	169	27	7	17	59	89	11	9	.292	.359	.452	.164	.313	.375	.491	.173	49.1	140-CF -3
2003	SDP	NL	27	482	128	28	4	7	56	82	6	3	.266	.343	.384	.034	.279	.354	.409	-.010	16.5	125-CF 6
2004	OAK	AL	28	439	121	24	3	13	48	68	7	4	.275	.347	.433	.032	.284	.360	.452	.061	19.6	116-CF 0

Breakout: 11%   Improve: 44%   Collapse: 18%

A bad back hampered Kotsay, a spring breakout candidate, throughout the season, keeping him out of the lineup more than a quarter of the time and killing his power when he played. He was traded to Oakland in November in what appeared to be a good deal for both teams, but for the A's, it depends entirely on the condition on Kotsay's back. His defense makes him average even if the power never comes around; given the nature of back injuries, it probably won't.

KEITH LOCKHART   PH   Bats: L   Throws: R   Born: 10-Nov-64   Age: 39

YEAR	TM	LG	AGE	AB	H	2B	3B	HR	BB	SO	SB	CS	AVG	OBP	SLG	MLVR	EQBA	EQOBP	EQSLG	EQMLVR	VORP	DEFENSE
2001	ATL	NL	36	178	39	6	0	3	16	22	1	2	.219	.289	.303	-.300	.228	.297	.311	-.290	-5.7	33-2B 1
2002	ATL	NL	37	296	64	13	3	5	27	50	0	1	.216	.282	.331	-.206	.227	.290	.350	-.251	-5.9	69-2B 4
2003	SDP	NL	38	95	23	5	1	3	13	19	0	1	.242	.339	.411	.047	.258	.350	.443	.012	5.2	15-2B -3
2004	SDP	NL	39	93	19	4	1	2	10	18	0	0	.210	.295	.318	-.263	.216	.299	.335	-.246	-1.0	29-2B -3

Breakout: 16%   Improve: 41%   Collapse: 45%

Like Hansen, Lockhart has appeared in almost every edition of *Baseball Prospectus,* leaving little left to say about him. He's old enough to make his roster spot a tenuous one; veteran leadership is nice, but range, speed and pop are nicer. Last season was just the second time in six years that Lockhart actually helped his team. Don't bet on him doing it again at 39.

MARK LORETTA   2B   Bats: R   Throws: R   Born: 14-Aug-71   Age: 32

YEAR	TM	LG	AGE	AB	H	2B	3B	HR	BB	SO	SB	CS	AVG	OBP	SLG	MLVR	EQBA	EQOBP	EQSLG	EQMLVR	VORP	DEFENSE	
2001	MIL	NL	29	384	111	14	2	2	28	46	1	2	.289	.346	.352	-.086	.296	.352	.357	-.075	10.7	48-2B 3	31-3B -4
2002	MIL	NL	30	217	58	14	0	2	23	32	0	0	.267	.350	.359	-.022	.276	.353	.376	-.060	7.1	44-2B -2	
2002	HOU	NL	30	66	28	4	0	2	9	5	1	1	.424	.481	.576	.600	.418	.487	.582	.604	13.1		
2003	SDP	NL	31	589	185	28	4	13	54	62	5	4	.314	.372	.441	.219	.334	.391	.473	.196	53.2	140-2B 3	
2004	SDP	NL	32	398	112	20	2	6	38	46	3	2	.281	.349	.390	-.031	.289	.353	.410	-.002	21.7	106-2B -4	

Breakout: 2%   Improve: 27%   Collapse: 54%

His season was a little bit better than ones he'd put up in the past, but in this one he was the best player on a bad team. For that, he got a two-year contract extension worth $5.25 million. Loretta is a good utility infielder and a mediocre regular, and he will be hard-pressed to stay above league average as a second baseman for the duration of this deal.

GARY MATTHEWS   OF   Bats: B   Throws: R   Born: 25-Aug-74   Age: 29

YEAR	TM	LG	AGE	AB	H	2B	3B	HR	BB	SO	SB	CS	AVG	OBP	SLG	MLVR	EQBA	EQOBP	EQSLG	EQMLVR	VORP	DEFENSE	
2001	CHC	NL	26	258	56	9	1	9	38	55	5	3	.217	.320	.364	-.160	.221	.322	.374	-.160	-1.0	68-CF -7	12-LF 0
2001	PIT	NL	26	147	36	6	1	5	22	45	3	2	.245	.341	.401	-.063	.242	.339	.403	-.074	3.2	40-CF -1	
2002	BAL	AL	27	344	95	25	3	7	43	69	15	5	.276	.355	.427	.075	.311	.390	.486	.190	24.2	62-RF 1	12-LF 0
2003	BAL	AL	28	162	33	12	1	2	9	29	0	3	.204	.250	.327	-.310	.227	.275	.368	-.255	-8.3	35-CF 1	
2003	SDP	NL	28	306	83	19	1	4	34	66	12	5	.271	.346	.379	.038	.290	.361	.408	.010	8.3	24-RF -1	25-CF 0
2004	ATL	NL	29	284	66	15	2	5	29	51	5	3	.233	.305	.355	-.186	.236	.306	.367	-.179	-6.6	77-CF -6	

Breakout: 60%   Improve: 72%   Collapse: 19%

Matthews hits a little from both sides of the plate, gets on base, runs well enough to steal 15 bases and pinch-run. If his name was Brian Smith, he might have settled into a career by now, but the expectation that he can be more, like his father was, keep teams from seeing him for what he is. Matthews was picked up on waivers by the Braves, who have needed a good fourth outfielder for years and who now have a fragile right fielder in J. D. Drew; this could be a good match.

DONALDO MENDEZ   SS   Bats: R   Throws: R   Born: 07-Jun-78   Age: 26

YEAR	TM	LG	AGE	AB	H	2B	3B	HR	BB	SO	SB	CS	AVG	OBP	SLG	MLVR	EQBA	EQOBP	EQSLG	EQMLVR	VORP	DEFENSE			
2001	SDP	NL	23	118	18	2	1	1	5	37	1	2	.153	.206	.212	-.614	.176	.225	.244	-.555	-10.9	36-SS	-9		
2002	MOB	SOU	24	224	49	16	0	4	19	53	15	5	.219	.297	.344	-.119	.202	.255	.325	-.369	-11.5	55-SS	-1		
2002	POR	PCL	24	217	47	9	1	6	14	63	11	4	.217	.282	.350	-.218	.202	.258	.335	-.350	-9.8	59-SS	-5		
2003	POR	PCL	25	358	81	17	0	6	25	83	10	7	.226	.288	.324	-.214	.211	.269	.311	-.356	-16.0	56-SS	-11	22-3B	1
2003	SDP	NL	25	84	19	6	0	2	7	32	1	0	.226	.298	.369	-.097	.244	.313	.395	-.133	1.5	24-SS	-3		
2004	*PIT*	*NL*	*26*	*232*	*51*	*10*	*1*	*4*	*17*	*57*	*5*	*2*	*.218*	*.285*	*.331*	*-.261*	*.220*	*.286*	*.343*	*-.258*	*-1.5*	*64-SS*	*-7*		

Breakout: 48%   *Improve: 62%*   *Collapse: 29%*

A Rule 5 victim, or a glove man who never had a chance? You can see it both ways with Mendez, who was yanked out of the Midwest League by the Padres in 2001 and hasn't had an OBP above .300 since then. Then again, he hadn't really hit before, and his Rule 5 year was truncated by a torn knee tendon that required surgery, so he wasn't just stuck on the bench all year. Regardless, his chance at a career is pretty much gone.

XAVIER NADY   RF   Bats: R   Throws: R   Born: 14-Nov-78   Age: 25

YEAR	TM	LG	AGE	AB	H	2B	3B	HR	BB	SO	SB	CS	AVG	OBP	SLG	MLVR	EQBA	EQOBP	EQSLG	EQMLVR	VORP	DEFENSE	
2001	LEL	CAL	22	524	158	38	1	26	62	109	6	0	.302	.381	.527	.298	.233	.299	.411	-.145	-10.0	109-1B	-5
2002	LEL	CAL	23	169	47	6	3	13	28	40	2	0	.278	.382	.580	.342	.209	.291	.429	-.153	-1.5		
2002	POR	PCL	23	315	89	12	1	10	20	60	0	1	.283	.329	.422	.021	.262	.305	.394	-.136	-7.8	55-LF	-2
2003	POR	PCL	24	136	36	7	0	7	12	28	0	0	.265	.329	.471	.090	.241	.304	.445	-.082	-0.7	32-RF	-4
2003	SDP	NL	24	371	99	17	1	9	24	74	6	2	.267	.321	.391	.006	.282	.333	.414	-.040	3.6	93-RF	-7
2004	*SDP*	*NL*	*25*	*366*	*93*	*20*	*1*	*14*	*31*	*71*	*3*	*2*	*.254*	*.318*	*.426*	*-.056*	*.260*	*.322*	*.448*	*-.027*	*8.9*	*97-RF*	*-4*

Breakout: 38%   *Improve: 63%*   *Collapse: 17%*

It's time to recalibrate. As good a hitter as Nady was in college, he's been an ordinary player at every pro level above A-ball, not hitting for average or power, drawing walks, or running. Even at his best last year, he struck out in a quarter of his at-bats and twice as often as he walked. Talent is nice, but performance matters, and Nady's performance doesn't fit his status a franchise-type player for the Padres. Rather than commit to him for 2004, the Padres need to let him start the year in Triple-A and establish himself as more than a .330/.430 hitter.

PHIL NEVIN   3B/1B   Bats: R   Throws: R   Born: 19-Jan-71   Age: 33

YEAR	TM	LG	AGE	AB	H	2B	3B	HR	BB	SO	SB	CS	AVG	OBP	SLG	MLVR	EQBA	EQOBP	EQSLG	EQMLVR	VORP	DEFENSE			
2001	SDP	NL	30	546	167	31	0	41	71	147	4	4	.306	.388	.588	.363	.317	.397	.607	.377	86.3	137-3B	-6		
2002	SDP	NL	31	407	116	16	0	12	38	87	4	0	.285	.344	.413	.081	.303	.359	.446	.072	27.0	66-3B	-5	32-1B	-4
2003	SDP	NL	32	226	63	8	0	13	21	44	2	0	.279	.339	.487	.185	.293	.349	.517	.146	12.9	28-3B	1	25-RF	-2
2004	*SDP*	*NL*	*33*	*312*	*83*	*15*	*1*	*13*	*33*	*67*	*2*	*1*	*.268*	*.339*	*.447*	*.018*	*.274*	*.343*	*.471*	*.050*	*17.9*	*84-3B*	*-6*		

Breakout: 12%   *Improve: 37%*   *Collapse: 25%*

It's not clear why Nevin is considered a star. In nine big-league seasons, he's had two full, healthy years in which he's been productive. Lucky him, he strung them together for a lousy team and got a big contract out of it. He doesn't hurt the Padres at the plate, and anyone is better defensively at first base than Ryan Klesko, so he has a place. The gap between perception and reality, however, is very wide, and that's before even considering that he's not regarded as a particularly good guy. With Giles, Klesko, Nady, and Nevin, the Padres have one two many guys at the right end of the defensive spectrum, and no center fielder in the bunch. Flipping Nevin or Nady for a center fielder—remember, they tried to get Ken Griffey Jr. for Nevin last year—still looks like a great idea, though Nevin's no-trade clause makes it tough to do so. The outfield defense, as currently constituted, would be awful, and Nady isn't going to hit enough to make that worthwhile.

MARK QUINN   SOB   Bats: R   Throws: R   Born: 21-May-74   Age: 30

YEAR	TM	LG	AGE	AB	H	2B	3B	HR	BB	SO	SB	CS	AVG	OBP	SLG	MLVR	EQBA	EQOBP	EQSLG	EQMLVR	VORP	DEFENSE			
2001	KCR	AL	27	453	122	31	2	17	12	69	9	5	.269	.298	.459	-.036	.277	.307	.475	-.003	7.1	50-RF	0	49-LF	0
2002	KCR	AL	28	76	18	4	0	2	5	15	2	1	.237	.301	.368	-.163	.250	.310	.395	-.134	-1.3	12-RF	0		
2002	OMA	PCL	28	39	7	2	1	0	4	7	0	0	.179	.289	.282	-.328	.154	.253	.256	-.489	-4.3				
2003	DUR	INT	29	60	10	3	1	0	3	17	0	0	.167	.206	.250	-.457	.167	.206	.250	-.590	-8.2				
2003	POR	PCL	29	180	49	13	0	8	24	36	0	0	.272	.362	.478	.161	.246	.330	.443	-.034	1.2	35-LF	-2		
2004	*STL*	*NL*	*30*	*171*	*41*	*10*	*1*	*5*	*14*	*37*	*1*	*1*	*.242*	*.307*	*.389*	*-.132*	*.245*	*.309*	*.409*	*-.113*	*-0.8*	*49-LF*	*-2*		

Breakout: 43%   *Improve: 57%*   *Collapse: 26%*

As a general rule, the informed-outsider position means disregarding most things about a player that cannot be objectively confirmed. It doesn't claim that those things don't exist or don't have an impact, but it's an acknowledgement that much of what we know about players' personalities comes through at least one filter, and is rarely presented without bias. This doesn't mean that you can't jackass your way out of a lot of money. Mark Quinn might have had a little Carlos Lee-type career for himself. Now, he'll be lucky if they remember where to send his pension checks.

HUMBERTO QUINTERO								C				Bats: R			Throws: R						Born: 02-Aug-79		Age: 24
YEAR	TM	LG	AGE	AB	H	2B	3B	HR	BB	SO	SB	CS	AVG	OBP	SLG	MLVR	EQBA	EQOBP	EQSLG	EQMLVR	VORP	DEFENSE	
2001	KAN	SAL	21	197	53	7	1	1	8	20	7	3	.269	.321	.330	-.005	.233	.269	.287	-.378	-12.9	57-C	26
2001	WNS	CAR	21	154	37	6	0	0	5	19	9	3	.240	.268	.279	-.162	.217	.244	.255	-.482	-14.2	42-C	7
2002	WNS	CAR	22	160	31	1	1	0	8	23	2	3	.194	.247	.212	-.355	.179	.217	.198	-.634	-22.4	51-C	16
2002	CHR	INT	22	41	9	1	0	0	3	8	0	0	.220	.273	.244	-.330	.220	.273	.220	-.470	-3.7	12-C	3
2002	MOB	SOU	22	125	30	8	0	1	5	12	0	3	.240	.286	.328	-.145	.228	.250	.315	-.379	-7.6	32-C	5
2003	MOB	SOU	23	386	115	26	0	3	19	41	0	0	.298	.343	.389	.069	.271	.306	.361	-.175	-0.2	106-C	8
2003	SDP	NL	23	23	5	0	0	0	1	6	0	0	.217	.250	.217	-.408	.261	.292	.261	-.353	-1.5		
2004	*SDP*	*NL*	*24*	*215*	*50*	*9*	*1*	*2*	*10*	*29*	*1*	*1*	*.233*	*.279*	*.308*	*-.295*	*.239*	*.283*	*.324*	*-.278*	*-5.2*	*58-C*	*3*
Breakout: 27%		Improve: 44%			Collapse: 31%																		

Quintero brought a great defensive reputation with him from the White Sox system when he was acquired for D'Angelo Jimenez in 2002. He improved upon that at Mobile, throwing out more than a third of runners trying to steal on him. While his offense also appeared to improve—he hit .298 with some doubles—the underlying numbers were pretty poor, including a terrible walk rate. He should settle in as the backup for Hernandez, providing a cannon arm with late-career Brad Ausmus-like offense.

TODD SEARS								1B				Bats: R			Throws: R						Born: 23-Oct-75		Age: 28
YEAR	TM	LG	AGE	AB	H	2B	3B	HR	BB	SO	SB	CS	AVG	OBP	SLG	MLVR	EQBA	EQOBP	EQSLG	EQMLVR	VORP	DEFENSE	
2001	EDM	PCL	25	408	127	25	2	13	41	71	2	1	.311	.376	.478	.149	.273	.336	.420	-.033	6.1	103-1B	-1
2002	EDM	PCL	26	484	150	36	4	20	59	142	2	1	.310	.388	.525	.263	.272	.344	.463	.041	18.8	119-1B	-12
2003	ROC	INT	27	283	72	12	1	7	37	90	6	1	.254	.347	.378	-.009	.234	.323	.357	-.173	-8.0	52-1B	-6
2003	MIN	AL	27	65	16	2	0	2	7	15	0	0	.246	.324	.369	-.116	.262	.341	.400	-.060	-0.4	11-1B	-1
2004	*SDP*	*NL*	*28*	*168*	*42*	*9*	*1*	*5*	*18*	*47*	*1*	*1*	*.252*	*.330*	*.413*	*-.055*	*.259*	*.334*	*.434*	*-.027*	*5.7*	*49-1B*	*-4*
Breakout: 29%		Improve: 56%			Collapse: 28%																		

Stuck at Triple-A since 2001, Sears had nowhere to go in the Twins system. He looked like he had nowhere to go with the Padres too after getting non-tendered in December. He's a tall guy who's rarely hit for as much power as he's been expected to, and isn't anything special around the bag at first. He needs to find his way to a bad team and establish himself with one good year, like Randall Simon did. The Pads re-signed him a few days after the non-tender, so he'll probably need two injuries to get his shot.

RAMON VAZQUEZ								SS				Bats: L			Throws: R						Born: 21-Aug-76		Age: 27
YEAR	TM	LG	AGE	AB	H	2B	3B	HR	BB	SO	SB	CS	AVG	OBP	SLG	MLVR	EQBA	EQOBP	EQSLG	EQMLVR	VORP	DEFENSE	
2001	TAC	PCL	24	466	140	28	1	10	76	84	9	7	.300	.397	.429	.140	.266	.358	.380	-.053	22.2	127-SS	8
2001	SEA	AL	24	35	8	0	0	0	0	3	0	0	.229	.222	.229	-.495	.257	.257	.257	-.433	-2.5		
2002	SDP	NL	25	423	116	21	5	2	45	79	7	2	.274	.344	.362	.002	.294	.360	.389	-.016	17.9	62-2B 3	31-SS 1
2003	SDP	NL	26	422	110	17	4	3	52	88	10	3	.261	.342	.341	-.021	.277	.355	.365	-.071	16.0	100-SS	-10
2004	*SDP*	*NL*	*27*	*429*	*112*	*21*	*3*	*5*	*49*	*78*	*9*	*4*	*.260*	*.338*	*.361*	*-.101*	*.267*	*.343*	*.380*	*-.076*	*16.4*	*115-SS*	*-6*
Breakout: 15%		Improve: 36%			Collapse: 26%																		

Vazquez has a ton of potential uses for the Padres. He's Greene insurance, if the rookie continues to scuffle at the plate. He could be a platoon partner for Loretta at second base, should Loretta return to earth. He could be trade bait to one of the teams lacking a shortstop and needing some OBP. (The Blue Jays come immediately to mind.) If they just keep him around on the bench, he's an excellent early-inning pinch-hitter and fifth infielder.

PITCHERS

BRAD BAKER
Bats: R   **Throws: R**   Born: 06-Nov-80   Age: 23

YEAR	TM	LG	AGE	G	GS	IP	H	BB	SO	HR	ERA	EQERA	EQH9	EQBB9	EQSO9	EQHR9	PERA	VORP	STF
2001	SAR	FLA	20	24	23	120.0	132	64	103	8	4.72	6.73	10.9	5.6	5.3	1.4	6.53	-13.9	-1
2002	SAR	FLA	21	12	12	61.3	53	25	65	4	2.79	4.61	10.2	4.6	6.8	1.3	5.83	6.0	13
2002	MOB	SOU	21	12	12	64.3	47	45	57	5	4.48	5.58	7.5	6.6	5.9	1.4	5.24	0.1	4
2003	LEL	CAL	22	27	4	44.7	31	14	69	2	2.01	3.15	8.3	3.8	9.2	0.9	4.26	10.9	28
2003	MOB	SOU	22	17	9	50.7	50	36	53	3	5.68	6.95	11.1	7.5	6.6	1.2	6.85	-6.8	-12
2004	*SDP*	*NL*	*23*	*10*	*7*	*36.0*	*39*	*25*	*30*	*5*	*5.97*	*6.54*	*9.8*	*5.5*	*6.6*	*1.2*	*6.52*	*-1.4*	*-8*

Breakout: 23%   *Improve: 55%*   *Collapse: 24%*

Closer prospect who came over for Alan Embree in 2002. Baker has the pedigree of a #1 pick, but his career ERA at Double-A is 5.01 and he had to be sent back to the Cal League to get himself together last year. The Padres have a fair number of pitching prospects coming up behind Baker, such as Gabe Ribas, Wilmer Villatoro, and Javier Martinez, so he has to hit the ground running this year. He seemed to take to relief at Lake Elsinore, so that's something.

ROD BECK
Bats: R   **Throws: R**   Born: 03-Aug-68   Age: 35

YEAR	TM	LG	AGE	G	GS	IP	H	BB	SO	HR	ERA	EQERA	EQH9	EQBB9	EQSO9	EQHR9	PERA	VORP	STF
2001	BOS	AL	32	68	0	80.7	77	28	63	15	3.90	4.08	8.1	2.8	6.5	1.5	4.51	13.4	-9
2003	IOW	PCL	34	21	0	30.7	25	7	26	2	0.59	1.88	7.8	2.5	6.6	0.9	3.75	11.9	6
2003	SDP	NL	34	36	0	35.3	25	11	32	4	1.78	2.38	6.6	2.6	7.1	1.1	3.33	14.5	11
2004	*SDP*	*NL*	*35*	*81*	*0*	*50.0*	*44*	*17*	*43*	*5*	*3.32*	*3.63*	*8.0*	*2.8*	*6.9*	*0.9*	*3.79*	*11.3*	*3*

Breakout: 32%   *Improve: 56%*   *Collapse: 25%*

One of the small things that argues in favor of baseball being better today than it ever was before is medicine, or more accurately, surgical procedures. Thirty years ago, maybe even 15 years ago, a 33-year-old with a blown-out elbow was done in baseball. Now, he can have reconstructive surgery, spend a few months getting himself together in Iowa, and come back almost as good as he ever was. Modern diagnostic and repair techniques keep talented people in the game longer, raising the level of play. Beck will be back in San Diego, setting up Trevor Hoffman and acting as insurance on the Pads' longtime closer.

MATT BRUBACK
Bats: R   **Throws: R**   Born: 12-Jan-79   Age: 25

YEAR	TM	LG	AGE	G	GS	IP	H	BB	SO	HR	ERA	EQERA	EQH9	EQBB9	EQSO9	EQHR9	PERA	VORP	STF
2001	DAY	FLA	22	14	14	84.0	70	21	87	3	3.00	4.11	9.2	2.7	6.1	0.8	4.30	12.7	24
2001	WTN	SOU	22	9	9	38.0	58	20	43	3	9.00	11.16	15.8	5.5	7.0	1.3	8.45	-21.4	-17
2002	WTN	SOU	23	28	28	174.0	157	48	158	9	3.16	4.62	10.0	2.7	5.9	1.0	4.84	17.2	14
2003	IOW	PCL	24	20	19	125.0	120	33	90	10	3.96	4.77	9.1	2.8	5.5	1.1	4.56	10.8	7
2003	NAS	PCL	24	4	4	22.0	18	12	16	3	4.91	5.40	8.6	5.8	5.8	1.8	5.98	0.4	-21
2003	POR	PCL	24	2	2	10.3	12	4	6	1	2.62	4.66	11.2	3.7	4.7	0.9	5.65	1.0	-3
2004	*SDP*	*NL*	*25*	*19*	*14*	*85.3*	*88*	*33*	*65*	*10*	*4.54*	*4.98*	*9.4*	*3.0*	*6.1*	*1.0*	*4.86*	*6.2*	*5*

Breakout: 13%   *Improve: 40%*   *Collapse: 28%*

One minute, you're making progress in your career, holding your own in your first exposure to Triple-A. The next, you've been traded, subsequently waived, and are clinging to your professional life in Portland. Bruback, a tall guy who doesn't throw terribly hard, didn't have a bad year despite the three addresses. While he's far from a top prospect, he will probably end up in San Diego during the year and could hold onto a low-leverage job for a while.

MIKE BYNUM
Bats: L   **Throws: L**   Born: 20-Mar-78   Age: 26

YEAR	TM	LG	AGE	G	GS	IP	H	BB	SO	HR	ERA	EQERA	EQH9	EQBB9	EQSO9	EQHR9	PERA	VORP	STF
2001	MOB	SOU	23	16	15	84.3	90	35	69	14	5.02	7.17	11.9	4.4	5.1	2.5	8.05	-13.1	-43
2002	MOB	SOU	24	6	5	33.0	17	7	29	0	0.82	1.78	5.6	2.1	5.6	0.3	2.07	12.9	38
2002	POR	PCL	24	7	7	41.0	36	7	35	6	3.51	4.86	9.7	1.7	6.1	1.7	5.25	3.0	-1
2002	SDP	NL	24	14	3	27.3	33	15	17	3	5.27	5.67	10.3	4.3	4.7	1.0	5.51	-0.2	-13
2003	POR	PCL	25	24	23	125.3	130	60	106	11	4.81	5.79	10.0	5.1	6.6	1.2	5.76	-2.5	-12
2003	SDP	NL	25	13	5	36.0	44	15	35	14	8.75	8.49	11.3	3.3	7.7	3.6	8.84	-15.6	-64
2004	*SDP*	*NL*	*26*	*21*	*13*	*73.7*	*73*	*36*	*60*	*8*	*4.58*	*5.02*	*9.0*	*3.9*	*6.5*	*1.0*	*5.03*	*4.2*	*2*

Breakout: 31%   *Improve: 53%*   *Collapse: 17%*

No pitcher had ever managed to give up 14 home runs while throwing fewer than 45 innings. Bynum buried that record in '03, craning his neck 14 times in just 36 frames with the Padres. His solid fastball/slider combination could still mean he replaces the non-tendered Mike Matthews in San Diego's bullpen this year.

ADAM EATON Bats: R Throws: R Born: 23-Nov-77 Age: 26

YEAR	TM	LG	AGE	G	GS	IP	H	BB	SO	HR	ERA	EQERA	EQH9	EQBB9	EQSO9	EQHR9	PERA	VORP	STF
2001	SDP	NL	23	17	17	116.7	108	40	109	20	4.32	4.63	8.4	2.9	7.1	1.4	4.62	12.1	23
2002	SDP	NL	24	6	6	33.3	28	17	25	5	5.41	4.96	7.4	3.9	5.8	1.4	4.42	2.3	4
2003	SDP	NL	25	31	31	183.0	173	68	146	20	4.08	4.49	8.7	3.0	6.4	1.0	4.37	15.6	14
2004	SDP	NL	26	29	29	185.0	180	71	140	22	4.33	4.74	8.8	3.0	6.1	1.1	4.60	19.7	10

Breakout: 15% Improve: 49% Collapse: 19%

Eaton is another data point in the argument that Tommy John surgery is just another stage in pitcher development. He was essentially the same pitcher in 2003 that he'd been in 2000–01, before the operation, with some improved command and a bit less endurance. Eaton makes a fine #2 starter behind Jake Peavy, and makes a great sleeper pick in your fantasy league this year.

JUSTIN GERMANO Bats: R Throws: R Born: 06-Aug-82 Age: 21

YEAR	TM	LG	AGE	G	GS	IP	H	BB	SO	HR	ERA	EQERA	EQH9	EQBB9	EQSO9	EQHR9	PERA	VORP	STF
2001	EUG	NWN	18	13	13	80.0	77	11	74	5	3.49	5.18	10.5	1.7	4.4	1.4	5.25	3.4	16
2001	FTW	MID	18	13	13	65.0	80	16	55	7	4.98	7.91	11.9	3.0	4.9	1.9	6.97	-15.5	0
2002	FTW	MID	19	24	24	155.7	166	19	119	14	3.18	5.82	11.7	1.5	4.4	2.2	6.76	-3.4	-2
2003	LEL	CAL	20	19	19	110.7	127	25	78	4	4.23	5.54	10.1	2.6	4.2	0.6	4.49	0.7	17
2003	MOB	SOU	20	9	9	58.0	60	13	44	6	4.34	5.87	10.2	2.3	5.0	1.7	5.67	-1.6	8
2004	SDP	NL	21	18	14	83.0	90	28	49	11	4.66	5.11	9.9	2.7	4.7	1.2	5.18	4.8	-3

Breakout: 1% Improve: 48% Collapse: 11%

Germano has emerged as a prospect, and been pushed through the system, largely on the basis of strong won-loss records and being liked within the organization. He doesn't miss a ton of bats with his average-plus stuff, and the ERAs you see above overstate his performance; he's given up 10–15 unearned runs a year. He's young, and not a big guy, so he's been working hard to post the results he has. It's unlikely that his steady march will continue; look for him suffer an injury or post an ugly ERA in 2004.

LUTHER HACKMAN Bats: R Throws: R Born: 10-Oct-74 Age: 29

YEAR	TM	LG	AGE	G	GS	IP	H	BB	SO	HR	ERA	EQERA	EQH9	EQBB9	EQSO9	EQHR9	PERA	VORP	STF
2001	MEM	PCL	26	16	0	22.7	21	1	12	2	2.78	3.38	8.4	0.4	3.4	0.8	3.36	5.3	-7
2001	STL	NL	26	35	0	35.7	28	14	24	7	4.29	4.76	7.4	3.2	5.3	1.6	4.45	3.2	-24
2002	STL	NL	27	43	6	81.0	90	39	46	7	4.11	5.49	10.8	3.9	4.6	0.8	5.38	0.9	-16
2003	SDP	NL	28	65	0	76.7	78	36	48	7	5.16	5.47	9.2	3.8	5.0	0.9	4.69	-7.5	-14
2004	CLE	AL	29	37	6	62.3	68	27	35	6	4.68	4.99	9.6	3.7	4.9	0.9	5.21	7.5	-13

Breakout: 31% Improve: 63% Collapse: 20%

Picked up in Brett Tomko trade, Hackman was an innings sponge during a period when the Padres' bullpen was bleeding from everywhere. There's little in his record or repertoire to indicate that he can be much better than this, although like most of this class, he could accidentally post a 2.53 ERA in front of a good defense and set himself up for life. There's not much difference between Hackman and someone like Antonio Alfonseca.

TREVOR HOFFMAN Bats: R Throws: R Born: 13-Oct-67 Age: 36

YEAR	TM	LG	AGE	G	GS	IP	H	BB	SO	HR	ERA	EQERA	EQH9	EQBB9	EQSO9	EQHR9	PERA	VORP	STF
2001	SDP	NL	33	62	0	60.3	48	21	63	10	3.43	3.86	7.3	2.9	7.9	1.4	4.03	11.3	1
2002	SDP	NL	34	61	0	59.3	52	18	69	2	2.73	3.26	7.8	2.3	9.0	0.3	3.01	15.1	37
2003	SDP	NL	35	9	0	9.0	7	3	11	1	2.00	3.12	7.3	3.1	9.3	1.0	3.71	3.5	20
2004	SDP	NL	36	44	0	49.7	44	17	50	6	3.32	3.64	8.1	2.7	8.0	1.1	4.08	11.0	10

Breakout: 23% Improve: 42% Collapse: 22%

(continued next page)

Trevor Hoffman *(continued)*

Hoffman missed most of the year because his October 2002 shoulder surgery, mostly to clear up fraying in his rotator cuff and labrum, didn't relieve his pain. A second operation, in which he had part of the collarbone shaved to make more room for the cuff, cleared things up. There are very few pitchers who have had the second procedure. He's pitching free and easy now and should see no problems. Hoffman re-signed with the Padres after the season.

BEN HOWARD · Bats: R · Throws: R · Born: 15-Jan-79 · Age: 25

YEAR	TM	LG	AGE	G	GS	IP	H	BB	SO	HR	ERA	EQERA	EQH9	EQBB9	EQSO9	EQHR9	PERA	VORP	STF
2001	LEL	CAL	22	18	18	101.7	86	32	107	4	2.83	4.67	9.9	3.8	5.5	0.7	4.83	9.4	14
2001	MOB	SOU	22	7	5	30.0	17	15	29	3	2.40	3.67	6.7	5.3	6.0	1.7	4.80	5.8	-1
2002	MOB	SOU	23	6	6	33.0	26	16	30	2	2.18	4.15	8.3	4.7	5.9	1.2	4.88	4.9	4
2002	POR	PCL	23	11	7	45.0	47	15	25	10	6.20	7.62	10.7	3.5	4.1	2.6	7.38	-9.3	-48
2002	SDP	NL	23	3	2	10.7	13	14	10	4	9.25	10.12	11.0	10.1	6.8	3.4	9.95	-5.4	-63
2003	POR	PCL	24	22	22	130.7	118	49	68	17	4.54	5.04	8.5	4.0	4.1	1.8	5.47	7.5	-23
2003	SDP	NL	24	6	6	34.7	31	15	24	10	3.63	5.13	8.1	3.5	5.7	2.7	6.18	3.2	-24
2004	*SDP*	*NL*	*25*	*17*	*12*	*69.3*	*74*	*34*	*44*	*10*	*5.31*	*5.82*	*9.7*	*3.9*	*5.1*	*1.3*	*5.80*	*0.9*	*-9*

Breakout: 24%   Improve: 50%   Collapse: 22%

It's likely that no matter what he does on the field, Howard is always going to be known as the player who survived the crash that killed Mike Darr in February of 2002. While his prospect status has slipped since then, that fact is unrelated to the crash; Howard actually opened '02 pitching well at Mobile. He has yet to be impressive above Double-A, however. The Padres' desire to win in 2004 will limit their patience with Howard, who may not get established for another year.

KEVIN JARVIS · Bats: R · Throws: R · Born: 01-Aug-69 · Age: 34

YEAR	TM	LG	AGE	G	GS	IP	H	BB	SO	HR	ERA	EQERA	EQH9	EQBB9	EQSO9	EQHR9	PERA	VORP	STF
2001	SDP	NL	31	32	32	193.3	189	49	133	37	4.80	4.87	8.6	2.1	5.2	1.6	4.73	15.1	-7
2002	SDP	NL	32	7	7	35.0	36	10	24	5	4.37	4.76	9.0	2.1	5.3	1.3	4.60	3.2	-3
2003	SDP	NL	33	16	16	92.0	113	32	49	15	5.87	6.39	11.2	2.8	4.3	1.5	6.09	-13.1	-23
2004	*SEA*	*AL*	*34*	*24*	*21*	*127.0*	*142*	*39*	*68*	*21*	*5.00*	*5.12*	*10.0*	*2.6*	*4.6*	*1.3*	*5.07*	*10.4*	*-2*

Breakout: 12%   Improve: 40%   Collapse: 21%

One of the worst contracts in recent memory goes on and on, as Jarvis is still due $4.25 million in 2004 and a $500,000 buyout in 2005. At the time of the deal, Jarvis had a career ERA of 5.91 and was coming off a career year in which he'd had a 4.80 ERA and given up 2,000 home runs. Since then, he's been alternately injured and ineffective. The financial commitment to him not only ties up funds better used on Mike Cameron or Greg Maddux or a *Rockwell's Greatest Hit* CD, it also means that he may have to be in the rotation, hurting the Pads' chances of being a surprise team in '04. Swapped to the Mariners for Jeff Cirillo in a deal designed to make familiar problems go away in exchange for new ones.

BRIAN LAWRENCE · Bats: R · Throws: R · Born: 14-May-76 · Age: 28

YEAR	TM	LG	AGE	G	GS	IP	H	BB	SO	HR	ERA	EQERA	EQH9	EQBB9	EQSO9	EQHR9	PERA	VORP	STF
2001	POR	PCL	25	9	8	45.0	42	17	42	3	3.80	4.75	9.3	4.1	6.3	0.6	4.57	3.9	8
2001	SDP	NL	25	27	15	114.7	107	34	84	10	3.45	3.98	8.4	2.4	5.5	0.7	3.78	19.9	14
2002	SDP	NL	26	35	31	210.0	230	52	149	16	3.69	4.27	9.5	1.9	5.5	0.7	4.10	30.3	17
2003	SDP	NL	27	33	33	210.7	206	57	116	27	4.19	4.50	8.9	2.2	4.5	1.2	4.41	16.6	-1
2004	*SDP*	*NL*	*28*	*29*	*28*	*174.7*	*182*	*53*	*108*	*18*	*4.10*	*4.50*	*9.5*	*2.4*	*5.0*	*0.9*	*4.55*	*20.1*	*6*

Breakout: 13%   Improve: 43%   Collapse: 15%

When the Padres looked like they were going to get Greg Maddux, it seemed like a great thing for Lawrence, who is a comparable, albeit inferior, pitcher. The idea of giving Lawrence the locker next to Maddux and a spiral notebook had a lot of merit. A command guy who lacks an out pitch against lefties, Lawrence is a reliable innings guy for a rotation fronted by two younger pitchers. A lot of his ratios went south in 2003, including big changes in his strikeout and groundball rates, so watch him carefully in the spring.

SCOTT LINEBRINK

Bats: R   **Throws: R**   Born: 04-Aug-76   Age: 27

YEAR	TM	LG	AGE	G	GS	IP	H	BB	SO	HR	ERA	EQERA	EQH9	EQBB9	EQSO9	EQHR9	PERA	VORP	STF
2001	NWO	PCL	24	50	0	72.0	52	24	72	4	3.50	3.78	7.3	3.6	6.6	0.7	3.56	13.5	10
2001	HOU	NL	24	9	0	10.3	6	6	9	0	2.62	2.70	5.4	4.5	6.3	0.0	2.39	3.2	30
2002	NWO	PCL	25	13	0	15.0	17	11	16	1	6.00	8.10	12.8	8.1	7.4	0.7	7.10	-3.7	-29
2002	HOU	NL	25	22	0	24.3	31	13	24	2	7.04	6.75	11.2	4.1	7.5	0.8	5.53	-3.1	0
2003	NWO	PCL	26	2	2	10.0	8	5	6	1	2.70	4.00	9.0	6.0	5.0	2.0	6.48	1.6	-44
2003	HOU	NL	26	9	6	31.7	38	14	17	4	4.26	5.04	11.3	3.6	4.5	1.2	5.95	5.4	-19
2003	SDP	NL	26	43	0	60.7	55	22	51	5	2.82	3.70	8.3	2.9	6.8	0.8	3.92	14.1	9
2004	SDP	NL	27	30	11	72.3	73	31	53	8	4.46	4.89	9.2	3.4	5.8	1.0	5.00	6.6	-4

Breakout: 23%   *Improve: 47%*   *Collapse: 26%*

Linebrink is best-suited for a role that really doesn't exist in MLB anymore, that of swingman. With most teams on a five-man rotation, and managers tending to leave their starters in for five innings in almost all circumstances, a guy who can start 10–15 times and provide 10–15 three-inning outings out of the bullpen doesn't really have a place. He ends up pitching in the sixth and seventh innings or the 12th and 13th innings. Given the Padres' outfield defense and the likelihood that Petco Park will be at least somewhat less friendly to flyball pitchers, Linebrink is a bad bet for 2004.

CARLTON LOEWER

Bats: B   **Throws: R**   Born: 24-Sep-73   Age: 30

YEAR	TM	LG	AGE	G	GS	IP	H	BB	SO	HR	ERA	EQERA	EQH9	EQBB9	EQSO9	EQHR9	PERA	VORP	STF
2001	POR	PCL	27	14	12	81.3	97	15	64	7	3.87	5.50	11.8	2.0	5.1	1.0	5.51	0.8	-4
2003	POR	PCL	29	23	23	125.0	161	28	57	9	5.40	6.34	12.3	2.4	3.5	1.0	5.92	-9.6	-21
2003	SDP	NL	29	5	5	21.7	35	8	11	3	6.64	7.71	14.6	3.0	3.9	1.3	7.42	-4.9	-34
2004	SDP	NL	30	15	9	49.7	57	27	-7	5	5.54	6.07	10.4	0.0	0.0	0.9	5.92	-0.7	-29

Breakout: 16%   *Improve: 43%*   *Collapse: 35%*

He lives! Loewer threw 15 big league innings in the years 2000–02, mostly because of injuries suffered after falling out of a tree while hunting. See, nature can defend itself. That he pitched at all can be considered an achievement, given that he was out of baseball in '02, but he had almost nothing, and will probably have to recast himself as a reliever to salvage any career. His story could get him an extra chance or two.

MIKE MATTHEWS

Bats: L   **Throws: L**   Born: 24-Oct-73   Age: 30

YEAR	TM	LG	AGE	G	GS	IP	H	BB	SO	HR	ERA	EQERA	EQH9	EQBB9	EQSO9	EQHR9	PERA	VORP	STF
2001	STL	NL	27	51	10	89.0	74	33	72	11	3.24	3.83	8.0	3.1	6.3	1.0	4.00	16.7	2
2002	STL	NL	28	43	0	41.7	40	22	32	5	3.88	5.22	9.3	4.3	6.1	1.1	5.15	1.7	-16
2002	MIL	NL	28	4	0	4.0	3	7	2	0	4.50	4.50	6.8	13.5	4.5	0.0	5.31	0.5	-28
2003	SDP	NL	29	77	0	64.7	65	29	44	4	4.45	4.76	9.2	3.6	5.5	0.6	4.35	3.5	-2
2004	CIN	NL	30	50	0	50.3	53	24	37	7	4.80	5.04	9.6	3.7	5.9	1.1	5.32	4.7	-10

Breakout: 30%   *Improve: 51%*   *Collapse: 25%*

He's been shoehorned into the specialist role, but there's no reason to think Matthews couldn't be more. Righties haven't hit him especially hard in his major league career (.268/.359/.439), and he took regular starts as recently as 2001. Non-tendered by the Padres, he'll no doubt take whatever role a team is willing to pay him $305,000 to fill. A team with some creativity and fearlessness could make a heck of a fifth starter out of him; naturally, the Reds are willing to try.

AKINORI OTSUKA

Bats: R   **Throws: R**   Born: 12-Jan-72   Age: 32

YEAR	TM	LG	AGE	G	GS	IP	H	BB	SO	HR	ERA	EQERA	EQH9	EQBB9	EQSO9	EQHR9	PERA	VORP	STF
2001	OSA	JPP	48	0	56.0	42	15	82	7	4.02	3.91	7.6	2.2	11.2	1.0	3.56	10.0	32	
2002	OSA	JPP	41	1	42.3	22	3	54	4	1.82	2.08	5.5	0.7	9.0	0.9	2.11	15.3	34	
2003	CHU	JPC	51	0	43.0	31	5	56	4	2.89	2.72	7.5	1.4	9.1	0.9	3.17	12.7	27	
2004	SDP	NL	32	58	0	46.7	37	8	52	4	2.29	2.51	7.2	1.4	9.0	0.7	2.63	15.4	24

Breakout: 33%   *Improve: 50%*   *Collapse: 10%*

If you had to pick one category of player to make a quick transition to major league baseball, it would be a two-pitch reliever who might go months before someone sees him a second time. In the same way that college relievers can often make a quick transition, Japanese relievers should be able to as well. Otsuka relies largely on a fastball and slider, and mixes in a change. His top PECOTA comps are Trevor Hoffman and John Wetteland, so that system likes him, and at $1.7 million for two years (plus a $300,000 posting fee), it's a small risk with some nice upside for the Padres.

CHRIS OXSPRING

Bats: L **Throws: R** Born: 13-May-77 Age: 27

YEAR	TM	LG	AGE	G	GS	IP	H	BB	SO	HR	ERA	EQERA	EQH9	EQBB9	EQSO9	EQHR9	PERA	VORP	STF
2001	FTW	MID	24	41	2	56.3	66	25	54	5	4.16	6.75	14.4	5.8	5.4	2.1	8.91	-6.1	-69
2002	LEL	CAL	25	15	1	26.3	24	8	30	2	4.79	5.87	11.7	3.5	5.9	1.6	6.55	-0.7	-42
2002	MOB	SOU	25	6	1	14.3	13	8	21	0	1.26	3.46	11.1	5.5	9.7	0.0	5.01	3.1	30
2003	MOB	SOU	26	40	18	135.7	106	62	129	6	2.92	4.03	9.3	4.9	5.9	0.9	5.08	21.1	-13
2004	SDP	NL	27	16	7	40.3	48	24	26	5	5.89	6.46	10.8	4.7	5.1	1.0	6.43	0.0	-16

Breakout: 24%   Improve: 43%   Collapse: 27%

An Australian who signed with the Padres out of the Frontier League, Oxspring is too old to rank high on prospect lists. That said, he has a very good performance record and an attention-getting slider. Shoulder problems that held him to 40 innings in 2002 appeared to be gone in '03. The Padres should be deep in the pen this year, so Oxspring may end up as trade bait, just as fellow independent-league refugee Cory Stewart was last year. Credit the Pads for mining talent from the indies.

DAVID PAULEY

Bats: R **Throws: R** Born: 17-Jun-83 Age: 21

YEAR	TM	LG	AGE	G	GS	IP	H	BB	SO	HR	ERA	EQERA	EQH9	EQBB9	EQSO9	EQHR9	PERA	VORP	STF
2001	IDA	PIO	18	15	15	68.7	88	24	53	8	6.03	7.59	12.1	4.5	3.5	2.2	7.86	-14.2	-25
2002	EUG	NWN	19	15	15	80.0	81	18	62	6	2.81	5.73	12.0	2.8	3.8	2.0	7.10	-1.0	-12
2003	FTW	MID	20	22	21	117.7	109	38	117	9	3.29	5.77	11.7	4.3	6.2	2.2	7.51	-1.9	-5
2004	SDP	NL	21	19	16	99.3	103	40	83	14	4.85	5.31	9.4	3.2	6.7	1.2	5.14	3.3	9

Breakout: 34%   Improve: 65%   Collapse: 5%

Pauley has been handled very carefully since being taken in the eighth round of the 2001 draft. In three pro seasons—two of them spent in short-season ball—he's thrown just 266 innings, averaging a shade above five innings a start. His best pitch is a curve, although he does get his fastball over 90. Like Germano, Pauley isn't a big guy, and may be someone who has trouble missing bats at higher levels. He needs to show something at Lake Elsinore this year.

JAKE PEAVY

Bats: R **Throws: R** Born: 31-May-81 Age: 23

YEAR	TM	LG	AGE	G	GS	IP	H	BB	SO	HR	ERA	EQERA	EQH9	EQBB9	EQSO9	EQHR9	PERA	VORP	STF
2001	LEL	CAL	20	19	19	105.3	76	33	144	6	3.08	4.42	8.9	3.7	7.5	1.0	4.61	12.3	36
2001	MOB	SOU	20	5	5	28.0	19	12	44	3	2.57	3.55	8.2	4.6	10.7	1.4	4.93	5.8	57
2002	MOB	SOU	21	14	14	80.3	65	30	89	4	2.80	3.98	8.3	3.5	7.5	0.8	4.14	13.4	39
2002	SDP	NL	21	17	17	97.7	106	33	90	11	4.51	4.91	9.5	2.6	7.2	1.0	4.66	7.3	40
2003	SDP	NL	22	32	32	194.7	173	82	156	33	4.11	4.60	8.2	3.4	6.4	1.5	4.80	19.6	21
2004	SDP	NL	23	24	23	148.3	146	59	121	19	4.33	4.75	8.9	3.2	6.6	1.2	4.83	14.6	11

Breakout: 10%   Improve: 41%   Collapse: 12%

Yummy. Peavy did a whole bunch of things right last season, including fighting through a dead-arm period in July to finish the year with good ratios in his last 11 starts (58 K, 25 BB in 65 2/3 IP). Bochy handled him fairly well; his PAP score wasn't in the game's top 50, and he had just one Category IV (122 or more pitches) start all season. You might be wary of him until the Padres get a center fielder, as he is a strong flyball pitcher, but that's a minor concern.

JOE ROA

Bats: R **Throws: R** Born: 11-Oct-71 Age: 32

YEAR	TM	LG	AGE	G	GS	IP	H	BB	SO	HR	ERA	EQERA	EQH9	EQBB9	EQSO9	EQHR9	PERA	VORP	STF
2001	PME	EAS	29	7	7	36.0	36	3	26	2	3.00	5.17	12.4	1.1	4.6	0.9	5.41	1.5	-5
2001	CLG	PCL	29	19	19	124.0	134	12	81	16	3.92	3.63	8.8	1.0	4.1	1.3	4.10	26.6	-3
2002	SWB	INT	30	17	17	111.0	83	16	74	4	1.86	2.81	7.7	1.6	5.0	0.5	3.05	31.7	23
2002	PHI	NL	30	14	11	71.3	78	13	35	11	4.04	4.68	10.3	1.5	3.9	1.5	5.23	6.9	-15
2003	PHI	NL	31	6	3	19.3	28	4	16	3	6.06	6.38	13.7	1.5	6.9	1.5	6.80	-1.7	-11
2003	IND	INT	31	5	4	24.7	32	3	18	3	4.74	5.96	13.1	1.2	5.2	1.6	6.61	-0.9	-23
2003	SDP	NL	31	18	1	25.3	34	6	18	5	6.76	7.03	12.2	1.8	5.5	1.8	6.67	-5.9	-36
2004	MIN	AL	32	26	12	76.7	90	15	41	13	4.81	4.70	10.1	1.6	4.8	1.3	4.75	10.3	-4

Breakout: 21%   Improve: 46%   Collapse: 31%

We're supposed to say that Joe Roa deserves the roster spot and innings that will go to Kevin Jarvis, because Roa's been bouncing around forever without getting a real chance in the majors. Truth is, though, he spent almost all of 2003 in the show and posted a 6.14 ERA. His strikeout-to-walk ratio was good, as it was in 2002 with the Phillies, but you can't give up a homer every six innings and keep your job... unless you're Jarvis, apparently. Roa starts '04 in the Twins' camp, and might stick as a long reliever if their kids continue to struggle.

| TIM STAUFFER | | Bats: R | Throws: R | Born: 2-Jun-82 | Age: 22 |

The Pads' #1 pick in the '03 draft, the fourth pick overall out of the University of Richmond, lost about $2 million when he reported shoulder weakness before signing. He did not undergo surgery, and while he didn't pitch professionally in 2003, he's expected to be ready for spring training. While conceding that Stauffer's self-reporting speaks well for him, it's clear that a 21-year-old with a shoulder problem is a risky investment.

DENNIS TANKERSLEY   Bats: R   Throws: R   Born: 24-Feb-79   Age: 25

YEAR	TM	LG	AGE	G	GS	IP	H	BB	SO	HR	ERA	EQERA	EQH9	EQBB9	EQSO9	EQHR9	PERA	VORP	STF
2001	LEL	CAL	22	9	8	52.3	29	12	68	1	0.52	1.74	7.3	2.7	6.8	0.4	3.03	20.0	45
2001	MOB	SOU	22	13	13	69.7	44	24	89	6	2.07	3.61	7.9	3.8	7.9	1.3	4.50	13.8	27
2002	MOB	SOU	23	10	10	50.7	47	21	56	1	3.02	4.63	9.8	3.9	7.1	0.4	4.46	5.0	28
2002	SDP	NL	23	17	9	51.3	59	40	39	10	8.07	7.59	10.1	6.0	5.8	1.8	6.67	-11.3	-20
2002	POR	PCL	23	9	9	51.0	43	30	51	6	3.88	5.98	8.9	6.2	7.3	1.3	5.67	-2.0	3
2003	POR	PCL	24	27	27	151.0	149	67	148	15	4.65	5.39	9.6	4.7	7.6	1.3	5.61	3.3	3
2003	SDP	NL	24	1	1	0.0	3	4	0	0	0.00	99.99	99.9	99.9	99.9	99.9	29.39	0.0	-999
2004	SDP	NL	25	21	16	90.3	89	48	79	10	4.77	5.23	9.0	4.2	7.0	1.0	5.28	5.1	5

Breakout: 20%   Improve: 50%   Collapse: 22%

Tankersley nearly set a dubious record last year. The most runs anyone has ever given up in a season without getting an out is eight, a mark set by Bob Kammeyer in 1979. Tankersley's April 9 outing at Pac Bell Park left him just shy of that, and helped him spend the rest of the year in Portland. With just two pitches and an awkward motion, he's probably best suited for relief work, at least in the short term

RUSTY TUCKER   Bats: R   Throws: L   Born: 15-Jul-80   Age: 23

YEAR	TM	LG	AGE	G	GS	IP	H	BB	SO	HR	ERA	EQERA	EQH9	EQBB9	EQSO9	EQHR9	PERA	VORP	STF
2001	IDA	PIO	20	30	0	35.3	41	50	43	4	7.14	11.62	13.2	20.7	6.3	2.5	11.58	-19.2	-94
2002	FTW	MID	21	31	0	35.7	19	10	50	2	1.01	3.19	7.8	3.5	7.8	1.5	4.54	8.3	11
2002	LEL	CAL	21	26	0	29.7	26	18	33	1	2.42	4.72	9.8	6.8	5.7	0.7	5.54	2.6	-2
2003	MOB	SOU	22	51	0	53.0	49	31	63	4	3.74	5.55	10.9	6.3	7.7	1.5	6.81	0.3	-10
2004	SDP	NL	23	12	2	17.3	22	18	10	3	8.48	9.29	11.6	8.2	4.8	1.5	9.18	-3.8	-41

Breakout: 18%   Improve: 52%   Collapse: 24%

Tucker comes with all the requisite caveats associated with minor league closers, and one more: He'll miss 2004 after Tommy John surgery in August. The Padres liked him enough to add him to the 40-man roster, anyway, as they love his mid-90s fastball and hard slider. As we've seen, Tommy John surgery can be just a step along the way for a pitcher, so check on Tucker's progress in 2005; he could be getting lefties out at Petco Park by the end of that season.

BRANDON VILLAFUERTE   Bats: R   Throws: R   Born: 17-Dec-75   Age: 28

YEAR	TM	LG	AGE	G	GS	IP	H	BB	SO	HR	ERA	EQERA	EQH9	EQBB9	EQSO9	EQHR9	PERA	VORP	STF
2001	OKL	PCL	25	38	0	63.7	63	26	65	4	2.83	3.97	9.8	4.4	6.7	0.6	4.82	10.7	1
2002	POR	PCL	26	47	0	58.0	43	22	54	2	2.02	3.44	8.4	4.0	6.5	0.5	4.00	12.6	4
2002	SDP	NL	26	31	0	32.0	29	12	25	2	1.41	2.59	7.8	2.9	6.0	0.6	3.46	10.5	12
2003	SDP	NL	27	31	0	40.7	39	26	34	7	4.20	5.22	8.8	5.2	6.6	1.6	5.68	3.7	-26
2003	POR	PCL	27	37	0	44.0	42	14	40	1	1.84	3.07	9.2	3.3	7.0	0.2	3.87	11.5	17
2004	SDP	NL	28	29	6	53.0	52	26	42	4	4.13	4.52	9.0	3.9	6.4	0.7	4.84	6.2	-2

Breakout: 23%   Improve: 43%   Collapse: 26%

(continued next page)

Brandon Villafuerte *(continued)*

Hyped as a closer candidate in the absence of Hoffman, Villafuerte was off to a decent start in the season's first two weeks. He was asked to pitch a mop-up inning April 18 in Colorado in 47-degree weather and gave up two runs. He was then brought back the next day and blew the save, giving up three more. At the end of April, he appeared in four straight games over five days, throwing 115 pitches. Two weeks later, he tossed 82 pitches on back-to-back days and ended up on the DL with a shoulder strain.

Sometimes, pitchers fail because they're not very good. Sometimes, they fail because they're asked to do too much. We report, you decide.

JAY WITASICK Bats: R Throws: R Born: 28-Aug-72 Age: 31

YEAR	TM	LG	AGE	G	GS	IP	H	BB	SO	HR	ERA	EQERA	EQH9	EQBB9	EQSO9	EQHR9	PERA	VORP	STF
2001	SDP	NL	28	31	0	38.7	31	15	53	3	1.86	3.38	7.7	3.1	10.4	0.7	3.59	9.2	34
2001	NYY	AL	28	32	0	40.3	47	18	53	5	4.69	5.40	10.1	3.6	10.8	0.9	4.98	0.9	22
2002	SFG	NL	29	44	0	68.3	58	21	54	3	2.37	3.32	8.2	2.5	6.2	0.4	3.38	16.5	18
2003	SDP	NL	30	46	0	45.7	42	25	42	6	4.53	4.87	8.5	4.5	7.3	1.2	4.90	2.5	-9
2004	SDP	NL	31	43	1	57.7	54	23	50	5	3.72	4.07	8.5	3.2	7.0	0.7	4.21	9.7	4

Breakout: 27%   Improve: 53%   Collapse: 29%

The two-run bump in his ERA between 2002 and 2003 was as much the result of context—park and defense—as anything he did. Witasick is a useful strikeout/groundball pitcher whose bouts of wildness keep him from being a high-leverage guy.

San Francisco Giants

Debby Boone. Men Without Hats. The Divinyls. And your 2004 San Francisco Giants.

No, the G-men haven't been spending their off-season recording nauseating pop ballads, new-wave synth, or pseudo-erotic pseudo-alternative rock. But they do have something in common with those erstwhile recording artists. They are baseball's one-hit wonders.

"One-hit" as in "one hitter." The Giants offense has been suddenly transformed from a strong ensemble cast anchored around a leading man to a one-man show. Barry Bonds has obviously been the club's main offensive force since his arrival in San Francisco in 1993. But Giants teams during his tenure have generally featured other good hitting performances, including stellar years by Jeff Kent, Rich Aurilia, Ellis Burks, Matt Williams, and others.

Last year, all that changed. With Kent's departure, Aurilia's decline, and disappointing showings by the new high-profile acquisitions (especially Edgardo Alfonzo), the Giants were left with very little offense in between PAs by #25. Bonds was once again the majors' best hitter, lapping the field in every advanced metric of offensive performance, and producing 92 runs more than an average left fielder according to Clay Davenport's numbers. But if Bonds got an A, no one else in the Giants lineup could grade much better than a C. Ray Durham was 13 runs better than an average second baseman; all the rest of the Giant regulars were right around league average, except Neifi Perez, who was considerably worse.

No other team in 2003 experienced anywhere near the discrepancy between the number one guy and everyone else. In fact, it's hard to recall a team in recent history that fit the Giants' profile of a single hitter carrying the rest of the offense to that extent. But that could just be a bad memory talking. So let's look at the issue more systematically. Where do the 2003 Giants rank among baseball's previous one-hit wonders, and what does the history of similar teams teach us about the Giants' future?

One way to measure one-hitter-wonder-ness is to look at how much one player's rate of offensive production exceeds the rate of production of his teammates. That is, divide the player's average offensive performance by the rest of the team's average offensive performance. We'll use OPS as an estimate for offensive production because (1) it's a good measure of overall offense, (2) it's widely known and easily understandable, and (3) since we're dividing

GIANTS PROSPECTUS

2003 record: 100–61; First place, NL West; Lost to Marlins in Division Series

Pythagenport record: 93–69

Runs scored per game: 4.7 (6th in NL)

Runs allowed per game: 4.0 (2nd in NL)

Team EqA: .269 (4th in NL)

2003 Batters Age: 32.7 (Oldest in NL)

2003 Pitchers Age: 28.7 (6th oldest in NL)

Ballpark: Pac Bell Park; Severe pitcher's park; Park Factor of 0.942

2003: A season of personal adversity for Barry Bonds didn't stop him from leading the Giants to another division title.

2004: Not as strong as in years past, but still a solid team, and Sabean's ability to upgrade on the fly is a plus.

player offense by team offense, most of the adjustments in the more sophisticated measures (park adjustments, league context adjustments, etc.) would be canceled out anyway. We'll only consider players with 500 or more plate appearances, and we'll use OPS without Hit By Pitches, Sacrifices, or Sacrifice Flies, just to keep things simple.

Table 1 shows the biggest single-player-influenced offenses by this measure. The column on the far right shows how much better the player was than the rest of the team; for example, Babe Ruth's 1.377 OPS in 1920 was 93.7% better than the non-Ruth Yankees' .711. It's a moderately interesting list to look at, but we can see right away that it isn't really measuring what we were getting at above. For one thing, a team can rate high in this measure even if they have two or three excellent hitters. For example, we see the 2001 and 2002 Giants rate higher than the 2003 version, even though both of the higher-ranked teams had players besides Bonds who put up exceptional numbers—Kent and Aurilia in 2001, and Kent in 2002. And we see (not listed in table 1) the 1927 Yankees show up high in the rankings twice—at #80 with Ruth, and at #117 with Gehrig—despite being the antithesis of a one-hit wonder. For another thing, because historically there is far more variability in individual player offense than there is in team offense, the measure gives much more weight to the performance of the individual than the team. Seven of the 10 seasons in

TABLE 1. OFFENSES MOST INFLUENCED BY A SINGLE PLAYER

Team	Year	Leading Hitter	Player OPS	Rest Of Team OPS	% Player > Team
New York Yankees	1920	Babe Ruth	1.377	.711	93.7%
San Francisco Giants	2002	Barry Bonds	1.376	.728	89.0%
San Francisco Giants	2001	Barry Bonds	1.373	.742	85.0%
New York Yankees	1923	Babe Ruth	1.306	.714	83.0%
Boston Red Sox	1957	Ted Williams	1.254	.699	79.5%
San Francisco Giants	2003	Barry Bonds	1.271	.718	77.0%
Boston Red Sox	1919	Babe Ruth	1.108	.628	76.4%
New York Yankees	1921	Babe Ruth	1.356	.773	75.4%
New York Yankees	1924	Babe Ruth	1.249	.718	74.0%
Boston Braves	1928	Rogers Hornsby	1.129	.653	73.0%

table 1 are among the top 10 individual season OPS totals, and Ruth's 1924 just misses at number 11.

To identify the one-hitter wonder teams from baseball history, what we want to measure is the hitter's dominance over *every* other hitter on the team, not just over the team as an aggregate. In other words, we want to measure how much the hitter's performance exceeded that of his team's second-best hitter. We can do that by dividing the best hitter's OPS by the second-best hitter's OPS.

Table 2 shows the teams most dominated by a single player by this measure. It seems to do a much better job of measuring what we're after: one great hitter, *and* little else of note on the team. It's still possible for a historic offensive year by one player to get a high ranking by itself—the 2001–2002 Giants are still here, for example—but those teams are now lower on the list, and the very highest teams feature mediocrity in the rest of the offense along with the one great player. The 2003 Giants rank fifth here,

TABLE 2. OFFENSES MOST DOMINATED BY A SINGLE PLAYER

Team	Year	Leading Hitter	Lead OPS	2nd Best Hitter	2nd Best OPS	% Leader > 2nd Best
New York Yankees	1920	Babe Ruth	1.377	Ping Bodie	.796	72.9%
New York Yankees	1923	Babe Ruth	1.306	Whitey Witt	.791	65.2%
San Francisco Giants	1996	Barry Bonds	1.079	Marvin Benard	.659	63.8%
Cleveland Naps	1910	Nap Lajoie	.955	George Stovall	.593	61.0%
San Francisco Giants	2003	Barry Bonds	1.271	Marquis Grissom	.791	60.1%
Chicago Cubs	2001	Sammy Sosa	1.177	Ricky Gutierrez	.741	58.7%
Boston Braves	1935	Wally Berger	.899	Billy Urbanski	.571	57.4%
Boston Red Sox	1919	Babe Ruth	1.108	Harry Hooper	.729	52.0%
Cleveland Naps	1911	Joe Jackson	1.051	Jack Graney	.692	51.8%
New York Giants	1957	Willie Mays	1.036	Daryl Spencer	.690	50.1%
Boston Red Sox	1957	Ted Williams	1.254	Jackie Jensen	.837	49.8%
New York Yankees	1921	Babe Ruth	1.356	Bob Meusel	.913	48.5%
San Francisco Giants	2002	Barry Bonds	1.376	Jeff Kent	.931	47.8%
Atlanta Braves	1984	Dale Murphy	.919	Rafael Ramirez	.623	47.4%
Pittsburgh Pirates	2002	Brian Giles	1.070	Kevin Young	.727	47.2%
New York Yankees	1957	Mickey Mantle	1.179	Gil McDougald	.801	47.2%
New York Yankees	1924	Babe Ruth	1.249	Bob Meusel	.854	46.2%
San Francisco Giants	2001	Barry Bonds	1.373	Rich Aurilia	.943	45.7%
Cleveland Naps	1913	Joe Jackson	1.007	Jack Graney	.695	44.9%
St. Louis Cardinals	1951	Stan Musial	1.062	Red Schoendienst	.737	44.2%

and their ranking could be even higher with different eligibility requirements. If we had pegged the cutoff for player inclusion at 400 PAs instead of 500, the 2003 Giants would rank first. All four teams ahead of them in table 2 had good offensive players who barely missed the 500-PA threshold, and that's certainly not the case with last year's Giants.

As with table 1, table 2 is dominated by Babe Ruth and the Yankees. It's easy to forget that not every Ruth Yankee team was like the 1927 version, and that the Yankee hitters of the early 20s other than Ruth were nothing to write home about. Ruth was only the first piece in the assembly of the Murderers Row offense, and none of the other pieces were fully in place for the 1920 team. That team finished second in the AL in run scoring despite the Babe having a season for the ages. Bob Meusel arrived full time in 1921, Lou Gehrig and Earle Combs in 1925, and Tony Lazzeri in 1926. After Gehrig came on the scene, of course, no Yankee team could ever really qualify as a one-hit wonder, no matter how monstrous a season Ruth had.

It's challenging to find a good parallel to the present-day Giants among the non-Giant teams in table 2. That's not surprising, as Barry Bonds is unique in many different ways. Naturally, most of the players in the "Leading Hitter" column were in mid-career, not entering their twilight at age 38. The teams that may give us some clue about possible future directions for the Giants are probably the Ruth Red Sox of 1919, the Cleveland Naps of 1910–1913, and the Ted Williams Red Sox of 1957. In hindsight, we know that all those teams were about to lose their offense-carrying superstar, just as the Giants are going to have to face the prospect of life after Bonds within in the next few years.

The message from those teams is mixed. The Red Sox were left with nothing after Harry Frazee's infamous sale of Ruth; they quickly sank to the bottom of the AL in run scoring, and stayed there for more than a decade. On the other hand, the Naps recovered quickly from the disastrous trade of Joe Jackson in 1915 (they were the Indians by then); they acquired Tris Speaker the next year and rode him to the top of the AL in run scoring through the early '20s. The Red Sox also dealt with the 1960 retirement of Williams gracefully; Carl Yastrzemski arrived on the scene the following season, and the Red Sox really suffered no dip in offense during the transition, slowly ascending the AL run-scoring rankings throughout the '60s.

There are obvious problems with drawing a team-building lesson from three historical examples, but if we did want to draw a lesson, it would be this: Barring Frazee-style neglect and incompetence on the part of ownership and management, the loss of a great hitter doesn't necessarily spell long-term catastrophe for the team's offense, even if he is the only worthwhile hitter they have at the moment. There are many ways of adding talent to the roster—that was true back in Joe Jackson's day, and it's doubly true now. While there may not be a new Barry Bonds right around the corner, it is possible to build a winning team without him. It's misguided to argue that the Giants need to completely abandon their future in order to win now with Bonds.

So what about the nearer term? Are the 2004 Giants destined to become another line in the one-hit wonders list? It sure looks that way. Unless they make a big late splash in the free agent or trade markets—at press time, A. J. Pierzynski was their most noteworthy addition—the offensive supporting cast will looks very similar to last year, only a year older. Edgardo Alfonzo is probably the best candidate to fill the Jeff Kent role, but with his age, injury history, and recent performance, even he has to be considered a long shot. Of course, the Giants' best chance of avoiding the list this year is something their fans don't want to contemplate: a steep Bonds decline. No one ever got rich betting against Barry Bonds, but he is 39, and age has to catch up with him one of these years.

The uncertainties surrounding the offense coupled with a shallow starting rotation combine to make this year the most challenging one for the Giants since the opening of Pac Bell Park in 2000. Their only consolation is that the NL West is suddenly challenging the AL Central for the title of weakest division in baseball. But even in a talent-poor division, a summer of watching a one-hit (or no-hit) offense and a weakened pitching staff in San Francisco could be painful. Not as painful as listening to Debby Boone, but painful.

HITTERS

EDGARDO ALFONZO 3B Bats: R Throws: R Born: 08-Nov-73 Age: 30

YEAR	TM	LG	AGE	AB	H	2B	3B	HR	BB	SO	SB	CS	AVG	OBP	SLG	MLVR	EQBA	EQOBP	EQSLG	EQMLVR	VORP	DEFENSE	
2001	NYM	NL	27	457	111	22	0	17	51	62	5	0	.243	.322	.403	-.076	.253	.332	.418	-.059	15.2	116-2B	-5
2002	NYM	NL	28	490	151	26	0	16	62	55	6	0	.308	.391	.459	.228	.321	.400	.486	.216	53.4	130-3B	4
2003	SFG	NL	29	514	133	25	2	13	58	41	5	2	.259	.334	.391	.007	.270	.346	.413	-.027	19.6	121-3B	-3
2004	SFG	NL	30	444	123	27	2	12	51	46	4	2	.278	.356	.425	.026	.278	.354	.438	.027	25.0	119-3B	-1

Breakout: 19%   Improve: 50%   Collapse: 18%

(continued next page)

Edgardo Alfonzo (continued)

Not everything Brian Sabean touches turns to gold. For the second year in a row, Alfonzo followed a disappointing first half with a relatively successful second half. The difference is that in 2003, the first half was a little more disappointing (read: it was disastrous) and the second half was a little less successful (read: it was mediocre). Alfonzo is a good bet for a bounceback season, even if he'll never again reach the lofty heights of his Mets heyday.

RICH AURILIA   SS   Bats: R   Throws: R   Born: 02-Sep-71   Age: 32

YEAR	TM	LG	AGE	AB	H	2B	3B	HR	BB	SO	SB	CS	AVG	OBP	SLG	MLVR	EQBA	EQOBP	EQSLG	EQMLVR	VORP	DEFENSE
2001	SFG	NL	29	636	206	37	5	37	47	83	1	3	.324	.369	.572	.328	.334	.379	.589	.346	92.9	143-SS 10
2002	SFG	NL	30	538	138	35	2	15	37	90	1	2	.257	.305	.413	-.014	.271	.317	.444	-.035	23.0	127-SS 1
2003	SFG	NL	31	505	140	26	1	13	36	82	2	2	.277	.325	.410	.031	.289	.336	.429	-.007	23.8	112-SS 1
2004	SEA	AL	32	444	119	23	2	15	32	70	2	2	.268	.318	.431	-.026	.272	.325	.444	-.019	21.3	114-SS -2

Breakout: 10%   Improve: 38%   Collapse: 30%

It's hard to know what to make of Aurilia's 2003. On one hand, two of the injuries that had a big impact on his offense—dry eyes and appendicitis—were fluky things that have little bearing on his future. On the other hand, Aurilia had his share of nagging injuries that suggest aging as well; his production even when healthy was nothing special, and his superstar 2001 got that much more distant in the rear-view mirror. Aurilia isn't the kind of hitter who'll get a big boost from moving out of Pac Bell Park; he's hit .312/.356/.486 in San Francisco the past three years, and only .267/.317/.460 away. At press time he signed a one-year deal with the Mariners.

MARVIN BENARD   OF   Bats: L   Throws: L   Born: 20-Jan-70   Age: 34

YEAR	TM	LG	AGE	AB	H	2B	3B	HR	BB	SO	SB	CS	AVG	OBP	SLG	MLVR	EQBA	EQOBP	EQSLG	EQMLVR	VORP	DEFENSE
2001	SFG	NL	31	392	104	19	2	15	29	66	10	5	.265	.320	.439	-.009	.278	.331	.460	.019	17.4	55-CF -3 22-RF -1
2002	SFG	NL	32	123	34	9	2	1	7	26	5	1	.276	.321	.407	.018	.294	.330	.437	-.001	2.0	11-RF 1
2003	SFG	NL	33	71	14	3	1	0	4	9	1	0	.197	.237	.268	-.384	.208	.250	.292	-.422	-5.3	14-LF 1
2004	CWS	AL	34	142	36	7	1	3	8	23	3	1	.251	.296	.383	-.139	.255	.303	.385	-.148	-1.8	40-LF 0

Breakout: 36%   Improve: 51%   Collapse: 33%

The expiration of Benard's three-year, $11.1 million mistake of a contract comes as a great relief to the Giants' front office, as he's spent the last two years of that contract mostly recovering from various knee surgeries. Still, now that he won't command a multi-million dollar salary, he could make a reasonable fifth outfielder for someone. He can play anywhere in the outfield (although you don't want him in center for any extended period), and, if he can get his knees healthy enough, he can still hit a little bit.

BARRY BONDS   LF   Bats: L   Throws: L   Born: 24-Jul-64   Age: 39

YEAR	TM	LG	AGE	AB	H	2B	3B	HR	BB	SO	SB	CS	AVG	OBP	SLG	MLVR	EQBA	EQOBP	EQSLG	EQMLVR	VORP	DEFENSE
2001	SFG	NL	36	476	156	32	2	73	177	93	13	3	.328	.515	.863	.905	.335	.517	.878	.904	155.1	125-LF 2
2002	SFG	NL	37	403	149	31	2	46	198	47	9	2	.370	.582	.799	.947	.378	.582	.828	.967	146.4	119-LF -2
2003	SFG	NL	38	390	133	22	1	45	148	58	7	0	.341	.529	.749	.832	.346	.529	.765	.794	111.7	113-LF 5
2004	SFG	NL	39	378	130	30	1	43	136	61	8	0	.343	.519	.772	.748	.343	.516	.795	.768	105.9	124-LF -2

Breakout: 4%   Improve: 50%   Collapse: 10%

By now, it's well known that Bonds can hold his own with baseball's all-time greats in both single-season and career performance. What's less well known (but shouldn't surprise anyone) is the extent to which Bonds dwarfs other players in his own age bracket. Here are the most productive hitters in baseball history between the ages of 36 and 38 (measured by a variant of Pete Palmer's Adjusted Batting Wins):

Player	ABW
Barry Bonds	38.7
Babe Ruth	25.7
Ted Williams	22.8
Edgar Martinez	18.5
Hank Aaron	16.3

A junk stat, sure, but it's still amazing that Bonds swamps the next closest player—Babe Ruth, no less—by more than 50%. The current flap over Balco will not have an impact on Bonds' season, but his increasingly sore body might.

JOSE CRUZ   OF   Bats: B   Throws: R   Born: 19-Apr-74   Age: 30

YEAR	TM	LG	AGE	AB	H	2B	3B	HR	BB	SO	SB	CS	AVG	OBP	SLG	MLVR	EQBA	EQOBP	EQSLG	EQMLVR	VORP	DEFENSE			
2001	TOR	AL	27	577	158	38	4	34	45	138	32	5	.274	.326	.530	.127	.288	.343	.562	.195	50.8	124-CF -11		11-LF	1
2002	TOR	AL	28	466	114	26	5	18	51	106	7	1	.245	.317	.438	-.025	.259	.334	.468	.019	9.1	54-LF	1	46-RF	1
2003	SFG	NL	29	539	135	26	1	20	102	121	5	8	.250	.366	.414	.086	.261	.376	.437	.054	15.2	152-RF 14			
2004	TBY	AL	30	446	114	25	2	17	58	99	8	3	.256	.341	.437012		.259	.348	.457	.027	13.1	120-RF	4		

Breakout: 22%   Improve: 51%   Collapse: 15%

What a weird year. One week, your play in right field is evoking memories of the great Roberto Clemente, the next it's evoking memories of Candy Maldonado's misadventures on the Busch Stadium Astroturf. Cruz's dropped fly ball in the 11th inning of Game 3 of the NLDS may not go down with Merkle's Boner or Buckner's wicket job—there are too many playoff games these days for one gaffe to take on such legendary status—but it will be long and bitterly remembered by Giants fans, much like the Maldonado misplay that was so costly in the 1987 playoffs. Cruz will never again win a Gold Glove Award, but we like his chances of boosting his raw offensive numbers, especially his power, in Tampa this year.

RAY DURHAM   2B   Bats: B   Throws: R   Born: 30-Nov-71   Age: 32

YEAR	TM	LG	AGE	AB	H	2B	3B	HR	BB	SO	SB	CS	AVG	OBP	SLG	MLVR	EQBA	EQOBP	EQSLG	EQMLVR	VORP	DEFENSE
2001	CWS	AL	29	611	163	42	10	20	64	110	23	10	.267	.337	.466	.057	.282	.355	.499	.120	48.6	146-2B 10
2002	CWS	AL	30	345	103	20	2	9	49	59	20	5	.299	.390	.446	.154	.325	.416	.486	.247	40.0	90-2B 0
2002	OAK	AL	30	219	60	14	4	6	24	34	6	2	.274	.350	.457	.092	.294	.370	.493	.149	18.6	11-2B 1
2003	SFG	NL	31	410	117	30	5	8	50	82	7	7	.285	.366	.441	.152	.298	.374	.464	.119	30.1	95-2B 11
2004	SFG	NL	32	445	125	29	4	11	56	81	10	5	.281	.363	.436	.055	.281	.361	.449	.057	28.8	121-2B -1

Breakout: 19%   Improve: 45%   Collapse: 16%

If you made out an all-underrated list for the past decade, Durham would have to be at or near the top. He stayed true to that form last year, holding the title of third-most valuable player—behind Bonds and Schmidt—on a 100-win club, while keeping completely out of the limelight. As much as we appreciate how underappreciated he is, though, it's time to get a little bearish on Durham. He's a player who's derived a fair amount of his value from his speed, and that speed is starting to go. That's not what Brian Sabean wants to hear about a player who's still owed almost $20 million for the next three years.

JASON ELLISON   CF   Bats: R   Throws: R   Born: 04-Apr-78   Age: 26

YEAR	TM	LG	AGE	AB	H	2B	3B	HR	BB	SO	SB	CS	AVG	OBP	SLG	MLVR	EQBA	EQOBP	EQSLG	EQMLVR	VORP	DEFENSE
2001	HAG	SAL	23	494	144	38	3	8	71	68	19	15	.291	.388	.429	.208	.213	.290	.323	-.296	-24.1	129-CF 3
2002	SJO	CAL	24	322	87	13	0	5	25	37	9	9	.270	.325	.357	-.048	.220	.263	.294	-.387	-23.3	79-CF -2
2002	FRE	PCL	24	196	61	8	1	3	21	28	16	3	.311	.389	.408	.090	.272	.344	.364	-.097	3.1	48-CF 2
2003	FRE	PCL	25	461	136	22	4	6	39	52	21	13	.295	.356	.399	.032	.263	.321	.363	-.149	-0.2	113-CF 1
2003	SFG	NL	25	10	1	0	0	0	0	1	0	0	.100	.100	.100	-.922	.200	.200	.200	-.660	-2.1	
2004	SFG	NL	26	194	48	9	1	3	17	27	5	2	.248	.315	.350	-.164	.248	.314	.361	-.167	-1.0	55-CF -1

Breakout: 37%   Improve: 56%   Collapse: 28%

Ellison is one of the best defensive center fielders in the Pacific Coast League. He has excellent speed, takes good routes to the ball, and has a strong, accurate arm. That's the good news. The bad news is that, unless he breaks through with some power, he's not going to hit well enough to show off that defensive ability regularly at the major league level.

PEDRO FELIZ   3B/1B   Bats: R   Throws: R   Born: 27-Apr-75   Age: 29

YEAR	TM	LG	AGE	AB	H	2B	3B	HR	BB	SO	SB	CS	AVG	OBP	SLG	MLVR	EQBA	EQOBP	EQSLG	EQMLVR	VORP	DEFENSE		
2001	SFG	NL	26	220	50	9	1	7	10	50	2	1	.227	.264	.373	-.238	.238	.275	.395	-.209	-1.6	55-3B -13		
2002	SFG	NL	27	146	37	4	1	2	6	27	0	0	.253	.281	.336	-.165	.275	.299	.362	-.184	-0.1	34-3B 0		
2003	SFG	NL	28	235	58	9	3	16	10	53	2	2	.247	.278	.515	.076	.259	.289	.544	.049	10.2	40-3B 2	11-LF	-1
2004	SFG	NL	29	181	45	9	1	7	12	41	2	1	.247	.294	.416	-.115	.247	.292	.428	-.116	4.7	50-3B -1		

Breakout: 20%   Improve: 37%   Collapse: 35%

(continued next page)

Pedro Feliz *(continued)*

A serious question for National League pitchers: How can you allow a man who will swing at anything that moves to hit 16 homers in 235 at-bats? Feliz had the third-lowest on-base percentage in the NL among players with as many ABs, yet he still managed to hit those 16 home runs, with nine doubles and three triples thrown in for good measure. He is the only player in major league history to combine a sub-.280 OBP with a SLG better than .500 (minimum 200 ABs). Actually, that PECOTA line gives us a pretty good idea of what NL pitchers' answer will be: "We won't let it happen again."

ANDRES GALARRAGA								1B		Bats: R			Throws: R						Born: 18-Jun-61		Age: 43	
YEAR	TM	LG	AGE	AB	H	2B	3B	HR	BB	SO	SB	CS	AVG	OBP	SLG	MLVR	EQBA	EQOBP	EQSLG	EQMLVR	VORP	DEFENSE
2001	TEX	AL	40	243	57	16	0	10	18	68	1	0	.235	.310	.424	-.082	.248	.323	.446	-.041	2.6	24-1B 0
2001	SFG	NL	40	156	45	12	1	7	13	49	0	3	.288	.351	.513	.172	.302	.364	.528	.196	11.7	34-1B -7
2002	MON	NL	41	292	76	12	0	9	30	81	2	2	.260	.344	.394	.007	.267	.348	.412	-.027	4.4	72-1B -4
2003	SFG	NL	42	272	82	15	0	12	19	61	1	3	.301	.352	.489	.212	.313	.360	.514	.181	18.6	58-1B -4
2004	*SFG*	*NL*	*43*	*170*	*45*	*9*	*0*	*6*	*16*	*41*	*1*	*1*	*.264*	*.336*	*.423*	*-.021*	*.264*	*.335*	*.435*	*-.020*	*5.0*	*48-1B -5*

Breakout: 21%   Improve: 29%   Collapse: 43%

Galarraga decided to return for 2003 largely to reach the 400 home-run milestone. El Gato Grande didn't quite make it—he's currently stuck on 398—but he did give the Giants far better production than they had a right to expect from a 42-year-old who had done very little the year before. He's unlikely to produce near his '03 level again. Here's hoping someone gives Galarraga a chance to hit his two homers and mash a few lefties off the bench, then lets him walk off into the sunset.

MARQUIS GRISSOM								CF		Bats: R			Throws: R						Born: 17-Apr-67		Age: 37			
YEAR	TM	LG	AGE	AB	H	2B	3B	HR	BB	SO	SB	CS	AVG	OBP	SLG	MLVR	EQBA	EQOBP	EQSLG	EQMLVR	VORP	DEFENSE			
2001	LAD	NL	34	448	99	17	1	21	16	107	7	5	.221	.250	.404	-.222	.235	.262	.431	-.184	-4.4	86-CF -4	23-LF 0		
2002	LAD	NL	35	343	95	21	4	17	22	68	5	1	.277	.321	.510	.170	.293	.334	.545	.162	27.5	53-CF -2	26-LF 0		
2003	SFG	NL	36	587	176	33	3	20	20	82	11	3	.300	.322	.468	.133	.311	.334	.488	.097	35.0	136-CF -8			
2004	*SFG*	*NL*	*37*	*410*	*110*	*24*	*2*	*14*	*22*	*67*	*5*	*2*	*.268*	*.306*	*.441*	*-.044*	*.268*	*.305*	*.454*	*-.044*	*6.1*	*104-CF -6*			

Breakout: 11%   Improve: 19%   Collapse: 28%

If there were no such thing as right-handed pitchers, Marquis Grissom would be a perennial MVP candidate. Over the past three years, he's posted a line of .305/.343/.592 against lefties, vs. a .253/.280/.402 line against righties; his 2003 split was an outrageous .364/.399/.657 vs. LH, .280/.298/.409 vs. RH At age 37, Grissom appears headed for a major decline, and the only way to delay it would be to severely cut back on his plate appearances against righties, via some heavy platooning with newly-acquired Michael Tucker.

JEFFREY HAMMONDS								OF		Bats: R			Throws: R						Born: 05-Mar-71		Age: 33			
YEAR	TM	LG	AGE	AB	H	2B	3B	HR	BB	SO	SB	CS	AVG	OBP	SLG	MLVR	EQBA	EQOBP	EQSLG	EQMLVR	VORP	DEFENSE			
2001	MIL	NL	30	174	43	11	1	6	14	42	5	3	.247	.314	.425	-.074	.250	.317	.426	-.078	3.4	46-CF -2			
2002	MIL	NL	31	448	115	26	5	9	52	86	4	5	.257	.332	.397	-.009	.264	.339	.415	-.042	13.0	61-CF 0	42-RF -3		
2003	MIL	NL	32	38	6	2	0	1	3	7	0	0	.158	.220	.289	-.431	.158	.220	.316	-.475	-3.9				
2003	FRE	PCL	32	36	12	1	0	2	3	3	1	0	.333	.385	.528	.294	.278	.333	.472	.040	1.8				
2003	SFG	NL	32	94	26	10	0	3	13	21	1	0	.277	.370	.479	.203	.292	.381	.500	.175	7.0	10-LF 0			
2004	*SFG*	*NL*	*33*	*201*	*50*	*12*	*1*	*5*	*21*	*38*	*2*	*1*	*.251*	*.325*	*.395*	*-.087*	*.251*	*.323*	*.407*	*-.088*	*1.3*	*56-CF -8*			

Breakout: 25%   Improve: 51%   Collapse: 27%

Brian Sabean's pickup of Brewers cast-off Hammonds at mid-season may not have sent shockwaves through the league, but it was a move that helped the club. Hammonds is a versatile outfielder with a career slugging average above .450 who is still young enough to be useful. That's not worth the $7 million per year contract Milwaukee gave him, but it is well worth the cost of a waiver claim that the Giants paid. As a decent fourth outfielder and platoon mate for Tucker, Hammonds is also worth the one-year, $1 million contract he signed to return for 2004.

TRAVIS ISHIKAWA — 1B — Bats: L — Throws: L — Born: 24-Sep-83 — Age: 20

YEAR	TM	LG	AGE	AB	H	2B	3B	HR	BB	SO	SB	CS	AVG	OBP	SLG	MLVR	EQBA	EQOBP	EQSLG	EQMLVR	VORP	DEFENSE
2002	SLO	NWN	18	88	27	2	1	1	5	22	1	1	.307	.347	.386	.120	.244	.272	.322	-.315	-10.8	21-1B -3
2003	HAG	SAL	19	194	40	5	0	3	33	69	3	4	.206	.329	.278	-.109	.157	.246	.216	-.555	-32.1	57-1B -4
2003	SLO	NWN	19	248	63	17	4	3	44	77	0	0	.254	.376	.391	.099	.171	.256	.271	-.456	-54.2	66-1B 0
2004	SFG	NL	20	263	50	11	2	4	23	87	1	1	.189	.262	.286	-.377	.189	.260	.294	-.385	-20.2	72-1B -8

Breakout: 38%   Improve: 58%   Collapse: 27%

Whatever else happens to Ishikawa from here on out, he'll have a place in history as the richest 21st-round pick ever. He had consensus second- or third-round talent coming out of high school, but his commitment to attend college dropped him to the 21st round of the 2002 draft, where the Giants snagged him. It took almost a million dollars to convince him that maybe higher education wasn't all it was cracked up to be. He struggled last year, but was still just a teenager, and showed good plate discipline and developing power amidst the low batting averages. He's worth following.

JUSTIN KNOEDLER — C — Bats: R — Throws: R — Born: 17-Jul-80 — Age: 23

YEAR	TM	LG	AGE	AB	H	2B	3B	HR	BB	SO	SB	CS	AVG	OBP	SLG	MLVR	EQBA	EQOBP	EQSLG	EQMLVR	VORP	DEFENSE
2002	HAG	SAL	21	280	72	16	2	5	37	56	6	5	.257	.349	.382	.052	.190	.258	.291	-.416	-22.0	81-C -24
2003	SJO	CAL	22	354	91	25	2	10	35	78	13	3	.257	.326	.424	.014	.198	.255	.335	-.358	-20.5	96-C 4
2004	SFG	NL	23	230	47	12	1	4	20	54	3	1	.207	.273	.322	-.301	.207	.271	.332	-.307	-6.1	63-C -6

Breakout: 38%   Improve: 51%   Collapse: 29%

Knoedler began his pro career as a relief pitcher, putting up a 1.24 ERA and striking out 11.8 batters per nine innings in the Northwest League in 2001. So naturally, he switched positions. Actually, Knoedler was a catcher in college, and he switched back largely to fill the organizational hole at the position. He's filling it nicely at the moment, showing decent power and speed and solid work behind the plate. We'll have to see him outside the hitting-crazy California League in '04 to get a better read; PECOTA suggests digging the resin bag out of mothballs.

FRED LEWIS — CF — Bats: L — Throws: R — Born: 09-Dec-80 — Age: 23

YEAR	TM	LG	AGE	AB	H	2B	3B	HR	BB	SO	SB	CS	AVG	OBP	SLG	MLVR	EQBA	EQOBP	EQSLG	EQMLVR	VORP	DEFENSE
2002	SLO	NWN	21	239	77	9	3	1	26	58	9	6	.322	.396	.397	.207	.238	.290	.302	-.311	-21.7	40-CF -6
2003	HAG	SAL	22	420	105	17	8	1	68	112	30	15	.250	.361	.336	.029	.190	.271	.261	-.430	-41.3	107-CF -12
2004	SFG	NL	23	233	48	10	2	2	22	67	5	3	.206	.278	.291	-.333	.206	.276	.299	-.340	-13.8	64-CF -9

Breakout: 32%   Improve: 53%   Collapse: 23%

The Giants' second pick in the 2002 draft, Lewis looks a little like Willie McGee on offense, with his slappy swing and speed on the basepaths. He was the typical tools-over-baseball-skills pick, and hasn't looked impressive to date. His batting average could go up as he rises through the system, but his walk rate should fall as he sees more pitchers who can throw strikes. The only thing that could turn him into a productive major leaguer is to develop some power, and with his current swing, that seems like a long shot.

TODD LINDEN — OF — Bats: B — Throws: R — Born: 30-Jun-80 — Age: 24

YEAR	TM	LG	AGE	AB	H	2B	3B	HR	BB	SO	SB	CS	AVG	OBP	SLG	MLVR	EQBA	EQOBP	EQSLG	EQMLVR	VORP	DEFENSE	
2002	SHV	TEX	22	392	123	26	2	12	61	101	9	5	.314	.419	.482	.314	.263	.352	.419	-.013	7.0	110-RF -5	
2002	FRE	PCL	22	100	25	2	1	3	20	35	2	0	.250	.380	.380	-.007	.208	.325	.327	-.224	-5.8	21-LF 0	
2003	FRE	PCL	23	471	131	24	3	11	40	105	14	4	.278	.356	.412	.038	.249	.319	.379	-.140	-10.7	106-RF -12	11-CF 0
2003	SFG	NL	23	38	8	1	0	1	1	8	0	0	.211	.231	.316	-.321	.237	.256	.342	-.322	-2.6		
2004	SFG	NL	24	245	60	13	2	6	26	62	4	2	.247	.330	.391	-.085	.247	.329	.403	-.086	2.4	69-RF -5	

Breakout: 22%   Improve: 48%   Collapse: 26%

On the face of it, Linden's 2003 was a big disappointment coming off his breakthrough 2002. But the depressed 2003 numbers were largely due to a catastrophic .210/.304/.222 April. After he got his feet wet, he put up a healthier .292/.367/.451 in the remainder of his Fresno campaign. He then topped off the year with a solid .316/.380/.531 line in the Arizona Fall League—though Andy Rooney could have cracked an AFL staff given the depths to which the league's pitching talent has sunk. He shows promise of developing power from both sides of the plate, and he's a fine outfielder with a good arm, even capable of playing a decent center field. We'd like to see what he can do given 450 major league ABs.

TREY LUNSFORD   C   Bats: R   Throws: R   Born: 25-May-79   Age: 25

YEAR	TM	LG	AGE	AB	H	2B	3B	HR	BB	SO	SB	CS	AVG	OBP	SLG	MLVR	EQBA	EQOBP	EQSLG	EQMLVR	VORP	DEFENSE	
2001	HAG	SAL	22	396	94	19	0	5	45	89	10	5	.237	.320	.323	-.046	.182	.248	.252	-.493	-40.4	108-C	-3
2002	SJO	CAL	23	51	13	3	0	1	3	5	2	0	.255	.321	.373	-.043	.212	.254	.327	-.363	-2.9	14-C	1
2002	SHV	TEX	23	210	59	13	0	1	29	42	5	2	.281	.379	.357	.063	.245	.321	.319	-.222	-3.4	62-C	-3
2002	FRE	PCL	23	57	10	0	0	2	6	15	0	0	.175	.258	.281	-.408	.158	.233	.263	-.520	-6.3	18-C	1
2003	FRE	PCL	24	206	59	10	1	2	17	33	0	1	.286	.341	.374	-.035	.254	.310	.337	-.213	-2.5	60-C	-7
2004	*SFG*	*NL*	*25*	*170*	*38*	*7*	*1*	*3*	*15*	*34*	*1*	*1*	*.223*	*.291*	*.318*	*-.265*	*.223*	*.289*	*.328*	*-.270*	*-4.0*	*48-C*	*-4*

Breakout: 25%   Improve: 45%   Collapse: 33%

Lunsford is a solid defensive catcher; last year he showed good ability to block pitches and threw out 27% of would-be basestealers. His hitting suggests a job as a future member of the Backup Catchers' Society. The acquisition of A. J. Pierzynski probably cost Lunsford his chance of opening the season as the Giants #2 receiver. He's next in line as an injury replacement.

LANCE NIEKRO   1B/3B   Bats: R   Throws: R   Born: 29-Jan-79   Age: 25

YEAR	TM	LG	AGE	AB	H	2B	3B	HR	BB	SO	SB	CS	AVG	OBP	SLG	MLVR	EQBA	EQOBP	EQSLG	EQMLVR	VORP	DEFENSE			
2001	SJO	CAL	22	163	47	11	0	3	4	14	4	2	.288	.298	.411	.001	.244	.257	.354	-.298	-5.5	32-3B	1		
2002	SHV	TEX	23	297	92	20	1	4	7	32	0	2	.310	.327	.424	.098	.281	.295	.395	-.138	-4.9	48-1B	-2	26-3B	-7
2003	FRE	PCL	24	381	115	15	2	4	19	39	3	3	.302	.334	.383	-.021	.272	.308	.352	-.183	-0.3	71-3B	-7	16-1B	-1
2003	SFG	NL	24	5	1	1	0	0	0	1	0	0	.200	.200	.400	-.263	.200	.200	.400	-.372	-0.2				
2004	*SFG*	*NL*	*25*	*219*	*58*	*12*	*1*	*3*	*11*	*27*	*1*	*1*	*.267*	*.303*	*.379*	*-.134*	*.267*	*.302*	*.390*	*-.136*	*2.9*	*58-3B*	*-5*		

Breakout: 31%   Improve: 48%   Collapse: 29%

The good news is that Niekro nearly doubled his career high in walks in 2003. The bad news is that his previous career high in walks was 11. His defense at third is not yet ready for prime time, so what that leaves is a first baseman who projects to produce, at best, an empty .300 batting average in the majors. He may get called up for a little light pinch-hitting duty in San Francisco this year; if they need him to do anything more, they've got a problem.

DANIEL ORTMEIER   OF   Bats: B   Throws: L   Born: 11-May-81   Age: 23

YEAR	TM	LG	AGE	AB	H	2B	3B	HR	BB	SO	SB	CS	AVG	OBP	SLG	MLVR	EQBA	EQOBP	EQSLG	EQMLVR	VORP	DEFENSE	
2002	SLO	NWN	21	195	57	9	1	5	18	37	3	0	.292	.352	.426	.165	.223	.264	.337	-.323	-28.4	27-LF	-1
2003	SJO	CAL	22	408	124	32	6	8	39	89	13	6	.304	.378	.471	.207	.238	.297	.377	-.193	-16.3	71-RF	-5
2004	*SFG*	*NL*	*23*	*261*	*59*	*15*	*2*	*5*	*20*	*62*	*4*	*2*	*.228*	*.289*	*.356*	*-.215*	*.227*	*.288*	*.367*	*-.219*	*-8.7*	*71-RF*	*-6*

Breakout: 23%   Improve: 48%   Collapse: 26%

Ortmeier is the Giants' second-best position player prospect after Todd Linden. If you've studied the Giants' minor league rosters, you know that's not saying much. Ortmeier showed a nice power surge in his first year in full-season ball, and he has a chance to develop more if some of those doubles become home runs. Unlike Linden, Ortmeier does not look comfortable tracking flies in the outfield, so he'll sink or swim primarily on his hitting. His performance at Norwich this year will tell us if he's for real.

NEIFI PEREZ   SS/2B   Bats: B   Throws: L   Born: 02-Jun-73   Age: 31

YEAR	TM	LG	AGE	AB	H	2B	3B	HR	BB	SO	SB	CS	AVG	OBP	SLG	MLVR	EQBA	EQOBP	EQSLG	EQMLVR	VORP	DEFENSE			
2001	COL	NL	28	382	114	19	8	7	16	49	6	2	.298	.326	.445	-.036	.282	.311	.421	-.070	13.2	87-SS	6		
2001	KCR	AL	28	199	48	7	1	1	10	19	3	4	.241	.277	.302	-.307	.247	.290	.313	-.291	-4.4	45-SS	1		
2002	KCR	AL	29	554	131	20	4	3	20	53	8	9	.236	.260	.303	-.324	.246	.274	.316	-.319	-16.0	135-SS	7		
2003	SFG	NL	30	328	84	19	4	1	14	23	3	2	.256	.285	.348	-.145	.267	.297	.366	-.188	0.2	44-2B	3	44-SS	5
2004	*SFG*	*NL*	*31*	*290*	*73*	*13*	*2*	*2*	*13*	*28*	*3*	*2*	*.251*	*.284*	*.329*	*-.247*	*.251*	*.282*	*.339*	*-.252*	*-2.6*	*76-SS*	*-2*		

Breakout: 28%   Improve: 44%   Collapse: 32%

Is Neifi Perez the worst hitter of all-time? We won't go into the detailed arguments here, but he has a case, along with Hal Lanier and a few others. He's still an excellent fielder, and he might be able to help a team if he's used mostly as a late-inning defensive sub. But regardless of how good a fielder he is, the thought of Neifi Perez breaking camp as the starting San Francisco shortstop should be terrifying to Giants fans.

CODY RANSOM SS Bats: R Throws: R Born: 17-Feb-76 Age: 28

YEAR	TM	LG	AGE	AB	H	2B	3B	HR	BB	SO	SB	CS	AVG	OBP	SLG	MLVR	EQBA	EQOBP	EQSLG	EQMLVR	VORP	DEFENSE	
2001	FRE	PCL	25	469	113	21	6	23	44	137	17	2	.241	.303	.458	-.089	.206	.269	.393	-.246	-6.7	133-SS	3
2002	FRE	PCL	26	449	93	18	4	13	47	151	6	4	.207	.283	.352	-.250	.178	.251	.305	-.417	-30.5	132-SS	0
2003	FRE	PCL	27	396	100	16	4	12	45	91	14	4	.253	.331	.404	-.035	.222	.296	.365	-.222	-2.3	109-SS	-9
2003	SFG	NL	27	27	6	1	0	1	1	11	0	0	.222	.250	.370	-.200	.222	.250	.407	-.251	-0.2		
2004	*SFG*	*NL*	*28*	*184*	*41*	*9*	*2*	*5*	*19*	*51*	*3*	*2*	*.226*	*.299*	*.376*	*-.173*	*.226*	*.297*	*.387*	*-.176*	*4.0*	*52-SS*	*-2*

Breakout: 52%   Improve: 63%   Collapse: 21%

Ransom worked hard with Fresno hitting coach Steve Decker in 2003 on controlling the strike zone, and the results were apparent in the numbers: a dramatically reduced strikeout rate, with no drop in his walk rate or power. Ransom is a slick fielder at short (or second), and with his decent pop and improving pitch selection, he wouldn't be a bad choice to fill the Giants shortstop hole on the cheap. Maybe an even better use for him would be as the right-handed end of a short-stop platoon. Please, just not with Neifi Perez.

BENITO SANTIAGO C Bats: R Throws: R Born: 09-Mar-65 Age: 39

YEAR	TM	LG	AGE	AB	H	2B	3B	HR	BB	SO	SB	CS	AVG	OBP	SLG	MLVR	EQBA	EQOBP	EQSLG	EQMLVR	VORP	DEFENSE	
2001	SFG	NL	36	477	125	25	4	6	23	78	5	4	.262	.295	.369	-.157	.276	.311	.390	-.120	6.6	121-C	0
2002	SFG	NL	37	478	133	24	5	16	27	73	4	2	.278	.315	.450	.072	.292	.329	.479	.056	27.7	120-C	-2
2003	SFG	NL	38	401	112	21	2	11	29	69	0	1	.279	.329	.424	.052	.291	.339	.445	.024	18.2	100-C	-8
2004	*KCR*	*AL*	*39*	*278*	*75*	*16*	*1*	*7*	*20*	*45*	*1*	*1*	*.271*	*.320*	*.414*	*-.042*	*.259*	*.313*	*.401*	*-.108*	*5.1*	*74-C*	*-4*

Breakout: 17%   Improve: 31%   Collapse: 36%

As expected, Santiago's hitting took a step back from his surprising 2002, largely because age-related aches and pains prevented him from playing as much. But the really noticeable decline in his game came on the defensive end—he just can't throw any more. He still does that cool throw-from-the-knees thing, but now the throws have a high, looping, Piazza-style arc on them. It's a little sad to watch, if you remember the cannon he used to have in the late 80s. He threw out 18.5% of would-be basestealers in 2003, which would have placed him just a hair out of last place in the majors if he'd had enough attempts to qualify. The Royals signed him to a two-year, $4.3 million contract that they'll soon regret.

NATE SCHIERHOLTZ 3B Bats: L Throws: R Born: 15-Feb-84 Age: 20

YEAR	TM	LG	AGE	AB	H	2B	3B	HR	BB	SO	SB	CS	AVG	OBP	SLG	MLVR	EQBA	EQOBP	EQSLG	EQMLVR	VORP	DEFENSE	
2003	SLO	NWN	19	124	38	6	2	3	12	15	0	1	.306	.382	.460	.232	.222	.278	.341	-.290	-7.4	31-3B	-2
2004	*SFG*	*NL*	*20*	*248*	*55*	*11*	*2*	*4*	*18*	*39*	*1*	*1*	*.222*	*.286*	*.332*	*-.256*	*.222*	*.284*	*.342*	*-.261*	*-3.9*	*68-3B*	*-5*

Breakout: 33%   Improve: 53%   Collapse: 30%

The Giants' second-round pick in '03 had a solid pro debut, putting up good numbers in the three major hitting areas—average, power, and patience—at the tender age of 19. There are questions about his fielding, although his defensive numbers in his brief stay at Salem-Keizer were nothing to complain about. Schierholtz's teammate, Brad Vericker, had an even more auspicious Northwest League debut, hitting .284/.404/.547, and finishing as the third-best hitter in the league by Clay Davenport's numbers. However, as someone who was undrafted and mostly played DH during the season, Vericker's a rung or two below Schierholtz on the prospect ladder.

J. T. SNOW 1B Bats: B Throws: L Born: 26-Feb-68 Age: 36

YEAR	TM	LG	AGE	AB	H	2B	3B	HR	BB	SO	SB	CS	AVG	OBP	SLG	MLVR	EQBA	EQOBP	EQSLG	EQMLVR	VORP	DEFENSE	
2001	SFG	NL	33	285	70	12	1	8	55	81	0	0	.246	.371	.379	-.010	.259	.382	.396	.009	7.8	78-1B	-5
2002	SFG	NL	34	422	104	26	2	6	59	90	0	0	.246	.344	.360	-.025	.263	.357	.390	-.043	4.6	113-1B	-6
2003	SFG	NL	35	330	90	18	3	8	55	55	1	2	.273	.387	.418	.146	.284	.394	.441	.110	17.0	94-1B	-1
2004	*SFG*	*NL*	*36*	*253*	*62*	*12*	*1*	*6*	*39*	*53*	*1*	*1*	*.245*	*.352*	*.373*	*-.071*	*.245*	*.350*	*.384*	*-.073*	*4.0*	*73-1B*	*-3*

Breakout: 18%   Improve: 34%   Collapse: 40%

Batting average is the potion that changes Snow from Dr. Jekyll into Mr. Hyde. When he hits around .280 (2000, 2003), he's Good J. T., a slick-fielding on-base machine with a little bit of pop. When he hits around .240 (2001, 2002), he's Evil J. T., an albatross of a first baseman with OBP and SLG both well south of .400. The Giants desperately need the former to show up in 2004; they've got no credible alternative at first. Given Snow's advancing age, we're more likely to see the latter.

TONY TORCATO   **OF**   **Bats: L**   **Throws: R**   Born: 25-Oct-79   Age: 24

YEAR	TM	LG	AGE	AB	H	2B	3B	HR	BB	SO	SB	CS	AVG	OBP	SLG	MLVR	EQBA	EQOBP	EQSLG	EQMLVR	VORP	DEFENSE			
2001	SJO	CAL	21	258	88	21	2	2	17	40	9	3	.341	.381	.461	.251	.276	.315	.379	-.128	-5.7	13-LF	-3		
2001	SHV	TEX	21	147	43	9	1	1	9	15	0	1	.293	.344	.388	.025	.257	.304	.345	-.211	-7.2	35-LF	0		
2001	FRE	PCL	21	150	48	8	1	2	2	20	0	1	.320	.329	.427	-.019	.286	.300	.374	-.156	-4.6	27-LF	2		
2002	FRE	PCL	22	490	142	23	3	13	29	65	4	6	.290	.330	.429	-.003	.255	.296	.379	-.180	-18.6	66-LF	-2	55-RF	-4
2003	FRE	PCL	23	423	125	18	2	3	6	33	4	0	.296	.304	.369	-.100	.270	.286	.342	-.242	-19.0	58-1B	-4	34-LF	-2
2004	*SFG*	*NL*	*24*	*237*	*62*	*14*	*1*	*3*	*13*	*29*	*2*	*1*	*.261*	*.302*	*.372*	*-.150*	*.261*	*.301*	*.383*	*-.152*	*-4.7*	*63-LF*	*-2*		

Breakout: 31%   *Improve: 52%*   *Collapse: 24%*

Torcato teased us a little bit in 2002 with his 13 homers, providing a tiny glimmer of hope that he would amount to more than an empty .290 batting average. But last year he dashed those hopes, reverting to the Torcato of old—limp power, and a hacker's mentality to rival Randall Simon. Corner outfielders with little defensive ability simply can't get by at the major league level by just hitting singles.

YORVIT TORREALBA   **C**   **Bats: R**   **Throws: R**   Born: 19-Jul-78   Age: 25

YEAR	TM	LG	AGE	AB	H	2B	3B	HR	BB	SO	SB	CS	AVG	OBP	SLG	MLVR	EQBA	EQOBP	EQSLG	EQMLVR	VORP	DEFENSE	
2001	FRE	PCL	22	394	108	23	3	8	19	65	2	3	.274	.313	.409	-.114	.239	.279	.355	-.258	-10.5	107-C	1
2002	SFG	NL	23	136	38	10	0	2	14	20	0	0	.279	.355	.397	.066	.295	.367	.424	.048	7.9	42-C	0
2003	SFG	NL	24	200	52	10	2	4	14	39	1	0	.260	.312	.390	-.033	.275	.323	.412	-.066	5.1	56-C	9
2004	*SFG*	*NL*	*25*	*239*	*63*	*14*	*2*	*5*	*17*	*40*	*2*	*1*	*.264*	*.320*	*.404*	*-.073*	*.264*	*.318*	*.416*	*-.074*	*11.2*	*65-C*	*1*

Breakout: 24%   *Improve: 38%*   *Collapse: 40%*

When the Giants traded for A. J. Pierzynski to replace the departing Benito Santiago at catcher, most reports ignored the home-grown catching alternative the Giants had on hand. Sure, Pierzynski is an upgrade over Torrealba, but how much of one? PECOTA projects an OBP/SLG (park neutral) of .318/.416 for Torrealba, and .336/.441 for Pierzynski. Are those 18 points of OBP and 25 points of SLG worth the extra $2 to $3 million Pierzynski will cost in a tight budget situation, not to mention the three decent young pitchers it took to get him? And that's not even considering Torrealba's defense, which is outstanding. Acknowledging that Pierzynski's longer track record makes for a more stable projection, the Giants don't appear to have upgraded much. On the bright side, the Giants can fashion a nifty platoon, with Torrealba spelling the lefty-swinging Pierzynski.

CARLOS VALDERRAMA   **OF**   **Bats: R**   **Throws: R**   Born: 30-Nov-77   Age: 26

YEAR	TM	LG	AGE	AB	H	2B	3B	HR	BB	SO	SB	CS	AVG	OBP	SLG	MLVR	EQBA	EQOBP	EQSLG	EQMLVR	VORP	DEFENSE			
2001	SHV	TEX	23	159	49	12	2	1	18	29	11	5	.308	.379	.428	.151	.261	.324	.360	-.149	-0.1	36-CF	-2		
2002	SJO	CAL	24	299	94	19	6	15	34	60	14	5	.314	.384	.569	.379	.245	.300	.444	-.088	3.5				
2002	SHV	TEX	24	135	33	3	1	4	10	23	4	0	.244	.304	.370	-.063	.219	.267	.350	-.301	-7.5				
2003	NRW	EAS	25	240	74	15	3	1	25	34	13	6	.308	.375	.408	.128	.263	.321	.358	-.156	-7.9	37-LF	-7	13-RF	-2
2003	FRE	PCL	25	202	56	5	0	3	12	28	7	8	.277	.324	.347	-.108	.249	.292	.313	-.285	-13.8	28-LF	-4		
2004	*SFG*	*NL*	*26*	*174*	*43*	*9*	*2*	*3*	*14*	*32*	*5*	*2*	*.247*	*.306*	*.371*	*-.154*	*.247*	*.304*	*.382*	*-.157*	*-0.9*	*49-LF*	*-4*		

Breakout: 34%   *Improve: 50%*   *Collapse: 32%*

Valderrama is pretty comparable to Tony Torcato—a little better glove, a little more plate discipline, a little less batting average, and a little older. We at BP often tend to favor players like Valderrama—capable of drawing walks—over players like Torcato. But the projection lines for the two suggest that there's really no difference in their expected production right now, and Torcato probably has the higher ceiling by virtue of being younger. Regardless, neither has done enough to merit a major league roster spot at the moment.

ERIC YOUNG   **2B**   **Bats: R**   **Throws: R**   Born: 18-May-67   Age: 37

YEAR	TM	LG	AGE	AB	H	2B	3B	HR	BB	SO	SB	CS	AVG	OBP	SLG	MLVR	EQBA	EQOBP	EQSLG	EQMLVR	VORP	DEFENSE	
2001	CHC	NL	34	603	168	43	4	6	42	45	31	14	.279	.333	.393	-.053	.283	.336	.399	-.055	20.0	137-2B	-2
2002	MIL	NL	35	496	139	29	3	3	39	38	31	11	.280	.338	.369	-.021	.288	.343	.381	-.063	14.7	119-2B	-5
2003	MIL	NL	36	404	105	18	1	15	48	34	25	7	.260	.344	.421	.027	.262	.344	.425	-.020	18.7	94-2B	-13
2003	SFG	NL	36	71	14	2	0	0	9	10	3	5	.197	.293	.225	-.331	.208	.303	.236	-.389	-4.9	17-2B	2
2004	*TEX*	*AL*	*37*	*335*	*89*	*18*	*2*	*5*	*33*	*37*	*15*	*6*	*.265*	*.336*	*.371*	*-.075*	*.258*	*.333*	*.362*	*-.124*	*8.0*	*91-2B*	*-6*

Breakout: 32%   *Improve: 59%*   *Collapse: 21%*

The Eric Young trade was a panic move, pure and simple. The Giants were coming off an 0–6 road trip, Ray Durham was on the DL nursing a strained hamstring, and Brian Sabean's stated reason for bringing in Young was to help reverse the team's slide. The only problem with that rationale is that it was late August, the Giants still held a gaudy 8 -game lead in first place, and Barry Bonds was about to return from bereavement leave. Predictably, the team's cushion turned out to be more than sufficient. Young made little difference and was even left off the postseason roster, and all the Giants have to show for the transaction is one less promising arm in their system. Control artist Greg Bruso is nobody's idea of an elite prospect, but he's still worth far more than a lame insurance policy. Young signed with Texas at press time.

PITCHERS

DAVID AARDSMA Bats: R Throws: R Born: 27-Dec-81 Age: 22

YEAR	TM	LG	AGE	G	GS	IP	H	BB	SO	HR	ERA	EQERA	EQH9	EQBB9	EQSO9	EQHR9	PERA	VORP	STF
2003	SJO	CAL	21	18	0	18.3	14	7	28	2	1.97	3.38	9.6	5.1	9.6	2.2	6.66	3.9	2

There were a few eyebrows raised when the Giants used their first-round pick on a reliever, even if he was the talented closer for the soon-to-be College World Series champion Rice Owls. But Aardsma did nothing to make the Giants doubt their selection in his brief pro debut in the California League. He showed a wicked mid-90s fastball with a good slider, and struck out an impressive 28 of the 74 batters he faced (38%). To answer questions about taking a closer in the first round, the Giants front office is fond of citing the example of Russ Ortiz, another college reliever who didn't convert to starting until his third year in pro ball.

BOOF BONSER Bats: R Throws: R Born: 14-Oct-81 Age: 22

YEAR	TM	LG	AGE	G	GS	IP	H	BB	SO	HR	ERA	EQERA	EQH9	EQBB9	EQSO9	EQHR9	PERA	VORP	STF
2001	HAG	SAL	19	27	27	134.0	91	61	178	7	2.49	4.46	8.8	6.3	7.2	1.1	5.37	14.6	27
2002	SHV	TEX	20	5	5	24.3	30	14	23	3	5.56	7.54	11.9	6.0	6.8	2.0	7.72	-4.9	-1
2002	SJO	CAL	20	23	23	128.3	89	70	139	9	2.88	4.76	8.0	6.2	5.9	1.2	5.13	10.8	14
2003	NRW	EAS	21	24	24	135.0	122	67	103	11	4.00	5.43	8.4	5.3	5.6	1.3	5.16	2.4	8
2003	FRE	PCL	21	4	4	23.0	17	8	28	4	3.13	4.50	6.1	3.7	10.6	2.0	4.37	2.7	45
2004	MIN	AL	22	16	9	52.7	55	29	40	8	5.53	5.40	9.1	4.7	6.7	1.2	5.31	2.6	-2

Breakout: 2%   Improve: 54%   Collapse: 17%

Bonser's stock has plummeted just as fast as his strikeout numbers as he's risen through the system: He struck out 33% of the batters he faced in Low-A, 26% in High-A, and 18% in Double-A. He's only 22, experienced a brief resurgence in Fresno at the end of last year, and his coaches there raved about him, so he could still offer Minnesota added value in the A. J. Pierzynski trade.

JIM BROWER Bats: R Throws: R Born: 29-Dec-72 Age: 31

YEAR	TM	LG	AGE	G	GS	IP	H	BB	SO	HR	ERA	EQERA	EQH9	EQBB9	EQSO9	EQHR9	PERA	VORP	STF
2001	CIN	NL	28	46	10	129.3	119	60	94	17	3.97	4.23	8.1	3.8	5.4	1.0	4.32	19.1	-5
2001	LOU	INT	28	2	2	11.0	12	2	11	1	4.09	5.40	11.7	1.8	7.2	0.9	5.27	0.2	10
2002	CIN	NL	29	22	0	39.3	38	10	24	2	3.89	3.82	8.8	1.9	4.8	0.5	3.60	7.5	7
2002	MON	NL	29	30	0	41.0	39	22	33	5	4.83	4.95	8.6	4.3	6.3	1.1	4.78	2.9	-11
2003	SFG	NL	30	51	5	100.0	90	39	65	8	3.96	4.55	8.7	3.2	5.3	0.8	4.19	11.7	-2
2004	SFG	NL	31	37	9	73.7	73	31	50	6	4.03	4.24	8.8	3.3	5.5	0.8	4.37	10.8	-4

Breakout: 29%   Improve: 58%   Collapse: 22%

The deal that brought Brower to the Giants in exchange for Livan Hernandez has been roundly lambasted in many circles, but that's pure hindsight. No one predicted that Hernandez would have a huge year in 2003; his career seemed to be heading in the opposite direction, and fast. And it's not like the Giants got nothing in return. Brower did a solid job in middle relief last year, and his ability to start made a big difference for the Giants as they fought through mid-season injuries in the rotation. He's been offered arbitration by the Giants, so look for more of the same in '04.

MATT CAIN

Bats: R **Throws: R** Born: 01-Oct-84 Age: 19

YEAR	TM	LG	AGE	G	GS	IP	H	BB	SO	HR	ERA	EQERA	EQH9	EQBB9	EQSO9	EQHR9	PERA	VORP	STF
2003	HAG	SAL	18	14	14	74.0	57	24	90	5	2.55	4.92	10.1	4.1	7.6	1.5	5.89	4.8	34
2004	SFG	NL	19	18	15	93.3	97	37	80	8	4.59	4.84	9.2	3.1	7.0	0.8	4.65	7.7	13

Breakout: 17%   Improve: 52%   Collapse: 14%

Baseball America named Cain the number-two prospect in the Giants' system. We don't rank him that high—chalk it up to squeamishness about 18-year-old pitchers who miss half a season with an elbow injury—but we understand the enthusiasm. Before the 2002 first-round pick's year was ended prematurely by a right elbow stress fracture, he dominated the Sally League, combining a mid-90s fastball with a changeup and curve that look surprisingly polished for a teenager. He struck out 30% of the batters he faced, and walked 8%, both impressive numbers. The elbow, and injuries in general, are the concerns, as is always the case for pitchers fresh out of high school.

JASON CHRISTIANSEN

Bats: R **Throws: L** Born: 21-Sep-69 Age: 34

YEAR	TM	LG	AGE	G	GS	IP	H	BB	SO	HR	ERA	EQERA	EQH9	EQBB9	EQSO9	EQHR9	PERA	VORP	STF
2001	STL	NL	31	30	0	19.3	15	10	19	4	4.66	4.82	7.2	4.3	7.2	1.4	4.51	1.6	-13
2001	SFG	NL	31	25	0	17.0	14	5	12	1	1.59	2.20	7.7	2.2	5.5	0.6	3.23	6.2	12
2002	SFG	NL	32	6	0	5.0	6	2	1	1	5.40	5.79	11.6	3.9	1.9	1.9	7.11	-0.1	-66
2003	SFG	NL	33	40	0	26.0	25	11	22	3	5.19	5.47	9.5	3.6	6.9	1.1	4.99	0.4	-9
2004	SFG	NL	34	28	1	37.3	39	16	26	5	4.77	5.03	9.2	3.4	5.8	1.2	5.01	2.8	-9

Breakout: 24%   Improve: 52%   Collapse: 19%

Christiansen completed the long road back from Tommy John surgery on June 4 when he stepped on a major league mound for the first time in more than a year. He got lefties out, but struggled against righties, especially toward the end of the season. Pitchers who've had Tommy John are often better the second year back after the surgery. The Giants hope that's the case with Christiansen—a return to his 2001 performance level would give a big boost to their iffy bullpen.

JEFF CLARK

Bats: R **Throws: R** Born: 06-May-80 Age: 24

YEAR	TM	LG	AGE	G	GS	IP	H	BB	SO	HR	ERA	EQERA	EQH9	EQBB9	EQSO9	EQHR9	PERA	VORP	STF
2001	HAG	SAL	21	27	27	148.0	152	15	131	18	3.65	6.63	12.7	1.4	4.5	2.7	7.84	-14.8	-29
2002	SJO	CAL	22	21	21	140.0	118	18	129	10	2.06	3.98	9.7	1.4	4.8	1.2	4.60	22.8	10
2002	SHV	TEX	22	6	6	35.7	45	2	20	5	5.04	6.61	12.9	0.6	3.9	2.5	7.53	-3.7	-28
2003	SJO	CAL	23	9	9	53.3	49	11	43	4	3.04	4.22	9.4	2.6	4.6	1.5	5.09	7.5	-6
2003	NRW	EAS	23	7	7	37.3	45	5	32	4	4.58	6.23	11.9	1.6	6.0	1.8	6.41	-2.4	-8
2004	SFG	NL	24	25	16	98.7	106	25	52	12	4.20	4.42	9.5	2.0	4.3	1.1	4.48	12.9	-4

Breakout: 21%   Improve: 57%   Collapse: 3%

The 2002 California League ERA champion's season was undone by a broken foot, so he'll likely have to try Double-A again this year. He's a control artist without a dominant fastball—his best pitch is a wicked curve—so he faces an uphill battle getting people to pay attention. But with strikeout-to-walk ratios like he's displayed in his four minor league seasons, he's still got a good chance at a major league career.

KEVIN CORREIA

Bats: R **Throws: R** Born: 24-Aug-80 Age: 23

YEAR	TM	LG	AGE	G	GS	IP	H	BB	SO	HR	ERA	EQERA	EQH9	EQBB9	EQSO9	EQHR9	PERA	VORP	STF
2002	SLO	NWN	21	10	8	37.7	37	14	31	1	4.54	6.89	12.1	4.7	4.1	0.8	6.23	-4.7	-13
2003	NRW	EAS	22	16	14	86.3	80	30	73	3	3.65	4.26	8.9	3.7	5.9	0.6	4.18	12.0	25
2003	SFG	NL	22	10	7	39.3	41	18	28	6	3.66	5.02	10.0	3.8	5.7	1.4	5.69	7.7	7
2003	FRE	PCL	22	3	3	19.0	16	2	23	3	2.84	3.44	7.4	1.0	9.8	2.0	4.07	4.4	43
2004	SFG	NL	23	22	16	97.0	100	42	74	13	4.52	4.76	9.1	3.4	6.2	1.3	5.15	12.6	3

Breakout: 19%   Improve: 45%   Collapse: 24%

If we had told you last off-season that Correia, a 2002 fourth-round draft pick with all of 37.2 Northwest League innings under his belt, would be in the Giants starting rotation by August, you would have laughed. After all, the Giants had tons of pitching prospects who were both better regarded and at more advanced levels than Correia—Boof Bonser, Noah Lowry, Jeff Clark, Ryan Hannaman, Francisco Liriano, and others. That Correia was the one who ended up getting the call says as much about the tough season the suffered by Giants' pitching prospects as it does about Correia. He's to be commended for responding well to being thrown into the fire, but there's little in his record so far that screams star potential.

SCOTT EYRE

Bats: L   **Throws: L**   Born: 30-May-72   Age: 32

YEAR	TM	LG	AGE	G	GS	IP	H	BB	SO	HR	ERA	EQERA	EQH9	EQBB9	EQSO9	EQHR9	PERA	VORP	STF
2001	SYR	INT	29	62	2	79.3	67	26	96	8	3.18	3.96	9.2	3.5	8.5	1.2	4.91	13.2	-2
2001	TOR	AL	29	17	0	15.7	15	7	16	1	3.44	3.52	8.2	3.5	8.8	0.6	3.82	3.5	24
2002	TOR	AL	30	49	3	63.3	69	29	51	4	4.98	4.65	9.6	3.8	7.0	0.4	4.38	6.5	11
2002	SFG	NL	30	21	0	11.3	11	7	7	0	1.59	4.22	9.3	5.1	5.1	0.0	4.21	1.6	3
2003	SFG	NL	31	74	0	57.0	60	26	35	4	3.32	4.64	10.1	3.8	5.0	0.7	4.90	11.3	-10
2004	*SFG*	*NL*	*32*	*45*	*0*	*54.7*	*57*	*24*	*37*	*5*	*4.35*	*4.58*	*9.3*	*3.4*	*5.5*	*0.8*	*4.78*	*6.1*	*-8*

Breakout: 22%   Improve: 41%   Collapse: 25%

Eyre has turned out to be an excellent situational lefty. He's neutralized left-handed hitters (.224/.297/.302 over the past three years), and at least keeps his head above water against righties when he has to face them. We have mixed feelings about the two-year, $2.45 million contract he signed with the Giants this off-season. On one hand, relief pitchers are so notoriously flaky, injury-prone, and replaceable that it's easy for a multi-year deal to go bad—witness Jason Christiansen's three-year, $6.8 million contract. On the other hand, unlike Christiansen's deal, Eyre's is for a small enough sum that the risk is pretty low.

JESSE FOPPERT

Bats: R   **Throws: R**   Born: 10-Jul-80   Age: 23

YEAR	TM	LG	AGE	G	GS	IP	H	BB	SO	HR	ERA	EQERA	EQH9	EQBB9	EQSO9	EQHR9	PERA	VORP	STF
2001	SLO	NWN	20	14	14	70.0	35	23	88	7	1.93	3.45	7.7	4.5	6.2	2.5	6.05	14.3	-7
2002	SHV	TEX	21	11	11	61.3	44	21	74	3	2.79	3.81	7.5	3.7	8.4	0.8	3.73	11.3	47
2002	FRE	PCL	21	14	14	79.0	71	35	109	12	3.99	4.62	8.1	4.4	10.7	1.4	4.81	8.3	52
2003	FRE	PCL	22	1	1	5.0	3	0	9	0	1.80	1.93	5.8	0.0	15.4	0.0	1.27	1.9	126
2003	SFG	NL	22	23	21	111.0	103	69	101	16	5.03	5.91	9.0	5.1	7.3	1.3	5.35	-3.7	20
2004	*SFG*	*NL*	*23*	*22*	*18*	*109.7*	*109*	*58*	*100*	*17*	*5.31*	*5.60*	*8.8*	*4.2*	*7.4*	*1.5*	*5.47*	*6.0*	*7*

Breakout: 8%   Improve: 43%   Collapse: 38%

Foppert's reputation took a slow and thorough beating in 2003. He started the year as one of the top pitching prospects in baseball, only to arrive in the majors in April showing disappointing velocity. He showed flashes of brilliance during the season, but his overall numbers were not what you'd like from a top prospect. To top off his fall from grace, he tore his ulnar collateral ligament in September while recovering from a nerve problem in the same elbow, and he's expected to miss the entire 2004 season following Tommy John surgery. He'll try to regain his lost prestige in 2005.

JAMES GARCIA

Bats: R   **Throws: R**   Born: 03-Feb-80   Age: 24

YEAR	TM	LG	AGE	G	GS	IP	H	BB	SO	HR	ERA	EQERA	EQH9	EQBB9	EQSO9	EQHR9	PERA	VORP	STF
2002	SLO	NWN	22	14	0	17.3	9	6	24	2	2.08	3.86	10.3	4.5	7.1	3.9	9.02	2.7	-66
2003	SJO	CAL	23	33	3	71.3	67	35	105	4	4.17	5.29	10.9	6.1	8.9	1.1	6.28	2.2	-2
2003	FRE	PCL	23	7	4	23.7	23	12	22	3	4.18	4.76	8.3	5.2	7.5	1.6	5.41	2.1	0
2004	*SFG*	*NL*	*24*	*12*	*4*	*27.3*	*28*	*16*	*25*	*4*	*5.17*	*5.45*	*9.1*	*4.8*	*7.5*	*1.3*	*5.67*	*1.0*	*-1*

Breakout: 10%   Improve: 40%   Collapse: 23%

An unheralded non-drafted free agent out of UC Santa Barbara, Garcia has attracted our attention because of his eye-popping strikeout totals—169 in 123 professional innings. He's done it with a good high-80s sinking fastball and a couple of slow breaking pitches that make minor league hitters look foolish. The Giants have taken notice of Garcia's performance as well, skipping him straight to Triple-A with a late-season promotion. It's possible he'll make an appearance in the big leagues some time this year.

JOSH HABEL

Bats: L   **Throws: L**   Born: 10-Sep-80   Age: 23

YEAR	TM	LG	AGE	G	GS	IP	H	BB	SO	HR	ERA	EQERA	EQH9	EQBB9	EQSO9	EQHR9	PERA	VORP	STF
2002	SLO	NWN	21	16	7	48.0	57	24	33	2	6.00	9.66	14.5	6.4	3.5	1.1	7.97	-18.5	-41
2003	HAG	SAL	22	37	16	122.0	90	35	127	9	2.36	4.60	11.2	3.7	6.0	2.0	6.89	11.3	-21
2004	*SFG*	*NL*	*23*	*15*	*8*	*44.3*	*52*	*24*	*29*	*7*	*5.82*	*6.13*	*10.3*	*4.2*	*5.3*	*1.5*	*6.31*	*0.9*	*-14*

Breakout: 26%   Improve: 55%   Collapse: 20%

Like Garcia, Habel was on no one's radar screen before this year, but he changed that by finishing third in the Sally League in ERA, and putting up solid peripheral numbers as well. He's not a power pitcher, but he's got a swing-and-miss changeup and an outstanding pickoff move. Hagerstown is a long way from the majors, but Habel has a chance to be a good lefty reliever down the road.

BRAD HENNESSEY Bats: R Throws: R Born: 07-Feb-80 Age: 24

YEAR	TM	LG	AGE	G	GS	IP	H	BB	SO	HR	ERA	EQERA	EQH9	EQBB9	EQSO9	EQHR9	PERA	VORP	STF
2001	SLO	NWN	21	9	9	34.0	28	11	22	1	2.38	4.40	8.8	4.1	2.9	0.6	4.35	4.1	-4
2003	HAG	SAL	23	15	15	79.3	81	27	44	6	4.20	7.99	14.2	4.4	3.2	2.2	8.73	-17.3	-62
2004	SFG	NL	24	19	13	67.3	94	49	38	10	7.77	8.19	12.4	5.8	4.6	1.4	8.20	-7.6	-26

Breakout: 23%   Improve: 63%   Collapse: 15%

One of the feel-good stories of 2003. A Giants' first-round pick three years ago, Hennessey missed all of 2002 because of a pair of cancerous tumors discovered in his back. He made it back to the mound, cancer-free, in June of 2003. His stuff wasn't terribly sharp and his numbers were unimpressive, but that's not surprising for someone who's been away from pro ball for a year and a half. He'll continue to try to regain his first-round form this year. At 24, his clock is ticking.

MATT HERGES Bats: L Throws: R Born: 01-Apr-70 Age: 34

YEAR	TM	LG	AGE	G	GS	IP	H	BB	SO	HR	ERA	EQERA	EQH9	EQBB9	EQSO9	EQHR9	PERA	VORP	STF
2001	LAD	NL	31	75	0	99.3	97	46	76	8	3.44	4.06	9.2	3.9	5.9	0.7	4.47	16.3	0
2002	MON	NL	32	62	0	64.7	80	26	50	10	4.03	5.29	11.1	3.1	6.0	1.4	6.01	2.2	-22
2003	SDP	NL	33	40	0	44.0	40	20	40	2	2.86	3.80	8.4	3.6	7.2	0.4	3.80	10.1	16
2003	SFG	NL	33	27	0	35.0	28	9	28	1	2.31	3.24	7.8	2.2	6.5	0.3	3.00	10.3	24
2004	SFG	NL	34	49	1	62.0	63	25	47	5	4.00	4.21	8.9	3.2	6.2	0.8	4.47	9.8	-2

Breakout: 21%   Improve: 37%   Collapse: 28%

We spent the Eric Young and Sidney Ponson comments giving Brian Sabean grief for his mid-season trades, so in the interest of equal time, we'll use this space to give him kudos for the Matt Herges deal. Herges addressed a real need for the club, and while the cost—23-year-old curveball artist Clay Hensley—wasn't zero, the Giants have a successful recent history of turning pitching prospects into valuable veterans at mid-season. The Giants avoided arbitration by signing him to a two-year, $2.5 million contract this off-season. Herges, not Felix Rodriguez, is the most likely candidate to collect saves if Robb Nen should falter.

DUSTIN HERMANSON Bats: R Throws: R Born: 21-Dec-72 Age: 31

YEAR	TM	LG	AGE	G	GS	IP	H	BB	SO	HR	ERA	EQERA	EQH9	EQBB9	EQSO9	EQHR9	PERA	VORP	STF
2001	STL	NL	28	33	33	192.3	195	73	123	34	4.45	5.41	9.5	3.2	4.9	1.4	5.30	3.9	-13
2002	BOS	AL	29	12	1	22.0	35	7	13	3	7.77	7.17	14.3	2.5	5.1	1.3	7.15	-3.7	-28
2002	PAW	INT	29	5	3	13.7	9	7	11	0	2.63	3.55	6.4	5.7	6.4	0.0	3.12	2.9	17
2003	STL	NL	30	23	0	29.7	35	14	12	4	5.45	5.97	10.7	3.8	3.1	1.3	5.84	0.1	-39
2003	FRE	PCL	30	4	4	26.0	29	3	17	2	4.85	4.74	10.2	1.1	4.7	1.1	4.64	2.4	-1
2003	SFG	NL	30	9	6	39.0	35	10	27	5	3.00	3.89	8.5	2.2	5.6	1.2	4.27	9.6	1
2004	SFG	NL	31	25	14	81.3	90	30	47	10	4.78	5.04	9.8	2.9	4.7	1.2	5.18	7.3	-8

Breakout: 18%   Improve: 44%   Collapse: 29%

The Giants' July pickup of Hermanson paid surprising dividends for the club, as he gave them six good starts during a time when much of the rest of the rotation was scuffling. We're skeptical that he can keep up that level of performance over a full season, though, as his strikeout rates have fallen off a cliff. The Giants signed him to a one-year contract and plan to have him in the 2004 rotation...yikes.

RYAN JENSEN Bats: R Throws: R Born: 17-Sep-75 Age: 28

YEAR	TM	LG	AGE	G	GS	IP	H	BB	SO	HR	ERA	EQERA	EQH9	EQBB9	EQSO9	EQHR9	PERA	VORP	STF
2001	FRE	PCL	25	20	17	106.0	97	34	95	11	3.48	3.99	8.7	3.4	5.9	1.1	4.58	17.8	1
2001	SFG	NL	25	10	7	42.3	44	25	26	5	4.26	5.05	9.4	4.8	4.6	0.9	5.11	2.5	-8
2002	SFG	NL	26	32	30	171.7	183	66	105	21	4.51	5.57	10.2	3.1	4.8	1.2	5.27	0.5	-9
2003	FRE	PCL	27	27	18	103.7	114	36	50	14	5.29	5.64	10.0	3.7	3.7	1.8	6.17	-0.4	-48
2003	SFG	NL	27	6	2	13.3	21	5	3	6	10.83	11.37	14.9	2.8	2.1	4.3	11.58	-8.6	-138
2004	SFG	NL	28	17	12	71.7	79	31	41	11	5.09	5.37	9.7	3.4	4.7	1.4	5.56	3.3	-9

Breakout: 26%   Improve: 52%   Collapse: 25%

Jensen's season was such a disaster by September, it was hard to remember that he started April in the Giants' rotation. We couldn't keep track of all the reasons given for the appalling numbers: loss of velocity, bad back, bad mechanics, bad conditioning, etc. Given that his peripheral numbers weren't all that special to begin with, even in his successful 2002, it will be a struggle for him just to make it back to the big leagues.

FRANCISCO LIRIANO Bats: L Throws: L Born: 26-Oct-83 Age: 20

YEAR	TM	LG	AGE	G	GS	IP	H	BB	SO	HR	ERA	EQERA	EQH9	EQBB9	EQSO9	EQHR9	PERA	VORP	STF
2001	SLO	NWN	17	2	2	9.0	7	1	12	2	5.00	7.04	11.7	1.2	7.0	4.7	10.15	-1.2	-13
2002	HAG	SAL	18	16	16	80.0	61	31	85	6	3.49	5.25	8.2	4.8	6.2	1.5	5.18	2.8	22
2003	SJO	CAL	19	1	1	0.7	5	2	0	0	51.43	54.00	54.0	27.0	0.0	0.0	18.92	-3.8	-207

Scouts love Liriano's arm, but he can't keep it healthy. He missed the latter half of 2002 with shoulder problems, and then experienced more shoulder pain in 2003 after throwing all of two-thirds of an inning in San Jose. He made it back to the Giants' Arizona Rookie League affiliate at the end of the year, where he struck out nine and walked six in 8.1 innings. There's some upside here, but with that injury history, he's a low probability guy. Traded to the Twins as part of the Pierzynski package.

NOAH LOWRY Bats: L Throws: L Born: 10-Oct-80 Age: 23

YEAR	TM	LG	AGE	G	GS	IP	H	BB	SO	HR	ERA	EQERA	EQH9	EQBB9	EQSO9	EQHR9	PERA	VORP	STF
2001	SLO	NWN	20	8	7	25.0	26	8	28	2	3.60	7.89	12.9	4.2	5.4	2.1	7.86	-5.5	-26
2002	SJO	CAL	21	15	12	58.7	38	20	62	4	2.15	4.30	7.9	4.0	5.5	1.2	4.49	7.6	6
2003	NRW	EAS	22	23	23	118.3	127	47	97	7	4.72	5.50	10.3	4.3	5.8	1.0	5.45	1.2	8
2003	FRE	PCL	22	4	4	19.0	15	6	13	0	2.37	2.45	6.4	3.4	5.4	0.0	2.51	6.4	40
2003	SFG	NL	22	4	0	6.3	1	2	5	0	0.00	1.50	1.5	3.0	6.0	0.0	0.61	4.0	46
2004	*SFG*	*NL*	*23*	*16*	*11*	*65.0*	*67*	*31*	*48*	*8*	*4.75*	*5.00*	*9.1*	*3.8*	*6.0*	*1.1*	*5.09*	*5.6*	*0*

Breakout: 23%   Improve: 49%   Collapse: 23%

A first-round pick in 2001 (do the Giants *ever* spend high picks on hitters?), Lowry moved quickly last year, even pitching a handful of scoreless September innings in San Francisco. His strength is his changeup; he uses his high-80s fastball mainly as a tool to set the hitter up for the change. His curve is erratic and needs work if he wants to be a big league starter. In the meantime, he's got the makings of a quality situational lefty.

JOE NATHAN Bats: R Throws: R Born: 22-Nov-74 Age: 29

YEAR	TM	LG	AGE	G	GS	IP	H	BB	SO	HR	ERA	EQERA	EQH9	EQBB9	EQSO9	EQHR9	PERA	VORP	STF
2001	SHV	TEX	26	21	7	62.3	73	37	33	11	6.93	8.61	13.4	6.8	3.5	3.0	9.91	-18.2	-118
2001	FRE	PCL	26	10	10	46.3	63	33	21	13	7.78	9.49	12.9	7.6	3.0	3.0	9.82	-18.5	-113
2002	FRE	PCL	27	31	25	146.3	167	74	117	20	5.60	6.45	11.3	5.3	5.5	1.6	6.85	-12.8	-39
2003	SFG	NL	28	78	0	79.0	51	33	83	7	2.96	3.23	6.5	3.5	8.5	0.8	3.26	21.9	19
2004	*MIN*	*AL*	*29*	*40*	*5*	*61.3*	*63*	*32*	*48*	*10*	*5.27*	*5.14*	*8.8*	*4.4*	*7.0*	*1.3*	*5.22*	*5.8*	*-5*

Breakout: 27%   Improve: 56%   Collapse: 16%

Nathan's numbers made a huge leap forward in 2003. He put up strikeout and hit rates that were totally out of line with anything he had ever done before, in the majors or minors. His stuff is impressive, with a mid-90s fastball and a sharp breaking slider. Still, we're skeptical that he'll continue to outperform his previous record by such a wide margin— PECOTA sees a nearly two-run increase in his ERA. Gone to Minnesota in the Pierzynski deal; this was a good time to trade him.

ROBB NEN Bats: R Throws: R Born: 28-Nov-69 Age: 34

YEAR	TM	LG	AGE	G	GS	IP	H	BB	SO	HR	ERA	EQERA	EQH9	EQBB9	EQSO9	EQHR9	PERA	VORP	STF
2001	SFG	NL	31	79	0	77.7	58	22	93	6	3.01	3.15	7.1	2.4	9.2	0.6	3.04	20.2	32
2002	SFG	NL	32	68	0	73.7	64	20	81	2	2.20	3.09	8.5	2.2	8.7	0.3	3.25	19.5	38
2004	*SFG*	*NL*	*34*	*43*	*0*	*55.3*	*46*	*18*	*57*	*4*	*3.13*	*3.30*	*7.4*	*2.5*	*8.3*	*0.8*	*3.20*	*14.0*	*16*

Breakout: 20%   Improve: 40%   Collapse: 30%

Nen is coming off a trio of shoulder surgeries that nixed his entire 2003 season. The Giants say he's on track to pitch in spring training, but don't expect the old Robb Nen this year.

SIDNEY PONSON   Bats: R   Throws: R   Born: 02-Nov-76   Age: 27

YEAR	TM	LG	AGE	G	GS	IP	H	BB	SO	HR	ERA	EQERA	EQH9	EQBB9	EQSO9	EQHR9	PERA	VORP	STF
2001	BAL	AL	24	23	23	138.3	161	37	84	21	4.95	5.17	10.3	2.2	5.1	1.3	5.19	6.4	5
2002	BAL	AL	25	28	28	176.0	172	63	120	26	4.09	4.60	8.8	3.0	5.9	1.3	4.71	18.9	6
2003	BAL	AL	26	21	21	148.0	147	43	100	10	3.77	3.78	8.4	2.5	5.9	0.6	3.60	29.6	25
2003	SFG	NL	26	10	10	68.0	64	18	34	6	3.71	4.34	9.0	2.2	4.1	0.8	4.12	11.8	4
2004	BAL	AL	27	29	29	184.0	198	55	113	22	4.31	4.49	9.6	2.6	5.3	0.9	4.58	24.8	7

Breakout: 15%   Improve: 50%   Collapse: 12%

We never thought we'd be writing this, but Brian Sabean was really taken to the cleaners by the Orioles—yes, the Orioles—on this one. Baltimore co-GMs Jim Beattie and Mike Flanagan made the ultimate "buy low, sell high" trade, shipping Ponson off in the middle of a career year and getting back two promising young pitchers—Kurt Ainsworth and Ryan Hannaman—while they were on the DL, as well as Damian Moss. What's more, the Giants really didn't have much use for Ponson. They had already sewn up the division for all intents and purposes when they got him, so he was being brought in for, at best, a handful of postseason starts. The difference between Dustin Hermanson and Sidney Ponson in an October start or two is not worth several years of Ainsworth and Hannaman, even with the Giants' window rapidly closing. As it turned out, it was worth nothing at all. Now he's back in Baltimore, and the Giants didn't even get picks for him, having failed to offer him arbitration. Ouch. Just ouch.

FELIX RODRIGUEZ   Bats: R   Throws: R   Born: 09-Sep-72   Age: 31

YEAR	TM	LG	AGE	G	GS	IP	H	BB	SO	HR	ERA	EQERA	EQH9	EQBB9	EQSO9	EQHR9	PERA	VORP	STF
2001	SFG	NL	28	80	0	80.3	53	27	91	5	1.68	2.22	6.3	2.8	8.6	0.5	2.67	28.9	35
2002	SFG	NL	29	71	0	69.0	53	29	58	5	4.17	4.23	7.5	3.4	6.7	0.7	3.59	10.0	7
2003	SFG	NL	30	68	0	61.0	59	29	46	5	3.10	4.17	9.3	3.9	6.2	0.8	4.62	15.9	-2
2004	SFG	NL	31	52	0	54.0	52	23	42	6	4.12	4.35	8.5	3.3	6.3	1.1	4.59	7.8	-4

Breakout: 21%   Improve: 49%   Collapse: 31%

Giants fans have slowly come to accept that the Felix Rodriguez of 2000–01 isn't likely to reappear on the mound ever again. Today's Felix Rodriguez shows less velocity and less command than the Future Closer of three or four years ago. It's most noticeable in his inability to put batters away. From 2001 to 2003, the percentage of batters Rodriguez put in a 1–2 count fell moderately, from 38% to 30%. But the percentage of those 1–2 counts that Rodriguez was able to finish off with a strikeout fell much more dramatically, from 48% to 30%. You see similar results with the other two-strike counts. He's just a shadow of his former self.

KIRK RUETER   Bats: L   Throws: L   Born: 01-Dec-70   Age: 33

YEAR	TM	LG	AGE	G	GS	IP	H	BB	SO	HR	ERA	EQERA	EQH9	EQBB9	EQSO9	EQHR9	PERA	VORP	STF
2001	SFG	NL	30	34	34	195.3	213	66	83	25	4.42	5.04	9.8	2.8	3.2	1.1	4.93	11.7	-12
2002	SFG	NL	31	33	33	203.7	204	54	76	22	3.23	4.49	9.5	2.2	3.0	1.0	4.56	23.7	-8
2003	SFG	NL	32	27	27	147.0	170	47	41	14	4.53	5.44	10.9	2.7	2.3	0.9	5.28	10.4	-18
2004	SFG	NL	33	23	20	118.0	141	37	38	15	4.96	5.23	10.6	2.5	2.6	1.2	5.41	5.8	-15

Breakout: 14%   Improve: 56%   Collapse: 19%

Last season, Rueter struck out 41 batters in 147 innings, for a strikeout rate of 2.51 per nine innings. The last time anyone had a strikeout rate so low in 120 or more innings was 1989, when Mike Flanagan struck out 2.46 per nine in 171.2 frames. It's tempting to think that a miniscule and falling strikeout rate doesn't mean that much to a pure junkballer like Rueter, who's never relied much on strikeouts anyway. On the other hand, it did signal the beginning of the end for Flanagan, as he only pitched 153.1 more innings after that.

JASON SCHMIDT   Bats: R   Throws: R   Born: 29-Jan-73   Age: 31

YEAR	TM	LG	AGE	G	GS	IP	H	BB	SO	HR	ERA	EQERA	EQH9	EQBB9	EQSO9	EQHR9	PERA	VORP	STF
2001	PIT	NL	28	14	14	84.0	81	28	77	11	4.61	4.22	8.8	2.8	7.0	1.0	4.31	12.4	17
2001	SFG	NL	28	11	11	66.3	57	33	65	2	3.39	3.82	8.2	4.1	7.5	0.3	3.70	12.6	35
2002	SFG	NL	29	29	29	185.3	148	73	196	15	3.45	4.07	7.9	3.2	8.4	0.8	3.74	30.1	32
2003	SFG	NL	30	29	29	207.7	152	46	208	14	2.34	2.88	7.2	1.8	8.2	0.6	2.94	70.7	43
2004	SFG	NL	31	28	28	190.0	166	56	180	18	3.41	3.59	7.8	2.3	7.7	0.9	3.44	43.3	26

Breakout: 11%   Improve: 48%   Collapse: 17%

Last year we wrote about Schmidt: "If he can keep his right arm from falling off—always the big 'if' with Schmidt—and can tone down the 'Hit this!' machismo a bit away from SF, he could step up to become one of the NL's premiere pitchers this year." Schmidt held up his part of that prediction, cutting his road ERA from 5.02 to 2.44, while keeping his home ERA steady. He also kept intact the chicken wire and duct tape that holds his right arm together, but just barely; Schmidt underwent surgery immediately after the season to repair a torn tendon in his elbow. The Giants expect him to be ready to pitch Opening Day, but the injury still adds a big dose of uncertainty to an already uncertain rotation.

MERKIN VALDEZ   Bats: R   Throws: R   Born: 05-Nov-81   Age: 22

YEAR	TM	LG	AGE	G	GS	IP	H	BB	SO	HR	ERA	EQERA	EQH9	EQBB9	EQSO9	EQHR9	PERA	VORP	STF
2003	HAG	SAL	21	26	26	156.0	119	49	166	11	2.25	4.52	11.0	4.0	6.2	1.9	6.67	15.8	0
2004	SFG	NL	22	17	11	66.3	71	30	51	10	5.28	5.56	9.5	3.6	6.3	1.4	5.42	1.5	-1

Breakout: 5%   Improve: 45%   Collapse: 25%

Acquired from Atlanta in the Russ Ortiz trade, El Mago (The Magician) exploded on the prospect scene in Low-A Hagerstown, finishing the season as the top pitching prospect in the Sally League, and one of the better pitching prospects anywhere. He's got a devastating mid-90s sinking fastball, but his slider and (especially) changeup need work before they're major league ready. Because of the lack of a credible third pitch, there's talk about converting him to relief at some point.

JEROME WILLIAMS   Bats: R   Throws: R   Born: 04-Dec-81   Age: 22

YEAR	TM	LG	AGE	G	GS	IP	H	BB	SO	HR	ERA	EQERA	EQH9	EQBB9	EQSO9	EQHR9	PERA	VORP	STF
2001	SHV	TEX	19	23	23	130.0	116	34	84	14	3.95	5.40	8.1	2.8	4.6	1.3	4.37	2.7	17
2002	FRE	PCL	20	28	28	160.7	140	50	130	16	3.58	4.27	7.1	3.1	6.2	0.9	3.50	23.1	37
2003	FRE	PCL	21	10	10	57.0	52	16	40	3	2.68	3.20	6.7	2.9	5.9	0.5	2.91	15.0	41
2003	SFG	NL	21	21	21	131.0	116	49	88	10	3.30	4.19	8.5	3.1	5.5	0.7	4.03	24.8	33
2004	SFG	NL	22	24	21	133.0	130	52	92	14	4.14	4.37	8.7	3.1	5.6	1.0	4.38	18.6	7

Breakout: 10%   Improve: 38%   Collapse: 33%

In most other years, Williams would have been a strong Rookie of the Year candidate, but last year he was overshadowed by the outstanding campaigns of fellow rookie starters Brandon Webb (the winner of BP's Internet Baseball Awards) and Dontrelle Willis (the BBWAA winner). He doesn't have overpowering stuff—Williams lived in the high 80s most of the year—but he's got a broad repertoire and he'll throw any of his pitches on any count. His peripheral numbers didn't really support a 3.30 ERA last year, so he'll likely consolidate his gains a bit in '04, on the way to a long and successful career.

TIM WORRELL   Bats: R   Throws: R   Born: 05-Jul-67   Age: 36

YEAR	TM	LG	AGE	G	GS	IP	H	BB	SO	HR	ERA	EQERA	EQH9	EQBB9	EQSO9	EQHR9	PERA	VORP	STF
2001	SFG	NL	34	73	0	78.3	71	33	63	4	3.45	3.82	8.4	3.5	6.1	0.5	3.81	14.9	8
2002	SFG	NL	35	80	0	72.0	55	30	55	3	2.25	3.28	7.5	3.3	6.0	0.4	3.28	17.7	13
2003	SFG	NL	36	76	0	78.3	74	28	65	5	2.87	4.46	9.2	2.9	6.8	0.6	4.12	11.9	8
2004	PHI	NL	36	53	0	60.7	59	24	46	6	3.75	3.94	8.7	3.1	6.2	0.8	4.25	11.6	-2

Breakout: 42%   Improve: 62%   Collapse: 21%

The talk after Worrell's off-season signing of a two-year, $5.5 million deal with the Phillies is that he's returning to the role for which he's ideally suited: setup man. Actually, he was pretty well suited to be a closer. The one thing that has characterized Worrell's recent career is his inability to strand inherited runners—he's the majors' worst reliever at handling inherited runners over the past six seasons, according to Michael Wolverton's Inherited Runs Prevented stat. As a closer last year, Worrell's burden on that front was lessened substantially; he inherited only .37 runners per appearance, easily the lowest total among the Giants' full-time relievers, and about half as many as setup man Joe Nathan. As he gets back to seeing more runners on base when he comes in, it will be interesting to keep an eye on his strand rate.

CHAD ZERBE   Bats: L   Throws: L   Born: 27-Apr-72   Age: 32

YEAR	TM	LG	AGE	G	GS	IP	H	BB	SO	HR	ERA	EQERA	EQH9	EQBB9	EQSO9	EQHR9	PERA	VORP	STF
2001	FRE	PCL	29	17	0	25.3	28	9	17	2	3.56	4.94	10.3	3.8	4.2	0.8	5.09	1.7	-22
2001	SFG	NL	29	27	1	39.0	41	10	22	3	3.92	4.58	9.6	2.2	4.3	0.7	4.30	4.2	-6
2002	SFG	NL	30	50	0	56.3	52	21	26	3	3.04	4.19	8.7	3.0	3.7	0.5	3.91	8.4	-6
2002	FRE	PCL	30	3	3	10.3	8	3	5	0	0.00	0.00	7.4	2.8	3.7	0.0	2.81	6.0	25
2003	SFG	NL	31	33	1	49.7	60	14	17	3	4.71	5.36	11.5	2.3	2.9	0.6	5.06	3.5	-17
2003	FRE	PCL	31	7	0	10.3	11	1	7	3	2.62	5.59	10.2	0.9	5.6	3.7	7.92	0.0	-85
2004	SFG	NL	32	36	4	54.0	61	18	24	5	4.47	4.71	10.0	2.7	3.7	0.9	4.86	5.1	-16

Breakout: 24%   Improve: 52%   Collapse: 17%

Zerbe seems to be conducting a bizarre experiment to see how few batters a pitcher can strike out while holding onto a major league job. His major league K/9 numbers for the past four years: 7.5, 5.1, 4.2, 3.1. He won't hold on to a major league job for much longer if he continues to struggle against lefties to boot. From 2001–03, right-handed batters hit .249/.303/.386 against him, but lefties hit a robust .325/.369/.453.

Anaheim Angels

On May 23, 2003, the Anaheim Angels were officially sold to Arte Moreno, ending Disney's eight-year dalliance with the national pastime. As little as the Mouse seemed to enjoy baseball, it did preside over a successful ballpark renovation, the development of a number of good players, and the franchise's only championship in 44 seasons. Despite some missteps—the cheerleaders/dance squad that left everyone over the age of 19 feeling vaguely unclean, the periwinkle-accented uniforms, Mo Vaughn—the world leader in family entertainment will always have a place in the hearts of Southern California baseball fans.

Moreno, who traces his heritage to Mexico and who made his money in billboards, becomes the first minority owner of a Major League Baseball franchise, and one of just two minority owners in North American professional sports. Increasing minority presence in the game's front offices and boardrooms has been a goal of commissioner Bud Selig, and while *Baseball Prospectus* has taken issue with any number of Selig's policies and practices over the years, his emphasis on this point, and the progress the game has made in this area, is his greatest contribution to the industry.

Unfortunately for Moreno, he took over the Angels in the midst of its post-title honeymoon. By June, fans had seen the team without its makeup on, the lace had been replaced by flannel, and the champagne had run out, replaced by Pabst. While ticket sales surpassed the three-million mark for the first time ever, the crowds at Edison Field (now Angels Stadium, after energy company Edison International opted out of its naming-rights deal) dwindled to 2001 levels. Moreno tried to stem the tide with such populist moves as lowering concession prices and eliminating variable ticket pricing, efforts that won him goodwill and good press without changing the ease of seat-hopping in September. The Angels became the first World Series champion since the 1998 Marlins to finish the next year under .500.

The 2004 season will bring more of the same, as the Angels may have already seen their window for success in a tough division close. The team is older than you think, with all their best players save Troy Glaus exiting their primes. While they have three of the game's top 20 prospects coming through the farm system, there is little help immediately available. Meanwhile, they have major salary commitments to non-contributors and disappointments

ANGELS PROSPECTUS

2003 record: 77–85; Third place, AL West

Pythagenport record: 80–82

Runs scored per game: 4.5 (11th in AL)

Runs allowed per game: 4.6 (5th in AL)

Team EqA: .255 (8th in AL)

2003 Batters Age: 29.7 (5th oldest in AL)

2003 Pitchers Age: 29.1 (6th oldest in AL)

Ballpark: Edison International Field; Slight pitcher's park; Park Factor of 0.987

2003: The defending champions' magic feather ran out of power as almost all of their position players regressed.

2004: New owner Arte Moreno's high-risk, high-reward free agent signings could have the Angels back in the thick of it.

such as Kevin Appier and Darin Erstad, and face difficult negotiations after '04 with Glaus and Garret Anderson.

The next choir of Angels is on the way, however. There's no organization in the game with three hitters the caliber of catcher Jeff Mathis, third baseman Dallas McPherson and first baseman Casey Kotchman, all of whom have shown tremendous offensive potential as high as Double-A. Ervin Santana is a young pitching prospect who made our Top 50 list, as did the newly-dedicated Bobby Jenks, and 2003 #1 pick Brandon Wood could come quickly in an organization that lacks middle infielders. That's a core of talent that rivals any team's, and sets up the Angels to be a threat throughout the last half of this decade.

To bridge the gap between the championship season and the youth of '06, Moreno appears to be trying something new: appealing to the burgeoning Latino community that surrounds his ballpark.

The city of Anaheim sits in the middle of Orange County. Those two words call to mind oceans of white people sitting slightly to the right of Ghengis Khan, sunning themselves poolside while listening to the sweet sounds of Rush Limbaugh and nibbling on finger sandwiches. Their children you may be familiar with, if you've seen Fox's documentary series, "The O.C."

In truth, however, Angels Stadium abuts a thriving Latino community. The cities of Santa Ana and Anaheim include tens of thousands of immigrants and first-generation Americans, many from Mexico and other Latin American countries in which baseball is more than diversion, more than pastime. The Angels have never been able to reach this audience, and to be honest, have never devoted considerable time to doing so. Even Moreno, making the rounds after buying the team, was circumspect about what he would do to bring more Latino fans to the ballpark. He was understandably reluctant to be pigeonholed as a "Latino owner," and careful to not appear to be pandering to any audience other than baseball fans.

His actions this off-season, however, appear to be directly geared towards giving the large Hispanic audience players of similar heritage to cheer. The Angels made four free-agent signings, committing $145.5 million to Bartolo Colon, Kelvim Escobar, Jose Guillen, and most significantly, Vlad Guerrero. The moves had a baseball component, to be sure, but in the first three cases, Moreno appeared to overpay:

- In November, Colon had rejected a three-year, $36-million offer from the White Sox, a decision that caused fans with long memories to wonder if he was being advised by Jody Reed. The four-year, $51-million contract he eventually signed was one of just two four-year deals signed by free-agent pitchers this winter. The $51 million represents the most money committed to any pitcher since the winter of 2000–01. All this for a pitcher with a career ERA of 3.86 and just one season with an ERA below 2003's 3.87. By comparison, Javier Vazquez signed a four-year deal for $45 million with the Yankees; admittedly that contract covers his last pre-free agency season, but Vazquez has been a better pitcher than Colon in two of the past three seasons, is younger, and has much stronger peripherals.

- The Escobar signing looks even stranger. Despite finishing the year as the Blue Jays' #2 starter, he wound up with a 4.29 ERA, not far from his career mark of 4.58. He's never reached 200 innings in a season, and in fact, has never held the same role through consecutive seasons. His three-year, $18.5-million deal looks high as opposed to, say, the two-year, $7-million contract Jason Johnson eventually received as a non-tender, or the same contract John Thomson got from the Braves, or the three-year, $13.5-million deal the Blue Jays, Escobar's old team, reached with Miguel Batista.

- Guillen's contract was in line with what other outfielders of his stature received. Reggie Sanders, Jose Cruz Jr. and Rondell White all got two-year deals for $6 million total, while Carl Everett and Kenny Lofton fell in the same range. Why the

Angels chose Guillen, whose career year was really only a career three months, and who has never before been an adequate player, rather than one of the others, can be partially explained by looking at the overall pattern. You can argue that Guillen's approach fits the rake-and-rake Angels, but the decision to choose him certainly seems more like the ones that brought in Colon and Escobar for more money than players of their caliber were making.

- When it looked like Moreno was done for the winter, he made the offseason's biggest surprise move by signing Vladimir Guerrero to a five-year, $70-million contract. Unlike the other three contracts, Guerrero's deal is a bargain, his price held down by overwrought concerns about his back. Signing him adds to the Angels' cadre of Spanish-speaking stars, but more importantly, improves the team on the field more than the other three players combined, enough to vault the Angels ahead of the Mariners and close to the A's in the always-tough AL West.

This certainly changes the look of the team. The last few seasons, the Angels' most significant Latino presence was the battery of Ramon Ortiz and Bengie Molina, although Francisco Rodriguez certainly provided some great moments. Vlad Guerrero or Bartolo Colon should become the most accomplished Latin players in franchise history (Jose Cardenal? Sandy Alomar? OK, Luis Tiant and Fernando Valenzuela were both Angels for a few minutes) the day they put on the uniform.

Is this approach pandering? There's an argument for it, although few of Moreno's moves in his first season as Angels' owner indicated a desire to change the world. The evidence that teams with stars of a particular ethnicity attract more fans of that ethnicity is flimsy, although this is a hard thing to track from the outside. Having Spanish-speaking stars may help the Angels reach out to their potential fan base; they can use Guerrero, Colon, Escobar, and Guillen in radio and Spanish-language radio and television ads, as well as in the occasional ballpark between-innings fodder. If they can get these players into the community, and build an affinity for the team through a connection with those players, all the better.

If you view the signings as merely baseball signings, it's easy to pan them. The Angels committed a lot of money to pitchers who come to Southern California with holes in their performance record and questions about their value going forward. If you view the signings as an appeal for short-term interest from Latino fans, it's easy to see them as a gimmick doomed to fail, something worthy of the previous regime.

But if you look at the moves as the first steps in a long-term strategy to connect Orange County's team with Orange County's growing Latin contingent, then the deals make some sense. If just a small number of new fans come to see Colon pitch or Guerrero hit because they want to root for a Spanish-speaking player, they may discover that not only did they enjoy the experience—the revamped Angels Stadium is a nice place to watch a game—but that they'll come back for more than just those players. Live baseball can be an addictive thing; the game is so much

better in person than on television that just getting a fan to the ballpark for the first time is the biggest step.

Maybe Moreno doesn't want to be a Latino owner. Maybe he simply wants to win and make money at the same time. If so, he'll quickly become more than just the answer to a trivia question. He'll stand alongside the world's biggest entertainment company in the eyes of Angels' fans, and be an example of the kind of ownership baseball needs in the 21st century.

HITTERS

JARED ABRUZZO — C — Bats: B — Throws: R — Born: 15-Nov-81 — Age: 22

YEAR	TM	LG	AGE	AB	H	2B	3B	HR	BB	SO	SB	CS	AVG	OBP	SLG	MLVR	EQBA	EQOBP	EQSLG	EQMLVR	VORP	DEFENSE		
2001	CDR	MID	19	323	78	20	0	10	44	104	1	1	.241	.340	.396	.036	.180	.253	.302	-.416	-25.9	65-C -12		
2001	RCU	CAL	19	101	21	1	0	2	9	30	1	0	.208	.270	.277	-.294	.165	.211	.223	-.617	-13.8	21-C -7		
2002	RCU	CAL	20	385	94	27	0	16	30	124	1	1	.244	.300	.439	-.005	.197	.241	.356	-.357	-21.2	56-C -19		
2003	CDR	MID	21	468	127	30	1	13	59	99	1	0	.271	.352	.423	.151	.207	.272	.341	-.311	-20.9	88-C -14		
2004	ANA	AL	22	259	52	12	1	7	21	67	1	1	.199	.262	.327	-.300	.206	.272	.351	-.280	-9.2	70-C -16		

Breakout: 38%   Improve: 61%   Collapse: 19%

The Angels' #2 pick in the 2000 draft, Abruzzo was lapped by Jeff Mathis this year, which forced him back to the Midwest League. He handled it well, showing improved plate discipline and making the league's All-Star team. A high-school draftee, he's young enough to come through the system and eventually have a career as a backup, a role that will almost certainly come in a different organization.

ALFREDO AMEZAGA — SS — Bats: B — Throws: R — Born: 16-Jan-78 — Age: 26

YEAR	TM	LG	AGE	AB	H	2B	3B	HR	BB	SO	SB	CS	AVG	OBP	SLG	MLVR	EQBA	EQOBP	EQSLG	EQMLVR	VORP	DEFENSE		
2001	ARK	TEX	23	285	89	10	5	4	22	55	24	15	.312	.370	.425	.120	.259	.307	.360	-.183	1.8	69-SS 1		
2001	SLC	PCL	23	200	50	5	4	1	14	45	9	6	.250	.307	.330	-.265	.208	.264	.274	-.419	-12.4	49-SS -3		
2002	SLC	PCL	24	518	130	25	7	6	45	100	23	14	.251	.317	.361	-.161	.212	.275	.309	-.346	-21.6	126-SS 1		
2003	SLC	PCL	25	317	110	20	5	3	20	39	14	8	.347	.391	.470	.205	.299	.345	.415	-.002	18.2	64-SS 11	10-2B 2
2003	ANA	AL	25	105	22	3	2	2	9	23	2	2	.210	.278	.333	-.259	.229	.300	.362	-.214	-2.6	21-SS 0	13-3B -1
2004	ANA	AL	26	255	61	11	3	3	18	43	7	3	.238	.295	.343	-.200	.247	.306	.368	-.171	4.5	69-SS 1		

Breakout: 31%   Improve: 47%   Collapse: 31%

This is what a prospect looked like in the Angels' system as recently as a year ago. Now, with the three top guys coming along, plus a first-round pick in Brandon Wood who looks like he can play and even a hard thrower like Ervin Santana, Amezaga looks more like what he is: a utility infielder-to-be. Amezaga enters camp battling with David Eckstein for the shortstop job. He's not an asset outside of the marketing department.

GARRET ANDERSON — LF — Bats: L — Throws: L — Born: 30-Jun-72 — Age: 32

YEAR	TM	LG	AGE	AB	H	2B	3B	HR	BB	SO	SB	CS	AVG	OBP	SLG	MLVR	EQBA	EQOBP	EQSLG	EQMLVR	VORP	DEFENSE		
2001	ANA	AL	29	672	194	39	2	28	27	100	13	6	.289	.314	.478	.061	.308	.338	.513	.138	32.6	139-LF 0	11-CF 1
2002	ANA	AL	30	638	195	56	3	29	30	80	6	4	.306	.332	.539	.206	.326	.358	.579	.289	54.6	132-LF -4	11-CF 2
2003	ANA	AL	31	638	201	49	4	29	31	83	6	3	.315	.345	.541	.235	.333	.367	.578	.310	45.1	140-LF 16		
2004	ANA	AL	32	552	158	35	2	22	30	75	6	3	.286	.321	.477	.056	.297	.334	.513	.111	26.2	138-LF 3		

Breakout: 2%   Improve: 19%   Collapse: 36%

Anderson is one of those anomalies who makes being an analyst frustrating and makes being a fan exhilarating. Always a free swinger, Anderson has had his two best seasons in 2002 and 2003 while seeing the fewest pitches per plate appearance of his career. The undisciplined hitter became less disciplined and got better. Go figure. He's down to about 20 unintentional walks a year, or less than one a week, which works for him but does serve to keep his OBP a bit low and his MVP cases weak. He'll be an interesting free agent after the season.

ERIC AYBAR SS Bats: B Throws: R Born: 14-Jan-84 Age: 20

YEAR	TM	LG	AGE	AB	H	2B	3B	HR	BB	SO	SB	CS	AVG	OBP	SLG	MLVR	EQBA	EQOBP	EQSLG	EQMLVR	VORP	DEFENSE	
2002	PRO	PIO	18	273	89	15	6	4	21	43	15	10	.326	.395	.469	.240	.226	.267	.333	-.320	-17.0	63-SS	8
2003	CDR	MID	19	496	153	30	10	6	17	54	32	9	.308	.346	.446	.203	.258	.285	.397	-.172	4.5	120-SS	-11
2004	ANA	AL	20	325	77	17	3	4	14	47	10	4	.238	.277	.350	-.224	.246	.288	.375	-.195	3.0	84-SS	-6

Breakout: 25% Improve: 47% Collapse: 32%

Aybar is a flashy young shortstop who impressed observers with his tools, including an excellent arm. Paired with second baseman Alberto Callaspo through two levels, he would do well to pick up his double-play partner's plate discipline. With just 38 walks over two seasons (792 at-bats), Aybar will have to keep hitting .300 with some power to progress. In the long term, he's likely to get stuck behind 2003 #1 Brandon Wood, and end up as a utility infielder.

ALBERTO CALLASPO 2B Bats: B Throws: R Born: 19-Apr-83 Age: 21

YEAR	TM	LG	AGE	AB	H	2B	3B	HR	BB	SO	SB	CS	AVG	OBP	SLG	MLVR	EQBA	EQOBP	EQSLG	EQMLVR	VORP	DEFENSE	
2002	PRO	PIO	19	299	101	16	10	3	17	14	13	4	.338	.374	.488	.250	.237	.261	.353	-.297	-18.9	68-2B	6
2003	CDR	MID	20	514	168	38	4	2	42	28	20	6	.327	.377	.428	.234	.259	.302	.353	-.202	-4.4	120-2B	-9
2004	ANA	AL	21	319	77	16	2	3	17	27	6	2	.242	.284	.331	-.233	.251	.295	.356	-.205	-1.2	83-2B	-6

Breakout: 26% Improve: 46% Collapse: 23%

Slap-hitting second baseman who led the Midwest League in batting average and doubles. The biggest mark against Callaspo is that he's already a second baseman at age 21, with mixed evaluations of his range at the position but consensus on his double-play ability. He's going to have to keep hitting, and maybe turn some of those doubles into homers, to make progress. Callaspo has been handcuffed to Aybar so far, but that might not last as Brandon Wood and Sean Rodriguez began to move up.

JEFF DaVANON OF Bats: B Throws: R Born: 08-Dec-73 Age: 30

YEAR	TM	LG	AGE	AB	H	2B	3B	HR	BB	SO	SB	CS	AVG	OBP	SLG	MLVR	EQBA	EQOBP	EQSLG	EQMLVR	VORP	DEFENSE			
2001	SLC	PCL	27	256	80	19	8	10	32	57	8	3	.313	.390	.566	.260	.258	.339	.464	.021	6.7	54-RF	2	12-CF	0
2001	ANA	AL	27	88	17	2	1	5	11	29	1	3	.193	.280	.409	-.167	.205	.300	.432	-.135	-1.7	13-RF	-1		
2002	SLC	PCL	28	100	33	10	1	5	17	24	5	3	.330	.429	.600	.410	.263	.363	.485	.097	7.7	23-CF	-2		
2003	SLC	PCL	29	60	18	4	1	2	9	9	4	1	.300	.400	.500	.216	.250	.335	.433	-.035	2.1	11-CF	-4		
2003	ANA	AL	29	330	93	16	1	12	42	59	17	5	.282	.360	.445	.092	.304	.387	.488	.180	16.7	63-RF	-3	26-CF	-1
2004	ANA	AL	30	331	82	19	3	10	39	66	10	4	.247	.328	.410	-.050	.256	.341	.440	-.008	9.7	91-RF	2		

Breakout: 10% Improve: 30% Collapse: 31%

DaVanon is a useful fourth outfielder who had to play a bit too much last year. His performance did validate the decision to non-tender Orlando Palmeiro, who'd played a similar role for the Angels from 1999–2002. The power numbers he displayed in '03 were out of line, and mostly reflect three days in June in which he turned into Jim Thome in the bandbox of San Juan's Hiram Bithorn Stadium. Given his age, even projecting a Stan Javier future is optimistic.

WILSON DELGADO IF Bats: B Throws: R Born: 15-Jul-72 Age: 31

YEAR	TM	LG	AGE	AB	H	2B	3B	HR	BB	SO	SB	CS	AVG	OBP	SLG	MLVR	EQBA	EQOBP	EQSLG	EQMLVR	VORP	DEFENSE			
2001	OMA	PCL	28	255	63	11	2	4	16	43	8	3	.247	.293	.353	-.228	.220	.268	.315	-.347	-13.0	40-2B	-5	17-3B	-2
2001	KCR	AL	28	25	3	0	0	0	3	10	0	0	.120	.214	.120	-.705	.160	.250	.160	-.620	-3.3				
2002	MEM	PCL	29	365	95	19	2	7	23	54	2	5	.260	.309	.381	-.093	.243	.289	.354	-.237	-3.8	94-SS	7		
2002	STL	NL	29	20	4	2	0	2	0	6	0	0	.200	.200	.600	.010	.200	.200	.650	-.011	0.6				
2003	MEM	PCL	30	86	20	2	0	2	10	15	2	1	.233	.313	.326	-.158	.218	.292	.310	-.307	-2.8	25-SS	1		
2003	STL	NL	30	77	13	3	0	0	3	10	0	0	.169	.207	.208	-.550	.179	.218	.231	-.586	-7.2				
2003	ANA	AL	30	50	16	0	0	0	8	8	0	0	.320	.414	.320	.047	.353	.441	.353	.131	3.1				
2004	STL	NL	31	156	36	7	1	2	13	26	1	1	.229	.290	.317	-.265	.233	.292	.334	-.252	-1.6	44-SS	-5		

Breakout: 33% Improve: 51% Collapse: 34%

Delgado has now played in the major leagues in eight straight seasons, putting him on track for one of these weird Tom Prince careers in which he never actually has a major league role, never makes any memorable contribution, yet plays for 20 years. Hitting .320, no matter how empty or how few the at-bats, helps the cause. He's scatted back to whence he came.

DAVID ECKSTEIN
SS **Bats: R** **Throws: R** Born: 20-Jan-75 Age: 29

YEAR	TM	LG	AGE	AB	H	2B	3B	HR	BB	SO	SB	CS	AVG	OBP	SLG	MLVR	EQBA	EQOBP	EQSLG	EQMLVR	VORP	DEFENSE			
2001	ANA	AL	26	582	166	26	2	4	43	60	29	4	.285	.355	.357	-.036	.308	.374	.386	.017	33.3	115-SS	1	12-2B	-1
2002	ANA	AL	27	608	178	22	6	8	45	44	21	13	.293	.363	.388	.039	.322	.391	.430	.123	50.5	139-SS	6		
2003	ANA	AL	28	452	114	22	1	3	36	45	16	5	.252	.325	.325	-.156	.280	.351	.363	-.080	3.9	112-SS	11		
2004	ANA	AL	29	465	125	22	2	4	39	44	15	6	.269	.342	.353	-.086	.278	.355	.379	-.048	20.7	125-SS	1		

Breakout: 19%   Improve: 52%   Collapse: 18%

Scrappy only gets you so far. Eckstein, who was the darling of the 2002 champs, lost 40 points of batting average that he couldn't afford to lose, winding up a pretty mediocre player. His days as an everyday shortstop may be over—is there any sight sillier than Eckstein's four-step throws to first base?—but he'd help any number of teams as a utility infielder or platoon second baseman. He'll battle Amezaga for the shortstop job this spring.

DARIN ERSTAD
CF **Bats: L** **Throws: L** Born: 04-Jun-74 Age: 30

YEAR	TM	LG	AGE	AB	H	2B	3B	HR	BB	SO	SB	CS	AVG	OBP	SLG	MLVR	EQBA	EQOBP	EQSLG	EQMLVR	VORP	DEFENSE	
2001	ANA	AL	27	631	163	35	1	9	62	113	24	10	.258	.331	.360	-.095	.281	.355	.393	-.029	19.8	139-CF	11
2002	ANA	AL	28	625	177	28	4	10	27	67	23	3	.283	.313	.389	-.056	.305	.337	.419	-.005	22.0	137-CF	23
2003	ANA	AL	29	258	65	7	1	4	18	40	9	1	.252	.309	.333	-.177	.274	.331	.363	-.122	-2.4	65-CF	-1
2004	ANA	AL	30	376	98	17	3	5	27	52	9	4	.261	.315	.362	-.126	.270	.327	.389	-.090	1.5	98-CF	0

Breakout: 19%   Improve: 49%   Collapse: 17%

Erstad is now three years removed from his .355 batting average in 2000. His average, OBP and slugging since then are .268/.320/.367, and looks a lot closer to Gary Pettis in terms of value. Moving him to first base would be an unthinkably bad decision. Most of Erstad's value is in his defense, which is excellent. Whatever added benefit there would be to keeping him healthy would be a net negative, because he'd be among the worst first basemen in baseball.

Here's a question: If Erstad's leadership was such a critical part of the Angels' 2002 season, and he possesses some quality that gives him value beyond his performance record, what can you make of the fact that other than '02, Erstad's teams have ranged from average to crappy? If leadership matters, why is it only mentioned when a player has guys around him having really good seasons? Who led the '01 Angels, or the '98 version? Intangibles arguments are rife with inconsistencies. This is just one of the more obvious ones.

CHONE FIGGINS
UT **Bats: B** **Throws: R** Born: 22-Jan-78 Age: 26

YEAR	TM	LG	AGE	AB	H	2B	3B	HR	BB	SO	SB	CS	AVG	OBP	SLG	MLVR	EQBA	EQOBP	EQSLG	EQMLVR	VORP	DEFENSE			
2001	CAR	SOU	23	332	73	14	5	2	40	73	27	8	.220	.306	.310	-.174	.194	.263	.279	-.420	-27.5	77-2B	-7		
2001	ARK	TEX	23	138	37	12	2	0	14	26	7	2	.268	.329	.384	-.037	.223	.285	.324	-.299	-5.5	34-2B	-6		
2002	SLC	PCL	24	511	156	25	18	7	53	83	39	8	.305	.364	.466	.104	.261	.322	.401	-.095	12.1	117-2B	-4		
2003	SLC	PCL	25	285	89	14	15	4	29	36	16	6	.312	.379	.509	.208	.266	.330	.443	-.017	13.3	34-2B	-2	27-SS	-2
2003	ANA	AL	25	240	71	9	4	0	20	38	13	7	.296	.345	.367	-.033	.318	.373	.393	.034	6.0	37-CF	-1	11-2B	-1
2004	ANA	AL	26	362	91	17	6	4	30	58	16	5	.252	.311	.363	-.138	.261	.323	.390	-.103	9.9	96-2B	-4		

Breakout: 16%   Improve: 35%   Collapse: 29%

Figgins's slugging average is a bit inflated, because he hits a lot of triples that have more to do with his speed than his power. It doesn't distort evaluations of his value, however; that same speed means that his OBP is more valuable than that of a player with average speed, because Figgins is more likely to take extra bases on other peoples' hits. The two factors more or less cancel out for players of this type. Figgins will get plenty of playing time for the 2004 Angels, with a shot at the everyday job in center. Defensively, he's an infielder though, and why the Angels would move a great center fielder like Erstad to first base so they can put a converted shortstop in center field . . . the mind boggles.

BRAD FULLMER
DH **Bats: L** **Throws: R** Born: 17-Jan-75 Age: 29

YEAR	TM	LG	AGE	AB	H	2B	3B	HR	BB	SO	SB	CS	AVG	OBP	SLG	MLVR	EQBA	EQOBP	EQSLG	EQMLVR	VORP	DEFENSE	
2001	TOR	AL	26	522	143	31	2	18	38	88	5	2	.274	.326	.444	.011	.287	.345	.467	.062	25.1		
2002	ANA	AL	27	429	124	35	6	19	32	44	10	3	.289	.357	.531	.217	.312	.378	.577	.300	42.0	21-1B	0
2003	ANA	AL	28	206	63	9	2	9	26	31	5	4	.306	.387	.500	.234	.332	.412	.543	.328	18.7	18-1B	2
2004	TEX	AL	29	359	107	22	3	17	37	50	7	3	.297	.369	.515	.191	.289	.366	.502	.141	24.9		

Breakout: 8%   Improve: 35%   Collapse: 36%

(continued next page)

Brad Fullmer *(continued)*

For years, analysts have tried to make the point that the vast majority of baseball players are replaceable talents, or at least, replaceable once you need to pay them a certain amount of money. The concept took a long time to make headway, but over the past couple of seasons, more and more teams are grasping the idea that you don't need to spend a lot on players who aren't worth at least four or five wins above replacement level.

Fullmer is a good illustration of how baseball's new economy is working. Following his strong 2002 season for the champs, he expected to do pretty well for himself. Instead, he was non-tendered and, finding the market limited for poor defensive first basemen who didn't show a lot of sock, re-signed with the Angels for a million bucks. Off to a great start in 2003, he blew out his knee in June and missed the rest of the year. He signed a one-year deal for $1 million with the Rangers in December. The new market probably cost Fullmer between $6 million and $8 million over two years, and it's probably not done with him yet.

TROY GLAUS 3B Bats: R Throws: R Born: 03-Aug-76 Age: 27

YEAR	TM	LG	AGE	AB	H	2B	3B	HR	BB	SO	SB	CS	AVG	OBP	SLG	MLVR	EQBA	EQOBP	EQSLG	EQMLVR	VORP	DEFENSE	
2001	ANA	AL	24	588	147	38	2	41	107	158	10	3	.250	.367	.531	.184	.269	.387	.574	.262	74.5	156-3B	-6
2002	ANA	AL	25	569	142	24	1	30	88	144	10	3	.250	.352	.453	.071	.271	.375	.496	.140	50.0	147-3B	12
2003	ANA	AL	26	319	79	17	2	16	46	73	7	2	.248	.343	.464	.060	.265	.362	.505	.124	19.7	85-3B	-9
2004	*ANA*	*AL*	*27*	*442*	*111*	*23*	*2*	*25*	*67*	*105*	*7*	*3*	*.252*	*.352*	*.479*	*.079*	*.261*	*.366*	*.514*	*.131*	*39.1*	*122-3B*	*0*

Breakout: 10%   *Improve: 48%*   *Collapse: 20%*

Glaus is beginning to run into expectation issues, brought on by his early career year in 2000. Take that year out of his career, and he looks like a productive third baseman who contributes consistently on both sides of the ball. He's still just 27, and played deep into '03 with a painful torn right rotator cuff before shutting it down in July. He did not undergo surgery over the winter, however, which leaves it as a possibility that would cost him the 2004 season. If healthy for '04, he's a great bounceback candidate and a threat to pull mid-ballot MVP votes for the next five years, but he's a huge risk. Glaus might play some first base to lessen the strain on his throwing shoulder.

NICK GORNEAULT OF Bats: R Throws: R Born: 19-Apr-79 Age: 25

YEAR	TM	LG	AGE	AB	H	2B	3B	HR	BB	SO	SB	CS	AVG	OBP	SLG	MLVR	EQBA	EQOBP	EQSLG	EQMLVR	VORP	DEFENSE			
2001	PRO	PIO	22	168	53	12	4	6	11	65	5	2	.315	.373	.542	.284	.217	.251	.373	-.301	-13.6	20-CF	0	16-LF	0
2002	CDR	MID	23	346	100	17	7	10	30	106	12	5	.289	.346	.465	.202	.228	.274	.379	-.241	-19.5	50-LF	-1	46-RF	-3
2003	RCU	CAL	24	374	120	36	2	14	20	82	11	6	.321	.362	.540	.284	.251	.286	.434	-.123	-7.5	68-LF	-2	22-CF	0
2003	ARK	TEX	24	110	38	6	4	2	8	25	2	0	.345	.395	.527	.339	.291	.331	.455	.024	3.0	28-RF	3		
2004	*ANA*	*AL*	*25*	*253*	*63*	*15*	*2*	*8*	*15*	*66*	*4*	*2*	*.250*	*.296*	*.418*	*-.093*	*.259*	*.307*	*.449*	*-.053*	*4.9*	*67-LF*	*2*		

Breakout: 45%   *Improve: 61%*   *Collapse: 23%*

Gorneault is a stealth prospect (a 19th-round pick out of UMass) who doesn't have the pedigree of the big three hitters in this system but has matched them rope for rope over the past couple of seasons. His problem is plate discipline: a career 4:1 strikeout-to-walk ratio that hasn't hurt his numbers so far, but may present a problem against advanced pitching. Time isn't on his side, nor is the rest of his game. Gorneault will have to hit his way to the majors, and do it quickly.

GARY JOHNSON OF Bats: L Throws: L Born: 29-Oct-75 Age: 28

YEAR	TM	LG	AGE	AB	H	2B	3B	HR	BB	SO	SB	CS	AVG	OBP	SLG	MLVR	EQBA	EQOBP	EQSLG	EQMLVR	VORP	DEFENSE			
2001	ARK	TEX	25	466	114	24	2	11	60	93	8	7	.245	.336	.376	-.052	.201	.279	.315	-.336	-43.2	70-LF	-6	32-RF	-2
2002	SLC	PCL	26	143	38	9	3	5	15	49	1	1	.266	.341	.476	.045	.225	.298	.408	-.157	-3.9	18-RF	-1	18-LF	1
2003	SLC	PCL	27	447	114	23	7	12	61	112	4	2	.255	.346	.418	-.014	.216	.303	.362	-.216	-22.0	71-LF	4	17-RF	-1
2004	*ANA*	*AL*	*28*	*145*	*32*	*7*	*1*	*4*	*15*	*38*	*1*	*1*	*.221*	*.296*	*.370*	*-.173*	*.229*	*.308*	*.398*	*-.141*	*0.1*	*43-LF*	*-1*		

Breakout: 36%   *Improve: 52%*   *Collapse: 35%*

In a year when everything goes right, a team uses 16 position players all season and guys like Gary Johnson never see the majors. A fourth-outfielder type, Johnson got a late-season call-up as part of the Angels' not-so-perfect '03. He's not a prospect, although he could do the same job DaVanon did without anyone noticing the difference. If the Angels follow through on their ill-advised plan to move Erstad to first base, Johnson's outlook becomes much brighter.

ADAM KENNEDY   2B   Bats: L   Throws: R   Born: 10-Jan-76   Age: 28

YEAR	TM	LG	AGE	AB	H	2B	3B	HR	BB	SO	SB	CS	AVG	OBP	SLG	MLVR	EQBA	EQOBP	EQSLG	EQMLVR	VORP	DEFENSE	
2001	ANA	AL	25	478	129	25	3	6	27	71	12	7	.270	.318	.372	-.094	.292	.343	.406	-.024	18.4	123-2B	2
2002	ANA	AL	26	474	148	32	6	7	19	80	17	4	.312	.345	.449	.108	.336	.370	.484	.179	41.5	127-2B	17
2003	ANA	AL	27	449	121	17	1	13	45	73	22	9	.269	.344	.399	-.009	.292	.368	.438	.066	18.8	128-2B	15
2004	ANA	AL	28	424	116	23	3	9	33	66	13	5	.275	.335	.405	-.026	.284	.348	.435	.019	23.4	112-2B	6

Breakout: 11%   Improve: 37%   Collapse: 28%

While the shape of Kennedy's performance has been all over the place, the value has been fairly consistent. His walk rate spiked in '03, but he wasn't seeing more pitches (3.77 per PA, vs. 3.79 in '02 and 3.77 in '01), so it may have just been a blip. The Angels committed to him over the winter with a three-year, $8.85 million contract. Given that he's just 28 and has shown a number of skills at various times, that seems like a very good deal for them. Kennedy is unlikely to hurt them, and could peak around .330/.370/.490 during the contract.

CASEY KOTCHMAN   1B   Bats: L   Throws: L   Born: 22-Feb-83   Age: 21

YEAR	TM	LG	AGE	AB	H	2B	3B	HR	BB	SO	SB	CS	AVG	OBP	SLG	MLVR	EQBA	EQOBP	EQSLG	EQMLVR	VORP	DEFENSE	
2002	CDR	MID	19	288	81	30	1	5	48	37	2	1	.281	.390	.444	.226	.211	.297	.343	-.256	-16.2	72-1B	0
2003	RCU	CAL	20	206	72	12	0	8	30	16	2	0	.350	.441	.524	.405	.256	.335	.396	-.081	0.1	45-1B	0
2004	ANA	AL	21	263	62	15	1	5	26	32	1	1	.236	.309	.350	-.167	.245	.321	.376	-.136	-1.3	72-1B	-5

Breakout: 10%   Improve: 42%   Collapse: 31%

Health is a skill, and Kotchman doesn't have it. His injuries are a mix of flukes—getting hit in the mouth with a ground ball, getting hit on the hand by a pitch—and ones that might indicate fragility, like the torn hamstring he suffered last year that cost him the first half of the season, or the wrist problems that limited him to 288 at-bats the season prior. Just on ability, he's a top first-base prospect, but he needs to play a full season to justify the hype that surrounds him.

JEFF MATHIS   C   Bats: R   Throws: R   Born: 31-Mar-83   Age: 21

YEAR	TM	LG	AGE	AB	H	2B	3B	HR	BB	SO	SB	CS	AVG	OBP	SLG	MLVR	EQBA	EQOBP	EQSLG	EQMLVR	VORP	DEFENSE	
2001	PRO	PIO	18	77	23	6	3	0	11	13	1	0	.299	.387	.455	.164	.182	.255	.299	-.415	-10.5	19-C	-2
2002	CDR	MID	19	491	141	41	3	10	40	75	7	4	.287	.346	.444	.171	.230	.277	.366	-.252	-11.6	78-C	2
2003	RCU	CAL	20	378	122	28	3	11	35	74	5	3	.323	.384	.500	.260	.243	.296	.389	-.174	-0.1	81-C	-2
2003	ARK	TEX	20	95	27	11	0	2	12	16	1	2	.284	.364	.463	.148	.229	.299	.385	-.184	-0.3	23-C	0
2004	ANA	AL	21	299	66	15	1	6	21	58	2	1	.221	.277	.344	-.241	.229	.287	.370	-.215	-1.5	80-C	-8

Breakout: 17%   Improve: 38%   Collapse: 33%

In two years, one of the Molina brothers will be backing up this guy, one of the two best catching prospects in the game (along with Guillermo Quiroz) not named Joe Mauer. Mathis pounded the Midwest League at 19 and had a very good month in Double-A at 20, great age-for-league performance. He's still getting reps behind the plate—Mathis wasn't a full-time catcher until reaching the pros—but his defense is already considered an asset. That he was a shortstop in high school also may mitigate the usual concerns about the development of high-school catchers. He may be the best of the big four Angels prospects.

DALLAS McPHERSON   3B   Bats: L   Throws: R   Born: 23-Jul-80   Age: 23

YEAR	TM	LG	AGE	AB	H	2B	3B	HR	BB	SO	SB	CS	AVG	OBP	SLG	MLVR	EQBA	EQOBP	EQSLG	EQMLVR	VORP	DEFENSE	
2001	PRO	PIO	20	124	49	11	0	5	12	22	1	0	.395	.449	.605	.580	.256	.297	.405	-.140	2.7	21-3B	-5
2002	CDR	MID	21	499	138	24	3	15	78	128	30	6	.277	.381	.427	.188	.208	.288	.331	-.292	-17.9	118-3B	-10
2003	RCU	CAL	22	292	90	21	6	18	41	79	12	6	.308	.404	.606	.419	.224	.301	.444	-.103	7.2	67-3B	0
2003	ARK	TEX	22	102	32	9	1	5	19	25	4	0	.314	.426	.569	.401	.243	.348	.447	.002	6.2	18-3B	-2
2004	ANA	AL	23	258	58	14	1	8	27	69	5	2	.224	.302	.376	-.153	.232	.314	.404	-.120	5.6	71-3B	-6

Breakout: 23%   Improve: 54%   Collapse: 21%

Sorry, but that's not a third baseman's name. It's the name of the ruggedly handsome good guy on a quickly cancelled soap opera, or a weatherman in Billings, Montana. There's a chance it won't be a third baseman's name for much longer, as the presence of Glaus as well as McPherson's so-so defense may push the prospect to right field. His bat can handle a switch; McPherson has major league power and, like Mathis, kept hitting with an improved strikeout-to-walk ratio when pushed to Double-A at midseason. The bulging disks that delayed the start of McPherson's 2003 season didn't impact his play, but are worth keeping in the back of your mind as he progresses. High concept? A left-handed Tim Salmon.

BENGIE MOLINA   C   Bats: R   Throws: R   Born: 20-Jul-74   Age: 29

YEAR	TM	LG	AGE	AB	H	2B	3B	HR	BB	SO	SB	CS	AVG	OBP	SLG	MLVR	EQBA	EQOBP	EQSLG	EQMLVR	VORP	DEFENSE	
2001	ANA	AL	26	317	80	10	0	6	16	50	0	1	.252	.301	.341	-.180	.274	.323	.371	-.126	3.8	85-C	-1
2002	ANA	AL	27	428	105	18	0	5	15	34	0	0	.245	.274	.322	-.244	.269	.300	.355	-.197	-2.4	112-C	10
2003	ANA	AL	28	409	115	24	0	14	13	31	1	1	.281	.304	.443	-.009	.299	.326	.474	.051	14.7	109-C	11
2004	ANA	AL	29	329	84	16	0	7	15	33	1	1	.256	.292	.366	-.163	.265	.304	.393	-.129	4.9	85-C	2

Breakout: 13%   Improve: 39%   Collapse: 32%

Molina's defensive reputation and association with a championship team means that he's not in danger of losing his job even when he hits like he did in 2001 and 2002. A year like '03, when he found his stroke against lefties and drove some balls over the wall, is his upside. The broken left wrist he suffered while blocking the plate in September is not expected to impact his 2004 season.

JOSE MOLINA   C   Bats: R   Throws: R   Born: 03-Jun-75   Age: 29

YEAR	TM	LG	AGE	AB	H	2B	3B	HR	BB	SO	SB	CS	AVG	OBP	SLG	MLVR	EQBA	EQOBP	EQSLG	EQMLVR	VORP	DEFENSE	
2001	SLC	PCL	26	213	64	11	1	5	14	49	1	2	.300	.349	.432	-.008	.254	.301	.368	-.186	-0.8	61-C	4
2001	ANA	AL	26	45	15	4	0	2	3	9	0	0	.333	.375	.556	.316	.356	.408	.600	.434	7.1	14-C	2
2002	SLC	PCL	27	290	89	14	2	4	12	60	0	3	.307	.341	.410	-.011	.269	.302	.360	-.185	-1.0	76-C	12
2002	ANA	AL	27	70	19	3	0	0	5	15	0	2	.271	.312	.314	-.169	.296	.342	.352	-.101	1.3	24-C	2
2003	ANA	AL	28	114	21	4	0	0	1	26	0	0	.184	.210	.219	-.561	.211	.240	.246	-.506	-11.6	34-C	0
2004	ANA	AL	29	163	39	8	1	2	7	34	1	1	.237	.273	.333	-.252	.246	.284	.358	-.226	-1.7	45-C	1

Breakout: 53%   Improve: 61%   Collapse: 23%

Gauging catchers' defense is an inexact science. We can measure aspects of it, but there's enough gray area to make pure opinion a part of any analysis. So consider that a number of people think that Jose, the middle brother of the Backstopping Molinas, is a better defender than his Gold Glove-laden sibling. Although the two make a great story, the Angels would be better served by having at least one catcher who can hit right-handers and outrun the manager.

ERIC OWENS   OF   Bats: R   Throws: R   Born: 03-Feb-71   Age: 33

YEAR	TM	LG	AGE	AB	H	2B	3B	HR	BB	SO	SB	CS	AVG	OBP	SLG	MLVR	EQBA	EQOBP	EQSLG	EQMLVR	VORP	DEFENSE			
2001	FLA	NL	30	400	101	16	1	5	29	59	8	6	.253	.302	.335	-.204	.263	.312	.349	-.186	-13.3	61-RF	-6	31-CF	-1
2002	FLA	NL	31	385	104	15	5	4	31	33	26	9	.270	.324	.366	-.044	.285	.334	.389	-.071	-1.6	58-LF	0	30-RF	-3
2003	ANA	AL	32	241	65	6	0	1	10	24	11	8	.270	.300	.307	-.218	.293	.326	.331	-.165	-8.0	34-CF	-2	27-RF	-2
2004	ANA	AL	33	155	39	6	1	1	9	18	5	2	.252	.294	.332	-.209	.261	.305	.356	-.180	-3.7	44-RF	0		

Breakout: 28%   Improve: 46%   Collapse: 33%

Owens was more valuable when he could play the infield once in a while. Now, he's a fifth outfielder with a little speed and pop, a guy who can't play regularly for a week without hurting you. He killed the Angels for four months last year before picking it up a bit as they were playing out the string. A free agent as of early 2004, he'll probably make a roster on the strength of his speed and sheen of scrappiness.

ROBB QUINLAN   LF/1B   Bats: R   Throws: R   Born: 17-Mar-77   Age: 27

YEAR	TM	LG	AGE	AB	H	2B	3B	HR	BB	SO	SB	CS	AVG	OBP	SLG	MLVR	EQBA	EQOBP	EQSLG	EQMLVR	VORP	DEFENSE			
2001	ARK	TEX	24	492	145	33	7	14	53	84	0	4	.295	.366	.476	.168	.242	.306	.397	-.145	-9.8	112-1B	4		
2002	SLC	PCL	25	528	176	31	13	20	41	93	8	2	.333	.376	.555	.275	.283	.333	.475	.049	15.8	98-LF	-2		
2003	SLC	PCL	26	393	122	18	4	9	25	59	10	3	.310	.352	.445	.076	.271	.313	.395	-.113	-3.3	57-1B	3	24-LF	0
2003	ANA	AL	26	94	27	4	2	0	6	16	1	2	.287	.330	.372	-.058	.309	.356	.394	-.004	-0.1	19-1B	-1		
2004	ANA	AL	27	200	51	10	2	5	15	35	2	1	.254	.309	.393	-.100	.263	.321	.422	-.061	4.5	55-1B	-1		

Breakout: 26%   Improve: 42%   Collapse: 36%

Old for his leagues, Quinlan keeps advancing one level a year by hitting .300 with good power and some walks. His command of the strike zone hasn't kept pace with the rest of his game above Double-A, and his power hit a wall in '03, so there are reasons to be concerned. An outfielder in the minors, Quinlan played first base almost exclusively with the Angels, and will be at least a part-timer there in '04 with Scott Spiezio and Shawn Wooten gone.

TIM SALMON RF/DH Bats: R Throws: R Born: 24-Aug-68 Age: 35

YEAR	TM	LG	AGE	AB	H	2B	3B	HR	BB	SO	SB	CS	AVG	OBP	SLG	MLVR	EQBA	EQOBP	EQSLG	EQMLVR	VORP	DEFENSE	
2001	ANA	AL	32	475	108	21	1	17	96	121	9	3	.227	.365	.383	-.022	.247	.383	.418	.031	13.4	125-RF	2
2002	ANA	AL	33	483	138	37	1	22	71	102	6	3	.286	.380	.503	.213	.309	.405	.548	.298	47.9	102-RF	-4
2003	ANA	AL	34	528	145	35	4	19	77	93	3	1	.275	.374	.464	.127	.297	.397	.506	.215	31.2	66-RF	-6
2004	ANA	AL	35	407	105	21	2	15	62	80	4	2	.257	.359	.430	.034	.266	.373	.462	.081	21.9	113-RF	-5

Breakout: 14%   Improve: 36%   Collapse: 34%

Good hitter who seems like the kind of guy who isn't going to stay too much longer. Salmon has put up numbers, made some money and been atop a dogpile in October. He suffers enough minor injuries to make playing the game a painful experience. He's played his entire career in Anaheim and his wife is very involved in the community, so it doesn't seem like he'd want to go elsewhere and play for a check. He may not enjoy the '04 season much, as it appears he's slated to DH after the additions of Vlad Guerrero and Jose Guillen. While he filled that role in '03 after the team's loss of Fullmer, Salmon is on the record as preferring right field. Watch this carefully in March.

SCOTT SPIEZIO 1B/3B Bats: B Throws: R Born: 21-Sep-72 Age: 31

YEAR	TM	LG	AGE	AB	H	2B	3B	HR	BB	SO	SB	CS	AVG	OBP	SLG	MLVR	EQBA	EQOBP	EQSLG	EQMLVR	VORP	DEFENSE			
2001	ANA	AL	28	457	124	29	4	13	34	65	5	2	.271	.326	.438	.010	.290	.346	.468	.068	18.0	91-1B	11		
2002	ANA	AL	29	491	140	34	2	12	67	52	6	7	.285	.371	.436	.110	.314	.401	.481	.204	38.1	125-1B	2	13-3B	-1
2003	ANA	AL	30	521	138	36	7	16	46	66	6	3	.265	.326	.453	.033	.288	.354	.496	.120	17.8	88-1B	-1	40-3B	-2
2004	SEA	AL	31	427	120	26	3	13	39	55	5	3	.281	.344	.449	.051	.285	.352	.463	.062	20.9	113-1B	0		

Breakout: 15%   Improve: 46%   Collapse: 28%

Spiezio is valuable if he's coming off the bench, playing a few positions and not making very much money. He's an albatross as an everyday player at a position he doesn't play well, making $3 million a year. Bill Bavasi may have won the "GM who looks most like his team's popular former player" contest, but signing Spiezio to be the Mariners' third baseman in 2004 (and the successor to John Olerud after that) may make the team's fans wonder why they can't just get Bone himself to run the team.

BRANDON WOOD SS Bats: R Throws: R Born: 02-Mar-85 Age: 19

YEAR	TM	LG	AGE	AB	H	2B	3B	HR	BB	SO	SB	CS	AVG	OBP	SLG	MLVR	EQBA	EQOBP	EQSLG	EQMLVR	VORP	DEFENSE	
2003	PRO	PIO	18	162	45	13	2	5	16	48	1	1	.278	.348	.475	.112	.174	.230	.304	-.463	-22.7	33-SS	-5
2004	ANA	AL	19	233	42	13	1	4	16	75	1	1	.182	.239	.293	-.395	.188	.248	.315	-.382	-11.1	63-SS	-11

Breakout: 38%   Improve: 57%   Collapse: 24%

The Angels' #1 pick last year could come quickly in an organization that lacks talent up the middle. The lanky 18-year-old out of Scottsdale, Ariz. held his own after a promotion to the Pioneer League, showing fair power with a wood bat at Provo. The Angels also selected shortstop Sean Rodriguez in the third round, who didn't play as well and is the more likely of the two to move away from shortstop. The two might even end up as a double-play combination in a few years, providing the Angels with the high-upside middle infielders they haven't developed in decades.

SHAWN WOOTEN 1B/C Bats: R Throws: R Born: 24-Jul-72 Age: 31

YEAR	TM	LG	AGE	AB	H	2B	3B	HR	BB	SO	SB	CS	AVG	OBP	SLG	MLVR	EQBA	EQOBP	EQSLG	EQMLVR	VORP	DEFENSE			
2001	ANA	AL	28	221	69	8	1	8	5	42	2	0	.312	.332	.466	.097	.329	.353	.495	.159	18.2	19-C	-1	15-1B	1
2002	ANA	AL	29	113	33	8	0	3	6	24	2	0	.292	.331	.442	.056	.316	.354	.482	.128	7.2				
2003	ANA	AL	30	272	66	8	0	7	24	45	0	4	.243	.303	.349	-.170	.264	.330	.381	-.106	-4.7	26-1B	-1	12-C	-4
2004	PHI	NL	31	195	49	10	1	5	16	37	1	1	.250	.310	.383	-.128	.252	.310	.392	-.130	1.4	54-1B	0		

Breakout: 19%   Improve: 45%   Collapse: 33%

There are a number of guys like Wooten floating around baseball right now, hitters who have the ability to play catcher but shouldn't be back there for 1,000 innings. As recently as five years ago, most of these guys weren't being allowed to catch. Now, players like Wooten, Craig Wilson and Matt LeCroy are donning the tools of ignorance once or twice a week. Non-tendered and signed by the Phillies, Wooten should bounce back from his awful second half (.213/.277/.280) to help them in '04.

PITCHERS

STEVE ANDRADE   Bats: R   Throws: R   Born: 06-Feb-78   Age: 26

YEAR	TM	LG	AGE	G	GS	IP	H	BB	SO	HR	ERA	EQERA	EQH9	EQBB9	EQSO9	EQHR9	PERA	VORP	STF
2001	CDR	MID	23	20	0	29.0	33	8	31	3	6.52	7.92	14.4	3.6	6.1	2.5	8.94	-6.4	-61
2002	CDR	MID	24	46	0	54.3	30	16	93	1	1.16	2.56	9.5	3.7	9.9	0.6	4.42	15.4	24
2003	ARK	TEX	25	36	0	51.0	26	19	74	2	2.65	2.78	6.8	4.4	9.7	0.8	3.59	14.2	19
2004	*ANA*	*AL*	*26*	*25*	*5*	*47.0*	*41*	*20*	*49*	*4*	*3.61*	*3.85*	*7.7*	*3.7*	*9.0*	*0.8*	*3.91*	*10.0*	*16*

Breakout: 34%   Improve: 59%   Collapse: 20%

Strictly a performance listing, and quite possibly the only time he'll make the book, but Andrade has 174 strikeouts and just 38 walks in his last 108 ⅓ innings. That's pretty good for a 32nd-round pick. He was added to the 40-man roster over the winter, and is worth remembering as a guy who could be trade bait come July.

CHRIS BOOTCHECK   Bats: R   Throws: R   Born: 24-Oct-78   Age: 25

YEAR	TM	LG	AGE	G	GS	IP	H	BB	SO	HR	ERA	EQERA	EQH9	EQBB9	EQSO9	EQHR9	PERA	VORP	STF
2001	RCU	CAL	22	15	14	87.0	84	23	86	11	3.93	5.61	10.6	3.1	5.0	2.2	6.67	-0.1	-20
2001	ARK	TEX	22	6	6	36.3	39	11	22	3	5.45	6.15	10.7	3.2	3.7	1.3	5.77	-2.1	-9
2002	ARK	TEX	23	19	19	116.0	130	35	90	11	4.81	6.08	11.4	3.2	5.2	1.7	6.47	-5.7	-13
2002	SLC	PCL	23	9	9	58.0	64	16	38	5	3.88	4.50	9.3	2.7	4.5	0.8	4.39	6.8	11
2003	SLC	PCL	24	28	26	171.3	194	43	82	19	4.26	5.15	10.1	2.7	3.7	1.4	5.38	8.1	-14
2003	ANA	AL	24	4	1	10.3	16	6	7	5	9.61	10.80	13.5	5.4	6.3	3.6	10.36	-6.4	-75
2004	*ANA*	*AL*	*25*	*17*	*11*	*63.3*	*69*	*20*	*34*	*9*	*4.84*	*5.17*	*9.7*	*2.7*	*4.7*	*1.2*	*5.00*	*4.7*	*-6*

Breakout: 17%   Improve: 47%   Collapse: 24%

The Angels' #1 pick in 2000 has been a disappointment. Bootcheck hasn't had a good strikeout rate since his pro debut in the Cal League, in part because he never added the velocity he was projected to. That makes him a guy who doesn't miss enough bats to be successful. His ERA at Salt Lake is deceptive; more than 20% of the runs he allowed were unearned, so he was actually pitching at a 5.30 RA level or so. He's blocked in Anaheim, anyway, and may need to become a Rule 5 pick or a six-year free agent to get his next chance.

BRENDAN DONNELLY   Bats: R   Throws: R   Born: 04-Jul-71   Age: 32

YEAR	TM	LG	AGE	G	GS	IP	H	BB	SO	HR	ERA	EQERA	EQH9	EQBB9	EQSO9	EQHR9	PERA	VORP	STF
2001	ARK	TEX	30	27	0	29.0	21	13	37	2	2.48	3.16	8.8	5.3	8.4	1.1	5.03	7.0	-8
2001	SLC	PCL	30	29	0	41.3	38	8	50	4	2.40	2.84	9.7	2.1	8.1	0.9	4.48	11.7	10
2002	SLC	PCL	31	25	0	33.7	27	11	42	5	3.47	3.45	8.3	3.4	8.6	1.7	5.04	7.5	-12
2002	ANA	AL	31	46	0	49.7	32	19	54	2	2.17	2.64	6.4	3.2	9.4	0.4	2.74	15.7	40
2003	ANA	AL	32	63	0	74.0	55	24	79	2	1.58	2.13	6.8	2.8	9.5	0.3	2.66	34.5	47
2004	*ANA*	*AL*	*32*	*50*	*6*	*80.7*	*69*	*29*	*73*	*8*	*3.30*	*3.52*	*7.5*	*3.1*	*7.9*	*0.9*	*3.72*	*21.2*	*11*

Breakout: 18%   Improve: 52%   Collapse: 29%

Donnelly was completely dominant for three months, one of the most effective stretches of relief pitching ever. He pitched with bone chips in his elbow for much of the second half and still posted a 3.81 ERA with nearly a strikeout an inning. Minor surgery after the season cleared up the problem, so Donnelly should be healthy in '04. There's no obvious reason why he can't keep pitching well, although expecting him to maintain a career ERA under 2.00 is a bit optimistic.

GARY GLOVER   Bats: R   Throws: R   Born: 03-Dec-76   Age: 27

YEAR	TM	LG	AGE	G	GS	IP	H	BB	SO	HR	ERA	EQERA	EQH9	EQBB9	EQSO9	EQHR9	PERA	VORP	STF
2001	CHR	INT	24	6	6	38.3	21	5	29	3	1.88	2.27	5.6	1.3	5.3	1.0	2.41	13.2	25
2001	CWS	AL	24	46	11	100.3	98	32	63	16	4.94	4.75	8.8	2.7	5.3	1.3	4.64	9.1	-3
2002	CWS	AL	25	41	22	138.3	136	52	70	21	5.21	4.94	9.0	3.2	4.4	1.2	4.82	9.8	-12
2003	CWS	AL	26	24	0	35.7	43	14	23	3	4.54	4.72	11.0	3.4	5.8	0.8	5.31	5.8	-4
2003	ANA	AL	26	18	0	27.0	34	8	14	3	5.00	5.19	11.4	2.4	4.5	1.0	5.54	2.6	-17
2004	*CHC*	*NL*	*27*	*30*	*8*	*59.3*	*66*	*22*	*37*	*9*	*4.98*	*5.31*	*10.0*	*2.9*	*5.0*	*1.3*	*5.38*	*4.0*	*-11*

Breakout: 30%   Improve: 55%   Collapse: 22%

Glover is a low-leverage pitcher who would have had more value on a staff with a weaker bullpen. Brought in from Chicago in the Scott Schoeneweis dump, he had virtually no role for the Angels: 15 of the 18 appearances he made for them were in losses, and two of the others were in blowout wins. The Cubs, who invited him to spring training, have more use for a left-handed swingman than a right-handed one, so Glover will probably spend time in Triple-A this year.

STEVE GREEN   Bats: R   Throws: R   Born: 26-Jan-78   Age: 26

YEAR	TM	LG	AGE	G	GS	IP	H	BB	SO	HR	ERA	EQERA	EQH9	EQBB9	EQSO9	EQHR9	PERA	VORP	STF
2001	SLC	PCL	23	10	10	59.0	59	13	40	3	3.66	4.15	8.8	2.2	4.6	0.5	3.67	9.1	22
2003	SLC	PCL	25	21	21	110.0	120	47	70	6	4.66	5.00	9.7	4.5	4.8	0.7	4.91	7.0	-3
2004	ANA	AL	26	20	12	69.7	76	33	40	7	4.88	5.20	9.6	4.1	4.9	0.9	5.32	4.2	-9

Breakout: 18%   Improve: 49%   Collapse: 31%

Green is probably best known as the player whose presence on the 40-man roster enabled the Angels to get Francisco Rodriguez onto the playoff roster in 2002. In 2003, he made a successful comeback from Tommy John surgery. Command is what comes back last, and Green had pretty good command before the surgery, so he may take another step forward in '04 and regain his prospect status. Okay, the Montreal native is really just here as a sop to Jonah Keri, BP's token Quebecois.

KEVIN GREGG   Bats: R   Throws: R   Born: 20-Jun-78   Age: 26

YEAR	TM	LG	AGE	G	GS	IP	H	BB	SO	HR	ERA	EQERA	EQH9	EQBB9	EQSO9	EQHR9	PERA	VORP	STF
2001	MID	TEX	23	44	1	81.3	88	40	72	5	4.54	5.80	10.3	5.3	5.6	0.8	5.56	-1.7	-11
2002	MID	TEX	24	11	4	37.7	31	18	45	3	4.30	5.03	9.3	5.0	8.2	1.6	5.78	2.2	-9
2002	SAC	PCL	24	16	8	58.7	82	23	45	7	7.51	7.67	12.3	3.8	5.1	1.3	6.57	-12.9	-24
2003	ARK	TEX	25	15	11	66.3	60	19	60	2	3.53	4.25	10.3	3.3	6.1	0.6	4.78	8.9	6
2003	SLC	PCL	25	15	15	91.7	90	18	75	10	4.02	4.26	9.0	2.1	6.2	1.4	4.62	12.9	3
2003	ANA	AL	25	5	3	24.7	18	8	14	3	3.28	3.04	6.5	2.7	4.9	1.1	3.38	7.1	8
2004	ANA	AL	26	22	13	79.7	81	31	57	10	4.61	4.92	9.0	3.4	6.2	1.1	4.82	8.1	2

Breakout: 15%   Improve: 43%   Collapse: 20%

Every year, a few guys make the book because their major league performance warrants it, even though that performance doesn't really reflect their status. Gregg is one of those guys; called up in September, he posted a low ERA in enough innings that he really has to be included here. He's a journeyman, and despite good command of mediocre stuff, isn't likely to be back in the majors in 2004.

BOBBY JENKS   Bats: R   Throws: R   Born: 14-Mar-81   Age: 23

YEAR	TM	LG	AGE	G	GS	IP	H	BB	SO	HR	ERA	EQERA	EQH9	EQBB9	EQSO9	EQHR9	PERA	VORP	STF
2001	CDR	MID	20	21	21	99.0	90	64	98	10	5.27	7.49	10.8	8.4	5.6	2.2	8.11	-17.9	-27
2002	RCU	CAL	21	11	10	65.3	50	46	64	4	4.82	5.49	8.2	7.9	5.0	1.1	5.60	0.7	-2
2002	ARK	TEX	21	10	10	58.0	49	44	58	2	4.66	5.83	8.2	7.8	7.0	0.5	4.92	-1.4	25
2003	ARK	TEX	22	16	16	83.0	56	51	103	2	2.17	3.28	7.7	7.2	8.5	0.5	4.49	19.1	37
2004	ANA	AL	23	20	15	82.3	78	58	68	10	5.50	5.87	8.4	6.0	7.2	1.0	5.62	2.8	-1

Breakout: 23%   Improve: 60%   Collapse: 27%

You can look at Jenks's checkered personal history as either proof that he's a head case not worthy of the risk, or evidence that he's capable of addressing his demons, and therefore someone of strong character. While skepticism that he's put his problems with alcohol and temperament completely behind him is warranted, Jenks's 2003 performance at Arkansas was the kind of dominant work that cannot be ignored. His overpowering fastball marks him as a candidate for the major league bullpen, perhaps as soon as this summer.

JOHN LACKEY

Bats: R **Throws: R** Born: 23-Oct-78 Age: 25

YEAR	TM	LG	AGE	G	GS	IP	H	BB	SO	HR	ERA	EQERA	EQH9	EQBB9	EQSO9	EQHR9	PERA	VORP	STF
2001	ARK	TEX	22	18	18	127.3	106	29	94	11	3.46	4.14	8.6	2.5	4.7	1.3	4.52	19.0	7
2001	SLC	PCL	22	10	10	57.7	75	16	42	5	6.71	6.43	10.9	2.9	5.0	0.8	5.17	-5.2	11
2002	SLC	PCL	23	16	16	101.7	89	28	82	5	2.57	3.13	7.6	2.8	5.6	0.5	3.24	26.8	32
2002	ANA	AL	23	18	18	108.3	113	33	69	10	3.66	4.73	10.1	2.6	5.6	0.8	4.68	9.9	23
2003	ANA	AL	24	33	33	204.0	223	66	151	31	4.63	5.05	9.8	2.8	6.6	1.2	5.04	15.7	15
2004	ANA	AL	25	28	26	169.3	170	53	115	20	4.15	4.43	8.9	2.7	5.9	1.1	4.46	25.1	10

Breakout: 17%   Improve: 48%   Collapse: 10%

Like the other two homegrown starters in the Angels' rotation, Lackey puts the ball in the strike zone and in the air. His 2003 statistics were ruined by an April from the Navarro Collection, which drove the perception that he was a disappointment. Lackey was actually the Angels' best starter after that month, with strong peripherals (130 strikeouts and 47 walks in 172.2 innings) and an average of more than 6.1 innings per start. Expect some improvement, perhaps a lot of it if Erstad is back in center field.

BART MIADICH

Bats: R **Throws: R** Born: 03-Feb-76 Age: 28

YEAR	TM	LG	AGE	G	GS	IP	H	BB	SO	HR	ERA	EQERA	EQH9	EQBB9	EQSO9	EQHR9	PERA	VORP	STF
2001	SLC	PCL	25	55	0	59.0	40	29	73	4	2.44	2.98	7.1	5.3	8.3	0.7	3.92	15.8	11
2001	ANA	AL	25	11	0	10.0	6	8	11	2	4.50	4.66	5.6	6.5	9.3	1.9	4.77	1.0	-9
2002	SLC	PCL	26	59	0	80.7	60	64	92	5	3.68	4.46	7.5	8.2	7.8	0.7	4.92	9.5	-12
2003	SLC	PCL	27	46	0	51.3	39	41	65	4	3.68	4.18	7.6	8.6	9.9	1.0	5.26	7.5	-8
2004	SDP	NL	28	18	3	31.0	26	23	35	2	4.34	4.75	7.6	6.0	9.1	0.6	4.91	4.8	8

Breakout: 47%   Improve: 65%   Collapse: 14%

Given that the Angels have assembled championship-caliber bullpens from guys who had all the big league pedigree of your average house pet, a true minor league closer doesn't impress them much. Miadich saved 57 games at Salt Lake the last three years, with a less impressive performance record each time around. The Padres invited him to camp, but they're so deep in right-handed relievers that it's hard to see Miadich making the team.

RAMON ORTIZ

Bats: **Throws:** Born: 23-May-73 Age: 31

YEAR	TM	LG	AGE	G	GS	IP	H	BB	SO	HR	ERA	EQERA	EQH9	EQBB9	EQSO9	EQHR9	PERA	VORP	STF
2001	ANA	AL	28	32	32	208.7	223	76	135	25	4.36	4.87	9.7	3.1	5.5	1.0	4.82	16.3	4
2002	ANA	AL	29	32	32	217.3	188	68	162	40	3.77	4.39	8.3	2.7	6.6	1.6	4.67	27.8	2
2003	ANA	AL	30	32	32	180.0	209	63	94	28	5.20	5.69	10.4	3.0	4.7	1.3	5.50	-4.1	-12
2004	ANA	AL	31	26	23	140.7	155	56	74	20	5.20	5.55	9.8	3.4	4.6	1.3	5.50	9.9	-6

Breakout: 18%   Improve: 49%   Collapse: 24%

It was a historic season for Ortiz, who became just the fifth pitcher to win at least 16 games with an ERA of 5.20 or higher, the first since Bobby Witt and Kevin Ritz each turned the trick in 1996. Broadening the category, Ortiz became the 19th pitcher to win at least 15 games with an ERA of at least 5.00. Ortiz got the fourth-best run support in the league—6.35 per nine innings—on a team that ranked just 11th in runs, and pitched in front of a bullpen that preserved nearly every lead he left to it.

More telling than the wins is that Ortiz became an even more extreme flyball pitcher and lost nearly a third of his strikeout rate last year. He would make great trade bait, as the Angels have a younger, less expensive version of him with a bit more upside in Lackey. That notion doesn't seem to fit with everything else the Angels did this off-season, however. Ortiz comes with a high risk of implosion this year, and an ERA in the low 6.00s is as likely as one in the low 4.00s.

JOEL PERALTA

Bats: R **Throws: R** Born: 23-Mar-76 Age: 28

YEAR	TM	LG	AGE	G	GS	IP	H	BB	SO	HR	ERA	EQERA	EQH9	EQBB9	EQSO9	EQHR9	PERA	VORP	STF
2001	CDR	MID	25	41	0	42.3	27	5	53	3	2.13	2.95	9.3	1.5	6.9	1.7	4.98	10.8	-22
2002	ARK	TEX	26	12	0	17.7	25	10	11	5	6.61	9.60	17.4	6.6	4.2	6.0	15.65	-6.7	-215
2002	CDR	MID	26	41	0	47.3	28	11	53	2	0.95	2.92	9.2	2.9	6.3	1.4	4.95	11.9	-25
2003	ARK	TEX	27	47	0	52.3	39	12	48	3	2.24	2.89	8.7	2.7	6.2	1.2	4.42	14.1	-12
2004	ANA	AL	28	17	1	23.7	24	9	16	3	4.49	4.79	9.0	3.1	5.9	1.2	4.88	2.7	-7

Breakout: 28%   Improve: 49%   Collapse: 24%

Another minor league closer, Peralta's days as a prospect may have ended when he got caught up in AgeGate. He went from 23 to 27 over the previous winter, making his monster 2002 season in the Midwest League look even less impressive. He's one of many advanced-age relievers trying to make headway in an organization very deep in right-handed bullpen help. For what it's worth, the Angels had nearly 30 players pick up new birth dates in the scandal (as reported by *Baseball America*), a total that was only approached by the A's and Padres.

TROY PERCIVAL   Bats: R   Throws: R   Born: 09-Aug-69   Age: 34

YEAR	TM	LG	AGE	G	GS	IP	H	BB	SO	HR	ERA	EQERA	EQH9	EQBB9	EQSO9	EQHR9	PERA	VORP	STF
2001	ANA	AL	31	57	0	57.7	39	18	71	3	2.65	2.59	6.3	2.6	10.3	0.5	2.60	18.6	46
2002	ANA	AL	32	58	0	56.3	38	25	68	5	1.92	2.65	6.6	3.6	10.4	0.7	3.19	17.8	37
2003	ANA	AL	33	52	0	49.3	33	23	48	7	3.47	3.56	6.0	3.9	8.6	1.1	3.47	10.2	12
2004	ANA	AL	34	55	0	58.0	44	24	59	6	3.21	3.42	6.7	3.6	8.9	1.0	3.56	16.1	14

Breakout: 35%   Improve: 49%   Collapse: 10%

Percival is an example of how the closer-centric bullpen often funnels saves, money and glory to a guy who isn't the best performer on his team. By just about any measure, the Angels' closer hasn't been as good a pitcher as Donnelly or Ben Weber over the last two seasons, and he was arguably not as good as Francisco Rodriguez last year. His career ERA of 3.00 isn't impressive for a short reliever, and he's had more years above that mark than below it. Percival has often said that he will retire after 2004, so keep that in mind as you watch him this year.

FRANCISCO RODRIGUEZ   Bats: R   Throws: R   Born: 07-Jan-82   Age: 22

YEAR	TM	LG	AGE	G	GS	IP	H	BB	SO	HR	ERA	EQERA	EQH9	EQBB9	EQSO9	EQHR9	PERA	VORP	STF
2001	RCU	CAL	19	20	20	113.7	127	55	147	13	5.38	7.16	11.4	5.6	7.2	1.7	7.08	-18.1	15
2002	ARK	TEX	20	23	0	41.3	32	15	61	2	1.96	3.49	7.9	3.7	10.7	0.7	3.82	9.1	60
2002	SLC	PCL	20	27	0	42.0	30	13	59	1	2.57	2.43	6.2	3.1	10.8	0.2	2.46	14.3	76
2002	ANA	AL	20	5	0	5.7	3	2	13	0	0.00	1.59	4.8	3.2	17.5	0.0	1.68	2.5	142
2003	ANA	AL	21	59	0	86.0	50	35	95	12	3.03	2.90	5.2	3.4	9.8	1.2	2.98	26.2	53
2004	ANA	AL	22	43	15	107.7	92	46	108	12	3.89	4.15	7.6	3.7	8.7	1.0	3.98	20.1	15

Breakout: 13%   Improve: 36%   Collapse: 44%

K-Rod's amazing 2002 postseason may have raised expectations a bit too high. After all, he had precious little experience above A-ball, and as good as his two pitches were, he still had a lot of work to do developing them. Credit Mike Scioscia—who has shown himself to be a master with relievers—with being patient with Rodriguez through a rough start. The rookie was unhittable after May, allowing just 29 knocks in 70 innings. He could be the AL's best reliever this year.

ERVIN SANTANA   Bats: R   Throws: R   Born: 10-Jan-83   Age: 21

YEAR	TM	LG	AGE	G	GS	IP	H	BB	SO	HR	ERA	EQERA	EQH9	EQBB9	EQSO9	EQHR9	PERA	VORP	STF
2002	CDR	MID	19	27	27	147.0	133	48	146	10	4.16	6.80	11.1	4.1	5.9	1.7	6.53	-17.1	7
2003	RCU	CAL	20	20	20	124.7	98	36	130	9	2.53	3.89	8.5	3.6	6.4	1.3	4.71	21.5	26
2003	ARK	TEX	20	6	6	29.7	23	12	23	4	3.94	5.00	8.0	4.7	5.7	2.0	5.62	1.8	3
2004	ANA	AL	21	19	17	100.3	99	48	73	12	4.55	4.86	8.7	4.1	6.3	1.0	4.93	9.3	5

Breakout: 24%   Improve: 53%   Collapse: 11%

It's a funny thing about AgeGate: While some guys lost a ton of value, or perceived value, amidst the controversy, there were players who actually came out of it looking better thanks to the additional year. Santana is one of those; he added one baseball year—about 10 actual months—and a new first name (formerly Johan) in the crackdown, but since that year moved him from 19 to 20, it's actually a positive. He's one year closer to getting through the Injury Nexus, and his innings totals looked a bit better on a pitcher one year more mature. Santana gets his fastball into the high-90s and has a great slider. His approach on the mound and developing change-up mean that he's expected to remain a starter as he moves through the system. Shut down in August as a precaution, Santana is healthy going into 2004.

AARON SELE

			Bats: R				Throws: R							Born: 25-Jun-70			Age: 34	
YEAR	TM	LG	AGE	G	GS	IP	H	BB	SO	HR	ERA	EQERA	EQH9	EQBB9	EQSO9	EQHR9	PERA	VORP	STF
2001	SEA	AL	31	34	33	215.0	216	51	114	25	3.60	4.48	10.0	2.1	4.6	1.0	4.72	25.0	3
2002	ANA	AL	32	26	26	160.0	190	49	82	21	4.89	5.65	11.4	2.6	4.6	1.1	5.69	-0.8	-7
2003	ANA	AL	33	25	25	121.7	135	58	53	17	5.77	5.74	9.9	4.1	3.9	1.1	5.46	-3.0	-19
2004	ANA	AL	34	23	19	109.3	125	44	52	16	5.28	5.64	10.1	3.4	4.1	1.3	5.68	2.5	-11

Breakout: 17%   Improve: 45%   Collapse: 27%

Pitchers who didn't complete their starts used to be called "seven-inning pitchers." Sele may cause the introduction of the term "five-inning pitcher"—he actually averaged less than that in 2003 while coming back from a torn rotator cuff. Every indicator is going the wrong way, and if the Angels didn't have to pay him $8.5 million in 2004, he'd be looking for an employer. There's no role for him in Anaheim and no trade interest in him elsewhere, so Aaron Sele:Arte Moreno: David Ovitz:Disney.

STEVEN SHELL

			Bats: R				Throws: R							Born: 10-Mar-83			Age: 21	
YEAR	TM	LG	AGE	G	GS	IP	H	BB	SO	HR	ERA	EQERA	EQH9	EQBB9	EQSO9	EQHR9	PERA	VORP	STF
2001	PRO	PIO	18	14	4	37.7	52	15	33	3	7.16	9.79	14.3	5.3	4.2	1.6	8.19	-15.8	-25
2002	CDR	MID	19	22	21	121.0	119	26	86	12	3.72	6.96	11.8	2.7	4.2	2.4	7.41	-16.0	-14
2003	RCU	CAL	20	22	21	127.3	123	26	100	13	4.24	5.32	10.0	2.5	4.8	1.8	5.69	3.6	2
2004	ANA	AL	21	20	17	106.0	114	34	63	15	4.52	4.83	9.5	2.7	5.2	1.2	4.92	11.0	1

Breakout: 25%   Improve: 63%   Collapse: 2%

The Angels were touched by one in the 2001 draft, picking up their current top three hitting prospects in the first two rounds, then adding two credible starting pitchers in the third. Shell, a high-school draftee, has shown excellent command of a low-90s fastball so far. He was shut down last year with some elbow soreness, and given his age and the soreness with a relatively light workload, you have to be concerned. Jake Woods, the Angels' other third-rounder in '01, has been more durable but less effective while matching Shell's progress through the system. Both fall in well behind Santana for the rank of best Angels pitching prospect.

SCOT SHIELDS

			Bats: R				Throws: R							Born: 22-Jul-75			Age: 28	
YEAR	TM	LG	AGE	G	GS	IP	H	BB	SO	HR	ERA	EQERA	EQH9	EQBB9	EQSO9	EQHR9	PERA	VORP	STF
2001	SLC	PCL	25	21	21	137.7	141	31	104	24	4.97	5.16	9.7	2.4	5.0	1.7	5.50	6.3	-19
2002	SLC	PCL	26	28	1	47.0	39	6	50	5	3.06	3.07	8.2	1.2	7.2	1.2	3.81	12.4	3
2002	ANA	AL	26	29	1	49.0	31	21	30	4	2.20	2.89	6.2	3.7	5.4	0.8	3.18	14.1	4
2003	ANA	AL	27	44	13	148.3	138	38	111	12	2.85	3.46	8.4	2.2	6.7	0.7	3.65	40.9	20
2004	ANA	AL	28	32	18	108.7	107	31	75	12	3.70	3.94	8.7	2.5	6.0	1.0	4.13	22.0	5

Breakout: 21%   Improve: 41%   Collapse: 25%

While Shields pitched well enough as a starter for the Angels (closing the year with three straight excellent outings) for them to entertain the idea of keeping him in the rotation, the shopping they did over the winter pushes him back into the bullpen. He's actually most valuable as trade bait, with less than two years of service time and far too much stuff to be stuck in low-leverage relief work. He's 28, so there's limited upside, but he could be a mid-rotation starter for a good team.

JOE TORRES

			Bats: L				Throws: L							Born: 03-Sep-82			Age: 21	
YEAR	TM	LG	AGE	G	GS	IP	H	BB	SO	HR	ERA	EQERA	EQH9	EQBB9	EQSO9	EQHR9	PERA	VORP	STF
2001	PRO	PIO	18	9	8	31.3	32	15	39	2	4.03	7.16	11.7	6.5	6.2	1.3	6.98	-4.8	3
2001	CDR	MID	18	4	4	17.0	16	14	14	0	5.82	7.04	8.8	10.6	4.7	0.6	6.01	-2.4	2
2002	CDR	MID	19	25	25	133.0	125	66	87	7	3.52	7.62	10.5	6.2	3.8	1.3	6.45	-26.3	-9
2003	RCU	CAL	20	8	7	33.7	47	20	17	1	5.88	9.00	12.8	7.3	3.2	0.6	6.89	-11.7	-19

Torres was the Angels' #1 pick in the 2000 draft, a high schooler out of Florida who has been a disappointment as a pro. His performance record is unimpressive, and he's frustrated the organization at times with both his preparation and the loss of 5–6 mph on his fastball as compared to high school. He suffered shoulder pain last year that cost him part of the season. Torres is still just 22, but until he gets back the missing fastball, he's a non-prospect.

DERRICK TURNBOW Bats: R Throws: R Born: 25-Jan-78 Age: 26

YEAR	TM	LG	AGE	G	GS	IP	H	BB	SO	HR	ERA	EQERA	EQH9	EQBB9	EQSO9	EQHR9	PERA	VORP	STF
2001	ARK	TEX	23	3	3	14.0	12	5	11	0	2.57	3.46	9.0	4.2	4.8	0.0	3.84	3.1	23
2002	RCU	CAL	24	13	0	12.0	16	9	14	1	5.25	8.71	15.7	8.7	6.1	1.7	9.60	-3.6	-74
2003	ARK	TEX	25	7	0	14.0	4	5	19	0	0.00	0.00	4.3	4.3	9.2	0.0	1.84	7.9	51
2003	SLC	PCL	25	35	0	55.0	68	24	63	5	5.73	5.92	11.7	4.7	8.9	1.2	6.35	-1.8	-10
2003	ANA	AL	25	11	0	15.3	7	3	15	0	0.59	0.61	4.3	1.8	8.6	0.0	1.24	9.1	60
2004	ANA	AL	26	19	5	38.0	37	17	34	4	4.20	4.48	8.6	3.9	7.8	0.8	4.53	5.2	6

Breakout: 26%   Improve: 51%   Collapse: 20%

The Angels selected Turnbow from the Phillies in the 1999 Rule 5 draft, and carried him through the 2000 season. Allowed to send him to the minors in 2001, they watched him make just three starts before blowing out his elbow and missing most of '01 and '02. His ERAs belie good peripherals generated with a high-90s fastball and effective slider, and he was good in two brief major league stints last year. Turnbow failed a steroid test while playing for Team USA in the Olympic qualifying tournament, but won't face a suspension.

JARROD WASHBURN Bats: L Throws: L Born: 13-Aug-74 Age: 29

YEAR	TM	LG	AGE	G	GS	IP	H	BB	SO	HR	ERA	EQERA	EQH9	EQBB9	EQSO9	EQHR9	PERA	VORP	STF
2001	ANA	AL	26	30	30	193.3	196	54	126	25	3.77	4.25	9.1	2.4	5.5	1.1	4.45	27.9	8
2002	ANA	AL	27	32	32	206.0	183	59	139	19	3.15	3.73	8.6	2.4	6.0	0.8	3.93	40.6	20
2003	ANA	AL	28	32	32	207.3	205	54	118	34	4.43	4.45	8.8	2.2	5.1	1.4	4.59	29.1	-1
2004	ANA	AL	29	28	26	169.0	174	49	97	24	4.33	4.62	9.1	2.5	5.0	1.3	4.73	23.0	3

Breakout: 12%   Improve: 51%   Collapse: 17%

You would think that Washburn, an extreme flyball pitcher, would have missed Darin Erstad as much as any Angel, and that the jump in his ERA could be traced to the great flycatcher's absence. In fact, Washburn gave up fewer doubles and triples, both in total and by rate, than he did in '02. The problem was they became home runs: 34 in all, the highest figure in the AL. He's going to have years like that, and as long as the Angels don't overreact to them, they'll have a valuable mid-rotation starter.

BEN WEBER Bats: R Throws: R Born: 17-Nov-69 Age: 34

YEAR	TM	LG	AGE	G	GS	IP	H	BB	SO	HR	ERA	EQERA	EQH9	EQBB9	EQSO9	EQHR9	PERA	VORP	STF
2001	ANA	AL	31	56	0	68.3	66	31	40	4	3.43	3.95	8.7	3.8	4.9	0.5	4.16	12.1	-1
2002	ANA	AL	32	63	0	78.0	70	22	43	4	2.54	3.42	8.8	2.4	4.9	0.5	3.74	17.9	6
2003	ANA	AL	33	62	0	80.3	84	22	46	7	2.69	3.49	9.4	2.3	5.1	0.7	4.20	26.5	2
2004	ANA	AL	34	45	2	61.3	65	20	36	5	3.71	3.96	9.4	2.8	5.1	0.7	4.35	12.8	-6

Breakout: 28%   Improve: 51%   Collapse: 24%

In a bullpen with fireballers like Rodriguez, Percival and Donnelly, Weber gets a bit lost in the shuffle. He's an important cog though, the guy who gets used to keep tie games tied and get out of runners-on, less-than-two-outs situations. He hides the ball well and keeps it down, getting three times as many ground balls as fly balls.

Where do bullpens come from? Well, Weber pitched in Taiwan for two years, Donnelly spent time in two different independent leagues, Percival is a converted catcher, Turnbow was a Rule 5 pick who missed two years to injury. K-Rod is the only guy in this group with both a pedigree and performance. Keep that in mind when you consider the contracts still being handed out to guys for their next 60 or 120 innings.

Baltimore Orioles

With Jim Beattie and Mike Flanagan being installed just a season ago as an organizational duumvirate to steer the Orioles out of the aimlessness of the Thrift years, it might be premature to get really excited about the results.

That said, player development finally seems to be getting the attention it deserves. When asked, Beattie and Flanagan say the right sorts of things about valuing on-base percentage, even claiming that players had been demoted or released for not getting with the program (Gary Matthews and Geronimo Gil being particularly singled out). The real question is whether or not we're seeing a new Oriole Way being forged, one that shares the name but not the precepts of the old Earl Weaver brand of baseball. If the farm system really is on is way back, it could combine with the open-wallet policy Peter Angelos showed this off-season in signing Miguel Tejada and Javy Lopez (and fruitlessly pursuing Vladimir Guerrero), to signal the start of an Oriole rebirth.

In fact, some would argue the O's began turning the ship around last year, with improvements by several young hitters. But a closer look reveals a rare occurrence may have played a huge role in their offensive progress:

In 2002, the Baltimore Orioles hit 850 singles, the lowest total in the majors.

In 2003, the Orioles hit 1,063 singles, more than any other team in the majors.

No team in history has ever gone worst to first in the majors before, although a handful of others have done it within their own league: The 1882 Buffalo Bisons, 1903 Detroit Tigers, 1921 Cubs, 1927 Athletics, 1935 Giants, and 1953 Tigers all did it, and then there was a nearly 50-year gap before the 2001 Mariners did it.

Now that the Orioles have done it, what can we expect?

At every position, the Orioles' regulars improved their singles rate (singles per at-bat) over their 2002 counterpart (see table 1).

All of the other teams that went worst to first in their leagues had a player who was among the three best singles-hitters in the league (based on 250 AB): The 2001 Mariners had Ichiro!, the Giants had Bill Terry, the A's had Ty Cobb, and the Cubs had George Maisel, all of whom led the league in singles rate. Dan Brouthers of the 1882 Bisons, Richie Ashburn of the Phils, and Harvey Kuenn of the '53 Tigers all finished second in the league, while Jimmy Bar-

rett of the 1903 Tigers was third. By contrast, the Orioles' best singles hitter, Melvin Mora, was only sixth in the league, but they made up for it by then running the top 10 table (see table 2).

While no one says so, at least not publicly, the Orioles appear to be aping baseball's latest phenomenon: the 2002 Angels. Much was written last winter about the Angels' "put it in play" approach at the plate, and that this was supposedly a new trend that would set performance analysis on its ear. There are a couple of problems with that idea, and the way the Orioles went about it.

First, an offense based on singles is going to be more variable than an offense based on an approach focused on homers and walks. All events on a baseball field are a combination of skill and luck, defining skill as events within the player's control, and luck as events outside of his control (frequently, in some other player's control). Events that come primarily from a player's own skill will be very highly correlated for the same player from one season to the next; events that are mostly luck will have low correlations (see table 3).

Strikeouts, walks, and homers, the three events for which the opposing fielders are irrelevant, have the highest correlations; stolen bases are almost all about speed, which is most definitely a skill controlled by the player doing the running. The more a player's value is concentrated in those

ORIOLES PROSPECTUS

2003 record: 71–91; Fourth place, AL East

Pythagenport record: 73–89

Runs scored per game: 4.6 (10th in AL)

Runs allowed per game: 5.1 (9th in AL)

Team EqA: .255 (8th in AL)

2003 Batters Age: 29.9 (4th oldest in AL)

2003 Pitchers Age: 29.7 (5th oldest in AL)

Ballpark: Oriole Park; Severe pitcher's park; Park Factor of 0.959

2003: Is finishing second-to-last in a division with the Devil Rays really different than finishing dead last anywhere else?

2004: Spent an enormous wad of cash on free agents, but might not even get third place to show for it.

TABLE 1. 2003 REGULARS' SINGLES RATE VS. 2002 REGULARS' SINGLES RATE

Position	2003 Regular	Singles Average	2002 Regular	Singles Average	Gain
C	Fordyce	.216	Gil	.159	+.057
1B	Conine	.187	Conine	.173	+.014
2B	Roberts	.202	Hairston	.190	+.012
3B	Batista	.160	Batista	.133	+.027
SS	Cruz	.177	Bordick	.150	+.027
LF	Mora	.221	Mora	.138	+.083
CF	Matos	.214	Matthews	.174	+.040
RF	Gibbons	.174	Gibbons	.129	+.045
4th OF	Bigbie	.216	Singleton	.165	+.051
5th OF	Surhoff	.216	Cordova	.155	+.061

TABLE 2. TOP SINGLES/AB HITTERS, AMERICAN LEAGUE, 2003, 250+ AB

Rank	Player	2003 Singles Rate
1.	Derek Jeter, New York	.245
2.	Alex Sanchez, Detroit	.241
3.	Ichiro Suzuki, Seattle	.239
4.	Carl Crawford, Tampa Bay	.230
5.	Michael Young, Texas	.222
6.	Melvin Mora, Baltimore	.221
7.	B. J. Surhoff, Baltimore	.216
8.	Larry Bigbie, Baltimore	.216
9.	Brook Fordyce, Baltimore	.216
10.	Luis Matos, Baltimore	.214

TABLE 3. CORRELATIONS FOR BATTERS, PER PA, CONSECUTIVE SEASONS >200 AB, ALL PLAYERS 1969–2003

Strikeouts	.837
Stolen bases	.829
Walks	.751
Home runs	.750
Singles	.585
Batting outs	.583
Hits	.450
Triples	.412
Doubles	.384

is −.460. The 2002 Angels were third in doubles, fifth in steals, and 14th in triples. So despite being 21st in home runs and 26th in walks, they were a good offensive team overall, finishing fourth in runs scored.

In contrast, the 2003 Orioles were *all* about singles. They got 45.9% of their offense from singles, easily the highest total in the majors last year (San Diego was second, at 44.6%). They were 11th in the majors in stolen bases, the only other major category where they cracked the top two-thirds, since they finished 21st in doubles, 22nd in homers, 26th in triples, and 28th in walks. Without any kickers to all those singles, they weren't a good offensive team, and finished 18th in runs overall. In terms of Isolated Power (slugging percentage minus batting average), they finished second-to-last in the AL, ahead of only the Tigers.

If they were returning the same group of players, we'd be strongly pessimistic about their chances of having a better offense in 2003, given they're unlikely to repeat their singles title. Since the Orioles were one of the few teams willing to show Jerry Maguire and his ilk the money this off-season, a significantly different team will take the field in 2004. By signing up Tejada from Oakland and Lopez from the Braves, on paper they've added considerable power, and they've done it at a pair of positions where top-notch offense isn't easily acquired. The Isolated Power of both players was tremendous in 2003, .359 for Lopez (second in baseball behind Barry Bonds, though seven plate appearances short of qualifying as a full-time player), and .194 for Tejada.

But just as interesting, Tejada and Lopez aren't walk-drawing offensive dynamos. Much of their value is tied up in their power. But like their new teammates, a lot of their OBP is tied up in their ability to hit for average; Lopez drew only 28 walks on his own in 495 plate appearances, while Tejada drew only 46 unintentional free passes in 703 PA.

high-correlation categories, the more certain you can be that a player will repeat his performance. The top five teams in singles in 2002 finished 3-8-9-25-26 in singles in 2003; the top five home run teams of 2002 were 1-4-5-13-14 in 2003. Put simply, players and teams that rely on singles and doubles for their offense are going to make larger bounces between good and bad.

Second, Anaheim wasn't only about singles. The Angels got 43.5% of their offense in 2002 from singles, an above-average amount, but only good for fifth in the majors, behind the Tigers, Padres, Mets, and Dodgers. Teams that lead the league in singles as a proportion of total offense are almost always poor offensive teams; the correlation between a team's rank in singles proportion and runs scored

That isn't meant to minimize their value to their new team. If the ability to hit was as frozen as a set of video game settings or a Strat card, and you have one guy whose OBP is heavily dependent on walks, and another who gets on base at the same clip on balls hit with authority, you're going to want the hitter. Real life isn't frozen that way, of course, and as we've shown above, getting the ball in play safely isn't as reliable a skill set as hammering the ball or drawing walks.

The Orioles were also foremost among Vlad Guerrero's suitors this winter. Whereas there's a question as to how much value Lopez and Tejada will retain over the life of their contracts, Guerrero was the most desirable free agent since A-Rod, in terms of being an offensive superstar becoming a free agent while still in a hitter's traditional peak range of 25–29. Like Tejada and Lopez, a lot of Guerrero's value is tied up in his ability to hammer the ball into play, with an Isolated Power figure of .256, a singles average of .208, and 42 unintentional walks in 467 PA. But now he's an Angel, and the O's missed out on acquiring a true star hitter who fits into the program.

All of which is not to say that Beattie and Flanagan are thinking about these sort of things. Sensibly enough, they're probably thinking in terms of simply improving a lineup that needs improvement. A happy side effect is that it means they won't have to pretend that their previous free agent pickups, washouts David Segui and Marty Cordova, have to play major roles in the team's offense. At press time, the team was still trying to convince Segui to sit out the last year of his contract to recover from wrist surgery. Potential playing time for Jack Cust at DH and Larry Bigbie in the outfield rides on getting Segui out of the way. If fully healthy, Cordova would still come in handy as a part-time lefty-masher, spotting for Cust, Bigbie, or Jay Gibbons in the lineup but otherwise yielding to younger hitters with more upside.

Managing to sort out the veteran-related pictures can lead you to overlook some small bits of homegrown happiness in the lineup. Luis Matos finally broke through to claim the job in center field. Jerry Hairston looked like he was breaking through; when he broke down, Brian Roberts demonstrated that he's a useful alternative. Dealing one of the two second basemen makes sense, especially with Mike Fontenot on the way up. Bigbie showed real promise, and Cust encouraged those who think he'll make a nifty DH.

If there are questions about the Orioles' off-season, they relate to the virtues of their spending on one hand, and the state of the pitching staff on the other. Improving their lineup might be one response to the team mired in fourth place on a semi-permanent-basis, but they may still not move up. That's the price of being in a division where the Yankees and Red Sox are strong, well-run organizations,

and where the Blue Jays have a significant head start in their rebuild. Spending almost $100 million of Peter Angelos's dollars on Lopez and Tejada is not enough: The smart money has the O's finishing near a .500 record, give or take a couple games. That raises the worthwhile question of whether or not the expense is worth it; the Orioles could finish fourth without Lopez and Tejada still.

But there's more in play here than trying to clamber up the standings. Attendance has dropped to two-thirds of its heyday, and 2003 was the team's lowest draw since it moved to Camden Yards. There was plenty of conspiracy-minded speculation that it was all part of some nefarious plot to drive attendance down, to prove that the Orioles couldn't survive a National League neighbor in Washington, D.C. Put a crummy team on the field, driving people away from the park, and presto, baseball endures in Montreal. Such second-guessing is usually ill-conceived, and the commitments to Lopez and Tejada should squelch them. The question is whether the excitement generated by fielding a more competitive product will keep people interested in a team that still has no shot at the division.

One reason the Orioles have little hope for the foreseeable future is a questionable group of starting pitchers. The notional veteran anchors are Rodrigo Lopez and Omar Daal. Barring a significant veteran pickup—and at press time, only Maddux was left—the rotation will probably be rounded out by Eric DuBose, Matt Riley, Kurt Ainsworth, and perhaps Rick Bauer or John Stephens. So that shapes up as a rotation where the upside is entirely with the kids, and the vets can barely hold their own. Some teams win with that set-up, but this would be the first full seasons in a big league rotation for any of the young'uns, and the Yankees and Red Sox aren't about to go on a two-year vacation to the Marshall Islands. (Although youneverknow, Bud Selig's madcap internationalization schemes *could* get even sillier.) Ainsworth and Riley certainly have great promise, and DuBose is a wonderful little comeback story, but that's just a good place to start, not a great rotation of the here and now. A bullpen that might aspire to mediocrity and a manager who has yet to prove his chops in managing a pitching staff aren't very reassuring, either.

But if the objective is to hold people's interest in the meantime, that puts the responsibility back on Beattie and Flanagan to revamp a farm system that needs all the vamping it can get. They haven't been afraid to use the organization's overall weakness to their advantage, dipping into the Rule 5 draft. They've kept an extra short-season affiliate, not merely out of loyalty to Cal Ripken's Aberdeen franchise, but because when you're hard-up, it makes sense to look at as many warm bodies as possible. Pitch counts are being watched, perhaps even too stringently, as the Orioles tried to keep everyone at every level at 150 IP or less. Defensive instruction seems to have been given particular attention. Overall, the winning percentage of the organization's affiliates jumped over 50 points in '03, up to .486. The last couple of drafts have been promising, especially with the additions of Adam Loewen and Nick Markakis.

Entering the front office tag team's second season, it seems clear that progress is being made. A jump in the standings seems unlikely, not unless something goes wrong in Toronto, but a win total in the low 80s should do wonders at the box office. As long as it buys more time for Beattie and Flanagan to rebuild the rest of the organization, it's time well spent.

HITTERS

TOMMY ARKO C Bats: R Throws: R Born: 28-Jul-82 Age: 21

YEAR	TM	LG	AGE	AB	H	2B	3B	HR	BB	SO	SB	CS	AVG	OBP	SLG	MLVR	EQBA	EQOBP	EQSLG	EQMLVR	VORP	DEFENSE	
2001	BLU	APP	18	124	24	4	1	5	13	47	0	1	.194	.271	.363	-.131	.118	.178	.228	-.696	-43.1	33-C	-3
2002	BLU	APP	19	181	48	11	0	14	35	58	0	1	.265	.387	.558	.254	.147	.232	.304	-.472	-36.2	34-C	-1
2002	DEL	SAL	19	63	8	3	0	0	7	28	0	0	.127	.236	.175	-.413	.123	.195	.169	-.737	-11.5	19-C	-2
2003	ABE	NYP	20	43	11	3	1	4	6	19	0	0	.256	.360	.651	.455	.174	.245	.457	-.227	-1.4	13-C	0
2003	DEL	SAL	20	152	31	5	0	4	20	50	1	2	.204	.316	.316	-.064	.169	.245	.269	-.482	-15.8	46-C	-1
2003	FRD	CAR	20	113	21	3	0	6	8	40	0	0	.186	.244	.372	-.161	.157	.202	.322	-.504	-12.1	34-C	0
2004	BAL	AL	21	240	41	9	0	8	20	81	0	0	.171	.240	.312	-.374	.176	.249	.327	-.371	-13.4	66-C	-8

Breakout: 68%   Improve: 77%   Collapse: 11%

A catcher with some skills—power, an arm—and some serious liabilities: He's dead slow, a free swinger, and has poor footwork behind the plate. He'll need to learn to wait for better pitches to hit, because a sub-Mendoza line in the minors won't get him a promotion, no matter how far he hits the ball when he makes contact.

TONY BATISTA 3B Bats: R Throws: R Born: 09-Dec-73 Age: 30

YEAR	TM	LG	AGE	AB	H	2B	3B	HR	BB	SO	SB	CS	AVG	OBP	SLG	MLVR	EQBA	EQOBP	EQSLG	EQMLVR	VORP	DEFENSE			
2001	TOR	AL	27	271	56	11	1	13	13	66	0	1	.207	.251	.399	-.235	.218	.264	.428	-.198	-1.2	71-3B	3		
2001	BAL	AL	27	308	82	16	5	12	19	47	5	1	.266	.305	.468	.022	.284	.329	.506	.087	21.4	28-3B	0	20-SS	3
2002	BAL	AL	28	615	150	36	1	31	50	107	5	4	.244	.309	.457	.011	.268	.335	.506	.082	42.8	153-3B	9		
2003	BAL	AL	29	631	148	20	1	26	28	102	4	3	.235	.270	.393	-.155	.256	.295	.432	-.105	-0.6	152-3B	5		
2004	MON	NL	30	493	133	27	2	24	35	83	3	2	.270	.323	.483	.041	.254	.306	.446	-.063	14.1	127-3B	3		

Breakout: 30%   Improve: 60%   Collapse: 15%

You couldn't get through a week last summer without hearing about another trade rumor involving Batista and whichever team had a third baseman in a slump, but he stayed in Charm City all year. Maybe it was because the Orioles couldn't afford to trade him, since by August all of their in-house choices to take over for him at third had gotten hurt, and maybe it was because the other GMs were smart enough to see that he was slumping just as badly as whomever they already had. In any event, his contract with the Orioles ended, and he signed a one-year deal with the Expos, but not before performing one last service: As godfather of Miguel Tejada's children, he spent the last three years telling Tejada what a great place Baltimore is to play baseball. The Orioles thank you, Tony.

LARRY BIGBIE LF Bats: L Throws: L Born: 04-Nov-77 Age: 26

YEAR	TM	LG	AGE	AB	H	2B	3B	HR	BB	SO	SB	CS	AVG	OBP	SLG	MLVR	EQBA	EQOBP	EQSLG	EQMLVR	VORP	DEFENSE			
2001	BOW	EAS	23	262	77	13	3	8	40	54	10	7	.294	.386	.458	.215	.245	.331	.388	-.108	-3.7	69-RF	-5		
2001	ROC	INT	23	42	13	4	0	1	3	8	1	1	.310	.356	.476	.183	.279	.326	.442	-.015	1.4				
2001	BAL	AL	23	131	30	6	0	2	17	42	4	1	.229	.318	.321	-.181	.250	.340	.356	-.131	0.6	14-CF	0	13-RF	0
2002	ROC	INT	24	348	105	23	2	2	35	79	7	3	.302	.363	.397	.078	.281	.346	.372	-.076	-2.2	30-LF	0	24-CF	1
2002	BAL	AL	24	34	6	1	0	0	1	11	1	0	.176	.194	.206	-.580	.206	.229	.235	-.547	-3.6				
2003	OTT	INT	25	117	41	14	4	3	14	31	0	0	.350	.421	.615	.516	.317	.387	.575	.317	13.4	20-LF	-1		
2003	BAL	AL	25	287	87	15	1	9	29	60	7	1	.303	.365	.456	.167	.328	.393	.493	.222	16.4	73-LF	0		
2004	BAL	AL	26	294	78	18	2	7	31	66	4	2	.265	.335	.414	-.021	.274	.347	.434	.008	9.8	80-LF	1		

Breakout: 9%   Improve: 31%   Collapse: 34%

(continued next page)

Larry Bigbie (continued)

Starting the season, there was no reason to believe that Bigbie would be anything more than a marginal outfielder, destined to shuttle between Ottawa and Baltimore. After he hit .239 in April and May, there was still no reason. He strained his shoulder at the end of May, hit the DL for two months, and a different hitter came back when he came off it. The new Bigbie hit .370 in Ottawa, got called up, and hit .329 the rest of the way. With power. Against the toughest part of the Orioles schedule. PECOTA doesn't think the spike is for real.

GARY CATES UT — Bats: R — Throws: R — Born: 03-Jul-81 — Age: 22

YEAR	TM	LG	AGE	AB	H	2B	3B	HR	BB	SO	SB	CS	AVG	OBP	SLG	MLVR	EQBA	EQOBP	EQSLG	EQMLVR	VORP	DEFENSE		
2001	DEL	SAL	20	342	100	14	3	2	17	30	16	8	.292	.341	.368	.101	.251	.287	.324	-.278	-10.8	62-2B -4	16-SS	-8
2001	FRD	CAR	20	91	22	4	0	0	4	16	0	1	.242	.274	.286	-.143	.215	.247	.258	-.473	-8.3	24-2B -2		
2002	DEL	SAL	21	317	90	18	1	2	16	36	12	6	.284	.324	.366	.047	.240	.268	.320	-.328	-14.9	77-2B -15		
2002	FRD	CAR	21	126	25	6	0	0	7	18	2	2	.198	.239	.246	-.325	.173	.211	.213	-.628	-17.1	12-3B 0		
2003	FRD	CAR	22	355	112	23	3	3	21	40	11	12	.315	.361	.423	.166	.261	.296	.364	-.197	-2.5	38-2B -4	33-LF	-4
2003	BOW	EAS	22	46	13	4	1	0	5	3	2	0	.283	.364	.413	.091	.239	.328	.370	-.142	-0.2			
2004	BAL	AL	22	246	58	12	1	3	13	32	4	2	.238	.282	.328	-.243	.245	.292	.344	-.229	-5.2	66-2B -12		

Breakout: 27%   Improve: 55%   Collapse: 24%

PECOTA will say he's no prospect, but what he is is fun. Cates is listed (generously) at 5'7", and, as you would expect from a player that size, he is a pest. His specialties are bunting, bat control, wearing out opposing pitchers with Nomar-like batting glove adjustments, testing which brand of laundry detergent does best on his numerous grass stains, and burning outfielders who see this little guy at the plate and creep in too close.

WOODY CLIFFORDS CF — Bats: L — Throws: R — Born: 02-Dec-80 — Age: 23

YEAR	TM	LG	AGE	AB	H	2B	3B	HR	BB	SO	SB	CS	AVG	OBP	SLG	MLVR	EQBA	EQOBP	EQSLG	EQMLVR	VORP	DEFENSE		
2001	BLU	APP	20	198	55	13	2	6	32	40	8	1	.278	.381	.455	.186	.170	.241	.277	-.479	-58.8	25-LF -3	14-RF	-1
2002	DEL	SAL	21	314	83	21	1	1	53	57	15	5	.264	.385	.347	.100	.205	.293	.277	-.356	-22.4	56-CF -6	26-LF	-3
2003	FRD	CAR	22	440	124	29	1	8	71	77	16	10	.282	.390	.407	.159	.218	.305	.330	-.254	-16.5	91-CF -1	26-RF	-1
2004	BAL	AL	23	227	48	11	1	4	24	48	4	2	.213	.292	.329	-.236	.220	.303	.346	-.223	-7.5	64-CF -8		

Breakout: 34%   Improve: 63%   Collapse: 19%

Even though his numbers have been fairly unimpressive to date, Cliffords has several positives that suggest he'll do better than expected. For one, he's a good defensive outfielder, thanks in large part to his speed. He's got an athletic body and he knows the strike zone—all traits that PECOTA normally finds encouraging. He's smart enough to collect and study videos of good hitters.

MARTY CORDOVA LF — Bats: R — Throws: R — Born: 10-Jul-69 — Age: 34

YEAR	TM	LG	AGE	AB	H	2B	3B	HR	BB	SO	SB	CS	AVG	OBP	SLG	MLVR	EQBA	EQOBP	EQSLG	EQMLVR	VORP	DEFENSE		
2001	CLE	AL	31	409	123	20	2	20	23	81	0	3	.301	.348	.506	.164	.317	.365	.537	.228	28.8	74-LF -1	26-RF	-1
2002	BAL	AL	32	458	116	25	2	18	47	111	1	6	.253	.325	.434	.015	.282	.354	.489	.104	19.7	62-LF -1		
2003	BAL	AL	33	30	7	1	0	1	8	5	1	0	.233	.410	.367	.066	.267	.447	.400	.142	1.6			
2004	BAL	AL	34	218	54	10	1	8	25	46	2	1	.250	.331	.413	-.040	.258	.343	.433	-.013	5.6	61-LF -2		

Breakout: 21%   Improve: 47%   Collapse: 30%

Three million dollars for nine games played . . . compared to Albert Belle, that's a bargain. Cordova came out of spring training with a bad back, and before April was over he was having bone chips taken out of his elbow. Just when it looked like he was ready to return, he went back on the table, same elbow, ligament replacement surgery. In the meantime, Matos and Bigbie played themselves into 2004 starting jobs, leaving Cordova without an obvious place to play for the final year of his contract.

DEIVI CRUZ SS — Bats: R — Throws: R — Born: 06-Nov-72 — Age: 31

YEAR	TM	LG	AGE	AB	H	2B	3B	HR	BB	SO	SB	CS	AVG	OBP	SLG	MLVR	EQBA	EQOBP	EQSLG	EQMLVR	VORP	DEFENSE
2001	DET	AL	28	414	106	28	1	7	17	46	4	1	.256	.291	.379	-.136	.276	.314	.413	-.081	12.8	102-SS -14
2002	SDP	NL	29	514	135	28	2	7	22	58	2	3	.263	.294	.366	-.088	.281	.311	.397	-.106	12.5	130-SS -9
2003	BAL	AL	30	548	137	24	2	14	13	49	1	2	.250	.269	.378	-.167	.272	.295	.414	-.118	1.1	144-SS -2
2004	TBY	AL	31	396	100	21	1	6	15	42	1	1	.254	.284	.362	-.184	.257	.289	.379	-.180	3.0	100-SS -3

Breakout: 12%   Improve: 37%   Collapse: 30%

Cruz was the first player signed by the Beattie/Flanagan GM tandem last December, after they decided not to re-sign Mike Bordick. Cruz was anything but an inspiring acquisition at the time, and when he was hitting .167 in May it looked even worse. He did rebound from that (for a six-week stretch from the second half of May through the end of July he was a pretty good hitter, with a .290 EqA), but this was nothing more than a one-year rental keeping the position warm for a real solution, which turned out to be Tejada. He's a perfect castaway on Lou Piniella's Island of Oldish Misfit Mediocrities.

JACK CUST								DH		Bats: L			Throws: R						Born: 16-Jan-79			Age: 25	
YEAR	TM	LG	AGE	AB	H	2B	3B	HR	BB	SO	SB	CS	AVG	OBP	SLG	MLVR	EQBA	EQOBP	EQSLG	EQMLVR	VORP	DEFENSE	
2001	TUC	PCL	22	442	123	24	2	27	102	160	6	3	.278	.415	.525	.211	.220	.351	.410	-.058	1.2	68-RF -5	37-LF -2
2002	CSP	PCL	23	359	95	24	0	23	83	121	6	3	.265	.407	.524	.202	.209	.341	.415	-.078	-2.8	49-LF -3	40-RF -5
2002	COL	NL	23	65	11	2	0	1	12	32	0	1	.169	.295	.246	-.346	.154	.286	.231	-.452	-7.4	13-LF -1	
2003	OTT	INT	24	333	95	18	1	9	80	94	5	2	.285	.422	.426	.211	.257	.387	.393	.013	7.8	74-LF -5	
2003	BAL	AL	24	73	19	7	0	4	10	25	0	0	.260	.357	.521	.191	.284	.375	.581	.268	6.0		
2004	BAL	AL	25	256	63	13	1	12	41	71	4	2	.245	.356	.439	.031	.254	.369	.460	.063	14.5	74-LF -2	
Breakout: 40%		Improve: 64%			Collapse: 18%																		

Cust is a pure masher at the plate who brings nothing else to a baseball diamond. He can't field and can't run, and as much as we love selectivity, he may be too selective at the plate: He's not just waiting for a plain old Good Pitch To Hit, he's waiting for THE great pitch he can cream. The D-Backs and Rockies soured on him after realizing the extent of his deficiencies; at least the Orioles have the option of making him a DH, having stolen him away from the Rockies for the rarely available Chris Richard. Signing Raffy Palmeiro could leave him crowded out of the picture, but if he gets a shot at the better half of a DH platoon, he'll produce.

MIKE FONTENOT								2B		Bats: L			Throws: R						Born: 09-Jun-80			Age: 24
YEAR	TM	LG	AGE	AB	H	2B	3B	HR	BB	SO	SB	CS	AVG	OBP	SLG	MLVR	EQBA	EQOBP	EQSLG	EQMLVR	VORP	DEFENSE	
2002	FRD	CAR	22	481	127	16	4	8	42	117	13	9	.264	.333	.364	.010	.214	.270	.308	-.356	-27.3	112-2B -11	
2003	BOW	EAS	23	449	146	24	5	12	50	89	16	5	.325	.399	.481	.276	.276	.340	.424	-.017	22.9	112-2B 3	
2004	BAL	AL	24	253	62	12	2	6	21	57	4	2	.244	.307	.373	-.136	.252	.319	.391	-.115	6.7	69-2B -4	
Breakout: 25%		Improve: 54%			Collapse: 23%																		

Fontenot was the Orioles' first-round draft pick in 2001 after a brilliant sophomore season at LSU. His 2002 season was a great disappointment, and his first 101 at-bats of 2002 looked like this:

TEAM	AB	H	2B	3B	HR	BB	SO		AVG	OBP	SLG
Bowie	101	20	3	1	2	9	28		.198	.268	.307

Then, he did something remarkable, something that is hard to believe wasn't detected by the Oriole medical staff: He got a set of contact lenses. Once he could see, he had this line for the rest of the season:

Bowie	348	126	21	4	10	41	61		.362	.429	.532

For a guy a year out of college, that's a flat-out excellent season, or at least three-quarters of a season. It is a performance that, at Double-A, equals what Hairston and Roberts did at second base for the Orioles this year. With those incumbents creating a logjam ahead of him, he'll get a long look at Triple-A.

BROOK FORDYCE								C		Bats: R			Throws: R						Born: 07-May-70			Age: 34
YEAR	TM	LG	AGE	AB	H	2B	3B	HR	BB	SO	SB	CS	AVG	OBP	SLG	MLVR	EQBA	EQOBP	EQSLG	EQMLVR	VORP	DEFENSE	
2001	BAL	AL	31	292	61	18	0	5	21	56	1	2	.209	.268	.322	-.286	.229	.290	.358	-.239	-5.0	88-C -13	
2002	BAL	AL	32	130	30	8	0	1	9	19	1	0	.231	.301	.315	-.202	.260	.328	.351	-.154	0.7	41-C -9	
2003	BAL	AL	33	348	95	12	2	6	19	44	2	3	.273	.311	.371	-.099	.296	.337	.405	-.034	4.5	97-C -3	
2004	TBY	AL	34	208	52	11	1	3	14	32	2	1	.252	.305	.355	-.157	.255	.311	.372	-.152	1.9	57-C -2	
Breakout: 28%		Improve: 52%			Collapse: 31%																		

After two miserable seasons on a three-year contract, Fordyce reclaimed the starting catching job for the Orioles. He didn't force the Orioles' hand with stellar play; he was just a little less mediocre than he had been the previous two years, and that looked a little better than Geronimo Gil's stinkiness. The Orioles still didn't pick up their option on Fordyce for 2004, and he's off to Tampa, hoping to steal at-bats away from Toby Hall while keeping a far more deserving Pete LaForest chained to Triple-A.

JAY GIBBONS   **RF/1B?**   **Bats: L**   **Throws: L**   Born: 02-Mar-77   Age: 27

YEAR	TM	LG	AGE	AB	H	2B	3B	HR	BB	SO	SB	CS	AVG	OBP	SLG	MLVR	EQBA	EQOBP	EQSLG	EQMLVR	VORP	DEFENSE			
2001	BAL	AL	24	225	53	10	0	15	17	39	0	1	.236	.301	.480	.004	.252	.319	.522	.061	6.8	27-LF	0		
2002	BAL	AL	25	490	121	29	1	28	45	66	1	3	.247	.311	.482	.049	.270	.335	.532	.120	24.3	87-RF	6	24-1B	-2
2003	BAL	AL	26	625	173	39	2	23	49	89	0	1	.277	.330	.456	.076	.300	.355	.499	.138	19.6	143-RF	-10	11-1B	0
2004	*BAL*	*AL*	*27*	*521*	*140*	*29*	*1*	*24*	*47*	*75*	*1*	*1*	*.268*	*.331*	*.469*	*.046*	*.277*	*.343*	*.493*	*.081*	*19.7*	*136-RF*	*-2*		

Breakout: 25%   Improve: 51%   Collapse: 21%

Gibbons was named Oriole MVP by the local beat writers (a bad choice owed to counting stats; Mora or Matos would have been better), but we expected more now that he was fully recovered from his 2002 wrist surgeries. As in prior years, he was an average bat for right field, but below average with the glove. After Jeff Conine was traded, Gibbons played a little first base, where, in the minors, he rated as a reasonably good fielder. Although Segui's elbow plays a major part in the equation, first figures to be Gibbons's primary position in 2004.

GERONIMO GIL   **C**   **Bats: R**   **Throws: R**   Born: 07-Aug-75   Age: 28

YEAR	TM	LG	AGE	AB	H	2B	3B	HR	BB	SO	SB	CS	AVG	OBP	SLG	MLVR	EQBA	EQOBP	EQSLG	EQMLVR	VORP	DEFENSE			
2001	LVG	PCL	25	281	83	15	0	9	16	56	0	1	.295	.334	.445	-.010	.256	.298	.386	-.165	0.7	63-C	3	13-1B	1
2001	ROC	INT	25	82	22	6	1	2	0	23	0	0	.268	.271	.439	-.037	.256	.271	.427	-.156	0.4	23-C	0		
2001	BAL	AL	25	58	17	2	0	0	5	7	0	0	.293	.369	.328	-.035	.322	.390	.356	.015	2.9	17-C	1		
2002	BAL	AL	26	422	98	19	0	12	21	88	2	2	.232	.270	.363	-.195	.256	.295	.404	-.145	3.1	119-C	7		
2003	BAL	AL	27	169	40	4	0	3	12	34	0	0	.237	.299	.314	-.215	.265	.326	.347	-.160	-2.7	52-C	1		
2003	OTT	INT	27	134	47	10	0	1	7	28	0	3	.351	.386	.448	.239	.326	.370	.430	.089	10.2	29-C	3		
2004	*BAL*	*AL*	*28*	*218*	*53*	*10*	*1*	*6*	*14*	*43*	*1*	*1*	*.245*	*.295*	*.373*	*-.156*	*.253*	*.306*	*.392*	*-.136*	*2.3*	*59-C*	*0*		

Breakout: 28%   Improve: 51%   Collapse: 35%

Gil started the season as the Orioles' #1 catcher, but his offensive and defensive lapses quickly forced him out, initially into a time-sharing role with Fordyce and ultimately to Ottawa. He was shocked by his July demotion, but apparently it got his attention in a way no talks from his manager had managed to do; he raked International League pitchers, but still didn't get much playing time when he came back to Baltimore. In 2004, he'll be Javy Lopez's backup.

JERRY HAIRSTON   **2B**   **Bats: R**   **Throws: R**   Born: 29-May-76   Age: 28

YEAR	TM	LG	AGE	AB	H	2B	3B	HR	BB	SO	SB	CS	AVG	OBP	SLG	MLVR	EQBA	EQOBP	EQSLG	EQMLVR	VORP	DEFENSE	
2001	BAL	AL	25	532	124	25	5	8	44	73	29	11	.233	.305	.344	-.171	.261	.331	.386	-.099	10.7	154-2B	8
2002	BAL	AL	26	426	114	25	3	5	34	55	21	6	.268	.329	.376	-.046	.303	.363	.426	.050	25.4	116-2B	2
2003	BAL	AL	27	218	59	12	2	2	23	25	14	5	.271	.353	.372	-.009	.300	.381	.418	.069	8.9	48-2B	-2
2004	*BAL*	*AL*	*28*	*386*	*101*	*20*	*2*	*6*	*36*	*49*	*17*	*6*	*.261*	*.334*	*.370*	*-.083*	*.269*	*.346*	*.388*	*-.058*	*16.8*	*105-2B*	*-2*

Breakout: 14%   Improve: 38%   Collapse: 33%

Hairston was off to an All-Star start, hitting .287/.387/.382 with 14 stolen bases through May 20. Unfortunately, he then fouled a pitch off his foot, and even though the ball didn't break anything, it made him hop around in pain, in the course of which he landed wrong and broke his foot. He was supposed to miss six to eight weeks, but it was 14 weeks before he got back, and even then his bat stayed behind (just .230/.254/.344). In the meantime, Roberts filled in well, and Mike Fontenot lit things up in Bowie. Hairston is likely to start the season in Baltimore, but is a strong candidate to be dealt by the July 31 deadline, if not earlier.

MIKE HUGGINS   **1B**   **Bats: R**   **Throws: R**   Born: 29-Aug-80   Age: 23

YEAR	TM	LG	AGE	AB	H	2B	3B	HR	BB	SO	SB	CS	AVG	OBP	SLG	MLVR	EQBA	EQOBP	EQSLG	EQMLVR	VORP	DEFENSE	
2002	ABE	NYP	21	271	71	15	2	1	31	55	9	4	.262	.340	.343	.047	.197	.254	.268	-.453	-58.9	71-1B	-6
2003	FRD	CAR	22	454	133	32	0	13	55	93	3	3	.293	.367	.449	.191	.232	.295	.371	-.209	-19.3	113-1B	-6
2004	*BAL*	*AL*	*23*	*254*	*54*	*12*	*1*	*7*	*21*	*61*	*2*	*1*	*.213*	*.277*	*.342*	*-.247*	*.220*	*.287*	*.359*	*-.234*	*-8.9*	*69-1B*	*-6*

Breakout: 32%   Improve: 54%   Collapse: 21%

Huggins was the best first baseman in the Oriole system, which is not much of a compliment. A 13th-round pick out of Baylor, he discovered a power stroke that was totally absent in 2002, thanks to devoted attention to the workout program the O's designed for him. Or perhaps there was something else at play: He did have 10 home runs in his final college season, and Aberdeen just kills home runs. He doesn't project as a major league player with what he's shown so far, so he's doing the right thing by going back to finish his marketing degree in the off-season.

TRIPPER JOHNSON

TRIPPER JOHNSON   3B   **Bats: R**   **Throws: R**   Born: 28-Apr-82   Age: 22

YEAR	TM	LG	AGE	AB	H	2B	3B	HR	BB	SO	SB	CS	AVG	OBP	SLG	MLVR	EQBA	EQOBP	EQSLG	EQMLVR	VORP	DEFENSE	
2001	BLU	APP	19	157	41	6	1	2	11	37	4	0	.261	.312	.350	-.049	.182	.220	.245	-.561	-38.5	14-3B	-2
2002	DEL	SAL	20	493	128	32	6	11	62	88	19	6	.260	.349	.416	.133	.202	.269	.334	-.329	-24.1	131-3B	7
2003	FRD	CAR	21	417	114	25	3	5	46	92	7	8	.273	.359	.384	.079	.218	.284	.319	-.311	-18.2	116-3B	-3
2004	*BAL*	*AL*	*22*	*256*	*53*	*12*	*1*	*5*	*19*	*57*	*3*	*1*	*.206*	*.268*	*.318*	*-.298*	*.212*	*.278*	*.334*	*-.289*	*-6.5*	*70-3B*	*-5*

Breakout: 34%   Improve: 52%   Collapse: 27%

Following a storybook high school career, Nelson Alexander Johnson III—"Tripper" comes from "triple," but in the sense of his being the third—came to the O's in the first round of the 2000 draft. A sensational all-around athlete, as a pro he projects as all-around average; average batting average, average power, average walks, average speed, playing a position right smack in the middle of the defensive spectrum. He tailed off badly in the second half of the season, including a brutal month-long stretch where he hit .230 with zero extra-base hits.

JOSE LEON

JOSE LEON   1B/3B   **Bats: R**   **Throws: R**   Born: 08-Dec-76   Age: 27

YEAR	TM	LG	AGE	AB	H	2B	3B	HR	BB	SO	SB	CS	AVG	OBP	SLG	MLVR	EQBA	EQOBP	EQSLG	EQMLVR	VORP	DEFENSE	
2001	BOW	EAS	24	95	34	9	1	4	8	21	1	1	.358	.413	.600	.503	.306	.356	.520	.176	10.5	21-3B	-6
2001	ROC	INT	24	416	116	20	4	12	25	96	7	3	.279	.325	.433	.050	.264	.311	.417	-.090	10.9	107-3B	4
2002	BAL	AL	25	89	22	2	0	3	3	20	1	0	.247	.280	.371	-.156	.278	.307	.411	-.095	-0.3	15-1B	0
2002	ROC	INT	25	312	87	16	1	8	18	54	0	0	.279	.319	.413	.011	.262	.307	.396	-.129	4.6	79-3B	6
2003	OTT	INT	26	309	82	19	2	4	15	47	1	1	.265	.305	.379	-.055	.254	.296	.373	-.189	-0.8	65-3B	1
2003	BAL	AL	26	54	13	1	0	0	3	18	0	0	.241	.305	.259	-.275	.259	.329	.296	-.230	-2.1	10-3B	0
2004	*BAL*	*AL*	*27*	*197*	*49*	*10*	*1*	*6*	*13*	*39*	*1*	*1*	*.248*	*.299*	*.392*	*-.122*	*.257*	*.310*	*.411*	*-.100*	*7.1*	*54-3B*	*-1*

Breakout: 34%   Improve: 47%   Collapse: 30%

Leon's season ended a little early last year, courtesy of a thrown ball that hit him in the face and the broken bone that came with it. He has spent the last few years as the Orioles' emergency third baseman, spending most of that time stashed away at Triple-A. He was cut from the 40-man roster after the season and almost immediately re-signed to an Ottawa contract, so he'll keep playing the understudy. Since Baltimore's third-base position looks muddled for 2004, he may get a chance to fill in a little more often.

ROBERT MACHADO

ROBERT MACHADO   C   **Bats: R**   **Throws: R**   Born: 03-Jun-73   Age: 31

YEAR	TM	LG	AGE	AB	H	2B	3B	HR	BB	SO	SB	CS	AVG	OBP	SLG	MLVR	EQBA	EQOBP	EQSLG	EQMLVR	VORP	DEFENSE	
2001	IOW	PCL	28	180	51	11	0	8	11	36	0	0	.283	.332	.478	.056	.257	.305	.430	-.089	4.7	45-C	1
2001	CHC	NL	28	135	30	10	0	2	7	26	0	0	.222	.266	.341	-.295	.228	.270	.353	-.285	-4.1	37-C	1
2002	CHC	NL	29	58	16	4	0	1	5	11	0	0	.276	.333	.397	.017	.288	.344	.424	-.000	2.6	15-C	5
2002	MIL	NL	29	153	39	10	1	2	12	30	0	0	.255	.310	.373	-.082	.265	.321	.387	-.114	2.4	43-C	1
2003	OTT	INT	30	221	74	17	0	8	17	36	0	0	.335	.390	.520	.329	.308	.362	.496	.153	21.5	40-C	8
2003	BAL	AL	30	49	13	1	0	1	6	12	0	0	.265	.345	.347	-.009	.300	.375	.380	.004	1.9	14-C	2
2004	*BAL*	*AL*	*31*	*177*	*43*	*9*	*0*	*5*	*13*	*33*	*0*	*0*	*.244*	*.298*	*.384*	*-.138*	*.252*	*.309*	*.403*	*-.117*	*3.0*	*49-C*	*0*

Breakout: 13%   Improve: 28%   Collapse: 53%

Machado finished 2002 expecting to be Milwaukee's starting catcher in 2003. Ah, but the Brewers got themselves a new manager, and Machado had the misfortune to pull a hammy in spring training, and he got dumped. The Orioles picked him up and sent him to Ottawa. He's always been a good defensive catcher, but he's never, ever hit the way he did for the Lynx last year, and it's not likely he ever will again. He was sparingly used when they called him up to replace Gil, mostly backing up Fordyce, and declared free agency after the season.

VAL MAJEWSKI

VAL MAJEWSKI   CF   **Bats: L**   **Throws: L**   Born: 19-Jun-81   Age: 23

YEAR	TM	LG	AGE	AB	H	2B	3B	HR	BB	SO	SB	CS	AVG	OBP	SLG	MLVR	EQBA	EQOBP	EQSLG	EQMLVR	VORP	DEFENSE			
2002	ABE	NYP	21	110	33	7	4	1	13	14	8	4	.300	.376	.464	.276	.216	.269	.353	-.295	-9.6	26-CF	0		
2003	DEL	SAL	22	208	63	15	8	7	28	20	10	1	.303	.383	.553	.401	.232	.294	.427	-.133	-4.7	36-RF	-6	21-CF	-2
2003	FRD	CAR	22	159	46	18	1	5	7	23	0	0	.289	.321	.509	.209	.242	.267	.441	-.155	-0.4	27-CF	-6		
2004	*BAL*	*AL*	*23*	*281*	*67*	*16*	*4*	*7*	*19*	*41*	*5*	*2*	*.240*	*.291*	*.396*	*-.137*	*.248*	*.301*	*.416*	*-.115*	*1.3*	*75-CF*	*-10*		

Breakout: 28%   Improve: 59%   Collapse: 18%

(continued next page)

Val Majewski *(continued)*

Majewski is a scout's dream: Besides the athletic body, he has a certain presence about him that seems to give everybody the idea that he can't miss—must be "the good face" or something. His performance doesn't support that conclusion however, at least not yet. While his numbers look good at Delmarva, at 22 he was old for the competition, and so far, he projects to be fairly average. He did miss time with a stress fracture in his leg, which shows up as missing speed in Frederick.

NICK MARKAKIS — RF — Bats: L — Throws: L — Born: 17-Nov-83 — Age: 20

YEAR	TM	LG	AGE	AB	H	2B	3B	HR	BB	SO	SB	CS	AVG	OBP	SLG	MLVR	EQBA	EQOBP	EQSLG	EQMLVR	VORP	DEFENSE			
2003	ABE	NYP	19	205	58	14	3	1	30	33	13	5	.283	.372	.395	.177	.206	.274	.303	-.359	-36.7	44-RF	-5	11-CF	-1
2004	BAL	AL	20	243	50	11	2	3	18	47	6	3	.204	.260	.299	-.337	.211	.270	.314	-.330	-15.2	66-RF	-5		

Breakout: 28% Improve: 48% Collapse: 29%

The Orioles grabbed Markakis with the seventh overall pick in last year's draft. He'd previously gone 12–0 as a juco pitcher in 2003, striking out nearly 15 batters per 9 innings, and was considered one of the top pitchers in the draft. However, since he also hit .439 in college, with 21 homers and a nation-leading 92 RBI, the Orioles took him as a right fielder, and he responded by taking top prospect honors in the New York-Penn League.

One of Peter Angelos' pet projects right now is sponsoring the Greek national baseball team for the 2004 Olympics. Markakis happens to be of Greek descent, close enough for Greece's loose eligibility rules to qualify him for their national team. This provoked protests from other nations, chiefly Germany, whose rules are considerably stricter about defining "citizens." He missed three weeks playing in the European championships (batting cleanup, hitting .323), and is expected play in the Olympics . . . after the upset loss to Mexico, the only way Americans will play in the Olympics this year is to play for somebody else.

LUIS MATOS — CF — Bats: R — Throws: R — Born: 30-Oct-78 — Age: 25

YEAR	TM	LG	AGE	AB	H	2B	3B	HR	BB	SO	SB	CS	AVG	OBP	SLG	MLVR	EQBA	EQOBP	EQSLG	EQMLVR	VORP	DEFENSE			
2001	BOW	EAS	22	46	14	5	0	1	5	7	0	1	.304	.385	.478	.247	.271	.334	.417	-.042	1.2				
2001	BAL	AL	22	98	21	7	0	4	11	30	7	0	.214	.300	.408	-.109	.242	.323	.455	-.033	3.0	17-CF	0		
2002	BOW	EAS	23	218	60	14	2	9	32	45	14	4	.275	.370	.482	.192	.233	.316	.408	-.117	2.2	33-CF	-4	14-RF	-1
2003	OTT	INT	24	175	53	16	4	1	13	34	6	1	.303	.347	.457	.149	.282	.334	.441	.001	3.4	23-RF	-1	21-CF	-1
2003	BAL	AL	24	439	133	23	3	13	28	90	15	7	.303	.353	.458	.140	.332	.383	.506	.228	29.8	105-CF	0		
2004	BAL	AL	25	483	129	29	3	17	41	100	15	5	.268	.331	.444	.013	.277	.343	.466	.045	22.5	127-CF	-4		

Breakout: 17% Improve: 49% Collapse: 19%

BP has liked Matos for years, without much to show for it. He hit for average and some power, with speed and good center field defense, and could have provided a measure of youth to a team that qualified for pharmaceutical discounts. The problem was, he couldn't stay healthy. In 2003, he was healthy, and showed what he could do when given the chance and some health. With the 30 pounds he's added over the last three years, hopefully he'll stay in the lineup and off the DL.

DARNELL McDONALD — CF — Bats: R — Throws: R — Born: 17-Nov-78 — Age: 25

YEAR	TM	LG	AGE	AB	H	2B	3B	HR	BB	SO	SB	CS	AVG	OBP	SLG	MLVR	EQBA	EQOBP	EQSLG	EQMLVR	VORP	DEFENSE			
2001	BOW	EAS	22	117	33	7	1	3	9	28	3	3	.282	.336	.436	.100	.250	.300	.383	-.170	-4.2	25-LF	-3		
2001	ROC	INT	22	391	93	19	2	2	29	75	13	9	.238	.291	.312	-.195	.225	.279	.299	-.345	-22.8	63-CF	1	31-LF	-2
2002	BOW	EAS	23	144	42	9	1	4	22	27	9	3	.292	.393	.451	.200	.243	.326	.385	-.123	1.2	14-CF	-1	10-LF	0
2002	ROC	INT	23	332	96	21	6	6	32	78	11	3	.289	.353	.443	.113	.266	.331	.421	-.046	10.0	88-CF	2		
2003	OTT	INT	24	152	45	7	1	0	18	27	5	7	.296	.374	.355	.051	.271	.346	.329	-.143	0.2	23-CF	-1	14-RF	0
2004	BAL	AL	25	191	47	10	1	4	16	37	4	2	.248	.310	.374	-.127	.256	.322	.392	-.105	2.2	53-CF	-4		

Breakout: 25% Improve: 47% Collapse: 32%

We thought that maybe the former #1 draft pick had turned a corner in 2002, finally capitalizing on his prodigious tools to become a good baseball player. It is hard to know whether that was true or not, because he barely played a month before shoulder surgery ended his season. His walk and strikeout rates continued to show improvement in that small sample, but his power was non-existent. He projects as a decent backup center fielder, and little more.

CARLOS MENDEZ 1B Bats: R Throws: R Born: 18-Jun-74 Age: 30

YEAR	TM	LG	AGE	AB	H	2B	3B	HR	BB	SO	SB	CS	AVG	OBP	SLG	MLVR	EQBA	EQOBP	EQSLG	EQMLVR	VORP	DEFENSE			
2001	TOL	INT	27	398	98	27	1	18	9	53	0	0	.246	.268	.455	-.039	.236	.262	.441	-.169	-9.4	52-1B	-1	38-C	-2
2002	SAC	PCL	28	404	131	26	1	12	12	52	3	1	.324	.348	.483	.163	.296	.319	.445	-.007	18.0	59-C	-8	15-1B	0
2003	OTT	INT	29	248	86	18	4	4	11	28	1	2	.347	.375	.500	.293	.324	.359	.480	.142	16.1	58-1B	1		
2003	BAL	AL	29	45	10	2	0	0	0	12	0	0	.222	.217	.267	-.450	.244	.244	.311	-.387	-3.5				
2004	*BAL*	*AL*	*30*	*199*	*51*	*10*	*1*	*5*	*8*	*29*	*1*	*1*	*.259*	*.291*	*.403*	*-.114*	*.267*	*.302*	*.423*	*-.091*	*2.1*	*53-1B*	*2*		

Breakout: 13%   Improve: 29%   Collapse: 32%

After 12 years in the minor leagues, including six at Triple-A, Mendez finally made it to the majors. Throughout his minor-league career, he's been a high-average but impatient hitter, averaging less than one walk for every 25 at-bats, and 2004 was no different: After 42 games in Ottawa he was hitting .384, but his OBP was still only .412. He'll remain in Ottawa as the team's first baseman and emergency catcher for 2004.

MELVIN MORA 3B/LF Bats: R Throws: R Born: 02-Feb-72 Age: 32

YEAR	TM	LG	AGE	AB	H	2B	3B	HR	BB	SO	SB	CS	AVG	OBP	SLG	MLVR	EQBA	EQOBP	EQSLG	EQMLVR	VORP	DEFENSE			
2001	BAL	AL	29	436	109	28	0	7	41	91	11	4	.250	.329	.362	-.091	.280	.360	.408	.000	17.2	80-CF	-2	41-SS	2
2002	BAL	AL	30	557	130	30	4	19	70	108	16	10	.233	.338	.404	-.016	.266	.366	.463	.075	19.9	73-LF	5	35-SS	-3
2003	BAL	AL	31	344	109	17	1	15	49	71	6	3	.317	.418	.503	.322	.355	.451	.570	.452	38.0	56-LF	5	11-RF	-2
2004	*BAL*	*AL*	*32*	*365*	*96*	*19*	*1*	*12*	*44*	*71*	*6*	*2*	*.264*	*.355*	*.425*	*.027*	*.273*	*.369*	*.446*	*.059*	*18.6*	*101-LF*	*3*		

Breakout: 12%   Improve: 32%   Collapse: 34%

On July 7 last season, Melvin Mora was named to the AL All-Star team. It was an easy choice: At the time, he was first in the AL in batting average (.361), first in on-base average (.457), and second in slugging (.591). It looks like the All-Star Game was what Mr. Applegate promised him, because as soon as he was named to the team his season turned ugly. He'd been hit on the hand by a pitch in June, then sat out a couple of games and came back, seemingly without any problem. But a deep bruise was in there that just kept getting worse, and eventually sent him to the DL for a month; a knee injury ended his season in mid-September. From July 8 to the end of the season, Mora batted just 107 more times, for a feeble .196 batting average and .261 slugging average. The Orioles intend to play him at third base in 2004, even though he hasn't played there in 10 years, and it remains to be seen whether he has the stamina to produce in the second half.

JOSE MORBAN SS Bats: R Throws: R Born: 02-Dec-79 Age: 24

YEAR	TM	LG	AGE	AB	H	2B	3B	HR	BB	SO	SB	CS	AVG	OBP	SLG	MLVR	EQBA	EQOBP	EQSLG	EQMLVR	VORP	DEFENSE	
2001	SAV	SAL	21	474	119	20	11	8	42	119	46	18	.251	.313	.390	.052	.202	.252	.322	-.380	-27.3	115-SS	1
2002	PCH	FLA	22	485	126	27	12	8	46	111	21	9	.260	.326	.414	.073	.216	.268	.355	-.294	-13.6	119-SS	-4
2003	BAL	AL	23	71	10	0	0	2	3	21	8	0	.141	.187	.225	-.605	.155	.198	.282	-.567	-6.9		
2004	*BAL*	*AL*	*24*	*166*	*40*	*7*	*1*	*4*	*13*	*39*	*11*	*2*	*.240*	*.302*	*.382*	*-.136*	*.248*	*.313*	*.401*	*-.115*	*7.2*	*47-SS*	*-4*

Breakout: 76%   Improve: 82%   Collapse: 8%

Morban was a Rule 5 selection from the Twins' system, and the Orioles (who have no good shortstops in their system) decided to keep him. He was mainly used as a pinch-runner; the times he got to play in the field were when injuries had left the Orioles desperate for any warm body, and his batting performance left little doubt that that's about all he's good for. He was clearly overmatched by major league pitching, and he'll go back to the minors next year, where, weak as he is, he'll still be the best shortstop in the system.

TIM RAINES JR. CF Bats: R Throws: R Born: 31-Aug-79 Age: 24

YEAR	TM	LG	AGE	AB	H	2B	3B	HR	BB	SO	SB	CS	AVG	OBP	SLG	MLVR	EQBA	EQOBP	EQSLG	EQMLVR	VORP	DEFENSE			
2001	FRD	CAR	21	84	21	3	1	3	13	23	14	4	.250	.351	.417	.132	.202	.283	.348	-.283	-3.9	19-CF	-2		
2001	BOW	EAS	21	254	74	14	1	4	34	60	29	10	.291	.380	.402	.132	.250	.330	.352	-.156	-0.7	64-CF	0		
2001	ROC	INT	21	133	34	5	1	2	11	30	11	3	.256	.313	.353	-.092	.244	.297	.341	-.239	-3.6	34-CF	-8		
2002	BOW	EAS	22	491	128	17	4	5	34	101	33	15	.261	.310	.342	-.102	.231	.272	.310	-.340	-29.5	88-CF	-10	25-LF	-2
2003	BOW	EAS	23	247	76	15	4	4	21	40	28	6	.308	.371	.449	.174	.266	.323	.403	-.086	4.7	49-CF	-4		
2003	OTT	INT	23	214	64	11	5	3	19	37	23	9	.299	.357	.439	.137	.276	.337	.415	-.036	7.2	51-CF	0		
2003	BAL	AL	23	43	6	1	1	0	2	12	0	0	.140	.196	.209	-.609	.163	.214	.256	-.566	-5.2	12-CF	0		
2004	*BAL*	*AL*	*24*	*255*	*65*	*12*	*2*	*5*	*20*	*50*	*14*	*5*	*.253*	*.311*	*.379*	*-.115*	*.262*	*.322*	*.398*	*-.092*	*3.3*	*69-CF*	*-5*		

Breakout: 37%   Improve: 61%   Collapse: 16%

(continued next page)

Tim Raines Jr. *(continued)*

After a miserable 2002 season, Raines was dropped from the 40-man roster in December '02 and cleared waivers. The idea that nobody thought he was worth taking apparently bothered him, as he rededicated himself to baseball, stayed out of bar fights, listened to what his coaches were telling him, and put himself back on the prospect board with a breakout season at the plate and in the field. He's still a weak prospect, mind you—he doesn't walk enough to use his speed as effectively as his dad did—but that's better than where he was last year.

BRIAN ROBERTS   **2B**   **Bats: B**   **Throws: R**   Born: 09-Oct-77   Age: 26

YEAR	TM	LG	AGE	AB	H	2B	3B	HR	BB	SO	SB	CS	AVG	OBP	SLG	MLVR	EQBA	EQOBP	EQSLG	EQMLVR	VORP	DEFENSE	
2001	BOW	EAS	23	81	24	7	0	1	9	12	10	0	.296	.366	.420	.136	.262	.330	.369	-.124	1.3	19-2B	0
2001	ROC	INT	23	161	43	4	1	1	28	22	23	3	.267	.376	.323	-.015	.255	.356	.309	-.160	2.2	44-SS	-7
2001	BAL	AL	23	273	69	12	3	2	13	36	12	3	.253	.284	.341	-.204	.280	.315	.378	-.126	5.3	48-SS	-6
2002	ROC	INT	24	313	86	9	7	3	40	46	22	4	.275	.361	.377	.030	.258	.339	.358	-.125	4.8	69-2B	-5
2002	BAL	AL	24	128	29	6	0	1	15	21	9	2	.227	.308	.297	-.214	.254	.335	.331	-.172	0.1	25-2B	1
2003	OTT	INT	25	178	56	13	1	0	27	12	19	6	.315	.401	.399	.165	.286	.375	.374	-.014	9.1	36-2B	-4
2003	BAL	AL	25	460	124	22	4	5	46	58	23	6	.270	.337	.367	-.058	.297	.366	.409	.026	13.3	102-2B	6
2004	*BAL*	*AL*	*26*	*413*	*108*	*19*	*4*	*5*	*42*	*52*	*21*	*6*	*.262*	*.334*	*.361*	*-.093*	*.271*	*.346*	*.378*	*-.069*	*15.3*	*110-2B*	*-2*

Breakout: 17%   Improve: 46%   Collapse: 21%

For the second year in a row, Roberts came into the season playing second fiddle to Jerry Hairston, and for the second time it wasn't clear who the better player was, or is. Roberts's regular season was just a continuation of a strong performance in the Puerto Rican league last winter (translated .306/.391/.446). Between Roberts, Hairston, and now Fontenot, the Orioles are facing a second base glut. There was a lot of talk about moving Roberts back to short, but they only managed to test that out for two games in September, and the Tejada signing torpedoes the idea entirely.

DAVID SEGUI   **DH/1B**   **Bats: B**   **Throws: L**   Born: 19-Jul-66   Age: 37

YEAR	TM	LG	AGE	AB	H	2B	3B	HR	BB	SO	SB	CS	AVG	OBP	SLG	MLVR	EQBA	EQOBP	EQSLG	EQMLVR	VORP	DEFENSE
2001	BAL	AL	34	292	88	18	1	10	49	61	1	1	.301	.406	.473	.231	.328	.432	.517	.319	33.5	60-1B -9
2002	BAL	AL	35	95	25	4	0	2	11	22	0	0	.263	.336	.368	-.045	.292	.370	.406	.025	3.9	
2003	BAL	AL	36	224	59	10	1	5	26	47	1	0	.263	.341	.384	-.020	.288	.368	.420	.038	6.1	
2004	*BAL*	*AL*	*37*	*182*	*46*	*8*	*0*	*5*	*22*	*40*	*1*	*0*	*.253*	*.335*	*.380*	*-.074*	*.261*	*.347*	*.398*	*-.048*	*3.4*	

Breakout: 16%   Improve: 36%   Collapse: 40%

In *BP2002,* we set the over-under for "Segui plate appearances on remaining contract in 2003 and 2004" at 500; with 252 last year, we're on target so far. Segui's tale of the medical tape, 2003 edition: (1) March 12, broke his thumb fielding a batting practice ground ball; out four weeks. (2) April 17, strained hamstring; out 15 days. (3) May 23, left game with sinus infection. (4) June 12, fouled ball off foot; missed three games. (5) Approx. June 30, knee stiffens up, out nine games except for two pinch-hit appearances. (6) July 26, sprained wrist on check-swing, tore same tendon he did in 2002, required surgery September 8, out until spring training 2004, and perhaps longer. The Orioles have made it perhaps too obvious that they hope Segui's out for the year, while Segui seems determined to play.

B. J. SURHOFF   **LF**   **Bats: L**   **Throws: R**   Born: 04-Aug-64   Age: 39

YEAR	TM	LG	AGE	AB	H	2B	3B	HR	BB	SO	SB	CS	AVG	OBP	SLG	MLVR	EQBA	EQOBP	EQSLG	EQMLVR	VORP	DEFENSE	
2001	ATL	NL	36	484	131	33	1	10	38	48	9	3	.271	.321	.405	-.065	.277	.330	.415	-.048	0.9	116-LF	-3
2002	ATL	NL	37	75	22	5	0	0	9	5	1	3	.293	.369	.360	.032	.289	.365	.368	-.039	1.7		
2003	BAL	AL	38	319	94	20	0	5	29	29	2	2	.295	.353	.404	.044	.317	.378	.441	.111	10.4	20-LF -2	19-1B -1
2004	*BAL*	*AL*	*39*	*299*	*79*	*16*	*1*	*5*	*25*	*29*	*3*	*2*	*.265*	*.321*	*.370*	*-.103*	*.273*	*.333*	*.388*	*-.079*	*0.3*	*80-LF*	*-2*

Breakout: 2%   Improve: 36%   Collapse: 20%

A nice last-hurrah season for one of the game's nice guys. Surhoff hit the cover off the ball for two months last June and July, but faded with the rest of the team through a brutal August/September schedule. He wanted to come back for another year, and management willingly signed him up, but there's very little room in the Oriole outfield for him to play.

PITCHERS

KURT AINSWORTH
Bats: R   Throws: R   Born: 09-Sep-78   Age: 25

YEAR	TM	LG	AGE	G	GS	IP	H	BB	SO	HR	ERA	EQERA	EQH9	EQBB9	EQSO9	EQHR9	PERA	VORP	STF
2001	FRE	PCL	22	27	26	149.0	139	54	157	22	5.07	5.17	8.2	3.8	7.4	1.3	4.67	6.8	22
2002	FRE	PCL	23	20	19	116.0	101	43	119	7	3.41	3.94	8.1	3.8	7.3	0.7	3.94	20.2	33
2002	SFG	NL	23	6	4	25.7	22	12	15	1	2.10	3.33	8.1	3.7	4.8	0.4	3.69	6.1	22
2003	SFG	NL	24	11	11	66.0	66	26	48	7	3.82	4.86	9.6	3.3	5.9	1.0	4.85	8.5	13
2004	BAL	AL	25	23	19	113.7	117	46	83	14	4.52	4.71	9.2	3.5	6.3	1.0	4.76	13.2	7

Breakout: 16%   Improve: 41%   Collapse: 21%

Ainsworth was the key to the Sidney Ponson trade, even though his stock has fallen sharply in the last couple of years. He spent most of the year sidelined with a freak injury—what was originally diagnosed as a strained muscle in his upper back turned out to be a fractured shoulder blade, virtually unheard-of in baseball. It's thought that he'll be fine by the spring, which means he'll step right into the Oriole rotation. With this rag-tag bunch, it wouldn't be a shock to see Ainsworth or Matt Riley emerge as the staff ace by the All-Star break.

RICK BAUER
Bats: R   Throws: R   Born: 10-Jan-77   Age: 27

YEAR	TM	LG	AGE	G	GS	IP	H	BB	SO	HR	ERA	EQERA	EQH9	EQBB9	EQSO9	EQHR9	PERA	VORP	STF
2001	BOW	EAS	24	9	9	61.0	52	10	34	8	3.54	4.72	9.1	2.0	3.4	2.0	5.37	5.4	-26
2001	ROC	INT	24	19	18	113.3	119	28	89	10	3.89	4.81	9.9	2.5	5.4	1.0	4.80	9.4	8
2001	BAL	AL	24	6	6	33.0	35	9	16	7	4.64	5.34	9.3	2.2	4.2	1.7	5.21	0.9	-10
2002	BAL	AL	25	56	1	83.7	84	36	45	12	3.98	4.78	9.0	3.6	4.7	1.2	4.92	7.4	-17
2003	OTT	INT	26	7	7	36.7	31	13	21	1	2.45	3.48	8.3	4.0	4.0	0.3	3.76	7.9	9
2003	BAL	AL	26	35	0	61.3	58	24	43	5	4.55	4.48	7.9	3.3	6.1	0.6	3.67	2.8	8
2004	BAL	AL	27	25	10	64.7	69	25	40	9	4.76	4.96	9.6	3.3	5.4	1.1	5.10	6.5	-7

Breakout: 25%   Improve: 47%   Collapse: 30%

A failed—well, failed is such a strong word, let's try unsuccessful—starter throughout his minor league career, Bauer has emerged as a capable middle reliever, although he still wants to start. He had a huge split last year between men on (.845 OPS) and bases empty (.589), which explains the gap between his EqERA and PERA; that hasn't been a problem for him before, and isn't likely to continue. If all of the other kids struggle in camp, he might get a shot at the rotation, but don't hold your breath.

DENNY BAUTISTA
Bats: R   Throws: R   Born: 23-Oct-82   Age: 21

YEAR	TM	LG	AGE	G	GS	IP	H	BB	SO	HR	ERA	EQERA	EQH9	EQBB9	EQSO9	EQHR9	PERA	VORP	STF
2001	UTI	NYP	18	7	7	39.0	25	6	31	0	2.08	3.89	7.8	2.1	4.2	0.3	2.98	6.6	33
2001	KNE	MID	18	8	7	39.3	43	14	20	2	4.35	7.43	10.4	4.5	3.0	1.0	5.61	-7.4	-4
2002	JUP	FLA	19	19	15	88.3	80	40	79	6	4.99	6.89	9.3	5.0	6.1	1.3	5.57	-11.6	13
2003	JUP	FLA	20	14	14	84.0	68	35	77	2	3.21	5.21	8.6	4.7	6.0	0.7	4.52	3.3	27
2003	CAR	SOU	20	11	11	53.3	45	35	61	5	3.71	6.89	9.3	6.9	7.8	1.7	6.40	-6.9	14
2004	BAL	AL	21	19	15	87.0	86	50	68	10	4.87	5.08	8.8	4.9	6.8	0.9	5.17	7.2	4

Breakout: 27%   Improve: 57%   Collapse: 17%

Pedro Martinez. The first thing that's always mentioned with Bautista is that he's a good friend of Pedro's, who's been a sort of pitching coach and general advisor to the young man. Bautista's numbers aren't nearly as good as Pedro's at the same age (Pedro had some of the best translations ever seen coming up through the minors), but they are still very good. The Orioles traded Jeff Conine away to get him, but it was too late in the season for the O's to see his 95-mph fastball for themselves. Needs to harness his control to further tap into his raw talent.

ERIK BEDARD

Bats: L **Throws: L** Born: 06-Mar-79 Age: 25

YEAR	TM	LG	AGE	G	GS	IP	H	BB	SO	HR	ERA	EQERA	EQH9	EQBB9	EQSO9	EQHR9	PERA	VORP	STF
2001	FRD	CAR	22	17	17	96.3	68	26	130	4	2.15	3.95	9.1	3.5	7.5	1.0	4.61	15.5	27
2002	BOW	EAS	23	13	12	68.7	43	30	66	0	1.97	2.67	6.2	4.5	6.3	0.3	2.96	20.8	34
2003	ABE	NYP	24	2	2	7.7	7	1	13	0	2.34	4.26	14.2	1.4	8.5	0.0	5.31	0.9	37
2003	FRD	CAR	24	1	1	3.7	5	1	2	1	7.30	9.00	18.0	3.0	3.0	6.0	15.52	-1.1	-179
2004	BAL	AL	25	17	13	75.0	79	28	54	9	4.55	4.74	9.5	3.1	6.3	1.0	4.77	8.9	6

Breakout: 19%   Improve: 53%   Collapse: 24%

Bedard had Tommy John surgery in September of 2002, and was able to rehab and get in a few minor league starts just before the season ended. His rehab apparently went well: His fastball was reportedly back its to full 92–93-mph speed, and he was surprised to find that he still had a feel for his curveball—a good thing, because it was his best pitch. While he's been an outstanding pitcher throughout his pro career, he's been exceptionally dominant against left-handed hitters. In a couple of years, the O's could have a mighty interesting core of young starters between Ainsworth, Batista, Bedard, and Riley.

HECTOR CARRASCO

Bats: R **Throws: R** Born: 22-Oct-69 Age: 34

YEAR	TM	LG	AGE	G	GS	IP	H	BB	SO	HR	ERA	EQERA	EQH9	EQBB9	EQSO9	EQHR9	PERA	VORP	STF
2001	MIN	AL	31	56	0	73.7	77	30	70	8	4.64	4.52	9.4	3.4	7.9	0.9	4.64	8.6	9
2003	OTT	INT	33	33	0	44.7	32	20	47	2	2.21	3.10	7.5	5.1	7.5	0.7	4.05	11.3	5
2003	BAL	AL	33	40	0	38.3	40	20	27	5	4.93	4.97	8.8	4.3	6.2	0.9	4.69	2.3	-8
2004	BAL	AL	34	78	0	44.0	44	21	35	5	4.31	4.49	8.9	4.2	6.9	0.8	4.75	6.5	-4

Breakout: 38%   Improve: 58%   Collapse: 17%

After missing all of 2002 with rotator cuff surgery, the Orioles took a chance on Carrasco and set him up with the Triple-A Lynx. He started strong, and was soon Ottawa's closer. When Willis Roberts's injury opened up a spot in the pen, Carrasco came up and held it for the rest of the year, even though he wasn't very effective. He's been a lot better in the past, and as a free agent he could still be a nice addition to the back of somebody's bullpen.

OMAR DAAL

Bats: L **Throws: L** Born: 23-Feb-72 Age: 32

YEAR	TM	LG	AGE	G	GS	IP	H	BB	SO	HR	ERA	EQERA	EQH9	EQBB9	EQSO9	EQHR9	PERA	VORP	STF
2001	PHI	NL	29	32	32	185.7	199	56	107	26	4.46	5.07	9.8	2.5	4.4	1.2	4.96	10.5	-6
2002	LAD	NL	30	39	23	161.3	142	54	105	20	3.91	4.69	8.8	2.7	5.2	1.2	4.56	15.3	-5
2003	BAL	AL	31	19	17	93.7	134	30	53	11	6.34	6.34	12.1	2.7	5.0	1.0	5.84	-10.3	-7
2004	BAL	AL	32	24	17	101.7	121	34	54	16	5.24	5.47	10.7	2.9	4.6	1.2	5.61	4.7	-7

Breakout: 6%   Improve: 48%   Collapse: 22%

The Orioles signed Daal to a two-year, $7.5 million deal, with the idea that he'd be their #2 starter. That didn't work. Daal has been very streaky since moving into the Dodger rotation in May 2002: A good game (arbitrarily defined as having three more innings pitched than runs allowed) has been more than twice as likely to be followed by another good game, and a bad game has been almost twice as likely to be followed by another bad game. Both results were on the order of one in 14 chances. You can expect similar streakiness in the second year of his contract.

SEAN DOUGLASS

Bats: R **Throws: R** Born: 28-Apr-79 Age: 25

YEAR	TM	LG	AGE	G	GS	IP	H	BB	SO	HR	ERA	EQERA	EQH9	EQBB9	EQSO9	EQHR9	PERA	VORP	STF
2001	ROC	INT	22	27	27	162.3	160	61	156	13	3.49	4.49	8.5	3.8	7.1	0.8	4.26	19.3	33
2001	BAL	AL	22	4	4	20.3	21	11	17	3	5.32	4.95	9.0	4.5	6.8	1.4	5.28	1.4	20
2002	ROC	INT	23	14	13	66.7	66	35	71	4	4.72	5.40	9.0	5.5	8.2	0.7	4.84	1.4	25
2002	BAL	AL	23	15	8	53.3	58	35	44	10	6.08	6.75	9.9	5.4	7.1	1.6	6.14	-6.6	0
2003	OTT	INT	24	27	27	143.0	142	58	118	6	3.40	4.92	9.7	4.5	5.9	0.6	4.84	10.0	11
2003	BAL	AL	24	3	0	8.0	14	6	3	2	13.50	11.25	14.6	6.8	3.4	2.2	9.48	-7.2	-73
2004	MIN	AL	25	21	15	89.0	94	46	65	10	5.16	5.03	9.1	4.4	6.5	0.9	4.90	7.6	3

Breakout: 21%   Improve: 53%   Collapse: 24%

Douglass went into 2003 with a slim hope of landing the fifth starter's job, but a lousy spring put a stop to that. Instead he became the #2 starter in Ottawa, struggling through most of the season before finishing the year strong (4.43 ERA after 16 starts, 2.04 over his last 12). Called up in September, he only appeared in three games, and was later claimed by the

Twins when the O's tried to move him off the 40-man roster. Nothing in his track record suggests he'll be more than a middle relief mop-up guy, although those final 12 starts raise hopes a bit.

TRAVIS DRISKILL   Bats: R   Throws: R   Born: 01-Aug-71   Age: 32

YEAR	TM	LG	AGE	G	GS	IP	H	BB	SO	HR	ERA	EQERA	EQH9	EQBB9	EQSO9	EQHR9	PERA	VORP	STF
2001	NWO	PCL	29	28	28	178.7	175	33	145	21	3.78	4.86	10.0	2.0	5.4	1.4	5.09	13.5	-8
2002	ROC	INT	30	4	4	22.0	17	1	15	1	1.64	3.05	7.4	0.4	5.2	0.4	2.47	5.9	30
2002	BAL	AL	30	29	19	132.7	150	48	78	21	4.95	5.54	10.2	3.0	5.1	1.3	5.43	0.9	-12
2003	OTT	INT	31	9	9	50.7	46	6	36	8	2.84	3.91	9.6	1.4	5.1	2.3	5.88	8.6	-30
2003	BAL	AL	31	20	0	48.0	62	9	33	8	6.00	5.89	10.8	1.5	6.1	1.3	5.30	-4.9	-9
2004	*COL*	*NL*	*32*	*22*	*11*	*68.7*	*79*	*21*	*43*	*12*	*5.19*	*4.92*	*10.1*	*2.3*	*5.2*	*1.3*	*4.94*	*6.3*	*-4*

Breakout: 20%   Improve: 39%   Collapse: 38%

With Driskill, it is very simple: If his splitter isn't working, he's toast. If it is working, you can leave him in for three, four, even five innings with relative comfort. This makes him a tantalizing pitcher for coaches, who always think they can fix something that will allow him to have it all the time, but it just never works out. He chose free agency after the season, but unfortunately landed in Colorado.

ERIC DuBOSE   Bats: L   Throws: L   Born: 15-May-76   Age: 28

YEAR	TM	LG	AGE	G	GS	IP	H	BB	SO	HR	ERA	EQERA	EQH9	EQBB9	EQSO9	EQHR9	PERA	VORP	STF
2002	BOW	EAS	26	41	0	64.7	46	21	66	2	2.50	3.02	7.4	3.5	6.6	0.5	3.34	17.1	10
2003	OTT	INT	27	19	19	114.0	112	34	107	7	3.39	4.59	10.2	3.4	6.8	0.9	5.00	11.7	9
2003	BAL	AL	27	17	10	73.7	60	25	44	6	3.79	3.48	6.7	2.9	5.2	0.6	3.05	14.1	15
2004	*BAL*	*AL*	*28*	*25*	*17*	*98.0*	*103*	*38*	*64*	*11*	*4.45*	*4.64*	*9.4*	*3.3*	*5.7*	*0.9*	*4.74*	*12.7*	*1*

Breakout: 15%   Improve: 36%   Collapse: 30%

A first-round pick for the A's in 1997, DuBose saw his career apparently derailed by shoulder surgery that not only caused him to miss the entire 2001 season, but got him released by three organizations. The Orioles signed him in 2002, getting excellent work from him as a reliever in Bowie, and then challenged him as a starter this year. He doesn't throw as hard as he did pre-surgery, but he's developed an outstanding changeup—as long as he keeps it down, he's even better against right-handed hitters than he is against lefties. Sleeper material.

BRIAN FINCH   Bats: R   Throws: R   Born: 27-Sep-81   Age: 22

YEAR	TM	LG	AGE	G	GS	IP	H	BB	SO	HR	ERA	EQERA	EQH9	EQBB9	EQSO9	EQHR9	PERA	VORP	STF
2003	ABE	NYP	21	8	5	28.0	19	5	29	0	1.93	4.01	8.4	2.6	5.1	0.4	3.47	4.4	20

Most draft observers thought the Orioles were nuts when they took Finch with their second-round pick last year. Yes, his fastball sinks and can reach the mid-90s, yes, he's a big horse of a pitcher, and yes, he's got a pretty good changeup for this stage of his career. But he had a 5.40 ERA at Texas A&M, and those college guys hit better than .300 off him. In his first taste of pro ball, he held opposing hitters to a .183 average with excellent numbers across the board. The only flaw so far is that the O's had to shut him down early with elbow stiffness.

BUDDY GROOM   Bats: L   Throws: L   Born: 10-Jul-65   Age: 38

YEAR	TM	LG	AGE	G	GS	IP	H	BB	SO	HR	ERA	EQERA	EQH9	EQBB9	EQSO9	EQHR9	PERA	VORP	STF
2001	BAL	AL	36	70	0	66.0	64	9	54	4	3.55	3.39	8.6	1.1	6.9	0.6	3.32	15.6	22
2002	BAL	AL	37	70	0	62.0	44	12	48	4	1.60	2.11	6.5	1.7	6.8	0.6	2.56	23.2	25
2003	BAL	AL	38	60	0	45.3	58	14	34	7	5.36	5.44	10.9	2.6	6.6	1.2	5.48	1.7	-10
2004	*BAL*	*AL*	*38*	*52*	*0*	*46.3*	*47*	*14*	*33*	*5*	*3.94*	*4.10*	*9.1*	*2.6*	*6.2*	*0.9*	*4.22*	*8.9*	*-2*

Breakout: 25%   Improve: 43%   Collapse: 26%

Groom's seven-year streak of pitching 70 games or more finally came to an end last year, not due to injury but rather ineffectiveness. His mechanics deserted him after a typical Groom-like April, and he left pitches up and got hammered. His home run rate was the worst of his career; his hit rate was the highest in eight years; his ground/fly rate was the lowest in 10 years. However, all was not lost. He did an excellent job holding back inherited runners, and according to Michael Wolverton's rankings was the most underrated reliever in baseball. The O's have three million reasons to hope he gets straightened out in 2004.

RYAN HANNAMAN   Bats: L   Throws: L   Born: 28-Aug-81   Age: 22

YEAR	TM	LG	AGE	G	GS	IP	H	BB	SO	HR	ERA	EQERA	EQH9	EQBB9	EQSO9	EQHR9	PERA	VORP	STF
2002	HAG	SAL	20	24	24	131.7	129	46	145	9	2.80	5.21	11.4	4.4	6.0	1.6	6.71	5.0	4
2003	SJO	CAL	21	13	13	63.0	66	32	77	7	4.71	6.75	11.6	6.4	7.4	2.1	7.78	-7.2	-10
2003	FRD	CAR	21	5	5	19.0	14	17	22	2	3.79	6.06	9.4	11.0	7.7	2.8	8.68	-0.8	-34
2004	*BAL*	*AL*	*22*	*12*	*9*	*48.7*	*59*	*34*	*36*	*11*	*7.44*	*7.75*	*10.8*	*6.0*	*6.4*	*1.8*	*7.64*	*-1.6*	*-15*

Breakout: 17%   *Improve: 59%*   *Collapse: 16%*

The Orioles acquired Hannaman as a throw-in from the Sidney Ponson trade. A left-handed pitcher with a strong arm, Hannaman struggled with bicep tendinitis during the season and missed a month. His control was a problem before the injury, and became critical afterwards. His future will probably include a move to the bullpen.

PAT HENTGEN   Bats: R   Throws: R   Born: 13-Nov-68   Age: 35

YEAR	TM	LG	AGE	G	GS	IP	H	BB	SO	HR	ERA	EQERA	EQH9	EQBB9	EQSO9	EQHR9	PERA	VORP	STF
2001	BAL	AL	32	9	9	62.3	51	19	33	7	3.47	3.45	7.2	2.5	4.5	0.9	3.46	14.3	10
2002	BAL	AL	33	4	4	22.0	31	10	11	6	7.77	8.44	12.7	3.8	4.2	2.1	7.75	-6.7	-50
2003	BAL	AL	34	28	22	160.7	150	58	100	25	4.09	4.16	7.7	3.1	5.5	1.3	4.21	26.3	2
2004	*TOR*	*AL*	*35*	*25*	*23*	*140.7*	*159*	*49*	*80*	*23*	*5.06*	*4.80*	*9.7*	*2.9*	*5.0*	*1.2*	*4.91*	*16.1*	*1*

Breakout: 16%   *Improve: 48%*   *Collapse: 18%*

After losing most of 2001 and 2002 to injury, Hentgen started 2003 by getting shelled up and down the length of Florida in March, which bumped him from the rotation to the pen. He logged a few starts in the first half, filling in for injured pitchers, but just before the All-Star break his ERA stood at 5.40. As he approached the two-year anniversary of his Tommy John surgery, he started reeling off quality start after quality start, 11 in his last 15 games, producing a second-half ERA of 3.10. The Orioles declined an option for 2004; they still wanted him at a lower price, but he jumped ship for Toronto, where he should make a decent fourth starter, even if the improvement doesn't fully stick.

JASON JOHNSON   Bats: R   Throws: R   Born: 27-Oct-73   Age: 30

YEAR	TM	LG	AGE	G	GS	IP	H	BB	SO	HR	ERA	EQERA	EQH9	EQBB9	EQSO9	EQHR9	PERA	VORP	STF
2001	BAL	AL	27	32	32	196.0	194	77	114	28	4.09	4.69	8.7	3.3	4.9	1.2	4.68	19.2	-3
2002	BAL	AL	28	22	22	131.3	141	41	97	19	4.59	4.96	9.7	2.6	6.4	1.2	4.93	9.0	6
2003	BAL	AL	29	32	32	189.7	216	80	118	22	4.18	4.86	9.6	3.6	5.4	1.0	4.90	20.6	3
2004	*DET*	*AL*	*30*	*27*	*26*	*158.3*	*173*	*64*	*96*	*20*	*4.83*	*5.03*	*9.7*	*3.5*	*5.3*	*1.1*	*5.15*	*11.8*	*2*

Breakout: 9%   *Improve: 43%*   *Collapse: 19%*

On a team with a boatload of up-and-coming pitching prospects, Johnson was the odd man out, and was non-tendered in December. He's an average or slightly below-average major league starter, with moderate (but not great) durability, a battler who's had to fight his way past a severe obstacle (diabetes) to become a major leaguer. He was also being paid almost $3 million to be an average-to-slightly below starter, which makes him a textbook example of the type of player who should be non-tendered to avoid arbitration.

JORGE JULIO   Bats: R   Throws: R   Born: 03-Mar-79   Age: 25

YEAR	TM	LG	AGE	G	GS	IP	H	BB	SO	HR	ERA	EQERA	EQH9	EQBB9	EQSO9	EQHR9	PERA	VORP	STF
2001	ROC	INT	22	34	0	43.3	39	19	48	4	3.74	5.01	8.1	4.6	8.3	0.9	4.34	2.7	22
2001	BAL	AL	22	18	0	21.3	25	9	22	2	3.80	5.23	10.5	3.5	8.7	0.9	5.10	0.9	32
2002	BAL	AL	23	67	0	68.0	55	27	55	5	1.99	3.29	7.4	3.3	7.0	0.7	3.51	16.9	25
2003	BAL	AL	24	64	0	61.7	60	34	52	10	4.38	5.02	8.1	4.6	7.4	1.3	4.86	3.0	0
2004	*BAL*	*AL*	*25*	*45*	*9*	*80.7*	*79*	*35*	*65*	*10*	*4.39*	*4.58*	*8.8*	*3.7*	*6.9*	*1.0*	*4.64*	*10.5*	*1*

Breakout: 25%   *Improve: 52%*   *Collapse: 21%*

Winding up at 0–7 with a 4.38 ERA is an ugly line for a closer, but Julio is still the same pitcher he was coming into last season: a pitcher whose skills are somewhat borderline for a traditional closer. He doesn't have command of his fastball to use it exclusively, but too often that is exactly what he tries to do. He'll remain the Oriole closer into 2004, primarily because no one else is in any position to take the job away from him, but he's a risky long-term gamble.

DON LEVINSKI
Bats: R   Throws: R   Born: 20-Oct-82   Age: 21

YEAR	TM	LG	AGE	G	GS	IP	H	BB	SO	HR	ERA	EQERA	EQH9	EQBB9	EQSO9	EQHR9	PERA	VORP	STF
2002	CLN	MID	19	21	21	119.3	92	55	125	6	3.02	4.71	8.5	5.6	6.1	1.2	5.20	10.6	21
2003	JUP	FLA	20	21	21	87.0	75	70	77	1	4.03	7.27	8.9	9.3	5.9	0.3	5.47	-14.5	8
2004	BAL	AL	21	15	12	61.3	69	66	50	12	7.96	8.30	10.1	9.2	7.1	1.5	8.31	-10.6	-21

Breakout: 35%   Improve: 61%   Collapse: 24%

Levinski came with over Bautista in the Conine trade with the Marlins. He's a sinkerball pitcher, and a good one when healthy. Unfortunately, he's had rotator cuff problems for two years running, and the latest report is that it's a partial tear. He was also been ridiculously wild last season, but that's probably a byproduct of the shaky shoulder.

ROMMIE LEWIS
Bats: L   Throws: L   Born: 02-Sep-82   Age: 21

YEAR	TM	LG	AGE	G	GS	IP	H	BB	SO	HR	ERA	EQERA	EQH9	EQBB9	EQSO9	EQHR9	PERA	VORP	STF
2002	DEL	SAL	19	53	0	71.0	50	20	77	1	2.15	4.10	8.1	3.4	6.1	0.3	3.46	10.6	27
2003	FRD	CAR	20	26	20	113.3	108	60	69	9	3.34	5.89	9.6	6.2	4.0	1.8	6.53	-3.3	-18
2004	BAL	AL	21	17	12	66.3	71	38	40	10	5.70	5.94	9.6	4.9	5.2	1.2	5.96	-0.1	-11

Breakout: 28%   Improve: 52%   Collapse: 15%

A fourth-rounder from the 2001 draft, Lewis worked out of the bullpen in 2002, overpowering Sally League hitters with a moving 93-mph fastball. In 2003, working as a starter, his fastball dropped off to about 85, his control went south, and High-A hitters took advantage. He moved to the bullpen late in the season to make sure he didn't throw too many innings—a preventative measure the O's also took with some of their college picks.

KERRY LIGTENBERG
Bats: R   Throws: R   Born: 11-May-71   Age: 33

YEAR	TM	LG	AGE	G	GS	IP	H	BB	SO	HR	ERA	EQERA	EQH9	EQBB9	EQSO9	EQHR9	PERA	VORP	STF
2001	ATL	NL	30	53	0	59.7	50	30	56	4	3.02	3.79	8.1	4.3	7.3	0.5	3.87	11.5	13
2002	ATL	NL	31	52	0	66.7	52	33	51	6	2.97	3.86	8.0	4.0	6.1	0.9	4.17	12.2	-1
2003	BAL	AL	32	68	0	59.3	60	14	47	9	3.34	3.86	8.5	2.0	6.9	1.2	4.20	15.1	1
2004	TOR	AL	33	51	0	54.3	56	20	40	8	4.28	4.07	8.9	3.1	6.5	1.1	4.48	11.1	-2

Breakout: 29%   Improve: 56%   Collapse: 19%

If there were such a thing as a Right-handed One-Out GuY, Kerry would be it. His left/right splits this year were staggering, even for a guy with a pronounced platoon history: lefties hit .356/.424/.529, while he limited righties to .206/.230/.362. As the season progressed, and more teams caught on to his struggles against lefties, he tended to face fewer batters per game, dropping from 5.8 batters per game in the first month to less than three in July and August. He's useful, but limited. As happened with Hentgen, the Orioles declined their option on him, and he promptly signed with Toronto.

ADAM LOEWEN
Bats: L   Throws: L   Born: 09-Apr-84   Age: 20

YEAR	TM	LG	AGE	G	GS	IP	H	BB	SO	HR	ERA	EQERA	EQH9	EQBB9	EQSO9	EQHR9	PERA	VORP	STF
2003	ABE	NYP	19	7	7	23.3	13	9	25	0	2.70	3.98	7.1	5.3	5.8	0.4	3.73	3.7	24

Loewen was the prize pitching prospect from the 2003 draft, a draft-and-follow who was being touted as the overall #1 pick for 2004 if the Orioles let him go back into the draft. The Orioles met his demands just before the signing deadline, giving Loewen a $4 million bonus and major league contract. They were extremely protective of him this season, limiting him to three innings per outing and shutting him down completely in early August, but what little they saw was very, very good: a mid-90s fastball, and a good split-finger, slider, and curve. If there are worries at this point, they'd be control, stamina, and the usual TINSTAAP pitfalls.

RODRIGO LOPEZ Bats: R Throws: R Born: 14-Dec-75 Age: 28

YEAR	TM	LG	AGE	G	GS	IP	H	BB	SO	HR	ERA	EQERA	EQH9	EQBB9	EQSO9	EQHR9	PERA	VORP	STF
2001	POR	PCL	25	11	8	52.3	45	15	37	7	3.44	4.44	8.3	3.1	4.6	1.5	4.77	6.3	-17
2002	BAL	AL	26	33	28	196.7	172	62	136	23	3.57	3.89	7.9	2.7	6.0	1.0	3.89	36.0	14
2003	BAL	AL	27	26	26	147.0	188	43	103	24	5.82	5.90	10.8	2.5	6.1	1.3	5.52	-8.6	-2
2004	BAL	AL	28	22	19	119.0	130	38	76	16	4.63	4.83	9.8	2.7	5.5	1.1	4.92	12.8	5

Breakout: 13%   Improve: 41%   Collapse: 25%

There was the pitcher who was the runner-up for the Rookie of the Year Award, and then there was the pitcher we saw last year. Lopez threw a ton of innings in 2002, where a ton is defined as "338 innings between the start of winter ball in October 2001 and the end of the regular season in 2002." Lopez came into 2003 apparently worn out, and has yet to recover, as the 5.50 ERA he carried through his last six starts of 2002 extended through his 2003 season and into winter ball.

JOHN MAINE Bats: R Throws: R Born: 08-May-81 Age: 23

YEAR	TM	LG	AGE	G	GS	IP	H	BB	SO	HR	ERA	EQERA	EQH9	EQBB9	EQSO9	EQHR9	PERA	VORP	STF
2002	ABE	NYP	21	4	2	10.3	6	3	21	0	1.75	3.12	9.3	4.2	10.4	0.0	3.90	2.4	57
2002	DEL	SAL	21	6	5	33.0	21	4	39	0	1.36	3.38	8.0	1.5	6.4	0.3	2.91	7.2	45
2003	DEL	SAL	22	14	14	76.3	43	18	108	1	1.53	2.84	8.0	2.8	7.8	0.4	3.35	20.5	45
2003	FRD	CAR	22	12	12	70.3	48	20	77	5	3.07	4.02	8.2	3.3	6.9	1.7	4.97	11.0	9
2004	BAL	AL	23	22	16	95.3	92	32	78	11	4.06	4.23	8.7	2.8	7.1	0.9	4.19	16.6	13

Breakout: 10%   Improve: 38%   Collapse: 24%

Maine's run through the low minors was so staggeringly good, despite not having knock-scouts-over-with-feathers stuff, that some prospect mavens are falling over themselves to tell you how he's not as good as his stats. There may be something to that. Maine was a little old for the South Atlantic League, and while no 22 year-old of recent vintage has matched his performance in that or the comparable Midwest league, the ones who came closest (Adam Walker, Britt Reames, Denny Stark, Matt Smith, all a long way behind Maine's performance) have had less than inspiring later careers. So despite a league-leading 185 strikeouts and a career .176 batting average hit against him, keep the hype in reserve. If he makes a strong run through Double-A in '04, start getting excited.

DAMIAN MOSS Bats: R Throws: L Born: 24-Nov-76 Age: 27

YEAR	TM	LG	AGE	G	GS	IP	H	BB	SO	HR	ERA	EQERA	EQH9	EQBB9	EQSO9	EQHR9	PERA	VORP	STF
2001	RIC	INT	24	17	16	88.7	75	38	94	10	3.15	4.32	8.9	4.5	7.5	1.4	5.31	11.6	5
2002	ATL	NL	25	33	29	179.0	140	89	111	20	3.42	4.46	7.9	4.0	4.9	1.1	4.34	21.4	0
2003	SFG	NL	26	21	20	115.0	121	63	57	12	4.70	5.58	10.0	4.5	4.0	1.0	5.41	6.3	-15
2003	BAL	AL	26	10	9	50.7	63	29	22	12	6.21	6.84	10.4	4.9	3.8	2.0	6.85	-8.4	-47
2004	BAL	AL	27	21	18	102.0	116	55	53	15	5.68	5.92	10.2	4.6	4.5	1.2	6.07	0.4	-12

Breakout: 11%   Improve: 44%   Collapse: 24%

Moss, like Ainsworth and Hannaman, came to Baltimore in the Ponson trade. A casual glance might lead you to believe that, as the owner of a 21–13 lifetime record at the time, he was the key to the deal, but he was non-tendered in December. He was dreadful as an Oriole, primarily because he couldn't throw strikes, but also perhaps because he was 30 pounds overweight. He reportedly hired personal trainers for off-season workouts, and at press time was still searching for a new employer.

JOHN PARRISH Bats: L Throws: L Born: 26-Nov-77 Age: 26

YEAR	TM	LG	AGE	G	GS	IP	H	BB	SO	HR	ERA	EQERA	EQH9	EQBB9	EQSO9	EQHR9	PERA	VORP	STF
2001	ROC	INT	23	26	19	133.0	115	51	126	11	3.52	4.29	7.9	4.0	6.9	0.9	4.17	18.3	21
2001	BAL	AL	23	16	1	22.0	22	17	20	5	6.14	6.65	8.7	6.2	7.5	1.7	5.96	-2.5	-6
2003	BOW	EAS	25	49	0	76.3	58	33	85	5	2.01	3.74	9.2	4.9	8.2	1.2	5.32	13.9	-9
2003	BAL	AL	25	14	0	23.7	17	8	15	2	1.90	2.70	5.8	2.7	5.4	0.8	2.72	8.3	11
2004	BAL	AL	26	29	3	43.0	42	20	35	5	4.38	4.56	8.7	4.0	7.0	1.0	4.72	5.9	-1

Breakout: 27%   Improve: 50%   Collapse: 24%

Parrish's eye-popping numbers had a lot of people wondering what he was doing at Bowie. It turned out to be an unforeseen problem with their new Triple-A affiliate: Canadian immigration wouldn't issue him a work permit because of a two-year-old DUI incident, so the team had little choice but to work him out in Bowie. After missing all of 2002 with a torn knee ligament, Parrish converted completely to relief, usually in a multi-inning role. He could help the Baltimore pen this year.

MATT RILEY   Bats: L   Throws: L   Born: 02-Aug-79   Age: 24

YEAR	TM	LG	AGE	G	GS	IP	H	BB	SO	HR	ERA	EQERA	EQH9	EQBB9	EQSO9	EQHR9	PERA	VORP	STF
2002	BOW	EAS	22	22	22	109.3	136	48	105	12	6.34	7.37	12.3	4.6	6.4	1.7	7.24	-19.9	-10
2003	BOW	EAS	23	14	14	72.3	56	23	73	4	3.11	3.99	8.7	3.6	7.3	1.0	4.45	11.7	22
2003	OTT	INT	23	13	13	70.3	70	28	77	4	3.58	4.66	9.6	4.4	8.2	0.7	4.78	6.9	32
2003	BAL	AL	23	2	2	10.0	7	5	8	1	1.80	2.70	5.4	4.5	7.2	0.9	3.17	4.5	35
2004	*BAL*	*AL*	*24*	*20*	*13*	*76.0*	*79*	*36*	*63*	*10*	*4.89*	*5.10*	*9.3*	*4.1*	*7.2*	*1.1*	*5.18*	*6.8*	*6*

Breakout: 18%   Improve: 52%   Collapse: 28%

As noted in last year's edition, Riley made a significant improvement in the second half of 2002, then continued to improve in '03, so much that you can legitimately say that he's back. His translated statistics from last year are just as good as his 1998–99 numbers. His fastball didn't quite come all the way back to 95, but it still clears 90, and he once again has a killer curve ball. He's not a sure thing for the 2004 rotation, but he sure looks probable.

WILLIS ROBERTS   Bats: R   Throws: R   Born: 19-Jun-75   Age: 29

YEAR	TM	LG	AGE	G	GS	IP	H	BB	SO	HR	ERA	EQERA	EQH9	EQBB9	EQSO9	EQHR9	PERA	VORP	STF
2001	BAL	AL	26	46	18	132.0	142	55	95	15	4.91	4.84	9.5	3.5	6.0	0.9	4.80	10.8	0
2002	BAL	AL	27	66	0	75.0	79	32	51	5	3.36	4.46	9.5	3.6	5.9	0.6	4.52	9.2	1
2003	BAL	AL	28	26	0	39.3	41	16	26	7	5.73	5.35	8.8	3.5	5.8	1.4	5.00	-1.2	-18
2004	*BAL*	*AL*	*29*	*39*	*4*	*59.0*	*59*	*22*	*40*	*7*	*4.30*	*4.49*	*9.0*	*3.2*	*5.9*	*1.0*	*4.62*	*8.9*	*-4*

Breakout: 31%   Improve: 51%   Collapse: 23%

Roberts has gone from a Caribbean find to a closer to a setup man to released, all within three seasons. His problems last year could be traced to a torn elbow ligament; he blew it out in June after about five weeks of poor outings. Like many bullpen pitchers, he is a hard thrower who lacks any complementary off-speed pitches. He was released from the 40-man roster after the season and dispatched to Ottawa.

EDDY RODRIGUEZ   Bats: R   Throws: R   Born: 08-Aug-81   Age: 22

YEAR	TM	LG	AGE	G	GS	IP	H	BB	SO	HR	ERA	EQERA	EQH9	EQBB9	EQSO9	EQHR9	PERA	VORP	STF
2001	DEL	SAL	19	41	0	61.0	58	23	64	4	3.39	6.24	11.0	5.1	5.6	1.4	6.36	-3.8	-5
2002	FRD	CAR	20	38	0	48.3	28	20	58	3	2.24	3.09	6.4	4.9	7.8	1.2	4.07	12.2	22
2003	BOW	EAS	21	56	0	73.0	49	35	66	3	2.34	3.92	7.0	5.3	6.9	0.7	3.90	12.5	19
2004	*BAL*	*AL*	*22*	*21*	*3*	*31.3*	*34*	*22*	*25*	*4*	*6.06*	*6.32*	*9.6*	*6.0*	*6.8*	*1.0*	*6.13*	*1.3*	*-12*

Breakout: 23%   Improve: 52%   Collapse: 30%

E-Rod (rule 12.04g now requires that every player named Rodriguez be given a dash-Rod nickname, and E isn't taken) has spent much of the last two years as his team's closer, or at least co-closer. His repertoire isn't overwhelming—a pretty good low-90s fastball is his only really good pitch—but he's got a funky delivery that makes it hard for hitters to time. He's held minor league hitters to a .182 average over the last two years, a good 20 hits fewer than expected—a remarkably high number for only about 120 innings.

B. J. RYAN   **Bats: L**   **Throws: L**   **Born: 28-Dec-75**   **Age: 28**

YEAR	TM	LG	AGE	G	GS	IP	H	BB	SO	HR	ERA	EQERA	EQH9	EQBB9	EQSO9	EQHR9	PERA	VORP	STF
2001	BAL	AL	25	61	0	53.0	47	30	54	6	4.25	4.70	8.0	4.7	8.5	0.9	4.35	5.2	11
2002	BAL	AL	26	67	0	57.7	51	33	56	7	4.68	4.79	8.0	4.8	8.3	1.0	4.46	5.1	4
2003	BAL	AL	27	76	0	50.3	42	27	63	1	3.40	3.26	7.2	4.5	10.9	0.2	3.27	13.3	45
2004	BAL	AL	28	59	0	72.3	60	35	79	5	3.46	3.61	7.4	4.1	9.5	0.6	3.67	17.7	18

Breakout: 27%   Improve: 54%   Collapse: 16%

Ryan, by month, over his career since 2000:

Month	IP	R	RA
April/March	42.3	11	2.34
May	27.7	34	11.06
June	21.7	27	11.21
July	17.3	3	1.56
August	46.0	12	2.35
Sept./Oct.	45.3	10	1.99

For four months of the season, he's Rollie Fingers; for the other two, he's Freddy Got Fingered. Considering the Orioles have Groom and Parrish, and both border on untradable, Ryan might join the loser of the second base battle as trade bait.

JOHN STEPHENS   **Bats: R**   **Throws: R**   **Born: 15-Nov-79**   **Age: 24**

YEAR	TM	LG	AGE	G	GS	IP	H	BB	SO	HR	ERA	EQERA	EQH9	EQBB9	EQSO9	EQHR9	PERA	VORP	STF
2001	BOW	EAS	21	18	17	132.0	95	21	130	10	1.84	3.03	7.5	1.9	6.3	1.0	3.46	34.8	37
2001	ROC	INT	21	9	9	58.0	52	19	61	5	4.03	4.47	7.5	3.4	8.1	0.8	3.67	7.1	49
2002	ROC	INT	22	21	21	142.7	126	23	118	10	3.03	3.45	7.4	1.6	6.6	0.8	3.10	33.0	41
2002	BAL	AL	22	12	11	65.0	68	22	56	13	6.09	5.71	9.4	2.9	7.4	1.7	5.42	-0.8	22
2003	OTT	INT	23	27	27	158.7	155	39	132	15	3.97	4.85	9.3	2.7	6.2	1.2	4.78	12.4	14
2004	BAL	AL	24	23	17	103.7	104	32	76	15	4.38	4.56	9.0	2.7	6.4	1.2	4.53	15.7	8

Breakout: 18%   Improve: 46%   Collapse: 26%

Stephens broke his foot some time during the 2002 season, maybe in spring; nobody is quite sure when, because he pitched through it. He had surgery in the fall, and it was still sore well into spring 2003. He's a tough bloke, though, this Aussie, and he pitched through it again, but it wasn't until the second half that he pitched like the John Stephens of old:

Stint	IP	ERA	H/9	BB/9	SO/9	STUF
2003 Ottawa, first 14 starts, translated:	72.7	5.82	10.3	3.1	5.4	5
2003 Ottawa, last 13 starts, translated:	75.7	3.81	8.2	2.3	6.9	23

He still has to beat scouting biases against his lack of velocity, but he'll have a shot at the fifth starter's job in camp.

Boston Red Sox

As this is written, the Red Sox are in the midst of one of the more eventful off-seasons in their storied history. Within a few weeks of reaching the seventh game of the ALCS, the team hired a new manager (Terry Francona), and acquired the best starting pitcher (Curt Schilling) and relief pitcher (Keith Foulke) available.

That all seemed like plenty. But the story that grabbed headlines this off-season—aside from Pete Rose's questionable stab at contrition—was the A-Rod deal. Or rather, the A-Rod non-deal. As *BP2004* went to press, the trade that would have sent Manny Ramirez to Texas for Alex Rodriguez and cash considerations looked nearly dead in the water. The two teams could still head back to the negotiating table, especially given all the deadlines and new deadlines put into place by the Sox, Rangers, Bud Selig, and seemingly everyone within a 100-mile radius of Beantown or the Metroplex. But Texas' acquisitions of Brian Jordan and David Dellucci, plus comments by the two team's front offices, indicate that both clubs have moved on.

The trade would have ended the Red Sox tenure of two team superstars—Nomar Garciaparra was expected to be subsequently shipped off for pitching and young talent if A-Rod were acquired—would in exchange have brought them the best player in the world. Regardless of whether or not they pull off the deal, the Red Sox have signaled to the baseball world that they (a) are willing and able to spend a lot of money, and (b) know how to spend it wisely. That's not everything, but it's a hell of start.

On November 27, 2002, the Red Sox hired 28-year-old Theo Epstein to be their general manager, a move that dramatically signaled a new direction for the club. Epstein is bright, energetic, open to new ideas, a strong believer in player development, a consensus builder. He grew up reading baseball analysts, who instilled in him the confidence to challenge the way things have always been done, to search for the truth above all else. The Red Sox employ a team of analysts, including Bill James, but also surround Epstein with experienced baseball traditionalists, like Bill LaJoie and Lee Thomas. From all accounts, Epstein listens to everyone.

Upon getting the job, Epstein immediately set his sights on acquiring a big-name starting pitcher, but his reluctance to part with Casey Fossum apparently cost the team Bartolo Colon or Kevin Millwood, and the Yankees

RED SOX PROSPECTUS

2003 record: 95–67; Second place, AL East; Lost to Yankees in Championship Series

Pythagenport record: 94–68

Runs scored per game: 5.9 (1st in AL)

Runs allowed per game: 5.0 (8th in AL)

Team EqA: .285 (1st in AL)

2003 Batters Age: 30.2 (2nd oldest in AL)

2003 Pitchers Age: 32.0 (Oldest in AL)

Ballpark: Fenway Park; Slight hitter's park; Park Factor of 1.010

2003: A heavily redesigned roster and a new management group took Boston to the World Series doorstep.

2004: Even without A-Rod, the Sox have a deep, championship-quality team on their hands.

outbid the Red Sox on Jose Contreras. Wisely, Epstein resisted the temptation to sign local product Tom Glavine or overpay for another veteran, instead standing pat. He famously did not offer a contract to closer Ugueth Urbina, replacing him with . . . no one. More on this later.

Turning to the offense, Epstein non-tendered Brian Daubach, politely controlled his glee as Cliff Floyd refused arbitration, and used the money freed up to haul in Bill Mueller, Jeremy Giambi, Kevin Millar, David Ortiz, and Todd Walker, paying about $11.5 million (for 2003) for the quintet. The team's internal estimate had the 2003 Sox scoring 900 runs.

In fact, the offense spent much of the year on pace for 1000 runs, settling for 961. It was an amazing group of hitters, combining power (a franchise record 238 home runs, and an all-time record .491 slugging percentage) and patience (a major league-best .360 on base percentage), while also pacing the majors in doubles and sacrifice flies. Pitchers are supposed to feel good walking out at the start of an inning to face the bottom of a team's order. The Red Sox offered no such break with their most common trio (see table 1).

So how do we grade the first year of the Theo Epstein era? At the major league level, it depends largely on what part of the team you focus on. Although the composition of the roster and the nature of the games played were

TABLE 1.

Player	HR	AVG	OBP	SLG	EqA
Trot Nixon	28	.306	.396	.578	.325
Bill Mueller	19	.326	.398	.540	.317
Jason Varitek	25	.273	.351	.512	.293

dramatically different, the 2003 Red Sox were actually no better than they had been in 2002. Sure, they won two more games (93 to 95) but the 2002 club was very unlucky, as their runs scored and allowed totals reflected a 100-win team. Yes, they made the playoffs in 2003, but this was partly because their primary Wild Card competition (the Angels and Mariners) fell off down the stretch.

Although the offense improved by 103 runs, the pitching and defense regressed by 144, keeping the team in second place for the sixth straight year. Pinpointing the culprit is not easy, since the starting pitching, relief pitching, and defense were all significantly worse. Although it did not receive as much negative attention, the rotation actually fell off much more than the bullpen (see table 2).

Connie Mack once said that pitching was 90% of baseball. Fortunately for the 2003 Red Sox, Mack was misinformed.

With Derek Lowe struggling in his second year as a full-time starter, and Tim Wakefield predictably regressing to third-starter/innings-eater status with his return to the rotation full-time, the ineptitude of the other 40% of the rotation could not be papered over this time around. Fossum and mid-season acquisition Jeff Suppan disappointed, and John Burkett, sporting a shiny 5.15 ERA over 180 innings, was actually called upon to pitch big games in October. The Red Sox gave 62 starts to pitchers with ERAs over 5.00, a situation that cost them at least a division title.

The Red Sox also had problems catching the ball. While it is difficult to properly separate the contributions of pitching and defense, the Red Sox DER (which measures the percentage of balls in play that are turned into outs) decreased from .719 (4th in the league) to .700 (10th). Derek Lowe, who makes his living getting players to hit ground balls, was especially hurt by a newly porous right side of the infield.

TABLE 2.

ERA	SP	RP	Total
2002	3.53	4.25	3.75
2003	4.30	4.83	4.48
Diff	−.77	−.58	−.73

The biggest story surrounding the Red Sox all summer, you may have heard, was the failure of the bullpen. The media's term for Boston's early-season strategy was "bullpen-by-committee," a phrase that could be, and therefore was, misinterpreted. Epstein wanted a flexible bullpen whose use depended on (1) the strengths of the pitcher, (2) the strengths of the hitters, and (3) an understanding of which game situations are most critical. He believes, and we agree with him, that saving your best reliever for ninth-inning save opportunities, often to protect two or three-run leads, is a waste of available resources.

Rather than signing Urbina or acquiring another experienced closer, Epstein tried to build a bullpen filled with pitchers who had shown an ability to assume larger roles. To holdovers Alan Embree and Bob Howry, both mid-2002 pickups, Epstein added Ramiro Mendoza, Mike Timlin and Chad Fox, and filled the organization with assorted lesser signings. He then handed the keys to Grady Little.

There were at least two problems with the execution. First, any debate over how to use a bullpen presupposes that you have good pitchers. Tony La Russa's use of Dennis Eckersley may have been sub-optimal, but not enough to offset the fact that he had Eckersley in the first place. Epstein did not have Eckersley. He had Chad Fox, and no matter how brilliant your use of Chad Fox is, when you hand him the ball he's still going to be Chad Fox. The Red Sox collected a bunch of journeymen relievers, and gave some of them a lot of money. As it turned out, Embree and Timlin pitched at least as well as could have expected, Fox was OK but predictably got hurt, Howry struggled and was quickly exiled, and Ramiro spent the year battling his very own Mendoza line—a 7.00 ERA. There were scores of others who were tried for two days or two weeks, and for the most part they pitched terribly.

The second problem was entrusting this bullpen to Grady Little. One of the reasons managers like to have relievers with set roles is that it unburdens the skipper of difficult in-game decisions. Having a "closer" and "set-up men" might be a crutch, but it is a crutch that Grady Little wanted and needed. To extend this analogy, Theo Epstein removed Grady Little's crutch and pushed him out into a busy hallway. Little said all the right things in the spring, but with an expiring contract and brand new boss, what else could he say?

On Opening Day in St. Petersburg, Pedro Martinez departed after seven innings with a 4–1 lead. Mendoza pitched a perfect eighth but was removed, apparently because Little interpreted the new bullpen strategy as "Everyone Gets To Pitch." Embree and Fox gave up two-run home runs to lose the game. The next night, it was Howry who allowed an eight- inning bomb, in a game the Sox had to win in the 16th. It was just two games, and only one loss, but it was plenty. With the local media firmly in his corner, Grady Little spent the next six months desperately looking for a closer, and never found one to his liking.

Little regularly removed pitchers who were pitching well, thereby maximizing his chances of discovering someone having a bad day. It wasn't too long ago that relief pitchers who entered the game in the seventh inning would keep pitching until they provided some indication that they no longer could. Twelve-man pitching staffs are not the result of starters not pitching enough innings; it is the relievers who are being unnecessarily pampered. This endless carousel has led to larger staffs populated by lesser pitchers, and results in good pitchers having a bad few innings turn into a six-week slump. The Red Sox were victimized by both of these phenomena.

In late May, Epstein acquired Byung-Hyun Kim, whom Arizona had moved to the rotation in the spring at Kim's urging. Although the Red Sox desperately needed a starting pitcher, the temptation to put Kim in the bullpen—in a role he did not want and had not been physically training for—was too much for Little. After five starts, Kim was anointed the team's full-time closer. Although he accumulated 16 saves in half a season, Little actually used Kim creatively at times, bringing him into a lot of tie games. He ended the regular season on a high, allowing just one hit and one walk in his final eight appearances.

At the trading deadline the Red Sox acquired Scott Williamson, the perfect relief pitcher for a flexible bullpen, with no platoon split and the ability to pitch multiple high-quality innings per outing. Little turned him into a one-inning setup man. To be fair, Williamson did not pitch well in the regular season with the Sox, but it was only 20 innings.

When Kim struggled to close out the first game of the ALDS in Oakland, Little brought in Embree, who promptly allowed a run-scoring single to Erubiel Durazo. This removal was not well received by the emotional Kim, who flipped off the crowd at Fenway Park while being introduced a few days later. Despite entering October pitching his best baseball of the year, after one outing (walk, fly ball, hit batter, strikeout), he was done for the playoffs.

Above any other sin, Little is most guilty of allowing the bullpen drama to take over the team. Bullpens are not perfect, and the Boston version surely had its problems, but the manager was so busy complaining about it that he failed to notice when pitchers were going well. In this particular instance, Little could have said, "B.K. has been pitching great and I think the umpire squeezed him a little bit tonight. I have tremendous confidence in him, I just thought Embree was a better matchup against a tough left-handed hitter." Instead, the story was that Kim choked and the Red Sox bullpen was (again) a failure.

Deprived of their ace, the remaining relief pitchers—Williamson, Timlin, and Embree—were nearly perfect, allowing just one run in 24 appearances in the post-season. Ironically, Little had finally found the bullpen he wanted, one that never gave up any runs, and he managed it pretty well until the seventh game of the ALCS. The memory of Pedro Martinez giving up three singles, three doubles, and a home run to his final nine batters will always be the painful epitaph to Little's two-year run in Boston.

So the first year of the Theo Epstein era was a mixed bag at the major league level: a great offense, but large regressions on defense and on the mound. The Schilling acquisition, along with the new, low-cost offense/defense combo of Mark Bellhorn and Pokey Reese at second base, should help. But the true effect of Boston's new management team will come when its increased emphasis on the minor league organization begins to pay off. Epstein inherited a system in tatters, one generally ranked at or near the bottom of the heap. The Red Sox got solid marks for its 2003 draft, one heavily focused on college selections that can get to the upper levels of the system quickly. The Red Sox could use a steady influx of low-priced talent, both to play in Fenway Park and for Epstein to use to acquire talent from other organizations. As good as some of his deals were, they are even more impressive when considering that he had so little minor league talent to offer.

Red Sox fans and media had focused on 2004 as the last year in a "window of opportunity," with the expiration of their contracts with Pedro Martinez, Derek Lowe, Nomar Garciaparra, and Jason Varitek. This is overstated nonsense, as the team's management is well aware. As great as Pedro Martinez has been, and still is, if he and the team cannot reach an agreement for 2005 and beyond, his loss would be compensated by an additional $17.5 million (his 2004 salary) to spend on someone else or, presumably, multiple players. With $120 million of payroll, it is more important that the team not squander its advantage by taking on crippling contracts.

Even before the acquisitions of Schilling and Foulke, it had been a promising start. The last few years of the Dan Duquette era were reckless ones, both for the minor league system and for the prevalence of bloated contracts. Epstein and his staff have made a lot of progress in both areas. With one of the highest payrolls in baseball, a new-found understanding of the game's economics, an increased ability to wring new revenue from their old ballpark, and a commitment to player development, the Red Sox should be able to compete for championships nearly every year well into the future.

HITTERS

ANDY ABAD   1B/OF   Bats: L   Throws: L   Born: 25-Aug-72   Age: 31

YEAR	TM	LG	AGE	AB	H	2B	3B	HR	BB	SO	SB	CS	AVG	OBP	SLG	MLVR	EQBA	EQOBP	EQSLG	EQMLVR	VORP	DEFENSE			
2001	SAC	PCL	28	462	139	19	2	19	58	67	4	2	.301	.379	.474	.149	.265	.340	.418	-.035	4.3	56-RF	-7	13-LF	-1
2002	CLG	PCL	29	352	106	28	2	11	57	44	0	3	.301	.402	.486	.170	.242	.340	.392	-.087	-3.9	37-LF	0	36-RF	-1
2003	PAW	INT	30	504	153	35	3	13	55	67	0	3	.304	.372	.462	.191	.279	.351	.438	.025	17.1	87-1B	-1	16-RF	0
2003	BOS	AL	30	17	2	0	0	0	2	5	0	1	.118	.211	.118	-.719	.176	.263	.176	-.566	-3.1				
2004	PIT	NL	31	166	41	9	1	4	19	25	0	1	.247	.330	.382	-.098	.249	.331	.396	-.090	1.2	48-1B	-4		

Breakout: 23%   *Improve: 38%*   *Collapse: 44%*

Back in Pawtucket after a three-year all-expenses-paid world tour, Abad's fine season earned him a few key at-bats in the major league pennant race. While he has the good fortune to be in an organization smart enough to value his skills (plate discipline and power), he is also in one that can afford better players at offensive positions. Were he a Tiger, he would be one of their better hitters.

CLAUDIO ARIAS   3B/OF   Bats: R   Throws: R   Born: 09-May-82   Age: 22

YEAR	TM	LG	AGE	AB	H	2B	3B	HR	BB	SO	SB	CS	AVG	OBP	SLG	MLVR	EQBA	EQOBP	EQSLG	EQMLVR	VORP	DEFENSE	
2003	LOW	NYP	21	187	49	9	1	5	7	55	3	3	.262	.293	.401	.044	.205	.228	.332	-.411	-24.3	46-3B	-12
2004	BOS	AL	22	233	46	10	1	5	8	70	2	2	.199	.232	.318	-.366	.196	.231	.320	-.403	-13.9	61-3B	-8

Breakout: 29%   *Improve: 50%*   *Collapse: 23%*

In 2002 he was Luis Herrera and thought to be 18. Arias's new age hurt his prospect status a lot. His one tool—raw power—keeps him on prospect lists despite his complete lack of plate discipline. His so-so defense at third caused a move to the outfield for 2004. He crushes good fastballs, and the organization is hoping to help him develop the rest.

ADRIAN BROWN   OF   Bats: B   Throws: R   Born: 07-Feb-74   Age: 30

YEAR	TM	LG	AGE	AB	H	2B	3B	HR	BB	SO	SB	CS	AVG	OBP	SLG	MLVR	EQBA	EQOBP	EQSLG	EQMLVR	VORP	DEFENSE			
2001	PIT	NL	27	31	6	0	0	1	3	3	2	1	.194	.265	.290	-.390	.194	.265	.290	-.401	-2.5				
2002	NAS	PCL	28	184	62	7	1	3	23	18	22	6	.337	.409	.435	.232	.305	.375	.396	.031	5.6	38-RF	-5		
2002	PIT	NL	28	208	45	10	2	1	19	34	10	6	.216	.284	.298	-.252	.223	.287	.308	-.317	-9.6	48-CF	-5		
2003	PAW	INT	29	482	136	16	3	5	48	81	34	11	.282	.347	.359	-.001	.266	.330	.342	-.159	-1.8	80-CF	-7	27-RF	-2
2003	BOS	AL	29	15	3	0	0	0	1	4	2	0	.200	.250	.200	-.510	.200	.250	.200	-.554	-1.0				
2004	BOS	AL	30	204	54	9	2	3	19	33	9	4	.264	.327	.367	-.097	.259	.326	.369	-.127	1.0	57-CF	-8		

Breakout: 35%   *Improve: 53%*   *Collapse: 27%*

Brown's career is an example of the collateral damage from the emergence of the "second situational lefty." Twenty years ago, when teams had seven- or eight-man benches, Brown would have had a 12-year career as a fifth outfielder and pinch-runner. With today's 12-man pitching staffs, he has to spend most of his prime baseball years bouncing around the high minors. Naturally, when the Red Sox went with a 10-man staff for the Division Series, Brown made the roster. That's nice and all, but a generation ago he could have been Herm Winningham.

LOU COLLIER   UT   Bats: R   Throws: R   Born: 21-Aug-73   Age: 30

YEAR	TM	LG	AGE	AB	H	2B	3B	HR	BB	SO	SB	CS	AVG	OBP	SLG	MLVR	EQBA	EQOBP	EQSLG	EQMLVR	VORP	DEFENSE			
2001	IND	INT	27	312	90	17	2	14	24	64	9	3	.288	.350	.490	.170	.269	.328	.465	.013	14.8	45-CF	-1	14-2B	0
2001	MIL	NL	27	127	32	8	1	2	17	30	5	1	.252	.340	.378	-.086	.256	.346	.380	-.082	3.6	14-3B	-2		
2002	OTT	INT	28	307	97	26	6	6	37	69	5	2	.316	.394	.498	.288	.291	.372	.470	.117	16.9	23-LF	0	17-3B	-2
2003	PAW	INT	29	392	115	19	4	14	32	94	8	7	.293	.354	.469	.164	.270	.335	.447	.001	6.6	71-LF	2	19-SS	-1
2004	BOS	AL	30	174	46	10	1	5	17	39	2	1	.261	.334	.421	-.016	.256	.333	.423	-.044	4.9	50-LF	2		

Breakout: 19%   *Improve: 32%*   *Collapse: 33%*

He was one of three PawSox (along with Abad and Arroyo) to make the International League's post-season All-Star team, something sure to thrill the Collier grandchildren someday. Pawtucket dominated the International League with players like this, minor league veterans ready to be called up for two-week emergency stints. Lou can play the middle infield and outfield, knows the strike zone and hits some doubles, so he might find a job on someone's major league roster. He signed a minor league deal with the Phillies, who are unlikely to have room for him.

CESAR CRESPO

UT   **Bats: B**   **Throws: R**   Born: 23-May-79   Age: 25

YEAR	TM	LG	AGE	AB	H	2B	3B	HR	BB	SO	SB	CS	AVG	OBP	SLG	MLVR	EQBA	EQOBP	EQSLG	EQMLVR	VORP	DEFENSE			
2001	POR	PCL	22	273	71	18	3	8	39	66	23	3	.260	.354	.436	.027	.232	.320	.391	-.134	3.7	32-2B	0	12-SS	1
2001	SDP	NL	22	153	32	6	0	4	25	50	6	2	.209	.320	.327	-.197	.229	.335	.350	-.162	0.6	27-2B	-3		
2002	CAR	PRL	23	155	42	7	4	3	32	28	4	3	.271	.402	.426	.212	.244	.355	.402	-.044	11.8				
2002	POR	PCL	23	322	83	17	2	9	50	78	21	7	.258	.363	.407	.039	.232	.326	.369	-.152	2.5	34-2B	1	21-SS	0
2003	PAW	INT	24	465	124	31	3	9	40	93	13	8	.267	.323	.404	.007	.247	.306	.385	-.158	-13.2	79-RF	-4	42-2B	-4
2004	*BOS*	*AL*	*25*	*216*	*56*	*13*	*1*	*5*	*22*	*43*	*8*	*2*	*.260*	*.329*	*.407*	*-.044*	*.255*	*.328*	*.409*	*-.073*	*7.3*	*60-RF*	*3*		

Breakout: 34%   Improve: 58%   Collapse: 23%

One of the early small moves of the new regime was to acquire Crespo from the Padres, for whom Epstein had previously worked. Crespo can play several positions, has above-average power for a middle infielder and a good eye at the plate. His youth and versatility will likely bring him back to the big leagues, probably in 2004. In the era of 12-man pitching staffs, versatility is everything.

JOHNNY DAMON

OF   **Bats: L**   **Throws: L**   Born: 05-Nov-73   Age: 30

YEAR	TM	LG	AGE	AB	H	2B	3B	HR	BB	SO	SB	CS	AVG	OBP	SLG	MLVR	EQBA	EQOBP	EQSLG	EQMLVR	VORP	DEFENSE			
2001	OAK	AL	27	644	165	34	4	9	61	70	27	12	.256	.324	.363	-.105	.277	.346	.394	-.048	16.5	86-CF	5	67-LF	3
2002	BOS	AL	28	623	178	34	11	14	65	70	31	6	.286	.356	.443	.089	.311	.382	.486	.176	52.4	145-CF	3		
2003	BOS	AL	29	608	166	32	6	12	68	74	30	6	.273	.345	.405	-.015	.292	.367	.438	.065	20.4	142-CF	2		
2004	*BOS*	*AL*	*30*	*574*	*162*	*33*	*6*	*12*	*59*	*65*	*21*	*8*	*.282*	*.351*	*.421*	*.028*	*.277*	*.350*	*.424*	*.001*	*14.7*	*151-CF*	*-1*		

Breakout: 12%   Improve: 50%   Collapse: 19%

Grady Little batted the team's worst three OBPs first, second and third in the batting order, which helped the Red Sox miss its expected runs total by 47 (1008 EqR vs. 961 actual runs). Damon's greatest asset at this point is his defense, especially crucial patrolling center field between two sluggish sluggers. The club still owes him $16.5 million over the next two years, money he earned long ago in Missouri. Mercifully he had the good sense not to join his teammates in their October head shaving, which would have cost him any chance he had of appearing on "That 70s Show."

NOMAR GARCIAPARRA

SS   **Bats: R**   **Throws: R**   Born: 23-Jul-73   Age: 30

YEAR	TM	LG	AGE	AB	H	2B	3B	HR	BB	SO	SB	CS	AVG	OBP	SLG	MLVR	EQBA	EQOBP	EQSLG	EQMLVR	VORP	DEFENSE	
2001	BOS	AL	27	83	24	3	0	4	7	9	0	1	.289	.352	.470	.106	.301	.368	.494	.154	7.7	21-SS	0
2002	BOS	AL	28	635	197	56	5	24	41	63	5	2	.310	.352	.528	.220	.330	.377	.564	.301	80.3	151-SS	-5
2003	BOS	AL	29	658	198	37	13	28	39	61	19	5	.301	.345	.524	.178	.321	.370	.565	.281	59.6	151-SS	-8
2004	*BOS*	*AL*	*30*	*584*	*181*	*38*	*5*	*22*	*42*	*59*	*10*	*4*	*.310*	*.360*	*.505*	*.177*	*.304*	*.359*	*.507*	*.152*	*52.1*	*150-SS*	*-4*

Breakout: 12%   Improve: 37%   Collapse: 28%

Although well off the rarified peak of 1999–2000, Garciaparra is still a fine player. He is entering the last year of a seven-year, $44.5 million contract, one that has been a relative bargain for the Red Sox. The way these things work, his next deal will likely overpay him for his wonderful past. "Nomah" is beloved in Boston, but he seemed to grow wary of the oppressive local media in 2003, raising some doubt that he and Mia will be raising their gifted progeny in the Hub.

JEREMY GIAMBI

1B/OF   **Bats: L**   **Throws: L**   Born: 30-Sep-74   Age: 29

YEAR	TM	LG	AGE	AB	H	2B	3B	HR	BB	SO	SB	CS	AVG	OBP	SLG	MLVR	EQBA	EQOBP	EQSLG	EQMLVR	VORP	DEFENSE			
2001	OAK	AL	26	371	105	26	0	12	63	83	0	1	.283	.391	.450	.150	.302	.410	.487	.216	28.8	26-RF	-2		
2002	OAK	AL	27	157	43	7	0	8	27	40	0	0	.274	.390	.471	.179	.296	.409	.509	.238	12.7	33-LF	0		
2002	PHI	NL	27	156	38	10	0	12	52	54	0	1	.244	.435	.538	.333	.248	.434	.559	.299	18.8	18-1B	-1	14-RF	-3
2003	BOS	AL	28	127	25	5	0	5	26	42	1	0	.197	.342	.354	-.132	.213	.357	.386	-.082	-0.5				
2003	PAW	INT	28	35	8	4	0	1	7	15	0	0	.229	.357	.429	.067	.222	.333	.389	-.118	0.1				
2004	*LAD*	*NL*	*29*	*184*	*45*	*8*	*0*	*10*	*34*	*56*	*1*	*0*	*.247*	*.367*	*.458*	*.063*	*.257*	*.376*	*.472*	*.092*	*11.9*				

Breakout: 22%   Improve: 58%   Collapse: 25%

"Little G" was the one hitter Epstein brought in that did not work out; PECOTA didn't like his long-term outlook heading into 2003 and projected a huge drop from his '02 level, though not nearly huge enough. Giambi tried to play through a left shoulder injury, struggled badly, and was finally discovered to have a torn labrum. The Red Sox didn't miss him much, in large part because their regulars were injury-free. He should be healthy in the spring but will be attempting his comeback outside of New England.

JOHN HATTIG 3B Bats: B Throws: R Born: 27-Feb-80 Age: 24

YEAR	TM	LG	AGE	AB	H	2B	3B	HR	BB	SO	SB	CS	AVG	OBP	SLG	MLVR	EQBA	EQOBP	EQSLG	EQMLVR	VORP	DEFENSE			
2001	LOW	NYP	21	45	5	0	1	1	3	7	1	0	.111	.184	.222	-.424	.109	.153	.217	-.766	-15.4				
2001	AUG	SAL	21	179	51	9	1	1	22	42	4	1	.285	.371	.363	.118	.228	.292	.291	-.328	-14.5	26-1B	-3	11-3B	-1
2002	AUG	SAL	22	347	98	20	0	7	52	73	1	2	.282	.377	.401	.147	.208	.281	.307	-.339	-19.2	82-3B	1		
2002	SAR	FLA	22	85	21	6	0	0	7	16	0	0	.247	.301	.318	-.103	.207	.250	.276	-.445	-8.7				
2003	PME	EAS	23	32	7	2	0	0	2	11	0	0	.219	.265	.281	-.312	.188	.235	.250	-.521	-3.8				
2003	SAR	FLA	23	400	118	29	2	6	59	70	9	7	.295	.385	.422	.206	.235	.310	.357	-.197	-2.4	97-3B	-2		
2004	*BOS*	*AL*	*24*	*245*	*58*	*14*	*1*	*5*	*23*	*51*	*2*	*1*	*.236*	*.305*	*.364*	*-.157*	*.231*	*.304*	*.366*	*-.188*	*0.0*	*68-3B*	*-4*		

Breakout: 43%   Improve: 68%   Collapse: 17%

Trying to become the first Guam native to reach the major leagues, Hattig saved his season with a .393/.449/.628 performance over his last 99 at-bats at Sarasota, which earned him a promotion to Portland. He has a measured approach at the plate, and the strike zone command that the organization values. He needs to hit in Portland this season to have a chance.

DAMIAN JACKSON 2B/OF Bats: R Throws: R Born: 16-Aug-73 Age: 30

YEAR	TM	LG	AGE	AB	H	2B	3B	HR	BB	SO	SB	CS	AVG	OBP	SLG	MLVR	EQBA	EQOBP	EQSLG	EQMLVR	VORP	DEFENSE	
2001	SDP	NL	27	440	106	21	6	4	44	128	23	6	.241	.316	.343	-.163	.258	.331	.367	-.128	5.8	116-2B	6
2002	DET	AL	28	245	63	20	1	1	21	36	12	3	.257	.320	.359	-.094	.290	.354	.407	-.004	11.5	51-2B	-2
2003	BOS	AL	29	161	42	7	0	1	8	28	16	8	.261	.294	.323	-.226	.273	.312	.335	-.199	-3.3	16-2B	-1
2004	*COL*	*NL*	*30*	*148*	*40*	*8*	*1*	*2*	*13*	*27*	*8*	*4*	*.268*	*.331*	*.379*	*-.086*	*.259*	*.320*	*.362*	*-.145*	*1.8*	*43-2B*	*-2*

Breakout: 22%   Improve: 47%   Collapse: 31%

It was hoped that Jackson would be able to provide a platoon option at second base, but he did not hit at all. His 2003 value was that he played a better keystone than Walker, a trait he shares with several million other mammals. His versatility keeps him around, but it's hard to see what he does that Crespo couldn't do better and cheaper. The Sox wisely non-tendered him. Signed with the Rockies, where he'll battle Benji Gil for a utility job.

GABE KAPLER OF Bats: R Throws: R Born: 31-Jul-75 Age: 28

YEAR	TM	LG	AGE	AB	H	2B	3B	HR	BB	SO	SB	CS	AVG	OBP	SLG	MLVR	EQBA	EQOBP	EQSLG	EQMLVR	VORP	DEFENSE			
2001	TEX	AL	25	483	129	29	1	17	61	70	23	6	.267	.348	.437	.027	.278	.365	.456	.074	28.2	131-CF	-6		
2002	TEX	AL	26	196	51	12	1	0	8	30	5	2	.260	.285	.332	-.218	.276	.307	.352	-.182	-6.2	26-LF	0	17-CF	1
2002	COL	NL	26	119	37	4	3	2	8	23	6	2	.311	.359	.445	.093	.303	.346	.429	.024	2.7	18-RF	2	12-LF	0
2003	COL	NL	27	67	15	2	0	0	8	18	2	0	.224	.307	.254	-.343	.209	.293	.239	-.406	-4.4	10-RF	-1		
2003	BOS	AL	27	158	46	11	1	4	14	23	4	2	.291	.349	.449	.070	.304	.364	.475	.123	5.6	22-RF	-2	12-LF	-1
2004	*BOS*	*AL*	*28*	*193*	*53*	*10*	*2*	*4*	*21*	*34*	*7*	*2*	*.274*	*.345*	*.409*	*-.004*	*.269*	*.344*	*.412*	*-.032*	*5.2*	*55-RF*	*1*		

Breakout: 30%   Improve: 53%   Collapse: 25%

The best player on the Red Sox bench after his mid-season signing, he saw quite a bit of playing time, especially after Nixon's calf injury in September. Kapler can play all three outfield positions well, and hits lefties much better than Nixon or Ortiz, so he has quite a bit of value on this team. He'll likely be looking for more playing time in 2004, and the Red Sox would do well to give it to him, especially against lefties. Female Sox fans in particular applauded the one-year deal Boston dished out to bring "Gabe the Babe" back.

DAVE McCARTY 1B Bats: R Throws: L Born: 23-Nov-69 Age: 34

YEAR	TM	LG	AGE	AB	H	2B	3B	HR	BB	SO	SB	CS	AVG	OBP	SLG	MLVR	EQBA	EQOBP	EQSLG	EQMLVR	VORP	DEFENSE	
2001	KCR	AL	31	200	50	10	0	7	24	45	0	0	.250	.328	.405	-.072	.256	.341	.422	-.034	2.6	49-1B	-1
2002	DUR	INT	32	114	37	7	1	8	14	33	0	1	.325	.398	.614	.442	.293	.364	.560	.232	11.2	25-1B	1
2002	KCR	AL	32	32	3	1	0	1	2	10	0	0	.094	.147	.219	-.703	.094	.147	.250	-.740	-5.0		
2002	TBY	AL	32	34	6	0	0	1	4	9	0	0	.176	.300	.265	-.303	.206	.319	.294	-.280	-1.4		
2003	OAK	AL	33	26	7	2	0	0	1	7	0	0	.269	.286	.346	-.200	.269	.296	.385	-.161	-1.0		
2003	SAC	PCL	33	352	95	23	2	15	44	71	4	1	.270	.351	.474	.121	.239	.318	.428	-.082	0.1	60-1B	2
2003	BOS	AL	33	27	11	3	0	1	2	7	0	0	.407	.448	.630	.610	.444	.483	.667	.770	4.4		
2004	*BOS*	*AL*	*34*	*114*	*28*	*6*	*0*	*4*	*12*	*29*	*1*	*0*	*.243*	*.320*	*.408*	*-.069*	*.238*	*.319*	*.410*	*-.099*	*1.9*	*35-1B*	*-3*

Breakout: 26%   Improve: 40%   Collapse: 44%

A former uberprospect in Minnesota, McCarty has been reduced to journeyman status for several years. He hit pretty well for Boston after his July acquisition, and somehow made the post-season roster. That said, the Red Sox were fortunate in the quality and health of their regulars, and might need a better bench option going forward. He's been re-signed to a minor league deal, and reportedly is trying to add "pitcher" to his resume.

LOU MERLONI   IF   Bats: R   Throws: R   Born: 06-Apr-71   Age: 33

YEAR	TM	LG	AGE	AB	H	2B	3B	HR	BB	SO	SB	CS	AVG	OBP	SLG	MLVR	EQBA	EQOBP	EQSLG	EQMLVR	VORP	DEFENSE			
2001	PAW	INT	30	195	51	12	0	4	15	37	2	0	.262	.330	.385	-.014	.253	.313	.374	-.156	2.8	28-SS	-4	18-2B	-1
2001	BOS	AL	30	146	39	10	0	3	6	31	2	1	.267	.306	.397	-.091	.281	.324	.425	-.041	5.9	37-SS	1		
2002	BOS	AL	31	194	48	12	2	4	20	35	1	2	.247	.332	.392	-.050	.272	.355	.431	.016	9.7	51-2B	-2		
2003	SDP	NL	32	151	41	7	2	1	22	33	2	3	.272	.362	.364	.045	.290	.381	.387	.018	7.4	19-3B	-2	19-SS	-3
2003	BOS	AL	32	30	7	1	0	0	4	8	0	0	.233	.324	.267	-.260	.267	.353	.300	-.171	-0.8				
2004	CLE	AL	33	150	36	7	1	3	14	31	1	1	.238	.312	.349	-.162	.247	.325	.378	-.125	5.7	44-2B	-3		

Breakout: 22%   Improve: 48%   Collapse: 32%

Beaten out by Jackson for the utility role, Merloni was dealt to San Diego in the spring and reacquired later in the summer. For someone who has spent so much time bouncing between Triple-A and the majors, he's a pretty consistent player, playing three infield positions and hitting a little. Merloni looked like a decent platoon option for Walker, but Jackson trumped him by being able to play the outfield and pinch-run. We'll chalk his weird reverse '03 splits (.337/.404/.427 vs. RH, .196/.308/.272 vs. LH) up to small sample size given his historical preference for hitting southpaws.

KEVIN MILLAR   1B/OF   Bats: R   Throws: R   Born: 24-Sep-71   Age: 32

YEAR	TM	LG	AGE	AB	H	2B	3B	HR	BB	SO	SB	CS	AVG	OBP	SLG	MLVR	EQBA	EQOBP	EQSLG	EQMLVR	VORP	DEFENSE			
2001	FLA	NL	29	449	141	39	5	20	39	70	0	0	.314	.374	.557	.294	.322	.381	.571	.308	46.6	56-RF	-5	21-LF	0
2002	FLA	NL	30	438	134	41	0	16	40	74	0	2	.306	.366	.509	.251	.315	.375	.531	.233	32.9	75-LF	0	18-RF	-2
2003	BOS	AL	31	544	150	30	1	25	60	108	3	2	.276	.348	.472	.086	.291	.369	.505	.161	20.8	95-1B	9	19-LF	-1
2004	BOS	AL	32	466	135	30	2	20	47	86	3	2	.289	.357	.492	.136	.284	.356	.495	.111	24.6	123-1B	-1		

Breakout: 14%   Improve: 40%   Collapse: 21%

Last winter Millar was the center of a six-week multinational tug of war involving the Red Sox, the Marlins, and the Chunichi Dragons, which ultimately landed him where he wanted to be. After the Hillenbrand trade, Millar settled into his everyday job at first base and became the media's symbol of the Red Sox's happy clubhouse. A bruised hand and tweaked quad coincided with his second-half fade (.251/.331/.421, vs. a .294/.361/.511 first half). The Sox could use a left-handed bat to spell Millar against tough righties.

DOUG MIRABELLI   C   Bats: R   Throws: R   Born: 18-Oct-70   Age: 33

YEAR	TM	LG	AGE	AB	H	2B	3B	HR	BB	SO	SB	CS	AVG	OBP	SLG	MLVR	EQBA	EQOBP	EQSLG	EQMLVR	VORP	DEFENSE	
2001	BOS	AL	30	141	38	8	0	9	17	36	0	0	.270	.360	.518	.165	.284	.377	.553	.233	15.3	42-C	2
2001	TEX	AL	30	49	5	2	0	2	10	21	0	0	.102	.254	.265	-.450	.122	.271	.286	-.426	-3.5	14-C	7
2002	BOS	AL	31	151	34	7	0	7	17	33	0	0	.225	.312	.411	-.075	.243	.333	.447	-.025	5.9	40-C	0
2003	BOS	AL	32	163	42	13	0	6	11	36	0	0	.258	.307	.448	-.033	.270	.323	.479	.025	4.8	43-C	-7
2004	BOS	AL	33	137	33	8	0	6	16	32	0	0	.243	.326	.422	-.041	.239	.326	.424	-.069	4.4	41-C	-2

Breakout: 24%   Improve: 56%   Collapse: 27%

Mirabelli usually has a huge platoon split, but he didn't last season. Because he's been Tim Wakefield's catcher, the Red Sox have not gotten any benefit out of this split—he starts against whoever happens to be pitching that day. He edged out Jorge Posada for the league lead in passed balls (14–13), although, trying to catch Wakefield's knuckler, he has a pretty good excuse.

BILL MUELLER   3B   Bats: B   Throws: R   Born: 17-Mar-71   Age: 33

YEAR	TM	LG	AGE	AB	H	2B	3B	HR	BB	SO	SB	CS	AVG	OBP	SLG	MLVR	EQBA	EQOBP	EQSLG	EQMLVR	VORP	DEFENSE	
2001	CHC	NL	30	210	62	12	1	6	37	19	1	1	.295	.403	.448	.163	.298	.407	.456	.166	22.0	57-3B	-2
2002	CHC	NL	31	353	94	19	4	7	51	41	0	0	.266	.355	.402	.053	.277	.365	.424	.029	20.3	99-3B	-1
2002	SFG	NL	31	13	2	0	0	0	1	1	0	0	.154	.214	.154	-.580	.231	.286	.231	-.422	-1.0		
2003	BOS	AL	32	524	171	45	5	19	59	77	1	4	.326	.398	.540	.308	.349	.422	.584	.422	61.2	121-3B	-2
2004	BOS	AL	33	391	108	22	2	10	45	49	1	2	.275	.352	.423	.027	.270	.351	.425	.000	22.1	106-3B	-4

Breakout: 8%   Improve: 30%   Collapse: 41%

(continued next page)

Bill Mueller *(continued)*

The Red Sox had four regulars exceed their 90th-percentile PECOTA projection, but Mueller was the most surprising of all. When he signed it wasn't clear where he would play, and he had just 54 at-bats at the end of April, getting time at both second and third base. He settled in at the hot corner when Hillenbrand was dealt, and just kept hitting. The most likely Red Sock to regress significantly, likely back to the still-fine player the Sox thought they had signed.

DAVID MURPHY   CF   Bats: L   Throws: L   Born: 18-Oct-81   Age: 22

YEAR	TM	LG	AGE	AB	H	2B	3B	HR	BB	SO	SB	CS	AVG	OBP	SLG	MLVR	EQBA	EQOBP	EQSLG	EQMLVR	VORP	DEFENSE	
2003	LOW	NYP	21	78	27	4	0	0	16	9	4	1	.346	.453	.397	.302	.229	.319	.277	-.292	-7.4	20-CF	-1
2003	SAR	FLA	21	153	37	5	1	1	20	33	6	2	.242	.329	.307	-.046	.208	.276	.270	-.400	-13.8	40-CF	-4
2004	*BOS*	*AL*	*22*	*221*	*48*	*10*	*2*	*2*	*21*	*46*	*5*	*2*	*.217*	*.287*	*.301*	*-.279*	*.213*	*.286*	*.302*	*-.313*	*-12.1*	*61-CF*	*-5*

Breakout: 26%   *Improve: 61%*   *Collapse: 17%*

The first draft pick of the Epstein era is about what you would expect: a polished college hitter with command of the strike zone. Murphy is also a fine athlete who can play an above-average center field. (He played right field at Baylor beside Chad Durbin, the team's 10th-round pick.) Murphy's performance in Lowell earned him a double-promotion to the FSL, where he rebounded after a poor start. He needs to develop some power to be a star, but even without it he could have a career.

MATT MURTON   LF   Bats: R   Throws: R   Born: 03-Oct-81   Age: 22

YEAR	TM	LG	AGE	AB	H	2B	3B	HR	BB	SO	SB	CS	AVG	OBP	SLG	MLVR	EQBA	EQOBP	EQSLG	EQMLVR	VORP	DEFENSE	
2003	LOW	NYP	21	189	54	11	2	2	27	39	9	3	.286	.374	.397	.160	.206	.277	.296	-.363	-36.1	47-LF	-6
2004	*BOS*	*AL*	*22*	*211*	*45*	*10*	*2*	*3*	*18*	*51*	*5*	*2*	*.214*	*.281*	*.316*	*-.273*	*.210*	*.280*	*.318*	*-.307*	*-12.3*	*59-LF*	*-5*

Breakout: 35%   *Improve: 57%*   *Collapse: 13%*

Boston's sandwich pick last summer, Murton is often lumped with Murphy, his teammate on two championship teams in the Cape Cod League. Unlike Murphy, he is not a plus defensive player, and will have to continually work to become a decent left fielder. That said, his power development has put him ahead of Murphy with many observers. He is a true student of hitting, working long hours, taking detailed notes on opposing pitchers and regularly poring over a dog-eared copy of Ted Williams's classic "The Science of Hitting." Will likely get bumped to Sarasota in 2004.

TROT NIXON   RF   Bats: L   Throws: L   Born: 11-Apr-74   Age: 30

YEAR	TM	LG	AGE	AB	H	2B	3B	HR	BB	SO	SB	CS	AVG	OBP	SLG	MLVR	EQBA	EQOBP	EQSLG	EQMLVR	VORP	DEFENSE			
2001	BOS	AL	27	535	150	31	4	27	79	113	7	4	.280	.376	.505	.185	.300	.398	.544	.272	49.5	75-RF	-3	67-CF	-1
2002	BOS	AL	28	532	136	36	3	24	65	109	4	2	.256	.338	.470	.069	.274	.359	.509	.133	27.9	136-RF	4	12-CF	1
2003	BOS	AL	29	441	135	24	6	28	65	96	4	2	.306	.396	.578	.336	.325	.418	.616	.431	44.4	119-RF	-3		
2004	*BOS*	*AL*	*30*	*431*	*122*	*26*	*3*	*22*	*59*	*88*	*4*	*2*	*.284*	*.372*	*.511*	*.178*	*.278*	*.371*	*.513*	*.154*	*28.5*	*118-RF*	*1*		

Breakout: 7%   *Improve: 31%*   *Collapse: 27%*

Nixon was drafted back in the Lou Gorman era, and prior to last season, New England had been disappointed in his output. If Nixon had stayed a little healthier and hit lefties at all, he would have been an MVP candidate, since he brutalized northpaws (.330/.423/.635). Unfortunately, with a left-hander on the mound, Nixon has hit .220/.306/.349 over the past four seasons; you'd be better off with Rey Ordonez up there. Nixon is a good defensive player, although the extra 30 pounds he put on last year cut down on his range in Fenway's vast right field. He is about to get very expensive, so he is no longer the trading chip that he once was.

DAVID ORTIZ   1B/DH   Bats: L   Throws: L   Born: 18-Nov-75   Age: 28

YEAR	TM	LG	AGE	AB	H	2B	3B	HR	BB	SO	SB	CS	AVG	OBP	SLG	MLVR	EQBA	EQOBP	EQSLG	EQMLVR	VORP	DEFENSE	
2001	MIN	AL	25	303	71	17	1	18	40	68	1	0	.234	.324	.475	.014	.244	.338	.502	.059	15.3		
2002	MIN	AL	26	412	112	32	1	20	43	87	1	2	.272	.339	.500	.118	.287	.361	.534	.184	29.3	12-1B	0
2003	BOS	AL	27	448	129	39	2	31	58	83	0	0	.288	.369	.592	.293	.304	.387	.631	.380	45.1	39-1B	0
2004	*BOS*	*AL*	*28*	*414*	*115*	*27*	*1*	*25*	*54*	*81*	*0*	*1*	*.278*	*.361*	*.533*	*.184*	*.273*	*.360*	*.536*	*.161*	*28.7*	*112-DH*	*0*

Breakout: 11%   *Improve: 34%*   *Collapse: 27%*

Like Nixon, had an outstanding year despite utter ineptitude against southpaws. Early on, he was the odd man out in the first base/DH surplus, finally settling in after Hillenbrand and Giambi were voted off the island. Through June, he was hitting .294 with four home runs, prompting Manny Ramirez to regularly refer to David as "Juan Pierre." Suitably chastened, Ortiz was the best hitter in the league for the second half (.284, .360, .661, with 27 home runs), even if he wasn't a legitimate MVP candidate, as some postulated.

JEREMY OWENS   CF   Bats: R   Throws: R   Born: 09-Dec-76   Age: 27

YEAR	TM	LG	AGE	AB	H	2B	3B	HR	BB	SO	SB	CS	AVG	OBP	SLG	MLVR	EQBA	EQOBP	EQSLG	EQMLVR	VORP	DEFENSE		
2001	LEL	CAL	24	91	18	1	1	3	7	39	4	2	.198	.260	.330	-.243	.163	.218	.261	-.551	-10.9	12-CF	6	
2001	MOB	SOU	24	395	85	20	6	7	55	149	33	12	.215	.311	.349	-.119	.184	.264	.307	-.386	-31.6	95-CF	0	13-RF -1
2002	LEL	CAL	25	418	96	21	4	13	39	148	23	9	.230	.299	.392	-.077	.185	.236	.319	-.425	-44.6	60-RF	0	46-CF 1
2003	PME	EAS	26	471	124	25	8	21	41	161	15	7	.263	.326	.484	.090	.219	.273	.414	-.200	-7.6	136-CF -1		
2004	BOS	AL	27	182	43	9	2	6	16	58	5	2	.235	.298	.406	-.116	.231	.297	.408	-.147	-0.5	51-CF -3		

Breakout: 51%   *Improve: 67%*   *Collapse: 23%*

The Red Sox love J.O., and it isn't hard to find reasons for their affection. Owens hits with power, plays a solid defensive center field, and runs the bases well. Unfortunately, he has a ghastly all-or-nothing swing, resulting in a whiff every three trips to the dish. His work ethic and attitude give the organization hope that he can develop the moderate plate discipline that could bring him to the big leagues, but time is quickly running out.

HANLEY RAMIREZ   SS   Bats: B   Throws: R   Born: 23-Dec-83   Age: 20

YEAR	TM	LG	AGE	AB	H	2B	3B	HR	BB	SO	SB	CS	AVG	OBP	SLG	MLVR	EQBA	EQOBP	EQSLG	EQMLVR	VORP	DEFENSE
2002	LOW	NYP	18	97	36	9	2	1	4	14	4	3	.371	.400	.536	.448	.283	.310	.424	-.066	7.2	22-SS -3
2003	AUG	SAL	19	422	116	24	3	8	32	73	36	13	.275	.327	.403	.083	.221	.259	.339	-.331	-17.9	102-SS -13
2004	BOS	AL	20	297	72	17	2	5	16	51	12	5	.243	.285	.365	-.186	.239	.284	.367	-.218	1.8	78-SS -8

Breakout: 32%   *Improve: 48%*   *Collapse: 26%*

Rated by most observers as the best prospect in the system a year ago, Ramirez's off-year and continued attitude problems (he was suspended three times) have cooled the hoopla a bit. As the organization views it, he's not a bad kid, just an immature one who didn't handle all the attention and accolades. His good second half and strong instructional league showing are positive signs. A switch-hitting shortstop with power and speed, he still has more upside than any other player in the organization. If 2003 was just the speed bump he needed, Hanley could be back atop prospect lists by mid-season. If he continues to try to follow his own rules, he might need to change organizations.

MANNY RAMIREZ   LF   Bats: R   Throws: R   Born: 30-May-72   Age: 32

YEAR	TM	LG	AGE	AB	H	2B	3B	HR	BB	SO	SB	CS	AVG	OBP	SLG	MLVR	EQBA	EQOBP	EQSLG	EQMLVR	VORP	DEFENSE
2001	BOS	AL	29	529	162	33	2	41	81	147	0	1	.306	.405	.609	.391	.323	.420	.647	.474	77.0	52-LF 3
2002	BOS	AL	30	436	152	31	0	33	73	85	0	0	.349	.450	.647	.563	.371	.469	.695	.672	87.2	59-LF -4
2003	BOS	AL	31	569	185	36	1	37	97	94	3	1	.325	.427	.587	.413	.346	.448	.628	.517	70.5	116-LF -3
2004	BOS	AL	32	514	161	34	1	34	81	99	2	1	.314	.410	.582	.354	.308	.409	.585	.334	57.1	142-LF -2

Breakout: 8%   *Improve: 30%*   *Collapse: 38%*

Although his contract is a quaint reminder of an age gone by, Manny's production has not ebbed. He took some heat in New England for driving in "only" 104 runs, though critics conveniently ignored Grady Little's stacking of the team's three worst OBPs at the top of the lineup. Little was given a lot of credit for his "handling" of Ramirez, but Manny had the same year he always has. Ramirez's manager should count on an annual off-the-field incident, like last September's "head cold," and an occasional jog down to first base on a ground ball. He should also be able to count on someone who shows up early to look at film, works hard on his defense, takes hours of extra batting practice, and is one of the top 10 hitters in baseball every year.

JUSTIN SHERROD   RF   Bats: R   Throws: R   Born: 11-Jan-78   Age: 26

YEAR	TM	LG	AGE	AB	H	2B	3B	HR	BB	SO	SB	CS	AVG	OBP	SLG	MLVR	EQBA	EQOBP	EQSLG	EQMLVR	VORP	DEFENSE		
2001	AUG	SAL	23	307	89	24	3	11	34	102	16	7	.290	.396	.495	.314	.226	.301	.393	-.171	0.9	45-3B -8	18-RF -2	
2001	SAR	FLA	23	141	43	8	3	7	11	37	5	1	.305	.357	.553	.333	.250	.289	.472	-.064	5.1	33-3B -9		
2002	TRN	EAS	24	243	62	19	1	9	29	81	8	4	.255	.343	.453	.090	.218	.291	.395	-.193	-9.8	59-RF -5	13-LF -1	
2003	PME	EAS	25	448	116	28	2	15	47	143	6	5	.259	.346	.431	.047	.214	.286	.370	-.239	-24.3	123-RF -2		
2004	BOS	AL	26	185	44	11	1	7	16	58	2	1	.236	.308	.420	-.079	.232	.307	.422	-.109	1.7	53-RF -2		

Breakout: 39%   *Improve: 56%*   *Collapse: 22%*

(continued next page)

Justin Sherrod (*continued*)

Posts similar offensive lines to Jeremy Owens, as the two players have shown similar Dom DeLuise-like plate discipline. The Red Sox believe there is a subset of players who can improve this critical part of their game in the minor leagues, and that the trick is finding those players and guiding them. Sherrod is an otherwise solid all-around player who seems to be receptive to instruction, but he's stalled largely because he strikes out in 30% of his plate appearances.

KELLY SHOPPACH   C   **Bats: R**   **Throws: R**   Born: 29-Apr-80   Age: 24

YEAR	TM	LG	AGE	AB	H	2B	3B	HR	BB	SO	SB	CS	AVG	OBP	SLG	MLVR	EQBA	EQOBP	EQSLG	EQMLVR	VORP	DEFENSE
2002	SAR	FLA	22	414	112	35	1	10	59	112	2	1	.271	.369	.432	.157	.214	.292	.357	-.245	-10.1	92-C -4
2003	PME	EAS	23	340	96	30	2	12	35	83	0	0	.282	.353	.488	.154	.232	.296	.415	-.146	2.9	82-C 3
2004	BOS	AL	24	218	50	13	1	6	20	56	0	0	.228	.297	.376	-.160	.223	.296	.378	-.192	-1.2	61-C -6

Breakout: 20%   Improve: 38%   Collapse: 35%

The team's top 2001 draft pick made it to Triple-A in his second professional season, despite shoulder surgery last fall which delayed his 2003 debut. Shoppach is highly regarded as an agile defensive catcher with a good arm and a quick release. He has also hit well, with gap power to all fields. His patience regressed a bit from its '02 level, and the Sox hope Shoppach can reclaim better command of the strike zone. With Varitek's contract running out after the 2004 season, Shoppach could find the starting job waiting for him.

CHAD SPANN   3B   **Bats: R**   **Throws: R**   Born: 25-Oct-83   Age: 20

YEAR	TM	LG	AGE	AB	H	2B	3B	HR	BB	SO	SB	CS	AVG	OBP	SLG	MLVR	EQBA	EQOBP	EQSLG	EQMLVR	VORP	DEFENSE
2003	AUG	SAL	19	414	129	21	3	5	40	64	9	5	.312	.379	.413	.194	.243	.293	.332	-.260	-11.1	100-3B -4
2004	BOS	AL	20	289	68	14	2	4	19	51	3	2	.235	.286	.332	-.233	.230	.285	.333	-.266	-4.5	77-3B -6

Breakout: 23%   Improve: 45%   Collapse: 39%

A bright spot on a miserable Augusta team, he made a big leap forward after a poor 2002 in the Gulf Coast League. Spann needed a great spring just to make the Augusta roster, but he is now one of the brighter prospects in the system. In an organization that wants to show that plate discipline can be developed, Spann was their crowning achievement in 2003—at one walk for every 11 times up, it tells you how far he's had to come. Now that he is a good third baseman with better-rounded offensive skills, Spann will be given every opportunity to advance quickly up the ladder.

JASON VARITEK   C   **Bats: B**   **Throws: R**   Born: 11-Apr-72   Age: 32

YEAR	TM	LG	AGE	AB	H	2B	3B	HR	BB	SO	SB	CS	AVG	OBP	SLG	MLVR	EQBA	EQOBP	EQSLG	EQMLVR	VORP	DEFENSE
2001	BOS	AL	29	174	51	11	1	7	21	35	0	0	.293	.371	.489	.166	.306	.387	.520	.227	18.7	50-C 4
2002	BOS	AL	30	467	124	27	1	10	41	95	4	3	.266	.332	.392	-.037	.285	.352	.425	.013	22.4	122-C -2
2003	BOS	AL	31	451	123	31	1	25	51	106	3	2	.273	.351	.512	.142	.288	.371	.546	.218	34.4	118-C -3
2004	BOS	AL	32	349	93	21	1	14	37	74	3	1	.268	.343	.456	.048	.263	.342	.458	.021	21.0	95-C -4

Breakout: 15%   Improve: 43%   Collapse: 30%

Varitek's great season was not a fluke—he was having a similar one in 2001 until he broke his elbow, and it took him a year and a half to fully recover. He and his hefty 2001-era contract (three years/$14.9 million) could have been had cheaply all last winter, but the Red Sox got their money's worth out of their #9 hitter. With his contract expiring at the end of 2004, and with the popular backstop approaching his mid-30s, a lot of people are already handing Shoppach the 2005 catcher's job.

TODD WALKER   2B   **Bats: L**   **Throws: R**   Born: 25-May-73   Age: 31

YEAR	TM	LG	AGE	AB	H	2B	3B	HR	BB	SO	SB	CS	AVG	OBP	SLG	MLVR	EQBA	EQOBP	EQSLG	EQMLVR	VORP	DEFENSE
2001	COL	NL	28	290	86	18	2	12	25	40	1	3	.297	.349	.497	.073	.278	.335	.465	.033	16.3	72-2B -5
2001	CIN	NL	28	261	77	17	0	5	26	42	0	5	.295	.361	.418	.029	.292	.357	.409	.006	13.1	61-2B -1
2002	CIN	NL	29	612	183	42	3	11	50	81	8	5	.299	.353	.431	.090	.300	.352	.436	.042	34.6	147-2B 6
2003	BOS	AL	30	587	166	38	4	13	48	54	1	1	.283	.333	.428	.005	.299	.355	.455	.074	22.6	134-2B -18
2004	CHC	NL	31	507	138	31	2	11	46	59	2	2	.272	.332	.405	-.046	.275	.333	.416	-.040	18.4	132-2B -6

Breakout: 18%   Improve: 34%   Collapse: 21%

After a brutal stretch in July and August, Walker came back huge in September and October, hitting close to .350 with power in each month, with several dramatic home runs mixed in for good measure. Unfortunately, he offered defense on par with the Maginot Line, causing Little to bench him when Derek Lowe was on the hill. He would be a more valuable player on a team where he did not have to play 150 games at second base. The Cubs obliged, setting up a platoon with Mark Grudzielanek after signing Walker to a bargain-basement, one-year, $1.75 million deal. Mark Bellhorn and Pokey Reese should combine with Bill Mueller to provide a good blend of offense and defense at second and third in Boston.

KEVIN YOUKILIS   3B   Bats: R   Throws: R   Born: 15-Mar-79   Age: 25

YEAR	TM	LG	AGE	AB	H	2B	3B	HR	BB	SO	SB	CS	AVG	OBP	SLG	MLVR	EQBA	EQOBP	EQSLG	EQMLVR	VORP	DEFENSE			
2001	LOW	NYP	22	183	58	14	2	3	70	28	4	3	.317	.512	.464	.433	.150	.290	.227	-.450	-34.1	58-3B	-4		
2002	AUG	SAL	23	53	15	5	0	0	13	8	0	0	.283	.433	.377	.198	.193	.297	.281	-.348	-3.4	15-3B	0		
2002	SAR	FLA	23	268	79	16	0	3	49	37	0	2	.295	.422	.388	.193	.236	.337	.318	-.196	-10.6	40-1B	-4	33-3B	-2
2002	TRN	EAS	23	160	55	10	0	5	31	18	5	4	.344	.462	.500	.406	.279	.379	.412	.040	11.8	44-3B	-5		
2003	PAW	INT	24	109	18	3	0	2	18	21	0	1	.165	.295	.248	-.291	.162	.285	.243	-.436	-9.2	29-3B	-3		
2003	PME	EAS	24	312	102	23	1	6	86	40	7	0	.327	.487	.465	.356	.245	.387	.362	-.035	16.4	92-3B	1		
2004	*BOS*	*AL*	*25*	*231*	*55*	*12*	*1*	*4*	*31*	*37*	*2*	*1*	*.237*	*.339*	*.351*	*-.112*	*.232*	*.338*	*.353*	*-.142*	*4.7*	*67-3B*	*-4*		

Breakout: 22%   *Improve: 42%*   *Collapse: 29%*

He's steadily advanced up the ladder based on his Bonds-like ability to draw walks, with the hope that other skills (especially defense and power) would evolve. So far, they haven't. In his first taste of Triple-A pitching, the Greek God of Walks was fed a steady stream of high fastballs that he usually took for strikes, resulting in a lot of pitcher's counts and weakly batted balls. Optimists compare Youkilis to Wade Boggs, who was a much better defender and hit .361/.444/.486 in the major leagues at this age. A career resembling Ken Oberkfell's or Dave Magadan's, with less defense, looks more likely.

PITCHERS

ABE ALVAREZ   Bats: L   Throws: L   Born: 17-Oct-82   Age: 21

YEAR	TM	LG	AGE	G	GS	IP	H	BB	SO	HR	ERA	EQERA	EQH9	EQBB9	EQSO9	EQHR9	PERA	VORP	STF
2003	LOW	NYP	20	9	9	19.0	9	2	19	0	0.00	1.59	6.4	1.6	5.3	0.5	2.43	7.6	28

The team's second round pick in 2003, Alvarez is essentially the pitching version of David Murphy. A polished and well-rounded lefty, he has no overpowering pitch, but mixes an 86-mph sinking fastball with a good curveball and changeup. The Red Sox believe he has near major league quality stuff, and just needs to pitch. Expect him to start at Sarasota, but the Red Sox will not hesitate to promote him rapidly.

BRONSON ARROYO   Bats: R   Throws: R   Born: 24-Feb-77   Age: 27

YEAR	TM	LG	AGE	G	GS	IP	H	BB	SO	HR	ERA	EQERA	EQH9	EQBB9	EQSO9	EQHR9	PERA	VORP	STF
2001	NAS	PCL	24	9	9	66.3	63	15	49	6	3.94	4.70	9.4	2.5	4.8	1.0	4.59	6.1	4
2001	PIT	NL	24	24	13	88.3	99	34	39	12	5.10	4.96	9.9	3.2	3.4	1.1	5.09	6.1	-11
2002	NAS	PCL	25	22	21	143.0	126	28	116	10	2.96	3.92	8.6	2.0	5.6	0.8	3.86	24.9	15
2002	PIT	NL	25	9	4	27.0	30	15	22	1	4.00	5.13	10.3	4.4	6.2	0.3	4.78	1.4	10
2003	PAW	INT	26	24	24	149.7	148	23	155	9	3.43	4.31	10.3	1.7	7.5	0.8	4.52	19.7	21
2003	BOS	AL	26	6	0	17.3	10	4	14	0	2.08	1.59	4.8	2.1	6.9	0.0	1.49	6.5	47
2004	*BOS*	*AL*	*27*	*21*	*15*	*89.7*	*98*	*25*	*63*	*11*	*4.35*	*4.13*	*9.2*	*2.4*	*6.3*	*1.0*	*4.22*	*16.7*	*9*

Breakout: 18%   *Improve: 45%*   *Collapse: 25%*

After a fine campaign for the PawSox (including a perfect game), Arroyo's solid September showing with the big club earned him a spot on the post-season roster. His stuff is not overpowering, but he mixes his pitches well and avoids the base on balls. He's a candidate for the fifth starter's job, and could fill it ably if selected.

JAMIE BROWN

			Bats: R				Throws: R					Born: 31-Mar-77			Age: 27	

YEAR	TM	LG	AGE	G	GS	IP	H	BB	SO	HR	ERA	EQERA	EQH9	EQBB9	EQSO9	EQHR9	PERA	VORP	STF
2001	AKR	EAS	24	4	4	19.7	22	7	12	2	5.03	6.62	11.7	4.6	3.6	1.5	6.84	-2.0	-38
2002	AKR	EAS	25	18	17	103.7	98	17	72	5	2.78	4.76	10.8	1.7	4.7	0.8	4.76	8.7	2
2003	BUF	INT	26	13	10	61.3	45	17	26	4	3.52	3.81	7.0	3.0	3.0	1.0	3.57	11.3	-11
2003	PAW	INT	26	18	3	51.7	40	5	39	1	2.26	3.00	7.7	1.1	5.4	0.2	2.58	13.9	26
2004	BOS	AL	27	18	9	53.7	61	17	28	7	4.66	4.43	9.6	2.6	4.6	1.1	4.58	8.4	-6

Breakout: 26%   Improve: 50%   Collapse: 23%

Acquired in mid-summer from the Indians, Brown was moved to the bullpen by the PawSox, where he pitched well. Brown reached Double-A in his first full season back in 1998, but has been beset by a slew of injury problems, including Tommy John surgery in 2001. His assets are a low-90s fastball and excellent control. After his first healthy professional season, he was added to the 40-man roster in October on the strong recommendation of Bill Haselman, who caught him in Pawtucket.

JOHN BURKETT

			Bats: R				Throws: R					Born: 28-Nov-64			Age: 39	

YEAR	TM	LG	AGE	G	GS	IP	H	BB	SO	HR	ERA	EQERA	EQH9	EQBB9	EQSO9	EQHR9	PERA	VORP	STF
2001	ATL	NL	36	34	34	219.3	187	70	187	17	3.04	3.62	8.2	2.7	6.6	0.6	3.64	45.9	26
2002	BOS	AL	37	29	29	173.0	199	50	124	25	4.53	4.74	10.5	2.4	6.3	1.2	5.21	16.0	6
2003	BOS	AL	38	32	30	181.7	202	47	107	20	5.15	4.27	9.2	2.2	5.1	0.9	4.21	12.6	10
2004	BOS	AL	39	30	24	147.3	167	44	89	19	4.93	4.68	9.6	2.6	5.4	1.1	4.60	17.8	4

Breakout: 10%   Improve: 33%   Collapse: 26%

With the expiration of his two-year, $11 million deal, Burkett may retire, perhaps to energize the floundering Pro Bowlers' Tour. A large subplot of Boston's post-season was how the team could delay, or avoid, Burkett's turn in the rotation. Ironically, the Sox ended up winning both of his starts (rallying after he had left), each time setting up a winner-take-all game the next day. A serious upgrade here was the club's largest need heading into the off-season. Curt Schilling will do.

BRUCE CHEN

			Bats: L				Throws: L					Born: 19-Jun-77			Age: 27	

YEAR	TM	LG	AGE	G	GS	IP	H	BB	SO	HR	ERA	EQERA	EQH9	EQBB9	EQSO9	EQHR9	PERA	VORP	STF
2001	PHI	NL	24	16	16	86.3	90	31	79	19	5.01	5.64	9.7	3.0	6.9	1.7	5.61	-0.4	2
2001	NYM	NL	24	11	11	59.7	56	28	47	10	4.67	5.31	8.6	3.9	5.9	1.4	5.00	1.9	1
2002	MON	NL	25	15	5	37.3	47	23	43	9	7.00	7.36	11.5	4.7	8.8	2.2	7.44	-7.2	-26
2002	CIN	NL	25	39	1	39.7	37	20	37	7	4.31	5.12	8.6	4.0	7.2	1.6	5.25	2.1	-14
2003	HOU	NL	26	11	0	12.0	14	8	8	2	6.00	6.17	10.8	5.4	5.4	1.5	6.60	-0.2	-39
2003	BOS	AL	26	5	2	12.3	12	2	12	4	5.12	5.11	8.0	1.5	8.0	2.2	4.85	0.2	-10
2003	PAW	INT	26	16	15	85.0	80	15	73	12	4.24	4.87	9.8	2.0	6.3	2.1	5.83	6.3	-23
2004	TOR	AL	27	25	13	77.3	82	27	56	14	4.82	4.57	9.2	2.9	6.5	1.3	4.72	12.0	2

Breakout: 30%   Improve: 57%   Collapse: 18%

Having hurled for seven major league teams at age 26, he is a full three teams ahead of Mike Morgan's pace. As long as he keeps piling up 73/15 strikeout-to-walk ratios in Triple-A, Chen is going to get chances. His gopheritis—12 home runs allowed in 85 Triple-A innings—remains a big stumbling block. Scouts still love his stuff, but several major league teams have given up waiting for him to develop the consistency he desperately needs. The Blue Jays are next in line, having signed him to a minor league deal.

JORGE DE LA ROSA

			Bats: L				Throws: L					Born: 05-Apr-81			Age: 23	

YEAR	TM	LG	AGE	G	GS	IP	H	BB	SO	HR	ERA	EQERA	EQH9	EQBB9	EQSO9	EQHR9	PERA	VORP	STF
2001	SAR	FLA	20	12	0	29.7	13	12	27	0	1.21	2.28	4.6	4.2	5.5	0.3	2.24	10.2	31
2001	TRN	EAS	20	29	0	37.0	56	20	27	4	5.84	9.34	12.6	6.1	4.8	1.3	7.26	-14.8	-21
2002	SAR	FLA	21	23	23	120.7	105	52	95	10	3.65	5.27	10.0	4.8	5.0	1.8	6.36	3.9	-9
2002	TRN	EAS	21	4	4	18.0	17	9	15	0	5.50	5.29	8.5	5.3	5.8	0.0	3.91	0.6	29
2003	PME	EAS	22	22	20	99.7	87	36	102	6	2.80	4.04	9.1	3.9	7.4	1.0	4.75	15.8	24
2003	PAW	INT	22	5	5	24.0	27	12	17	0	3.75	5.56	9.5	5.6	5.6	0.4	4.83	0.1	16
2004	MIL	NL	23	15	11	60.0	64	34	48	9	5.83	5.98	9.7	4.4	6.5	1.2	5.78	1.6	-2

Breakout: 14%   Improve: 45%   Collapse: 29%

Dan Duquette called De la Rosa the "Mexican John Rocker," fortunately more for the liveliness of his left arm than for his volatility. Although most scouts project him as a relief hurler, the Red Sox turned him into a starter in 2002, and he has pitched well since. He had a great year in Portland, and a primo series of starts late in the season got him promoted to Triple-A. He throws a fastball that can get to 94 mph, and a hard slider. After his fine 2003 season, he was the best pitching prospect in the system, and was part of the swag needed to bring in Curt Schilling. As part of the three-way deal, De la Rosa wound up with the Brewers.

MANNY DELCARMEN

Bats: R **Throws: R** Born: 16-Feb-82 Age: 22

YEAR	TM	LG	AGE	G	GS	IP	H	BB	SO	HR	ERA	EQERA	EQH9	EQBB9	EQSO9	EQHR9	PERA	VORP	STF
2002	AUG	SAL	20	26	24	136.0	124	56	136	15	4.10	7.02	11.5	5.2	5.6	2.7	8.28	-18.4	-25
2003	SAR	FLA	21	4	3	23.0	16	7	16	1	3.13	4.35	7.8	3.5	4.4	1.3	4.45	2.9	4
2004	BOS	AL	22	18	12	65.0	84	25	30	11	6.58	6.25	10.9	3.3	4.1	1.5	6.10	2.7	-16

Breakout: 27%   Improve: 53%   Collapse: 19%

His overpowering stuff, including a 94-mph moving fastball, a hard sinker, a curve, and a changeup, had the BoSox salivating last spring. Unfortunately, after a few impressive starts for Sarasota, Delcarmen had Tommy John surgery and was through for the year. The Red Sox are pleased with his training regimen while recuperating, and intend to take things slowly. Following surgery in May '03, look for a mid-summer return or later for this Boston native.

ALAN EMBREE

Bats: L **Throws: L** Born: 23-Jan-70 Age: 34

YEAR	TM	LG	AGE	G	GS	IP	H	BB	SO	HR	ERA	EQERA	EQH9	EQBB9	EQSO9	EQHR9	PERA	VORP	STF
2001	SFG	NL	31	22	0	20.0	34	10	25	7	11.25	10.98	15.6	4.1	9.2	2.7	9.74	-11.8	-62
2001	CWS	AL	31	39	0	34.0	31	7	34	7	5.03	4.64	8.2	1.6	8.5	1.6	4.34	3.5	1
2002	SDP	NL	32	36	0	28.7	23	9	38	2	0.94	2.89	7.4	2.6	10.3	0.6	3.21	8.4	38
2002	BOS	AL	32	32	0	33.3	24	11	43	4	2.97	3.06	6.7	2.8	11.1	1.1	3.39	9.1	33
2003	BOS	AL	33	65	0	55.0	49	16	45	5	4.25	3.31	7.3	2.5	7.1	0.7	3.20	10.5	17
2004	BOS	AL	34	53	0	53.7	53	16	49	6	4.05	3.85	8.3	2.6	8.3	1.0	3.74	11.7	12

Breakout: 22%   Improve: 50%   Collapse: 20%

Little tried to use Embree as a situational lefty, although he doesn't show much of a platoon advantage. In fact, his season was hurt by a couple of big homers allowed to left-handed hitters. He pitched well in the post-season when Little finally began to trust his bullpen, and had a nice seat in Yankee Stadium during Pedro's valiant struggles in Game 7. Embree should be a key part of the pen again in 2004.

CASEY FOSSUM

Bats: B **Throws: L** Born: 09-Jan-78 Age: 26

YEAR	TM	LG	AGE	G	GS	IP	H	BB	SO	HR	ERA	EQERA	EQH9	EQBB9	EQSO9	EQHR9	PERA	VORP	STF
2001	TRN	EAS	23	20	20	117.7	102	28	130	5	2.83	3.78	8.5	2.8	6.6	0.6	3.78	22.2	32
2001	BOS	AL	23	13	7	44.3	44	20	26	4	4.88	4.33	8.2	3.7	4.9	0.6	3.98	6.2	14
2002	BOS	AL	24	43	12	106.7	113	30	101	12	3.46	4.37	9.7	2.4	8.2	1.0	4.55	14.1	25
2003	PAW	INT	25	5	4	13.0	11	5	14	1	3.46	3.75	8.2	4.5	7.5	0.8	4.29	2.5	9
2003	BOS	AL	25	19	14	79.0	82	34	63	9	5.47	4.73	8.7	3.6	6.9	0.9	4.40	-2.5	12
2004	ARI	NL	26	23	14	81.3	84	35	69	11	4.98	4.76	9.0	3.3	7.1	1.1	4.61	8.8	7

Breakout: 21%   Improve: 38%   Collapse: 28%

A reluctance to part with Fossum supposedly cost the Red Sox either Kevin Millwood or Bartolo Colon. With that pressure, Fossum was handed a job in the rotation, and alternated between ineffective and hurt the entire season. In October, he had arthroscopic surgery on his rotator cuff, but should be back in the spring. Scouts are still high on his lively left arm, but he might need some innings in the bullpen before he is handed another starting job. The Snakes will likely have a spot for him.

JEROME GAMBLE

Bats: R **Throws: R** Born: 05-Apr-80 Age: 24

YEAR	TM	LG	AGE	G	GS	IP	H	BB	SO	HR	ERA	EQERA	EQH9	EQBB9	EQSO9	EQHR9	PERA	VORP	STF
2002	AUG	SAL	22	14	14	49.3	34	22	42	2	1.83	3.95	8.1	5.6	4.6	1.0	4.89	7.9	-9
2003	PME	EAS	23	2	2	11.0	10	1	11	0	4.91	4.35	9.6	0.9	7.0	0.0	3.14	1.4	49
2003	SAR	FLA	23	17	14	76.3	68	21	51	2	3.66	5.56	10.1	3.2	4.2	0.8	4.85	0.3	-4
2004	BOS	AL	24	21	13	75.0	91	35	38	11	5.89	5.60	10.3	3.9	4.6	1.3	5.62	4.7	-13

Breakout: 18%   Improve: 44%   Collapse: 31%

(continued next page)

Jerome Gamble *(continued)*

Selected by the Reds in the 2002 Rule 5 draft, Gamble was returned to the Red Sox in the spring. His great stuff—including a 93-mph fastball—and heady approach on the mound make him popular with the organization. He is a Tommy John recovery case, and still experiences soreness when he throws a curveball. A big injury risk, otherwise one of the best pitching prospects in the system. He'll start the season in Portland, and the team will continue to be cautious for at least another year.

DICKY GONZALEZ   Bats: R   Throws: R   Born: 21-Dec-78   Age: 25

YEAR	TM	LG	AGE	G	GS	IP	H	BB	SO	HR	ERA	EQERA	EQH9	EQBB9	EQSO9	EQHR9	PERA	VORP	STF
2001	NOR	INT	22	17	16	96.0	96	20	70	10	3.09	4.61	8.8	2.2	5.5	1.1	4.27	10.1	19
2001	NYM	NL	22	16	7	59.0	72	17	31	4	4.88	5.08	11.1	2.4	4.0	0.5	4.78	3.3	11
2002	OTT	INT	23	22	22	119.7	137	33	72	10	3.76	5.94	11.3	3.0	4.8	1.1	5.66	-4.2	0
2003	PAW	INT	24	27	25	151.7	180	29	104	13	4.03	5.36	11.5	2.1	4.9	1.2	5.67	3.8	-2
2004	TBY	AL	25	15	10	61.3	72	18	33	9	4.94	4.92	10.2	2.4	4.7	1.2	5.02	6.8	-4

Breakout: 15%   Improve: 42%   Collapse: 29%

Like most of the minor league veteran pitchers acquired last winter, Gonzalez has exceptional control, a fastball in the low 90s, and a good changeup. He was acquired in late March and almost made the team, but was one of the rare PawSox pitchers not hauled up during the summer. He needs to develop a good breaking pitch to get back to the majors. He was signed to a minor league contract by the Devil Rays.

BOBBY HOWRY   Bats: L   Throws: R   Born: 04-Aug-73   Age: 30

YEAR	TM	LG	AGE	G	GS	IP	H	BB	SO	HR	ERA	EQERA	EQH9	EQBB9	EQSO9	EQHR9	PERA	VORP	STF
2001	CWS	AL	27	69	0	78.7	85	30	64	11	4.69	4.62	9.8	3.2	6.9	1.2	5.12	8.3	-5
2002	CWS	AL	28	47	0	50.7	45	17	31	7	3.91	3.88	8.1	2.8	5.4	1.1	4.16	9.3	-7
2002	BOS	AL	28	20	0	18.0	22	4	14	2	5.00	5.71	11.4	2.1	6.7	1.0	5.39	-0.2	-4
2003	BOS	AL	29	4	0	4.3	11	3	4	1	12.56	12.46	20.8	6.2	8.3	2.1	11.38	-3.1	-66
2003	PAW	INT	29	13	0	17.0	14	1	10	1	1.06	2.30	8.0	0.6	4.0	0.6	2.95	5.8	7
2004	CLE	AL	30	46	0	38.0	42	13	24	5	4.87	5.19	9.8	2.9	5.4	1.3	5.31	4.6	-12

Breakout: 27%   Improve: 51%   Collapse: 29%

The Red Sox spent $2 million for those four innings, and will not be so inclined again. Howry's season was curtailed by a damaged ulnar nerve, which should be healed by the spring. The Indians gave him a minor league deal and a spring training invite.

TODD JONES   Bats: R   Throws: R   Born: 24-Apr-68   Age: 36

YEAR	TM	LG	AGE	G	GS	IP	H	BB	SO	HR	ERA	EQERA	EQH9	EQBB9	EQSO9	EQHR9	PERA	VORP	STF
2001	DET	AL	33	45	0	48.7	60	22	39	6	4.62	5.40	10.2	3.7	6.5	0.9	5.19	1.1	-6
2001	MIN	AL	33	24	0	19.3	27	7	15	3	3.26	4.82	12.5	2.9	6.8	1.4	6.59	1.6	-17
2002	COL	NL	34	79	0	82.3	84	28	73	10	4.70	4.29	9.3	2.7	6.9	1.0	4.54	11.6	0
2003	COL	NL	35	33	1	39.3	61	18	28	8	8.24	7.62	13.2	3.7	5.5	1.6	7.31	-10.0	-41
2003	BOS	AL	35	26	0	29.3	32	13	31	2	5.53	4.66	9.3	3.7	9.3	0.6	4.39	0.5	22
2004	TBY	AL	36	49	0	57.3	61	22	43	6	4.47	4.45	9.1	3.3	6.7	0.9	4.42	8.6	0

Breakout: 25%   Improve: 52%   Collapse: 30%

Jones caused a stir in April when he said he would not want to have a gay teammate, especially if "he's rubbing it in our face." Moving right along...Jones's 7.08 ERA might ordinarily spell the end of a 36-year-old's career, but since he once saved 40 games he will likely get several more chances. In fact, this is a little-known clause of the new CBA.

BYUNG-HYUN KIM   Bats: R   Throws: R   Born: 21-Jan-79   Age: 25

YEAR	TM	LG	AGE	G	GS	IP	H	BB	SO	HR	ERA	EQERA	EQH9	EQBB9	EQSO9	EQHR9	PERA	VORP	STF
2001	ARI	NL	22	78	0	98.0	58	44	113	10	2.94	2.79	5.9	3.7	8.8	0.8	3.01	29.3	44
2002	ARI	NL	23	72	0	84.0	64	26	92	5	2.04	2.45	7.3	2.5	8.6	0.6	3.06	28.2	44
2003	ARI	NL	24	7	7	43.0	34	15	33	6	3.56	3.24	6.9	2.8	6.0	1.1	3.55	10.9	22
2003	BOS	AL	24	49	5	79.3	70	18	69	6	3.18	3.12	7.3	2.0	7.6	0.6	2.96	14.6	34
2004	BOS	AL	25	42	19	123.3	112	37	101	12	3.48	3.31	7.6	2.6	7.4	0.8	3.34	33.9	14

Breakout: 21%   Improve: 43%   Collapse: 14%

Heisted from the Snakes for Shea Hillenbrand, Kim was first put in the rotation, where he wanted to be, before being asked to rescue the bullpen. He pitched well, but Little lost confidence in him after a few pitches missed the corner in October, leaving his future in limbo. The team's off-season dilemma is that an arbiter will likely reward Kim $3 million or more based on his record as a closer, which is a steep price for an unproven starter. They offered him arbitration, so he will likely get a shot at the fifth spot in the rotation.

JON LESTER Bats: L Throws: L Born: 07-Jan-84 Age: 20

YEAR	TM	LG	AGE	G	GS	IP	H	BB	SO	HR	ERA	EQERA	EQH9	EQBB9	EQSO9	EQHR9	PERA	VORP	STF
2003	AUG	SAL	19	24	21	106.0	102	44	71	7	3.65	5.89	9.7	4.9	3.8	1.5	5.95	-3.1	-8

The team's top 2002 pick was a late signing, but a fine spring got him onto the roster at Augusta. The pride of Puyallup, Washington, mixes a 93-mph fastball with a curve and changeup. As a tall left-hander with good command and composure, he has the smooth repeatable delivery that scouts love. He'll need to improve his peripheral numbers to find success as he climbs the ladder. We'll keep you posted.

DEREK LOWE Bats: Throws: Born: 01-Jun-73 Age: 31

YEAR	TM	LG	AGE	G	GS	IP	H	BB	SO	HR	ERA	EQERA	EQH9	EQBB9	EQSO9	EQHR9	PERA	VORP	STF
2001	BOS	AL	28	67	3	91.7	103	29	82	7	3.53	3.70	9.7	2.6	7.4	0.6	4.26	19.0	17
2002	BOS	AL	29	32	32	219.7	166	48	127	12	2.58	2.48	6.9	1.8	5.1	0.5	2.69	72.9	30
2003	BOS	AL	30	33	33	203.3	216	72	110	17	4.47	4.04	8.8	3.0	4.7	0.7	4.10	21.9	11
2004	*BOS*	*AL*	*31*	*31*	*27*	*161.3*	*178*	*56*	*89*	*13*	*4.28*	*4.07*	*9.3*	*2.9*	*5.0*	*0.7*	*4.17*	*27.9*	*4*
Breakout: 13%		*Improve: 54%*			*Collapse: 20%*														

The biggest victim of Boston's poor infield defense was Lowe, who likely grew tired of watching 12-hop grounders dribble through to right field. Lowe's first-half troubles may have been partly caused by off-field worries: He had surgery to remove a cancerous growth from his nose last off-season, and then in June had to deal with a second growth, which turned out to be benign. Lowe improved as the season progressed and was excellent in September and October. While hoping for more, the Red Sox would be happy to see D-Lowe split the difference between his 2002 and 2003 numbers. Pokey Reese's signing could push that goal closer to fruition.

BRANDON LYON Bats: R Throws: R Born: 10-Aug-79 Age: 24

YEAR	TM	LG	AGE	G	GS	IP	H	BB	SO	HR	ERA	EQERA	EQH9	EQBB9	EQSO9	EQHR9	PERA	VORP	STF
2001	TEN	SOU	21	9	9	58.7	57	9	45	7	3.68	5.26	10.7	1.7	4.9	1.7	5.74	2.0	4
2001	SYR	INT	21	11	11	68.3	68	10	53	7	3.69	4.61	8.3	1.5	6.0	0.9	3.67	7.3	33
2001	TOR	AL	21	11	11	63.0	63	15	35	6	4.29	3.94	8.3	2.0	4.7	0.7	3.65	11.4	30
2002	SYR	INT	22	14	14	75.7	99	19	35	4	5.11	6.53	11.1	2.6	3.7	0.6	4.99	-7.5	5
2002	TOR	AL	22	15	10	62.0	78	19	30	14	6.53	6.08	10.8	2.5	4.2	1.8	6.15	-3.2	-9
2003	BOS	AL	23	49	0	59.0	73	19	50	6	4.12	4.47	10.3	2.8	7.4	0.8	4.78	6.2	22
2004	*ARI*	*NL*	*24*	*33*	*11*	*76.0*	*84*	*25*	*57*	*11*	*4.92*	*4.71*	*9.6*	*2.5*	*6.2*	*1.1*	*4.60*	*8.8*	*0*
Breakout: 15%		*Improve: 40%*			*Collapse: 34%*														

In a period of a few weeks beginning in late July, Lyon was (1) traded to the Pirates (as part of the Sauerbeck deal), (2) determined to have a bad elbow, (3) disabled, (4) returned to the Red Sox (as part of the Suppan deal), and (5) determined to be healthy. For the first few months of the season the Red Sox's closer was whoever had pitched well yesterday, and in that environment Lyon held the job as long as anyone. A rough patch in June put him in the doghouse, and he never really got out of it. He was sent to the Diamondbacks as part of the Schilling trade.

ANASTACIO MARTINEZ Bats: R Throws: R Born: 03-Nov-78 Age: 25

YEAR	TM	LG	AGE	G	GS	IP	H	BB	SO	HR	ERA	EQERA	EQH9	EQBB9	EQSO9	EQHR9	PERA	VORP	STF
2001	SAR	FLA	22	25	24	145.0	130	39	123	12	3.35	4.70	9.8	2.9	5.0	1.8	5.78	13.2	-7
2002	TRN	EAS	23	27	27	139.0	152	75	127	12	5.31	6.54	10.6	5.6	6.1	1.3	6.21	-13.5	-9
2003	PME	EAS	24	34	0	40.0	31	24	37	3	2.25	3.75	8.2	6.8	6.8	1.2	5.45	7.4	-18
2003	PAW	INT	24	8	0	14.0	12	3	15	2	1.93	3.46	9.0	2.1	7.6	2.1	5.40	3.1	-8
2004	*BOS*	*AL*	*25*	*19*	*5*	*35.3*	*40*	*18*	*24*	*5*	*5.60*	*5.32*	*9.5*	*4.3*	*6.1*	*1.1*	*5.24*	*2.3*	*-9*
Breakout: 19%		*Improve: 51%*			*Collapse: 25%*														

(continued next page)

Anastacio Martinez *(continued)*

Like Lyon, Martinez spent nine days in the Pirates' organization before coming back (due to Lyon's "injury"). He had a decent season in the bullpen for Portland and Pawtucket and could find a role for himself in Boston in 2004, depending on what the roster looks like in April. Has three good pitches, none of them overpowering, plus some control problems. The Sox need the promising young starter who posted a 3:1 strikeout to walk ratio at Sarasota in 2001 to reemerge for Martinez to have a real future.

PEDRO MARTINEZ   Bats: R   Throws: R   Born: 25-Oct-71   Age: 32

YEAR	TM	LG	AGE	G	GS	IP	H	BB	SO	HR	ERA	EQERA	EQH9	EQBB9	EQSO9	EQHR9	PERA	VORP	STF
2001	BOS	AL	29	18	18	116.7	84	25	163	5	2.39	2.13	6.4	1.8	11.7	0.3	2.26	44.0	78
2002	BOS	AL	30	30	30	199.3	144	40	239	13	2.26	2.48	6.7	1.7	10.4	0.5	2.52	66.8	64
2003	BOS	AL	31	29	29	186.7	147	47	206	7	2.22	2.21	6.6	2.1	9.7	0.3	2.42	71.4	63
2004	BOS	AL	32	28	27	182.7	145	42	188	13	2.49	2.37	6.7	1.9	9.3	0.6	2.39	70.0	40

Breakout: 41%   Improve: 63%   Collapse: 9%

For 100 pitches per game, there is still no pitcher you'd rather have on the mound than Martinez. Pedro is entering the final year of what will have been a seven-year, $90 million contract, one which both parties should feel good about. That said, with a shoulder that is one hard slider away from the surgeon's knife, the team will be reluctant to give him another long-term commitment, making it possible that he will not be in Boston in 2005. Martinez believes that the team owes him for his past brilliance, and has been known to whine about it in the media. If this is the end of the ride, let's hope both sides handle it better than the Clemens debacle of 1996.

RAMIRO MENDOZA   Bats: R   Throws: R   Born: 15-Jun-72   Age: 32

YEAR	TM	LG	AGE	G	GS	IP	H	BB	SO	HR	ERA	EQERA	EQH9	EQBB9	EQSO9	EQHR9	PERA	VORP	STF
2001	NYY	AL	29	56	2	100.7	89	23	70	9	3.75	3.29	7.4	1.9	5.8	0.7	3.18	25.2	12
2002	NYY	AL	30	62	0	91.7	102	16	61	8	3.44	3.93	9.6	1.4	5.7	0.7	4.00	16.6	8
2003	BOS	AL	31	37	5	66.7	98	20	36	10	6.75	6.00	12.3	2.5	4.6	1.2	6.15	-6.6	-23
2004	BOS	AL	32	37	8	70.7	83	19	39	8	4.57	4.34	9.9	2.3	4.9	0.9	4.46	11.4	-6

Breakout: 19%   Improve: 49%   Collapse: 19%

Continued his fine work for the Yankees in 2003, only this time Mendoza did so wearing Red Sox garb. He was equally horrific out of the pen and during a stint in the rotation. He did two stints on the DL for right knee tendinitis, but his confidence and mechanics were his primary problems. Mendoza will get another shot, because the Sox are still on the hook for (gulp) $3.6 million.

ROBERT PERSON   Bats: R   Throws: R   Born: 08-Jan-69   Age: 35

YEAR	TM	LG	AGE	G	GS	IP	H	BB	SO	HR	ERA	EQERA	EQH9	EQBB9	EQSO9	EQHR9	PERA	VORP	STF
2001	PHI	NL	32	33	33	208.3	179	80	183	34	4.19	4.46	8.0	3.2	6.7	1.3	4.41	25.3	6
2002	PHI	NL	33	16	16	87.7	79	51	61	13	5.44	5.66	8.6	4.6	5.4	1.4	5.22	-0.6	-14
2003	BOS	AL	34	7	0	11.7	11	8	10	0	7.69	4.63	7.7	5.4	7.7	0.0	3.58	-2.2	24
2004	CWS	AL	35	22	13	70.7	94	32	49	25	8.16	8.23	12.0	3.8	6.0	2.5	8.19	-11.9	-18

Breakout: 17%   Improve: 41%   Collapse: 28%

The Sox were hoping that Person would compete for a spot in the rotation, but he had not sufficiently recovered from elbow and shoulder problems when the team broke camp. Once he was ready, he was anointed the closer, since everyone else in the city had had a turn. That did not go well, and he was soon disabled with an inflamed right hip and never heard from again. There were loud whispers about his poor conditioning, but it hardly matters at this point. At his advanced age, Person's just about at the end of the line.

RYAN RUPE   Bats: R   Throws: R   Born: 31-Mar-75   Age: 29

YEAR	TM	LG	AGE	G	GS	IP	H	BB	SO	HR	ERA	EQERA	EQH9	EQBB9	EQSO9	EQHR9	PERA	VORP	STF
2001	TBY	AL	26	28	26	143.3	161	48	123	30	6.59	5.63	9.7	2.8	7.2	1.7	5.45	-0.5	-4
2002	TBY	AL	27	15	15	90.0	83	25	67	11	5.60	4.41	8.0	2.3	6.5	1.0	3.84	11.6	16
2003	BOS	AL	28	4	1	10.0	13	1	7	4	6.30	7.20	10.8	0.9	6.3	2.7	6.77	-2.3	-42
2003	PAW	INT	28	20	18	102.0	93	19	77	11	3.26	4.52	9.3	2.1	5.5	1.5	4.99	11.2	-12
2004	BOS	AL	29	26	18	111.0	118	28	77	15	4.58	4.36	9.0	2.2	6.3	1.1	4.13	17.7	9

Breakout: 21%   Improve: 59%   Collapse: 16%

Let go by Tampa Bay in a cost-cutting move, Rupe would have been one of the Devil Rays' better pitchers. The Red Sox like him because he throws strikes, and he showed his usual solid command in Pawtucket. He deserves another chance, though he will not get it here. At this writing, he was close to signing a deal with the Nippon Ham Fighters.

SCOTT SAUERBECK　　　　　　　　　Bats: R　　Throws: L　　　　　　　Born: 09-Nov-71　　Age: 32

YEAR	TM	LG	AGE	G	GS	IP	H	BB	SO	HR	ERA	EQERA	EQH9	EQBB9	EQSO9	EQHR9	PERA	VORP	STF
2001	PIT	NL	29	70	0	62.7	61	40	79	4	5.60	4.87	9.1	5.3	9.4	0.4	4.57	4.9	19
2002	PIT	NL	30	78	0	62.7	50	27	70	4	2.30	3.13	7.6	3.4	8.8	0.6	3.53	16.5	25
2003	PIT	NL	31	53	0	40.0	30	25	32	5	4.05	4.15	6.7	5.1	6.2	1.2	4.19	5.2	-12
2003	BOS	AL	31	26	0	16.7	17	18	18	1	6.47	5.94	8.6	9.2	9.2	0.5	5.46	-2.9	-1
2004	*BOS*	*AL*	*32*	*60*	*0*	*62.3*	*59*	*32*	*52*	*5*	*4.08*	*3.88*	*8.0*	*4.4*	*7.5*	*0.7*	*4.05*	*13.0*	*3*

Breakout: 39%　　Improve: 60%　　Collapse: 8%

After an excellent 2002 and a fair first half of 2003, he came to Boston and stunk up the joint. In October he revealed that he had been suffering from a strained oblique muscle, but by that time the Boston mob was ready to dump him into the harbor like a sack of tea. Someone who has serious control problems has limited value as a situational pitcher, and his large platoon split makes it harder to leave him in for more than a few batters. He will be moving on, sans parting gifts.

JOSHUA STEVENS　　　　　　　　　Bats: R　　Throws: R　　　　　　　Born: 06-Jun-79　　Age: 25

YEAR	TM	LG	AGE	G	GS	IP	H	BB	SO	HR	ERA	EQERA	EQH9	EQBB9	EQSO9	EQHR9	PERA	VORP	STF
2001	GRB	SAL	22	19	2	36.7	29	9	42	3	2.94	4.88	10.6	3.4	6.0	2.0	6.54	2.5	-25
2002	NRW	EAS	23	24	0	40.0	50	8	33	2	3.83	5.84	12.4	2.2	5.6	0.7	5.55	-1.0	-1
2002	TAM	FLA	23	21	1	37.3	34	8	41	1	2.90	4.28	10.4	2.4	6.7	0.5	4.48	4.9	14
2003	PME	EAS	24	25	24	154.3	163	19	96	11	3.85	4.65	10.8	1.3	4.5	1.2	5.14	14.9	-1
2004	*BOS*	*AL*	*25*	*19*	*13*	*79.3*	*96*	*18*	*45*	*11*	*5.13*	*4.88*	*10.2*	*1.9*	*5.1*	*1.2*	*4.78*	*9.8*	*1*

Breakout: 12%　　Improve: 35%　　Collapse: 30%

Ladies and gentlemen, your Portland Sea Dogs Pitcher of the Year. The Red Sox signed Stevens as a minor league free agent based solely on his numbers. His value, like most of the pitchers brought into the organization last year, is in his avoidance of walks (19 in 146 innings). His stuff (stop us if you've heard this before) is not overpowering, but he may get a chance to move up to Pawtucket.

JEFF SUPPAN　　　　　　　　　Bats: R　　Throws: R　　　　　　　Born: 02-Jan-75　　Age: 29

YEAR	TM	LG	AGE	G	GS	IP	H	BB	SO	HR	ERA	EQERA	EQH9	EQBB9	EQSO9	EQHR9	PERA	VORP	STF
2001	KCR	AL	26	34	34	218.3	227	74	120	26	4.37	4.42	9.1	2.8	4.6	0.9	4.48	27.8	3
2002	KCR	AL	27	33	33	208.0	229	68	109	32	5.32	4.85	9.4	2.7	4.5	1.2	4.81	17.0	-4
2003	PIT	NL	28	21	21	141.0	147	31	78	11	3.57	3.78	9.3	1.8	4.4	0.7	3.96	31.9	14
2003	BOS	AL	28	11	10	63.0	70	20	32	12	5.57	4.91	9.1	2.6	4.5	1.4	4.94	0.9	-11
2004	*STL*	*NL*	*29*	*28*	*27*	*169.7*	*180*	*50*	*93*	*19*	*4.32*	*4.71*	*9.6*	*2.4*	*4.4*	*1.1*	*4.70*	*16.7*	*2*

Breakout: 13%　　Improve: 51%　　Collapse: 23%

When Suppan was acquired at the trading deadline, fans and media cheered the pick-up. By September, any Sox die-hard would have gladly reversed the deal. Grady Little was given a lot of credit in the local media for creating an atmosphere that allowed his team to excel, a judgment that ignores the long line of pitchers who showed up at his door step and struggled with their mechanics and confidence. The Sox declined Suppan's option, and he signed a two-year deal with the pitching-desperate Cardinals.

MIKE TIMLIN　　　　　　　　　Bats: R　　Throws: R　　　　　　　Born: 10-Mar-66　　Age: 38

YEAR	TM	LG	AGE	G	GS	IP	H	BB	SO	HR	ERA	EQERA	EQH9	EQBB9	EQSO9	EQHR9	PERA	VORP	STF
2001	STL	NL	35	67	0	72.7	78	19	47	6	4.09	4.72	10.2	2.2	5.0	0.7	4.50	6.7	-3
2002	PHI	NL	36	30	0	35.7	27	7	15	6	3.78	3.74	7.2	1.6	3.5	1.6	3.93	7.0	-25
2002	STL	NL	36	42	1	61.0	48	7	35	9	2.51	3.30	7.7	0.9	4.6	1.4	3.73	14.6	-10
2003	BOS	AL	37	72	0	83.7	77	9	65	11	3.55	3.17	7.5	0.9	6.8	1.1	3.27	18.4	12
2004	*BOS*	*AL*	*38*	*53*	*0*	*61.3*	*64*	*12*	*38*	*7*	*3.83*	*3.64*	*8.7*	*1.7*	*5.6*	*1.0*	*3.68*	*14.8*	*-1*

Breakout: 23%　　Improve: 48%　　Collapse: 25%

(continued next page)

Mike Timlin *(continued)*

Amidst the carnage that was the 2003 Red Sox bullpen, Timlin was a bright spot, hurling 83 good innings and pitching consistently well the whole season. And, of course, he was dominant in October. The Red Sox inked him to a new one-year deal with a 2005 option that will kick in if he stays healthy and effective. Timlin will play a big role in the '04 pen.

TIM WAKEFIELD   Bats: R   Throws: R   Born: 02-Aug-66   Age: 37

YEAR	TM	LG	AGE	G	GS	IP	H	BB	SO	HR	ERA	EQERA	EQH9	EQBB9	EQSO9	EQHR9	PERA	VORP	STF
2001	BOS	AL	34	45	17	168.7	156	73	148	13	3.89	3.69	7.9	3.6	7.3	0.6	3.75	35.2	22
2002	BOS	AL	35	45	15	163.3	121	51	134	15	2.81	2.86	6.8	2.6	7.2	0.7	3.08	47.9	25
2003	BOS	AL	36	35	33	202.3	193	71	169	23	4.09	3.79	7.9	3.0	7.3	0.9	3.87	28.2	23
2004	*BOS*	*AL*	*37*	*31*	*25*	*152.3*	*153*	*55*	*120*	*19*	*4.44*	*4.22*	*8.5*	*3.0*	*7.1*	*1.0*	*4.15*	*26.8*	*14*
Breakout: 12%			*Improve: 40%*				*Collapse: 25%*												

Two hundred innings of Wakefield is a bargain at just over $4 million per year. There are a lot of reasons to root for him, not least of which is that he is a joy to watch. In an era of relative sameness amongst the game's pitchers, Wakefield is the only good pitcher who regularly throws a knuckleball, one that is nearly unhittable when it's dancing. He is a better athlete than many of the knuckleballers of the 1970s, and pitches with a unique stiff, upright style. Hopefully there were thousands of teenagers watching him in the ALCS, who then headed outside to play catch. If he takes care of himself he could have several more productive years left.

SCOTT WILLIAMSON   Bats: R   Throws: R   Born: 17-Feb-76   Age: 28

YEAR	TM	LG	AGE	G	GS	IP	H	BB	SO	HR	ERA	EQERA	EQH9	EQBB9	EQSO9	EQHR9	PERA	VORP	STF
2002	CIN	NL	26	63	0	74.0	46	36	84	5	2.92	3.01	5.9	3.9	8.9	0.6	2.94	20.6	27
2003	CIN	NL	27	42	0	42.3	34	25	53	6	3.19	3.70	7.4	4.8	10.0	1.3	4.52	11.5	9
2003	BOS	AL	27	24	0	20.3	20	9	21	1	6.21	4.50	8.6	3.6	9.0	0.4	3.85	-1.5	25
2004	*BOS*	*AL*	*28*	*42*	*5*	*66.7*	*61*	*34*	*61*	*7*	*4.11*	*3.90*	*7.7*	*4.3*	*8.3*	*0.8*	*4.07*	*14.9*	*9*
Breakout: 28%			*Improve: 44%*				*Collapse: 32%*												

Struggled in a strict set-up role for two months before blossoming in the playoffs. Williamson could be one of the most valuable relief pitchers in baseball, but that value is squandered in a one-inning role. He had a difficult time personally, as his wife and newborn son were both hospitalized after a difficult birth. All are now doing well, and the Sox should reward Williamson with a bigger role in 2004. Instead, rumors have swirled that he'll be traded before Opening Day, though he remained a Red Sock at press time.

CHARLIE ZINK   Bats: R   Throws: R   Born: 26-Aug-79   Age: 24

YEAR	TM	LG	AGE	G	GS	IP	H	BB	SO	HR	ERA	EQERA	EQH9	EQBB9	EQSO9	EQHR9	PERA	VORP	STF
2002	AUG	SAL	22	26	0	48.3	42	16	48	1	1.68	4.85	10.1	4.0	5.3	0.4	4.70	3.6	2
2003	SAR	FLA	23	24	19	136.0	123	64	94	10	3.90	6.44	11.1	5.7	4.4	2.2	7.65	-10.9	-45
2003	PME	EAS	23	6	6	39.3	21	14	18	1	3.44	2.97	5.0	4.0	3.2	0.5	2.51	10.6	13
2004	*BOS*	*AL*	*24*	*19*	*11*	*55.7*	*73*	*47*	*31*	*11*	*8.20*	*7.80*	*11.0*	*7.2*	*5.1*	*1.8*	*7.69*	*-4.3*	*-30*
Breakout: 24%			*Improve: 55%*				*Collapse: 21%*												

As the only knuckleballer in the high minors, Zink has as good a chance at a long career as anyone in the minor leagues. He began experimenting with the knuckleball with Augusta in 2002 before the organization converted him completely last spring. A solid four months in Sarasota got him promoted to Portland, where he twice flirted with no-hitters. He is probably slated to start back with Portland, but by September he might end up a rung or two higher.

Because of his long fingers, Zink actually throws the pitch with one fingertip (his middle one) rather than the usual two, keeping his index finger fully knuckled. He is a true student of the pitch, constantly reviewing the tapes of Wakefield that the Red Sox provide. He still uses his fastball when he gets behind in the count, but he has a lot of confidence in his knuckler, which causes some pretty ghastly swings. He struggled at first in the dead air of the Arizona Fall League, but later came on strong. One to watch.

Chicago White Sox

On January 31, 2003, the White Sox announced that they had reached an agreement to change the name of Comiskey Park to U.S. Cellular Field. The name Comiskey had been associated with the ballpark at 35th and Shields nearly since the opening of the original facility; in one well-choreographed press conference in the dingiest days of the Chicago winter, the Sox had undone 90 years' worth of tradition.

We don't begrudge a team for doing what it can to increase its revenue. On the contrary, we've frequently argued that if baseball clubs are run like any other profit-maximizing business, the product on the field will ultimately be improved. And the Sox had ample reason to execute the name change—the deal with U.S. Cellular will pay them $68 million over the next 20 seasons. It's easy to understand why a team might want to accept a naming rights deal.

What's more difficult to fathom is why it *wouldn't.* Yet the four major league clubs with the strongest recurring revenue bases—the Yankees, Dodgers, Red Sox, and Cubs—have staunchly resisted any suggestion of a corporate appendage to their beloved ballparks, even though the deals they'd secure would surely be record breaking. *Sprint PCS Grounds at Chavez Ravine:* Where the scoreboard is as clear as your phone calls!

The reason, of course, is that tradition is worth something; if Fenway Park and Wrigley Field were unveiled as *CITGO Station* and *Tribune Field,* it would cause irreparable damage to the brand equity of the Red Sox and Cubs, ultimately harming their bottom lines.

The White Sox? The franchise doesn't have $68 million worth of cachet. And that's part of the problem.

This season will be the Sox's 14th as tenants of U.S. Cellular Field, and the team is in the midst of a full-fledged pimples-and-wet dreams identity crisis. The Sox have behaved like an erratic middle child, stuck between the big-brother Cubs 70 city blocks above them, and the runts that make up the A.L. Central beneath them. Since Ken Williams took over as general manager in October 2000, the team has reversed its direction as often as a freshman changes his major:

- **Winter 2000–2001.** Coming off a division title, the Sox trade for the big belly and big contract of David Wells, while adding other veteran parts like Royce Clayton, and Sandy Alomar. The White

WHITE SOX PROSPECTUS

2003 record: 86–76; Second place, AL Central

Pythagenport record: 88–74

Runs scored per game: 4.9 (6th in AL)

Runs allowed per game: 4.4 (3rd in AL)

Team EqA: .261 (6th in AL)

2003 Batters Age: 30.2 (3rd oldest in AL)

2003 Pitchers Age: 28.4 (5th youngest in AL)

Ballpark: U.S. Cellular Field; Slight hitter's park; Park Factor of 1.018

2003: Aggressive in-season roster revisions weren't enough to prevent a second straight second-place finish.

2004: In a division without an elite team, the White Sox are still a verifiable threat.

Flag Era, a.k.a. The Kids Can Play, at last appears to be over. *Zig.*

- **July 2002.** Hopelessly behind the juggernaut Twins, the Sox trade Ray Durham, Kenny Lofton, Alomar, and Bob Howry in a series of deadline deals, bringing in little in return save for a slew of minor league relief arms. *Zag.*

- **January 2003.** After spending much of the winter sitting on his hands, Ken Williams seizes his opportunity to grab Bartolo Colon at a discount price. *Zig.*

- **July 2003.** With the Sox locked in a horse race with the Twins and Royals, Williams grabs Robby Alomar, Carl Everett, Scott Sullivan, and Scott Schoeneweis on the trade market, exchanging prospects and cash in the deals. *Double Zig.*

Taken on their own merits, did these courses of action make sense? Sure they did, and for the most part, Williams executed them satisfactorily. Wells's conditioning had always worried his employers, but 2001 was the only season in the past nine in which he failed to make at least 29 starts; he was a defensible acquisition for a team looking have a big year. The Sox weren't going to catch the Twins in 2002. Colon came too cheaply to turn down. Adding a couple of bats for last year's stretch run was a reasonable gambit against a pair of financially strapped opponents.

What's been lacking, however, is a grander sense of purpose and design. Do the Sox want to play with the big boys, treating their pals in the AL Central as mere potholes on the road to the post-season? Or, in spite of their big-city pedigree, do they see themselves as a middle-market franchise that needs to construct many of their building blocks from within?

That brings us to the present. The Sox sat idle this winter, outbid by the Angels for Bartolo Colon, declining to offer contracts to Alomar, Everett, and Sullivan, watching as Tony Graffanino and Tom Gordon wound up in other uniforms. The only significant player the Sox have added is Jose Uribe, who will compete with Willie Harris for the second base job. Tellingly, the most noise that the team made was as the potential third wheel in the Big Trade that Wasn't which would have brought them Nomar.

Zag.

Particularly bizarre was the course of action involving Colon. Published reports had the Sox willing to offer $36 million over three years to the big right-hander. When Colon found another team that would overpay him more, shouldn't the Sox have sought to replace his contribution by signing Sidney Ponson, trading for Javy Vazquez, or patching up center field and second base? Thirty-six million is a lot of chips to bring to the table

Instead, the Sox folded their hand, deciding that what they needed wasn't a center fielder or a right-handed starter, but a personality transplant. As Williams told the *Chicago Sun Times* on January 6:

> You're always, as a GM, looking to make a team as good as it can be on paper heading into the season—the key phrase being "on paper".... As good as we have been on paper, we haven't brought home the prize.... People want to look at this team as being stripped down ... and we certainly, based on how we ended the season last year, appear on paper not to be as strong. But the one thing you have to be mindful of in the sports arena is how much desire, heart, and determination your guys have. From that standpoint, I feel good about what we are taking down to spring training.

It's hard to tell whether the man was bluffing. Certainly, Williams has jiggered the roster many times over. And just as certainly, the Sox's string of bridesmaid finishes has been frustrating. A healthier elbow here, a more favorable schedule there, and the outcome might have been much different.

But is that any reason to quit trying? Why, with the economy improving and home attendance having increased by 15% last year, does the team suddenly feel the need to trim payroll? And what prohibits the Sox from improving their roster at the same time that they address their perceived lack of leadership?

Chicago has made one significant addition, of course, replacing Jerry Manuel with Ozzie Guillen. As a player, Guillen didn't perform very well "on paper"—his lifetime Equivalent Average of .228 is among the worst of any player of comparable career length.

But golly if Ozzie wasn't full of desire, heart, and determination. In those departments, Guillen is a Hall of Famer, and the veritable opposite of Manuel, a solemn, aloof man who finished his tenure with the White Sox with a 500–471 record over six seasons. Chicagoans can handle an overbearing personality like Mike Ditka or Doug Collins, a cuddly one like Dusty Baker, even a vaguely rebellious geek like Phil Jackson. But a man who sits passively in the face of criticism and adversity, quoting bible verses and chomping sunflower seeds in the dugout? Well, that's another story. Rightly or wrongly, Manuel's introversion was read as indifference.

Baseball, more manifestly than other sports, is a game infused with randomness; it is the only activity, so the cliché goes, in which a man who succeeds at his task three times out of 10 is considered wildly successful. Many factors that affect the fate of a ballclub—injuries, career years, the whimsy of a particular free agent—lie outside of its immediate sphere of control.

This is the source of Ken Williams's frustration: He had a good plan, he executed it, and it didn't work. From Williams's perspective, the manager's job isn't about knowing whom to platoon with whom, or when to lay down the suicide squeeze. Rather, the manager is the guy who channels the animal spirits to make order out of the void. Manuel's tragic flaw wasn't so much the failure to exercise leadership as the failure to *appear* to exercise leadership.

What can we expect from his successor? Guillen is eager, gregarious, charming. He has already made a public spectacle of demanding hustle and clubhouse harmony— an implicit dig at Frank Thomas, with whom he feuded when the two were teammates.

It is natural to assume that, as a field general, Guillen will prefer the same style of play that he practiced. And Ozzie Guillen, though a smart, eloquent man, was one wicked stupid baseball player, running reckless on the basepaths, swinging at any pitch within a foot of the plate. That approach, of course, would be disastrous for the Pale Hose, whose aging collection of sluggers is far more Southside Hitman than Go-Go Sock.

But is such a presumption fair? Do dumb ballplayers necessarily make for dumb managers? Years ago, Bill James introduced something called Baseball IQ, a metric that, in a rare bout of political correctness, he later renamed "Percentage Player Index." The statistic takes into account four components—fielding percentage relative to league and position norms, stolen-base percentage, strikeout-to-walk ratio, and walk frequency—that are generally associated with smart baseball.

We took all players who accumulated at least 2,000 plate appearances since 1951 (prior to that season, the National League had been erratic about keeping track of times caught stealing, compromising one of the components of our metric) and ranked them in percentiles according to the four categories. By adding the four percentile scores and dividing by two, we come up with a score on the same scale as the original intelligence quotient, in which 100 is average, and scores above 140 indicate "genius." Table 1, for example, is Guillen's tally.

No Stephen J. Hawking on the baseball diamond, he.

Thirty-nine players in our sample eventually went on to manage at least 500 games in the big leagues. The highest and lowest Baseball IQs among them are provided in table 2.

(Hal McRae originally held the last spot on the "dumbest" list, but only because the system punished him significantly for playing DH; both McRae's bad knees and his managerial tenure have caused him plenty of grief, so we'll give the man a break).

Which group would you rather select your manager from? Both contain their share of successes and failures (see table 3).

The "smart" managers won six pennants between them, the "dumb" ones 10. The "dumb" group managed their teams to a higher winning percentage, but both exceeded their Pythagorean W–L percentages. The conclusion? Players of all types have gone on to be great managers, as well as terrible ones.

Results are one thing, of course; and tactics are another; we can also compare the two groups according to statistics that might reveal something about their preferred strategies. To do this correctly, we need to evaluate our groups against the average results for the leagues in which they were managing (see table 4).

For the most part, the results don't reveal much of anything. Both groups of managers had their players attempt steals at a rate slightly higher than the league norm. Both were about average in their propensity to lay down the sacrifice bunt.

The one significant exception is in the area of plate discipline. While the teams managed by the "dumb" players drew around 14 walks fewer per season than their league norms, the teams managed by the "smart" players exceeded the league average walk rate by a substantial margin, while also striking out more frequently. While we can't be certain that the managers are at the root of them, the differences are statistically significant. There may be something to the notion that a manager who exercised good plate discipline can encourage his players to do the same.

TABLE 1. BASEBALL IQ CALCULATION FOR OZZIE GUILLEN

Metric	Result	Percentile
Fielding Percentage	.974	75
Stolen Base %	61.0%	53
K/BB Ratio	.468	22
Walk Rate	3.4%	1
Baseball IQ = (7553221) / 2 =		75

TABLE 2. MANAGERS WITH HIGHEST AND LOWEST BASEBALL IQ SCORES

"Smart"

Dick Howser	171
Frank Robinson	157
Ted Williams	153
Pete Rose	142
Dusty Baker	142
Mike Scioscia	135
Larry Bowa	135
Gil Hodges	130
Red Schoendienst	129
Art Howe	129

"Dumb"

Cito Gaston	42
Russ Nixon	44
Buck Rodgers	57
Don Zimmer	58
Billy Gardner	62
Billy Martin	64
Lou Piniella	65
Bob Lillis	68
Dick Williams	77
Felipe Alou	83

TABLE 3. COMPARISON OF MANAGER TYPES: RECORDS

	Seasons	Pennants	Wins / 162 G	Pythagorean	Wins
"Smart"	79	6		81.5	80.9
"Dumb"	99	10		83.5	83.0

TABLE 4. COMPARISON OF MANAGER TYPES: TACTICS

Totals per 162 G	RS	RA	HR	BB	K	SB	CS	SB%	SH
Smart	698	699	139	548	967	107	50	68%	64
League Average	681	681	137	514	921	98	49	67%	63
Dumb	717	699	144	523	912	118	56	68%	61
League Average	710	710	138	537	904	114	57	67%	63

Nevertheless, it is clear that one cannot presume the sort of team a manager will craft based on his profile as a player, and Guillen deserves the benefit of the doubt. Williams, on the other hand, has established a track record, and we can afford to make some more substantive judgments on his behalf. One of our complaints is that the White Sox could stand to spend more to improve their roster; since most general managers have their payrolls imposed upon them by ownership, it is not fair to blame Williams for that. Williams has also, contrary to the popular image, become a capable evaluator of talent; while he scores poorly on deals like Keith Foulke-for-Billy Koch, a more objective review of the team's transaction logs reveals steady improvement, and as many successes as failures.

Where Williams comes up wanting, however, is in the vision category. The solution to the periodic crises of confidence that a baseball franchise endures isn't some old-fangled mysticism about desire and hustle. Nor is it hiring a new manager, any more so than the way to resolve an identity crisis is by getting a new haircut. Rather, the solution involves laying out an organizational architecture that provides context for the team's successes and failures. As impolitic as it might have been of Billy Beane to say that his "s*** doesn't work in the playoffs," his thought process reflects an understanding of his methods and goals, and the vulnerabilities thereof. Williams has done a good job of reacting to the situations that the Sox find themselves in, but the GM position requires being proactive too.

The White Sox will be competitive this year, at least in a nominal sense, because of the paltry quality of competition in their division. A preliminary analysis by our PECOTA system projects the Sox, Twins and Royals all to finish within a game or two of the .500 mark given their rosters as of mid-January press time, with the Indians behind them mired around 70 wins. It is likely that the Sox will find themselves in their customary position at the trade deadline, stuck between contender and pretender by the thinnest of margins.

Magglio Ordonez's three-year deal will expire at the end of the season, relieving the Sox of their most expensive contract but also their best player. Esteban Loaiza, their best pitcher, will be a free agent too, and surely will command more money this time around. It is not clear that the Sox have the resources to replace their contributions from within: The farm system, once considered strong, has thinned out behind Jeremy Reed and Kris Honel, triggering a series of shakeups in the team's scouting and development staff.

It will be a tough position for Ken Williams to be in, but also a moment of opportunity to dictate the franchise's direction for the balance of the decade, one that will require some serious thought about the team's longer-term aspirations and identity. Williams has demonstrated solid growth thus far, and we wish him the best in navigating the storm.

HITTERS

SANDY ALOMAR C Bats: R Throws: R Born: 18-Jun-66 Age: 38

YEAR	TM	LG	AGE	AB	H	2B	3B	HR	BB	SO	SB	CS	AVG	OBP	SLG	MLVR	EQBA	EQOBP	EQSLG	EQMLVR	VORP	DEFENSE	
2001	CWS	AL	35	220	54	8	1	4	12	17	1	2	.245	.288	.345	-.209	.259	.305	.368	-.175	-0.1	62-C	0
2002	CWS	AL	36	167	48	10	1	7	5	14	0	0	.287	.309	.485	.063	.304	.327	.518	.123	12.3	47-C	-3
2002	COL	NL	36	116	31	4	0	0	4	19	0	0	.267	.292	.302	-.240	.259	.277	.293	-.338	-4.8	32-C	-2
2003	CWS	AL	37	194	52	12	0	5	4	17	0	0	.268	.281	.407	-.131	.284	.302	.428	-.074	1.1	55-C	-1
2004	CWS	AL	38	135	32	6	0	2	6	15	0	0	.237	.270	.325	-.269	.241	.277	.327	-.284	-4.3	38-C	-4

Breakout: 5% Improve: 26% Collapse: 50%

How some guys get reputations as malingerers while Sandy Alomar builds a career out of 70-game seasons boggles the mind. Nevertheless, Alomar was re-signed by the White Sox, who are keen on his veteran presence and success in working with Mark Buehrle. He'll be available for 105 games, play in 60 of those, and post a sub-.300 OBP. Alomar's career illustrates the problems tall catchers can have, a developmental point we would do well to keep in mind as we drool over Joe Mauer.

ROBERTO ALOMAR   2B   Bats: B   Throws: R   Born: 05-Feb-68   Age: 36

YEAR	TM	LG	AGE	AB	H	2B	3B	HR	BB	SO	SB	CS	AVG	OBP	SLG	MLVR	EQBA	EQOBP	EQSLG	EQMLVR	VORP	DEFENSE	
2001	CLE	AL	33	575	193	34	12	20	80	71	30	6	.336	.415	.541	.352	.359	.442	.584	.464	99.1	148-2B	3
2002	NYM	NL	34	590	157	24	4	11	57	83	16	4	.266	.331	.376	-.016	.280	.341	.400	-.046	20.3	138-2B	-3
2003	NYM	NL	35	263	69	17	1	2	29	40	6	0	.262	.336	.357	-.041	.272	.347	.377	-.073	7.7	65-2B	-1
2003	CWS	AL	35	253	64	11	1	3	30	37	6	2	.253	.330	.340	-.146	.269	.353	.368	-.076	0.4	62-2B	-2
2004	ARI	NL	36	423	121	24	4	8	49	59	11	3	.285	.360	.418	.029	.275	.348	.406	-.027	21.8	115-2B	-5

Breakout: 22%   Improve: 47%   Collapse: 21%

It's never much fun to eulogize a guy before he's hung up his spikes, especially when he's a no-brainer Hall of Famer, but Alomar's days as a championship-caliber player are past him. His power is gone, and when a guy who has spent the better part of 15 years turning the pivot loses his power, it isn't likely to come back. Alomar still tries his darndest to get on base: He averaged more than 4.1 pitches per plate appearance last season, but his walk rate has dropped to well off his career highs, as pitchers have less incentive to throw to him carefully. He hit like Hal Lanier from the right side last year—though his hip problems might have had something to do with that—and his defense, always overrated, is now outright sub-par. There are a lot of negatives here, and a team thinking about signing him needs to consider an incentive-heavy contract, as well as the quality of its training staff. Predictably, he'll be a Diamondback.

GABE ALVAREZ   1B   Bats: R   Throws: R   Born: 06-Mar-74   Age: 30

YEAR	TM	LG	AGE	AB	H	2B	3B	HR	BB	SO	SB	CS	AVG	OBP	SLG	MLVR	EQBA	EQOBP	EQSLG	EQMLVR	VORP	DEFENSE			
2001	CHT	SOU	27	336	85	23	1	16	61	82	4	4	.253	.377	.470	.162	.210	.313	.391	-.162	2.2	67-3B	-23	15-1B	-2
2002	HUN	SOU	28	94	19	3	0	1	18	24	0	0	.202	.336	.266	-.158	.184	.283	.255	-.416	-7.6	25-3B	-7		
2003	BIR	SOU	29	410	127	34	0	11	58	87	2	5	.310	.401	.473	.290	.266	.343	.419	-.027	7.8	80-1B	-6	10-3B	-1
2004	CWS	AL	30	128	29	6	0	5	14	31	0	0	.231	.316	.393	-.103	.235	.324	.396	-.111	1.5	39-1B	-1		

Breakout 37%   Improve 51%   Collapse 33%

Not since Michael Jordan has such a well-traveled 30-year-old found his way to Hoover Metropolitan Stadium. Alvarez was signed by the White Sox after spending 2002 languishing in Huntsville and Mexico, and rode a .401 OBP to a spot on the Southern League's All-Star team. He's a good working example of freely available talent, and would beat that PECOTA with regular playing time. Alvarez once single-handedly crippled a Scoresheet Baseball league by being traded for Eric Chavez after a hot couple of weeks in Detroit.

BRIAN ANDERSON   CF   Bats: R   Throws: R   Born: 11-Mar-82   Age: 22

YEAR	TM	LG	AGE	AB	H	2B	3B	HR	BB	SO	SB	CS	AVG	OBP	SLG	MLVR	EQBA	EQOBP	EQSLG	EQMLVR	VORP	DEFENSE	
2003	GRF	PIO	21	49	19	2	1	2	9	10	3	1	.388	.492	.592	.613	.224	.313	.347	-.212	-1.9	12-CF	0
2004	CWS	AL	22	213	44	6	0	7	24	54	4	2	.206	.283	.341	-.241	.210	.290	.344	-.255	-8.2	59-CF	-4

Breakout: 19%   Improve: 40%   Collapse: 28%

The team's 2003 first-round pick, Anderson looked like a glorified tools player while at the University of Arizona, so it was encouraging to see that he exercised fine plate discipline, even in a short Pioneer League debut. His season was ended early by wrist surgery—never a good sign for a developing hitter—but Anderson is expected to be 100% in the spring. He has several different paths that he can take toward becoming a good big leaguer, potentially in the Andy Van Slyke mold.

JOE BORCHARD   CF   Bats: B   Throws: R   Born: 25-Nov-78   Age: 25

YEAR	TM	LG	AGE	AB	H	2B	3B	HR	BB	SO	SB	CS	AVG	OBP	SLG	MLVR	EQBA	EQOBP	EQSLG	EQMLVR	VORP	DEFENSE	
2001	BIR	SOU	22	515	152	27	1	27	67	158	5	4	.295	.384	.509	.279	.253	.327	.445	-.031	18.8	133-CF	-5
2002	CHR	INT	23	438	119	35	2	20	49	139	2	4	.272	.349	.498	.163	.246	.322	.460	-.025	16.9	108-CF	-2
2002	CWS	AL	23	36	8	0	0	2	1	14	0	0	.222	.243	.389	-.233	.250	.270	.417	-.177	-0.5		
2003	CHR	INT	24	435	110	20	2	13	27	103	2	4	.253	.307	.398	-.032	.240	.295	.386	-.182	-4.6	108-CF	-1
2003	CWS	AL	24	49	9	1	0	1	5	18	0	1	.184	.246	.265	-.441	.204	.278	.286	-.375	-4.6	13-CF	0
2004	CWS	AL	25	285	71	14	1	14	25	72	2	1	.251	.318	.457	-.006	.255	.326	.459	-.011	11.1	77-CF	-1

Breakout: 42%   Improve: 65%   Collapse: 18%

(continued next page)

Joe Borchard *(continued)*

One of the traps that we fall into in prospect evaluation is to focus almost exclusively on a minor leaguer's most recent campaign. Borchard had as difficult a year as he could in 2003, persistently tinkering with his swing and his hitting approach as his plate discipline and confidence collapsed; an ill-advised call-up to Chicago in May did not help matters. Still, Borchard posted EqSLG numbers of .445 and .460 at ages 22 and 23, and is a good enough center fielder to handle the position in the bigs—those skills are his to keep, even if he's hit a bankrupt spot.

One of the problems Borchard has is that he's a very tall guy with a very upright batting stance, and that makes for a very large strike zone. For that reason, his taking a lot of pitches can have its downside: Pitchers have a lot of room to play with if he's fallen behind in the count. In the near term, it might be wise to focus on getting him comfortable at the plate again, letting him swing at the first meaty pitch that he sees. Many of Borchard's PECOTA comparables were late bloomers in the Jay Buhner mold; once Borchard starts mashing those meatballs again, his walks will come, as Buhner's did.

JAMIE BURKE			C						Bats: R			Throws: R					Born: 24-Sep-71			Age: 32	
YEAR	TM	LG	AGE	AB	H	2B	3B	HR	BB	SO	SB	CS	AVG	OBP	SLG	MLVR	EQBA	EQOBP	EQSLG	EQMLVR	VORP	DEFENSE
2001	SLC	PCL	29	215	47	10	3	0	19	28	1	0	.219	.292	.293	-.362	.183	.254	.249	-.485	-19.6	36-C -2 13-3B 1
2002	SLC	PCL	30	316	96	12	4	8	20	37	1	3	.304	.350	.443	.048	.263	.308	.385	-.142	2.8	31-C -5 31-3B -1
2003	CHR	INT	31	323	104	13	0	6	20	39	1	1	.322	.363	.418	.139	.306	.353	.404	.003	17.3	72-C 2
2004	*CWS*	*AL*	*32*	*131*	*32*	*5*	*1*	*3*	*10*	*19*	*1*	*0*	*.244*	*.303*	*.348*	*-.174*	*.248*	*.311*	*.351*	*-.185*	*-0.8*	*38-C -5*
Breakout: 16%			*Improve: 36%*			*Collapse: 39%*																

Burke had some glossy numbers at Charlotte, but .322 batting averages by 31-year-old catchers in their fifth Triple-A season have roughly as much chance of holding up well as Greta Van Susteren's facelift. Still, Burke might well be every bit as effective as Sandy Alomar, and the team could use the $500,000 savings toward something useful, like hiring one of the Queer Eye guys to lend a hand to William Ligue Jr.

JOE CREDE			3B						Bats: R			Throws: R					Born: 26-Apr-78			Age: 26	
YEAR	TM	LG	AGE	AB	H	2B	3B	HR	BB	SO	SB	CS	AVG	OBP	SLG	MLVR	EQBA	EQOBP	EQSLG	EQMLVR	VORP	DEFENSE
2001	CHR	INT	23	463	128	34	1	17	46	88	2	1	.276	.349	.464	.121	.256	.326	.437	-.041	19.6	123-3B 7
2001	CWS	AL	23	50	11	1	1	0	3	11	1	0	.220	.273	.280	-.341	.240	.293	.300	-.307	-1.6	12-3B -1
2002	CHR	INT	24	359	112	21	0	24	26	48	0	1	.312	.359	.571	.315	.285	.337	.533	.141	35.0	92-3B 5
2002	CWS	AL	24	200	57	10	0	12	8	40	0	2	.285	.311	.515	.106	.303	.333	.547	.174	17.8	48-3B 0
2003	CWS	AL	25	536	140	31	2	19	32	75	1	1	.261	.308	.433	-.054	.274	.324	.461	.004	14.3	150-3B 5
2004	*CWS*	*AL*	*26*	*461*	*123*	*25*	*1*	*22*	*34*	*72*	*2*	*1*	*.266*	*.320*	*.467*	*.024*	*.271*	*.328*	*.470*	*.020*	*26.5*	*119-3B 2*
Breakout: 25%			*Improve: 52%*			*Collapse: 25%*																

Up until the 15th of July, Crede looked like the biggest disappointment since *The Phantom Menace,* the long years of waiting having produced a B-grade hitter who wasn't the second coming of Greg Norton, let alone Bill Melton. Fortunately, Crede turned things around with a .308/.349/.543 line in the second half, showing renewed confidence and aggression at the plate after he was reunited with Greg Walker, his long-time hitting instructor in the minors. Crede's defense at third base is rock-solid, with excellent range and a natural instinct for the position. He's not going to be a superstar, but is capable of putting together a couple of seasons in line with his post-break averages, and a good bet to beat his PECOTA.

BRIAN DAUBACH			1B/DH						Bats: L			Throws: R					Born: 11-Feb-72			Age: 32	
YEAR	TM	LG	AGE	AB	H	2B	3B	HR	BB	SO	SB	CS	AVG	OBP	SLG	MLVR	EQBA	EQOBP	EQSLG	EQMLVR	VORP	DEFENSE
2001	BOS	AL	29	407	107	28	3	22	53	108	1	0	.263	.350	.509	.132	.279	.370	.542	.201	31.3	101-1B 4
2002	BOS	AL	30	444	118	24	2	20	51	126	2	1	.266	.348	.464	.086	.286	.367	.504	.151	27.3	51-1B -1 27-LF 0
2003	CWS	AL	31	183	42	11	0	6	34	54	1	0	.230	.352	.388	-.058	.245	.365	.424	.004	1.4	29-1B 0
2004	*BOS*	*AL*	*32*	*149*	*37*	*8*	*1*	*7*	*22*	*40*	*1*	*0*	*.249*	*.350*	*.456*	*.045*	*.245*	*.349*	*.459*	*.019*	*8.1*	*45-1B -3*
Breakout: 21%			*Improve: 44%*			*Collapse: 40%*																

Not a bad acquisition by Kenny Williams, but Daubach had a rough season in Chicago, the sort of year that might get him stuck with minor league contracts for the balance of his career. The trouble with Daubach is that gets out of sync when used sporadically—he's just 5-for-38 in pinch-hitting appearances since 2001—but isn't quite good enough to pencil into the lineup every day. The Red Sox have signed him to a minor league deal, where he'll provide a nice OBP off the bench, but not much else.

CARL EVERETT   OF   Bats: B   Throws: R   Born: 03-Jun-71   Age: 33

YEAR	TM	LG	AGE	AB	H	2B	3B	HR	BB	SO	SB	CS	AVG	OBP	SLG	MLVR	EQBA	EQOBP	EQSLG	EQMLVR	VORP	DEFENSE			
2001	BOS	AL	30	409	105	24	4	14	27	104	9	2	.257	.323	.438	-.014	.273	.335	.471	.037	19.2	80-CF	-3		
2002	TEX	AL	31	374	100	16	0	16	33	77	2	3	.267	.333	.439	.015	.283	.350	.469	.070	13.0	30-RF	-2	26-CF	-1
2003	TEX	AL	32	270	74	13	3	18	31	48	4	1	.274	.356	.544	.162	.286	.372	.572	.253	16.2	31-LF	-2	28-RF	0
2003	CWS	AL	32	256	77	14	0	10	22	36	4	3	.301	.377	.473	.151	.323	.396	.510	.246	18.4	56-CF	-3		
2004	MON	NL	33	405	119	23	2	19	41	75	4	3	.293	.368	.503	.162	.276	.349	.465	.053	15.2	109-CF	-9		

Breakout: 17%   Improve: 47%   Collapse: 22%

It isn't often that the Expos get to have a big press conference, but there they were in December, signing free agent Everett to a two-year deal. While no one can replace Vladimir Guerrero, Everett does provide real power and a good OBP. He hasn't done anything from the right side of the plate in years, so platooning him—or encouraging him to drop switch-hitting—would have merit. He also needs to be kept far away from center field, as his poor range and arm were notably costly to the Sox down the stretch. While Everett carries a reputation and some entertaining b-roll with him to Canada, it's been some time since he made a headline for anything other than his strong play. "Jurassic Carl" jokes—and worse ones—should be consigned to the dustbin.

ROSS GLOAD   1B/DH   Bats: L   Throws: L   Born: 05-Apr-76   Age: 28

YEAR	TM	LG	AGE	AB	H	2B	3B	HR	BB	SO	SB	CS	AVG	OBP	SLG	MLVR	EQBA	EQOBP	EQSLG	EQMLVR	VORP	DEFENSE			
2001	IOW	PCL	25	475	141	32	10	15	35	88	9	7	.297	.344	.501	.126	.264	.314	.445b	-.045	5.6	46-1B	4	44-RF	1
2002	CSP	PCL	26	442	139	28	6	16	18	59	9	4	.314	.338	.514	.126	.270	.299	.446	-.065	2.2	86-1B	5		
2003	CHR	INT	27	508	160	40	6	18	29	60	6	3	.315	.349	.524	.258	.294	.337	.501	.104	28.7	102-1B	-6	13-LF	0
2004	CWS	AL	28	227	60	13	2	8	15	36	2	2	.265	.312	.450	-.012	.270	.320	.453	-.017	7.6	61-1B	-1		

Breakout: 16%   Improve: 34%   Collapse: 34%

Gload is your classic Pedro Cerrano slugger, swinging from his heels and hitting fastballs a long way, but struggling with tricky breaking pitches. With Brian Daubach departed, he'd suffice as a left-handed bat off the bench for a couple of years, provided it's at the league minimum.

TONY GRAFFANINO   IF   Bats: R   Throws: R   Born: 06-Jun-72   Age: 32

YEAR	TM	LG	AGE	AB	H	2B	3B	HR	BB	SO	SB	CS	AVG	OBP	SLG	MLVR	EQBA	EQOBP	EQSLG	EQMLVR	VORP	DEFENSE			
2001	CWS	AL	29	145	44	9	0	2	16	29	4	1	.303	.370	.407	.063	.329	.398	.438	.153	13.1	22-3B	-3	16-2B	2
2002	CWS	AL	30	229	60	12	4	6	22	38	2	1	.262	.329	.428	-.001	.278	.348	.457	.045	13.6	31-3B	1	19-2B	0
2003	CWS	AL	31	250	65	15	3	7	24	37	8	0	.260	.331	.428	-.021	.272	.346	.456	.035	11.4	27-SS	1	27-2B	0
2004	KCR	AL	32	218	58	12	2	4	20	34	4	2	.266	.330	.398	-.049	.254	.322	.386	-.115	8.3	61-2B	-3		

Breakout: 8%   Improve: 21%   Collapse: 55%

The line between starters and reserves can be pretty thin, and one wonders whether Graffanino's versatility has actually worked to his disadvantage. Graffanino combines a league-average bat with steady defense at all three infield positions, and a healthy dose of scrappiness. A good signing by the Royals; he and Desi Relaford should provide one of the more productive second-base positions in the league.

WILLIE HARRIS   2B/CF   Bats: L   Throws: R   Born: 22-Jun-78   Age: 26

YEAR	TM	LG	AGE	AB	H	2B	3B	HR	BB	SO	SB	CS	AVG	OBP	SLG	MLVR	EQBA	EQOBP	EQSLG	EQMLVR	VORP	DEFENSE			
2001	BOW	EAS	23	525	160	27	4	9	46	71	54	16	.305	.364	.423	.144	.269	.325	.376	-.119	9.2	90-2B	-5	40-CF	0
2002	CHR	INT	24	360	102	16	5	5	33	61	32	14	.283	.345	.397	.035	.259	.321	.372	-.139	4.0	82-2B	0		
2002	CWS	AL	24	163	38	4	0	2	9	21	8	0	.233	.270	.294	-.304	.250	.289	.317	-.285	-4.6	37-2B	0		
2003	CHR	INT	25	100	38	6	1	6	17	20	9	3	.380	.470	.640	.649	.340	.429	.592	.432	20.3	17-2B	2		
2003	CWS	AL	25	137	28	3	1	0	10	28	12	2	.204	.259	.241	-.440	.219	.277	.263	-.402	-9.0	34-CF	-1		
2004	CWS	AL	26	225	57	10	2	5	19	38	12	4	.253	.313	.380	-.111	.257	.321	.383	-.119	5.2	62-CF	0		

Breakout: 20%   Improve: 42%   Collapse: 37%

It's hard to tell whether Harris is one of those players whose skills don't translate from Triple-A to the bigs, or if he needs regular playing time to remain effective. Either way, his career .213/.255/.262 line at the major league level is abominable. In a perfect world, the Sox would give him a block of 250 plate appearances to find out, and with no incumbent, next year will be his best chance. Harris doesn't need to be Tony Phillips to be a useful player, but he can't be Donnie Sadler, either.

PAUL KONERKO   **1B**   **Bats: R**   **Throws: R**   Born: 05-Mar-76   Age: 28

YEAR	TM	LG	AGE	AB	H	2B	3B	HR	BB	SO	SB	CS	AVG	OBP	SLG	MLVR	EQBA	EQOBP	EQSLG	EQMLVR	VORP	DEFENSE
2001	CWS	AL	25	582	164	35	0	32	54	89	1	0	.282	.349	.507	.144	.297	.366	.539	.210	45.5	141-1B -2
2002	CWS	AL	26	570	173	30	0	27	44	72	0	0	.304	.359	.498	.177	.322	.380	.531	.249	49.1	135-1B -9
2003	CWS	AL	27	444	104	19	0	18	43	50	0	0	.234	.305	.399	-.128	.248	.323	.426	-.068	-6.3	108-1B 7
2004	CWS	AL	28	416	113	22	0	19	38	56	0	0	.271	.337	.465	.054	.276	.346	.468	.052	15.7	110-1B 0

Breakout: 25%   Improve: 53%   Collapse: 18%

It's not often that we say this about a player, but Konerko's struggles in the first half might well have resulted from his taking too many pitches. He's always been a good hitter early in the count, but he'd defaulted into an overly tentative approach at the plate, improving his walk rate slightly but harming the rest of his game substantially, as he often found himself stuck making weak contact on 1–2 pitches that his slightly long swing wasn't optimally designed to deal with. His second-half line of .275/.346/.507 was almost exactly in line with what we've come to expect of him, and a reasonable benchmark for what he should produce next season, though it's worth keeping in mind that Konerko's baseball age is running a few years ahead of his biological one.

CARLOS LEE   **LF**   **Bats: R**   **Throws: R**   Born: 20-Jun-76   Age: 28

YEAR	TM	LG	AGE	AB	H	2B	3B	HR	BB	SO	SB	CS	AVG	OBP	SLG	MLVR	EQBA	EQOBP	EQSLG	EQMLVR	VORP	DEFENSE
2001	CWS	AL	25	558	150	33	3	24	38	85	17	7	.269	.321	.468	.033	.284	.338	.497	.090	21.0	108-LF 3
2002	CWS	AL	26	492	130	26	2	26	75	73	1	4	.264	.359	.484	.124	.285	.383	.525	.206	35.5	113-LF 9
2003	CWS	AL	27	623	181	35	1	31	37	91	18	4	.291	.331	.499	.103	.304	.349	.527	.172	24.2	149-LF 1
2004	CWS	AL	28	528	145	29	2	26	49	81	11	5	.274	.337	.484	.081	.279	.346	.487	.079	19.0	137-LF 1

Breakout: 15%   Improve: 43%   Collapse: 21%

One of the jabs you hear when you do performance analysis is that players aren't stat-generating robots. Now, we know this, but it's always nice to have someone like Carlos Lee tattoo the lesson in a sensitive place. Lee's 2002 line sticks out from his other four seasons like a sore thumb: nearly as many walks as in his next two best seasons combined, the only K/BB ratio under 2.0 of his career, and the one year in four in which he didn't steal bases. There's no obvious explanation for the difference, other than that Lee is human.

Lee regressed in some important ways in 2003. At the same time, he leveraged a career high in playing time, some extra balls falling in, and the big OBPs in front of him into 113 RBIs and a two-year, $15-million contract. He's not a bad player, and his underrated play in left field adds to his value. Coming into his age-27 season, he may show a power spike that makes him a popular MVP choice in a misguided, Shannon Stewart kind of way, should the White Sox ever pull it together for six months.

AARON MILES   **2B**   **Bats: B**   **Throws: R**   Born: 15-Dec-76   Age: 27

YEAR	TM	LG	AGE	AB	H	2B	3B	HR	BB	SO	SB	CS	AVG	OBP	SLG	MLVR	EQBA	EQOBP	EQSLG	EQMLVR	VORP	DEFENSE		
2001	BIR	SOU	24	343	89	16	3	8	26	35	3	5	.259	.313	.394	-.014	.231	.276	.359	-.263	-8.5	22-3B -9	15-2B	-4
2002	BIR	SOU	25	531	171	39	1	9	40	45	25	16	.322	.369	.450	.227	.287	.322	.416	-.053	20.3	125-2B -20		
2003	CHR	INT	26	546	166	34	5	11	40	52	8	9	.304	.351	.445	.142	.284	.334	.427	-.017	26.4	120-2B -2		
2004	COL	NL	27	243	67	14	1	5	19	26	3	2	.278	.332	.415	-.028	.269	.321	.397	-.090	7.5	66-2B -5		

Breakout: 25%   Improve: 44%   Collapse: 35%

Miles is a tiny little dude and a slap hitter, which leads to all the inevitable comparisons with David Eckstein. Eckstein reached the majors at 26 after his original organization waived him, and gave his new team a couple of good years. Miles was traded to the Rockies over the winter, and with little competition in camp, he could be their Opening Day second baseman. Achieving Eckstein's cult-like following, of course, will also require Miles to replicate some of Eckstein's success—so far as we're aware, Craig Grebeck never had a fan club. And that could be, if you'll pardon the pun, a tall order. Miles does not possess Eckstein's above-average batting eye, and while he has a hair more power, PECOTA intuits that his short stature cuts against the potential for a power breakout.

MIGUEL OLIVO   **C**   **Bats: R**   **Throws: R**   Born: 15-Jul-78   Age: 25

YEAR	TM	LG	AGE	AB	H	2B	3B	HR	BB	SO	SB	CS	AVG	OBP	SLG	MLVR	EQBA	EQOBP	EQSLG	EQMLVR	VORP	DEFENSE
2001	BIR	SOU	22	316	82	23	1	14	37	62	6	3	.259	.347	.472	.144	.227	.298	.417	-.143	3.0	90-C -1
2002	BIR	SOU	23	359	110	24	10	6	40	66	29	13	.306	.381	.479	.269	.266	.324	.431	-.045	14.9	99-C -2
2003	CWS	AL	24	317	75	19	1	6	19	80	6	4	.237	.287	.360	-.210	.252	.305	.388	-.152	-5.5	101-C 3
2004	CWS	AL	25	301	75	16	2	9	23	63	7	3	.248	.307	.406	-.090	.252	.315	.409	-.098	9.9	80-C 0

Breakout: 26%   Improve: 50%   Collapse: 34%

Olivo has more pop in his bat than he demonstrated last year, but catcher development patterns are odd, and while there's the possibility that he'll go Ramon Hernandez on the league, it's hardly a foregone conclusion. Particularly troublesome was Olivo's declining plate discipline, hardly the sign of a late-blooming hitter. He'll be the starter next year, and has an outstanding arm, but Sox fans are hoping for something more than a catch-and-throw guy.

MAGGLIO ORDONEZ   RF   **Bats: R**   **Throws: R**   Born: 28-Jan-74   Age: 30

YEAR	TM	LG	AGE	AB	H	2B	3B	HR	BB	SO	SB	CS	AVG	OBP	SLG	MLVR	EQBA	EQOBP	EQSLG	EQMLVR	VORP	DEFENSE	
2001	CWS	AL	27	593	181	40	1	31	70	70	25	7	.305	.382	.533	.254	.323	.400	.570	.337	65.2	150-RF	-3
2002	CWS	AL	28	590	189	47	1	38	53	77	7	5	.320	.381	.597	.362	.343	.404	.643	.473	83.3	146-RF	0
2003	CWS	AL	29	606	192	46	3	29	57	73	9	5	.317	.380	.546	.272	.337	.402	.586	.380	51.6	150-RF	12
2004	*CWS*	*AL*	*30*	*517*	*155*	*32*	*2*	*29*	*54*	*69*	*8*	*3*	*.299*	*.368*	*.538*	*.221*	*.304*	*.377*	*.541*	*.226*	*40.8*	*136-RF*	*3*

Breakout: 8%   Improve: 42%   Collapse: 24%

Even great players have their peaks and valleys, but Ordonez has performed within a microscopic range in all his rate stats for the last four seasons. He doesn't miss much playing time, and his defense in right field has also been consistent, with an outstanding year afield in 2003. Expect more of the same in '04. As good as he is, and as unimpressive as his teammates have been, it's surprising that Ordonez has drawn just three intentional walks over the past two years.

The Sox's attempt to trade Magglio illustrates one of the ambiguities that teams face when signing players to multi-year contracts. Ordonez is due $14 million this year, the last season of a three-year deal that averages $9.8 million per. Major league teams have a variety of financing instruments available to them, and when they sign a player to a back-loaded contract, they need to plan and prepare accordingly. Instead, the Sox will count the entire $14 million against their payroll budget, undermining their opportunity to sign another player who might help them win a pennant in what will likely be the last year of Ordonez's fine run in Chicago.

JEREMY REED   RF   **Bats: L**   **Throws: L**   Born: 15-Jun-81   Age: 23

YEAR	TM	LG	AGE	AB	H	2B	3B	HR	BB	SO	SB	CS	AVG	OBP	SLG	MLVR	EQBA	EQOBP	EQSLG	EQMLVR	VORP	DEFENSE			
2002	KAN	SAL	21	210	67	15	0	4	11	24	17	5	.319	.377	.448	.242	.257	.298	.379	-.174	-6.9	35-RF	-2	19-CF	0
2003	BIR	SOU	22	242	99	17	3	7	29	19	18	13	.409	.474	.591	.644	.339	.395	.506	.256	25.8	41-RF	1	21-CF	0
2003	WNS	CAR	22	222	74	18	1	4	41	17	27	6	.333	.431	.477	.352	.255	.342	.381	-.089	-1.9	44-RF	-2	21-CF	0
2004	*CWS*	*AL*	*23*	*298*	*83*	*16*	*2*	*9*	*28*	*34*	*14*	*4*	*.279*	*.347*	*.433*	*.035*	*.284*	*.356*	*.436*	*.033*	*15.2*	*81-RF*	*1*		

Breakout: 27%   Improve: 51%   Collapse: 19%

We'll be the first to tell you that batting average is the most overrated metric out there, but sustaining a .409 AVG for half a season against professional pitching is an impressive feat however you slice it, especially for a 22-year-old in his first exposure to Double-A. Nor is it as though there aren't other facets to Reed's game: He runs well, had twice as many walks as strikeouts, and while his swing as it stands now is geared toward producing line drives, he possesses the sort of doubles power that could turn into something more as he adds strength. Reed could be a Rusty Greer type of player next year, with further upward potential above and beyond that—two of his top six PECOTA comparables are Tony Gwynn and Don Mattingly. Tempting as it might be to stick him in center field next year, the position stretches his abilities.

ARMANDO RIOS   OF   **Bats: L**   **Throws: L**   Born: 13-Sep-71   Age: 32

YEAR	TM	LG	AGE	AB	H	2B	3B	HR	BB	SO	SB	CS	AVG	OBP	SLG	MLVR	EQBA	EQOBP	EQSLG	EQMLVR	VORP	DEFENSE			
2001	SFG	NL	29	316	82	17	3	14	34	73	3	2	.259	.330	.465	.040	.269	.339	.480	.053	10.3	64-RF	3	13-LF	0
2002	CAR	PRL	30	86	22	5	0	1	8	10	6	2	.256	.326	.349	.005	.247	.307	.348	-.208	-6.0				
2002	PIT	NL	30	208	55	11	0	1	16	39	1	1	.264	.319	.332	-.119	.275	.326	.346	-.155	-5.0	39-RF	2		
2003	CWS	AL	31	104	22	3	0	2	5	13	0	1	.212	.245	.298	-.385	.231	.266	.327	-.328	-7.7	16-CF	0		
2003	CHR	INT	31	155	50	9	1	6	14	30	5	6	.323	.389	.510	.303	.291	.359	.475	.102	8.1	34-RF	-3		
2004	*CWS*	*AL*	*32*	*153*	*38*	*6*	*1*	*4*	*16*	*29*	*2*	*1*	*.247*	*.320*	*.374*	*-.111*	*.251*	*.328*	*.376*	*-.119*	*-1.9*	*-24845 RF*	*-1*		

Breakout: Improve: Collapse:

A fine fourth outfielder in his day, Rios has struggled since blowing out his knee at the end of 2001, but on an up note with a couple of strong couple of months at Charlotte. Unfortunately, Rios has reached the point where his age will begin to work against him, so coming back to full strength could be a Sisyphusian chore. Having refused the Sox's minor league assignment, he'll take his chances as an NRI.

MIKE RIVERA C Bats: R Throws: R Born: 08-Sep-76 Age: 27

YEAR	TM	LG	AGE	AB	H	2B	3B	HR	BB	SO	SB	CS	AVG	OBP	SLG	MLVR	EQBA	EQOBP	EQSLG	EQMLVR	VORP	DEFENSE	
2001	ERI	EAS	24	415	120	19	1	33	44	96	2	2	.289	.368	.578	.307	.239	.311	.480	-.023	19.2	108-C	-5
2002	DET	AL	25	132	30	8	1	1	4	35	0	0	.227	.254	.326	-.280	.256	.282	.361	-.232	-2.0	37-C	-2
2002	TOL	INT	25	265	66	11	1	20	35	64	0	1	.249	.341	.525	.165	.227	.314	.487	-.018	12.6	63-C	2
2003	SDP	NL	26	53	9	1	0	1	5	11	0	0	.170	.241	.245	-.406	.185	.254	.278	-.444	-3.9	18-C	0
2003	CHR	INT	26	245	76	11	0	12	16	50	0	1	.310	.373	.502	.258	.290	.351	.484	.100	20.3	34-C	-6
2004	CWS	AL	27	197	47	9	0	9	17	46	0	1	.238	.308	.429	-.066	.243	.316	.432	-.073	8.6	55-C	-5

Breakout: 27%   Improve: 51%   Collapse: 33%

Any catcher who has a season with 33 home runs is going to get at least a couple of chances, and the Sox did not hesitate to pick up Rivera after failed trials in Detroit and San Diego. While his solid numbers in Charlotte do not suggest a player who has learned any new tricks—his high batting average, unaccompanied by improvement to his plate discipline, looks like a fluke—Rivera's power is legit, and he'd be an overqualified backup for a team willing to give him a chance. Fairly or not, he has gained a reputation for having a poor rapport with his pitchers.

AARON ROWAND CF Bats: R Throws: R Born: 29-Aug-77 Age: 26

YEAR	TM	LG	AGE	AB	H	2B	3B	HR	BB	SO	SB	CS	AVG	OBP	SLG	MLVR	EQBA	EQOBP	EQSLG	EQMLVR	VORP	DEFENSE			
2001	CHR	INT	23	329	97	28	0	16	21	47	8	2	.295	.353	.526	.224	.274	.329	.497	.065	12.6	73-RF	-2		
2001	CWS	AL	23	123	36	5	0	4	15	28	5	1	.293	.385	.431	.112	.317	.408	.463	.194	8.4	17-LF	2	19-CF	1
2002	CWS	AL	24	302	78	16	2	7	12	54	0	1	.258	.298	.394	-.104	.277	.317	.422	-.061	6.5	62-CF	-3	28-LF	2
2003	CWS	AL	25	157	45	8	0	6	7	21	0	0	.287	.327	.452	.028	.299	.343	.478	.086	5.6	41-CF	3		
2003	CHR	INT	25	120	29	9	0	3	11	12	0	0	.242	.316	.392	-.033	.230	.295	.385	-.191	-1.6	21-CF	1	11-RF	-1
2004	CWS	AL	26	130	34	7	0	5	10	21	1	0	.262	.323	.429	-.024	.267	.331	.432	-.029	4.5	38-CF	-4		

Breakout: 24%   Improve: 47%   Collapse: 34%

Making Rowand, who can't hit right-handers, the starting center fielder in April worked about as poorly as you'd expect and earned the overmatched 25-year-old a month in Charlotte. Upon his return, with Carl Everett having arrived, Rowand was able to be the lefty-mashing fourth outfielder his product specifications described: .381/.412/.629 in limited playing time. He's a championship-caliber reserve, and a replacement-level regular . . . we'll see if Ozzie Guillen knows the difference.

FRANK THOMAS DH Bats: R Throws: R Born: 27-May-68 Age: 36

YEAR	TM	LG	AGE	AB	H	2B	3B	HR	BB	SO	SB	CS	AVG	OBP	SLG	MLVR	EQBA	EQOBP	EQSLG	EQMLVR	VORP	DEFENSE	
2001	CWS	AL	33	68	15	3	0	4	10	12	0	0	.221	.316	.441	-.048	.235	.333	.471	.001	2.4		
2002	CWS	AL	34	523	132	29	1	28	88	115	3	0	.252	.361	.472	.103	.271	.383	.510	.172	43.8		
2003	CWS	AL	35	546	146	35	0	42	100	115	0	0	.267	.390	.562	.258	.285	.406	.602	.346	58.2	24-1B	-2
2004	CWS	AL	36	452	116	22	0	29	80	98	1	1	.256	.371	.496	.134	.261	.380	.499	.136	29.3	127-DH	-2

Breakout: 26%   Improve: 40%   Collapse: 30%

The absurdity of the first half of Big Frank's career has obscured the effectiveness of the second: His worst full-season EqAs are .290, .301, and .303, and you can find any number of "stars" who don't have two numbers that high on their player card. It would be nice to see Thomas get a chance to go nuts on a big stage in October, a la Barry Bonds, but he doesn't need that to validate his status as an inner-circle Hall of Famer.

One of Thomas's most unheralded skills is his ability to foul off pitches. Certainly, his prodigious walk rates have resulted partly from the respect that pitchers must afford to his power, but he also has one of the largest strike zones in baseball, and without knowing how to defend it appropriately, he would not be the same caliber of hitter. For those of you who subscribe to MLB.com's clips service, Thomas's 10-pinch battle against Pedro Martinez (5th inning, June 16) was one of the best confrontations of the season, complete with a brushback pitch, a light tower shot that just went foul, and a big, beautiful curveball to end it.

JOSE VALENTIN SS Bats: B Throws: R Born: 12-Oct-69 Age: 34

YEAR	TM	LG	AGE	AB	H	2B	3B	HR	BB	SO	SB	CS	AVG	OBP	SLG	MLVR	EQBA	EQOBP	EQSLG	EQMLVR	VORP	DEFENSE			
2001	CWS	AL	31	438	113	22	2	28	50	114	9	6	.258	.336	.509	.104	.273	.353	.542	.167	41.5	60-3B	-8	40-SS	-1
2002	CWS	AL	32	474	118	26	4	25	43	99	3	3	.249	.311	.479	.025	.265	.330	.511	.077	32.1	83-3B	0	46-SS	-3
2003	CWS	AL	33	503	119	26	2	28	54	114	8	3	.237	.313	.463	-.023	.252	.330	.500	.050	21.8	135-SS	3		
2004	CWS	AL	34	354	88	16	2	19	40	78	5	2	.248	.326	.466	.018	.252	.334	.469	.014	23.0	96-SS	-4		

Breakout: 40%   Improve: 60%   Collapse: 20%

As any member in good standing of the Chicago press corps can tell you, Valentin is a chatterbox fully worthy of Popeye on a spinach bender, and like the erstwhile sailor, he 'ams what he 'ams. Valentin has long taken his share of criticism for his low batting average and high error rates, but he hits right-handed pitchers for more power than any shortstop this side of A-Rod, draws his share of walks, and saves far more plays than he muffs with his fine arm and footwork. In short, he's been an underrated player for a long time, and the Sox dodged a bullet by picking up his option.

ROB VALIDO   SS   Bats: R   Throws: R   Born: 16-May-85   Age: 19

YEAR	TM	LG	AGE	AB	H	2B	3B	HR	BB	SO	SB	CS	AVG	OBP	SLG	MLVR	EQBA	EQOBP	EQSLG	EQMLVR	VORP	DEFENSE
2003	BRI	APP	18	215	66	15	2	6	17	28	17	6	.307	.364	.479	.259	.214	.253	.345	-.338	-20.4	58-SS -5
2004	CWS	AL	19	267	58	13	2	5	13	44	11	3	.217	.261	.341	-.274	.221	.268	.343	-.290	-5.1	71-SS -9

Breakout: 34%   Improve: 55%   Collapse: 22%

Another member of the Sox's promising 2003 amateur draft class, Valido hails from the same high school as Cubs' infield prospect Luis Montanez. Like Montanez, Valido came out of the amateur ranks with the reputation as a glove guy first, but surprised observers by posting big, well-rounded offensive numbers in his professional debut. He could be a solid prospect a year from now, or, like Montanez, completely forgotten about.

PITCHERS

JON ADKINS   Bats: L   Throws: R   Born: 30-Aug-77   Age: 26

YEAR	TM	LG	AGE	G	GS	IP	H	BB	SO	HR	ERA	EQERA	EQH9	EQBB9	EQSO9	EQHR9	PERA	VORP	STF
2001	MID	TEX	23	24	24	137.3	147	36	74	9	4.46	5.10	9.6	2.8	3.3	0.9	4.64	7.3	-3
2002	SAC	PCL	24	20	20	97.0	139	33	76	9	6.03	6.73	12.5	3.4	5.2	1.1	6.28	-11.8	-10
2002	CHR	INT	24	8	7	46.3	47	12	31	4	3.69	4.78	9.8	2.7	5.0	1.0	4.83	3.9	3
2003	CHR	INT	25	26	19	122.7	119	34	59	11	3.96	5.23	9.2	3.1	3.5	1.3	4.95	4.7	-22
2004	CWS	AL	26	16	9	51.0	60	19	26	8	5.49	5.54	10.6	3.2	4.4	1.2	5.57	2.5	-12

Breakout: 27%   Improve: 45%   Collapse: 25%

The bounty, such as it was, for two months of Ray Durham and a pair of draft picks. Adkins was not a top-flight prospect at the time of his acquisition, and is not a top prospect today. While his ERA was lower in his second turn at Triple-A, his strikeout rate was down a bit, and it's evident that his combination of a straight, low-90s fastball, hittable curve, and flat slider ain't fooling anyone. That he's been kept on the 40-man roster suggests that the Sox are an organization that makes up in stubbornness what it lacks in depth.

BYEONG AN   Bats: L   Throws: L   Born: 01-Jul-80   Age: 24

YEAR	TM	LG	AGE	G	GS	IP	H	BB	SO	HR	ERA	EQERA	EQH9	EQBB9	EQSO9	EQHR9	PERA	VORP	STF
2001	SAR	FLA	21	23	21	119.3	122	42	84	10	3.62	5.77	10.1	3.7	4.3	1.7	6.02	-2.1	-5
2002	SAR	FLA	22	25	12	98.0	102	33	58	8	5.33	6.85	11.5	3.8	3.7	1.7	6.75	-12.2	-26
2003	WNS	CAR	23	12	12	68.3	66	27	45	5	3.16	6.07	11.5	4.7	4.2	1.8	7.11	-3.1	-25
2003	BIR	SOU	23	16	14	80.0	76	34	45	4	3.94	5.50	9.4	4.4	3.4	1.0	5.11	0.8	-8
2004	CWS	AL	23	20	12	65.7	76	30	33	12	5.81	5.86	10.5	3.9	4.4	1.3	5.98	1.5	-16

Breakout: 31%   Improve: 53%   Collapse: 24%

An, the first Korean national to play in the White Sox organization, is a pitcher more along the lines of Shigetoshi Hasegawa than Hideo Nomo or Byung Kim, throwing in the upper 80s and experiencing mild success when he keeps the ball down. If he surfaces in the big leagues, it will likely be as a middle reliever.

JEFF BAJENARU   Bats: R   Throws: R   Born: 21-Mar-78   Age: 26

YEAR	TM	LG	AGE	G	GS	IP	H	BB	SO	HR	ERA	EQERA	EQH9	EQBB9	EQSO9	EQHR9	PERA	VORP	STF
2001	WNS	CAR	23	35	0	40.3	32	21	51	3	3.35	5.56	10.6	7.1	7.1	1.9	7.26	0.2	-37
2003	BIR	SOU	25	50	0	64.7	53	28	62	2	3.20	4.78	9.1	4.6	5.9	0.6	4.61	5.3	-10
2004	CWS	AL	26	17	2	24.3	25	14	17	3	5.22	5.26	9.4	4.8	6.2	1.0	5.38	1.5	-10

Breakout: 18%   Improve: 48%   Collapse: 17%

(continued next page)

Jeff Bajenaru *(continued)*

Bajenaru returned from a year lost to elbow injury to put together a reasonable campaign as Birmingham's closer despite some occasional bouts of the wilds. But minor league closers are a dime a dozen; what's more interesting is that Bajenaru was an accomplished two-way player at the University of Oklahoma, earning first-team All-Big 12 honors for his work as an outfielder. Why not let the guy handle the bat when his turn in the bullpen isn't up? The Brooks Kieschnick thing has gone pretty well all things considered, no?

MARK BUEHRLE — Bats: L — Throws: L — Born: 23-Mar-79 — Age: 25

YEAR	TM	LG	AGE	G	GS	IP	H	BB	SO	HR	ERA	EQERA	EQH9	EQBB9	EQSO9	EQHR9	PERA	VORP	STF
2001	CWS	AL	22	32	32	221.3	188	48	126	24	3.29	3.31	7.6	1.8	4.8	0.9	3.42	54.0	29
2002	CWS	AL	23	34	34	239.0	236	61	134	25	3.58	3.81	9.1	2.2	4.9	0.9	4.17	45.5	22
2003	CWS	AL	24	35	35	230.3	250	61	119	22	4.14	4.45	9.9	2.3	4.6	0.8	4.50	29.8	14
2004	CWS	AL	25	29	29	202.3	216	55	111	28	4.42	4.46	9.6	2.3	4.8	1.0	4.41	28.6	5

Breakout: 20%   Improve: 52%   Collapse: 17%

Left-hander genealogies can be every bit as incestuous as something you'd see on Jerry Springer, and the results of the paternity test reveal that Buehrle is a hybrid of Tom Glavine and Tommy John, possessing the former's feel for mixing pitches and speeds—Buehrle routinely hits every number on the radar gun from 80 to 89 during the course of one of his starts—with the latter's plebian efficiency, working quickly and rarely issuing walks. He doesn't possess John's uncanny ability to keep the ball down, however, which is the main reason that PECOTA thinks his ERA will increase for the third consecutive season.

BARTOLO COLON — Bats: R — Throws: R — Born: 24-May-73 — Age: 31

YEAR	TM	LG	AGE	G	GS	IP	H	BB	SO	HR	ERA	EQERA	EQH9	EQBB9	EQSO9	EQHR9	PERA	VORP	STF
2001	CLE	AL	28	34	34	222.3	220	90	201	26	4.09	3.78	8.0	3.3	7.4	0.9	4.03	44.8	22
2002	CLE	AL	29	16	16	116.3	104	31	75	11	2.55	2.74	7.2	2.2	5.5	0.8	3.22	36.5	22
2002	MON	NL	29	17	17	117.0	115	39	74	9	3.31	3.90	8.8	2.6	4.9	0.7	4.01	21.3	12
2003	CWS	AL	30	34	34	242.0	223	67	173	30	3.87	3.75	8.4	2.4	6.4	1.0	4.03	54.2	18
2004	ANA	AL	31	30	30	203.0	196	64	137	22	3.85	4.11	8.6	2.7	5.9	0.9	4.11	37.8	11

Breakout: 20%   Improve: 53%   Collapse: 17%

There was a lot of fuss within sabermetric circles about how to read Colon's 2002 numbers, which combined a career-best ERA with a career-worst strikeout rate. In the end, the debate turned out to be much ado about nothing, as Colon turned in a 2003 season that was pretty much a dead ringer for one of his vintage campaigns in Cleveland—lots of innings and an ERA around 4. Oh sure, Colon's peripheral numbers have changed their shape ever since Indians pitching coach Mike Brown altered his delivery two spring trainings ago, but he was a good pitcher before and has been a good pitcher since, if not quite the mega-ace that the Angels are paying for. It's a bit alarmist to speculate that a guy is on the brink of disaster when he's still throwing 99 and has cut his walk rate by 50%. What holds Colon back from being Roger Clemens is the same thing that always has: the lack of a killer breaking pitch.

NEAL COTTS — Bats: L — Throws: L — Born: 25-Mar-80 — Age: 24

YEAR	TM	LG	AGE	G	GS	IP	H	BB	SO	HR	ERA	EQERA	EQH9	EQBB9	EQSO9	EQHR9	PERA	VORP	STF
2001	VAN	NWN	21	9	7	35.0	28	13	44	2	3.09	5.52	11.4	5.2	6.1	1.5	6.77	0.3	-10
2001	VIS	CAL	21	7	7	31.0	27	15	34	0	2.32	4.40	8.8	5.7	5.7	0.3	4.45	3.8	20
2002	MOD	CAL	22	28	28	137.7	123	87	178	5	4.12	6.06	10.1	7.2	6.8	0.7	5.75	-6.3	7
2003	BIR	SOU	23	21	21	108.3	67	56	133	2	2.16	3.56	6.9	5.4	7.7	0.4	3.58	22.4	34
2003	CWS	AL	23	4	4	13.3	15	17	10	1	8.12	7.62	10.4	11.1	6.9	0.7	6.83	-3.0	-4
2004	CWS	AL	24	19	13	69.0	73	53	57	11	6.39	6.45	9.5	6.6	7.1	1.1	6.28	3.9	-7

Breakout: 19%   Improve: 36%   Collapse: 26%

Cotts has two big strikes against him: First, high walk rates that show he's not ready for prime time, and second, a whipping, violent delivery that places a tremendous amount of strain on his elbow. BP's Will Carroll, who has a book coming out on pitching mechanics, is as down on Cotts's delivery as any in pro ball. Those two problems might well be related, since the essence of a good delivery is that it's repeatable, and the essence of good control is being able to hit one's spots on demand. Certainly, Cotts has some things going for him—his fastball moves well, he keeps the ball down, and changes speeds effectively—but he's in a higher risk bracket than those kids from Jackass.

FELIX DIAZ   Bats: R   Throws: R   Born: 27-Jul-80   Age: 23

YEAR	TM	LG	AGE	G	GS	IP	H	BB	SO	HR	ERA	EQERA	EQH9	EQBB9	EQSO9	EQHR9	PERA	VORP	STF
2001	HAG	SAL	20	15	12	51.7	49	16	56	4	3.66	6.70	11.8	4.3	5.7	1.6	6.83	-5.4	-8
2002	BIR	SOU	21	7	6	31.0	25	8	30	4	3.48	5.20	9.4	2.6	6.8	2.3	6.03	1.2	1
2002	SHV	TEX	21	12	12	60.0	54	23	48	1	2.70	4.31	8.3	4.0	5.6	0.3	3.79	8.1	29
2003	CHR	INT	22	27	18	115.7	122	33	83	12	3.97	5.48	9.2	3.1	5.6	1.2	4.90	1.5	7
2004	CWS	AL	23	18	11	63.3	67	24	41	10	4.83	4.87	9.5	3.3	5.6	1.2	4.99	7.8	-2

Breakout: 24%   Improve: 56%   Collapse: 17%

Diaz has what you'd call a classic Dominican repertoire, featuring a mid-90s fastball and a power slider. Completing the stereotype, he's an undersized guy (6′1″, 180) who has had some injury troubles, and added a year to his birth certificate during AgeGate. Diaz made some strides with his control last season, and is being talked up as a rotation candidate, but like Juan Cruz eight miles north, his body type and pitch assortment may be best suited to the bullpen.

SCOTT DUNN   Bats: R   Throws: R   Born: 23-May-78   Age: 26

YEAR	TM	LG	AGE	G	GS	IP	H	BB	SO	HR	ERA	EQERA	EQH9	EQBB9	EQSO9	EQHR9	PERA	VORP	STF
2001	MUD	CAL	23	10	10	59.7	45	31	73	2	2.11	4.27	9.1	6.3	6.3	0.7	5.10	7.8	9
2001	CHT	SOU	23	17	17	98.3	96	71	87	10	4.12	6.20	10.0	7.6	5.4	1.5	6.75	-6.0	-22
2002	CHT	SOU	24	37	12	110.3	99	54	114	10	3.92	5.27	9.8	4.7	6.6	1.7	6.13	3.7	-24
2003	CHT	SOU	25	31	0	40.3	31	16	54	3	3.80	5.00	9.5	4.2	8.2	1.5	5.58	2.4	-19
2003	BIR	SOU	25	8	0	10.7	8	5	14	0	1.68	2.79	9.3	4.7	8.4	0.0	4.05	3.0	26
2004	CWS	AL	26	12	6	35.3	38	23	29	6	6.01	6.06	9.7	5.5	7.2	1.2	6.03	-0.6	-5

Breakout: 12%   Improve: 37%   Collapse: 28%

The prospect acquired in the D'Angelo Jimenez trade, Dunn's career as a starter was undone by control problems. He's improved his ratios substantially since converting to relief, and has more upside than PECOTA suggests. There are some reports that Dunn throws a knuckleball to complement his 94-mph heater, but the pitch is really more of a knuckle-curve, and even then, he throws it only occasionally. We're still waiting for the guy that alternates between 94 and 54 with aplomb, driving opposing hitters into the sort of fits that have previously been observed only in highly classified experiments involving Kaopectate, Gilbert Gottfried, and a troop of rhesus monkeys.

JON GARLAND   Bats: R   Throws: R   Born: 27-Sep-79   Age: 24

YEAR	TM	LG	AGE	G	GS	IP	H	BB	SO	HR	ERA	EQERA	EQH9	EQBB9	EQSO9	EQHR9	PERA	VORP	STF
2001	CHR	INT	21	5	5	33.0	31	11	26	1	2.73	3.69	8.0	3.4	6.3	0.3	3.42	6.7	44
2001	CWS	AL	21	35	16	117.0	123	55	61	16	3.69	4.62	9.5	4.0	4.4	1.1	5.16	12.3	7
2002	CWS	AL	22	33	33	192.7	188	83	112	23	4.58	4.65	9.0	3.6	5.1	1.0	4.65	19.6	19
2003	CWS	AL	23	32	32	191.7	188	74	108	28	4.51	4.53	8.9	3.3	5.0	1.2	4.75	25.0	12
2004	CWS	AL	24	27	24	148.7	156	61	89	22	4.76	4.80	9.4	3.5	5.2	1.1	4.95	15.9	1

Breakout: 25%   Improve: 51%   Collapse: 17%

His heavy sinker has long been reputed to be a great out pitch, but Garland has yet to figure out how to make it do the nasty things that Kevin Brown's does, or to leverage it into big strikeout numbers. He also lacks Brown's breaking stuff, as his over-the-top delivery leads his curve to float on him, rather than break. In any event, Garland's lack of progress speaks for itself: He's not a bad pitcher by any means, and has made modest improvements to his control, but odds are that he gets expensive before he really turns the corner.

MATT GINTER   Bats: R   Throws: R   Born: 24-Dec-77   Age: 26

YEAR	TM	LG	AGE	G	GS	IP	H	BB	SO	HR	ERA	EQERA	EQH9	EQBB9	EQSO9	EQHR9	PERA	VORP	STF
2001	CHR	INT	23	22	10	76.3	62	24	67	3	2.60	3.64	7.8	3.3	6.4	0.4	3.39	15.6	28
2001	CWS	AL	23	20	0	39.7	34	14	24	2	5.21	4.03	7.8	3.1	5.2	0.5	3.46	6.6	17
2002	CHR	INT	24	13	0	16.0	20	10	9	3	3.94	6.75	12.3	6.8	4.3	2.5	8.71	-1.9	-71
2002	CWS	AL	24	33	0	54.3	59	21	37	6	4.48	5.16	10.0	3.3	6.0	0.9	4.87	2.6	4
2003	CHR	INT	25	49	0	68.3	66	22	52	2	3.03	4.41	9.2	3.6	5.5	0.4	4.18	8.4	1
2004	CWS	AL	26	23	6	46.0	50	18	30	7	5.11	5.15	9.8	3.3	5.7	1.1	5.08	4.1	-7

Breakout: 22%   Improve: 51%   Collapse: 25%

(continued next page)

Matt Ginter (continued)

Ginter spent virtually the entire season in Charlotte after having struggled mightily against left-handed hitters in 2002, a characteristic that makes him difficult to use in high-leverage situations. Unfortunately, there isn't much evidence that he's corrected his problems, as lefties hit .343 off him in Triple-A, vs. righties' .193 clip. Even in these days of bullpen specialization, there isn't much room for ROOGYs, and Ginter's future will remain very much in doubt until he learns how to handle southpaws.

TOM GORDON   Bats: R   Throws: R   Born: 18-Nov-67   Age: 36

YEAR	TM	LG	AGE	G	GS	IP	H	BB	SO	HR	ERA	EQERA	EQH9	EQBB9	EQSO9	EQHR9	PERA	VORP	STF
2001	CHC	NL	33	47	0	45.3	32	16	67	4	3.38	3.09	6.8	2.9	11.1	0.6	3.00	12.2	43
2002	CHC	NL	34	19	0	23.7	27	10	31	1	3.42	4.70	10.6	3.1	10.2	0.4	4.53	2.3	33
2002	HOU	NL	34	15	0	19.0	15	6	17	2	3.32	3.44	6.9	2.5	6.9	1.0	3.32	4.4	9
2003	CWS	AL	35	66	0	74.0	57	31	91	4	3.16	3.12	7.1	3.6	10.9	0.4	3.14	21.2	45
2004	NYY	AL	36	48	8	85.3	71	35	88	8	3.22	3.32	7.3	3.5	9.1	0.8	3.58	25.3	18

Breakout: 34%   Improve: 48%   Collapse: 21%

Gordon's big curve is still one of the best in the game, and even if the U.S. Cellular radar gun is exaggerating when it puts his fastball velocity at 98, there's little doubt that he's got enough stuff to be a real asset in the bullpen. Gordon's beyond the point where his Tommy John surgery should really be a concern, and given his high strikeout rates, he's the right kind of reliever to put in front of a porous Yankee defense.

KRIS HONEL   Bats: R   Throws: R   Born: 07-Nov-82   Age: 21

YEAR	TM	LG	AGE	G	GS	IP	H	BB	SO	HR	ERA	EQERA	EQH9	EQBB9	EQSO9	EQHR9	PERA	VORP	STF
2001	BRI	APP	18	8	8	46.0	41	9	45	4	3.13	6.41	11.9	2.7	4.1	2.3	7.35	-3.5	-10
2002	KAN	SAL	19	26	26	153.3	128	52	152	12	2.82	5.20	9.9	4.2	5.7	1.8	6.14	6.0	9
2003	WNS	CAR	20	24	24	133.0	122	42	122	7	3.11	5.34	10.4	3.7	6.2	1.1	5.53	3.4	19
2003	BIR	SOU	20	2	2	12.0	9	6	13	2	3.75	5.73	8.2	4.9	7.4	3.3	7.30	-0.2	-4
2004	CWS	AL	21	18	15	89.7	90	38	69	13	4.71	4.75	9.1	3.6	6.7	1.0	4.77	10.6	9

Breakout: 31%   Improve: 59%   Collapse: 8%

Honel might have been passed over by Neal Cotts on the hype meter, but he's the better pitching prospect, possessing a tremendous knuckle-curve, a fastball that hovers around 88 mph but moves well, solid mechanics, and a good feel for pitching. He's a similar prospect to St. Louis' Adam Wainwright, and like Wainwright, projects as a solid #2/#3 starter if he can continue to make improvements to his command.

BILL KOCH   Bats: R   Throws: R   Born: 14-Dec-74   Age: 29

YEAR	TM	LG	AGE	G	GS	IP	H	BB	SO	HR	ERA	EQERA	EQH9	EQBB9	EQSO9	EQHR9	PERA	VORP	STF
2001	TOR	AL	26	69	0	69.3	69	33	55	7	4.81	4.48	8.4	4.0	6.6	0.8	4.28	8.5	1
2002	OAK	AL	27	84	0	93.7	73	46	93	7	3.27	3.56	7.1	4.1	8.6	0.6	3.49	20.6	23
2003	CWS	AL	28	55	0	53.0	59	28	42	10	5.77	5.79	10.2	4.6	7.0	1.6	6.09	-0.5	-24
2004	CWS	AL	29	51	0	55.7	54	26	45	7	4.51	4.55	8.8	4.0	7.0	0.9	4.59	7.5	-1

Breakout: 25%   Improve: 56%   Collapse: 19%

Koch has always been heavily dependent on his fastball velocity: His heater doesn't move much, and he doesn't know where it's going, so unless he can throw it by people, he's going to get into trouble. Whether on account of his elbow problems, his heavy usage in 2002, or something else, Koch's fastball diminished last year from its customary 99 to a more hittable 95, and that was enough to send his HR rate and ERA soaring.

We've tried to give Ken Williams credit for his good moves, and he's made a few of them, but the challenge trade that brought Koch to Chicago for Keith Foulke looked like a bad deal at the time, and it looks even worse now. The only department in which Koch had outpaced Foulke was in saves, a statistic that has little meaning in the present, and even less predictive value going forward. Health willing, Koch can still be a good pitcher—he's never been a great pitcher—but the Sox need to ease him back into high-leverage situations, as his confidence was shot by mid-summer, further contributing to his struggles.

ESTEBAN LOAIZA — Bats: R — Throws: R — Born: 31-Dec-71 — Age: 32

YEAR	TM	LG	AGE	G	GS	IP	H	BB	SO	HR	ERA	EQERA	EQH9	EQBB9	EQSO9	EQHR9	PERA	VORP	STF
2001	TOR	AL	29	36	30	190.0	239	40	110	27	5.02	5.06	10.6	1.7	4.8	1.1	5.01	11.2	-1
2002	TOR	AL	30	25	25	151.3	192	38	87	18	5.71	5.30	11.0	2.1	4.9	1.0	5.15	4.9	2
2003	CWS	AL	31	34	34	226.3	196	56	207	17	2.90	2.97	7.9	2.1	8.2	0.6	3.34	75.3	42
2004	CWS	AL	32	31	30	200.7	206	48	148	28	3.93	3.97	9.2	2.1	6.4	1.0	4.16	40.4	16

Breakout: 19%   Improve: 40%   Collapse: 12%

Loaiza's breakout campaign is sure to be classified with the likes of Steve Stone's 1980 or Mike Caldwell's 1978, the implication being that he's going to forfeit whatever success he had as soon as his deal with Denny McLain runs out. In Loaiza's case, however, there are real reasons to believe that his improvements are sustainable. He was free of off-the-field troubles (a nasty divorce case and a life-threatening injury to his new girlfriend) for the first time in several seasons, and perhaps more importantly, had added a sharp cut fastball to his arsenal. Loaiza's command has always been good, and with the new pitch, he's become a genuinely impressive pitcher to watch. Assuming that the rough landing that cost him the Cy Young was nothing more than a simple case of fatigue, he should beat that PECOTA in '04.

GARY MAJEWSKI — Bats: R — Throws: R — Born: 26-Feb-80 — Age: 24

YEAR	TM	LG	AGE	G	GS	IP	H	BB	SO	HR	ERA	EQERA	EQH9	EQBB9	EQSO9	EQHR9	PERA	VORP	STF
2001	VRO	FLA	21	23	13	75.0	103	36	41	9	6.24	9.68	15.5	5.3	3.4	2.7	10.17	-29.9	-65
2001	WNS	CAR	21	9	6	43.0	42	10	31	3	2.93	5.21	10.9	3.1	4.0	1.7	6.20	1.6	-12
2002	BIR	SOU	22	57	1	74.7	61	34	75	3	2.65	4.92	9.3	4.4	6.5	0.8	4.81	5.1	6
2003	CHR	INT	23	42	1	72.7	62	29	72	3	3.96	4.50	7.9	4.4	7.4	0.5	3.90	8.3	21
2004	CWS	AL	24	17	7	42.0	43	20	32	6	4.91	4.95	9.3	4.1	6.7	1.0	5.04	4.5	-1

Breakout: 24%   Improve: 52%   Collapse: 20%

The Blue Jays selected Majewski in last year's Rule 5 draft but returned him after Aquilino Lopez impressed them more, all of which goes to show that minor league relievers with good strikeout rates and mediocre control are expendable commodities. There are reports that Majewski's velocity is down from his earlier days as a starter, and he struggled in his AFL campaign, so there are some flashing yellows here.

CORWIN MALONE — Bats: R — Throws: L — Born: 03-Jul-80 — Age: 23

YEAR	TM	LG	AGE	G	GS	IP	H	BB	SO	HR	ERA	EQERA	EQH9	EQBB9	EQSO9	EQHR9	PERA	VORP	STF
2001	KAN	SAL	21	18	18	112.3	83	44	119	2	2.00	4.53	9.1	5.4	5.5	0.4	4.55	11.6	26
2001	WNS	CAR	21	5	5	36.7	25	10	38	1	1.72	3.82	7.6	3.5	6.0	0.5	3.57	6.5	37
2001	BIR	SOU	21	4	4	19.3	8	12	20	2	2.33	3.06	4.6	6.6	7.1	1.5	4.03	5.0	24
2002	BIR	SOU	22	22	22	124.3	116	89	89	6	4.71	7.06	9.7	6.8	4.9	0.9	5.72	-18.6	0
2003	KAN	SAL	23	5	5	24.7	27	10	29	2	5.10	8.71	14.8	5.2	7.0	2.2	9.02	-7.2	-33
2003	BIR	SOU	23	8	8	40.0	50	28	28	2	5.40	7.85	12.5	7.4	4.4	1.0	7.22	-9.2	-20
2004	CWS	AL	23	13	10	52.3	64	36	31	11	7.25	7.31	11.0	5.9	5.1	1.5	7.28	-3.5	-20

Breakout: 26%   Improve: 66%   Collapse: 20%

Malone's stock has dropped mightily after two rough seasons, as he's struggled first with his control and then with elbow problems. What's more, his velocity is down, his curveball hasn't come, and the reports on his delivery aren't encouraging. Malone began his professional career as a reliever, and it's possible that the big 2001 campaign that put him on the radar, in which he logged 170 innings between three levels as a 21-year-old, will prove to be his undoing. Much as it seems like a no-lose proposition to suggest that every kid with a live arm make a go of it as a starter, some pitchers have physiques and repertoires that are better suited to the bullpen, and every pitcher warrants careful handling until his body has matured.

DAMASO MARTE — Bats: L — Throws: L — Born: 14-Feb-75 — Age: 29

YEAR	TM	LG	AGE	G	GS	IP	H	BB	SO	HR	ERA	EQERA	EQH9	EQBB9	EQSO9	EQHR9	PERA	VORP	STF
2001	NRW	EAS	26	23	0	36.0	29	7	36	3	3.50	4.50	9.6	2.5	6.2	1.4	5.07	3.9	-23
2001	PIT	NL	26	23	0	36.3	34	12	39	5	4.71	4.37	8.7	2.8	8.2	1.0	4.32	4.8	10
2002	CWS	AL	27	68	0	60.3	44	18	72	5	2.84	2.78	6.8	2.5	10.3	0.6	2.89	18.3	41
2003	CWS	AL	28	71	0	79.7	50	34	87	3	1.58	1.99	5.8	3.6	9.7	0.4	2.58	35.7	44
2004	CWS	AL	29	55	2	75.3	60	28	78	8	3.11	3.14	7.2	3.2	8.9	0.8	3.34	22.9	18

Breakout: 36%   Improve: 61%   Collapse: 22%

(continued next page)

Damaso Marte *(continued)*

Marte is one nasty pitcher, capable of just as much dominance as a vintage Arthur Rhodes or Michele Foucault. He's unafraid to send cutters and sliders darting to every corner of the strike zone, a combination that makes him highly effective against lefties and righties alike. Marte has his wild nights, and probably won't post a 1.58 ERA again, but if Ozzie Guillen does anything other than use him in the team's highest-leverage situations, he'll be making a mistake.

RYAN MEAUX Bats: R Throws: L Born: 05-Oct-78 Age: 25

YEAR	TM	LG	AGE	G	GS	IP	H	BB	SO	HR	ERA	EQERA	EQH9	EQBB9	EQSO9	EQHR9	PERA	VORP	STF
2001	SLO	NWN	22	17	3	29.0	39	11	27	4	5.59	10.12	17.6	5.2	4.5	3.8	12.32	-12.1	-108
2002	HAG	SAL	23	44	0	54.7	41	12	44	1	2.63	3.86	8.4	2.8	4.2	0.4	3.57	9.5	0
2002	KAN	SAL	23	10	0	13.3	19	0	13	1	1.35	9.00	18.0	0.8	5.7	1.6	8.78	-4.2	-41
2003	WNS	CAR	24	32	0	55.0	49	3	43	2	1.15	3.94	11.1	0.6	5.1	0.9	4.71	8.9	-3
2003	BIR	SOU	24	26	0	38.0	39	3	29	0	2.13	3.86	10.5	0.8	4.6	0.3	3.83	6.8	11
2004	*CWS*	*AL*	*25*	*18*	*4*	*35.7*	*41*	*6*	*18*	*6*	*4.56*	*4.60*	*10.3*	*1.5*	*4.4*	*1.1*	*4.67*	*5.5*	*-8*

Breakout: 16%   Improve: 50%   Collapse: 27%

Meaux is a smart pitcher who is able to locate his sweeping curveball at any point in the strike zone with impeccable command, a combination that has produced an Eckersley-like 85:6 strikeout-to-walk ratio since he came to the White Sox organization in the Kenny Lofton deal. He doesn't throw hard, and as PECOTA suggests, it's probable that big league hitters will be able to tee off on a few of his juicier offerings, but Meaux has a better chance to contribute at the major league level than any of the unpolished power arms that dominate the team's minor league relief ranks. The last name is pronounced "Mo," as in Money, or Vaughn.

ARNALDO MUNOZ Bats: L Throws: L Born: 21-Jun-82 Age: 22

YEAR	TM	LG	AGE	G	GS	IP	H	BB	SO	HR	ERA	EQERA	EQH9	EQBB9	EQSO9	EQHR9	PERA	VORP	STF
2001	KAN	SAL	19	60	0	79.7	41	42	115	2	2.48	4.26	7.2	7.3	8.0	0.5	4.37	10.1	29
2002	BIR	SOU	20	51	0	72.3	62	29	78	6	2.61	5.00	9.2	3.8	7.7	1.4	5.15	4.4	19
2003	CHR	INT	21	49	0	55.0	52	27	63	7	4.75	6.23	8.5	5.4	9.3	1.4	5.27	-3.6	22
2004	*CWS*	*AL*	*22*	*23*	*3*	*35.3*	*32*	*21*	*35*	*5*	*4.77*	*4.81*	*8.1*	*5.0*	*8.5*	*1.0*	*4.77*	*3.8*	*5*

Breakout: 7%   Improve: 47%   Collapse: 11%

Munoz generated a lot of buzz after a tremendous Winter League season in Venezuela in which he posted a 74:11 strikeout-to-walk ratio in 40 IP. The extra innings might have taken their toll, as his command regressed once he returned to the States; Munoz is taking the winter off this time around. He's still a good prospect, earning all sorts of superlatives with his big overhand curve, but the talk of making him a starter is premature, as his performance has declined in longer outings.

ENEMENCIO PACHECO Bats: R Throws: R Born: 31-Aug-78 Age: 25

YEAR	TM	LG	AGE	G	GS	IP	H	BB	SO	HR	ERA	EQERA	EQH9	EQBB9	EQSO9	EQHR9	PERA	VORP	STF
2001	ASH	SAL	22	7	7	36.3	38	9	34	0	4.21	6.19	12.1	3.4	4.8	0.3	5.27	-2.1	10
2001	SLM	CAR	22	27	3	42.3	55	18	29	4	4.68	8.76	14.4	5.6	3.9	2.2	9.03	-13.0	-64
2002	SLM	CAR	23	41	0	51.3	52	26	31	1	3.16	6.11	10.6	6.3	3.7	0.4	5.54	-2.6	-23
2002	WNS	CAR	23	8	4	24.7	31	8	24	1	4.74	7.89	14.1	4.2	6.2	0.8	6.92	-5.5	-13
2003	BIR	SOU	24	30	24	151.3	131	51	116	5	2.56	4.23	9.0	3.5	4.7	0.7	4.33	21.1	5
2004	*CWS*	*AL*	*25*	*17*	*10*	*55.7*	*63*	*26*	*31*	*7*	*5.27*	*5.31*	*10.2*	*4.0*	*4.8*	*0.9*	*5.41*	*2.7*	*-10*

Breakout: 26%   Improve: 52%   Collapse: 24%

Yes, kids, Enemencio is Spanish for Eminem! ¿Dónde está el baño? Pacheco improved his command substantially last season, but still rates as a fringe prospect, as he was old for his level, with a pedestrian strikeout rate. The Rox were willing to give him up for a couple of months of Sandy Alomar, a fact that spoke to their annoyance with his inability to develop a consistent second pitch. Pacheco has been added to the 40-man roster, but will need to follow up with another solid season to have a shot at a big league career.

JON RAUCH   Bats: R   Throws: R   Born: 27-Sep-78   Age: 25

YEAR	TM	LG	AGE	G	GS	IP	H	BB	SO	HR	ERA	EQERA	EQH9	EQBB9	EQSO9	EQHR9	PERA	VORP	STF
2001	CHR	INT	22	6	6	28.0	28	7	27	8	5.79	6.84	9.6	2.7	7.5	3.1	7.13	-3.6	-15
2002	CHR	INT	23	19	19	109.3	91	42	97	14	4.28	5.08	7.8	4.0	7.0	1.6	4.84	5.9	9
2002	CWS	AL	23	8	6	28.7	28	14	19	7	6.59	6.51	8.8	4.2	5.9	2.0	5.81	-2.8	-11
2003	CHR	INT	24	24	23	124.7	121	35	94	16	4.11	5.18	9.7	3.1	5.5	1.8	5.80	5.4	-15
2004	CWS	AL	25	21	14	83.0	83	34	59	15	5.14	5.18	9.0	3.5	6.1	1.3	4.97	5.6	0

Breakout: 22%   Improve: 40%   Collapse: 17%

Ever since Randy Johnson became Randy Johnson, baseball people have developed something of a fetish for very tall pitchers, a fact that obscures the hundreds of D'Amicos and Judens that litter the landscape. Height alone does not intrinsically provide a pitcher with an advantage; it can become an advantage if he's able to leverage it by throwing pitches from tricky angles or with tricky movement. That doesn't really describe Rauch, since while he stands at 6'11", his fastball is relatively flat, and as evidenced by his high HR rates, he has trouble fooling hitters. He's got good enough command and pitch selection to have a shot at being a #3 starter, but if it weren't for his tremendous height, he'd be a right-handed John Halama.

DAVID SANDERS   Bats: L   Throws: L   Born: 29-Aug-79   Age: 24

YEAR	TM	LG	AGE	G	GS	IP	H	BB	SO	HR	ERA	EQERA	EQH9	EQBB9	EQSO9	EQHR9	PERA	VORP	STF
2001	BIR	SOU	21	36	0	34.0	27	25	25	1	2.65	4.88	7.8	7.8	4.6	0.3	4.56	2.5	-2
2002	BIR	SOU	22	47	0	63.7	56	28	61	3	1.84	4.24	10.0	4.2	6.3	0.9	5.26	8.7	3
2003	CHR	INT	23	19	0	22.0	23	6	25	3	3.68	4.87	10.2	3.1	8.4	1.8	5.88	1.6	0
2003	CWS	AL	23	20	0	22.0	25	11	14	5	6.14	6.33	10.1	4.2	5.5	1.7	6.14	-1.2	-17
2004	CWS	AL	24	21	3	33.7	35	17	25	5	5.18	5.22	9.2	4.2	6.6	1.2	5.28	3.2	-6

Breakout: 25%   Improve: 55%   Collapse: 26%

Sanders was decidedly unimpressive in a three-month stint in the bigs, failing to demonstrate the command that you'd associate with a trusty reliever. That, of course, might have been predicted by the high walk rates that he'd posted in the minor leagues, but the small sample sizes associated with relief pitchers give every team its share of phantom prospects, and Sanders's ERA had been good at Birmingham. With Meaux and Munoz also in the organization, not to mention Wunsch and Marte, he may be buried.

SCOTT SCHOENEWEIS   Bats: L   Throws: L   Born: 02-Oct-73   Age: 30

YEAR	TM	LG	AGE	G	GS	IP	H	BB	SO	HR	ERA	EQERA	EQH9	EQBB9	EQSO9	EQHR9	PERA	VORP	STF
2001	ANA	AL	27	32	32	205.3	227	77	104	21	5.09	5.14	10.0	3.2	4.3	0.8	4.83	10.1	0
2002	ANA	AL	28	54	15	118.0	119	49	65	17	4.88	5.38	9.7	3.5	4.9	1.2	5.23	2.7	-19
2003	ANA	AL	29	39	0	38.7	37	10	29	2	3.95	3.86	8.7	2.2	6.8	0.5	3.57	6.2	17
2003	CWS	AL	29	20	0	26.0	26	9	27	1	4.50	4.32	9.4	2.9	9.4	0.4	3.91	1.4	33
2004	CWS	AL	30	41	8	72.0	75	27	49	9	4.55	4.59	9.4	3.2	5.9	0.9	4.61	10.1	-4

Breakout: 21%   Improve: 44%   Collapse: 28%

The Sox were expected to non-tender Schoeneweis, but reversed course at the last minute, apparently hoping that he'll be worth his arbitration payout if returned to a starter's role. It wasn't a bad thought, but Schoeneweis showed real potential as a reliever last year, upping his strikeout rate significantly while limiting left-handers to a .227/.293/.277 line. He isn't likely to match that PECOTA projection if left in the rotation, where his lack of a change-up leaves him exposed.

JOSH STEWART   Bats: L   Throws: L   Born: 05-Dec-78   Age: 25

YEAR	TM	LG	AGE	G	GS	IP	H	BB	SO	HR	ERA	EQERA	EQH9	EQBB9	EQSO9	EQHR9	PERA	VORP	STF
2001	BIR	SOU	22	16	16	82.3	110	42	47	7	6.67	8.96	13.4	5.4	3.5	1.3	7.52	-28.1	-31
2001	WNS	CAR	22	12	12	63.7	64	28	38	6	3.81	7.81	11.2	5.9	3.4	2.1	7.64	-13.6	-47
2002	BIR	SOU	23	26	26	150.3	145	56	92	11	3.53	5.52	10.6	3.7	4.1	1.4	5.93	1.2	-14
2003	CHR	INT	24	5	5	26.3	38	6	10	4	6.16	7.77	14.1	2.6	2.6	2.2	8.28	-5.9	-55
2003	CWS	AL	24	5	5	25.7	28	16	13	4	5.95	5.84	9.9	5.5	4.4	1.1	5.71	-0.8	-10
2004	CWS	AL	25	20	13	70.3	95	40	35	16	7.56	7.62	12.2	4.8	4.3	1.6	7.51	-6.9	-24

Breakout: 21%   Improve: 53%   Collapse: 25%

(continued next page)

Josh Stewart *(continued)*

Stewart's credentials as a prospect were specious to begin with, and after five bad starts in Chicago and a slew of injury troubles—including circulatory problems after a Jeff Conine line drive produced a blood clot in his shoulder—he'll likely have to content himself with Charlotte's high Waffle House-to-minor league pitcher ratio.

SCOTT SULLIVAN Bats: R Throws: R Born: 13-Mar-71 Age: 33

YEAR	TM	LG	AGE	G	GS	IP	H	BB	SO	HR	ERA	EQERA	EQH9	EQBB9	EQSO9	EQHR9	PERA	VORP	STF
2001	CIN	NL	30	79	0	103.3	94	36	82	10	3.31	3.60	8.1	2.9	6.0	0.7	3.76	22.2	6
2002	CIN	NL	31	71	0	78.7	93	31	78	15	6.06	6.37	10.8	3.1	7.7	1.7	6.07	-6.5	-19
2003	CIN	NL	32	50	0	49.7	39	26	43	4	3.62	3.72	7.1	4.3	6.9	0.7	3.71	9.1	5
2003	CWS	AL	32	15	0	14.3	9	6	13	2	3.78	3.21	5.8	3.9	7.7	1.3	3.52	3.5	4
2004	*KCR*	*AL*	*33*	*46*	*0*	*51.7*	*54*	*23*	*39*	*8*	*4.97*	*4.38*	*8.6*	*3.7*	*7.0*	*1.2*	*4.52*	*8.8*	*-2*

Breakout: 25%   Improve: 49%   Collapse: 24%

The brief stretch of time when the Sox had sidearmers Sullivan and Kelly Wunsch on the roster was a lot of fun, but it's looking more and more as though the four consecutive years of 100 IP that Sullivan endured from 1998–2001 have taken their toll, as 2003 featured the highest walk rate of his career. He's a riskier pickup than he appears for the Royals.

RYAN WING Bats: L Throws: L Born: 01-Feb-82 Age: 22

YEAR	TM	LG	AGE	G	GS	IP	H	BB	SO	HR	ERA	EQERA	EQH9	EQBB9	EQSO9	EQHR9	PERA	VORP	STF
2001	BRI	APP	19	1	0	1.0	1	0	2	0	9.00	0.00	13.5	0.0	13.5	0.0	4.51	0.4	97
2002	KAN	SAL	20	25	21	123.7	111	60	109	6	3.78	6.52	10.4	6.1	4.8	1.2	6.22	-11.0	-4
2003	WNS	CAR	21	26	26	145.0	116	67	107	9	2.98	5.57	9.6	5.6	4.8	1.5	6.09	0.4	-8
2004	*CWS*	*AL*	*22*	*11*	*7*	*36.7*	*45*	*28*	*22*	*8*	*7.75*	*7.82*	*11.1*	*6.6*	*5.3*	*1.6*	*7.66*	*-4.5*	*-25*

Breakout: 5%   Improve: 50%   Collapse: 29%

Wing is better liked by scouts than you'd guess from his raw numbers; they commend the movement on his cut fastball and an arm action that's tough on left-handed batters. We can't recommend him until he demonstrates better control.

DANNY WRIGHT Bats: R Throws: R Born: 14-Dec-77 Age: 26

YEAR	TM	LG	AGE	G	GS	IP	H	BB	SO	HR	ERA	EQERA	EQH9	EQBB9	EQSO9	EQHR9	PERA	VORP	STF
2001	BIR	SOU	23	20	20	134.0	112	41	128	6	2.82	4.41	9.0	3.2	5.8	0.7	4.21	16.2	20
2001	CWS	AL	23	13	12	66.3	78	39	36	12	5.70	6.02	10.6	4.9	4.6	1.4	6.25	-3.0	-8
2002	CWS	AL	24	33	33	196.3	200	71	136	32	5.18	5.09	9.3	3.0	6.0	1.3	5.02	10.7	9
2003	CWS	AL	25	20	15	86.3	91	46	47	16	6.15	5.83	9.5	4.6	4.9	1.5	5.78	-5.1	-22
2003	CHR	INT	25	8	7	33.0	25	10	25	5	4.64	4.75	7.7	3.3	5.6	2.1	5.17	2.9	-28
2004	*CWS*	*AL*	*26*	*24*	*18*	*102.0*	*109*	*45*	*65*	*17*	*5.44*	*5.49*	*9.6*	*3.8*	*5.5*	*1.2*	*5.32*	*3.9*	*-4*

Breakout: 22%   Improve: 43%   Collapse: 25%

We predicted last season that Wright was on the verge of a breakout, but instead he stumbled badly, undone by faulty command, a high gopher ball rate, and bouts of elbow soreness. He's a big, tall Texan who throws hard, so he'll probably get at least one more chance, but he hasn't shown much indication that he's a pitcher.

KELLY WUNSCH Bats: L Throws: L Born: 12-Jul-72 Age: 31

YEAR	TM	LG	AGE	G	GS	IP	H	BB	SO	HR	ERA	EQERA	EQH9	EQBB9	EQSO9	EQHR9	PERA	VORP	STF
2001	CWS	AL	28	33	0	22.3	21	9	16	4	7.67	5.82	8.3	3.3	6.2	1.2	4.53	-0.5	-14
2002	CHR	INT	29	10	2	12.0	13	5	9	0	2.25	4.09	10.6	4.9	5.7	0.0	4.73	1.8	4
2002	CWS	AL	29	50	0	31.7	26	19	22	3	3.41	3.52	7.6	5.0	6.2	0.9	4.31	7.1	-5
2003	CWS	AL	30	43	0	36.0	17	25	33	1	2.75	2.57	4.4	5.9	8.2	0.3	2.54	10.9	27
2004	*CWS*	*AL*	*31*	*43*	*0*	*46.7*	*42*	*25*	*38*	*5*	*4.38*	*4.42*	*8.0*	*4.5*	*7.0*	*0.8*	*4.48*	*6.8*	*-2*

Breakout: 26%   Improve: 49%   Collapse: 27%

We love the guy too, but in spite of the low ERA, it's clear that Wunsch isn't the same pitcher that he was before undergoing Tommy John Surgery in 2001. His Frisbees were really floating on him last season, especially toward the end of the year, and he spent time on the shelf with a muscle strain. Wunsch has consistently posted very low hit rates on balls in play against him; knuckleballers have been revealed to do especially well in that department, so one wonders whether sidearmers are capable of the same magic.

TETSU YOFU										**Bats: R**		**Throws: R**				**Born: 26-Jun-73**		**Age: 31**
YEAR	TM	LG	AGE	G	GS	IP	H	BB	SO	HR	ERA	EQERA	EQH9	EQBB9	EQSO9	EQHR9	PERA	VORP	STF
2003	BIR	SOU	30	29	20	131.0	117	37	114	8	3.50	4.90	10.1	3.0	5.4	1.3	5.35	9.2	-19
2004	CWS	AL	31	16	9	50.0	58	19	33	10	5.65	5.69	10.4	3.2	5.8	1.4	5.70	3.1	-6

Breakout: 24%   Improve: 53%   Collapse: 30%

He sounds like the villain from a poorly transliterated Nintendo game, but instead he's a Japanese-born pitcher who had been the staff ace of the Brother Elephants, Taiwan's most popular major league team, before coming to the U.S. Yofu isn't really a top prospect, but he throws strikes and mixes his pitches well enough to have a shot of breaking camp with the big club in a swingman role.

Cleveland Indians

Last year, we were pretty sunny on all things Cleveland, and it's easy to see why. Aside from the light at the end of the tunnel or whatever other tireless, tiresome literary devices might be employed, Mark Shapiro's charges hit bottom, and should be moving up.

They're a year into their long-overdue rebuilding project, and all's well, right? Young talent is getting broken in, and nobody else in the division resembles a burgeoning dynasty, not yet at any rate. The Twins and White Sox have failed to capitalize on their recent opportunities, and going forward seem determined to find new and interesting ways to come up short. The Royals' leap from 100 losses to contention has to be encouraging for the Indians, and while the Royals' group of young talent is slightly more advanced than Cleveland's they don't look like a powerhouse. If Allard Baird can whip up a competitive team that quickly, you'd think that Shapiro shouldn't be far behind. Another couple of years, and it's going to be just like John Hart's tremendously successful building-up of the franchise, right?

The problem is that the Tribe isn't really out of their trough, not yet. And although the people involved know their business, and the talent in the organization is very promising, there are a few flawed assumptions in play.

The first is that rebuilding projects simply work because you want them to; in reality, not all of them make it. History is littered with false starts. It's easy to chortle over Randy Smith's recent, disastrous attempt to rebuild the Tigers—a lot of analysts are guilty of schadenfreude when it comes to some guys. But the rebuilds of the Brewers in the mid-'80s or the A's during their brief Billyball rebound of '80–'81 didn't amount to much. The Royals thought they were going places in the late '80s, and the Twins and Pirates thought they were bouncing back well in the mid-'90s. The White Sox are currently stalled in one of the most exasperating and unsuccessful rebuilding efforts imaginable. Tribe fans should never forget the false promise that 1986 inspired.

All those teams had some young talent, and some featured some of the best players in the game. Every one of them wound up falling short of expectations.

It's important to remember rebuilding projects that didn't work, in part because we're operating in the post-*Moneyball* landscape. Beyond the real wisdom contained therein, there's the real-world problem that one size does

INDIANS PROSPECTUS

2003 record: 68–94; Fourth place, AL Central

Pythagenport record: 72–90

Runs scored per game: 4.3 (13th in AL)

Runs allowed per game: 4.8 (7th in AL)

Team EqA: .244 (13th in AL)

2003 Batters Age: 27.7 (3rd youngest in AL)

2003 Pitchers Age: 28.4 (6th youngest in AL)

Ballpark: Jacobs Field; Neutral park; Park Factor of 0.997

2003: One of the league's youngest organizations suffered through some acute growing pains.

2004: A promising future, but only some of the kids will to be ready to contribute this year.

not fit all. Only occasionally does a rebuilding project produce a crescendo nearly perfect as the Yankees of the early-to-mid '90s. It's easy for those of us in the analyst community to prescribe a commitment to simple ideas like scoring runs by getting on base, drafting college talent, being thrifty, buying low and sell high, and not overworking young pitchers. None of these ideas are particularly original; you can trace their roots to Branch Rickey or Connie Mack or Earl Weaver or Ben Franklin or J. P. Morgan, as you see fit.

Things are a bit messier and contingent in the real world, where there are no formulaic cycles. Critical elements of a team's core might not develop, or insist on getting out of Dodge to join some other team as soon as possible. Star pitchers flame out, and while modern surgical techniques seem to be able to resurrect almost anybody, it involves playing time lost and service time accrued. The inflationary engine of salary arbitration and the general accumulation of minor league talent create pressures on the bottom line and roster makeup that are more acute today, especially in an industry that's becoming more and more aggressively cannibalistic when it comes to talent. Combined, those factors make team construction an exercise in Darwinian selection and demand constant mutations in response to new adaptive pressures. That means accepting the idea that beyond a team's core, everyone else is interchangeable.

The other assumption is that this rebuilding project bears any resemblance to the contender Hart built. That team had a talented young outfield, and so does this one. After the acquisition on Omar Vizquel, that team had a middle infield combo that put runs on the board—remember how life was before A-Rod and the league's shortstop trinity?—and picking up Brandon Phillips was supposed to give this team a middle infield that puts runs on the board. That team had Sandy Alomar, always creaky, but snapping off a .500 slugging percentage once in a while to remind you what he was for; this team has Victor Martinez, who we considered one of the five best prospects in baseball going into 2003. Although the '90s Indians relied heavily on veteran starting pitchers like Dennis Martinez, Orel Hershiser, and Dave Burba, Hart's era also saw the system crank out Bartolo Colon, Charles Nagy, Chad Ogea, and Jaret Wright. Shapiro's Indians have promise in C. C. Sabathia, Jason Davis, and Cliff Lee. So we're supposedly comparing apples to apples, and this team's going places.

Not quite. These are not your older brother's Indians, at least not yet. A total of 68 wins doesn't sound so bad for a team hitting bottom. The problem is that the Indians followed Lou Boudreau's advice: They beat the snot out of the hapless Tigers and D-Rays, and managed a far less impressive 51–85 (a .375 winning percentage) against the real ballclubs. They didn't finish the year strong, instead getting cuffed around by their stronger divisional brethren.

There are other uninspiring indicators. Although the Indians finished fifth in the league in ERA, they were seventh in runs allowed. Blame a leaky defense, but with a ballpark that doesn't hurt the pitching staff, that's mediocre. Don't knock it—mediocrity is something the offense can aspire to. Fielding the worst lineup in the league not named the Tigers, this team is decisively different from the ones that Hart built. Shapiro likes to point out that before they were stars, the core of the Hart teams weren't great hitters, which technically isn't true, for a couple of reasons. The stars of the Hart teams were younger when they arrived, and came up with outstanding minor league track records. By comparison, this first Shapiro rebuild is already near its prime, and you can see how many wins that adds up to.

What went wrong with the lineup? First, there was Brandon Phillips's deafening implosion. Second base is a demanding enough position as is, and claims its share of victims to injury and stalled careers. Phillips was expected to be the perfect inheritor to the position of Robbie Alomar and Carlos Baerga, and instead made fans wonder whatever happened to good old Duane Kuiper. Phillips might get his career turned around, but if you were somebody who spent time waiting on Carlos Febles or Warren Morris or Brent Gates or Geronimo Pena in years past, you know how fragile greatness can be at the keystone. It doesn't help that Omar Vizquel is done and won't go, having first

rejected a trade, and failing a physical to put the kibosh on a subsequent trade attempt. It was so much easier to move aside Felix Fermin, back in the day.

Second, as promising as the Indians' current collection of raw materials is, the Hart Indians developed not just merely good major league players, but great ones. Start with the outfield. The five outfielders that the Shapiro's Indians have to sort through might seem like a good group on the face of it: Milton Bradley looks like a future very good player, Jody Gerut's here to stay, and between Coco Crisp, Alex Escobar, and Ryan Ludwick, you could reasonably expect that somebody's going to turn out well. That isn't the problem. What's impossible to overcome is that none of the outfielders on this Indians incarnation resembles a potentially great player, with Bradley the only one who projects to even come close.

Compare them to the devastating trio of Albert Belle, Manny Ramirez, and Kenny Lofton; nobody's even close in terms of enjoying comparable long term upside. Bradley is about to turn 26; at that age, Lofton was an established leadoff star, Ramirez had thwacked more than 100 home runs, and Belle was one of the game's top star sluggers. Gerut's already 27, which means he's useful now, but likely to be much less so in three or four years.

And that's the way it is with this team, pretty much across the board. Ben Broussard and Travis Hafner are nice players, and if they're playing second fiddle to some actual top-tier offensive star, they're assets. They're also both 27 already. It almost goes without saying that they're not going to grow up to be Jim Thome. The only hitter above A-ball who might develop into an offensive fulcrum is Victor Martinez, and the odds of that aren't all that good. Grady Sizemore, Jason Cooper, and Michael Aubrey look good, but won't arrive in time for them to step into a lineup that can count on most of today's regulars hitting their peak.

Where Shapiro's Indians deserve comparison with Hart's is in the front office. Just as Hart was crafty in his heyday, swinging a few good deals (and the more famously ill-advised ones of his later career), Shapiro has been able to add talent to the organization without surrendering too much in return. He got solid swag for Colon—much better than what Omar Minaya got for him—and if Phillips never develops and the Indians only get good work out of Sizemore and Cliff Lee, they still come out feeling good. Adding Gerut and Josh Bard for Karim Garcia—perennial minor league free agent Karim Garcia!—was a particularly nifty piece of work. If there was a misstep, it was not trading Danys Baez down the stretch last year, but hindsight's 20–20, and at the time they felt they might keep him. Shapiro has proven he can do some quality talent mining. As long as he doesn't strut Bowden-style, he should be able to continue to add talent when opportunities present themselves.

The other aspect of Shapiro's administration that deserves credit is the outstanding player development system that he's put together. From his early start at Hart's side, Shapiro tried to institute some changes; the results were mixed, and the drafts produced guys like Scott Pratt and Zach Sorensen and Jon Hamilton. Shapiro seems to have learned from the experience. His staff—Assistant GM Chris Antonetti, farm director John Farrell, and scouting director John Mirabelli—are doing an outstanding job of assembling talent through the draft, while also keeping a collective toe in international waters. Although the offensive talent seems merely good, the breadth and depth of pitching in the organization holds the promise of producing a better staff than any the Hart regime home-brewed. As part of a general trend in the industry, the Indians seem to favor command, but they're not relying on a formula of only gunning for college pitchers, seeking value first and foremost. You need to look everywhere for pitching, and a number of their farmhands are international draftees or high school products.

The Indians' ability to accumulate talent is already placing pressure on the organization from below. While the winter meetings were a debacle for the Pirates, the Indians were also bloodied. Rule 5 cost them Hector Luna, Willy Taveras, lefty Matt White, flamethrower Lino Urdaneta, and five other bodies. Although there were a couple of noggin-scratchers on the 40-man roster (Jack Cressend? Tim Laker?), there wasn't much to be done overall to prevent the pillaging. It's the penalty for running a good farm system, and it's easier for other teams to interpret minor league stats than it is to scout and project amateur talent.

The real problem here is expectations, created by unfair comparisons and a few too many worst-to-first Cinderella stories in recent memory. The Indians aren't going to pounce on the division the way the Royals did. They're not poised to challenge the current troika above them in the standings. They're making progress, but it's going to be slow going, and the results aren't guaranteed. Building a pitching pipeline to the majors is sensible; pitching is always the bartering chip of choice, and dealing from depth has given the Braves remarkable staying power. It's easier to assemble a good lineup than a good pitching staff, so as long as Shapiro doesn't get too caught up on the virtues of today's lineup, they may eventually challenge. It's just going to take a while.

HITTERS

MIKE AUBREY   1B   Bats: L   Throws: L   Born: 15-Apr-82   Age: 22

YEAR	TM	LG	AGE	AB	H	2B	3B	HR	BB	SO	SB	CS	AVG	OBP	SLG	MLVR	EQBA	EQOBP	EQSLG	EQMLVR	VORP	DEFENSE
2003	LKC	SAL	21	138	48	13	0	5	14	22	0	0	.348	.409	.551	.469	.264	.314	.438	-.055	1.2	37-1B 3
2004	CLE	AL	22	260	62	15	0	7	19	50	0	0	.239	.290	.375	-.166	.248	.302	.406	-.128	-1.6	69-1B -3

Breakout: 15%   Improve: 34%   Collapse: 41%

The Tribe's top pick of 2003, Aubrey was labeled the best college hitter available after Rickie Weeks. While they didn't rush him up to the big leagues in some desperate ploy to inspire hope, to their credit, the Tribe didn't stick him in a short-season league either. They let him face kids in Low-A, and he predictably drubbed them. The Indians like to do mid-season promotions, so Cap'n Jack could wind up in Double-A in pretty short order. If he isn't on big league radar in 2005, something will have gone amiss.

JOSH BARD   C   Bats: B   Throws: R   Born: 30-Mar-78   Age: 26

YEAR	TM	LG	AGE	AB	H	2B	3B	HR	BB	SO	SB	CS	AVG	OBP	SLG	MLVR	EQBA	EQOBP	EQSLG	EQMLVR	VORP	DEFENSE
2001	CAR	SOU	23	124	32	13	0	1	19	23	0	1	.258	.359	.387	.036	.219	.303	.336	-.249	-3.3	35-C 3
2001	AKR	EAS	23	194	54	11	0	4	16	27	0	0	.278	.338	.397	.047	.246	.299	.357	-.211	-2.3	40-C 1
2002	BUF	INT	24	344	102	26	2	6	20	45	0	0	.297	.332	.436	.082	.277	.319	.419	-.062	11.1	93-C 2
2002	CLE	AL	24	90	20	5	0	3	4	13	0	0	.222	.255	.378	-.220	.233	.274	.411	-.192	-0.4	23-C 2
2003	CLE	AL	25	303	74	13	1	8	22	53	0	2	.244	.293	.373	-.163	.263	.315	.401	-.107	-1.5	81-C 7
2003	BUF	INT	25	115	38	7	0	5	14	17	1	2	.330	.408	.522	.344	.299	.373	.487	.150	11.9	29-C 2
2004	CLE	AL	26	303	74	17	1	7	24	48	1	1	.245	.302	.380	-.135	.255	.314	.412	-.094	9.6	81-C 1

Breakout: 25%   Improve: 41%   Collapse: 36%

Suddenly no longer the big part of the Jacob Cruz deal of '99, but still a bit of an organizational favorite for his hustle and his catching skills. Bard still struggles to hit breaking stuff, and will probably never hit well enough to stick as a regular, not unless you're using the Matheny Scale. He will make a fine part-time player, sharing the job with Victor Martinez until Martinez hits well enough to claim an even larger share of the at-bats.

CASEY BLAKE   **3B**   **Bats: R**   **Throws: R**   Born: 23-Aug-73   Age: 30

YEAR	TM	LG	AGE	AB	H	2B	3B	HR	BB	SO	SB	CS	AVG	OBP	SLG	MLVR	EQBA	EQOBP	EQSLG	EQMLVR	VORP	DEFENSE			
2001	EDM	PCL	27	375	116	24	6	10	34	66	14	3	.309	.376	.485	.158	.271	.335	.426	-.028	17.0	82-3B	-1		
2001	MIN	AL	27	22	7	1	0	0	3	8	1	0	.318	.400	.364	.065	.318	.400	.409	.106	1.4				
2001	BAL	AL	27	15	2	0	0	1	1	4	2	0	.133	.188	.333	-.466	.133	.187	.400	-.441	-1.2				
2002	EDM	PCL	28	482	149	25	3	19	54	78	24	9	.309	.383	.492	.209	.271	.342	.435	-.003	26.6	110-3B	1		
2002	MIN	AL	28	20	4	1	0	0	2	7	0	0	.200	.273	.250	-.372	.200	.273	.300	-.369	-1.3				
2003	CLE	AL	29	557	143	35	0	17	38	109	7	9	.257	.312	.411	-.067	.275	.334	.445	.000	9.2	132-3B	8	15-1B	2
2004	CLE	AL	30	405	100	22	2	10	33	76	7	3	.246	.307	.384	-.121	.255	.320	.416	-.079	12.8	107-3B	0		

Breakout: 12%   Improve: 41%   Collapse: 29%

I suppose if Blake wasn't so busy explaining to Clevelanders that he was the team's third baseman, he might have had a really big year, because 15 of his 17 home runs were hit on the road. That's one of those fun fluky stats, not an indication that Blake's ever going to pop 30. He and Tom Evans came up through the Jays' chain around the same time, and statheads generally pegged Evans as the one who might make it. Instead, it was Blake who finally got a chance, and did a thoroughly adequate job with his first shot at a regular major league job. With Corey Smith and Matt Whitney's troubles, Blake might actually have a surprising bit of job security, at least for 2004.

MILTON BRADLEY   **CF**   **Bats: B**   **Throws: R**   Born: 15-Apr-78   Age: 26

YEAR	TM	LG	AGE	AB	H	2B	3B	HR	BB	SO	SB	CS	AVG	OBP	SLG	MLVR	EQBA	EQOBP	EQSLG	EQMLVR	VORP	DEFENSE			
2001	MON	NL	23	220	49	16	3	1	19	62	7	4	.223	.287	.336	-.267	.221	.285	.338	-.281	-8.4	52-CF	0	13-LF	0
2001	OTT	INT	23	136	37	7	2	2	23	30	14	1	.272	.383	.397	.096	.257	.359	.379	-.058	3.9	34-CF	0		
2001	BUF	INT	23	114	29	3	0	5	19	31	9	2	.254	.361	.412	.066	.231	.333	.385	-.118	1.1	27-CF	-2		
2001	CLE	AL	23	18	4	1	0	0	2	3	1	1	.222	.300	.278	-.287	.222	.300	.333	-.258	-0.6				
2002	CLE	AL	24	325	81	18	3	9	32	58	6	3	.249	.317	.406	-.054	.266	.335	.434	-.021	11.0	91-CF	-6		
2003	CLE	AL	25	377	121	34	2	10	64	73	17	7	.321	.421	.501	.297	.345	.448	.542	.397	45.7	93-CF	0		
2004	CLE	AL	26	424	113	24	3	11	54	80	14	5	.266	.350	.418	.011	.276	.365	.453	.064	21.2	115-CF	-1		

Breakout: 5%   Improve: 31%   Collapse: 30%

Not that he's going anywhere, but Giants fans with a sense of nostalgia should take to Milton; he's gifted with both Chili Davis's promise at the plate and Jeff Leonard's ability to scare the bejeezus out of whitey. After two years marred by nagging hurts, a healthy Bradley is poised to surprise some people with what he can do over a full season. He's not a young maybe anymore, but last year was the first one to hint at the talent many have expected. He faces criminal charges, essentially for not showing much respect to the boys in blue—the ones in patrol cars, not calling balls or strikes—during a traffic stop. It probably falls short of earning him any street cred, but at least he was in character.

BEN BROUSSARD   **1B**   **Bats: L**   **Throws: L**   Born: 24-Sep-76   Age: 27

YEAR	TM	LG	AGE	AB	H	2B	3B	HR	BB	SO	SB	CS	AVG	OBP	SLG	MLVR	EQBA	EQOBP	EQSLG	EQMLVR	VORP	DEFENSE			
2001	MUD	CAL	24	102	25	5	0	5	16	31	0	0	.245	.360	.441	.115	.189	.282	.349	-.291	-6.9	30-1B	1		
2001	CHT	SOU	24	353	113	27	0	23	61	69	10	3	.320	.428	.592	.451	.258	.351	.479	.063	18.1	92-1B	-7		
2002	LOU	INT	25	187	51	14	1	11	31	50	4	1	.273	.396	.535	.276	.242	.362	.484	.075	9.3	43-1B	-1		
2002	BUF	INT	25	153	37	8	0	5	24	30	0	0	.242	.354	.392	.018	.224	.329	.372	-.147	-4.5	18-LF	-1	16-RF	0
2002	CLE	AL	25	112	27	4	0	4	7	25	0	0	.241	.292	.384	-.134	.265	.313	.416	-.087	-1.0	25-LF	-2		
2003	BUF	INT	26	120	30	2	1	3	9	29	3	0	.250	.303	.358	-.101	.240	.296	.347	-.235	-5.6	23-1B	1		
2003	CLE	AL	26	386	96	21	3	16	32	75	5	2	.249	.312	.443	-.029	.266	.332	.475	.031	3.9	101-1B	-2		
2004	CLE	AL	27	381	92	19	2	14	39	81	6	2	.242	.319	.413	-.065	.251	.332	.447	-.019	10.0	103-1B	0		

Breakout: 25%   Improve: 46%   Collapse: 16%

Once upon a time, or right around this time two years ago, BP was coming off of a particularly bitter internal debate on the virtues of Ken Harvey. It got rough, perhaps a bit unnecessarily, with people who like Harvey pointing out he could be something special, while others pointed out he might grow up to be the illegitimate love child of Pat Tabler and Floyd Rayford, with less defensive skill than either parent. One riposte pointed out that if Harvey was a prospect, so was Broussard, which is sort of like trumping Pat Tabler with a Greg Brock reference: It's not really a trump, and all it does is reflect on how silly the debate was. Harvey might grow up to be Bill Madlock, with less defensive skill, and Broussard might grow up to be Paul Sorrento. Don't hold your breath on either's account. You could pass out or choke on a pretzel or something.

ELLIS BURKS   DH   Bats: R   Throws: R   Born: 11-Sep-64   Age: 39

YEAR	TM	LG	AGE	AB	H	2B	3B	HR	BB	SO	SB	CS	AVG	OBP	SLG	MLVR	EQBA	EQOBP	EQSLG	EQMLVR	VORP	DEFENSE	
2001	CLE	AL	36	439	123	29	1	28	62	85	5	1	.280	.369	.542	.225	.297	.391	.580	.307	42.9	13-LF	0
2002	CLE	AL	37	518	156	28	0	32	44	108	2	3	.301	.362	.541	.246	.323	.383	.581	.327	62.1		
2003	CLE	AL	38	198	52	11	1	6	27	46	1	1	.263	.360	.419	.015	.281	.377	.452	.092	7.1		
2004	*CLE*	*AL*	*39*	*297*	*77*	*17*	*1*	*13*	*36*	*64*	*2*	*1*	*.261*	*.344*	*.449*	*.035*	*.271*	*.358*	*.486*	*.091*	*16.2*		

Breakout: 4%   Improve: 58%   Collapse: 17%

As classy an act as Burks is, he's close to done. In part, it's because the world isn't sympathetic to DHs who struggle to slug .400. But a more basic problem is that as of early January, every AL team had a starting DH in place, and while someone like Oakland could use a right-handed bat off the bench, it's hard to fit a backup DH into today's rosters.

RYAN CHURCH   OF   Bats: L   Throws: L   Born: 14-Oct-78   Age: 25

YEAR	TM	LG	AGE	AB	H	2B	3B	HR	BB	SO	SB	CS	AVG	OBP	SLG	MLVR	EQBA	EQOBP	EQSLG	EQMLVR	VORP	DEFENSE			
2001	CGA	SAL	22	363	104	23	3	17	54	79	4	6	.287	.385	.507	.298	.206	.285	.373	-.242	-21.5	96-RF	3		
2001	KIN	CAR	22	83	20	7	0	5	18	23	1	0	.241	.379	.506	.271	.178	.291	.378	-.241	-5.0	13-RF	-1		
2002	KIN	CAR	23	181	59	12	1	10	31	51	4	4	.326	.433	.569	.472	.243	.334	.434	-.041	1.5	33-RF	-3	11-CF	-2
2002	AKR	EAS	23	291	86	17	4	12	12	58	1	0	.296	.325	.505	.171	.259	.284	.454	-.091	4.7	37-CF	2	31-RF	2
2003	AKR	EAS	24	371	97	17	3	13	32	64	4	3	.261	.325	.429	.029	.223	.277	.378	-.240	-19.7	82-RF	0	16-CF	2
2004	*MON*	*NL*	*25*	*182*	*47*	*10*	*1*	*8*	*17*	*39*	*2*	*1*	*.256*	*.324*	*.465*	*.007*	*.241*	*.307*	*.429*	*-.094*	*1.4*	*51-RF*	*2*		

Breakout: 46%   Improve: 58%   Collapse: 23%

Church isn't a sleeper as much as very underrated. He's got a great arm, and he can hit most of the people most of the time. His problem is that he can't hit lefties, and shouldn't be in the lineup against them. It's OK for Akron—after all, the minors are there to find out what people can't do as much as finding out what they can. Church could be the next Trot Nixon, without the hype, and that's handy. He's an outstanding pickup for the Expos, especially since that projection makes no allowance for his platoon splits.

JASON COOPER   LF   Bats: L   Throws: L   Born: 06-Dec-80   Age: 23

YEAR	TM	LG	AGE	AB	H	2B	3B	HR	BB	SO	SB	CS	AVG	OBP	SLG	MLVR	EQBA	EQOBP	EQSLG	EQMLVR	VORP	DEFENSE	
2002	CGA	SAL	21	55	14	5	0	4	6	17	0	0	.255	.339	.564	.272	.193	.251	.421	-.251	-2.2		
2003	LKC	SAL	22	263	78	17	7	12	32	52	3	2	.297	.385	.551	.388	.228	.291	.431	-.136	-6.9	57-LF	-3
2003	KIN	CAR	22	218	67	17	2	9	25	46	3	0	.307	.380	.528	.340	.244	.305	.431	-.098	-3.1	36-LF	-2
2004	*CLE*	*AL*	*23*	*267*	*62*	*15*	*2*	*9*	*23*	*64*	*2*	*1*	*.231*	*.296*	*.396*	*-.133*	*.240*	*.309*	*.429*	*-.092*	*0.8*	*72-LF*	*-4*

Breakout: 30%   Improve: 64%   Collapse: 18%

It might seem a bit goofy to see a guy from Stanford in the Sally League, but the Indians had Cooper go back to his old high school hitting style after a moderately disappointing college career as a slugger. The new stance helped him generate much better power, and now he's a college-experienced hitter with a shot to move up fast.

COCO CRISP   OF   Bats: B   Throws: R   Born: 01-Nov-79   Age: 24

YEAR	TM	LG	AGE	AB	H	2B	3B	HR	BB	SO	SB	CS	AVG	OBP	SLG	MLVR	EQBA	EQOBP	EQSLG	EQMLVR	VORP	DEFENSE			
2001	POT	CAR	21	530	162	23	3	11	52	64	39	21	.306	.368	.423	.185	.242	.298	.348	-.229	-29.9	124-LF	-6	11-CF	-1
2002	NHV	EAS	22	355	107	16	1	9	36	56	26	10	.301	.365	.428	.146	.264	.319	.380	-.128	2.1	79-CF	2		
2002	CLE	AL	22	127	33	9	2	1	11	19	4	1	.260	.314	.386	-.078	.281	.338	.414	-.031	3.9	31-CF	-2		
2003	BUF	INT	23	225	81	19	6	1	26	24	20	8	.360	.434	.511	.397	.328	.402	.472	.207	25.3	51-CF	5		
2003	CLE	AL	23	414	110	15	6	3	23	51	15	9	.266	.302	.353	-.159	.284	.325	.378	-.105	-8.2	49-CF	-4	39-LF	2
2004	*CLE*	*AL*	*24*	*452*	*119*	*22*	*4*	*7*	*37*	*59*	*18*	*6*	*.263*	*.321*	*.376*	*-.096*	*.273*	*.334*	*.407*	*-.052*	*7.4*	*118-CF*	*-3*		

Breakout: 25%   Improve: 46%   Collapse: 26%

Crisp showed improved command of the strike zone in the first half in Buffalo, working counts and doing those lead-off things that could make him a very rich man. The problem is that Crisp's improvement was to get up to walking in almost 10% of his plate appearances, or the cusp of respectability; once brought up, he went back to flailing. His arm isn't going to help him stay in center, and until he shows any ability to really take command of the strike zone, he's more Thomas Howard than Kenny Lofton.

ALEX ESCOBAR   OF   Bats: R   Throws: R   Born: 06-Sep-78   Age: 25

YEAR	TM	LG	AGE	AB	H	2B	3B	HR	BB	SO	SB	CS	AVG	OBP	SLG	MLVR	EQBA	EQOBP	EQSLG	EQMLVR	VORP	DEFENSE		
2001	NOR	INT	22	397	106	21	4	12	35	146	18	3	.267	.327	.431	.054	.257	.316	.420	-.083	8.1	78-CF	-1	22-RF -2
2001	NYM	NL	22	50	10	1	0	3	3	19	1	0	.200	.245	.400	-.258	.216	.259	.412	-.231	-1.4			
2003	BUF	INT	24	439	110	21	2	24	24	133	8	3	.251	.296	.472	.038	.236	.286	.454	-.107	-5.5	89-RF	-4	
2003	CLE	AL	24	99	27	2	0	5	7	33	1	0	.273	.324	.444	.014	.293	.351	.475	.090	1.8	25-RF	4	
2004	CLE	AL	25	298	72	16	1	11	23	83	5	2	.241	.302	.418	-.089	.251	.314	.453	-.043	6.2	80-RF	0	

Breakout: 26%   Improve: 58%   Collapse: 29%

Escobar still has power, and still has a great arm, but he's lost two of the last five years to injuries. The knee injury that cost him 2002 was not a problem in 2003, and despite his problems, he should be a little more durable than his main competition for the open job in an outfield corner, either Lawton or Ludwick. He has the arm for right, and a healthy amount of power. You might want to compare him to Ellis Valentine for those things, but Valentine had cracked almost 80 home runs in the big leagues by the age that Escobar's at now.

JODY GERUT   OF   Bats: L   Throws: L   Born: 18-Sep-77   Age: 26

YEAR	TM	LG	AGE	AB	H	2B	3B	HR	BB	SO	SB	CS	AVG	OBP	SLG	MLVR	EQBA	EQOBP	EQSLG	EQMLVR	VORP	DEFENSE		
2002	AKR	EAS	24	256	72	15	2	9	34	30	17	8	.281	.368	.461	.161	.234	.307	.395	-.151	-0.3	54-CF	-3	
2002	BUF	INT	24	183	59	7	2	1	23	20	3	5	.322	.401	.399	.162	.296	.372	.371	-.017	7.4	28-CF	2	17-LF 1
2003	BUF	INT	25	65	18	5	0	5	11	11	4	0	.277	.377	.585	.327	.254	.351	.537	.138	5.7			
2003	CLE	AL	25	480	134	33	2	22	35	70	4	5	.279	.336	.494	.108	.301	.358	.535	.195	19.1	61-RF	3	36-LF -1
2004	CLE	AL	26	476	126	28	2	16	44	69	8	4	.265	.331	.435	.000	.275	.345	.471	.053	17.3	125-RF	2	

Breakout: 15%   Improve: 42%   Collapse: 27%

After losing 2001 to a knee injury, he was tossed into the '02 deal for Karim Garcia. His response to a fourth outfielder label was an intense conditioning program. That's what really happens to fourth outfielders when they get the label early on: They either stay in Triple-A, or they win big league jobs, but they very rarely graduate to fourth outfielderdom before they're pushing 30. Gerut showed enough power to stick as a regular, not as a star, but not as a fourth either. Although he doesn't get talked up for it (beat writers generally chat up veterans, or rely on old relationships), he's one of the brightest players in the game today.

RICKY GUTIERREZ   IF   Bats: R   Throws: R   Born: 23-May-70   Age: 34

YEAR	TM	LG	AGE	AB	H	2B	3B	HR	BB	SO	SB	CS	AVG	OBP	SLG	MLVR	EQBA	EQOBP	EQSLG	EQMLVR	VORP	DEFENSE	
2001	CHC	NL	31	528	153	23	3	10	40	56	4	3	.290	.345	.402	-.011	.299	.356	.412	.014	31.7	139-SS	-5
2002	CLE	AL	32	353	97	13	0	4	20	48	0	1	.275	.325	.346	-.102	.298	.347	.376	-.055	10.9	91-2B	-4
2003	BUF	INT	33	65	19	2	1	0	4	5	4	1	.292	.338	.354	-.020	.277	.335	.338	-.148	-0.4		
2003	CLE	AL	33	50	13	3	0	0	3	5	0	0	.260	.309	.320	-.195	.280	.331	.360	-.122	-0.3		
2004	CLE	AL	34	225	58	10	1	2	16	27	3	1	.259	.317	.342	-.150	.269	.330	.371	-.111	9.0	62-SS	-5

Breakout: 27%   Improve: 48%   Collapse: 34%

It might be a point of pride that he isn't going to let his potentially crippling neck injury end his career, and with $4 million still coming his way in 2004, he's gamely talking up his chances of claiming the job at second base. It might be mean-spirited to mention, but he was in decline before he signed with the Tribe, and his defensive shortcomings should be the last thing they want to inflict on a young staff.

TRAVIS HAFNER   1B   Bats: L   Throws: R   Born: 03-Jun-77   Age: 27

YEAR	TM	LG	AGE	AB	H	2B	3B	HR	BB	SO	SB	CS	AVG	OBP	SLG	MLVR	EQBA	EQOBP	EQSLG	EQMLVR	VORP	DEFENSE	
2001	TUL	TEX	24	323	91	25	0	20	59	82	3	1	.282	.396	.545	.301	.227	.326	.441	-.059	2.6	78-1B	-4
2002	OKL	PCL	25	401	137	22	1	21	79	76	2	1	.342	.463	.559	.483	.298	.406	.493	.214	37.1	62-1B	-2
2002	TEX	AL	25	62	15	4	1	1	8	15	0	1	.242	.329	.387	-.078	.258	.343	.419	-.033	1.5		
2003	BUF	INT	26	100	27	4	0	2	25	26	2	1	.270	.421	.370	.125	.240	.376	.346	-.080	0.1	24-1B	-1
2003	CLE	AL	26	291	74	19	3	14	22	81	2	1	.254	.327	.485	.058	.274	.343	.527	.131	11.9	39-1B	-2
2004	CLE	AL	27	369	93	20	1	15	47	88	3	1	.252	.344	.436	.012	.261	.358	.472	.065	19.4	101-1B	-2

Breakout: 16%   Improve: 36%   Collapse: 28%

(continued next page)

Travis Hafner (*continued*)

Burdened with high expectations from people like us, Hafner struggled at the start, earned a trip to go see a Buffalo summer, made adjustments, and earned a recall. The only person who might not be happy about that could be Ben Broussard, but Hafner's tireless when it comes to making himself a better hitter. Last year put a dent in his career, but that projection doesn't allow for his hitting after he came back (.273/.348/.519) or his value as a platoon hitter (he slugged .541 against right-handers on the year). He'll continue to share the duties at first and DH with Broussard for the next year, but the odds of both being part of the next Tribe contender are remote.

JOE INGLETT — 2B — Bats: L — Throws: R — Born: 29-Jun-78 — Age: 26

YEAR	TM	LG	AGE	AB	H	2B	3B	HR	BB	SO	SB	CS	AVG	OBP	SLG	MLVR	EQBA	EQOBP	EQSLG	EQMLVR	VORP	DEFENSE		
2001	CGA	SAL	23	237	71	9	2	2	24	22	5	3	.300	.361	.380	.122	.231	.283	.296	-.338	-12.4	52-2B -3		
2002	CGA	SAL	24	235	73	18	5	2	28	25	5	3	.311	.389	.455	.247	.231	.292	.355	-.238	-4.4	33-3B -1	13-2B	-4
2002	KIN	CAR	24	238	67	12	0	0	29	38	5	2	.282	.362	.332	.033	.232	.297	.280	-.331	-11.8	54-2B 0		
2003	KIN	CAR	25	85	28	10	1	0	20	14	1	0	.329	.454	.471	.378	.244	.349	.367	-.102	2.3	17-2B 2		
2003	AKR	EAS	25	276	78	16	1	4	37	36	1	2	.283	.377	.391	.077	.237	.318	.337	-.208	-2.9	66-2B -6		
2004	CLE	AL	26	159	37	8	1	2	14	25	1	1	.231	.302	.326	-.213	.240	.314	.353	-.180	2.2	46-2B -4		

Breakout: 36%   Improve: 50%   Collapse: 33%

Inglett is an on-base pest drafted out of the University of Nevada-Reno in 2000. He's slowly slid into the career of an organizational soldier, struggling to get noticed amidst the organization's bevy of shortstops. With Ron Belliard coming in, you could foresee his having value as a lefty alternative, but he's not a platoon hitter. Still, Craig Counsell came from somewhere, and it wasn't until he was almost 27. If Inglett keeps getting on base, he'll get up at some point.

TIM LAKER — C — Bats: R — Throws: R — Born: 27-Nov-69 — Age: 34

YEAR	TM	LG	AGE	AB	H	2B	3B	HR	BB	SO	SB	CS	AVG	OBP	SLG	MLVR	EQBA	EQOBP	EQSLG	EQMLVR	VORP	DEFENSE		
2001	BUF	INT	31	320	79	13	0	20	28	53	2	1	.247	.314	.475	.064	.231	.296	.451	-.097	7.5	78-C -4		
2001	CLE	AL	31	33	6	0	0	1	6	8	0	0	.182	.308	.273	-.295	.212	.333	.303	-.237	-1.0			
2002	BUF	INT	32	216	49	10	0	4	21	52	2	0	.227	.303	.329	-.159	.216	.288	.317	-.307	-8.7	30-C -2	18-1B	-1
2003	CLE	AL	33	162	39	11	0	3	9	38	2	2	.241	.281	.364	-.199	.259	.302	.395	-.142	-2.1	43-C -1		
2004	CLE	AL	34	181	41	8	0	5	15	43	2	1	.225	.292	.357	-.194	.234	.304	.387	-.159	1.6	51-C -4		

Breakout: 47%   Improve: 55%   Collapse: 30%

Laker's got slightly more pop than your average backup, but he isn't Todd Pratt. Normally, you'd expect the Devil Rays to have wildly overpaid him by now, but Brook Fordyce won that particular jackpot. Instead, Laker gets the full benefit of being frequently mistaken for Tom Prince, and sometimes Mark Parent.

MATT LAWTON — OF — Bats: L — Throws: R — Born: 03-Nov-71 — Age: 32

YEAR	TM	LG	AGE	AB	H	2B	3B	HR	BB	SO	SB	CS	AVG	OBP	SLG	MLVR	EQBA	EQOBP	EQSLG	EQMLVR	VORP	DEFENSE		
2001	MIN	AL	29	376	110	25	0	10	63	46	19	6	.293	.396	.439	.138	.308	.413	.467	.200	28.1	85-RF 3		
2001	NYM	NL	29	183	45	11	1	3	22	34	10	2	.246	.352	.366	-.067	.262	.360	.390	-.038	1.4	47-RF -1		
2002	CLE	AL	30	416	98	19	2	15	59	34	8	9	.236	.342	.399	-.028	.260	.361	.440	.030	11.0	85-RF -2	23-LF	0
2003	CLE	AL	31	374	93	19	0	15	47	47	10	3	.249	.343	.420	-.006	.271	.364	.463	.076	5.4	55-LF -1	11-RF	-1
2004	CLE	AL	32	353	88	18	1	10	47	47	8	3	.249	.345	.393	-.042	.258	.359	.425	.005	10.0	98-LF -1		

Breakout: 24%   Improve: 59%   Collapse: 20%

Lawton gets sympathy for his fall from goodness, but not a lot; that's the way people let salaries pervert their sense of cosmic injustice. The shoulder injury that ruined his 2002 came at a time when non-stars normally decline. As an athletic player and superb glove, you could have reasonably hoped that Lawton would age gracefully. He managed to get back from his shoulder early, only to break down with a dislocated finger. He's also required knee surgery, but he's supposed to be healthy in camp. He's not a joke in the outfield and he can still get on base against and occasionally hurt right-handed pitching, so he still has value. It's sad to think on 1998 or 2000, when he might have been the most underrated player in the game, only to be thoughtlessly discarded to the Mets later.

RYAN LUDWICK

OF **Bats: R** **Throws: L** Born: 13-Jul-78 Age: 25

YEAR	TM	LG	AGE	AB	H	2B	3B	HR	BB	SO	SB	CS	AVG	OBP	SLG	MLVR	EQBA	EQOBP	EQSLG	EQMLVR	VORP	DEFENSE			
2001	MID	TEX	22	443	119	23	3	25	56	113	9	10	.269	.356	.503	.148	.213	.290	.404	-.186	-5.3	115-CF	-11		
2002	OKL	PCL	23	305	87	27	4	15	38	76	2	2	.285	.370	.548	.264	.256	.333	.495	.052	17.8	54-CF	-5	22-RF	-2
2002	TEX	AL	23	81	19	6	0	1	7	24	2	1	.235	.295	.346	-.195	.247	.307	.370	-.177	-0.6	14-CF	1		
2003	OKL	PCL	24	317	96	24	3	17	33	71	1	1	.303	.372	.558	.318	.272	.342	.512	.106	16.6	50-RF	-2		
2003	TEX	AL	24	26	4	1	0	0	4	9	0	0	.154	.267	.192	-.517	.154	.267	.231	-.492	-3.3				
2003	CLE	AL	24	136	36	7	1	7	8	39	2	0	.265	.306	.485	.032	.279	.324	.515	.087	3.4	19-RF	2	13-LF	0
2004	CLE	AL	25	292	70	17	1	11	29	72	2	1	.240	.313	.418	-.072	.249	.325	.452	-.025	8.5	79-RF	2		

Breakout: 25%   Improve: 50%   Collapse: 28%

You could believe both sides were pleased by the Ludwick for Ricardo Rodriguez deal, except both guys got hurt, squelching any early start to bragging rights. Ludwick had off-season knee surgery, but he's expected to be healthy by spring training. Still, persistent questions about his hip should temper people's enthusiasm for his shot at becoming an everyday player. As another good glove with decent power amidst the Tribe's small horde of the similarly useful, Ludwick will have to fight for at-bats.

HECTOR LUNA

SS **Bats: R** **Throws: R** Born: 01-Feb-80 Age: 24

YEAR	TM	LG	AGE	AB	H	2B	3B	HR	BB	SO	SB	CS	AVG	OBP	SLG	MLVR	EQBA	EQOBP	EQSLG	EQMLVR	VORP	DEFENSE	
2001	CGA	SAL	21	241	64	8	3	3	23	48	15	4	.266	.339	.361	.047	.208	.267	.288	-.393	-14.7	63-SS	4
2002	KIN	CAR	22	468	129	15	6	11	39	79	32	11	.276	.334	.404	.082	.228	.275	.351	-.278	-10.9	122-SS	-7
2003	AKR	EAS	23	462	137	19	2	2	48	64	17	5	.297	.368	.359	.029	.256	.317	.316	-.227	-3.5	125-SS	-15
2004	STL	NL	24	231	56	11	1	3	21	39	6	2	.241	.309	.338	-.195	.244	.311	.356	-.180	3.7	64-SS	-6

Breakout: 45%   Improve: 65%   Collapse: 19%

How is it that 35 errors for Luna kept him off the 40-man roster; while 45 by Corey Smith doesn't? Much of it has to do with what was surrounding Luna in the organization, with Jhonny Peralta ahead and Ivan Ochoa coming up behind. Luna has the physical skills to play defense, as he's gifted with a strong arm and quick feet, and he can hit a little. Nabbed via Rule 5 for the second consecutive year, this time by the Cardinals, where he'll get a look at second base.

VICTOR MARTINEZ

C **Bats: B** **Throws: R** Born: 23-Dec-78 Age: 25

YEAR	TM	LG	AGE	AB	H	2B	3B	HR	BB	SO	SB	CS	AVG	OBP	SLG	MLVR	EQBA	EQOBP	EQSLG	EQMLVR	VORP	DEFENSE			
2001	KIN	CAR	22	420	138	33	2	10	39	60	3	3	.329	.394	.488	.342	.268	.323	.415	-.068	13.7	106-C	-11		
2002	AKR	EAS	23	443	149	40	0	22	58	62	3	3	.336	.417	.576	.439	.279	.353	.486	.095	37.1	101-C	1		
2002	CLE	AL	23	32	9	1	0	1	3	2	0	0	.281	.333	.406	-.001	.312	.371	.438	.090	1.8				
2003	BUF	INT	24	274	90	19	0	7	26	32	3	5	.328	.395	.474	.261	.302	.371	.446	.092	22.6	56-C	-11	13-1B	-2
2003	CLE	AL	24	159	46	4	0	1	13	21	1	1	.289	.345	.333	-.091	.306	.365	.356	-.044	2.5	39-C	1		
2004	CLE	AL	25	313	81	18	1	8	27	43	3	1	.261	.326	.399	-.058	.270	.339	.432	-.011	17.2	84-C	-7		

Breakout: 14%   Improve: 37%   Collapse: 33%

Martinez went into camp expected to win the job at catcher, but like that too-good-to-be-true beauty in the bar, he lost the popularity contest to the more easily appreciated and homely Josh Bard. Banished and not happy about it, he stumbled to a slow start in Buffalo, but eventually bounced back. He's improving his English, which helps with his game-calling, but struggled to control the running game in the minors. However, once he got to the big leagues, he was better off, and having pitchers like Sabathia and Davis, who do a great job of holding runners, will help. The real problem is that he has to be the hitter we saw in 2002 to hack it as a big league regular. If he doesn't, he'll be an even bigger letdown than Sandy Alomar in the Tribe's history of catching disappointments.

JOHN McDONALD

2B/SS **Bats: R** **Throws: R** Born: 24-Sep-74 Age: 29

YEAR	TM	LG	AGE	AB	H	2B	3B	HR	BB	SO	SB	CS	AVG	OBP	SLG	MLVR	EQBA	EQOBP	EQSLG	EQMLVR	VORP	DEFENSE			
2001	BUF	INT	26	410	100	17	1	2	33	72	17	10	.244	.305	.305	-.173	.234	.295	.294	-.315	-13.9	110-SS	7		
2001	CLE	AL	26	22	2	1	0	0	1	7	0	0	.091	.167	.136	-.780	.136	.200	.182	-.705	-3.2				
2002	CLE	AL	27	264	66	11	3	1	10	50	3	0	.250	.288	.326	-.213	.272	.311	.355	-.173	0.1	56-2B	3	16-SS	-1
2003	CLE	AL	28	214	46	9	1	1	11	31	3	3	.215	.258	.280	-.386	.238	.284	.308	-.315	-12.4	28-2B	4	21-SS	-3
2004	CLE	AL	29	203	47	8	1	1	13	34	3	2	.230	.283	.304	-.276	.238	.295	.329	-.249	-2.7	56-2B	0		

Breakout: 47%   Improve: 59%   Collapse: 22%

(continued next page)

John McDonald (continued)

Ah, the miseries of completism. When you're young, if you set yourself an ambition, is it something bold? Something involving being the best at something, or famous, or wealthy? Chances are, you were disappointed in those ambitions, maybe not entirely, but hopefully you found a measure of happiness and success. Then there are careers like McDonald's. He's a nifty utility infielder, and if you had the Yankees' middle infield, he'd be a leatherly godsend. He could dream of being Rey Sanchez someday, but that ambition looks thwarted. Hopefully, he's accommodated himself to settling.

IVAN OCHOA SS Bats: R Throws: R Born: 16-Dec-82 Age: 21

YEAR	TM	LG	AGE	AB	H	2B	3B	HR	BB	SO	SB	CS	AVG	OBP	SLG	MLVR	EQBA	EQOBP	EQSLG	EQMLVR	VORP	DEFENSE			
2001	BNC	APP	18	176	38	2	0	0	24	57	14	5	.216	.346	.227	-.132	.162	.237	.173	-.630	-51.0	37-SS	1	13-2B	-1
2002	CGA	SAL	19	391	85	9	3	0	54	87	47	10	.217	.324	.256	-.156	.170	.248	.202	-.565	-47.0	125-SS	11		
2003	KIN	CAR	20	296	75	12	3	0	31	67	28	10	.253	.336	.314	-.044	.217	.279	.276	-.381	-17.3	80-SS	0		
2004	CLE	AL	21	248	48	9	2	1	20	59	11	4	.192	.261	.255	-.397	.199	.272	.276	-.382	-9.1	68-SS	-4		

Breakout: 38%   Improve: 58%   Collapse: 18%

Ochoa had his Ozzie versus Niedenfuer moment in the Carolina League playoffs, launching his first professional home run. His defensive work is outstanding, and the team added him to the 40-man roster on the theory that he could be the next Vizquel. He's relatively patient and runs well, but that's the extent of his offensive abilities. Pushing him to Double-A would be ambitious, especially with the Peralta vs. Vizquel situation still to be played out.

JHONNY PERALTA SS Bats: R Throws: R Born: 28-May-82 Age: 22

YEAR	TM	LG	AGE	AB	H	2B	3B	HR	BB	SO	SB	CS	AVG	OBP	SLG	MLVR	EQBA	EQOBP	EQSLG	EQMLVR	VORP	DEFENSE	
2001	KIN	CAR	19	441	106	24	2	7	58	148	4	8	.240	.328	.351	.022	.196	.271	.297	-.379	-24.9	124-SS	-13
2002	AKR	EAS	20	470	132	28	5	15	45	97	4	2	.281	.343	.457	.118	.241	.298	.398	-.159	6.2	128-SS	10
2003	BUF	INT	21	237	61	12	1	1	15	45	1	3	.257	.310	.329	-.123	.244	.297	.315	-.276	-5.2	60-SS	13
2003	CLE	AL	21	242	55	10	1	4	20	65	1	3	.227	.295	.326	-.233	.247	.315	.362	-.173	-4.1	66-SS	2
2004	CLE	AL	22	351	81	19	1	7	29	79	3	2	.230	.293	.351	-.198	.238	.305	.380	-.163	5.3	93-SS	0

Breakout: 37%   Improve: 55%   Collapse: 30%

Vizquel's injury forced Peralta to arrive in the majors a good year early, so he shouldn't be criticized for his struggles. He wasn't ready, but he showed that he can play a decent short nonetheless. Spending a good chunk of 2004 in Buffalo will put him in an interesting position: Will he get the job in 2005, once Vizquel's contract runs out? Or will he be trade bait? The Indians' system is rich in talent at short, but Peralta is clearly the pick of the litter, the puppy you keep for yourself while foisting all the others off on people who have something you want. He'll hit for power, and he can play the position. He won't be a star, but he will be a good answer for four or five years.

BRANDON PHILLIPS 2B Bats: R Throws: R Born: 28-Jun-81 Age: 23

YEAR	TM	LG	AGE	AB	H	2B	3B	HR	BB	SO	SB	CS	AVG	OBP	SLG	MLVR	EQBA	EQOBP	EQSLG	EQMLVR	VORP	DEFENSE			
2001	JUP	FLA	20	194	55	12	2	4	38	45	17	3	.284	.414	.428	.241	.229	.327	.361	-.163	2.7	55-SS	-2		
2001	HAR	EAS	20	265	79	19	0	7	12	42	13	6	.298	.337	.449	.113	.261	.298	.399	-.143	4.9	61-SS	4		
2002	HAR	EAS	21	245	80	13	2	9	16	33	6	3	.327	.380	.506	.270	.276	.320	.439	-.032	12.3	53-SS	-9		
2002	OTT	INT	21	35	9	4	0	1	2	6	0	0	.257	.297	.457	.030	.257	.297	.429	-.105	0.2				
2002	BUF	INT	21	223	63	14	0	8	14	39	8	2	.283	.321	.453	.075	.263	.312	.429	-.072	8.5	44-SS	4	11-2B	2
2002	CLE	AL	21	31	8	3	1	0	3	6	0	0	.258	.343	.419	.015	.290	.368	.452	.084	1.7				
2003	CLE	AL	22	370	77	18	1	6	14	77	4	5	.208	.242	.311	-.365	.227	.264	.343	-.312	-20.6	108-2B	-1		
2003	BUF	INT	22	154	27	7	0	3	12	22	7	3	.175	.247	.279	-.340	.168	.237	.277	-.488	-14.8	42-2B	-1		
2004	CLE	AL	23	345	83	18	1	9	25	62	10	3	.241	.298	.377	-.149	.250	.310	.408	-.109	13.4	91-2B	-1		

Breakout: 43%   Improve: 71%   Collapse: 15%

He went from can't miss to did, and nobody knows if the spatula has yet been made that can scrape him up from last season's epic tumble from the heights of prospectdom. His failures were worsened by Phillips's reputation as a showboat; there's a thin line between being charismatic and being a nuisance. At least Pokey Reese pokerized pitches for a season before reverting to mud—Phillips hasn't even done that much. He's clearly young enough to fix his problems, but the organization has threatened him with the need to improve, and he hasn't. They've already said he's Buffalo-bound to start '04, and it will be up to him to earn his way back.

GRADY SIZEMORE OF Bats: L Throws: L Born: 02-Aug-82 Age: 21

YEAR	TM	LG	AGE	AB	H	2B	3B	HR	BB	SO	SB	CS	AVG	OBP	SLG	MLVR	EQBA	EQOBP	EQSLG	EQMLVR	VORP	DEFENSE	
2001	CLN	MID	18	451	121	16	4	2	81	92	32	11	.268	.381	.335	.026	.188	.278	.237	-.448	-45.8	90-CF -11	24-LF -4
2002	BRV	FLA	19	256	66	15	4	0	36	41	9	9	.258	.351	.348	.037	.213	.285	.295	-.344	-25.6	64-LF -9	
2002	KIN	CAR	19	172	59	9	3	3	33	30	14	7	.343	.451	.483	.400	.260	.348	.376	-.081	-1.6	39-LF -5	
2003	AKR	EAS	20	496	151	26	11	13	46	73	10	9	.304	.373	.480	.209	.257	.316	.418	-.085	9.4	111-CF -17	11-LF 1
2004	CLE	AL	21	291	66	15	2	5	25	53	5	2	.226	.292	.342	-.213	.234	.304	.370	-.180	-5.8	79-CF -14	

Breakout: 14%   Improve: 39%   Collapse: 29%

Talented, and the latest great hope for closet pigskin fans who scout. Unlike so many of the others of that ilk, Sizemore does not have a great arm. He's a natural athlete, but he's not an effortless flycatcher in center—they're hoping he grows into the role. What Sizemore does really well is make contact with a quick stroke; some wonder how much more power he'll have when or if he improves his ability to kill his pitch. People who successfully make the jump to Double-A while continuing to improve aren't common, but Sizemore's still a diamond in the rough.

COREY SMITH Top Draft Choice Bats: R Throws: R Born: 15-Apr-82 Age: 22

YEAR	TM	LG	AGE	AB	H	2B	3B	HR	BB	SO	SB	CS	AVG	OBP	SLG	MLVR	EQBA	EQOBP	EQSLG	EQMLVR	VORP	DEFENSE
2001	CGA	SAL	19	500	130	26	5	18	37	149	10	7	.260	.312	.440	.102	.204	.249	.353	-.341	-25.2	113-3B -20
2002	KIN	CAR	20	505	129	29	2	13	59	141	7	2	.255	.341	.398	.071	.207	.276	.338	-.307	-20.3	130-3B -22
2003	AKR	EAS	21	473	128	27	3	9	50	99	7	2	.271	.340	.397	.017	.229	.288	.346	-.259	-11.5	122-3B -28
2004	CLE	AL	22	260	55	13	1	6	20	64	3	1	.213	.274	.341	-.254	.221	.285	.369	-.224	-1.5	70-3B -15

Breakout: 32%   Improve: 49%   Collapse: 20%

It's not really an accurate comparison, but Smith shares a lot of career path mishaps with Dmitri Young, despite Smith not being a switch-hitter. Like Young, Smith has tremendously quick wrists, and like Young, he was a high school shortstop who doesn't have a position. Like Young, he can't play third, but he does have a great arm. He's on the 40-man because he has to be, but it's anybody's guess where he'll wind up. As a hitter, he's improved his command of the strike zone and avoided setbacks, but he hasn't broken out. He'll get that breakout some time soon, just as Young did.

ZACH SORENSEN UT Bats: B Throws: R Born: 03-Jan-77 Age: 27

YEAR	TM	LG	AGE	AB	H	2B	3B	HR	BB	SO	SB	CS	AVG	OBP	SLG	MLVR	EQBA	EQOBP	EQSLG	EQMLVR	VORP	DEFENSE	
2001	AKR	EAS	24	194	45	6	1	5	11	30	10	8	.232	.273	.351	-.150	.203	.245	.310	-.410	-12.1	45-SS 1	
2002	BUF	INT	25	455	120	12	12	7	24	72	13	6	.264	.300	.389	-.062	.249	.289	.374	-.204	-3.9	62-2B 6	54-SS 2
2003	BUF	INT	26	238	57	12	3	3	22	42	12	5	.239	.299	.353	-.121	.221	.286	.338	-.279	-7.7	30-2B -1	
2003	CLE	AL	26	37	5	1	0	1	7	13	0	3	.135	.273	.243	-.424	.162	.295	.270	-.380	-3.5		
2004	CLE	AL	27	184	44	8	2	3	14	33	6	2	.237	.292	.359	-.185	.246	.304	.389	-.149	3.9	51-2B -1	

Breakout: 51%   Improve: 70%   Collapse: 17%

A one-time prospect in this organization, it's to Shapiro and company's credit that they're loyal to him, but only up to a point. Sorensen really only got a look because similarly limited organizational pet John McDonald kept breaking down. As a last man off the bench, he might get to hang around in a Hocking-like existence.

WILLY TAVERAS CF Bats: R Throws: R Born: 25-Dec-81 Age: 22

YEAR	TM	LG	AGE	AB	H	2B	3B	HR	BB	SO	SB	CS	AVG	OBP	SLG	MLVR	EQBA	EQOBP	EQSLG	EQMLVR	VORP	DEFENSE	
2001	CGA	SAL	19	395	107	15	7	3	22	73	29	9	.271	.317	.367	.025	.225	.262	.309	-.365	-26.5	82-CF -5	14-LF -1
2002	CGA	SAL	20	313	83	14	1	4	45	68	54	12	.265	.385	.355	.083	.210	.295	.290	-.332	-19.3	81-CF -12	
2003	KIN	CAR	21	397	112	9	6	2	52	68	57	12	.282	.381	.350	.088	.241	.315	.307	-.253	-14.0	104-CF -8	
2004	HOU	NL	22	262	61	11	2	3	22	52	14	4	.235	.306	.326	-.221	.232	.302	.324	-.246	-7.5	72-CF -7	

Breakout: 19%   Improve: 44%   Collapse: 25%

Speed on the bases, grace in the field, and patience at the plate, you could say Taveras has several things going for him. It's enough to get him listed as the best prospect on Kinston, but he was available in the Rule 5 draft. There, he was snagged by the Astros, where he might stick in their "Biggio's Legs" roster spot.

OMAR VIZQUEL

																	MLVR	EQBA	EQOBP	EQSLG	EQMLVR	VORP		DEFENSE

OMAR VIZQUEL   SS   Bats: B   Throws: R   Born: 24-Apr-67   Age: 37

YEAR	TM	LG	AGE	AB	H	2B	3B	HR	BB	SO	SB	CS	AVG	OBP	SLG	MLVR	EQBA	EQOBP	EQSLG	EQMLVR	VORP	DEFENSE	
2001	CLE	AL	34	611	156	26	8	2	61	72	13	9	.255	.323	.334	-.151	.274	.344	.361	-.100	16.4	147-SS	8
2002	CLE	AL	35	582	160	31	5	14	56	64	18	10	.275	.341	.418	.023	.300	.369	.457	.102	47.5	146-SS	11
2003	CLE	AL	36	250	61	13	2	2	29	20	8	3	.244	.321	.336	-.150	.267	.345	.367	-.095	2.6	64-SS	7
2004	CLE	AL	37	314	79	15	2	3	34	34	9	3	.251	.326	.341	-.139	.261	.339	.370	-.100	11.9	86-SS	1

Breakout: 30%   Improve: 63%   Collapse: 17%

The sands are running out on Leetle O's career. He's hobbled by a knee that kept him from being traded back to the Mariners, and he doesn't hit for power or run as much as he used to. At the plate, that reduces him to the player he was when he first came up, a twist of everyday irony unlikely to be made into a screenplay. He'll get his 2000th hit (18 to go) and his next stolen base will be his 300th, and he can still boast he's the best-fielding big league shortstop in Ohio. That's little better than kicking one of Barry Larkin's crutches out from under him, but Larkin's earned a trip to Cooperstown, while Vizquel should be satisfied with seeing his number retired.

PITCHERS

DANNY BAEZ   Bats: R   Throws: R   Born: 10-Sep-77   Age: 26

YEAR	TM	LG	AGE	G	GS	IP	H	BB	SO	HR	ERA	EQERA	EQH9	EQBB9	EQSO9	EQHR9	PERA	VORP	STF
2001	BUF	INT	23	16	0	25.3	18	9	30	2	3.20	3.80	7.2	3.8	8.7	0.8	3.63	4.7	29
2001	CLE	AL	23	43	0	50.3	34	20	52	5	2.50	2.88	5.4	3.2	8.5	0.7	2.62	15.1	39
2002	CLE	AL	24	39	26	165.3	160	82	130	14	4.41	3.89	7.9	4.1	6.6	0.7	3.95	31.2	23
2003	CLE	AL	25	73	0	75.7	65	23	66	9	3.80	3.68	7.7	2.6	7.7	1.0	3.74	13.7	15
2004	TBY	AL	26	42	14	99.3	89	37	81	10	3.73	3.71	7.8	3.2	7.3	0.9	3.74	22.4	9

Breakout: 33%   Improve: 59%   Collapse: 19%

Baez turned out to be a lot of hype, but nevertheless a useful pitcher. He's still a splitter/fastball pitcher with little commitment to changing speeds, but he's been adequate starting or relieving. Blowing 10 of 35 save opportunities shouldn't have put him high on anyone's list of potentially dominating closers, but the Devil Fishies handed him a moronic two-year, $6 million deal to finish games in Tampa. See, cash doesn't evaporate, it just disappears in reasonably explained senseless gestures, like overtipping a waitress at Hooters.

JASON BERE   Bats: R   Throws: R   Born: 26-May-71   Age: 33

YEAR	TM	LG	AGE	G	GS	IP	H	BB	SO	HR	ERA	EQERA	EQH9	EQBB9	EQSO9	EQHR9	PERA	VORP	STF
2001	CHC	NL	30	32	32	188.0	171	77	175	24	4.31	4.35	8.2	3.4	7.0	1.0	4.26	25.3	14
2002	CHC	NL	31	16	16	85.7	98	28	65	13	5.67	5.75	10.3	2.6	6.0	1.4	5.45	-1.4	-7
2003	BUF	INT	32	3	3	14.7	9	3	17	0	0.61	1.32	6.6	2.0	7.9	0.0	2.17	6.5	56
2003	CLE	AL	32	2	2	6.7	5	2	1	0	4.03	2.84	7.1	2.8	1.4	0.0	2.70	1.4	4
2004	CLE	AL	33	24	17	98.7	103	35	67	14	4.91	5.24	9.2	3.1	5.9	1.4	4.97	8.9	0

Breakout: 21%   Improve: 44%   Collapse: 29%

One of the club's madding herd of retreads, Bere will be pushing among Jason Stanford and Jeff D'Amico (the big one) for the fifth slot in the rotation. He's supposed to be recovered from last June's shoulder surgery, but since his shoulder is always a source of concern, it would be a bit much to expect him to put up a year like his '01 campaign.

RAFAEL BETANCOURT   Bats: R   Throws: R   Born: 29-Apr-75   Age: 29

YEAR	TM	LG	AGE	G	GS	IP	H	BB	SO	HR	ERA	EQERA	EQH9	EQBB9	EQSO9	EQHR9	PERA	VORP	STF
2001	TRN	EAS	26	16	0	24.0	28	3	27	0	5.63	5.32	12.3	1.6	7.0	0.4	4.97	0.7	6
2003	AKR	EAS	28	31	0	45.3	33	13	75	0	1.39	2.66	8.9	3.1	12.0	0.2	3.58	13.3	48
2003	BUF	INT	28	4	0	6.7	6	2	6	1	4.03	4.50	9.0	3.0	6.0	1.5	5.04	0.7	-22
2003	CLE	AL	28	33	0	38.0	27	13	36	5	2.13	2.68	6.3	2.9	8.3	1.0	3.17	14.0	20
2004	CLE	AL	29	40	3	58.3	51	20	57	6	3.47	3.70	7.7	2.9	8.5	1.0	3.78	14.2	14

Breakout: 32%   Improve: 55%   Collapse: 29%

The new Josias Manzanillo, non-optional cup included. Like Manzanillo once upon a time, Betancourt has a great arm, and he's someone we've heard about for years. Like Felix Rodriguez and Guillermo Mota, he's a converted position player. Of course, if you're pushing 30, have yet to pitch a full year in the majors, and signed your first pro contract in 1993, chances are you've been just about everything at one time or another. Once the Tribe moves beyond various veteran gateway relievers, Betancourt will be a key part of a quality pen.

JASON BOYD | Bats: R | Throws: R | Born: 23-Feb-73 | Age: 31

YEAR	TM	LG	AGE	G	GS	IP	H	BB	SO	HR	ERA	EQERA	EQH9	EQBB9	EQSO9	EQHR9	PERA	VORP	STF
2001	SWB	INT	28	52	0	59.3	44	22	66	4	1.97	3.69	8.4	4.0	7.9	0.8	4.30	11.4	3
2002	POR	PCL	29	19	0	26.0	19	7	22	2	1.04	2.70	8.5	2.7	6.2	1.2	4.33	7.5	-6
2002	SDP	NL	29	23	0	28.3	33	15	18	6	7.95	7.71	10.0	4.2	4.8	1.9	6.36	-6.6	-51
2003	BUF	INT	30	9	0	14.7	12	2	14	0	1.22	2.63	8.6	1.3	6.6	0.0	2.83	4.5	33
2003	CLE	AL	30	44	0	52.3	38	26	31	4	4.30	3.55	6.6	4.3	5.3	0.7	3.47	9.4	0
2004	PIT	NL	31	29	8	59.0	57	27	45	6	4.62	4.90	8.7	3.7	6.2	0.9	4.61	5.1	-3

Breakout: 31%   Improve: 56%   Collapse: 28%

Shapiro has shown a tremendous ability to learn from his mistakes, but that doesn't mean he doesn't still make a few. Why Boyd was on the roster for most of the season defies description. Sure, he was healthy and standing around, but his big league career has been a litany of disappointments and bleacher bombardments. He's wild without fooling all that many people. Although he had the best year of his career, Shapiro at least didn't get hung up on it, cutting bait and moving on. Sometimes, you can ask for lightning in a bottle a bit too insistently.

FERNANDO CABRERA | Bats: R | Throws: R | Born: 16-Nov-81 | Age: 22

YEAR	TM	LG	AGE	G	GS	IP	H	BB	SO	HR	ERA	EQERA	EQH9	EQBB9	EQSO9	EQHR9	PERA	VORP	STF
2001	CGA	SAL	19	20	20	94.7	89	37	96	7	3.61	7.05	11.4	5.4	5.5	1.5	6.84	-13.2	0
2002	KIN	CAR	20	21	21	110.0	83	40	107	7	3.52	5.25	8.6	4.5	6.4	1.4	5.13	3.8	16
2002	AKR	EAS	20	7	4	27.0	26	12	29	1	5.33	6.48	9.7	4.7	7.9	0.4	4.59	-2.4	39
2003	AKR	EAS	21	36	15	109.0	96	40	115	8	2.97	4.28	8.8	3.9	7.8	1.2	4.81	14.8	24
2004	CLE	AL	22	15	8	47.3	48	23	39	6	4.90	5.23	8.9	4.1	7.2	1.1	5.13	3.3	3

Breakout: 2%   Improve: 37%   Collapse: 31%

Cabrera is doubly cursed: It's easy to lose sight of him amidst the Tribe's cornucopia of talented young pitchers, and he's a Cabrera. How are you supposed keep track? There are more Cabreras flying around these days than Wallendas in the circus. Consistent low-90s heat produced expectations that he'd eventually transition into a relief role, with the Indians finally initiating the process last year.

FAUSTO CARMONA | Bats: R | Throws: R | Born: 07-Dec-83 | Age: 20

YEAR	TM	LG	AGE	G	GS	IP	H	BB	SO	HR	ERA	EQERA	EQH9	EQBB9	EQSO9	EQHR9	PERA	VORP	STF
2002	BNC	APP	18	13	11	76.3	89	10	42	4	3.30	6.52	12.5	1.6	2.6	1.2	6.01	-7.1	-3
2003	LKC	SAL	19	24	24	148.3	117	14	83	10	2.06	5.13	9.4	1.2	3.2	1.6	4.90	6.9	1
2003	AKR	EAS	19	1	1	6.0	8	0	3	1	4.50	6.35	11.1	0.0	4.8	1.6	5.32	-0.5	16
2004	CLE	AL	20	18	15	98.0	111	12	39	10	4.23	4.52	10.0	1.0	3.5	0.9	4.18	12.9	0

Breakout: 11%   Improve: 61%   Collapse: 4%

The minor league leader in wins with 17, Carmona put himself on the map as the Sally League's best control pitcher. Beyond the great command, he's got a high velocity sinker and some decent breaking stuff that combine to force plenty of grounders, and he knows how and when to mix in a changeup. With his youth, the Indians are being sensibly cautious; it might make sense to pair him with Ivan Ochoa at Kinston, so that he works with a plus shortstop while also learning how to finish hitters.

JACK CRESSEND | Bats: R | Throws: R | Born: 13-May-75 | Age: 29

YEAR	TM	LG	AGE	G	GS	IP	H	BB	SO	HR	ERA	EQERA	EQH9	EQBB9	EQSO9	EQHR9	PERA	VORP	STF
2001	MIN	AL	26	44	0	56.3	50	16	40	6	3.68	3.48	8.0	2.3	6.0	0.8	3.64	12.8	6
2002	MIN	AL	27	23	0	32.0	40	19	22	6	5.91	6.89	11.2	4.9	6.0	1.4	6.51	-4.5	-31
2003	CLE	AL	28	33	0	43.0	40	9	28	1	2.51	2.61	8.5	1.7	5.9	0.2	3.13	16.3	25
2004	CLE	AL	29	45	1	58.7	61	19	36	6	4.10	4.37	9.2	2.7	5.3	1.0	4.57	9.6	-7

Breakout: 25%   Improve: 55%   Collapse: 21%

(continued next page)

Jack Cressend *(continued)*

After snagging him on waivers, Cressend was a perfectly adequate middle reliever. The mystery is why he was retained on the 40-man roster, especially considering the talent the team lost in the Rule 5 draft. The answer lies in the peripherals: He's a decent righty-getter, he's good at keeping runners close, he changes speeds well, and he's effective pitching from the stretch. These are good things, but if he gets put on waivers at the end of camp, it's also a terrible waste of a roster spot.

FRANCISCO CRUCETA

Bats: R **Throws: R** Born: 04-Jul-81 Age: 22

YEAR	TM	LG	AGE	G	GS	IP	H	BB	SO	HR	ERA	EQERA	EQH9	EQBB9	EQSO9	EQHR9	PERA	VORP	STF
2002	SGA	SAL	21	20	20	112.7	98	34	111	7	2.80	5.18	10.9	3.8	5.5	1.5	6.15	4.5	6
2002	KIN	CAR	21	7	7	39.7	31	25	37	2	2.49	5.14	8.5	8.0	6.2	1.0	5.65	1.8	13
2003	AKR	EAS	22	27	25	163.3	141	66	134	7	3.09	4.49	8.2	4.3	6.1	0.6	4.12	18.8	30
2004	*CLE*	*AL*	*22*	*19*	*13*	*74.3*	*83*	*42*	*49*	*10*	*5.84*	*6.23*	*9.9*	*4.8*	*5.7*	*1.3*	*6.04*	*0.5*	*-9*

Breakout: 9% *Improve: 46%* *Collapse: 31%*

Cruceta was part of the goody bag from the Dodgers brought over in exchange for the occasionally healthy Paul Shuey. He came into Double-A with 90+ heat and very little pro experience. While holding tremendous promise, his season yielded mixed results. He continued to overpower hitters, rarely letting hits get into the outfield. However, his walk rate jumped significantly. He was working on ironing out inconsistent deliveries that tipped his breaking stuff; until he regains that margin of control, he won't make it.

JASON DAVIS

Bats: R **Throws: R** Born: 08-May-80 Age: 24

YEAR	TM	LG	AGE	G	GS	IP	H	BB	SO	HR	ERA	EQERA	EQH9	EQBB9	EQSO9	EQHR9	PERA	VORP	STF
2001	CGA	SAL	21	27	27	160.0	147	51	115	9	2.70	6.30	10.8	4.3	3.7	1.2	6.03	-10.8	-11
2002	KIN	CAR	22	17	17	99.7	107	31	68	7	4.15	7.57	12.0	3.9	4.3	1.6	6.88	-19.3	-22
2002	AKR	EAS	22	10	10	59.0	63	16	45	2	3.51	5.53	11.4	2.9	5.2	0.5	5.05	0.4	19
2002	CLE	AL	22	3	2	14.7	12	4	11	1	1.84	1.88	6.9	2.5	6.3	0.6	3.02	5.9	43
2003	CLE	AL	23	27	27	165.3	172	47	85	25	4.68	4.86	9.3	2.4	4.6	1.2	4.77	7.5	8
2004	*CLE*	*AL*	*24*	*24*	*21*	*129.0*	*147*	*50*	*72*	*16*	*5.10*	*5.44*	*10.0*	*3.3*	*4.9*	*1.1*	*5.37*	*4.9*	*-3*

Breakout: 12% *Improve: 46%* *Collapse: 24%*

As expected, Davis was good enough to pitch in the majors. The real question is if he's good enough to stick. The blazing heat and fall-off-the-table splitter could be the stuff of greatness, but he made too many mistakes inside the strike zone. He needs to find a breaking pitch or a changeup to freeze right-handed hitters. All that aside, he made quality starts more than half the time (14 in 27, with three blown after the sixth inning). He wore down with a sore shoulder, missing most of the last six weeks, which raises alarms for 2004. Was it the attempt to give him his first shutout on Aug. 8? He lost it and the game in the ninth, throwing a season-high 123 pitches. Is a personal milestone really that important?

DAN DENHAM

Bats: R **Throws: R** Born: 24-Dec-82 Age: 21

YEAR	TM	LG	AGE	G	GS	IP	H	BB	SO	HR	ERA	EQERA	EQH9	EQBB9	EQSO9	EQHR9	PERA	VORP	STF
2001	BNC	APP	18	8	8	30.7	30	26	31	5	4.40	10.65	14.1	13.7	4.6	4.6	13.35	-13.3	-89
2002	CGA	SAL	19	28	28	124.7	123	65	109	7	4.76	7.34	10.7	6.4	5.0	1.2	6.46	-21.3	-2
2003	LKC	SAL	20	14	14	73.0	75	22	63	4	3.08	6.75	12.9	3.7	4.9	1.4	7.02	-8.0	-4
2003	KIN	CAR	20	14	14	72.0	82	27	39	2	4.50	7.54	11.2	4.2	3.6	0.5	5.43	-14.2	0
2004	*CLE*	*AL*	*21*	*16*	*12*	*69.0*	*79*	*39*	*39*	*8*	*5.70*	*6.08*	*10.1*	*4.9*	*4.9*	*1.1*	*6.10*	*-3.7*	*-12*

Breakout: 23% *Improve: 55%* *Collapse: 6%*

It's worth remembering that pitchers picked out of high school have promise too. Denham is an aspiring sinker-slider power groundball guy, and he's made slow progress through the system. He can afford to take the slow path; he may not allow many extra-base hits, but he's still hittable. Getting him geared to successfully make the jump to Double-A later in the year makes sense, since the Tribe has no shortage of young pitching talent that would force him to move up any faster.

KYLE DENNEY Bats: R   Throws: R   Born: 27-Jul-77   Age: 26

YEAR	TM	LG	AGE	G	GS	IP	H	BB	SO	HR	ERA	EQERA	EQH9	EQBB9	EQSO9	EQHR9	PERA	VORP	STF
2001	KIN	CAR	23	11	10	57.0	32	13	80	2	2.05	3.47	8.0	3.1	7.8	0.9	3.95	11.7	27
2002	KIN	CAR	24	15	14	85.0	76	41	68	5	3.60	6.04	10.8	6.2	5.1	1.5	6.75	-3.6	-32
2002	AKR	EAS	24	6	5	34.7	23	5	32	2	1.56	2.87	7.8	1.4	6.3	0.9	3.31	9.5	27
2003	AKR	EAS	25	18	18	104.0	97	24	87	7	2.42	3.93	10.1	2.6	5.9	1.2	5.18	17.4	-1
2003	BUF	INT	25	6	6	30.7	35	10	26	4	5.28	6.11	11.6	3.5	6.1	1.9	6.90	-1.6	-29
2004	*CLE*	*AL*	*26*	*20*	*13*	*74.7*	*78*	*28*	*52*	*9*	*4.52*	*4.82*	*9.2*	*3.2*	*6.1*	*1.1*	*4.83*	*8.4*	*2*

Breakout: 22%   Improve: 45%   Collapse: 22%

Considered the Eastern League's top control pitcher, Denney is the organization's right-handed doppelganger of Jason Stanford. A college pitcher drafted out of Oklahoma in '99 and something of a finesse guy, he's not considered a top prospect. However, if he keeps pitching well and moving up and avoiding a career-altering injury, at some point he'll get a shot—the survivors almost always do.

JAKE DITTLER Bats: R   Throws: R   Born: 24-Nov-82   Age: 21

YEAR	TM	LG	AGE	G	GS	IP	H	BB	SO	HR	ERA	EQERA	EQH9	EQBB9	EQSO9	EQHR9	PERA	VORP	STF
2001	BNC	APP	18	6	5	22.0	25	12	20	0	3.68	9.16	13.5	8.2	3.9	0.5	7.28	-7.4	-13
2002	CGA	SAL	19	25	25	128.3	127	51	108	4	4.28	6.79	10.4	4.8	4.7	0.7	5.35	-15.2	11
2003	LKC	SAL	20	17	17	89.0	86	20	82	4	2.63	6.78	12.2	2.8	5.3	1.2	6.11	-10.1	6
2003	KIN	CAR	20	8	8	48.7	47	11	32	2	2.40	5.08	9.9	2.6	4.3	0.8	4.67	2.6	16
2004	*CLE*	*AL*	*21*	*19*	*14*	*81.3*	*91*	*35*	*46*	*8*	*4.88*	*5.20*	*9.9*	*3.6*	*5.0*	*0.9*	*5.25*	*3.8*	*-5*

Breakout: 17%   Improve: 58%   Collapse: 6%

It's OK, you're right, his name does sound like a discarded alternative for Mark Wahlberg's character in *Boogie Nights*. As he matures, he's picking up velocity and learning touch on his change. If he masters his breaking stuff, he could explode up through Double-A and beyond. You can say that about a lot of guys, of course, but Dittler is clearly not a finished product, and he already holds tremendous promise.

SHEA DOUGLAS Bats: L   Throws: L   Born: 03-Feb-81   Age: 23

YEAR	TM	LG	AGE	G	GS	IP	H	BB	SO	HR	ERA	EQERA	EQH9	EQBB9	EQSO9	EQHR9	PERA	VORP	STF
2002	BNC	APP	21	12	0	33.0	26	10	49	1	1.36	4.50	11.6	3.9	7.1	0.6	5.50	3.4	14
2003	LKC	SAL	22	34	0	85.7	46	30	104	2	1.37	3.30	7.9	4.4	6.8	0.6	4.00	18.8	17
2004	*CLE*	*AL*	*23*	*21*	*9*	*58.3*	*59*	*27*	*46*	*5*	*4.59*	*4.90*	*8.8*	*4.0*	*6.8*	*0.9*	*4.76*	*6.0*	*2*

Breakout: 11%   Improve: 48%   Collapse: 25%

One of several college-bred stars working in Lake County's dominant pen. The Captains romped to a 97–43 record, tossing 21 shutouts (only one a complete game), while also fielding one of the best lineups in low A-ball. Douglas was a successful college starter at Southern Miss, but lefties whose out pitch is a changeup are basically begging for a move to the pen. His change is one of the best in the minors, and should help put him in a position to fight for a big league job by 2005.

TRAVIS FOLEY Bats: R   Throws: R   Born: 11-Mar-83   Age: 21

YEAR	TM	LG	AGE	G	GS	IP	H	BB	SO	HR	ERA	EQERA	EQH9	EQBB9	EQSO9	EQHR9	PERA	VORP	STF
2001	BNC	APP	18	10	10	45.0	26	15	59	4	2.80	4.58	9.4	5.1	5.5	2.4	6.90	4.2	-5
2002	CGA	SAL	19	26	26	137.3	108	44	138	9	2.82	4.59	9.2	4.0	5.7	1.5	5.39	13.7	15
2003	KIN	CAR	20	24	24	126.7	115	54	96	7	3.69	5.86	9.7	5.0	5.0	1.3	5.67	-3.3	3
2004	*CLE*	*AL*	*21*	*17*	*15*	*91.0*	*91*	*46*	*59*	*10*	*4.81*	*5.13*	*8.8*	*4.4*	*5.6*	*1.1*	*5.09*	*4.8*	*0*

Breakout: 27%   Improve: 66%   Collapse: 7%

Foley continues to impress as he clambers up one rung after another. This year, he dramatically improved during the season, learning to change speeds to complement a 90ish fastball and solid breaking stuff. He's got an especially tasty Krukow-like big-bending curve, with the concern being that he likes it too much. He'll need to improve his control while making the jump to Double-A, no easy feat, so an initial repeat at high A-ball might make sense.

JEREMY GUTHRIE   Bats: B   Throws: R   Born: 08-Apr-79   Age: 25

YEAR	TM	LG	AGE	G	GS	IP	H	BB	SO	HR	ERA	EQERA	EQH9	EQBB9	EQSO9	EQHR9	PERA	VORP	STF
2003	AKR	EAS	24	10	9	62.7	44	14	35	0	1.44	2.33	6.8	2.5	3.9	0.3	2.72	21.1	24
2003	BUF	INT	24	18	18	96.7	129	30	62	15	6.51	7.79	13.1	3.4	4.7	2.2	8.01	-21.7	-43
2004	CLE	AL	25	17	10	57.3	72	25	34	10	6.13	6.54	11.0	3.7	5.2	1.6	6.43	-1.6	-13

Breakout: 16%   Improve: 45%   Collapse: 31%

Clearly not ready for the majors in his first pro season since being picked in the first round out of Stanford, Guthrie's nevertheless on the fast track, and should turn up in the big leagues by the end of 2004. He has good stuff and merely needs the repetition to learn to avoid mistakes inside the strike zone to veteran hitters. He's gaining touch on a slider and change to support the heat that's consistently in the low 90s. Considering his struggles in Buffalo, he's a dark horse to break camp with the team, but once the D'Amicos and Beres excuse themselves, Guthrie should be ready to become part of the next good Indians rotation.

ALEX HERRERA   Bats: L   Throws: L   Born: 05-Nov-76   Age: 27

YEAR	TM	LG	AGE	G	GS	IP	H	BB	SO	HR	ERA	EQERA	EQH9	EQBB9	EQSO9	EQHR9	PERA	VORP	STF
2001	AKR	EAS	24	15	0	28.7	24	9	22	1	2.82	4.21	9.1	3.9	4.9	0.4	4.15	4.0	2
2001	KIN	CAR	24	28	0	59.7	36	18	83	1	0.60	2.63	8.4	4.0	7.7	0.4	3.84	16.9	22
2002	AKR	EAS	25	30	0	61.3	47	30	65	8	3.38	5.03	9.7	5.4	7.4	2.2	6.80	3.4	-45
2002	BUF	INT	25	5	0	7.0	10	8	5	0	11.57	11.37	14.2	12.8	5.7	0.0	7.98	-4.0	-50
2002	CLE	AL	25	5	0	5.3	3	1	5	0	0.00	1.69	5.1	1.7	8.4	0.0	1.48	2.3	54
2003	BUF	INT	26	34	0	56.0	51	45	46	9	5.30	7.02	9.5	9.4	6.1	2.3	7.93	-7.9	-80
2003	CLE	AL	26	10	0	7.0	7	8	6	3	9.00	9.00	9.0	9.0	7.7	3.9	9.46	-2.4	-101
2004	COL	NL	27	11	1	10.7	21	18	2	4	13.07	12.37	16.9	12.8	1.6	2.6	15.46	-2.4	-94

Breakout: 35%   Improve: 47%   Collapse: 42%

Lefties who throw in the mid-90s have a way of getting noticed, but Herrera's Wild Thing tendencies wore thin, and he's made no progress in terms of becoming consistent in his mechanics or picking up on skills like holding baserunners. An organization already overloaded on possibilities for the 40-man roster couldn't find a way to keep a single pitch, no matter how hard or left-handed, on it. He was promptly claimed by the Rockies, where he'll get a look, but is a wild spot reliever really going to get himself ironed out a mile up?

DAVID LEE   Bats: R   Throws: R   Born: 12-Mar-73   Age: 31

YEAR	TM	LG	AGE	G	GS	IP	H	BB	SO	HR	ERA	EQERA	EQH9	EQBB9	EQSO9	EQHR9	PERA	VORP	STF
2001	POR	PCL	28	9	0	12.0	5	5	14	0	0.75	1.64	4.9	4.9	7.4	0.0	2.29	4.8	29
2001	SDP	NL	28	41	0	48.7	52	27	42	6	3.70	4.56	9.7	4.6	6.5	1.0	5.19	5.5	-8
2002	EDM	PCL	29	51	0	64.7	80	31	70	5	4.59	6.23	11.9	4.9	7.3	0.9	6.16	-4.2	-19
2003	LVG	PCL	30	56	0	60.3	47	36	61	4	3.13	3.70	7.6	6.4	7.7	0.8	4.57	11.8	-6
2003	CLE	AL	30	8	0	7.7	4	6	7	1	4.68	3.68	4.9	7.4	8.6	1.2	4.06	1.0	-2
2004	CLE	AL	31	26	2	36.7	35	22	32	4	4.63	4.94	8.3	5.1	7.6	1.0	5.25	4.1	-2

Breakout: 38%   Improve: 65%   Collapse: 20%

The current wishful claimant of the Fastball Flyer Roster Spot previously held by Jason Boyd and Chad Paronto, he has to hope for better results. He'll be in camp as a spring training NRI, having passed through waivers and re-signing, but he'll have to push past Cressend, Betancourt, and Matt Miller to crack the squad.

CLIFF LEE   Bats: L   Throws: L   Born: 30-Aug-78   Age: 25

YEAR	TM	LG	AGE	G	GS	IP	H	BB	SO	HR	ERA	EQERA	EQH9	EQBB9	EQSO9	EQHR9	PERA	VORP	STF
2001	JUP	FLA	22	21	20	109.7	78	46	129	13	2.79	5.25	10.1	4.8	7.4	2.9	7.66	3.7	-23
2002	HAR	EAS	23	15	15	86.3	61	23	105	12	3.23	3.94	8.5	2.9	8.3	2.1	5.37	14.3	9
2002	AKR	EAS	23	3	3	16.7	11	10	18	1	5.39	6.00	7.8	6.6	7.2	1.2	5.14	-0.7	2
2002	BUF	INT	23	8	8	43.0	36	22	30	7	3.77	5.22	8.2	5.4	5.7	2.0	5.97	1.7	-16
2002	CLE	AL	23	2	2	10.3	6	8	6	0	1.75	1.74	4.4	6.1	5.2	0.0	2.41	4.4	37
2003	BUF	INT	24	11	11	63.3	62	31	61	4	3.27	4.66	9.8	5.4	7.0	0.9	5.43	6.1	10
2003	CLE	AL	24	9	9	52.3	41	20	44	7	3.61	3.91	7.1	3.2	7.5	1.1	3.72	6.4	29
2004	CLE	AL	25	19	15	92.0	89	43	71	12	4.79	5.11	8.6	4.0	6.7	1.2	4.96	7.0	6

Breakout: 19%   Improve: 41%   Collapse: 21%

Lee strained his abdomen in camp, losing an early shot at a job in the rotation, and eventually required hernia surgery after the season. As you can see, once he was able to pitch, he didn't spend the year marooned in Buffalo. He's almost El Sid-like in his ability to beat people without blazing heat. Although he does get up over 90, it's his delivery, movement, and slider that combine to make him such a challenge to make contact against. He could wind up anywhere between Steve Trout and Fernandez, either merely succeeding or flat-out torching the league, but it'll be fun to see which way he goes, starting this year.

TERRY MULHOLLAND Bats: R   Throws: L   Born: 09-Mar-63   Age: 41

YEAR	TM	LG	AGE	G	GS	IP	H	BB	SO	HR	ERA	EQERA	EQH9	EQBB9	EQSO9	EQHR9	PERA	VORP	STF
2001	PIT	NL	38	22	1	36.3	38	10	17	5	3.72	3.86	9.3	2.3	3.6	1.0	4.50	6.8	-15
2001	LAD	NL	38	19	3	29.3	40	7	25	7	5.84	6.75	12.5	1.9	6.4	1.9	6.92	-3.6	-32
2002	LAD	NL	39	21	0	32.0	45	7	17	10	7.31	9.00	13.8	1.8	4.2	3.0	8.95	-11.3	-81
2002	CLE	AL	39	16	3	47.0	56	14	21	5	4.60	4.44	9.6	2.5	3.9	0.8	4.46	6.0	-6
2003	CLE	AL	40	45	3	99.0	117	37	42	17	4.91	5.36	10.5	3.2	3.8	1.4	5.78	5.0	-31
2004	CLE	AL	41	41	8	70.7	90	25	28	11	5.90	6.30	11.2	3.0	3.5	1.5	6.57	0.3	-26

Breakout: 12%   Improve: 57%   Collapse: 10%

Although he's starting to resemble a toothless extra from a Sergio Leone western to be named later, Mulholland has his uses. He still has one of the best pickoff moves in the history of the game, and he's still rubber-armed. If you're expecting a long, ugly season, and need an 11th pitcher who can soak up innings, Mulholland's your guy. You'd think the Rangers would be all over him.

DAVID RISKE Bats: R   Throws: R   Born: 23-Oct-76   Age: 27

YEAR	TM	LG	AGE	G	GS	IP	H	BB	SO	HR	ERA	EQERA	EQH9	EQBB9	EQSO9	EQHR9	PERA	VORP	STF
2001	BUF	INT	24	38	0	53.3	45	17	72	2	2.36	3.65	8.9	3.5	9.5	0.5	4.07	10.7	32
2001	CLE	AL	24	26	0	27.3	20	18	29	3	1.98	2.63	5.9	5.3	8.6	1.0	3.69	9.0	22
2002	CLE	AL	25	51	0	51.3	49	35	65	8	5.26	4.91	8.1	5.4	10.7	1.2	4.90	3.9	14
2003	CLE	AL	26	68	0	74.7	52	20	82	9	2.29	2.49	6.2	2.2	9.7	1.0	2.93	28.1	32
2004	CLE	AL	27	44	6	75.7	62	27	77	8	3.15	3.36	7.3	3.0	8.9	1.0	3.61	20.7	17

Breakout: 30%   Improve: 55%   Collapse: 27%

The wicked giddy-up and movement on his fastball is the stuff of Charlie Sheen's best impressions of a pitcher, but after years of hunting for an effective alternative, Riske finally picked up a splitter to give him that extra hammer that should make him an elite reliever into the future. Technically, Riske is slated to lose the closer's job now that Wickman is back and Baez is a D-Ray, but Wickman's not a young man or one known for his commitment to conditioning. Don't act surprised if it's July and Riske's calling the ninth inning home again.

C. C. SABATHIA Bats: L   Throws: L   Born: 21-Jul-80   Age: 23

YEAR	TM	LG	AGE	G	GS	IP	H	BB	SO	HR	ERA	EQERA	EQH9	EQBB9	EQSO9	EQHR9	PERA	VORP	STF
2001	CLE	AL	20	33	33	180.3	149	95	171	19	4.39	3.66	6.7	4.3	7.8	0.9	3.62	38.7	54
2002	CLE	AL	21	33	33	210.0	198	88	149	17	4.37	3.72	7.7	3.4	6.0	0.6	3.66	43.5	40
2003	CLE	AL	22	30	30	197.7	190	66	141	19	3.60	3.77	8.7	2.9	6.4	0.8	4.10	44.8	37
2004	CLE	AL	23	27	27	172.0	168	68	128	17	4.18	4.46	8.6	3.4	6.5	0.9	4.43	25.7	12

Breakout: 22%   Improve: 51%   Collapse: 24%

Despite dire expectations and an early-season elbow tweak that had statheads ready to bellow "told you so," Sabathia has yet to break down, and he managed quality starts in 21 of 30 games (losing two of them after the sixth). As for making only 30 starts, he lost a couple to a sprained ankle and food poisoning, and the team was sensible in seeking to rest him down the stretch. Although you should be as concerned about his long-term future, he's been Livan-like in his ability to thumb his nose at workload concerns. More importantly, he's not the Swindellian flounder he was when he came up, having gotten more serious about keeping himself in shape. He's got another couple of years to worry about before he's really out of the injury nexus, and his ability to pack on poundage easily is a permanent source of concern, but he might be mixing his mid-90s heat and hammer curve for quite some time to come.

JOSE SANTIAGO

Bats: R   **Throws: R**   Born: 05-Nov-74   Age: 29

YEAR	TM	LG	AGE	G	GS	IP	H	BB	SO	HR	ERA	EQERA	EQH9	EQBB9	EQSO9	EQHR9	PERA	VORP	STF
2001	KCR	AL	26	20	0	29.3	40	9	15	2	6.76	5.72	12.1	2.5	4.4	0.6	5.42	-0.4	-10
2001	PHI	NL	26	53	0	62.3	66	13	28	3	3.61	3.94	9.7	1.8	3.5	0.5	3.97	10.9	-2
2002	PHI	NL	27	42	0	47.0	56	15	30	7	6.70	6.45	11.3	2.6	5.0	1.4	5.94	-4.2	-29
2002	SWB	INT	27	22	0	28.0	28	7	21	0	1.29	3.51	10.5	2.8	5.6	0.4	4.47	6.0	5
2003	BUF	INT	28	25	4	66.7	79	22	33	1	2.43	4.67	11.2	3.6	3.5	0.1	4.85	6.4	-5
2003	CLE	AL	28	25	0	31.7	37	14	15	2	2.84	3.82	10.6	3.8	4.1	0.6	5.04	9.8	-9
2004	CLE	AL	29	73	0	47.0	57	18	23	4	4.90	5.23	10.7	3.3	4.2	0.9	5.45	3.4	-19

Breakout: 27%   Improve: 54%   Collapse: 26%

There was once a point when Santiago was considered a relief prospect, oxymoron though that may be. He shuttling up and down the Lake Erie coast, which might conjure up romantic images of tramp steamers and bumptious fur traders or something, but more likely involves traffic and lunch in Erie, Pennsylvania. A minor league free agent, and still someone who might get turned around, but it would almost certainly have to involve the splitter or a trick pitch. Or a battalion of rabid giant anteaters that obey his every command.

JASON STANFORD

Bats: L   **Throws: L**   Born: 23-Jan-77   Age: 27

YEAR	TM	LG	AGE	G	GS	IP	H	BB	SO	HR	ERA	EQERA	EQH9	EQBB9	EQSO9	EQHR9	PERA	VORP	STF
2001	AKR	EAS	24	24	24	141.7	152	32	108	11	4.06	5.88	11.7	2.8	4.7	1.1	5.86	-4.0	-8
2002	AKR	EAS	25	18	18	102.3	108	33	86	3	3.43	5.54	12.2	3.6	5.7	0.5	5.55	0.6	4
2002	BUF	INT	25	6	5	35.7	33	11	23	5	2.77	4.41	9.4	3.3	5.0	1.9	5.83	4.3	-24
2003	BUF	INT	26	20	20	126.0	124	25	108	13	3.43	4.67	10.1	2.3	6.1	1.5	5.33	12.0	-6
2003	CLE	AL	26	13	8	50.0	48	16	30	5	3.60	3.72	8.6	2.8	5.4	0.7	3.98	12.8	9
2004	CLE	AL	27	22	14	80.3	88	27	51	11	4.67	4.98	9.7	2.9	5.5	1.2	5.11	8.1	-2

Breakout: 19%   Improve: 46%   Collapse: 28%

Another lefty junkballer, but not one to thoughtlessly condemn to Quadruple-A-dom. Stanford has kept honing his command to the point that he might actually be one of the few who deserves those quick Moyer comparisons that get slapped on every minor league lefty with dreams of a better life. Now that Traber and Tallet are out of the picture for 2004, Stanford might finally get his crack at a big league rotation, but he'll have to beat out the veteran non-roster invitees to get there.

KAZ TADANO

Bats: R   **Throws: R**   Born: 25-Apr-80   Age: 24

YEAR	TM	LG	AGE	G	GS	IP	H	BB	SO	HR	ERA	EQERA	EQH9	EQBB9	EQSO9	EQHR9	PERA	VORP	STF
2003	KIN	CAR	23	7	1	19.0	13	3	28	0	1.89	3.24	9.2	1.6	9.2	0.5	3.66	4.4	41
2003	AKR	EAS	23	31	0	72.7	62	15	78	4	1.24	2.96	8.9	2.3	7.7	0.9	4.13	19.7	22
2003	BUF	INT	23	2	0	7.0	6	4	6	0	3.86	4.26	8.5	7.1	7.1	0.0	4.39	0.9	26
2004	CLE	AL	24	21	9	59.7	58	18	51	6	3.65	3.89	8.5	2.6	7.4	0.9	4.05	13.7	12

Breakout: 25%   Improve: 48%   Collapse: 29%

Tadano was one of the best amateur talents in Japan, but his appearance in a porn film apparently didn't fly there. The Tribe stepped into the breach, signing him for $67,000. Maybe it's because we live in a world where everyone's seen Tommy Lee and Pamela Anderson, but he discussed it frankly with each of his new sets of teammates with each promotion. To the general credit of the open-mindedness of the young, nobody was upset. And why not? He deals heat in the low 90s and has four pitches he can throw for strikes. As some argue was the case with Jackie Robinson and Branch Rickey, it could just be that the Indians wanted a good baseball player.

BILLY TRABER

Bats: L   **Throws: L**   Born: 18-Sep-79   Age: 24

YEAR	TM	LG	AGE	G	GS	IP	H	BB	SO	HR	ERA	EQERA	EQH9	EQBB9	EQSO9	EQHR9	PERA	VORP	STF
2001	SLU	FLA	21	18	18	101.7	85	23	79	2	2.65	4.06	8.9	2.4	4.5	0.5	3.78	15.9	24
2001	BIN	EAS	21	8	8	42.7	50	13	45	4	4.43	6.30	11.0	3.6	6.5	1.1	5.72	-3.1	16
2002	AKR	EAS	22	18	17	107.7	99	20	82	8	2.76	4.61	10.0	2.0	5.2	1.1	4.84	10.7	14
2002	BUF	INT	22	9	9	54.7	58	12	33	3	3.29	4.82	9.3	2.2	5.0	0.7	4.10	4.5	23
2003	CLE	AL	23	33	18	111.7	132	40	88	15	5.24	5.23	10.6	3.1	7.0	1.1	5.34	6.3	17
2004	CLE	AL	24	30	20	119.7	128	41	85	12	4.28	4.56	9.4	2.9	6.2	1.0	4.69	16.5	5

Breakout: 18%   Improve: 51%   Collapse: 24%

You can ignore the projection, as Traber's out for the year after Tommy John surgery. Ditto for Brian Tallet, but he's less of a prospect, so of the two, it's probably better for you to keep Traber in mind for the future. Traber has had elbow trouble since he was drafted, so if anything, it's good to finally get this out of the way. The question is going to be if he can use his splitter consistently, or if the pitch places too much stress on his elbow.

JAKE WESTBROOK

Bats: R **Throws: R** Born: 29-Sep-77 Age: 26

YEAR	TM	LG	AGE	G	GS	IP	H	BB	SO	HR	ERA	EQERA	EQH9	EQBB9	EQSO9	EQHR9	PERA	VORP	STF
2001	BUF	INT	23	12	12	64.7	60	23	45	2	3.20	4.57	8.6	3.7	5.0	0.3	3.80	7.0	22
2001	CLE	AL	23	23	6	64.7	79	22	48	6	5.84	4.76	9.9	2.8	6.2	0.7	4.55	6.0	19
2002	CLE	AL	24	11	4	41.7	50	12	20	6	5.83	5.01	9.8	2.4	4.1	1.1	4.83	2.7	-3
2003	CLE	AL	25	34	22	133.0	142	56	58	9	4.33	4.50	9.6	3.7	3.9	0.6	4.56	17.3	0
2004	CLE	AL	26	29	18	103.0	117	42	51	9	4.79	5.11	10.0	3.5	4.3	0.8	5.16	6.5	-10

Breakout: 20%   Improve: 43%   Collapse: 26%

Now that Miguel Batista's gone and become a full-blown good big league starter, the term "utility pitcher" can revert to someone more appropriate, someone like Westbrook. An extreme groundball pitcher, he's not a rubber-armed workhorse as much as he's the sort you can stick in any role for a stretch. He opened the year starting, went to the pen, then got plugged back into the rotation. He'll compete for the fourth or fifth slot in the rotation, but if he loses, he'll mop up in the starts of the winners, and eventually stand in for whoever flops.

BOB WICKMAN

Bats: R **Throws: R** Born: 06-Feb-69 Age: 35

YEAR	TM	LG	AGE	G	GS	IP	H	BB	SO	HR	ERA	EQERA	EQH9	EQBB9	EQSO9	EQHR9	PERA	VORP	STF
2001	CLE	AL	32	70	0	67.7	61	14	66	4	2.39	2.28	7.3	1.7	8.1	0.4	2.72	24.7	36
2002	CLE	AL	33	36	0	34.3	42	10	36	3	4.46	4.76	10.3	2.4	9.0	0.8	4.65	3.2	18
2004	CLE	AL	35	35	0	35.3	36	10	31	3	3.76	4.02	9.0	2.5	7.6	0.7	4.11	7.0	9

Breakout: 31%   Improve: 55%   Collapse: 26%

Wickman put in a few minor league innings to show that his rehab from Tommy John surgery was on track, so the big beastie should be fully prepped for challenging Riske for the closer's job. Although Riske is and should continue to be the better pitcher, from a level of pure pragmatism, it would probably work out for the best if Wickman gets the glory role. That way, Riske can actually protect leads earlier on, increasing the likelihood that those leads make it to the ninth.

MARK WOHLERS

Bats: R **Throws: R** Born: 23-Jan-70 Age: 34

YEAR	TM	LG	AGE	G	GS	IP	H	BB	SO	HR	ERA	EQERA	EQH9	EQBB9	EQSO9	EQHR9	PERA	VORP	STF
2001	CIN	NL	31	30	0	32.0	36	7	21	5	3.94	4.94	9.9	1.7	4.9	1.2	4.74	2.3	-14
2001	NYY	AL	31	31	0	35.7	33	18	33	3	4.54	4.37	8.0	4.1	7.7	0.8	4.08	4.8	9
2002	CLE	AL	32	64	0	71.3	71	26	46	6	4.80	3.95	8.2	2.9	5.5	0.6	3.73	13.0	3
2004	CLE	AL	34	60	0	48.0	52	18	31	5	4.82	5.14	9.5	3.2	5.6	1.1	4.98	4.1	-10

Breakout: 17%   Improve: 37%   Collapse: 30%

Technically, Wohlers joins Wickman on the rehabbed reinforcement front. Although he's "back," in that he's sort of beaten the Steve Blass Disease rap, he also had Tommy John surgery in June; even on an accelerated schedule, he might only pitch after the All-Star break. Beyond all that, he's also not an incredibly valuable relief asset. If he makes the team, he's likely to be shunted off to low-leverage innings involving insurmountable leads.

Detroit Tigers

We're not ordinarily fond of looking backwards at BP. We assume that most of our readers buy this book to learn things they don't already know, and we're not going to break any new ground by rehashing seasons past.

Except...sometimes things happen which are so extraordinary, so outside the realm of common experience, that trying to figure out what comes next requires more divination than contemplation. And sometimes the only way to divine the future is to examine the past.

One hundred nineteen losses qualify as "things happen." The Tigers were at least 10 games worse than every team since the 1960s. The Tigers were as far removed from a 100-loss team as a 100-loss team is from .500. So yes, some perspective is in order.

Table 1 shows the nine worst teams since 1900.

Of the five teams ahead of them on this list, two (the 1916 and 1919 A's) were the product of the Great Philadelphia Fire Sale after Connie Mack, faced with higher salary demands brought on by competition from the Federal League, sold his team off en masse after their 1914 pennant. The 1962 Mets were an expansion team. The 1935 Braves had the greatest fluke season of all-time; they were over .500 the year before, and would make it back over .500 two years later.

The Tigers, with stable ownership, a storied history, and a new retroplex ballpark, have no such extenuating circumstances. The 2003 Tigers came about their record the hard way: by earning every last one of their 119 losses. They were the worst major-league baseball team without an excuse in 100 years.

There is no easy explanation for what happened. There can't be; no single error in judgment is strong enough to push a team 38 full games under .500. But to use a sweeping generalization, what felled the Tigers is the same combination of factors that has plagued all the bad teams of the last generation, only more so.

Criminal neglect of the farm system? Check. Over the past 20 years, the Tigers' farm system has probably been the least fruitful in the game.

Poor free agent signings? Randy Smith would have been better off delegating the job of signing free agents to one of those monkeys that the Wall Street Journal trots out to make stock picks.

TIGERS PROSPECTUS

2003 record: 43–119; Fifth place, AL Central

Pythagenport record: 47–115

Runs scored per game: 3.6 (14th in AL)

Runs allowed per game: 5.7 (13th in AL)

Team EqA: .235 (14th in AL)

2003 Batters Age: 27.9 (4th youngest in AL)

2003 Pitchers Age: 25.9 (Youngest in AL)

Ballpark: Comerica Park; Moderate pitcher's park; Park Factor of 0.966

2003: Motor City favorite son Alan Trammell returned to preside over the worst team in Tigers history.

2004: The system's barren and the free-agent supplements are mediocre; look for another 100-loss season.

Bad trades? The Tigers traded six players to get Juan Gonzalez.

But it goes deeper than that. Everything said in the last three paragraphs can apply to any team that loses 100 games. What made the 2003 Tigers such a historic example of incompetence was the extreme to which their incompetence was manifest.

Randy Smith had many shortcomings, but his biggest was that he was unable to keep a healthy distance emotionally from his ballplayers. It's a GM's job to see the shortcomings in his own players, and Smith was unable to do that. He thought Damion Easley was a star, and paid *him* like one. He thought Bobby Higginson was a superstar, and paid him like one. He ignored the fact that Matt Anderson was too unreliable, and Danny Patterson was too generic, to merit three-year contracts each. As it turned out, both of them blew out their arms within a dozen innings of signing their deals.

The Tigers had nine players on their payroll last year making $2 million or more. (See table 2.)

That might just be the greatest waste of payroll in major league history. For over $48 million—about $4 million less than the World Champion Marlins spent on their whole roster—the Tigers got Dmitri Young and eight players who would have been overpaid at the major league minimum.

TABLE 1. NINE WORST TEAMS SINCE 1900

Year	Team	W	L	Pct.
1916	Philadelphia A's	36	117	.235
1935	Boston Braves	38	115	.248
1962	New York Mets	40	120	.250
1904	Washington Senators	38	113	.252
1919	Philadelphia A's	36	104	.257
2003	*Detroit Tigers*	*43*	*119*	*.265*
1952	Pittsburgh Pirates	42	112	.273
1909	Washington Senators	42	110	.276
1942	Philadelphia Phillies	42	109	.278

TABLE 2. TIGERS' PLAYERS ≥$2 MILLION, 2003

Bobby Higginson:	$11.85 million
Dean Palmer:	$8.5 million
Dmitri Young:	$6.75 million
Damion Easley:	$6.5 million
Steve Sparks:	$4.5 million
Matt Anderson:	$3.2 million
Craig Paquette:	$2.625 million
Danny Patterson:	$2.5 million
Shane Halter:	$2.15 million

As disastrous as their free agent campaigns have been, the Tigers can at least take solace in the fact that the drain on its payroll will come to an end shortly. (Only Higginson and Young are under contract beyond this season, and they come off the books after 2005.) Unfortunately, while their free agents were chiefly responsible for the depths to which the franchise has fallen, it's the remainder of the roster that gives reason to believe their climb back to respectability will be a long, arduous one.

The remainder of the roster may not have represented a waste of money, but almost to a man represented a waste of roster space. It is here that the Tigers differentiate themselves from the crowd of 100-loss teams. Their young talent wasn't just bad; it was, in many cases, below replacement level. This not only hurt the Tigers on the field in 2003, it hurts them into the future, because their young players were so bad that few of them ever *project* to reach mediocrity.

That's the difference between a team that loses 105 or 106 games, like the 1991 Indians (that had a nucleus of Carlos Baerga, Albert Belle, and Sandy Alomar) or the 1988 Braves (Ron Gant, Tom Glavine, John Smoltz), and a team that loses 119 games. The Tigers have no young players to build around.

Their roster wasn't particularly young to begin with. Only two of the 19 players who batted at least 50 times were under the age of 25. (Those two players, Ramon Santiago and Omar Infante, were the first keystone combination since the 1989 Pirates in which neither player (min: 200 PA) mustered either a .300 OBP *or* a .300 slugging average.) Four Tiger pitchers under the age of 25 threw at least 50 innings. Two of them, Wil Ledezma and Matt Roney, were Rule 5 picks who pitched like it. Another, Nate Cornejo, finished with the lowest strikeout rate (2.13 per 9 IP) by a qualifying pitcher in 50 years.

That leaves exactly one player, Jeremy Bonderman, with any star potential whatsoever.

It's instructive to look at the road to respectability followed by the other members of the sub-.280 club. Eliminating duplications, we have table 3.

It's actually pretty remarkable that five of the six worst teams of the last century—without benefit of free agency or the draft (the Mets did have the draft for a few years)—worked their way back into contention, "contention" being defined as a .550 winning percentage, in

TABLE 3. TEAMS THAT MOVED TO RESPECTABILITY AFTER BEING <.280

Team	Year	Record	.500	.550	Holdovers
Washington Senators	1904	38–113	1912	1912	Tom Hughes
Philadelphia A's	1916	36–117	1925	1925	None
Boston Braves	1935	38–115	1937	1947	None
Philadelphia Phillies	1942	42–109	1949	1950	None
Pittsburgh Pirates	1952	42–112	1958	1960	Bob Friend, Dick Groat
New York Mets	1962	40–120	1969	1969	Al Jackson, Ed Kranepool

less than a decade. (And the sixth team, the 1935 Braves, was back over .500 in two years.)

But it's the last column which is most pertinent. "Holdovers" lists which players appeared on both the all-time loser squad and the team which played .550-ball. The qualifications aren't particularly sticky; any player who made even a single appearance on both teams is listed. The six teams combined for just five holdovers, or less than one per team.

The point here is that the Tigers have to approach the future with the assumption that no one who played for them last year, save possibly Jeremy Bonderman, is going to still be with the team the next time they're good. A few other players—Carlos Pena, Eric Munson, Cody Ross, and maybe Franklyn German—have a more modest upside. Everyone else is just a place-holder.

It's fashionable to praise a team that finally gets off the 72-win track and commits to a full-blown rebuilding project, even if it means getting worse before they get better. That praise is predicated on the assumption that in the process of rebuilding, a team receives an infusion of young players that have a better chance at relevance than the veterans they replaced. That assumption simply doesn't hold true for the Tigers. Nearly a decade into their rebuilding phase, they are as strapped for prospects as they were when they started.

It is absolutely crucial that the Tigers' front office—and their owner—understand this fact. A decade after their last winning season, it's tempting for Ilitch to think that his franchise is somehow farther along in the rebuilding process than at Ground Zero. They're not. Dave Dombrowski inherited a situation so disastrous that he simply can't be held to a normal rebuilding timetable.

Already, some members of the Detroit media have called for Dombrowski's head, reasoning that no rebuilding job can excuse a 119-loss season. That sentiment is both misguided and destructive. As hard as it is to believe that Dombrowski is essentially blameless for the 2003 Tigers—given that he fired Randy Smith and took over as GM the previous April—that is exactly the case.

In the strictest sense, you can blame Dombrowski for the fact that the Tigers lost 119 games and not, say, 110. He jettisoned Mark Redman, who would have been the ace of his staff, to the Marlins in exchange for prospects. Robert Fick was waived after he refused to agree to the Tigers' contract offer. Randall Simon was shipped to Pittsburgh for more minor league depth. And, of course, Jeff Weaver was traded to the Yankees in a controversial deal.

But each of those moves were made because Dombrowski realized that the franchise's contention horizon was so distant that none of these players would still be productive and under contract at that point. For his efforts Dombrowski saved the team close to $10 million while

bringing in a bunch of young players who might be worth something someday; the sort of moves, in other words, that Randy Smith should have been making all along.

Of the five players on the 2003 Tigers who might have a long-term future with the team, three of them—Bonderman, Pena, and German—were acquired for Weaver alone. A fourth, Eric Munson, was another failed top prospect until the new administration made the gutsy decision to move him to third base.

As Dombrowski is fond of saying when questioned about his decision to trade Weaver et al: "I've had to break up a World Championship team before. Believe me, this isn't the same thing." Indeed, the success of last year's Marlins should serve as the definitive proof that Dombrowski can do this job, because he's done it before.

The 1998 Marlins are one of only three teams since 1980 to lose twice as many games as they won. The 2003 Marlins, rebuilt largely by Dombrowski before he left Miami, are only the third team in history to win a World Series within five years of a season in which they lost two-thirds of their games. (The other teams to accomplish the feat, the 1914 Braves and 1969 Mets, both use "Miracle" as their middle name.)

Conventional wisdom states that using a first-round pick on a high school pitcher is folly—but Josh Beckett, taken with the #2 overall pick in 1999, is one of the brightest lights in the game. Conventional wisdom states that the big-ticket amateur free agents abroad are almost always busts—but the Marlins spent $1.6 million on Miguel Cabrera (outbidding the Yankees) and today there aren't a dozen players in baseball who you'd rather build your franchise around.

When you have great scouts, you can flout conventional wisdom and get away with it. And Dombrowski has always surrounded himself with great scouts. With them, he built a winner in Montreal, he built a winner in Florida—twice—so there's no reason to think, given enough time, he can't do it in Detroit as well.

But it's going to take time. For one thing, unlike his move from Montreal to Florida, this time Dombrowski has had to build his staff almost from scratch. The Latin America staff that was so successful at finding players like Cabrera and Edgar Renteria largely accompanied John Henry to Boston. The minor league development staff that Dombrowski inherited was left largely intact for the last two years, as the new administration figured out which coaches were worth keeping and which weren't. (That process was finally completed with an end-of-season purge.)

Another complicating factor is that the best-laid plans of a GM can always be torpedoed by ownership. Mike Ilitch is trying to meddle with the rebuilding process by throwing his millions around to sign free agents. Dombrowski's previous history on the free-agent market (Kevin Brown, Al Leiter) is reassuring. The problem, as the Tigers discovered when they tried to bid on Miguel Tejada, is that the only free agents that are going to be tempted to join a 43-win team are those with precious few other options. The Tigers were willing to match the Orioles' offer on Tejada, but stopped their bidding at five years and $45 million after they determined they were just being used as a tool to jack up his price. Instead, the Tigers overpaid for the likes of Fernando Vina and Rondell White, who are nothing more than worn band-aids over a bullet wound.

The most obvious reason why it's going to take so much time, of course, is simply how high the mountain is that the Tigers have to climb. The Marlins won the World Series by improving on their atrocious 1998 squad by 36 games. If five years from now, the Tigers have improved upon their 2003 record by 36 games, they'll still be under .500.

HITTERS

BRENT CLEVLEN
RF   Bats: R   Throws: R   Born: 27-Oct-83   Age: 20

YEAR	TM	LG	AGE	AB	H	2B	3B	HR	BB	SO	SB	CS	AVG	OBP	SLG	MLVR	EQBA	EQOBP	EQSLG	EQMLVR	VORP	DEFENSE	
2003	WMI	MID	19	481	125	22	7	12	72	111	6	3	.260	.359	.410	.141	.198	.274	.329	-.328	-42.2	132-RF	-8
2004	DET	AL	20	284	54	11	2	5	23	75	2	2	.190	.255	.293	-.361	.198	.266	.315	-.343	-19.4	76-RF	-8

Breakout: 19%   Improve: 37%   Collapse: 38%

Clevlen, the Tigers' second-round pick out of a Texas high school in 2002, is probably the most complete hitting prospect in the organization. His offensive numbers are even more impressive considering the context; he hit 63 points higher, and 10 of his 12 homers, on the road. Defensively, he makes up for only adequate range with a strong arm. Don't get too excited, Tiger fans; this is as good as this chapter gets. And it's not that good.

DAVID ESPINOSA
OF   Bats: B   Throws: R   Born: 16-Dec-81   Age: 22

YEAR	TM	LG	AGE	AB	H	2B	3B	HR	BB	SO	SB	CS	AVG	OBP	SLG	MLVR	EQBA	EQOBP	EQSLG	EQMLVR	VORP	DEFENSE			
2001	DYT	MID	19	493	129	29	8	7	55	120	15	10	.262	.340	.396	.033	.191	.253	.298	-.416	-33.6	120-SS	-25		
2002	STO	CAL	20	367	90	13	7	7	62	104	26	17	.245	.356	.376	.027	.188	.276	.293	-.378	-24.1	94-2B	-10		
2003	LAK	FLA	21	350	95	18	7	4	50	78	13	10	.271	.359	.397	.120	.214	.288	.332	-.287	-17.0	57-CF	-9	34-RF	-5
2004	DET	AL	22	237	49	11	2	4	21	57	5	2	.206	.275	.322	-.280	.215	.287	.346	-.256	-8.3	65-CF	-11		

Breakout: 34%   Improve: 57%   Collapse: 17%

You couldn't count on the Jim Bowden Reds to be all that good, but you could always count on them to find original ways to cut costs. They gave Espinosa, their first-round pick in 2000, an eight-year major league contract to spread out his bonus money, then traded him to Detroit for Brian Moehler having paid him just a fraction of it. The Tigers are still on the hook for the rest of the bonus even though they outrighted him off the 40-man roster last season. Though his days in the middle infield are a distant memory, he's still young enough, with enough breadth of skills, to harbor continued dreams of relevance someday.

TONY GIARRATANO
SS   Bats: B   Throws: R   Born: 29-Nov-82   Age: 21

YEAR	TM	LG	AGE	AB	H	2B	3B	HR	BB	SO	SB	CS	AVG	OBP	SLG	MLVR	EQBA	EQOBP	EQSLG	EQMLVR	VORP	DEFENSE	
2003	ONE	NYP	20	189	62	11	4	3	12	22	9	4	.328	.369	.476	.285	.242	.275	.371	-.240	-4.0	44-SS	-2
2004	DET	AL	21	276	63	13	2	4	12	40	5	3	.228	.263	.337	-.271	.237	.275	.362	-.243	-2.4	72-SS	-6

Breakout: 21%   Improve: 38%   Collapse: 29%

A third-round pick out of Tulane, Giarratano was arguably the best defensive collegiate shortstop in the draft. His offense after signing was a pleasant surprise, and he was named the New York-Penn League's #3 prospect, the highest ranking of any Tiger. His teammate Kody Kirkland, a former 30th-round pick acquired in the Randall Simon trade, was ranked #4. Both are mentioned here simply as proof that the Dombrowski regime is already bringing in young talent at a rate that Randy Smith could only dream about.

CURTIS GRANDERSON

OF   **Bats: L**   **Throws: R**   Born: 16-Mar-81   Age: 23

YEAR	TM	LG	AGE	AB	H	2B	3B	HR	BB	SO	SB	CS	AVG	OBP	SLG	MLVR	EQBA	EQOBP	EQSLG	EQMLVR	VORP	DEFENSE			
2002	ONE	NYP	21	212	73	15	4	3	20	35	9	2	.344	.417	.495	.374	.243	.297	.367	-.203	-17.9	50-LF	-2		
2003	LAK	FLA	22	476	136	29	10	11	49	91	10	7	.286	.365	.458	.215	.233	.295	.394	-.176	-4.6	75-CF	0	51-LF	-3
2004	DET	AL	23	269	65	14	3	6	20	57	4	2	.242	.304	.385	-.128	.252	.317	.413	-.088	3.3	73-CF	-9		

Breakout: 39%   Improve: 62%   Collapse: 11%

Granderson answered the doubts that come with playing at a small-time college program (University of Illinois-Chicago) by holding his own in the Florida State League in his first full pro season. Asked to be a stopgap in center field, he played so well that the Tigers now think he can reach the majors without moving to a corner. He's the sort of low-ceiling, tools-indifferent player that helps win ballgames by hitting the snot out of the ball for a few years in the majors.

SHANE HALTER

IF   **Bats: R**   **Throws: R**   Born: 08-Nov-69   Age: 34

YEAR	TM	LG	AGE	AB	H	2B	3B	HR	BB	SO	SB	CS	AVG	OBP	SLG	MLVR	EQBA	EQOBP	EQSLG	EQMLVR	VORP	DEFENSE			
2001	DET	AL	31	450	128	32	7	12	37	100	3	3	.284	.344	.467	.103	.306	.369	.504	.175	42.1	68-3B	-4	60-SS	-7
2002	DET	AL	32	410	98	22	6	10	39	92	0	4	.239	.309	.395	-.079	.263	.332	.439	-.022	20.5	79-SS	-8	24-3B	0
2003	DET	AL	33	360	78	5	2	12	27	77	2	3	.217	.269	.342	-.249	.240	.297	.384	-.181	-9.8	43-3B	2	20-SS	-2
2004	ANA	AL	34	230	54	10	1	6	20	54	1	1	.236	.299	.366	-.163	.244	.311	.394	-.131	5.3	63-3B	1		

Breakout: 31%   Improve: 45%   Collapse: 38%

What is there to say about Halter that hasn't already been said before? He hits like a utility infielder and fields like a DH. He plays in a ballpark uniquely ill-suited for his one offensive asset, right-handed power. He had the third-lowest OBP in the majors of anyone who batted 300 or more times. And because Randy Smith decided to reward him with a multi-year contract after the only good season of his career, he got paid more than Bill Mueller did. Don't expect that to happen as an NRI, Shane. As an Angel in the infield, he'll be hard-pressed to stick.

JACK HANNAHAN

3B   **Bats: L**   **Throws: R**   Born: 04-Mar-80   Age: 24

YEAR	TM	LG	AGE	AB	H	2B	3B	HR	BB	SO	SB	CS	AVG	OBP	SLG	MLVR	EQBA	EQOBP	EQSLG	EQMLVR	VORP	DEFENSE	
2001	WMI	MID	21	170	54	11	0	1	26	39	4	2	.318	.409	.400	.215	.242	.313	.309	-.253	-4.1	45-3B	2
2002	LAK	FLA	22	246	67	11	1	6	36	44	9	3	.272	.362	.398	.106	.216	.292	.325	-.288	-8.8	63-3B	8
2002	ERI	EAS	22	226	54	12	1	3	21	50	2	1	.239	.309	.341	-.143	.202	.257	.294	-.408	-16.0	64-3B	12
2003	ERI	EAS	23	471	121	18	0	9	48	78	2	0	.257	.328	.352	-.085	.216	.276	.302	-.351	-25.1	132-3B	15
2004	DET	AL	24	210	47	9	1	4	18	42	1	1	.224	.288	.328	-.239	.233	.301	.352	-.211	-0.4	58-3B	5

Breakout: 49%   Improve: 71%   Collapse: 16%

He's pretty much fallen off all the prospect lists after his second straight disappointing season, but Hannahan is listed here because his defensive numbers at third base are so exceptional that if he ever does find his bat, he could resurrect his career quickly. There's nothing about his approach at the plate that's incurable; he simply hasn't developed power like expected. Realistically, he probably never will.

BOBBY HIGGINSON

RF   **Bats: L**   **Throws: R**   Born: 18-Aug-70   Age: 33

YEAR	TM	LG	AGE	AB	H	2B	3B	HR	BB	SO	SB	CS	AVG	OBP	SLG	MLVR	EQBA	EQOBP	EQSLG	EQMLVR	VORP	DEFENSE	
2001	DET	AL	30	541	150	28	6	17	80	65	20	12	.277	.367	.445	.107	.302	.396	.490	.197	38.0	138-LF	7
2002	DET	AL	31	444	125	24	3	10	41	45	12	5	.282	.345	.417	.047	.307	.373	.458	.117	21.0	113-LF	-8
2003	DET	AL	32	469	110	13	4	14	59	73	8	8	.235	.320	.369	-.104	.260	.347	.412	-.034	-7.8	111-RF	2
2004	DET	AL	33	394	102	19	2	10	45	55	7	4	.258	.335	.396	-.049	.269	.349	.426	-.004	8.3	106-RF	-3

Breakout: 18%   Improve: 48%   Collapse: 20%

It wouldn't be a shock if Higginson rebounded this season; he suffered through a season-long struggle with his hamstrings, and after his last bad season (1999, when he hit just .239/.351/.382) he bounced back with one of his best years in 2000. But more and more, Higginson looks like a man who's just seen enough losing: His streak of playing for sub-.500 teams (counting the majors, minor leagues, and college) now stands at 15 seasons in a row. As we've said for years, he needs a change of scenery badly, but his albatross of a contract continues to make that next to impossible.

A. J. HINCH C Bats: R Throws: R Born: 15-May-74 Age: 30

YEAR	TM	LG	AGE	AB	H	2B	3B	HR	BB	SO	SB	CS	AVG	OBP	SLG	MLVR	EQBA	EQOBP	EQSLG	EQMLVR	VORP		DEFENSE	
2001	OMA	PCL	27	168	54	14	0	10	11	33	1	0	.321	.365	.583	.305	.281	.328	.515	.096	13.4		24-C	0
2001	KCR	AL	27	121	19	3	0	6	8	26	1	1	.157	.226	.331	-.409	.167	.238	.342	-.400	-7.1		37-C	-2
2002	KCR	AL	28	197	49	7	1	7	18	35	3	3	.249	.321	.401	-.079	.259	.329	.421	-.056	6.1		59-C	-5
2003	TOL	INT	29	185	48	15	1	4	13	38	0	1	.259	.320	.416	.008	.242	.301	.403	-.146	1.6		48-C	-7
2003	DET	AL	29	74	15	3	1	3	3	18	0	0	.203	.247	.392	-.231	.216	.271	.432	-.181	-1.5		21-C	-6
2004	PHI	NL	30	153	37	8	1	5	12	33	1	1	.239	.302	.399	-.130	.241	.301	.408	-.132	3.6		44-C	-4

Breakout: 30%   Improve: 55%   Collapse: 28%

It's about time to let go of the notion that Hinch can ever get past Quadruple-A status. He now has over 1,000 plate appearances in the majors with a career line of .220/.281/.357, and he turns 30 in May. Interestingly, Hinch himself may be coming to that conclusion: The Stanford grad was seen networking at the general manager meetings in Arizona and is thought by many to be future GM material. The Tigers' other backup catcher, Matt Walbeck, retired after the Tigers offered him the manager's job at West Michigan. Given that Walbeck's clubhouse presence and handling of pitchers kept him in the majors for 11 years despite a lifetime line of .233/.280/.315, his talents are a much better fit for his new job than his old one.

OMAR INFANTE SS Bats: R Throws: R Born: 26-Dec-81 Age: 22

YEAR	TM	LG	AGE	AB	H	2B	3B	HR	BB	SO	SB	CS	AVG	OBP	SLG	MLVR	EQBA	EQOBP	EQSLG	EQMLVR	VORP		DEFENSE	
2001	ERI	EAS	19	540	163	21	4	2	46	87	27	12	.302	.355	.367	.028	.257	.313	.314	-.238	-5.7		130-SS	4
2002	TOL	INT	20	436	117	16	8	4	28	49	19	15	.268	.309	.369	-.074	.247	.292	.347	-.238	-4.5		119-SS	-1
2002	DET	AL	20	72	24	3	0	1	3	10	0	1	.333	.360	.417	.116	.370	.395	.452	.210	7.8		16-SS	-2
2003	TOL	INT	21	224	50	10	0	2	22	32	22	4	.223	.299	.295	-.207	.212	.288	.283	-.355	-10.9		62-SS	-7
2003	DET	AL	21	221	49	6	1	0	18	37	6	3	.222	.278	.258	-.345	.252	.311	.293	-.274	-9.6		63-SS	2
2004	DET	AL	22	337	82	15	2	4	27	47	14	4	.244	.304	.337	-.188	.255	.317	.362	-.155	8.5		90-SS	-3

Breakout: 42%   Improve: 63%   Collapse: 17%

After being talked about as one of the Tigers' most exciting prospects for three years, he fell out of favor with the team in less than three months. He didn't hit, he didn't field, and after not running out a flyball, he didn't have a job. The team tried to send a signal by not recalling him in September, but an injury to Halter forced Detroit to bring him up for the final week. The Tigers think they may have gotten through to him, and he was hitting extremely well in Venezuela as we went to press. At his age quantum leaps forward are not entirely impossible, but he's already played himself out of the Tigers' good graces once, and he may not even get the chance to do it twice.

BRANDON INGE C Bats: R Throws: R Born: 19-May-77 Age: 27

YEAR	TM	LG	AGE	AB	H	2B	3B	HR	BB	SO	SB	CS	AVG	OBP	SLG	MLVR	EQBA	EQOBP	EQSLG	EQMLVR	VORP		DEFENSE	
2001	TOL	INT	24	90	26	11	1	2	7	24	1	0	.289	.337	.500	.167	.264	.321	.473	.007	4.7		25-C	2
2001	DET	AL	24	189	34	11	0	0	9	41	1	4	.180	.215	.238	-.517	.205	.241	.279	-.460	-13.8		59-C	10
2002	DET	AL	25	321	65	15	3	7	24	101	1	3	.202	.266	.333	-.262	.231	.293	.383	-.197	-2.0		93-C	0
2003	TOL	INT	26	142	39	9	0	5	11	23	3	1	.275	.327	.444	.066	.252	.305	.427	-.097	3.4		35-C	7
2003	DET	AL	26	330	67	15	3	8	24	79	4	4	.203	.265	.339	-.268	.227	.291	.384	-.202	-11.0		100-C	11
2004	DET	AL	27	236	53	12	1	6	18	53	2	1	.227	.289	.373	-.178	.236	.302	.401	-.143	4.4		64-C	4

Breakout: 45%   Improve: 64%   Collapse: 22%

To the Tigers' credit, at least they were right about Inge's power potential: After going homerless in his major league debut, he has hit 15 homers in 651 at-bats the last two years. That lifetime .198 average is a problem, though. His throwing touch came back last year, as he nailed 30% of attempted basestealers. In a more forgiving ballpark, Inge might make a useful backup out of the Mark Parent mold. There's still some upside here. There better be, if he wants to hold off Rule 5 stud Chris Shelton.

DONALD KELLY IF Bats: L Throws: R Born: 15-Feb-80 Age: 24

YEAR	TM	LG	AGE	AB	H	2B	3B	HR	BB	SO	SB	CS	AVG	OBP	SLG	MLVR	EQBA	EQOBP	EQSLG	EQMLVR	VORP	DEFENSE		DEFENSE	
2001	ONE	NYP	21	262	75	8	3	0	25	16	8	5	.286	.345	.340	.037	.211	.258	.252	-.460	-40.0	65-SS	-1		
2002	WMI	MID	22	455	130	21	5	1	59	40	9	6	.286	.368	.360	.106	.229	.293	.294	-.321	-17.0	111-SS	2		
2003	LAK	FLA	23	303	96	17	4	1	45	25	15	2	.317	.401	.409	.223	.254	.328	.343	-.169	1.2	32-3B	-1	19-SS	1
2003	ERI	EAS	23	83	22	5	1	1	15	9	0	0	.265	.378	.386	.045	.214	.312	.321	-.254	-1.4	20-SS	0		
2004	DET	AL	24	238	57	12	1	2	23	26	4	2	.237	.306	.323	-.207	.247	.319	.346	-.176	1.7	66-SS	-6		

Breakout: 35%   Improve: 57%   Collapse: 24%

The closest player the Tigers have to a real sleeper. Kelly is a left-handed hitter who's posted more walks than strikeouts every season of his career, and can play all over the infield. The Tigers have grown awfully fond of him, and they think he can make a fine utility player, if not a starter somewhere in the infield (most likely third base). Much like Granderson, the only thing he seems to do well on the field is play baseball.

GENE KINGSALE CF Bats: B Throws: R Born: 20-Aug-76 Age: 27

YEAR	TM	LG	AGE	AB	H	2B	3B	HR	BB	SO	SB	CS	AVG	OBP	SLG	MLVR	EQBA	EQOBP	EQSLG	EQMLVR	VORP	DEFENSE		DEFENSE	
2001	ROC	INT	24	244	49	12	2	0	26	44	16	2	.201	.283	.266	-.285	.198	.272	.266	-.418	-20.1	26-CF	0	24-LF	-1
2001	TAC	PCL	24	215	63	14	4	3	8	25	12	4	.293	.327	.437	.015	.270	.302	.409	-.114	2.0	47-CF	0		
2002	TAC	PCL	25	188	49	15	3	6	15	30	10	3	.261	.317	.468	.042	.238	.293	.429	-.127	-3.7	26-RF	-3	19-LF	-2
2002	SDP	NL	25	216	60	10	3	2	20	47	9	2	.278	.346	.380	.032	.297	.360	.410	.017	4.7	34-RF	-4	17-LF	-1
2003	TOL	INT	26	160	39	6	5	0	11	24	9	5	.244	.297	.344	-.136	.230	.285	.329	-.288	-7.0	25-CF	-2	14-LF	0
2003	DET	AL	26	120	25	3	1	1	10	17	1	3	.208	.265	.275	-.353	.231	.290	.314	-.299	-8.6	19-CF	-2		
2004	SDP	NL	27	275	73	14	3	3	21	41	9	3	.266	.320	.368	-.121	.273	.324	.387	-.096	3.0	74-CF	-7		

Breakout: 21%   Improve: 34%   Collapse: 40%

It was a worthwhile ploy. Kingsale, at least, plays the great defense in center field that is a prerequisite for success in Comerica Park, and he did have a .350 OBP in 2002. He ended up failing miserably at his last good shot at a starting job, and signed back with the Padres after the season. At least he lasted longer with his new team than the man he was traded for, Mike Rivera, who was flushed out of the Padres' organization after 50 at-bats. You'd imagine it's some solace for Dombrowski, knowing that it's hard to get taken in a trade when you have nothing worth trading for.

DANNY KLASSEN IF Bats: R Throws: R Born: 22-Sep-75 Age: 28

YEAR	TM	LG	AGE	AB	H	2B	3B	HR	BB	SO	SB	CS	AVG	OBP	SLG	MLVR	EQBA	EQOBP	EQSLG	EQMLVR	VORP	DEFENSE		DEFENSE	
2002	TUC	PCL	26	361	83	20	5	2	22	106	6	1	.230	.277	.330	-.291	.198	.245	.289	-.442	-25.3	79-SS	0	24-3B	7
2003	TOL	INT	27	407	100	19	4	11	28	110	12	5	.246	.303	.393	-.061	.230	.289	.379	-.211	-1.0	75-SS	-5	30-2B	8
2003	DET	AL	27	73	18	3	1	1	4	26	0	1	.247	.286	.356	-.178	.260	.308	.384	-.146	-0.6	13-3B	0		
2004	DET	AL	28	235	52	11	2	5	17	64	4	2	.221	.282	.348	-.226	.231	.295	.374	-.196	4.2	64-SS	-1		

Breakout: 39%   Improve: 57%   Collapse: 26%

Klassen is a swing-from-the-heels hitter without the power to make it work. He was signed as a minor league free agent last winter; of the 19 players who batted 50 or more times for the Tigers last season, seven of them were originally signed as minor league free agents or NRIs. In some organizations, that would be a sign of financial prudence. In Detroit, it's a sign of a talent bankruptcy.

NOOK LOGAN CF Bats: B Throws: R Born: 28-Nov-79 Age: 24

YEAR	TM	LG	AGE	AB	H	2B	3B	HR	BB	SO	SB	CS	AVG	OBP	SLG	MLVR	EQBA	EQOBP	EQSLG	EQMLVR	VORP	DEFENSE	
2001	WMI	MID	21	522	137	19	8	1	53	129	67	19	.262	.330	.335	-.031	.214	.268	.277	-.403	-42.0	123-CF	-7
2002	LAK	FLA	22	506	136	14	7	2	40	111	55	16	.269	.321	.336	-.036	.232	.272	.295	-.361	-33.8	121-CF	-3
2003	ERI	EAS	23	514	129	16	7	4	51	103	37	13	.251	.316	.333	-.135	.211	.270	.285	-.390	-38.8	128-CF	5
2004	DET	AL	24	209	47	8	2	2	15	46	10	3	.224	.276	.309	-.285	.233	.288	.332	-.260	-8.7	57-CF	-3

Breakout: 42%   Improve: 68%   Collapse: 15%

One of Randy Smith's biggest weaknesses as a scout was his fetish for outfielders who run like the wind, even if, like Nook Logan, they hit seven homers in their first four pro seasons. Logan makes a great center fielder in every phase of the game save the one that uses a bat. Barring a sudden market bubble for Gary Pettis types, his major league career is likely to be short and, um, swift.

CRAIG MONROE LF Bats: R Throws: R Born: 27-Feb-77 Age: 27

YEAR	TM	LG	AGE	AB	H	2B	3B	HR	BB	SO	SB	CS	AVG	OBP	SLG	MLVR	EQBA	EQOBP	EQSLG	EQMLVR	VORP		DEFENSE			
2001	OKL	PCL	24	410	115	25	5	20	46	85	10	8	.280	.358	.512	.158	.247	.321	.450	-.040	1.8		64-LF	2	23-RF	-2
2001	TEX	AL	24	52	11	1	0	2	6	18	2	0	.212	.293	.346	-.228	.231	.310	.365	-.189	-1.7		16-RF	1		
2002	TOL	INT	25	358	115	30	4	10	35	57	7	3	.321	.379	.511	.272	.293	.356	.475	.098	16.3		67-LF	-1	10-CF	-1
2003	DET	AL	26	425	102	18	1	23	27	89	4	2	.240	.287	.449	-.050	.262	.313	.494	.021	0.3		68-LF	-1	34-RF	-2
2004	*DET*	*AL*	*27*	*423*	*109*	*23*	*2*	*17*	*36*	*83*	*5*	*3*	*.258*	*.318*	*.443*	*-.016*	*.269*	*.332*	*.476*	*.033*	*13.0*		*111-LF*	*-1*		

Breakout: 21%   Improve: 46%   Collapse: 20%

Two years ago, one of us had the opportunity to speak at the first annual Detroit Tigers Baseball Dinner, and was seated between then-GM Randy Smith and Tigers fan (and best-selling author) Dave Chilton. After ribbing Smith mercilessly for an hour, Chilton applauded the decision earlier that week to claim Monroe off waivers. "In fact," Chilton leaned in conspiratorially, "I'm willing to bet you that Monroe drives in more runs for the Tigers than (free-agent signing) Craig Paquette." Armed with the knowledge that he had some influence on the playing time of the two combatants, Smith almost leaped out of his seat to shake hands on the deal. Six games into the season, Smith was fired; by the end of Paquette's contract, the final score was: Chilton 71, Smith 20. Dave, I'll testify that Randy owes you dinner. But you'll have to fly to San Diego to collect.

SCOTT MOORE 3B Bats: L Throws: R Born: 17-Nov-83 Age: 20

YEAR	TM	LG	AGE	AB	H	2B	3B	HR	BB	SO	SB	CS	AVG	OBP	SLG	MLVR	EQBA	EQOBP	EQSLG	EQMLVR	VORP	DEFENSE
2003	WMI	MID	19	372	89	16	6	6	41	110	2	4	.239	.325	.363	.022	.189	.252	.303	-.413	-27.8	95-3B -21
2004	*DET*	*AL*	*20*	*253*	*45*	*10*	*2*	*4*	*17*	*80*	*1*	*1*	*.180*	*.237*	*.283*	*-.412*	*.187*	*.247*	*.304*	*-.398*	*-14.0*	*68-3B -12*

Breakout: 26%   Improve: 45%   Collapse: 36%

After his first full pro season, Moore is on the path to becoming another failed first-round pick for a franchise that knows no other type. Moore wasn't drafted for his glove—although his defensive slide from shortstop to third base will probably stop there—so his tepid showing with the bat so far has been disappointing. He's still way too young to be written off yet.

WARREN MORRIS 2B Bats: L Throws: R Born: 11-Jan-74 Age: 30

YEAR	TM	LG	AGE	AB	H	2B	3B	HR	BB	SO	SB	CS	AVG	OBP	SLG	MLVR	EQBA	EQOBP	EQSLG	EQMLVR	VORP	DEFENSE
2001	NAS	PCL	27	223	68	16	2	5	12	21	3	4	.305	.342	.462	.091	.278	.319	.422	-.057	8.1	46-2B -2
2001	PIT	NL	27	103	21	6	0	2	3	9	2	3	.204	.239	.320	-.396	.202	.236	.327	-.404	-6.4	22-2B -2
2002	EDM	PCL	28	92	24	6	2	2	3	16	2	1	.261	.281	.435	-.088	.239	.263	.402	-.221	-1.2	24-2B -5
2002	MEM	PCL	28	100	26	4	1	2	8	12	0	1	.260	.306	.380	-.099	.238	.287	.356	-.241	-2.1	22-2B 1
2002	PAW	INT	28	164	50	11	2	3	11	22	2	1	.305	.352	.451	.146	.289	.342	.434	.011	9.0	19-2B 0
2003	TOL	INT	29	206	57	13	4	2	16	26	4	1	.277	.330	.408	.026	.260	.315	.389	-.126	3.2	44-2B 2
2003	DET	AL	29	346	94	13	2	6	23	42	4	2	.272	.316	.373	-.080	.299	.347	.411	-.004	7.1	85-2B 3
2004	*DET*	*AL*	*30*	*361*	*90*	*18*	*2*	*6*	*23*	*49*	*4*	*2*	*.250*	*.297*	*.364*	*-.162*	*.260*	*.310*	*.391*	*-.126*	*7.5*	*94-2B -2*

Breakout: 18%   Improve: 46%   Collapse: 33%

From College World Series hero to a member of the '03 Tigers—Morris has seen the valley from the mountaintop and the mountaintop from the valley. Like most sufferers of Brent Gates Syndrome, the prognosis is terminal; you can't be a utility player if you can't play shortstop, and Morris doesn't hit enough to be anything more than a utility player. None of this stopped Shane Halter, mind you.

ERIC MUNSON 3B Bats: L Throws: R Born: 03-Oct-77 Age: 26

YEAR	TM	LG	AGE	AB	H	2B	3B	HR	BB	SO	SB	CS	AVG	OBP	SLG	MLVR	EQBA	EQOBP	EQSLG	EQMLVR	VORP	DEFENSE
2001	ERI	EAS	23	519	135	35	1	26	84	141	0	3	.260	.371	.482	.167	.213	.313	.398	-.150	-11.3	128-1B -13
2001	DET	AL	23	66	10	3	1	1	3	21	0	1	.152	.188	.273	-.536	.182	.217	.318	-.466	-6.4	16-1B 1
2002	TOL	INT	24	477	125	30	4	24	77	114	1	3	.262	.367	.493	.176	.237	.340	.451	-.012	10.7	129-1B -8
2002	DET	AL	24	59	11	0	0	2	6	11	0	0	.186	.269	.288	-.323	.217	.297	.333	-.266	-2.3	
2003	DET	AL	25	313	75	9	0	18	35	61	3	0	.240	.312	.441	-.018	.260	.340	.483	.051	12.8	83-3B -15
2004	*DET*	*AL*	*26*	*356*	*86*	*18*	*1*	*16*	*43*	*76*	*2*	*1*	*.242*	*.327*	*.430*	*-.031*	*.252*	*.341*	*.461*	*.016*	*19.0*	*97-3B -8*

Breakout: 23%   Improve: 55%   Collapse: 21%

(continued next page)

Eric Munson (*continued*)

Given Munson's agility, the new administration figured it had nothing to lose by trying him at third base. After promising stints in Instructional League and in Puerto Rico last winter, he was handed the job out of spring training, and played the position better than anyone had the right to expect. He was still very rough, but he hit .257/.324/.470 after April, and besides, how can anyone play third as poorly as . . .

DEAN PALMER DH Bats: R Throws: R Born: 27-Dec-68 Age: 35

YEAR	TM	LG	AGE	AB	H	2B	3B	HR	BB	SO	SB	CS	AVG	OBP	SLG	MLVR	EQBA	EQOBP	EQSLG	EQMLVR	VORP	DEFENSE
2001	DET	AL	32	216	48	11	0	11	27	59	4	1	.222	.317	.426	-.049	.243	.335	.468	.007	7.8	
2003	DET	AL	34	86	12	2	0	0	9	28	0	0	.140	.235	.163	-.590	.163	.262	.198	-.543	-11.2	
2004	DET	AL	35	137	24	5	0	3	18	45	1	0	.176	.282	.288	-.323	.183	.295	.309	-.303	-8.8	41-DH -2

Breakout: 79%   Improve: 84%   Collapse: 13%

. . . who, the last time he was healthy enough to play third, fielded .914? And has two of the five worst fielding percentages at third base (min: 90 G) since 1990? And who cost his teams 124 fielding runs at third base over his career? After struggling to return from his devastating shoulder injury in 2001—a struggle which yielded 12 hits and no homers—Palmer has earned a nice, quiet, pain-free retirement. He's refusing to go gently into that good night, signing a minor-league deal with the Tigers. He's lucky the Tigers don't play in Oregon, or his career would have been euthanized over the winter.

CARLOS PENA 1B Bats: L Throws: L Born: 17-May-78 Age: 26

YEAR	TM	LG	AGE	AB	H	2B	3B	HR	BB	SO	SB	CS	AVG	OBP	SLG	MLVR	EQBA	EQOBP	EQSLG	EQMLVR	VORP	DEFENSE
2001	OKL	PCL	23	431	124	38	3	23	80	127	11	3	.288	.408	.550	.304	.251	.362	.475	.071	21.5	115-1B -1
2001	TEX	AL	23	62	16	4	1	3	10	17	0	0	.258	.361	.500	.122	.274	.375	.532	.191	4.6	16-1B 2
2002	OAK	AL	24	124	27	4	0	7	15	38	0	0	.218	.305	.419	-.076	.240	.330	.456	-.021	2.0	38-1B 6
2002	SAC	PCL	24	175	42	10	1	10	24	49	3	0	.240	.340	.480	.066	.215	.306	.429	-.121	-1.9	40-1B 3
2002	DET	AL	24	273	69	13	4	12	26	73	2	2	.253	.321	.462	.042	.275	.343	.507	.104	14.1	70-1B -2
2003	DET	AL	25	452	112	21	6	18	53	123	4	5	.248	.332	.440	.015	.274	.358	.491	.106	8.7	123-1B -11
2004	DET	AL	26	431	109	24	3	19	52	109	5	3	.253	.339	.454	.028	.264	.354	.488	.081	22.4	116-1B -1

Breakout: 27%   Improve: 55%   Collapse: 21%

Three bad months with the A's in 2002 gets you traded to Detroit? Alan Dershowitz has written books on cases that were less egregious miscarriages of justice. Those of you who are skeptical about our defensive metrics should note that Pena's awful showing last year corresponds to a season-long defensive slump that got him benched to clear his head on multiple occasions. Like the team as a whole, Pena deserves a mulligan. He's a better player than he showed last year, and his final numbers weren't that bad for his ballpark. Derrek Lee, who Pena compares favorably to in terms of power and defensive potential, suffered through similar struggles before he broke through.

BEN PETRICK OF/"C" Bats: R Throws: R Born: 07-Apr-77 Age: 27

YEAR	TM	LG	AGE	AB	H	2B	3B	HR	BB	SO	SB	CS	AVG	OBP	SLG	MLVR	EQBA	EQOBP	EQSLG	EQMLVR	VORP	DEFENSE	
2001	COL	NL	24	244	58	15	3	11	31	67	3	3	.238	.327	.459	-.063	.222	.314	.428	-.102	4.9	67-C -7	
2002	CSP	PCL	25	265	85	18	4	16	40	77	10	6	.321	.406	.600	.354	.260	.346	.489	.070	10.4	31-LF -2	18-CF -2
2002	COL	NL	25	95	20	3	1	5	9	33	0	1	.211	.283	.421	-.134	.200	.268	.411	-.227	-1.4	14-C -1	
2003	CSP	PCL	26	228	59	16	3	11	26	53	4	4	.259	.333	.500	.064	.212	.287	.416	-.176	-8.6	18-LF 1	20-1B -1
2003	DET	AL	26	120	27	6	0	4	8	30	0	0	.225	.273	.375	-.190	.248	.295	.413	-.138	-3.1	15-LF -1	11-CF 0
2004	DET	AL	27	150	33	8	1	6	15	42	2	1	.224	.298	.402	-.127	.233	.311	.432	-.088	4.0	43-LF 2	

Breakout: 45%   Improve: 61%   Collapse: 26%

It didn't work out all that well, but Petrick is exactly the sort of player a team in Detroit's position should be taking chances on. He had reached a crisis of confidence after repeated failures with the Rockies, and his defense behind the plate is always going to have teams looking for another position to hide him at. But he's cheap, he's young, and not so long ago we all thought he could hit. Turns out he probably can't, but all it cost the Tigers to find out was Adam Bernero.

RYAN RABURN   3B   Bats: R   Throws: R   Born: 17-Apr-81   Age: 23

YEAR	TM	LG	AGE	AB	H	2B	3B	HR	BB	SO	SB	CS	AVG	OBP	SLG	MLVR	EQBA	EQOBP	EQSLG	EQMLVR	VORP	DEFENSE
2001	ONE	NYP	20	171	62	17	8	8	17	42	1	3	.363	.418	.696	.661	.249	.293	.486	-.038	14.5	41-3B -17
2002	WMI	MID	21	150	33	10	1	6	16	46	0	2	.220	.306	.420	.049	.179	.242	.346	-.379	-9.2	17-3B -5
2003	LAK	FLA	22	325	72	14	3	12	45	89	2	1	.222	.332	.394	.049	.181	.266	.338	-.342	-18.1	82-3B -5
2004	*DET*	*AL*	*23*	*253*	*53*	*13*	*1*	*8*	*20*	*72*	*1*	*1*	*.210*	*.278*	*.366*	*-.217*	*.219*	*.290*	*.394*	*-.186*	*-0.2*	*69-3B -7*

Breakout: 35%   *Improve: 67%*   *Collapse: 14%*

Raburn is a secondary-skills goof whose prospect status has been hurt by his inconsistent batting average, which given the natural variance in that stat makes him a good candidate for a breakthrough this year. He has now fully recovered from a hip injury and lost some weight, and given the organizational depth at third base the Tigers moved him to second in instructional league. A middle infielder with pop would be a welcome development in this organization.

CODY ROSS   OF   Bats: R   Throws: L   Born: 23-Dec-80   Age: 23

YEAR	TM	LG	AGE	AB	H	2B	3B	HR	BB	SO	SB	CS	AVG	OBP	SLG	MLVR	EQBA	EQOBP	EQSLG	EQMLVR	VORP	DEFENSE		
2001	LAK	FLA	20	482	133	34	5	15	44	96	28	5	.276	.337	.461	.148	.228	.275	.396	-.215	-24.6	116-LF 4		
2002	ERI	EAS	21	400	112	28	3	19	44	86	16	2	.280	.352	.507	.172	.231	.295	.422	-.139	-10.6	84-LF -2	18-CF 0
2003	TOL	INT	22	470	135	35	6	20	32	86	15	6	.287	.333	.515	.182	.264	.317	.484	.016	11.8	96-RF 2	16-CF -1
2004	*DET*	*AL*	*23*	*317*	*80*	*18*	*2*	*12*	*24*	*61*	*9*	*3*	*.253*	*.309*	*.433*	*-.048*	*.264*	*.323*	*.466*	*-.001*	*11.1*	*84-RF -1*		

Breakout: 30%   *Improve: 59%*   *Collapse: 21%*

The height bias doesn't just work against pitchers. Ross, who's probably the Tigers' best prospect in the high minors even though his season ended with a torn ACL, was marked down for his performance because, in the words of one observer, he's "a little man trying to play a big man's game." He plays the big man's game pretty well, actually, unless you're not impressed by a .515 slugging average in Triple-A at age 22. The Tigers themselves are divided as to whether he'll make it as a starter or as a fourth outfielder. I guess they'd rather he emulate the game of...

ALEX SANCHEZ   CF   Bats: L   Throws: L   Born: 26-Aug-76   Age: 27

YEAR	TM	LG	AGE	AB	H	2B	3B	HR	BB	SO	SB	CS	AVG	OBP	SLG	MLVR	EQBA	EQOBP	EQSLG	EQMLVR	VORP	DEFENSE		
2001	IND	INT	24	335	105	14	5	1	22	44	27	8	.313	.359	.394	.077	.295	.340	.375	-.072	7.4	72-CF -9		
2001	MIL	NL	24	68	14	3	2	0	5	13	6	2	.206	.260	.309	-.364	.203	.257	.319	-.373	-4.7			
2002	MIL	NL	25	394	114	10	7	1	31	62	37	14	.289	.343	.358	-.021	.292	.345	.365	-.079	7.1	86-CF 0	16-LF 0
2003	MIL	NL	26	163	46	10	3	0	7	28	8	6	.282	.316	.380	-.058	.285	.320	.382	-.107	1.2	36-CF 1	
2003	DET	AL	26	394	114	13	5	1	18	46	44	18	.289	.320	.355	-.086	.310	.344	.383	-.041	6.3	98-CF -6	
2004	*DET*	*AL*	*27*	*467*	*124*	*19*	*6*	*3*	*26*	*66*	*31*	*10*	*.266*	*.309*	*.353*	*-.145*	*.277*	*.322*	*.379*	*-.107*	*3.1*	*119-CF -1*		

Breakout: 15%   *Improve: 32%*   *Collapse: 40%*

...who is a great example of the difference between speed as a *tool* and speed as a *skill*. Sanchez is very, very fast. But in the outfield, his speed is negated by horrible defensive instincts—there hasn't been a player with a higher ratio of speed to defensive ability since Luis Polonia. Offensively, the value of his speed is compromised by his poor OBP, and when he does reach base he gets poor jumps and uses worse judgment, which is why his career stolen base percentage is a break-even 70%. His performance is 99% motion and 1% movement. The trade of actual, live, breathing minor league players to get him is the single most compelling reason to doubt Dombrowski's competence, if not sanity.

RAMON SANTIAGO   2B/SS   Bats: B   Throws: R   Born: 31-Aug-79   Age: 24

YEAR	TM	LG	AGE	AB	H	2B	3B	HR	BB	SO	SB	CS	AVG	OBP	SLG	MLVR	EQBA	EQOBP	EQSLG	EQMLVR	VORP	DEFENSE		
2001	LAK	FLA	21	429	115	15	3	2	54	60	34	8	.268	.361	.331	.009	.222	.291	.281	-.347	-31.1			
2002	ERI	EAS	22	75	21	0	2	1	3	12	6	0	.280	.329	.373	-.041	.253	.288	.333	-.262	-1.3	20-SS 0	
2002	DET	AL	22	222	54	5	5	4	13	48	8	5	.243	.306	.365	-.120	.272	.333	.415	-.046	9.3	63-SS 0	
2003	DET	AL	23	444	100	18	1	2	33	66	10	4	.225	.292	.284	-.279	.249	.316	.316	-.233	-12.3	76-SS 4	50-2B -5
2004	*SEA*	*AL*	*24*	*360*	*89*	*14*	*3*	*4*	*29*	*56*	*10*	*4*	*.248*	*.317*	*.339*	*-.161*	*.252*	*.324*	*.349*	*-.162*	*6.3*	*98-SS -5*		

Breakout: 40%   *Improve: 55%*   *Collapse: 24%*

Two decades ago, the story was that Alan Trammell and Lou Whitaker were so intimately connected that karmic forces prevented either of them from outplaying the other for very long. The same forces appear to have returned to play a joke on the Tigers. After two seasons in the majors, Santiago and Infante are almost indistinguishable statistically. Their

(continued next page)

Ramon Santiago (*continued*)

career OBPs are identical; Santiago has a 14-point edge in slugging, Infante the 18-point edge in batting average. Of course, they're both so bad that a force greater than karma—call it "survival of the fittest"—will likely sweep both of them out of Detroit before long. Santiago was the first to go, traded to Seattle along with middle infield prospect Juan Gonzalez for Carlos Guillen, finally bringing the Tigers an actual big league shortstop.

JUAN TEJEDA   1B   Bats: R   Throws: R   Born: 26-Jan-82   Age: 22

YEAR	TM	LG	AGE	AB	H	2B	3B	HR	BB	SO	SB	CS	AVG	OBP	SLG	MLVR	EQBA	EQOBP	EQSLG	EQMLVR	VORP	DEFENSE	
2002	WMI	MID	20	524	157	34	6	11	60	89	5	1	.300	.372	.450	.240	.234	.293	.366	-.218	-22.1	134-1B -6	
2003	LAK	FLA	21	461	129	28	4	10	56	68	6	3	.280	.360	.423	.160	.229	.293	.365	-.223	-22.0	109-1B -14	
2004	DET	AL	22	256	58	13	1	6	20	47	2	1	.226	.286	.353	-.209	.235	.299	.379	-.178	-4.2	70-1B -8	

Breakout: 30%   Improve: 48%   Collapse: 23%

The Tigers' 2002 Minor League Player of the Year had arguably a more impressive season last year, given how tough it is to hit for power in the Florida State League. He's going to have to continue to hit well, because this slow first baseman will go only as far as his bat carries him. He's not in the Clevlen/Granderson class of Tiger prospect, but in this organization anyone with a pulse has a chance to surface in Detroit.

ANDRES TORRES   CF   Bats: R   Throws: R   Born: 26-Jan-78   Age: 26

YEAR	TM	LG	AGE	AB	H	2B	3B	HR	BB	SO	SB	CS	AVG	OBP	SLG	MLVR	EQBA	EQOBP	EQSLG	EQMLVR	VORP	DEFENSE			
2001	ERI	EAS	23	252	74	16	3	1	36	50	19	11	.294	.391	.393	.114	.243	.331	.324	-.196	-3.9	54-CF -1			
2002	TOL	INT	24	462	123	17	8	4	53	116	42	12	.266	.345	.364	-.021	.248	.325	.342	-.180	-4.6	115-CF -13			
2002	DET	AL	24	70	14	1	1	0	6	16	2	2	.200	.266	.243	-.381	.239	.306	.282	-.306	-3.1	18-CF -2			
2003	TOL	INT	25	271	69	13	3	2	18	61	27	11	.255	.301	.347	-.119	.239	.289	.331	-.272	-10.5	70-CF -3			
2003	DET	AL	25	168	37	4	3	1	10	35	5	5	.220	.263	.298	-.321	.243	.289	.331	-.270	-9.9	29-CF -2	11-RF	1
2004	DET	AL	26	260	62	11	3	4	21	58	13	5	.238	.299	.346	-.189	.247	.312	.371	-.156	-0.4	71-CF -4			

Breakout: 42%   Improve: 57%   Collapse: 29%

Nook Logan, take a look: This could be your career in two years. Ordinarily, Torres would have no business ever playing regularly in the major leagues. But given that none of their center field options are going to be with the team for long, the Tigers might as well suck it up offensively with the player whose glove gives their young pitchers the best chance to develop.

KEVIN WITT   1B   Bats: L   Throws: R   Born: 05-Jan-76   Age: 28

YEAR	TM	LG	AGE	AB	H	2B	3B	HR	BB	SO	SB	CS	AVG	OBP	SLG	MLVR	EQBA	EQOBP	EQSLG	EQMLVR	VORP	DEFENSE			
2001	POR	PCL	25	456	132	28	5	27	22	127	1	1	.289	.322	.550	.164	.264	.302	.501	.014	13.4	76-1B -5	16-RF	-2
2002	LOU	INT	26	509	134	32	1	24	34	140	0	1	.263	.314	.472	.063	.245	.297	.446	-.091	-1.1	64-1B -3	24-LF	0
2003	TOL	INT	27	133	42	10	0	9	16	36	0	0	.316	.391	.594	.397	.281	.356	.548	.189	11.8	24-1B -3	12-3B	-2
2003	DET	AL	27	270	71	9	0	10	15	68	1	1	.263	.301	.407	-.065	.283	.325	.445	-.009	2.3	24-1B 1			
2004	STL	NL	28	265	64	14	1	10	22	74	1	1	.242	.303	.418	-.101	.246	.305	.439	-.081	3.4	71-1B -4			

Breakout: 18%   Improve: 35%   Collapse: 45%

According to the Tigers' media guide, in 1994 Witt "topped all Pioneer League shortstops with 99 assists." Which begs the question, how bad were the other shortstops in that league? Witt deservedly got his first extended shot in the majors after hitting at least 23 home runs for six straight minor league seasons. After being released by the Tigers, he signed a minor league deal with St. Louis. If he gets a chance to play, he's almost even money to post a higher slugging average this year than Tino Martinez.

DMITRI YOUNG   Hitter   Bats: B   Throws: R   Born: 11-Oct-73   Age: 30

YEAR	TM	LG	AGE	AB	H	2B	3B	HR	BB	SO	SB	CS	AVG	OBP	SLG	MLVR	EQBA	EQOBP	EQSLG	EQMLVR	VORP	DEFENSE			
2001	CIN	NL	27	540	163	28	3	21	37	77	8	5	.302	.350	.481	.106	.299	.348	.477	.093	21.6	70-LF -1	25-1B	1
2002	DET	AL	28	201	57	14	0	7	12	39	2	0	.284	.329	.458	.076	.309	.352	.505	.151	12.6	14-1B -2			
2003	DET	AL	29	562	167	34	7	29	58	130	2	1	.297	.372	.537	.269	.322	.396	.586	.352	55.4	58-LF 1	16-3B	-3
2004	DET	AL	30	439	123	25	2	19	37	89	3	1	.279	.340	.475	.077	.291	.355	.510	.136	28.2	115-DH 0			

Breakout: 2%   Improve: 20%   Collapse: 36%

Wally Berger and Richie Ashburn welcome Young to the exclusive club of hitters who had great seasons on awful teams. Here's a list of the five players since 1900 whose EqA most exceeded their team's winning percentage (min: 450 PA):

Year	Team	Pct.	Player	EqA	Difference
1916	Philadelphia A's	.235	Amos Strunk	.308	.073
1935	Boston Braves	.248	Wally Berger	.320	.072
1928	Boston Braves	.327	Rogers Hornsby	.383	.056
1962	New York Mets	.250	Richie Ashburn	.303	.053
2003	Detroit Tigers	.265	Dmitri Young	.312	.047

Speaking of famous performances for legendarily bad teams, why doesn't anyone talk about Dmitri's time at the hot corner last season in the same hushed tones that delivered Marv Throneberry's reviews for the '62 Mets? Young was only the third player in the last 30 years to handle 50 chances at third base with a fielding percentage under .850. Nevertheless, he had a better season than trendy MVP candidates like David Ortiz and Shannon Stewart, and is the one player the Tigers can cash in for some real building blocks. His contract is not nearly as unmovable as it once was, following his '03 performance.

PITCHERS

MATT ANDERSON

Bats: R　　Throws: R　　Born: 17-Aug-76　　Age: 27

YEAR	TM	LG	AGE	G	GS	IP	H	BB	SO	HR	ERA	EQERA	EQH9	EQBB9	EQSO9	EQHR9	PERA	VORP	STF
2001	DET	AL	24	62	0	56.0	56	18	52	2	4.82	4.09	8.5	2.6	7.7	0.3	3.46	9.2	31
2002	DET	AL	25	12	0	11.0	17	8	8	1	9.00	8.18	13.1	5.7	5.7	0.8	6.86	-3.2	-25
2003	TOL	INT	26	23	5	38.0	50	8	31	4	3.79	6.49	13.5	2.3	6.0	1.6	7.04	-3.4	-35
2003	DET	AL	26	23	0	23.3	25	9	13	5	5.41	5.48	9.0	3.1	4.7	1.6	5.18	-2.2	-30
2004	DET	AL	27	25	0	27.0	31	10	17	5	5.57	5.80	10.1	3.1	5.6	1.4	5.65	2.0	-13

Breakout: 28%　　Improve: 57%　　Collapse: 22%

It's not completely fair to blast the Tigers for using the #1 overall pick on him in 1997—*Baseball America* ranked him as the best pitching prospect in college that year—but how can you think that any reliever is worthy of the #1 pick? After a muscle tear in his right shoulder shelved him for most of 2002, he lost about 5 mph on his fastball when he returned. Since Anderson's entire repertoire revolved around throwing his fastball harder than all but a few men on earth, if he doesn't get it back, he's probably toast.

KENNY BAUGH

Bats: R　　Throws: R　　Born: 05-Feb-79　　Age: 25

YEAR	TM	LG	AGE	G	GS	IP	H	BB	SO	HR	ERA	EQERA	EQH9	EQBB9	EQSO9	EQHR9	PERA	VORP	STF
2001	WMI	MID	22	6	6	34.0	31	10	39	0	1.59	5.16	11.2	3.9	6.4	0.3	5.03	1.5	24
2001	ERI	EAS	22	5	5	30.3	23	6	30	5	2.97	4.94	8.6	2.3	6.3	2.3	5.56	2.0	-2
2003	LAK	FLA	24	4	4	21.0	21	11	12	2	3.86	7.36	11.8	6.4	3.4	2.9	9.06	-3.6	-88
2003	ERI	EAS	24	19	19	109.7	111	32	58	16	4.59	6.45	11.2	3.3	3.9	2.6	7.53	-9.2	-53
2004	DET	AL	25	14	8	43.3	57	25	20	9	7.40	7.72	11.7	4.9	4.1	1.8	7.57	-5.8	-28

Breakout: 29%　　Improve: 43%　　Collapse: 26%

Pitch counts have taken a dramatic decline in the major leagues over the past five years, but the changes made at the collegiate level have been much more modest. Baugh is sad testimony to the fact that no matter how proactive professional teams are at protecting their young pitchers, occasionally you find out that you drafted damaged goods. Upon his return from rotator cuff surgery, he was throwing only 2 mph slower than before, but sometimes the difference between 89 and 91 makes all the difference in the world.

JEREMY BONDERMAN
Bats: R   Throws: R   Born: 28-Oct-82   Age: 21

YEAR	TM	LG	AGE	G	GS	IP	H	BB	SO	HR	ERA	EQERA	EQH9	EQBB9	EQSO9	EQHR9	PERA	VORP	STF
2002	MOD	CAL	19	25	25	144.7	129	55	160	15	3.61	5.96	9.0	4.2	6.2	1.5	5.44	-5.4	18
2003	DET	AL	20	33	28	162.0	193	58	108	23	5.56	5.62	10.3	3.1	5.8	1.2	5.32	-15.5	26
2004	DET	AL	21	24	23	141.0	147	55	102	18	4.67	4.87	9.2	3.4	6.3	1.1	4.83	13.6	9

Breakout: 23%   Improve: 55%   Collapse: 10%

Okay, so Bonderman survived his trial by fire without getting hurt or being admitted to a sanitarium. But what pressing emergency required the Tigers to rush a 20-year-old pitcher to the majors without having spent a single day in Double-A or Triple-A? The Tigers claimed they wanted Bonderman to work with Bob Cluck all season, but what does that say about your minor league development guys when you don't trust them to not ruin your most promising arm in the span of a few months?

The Tigers would have lost nothing by starting Bonderman in Triple-A and promoting him as soon as he got comfortable. What they lost by keeping him in the majors all season was a year of service time. In essence, the Tigers decided that a year of Bonderman pitching for a hopeless team at age 20 was more valuable than a year of Bonderman at age 26 pitching for a team that might be in contention. Or maybe they didn't think about it much at all. The Tigers would be smart to send him back to Triple-A to start this season, rebuilding his confidence while delaying his free agency by a year. Even smart GMs sometimes have trouble admitting they've made a mistake.

ADRIAN BURNSIDE
Bats: R   Throws: L   Born: 15-Mar-77   Age: 27

YEAR	TM	LG	AGE	G	GS	IP	H	BB	SO	HR	ERA	EQERA	EQH9	EQBB9	EQSO9	EQHR9	PERA	VORP	STF
2001	JAX	SOU	24	13	12	67.7	44	30	67	6	2.66	4.22	8.3	4.8	6.2	1.4	5.07	9.2	-5
2001	ALT	EAS	24	6	6	32.3	28	14	32	3	3.62	5.34	9.7	5.3	6.3	1.3	5.75	0.8	-9
2002	ALT	EAS	25	32	23	130.7	120	67	122	18	4.54	6.28	10.7	5.6	6.4	2.3	7.51	-8.8	-55
2003	ERI	EAS	26	15	11	67.3	81	27	46	9	6.29	8.24	13.9	4.6	5.0	2.4	8.87	-17.3	-77
2004	DET	AL	27	16	5	33.7	39	23	20	6	6.66	6.94	10.3	5.8	5.2	1.6	6.94	-0.4	-24

Breakout: 32%   Improve: 56%   Collapse: 21%

You'd never know it by the numbers above, but teams are drawn to Burnside like an adolescent male to Hilary Duff. He was selected in the Rule 5 draft by the Reds in 1999 (but returned to the Dodgers); the Pirates insisted on him in the Terry Mulholland deal; the Tigers got him in the Randall Simon trade. The combination of being left-handed and Australian is apparently impossible to resist. Of course, for each team that's acquired him, another one is getting rid of him, which suggests that he looks a lot better from a distance than in person.

JON CONNOLLY
Bats: R   Throws: L   Born: 24-Aug-83   Age: 20

YEAR	TM	LG	AGE	G	GS	IP	H	BB	SO	HR	ERA	EQERA	EQH9	EQBB9	EQSO9	EQHR9	PERA	VORP	STF
2002	ONE	NYP	18	14	14	85.3	102	10	50	7	4.01	8.48	14.2	1.6	3.1	2.4	8.33	-23.8	-22
2003	WMI	MID	19	25	25	166.0	128	38	104	4	1.41	3.54	7.8	2.8	3.9	0.6	3.58	34.9	24
2004	DET	AL	20	22	20	129.7	144	31	70	17	4.49	4.68	9.8	2.0	4.7	1.1	4.63	15.1	4

Breakout: 31%   Improve: 74%   Collapse: 0%

Ladies and gentlemen, presenting your minor league ERA leader for 2003! Never mind the portly physique—Connolly has roughly the body of a 20-year-old Sid Fernandez—or the mid-80s fastball. The Tigers shut him down early simply for reaching his innings quota for the year, which means, if nothing else, that they're protecting his arm like he's a prospect. Every pitcher cut from this cloth gets compared to Jamie Moyer. Given that Connolly's biggest assets are his changeup and his control, the pitcher he might compare best with is Glendon Rusch.

NATE CORNEJO
Bats: R   Throws: R   Born: 24-Sep-79   Age: 24

YEAR	TM	LG	AGE	G	GS	IP	H	BB	SO	HR	ERA	EQERA	EQH9	EQBB9	EQSO9	EQHR9	PERA	VORP	STF
2001	ERI	EAS	21	19	19	124.3	107	41	105	12	2.68	4.59	8.7	4.0	5.5	1.2	4.85	12.8	15
2001	TOL	INT	21	4	4	29.7	24	7	22	1	2.12	2.79	6.2	2.5	5.6	0.3	2.43	9.1	45
2001	DET	AL	21	10	10	42.7	63	28	22	10	7.38	7.80	12.2	5.3	4.2	1.9	7.66	-10.4	-16
2002	TOL	INT	22	21	20	132.3	163	31	86	11	4.42	5.77	10.5	2.4	5.2	0.9	4.97	-2.4	16
2002	DET	AL	22	9	9	50.0	63	18	23	6	5.04	5.29	10.6	2.9	3.8	0.9	5.16	1.7	8
2003	DET	AL	23	32	32	194.7	236	58	46	18	4.67	4.75	10.4	2.6	2.1	0.8	4.85	13.2	-1
2004	DET	AL	24	28	23	137.3	164	52	52	17	5.21	5.44	10.5	3.3	3.3	1.1	5.54	3.2	-13

Breakout: 6%   Improve: 51%   Collapse: 13%

Mike Maroth may have had the 21 losses, but Cornejo had the more historic season. Not only was his strikeout rate the lowest in 50 years, it occurred in the most prolific strikeout era of all-time. Cornejo struck out 3.98 fewer batters per nine innings than the league did as a whole. That's the greatest disparity in major league history, and it's not close (min: 150 IP):

Year	Pitcher	K/9	League	Difference
2003	Nate Cornejo	2.13	6.11	3.98
1969	Joe Niekro	2.45	6.02	3.57
2002	Kirk Rueter	3.36	6.77	3.41
1999	Scott Karl	3.37	6.69	3.32
1972	Steve Kline	2.21	5.50	3.29

Cornejo didn't compensate for his strikeout rate elsewhere: His control was good but not great, and his home run rate was below league average only because of his home ballpark. Yet his final ERA was only slightly above league average. When scouts evaluate his stuff, his fastball grades out at 50, his changeup grades out at 50, and his Jedi Mind Trick grades out at 80. His performance last season is about as sustainable as anti-matter.

ERIC ECKENSTAHLER   Bats: L   Throws: L   Born: 17-Dec-76   Age: 27

YEAR	TM	LG	AGE	G	GS	IP	H	BB	SO	HR	ERA	EQERA	EQH9	EQBB9	EQSO9	EQHR9	PERA	VORP	STF
2001	ERI	EAS	24	46	0	64.7	65	31	73	7	3.89	5.88	11.6	6.0	7.1	1.6	7.12	-1.8	-31
2002	TOL	INT	25	52	0	67.0	57	35	69	8	4.43	5.25	8.6	5.7	7.9	1.6	5.69	2.4	-24
2003	DET	AL	26	20	0	15.7	9	15	12	0	2.87	2.93	5.3	8.2	6.5	0.0	3.34	4.1	10
2003	TOL	INT	26	39	0	42.7	32	25	40	2	3.16	4.66	7.7	6.8	6.8	0.7	4.62	4.0	-13
2004	DET	AL	27	26	0	29.0	29	19	26	4	4.98	5.19	8.9	5.5	7.8	1.1	5.63	3.4	-4

Breakout: 39%   Improve: 48%   Collapse: 43%

He's a left-hander who can throw in the low 90s, he throws an occasionally-plus curveball, and struggles with his command: Man, there are *a lot* of guys like Eckenstahler trying to stick in the majors. The former 32nd-round pick would be a generic reliever in any other organization, but his strikeout rate—he's whiffed a man an inning at every level—makes him one of the better pitching prospects in the Tigers' system. Which is very sad indeed.

FRANKLYN GERMAN   Bats: R   Throws: R   Born: 20-Jan-80   Age: 24

YEAR	TM	LG	AGE	G	GS	IP	H	BB	SO	HR	ERA	EQERA	EQH9	EQBB9	EQSO9	EQHR9	PERA	VORP	STF
2001	VIS	CAL	21	53	0	63.3	67	31	93	7	3.98	6.07	12.0	5.9	7.7	1.9	7.63	-2.9	-15
2002	MID	TEX	22	37	0	41.3	28	27	59	0	3.05	3.58	7.6	6.9	9.6	0.2	4.16	8.5	36
2002	TOL	INT	22	23	0	22.7	15	7	31	0	1.59	2.11	6.3	3.4	11.4	0.0	2.40	8.3	73
2003	TOL	INT	23	24	0	29.3	21	9	32	2	2.46	3.29	6.9	3.3	8.2	1.0	3.57	7.0	23
2003	DET	AL	23	45	0	44.7	47	45	41	5	6.04	6.09	9.1	8.5	7.9	0.8	5.81	-3.7	5
2004	DET	AL	24	35	5	56.3	50	33	58	4	4.15	4.32	7.8	5.0	9.0	0.7	4.39	9.9	11

Breakout: 28%   Improve: 53%   Collapse: 23%

When you consider he's the window dressing in the Jeff Weaver deal, it was a hell of a trade for Detroit. He's reminiscent of Armando Benitez in his body type and his fastball-splitter repertoire, and Benitez's development as a closer was also hampered by severe struggles with his command. Like Benitez, German is capable of absolutely unhittable stretches, but he's likely always going to give up too many walks to let his manager feel completely at ease.

SETH GREISINGER   Bats: R   Throws: R   Born: 29-Jul-75   Age: 28

YEAR	TM	LG	AGE	G	GS	IP	H	BB	SO	HR	ERA	EQERA	EQH9	EQBB9	EQSO9	EQHR9	PERA	VORP	STF
2002	ERI	EAS	26	4	4	21.0	12	9	21	1	1.29	2.33	6.1	4.7	6.5	0.9	3.55	7.0	7
2002	DET	AL	26	8	8	37.7	46	13	14	4	6.21	5.11	10.2	2.9	3.2	1.0	5.07	2.0	-14
2003	TOL	INT	27	25	21	136.0	154	23	80	16	3.97	5.70	11.4	1.9	4.3	1.7	6.19	-1.4	-30
2004	MIN	AL	28	18	10	60.7	72	18	30	10	5.27	5.15	10.3	2.5	4.5	1.3	5.25	4.9	-9

Breakout: 19%   Improve: 46%   Collapse: 23%

(continued next page)

Seth Greisinger *(continued)*

Greisinger needed nearly three years to return to the mound after Tommy John surgery, which has to be the most circuitous recovery this side of Jose Rijo. Greisinger had a disappointing career for a #1 pick even before the injury, so even though he appears to have topped out as a good finesse pitcher in Triple-A, the surgery is less to blame for that than the fact that he wasn't as good as everyone thought to begin with. Signed with the Twins as a six-year minor league free agent.

ROB HENKEL											Bats: R		Throws: L				Born: 03-Aug-78		Age: 25
YEAR	TM	LG	AGE	G	GS	IP	H	BB	SO	HR	ERA	EQERA	EQH9	EQBB9	EQSO9	EQHR9	PERA	VORP	STF
2002	JUP	FLA	23	14	12	75.3	55	22	82	4	2.51	4.03	9.1	3.4	6.9	1.2	4.87	11.7	11
2002	PME	EAS	23	13	13	70.0	54	27	68	6	3.86	4.26	8.7	4.1	6.7	1.3	4.95	9.4	8
2003	ERI	EAS	24	16	16	82.7	67	27	70	7	3.37	4.24	9.1	3.6	6.2	1.5	5.21	11.2	-4
2004	DET	AL	25	21	14	80.7	84	36	59	10	4.87	5.08	9.2	3.8	6.4	1.1	5.02	5.8	2

Breakout: 17%   Improve: 47%   Collapse: 23%

Mark Redman won a World Series, but Rob Henkel is now the Tigers' best pitching prospect in the high minors. It makes sense that the Tigers would try to raid the Marlins' farm system for prospects, given that their front office was more familiar with it than the Marlins were. Henkel did miss half the season with assorted injuries—a rib strain, a biceps injury, some back pain—none of them considered serious. He's already 25, but a lot of left-handed pitchers who reach the majors at that age go on to have long careers. Jeff Fassero didn't debut until he was 28.

GARY KNOTTS											Bats: R		Throws: R				Born: 12-Feb-77		Age: 27
YEAR	TM	LG	AGE	G	GS	IP	H	BB	SO	HR	ERA	EQERA	EQH9	EQBB9	EQSO9	EQHR9	PERA	VORP	STF
2001	CLG	PCL	24	21	21	118.7	136	43	104	16	5.46	4.99	9.4	3.7	5.5	1.2	5.19	7.8	-2
2002	CLG	PCL	25	42	0	53.0	53	32	44	4	4.25	4.89	9.4	6.2	5.6	0.7	5.28	3.9	-18
2002	FLA	NL	25	28	0	30.7	21	16	21	6	4.40	4.25	6.4	4.2	5.5	1.8	4.52	4.5	-25
2003	TOL	INT	26	13	13	79.0	98	28	63	15	5.13	7.23	13.2	4.1	5.8	2.8	8.86	-12.9	-64
2003	DET	AL	26	20	18	95.3	111	47	51	14	6.04	5.77	10.0	4.1	4.7	1.2	5.47	-9.7	-15
2004	DET	AL	27	23	16	92.3	108	43	55	17	6.05	6.31	10.3	4.0	5.2	1.6	6.19	-0.5	-12

Breakout: 26%   Improve: 46%   Collapse: 28%

The Tigers also acquired Knotts in the Redman deal, though they'd probably like to keep that on the down-low. As long as they're going to get their brains beat in for a few more years, the Tigers would be better off using their pitching staff as a sort of proving grounds for alternative pitchers—knuckleballers, sidearmers, that Japanese pitcher who throws a gyroball, whatever. Giving innings to a guy like Knotts, who throws just like a major league pitcher, only worse, isn't going to accomplish anything now or in the future.

PRESTON LARRISON											Bats: R		Throws: R				Born: 19-Nov-80		Age: 23
YEAR	TM	LG	AGE	G	GS	IP	H	BB	SO	HR	ERA	EQERA	EQH9	EQBB9	EQSO9	EQHR9	PERA	VORP	STF
2001	ONE	NYP	20	10	8	47.3	37	21	50	1	2.47	5.01	9.1	5.9	5.4	0.7	5.01	2.7	12
2002	LAK	FLA	21	21	19	120.3	86	45	92	6	2.39	4.30	8.7	4.2	4.9	1.1	4.83	15.4	9
2003	ERI	EAS	22	24	24	126.7	161	59	53	10	5.61	7.69	12.8	5.1	3.1	1.3	7.23	-26.6	-29
2004	DET	AL	23	16	10	50.7	71	36	15	9	8.03	8.37	12.4	6.1	2.5	1.6	8.32	-10.0	-42

Breakout: 17%   Improve: 45%   Collapse: 34%

His arm hurt when he showed up in camp, and after starting his season a month late, he pitched like it. Larrison is emblematic of the dangers of evaluating a draft class on the basis of their first three months. At the end of the 2001 season, the Tigers' first six draft picks that summer all looked like potential stars. Since then, Baugh and Larrison got hurt, Matt Coenen was traded to the Braves for a Rule 5 pick, and Hannahan, Michael Woods, and Mike Rabelo have failed to develop at all. Drafting college players only lowers your risk; it doesn't eliminate it.

WIL LEDEZMA											Bats: L		Throws: L				Born: 21-Jan-81		Age: 23
YEAR	TM	LG	AGE	G	GS	IP	H	BB	SO	HR	ERA	EQERA	EQH9	EQBB9	EQSO9	EQHR9	PERA	VORP	STF
2002	AUG	SAL	21	5	5	23.7	23	8	38	0	3.80	5.66	12.2	4.4	8.7	0.4	5.64	-0.1	36
2003	DET	AL	22	34	8	84.0	99	35	49	12	5.79	5.36	10.2	3.5	5.1	1.2	5.42	-1.6	3
2004	DET	AL	23	27	13	75.3	93	41	43	13	6.48	6.75	10.8	4.6	5.0	1.5	6.79	0.7	-19

Breakout: 20%   Improve: 49%   Collapse: 21%

Ledezma was about as scouty a pick as any Rule 5'er ever. Limited by an elbow stress fracture, he had thrown just 27 innings the two previous years, and had never pitched above the South Atlantic League. But he pitched for Phil Regan (the Tigers' manager in the Midwest League) in winter ball, showed a mid-90s fastball with an excellent change, and that was enough to get him picked. He had a pretty good season for a guy who jumped four levels. The Tigers are still high on him, but it will be a few years before we have any idea if he's got the goods or not.

SHANE LOUX Bats: R Throws: R Born: 31-Aug-79 Age: 24

YEAR	TM	LG	AGE	G	GS	IP	H	BB	SO	HR	ERA	EQERA	EQH9	EQBB9	EQSO9	EQHR9	PERA	VORP	STF
2001	TOL	INT	21	28	27	151.0	203	73	72	22	5.78	7.56	10.2	4.7	3.6	1.4	6.01	-32.7	-11
2002	DET	AL	22	3	3	14.0	19	3	7	4	9.00	7.90	11.2	2.0	4.6	2.6	7.23	-3.5	-22
2002	TOL	INT	22	26	26	158.3	196	38	87	11	4.72	6.05	10.4	2.5	4.4	0.8	4.80	-7.7	12
2003	DET	AL	23	11	4	30.3	37	12	8	4	7.13	6.07	10.3	3.3	2.4	1.2	5.52	-4.9	-23
2003	TOL	INT	23	21	20	128.0	129	30	58	5	3.02	4.39	8.9	2.5	3.3	0.5	3.85	16.3	11
2004	*DET*	*AL*	*24*	*20*	*13*	*72.7*	*87*	*31*	*35*	*10*	*5.56*	*5.80*	*10.5*	*3.7*	*4.1*	*1.2*	*5.76*	*1.6*	*-15*

Breakout: 14%   Improve: 50%   Collapse: 27%

A member of that maddening group of pitchers whose fastball looks good to the scouts and better to the hitters. Loux, like a lot of pitchers drafted in the Randy Smith era, throws 89–92 with a little sink, but if it's not 92, it tends to get crushed. This has led to criminally low strikeout rates and inconsistent success despite his ability to limit homers and walks. Realistically, his upside is at the Tanyon Sturtze/Don Wengert level that epitomizes this group, which is to say, the Tigers might be better off if he never develops to that point at all.

MIKE MAROTH Bats: L Throws: L Born: 17-Aug-77 Age: 26

YEAR	TM	LG	AGE	G	GS	IP	H	BB	SO	HR	ERA	EQERA	EQH9	EQBB9	EQSO9	EQHR9	PERA	VORP	STF
2001	TOL	INT	23	24	23	131.7	158	50	63	11	4.65	6.02	10.1	3.8	3.4	0.9	5.19	-5.9	-8
2002	DET	AL	24	21	21	128.7	136	36	58	7	4.48	3.85	8.8	2.3	3.8	0.4	3.64	24.6	19
2002	TOL	INT	24	11	11	73.3	53	22	51	7	2.82	3.56	7.0	3.2	5.3	1.2	3.81	15.5	8
2003	DET	AL	25	33	33	193.3	231	50	87	34	5.73	5.39	10.2	2.2	4.0	1.4	5.36	-8.4	-12
2004	*DET*	*AL*	*26*	*25*	*21*	*129.3*	*153*	*40*	*57*	*19*	*5.27*	*5.50*	*10.5*	*2.7*	*3.9*	*1.3*	*5.40*	*5.2*	*-8*

Breakout: 10%   Improve: 41%   Collapse: 24%

The Tigers did do some positive things for baseball. Thanks to Maroth, we are no longer subject to Brian Kingman watches every September. He'll do as a placeholder, but the Tigers need to resist the temptation to believe the dictum that "you have to be a pretty good pitcher to lose 20 games." Actually, you only have to be pretty durable. Maroth surrendered a league-high 34 homers in the toughest home-run park in the league, and that's one number his teammates didn't have a hand in. He's a poor man's Brian Anderson, and the real thing has enough flaws as it is.

CHRIS MEARS Bats: R Throws: R Born: 20-Jan-78 Age: 26

YEAR	TM	LG	AGE	G	GS	IP	H	BB	SO	HR	ERA	EQERA	EQH9	EQBB9	EQSO9	EQHR9	PERA	VORP	STF
2001	SBR	CAL	23	38	12	107.0	104	49	74	10	4.46	6.89	11.3	5.6	3.6	1.7	7.12	-13.5	-51
2002	SAN	TEX	24	30	20	143.3	138	38	103	16	3.14	5.41	11.5	2.9	5.0	2.3	7.16	2.7	-38
2003	TOL	INT	25	25	5	58.3	53	19	28	5	2.78	4.00	8.7	3.7	3.5	1.2	4.76	9.6	-25
2003	DET	AL	25	29	3	41.3	50	11	21	5	5.45	5.13	10.5	2.2	4.5	0.9	4.89	-1.8	-9
2004	*DET*	*AL*	*26*	*23*	*7*	*49.0*	*56*	*19*	*28*	*7*	*5.28*	*5.50*	*10.0*	*3.2*	*4.9*	*1.3*	*5.42*	*2.6*	*-13*

Breakout: 27%   Improve: 54%   Collapse: 15%

Fifty pitchers saved at least five games in the majors last season, and Mears might have been the most unlikely. He was signed as a minor league free agent—sense a trend here?—last December. Mears slings the ball from a near-sidearm angle that yields just average velocity but terrific movement. As you would expect, he ate up right-handed hitters (.230/.299/.310) while getting abused by left-handers (.395/.432/.645). The list of pitchers that fit Mears's profile—Steve Reed, Chad Bradford, etc.—were all similarly unwanted at some point in their careers. Mears is probably still years away from his peak.

DANNY PATTERSON   Bats: R   Throws: R   Born: 17-Feb-71   Age: 33

YEAR	TM	LG	AGE	G	GS	IP	H	BB	SO	HR	ERA	EQERA	EQH9	EQBB9	EQSO9	EQHR9	PERA	VORP	STF
2001	DET	AL	30	60	0	64.7	64	12	27	4	3.06	3.13	8.1	1.6	3.4	0.6	3.27	17.4	0
2003	TOL	INT	32	10	0	11.0	8	5	6	0	2.45	2.70	7.2	5.4	3.6	0.0	3.43	3.2	-1
2003	DET	AL	32	19	0	17.7	15	4	19	1	4.07	3.12	7.3	2.1	9.3	0.5	2.91	3.3	37
2004	*DET*	*AL*	*33*	*62*	*0*	*39.7*	*42*	*12*	*25*	*3*	*4.14*	*4.32*	*9.4*	*2.7*	*5.5*	*0.7*	*4.27*	*6.2*	*-6*

Breakout: 29%   *Improve: 51%*   *Collapse: 32%*

Tommy John surgery has made his contract an albatross, but Patterson is an underrated middle reliever who generates groundballs and throws strikes when healthy. Upon his return from surgery, Patterson—who struck out less than a batter every other inning in 2000 and 2001—fanned 19 in 18 innings. That could be a function of small sample size, or perhaps a sign that he was pitching with an elbow problem long before surgery. If true, he could be a much better pitcher in his rebuilt form. Much like the man whose role he essentially took in Detroit, Doug Brocail, Patterson is a luxury on a bad team. Assuming the Tigers pick up most of his salary, he's one of their few commodities that a savvy team ought to inquire about.

ADAM PETTYJOHN   Bats: R   Throws: L   Born: 11-Jun-77   Age: 27

YEAR	TM	LG	AGE	G	GS	IP	H	BB	SO	HR	ERA	EQERA	EQH9	EQBB9	EQSO9	EQHR9	PERA	VORP	STF
2001	TOL	INT	24	17	17	107.3	107	26	78	9	3.44	4.60	9.1	2.5	5.0	1.0	4.40	11.3	8
2001	DET	AL	24	16	9	65.0	81	21	40	10	5.82	5.88	10.4	2.7	5.0	-1.3	5.34	-2.0	-4
2003	ERI	EAS	26	19	10	81.0	87	18	49	9	4.00	5.53	12.2	2.5	4.4	2.0	7.07	0.6	-49
2004	*SFG*	*NL*	*27*	*23*	*7*	*50.3*	*56*	*17*	*30*	*7*	*4.71*	*4.96*	*9.9*	*2.6*	*4.8*	*1.2*	*5.00*	*5.0*	*-10*

Breakout: 28%   *Improve: 54%*   *Collapse: 20%*

Having made a complete recovery after ulcerative colitis sent him to numerous surgeries, frightening weight loss and the near loss of his life, you'd imagine that Pettyjohn regards anything he accomplishes in his baseball career as mere gravy. He returned to the mound last summer and acquitted himself well in Double-A. We obviously don't have an extensive track record of pitchers recovering from near-death experiences to compare him to. Never underestimate a man who regards every sunrise as a blessing and every pitch as a gift. He signed a minor-league deal with the Giants.

NATE ROBERTSON   Bats: R   Throws: L   Born: 03-Sep-77   Age: 26

YEAR	TM	LG	AGE	G	GS	IP	H	BB	SO	HR	ERA	EQERA	EQH9	EQBB9	EQSO9	EQHR9	PERA	VORP	STF
2001	BRV	FLA	23	19	19	106.3	95	43	67	3	2.88	5.46	9.9	4.3	3.8	0.7	4.96	1.5	-4
2002	PME	EAS	24	27	27	163.0	156	50	109	12	3.42	4.83	10.3	3.3	4.5	1.2	5.40	12.6	-7
2003	TOL	INT	25	24	23	155.0	145	47	102	14	3.14	4.41	9.1	3.4	4.8	1.3	4.98	18.9	-8
2003	DET	AL	25	8	8	44.7	55	23	33	6	5.44	5.32	10.6	4.3	6.5	1.0	5.62	1.4	5
2004	*DET*	*AL*	*26*	*21*	*15*	*86.0*	*98*	*39*	*49*	*11*	*5.21*	*5.44*	*10.1*	*3.9*	*5.0*	*1.1*	*5.53*	*3.5*	*-7*

Breakout: 19%   *Improve: 45%*   *Collapse: 26%*

Like Knotts, he was essentially ballast in the Redman-for-Henkel deal. Robertson is a Wichita State alumnus who, in keeping with contractual obligations all pitchers make to the university, underwent major arm surgery—in his case, Tommy John—soon after he was drafted. While the organization is still somewhat optimistic that he could be a late-bloomer a la Mark Redman, there's little to recommend here even if he stays healthy.

FERNANDO RODNEY   Bats: R   Throws: R   Born: 18-Mar-77   Age: 27

YEAR	TM	LG	AGE	G	GS	IP	H	BB	SO	HR	ERA	EQERA	EQH9	EQBB9	EQSO9	EQHR9	PERA	VORP	STF
2001	LAK	FLA	24	16	9	55.3	53	19	44	2	3.42	5.88	11.4	3.9	4.8	0.9	5.77	-1.5	-18
2002	ERI	EAS	25	21	0	20.3	14	5	18	0	1.33	2.37	7.1	2.4	5.7	0.5	2.93	6.8	11
2002	TOL	INT	25	20	0	22.3	13	9	25	1	0.81	2.18	6.1	4.4	8.7	0.4	2.98	7.9	28
2002	DET	AL	25	20	0	18.0	25	10	10	2	6.00	6.50	11.5	4.5	4.5	1.0	6.09	-1.8	-27
2003	TOL	INT	26	38	0	40.7	22	13	58	0	1.33	1.95	6.3	3.6	10.5	0.2	2.69	15.0	44
2003	DET	AL	26	27	0	29.7	35	17	33	2	6.06	5.52	10.1	4.9	9.8	0.6	5.05	-1.2	17
2004	*DET*	*AL*	*27*	*36*	*4*	*52.7*	*51*	*26*	*48*	*5*	*4.46*	*4.65*	*8.6*	*4.2*	*7.9*	*0.9*	*4.69*	*8.1*	*4*

Breakout: 29%   *Improve: 53%*   *Collapse: 22%*

Along with German, Rodney gives the Tigers two prototypical, fire-breathing, wild-as-sin minor league relievers who are struggling to make the transition to the major leagues. Whereas German tries to bury hitters with a splitter, Rodney relies on what teams call a Bugs Bunny-changeup. Attention rotoheads: He also goes into spring training with a head start on the closer's job. Keep in mind, the track record of minor league closers is gruesome, as command or health issues prevent most of them from major league success. Just as the best way to develop a starting pitcher remains to start with five minor league starters, the best way to develop a relief pitcher remains to start with five minor league starters.

MATT RONEY						Bats: R			Throws: R						Born: 10-Jan-80		Age: 24
YEAR	TM	LG	AGE	G	GS	IP	H	BB	SO	HR	ERA	EQERA	EQH9	EQBB9	EQSO9	EQHR9	PERA	VORP	STF
2001	ASH	SAL	21	23	23	121.0	131	43	115	16	4.98	7.34	13.4	5.0	5.0	2.8	9.20	-19.9	-43
2002	ASH	SAL	22	14	14	82.7	82	25	88	7	3.48	5.33	11.6	3.7	5.7	2.0	7.06	2.2	-16
2002	CAR	SOU	22	13	13	70.7	73	33	61	6	6.11	6.44	11.2	4.5	5.6	1.5	6.53	-6.0	-7
2003	DET	AL	23	45	11	100.7	102	48	47	17	5.45	5.20	8.6	4.0	4.1	1.4	5.03	-3.1	-13
2004	DET	AL	24	33	12	72.0	94	48	47	18	8.04	8.38	11.5	5.7	5.7	2.2	8.22	-16.9	-28

Breakout: 16%   Improve: 52%   Collapse: 18%

Another Rule 5 pick, Roney was a former first-rounder discarded by the Rockies. Unlike Ledezma, Roney did have some upper-level minor-league experience, but his upside is decidedly smaller. In many ways, he resembles Jeff Farnsworth, who the Tigers took in the Rule 5 draft in 2002. Farnsworth didn't resurface last year, and the team's protestations that he has a higher ceiling aside, Roney can expect to meet the same fate.

KYLE SLEETH	Bats: R	Throws: R	Born: 20-Dec-81	Age: 22

As if the Tigers hadn't suffered enough, in the 2003 amateur draft that contained only two obvious franchise talents, Delmon Young and Rickie Weeks, the Tigers picked third. (Because the leagues alternate the first pick, the Tigers won't have the first pick this year even after 119 losses.) Sleeth was their default pick, the best collegiate pitcher in the draft. While he signed too late to pitch in the minors, the Tigers are happy with his ability to throw four pitches for strikes and think he can move quickly.

CHRIS SPURLING						Bats: R			Throws: R						Born: 28-Jun-77		Age: 27
YEAR	TM	LG	AGE	G	GS	IP	H	BB	SO	HR	ERA	EQERA	EQH9	EQBB9	EQSO9	EQHR9	PERA	VORP	STF
2001	ALT	EAS	24	34	15	121.7	133	28	63	9	3.11	5.37	11.1	2.8	3.2	1.1	5.55	2.8	-22
2002	ALT	EAS	25	51	0	70.0	54	12	60	8	2.19	3.57	8.9	1.9	5.7	1.9	5.05	14.2	-28
2003	DET	AL	26	66	0	77.0	78	22	38	9	4.68	4.20	8.6	2.4	4.3	1.0	4.15	7.2	-10
2004	DET	AL	27	36	7	62.3	71	19	35	9	5.11	5.33	10.1	2.7	4.9	1.3	5.22	3.9	-12

Breakout: 22%   Improve: 39%   Collapse: 22%

The Tigers got their third Rule 5 pick courtesy of the Braves, who initially drafted him away from Pittsburgh before thinking better of it. Spurling has the least upside but the most polish of the three, and is the only one who is likely to spend most of this season in the Tigers' bullpen. Despite excellent control, it's unlikely he'll ever strike out enough hitters to find sustained major league success.

ANDY VAN HEKKEN						Bats: R			Throws: L						Born: 31-Jul-79		Age: 24
YEAR	TM	LG	AGE	G	GS	IP	H	BB	SO	HR	ERA	EQERA	EQH9	EQBB9	EQSO9	EQHR9	PERA	VORP	STF
2001	LAK	FLA	21	19	19	110.7	105	33	82	8	3.17	5.36	10.8	3.3	4.5	1.6	6.18	2.6	-5
2001	ERI	EAS	21	8	8	48.0	63	8	29	5	4.69	7.05	12.5	2.0	3.8	1.2	6.13	-7.2	-2
2002	ERI	EAS	22	21	21	134.0	138	34	97	10	3.83	4.92	9.5	2.6	4.8	1.1	4.75	9.5	9
2002	TOL	INT	22	7	7	49.3	41	11	19	4	1.83	3.26	7.1	2.3	3.1	1.0	3.41	12.2	10
2002	DET	AL	22	5	5	30.0	38	6	5	2	3.00	3.99	10.4	1.5	1.5	0.6	4.42	5.2	4
2003	ERI	EAS	23	13	13	80.7	89	18	32	13	4.01	5.94	11.6	2.5	2.8	2.7	7.77	-2.7	-50
2003	TOL	INT	23	13	12	72.0	93	18	25	11	5.88	6.92	11.7	2.8	2.5	2.0	6.95	-9.9	-37
2004	DET	AL	24	16	11	54.3	79	34	18	6	7.23	7.54	12.8	5.3	2.9	0.9	7.46	-4.2	-31

Breakout: 11%   Improve: 46%   Collapse: 32%

(continued next page)

Andy Van Hekken (continued)

He's a Michigan native who the Tigers acquired from the Mariners in the Brian Hunter trade to make up for missing him in the draft. Van Hekken is a perfectly competent minor league southpaw who suffers from the same problem as nearly every other starter in the organization: He doesn't miss many bats. The Tigers struck out just 764 batters, the fewest by any team in a full season since the 1992 Tigers whiffed just 693. The farm system is similarly bereft of starters with above-average strikeout rates. Dombrowski has an enviable track record of developing power pitchers, which is good, because he got exactly zero help from his predecessor in that department.

JAMIE WALKER Bats: L Throws: L Born: 01-Jul-71 Age: 33

YEAR	TM	LG	AGE	G	GS	IP	H	BB	SO	HR	ERA	EQERA	EQH9	EQBB9	EQSO9	EQHR9	PERA	VORP	STF
2001	BUF	INT	30	38	8	93.0	104	27	51	12	3.87	5.70	11.3	3.1	3.9	1.6	6.29	-0.9	-42
2002	TOL	INT	31	10	0	13.7	7	3	9	2	1.97	2.13	5.0	2.1	5.0	2.1	3.52	4.9	-29
2002	DET	AL	31	57	0	43.7	32	9	40	9	3.71	3.14	6.1	1.7	7.7	1.7	3.38	11.8	2
2003	DET	AL	32	78	0	65.0	61	17	45	9	3.32	3.69	8.0	2.3	6.1	1.1	3.94	11.7	-1
2004	DET	AL	32	41	0	50.3	53	16	34	9	4.71	4.91	9.3	2.7	5.9	1.5	4.99	5.7	-8

Breakout: 17%   Improve: 41%   Collapse: 32%

Give opportunities to enough replacement-level players, and a few will stick to the wall by sheer chance. Walker washed out of the Royals system in 2000—something nearly impossible for a pitcher to do at the time—but has enjoyed a nice rebirth out of the Tigers' bullpen the last two years. Even so, he forever lives on the edge; 18 homers in 109 innings over the last two years, in the game's most spacious park for lefties, translates into disaster almost anywhere else. Given his low margin for error, the Tigers would do well to cash him in now for whatever they can get.

JOEL ZUMAYA Bats: R Throws: R Born: 09-Nov-84 Age: 19

YEAR	TM	LG	AGE	G	GS	IP	H	BB	SO	HR	ERA	EQERA	EQH9	EQBB9	EQSO9	EQHR9	PERA	VORP	STF
2003	WMI	MID	18	19	19	90.3	69	38	126	3	2.79	5.02	8.8	5.4	9.3	0.8	4.78	5.2	56

The inherent unpredictability of pitchers can cut both ways. For every Ryan Anderson, there's a Joel Zumaya, an 11th-round draft pick that was throwing 88 in high school but showed up in camp throwing 93. Presto, chango: You've got the best pitching prospect in the organization, even though he did miss six weeks with back pain last summer. He's the only starter in the organization with an eye-opening strikeout rate, and he now sits comfortably at 94–96. The Tigers can only hope that Zumaya's emergence is the start of a trend even as they acknowledge that it was an anomaly.

Kansas City Royals

An important scientific innovation rarely makes its way by gradually winning over and converting its opponents. What does happen is that its opponents gradually die out, and that the growing generation is familiarized with the ideas from the beginning.

MAX PLANCK

The best revolutions don't happen overnight. Progress is best made when old ideas are gradually replaced by new ones. Try to rush the process, and the end result is usually violent and bloody. Ask the Russians and French how their Revolutions went.

So it shouldn't disappoint anyone that the sabermetric revolution is moving at its own pace. We're not going to wake up one morning and find that all 30 major league teams are suddenly enamored with on-base percentage, understand the importance of replacement level, and evaluate minor league players on their performance more than their tools. The revolution occurs haltingly, one team at a time, as a believer gets promoted here and a grizzled old-schooler retires there.

Let us welcome the newest team to the party. A team that previously was so possessed with Neanderthal ideas from baseball past that its progress, to this point, has been written off as a natural regression to the pack. Make no mistake, though: The Kansas City Royals have joined the revolution, and the results figure to turn baseball on its ear in the Midwest.

As in Oakland and Toronto, the Royals' new-found philosophy can be essentially traced to the influence of one man. But in complete contradistinction to Billy Beane and J. P. Ricciardi, Allard Baird has never been considered one of the leading lights of sabermetric thought within baseball. With good reason; whereas Beane and Ricciardi were already disciples of sabermetric thinking before they were made general managers, Baird's path to becoming a believer had only begun when he was named to run the Royals. He is the exception that proves Planck's rule.

The ongoing education of Allard Baird is the most satisfying explanation for the dichotomy, until recently, between his words and his deeds. From the moment he was hired, Baird issued proclamations on the importance of plate discipline that had never before been heard from anyone associated with the Royals. His words were drowned out by a series of trades that seemed to betray common

ROYALS PROSPECTUS

2003 record: 83–79; Third place, AL Central

Pythagenport record: 78–84

Runs scored per game: 5.2 (4th in AL)

Runs allowed per game: 5.4 (12th in AL)

Team EqA: .251 (11th in AL)

2003 Batters Age: 29.6 (7th oldest in AL)

2003 Pitchers Age: 28.4 (4th youngest in AL)

Ballpark: Kaufmann Stadium; Severe hitter's park; Park Factor of 1.100

2003: The feel-good story of the American League before falling behind the Twins after the break.

2004: It'll take some luck for the Royals to run with the Twins and White Sox again.

sense, let alone a sabermetric viewpoint, and for a time made Baird the laughingstock of baseball.

A re-examination of his two most notorious trades are in order, because understanding why he made them is key to understanding what's really going on in Kansas City. Three years ago, Baird traded Johnny Damon (and Mark Ellis) in a three-way deal that netted him Roberto Hernandez (and Angel Berroa). At the time, Baird was blasted for trading an All-Star centerfielder for an aging closer whose value was more opportunity than performance. And deservedly so, but what was not seen at the time was that the secondary exchange of prospects, which appeared equal at the time, was not. Mark Ellis appears to have topped out offensively at a marginal level for a second baseman. Berroa is the AL Rookie of the Year. It's hard to say that Baird got taken by Billy Beane when he ended up with the best player in the deal.

Eighteen months later, he traded Jermaine Dye for Neifi Perez, a deal that defies analysis or explanation, but at least comes with an excuse: Baird was forced by owner David Glass to trade Dye for the best offer on the table. We're not sure what twisted set of circumstances could combine to make Neifi Perez the best *anything,* but trading under duress has torpedoed plenty of other teams too.

While those two trades certainly symbolized Baird's failure as a GM, a third transaction didn't trail by much. After standing by Tony Muser long past the point of merit, Baird bypassed the obvious choice to replace him, Buck Showalter, to take a chance on another first-time manager in Tony Pena. At the time, this looked like another nail in the coffin over Baird's claims to believe in the importance of plate discipline and OBP. Pena's singular weakness throughout his major league career was his poor strike zone judgment, and on the theory that most managers mold their team in their own image, it appeared to be more of the same in Kansas City. The back-story is that Pena himself admitted to Baird, before he was hired, that his inability to control the strike zone was his biggest weakness as a player. He fully supported an organizational approach to better plate discipline; he wouldn't have been hired if he hadn't. Two years later, Pena is the reigning Manager of the Year, while Showalter can't get along with the best player in the league.

Suddenly, Baird appears in a much more favorable light. He looks less like a man with a schizophrenic understanding of baseball and more like a GM trying to improve his craft over time, who has made a few obvious and highly publicized mistakes in the process of doing so.

Baird's task as GM has been complicated by the organization he was put in charge of. The Royals don't have a history of enlightened management for Baird to build upon. Whereas Billy Beane benefited from Sandy Alderson's previous association with the A's, Baird is starting the process completely fresh.

This caused problems when the organization initially failed to embrace Baird's enthusiasm for plate discipline; few of the old coaches at any level of the farm system could adjust to their boss' new thinking. The tide only started to turn organizationally last winter, when major league hitting coach Lamar Johnson, who had chafed at the new philosophy, was let go. Baird contacted Jeff Pentland, the man credited with turning Sammy Sosa's career around, almost as soon as he was fired by the Cubs. And after years of being told by his minor league coaches that they didn't want to "take away a hitter's aggressiveness" by emphasizing walks, Baird worked around the problem by telling them to emphasize the importance of getting into good hitter's counts to allow those hitters to "unleash their aggressiveness." Baird's efforts are slowly starting to bear fruit. Over the past two seasons the Royals have ranked eighth and ninth in walks, after finishing higher than 10th just once in the previous 22 years. There's still a long way to go, but at least they're making decent progress.

Of course, there's more to modern baseball thinking than simply acknowledging the importance of OBP. Baird's influence in other areas is easier to track. Under Herk Robinson, the Royals essentially ignored the minor league free agent market as a source of talent. Under Baird, they have been among the most active teams in baseball. This winter, for instance, they signed Calvin Pickering and Joe Dawley, two of the best performers in Triple-A the last few years.

The Royals' thirst for alternative talent sources goes beyond minor league free agents. K.C. has drafted a quality pitching prospect in each of the last two Rule 5 drafts; Miguel Asencio and D. J. Carrasco both figure to feature prominently this season. Baird snagged Darrell May out of Japan and Aaron Guiel out of Mexico. Last summer, Baird added the Indy leagues to his resume, turning Jose Lima from the ace of the Newark Bears to a contributing starter on a team that stayed in first place longer than anyone expected. Emboldened by the success of that move, and recognizing an acute organizational need for catchers, this winter Baird signed Kirk Pierce and Charles Alley, the first- and second-team catchers on *Baseball America*'s Independent League All-Star squad.

In addition to learning new ideas, Baird has done a masterful job of admitting his past mistakes in the most eloquent way possible: by not repeating them. While Berroa rescued the Damon trade, the fact remains that Baird made the trade for the wrong reason: to acquire an established closer. Did he learn from his mistake? Consider that last season, the Royals made the rare move of entrusting the job to a rookie on Opening Day. Mike MacDougal had never even pitched in relief regularly until the August '02. But for the major league minimum, Baird got roughly the same level of performance from MacDougal that Hernandez had delivered for $6 million a year.

In the immensely-talented 2001 draft, new scouting director Deric Ladnier completely screwed the pooch by selecting raw, risky high school talent with almost every pick. First-rounder Colt Griffin still can't throw strikes, but his pick looks like genius compared to second-rounder Roscoe Crosby, who collected $1.25 million—without ever playing in a minor league game—before bolting for college football. Since that debacle, the Royals have been much more judicious with their high school picks; last season they selected high school players with just four of their first 23 picks. Overall, their 2003 draft was one of the five most college-focused in the game.

Best of all, the mistakes Baird made—like nearly every GM in baseball—by spending millions of dollars on mediocre veterans whose market value plummeted after the 2001 season, have finally come off the books. As a result, the Royals went into this off-season with just two players earning guaranteed money in 2004: Desi Relaford (at $900,000) and Mike Sweeney.

There were approximately 29 teams in baseball that had at least one albatross contract they were looking to unload this winter. The A's had Jermaine Dye at $13.5 million for another season; Boston couldn't waive Manny Ramirez's $20 million-a-year contract. Even the Blue Jays are paying Carlos Delgado millions more than he would get on the open market. Virtually alone in baseball, the Royals suddenly had no dead weight on the payroll, and instead had the financial flexibility to pick up quality free agents who are undervalued in today's market because no one has any money to spend.

The irony is that the Royals' performance on the field last season, in which they held first place for 106 days and led the division by seven games at the All-Star Break, garnered Baird the right attention for all the wrong reasons. The Royals were not a good team last year; they were a 73-win team that rode a fluky performance with runners in scoring position and a weak schedule to a winning record. But it says something about Baird that, privately at least, he concedes that the Royals were playing way over their head last season.

He entered this off-season at the helm of a franchise that could improve structurally in 2004 and still win only 77 games, while working for an owner that refused to believe that his team's winning record last season was a fluke. Working from such an unenviable position, Baird did an impressive job of threading the needle, improving the Royals in the short-term without jeopardizing their long-term plans in the slightest. Happily, the market for mid-tier free agents has cratered, and the Royals were one of the few teams poised to take advantage of it. The Royals signed no less than ten free agents by mid-December, yet not one signed for more than $3.25 million a season, not one got a guaranteed contract longer than two years, and not one

required the Royals to give up a draft pick. Compare what the Royals are paying these 11 free agents to what they paid some of their players last season in table 1.

Factoring in the major league minimum for the four additional roster spots, the second column of players, featuring talent upgrades at seven spots, will cost just $1.8 million more than the first. Even accounting for arbitration-induced raises for Beltran and Darrell May, Baird was able to dramatically upgrade his mid-tier talent without significantly increasing payroll.

And in another sign of the Bizarro World we've suddenly entered, the Royals were the prime beneficiaries of other teams' madness. Despite announcing to the world that none of their free agents would be offered arbitration, the Royals got a pair of draft picks for Raul Ibanez when the Mariners couldn't contain themselves. They again got draft pick compensation when, hours before the deadline, the Giants signed Michael Tucker, deliberately giving away their first-round pick rather than bear the thought of drafting a top-quality player.

The Royals still have a long way to go, and Baird still has plenty of room for improvement. His biggest weakness, his loyalty (also viewed by some as his biggest virtue), needs to be put to the test. Baird's first challenge on that front came after the team's medical staff presided over far too many injuries—large and small, mundane and bizarre, unexpected and predictable—last season. As unimpressive as the Royals were on paper, they may have held onto their seven-game lead at the All-Star Break had they been able to keep Sweeney healthy, or Relaford, or at least a couple of their starting pitchers.

Going forward, the Royals' greatest asset in terms of talent resides in a cheap, promising pitching staff, filled with pitchers like Jeremy Affeldt and MacDougal, who have

TABLE 1.

2003		2004	
Joe Randa:	$4.5 million	Juan Gonzalez:	$4 million
Raul Ibanez:	$3 million	Joe Randa:	$3.25 million
Brent Mayne:	$2.75 million	Brian Anderson:	$3.25
Michael Tucker:	$2.75 million	Benito Santiago:	$2.15
Jason Grimsley:	$2 million	Scott Sullivan:	$2.1 million
Albie Lopez:	$1.5 million	Curtis Leskanic:	$1.5 million
Mike DiFelice:	$650,000	Tony Graffanino:	$1.1 million
		Matt Stairs:	$1 million
		Jason Grimsley:	$1 million
		Kelly Stinnett:	$500,000
		Kevin Appier:	$300,000
Total:	$17.15 million	Total:	$20.15 million

tremendous breakout potential and are not yet arbitration-eligible. The Royals already lost one of those pitchers, Runelvys Hernandez, to Tommy John surgery. They can't afford to lose any more and still remain competitive the next few years.

In the short term, this is an organization that may need to regroup a little, though with the Twins and White Sox going to great lengths to keep the division up for grabs, the Royals could be a surprise contender for a second straight year. In the long term, baseball in Kansas City looks rosier than it has since the Royals put away the Cardinals in 1985.

HITTER

CARLOS BELTRAN CF Bats: B Throws: R Born: 24-Apr-77 Age: 27

YEAR	TM	LG	AGE	AB	H	2B	3B	HR	BB	SO	SB	CS	AVG	OBP	SLG	MLVR	EQBA	EQOBP	EQSLG	EQMLVR	VORP	DEFENSE	
2001	KCR	AL	24	617	189	32	12	24	52	120	31	1	.306	.362	.514	.178	.314	.374	.533	.233	61.5	149-CF	14
2002	KCR	AL	25	637	174	44	7	29	71	135	35	7	.273	.346	.501	.111	.283	.360	.520	.159	52.1	146-CF	4
2003	KCR	AL	26	521	160	14	10	26	72	81	41	4	.307	.389	.522	.181	.310	.398	.531	.265	49.5	129-CF	5
2004	KCR	AL	27	532	161	31	7	24	64	93	28	7	.302	.377	.522	.216	.288	.368	.505	.148	36.8	142-CF	1

Breakout: 13%   Improve: 39%   Collapse: 18%

One of the top seven or eight franchise talents in baseball right now. With the exception of an injury-marred sophomore campaign, Beltran has made incremental improvements on his Rookie of the Year season every year since. Last year, he set another career high in walks while cutting his strikeout rate by 27%; he set career highs in the three major rate categories; and he improved upon a stolen-base percentage that was already the best in major league history.

A recent study by Nate Silver showed that players that excel at both power and speed have greater longevity than players with either skill alone. Beltran has the greatest power-speed package of any active player under the age of 30. He's entering his age 27 season, which is responsible for more career years than any other age. The possibility of an MVP-caliber season from Beltran single-handedly makes the Royals' hopes of contending this season somewhat realistic. Unless he can fetch Alfonso Soriano, it makes sense for them to hold onto him and settle for draft picks as compensation when he hits free agency at season's end.

BRANDON BERGER OF Bats: R Throws: R Born: 21-Feb-75 Age: 29

YEAR	TM	LG	AGE	AB	H	2B	3B	HR	BB	SO	SB	CS	AVG	OBP	SLG	MLVR	EQBA	EQOBP	EQSLG	EQMLVR	VORP	DEFENSE			
2001	WIC	TEX	26	454	140	28	3	40	43	91	14	6	.308	.383	.648	.449	.255	.318	.537	.083	19.6	38-LF	-2	29-RF	-3
2002	OMA	PCL	27	261	76	16	1	13	25	43	11	2	.291	.363	.510	.189	.260	.324	.458	-.012	3.3	30-LF	2	22-RF	-1
2002	KCR	AL	27	134	27	5	1	6	8	32	1	0	.201	.255	.388	-.242	.209	.262	.410	-.234	-5.8	15-RF	1	11-LF	0
2003	OMA	PCL	28	226	61	16	3	12	31	58	6	1	.270	.367	.527	.213	.237	.328	.474	-.003	4.3	30-RF	3		
2004	KCR	AL	29	186	49	10	1	9	20	41	3	1	.262	.340	.470	.058	.250	.332	.456	-.009	6.5	53-RF	-3		

Breakout: 31%   Improve: 52%   Collapse: 22%

Berger was shipped out to Triple-A after just 32 at-bats, and Aaron Guiel's emergence kept him there even though Berger was the best hitter in Omaha for most of the season. Berger is capable of contributing as a fourth outfielder and a lefty-masher off the bench, but his skills are replaceable enough that whether he gets that shot depends less on him than on how the team decides to address its openings on the outfield corners. Based on their moves in the off-season, that means he's probably buried for another year.

ANGEL BERROA SS Bats: R Throws: R Born: 27-Jan-78 Age: 26

YEAR	TM	LG	AGE	AB	H	2B	3B	HR	BB	SO	SB	CS	AVG	OBP	SLG	MLVR	EQBA	EQOBP	EQSLG	EQMLVR	VORP	DEFENSE	
2001	WIL	CAR	23	199	63	18	4	6	9	41	10	6	.317	.382	.538	.380	.267	.313	.476	.000	12.0	51-SS	-4
2001	WIC	TEX	23	304	90	20	4	8	17	55	15	6	.296	.373	.467	.176	.259	.315	.420	-.083	11.0	78-SS	0
2001	KCR	AL	23	53	16	2	0	0	3	10	2	0	.302	.339	.340	-.103	.321	.357	.358	-.045	2.1	12-SS	0
2002	OMA	PCL	24	297	64	11	4	8	15	84	6	4	.215	.277	.360	-.229	.199	.251	.337	-.362	-13.6	77-SS	0
2002	KCR	AL	24	75	17	7	1	0	7	10	3	0	.227	.301	.347	-.197	.240	.312	.373	-.168	0.7	20-SS	2
2003	KCR	AL	25	567	163	28	7	17	29	100	21	5	.287	.338	.451	-.004	.292	.345	.464	.062	28.2	157-SS	8
2004	KCR	AL	26	506	139	30	6	13	30	90	15	6	.275	.331	.432	.003	.263	.323	.418	-.064	21.1	132-SS	3

Breakout: 26%   Improve: 51%   Collapse: 20%

While his walk rate doesn't show it, Berroa made some solid strides in his plate discipline last year. His average of 3.68 pitches per PA was just a tick under the major league average of 3.75. The stat that would best show the transformation in his approach, Sliders Down and Away that were Spit On, is not officially recognized yet. At age 25, Berroa was pretty old for a traditional Rookie of the Year player, but the potential for continued improvement in strike zone judgment gives him additional upside. If he can simply maintain his rookie performance from now until free agency, he'll be the best shortstop in franchise history.

ANDRES BLANCO   **SS**   **Bats: B**   **Throws: R**   Born: 11-Apr-84   Age: 20

YEAR	TM	LG	AGE	AB	H	2B	3B	HR	BB	SO	SB	CS	AVG	OBP	SLG	MLVR	EQBA	EQOBP	EQSLG	EQMLVR	VORP	DEFENSE
2003	WIL	CAR	19	394	96	11	3	0	44	50	13	7	.244	.330	.287	-.101	.205	.270	.247	-.445	-30.3	106-SS -14
2004	KCR	AL	20	271	57	11	2	2	21	43	5	3	.211	.273	.281	-.333	.201	.267	.272	-.395	-12.6	73-SS -9

Breakout: 35%   Improve: 52%   Collapse: 27%

Though you'd never guess it from the numbers above, Blanco is widely considered one of the Royals' best prospects. In reality, he's about as good as a prospect can be without actually hitting; he played the entire season in the Carolina League at age 19, he has pretty good plate discipline, and his defensive tools are highly regarded. If he can take on a steady growth curve with the bat, he might be a player someday. With Berroa entrenched at shortstop for the next five years, the Royals can afford to wait and see.

DEE BROWN   **OF**   **Bats: L**   **Throws: R**   Born: 27-Mar-78   Age: 26

YEAR	TM	LG	AGE	AB	H	2B	3B	HR	BB	SO	SB	CS	AVG	OBP	SLG	MLVR	EQBA	EQOBP	EQSLG	EQMLVR	VORP	DEFENSE	
2001	KCR	AL	23	380	93	19	0	7	22	81	5	3	.245	.286	.350	-.222	.251	.297	.362	-.205	-14.6	74-LF -1	
2002	OMA	PCL	24	458	126	23	1	17	44	111	10	4	.275	.344	.441	.047	.248	.312	.398	-.128	-10.0	79-LF -3	
2002	KCR	AL	24	51	12	3	1	1	4	20	0	0	.235	.291	.392	-.152	.255	.309	.412	-.108	0.2		
2003	KCR	AL	25	132	30	7	0	2	8	37	1	1	.227	.280	.326	-.315	.229	.287	.336	-.275	-8.3	17-RF 2	11-LF -2
2004	KCR	AL	26	169	43	9	1	5	14	39	2	1	.256	.321	.413	-.053	.244	.313	.400	-.119	0.0	48-LF -2	

Breakout: 40%   Improve: 56%   Collapse: 24%

At some point, you have to cut bait. Brown had only sporadic playing time for the second straight year, but he now has 616 at-bats in the majors, with a career .229 average, 10 homers and 39 walks. Since his breakout minor league season—which occurred last century—he hasn't even put up impressive numbers in the minors. Brown will probably hit somewhere, someday, but it's not going to be Kansas City, 2004. The acquisition of Rich Thompson in the Rule 5 draft should be the final nail in the coffin.

DAVID DeJESUS   **CF**   **Bats: L**   **Throws: L**   Born: 20-Dec-79   Age: 24

YEAR	TM	LG	AGE	AB	H	2B	3B	HR	BB	SO	SB	CS	AVG	OBP	SLG	MLVR	EQBA	EQOBP	EQSLG	EQMLVR	VORP	DEFENSE
2002	WIL	CAR	22	334	99	22	6	4	48	42	15	6	.296	.400	.434	.226	.234	.317	.361	-.179	-3.4	74-CF -5
2002	WIC	TEX	22	79	20	5	2	2	8	10	3	1	.253	.347	.443	.103	.225	.308	.387	-.167	-0.5	19-CF -1
2003	WIC	TEX	23	71	24	4	0	2	9	8	1	3	.338	.422	.479	.326	.278	.351	.403	-.025	2.8	17-CF 0
2003	OMA	PCL	23	215	64	16	3	5	34	30	8	4	.298	.412	.470	.234	.263	.367	.419	.015	10.8	50-CF -7
2004	KCR	AL	24	260	73	17	3	6	28	38	6	3	.280	.362	.439	.068	.267	.354	.425	.002	11.3	73-CF -3

Breakout: 31%   Improve: 53%   Collapse: 24%

DeJesus slipped under the radar screen of most prospect mavens, largely because assorted elbow and shoulder problems delayed his pro debut by 18 months (and cost him the first six weeks of last season). But as a line-drive hitter with good plate discipline, he's reached a .400 OBP in three of four minor league stops, is finally getting taken seriously as one of the best outfield prospects in the game, and made it all the way to the majors for a seven-AB cup o' joe last year. He's heir apparent to Beltran in center field, and would have been a capable apprentice in left field for a year, before the Royals signed Matt Stairs and Juan Gonzalez. To give you an idea of his upside, here are PECOTA's 75th-percentile EqA (Equivalent Average) projections for DeJesus, 2004-2008: .289/.299/.305/.315/.308.

MIKE DiFELICE   C   Bats: R   Throws: R   Born: 28-May-69   Age: 35

YEAR	TM	LG	AGE	AB	H	2B	3B	HR	BB	SO	SB	CS	AVG	OBP	SLG	MLVR	EQBA	EQOBP	EQSLG	EQMLVR	VORP	DEFENSE	
2001	TBY	AL	32	149	31	5	1	2	8	39	1	1	.208	.259	.295	-.348	.228	.282	.322	-.305	-5.1	45-C	4
2002	STL	NL	33	174	40	11	0	4	17	42	0	0	.230	.297	.362	-.128	.243	.309	.384	-.156	0.8	49-C	3
2003	KCR	AL	34	189	48	16	1	3	9	30	1	0	.254	.299	.397	-.172	.261	.305	.415	-.107	-0.7	55-C	2
2004	DET	AL	35	134	28	6	0	3	9	31	1	0	.212	.270	.326	-.281	.220	.282	.350	-.256	-3.0	39-C	1

Breakout: 31%   *Improve: 45%*   *Collapse: 38%*

A card-carrying member of the Backup Catchers Guild, DiFelice has nothing to distinguish him other than a tendency for brutish behavior (as when he was arrested for assaulting two women in a nightclub back in 2001). His garbage-tossing, cooler-breaking tirade after being tossed out of a game on national TV last August was reason enough to cut him loose. Backup catchers with less emotional baggage are easy to find. But apparently, they're not easy to lure to Detroit, because the Tigers signed him to a one-year deal.

DAMASO ESPINO   3B   Bats: B   Throws: R   Born: 08-May-83   Age: 21

YEAR	TM	LG	AGE	AB	H	2B	3B	HR	BB	SO	SB	CS	AVG	OBP	SLG	MLVR	EQBA	EQOBP	EQSLG	EQMLVR	VORP	DEFENSE
2003	BUR	MID	20	480	137	25	3	3	69	76	8	4	.285	.377	.369	.120	.218	.291	.292	-.334	-23.9	114-3B -19
2004	KCR	AL	21	290	67	13	2	3	23	52	3	2	.231	.292	.319	-.240	.221	.285	.309	-.304	-8.8	78-3B -10

Breakout: 22%   *Improve: 44%*   *Collapse: 28%*

Espino, acquired from the Reds for Jeff Austin before the season, is one of the clearest signs that the revolution has reached the lowest levels of the Royals' organization. He joined the Royals as more promise than production, but bought into the program, leading Burlington in walks. He's young enough to translate that plate discipline into a power surge over the next few years.

CARLOS FEBLES   2B   Bats: R   Throws: R   Born: 24-May-76   Age: 28

YEAR	TM	LG	AGE	AB	H	2B	3B	HR	BB	SO	SB	CS	AVG	OBP	SLG	MLVR	EQBA	EQOBP	EQSLG	EQMLVR	VORP	DEFENSE
2001	OMA	PCL	25	98	33	7	1	2	9	14	6	2	.337	.414	.490	.269	.296	.365	.439	.066	7.2	22-2B 2
2001	KCR	AL	25	292	69	9	2	8	22	58	5	2	.236	.291	.363	-.201	.244	.301	.378	-.179	-0.3	69-2B 0
2002	KCR	AL	26	351	86	16	4	4	41	63	16	5	.245	.336	.348	-.123	.257	.346	.366	-.101	7.0	100-2B 4
2003	KCR	AL	27	196	46	5	0	0	13	30	8	2	.235	.299	.260	-.360	.246	.306	.272	-.317	-9.6	55-2B 2
2004	KCR	AL	28	227	59	12	2	3	21	36	7	3	.258	.330	.365	-.097	.246	.323	.353	-.161	5.4	64-2B -1

Breakout: 32%   *Improve: 58%*   *Collapse: 25%*

The final stage of Brent Gates Syndrome is always difficult to watch. Febles, who hit 10 homers as a 23-year-old rookie, slugged just .260 last season. He still plays excellent defense, and could still hang on somewhere in a Rafael Belliard role if he can prove he can move around the diamond. The Dodgers are apparently interested in him, and he would fit perfectly into their offensive philosophy of trying to score as few runs as possible.

BYRON GETTIS   OF   Bats: R   Throws: R   Born: 13-Mar-80   Age: 24

YEAR	TM	LG	AGE	AB	H	2B	3B	HR	BB	SO	SB	CS	AVG	OBP	SLG	MLVR	EQBA	EQOBP	EQSLG	EQMLVR	VORP	DEFENSE
2001	BUR	MID	21	140	44	9	2	5	14	25	4	3	.314	.385	.514	.300	.238	.295	.392	-.175	-5.5	37-LF 9
2001	WIL	CAR	21	303	76	21	2	6	20	70	4	5	.251	.321	.393	.069	.217	.268	.358	-.289	-21.6	75-LF -4
2002	WIL	CAR	22	449	127	33	2	8	48	103	10	5	.283	.364	.419	.146	.228	.293	.351	-.243	-24.9	109-RF -9
2003	WIC	TEX	23	510	154	31	4	16	55	110	15	11	.302	.377	.473	.218	.252	.322	.411	-.088	-3.6	128-RF -3
2004	KCR	AL	24	274	71	17	2	9	23	58	5	2	.259	.328	.428	-.019	.248	.320	.414	-.085	2.5	75-RF -3

Breakout: 34%   *Improve: 52%*   *Collapse: 24%*

A former college football recruit who signed with the Royals as a non-drafted free agent, Gettis had his best season in his first exposure to Double-A. He projects as a classic tweener, with not quite enough glove to play center and not quite enough bat to play the corners. He's got more upside than a player with similar numbers but less athleticism, but not enough that the Royals should regard him as a future cog in their lineup instead of as a trading chit to acquire what they need if they're still in contention at the trading deadline.

ALEXIS GOMEZ

ALEXIS GOMEZ CF Bats: L Throws: L Born: 08-Aug-78 Age: 25

YEAR	TM	LG	AGE	AB	H	2B	3B	HR	BB	SO	SB	CS	AVG	OBP	SLG	MLVR	EQBA	EQOBP	EQSLG	EQMLVR	VORP	DEFENSE		
2001	WIL	CAR	22	169	51	8	2	1	11	43	7	3	.302	.348	.391	.137	.257	.299	.343	-.224	-3.9	45-CF	-3		
2001	WIC	TEX	22	342	96	15	6	4	27	70	16	10	.281	.337	.395	.007	.238	.290	.337	-.262	-12.1	83-CF	-5		
2002	WIC	TEX	23	461	136	21	8	14	45	84	36	24	.295	.359	.466	.185	.245	.300	.403	-.145	0.3	86-CF	-6	24-RF	-3
2003	OMA	PCL	24	457	123	23	8	8	26	92	4	5	.269	.307	.407	-.049	.243	.284	.377	-.214	-8.7	75-CF	-6	44-RF	1
2004	KCR	AL	25	209	55	12	2	5	16	40	4	2	.261	.315	.409	-.064	.249	.307	.397	-.130	-0.3	57-CF	-5		

Breakout: 31% Improve: 56% Collapse: 27%

After years of being the frontrunner to succeed Beltran in center field, Gomez saw his candidacy dogged by a pair of skeletons in his closet: One, that he was two years older than previously listed, and two, that he's not very good. His campaign was finally done in by the revelation that DeJesus is the better (and younger) player. Gomez may still surface one day as an extra outfielder, especially if Jim Bowden resurfaces with another GM job somewhere.

RUBEN GOTAY

RUBEN GOTAY 2B Bats: B Throws: R Born: 25-Dec-82 Age: 21

YEAR	TM	LG	AGE	AB	H	2B	3B	HR	BB	SO	SB	CS	AVG	OBP	SLG	MLVR	EQBA	EQOBP	EQSLG	EQMLVR	VORP	DEFENSE	
2002	BUR	MID	19	509	145	42	9	9	73	110	5	4	.285	.377	.456	.223	.213	.288	.352	-.261	-14.0	115-2B	4
2003	WIL	CAR	20	502	131	31	2	9	60	97	8	1	.261	.343	.384	.053	.211	.278	.324	-.320	-23.3	123-2B	-5
2004	KCR	AL	21	282	65	16	2	5	24	59	2	1	.229	.294	.356	-.191	.218	.287	.344	-.255	-5.9	76-2B	-7

Breakout: 23% Improve: 47% Collapse: 28%

He's no favorite with the scouts, but Gotay has displayed impressive secondary skills as one of the youngest players in his league in back-to-back seasons. It's a testament to the Royals' new philosophy that they consider Gotay one of the team's best prospects, even though the emergence of Donald Murphy a rung below him may convince them to move Gotay to third base. A lot of good hitters have put up mediocre numbers at Wilmington, so look for a breakout season for Gotay at Double-A this year.

AARON GUIEL

AARON GUIEL RF Bats: L Throws: R Born: 05-Oct-72 Age: 31

YEAR	TM	LG	AGE	AB	H	2B	3B	HR	BB	SO	SB	CS	AVG	OBP	SLG	MLVR	EQBA	EQOBP	EQSLG	EQMLVR	VORP	DEFENSE	
2001	OMA	PCL	28	442	118	27	3	21	51	92	6	4	.267	.355	.484	.089	.235	.320	.424	-.087	-2.9	112-RF	-2
2002	OMA	PCL	29	215	76	11	1	9	29	34	8	1	.353	.443	.540	.423	.310	.396	.472	.179	16.2	54-RF	1
2002	KCR	AL	29	240	56	13	0	4	19	61	1	5	.233	.296	.338	-.215	.246	.310	.354	-.194	-8.0	57-RF	-4
2003	OMA	PCL	30	190	53	9	2	8	33	43	3	0	.279	.408	.474	.217	.245	.361	.422	-.006	3.6	47-RF	3
2003	KCR	AL	30	354	98	30	0	15	27	63	3	5	.277	.346	.489	.044	.282	.354	.499	.118	7.7	82-RF	5
2004	KCR	AL	31	306	80	17	1	11	32	63	4	2	.263	.346	.438	.025	.251	.338	.424	-.040	4.3	84-RF	0

Breakout: 19% Improve: 43% Collapse: 32%

A Ken Phelps All-Star made good. Guiel had been a secondary-skills star in the minors for years, but didn't make his major league debut until he was nearly 30. He got a second chance last season and finished behind only Beltran and Sweeney in EqA. He's also an example of what appears to be a new organizational fetish with hit-by-pitches, getting hit 13 times in less than 400 plate appearances last season. (Berroa tied a franchise record with 18; DeJesus has been hit 29 times in just 185 minor league games.) Guiel's role could be reduced with Matt Stairs and Juan Gonzalez around, but he'll still get a chance to hit righties in key spots.

KEN HARVEY

KEN HARVEY 1B Bats: R Throws: R Born: 01-Mar-78 Age: 26

YEAR	TM	LG	AGE	AB	H	2B	3B	HR	BB	SO	SB	CS	AVG	OBP	SLG	MLVR	EQBA	EQOBP	EQSLG	EQMLVR	VORP	DEFENSE	
2001	WIL	CAR	23	137	52	9	1	6	13	21	3	1	.380	.455	.591	.592	.303	.362	.490	.140	9.6	20-1B	0
2001	WIC	TEX	23	314	106	20	3	9	18	60	3	0	.338	.372	.506	.271	.289	.325	.441	-.009	7.0	52-1B	1
2002	OMA	PCL	24	488	135	30	1	20	42	87	8	3	.277	.342	.465	.079	.249	.310	.421	-.099	-2.2	109-1B	-9
2003	KCR	AL	25	485	129	30	0	13	29	94	2	3	.266	.313	.408	-.125	.270	.320	.418	-.068	-6.6	91-1B	5
2004	KCR	AL	26	424	119	28	1	16	31	78	3	2	.280	.333	.463	.051	.267	.325	.448	-.017	11.4	110-1B	-1

Breakout: 42% Improve: 66% Collapse: 13%

OK, now we know why scouts were so unimpressed with him even as he hit .479 in the AFL last year. His groundball/flyball ratio of 2.49 ranked fourth in the majors, behind only Luis Castillo, Juan Pierre, and Jacque Jones; Harvey fits in that group like Donald Rumsfeld at an anti-war protest. He did hit lefties pretty well (.333/.377/.564), which means the Royals can platoon him with Stairs, giving him 200 at-bats this season to see if he can figure out his swing without crippling the team in the process.

RAUL IBANEZ   LF   Bats: L   Throws: R   Born: 02-Jun-72   Age: 32

YEAR	TM	LG	AGE	AB	H	2B	3B	HR	BB	SO	SB	CS	AVG	OBP	SLG	MLVR	EQBA	EQOBP	EQSLG	EQMLVR	VORP	DEFENSE			
2001	KCR	AL	29	279	78	11	5	13	32	51	0	2	.280	.353	.495	.112	.288	.363	.511	.156	16.6	17-RF	-1	12-LF	-1
2002	KCR	AL	30	497	146	37	6	24	40	76	5	3	.294	.346	.537	.178	.304	.361	.558	.237	41.3	42-1B	0	32-LF	-1
2003	KCR	AL	31	608	179	33	5	18	49	81	8	4	.294	.345	.454	.016	.299	.356	.463	.087	9.9	116-LF	-8	19-1B	2
2004	SEA	AL	32	442	117	23	3	15	39	69	4	2	.264	.324	.431	-.018	.268	.331	.444	-.011	8.6	115-LF	-3		

Breakout: 12%   Improve: 40%   Collapse: 31%

The best pickup of the Baird Administration, complete with the appropriate ending: letting him cash in on his free-agent millions elsewhere. Ibanez is a left fielder who's barely league average, who's also on the wrong side of 30; David DeJesus is already a comparable player at 10% the price tag, and he'll get better. Ibanez's bat speed tailed off toward the season's end to boot. The Mariners are going to be staring at a lot of wasted salary by the end of his awful three-year, $13 million contract.

MENDY LOPEZ   IF   Bats: R   Throws: R   Born: 15-Oct-73   Age: 30

YEAR	TM	LG	AGE	AB	H	2B	3B	HR	BB	SO	SB	CS	AVG	OBP	SLG	MLVR	EQBA	EQOBP	EQSLG	EQMLVR	VORP	DEFENSE			
2001	NWO	PCL	27	208	58	11	1	14	18	49	2	2	.279	.343	.543	.199	.257	.319	.495	.028	13.8	33-2B	8	13-SS	-1
2001	PIT	NL	27	43	10	3	1	0	4	16	0	0	.233	.292	.349	-.236	.233	.298	.349	-.233	-1.3				
2002	NAS	PCL	28	385	97	26	0	11	34	99	4	1	.252	.309	.405	-.060	.234	.293	.378	-.202	0.1	59-SS	-5	39-3B	2
2003	KCR	AL	29	94	26	5	1	3	4	28	2	0	.277	.306	.447	-.077	.280	.316	.452	-.017	1.8				
2004	KCR	AL	30	148	37	8	1	5	11	38	2	1	.246	.302	.409	-.097	.235	.295	.396	-.163	1.6	42-3B	1		

Breakout: 21%   Improve: 44%   Collapse: 36%

The Royals had a lot of hitters in their second stint with the team. Unlike Randa or Mayne or Tucker, Lopez's first time around had been forgotten by all but the most ardent fans, but bringing him back certainly made more sense than recycling Tucker and Mayne. Lopez hits with more pop than your typical utility infielder without giving away anything on defense. The Royals wisely gave him a Triple-A contract and an NRI, and he'll compete with Desi Relaford and Tony Graffanino for time at second base and as a utility infielder.

CHRIS LUBANSKI   CF   Bats: L   Throws: L   Born: 24-Mar-85   Age: 19

The #5 pick in last year's draft was a legitimate pick based on his talent, but his imminent signability—he was under contract less than 24 hours after he was drafted—didn't hurt. No doubt helped by the quick negotiations, Lubanski was named the #1 prospect in the Arizona League by Baseball America after hitting .326/.382/.452. He's a Johnny Damon clone, a line-drive hitter with exceptional speed, and the Royals have done well developing this type of player over the last 10 years.

JULIUS MATOS   UT   Bats: R   Throws: R   Born: 12-Dec-74   Age: 29

YEAR	TM	LG	AGE	AB	H	2B	3B	HR	BB	SO	SB	CS	AVG	OBP	SLG	MLVR	EQBA	EQOBP	EQSLG	EQMLVR	VORP	DEFENSE			
2001	MOB	SOU	26	67	22	6	0	0	1	5	1	2	.328	.343	.418	.106	.294	.300	.382	-.138	1.3	11-SS	-1		
2001	POR	PCL	26	383	107	12	2	7	15	48	6	8	.279	.314	.376	-.118	.254	.291	.343	-.241	-4.5	95-SS	-8		
2002	POR	PCL	27	186	58	17	0	4	9	20	1	2	.312	.345	.468	.142	.289	.322	.439	-.017	10.4	46-SS	-5		
2002	SDP	NL	27	185	44	3	0	2	9	33	1	1	.238	.279	.286	-.240	.265	.301	.317	-.252	-3.6	35-2B	-1		
2003	OMA	PCL	28	370	107	19	0	7	13	31	10	5	.289	.325	.397	-.016	.266	.303	.375	-.164	4.0	66-SS	-6	14-LF	-1
2003	KCR	AL	28	57	15	1	0	2	1	12	1	0	.263	.276	.386	-.221	.263	.276	.404	-.175	-0.7				
2004	KCR	AL	29	184	49	9	1	3	8	24	2	1	.263	.302	.372	-.134	.252	.295	.360	-.200	-1.4	50-SS	-8		

Breakout: 22%   Improve: 44%   Collapse: 30%

This is what a utility infielder normally hits like. That's to take nothing away from Matos, who's in good standing in the fraternity of sixth infielders, but he's a step down from Lopez. The amount of time Matos spends on a major league diamond is inversely proportional to the health record of the starting infield, so the Royals hope this is one insurance policy they won't have to make a claim on. The re-upping of Lopez and signing of Graffanino—one of the best utility infielders in the game—make it unlikely that they'll have to.

BRENT MAYNE C Bats: L Throws: R Born: 19-Apr-68 Age: 36

YEAR	TM	LG	AGE	AB	H	2B	3B	HR	BB	SO	SB	CS	AVG	OBP	SLG	MLVR	EQBA	EQOBP	EQSLG	EQMLVR	VORP	DEFENSE	
2001	COL	NL	33	160	53	7	0	0	16	24	0	0	.331	.385	.375	-.002	.314	.377	.352	-.021	6.7	44-C	5
2001	KCR	AL	33	166	40	4	1	2	10	17	1	2	.241	.283	.313	-.279	.248	.298	.321	-.263	-3.8	46-C	-2
2002	KCR	AL	34	326	77	8	2	4	34	54	4	4	.236	.309	.310	-.225	.246	.322	.326	-.209	-3.1	94-C	2
2003	KCR	AL	35	372	91	17	1	6	32	59	0	2	.245	.307	.344	-.232	.249	.317	.352	-.181	-8.3	106-C	1
2004	ARI	NL	36	234	57	9	1	2	22	38	1	1	.242	.307	.318	-.224	.233	.297	.309	-.274	-5.7	64-C	-2

Breakout: 25%   Improve: 43%   Collapse: 31%

For all the talk about how the Royals were lucky to win 83 games last season, it's not hard to see how they can still improve on their record. Mayne batted nearly 800 times the last two seasons even though he was washed up before he ever returned to Kansas City. Benito Santiago is no star, but his numbers the last two seasons tower over Mayne's, despite playing in a much, much more difficult home park. Over the last two seasons, Santiago has hit .290/.337/.480 on the road; Mayne has hit .224/.299/.331. He's Arizona's problem now, after the Snakes inked him to a one-year, $800,000 deal.

TYDUS MEADOWS OF Bats: R Throws: R Born: 05-Sep-77 Age: 26

YEAR	TM	LG	AGE	AB	H	2B	3B	HR	BB	SO	SB	CS	AVG	OBP	SLG	MLVR	EQBA	EQOBP	EQSLG	EQMLVR	VORP	DEFENSE	
2001	WTN	SOU	23	197	53	10	3	10	40	57	0	2	.269	.412	.503	.286	.222	.336	.420	-.072	-1.2	49-LF	-4
2002	WIL	CAR	24	339	100	19	4	11	54	83	13	3	.295	.402	.472	.276	.227	.315	.378	-.164	-12.1	66-LF	-1
2002	WIC	TEX	24	119	41	12	3	4	14	23	4	2	.345	.421	.597	.498	.281	.351	.504	.119	6.5	17-LF	0
2003	WIC	TEX	25	421	122	27	4	17	41	75	14	8	.290	.368	.494	.223	.245	.313	.428	-.086	-4.2	63-LF	-2
2004	TEX	AL	26	192	49	11	1	8	19	42	3	1	.257	.334	.451	.018	.250	.331	.440	-.032	5.7	55-LF	-2

Breakout: 37%   Improve: 54%   Collapse: 25%

A minor league veteran whose primary role in the organization was to provide protection for Byron Gettis in Wichita's lineup. Meadows was a shrewd pickup in the minor league Rule 5 draft two years ago. He's here more for what he represents—a growing organizational focus on acquiring free talent—than for his major league prospects, which are slim to none. Ironically, he was selected again in the minor league Rule 5 draft, this time by the Rangers.

DONALD MURPHY 2B Bats: R Throws: R Born: 10-Mar-83 Age: 21

YEAR	TM	LG	AGE	AB	H	2B	3B	HR	BB	SO	SB	CS	AVG	OBP	SLG	MLVR	EQBA	EQOBP	EQSLG	EQMLVR	VORP	DEFENSE			
2002	SPO	NWN	19	109	33	10	2	0	6	17	0	0	.303	.356	.431	.193	.241	.274	.357	-.263	-3.5	23-SS	-1		
2002	BUR	MID	19	120	27	6	3	0	11	31	0	2	.225	.300	.325	-.090	.185	.240	.274	-.479	-10.1	31-SS	-2		
2003	BUR	MID	20	504	158	29	6	5	65	78	15	6	.313	.397	.425	.238	.239	.307	.337	-.228	-8.6	82-2B	4	40-SS	-2
2004	KCR	AL	21	306	74	17	3	4	23	57	4	2	.240	.300	.353	-.176	.229	.293	.342	-.240	-2.4	82-2B	-4		

Breakout: 27%   Improve: 43%   Collapse: 28%

A fifth-round pick out of a community college in 2002, Murphy emerged as one of the hardest-working players in the Midwest League last season. A number of observers compared him to a young Craig Biggio, which is absurd, but he does compare favorably to one-time Royals' second-base prospect Mark Ellis. Murphy is a better player than Ellis at the same age; he was a Midwest League All-Star at age 20, while Ellis wasn't even drafted until he was 22. Between Murphy and Gotay, the Royals can take the quantity-is-quality approach to developing a second baseman, hoping that one of them will emerge as a quality major leaguer.

JARROD PATTERSON 3B/1B Bats: L Throws: R Born: 07-Sep-73 Age: 30

YEAR	TM	LG	AGE	AB	H	2B	3B	HR	BB	SO	SB	CS	AVG	OBP	SLG	MLVR	EQBA	EQOBP	EQSLG	EQMLVR	VORP	DEFENSE			
2001	ERI	EAS	27	70	28	5	1	7	11	11	0	0	.400	.476	.800	.853	.306	.390	.625	.378	12.6	20-3B	-3		
2001	TOL	INT	27	213	63	15	2	7	30	47	2	1	.296	.381	.484	.217	.271	.355	.450	.042	14.5	37-3B	1		
2001	DET	AL	27	41	11	1	1	2	0	4	0	1	.268	.302	.488	.047	.293	.318	.537	.124	2.5				
2002	TOL	INT	28	447	132	34	6	13	46	71	3	1	.295	.364	.485	.190	.270	.339	.454	.018	26.5	68-3B	0	40-2B	-10
2003	OMA	PCL	29	478	123	33	2	18	51	92	4	1	.257	.329	.448	.035	.229	.298	.406	-.157	3.4	71-3B	-1	28-1B	-6
2004	KCR	AL	30	170	45	11	1	6	17	34	1	1	.262	.332	.437	.001	.250	.324	.423	-.065	6.8	49-3B	-5		

Breakout: 26%   Improve: 49%   Collapse: 30%

A long-time minor league star whose glove at third base has held him back, Patterson nearly made the team out of spring training, only to slump to his worst season in the minors since the mid-90s. The Royals still like his bat, and he played outfield in winter ball to enhance his versatility, which now that Joe Randa has signed may be his only way to sell the team on his merits.

BRANDON POWELL 2B **Bats: L** **Throws: R** Born: 15-Aug-80 Age: 23

If the triple is the most exciting play in baseball, then Powell was the most exciting player in the game last year, hitting 15 three-baggers in just 52 rookie-league games while hitting .330/.402/.583. Powell, like a lot of his teammates, shouldn't have been in the league to begin with. The Royals lost the annual game of organizational musical chairs and were without a high-level rookie affiliate, forcing them to play two minor league teams in the same league. Powell, along with Division II Player of the Year Mike Aviles (.363/.404/.585 and the league MVP) and first-rounder Mitch Maier (.350/.403/.507), led the team to the Arizona League championship.

Powell and Aviles were both college seniors, and both were drafted largely for economic reasons. The Royals used their fifth- through ninth-round picks on college seniors, and gave each player a take-it-or-leave-it offer of $1,000 to sign. With no leverage to speak of, all five signed quickly, even though only two other players drafted in those five rounds signed for less than five figures. Whether the Royals are poised to start a new trend or if this is just a one-year aberration, the fact is they managed to save nearly $600,000 in those five rounds while taking just a marginal hit, if any, in prospect quality.

JOE RANDA 3B **Bats: R** **Throws: R** Born: 18-Dec-69 Age: 34

YEAR	TM	LG	AGE	AB	H	2B	3B	HR	BB	SO	SB	CS	AVG	OBP	SLG	MLVR	EQBA	EQOBP	EQSLG	EQMLVR	VORP	DEFENSE	
2001	KCR	AL	31	581	147	34	2	13	42	80	3	2	.253	.307	.386	-.132	.261	.320	.401	-.099	12.3	134-3B	13
2002	KCR	AL	32	549	155	36	5	11	46	69	2	1	.282	.341	.426	.013	.292	.357	.445	.057	33.9	126-3B	-3
2003	KCR	AL	33	502	146	31	1	16	41	61	1	0	.291	.348	.452	.011	.295	.358	.464	.088	22.4	123-3B	-1
2004	KCR	AL	34	393	107	22	1	9	33	52	2	1	.272	.333	.405	-.031	.260	.325	.392	-.097	10.3	104-3B	-2

Breakout: 13% Improve: 41% Collapse: 33%

Rumors of his demise were greatly exaggerated. Randa arrested three years of decline by hitting .344 after the All-Star Break and finished with his best performance since 1999. He made only seven errors all year, though this was partly due to an official scorer only slightly less generous than the Bill and Melinda Gates Foundation. Even at age 34, Randa was the best internal option to man third base, and convincing him to re-up on an affordable two-year deal (the second year is a mutual option) was a minor coup for Baird.

DESI RELAFORD IF **Bats: B** **Throws: R** Born: 16-Sep-73 Age: 30

YEAR	TM	LG	AGE	AB	H	2B	3B	HR	BB	SO	SB	CS	AVG	OBP	SLG	MLVR	EQBA	EQOBP	EQSLG	EQMLVR	VORP	DEFENSE			
2001	NYM	NL	27	301	91	27	0	8	27	65	13	5	.302	.364	.472	.146	.312	.375	.490	.171	29.2	44-2B	-6	17-SS	-1
2002	SEA	AL	28	329	88	13	2	6	33	51	10	3	.267	.339	.374	-.025	.299	.372	.418	.052	21.6	33-SS	-3	26-3B	-1
2003	KCR	AL	29	500	127	27	5	8	40	70	20	4	.254	.315	.376	-.171	.258	.322	.385	-.120	-1.8	85-2B	-7	28-3B	-1
2004	KCR	AL	30	370	104	21	3	7	33	54	12	4	.281	.344	.413	.006	.268	.336	.400	-.060	12.8	99-2B	-5		

Breakout: 13% Improve: 52% Collapse: 24%

A wrist injury which prevented him from swinging the bat right-handed for the season's second half ruined his season, and maybe the Royals' year too: Relaford hit just .207/.279/.293 after the break. With a healthy wrist before in the first half, he hit .288/.341/.435, which is right around his performance level in 2001 and 2002. Relaford's talents are still more suited to a super-utility role than as the starting second baseman, but if he's the worst regular in the Royals' lineup, it will be their best offense in a while.

MIKE SWEENEY 1B **Bats: R** **Throws: R** Born: 22-Jul-73 Age: 30

YEAR	TM	LG	AGE	AB	H	2B	3B	HR	BB	SO	SB	CS	AVG	OBP	SLG	MLVR	EQBA	EQOBP	EQSLG	EQMLVR	VORP	DEFENSE	
2001	KCR	AL	27	559	170	46	0	29	64	64	10	3	.304	.374	.542	.232	.312	.387	.562	.293	56.6	105-1B	-5
2002	KCR	AL	28	471	160	31	1	24	61	46	9	7	.340	.417	.563	.364	.350	.431	.582	.434	66.2	100-1B	7
2003	KCR	AL	29	392	115	18	1	16	64	56	3	2	.293	.391	.467	.102	.298	.401	.478	.185	21.3	43-1B	2
2004	KCR	AL	30	430	132	28	1	19	59	55	5	2	.306	.389	.513	.228	.292	.380	.497	.160	30.9	117-1B	-1

Breakout: 14% Improve: 45% Collapse: 23%

OK, the injury that really sank the Royals' season was the one to Sweeney's neck, which apparently happened after too many teammates whacked him on the helmet following a game-winning hit against the Giants on Father's Day. Before going on the DL, Sweeney was hitting his usual .321/.440/.540; after missing six weeks, Sweeney hit just .260/.325/.379 to finish with his worst numbers as a regular. Sweeney has missed 105 games the last three years, and his durability is calling into question the wisdom of his $11 million-a-year contract. He's still the best hitter on the team along with Beltran, and will probably finish his career as one of the five best Royals ever.

MIKE TONIS   C   Bats: R   Throws: R   Born: 09-Feb-79   Age: 25

YEAR	TM	LG	AGE	AB	H	2B	3B	HR	BB	SO	SB	CS	AVG	OBP	SLG	MLVR	EQBA	EQOBP	EQSLG	EQMLVR	VORP	DEFENSE	
2001	WIL	CAR	22	123	31	8	0	3	15	34	0	0	.252	.343	.390	.096	.209	.281	.341	-.292	-4.7	31-C	1
2001	WIC	TEX	22	226	61	11	1	9	22	41	1	1	.270	.344	.447	.080	.228	.290	.382	-.206	-2.3	59-C	0
2003	WIC	TEX	24	307	73	18	0	2	23	52	3	1	.238	.296	.316	-.175	.210	.262	.285	-.407	-21.8	80-C	0
2004	KCR	AL	25	174	41	9	1	4	13	32	2	1	.237	.295	.362	-.175	.227	.288	.351	-.240	-3.5	49-C	-4

Breakout: 50%   Improve: 71%   Collapse: 13%

After a 2002 campaign that was almost entirely lost to injury, Tonis returned last season a shell of his former self. His power potential is still on the DL; he hit only two homers all season after belting 12 the year before his injury. Not even a trip to the hitter-friendly AFL could revive his bat, and at this point the Royals need to work from the assumption that their one-time catcher of the future doesn't have one.

MICHAEL TUCKER   OF   Bats: L   Throws: R   Born: 25-Jun-71   Age: 33

YEAR	TM	LG	AGE	AB	H	2B	3B	HR	BB	SO	SB	CS	AVG	OBP	SLG	MLVR	EQBA	EQOBP	EQSLG	EQMLVR	VORP	DEFENSE			
2001	CIN	NL	30	231	56	10	1	7	23	55	12	5	.242	.308	.385	-.153	.240	.311	.378	-.163	-7.0	23-LF	1	22-CF	-1
2001	CHC	NL	30	205	54	9	7	5	23	47	4	3	.263	.339	.449	.023	.269	.344	.452	.023	10.0	31-CF	-2	21-LF	2
2002	KCR	AL	31	475	118	27	6	12	56	105	23	9	.248	.330	.406	-.056	.255	.339	.422	-.039	3.4	62-RF	2	31-LF	-1
2003	KCR	AL	32	389	102	20	5	13	39	88	8	10	.262	.331	.440	-.059	.264	.336	.448	-.001	-0.6	39-RF	2	23-CF	-2
2004	SFG	NL	33	197	48	10	2	4	24	48	7	2	.242	.328	.379	-.108	.242	.326	.390	-.110	0.3	57-RF	-2		

Breakout: 28%   Improve: 48%   Collapse: 28%

The very picture of mediocrity, Tucker has had an OPS between 700 and 800 in eight of his nine major league seasons. Given how far the price of mediocrity has plummeted on the open market, Tucker did well to get two years and $3.5 million from the Giants. (The Royals did even better to get a first-round pick as compensation.) His swing still has the power of seduction, but let's be straight here: Over the last two seasons, Tucker hit .195/.267/.311 away from Kauffman Stadium. The Giants should be happy if he performs to the standards of a good fourth outfielder this year.

RONDELL WHITE   LF   Bats: R   Throws: R   Born: 23-Feb-72   Age: 32

YEAR	TM	LG	AGE	AB	H	2B	3B	HR	BB	SO	SB	CS	AVG	OBP	SLG	MLVR	EQBA	EQOBP	EQSLG	EQMLVR	VORP	DEFENSE	
2001	CHC	NL	29	323	99	19	1	17	26	56	1	0	.307	.371	.529	.231	.313	.372	.538	.236	26.1	67-LF	5
2002	NYY	AL	30	455	109	21	0	14	25	86	1	2	.240	.288	.378	-.145	.260	.310	.415	-.098	-4.9	109-LF	6
2003	SDP	NL	31	413	115	17	3	10	25	71	1	4	.278	.330	.465	.129	.296	.345	.498	.115	14.5	95-LF	-2
2003	KCR	AL	31	75	26	6	1	4	6	8	0	0	.347	.400	.613	.360	.351	.419	.622	.475	8.3	17-LF	1
2004	DET	AL	32	390	103	20	1	14	28	65	1	1	.264	.321	.429	-.026	.275	.335	.461	.023	10.4	102-LF	-1

Breakout: 11%   Improve: 32%   Collapse: 36%

His arrival came too late to save the Royals' playoff hopes, but White finished the season strongly enough that the Royals entertained thoughts of bringing him back for 2004. He's surprisingly consistent with the bat for someone who's so inconsistently in the lineup; his disaster with the Yankees in 2002 is really the only off-season of his career. The difference between White and Shannon Stewart is a lot smaller than you think. In Detroit, he could hit like Rogers Hornsby this year and it still won't matter.

PITCHERS

PAUL ABBOTT   Bats: R   Throws: R   Born: 15-Sep-67   Age: 36

YEAR	TM	LG	AGE	G	GS	IP	H	BB	SO	HR	ERA	EQERA	EQH9	EQBB9	EQSO9	EQHR9	PERA	VORP	STF
2001	SEA	AL	33	28	27	163.0	145	87	118	21	4.25	4.90	8.9	4.6	6.2	1.1	5.00	12.0	1
2002	SEA	AL	34	7	5	26.3	40	20	22	5	11.98	10.73	13.5	6.2	7.3	1.7	8.15	-14.8	-43
2003	TUC	PCL	35	11	8	54.7	63	12	50	3	3.95	4.35	10.8	2.3	7.0	0.7	4.78	7.2	15
2003	KCR	AL	35	10	8	47.7	47	26	32	8	5.28	4.79	8.2	4.6	5.9	1.3	4.96	5.0	-8
2004	TBY	AL	36	23	17	96.3	118	45	65	21	6.24	6.21	10.5	3.9	6.0	1.9	6.50	2.4	-8

Breakout: 25%   Improve: 70%   Collapse: 11%

Only the 37th pitcher that Allard Baird traded for as the Royals' rotation disintegrated down the stretch. Abbott, as he usually is, was unhittable at times; unfortunately, he gives up so many walks and home runs that he generally has to be close to unhittable to be effective. His style plays best in a really big park like Safeco Field. Instead he signed with the Devil Rays, reuniting with Lou Piniella, for whom he won 17 games in Seattle in 2001.

JEREMY AFFELDT

						Bats: L				Throws: L					Born: 06-Jun-79		Age: 25

YEAR	TM	LG	AGE	G	GS	IP	H	BB	SO	HR	ERA	EQERA	EQH9	EQBB9	EQSO9	EQHR9	PERA	VORP	STF
2001	WIC	TEX	22	25	25	145.3	153	46	128	9	3.90	5.90	11.1	3.5	5.7	0.9	5.54	-4.4	10
2002	KCR	AL	23	34	7	77.7	85	37	67	8	4.63	4.34	9.4	3.9	7.4	0.8	4.71	10.7	23
2003	KCR	AL	24	36	18	126.0	126	38	98	12	3.93	3.65	8.5	2.6	6.9	0.7	3.86	30.2	26
2004	KCR	AL	25	30	20	118.7	130	44	87	15	4.69	4.14	9.1	3.1	6.7	1.0	4.26	22.8	9

Breakout: 16%   Improve: 42%   Collapse: 24%

After battling with a blister problem on his middle finger for nearly two seasons, Affeldt is seriously considering having a procedure known as a partial nail avulsion, in which the medial portion of the fingernail is removed all the way to the matrix (where the nail is formed), and a caustic chemical is then applied to the matrix to make sure that portion of the nail never grows again.

The reason for sharing this level of medical detail is simple: His propensity for blisters is the only reason Affeldt is not yet a household name. He throws his fastball harder than all but a handful of lefties in the game, and it's a secondary pitch to his 12-6 yakker. After his blister problem forced him to move to the bullpen, he gave up just 31 baserunners in 32 innings, with 35 strikeouts. The Royals plan on giving him one more shot at the starting rotation, so if his procedure is successful, he's a great candidate to grab the staff ace mantle and 15–18 wins this season.

BRIAN ANDERSON

						Bats: B				Throws: L					Born: 26-Apr-72		Age: 32

YEAR	TM	LG	AGE	G	GS	IP	H	BB	SO	HR	ERA	EQERA	EQH9	EQBB9	EQSO9	EQHR9	PERA	VORP	STF
2001	ARI	NL	29	29	22	133.3	156	30	55	25	5.20	5.88	10.7	1.9	3.2	1.5	5.60	-4.0	-27
2002	ARI	NL	30	35	24	156.0	174	32	81	23	4.79	4.75	10.0	1.6	4.1	1.3	4.98	14.1	-12
2003	CLE	AL	31	25	24	148.0	162	32	72	21	3.71	4.81	9.8	1.9	4.4	1.1	4.74	9.1	-1
2003	KCR	AL	31	7	7	49.7	50	11	15	6	3.98	3.54	8.6	1.9	2.6	0.9	3.95	12.7	-2
2004	KCR	AL	32	28	24	145.0	184	33	63	26	5.50	4.85	10.5	1.9	4.0	1.4	4.85	16.6	-4

Breakout: 14%   Improve: 53%   Collapse: 20%

Like White, Anderson's one-month audition with the Royals impressed the team enough that they wanted to re-sign him, and his one month in the low-stress atmosphere of Kansas City impressed Anderson enough that he shocked everyone by not returning to his native Ohio. Anderson's career-best ERA is an illusion created by 27 unearned runs, nine more than anyone else in the majors. He is what he is: a .500 pitcher who gives up tons of flyballs, relying on his defense and good control. There's value in that, but the Royals already have such a pitcher in Darrell May, and it's an open question whether they really need two of them.

KEVIN APPIER

						Bats: R				Throws: R					Born: 06-Dec-67		Age: 36

YEAR	TM	LG	AGE	G	GS	IP	H	BB	SO	HR	ERA	EQERA	EQH9	EQBB9	EQSO9	EQHR9	PERA	VORP	STF
2001	NYM	NL	33	33	33	206.7	181	64	172	22	3.57	3.86	8.1	2.6	6.4	0.9	3.81	38.3	19
2002	ANA	AL	34	32	32	188.3	191	64	132	23	3.92	4.73	9.8	2.9	6.2	1.0	4.84	17.3	9
2003	ANA	AL	35	19	19	92.7	105	36	50	17	5.63	5.72	10.1	3.3	4.8	1.5	5.71	0.2	-19
2003	KCR	AL	35	4	4	19.0	15	7	5	4	4.26	3.86	6.3	2.9	2.4	1.4	3.71	4.3	-21
2004	KCR	AL	36	25	20	114.7	130	42	66	19	5.12	4.51	9.3	3.1	5.2	1.3	4.73	17.3	-1

Breakout: 18%   Improve: 50%   Collapse: 14%

The prodigal son returned, and his six shutout innings in an 11–0 pasting of the Yankees in mid-August was the highest of many high points in the Royals' season. But he was already living on borrowed time, pitching with a partial tear in his ulnar collateral ligament, and inevitably the ligament deteriorated, prompting surgery which should keep him out until May. The Royals are bringing him back for the major league minimum, but it would be an upset if he ever started regularly again. With his deceptive motion and a slider that's still nasty when he's on, a mild renaissance as a reliever isn't out of the question.

MIGUEL ASENCIO

						Bats: R				Throws: R					Born: 29-Sep-80		Age: 23

YEAR	TM	LG	AGE	G	GS	IP	H	BB	SO	HR	ERA	EQERA	EQH9	EQBB9	EQSO9	EQHR9	PERA	VORP	STF
2001	CLR	FLA	20	28	21	155.3	124	70	123	7	2.84	4.92	8.3	4.8	4.9	0.9	4.64	10.8	14
2002	KCR	AL	21	31	21	123.3	136	64	58	17	5.11	4.82	9.3	4.2	4.0	1.0	5.09	10.5	6
2003	KCR	AL	22	8	8	48.3	54	21	27	4	5.22	4.56	9.5	3.6	4.9	0.6	4.48	5.4	25
2004	KCR	AL	23	20	17	96.3	113	46	55	14	5.61	4.95	9.7	4.0	5.2	1.1	5.02	9.2	-3

Breakout: 16%   Improve: 39%   Collapse: 22%

Asencio was the Royals' first starter to go down, and his loss became more and more painful as the team entered areas on its depth chart that it didn't know existed. A year after he was rushed into service as a Rule 5 pick, Asencio made significant strides before being felled by bone chips, reversing his strikeout-to-walk ratio and cutting his home-run rate significantly. He successfully rehabbed in September and should be in the rotation this season. While Affeldt a lot of the hype, Asencio (who's more than a year younger) is a breakout candidate of his own.

BRIAN BASS Bats: R Throws: R Born: 06-Jan-82 Age: 22

YEAR	TM	LG	AGE	G	GS	IP	H	BB	SO	HR	ERA	EQERA	EQH9	EQBB9	EQSO9	EQHR9	PERA	VORP	STF
2001	BUR	MID	19	26	26	139.3	138	53	75	16	4.65	6.79	10.1	4.8	3.1	2.1	6.88	-16.7	-23
2002	BUR	MID	20	20	20	110.3	103	31	60	8	3.83	5.79	10.6	3.5	3.0	1.8	6.39	-2.1	-19
2003	WIL	CAR	21	26	26	152.3	129	43	119	7	2.84	5.09	9.9	3.3	5.0	1.1	5.12	7.6	10
2004	KCR	AL	22	17	11	61.0	76	27	33	12	6.56	5.78	10.3	3.8	4.9	1.5	5.63	1.9	-12

Breakout: 7%   Improve: 38%   Collapse: 34%

Every year, the ballpark in Wilmington turns a pitching suspect into a prospect. Brian Bass got the wind beneath his wings last season. There's reason to think he's not just a ballpark illusion, given his youth and history of success even before last year. There are prospects, there are sleepers, and then, like Affeldt two years ago and Bass today, there are the guys so deeply in REM that their dreams would have made Timothy Leary jealous.

RYAN BUKVICH Bats: R Throws: R Born: 13-May-78 Age: 26

YEAR	TM	LG	AGE	G	GS	IP	H	BB	SO	HR	ERA	EQERA	EQH9	EQBB9	EQSO9	EQHR9	PERA	VORP	STF
2001	WIL	CAR	23	37	0	57.7	41	31	80	1	1.72	4.44	9.6	7.4	8.0	0.4	5.27	6.3	7
2002	WIC	TEX	24	23	0	34.3	17	15	47	0	1.31	2.93	6.5	4.7	9.4	0.3	3.10	9.1	34
2002	OMA	PCL	24	12	0	13.7	4	7	17	0	0.00	0.00	3.6	5.0	8.5	0.0	1.76	7.9	48
2002	KCR	AL	24	26	0	25.0	26	19	20	2	6.12	5.47	9.1	6.2	6.9	0.7	5.14	0.4	1
2003	OMA	PCL	25	34	0	36.7	39	25	44	2	4.90	6.15	10.7	7.5	9.4	0.8	6.16	-2.1	-9
2003	KCR	AL	25	9	0	10.3	12	9	8	2	9.61	7.84	9.6	7.0	7.0	1.7	6.64	-3.2	-37
2004	KCR	AL	26	17	1	21.0	23	15	18	3	6.02	5.31	9.0	6.1	8.0	1.0	5.32	1.8	-4

Breakout: 24%   Improve: 44%   Collapse: 43%

Bukvich entered last season as the Royals' alternate closer in case MacDougal failed, but the twin bugaboos of power relievers—control problems and arm soreness—ruined his season. He started to find his old form in Omaha late in the year. Bukvich's fastball should get him plenty of second chances to stick in the majors and cause announcers nationwide to tread very, very carefully when pronouncing his last name.

DANNY CARRASCO Bats: R Throws: R Born: 12-Apr-77 Age: 27

YEAR	TM	LG	AGE	G	GS	IP	H	BB	SO	HR	ERA	EQERA	EQH9	EQBB9	EQSO9	EQHR9	PERA	VORP	STF
2001	LYN	CAR	24	22	0	36.0	18	14	40	0	1.50	2.59	6.6	5.2	6.0	0.3	3.34	10.5	10
2001	ALT	EAS	24	27	1	37.0	34	25	35	2	4.14	6.61	9.9	8.3	6.1	0.8	6.13	-3.7	-28
2002	LYN	CAR	25	55	0	72.7	52	18	83	1	1.61	3.27	9.2	3.1	7.1	0.3	3.89	16.4	14
2003	KCR	AL	26	50	2	80.3	82	40	57	8	4.82	4.33	8.8	4.2	6.3	0.8	4.52	12.9	0
2004	KCR	AL	27	37	11	75.7	83	37	51	8	5.02	4.42	9.1	4.1	6.1	0.8	4.52	12.7	-3

Breakout: 19%   Improve: 49%   Collapse: 21%

Like Asencio before him, Carrasco was a Rule 5 pick made good. Unlike Asencio, Carrasco was a fairly low-risk, low-upside selection, and lived up to both labels: He was a decent middle reliever all season, and kept the bullpen together when MacDougal and Grimsley hit a rough patch in May, but 2003 pretty much represents the limits of his success. As the Royals have proven the last two years, there is no easier and cheaper way to add to your team's pitching depth than through Rule 5.

JOEY DAWLEY Bats: R Throws: R Born: 19-Sep-71 Age: 32

YEAR	TM	LG	AGE	G	GS	IP	H	BB	SO	HR	ERA	EQERA	EQH9	EQBB9	EQSO9	EQHR9	PERA	VORP	STF
2001	GRN	SOU	29	22	21	127.3	95	46	130	15	3.04	4.21	9.1	3.9	6.3	1.9	5.78	17.5	-27
2002	RIC	INT	30	24	23	140.3	113	36	136	10	2.63	3.52	8.1	2.8	7.3	1.0	3.98	30.1	17
2003	RIC	INT	31	46	4	56.7	47	23	73	4	3.33	4.35	8.7	4.5	9.4	1.0	4.78	7.2	2
2004	KCR	AL	32	17	8	49.3	51	22	43	8	5.29	4.66	8.6	3.7	7.9	1.2	4.46	6.8	9

Breakout: 24% Improve: 49% Collapse: 30%

(continued next page)

Joey Dawley *(continued)*

Dawley doesn't have much of a scouting report—his fastball moves, but doesn't hit 90, and his curve and change are both below-average—but he's consistently racked up high strikeout totals in the minor leagues, including some great numbers last year in Richmond. It is rare to find the hitter whose success doesn't translate between Triple-A and the majors, and less rare to find the pitcher, but Dawley was worth a flier for a team looking for pitching depth. He's yet another example of the Royals' new creative bent.

NATE FIELD   **Bats: R**   **Throws: R**   Born: 11-Dec-75   Age: 28

YEAR	TM	LG	AGE	G	GS	IP	H	BB	SO	HR	ERA	EQERA	EQH9	EQBB9	EQSO9	EQHR9	PERA	VORP	STF
2001	WIC	TEX	25	52	0	73.0	61	18	67	3	1.48	3.27	9.4	2.7	5.9	0.7	4.28	17.1	0
2002	OMA	PCL	26	18	0	16.3	22	8	13	0	3.31	6.60	13.8	5.4	5.4	0.0	6.21	-1.7	-13
2002	COH	INT	26	21	2	38.7	46	21	25	6	6.74	6.69	10.9	5.7	4.7	2.0	7.26	-4.4	-64
2003	WIC	TEX	27	15	0	20.0	20	8	20	2	3.60	5.60	11.7	4.6	6.6	2.0	7.36	0.0	-56
2003	OMA	PCL	27	19	0	22.7	15	4	17	4	3.17	3.48	7.0	1.7	5.7	2.6	4.96	4.9	-45
2003	KCR	AL	27	19	0	21.7	19	14	19	3	4.15	3.80	7.6	5.5	7.6	1.3	4.80	5.2	-6
2004	*KCR*	*AL*	*28*	*19*	*2*	*28.3*	*32*	*13*	*20*	*4*	*5.30*	*4.67*	*9.3*	*3.9*	*6.5*	*1.2*	*4.85*	*4.2*	*-5*

Breakout: 24%   Improve: 49%   Collapse: 22%

Sometimes an organization will have a fetish for a marginal prospect for no apparent reason. The Royals were happy to sign Field as a minor league free agent in 2001, and after he got away on waivers, they reclaimed him last winter. Field did nothing in his short stint with the club last year to change his outlook one way or another. He is the very face of the replacement-level reliever, but keep in mind that teams are more likely to get a positive contribution from a reliever once thought of as replacement-level than from any other position.

CHRIS GEORGE   **Bats: L**   **Throws: L**   Born: 16-Sep-79   Age: 24

YEAR	TM	LG	AGE	G	GS	IP	H	BB	SO	HR	ERA	EQERA	EQH9	EQBB9	EQSO9	EQHR9	PERA	VORP	STF
2001	OMA	PCL	21	20	20	117.3	103	51	84	14	3.53	4.69	7.1	4.4	5.2	1.0	4.07	11.5	18
2001	KCR	AL	21	13	13	74.0	83	18	32	14	5.59	5.15	9.8	2.0	3.6	1.5	5.20	3.6	5
2002	OMA	PCL	22	22	21	127.3	145	65	94	15	5.87	6.62	9.8	5.1	5.4	1.2	5.64	-13.9	2
2002	KCR	AL	22	6	6	27.3	37	8	13	2	5.60	5.06	11.8	2.4	4.1	0.7	5.31	1.6	11
2003	OMA	PCL	23	10	10	54.3	71	22	28	8	7.29	8.53	12.3	4.3	4.3	1.8	7.27	-16.5	-32
2003	KCR	AL	23	18	18	93.7	120	44	39	22	7.11	6.34	10.8	4.0	3.6	1.8	6.54	-6.5	-20
2004	*KCR*	*AL*	*24*	*25*	*20*	*113.0*	*139*	*57*	*59*	*18*	*6.24*	*5.50*	*10.2*	*4.2*	*4.7*	*1.3*	*5.50*	*5.9*	*-9*

Breakout: 15%   Improve: 56%   Collapse: 21%

One of the great anomalies of the 2003 season. George was the first pitcher in major league history to win seven or more games, with a winning record, despite an ERA over seven. The Royals sent him down in July and kept him in Triple-A even as they shuffled through a dozen more starting pitchers. Fourteen years ago, when the Royals opened the vault to sign Storm Davis (who went 19–7 despite a worse-than-league-average ERA), pitching coach Frank Funk stated: "We don't want pitchers with good ERAs. We want pitchers with wins." The organization has come a long way.

JIMMY GOBBLE   **Bats: L**   **Throws: L**   Born: 19-Jul-81   Age: 22

YEAR	TM	LG	AGE	G	GS	IP	H	BB	SO	HR	ERA	EQERA	EQH9	EQBB9	EQSO9	EQHR9	PERA	VORP	STF
2001	WIL	CAR	19	27	27	162.3	134	33	154	8	2.55	4.84	8.9	2.6	5.6	1.0	4.30	12.4	30
2002	WIC	TEX	20	13	13	69.3	71	19	52	3	3.38	5.43	9.9	2.8	5.4	0.7	4.53	1.2	26
2003	WIC	TEX	21	22	22	132.7	128	40	100	11	3.19	5.36	9.5	3.4	5.2	1.4	5.27	3.3	8
2003	KCR	AL	21	9	9	52.7	56	15	31	8	4.61	4.53	9.1	2.4	5.2	1.2	4.61	5.6	24
2004	*KCR*	*AL*	*22*	*21*	*18*	*103.0*	*119*	*39*	*65*	*18*	*5.80*	*5.11*	*9.6*	*3.2*	*5.8*	*1.4*	*4.97*	*9.6*	*1*

Breakout: 9%   Improve: 39%   Collapse: 26%

Gobble, who had followed the Chris George career track since he was drafted (both were high-school left-handers taken in the supplemental first round, a year apart), smartly diverged from the path last season. He throws harder and has a much better curveball, and he showed flashes of greatness after being abruptly thrown into a pennant race straight out of Double-A last August. He is an extreme flyball pitcher, even more so than Anderson and Darrell May. The potential is there for the Royals' leftfielder to record an insane amount of putouts this season, a big reason why the Royals would be well-served to give a starting corner-outfield job to DeJesus.

ZACK GREINKE   Bats: R   Throws: R   Born: 21-Oct-83   Age: 20

YEAR	TM	LG	AGE	G	GS	IP	H	BB	SO	HR	ERA	EQERA	EQH9	EQBB9	EQSO9	EQHR9	PERA	VORP	STF
2003	WIL	CAR	19	14	14	87.0	56	13	78	5	1.14	2.97	7.3	1.7	6.2	1.1	3.48	23.0	40
2003	WIC	TEX	19	9	9	53.0	58	5	34	5	3.23	5.12	9.5	1.1	4.8	1.4	4.65	2.7	21
2004	*KCR*	*AL*	*20*	*20*	*17*	*110.3*	*125*	*18*	*71*	*14*	*4.36*	*3.84*	*9.4*	*1.4*	*5.9*	*1.0*	*3.79*	*24.4*	*15*

Breakout: 16%   *Improve: 61%*   *Collapse: 7%*

This is why teams persist in drafting high school pitchers in the first round. A year after he was drafted with the fifth overall pick, Greinke is now one of the best pitching prospects in baseball. You'd be hard-pressed to name another teenage pitcher in the last two decades who had a better ability to throw strikes with four pitches, change speeds, and attack each hitter's weaknesses with such precision. He has tremendous mechanics, enough poise to pitch well as the youngest American ever to pitch in the Puerto Rican winter league, and no injury history to speak of. The Royals actually drew criticism for not throwing him into a pennant race last September at age 19. If a potential MVP season from Beltran is reason #1 why the Royals have a legitimate chance to improve on 83 wins this season, Greinke is reason #2.

COLT GRIFFIN   Bats: R   Throws: R   Born: 29-Sep-82   Age: 21

YEAR	TM	LG	AGE	G	GS	IP	H	BB	SO	HR	ERA	EQERA	EQH9	EQBB9	EQSO9	EQHR9	PERA	VORP	STF
2002	BUR	MID	19	19	19	90.7	75	82	66	1	5.36	7.43	8.4	11.2	4.3	0.2	5.67	-16.3	0
2003	BUR	MID	20	27	27	149.7	127	97	107	7	3.91	7.07	10.2	8.6	4.5	1.3	6.96	-20.8	-15

Amazingly, some say Griffin has a higher upside than the pitcher above, which just goes to show you how overrated "upside" can be. The first high school pitcher to hit 100 on the radar gun—a curse which will follow him the rest of his life—Griffin is making slow, deliberate progress toward becoming a pitcher. Most pitchers with Griffin's profile tend to break down just as they're about to break out. If he avoids that downfall, the switch may flicker on, a la Bobby Jenks, any year now.

JASON GRIMSLEY   Bats: R   Throws: R   Born: 07-Aug-67   Age: 36

YEAR	TM	LG	AGE	G	GS	IP	H	BB	SO	HR	ERA	EQERA	EQH9	EQBB9	EQSO9	EQHR9	PERA	VORP	STF
2001	KCR	AL	33	73	0	80.3	71	28	61	8	3.03	3.35	7.8	2.9	6.3	0.8	3.73	19.5	7
2002	KCR	AL	34	70	0	71.3	64	37	59	4	3.91	3.47	7.7	4.2	7.1	0.4	3.63	16.6	16
2003	KCR	AL	35	76	0	75.0	88	36	58	6	5.16	4.89	10.1	4.0	6.7	0.6	4.88	6.6	2
2004	*KCR*	*AL*	*36*	*55*	*0*	*62.7*	*64*	*29*	*47*	*4*	*3.99*	*3.52*	*8.4*	*3.9*	*6.9*	*0.5*	*3.78*	*15.8*	*3*

Breakout: 44%   *Improve: 67%*   *Collapse: 19%*

After being called upon to pitch every other hour in April and May, Grimsley was hammered the rest of the season, and allowed exactly half of his 56 inherited runners to score. Grimsley has only two settings: unhittable and 93 Octane, depending on whether his sinker is biting or not. How a pitcher with such nasty stuff can have such an ordinary record is hard to fathom; the Royals are hoping that his struggles last year were the result of a combination of overwork and bad luck. He's not a bad gamble to bring back at $1 million, especially now that Scott Sullivan has been signed to soak up some of his innings.

RUNELVYS HERNANDEZ   Bats: R   Throws: R   Born: 27-Apr-78   Age: 26

YEAR	TM	LG	AGE	G	GS	IP	H	BB	SO	HR	ERA	EQERA	EQH9	EQBB9	EQSO9	EQHR9	PERA	VORP	STF
2001	BUR	MID	23	17	17	100.7	94	29	100	5	3.40	5.20	11.2	3.7	5.4	1.1	5.85	3.9	-3
2002	WIC	TEX	24	16	14	106.3	96	24	86	3	2.71	4.52	10.2	2.4	5.5	0.6	4.43	11.5	17
2002	KCR	AL	24	12	12	74.3	79	22	45	8	4.36	3.96	9.0	2.5	5.2	0.9	4.24	13.2	18
2003	KCR	AL	25	16	16	91.7	87	37	48	9	4.61	4.01	8.0	3.4	4.6	0.8	3.99	14.0	8
2004	*KCR*	*AL*	*26*	*23*	*18*	*101.7*	*122*	*42*	*57*	*14*	*5.69*	*5.02*	*10.0*	*3.4*	*5.1*	*1.1*	*4.95*	*9.7*	*-3*

Breakout: 16%   *Improve: 46%*   *Collapse: 26%*

Moron, n: A pitcher who refuses to admit that he is pitching in pain. See also Hernandez, Runelvys.

After starting the season as one of the best pitchers in the league in April, Hernandez struggled before finally admitting that his arm hurt, and he was shut down for two months. Upon his return, it was obvious that he didn't have the same stuff as before: His velocity still touched the low 90s, but his pitches had next to no movement, and his ERA shot up. Finally, after giving up nine runs in three innings to the Twins, the Royals decided to try some tough love and

(continued next page)

Runelvys Hernandez *(continued)*

optioned Hernandez to Double-A to get him to fess up. He did—nothing like losing major league service time to get a player to notice the throbbing in his elbow. An MRI then showed that Hernandez *had been pitching with a torn ligament in his elbow,* and needed Tommy John surgery. He should be back in 2005, and who knows? Maybe with a healthy new ligament, he'll be better than ever. It will help if he uses the time off to rehab his brain as well as his elbow.

CURT LESKANIC   Bats: R   Throws: R   Born: 02-Apr-68   Age: 36

YEAR	TM	LG	AGE	G	GS	IP	H	BB	SO	HR	ERA	EQERA	EQH9	EQBB9	EQSO9	EQHR9	PERA	VORP	STF
2001	MIL	NL	33	70	0	69.3	63	31	64	11	3.64	4.32	8.5	3.8	7.0	1.2	4.70	9.5	-6
2003	MIL	NL	35	26	0	26.7	22	18	28	1	2.70	3.08	7.5	5.5	8.2	0.3	3.83	8.7	20
2003	KCR	AL	35	27	0	26.0	16	11	22	1	1.73	2.13	5.3	3.6	7.5	0.4	2.38	10.7	29
2004	KCR	AL	36	59	0	55.3	52	30	49	5	4.07	3.59	7.8	4.6	8.1	0.7	3.89	14.5	6

Breakout: 35%   Improve: 58%   Collapse: 19%

Allard Baird finally found his grail: a reliever that could get guys out. Leskanic's style is about as subtle as Jim Carrey: a fastball at 95, a slider at 85, and a tip of the cap if you can hit either one. He's one of the more underrated relievers in the game, as one of the few pitchers to have tamed Coors Field *and* make a full recovery from rotator cuff surgery. He'll be back for another year in the set-up role, but he brings with him closer insurance in case MacDougal struggles again.

AL LEVINE   Bats: L   Throws: R   Born: 22-May-68   Age: 36

YEAR	TM	LG	AGE	G	GS	IP	H	BB	SO	HR	ERA	EQERA	EQH9	EQBB9	EQSO9	EQHR9	PERA	VORP	STF
2001	ANA	AL	33	64	1	75.7	71	28	40	7	2.38	3.45	8.4	3.1	4.4	0.7	4.00	17.4	-4
2002	ANA	AL	34	52	0	63.7	61	34	40	8	4.24	5.19	9.2	4.6	5.5	1.0	5.09	2.8	-17
2003	TBY	AL	35	36	0	49.7	45	18	25	7	2.90	4.15	8.3	3.2	4.5	1.1	4.41	9.6	-15
2003	KCR	AL	35	18	0	21.3	22	11	5	2	2.54	3.00	8.6	4.3	2.1	0.9	4.59	8.6	-25
2004	DET	AL	36	48	0	48.7	57	25	26	7	5.65	5.89	10.4	4.4	4.7	1.2	6.01	1.4	-22

Breakout: 20%   Improve: 43%   Collapse: 41%

As transactions go, seeing your name next to the word "sold," as in "we wanted to trade you, but the only name that any team would agree to was Ben Franklin," has to be among the most deflating. Levine, almost unique among major league pitchers, consistently gives up fewer hits than his other numbers would predict, and finishes with better ERAs than his peripheral numbers would suggest, in a sample size that has grown so large that it must be taken seriously. His stuff, like his numbers, only seem to inspire confidence after the fact, which is why Levine and his 3.08 ERA over the last three years had to settle for a one-year, six-figure contract with the Tigers.

JOSE LIMA   Bats: R   Throws: R   Born: 30-Sep-72   Age: 31

YEAR	TM	LG	AGE	G	GS	IP	H	BB	SO	HR	ERA	EQERA	EQH9	EQBB9	EQSO9	EQHR9	PERA	VORP	STF
2001	HOU	NL	28	14	9	53.0	77	16	41	12	7.30	7.54	13.0	2.5	5.8	1.8	7.07	-11.1	-30
2001	DET	AL	28	18	18	112.7	120	22	43	23	4.71	4.72	8.6	1.6	3.2	1.6	4.66	10.8	-18
2002	DET	AL	29	20	12	68.3	86	21	33	12	7.77	6.15	10.6	2.5	4.1	1.5	5.66	-4.1	-26
2003	KCR	AL	30	14	14	73.3	80	26	32	7	4.91	4.27	9.3	3.0	3.9	0.8	4.42	11.9	0
2004	KCR	AL	31	24	17	95.0	127	33	41	19	6.77	5.97	11.1	2.9	3.9	1.6	5.79	3.5	-15

Breakout: 16%   Improve: 42%   Collapse: 26%

At the All-Star Break, which part of this sentence was most stupefying: "The Royals, led by staff ace Jose Lima, lead the AL Central by seven games." Lima's regression in the second half had a lot to do with that of the team as a whole, and a strained groin—plus the questionable decision to try to let him pitch through it—serves as another condemnation of the Royals' medical staff. He'll latch on again somewhere this year. The trick with Lima is that he's best sampled, both on the mound and in the clubhouse, in small doses.

GRAEME LLOYD Bats: L   Throws: L   Born: 09-Apr-67   Age: 37

YEAR	TM	LG	AGE	G	GS	IP	H	BB	SO	HR	ERA	EQERA	EQH9	EQBB9	EQSO9	EQHR9	PERA	VORP	STF
2001	MON	NL	34	84	0	70.3	74	21	44	6	4.35	4.21	9.1	2.5	4.7	0.7	4.06	10.5	-3
2002	MON	NL	35	41	0	30.7	41	8	17	5	5.86	6.07	11.8	2.1	4.2	1.5	6.20	-1.6	-36
2002	FLA	NL	35	25	0	26.3	26	11	20	1	4.45	4.21	8.8	3.2	6.0	0.4	3.78	4.0	10
2003	NYM	NL	36	36	0	35.3	39	7	17	2	3.31	4.24	9.8	1.6	4.0	0.5	4.01	5.3	-2
2003	KCR	AL	36	16	0	12.3	29	7	8	0	10.98	10.50	21.0	4.5	6.0	0.0	8.86	-8.2	-20
2004	*KCR*	*AL*	*37*	*49*	*0*	*36.3*	*49*	*12*	*17*	*5*	*5.74*	*5.06*	*11.2*	*2.8*	*4.2*	*1.1*	*5.32*	*5.4*	*-18*

Breakout: 26%   Improve: 56%   Collapse: 25%

Make enough mid-season trades for pitching and inevitably one of them is going to end up a turkey. There was nothing in Lloyd's record that suggested he would give up 29 hits in 64 at-bats, so chalk his time in Kansas City up to DIPS theory gone wild. Still one of the more reliable relievers in the game at retiring his left-handed brethren, he'll make a good NRI somewhere.

SEAN LOWE Bats: R   Throws: R   Born: 29-Mar-71   Age: 33

YEAR	TM	LG	AGE	G	GS	IP	H	BB	SO	HR	ERA	EQERA	EQH9	EQBB9	EQSO9	EQHR9	PERA	VORP	STF
2001	CWS	AL	30	45	11	127.0	123	32	71	12	3.61	3.69	8.8	2.1	4.7	0.7	3.90	25.9	4
2002	NAS	PCL	31	5	5	22.0	29	3	21	0	5.73	5.75	13.7	1.3	6.6	0.4	5.58	-0.3	13
2002	PIT	NL	31	43	1	69.0	85	34	57	8	5.35	6.08	11.5	3.9	6.5	1.1	5.96	-3.6	-14
2003	OMA	PCL	32	14	7	52.7	54	19	27	3	3.24	4.66	10.2	3.9	3.9	0.7	5.10	5.0	-15
2003	KCR	AL	32	28	0	44.7	55	21	28	7	6.24	5.73	10.4	3.9	5.5	1.2	5.67	0.3	-20
2004	*KCR*	*AL*	*33*	*26*	*7*	*50.7*	*62*	*21*	*27*	*6*	*5.45*	*4.81*	*10.2*	*3.5*	*4.9*	*0.9*	*4.89*	*5.9*	*-11*

Breakout: 25%   Improve: 46%   Collapse: 29%

Included only because he'll probably surface somewhere, giving up too many runs for another team this season. Lowe is proof that being a groundball pitcher doesn't automatically make you an effective one.

MIKE MacDOUGAL Bats: B   Throws: R   Born: 05-Mar-77   Age: 27

YEAR	TM	LG	AGE	G	GS	IP	H	BB	SO	HR	ERA	EQERA	EQH9	EQBB9	EQSO9	EQHR9	PERA	VORP	STF
2001	OMA	PCL	24	28	27	144.3	144	76	110	13	4.68	5.90	9.4	5.6	5.0	0.9	5.36	-4.5	-9
2001	KCR	AL	24	3	3	15.3	18	4	7	2	4.71	4.91	10.4	2.5	3.7	1.2	5.31	1.1	-6
2002	WIC	TEX	25	4	4	17.7	11	24	14	1	3.05	7.63	7.6	15.3	5.3	1.2	7.21	-3.5	-70
2002	OMA	PCL	25	12	10	53.0	52	55	30	4	5.60	7.53	9.2	10.8	3.9	0.9	6.60	-10.5	51
2003	KCR	AL	26	68	0	64.0	64	32	57	4	4.08	4.14	8.6	4.3	7.9	0.4	4.05	9.4	17
2004	*KCR*	*AL*	*27*	*37*	*6*	*56.7*	*61*	*35*	*42*	*6*	*5.38*	*4.74*	*9.0*	*5.2*	*6.8*	*0.8*	*4.74*	*6.6*	*-4*

Breakout: 18%   Improve: 43%   Collapse: 28%

His breaking ball—somewhere between a curve and a slider—may just be the best pitch in baseball. Certainly, no other pitch froze Frank Thomas, Albert Pujols, *and* Barry Bonds for strike three last season. His mechanics are more high-maintenance than J-Lo, but they're worth the trouble. His freakish ability to keep the ball down (his career G/F ratio is over 3) means that hitters are unlikely to beat him on their own. Which is why it's such a good sign that, from July 27 on, MacDougal walked only five batters in 20 innings. If MacDougal can maintain similarly impressive control in the future, he's going to be a stud.

DARRELL MAY Bats: L   Throws: L   Born: 13-Jun-72   Age: 32

YEAR	TM	LG	AGE	G	GS	IP	H	BB	SO	HR	ERA	EQERA	EQH9	EQBB9	EQSO9	EQHR9	PERA	VORP	STF
2001	YOM	JPC	29	26	26	159.0	160	45	168	24	4.13	5.33	9.7	2.6	7.7	1.6	5.37	4.5	-3
2002	KCR	AL	30	30	21	131.3	144	50	95	28	5.35	5.08	9.3	3.1	6.2	1.7	5.42	7.5	-12
2003	KCR	AL	31	35	32	210.0	197	53	115	31	3.77	3.64	7.9	2.2	4.8	1.1	3.91	49.1	6
2004	*KCR*	*AL*	*32*	*30*	*25*	*151.3*	*169*	*44*	*90*	*26*	*5.03*	*4.44*	*9.2*	*2.4*	*5.5*	*1.3*	*4.38*	*24.5*	*4*

Breakout: 16%   Improve: 56%   Collapse: 19%

If the success of players like Hideo Nomo and Ichiro Suzuki hasn't convinced you that Japanese baseball is directly comparable to the major leagues, then Darrell May should. Baird took a chance on bringing May back to this side of the Pacific largely because of his track record in Japan. Last season, not only did May pitch as well as his statistical record in Japan suggested he would, but his success had the same shape: As he was in Japan, he had good control, a decent strikeout rate for a southpaw, and a few too many homers allowed. The more distant fences this year should cut his homer total enough to make up for any regression elsewhere.

KYLE SNYDER

Bats: B   **Throws: R**   Born: 09-Sep-77   Age: 26

YEAR	TM	LG	AGE	G	GS	IP	H	BB	SO	HR	ERA	EQERA	EQH9	EQBB9	EQSO9	EQHR9	PERA	VORP	STF
2002	WIL	CAR	24	15	15	48.3	49	11	48	1	2.98	5.53	12.1	2.8	6.2	0.4	5.24	0.3	6
2002	WIC	TEX	24	6	6	25.7	21	7	18	4	4.20	5.64	10.1	3.2	4.8	3.2	7.80	-0.1	-64
2003	OMA	PCL	25	5	5	29.0	28	6	15	3	2.79	4.00	9.3	2.3	4.0	1.3	4.87	4.8	-11
2003	KCR	AL	25	15	15	85.3	94	21	39	11	5.17	4.54	9.4	2.1	4.0	1.0	4.42	8.9	2
2004	KCR	AL	26	22	16	91.0	118	32	46	15	6.26	5.51	10.7	2.9	4.7	1.3	5.26	6.2	-7

Breakout: 16%   *Improve: 37%*   *Collapse: 27%*

After having his career derailed by elbow problems almost from the moment he was drafted, Snyder came down with a shoulder ailment just as he was establishing himself in the majors. Life isn't fair. He had a minor arthroscopic clean-up after the season, and should be ready for spring training. Even before the injury, Snyder was more of a finesse pitcher than his 6′9″ frame and first-round pedigree would have you believe, so he can't afford to lose anything more off his fastball.

JORGE VASQUEZ

Bats: R   **Throws: R**   Born: 16-Jul-78   Age: 25

YEAR	TM	LG	AGE	G	GS	IP	H	BB	SO	HR	ERA	EQERA	EQH9	EQBB9	EQSO9	EQHR9	PERA	VORP	STF
2001	SPO	NWN	22	10	8	50.3	50	13	67	3	5.01	6.28	13.2	3.6	6.5	1.7	7.33	-3.2	-13
2002	BUR	MID	23	22	0	46.0	22	15	55	3	1.57	2.52	7.6	4.1	6.9	1.8	5.03	13.4	-13
2003	WIL	CAR	24	17	0	23.0	19	14	31	1	1.96	5.12	11.2	7.4	8.8	0.9	6.50	1.0	-12
2003	WIC	TEX	24	36	0	51.7	39	18	52	3	1.91	3.47	8.3	4.0	6.8	1.2	4.62	11.1	-4
2004	KCR	AL	25	18	5	33.7	39	17	26	5	5.87	5.18	9.5	4.2	7.1	1.2	5.08	2.1	-2

Breakout: 15%   *Improve: 45%*   *Collapse: 25%*

After years as a non-descript pitcher in the Dominican Summer League, Vasquez came stateside and climbed to Double-A within two years. It's the same recipe for success that got Runelvys Hernandez to the majors, and the Royals recognize the formula well enough that Vasquez might get a shot in the back of the bullpen by the end of the year.

BRAD VOYLES

Bats: R   **Throws: R**   Born: 30-Dec-76   Age: 27

YEAR	TM	LG	AGE	G	GS	IP	H	BB	SO	HR	ERA	EQERA	EQH9	EQBB9	EQSO9	EQHR9	PERA	VORP	STF
2001	GRN	SOU	24	15	0	16.7	11	10	25	0	1.08	2.45	8.6	6.8	9.2	0.0	4.29	5.1	30
2001	WIC	TEX	24	11	0	15.3	8	10	19	0	0.00	0.00	6.6	7.2	7.9	0.0	3.60	8.5	30
2002	OMA	PCL	25	26	0	32.3	29	22	34	2	4.18	4.80	9.0	6.9	7.2	0.6	5.13	2.7	-8
2002	KCR	AL	25	22	0	27.7	31	18	26	5	6.50	5.93	9.5	5.3	7.9	1.3	5.68	-1.0	-9
2003	OMA	PCL	26	29	9	81.3	68	24	69	5	2.99	3.62	8.6	3.3	6.6	0.8	4.19	16.4	3
2003	KCR	AL	26	11	3	31.3	47	18	24	6	7.48	7.26	12.8	4.9	6.7	1.5	7.22	-5.7	-26
2004	KCR	AL	27	21	10	57.7	61	29	44	8	5.17	4.56	8.8	4.2	7.0	1.1	4.73	9.3	1

Breakout: 26%   *Improve: 50%*   *Collapse: 28%*

A failed starter getting an audition in relief is about as newsworthy as the cancellation of whichever new FOX series gets the most promotional time in the World Series. (*Skin,* anyone?) A career reliever moving to the rotation is much less common, but after noticing that Voyles tends to get too amped and struggle in his first inning, the Royals made him a starter at mid-season. The early results were promising, but as in relief, Voyles was considerably less successful in his major league auditions. In either role, he lacks the hop on his fastball or the command of his big-breaking curveball to project much beyond replacement-level quality.

LES WALROND

Bats: L   **Throws: L**   Born: 07-Nov-76   Age: 27

YEAR	TM	LG	AGE	G	GS	IP	H	BB	SO	HR	ERA	EQERA	EQH9	EQBB9	EQSO9	EQHR9	PERA	VORP	STF
2001	NHV	EAS	24	16	16	81.3	68	46	67	5	3.87	5.47	9.0	7.0	5.1	0.9	5.45	1.0	-13
2002	NHV	EAS	25	4	4	22.3	19	10	31	2	2.42	4.58	10.5	5.0	9.6	1.4	6.08	2.2	3
2002	MEM	PCL	25	28	18	123.0	127	63	111	20	4.98	6.95	10.6	5.4	6.3	2.0	7.02	-16.9	-42
2003	MEM	PCL	26	10	1	17.3	12	7	14	0	1.04	2.25	7.3	4.5	6.2	0.0	3.19	6.0	20
2003	OMA	PCL	26	18	0	25.7	19	9	20	1	2.45	3.42	7.6	3.8	6.1	0.4	3.47	5.7	7
2004	KCR	AL	27	15	3	24.3	29	15	16	4	6.20	5.46	9.7	5.3	6.1	1.3	5.52	2.6	-14

Breakout: 23%   *Improve: 44%*   *Collapse: 33%*

The only thing worse than the Royals' right-handed relievers over the past five years has been their left-handers. Walrond was a waiver-wire pickup from the Cardinals who immediately took to relief in Triple-A and was brought to the Show in the hope he might be the answer to their woes. Eight innings and nine runs later, Walrond was back to being an afterthought. If Affeldt moves into the rotation this year, Walrond could get another chance to meet the Royals' bullpen quota from the left side.

KRIS WILSON Bats: R Throws: R Born: 06-Aug-76 Age: 27

YEAR	TM	LG	AGE	G	GS	IP	H	BB	SO	HR	ERA	EQERA	EQH9	EQBB9	EQSO9	EQHR9	PERA	VORP	STF
2001	OMA	PCL	24	6	5	29.0	31	6	18	2	2.79	3.95	9.9	2.3	4.0	0.7	4.39	5.0	5
2001	KCR	AL	24	29	15	109.3	132	32	67	26	5.19	5.84	10.6	2.5	5.2	1.9	6.09	-2.8	-16
2002	WIC	TEX	25	13	7	48.0	47	4	33	4	1.88	4.68	11.7	0.9	4.7	1.7	5.99	4.3	-26
2002	OMA	PCL	25	8	3	26.3	38	1	17	0	3.08	4.38	13.9	0.4	4.4	0.4	5.35	3.3	8
2002	KCR	AL	25	12	0	18.7	29	5	10	7	8.18	7.85	13.3	2.0	4.4	2.9	8.65	-4.6	-68
2003	KCR	AL	26	29	4	72.7	92	16	42	13	5.32	5.30	10.7	1.9	5.0	1.4	5.44	3.3	-16
2004	KCR	AL	27	27	11	71.0	88	16	39	12	5.25	4.63	10.2	1.9	5.0	1.3	4.71	9.6	-5

Breakout: 19%   Improve: 47%   Collapse: 22%

Every team needs a pitcher like Wilson, a strike-throwing machine with enough of a breaking pitch to keep hitters honest. Wilson can be better than that; right now he's no different than Bob Tewksbury or Rick Reed at the same age, except they were still toiling in the minors. He's the sort of pitcher who could shock the world by winning 15 games if he gets the stars, his defense, and his ballpark all in alignment. The Royals gave Wilson a Triple-A deal and an NRI, may improve their defense with the right moves, and moved the fences back for the '04 season. At press time they were negotiating with a team of astronomers.

JAMEY WRIGHT Bats: R Throws: R Born: 24-Dec-74 Age: 29

YEAR	TM	LG	AGE	G	GS	IP	H	BB	SO	HR	ERA	EQERA	EQH9	EQBB9	EQSO9	EQHR9	PERA	VORP	STF
2001	MIL	NL	26	33	33	194.7	201	98	129	26	4.90	5.32	9.4	4.2	5.0	1.1	5.12	5.8	-6
2002	MIL	NL	27	19	19	114.3	115	63	69	15	5.35	5.53	9.2	4.3	4.7	1.2	5.22	0.9	-12
2002	STL	NL	27	4	3	15.0	15	12	8	2	4.80	5.65	10.0	6.3	4.4	1.3	6.19	-0.1	-31
2003	IND	INT	28	7	4	22.0	32	10	17	5	7.36	9.15	15.1	5.0	5.5	3.2	10.47	-7.8	-100
2003	OKL	PCL	28	7	7	39.3	38	21	40	1	4.12	4.91	9.3	5.6	7.9	0.2	4.57	2.8	20
2003	OMA	PCL	28	13	12	76.7	70	38	65	10	3.64	5.17	9.6	5.4	6.7	1.8	6.31	3.3	-27
2003	KCR	AL	28	4	4	25.3	23	11	19	1	4.27	3.65	7.7	3.6	6.6	0.4	3.43	3.9	30
2004	CHC	NL	29	34	18	104.7	105	58	79	10	4.66	4.96	9.0	4.4	6.1	0.9	5.13	6.9	-3

Breakout: 21%   Improve: 47%   Collapse: 18%

The one-time Rockies pitching prospect (is there any other kind?) turned heads with a collection of fine September starts. Of course, if you take away his shutout against the Tigers, he had a 6.61 ERA. Which, unless he regains even more velocity on his sinker, is a good approximation of what might happen this season. He signed a minor-league deal with the Cubs.

Minnesota Twins

Not a bad year at Cirque du Pohlad.

On the ownership side, things went about as well as could be hoped. The Twins generated lots of free publicity and even some fan support as they lost a court case, then settled with local authorities by agreeing to continue to exist. The more cynical public never really thought there was ever any real threat of contraction, and that the contraction noises were really just an attempt to boot the legislature and the populace in the butt and get them to cough up some dough for a new stadium. So far, it looks like Carl and Bud were successful; the debate in Minnesota is moving forward with a basic question of "How do we build the new sports facilities?", rather than "Should we build the new sports facilities?" All the familiar sound bites have already started flying, as Twins President Jerry Bell has already brought out some old-school PR: "What a new ballpark and its revenues do is allow us to keep that talent here after it's been developed."

Perhaps Bell's assertion is true, but it'd be closer to the mark if he'd gone with "What a new ballpark and its revenues do is allow us to frantically and reflexively overpay selected players just after they have their fluke season." The Twins have some really well-developed chops on the baseball side. Scouting and player development do an outstanding job of drafting and developing ballplayers. The Twins' farm system has been truly outstanding for several years, providing a steady stream of talent to the big league club. Twins' Director of Minor League Operations Jim Rantz is probably the most effective baseball exec no one's ever heard of. Minnesota's back-to-back AL Central titles have been won primarily with homegrown talent on a relatively modest budget, and in terms of homegrown talent, the best is yet to come, with Justin Morneau and Joe Mauer likely to break out over the next couple of years. This club has definitely overbuilt their foundation.

The structure on top of the foundation is a little less certain however. For all the good work the Twins have done in terms of drafting and developing talent, they haven't been particularly adept at making the best possible use of it at the major league level. If the job of the minor leagues is to nurture young players and get them ready for the majors, the executives at the big league level have the responsibility of finding the best way to utilize those resources. The San Francisco Giants are a perfect example of that; they develop reasonable pitching prospects by the bushel, but haven't developed a reasonable hitter in years. So GM Brian Sabean uses the pitching developed by the farm system as currency to trade for needed offensive players, in order to make the team as a whole as productive as possible. That hasn't happened here.

GM Terry Ryan and Assistant GM Wayne Krivsky aren't the most active traders on the block. That's not necessarily a bad thing. But it is a bad thing when a team is clearly unbalanced, with tremendous surpluses in one area, and gaping, enormous voids that are holding the club back in others. When that's the case, the front office needs to step up and aggressively address the problem. The Twins have enough major-league caliber outfielders to stock at least two major league clubs, and yet, the club has significant holes that could be fixed—or at least patched—if Ryan would be more proactive about trading with other clubs.

The Twins need to learn and embrace the ideas of marginal production and marginal cost. After the 2003 season, there is no organization in MLB that needed Shannon Stewart less than the Minnesota Twins. With corner outfield options overflowing from their own system, the Twins signed Stewart to a three-year deal worth $6 million annually. This doesn't build confidence in the front office's ability to identify their own strengths and weaknesses, much less their ability to manage a budget that's more constrained than most. It's not that Stewart's a bad

TWINS PROSPECTUS

2003 record: 90–72; First place, AL Central; Lost to Yankees in Division Series

Pythagenport record: 85–77

Runs scored per game: 4.9 (6th in AL)

Runs allowed per game: 4.7 (6th in AL)

Team EqA: .262 (5th in AL)

2003 Batters Age: 27.6 (2nd youngest in AL)

2003 Pitchers Age: 30.1 (3rd oldest in AL)

Ballpark: Metrodome; Neutral park; Park Factor of 1.009

2003: Overcame some glaring weak spots with a consistent, balanced team effort to take the Central.

2004: A fruitful farm system separates the Twins from their division rivals and makes them the favorite to repeat.

ballplayer; he's actually a fine outfielder with a reasonable if unspectacular bat, and he's good enough to help a championship club in a starting role. The problem is that the marginal gain you get from having Shannon Stewart on the field instead of the likes of Michael Restovich, Dustan Mohr, Michael Cuddyer, or Lew Ford isn't very much, especially considering the marginal cost is millions of dollars. Every club needs to maximize their return on investment to some extent, and for a club in a market with limited local broadcast revenue, the need is that much more acute.

And the Twins have places they could spend those dollars. The middle infield has been approximately as useful as a deranged street performer suspended over a European metropolis. The tandem of Guzman and Rivas is still young, but neither one has done anything that leads you to believe that they're going to be players who push a club towards a championship. Where they once were promising prospects who looked like they might turn into Edgar Renteria, both now appear more likely to end up like Edgar Bergen. The Twins have been good enough to win in baseball's easiest division, but they're not going to take a step forward until they address the giant hole that is their middle infield.

Financial management hasn't really been the Twins' strong point. Terry Ryan's had an unfortunate tendency to sign players immediately after their best season, usually to a long-term contract that's far more expensive than the player's performance, or more accurately his future expected performance, is going to be worth. Table 1 is an example.

That list doesn't include Rick Reed, who was already signed to a bowlclimber of a contract (first year of a three-year, $21.75 million deal) when he was acquired from the New York Mets for Matt Lawton in July of 2001. The Milton contract delay was more a question of the Twins losing their rights to unilaterally renew his contract. The Twins like that four-year deal for guys from their own system; but in each of those cases, the expected future performance wasn't worth the money paid. Ryan's weakness for a great season in the most recent year, even in the face of peripheral stats that say "danger" for the future, means that Pretty Good Players get paid like stars. That's not a

recipe any team wants to follow, much less one in a market whose local television broadcasts are saturated with ads for All-American Recreation and Menards, instead of Coke, Budweiser, and Toyota.

For the 2004 season, though, it's all water under the bridge. Eric Milton and his $9 million-encumbrance have been shipped off, A. J. Pierzynski's a Giant, and the Twins' bullpen has suffered the loss of LaTroy Hawkins and Eddie Guardado, two of the better and more reliable relievers in baseball; Jesse Crain should be able to take over and give the Twins 80 very good innings to mitigate the effects of those losses. The offense is solid with the potential to be better than that, and the starting rotation is something of a question mark after Johan Santana's turn. The Twins should be a better team than they were last year, and there's help on the way from the farm system. A GM's made his job much easier if the passage of time makes his team better rather than worse, and that's the case with the 2004 Twins.

In the rotation, Santana's a capable ace, and if the Twins stick with Grant Balfour, they've got a shot at developing a legitimate 1–2 punch by the end of the season. Kyle Lohse is a capable rotation filler with some semblance of upside, and Brad Radke's $10 million worth of a legitimate #3/4 starter. The fifth spot needs to be filled; if the Twins can't find a good, affordable gamble on the free agent market, the spot could go to Joe Nathan, acquired from the Giants in the Pierzynski deal, or possibly the likes of Carlos Pulido. It's not a strong rotation, and it's one of many places where the Twins could have better spent the money they gave to Shannon Stewart. The Twins would be better positioned with Lew Ford and Miguel Batista getting playing time, rather than say, Stewart and Nathan.

The offense is a starless bunch, with several good players but no true juggernauts. There are capable hitters throughout the lineup, from Matt LeCroy and Torii Hunter to Corey Koskie and Shannon Stewart. The Twins have a bunch of young players—Michael Cuddyer and Justin Morneau for instance—capable of breaking out and having a big offensive season, and it's a good bet that at least one of them will. They'd better, because the middle infield's become an offensive sinkhole. The tandem of Rivas and Guzman have been nothing short of miserable with the bat, though at least they're now moving into the age bracket where significant improvement could occur at any time. Defensively, they're not good enough to make up for their anemic offense with their gloves, so they need to take a step forward if the Twins are going to compete with the better teams in the AL.

One luxury the Twins have that other World Series contenders don't is time. Minnesota can take some chances during the season, because the unbalanced schedule means the team plays considerably weaker competition than non-Central clubs. The Twins were able to ride out Lohse's

TABLE 1. TWINS' RE-SIGNS FOLLOWING PLAYER'S BEST SEASON

Player	Best Season	Contract Signed
Brad Radke	1999	Jul 2000 – 4 years, $36 million
Torii Hunter	2002	Jan 2003 – 4 years, $32 million
Joe Mays	2001	Jan 2002 – 4 years, $20 million
Eric Milton	1999	Feb 2001 – 4 years, $21 million

miserable stretch during the 2003 season, and they were rewarded with some pretty decent pitching down the stretch. This year, they're going to have to take some chances in the rotation, and if they can risk five starts on Grant Balfour and end up with a very good pitcher as a result, that's a competitive advantage not available to teams like the Red Sox, Mariners, or Blue Jays, who won't have the time to be patient and let someone develop during the season.

The Twins should be right there at the top of the AL Central at the end of the season. Ron Gardenhire's got a team that's a year better, rather than a year more frail or a year older, and that's a nice thing for a manager to work with. But the Twins need to improve if they want to be in the top tier of teams in the AL. Terry Ryan and Wayne Krivsky need to start getting active, move some of the surplus outfielders out of town, and shore up the team's weaknesses. Is Lew Ford really valuable if he's never going to play for you? A lot of teams can use a player like Ford, and have valuable talent to send in return.

Over the next few months, Ryan needs to learn to identify and anticipate his team's real needs, and work the phones to find players to meet those needs. That doesn't mean a marginal upgrade at positions where the Twins are already strong. It means getting guys who can provide meaningful production where the team currently lacks it. If the Twins can do that, there's no reason they can't play with the big kids in the AL.

HITTERS

SHANE ANDREWS   3B/1B   Bats: R   Throws: R   Born: 28-Aug-71   Age: 32

YEAR	TM	LG	AGE	AB	H	2B	3B	HR	BB	SO	SB	CS	AVG	OBP	SLG	MLVR	EQBA	EQOBP	EQSLG	EQMLVR	VORP	DEFENSE			
2001	MEM	PCL	29	193	42	9	1	9	33	63	2	0	.218	.341	.415	-.060	.194	.304	.362	-.227	-9.4	42-1B	-3	12-3B	0
2002	PAW	INT	30	390	100	19	1	22	52	123	1	1	.256	.348	.479	.137	.237	.324	.453	-.038	17.4	76-3B	-5	13-1B	1
2003	ROC	INT	31	445	114	31	2	11	43	126	2	2	.256	.327	.409	-.000	.234	.304	.384	-.172	1.1	105-3B	3	11-1B	-4
2004	MIN	AL	32	124	28	6	1	4	13	36	1	0	.228	.307	.395	-.119	.228	.310	.401	-.134	3.9	37-3B	-3		

Breakout: 32%   Improve: 55%   Collapse: 29%

He's gotta love the game. Andrews has made at least a few bucks in the majors, but he's spent the bulk of the last two seasons waiting for an opportunity at Triple-A. There are teams running some pretty bad third basemen out there, so Andrews may get an opportunity if he's willing to scour the Arizona and Florida fields in February. Might make sense to hang around that Seattle club, or perhaps Los Angeles.

JASON BARTLETT   SS   Bats: R   Throws: R   Born: 30-Oct-79   Age: 24

YEAR	TM	LG	AGE	AB	H	2B	3B	HR	BB	SO	SB	CS	AVG	OBP	SLG	MLVR	EQBA	EQOBP	EQSLG	EQMLVR	VORP	DEFENSE	
2001	EUG	NWN	21	267	80	12	4	3	28	47	12	4	.300	.375	.408	.160	.222	.276	.309	-.339	-20.8	67-SS	-2
2002	FTM	FLA	22	145	38	7	0	2	17	24	11	2	.262	.348	.352	.038	.232	.292	.311	-.298	-4.6	28-SS	-4
2002	LEL	CAL	22	308	77	14	4	1	32	53	24	5	.250	.330	.331	-.093	.204	.263	.274	-.423	-20.3	75-SS	-11
2003	NBR	EAS	23	548	162	31	8	8	58	67	41	24	.296	.383	.425	.146	.250	.319	.371	-.151	9.0	139-SS	1
2004	MIN	AL	24	234	60	12	2	4	19	36	9	3	.255	.321	.376	-.101	.255	.324	.382	-.115	8.6	65-SS	-5

Breakout: 53%   Improve: 68%   Collapse: 20%

Bartlett made a big jump in 2003, improving his footwork in the field, and showing significant improvement at the plate. His .296/.380/.425 line at New Britain was by far his best season at the plate, and he reached base 20 times on HBP. That's dedication. He's a bit old to be considered a top-flight prospect, but with his speed, defense, and ability to get on base, he could end up being a valuable option for the Twins fairly soon, especially considering the current state of affairs in the middle infield. Not a bad pickup for Brian Buchanan; this is the kind of deal the Twins should be doing more of. It's not clear that Cristian Guzman's a better option right now.

ROB BOWEN   C   Bats: B   Throws: R   Born: 24-Feb-81   Age: 23

YEAR	TM	LG	AGE	AB	H	2B	3B	HR	BB	SO	SB	CS	AVG	OBP	SLG	MLVR	EQBA	EQOBP	EQSLG	EQMLVR	VORP	DEFENSE	
2001	QUD	MID	20	385	98	18	2	18	37	112	4	0	.255	.323	.452	.083	.191	.244	.344	-.371	-24.1	98-C	-6
2002	FTM	FLA	21	342	63	12	1	10	38	69	1	0	.184	.275	.313	-.166	.161	.227	.280	-.508	-37.5	83-C	3
2003	NBR	EAS	22	134	41	13	0	1	13	24	0	0	.306	.376	.425	.143	.267	.322	.378	-.123	2.1	37-C	0
2003	ROC	INT	22	105	27	7	0	6	11	25	0	0	.257	.333	.495	.120	.236	.312	.453	-.061	3.7	26-C	2
2004	MIN	AL	23	246	51	12	1	6	20	55	1	0	.207	.270	.338	-.268	.206	.273	.343	-.289	-7.8	67-C	-5

Breakout: 19%   Improve: 48%   Collapse: 28%

Bowen's not a bad catching prospect, really. He's not going to be a star, but in a league where Dan Wilson makes $4.5 million, and luck is just as important as merit in having a job as a backup, Bowen may well have a long career. Defensively, he's middling. Offensively, he's got some difficulties controlling the strike zone, but will occasionally kill a ball. He's taken some steps forward with the bat, and if he can take a couple more, he'll be able to have a career of some length. Of course, it won't be as a starter in this organization.

MIKE CUDDYER

RF   Bats: R   Throws: R   Born: 27-Mar-79   Age: 25

YEAR	TM	LG	AGE	AB	H	2B	3B	HR	BB	SO	SB	CS	AVG	OBP	SLG	MLVR	EQBA	EQOBP	EQSLG	EQMLVR	VORP		DEFENSE		
2001	NBR	EAS	22	509	153	36	3	30	75	106	5	9	.301	.397	.560	.361	.249	.335	.468	.012	31.5		75-3B	-1	53-1B	-3
2002	EDM	PCL	23	330	102	16	9	20	36	79	12	7	.309	.382	.594	.349	.269	.335	.520	.102	17.1		73-RF	1		
2002	MIN	AL	23	112	29	7	0	4	8	30	2	0	.259	.314	.429	-.029	.277	.335	.455	.018	2.4		21-RF	0		
2003	ROC	INT	24	186	57	17	0	3	25	49	5	4	.306	.392	.446	.187	.271	.356	.410	-.012	3.2		26-RF	-2		
2003	MIN	AL	24	102	25	1	3	4	12	19	1	1	.245	.325	.431	-.039	.255	.339	.461	.015	1.3		11-RF	1		
2004	*MIN*	*AL*	*25*	*312*	*86*	*18*	*2*	*13*	*33*	*61*	*5*	*2*	*.276*	*.348*	*.477*	*.090*	*.275*	*.351*	*.485*	*.083*	*19.8*		*85-RF*	*0*		

Breakout: 27%   Improve: 64%   Collapse: 15%

Cuddyer's probably a little overripe as a prospect. His skill set's pretty clear—some power, reasonable plate discipline, and a good arm. He's going to be a pretty good ballplayer, but those of you who dreamed of seeing him on the left side of the infield are never going to have that wish fulfilled. Cuddyer's well regarded for his work ethic and ability to adjust, and could well take a big step forward offensively this year. The Twins need a legitimate bopper, and Cuddyer could well be the guy; in his brief career, there's no evidence of a big platoon split, and he has hit for significant power in the minors.

JEFF DEARDORFF

1B   Bats: R   Throws: R   Born: 14-Aug-78   Age: 25

YEAR	TM	LG	AGE	AB	H	2B	3B	HR	BB	SO	SB	CS	AVG	OBP	SLG	MLVR	EQBA	EQOBP	EQSLG	EQMLVR	VORP		DEFENSE		
2001	HDS	CAL	22	260	79	18	1	15	22	70	5	4	.304	.365	.554	.242	.221	.270	.407	-.214	-10.0		29-1B	-3	25-RF	-3
2001	HUN	SOU	22	201	56	11	1	14	13	66	1	1	.279	.329	.552	.228	.245	.284	.485	-.059	0.4		26-RF	-1	11-LF	0
2002	HUN	SOU	23	425	108	23	1	19	60	131	13	6	.254	.356	.447	.132	.220	.297	.398	-.176	-17.1		54-LF	-3	32-1B	2
2003	NBR	EAS	24	412	130	28	2	17	41	110	16	5	.316	.380	.517	.286	.263	.319	.443	-.040	5.6		96-1B	-5		
2003	ROC	INT	24	67	20	6	2	2	3	20	2	1	.299	.329	.537	.207	.284	.314	.507	.063	3.7					
2004	*MIN*	*AL*	*25*	*218*	*53*	*12*	*1*	*9*	*18*	*58*	*4*	*2*	*.245*	*.307*	*.440*	*-.048*	*.245*	*.310*	*.448*	*-.060*	*5.0*		*60-1B*	*-3*		

Breakout: 26%   Improve: 54%   Collapse: 26%

The numbers aren't bad, but the Twins have no interest in him in the long-term. Deardorff's at the bottom of the totem pole of reasonable outfield options, and he's just got too many holes in his game to make a serious run at a career in Minnesota. There are guys who play better defense, run better, hit for more average, more power... Deardorff couldn't be in an organization that's a worse fit for him. If he finds the right opportunity, he could well have a big league career. He's like an edgy performance artist hanging out in Branson, hurling raw meat at an audience that just doesn't understand.

LEW FORD

CF/LF   Bats: R   Throws: R   Born: 12-Aug-76   Age: 27

YEAR	TM	LG	AGE	AB	H	2B	3B	HR	BB	SO	SB	CS	AVG	OBP	SLG	MLVR	EQBA	EQOBP	EQSLG	EQMLVR	VORP		DEFENSE		
2001	FTM	FLA	24	265	79	15	2	2	21	30	19	9	.298	.376	.392	.155	.264	.313	.359	-.169	-1.8		59-CF	-3		
2001	NBR	EAS	24	252	55	9	3	7	20	35	5	5	.218	.291	.361	-.115	.195	.256	.327	-.369	-16.9		58-CF	-7		
2002	EDM	PCL	25	193	64	11	2	5	13	21	11	1	.332	.392	.487	.239	.297	.350	.438	.039	10.7		37-CF	1		
2002	NBR	EAS	25	373	116	27	2	15	49	47	17	5	.311	.402	.515	.311	.262	.338	.444	-.005	17.2		93-CF	-8		
2003	ROC	INT	26	211	64	18	2	3	10	28	4	5	.303	.358	.450	.138	.280	.332	.427	-.024	7.6		27-CF	-3	10-LF	0
2003	MIN	AL	26	73	24	7	1	3	8	9	2	0	.329	.402	.575	.359	.342	.420	.603	.437	9.1					
2004	*MIN*	*AL*	*27*	*225*	*60*	*14*	*2*	*6*	*16*	*32*	*5*	*2*	*.267*	*.326*	*.418*	*-.028*	*.267*	*.330*	*.425*	*-.040*	*7.5*		*62-CF*	*-4*		

Breakout: 17%   Improve: 33%   Collapse: 42%

We at BP love Shannon Stewart as much as anyone, but when's Lew Ford going to get a little love? Ford's a legitimate major league outfielder right now. Defensively, he's stretched in center, but unlike the Tweeners (guys who can't hit enough to play a corner spot, but can't defend well enough to play center), Ford has some offensive upside. He's hit for average, shown some power, controls the strike zone, and runs pretty well. Unfortunately for him, he's in an organization with so many decent options in the OF that he's just kind of been lost in the shuffle.

B. J. GARBE   CF/RF   Bats: R   Throws: R   Born: 03-Feb-81   Age: 23

YEAR	TM	LG	AGE	AB	H	2B	3B	HR	BB	SO	SB	CS	AVG	OBP	SLG	MLVR	EQBA	EQOBP	EQSLG	EQMLVR	VORP	DEFENSE			
2001	FTM	FLA	20	463	112	14	4	6	51	86	13	7	.242	.333	.328	-.029	.209	.272	.294	-.374	-45.1	107-RF	-8	25-CF	-2
2002	FTM	FLA	21	427	102	13	2	5	36	89	18	6	.239	.309	.314	-.084	.211	.262	.286	-.405	-35.2	78-CF	-2	27-RF	-3
2003	NBR	EAS	22	225	40	9	1	3	16	60	5	3	.178	.242	.267	-.378	.159	.210	.251	-.583	-29.9	66-CF	6		
2004	*MIN*	*AL*	*23*	*205*	*43*	*9*	*1*	*4*	*14*	*48*	*4*	*2*	*.211*	*.270*	*.318*	*-.292*	*.210*	*.272*	*.324*	*-.313*	*-10.3*	*57-CF*	*-8*		

Breakout: 51%   *Improve: 71%*   *Collapse: 15%*

He's hit the wall. The fifth pick in the 1999 draft, Garbe has simply never put it together. He's got tools and he's been improving defensively, but he's had a slow bat, and hasn't been able to identify pitches or control the strike zone. He's still young enough that he can have a reasonable career, but he needs a big skills consolidation and breakout season all in one.

CHRIS GOMEZ   SS   Bats: R   Throws: R   Born: 16-Jun-71   Age: 33

YEAR	TM	LG	AGE	AB	H	2B	3B	HR	BB	SO	SB	CS	AVG	OBP	SLG	MLVR	EQBA	EQOBP	EQSLG	EQMLVR	VORP	DEFENSE			
2001	SDP	NL	30	112	21	3	0	0	9	14	1	0	.188	.248	.214	-.509	.211	.268	.237	-.460	-7.8	25-SS	-6		
2001	TBY	AL	30	189	57	16	0	8	8	24	3	0	.302	.337	.513	.159	.321	.357	.547	.234	21.1	51-SS	-3		
2002	TBY	AL	31	461	122	31	3	10	21	58	1	3	.265	.307	.410	-.053	.284	.326	.444	-.007	22.7	123-SS	7		
2003	MIN	AL	32	175	44	9	3	1	7	13	2	1	.251	.280	.354	-.222	.269	.301	.383	-.154	-2.3	20-2B	0	17-3B	1
2004	*TOR*	*AL*	*33*	*202*	*53*	*11*	*1*	*4*	*11*	*22*	*2*	*1*	*.263*	*.305*	*.387*	*-.109*	*.259*	*.305*	*.384*	*-.143*	*4.7*	*55-SS*	*-3*		

Breakout: 30%   *Improve: 49%*   *Collapse: 27%*

Missed some time with a knee injury and back pain, but neither of those affected his freakish resemblance to Tim Allen. Gomez is at a point in his career where he'd be a reasonable backup on a contending team. He can play any infield position well enough to keep it warm for a few days, can provide the occasional home run off the bench, and keep the local press mollified. Signed a one-year, $750,000 deal with the Blue Jays to fill the Mike Bordick role.

CRISTIAN GUZMAN   SS   Bats: B   Throws: R   Born: 21-Mar-78   Age: 26

YEAR	TM	LG	AGE	AB	H	2B	3B	HR	BB	SO	SB	CS	AVG	OBP	SLG	MLVR	EQBA	EQOBP	EQSLG	EQMLVR	VORP	DEFENSE	
2001	MIN	AL	23	493	149	28	14	10	21	78	25	8	.302	.337	.477	.097	.316	.352	.501	.152	44.1	116-SS	-3
2002	MIN	AL	24	623	170	31	6	9	17	79	12	13	.273	.294	.385	-.112	.290	.312	.411	-.076	19.6	142-SS	5
2003	MIN	AL	25	534	143	15	14	3	30	79	18	9	.268	.313	.365	-.145	.286	.332	.391	-.071	5.3	138-SS	2
2004	*MIN*	*AL*	*26*	*533*	*149*	*25*	*8*	*7*	*28*	*73*	*16*	*7*	*.279*	*.318*	*.397*	*-.061*	*.279*	*.321*	*.404*	*-.074*	*20.2*	*136-SS*	*1*

Breakout: 19%   *Improve: 48%*   *Collapse: 14%*

You don't typically see this kind of career stagnation without invoking the name of Steven Seagal. Guzman's either been flatlining or declining for some time now. Players with this kind of speed who get a lot of leg doubles might not see as many of those doubles morph into home runs as they mature, and Guzman's turning into such an extreme slap hitter that it's hard to keep opposing defenses honest. He's a player that probably should be replaced, and if he does end up tearing off a big 2004 season, he's going to become suddenly very expensive.

DENNY HOCKING   UT   Bats: B   Throws: R   Born: 02-Apr-70   Age: 34

YEAR	TM	LG	AGE	AB	H	2B	3B	HR	BB	SO	SB	CS	AVG	OBP	SLG	MLVR	EQBA	EQOBP	EQSLG	EQMLVR	VORP	DEFENSE			
2001	MIN	AL	31	327	82	16	2	3	29	67	6	1	.251	.316	.339	-.167	.263	.330	.358	-.139	5.5	40-SS	2	12-2B	-2
2002	MIN	AL	32	260	65	13	0	2	24	44	0	2	.250	.316	.323	-.171	.268	.334	.345	-.146	2.0	46-2B	-3	18-SS	-1
2003	MIN	AL	33	188	45	10	2	3	15	37	0	1	.239	.296	.362	-.196	.255	.314	.394	-.124	-2.6	15-2B	0	18-3B	-1
2004	*COL*	*NL*	*34*	*118*	*30*	*6*	*1*	*2*	*12*	*24*	*1*	*1*	*.250*	*.318*	*.355*	*-.151*	*.241*	*.308*	*.340*	*-.208*	*0.7*	*36-2B*	*-4*		

Breakout: 28%   *Improve: 49%*   *Collapse: 38%*

There are worse utility infielders. Hocking's a line-drive hitter who won't kill you with the glove, and he's well regarded for his work ethic and willingness to be a solid clubhouse guy. He's precisely the kind of player who's likely to get his contract squeezed as a result of increased use of analysis in front offices, but there's also some value here in his not being particularly risky.

TORII HUNTER CF **Bats: R** **Throws: R** Born: 18-Jul-75 Age: 28

YEAR	TM	LG	AGE	AB	H	2B	3B	HR	BB	SO	SB	CS	AVG	OBP	SLG	MLVR	EQBA	EQOBP	EQSLG	EQMLVR	VORP	DEFENSE	
2001	MIN	AL	25	564	147	32	5	27	29	125	9	6	.261	.306	.479	.011	.275	.319	.507	.063	30.1	147-CF	17
2002	MIN	AL	26	561	162	37	4	29	35	118	23	8	.289	.336	.524	.162	.309	.355	.562	.239	55.4	134-CF	-5
2003	MIN	AL	27	581	145	31	4	26	50	106	6	7	.250	.314	.451	-.032	.266	.332	.485	.045	12.8	145-CF	3
2004	MIN	AL	28	501	138	29	3	26	40	95	10	3	.275	.332	.500	.093	.274	.335	.508	.086	25.6	129-CF	-2

Breakout: 24%   Improve: 51%   Collapse: 14%

Seeing a trend in terms of the Twins' front office signing guys immediately after their best year? Hunter will receive $25 million-plus over the next three years for a deal he signed after his 2002 career year. He's got some holes in his swing, but he did step forward a bit in plate discipline this year, and he plays an acrobatic and effective center field. The golden age of defensive centerfielders we're currently in is absolutely a blast. If you're not chasing down the video of players like Hunter, Cameron, and Carlos Beltran every day, you should be.

JACQUE JONES LF **Bats: L** **Throws: L** Born: 25-Apr-75 Age: 29

YEAR	TM	LG	AGE	AB	H	2B	3B	HR	BB	SO	SB	CS	AVG	OBP	SLG	MLVR	EQBA	EQOBP	EQSLG	EQMLVR	VORP	DEFENSE	
2001	MIN	AL	26	475	131	25	0	14	39	92	12	9	.276	.335	.417	-.012	.288	.348	.438	.027	10.1	121-LF	-8
2002	MIN	AL	27	577	173	37	2	27	37	129	6	7	.300	.344	.511	.168	.319	.364	.547	.243	44.0	131-LF	7
2003	MIN	AL	28	517	157	33	1	16	21	105	13	1	.304	.336	.464	.069	.319	.352	.492	.142	18.1	83-LF	-5
2004	MIN	AL	29	498	141	29	2	19	33	97	10	4	.282	.329	.464	.049	.282	.332	.472	.040	14.8	127-LF	-1

Breakout: 4%   Improve: 24%   Collapse: 31%

Jones hit just .269/.310/.393 against lefties, but that's a considerable improvement over the .231/.274/.336 he's managed over the last three years. Jones has some speed, some power, plays defense well, but doesn't draw many walks. He's one of a number of imperfect options the Twins have for their corner OF spots. There simply aren't two players who can do it all in LF and RF for the Twins; Gardenhire needs to pick and choose his spots for offense and defense against specific opponents. He's juggled pretty well so far, and most of the choices are fairly stark.

COREY KOSKIE 3B **Bats: L** **Throws: R** Born: 28-Jun-73 Age: 31

YEAR	TM	LG	AGE	AB	H	2B	3B	HR	BB	SO	SB	CS	AVG	OBP	SLG	MLVR	EQBA	EQOBP	EQSLG	EQMLVR	VORP	DEFENSE	
2001	MIN	AL	28	562	155	37	2	26	68	118	27	6	.276	.366	.488	.136	.293	.380	.522	.205	58.6	148-3B	6
2002	MIN	AL	29	490	131	37	3	15	72	127	10	11	.267	.371	.447	.099	.286	.387	.483	.156	45.6	134 3B	9
2003	MIN	AL	30	469	137	29	2	14	77	113	11	5	.292	.400	.452	.143	.316	.420	.494	.256	39.7	124-3B	4
2004	MIN	AL	31	454	125	28	2	18	66	103	11	5	.276	.373	.468	.119	.276	.377	.476	.113	38.8	125-3B	1

Breakout: 13%   Improve: 44%   Collapse: 19%

A very underrated player. While Eric Chavez has hit like Helen Keller against lefties, Koskie's fared considerably better—as well as a Don Knotts, Jim Nabors, or perhaps even Rey Ordonez. Koskie kills right-handers, plays good defense, draws his walks, and can even steal the occasional base. He doesn't get much attention, but in the AL, there's no one who's clearly better with the bat, at least until either Troy Glaus stops flailing against curveballs from right-handers or Eric Chavez shows he can hit lefties at least marginally well.

JASON KUBEL RF **Bats: L** **Throws: R** Born: 25-May-82 Age: 22

YEAR	TM	LG	AGE	AB	H	2B	3B	HR	BB	SO	SB	CS	AVG	OBP	SLG	MLVR	EQBA	EQOBP	EQSLG	EQMLVR	VORP	DEFENSE	
2002	QUD	MID	20	424	136	26	4	17	41	48	3	5	.321	.382	.521	.333	.239	.287	.402	-.176	-15.1	106-RF	-11
2003	FTM	FLA	21	420	125	20	4	5	48	54	4	6	.298	.371	.400	.183	.253	.310	.353	-.191	-17.4	106-RF	-4
2004	MIN	AL	22	269	65	14	2	6	21	41	1	1	.241	.298	.372	-.155	.240	.301	.378	-.172	-5.8	73-RF	-6

Breakout: 24%   Improve: 44%   Collapse: 27%

His power lapsed against the tougher competition of the Florida State League, but within the context of the league, he performed well. Kubel was a 12th-round pick in the 2000 draft, which means he's way ahead of expectations. He's got a short stroke, controls the strike zone fairly well, and if he starts off well in New Britain, he could end up fast-tracked for an opportunity in Minnesota. I mean, it's not as if you can ever have too many outfielders.

DAVID LAMB
SS Bats: B Throws: R Born: 06-Jun-75 Age: 29

YEAR	TM	LG	AGE	AB	H	2B	3B	HR	BB	SO	SB	CS	AVG	OBP	SLG	MLVR	EQBA	EQOBP	EQSLG	EQMLVR	VORP	DEFENSE	
2001	CAR	SOU	26	287	78	16	0	5	37	39	2	3	.272	.363	.380	.042	.234	.307	.332	-.238	-3.5	69-SS	5
2001	CLG	PCL	26	67	20	6	0	1	11	11	0	0	.299	.412	.433	.090	.242	.344	.348	-.139	0.8	13-2B	-1
2002	EDM	PCL	27	440	136	25	3	10	45	57	2	6	.309	.381	.448	.145	.274	.338	.401	-.055	20.0	114-SS	-10
2003	ROC	INT	28	405	105	15	2	2	49	60	2	6	.259	.351	.321	-.071	.240	.326	.298	-.243	-5.2	88-SS	-1
2004	*MIN*	*AL*	*29*	*153*	*38*	*7*	*1*	*2*	*15*	*24*	*1*	*1*	*.246*	*.320*	*.345*	*-.148*	*.246*	*.323*	*.351*	*-.164*	*1.3*	*44-SS*	*-4*

Breakout: 32%   Improve: 45%   Collapse: 37%

On a team with bushels of unappealing choices to play the middle infield, Lamb's definitely one of them. He's not quite enough of a hitter to make a big club, even one with a major hole. Defensively, he's not really a long-term solution in the middle infield, and there's no way he's going to hit enough to help a club at a corner spot. In short, he's a classic infield tweener.

MATT LeCROY
DH/C/1B Bats: R Throws: R Born: 13-Dec-75 Age: 28

YEAR	TM	LG	AGE	AB	H	2B	3B	HR	BB	SO	SB	CS	AVG	OBP	SLG	MLVR	EQBA	EQOBP	EQSLG	EQMLVR	VORP	DEFENSE			
2001	EDM	PCL	25	396	130	17	0	20	36	95	0	2	.328	.393	.523	.260	.284	.346	.457	.047	25.8	20-C	-3	10-1B	-2
2001	MIN	AL	25	40	17	5	0	3	0	8	0	1	.425	.439	.775	.840	.450	.460	.825	1.011	11.0				
2002	EDM	PCL	26	174	61	7	1	12	17	34	2	0	.351	.421	.609	.477	.305	.368	.540	.223	21.1	10-C	0		
2002	MIN	AL	26	181	47	11	1	7	13	38	0	2	.260	.309	.448	-.011	.280	.328	.484	.050	8.2				
2003	MIN	AL	27	345	99	19	0	17	25	82	0	1	.287	.342	.490	.105	.303	.359	.520	.178	19.3	16-C	-4	12-1B	-2
2004	*MIN*	*AL*	*28*	*320*	*84*	*17*	*1*	*14*	*25*	*74*	*1*	*1*	*.263*	*.322*	*.450*	*.002*	*.262*	*.325*	*.458*	*-.008*	*10.9*				

Breakout: 5%   Improve: 23%   Collapse: 49%

With the trade of Pierzynski to the Giants, it's not yet clear whether or not LeCroy will have the starting job at the start of the season. He's not the catcher of the future, but he is a solid right-handed bat, and if he can keep the position warm until Joe Mauer's really ready, the Twins' offense could certainly benefit from having him at C and one of the outfielders at DH. Defensively, LeCroy's a liability at catcher. But he's an underrated hitter with good power, and could put up 450 very productive plate appearances, with 25 homers, from the C, 1B, and DH spots.

JOE MAUER
C Bats: L Throws: R Born: 19-Apr-83 Age: 21

YEAR	TM	LG	AGE	AB	H	2B	3B	HR	BB	SO	SB	CS	AVG	OBP	SLG	MLVR	EQBA	EQOBP	EQSLG	EQMLVR	VORP	DEFENSE			
2001	ELZ	APP	18	110	44	6	2	0	19	10	4	0	.400	.492	.491	.528	.256	.327	.316	-.207	-3.0	19-C	-3		
2002	QUD	MID	19	411	124	23	1	4	61	42	0	0	.302	.395	.392	.168	.227	.299	.300	-.302	-17.8	81-C	12	12-1B	0
2003	FTM	FLA	20	233	78	13	1	1	24	24	3	0	.335	.399	.412	.265	.287	.337	.361	-.104	5.3	39-C	11		
2003	NBR	EAS	20	276	94	17	1	4	25	25	0	0	.341	.405	.453	.257	.292	.346	.397	-.032	12.1	58-C	3		
2004	*MIN*	*AL*	*21*	*307*	*77*	*16*	*1*	*4*	*23*	*37*	*1*	*1*	*.250*	*.306*	*.346*	*-.168*	*.249*	*.310*	*.352*	*-.185*	*0.7*	*82-C*	*-4*		

Breakout: 11%   Improve: 28%   Collapse: 46%

Here he is. The Twins received a lot of flak from analysts, including us, for not drafting Mark Prior with the first selection in the 2001 draft, and instead drafting The Local Boy. Since then, they've acquitted themselves very nicely, thank you. Mauer's hit for average, shown some doubles power, received raves for his defense behind the plate, and performed well against competition well beyond his years at each stop through the minors. With the trade of Pierzynski, it's clear that the Twins believe his time is just about here. Mauer projects as a pre-injury Jason Kendall player: He's got a broad set of skills, and he's going to be outstanding—a good defensive catcher with a high average, walks, and power. Twins fans, begin salivating.

DOUG MIENTKIEWICZ
1B Bats: L Throws: R Born: 19-Jun-74 Age: 30

YEAR	TM	LG	AGE	AB	H	2B	3B	HR	BB	SO	SB	CS	AVG	OBP	SLG	MLVR	EQBA	EQOBP	EQSLG	EQMLVR	VORP	DEFENSE	
2001	MIN	AL	27	543	166	39	1	15	67	92	2	6	.306	.391	.464	.173	.322	.406	.493	.237	47.2	143-1B	12
2002	MIN	AL	28	467	122	29	1	10	74	69	1	2	.261	.369	.392	.021	.281	.386	.421	.066	19.5	131-1B	7
2003	MIN	AL	29	487	146	38	1	11	74	55	4	1	.300	.398	.450	.147	.318	.414	.482	.231	27.0	126-1B	-1
2004	*MIN*	*AL*	*30*	*417*	*118*	*27*	*1*	*11*	*58*	*56*	*2*	*2*	*.284*	*.374*	*.436*	*.087*	*.284*	*.378*	*.443*	*.080*	*20.3*	*114-1B*	*0*

Breakout: 12%   Improve: 38%   Collapse: 18%

The Twins just don't need this guy. He's a slick fielder, but his bat isn't worth the extra expense and waste of other talent the Twins must suffer through if they keep him as their starting first baseman. Just as the Cub faithful canonized Mark Grace and were saddled with him as a result, the Twins have exactly the same situation going on with Minky. Minnesota would be better off with a one-year stopgap of LeCroy and a cheap free agent, working Morneau into the job gradually towards the end of the year. If they can keep Mientkiewicz on a one-year deal, he'll still help the team and make good trade bait to boot. Credit Terry Ryan and company for handing out one of their famous four-year, overpay deals here.

DUSTAN MOHR RF/LF Bats: R Throws: R Born: 19-Jun-76 Age: 28

YEAR	TM	LG	AGE	AB	H	2B	3B	HR	BB	SO	SB	CS	AVG	OBP	SLG	MLVR	EQBA	EQOBP	EQSLG	EQMLVR	VORP	DEFENSE			
2001	NBR	EAS	25	518	174	41	3	24	49	111	9	9	.336	.398	.566	.407	.285	.343	.483	.079	36.0	68-CF	-3	67-LF	0
2001	MIN	AL	25	51	12	2	0	0	5	17	1	1	.235	.304	.275	-.284	.255	.321	.294	-.251	-2.5	13-RF	1		
2002	MIN	AL	26	383	103	23	2	12	31	86	6	3	.269	.325	.433	.004	.288	.344	.468	.063	12.8	82-RF	3	21-LF	2
2003	MIN	AL	27	348	87	22	0	10	33	106	5	2	.250	.317	.399	-.097	.266	.335	.433	-.022	-3.8	70-RF	3	23-LF	-2
2004	SFG	NL	28	304	79	18	2	10	29	82	4	2	.261	.326	.434	-.026	.261	.324	.447	-.025	7.4	82-RF	1		

Breakout: 28%   Improve: 43%   Collapse: 31%

Another one of Minnesota's endless supply of Pretty Good Outfielders. OK, so over the last couple of years, the Twins have had Cuddyer, Mohr, Ford, Kielty, Stewart, Buchanan, Jones, Hunter, Restovich . . . good lord. While other teams try to make due with the remains of Ruben Sierra, Marvin Benard, or Terrence Long, the Twins are loaded with players with some limitations, who can still contribute or have significant promise. Mohr's fully capable of having a big year; he's kind of where Bubba Trammell was a few years ago, where he should try to find a spot to play, even if it's for minimal dollars, if he can find 500 PA. Mohr can play defense and hit lefties. Seven years from now, he might look back and find he's had Greg Colbrunn's career.

JUSTIN MORNEAU 1B BATS: L THROWS: R Born: 15-May-81 Age: 23

YEAR	TM	LG	AGE	AB	H	2B	3B	HR	BB	SO	SB	CS	AVG	OBP	SLG	MLVR	EQBA	EQOBP	EQSLG	EQMLVR	VORP	DEFENSE	
2001	FTM	FLA	20	197	58	10	3	4	24	41	0	0	.294	.393	.437	.234	.249	.318	.380	-.141	-3.6	47-1B	-2
2001	QUD	MID	20	236	84	17	2	12	26	38	0	0	.356	.426	.597	.511	.257	.315	.440	-.056	2.0	57-1B	-1
2002	NBR	EAS	21	494	147	31	4	16	42	88	7	0	.298	.360	.474	.182	.256	.308	.416	-.104	-3.1	124-1B	-10
2003	NBR	EAS	22	79	26	3	1	6	7	14	0	0	.329	.384	.620	.451	.266	.318	.532	.087	4.2	20-1B	2
2003	ROC	INT	22	265	71	11	1	16	28	56	0	2	.268	.347	.498	.153	.243	.319	.464	-.027	4.6	58-1B	-3
2003	MIN	AL	22	106	24	4	0	4	9	30	0	0	.226	.287	.377	-.192	.236	.302	.406	-.144	-1.6		
2004	MIN	AL	23	336	88	19	2	14	30	67	2	1	.262	.327	.453	.013	.261	.330	.461	.003	12.3	90-1B	-3

Breakout: 38%   Improve: 59%   Collapse: 17%

What do the Twins do best? Drafting and player development. No organization is better at it than the Twins. In most organizations, Morneau would draw so much attention that he'd suck the oxygen out of the virtual prospect room. In this organization, he's far behind Mauer in terms of recognition. Morneau's not just going to be a good hitter; he's going to be positively great. How great? Healthy, prime Fred McGriff great. He's got a quick, compact stroke, and if he gets the playing time, he's going to be very good very soon.

A. J. PIERZYNSKI C Bats: L Throws: R Born: 30-Dec-76 Age: 27

YEAR	TM	LG	AGE	AB	H	2B	3B	HR	BB	SO	SB	CS	AVG	OBP	SLG	MLVR	EQBA	EQOBP	EQSLG	EQMLVR	VORP	DEFENSE	
2001	MIN	AL	24	381	110	33	2	7	16	57	1	7	.289	.324	.441	.014	.299	.336	.462	.050	21.5	100-C	0
2002	MIN	AL	25	440	132	31	6	6	13	61	1	2	.300	.336	.439	.055	.317	.352	.468	.105	30.3	115-C	1
2003	MIN	AL	26	487	152	35	3	11	24	55	3	1	.312	.363	.464	.121	.330	.379	.496	.205	33.6	131-C	5
2004	SFG	NL	27	408	118	27	3	8	22	51	2	2	.289	.339	.430	.012	.289	.337	.443	.014	22.5	106-C	0

Breakout: 12%   Improve: 28%   Collapse: 39%

The AL's favorite red-ass has moved to the Giants, where he'll take over for Benito Santiago. Pierzynski's a solid hitter with moderate power, and will add a much needed reliable bat to the Giant offense. He's going to make a lot of free agent money when he hits the market, and should have a career close to Terry Steinbach's.

TOM PRINCE

C   **Bats: R**   **Throws: R**   Born: 13-Aug-64   Age: 39

YEAR	TM	LG	AGE	AB	H	2B	3B	HR	BB	SO	SB	CS	AVG	OBP	SLG	MLVR	EQBA	EQOBP	EQSLG	EQMLVR	VORP	DEFENSE
2001	MIN	AL	36	196	43	4	1	7	12	39	3	1	.219	.285	.357	-.219	.235	.297	.383	-.186	-0.7	61-C 11
2002	MIN	AL	37	125	28	7	1	4	14	26	1	3	.224	.322	.392	-.087	.246	.337	.429	-.040	4.5	40-C 3
2003	MIN	AL	38	40	8	2	0	2	5	7	1	0	.200	.319	.400	-.120	.225	.334	.450	-.034	0.6	13-C 2
2003	OMA	PCL	38	91	28	10	0	1	14	15	0	1	.308	.422	.451	.234	.272	.372	.413	.023	5.5	27-C 2
2004	*MIN*	*AL*	*39*	*101*	*23*	*6*	*0*	*3*	*10*	*19*	*0*	*0*	*.231*	*.330*	*.372*	*-.105*	*.231*	*.333*	*.379*	*-.119*	*2.8*	*32-C -3*

Breakout: 35%   Improve: 67%   Collapse: 19%

Receiverus Secundi, in its natural habitat. Is there another player who more embodies the very spirit of the backup catcher? Mark Parent? Junior Ortiz? Prince has hit the lottery, and had a long career despite not having a ton of natural talent, or really ever having a big season. Somewhere along the line, he got the "Proven MLB Backup Catcher" glow.

MIKE RESTOVICH

OF   **Bats: R**   **Throws: R**   Born: 03-Jan-79   Age: 25

YEAR	TM	LG	AGE	AB	H	2B	3B	HR	BB	SO	SB	CS	AVG	OBP	SLG	MLVR	EQBA	EQOBP	EQSLG	EQMLVR	VORP	DEFENSE		
2001	NBR	EAS	22	501	135	33	4	23	54	125	15	7	.269	.348	.489	.173	.233	.302	.426	-.119	-8.3	138-RF 1		
2002	EDM	PCL	23	518	148	32	7	29	53	151	11	7	.286	.357	.542	.213	.250	.316	.476	-.010	8.8	60-RF -1	61-LF -2
2003	ROC	INT	24	454	125	34	2	16	47	117	10	3	.275	.349	.465	.119	.251	.322	.434	-.057	1.2	93-RF 6	17-LF 3
2003	MIN	AL	24	53	15	3	2	0	10	12	0	0	.283	.406	.415	.111	.302	.429	.434	.178	2.6			
2004	*MIN*	*AL*	*25*	*304*	*81*	*19*	*2*	*13*	*29*	*68*	*6*	*2*	*.267*	*.335*	*.474*	*.059*	*.267*	*.339*	*.482*	*.050*	*14.3*	*82-RF 1*		

Breakout: 36%   Improve: 69%   Collapse: 12%

Restovich might be the prospect most likely to be the next Rob Deer. He's got significant power, is mechanical but effective defensively, has a frame that makes you believe his modest speed isn't going to last more than another couple of years, and piles up the Ks. He definitely has the stroke to have a successful major league career. Depending on how the Twins' outfield melange ends up, he could be moved in a deal to restock the bullpen. He's got a .550 SLG peak in him if he gets the opportunity.

LUIS RIVAS

2B   **Bats: R**   **Throws: R**   Born: 30-Aug-79   Age: 24

YEAR	TM	LG	AGE	AB	H	2B	3B	HR	BB	SO	SB	CS	AVG	OBP	SLG	MLVR	EQBA	EQOBP	EQSLG	EQMLVR	VORP	DEFENSE
2001	MIN	AL	21	563	150	21	6	7	40	99	31	11	.266	.322	.362	-.115	.281	.337	.382	-.079	14.0	145-2B -16
2002	MIN	AL	22	316	81	23	4	4	19	51	9	4	.256	.305	.392	-.096	.274	.322	.426	-.049	10.2	87-2B -1
2003	MIN	AL	23	475	123	16	9	8	30	65	17	7	.259	.310	.381	-.127	.277	.328	.412	-.056	3.4	125-2B -1
2004	*MIN*	*AL*	*24*	*432*	*113*	*21*	*4*	*8*	*32*	*61*	*15*	*5*	*.262*	*.317*	*.386*	*-.089*	*.261*	*.320*	*.393*	*-.103*	*12.1*	*113-2B 0*

Breakout: 22%   Improve: 47%   Collapse: 20%

Not exactly Whitaker and Trammell. Rivas, like Guzman, appears to have his career stuck in neutral. He hasn't hit, he's not showing noticeable development, and defensively, he's been acceptable but neither impressive or improving. The Twins have done a fantastic job creating and expanding a window of opportunity for this team to win a championship. The marginal gain they could realize by replacing either of Rivas or Guzman with an impact player is truly enormous. They'd like to realize that gain through normal development and maturation, but the team's operating at a sub-optimal level while they wait.

MIKE RYAN

OF   **Bats: L**   **Throws: R**   Born: 06-Jul-77   Age: 26

YEAR	TM	LG	AGE	AB	H	2B	3B	HR	BB	SO	SB	CS	AVG	OBP	SLG	MLVR	EQBA	EQOBP	EQSLG	EQMLVR	VORP	DEFENSE		
2001	EDM	PCL	24	527	152	36	7	18	52	121	1	6	.288	.355	.486	.101	.251	.314	.422	-.088	-3.6	75-RF -6	36-2B -8
2002	EDM	PCL	25	540	141	36	6	31	55	124	4	5	.261	.332	.522	.120	.231	.295	.459	-.088	-5.5	60-LF -4	45-CF -7
2003	ROC	INT	26	408	92	20	4	15	38	89	6	1	.225	.293	.404	-.083	.207	.276	.378	-.252	-24.8	72-LF -7	11-CF -1
2003	MIN	AL	26	61	24	7	0	5	6	12	2	1	.393	.448	.754	.752	.410	.471	.787	.874	13.3	12-RF 2		
2004	*MIN*	*AL*	*26*	*221*	*55*	*12*	*2*	*9*	*20*	*45*	*3*	*1*	*.251*	*.314*	*.441*	*-.031*	*.250*	*.318*	*.449*	*-.042*	*5.6*	*61-LF -2*		

Breakout: 40%   Improve: 63%   Collapse: 20%

Sorry, kid. This is the wrong organization for you. Ryan's a Quadruple-A outfielder with a chance to get good enough for a semi-regular role on a bad team. The Twins have so many outfielders who are legitimately good that they'd have to have some sort of Stalinist purge for Ryan to get any sort of opportunity. Of course, he did bash the snot out of the ball in just under 70 PA, so he might get a look in the spring.

SHANNON STEWART — LF   Bats: R   Throws: R   Born: 25-Feb-74   Age: 30

YEAR	TM	LG	AGE	AB	H	2B	3B	HR	BB	SO	SB	CS	AVG	OBP	SLG	MLVR	EQBA	EQOBP	EQSLG	EQMLVR	VORP	DEFENSE		
2001	TOR	AL	27	640	202	44	7	12	46	72	27	10	.316	.372	.463	.148	.331	.386	.487	.205	42.4	128-LF	3	
2002	TOR	AL	28	577	175	38	6	10	54	60	14	2	.303	.372	.442	.121	.322	.389	.471	.178	35.0	92-LF	0	
2003	TOR	AL	29	303	89	22	2	7	27	30	1	2	.294	.355	.449	.028	.310	.372	.475	.142	4.6	69-LF	8	
2003	MIN	AL	29	270	87	22	0	6	25	36	3	4	.322	.388	.470	.179	.343	.409	.502	.277	14.7	45-LF	1	14-RF 1
2004	*MIN*	*AL*	*30*	*543*	*159*	*35*	*3*	*12*	*49*	*63*	*8*	*4*	*.293*	*.357*	*.436*	*.065*	*.293*	*.360*	*.443*	*.057*	*17.7*	*142-LF*	*1*	

Breakout: 8%   *Improve: 35%*   *Collapse: 26%*

A good and consistent player. The campaign to get him some AL MVP consideration was ill-advised, though. He's a solid ballplayer, but the Twins' tear once Shannon Stewart arrived was more the result of a soft schedule, including plenty-o-games against such stalwart opponents as the Detroit Tigers and Cleveland Indians, than some magic inspirational voodoo Stewart brought along. He hits for average, controls the strike zone well, and has some pop. Defensively, a shoulder held together by good intentions, bailing wire, and mucilage means that runners are free to go on him at any time, but he covers a lot of ground for a corner OF, which makes up for most of the shortcomings with his arm. Re-signed with the Twins for three years, $18 million, more than they should have paid.

KEVIN YOUNG — 1B   Bats: R   Throws: R   Born: 16-Jun-69   Age: 35

YEAR	TM	LG	AGE	AB	H	2B	3B	HR	BB	SO	SB	CS	AVG	OBP	SLG	MLVR	EQBA	EQOBP	EQSLG	EQMLVR	VORP	DEFENSE	
2001	PIT	NL	32	449	104	33	0	14	42	119	15	11	.232	.313	.399	-.129	.230	.307	.397	-.151	-8.8	120-1B	7
2002	PIT	NL	33	468	115	26	1	16	50	101	4	6	.246	.324	.408	-.021	.251	.323	.423	-.070	1.7	130-1B	0
2003	PIT	NL	34	84	17	4	0	2	12	25	1	0	.202	.302	.321	-.225	.200	.299	.329	-.277	-3.5	22-1B	0
2004	*MIN*	*AL*	*35*	*194*	*45*	*10*	*1*	*6*	*22*	*48*	*2*	*1*	*.233*	*.317*	*.386*	*-.109*	*.233*	*.320*	*.393*	*-.124*	*-0.4*	*55-1B*	*-2*

Breakout: 40%   *Improve: 58%*   *Collapse: 27%*

Young had to leave the Twins in July to attend to his wife, whom we at BP wish the best of health and good fortune. Young's a free agent, and will be looking for an opportunity to hook on somewhere with a minor league deal if he chooses to extend his career. Many years ago, Kevin Young was a hot young third base prospect, and the subject of heated debate online, along with players like Willie Greene, Kal Daniels, and dozens of others. The defensive spectrum can be a very demanding taskmaster. The slide from shortstop to first baseman or corner outfield can strongly resemble a Hobbesian dystopia—nasty, brutish, and short.

PITCHERS

JAMES BALDWIN — Bats: R   Throws: R   Born: 15-Jul-71   Age: 32

YEAR	TM	LG	AGE	G	GS	IP	H	BB	SO	HR	ERA	EQERA	EQH9	EQBB9	EQSO9	EQHR9	PERA	VORP	STF
2001	CWS	AL	29	17	16	95.7	109	38	42	15	4.61	5.17	10.2	3.3	3.7	1.3	5.51	4.4	-17
2001	LAD	NL	29	12	12	79.3	82	25	53	10	4.20	4.64	9.6	2.6	5.1	1.1	4.78	8.1	2
2002	SEA	AL	30	30	23	150.0	179	49	88	26	5.28	5.90	10.7	2.7	5.1	1.5	5.80	-4.8	-16
2003	OMA	PCL	31	8	8	46.3	48	13	24	3	4.08	5.27	10.3	3.0	4.0	0.8	4.98	1.6	-9
2003	ROC	INT	31	5	5	29.7	25	3	18	2	2.42	3.21	7.7	1.0	4.2	1.0	3.29	7.4	8
2003	MIN	AL	31	10	0	15.0	21	4	7	6	5.40	6.75	11.7	2.5	4.3	3.1	8.18	0.0	-73
2004	*MIN*	*AL*	*32*	*35*	*15*	*96.0*	*111*	*28*	*50*	*15*	*5.02*	*4.90*	*10.0*	*2.5*	*4.6*	*1.2*	*4.99*	*11.5*	*-9*

Breakout: 29%   *Improve: 57%*   *Collapse: 36%*

Baldwin was distinctly and unambiguously awful for the Twins, who quickly sent him down, since they already had plenty of guys like that to start games. He refused the assignment and became a free agent, after having already been rejected by the pitching-rich Royals. Baldwin's career ended in 2002 in Seattle, as amply demonstrated by his home/road splits. He'll be trolling for a job come spring training time, but realistically, a career that had some bright spots has come to an end.

GRANT BALFOUR

Bats: R **Throws: R** Born: 30-Dec-77 Age: 26

YEAR	TM	LG	AGE	G	GS	IP	H	BB	SO	HR	ERA	EQERA	EQH9	EQBB9	EQSO9	EQHR9	PERA	VORP	STF
2001	NBR	EAS	23	35	0	50.0	26	22	72	1	1.08	2.23	6.5	5.5	9.1	0.2	3.25	16.6	39
2001	EDM	PCL	23	11	0	16.3	18	10	17	2	5.52	6.32	9.2	6.3	6.9	1.1	5.64	-1.3	-10
2002	EDM	PCL	24	58	0	71.3	60	30	88	3	4.17	4.01	8.0	4.3	8.4	0.5	3.90	11.9	21
2003	ROC	INT	25	21	11	71.0	48	16	87	6	2.41	2.71	6.8	2.4	8.7	1.1	3.35	21.3	24
2003	MIN	AL	25	17	1	26.0	23	14	30	4	4.15	4.21	7.7	4.6	10.2	1.1	4.33	5.2	22
2004	MIN	AL	26	26	11	75.3	65	29	73	8	3.57	3.48	7.5	3.2	8.6	0.9	3.56	19.4	19

Breakout: 32%   Improve: 57%   Collapse: 18%

The "Hey, let's move him back into the rotation" idea worked out pretty well there. Balfour's got a live fastball, which he harnessed at Rochester. Once promoted to the bigs though, he was Dr. Jekyll and Mr. Acker, mixing innings where he looked completely and totally dominant with innings where it looked like he had no clue what he was doing. His arm appears to be healthy, and Balfour will be in the mix for a shot at making the staff out of spring training. Those peripheral numbers have been outstanding from time to time—those K rates are pretty amazing—and Balfour's a candidate to follow the Johan Santana career path if things break his way. A legal name change wouldn't kill the guy; people wouldn't hurry to a physician named "Rick Tusofdeth" or something.

JESSE CRAIN

Bats: R **Throws: R** Born: 05-Jul-81 Age: 22

YEAR	TM	LG	AGE	G	GS	IP	H	BB	SO	HR	ERA	EQERA	EQH9	EQBB9	EQSO9	EQHR9	PERA	VORP	STF
2002	ELZ	APP	21	9	0	15.7	4	7	18	0	0.57	1.32	4.0	5.3	5.3	0.0	2.03	6.5	27
2002	QUD	MID	21	9	0	12.0	6	4	11	0	1.50	3.38	5.9	4.2	5.1	0.0	2.54	2.6	23
2003	FTM	FLA	22	10	0	19.0	10	5	25	0	2.84	3.71	6.9	3.2	8.5	0.0	2.61	3.6	49
2003	NBR	EAS	22	22	0	39.0	13	10	56	0	0.69	1.25	4.0	2.8	10.8	0.2	1.52	17.4	74
2003	ROC	INT	22	23	0	26.0	24	10	33	0	3.12	3.60	7.6	4.0	10.1	0.4	3.42	5.6	56
2004	MIN	AL	22	23	10	64.7	52	23	63	6	3.15	3.08	7.0	3.1	8.6	0.7	3.06	19.0	21

Breakout: 20%   Improve: 53%   Collapse: 34%

Half the AL executives we spoke with during the season were interested in acquiring Jesse Crain. He's got a particularly nasty slider and a plus fastball, and does a good job of mixing the two up and making batters look more confounded than James Lipton interviewing a Grey Goose-bearing Bill Shatner. In Double-A and Triple-A, Crain fanned 89 in 65 innings, which bodes exceptionally well for the future; those 13 hits allowed in 39 Double-A innings isn't a typo either. The amount of time it takes him to break into the Minnesota pen, and then into the closer role, could be breathtakingly short. He'll be needed, with Guardado and Hawkins gone.

J. D. DURBIN

Bats: R **Throws: R** Born: 24-Feb-82 Age: 22

YEAR	TM	LG	AGE	G	GS	IP	H	BB	SO	HR	ERA	EQERA	EQH9	EQBB9	EQSO9	EQHR9	PERA	VORP	STF
2001	ELZ	APP	19	8	7	33.7	23	17	39	2	1.87	6.18	9.8	7.8	4.9	1.6	6.86	-1.8	-16
2002	QUD	MID	20	27	27	161.0	144	51	163	14	3.19	5.91	11.6	4.0	5.8	2.2	7.37	-4.8	-5
2003	FTM	FLA	21	14	14	87.3	73	22	69	3	3.09	5.19	9.6	2.9	5.0	1.0	4.80	3.6	12
2003	NBR	EAS	21	14	14	94.7	102	29	70	10	3.14	5.22	10.3	3.3	5.5	1.6	5.92	3.7	6
2004	MIN	AL	22	16	12	69.0	78	28	44	13	5.73	5.60	9.8	3.5	5.6	1.5	5.43	3.2	-4

Breakout: 12%   Improve: 40%   Collapse: 35%

He's received a fair amount of ink given his performance record. Durbin's a prospect in the same way that the Twins have reliable starters; that is, they've got a bunch of guys who can be a soft #2 if they have their best year, all lined up behind Johan Santana. Durbin's young, and may add a couple of mph to his fastball and improve his breaking stuff, so he's got a higher ceiling than say, Joe Mays, but the K rate's not outstanding, the control's not outstanding, and the radar gun's not lighting up. A year from now, maybe he'll be fanning a guy per inning in Triple-A. More likely, he'll post an ERA in the low 4s in the PCL with 6 Ks per nine innings. In other words, he's a C prospect with a chance to be a B-.

TONY FIORE

Bats: R **Throws: R** Born: 12-Oct-71 Age: 32

YEAR	TM	LG	AGE	G	GS	IP	H	BB	SO	HR	ERA	EQERA	EQH9	EQBB9	EQSO9	EQHR9	PERA	VORP	STF
2001	EDM	PCL	29	32	6	80.7	85	25	58	4	3.68	4.07	9.1	3.3	4.5	0.5	4.08	13.1	-2
2002	MIN	AL	30	48	2	91.0	74	43	55	10	3.16	3.46	7.2	4.0	5.2	0.9	3.89	21.0	-3
2003	ROC	INT	31	16	11	84.3	80	21	48	5	3.95	4.33	8.7	2.7	4.0	0.8	4.09	11.1	-2
2003	MIN	AL	31	21	0	36.0	32	21	23	5	5.50	5.09	7.6	4.8	5.6	1.0	4.43	-1.1	-12
2004	HOU	NL	32	34	12	78	83	35	45	10	4.87	4.96	9.5	3.5	4.7	1.1	5.10	5.8	-12

Breakout: 18%   Improve: 49%   Collapse: 20%

The scary thing is that as much of a minor league vet as Fiore is, his 2003 performance record and expected effectiveness weren't that far from Twins' starters not named Santana, despite the several-million-dollar gap in salaries. Fiore's going to be battling for one of the final two spots on a roster for the rest of his career. He's an extreme junkballer, and best suited for long relief.

EDDIE GUARDADO   Bats: R   Throws: L   Born: 02-Oct-70   Age: 33

YEAR	TM	LG	AGE	G	GS	IP	H	BB	SO	HR	ERA	EQERA	EQH9	EQBB9	EQSO9	EQHR9	PERA	VORP	STF
2001	MIN	AL	30	67	0	66.7	47	23	67	5	3.51	3.06	6.4	2.9	8.5	0.6	2.82	18.3	29
2002	MIN	AL	31	68	0	67.7	53	18	70	9	2.92	3.02	7.0	2.2	8.9	1.1	3.37	18.8	21
2003	MIN	AL	32	66	0	65.3	50	14	60	7	2.89	2.83	6.6	1.8	8.1	0.8	2.89	21.2	24
2004	SEA	AL	33	50	0	58.7	51	15	53	7	3.35	3.42	7.8	2.2	7.9	1.0	3.47	16.3	12

Breakout: 41%   Improve: 57%   Collapse: 24%

Predictable, quality pitching isn't easy to find, but Eddie's been doing it for a long time. He's been effective against righties over the years, but absolutely devastating against lefties, holding them to a .195 average with only seven walks and two home runs in the last *three seasons.* He's finally on the free agent market, and will draw interest from a large number of clubs. He's likely to continue at his current level of performance over the life of the three-year deal he signed with Seattle.

LaTROY HAWKINS   Bats: R   Throws: R   Born: 21-Dec-72   Age: 31

YEAR	TM	LG	AGE	G	GS	IP	H	BB	SO	HR	ERA	EQERA	EQH9	EQBB9	EQSO9	EQHR9	PERA	VORP	STF
2001	MIN	AL	28	62	0	51.3	59	39	36	3	5.96	5.72	10.2	6.3	5.9	0.5	5.44	-0.7	-12
2002	MIN	AL	29	65	0	80.3	63	15	63	5	2.13	2.56	7.0	1.5	6.9	0.5	2.61	26.1	28
2003	MIN	AL	30	74	0	77.3	69	15	75	4	1.86	2.51	7.8	1.7	8.6	0.4	2.88	31.1	40
2004	CHC	NL	31	52	1	67.0	62	23	60	6	3.37	3.58	8.4	2.7	7.3	0.8	3.84	15.0	8

Breakout: 30%   Improve: 54%   Collapse: 23%

Hawkins, who once made a cottage industry out of raising Tom Kelly's ire and blood pressure, has finally found his niche as one of the nastiest setup men in the league. He's pretty much been the right-handed Arthur Rhodes—didn't work out as a starter despite tremendous stuff. But once he found a spot in the bullpen and added just a touch more control, he became almost unhittable. Everything about his performance profile says he's going to continue to be successful. The Cubs gave him a three-year, $11.2 million payday.

ADAM JOHNSON   Bats: R   Throws: R   Born: 12-Jul-79   Age: 24

YEAR	TM	LG	AGE	G	GS	IP	H	BB	SO	HR	ERA	EQERA	EQH9	EQBB9	EQSO9	EQHR9	PERA	VORP	STF
2001	EDM	PCL	21	4	4	23.7	19	10	25	0	5.70	4.30	6.3	4.3	7.8	0.0	2.67	3.3	58
2001	MIN	AL	21	7	4	25.0	32	13	17	6	8.28	7.77	11.5	4.4	5.5	1.8	7.01	-5.9	-4
2001	NBR	EAS	21	18	18	113.0	105	39	110	10	3.82	5.61	9.6	4.1	6.3	1.1	5.25	-0.1	19
2002	EDM	PCL	22	27	27	151.3	182	55	112	25	5.47	6.11	9.7	3.6	5.3	1.6	5.63	-8.4	-1
2003	ROC	INT	23	28	17	114.3	128	48	78	7	5.35	5.70	9.6	4.5	5.0	0.7	4.94	-1.2	1
2004	MIN	AL	24	14	11	58.7	69	36	40	10	6.54	6.38	10.2	5.1	6.0	1.4	6.21	-0.7	-9

Breakout: 22%   Improve: 54%   Collapse: 25%

Johnson seems to have been around forever as a "sleeper" in the analyst community, but he really hasn't pitched well now in nearly four years. He's still only 24 years old, but he's not headed in a good direction. In November, he left his winter league team after being roundly pelted in limited action. He definitely has better stuff than a lot of guys who have a major league career, but he hasn't put it together yet. Sometimes, it can take years, and sometimes, it never happens.

BEAU KEMP   Bats: R   Throws: R   Born: 31-Oct-80   Age: 23

YEAR	TM	LG	AGE	G	GS	IP	H	BB	SO	HR	ERA	EQERA	EQH9	EQBB9	EQSO9	EQHR9	PERA	VORP	STF
2001	QUD	MID	20	31	0	43.0	29	15	46	4	2.51	4.86	9.0	4.6	6.1	1.9	6.01	3.0	-11
2002	FTM	FLA	21	59	0	68.3	49	18	49	0	0.66	3.14	7.4	2.9	4.4	0.3	3.06	17.2	14
2003	FTM	FLA	22	22	0	26.3	30	7	16	3	3.76	7.54	13.9	3.2	4.0	3.6	10.12	-4.9	-82
2003	NBR	EAS	22	36	0	52.0	63	23	38	1	3.98	6.70	11.5	4.8	5.2	0.4	5.50	-5.9	-2
2004	MIN	AL	23	12	2	18.7	22	9	11	3	5.71	5.57	10.1	4.2	5.0	1.3	5.61	1.4	-17

Breakout: 22%   Improve: 50%   Collapse: 23%

Not the best possible followup. Kemp was lights-out in 2002, but followed up with a 3.98 ERA in New Britain, along with a pretty pedestrian set of peripheral numbers. He's a relief prospect, but probably not one that's going to be noteworthy enough to follow real closely.

KYLE LOHSE

Bats: R   **Throws: R**   Born: 04-Oct-78   Age: 25

YEAR	TM	LG	AGE	G	GS	IP	H	BB	SO	HR	ERA	EQERA	EQH9	EQBB9	EQSO9	EQHR9	PERA	VORP	STF
2001	NBR	EAS	22	6	6	38.0	32	4	32	5	2.37	3.93	9.4	1.3	5.2	1.8	5.16	6.4	4
2001	EDM	PCL	22	8	8	49.0	50	13	48	3	3.12	3.91	8.0	2.6	6.7	0.6	3.47	9.1	40
2001	MIN	AL	22	19	16	90.3	102	29	64	16	5.68	5.44	10.0	2.7	6.0	1.4	5.33	1.6	14
2002	MIN	AL	23	32	31	180.7	181	70	124	26	4.23	4.56	8.9	3.2	5.9	1.2	4.72	20.3	17
2003	MIN	AL	24	33	33	201.0	211	45	130	28	4.61	4.37	9.1	1.9	5.7	1.1	4.33	26.2	17
2004	*MIN*	*AL*	*25*	*29*	*27*	*173.0*	*183*	*46*	*110*	*25*	*4.46*	*4.35*	*9.1*	*2.3*	*5.7*	*1.1*	*4.32*	*27.9*	*10*

Breakout: 16%   *Improve: 52%*   *Collapse: 10%*

Probably the streakiest of the rotation's four dwarves. Lohse's got more headroom than the rest of the bunch. His K rate is at least in an area where you might expect some improvement, he's young, and he does have a tendency to show up and look very good in stretches. Too often, of course, those stretches are against weak sister opponents. If the Twins can get 200 innings of league average ball out of Lohse, they'll be happy.

JOE MAYS

Bats: B   **Throws: R**   Born: 10-Dec-75   Age: 28

YEAR	TM	LG	AGE	G	GS	IP	H	BB	SO	HR	ERA	EQERA	EQH9	EQBB9	EQSO9	EQHR9	PERA	VORP	STF
2001	MIN	AL	25	34	34	233.7	205	64	123	25	3.16	3.32	7.7	2.3	4.5	0.9	3.62	57.1	13
2002	MIN	AL	26	17	17	95.3	113	25	38	14	5.38	5.38	10.6	2.2	3.4	1.2	5.23	2.2	-13
2003	MIN	AL	27	31	21	130.0	159	39	50	21	6.30	5.76	10.5	2.6	3.4	1.3	5.45	-5.6	-23
2004	*MIN*	*AL*	*28*	*27*	*18*	*102.3*	*122*	*33*	*44*	*16*	*5.29*	*5.16*	*10.4*	*2.7*	*3.8*	*1.2*	*5.17*	*7.2*	*-12*

Breakout: 14%   *Improve: 45%*   *Collapse: 24%*

"Buy low, sell high" may sound painfully obvious for handling baseball talent, but when it comes to the contracts in the starting rotation, it's a maxim the Twins would do well to tattoo on their foreheads. The rotation's jam-packed with economic derelictions of duty, but of all the contracts stinking up the HumptyDome, Mays's might be the most egregious: The Twins tossed him a four-year deal worth $20 million after the 2001 season. (If you check out the stat lines above, it's the one that sticks out like a sore thumb, both for quality and number of innings pitched.) Since having a fluke season in which he pitched a career-high 233 innings, Mays has been predictably ineffective and injured in approximately equal dollops. The Twins' inability to identify fluke or career years, and their propensity to time contract negotiations badly, borders on the preternatural.

ERIC MILTON

Bats: L   **Throws: L**   Born: 04-Aug-75   Age: 28

YEAR	TM	LG	AGE	G	GS	IP	H	BB	SO	HR	ERA	EQERA	EQH9	EQBB9	EQSO9	EQHR9	PERA	VORP	STF
2001	MIN	AL	25	35	34	220.7	222	61	157	35	4.32	4.30	8.9	2.3	6.0	1.3	4.55	30.9	9
2002	MIN	AL	26	29	29	171.0	173	30	121	24	4.84	4.46	9.0	1.5	6.2	1.1	4.19	20.9	13
2003	MIN	AL	27	3	3	17.0	15	1	7	2	2.65	2.76	7.7	0.6	3.9	1.1	3.30	6.2	9
2004	*PHI*	*NL*	*28*	*37*	*20*	*126.7*	*129*	*30*	*81*	*19*	*4.25*	*4.47*	*9.1*	*1.9*	*5.2*	*1.3*	*4.40*	*17.5*	*0*

Breakout: 22%   *Improve: 63%*   *Collapse: 15%*

Milton came back from knee surgery late in the season, and pitched well against weak competition. Milton never really performed as well as many scouts and analysts had hoped. His peripheral numbers have been either flat or declining for a while, and at this point, the best chance for him becoming a front-of-the-rotation guy is that his arm got reinvigorated during a season off. More likely, he'll be a league average starter or so for $9 million. The Twins got a bunch of flotsam in Carlos Silva, Nick Punto, and a PTBNL for Milton, but deleting his salary while also opening a rotation spot for a comer like Grant Balfour should pay off nicely.

MIKE NAKAMURA

Bats: R   **Throws: R**   Born: 06-Sep-76   Age: 27

YEAR	TM	LG	AGE	G	GS	IP	H	BB	SO	HR	ERA	EQERA	EQH9	EQBB9	EQSO9	EQHR9	PERA	VORP	STF
2001	NBR	EAS	24	48	1	86.3	75	24	109	3	1.77	3.62	10.2	3.4	7.8	0.5	4.55	16.9	19
2002	EDM	PCL	25	46	4	87.3	85	22	80	7	4.74	4.66	8.9	2.5	6.2	0.9	4.16	8.7	0
2003	ROC	INT	26	43	0	78.3	71	28	95	4	2.99	3.72	9.0	4.0	8.7	0.7	4.47	15.2	12
2003	MIN	AL	26	12	0	12.7	20	2	14	4	7.80	7.30	13.9	1.5	9.5	2.2	7.65	-2.6	-20
2004	*MIN*	*AL*	*27*	*20*	*4*	*36.0*	*36*	*13*	*31*	*4*	*4.07*	*3.97*	*8.6*	*3.1*	*7.6*	*0.9*	*4.15*	*7.9*	*8*

Breakout: 28%   *Improve: 56%*   *Collapse: 19%*

Better than he showed during his brief stint with the Twins. Nakamura changes speeds fairly well, but he's going to have to scramble for a shot after getting pasted and losing his roster spot to fellow Aussie Balfour. He hasn't been asked to start for several years, and is unlikely ever to return to that role. Most likely he'll land at Triple-A and hope for an opportunity at a promotion, along with 10 to 12 score other guys in the same boat.

JESSE OROSCO   Bats: R   Throws: L   Born: 21-Apr-57   Age: 47

YEAR	TM	LG	AGE	G	GS	IP	H	BB	SO	HR	ERA	EQERA	EQH9	EQBB9	EQSO9	EQHR9	PERA	VORP	STF
2001	LAD	NL	44	35	0	16.0	17	7	21	3	3.94	4.70	10.0	3.5	10.0	1.8	5.85	1.5	-4
2002	LAD	NL	45	56	0	27.0	24	12	22	4	3.00	4.56	8.8	3.5	6.3	1.4	4.96	3.0	-17
2003	SDP	NL	46	42	0	25.0	33	10	22	4	7.56	7.40	12.2	3.3	7.0	1.5	6.58	-8.3	-26
2003	NYY	AL	46	15	0	4.3	4	6	4	0	10.47	8.31	8.3	12.5	8.3	0.0	5.60	-3.3	-14
2003	MIN	AL	46	8	0	4.3	4	5	3	0	6.28	6.23	8.3	10.4	6.2	0.0	5.15	0.1	-13
2004	ARI	NL	47	48	0	51.3	54	22	34	7	5.16	4.93	9.2	3.4	5.5	1.1	4.83	2.6	-10

Breakout: 55%   Improve: 55%   Collapse: 0%

All hail He Who Cheats Mictlantecuhtli! When Jesse Orosco played his first MLB game, Jimmy Carter was President of the United States. Nolan Ryan was 15 years away from retirement. Josh Beckett hadn't yet been conceived. The top-rated show on American TV was, inexplicably, *Laverne and Shirley*. Fittingly, Gloria Gaynor's "I Will Survive" was the #1 single in the U.S. Not surprisingly, Orosco has signed a minor league deal with the Diamondbacks, where GM Joe Garagiola Jr. apparently has delusions of being Saint Peter.

CARLOS PULIDO   Bats: L   Throws: L   Born: 05-Aug-71   Age: 32

YEAR	TM	LG	AGE	G	GS	IP	H	BB	SO	HR	ERA	EQERA	EQH9	EQBB9	EQSO9	EQHR9	PERA	VORP	STF
2003	ROC	INT	31	25	25	149.3	145	40	87	13	3.56	4.25	9.0	3.0	4.1	1.2	4.75	21.0	-12
2003	MIN	AL	31	7	1	15.7	15	3	6	0	4.01	3.60	8.4	1.8	3.6	0.0	2.94	1.4	15
2004	MIN	AL	32	19	10	59.7	72	21	28	10	5.60	5.46	10.4	3.0	4.2	1.4	5.50	3.7	-14

Breakout: 23%   Improve: 52%   Collapse: 29%

Pulido, healthy and back from Japan, got an opportunity for some mop-up time with the big club, and really didn't pitch too badly. He's not a good bet to have anything resembling consistent success, but he's probably earned a few looks as a potential reflexive lefty from the occasional desperate club. He may get a shot at the #5 starter's job in spring training.

BRAD RADKE   Bats: R   Throws: R   Born: 27-Oct-72   Age: 31

YEAR	TM	LG	AGE	G	GS	IP	H	BB	SO	HR	ERA	EQERA	EQH9	EQBB9	EQSO9	EQHR9	PERA	VORP	STF
2001	MIN	AL	28	33	33	226.0	235	26	137	24	3.94	3.85	9.2	1.0	5.1	0.9	3.89	42.3	17
2002	MIN	AL	29	21	21	118.3	124	20	62	12	4.72	4.34	9.3	1.4	4.6	0.9	4.07	16.0	9
2003	MIN	AL	30	33	33	212.3	242	28	120	32	4.49	4.49	9.9	1.1	5.0	1.2	4.62	29.7	4
2004	MIN	AL	31	28	26	167.3	189	28	89	25	4.50	4.39	9.8	1.4	4.7	1.2	4.36	27.7	6

Breakout: 17%   Improve: 54%   Collapse: 21%

Radke will receive a total of $11.5 million for the 2004 season: $10 million in salary, $1.5 million in deferred bonuses. He's not likely to be worth even a third of that money. He's an innings-eater at this point, lacking the stuff to keep good hitters off balance or particularly afraid. His unadjusted ERA of 4.49 is, on the surface, league average. But when considering strength of opponent, particularly the nine starts he made against Cleveland, Detroit, and Baltimore, it's not only nothing special—it's not really of any significant value. His peripheral numbers don't do anything to portend future success, either. Radke's pushing the limits of the "consistency is inherently valuable" concept, much like the CBS Television Network.

RICK REED   Bats: R   Throws: R   Born: 16-Aug-65   Age: 38

YEAR	TM	LG	AGE	G	GS	IP	H	BB	SO	HR	ERA	EQERA	EQH9	EQBB9	EQSO9	EQHR9	PERA	VORP	STF
2001	NYM	NL	35	20	20	134.7	119	17	99	16	3.47	3.51	8.1	1.1	5.7	1.0	3.47	29.8	19
2001	MIN	AL	35	12	12	67.7	92	14	43	12	5.18	5.89	12.1	1.8	5.3	1.4	6.02	-2.1	-8
2002	MIN	AL	36	33	32	188.0	192	26	121	32	3.78	4.21	9.1	1.1	5.6	1.4	4.41	28.1	5
2003	MIN	AL	37	27	21	135.0	155	29	71	21	5.07	4.93	9.9	1.9	4.7	1.2	4.89	9.6	-5
2004	MIN	AL	38	24	19	117.7	133	26	62	18	4.71	4.59	9.8	1.9	4.7	1.2	4.56	16.8	1

Breakout: 20%   Improve: 39%   Collapse: 16%

(continued next page)

Rick Reed (*continued*)

Right about now, Terry Ryan's gotta look and feel like someone coming up for a desperation breath in a deep-sea thriller. Reed's hideous, idiotic contract has finally come to a merciful end, after chewing up a cool $8 million in 2003. Hard to believe the Twins didn't want to pick up that $8 million option for 2004, yes? His option would have kicked in at 197.1 innings, a mark he was never in danger of reaching due to a disk problem in his lower back. Reed's a bad pitcher: He's got no stuff to speak of, and his one skill, the ability to place the ball in the strike zone, is pretty much offset by the fact that major league hitters start salivating like a Pavlovian terrier at a Mike Oldfield concert at the prospect of facing his stuff.

JUAN RINCON   Bats: R   Throws: R   Born: 23-Jan-79   Age: 25

YEAR	TM	LG	AGE	G	GS	IP	H	BB	SO	HR	ERA	EQERA	EQH9	EQBB9	EQSO9	EQHR9	PERA	VORP	STF
2001	NBR	EAS	22	29	23	153.3	130	57	133	9	2.88	4.83	9.1	4.5	5.4	0.8	4.80	11.8	11
2002	EDM	PCL	23	19	16	101.7	111	35	75	12	4.78	5.13	9.2	3.4	5.1	1.2	4.95	5.1	2
2002	MIN	AL	23	10	3	28.7	44	9	21	5	6.27	7.07	13.8	2.6	6.4	1.3	6.91	-4.6	0
2003	MIN	AL	24	58	0	85.7	74	38	63	5	3.68	3.66	7.5	3.8	6.5	0.4	3.47	18.7	21
2004	MIN	AL	25	35	13	86.0	91	38	58	10	4.79	4.68	9.1	3.8	6.0	1.0	4.74	11.0	-3

Breakout: 23%   Improve: 55%   Collapse: 19%

The Twins have been able to lean very heavily on the bullpen, and it's a strategy that's worked well for them. If a club's going to do that, they need to have a solid, reliable closer, a nasty setup guy or two, at least one rubber-armed guy that can actually pitch, and perhaps a lefty specialist that can pitch five times a week. Rincon's durable and reliable, and he's got good enough stuff to be an important member of the pen for some time. He's not likely to get a shot at the closer role, but he may end up throwing 90 fairly important innings.

KENNY ROGERS   Bats: L   Throws: L   Born: 10-Nov-64   Age: 39

YEAR	TM	LG	AGE	G	GS	IP	H	BB	SO	HR	ERA	EQERA	EQH9	EQBB9	EQSO9	EQHR9	PERA	VORP	STF
2001	TEX	AL	36	20	20	120.7	150	49	74	18	6.19	5.53	10.1	3.3	5.0	1.1	5.24	0.9	-5
2002	TEX	AL	37	33	33	210.7	212	70	107	21	3.84	3.88	8.5	2.7	4.4	0.8	4.00	39.4	8
2003	MIN	AL	38	33	31	195.0	227	50	116	22	4.57	4.74	10.1	2.2	5.3	0.9	4.68	21.3	8
2004	TEX	AL	39	30	25	149.7	182	48	82	22	5.32	4.81	10.2	2.7	5.0	1.1	4.88	16.3	0

Breakout: 18%   Improve: 48%   Collapse: 29%

Well, he was brought in as a guy to fill the rotation, and he did that, albeit probably not quite as well as the Minnesota brain trust had hoped. A championship team can have one guy like this in the rotation, maybe two if they're number four and five. Having four of them means a lot of dependence on either a tremendous bullpen or a nasty offense. But hey, Terry Ryan and crew picked up 31 generic starts for $2 million, and that's not bad. It's not enough to counter the confluence of big money and weak performance in the rest of the rotation, but it's not bad. By way of contrast, now that he's with the Rangers, he's their ace, which is not good.

J. C. ROMERO   Bats: B   Throws: L   Born: 04-Jun-76   Age: 28

YEAR	TM	LG	AGE	G	GS	IP	H	BB	SO	HR	ERA	EQERA	EQH9	EQBB9	EQSO9	EQHR9	PERA	VORP	STF
2001	EDM	PCL	25	12	10	63.7	67	24	55	4	3.67	4.72	9.0	4.0	5.5	0.6	4.36	6.0	6
2001	MIN	AL	25	14	11	65.0	71	24	39	10	6.23	5.57	9.7	3.1	5.0	1.3	5.20	0.2	-9
2002	MIN	AL	26	81	0	81.0	62	36	76	3	1.89	2.40	7.0	3.7	8.1	0.3	3.09	28.0	30
2003	MIN	AL	27	73	0	63.0	66	42	50	7	5.00	5.08	9.1	5.7	7.0	0.9	5.15	4.8	-8
2004	MIN	AL	28	45	0	52.0	54	28	37	5	4.59	4.48	8.9	4.5	6.4	0.8	4.74	8.0	-6

Breakout: 25%   Improve: 42%   Collapse: 32%

You think you had a particularly rough year? Consider the year of J. C. Romero, then count your blessings. His ERA and HR rate both more than doubled from the previous year. In September, he sat on a knife, forcing him to get stitches in his butt. In August, Ben Broussard whacked him on the head with a foul ball in batting practice. He probably got audited. There's a good chance he had to sit through "The Cat in the Hat" in the Cineplex around Christmastime, and his pal Sam Waksal was convicted and headed for jail. Don't complain to Romero about your problems. He doesn't need to hear it. Is he likely to have another year that bad? On the field, 2002 looks like an anomaly; he had never reached those levels of performance before, and he's not likely to ever match them. But he does have some strength in his peripherals; he'll probably be at or near league average. As for the rest of it, you have to think he'll find a crisp $20 bill somewhere this year.

JOHAN SANTANA

Bats: L **Throws: L** Born: 13-Mar-79 Age: 25

YEAR	TM	LG	AGE	G	GS	IP	H	BB	SO	HR	ERA	EQERA	EQH9	EQBB9	EQSO9	EQHR9	PERA	VORP	STF
2002	EDM	PCL	23	11	9	48.7	37	27	75	7	3.14	4.53	7.5	5.7	11.0	1.6	5.08	5.4	27
2001	MIN	AL	22	15	4	43.7	50	16	28	6	4.74	5.10	10.2	3.0	5.3	1.1	5.13	2.4	10
2002	MIN	AL	23	27	14	108.3	84	49	137	7	2.99	3.23	7.0	3.7	10.9	0.5	3.26	27.9	65
2003	MIN	AL	24	45	18	158.3	127	47	169	17	3.07	3.08	7.0	2.5	9.4	0.9	3.23	48.7	45
2004	*MIN*	*AL*	*25*	*33*	*20*	*125.3*	*109*	*40*	*125*	*16*	*3.75*	*3.66*	*7.5*	*2.7*	*8.8*	*1.0*	*3.53*	*30.5*	*24*

Breakout: 30%   *Improve: 44%*   *Collapse: 19%*

Santana wasn't moved to the rotation full-time until July. When given the opportunity, he was as dominant as any AL starter who didn't attend Ohio Dominican, posting a 2.89 ERA over 18 starts and 110 innings, allowing only 83 hits and 27 walks. One AL Exec likened Santana to a left-handed Pedro, and the comparison's apt. Santana works off of a plus fastball and has a devastating changeup. If he has a weakness, it's the occasional meaty change, but there's no reason to expect him to falter in '04. He'll be in the running for the Cy Young award—in part because he's an outstanding pitcher, in part because he's got a very good defense behind him, and in part because he'll get a bunch of starts against the Indians and Tigers. Probably a Top 15 starter in the AL—he'll pitch a lot more innings than PECOTA projects—but with a high level of potential variance.

MANNY TEJADA

Bats: R **Throws: R** Born: 16-Apr-82 Age: 22

YEAR	TM	LG	AGE	G	GS	IP	H	BB	SO	HR	ERA	EQERA	EQH9	EQBB9	EQSO9	EQHR9	PERA	VORP	STF
2001	ELZ	APP	19	11	10	56.3	43	20	87	6	3.20	6.75	12.7	5.6	6.8	3.0	9.21	-5.8	-21
2002	QUD	MID	20	14	14	91.3	70	23	78	9	2.76	5.01	10.0	3.2	4.9	2.5	6.82	5.2	-12
2003	FTM	FLA	21	8	6	24.0	9	20	20	1	1.88	3.86	4.7	9.9	5.1	1.3	4.79	4.1	-13
2004	*MIN*	*AL*	*22*	*15*	*10*	*53.0*	*56*	*43*	*39*	*10*	*6.74*	*6.58*	*9.1*	*6.9*	*6.5*	*1.6*	*6.60*	*-1.4*	*-14*

Breakout: 29%   *Improve: 56%*   *Collapse: 9%*

Tejada's got good velocity, in the same tradition of Brad Pennington, Steve Dalkowski, and, more recently, Rick Ankiel. Batters don't come close to digging in against him, as they really should be ready to bail out at a moment's notice. Tejada doesn't so much hit spots as present an interesting intellectual exercise in the nature of random vectors. He's got several years to figure out how to throw strikes, but the numbers don't lie—most guys like this never get close to being useful major league pitchers.

BRAD THOMAS

Bats: L **Throws: L** Born: 12-Oct-77 Age: 26

YEAR	TM	LG	AGE	G	GS	IP	H	BB	SO	HR	ERA	EQERA	EQH9	EQBB9	EQSO9	EQHR9	PERA	VORP	STF
2001	NBR	EAS	23	19	19	119.3	91	26	97	4	1.96	3.73	8.1	2.7	5.1	0.5	3.50	22.6	24
2002	EDM	PCL	24	28	27	152.0	175	54	97	20	5.74	6.27	10.2	3.5	4.3	1.5	5.78	-10.8	-21
2003	ROC	INT	25	15	11	58.7	68	10	50	3	3.53	4.20	10.7	1.8	6.0	0.6	4.55	8.7	12
2003	MIN	AL	25	3	0	4.7	6	3	2	1	7.66	7.71	11.6	5.8	3.9	1.9	7.54	-0.9	-59
2004	*MIN*	*AL*	*26*	*16*	*9*	*55.3*	*61*	*19*	*34*	*7*	*4.78*	*4.66*	*9.6*	*2.9*	*5.5*	*1.0*	*4.66*	*7.2*	*-1*

Breakout: 26%   *Improve: 47%*   *Collapse: 23%*

If Thomas were right-handed, he would have shuffled through eight organizations by now, and likely ended up a Tiger. Everything about his performance record is all over the map. He hasn't really had a shot at the majors on a sustained basis, but he also hasn't earned it. The Twins need to stick him at Triple-A and either give him 50 relief appearances or 25 starts, and find out whether or not he's part of their future.

New York Yankees

The law of unintended consequences, often cited but rarely defined, is that actions of people—and especially of government—always have effects that are unanticipated or "unintended."

ROB NORTON, http://www.econlib.org

During the negotiations that led to a new Collective Bargaining Agreement in 2002, management's refrain was that a broken system needed to be fixed. Led by Commissioner Bud Selig, the owners wanted to establish rules that would redistribute money from high-revenue teams to low-revenue ones, while also constraining teams from spending money on players. These rules were deemed necessary to protect competitive balance, which was perceived to be a problem under the last CBA.

As was well-covered at baseballprospectus.com in 2002, the primary motivation of the owners wasn't promoting competitive balance, but lowering labor costs. As you can see in table 1, the top payrolls in the game were on the rise in the period leading up to the new CBA. In this period, the Yankees' payroll tracked reasonably well with the payrolls of their closest competitors. Except in 2002, the gap between the Yankees' payroll and that of the next team was insignificant, and the gap between the Yankees' payroll and the average of the top-five teams other than the Yankees was small.

Thanks to considerable press and public pressure, the owners won the 2002 round of negotiations. The current CBA includes provisions for significantly increased sharing of local revenue and an investment tax that penalizes teams that incur labor costs above a certain level. The rules have had exactly the effects predicted by analysts such as Doug Pappas: They have lowered the value and the cost of labor—a player's marginal revenue product is lessened as teams keep only 66% of the marginal revenue he creates—and provided a significant disincentive for teams to spend past the penalty point.

Twenty-nine teams, anyway. Those 29 teams are playing by a set of rules, while one team just doesn't care. Whereas the Yankees' payroll advantage used to be small, it's grown exponentially in just two years, and shows no signs of diminishing.

On Opening Day, 2003, the Yankees had a payroll of $149.7 million. The next closest payroll was that of the Mets at $116.9 million, a figure they spent a good chunk of

YANKEES PROSPECTUS

2003 record: 101–61; First place, AL East; Lost to Marlins in World Series

Pythagenport record: 96–66

Runs scored per game: 5.4 (3rd in AL)

Runs allowed per game: 4.4 (3rd in AL)

Team EqA: .280 (2nd in AL)

2003 Batters Age: 29.7 (6th oldest in AL)

2003 Pitchers Age: 31.9 (2nd oldest in AL)

Ballpark: Yankee Stadium; Slight pitcher's park; Park Factor of 0.976

2003: The veteran squad didn't miss a beat until falling to the Marlins in the World Series.

2004: A productive off-season helps patch over age-related holes on the roster for at least one more year.

their summer lowering in an effort to avoid the investment tax. The average payroll of the top five non-Yankee teams barely edged up, to $103.8 million.

The situation that had not existed prior to 2003—one team spending its competition into oblivion—was created by the new CBA. The Yankees, rather than being constrained by massive revenue-sharing payments and the threat of an eight-figure tax hit, acted as if those measures didn't exist. With all of their competitors trying to avoid the tax, the gap between the Yankees' payroll and everyone else's grew at a staggering rate.

Well, it was just one season, and a number of teams were trying hard to avoid setting up multiple-offender penalties that apply to teams going over the tax threshold more than once before 2006. Given that the Yankees paid just over $60 million in success tax last year ($48.8 million into the revenue-sharing pool, $11.8 million in investment tax) there's no way they could continue outspending their nearest opponents by $30 million or more.

TABLE 1. YANKEES' OPENING-DAY PAYROLL RELATIVE TO OTHERS (IN MILLIONS)

Year	Yankees	Top Non-Yankees Payroll	Avg of Top 5 Non-Yankees Payrolls
1998	$63.5	$69.0 (Orioles)	$59.2
1999	$85.0	$79.3 (Dodgers)	$74.9
2000	$92.5	$88.1 (Dodgers)	$82.6
2001	$109.8	$109.6 (Red Sox)	$99.1
2002	$125.9	$108.4 (Red Sox)	$101.2

Could they?

We got our answer in December. In short succession, the Yankees traded for two starting pitchers, Kevin Brown and Javier Vazquez, who will combine to make $23.5 million in 2004. They signed two free-agent outfielders, Gary Sheffield and Kenny Lofton, for $16 million in '04. For good measure, they added two relievers, Paul Quantrill and Tom Gordon, for $7 million in '04. In addition to pushing the Yankees' 2004 payroll into the stratosphere, the signings also ballooned what was already the game's most significant commitment for the years 2005 through 2007, and made one thing very clear: The Yankees aren't playing by everyone else's rules.

The Yankees' projected 2004 Opening Day payroll is $164 million for 23 players, and that's before arbitration awards for Alfonso Soriano and Gabe White, or settlements in advance of a hearing, bump that figure up another $4 million to $6 million. The #2 projected team, the Red Sox, is likely to be somewhere in the $115 million–$120 million range, just under the $120.5 million tax threshold. No other team is projected to approach the threshold. It is possible that the Yankees' Opening Day payroll will be $50 million higher than the #2 team, and $65 million higher than the average of the next five teams.

That wasn't the case in 1992, or in 2002, but it is the case now, and it can be directly traced to a Collective Bargaining Agreement that was drawn up to address a problem that didn't exist. The 2002 CBA created rules that all but invited the Law of Unintended Consequences to dinner. Barring a sea change in George Steinbrenner's approach or in the way other owners treat the luxury-tax threshold, this situation will probably hold for 2005. We may see the gap close after that; in 2006, there is no tax for teams crossing the threshold for the first time, and in 2007, there is no tax.

Regardless, the Yankees can expect to set the payroll pace for some time to come. They already have $120 million in guaranteed money committed for 2005, $90 million for 2006, and at least some salary commitments out to 2010, when Derek Jeter's contract expires.

The new rules have created chaos at the top of the payroll scale, while not doing anything to encourage investment by teams at the bottom of it. At least two teams, the Brewers and the Devil Rays, are projected to have payrolls that come to less than the total amount of money they'll receive just from the central fund—revenue-sharing money plus national-TV money.

The only tangible effect of the new rules on the game on the field is to create exactly the kind of imbalance the rules were theoretically supposed to stop. In two years, we will no doubt be hearing how new, more stringent rules are needed to address the Yankees' dominance in the payroll standings, with no acknowledgment that the problem was created by the very rules that the owners worked so hard to get.

There's already precedent for this. The Collective Bargaining Agreement that was reached in 1996 included revenue-redistribution agreements that tied disbursements to payroll. The less you spent on players, the more money you made from the pool. The Twins and Expos, owned by Carl Pohlad and a consortium headed by Claude Brochu, quickly surmised that it made more sense to cut payroll to the bone than to spend money on players. The first plan produced about the same amount of money with much less risk.

When contraction entered the national lexicon in November, 2001, it was the Twins and Expos who were targeted for extinction, because both franchises had fallen into disarray. But there was no mention of why that had happened—that the previous agreement's fatal flaw had caused each team's owner to pursue revenue-sharing money instead of wins.

The owners have already tried capitalizing on a poorly-crafted rule's unintended consequences—coupled with the crude, misinformed way in which the finances of baseball are understood and reported by the media—to bring about the kind of change that benefits them and hurts the game. There is no doubt that, come 2007, they will make a similarly flawed argument to demand further concessions from the MLBPA.

The true lesson, however, is that any set of rules is only as good as the people they are applied to. In the case of the previous CBA, the fatal flaw of the agreement was exploited by two men who didn't have the key ingredient that makes a great sports owner: a desire to win. In the current case, the Yankees are owned by a man who has both that desire, and the willingness to plow the money the team generates back into the team, bucking the trend of his compatriots.

Baseball doesn't need industry-wide agreements to control labor costs. It needs owners like Steinbrenner, like Arte Moreno, like Peter Angelos, who want to win more than they want to be liked by their fellow owners, or win labor battles, or make a short-term profit.

TABLE 2. EQUIVALENT STRIKEOUT RATES

New Pitcher	PECOTA Projected EqK/9	Old Pitcher	2003 EqK/9
Jose Contreras	8.2	Roger Clemens	8.1
Javier Vazquez	7.9	Andy Pettitte	7.8
Kevin Brown	6.3	Jeff Weaver	5.3
Jon Lieber	4.6	David Wells	4.3

TABLE 3. PROJECTED EQUIVALENT RUNS, 2004 YANKEES

Player	EqR
Kenny Lofton	65
Derek Jeter	83
Gary Sheffield	102
Jason Giambi	111
Jorge Posada	73
Bernie Williams	73
Hideki Matsui	82
Alfonso Soriano	109
Aaron Boone	70
John Flaherty	17
Tony Clark	21
Ruben Sierra	27
Enrique Wilson	14
Miguel Cairo	29
Total	877

Steinbrenner has a bigger problem than the industry, however. It's not clear whether all the money he's spending will make a difference on the field. For while they've gotten more expensive, the Yankees have also gotten older, and they have done absolutely nothing to address their key flaw: a defense that doesn't make plays. In fact, by trading away their one superior defender in Nick Johnson, the Yankees have made themselves worse in that area in '04.

Indirectly, the Yankees have addressed their dreadful defense by adding pitchers who get strikeouts. Kevin Brown, Javier Vazquez, and Tom Gordon all have above-average strikeout rates. Jose Contreras struck out 9.1 men per nine innings last season and will claim a full-time role in the rotation in '04. Table 2 shows that the Yankee rotation in 2004 should strike out more batters than it did in 2003.

A rotation that keeps the ball out of play will help, but the Yankees don't need to have a world-beating pitching staff. They're going to be among the league leaders in runs scored, led once again by three of the biggest competitive advantages in the game: Derek Jeter, Alfonso Soriano, and Jorge Posada. There's no other team in baseball that has hitters of that caliber playing every day at those spots. The key to the Yankee dynasty, from 1996 through today, has been their day-in, day-out offensive edge up the middle.

Adding Sheffield to play right field will make a huge difference, more than enough to offset replacing Nick Johnson with Kenny Lofton. While you can expect some backsliding from Posada, and the bench is weak, this is an elite offense. Table 3 shows the projected contributions of the team's top 13 players. It leaves a fair number of plate appearances by injury replacements, September call-ups, and 14th hitters unaccounted for that should get the team to 900 runs, but you can see the core's strength.

It's been more than three years since the Yankees last won the World Series, a drought that isn't going to generate much sympathy in Boston or Chicago, but which seems like forever coming on the heels of four titles in five years. If this winter's massive investments in talent don't yield the 27th championship in franchise history—and you can argue that all the moves don't even make the Yankees the best team in the AL East—who knows what Steinbrenner might do next winter?

HITTERS

ERICK ALMONTE   SS   Bats: R   Throws: R   Born: 01-Feb-78   Age: 26

YEAR	TM	LG	AGE	AB	H	2B	3B	HR	BB	SO	SB	CS	AVG	OBP	SLG	MLVR	EQBA	EQOBP	EQSLG	EQMLVR	VORP	DEFENSE
2001	COH	INT	23	345	99	19	3	12	44	90	4	5	.287	.369	.464	.172	.263	.342	.436	-.008	21.1	94-SS -9
2002	NRW	EAS	24	187	45	7	0	8	30	59	10	2	.241	.342	.406	.029	.207	.295	.358	-.243	-2.5	50-SS 4
2002	COH	INT	24	221	52	10	1	9	15	60	2	1	.235	.282	.412	-.084	.221	.270	.396	-.229	-1.8	60-SS -12
2003	NYY	AL	25	100	26	6	0	1	8	24	1	0	.260	.321	.350	-.118	.287	.344	.386	-.055	1.8	31-SS -12
2003	COH	INT	25	179	43	11	1	4	17	46	4	3	.240	.310	.380	-.067	.221	.290	.365	-.234	-1.7	46-SS 3
2004	NYY	AL	26	249	59	13	1	7	24	60	4	2	.237	.306	.381	-.132	.242	.314	.396	-.125	6.0	68-SS -5

Breakout: 35%   Improve: 55%   Collapse: 31%

Given six weeks to establish himself as credible trade bait, Almonte showed himself to be inadequate as a starting shortstop, which didn't help the Yankees when they were looking for help in late July. He should spend the 2004 season in the Bronx as a backup middle infielder, a position with a very high salary-to-work ratio, and one in which his lack of major league skills won't affect the team much, but he'll be boxed out by Miguel Cairo.

AARON BOONE 3B Bats: R Throws: R Born: 09-Mar-73 Age: 31

YEAR	TM	LG	AGE	AB	H	2B	3B	HR	BB	SO	SB	CS	AVG	OBP	SLG	MLVR	EQBA	EQOBP	EQSLG	EQMLVR	VORP	DEFENSE			
2001	CIN	NL	28	381	112	26	2	14	29	71	6	3	.294	.351	.483	.102	.294	.351	.481	.099	29.0	102-3B	-6		
2002	CIN	NL	29	606	146	38	2	26	56	111	32	8	.241	.314	.439	-.009	.242	.311	.444	-.070	17.6	144-3B	15	13-SS	-2
2003	CIN	NL	30	403	110	19	3	18	35	74	15	3	.273	.339	.469	.083	.277	.339	.478	.058	24.4	82-3B	3	19-2B	5
2003	NYY	AL	30	189	48	13	0	6	11	30	8	0	.254	.302	.418	-.048	.274	.325	.453	-.005	6.2	53-3B	5		
2004	*NYY*	*AL*	*31*	*480*	*128*	*28*	*2*	*16*	*36*	*82*	*16*	*4*	*.268*	*.324*	*.437*	*-.008*	*.272*	*.333*	*.453*	*.007*	*26.1*	*125-3B*	*5*		

Breakout: 18%   Improve: 50%   Collapse: 19%

By the end of October, it was hard for Yankee fans to be rational about Boone. In the vast majority of his postseason at-bats, he showed little more than a weakness for fastballs above his head and sliders off the plate. Not only was he unproductive—.170/.196/.302 in October—he looked awful in the attempt. But he had this one swing, against a hanging knuckleball late on a Thursday night in New York . . . maybe it didn't erase all of the bad, but it sure made booing him feel a bit strange.

Boone is the kind of player—average, maybe a little above—who has been finding himself on the free-agent market the past two seasons. The Yankees' void at third base and vast reserves of cash caused them to offer him arbitration and bring him back at $6 million. He won't hurt them. Boone is the best defensive middle infielder on the Yankees' 40-man roster.

ROBINSON CANO 2B Bats: L Throws: R Born: 22-Oct-82 Age: 21

YEAR	TM	LG	AGE	AB	H	2B	3B	HR	BB	SO	SB	CS	AVG	OBP	SLG	MLVR	EQBA	EQOBP	EQSLG	EQMLVR	VORP	DEFENSE			
2002	GRB	SAL	19	474	131	20	9	14	29	78	2	1	.276	.321	.445	.116	.218	.251	.363	-.314	-15.9	57-SS	-7	54-2B	-9
2002	STA	NYP	19	87	24	5	1	1	4	8	6	1	.276	.308	.391	.059	.213	.239	.326	-.393	-10.6	19-2B	0		
2003	TAM	FLA	20	366	101	16	3	5	17	49	1	1	.276	.313	.377	.055	.245	.275	.355	-.261	-10.1	88-2B	-6		
2003	TRN	EAS	20	164	46	9	1	1	9	16	0	0	.280	.341	.366	-.021	.250	.294	.335	-.250	-3.7	43-2B	-5		
2004	*NYY*	*AL*	*21*	*296*	*68*	*14*	*2*	*5*	*13*	*46*	*1*	*1*	*.229*	*.268*	*.343*	*-.253*	*.234*	*.275*	*.356*	*-.254*	*-5.4*	*77-2B*	*-10*		

Breakout: 25%   Improve: 42%   Collapse: 29%

His age and the organizational affection for him mark Cano as a prospect, but there's not much here. Forget how BP likes plate discipline and how Cano doesn't walk. Having been moved off of shortstop in 2003, he's a second baseman who isn't fast and who hasn't hit for very high averages. His prospect status is almost entirely a scouting thing, where they like the way he looks at the plate and project that he'll fill out his six-foot frame with time. That might happen, but for now, Cano looks like he needs at least one full season in Double-A and lots of improvement. Trade bait.

DAVID DELLUCCI OF Bats: L Throws: L Born: 31-Oct-73 Age: 30

YEAR	TM	LG	AGE	AB	H	2B	3B	HR	BB	SO	SB	CS	AVG	OBP	SLG	MLVR	EQBA	EQOBP	EQSLG	EQMLVR	VORP	DEFENSE			
2001	ARI	NL	27	217	60	10	2	10	22	52	2	1	.276	.349	.479	.074	.274	.345	.475	.061	7.5	23-RF	-1	13-CF	0
2002	ARI	NL	28	229	56	11	2	7	28	55	2	4	.245	.326	.402	-.038	.242	.324	.403	-.103	-2.3	34-RF	-3	15-LF	-1
2003	ARI	NL	29	165	40	11	3	2	19	45	9	0	.242	.328	.382	-.102	.241	.324	.380	-.135	-0.5	38-RF	-3		
2003	NYY	AL	29	51	9	1	0	1	4	13	3	0	.176	.263	.255	-.404	.196	.275	.294	-.375	-4.0	14-RF	1		
2004	*TEX*	*AL*	*30*	*174*	*43*	*8*	*1*	*5*	*18*	*41*	*5*	*2*	*.250*	*.327*	*.407*	*-.055*	*.244*	*.324*	*.397*	*-.104*	*-0.3*	*50-RF*	*-1*		

Breakout: 43%   Improve: 58%   Collapse: 24%

Serviceable extra outfielder who just hasn't hit as much as was expected. The hand injury that cost him most of 2000 lowered expectations, but he hasn't even been able to sustain his good 2001 performance. The Rangers have picked him up; given how they're relying on very young outfielders at the start of the year, Dellucci could end up with 300 at-bats and a decent little year.

ERIC DUNCAN 3B Bats: L Throws: R Born: 07-Dec-84 Age: 19

YEAR	TM	LG	AGE	AB	H	2B	3B	HR	BB	SO	SB	CS	AVG	OBP	SLG	MLVR	EQBA	EQOBP	EQSLG	EQMLVR	VORP	DEFENSE
2003	STA	NYP	18	59	22	5	4	2	2	11	1	0	.373	.413	.695	.708	.295	.315	.557	.151	11.0	13-3B	-3

The Yankees' #1 pick in the 2003 draft, Duncan was voted the #1 prospect in the Gulf Coast League, and tore up the New York Penn circuit in three weeks there. He's going to have to hit, because while he played third last year, his glove isn't going to let him stay there much longer. Comparisons to Jim Thome are premature, especially given the walk rate at Staten Island. The Yankees have been pushing guys, so Duncan could open the year at Tampa.

JOHN FLAHERTY C Bats: R Throws: R Born: 21-Oct-67 Age: 36

YEAR	TM	LG	AGE	AB	H	2B	3B	HR	BB	SO	SB	CS	AVG	OBP	SLG	MLVR	EQBA	EQOBP	EQSLG	EQMLVR	VORP	DEFENSE	
2001	TBY	AL	33	248	59	17	1	4	10	33	1	0	.238	.269	.363	-.220	.254	.291	.387	-.178	-0.3	70-C	-6
2002	TBY	AL	34	281	73	20	0	4	15	50	2	2	.260	.296	.374	-.126	.279	.320	.403	-.082	6.5	75-C	0
2003	NYY	AL	35	105	28	8	0	4	4	19	0	0	.267	.297	.457	-.016	.286	.323	.486	.050	3.4	27-C	-1
2004	NYY	AL	36	153	38	8	0	4	8	24	0	0	.250	.288	.383	-.152	.254	.295	.398	-.146	2.9	43-C	-1

Breakout: 25%   Improve: 47%   Collapse: 33%

Flaherty is a fair receiver who doesn't hurt the team in his 20 day-game-after-night-game starts. If anything ever happened to Jorge Posada, though, the Yankees would be doomed. Brought back for $775,000, Flaherty will be the first player to hold the Yankees' backup-catcher job for consecutive seasons since Joe Girardi was allowed to leave.

KARIM GARCIA OF Bats: L Throws: L Born: 29-Oct-75 Age: 28

YEAR	TM	LG	AGE	AB	H	2B	3B	HR	BB	SO	SB	CS	AVG	OBP	SLG	MLVR	EQBA	EQOBP	EQSLG	EQMLVR	VORP	DEFENSE			
2001	BUF	INT	25	462	122	16	4	31	44	106	4	4	.264	.326	.517	.153	.243	.308	.484	-.019	6.5	97-RF	-4	12-LF	0
2001	CLE	AL	25	45	14	3	0	5	3	13	0	0	.311	.360	.711	.478	.333	.385	.756	.597	8.2				
2002	COH	INT	26	288	78	16	3	12	20	48	1	5	.271	.316	.472	.081	.248	.297	.445	-.089	5.0	27-CF	-1	17-LF	0
2002	BUF	INT	26	91	36	7	2	3	9	14	0	1	.396	.450	.615	.604	.359	.416	.576	.415	15.5	17-CF	-2		
2002	CLE	AL	26	197	59	8	0	16	6	40	0	3	.299	.317	.584	.236	.318	.341	.626	.323	19.3	41-RF	-1		
2003	CLE	AL	27	93	18	1	0	5	5	20	0	0	.194	.238	.366	-.308	.204	.258	.398	-.261	-5.7	15-RF	-4		
2003	BUF	INT	27	60	16	6	0	0	2	17	2	1	.267	.290	.367	-.100	.250	.286	.333	-.268	-3.6	11-RF	0		
2003	NYY	AL	27	151	46	5	0	6	9	32	0	2	.305	.342	.457	.099	.329	.370	.493	.185	4.8	30-RF	0	13-LF	1
2004	NYM	NL	28	270	67	14	1	10	22	62	2	2	.249	.305	.425	-.081	.252	.307	.445	-.065	2.2	72-RF	-2		

Breakout: 22%   Improve: 45%   Collapse: 31%

Garcia is a useful left-handed power bat who has spent the last few years pinballing between Cleveland and New York. His career slugging average is .432, which breaks down as .540 for the Tribe, and .390 for everyone else. Although he signed with the Mets as a free agent after being non-tendered, it would be fun to see him spend part of a fourth straight season by the lake. It wouldn't be surprising to see him have a few good years as a platoon player for a non-contender.

JASON GIAMBI 1B/DH Bats: L Throws: R Born: 08-Jan-71 Age: 33

YEAR	TM	LG	AGE	AB	H	2B	3B	HR	BB	SO	SB	CS	AVG	OBP	SLG	MLVR	EQBA	EQOBP	EQSLG	EQMLVR	VORP	DEFENSE	
2001	OAK	AL	30	520	178	47	2	38	129	83	2	0	.342	.477	.660	.609	.366	.501	.712	.725	123.6	127-1B	2
2002	NYY	AL	31	560	176	34	1	41	109	112	2	2	.314	.435	.598	.449	.342	.460	.654	.563	101.0	86-1B	3
2003	NYY	AL	32	535	134	25	0	41	129	140	2	1	.250	.412	.527	.256	.277	.434	.586	.360	54.2	83-1B	-6
2004	NYY	AL	33	472	133	26	0	34	96	108	2	0	.282	.414	.557	.297	.287	.425	.578	.327	59.6	137-1B	-3

Breakout: 13%   Improve: 38%   Collapse: 15%

Giambi's "off year," in which he was a top-five American Leaguer according to Equivalent Average (EqA) and Equivalent Runs (EqR), has been blamed on his left knee problem. The patellar tendinitis in the joint isn't going away, and you may remember what a similar injury did to Mark McGwire a few years ago. Post-season surgery didn't fix the problem so much as make it manageable. Look for Giambi to stay productive without approaching the heights of 2000–02, and be a full-time DH who can't run by the end of his contract.

RUDY GUILLEN OF Bats: R Throws: R Born: 23-Nov-83 Age: 20

YEAR	TM	LG	AGE	AB	H	2B	3B	HR	BB	SO	SB	CS	AVG	OBP	SLG	MLVR	EQBA	EQOBP	EQSLG	EQMLVR	VORP	DEFENSE			
2003	BCR	MID	19	493	128	29	4	13	32	87	13	6	.260	.311	.414	.070	.211	.251	.352	-.334	-28.8	95-CF	-14	31-RF	-3
2004	NYY	AL	20	294	61	13	2	6	15	61	5	2	.208	.250	.327	-.318	.212	.256	.340	-.322	-15.9	77-CF	-12		

Breakout: 26%   Improve: 46%   Collapse: 36%

A scout's favorite who might be worth getting excited about, Guillen has two things in his favor. One is that he hits the ball: 126 strikeouts in 712 at-bats isn't excessive, and he's drawn 46 walks in that time. For a kid from the Dominican at ages 18 and 19, that qualifies as patient. Second, he's a center fielder, which means that he won't have to be a .280 EqA hitter to contribute. He's 6′ 3″ and adding weight, so his power could come quickly over the next few years. In an organization as thin as this one, he looks like a strong prospect.

DREW HENSON 3B/QB Bats: R Throws: R Born: 13-Feb-80 Age: 24

YEAR	TM	LG	AGE	AB	H	2B	3B	HR	BB	SO	SB	CS	AVG	OBP	SLG	MLVR	EQBA	EQOBP	EQSLG	EQMLVR	VORP	DEFENSE
2001	COH	INT	21	270	60	6	0	11	10	85	2	1	.222	.249	.367	-.201	.214	.245	.362	-.330	-11.6	66-3B -10
2002	COH	INT	22	471	113	30	4	18	37	151	2	1	.240	.301	.435	-.018	.224	.286	.416	-.169	1.6	124-3B -32
2003	COH	INT	23	483	113	40	2	14	32	122	8	4	.234	.291	.412	-.061	.222	.282	.399	-.202	-3.0	132-3B -26
2004	NYY	AL	24	258	61	15	1	9	18	65	3	1	.235	.293	.409	-.119	.239	.301	.425	-.111	6.3	70-3B -13

Breakout: 35%   Improve: 60%   Collapse: 18%

Apologists can be found everywhere, but Henson has established that he's the International League's version of Jim Presley, only with less power. He very much wants to be a baseball player, and as long as the Yankees will keep him around, he'll pursue the dream. They're invested in him through '06, so he's going to keep getting chances. His current pace of incremental improvement could have him hitting .260/.315/.455 in the majors at his peak, with poor hot-corner defense. What's the point?

MICHEL HERNANDEZ C Bats: R Throws: R Born: 12-Aug-78 Age: 25

YEAR	TM	LG	AGE	AB	H	2B	3B	HR	BB	SO	SB	CS	AVG	OBP	SLG	MLVR	EQBA	EQOBP	EQSLG	EQMLVR	VORP	DEFENSE
2001	NRW	EAS	22	128	29	6	0	2	10	20	1	0	.227	.291	.320	-.156	.206	.263	.298	-.389	-8.2	38-C 1
2002	NRW	EAS	23	61	19	6	0	1	5	6	0	1	.311	.358	.459	.182	.274	.318	.403	-.089	1.6	14-C 0
2002	COH	INT	23	121	34	5	1	1	8	13	1	3	.281	.336	.364	-.025	.262	.315	.344	-.188	-0.5	31-C -8
2003	COH	INT	24	282	79	14	0	4	37	35	0	2	.280	.367	.372	.046	.261	.346	.352	-.117	4.9	82-C 0
2004	BOS	AL	25	183	48	9	1	4	17	24	1	1	.263	.333	.382	-.067	.258	.333	.384	-.096	6.4	52-C -2

Breakout: 33%   Improve: 52%   Collapse: 28%

About the only thing Flaherty has on Hernandez is service time, but that makes a big difference to people within the game when it comes to picking a backup catcher. Hernandez isn't a prospect any longer, but his defense is good enough to make him an asset as a major league backup, and he certainly wouldn't hit worse than the Flahertys of the world. The Red Sox claimed him off waivers.

DEREK JETER SS Bats: R Throws: R Born: 26-Jun-74 Age: 30

YEAR	TM	LG	AGE	AB	H	2B	3B	HR	BB	SO	SB	CS	AVG	OBP	SLG	MLVR	EQBA	EQOBP	EQSLG	EQMLVR	VORP	DEFENSE
2001	NYY	AL	27	614	191	35	3	21	56	99	27	3	.311	.377	.480	.199	.335	.400	.521	.281	77.8	143-SS -17
2002	NYY	AL	28	644	191	26	0	18	73	114	32	3	.297	.373	.421	.103	.321	.396	.459	.172	62.7	152-SS -19
2003	NYY	AL	29	482	156	25	3	10	43	88	11	5	.324	.393	.450	.203	.357	.423	.499	.311	47.4	112-SS -15
2004	NYY	AL	30	517	151	27	3	13	51	90	14	4	.292	.364	.433	.073	.297	.373	.450	.092	41.4	137-SS -10

Breakout: 7%   Improve: 29%   Collapse: 34%

The debate over Jeter's defense would seem to be the debate over defensive evaluation writ small, a battle between observation and statistics. It's not, though; in addition to having awful numbers, Jeter looks bad defensively. While he's athletic, which enables him to make two specific types of plays—a jump throw from the 5–6 hole, and any play on which he dives and reaches the ball—his lack of a first step or good footwork causes many, many balls to get past him, especially to his left. How so many people watching Jeter cannot see him for the poor gloveman he is would make a tremendous research project for a psychology journal. That's one butt-nekkid emperor, folks.

NICK JOHNSON 1B Bats: L Throws: L Born: 19-Sep-78 Age: 25

YEAR	TM	LG	AGE	AB	H	2B	3B	HR	BB	SO	SB	CS	AVG	OBP	SLG	MLVR	EQBA	EQOBP	EQSLG	EQMLVR	VORP	DEFENSE
2001	COH	INT	22	359	92	20	0	18	81	105	9	2	.256	.407	.462	.206	.233	.372	.429	.015	12.0	109-1B 0
2001	NYY	AL	22	67	13	2	0	2	7	15	0	0	.194	.308	.313	-.230	.209	.321	.358	-.190	-1.9	11-1B 0
2002	NYY	AL	23	378	92	15	0	15	48	98	1	3	.243	.347	.402	-.005	.267	.365	.445	.050	13.2	62-1B 3
2003	NYY	AL	24	324	92	19	0	14	70	57	5	2	.284	.422	.472	.242	.311	.444	.518	.323	29.9	58-1B -2
2004	MON	NL	25	394	118	25	1	25	73	80	5	2	.300	.421	.558	.319	.282	.400	.515	.206	37.4	114-1B -1

Breakout: 33%   Improve: 64%   Collapse: 10%

Traded to the Expos, Johnson will be more valuable to them than he would have been to the Yankees because he'll be able to play first base full-time. A decent chunk of his value is defensive, and splitting time at the bag with Jason Giambi wasn't helping him or the Yankees. Johnson has to prove he can stay healthy for a full season, avoiding the hand and wrist problems that have followed him his entire career. When he plays, he'll be very valuable, and PECOTA's projecting a big—albeit injury-limited—2004.

HIDEKI MATSUI   OF   Bats: L   Throws: R   Born: 12-Jun-74   Age: 30

YEAR	TM	LG	AGE	AB	H	2B	3B	HR	BB	SO	SB	CS	AVG	OBP	SLG	MLVR	EQBA	EQOBP	EQSLG	EQMLVR	VORP	DEFENSE			
2001	YOM	JPC	27	481	160	23	3	36	120	96	3	0	.333	.466	.617	.545	.303	.395	.485	.189	52.9				
2002	YOM	JPC	28	500	167	27	1	50	114	104	3	0	.334	.463	.692	.630	.309	.405	.512	.249	68.3				
2003	NYY	AL	29	623	179	42	1	16	63	86	2	2	.287	.353	.435	.078	.309	.378	.471	.146	21.7	111-LF	-9	44-CF	-2
2004	NYY	AL	30	501	140	30	2	17	62	87	3	2	.279	.360	.451	.079	.284	.369	.469	.098	26.8	135-LF	0		

Breakout: 12%   Improve: 41%   Collapse: 19%

"Godzilla" didn't hit for power, and in fact was a groundball hitter in his first season stateside. The reputation he developed as a clutch hitter was almost entirely due to his RBI count, which itself was a function of his lineup position and durability. He wasn't the team MVP; he wasn't one of the top seven candidates. Look for him to make adjustments—he did hit start getting the ball in the air in the second half—and come back with a .500 slugging average this year.

BRIAN MYROW   3B/2B   Bats: L   Throws: R   Born: 04-Sep-76   Age: 27

YEAR	TM	LG	AGE	AB	H	2B	3B	HR	BB	SO	SB	CS	AVG	OBP	SLG	MLVR	EQBA	EQOBP	EQSLG	EQMLVR	VORP	DEFENSE			
2001	WIN	NTH	24	88	34	9	0	10	31	11	2	0	.386	.554	.830	.959	.228	.376	.478	.081	10.1				
2001	TAM	FLA	24	149	38	11	1	3	32	29	5	1	.255	.399	.403	.166	.209	.318	.335	-.227	-2.4	27-3B	-10		
2002	TAM	FLA	25	225	63	12	1	5	42	45	0	0	.280	.409	.409	.211	.227	.327	.345	-.185	-0.4	19-3B	0		
2002	NRW	EAS	25	188	57	16	0	3	41	42	5	0	.303	.441	.436	.269	.250	.364	.367	-.069	7.4	45-3B	-7		
2003	TRN	EAS	26	461	141	31	8	18	107	113	6	3	.306	.447	.525	.371	.237	.361	.419	-.016	26.9	86-3B	-22	23-2B	-4
2004	NYY	AL	27	207	50	11	1	7	27	49	2	1	.241	.340	.409	-.035	.246	.349	.425	-.023	12.3	60-3B	-9		

Breakout: 31%   Improve: 52%   Collapse: 18%

It can't be easy to find people who would look upon a year and a half in Trenton, New Jersey as an upgrade, but after two years in Winnipeg, it had to seem pretty good to Myrow. He's not a prospect, but anyone with a career Double-A OBP of .445 is going to get mentioned in this book. Look at that PECOTA projection; for a team that never uses its backup infielder on defense, wouldn't Myrow be a better use of a roster spot than Almonte, or even Miguel Cairo?

DIONER NAVARRO   C   Bats: B   Throws: R   Born: 09-Feb-84   Age: 20

YEAR	TM	LG	AGE	AB	H	2B	3B	HR	BB	SO	SB	CS	AVG	OBP	SLG	MLVR	EQBA	EQOBP	EQSLG	EQMLVR	VORP	DEFENSE	
2002	GRB	SAL	18	328	78	12	2	8	39	61	1	2	.238	.326	.360	-.014	.180	.245	.284	-.457	-29.4	79-C	1
2003	TAM	FLA	19	197	59	16	4	3	17	27	1	0	.299	.364	.467	.258	.255	.306	.417	-.107	4.3	50-C	-1
2003	TRN	EAS	19	208	71	15	0	4	18	26	2	3	.341	.388	.471	.250	.288	.338	.409	-.033	9.1	40-C	-2
2004	NYY	AL	20	315	71	15	1	6	23	52	2	1	.224	.282	.342	-.233	.228	.289	.355	-.232	-3.1	84-C	-7

Breakout: 20%   Improve: 40%   Collapse: 44%

Navarro's huge 2003 season has him all over prospect lists, and as a catcher who hit .341 in the Eastern League and just turned 20, there's a lot to like. When you look deeper, though, you see some problems. Most of his offensive value is in his batting average; he doesn't walk a lot, although his strikeout-to-walk ratio is acceptable. His isolated power was OK given his age, but his power potential is limited by his size (his listed height of 5'10" is generous). He is almost certain to be less productive in 2004 than he was last year, so keep expectations down and see how the rest of his offense develops before buying into the hype.

JORGE POSADA   C   Bats: B   Throws: R   Born: 17-Aug-71   Age: 32

YEAR	TM	LG	AGE	AB	H	2B	3B	HR	BB	SO	SB	CS	AVG	OBP	SLG	MLVR	EQBA	EQOBP	EQSLG	EQMLVR	VORP	DEFENSE	
2001	NYY	AL	29	484	134	28	1	22	62	132	2	6	.277	.363	.475	.136	.303	.388	.526	.234	53.4	124-C	-4
2002	NYY	AL	30	511	137	40	1	20	81	143	1	0	.268	.370	.468	.136	.290	.392	.511	.207	52.6	134-C	-2
2003	NYY	AL	31	481	135	24	0	30	93	110	2	4	.281	.405	.518	.270	.312	.433	.581	.390	55.9	135-C	1
2004	NYY	AL	32	417	109	22	1	20	67	101	3	1	.261	.368	.460	.089	.266	.377	.478	.108	35.3	116-C	-4

Breakout: 5%   Improve: 31%   Collapse: 23%

One of the real player-development highlights for the Yankees in the past 20 years, Posada has gone from minor league infielder to MVP-candidate catcher. It's nice to see that his defensive reputation, while not great, hasn't gone the way of most catchers who hit well. Because he didn't catch as a young player, it's reasonable to think he will hold up better in his early 30s as well, with less wear and tear on his knees. All signs point to Posada maintaining his recent performance level, which gives the Yankees a significant competitive advantage in the catcher-thin American League.

JUAN RIVERA RF/LF Bats: R Throws: R Born: 03-Jul-78 Age: 25

YEAR	TM	LG	AGE	AB	H	2B	3B	HR	BB	SO	SB	CS	AVG	OBP	SLG	MLVR	EQBA	EQOBP	EQSLG	EQMLVR	VORP	DEFENSE			
2001	NRW	EAS	23	316	101	18	3	14	15	50	5	7	.320	.353	.528	.290	.279	.316	.467	.004	6.3	76-RF	5		
2001	COH	INT	23	199	65	11	1	14	15	31	4	5	.327	.372	.603	.403	.297	.348	.559	.209	16.3	55-RF	1		
2002	COH	INT	24	265	86	21	1	8	13	39	5	1	.325	.355	.502	.231	.301	.337	.477	.076	11.0	64-RF	-5		
2002	NYY	AL	24	83	22	5	0	1	6	10	1	1	.265	.311	.361	-.109	.286	.333	.393	-.066	0.0	14-RF	0	13-LF	0
2003	COH	INT	25	308	100	21	0	7	26	37	1	3	.325	.374	.461	.209	.301	.355	.436	.048	10.3	54-RF	-2	24-LF	1
2003	NYY	AL	25	173	46	14	0	7	10	27	0	0	.266	.304	.468	.022	.282	.324	.506	.077	2.7	32-LF	-4	14-RF	0
2004	MON	NL	25	313	92	20	1	13	24	43	3	1	.295	.347	.493	.116	.277	.329	.455	.007	9.7	83-RF	-3		

Breakout: 20%   Improve: 47%   Collapse: 36%

Rivera was traded to the Expos along with Johnson and Randy Choate in the Javier Vazquez deal. Whereas Johnson will be given the first-base job, Rivera's path to playing time is less clear. He'll likely battle Terrmel Sledge and, in effect, Endy Chavez for the left-field job, though he could also become Carl Everett's platoon partner in right field. Rivera isn't going to be a star, but he could have Carlos Lee's '02–'03 peak over the next few years, and that's not bad for $300,000.

BRONSON SARDINHA It depends Bats: L Throws: R Born: 06-Apr-83 Age: 21

YEAR	TM	LG	AGE	AB	H	2B	3B	HR	BB	SO	SB	CS	AVG	OBP	SLG	MLVR	EQBA	EQOBP	EQSLG	EQMLVR	VORP	DEFENSE			
2002	GRB	SAL	19	342	90	13	0	12	34	78	15	6	.263	.334	.406	.073	.202	.256	.325	-.367	-17.5	63-SS	-21	12-LF	-2
2002	STA	NYP	19	124	40	8	0	4	24	36	4	1	.323	.433	.484	.371	.212	.299	.333	-.265	-16.7	26-LF	-3		
2003	BCR	MID	20	269	74	16	0	8	40	40	5	3	.275	.374	.424	.178	.206	.284	.335	-.296	-21.9	32-LF	-4	16-RF	-2
2003	TAM	FLA	20	212	41	8	2	1	24	57	8	2	.193	.279	.264	-.185	.177	.243	.250	-.509	-26.0	57-CF	-7		
2004	NYY	AL	21	273	56	11	1	5	23	63	4	2	.204	.272	.314	-.297	.208	.279	.326	-.300	-14.3	74-CF	-17		

Breakout: 44%   Improve: 63%   Collapse: 17%

Sardinha has had a very strange trip through his first three professional seasons. Drafted with a supplemental #1 pick in 2001, he opened '02 as a shortstop in the Sally League and ended it as an outfielder in the New York-Penn League. Last year he started the season in the Florida State League and didn't hit, earning a demotion to the Midwest League, where he did. The way he hits after demotions indicates that at least part of the problem is that he's being rushed. He'll open '04 as a third baseman at Tampa; his bat is best suited to that spot, and he has the hands and arm for the position. He'll come as quickly as his power lets him.

FERNANDO SEGUIGNOL DH Bats: B Throws: R Born: 19-Jan-75 Age: 29

YEAR	TM	LG	AGE	AB	H	2B	3B	HR	BB	SO	SB	CS	AVG	OBP	SLG	MLVR	EQBA	EQOBP	EQSLG	EQMLVR	VORP	DEFENSE	
2001	OTT	INT	26	242	75	12	0	14	15	49	0	1	.310	.363	.533	.275	.290	.339	.506	.110	13.7	51-1B	1
2001	MON	NL	26	50	7	2	0	0	2	17	0	0	.140	.185	.180	-.721	.140	.186	.200	-.710	-7.9		
2002	ORX	JPP	27	280	57	8	0	23	40	104	1	0	.204	.316	.479	.052	.202	.309	.463	-.080	4.3		
2003	COH	INT	28	402	137	28	1	28	34	81	0	0	.341	.401	.624	.485	.310	.371	.580	.291	44.4	26-1B	0
2004	NYY	AL	29	226	58	11	1	11	21	51	0	0	.255	.324	.461	.015	.260	.333	.479	.030	9.7		

Breakout: 13%   Improve: 41%   Collapse: 34%

Rather than trading for Garcia and Ruben Sierra, the Yankees should have just called up Seguignol, who was having yet another big year at Triple-A. He's just a power source, but a very good one, someone who might hit 30 bombs and slug .525 in the majors. Half the teams in the AL don't have a DH this good. Unfortunately for him, the Yankees do, whether it ends up being Giambi or Bernie Williams. Rather than wait around for someone to wise up, he's gone back to Japan.

RUBEN SIERRA PH Bats: B Throws: R Born: 06-Oct-65 Age: 38

YEAR	TM	LG	AGE	AB	H	2B	3B	HR	BB	SO	SB	CS	AVG	OBP	SLG	MLVR	EQBA	EQOBP	EQSLG	EQMLVR	VORP	DEFENSE	
2001	OKL	PCL	35	94	25	2	1	3	10	14	2	0	.266	.337	.404	-.046	.242	.308	.358	-.195	-2.0		
2001	TEX	AL	35	344	100	22	1	23	19	52	2	0	.291	.322	.561	.173	.300	.341	.583	.236	25.7	29-RF	-5
2002	SEA	AL	36	419	113	23	0	13	31	66	4	0	.270	.319	.418	.001	.296	.347	.461	.065	12.7	42-LF	-1
2003	TEX	AL	37	133	35	9	0	3	14	27	1	1	.263	.333	.398	-.076	.278	.347	.421	-.007	0.0	12-LF	-1
2003	NYY	AL	37	174	48	8	1	6	13	20	1	0	.276	.323	.437	.027	.297	.349	.469	.081	6.1		
2004	NYY	AL	38	220	56	11	1	7	17	36	2	1	.255	.309	.408	-.080	.260	.317	.423	-.070	2.0		

Breakout: 22%   Improve: 35%   Collapse: 39%

(continued next page)

Ruben Sierra *(continued)*

Sierra doesn't hit enough to lay claim to a regular job any longer, but the way in which he can still turn on a fastball from the left side may make him a credible pinch-hitter. He had two postseason hits for the Yankees, cranking fastballs from Scott Williamson and Ugueth Urbina for a homer and a triple. He'll get most of his playing time in that role in '04, having signed a one-year, $1 million contract with the Yanks.

ALFONSO SORIANO 2B Bats: R Throws: R Born: 07-Jan-78 Age: 26

YEAR	TM	LG	AGE	AB	H	2B	3B	HR	BB	SO	SB	CS	AVG	OBP	SLG	MLVR	EQBA	EQOBP	EQSLG	EQMLVR	VORP	DEFENSE
2001	NYY	AL	23	574	154	34	3	18	29	125	43	14	.268	.304	.432	-.031	.288	.328	.468	.035	30.3	152-2B -19
2002	NYY	AL	24	696	209	51	2	39	23	157	41	13	.300	.332	.547	.214	.326	.360	.598	.320	83.2	154-2B -12
2003	NYY	AL	25	682	198	36	5	38	38	130	35	8	.290	.338	.525	.182	.316	.364	.576	.281	58.3	154-2B -5
2004	NYY	AL	26	624	181	38	4	31	41	118	31	9	.290	.340	.513	.138	.295	.349	.533	.161	55.5	159-2B -4

Breakout: 9%   Improve: 32%   Collapse: 22%

Sammy or Samuel? That's the question you have to ask about Soriano, who had another strong season despite his poor plate discipline. He did improve in 2003, striking out less and taking a few more walks, although nearly 20% of his 38 were intentional passes. Soriano doesn't have to walk even 50 times a year to be a productive player, because his power is exceptional. You'd like to see him work his way into more hitter's counts, however. Stepping back from the numbers for a second, his postseason showed a susceptibility to the classic fastball-up, fastball-up, breaking ball-away sequence that has been burying hitters since the Wilson administration.

At 26, Sammy Sosa's walk rate spiked in the strike-shortened 1994 season, and while he went back and forth over the next few seasons, he eventually emerged as Sammy! in 1998. Juan Samuel also had a big age-26 season in 1987, including a career-best walk rate, but never again came close to that performance. Watch to see if Soriano shows a similar spike in '04, and if he appears to have learned anything from his painful October.

JON-MARK SPROWL C Bats: L Throws: R Born: 01-Aug-80 Age: 23

YEAR	TM	LG	AGE	AB	H	2B	3B	HR	BB	SO	SB	CS	AVG	OBP	SLG	MLVR	EQBA	EQOBP	EQSLG	EQMLVR	VORP	DEFENSE		
2001	LNS	MID	20	155	34	9	0	3	18	24	0	3	.219	.311	.335	-.115	.158	.229	.247	-.549	-18.4	13-C -7		
2002	LNC	CAL	21	230	64	12	1	6	43	42	2	4	.278	.404	.417	.104	.190	.290	.289	-.354	-13.3	22-C -10	11-LF	0
2003	SBN	MID	22	321	95	22	3	4	54	31	5	4	.296	.402	.421	.230	.217	.302	.323	-.270	-10.6	64-C -17		
2003	BCR	MID	22	97	39	8	0	1	17	8	0	1	.402	.500	.515	.556	.294	.378	.382	.008	6.1	18-C -2		
2004	NYY	AL	23	243	53	13	1	4	24	38	1	1	.220	.298	.334	-.216	.224	.305	.347	-.214	-3.5	68-C -14		

Breakout: 29%   Improve: 57%   Collapse: 23%

As if getting rid of Raul Mondesi wasn't enough—addition by subtraction and all that—the Yankees picked up a fun prospect from the Diamondbacks. Sprowl has shown excellent plate discipline in his five professional seasons, but until 2002 had yet to mix in much else. He's not much of a defensive catcher, and at 24, he'll have to start making some progress if he's going to have a career. His upside is a second catcher who can start 60 times and also be a good bat off the bench, one of the Greg Myers/Ron Hassey class of left-handed-hitting receivers.

FERDIN TEJEDA SS Bats: R Throws: R Born: 15-Sep-82 Age: 21

YEAR	TM	LG	AGE	AB	H	2B	3B	HR	BB	SO	SB	CS	AVG	OBP	SLG	MLVR	EQBA	EQOBP	EQSLG	EQMLVR	VORP	DEFENSE
2002	STA	NYP	19	181	50	7	2	0	11	33	11	3	.276	.316	.337	.000	.216	.249	.270	-.451	-25.5	46-SS -1
2003	TAM	FLA	20	217	64	9	5	0	6	38	4	3	.295	.320	.382	.086	.270	.288	.360	-.212	-0.6	48-SS 10
2004	NYA	AL	21	267	60	11	3	2	9	48	4	2	.227	.259	.310	-.315	.231	.265	.322	-.319	-7.7	70-SS -5

Breakout: 11%   Improve: 26%   Collapse: 44%

Tejeda may be 20 years too late. His combination of singles and slick fielding would have made him a top prospect in the 1980s, but now, we expect shortstops to do more. Almost all of his offensive contribution is in his batting average: he's rarely walked or picked up an extra-base hit in his two seasons in the U.S. He'll move to the Eastern League in 2004, and he'll cease to be a prospect the next time his average falls into the .270s. He's been susceptible to leg injuries, a bad sign for a young player.

BERNIE WILLIAMS — CF/DH — Bats: B — Throws: R — Born: 13-Sep-68 — Age: 35

YEAR	TM	LG	AGE	AB	H	2B	3B	HR	BB	SO	SB	CS	AVG	OBP	SLG	MLVR	EQBA	EQOBP	EQSLG	EQMLVR	VORP	DEFENSE		
2001	NYY	AL	32	540	166	38	0	26	78	67	11	5	.307	.395	.522	.280	.337	.428	.577	.406	82.1	144-CF -4		
2002	NYY	AL	33	612	204	37	2	19	83	97	8	4	.333	.415	.493	.302	.359	.438	.535	.389	87.0	147-CF -12		
2003	NYY	AL	34	445	117	19	1	15	71	61	5	0	.263	.367	.411	.059	.285	.389	.450	.114	22.9	113-CF -5		
2004	NYY	AL	35	436	124	24	2	14	61	61	6	2	.285	.374	.440	.091	.290	.383	.457	.111	25.9	119-CF -5		

Breakout: 10%   Improve: 36%   Collapse: 25%

Anyone who has watched the Yankees over the past few years recognized that Williams needed to be moved from center field. Making him the DH and installing Kenny Lofton in center really wasn't much of a solution, however; Lofton has lost a lot of range, and is one of the few outfielders Williams might be able to take in a throwing contest. We've argued in the past that getting Williams out of center field could help his bat, so this is the year we find out if that's true. He'll vault past that PECOTA projection, and may have a career year for power and walks. Given Giambi's knee problem, it might be worth it to see if Williams can play some first base.

ENRIQUE WILSON — IF — Bats: B — Throws: R — Born: 27-Jul-73 — Age: 30

YEAR	TM	LG	AGE	AB	H	2B	3B	HR	BB	SO	SB	CS	AVG	OBP	SLG	MLVR	EQBA	EQOBP	EQSLG	EQMLVR	VORP	DEFENSE		
2001	PIT	NL	27	129	24	3	0	1	3	23	0	3	.186	.203	.233	-.597	.185	.203	.238	-.605	-13.9	23-SS -1		
2001	NYY	AL	27	99	24	5	1	1	6	14	0	2	.242	.283	.343	-.211	.270	.311	.380	-.139	1.6	11-SS -2	13-3B	3
2002	NYY	AL	28	105	19	2	2	2	8	22	1	1	.181	.239	.295	-.379	.208	.263	.340	-.329	-3.9	14-3B -1		
2003	NYY	AL	29	135	31	9	0	3	7	14	3	1	.230	.276	.363	-.213	.252	.301	.400	-.143	-1.2	20-SS -3	12-3B	2
2004	NYY	AL	30	141	34	6	1	3	9	20	2	2	.238	.287	.351	-.204	.243	.294	.364	-.201	1.3	41-SS -7		

Breakout: 45%   Improve: 65%   Collapse: 25%

The depths of Yankee-fan frustration with Boone and Soriano in October were illustrated by the calls for one of them to be benched in favor of Wilson, who hasn't had a .300 OBP since 2000. Other than the weird Pedro Martinez thing— Wilson's at .500/.524/.700 against the Sox ace in 21 PAs—he's a player of minimal value. He'll be back in '04, however.

PITCHERS

ANDY BEAL — Bats: L — Throws: L — Born: 31-Oct-78 — Age: 25

YEAR	TM	LG	AGE	G	GS	IP	H	BB	SO	HR	ERA	EQERA	EQH9	EQBB9	EQSO9	EQHR9	PERA	VORP	STF
2001	TAM	FLA	22	17	17	99.0	101	30	72	6	3.00	6.28	10.8	3.2	4.3	1.4	5.85	-6.8	-10
2002	TAM	FLA	23	10	10	54.3	59	13	37	0	2.65	4.93	11.7	2.7	4.2	0.4	5.01	3.7	9
2002	NRW	EAS	23	10	10	62.7	56	22	61	3	3.30	4.37	9.2	3.7	6.6	0.8	4.56	7.9	21
2002	COH	INT	23	8	8	44.7	50	21	31	6	6.04	6.23	9.1	4.8	5.4	1.7	5.81	-3.0	-11
2003	TRN	EAS	24	17	12	74.3	76	20	64	4	3.51	4.37	9.4	2.8	5.9	0.9	4.52	9.6	6
2003	COH	INT	24	8	8	38.7	51	11	25	8	7.44	8.41	13.2	3.3	4.8	3.1	9.11	-11.0	-64
2004	NYY	AL	25	15	10	55.7	63	20	34	8	5.07	5.23	10.0	3.1	5.4	1.2	5.29	4.8	-4

Breakout: 20%   Improve: 53%   Collapse: 25%

Another of the Yankees' college draftees, Beal has struggled in the transition from Double-A to Triple-A, not unusual for a pitcher without a fastball. As you read through the next few pages, you'll see a lot of guys like this, Yankee draftees who haven't been able to make the transition from college and low minor league success to major league performance. Whether it's a weakness in drafting or development is unclear, but it's certain that the Yankees aren't getting anything out of their system right now, which is one of the reasons they have an astronomical payroll.

COLTER BEAN — Bats: R — Throws: R — Born: 16-Jan-77 — Age: 27

YEAR	TM	LG	AGE	G	GS	IP	H	BB	SO	HR	ERA	EQERA	EQH9	EQBB9	EQSO9	EQHR9	PERA	VORP	STF
2001	TAM	FLA	24	32	0	49.3	27	18	77	0	1.46	2.47	7.6	3.9	9.3	0.2	3.30	15.2	36
2002	TAM	FLA	25	46	0	54.7	34	21	78	2	1.97	3.78	8.7	4.5	8.9	0.9	4.67	9.6	-1
2003	TRN	EAS	26	3	0	4.7	2	2	9	0	0.00	2.08	6.2	4.2	12.5	0.0	2.56	1.7	58
2003	COH	INT	26	50	0	69.0	53	27	70	5	2.87	4.29	8.0	4.4	7.3	1.0	4.42	9.2	-6
2004	BOS	AL	27	20	3	30.7	31	16	27	3	4.58	4.35	8.4	4.3	7.8	1.0	4.53	5.3	4

Breakout: 32%   Improve: 49%   Collapse: 35%

(continued next page)

Colter Bean *(continued)*

He wouldn't have had a role in New York, but after being taken by the Red Sox in the Rule 5 draft, Bean might stick and become a fan favorite in Boston. He comes in around .9 Garces, and ate up right-handed batters at Triple-A last year. He's not a power pitcher like El Guapo, but a finesse guy who comes from the side. He'd be helped if Scott Williamson was somewhere else by Opening Day.

DANNY BORRELL   Bats: L   Throws: L   Born: 24-Jan-79   Age: 25

YEAR	TM	LG	AGE	G	GS	IP	H	BB	SO	HR	ERA	EQERA	EQH9	EQBB9	EQSO9	EQHR9	PERA	VORP	STF
2001	TAM	FLA	22	22	20	111.0	109	38	84	6	3.97	5.95	10.4	3.6	4.4	1.2	5.63	-3.9	-8
2002	TAM	FLA	23	7	6	38.7	33	10	44	0	2.33	3.89	10.1	2.9	7.0	0.3	4.19	6.6	35
2002	NRW	EAS	23	21	20	128.3	116	39	91	5	2.31	3.93	8.9	3.2	4.7	0.6	4.13	22.1	16
2003	COH	INT	24	10	10	55.3	55	22	30	4	2.93	4.73	9.3	4.4	3.9	1.1	5.13	5.0	-10
2004	*NYY*	*AL*	*25*	*19*	*14*	*77.3*	*89*	*34*	*42*	*10*	*5.41*	*5.58*	*10.2*	*3.8*	*4.7*	*1.1*	*5.58*	*1.9*	*-9*

Breakout: 17%   *Improve: 47%*   *Collapse: 28%*

Borrell's steady march through the Yankee system was derailed in June when he was diagnosed with a torn left labrum. The resulting surgery ended his '03 season and will likely render him a non-factor until 2005 at the earliest. Before the injury, the Yankees' #2 pick in 2000 had been successful with a low-90s fastball and an effective curve and change-up.

YHENCY BRAZOBAN   Bats: R   Throws: R   Born: 11-Jun-80   Age: 24

YEAR	TM	LG	AGE	G	GS	IP	H	BB	SO	HR	ERA	EQERA	EQH9	EQBB9	EQSO9	EQHR9	PERA	VORP	STF
2003	TAM	FLA	23	24	0	28.7	27	12	34	0	2.82	5.76	11.5	5.0	7.6	0.4	5.48	-0.4	6
2003	TRN	EAS	23	20	0	27.7	33	14	19	5	7.80	8.06	11.2	5.6	4.9	3.2	8.85	-7.0	-77
2004	*LAD*	*NL*	*24*	*15*	*1*	*20.7*	*22*	*12*	*15*	*3*	*5.53*	*6.19*	*10.1*	*4.5*	*5.8*	*1.3*	*6.38*	*0.0*	*-16*

Breakout: 32%   *Improve: 62%*   *Breakout: 13%*

The converted outfielder—picture a tools guy without much speed—took to the mound in 2002 and impressed the Yankees with a high-90s fastball. The rest of the package is still coming, and with a career ERA of 5.34 in 64 innings, it's coming slowly. The Yankees packaged Brazoban in the Kevin Brown deal; the Dodgers can plunk him down in Jacksonville and let him work on his command and his slider. Be patient.

RANDY CHOATE   Bats: L   Throws: L   Born: 05-Sep-75   Age: 28

YEAR	TM	LG	AGE	G	GS	IP	H	BB	SO	HR	ERA	EQERA	EQH9	EQBB9	EQSO9	EQHR9	PERA	VORP	STF
2001	NYY	AL	25	37	0	48.3	34	27	35	0	3.35	3.06	6.1	4.6	6.1	0.2	2.88	13.3	20
2002	COH	INT	26	31	0	36.7	25	15	32	0	1.72	2.08	6.0	4.4	6.5	0.3	2.82	13.6	17
2002	NYY	AL	26	18	0	22.3	18	15	17	1	6.05	4.91	7.0	5.3	6.5	0.4	3.63	1.7	6
2003	COH	INT	27	54	3	71.3	75	24	56	4	3.91	5.07	10.4	3.7	5.6	0.8	5.16	3.9	-15
2004	*MON*	*NL*	*28*	*16*	*2*	*24.3*	*26*	*12*	*17*	*3*	*5.34*	*4.77*	*9.3*	*3.9*	*5.8*	*0.9*	*4.68*	*2.9*	*-7*

Breakout: 24%   *Improve: 49%*   *Collapse: 28%*

The other guy in the Javier Vazquez trade, Choate was never able to establish himself under Joe Torre. He struggles to locate his stuff, which makes him prone to walking guys, not a good quality in a specialist. The Expos' trade of Scott Stewart clears space for him in Montreal, and if allowed to throw complete innings and multiple innings, he could be valuable.

ROGER CLEMENS   Bats: R   Throws: R   Born: 04-Aug-62   Age: 41

YEAR	TM	LG	AGE	G	GS	IP	H	BB	SO	HR	ERA	EQERA	EQH9	EQBB9	EQSO9	EQHR9	PERA	VORP	STF
2001	NYY	AL	38	33	33	220.3	205	72	213	19	3.51	3.54	8.0	2.7	8.0	0.7	3.62	49.4	35
2002	NYY	AL	39	29	29	180.0	172	63	192	18	4.35	4.02	8.3	2.9	9.1	0.8	3.90	31.0	37
2003	NYY	AL	40	33	33	211.7	199	58	190	24	3.91	3.66	7.8	2.3	7.8	0.9	3.59	37.9	31
2004	*HOU*	*NL*	*41*	*28*	*26*	*166.7*	*154*	*54*	*153*	*16*	*3.69*	*3.75*	*8.3*	*2.6*	*7.5*	*0.8*	*3.68*	*32.8*	*23*

Breakout: 16%   *Improve: 48%*   *Collapse: 14%*

It's silly to get too worked up about it, but if Clemens unretires to play for the Astros in '04 (and we're including a Houston PECOTA, even though Clemens was still technically retired as of press time) Yankee fans definitely have to feel a bit snookered. They invested a lot of emotional energy in Clemens' last outings, most notably his Game Four start in the World Series. You can't stop a man from pursuing his happiness, but you also can't blame pinstripe loyalists if they feel a bit cheated.

Now that he's an Astro, he could easily tip the balance in the NL Central. He's still a credible #2 starter and a huge upgrade over Jeriome Robertson or whoever he'd be replacing in Houston's rotation. He would have retired as one of the best pitchers ever, right there with Lefty Grove, Walter Johnson, and Greg Maddux, but that's still on his c.v.

JOSE CONTRERAS Bats: R Throws: R Born: 06-Dec-71 Age: 32

YEAR	TM	LG	AGE	G	GS	IP	H	BB	SO	HR	ERA	EQERA	EQH9	EQBB9	EQSO9	EQHR9	PERA	VORP	STF
2003	NYY	AL	31	18	9	71.0	52	30	72	4	3.30	2.96	6.0	3.6	8.9	0.5	2.82	19.1	40
2003	COH	INT	31	3	3	15.0	10	2	18	1	1.20	1.93	7.1	1.3	8.4	0.6	2.72	5.7	43
2004	NYY	AL	32	31	16	101.3	88	45	95	9	3.56	3.67	7.7	3.8	8.2	0.7	3.84	24.4	16

Breakout: 24% Improve: 56% Collapse: 30%

Contreras showed electric stuff at times, but also had some trouble commanding it, a flaw that caused him to struggle against the more patient teams he faced. Fortunately for him, six of his nine starts were against the Devil Rays, Tigers, Orioles, and Reds, and he had a 1.48 ERA against those teams. He misses bats, which is a big plus in front of a defense that misses balls. Contreras will likely settle in as a mid-rotation starter, but an inconsistent one, mixing game scores of 91 and 19 with frustrating frequency.

JORGE DE PAULA Bats: R Throws: R Born: 10-Nov-78 Age: 25

YEAR	TM	LG	AGE	G	GS	IP	H	BB	SO	HR	ERA	EQERA	EQH9	EQBB9	EQSO9	EQHR9	PERA	VORP	STF
2003	COH	INT	24	27	27	167.7	168	57	125	22	4.35	5.42	9.9	3.8	5.4	1.9	6.11	3.1	-17
2003	NYY	AL	24	4	1	11.3	3	1	7	1	0.80	0.82	1.6	0.8	5.7	0.8	0.61	6.4	36
2004	NYY	AL	25	16	11	64.7	72	27	40	11	5.41	5.57	9.8	3.5	5.5	1.4	5.48	3.2	-6

Breakout: 23% Improve: 49% Collapse: 22%

Listed previously as Julio De Paula, the right-hander reached the majors this season and might have warranted a spot on the playoff roster, especially for the World Series. He's a fastball/change-up pitcher who hasn't yet mastered a third pitch, a flaw that will limit him to bullpen work. Actually, given the Yankee roster, it will probably limit him to mid-rotation work at Columbus and a mid-season trade. He'll have some good years in relief.

ALEX GRAMAN Bats: L Throws: L Born: 17-Nov-77 Age: 26

YEAR	TM	LG	AGE	G	GS	IP	H	BB	SO	HR	ERA	EQERA	EQH9	EQBB9	EQSO9	EQHR9	PERA	VORP	STF
2001	NRW	EAS	23	28	28	166.3	174	60	138	10	3.52	5.69	10.9	4.4	5.1	0.8	5.59	-1.5	2
2002	NRW	EAS	24	8	8	50.0	46	13	31	2	2.88	4.11	9.2	2.7	4.1	0.6	4.12	7.6	9
2002	COH	INT	24	20	20	124.0	141	37	98	11	4.65	4.99	9.9	3.1	5.8	1.1	5.10	8.1	5
2003	COH	INT	25	26	26	142.7	135	63	110	14	4.48	5.28	9.2	4.9	5.6	1.4	5.54	4.7	-16
2004	NYY	AL	26	18	12	66.0	79	33	42	9	5.95	6.13	10.6	4.3	5.6	1.2	6.06	0.4	-8

Breakout: 21% Improve: 50% Collapse: 26%

Look around the Yankee organization and you see more scalpel marks than in a whole season of "ER." Graman is one of the lucky ones, having made it to Triple-A without undergoing general anesthesia. He's not as polished as Borrell or as exciting as Chien-Ming Wang, but he keeps the ball down and could eventually snag a role as a fifth starter or swingman, most likely in another system.

CHRIS HAMMOND Bats: L Throws: L Born: 21-Jan-66 Age: 38

YEAR	TM	LG	AGE	G	GS	IP	H	BB	SO	HR	ERA	EQERA	EQH9	EQBB9	EQSO9	EQHR9	PERA	VORP	STF
2001	BUF	INT	35	28	4	51.7	53	20	54	5	3.31	5.17	10.9	4.2	7.5	1.1	5.84	2.2	-14
2001	RIC	INT	35	21	0	30.7	32	4	29	0	2.35	3.54	10.9	1.3	6.8	0.3	4.18	6.4	19
2002	ATL	NL	36	63	0	76.0	53	31	63	1	0.95	2.64	7.2	3.3	6.7	0.1	2.89	23.6	27
2003	NYY	AL	37	62	0	63.0	65	11	45	5	2.86	3.19	8.6	1.5	6.2	0.6	3.42	17.9	17
2004	OAK	AL	38	39	1	53.0	52	16	36	5	3.57	3.77	8.9	2.5	5.8	0.8	4.13	12.3	-1

Breakout: 34% Improve: 44% Collapse: 27%

Hammond didn't pitch poorly for the Yankees, but he didn't do what they needed him to do, which was get left-handed batters out. Lefties hit .292/.337/.461 against him, and it was a Johnny Damon homer off of Hammond on July 27 that sealed his fate. Once the Yankees picked up Gabe White and Felix Heredia, Hammond was relegated to mop-up duty. He was dealt to the A's over the winter; don't expect him to have much of a role for a team with two better lefty relievers, three left-handed starters, and a left-handed Rule 5 pick in Frank Brooks.

SEAN HENN

Bats: R | Throws: L | Born: 23-Apr-81 | Age: 23

YEAR	TM	LG	AGE	G	GS	IP	H	BB	SO	HR	ERA	EQERA	EQH9	EQBB9	EQSO9	EQHR9	PERA	VORP	STF
2001	STA	NYP	20	9	8	42.0	26	15	49	3	3.00	4.93	9.9	5.2	6.2	2.3	7.04	2.6	-12
2003	TAM	FLA	22	16	16	72.3	69	37	52	3	3.61	6.08	10.9	6.1	4.5	1.3	6.53	-3.4	-19
2004	NYY	AL	23	15	10	53.3	68	39	32	11	7.81	8.05	11.3	6.2	5.2	1.8	7.92	-4.2	-25

Breakout: 25%   Improve: 59%   Collapse: 21%

Henn made headlines in 2001 for being the most expensive draft-and-follow ever, signing for a $1.7 million bonus just before the draft. Not bad for a 26th-rounder. After a great debut that year, he missed all of 2002 following—wait for it—Tommy John surgery. He was OK at Tampa this year, but he missed some time with a sore shoulder that also dragged down his stats. He's worth keeping an eye on, as he's still one of the top two or three pitching prospects in a weak system.

FELIX HEREDIA

Bats: L | Throws: L | Born: 18-Jun-75 | Age: 29

YEAR	TM	LG	AGE	G	GS	IP	H	BB	SO	HR	ERA	EQERA	EQH9	EQBB9	EQSO9	EQHR9	PERA	VORP	STF
2001	CHC	NL	26	48	0	35.0	45	16	28	6	6.17	6.62	11.4	3.7	6.1	1.3	6.15	-3.9	-26
2002	TOR	AL	27	53	0	52.3	51	26	31	5	3.61	4.38	8.4	4.0	5.1	0.7	4.23	7.0	-6
2003	CIN	NL	28	57	0	72.0	61	28	41	9	3.00	3.47	7.5	3.1	4.5	1.0	3.86	18.1	-10
2003	NYY	AL	28	12	0	15.0	13	5	4	1	1.20	3.07	6.8	3.1	2.5	0.6	3.16	4.7	-10
2004	NYY	AL	29	40	4	58.0	66	26	31	8	5.34	5.51	10.1	3.9	4.6	1.2	5.62	3.1	-18

Breakout: 22%   Improve: 40%   Collapse: 34%

Heredia was acquired on waivers because GM Brian Cashman didn't want him going to another team, not because he actually wanted Yet Another Lefty Reliever. It worked out, though; Heredia quickly gained Joe Torre's confidence and moved from #3 to #1 on the lefty depth chart in five weeks, even pushing Chris Hammond off the LCS roster. He can pitch a lot, so Torre would be best served to use him for full innings or even as a long man, with Gabe White in the specialist role.

STEVE KARSAY

Bats: R | Throws: R | Born: 24-Mar-72 | Age: 32

YEAR	TM	LG	AGE	G	GS	IP	H	BB	SO	HR	ERA	EQERA	EQH9	EQBB9	EQSO9	EQHR9	PERA	VORP	STF
2001	CLE	AL	29	31	0	43.3	29	8	44	1	1.25	1.27	5.3	1.5	8.4	0.2	1.66	20.5	51
2001	ATL	NL	29	43	0	44.7	44	17	39	4	3.42	4.43	9.3	3.2	6.8	0.6	4.28	5.6	7
2002	NYY	AL	30	78	0	88.3	87	30	65	7	3.26	3.44	8.4	2.8	6.4	0.6	3.80	20.7	11
2004	NYY	AL	32	60	0	59.7	59	19	42	5	3.62	3.73	8.8	2.8	6.1	0.6	3.90	14.0	0

Breakout: 28%   Improve: 45%   Collapse: 27%

Karsay missed the entire 2003 season following arthroscopic shoulder surgery. The attempt to avoid surgery by rehabbing the shoulder pushed the operation back to May, so Karsay may not be ready to start the season. Given the Yankees' free-agent signings this winter, they can let Karsay take his time with an eye towards coming out of the bullpen in the playoffs.

JON LIEBER

Bats: L | Throws: R | Born: 02-Apr-70 | Age: 34

YEAR	TM	LG	AGE	G	GS	IP	H	BB	SO	HR	ERA	EQERA	EQH9	EQBB9	EQSO9	EQHR9	PERA	VORP	STF
2001	CHC	NL	31	34	34	232.3	226	41	148	25	3.80	3.75	8.6	1.5	4.8	0.9	3.75	45.9	13
2002	CHC	NL	32	21	21	141.0	153	12	87	15	3.70	3.92	9.6	0.7	4.9	1.0	4.14	25.3	11
2004	NYY	AL	34	36	25	153.7	178	23	80	21	4.44	4.57	10.2	1.3	4.6	1.1	4.51	21.1	1

Breakout: 18%   Improve: 29%   Collapse: 34%

Lieber was paid $550,000 by the Yankees last year to rehab from Tommy John surgery. By all accounts it went well, and he even made a few minor league starts at the end of the year. True to his nature, he struck out 10 and walked none in eight innings. Command is everything for Lieber, who throws strikes and puts the ball in the air. While that's worked for him, it may not be the best plan for success in front of this Yankee defense. He could win 15 games with an ERA in the mid-4.00s.

MIKE MUSSINA

Bats: R | Throws: R | Born: 08-Dec-68 | Age: 35

YEAR	TM	LG	AGE	G	GS	IP	H	BB	SO	HR	ERA	EQERA	EQH9	EQBB9	EQSO9	EQHR9	PERA	VORP	STF
2001	NYY	AL	32	34	34	228.7	202	42	214	20	3.15	3.06	7.5	1.5	7.8	0.7	3.09	63.0	40
2002	NYY	AL	33	33	33	215.7	208	48	182	27	4.05	3.80	8.3	1.8	7.3	1.0	3.82	42.2	25
2003	NYY	AL	34	31	31	214.7	192	40	195	21	3.40	3.15	7.4	1.6	8.0	0.8	3.09	50.9	39
2004	NYY	AL	35	30	30	213.3	195	44	185	24	3.31	3.41	8.1	1.8	7.6	0.9	3.35	56.3	26

Breakout: 27%   Improve: 59%   Collapse: 15%

Mussina keeps working on a "best pitcher to never win a Cy Young"-type career. He just keeps racking up innings and strikeouts, and despite a lousy postseason rep, has some tremendous October work on his resume. He added to that with three shutout innings in Game Seven of the ALCS, innings that kept the Yankees in a game they would eventually win in extra innings. Already a fringe Hall of Fame candidate, he's two years from being a serious one.

JEFF NELSON Bats: R Throws: R Born: 17-Nov-66 Age: 37

YEAR	TM	LG	AGE	G	GS	IP	H	BB	SO	HR	ERA	EQERA	EQH9	EQBB9	EQSO9	EQHR9	PERA	VORP	STF
2001	SEA	AL	34	69	0	65.3	30	44	88	3	2.76	2.87	4.9	5.7	11.5	0.4	2.81	19.0	43
2002	SEA	AL	35	41	0	45.7	36	27	55	4	3.94	4.03	7.3	4.8	10.3	0.8	3.95	7.8	24
2003	SEA	AL	36	46	0	37.7	34	14	47	3	3.34	4.21	8.7	3.2	11.1	0.7	4.05	7.9	34
2003	NYY	AL	36	24	0	17.7	17	10	21	1	4.58	4.08	8.2	4.6	10.2	0.5	3.99	2.4	29
2004	TEX	AL	37	63	0	49.7	43	27	53	5	3.94	3.55	7.2	4.6	9.7	0.8	3.81	13.3	15

Breakout: 31%   Improve: 51%   Collapse: 36%

Nelson is the closest thing to a righty specialist that we've seen. Five times in the last six seasons, he's averaged less than an inning per appearance, a period in which he's become more and more susceptible to left-handed batters—well, to walking them, anyway. A good manager, especially one in, say, the righty-heavy NL Central, could make excellent use of Nelson and his frisbee slider. The Cardinals might be well-served to pick him up just to use him against the Cubs 19 times. Instead, he's in Texas, where he'll struggle to get full innings of work against divisional opponents.

ANTONIO OSUNA Bats: R Throws: R Born: 12-Apr-73 Age: 31

YEAR	TM	LG	AGE	G	GS	IP	H	BB	SO	HR	ERA	EQERA	EQH9	EQBB9	EQSO9	EQHR9	PERA	VORP	STF
2001	CWS	AL	28	4	0	4.3	8	2	6	3	20.93	16.62	16.6	4.2	10.4	6.2	15.09	-5.3	-158
2002	CWS	AL	29	59	0	67.7	64	28	66	1	3.86	3.86	8.8	3.4	8.5	0.1	3.63	12.6	32
2003	NYY	AL	30	48	0	50.7	58	20	47	3	3.73	3.93	9.5	3.2	8.0	0.5	4.26	10.8	19
2004	NYY	AL	31	48	2	64.7	64	24	56	8	4.40	4.54	8.7	3.2	7.6	1.1	4.60	10.3	4

Breakout: 29%   Improve: 58%   Collapse: 20%

As usual, Osuna was effective when healthy, getting righties out and striking out nearly a man an inning. A right groin strain kept him on and off the DL for much of the summer, continuing his history of injuries. He should have been on the World Series roster, and he certainly would have been a better choice late in Game Four of the World Series than Jeff Weaver was. His option wasn't picked up, and he remained a free agent at press time.

ANDY PETTITTE Bats: L Throws: L Born: 15-Jun-72 Age: 32

YEAR	TM	LG	AGE	G	GS	IP	H	BB	SO	HR	ERA	EQERA	EQH9	EQBB9	EQSO9	EQHR9	PERA	VORP	STF
2001	NYY	AL	29	31	31	200.7	224	41	164	14	3.99	4.03	9.6	1.7	6.8	0.6	3.91	34.2	31
2002	NYY	AL	30	22	22	134.7	144	32	97	6	3.27	3.56	9.3	2.0	6.2	0.3	3.65	29.8	33
2003	NYY	AL	31	33	33	208.3	227	50	180	21	4.02	4.15	9.0	2.0	7.5	0.8	4.03	25.4	28
2004	HOU	NL	32	27	27	179.3	183	47	143	18	3.79	3.86	9.1	2.0	6.5	0.8	3.92	34.6	19

Breakout: 17%   Improve: 45%   Collapse: 21%

Much was made of Pettitte feeling slighted by the Yankees as he was trying to decide whether to leave New York. It was overblown; Pettitte was never a New York guy, and any story attached to his departure begins and ends with one point—he wanted to be closer to home. The Astros get a groundball-throwing innings guy who should benefit by getting away from Derek Jeter. Nevertheless, they think they're getting an ace, when in fact Pettitte is more of a #2/#3 guy, so there's the potential for disappointment here.

JUSTIN POPE Bats: B Throws: R Born: 08-Nov-79 Age: 24

YEAR	TM	LG	AGE	G	GS	IP	H	BB	SO	HR	ERA	EQERA	EQH9	EQBB9	EQSO9	EQHR9	PERA	VORP	STF
2001	NWJ	NYP	21	15	15	69.3	64	14	66	6	2.60	6.63	12.8	2.8	4.9	2.9	8.60	-6.7	-43
2002	PEO	MID	22	12	12	78.3	48	12	72	3	1.38	3.13	8.1	2.0	5.1	1.0	3.83	18.9	17
2003	PMB	FLA	23	20	18	106.0	123	33	69	9	4.92	7.53	13.8	3.7	4.2	2.6	8.92	-19.7	-57
2004	NYY	AL	24	15	10	52.0	74	28	37	15	8.38	8.63	12.6	4.6	6.2	2.5	8.43	-8.0	-19

Breakout: 10%   Improve: 42%   Collapse: 19%

The Cardinals' #1 pick in 2001 was swapped to the Yankees for 10 weeks of Sterling Hitchcock. Pope wasn't able to build on his excellent 2002 performance last year. He's a command guy with a so-so fastball who mixes in a slider and change-up. He doesn't have much upside, but should advance to Triple-A quickly in this system and establish himself as . . . oh, who are we kidding . . . trade bait. He needs to find the 3-4 mph on his fastball that went missing between '02 and '03.

SCOTT PROCTOR

Bats: R   Throws: R   Born: 02-Jan-77   Age: 27

YEAR	TM	LG	AGE	G	GS	IP	H	BB	SO	HR	ERA	EQERA	EQH9	EQBB9	EQSO9	EQHR9	PERA	VORP	STF
2001	VRO	FLA	24	15	15	90.7	73	30	79	8	2.48	4.56	10.5	3.6	5.4	2.2	6.73	9.1	-31
2001	JAX	SOU	24	10	9	49.7	39	31	48	6	4.16	6.44	10.0	6.9	6.0	1.9	6.96	-4.0	-37
2002	JAX	SOU	25	26	25	133.3	111	85	131	10	3.51	6.44	11.0	6.4	6.6	1.6	6.94	-10.8	-34
2003	JAX	SOU	26	17	0	27.0	20	7	24	0	1.00	2.96	8.1	2.6	5.5	0.4	3.36	7.1	8
2003	LVG	PCL	26	24	0	39.3	35	13	35	2	3.66	3.89	8.5	3.4	6.8	0.7	4.10	7.0	2
2003	COH	INT	26	10	0	19.0	13	3	26	2	1.42	2.08	7.8	1.6	9.9	1.6	4.02	6.8	15
2004	NYY	AL	27	11	6	34.3	35	16	27	5	4.73	4.88	9.0	3.9	6.8	1.1	4.94	4.1	3

Breakout: 27%   Improve: 50%   Collapse: 30%

One of two C prospects acquired from the Dodgers for Robin Ventura, Proctor adapted well to relief, dramatically improving his command while pushing his velocity into the high 90s. Before the winter shopping spree, he looked like a candidate for a set-up job. Steve Karsay and Tom Gordon are almost never healthy at the same time, though, so Proctor should have some role in the Yankees' pen.

RAMON RAMIREZ

Bats: R   Throws: R   Born: 31-Aug-81   Age: 22

YEAR	TM	LG	AGE	G	GS	IP	H	BB	SO	HR	ERA	EQERA	EQH9	EQBB9	EQSO9	EQHR9	PERA	VORP	STF
2003	TRN	EAS	21	4	3	21.3	18	8	21	3	1.69	4.05	7.7	4.1	7.2	2.2	5.53	3.4	9
2003	TAM	FLA	21	14	14	74.3	88	20	70	7	5.21	7.92	14.8	3.3	6.2	3.0	9.65	-16.4	-31
2004	NYY	AL	22	15	9	52.3	63	22	38	11	6.35	6.54	10.6	3.6	6.3	1.8	6.34	-1.8	-6

Breakout: 7%   Improve: 44%   Collapse: 30%

One way for small right-handers to get respect is by being international free agents. Ramirez, a Dominican who failed as an outfield prospect, recast himself as a pitcher, worked his way over to Japan and was signed by the Yankees in the spring of 2003. He throws a mid-90s fastball and a power curve, but his performance last year was unimpressive until a 1.44 ERA in the Arizona Fall League opened some eyes. He's best-suited for relief work, although he'll continue to start for the foreseeable future.

AL REYES

Bats: R   Throws: R   Born: 10-Apr-70   Age: 34

YEAR	TM	LG	AGE	G	GS	IP	H	BB	SO	HR	ERA	EQERA	EQH9	EQBB9	EQSO9	EQHR9	PERA	VORP	STF
2001	LVG	PCL	31	19	0	29.3	24	10	37	3	3.38	3.29	8.2	3.6	8.2	1.0	4.27	7.0	5
2001	LAD	NL	31	19	0	25.7	28	13	23	3	3.85	5.11	10.2	4.4	6.9	1.1	5.52	1.3	-10
2002	NAS	PCL	32	43	0	66.7	40	22	90	5	2.70	2.95	6.8	3.4	9.3	0.9	3.42	18.0	18
2002	PIT	NL	32	15	0	17.0	9	7	21	1	2.65	2.76	5.5	3.3	9.9	0.6	2.52	5.1	39
2003	COH	INT	33	15	0	17.0	16	5	21	1	3.71	4.02	9.8	3.4	8.6	0.6	4.48	2.8	14
2003	NYY	AL	33	13	0	17.0	13	9	9	1	3.18	3.24	5.9	4.3	4.9	0.5	3.06	4.0	2
2004	TBY	AL	34	27	4	42.3	41	19	34	5	4.23	4.21	8.4	3.8	7.0	0.9	4.34	8.0	1

Breakout: 24%   Improve: 47%   Collapse: 27%

Reyes continues to pitch well and not get respect. After his 17 innings last year, he now has a career ERA of 4.15 in 267 innings. In fact, his career line looks a bit like a Jack Morris season, with 255 strikeouts and 142 walks (OK, that's high), as well as a 15–8 record. Now 33, Reyes will be back in Triple-A in 2004, waiting for the right combination of injuries and poor performance by Yankee incumbents to create another opportunity. There just isn't millions of dollars' worth of difference between Reyes and Tom Gordon or Paul Quantrill.

MARIANO RIVERA

Bats: R   Throws: R   Born: 29-Nov-69   Age: 34

YEAR	TM	LG	AGE	G	GS	IP	H	BB	SO	HR	ERA	EQERA	EQH9	EQBB9	EQSO9	EQHR9	PERA	VORP	STF
2001	NYY	AL	31	71	0	80.7	61	12	83	5	2.34	2.29	6.5	1.3	8.6	0.5	2.31	28.9	41
2002	NYY	AL	32	45	0	46.0	35	11	41	3	2.74	2.60	6.6	2.0	7.6	0.6	2.69	15.0	27
2003	NYY	AL	33	64	0	70.7	61	10	63	3	1.65	2.08	7.1	1.2	7.8	0.4	2.50	31.1	38
2004	NYY	AL	34	63	0	62.3	57	12	52	6	2.97	3.06	8.0	1.7	7.2	0.8	3.15	19.8	11

Breakout: 24%   Improve: 47%   Collapse: 34%

Rivera is, without question, the best one-pitch pitcher ever. He just keeps throwing that unhittable cutter to different spots and tying up hitters. Even though his career totals are ridiculously low for a Hall of Famer, he has to be taken seriously as a candidate once he becomes eligible by pitching this year. His postseason performance has been otherworldly: 96 innings with an ERA of 0.75. That matters when considering greatness, regardless of how contrived the closer role is. Expect more of the same in 2004.

CHIEN-MING WANG   Bats: R   Throws: R   Born: 31-Mar-80   Age: 24

YEAR	TM	LG	AGE	G	GS	IP	H	BB	SO	HR	ERA	EQERA	EQH9	EQBB9	EQSO9	EQHR9	PERA	VORP	STF
2002	STA	NYP	22	13	13	78.3	63	14	64	2	1.72	4.81	10.7	2.5	4.3	0.9	5.12	5.9	2
2003	TRN	EAS	23	21	21	122.0	143	32	84	7	4.65	5.25	10.2	2.8	4.8	0.9	4.93	4.5	5
2004	NYY	AL	24	22	15	88.0	104	33	45	14	5.43	5.59	10.4	3.2	4.5	1.3	5.59	5.0	-10

Breakout: 11%   Improve: 47%   Collapse: 30%

Wang missed all of 2001 following shoulder surgery. While he seems to have mastered the New York-Penn League (10–5, 2.12 ERA in 27 career starts), he wasn't able to carry that through a full season at Double-A, getting hit hard down the stretch in '03. If the Yankees had more depth, or if Wang wasn't an expensive international signing from Taiwan, he probably wouldn't be listed here. He may need to move to the bullpen to reach the majors, because there's no third pitch so far.

JEFF WEAVER   Bats: R   Throws: R   Born: 22-Aug-76   Age: 27

YEAR	TM	LG	AGE	G	GS	IP	H	BB	SO	HR	ERA	EQERA	EQH9	EQBB9	EQSO9	EQHR9	PERA	VORP	STF
2001	DET	AL	24	33	33	229.3	235	68	152	19	4.08	4.03	8.5	2.4	5.5	0.7	3.78	39.4	25
2002	DET	AL	25	17	17	121.7	112	33	75	4	3.18	3.09	7.7	2.3	5.3	0.3	3.01	33.3	32
2002	NYY	AL	25	15	8	78.0	81	15	57	12	4.04	4.01	8.8	1.5	6.2	1.3	4.31	13.5	12
2003	NYY	AL	26	32	24	159.3	211	47	93	16	5.99	5.54	11.0	2.5	5.1	0.8	5.08	-10.9	2
2004	LAD	NL	27	28	25	159.3	159	50	99	18	4.07	4.56	9.5	2.5	4.9	0.9	4.56	17.9	5

Breakout: 17%   Improve: 53%   Collapse: 12%

Probably the most unpopular Yankee since Ed Whitson, Weaver ends his pinstriped career with a 5.35 ERA, one unfortunate World Series appearance, and, you'd imagine, one heck of a smile on his face. After Whitson was sent away from New York in 1986, he went on to have a number of good seasons with the Padres. Weaver has been dropped into a great situation in L.A., with a good infield defense in a pitcher's park. His ERA could drop under 4.00 just based on that alone. He's a great fantasy pick in '04.

DAVID WELLS   Bats: L   Throws: L   Born: 20-May-63   Age: 41

YEAR	TM	LG	AGE	G	GS	IP	H	BB	SO	HR	ERA	EQERA	EQH9	EQBB9	EQSO9	EQHR9	PERA	VORP	STF
2001	CWS	AL	38	16	16	100.7	120	21	59	12	4.47	4.75	10.8	1.8	5.0	0.9	4.93	9.1	6
2002	NYY	AL	39	31	31	206.3	210	45	137	21	3.75	3.84	8.7	1.8	5.7	0.8	3.86	39.4	18
2003	NYY	AL	40	31	30	213.0	242	20	101	24	4.14	3.87	9.3	0.8	4.2	0.9	3.93	36.7	10
2004	SDP	NL	41	27	27	174.7	186	37	93	16	3.68	4.03	9.7	1.7	4.3	0.8	4.27	29.5	5

Breakout: 12%   Improve: 76%   Collapse: 0%

For the second time in three winters, Wells broke an agreement with one team to sign with another. This time, it was the Yankees left holding the bag, as Wells returned to his boyhood home in San Diego on a one-year deal for less than $2 million. It's not a good pairing; Wells throws strikes and relies on his defense, and the Padres may have the worst collective range in the NL, certainly in the outfield. That and Wells' back problems could combine to make this a forgettable season for Boomer.

GABE WHITE   Bats: L   Throws: L   Born: 20-Nov-71   Age: 32

YEAR	TM	LG	AGE	G	GS	IP	H	BB	SO	HR	ERA	EQERA	EQH9	EQBB9	EQSO9	EQHR9	PERA	VORP	STF
2001	COL	NL	29	69	0	67.7	70	26	47	18	6.25	5.45	9.0	3.1	5.2	1.9	5.57	1.1	-37
2002	CIN	NL	30	62	0	54.3	49	10	41	3	2.98	3.12	8.3	1.4	5.9	0.5	3.23	14.3	16
2003	CIN	NL	31	34	0	34.3	36	6	23	5	3.94	4.09	9.3	1.4	5.5	1.4	4.55	6.5	-11
2003	NYY	AL	31	12	0	12.3	8	2	6	2	4.39	3.00	5.2	1.5	4.5	1.5	2.81	0.9	-10
2004	NYY	AL	32	67	0	38.7	41	9	23	6	4.46	4.60	9.3	2.1	5.3	1.3	4.62	6.0	-10

Breakout: 24%   Improve: 48%   Collapse: 30%

Things you do when you have far too much money and time on your hands: build planes that won't fly; purchase media companies; make bad porn and release it on the Internet; give away a million bucks for an injured pitcher. The Yankees bought—excuse me, "traded for"—White in early August even though he was still on the DL. He made 12 appearances for them and lost whatever role he might have had to waiver claim Felix Heredia. White throws strikes and isn't as nasty on lefties as his perpetual placement in the specialist role would have you believe.

Oakland Athletics

Stop me if you've heard this one. It's about a financially constrained club that's a perpetual second banana in a two-team market. The front office talent is generally and rightfully regarded as the very best in baseball. During the second half of the season, the team plays like it's possessed by the '27 Yankees, and romps through a difficult schedule like a hot knife through butter. The team makes the playoffs and builds an early lead in the first postseason series, only to lose the series to a Big Market East Coast team with an enormous payroll. Then, after the season, the story around the club becomes the impending departure of one of its biggest stars, a recent MVP, because he's simply going to be too expensive to retain.

OK, so there was a little variance. The Oakland A's played well in both halves of the season, instead of spending the first 10 weeks digging a hole to climb out of. That's something of a change from the previous two years (see table 1).

Is it just dumb luck that the A's tend to clean up after the All-Star break? Probably not. Despite the financial limitations that go with the job, the A's front office always seems to find a stretch-drive deal to improve the club. Sometimes, the move is to bring up a Tim Hudson or a Barry Zito. Sometimes, it's grabbing Ray Durham from the White Sox, or Jose Guillen to provide some much-needed right-handed power. Billy Beane, Paul DePodesta, David Forst, and the entire crew in the A's front office do a better job of managing information about who's available and what the players are likely to do on the field than anyone else. While the A's main competition in the Emerald City contemplates their navel as the trade deadline passes, counting profits and watching the Mariner offense nosedive, the A's find a way to identify their key weakness and get the help they need.

Once again this season, the help the A's needed was a bat, hence the trade for Guillen. It's a little strange that the A's get criticized by some in the media for depending too much on the three-run homer; the same pundits who make that claim always talk about the merits of pitching and defense, seemingly oblivious to the fact that pitching and defense are precisely what the A's are constructed on. They were second in the AL in defensive efficiency, led by Eric Chavez, who had one of the greatest defensive seasons ever by a third baseman. On the mound, the A's served up tons of ground balls and strikeouts, which led to the team allowing the second fewest runs in the AL,

ATHLETICS PROSPECTUS

2003 record: 96–66; First place, AL West; Lost to Red Sox in Division Series

Pythagenport record: 94–68

Runs scored per game: 4.7 (9th in AL)

Runs allowed per game: 4.0 (2nd in AL)

Team EqA: .255 (8th in AL)

2003 Batters Age: 28.5 (5th youngest in AL)

2003 Pitchers Age: 27.6 (3rd youngest in AL)

Ballpark: Network Associates Coliseum; Neutral park; Park Factor of 1.003

2003: Amidst rumors of Billy Beane leaving town, the team won another divisional pennant before flopping in the playoffs.

2004: These aren't your father's walk-and-homer Athletics, but the best pitching staff in the West should be enough for a repeat.

with an assist from the massive foul ground and offense-dampening effects of the Oakland Coliseum. Beane's pre-2003 acquisition of Chris Singleton was driven almost entirely by Singleton's ability to cover ground in the outfield; defense is obviously of tremendous importance to the A's. Sometimes, you can't please the Luddites.

Offensively, though, the A's were no great shakes. Erubiel Durazo, whom the Diamondbacks estimated was worth slightly less than Elmer "5.07" Dessens, was acceptable but not overwhelming offensively. Mark Ellis, Scott Hatteberg, and Miguel Tejada all regressed a bit towards the mean, and the rotation of A's outfielders was a mixture of great and mediocre, with a heaping helping of atrocious. The biggest disappointments came from Jermaine Dye, whose game has never been the same since his broken leg, and the execrable Terrence Long, who managed to crest a .300 on-base percentage during only two of the season's six months, despite playing 140 games. Only one A's regular, Durazo, had an OBP higher than .350, and the virtues of patience espoused so consistently by the A's organization were practiced only by Durazo, and to a lesser extent, Hatteberg and Chavez. Oakland got to the postseason, but it was in spite of their offense, not because of it.

The 2004 A's will look considerably different than the 2003 edition. They've improved their outfield offense

TABLE 1. A'S SECOND HALF VS. FIRST HALF, 2001–2003

Year	Pre-Break WP	Post-Break WP
2001	.506	.773
2002	.568	.716
2003	.581	.609

and defense through the additions of Bobby Kielty from Toronto, and Mark Kotsay from San Diego. Kielty's plate discipline and power will be a welcome addition to the club, as will Kotsay's defense and broad offensive skill set. Catcher remained open at the time of this writing, but there are some decent options available in the second and third tier of the free agent market, and the cost of Ted Lilly and Ramon Hernandez for the marginal gains of Kielty and Kotsay over Long and Singleton is a reasonable price to pay. The most obvious change will be at short, where Miguel Tejada will be replaced by Bobby Crosby, who's likely to make A's fans forget about Tejada by mid-2005. The offense should be able to improve, possibly substantially, on the 768 runs scored in 2003.

On the mound, the A's will feature a rotation that induces night sweats in opposing hitting coaches. Ted Lilly's gone, but the front three of Hudson, Mulder, and Zito are still in place, joined by Rich Harden, who will likely claw his way into the #2 slot in the rotation by August. Harden's every bit the pitching prospect Zito and Hudson were, and will fill the #4 spot with ease.

The fifth spot in the rotation looked like a question mark until Oakland traded for Mark Redman, then signed him to a three-year contract. Redman was one of the National League's best lefties for much of 2003, before faltering a bit in the season's dog days and in the playoffs with Florida; that he was one of the most overworked pitchers in baseball as measured by BP's Pitcher Abuse Points (found at www.baseballprospectus.com) may have played a role in his struggles. Nonetheless, if Redman can return to the form he showed through most of '03, he'll allow the A's to ease Harden into the flow. There are concerns that Mark Mulder's hip fracture may be slow to heal. Justin Duchscherer and Mike Wood would likely get the call if Mulder's rehab goes slower than expected, both surviving through the use of a middling fastball and an assortment of pitches that move down and out of the strike zone. The rotation remains the bedrock on which the club is built, and it could be even better this season.

The bullpen's a different story. The anchor of the 2003 pen was the incredible Keith Foulke, but he bolted for a three-year deal with Boston. The A's still have Chad Bradford from the right side and Ricardo Rincon from the left;

they're also in the unfortunate position of being committed to Jim Mecir for one more year at $3.3 million. That wouldn't be so bad if Mecir were younger and/or healthier, but his performance has declined, and even though he's likely to rebound somewhat from a very bad 2003, he's not likely to be much better than really expensive filler. The A's will probably hope Chad Harville, now fully recovered from his injuries, steps up and become a reliable arm. The bullpen looks like Oakland's biggest weakness. And if you're going to pick one place to have a relative weakness, the bullpen's a good one, especially with Beane's ability to pick up good arms cheaply through the rest of the off-season and in-season via various scrap heaps. With limited resources, you do have to pick your spots.

The coaching staff looks dramatically different than it did just 12 months ago. Ken Macha's bench coach, Terry Francona, will manage the Boston Red Sox, while Oakland's professorial pitching coach, Rick Peterson, reunites with Art Howe at Shea Stadium. Former A's junkballer Curt Young takes over as pitching coach, leading some in baseball to predict a drop-off in the performance of the A's rotation. "People don't understand how much those guys relied on Rick Peterson," said one AL GM, "and there's no question there's going to be a drop-off in that staff." It's probably not that cut and dried; the effects of various coaches has never really been definitively studied, and it's hard to believe that pitchers like Hudson, Bradford, and Zito don't have the capability to perform at their best under another coach—especially one imbued with Peterson's teachings, as Young is.

The A's are well positioned for another run at the postseason. They still have the best rotation in the division, and possibly in baseball, even after Boston's acquisition of Curt Schilling. Miguel Tejada's departure will be adequately covered by Bobby Crosby, the influx of new outfielders and the departure of Terrence Long should lead to increased run scoring. Beane, DePodesta, and the rest of the A's front office haven't fallen victim to the delusion that activity in the off-season is equal to improvement in the off-season: The moves that have been made make sense from a baseball perspective, and address the A's most pressing needs. Few teams, if any, are better at using baseball's discard pile as a source of inexpensive and underutilized talent, and the A's expect to have one-time pile pickups Billy McMillon and Adam Melhuse back, anchoring baseball's most underrated pinch-hitting corps. In the minors, they have Crosby ready now, and hope Joe Blanton will be able to join the team in August, à la Hudson and Zito. A step behind those two are Omar Quintanilla and Jeremy Brown, both of whom should move up on prospect lists during the 2004 season. Overall, the A's are in good shape, still well-run, and remain the favorites to win the AL West.

If A's fans need something to worry about, they should focus on ownership and the front office. The Hofmann/Schott ownership group has always been fairly parsimonious; it's been the front office staff, led by Beane after tutelage from his GM predecessor Sandy Alderson, that has excelled at putting a winning team on the field. But as anyone who constructs a payroll on a regular basis knows, you can't grow or sustain a business if you don't keep excellent people happy. And it's hard to believe that any exec in the A's front office qualifies as ecstatic.

Any free agent considering Oakland has to know that there's a good chance that Beane, DePodesta, and Forst may all be gone, possibly as early as this year. People who are great at what they do need to have great projects to work on, and the resources they need to do their job. Great engineers gravitate towards interesting problems. Great product managers move heaven and earth to work on fantastic, cutting-edge products. Does any reasonable person think that, with all the ownership churn in baseball, and the number of teams who could use the services of a Billy Beane, that he or any of the A's gifted staff is going to hang around instead of going where they have more money to spend and an ownership group more dedicated to the team on the field? This isn't rocket science. The rumors are already flying. Rebuilding a front office like the A's currently have could be far more challenging than building a winner on the field. If two or three key decisions or breaks go the wrong way, it could be 1977 all over again in Oakland.

With all due respect to Mickey Klutts, that's not a scenario A's fans are particularly sanguine about. With Arte Moreno taking over in Anaheim, Hiroshi Yamauchi running a tight ship on the business side in Seattle, and Tom Hicks clearly willing to spend money in Texas, Oakland has a persistent handicap in the AL West. For the last several years, Beane, DePodesta, and the rest of the A's front office have done a great job patching together a fantastic team despite having fewer people and less money to work with than their opponents. But the rest of baseball knows how important those people are to Oakland, and they know they could succeed elsewhere. Beane turned down the position in Boston last year; he probably won't turn down the next offer, especially if it comes from a team like the Dodgers, who do need a new GM, despite Dan Evans's statements to the contrary. However, Hofmann and Schott aren't ready to rebuild the talent in the front office should there be a mass exodus to greener pastures.

The A's front office is focused on making sure the team on the field is ready to compete for a world championship—we know they'll do their job. The real question is whether or not Hofmann and Schott are prepared to step up and do their jobs—either invest more money in the club, sell it, or develop a system for replacing front office talent that's as solid as the A's current system for replacing on-field talent. They're going to have to do one of those things, and sooner than they'd probably like.

HITTERS

MATT ALLEGRA   RF   **Bats: R**   **Throws: R**   Born: 10-Jul-81   Age: 22

YEAR	TM	LG	AGE	AB	H	2B	3B	HR	BB	SO	SB	CS	AVG	OBP	SLG	MLVR	EQBA	EQOBP	EQSLG	EQMLVR	VORP	DEFENSE			
2001	MOD	CAL	19	153	32	3	2	2	21	61	3	1	.209	.320	.294	-.181	.166	.246	.236	-.526	-22.2	32-LF	-3	13-CF	-1
2001	VAN	NWN	19	273	60	16	2	11	30	104	5	6	.220	.308	.414	.038	.162	.224	.313	-.469	-51.0	70-CF	-2		
2002	VIS	CAL	20	494	139	35	3	20	47	160	9	9	.281	.356	.486	.168	.218	.273	.382	-.245	-14.2	58-CF	-5	55-RF	-5
2003	MID	TEX	21	452	108	22	2	14	33	156	5	2	.239	.299	.389	-.092	.197	.250	.335	-.368	-40.0	115-RF	-2		
2004	OAK	AL	22	253	51	12	1	8	18	78	2	1	.201	.260	.348	-.276	.207	.269	.364	-.269	-12.6	68-RF	-4		

Breakout: 36%   Improve: 62%   Collapse: 14%

Allegra's a future corner OF who can do a little bit of everything. His strike zone judgment has become a significant problem though, including a nearly 5:1 K:BB ratio last year. Still, he was young for the Texas League, and may simply need a little time to consolidate his skills. He's got exciting power potential if he can improve that pitch selection.

JEREMY BROWN   C   **Bats: R**   **Throws: R**   Born: 25-Oct-79   Age: 24

YEAR	TM	LG	AGE	AB	H	2B	3B	HR	BB	SO	SB	CS	AVG	OBP	SLG	MLVR	EQBA	EQOBP	EQSLG	EQMLVR	VORP	DEFENSE	
2002	VIS	CAL	22	187	58	14	0	10	44	49	1	1	.310	.446	.545	.403	.216	.324	.381	-.150	1.4	48-C	-4
2003	MID	TEX	23	233	64	10	1	5	41	38	3	0	.275	.390	.391	.079	.220	.318	.322	-.238	-4.8	61-C	-9
2004	OAK	AL	24	192	41	8	1	4	21	38	1	1	.214	.300	.327	-.224	.220	.311	.342	-.213	-1.0	56-C	-6

Breakout: 16%   Improve: 39%   Collapse: 26%

Yes, he's one of the more famous prospects in baseball, but Brown's performance hasn't lived up to the hype. He's got old player's skills—he draws walks and hits for some pop. But reviews on his defense are somewhat mixed, more positive within the A's organization than outside of it. He'll get the opportunity to spend a year working on making more solid contact; the injury to his left thumb did interrupt a promising season. If he hits .290 at a combination of Double and Triple-A, he'll make it to Oakland pretty quickly. The door's wide open with the big league catching job likely to be stocked on a patchwork basis in the foreseeable future.

ERIC BYRNES   OF   Bats: R   Throws: R   Born: 16-Feb-76   Age: 28

YEAR	TM	LG	AGE	AB	H	2B	3B	HR	BB	SO	SB	CS	AVG	OBP	SLG	MLVR	EQBA	EQOBP	EQSLG	EQMLVR	VORP	DEFENSE			
2001	SAC	PCL	25	415	120	23	2	20	33	66	25	3	.289	.349	.499	.120	.258	.315	.447	-.046	1.1	62-LF	-2	30-CF	-1
2002	SAC	PCL	26	119	31	7	0	4	7	15	5	1	.261	.302	.420	-.066	.235	.278	.387	-.217	-5.3	17-LF	0	13-CF	-2
2002	OAK	AL	26	94	23	4	2	3	4	17	3	0	.245	.297	.426	-.063	.263	.310	.474	-.012	1.0	17-LF	0		
2003	OAK	AL	27	414	109	27	9	12	42	71	10	2	.263	.334	.459	.034	.280	.352	.489	.099	15.3	75-CF	1	32-LF	1
2004	OAK	AL	28	420	110	22	4	16	36	70	11	4	.262	.323	.445	-.003	.270	.334	.465	.023	15.0	110-CF	-5		

Breakout: 23%   Improve: 47%   Collapse: 24%

If there was a streakier player in 2003, he must have been playing in Asia. A's fans, starved for an outfielder to root for, rallied behind the hustling, telegenic Byrnes during the early season. He played an outwardly lively game, and hit the snot out of the ball for two months, including hitting for the cycle against the hated Giants. Then, just as quickly as NBC canned "The Lyon's Den," Byrnes fell off a cliff:

Month	BA	OBP	SLG
May	.356	.405	.625
June	.322	.395	.583
July	.095	.152	.176
Aug	.167	.167	.367
Sept	.208	.333	.340

The A's are notoriously secretive about injuries on their club, and the natural inclination on seeing a performance record like this is to assume that Byrnes had some sort of minor injury—like internal bleeding and multiple fractures—that caused that kind of drop-off.

ERIC CHAVEZ   3B   Bats: L   Throws: R   Born: 07-Dec-77   Age: 26

YEAR	TM	LG	AGE	AB	H	2B	3B	HR	BB	SO	SB	CS	AVG	OBP	SLG	MLVR	EQBA	EQOBP	EQSLG	EQMLVR	VORP	DEFENSE	
2001	OAK	AL	23	552	159	43	0	32	41	99	8	2	.288	.342	.540	.193	.306	.360	.577	.265	62.2	146-3B	20
2002	OAK	AL	24	585	161	31	3	34	65	119	8	3	.275	.349	.513	.166	.296	.370	.553	.235	63.8	138-3B	3
2003	OAK	AL	25	588	166	39	5	29	62	89	8	3	.282	.352	.514	.155	.303	.373	.557	.253	48.9	152-3B	25
2004	OAK	AL	26	542	152	31	3	30	59	90	7	3	.280	.350	.513	.144	.289	.363	.536	.181	50.7	143-3B	7

Breakout: 16%   Improve: 45%   Collapse: 19%

One of the most consistent, yet maddening players in the majors. Chavez is far and away the best defensive 3B in baseball, and has a beautiful left-handed stroke that repeatedly punishes right-handed pitchers. Over the past three years, playing in one of the worst offensive parks in baseball, Chavez has lit up righties at a .306/.375/.579 pace. But against southpaws, he's almost helpless, posting a .229/.278/.395 line. If he can become a league-average hitter against lefties, he'll be a top-tier MVP candidate on a regular basis. As it is, he hasn't gotten that kind of attention, largely because he plays in a park that dampens his offensive numbers, and because he's not a particularly visible player. From the A's perspective, don't sweat the losses of Giambi and Tejada—Chavez is the guy they really want to keep around, and he's a free agent after this season, when he'll make $5.2 million.

BOBBY CROSBY

SS   **Bats: R**   **Throws: R**   Born: 12-Jan-80   Age: 24

YEAR	TM	LG	AGE	AB	H	2B	3B	HR	BB	SO	SB	CS	AVG	OBP	SLG	MLVR	EQBA	EQOBP	EQSLG	EQMLVR	VORP	DEFENSE	
2001	MOD	CAL	21	38	15	5	0	1	3	8	0	0	.395	.439	.605	.589	.316	.350	.474	.109	2.6		
2002	MID	TEX	22	228	64	16	0	7	19	41	9	2	.281	.336	.443	.083	.236	.283	.380	-.217	-0.9	57-SS	-2
2002	MOD	CAL	22	280	86	17	2	2	33	43	5	0	.307	.394	.404	.148	.242	.308	.319	-.249	-3.9	70-SS	0
2003	SAC	PCL	23	465	143	32	6	22	63	110	24	4	.308	.398	.544	.324	.273	.356	.490	.100	42.3	120-SS	-1
2004	*OAK*	*AL*	*24*	*291*	*74*	*16*	*2*	*10*	*27*	*63*	*8*	*2*	*.254*	*.323*	*.421*	*-.040*	*.262*	*.335*	*.439*	*-.016*	*18.1*	*79-SS*	*-1*

Breakout: 21%   *Improve: 48%*   *Collapse: 26%*

Meet the man who makes Miguel Tejada expendable. Crosby's capable defensively, hits well, and is actually fairly reminiscent of Tejada at the same age. With Tejada off to Baltimore, Crosby's ready to step in and contribute at a reasonable level immediately. He'll hit for some average, moderate power, and draw a few more walks than Tejada. Crosby's a quality ballplayer, and can contribute on a potential championship club. Offensively, his peak should look something like .300/.380/.520 in a neutral park.

ERUBIEL DURAZO

DH   **Bats: L**   **Throws: L**   Born: 23-Jan-74   Age: 30

YEAR	TM	LG	AGE	AB	H	2B	3B	HR	BB	SO	SB	CS	AVG	OBP	SLG	MLVR	EQBA	EQOBP	EQSLG	EQMLVR	VORP	DEFENSE	
2001	ARI	NL	27	175	47	11	0	12	28	49	0	0	.269	.376	.537	.190	.266	.371	.531	.175	13.1	31-1B	-1
2002	ARI	NL	28	222	58	12	2	16	49	60	0	1	.261	.399	.550	.276	.258	.390	.547	.220	19.5	50-1B	-2
2003	OAK	AL	29	537	139	29	0	21	100	105	1	1	.259	.377	.430	.064	.276	.393	.465	.134	26.0	31-1B	-7
2004	*OAK*	*AL*	*30*	*401*	*102*	*21*	*1*	*20*	*64*	*84*	*1*	*1*	*.254*	*.358*	*.460*	*.067*	*.262*	*.371*	*.480*	*.097*	*22.6*		

Breakout: 13%   *Improve: 39%*   *Collapse: 20%*

OK, so the emancipation proclamation was read, and Durazo certainly wasn't bad, but he wasn't all that tremendous, either. Defensively, it was clear from inning one that he was downright awful at first base, to the point where you don't want him manning the bag at all. With the bat, he was OK, drawing 100 walks, but not hitting for the kind of average and power the A's were looking for. On the bright side, he was healthy, and at times, he looked like an unchained beast at the plate. Look for an improvement, particularly in HR, in 2004.

JERMAINE DYE

RF   **Bats: R**   **Throws: R**   Born: 28-Jan-74   Age: 30

YEAR	TM	LG	AGE	AB	H	2B	3B	HR	BB	SO	SB	CS	AVG	OBP	SLG	MLVR	EQBA	EQOBP	EQSLG	EQMLVR	VORP	DEFENSE	
2001	KCR	AL	27	367	100	14	0	13	30	68	7	1	.272	.337	.417	-.022	.282	.347	.433	.013	7.5	85-RF	0
2001	OAK	AL	27	232	69	17	1	13	27	44	2	0	.297	.373	.547	.263	.316	.391	.590	.343	24.9	61-RF	2
2002	OAK	AL	28	488	123	27	1	24	52	108	2	0	.252	.336	.459	.055	.274	.354	.503	.116	23.1	101-RF	-3
2003	OAK	AL	29	221	38	6	0	4	25	42	1	0	.172	.265	.253	-.426	.190	.282	.285	-.375	-22.2	52-RF	7
2004	*OAK*	*AL*	*30*	*281*	*68*	*14*	*1*	*10*	*29*	*56*	*1*	*1*	*.242*	*.317*	*.407*	*-.078*	*.249*	*.328*	*.425*	*-.056*	*3.8*	*77-RF*	*-1*

Breakout: 30%   *Improve: 60%*   *Collapse: 20%*

The contract light's at the end of the tunnel. Dye's never been the same since breaking his leg during that fateful playoff game. He doesn't have the same kind of torque in his swing, he doesn't cover as much ground in the outfield, and he lacks the grace and fluidity he showed before he got hurt. There were no hopeful signs in his performance record; he failed to reach a .200 average during any month of the season, and the only value he really had on the field was in the form of his arm. Hopefully, he'll be at least closer to healthy, since the A's will likely have more than 20% of their payroll—$11 million—going to Dye during the 2004 season. There are rumors of Billy Beane possibly being able to ship Dye's contract out of town; if that occurs, Beane should be immediately inducted into Cooperstown.

MIKE EDWARDS

LF/RF   **Bats: R**   **Throws: R**   Born: 24-Nov-76   Age: 27

YEAR	TM	LG	AGE	AB	H	2B	3B	HR	BB	SO	SB	CS	AVG	OBP	SLG	MLVR	EQBA	EQOBP	EQSLG	EQMLVR	VORP	DEFENSE			
2001	MHV	NYP	24	71	26	5	0	6	12	7	0	1	.366	.464	.690	.679	.230	.308	.432	-.102	1.1				
2001	AKR	EAS	24	111	37	7	3	6	13	26	0	0	.333	.403	.613	.474	.278	.346	.513	.120	7.2	17-1B	0		
2002	CHT	SOU	25	424	130	19	2	11	41	57	9	11	.307	.381	.439	.195	.266	.319	.394	-.107	-5.4	54-RF	-9	42-1B	-1
2002	LOU	INT	25	57	23	5	1	2	6	9	0	0	.404	.460	.632	.636	.362	.413	.586	.429	9.4				
2003	SAC	PCL	26	436	130	23	4	14	60	78	5	2	.298	.390	.466	.197	.266	.350	.423	-.009	6.0	65-LF	2	21-RF	-2
2004	*OAK*	*AL*	*27*	*189*	*48*	*9*	*1*	*6*	*17*	*33*	*1*	*1*	*.256*	*.325*	*.418*	*-.039*	*.264*	*.337*	*.437*	*-.015*	*7.2*	*53-LF*	*-2*		

Breakout: 22%   *Improve: 39%*   *Collapse: 36%*

Nice acquisition by the A's. Edwards gets no attention, but take a look at his performance record. He hits for a little bit of average, draws a few walks, and hits for some power, all while playing acceptably in a corner OF spot. With Beane overhauling the A's outfield this off-season, it's unlikely Edwards will get the opportunity to play in Oakland. If Detroit or Tampa wanted to take a chance on a guy like Edwards for a fourth OF spot, they wouldn't be disappointed.

MARK ELLIS 2B **Bats: R** **Throws: R** Born: 06-Jun-77 Age: 27

YEAR	TM	LG	AGE	AB	H	2B	3B	HR	BB	SO	SB	CS	AVG	OBP	SLG	MLVR	EQBA	EQOBP	EQSLG	EQMLVR	VORP	DEFENSE
2001	SAC	PCL	24	472	129	38	0	10	54	78	21	7	.273	.354	.417	.001	.241	.315	.369	-.167	5.0	130-SS 0
2002	SAC	PCL	25	84	25	10	1	0	6	13	4	0	.298	.372	.440	.118	.274	.340	.405	-.046	3.7	21-SS 2
2002	OAK	AL	25	345	94	16	4	6	44	54	4	2	.272	.361	.394	.029	.295	.381	.433	.085	23.9	83-2B -11
2003	OAK	AL	26	553	137	31	5	9	48	94	6	2	.248	.316	.371	-.131	.265	.333	.399	-.074	3.4	147-2B -4
2004	OAK	AL	27	458	117	23	3	9	43	74	8	3	.255	.325	.378	-.092	.263	.336	.395	-.071	15.4	122-2B -2

Breakout: 18% Improve: 45% Collapse: 19%

One thing about the A's front office is that they actually have some pretty interesting internal metrics that they use to value performance. Their defensive system is something they rely on pretty heavily, and usually, it's pretty close to the system we use here at BP. In the case of Ellis, though, the differences are profound. The A's rate Ellis as an elite second baseman defensively, well above the majority of guys at the position. That makes him a valuable player in Oakland's eyes, as the defensive contribution is enough to offset Ellis's limited offensive contributions. Our metrics show him as below-average defensively, making the second base position a candidate for an upgrade, rather than a point of strength. Ellis is a better hitter than he showed in 2003; no matter what he does defensively in 2004, look for an improvement with the bat.

RON GANT LF **Bats: R** **Throws: R** Born: 02-Mar-65 Age: 39

YEAR	TM	LG	AGE	AB	H	2B	3B	HR	BB	SO	SB	CS	AVG	OBP	SLG	MLVR	EQBA	EQOBP	EQSLG	EQMLVR	VORP	DEFENSE
2001	COL	NL	36	171	44	8	2	8	24	56	3	1	.257	.349	.468	.001	.235	.330	.435	-.053	0.1	44-LF 0
2001	OAK	AL	36	81	21	5	1	2	11	24	2	0	.259	.348	.420	.017	.280	.366	.451	.070	4.3	
2002	SDP	NL	37	309	81	14	1	18	36	59	4	6	.262	.343	.489	.162	.280	.354	.528	.157	17.5	69-LF -3
2003	OAK	AL	38	41	6	0	0	1	2	9	0	0	.146	.186	.220	-.638	.171	.209	.244	-.590	-5.5	
2004	OAK	AL	39	139	33	6	1	5	15	31	1	1	.234	.311	.399	-.104	.242	.322	.416	-.084	-0.6	41-LF -1

Breakout: 24% Improve: 58% Collapse: 22%

Not a bad run. Thanks for the memories and the class, Ron. From underachieving second baseman in the Atlanta Braves organization to very productive outfielder for a number of championship teams, Gant was a reliable and productive hitter, particularly against left-handers, who he hit pretty well right until the end. Good luck, Mr. Gant.

ESTEBAN GERMAN 2B **Bats: R** **Throws: R** Born: 26-Jan-78 Age: 26

YEAR	TM	LG	AGE	AB	H	2B	3B	HR	BB	SO	SB	CS	AVG	OBP	SLG	MLVR	EQBA	EQOBP	EQSLG	EQMLVR	VORP	DEFENSE
2001	MID	TEX	23	335	95	20	3	6	63	66	31	11	.284	.415	.415	.139	.224	.331	.335	-.192	-1.9	78-2B 0
2001	SAC	PCL	23	150	56	8	0	4	18	20	17	2	.373	.460	.507	.410	.333	.411	.453	.200	16.9	35-2B -2
2002	SAC	PCL	24	458	126	16	4	2	78	66	26	14	.275	.390	.341	-.002	.241	.344	.300	-.204	-4.0	115-2B -5
2003	SAC	PCL	25	467	143	20	8	3	56	64	32	8	.306	.383	.403	.106	.277	.348	.368	-.080	13.1	110-2B -6
2004	OAK	AL	26	221	55	9	2	3	22	37	10	3	.247	.326	.347	-.133	.255	.338	.363	-.116	9.6	62-2B -4

Breakout: 20% Improve: 41% Collapse: 34%

Think Luis Castillo Unbelievably Freaking Lite, and that's German. He's got tremendous speed, not enough power to keep defenses honest, and is going to have to learn how to play the outfield to have a major league career as a utility guy who lives off his speed.

JASON GRABOWSKI RF/1B **Bats: L** **Throws: R** Born: 24-May-76 Age: 28

YEAR	TM	LG	AGE	AB	H	2B	3B	HR	BB	SO	SB	CS	AVG	OBP	SLG	MLVR	EQBA	EQOBP	EQSLG	EQMLVR	VORP	DEFENSE	
2001	TAC	PCL	25	394	117	32	3	9	61	94	7	4	.297	.394	.462	.176	.262	.354	.410	-.022	19.6	58-3B -9	18-1B 0
2002	SAC	PCL	26	265	78	22	3	12	39	56	6	4	.294	.387	.536	.269	.257	.342	.466	.029	7.4	20-RF -2	14-C -6
2003	SAC	PCL	27	250	73	13	2	9	31	46	7	2	.292	.370	.468	.162	.262	.336	.425	-.035	2.3	45-RF -5	
2004	OAK	AL	28	171	43	9	1	6	18	36	3	1	.249	.321	.426	-.040	.257	.333	.445	-.016	7.0	49-RF -1	

Breakout: 24% Improve: 39% Collapse: 29%

When we talk about readily available substitute players, this is the kind of guy we're talking about. Grabowski's a major league-quality player—maybe even good enough to be a regular under the right circumstances. He can hit for a little average, has some pop with the bat, and has pretty good plate discipline. There are worse players starting all over the place at 1B and corner OF spots in major league baseball, many of whom make a ton of money. When teams like the Devil Rays run Jason Tyner out to the field, the Grabowski family is fully justified in throwing socks at the television in anger.

JOSE GUILLEN
RF   Bats: R   Throws: R   Born: 17-May-76   Age: 28

YEAR	TM	LG	AGE	AB	H	2B	3B	HR	BB	SO	SB	CS	AVG	OBP	SLG	MLVR	EQBA	EQOBP	EQSLG	EQMLVR	VORP	DEFENSE	
2001	DUR	INT	25	119	35	9	0	7	3	28	0	0	.294	.311	.546	.198	.275	.293	.525	.045	3.7	26-RF -1	
2001	TBY	AL	25	135	37	5	0	3	6	26	2	3	.274	.319	.378	-.083	.289	.335	.407	-.040	0.9	36-RF 5	
2002	ARI	NL	26	131	30	4	0	4	7	25	3	4	.229	.279	.351	-.194	.227	.270	.356	-.282	-7.1	28-RF -1	
2002	CIN	NL	26	109	27	3	0	4	7	18	1	1	.248	.299	.385	-.099	.245	.296	.391	-.170	-2.9	19-RF 0	
2003	CIN	NL	27	315	106	21	1	23	17	63	1	3	.337	.387	.629	.454	.335	.382	.636	.421	38.7	61-RF 3	17-LF -4
2003	OAK	AL	27	170	45	7	1	8	7	32	0	0	.265	.313	.459	-.001	.282	.329	.494	.068	2.3	27-RF -1	
2004	*ANA*	*AL*	*28*	*377*	*100*	*21*	*1*	*14*	*20*	*72*	*3*	*2*	*.265*	*.313*	*.435*	*-.031*	*.275*	*.325*	*.467*	*.015*	*10.8*	*98-RF -2*	

Breakout: 11%   *Improve: 35%*   *Collapse: 30%*

A very nice pickup by the A's front office down the stretch—one that caused Mariner fans to curse "Stand" Pat Gillick one final time, particularly when the A's only gave up Aaron Harang and Joe Valentine. Guillen gave the A's the right-handed pop they needed down the stretch, and played pretty well, even through a broken hamate bone. He's a free agent now, and one who's really only had one good year. He's probably not going to play as well next year as he did in 2003, but the Angels bet two years, $6 million on him to find out.

SCOTT HATTEBERG
1B   Bats: L   Throws: R   Born: 14-Dec-69   Age: 34

YEAR	TM	LG	AGE	AB	H	2B	3B	HR	BB	SO	SB	CS	AVG	OBP	SLG	MLVR	EQBA	EQOBP	EQSLG	EQMLVR	VORP	DEFENSE
2001	BOS	AL	31	278	68	19	0	3	33	26	1	1	.245	.333	.345	-.125	.260	.347	.372	-.089	6.3	64-C -29
2002	OAK	AL	32	492	138	22	4	15	68	56	0	0	.280	.375	.433	.108	.303	.395	.473	.172	33.8	83-1B 9
2003	OAK	AL	33	541	137	34	0	12	66	53	0	1	.253	.344	.383	-.058	.271	.360	.414	.001	1.4	125-1B -4
2004	*OAK*	*AL*	*34*	*382*	*99*	*19*	*1*	*9*	*49*	*42*	*1*	*1*	*.259*	*.347*	*.385*	*-.041*	*.267*	*.360*	*.402*	*-.017*	*8.8*	*105-1B -1*

Breakout: 27%   *Improve: 51%*   *Collapse: 23%*

A good ballplayer, but not someone who gives the A's a competitive advantage at first base. Hatteberg works the count, but has only moderate power. The A's made a pretty sizable mistake in signing him to a contract extension in July. He's signed through his age 34 and 35 seasons, with an option on his age 36 season, for about $2.5 million annually. Bad idea. Hatteberg's likely performance over the next two seasons is more likely to resemble his 2003 than his 2002, and the A's will have to make up the ground they're giving at that position elsewhere.

RAMON HERNANDEZ
C   Bats: R   Throws: R   Born: 20-May-76   Age: 28

YEAR	TM	LG	AGE	AB	H	2B	3B	HR	BB	SO	SB	CS	AVG	OBP	SLG	MLVR	EQBA	EQOBP	EQSLG	EQMLVR	VORP	DEFENSE
2001	OAK	AL	25	453	115	25	0	15	37	68	1	1	.254	.319	.408	-.055	.273	.336	.442	-.002	19.8	128-C 1
2002	OAK	AL	26	403	94	20	0	7	43	64	0	0	.233	.315	.335	-.158	.256	.336	.369	-.117	6.0	120-C 8
2003	OAK	AL	27	483	132	24	1	21	33	79	0	0	.273	.335	.458	.047	.291	.352	.492	.114	25.0	133-C 2
2004	*SDP*	*NL*	*28*	*367*	*92*	*19*	*1*	*11*	*34*	*61*	*0*	*1*	*.250*	*.323*	*.395*	*-.091*	*.256*	*.327*	*.415*	*-.065*	*13.0*	*99-C 1*

Breakout: 17%   *Improve: 38%*   *Collapse: 30%*

Look! It's Terry Steinbach! Hernandez is a perfectly fine catcher who hits a lot of balls in the 5–6 hole for singles, and pops the more-than-occasional home run. Defensively, he's solid, and he'll be a nice upgrade for a San Diego team that's grown far too accustomed to seeing the likes of Wiki Gonzalez on the field. Is he enough of an upgrade to give up Kotsay and take on the overpaid, light-hitting Terrence Long? Remains to be seen, but Terrence Long's a pretty bad ballplayer.

DAN JOHNSON
1B   Bats: L   Throws: R   Born: 10-Aug-79   Age: 24

YEAR	TM	LG	AGE	AB	H	2B	3B	HR	BB	SO	SB	CS	AVG	OBP	SLG	MLVR	EQBA	EQOBP	EQSLG	EQMLVR	VORP	DEFENSE
2001	VAN	NWN	21	247	70	15	2	11	27	63	0	0	.283	.359	.494	.262	.209	.263	.372	-.284	-28.8	54-1B -6
2002	MOD	CAL	22	426	125	23	1	21	57	87	4	1	.293	.377	.500	.241	.225	.290	.385	-.204	-15.7	79-1B 0
2003	MID	TEX	23	538	156	26	4	27	68	82	7	4	.290	.372	.504	.210	.233	.306	.419	-.121	-6.2	107-1B -1
2004	*OAK*	*AL*	*24*	*279*	*68*	*15*	*1*	*11*	*25*	*51*	*2*	*1*	*.242*	*.306*	*.419*	*-.080*	*.250*	*.317*	*.437*	*-.059*	*3.1*	*75-1B -1*

Breakout: 42%   *Improve: 64%*   *Collapse: 17%*

He's making his way up. Johnson's been added to the 40-man roster after, and he was great in the Arizona Fall League following a good year at Midland and a four-AB stint at Triple-A. Defensively, he's relatively agile. He'll start the year in Sacramento, and if he continues to make adjustments, he's a candidate to turn into a reasonable prospect. It's not out of the question that he'll have a big 2004, and become the default replacement for Erubiel Durazo if Ruby gets too expensive.

MARK JOHNSON

MARK JOHNSON				**C**			**Bats: L**		**Throws: R**							**Born: 12-Sep-75**				**Age: 28**		

YEAR	TM	LG	AGE	AB	H	2B	3B	HR	BB	SO	SB	CS	AVG	OBP	SLG	MLVR	EQBA	EQOBP	EQSLG	EQMLVR	VORP	DEFENSE
2001	CHR	INT	25	196	53	5	2	4	29	34	2	1	.270	.364	.378	.031	.250	.339	.350	-.141	2.0	47-C -6
2001	CWS	AL	25	173	43	6	1	5	23	31	2	1	.249	.343	.382	-.057	.266	.360	.410	-.008	7.9	55-C 4
2002	CWS	AL	26	263	55	8	1	4	30	52	0	0	.209	.297	.293	-.266	.227	.314	.322	-.242	-4.8	79-C 4
2003	SAC	PCL	27	162	37	11	1	3	35	23	0	1	.228	.375	.364	-.012	.200	.333	.321	-.220	-2.4	49-C -4
2004	*MIL*	*NL*	*28*	*163*	*39*	*8*	*1*	*4*	*21*	*29*	*1*	*1*	*.239*	*.333*	*.364*	*-.120*	*.240*	*.333*	*.365*	*-.131*	*4.4*	*49-C -3*

Breakout: 50%   Improve: 65%   Collapse: 26%

OK, we admit it. He's not going to pan out. Long a favorite of analysts because of his plate discipline and occasional flashes of power, Johnson's never put it all together. He continues to draw walks, but his offensive game everywhere else has been completely flat. He's going to have to accept a minor league gig somewhere and actually hit for a decent average in order to get another shot at a major league job. The Brewers took a flyer, and he's got a shot at a backup job with the anemic Gary Bennett as competition.

GRAHAM KOONCE				**1B**			**Bats: L**		**Throws: L**							**Born: 15-May-75**				**Age: 29**		

YEAR	TM	LG	AGE	AB	H	2B	3B	HR	BB	SO	SB	CS	AVG	OBP	SLG	MLVR	EQBA	EQOBP	EQSLG	EQMLVR	VORP	DEFENSE	
2001	MOB	SOU	26	320	85	18	0	13	89	83	0	0	.266	.431	.444	.223	.207	.345	.349	-.156	-8.8	50-1B -5	20-LF -4
2002	MID	TEX	27	470	129	28	0	24	133	117	2	0	.274	.444	.487	.288	.205	.347	.370	-.126	-7.2	116-1B -8	
2003	SAC	PCL	28	480	133	23	1	34	98	119	0	0	.277	.411	.542	.309	.237	.358	.472	.048	20.1	80-1B 2	
2004	*OAK*	*AL*	*29*	*168*	*37*	*7*	*0*	*8*	*26*	*45*	*0*	*0*	*.220*	*.328*	*.401*	*-.080*	*.227*	*.339*	*.419*	*-.060*	*1.9*	*50-1B -3*	

Breakout: 16%   Improve: 46%   Collapse: 34%

A fan favorite, and there might not be anyone in organized baseball not named Bonds who sees more pitches. Koonce is an extreme take-and-rake hitter, and an indifferent defender around the bag. He's good enough for a bench job in the majors, but it's really hard for a manager to accept the low batting average he's going to put up, even with the homers and the walks.

TERRENCE LONG			**Headache**			**Bats: L**		**Throws: L**								**Born: 29-Feb-76**				**Age: 28**		

YEAR	TM	LG	AGE	AB	H	2B	3B	HR	BB	SO	SB	CS	AVG	OBP	SLG	MLVR	EQBA	EQOBP	EQSLG	EQMLVR	VORP	DEFENSE	
2001	OAK	AL	25	629	178	37	4	12	52	103	9	3	.283	.338	.412	.006	.300	.356	.441	.056	32.7	71-CF 3	61-LF 0
2002	OAK	AL	26	587	141	32	4	16	48	96	3	6	.240	.300	.390	-.108	.264	.323	.432	-.047	15.0	158-CF 6	
2003	OAK	AL	27	486	119	22	2	14	31	67	4	1	.245	.294	.385	-.151	.261	.311	.415	-.096	-12.9	64-LF 3	70-RF 6
2004	*SDP*	*NL*	*28*	*424*	*108*	*23*	*2*	*10*	*37*	*64*	*3*	*2*	*.256*	*.317*	*.391*	*-.103*	*.262*	*.321*	*.411*	*-.077*	*1.0*	*110-LF 0*	

Breakout: 29%   Improve: 60%   Collapse: 18%

On behalf of Oakland A's fans everywhere, *Bon Voyage.* On behalf of San Diego Padre fans everywhere, NOOOOOOO-OOOO!!!! Long's an awful ballplayer. He doesn't hit for average, doesn't have much power, doesn't work the strike zone well, and, best of all, spoke out after the season about how he deserved more playing time. That might be true, if he were playing for say, the Modesto A's. Long's a tweener, and on the low end of even that unchallenging scale. More important, he's shown absolutely no development whatsoever. The A's will absolutely not miss Long in any way, shape, or form, and getting rid of him at all was a major coup for Billy Beane. Instead of Beane, it'll now be Kevin Towers doodling things like "The Top 10 Uses for Terrence Long" on his desktop notepad. Note to Kevin: Paperweight.

BILLY McMILLON			**OF/PH**			**Bats: L**		**Throws: L**								**Born: 17-Nov-71**				**Age: 32**		

YEAR	TM	LG	AGE	AB	H	2B	3B	HR	BB	SO	SB	CS	AVG	OBP	SLG	MLVR	EQBA	EQOBP	EQSLG	EQMLVR	VORP	DEFENSE
2001	DET	AL	29	34	3	1	0	1	2	12	0	0	.088	.162	.206	-.697	.118	.184	.265	-.635	-4.5	
2001	OAK	AL	29	58	17	7	1	0	5	13	1	0	.293	.359	.448	.102	.310	.382	.483	.171	3.3	10-LF -1
2002	COH	INT	30	442	133	32	3	8	59	71	2	5	.301	.391	.441	.182	.276	.360	.411	.001	7.8	71-LF -7
2003	OAK	AL	31	153	41	11	0	6	19	36	0	0	.268	.356	.458	.073	.286	.370	.494	.142	6.8	30-LF -1
2003	SAC	PCL	31	153	51	10	0	8	17	30	1	1	.333	.404	.556	.376	.292	.358	.494	.128	8.7	25-RF -4
2004	*OAK*	*AL*	*32*	*182*	*45*	*9*	*1*	*6*	*20*	*40*	*1*	*1*	*.249*	*.328*	*.411*	*-.048*	*.257*	*.340*	*.429*	*-.025*	*4.2*	*52-LF -4*

Breakout: 18%   Improve: 40%   Collapse: 37%

This is the guy who should be getting ABs in place of that mediocre, expensive ballplayer on your club. McMillon's a fine ballplayer, and one tough SOB, coming back from what should have been career-ending shoulder trouble. He never got the opportunity to start, but when he's been given a shot, all he's done is hit, hit, hit. The A's want to bring him back as a bench player for the 2004 season; if they can't use him, he'd be a productive platoon OF that a lot of clubs could really use. A very underrated player throughout his career—we're downright giddy to see him getting some playing time and making a few bucks.

ADAM MELHUSE   **C**   **Bats: B**   **Throws: R**   Born: 27-Mar-72   Age: 32

YEAR	TM	LG	AGE	AB	H	2B	3B	HR	BB	SO	SB	CS	AVG	OBP	SLG	MLVR	EQBA	EQOBP	EQSLG	EQMLVR	VORP	DEFENSE		
2001	CSP	PCL	29	184	49	10	1	7	31	42	0	1	.266	.378	.446	.028	.214	.320	.357	-.191	-1.1	35-C	-5	
2001	COL	NL	29	71	13	2	0	1	6	18	1	0	.183	.247	.254	-.510	.169	.234	.225	-.564	-7.5	16-C	-6	
2002	CSP	PCL	30	115	40	10	1	6	16	23	2	1	.348	.427	.609	.427	.283	.362	.496	.129	10.8	25-C	-2	
2002	IOW	PCL	30	226	66	19	0	7	28	47	2	3	.292	.370	.469	.149	.259	.329	.421	-.056	8.2	45-C	-4	11-3B -2
2003	SAC	PCL	31	147	42	9	0	3	26	32	0	1	.286	.397	.408	.120	.248	.351	.362	-.102	3.2	27-C	7	
2003	OAK	AL	31	77	23	7	0	5	9	19	0	0	.299	.372	.584	.303	.312	.391	.623	.384	9.5	20-C	0	
2004	*OAK*	*AL*	*32*	*150*	*35*	*7*	*0*	*6*	*18*	*34*	*0*	*1*	*.233*	*.317*	*.403*	*-.088*	*.241*	*.328*	*.421*	*-.067*	*5.3*	*44-C*	*-4*	

Breakout: 24%   *Improve: 46%*   *Collapse: 29%*

Along with McMillon, one of the Ken Phelps All-Stars that provided a lot of offense off the bench. Melhuse is going to have an opportunity to play a bit more now that Hernandez is gone. He'll hit. The A's will likely go out and get a Josh Bard-type, and Melhuse will fill in the gaps as a corner guy, backup catcher, and pinch-hitter. He'll produce in that role.

FRANK MENECHINO   **2B**   **Bats: R**   **Throws: R**   Born: 07-Jan-71   Age: 33

YEAR	TM	LG	AGE	AB	H	2B	3B	HR	BB	SO	SB	CS	AVG	OBP	SLG	MLVR	EQBA	EQOBP	EQSLG	EQMLVR	VORP	DEFENSE	
2001	OAK	AL	30	471	114	22	2	12	79	97	2	3	.242	.373	.374	-.009	.264	.388	.411	.044	28.4	131-2B	0
2002	OAK	AL	31	132	27	7	0	3	20	32	0	0	.205	.314	.326	-.187	.226	.335	.361	-.149	0.9	27-2B	0
2002	SAC	PCL	31	314	78	12	0	6	46	58	10	3	.248	.359	.344	-.073	.223	.319	.314	-.245	-3.9	68-SS	-11
2003	OAK	AL	32	83	16	0	0	2	19	16	0	0	.193	.368	.265	-.196	.217	.388	.301	-.125	-0.7	14-2B	0
2004	*OAK*	*AL*	*33*	*169*	*38*	*7*	*0*	*3*	*26*	*34*	*1*	*1*	*.227*	*.342*	*.334*	*-.133*	*.234*	*.354*	*.348*	*-.116*	*4.5*	*52-2B*	*-2*

Breakout: 39%   *Improve: 65%*   *Collapse: 19%*

About halfway through the 2001 season, Frank Menechino suffered an elbow injury. Since that time, he's been absolutely awful at the plate. His once surprising pop has abated, and his ability to hit for average has gone the way of the dodo. He's now an updated version of Randy Ready towards the end of his career, and he'll be hard-pressed to find a club to give him an opportunity to play a whole heck of a lot. He basically brings two skills to the table: the ability to draw walks, and the ability to passably play the middle infield. The A's brought him back for a year.

ADAM MORRISSEY   **3B/2B**   **Bats: R**   **Throws: R**   Born: 08-Jun-81   Age: 23

YEAR	TM	LG	AGE	AB	H	2B	3B	HR	BB	SO	SB	CS	AVG	OBP	SLG	MLVR	EQBA	EQOBP	EQSLG	EQMLVR	VORP	DEFENSE		
2001	LNS	MID	20	418	129	26	11	14	80	82	10	9	.309	.429	.524	.355	.210	.305	.360	-.219	-6.1	44-2B	-2	27-3B -9
2002	MOD	CAL	21	141	41	7	1	3	20	28	4	3	.291	.383	.418	.137	.222	.298	.319	-.281	-4.6	28-2B	-7	
2002	MID	TEX	21	302	71	15	1	2	38	71	4	2	.235	.323	.311	-.141	.196	.269	.265	-.426	-23.5	83-2B	-18	
2003	MID	TEX	22	469	125	27	2	5	50	99	9	1	.267	.340	.365	-.041	.221	.285	.311	-.318	-19.5	105-3B	-10	16-2B -5
2004	*OAK*	*AL*	*23*	*236*	*52*	*11*	*1*	*5*	*22*	*53*	*3*	*2*	*.218*	*.289*	*.335*	*-.232*	*.225*	*.299*	*.350*	*-.221*	*0.2*	*65-3B*	*-9*	

Breakout: 41%   *Improve: 63%*   *Collapse: 19%*

The A's were happy to grab him from the Cubs, but since coming over, he hasn't really shown much. His power's fallen off, he's been somewhere between bad and yecch defensively, and even his plate discipline's slipped a bit. He needs to spend a year rediscovering his skills to get his career back on track. He's still only 23 years old this season, and if he can hit .290/.400/.500 in the Texas League, he'll be back on the horse.

JASON PERRY   **OF/DH**   **Bats: L**   **Throws: R**   Born: 18-Aug-80   Age: 23

YEAR	TM	LG	AGE	AB	H	2B	3B	HR	BB	SO	SB	CS	AVG	OBP	SLG	MLVR	EQBA	EQOBP	EQSLG	EQMLVR	VORP	DEFENSE	
2002	MED	PIO	21	106	45	6	2	10	12	19	0	2	.425	.508	.802	.984	.269	.320	.510	.063	9.1	18-1B	-1
2002	DUN	FLA	21	45	13	3	0	1	5	11	0	0	.289	.396	.422	.176	.239	.319	.348	-.189	-0.9		
2003	DUN	FLA	22	135	41	11	1	1	10	32	1	0	.304	.361	.422	.206	.264	.309	.386	-.138	-3.6	11-LF	-2
2003	MOD	CAL	22	190	58	9	1	4	21	46	0	1	.305	.394	.426	.170	.240	.305	.339	-.229	-9.2	31-RF	-6
2004	*OAK*	*AL*	*23*	*217*	*52*	*11*	*2*	*6*	*16*	*54*	*1*	*1*	*.239*	*.302*	*.387*	*-.130*	*.247*	*.313*	*.404*	*-.112*	*-0.5*		

Breakout: 19%   *Improve: 50%*   *Collapse: 24%*

The PTBNL in the deal that sent John-Ford Griffin to Toronto, Perry's a similar player who didn't have a particularly good year. He's got a good eye, a stroke reminiscent of former Dodger farmhand Brian Traxler, and limited speed. Defensively, Perry's as adept with the glove as Jon "Jerry Curl" Butcher is at writing and performing the gritty chronicles of the urban street. A long shot to make it to the majors, but he may yet show enough pop to get there.

OMAR QUINTANILLA

OMAR QUINTANILLA   SS   **Bats: L**   **Throws: R**   Born: 24-Oct-81   Age: 22

YEAR	TM	LG	AGE	AB	H	2B	3B	HR	BB	SO	SB	CS	AVG	OBP	SLG	MLVR	EQBA	EQOBP	EQSLG	EQMLVR	VORP	DEFENSE			
2003	VAN	NWN	21	129	44	5	4	0	12	20	7	1	.341	.401	.442	.299	.263	.302	.346	-.210	-0.5	29-SS	-1		
2003	MOD	CAL	21	36	15	3	0	2	3	6	0	0	.417	.462	.667	.748	.306	.342	.528	.165	3.0				
2004	*OAK*	*AL*	*22*	*261*	*65*	*12*	*4*	*4*	*15*	*47*	*5*	*2*	*.247*	*.292*	*.359*	*-.178*	*.255*	*.303*	*.375*	*-.163*	*5.4*	*69-SS*	*-7*		
Breakout: 19%			Improve: 33%				Collapse: 39%																		

The University of Texas product performed well right off the bat, pelting Northwest League pitching, and finishing the year hitting .400 during the last few days in Modesto. Quintanilla's already reasonably polished, has quick hands, and even played decent defense at Vancouver before a quick burst of errors at Modesto. Quintanilla will be fast-tracked: He'll likely start the season at Modesto, but will jump up quickly with a hot start, and a September callup's not out of the question.

OLMEDO SAENZ

OLMEDO SAENZ   PH   **Bats: R**   **Throws: R**   Born: 08-Oct-70   Age: 33

YEAR	TM	LG	AGE	AB	H	2B	3B	HR	BB	SO	SB	CS	AVG	OBP	SLG	MLVR	EQBA	EQOBP	EQSLG	EQMLVR	VORP	DEFENSE			
2001	OAK	AL	30	305	67	21	1	9	19	64	0	1	.220	.294	.384	-.157	.242	.309	.422	-.104	-1.6	21-1B	-2		
2002	OAK	AL	31	156	43	10	1	6	13	31	1	1	.276	.358	.468	.122	.299	.377	.510	.189	10.9	20-1B	1	15-3B	-3
2004	*OAK*	*AL*	*33*	*133*	*32*	*7*	*0*	*3*	*10*	*28*	*1*	*0*	*.242*	*.312*	*.370*	*-.132*	*.249*	*.323*	*.386*	*-.115*	*2.5*	*39-1B*	*-1*		
Breakout: 17%			Improve: 40%				Collapse: 46%																		

Don't completely forget about this guy. During his four years with the A's, he was very productive as a part-time player in three of those seasons, hitting vicious line drives for average and power. He suffered a nasty ruptured Achilles tendon that caused him to miss the 2003 season, but he'll be pounding the pavement looking for a job as a backup corner infielder and right-handed pinch-hitter. He can still hit.

CHRIS SINGLETON

CHRIS SINGLETON   CF   **Bats: L**   **Throws: L**   Born: 15-Aug-72   Age: 31

YEAR	TM	LG	AGE	AB	H	2B	3B	HR	BB	SO	SB	CS	AVG	OBP	SLG	MLVR	EQBA	EQOBP	EQSLG	EQMLVR	VORP	DEFENSE			
2001	CWS	AL	28	392	117	21	5	7	20	61	12	11	.298	.334	.431	.030	.310	.348	.450	.064	21.3	106-CF	3	14-LF	2
2002	BAL	AL	29	466	122	30	6	9	21	83	20	2	.262	.299	.410	-.056	.287	.324	.450	.001	17.7	112-CF	-6		
2003	OAK	AL	30	306	75	24	1	1	26	55	7	2	.245	.306	.340	-.198	.264	.325	.365	-.138	-5.1	83-CF	-1		
2004	*OAK*	*AL*	*31*	*236*	*60*	*12*	*2*	*4*	*16*	*41*	*6*	*2*	*.253*	*.300*	*.372*	*-.143*	*.261*	*.311*	*.388*	*-.126*	*0.9*	*64-CF*	*-3*		
Breakout: 18%			Improve: 40%				Collapse: 36%																		

The real mystery about Singleton's career is where the hell his power went. Early in his career, he had moderate home run power, as well as the power and speed to pile up a few doubles and triples. As time went on, his pop faded pretty dramatically, which is pretty odd considering he was entering his late-20s and early-30s. He's a fairly smart ballplayer at this point, and probably has a few years in him as a fourth outfielder bouncing around the league.

NICK SWISHER

NICK SWISHER   CF   **Bats: B**   **Throws: L**   Born: 25-Nov-80   Age: 23

YEAR	TM	LG	AGE	AB	H	2B	3B	HR	BB	SO	SB	CS	AVG	OBP	SLG	MLVR	EQBA	EQOBP	EQSLG	EQMLVR	VORP	DEFENSE
2002	VAN	NWN	21	44	11	3	0	2	13	11	3	0	.250	.441	.455	.310	.163	.289	.286	-.372	-6.6	12-CF -2
2002	VIS	CAL	21	183	44	13	2	4	26	48	3	1	.240	.341	.399	-.002	.182	.261	.305	-.395	-13.9	38-CF -6
2003	MOD	CAL	22	189	56	14	2	10	41	49	0	2	.296	.427	.550	.377	.205	.311	.385	-.177	-1.8	33-CF -5
2003	MID	TEX	22	287	66	24	2	5	37	76	0	1	.230	.330	.380	-.060	.187	.271	.318	-.355	-18.3	61-CF -8
2004	*OAK*	*AL*	*23*	*256*	*51*	*14*	*1*	*6*	*26*	*70*	*1*	*1*	*.199*	*.279*	*.336*	*-.258*	*.206*	*.289*	*.351*	*-.249*	*-8.7*	*71-CF -10*
Breakout: 33%			Improve: 60%				Collapse: 23%															

Another *Moneyball* Prospect, Swisher played pretty well at Single-A Modesto, but had a tough time when exposed to better pitching in the Texas League. At both stops he was vulnerable to the strikeout, but showed pretty good power to go along with what will end up being corner OF defense. Swisher's a good prospect, but not one of the top OF prospects in the minors. That said, he may well have a big consolidation year and climb the prospect lists.

MIGUEL TEJADA

MIGUEL TEJADA   SS   **Bats: R**   **Throws: R**   Born: 25-May-76   Age: 28

YEAR	TM	LG	AGE	AB	H	2B	3B	HR	BB	SO	SB	CS	AVG	OBP	SLG	MLVR	EQBA	EQOBP	EQSLG	EQMLVR	VORP	DEFENSE
2001	OAK	AL	25	622	166	31	3	31	43	89	11	5	.267	.327	.476	.062	.290	.348	.518	.143	54.1	159-SS -7
2002	OAK	AL	26	662	204	30	0	34	38	84	7	2	.308	.356	.508	.202	.332	.377	.549	.282	80.2	157-SS -9
2003	OAK	AL	27	636	177	42	0	27	53	65	10	0	.278	.340	.472	.070	.295	.357	.505	.145	43.3	158-SS -7
2004	*BAL*	*AL*	*28*	*562*	*157*	*31*	*2*	*24*	*47*	*68*	*7*	*3*	*.280*	*.341*	*.472*	*.076*	*.289*	*.354*	*.495*	*.113*	*46.1*	*146-SS -7*
Breakout: 11%			Improve: 42%				Collapse: 19%															

(continued next page)

Miguel Tejada (*continued*)

Tejada is a very fine player whom the A's did well to let walk. He's got significant power, he's pretty reasonable defensively, and he even shows the occasional flash of plate discipline. But a contract similar to the $72 million deal he got with the Orioles would have cost more than he's worth to the A's, particularly when they have Crosby ready to take over the major league SS job. Tejada might be one of those guys who's very sensitive to the park he's in, and becomes a creature of it. After landing in another pitcher's park in Baltimore, his raw stats may not look markedly different.

PITCHERS

JOE BLANTON
Bats: R Throws: R Born: 11-Dec-80 Age: 23

YEAR	TM	LG	AGE	G	GS	IP	H	BB	SO	HR	ERA	EQERA	EQH9	EQBB9	EQSO9	EQHR9	PERA	VORP	STF
2002	MOD	CAL	21	2	1	6.0	8	6	6	1	7.50	11.81	15.2	11.8	5.1	3.4	11.95	-3.7	-91
2002	VAN	NWN	21	4	2	14.3	11	2	15	0	3.15	4.26	9.9	1.4	5.0	0.0	3.49	1.9	28
2003	KNE	MID	22	21	21	133.0	110	19	144	6	2.57	4.80	10.7	1.9	6.7	1.4	5.38	10.3	13
2003	MID	TEX	22	7	5	35.7	21	7	30	1	1.26	1.87	5.3	2.1	5.3	0.5	2.16	14.0	36
2004	OAK	AL	23	21	15	91.3	95	25	65	13	4.36	4.61	9.3	2.4	6.1	1.1	4.52	12.5	7

Breakout: 13%   Improve: 39%   Collapse: 21%

Far and away the best pitching prospect in the A's system, and one of the better ones in all of baseball. Blanton's got solid but not eye-popping stuff, and very advanced control for a pitcher his age. He has good control of his fastball, a plus curve, and his changeup's still a work in progress. Once he gets that last pitch under control, look out. He could be the next Hudson/Zito in terms of coming up in July and immediately turning into a front-of-the-rotation starter. He'll make Mark Mulder expendable sooner than you think.

MICAH BOWIE
Bats: L Throws: L Born: 10-Nov-74 Age: 29

YEAR	TM	LG	AGE	G	GS	IP	H	BB	SO	HR	ERA	EQERA	EQH9	EQBB9	EQSO9	EQHR9	PERA	VORP	STF
2001	SAC	PCL	26	38	10	116.0	123	44	102	13	5.04	5.42	10.2	4.1	5.8	1.2	5.62	2.2	-23
2002	SAC	PCL	27	46	0	54.7	40	24	64	2	3.13	3.14	7.0	4.5	7.8	0.3	3.34	14.1	17
2002	OAK	AL	27	13	0	12.0	12	8	8	1	1.50	3.09	9.3	5.4	5.4	0.8	5.06	3.3	-8
2003	OAK	AL	28	6	0	8.3	13	2	4	1	7.59	6.75	14.6	2.2	4.5	1.1	7.05	-1.5	-28
2004	OAK	AL	29	24	4	41.7	42	16	30	5	3.98	4.21	9.0	3.3	6.1	0.9	4.61	7.9	-2

Breakout: 27%   Improve: 56%   Collapse: 14%

Yet another lefty who's going to be bouncing around for the next several years. Bowie's got the typical lefty reliever repertoire, and does what he's supposed to do: keep the ball down and away, and let the hitter swing at a pitch he can't drive. He's got some career left as a second lefty, but if he has a great 50 innings some year, and he signs with some team for too many years and too much money, find a way to short that team's stock.

CHAD BRADFORD
Bats: R Throws: R Born: 14-Sep-74 Age: 29

YEAR	TM	LG	AGE	G	GS	IP	H	BB	SO	HR	ERA	EQERA	EQH9	EQBB9	EQSO9	EQHR9	PERA	VORP	STF
2001	SAC	PCL	26	12	0	23.7	15	2	24	0	0.38	1.23	6.5	0.8	6.5	0.4	2.17	10.7	32
2001	OAK	AL	26	35	0	36.7	41	6	34	6	2.70	3.82	10.2	1.3	7.9	1.3	4.81	7.0	7
2002	OAK	AL	27	75	0	75.3	73	14	56	2	3.11	3.36	8.8	1.6	6.5	0.2	3.26	18.0	25
2003	OAK	AL	28	72	0	77.0	67	30	62	7	3.04	3.53	8.1	3.4	7.2	0.7	3.92	22.8	11
2004	OAK	AL	29	55	2	75.3	71	25	57	5	3.10	3.28	8.5	2.8	6.5	0.6	3.72	20.7	5

Breakout: 26%   Improve: 55%   Collapse: 15%

We hope Mr. Bradford understands the compliment we intend when we call him one of the most boring relievers in baseball. All he does is come in and drive right-handed batters to the edge of suicide as they weakly ground out to the left side or hit a tailor-made double play ball. Bradford's extreme submarine delivery makes him both effective and dependable, since he doesn't put a tremendous amount of strain on his elbow or shoulder. Don't be fooled by his ERA; Bradford had a truly great 2003. He was the best reliever in baseball at keeping runners he inherited from scoring—check out the statistical reports at www.baseballprospectus.com for all the details. It'd be nice if he could better handle lefties, but that's small beer given all his other qualities. Chad Bradford just plain rocks.

FRANK CASTILLO

Bats: R   Throws: R   Born: 01-Apr-69   Age: 35

YEAR	TM	LG	AGE	G	GS	IP	H	BB	SO	HR	ERA	EQERA	EQH9	EQBB9	EQSO9	EQHR9	PERA	VORP	STF
2001	BOS	AL	32	26	26	136.7	138	35	89	14	4.21	3.84	8.6	2.2	5.5	0.8	3.86	26.1	14
2002	BOS	AL	33	36	23	163.3	174	58	112	19	5.07	4.85	9.7	3.0	6.0	1.0	4.78	13.1	4
2003	RIC	INT	34	4	3	18.0	23	4	14	1	1.50	4.32	12.4	2.7	5.4	0.5	5.50	2.4	4
2003	SAC	PCL	34	19	16	96.0	104	34	59	12	4.13	5.42	10.9	3.9	4.8	1.7	6.51	1.8	-36
2004	OAK	AL	35	48	14	102.3	114	39	60	17	5.24	5.55	10.0	3.2	5.1	1.3	5.55	3.7	-12

Breakout: 13%   Improve: 38%   Collapse: 31%

The A's picked up Castillo as a castoff from Boston in spring training, and he spent a good chunk of the year in Sacramento chewing up unimpressive innings. He'll spend the spring looking for a spot starter/last guy in the pen gig in Florida and Arizona. He's not that far removed from a couple of acceptable seasons, but it's hard to imagine that he'll be the best option for any specific team. Never really had the year a lot of analysts expected based on his early career, but if he's at the end, it was a pretty good run.

JUSTIN DUCHSCHERER

Bats: R   Throws: R   Born: 19-Nov-77   Age: 26

YEAR	TM	LG	AGE	G	GS	IP	H	BB	SO	HR	ERA	EQERA	EQH9	EQBB9	EQSO9	EQHR9	PERA	VORP	STF
2001	TRN	EAS	23	12	12	73.7	49	14	69	6	2.44	3.01	6.4	2.2	5.6	1.2	3.26	19.8	19
2001	TUL	TEX	23	6	6	43.3	39	10	55	3	2.08	3.86	10.0	2.5	8.2	1.1	4.91	7.7	29
2001	OKL	PCL	23	7	7	50.7	48	10	52	6	2.84	4.15	9.1	2.1	7.0	1.1	4.38	7.7	25
2001	TEX	AL	23	5	2	14.7	24	4	11	5	12.24	9.20	13.5	2.5	6.1	2.5	8.18	-5.9	-28
2002	SAC	PCL	24	14	11	63.0	73	17	52	7	5.57	5.64	10.1	2.7	5.5	1.2	5.13	-0.3	-4
2003	SAC	PCL	25	24	23	155.0	151	18	117	12	3.25	3.98	9.5	1.2	5.8	1.1	4.26	26.0	12
2003	OAK	AL	25	4	3	16.3	17	3	15	1	3.31	4.02	9.8	1.7	8.0	0.6	4.00	3.8	35
2004	OAK	AL	26	23	14	84.0	85	19	56	11	4.13	4.37	9.1	2.0	5.8	1.0	4.18	13.9	5

Breakout: 14%   Improve: 35%   Collapse: 28%

Pitched pretty well for the RiverCats and filled in a little bit in Oakland. Duchscherer doesn't have overpowering stuff; he needs to survive by changing speeds and moving around in the strike zone. With Ted Lilly gone, he'd have been one of the guys in the running for the #5 spot in the rotation, but the trade for Mark Redman likely means more time in Sacramento, unless Mulder's not healthy by Opening Day.

JEREMY FIKAC

Bats: R   Throws: R   Born: 08-Apr-75   Age: 29

YEAR	TM	LG	AGE	G	GS	IP	H	BB	SO	HR	ERA	EQERA	EQH9	EQBB9	EQSO9	EQHR9	PERA	VORP	STF
2001	MOB	SOU	26	53	0	68.7	54	20	75	3	1.97	3.25	9.6	3.1	6.6	0.7	4.51	15.9	-1
2001	SDP	NL	26	23	0	26.3	15	5	19	2	1.37	2.13	5.0	1.4	5.3	0.7	1.94	9.8	16
2002	SDP	NL	27	65	0	69.0	74	34	66	13	5.48	6.25	9.6	3.9	7.3	1.7	5.79	-4.9	-24
2003	OAK	AL	28	14	0	16.0	14	11	9	4	4.50	5.28	8.2	5.9	5.3	1.8	5.80	2.6	-39
2003	SAC	PCL	28	42	0	56.0	40	13	50	4	2.25	3.31	7.3	2.4	7.0	1.0	3.58	13.2	1
2004	MON	NL	29	32	2	43.7	45	19	36	7	4.92	4.40	8.9	3.3	7.0	1.1	4.49	7.0	1

Breakout: 31%   Improve: 51%   Collapse: 23%

Fikac is pretty much a one-trick pony out of the pen, and he's good enough to land a major league bullpen job—he's just never managed to stay effective for any stretch of time in the majors. He was effective in Sacramento, not disastrous in Oakland, and the Expos will give him a chance to crack the back of their bullpen. Worse relievers make millions.

KEITH FOULKE

Bats: R   Throws: R   Born: 19-Oct-72   Age: 31

YEAR	TM	LG	AGE	G	GS	IP	H	BB	SO	HR	ERA	EQERA	EQH9	EQBB9	EQSO9	EQHR9	PERA	VORP	STF
2001	CWS	AL	28	72	0	81.0	57	22	75	3	2.33	2.31	6.5	2.3	7.8	0.3	2.50	28.5	35
2002	CWS	AL	29	65	0	77.7	65	13	58	7	2.90	2.91	7.7	1.5	6.5	0.7	3.18	22.2	18
2003	OAK	AL	30	72	0	86.7	57	20	88	10	2.08	2.38	6.2	1.9	9.1	1.0	2.80	36.1	30
2004	BOS	AL	31	55	1	74.7	67	19	64	9	3.15	2.99	7.6	2.2	7.7	1.0	3.33	24.8	12

Breakout: 36%   Improve: 65%   Collapse: 19%

He's already one of the best relievers ever to play the game, and he did nothing in 2003 but strengthen his credentials. He can throw his fastball into a thimble, with a changeup that makes right-handers beg for a quick and painless death. He'll continue to be one of the best relievers in baseball for the next three seasons in Boston; we had him ranked as the 6th-best reliever in the game last year, and that's really nothing new. An amazing pitcher, we'll be debating his Hall of Fame chances a few years from now.

BEN FRITZ

	Bats: R		Throws: R								Born: 29-Mar-81				Age: 23	

YEAR	TM	LG	AGE	G	GS	IP	H	BB	SO	HR	ERA	EQERA	EQH9	EQBB9	EQSO9	EQHR9	PERA	VORP	STF
2002	VAN	NWN	21	9	9	39.7	29	14	33	1	2.95	5.19	9.1	4.4	4.2	0.8	4.74	1.6	-1
2002	VIS	CAL	21	3	3	17.0	15	6	16	1	3.71	4.60	9.2	4.0	4.6	1.1	5.07	1.7	5
2003	MOD	CAL	22	15	15	77.0	83	34	77	3	4.91	6.17	10.9	5.4	5.9	0.8	5.78	-4.4	3
2004	OAK	AL	23	20	13	69.3	80	45	41	10	6.41	6.78	10.4	5.5	5.1	1.2	6.54	-3.3	-17

Breakout: 13%   Improve: 45%   Collapse: 27%

Fritz struggled in Modesto, but did manage to strike out a hitter per inning. He might begin the season in the California League again—Fritz didn't really look particularly good all season. The movement and velocity on his pitches were both off. If he's going to have a major league career, he needs to take a step forward pretty quickly.

JOHN HALAMA

	Bats: L		Throws: L								Born: 22-Feb-72				Age: 32	

YEAR	TM	LG	AGE	G	GS	IP	H	BB	SO	HR	ERA	EQERA	EQH9	EQBB9	EQSO9	EQHR9	PERA	VORP	STF
2001	SEA	AL	29	31	17	110.3	132	26	50	18	4.73	6.12	11.9	2.0	3.9	1.4	6.06	-6.0	-25
2002	SEA	AL	30	31	10	101.0	112	33	70	9	3.56	4.52	10.0	2.8	6.0	0.7	4.64	11.7	7
2003	OAK	AL	31	35	13	108.7	117	36	51	18	4.22	5.38	10.0	2.9	4.3	1.4	5.39	3.7	-22
2004	TBY	AL	32	32	16	97.7	116	30	48	13	5.05	5.03	10.3	2.6	4.3	1.2	5.07	8.2	-10

Breakout: 11%   Improve: 47%   Collapse: 22%

Another soft-tossing lefty who hopes to end up as a starter in the back of the rotation. Halama's indistinguishable from three dozen other guys whom their agents tout as a possible Jamie Moyer. He won't be completely awful in the rotation, but his value lies exclusively in his ability to chew up a bunch of innings. In a more hitter-friendly park he could post an ERA well into the fives, and he may well get that opportunity, having signed with the Devil Rays.

RICH HARDEN

	Bats: L		Throws: R								Born: 30-Nov-81				Age: 22	

YEAR	TM	LG	AGE	G	GS	IP	H	BB	SO	HR	ERA	EQERA	EQH9	EQBB9	EQSO9	EQHR9	PERA	VORP	STF
2001	VAN	NWN	19	18	14	74.3	47	38	100	3	3.39	5.17	9.0	7.2	6.8	1.1	5.81	3.0	13
2002	VIS	CAL	20	12	12	67.7	49	24	85	4	2.92	4.06	8.0	3.9	6.7	0.9	4.15	10.6	33
2002	MID	TEX	20	16	16	85.3	67	52	102	2	2.95	4.26	7.4	6.3	8.6	0.3	3.98	12.0	53
2003	MID	TEX	21	2	2	13.0	0	0	17	0	0.00	0.00	0.8	0.8	9.0	0.0	0.09	7.5	91
2003	SAC	PCL	21	16	14	88.7	72	35	91	6	3.15	3.92	7.0	4.1	8.9	0.7	3.59	15.9	53
2003	OAK	AL	21	15	13	74.7	72	40	67	5	4.46	4.50	9.0	4.6	8.0	0.5	4.40	11.3	50
2004	OAK	AL	22	25	19	110.3	98	59	104	12	4.33	4.58	8.0	4.6	8.2	0.9	4.50	15.3	14

Breakout: 7%   Improve: 33%   Collapse: 35%

He got a little tired towards the end of the year, but man, what a pitcher this guy's going to be. Tremendous four-seam fastball that he throws as hard as 97–98, a two-seamer that moves a bit more at 92–93, and an improving array of hard breaking stuff and a changeup. Even if the A's actually manage to retain Hudson, Zito, and Mulder, Harden will still be Starter #1A by the start of the '05 season. He's that good.

CHAD HARVILLE

	Bats: R		Throws: R								Born: 16-Sep-76				Age: 27	

YEAR	TM	LG	AGE	G	GS	IP	H	BB	SO	HR	ERA	EQERA	EQH9	EQBB9	EQSO9	EQHR9	PERA	VORP	STF
2001	SAC	PCL	24	33	0	40.7	35	12	55	5	3.98	4.26	8.8	3.1	8.8	1.2	4.55	5.7	11
2002	SAC	PCL	25	24	0	30.0	32	13	26	5	5.40	5.65	9.4	4.4	6.0	1.9	6.08	-0.2	-41
2003	SAC	PCL	26	48	0	57.0	42	21	57	5	2.05	3.27	7.7	4.0	7.7	1.2	4.37	13.5	-5
2003	OAK	AL	26	21	0	21.7	25	17	18	3	5.81	6.43	10.7	6.9	7.3	1.3	6.59	-0.7	-26
2004	OAK	AL	27	21	2	30.0	29	15	25	4	4.36	4.61	8.6	4.2	7.2	1.0	4.81	4.5	0

Breakout: 20%   Improve: 47%   Collapse: 28%

The whole right-handed Billy Wagner thing just hasn't worked out. Harville, once renowned for his small stature and tremendous fastball, pitched well for the RiverCats, but once again didn't look particularly great in Oakland. He still throws very hard, but didn't look completely comfortable with his improving curveball, and occasionally couldn't find the strike zone with a sherpa and a GPS unit. He's out of options, so he has to make the club out of spring training if the A's want to keep him, and he's still a reasonable bet to be a good pitcher in some role. If and when that actually happens is a matter of speculation.

ERIK HILJUS

Bats: R **Throws: R** Born: 25-Dec-72 Age: 31

YEAR	TM	LG	AGE	G	GS	IP	H	BB	SO	HR	ERA	EQERA	EQH9	EQBB9	EQSO9	EQHR9	PERA	VORP	STF
2001	SAC	PCL	28	15	15	101.7	79	26	108	18	3.63	4.01	7.8	2.8	7.0	1.9	4.85	16.7	-10
2001	OAK	AL	28	16	11	66.0	70	21	67	7	3.41	4.24	9.8	2.7	8.6	0.8	4.54	9.6	25
2002	OAK	AL	29	9	9	45.7	52	21	29	11	6.50	6.70	10.2	3.9	5.5	2.0	6.46	-5.4	-32
2002	SAC	PCL	29	9	6	37.7	54	15	30	3	7.64	7.25	13.0	4.0	5.2	1.0	6.61	-6.6	-25
2003	SAC	PCL	30	29	29	174.7	174	52	129	28	4.69	5.82	10.3	3.2	5.8	2.3	6.65	-3.9	-39
2004	*OAK*	*AL*	*31*	*11*	*9*	*52.3*	*57*	*20*	*35*	*10*	*5.57*	*5.89*	*9.7*	*3.3*	*5.7*	*1.6*	*5.75*	*1.3*	*-2*

Breakout: 14%   *Improve: 39%*   *Collapse: 35%*

The A's got the best stretch of his career during the 2001 season, when he capably filled in as a back-of-the-rotation arm for a few weeks. Hiljus is a big guy without great stuff, and he needs to really keep that walk rate down to be successful. He's a long shot to have a career from here on out.

TIM HUDSON

Bats: R **Throws: R** Born: 14-Jul-75 Age: 28

YEAR	TM	LG	AGE	G	GS	IP	H	BB	SO	HR	ERA	EQERA	EQH9	EQBB9	EQSO9	EQHR9	PERA	VORP	STF
2001	OAK	AL	25	35	35	235.0	216	71	181	20	3.37	3.79	8.5	2.6	6.5	0.7	3.82	45.4	27
2002	OAK	AL	26	34	34	238.3	237	62	152	19	2.98	3.61	9.1	2.2	5.6	0.7	3.96	50.7	20
2003	OAK	AL	27	34	34	240.0	197	61	162	15	2.70	3.10	7.7	2.2	6.1	0.5	3.18	74.2	31
2004	*OAK*	*AL*	*28*	*31*	*31*	*215.0*	*213*	*58*	*140*	*18*	*3.54*	*3.74*	*8.9*	*2.3*	*5.6*	*0.7*	*3.84*	*45.6*	*13*

Breakout: 21%   *Improve: 55%*   *Collapse: 13%*

Yes, his strikeout rate has dipped. Yes, he's thrown an awful lot of innings. But consider this: His control's consistently improved since he's reached the majors, to the point now where he's among the stingiest pitchers in baseball in terms of the free pass, in addition to being tough to hit. How has he managed to mitigate the damage from that declining K rate? Why, with the help of his buddy Eric Chavez, of course. Hudson's allowed less than half as many fly balls as ground balls, and ground balls don't fly out of the park. One of the best three or four pitchers in the American League, and fully capable of running off five or six years of Greg Madduxness from 2004–2009 or so.

SHANE KOMINE

Bats: R **Throws: R** Born: 18-Oct-80 Age: 23

YEAR	TM	LG	AGE	G	GS	IP	H	BB	SO	HR	ERA	EQERA	EQH9	EQBB9	EQSO9	EQHR9	PERA	VORP	STF
2002	VIS	CAL	21	18	0	25.7	23	20	22	2	5.95	7.71	9.3	8.9	4.2	1.2	6.40	-5.5	-35
2003	KNE	MID	22	8	8	54.3	45	9	50	1	1.82	3.91	9.9	2.0	5.6	0.6	4.17	9.1	26
2003	MID	TEX	22	19	18	103.3	108	30	75	6	3.75	4.73	9.6	3.2	4.7	1.0	4.92	9.4	6
2004	*OAK*	*AL*	*23*	*19*	*12*	*72.3*	*78*	*32*	*39*	*11*	*5.11*	*5.41*	*9.7*	*3.8*	*4.7*	*1.2*	*5.46*	*5.3*	*-11*

Breakout: 20%   *Improve: 46%*   *Collapse: 19%*

Komine posted a 3.75 ERA at Midland, but his peripheral numbers were less than encouraging. His control has developed some, but he's still not keeping hitters off balance particularly well, and he gave up a large number of unearned runs that don't show up in his ERA. He's got good enough stuff to possibly make it to the majors, but he's going to have to dramatically improve his command in order to have a chance at a big league career.

TED LILLY

Bats: L **Throws: L** Born: 04-Jan-76 Age: 28

YEAR	TM	LG	AGE	G	GS	IP	H	BB	SO	HR	ERA	EQERA	EQH9	EQBB9	EQSO9	EQHR9	PERA	VORP	STF
2001	NYY	AL	25	26	21	120.7	126	51	112	20	5.37	5.22	8.9	3.5	7.7	1.4	4.95	5.0	8
2002	NYY	AL	26	16	11	76.7	57	24	59	10	3.40	3.12	6.4	2.6	6.6	1.1	3.24	20.7	17
2002	OAK	AL	26	6	5	23.3	23	7	18	5	4.64	4.76	8.7	2.4	6.8	1.6	4.82	2.1	-3
2003	OAK	AL	27	32	31	178.3	179	58	147	24	4.34	4.57	9.4	2.8	7.4	1.1	4.70	25.7	15
2004	*TOR*	*AL*	*28*	*27*	*22*	*134.3*	*144*	*46*	*98*	*23*	*5.07*	*4.81*	*9.2*	*2.9*	*6.5*	*1.3*	*4.70*	*15.7*	*8*

Breakout: 5%   *Improve: 34%*   *Collapse: 25%*

Velocity improved late in the year, as did the movement on his curveball. Lilly's always had good peripheral numbers, all the way back to his time as a farmhand in the Los Angeles and Montreal systems. He's still got a chance to be a front-of-the-rotation guy, but more likely, he spends the balance of his career as a #3 starter. He's always going to have an issue with leaving a meaty hanging curve in the middle of the plate against right-handers; the challenge will be making sure that they're solo shots. Traded to Toronto in a deal that brings Bobby Kielty to Oakland, a good trade for both clubs.

JIM MECIR   Bats: B   Throws: R   Born: 16-May-70   Age: 34

YEAR	TM	LG	AGE	G	GS	IP	H	BB	SO	HR	ERA	EQERA	EQH9	EQBB9	EQSO9	EQHR9	PERA	VORP	STF
2001	OAK	AL	31	54	0	63.0	54	26	61	4	3.43	3.56	8.0	3.4	8.2	0.6	3.71	13.8	21
2002	OAK	AL	32	61	0	67.7	68	29	53	5	4.25	4.55	9.2	3.6	6.7	0.6	4.29	7.6	8
2003	OAK	AL	33	41	0	37.0	40	16	25	4	5.59	5.60	10.2	3.8	6.1	0.8	5.02	-0.6	-6
2004	OAK	AL	34	83	0	38.3	40	16	27	4	4.57	4.84	9.3	3.5	6.0	0.9	4.83	4.7	-8

Breakout: 23%   Improve: 44%   Collapse: 29%

As happens with age, the injuries come a little more frequently, take a little longer to heal, and recovery's never 100%. The A's long ago made the mistake of picking up his $3.3 million option for 2004, so they'll hope the stretches of health and effectiveness are more in line with 2001 than 2003. The weakened bullpen could use a mild renaissance.

MARK MULDER   Bats: L   Throws: L   Born: 05-Aug-77   Age: 26

YEAR	TM	LG	AGE	G	GS	IP	H	BB	SO	HR	ERA	EQERA	EQH9	EQBB9	EQSO9	EQHR9	PERA	VORP	STF
2001	OAK	AL	23	34	34	229.3	214	51	153	16	3.45	3.56	8.6	1.9	5.7	0.6	3.54	49.8	35
2002	OAK	AL	24	30	30	207.3	182	55	159	21	3.47	3.65	8.0	2.2	6.7	0.9	3.63	43.3	32
2003	OAK	AL	25	26	26	186.7	180	40	128	15	3.13	3.44	9.1	1.9	6.2	0.7	3.84	57.1	28
2004	OAK	AL	26	28	28	183.7	186	47	121	19	3.76	3.97	9.1	2.2	5.7	0.8	4.02	35.6	13

Breakout: 15%   Improve: 39%   Collapse: 21%

He's not really in the same effectiveness category with Hudson or Zito during a good year, but he's still a very good #3 starter. His hip injury (stress fracture) kept him out of action during the late part of the season and in Oakland's abbreviated postseason. Mulder supposedly would have been ready for long relief had the A's made the ALCS, but no one knows for sure how healthy he is outside of the organization. They're saying he'll be ready for spring training, despite some reports that his hip injury may be lingering.

MICHAEL NEU   Bats: B   Throws: R   Born: 09-Mar-78   Age: 26

YEAR	TM	LG	AGE	G	GS	IP	H	BB	SO	HR	ERA	EQERA	EQH9	EQBB9	EQSO9	EQHR9	PERA	VORP	STF
2001	MUD	CAL	23	53	0	64.7	50	30	102	3	2.36	4.50	10.3	5.6	8.4	1.0	5.71	6.8	0
2002	CHT	SOU	24	21	0	27.0	22	9	38	0	1.33	2.55	9.1	3.3	9.1	0.4	3.93	8.4	33
2002	LOU	INT	24	40	0	40.3	35	18	47	4	4.02	4.54	8.6	4.8	8.8	1.2	4.97	4.4	5
2003	OAK	AL	25	32	0	42.0	43	26	20	2	3.64	4.46	9.6	5.4	4.2	0.4	4.88	9.7	-9
2004	FLO	NL	26	39	0	45.3	45	25	33	3	4.23	4.72	9.1	4.4	5.9	0.6	5.07	4.0	-8

Breakout: 26%   Improve: 54%   Collapse: 16%

Hey, not too bad for a Rule 5 guy. Neu's a good candidate to bounce back considerably and be effective in 2004. Take a look at those K rate: His low rate in 2003 is really an anomaly, and he still pitched pretty well in mop-up duty with the A's. Traded to Florida in the Mark Redman deal, he should find a job with Looper and company signing elsewhere.

JOHN RHEINECKER   Bats: L   Throws: L   Born: 29-May-79   Age: 25

YEAR	TM	LG	AGE	G	GS	IP	H	BB	SO	HR	ERA	EQERA	EQH9	EQBB9	EQSO9	EQHR9	PERA	VORP	STF
2001	VAN	NWN	22	6	5	22.7	13	4	17	0	1.59	3.10	7.1	2.2	3.5	0.4	2.88	5.6	11
2002	VIS	CAL	23	9	9	50.7	41	10	62	2	2.31	3.52	9.4	2.2	6.3	0.6	4.00	10.6	27
2002	MID	TEX	23	20	20	128.0	137	24	100	7	3.38	4.99	10.5	2.0	5.2	1.0	4.91	8.1	10
2003	MID	TEX	24	23	23	142.3	186	32	89	13	4.74	6.20	12.6	2.5	4.1	1.6	6.82	-8.8	-26
2003	SAC	PCL	24	6	6	38.0	47	12	26	1	3.79	5.55	11.6	3.3	5.3	0.3	4.99	0.2	17
2004	OAK	AL	25	18	12	71.0	81	22	39	10	4.93	5.22	10.3	2.6	4.7	1.2	5.23	5.3	-5

Breakout: 10%   Improve: 47%   Collapse: 30%

One of Oakland's more pedestrian pitching prospects, a la Chris Enochs. Rheinecker's already found his command to a large extent, but there's not a lot in his performance record to suggest he's going to be effective in the majors. He doesn't have electric stuff and his peripherals are nothing special. If he's going to have a career in the majors, it's most likely as a lefty specialist.

RICARDO RINCON

Bats: L   Throws: L   Born: 13-Apr-70   Age: 34

YEAR	TM	LG	AGE	G	GS	IP	H	BB	SO	HR	ERA	EQERA	EQH9	EQBB9	EQSO9	EQHR9	PERA	VORP	STF
2001	CLE	AL	31	67	0	54.0	44	21	50	3	2.83	2.68	6.5	3.2	7.5	0.5	2.92	17.4	24
2002	CLE	AL	32	46	0	35.7	36	8	30	3	4.79	3.82	8.4	1.8	7.1	0.8	3.61	7.0	14
2002	OAK	AL	32	25	0	20.3	11	3	19	1	3.10	2.29	5.0	1.4	8.2	0.5	1.73	7.2	39
2003	OAK	AL	33	64	0	55.3	45	32	40	4	3.25	3.71	7.6	5.1	6.4	0.5	3.94	15.5	5
2004	OAK	AL	34	58	0	56.7	54	26	41	6	4.07	4.31	8.6	3.9	6.2	0.8	4.53	9.4	-6

Breakout: 28%   Improve: 52%   Collapse: 21%

Another year under the belt, as Jesse Orosco Mark II moves happily along his career path. Like Orosco, Rincon mows down lefties, yielding a torrid .205/.251/.305 line to them over the past three years. He backs off considerably against righties these days, pitching around even average hitters. The A's inked him to a two-year, $3.65 million deal. No truth to the rumor that Beane was close to moving him for Brian Giles.

BERT SNOW

Bats: R   Throws: R   Born: 23-Mar-77   Age: 27

YEAR	TM	LG	AGE	G	GS	IP	H	BB	SO	HR	ERA	EQERA	EQH9	EQBB9	EQSO9	EQHR9	PERA	VORP	STF
2002	MID	TEX	25	24	0	21.7	21	11	29	1	4.98	5.59	11.2	5.6	8.8	0.9	6.04	0.0	-12
2002	VIS	CAL	25	12	1	18.0	8	7	25	1	1.00	1.69	6.2	4.5	7.3	1.1	3.74	7.0	-4
2003	MID	TEX	26	32	0	37.0	34	27	41	2	6.08	6.27	9.8	8.5	7.4	1.1	6.39	-2.5	-41
2003	SAC	PCL	26	12	0	15.3	18	4	5	3	5.29	6.43	11.6	2.6	2.6	2.6	7.56	-1.3	-83
2004	OAK	AL	27	14	1	17.3	21	12	10	3	6.66	7.05	11.0	5.9	5.2	1.3	6.99	-0.3	-26

Breakout: 24%   Improve: 38%   Collapse: 39%

He'll be in the running for a spot at the back end of the bullpen. Snow's got good stuff, but has occasional problems finding the strike zone. Until he can find some way to consistently throw at least one of his pitches for strikes, he's not going to have any semblance of a career.

STEVE SPARKS

Bats: R   Throws: R   Born: 02-Jul-65   Age: 38

YEAR	TM	LG	AGE	G	GS	IP	H	BB	SO	HR	ERA	EQERA	EQH9	EQBB9	EQSO9	EQHR9	PERA	VORP	STF
2001	DET	AL	36	35	33	232.0	244	64	116	22	3.65	3.99	8.6	2.3	4.1	0.8	3.94	40.8	7
2002	DET	AL	37	32	30	189.0	238	67	98	23	5.52	5.45	10.6	2.9	4.4	1.0	5.24	3.1	-5
2003	DET	AL	38	42	0	89.7	95	34	49	11	4.72	4.83	9.0	3.2	4.8	1.0	4.62	0.0	-11
2003	OAK	AL	38	9	0	17.3	19	3	5	2	5.72	4.96	10.5	1.7	2.8	1.1	4.98	0.4	-23
2004	ARI	NL	38	30	15	91.3	104	35	47	11	5.10	4.88	9.9	3.0	4.3	0.9	4.77	8.5	-10

Breakout: 31%   Improve: 52%   Collapse: 30%

A very good pickup by the A's front office, nabbing some injury insurance for nothing. There are no surprises here; Sparks is a knuckleballer, with all the plusses and minuses that come with that label. Just as you know what you're going to get when you hear the term "CBS Made-for-TV Movie," you know what you're going to get when you hear "Steve Sparks." Arizona signed him to a one-year deal, where he'll serve as injury insurance and make a few hundred thousand bucks. It's all good.

MIKE WOOD

Bats: R   Throws: R   Born: 26-Apr-80   Age: 24

YEAR	TM	LG	AGE	G	GS	IP	H	BB	SO	HR	ERA	EQERA	EQH9	EQBB9	EQSO9	EQHR9	PERA	VORP	STF
2001	VAN	NWN	21	5	2	21.7	17	4	24	0	1.24	3.32	10.4	2.4	5.2	0.5	4.44	4.8	22
2001	MOD	CAL	21	10	9	58.3	46	10	52	6	3.09	3.88	8.6	2.0	4.6	1.7	4.81	10.2	3
2002	MOD	CAL	22	7	7	41.3	41	6	50	4	3.49	5.06	11.3	1.7	6.3	1.7	5.99	2.2	4
2002	MID	TEX	22	17	17	105.7	103	29	63	8	3.15	4.41	9.5	2.8	3.9	1.3	5.02	13.0	0
2003	SAC	PCL	23	16	16	91.3	87	23	59	5	3.06	4.07	8.7	2.6	5.2	0.7	3.96	14.7	19
2003	OAK	AL	23	7	1	13.7	24	7	15	1	10.51	9.45	16.2	4.1	9.4	0.7	7.51	-8.0	19
2004	OAK	AL	24	21	15	87.0	93	29	53	13	4.73	5.00	9.6	2.9	5.2	1.2	4.94	9.5	-2

Breakout: 13%   Improve: 47%   Collapse: 29%

Keeps the ball down, down, down. When he doesn't, it goes deep, deep, deep. Wood doesn't have overpowering stuff—he's kind of in the Vicente Padilla mode of pitchers, throwing eight flavors of a ball that moves down and/or away. He keeps hitters off balance, and he's still learning his craft. Wood's been underestimated along the way, but he's managed to be successful. He could well have a pretty good career as either a starter or a swingman. In many ways, the A's are perfect for him: They value infield defense, and so does he.

ED YARNALL   Bats: L   Throws: L   Born: 04-Dec-75   Age: 28

YEAR	TM	LG	AGE	G	GS	IP	H	BB	SO	HR	ERA	EQERA	EQH9	EQBB9	EQSO9	EQHR9	PERA	VORP	STF
2001	ORX	JPP	25	15	14	73.3	52	47	82	7	3.93	4.13	7.2	5.3	8.5	0.8	4.07	11.4	20
2002	ORX	JPP	26	25	1	164.3	149	62	120	13	3.61	4.66	9.2	4.4	5.2	0.8	4.77	15.5	0
2003	SAC	PCL	27	18	13	64.7	72	30	46	6	3.76	5.34	11.3	5.0	5.6	1.4	6.52	1.7	-31
2004	OAK	AL	28	15	9	51.7	55	27	34	7	5.37	5.68	9.6	4.4	5.7	1.2	5.68	2.5	-7

Breakout: 24%   Improve: 56%   Collapse: 23%

Here we are, four years removed from Columbus, and Yarnall's pretty much at the same point as he was then. He's still young enough to have a career, still throws lefty, and could go either way if given a major role on a major league club. His velocity's not what it once was, but he's adapted fairly well. He's in the Halama/Hiljus/Harang class of pitchers, and in this organization, he's probably not going to get a clear shot at the big league level. Still, there are clubs paying for Rick Reed's services, so there's a place for Ed Yarnall somewhere.

BARRY ZITO   Bats: L   Throws: L   Born: 13-May-78   Age: 26

YEAR	TM	LG	AGE	G	GS	IP	H	BB	SO	HR	ERA	EQERA	EQH9	EQBB9	EQSO9	EQHR9	PERA	VORP	STF
2001	OAK	AL	23	35	35	214.3	184	80	205	18	3.49	3.70	7.9	3.1	8.1	0.7	3.70	43.6	47
2002	OAK	AL	24	35	35	229.3	182	78	182	24	2.75	3.21	7.2	2.8	6.9	0.9	3.48	58.8	33
2003	OAK	AL	25	35	35	231.7	186	88	146	19	3.30	3.58	7.5	3.3	5.7	0.7	3.60	54.8	21
2004	OAK	AL	26	32	31	202.0	189	71	143	25	4.02	4.25	8.4	3.0	6.1	1.0	4.22	33.5	11

Breakout: 14%   Improve: 49%   Collapse: 12%

He didn't win the Cy Young in 2003, but he still pitched very well. Analysts are more than a little worried about the trend in his K rate. Zito walks a few guys, has a tendency to throw a fair number of flyballs, and he's thrown a pretty big number of innings over the last three years. Some interesting metrics for Zito over the last three seasons:

Year	K/9	GB/FB
2001	8.61	0.85
2002	7.14	0.74
2003	5.67	0.89

That K rate's gone from among the league's best to below league average, and it's not as if Zito, who works to change the eye-plane of the hitter from high to low, has suddenly become Chad Bradford. A high K rate is an indicator of a low future ERA. Zito's performance record is certainly outstanding, but there is a non-negligible risk of a precipitous decline. PECOTA sees regression on the way.

Seattle Mariners

Those of you living on the East Coast may not have noticed, but the AL West has become quite a killing grounds. There's your budget efficiency machine in Oakland, Bill Stoneman's "Anaheim Abattoir" Bullpen, A-Rod's Mini-Coors Adventure, and, up in Seattle, that rarest of creatures in baseball: the company that invests in itself, and does it well, at least above the level of general manager.

This crucible causes fans in AL Central cities to breathe easy, seeing bursts of Cleveland and Detroit on the schedule, and fans of the Red Sox, Blue Jays, and Yankees to cherish their 5,169 games against Tampa Bay and Baltimore, while watching their Wild Card competitors machete each other to death in a greased-down death match up and down the Pacific Coast, with occasional visits to Tom Hicks' Magical Offensive Kingdom for a quick cage match.

In MLB's equivalent of Antietam, the Mariners and Athletics have become bitter rivals, and far better baseball teams than denizens of the lesser (read: suit-wearing) coast realize. Despite having dramatically different approaches to how they run their respective clubs, both have been quite successful. Going into 2004, Seattle and Oakland are once again likely to be battling each other for the top spot in the West, with a beefed-up Angels team vying to join the dance. Oakland's basically powered by efficiency and guile, where Seattle's powered, at least for 2004, by money, and a thus-far friendly hand of fate.

The good news for Mariner fans is that while Billy Beane gets, and earns, tremendous press for building a winner under a mountain of wet carpet in Oakland, he's still operating under a mountain of wet carpet. The A's ownership group of Steve Schott and Ken Hofmann has made it clear that they're not going to increase their investment in the club—period. Contrast that to the Mariners, who have a distinct and sustainable advantage off the field that directly translates to wins on it: a dedicated ownership group led by Hiroshi Yamauchi.

This off-season, a lot of attention has been paid to the transition in the Mariner GM chair. Pat Gillick, architect of two World Series winners in Toronto, has stepped down and been replaced by Bill Bavasi. Despite the Mariners' success, fans didn't exactly lament Gillick's departure. Gillick's critics point out that he's earned his nickname of "Stand Pat," refusing to make a deal at the deadline to shore up obvious weaknesses in the outfield and at third base,

MARINERS PROSPECTUS

2003 record: 93–69; Second place, AL West

Pythagenport record: 98–64

Runs scored per game: 4.9 (6th in AL)

Runs allowed per game: 3.9 (1st in AL)

Team EqA: .268 (3rd in AL)

2003 Batters Age: 32.6 (Oldest in AL)

2003 Pitchers Age: 30.0 (4th oldest in AL)

Ballpark: Safeco Field; Severe pitcher's park; Park Factor of 0.949

2003: Another strong squad missed the postseason, in part due to chronic inability to improve at the trade deadline.

2004: The roster isn't aging well, and Bill Bavasi's bizarre off-season moves aren't a good sign for Mariner faithful.

while watching the financially-strapped A's come up with genuine contributors at a reasonable cost. His detractors in baseball point out that his success in Toronto was the result of an environment in which the Blue Jays sold out every game and had a nearly unlimited budget. One NL GM points out that "in Seattle, Gillick was in the right place at the right time. They got Kaz Sasaki and Ichiro because of their owner and their scouting guys, not because of Pat."

That may or may not be the case, but it's all in the past now. Gillick may not have had a penchant for the in-season move to shore up a weakness, but he leaves behind an effective and professional front office filled with people like Roger Jongewaard and Hide Sueyoshi, and a farm system with a number of promising prospects on both sides of the ball. New GM Bill Bavasi steps into what one AL exec calls "the best pure general manager job out there." Given that he's got a big budget, a pretty good farm system, and inherits a team that's won 93 games in each of the last two seasons, Bavasi's got some pretty expectations to live up to right off the bat. So what's he got to work with?

The Mariners are a good team. But they're old. The Mariners' stars are all long in the tooth. Mr. Mariner, Edgar Martinez, will start next season at age 41, as will rotation anchor Jamie Moyer. Bret Boone turns 35 a week into the 2004 season; John Olerud's already there. Let's take a look at the severity of the problem, relative to the rest of the competition in the AL West. Baseball Prospectus has a

FIGURE 1. PITCHING VORP BY PITCHER AGE

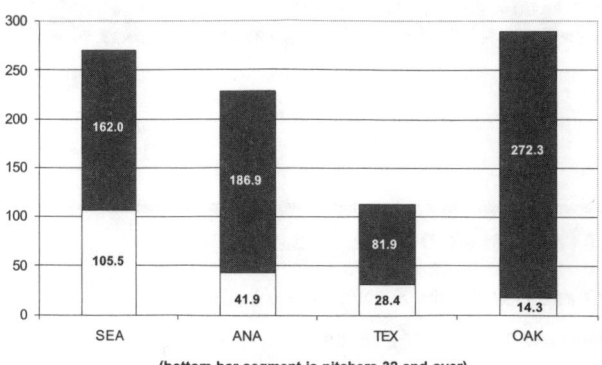

(bottom bar segment is pitchers 32 and over)

FIGURE 2. OFFENSIVE VORP BY HITTER AGE

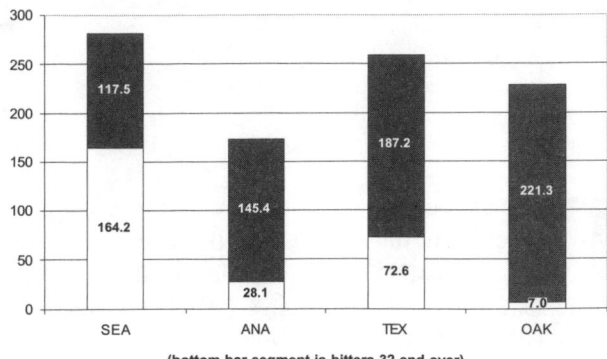

(bottom bar segment is hitters 32 and over)

measurement called Value Over Replacement Player (VORP) that measures how many more runs a player is worth than an easily-acquirable substitute. (You can find more details about VORP in the essay at the front of this book.)

Figure 1 shows the Total Value Over Replacement Player (VORP) for each pitching staff in the AL West. This doesn't include players who have a negative VORP; if a team's management can't or doesn't identify players below replacement level, that team has bigger worries than being excessively vulnerable to the ravages of age. The bottom part of each team's bar is the proportion of VORP contributed by players 32 years of age or younger; the upper section represents the VORP contributed by players 31 years of age and younger. Seattle and Oakland both had outstanding pitching staffs in the 2003 season, but the Mariners, led by Jamie Moyer, had a far greater proportion of its quality innings come from older pitchers than did Oakland, to the tune of about 40% for the Mariners, and less than 5% for the Athletics. That's what happens when you extract the best season ever from Shigetoshi Hasegawa and get 215 innings from Jamie Moyer, affectionately known as Methusaleh's Pitching Coach. Of course, it could be worse—Bavasi could have inherited that Chan Ho-riffic Ranger staff.

Figure 2 shows the same calculations, but on the offensive side. Once again, the Mariners are right at the top, both in terms of total production and the age of the people who provided it: 58% of the Mariners' potent offense came from older players, most of that concentrated into Bret Boone and Edgar Martinez. In terms of both run creation and prevention, the 2003 Mariners were very effective and very old relative to their competition.

Is that necessarily a bad thing? No. On a one-season basis, the important thing is getting the production, not worrying about how the same players might perform down the road. But running a ballclub is never strictly a one-season proposition, even when a Cinderella's gunning for a ring. No matter what the circumstances a team finds

itself in, everything that can possibly be done to improve must necessarily be done in the future. It's the job of the GM and the executive staff to have a long-term plan, even if it is put aside or de-prioritized from time to time—because aging happens. Sometimes, it happens very suddenly; a player's production can just drop off a cliff, or an insidious decline can set in. Most players have seen their best seasons by the age of 30, so a team that's heavily dependent on a core of old players is at risk to have a disappointing season. The Mariners fit that profile precisely.

What else does Bavasi get to deal with? Well, it'd be nice if the Mariners had a reasonable bench. In 2003, Greg Colbrunn and John Mabry were supposed to be the offensive oomph available to manager Bob Melvin. Instead, Mabry predictably reverted to form, and Colbrunn's season was cut short by injury. What about the rest of the bench? It was, in a word, dreadful. A clearly finished Mark McLemore somehow managed to accumulate more than 350 AB, while fan favorite Willie Bloomquist hustled ineffectually, as is his pattern. The Mariner bench posed no threat to opposing managers, leaving Melvin at a tactical disadvantage. Coming into the GM chair, if Bavasi could avoid Gillick's weakness for veterans coming off a fluke year, and not award long-term contracts when they're not necessary or advisable, it would have warmed the hearts of Mariner fans everywhere.

But since Gillick's "departure," it's clear that he's never really departed, and the front office's moves can best be described as puzzling. Offering a 40-year-old Pat Borders arbitration? What possible explanation is there for that? According to Bavasi, it's "because the club has a special relationship with this guy." Huh? Borders has played a grand total of 21 games for the Mariners, logging a grand total of 24 at-bats over a three-year period. Is it really that he's developed a special relationship with the Mariners, or that he's got a long relationship with Pat Gillick that goes back to Toronto? And if that's the case, is it likely that a new regime, free of Gillick's hand, would cough up what amounts to a generous severance package? Would the Clubbie even recognize Borders? Who's really in charge?

It's hard enough to get a front office going in one direction with a single individual in charge. When a GM with a big reputation moves into a "consulting role", you can end up with more fiefdoms, turf wars, confusion, and goal divergence than the Argentinian Parliament. Bavasi's track record as GM in Anaheim wasn't particularly noteworthy, and he's not coming in with a mandate to overhaul a moribund organization. In baseball, the loyalty that comes with a hiring often goes to the individual who made the hire rather than the club, so if Bavasi and Gillick and/or his underlings start to disagree, the strengths of the Mariner front office may not be enough to overcome any potential discord. Bill Walsh might be the greatest despot in the history of professional sports, but the front office hasn't functioned in anything resembling a unified fashion since he's been in the position of staring over the shoulder of other execs with the San Francisco 49ers. And Pat Gillick is no Bill Walsh.

The early returns aren't encouraging for Mariner fans. Bavasi's been saved from himself on one occasion, when, longing for the days of the first Clinton administration, he agreed to trade Carlos Guillen, who's been a pretty good if not superlative player when healthy, for Omar Vizquel, who, well, was overrated many years ago, and was considerably worse in 2003. Vizquel's contract might be the only thing even keeping him in the league: It entitles him to $7 million in guaranteed cash for the 2004 season and a personal services deal, which is precisely the sort of thing you'd like to add into a deal where you pick up a shortstop with bad wheels who can't hit and turns 37 in April.

If this kind of activity causes you to slap your head in stunned disbelief, something like the feeling you get when you discover you've bought tickets to see Wayland Flowers and Madame, you're not alone. Consider the case of Raul Ibanez. Ibanez turns 32 in June. He plays a capable corner OF or 1B. Last season, playing in Kauffman Stadium, one of the best couple of hitter's parks in the AL, he hit .296/.346/.456. He was pretty much the definition of a replaceable corner OF. Naturally, since the Mariners needed to get rid of one of the best center fielders in the game in Mike Cameron because he strikes out too much, they signed Ibanez to a three-year deal worth $13 million. Not to get overly technical, but that classifies as *meshugenah*. Ibanez is utterly replaceable for near the league minimum, and the failure of Bavasi to recognize that should cause Mariner fans to tremble each and every off-season.

Wait, there's much, much more:

- Desperate to erase the painful memory of Jeff Cirillo's flailing, Bavasi signed Scott Spiezio, a league-average hitter who turns 32 this year and a liability waiting to happen as an everyday third baseman, to a three-year, $9 million deal.

- Rather than non-tender Freddy Garcia and admit he's no more than an innings-eater at this stage, he chucked nearly $7 million at him for the '04 season.

- Unhappy with a lefty-mashing—albeit injury-prone—first baseman who'd fit perfectly platooning with the fading John Olerud, Bavasi shipped Greg Colbrunn to Arizona for Quinton ".219/.275/.313, .309/.368/.458, .227/.276/.275 the last three years, guess which one was the outlier" McCracken.

- Figuring the team wasn't old enough, he signed 32-year-old Rich Aurilia to a one-year deal for $3.5 million, then flipped Carlos Guillen, a 28-year-old already Aurilia's equal, more likely to improve, and making $1 million less, to Detroit for HACKING MASSter Ramon Santiago and non-prospect SS Juan Gonzalez.

After a while Mariners fans must have figured Billy Beane, Bill Stoneman, and John Hart snuck into Bavasi's office, put him under hypnosis for the entire off-season, then giggled away as one inane move topped the next.

At least there's a bright side. The Mariners have a very strong farm system, with some tremendous arms that could be in Seattle and really contributing soon. Just on the major league roster, they've got a probable impact starter in Rafael Soriano, meaning they have a level of flexibility not available to many other clubs. The Mariners also have a large and diversified revenue base. They draw big crowds who pay high ticket prices. They've invested in their organization by marketing the Mariners in Japan, where games are broadcast every day. They've got great out-of-home sponsorship sales, as well as reasonable local broadcast rights contracts, and a share of the national money. They're not hurting for revenue. The Mariners also have the best overseas scouting organization in baseball. Not only does this mean that the M's were first in the wave of bringing Asian stars to the U.S., it also means they have a base in place to continue importing talent to fill needs. Other teams should note that this is a chicken-and-egg issue; the Mariners made a conscious effort to expand their business, and made the necessary investments of time and money. There's nothing preventing every other club in MLB from taking similar steps, except their own aversion to anything remotely resembling risk.

So where are the Mariners overall? Well, they're not young, but they were right at the top of the division in offense and defense just a year ago. They have an exceptionally stable and effective ownership group, a loyal fan base, good revenue streams, a starting rotation that's already pretty good, with lots of young talent available to join it quickly if need be. Offensively, they've got two middle infielders in Aurilia and Boone who can probably hit, a few weak spots/designated outs that aren't hard to identify, an excellent right fielder in Ichiro Suzuki, and a should-be future HoFer in Edgar Martinez—a reasonable bet to hit .300/.400/.500 into his mid-50s, even if only for a few games a year. Like the World Champion 2002 Angels, the '03 Mariners were heavily dependent upon their bullpen, as Rafael Soriano and Shigetoshi Hasegawa made up for off years from Arthur Rhodes and Kaz Sasaki, mak-

ing the Mariner bullpen the fourth most effective in baseball.

Given the flaws in their competitors, it's reasonable to expect the Mariners to compete for the AL West title. There are some risks, and if things break the wrong way, they could drop precipitously. Even if they don't win the division in 2004, they're a better bet than Oakland for success in the long term, given both clubs' ownership. The infrastructure's just better-built in Seattle, and Yamauchi isn't likely to let that change.

It may take the M's a while to find the right general manager, though. And until that happens, it'll be white-knuckle time in Woodinville.

HITTERS

WILLIE BLOOMQUIST   UT   Bats: R   Throws: R   Born: 27-Nov-77   Age: 26

YEAR	TM	LG	AGE	AB	H	2B	3B	HR	BB	SO	SB	CS	AVG	OBP	SLG	MLVR	EQBA	EQOBP	EQSLG	EQMLVR	VORP	DEFENSE			
2001	SAN	TEX	23	491	125	23	2	0	28	55	34	9	.255	.296	.310	-.175	.235	.269	.287	-.377	-25.4	70-SS	-4	50-2B	0
2002	SEA	AL	24	33	15	4	0	0	5	2	3	1	.455	.526	.576	.741	.500	.575	.618	.891	9.1				
2002	TAC	PCL	24	337	91	14	3	6	29	44	20	10	.270	.333	.383	-.041	.247	.304	.353	-.207	-3.4	26-2B	-1	26-LF	-3
2003	SEA	AL	25	196	49	7	2	1	19	39	4	1	.250	.319	.321	-.121	.278	.346	.354	-.103	1.9	29-3B	0	15-SS	0
2004	SEA	AL	26	223	55	9	2	3	17	35	6	2	.247	.303	.341	-.182	.251	.310	.351	-.184	0.6	61-3B	0		

Breakout: 28%   Improve: 47%   Collapse: 33%

This is a dangerous ballplayer. He's a hustling crowd favorite, and likely to result in lots of banners singing his praises around the ballpark, but between the lines, he's a mediocre utility infielder with offensive potency comparable to guys like Lou Merloni, Jorge Velandia, and James Garner. With Jeff Cirillo's time-lapse decay, Bloomquist had a slight window of opportunity to seize the 3B job, have 600 career plate appearances where he hits at a league average, and become a complete lead weight around the neck of the franchise. Overpaying Scott Spiezio over three years at least solves that problem.

BRET BOONE   2B   Bats: R   Throws: R   Born: 06-Apr-69   Age: 35

YEAR	TM	LG	AGE	AB	H	2B	3B	HR	BB	SO	SB	CS	AVG	OBP	SLG	MLVR	EQBA	EQOBP	EQSLG	EQMLVR	VORP	DEFENSE	
2001	SEA	AL	32	623	206	37	3	37	40	110	5	5	.331	.379	.578	.366	.354	.402	.624	.458	97.6	152-2B	7
2002	SEA	AL	33	608	169	34	3	24	53	102	12	5	.278	.342	.462	.108	.306	.368	.513	.186	56.1	144-2B	0
2003	SEA	AL	34	622	183	35	5	35	68	125	16	3	.294	.370	.535	.316	.321	.395	.589	.354	79.2	155-2B	12
2004	SEA	AL	35	546	154	30	3	26	53	99	10	4	.282	.349	.493	.118	.286	.357	.508	.132	44.3	143-2B	1

Breakout: 7%   Improve: 28%   Collapse: 28%

A late bloomer, a fantastic ballplayer, would have been a deserving MVP last season. The only thing Boone didn't do well before last year was draw a bunch of walks. Now he does that, too. The three-year, $25 million deal he signed in January 2002 has been a heck of a bargain for the Mariners, especially considering the state of 2B in the AL. Defensively, Boone's range, particularly back and to his left, is phenomenal. He's not likely to put up numbers quite as good as he did last season, but he's still potentially the core of a championship club.

PAT BORDERS   C   Bats: R   Throws: R   Born: 14-May-63   Age: 41

YEAR	TM	LG	AGE	AB	H	2B	3B	HR	BB	SO	SB	CS	AVG	OBP	SLG	MLVR	EQBA	EQOBP	EQSLG	EQMLVR	VORP	DEFENSE	
2001	DUR	INT	38	313	74	15	1	2	16	61	3	2	.236	.278	.310	-.221	.229	.271	.302	-.355	-16.5	40-C	4
2002	TAC	PCL	39	317	84	16	1	12	11	47	3	2	.265	.290	.435	-.049	.246	.271	.410	-.189	-1.5	78-C	12
2003	TAC	PCL	40	293	92	27	1	12	20	54	1	2	.314	.366	.536	.292	.288	.337	.502	.099	23.9	66-C	-1
2003	SEA	AL	40	14	2	1	0	0	1	5	0	0	.143	.200	.214	-.567	.143	.200	.286	-.563	-1.4		
2004	SEA	AL	41	100	25	5	1	2	5	20	1	0	.250	.291	.386	-.143	.254	.297	.397	-.143	-0.1	30-C	-2

Breakout: 25%   Improve: 62%   Collapse: 17%

Borders made it back to the bigs for a little bit. He wasn't a particularly great player over the course of his career, but he had some great moments, outlasted everyone's expectations, and wears the jewelry of a champion. He's been offered arbitration, a bizarre decision on the part of the Mariners caused by excessive loyalty. Perhaps the career-ending arbitration offer will become known as a "Gillick."

MIKE CAMERON   CF   Bats: R   Throws: R   Born: 08-Jan-73   Age: 31

YEAR	TM	LG	AGE	AB	H	2B	3B	HR	BB	SO	SB	CS	AVG	OBP	SLG	MLVR	EQBA	EQOBP	EQSLG	EQMLVR	VORP	DEFENSE
2001	SEA	AL	28	540	144	30	5	25	69	155	34	5	.267	.360	.480	.134	.299	.388	.540	.249	56.1	144-CF 12
2002	SEA	AL	29	545	130	26	5	25	79	176	31	8	.239	.342	.442	.050	.274	.374	.513	.164	45.6	146-CF 7
2003	SEA	AL	30	534	135	31	5	18	70	137	17	7	.253	.345	.431	.087	.281	.372	.485	.129	30.9	144-CF 21
2004	NYM	NL	31	465	123	25	4	20	69	129	16	5	.265	.366	.464	.083	.269	.367	.486	.104	25.6	128-CF 6

Breakout: 26%   Improve: 59%   Collapse: 12%

Cameron's everything you could want in a ballplayer. He's durable, hits for some average, pretty good power, draws some walks, and plays all-world defense at a key position. His value on the free agent market was slightly depressed compared to his real value, but that's a problem with front offices working with imperfect information, not an indictment of Cameron. The Mets got a steal at three years, $19.5 million, and a couple dozen other teams missed out on a huge upgrade.

RUBEN CASTILLO   SS   Bats: R   Throws: R   Born: 16-Aug-78   Age: 25

YEAR	TM	LG	AGE	AB	H	2B	3B	HR	BB	SO	SB	CS	AVG	OBP	SLG	MLVR	EQBA	EQOBP	EQSLG	EQMLVR	VORP	DEFENSE
2001	SBR	CAL	22	270	60	7	2	1	5	53	10	2	.222	.245	.274	-.331	.196	.211	.244	-.575	-27.9	75-SS -12
2001	SAN	TEX	22	126	25	4	0	0	7	27	1	0	.198	.246	.230	-.408	.195	.228	.227	-.564	-13.5	39-SS -3
2002	SAN	TEX	23	394	86	12	4	3	16	86	10	7	.218	.252	.292	-.257	.210	.235	.287	-.458	-29.7	113-SS 1
2003	TAC	PCL	24	337	71	14	0	0	22	71	17	10	.211	.263	.252	-.367	.201	.250	.245	-.491	-28.9	105-SS -7
2004	SEA	AL	25	157	34	6	1	2	7	32	4	2	.217	.257	.298	-.339	.220	.262	.307	-.350	-5.1	44-SS -3

Breakout: 61%   Improve: 69%   Collapse: 21%

Sometimes, the stat lines really don't make much sense when it comes to narrative. Castillo's progressed steadily through the minors, bumping up pretty much a level a year, which is usually a sign that someone has some shot at being a productive major leaguer. But in the case of Castillo, his consistent promotion is actually a compelling riddle. He's never hit well at any level in any amount of playing time, and his fielding is indifferent at best. Have we discovered the Chauncey Gardener of middle infielders?

SHIN-SOO CHOO   OF   Bats: L   Throws: L   Born: 13-Jul-82   Age: 21

YEAR	TM	LG	AGE	AB	H	2B	3B	HR	BB	SO	SB	CS	AVG	OBP	SLG	MLVR	EQBA	EQOBP	EQSLG	EQMLVR	VORP	DEFENSE	
2002	WIS	MID	19	420	127	24	8	6	70	98	34	21	.302	.417	.440	.268	.220	.307	.331	-.248	-14.4	69-CF -11	37-RF -4
2003	SBR	CAL	20	412	118	18	13	9	44	84	18	10	.286	.368	.459	.159	.221	.286	.361	-.247	-24.6	62-LF -4	33-RF -1
2004	SEA	AL	21	260	58	13	3	5	22	58	6	3	.223	.291	.347	-.210	.227	.297	.358	-.213	-9.1	71-LF -5	

Breakout: 14%   Improve: 42%   Collapse: 26%

Choo's an interesting prospect. He's got some patience at the plate, runs well, and has pretty reasonable gap power that will probably develop into some legitimate HR power down the road. He's kind of Johnny Damonish. He has the physical tools to play CF, but doesn't have the best instincts in the outfield. He's one of the faster players in organized ball, and could end up as a legitimate speed threat with some plate discipline and power. His 2004 campaign will go a long way towards establishing a likely career path; if he goes to Double-A and plays well, he's a potential plus starter in the majors. If he struggles significantly, he's going to lose a lot of sheen very quickly.

RYAN CHRISTIANSON   C?   Bats: R   Throws: R   Born: 21-Apr-81   Age: 23

YEAR	TM	LG	AGE	AB	H	2B	3B	HR	BB	SO	SB	CS	AVG	OBP	SLG	MLVR	EQBA	EQOBP	EQSLG	EQMLVR	VORP	DEFENSE
2001	SBR	CAL	20	528	131	42	5	12	53	112	3	2	.248	.320	.415	.010	.197	.254	.332	-.365	-30.2	108-C 8
2002	SAN	TEX	21	190	48	11	0	5	16	36	0	2	.253	.317	.389	.007	.231	.279	.364	-.250	-4.5	45-C 4
2002	SBR	CAL	21	71	20	5	1	1	4	17	1	0	.282	.346	.423	.088	.236	.281	.361	-.247	-1.5	17-C 1
2004	SEA	AL	23	67	17	4	0	3	5	13	1	0	.257	.315	.444	-.021	.261	.322	.457	-.015	9.1	22-C -3

Breakout: 69%   Improve: 83%   Collapse: 8%

(continued next page)

Ryan Christianson (*continued*)

He's been hit by a spate of injuries, including serious shoulder problems that make it unlikely he'll have a career in the majors as a catcher. Christianson hasn't hit particularly well, he's a big guy, and he hasn't been able to stay healthy, so there's a bunch of obstacles stacked against his staying on the good side of the defensive spectrum.

JEFF CIRILLO   **3B**   **Bats: R**   **Throws: R**   Born: 23-Sep-69   Age: 34

YEAR	TM	LG	AGE	AB	H	2B	3B	HR	BB	SO	SB	CS	AVG	OBP	SLG	MLVR	EQBA	EQOBP	EQSLG	EQMLVR	VORP	DEFENSE
2001	COL	NL	31	528	165	26	4	17	43	63	12	2	.313	.370	.473	.090	.295	.352	.448	.055	33.4	136-3B 22
2002	SEA	AL	32	485	121	20	0	6	31	67	8	4	.249	.307	.328	-.158	.281	.336	.369	-.099	9.9	126-3B 8
2003	SEA	AL	33	258	53	11	0	2	24	32	1	1	.205	.286	.271	-.284	.235	.311	.312	-.257	-8.7	74-3B -2
2004	SDP	NL	34	212	53	10	1	3	20	29	2	1	.249	.321	.342	-.164	.256	.326	.359	-.142	3.4	59-3B -1

Breakout: 39%   Improve: 56%   Collapse: 22%

"Other than that, Mrs. Lincoln, how'd you like the play?" Cirillo's value at this point is freakishly concentrated in the morbid curiosity of whether he can find another facet of the game, and dramatically decay in that, too. In 1997–1999, Jeff Cirillo was pretty much the same ballplayer as Bill Mueller in 2003. What happened? Cirillo's been a complete disaster at the plate, his defense has gone from outstanding to indifferent on a good day, and he's just plain completely lost. Bavasi miraculously found a taker for him, though the M's got back two other albatrosses in Kevin Jarvis and Wiki Gonzalez and had to kick in nearly $5 million in 2005 to even out salaries as part of a six-player deal with the Padres.

GREG COLBRUNN   **1B**   **Bats: R**   **Throws: R**   Born: 26-Jul-69   Age: 34

YEAR	TM	LG	AGE	AB	H	2B	3B	HR	BB	SO	SB	CS	AVG	OBP	SLG	MLVR	EQBA	EQOBP	EQSLG	EQMLVR	VORP	DEFENSE
2001	ARI	NL	31	97	28	8	0	4	9	14	0	0	.289	.373	.495	.147	.286	.365	.500	.142	7.1	
2002	ARI	NL	32	171	57	16	2	10	13	19	0	0	.333	.380	.626	.427	.329	.373	.624	.382	20.3	32-1B -2
2003	SEA	AL	33	58	16	1	1	3	4	16	0	1	.276	.323	.483	.147	.305	.349	.542	.195	3.1	11-1B -2
2004	ARI	NL	34	176	50	10	1	9	15	33	0	1	.284	.343	.502	.112	.274	.332	.487	.052	11.0	49-1B -2

Breakout: 11%   Improve: 32%   Collapse: 41%

Colbrunn's a lefty masher who'd be a perfect platoon mate at first base as John Olerud's decline takes hold. Pat Gillick probably could have waited a few days longer to sign him and dodged the compensation cost he incurred. Injuries are now a serious concern, as torn cartilage in the wrist isn't something a hitter ever wants to deal with. Though the injury risk remains significant for '04, flipping Colbrunn to the Diamondbacks for Quinton Freakin' McCracken is your basic low-risk, zero-reward proposition.

BEN DAVIS   **C**   **Bats: B**   **Throws: R**   Born: 10-Mar-77   Age: 27

YEAR	TM	LG	AGE	AB	H	2B	3B	HR	BB	SO	SB	CS	AVG	OBP	SLG	MLVR	EQBA	EQOBP	EQSLG	EQMLVR	VORP	DEFENSE
2001	SDP	NL	24	448	107	20	0	11	66	112	4	4	.239	.342	.357	-.096	.253	.351	.377	-.079	12.2	120-C 2
2002	SEA	AL	25	228	59	10	1	7	18	58	1	1	.259	.319	.404	-.027	.286	.344	.450	.035	12.1	62-C 4
2003	SEA	AL	26	246	58	18	0	6	18	61	0	0	.236	.288	.382	-.108	.258	.311	.423	-.087	3.0	68-C 0
2004	SEA	AL	27	245	60	13	1	8	24	58	1	1	.246	.314	.401	-.087	.249	.321	.413	-.083	8.9	67-C -2

Breakout: 28%   Improve: 46%   Collapse: 28%

Took a step back offensively, losing some power and some plate discipline. Davis is a big guy, but doesn't have the quickest bat in the world. With Dan Wilson making more money than he really should, Davis is going to have to scramble for playing time, and Wiki Gonzalez's arrival may make things even tougher. He probably shouldn't switch-hit; Davis has never hit righties particularly well, and really struggled against them last season. Draws raves from Curt Schilling for his little ball game.

MICHAEL GARCIAPARRA   **SS**   **Bats: R**   **Throws: R**   Born: 02-Apr-83   Age: 21

YEAR	TM	LG	AGE	AB	H	2B	3B	HR	BB	SO	SB	CS	AVG	OBP	SLG	MLVR	EQBA	EQOBP	EQSLG	EQMLVR	VORP	DEFENSE
2002	EVE	NWN	19	31	5	2	0	0	4	15	0	1	.161	.257	.226	-.291	.094	.171	.156	-.812	-12.1	
2003	WIS	MID	20	440	107	12	1	2	38	80	14	4	.243	.316	.289	-.099	.200	.253	.242	-.489	-39.4	122-SS -26
2004	SEA	AL	21	256	49	9	1	2	16	61	4	2	.191	.246	.259	-.419	.194	.252	.267	-.434	-15.1	69-SS -12

Breakout: 49%   Improve: 66%   Collapse: 20%

If you haven't had a chance to see Nomar's little brother play shortstop, and want to know people's subjective opinions about his ability to handle the position, head to the Internet Movie Database and check the reviews for *Manos, The Hands of Fate.* Garciaparra was singularly unimpressive in the field, handling balls approximately as deftly as Joey Buttafuoco handles queries about "DeBrett's Peerage and Baronetage." With the bat, there were occasionally flashes of promise, but nothing overwhelming, and certainly no signs of what the Mariners were hoping for when he was drafted and signed. He's got a lot of time still to develop, but one year into his pro career, things could certainly look better.

CARLOS GUILLEN   SS   Bats: B   Throws: R   Born: 30-Sep-75   Age: 28

YEAR	TM	LG	AGE	AB	H	2B	3B	HR	BB	SO	SB	CS	AVG	OBP	SLG	MLVR	EQBA	EQOBP	EQSLG	EQMLVR	VORP		DEFENSE		
2001	SEA	AL	25	456	118	21	4	5	53	89	4	1	.259	.337	.355	-.079	.284	.361	.390	-.020	21.6		123-SS	4	
2002	SEA	AL	26	475	124	24	6	9	46	91	4	5	.261	.328	.394	-.023	.296	.361	.447	.070	33.4		126-SS	-20	
2003	SEA	AL	27	388	107	19	3	7	52	64	4	4	.276	.363	.394	.083	.308	.394	.440	.129	26.1		70-SS	-3	31-3B -1
2004	DET	AL	28	385	99	18	3	8	45	67	4	3	.258	.336	.380	-.068	.269	.350	.408	-.024	21.4		104-SS	-6	

Breakout: 19%   Improve: 39%   Collapse: 29%

A very underrated ballplayer. Guillen's an acceptable defensive player, hits for a reasonable average, has some pop, and pretty good control of the strike zone. He's fully capable of playing a championship-caliber shortstop, and no player's recognition is more dampened by his home park. The Mariners proved their inability to recognize Guillen's talent, jettisoning him to Detroit for some flotsam and signing Rich Aurilia to take his place.

JUSTIN LEONE   3B   Bats: R   Throws: R   Born: 09-Mar-77   Age: 27

YEAR	TM	LG	AGE	AB	H	2B	3B	HR	BB	SO	SB	CS	AVG	OBP	SLG	MLVR	EQBA	EQOBP	EQSLG	EQMLVR	VORP		DEFENSE	
2001	SBR	CAL	24	485	113	27	4	22	57	158	4	3	.233	.320	.441	.033	.183	.250	.348	-.359	-26.3		126-3B	-3
2002	SBR	CAL	25	358	89	20	5	18	57	98	6	0	.249	.360	.483	.162	.192	.277	.370	-.271	-10.4		96-3B	1
2003	SAN	TEX	26	455	131	38	7	21	92	104	20	6	.288	.411	.541	.367	.235	.341	.455	-.006	26.9		121-3B	1
2004	SEA	AL	27	224	52	12	1	9	25	56	3	1	.232	.311	.418	-.081	.235	.318	.430	-.078	8.0		63-3B	-2

Breakout: 32%   Improve: 54%   Collapse: 25%

Is he good enough to be a major league regular and help a club? No. Is he good enough to help a club if its current regular is Jeff Cirillo? He might have been, before the M's signed Spiezio. Leone's 2003 was probably at the top of his range, and it translates to something like Rob Deer's younger brother's high school stats. His ability to contribute at the big league level will depend on whether he can sustain his '03 gains.

JOSE LOPEZ   SS   Bats: R   Throws: R   Born: 24-Nov-83   Age: 20

YEAR	TM	LG	AGE	AB	H	2B	3B	HR	BB	SO	SB	CS	AVG	OBP	SLG	MLVR	EQBA	EQOBP	EQSLG	EQMLVR	VORP		DEFENSE		
2001	EVE	NWN	17	289	74	15	0	2	13	44	13	6	.256	.311	.329	-.083	.199	.233	.261	-.505	-46.4		61-SS	9	
2002	SBR	CAL	18	522	169	39	5	8	27	45	31	13	.324	.363	.464	.210	.271	.298	.392	-.145	8.8		116-SS	-21	
2003	SAN	TEX	19	538	139	35	2	13	27	56	18	8	.258	.306	.403	-.004	.234	.274	.379	-.237	-5.4		88-SS	-14	34-2B 0
2004	SEA	AL	20	318	78	18	1	6	16	37	9	3	.246	.287	.368	-.176	.250	.294	.379	-.177	3.7		83-SS	-13	

Breakout: 32%   Improve: 49%   Collapse: 31%

Lopez flashed some serious bat speed during the 2003 season, as well as a penchant for putting the ball in play. His swing isn't what you'd expect from a guy with so few Ks; it's a little uncontrolled and jerky. He's filling out physically, and it wouldn't be surprising to see him start to move down the defensive spectrum pretty quickly, but he's definitely got some chance of turning into an interesting hitter. He'll play at least part of the 2004 season in Triple-A at the age of 20. Anyone who can do that and hold their own has a pretty good shot at a solid major league career.

JOHN MABRY   OF   Bats: L   Throws: R   Born: 17-Oct-70   Age: 33

YEAR	TM	LG	AGE	AB	H	2B	3B	HR	BB	SO	SB	CS	AVG	OBP	SLG	MLVR	EQBA	EQOBP	EQSLG	EQMLVR	VORP		DEFENSE		
2001	FLA	NL	30	147	32	7	0	6	13	44	1	0	.218	.303	.388	-.153	.228	.307	.409	-.137	-2.9		23-RF	-4	
2002	PHI	NL	31	21	6	0	0	0	1	5	0	0	.286	.318	.286	-.155	.286	.318	.286	-.251	-0.6				
2002	OAK	AL	31	193	53	13	1	11	14	37	1	1	.275	.327	.523	.145	.297	.347	.569	.222	14.9		15-1B	1	27-LF 1
2003	SEA	AL	32	104	22	6	0	3	15	21	0	0	.212	.328	.356	-.077	.238	.352	.400	-.057	1.0				
2004	SEA	AL	33	131	31	6	0	3	13	27	0	0	.233	.307	.351	-.172	.236	.314	.361	-.174	-3.7		39-RF	-3	

Breakout: 35%   Improve: 54%   Collapse: 33%

(continued next page)

John Mabry (*continued*)

So Mabry has the best two months of his life in Oakland after being acquired as an object lesson for Jeremy Giambi, and Pat Gillick decides to pick him up as a lefty bat, figuring he'd fill the Mariners' needs. Well, he was pretty much a fungible Quadruple-A commodity, as he's been for years, and the Mariners' squishy bench was all the more doughy for it. Gillick's inability to identify fluke seasons or the expected effects of age won't be missed in the Emerald City, though his successor's done a fine job of carrying on the legacy thus far. In a shocking move, Mabry's 2004 option was declined by the Mariners, who decided a $250,000 buyout was a bargain.

EDGAR MARTINEZ   DH   Bats: R   Throws: R   Born: 02-Jan-63   Age: 41

YEAR	TM	LG	AGE	AB	H	2B	3B	HR	BB	SO	SB	CS	AVG	OBP	SLG	MLVR	EQBA	EQOBP	EQSLG	EQMLVR	VORP	DEFENSE
2001	SEA	AL	38	470	144	40	1	23	93	90	4	1	.306	.430	.543	.367	.333	.451	.596	.461	76.8	
2002	SEA	AL	39	328	91	23	0	15	67	69	1	1	.277	.409	.485	.249	.312	.437	.548	.352	44.4	
2003	SEA	AL	40	497	146	25	0	24	92	95	0	1	.294	.411	.489	.315	.323	.436	.543	.356	61.1	
2004	SEA	AL	41	395	107	21	0	20	72	79	1	1	.272	.390	.476	.153	.276	.399	.490	.168	27.8	

Breakout: 28%   Improve: 35%   Collapse: 42%

Thankfully, he'll be back for another season. At BP, we don't understand why there's even any sort of discussion about whether or not Edgar Martinez belongs in the Hall of Fame. If the Hall of Fame doesn't exist to honor the very best, classiest players in the game, what's it for? To create a mead-hall for gangs of myopic buddies to cram with the sepia-toned undeserving? Debates about the Hall of Fame often do two things: First, they focus on a player's peak versus career performances. Second, they miss the point—usually, the debate illustrates how useless and pointless the Hall has truly become, thanks to additions like Phil Rizzuto and Tony Perez. In the case of Edgar Martinez, the debate has become a proxy for the place of the DH in baseball. But take a look at Edgar's performance since getting a regular gig:

Year	Games	AVG	OBP	SLG	Year	Games	AVG	OBP	SLG
1990	144	.302	.397	.433	1997	155	.330	.456	.554
1991	150	.307	.405	.452	1998	154	.322	.429	.565
1992	135	.343	.404	.544	1999	142	.337	.447	.554
1993	42	.237	.366	.378	2000	153	.324	.423	.579
1994	89	.285	.387	.482	2001	132	.306	.423	.543
1995	145	.356	.479	.628	2002	97	.277	.403	.485
1996	139	.327	.464	.595	2003	145	.294	.406	.489

How can one make a reasoned argument to keep Edgar Martinez out of the Hall of Fame? The only thing to hang one's hat on is that he's been a DH, which means the person making the argument is arguing what baseball should be, not what it is. And if someone's arguing that Edgar Martinez isn't what baseball should be, just walk away, because that person's a fool.

MARK McLEMORE   UT   Bats: B   Throws: R   Born: 04-Oct-64   Age: 39

YEAR	TM	LG	AGE	AB	H	2B	3B	HR	BB	SO	SB	CS	AVG	OBP	SLG	MLVR	EQBA	EQOBP	EQSLG	EQMLVR	VORP	DEFENSE			
2001	SEA	AL	36	409	117	16	9	5	69	84	39	7	.286	.389	.406	.103	.320	.420	.455	.207	29.0	31-LF	0	28-3B	-3
2002	SEA	AL	37	337	91	17	2	7	61	63	18	10	.270	.383	.395	.085	.305	.415	.451	.179	21.9	66-LF	1		
2003	SEA	AL	38	309	72	15	2	2	38	71	5	5	.233	.321	.314	-.139	.263	.350	.356	-.103	-0.1	33-SS	3	28-3B	3
2004	SEA	AL	39	264	64	12	3	5	37	53	10	3	.244	.337	.359	-.101	.247	.345	.370	-.099	5.9	74-LF	3		

Breakout: 4%   Improve: 60%   Collapse: 17%

If you were curious what 40% of the player Rickey Henderson was looked like at age 38, hope you were paying attention. McLemore looked totally overmatched at the plate all season. His role, which was primarily to provide Bob Melvin with the second half of a Hobson's Choice at third base and fill in where needed, is something the Mariners still need, but McLemore's interested in greener pastures and more playing time, and the team that gives it to him will be making a mistake.

CHAD MEYERS UT **Bats: R** **Throws: R** Born: 08-Aug-75 Age: 28

YEAR	TM	LG	AGE	AB	H	2B	3B	HR	BB	SO	SB	CS	AVG	OBP	SLG	MLVR	EQBA	EQOBP	EQSLG	EQMLVR	VORP	DEFENSE			
2001	IOW	PCL	25	446	134	31	5	9	58	72	27	9	.300	.411	.453	.181	.266	.364	.400	-.014	23.5	99-2B-18	13-RF	-1	
2002	MEM	PCL	26	358	96	19	1	8	51	54	43	9	.268	.389	.394	.080	.250	.352	.368	-.091	6.6	30-CF	-1	18-2B	0
2003	TAC	PCL	27	377	113	20	3	4	30	46	37	12	.300	.362	.401	.079	.279	.336	.379	-.086	7.0	49-CF	-4	25-LF	-2
2004	SEA	AL	28	172	44	9	1	3	16	27	9	3	.257	.337	.378	-.070	.261	.344	.390	-.066	5.9	50-CF	-7		

Breakout: 22%   Improve: 46%   Collapse: 31%

He's a utility guy with some speed who draws some walks, has the power of a Freshman Congressional Democrat, and is no worse than most of the 25th guys on major league rosters. He's free to sign with anyone looking for a pinch-runner with a pretty good batting eye who can play outfield or second base.

JOHN OLERUD 1B **Bats: L** **Throws: L** Born: 05-Aug-68 Age: 35

YEAR	TM	LG	AGE	AB	H	2B	3B	HR	BB	SO	SB	CS	AVG	OBP	SLG	MLVR	EQBA	EQOBP	EQSLG	EQMLVR	VORP	DEFENSE	
2001	SEA	AL	32	572	173	32	1	21	94	70	3	1	.302	.405	.472	.231	.329	.428	.516	.313	61.3	150-1B	-4
2002	SEA	AL	33	553	166	39	0	22	98	66	0	0	.300	.410	.490	.278	.333	.438	.549	.378	70.6	147-1B	1
2003	SEA	AL	34	539	145	35	0	10	84	67	0	1	.269	.374	.390	.095	.295	.397	.432	.113	22.7	144-1B	8
2004	SEA	AL	35	446	126	27	0	14	72	53	1	1	.283	.385	.441	.109	.287	.393	.455	.123	27.7	124-1B	1

Breakout: 18%   Improve: 49%   Collapse: 19%

Olerud's 2003 had to be horrifying for Mariners fans and front office execs alike. Having watched another patient first baseman without speed drop off the face of the earth in the late 80s, they've got to have the words "Alvin Davis" in the back of their minds. Olerud's power outage may be the scariest part of his 2003; it's hard to compete in a division like the AL West with a first baseman who can't mash. If Olerud can't bounce back, the Mariners will find it that much harder to take advantage of the vulnerability Oakland's chosen to take on at that particular position. Olerud's in the last year of his deal; his chances at the HoF and a big contract are highly dependent on his ability to rediscover about 20 extra-base hits.

RENE RIVERA C **Bats: R** **Throws: R** Born: 31-Jul-83 Age: 20

YEAR	TM	LG	AGE	AB	H	2B	3B	HR	BB	SO	SB	CS	AVG	OBP	SLG	MLVR	EQBA	EQOBP	EQSLG	EQMLVR	VORP	DEFENSE	
2001	EVE	NWN	17	45	4	1	0	2	1	19	0	0	.089	.109	.244	-.580	.067	.087	.200	-.940	-17.9	12-C	0
2002	EVE	NWN	18	227	55	18	1	1	16	38	5	2	.242	.317	.344	-.030	.190	.233	.276	-.488	-38.5	57-C	2
2003	WIS	MID	19	407	112	19	0	9	38	81	2	2	.275	.347	.388	.090	.213	.268	.319	-.346	-22.1	107-C	11
2004	SEA	AL	20	270	53	11	0	6	15	58	1	1	.195	.243	.302	-.369	.197	.248	.311	-.382	-13.9	72-C	-4

Breakout: 31%   Improve: 50%   Collapse: 27%

Rivera, a second-round pick in 2001 out of high school in Puerto Rico, just looks like a catcher. He's not one of these guys who's 6'5" and backstopping in the low minors. He's a good defensive catcher who showed pretty good development with the bat. Rivera's young enough to have a shot at a solid career; another season like 2003 will put him onto some prospect lists for the 2005 season.

REY SANCHEZ SS/2B **Bats: R** **Throws: R** Born: 05-Oct-67 Age: 36

YEAR	TM	LG	AGE	AB	H	2B	3B	HR	BB	SO	SB	CS	AVG	OBP	SLG	MLVR	EQBA	EQOBP	EQSLG	EQMLVR	VORP	DEFENSE	
2001	KCR	AL	33	390	118	14	5	0	11	34	9	1	.303	.325	.364	-.094	.312	.337	.376	-.063	13.6	94-SS	27
2001	ATL	NL	33	154	35	4	1	0	4	15	2	0	.227	.247	.266	-.434	.237	.252	.282	-.417	-8.7	45-SS	10
2002	BOS	AL	34	357	102	12	3	1	17	31	2	2	.286	.322	.345	-.105	.306	.344	.368	-.066	9.6	90-2B	6
2003	NYM	NL	35	174	36	3	1	0	8	18	1	1	.207	.242	.236	-.397	.222	.255	.256	-.456	-11.0	36-SS	6
2003	SEA	AL	35	170	50	5	1	0	8	21	1	0	.294	.333	.335	-.044	.320	.359	.366	-.030	6.0	44-SS	2
2004	TBY	AL	36	204	49	7	1	0	10	23	2	1	.242	.279	.292	-.294	.245	.284	.305	-.297	-2.8	55-SS	-2

Breakout: 19%   Improve: 46%   Collapse: 40%

Certainly good at what he does, which is field well and slap the ball. But when he's among the most threatening bats on your bench, that's a situation that needs to be addressed. Sanchez can still pick it pretty well at shortstop, and grab a single off the bench. He's a decent guy to have in the backup infielder role, if you prefer the defense/empty batting average model to the Mark Bellhorn (in a good year) model.

CHRIS SNELLING   LF   Bats: L   Throws: L   Born: 03-Dec-81   Age: 22

YEAR	TM	LG	AGE	AB	H	2B	3B	HR	BB	SO	SB	CS	AVG	OBP	SLG	MLVR	EQBA	EQOBP	EQSLG	EQMLVR	VORP	DEFENSE				
2001	SBR	CAL	19	450	151	29	10	7	45	63	12	5	.336	.421	.491	.345	.266	.328	.392	-.093	-5.1	84-LF	0	18-CF	-2	
2002	SAN	TEX	20	89	29	9	2	1	12	11	5	1	.326	.429	.506	.392	.283	.366	.457	.081	6.5	11-CF	0	10-LF	1	
2003	SAN	TEX	21	186	62	12	2	3	8	30	1	7	.333	.377	.468	.266	.293	.328	.426	-.022	2.4	15-RF	-1	11-LF	1	
2003	TAC	PCL	21	67	18	2	0	3	5	12	1	0	.269	.338	.433	.057	.254	.318	.403	-.105	-0.8	11-RF	1			
2004	SEA	AL	22	234	62	14	1	5	20	37	4	1	.263	.334	.401	-.041	.267	.341	.413	-.035	7.4	65-LF	-1			

Breakout: 25%   Improve: 43%   Collapse: 30%

There exists a subset of Mariner fans who remember watching a certain third base coach doing his best to make Snelling do a Mr. Bill impersonation after rounding third particularly hard. Not surprisingly, Snelling was hurt pretty bad, which is one of the things he does best. He's building a nice Fred Lynn/Rusty Greer lite career path, but without actually getting in a healthy season; he's a good bet to have continued health problems too. If he can somehow find a way to get healthy and stay that way, he's going to be a very good major leaguer. Snelling can hit, has good baseball instincts, and tremendous tools. But he could use a little lucky mojo. Send the guy a rabbit's foot, for Pete's sake.

JAMAL STRONG   CF   Bats: R   Throws: R   Born: 05-Aug-78   Age: 25

YEAR	TM	LG	AGE	AB	H	2B	3B	HR	BB	SO	SB	CS	AVG	OBP	SLG	MLVR	EQBA	EQOBP	EQSLG	EQMLVR	VORP	DEFENSE	
2001	WIS	MID	22	184	65	12	1	0	40	27	35	4	.353	.480	.429	.361	.249	.347	.306	-.185	-2.4	42-CF	-5
2001	SBR	CAL	22	331	103	11	2	0	51	60	47	8	.311	.411	.356	.128	.243	.323	.279	-.274	-13.1	81-CF	-7
2002	SAN	TEX	23	503	140	16	5	1	62	87	46	16	.278	.369	.336	.036	.252	.324	.310	-.224	-12.3	123-CF	0
2003	TAC	PCL	24	210	64	6	1	2	25	38	26	11	.305	.392	.371	.094	.282	.358	.347	-.087	4.0	53-CF	-5
2004	SEA	AL	25	210	52	9	2	2	19	38	12	4	.249	.319	.342	-.152	.252	.326	.352	-.152	1.3	59-CF	-2

Breakout: 23%   Improve: 41%   Collapse: 36%

Tools hounds love his grace and speed. Strong's blazingly fast, but has little else to offer, except perhaps instruction on how to take a brutally asymptotic path to fly balls. His 15 minutes in the prospect spotlight have expired, and he'll spend the rest of his career trying to have Brian L. Hunter's 1997.

ICHIRO SUZUKI   RF   Bats: L   Throws: R   Born: 22-Oct-73   Age: 30

YEAR	TM	LG	AGE	AB	H	2B	3B	HR	BB	SO	SB	CS	AVG	OBP	SLG	MLVR	EQBA	EQOBP	EQSLG	EQMLVR	VORP	DEFENSE	
2001	SEA	AL	27	692	242	34	8	8	30	53	56	14	.350	.384	.457	.220	.381	.415	.499	.326	65.7	146-RF	11
2002	SEA	AL	28	647	208	27	8	8	68	62	31	15	.321	.390	.425	.177	.362	.428	.480	.297	61.0	146-RF	3
2003	SEA	AL	29	679	212	29	8	13	36	69	34	8	.312	.352	.436	.165	.345	.385	.485	.215	39.0	155-RF	4
2004	SEA	AL	30	604	187	32	7	8	36	54	23	8	.309	.351	.423	.052	.313	.359	.436	.063	22.4	152-RF	1

Breakout: 2%   Improve: 23%   Collapse: 36%

This is the player that people think Tony Gwynn was. Suzuki's value is overrated by Mariner fans, and underrated by the analyst community, who don't seem to pay attention to park effects when it comes to evaluating his performance. Suzuki's seminal skill is hitting singles, something that is generally overrated by the general public. Analysts point to his lack of walks and significant power, and scoff at Ichiro's support for major awards like MVP. But considering the environment in which he's performed, he's been truly outstanding—check out those translated batting averages. Add in his defensive prowess (which is good but not as good as everyone thinks), and his ability to steal a base, and you've got a very valuable ballplayer. Is he in the same category as Barry Bonds and Alex Rodriguez? No. But the bar isn't set there, at least while the likes of Terrence Long walk the earth. Suzuki's a great ballplayer, and more valuable than his numbers because of the additional marginal revenue the Mariners reap from the Japanese market.

LUIS UGUETO   Running Joke   Bats: B   Throws: R   Born: 15-Feb-79   Age: 25

YEAR	TM	LG	AGE	AB	H	2B	3B	HR	BB	SO	SB	CS	AVG	OBP	SLG	MLVR	EQBA	EQOBP	EQSLG	EQMLVR	VORP	DEFENSE				
2001	BRV	FLA	22	392	103	12	5	3	38	96	22	7	.263	.331	.342	-.001	.230	.278	.309	-.330	-16.0	107-SS	-1	14-2B	-1	
2002	TAC	PCL	23	51	13	1	0	0	3	13	2	1	.255	.296	.275	-.275	.235	.278	.255	-.404	-3.2	12-SS	4			
2003	SAN	TEX	24	350	91	12	2	1	27	75	25	10	.260	.315	.314	-.113	.237	.284	.290	-.341	-17.6	45-2B	-5	44-SS	-7	
2003	TAC	PCL	24	26	8	3	0	2	5	4	2	0	.308	.419	.654	.521	.259	.355	.556	.175	2.6					
2004	SEA	AL	25	219	52	9	1	3	17	47	10	3	.239	.295	.335	-.210	.243	.301	.345	-.214	0.9	60-SS	-5			

Breakout: 44%   Improve: 62%   Collapse: 22%

Let's play Rule 5 Roulette! Ugueto, having served his time as a designated pinch runner and out under Lou Piniella in 2002, was allowed to learn his craft at San Antonio, where he picked up his career where he left off—not hitting, not fielding particularly well, and failing to turn his prodigious speed into baseball value. Look for him in the agate type of John Sickels's 2006 Prospect Book.

DAN WILSON C Bats: R Throws: R Born: 25-Mar-69 Age: 35

YEAR	TM	LG	AGE	AB	H	2B	3B	HR	BB	SO	SB	CS	AVG	OBP	SLG	MLVR	EQBA	EQOBP	EQSLG	EQMLVR	VORP	DEFENSE
2001	SEA	AL	32	377	100	20	1	10	20	69	3	2	.265	.306	.403	-.066	.287	.328	.437	-.011	15.0	104-C 6
2002	SEA	AL	33	359	106	16	1	6	18	81	1	0	.295	.332	.396	.015	.326	.362	.436	.084	22.8	100-C 1
2003	SEA	AL	34	316	76	15	2	4	15	52	0	0	.241	.275	.339	-.189	.264	.301	.374	-.171	-2.8	90-C 1
2004	SEA	AL	35	226	56	11	1	4	13	45	1	1	.249	.290	.364	-.175	.253	.296	.375	-.176	1.2	61-C -1

Breakout: 27%   Improve: 36%   Collapse: 32%

Gillick's decision to sign Wilson to a two-year deal after the 2002 season was met with glee, at least among A's fans. Wilson's an average catch-and-throw guy who's no threat with the bat, having seen his offensive prime pass some time ago. He's signed for the 2004 season, and if the Mariners expect to have an offense that can keep them strongly in contention, they either need Wilson to be possessed by whatever snatched Javy Lopez's body in 2003, or for him to see no more than a couple of games a week behind a catcher who's not currently in the organization. Fat chance of either happening.

RANDY WINN LF/CF Bats: B Throws: R Born: 09-Jun-74 Age: 30

YEAR	TM	LG	AGE	AB	H	2B	3B	HR	BB	SO	SB	CS	AVG	OBP	SLG	MLVR	EQBA	EQOBP	EQSLG	EQMLVR	VORP	DEFENSE	
2001	TBY	AL	27	429	117	25	6	6	38	81	12	10	.273	.340	.401	-.014	.290	.357	.432	.036	11.6	60-RF -5	45-CF -4
2002	TBY	AL	28	607	181	39	9	14	55	109	27	8	.298	.362	.461	.138	.325	.387	.506	.227	59.7	132-CF -3	
2003	SEA	AL	29	600	177	37	4	11	41	108	23	5	.295	.348	.425	.121	.321	.373	.465	.141	28.0	135-LF 2	18-CF 3
2004	SEA	AL	30	471	129	26	4	10	40	85	15	6	.275	.336	.413	-.013	.279	.344	.425	-.006	10.2	123-LF 5	

Breakout: 7%   Improve: 28%   Collapse: 36%

Winn's developed into a good ballplayer, and is more than ample compensation for the loss of Mt. Piniella. He's got speed, hits for moderate power and a solid average, and can play left field or center field more than well enough for most clubs, with center beckoning in Seattle following Mike Cameron's departure. His basestealing technique's improved dramatically, as his use of the phantom first step has gone from "nearly every friggin' time he steals" to "rarely, and usually only against Mike Piazza." The M's signed him to a two-year, $7.25 million deal with a $5 million dual option for 2006, avoiding arbitration.

PITCHERS

CRAIG ANDERSON Bats: L Throws: L Born: 30-Oct-80 Age: 23

YEAR	TM	LG	AGE	G	GS	IP	H	BB	SO	HR	ERA	EQERA	EQH9	EQBB9	EQSO9	EQHR9	PERA	VORP	STF
2001	SBR	CAL	20	28	28	179.0	142	39	178	16	2.26	4.57	9.1	2.6	5.4	1.5	5.01	18.5	15
2002	SAN	TEX	21	27	27	152.0	143	64	94	12	3.20	5.53	9.8	4.5	4.4	1.4	5.81	1.1	-3
2003	TAC	PCL	22	28	27	177.0	187	46	67	27	3.56	5.73	9.3	2.7	3.2	1.8	5.53	-2.4	-16
2004	SEA	AL	23	18	13	75.3	83	30	37	14	5.23	5.35	9.8	3.4	4.3	1.4	5.48	5.7	-12

Breakout: 23%   Improve: 53%   Collapse: 19%

Scouts admire his poise and ability to nibble at the corners, but no one thinks much of his stuff. Anderson could well bounce around for another 10 years and end up as a serviceable one-out lefty. The comparisons to Jamie Moyer are inevitable, but premature. Much more likely to have a career out of the pen once he perfects his Ricardo Rincon/Jesse Orosco pitch than he is to ever succeed in a big league rotation.

RYAN ANDERSON Bats: L Throws: L Born: 12-Jul-79 Age: 24

The "Little Unit" has completed his transformation into the "Orthopedic Unit." His left shoulder could never stand up to the tremendous stresses he generated while pitching, and he's missed three consecutive seasons with major shoulder injuries and surgery. Despite the setbacks, Anderson intends to come back and pitch, and Dr. Larry Pedagana believes such a thing is possible. We certainly wish him the best of luck.

CHA BAEK

Bats: R   **Throws: R**   Born: 29-May-80   Age: 24

YEAR	TM	LG	AGE	G	GS	IP	H	BB	SO	HR	ERA	EQERA	EQH9	EQBB9	EQSO9	EQHR9	PERA	VORP	STF
2001	SBR	CAL	21	5	4	21.0	17	2	16	2	3.43	5.21	9.5	0.9	3.8	1.9	5.17	0.8	-13
2003	SBR	CAL	23	13	10	56.7	55	9	50	3	3.65	5.12	10.9	1.9	5.1	1.1	5.18	2.7	-1
2003	SAN	TEX	23	9	9	56.0	49	17	46	2	2.57	4.65	9.5	3.6	5.5	0.7	4.59	5.3	15
2004	SEA	AL	24	22	15	87.0	95	28	50	13	4.72	4.82	9.7	2.8	5.0	1.2	4.88	11.0	-3

Breakout: 14%   Improve: 49%   Collapse: 23%

Baek's another one of Seattle's good grabs from overseas. He throws a fastball in the vicinity of 93, mixes in a slider, and is working on filling out his repertoire. Baek struck out 50 against nine walks at Ye Olde Inland Empire last year, then went to San Antonio, dropped his ERA by a run, and managed a 46:17 K:BB ratio in nine starts. Baek's a very good pitching prospect; in many organizations, he'd be the best prospect by a fair margin. In this one, he's part of a crowd.

ARMANDO BENITEZ

Bats: R   **Throws: R**   Born: 03-Nov-72   Age: 31

YEAR	TM	LG	AGE	G	GS	IP	H	BB	SO	HR	ERA	EQERA	EQH9	EQBB9	EQSO9	EQHR9	PERA	VORP	STF
2001	NYM	NL	28	73	0	76.3	59	40	93	12	3.77	4.03	7.3	4.4	9.3	1.2	4.30	12.9	8
2002	NYM	NL	29	62	0	67.3	46	25	79	8	2.27	3.06	6.7	2.9	9.2	1.1	3.46	18.3	19
2003	NYM	NL	30	45	0	49.3	41	24	50	5	3.10	3.75	7.7	3.9	8.1	0.9	4.06	12.0	9
2003	NYY	AL	30	9	0	9.3	8	6	10	0	1.94	3.86	7.7	5.8	9.6	0.0	3.66	2.0	35
2003	SEA	AL	30	15	0	14.3	10	11	15	1	3.15	3.95	6.6	6.6	9.2	0.7	4.02	4.2	14
2004	FLO	NL	31	47	2	62.7	53	29	66	6	3.66	4.09	7.7	3.6	8.4	1.0	4.25	10.6	9

Breakout: 33%   Improve: 50%   Collapse: 33%

A better pitcher than he gets credit for. Fans of the teams he's pitched for tend to remember his worst moments, like giving up a bomb to J. T. Snow in the postseason, or one of a number of key singles, walks, and bombs to blow a save. Benitez isn't a bad pitcher, but the expectations put on him are always very high, in part because he's got such nasty stuff. There's not a ton of variance in his performance from year to year; he's a solid bullpen guy, but he's not in the same class as Mariano Rivera, Billy Wagner, and Eric Gagne. The Marlins will pay him accordingly, with a one-year, $3.5 million deal.

TRAVIS BLACKLEY

Bats: L   **Throws: L**   Born: 04-Nov-82   Age: 21

YEAR	TM	LG	AGE	G	GS	IP	H	BB	SO	HR	ERA	EQERA	EQH9	EQBB9	EQSO9	EQHR9	PERA	VORP	STF
2001	EVE	NWN	18	14	14	78.7	60	29	90	7	3.32	4.85	9.6	5.0	5.8	2.0	6.41	5.7	10
2002	SBR	CAL	19	21	20	121.3	102	44	152	11	3.49	4.96	9.3	4.1	7.1	1.4	5.32	7.9	30
2003	SAN	TEX	20	27	27	162.3	125	62	144	11	2.61	4.61	7.9	4.4	6.6	1.2	4.53	16.3	29
2004	SEA	AL	21	18	16	95.7	89	50	78	13	4.49	4.59	8.3	4.4	7.1	1.1	4.73	13.1	10

Breakout: 37%   Improve: 54%   Collapse: 11%

Ripped up the Texas League. Blackley showed tremendous command of his stuff, allowing only 125 hits in 162 innings, and striking out 144. He's not blessed with a tremendous fastball, but he fields his position exceptionally well, and has a consistent delivery from pitch to pitch, leaving a number of hitters way out on their front foot. He'll start the season at Triple-A, but there's no shortage of opportunities on the big club. If Blackley pitches well, he'll get a shot at the rotation soon enough.

GIOVANNI CARRARA

Bats: R   **Throws: R**   Born: 04-Mar-68   Age: 36

YEAR	TM	LG	AGE	G	GS	IP	H	BB	SO	HR	ERA	EQERA	EQH9	EQBB9	EQSO9	EQHR9	PERA	VORP	STF
2001	LAD	NL	33	47	3	85.3	73	24	70	12	3.17	3.54	8.0	2.3	6.3	1.2	4.04	18.6	0
2002	LAD	NL	34	63	1	90.7	83	32	56	14	3.27	4.54	9.2	2.8	5.0	1.5	5.08	10.0	-22
2003	TAC	PCL	35	18	0	27.7	28	9	27	2	4.22	5.33	10.7	3.6	7.5	1.1	5.46	0.8	-11
2003	SEA	AL	35	23	0	29.0	40	14	13	6	6.83	7.81	13.0	4.2	3.9	1.6	7.44	-4.1	-53
2004	CLE	AL	36	57	0	53.7	57	20	35	6	4.29	4.58	9.4	3.1	5.6	1.1	4.95	7.8	-9

Breakout: 28%   Improve: 58%   Collapse: 23%

Always among the very warmest of bodies, Carrara, who was once a Ken Phelps All Star, finally got his shot in MLB at an advanced age, and has managed a brief career. And there's nothing quite like getting lit up to make sure one's career stays brief. Carrara can still probably pitch under the right circumstances, and the Indians will give him a shot.

KEN CLOUDE

Bats: R **Throws: R** Born: 09-Jan-75 Age: 29

YEAR	TM	LG	AGE	G	GS	IP	H	BB	SO	HR	ERA	EQERA	EQH9	EQBB9	EQSO9	EQHR9	PERA	VORP	STF
2002	TAC	PCL	27	15	15	92.7	73	20	52	9	2.33	3.00	7.3	2.2	3.8	1.1	3.66	25.1	-2
2003	TAC	PCL	28	21	17	75.7	88	37	39	15	5.94	7.81	12.2	5.4	4.1	2.9	8.95	-16.7	-93
2004	TBY	AL	34	13	8	44.0	60	24	19	12	7.78	7.74	11.8	4.6	3.9 2.3	7.91	-5.7	-31	

Breakout: 24%   Improve: 53%   Collapse: 10%

It'd be easy to blame Lou Piniella for snuffing out Cloude's promise. Doesn't necessarily mean it'd be wrong, but Cloude apparently doesn't think that way. He's signed on with the Devil Rays organization, but it's not clear he'll be invited to spring training. His odds of having a major league career are still slightly better than those of Tito Jackson, but not so much that you'd notice.

BRIAN FALKENBORG

Bats: R **Throws: R** Born: 18-Jan-78 Age: 26

YEAR	TM	LG	AGE	G	GS	IP	H	BB	SO	HR	ERA	EQERA	EQH9	EQBB9	EQSO9	EQHR9	PERA	VORP	STF
2001	SAN	TEX	23	12	12	66.0	80	24	56	9	5.45	7.67	12.1	4.0	5.5	2.2	7.63	-14.0	-33
2001	TAC	PCL	23	8	8	48.3	50	18	27	6	4.47	5.76	9.5	4.0	3.8	1.2	5.27	-0.8	-9
2002	TAC	PCL	24	9	9	49.3	51	13	42	3	2.74	4.47	9.7	2.7	5.8	0.8	4.52	5.8	14
2003	TAC	PCL	25	17	14	79.7	66	26	62	7	2.94	4.03	8.2	3.5	6.1	1.2	4.51	12.9	-2
2004	LAD	NL	26	17	12	69.3	67	29	53	9	4.49	5.03	9.1	3.4	6.1	1.0	4.91	4.0	2

Breakout: 21%   Improve: 43%   Collapse: 18%

He'll likely get an opportunity to make the rotation at some point during the 2004 season. Falkenborg doesn't have the fastball he once had with the Oriole organization, but he's been working hard and the trend at Tacoma isn't hard to identify—he keeps getting better. When he gets the crack at the big league staff, Falkenborg better take advantage of it. This system's too loaded with guys who deserve a shot to guarantee a second opportunity should the first one be missed. But hey, there's always Tampa!

RYAN FRANKLIN

Bats: R **Throws: R** Born: 05-Mar-73 Age: 31

YEAR	TM	LG	AGE	G	GS	IP	H	BB	SO	HR	ERA	EQERA	EQH9	EQBB9	EQSO9	EQHR9	PERA	VORP	STF
2001	SEA	AL	28	38	0	78.3	76	24	60	13	3.56	4.52	9.7	2.7	6.6	1.5	5.21	8.8	-9
2002	SEA	AL	29	41	12	118.7	117	22	65	14	4.02	4.42	8.9	1.6	4.8	1.0	4.10	14.9	-1
2003	SEA	AL	30	32	32	212.0	199	61	99	34	3.57	4.53	9.0	2.5	4.3	1.4	4.80	41.5	-8
2004	SEA	AL	31	30	25	153.7	167	48	76	26	4.97	5.08	9.7	2.7	4.3	1.4	5.11	14.7	-5

Breakout: 15%   Improve: 47%   Collapse: 23%

No offense meant to Franklin, but he's pretty much the new Walt Terrell. He survives by throwing annoyingly accurate pitches, and then watches hitters repeatedly "just miss" what they perceive as mediocre offerings. His sub-4 ERA is down that low only because of Safeco Field and the Seattle defense. Franklin's valuable, in that anyone who can throw a full season's worth of starts as a league-average pitcher is always valuable. The Mariners would be thrilled to see Franklin repeat his 2003 again and again. Signed a two-year, $4.3 million deal in December.

FREDDY GARCIA

Bats: R **Throws: R** Born: 10-Jun-76 Age: 28

YEAR	TM	LG	AGE	G	GS	IP	H	BB	SO	HR	ERA	EQERA	EQH9	EQBB9	EQSO9	EQHR9	PERA	VORP	STF
2001	SEA	AL	25	34	34	238.7	199	69	163	16	3.05	3.62	8.4	2.5	6.0	0.6	3.64	49.2	27
2002	SEA	AL	26	34	34	223.7	227	63	181	30	4.39	4.58	9.2	2.4	7.0	1.1	4.52	24.5	15
2003	SEA	AL	27	33	33	201.3	196	71	144	31	4.52	5.17	9.3	3.1	6.5	1.3	5.00	17.7	2
2004	SEA	AL	28	28	28	178.0	178	59	122	22	4.21	4.30	8.9	2.8	6.0	1.0	4.32	28.3	11

Breakout: 19%   Improve: 46%   Collapse: 19%

By all rights, Garcia should look a little bit more like Jack Cassidy in The Eiger Sanction. He's noted as much for eccentricities as performance, has a bit of the air of a cheesy gadfly villain, and there's a definite limit to how much screen time you really want him to have on your club. He's slipped from a solid #2 starter to an innings guy, kind of a hard-throwing Rick Reed. The Mariners would have been better off non-tendering him and trying to sign him at a reduced rate, or even letting him go entirely, than gift-wrapping a $6.875 million salary for '04.

SHIGETOSHI HASEGAWA   **Bats: R**   **Throws: R**   Born: 01-Aug-68   Age: 35

YEAR	TM	LG	AGE	G	GS	IP	H	BB	SO	HR	ERA	EQERA	EQH9	EQBB9	EQSO9	EQHR9	PERA	VORP	STF
2001	ANA	AL	32	46	0	55.7	52	20	41	5	4.04	4.19	8.6	3.0	6.2	0.7	3.95	8.4	6
2002	SEA	AL	33	53	0	70.3	60	30	39	4	3.20	3.57	7.7	3.6	4.8	0.5	3.60	15.3	1
2003	SEA	AL	34	63	0	73.0	62	18	32	5	1.48	2.48	8.2	2.2	4.0	0.5	3.46	35.4	4
2004	SEA	AL	35	50	0	56.7	60	19	31	7	4.28	4.38	9.4	2.9	4.7	1.0	4.61	9.9	-12

Breakout: 28%   Improve: 48%   Collapse: 32%

Take a careful look at that performance record up above. Shiggy's K rate didn't improve, his home runs allowed didn't improve, and yet, his ERA was both microscopic and way out of line with his career record and reasonable expectations. Why? He posted a career-low walk rate, and a career-high groundball:flyball ratio of 1.47. He played in a fantastic pitcher's park in Safeco. Most important, he was luckier than any human being has any right to be. Bill Bavasi paid for fluky past performance rather than reasonable future expectations, signing him to a two-year, $6.3 million contract. Look for Hasegawa's numbers to be much closer to his career norms in 2004.

JEFF HEAVERLO   **Bats: R**   **Throws: R**   Born: 13-Jan-78   Age: 26

YEAR	TM	LG	AGE	G	GS	IP	H	BB	SO	HR	ERA	EQERA	EQH9	EQBB9	EQSO9	EQHR9	PERA	VORP	STF
2001	SAN	TEX	23	27	27	178.7	164	40	173	12	3.12	4.47	9.1	2.4	6.1	1.0	4.41	21.0	17
2003	TAC	PCL	25	24	24	123.7	150	38	75	8	5.38	6.51	11.7	3.3	4.7	0.9	5.70	-11.6	-12
2004	SEA	AL	26	25	8	56.0	64	20	32	7	4.97	5.08	10.1	3.1	5.0	1.0	5.11	4.3	-9

Breakout: 21%   Improve: 43%   Collapse: 26%

To pre-empt the question: No, you don't necessarily have to have your labrum surgically repaired to pitch in the Mariners' organization, but apparently, it helps. Heaverlo was clearly not back to anywhere near 100% at any point during the season. He'll begin the season at Triple-A, and he'll have to show some semblance of health and effectiveness to regain a spot on the Prospect Zeitgeist.

FELIX HERNANDEZ   **Bats: R**   **Throws: R**   Born: 08-Apr-86   Age: 18

YEAR	TM	LG	AGE	G	GS	IP	H	BB	SO	HR	ERA	EQERA	EQH9	EQBB9	EQSO9	EQHR9	PERA	VORP	STF
2003	EVE	NWN	17	11	7	55.0	43	24	73	2	2.29	4.17	8.7	5.3	7.6	0.9	4.86	7.9	47
2003	WIS	MID	17	2	2	14.0	9	3	18	1	1.93	3.55	7.1	2.8	9.2	1.4	3.94	2.9	67

This is probably the best prospect you've never heard of; the closest analog for him is probably the Angels' Francisco Rodriguez. Hernandez throws ridiculously hard, has pretty good control, and an impressive performance record under his belt at the tender age of 17. The organization loves him, and why not? He throws a legitimate 94 mph with no apparent effort. Best of all, it's not a straight fastball, but rather one of those pacts-with-Satan things that has a natural tail in to right-handed batters. Hernandez will be a Mariner much sooner than you think.

RETT JOHNSON   **Bats: L**   **Throws: R**   Born: 06-Jul-79   Age: 24

YEAR	TM	LG	AGE	G	GS	IP	H	BB	SO	HR	ERA	EQERA	EQH9	EQBB9	EQSO9	EQHR9	PERA	VORP	STF
2001	WIS	MID	22	16	16	99.3	92	30	96	4	2.27	4.79	10.6	3.9	5.3	0.8	5.29	7.9	14
2001	SBR	CAL	22	12	12	66.0	56	33	70	5	4.09	6.24	10.3	6.1	5.6	1.4	6.39	-4.1	-4
2002	SBR	CAL	23	7	7	37.0	27	11	34	1	3.65	4.28	8.0	3.2	4.8	0.5	3.66	4.9	17
2002	SAN	TEX	23	21	21	117.0	107	53	104	5	3.62	6.15	10.2	4.9	6.1	0.9	5.39	-6.4	10
2003	SAN	TEX	24	14	14	83.0	74	21	63	7	3.04	5.09	10.0	2.9	5.2	1.6	5.62	4.2	-5
2003	TAC	PCL	24	11	10	71.0	63	18	49	2	2.15	3.90	8.1	2.7	5.5	0.4	3.39	12.7	30
2004	SEA	AL	24	20	16	94.7	98	37	62	12	4.64	4.75	9.2	3.4	5.7	1.0	4.76	11.4	3

Breakout: 22%   Improve: 54%   Collapse: 22%

Needed to take a step forward with his control to be a real prospect, and he did exactly that. Pitched well at two levels, using his sinking fastball as a base pitch, and inducing soul-draining groundballs from both Texas League and PCL hitters. Johnson also features a slider, but rarely, if ever, works up in the strike zone. One of a number of reasonable options the Mariners have for a deep-in-the-rotation starter.

RYAN KETCHNER **Bats: L** **Throws: L** **Born: 19-Apr-82** **Age: 22**

YEAR	TM	LG	AGE	G	GS	IP	H	BB	SO	HR	ERA	EQERA	EQH9	EQBB9	EQSO9	EQHR9	PERA	VORP	STF
2001	EVE	NWN	19	20	5	52.3	38	18	58	3	2.93	4.14	9.1	4.7	5.3	1.4	5.44	7.4	2
2002	WIS	MID	20	31	12	111.0	75	39	118	3	2.59	3.92	8.1	4.3	5.9	0.6	4.09	18.4	22
2003	SBR	CAL	21	31	22	156.7	133	33	159	10	3.45	4.54	9.7	2.6	6.1	1.2	4.93	16.6	16
2004	SEA	AL	22	18	12	69.3	72	27	47	10	4.66	4.77	9.2	3.4	5.9	1.1	4.84	8.6	0

Breakout: 11%   Improve: 41%   Collapse: 28%

At any level, anyone who strikes out more than a guy per inning and posts a K:BB ratio of around 5:1 deserves some notice. People will latch onto the easy human interest story here (Ketchner was born deaf), but the real story is that this guy is dusting people fairly convincingly with an 87-mph fastball. His pitching pattern is reminiscent of Barry Zito's; hitters get used to looking for a featured pitch aside from the fastball (in Zito's case the curve, in Ketchner's, the changeup), then are way behind a fastball they'd normally have a good swing at. He'll face the Double-A testing grounds next year.

AARON LOOPER **Bats: R** **Throws: R** **Born: 07-Sep-76** **Age: 27**

YEAR	TM	LG	AGE	G	GS	IP	H	BB	SO	HR	ERA	EQERA	EQH9	EQBB9	EQSO9	EQHR9	PERA	VORP	STF
2001	SBR	CAL	24	56	0	71.0	59	22	77	1	2.79	5.20	10.4	3.8	5.6	0.3	4.61	2.8	-1
2002	SAN	TEX	25	57	0	90.7	76	30	73	4	2.28	4.71	10.0	3.6	5.5	0.9	5.01	7.9	-16
2003	TAC	PCL	26	46	0	75.3	72	26	67	10	3.11	4.59	10.1	3.8	6.9	2.0	6.30	7.7	-36
2004	SEA	AL	27	15	4	30.0	30	11	22	4	4.45	4.56	9.0	3.3	6.4	1.0	4.65	4.7	-1

Breakout: 31%   Improve: 55%   Collapse: 25%

Made the big club, and not just as a favor to his dad. Looper doesn't have tremendous stuff, but he's made some sort of progress every year, and the whole package is now a pretty reasonable pitcher. He'll be fighting for a job in the spring, and probably for several springs after that.

ROBERT MADRITSCH **Bats: L** **Throws: L** **Born: 28-Feb-76** **Age: 28**

YEAR	TM	LG	AGE	G	GS	IP	H	BB	SO	HR	ERA	EQERA	EQH9	EQBB9	EQSO9	EQHR9	PERA	VORP	STF
2003	SAN	TEX	27	27	27	158.7	133	67	154	11	3.63	5.73	10.3	5.1	6.7	1.4	6.12	-2.0	-23
2004	SEA	AL	28	17	9	53.0	56	32	38	7	5.50	5.63	9.5	5.1	6.2	1.1	5.68	2.0	-7

Breakout: 21%   Improve: 45%   Collapse: 25%

It took him a while to settle in, but Madritsch ended his season in fine form in the Texas League. He spent the 2002 devastating the Northern League before rolling along nicely in San Antonio, despite not having pinpoint control. He'll start the season in Triple-A, but may end up in Seattle either out of the pen or in a spot-starting role.

JULIO MATEO **Bats: R** **Throws: R** **Born: 02-Aug-77** **Age: 26**

YEAR	TM	LG	AGE	G	GS	IP	H	BB	SO	HR	ERA	EQERA	EQH9	EQBB9	EQSO9	EQHR9	PERA	VORP	STF
2001	SBR	CAL	23	56	0	66.0	58	16	79	5	2.86	5.15	11.2	3.0	6.2	1.4	5.97	2.9	-17
2002	SAN	TEX	24	12	0	17.3	7	3	18	2	0.52	2.35	5.9	1.8	7.0	2.3	4.05	5.5	-16
2002	TAC	PCL	24	20	0	31.0	39	7	23	2	4.06	5.22	11.7	2.1	4.9	0.6	5.09	1.2	-3
2002	SEA	AL	24	12	0	21.0	20	12	15	2	4.29	4.43	8.9	4.9	6.2	0.9	4.83	2.6	3
2003	SEA	AL	25	50	0	85.7	69	13	71	14	3.15	3.64	7.7	1.3	7.5	1.4	3.82	22.7	10
2004	SEA	AL	26	41	11	90.7	87	22	71	14	3.86	3.95	8.6	2.1	6.8	1.2	4.08	20.1	7

Breakout: 27%   Improve: 52%   Collapse: 21%

Mateo's velocity picked up in 2003, and he matured into a very good bullpen pitcher. He works high in the strike zone and lets the outfielders camp under a bunch of flyballs—a strategy particularly well-suited to playing half your games at Safeco. Mateo's ERA was considerably better on the road, but that's largely a function of luck, as his peripheral numbers were better at home. There's still room for further improvement; Mateo's improved control resulted in fewer walks in 2003, and his stuff could get even better if he can learn to be sharper within the strike zone.

GIL MECHE

Bats: R   **Throws: R**   Born: 08-Sep-78   Age: 25

YEAR	TM	LG	AGE	G	GS	IP	H	BB	SO	HR	ERA	EQERA	EQH9	EQBB9	EQSO9	EQHR9	PERA	VORP	STF
2002	SAN	TEX	23	25	13	65.0	68	32	56	8	6.51	8.32	12.2	5.3	6.0	2.4	8.19	-17.3	-49
2003	SEA	AL	24	32	32	186.3	187	63	130	30	4.59	5.13	9.6	2.9	6.3	1.4	5.16	20.4	9
2004	SEA	AL	25	27	23	142.3	149	52	97	22	4.73	4.84	9.3	3.1	5.9	1.2	4.88	15.0	5

Breakout: 13%   Improve: 46%   Collapse: 14%

You just can't stop Meche. He's been under the knife more often than Joan Rivers, and he just keeps coming. Meche's injuries and therapies have been profound, and yet, he pitched great during the first half of the season. In the second half, he appeared to just plain run out of gas, struggling with the location of his pitches and his mechanics. He's always outperformed expectations, performing well even when he wasn't the anointed prospect. The Mariners need to work harder to keep him healthy, because he's fighting long odds with each post-torn labrum pitch he throws.

JAMIE MOYER

Bats: L   **Throws: L**   Born: 18-Nov-62   Age: 41

YEAR	TM	LG	AGE	G	GS	IP	H	BB	SO	HR	ERA	EQERA	EQH9	EQBB9	EQSO9	EQHR9	PERA	VORP	STF
2001	SEA	AL	38	33	33	209.7	187	44	119	24	3.43	3.99	8.9	1.8	5.0	1.0	4.10	35.1	10
2002	SEA	AL	39	34	34	230.7	198	50	147	28	3.32	3.57	7.7	1.8	5.6	1.1	3.63	50.1	14
2003	SEA	AL	40	33	33	215.0	199	66	129	19	3.27	4.02	8.9	2.7	5.4	0.8	4.13	54.0	15
2004	SEA	AL	41	25	24	159.3	161	42	90	22	4.15	4.25	9.0	2.3	4.9	1.1	4.24	28.4	6

Breakout: 18%   Improve: 59%   Collapse: 12%

Is there any reason he couldn't pitch until he's 50? Everyone knows Moyer; he's good enough at what he does that every agent who represents a bunch of guys who can't throw hard can repeat his statistics from memory. He's a quality major league pitcher in the best possible situation, surrounded by a good defense in a big park. He's also the beneficiary, deserved or not, of a sizable strike zone that in the past belonged exclusively to the likes of Tom Glavine and Jimmy Key. With two years left on the three-year deal he signed after the '02 season, there's no reason to believe that Moyer's 2004 season is going to be much different than his 2003.

CLINT NAGEOTTE

Bats: R   **Throws: R**   Born: 25-Oct-80   Age: 23

YEAR	TM	LG	AGE	G	GS	IP	H	BB	SO	HR	ERA	EQERA	EQH9	EQBB9	EQSO9	EQHR9	PERA	VORP	STF
2001	WIS	MID	20	28	26	152.3	141	50	187	10	3.13	5.55	11.4	4.3	6.9	1.4	6.33	0.7	16
2002	SBR	CAL	21	29	29	164.7	153	68	214	10	4.54	6.23	11.2	4.7	6.8	1.0	5.99	-10.2	14
2003	SAN	TEX	22	27	27	154.0	127	67	157	6	3.10	5.03	9.3	5.1	7.0	0.7	4.90	8.7	23
2004	SEA	AL	23	16	12	69.3	72	35	55	9	5.05	5.17	9.3	4.3	6.9	1.1	5.19	6.3	4

Breakout: 17%   Improve: 50%   Collapse: 21%

Something of the "it" prospect in the Mariners' system. Nageotte possesses a lot of the qualities we like to see in a prospect: He has good stuff, racks up the Ks, doesn't give up many homers. He's not far off from the majors, and if he arrives with slightly better control, he's going to be outstanding. Even if he doesn't, he could still be very good. The Mariners have been wise not to work him quite as hard as they could have; it'd be nice if Nageotte could avoid the fate of Meche, Anderson, and the others who've had labrums fail on them.

JOEL PINEIRO

Bats: R   **Throws: R**   Born: 25-Sep-78   Age: 25

YEAR	TM	LG	AGE	G	GS	IP	H	BB	SO	HR	ERA	EQERA	EQH9	EQBB9	EQSO9	EQHR9	PERA	VORP	STF
2001	TAC	PCL	22	18	10	77.0	68	33	64	8	3.62	4.58	7.9	4.5	5.9	1.0	4.41	8.2	13
2001	SEA	AL	22	17	11	75.3	50	21	56	2	2.03	2.80	6.8	2.4	6.5	0.3	2.59	22.0	48
2002	SEA	AL	23	37	28	194.3	189	54	136	24	3.24	3.93	8.8	2.3	6.1	1.1	4.25	34.8	24
2003	SEA	AL	24	32	32	211.7	192	76	151	19	3.78	4.29	8.7	3.1	6.4	0.8	4.15	40.3	26
2004	SEA	AL	25	29	28	180.0	172	60	126	21	3.91	4.00	8.5	2.8	6.1	0.9	4.03	36.0	13

Breakout: 24%   Improve: 54%   Collapse: 13%

A tale of two distinct seasons:

Before the All-Star break: 129 IP, 3.28 ERA

After the All-Star break: 82.2 IP, 4.57 ERA

Pineiro had an amazing July, posting a 1.44 ERA for the month to go with a 5–0 record, then flipped and had a miserable August, with an ERA in excess of 8. By the end of the season, he looked worn down. Pineiro's stuff is very good, particularly his two-seam fastball, which can reach 91–92 with good movement, and has that Tim Hudsonesque "dodge" of the hitter's bat. Pineiro's fully capable of contending for the Cy Young award in front of a good defense and pitching in this park, assuming he can shake off the second-half malaise.

J. J. PUTZ — Bats: R — Throws: R — Born: 22-Feb-77 — Age: 27

YEAR	TM	LG	AGE	G	GS	IP	H	BB	SO	HR	ERA	EQERA	EQH9	EQBB9	EQSO9	EQHR9	PERA	VORP	STF
2001	SAN	TEX	24	27	26	148.0	145	59	135	11	3.83	5.68	10.0	4.4	5.7	1.2	5.54	-1.2	-8
2002	SAN	TEX	25	15	15	84.0	84	28	60	7	3.64	6.11	12.0	3.7	4.9	1.7	6.89	-4.2	-36
2002	TAC	PCL	25	9	9	54.0	51	21	39	4	3.83	4.44	8.7	3.9	5.0	0.9	4.52	6.5	0
2003	TAC	PCL	26	41	0	86.0	69	34	60	4	2.51	3.87	8.0	4.3	5.5	0.7	4.09	15.2	-6
2003	SEA	AL	26	3	0	3.7	4	3	3	0	4.86	5.40	10.8	8.1	8.1	0.0	5.56	0.3	8
2004	SEA	AL	27	14	8	45.0	47	21	28	6	4.93	5.04	9.4	3.9	5.5	1.1	5.14	4.5	-6

Breakout: 25%   Improve: 49%   Collapse: 26%

Starting wasn't working, so the Mariners moved Putz to the pen, and the results were promising. He's not going to be a tremendous closer or anything, but he should have a clean shot at a bullpen job to start the season. Strictly back-of-the-bullpen material.

ARTHUR RHODES — Bats: L — Throws: L — Born: 24-Oct-69 — Age: 34

YEAR	TM	LG	AGE	G	GS	IP	H	BB	SO	HR	ERA	EQERA	EQH9	EQBB9	EQSO9	EQHR9	PERA	VORP	STF
2001	SEA	AL	31	72	0	68.0	46	12	83	5	1.72	2.38	6.9	1.5	10.5	0.6	2.60	23.0	49
2002	SEA	AL	32	66	0	69.7	45	13	81	4	2.32	2.27	5.9	1.6	10.2	0.5	2.18	24.9	49
2003	SEA	AL	33	67	0	54.0	53	18	48	4	4.17	4.38	9.5	3.0	8.1	0.7	4.36	9.2	14
2004	OAK	AL	34	58	0	65.7	57	19	62	6	3.13	3.31	7.8	2.4	8.2	0.7	3.32	18.1	15

Breakout: 31%   Improve: 51%   Collapse: 22%

Do not mess with a man's earring. Rhodes had his worst season in recent memory, but the basics are still in place. He still throws very hard, he's not hurt, and he's going to be back to form in 2004. His 2003 season stands out as a fluke, and the smart money is that he'll be back to his typical dominant self, blowing lefties and righties away in a setup role. Could be one of the very best bargains of the available relievers; his 2003 screams "fluke," and his performance record screams "nasty." The A's ventured three years, $9.2 million on "nasty."

KAZUHIRO SASAKI — Bats: R — Throws: R — Born: 22-Feb-68 — Age: 36

YEAR	TM	LG	AGE	G	GS	IP	H	BB	SO	HR	ERA	EQERA	EQH9	EQBB9	EQSO9	EQHR9	PERA	VORP	STF
2001	SEA	AL	33	69	0	66.7	48	11	62	6	3.24	3.16	7.3	1.4	8.0	0.7	2.95	17.0	27
2002	SEA	AL	34	61	0	60.7	44	20	73	6	2.52	3.36	6.7	2.7	10.4	0.8	3.07	14.7	36
2003	SEA	AL	35	35	0	33.3	31	15	29	2	4.05	4.78	9.0	3.9	7.9	0.6	4.28	4.0	13
2004	SEA	AL	36	61	0	38.3	33	12	34	5	3.61	3.69	7.8	2.7	7.8	1.0	3.73	9.2	8

Breakout: 30%   Improve: 69%   Collapse: 5%

Went on the DL with a rib injury in August, and it was plain that he wasn't healthy over much of the year. Often, when a player has a minor injury, he makes minor adjustments to his game to counter its effects. When that happens, the chance of another injury, sometimes in a weird spot like the ribs, goes up. Of course, in this case, it's that Sasaki cracked his ribs, ahem, "handling his luggage," which is approximately as credible as Babe Ruth's season-long "tummyache." The tremendous seasons by Hasegawa and Soriano lessened the impact of Sasaki's lack of effectiveness and availability. Last word on his injuries: He appears to be fine, has his velocity back, but at press time, the stunning news that Sasaki was going to stay in Japan in '04 had just broken.

RAFAEL SORIANO — Bats: R — Throws: R — Born: 19-Dec-79 — Age: 24

YEAR	TM	LG	AGE	G	GS	IP	H	BB	SO	HR	ERA	EQERA	EQH9	EQBB9	EQSO9	EQHR9	PERA	VORP	STF
2001	SBR	CAL	21	15	15	89.0	49	39	98	4	2.53	3.66	7.1	5.3	5.8	0.8	4.07	17.0	22
2001	SAN	TEX	21	8	8	48.3	34	14	53	5	3.35	3.80	7.2	3.2	7.2	1.6	4.33	9.0	26
2002	SAN	TEX	22	10	8	46.7	32	15	52	6	2.31	3.92	8.7	3.5	7.8	2.6	6.31	7.7	-3
2002	SEA	AL	22	10	8	47.3	45	16	32	8	4.57	4.73	8.7	2.8	5.9	1.4	4.68	4.4	17
2003	TAC	PCL	23	11	10	62.0	43	12	63	2	3.19	3.24	6.6	2.0	8.2	0.5	2.58	15.3	52
2003	SEA	AL	23	40	0	53.0	30	12	68	2	1.53	1.95	5.5	2.0	11.5	0.4	1.97	25.4	75
2004	SEA	AL	24	31	16	102.7	89	34	95	14	3.61	3.69	7.7	2.8	8.1	1.0	3.76	23.8	17

Breakout: 25%   Improve: 43%   Collapse: 26%

(continued next page)

Rafael Soriano *(continued)*

That clicking sound heard around the league was the sound of tremendous ability aligning with experience and knowledge. Soriano's got a positively otherworldly fastball, and he's now using it properly, weaving other pitches around it to create a smothering, Lovecraftian nightmare for opposing hitters. The Mariners will probably move him into the rotation in 2004, and there's no better candidate to absolutely explode on the league and turn into a dominant starter. Just as Johan Santana moved into the Minnesota rotation and became a legitimate #1 starter, so too will Soriano.

BRIAN SWEENEY Bats: R Throws: R Born: 13-Jun-74 Age: 30

YEAR	TM	LG	AGE	G	GS	IP	H	BB	SO	HR	ERA	EQERA	EQH9	EQBB9	EQSO9	EQHR9	PERA	VORP	STF
2001	SAN	TEX	27	37	9	104.3	117	23	96	8	3.80	5.36	11.8	2.4	5.7	1.3	5.99	2.6	-25
2002	TAC	PCL	28	30	23	142.0	157	28	113	16	3.80	4.90	10.8	2.0	5.4	1.4	5.48	10.3	-13
2003	TAC	PCL	29	29	21	141.0	165	32	115	17	4.28	6.09	12.2	2.4	6.4	1.7	6.67	-7.0	-25
2004	SDP	NL	30	16	8	46.7	52	14	35	6	4.55	4.99	10.1	2.4	5.9	1.1	5.11	4.5	0

Breakout: 21%   Improve: 43%   Collapse: 27%

Every organization has at least two or three guys like Brian Sweeney, and that's both a necessary and good thing. Need a spot start? No problem. Starter got knocked out in the third against the Red Sox, and you need five innings to save the pen? I'm on it, Skip. Going into the 12th inning and the bullpen's empty and tired? Sweeney to the rescue. Like literally dozens of other guys, he'll spend the rest of his career battling for one of the last two spots on the pitching staff, hoping to have the hot couple of months that will establish him firmly in the majors. The dream is the Kevin Jarvis career path, and Sweeney got traded for the real McCoy as part of the six-player Cirillo deal with San Diego.

AARON TAYLOR Bats: R Throws: R Born: 20-Aug-77 Age: 26

YEAR	TM	LG	AGE	G	GS	IP	H	BB	SO	HR	ERA	EQERA	EQH9	EQBB9	EQSO9	EQHR9	PERA	VORP	STF
2001	WIS	MID	23	28	0	29.3	19	11	50	1	2.46	3.65	9.9	5.1	9.9	0.7	5.10	5.4	17
2002	SAN	TEX	24	61	0	77.0	51	34	93	5	2.34	4.35	8.4	4.7	8.3	1.3	5.02	9.5	-4
2003	TAC	PCL	25	33	0	40.3	30	13	34	3	2.46	3.38	7.5	3.4	6.5	1.0	3.85	9.2	0
2003	SEA	AL	25	10	0	12.7	17	6	9	0	8.50	7.50	13.5	4.5	6.8	0.0	5.83	-4.3	6
2004	SEA	AL	26	26	5	46.0	44	19	36	6	4.53	4.64	8.5	3.6	6.9	1.0	4.46	5.4	1

Breakout: 27%   Improve: 54%   Collapse: 23%

Fastball/splitter pitcher, in the mold of former Angels closer Bryan Harvey. His fastball can reach 97, but usually is in the 92–94 range. He gets guys out by getting them to foul off or miss a couple of fastballs, then throws a splitter that's getting better and better. In an organization with fewer options available, he'd be a candidate for the closer's job. In Seattle, he's going to have to get lucky to get that opportunity.

MATT THORNTON Bats: L Throws: L Born: 15-Sep-76 Age: 27

YEAR	TM	LG	AGE	G	GS	IP	H	BB	SO	HR	ERA	EQERA	EQH9	EQBB9	EQSO9	EQHR9	PERA	VORP	STF
2001	SBR	CAL	24	27	27	157.0	126	60	192	9	2.52	4.72	10.8	4.7	6.5	1.1	5.92	13.2	-4
2002	SAN	TEX	25	12	12	62.0	52	29	44	3	3.63	5.73	9.8	5.1	4.9	1.0	5.45	-0.8	-19
2003	SAN	TEX	26	4	4	25.3	8	9	18	0	0.36	1.99	4.0	4.0	4.8	0.4	2.00	9.1	21
2004	SEA	AL	27	18	11	60.3	64	32	40	9	5.30	5.42	9.4	4.5	5.8	1.2	5.59	3.8	-8

Breakout: 23%   Improve: 46%   Collapse: 31%

Fallen off a lot of radar screens, and deserves more attention than he's gotten. Thornton underwent Tommy John surgery, came back and pitched well, throwing a variety of nameless pitches at less than impressive speeds, and somehow compelling hitters to spend most of their at-bat shifting their weight around. He then started having pretty serious problems with discs in his neck. He's expected to be healthy for the 2004 season, and he'll likely start the year confusing hitters in the PCL.

Tampa Bay Devil Rays

Another year passed, another year of futility for the Devil Rays.

Seeking to fire up the club, Chuck LaMar brings in Lou Piniella to manage, sending Randy Winn to Seattle for the right to hire Piniella as manager. Piniella accepts the job; it's near his home and family, and it's certainly a less stressful job than say, managing a contending club. The results weren't pretty. The Devil Rays weren't just bad—they were uninteresting and bad, a far greater sin in any entertainment business.

The obvious question is comparable to that posed by a Senator waking up surrounded by hookers in a foreign land: "How did this happen?" Well, let's go to the timeline:

The Timeline—Condensed for Brevity

March 9, 1995: The Tampa Bay Devil Rays begin operations as a Major League Baseball Franchise. Atlanta Braves Assistant GM Chuck LaMar is hired as general manager of the Rays, tasked to build a successful organization from the ground up.

November 18, 1997: MLB holds an expansion draft for its newest clubs, the Diamondbacks and the Devil Rays. The Ray front office, headed by LaMar and manager Larry Rothschild, who had served as the pitching coach for the Florida Marlins, performs moderately well in the draft, selecting a reasonable group of prospects, including Tony Saunders, Bobby Abreu, Dmitri Young, and Bubba Trammell.

November 18, 1997: Chuck LaMar completes a previous deal to acquire Mike Kelly from the Cincinnati Reds. The Reds receive Dmitri Young, who had been drafted away from the Reds organization earlier that day.

November 18, 1997: The Devil Rays send outfielder Bobby Abreu to the Philadelphia Phillies for shortstop Kevin Stocker.

December 13, 1999: Chuck LaMar signs 34-year old OF/DH Greg Vaughn to a 4-year, $34 million contract. Vaughn was coming off a season in which he hit .245/.347/.535 for the Reds. According to LaMar: "When Greg Vaughn signed that contract, we were heading in a different direction. We were headed toward a competitive, veteran type of team until the young kids are ready."

December 19, 1999: The D-Rays family of stars grows by one, as 32-year old OF Gerald Williams joins the club. Williams would earn in excess of $7 million over the next

DEVIL RAYS PROSPECTUS

2003 record: 63–99; Fifth place, AL East

Pythagenport record: 67–95

Runs scored per game: 4.4 (12th in AL)

Runs allowed per game: 5.3 (11th in AL)

Team EqA: .250 (12th in AL)

2003 Batters Age: 26.8 (Youngest in AL)

2003 Pitchers Age: 26.9 (2nd youngest in AL)

Ballpark: Tropicana Field; Neutral park; Park Factor of 0.997

2003: The team's two-season streak of triple-digit losses comes to an end, but Tampa finishes last again.

2004: Stuck in neutral as division rivals hit the nitrous. Devil Rays fans don't deserve this—Celine Dion fans don't even deserve this.

three seasons. That $7 million bought just under 1,000 plate appearances of a tidy .247 batting average, virtually unburdened by walks, power, or basestealing prowess—exactly in line with reasonable expectations.

December 15, 2002: The Rays relieve the Mets of an albatross, acquiring SS Rey Ordonez and enough cash to cover all but $2 million of his salary, for Russ Johnson and Josh Presley. At the time of the acquisition, Ordonez is 31 years of age with seven years of major league experience—not to mention eight career home runs, 123 non-intentional walks, and 151 total extra-base hits in approximately 3,000 career plate appearances.

November 21, 2003: The Rays acquire 1B Tino Martinez from the St. Louis Cardinals for RP prospect Evan Rust. The Cardinals include enough cash so that Martinez will cost Tampa $1.5 million guaranteed.

December 8, 2003: Chuck LaMar signs 34-year old Eduardo Perez to a two-year deal worth $1.7 million.

There are dozens of additional items that could be added here, but you get the point.

The Problem

The common thread linking all these moves is that there's no guiding principle behind any of them. Barring a through-the-looking-glass incarnation of Rachel Phelps, there's simply no logical explanation for these transactions. If you evaluate each move individually, you are repeatedly compelled to ask "Why was this done?" Even if the players acquired performed at the very top of reasonable expectations once they hit the Trop, the Devil Rays wouldn't be materially better off. They would have simply been more effective treading water.

When decisions are made and actions taken, it is presumably because there is some sort of desired outcome. Things might not work out perfectly, but there should be an expected result. If someone decides to go on a diet and exercise regimen to lose weight, and they follow it, they'll lose weight. If that person's overweight, the decision and action plan makes sense. If they're starving to death, it's a bad decision from the get-go, because the intended outcome itself isn't desirable. Why undertake an endeavor if, even if it works well, it doesn't leave you better off?

In short, forget about microdiscussions, like different methods of player evaluation. Putting aside the merits of differing views on how to forecast future performance, how about simply having a plan? Even a simple checklist of things the organization should do in the next 12 months would be nice. Ideally, there should be some goal at the end of the checklist, and the individual items on the list should contribute towards that goal. For starters, the goal can be just about anything baseball-related. A simple sentence, like "Win 81 games during the 2006 regular season" would be a quantum leap forward for this franchise.

Based on what the Devil Rays have done over the entirety of their existence, can you divine what the current sentence might say? "Don't lose 115 games in a single season"? "Make sure every mediocre ballplayer with no upside makes a comfortable living"? "Sign every player who ever had anything to do with Florida, even marginally"? It's certainly not something like "Maximize talent for every dollar we spend," or "Build and develop a talent base strong enough to win 85 games a year, minimum, for four years starting in 2005." This organization seems to believe that there's a significant difference between winning 64 games and winning 72 games, that the latter is some sort of noteworthy accomplishment. No achievement has ever taken place without a worthwhile goal.

The Case Study

Look at the Tino Martinez deal through that lens for a moment. What goal is Chuck LaMar trying to achieve? If everything works out perfectly, will the organization be better off? (See table 1.)

There's not a whole lot of mystery here. Martinez's 2004 production will cost the Rays $1.5 million. What will they get for their money? If everything breaks right, and Martinez has a shocking year, he'll play 155 games and hit .320/.390/.550. Granted, the chance of that happening is very near zero, but for the sake of discussion, let's say that pigs fly, hell freezes over, Canada invades Michigan, and

TABLE 1. TINO MARTINEZ'S LAST FOUR SEASONS

Year	Age	G	BA	OBP	SLG
2000	32	155	.258	.328	.422
2001	33	154	.280	.329	.501
2002	34	150	.262	.337	.438
2003	35	138	.273	.352	.429

Martinez hits like Don Mattingly in his prime. Martinez's theoretical miracle season would be worth somewhere around 50 runs better than a replacement player, a 30-run improvement over the 20 runs Travis Lee was worth in 2003. So the Rays would expect to be about three wins better at 1B than they were in 2003.

Then what? The 2003 Rays won 63 games, and 15 of those wins came against powerhouse clubs in Baltimore and Detroit. Martinez's miracle season might bring them to 66, maybe 67. Then Martinez is a year older, coming off a big year, and has an $8 million option for the 2005 season, one that he almost certainly won't be worth. The one upside is that when he leaves to play somewhere else, the Rays would receive a draft pick in the 2005 draft as compensation. Considering that the Devil Ray player acquisition and development system has a spotty history, the pick is cold comfort at best.

So why would this club want to go get Tino Martinez? For the same price, the Rays can acquire two or three Triple-A veterans and give them all jobs on the major league roster. If they work out, great; you get either a player to build around at a low cost, or a bargaining chip that can be used to bring much needed talent into the organization. If the player doesn't work out, the team can move onto another option. The cost is low, both in terms of dollars and wins, and if things work out, there's a gain for the organization.

But that's not happening. Instead, the Devil Rays are pursuing a course of action that, if successful, will leave the team no better off than it currently is.

The Good News

This organization makes the term "good news" highly relative. Remember, this is the organization that had two of its minor league prospects suffer gunshot wounds, and signed a high-profile amateur free agent, Toe Nash, who was later incarcerated for three counts of felony carnal knowledge of a juvenile. So, keeping that in mind, consider Aubrey Huff's consolation season. Huff posted a .311/.367/.555 line in 2003, building on his excellent 2002. Huff's become one of the very best hitters in baseball, and even with his defensive limitations, he's a championship caliber player. The Rays inked him to a three-year contract, buying out three arbitration years. On the mound, Victor Zambrano was relatively healthy and pitched well, finally demonstrating passable command of his considerable stuff.

In the minors, B. J. Upton started his professional career with a bang, playing well in the Sally League, and even holding his own offensively in 105 Double-A at-bats, just as he turned 19. He's nominally a shortstop, but scouts are split on whether or not he'll be able to stay in the middle infield. Whether or not he does is of secondary importance; Upton is the canary in the coal mine for Tampa's player development apparatus. The Rays have never really had an impact player come out of their own system. LaMar's penchant for drafting high schoolers hasn't been a good match for the instructional capabilities of the organization to date. If Upton, Baldelli, and Carl Crawford all work out, the Devil Rays will have shown they've figured out how to draft and develop young players. They still won't have the tactics of salary maximization down, but every organization has to start somewhere.

State of Affairs

Tampa Bay's transformed itself into a kind of Wonderland within major league baseball, where the unexpected and inexplicable become commonplace. It's not just the little things, like Ken Cloude choosing to reunite with his old buddy Lou Piniella, with whom he had such a great relationship in Seattle. It's not just the bizarre turf, or the catwalks that lead to pachinko-style caroms on hard-hit balls. There's a combination of events and entities that give the whole place a kind of Bermuda Triangle feel. Ben Grieve in a public argument with anyone, much less his manager? A team trying to hold to a budget going after Carl Everett in

the free agent market, when the only assets it really has are outfielders with some semblance of promise? While other teams are trying to put together winning ballclubs, either now or in the future, owner Vince Naimoli and crew seem headed for a re-enactment of the ending of *Magnolia*.

The Tampa Bay Devil Ray organization is completely and totally dysfunctional. There is nothing of lasting value here. In nine years of existence, the Rays haven't even managed a cave painting for which they might somehow be noticed, much less remembered. From the fractured and ineffectual ownership group through the incompetent front office, there is nothing of importance or interest in this organization. It is a complete and total wasteland. Fans of the Devil Rays, if any ever existed or remain, will have to wait until Naimoli and the other partners divest themselves of the club, and an ownership group takes over that has some idea of how to build a club before there's even a possibility of future success on the diamond.

This may sound like an overly harsh assessment of the personnel working for the Devil Rays. But it's not personal. The job security enjoyed by Chuck LaMar is really nothing short of inexcusable. Just as players are held accountable for their performance on the field, and end up unemployed or demoted if they don't perform, so too should general managers and front office executives be held accountable for their performance. The ownership group in Tampa should have replaced LaMar long ago. The miserable attendance and persistent lack of interest in the Devil Rays make it clear that the fans are at least doing their part, and holding Naimoli responsible.

HITTERS

MARLON ANDERSON 2B Bats: L Throws: R Born: 06-Jan-74 Age: 30

YEAR	TM	LG	AGE	AB	H	2B	3B	HR	BB	SO	SB	CS	AVG	OBP	SLG	MLVR	EQBA	EQOBP	EQSLG	EQMLVR	VORP	DEFENSE
2001	PHI	NL	27	522	153	30	2	11	35	74	8	5	.293	.340	.421	.015	.301	.346	.433	.028	28.8	134-2B 8
2002	PHI	NL	28	539	139	30	6	8	42	71	5	1	.258	.317	.380	-.044	.273	.326	.405	-.073	14.1	130-2B -11
2003	TBY	AL	29	482	130	27	3	6	41	60	19	3	.270	.331	.376	-.075	.293	.354	.409	.001	12.1	123-2B -4
2004	STL	NL	30	399	106	21	3	6	30	51	8	3	.267	.320	.377	-.093	.271	.328	.399	-.074	13.8	104-2B -4

Breakout: 10%   Improve: 41%   Collapse: 30%

Once again, the Devil Rays demonstrate their commitment to revving the engine with the car in neutral. Anderson, who was perhaps the very definition of a player who was "present and breathing" in Philadelphia, was the very definition of "there" in Tampa Bay. He continued about average offensively and slightly below average with the glove, providing the perfect fuel for a team determined to play out the entire schedule. Again, the same question needs to be asked: What was the point? Anderson can be a backup to a good but fragile second baseman on a good team. But was there ever any upside for Tampa here? He only earned $600,000, but why pay more than the minimum if there's just no potential gain? The Cardinals signed him to an identical one year, $600,000 deal, and Anderson's the frontrunner to man the deuce in St. Louis in 2004.

ROCCO BALDELLI   CF   Bats: R   Throws: R   Born: 25-Sep-81   Age: 22

YEAR	TM	LG	AGE	AB	H	2B	3B	HR	BB	SO	SB	CS	AVG	OBP	SLG	MLVR	EQBA	EQOBP	EQSLG	EQMLVR	VORP	DEFENSE
2001	CSC	SAL	19	406	101	23	6	8	23	89	25	9	.249	.307	.394	.042	.208	.250	.337	-.359	-26.8	112-CF -8
2002	BAK	CAL	20	312	104	19	1	14	18	63	21	6	.333	.383	.535	.332	.265	.300	.435	-.084	5.8	62-CF -6
2002	ORL	SOU	20	70	26	3	1	2	5	11	3	2	.371	.429	.529	.456	.324	.370	.465	.138	6.3	12-CF -1
2002	DUR	INT	20	96	28	6	1	3	0	23	2	5	.292	.292	.469	.056	.271	.278	.438	-.114	0.9	19-CF -3
2003	TBY	AL	21	637	184	32	8	11	30	128	27	10	.289	.329	.416	-.007	.308	.349	.448	.061	20.8	150-CF 5
2004	TBY	AL	22	581	158	33	5	16	34	106	20	7	.272	.318	.426	-.028	.274	.324	.446	-.015	16.6	148-CF 1

Breakout: 32%   Improve: 55%   Collapse: 28%

That may have been the most expensive PR move in the Devil Rays' history. Baldelli made the jump from the California League to the bigs in just over a year, an ill-advised rush job by Tampa. He started off gangbusters, but the league quickly caught up with him, holding him to just a .270/.322/.378 line after the All-Star break. So instead of learning his craft in Double-A, he was earning his way out of the renewal category, and will now be eligible for free agency a year—maybe more—earlier than he should. That's just plain bad planning on the part of the front office, which is approximately as surprising as an Eastern sunrise. At least Baldelli did his part, which bodes well for his future. Even as he struggled throughout the season, he did take some steps forward in the second half, increasing his walk rate and showing far better judgment on the basepaths. Baldelli's going to help some team towards a title, but it's not going to be the Rays unless there's a change in the owner's box and front office.

WES BANKSTON   RF   Bats: R   Throws: R   Born: 23-Nov-83   Age: 20

YEAR	TM	LG	AGE	AB	H	2B	3B	HR	BB	SO	SB	CS	AVG	OBP	SLG	MLVR	EQBA	EQOBP	EQSLG	EQMLVR	VORP	DEFENSE
2002	PRI	APP	18	246	74	10	1	18	18	46	2	1	.301	.351	.569	.283	.204	.230	.384	-.334	-40.3	58-RF -5
2003	CSC	SAL	19	375	96	18	1	12	53	94	2	3	.256	.351	.405	.116	.195	.264	.320	-.362	-36.7	88-RF -13
2004	TBY	AL	20	268	54	12	1	6	18	63	2	1	.201	.254	.324	-.317	.204	.259	.339	-.321	-17.2	72-RF -10

Breakout: 34%   Improve: 51%   Collapse: 32%

Bankston's not gotten much attention, but he's got some promise. A 19-year-old playing fairly well in the Sally League is a nice accomplishment. He's got a long way to go, and there's concern that his swing is a little long, but he's got legitimate power, and enough strength that he'll be able to tweak his form a little bit without a major loss. If he can get the technique down in the outfield, he'll field well enough to play in the bigs. The Rays do draft guys with good tools. Now if they can get their player development skills down, guys like Bankston may well become very good big league players.

JAY CANIZARO   2B   Bats: R   Throws: R   Born: 04-Jul-73   Age: 30

YEAR	TM	LG	AGE	AB	H	2B	3B	HR	BB	SO	SB	CS	AVG	OBP	SLG	MLVR	EQBA	EQOBP	EQSLG	EQMLVR	VORP	DEFENSE
2002	EDM	PCL	29	247	71	11	2	14	30	46	6	3	.287	.371	.518	.206	.250	.326	.456	-.020	12.0	57-2B -8
2002	MIN	AL	29	112	24	8	1	0	10	22	0	1	.214	.285	.304	-.274	.232	.305	.330	-.246	-2.1	25-2B 0
2003	DUR	INT	30	92	22	7	0	4	9	19	2	0	.239	.307	.446	.008	.215	.284	.419	-.175	0.0	15-2B -6
2004	TBY	AL	30	112	27	6	1	3	11	22	2	1	.237	.308	.376	-.135	.240	.314	.394	-.128	3.4	34-2B -5

Breakout: 33%   Improve: 48%   Collapse: 31%

From time to time, Canizaro's shown some pretty impressive potential, and even pretty impressive results. He's not horrible with the glove, and yet, he's never really been given an extended trial, even when he played pretty well. At some point, you have to ask . . . why? Is he displaying anti-social behavior? Beheading teammates? What's the deal? He got hurt in May, then, once healthy, was released. He'll look around for a job, but you don't get the impression he's made enough friends to catch a break, and he's now on the wrong side of 30 to boot.

JORGE CANTU   SS/3B   Bats: R   Throws: R   Born: 30-Jan-82   Age: 22

YEAR	TM	LG	AGE	AB	H	2B	3B	HR	BB	SO	SB	CS	AVG	OBP	SLG	MLVR	EQBA	EQOBP	EQSLG	EQMLVR	VORP	DEFENSE	
2001	ORL	SOU	19	512	131	26	3	4	17	93	4	9	.256	.291	.342	-.132	.235	.259	.318	-.352	-23.1	119-SS -21	
2002	ORL	SOU	20	512	124	31	1	3	23	74	2	6	.242	.280	.324	-.149	.228	.249	.313	-.383	-28.6	95-SS -1	33-3B -4
2003	DUR	INT	21	200	59	16	1	4	8	21	2	1	.295	.319	.445	.086	.275	.314	.425	-.064	8.1	49-SS -8	
2003	ORL	SOU	21	158	34	10	0	3	9	27	0	3	.215	.262	.335	-.166	.199	.235	.317	-.422	-11.9	33-3B -3	
2004	TBY	AL	22	249	57	13	1	4	11	36	1	1	.230	.268	.332	-.267	.232	.273	.348	-.268	-4.6	66-SS -9	

Breakout: 27%   Improve: 46%   Collapse: 34%

Even in limited playing time, and no matter how choppy he may be at shortstop, Cantu did hit .295/.319/.445 in Triple-A at the age of 21. Yes, he showed all the plate discipline of Oscar Azocar after a Sudafed binge, but at least that's something. Even keeping that in mind, Cantu's not much of a prospect, and really should be at Double-A. He has no inkling of whether a pitch is going to be a ball or a strike, and he needs to learn a defensive position. He's likely to be a Grade B− prospect at 3B or OF a couple of years from now if things break his way. If they don't, he could be the next Kit Pellow.

CARL CRAWFORD

																							DEFENSE			
			LF			Bats: L			Throws: L							Born: 05-Aug-81				Age: 22						
YEAR	TM	LG	AGE	AB	H	2B	3B	HR	BB	SO	SB	CS	AVG	OBP	SLG	MLVR	EQBA	EQOBP	EQSLG	EQMLVR	VORP		DEFENSE			
2001	ORL	SOU	19	537	147	24	3	4	36	90	36	20	.274	.324	.352	-.050	.245	.284	.318	-.297	-25.0	116-CF	-3	15-LF	-1
2002	DUR	INT	20	353	105	17	9	7	20	69	26	8	.297	.339	.456	.116	.276	.319	.431	-.046	10.5	45-CF	-5	36-LF	-1
2002	TBY	AL	20	259	67	11	6	2	9	41	9	5	.259	.292	.371	-.138	.280	.312	.406	-.091	-2.4	63-LF	3		
2003	TBY	AL	21	630	177	18	9	5	26	102	55	10	.281	.311	.362	-.127	.302	.334	.391	-.055	-6.7	131-LF	3	11-CF	0
2004	TBY	AL	22	502	140	25	6	7	28	73	31	8	.278	.319	.396	-.062	.281	.326	.414	-.050	8.3	127-LF	1		

Breakout: 28%   Improve: 53%   Collapse: 25%

Another example of a guy who could well be a very good ballplayer down the road, at which time he'll either cost a fortune or be with another team. Crawford's extremely fast, is a hacker of the highest order, and is young enough so that he could end up being a truly outstanding player. If he improves his plate discipline 15%, he'll increase his average and power enough to be an outfielder of acceptable production. Any way LaMar can arrange for him to spend a month in a locked facility with Rickey Henderson? Sure, he might end up speaking of himself in the third person, but it'd be worth it.

MATT DIAZ

YEAR	TM	LG	AGE	AB	H	2B	3B	HR	BB	SO	SB	CS	AVG	OBP	SLG	MLVR	EQBA	EQOBP	EQSLG	EQMLVR	VORP		DEFENSE			
			OF			Bats: R			Throws: R							Born: 03-Mar-78				Age: 26						
2001	BAK	CAL	23	524	172	40	2	17	24	73	11	5	.328	.374	.510	.279	.265	.298	.419	-.111	-6.9	127-RF	-3		
2002	ORL	SOU	24	449	123	28	1	10	34	72	31	9	.274	.339	.408	.075	.249	.293	.389	-.175	-17.3	78-LF	-4	19-RF	-1
2003	ORL	SOU	25	227	87	21	0	5	19	24	9	5	.383	.449	.542	.511	.335	.385	.485	.204	19.6	57-RF	4		
2003	DUR	INT	25	253	83	18	3	8	16	45	6	2	.328	.386	.518	.301	.306	.360	.494	.145	15.9	53-RF	4	14-LF	1
2004	TBY	AL	26	264	70	15	2	6	16	41	6	2	.265	.318	.408	-.058	.268	.324	.427	-.046	7.1	71-RF	1		

Breakout: 17%   Improve: 39%   Collapse: 38%

When Ben Grieve went down with a blood clot, Matt Diaz got a deserved if brief nine-AB look in the bigs. He appears to have taken a huge step forward, showing more patience at the plate, working pitchers deep into counts, getting a ball to drive, and hitting it hard. He'll start the year at Triple-A, but he could be up in the bigs very quickly if the improvement's more than a mirage.

ELIJAH DUKES

YEAR	TM	LG	AGE	AB	H	2B	3B	HR	BB	SO	SB	CS	AVG	OBP	SLG	MLVR	EQBA	EQOBP	EQSLG	EQMLVR	VORP	DEFENSE
			LF			Bats: B			Throws: R							Born: 26-Jun-84				Age: 20		
2003	CSC	SAL	19	383	94	17	4	7	45	130	33	11	.245	.340	.366	.044	.198	.261	.308	-.383	-40.6	101-LF -11
2004	TBY	AL	20	284	55	13	2	4	19	92	11	4	.193	.256	.297	-.352	.195	.261	.311	-.358	-17.7	76-LF -10

Breakout: 26%   Improve: 47%   Collapse: 29%

Arrested on an assault charge for throwing a remote control at his children's mother. There's something to be said for just not drafting players who haven't been to college. Not that a college education means that someone's got an even keel, but young men between the ages of 18–21 are just hard to predict. In the case of someone who's been through school, the club has passed that risk onto the NCAA and the school in question. On the field, Dukes didn't have a bad start. He needs some seasoning both at the plate and in the field. If he can get his act together and perform well at High-A, perhaps exchanging 10 strikeouts for walks, he's got a shot at a career.

DAMION EASLEY

YEAR	TM	LG	AGE	AB	H	2B	3B	HR	BB	SO	SB	CS	AVG	OBP	SLG	MLVR	EQBA	EQOBP	EQSLG	EQMLVR	VORP	DEFENSE
			2B			Bats: R			Throws: R							Born: 11-Nov-69				Age: 34		
2001	DET	AL	31	585	146	27	7	11	52	90	10	5	.250	.325	.376	-.082	.277	.349	.419	-.007	26.0	151-2B 5
2002	DET	AL	32	304	68	14	1	8	27	43	1	3	.224	.310	.355	-.138	.251	.331	.401	-.086	7.5	84-2B 0
2003	TBY	AL	33	107	20	3	1	1	2	18	0	0	.187	.202	.262	-.521	.206	.220	.299	-.474	-9.3	19-3B -2
2004	TBY	AL	34	197	47	9	1	4	14	32	1	1	.237	.299	.347	-.189	.239	.305	.363	-.186	0.0	55-2B -2

Breakout: 47%   Improve: 66%   Collapse: 24%

(continued next page)

Damion Easley *(continued)*

A low-risk, low-reward signing by the Rays, as the Tigers were on the hook for the incredibly foolish contract they inked him to. Things didn't pan out, so Easley will either be trolling for work in the spring, or more likely, enjoying the last year of his Tiger contract by spending time with his family and friends.

JONNY GOMES   OF   Bats: R   Throws: R   Born: 22-Nov-80   Age: 23

YEAR	TM	LG	AGE	AB	H	2B	3B	HR	BB	SO	SB	CS	AVG	OBP	SLG	MLVR	EQBA	EQOBP	EQSLG	EQMLVR	VORP	DEFENSE		
2001	PRI	APP	20	206	60	11	2	16	33	73	15	4	.291	.449	.597	.472	.185	.277	.380	-.262	-16.8	60-CF -14		
2002	BAK	CAL	21	446	124	24	9	30	91	173	15	3	.278	.433	.574	.392	.200	.316	.410	-.138	-12.4	108-LF -15	11-RF	-2
2003	ORL	SOU	22	442	110	28	3	17	53	148	23	2	.249	.350	.441	.125	.220	.298	.402	-.169	-16.7	101-LF -18		
2004	*TBY*	*AL*	*23*	*250*	*55*	*14*	*1*	*9*	*26*	*78*	*7*	*2*	*.221*	*.307*	*.393*	*-.125*	*.223*	*.314*	*.411*	*-.118*	*0.1*	*70-LF -9*		

Breakout: 29%   *Improve: 50%*   *Collapse: 26%*

The Cardinals wanted Gomes as part of the ransom for Tino Martinez, which certainly falls under the heading of "Chutzpah, Extreme." Gomes is a pretty reasonable OF prospect, probably more so than Josh Hamilton ever really was. Defensively, he's best described as "rapid but unpredictable," which is kind of the opposite of Coach Wooden's "Be quick, but don't hurry." Gomes has power and a quick swing, but has a long way to go defensively. He's one of the hopes of the organization, and probably has as much upside as anyone in the system short of Upton.

BEN GRIEVE   OF/DH   Bats: Throws: Born: 04-May-76   Age: 28

YEAR	TM	LG	AGE	AB	H	2B	3B	HR	BB	SO	SB	CS	AVG	OBP	SLG	MLVR	EQBA	EQOBP	EQSLG	EQMLVR	VORP	DEFENSE		
2001	TBY	AL	25	542	143	30	2	11	87	159	7	1	.264	.374	.387	.022	.284	.390	.419	.073	21.4	62-RF -5	47-LF	0
2002	TBY	AL	26	482	121	30	0	19	69	121	8	2	.251	.354	.432	.047	.273	.373	.472	.105	22.6	114-RF -7		
2003	TBY	AL	27	165	38	7	0	4	32	41	0	0	.230	.374	.345	-.060	.247	.387	.380	-.010	2.5			
2004	*MIL*	*NL*	*28*	*287*	*74*	*15*	*1*	*14*	*48*	*75*	*2*	*1*	*.258*	*.371*	*.459*	*.078*	*.259*	*.370*	*.459*	*.068*	*14.6*	*82-RF -3*		

Breakout: 31%   *Improve: 53%*   *Collapse: 19%*

There aren't many players with this kind of trend:

Age	EqA	Age	EqA
21	.310	25	.280
22	.297	26	.284
23	.289	27	.268
24	.287		

That's not pretty. Hopefully, Grieve's over his blood clot problems, and can begin to rebuild his career. His falling out with Piniella was both predictable and tragic, and he needs to start over. He still has an old player's skill set, heavy on the batting eye, and he has little defensive value. But it's too early to completely write him off. Under the right circumstances, he can still be a .280/.400/.450 guy, it just may not be possible to find those circumstances. The Brewers signed him to a one-year deal.

TOBY HALL   C   Bats: R   Throws: R   Born: 21-Oct-75   Age: 28

YEAR	TM	LG	AGE	AB	H	2B	3B	HR	BB	SO	SB	CS	AVG	OBP	SLG	MLVR	EQBA	EQOBP	EQSLG	EQMLVR	VORP	DEFENSE
2001	DUR	INT	25	373	125	28	1	19	29	22	1	3	.335	.388	.568	.380	.306	.357	.530	.192	40.7	64-C 4
2001	TBY	AL	25	188	56	16	0	4	4	16	2	2	.298	.323	.447	.039	.317	.343	.481	.109	13.2	46-C 3
2002	DUR	INT	26	92	32	4	0	2	3	10	0	0	.348	.394	.457	.248	.326	.373	.435	.102	7.2	18-C -2
2002	TBY	AL	26	330	85	19	1	6	17	27	0	1	.258	.296	.376	-.124	.277	.316	.410	-.081	7.7	83-C 2
2003	TBY	AL	27	463	117	23	0	12	23	40	0	1	.253	.298	.380	-.140	.272	.317	.412	-.080	1.2	122-C 8
2004	*TBY*	*AL*	*28*	*339*	*90*	*20*	*1*	*9*	*21*	*33*	*0*	*1*	*.264*	*.313*	*.404*	*-.072*	*.267*	*.319*	*.423*	*-.061*	*10.7*	*89-C -1*

Breakout: 24%   *Improve: 46%*   *Collapse: 23%*

Can this organization really do anything more than tell guys "Sink or Swim?" Hall's been stagnant through a time when that really shouldn't happen, and that pattern's repeated with a bunch of players throughout the organization. It's not as if Hall was ever going to be Mike Piazza, but perhaps Matt LeCroy would have been nice. He's got Pete LaForest nipping at his heels now, so he'll have to show some production to keep his playing time up.

AUBREY HUFF								RF/1B/DH		Bats: L		Throws: R					Born: 20-Dec-76		Age: 27	
YEAR	TM	LG	AGE	AB	H	2B	3B	HR	BB	SO	SB	CS	AVG	OBP	SLG	MLVR	EQBA	EQOBP	EQSLG	EQMLVR	VORP	DEFENSE
2001	DUR	INT	24	66	19	6	0	3	5	7	0	0	.288	.338	.515	.188	.269	.319	.478	.015	3.8	16-3B 1	
2001	TBY	AL	24	411	102	25	1	8	23	72	1	3	.248	.288	.372	-.166	.267	.309	.403	-.112	7.3	68-3B -4	17-1B -2
2002	DUR	INT	25	126	41	9	0	3	12	13	0	0	.325	.388	.468	.234	.299	.363	.433	.056	5.3	25-1B 2	
2002	TBY	AL	25	454	142	25	0	23	37	55	4	1	.313	.366	.520	.238	.333	.387	.558	.312	46.7	44-1B -3	14-3B -2
2003	TBY	AL	26	636	198	47	3	34	53	80	2	3	.311	.372	.555	.270	.330	.391	.593	.365	55.8	95-RF -6	20-1B 2
2004	*TBY*	*AL*	*27*	*549*	*159*	*35*	*1*	*23*	*47*	*73*	*3*	*1*	*.290*	*.347*	*.486*	*.112*	*.293*	*.354*	*.508*	*.134*	*31.8*	*142-RF -2*	
Breakout: 4%			*Improve: 26%*				*Collapse: 30%*															

Although it may be shocking, this organization actually has a bona-fide good hitter. Huff's an outstanding offensive player who led all AL right fielders in Value Over Replacement Player (VORP) in '03. He puts the ball in play a huge percentage of the time, and has a very nice, compact swing that he uses to drive the ball all over the park. He was eligible for arbitration, but the Rays signed him to a three-year, $14.5 million deal, another shocking, but welcome development for Rays fans.

PETE LaFOREST								C		Bats: L		Throws: R					Born: 27-Jan-78		Age: 26	
YEAR	TM	LG	AGE	AB	H	2B	3B	HR	BB	SO	SB	CS	AVG	OBP	SLG	MLVR	EQBA	EQOBP	EQSLG	EQMLVR	VORP	DEFENSE
2002	ORL	SOU	24	359	97	18	1	20	60	94	9	6	.270	.378	.493	.240	.229	.313	.429	-.097	9.4	81-C -21
2002	DUR	INT	24	66	17	3	0	3	3	28	0	1	.258	.290	.439	-.017	.242	.275	.424	-.165	0.2	13-C -5
2003	ORL	SOU	25	72	18	8	0	3	16	17	0	0	.250	.393	.486	.241	.211	.323	.408	-.120	0.2	
2003	DUR	INT	25	201	54	14	2	14	36	56	2	1	.269	.385	.567	.304	.238	.347	.515	.087	17.3	45-C -4
2003	TBY	AL	25	48	8	2	0	0	1	14	0	0	.167	.200	.208	-.613	.188	.217	.250	-.558	-5.7	
2004	*TBY*	*AL*	*26*	*225*	*51*	*12*	*1*	*9*	*27*	*60*	*1*	*1*	*.225*	*.311*	*.400*	*-.108*	*.227*	*.317*	*.418*	*-.100*	*4.1*	*63-C -11*
Breakout: 23%			*Improve: 51%*				*Collapse: 24%*														

LaForest's not really that different from Toby Hall. He's got slightly better plate discipline and isolated power, but doesn't hit for quite the average. If both he and Hall are productive, both should be able to find playing time at the Trop; both have work to do to become an effective defensive catcher, and LaForest probably has a higher upside. Tampa's useless signing of Brook Fordyce likely leaves LaForest without a job, shooting the team in the foot yet again.

TRAVIS LEE								1B		Bats: L		Throws: L					Born: 26-May-75		Age: 29	
YEAR	TM	LG	AGE	AB	H	2B	3B	HR	BB	SO	SB	CS	AVG	OBP	SLG	MLVR	EQBA	EQOBP	EQSLG	EQMLVR	VORP	DEFENSE
2001	PHI	NL	26	555	143	34	2	20	71	109	3	4	.258	.346	.434	.015	.265	.351	.448	.027	17.6	153-1B -7
2002	PHI	NL	27	536	142	26	2	13	54	104	5	3	.265	.332	.394	.005	.277	.339	.418	-.027	7.9	135-1B 6
2003	TBY	AL	28	542	149	37	3	19	64	97	6	2	.275	.351	.459	.080	.292	.369	.494	.146	20.8	141-1B 14
2004	*TBY*	*AL*	*29*	*481*	*129*	*28*	*3*	*16*	*56*	*84*	*5*	*2*	*.267*	*.343*	*.435*	*.021*	*.270*	*.350*	*.455*	*.037*	*17.6*	*128-1B 4*
Breakout: 17%			*Improve: 45%*				*Collapse: 16%*														

Even his 2003 performance wasn't really all that. Given where Lee was a few years ago, it's hard to categorize an age-28 season of .275/.348/.459 as a big breakout. He's a solid defender, but as a first baseman, he's not going to push a club towards a championship as much as he is going to fill a gap and play a supporting role. Still, LaMar and Bonifay deserve credit for doing the right thing here—letting Lee put up good numbers, then declining his $2.5 million option, offering him less money or the right to walk. The Rays' signing of Rob Fick all but cinches Lee's departure.

JEFF LIEFER   **1B**   **Bats: L**   **Throws: R**   Born: 17-Aug-74   Age: 29

YEAR	TM	LG	AGE	AB	H	2B	3B	HR	BB	SO	SB	CS	AVG	OBP	SLG	MLVR	EQBA	EQOBP	EQSLG	EQMLVR	VORP	DEFENSE			
2001	CHR	INT	26	119	34	7	0	6	15	41	3	1	.286	.384	.496	.223	.264	.353	.455	.039	4.5	28-1B	1		
2001	CWS	AL	26	254	65	13	0	18	20	69	0	1	.256	.315	.520	.082	.268	.330	.547	.131	12.4	21-LF	1	11-3B	-3
2002	CWS	AL	27	204	47	8	0	7	19	60	0	0	.230	.296	.373	-.155	.244	.311	.400	-.130	-2.5	23-1B	-3	16-LF	1
2003	MON	NL	28	88	17	3	0	3	3	26	0	1	.193	.220	.330	-.423	.193	.220	.318	-.454	-8.2	16-1B	-1		
2003	DUR	INT	28	157	41	10	3	7	14	49	0	0	.261	.326	.497	.121	.241	.305	.468	-.049	0.3	23-LF	2		
2003	TBY	AL	28	25	3	1	0	1	3	13	0	0	.120	.214	.280	-.500	.120	.214	.320	-.501	-2.3				
2004	*MIL*	*NL*	*29*	*165*	*38*	*8*	*1*	*8*	*18*	*52*	*0*	*1*	*.232*	*.310*	*.433*	*-.076*	*.234*	*.310*	*.434*	*-.088*	*1.8*	*47-1B*	*-2*		

Breakout: 46%   Improve: 56%   Collapse: 31%

The Rays picked him off waivers after he had outlived his usefulness in Montreal. He didn't hit, so he was a free agent after being let go. GMs everywhere can look forward to receiving their custom DVD filled with highlights from Liefer's half season with the White Sox in '01 in the coming weeks, cut to the rippin', urgency-inspiring sounds of Frank Stallone's "Far From Over," with a voice-over by Shadoe Stevens. That was enough to perk up the Brewers' interest.

GEORGE LOMBARD   **OF**   **Bats: L**   **Throws: R**   Born: 14-Sep-75   Age: 28

YEAR	TM	LG	AGE	AB	H	2B	3B	HR	BB	SO	SB	CS	AVG	OBP	SLG	MLVR	EQBA	EQOBP	EQSLG	EQMLVR	VORP	DEFENSE			
2001	RIC	INT	25	44	14	2	1	4	6	14	3	2	.318	.423	.682	.558	.289	.389	.600	.322	5.4	11-LF	0		
2002	DET	AL	26	241	58	11	3	5	20	78	13	2	.241	.302	.373	-.119	.262	.323	.414	-.074	4.8	36-CF	-5	25-LF	-2
2003	DUR	INT	27	438	117	25	4	17	45	143	23	6	.267	.344	.459	.104	.246	.318	.433	-.069	10.5	64-CF	1	30-RF	2
2004	*TBY*	*AL*	*28*	*204*	*51*	*10*	*2*	*8*	*21*	*59*	*7*	*3*	*.250*	*.323*	*.438*	*-.021*	*.253*	*.330*	*.458*	*-.007*	*6.5*	*58-CF*	*-7*		

Breakout: 27%   Improve: 48%   Collapse: 31%

Lombard's a guy that can actually help a major league club. He can play reasonable defense, hit for a little power, and draw a few walks. No, he's not going to be Andruw Jones, but as a fourth outfielder, there are a lot of worse guys who have jobs. He's a tweener, to be sure, but why pay up for a fourth outfielder when you can get Lombard for the league minimum?

JULIO LUGO   **SS**   **Bats: R**   **Throws: R**   Born: 16-Nov-75   Age: 28

YEAR	TM	LG	AGE	AB	H	2B	3B	HR	BB	SO	SB	CS	AVG	OBP	SLG	MLVR	EQBA	EQOBP	EQSLG	EQMLVR	VORP	DEFENSE
2001	HOU	NL	25	513	135	20	3	10	46	116	12	11	.263	.330	.372	-.121	.257	.322	.364	-.150	7.5	124-SS	-3
2002	HOU	NL	26	322	84	15	1	8	28	74	9	3	.261	.324	.388	-.046	.262	.322	.391	-.108	7.9	79-SS -11
2003	HOU	NL	27	65	16	3	0	0	9	12	2	1	.246	.338	.292	-.206	.242	.324	.303	-.239	-0.8	18-SS	0
2003	TBY	AL	27	433	119	13	4	15	35	88	10	3	.275	.335	.427	.009	.297	.356	.464	.086	22.1	115-SS	5
2004	*TBY*	*AL*	*28*	*390*	*100*	*18*	*2*	*8*	*37*	*76*	*9*	*4*	*.256*	*.322*	*.373*	*-.103*	*.259*	*.328*	*.390*	*-.094*	*12.9*	*104-SS*	*-1*

Breakout: 16%   Improve: 42%   Collapse: 25%

The Rays exercised their $1.75 million option on him for the 2004 season. Lugo's not a bad ballplayer: He's a guy who can play the middle infield and hit a little, a la Chris Gomez. If the Rays work it right, maybe Lugo'll get hot, and they can move him for an arm or a prospect during the season, cut their salary a little in the process, and pick up a body who might turn into something for their next contending team. Sorry. I mean their first contending team.

AL MARTIN   **DH**   **Bats: L**   **Throws: L**   Born: 24-Nov-67   Age: 36

YEAR	TM	LG	AGE	AB	H	2B	3B	HR	BB	SO	SB	CS	AVG	OBP	SLG	MLVR	EQBA	EQOBP	EQSLG	EQMLVR	VORP	DEFENSE
2001	SEA	AL	33	283	68	15	2	7	37	59	9	3	.240	.332	.382	-.065	.269	.358	.427	.014	5.1	60-LF	-1
2003	TBY	AL	35	238	60	12	2	3	17	51	2	2	.252	.307	.357	-.152	.276	.331	.389	-.084	-1.8	
2004	*TBY*	*AL*	*36*	*160*	*39*	*8*	*1*	*3*	*17*	*35*	*2*	*1*	*.241*	*.316*	*.363*	*-.135*	*.244*	*.322*	*.380*	*-.129*	*-0.2*	

Breakout: 31%   Improve: 51%   Collapse: 31%

No, I don't know why they signed him. No, I don't know why they gave him that much playing time. No, I don't know where he's going next. No, I'm not surprised he was ineffective and innocuous in the DH spot. No, I'm not surprised that the only club that was interested in him was the Devil Rays. No, I don't know if he's officially retired. No, you shouldn't care.

REY ORDONEZ SS **Bats: R** **Throws: R** Born: 11-Jan-71 Age: 33

YEAR	TM	LG	AGE	AB	H	2B	3B	HR	BB	SO	SB	CS	AVG	OBP	SLG	MLVR	EQBA	EQOBP	EQSLG	EQMLVR	VORP	DEFENSE	
2001	NYM	NL	30	461	114	24	4	3	34	43	3	2	.247	.300	.336	-.208	.258	.309	.350	-.194	1.1	136-SS	7
2002	NYM	NL	31	460	117	25	2	1	24	46	2	2	.254	.294	.324	-.160	.273	.308	.348	-.188	1.7	129-SS	4
2003	TBY	AL	32	117	37	11	0	3	2	12	0	2	.316	.333	.487	.125	.333	.354	.513	.193	8.2	34-SS	4
2004	*SDP*	*NL*	*33*	*218*	*57*	*11*	*1*	*3*	*12*	*23*	*1*	*1*	*.260*	*.299*	*.356*	*-.178*	*.266*	*.303*	*.374*	*-.156*	*3.4*	*59-SS*	*0*

Breakout: 17% *Improve: 37%* *Collapse: 42%*

The left knee sprain Ordonez suffered may end up making him an awful lot of money. Instead of doing his normal routine where he hits miserably and plays slightly better than average defense, Ordonez had the month of his life in April, then went down for the season, leaving his numbers looking acceptable for a major league shortstop. Rather than re-signing St. Rey, who will play next season at age 33, and has never topped a normalized slugging of .350 in any year where he had significant playing time, they signed his HACKING MASS All-Star namesake Rey Sanchez to a one-year deal; so Sanchez will team with Julio Lugo up the middle. Look out Orioles! Meanwhile, Ordonez signed a minor league deal with the Pads, where he might earn defensive replacement work.

ANTONIO PEREZ 2B **Bats: R** **Throws: R** Born: 26-Jan-80 Age: 24

YEAR	TM	LG	AGE	AB	H	2B	3B	HR	BB	SO	SB	CS	AVG	OBP	SLG	MLVR	EQBA	EQOBP	EQSLG	EQMLVR	VORP	DEFENSE	
2002	SAN	TEX	22	240	62	8	2	2	11	64	15	9	.258	.318	.333	-.065	.246	.288	.320	-.285	-7.8	58-2B	-13
2003	ORL	SOU	23	81	22	5	1	2	18	18	3	1	.272	.427	.432	.239	.224	.349	.376	-.103	2.1	21-2B	-3
2003	DUR	INT	23	134	38	12	2	6	10	38	3	1	.284	.347	.537	.226	.259	.320	.511	.054	9.3	33-2B	0
2003	TBY	AL	23	125	31	6	1	2	18	34	4	1	.248	.347	.360	-.079	.278	.372	.397	.006	3.1	23-2B	-1
2004	*TBY*	*AL*	*24*	*296*	*75*	*16*	*2*	*7*	*27*	*71*	*7*	*3*	*.252*	*.327*	*.395*	*-.068*	*.255*	*.333*	*.414*	*-.058*	*15.6*	*81-2B*	*-3*

Breakout: 31% *Improve: 59%* *Collapse: 20%*

Perez came over in the deal that also brought Mt. Piniella. He's actually something of a prospect; he can play second base fairly well without getting completely shredded by incoming spikes, he's got a little bit of pop in his bat with the potential for much more, and he'll play this upcoming season at age 24, hopefully at Triple-A. If he can cut down his strikeouts just a bit, add a single here and there, and stay healthy, Perez can be a very good ballplayer.

ADAM PIATT LF **Bats: R** **Throws: R** Born: 08-Feb-76 Age: 28

YEAR	TM	LG	AGE	AB	H	2B	3B	HR	BB	SO	SB	CS	AVG	OBP	SLG	MLVR	EQBA	EQOBP	EQSLG	EQMLVR	VORP	DEFENSE	
2001	SAC	PCL	25	109	28	9	0	1	11	27	2	0	.257	.341	.367	-.105	.229	.306	.330	-.246	-5.8	19-RF	-2
2001	OAK	AL	25	95	20	5	1	0	13	26	0	0	.211	.306	.284	-.268	.232	.330	.305	-.230	-4.2	31-RF	0
2002	SAC	PCL	26	234	69	15	0	8	35	30	4	3	.295	.389	.462	.173	.258	.346	.403	-.050	1.1	40-RF	-7
2002	OAK	AL	26	137	32	8	0	5	12	33	2	1	.234	.305	.401	-.089	.261	.332	.442	-.019	1.2	27-LF	1
2003	OAK	AL	27	100	24	10	0	4	6	30	1	2	.240	.283	.460	-.074	.250	.299	.490	-.020	-0.8	24-LF	1
2003	TBY	AL	27	32	6	3	0	2	3	16	0	0	.188	.257	.469	-.149	.219	.286	.500	-.057	-0.7		
2004	*CLE*	*AL*	*28*	*149*	*34*	*8*	*0*	*5*	*15*	*43*	*2*	*1*	*.229*	*.303*	*.396*	*-.122*	*.238*	*.316*	*.429*	*-.081*	*1.2*	*43-LF*	*-1*

Breakout: 26% *Improve: 49%* *Collapse: 31%*

Piatt has power. He suffered a nasty illness a couple of years back that basically cost him two years of playing time and development, and probably several million dollars. If you take a look at his entire major league career, you end up with a .248/.323/.422 line. He's capable of considerably better than that, particularly as half a platoon. Defensively, he's not a bad corner outfielder. If the Rays give him 200 PA early in the season, he may turn into a valuable commodity to trade, or perhaps even someone to bat behind Aubrey Huff for a year or two. Instead the Indians will give him a shot.

DAMIAN ROLLS UT **Bats: R** **Throws: R** Born: 15-Sep-77 Age: 26

YEAR	TM	LG	AGE	AB	H	2B	3B	HR	BB	SO	SB	CS	AVG	OBP	SLG	MLVR	EQBA	EQOBP	EQSLG	EQMLVR	VORP	DEFENSE			
2001	TBY	AL	23	237	62	11	1	2	10	47	12	4	.262	.291	.342	-.193	.282	.313	.370	-.140	2.1	40-2B	0	14-CF	-3
2002	DUR	INT	24	244	65	6	4	6	21	43	15	0	.266	.337	.398	.011	.248	.316	.378	-.148	0.0	43-CF	-3	12-RF	0
2002	TBY	AL	24	89	26	6	1	0	3	16	2	5	.292	.330	.382	-.031	.311	.345	.411	.003	1.5	13-RF	-1		
2003	DUR	INT	25	77	19	4	1	0	4	15	4	2	.247	.284	.325	-.184	.234	.280	.299	-.338	-4.8				
2003	TBY	AL	25	373	95	20	0	7	19	84	11	3	.255	.303	.365	-.150	.278	.326	.398	-.079	-1.6	72-3B	2	23-RF	-2
2004	*TBY*	*AL*	*26*	*338*	*86*	*16*	*2*	*6*	*22*	*67*	*11*	*4*	*.255*	*.309*	*.375*	*-.124*	*.258*	*.315*	*.392*	*-.117*	*4.8*	*89-3B*	*-2*		

Breakout: 31% *Improve: 54%* *Collapse: 23%*

(continued next page)

Damian Rolls (continued)

The Rays have really gathered up a whole bunch of warm bodies. Rolls is another below-average player, albeit one with some speed. He's a middle-of-the-road defender at third base, and can fill in should someone get hurt in the outfield. With the bat, he's neither selective nor particularly powerful, and when he's shown a solid batting average in the past, it's been emptier than Jerry Bruckheimer's Artistic Soul. Rolls is, in many ways, the perfect Devil Ray.

JARED SANDBERG 3B Bats: R Throws: R Born: 02-Mar-78 Age: 26

YEAR	TM	LG	AGE	AB	H	2B	3B	HR	BB	SO	SB	CS	AVG	OBP	SLG	MLVR	EQBA	EQOBP	EQSLG	EQMLVR	VORP	DEFENSE	
2001	DUR	INT	23	322	77	16	0	16	38	81	0	1	.239	.331	.438	.035	.226	.308	.415	-.128	5.2	89-3B	7
2001	TBY	AL	23	136	28	7	0	1	10	45	1	0	.206	.265	.279	-.358	.221	.283	.309	-.325	-5.2	38-3B	0
2002	DUR	INT	24	114	32	9	0	4	14	42	1	0	.281	.369	.465	.161	.259	.341	.440	-.007	6.1	20-3B	-1
2002	TBY	AL	24	358	82	21	1	18	39	139	3	2	.229	.307	.444	-.035	.247	.323	.485	.012	18.4	96-3B	-3
2003	DUR	INT	25	272	63	17	1	12	30	95	1	0	.232	.313	.434	-.004	.215	.293	.411	-.169	0.9	59-3B	3
2003	TBY	AL	25	136	29	10	1	6	16	52	0	0	.213	.305	.434	-.088	.228	.321	.471	-.027	2.6	40-3B	-2
2004	TBY	AL	26	193	45	11	1	8	20	59	1	1	.232	.310	.419	-.080	.235	.317	.438	-.070	9.4	55-3B	-3

Breakout: 24%   Improve: 48%   Collapse: 27%

Having to make some sort of Sophie's Choice between Damian Rolls and Jared Sandberg is a little like agonizing in the local Blockbuster over whether to grab "Along Came a Spider" or "Enough." Yes, you can spend a fair amount of time thinking about the decision, or you can just admit that you're saddling yourself with a sticky, ineffectual mediocrity, and get the hell out of the store. To be fair, Sandberg's shown some ability to hit for power, and even if he doesn't work out, at least you're gambling on some hope of an upside. He has a chance to be the next Scott Spiezio, if everything breaks his way.

TERRY SHUMPERT UT Bats: R Throws: R Born: 16-Aug-66 Age: 37

YEAR	TM	LG	AGE	AB	H	2B	3B	HR	BB	SO	SB	CS	AVG	OBP	SLG	MLVR	EQBA	EQOBP	EQSLG	EQMLVR	VORP	DEFENSE			
2001	COL	NL	34	242	70	14	5	4	15	44	14	3	.289	.338	.438	-.031	.274	.320	.415	-.069	6.8	26-2B	-2	22-LF	0
2002	COL	NL	35	234	55	12	1	6	21	41	4	1	.235	.309	.372	-.137	.226	.297	.359	-.225	-3.1	47-2B	-3		
2003	TBY	AL	36	84	16	5	2	2	10	17	1	0	.190	.292	.369	-.208	.202	.306	.405	-.162	-1.4	10-2B	-2		
2004	BOS	AL	37	109	26	5	1	2	10	21	2	1	.236	.304	.355	-.170	.231	.303	.357	-.202	-0.5	33-2B	-5		

Breakout: 26%   Improve: 48%   Collapse: 35%

Of course Terry Shumpert's here! Where else would he be? Shumpert missed a fair amount of time with a bad hamstring during the season, but returned for the final few games of the year. The St. Petersburg Times published the following on September 29th, 2003, presented for your consumption without comment:

CLASSY MOVE: Piniella showed some class Sunday by using veteran Terry Shumpert, 37, at designated hitter. It likely was Shumpert's last game with the Rays and possibly his last game in the majors after playing parts of 14 seasons with six teams.
"What a classy young man, what a pro," Piniella said. "It has been a pleasure having him here all year. He has helped our younger kids. He has helped bring some professionalism to our clubhouse."
Piniella said the same of veteran Al Martin.

JASON TYNER OF Bats: L Throws: L Born: 23-Apr-77 Age: 27

YEAR	TM	LG	AGE	AB	H	2B	3B	HR	BB	SO	SB	CS	AVG	OBP	SLG	MLVR	EQBA	EQOBP	EQSLG	EQMLVR	VORP	DEFENSE			
2001	DUR	INT	24	157	49	2	1	0	15	10	11	5	.312	.379	.338	.037	.294	.356	.312	-.132	0.7	38-CF	-2		
2001	TBY	AL	24	396	111	8	5	0	15	42	31	6	.280	.312	.326	-.165	.302	.335	.353	-.108	-5.4	45-LF	0	44-CF	-5
2002	DUR	INT	25	351	102	12	4	0	34	27	20	7	.291	.363	.348	.006	.270	.340	.330	-.154	-10.6	72-LF	-1	13-CF	-1
2002	TBY	AL	25	168	36	2	1	0	7	19	7	1	.214	.250	.238	-.420	.237	.270	.266	-.403	-14.7	38-LF	0		
2003	DUR	INT	26	275	89	11	5	0	22	25	10	7	.324	.376	.400	.123	.300	.355	.372	-.044	8.6	61-CF	-3		
2003	TBY	AL	26	90	25	7	0	0	10	12	2	1	.278	.350	.356	-.056	.300	.376	.378	.004	0.5	15-RF	-1		
2004	TEX	AL	27	254	70	11	3	1	20	27	9	3	.275	.332	.357	-.093	.268	.329	.348	-.143	-1.2	69-CF	-7		

Breakout: 24%   Improve: 41%   Collapse: 32%

Tyner's a speed burner with no other skills—an extreme slap hitter without sufficient power to keep the infielders honest, much less the outfielders. Entering his prime, he might be able to find a 25th-man job somewhere as a defensive replacement/pinch-runner, but a strong team just doesn't have a major league roster spot for this type of player. The Rangers signed him to a minor league deal, proving just how desperate they are for a center fielder.

B. J. UPTON   SS   Bats: R   Throws: R   Born: 21-Aug-84   Age: 19

YEAR	TM	LG	AGE	AB	H	2B	3B	HR	BB	SO	SB	CS	AVG	OBP	SLG	MLVR	EQBA	EQOBP	EQSLG	EQMLVR	VORP	DEFENSE
2003	CSC	SAL	18	384	116	22	6	7	57	80	38	17	.302	.399	.445	.265	.225	.297	.347	-.243	-5.1	94-SS -25
2003	ORL	SOU	18	105	29	8	0	1	16	25	2	4	.276	.382	.381	.114	.239	.321	.339	-.198	0.2	27-SS -10
2004	TBY	AL	19	317	69	15	2	4	28	72	12	5	.216	.284	.321	-.259	.219	.290	.336	-.261	-2.3	85-SS -15

Breakout: 27%   Improve: 41%   Collapse: 35%

If you've read this far through the D-Ray player comments, this is probably the guy you're looking for, an oasis after trudging through the veritable desert of offensive talent on the club. Upton's first season can really only be categorized as a big success. He played well at Charleston, hitting for average and some power, with slightly choppy defense. He was promoted all the way to Double-A Orlando, where he wasn't overmatched, hitting .276 with 16 walks in a little over 120 plate appearances. He'll begin next season as one of the youngest players in Double-A, with a track record that includes plate discipline and power, and he'll spend a year working on his defense. Upton's a truly outstanding prospect, and could be the best prospect in baseball by this time next year.

JAVIER VALENTIN   C   Bats: B   Throws: R   Born: 19-Sep-75   Age: 28

YEAR	TM	LG	AGE	AB	H	2B	3B	HR	BB	SO	SB	CS	AVG	OBP	SLG	MLVR	EQBA	EQOBP	EQSLG	EQMLVR	VORP	DEFENSE	
2001	EDM	PCL	25	431	121	29	2	17	47	108	0	1	.281	.357	.476	.083	.246	.317	.418	-.092	10.6	49-C 1	25-3B -4
2002	EDM	PCL	26	455	130	33	1	21	41	96	0	1	.286	.351	.501	.148	.253	.313	.444	-.058	16.0	69-C -2	
2003	TBY	AL	27	135	30	7	1	3	5	31	0	0	.222	.255	.356	-.272	.237	.274	.385	-.226	-4.0	37-C 0	
2004	CIN	NL	28	194	48	11	1	7	16	44	0	0	.246	.309	.422	-.081	.244	.304	.420	-.104	4.7	54-C -6	

Breakout: 29%   Improve: 55%   Collapse: 29%

It didn't work out great, but this was a good gamble on the part of the Rays. Valentin's shown flashes of offensive skills at various points through the years, he was coming into his age-27 season, and his defense is acceptable for a major league catcher, something that wasn't often said of Toby Hall. Valentin didn't get much playing time and didn't hit, but he makes a nifty alternative for the Reds, because there's still something to like here. He can hit the ball over the fence, and he's not too bad defensively, which puts him ahead of a lot of backups who have jobs.

PITCHERS

BRANDON BACKE   Bats: R   Throws: R   Born: 05-Apr-78   Age: 26

YEAR	TM	LG	AGE	G	GS	IP	H	BB	SO	HR	ERA	EQERA	EQH9	EQBB9	EQSO9	EQHR9	PERA	VORP	STF
2001	BAK	CAL	23	17	0	24.7	13	8	33	1	1.09	2.86	6.5	3.7	7.0	0.8	3.37	6.7	12
2001	CSC	SAL	23	16	0	24.7	17	7	20	2	2.91	4.22	8.9	3.8	4.2	2.1	5.96	3.3	-45
2001	ORL	SOU	23	14	0	22.0	20	11	20	1	5.73	5.85	9.4	5.4	5.4	0.9	5.28	-0.6	-14
2002	ORL	SOU	24	20	14	92.3	91	37	45	9	4.68	6.48	10.7	3.9	3.1	1.9	6.69	-8.1	-48
2002	TBY	AL	24	9	0	13.0	15	7	6	3	6.92	6.39	9.9	4.3	4.3	2.1	6.63	-1.1	-42
2003	DUR	INT	25	16	2	33.0	33	13	27	1	4.64	5.93	10.1	4.5	5.9	0.3	4.67	-1.1	0
2003	TBY	AL	25	28	0	44.7	40	25	36	6	5.44	5.02	8.4	4.8	7.1	1.0	4.75	1.3	-1
2004	HOU	NL	26	17	7	43.0	44	22	32	6	5.13	5.22	9.1	4.0	6.1	1.2	5.19	2.1	-5

Breakout: 24%   Improve: 51%   Collapse: 17%

A converted outfielder, Backe's still got a lot of learning to do. He suffered through some elbow tenderness at the end of last season, and didn't demonstrate any kind of control to speak of, though he does have a live arm. It's something of a mystery why he's in the majors rather than in Triple-A or Double-A learning how to pitch. Traded to the Astros for Geoff Blum.

ROB BELL   Bats: R   Throws: R   Born: 17-Jan-77   Age: 27

YEAR	TM	LG	AGE	G	GS	IP	H	BB	SO	HR	ERA	EQERA	EQH9	EQBB9	EQSO9	EQHR9	PERA	VORP	STF
2001	CIN	NL	24	9	9	44.3	46	17	33	9	5.49	5.23	9.0	3.1	5.7	1.7	5.29	1.8	-5
2001	LOU	INT	24	5	4	27.0	32	4	26	4	3.33	5.04	11.9	1.4	6.8	1.8	6.31	1.6	-1
2001	TEX	AL	24	18	18	105.3	130	47	64	23	7.18	6.24	9.9	3.6	5.0	1.7	5.91	-7.5	-12
2002	OKL	PCL	25	12	11	75.3	70	25	55	10	4.06	4.42	8.5	3.4	4.9	1.5	4.94	9.3	-14
2002	TEX	AL	25	17	15	94.0	113	35	70	16	6.22	5.63	10.2	3.0	6.3	1.4	5.45	-0.3	0
2003	DUR	INT	26	12	12	71.7	72	15	48	10	4.02	5.15	10.7	2.4	4.9	2.1	6.41	3.2	-33
2003	TBY	AL	26	19	18	101.0	103	39	44	15	5.52	5.21	9.4	3.4	3.9	1.2	5.06	2.3	-14
2004	TBY	AL	27	22	16	93.3	106	34	51	15	5.34	5.31	9.8	3.1	4.9	1.3	5.21	5.7	-6

Breakout: 17%   Improve: 44%   Collapse: 27%

(continued next page)

Rob Bell *(continued)*

His celebrated curveball has never really been enough to get major league hitters out, since they can basically wait for a hanger or hammer his other pitches like emerging rodents in a carnival game. Bell's trying to have a career with 70% of Tom Gordon's stuff, and that's no easy task. He did have 11 quality starts during 2003, but five of them lasted exactly six innings, and others stretched the definition in ways that can't be mentioned in polite company. Bell hasn't been a good pitcher in the past, he wasn't good in 2003, and he won't be good in 2004 and beyond.

DEWON BRAZELTON   Bats: R   Throws: R   Born: 16-Jun-80   Age: 24

YEAR	TM	LG	AGE	G	GS	IP	H	BB	SO	HR	ERA	EQERA	EQH9	EQBB9	EQSO9	EQHR9	PERA	VORP	STF
2002	ORL	SOU	22	26	26	146.0	129	67	109	7	3.33	5.24	9.3	4.4	4.8	0.9	4.90	5.4	6
2002	TBY	AL	22	2	2	13.0	12	6	5	3	4.85	4.97	7.8	3.6	3.6	2.1	5.42	0.9	-11
2003	TBY	AL	23	10	10	48.3	57	23	24	9	6.89	7.38	10.9	4.1	4.5	1.6	6.33	-17.3	-14
2003	DUR	INT	23	5	5	25.7	23	11	18	1	4.20	5.32	8.4	4.9	5.3	0.4	4.14	0.7	15
2003	BAK	CAL	23	9	9	49.7	62	19	42	4	5.25	7.46	13.1	4.8	5.0	1.6	7.57	-9.2	-31
2004	*TBY*	*AL*	*24*	*21*	*15*	*84.7*	*100*	*47*	*47*	*13*	*6.42*	*6.39*	*10.2*	*4.8*	*5.0*	*1.4*	*6.11*	*-1.2*	*-14*

Breakout: 21%   *Improve: 51%*   *Collapse: 20%*

Brazelton's got live stuff, but his performance record is just plain ugly. He's never piled up strikeouts like a real pitching prospect. He's never demonstrated the kind of control you'd like out of someone who's a promising candidate for the rotation. It's not clear where, along the line, it was decided that Brazelton's a pitching prospect. Until he actually performs on the field, there's not really any reason to buy into the line of thinking that he's going to be a part of a successful Devil Ray club.

LANCE CARTER   Bats: R   Throws: R   Born: 18-Dec-74   Age: 29

YEAR	TM	LG	AGE	G	GS	IP	H	BB	SO	HR	ERA	EQERA	EQH9	EQBB9	EQSO9	EQHR9	PERA	VORP	STF
2002	DUR	INT	27	33	18	132.0	111	12	90	15	2.80	3.50	8.2	0.9	5.1	1.5	4.12	28.8	-8
2002	TBY	AL	27	8	0	20.3	15	5	14	2	1.33	1.83	6.4	1.8	5.9	0.9	2.87	8.3	17
2003	TBY	AL	28	62	0	79.0	72	19	47	12	4.33	4.04	8.3	2.1	5.4	1.3	4.27	12.9	-10
2004	*TBY*	*AL*	*29*	*38*	*8*	*72.7*	*77*	*17*	*44*	*12*	*4.33*	*4.31*	*9.1*	*1.9*	*5.4*	*1.4*	*4.42*	*13.5*	*-5*

Breakout: 24%   *Improve: 48%*   *Collapse: 22%*

Carter's newfound control has been a key to his modest success over the last couple of years. His K:BB ratio's solid if not overwhelming, he doesn't give up a ton of hits, and his peripheral ERA isn't way out of line with his actual ERA. Still, he's not particularly valuable, and certainly not as good as some of the filler relievers in places like Minnesota, Seattle, or Oakland. If he ends up making a lot of money, it'll say more about the organization that signs him as a closer than it will about Carter.

JESUS COLOME   Bats: R   Throws: R   Born: 23-Dec-77   Age: 26

YEAR	TM	LG	AGE	G	GS	IP	H	BB	SO	HR	ERA	EQERA	EQH9	EQBB9	EQSO9	EQHR9	PERA	VORP	STF
2001	TBY	AL	23	30	0	48.7	37	25	31	8	3.33	3.59	6.4	4.3	5.3	1.3	4.04	10.7	0
2002	DUR	INT	24	18	0	29.0	18	13	30	1	2.17	3.00	6.0	4.7	8.0	0.3	2.95	7.8	29
2002	TBY	AL	24	32	0	41.3	56	33	33	6	8.28	7.68	11.9	6.6	6.8	1.1	6.82	-9.5	-15
2003	TBY	AL	25	54	0	74.0	69	46	69	9	4.50	4.65	8.7	5.4	8.3	1.0	4.98	11.6	5
2004	*TBY*	*AL*	*26*	*36*	*10*	*75.0*	*74*	*39*	*61*	*10*	*4.72*	*4.69*	*8.5*	*4.4*	*7.2*	*1.1*	*4.87*	*9.0*	*0*

Breakout: 24%   *Improve: 51%*   *Collapse: 15%*

He still throws really hard. Colome's arm's caused drooling among scouts since before he was signed, but he's never really pitched that well. If things go his way, he could end up following the LaTroy Hawkins career path; they've got similar stuff, and it took Hawkins until his late-mid 20s to harness everything. More likely, Colome will follow the Reggie Harris career path.

BARTOLOME FORTUNATO

Bats: R   **Throws: R**   Born: 24-Aug-74   Age: 29

YEAR	TM	LG	AGE	G	GS	IP	H	BB	SO	HR	ERA	EQERA	EQH9	EQBB9	EQSO9	EQHR9	PERA	VORP	STF
2001	HUD	NYP	26	16	9	59.7	70	29	53	3	5.13	8.56	17.1	7.2	4.8	2.1	10.33	-15.6	-105
2002	BAK	CAL	27	25	5	60.7	58	25	85	3	4.00	5.17	11.3	4.7	7.2	1.0	5.99	2.6	-22
2002	ORL	SOU	27	10	2	25.7	16	11	34	2	2.10	3.57	8.3	4.4	8.7	1.6	5.16	5.1	-13
2003	ORL	SOU	28	35	1	53.0	48	20	63	4	3.06	5.24	11.3	4.1	7.6	1.6	6.42	1.9	-31
2003	DUR	INT	28	5	4	21.7	15	11	20	3	3.32	5.12	7.9	6.1	7.0	1.9	5.78	1.0	-31
2004	*TBY*	*AL*	*29*	*13*	*4*	*28.0*	*32*	*17*	*23*	*4*	*5.63*	*5.60*	*9.9*	*5.1*	*7.2*	*1.2*	*5.92*	*1.7*	*-5*

Breakout: 32%   *Improve: 58%*   *Collapse: 18%*

Fortunato's age is apparently a greater mystery than the continued perception of the virtuosity of the Dave Matthews Band. According to one source, the Rays signed him as a 16-year old free agent in 1996, which means he'd be 24 this coming year, but most say he'll celebrate his 30th birthday next year. No matter what his age, Fortunato has the stuff to make it in the big leagues. He keeps hitters off balance, and he's been effective in limited stints along the way, with peripheral numbers that show some promise, including striking out nearly a batter per inning at Durham and better than that at Orlando. He'd have been a decent long shot to save some games for Tampa in 2004 until the Rays one-upped their own stupidity by shelling out $6 million for two years of Danys Baez as closer.

CHAD GAUDIN

Bats: R   **Throws: R**   Born: 24-Mar-83   Age: 21

YEAR	TM	LG	AGE	G	GS	IP	H	BB	SO	HR	ERA	EQERA	EQH9	EQBB9	EQSO9	EQHR9	PERA	VORP	STF
2002	CSC	SAL	19	26	17	119.3	106	37	106	5	2.26	4.92	9.3	3.8	4.9	0.9	4.80	8.2	15
2003	BAK	CAL	20	14	14	80.3	63	23	70	2	2.13	3.35	7.3	3.5	5.3	0.5	3.34	18.8	33
2003	ORL	SOU	20	3	3	19.0	8	3	23	0	0.47	1.02	4.6	1.5	8.2	0.0	1.27	9.0	80
2003	TBY	AL	20	15	3	40.0	37	16	23	4	3.60	3.99	8.5	3.5	5.2	0.9	4.35	8.3	22
2004	*TBY*	*AL*	*21*	*23*	*17*	*102.0*	*101*	*40*	*66*	*10*	*4.26*	*4.24*	*8.5*	*3.3*	*5.7*	*0.8*	*4.18*	*17.1*	*4*

Breakout: 19%   *Improve: 65%*   *Collapse: 11%*

Gaudin's a small righty with solid control and good stuff. So what the hell is he doing in the major leagues at age 20? Was there a pennant race going on that we somehow missed? Are the Devil Rays so worried about their minor league instructors screwing kids up that they'll pull them out of the minors to join a moribund major league club and burn their early service time? Is the goal here to make sure that any player who turns out to be good quickly becomes too expensive to keep around?

His peripheral numbers are pretty good, and Gaudin's got a chance to be a contributor to a major league club. Why they moved him from High-A to Double-A is pretty clear. Why they moved him from Double-A to the bigs after a perfect game is less clear, and borderline nuts. The Rays should put Gaudin at Triple-A to start next season, and let him learn how to pitch, and control the load on his arm.

JEREMI GONZALEZ

Bats: R   **Throws: R**   Born: 08-Jan-75   Age: 29

YEAR	TM	LG	AGE	G	GS	IP	H	BB	SO	HR	ERA	EQERA	EQH9	EQBB9	EQSO9	EQHR9	PERA	VORP	STF
2002	OKL	PCL	27	46	5	92.0	86	39	93	8	3.33	4.29	9.1	4.4	6.9	1.0	4.97	12.5	-10
2003	DUR	INT	28	7	6	32.0	24	6	33	2	2.53	3.38	8.0	2.1	7.4	0.9	3.67	7.2	18
2003	TBY	AL	28	25	25	156.3	131	69	97	18	3.92	3.90	7.7	3.8	5.6	1.0	4.12	31.7	8
2004	*TBY*	*AL*	*29*	*26*	*22*	*130.3*	*130*	*56*	*89*	*17*	*4.65*	*4.63*	*8.6*	*3.7*	*6.0*	*1.1*	*4.69*	*17.1*	*4*

Breakout: 14%   *Improve: 51%*   *Collapse: 16%*

Finally showed why the statheads have always loved him. After approximately 914 surgeries and rehab stints, he was solid in the D-Ray rotation, posting a 3.91 ERA over 25 starts. His health is always going to be a concern, and his peripherals are only average, but Gonzalez at least got a moment in the sun. He could have a run of a couple years as an effective starter at the back end of some team's rotation, hoping to get a little of that Willie Blair Luck® that he's karmically due.

TRAVIS HARPER

Bats: L   **Throws: R**   Born: 21-May-76   Age: 28

YEAR	TM	LG	AGE	G	GS	IP	H	BB	SO	HR	ERA	EQERA	EQH9	EQBB9	EQSO9	EQHR9	PERA	VORP	STF
2001	DUR	INT	25	25	25	155.7	140	38	115	25	3.70	5.06	9.4	2.6	5.2	2.0	5.68	8.5	-22
2002	DUR	INT	26	4	4	19.3	31	3	17	5	6.99	8.66	16.8	1.5	6.6	3.6	10.95	-6.0	-84
2002	TBY	AL	26	37	7	85.7	101	27	60	14	5.46	5.25	10.2	2.6	6.0	1.3	5.24	3.3	-10
2003	TBY	AL	27	61	0	93.0	86	31	64	9	3.77	4.03	8.6	2.9	6.1	0.8	4.07	16.1	4
2004	*TBY*	*AL*	*28*	*30*	*9*	*66.0*	*71*	*22*	*42*	*9*	*4.71*	*4.69*	*9.3*	*2.9*	*5.6*	*1.2*	*4.76*	*8.8*	*-5*

Breakout: 23%   *Improve: 45%*   *Collapse: 26%*

(continued next page)

Travis Harper *(continued)*

Harper's pretty much the definition of a league-average pitcher. Everything about his 2003 season was pretty much the middle of the road—walk rate, K rate, hit rate, Expected Runs Prevented. The Ray bullpen was pretty non-descript, which some teams would have killed for. Harper's likely to continue as a third or fourth guy out of the pen role for the next few years. He's got good enough stuff to take a step forward, either in terms of control or K rate; doing so would result in him making a whole bunch more money than he would otherwise.

JOE KENNEDY   Bats: R   Throws: L   Born: 24-May-79   Age: 25

YEAR	TM	LG	AGE	G	GS	IP	H	BB	SO	HR	ERA	EQERA	EQH9	EQBB9	EQSO9	EQHR9	PERA	VORP	STF
2001	DUR	INT	22	4	4	26.0	22	9	23	2	2.42	4.07	8.1	3.7	6.7	0.7	4.02	4.1	33
2001	ORL	SOU	22	7	7	47.0	29	3	52	0	0.19	1.26	6.9	0.6	6.7	0.2	2.11	20.7	60
2001	TBY	AL	22	20	20	117.7	122	34	78	16	4.44	4.16	8.9	2.4	5.6	1.1	4.42	18.4	25
2002	TBY	AL	23	30	30	196.7	204	55	109	23	4.53	4.41	9.0	2.3	4.8	0.9	4.24	25.3	18
2003	TBY	AL	24	32	22	133.7	167	47	77	19	6.13	6.17	11.5	3.0	5.2	1.2	5.89	-13.3	-4
2004	COL	NL	25	26	21	125.3	144	43	79	21	5.41	5.12	10.1	2.7	5.3	1.2	5.04	8.8	0

Breakout: 9%   Improve: 44%   Collapse: 25%

Early in the 2001 season, there was no better pitching prospect than Joe Kennedy. He had a run at Double-A Orlando reminiscent of Rich Harden's start to the 2003 season—complete and utter dominance. In his first seven starts, Kennedy threw 47 innings, in which he allowed 29 hits and three walks, with 52 strikeouts, all neatly wrapped up in a 0.19 ERA. He was promoted to Triple-A, where he was still excellent, making four starts, walking nine, and striking out 23, yielding a 2.42 ERA. He was called up to the big club, where he made 20 league-average starts with reasonable if unspectacular peripherals. Nearly 190 innings at the age of 22 was a pretty heavy workload, but Kennedy looked like a star in the making. His fastball was live, and his other pitches were good enough to fill out a major league-quality repertoire.

In the 2002 season, Kennedy pitched pretty well in the first half, but completely ran out of gas at the beginning of the summer. His K rate dropped from 5.8 to 3.8, and his ERA increased by half a run. He was obviously tired at the very least, and the Devil Rays were careening towards another irrelevant finish in the AL East. He ended up throwing 196.2 innings, for a total of 386 innings over two years at the ages of 22 and 23.

We don't know whether or not the heavy workload endured by Kennedy was responsible for his lack of development to date. He may still end up being a great pitcher, and different pitcher use may not have helped anyway. But those 80 innings didn't make a bit of difference in the short term for the Rays. So why take the chance with a guy who might well have been the best player in the organization? Traded to the Rockies in a three-way deal, Kennedy's odds for a turnaround just got a bit longer.

MARK MALASKA   Bats: L   Throws: L   Born: 17-Jan-78   Age: 26

YEAR	TM	LG	AGE	G	GS	IP	H	BB	SO	HR	ERA	EQERA	EQH9	EQBB9	EQSO9	EQHR9	PERA	VORP	STF
2001	BAK	CAL	23	3	3	17.7	14	5	13	1	4.07	4.41	7.7	3.3	3.9	1.1	4.14	2.2	-3
2001	CSC	SAL	23	25	25	157.0	153	35	152	11	2.92	5.85	12.2	3.1	4.9	1.7	6.80	-3.8	-21
2002	BAK	CAL	24	15	15	91.3	98	12	94	5	2.96	4.98	11.0	1.5	5.1	1.0	4.97	5.9	3
2002	ORL	SOU	24	12	11	70.7	82	28	49	4	3.69	6.33	12.4	3.8	4.5	1.1	6.44	-5.2	-16
2003	ORL	SOU	25	19	0	25.0	21	4	22	2	2.16	3.22	10.1	1.6	5.6	1.6	5.29	5.9	-22
2003	DUR	INT	25	15	0	23.0	24	8	22	1	4.30	5.57	10.7	3.9	6.9	0.4	4.90	0.1	3
2003	TBY	AL	25	22	0	16.0	13	12	17	0	2.81	3.52	7.6	6.5	9.4	0.0	3.81	3.5	34
2004	TBY	AL	26	16	9	51.0	56	19	36	6	4.69	4.67	9.4	3.3	6.2	0.9	4.71	6.4	2

Breakout: 25%   Improve: 49%   Collapse: 19%

Malaska's turned the corner, and become a reasonable lefty relief prospect. His control can bail out from time to time, but he's got reasonable stuff, and he could have a nice career as a bullpen lefty. His total line for 2003, at Double-A, Triple-A, and the majors, included 64 innings pitched, 58 hits, 24 walks, 61 strikeouts, and an ERA of 3.09. So naturally, the Devil Rays waived him, and he was picked up by a competent club, the Red Sox.

JAROD MATTHEWS   Bats: R   Throws: R   Born: 10-Nov-82   Age: 21

YEAR	TM	LG	AGE	G	GS	IP	H	BB	SO	HR	ERA	EQERA	EQH9	EQBB9	EQSO9	EQHR9	PERA	VORP	STF
2002	CSC	SAL	19	24	24	137.7	131	37	115	7	3.59	5.83	9.9	3.2	4.6	1.1	5.08	-3.2	13
2003	BAK	CAL	20	23	21	121.0	131	27	109	12	4.02	5.85	10.7	2.7	5.4	1.7	5.98	-3.1	4
2004	TBY	AL	21	16	13	80.7	87	29	51	10	4.61	4.59	9.3	3.0	5.6	1.1	4.66	11.4	3

Breakout: 15%   Improve: 56%   Collapse: 12%

Pitched pretty well in Bakersfield, certainly well enough to earn a promotion to Double-A. His strikeout rate wasn't great, but he's got good poise, reasonable control of his entire repertoire, and may well be able to survive the Double-A Trial By Fire after getting through the pitcher-crushing Cal League. If he were in an organization that had a good track record for developing pitching, he could turn into a very good prospect.

SETH McCLUNG Bats: R Throws: R Born: 07-Feb-81 Age: 23

YEAR	TM	LG	AGE	G	GS	IP	H	BB	SO	HR	ERA	EQERA	EQH9	EQBB9	EQSO9	EQHR9	PERA	VORP	STF
2001	CSC	SAL	20	28	28	164.3	142	53	165	6	2.79	5.41	10.0	4.4	5.0	0.8	5.13	3.1	14
2002	BAK	CAL	21	7	7	37.0	35	11	48	1	2.92	4.46	9.7	3.1	6.6	0.5	4.35	4.3	32
2002	ORL	SOU	21	20	19	114.0	138	53	64	12	5.37	7.58	11.9	4.4	3.7	1.9	7.30	-23.3	-23
2003	TBY	AL	22	12	5	38.7	33	25	25	6	5.35	5.06	8.0	5.5	5.8	1.2	4.96	2.4	7
2004	TBY	AL	23	22	15	78.3	98	47	48	16	7.15	7.12	10.8	5.1	5.4	1.8	7.10	-5.9	-18

Breakout: 12%   Improve: 60%   Collapse: 24%

Flamethrower, brought to the majors before he was ready. By June he'd hit Dr. Lewis Yocum's operating table for Tommy John surgery. He'll be back late in the 2004 season at the earliest. Considering McClung wasn't ready for the majors when he was called up before, it's unreasonable to expect him to be an effective major league pitcher until at least 2006.

JIM PARQUE Bats: L Throws: L Born: 08-Feb-76 Age: 28

YEAR	TM	LG	AGE	G	GS	IP	H	BB	SO	HR	ERA	EQERA	EQH9	EQBB9	EQSO9	EQHR9	PERA	VORP	STF
2001	CWS	AL	25	5	5	28.0	36	10	15	7	8.04	7.33	11.7	3.0	4.7	2.0	6.93	-5.2	-32
2002	CHR	INT	26	20	20	105.7	131	38	63	21	6.47	7.63	12.6	3.9	4.6	2.7	8.48	-21.8	-71
2002	CWS	AL	26	8	4	25.3	34	16	13	11	9.96	9.49	12.0	5.1	4.4	3.6	9.79	-10.7	-101
2003	DUR	INT	27	21	21	121.3	132	47	49	13	4.08	5.83	11.1	4.4	3.0	1.6	6.56	-2.8	-43
2003	TBY	AL	27	5	5	17.3	27	16	8	2	11.97	10.26	14.6	8.1	4.3	1.1	8.34	-11.7	-54

When Jamie Moyer, Steve Sparks, and Clara Peller all start making fun of your fastball, maybe it's time to move on to your next career. Parque's done, released from Durham late in the season. It's unlikely his playing career will continue.

STEVE PARRIS Bats: R Throws: R Born: 17-Dec-67 Age: 36

YEAR	TM	LG	AGE	G	GS	IP	H	BB	SO	HR	ERA	EQERA	EQH9	EQBB9	EQSO9	EQHR9	PERA	VORP	STF
2001	TOR	AL	33	19	19	105.7	126	41	49	18	4.60	5.18	9.9	3.2	3.8	1.4	5.45	4.9	-18
2002	TOR	AL	34	14	14	75.3	96	35	48	13	5.98	5.84	11.1	3.8	5.5	1.3	6.05	-2.0	-13
2003	TBY	AL	35	10	7	43.7	60	13	14	12	6.18	6.86	12.4	2.6	2.8	2.4	7.69	-3.4	-59
2004	TBY	AL	36	34	14	90.7	105	30	39	14	4.62	4.60	10.0	2.8	3.8	1.3	5.21	11.1	-15

Breakout: 39%   Improve: 68%   Collapse: 4%

Parris' playing career is probably over. His shoulder really hasn't come back close to where it once was, and he's been spending his time trying to strengthen it, but it's unlikely he's going to find anyone to give him a shot at a job, even as an NRI.

JOHN ROCKER Bats: R Throws: L Born: 17-Oct-74 Age: 29

YEAR	TM	LG	AGE	G	GS	IP	H	BB	SO	HR	ERA	EQERA	EQH9	EQBB9	EQSO9	EQHR9	PERA	VORP	STF
2001	ATL	NL	26	30	0	32.0	25	16	36	2	3.09	3.82	7.6	4.1	8.5	0.6	3.73	6.1	19
2001	CLE	AL	26	38	0	34.7	33	25	43	2	5.45	4.67	8.0	6.0	10.1	0.5	4.33	3.6	22
2002	TEX	AL	27	30	0	24.3	29	13	30	5	6.67	6.29	10.4	4.4	10.4	1.5	5.95	-1.9	-1
2003	ORL	SOU	28	17	0	19.7	23	26	20	4	9.14	12.12	15.4	15.4	6.6	4.4	13.75	-11.8	-196
2004	TBY	AL	29	11	1	12.7	17	17	11	3	9.62	9.58	11.3	11.5	7.6	1.8	9.73	-2.3	-38

Breakout: 24%   Improve: 56%   Collapse: 27%

Okay, all those who thought, at the end of the 1999 season, that John Rocker would become the punchline for a number of jokes, and pitch his way out of baseball within three years, raise your hand, and start telling fortunes for a living. He's not the most sympathetic character in the world, but man, it's hard to argue that he hasn't hit an amazing streak of bad luck. He's no longer with the organization, and will be trolling for work, but he's left-handed, and he's still under 30 years of age. If he were Steve Ontiveros and not John Rocker, you'd still be looking for him in 2015.

BOBBY SEAY
Bats: L   **Throws: L**   Born: 20-Jun-78   Age: 26

YEAR	TM	LG	AGE	G	GS	IP	H	BB	SO	HR	ERA	EQERA	EQH9	EQBB9	EQSO9	EQHR9	PERA	VORP	STF
2001	ORL	SOU	23	15	13	64.7	81	26	49	9	5.98	8.13	13.0	4.3	4.6	2.1	8.08	-16.5	-45
2001	TBY	AL	23	12	0	13.0	13	5	12	3	6.23	5.68	8.5	3.6	7.8	2.1	5.66	-0.1	-3
2002	ORL	SOU	24	15	3	35.7	31	15	24	2	3.28	5.01	9.5	4.2	4.5	1.1	5.20	2.1	-22
2002	DUR	INT	24	10	0	15.0	15	2	14	1	6.00	5.14	9.6	1.3	7.1	0.6	3.91	0.7	17
2003	DUR	INT	25	25	0	30.0	23	15	29	1	2.10	3.95	7.9	5.6	6.9	0.3	4.04	5.0	7
2003	TBY	AL	25	12	0	9.0	7	6	5	0	3.00	3.12	7.3	6.2	5.2	0.0	3.66	2.9	9
2004	*TBY*	*AL*	*26*	*18*	*6*	*39.3*	*42*	*21*	*28*	*5*	*5.31*	*5.29*	*9.3*	*4.6*	*6.4*	*1.0*	*5.17*	*2.7*	*-6*

Breakout: 15%   *Improve: 43%*   *Collapse: 31%*

Once a bonus baby, now one of many fungible lefties. Seay's once-ballyhooed stuff still hasn't been fully harnessed, even though there's some velocity gone from the fastball. He missed most of the 2002 season with an injury, but pitched well when he took the mound in 2003. Of course, he wasn't able to take the mound very often because of shoulder tendinitis, so his future's as cloudy as it ever was.

JORGE SOSA
Bats: B   **Throws: R**   Born: 28-Apr-77   Age: 27

YEAR	TM	LG	AGE	G	GS	IP	H	BB	SO	HR	ERA	EQERA	EQH9	EQBB9	EQSO9	EQHR9	PERA	VORP	STF
2001	EVE	NWN	24	21	7	58.7	45	19	57	2	1.69	4.29	10.2	4.5	4.6	0.9	5.37	7.3	-21
2002	TBY	AL	25	31	14	99.3	88	54	48	16	5.53	4.81	7.6	4.4	4.2	1.3	4.60	8.5	-18
2003	TBY	AL	26	29	19	128.7	137	60	72	14	4.62	4.95	9.8	4.0	5.0	0.9	5.05	13.5	-4
2004	*TBY*	*AL*	*27*	*23*	*16*	*89.3*	*108*	*43*	*43*	*12*	*5.75*	*5.73*	*10.4*	*4.1*	*4.3*	*1.1*	*5.76*	*1.9*	*-14*

Breakout: 19%   *Improve: 44%*   *Collapse: 30%*

The numbers aren't tremendous, but there is a lot to like here. Sosa's got a solid arm, and managed to pitch about as well as average in the majors. Is that anything to write home about? Well, perhaps not, but Sosa's only been pitching since the 2001 season. Before that, he was a strong-armed outfielder who wasn't going to make the bigs with his bat. He's got a shot to be a good pitcher; a small improvement in his command could result in fewer hits, fewer walks, and more strikeouts, all at once, which would make his future look considerably rosier.

JASON STANDRIDGE
Bats: R   **Throws: R**   Born: 09-Nov-78   Age: 25

YEAR	TM	LG	AGE	G	GS	IP	H	BB	SO	HR	ERA	EQERA	EQH9	EQBB9	EQSO9	EQHR9	PERA	VORP	STF
2001	DUR	INT	22	20	20	102.3	130	50	48	13	5.28	7.89	11.3	5.0	3.5	1.3	6.50	-24.7	-20
2001	TBY	AL	22	9	1	19.3	19	14	9	5	4.66	5.21	8.5	6.2	3.8	1.9	6.21	0.8	-25
2002	DUR	INT	23	29	29	173.0	168	64	111	12	3.12	4.55	8.5	3.9	5.0	0.8	4.38	19.2	12
2003	DUR	INT	24	12	10	60.0	62	28	37	5	4.50	5.76	10.4	5.3	4.4	1.2	5.95	-1.0	-17
2003	TBY	AL	24	8	7	35.3	38	16	20	7	6.37	5.82	9.8	4.0	5.0	1.6	5.82	-1.8	-13
2004	*TBY*	*AL*	*25*	*21*	*15*	*85.3*	*97*	*40*	*48*	*11*	*5.28*	*5.26*	*9.8*	*4.0*	*4.9*	*1.1*	*5.34*	*5.7*	*-7*

Breakout: 18%   *Improve: 56%*   *Collapse: 25%*

Standridge, you may remember, was a first-round pick, and he's spent most of his career trying to gain control of the strike zone. He didn't make much progress in 2003. His fastball's mediocre, and he doesn't have good control of his breaking stuff. His opportunity to have a career in the bigs is effectively gone; the Jeff Bittiger or Billy Taylor route are realistically his best opportunities for a career playing baseball at this point.

BRIAN STOKES
Bats: R   **Throws: R**   Born: 07-Sep-79   Age: 24

YEAR	TM	LG	AGE	G	GS	IP	H	BB	SO	HR	ERA	EQERA	EQH9	EQBB9	EQSO9	EQHR9	PERA	VORP	STF
2001	BAK	CAL	21	32	20	128.7	118	64	92	11	3.92	5.80	9.1	5.7	3.7	1.4	5.84	-2.6	-21
2002	BAK	CAL	22	28	28	165.7	156	57	152	13	3.26	4.90	8.9	3.7	4.6	1.3	4.96	12.1	-1
2003	ORL	SOU	23	10	10	50.7	55	13	33	2	3.20	5.63	11.1	2.7	4.1	0.8	5.18	-0.2	-1
2004	*TBY*	*AL*	*24*	*20*	*14*	*77.3*	*93*	*41*	*43*	*14*	*6.19*	*6.16*	*10.3*	*4.5*	*4.9*	*1.5*	*6.18*	*1.5*	*-15*

Breakout: 20%   *Improve: 55%*   *Collapse: 23%*

Stokes pitched well in limited duty at Orlando, posting a 3.30 ERA with a reasonable K/BB rate, albeit a strikeout rate that didn't knock anyone out. He's gained more command and control of his stuff as he's matured, and he hasn't crumbled under anything they've asked him to do yet. At the very least, he's earned an opportunity to make 30 starts at Double-A and see what happens. Unfortunately, that will have to wait until his elbow's healed up.

JON SWITZER Bats: L Throws: L Born: 13-Aug-79 Age: 24

YEAR	TM	LG	AGE	G	GS	IP	H	BB	SO	HR	ERA	EQERA	EQH9	EQBB9	EQSO9	EQHR9	PERA	VORP	STF
2001	HUD	NYP	21	5	0	14.3	9	2	20	0	0.63	2.92	8.8	2.2	7.3	0.0	3.15	3.7	44
2002	BAK	CAL	22	20	20	103.3	108	26	129	8	4.27	5.34	10.8	2.7	6.3	1.3	5.59	2.8	6
2003	ORL	SOU	23	22	22	126.0	117	32	100	10	3.43	5.13	10.2	2.7	5.0	1.6	5.63	6.0	-7
2003	TBY	AL	23	5	0	9.7	13	3	7	2	7.42	6.75	12.5	2.9	6.8	1.9	7.16	-1.7	-10
2004	TBY	AL	24	19	12	68.0	76	21	44	10	4.82	4.80	9.6	2.7	5.7	1.2	4.84	8.7	0

Breakout: 13% Improve: 47% Collapse: 31%

Not a bad season. Switzer posted a K:BB ratio of better than 3:1 at Orlando, striking out 100 and walking 32 in 126 innings. He's not going to be a #1 starter, but he's making progress, and he'll start the season in Triple-A with a chance to end it in the bigs.

MIKE VENAFRO Bats: L Throws: L Born: 02-Aug-73 Age: 30

YEAR	TM	LG	AGE	G	GS	IP	H	BB	SO	HR	ERA	EQERA	EQH9	EQBB9	EQSO9	EQHR9	PERA	VORP	STF
2001	TEX	AL	27	70	0	60.0	54	28	29	2	4.80	3.79	7.1	3.8	3.9	0.3	3.22	11.9	0
2002	OAK	AL	28	47	0	37.0	45	14	16	5	4.62	5.55	11.1	3.3	3.8	1.0	5.61	0.2	-27
2003	NWO	PCL	29	23	0	28.0	35	5	11	0	3.54	5.33	12.8	2.1	3.2	0.4	5.36	0.8	-15
2003	TBY	AL	29	24	0	19.0	24	3	9	1	4.74	4.50	12.0	1.5	4.5	0.5	4.95	2.5	-1
2004	KCR	AL	30	39	0	34.3	43	12	15	4	5.10	4.49	10.5	2.9	3.9	0.8	4.77	5.7	-17

Breakout: 34% Improve: 59% Collapse: 17%

Still around, and still good enough to work. Venafro's a classic lefty specialist, but with the luxury package, since he also makes the running game exceptionally dangerous. He'll probably never get even close to averaging one inning per outing again, but he should be a functional last man out of the pen for the Royals in '04.

DOUG WAECHTER Bats: R Throws: R Born: 28-Jan-81 Age: 23

YEAR	TM	LG	AGE	G	GS	IP	H	BB	SO	HR	ERA	EQERA	EQH9	EQBB9	EQSO9	EQHR9	PERA	VORP	STF
2001	CSC	SAL	20	26	26	153.3	179	38	107	14	4.34	7.91	13.0	3.3	3.5	2.0	7.65	-34.7	-24
2002	CSC	SAL	21	7	7	36.3	39	16	36	2	3.47	7.03	12.1	5.3	5.3	1.4	7.01	-5.1	-11
2002	BAK	CAL	21	17	17	108.3	114	29	101	9	2.66	4.66	10.0	2.9	4.7	1.3	5.33	10.7	5
2002	ORL	SOU	21	4	4	18.0	27	13	18	4	9.00	12.12	16.5	7.2	6.6	3.9	12.26	-11.8	-65
2003	ORL	SOU	22	13	12	76.3	74	19	45	6	4.13	5.32	10.3	2.6	3.6	1.6	5.65	2.2	-10
2003	DUR	INT	22	10	10	51.3	51	12	35	9	3.33	5.44	9.4	2.6	5.4	2.1	5.78	0.9	-5
2003	TBY	AL	22	6	5	35.3	29	15	29	4	3.31	3.44	7.7	3.7	7.4	1.1	4.12	10.2	40
2004	TBY	AL	23	22	16	89.7	106	37	52	17	5.90	5.87	10.2	3.5	5.1	1.6	5.92	3.3	-10

Breakout: 16% Improve: 49% Collapse: 17%

That's a nice season. Waechter marched his way up through the minors, then pitched great once he got to the bigs. He's probably the protagonist in a large number of the Seattle Mariners' nightmares, as he completely chewed them up during a 10-day period at the end of August, when Seattle still had dreams of making the postseason. Waechter helped disabuse them of that notion, winning two games by throwing 11.2 shutout innings during which he looked like Jamie Moyer's right-handed doppelganger. Waechter will start the 2004 season in the Devil Ray rotation, but then again, the same might be said for you.

VICTOR ZAMBRANO Bats: R Throws: R Born: 06-Aug-75 Age: 28

YEAR	TM	LG	AGE	G	GS	IP	H	BB	SO	HR	ERA	EQERA	EQH9	EQBB9	EQSO9	EQHR9	PERA	VORP	STF
2001	DUR	INT	25	29	0	30.3	26	12	29	2	2.08	4.23	9.1	4.2	6.8	0.7	4.51	4.2	1
2001	TBY	AL	25	36	0	51.3	38	18	58	6	3.16	3.04	6.4	2.9	9.5	0.9	3.12	14.3	32
2002	TBY	AL	26	42	11	114.0	120	68	73	15	5.53	5.38	9.1	4.9	5.5	1.0	5.13	2.7	-14
2003	TBY	AL	27	34	28	188.3	165	106	132	21	4.21	4.41	8.1	4.9	6.2	0.9	4.48	26.7	7
2004	TBY	AL	28	28	22	128.3	132	66	88	16	5.01	4.99	8.9	4.4	6.1	1.1	5.00	10.7	0

Breakout: 10% Improve: 45% Collapse: 24%

It's palpitation-tastic! Zambrano rides the lightning from the time the game starts until he leaves it, often soaked in the sweat of a man who lives on the edge. He's tough to hit, but gives up walks by the bushel. One moment, he looks unhittable, but he can go all Dave Burba on you faster than viewers can grimace watching Janice and Ralphie on the Sopranos. Zambrano's effective as it is, but if he can improve his control just a little bit, he could be considerably better, perhaps even a legitimate #2 starter on a good team.

Texas Rangers

You can read a thousand articles from the past half-decade analyzing the Rangers' woes, but you'll find only one story: The offense is fine, their problem is pitching. It's become a cliché.

Normally, clichés are lazy, simplistic ways of presenting a more complex story. But not this one. Pitching ineptitude is *the* defining characteristic of Ranger teams of the past few seasons. The pitching hasn't just been bad, it's been historically bad. No team in the post-war era has allowed as many runs over a four-year period as the 2000–2003 Rangers. Not even the Rockies. Only 15 teams during that era (and only 12 teams outside of Planet Coors) have allowed more than six runs per nine innings over a season. Three of those teams are Rangers clubs from the past four years (2000, 2001, and 2003). Since 2000, Texas has had by far the most major league pitchers with season ERAs over 5.00 (27), and the fewest with ERAs under 4.00 (six; minimum 50 innings). During those same four years, they've had an astonishing seven pitchers put up ERAs over 7.00.

Saying the Rangers' problem is all pitching is an easy diagnosis, but it really just begs another, much more interesting question: Why? This is a well-financed team whose recent management—John Hart and Grady Fuson of late, current Brewers GM Doug Melvin preceding them, and current Reds GM Dan O'Brien spanning both regimes—is well regarded. That's generally not a formula that leads to perpetual failure in one-half of the game. So why can't the Rangers prevent runs?

It's not like there's a shortage of answers to that question. You can't read the baseball press for more than a week without stumbling across another new theory advanced by one pundit or another, each trying to give an answer a little more nuanced than "They just suck." Most are of the spread-the-blame variety, placing some of the responsibility on someone or something other than the guys who stand on the mound. Many of these theories sound plausible enough on their face, but they're also generally tossed off without a great deal of investigation and evidence behind them. So let's take a more careful look at the most prominent of these theories, and see whether any of them really explain the Rangers' pitching problems.

Theory #1: It's the park. There's no question that The Ballpark in Arlington (TBiA) is friendly to hitters. Over the

RANGERS PROSPECTUS

2003 record: 71–91; Fourth place, AL West

Pythagenport record: 68–94

Runs scored per game: 5.1 (5th in AL)

Runs allowed per game: 6.0 (14th in AL)

Team EqA: .259 (7th in AL)

2003 Batters Age: 29.0 (7th youngest in AL)

2003 Pitchers Age: 28.6 (7th youngest in AL)

Ballpark: Ballpark In Arlington; Severe hitter's park; Park Factor of 1.053

2003: Buck Showalter's first season as skipper ended as Jerry Narron's last did—in the basement.

2004: Some good young hitters will keep the offense solid, but they've got to find a few starters who can pitch in Arlington.

past four years, the Rangers and their opponents have scored 5.97 runs per nine innings in Texas home games, and 5.27 runs per nine in road games. That's a 13% inflation rate for run scoring in Arlington, the fourth-highest figure during that time in the majors, behind Colorado (45%), Kansas City (21%), and Arizona (14%).

But the 13% figure is hardly unusual. Besides the three teams mentioned above, the Astros (12%) and Expos (11%) are also in the Rangers' neighborhood. And the idea that TBiA has some special, disproportionate impact on Ranger hurlers—turning otherwise decent pitchers into cannon fodder when they pitch there—doesn't withstand even the most superficial scrutiny.

For one thing, the Rangers show absolutely no ability to pitch away from Arlington. They were 29th in the majors in road runs allowed per inning in 2000, 30th in 2001, 20th in 2002, and 28th last year. Over the four years combined, they were second-to-last in the majors in runs allowed per inning on the road; only the lowly Tigers kept them out of the basement. This was despite the fact that Texas plays a disproportionate number of its road games in three pretty good pitcher's parks (Seattle, Oakland, and Anaheim).

In fact, over the past four years Ranger pitchers have given up runs at a slightly higher rate on the road than at home. Now granted, most teams do this—they don't call it "home-field advantage" for nothing—so it doesn't mean that Ranger pitchers aren't impacted by the park. But it does distinguish the Rangers from those few teams whose park effect is extreme enough to cause the pitching staff to give up more runs at home—Colorado, Kansas City, and Arizona among them. And it belies the idea that the Rangers' problem is that the pitchers are poorly suited to their park.

This whole notion of park suitability is worth delving into in a little more detail. There's a quick-and-dirty way of measuring a team's suitability to its home park: Divide the park's effect on the team's hitters by the park's effect on the team's pitchers, where the park's effect on hitters is the ratio of runs scored at home to runs scored on the road (and similarly for pitchers). This number will be high when the park helps the team's hitters more than it hurts the team's pitchers. (Or, in the case of a pitcher's park, hurts the team's hitters less than it helps the team's pitchers.) And it will be low when . . . well, you get the idea.

Table 1 shows the teams best suited to their home parks over the past four years. The Rangers show up at number six on the list, which tells you that the Rangers' problem is not being poorly tailored to their ballpark. Put another way, it tells us that TBiA rates as a hitter's park not so much because the Rangers can't pitch there, but more because the Ranger offense is well suited to hit there.

So the park's effect on pitchers is not the club's problem. If anything, it could be the misguided preoccupation with the park that contributes to the club's pitching difficulties, rather than the park itself. Like the Rockies with Coors Field (number one on the list), the Ranger brass may be fixating on finding the mythical Pitcher Who Can Pitch in Arlington rather than pitchers who can pitch anywhere, and in the process are stocking the team with pitchers who can pitch nowhere.

TABLE 1. TEAMS BEST-SUITED TO THEIR HOME PARKS, 2000–2003

Team	Hitting Effect	Pitching Effect	Suitability
Colorado	1.78	1.18	1.51
Florida	1.10	0.75	1.47
St. Louis	1.09	0.83	1.32
Chicago (AL)	1.21	0.92	1.31
Montreal	1.28	0.98	1.31
TEXAS	1.29	1.00	1.29
San Francisco	0.97	0.76	1.28
Oakland	1.05	0.83	1.26
Philadelphia	1.02	0.84	1.22
Baltimore	0.98	0.83	1.19

Theory #2: It's the fielding. Nobody is going to confuse the 2003 Rangers with the 1969 Orioles. But there seems to be a growing line of thought that the Ranger fielders are so uniquely bad that the atrocities seemingly committed by the pitching staff in recent years were actually due in large part—maybe even primarily—to the fielding. It's an interesting idea, but there doesn't seem to be a lot of evidence to support it.

For one thing, it's hard to see how the Ranger fielders have been all that bad, at least not at the level that would cause the stratospheric opponent run totals Texas has seen. We won't spend any time defending the Ranger outfield, which has seen its share of recent occupants—Juan Gonzalez, Kevin Mench, Carl Everett, etc.—who don't exactly evoke memories of Willie Mays. But Texas has compensated in the infield, where they've had the consensus best fielding shortstop in the AL (Alex Rodriguez) and a second baseman with an outstanding reputation and at least decent numbers (Michael Young).

Various statistical measures of team fielding have tended to rate recent Ranger clubs as below average, but usually not at the very bottom of the league. Of course, it's hard to know how much stock to put in those measures anyway; the extent to which they're actually measuring fielding as opposed to pitching (and luck) is still very much open to question. What isn't questionable is that the fielders have virtually nothing to do with strikeouts, walks, and home runs—those are entirely the responsibility of the pitching staff. And those numbers do not paint a pretty picture of the Ranger hurlers.

Over the past four years the Rangers ranked 29th, 27th, and 27th in the majors in walks, strikeouts, and home runs respectively (per batter faced, in all cases). The breadth of Texas' bad pitching performance is unmatched in baseball—all other teams ranked better than 27th in at least one of the three pitching-only categories. On the road, the Rangers ranked 29th, 24th, and 24th, with only the lowly Devil Rays and Royals matching the Rangers' level of consistency.

The bottom line: While it's possible that Ranger fielders are costing the team a few runs a year, to fixate on fielding is really missing the elephant in the room. The Ranger pitchers would allow tons of runs even if they played in front of Brooks Robinson and company.

Theory #3: It's the catcher. No one believes this one any more, but a few years ago it was popular to blame part of the Rangers' problems on Pudge Rodriguez's supposed inability to work with pitchers, especially after some overpublicized remarks by Todd Stottlemyre. But when Pudge missed half of 2000, 2001, and 2002 with injuries, and the Rangers' pitching didn't take a noticeable turn for the better in his absence, the theory began to lose its appeal. And when Pudge left last year, only to catch the young Marlins staff in a tremendous season-long performance—while the Rangers stunk worse than ever with Einar Diaz behind the plate—the theory was shot.

Theory #4: It's the lack of lefties. This is really a variant on the "It's the park" theory. An idea that's gaining steam in the media, based largely on the short right-field porch and the recent success of Kenny Rogers, is that left-handed pitchers are uniquely suited to success in The Ballpark at Arlington. And it may not only be members of the media who subscribe to this idea: The Texas front office has loaded the minor league system with lefty soft-tossers. Double-A Frisco started the season with an all-lefty starting rotation.

But as with the other theories we've looked at, the evidence supporting this one is skimpy at best. Sure, Rogers was quite good during his Ranger years, but that's because he's a good pitcher, not because he's a lefty. Rogers has had six different home parks during his 15-year career—two in Texas, two in New York, and one each in Oakland and Minnesota—and he's been effective (and underrated) nearly everywhere he's pitched; his career year came while pitching for Oakland. And while the recency effect may make it tempting to generalize from the Rogers example, it only takes a slightly longer memory to see that righties can succeed in the park just as well as lefties. Virtually all of the most successful Ranger pitchers during the TBiA era other than Rogers are righties: Ken Hill, Aaron Sele, Rick Helling, John Wetteland, and Jeff Zimmerman among them.

In fact, contrary to common belief, the Rangers have not always been a pitching disaster since TBiA opened. Their 1996 pitching staff was among the best in the AL, allowing half a run per game less than league average. That staff was heavily right-handed, with lefties accounting for only 20% of Ranger innings that year. It's good pitchers the Rangers lack, not ones who throw left, right, or center.

Theory #5: It's the coaching. It's always easy to point the finger at middle management when there's a breakdown among the worker bees, and the Ranger pitching breakdown has produced a level of scapegoating not seen since the Nixon administration. Since Opening Day 2000, the Rangers have gone through five pitching coaches: Dick Bosman, Larry Hardy, Bobby Cuellar, Oscar Acosta, and Orel Hershiser. There certainly isn't much evidence that any of these guys is a miracle worker in the Mazzone/Duncan/Kerrigan mold (although a weak case could be made for Acosta), but it would represent an astonishing run of bad luck if they were *all* incompetent enough to cause the consistently disastrous pitching we've seen from Texas the past few years.

Even more telling is the fact that Ranger pitchers generally haven't suddenly become more effective when they became ex-Rangers. Most of the pitchers who've left the club—Rogers, Sele, Helling, Darren Oliver, Esteban Loaiza, etc.—continued to pitch at about the same level immedi-

ately after leaving as they did immediately before. Yes, Loaiza had a career year in 2003, but that was after two-and-a-half seasons of mediocrity in Toronto. The young pitchers who flamed out in Texas—Ryan Glynn, Aaron Myette, Rob Bell, etc.—haven't set the world on fire since leaving. That strongly suggests that recent Ranger hurlers were not innately talented pitchers who were held back by poor instruction.

So we've ruled out park effects, fielding, catching, handedness, and coaching as significant causes of the Rangers run prevention problems. What does that leave us? Exactly what the overthinkers were trying to avoid. Occam's Razor triumphs again: They just suck.

More specifically, the Ranger brain trust has done a miserable job of evaluating pitching talent in the past five years. They've made all the classic mistakes. They over-relied on, and in many cases overpaid for, second- and third-tier free agent starters (Chan-Ho Park, Darren Oliver, Dave Burba, John Thomson). They spent millions on mediocre middle relievers (Jay Powell, Todd Van Poppel, Dan Miceli, Esteban Yan). They gave significant major league innings to "prospects" who had demonstrated no major league ability (Ryan Glynn, Aaron Myette, Matt Perisho, Tony Mounce). And they misjudged and ultimately gave away the only proven major league starting talent their system has produced in the past five years (Doug Davis).

Can we find a silver lining? Maybe if we squint really hard. While the 2004 Rangers aren't shaping up to have much more talent than the 2000–2003 versions, Ranger fans can take heart that pitching is notoriously variable. Chan Ho Park and Colby Lewis both have more ability than they've shown the past two years. They could form a respectable front two if things break right. Francisco Cordero could harness his raw materials to become one of the league's top closers. And Joaquin Benoit, Juan Dominguez, Erasmo Ramirez, Brian Shouse, and a few shrewdly chosen journeymen could round out a respectable staff.

That's a wildly optimistic scenario, of course. A more likely outcome is for the Rangers to once again get buried near the bottom of the league in run prevention, and to hope that their offense can manage to score more runs than their pitchers allow. Therein lies the real silver lining—the fact that their team gets to spend half of every game on offense. The prospect of pitching to a middle of the lineup consisting of Alex Rodriguez (at press time at least, he's still a Ranger), Mark Teixeira, and Hank Blalock for the next five years should have AL West pitchers sweating bullets. A handful of solid young players with less star power—Laynce Nix, Kevin Mench, Adrian Gonzalez, and others—promise to help in the near future as well. And that's a good thing, because with pitching like the Rangers', they're gonna need all the help they can get.

HITTERS

HANK BLALOCK — 3B — Bats: L — Throws: L — Born: 21-Nov-80 — Age: 23

YEAR	TM	LG	AGE	AB	H	2B	3B	HR	BB	SO	SB	CS	AVG	OBP	SLG	MLVR	EQBA	EQOBP	EQSLG	EQMLVR	VORP	DEFENSE	
2001	PCH	FLA	20	237	90	19	1	7	26	31	7	4	.380	.437	.557	.517	.300	.352	.457	.072	19.6	62-3B	8
2001	TUL	TEX	20	272	89	18	4	11	39	38	3	3	.327	.413	.544	.372	.264	.340	.444	.001	15.7	66-3B	-1
2002	TEX	AL	21	147	31	8	0	3	20	43	0	0	.211	.306	.327	-.214	.224	.325	.347	-.188	-0.3	39-3B	-3
2002	OKL	PCL	21	387	119	32	1	8	34	61	2	1	.307	.363	.457	.149	.279	.333	.418	-.036	15.8	89-3B	-11
2003	TEX	AL	22	567	170	33	3	29	44	97	2	3	.300	.350	.522	.147	.312	.365	.545	.233	43.2	131-3B	0
2004	TEX	AL	23	516	150	33	2	23	48	84	4	2	.291	.352	.499	.139	.284	.349	.487	.089	37.4	135-3B	-2

Breakout: 19%   Improve: 61%   Collapse: 14%

At the tender age of 22, Blalock's .872 OPS was 18th in the AL, and 15% better than the AL average of .757. The list of third basemen who exceeded league OPS by 10% or more at as young an age is short and, for Blalock, pretty sweet. It features immortals such as Eddie Matthews, George Brett, Ron Santo, and Dick Allen. But it also has more than its share of early flameouts—Bob Horner, Richie Hebner, and Jim Ray Hart, to name a few. To stay out of the latter group, Blalock will need to improve his performance against left-handed pitching over the next few years; he hit a Chavezian .209/.245/.295 against them in 2003.

JASON BOTTS — DH/1B/OF — Bats: B — Throws: R — Born: 26-Jul-80 — Age: 23

YEAR	TM	LG	AGE	AB	H	2B	3B	HR	BB	SO	SB	CS	AVG	OBP	SLG	MLVR	EQBA	EQOBP	EQSLG	EQMLVR	VORP	DEFENSE			
2001	SAV	SAL	20	392	121	24	2	9	53	88	13	7	.309	.416	.449	.304	.240	.319	.355	-.179	-12.8	57-1B	-4	39-RF	-6
2002	PCH	FLA	21	401	102	22	5	9	75	99	7	2	.254	.387	.401	.140	.204	.306	.333	-.256	-25.4	86-RF	-3		
2003	STO	CAL	22	283	89	14	2	9	45	59	12	3	.314	.409	.473	.275	.235	.315	.360	-.183	-9.0	72-1B	-9		
2003	FRI	TEX	22	194	51	11	1	4	21	45	6	1	.263	.341	.392	.025	.228	.295	.350	-.241	-10.7	23-RF	-1	10-1B	0
2004	TEX	AL	23	268	62	15	1	7	28	61	4	1	.231	.314	.375	-.129	.225	.311	.366	-.178	-5.4	74-1B	-7		

Breakout: 25%   Improve: 55%   Collapse: 24%

Jason Botts is a *biiiig* man. Whether he's a major league regular is still an open question. He put up nice numbers in Stockton, but that doesn't mean too much given that he was repeating High-A at a relatively advanced age. Defensively, he hasn't shown that he's anything more than a DH. There's still promise here, but he needs a breakthrough in some area—power, outfield defense, or (preferably) both.

JASON BOURGEOIS — 2B/SS? — Bats: R — Throws: R — Born: 04-Jan-82 — Age: 22

YEAR	TM	LG	AGE	AB	H	2B	3B	HR	BB	SO	SB	CS	AVG	OBP	SLG	MLVR	EQBA	EQOBP	EQSLG	EQMLVR	VORP	DEFENSE			
2001	PUL	APP	19	251	78	12	2	7	26	47	21	7	.311	.387	.458	.254	.208	.258	.312	-.378	-33.1	61-2B	-6		
2002	SAV	SAL	20	522	133	21	5	8	40	66	22	11	.255	.318	.360	-.003	.206	.251	.303	-.406	-32.7	97-SS	-22	20-2B	1
2003	STO	CAL	21	277	91	22	3	4	36	33	16	3	.329	.416	.473	.299	.256	.328	.374	-.125	4.3	51-2B	-7	13-SS	-4
2003	FRI	TEX	21	202	51	5	4	4	16	45	3	1	.252	.308	.376	-.057	.221	.274	.343	-.296	-7.5	53-2B	-9		
2004	TEX	AL	22	280	67	15	2	5	20	45	6	2	.241	.297	.363	-.168	.234	.295	.354	-.219	-1.4	75-2B	-12		

Breakout: 34%   Improve: 53%   Collapse: 22%

A recent conversation with a member of the Rangers' minor league staff tells you everything you need to know about Bourgeois: "What do you think of Bourgeois?" "He's an exciting offensive talent." "And how's his defense?" "He's an exciting offensive talent." Bourgeois's on-base skills and speed *are* moderately exciting—for a middle infielder. But he'll grow dull as dishwater if he keeps having to move left on the defensive spectrum.

PATRICK BOYD — CF — Bats: B — Throws: R — Born: 07-Sep-78 — Age: 25

YEAR	TM	LG	AGE	AB	H	2B	3B	HR	BB	SO	SB	CS	AVG	OBP	SLG	MLVR	EQBA	EQOBP	EQSLG	EQMLVR	VORP	DEFENSE	
2002	SAV	SAL	23	257	62	15	2	5	24	68	8	4	.241	.313	.374	-.001	.189	.238	.306	-.437	-23.3	55-CF	-5
2003	STO	CAL	24	221	65	17	0	13	29	68	11	1	.294	.381	.548	.314	.222	.295	.422	-.146	0.1	56-CF	-5
2003	FRI	TEX	24	160	31	5	3	3	16	39	9	3	.194	.278	.319	-.222	.167	.240	.290	-.465	-15.9	46-CF	4
2004	TEX	AL	25	187	42	10	1	6	17	52	5	2	.224	.293	.395	-.146	.218	.290	.385	-.196	-3.5	53-CF	-4

Breakout: 48%   Improve: 66%   Collapse: 20%

Last year Boyd finally put a series of injuries behind him and rediscovered some of the power he last displayed four years earlier during his stellar sophomore year at Clemson. Couple that with his solid work in center field, and you could being to tout him as a dark horse candidate to fill the Rangers' hole at that position in another year or so. That is until you consider that he was nearly 25 in A-ball last year, in the hitter-friendly Cal League to boot. Boyd needs a big year at Double-A in '04 to get taken seriously as a prospect.

JEREMY CLEVELAND   **OF**   **Bats: R**   **Throws: R**   Born: 10-Sep-81   Age: 22

YEAR	TM	LG	AGE	AB	H	2B	3B	HR	BB	SO	SB	CS	AVG	OBP	SLG	MLVR	EQBA	EQOBP	EQSLG	EQMLVR	VORP	DEFENSE
2003	SPO	NWN	21	245	79	20	3	7	40	50	5	1	.322	.432	.514	.392	.220	.300	.366	-.214	-20.8	53-RF -5
2004	TEX	AL	22	232	55	14	1	6	20	54	2	2	.237	.310	.388	-.116	.230	.307	.379	-.166	-3.3	65-RF -4

Breakout: 22%   Improve: 51%   Collapse: 19%

A 2003 8th-round draft pick out of the University of North Carolina, Cleveland exploded onto the pro ball scene as the best hitter in the Northwest League according to Clay Davenport's Equivalent Average (EqA). Cleveland's outfield-mates and fellow 2003 college draftees, Dane Bubela (22nd round out of Rice) and Andrew Wishy (12th round out of Arkansas) were similarly dominant at Spokane, finishing second and fifth in the league respectively. All three should move quickly through the system this year to find a level that challenges them. None of them are stellar fielders, with Bubela the most accomplished of the three.

EINAR DIAZ   **C**   **Bats: R**   **Throws: R**   Born: 28-Dec-72   Age: 31

YEAR	TM	LG	AGE	AB	H	2B	3B	HR	BB	SO	SB	CS	AVG	OBP	SLG	MLVR	EQBA	EQOBP	EQSLG	EQMLVR	VORP	DEFENSE
2001	CLE	AL	28	437	121	34	1	4	17	44	1	2	.277	.328	.387	-.056	.295	.341	.416	-.011	17.4	124-C 15
2002	CLE	AL	29	320	66	19	0	2	17	27	0	1	.206	.258	.284	-.348	.227	.279	.318	-.317	-11.8	96-C -2
2003	TEX	AL	30	334	86	14	1	4	9	32	3	1	.257	.294	.341	-.227	.270	.307	.360	-.175	-6.2	100-C 1
2004	TEX	AL	31	250	66	13	1	3	12	25	2	1	.262	.315	.360	-.127	.255	.312	.351	-.178	0.1	68-C -1

Breakout: 43%   Improve: 57%   Collapse: 28%

It's not often a team replaces one of the best catchers in the game with one of the worst. How much did the Pudge/Einar flip cost the Rangers? VORP makes the offensive difference between the two a little more than 50 runs, and most measurements rate them as having roughly equal value defensively (Pudge's arm isn't the cannon it used to be). So the Rangers lost about 50 runs, or about five wins, by letting Pudge go without a solid replacement. That's not enough to have made a difference in the playoff race, but it's enough to highlight the need for a better Pudge alternative than this.

NATE GOLD   **1B/3B**   **Bats: R**   **Throws: R**   Born: 12-Jun-80   Age: 24

YEAR	TM	LG	AGE	AB	H	2B	3B	HR	BB	SO	SB	CS	AVG	OBP	SLG	MLVR	EQBA	EQOBP	EQSLG	EQMLVR	VORP	DEFENSE	
2002	PUL	APP	22	113	36	9	1	5	17	20	2	0	.319	.405	.549	.350	.193	.252	.333	-.369	-22.0	27-1B 0	
2002	SAV	SAL	22	142	27	7	0	5	11	38	0	2	.190	.258	.345	-.151	.158	.200	.288	-.554	-20.7	37-1B 2	
2003	CLN	MID	23	369	99	35	3	12	59	76	4	2	.268	.370	.477	.219	.193	.277	.355	-.290	-26.4	83-1B 2	18-3B -4
2004	TEX	AL	24	246	53	14	1	8	21	60	2	1	.214	.282	.369	-.204	.208	.279	.360	-.255	-8.5	67-1B -3	

Breakout: 34%   Improve: 67%   Collapse: 13%

The 2002 10th-round draft pick and former NCAA home run champ had a fine year at the plate, finishing fifth in the Midwest League in slugging, tied for third in doubles, and tied for fourth in EqA. He also showed good control of the strike zone, with a 77:59 K:BB ratio. The only thing missing was the batting average, the most fickle of stats. The next step would be finding success at a more age-appropriate level, starting this year.

ADRIAN GONZALEZ   **1B**   **Bats: L**   **Throws: L**   Born: 08-May-82   Age: 22

YEAR	TM	LG	AGE	AB	H	2B	3B	HR	BB	SO	SB	CS	AVG	OBP	SLG	MLVR	EQBA	EQOBP	EQSLG	EQMLVR	VORP	DEFENSE
2001	KNE	MID	19	516	161	37	1	17	57	83	5	5	.312	.382	.486	.275	.234	.291	.371	-.215	-20.8	116-1B -2
2002	PME	EAS	20	508	135	34	1	17	54	112	6	3	.266	.344	.437	.066	.222	.287	.374	-.227	-23.8	135-1B -2
2003	ABQ	PCL	21	139	30	5	1	1	14	25	1	0	.216	.286	.288	-.332	.175	.247	.234	-.523	-18.4	37-1B 1
2003	CAR	SOU	21	137	42	9	1	1	14	25	1	1	.307	.368	.409	.146	.264	.318	.364	-.153	-3.0	36-1B -4
2003	FRI	TEX	21	173	49	6	2	3	11	27	0	0	.283	.326	.393	.019	.247	.290	.356	-.230	-7.7	43-1B 3
2004	TEX	AL	22	261	62	14	1	7	20	49	1	1	.238	.297	.382	-.147	.231	.294	.373	-.197	-6.8	71-1B -5

Breakout: 25%   Improve: 51%   Collapse: 20%

The crown jewel of John Hart's mid-season acquisitions, Gonzalez spent the year recovering from off-season wrist surgery and putting up disappointing numbers as a result. But he improved throughout the year, capping his season with a solid .260/.396/.455 Arizona Fall League showing, albeit against AFL pitching that gets more horrendous every year as teams preserve their best young arms. With the wrist fully recovered, look for Gonzalez to reestablish himself as an elite prospect and break into the Rangers' lineup by 2005, if not sooner.

JUAN GONZALEZ   OF   Bats: R   Throws: R   Born: 16-Oct-69   Age: 34

YEAR	TM	LG	AGE	AB	H	2B	3B	HR	BB	SO	SB	CS	AVG	OBP	SLG	MLVR	EQBA	EQOBP	EQSLG	EQMLVR	VORP	DEFENSE	
2001	CLE	AL	31	532	173	34	1	35	41	94	1	0	.325	.370	.590	.341	.342	.396	.626	.436	68.0	111-RF	1
2002	TEX	AL	32	277	78	21	1	8	17	56	2	0	.282	.324	.451	.028	.295	.337	.478	.072	9.5	59-RF	4
2003	TEX	AL	33	327	96	17	1	24	14	73	1	1	.294	.329	.572	.182	.304	.342	.601	.269	20.1	50-RF	4
2004	KCR	AL	34	338	97	20	1	17	23	69	1	1	.286	.334	.502	.110	.273	.326	.486	.041	12.3	88-RF	-2

Breakout: 11%   Improve: 30%   Collapse: 34%

Gonzalez took plenty of flak for vetoing a trade to the then-contending Expos, with columnists across North America raising questions about his competitiveness. We've never understood how wanting to move to an already-good team makes you competitive. Why is it competitive to leech off the work done by others? Shouldn't it be just as competitive to stick with your current bunch through thick and thin, doing everything you can to make them better? Regardless, Gonzalez ended up doing neither, as shortly after the aborted trade his season was ended by yet another injury (this one a torn calf muscle). He'll help the Royals, though how much is open to debate:

Player	Projected 2004 EqBA/EqOBP/EqSLG
Juan Gonzalez	.273/.326/.486
David DeJesus	.267/.354/.425

TODD GREENE   C   Bats: R   Throws: R   Born: 08-May-71   Age: 33

YEAR	TM	LG	AGE	AB	H	2B	3B	HR	BB	SO	SB	CS	AVG	OBP	SLG	MLVR	EQBA	EQOBP	EQSLG	EQMLVR	VORP	DEFENSE			
2001	COH	INT	30	131	33	8	0	6	4	19	3	2	.252	.279	.450	-.016	.242	.268	.439	-.156	0.7	27-C	-3		
2001	NYY	AL	30	96	20	4	0	1	3	21	0	0	.208	.240	.281	-.398	.229	.266	.312	-.350	-4.2	23-C	-5		
2002	LVG	PCL	31	125	44	12	0	11	3	21	0	0	.352	.373	.712	.534	.309	.335	.626	.302	16.2	24-C	0		
2002	OKL	PCL	31	152	46	9	0	6	9	27	2	0	.303	.339	.480	.137	.281	.319	.444	-.023	6.3	23-C	-4		
2002	TEX	AL	31	112	30	5	0	10	2	23	0	0	.268	.282	.580	.124	.277	.294	.616	.183	7.2	12-1B	0	13-C	-2
2003	TEX	AL	32	205	47	10	1	10	2	47	0	0	.229	.243	.434	-.211	.240	.257	.456	-.153	-2.8	46-C	-3		
2004	COL	NL	33	266	71	16	1	12	13	57	1	1	.267	.304	.467	-.012	.258	.295	.447	-.077	7.3	70-C	-6		

Breakout: 30%   Improve: 59%   Collapse: 29%

¿Quién es mas macho, Soriano o Greene? Anybody can hit home runs if they meekly wait for a good pitch. But it takes a real man to crank them out of the park while hacking away at anything that moves. Alfonso Soriano is celebrated for this, but he's got nothing on Todd Greene. Greene is the all-time leader in HR-to-walk ratio, and it isn't close. He's the Bob Beamon of HR-to-walk ratio. His HR-to-walk ratio of 1.41 makes Soriano (second place with 1.08, and falling) look like Jackie Rexrode. Single season? Prior to 2002, no one with at least 10 HRs had ever had a HR-to-walk ratio higher than 3.25. Greene has now reached 5.0 two years in a row. *Si, Greene es mas macho!*

JASON JONES   OF   Bats: B   Throws: R   Born: 17-Oct-76   Age: 27

YEAR	TM	LG	AGE	AB	H	2B	3B	HR	BB	SO	SB	CS	AVG	OBP	SLG	MLVR	EQBA	EQOBP	EQSLG	EQMLVR	VORP	DEFENSE			
2001	PCH	FLA	24	375	106	26	2	15	56	48	1	3	.283	.374	.483	.243	.224	.297	.396	-.176	-11.8	98-1B	-5		
2001	TUL	TEX	24	107	23	6	0	2	3	17	0	0	.215	.243	.327	-.292	.187	.213	.299	-.498	-12.7	28-1B	-5		
2002	TUL	TEX	25	471	139	33	2	13	87	97	12	7	.295	.401	.456	.231	.243	.336	.387	-.101	-2.8	120-1B	-19	15-LF	-2
2003	OKL	PCL	26	375	108	29	0	9	50	80	7	2	.288	.374	.437	.139	.262	.341	.407	-.050	0.5	52-LF	-3	11-1B	-1
2003	TEX	AL	26	107	23	6	0	3	10	21	0	1	.215	.298	.355	-.195	.224	.305	.383	-.179	-3.9	10-LF	0	12-RF	-1
2004	TEX	AL	27	224	56	12	1	9	23	44	3	1	.249	.322	.427	-.038	.243	.319	.417	-.088	3.0	62-LF	-5		

Breakout: 30%   Improve: 49%   Collapse: 23%

Jason Jones is no one's idea of a great prospect, but he does have a well-rounded game: decent line-drive swing, decent plate discipline, decent gap power, and decent outfield defense. He's cheap, he can come off the bench from both sides of the plate, and he's just turning 27. That's a good resume for a fifth outfielder.

GERALD LAIRD

C | **Bats: R** | **Throws: R** | Born: 13-Nov-79 | Age: 24

YEAR	TM	LG	AGE	AB	H	2B	3B	HR	BB	SO	SB	CS	AVG	OBP	SLG	MLVR	EQBA	EQOBP	EQSLG	EQMLVR	VORP	DEFENSE	
2001	MOD	CAL	21	443	113	13	5	5	48	101	10	9	.255	.337	.341	-.065	.200	.266	.271	-.422	-33.2	81-C	8
2002	TUL	TEX	22	442	122	21	4	11	45	95	8	6	.276	.343	.416	.075	.238	.297	.371	-.201	-3.8	96-C	2
2003	OKL	PCL	23	338	88	20	5	9	37	61	9	3	.260	.344	.429	.053	.240	.315	.404	-.120	5.6	89-C	5
2003	TEX	AL	23	44	12	2	1	1	5	11	0	0	.273	.360	.432	.021	.295	.377	.455	.109	2.0	11-C	1
2004	*TEX*	*AL*	*24*	*237*	*59*	*12*	*2*	*7*	*21*	*46*	*4*	*2*	*.251*	*.318*	*.402*	*-.076*	*.244*	*.315*	*.392*	*-.126*	*4.4*	*65-C*	*-1*

Breakout: 35%   Improve: 52%   Collapse: 24%

There are no questions about Laird behind the plate—he's a tremendous defensive catcher. There are questions about the major league readiness of his bat, and on that front the 2003 returns are encouraging. He made the move to Triple-A without missing a beat, then capped off his season with a .273/.360/.432 audition in 44 at-bats in Arlington and an equally impressive showing with Team USA in the Arizona Fall League. He isn't the same caliber prospect as Joe Mauer, Jeff Mathis, or Victor Martinez, but he may be more ready than any of them to have a major league impact in 2004.

MIKE LAMB

3B/1B | **Bats: L** | **Throws: R** | Born: 09-Aug-75 | Age: 28

YEAR	TM	LG	AGE	AB	H	2B	3B	HR	BB	SO	SB	CS	AVG	OBP	SLG	MLVR	EQBA	EQOBP	EQSLG	EQMLVR	VORP	DEFENSE			
2001	OKL	PCL	25	273	81	19	3	8	13	31	0	2	.297	.331	.476	.076	.272	.312	.434	-.058	9.6	69-3B	-15		
2001	TEX	AL	25	284	87	18	0	4	14	27	2	1	.306	.348	.412	.023	.318	.363	.428	.066	17.3	68-3B	-8		
2002	TEX	AL	26	314	89	13	0	9	33	48	0	0	.283	.354	.411	.026	.298	.371	.435	.073	12.8	42-1B	-3	13-3B	-4
2003	OKL	PCL	27	274	79	19	4	9	42	45	1	1	.288	.383	.485	.219	.258	.348	.444	.010	16.6	65-3B	-1		
2003	TEX	AL	27	38	5	0	0	0	2	7	1	0	.132	.190	.132	-.753	.158	.215	.158	-.699	-5.6				
2004	*TEX*	*AL*	*28*	*189*	*51*	*10*	*1*	*5*	*18*	*31*	*1*	*1*	*.270*	*.338*	*.410*	*-.018*	*.263*	*.335*	*.400*	*-.068*	*6.1*	*53-3B*	*-4*		

Breakout: 19%   Improve: 35%   Collapse: 41%

The organization continued to sour on Lamb in 2003. You've heard this story hundreds of times before: A pretty good hitter can't quite stay far enough right on the defensive spectrum to justify a major league spot. Players like this are drawn by force of nature to the Sacramento River Cats.

MARSHALL McDOUGALL

IF | **Bats: R** | **Throws: R** | Born: 19-Dec-78 | Age: 25

YEAR	TM	LG	AGE	AB	H	2B	3B	HR	BB	SO	SB	CS	AVG	OBP	SLG	MLVR	EQBA	EQOBP	EQSLG	EQMLVR	VORP	DEFENSE			
2001	VIS	CAL	22	534	137	43	7	12	46	110	14	2	.257	.321	.431	.024	.203	.253	.344	-.346	-26.1	75-3B	-1	29-2B	0
2002	MID	TEX	23	323	98	22	5	9	38	57	7	4	.303	.374	.486	.214	.248	.313	.411	-.108	7.2	36-3B	-2	27-SS	-2
2003	FRI	TEX	24	418	108	16	3	13	43	68	18	3	.258	.328	.404	.018	.224	.287	.363	-.241	-5.0	90-SS	-5	16-3B	0
2003	OKL	PCL	24	111	30	4	2	2	13	21	1	1	.270	.341	.396	.012	.241	.315	.366	-.171	1.1	13-SS	1		
2004	*TEX*	*AL*	*25*	*234*	*60*	*13*	*2*	*7*	*20*	*41*	*4*	*2*	*.256*	*.318*	*.411*	*-.061*	*.249*	*.315*	*.401*	*-.111*	*7.0*	*64-SS*	*-8*		

Breakout: 36%   Improve: 64%   Collapse: 21%

Originally drafted by Grady Fuson when he was with the A's, McDougall came to Texas from Oakland via Cleveland through a complicated series of trades and Rule 5 maneuvers. McDougall shows some offensive and defensive promise at shortstop, but there's not much future at that position with the Rangers, for obvious reasons (barring any silly trades, that is). One possibility is that the Rangers could take advantage of his strong arm by moving him to catcher, to fill the organizational void of real prospects at that position. The Expos are trying a similar tack with Josh McKinley, and as with McKinley, it may give McDougall a shot at a useful big league career.

KEVIN MENCH

OF | **Bats: R** | **Throws: R** | Born: 07-Jan-78 | Age: 26

YEAR	TM	LG	AGE	AB	H	2B	3B	HR	BB	SO	SB	CS	AVG	OBP	SLG	MLVR	EQBA	EQOBP	EQSLG	EQMLVR	VORP	DEFENSE			
2001	TUL	TEX	23	475	126	34	2	26	34	76	4	6	.265	.319	.509	.123	.226	.273	.437	-.163	-13.8	112-RF	2		
2002	OKL	PCL	24	98	21	8	0	6	17	33	0	0	.214	.342	.480	.060	.190	.303	.430	-.143	-2.3	17-RF	0		
2002	TEX	AL	24	366	95	20	2	15	31	83	1	1	.260	.327	.448	.011	.272	.342	.477	.057	11.5	48-RF	2	49-LF	-1
2003	OKL	PCL	25	105	28	8	0	4	19	15	2	0	.267	.366	.457	.135	.234	.342	.421	-.050	0.5	16-RF	-2	12-LF	-1
2003	TEX	AL	25	125	40	12	0	2	10	17	1	1	.320	.381	.464	.138	.336	.396	.496	.240	5.8	29-LF	-2		
2004	*TEX*	*AL*	*26*	*270*	*72*	*18*	*1*	*11*	*27*	*50*	*2*	*1*	*.267*	*.340*	*.465*	*.054*	*.260*	*.337*	*.453*	*.004*	*8.8*	*74-LF*	*-2*		

Breakout: 32%   Improve: 57%   Collapse: 24%

Last year we said about Mench: "If he gets the ABs, he's a very strong candidate for a breakout year." Sometimes it pays to hedge. He didn't get the ABs, because a strained oblique muscle in March and a broken wrist in July conspired to limit him to a month and a half of fully healthy play. He did look like a breakout player during that month and a half, hitting a sizzling .355/.419/.527 during June and July. Wrist injuries have a way of hanging around, so get ready for another hedge: If the wrist is 100% by April, Mench should fulfill the promise we saw in him last year.

DREW MEYER   SS/CF   Bats: L   Throws: R   Born: 29-Aug-81   Age: 22

YEAR	TM	LG	AGE	AB	H	2B	3B	HR	BB	SO	SB	CS	AVG	OBP	SLG	MLVR	EQBA	EQOBP	EQSLG	EQMLVR	VORP	DEFENSE		
2002	SAV	SAL	20	214	52	5	4	1	10	53	7	6	.243	.274	.318	-.132	.202	.227	.271	-.501	-19.2	32-SS -4	19-2B	-1
2003	STO	CAL	21	398	112	16	9	5	32	92	24	10	.281	.330	.405	.019	.224	.268	.329	-.325	-14.4	92-SS 9		
2003	FRI	TEX	21	98	31	1	1	0	11	23	9	1	.316	.385	.347	.076	.273	.339	.303	-.192	0.3	26-SS 4		
2004	*TEX*	*AL*	*22*	*270*	*63*	*12*	*3*	*3*	*17*	*61*	*8*	*3*	*.234*	*.279*	*.338*	*-.237*	*.227*	*.276*	*.330*	*-.288*	*-5.5*	*72-SS -5*		

Breakout: 36%   *Improve: 59%*   *Collapse: 22%*

Meyer hasn't yet put up the numbers you'd like to see from a first-round pick (10th overall in 2002), but when you watch him play, it's easy to see what caught the Rangers' eye. He's the kind of player who's constantly drawing attention to himself on the field—hustling for the extra base, scrambling after Texas Leaguers, or sliding head first into a bag that no one is throwing to. But there's more to Meyer than getting his uniform dirty. His offense has improved with each promotion, his defense at short is already major league caliber, and he's drawing coaches' raves for his work in center field, where he's in the process of moving. Like Lenny Dykstra, Meyer is going to have a major league career largely through sheer force of will.

RAMON NIVAR   CF/2B   Bats: R   Throws: R   Born: 22-Feb-80   Age: 24

YEAR	TM	LG	AGE	AB	H	2B	3B	HR	BB	SO	SB	CS	AVG	OBP	SLG	MLVR	EQBA	EQOBP	EQSLG	EQMLVR	VORP	DEFENSE		
2001	PCH	FLA	21	515	124	20	1	2	28	65	28	18	.241	.286	.295	-.158	.213	.243	.269	-.466	-46.6	94-2B -5	34-SS	-8
2002	PCH	FLA	22	472	144	21	8	3	32	44	39	15	.305	.353	.403	.129	.263	.300	.354	-.202	-3.8	99-2B 7	13-SS	0
2003	FRI	TEX	23	317	110	17	4	4	20	23	9	9	.347	.387	.464	.271	.298	.336	.411	-.025	14.4	54-2B -1	17-SS	0
2003	OKL	PCL	23	89	30	2	2	2	5	5	6	1	.337	.368	.472	.226	.315	.351	.449	.073	5.7	20-CF 0		
2003	TEX	AL	23	90	19	1	2	0	4	10	4	2	.211	.253	.267	-.430	.222	.262	.289	-.395	-6.5	26-CF -1		
2004	*TEX*	*AL*	*24*	*290*	*78*	*14*	*2*	*4*	*17*	*30*	*9*	*3*	*.267*	*.312*	*.370*	*-.116*	*.260*	*.309*	*.361*	*-.166*	*0.8*	*77-2B 0*		

Breakout: 25%   *Improve: 49%*   *Collapse: 25%*

You won't find a better demonstration of the limitations of an empty batting average than Ramon Nivar. In 2003 he had as spectacular a breakthrough season as a prospect of his type can possibly have, and it's still hard to get excited about him. Despite the encouraging declining K rate, he's just not going to hit .350 consistently in the majors. And even if he does manage to consistently hit .300, a .300/.330/.420 center fielder is, well, it's Juan Pierre without the steals. His work in center field was predictably raw for a newly converted middle infielder with a weak arm. This would be the perfect time to trade him.

LAYNCE NIX   OF   Bats: L   Throws: L   Born: 30-Oct-80   Age: 23

YEAR	TM	LG	AGE	AB	H	2B	3B	HR	BB	SO	SB	CS	AVG	OBP	SLG	MLVR	EQBA	EQOBP	EQSLG	EQMLVR	VORP	DEFENSE		
2001	SAV	SAL	20	407	113	26	8	8	37	94	9	6	.278	.337	.440	.166	.219	.270	.353	-.291	-30.0	67-RF -5	36-CF	-3
2002	PCH	FLA	21	512	146	27	3	21	72	105	17	1	.285	.374	.473	.233	.229	.302	.389	-.173	-4.2	79-CF -4	28-LF	-1
2003	FRI	TEX	22	335	95	23	0	15	34	68	9	2	.284	.344	.487	.177	.241	.299	.429	-.114	3.5	70-CF -8		
2003	TEX	AL	22	184	47	10	0	8	9	53	3	0	.255	.289	.440	-.104	.262	.301	.459	-.050	-0.8	30-RF -3	20-CF	-1
2004	*TEX*	*AL*	*23*	*323*	*86*	*19*	*2*	*13*	*27*	*69*	*6*	*2*	*.267*	*.324*	*.456*	*.016*	*.259*	*.321*	*.445*	*-.035*	*6.9*	*86-CF -8*		

Breakout: 44%   *Improve: 71%*   *Collapse: 11%*

Did the Rangers rush Nix by giving him a starting major league job just a half year out of Single-A? We doubt it. We don't know of any evidence that shows how putting a young player in the majors before he's dominated the high minors stunts his development. In fact, as you can see from the translated statistics above, Nix actually hit better in Arlington than at Double-A Frisco, although it's worth noting that he faced almost no left-handed pitching there. His power is outstanding for a 22-year-old. Now he just needs to get back some control of the strike zone; his 6:1 K:BB ratio was second-worst in the AL (minimum 150 PAs). He's really stretched in center field, but even as a corner outfielder, he'll be a good one.

RAFAEL PALMEIRO   DH/1B   Bats: L   Throws: L   Born: 24-Sep-64   Age: 39

YEAR	TM	LG	AGE	AB	H	2B	3B	HR	BB	SO	SB	CS	AVG	OBP	SLG	MLVR	EQBA	EQOBP	EQSLG	EQMLVR	VORP	DEFENSE	
2001	TEX	AL	36	600	164	33	0	47	101	90	1	1	.273	.381	.563	.249	.285	.394	.592	.314	65.4	112-1B 1	
2002	TEX	AL	37	546	149	34	0	43	104	94	2	0	.273	.391	.571	.282	.288	.408	.606	.358	67.7	89-1B 6	
2003	TEX	AL	38	561	146	21	2	38	84	77	2	0	.260	.359	.508	.108	.271	.372	.534	.186	32.0	52-1B 4	
2004	*BAL*	*AL*	*39*	*406*	*103*	*20*	*0*	*26*	*66*	*65*	*1*	*1*	*.255*	*.361*	*.498*	*.120*	*.263*	*.375*	*.523*	*.158*	*28.4*		

Breakout: 14%   *Improve: 63%*   *Collapse: 14%*

(continued next page)

Rafael Palmeiro *(continued)*

Is Palmeiro the greatest player in Ranger history? Maybe, although Pudge Rodriguez has a strong case as well. In any event the key word is "history." In the present, father time is catching up to Palmeiro. His decline in 2003 was steep and wide-ranging. In all three major hitting areas—average, power, and patience—he had his worst year since he was an Oriole. He played less often in the field than any year since his Gold Glove (cough) season of 1999. He's clearly qualified for the Hall of Fame, but even if he doesn't get elected, millions of fathers will remember him fondly for the day they first heard the question "Dad, what's Viagra for?" He's an Oriole again, after signing a one-year deal with an option for a second.

HERBERT PERRY IF/DH Bats: R Throws: R Born: 15-Sep-69 Age: 34

YEAR	TM	LG	AGE	AB	H	2B	3B	HR	BB	SO	SB	CS	AVG	OBP	SLG	MLVR	EQBA	EQOBP	EQSLG	EQMLVR	VORP	DEFENSE
2001	CWS	AL	31	285	73	21	1	7	23	55	2	2	.256	.326	.411	-.046	.270	.340	.435	-.007	13.1	58-3B -7
2002	TEX	AL	32	450	124	24	1	22	34	66	4	2	.276	.333	.480	.077	.288	.346	.508	.123	34.7	106-3B -8
2003	TEX	AL	33	24	4	1	0	0	0	3	0	0	.167	.167	.208	-.692	.167	.167	.250	-.670	-3.2	
2004	*TEX*	*AL*	*34*	*185*	*48*	*10*	*0*	*6*	*16*	*31*	*1*	*1*	*.260*	*.326*	*.417*	*-.035*	*.253*	*.323*	*.407*	*-.085*	*6.0*	*52-3B -2*

Breakout: 33%   Improve: 48%   Collapse: 26%

It sounds malicious to say this, but the shoulder injury that cost Perry his 2003 was the best thing that could have happened to the Rangers. It cleared the way for full-time major league roles for both Blalock and Teixeira, roles for which they were clearly ready. Perry should be ready to play by spring training, probably mostly at DH or first as both the surgery and Blalock's entrenchment will make it tough for him to find time at third.

ALEX RODRIGUEZ SS Bats: R Throws: R Born: 27-Jul-75 Age: 28

YEAR	TM	LG	AGE	AB	H	2B	3B	HR	BB	SO	SB	CS	AVG	OBP	SLG	MLVR	EQBA	EQOBP	EQSLG	EQMLVR	VORP	DEFENSE
2001	TEX	AL	25	632	201	34	1	52	75	131	18	3	.318	.399	.622	.400	.331	.413	.652	.482	113.5	156-SS 10
2002	TEX	AL	26	624	187	27	2	57	87	122	9	4	.300	.392	.623	.377	.318	.410	.665	.478	114.3	157-SS 13
2003	TEX	AL	27	607	181	30	6	47	87	126	17	3	.298	.396	.600	.313	.314	.412	.634	.433	83.9	154-SS 9
2004	*TEX*	*AL*	*28*	*576*	*177*	*34*	*3*	*46*	*84*	*117*	*12*	*3*	*.307*	*.402*	*.619*	*.382*	*.299*	*.398*	*.604*	*.332*	*83.2*	*158-SS 1*

Breakout: 11%   Improve: 53%   Collapse: 8%

A-Rod takes all the fun out of the game. You used to be able to have an argument with your drinking buddies about which member of the SS trinity was the best. Now you'd be laughed out of the bar if you tried to make the case for Jeter or Garciaparra, or Tejada or anyone else for that matter. There used to be interesting and provocative columns each year debating the qualifications of various AL MVP candidates. Now any sportswriter with a beef against Rodriguez has to resort to increasingly convoluted and bizarre arguments for an alternative "candidate," culminating last September in the hilarious Shannon-Stewart-for-MVP campaign. With his next two home runs, Rodriguez will tie and break the career record for homers as a shortstop—at the age of 28. The Rangers would be making the biggest mistake in franchise history if they resurrect and follow through on their early-off-season plan to trade him.

VINCENT SINISI OF/1B Bats: L Throws: L Born: 07-Nov-81 Age: 22

YEAR	TM	LG	AGE	AB	H	2B	3B	HR	BB	SO	SB	CS	AVG	OBP	SLG	MLVR	EQBA	EQOBP	EQSLG	EQMLVR	VORP	DEFENSE
2003	STO	CAL	21	62	16	1	0	1	3	8	1	1	.258	.288	.323	-.191	.210	.246	.258	-.477	-6.2	

Texas was positively giddy to find Rice star Sinisi still available for their second-round draft pick. He signed late and didn't put up good numbers in his brief pro debut. But he did show a good approach at the plate, good gap power, and a credible corner outfield glove. The Rangers are anxious to see what he can do in a full minor league season.

WILL SMITH OF Bats: L Throws: R Born: 23-Oct-81 Age: 22

YEAR	TM	LG	AGE	AB	H	2B	3B	HR	BB	SO	SB	CS	AVG	OBP	SLG	MLVR	EQBA	EQOBP	EQSLG	EQMLVR	VORP	DEFENSE	
2001	KNE	MID	19	535	150	26	2	16	32	74	4	5	.280	.324	.426	.084	.221	.258	.346	-.323	-41.9	113-LF -11	
2002	JUP	FLA	20	549	164	30	12	14	31	75	8	3	.299	.336	.474	.214	.258	.288	.423	-.129	-12.1	86-LF -10	29-RF -3
2003	CAR	SOU	21	123	36	5	1	1	11	23	1	0	.293	.346	.374	.056	.262	.306	.341	-.210	-6.0	25-LF -1	
2003	FRI	TEX	21	130	26	6	1	4	5	28	0	0	.200	.226	.354	-.260	.177	.207	.323	-.482	-16.4	30-LF 0	
2004	*TEX*	*AL*	*22*	*228*	*56*	*12*	*1*	*6*	*13*	*38*	*1*	*1*	*.246*	*.288*	*.387*	*-.150*	*.239*	*.285*	*.378*	*-.202*	*-6.5*	*62-LF -5*	

Breakout: 30%   Improve: 53%   Collapse: 24%

Another part of the booty from the Ugueth Urbina deal, Smith was considered one of Florida's better prospects last off-season, but he had a lost year in Double-A. A broken hamate bone in April sapped him of his power (what is it with these Marlin prospects and wrist injuries?), and without power there's not much to him, as he doesn't walk and isn't a great outfielder. He was young for the level anyway, so he'll likely return to Frisco and try to regain his lost luster.

SHANE SPENCER OF Bats: R Throws: R Born: 20-Feb-72 Age: 32

YEAR	TM	LG	AGE	AB	H	2B	3B	HR	BB	SO	SB	CS	AVG	OBP	SLG	MLVR	EQBA	EQOBP	EQSLG	EQMLVR	VORP	DEFENSE			
2001	COH	INT	29	173	40	10	1	3	23	21	4	1	.231	.323	.353	-.085	.220	.308	.345	-.227	-9.4	30-LF	-1		
2001	NYY	AL	29	283	73	14	2	10	21	58	4	1	.258	.315	.428	-.027	.277	.336	.467	.037	6.7	44-LF	2	28-RF	1
2002	NYY	AL	30	288	71	15	2	6	31	62	0	3	.247	.324	.375	-.079	.268	.347	.409	-.032	2.5	47-RF	0	30-LF	0
2003	CLE	AL	31	210	57	10	0	8	18	52	2	0	.271	.328	.433	.004	.289	.350	.464	.068	4.1	28-RF	-3	13-LF	0
2003	TEX	AL	31	185	42	10	0	4	27	40	0	0	.227	.329	.346	-.175	.238	.340	.368	-.122	-6.7	41-LF	-4	11-RF	1
2004	TEX	AL	32	262	69	14	1	9	27	54	2	1	.263	.335	.427	-.005	.256	.332	.417	-.055	3.2	72-LF	-2		

Breakout: 32%   Improve: 52%   Collapse: 29%

Never underestimate the power of a first impression. We doubt that Spencer would have 1,600 major league plate appearances under his belt if he hadn't managed to slug .910 in the first 73 of those PAs. Even now, five years later, that celebrated 1998 September still dominates his career line; take it away, and his career OPS drops by 27 points. He's not going to make a living off it too much longer: Spencer's now well into his 30s, coming off two straight years of replacement-level performance.

MARK TEIXEIRA 1B Bats: B Throws: R Born: 11-Apr-81 Age: 23

YEAR	TM	LG	AGE	AB	H	2B	3B	HR	BB	SO	SB	CS	AVG	OBP	SLG	MLVR	EQBA	EQOBP	EQSLG	EQMLVR	VORP	DEFENSE			
2002	PCH	FLA	21	150	48	10	2	9	21	24	2	0	.320	.411	.593	.466	.250	.321	.474	-.004	8.5	36-3B	-9		
2002	TUL	TEX	21	171	54	11	3	10	25	36	3	2	.316	.415	.591	.445	.257	.340	.486	.052	13.0	47-3B	0		
2003	TEX	AL	22	529	137	29	5	26	44	120	1	2	.259	.331	.480	.017	.269	.342	.503	.091	11.8	105-1B	0	13-3B	-6
2004	TEX	AL	23	522	148	32	3	29	51	110	3	2	.283	.356	.522	.167	.275	.353	.509	.117	32.5	138-1B	0		

Breakout: 46%   Improve: 72%   Collapse: 9%

There seems to be a small air of disappointment surrounding Teixeira's rookie year, if only because he didn't immediately hit like Mickey Mantle at his peak. But unrealistic expectations aside, Teixeira gave us no real reason to be disappointed, and plenty of reasons to be excited. For one thing, he showed sensational power for a 22-year-old. The only recent players to put up better Isolated Power (SLG minus BA) numbers at as young an age are Albert Pujols, Alex Rodriguez, Juan Gonzalez, Vladimir Guerrero, Andruw Jones, and Ken Griffey Jr. The two names immediately below Teixeira on the list are Eric Chavez and Troy Glaus. Look for Teixeira's batting average to rise this year, and for him to make himself more at home with that company.

ANTHONY WEBSTER CF Bats: L Throws: R Born: 10-Apr-83 Age: 21

YEAR	TM	LG	AGE	AB	H	2B	3B	HR	BB	SO	SB	CS	AVG	OBP	SLG	MLVR	EQBA	EQOBP	EQSLG	EQMLVR	VORP	DEFENSE	
2002	BRI	APP	19	244	86	7	3	1	38	38	16	7	.352	.448	.418	.283	.220	.287	.264	-.379	-36.0	53-CF	-8
2003	KAN	SAL	20	363	105	18	1	2	31	58	20	12	.289	.353	.361	.084	.237	.282	.301	-.329	-21.8	86-CF	-12
2003	CLN	MID	20	74	20	7	0	1	0	8	4	1	.270	.286	.405	.019	.230	.239	.365	-.327	-3.9	13-CF	-2
2004	TEX	AL	21	284	66	12	2	3	17	50	7	4	.231	.283	.316	-.260	.225	.280	.308	-.311	-14.9	76-CF	-10

Breakout: 26%   Improve: 51%   Collapse: 22%

Webster is the best of the three prospects acquired from the White Sox in the Carl Everett deal, or at least the one with the highest ceiling. He's a classic tools guy: lots of athletic ability, but still a long way to go in terms of baseball skills. His 2003 was a little troubling because of the big drop in his walk rate; he topped off the year by drawing zero walks in 78 PAs in Clinton. He's young, and there's still plenty of room for improvement in lots of areas. In particular, there's a good chance he'll turn his raw strength into better power numbers this year in Stockton.

MICHAEL YOUNG 2B Bats: R Throws: R Born: 19-Oct-76 Age: 27

YEAR	TM	LG	AGE	AB	H	2B	3B	HR	BB	SO	SB	CS	AVG	OBP	SLG	MLVR	EQBA	EQOBP	EQSLG	EQMLVR	VORP	DEFENSE	
2001	OKL	PCL	24	189	55	8	0	8	20	34	3	3	.291	.358	.460	.096	.258	.324	.405	-.088	5.0	43-2B	-7
2001	TEX	AL	24	386	96	18	4	11	26	91	3	1	.249	.298	.402	-.123	.260	.314	.423	-.080	9.2	102-2B	3
2002	TEX	AL	25	573	150	26	8	9	41	112	6	7	.262	.308	.382	-.107	.275	.326	.406	-.070	15.3	142-2B	1
2003	TEX	AL	26	666	204	33	9	14	36	103	13	2	.306	.339	.446	.032	.316	.355	.464	.103	31.7	158-2B	-8
2004	TEX	AL	27	539	146	27	4	13	36	89	8	3	.271	.317	.407	-.057	.263	.314	.397	-.108	10.3	138-2B	-2

Breakout: 5%   Improve: 28%   Collapse: 38%

In a year when Young's offensive production took a huge step forward, his fielding took a step backward, raising questions about his reputation in some circles as a world-beating second baseman. Young's offensive spike came almost entirely from an uptick in singles—his isolated power rose only slightly, and his walk rate actually dropped—so there's a good chance he'll give some of it back this year.

PITCHERS

JOAQUIN BENOIT

Bats: R   **Throws: R**   Born: 26-Jul-77   Age: 26

YEAR	TM	LG	AGE	G	GS	IP	H	BB	SO	HR	ERA	EQERA	EQH9	EQBB9	EQSO9	EQHR9	PERA	VORP	STF
2001	TUL	TEX	23	4	4	21.7	23	6	23	1	3.32	4.50	10.8	3.2	6.8	0.9	5.25	2.4	17
2001	OKL	PCL	23	24	24	131.0	113	73	142	14	4.19	4.87	8.3	6.0	7.5	1.1	5.08	9.9	13
2002	OKL	PCL	24	16	16	98.7	74	37	103	8	3.56	3.58	7.2	3.8	7.1	1.0	3.82	20.9	22
2002	TEX	AL	24	17	13	84.7	91	58	59	6	5.31	4.95	9.3	5.6	5.9	0.5	4.85	6.0	14
2003	OKL	PCL	25	6	6	33.0	28	11	31	3	3.82	4.65	8.1	3.5	7.3	1.2	4.38	3.3	7
2003	TEX	AL	25	25	17	105.0	99	51	87	23	5.49	4.63	7.5	4.0	7.1	1.7	4.82	5.5	-3
2004	TEX	AL	26	24	16	95.0	98	46	75	15	5.22	4.72	8.7	4.1	7.1	1.2	4.66	12.8	6

Breakout: 26%   Improve: 50%   Collapse: 20%

You wouldn't know it from the 5.49 ERA, but Benoit may have turned a corner in 2003. His major league strikeout rate saw a big spike from 2002, and his walk rate improved as well. His big issue was the long ball (nearly one for every four innings!), but there's just nothing in his history to suggest that it'll become a chronic problem. The Rangers were disappointed with his second half, but given the lack of options, he'll be given every chance to establish himself in the 2004 rotation.

FRANCISCO CORDERO

Bats: R   **Throws: R**   Born: 11-May-75   Age: 29

YEAR	TM	LG	AGE	G	GS	IP	H	BB	SO	HR	ERA	EQERA	EQH9	EQBB9	EQSO9	EQHR9	PERA	VORP	STF
2002	TEX	AL	27	39	0	45.3	33	13	41	2	1.79	2.23	6.3	2.4	7.7	0.4	2.51	16.6	33
2003	TEX	AL	28	73	0	82.7	70	38	90	4	2.94	2.95	6.9	3.8	9.4	0.3	3.07	23.1	37
2004	TEX	AL	29	55	6	84.3	77	36	81	7	3.70	3.35	7.7	3.6	8.7	0.6	3.48	23.5	16

Breakout: 30%   Improve: 53%   Collapse: 33%

On the face of it, it seemed like a gross mismanagement of resources for the Rangers to spend $4.5 million on Proven Closer™ Ugueth Urbina when they had the 100-mph arm of Cordero ready to take over the role. But that ignores the inflated value attached to the Proven Closer™ throughout MLB front offices. When John Hart was able to convert Urbina into a top-notch package of prospects at mid-season, it turned out to be money well spent. Meanwhile, Cordero's still here, still cheap, and still throws 100 mph. The closer role looks to be his for real this time, but stranger things have happened.

JOHN DANKS

Bats: L   **Throws: L**   Born: 15-Apr-85   Age: 19

YEAR	TM	LG	AGE	G	GS	IP	H	BB	SO	HR	ERA	EQERA	EQH9	EQBB9	EQSO9	EQHR9	PERA	VORP	STF
2003	SPO	NWN	18	5	5	12.7	12	7	13	0	8.50	9.82	11.5	6.5	5.7	0.0	5.50	-5.2	12

In a game where on-field management is risk-averse to the point of absurdity, front offices continue to make huge wagers on baseball's ultimate long shots: high school pitchers. There's no question that Danks—taken with the ninth overall pick in the draft and signed with a $2.1 million signing bonus—has plenty of raw talent. He throws in the low 90s and has a sharp curve that belies his age. But predicting how an 18-year-old's body is going to develop over the next five to 10 years is as inexact a science as you're likely to find. By using their number one pick on Danks, the Rangers are giving traditional scouting a trust that it hasn't earned.

R. A. DICKEY

Bats: R   **Throws: R**   Born: 29-Oct-74   Age: 29

YEAR	TM	LG	AGE	G	GS	IP	H	BB	SO	HR	ERA	EQERA	EQH9	EQBB9	EQSO9	EQHR9	PERA	VORP	STF
2001	OKL	PCL	26	24	24	163.0	164	45	120	14	3.75	4.71	9.9	3.0	4.8	1.0	4.88	14.9	-4
2001	TEX	AL	26	4	0	12.0	13	7	4	3	6.75	6.00	8.2	4.5	3.0	2.2	6.06	-0.5	-58
2002	OKL	PCL	27	37	19	154.0	176	47	109	8	4.09	4.88	10.5	3.1	4.8	0.6	4.83	11.7	-3
2003	OKL	PCL	28	3	2	15.0	14	3	4	1	1.20	3.21	8.4	1.9	1.9	0.6	3.59	3.7	-5
2003	TEX	AL	28	38	13	116.7	135	38	94	16	5.09	4.41	9.4	2.7	7.0	1.1	4.65	12.2	6
2004	TEX	AL	29	31	15	91.0	107	33	59	13	5.13	4.63	9.9	3.1	5.9	1.1	4.85	12.8	-1

Breakout: 22%   Improve: 48%   Collapse: 22%

Dickey is a baseball writer's dream, with interesting stories from every angle: his history (first-round pick turned organizational soldier turned successful major leaguer); his repertoire (he throws a knuckle-splitter called "The Thang"); even his anatomy (he was born without an ulnar collateral ligament in his right elbow). But the real story from 2003 was his performance, which was the Rangers' most pleasant surprise of the year. He was above average as both a starter and reliever, and he led AL rookie pitchers in both K rate and K/BB ratio (minimum 100 innings). There's nothing in his seven-year minor league career to indicate that he has that kind of strikeout ability though, so don't expect a repeat performance in 2004.

JUAN DOMINGUEZ Bats: R Throws: R Born: 18-May-80 Age: 24

YEAR	TM	LG	AGE	G	GS	IP	H	BB	SO	HR	ERA	EQERA	EQH9	EQBB9	EQSO9	EQHR9	PERA	VORP	STF
2002	SAV	SAL	22	16	9	66.7	50	21	70	4	2.16	4.53	9.7	4.1	5.8	1.6	5.74	6.9	-9
2003	STO	CAL	23	16	9	63.3	55	16	72	3	2.84	4.63	10.2	3.2	6.7	1.0	5.06	6.1	7
2003	FRI	TEX	23	9	9	55.3	35	21	54	2	2.60	3.40	6.8	4.3	6.6	0.7	3.56	12.3	26
2003	OKL	PCL	23	3	3	18.0	15	3	14	1	3.50	3.63	7.3	1.6	6.2	0.5	2.81	3.8	38
2003	TEX	AL	23	6	3	16.3	16	12	13	5	7.18	6.06	7.7	6.1	6.6	2.2	6.09	-2.5	-16
2004	TEX	AL	24	19	12	69.0	77	29	49	11	5.14	4.64	9.4	3.5	6.4	1.2	4.83	9.3	3

Breakout: 21% Improve: 50% Collapse: 19%

Dominguez skyrocketed through the system in 2003, hitting every level between High-A and the majors. He struck out an impressive 24% of the batters he faced on the season, while walking just 8%. He combines a low-90s fastball with good movement with an outstanding changeup. His slider improved during the year, but it's still not major league quality. If he doesn't progress significantly with the breaking pitch, he still has a solid future in the bullpen.

RYAN DRESE Bats: R Throws: R Born: 05-Apr-76 Age: 28

YEAR	TM	LG	AGE	G	GS	IP	H	BB	SO	HR	ERA	EQERA	EQH9	EQBB9	EQSO9	EQHR9	PERA	VORP	STF
2001	AKR	EAS	25	14	13	86.0	64	29	73	4	3.35	4.34	8.6	4.1	5.3	0.7	4.32	10.7	3
2001	BUF	INT	25	11	10	60.7	60	17	52	7	4.00	5.14	10.0	3.1	6.1	1.4	5.45	2.9	-8
2001	CLE	AL	25	9	4	36.7	32	15	24	2	3.43	2.97	6.9	3.5	5.4	0.5	3.20	10.6	20
2002	BUF	INT	26	3	3	22.0	16	4	16	1	1.64	2.66	7.5	1.8	5.3	0.4	2.92	6.6	28
2002	CLE	AL	26	26	26	137.3	176	62	102	15	6.55	5.58	10.6	3.7	6.2	0.9	5.25	0.3	4
2003	TEX	AL	27	11	8	46.0	61	24	26	8	6.85	6.46	10.8	4.3	4.9	1.4	6.11	-9.6	-24
2003	OKL	PCL	27	20	20	122.0	143	39	68	8	4.65	5.76	11.1	3.4	4.3	0.9	5.54	-2.0	-14
2004	TEX	AL	28	19	14	78.7	99	34	43	12	6.00	5.42	10.6	3.7	5.0	1.1	5.42	4.7	-7

Breakout: 17% Improve: 48% Collapse: 26%

The Rangers were robbed when they gave up Travis Hafner in a trade with Cleveland that netted them Einar Diaz, but there was some hope at the time that the pitching portion of the deal (Aaron Myette for Drese) might mitigate some of the damage. That's not going to happen. Between his control problems and his flaky mechanics, Drese did nothing to inspire confidence. The Rangers got him to eliminate two pitches from his arsenal in order to focus on his three best—fastball, slider, and change—but it didn't help. It's going to take a very special pitching coach to fix Ryan Drese.

JUSTIN ECHOLS Bats: R Throws: R Born: 06-Oct-80 Age: 23

YEAR	TM	LG	AGE	G	GS	IP	H	BB	SO	HR	ERA	EQERA	EQH9	EQBB9	EQSO9	EQHR9	PERA	VORP	STF
2001	SAV	SAL	20	36	13	123.0	88	67	156	4	3.80	5.52	9.2	7.6	6.6	0.8	5.60	0.9	10
2002	PCH	FLA	21	46	11	112.3	94	54	117	6	3.93	6.10	10.9	5.6	6.8	1.2	6.29	-5.4	-1
2003	STO	CAL	22	25	13	98.0	74	43	98	4	2.85	4.64	8.5	5.5	6.0	0.8	4.76	9.3	5
2003	FRI	TEX	22	8	8	44.0	32	26	33	5	4.91	5.72	7.8	6.9	5.0	2.1	6.21	-0.5	-23
2004	TEX	AL	23	15	9	47.0	57	32	29	8	6.84	6.18	10.2	5.7	5.6	1.2	6.09	1.0	-15

Breakout: 25% Improve: 52% Collapse: 22%

A favorite of Texas minor league expert Jamey Newberg (www.newbergreport.com), Echols has been brought along slowly, spending two years in short-season ball and now two years in High-A. He saw a lot more press in 2003 because of his ERA—his 2.85 would have been good for third in the California League if he'd qualified by sticking around for another two or three outings—but he's always had good peripherals so there was no breakthrough here. He doesn't have an overpowering fastball, but he changes speeds very well. He's on the right track.

AARON FULTZ Bats: L Throws: L Born: 04-Sep-73 Age: 30

YEAR	TM	LG	AGE	G	GS	IP	H	BB	SO	HR	ERA	EQERA	EQH9	EQBB9	EQSO9	EQHR9	PERA	VORP	STF
2001	SFG	NL	27	66	0	71.0	70	21	67	9	4.56	4.76	9.1	2.5	7.1	1.1	4.46	6.3	1
2002	SFG	NL	28	43	0	41.3	47	19	31	4	4.79	5.67	10.9	3.6	5.9	0.9	5.45	-0.3	-13
2003	TEX	AL	29	64	0	67.3	75	27	53	9	5.22	4.68	9.0	3.3	6.8	1.1	4.63	3.5	-3
2004	MIN	AL	30	48	0	51.7	55	21	39	7	4.71	4.59	9.2	3.4	6.6	1.1	4.68	7.2	-3

Breakout: 30% Improve: 47% Collapse: 32%

(continued next page)

Aaron Fultz *(continued)*

OK, maybe the Ranger pitching staff *is* jinxed. Even when the team makes a decent pitching acquisition, something goes freakishly wrong. Fultz was one of the best left-handed relievers in the majors for the first half of the season, but then he hurt his shoulder by running into the outfield wall shagging flies in batting practice, and he was never the same after that. He'll be a solid situational lefty again in 2004; Fultz's .218/.289/.311 against left-handed batters was one of the better lines in the AL in 2003, and it wasn't out of line with what he's done the rest of his career.

ROSMAN GARCIA   **Bats: R**   **Throws: R**   Born: 03-Jan-79   Age: 25

YEAR	TM	LG	AGE	G	GS	IP	H	BB	SO	HR	ERA	EQERA	EQH9	EQBB9	EQSO9	EQHR9	PERA	VORP	STF
2001	TAM	FLA	22	26	7	59.7	56	22	42	2	3.47	5.56	9.5	3.9	4.1	0.8	4.83	0.2	-10
2002	TUL	TEX	23	53	0	74.7	75	32	38	1	3.01	5.45	9.6	4.4	3.4	0.3	4.46	1.2	-10
2003	TEX	AL	24	46	0	46.3	63	23	25	4	6.03	5.44	11.1	4.1	4.7	0.6	5.33	0.0	-6
2003	OKL	PCL	24	17	2	28.3	20	6	21	1	1.91	2.70	6.4	2.4	5.7	0.3	2.51	8.6	22
2004	*TEX*	*AL*	*25*	*31*	*6*	*51.3*	*63*	*24*	*26*	*6*	*5.54*	*5.00*	*10.4*	*3.9*	*4.6*	*0.9*	*5.18*	*4.2*	*-15*

Breakout: 21%   Improve: 48%   Collapse: 22%

Garcia transformed a strong two months in Oklahoma (16 innings) into a semi-regular spot in the majors in 2003, even though there was nothing in his seven-year pro career to indicate major league ability. The results were predictable. The Rangers were so desperate for right-handed middle relief by mid-season that Garcia was called the team's "hidden gem" by the *Dallas Morning News,* despite sporting a 4.91 ERA at the time. We're here to tell you: With his middling repertoire and inability to strike batters out, Garcia is no gem, hidden or otherwise.

KELVIN JIMENEZ   **Bats: R**   **Throws: R**   Born: 27-Oct-80   Age: 23

YEAR	TM	LG	AGE	G	GS	IP	H	BB	SO	HR	ERA	EQERA	EQH9	EQBB9	EQSO9	EQHR9	PERA	VORP	STF
2001	PUL	APP	20	4	4	14.3	24	4	10	2	6.29	13.50	21.0	4.5	3.0	3.8	13.55	-10.5	-102
2002	SAV	SAL	21	29	16	121.0	122	37	116	9	3.20	6.60	12.2	3.9	5.3	1.8	7.13	-11.7	-18
2003	STO	CAL	22	34	18	131.3	135	43	101	14	4.73	6.69	11.3	4.1	4.6	2.1	7.15	-14.2	-35
2004	*TEX*	*AL*	*23*	*15*	*8*	*41.3*	*56*	*22*	*24*	*8*	*6.88*	*6.22*	*11.4*	*4.5*	*5.2*	*1.4*	*6.36*	*0.4*	*-16*

Breakout: 25%   Improve: 65%   Collapse: 17%

A skinny hard-throwing kid with limbs flying every which way in his motion, Jimenez is the stereotypical Dominican pitcher. His numbers haven't been awe-inspiring so far—he struck out a decent but unspectacular 18% of the batters he faced in Stockton—but he's got good stuff and good control, and he's shown flashes of brilliance. He's got the best chance of all the second-tier Stockton pitchers—Jason Andrew, John Barnett, Kiki Bengochea, and Sam Narron—to emerge as a real prospect this year.

BEN KOZLOWSKI   **Bats: L**   **Throws: L**   Born: 16-Aug-80   Age: 23

YEAR	TM	LG	AGE	G	GS	IP	H	BB	SO	HR	ERA	EQERA	EQH9	EQBB9	EQSO9	EQHR9	PERA	VORP	STF
2001	MCN	SAL	20	26	23	145.3	134	27	147	8	2.48	5.41	11.5	2.6	5.2	1.2	5.77	2.7	11
2001	MYR	CAR	20	2	2	14.3	15	3	13	1	3.78	7.11	12.1	2.8	5.0	1.4	6.38	-2.1	3
2002	PCH	FLA	21	21	12	79.0	63	25	76	2	2.05	4.91	9.9	3.6	6.2	0.5	4.60	5.3	22
2002	TUL	TEX	21	8	8	52.0	28	22	41	3	1.90	3.00	5.4	4.5	5.6	0.9	3.24	13.9	27
2002	TEX	AL	21	2	2	10.0	11	11	6	3	6.30	6.30	9.0	9.0	5.4	2.7	8.07	-0.8	-20
2003	FRI	TEX	22	11	10	54.7	71	27	29	4	5.43	7.97	12.9	5.6	3.6	1.3	7.30	-13.1	-27
2004	*TEX*	*AL*	*23*	*21*	*14*	*74.0*	*95*	*39*	*43*	*13*	*6.49*	*5.86*	*10.9*	*4.4*	*5.2*	*1.3*	*6.01*	*2.4*	*-11*

Breakout: 23%   Improve: 51%   Collapse: 30%

After a meteoric rise through the system in 2002 that took him from A-ball all the way to Arlington, Kozlowski popped up on all kinds of top prospect lists last off-season. But his 2003 was derailed by a torn elbow ligament that resulted in Tommy John surgery in June. He's expected to resume tossing by spring training, but getting back to normal following Tommy John surgery generally takes more time than that. Don't expect a return to '02 form until 2005 at the earliest.

COLBY LEWIS

Bats: R   **Throws: R**   Born: 02-Aug-79   Age: 24

YEAR	TM	LG	AGE	G	GS	IP	H	BB	SO	HR	ERA	EQERA	EQH9	EQBB9	EQSO9	EQHR9	PERA	VORP	STF
2001	TUL	TEX	21	25	25	156.0	150	62	162	15	4.50	5.55	9.7	4.4	6.9	1.4	5.60	0.8	18
2002	OKL	PCL	22	20	20	106.7	100	28	99	4	3.63	3.89	7.7	2.6	6.8	0.3	3.13	19.8	42
2002	TEX	AL	22	15	4	34.3	42	26	28	4	6.30	6.09	10.6	6.1	6.9	0.8	5.82	-1.9	14
2003	OKL	PCL	23	7	7	47.7	36	19	43	6	3.02	3.83	7.1	4.2	7.3	1.6	4.57	8.8	13
2003	TEX	AL	23	26	26	127.0	163	70	88	23	7.30	6.06	10.3	4.6	5.9	1.4	5.99	-15.2	1
2004	*TEX*	*AL*	*24*	*24*	*21*	*121.7*	*135*	*60*	*91*	*18*	*5.49*	*4.96*	*9.3*	*4.1*	*6.8*	*1.1*	*4.91*	*11.8*	*7*

Breakout: 17%   *Improve: 46%*   *Collapse: 23%*

Does the disastrous start to Colby Lewis's major league career mean he won't live up to the considerable promise he showed in the minor leagues? Not necessarily. Just in the past couple of decades, Greg Maddux, Frank Viola, John Smoltz, and Jason Schmidt are a few of the pitchers whose successful careers started with catastrophic seasons. Lewis's catastrophe stems from his lack of a credible change-up, and his inability to control his (otherwise sharp) curve. Even as a one-trick pony, his one trick (fastball) is probably good enough to make him an effective reliever. But don't give up on him as a starter just yet. His performance record suggests he can harness his stuff and learn to get through a lineup several times, maybe as early as this year.

WES LITTLETON

Bats: R   **Throws: R**   Born: 02-Sep-82   Age: 21

YEAR	TM	LG	AGE	G	GS	IP	H	BB	SO	HR	ERA	EQERA	EQH9	EQBB9	EQSO9	EQHR9	PERA	VORP	STF
2003	SPO	NWN	20	12	8	52.0	36	8	47	2	1.56	3.35	9.1	2.0	4.9	1.2	4.45	11.4	13
2004	*TEX*	*AL*	*21*	*21*	*15*	*85.7*	*99*	*28*	*47*	*13*	*4.91*	*4.44*	*9.7*	*2.7*	*5.0*	*1.1*	*4.61*	*13.1*	*-2*

Breakout: 9%   *Improve: 57%*   *Collapse: 6%*

Littleton, a Cal State Fullerton product, was a first-round talent coming into the 2003 draft. But he slid to the fourth round, possibly because of worries over a team suspension that cost him a month of the college season. He's rewarded the Rangers' confidence in him so far, putting up a 1.56 ERA with tremendous control in his brief Northwest League stint. Littleton's the closest of the Rangers' 2003 pitching draftees to major league readiness, and he could move quickly through the system.

KAMERON LOE

Bats: R   **Throws: R**   Born: 10-Sep-81   Age: 22

YEAR	TM	LG	AGE	G	GS	IP	H	BB	SO	HR	ERA	EQERA	EQH9	EQBB9	EQSO9	EQHR9	PERA	VORP	STF
2002	PUL	APP	20	14	11	58.3	64	17	55	3	4.48	6.75	12.3	3.5	4.3	1.2	6.41	-6.6	-11
2003	CLN	MID	21	23	11	97.0	78	19	94	3	1.95	4.02	9.1	2.5	5.8	0.8	4.20	15.3	19
2003	STO	CAL	21	9	4	37.7	26	6	31	1	0.95	2.60	7.3	1.8	4.7	0.5	2.90	11.6	26
2004	*TEX*	*AL*	*22*	*22*	*14*	*81.3*	*99*	*23*	*46*	*11*	*5.30*	*4.79*	*10.2*	*2.4*	*5.1*	*1.0*	*4.62*	*9.9*	*-1*

Breakout: 12%   *Improve: 47%*   *Collapse: 26%*

Loe won't be the intimidator that his 6'8" frame suggests—he's a control/finesse artist. There could be a good major league career in his future, though, based on his 2003 performance. In addition to the excellent regular-season lines you see above, Loe topped off the year with two dominating starts in the California League playoffs, striking out 18 and walking just two in 12 innings. There's still a fair amount of healthy skepticism surrounding Loe because of his lack of velocity; he'll have to succeed in Double-A and onward to dispel it.

RON MAHAY

Bats: L   **Throws: L**   Born: 28-Jun-71   Age: 33

YEAR	TM	LG	AGE	G	GS	IP	H	BB	SO	HR	ERA	EQERA	EQH9	EQBB9	EQSO9	EQHR9	PERA	VORP	STF
2001	POR	PCL	30	14	0	16.7	13	5	18	2	3.77	4.70	8.2	3.5	7.0	1.2	4.45	1.5	-12
2001	IOW	PCL	30	36	0	46.7	29	10	52	5	2.31	2.72	6.7	2.3	7.3	1.3	3.46	13.8	1
2001	CHC	NL	30	17	0	20.7	14	15	24	4	2.61	3.54	6.2	5.8	8.9	1.3	4.28	4.6	0
2002	IOW	PCL	31	39	1	46.7	32	15	50	3	1.93	2.70	7.1	3.3	7.3	0.8	3.51	14.0	7
2002	CHC	NL	31	11	0	14.7	13	8	14	6	8.57	7.53	8.2	4.4	7.5	3.8	7.81	-3.1	-77
2003	OKL	PCL	32	26	0	42.7	36	10	51	5	4.22	4.54	8.6	2.5	9.1	1.6	4.75	4.7	-5
2003	TEX	AL	32	35	0	45.3	33	20	38	3	3.18	2.80	5.8	3.6	7.2	0.6	2.81	11.8	20
2004	*TEX*	*AL*	*33*	*34*	*5*	*57.7*	*56*	*23*	*49*	*9*	*4.66*	*4.21*	*8.2*	*3.4*	*7.6*	*1.1*	*4.12*	*10.5*	*6*

Breakout: 23%   *Improve: 58%*   *Collapse: 22%*

From the "descriptions we never thought we'd see" department: The *Dallas Morning News* referred to Mahay's 2003 as a "breakthrough" on one occasion and a "breakout" on another. How about "a pretty good 45-inning stretch by a journeyman reliever" instead? He's not your classic one-out lefty; over the past three years, left-handers have hit better against him than right-handers (.751 OPS vs. .679). Re-upped by the Rangers to a one-year deal.

A. J. MURRAY   Bats: B   Throws: L   Born: 17-Mar-82   Age: 22

YEAR	TM	LG	AGE	G	GS	IP	H	BB	SO	HR	ERA	EQERA	EQH9	EQBB9	EQSO9	EQHR9	PERA	VORP	STF
2002	PCH	FLA	20	19	14	83.3	77	20	68	4	3.03	5.09	10.8	2.7	5.4	1.0	5.20	4.2	16
2002	SAV	SAL	20	14	8	62.7	63	14	51	0	2.87	4.98	11.1	2.7	4.3	0.3	4.70	3.9	17
2003	FRI	TEX	21	27	25	144.0	134	63	90	13	3.63	5.44	9.0	5.0	4.4	1.6	5.73	2.4	-7
2004	TEX	AL	22	16	11	59.3	75	32	31	11	6.61	5.97	10.7	4.6	4.8	1.3	6.04	-0.2	-15

Breakout: 8%   Improve: 44%   Collapse: 28%

Murray is a typical crafty lefty, with a standard three-pitch repertoire that impresses no one, but with enough command so far to succeed in the minors. Actually, "succeed" may be too strong a term—he got some press last year based on a 10–4 record, but his ERA of 3.63 was only so-so, and his lousy peripheral numbers suggest that even that ERA was something of a fluke. He's still young, but there's nothing here so far to suggest future major league success.

CHAN HO PARK   Bats: R   Throws: R   Born: 30-Jun-73   Age: 31

YEAR	TM	LG	AGE	G	GS	IP	H	BB	SO	HR	ERA	EQERA	EQH9	EQBB9	EQSO9	EQHR9	PERA	VORP	STF
2001	LAD	NL	28	36	35	234.0	183	91	218	23	3.50	3.70	7.4	3.3	7.1	0.8	3.64	47.2	24
2002	TEX	AL	29	25	25	145.7	154	78	121	20	5.74	5.06	9.0	4.4	7.1	1.1	4.93	8.6	7
2003	TEX	AL	30	7	7	29.7	34	25	16	5	7.58	6.30	9.0	6.9	4.5	1.2	5.82	-5.2	-30
2004	TEX	AL	31	31	14	82.0	96	47	56	14	6.31	5.70	9.9	4.9	6.1	1.3	5.74	2.8	-10

Breakout: 17%   Improve: 41%   Collapse: 33%

If you're looking for the root cause of the Chan Ho Park disaster, you won't find it here. The text on the transactions lines last year read "DL: lower back strain," but the latest diagnosis points to the back—as well as his aches and pains in his rib cage and oblique muscles—as merely a byproduct of a two-year-old hamstring problem. Then there are the psychological effects of two years of catastrophic failure after signing a $65 million contract. In short, the man's a mess. We're still betting he can regroup and pitch well enough to justify a rotation spot, even if he won't justify that franchise-crippling contract.

JAY POWELL   Bats: R   Throws: R   Born: 09-Jan-72   Age: 32

YEAR	TM	LG	AGE	G	GS	IP	H	BB	SO	HR	ERA	EQERA	EQH9	EQBB9	EQSO9	EQHR9	PERA	VORP	STF
2001	HOU	NL	29	35	0	36.3	41	19	28	4	3.72	4.84	10.2	4.3	5.9	0.8	5.17	3.0	-8
2001	COL	NL	29	39	0	38.7	34	12	26	5	2.79	3.62	7.7	2.7	5.1	1.0	3.78	8.2	-5
2002	TEX	AL	30	51	0	49.7	50	24	35	5	3.44	4.41	8.6	4.0	6.1	0.7	4.35	6.5	-1
2003	TEX	AL	31	51	0	58.7	75	34	40	7	7.82	6.41	10.4	4.7	5.8	0.9	5.52	-16.5	-18
2004	TEX	AL	32	46	0	45.0	53	22	29	5	5.58	5.04	10.0	4.1	5.8	0.9	4.96	3.5	-10

Breakout: 24%   Improve: 51%   Collapse: 17%

We followed Powell's 2003 stretch run with kind of a sick fascination to see if he would achieve the distinction of allowing more than a run per inning. It's surprising how often it's been done in recent years, even by as big a name as Roy Halladay (in 2000). Anyway, Powell disappointed us by finishing strong with a newly unveiled sidearm delivery, and he ended up just missing with 58 runs in 58.2 IP. The Rangers owe him $3 million in 2004, but the John Hart regime has already shown with Todd Van Poppel that they know a sunk cost when they see it, so hopefully they'll do the right thing here too.

ERASMO RAMIREZ   Bats: L   Throws: L   Born: 29-Apr-76   Age: 28

YEAR	TM	LG	AGE	G	GS	IP	H	BB	SO	HR	ERA	EQERA	EQH9	EQBB9	EQSO9	EQHR9	PERA	VORP	STF
2001	SJO	CAL	25	17	0	31.7	23	5	33	2	3.41	4.55	9.8	2.0	5.5	1.3	4.89	3.2	-22
2001	SHV	TEX	25	22	1	33.3	25	5	39	1	2.16	3.30	9.0	1.8	7.5	0.6	3.71	7.7	17
2001	TUL	TEX	25	12	0	16.3	17	5	18	3	4.42	5.65	12.6	3.8	7.5	3.1	8.91	-0.1	-73
2002	TUL	TEX	26	34	0	54.0	51	8	34	1	3.00	4.56	9.9	1.6	4.2	0.4	3.88	5.7	-2
2002	OKL	PCL	26	25	0	21.0	15	4	17	0	1.29	2.29	6.9	1.8	5.5	0.5	2.66	7.2	13
2003	OKL	PCL	27	22	0	35.3	36	2	20	0	1.53	2.97	9.5	0.5	4.3	0.3	3.28	9.7	13
2003	TEX	AL	27	34	0	49.0	46	9	28	4	3.86	2.98	7.4	1.5	5.0	0.6	2.92	12.3	13
2004	TEX	AL	28	31	6	56.7	66	14	33	8	4.50	4.06	9.8	2.1	5.3	1.0	4.32	11.2	-3

Breakout: 21%   Improve: 50%   Collapse: 21%

A testament to the availability of free talent. Even after the excellent year Ramirez had in their system in 2002, The Rangers were slow to commit to a major league role for the minor league journeyman, preferring guys like C. J. Nitkowski and the Garcia twins for the bullpen in the first half. But when they called up the Eraser for keeps in late July, he performed like his minor league numbers suggested he would, throwing strikes, keeping the ball on the ground and runs off the board. As a lefty reliever, he only needs another 50 or so innings of performance like that to be given virtual major league tenure.

MARIO RAMOS Bats: L Throws: L Born: 19-Oct-77 Age: 26

YEAR	TM	LG	AGE	G	GS	IP	H	BB	SO	HR	ERA	EQERA	EQH9	EQBB9	EQSO9	EQHR9	PERA	VORP	STF
2001	MID	TEX	23	15	15	93.7	71	28	68	7	3.07	3.67	7.0	3.2	4.5	1.0	3.68	18.9	8
2001	SAC	PCL	23	13	13	80.3	74	27	82	5	3.14	3.89	8.3	3.5	7.0	0.6	3.87	14.5	33
2002	OKL	PCL	24	34	19	121.7	162	53	75	20	7.40	7.80	12.0	4.4	4.1	1.9	7.31	-28.2	-47
2003	FRI	TEX	25	19	19	121.3	130	28	103	9	3.86	5.48	12.0	2.7	5.7	1.5	6.35	1.4	-17
2003	OKL	PCL	25	5	5	32.3	39	12	22	1	6.41	6.46	10.9	3.8	5.3	0.3	4.84	-2.9	8
2003	TEX	AL	25	3	3	13.0	11	13	8	3	6.23	5.54	6.9	8.3	5.5	2.1	6.21	0.0	-39
2004	OAK	AL	26	20	12	71.7	77	30	45	10	5.03	5.32	9.6	3.6	5.5	1.2	5.32	5.3	-5

Breakout: 26% Improve: 48% Collapse: 28%

After a high-profile catastrophe of a season in 2002, Ramos was sent back to Double-A to start 2003, in part to bolster his confidence. He did pitch better there, leading Frisco in strikeouts and putting together a 3.7:1 K:BB ratio. But his performance was hardly awe-inspiring for a two-year Triple-A veteran, and he was terrible in his eight starts at Oklahoma and Arlington. He's headed back to the team that traded him in the big Carlos Pena deal, as the A's claimed him off waivers.

RICARDO RODRIGUEZ Bats: R Throws: R Born: 21-May-78 Age: 26

YEAR	TM	LG	AGE	G	GS	IP	H	BB	SO	HR	ERA	EQERA	EQH9	EQBB9	EQSO9	EQHR9	PERA	VORP	STF
2001	VRO	FLA	23	26	26	154.3	133	60	154	13	3.21	5.47	10.9	4.3	6.1	1.9	6.82	2.0	-18
2002	JAX	SOU	24	11	11	68.0	56	13	44	4	1.99	4.50	9.9	2.0	4.3	1.2	4.87	7.3	-3
2002	LVG	PCL	24	2	2	11.7	13	5	7	1	3.85	4.76	9.5	4.0	4.0	0.8	4.84	1.1	-1
2002	BUF	INT	24	4	4	25.0	26	7	14	1	3.60	4.63	10.0	3.1	4.2	0.4	4.39	2.5	13
2002	CLE	AL	24	7	7	41.3	40	18	24	5	5.67	4.39	7.9	3.5	4.8	0.9	4.03	5.5	12
2003	CLE	AL	25	15	15	81.7	89	28	41	16	5.73	5.58	9.7	3.0	4.4	1.6	5.50	-3.4	-16
2004	TEX	AL	26	21	17	96.0	113	37	57	15	5.59	5.05	9.9	3.2	5.4	1.1	4.90	7.4	-1

Breakout: 21% Improve: 50% Collapse: 17%

Rodriguez came over from Cleveland with Shane Spencer in exchange for hot-hitting outfield prospect Ryan Ludwick. For the Rangers, Rodriguez was the key player in that deal, partly because they think his ground ball tendencies will serve him well in The Ballpark in Arlington. Yeah, maybe, but we're more concerned with the strikeout rate, which has plummeted since his days in the Dodger system. Rodriguez had surgery to repair the torn labrum in his right hip that cost him half the season; he should be ready to compete for a rotation spot in spring training.

JOSH RUPE Bats: R Throws: R Born: 18-Aug-82 Age: 21

YEAR	TM	LG	AGE	G	GS	IP	H	BB	SO	HR	ERA	EQERA	EQH9	EQBB9	EQSO9	EQHR9	PERA	VORP	STF
2002	BRI	APP	19	17	2	37.7	38	22	40	4	5.25	8.90	13.5	7.5	5.5	2.6	9.51	-11.5	-45
2003	KAN	SAL	20	26	7	65.7	50	36	69	0	3.01	5.21	9.3	6.8	6.0	0.3	4.97	2.5	13
2003	CLN	MID	20	6	5	27.7	29	7	23	1	3.90	6.12	11.2	3.2	5.0	1.1	5.67	-1.4	5
2004	TEX	AL	21	16	8	45.3	56	30	33	7	6.87	6.21	10.5	5.7	6.5	1.2	6.27	-0.8	-10

Breakout: 21% Improve: 52% Collapse: 16%

Another part of the Carl Everett haul, Rupe is a 2002 third-round pick who brandishes a solid four-pitch selection, highlighted by a low-90s fastball and a sharp breaking ball. His numbers in his full-season pro debut in 2003 were impressive, even more so when you consider that 10 of the 41 runs he allowed came in a single lousy outing. As with almost any young pitcher, there are some caveats: his 1/90 HR/IP rate was fluky, his season ended with shoulder tendinitis, and he's still a long way from the majors. Still, there's promise here.

BRIAN SHOUSE Bats: L Throws: L Born: 26-Sep-68 Age: 35

YEAR	TM	LG	AGE	G	GS	IP	H	BB	SO	HR	ERA	EQERA	EQH9	EQBB9	EQSO9	EQHR9	PERA	VORP	STF
2001	NWO	PCL	32	56	1	53.0	51	15	56	4	2.89	4.44	10.0	3.1	7.0	0.9	4.89	6.3	-6
2002	NWO	PCL	33	19	0	21.0	17	3	20	2	3.43	4.74	9.5	1.4	6.6	1.4	4.70	1.8	-14
2002	KCR	AL	33	23	0	14.7	15	9	11	3	6.12	5.52	8.6	4.9	6.1	1.8	5.78	0.1	-35
2003	OKL	PCL	34	6	0	7.3	8	3	2	0	3.70	5.14	10.3	3.9	2.6	0.0	4.36	0.4	-13
2003	TEX	AL	34	62	0	61.0	62	14	40	1	3.10	2.83	8.2	1.9	5.7	0.1	3.00	17.4	23
2004	TEX	AL	35	41	5	62.7	70	20	41	6	4.43	4.00	9.4	2.7	5.9	0.7	4.05	12.8	-1

Breakout: 32% Improve: 55% Collapse: 34%

(continued next page)

Brian Shouse (continued)

At the end of the 2002 season, the Ranger front office was openly fretting about the lack of credible lefties in their bullpen. That changed in a hurry in 2003. Between Shouse, Ramirez, Mahay, and Fultz, Texas had the best-performing collection of lefty relievers in the league, and Shouse was the ace of the group. He was the second best left-handed reliever in the AL at preventing runs (behind only Damaso Marte) according to Michael Wolverton's Reliever Evaluation Tools report, available at www.baseballprospectus.com. It's not terribly surprising when a lefty sidearmer destroys left-handed hitters—they hit a pathetic .190/.230/.271 against him last year. Shouse's continued success in the majors will depend largely on his ability to hold his own against righties.

RYAN SNARE   Bats: L   Throws: L   Born: 08-Feb-79   Age: 25

YEAR	TM	LG	AGE	G	GS	IP	H	BB	SO	HR	ERA	EQERA	EQH9	EQBB9	EQSO9	EQHR9	PERA	VORP	STF
2001	DYT	MID	22	21	20	115.0	101	37	118	7	3.05	4.87	10.3	4.2	5.7	1.2	5.68	8.2	0
2002	STO	CAL	23	13	13	82.0	74	18	81	4	3.07	5.45	10.9	2.5	5.2	0.9	5.10	1.2	6
2002	PME	EAS	23	11	9	55.0	46	19	52	6	3.44	4.53	9.4	3.6	6.5	1.6	5.56	5.9	-1
2003	CAR	SOU	24	18	18	103.0	98	37	77	4	3.67	5.48	10.7	3.8	4.7	0.8	5.28	1.2	-2
2003	OKL	PCL	24	9	9	54.7	59	13	28	7	3.46	5.08	10.0	2.5	3.9	1.8	5.71	3.0	-20
2004	TEX	AL	25	19	12	67.0	84	27	37	11	5.94	5.36	10.6	3.4	5.0	1.3	5.45	5.0	-8

Breakout: 19%   Improve: 54%   Collapse: 23%

Snare came over from the Marlins in the Ugueth Urbina trade. Neither his stuff nor his peripheral numbers are inspiring; in particular, the falling strikeout rate is a concern. Still, he has that consistent run of 3.00-ish minor league ERAs working for him, and he has the traded-for-a-veteran glow to distinguish him from other soft-tossing minor leaguers (a double-dip of it, as he was involved in the 2002 Ryan Dempster deal as well), so there's a good chance we'll see him in a Ranger uniform this year.

ERIK THOMPSON   Bats: R   Throws: R   Born: 23-Jun-82   Age: 22

YEAR	TM	LG	AGE	G	GS	IP	H	BB	SO	HR	ERA	EQERA	EQH9	EQBB9	EQSO9	EQHR9	PERA	VORP	STF
2002	PUL	APP	20	3	3	17.0	19	2	16	0	3.18	4.70	12.3	1.2	4.1	0.6	5.12	1.5	16
2003	CLN	MID	21	14	7	57.7	49	5	52	6	2.81	4.62	10.7	1.1	5.5	2.8	6.96	5.5	-21
2003	STO	CAL	21	19	9	80.3	74	13	62	6	2.91	4.32	10.0	2.0	4.6	1.5	5.23	10.4	0
2004	TEX	AL	22	18	12	68.3	85	15	37	13	5.35	4.83	10.5	1.8	4.9	1.4	5.00	7.7	-3

Breakout: 3%   Improve: 49%   Collapse: 13%

Thompson is a little guy who's all about throwing strikes—he's walked just 22 batters in 193 professional innings. His half-season at Stockton was even more impressive than the line above shows, as he finished the year with a pair of outstanding starts in the California League playoffs: 13 innings, seven hits, no runs, no walks, 16 strikeouts. It will be interesting to see how Thompson, Loe, Jimenez, et al. make the transition to Frisco, where they will shift from the Texas low-minors tandem rotation system—eight pitchers alternating starts and relief appearances—to full-time starting. The initial returns from last year—Kozlowski, Murray, Wilson, Dominguez, and Echols—weren't encouraging on the whole, but those aren't enough data points to draw any real conclusions.

JOHN THOMSON   Bats: R   Throws: R   Born: 01-Oct-73   Age: 30

YEAR	TM	LG	AGE	G	GS	IP	H	BB	SO	HR	ERA	EQERA	EQH9	EQBB9	EQSO9	EQHR9	PERA	VORP	STF
2001	CSP	PCL	27	12	12	68.0	74	13	52	6	3.31	3.43	9.2	1.9	4.8	0.8	4.11	15.8	7
2001	COL	NL	27	14	14	93.7	84	25	68	15	4.03	3.69	8.0	2.2	5.5	1.2	3.99	19.2	8
2002	COL	NL	28	21	21	127.3	136	27	76	21	4.88	4.70	9.5	1.7	4.7	1.4	4.83	12.3	-5
2002	NYM	NL	28	9	9	54.3	65	17	31	7	4.31	6.23	11.1	2.4	4.5	1.2	5.57	-3.6	-11
2003	TEX	AL	29	35	35	217.0	234	49	136	27	4.85	4.01	8.6	1.9	5.4	1.0	3.95	24.1	13
2004	ATL	NL	30	29	27	174.3	173	47	113	19	4.03	4.37	9.0	2.1	5.2	1.0	4.16	24.0	9

Breakout: 14%   Improve: 55%   Collapse: 21%

Yes, ladies and gentlemen, this was your 2003 Texas Rangers ace. We shouldn't make fun, since Thomson actually did have a nice year, even if it wasn't up the standard of most teams' number-one starter. Now he'll be making the transition from two of the most unpleasant pitching environments in baseball (Colorado and Texas) to the Cox/Mazzone pitching factory in Atlanta. We expect good things.

ISMAEL VALDES

Bats: R   **Throws: R**   Born: 21-Aug-73   Age: 30

YEAR	TM	LG	AGE	G	GS	IP	H	BB	SO	HR	ERA	EQERA	EQH9	EQBB9	EQSO9	EQHR9	PERA	VORP	STF
2001	ANA	AL	27	27	27	163.7	177	50	100	20	4.45	4.62	9.8	2.6	5.2	1.0	4.77	17.2	4
2002	TEX	AL	28	23	23	146.7	135	36	75	19	3.93	3.52	7.7	2.0	4.4	1.0	3.64	33.1	8
2002	SEA	AL	28	8	8	49.3	59	11	27	7	4.93	5.48	10.8	1.9	4.7	1.1	5.18	0.6	-2
2003	TEX	AL	29	22	22	115.0	148	29	47	23	6.10	5.34	10.2	2.1	3.5	1.6	5.50	-3.1	-22
2004	SDP	NL	30	25	20	119.0	133	36	61	16	4.70	5.15	10.1	2.4	4.1	1.2	5.22	7.8	-6

Breakout: 14%   Improve: 46%   Collapse: 20%

Most of Valdes's problems in 2003 were injury-related. His early-season starts were hampered by a shoulder that was described as "barky" (gotta love Buck Showalter's vocabulary), and his mid-season was hampered by tendinitis in his knee. He's signed with San Diego, where better health and the park should help him get his ERA back down to the 4.00–4.50 range.

C. J. WILSON

Bats: L   **Throws: L**   Born: 18-Nov-80   Age: 23

YEAR	TM	LG	AGE	G	GS	IP	H	BB	SO	HR	ERA	EQERA	EQH9	EQBB9	EQSO9	EQHR9	PERA	VORP	STF
2001	PUL	APP	20	8	8	37.7	24	9	49	2	0.95	3.13	9.7	3.4	5.4	1.4	5.40	8.7	6
2001	SAV	SAL	20	5	5	34.0	30	9	26	2	3.18	5.10	10.2	3.6	3.9	1.2	5.49	1.7	2
2002	PCH	FLA	21	26	15	106.0	86	41	76	4	3.06	5.52	10.0	4.5	4.6	0.8	5.14	0.8	3
2002	TUL	TEX	21	5	5	30.0	23	12	17	0	1.80	3.21	7.1	4.2	3.9	0.3	3.32	7.4	24
2003	FRI	TEX	22	22	21	123.0	135	38	89	11	5.05	6.69	11.4	3.5	4.9	1.7	6.56	-13.5	-13
2004	TEX	AL	23	18	12	66.7	85	34	37	12	6.49	5.86	10.8	4.3	5.0	1.3	5.90	2.7	-11

Breakout: 19%   Improve: 49%   Collapse: 24%

It was tempting to combine the A. J. Murray and C. J Wilson entries into a single junkballing-lefties-with-no-first-names comment. Wilson's season didn't end as happily as Murray's, as he went down late in the year with elbow problems that resulted in Tommy John surgery. He was an overpublicized long-shot prospect to begin with, and the injury makes his shot that much longer.

JEFF ZIMMERMAN

Bats: R   **Throws: R**   Born: 09-Aug-72   Age: 31

YEAR	TM	LG	AGE	G	GS	IP	H	BB	SO	HR	ERA	EQERA	EQH9	EQBB9	EQSO9	EQHR9	PERA	VORP	STF
2001	TEX	AL	28	66	0	71.3	48	16	72	10	2.40	2.18	5.4	1.8	8.3	1.2	2.58	26.7	23
2004	TEX	AL	31	55	0	42.0	38	10	41	6	3.35	3.03	7.6	2.0	8.9	1.0	3.22	13.4	18

Breakout: 39%   Improve: 65%   Collapse: 19%

Ranger fans can be forgiven if they flashed back to Justin Thompson when reading stories about Zimmerman in the paper this fall. As with Thompson, the Zimmerman rehab has involved frequent reports of setbacks and new pains. But elbow injuries (Zimmerman) are generally far less serious than shoulder injuries (Thompson), so it's not likely that we're looking at the kind of perpetual hope and disappointment cycle we got with Thompson. Zimmerman will pitch this year, but don't expect him to get back to anywhere near his terrific '99–'01 level.

Toronto Blue Jays

The poet Tennyson's image of Nature as red in tooth in claw conveyed the image of a world defined by struggle, and a figurative stewpot take the hindmost. In a competitive landscape populated by the Yankees and Red Sox acting out their particularly expensive brand of Darwinian selection, you can be forgiven if you're beginning to wonder what blue jay tastes like, especially when the menu seems to always include always-fresh devil ray and oriole.

How does a team compete against the two titans? It isn't like the Red Sox and Yankees are spending money badly. They're not buying Ed Whitson or Steve Avery or a broken-down Andre Dawson. They're acquiring Kevin Brown and Curt Schilling and Keith Foulke and Gary Sheffield, stars on the short list for best players at their positions. New era economic sensibilities might inform both team's decision-making, and although both teams may have taken on considerable debt far into the distant future, neither seems likely to suddenly capsize from the top-heavy expense on star talent. How do you beat that?

You do it with something old and with something new, or in this case, with adaptive strategies both old and new.

The old strategy should be immediately recognizable to old-time Jays fans, because it resembles the slow build-up to respectability that the franchise Pat Gillick and Paul Beeston built achieved in the early '80s. That team was primarily forged through perceptive scouting and hard work, the nuts and bolts of player development. Consider their all-time leaders in terms of games played, which was entirely built on Gillick's watch, and how they were acquired (see table 1).

Similarly, some of the smaller moves wound up being the most canny pick-ups. For example, the Jays acquired Cecil Fielder from the Royals. In 1983. For a broken-down Leon Roberts. When they had a shot to dominate the AL East in the mid-'80s, Gillick pulled the trigger on a series of trades to fix their bullpen and DH problems. When they fell short of the brass ring with those teams, Gillick showed he'd learned a thing or two later on with a brilliant series of build-up deals in the early '90s, intended to make sure they won this time around. Of note, he added Robbie Alomar, Joe Carter, Devon White, Ricky Henderson, David Cone, and Tom Candiotti. It would cost him Fred McGriff and Tony Fernandez, but he managed to get Fernandez back for nothing a couple of seasons later. The only pros-

BLUE JAYS PROSPECTUS

2003 record: 86–76; Third place, AL East

Pythagenport record: 87–75

Runs scored per game: 5.5 (2nd in AL)

Runs allowed per game: 5.1 (9th in AL)

Team EqA: .268 (3rd in AL)

2003 Batters Age: 28.7 (6th youngest in AL)

2003 Pitchers Age: 29.0 (7th oldest in AL)

Ballpark: SkyDome; Moderate hitter's park; Park Factor of 1.034

2003: The new-look Jays gave the Yankees and Red Sox a scare before tailing off in the second half.

2004: The offense is intact, and the pitching is improved, but a nightmarish division will keep the Jays out of the playoffs.

pect of note he gave up was Jeff Kent; you could debate who the second-best prospect was, either Steve Karsay or Glenallen Hill, but we're not talking about irreplaceable talents at that point.

What's significant is that none of this initially involved playing the free agent market. Before 1990, Gillick had signed five major league free agents in the entire history of the franchise: Luis Gomez (1978), Dennis Lamp (1984), Gary Allenson (1985), Bob Brenly (1989), and Tom Lawless (also '89). None of them were intended to be key players. At that point, you could speculate that Toronto had many of the same problems with attracting free agents that the Expos had (as you've seen in the Expos essay), but Gillick's tremendous achievements in scouting and acquiring players before they became famous or expensive had put the franchise in a situation where they didn't have to worry about it. The organization's approach changed by the early '90s, as Gillick did some prodigious shopping, signing up eleven free agents in 1992–93 alone. He had to. At that point, many of the building blocks of his player development program weren't quite so remarkable any more. Everyone was dipping into Latin America by then, and more teams were perhaps doing both a better job of sorting out which players you protect on your 40-man roster, and which players you pick up via Rule 5. The menu of choices general managers could employ to tailor their player development pro-

TABLE 1. BLUE JAYS' ALL-TIME LEADERS

Player, Position	Path to Toronto	Games Played	Observation
Ernie Whitt, C	Expansion Draft, 1976	1159	He was stuck behind Carlton Fisk in Boston
Carlos Delgado, 1B	Amateur Free Agent, 1988	1048	Willie Upshaw is second on the list with 950 games; he was picked through the Rule 5 draft in 1977
Damaso Garcia, 2B	Trade, 1979	869	Trapped behind Willie Randolph in New York, he was thrown in on the Cerone trade
Kelly Gruber, 3B	Rule 5 draft, 1983	829	Ed Sprague, who they drafted in the 1st round of 1988, ranks second with 814
Tony Fernandez, SS	Amateur Free Agent, 1979	1104	The pride of the organization's once-fabled Dominican program; he signed at 17
Lloyd Moseby, OF	1st round pick, 1978	1349	Moseby was the second choice overall in the draft, out of an Arkansas high school
George Bell, OF	Rule 5 draft, 1980	1066	Nobody knows what the Phillies were thinking; they hadn't even made the Von Hayes deal yet
Jesse Barfield, OF	9th round pick, 1977	996	Joe Carter and Shannon Stewart finished 4–5 behind Barfield in games played in the outfield

grams had become more universal, crimping everyone's style when it came to mining a particular vein of talent. The subsequent planlessness of the Ash years squandered decades that had been spent building up the Jays in their market.

Despite some local caterwauling for one candidate or another to replace Ash, CEO Paul Godfrey broke with expectations and returned the franchise to its roots, hauling in J. P. Ricciardi. Ricciardi was a veteran of Billy Beane's chatty, clever kaffeeklatsch management style, and one equipped with an extensive player development background. Upon taking over in Toronto, he quickly moved to re-shape the organization in ways informed by his Oakland experience. Practically speaking, that has meant a lot of change in the organization. Although there has been plenty of sympathetic squawking in industry rags as he replaces much of the *ancien regime,* left behind by Pat Gillick to rot in various sinecures, in only two years, he's pared down and improved the scouting department. In turn, Ricciardi has managed to assemble a considerable amount of minor league talent through the amateur draft and on the margins of any deal he consummates, helping conjure up a mutually flattering comparison to the way things were done in Gillick's heyday.

As a product of the moves that have retooled the big league team, on paper, it's a team that should win 85–90 games, even with an unbalanced schedule that will leave them to face those same Yankees and Red Sox for a quarter of their schedule. Which is why, in part, Ricciardi understands the value of working in something new. If money alone determined outcomes, Oakland would have never overtaken Gillick's Mariners or Bavasi's Angels in years

past. He deliberately sought out a statistically-minded familiar to do for him some of what Paul DePodesta and Dave Forst do for Beane. That just happened to be BP graduate Keith Law. (A question about whether or not we're biased when it comes to assessing the Blue Jays is appropriate, but we're cannibalistic enough to eat our own, just on principle.) Admittedly, Ricciardi and Law are intelligent and likeable. But likeability in the management and analysis parts of operating a franchise are not particularly important when it comes to assessing performance and looking at a team's ultimate success; it might count, but for little. I'm sure that friends, family, co-workers, and the Knights of Columbus in Tampa have nothing but good things to say about Chuck LaMar, for example.

By bringing in a personal stathead, Ricciardi has not done something revolutionary or unique. The A's grow their own, and other organizations are starting to do likewise. John Henry bought himself a relatively famous big gun in Bill James, but Theo Epstein is more than a little acquainted with the state of performance analysis on his own, and notable analysts like Eddie Epstein and Craig Wright made livings as statistically-informed consultants long beforehand. Of course, the Red Sox have their old stathead legacy of Dan Duquette and Mike Gimbel. The point here is that the competitive environment has changed, and Ricciardi, and Beane, and Epstein, and several other GMs, know it. As the mathematician David Hilbert put is, we must know, we will know. To win in today's competitive environment, you need to know, and the winners will.

That said, performance analysis is not a substitute for baseball acumen. It is not a cure-all, and it does not replace traditional player development. Inspired by an Age of Reason sensibility, it only informs these aspects of the industry. Statistical analysis cannot replace scouting wholesale, nor do those who use it wish for it to be so. It is a tool. Edward Wilson, one of the greatest scientific minds alive today, and happily teaching entomology at the selfsame Harvard that seems to have gotten into the business of cranking out baseball executives, encourages his fellow man to transcend the boundaries of discrete bodies of knowledge to see the world as it really is. Similarly, the future of performance analysis or sabermetrics lies not in genius, but in collaboration. In the same poem where he had described the brutish vision of competition in Nature that fired up generations of cypto-Social Darwinists, Tennyson also encourages us with the advice that:

> Let knowledge grow from more to more,
> But more of reverence in us dwell

As long as more traditional industry types and statheads keep that in mind, and recognize a shared love of the game in each other, we should see the competitive environment become ever more enriched by arete, achieving excellence in a world stocked with excellent competition. And the Devil Rays.

Informed but not instructed by that sort of wisdom, Ricciardi is building a team that can run with their lessthrifty brethren in the AL East. In isolation, in terms of what's on the field right now, it's a pretty good team, a quality blend of homegrown goodies, productive shopping trips, and modestly-priced rentals. Offensively, the Jays believe they might field a lineup with four thirty home run players in it: beyond Carlos Delgado and Vernon Wells, they anticipate that healthy seasons from Phelps and Hinske will let them both join the first two. The other positions are stocked with talent that is both useful at the moment, and replaceable in the future. In the middle infield, Chris Woodward might be only be good enough to be the utility infielder of the next division-winning Jays team, and Orlando Hudson is turning into a slick glove instead of an offensive asset, but both of these guys can play. They have a productive job-sharing setup behind the plate, with Greg Myers and Kevin Cash doing their best Ernie Whitt/Buck Martinez impression. Frank Catalanotto and Reed Johnson will make a great platoon someday, but for the time being, they're fine regulars to flank Wells in the outfield.

What's important to keep in mind is that for the five positions beyond the lineup's core four, the Jays have young talent pressing up through the system, portending a team that should be able to contend into the future, and in a way that is much more resilient and enduring than the increasingly brittle Yankee and Red Sox organizations. Behind the plate, they have a potential star nearing readiness in Guillermo Quiroz. In the outfield, they have Alex Rios, Gabe Gross, and John-Ford Griffin coming up fast; all three should be ready by spring training 2005 at the latest. In the middle infield, they have Russ Adams, Aaron Hill, and Jorge Sequea, and while it's an open question as to whether any of them will wind up at short, the Jays really want Adams to stick there; Hill should wind up at second or third.

For now, the pitching staff is a little more of a mercenary jumble. Beyond homegrown ace Roy Halladay, the league's true workhorse, they've added a veteran trio of Pat Hentgen, Ted Lilly, and Miguel Batista. It might not be the stuff of history, but it beats the last two years' worth of jumbled rotations. The bullpen, a complete disaster last year, has been patched with Justin Speier, Terry Adams, Kerry Ligtenberg, and Valerio De Los Santos. But coming up behind, the Jays have Dustin McGowan and David Bush on the cutting edge of a host of promising possibilities cranked out by a reinvigorated player development program.

Treated to a franchise so-armed and so-informed, Blue Jays fans should get as enthusiastic for today's Jays as they were for Gillick's age of gold, promise, and trophies. The Jays probably won't win this year. Or next. But they have adapted, they are getting ready, and if the Yankees and Red Sox miss a beat, the Jays will be ready for them, red in tooth and claw, in this new era of competition and excellence.

HITTERS

RUSS ADAMS   SS   Bats: L   Throws: R   Born: 30-Aug-80   Age: 23

YEAR	TM	LG	AGE	AB	H	2B	3B	HR	BB	SO	SB	CS	AVG	OBP	SLG	MLVR	EQBA	EQOBP	EQSLG	EQMLVR	VORP	DEFENSE	
2002	AUB	NYP	21	113	40	7	3	0	24	11	13	1	.354	.464	.469	.417	.231	.323	.314	-.232	-2.1	30-SS	-1
2002	DUN	FLA	21	147	34	4	2	1	18	17	5	2	.231	.321	.306	-.109	.185	.254	.252	-.480	-12.9	35-SS	-2
2003	DUN	FLA	22	258	72	9	5	3	38	27	9	2	.279	.380	.388	.168	.239	.319	.346	-.192	0.9	66-SS	-6
2003	NHV	EAS	22	271	75	10	4	4	30	37	8	1	.277	.349	.387	.037	.240	.301	.345	-.228	-2.1	62-SS	-13
2004	TOR	AL	23	247	61	11	3	3	24	34	5	2	.245	.317	.352	-.144	.242	.318	.350	-.177	3.4	68-SS	-9

Breakout: 32%   Improve: 59%   Collapse: 21%

Despite the concerns that Adams's arm isn't good enough at short for another year, the organization still hasn't ruled out his capacity to handle the position. On a certain level, they have to: If Adams can't hack it as a shortstop, he goes from top prospect to a nifty second baseman, and they didn't pick him to be the new Craig Counsell. He's not a platoon hitter, so he will be an effective everyday player, but he's going to have to show improvement at short if he wants to avoid a career with plenty of stops.

JIMMY ALVAREZ   IF   Bats: B   Throws: R   Born: 04-Oct-79   Age: 24

YEAR	TM	LG	AGE	AB	H	2B	3B	HR	BB	SO	SB	CS	AVG	OBP	SLG	MLVR	EQBA	EQOBP	EQSLG	EQMLVR	VORP		DEFENSE		
2001	DUN	FLA	21	467	132	19	4	8	49	87	29	7	.283	.351	.392	.074	.231	.284	.332	-.285	-12.2		99-SS -19	14-2B	1
2002	TEN	SOU	22	497	138	32	3	8	79	121	20	11	.278	.383	.402	.111	.231	.316	.347	-.202	-4.2		109-2B -1		
2003	SYR	INT	23	342	88	13	7	4	45	92	11	5	.257	.342	.371	-.016	.236	.321	.349	-.186	1.8		62-SS -4	25-2B	-6
2004	BOS	AL	24	225	57	12	2	4	23	48	7	2	.255	.330	.385	-.073	.250	.329	.387	-.103	10.5		63-SS -7		

Breakout: 38%   Improve: 60%   Collapse: 21%

A Dominican picked up from the Twins in a minor trade in 2000, Alvarez is a good utility infielder in the making. He's improved his glovework at short, gets on base well enough, and has footspeed. His power spike in '02 was a bit of an anomaly, but he's young and might get it back. The Jays wanted to re-sign him, but he was appreciated by the Red Sox as well, and signed with them as a minor league free agent.

DAVE BERG   IF   Bats: R   Throws: R   Born: 03-Sep-70   Age: 33

YEAR	TM	LG	AGE	AB	H	2B	3B	HR	BB	SO	SB	CS	AVG	OBP	SLG	MLVR	EQBA	EQOBP	EQSLG	EQMLVR	VORP		DEFENSE		
2001	FLA	NL	30	215	52	12	1	4	14	39	0	1	.242	.292	.363	-.192	.252	.302	.376	-.175	0.0		29-2B -2	10-SS	-1
2002	TOR	AL	31	374	101	26	2	4	26	57	0	2	.270	.322	.382	-.070	.287	.342	.410	-.025	14.4		43-2B -2	17-3B	2
2003	TOR	AL	32	161	41	6	1	4	11	34	0	1	.255	.301	.379	-.155	.267	.318	.398	-.102	-0.8		17-2B -1	12-3B	-2
2004	TOR	AL	33	161	41	8	1	3	11	30	1	1	.255	.307	.371	-.132	.251	.307	.368	-.166	1.7		46-2B -6		

Breakout: 19%   Improve: 43%   Collapse: 42%

It was a misstep to hand Berg a two-year deal, but he has his uses. He could have gotten more playing time, as he did in 2002, but he suffered from some strange form of fatigue that left him dizzy and easily worn out; eventually it pushed him onto the DL. When he could play, he did mash lefties, but that hasn't been something he's done consistently. If that sticks, he might be able to wring a few more years out of his career.

KEVIN CASH   C   Bats: R   Throws: R   Born: 06-Dec-77   Age: 26

YEAR	TM	LG	AGE	AB	H	2B	3B	HR	BB	SO	SB	CS	AVG	OBP	SLG	MLVR	EQBA	EQOBP	EQSLG	EQMLVR	VORP		DEFENSE
2001	DUN	FLA	23	371	105	27	0	12	43	80	4	3	.283	.369	.453	.177	.227	.290	.375	-.216	-5.1		77-C 11
2002	TEN	SOU	24	213	59	15	1	8	36	44	5	2	.277	.381	.469	.194	.225	.309	.399	-.148	1.7		38-C 0
2002	SYR	INT	24	236	52	18	0	10	25	72	0	1	.220	.299	.424	-.059	.202	.279	.395	-.227	-3.8		57-C 8
2003	SYR	INT	25	326	88	28	2	8	29	81	1	0	.270	.331	.442	.065	.249	.313	.419	-.096	7.9		84-C 13
2003	TOR	AL	25	106	15	3	0	1	4	22	0	0	.142	.179	.198	-.684	.160	.197	.226	-.644	-13.6		28-C 2
2004	TOR	AL	26	224	53	13	1	8	19	50	1	1	.237	.303	.407	-.104	.234	.304	.403	-.138	3.8		62-C 2

Breakout: 40%   Improve: 58%   Collapse: 26%

A latter-day delight cut from the same cloth that gave us Jim Sundberg, Cash has been able to gun down more than 40% of opposing runners over the last two years. He's a nifty job-sharing partner with Myers in an offense-defense platoon, with the question being which half survives Quiroz's arrival in 2005. Cash would rot behind Quiroz, but after a year as a part-time starter, he'll have value in trade. As a regular, he'll be adequate, and seeing the sort of money that gets thrown at the less-than-adequate Brad Ausmus or Mike Matheny, he might just hit the jackpot.

FRANK CATALANOTTO   OF   Bats: L   Throws: R   Born: 27-Apr-74   Age: 30

YEAR	TM	LG	AGE	AB	H	2B	3B	HR	BB	SO	SB	CS	AVG	OBP	SLG	MLVR	EQBA	EQOBP	EQSLG	EQMLVR	VORP		DEFENSE		
2001	TEX	AL	27	463	153	31	5	11	39	55	15	5	.330	.391	.490	.225	.346	.406	.514	.293	40.9		69-LF -1	14-RF	0
2002	TEX	AL	28	212	57	16	6	3	25	27	9	5	.269	.364	.443	.075	.286	.378	.474	.129	10.3		19-LF -2	15-2B	0
2003	TOR	AL	29	489	146	34	6	13	35	62	2	2	.299	.351	.472	.094	.313	.367	.497	.168	18.4		50-LF 4	35-RF	-3
2004	TOR	AL	30	366	104	23	4	9	33	47	5	3	.285	.353	.445	.064	.281	.354	.442	.034	14.9		98-LF -1		

Breakout: 10%   Improve: 33%   Collapse: 25%

A complete hitter and delightfully enthusiastic ballplayer. Although Cat's not a righty-killer of the first order, when you can belt them at a .318/.368/.501 clip, nobody's asking questions. Like John Lowenstein before him, he might have started off as an infielder, but that's over and done with. It's a shame so much of his career was wasted on the Tigers organization or a Rangers team that only occasionally had a sense of direction. However, he got a head start on his life as a sub-star-level offensive weapon, and he should retain value as a platoon outfielder for several seasons to come.

VITO CHIARAVOLLOTI   1B   Bats: R   Throws: R   Born: 26-Oct-80   Age: 23

YEAR	TM	LG	AGE	AB	H	2B	3B	HR	BB	SO	SB	CS	AVG	OBP	SLG	MLVR	EQBA	EQOBP	EQSLG	EQMLVR	VORP		DEFENSE
2003	AUB	NYP	22	228	80	20	1	12	47	48	0	0	.351	.469	.605	.591	.224	.316	.398	-.137	-7.6		53-1B -8
2004	TOR	AL	23	248	57	13	0	10	28	62	0	0	.231	.317	.403	-.088	.228	.318	.400	-.121	0.2		70-1B -5

Breakout: 18%   Improve: 41%   Collapse: 23%

As a 15th-round pick in the '03 draft out of the University of Richmond, it might be easy to characterize Chiaravolloti as the new Jays' idea of an organizational soldier. He's more than that, however. In addition to winning a triple crown in his professional debut, he's a tremendous athlete and a former swimming champ, so we're not talking about some lump. He had to have surgery on an elbow this winter, but should be at full speed in camp.

HOWIE CLARK   UT   Bats: L   Throws: R   Born: 13-Feb-74   Age: 30

YEAR	TM	LG	AGE	AB	H	2B	3B	HR	BB	SO	SB	CS	AVG	OBP	SLG	MLVR	EQBA	EQOBP	EQSLG	EQMLVR	VORP	DEFENSE			
2001	YUC	MEX	27	493	164	42	7	5	43	47	5	4	.333	.388	.477	.286	.286	.330	.427	-.023	17.7				
2002	ROC	INT	28	418	129	21	4	7	41	28	3	4	.309	.369	.428	.135	.286	.348	.402	-.026	4.9	62-RF -9	16-1B -2		
2002	BAL	AL	28	53	16	5	0	0	3	6	0	0	.302	.362	.396	.067	.333	.386	.444	.144	3.7				
2003	SYR	INT	29	252	65	14	1	4	21	20	1	0	.258	.316	.369	-.063	.240	.303	.354	-.212	-2.9	51-2B -8			
2003	TOR	AL	29	70	25	3	1	0	3	6	0	1	.357	.400	.429	.167	.371	.410	.457	.243	5.0				
2004	TOR	AL	30	189	52	12	1	3	15	21	1	1	.272	.329	.399	-.044	.269	.330	.396	-.076	5.1	53-2B -12			

Breakout: 26%   Improve: 45%   Collapse: 36%

Another useful journeyman dug up by the Jays, but only semi-liberated from minor league chattelry. He can still fill in at five positions adequately, still hits lefty and well enough to be useful, and the chances that anyone's going to swipe him on waivers should you elect to yo-yo him on the Syracuse shuttle are remote. It's surprising an NL team doesn't want him for his qualities, but apparently he lacks that Lenny Harris verve.

CARLOS DELGADO   1B   Bats: L   Throws: R   Born: 25-Jun-72   Age: 32

YEAR	TM	LG	AGE	AB	H	2B	3B	HR	BB	SO	SB	CS	AVG	OBP	SLG	MLVR	EQBA	EQOBP	EQSLG	EQMLVR	VORP	DEFENSE
2001	TOR	AL	29	574	160	31	1	39	111	136	3	0	.279	.408	.540	.274	.295	.422	.576	.348	70.3	159-1B -4
2002	TOR	AL	30	505	140	34	2	33	102	126	1	0	.277	.406	.549	.289	.297	.426	.591	.376	66.5	140-1B 5
2003	TOR	AL	31	570	172	38	1	42	109	137	0	0	.302	.426	.593	.373	.319	.443	.630	.478	71.0	145-1B -1
2004	TOR	AL	32	517	149	31	1	36	93	123	1	1	.287	.405	.559	.291	.284	.406	.555	.266	50.3	147-1B 1

Breakout: 9%   Improve: 34%   Collapse: 29%

The second-best season for the greatest Blue Jay of all time. It was a superb ramp-up to the last year of his contract, but a major part of the difference was that Delgado significantly improved his hitting against lefties, reaching .284/.395/.475 against them after hitting .246/.338/.433 and .238/.325/.360 vs. LH the previous two seasons. The real question is whether he's going to be able to be pleased by the Jays under the game's new economics. The Jays are smart enough to know that a 30-something first baseman—no matter how good—isn't worth the $18.5 million he'll make in 2004. He also has a no-trade clause though, so he won't be flipped for goodies at the deadline.

SHAWN FAGAN   1B/3B   Bats: R   Throws: R   Born: 02-Mar-78   Age: 26

YEAR	TM	LG	AGE	AB	H	2B	3B	HR	BB	SO	SB	CS	AVG	OBP	SLG	MLVR	EQBA	EQOBP	EQSLG	EQMLVR	VORP	DEFENSE			
2001	DUN	FLA	23	475	143	18	5	10	86	114	7	2	.301	.407	.423	.205	.229	.315	.333	-.224	-6.9	114-3B -3			
2002	TEN	SOU	24	421	113	24	0	12	102	87	6	3	.268	.411	.411	.156	.211	.329	.338	-.200	-16.6	44-1B -6	44-3B 5		
2003	NHV	EAS	25	421	132	14	3	5	62	82	4	2	.314	.402	.397	.164	.268	.349	.345	-.117	-4.4	44-1B -6	28-3B -5		
2003	SYR	INT	25	58	12	3	0	0	2	22	1	0	.207	.230	.259	-.387	.207	.233	.259	-.504	-7.2	17-1B 5			
2004	TOR	AL	26	154	37	7	1	4	16	36	1	1	.239	.318	.364	-.132	.236	.318	.361	-.165	-1.4	45-1B -3			

Breakout: 30%   Improve: 45%   Collapse: 38%

Kevin Youkilis, but without the *Moneyball* karma, even less power, and an ability to play third that's no better than an urban legend. In assembling PECOTA, one of the things Nate Silver found is that guys like this, the high-walks players without a lot of power, generally don't develop into useful big leaguers. You could ask how many of them get legit shots to show what they can do, but the results are still hard to ignore. Fagan would be better off trying to pull a Kieschnick, resuming his career as a college closer, and offering his organization a combo 12th pitcher/spare bat, but the Kieschnick phenomenon doesn't seem to have inspired a wave of imitators.

TYRELL GODWIN

OF   **Bats: L**   **Throws: R**   Born: 10-Jul-79   Age: 24

YEAR	TM	LG	AGE	AB	H	2B	3B	HR	BB	SO	SB	CS	AVG	OBP	SLG	MLVR	EQBA	EQOBP	EQSLG	EQMLVR	VORP	DEFENSE	
2001	AUB	NYP	21	117	43	8	2	2	19	27	9	5	.368	.464	.521	.489	.244	.320	.358	-.171	-1.7	11-CF 0	
2002	CWV	SAL	22	185	52	8	5	0	20	23	10	2	.281	.364	.378	.099	.225	.284	.309	-.321	-15.4	29-LF -2	18-CF -2
2003	DUN	FLA	23	322	88	16	0	1	29	39	20	7	.273	.348	.332	.049	.248	.300	.310	-.274	-13.1	94-CF -5	
2003	NHV	EAS	23	123	38	6	3	1	3	27	6	1	.309	.328	.431	.093	.276	.297	.398	-.134	-2.4	27-RF -7	
2004	TOR	AL	24	228	59	11	3	3	16	39	7	3	.257	.314	.370	-.119	.254	.314	.367	-.153	-1.7	62-CF -7	

Breakout: 34%   Improve: 57%   Collapse: 17%

In days of yore, he'd get a nickname like "Slappy," because the odds of his getting a ball in play with a long liner seem unnaturally slim. He's a scout's sort of player, whippet-fast, and only one "o" short of being the third leg of the Goodwin trio. The low-wattage stylings of Tom and Curtis at the plate have entertained hometown fans wherever they visit, and Ty seems likely to join them. Given the Blue Jay regime change, you can count on Godwin being happily tossed into a deal.

JOHN-FORD GRIFFIN

LF   **Bats: L**   **Throws: L**   Born: 19-Nov-79   Age: 24

YEAR	TM	LG	AGE	AB	H	2B	3B	HR	BB	SO	SB	CS	AVG	OBP	SLG	MLVR	EQBA	EQOBP	EQSLG	EQMLVR	VORP	DEFENSE
2001	STA	NYP	21	238	74	17	1	5	40	41	10	4	.311	.413	.454	.291	.207	.285	.315	-.320	-38.1	60-LF -7
2002	TAM	FLA	22	255	68	16	1	3	29	45	1	0	.267	.344	.373	.062	.226	.287	.328	-.288	-19.9	45-LF -6
2002	NRW	EAS	22	67	22	3	0	5	8	13	0	1	.328	.400	.597	.449	.275	.333	.507	.087	3.1	16-LF -2
2003	NHV	EAS	23	373	104	23	3	13	49	85	2	0	.279	.361	.461	.159	.237	.310	.405	-.130	-8.7	61-LF -3
2004	TOR	AL	24	220	55	13	1	7	21	46	1	1	.249	.318	.415	-.060	.246	.318	.412	-.093	-0.4	61-LF -1

Breakout: 38%   Improve: 59%   Collapse: 25%

Griffin literally limped along, slowed with a broken foot that he didn't get checked out. You can sympathize a bit: He's probably the third of the three talented outfielders moving up together from Double-A, and with Vernon Wells part of the team's long-term plans, he's in a bit of a bind. He hits for more power than Gross, and doesn't have Gross's platoon issues, but he's really only going to be able to handle left. A healthy season in Syracuse will help sort out if he's their left fielder of the future, or a chit to bargain with, but I like his chances of having a monster year at the plate.

GABE GROSS

OF   **Bats: L**   **Throws: R**   Born: 21-Oct-79   Age: 24

YEAR	TM	LG	AGE	AB	H	2B	3B	HR	BB	SO	SB	CS	AVG	OBP	SLG	MLVR	EQBA	EQOBP	EQSLG	EQMLVR	VORP	DEFENSE	
2001	DUN	FLA	21	126	38	9	2	4	26	29	4	2	.302	.426	.500	.324	.221	.320	.382	-.153	-3.8	24-RF -5	10-LF -2
2001	TEN	SOU	21	41	10	1	0	3	6	12	0	1	.244	.373	.488	.156	.190	.301	.405	-.179	-0.7		
2002	TEN	SOU	22	403	96	17	5	10	53	71	8	2	.230	.333	.380	-.018	.204	.276	.336	-.311	-30.6	101-RF -1	
2003	NHV	EAS	23	310	99	23	3	7	52	53	3	2	.319	.423	.481	.313	.262	.353	.410	-.024	4.1	77-RF -3	
2003	SYR	INT	23	182	48	16	2	5	31	56	1	1	.264	.380	.456	.156	.237	.346	.425	-.036	1.8	42-RF 5	
2004	TOR	AL	24	265	67	16	2	9	30	54	2	1	.255	.336	.429	-.006	.251	.337	.426	-.038	5.7	74-RF 0	

Breakout: 35%   Improve: 58%   Collapse: 25%

In a non-news story, Gross was the starting right fielder for Team USA, which is another way of saying he's clean, and this year's return to power-hitting was all natural, lending that much more credence to the story that his struggles in 2002 were a matter of his pressing against advanced competition and a lack of baseball experience. He might only be a platoon hitter for the moment, but he's going to open the year in Triple-A, where he can work on it. He's also got a strong enough arm for right, creating a nice problem for the Jays if Gross, Rios, and Wells wind up in the same outfield.

AARON HILL

SS   **Bats: R**   **Throws: R**   Born: 21-Mar-82   Age: 22

YEAR	TM	LG	AGE	AB	H	2B	3B	HR	BB	SO	SB	CS	AVG	OBP	SLG	MLVR	EQBA	EQOBP	EQSLG	EQMLVR	VORP	DEFENSE
2003	AUB	NYP	21	122	44	4	0	4	16	20	1	1	.361	.446	.492	.438	.256	.324	.364	-.147	4.0	30-SS -5
2003	DUN	FLA	21	119	34	7	0	0	11	10	1	0	.286	.343	.345	.066	.250	.298	.315	-.270	-2.6	29-SS -7
2004	TOR	AL	22	242	58	11	1	4	18	38	1	1	.240	.301	.341	-.190	.236	.302	.339	-.224	-0.5	66-SS -7

Breakout: 25%   Improve: 43%   Collapse: 41%

Hill was the Jays' top pick in the 2003 draft after finishing his college career at LSU as the SEC's player of the year. As a hitter, he's everything they want: patient, able to kill his pitch, with significant power potential. It's expected that he will outgrow short; some think he's athletic enough to move to second, but third seems the more likely destination. It's a year or two away before he starts pushing other people's careers around; once he comes off of short, he's either going to push Hinske to first (assuming Delgado leaves), or keep Russ Adams at short if he can handle it, and somewhere else if he can't.

ERIC HINSKE   3B   Bats: L   Throws: R   Born: 05-Aug-77   Age: 26

YEAR	TM	LG	AGE	AB	H	2B	3B	HR	BB	SO	SB	CS	AVG	OBP	SLG	MLVR	EQBA	EQOBP	EQSLG	EQMLVR	VORP	DEFENSE
2001	SAC	PCL	23	436	123	27	1	25	54	113	20	7	.282	.373	.521	.185	.247	.330	.454	-.018	21.3	114-3B -11
2002	TOR	AL	24	566	158	38	2	24	77	138	13	1	.279	.365	.481	.139	.296	.384	.514	.203	59.0	142-3B -13
2003	TOR	AL	25	449	109	45	3	12	59	104	12	2	.243	.329	.437	-.037	.254	.344	.461	.023	16.0	121-3B -17
2004	TOR	AL	26	467	127	30	3	22	59	103	12	4	.272	.355	.486	.111	.269	.356	.483	.082	35.4	125-3B -6

Breakout: 22%   *Improve: 56%*   *Collapse: 12%*

Since being stolen from the Cubs—these days, he'd look pretty handy amidst their wall of right-handed bats—then heisted from the A's, Hinske has been remarkably consistent. Sure, his batting average jumped around last year, but despite playing through a hand injury that cost him a month and hampered his ability to drive the ball to all fields, his walk rates and power—his Isolated Slugging (SLG-AVG) was .202 in '02, .194 in '03—really didn't fluctuate. Less happily, Hinske hasn't made any progress at third, but once his wrist is healed, they hope he'll throw better. Everyone's expecting a rebound season, and that projected OBP is lower than what he'll do.

ORLANDO HUDSON   2B   Bats: B   Throws: R   Born: 12-Dec-77   Age: 26

YEAR	TM	LG	AGE	AB	H	2B	3B	HR	BB	SO	SB	CS	AVG	OBP	SLG	MLVR	EQBA	EQOBP	EQSLG	EQMLVR	VORP	DEFENSE		
2001	TEN	SOU	23	306	94	22	8	4	37	42	8	3	.307	.385	.471	.204	.254	.321	.399	-.105	6.7	66-2B	6	11-3B 3
2001	SYR	INT	23	194	59	14	3	4	23	34	11	3	.304	.378	.469	.192	.274	.351	.437	.019	11.4	50-2B	8	
2002	SYR	INT	24	417	127	27	3	10	35	54	8	5	.305	.363	.456	.150	.277	.335	.425	-.024	18.4	97-2B	5	
2002	TOR	AL	24	192	53	10	5	4	11	27	0	1	.276	.319	.443	.010	.295	.339	.472	.066	11.7	52-2B	5	
2003	TOR	AL	25	474	127	21	6	9	39	87	5	4	.268	.328	.395	-.076	.283	.345	.420	-.008	9.1	131-2B	20	
2004	TOR	AL	26	422	113	23	4	9	36	67	6	3	.268	.329	.403	-.043	.265	.330	.400	-.075	12.7	111-2B	6	

Breakout: 13%   *Improve: 35%*   *Collapse: 23%*

Last year, we jumped the gun by nominating Hudson for a career as the second-best second baseman in Jays' history; clearly, Damaso Garcia still has some pull with the fates. Hudson is wildly popular among some scouty types, and his career has not been hindered by the "pimp" gaffe. It's just that he's simply not that good. He's an ersatz switch-hitter, since he can't and doesn't hit lefties. However, he did have a breakthrough in terms of applying himself defensively, and he might be the best second baseman in the game when it comes to running down popups. He's a fun player, just one that's short of stardom.

REED JOHNSON   OF   Bats: R   Throws: R   Born: 08-Dec-76   Age: 27

YEAR	TM	LG	AGE	AB	H	2B	3B	HR	BB	SO	SB	CS	AVG	OBP	SLG	MLVR	EQBA	EQOBP	EQSLG	EQMLVR	VORP	DEFENSE		
2001	TEN	SOU	24	554	174	29	4	13	45	79	42	12	.314	.383	.451	.182	.271	.325	.395	-.090	-5.9	120-LF	-1	
2002	SYR	INT	25	159	37	8	3	2	12	23	1	4	.233	.317	.358	-.104	.214	.293	.340	-.267	-5.5	32-CF	1	11-LF 1
2003	SYR	INT	26	101	33	4	1	2	3	13	3	1	.327	.369	.446	.178	.307	.354	.436	.052	5.9	17-CF	0	
2003	TOR	AL	26	412	121	21	2	10	20	67	5	3	.294	.353	.427	.032	.313	.371	.459	.121	7.9	58-RF	-5	39-LF 1
2004	TOR	AL	27	395	109	22	3	9	27	59	7	4	.275	.338	.415	-.007	.272	.339	.412	-.039	6.4	105-RF	0	

Breakout: 26%   *Improve: 45%*   *Collapse: 26%*

We love to see organizational soldiers get chances and thrive, probably more so than anybody else, but Johnson seems to have been the victim of some hyperbole, as if he was somehow as handy as Jody Gerut or Scott Podsednik. He can hit well enough, he's happy to take a pitch off a shoulder for a base, he's a remarkably effective push-bunter, and he throws well and accurately. Those are fun qualities to have, but it's not the stuff of an everyday player in a corner. He's a very good fourth outfielder for a team that needs to use one.

BOBBY KIELTY   OF   Bats: B   Throws: R   Born: 05-Aug-76   Age: 27

YEAR	TM	LG	AGE	AB	H	2B	3B	HR	BB	SO	SB	CS	AVG	OBP	SLG	MLVR	EQBA	EQOBP	EQSLG	EQMLVR	VORP	DEFENSE		
2001	EDM	PCL	24	341	98	25	2	12	53	76	5	0	.287	.391	.478	.153	.246	.343	.409	-.056	9.8	74-CF	1	12-LF 0
2001	MIN	AL	24	104	26	8	0	2	8	25	3	0	.250	.297	.385	-.142	.269	.326	.413	-.064	0.0	12-RF	0	
2002	MIN	AL	25	289	84	14	3	12	52	66	4	1	.291	.405	.484	.221	.309	.424	.519	.290	29.1	35-RF	1	25-CF -1
2003	MIN	AL	26	238	60	13	0	9	42	56	6	2	.252	.370	.420	.037	.268	.385	.452	.096	8.7	28-RF	1	
2003	TOR	AL	26	189	44	13	1	4	29	36	2	1	.233	.342	.376	-.098	.249	.361	.407	-.023	-2.3	50-RF	-3	
2004	OAK	AL	27	383	97	21	2	15	54	83	6	2	.254	.351	.437	.027	.262	.364	.456	.055	16.7	106-RF	0	

Breakout: 17%   *Improve: 44%*   *Collapse: 23%*

Kielty's an asset, but the question is if he's really going to hit well enough to be an everyday starter, or just a crafted tool within a tailored arsenal. The Jays' concern was that he keeps getting worse against right-handed pitching, which is going to limit his utility. In Oakland, where teams like to try to stack their rotations with lefties, that could be a formula for what might look like a breakout season in terms of cumulative stats; the challenge is for the A's to get him back to hanging in against right-handed pitching.

RODNEY MEDINA OF Bats: B Throws: R Born: 17-Oct-81 Age: 22

YEAR	TM	LG	AGE	AB	H	2B	3B	HR	BB	SO	SB	CS	AVG	OBP	SLG	MLVR	EQBA	EQOBP	EQSLG	EQMLVR	VORP	DEFENSE		
2001	MED	PIO	19	195	60	7	0	7	19	29	6	2	.308	.375	.451	.149	.201	.246	.299	-.424	-40.3	20-LF -4	16-1B -1	
2002	CWV	SAL	20	339	97	12	7	3	33	44	11	10	.286	.354	.389	.103	.221	.272	.307	-.350	-30.9	29-LF -2	18-RF -2	
2003	CWV	SAL	21	452	128	23	8	11	45	44	6	4	.283	.349	.442	.175	.220	.270	.355	-.287	-35.2	116-LF -8		
2004	TOR	AL	22	252	58	12	2	5	17	35	2	1	.231	.280	.350	-.221	.228	.281	.347	-.258	-12.6	68-LF -6		

Breakout: 27% Improve: 54% Collapse: 20%

From a player development point of view, Medina was probably the sole reason Charleston played out its season after Brandon League was promoted. His best quality is his youth, which provides the hope that he's going to pick up some more power as he matures. If he's really going to be a prospect, he's going to need it.

GREG MYERS C Bats: L Throws: R Born: 14-Apr-66 Age: 38

YEAR	TM	LG	AGE	AB	H	2B	3B	HR	BB	SO	SB	CS	AVG	OBP	SLG	MLVR	EQBA	EQOBP	EQSLG	EQMLVR	VORP	DEFENSE
2001	BAL	AL	35	74	20	2	0	4	8	17	0	0	.270	.341	.459	.076	.293	.361	.507	.152	5.6	
2001	OAK	AL	35	87	16	1	0	7	13	21	0	0	.184	.290	.437	-.119	.195	.307	.471	-.078	2.2	23-C 1
2002	OAK	AL	36	144	32	5	0	6	26	36	0	0	.222	.341	.382	-.056	.247	.360	.425	-.002	6.9	41-C 0
2003	TOR	AL	37	329	101	19	0	15	37	57	0	3	.307	.374	.502	.179	.322	.394	.529	.268	27.4	69-C -11
2004	TOR	AL	38	135	32	7	0	5	17	28	0	0	.238	.323	.400	-.077	.235	.323	.397	-.110	3.1	40-C -6

Breakout: 9% Improve: 21% Collapse: 46%

It's sort of fun to see the legend of Ernie Whitt find an echo in modern times, and Myers wound up having so much fun on this team that he quickly killed talk of retiring after 2003; hopefully, Kevin Cash will turn out better than Pat Borders. Last year looks like a breakout, but his power has remained pretty consistent across the last three years. What changed was playing time, and with it, a big boost in his batting average. That screams fluke, but Myers is useful enough to share time, spot for Cash against the contenders and the tough righties, and perhaps earn himself a little more love in an appreciative city.

JOSH PHELPS DH Bats: R Throws: R Born: 12-May-78 Age: 26

YEAR	TM	LG	AGE	AB	H	2B	3B	HR	BB	SO	SB	CS	AVG	OBP	SLG	MLVR	EQBA	EQOBP	EQSLG	EQMLVR	VORP	DEFENSE
2001	TEN	SOU	23	486	142	36	1	31	80	127	3	3	.292	.406	.562	.337	.233	.330	.452	-.032	22.3	67-C -11
2002	SYR	INT	24	257	75	20	1	24	32	83	0	0	.292	.380	.658	.424	.258	.343	.588	.198	29.0	34-C -11
2002	TOR	AL	24	265	82	20	1	15	19	82	0	0	.309	.362	.562	.274	.327	.379	.594	.344	31.9	
2003	TOR	AL	25	396	106	18	1	20	39	115	1	2	.268	.358	.470	.075	.283	.369	.497	.142	19.9	
2004	TOR	AL	26	395	107	23	1	24	43	105	2	1	.272	.355	.520	.154	.268	.356	.516	.125	27.4	

Breakout: 26% Improve: 49% Collapse: 25%

It's been a fitful start to a career, but it's only the dead calm before he starts terrorizing bleacher denizens. Phelps is a devoted student of the art of hitting, and a dead pull hitter fully primed to kill any kind of offering at the plate. A full, healthy season for Phelps will mean more than 30 bombs. That isn't a case of our trying to whistle our way past the old cover curse, either...c'mon, Richard Hidalgo turned out OK. As you can see from this year's cover, we're condemning either all baseballs or statistical analysis. Or maybe the color blue. Hopefully not Michael Lewis.

SIMON POND INF Bats: L Throws: R Born: 27-Oct-76 Age: 27

YEAR	TM	LG	AGE	AB	H	2B	3B	HR	BB	SO	SB	CS	AVG	OBP	SLG	MLVR	EQBA	EQOBP	EQSLG	EQMLVR	VORP	DEFENSE		
2001	KIN	CAR	24	97	33	8	1	4	10	12	1	1	.340	.400	.567	.461	.265	.327	.461	.002	2.6	20-1B -1		
2001	AKR	EAS	24	388	104	29	3	11	30	70	2	3	.268	.320	.443	.071	.235	.289	.394	-.186	-12.3	71-1B -2		
2002	DUN	FLA	25	401	114	25	7	13	46	73	2	3	.284	.357	.479	.191	.222	.282	.383	-.224	-5.5	65-3B -3	27-1B -1	
2003	NHV	EAS	26	228	77	17	1	7	39	33	1	1	.338	.440	.513	.399	.279	.369	.442	.063	17.8	53-3B -6		
2003	SYR	INT	26	248	76	21	1	5	16	42	1	1	.306	.353	.460	.155	.284	.331	.440	-.004	13.3	30-3B -2	16-1B 1	
2004	TOR	AL	27	205	53	12	1	7	18	35	1	1	.259	.321	.426	-.032	.255	.322	.423	-.065	8.7	57-3B -5		

Breakout: 25% Improve: 40% Collapse: 31%

(continued next page)

Simon Pond *(continued)*

A solid example of the kind of free talent you can find floating around, the Jays signed him as a minor league free agent. What probably helped make him available was a funky, jerky swing that's downright cringe-worthy, but all he's done is continue to hit. Now he's the organization's internal patch if there's an injury at first base or DH. He's not much of a third baseman, but to help his chances of sticking, he's working out in the outfield.

GUILLERMO QUIROZ   C   Bats: R   Throws: R   Born: 29-Nov-81   Age: 22

YEAR	TM	LG	AGE	AB	H	2B	3B	HR	BB	SO	SB	CS	AVG	OBP	SLG	MLVR	EQBA	EQOBP	EQSLG	EQMLVR	VORP	DEFENSE	
2001	CWV	SAL	19	261	52	12	0	7	29	67	5	1	.199	.294	.326	-.088	.162	.231	.268	-.516	-30.0	79-C	5
2002	DUN	FLA	20	411	107	28	1	12	35	91	1	0	.260	.330	.421	.062	.213	.264	.354	-.305	-16.6	90-C	-1
2002	SYR	INT	20	45	10	4	0	1	3	14	0	0	.222	.271	.378	-.164	.200	.250	.356	-.338	-2.7		
2003	NHV	EAS	21	369	104	27	0	20	45	83	0	0	.282	.372	.518	.254	.240	.317	.453	-.049	14.1	96-C	2
2004	*TOR*	*AL*	*22*	*284*	*65*	*14*	*1*	*11*	*24*	*65*	*1*	*1*	*.227*	*.294*	*.398*	*-.138*	*.224*	*.294*	*.395*	*-.172*	*1.9*	*77-C*	*-6*

Breakout: 20%   *Improve: 41%*   *Collapse: 25%*

One of the things about signing Latin talent young is that you don't know what you'll get. Some people had written off Quiroz, years early considering his youth. Now, after two years of dramatic improvement at the plate, he's one of the best catching prospects in the game. The advantage of having the Myers-Cash arrangement in the big leagues ahead of him is that he'll get the time to consolidate his gains from the last two years. It's easy to get fired up and think "Lance Parrish": Quiroz has one of the best arms in the game, handles pitchers well, and while he won't match Joe Mauer's all-around potential, he has the 30-homer potential Mauer may never develop.

DOMINIC RICH   2B   Bats: L   Throws: R   Born: 22-Aug-79   Age: 24

YEAR	TM	LG	AGE	AB	H	2B	3B	HR	BB	SO	SB	CS	AVG	OBP	SLG	MLVR	EQBA	EQOBP	EQSLG	EQMLVR	VORP	DEFENSE	
2001	CWV	SAL	21	327	91	16	1	4	47	54	20	8	.278	.382	.370	.137	.213	.293	.288	-.338	-18.4	75-2B	-16
2002	DUN	FLA	22	377	130	14	5	8	57	49	8	6	.345	.437	.472	.335	.264	.339	.370	-.104	8.7	93-2B	9
2002	TEN	SOU	22	132	36	4	1	1	18	23	2	4	.273	.364	.341	.001	.231	.302	.291	-.306	-5.4	18-2B	-5
2003	NHV	EAS	23	390	101	22	2	3	30	48	1	4	.259	.326	.349	-.067	.231	.284	.320	-.302	-14.6	100-2B	4
2004	*TOR*	*AL*	*24*	*188*	*48*	*9*	*1*	*3*	*16*	*28*	*2*	*1*	*.253*	*.320*	*.364*	*-.120*	*.250*	*.320*	*.361*	*-.154*	*2.9*	*53-2B*	*-1*

Breakout: 43%   *Improve: 60%*   *Collapse: 22%*

Briefly bandied about as a prospect of note after he won the Florida State League batting title in 2002, Rich might eventually drift into the majors. Will he belong? He hangs tough on the deuce, and has solid range, but an action figure physique generally irks scouting-oriented mindsets. More importantly he's never really showed much power and he's only moderately patient. On the excuses front, he was apparently banged up in '01 and '03, but that sort of goes with the territory of being a second baseman.

ALEXIS RIOS   CF   Bats: R   Throws: R   Born: 18-Feb-81   Age: 23

YEAR	TM	LG	AGE	AB	H	2B	3B	HR	BB	SO	SB	CS	AVG	OBP	SLG	MLVR	EQBA	EQOBP	EQSLG	EQMLVR	VORP	DEFENSE			
2001	CWV	SAL	20	480	126	20	9	2	25	59	22	14	.263	.296	.354	-.015	.217	.249	.300	-.408	-52.3	97-RF	-8	24-CF	-3
2002	DUN	FLA	21	456	139	22	8	3	27	55	14	8	.305	.344	.408	.098	.254	.285	.347	-.247	-24.8	88-RF	-7	22-CF	-1
2003	NHV	EAS	22	514	181	32	11	11	39	85	11	3	.352	.402	.521	.377	.301	.346	.463	.071	33.1	120-CF	-12		
2004	*TOR*	*AL*	*23*	*322*	*86*	*18*	*3*	*7*	*20*	*52*	*5*	*2*	*.267*	*.314*	*.409*	*-.061*	*.264*	*.314*	*.406*	*-.095*	*4.1*	*85-CF*	*-9*		

Breakout: 15%   *Improve: 39%*   *Collapse: 33%*

An important distinction between plate discipline in theory and in practice is that you can get hung up on certain results without seeing what has actually worked out. Rios isn't a big walker, but he took to the organization's philosophy of learning to identify your pitch and whack it, and saw his numbers spike while making the jump to Double-A. Is he walking enough? Perhaps not, and perhaps not yet, but the positive reinforcement that success and coaching can provide have to be factored in somehow. Rios is a giant from the Dave Winfield mold, with an arm to match. The problem is that people see the size and talk about Juan Gonzalez; at 23, Gonzo had a couple of hundred big league games under his belt, and he was already hitting for power. That said, Rios was showing considerably more power in winter ball. Although the numbers don't reflect it, Rios is considered a plus glove in center, to the point that if Wells gets bigger, it might be Wells who goes to right.

JORGE SEQUEA   2B/SS   Bats: R   Throws: R   Born: 01-Oct-80   Age: 23

YEAR	TM	LG	AGE	AB	H	2B	3B	HR	BB	SO	SB	CS	AVG	OBP	SLG	MLVR	EQBA	EQOBP	EQSLG	EQMLVR	VORP		DEFENSE			
2001	LAK	FLA	20	328	81	16	1	6	32	47	9	7	.247	.318	.357	-.034	.203	.259	.304	-.390	-22.5	57-2B	4	31-SS	-9
2002	ERI	EAS	21	397	106	24	3	5	41	79	13	2	.267	.343	.380	-.018	.228	.292	.330	-.274	-12.3	89-2B	9		
2003	NHV	EAS	22	111	38	7	0	2	11	21	0	4	.342	.400	.459	.274	.286	.342	.402	-.037	5.5	11-SS	-4	11-2B	1
2003	SYR	INT	22	271	69	15	4	3	30	45	7	5	.255	.341	.373	-.018	.237	.319	.354	-.183	-0.6	50-2B	-9	10-SS	0
2004	*TOR*	*AL*	*23*	*225*	*55*	*11*	*1*	*4*	*20*	*39*	*4*	*2*	*.243*	*.314*	*.360*	*-.142*	*.239*	*.314*	*.358*	*-.175*	*2.8*	*63-2B*	*-5*		
Breakout: 29%		*Improve: 52%*			*Collapse: 29%*																				

Swiped from the Tigers in the minor league portion of the Rule 5 draft; predation on the weak and the sick is like that. A full year in Triple-A as the SkyChiefs' second baseman should prep him to be Dave Berg's replacement in a utility role where he actually gets some playing time, instead of rotting away, Stapleton-like, at the end of the bench.

VERNON WELLS   CF   Bats: R   Throws: R   Born: 08-Dec-78   Age: 25

YEAR	TM	LG	AGE	AB	H	2B	3B	HR	BB	SO	SB	CS	AVG	OBP	SLG	MLVR	EQBA	EQOBP	EQSLG	EQMLVR	VORP		DEFENSE			
2001	SYR	INT	22	413	116	27	4	12	29	68	15	11	.281	.333	.453	.080	.257	.310	.423	-.089	7.0	94-CF	-3		
2001	TOR	AL	22	96	30	8	0	1	5	15	5	0	.313	.350	.427	.059	.323	.367	.448	.107	6.1	27-CF	-3		
2002	TOR	AL	23	608	167	34	4	23	27	85	9	4	.275	.305	.457	.006	.289	.323	.485	.052	30.2	138-CF	1	12-RF	0
2003	TOR	AL	24	678	215	49	5	33	42	80	4	1	.317	.359	.550	.234	.330	.377	.578	.322	61.0	159-CF	0		
2004	*TOR*	*AL*	*25*	*611*	*180*	*39*	*4*	*27*	*43*	*80*	*8*	*3*	*.295*	*.344*	*.506*	*.139*	*.291*	*.345*	*.502*	*.109*	*32.8*	*156-CF*	*0*		
Breakout: 12%		*Improve: 42%*			*Collapse: 18%*																				

A terrific ballplayer, Wells gives the Jays a second identifiable star in the lineup beyond Delgado. Beyond a slow start in April and a tough July when he didn't have many people to drive in while still hitting, there really wasn't a wart on his breakout season. Don't let yourself fall into the temptation to compare him to Garret Anderson as a hitter who can hit without being overly patient: Wells is better. Not just because he's more patient, but because of his power and center-field defense. While you can expect his average to bounce around, the power will be a constant. He's filling out with age, which gets exaggerated by an organizational reluctance to run, but on a practical level, it might mean a move to an outfield corner in another year or two.

JAYSON WERTH   OF   Bats: R   Throws: R   Born: 20-May-79   Age: 25

YEAR	TM	LG	AGE	AB	H	2B	3B	HR	BB	SO	SB	CS	AVG	OBP	SLG	MLVR	EQBA	EQOBP	EQSLG	EQMLVR	VORP		DEFENSE			
2001	DUN	FLA	22	70	14	3	0	2	17	19	1	1	.200	.356	.329	-.043	.149	.267	.257	-.461	-8.3				
2001	TEN	SOU	22	369	105	23	1	18	63	93	12	3	.285	.387	.499	.224	.227	.318	.406	-.121	6.3	45-C	4	25-1B	-3
2002	SYR	INT	23	443	114	25	2	18	67	125	24	7	.257	.354	.445	.083	.229	.327	.405	-.104	-6.8	93-LF	0	21-C	-7
2002	TOR	AL	23	46	12	2	1	0	6	11	1	0	.261	.340	.348	-.090	.283	.365	.370	-.041	0.3	10-RF	1		
2003	DUN	FLA	24	62	23	5	0	4	3	14	1	0	.371	.388	.645	.621	.312	.343	.562	.223	5.5	12-RF	-1		
2003	SYR	INT	24	236	56	19	1	9	15	68	11	1	.237	.285	.441	-.034	.224	.277	.422	-.178	-2.2	33-CF	-1	16-RF	0
2003	TOR	AL	24	48	10	4	0	2	3	22	1	0	.208	.255	.417	-.218	.229	.275	.438	-.155	-1.6	14-RF	-1		
2004	*TOR*	*AL*	*25*	*269*	*71*	*16*	*1*	*13*	*27*	*68*	*8*	*2*	*.265*	*.333*	*.482*	*.063*	*.261*	*.334*	*.478*	*.033*	*12.3*	*73-RF*	*1*		
Breakout: 50%		*Improve: 74%*			*Collapse: 14%*																				

Setting aside the tools of ignorance, Werth has proven athletic enough to handle the outfield. Originally, the Jays moved him out from behind the plate because of anecdotal evidence that big men can't last at catcher; at 6'5", Werth would have been the biggest catcher around since Sandy Alomar Jr. and Andy Allanson. Now, whether or not Werth would have broken down is speculative, but as a corner outfielder, there's concern that he might flash some power, some speed, and not enough overall to actually help out as a regular.

TOM WILSON   C   Bats: R   Throws: R   Born: 19-Dec-70   Age: 33

YEAR	TM	LG	AGE	AB	H	2B	3B	HR	BB	SO	SB	CS	AVG	OBP	SLG	MLVR	EQBA	EQOBP	EQSLG	EQMLVR	VORP		DEFENSE
2001	SAC	PCL	30	259	73	15	1	8	49	62	0	1	.282	.394	.440	.113	.244	.356	.382	-.069	8.6	46-C	-7
2002	TOR	AL	31	265	68	10	0	8	28	79	0	0	.257	.334	.385	-.054	.274	.355	.414	-.006	11.7	53-C	-8
2003	TOR	AL	32	256	66	19	0	5	28	80	0	0	.258	.331	.391	-.083	.270	.346	.414	-.025	4.4	62-C	-7
2004	*SDP*	*NL*	*33*	*203*	*48*	*10*	*1*	*5*	*28*	*62*	*1*	*0*	*.237*	*.335*	*.365*	*-.116*	*.243*	*.340*	*.384*	*-.092*	*5.1*	*59-C*	*-6*
Breakout: 25%		*Improve: 56%*			*Collapse: 23%*																		

Wilson spent years knocking around the minors, but he was ready to play in the big leagues by '95 or '96. Finally given a chance to share a catching job, he showed decent power and he reached base well enough, but the reservations about his defense were appropriate. It's nice to finally break in and get appreciated for what you can do, but fungibility is a bitch if you're the fungi.

CHRIS WOODWARD — SS — Bats: R — Throws: R — Born: 27-Jun-76 — Age: 28

YEAR	TM	LG	AGE	AB	H	2B	3B	HR	BB	SO	SB	CS	AVG	OBP	SLG	MLVR	EQBA	EQOBP	EQSLG	EQMLVR	VORP	DEFENSE		
2001	SYR	INT	25	193	59	14	3	11	16	40	0	0	.306	.360	.580	.314	.277	.334	.533	.127	17.5	21-3B	2	12-SS -2
2001	TOR	AL	25	63	12	3	2	2	0	14	0	1	.190	.190	.397	-.358	.206	.206	.429	-.314	-2.1	13-2B	1	
2002	TOR	AL	26	312	86	13	4	13	26	72	3	0	.276	.330	.468	.062	.293	.354	.500	.130	26.9	79-SS	1	
2003	TOR	AL	27	349	91	22	2	7	28	72	1	2	.261	.316	.395	-.101	.275	.335	.418	-.036	6.6	100-SS	-3	
2004	TOR	AL	28	382	100	22	3	13	32	77	3	2	.261	.320	.430	-.028	.257	.321	.427	-.060	16.4	101-SS	-2	

Breakout: 13%   Improve: 37%   Collapse: 34%

Even though he's not going to slug .468 over a full season, Woodward is a perfectly handy placeholder until the organization generates a replacement. He effectively managed to lose his job to Mike Bordick in-season by annoying the powers that be with lapses afield and at the plate, but they seem ready to forgive and see if he can hold the job for another year, or at least until Adams is ready to push him aside. Newly-signed Chris Gomez may steal some time if Woodward struggles.

PITCHERS

JASON ARNOLD — Bats: R — Throws: R — Born: 02-May-79 — Age: 25

YEAR	TM	LG	AGE	G	GS	IP	H	BB	SO	HR	ERA	EQERA	EQH9	EQBB9	EQSO9	EQHR9	PERA	VORP	STF
2001	STA	NYP	22	10	10	66.0	35	15	74	2	1.50	3.21	8.4	3.2	5.8	1.0	4.23	14.9	17
2002	TAM	FLA	23	13	13	80.0	64	22	83	2	2.48	4.11	9.2	3.1	6.3	0.5	4.10	12.0	27
2002	NRW	EAS	23	3	3	17.3	17	5	18	1	4.16	6.19	10.1	2.8	6.8	1.1	5.09	-1.0	11
2002	MID	TEX	23	10	10	58.0	42	24	53	2	2.33	3.69	7.2	4.4	6.0	0.7	3.74	11.4	21
2003	NHV	EAS	24	6	6	35.3	18	11	33	2	1.53	2.23	5.3	3.3	6.7	1.1	2.99	12.1	21
2003	SYR	INT	24	21	20	120.7	121	46	82	16	4.32	5.48	9.5	4.3	4.9	1.9	6.08	1.5	-22
2004	TOR	AL	25	20	15	87.3	96	38	58	13	5.36	5.09	9.5	3.7	5.9	1.1	4.97	7.6	1

Breakout: 14%   Improve: 47%   Collapse: 26%

Arnold's name has been kicked around on prospect lists, but that's what happens when all the smart kids want to play with you. He did little in 2003 to help himself: He lost velocity, and while he was probably smart enough to fool minor league hitters up through Double-A, he apparently had real problems with hitters who'd had any big league exposure. He's good enough to be a fourth starter, but more than that was expected when he was acquired. He should challenge for a job during the summer, but if he fails to do so, he'll be swamped by the wave of young pitching surging through the system.

JOSHUA BANKS — Bats: R — Throws: R — Born: 18-Jul-82 — Age: 21

YEAR	TM	LG	AGE	G	GS	IP	H	BB	SO	HR	ERA	EQERA	EQH9	EQBB9	EQSO9	EQHR9	PERA	VORP	STF
2003	AUB	NYP	20	15	15	66.7	58	10	81	1	2.43	5.34	11.6	2.0	6.4	0.6	5.03	1.7	26

The most dominant pitcher on a dominant Auburn staff, Banks was a steal in the second round of the '03 draft. Relying on a low-90s fastball and great splitter, how quickly he moves up will depend on how well his change and other breaking pitches come along.

DAVID BUSH — Bats: R — Throws: R — Born: 09-Nov-79 — Age: 24

YEAR	TM	LG	AGE	G	GS	IP	H	BB	SO	HR	ERA	EQERA	EQH9	EQBB9	EQSO9	EQHR9	PERA	VORP	STF
2002	AUB	NYP	22	18	0	22.3	13	7	39	1	2.83	5.00	11.0	4.5	9.5	1.5	6.30	1.2	0
2002	DUN	FLA	22	7	0	13.3	10	2	9	1	2.03	3.00	8.2	1.5	4.5	1.5	4.27	3.5	-6
2003	DUN	FLA	23	14	14	77.0	64	9	75	6	2.81	5.00	11.1	1.4	6.2	2.4	6.69	4.4	-19
2003	NHV	EAS	23	14	14	81.0	73	19	73	4	2.78	3.82	8.8	2.5	6.3	0.8	4.11	14.9	24
2004	TOR	AL	24	21	13	79.7	87	22	57	13	4.82	4.57	9.4	2.4	6.4	1.2	4.51	12.0	7

Breakout: 19%   Improve: 47%   Collapse: 24%

A college closer turned starter picked out of Wake Forest in '02. After suffering from blood clots in his leg, Bush dropped into the second round, pleasing the Jays to no end. He was supposed to only be a two-pitch pitcher, but he's exceptionally efficient with his pitches, has yet to struggle, and he's picked up a change and improved his command of his darting slider with the repetition that comes from starting. He's also favored for his confidence and poise. A keeper.

GUSTAVO CHACIN
Bats: L **Throws: L** Born: 04-Dec-80 Age: 23

YEAR	TM	LG	AGE	G	GS	IP	H	BB	SO	HR	ERA	EQERA	EQH9	EQBB9	EQSO9	EQHR9	PERA	VORP	STF
2001	TEN	SOU	20	25	23	140.3	138	39	86	17	3.98	5.95	10.1	2.9	4.1	1.5	5.62	-5.0	1
2002	TEN	SOU	21	35	13	119.7	131	59	68	12	4.66	6.87	10.7	4.6	3.8	1.7	6.56	-15.7	-24
2003	NHV	EAS	22	46	2	69.3	78	29	55	1	4.16	5.85	10.6	4.5	5.6	0.3	4.87	-1.8	6
2004	*TOR*	*AL*	*23*	*10*	*6*	*30.7*	*38*	*17*	*18*	*5*	*6.33*	*6.01*	*10.7*	*4.7*	*5.1*	*1.3*	*6.08*	*1.0*	*-15*

Breakout: 25%   Improve: 55%   Collapse: 24%

If you're a reflexive believer in the concept that pitchers really only control walks, strikeouts, and home runs allowed, you might jump to the conclusion that Chacin is someone you want. If you talk to scouts or even a few analytically-minded types who have seen him, you'll find that everyone thinks he's just plain-old hittable. He doesn't own lefties, and he's a bit of a flyball pitcher. None of that adds up to a guy who's ready to be a good high-leverage lefty in the pen, though he could improve.

VINNY CHULK
Bats: R **Throws: R** Born: 19-Dec-78 Age: 25

YEAR	TM	LG	AGE	G	GS	IP	H	BB	SO	HR	ERA	EQERA	EQH9	EQBB9	EQSO9	EQHR9	PERA	VORP	STF
2001	DUN	FLA	22	16	1	34.7	38	13	50	2	3.11	5.58	13.2	4.1	8.8	1.2	6.83	0.1	9
2001	TEN	SOU	22	24	1	43.0	34	8	43	5	3.14	4.26	9.7	2.1	6.4	1.7	5.30	5.7	-1
2002	TEN	SOU	23	25	24	152.0	133	53	108	12	2.96	4.40	9.2	3.4	4.6	1.4	5.19	18.5	-5
2003	SYR	INT	24	23	21	119.3	118	46	90	14	4.22	5.45	9.4	4.3	5.4	1.6	5.78	1.8	-15
2003	TOR	AL	24	3	0	5.3	6	3	2	0	5.09	5.06	10.1	5.1	3.4	0.0	4.60	0.6	-1
2004	*TOR*	*AL*	*25*	*17*	*12*	*72.0*	*81*	*30*	*45*	*11*	*5.29*	*5.02*	*9.7*	*3.5*	*5.6*	*1.1*	*5.00*	*6.5*	*-1*

Breakout: 23%   Improve: 58%   Collapse: 18%

Chulk is a strike-thrower without really good stuff. He missed some time with a spur in his elbow, but it didn't require surgery in-season. His clock is ticking: With the wave of talent coming up behind him, he's probably the good arm most in danger of being swamped. He might hang on as a utility pitcher, and if the Jays suffer another wave of injuries as debilitating as those they endured in '02, he might get a shot at the rotation.

KELVIM ESCOBAR
Bats: R **Throws: R** Born: 11-Apr-76 Age: 28

YEAR	TM	LG	AGE	G	GS	IP	H	BB	SO	HR	ERA	EQERA	EQH9	EQBB9	EQSO9	EQHR9	PERA	VORP	STF
2001	TOR	AL	25	59	11	126.0	93	52	121	8	3.50	3.06	6.3	3.4	8.0	0.5	2.87	34.9	31
2002	TOR	AL	26	76	0	78.0	75	44	85	10	4.27	4.32	8.4	4.6	9.2	1.1	4.66	11.0	9
2003	TOR	AL	27	41	26	180.3	189	78	159	15	4.29	4.14	8.8	3.6	7.7	0.7	4.19	27.8	23
2004	*ANA*	*AL*	*28*	*33*	*22*	*130.3*	*122*	*53*	*104*	*12*	*3.92*	*4.18*	*8.3*	*3.5*	*6.9*	*0.8*	*4.20*	*22.4*	*10*

Breakout: 12%   Improve: 39%   Collapse: 29%

Take a good look at Escobar's career numbers some time. It's an instructive exercise. Fans like you and me have been taking it for granted for the last six or seven years that the Jays have had this great pitcher on their hands, only they never know quite what to do with him. But after seven years, he has a career ERA of 4.58, and he's allowed a hit per inning over his career and in every year of his career save 2001. In his single full season as a closer (2002), he threw tantrums over the suggestion that he could come into games in the 8th, and he wasn't all that special besides. For all of the expectations... no, for all of the assumptions that Escobar was a good pitcher, it's as if there's a continent-wide blind spot where he's concerned. The Angels demonstrated how big that blind spot has gotten, rewarding Escobar with more than $18 million over three years. It's not unreasonable to believe that, finally plugged into a single role and working for Mike Scioscia, he'll be fine, but the Angels can't afford him to be anything else, and it isn't something he's achieved to date.

BOB FILE
Bats: R **Throws: R** Born: 28-Jan-77 Age: 27

YEAR	TM	LG	AGE	G	GS	IP	H	BB	SO	HR	ERA	EQERA	EQH9	EQBB9	EQSO9	EQHR9	PERA	VORP	STF
2001	TOR	AL	24	60	0	74.3	57	29	38	6	3.27	3.10	6.3	3.2	4.2	0.6	2.99	20.2	5
2002	SYR	INT	25	33	0	36.3	39	15	23	2	5.95	6.42	10.4	4.5	4.8	0.8	5.39	-3.1	-25
2003	SYR	INT	26	11	0	10.7	10	2	7	0	4.21	3.60	9.0	1.8	4.5	0.0	3.19	2.2	13
2004	*TOR*	*AL*	*27*	*25*	*1*	*32.0*	*38*	*11*	*16*	*5*	*5.21*	*4.94*	*10.1*	*2.9*	*4.4*	*1.1*	*4.98*	*3.7*	*-15*

Breakout: 31%   Improve: 55%   Collapse: 22%

After missing much of the last two years to a surgery to reshape his collarbone, File will probably get reacquainted with his craft in Syracuse It helps that he has an option, and that they don't have to push him into action after picking up Justin Speier, Terry Adams, and Kerry Ligtenberg.

ROY HALLADAY

			Bats: R			**Throws: R**								**Born: 14-May-77**			**Age: 27**		

YEAR	TM	LG	AGE	G	GS	IP	H	BB	SO	HR	ERA	EQERA	EQH9	EQBB9	EQSO9	EQHR9	PERA	VORP	STF
2001	DUN	FLA	24	13	0	22.7	28	3	15	1	3.96	6.20	13.7	1.3	4.0	0.9	6.14	-1.4	-22
2001	TEN	SOU	24	5	5	34.0	25	6	29	2	2.12	3.30	9.0	1.8	5.4	0.9	4.06	7.7	16
2001	TOR	AL	24	17	16	105.3	97	25	96	3	3.16	3.06	7.9	2.0	7.6	0.3	2.94	29.1	53
2002	TOR	AL	25	34	34	239.3	223	62	168	10	2.93	3.13	8.1	2.2	6.1	0.3	3.18	63.9	36
2003	TOR	AL	26	36	36	266.0	253	32	204	26	3.25	3.13	7.9	1.0	6.7	0.8	3.13	67.7	33
2004	TOR	AL	27	32	32	223.7	238	44	154	22	3.91	3.71	9.2	1.7	6.1	0.7	3.60	48.5	18

Breakout: 5%   Improve: 30%   Collapse: 10%

Ah, the Great One, how sweet it is. There are few things tastier than an ace starter who knows it and acts like it. Not that he's Charles Barkley, but you're probably as tired of the GMC stock speech as anyone ("I'd like to thank God, Mom, and my Country. No, Rory, I don't often cry. Really, I don't.") Among big league starters, only Esteban Loaiza and Tim Hudson topped Halladay's 26 quality starts, although Toronto's weak pen helped flip five of those games into non-quality starts after the sixth. Halladay likes to pitch on short rest, and while it's not enough to make the Jays go to a four-man rotation, it's enough to have everyone else shuffle around Halladay taking his turn. It might seem greedy to consider Halladay has as good as a 30% shot of improving on last year, but he's the homegrown horse this team hasn't had since Pat Hentgen, and before that, Dave Stieb. Getting him signed up to a multi-year deal far outstrips re-inking Delgado as organizational priorities go.

D. J. HANSON

			Bats: R			**Throws: R**								**Born: 07-Aug-80**			**Age: 23**		

YEAR	TM	LG	AGE	G	GS	IP	H	BB	SO	HR	ERA	EQERA	EQH9	EQBB9	EQSO9	EQHR9	PERA	VORP	STF
2002	AUB	NYP	21	9	9	48.3	35	11	51	4	1.68	4.54	11.6	3.4	5.7	2.9	8.17	4.7	-30
2003	CWV	SAL	22	25	25	138.3	110	56	113	4	2.54	4.96	9.4	5.0	4.5	0.7	4.98	8.7	1
2004	TOR	AL	23	20	12	65.3	80	38	39	13	6.69	6.35	10.6	4.9	5.3	1.5	6.42	0.1	-16

Breakout: 32%   Improve: 63%   Collapse: 12%

A short pitcher with command who pre-dates the Ricciardi gang, Hanson is a former high school pick who has lost considerable time to multiple knee injuries. He finally logged his first full season since being drafted in '99 last year, the knee held up, and he improved dramatically as the season bounced along. He's got a nice curve and decent velocity, so if he can repeat the exercise in Dunedin, he'll merit a lot more attention.

JESSE HARPER

			Bats: R			**Throws: R**								**Born: 11-Nov-80**			**Age: 23**		

YEAR	TM	LG	AGE	G	GS	IP	H	BB	SO	HR	ERA	EQERA	EQH9	EQBB9	EQSO9	EQHR9	PERA	VORP	STF
2001	AUB	NYP	20	14	14	67.7	79	20	58	3	4.79	7.84	13.1	3.9	4.4	1.4	7.08	-14.9	-14
2002	CWV	SAL	21	21	14	112.7	98	25	97	4	2.16	4.57	10.0	2.7	4.7	0.8	4.68	11.5	12
2003	DUN	FLA	22	26	24	131.0	112	31	100	4	2.54	4.76	9.7	2.8	4.8	0.9	4.68	10.9	7
2004	TOR	AL	23	20	13	71.7	89	30	36	12	6.01	5.70	10.7	3.5	4.5	1.3	5.66	3.7	-13

Breakout: 12%   Improve: 43%   Collapse: 26%

Harper was the anchor of a Dunedin rotation that was in a constant state of flux despite being playoff-bound. The Jays like his moxie, but he has trouble finishing hitters despite a four-pitch assortment. None of his pitches are top-shelf by themselves, although there's some speculation that his assortment might improve if he headed to the pen. Expectations might be a bit high after a nifty won-loss record and a gaudy Florida State League ERA, especially since it was enough to get him onto the 40-man.

MARK HENDRICKSON

			Bats: L			**Throws: L**								**Born: 23-Jun-74**			**Age: 30**		

YEAR	TM	LG	AGE	G	GS	IP	H	BB	SO	HR	ERA	EQERA	EQH9	EQBB9	EQSO9	EQHR9	PERA	VORP	STF
2001	SYR	INT	27	38	6	73.3	80	18	33	13	4.67	6.01	11.0	2.7	3.2	2.1	6.72	-3.1	-62
2002	SYR	INT	28	19	14	92.0	90	22	68	12	3.52	4.38	10.1	2.6	5.7	1.7	5.71	11.4	-19
2002	TOR	AL	28	16	4	36.7	25	12	21	1	2.45	2.27	5.8	2.8	5.0	0.3	2.30	13.2	22
2003	TOR	AL	29	30	30	158.3	207	40	76	24	5.51	5.47	10.8	2.1	4.2	1.2	5.37	-3.1	-10
2004	TBY	AL	30	27	23	133.7	158	44	59	16	5.04	5.02	10.2	2.8	3.9	1.1	5.05	11.0	-7

Breakout: 8%   Improve: 55%   Collapse: 11%

For want of alternatives and on the strength of a nice cup of coffee in '02, the former hoops star slipped into the rotation. Although Hendrickson took his turn every fifth day, it was a lot less than you might have wished for. He's not likely to make it as a lefty reliever, with no effective breaking pitch, no real movement on any of his offerings, and little sense of how or when to change speeds. He's the fifth starter for a bad team. Naturally, Piniella really wanted him, reminding you that sometimes, be careful what you wish for.

JASON KERSHNER Bats: L Throws: L Born: 19-Dec-76 Age: 27

YEAR	TM	LG	AGE	G	GS	IP	H	BB	SO	HR	ERA	EQERA	EQH9	EQBB9	EQSO9	EQHR9	PERA	VORP	STF
2001	REA	EAS	24	26	19	123.7	147	26	70	18	4.80	7.18	13.0	2.6	3.5	2.1	7.63	-19.4	-50
2002	POR	PCL	25	31	12	86.0	65	26	83	8	3.03	3.92	8.5	3.2	6.8	1.2	4.50	14.6	-1
2002	SDP	NL	25	15	0	18.7	15	10	11	2	5.78	4.91	6.9	3.9	4.4	1.0	3.79	1.4	-14
2002	TOR	AL	25	10	0	5.3	5	4	7	1	1.70	3.38	8.4	6.8	11.8	1.7	5.89	1.3	9
2003	SYR	INT	26	24	0	45.7	42	9	30	1	2.36	3.38	8.6	2.1	4.6	0.2	3.31	10.5	11
2003	TOR	AL	26	40	0	54.0	43	15	32	5	3.17	2.89	6.5	2.4	5.3	0.7	2.84	15.2	9
2004	*TOR*	*AL*	*27*	*28*	*7*	*53.7*	*60*	*19*	*31*	*8*	*5.14*	*4.88*	*9.7*	*3.0*	*5.2*	*1.2*	*4.89*	*6.1*	*-9*

Breakout: 22%   *Improve: 56%*   *Collapse: 25%*

Usually, a big league lefty reliever has to have some sort of functioning breaking pitch, but most big league lefty relievers are squeezed into situational roles that leave little margin for error. Kershner's a different type. He makes a living off a great change-up, and he gets to stick as a long reliever. On a staff with only one consistent starter, there's work for a guy like Kershner, but he'll have to earn his job with Valerio De Los Santos and Bruce Chen in camp.

BRANDON LEAGUE Bats: R Throws: R Born: 16-Mar-83 Age: 21

YEAR	TM	LG	AGE	G	GS	IP	H	BB	SO	HR	ERA	EQERA	EQH9	EQBB9	EQSO9	EQHR9	PERA	VORP	STF
2001	MED	PIO	18	9	9	38.7	36	11	38	3	4.65	5.24	11.0	3.7	4.7	1.6	6.29	1.4	2
2002	AUB	NYP	19	16	16	85.7	80	23	72	2	3.15	7.09	11.7	3.8	4.4	0.7	5.71	-12.2	7
2003	CWV	SAL	20	12	12	70.7	58	18	61	1	1.91	3.55	9.2	3.0	4.7	0.3	3.90	14.4	31
2003	DUN	FLA	20	13	12	66.3	76	20	34	3	4.75	7.95	11.9	3.5	3.3	1.2	6.23	-15.7	-11
2004	*TOR*	*AL*	*21*	*18*	*14*	*80.7*	*97*	*31*	*41*	*9*	*5.30*	*5.03*	*10.4*	*3.3*	*4.5*	*0.9*	*5.02*	*5.7*	*-5*

Breakout: 11%   *Improve: 62%*   *Collapse: 1%*

League's mid-90s sinker was enough to get him named the Sally League's best flamethrower in *Baseball America*'s tools poll; the problem is that he has no other effective pitch. If he gets a second pitch, he'll be a dominant reliever; a third pitch, and he'll be a good big league starter. All assuming he stays healthy. Odds are, none of this will happen. He'll still be coveted for his heat for the next few years.

CORY LIDLE Bats: R Throws: R Born: 22-Mar-72 Age: 32

YEAR	TM	LG	AGE	G	GS	IP	H	BB	SO	HR	ERA	EQERA	EQH9	EQBB9	EQSO9	EQHR9	PERA	VORP	STF
2001	OAK	AL	29	29	29	188.0	170	47	118	23	3.59	3.89	8.2	2.1	5.3	1.0	3.89	34.3	12
2002	OAK	AL	30	31	30	192.0	191	39	111	17	3.89	4.00	9.0	1.7	5.1	0.7	3.88	32.8	16
2003	TOR	AL	31	31	31	192.7	216	60	112	24	5.74	4.93	9.3	2.6	5.1	1.0	4.53	-1.8	3
2004	*CIN*	*NL*	*32*	*27*	*26*	*163*	*170*	*49*	*101*	*19*	*4.32*	*4.54*	*9.6*	*2.4*	*5.0*	*0.9*	*4.45*	*18.3*	*6*

Breakout: 16%   *Improve: 51%*   *Collapse: 16%*

Sometimes, it doesn't pay to repeat a stroke of genius. Apparently it was Ricciardi who insisted on getting Lidle away from Tampa, which made Lidle a wealthy man. The last year of his contract was more expensive than Beane wanted to keep, so he was exported to Oakland North. Although Lidle pitched into some bad luck, he still took a major step backwards. He didn't produce a quality start half the time out, and at times he seemed to give in, especially with his splitter. A bad defense, small ballpark, and a bunch of right-handed power hitters in the division aren't going to help him much in Cincinnati.

AQUILINO LOPEZ Bats: R Throws: R Born: 21-Apr-75 Age: 29

YEAR	TM	LG	AGE	G	GS	IP	H	BB	SO	HR	ERA	EQERA	EQH9	EQBB9	EQSO9	EQHR9	PERA	VORP	STF
2001	SAN	TEX	26	42	0	62.7	48	25	79	4	3.01	4.13	8.7	4.4	8.1	1.1	4.86	9.3	-10
2002	TAC	PCL	27	34	11	109.3	89	27	103	6	2.39	3.18	8.0	2.6	6.4	0.7	3.61	27.4	12
2003	TOR	AL	28	72	0	73.7	58	34	64	5	3.42	3.22	6.6	3.8	7.6	0.5	3.11	18.5	21
2004	*TOR*	*AL*	*29*	*48*	*5*	*72.0*	*70*	*30*	*60*	*8*	*4.41*	*4.18*	*8.4*	*3.6*	*7.4*	*0.8*	*4.14*	*13.7*	*5*

Breakout: 31%   *Improve: 50%*   *Collapse: 27%*

When AgeGate put him closer to celebrating his 30th birthday, it spelled the end of Lopez's prospect status in some minds. For the Jays, he was an instant quality add-on through the Rule 5 draft. Lopez has great lateral movement on his slider, which he throws out of a delivery that leaves his shoulder way out in front, as if the pitch was pulling him off of the mound. It makes it almost impossible for a right-handed hitter to pick him up, but it makes some wonder how long he'll last. What can you say? Pitchers are flammable, and they can give you gas. In the end, Lopez was a great pickup, and as long as he's healthy, he'll be an asset.

DUSTIN McGOWAN

Bats: R   Throws: R   Born: 24-Mar-82   Age: 22

YEAR	TM	LG	AGE	G	GS	IP	H	BB	SO	HR	ERA	EQERA	EQH9	EQBB9	EQSO9	EQHR9	PERA	VORP	STF
2001	AUB	NYP	19	15	14	67.0	57	49	80	1	3.76	6.79	10.1	10.1	6.3	0.5	6.28	-7.5	10
2002	CWV	SAL	20	28	28	148.3	143	59	163	10	4.19	6.63	12.0	5.1	6.1	1.6	7.12	-14.6	0
2003	DUN	FLA	21	14	14	75.7	62	25	66	1	2.85	5.16	9.1	3.8	5.4	0.4	4.19	3.3	24
2003	NHV	EAS	21	14	14	76.7	78	19	72	1	3.17	4.21	9.3	2.6	6.8	0.2	3.74	11.2	45
2004	TOR	AL	22	18	13	70.0	80	37	51	10	5.64	5.35	9.9	4.5	6.5	1.1	5.44	4.4	-1

Breakout: 11%   Improve: 46%   Collapse: 28%

For some, the best pitcher above A-ball, and the one most likely to make an impact as a rookie this side of Edwin Jackson. The fate of Scott Elarton and TINSTAAPP theory should check anyone's enthusiasm, but let's face it, he's the sort of pitcher we're all supposed to get excited about. McGowan burns hitters with high-90s heat, a plus slider, and an improved change, showing particular touch setting up the change. Despite allowing only two home runs in 152.1 innings last year, he is not a groundball pitcher. He simply dominated his opposition; at higher levels, you can expect his home run rate to rise, but not so much that it affects his prospect status.

TREVER MILLER

Bats: R   Throws: L   Born: 29-May-73   Age: 31

YEAR	TM	LG	AGE	G	GS	IP	H	BB	SO	HR	ERA	EQERA	EQH9	EQBB9	EQSO9	EQHR9	PERA	VORP	STF
2001	PAW	INT	28	33	15	116.0	142	34	93	16	5.20	6.31	11.9	3.1	5.6	1.7	6.72	-8.5	-36
2002	LOU	INT	29	65	1	82.0	76	23	80	6	3.18	3.99	9.0	2.9	7.3	0.9	4.41	13.7	0
2003	TOR	AL	30	79	0	52.7	46	28	44	7	4.61	4.15	7.3	4.5	7.3	1.0	4.15	5.7	-1
2004	TBY	AL	31	42	2	55.7	55	23	44	6	4.48	4.45	8.5	3.6	7.1	1.0	4.41	8.7	1

Breakout: 29%   Improve: 56%   Collapse: 22%

Was it a successful year? Miller did stay up all season, and he did accrue service time. But as a lefty situational artist, he managed to give up six bombs to lefties, and may be best suited to pitching exclusively from the stretch. He's on the Jamie Walker career path, not quite the walk of the damned, but trying to make a living as a non-contender's situational lefty—especially after earning a guaranteed contract as part of a mini-exodus of Jays headed to Tampa.

JUSTIN MILLER

Bats: R   Throws: R   Born: 27-Aug-77   Age: 26

YEAR	TM	LG	AGE	G	GS	IP	H	BB	SO	HR	ERA	EQERA	EQH9	EQBB9	EQSO9	EQHR9	PERA	VORP	STF
2001	SAC	PCL	23	29	28	165.0	174	64	134	26	4.75	5.55	9.2	4.1	5.5	1.5	5.51	0.9	-5
2002	SYR	INT	24	8	8	44.7	34	16	29	0	1.61	2.83	7.4	3.9	5.0	0.2	3.28	12.7	26
2002	TOR	AL	24	25	18	102.3	103	66	68	12	5.54	5.27	8.7	5.3	5.6	0.9	4.88	3.7	2
2004	TOR	AL	26	23	16	91.0	105	46	56	13	5.79	5.50	10.0	4.3	5.5	1.0	5.44	4.6	-6

Breakout: 14%   Improve: 43%   Collapse: 27%

Another Oakland refugee from the player development program Ricciardi helped build, Miller is a contender for the fifth starter's job if and when he's ready. That may not be in time for camp, since he'll be rehabbing from shoulder surgery performed last May. Will he still have the big sinker when he's back? They have to wait and see what hell have left on the table. Even then, he's going to have to show improved command.

SANDY NIN

Bats: R   Throws: R   Born: 13-Aug-80   Age: 23

YEAR	TM	LG	AGE	G	GS	IP	H	BB	SO	HR	ERA	EQERA	EQH9	EQBB9	EQSO9	EQHR9	PERA	VORP	STF
2002	AUB	NYP	21	17	11	74.0	61	11	61	3	2.92	5.71	11.3	2.1	4.3	1.4	5.85	-0.8	-11
2003	CWV	SAL	22	23	23	131.0	124	19	87	4	2.89	5.00	10.7	1.8	3.6	0.8	4.73	7.8	4
2003	NHV	EAS	22	1	1	7.0	5	0	9	1	2.57	2.84	8.5	0.0	9.9	2.8	5.40	1.9	26
2004	COL	NL	23	21	13	77.3	98	24	35	14	5.77	5.46	11.1	2.4	3.8	1.4	5.51	5.1	-13

Breakout: 5%   Improve: 43%   Collapse: 18%

A holdover from the Jays' once-unparalleled Dominican program, Nin has some decent velocity, and this past year he picked up a good changeup. As a holdover from one of their previous theoretical infatuations, the Rockies love quality change-ups, so they were happy to get Nin in the three-way Justin Speier deal.

VINCE PERKINS

Bats: L **Throws: R** Born: 27-Sep-81 Age: 22

YEAR	TM	LG	AGE	G	GS	IP	H	BB	SO	HR	ERA	EQERA	EQH9	EQBB9	EQSO9	EQHR9	PERA	VORP	STF
2001	AUB	NYP	19	14	14	52.3	41	37	67	1	3.27	6.09	9.7	9.7	6.7	0.6	6.18	-2.4	11
2002	AUB	NYP	20	15	15	72.7	51	44	85	3	3.34	6.67	10.2	8.9	6.5	1.4	6.97	-7.1	-6
2003	CWV	SAL	21	8	8	44.3	19	22	60	1	1.83	2.79	6.3	6.1	7.7	0.5	3.58	12.1	40
2003	DUN	FLA	21	18	17	84.3	58	53	69	1	2.46	5.40	7.7	7.3	5.2	0.4	4.47	1.7	11
2004	TOR	AL	22	19	10	46.7	74	40	23	7	9.50	9.01	13.7	7.3	4.3	1.2	8.93	-9.1	-36

Breakout: 14%   Improve: 49%   Collapse: 25%

A big Canadian hurler, Perkins throws hard, clocking consistently in the high 90s. However, he really gives hitters the willies with a wild power slider that he doesn't have much consistency with yet. Without it, he might end up a quality reliever, but the Jays can afford to see if he's going to pick up control and avoid injury for a couple of seasons. He's a notch below McGowan and Bush in Toronto's pitching prospect hierarchy, but playing third fiddle to two of the best minor league pitchers around is far from faint praise.

ADAM PETERSON

Bats: R **Throws: R** Born: 18-May-79 Age: 25

YEAR	TM	LG	AGE	G	GS	IP	H	BB	SO	HR	ERA	EQERA	EQH9	EQBB9	EQSO9	EQHR9	PERA	VORP	STF
2002	AUB	NYP	23	18	0	31.3	29	9	19	2	2.30	5.96	13.3	4.2	3.2	2.5	8.62	-1.0	-77
2003	CWV	SAL	24	10	0	24.7	15	13	19	1	2.19	4.22	8.0	6.3	4.2	1.3	5.30	3.3	-37
2003	DUN	FLA	24	9	0	12.7	5	0	13	1	0.71	1.69	6.8	0.8	6.8	2.5	4.43	4.6	-22
2003	NHV	EAS	24	24	0	24.0	24	7	24	1	4.88	5.32	10.2	3.3	7.0	0.8	4.93	0.7	-1
2004	TOR	AL	25	19	4	31.0	41	21	21	7	7.94	7.54	11.4	5.7	5.9	1.8	7.38	-3.5	-24

Breakout: 18%   Improve: 48%   Collapse: 27%

A secondary starter with a great fastball out of Wichita State, the Jays converted him to relief. As a result, he's a near-term big leaguer, in that if he stays healthy and gets hot, he could be up by the All-Star break. Beyond the heat, he mixes in a good slider, but shoulder trouble crimped his style at the start of '03; rehab instead of surgery has served well so far, but it's a cautionary note to keep in mind.

CLIFF POLITTE

Bats: R **Throws: R** Born: 27-Feb-74 Age: 30

YEAR	TM	LG	AGE	G	GS	IP	H	BB	SO	HR	ERA	EQERA	EQH9	EQBB9	EQSO9	EQHR9	PERA	VORP	STF
2001	PHI	NL	27	23	0	26.0	24	8	23	2	2.42	3.28	8.8	2.6	6.9	0.7	3.96	6.4	12
2002	PHI	NL	28	13	0	16.3	19	9	15	0	3.87	5.74	11.5	4.6	7.5	0.0	4.98	-0.2	15
2002	TOR	AL	28	55	0	57.3	38	19	57	5	3.61	2.73	5.8	2.7	8.5	0.6	2.57	17.9	30
2003	TOR	AL	29	54	0	49.3	52	17	40	11	5.66	4.96	8.6	2.9	7.0	1.7	5.00	1.5	-15
2004	CWS	AL	30	47	2	63.7	61	22	51	10	4.19	4.22	8.7	3.0	7.0	1.1	4.34	11.9	2

Breakout: 27%   Improve: 53%   Collapse: 17%

Last spring, roto-fired hearts and minds were aflutter, wondering if saves would agglomerate in Politte's private stats stash after he was bumped into the closer's role to replace Escobar. We'll spare you the full argument, and leave you with the proposition that the save is a bastard born of an agent and an accountant, with MLB's historical artifact, Jerome Holtzman, on hand as midwife. After a good month in the closer's role, Politte came apart. He's a bit tightly wound, and it'll be interesting to see if that works well or badly with a manager in Ozzie Guillen who, as a player, was known for his corrosive tendency to carp.

TANYON STURTZE

Bats: R **Throws: R** Born: 12-Oct-70 Age: 33

YEAR	TM	LG	AGE	G	GS	IP	H	BB	SO	HR	ERA	EQERA	EQH9	EQBB9	EQSO9	EQHR9	PERA	VORP	STF
2001	TBY	AL	30	39	27	195.3	200	79	110	23	4.42	4.10	8.8	3.3	4.7	0.9	4.45	31.8	0
2002	TBY	AL	31	33	33	224.0	271	89	137	33	5.18	5.33	10.5	3.3	5.3	1.2	5.50	6.6	-5
2003	TOR	AL	32	40	8	89.3	107	43	54	14	5.95	5.79	9.9	4.1	5.3	1.2	5.49	-6.0	-20
2004	LAD	NL	33	23	13	77.0	82	34	47	13	5.44	6.09	10.1	3.5	4.8	1.3	5.90	-0.7	-12

Breakout: 23%   Improve: 40%   Collapse: 41%

Familiar to Ricciardi from his time in the A's system in the early-to-mid 90s, Sturtze opened 2003 in the Jays' rotation. He lost his job to Escobar in May, but he had big guaranteed money coming, so they carried him along, handing him mop-up work. Then he was entrusted with a 7–3 lead against the Red Sox on July 9th; a win would keep the Jays within four games. It took Sturtze 13 pitches to put three runs on the board without getting anybody out, and the Jays lost the game. He barely pitched after that, and I doubt he got a Christmas card from Canada.

COREY THURMAN
Bats: R **Throws: R** Born: 05-Nov-78 Age: 25

YEAR	TM	LG	AGE	G	GS	IP	H	BB	SO	HR	ERA	EQERA	EQH9	EQBB9	EQSO9	EQHR9	PERA	VORP	STF
2001	WIC	TEX	22	25	25	155.0	117	65	148	16	3.37	4.81	8.4	4.7	6.2	1.6	5.35	12.3	4
2002	TOR	AL	23	43	1	68.0	65	45	56	11	4.37	4.54	8.3	5.3	7.0	1.3	5.17	7.9	4
2003	SYR	INT	24	17	16	86.3	90	26	72	8	4.28	5.04	10.0	3.4	5.9	1.2	5.31	5.0	0
2003	TOR	AL	24	6	3	15.3	21	9	11	3	6.47	6.46	11.2	4.7	6.5	1.8	6.80	-0.5	-18
2004	CIN	NL	25	26	13	80.7	82	37	61	12	4.78	5.03	9.3	3.6	6.1	1.1	5.16	5.8	-2

Breakout: 17%   Improve: 50%   Collapse: 24%

The former Rule 5 success story slipped off the roster last season, and was afterwards outrighted off the 40-man. At that point, he elected for free agency, and has since caught on with the Reds. It's an open question as to whether he's worth the roster spot. He has the decent velocity that got him picked in the first place, but has no movement or sink on his fastball. The Jays taught him a change-up and he's added a new cutter, but if you think that sounds more like the assortment of a middle reliever and spare guy than a nascent prospect, you're right.

JOSH TOWERS
Bats: R **Throws: R** Born: 26-Feb-77 Age: 27

YEAR	TM	LG	AGE	G	GS	IP	H	BB	SO	HR	ERA	EQERA	EQH9	EQBB9	EQSO9	EQHR9	PERA	VORP	STF
2001	ROC	INT	24	6	6	41.0	40	8	27	2	3.51	3.69	8.8	2.1	4.6	0.5	3.60	8.3	22
2001	BAL	AL	24	24	20	140.3	165	16	58	21	4.49	4.67	10.3	0.9	3.5	1.3	4.87	13.9	0
2002	ROC	INT	25	15	13	69.0	109	14	43	16	7.57	8.91	15.0	2.1	4.7	2.9	9.46	-23.8	-73
2002	BAL	AL	25	5	3	27.3	42	5	13	11	7.91	8.54	13.7	1.4	4.1	3.4	9.37	-8.6	-70
2003	SYR	INT	26	21	20	132.7	133	20	76	10	3.32	4.06	9.4	1.7	4.1	1.1	4.45	21.2	-3
2003	TOR	AL	26	14	8	64.3	67	7	42	15	4.48	4.26	8.5	0.9	5.7	1.8	4.57	9.5	-7
2004	TOR	AL	27	22	16	96.0	116	17	52	19	5.04	4.78	10.4	1.5	4.8	1.5	5.00	11.6	-1

Breakout: 18%   Improve: 53%   Collapse: 18%

The fifth starter with a bullet going into camp, if that's the sort of thing you can brag about. If he ever got 30 or more starts, Towers could give up home runs at a rate that would put Bert Blyleven on the Brian Kingman sympathy circuit, fearing for his 50-tater mark. Bert can rest easy; the Jays skip their fifth starter pretty regularly. Even then, Towers's stranglehold on the job will only last until either Justin Miller or Josh Arnold show something in Syracuse. He has the job because of his control and his burgling instincts at getting outs, but Towers is already at his ceiling.

PETE WALKER
Bats: R **Throws: R** Born: 08-Apr-69 Age: 35

YEAR	TM	LG	AGE	G	GS	IP	H	BB	SO	HR	ERA	EQERA	EQH9	EQBB9	EQSO9	EQHR9	PERA	VORP	STF
2001	NOR	INT	32	26	26	168.3	145	46	106	12	2.99	4.35	8.6	2.9	4.4	0.9	4.25	21.6	-2
2002	TOR	AL	33	37	20	139.3	143	51	80	18	4.33	4.29	8.8	3.0	5.0	1.1	4.49	19.8	-4
2003	TOR	AL	34	23	7	55.3	59	24	29	11	4.88	4.77	8.7	3.6	4.6	1.5	5.10	6.4	-24
2004	TOR	AL	35	28	10	63.0	77	25	35	12	5.81	5.51	10.5	3.4	4.9	1.4	5.67	3.1	-14

Breakout: 16%   Improve: 48%   Collapse: 28%

A former prospect with almost as many scars as joints, Walker has managed to hang on long enough to get a wee bit of service time, showing a bit of learning along the way. He has one of the best pickoff moves to second base you'll see, for example. Really nothing more than an 11th pitcher, he can slip into a rotation that's plagued with injuries. He accepted a minor league deal with the Jays.

Thou Shalt Not Steal: Catchers and the Running Game

by Keith Woolner

How much does a good defensive catcher contribute to his team? That is a question that has long intrigued baseball analysts. Indeed, measuring the catcher's role in run prevention was #3 on the list of 21 Sabermetric "Hilbert" problems published in *Baseball Prospectus 2000*.

The primary defensive responsibilities of the catcher break down into four categories:

1. Catching pitches (preventing wild pitches/passed balls)

2. Fielding (handling pop-ups, fielding bunts, receiving throws to put out runners going home)

3. Negating the running game (throwing out basestealers, and preventing steal attempts)

4. Working with pitchers (game-calling, pitchframing, handling the pitching staff and other tasks that make pitchers more effective).

The last of these, handling pitchers, has been a topic frequently researched at Baseball Prospectus. In *Baseball Prospectus 1999* (and available online at http://www.baseballprospectus.com/news/20000110woolner.html), I presented an article entitled "Field General or Backstop: Evaluating the catcher's influence on pitcher performance," which presented evidence that the catcher does not, in fact, have much influence on pitcher performance, and that measures such as pitchers' ERA with a given catcher behind the plate (called catcher's ERA, or CERA) are not useful. Follow-up research has appeared on the BP web site, including "Catching Up With The General: A Postscript" (http://www.baseballprospectus.com/news/20000111woolner.html), which addressed some reader feedback on the original article, and "Simulating Catcher's ERA" (http://www.baseballprospectus.com/news/20020529aim.shtml), which dealt with a critique by Bill James of my research.

Suffice it to say here that the current state of evidence supports the theory that catchers exercise minimal (at best) influence on how well their pitchers perform versus opposing batters. "Calling a good game," "framing pitches

to get borderline calls," "keeping pitchers' heads in the game," and other commonly expressed ideas about what good catchers do can't be found in the box score.

In this article we turn to another category of catcher responsibilities—the running game.

The Runner's Decision and Decision Trees

The structure of the running game problem for the runner and catcher are not mirror-images of each other. Only the runner can make the decision of whether to make an attempt or not. The uncertainty of whether he'll be safe or not is the risk involved. There are three possible outcomes:

1. Runner successfully steals

2. Runner is thrown out stealing

3. Runner does not attempt a steal

We can represent the structure of the runner's decision (and of other situations throughout this article) using a decision tree.

A decision tree is a graphical representation of the alternatives a decision maker is facing, the uncertainties that make the choice difficult, the values of the resulting outcomes, and the order in which information and decisions are made. The tree is composed of nodes connected by arcs, where the shape of the node indicates the type of decision element it represents. Trees are typically structures running left to right that indicate the flow of time.

A square is a decision node—a place where the decision maker can choose among any of the arcs leading out of it.

A circle is an uncertainty node—any of the arcs coming out of this node may end up happening (with probabilities usually indicated on the branches coming out of the node itself), but the decision maker does not get to choose (or indeed influence at all) which outcome occurs.

A single thread of nodes and arcs leads to an outcome or a state of the world if those particular decisions and events happen. The value of the outcome is indicated as a number at the end of the thread.

FIGURE 1. RUNNER'S DECISION TREE

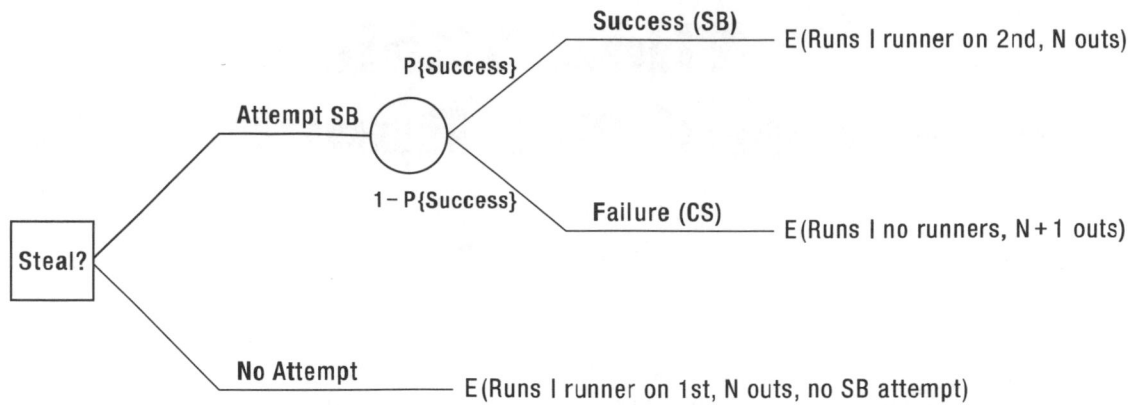

Let's look at a simple example of a decision tree in figure 1, representing the decision a runner on first base faces (and assuming no other runners are on base):

The runner faces a single decision, whether or not to steal, as shown in the "Steal?" decision node. If he chooses not to steal, the value of not attempting is the expected number of runs given that he stays on first base. Note that it is not necessary to explicitly model the rest of the inning to show all the possible outcomes of the batters' plate appearances following him (although in some circumstances it may be useful to do so).

If the runner decides to steal, he follows the "Attempt SB" arc coming from the "Steal?" node. There is then an uncertainty about whether the attempt will be successful, shown by the circle node. There is some chance of stealing the base, shown by the "Success (SB)" arc with a probability of P{Success}—the chance of the runner safely stealing second base. The other outcome, getting caught stealing, has the complementary probability of 1 − P{Success}. The values of these different outcomes are shown on the tree as well. They are the expected number of runs to be scored in the rest of the inning, with a runner on second (for the

SB outcome), or with no runners on base, but an additional out (for the CS outcome).

Let's plug in some numbers.

In Thorn & Palmer's "Hidden Game of Baseball," there's a matrix of expected runs from various combinations of runners on base and outs thus far in the inning. We can use the values here to help fill in the tree as shown in figure 2. In particular, the E(Runs | runner on 2nd, N outs) and E(Runs | no runners, N + 1 outs) can be taken directly from the table. For 0 outs, the values are 1.068 and 0.249, respectively.

Note that there are still missing values here. For starters, we need to know the value of P{Success}—the probability of a successful steal with no outs.

More importantly, note the ??? for the value following the "No Attempt" arc. Palmer's table has a value of 0.783 for runner on first, 0 outs, so why can't we use that value? The problem is that Palmer's table includes all situations where a runner was on first, including those where the runner eventually tried to steal a base. Since we're explicitly considering the case where a steal attempt was not made, we can't use that value here. Instead, the entire

FIGURE 2. RUNNER'S DECISION TREE, 0 OUTS

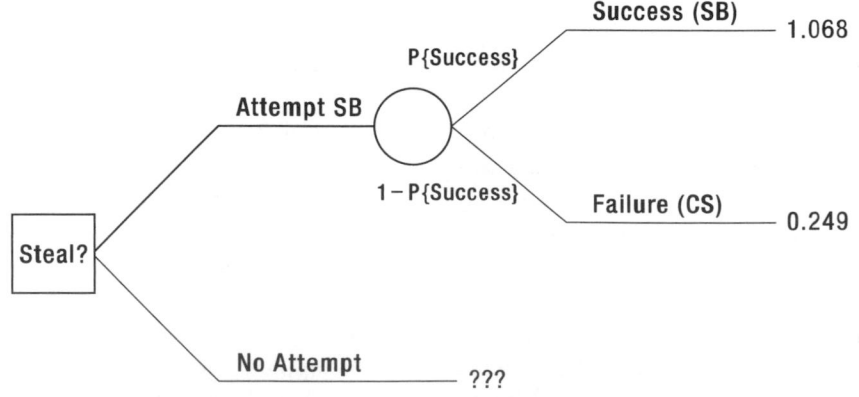

value of the tree must correspond to the 0.783 expected runs.

In order to estimate these missing values, we must turn to an analysis of play-by-play data. Thanks to the efforts of Retrosheet, Project Scoresheet, The Baseball Workshop, Gary Gillette, and others, we have complete play-by-play data for over 30 years of major league baseball that we can use to inform analyses such as this one.

The situation diagrammed in figure 2 has been faced by thousands of baserunners over many years, and each of them has made go/no-go decisions in each of them (or, in some cases, the manager has made them for him). By treating the decision not as an individual decision, but as an uncertainty created by the stream of decisions made over time, we can fill in the missing data, including the likelihood that a runner on first attempts a steal, and the likelihood of success in these situations, designated above by P{Success}.

For example, over the course of the seasons analyzed, 65.6% of runners who attempted a steal of second with nobody out were successful. That information allows us to fill in the probabilities of success and failure, resulting in figure 3.

With this information, we can determine the expected value of the entire SB attempt node, as it is the probability-weighted values of the various outcomes. Or...

$$\text{Value(SB attempt node)} = \text{Prob\{SB\}} \times \text{Value\{SB\}} + \text{Prob\{CS\}} \times \text{Value\{CS\}}$$

$$\text{Value(SB attempt node)} = 65.6\% \times 1.068 + 34.4\% \times 0.249 = 0.786$$

(See figure 4.)

Using the play-by-play data, we can also determine that a stolen base was attempted 12.8% of the time during a plate appearance when a runner was on first base and zero outs. Knowing the overall value of the "Steal?" node is 0.783 (from Palmer's expected runs table), we can figure out the value of not attempting a steal as shown in figure 5.

The value in attempting a steal, on average, is the difference between the Attempt and No Attempt threads, or .786-.78256 = or about 0.00344 runs. Very nearly zero.

FIGURE 4: UNCERTAINTY NODE FOR SB ATTEMPT, WITH THE EXPECTED VALUE OF THE NODE

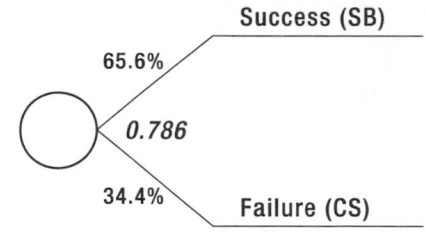

FIGURE 5: AGGREGATE TREE OF BASESTEALER DECISIONS, 0 OUT

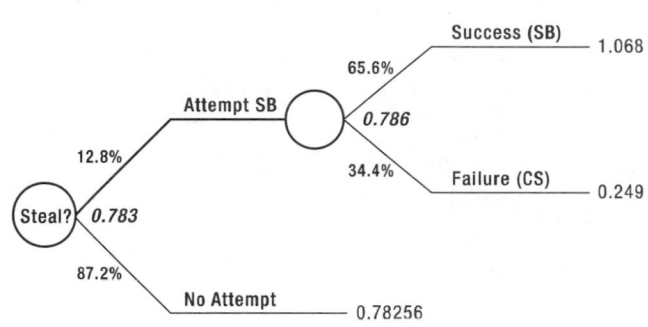

However, this only considers the case with one out. Let's look at the decision diagrams for 1 out and 2 outs in figures 6 and 7.

Using the three out-specific decision diagrams, we can compute the expected value (in runs) of a stolen base attempt by the number of outs, and the chance of successfully stealing a base that exactly balances the Attempt/No Attempt alternatives (see table 1).

Note that we are also discounting certain types of events: the possibility of an error on the SB attempt, a botched hit-and-run, steal attempts with a runner on third base, defensive indifference, and the like. These expected run values also only apply for situations where the

FIGURE 3: UNCERTAINTY NODE FOR SB ATTEMPT

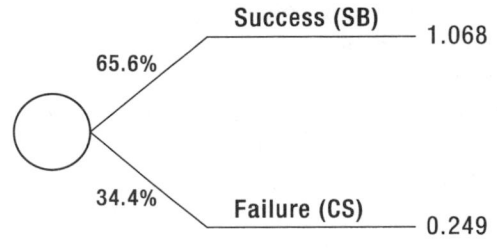

FIGURE 6: AGGREGATE TREE OF BASESTEALER DECISIONS, 1 OUT

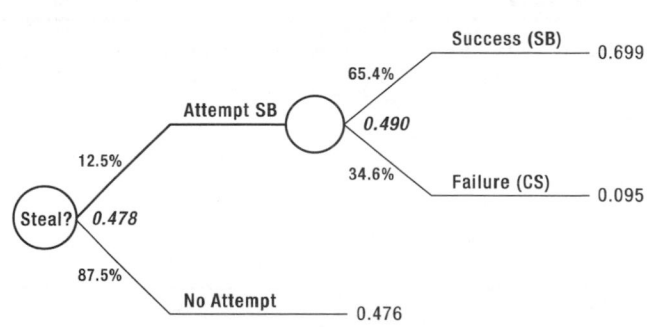

FIGURE 7: AGGREGATE TREE OF BASESTEALER DECISIONS, 2 OUTS

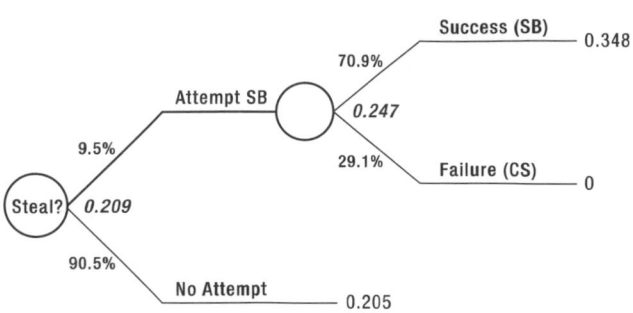

FIGURE 8: CATCHER'S "DECISION" TREE

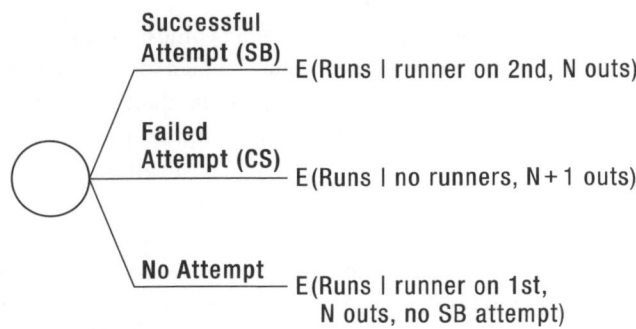

TABLE 1. VALUES OF SB ATTEMPT BY NUMBER OF OUTS

Outs	Run Value of SB Attempt	Breakeven SB Success %
0	0.003	65.1%
1	0.014	63.1%
2	0.042	58.9%

baserunner has an exactly average chance at successfully stealing the base compared to the historical norm. A better-than-average basestealer (or conversely, a worse-than-average catcher) will have increased values of attempting to steal across all out situations.

The fact that different out situations create different likelihoods to attempt a steal is something to consider as we develop a measure of the catcher's SB prevention. In particular, we will be using play-by-play analysis to look at how the actual runners on first base a catcher faced chose to steal or not steal depending on the number of outs in the situation. That will require an adjustment, or situational factor, similar to a park factor, to be applied to each attempt. These factors are relative to the overall average attempt and success rates, and are shown in table 2.

TABLE 2. SITUATIONAL FACTORS APPLIED TO SB ATTEMPTS

Outs	Attempt Rate	Attempt Factor	Success Rate	Success Factor
ALL	11.3%	1.00	67.5%	1.00
0	12.8%	1.13	65.6%	0.97
1	12.5%	1.11	65.4%	0.97
2	9.5%	0.84	70.9%	1.05

The Catcher's "Decision" and Measuring Value

For the catcher, the decision tree looks somewhat different. In fact, there is no decision to be made at all (ignoring the lesser question of whether to try to throw out the runner at all). The baserunner will either try to steal or not, and the catcher doesn't know whether he will try or not. The catcher is a reactor to the runner's decision, not a direct participant in it. For the catcher, the situation is an uncertainty with three outcomes as shown in figure 8.

Of the three possible outcomes of this uncertainty, the catcher has a definite, and seemingly obvious, order of preference:

1. Caught stealing (removes a baserunner, and generates an out)
2. No attempt (runner stays at first base, no out generated)
3. Successful stolen base (runners advances to second, no out generated)

The fact that both the best and worst outcomes for the catcher occur as a direct result of a decision by the runner leads to the odd effect that it is apparently not universally advantageous to reduce stolen base attempts. A catcher who can throw out baserunners a large percentage of the time benefits (in terms of expected runs) from having more runners try to run on him. Poor-throwing catchers want the opposite—they're hoping for fewer runners to try and run on them. And, of course, from the runner's point of view, he is more inclined to do exactly the opposite. Deception becomes key—enticing runners to attempt to steal because they underestimate their chances of getting thrown out by the catcher.

However, deception is not a long-term sustainable strategy. There is too much information, too much knowledge of a catcher's percentage of runners thrown out. There is no pattern a catcher can use to deceive a runner (short of deliberately not trying his best to throw out runners in less-than-key situations, a strategy his manager and teammates are not likely to be happy with).

TABLE 3.CHANCE OF A SINGLE RUN SCORING

Outs	Chance of Scoring at Least 1 Run with a Runner on 1st Base			Breakeven SB Success Rate for Scoring 1+ Runs
	SB	CS	No Attempt	
0	63.6%	17.8%	41.2%	51.1%
1	45.7%	8.4%	25.9%	46.9%
2	23.6%	0.0%	11.5%	48.7%

Furthermore, the goal of reducing expected runs is not always consistent with winning games. In some cases, particularly in the late innings of close games, maximizing the chance of a single run being scored can be more important for the team at bat than it would be in earlier innings (see table 3).

Given this information, I propose that it's total stolen base reduction relative to an average catcher that should be the basis for measuring the catcher's impact on the running game. Reductions in stolen base totals can occur either from throwing out runners or by preventing runners from attempting to steal in the first place by intimidation or reputation. Either method of SB reduction has the effect of eliminating a tool from the opponent's arsenal.

Do Park Factors Exist for SB/CS?

Many other aspects of baseball are affected by the environment the game is played in. It is easier to hit in Coors Field than in Oakland Coliseum, for example. Consequently, we often employ park factors to adjust the value of statistics posted by players, according to their home park or by the specific mix of parks they played in. These park effects are most commonly used in adjusting hitting and pitching performances.

But do parks influence the running game? Do park effects have relevance for stealing bases? And what does a "park effect" for basestealing mean? Answering the last question first, there are two relevant rates that could be affected by park: the attempt rate and the success rate. Note that this is different from hitting, where the equivalent of the "attempt" would be the plate appearance, whose frequency is not dictated by decisions, but by the rules of the game. A team cannot choose to bat more often—it must earn more opportunities through avoiding outs. For stolen bases, then, we need to consider two potential park factors—the attempt rate (how often do runners try to steal) and the success rate (how often are they safe when attempting a steal).

Most of the commonly cited park influences for hitting and pitching—hitting background, prevailing wind

direction and speeds, size of foul territory, thin atmosphere—do not apply to the same degree. There are a few factors that may contribute, most notably the surface of the field (turf/grass), and specifically whether the base paths are composed fully of dirt, or have turf across most of the infield area. Air density and winds might have a slight effect on the flight path of a thrown ball, but the amount of time the air has to act on a thrown ball is less than that of a fly ball or line drive, minimizing the total impact on its velocity and accuracy.

A different kind of park effect may arise indirectly from other causes. A park that depresses offense may cause teams that play there to employ "little-ball" and one-run strategies more often than at a more hitter-friendly stadium. Thus, teams may be more apt to steal at such parks, which could create a measurable park effect on attempt rate, and perhaps on success rate, depending on what kind of runners are systematically sent more often in such an environment.

Ultimately, the question of whether park effects exist or not becomes an empirical one—can we detect any? We can certainly look at the differences between attempt and success rates over a single season for a team's home and away games. However, declaring a park factor to exist because the home and away rates are not identical isn't sufficient, because you would expect variation, simply by chance. The true test of a park factor is whether it persists over time. That is, whether differences are attributable to the park itself by virtue of a sustained trend of inflating or deflating the statistics being examined.

I looked at each major league park over a 30-year period, and computed the attempt and success rate for each team's home and away games (considering both the team and its opponent), as is typical for park factor computations. To determine the attempt rate, I defined a stolen base opportunity as all situations where a runner was on first base, and second base was unoccupied. The stolen base attempt rate was then defined at (total attempts) / (stolen base opportunities). I aggregated the data into five-year groups. I then compared adjacent, non-overlapping time periods to see whether parks exhibited consistent park factors.

For example, I compared the attempt rate park factor for Fenway Park in Boston during 1980–1984 to that in 1985–1989, compared the factors for 1985–89 to 1990–94, and so on.

I was able to find mild evidence for a park factor on both attempt rate and success rate, with correlation coefficients of +0.412 and +0.476 respectively. These factors explain about 17% of the variance in park factors for attempt rate, and 23% of the variance for success rate. Figures 9 and 10 show the results in more detail

Based on this evidence, I opted to use five-year park factors for adjusting both attempt and success rates.

FIGURE 9. COMPARISON OF SB ATTEMPT RATE PARK FACTORS USING CONSECUTIVE, NONOVERLAPPING 5-YEAR PERIODS

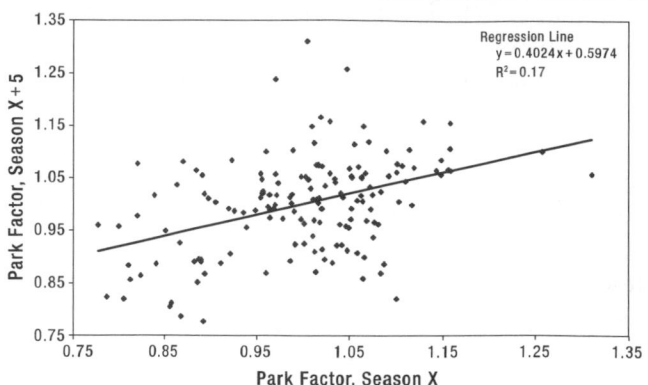

FIGURE 10. COMPARISON OF SB SUCCESS RATE PARK FACTORS USING CONSECUTIVE, NONOVERLAPPING 5-YEAR PERIODS

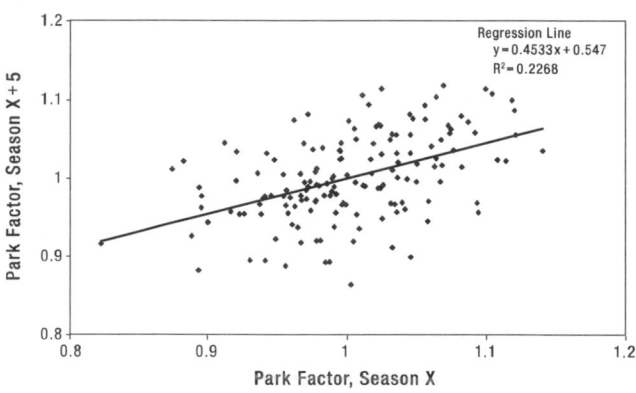

However, given the relative instability, and modest magnitude of most of the effects, a more casual analysis would not suffer much by omitting them entirely.

Complete SB attempt and success rate park factors will be available online at the Baseball Prospectus Web site (http://www.baseballprospectus.com) starting in 2004.

Quality of Runners Faced Composite Profile

Another factor that varies among catchers is how often they are faced with really good (or bad) baserunners, or teams that rely on the running game more than others. Particularly with the unbalanced schedule, having a divisional opponent mimicking the Whitey Herzog-era Cardinals creates a higher attempt rate against than would otherwise be expected. The same phenomenon appears in hitting stats, and especially pitching stats (since pitchers appear in fewer games than hitters do).

One approach I've used in the past to level the playing field (so to speak) is to create what I call a "composite opponent" who, instead of being league average, is instead

the average of all specific opponents the player faced: opposing pitchers for hitters, opposing hitters for pitchers, and opposing baserunners for catchers. By using a composite opposing runner profile, we can correct for a catcher who faced a set of runners who were unusually prone to stealing (not just versus this catcher, but all season long). For each baserunner faced in a SB opportunity, add the runner's seasonal attempt rate to the composite opposing runner's total. Similarly for the composite opposing runner's success rate.

An example may be more illustrative. Suppose that Carl Catcher faces 100 opposing runners, and 10 of them attempt to steal. Suppose also that the league average rate of steal attempts is 8%. We would assume that Carl's 10% rate of attempts is worse than average—runners are more likely to try to steal against him than against an average catcher.

But now let's suppose we look at the play-by-play data, and find that 60 of the runners whom Carl faced tried to steal in 10% of their chances that season, and the other 40 of whom attempted a steal in 12% of the time during the season. We would have expected 10.8 steal attempts with this particular set of opposing runners, so the fact that Carl had 10 attempts made against him actually means he was better than average! As it turns out, there is a fairly wide divergence of opposing runner attempt and success rates across major league catchers, and the value of including this adjustment is larger than this simplified example might make it seem.

SB Prevention Stats and Methods

I looked at every stolen base opportunity runners had against a given catcher, and computed the number of stolen base attempts and successes they had in those opportunities. I adjusted these rates for the catcher's home park and the out-situation to come up with the following numbers:

ATTDIFF: Difference in adjusted attempt rates between this catcher and an average catcher. Negative numbers indicate that fewer runners attempted to steal vs. this catcher

SBDIFF: Difference in adjusted success rates between this catcher and an average catcher. Negative numbers indicate that fewer attempts were successful vs. this catcher.

NETATT: Adjusted net difference in the number of attempts versus this catcher compared to an average catcher facing the same number of opportunities, adjusted for park and out-situation.

NETSB: Adjusted net difference in the number of successful steals versus this catcher compared to an average catcher facing the same number of attempts, adjusted for park and out-situation.

ADDOUTS: The number of additional outs a catcher generated in his stolen base opportunities versus a catcher with both average attempt rates and average success rates, adjusted for park and out-situation. Note that this number can be misleading, as a poor catcher can have a good ADDOUTS rating if his attempt rate is high.

E.g., League average is 10% attempt rate, 60% success rate.

Catcher faces 1,000 SB opportunities, 200 steal attempts, and 140 SB. His attempt rate is 20% and his opposing runner's success rate is 70%. Thus he allows both more attempts and better success to opposing runners).

This catcher generated 60 outs (200 attempts − 140 SB = 60 CS).

An average catcher would have generated $1000 \times 10\% \times (1 - 60\%) = 40$ outs in the same number of total opportunities. The effect of more attempts in those opportunities allows him to compile extra outs. Of course, he allowed 140 SB, whereas an average catcher would have allowed just 60 SB, which is a better reflection of how effective each was.

XSB: Extra Stolen Bases Allowed. Given the same number of stolen base opportunities, the number of extra stolen bases the catcher allowed versus a catcher with both average attempt rates and average success rates, adjusted for park and out-situation. This is the total measure of how much the catcher shut down the running game. Negative values indicate better stolen base prevention.

XSBR: Rate of XSB, or number of Extra Stolen Bases allowed per opportunity. Rate version of XSB.

The two tables, XSBR and XSB, are how we will evaluate catchers.

Seasonal Results

OK, enough theory. What most people reading this article want are the stats for the catchers themselves.

Remember, XSB is aggregate total SB prevented, and XSBR is the rate of prevention. SB_PA is the number of plate appearances in which a runner was on first while this catcher was behind the plate. Similarly, SBA is Stolen Base Attempts.

Ten best and worst catchers, by XSBR for each season 2000-2003 (min 800 SB_PA) are shown in table 4.

TABLE 4. 10 BEST AND WORST CATCHERS BY XSBR, 2000-2003

Name	SB_PA	SBA	SB	CS	ATTDIFF	SBDIFF	NETATT	NETSB	XSB	ADDOUTS	XSBR
						2000 Best					
Blanco, Henry	1177	58	24	34	−0.015	−0.192	−17.50	−11.16	−22.39	−4.89	−0.0190
Rodriguez, Ivan	1209	33	18	15	−0.025	−0.085	−29.64	−2.79	−21.57	8.07	−0.0178
Ausmus, Brad	1832	60	37	31	−0.017	−0.035	−30.72	−2.41	−19.83	10.88	−0.0108
Wilson, Dan	1018	48	30	18	−0.007	−0.024	−7.62	−1.16	−5.63	1.99	−0.0055
Lieberthal, Mike	1302	64	35	29	−0.010	0.004	−12.88	0.27	−6.72	6.16	−0.0052
Matheny, Mike	1441	89	44	45	0.002	−0.075	2.42	−6.64	−4.87	−7.29	−0.0034
Estalella, Bobby	1245	68	44	24	−0.012	0.092	−14.80	6.25	−2.02	12.78	−0.0016
Posada, Jorge	1788	91	60	31	−0.005	0.065	−9.10	5.95	0.85	9.94	0.0005
Gonzalez, Wiki	1058	62	39	23	−0.005	0.081	−5.30	5.05	1.84	7.14	0.0017
Johnson, Charles	1134	49	36	13	−0.010	0.179	−11.55	8.76	2.67	14.21	0.0024
						2000 Worst					
Fletcher, Darrin	1391	82	65	17	−0.001	0.178	−1.46	14.58	12.48	13.94	0.0090
Miller, Damian	1056	71	46	25	0.010	0.082	10.21	5.79	11.51	1.30	0.0109
Widger, Chris	1002	63	47	16	0.003	0.149	3.45	9.39	12.05	8.60	0.0120
Meluskey, Mitch	1233	77	59	18	−0.001	0.223	−1.70	17.15	15.29	17.00	0.0124
Mayne, Brent	1217	66	50	16	0.003	0.181	3.73	11.95	15.79	12.05	0.0130
Alomar Jr., Sandy	1315	87	67	20	0.006	0.150	7.47	13.06	17.76	10.30	0.0135
Flaherty, John	1379	102	75	27	0.023	0.179	31.18	18.24	37.23	6.05	0.0270
Hundley, Todd	1015	88	67	21	0.025	0.199	25.23	17.52	30.37	5.14	0.0299
Varitek, Jason	1368	110	79	31	0.033	0.160	45.04	17.57	46.41	1.37	0.0339
Piazza, Mike	1466	121	91	30	0.026	0.226	37.83	27.31	50.21	12.38	0.0342
						2001 Best					
Rodriguez, Ivan	1339	51	17	34	−0.026	−0.258	−34.48	−13.16	−34.95	−0.47	−0.0261
Matheny, Mike	1404	52	29	23	−0.020	0.054	−28.41	2.82	−11.77	16.64	−0.0084
Wilson, Dan	1224	49	36	13	−0.021	0.113	−25.54	5.53	−9.21	16.32	−0.0075
LaRue, Jason	1207	65	27	38	0.001	−0.104	1.01	−6.75	−6.72	−7.73	−0.0056
Pierzynski, A. J.	1140	58	38	20	−0.015	0.067	−17.34	3.88	−6.32	11.02	−0.0055
Blanco, Henry	1277	60	34	26	−0.008	−0.003	−10.70	−0.21	−5.97	4.73	−0.0047

(continued next page)

TABLE 4. 10 BEST AND WORST CATCHERS BY XSBR, 2000–2003 (continued)

Name	SB_PA	SBA	SB	CS	ATTDIFF	SBDIFF	NETATT	NETSB	XSB	ADDOUTS	XSBR
2001 Best (continued)											
Johnson, Charles	1593	75	49	26	−0.014	0.095	−22.59	7.10	−5.80	16.80	−0.0036
Ausmus, Brad	1442	74	41	33	−0.011	0.044	−15.87	3.23	−5.01	10.86	−0.0035
Diaz, Einar	1659	116	76	40	−0.006	0.035	−10.64	4.01	−2.43	8.22	−0.0015
Fletcher, Darrin	1459	94	65	29	−0.007	0.081	−10.51	7.61	0.87	11.39	0.0006
2001 Worst											
Santiago, Benito	1564	84	53	31	−0.005	0.130	−8.12	10.95	6.18	14.30	0.0039
Kendall, Jason	1652	84	59	25	−0.006	0.152	−10.17	12.81	7.69	17.86	0.0047
Molina, Ben	1114	76	50	26	0.003	0.048	2.88	3.65	5.98	3.10	0.0054
Davis, Ben	1573	96	63	33	0.000	0.157	0.30	15.03	14.40	14.11	0.0092
Lopez, Javy	1470	91	62	29	0.002	0.131	3.23	11.93	13.73	10.50	0.0093
Barrett, Michael	1609	93	75	18	0.001	0.221	2.06	20.56	22.81	20.76	0.0142
Miller, Damian	1259	96	62	34	0.018	0.088	22.13	8.44	20.52	−1.62	0.0163
Hernandez, Ramon	1527	125	86	39	0.014	0.092	21.23	11.54	25.34	4.12	0.0166
Fordyce, Brook	1075	103	84	19	0.023	0.209	25.19	21.51	36.93	11.73	0.0343
Piazza, Mike	1416	127	96	31	0.028	0.214	39.24	27.16	50.34	11.09	0.0355
2002 Best											
LaRue, Jason	1380	53	29	24	−0.020	−0.074	−28.14	−3.93	−20.64	7.50	−0.0150
Rodriguez, Ivan	1357	31	23	8	−0.031	0.154	−41.94	4.76	−19.62	22.31	−0.0145
Lampkin, Tom	1108	44	30	14	−0.024	0.121	−26.51	5.33	−10.35	16.16	−0.0093
Lieberthal, Mike	1605	67	45	22	−0.019	0.067	−30.85	4.50	−13.09	17.76	−0.0082
Hernandez, Ramon	1523	63	41	22	−0.016	0.083	−23.89	5.25	−8.21	15.68	−0.0054
Inge, Brandon	1214	48	34	14	−0.016	0.142	−19.51	6.81	−3.82	15.70	−0.0031
Pierzynski, A. J.	1393	58	42	16	−0.017	0.161	−23.49	9.31	−3.50	19.99	−0.0025
Molina, Ben	1401	71	41	30	−0.005	0.012	−6.90	0.86	−2.85	4.04	−0.0020
Mayne, Brent	1247	56	35	21	−0.004	0.077	−5.52	4.33	1.55	7.07	0.0012
Wilson, Dan	1193	52	40	12	−0.010	0.157	−11.37	8.14	1.85	13.22	0.0016
2002 Worst											
Matheny, Mike	1113	60	41	19	−0.001	0.125	−1.56	7.48	6.91	8.47	0.0062
Ausmus, Brad	1487	88	62	26	0.001	0.145	1.70	12.77	13.24	11.55	0.0089
Gil, Geronimo	1508	93	59	34	0.010	0.054	15.04	5.04	14.02	−1.02	0.0093
Lopez, Javy	1105	78	49	29	0.011	0.050	11.65	3.90	10.96	−0.69	0.0099
Johnson, Mark L.	1011	62	41	21	0.006	0.126	6.38	7.84	11.24	4.85	0.0111
Posada, Jorge	1604	99	72	27	0.006	0.146	9.78	14.49	20.22	10.44	0.0126
Lo Duca, Paul	1609	111	77	34	0.011	0.099	17.63	10.95	21.55	3.92	0.0134
Diaz, Einar	1298	105	73	32	0.015	0.107	18.95	11.27	22.36	3.41	0.0172
Varitek, Jason	1357	93	65	28	0.017	0.119	22.43	11.02	25.94	3.51	0.0191
Piazza, Mike	1438	134	111	23	0.033	0.235	47.08	31.54	60.65	13.57	0.0422
2003 Best											
Wilson, Dan	1114	34	23	11	−0.024	0.075	−26.85	2.54	−12.41	14.44	−0.0111
Hall, Toby	1728	64	38	26	−0.013	0.056	−23.23	3.61	−8.96	14.27	−0.0052
Olivo, Miguel	1105	48	30	18	−0.015	0.072	−16.24	3.48	−5.62	10.62	−0.0051
Schneider, Brian	1134	45	24	21	−0.008	0.002	−9.41	0.08	−4.64	4.76	−0.0041
Pierzynski, A. J.	1483	58	42	16	−0.019	0.165	−28.02	9.59	−5.81	22.21	−0.0039
Rodriguez, Ivan	1587	52	38	14	−0.017	0.201	−26.91	10.47	−4.32	22.59	−0.0027
Matheny, Mike	1492	47	34	13	−0.018	0.231	−27.49	10.84	−3.50	23.99	−0.0023
Wilson, Vance	1005	43	25	18	−0.011	0.080	−10.65	3.42	−2.00	8.64	−0.0020
Miller, Damian	1411	58	36	22	−0.010	0.106	−13.84	6.15	−1.45	12.39	−0.0010
Johnson, Charles	1417	54	34	20	−0.007	0.093	−10.19	5.02	0.25	10.44	0.0002
2003 Worst											
Mayne, Brent	1376	71	48	23	0.000	0.106	−0.56	7.52	7.52	8.08	0.0055
Ausmus, Brad	1666	96	61	35	0.002	0.095	2.63	9.12	10.68	8.05	0.0064
Varitek, Jason	1449	71	50	21	−0.002	0.189	−3.41	13.45	12.73	16.14	0.0088
Posada, Jorge	1555	86	61	25	0.005	0.157	8.23	13.54	18.60	10.37	0.0120
Bennett, Gary	1026	53	44	9	−0.006	0.319	−5.94	16.89	13.12	19.06	0.0128
Perez, Eddie	1315	71	54	17	0.006	0.202	7.96	14.32	19.34	11.37	0.0147
Lieberthal, Mike	1595	88	70	18	0.004	0.256	6.25	22.55	26.94	20.69	0.0169
Inge, Brandon	1365	94	61	33	0.017	0.118	22.66	11.14	23.64	0.98	0.0173
Fordyce, Brook	1313	80	61	19	0.012	0.223	15.91	17.83	26.40	10.49	0.0201
Lo Duca, Paul	1362	131	76	55	0.044	0.048	59.35	6.33	37.89	−21.46	0.0278

Next, the "all-time" 20 best and worst seasons by XSBR for the years we have data (1972–2003) in table 5.

TABLE 5. "ALL-TIME" 20 BEST AND WORST SEASONS BY XSBR, 1972–2003

Year Name	SB_PA	SBA	SB	CS	ATTDIFF	SBDIFF	NETATT	NETSB	XSB	ADDOUTS	XSBR
Best											
2001 Rodriguez, Ivan	1339	51	17	34	−0.026	−0.258	−34.48	−13.16	−34.95	−0.47	−0.0261
1988 Santiago, Benito	1526	88	51	37	−0.041	−0.016	−63.22	−1.42	−37.91	25.31	−0.0248
1998 Rodriguez, Ivan	1878	71	31	40	−0.031	−0.143	−58.65	−10.15	−44.41	14.24	−0.0237
1996 Johnson, Charles	1468	67	33	34	−0.026	−0.118	−38.83	−7.92	−32.20	6.63	−0.0219
1989 Santiago, Benito	1454	65	40	25	−0.036	0.027	−52.20	1.78	−28.39	23.81	−0.0195
2000 Blanco, Henry	1177	58	24	34	−0.015	−0.192	−17.50	−11.16	−22.39	−4.89	−0.0190
1997 Rodriguez, Ivan	1892	75	35	40	−0.027	−0.100	−50.30	−7.50	−34.76	15.54	−0.0184
1999 Rodriguez, Ivan	1804	72	33	39	−0.023	−0.111	−41.84	−8.01	−32.95	8.90	−0.0183
2000 Rodriguez, Ivan	1209	33	18	15	−0.025	−0.085	−29.64	−2.79	−21.57	8.07	−0.0178
1997 Ausmus, Brad	1495	81	41	40	−0.025	−0.064	−36.71	−5.22	−26.45	10.26	−0.0177
1998 Fasano, Sal	909	34	18	16	−0.029	−0.031	−26.19	−1.04	−15.75	10.44	−0.0173
1990 Santiago, Benito	1113	75	46	29	−0.026	−0.009	−29.05	−0.65	−18.65	10.40	−0.0168
2000 Kreuter, Chad	819	27	16	11	−0.029	0.025	−23.70	0.68	−12.49	11.21	−0.0153
2002 LaRue, Jason	1380	53	29	24	−0.020	−0.074	−28.14	−3.93	−20.64	7.50	−0.0150
1979 Munson, Thurman	966	57	30	27	−0.018	−0.079	−17.08	−4.53	−14.06	3.02	−0.0146
1983 Porter, Darrell	1512	104	61	43	−0.029	0.019	−44.23	2.00	−21.97	22.26	−0.0145
2002 Rodriguez, Ivan	1357	31	23	8	−0.031	0.154	−41.94	4.76	−19.62	22.31	−0.0145
1999 Valentin, Javier	835	40	20	20	−0.020	−0.066	−16.74	−2.65	−11.93	4.81	−0.0143
1994 Rodriguez, Ivan	1278	47	28	19	−0.027	0.026	−34.69	1.22	−18.26	16.43	−0.0143
1989 Berryhill, Damon	1012	57	32	25	−0.023	−0.006	−23.59	−0.36	−14.01	9.58	−0.0138
Worst											
1977 Kendall, Fred	1185	107	84	23	0.021	0.287	24.69	30.67	43.60	18.92	0.0368
1999 Varitek, Jason	1677	150	109	41	0.035	0.157	58.38	23.49	61.82	3.44	0.0369
1984 Benedict, Bruce	1124	105	81	24	0.015	0.284	16.35	29.78	42.00	25.66	0.0374
1990 Fitzgerald, Mike	990	112	89	23	0.030	0.166	29.93	18.61	37.34	7.41	0.0377
1977 Fosse, Ray	845	92	65	27	0.035	0.182	29.23	16.72	32.78	3.55	0.0388
1987 Ashby, Alan	1165	136	113	23	0.024	0.219	28.04	29.85	45.35	17.31	0.0389
1999 Nilsson, Dave	1161	114	92	22	0.028	0.216	32.89	24.67	45.22	12.32	0.0389
1978 Pocoroba, Biff	985	100	76	24	0.027	0.219	26.52	21.95	38.79	12.27	0.0394
1997 Haselman, Bill	898	80	60	20	0.036	0.204	32.46	16.32	36.01	3.55	0.0401
1995 Pena, Tony	930	78	63	15	0.027	0.305	25.07	23.76	38.23	13.15	0.0411
2002 Piazza, Mike	1438	134	111	23	0.033	0.235	47.08	31.54	60.65	13.57	0.0422
1990 Sasser, Mackey	823	114	80	34	0.046	0.103	37.50	11.77	35.20	−2.30	0.0428
1986 Virgil, Ozzie	1414	167	117	50	0.037	0.168	51.85	28.02	60.55	8.71	0.0428
1987 Fitzgerald, Mike	983	121	103	18	0.027	0.241	26.74	29.18	44.72	17.98	0.0455
1988 Carter, Gary	1254	144	118	26	0.028	0.246	34.97	35.47	58.52	23.55	0.0467
1998 Hoiles, Chris	948	108	86	22	0.041	0.189	38.63	20.39	44.71	6.08	0.0472
1979 Nolan, Joe	828	85	72	13	0.022	0.332	18.47	28.21	39.97	21.50	0.0483
1997 Widger, Chris	1044	116	100	16	0.039	0.245	40.21	28.42	52.19	11.98	0.0500
1992 Carter, Gary	879	120	86	34	0.059	0.157	51.44	18.90	47.49	−3.94	0.0540
2001 Hatteberg, Scott	872	106	98	8	0.061	0.377	52.77	39.97	74.77	21.99	0.0857

Now, the "all-time" 20 best and worst seasons by XSB (total SB prevention) for the years we have data (1972–2003) in table 6.

TABLE 6. "ALL-TIME" 20 BEST AND WORST SEASONS BY XSB, 1972–2003

Year Name	SB_PA	SBA	SB	CS	ATTDIFF	SBDIFF	NETATT	NETSB	XSB	ADDOUTS	XSBR
Best											
1998 Rodriguez, Ivan	1878	71	31	40	−0.031	−0.143	−58.65	−10.15	−44.41	14.4	−0.0237
1988 Santiago, Benito	1526	88	51	37	−0.041	−0.016	−63.22	−1.42	−37.91	25.31	−0.0248
2001 Rodriguez, Ivan	1339	51	17	34	−0.026	−0.258	−34.48	−13.16	−34.95	−0.47	−0.0261
1997 Rodriguez, Ivan	1892	75	35	40	−0.027	−0.100	−50.30	−7.50	−34.76	15.54	−0.0184
1999 Rodriguez, Ivan	1804	72	33	39	−0.023	−0.111	−41.84	−8.01	−32.95	8.90	−0.0183
1996 Johnson, Charles	1468	67	33	34	−0.026	−0.118	−38.83	−7.92	−32.20	6.63	−0.0219

(continued next page)

TABLE 6. "ALL-TIME" 20 BEST AND WORST SEASONS BY XSB, 1972–2003 (continued)

Year Name	SB_PA	SBA	SB	CS	ATTDIFF	SBDIFF	NETATT	NETSB	XSB	ADDOUTS	XSBR
					Best (continued)						
1989 Santiago, Benito	1454	65	40	25	−0.036	0.027	−52.20	1.78	−28.39	23.81	−0.0195
1997 Ausmus, Brad	1495	81	41	40	−0.025	−0.064	−36.71	−5.22	−26.45	10.26	−0.0177
1990 Daulton, Darren	1717	101	65	36	−0.027	0.035	−46.19	3.57	−23.51	22.68	−0.0137
1996 Rodriguez, Ivan	1949	85	42	43	−0.013	−0.097	−25.87	−8.25	−23.07	2.80	−0.0118
1995 Rodriguez, Ivan	1679	65	32	33	−0.020	−0.064	−33.64	−4.16	−22.68	10.96	−0.0135
2000 Blanco, Henry	1177	58	24	34	−0.015	−0.192	−17.50	−11.16	−22.39	4.89	−0.0190
1983 Porter, Darrell	1512	104	61	43	−0.029	0.019	−44.23	2.00	−21.97	22.26	−0.0145
2000 Rodriguez, Ivan	1209	33	18	15	−0.025	−0.085	−29.64	−2.79	−21.57	8.07	−0.0178
1986 Boone, Bob	1634	81	40	41	−0.020	−0.040	−32.67	−3.26	−21.40	11.27	−0.0131
1974 Bench, Johnny	1602	63	34	29	−0.026	0.001	41.64	0.09	−21.24	20.40	−0.0133
1982 Boone, Bob	1756	103	42	61	−0.015	−0.077	−27.15	−7.97	−21.15	6.00	−0.0120
1983 Carter, Gary	1660	148	83	65	−0.017	−0.030	−28.45	−4.49	−20.98	7.48	−0.0126
2002 LaRue, Jason	1380	53	29	24	−0.020	−0.074	−28.14	−3.93	−20.64	7.50	−0.0150
1993 Manwaring, Kirt	1561	96	52	44	−0.021	−0.017	−32.80	−1.59	−20.37	12.42	−0.0131
					Worst						
1983 Davis, Jody	1684	167	122	45	0.008	0.202	13.89	33.76	43.56	29.68	0.0259
1977 Kendall, Fred	1185	107	84	23	0.021	0.287	24.69	30.67	43.60	18.92	0.0368
1998 Hoiles, Chris	948	108	86	22	0.041	0.189	38.63	20.39	44.71	6.08	0.0472
1987 Fitzgerald, Mike	983	121	103	18	0.027	0.241	26.74	29.18	44.72	17.98	0.0455
1999 Nilsson, Dave	1161	114	92	22	0.028	0.216	32.89	24.67	45.22	12.32	0.0389
1987 Ashby, Alan	1165	136	113	23	0.024	0.219	28.04	29.85	45.35	17.31	0.0389
1978 Downing, Brian	1522	163	102	61	0.026	0.158	39.93	25.83	45.75	5.81	0.0301
2000 Varitek, Jason	1368	110	79	31	0.033	0.160	45.04	17.57	46.41	1.37	0.0339
1992 Carter, Gary	879	120	86	34	0.059	0.157	51.44	18.90	47.49	-3.94	0.0540
1999 Piazza, Mike	1619	131	100	31	0.019	0.233	30.95	30.58	49.33	18.38	0.0305
2000 Piazza, Mike	1466	121	91	30	0.026	0.226	37.83	27.31	50.21	12.38	0.0342
2001 Piazza, Mike	1416	127	96	31	0.028	0.214	39.24	27.16	50.34	11.09	0.0355
1987 Virgil, Ozzie	1616	155	123	32	0.012	0.234	19.27	36.34	52.06	32.79	0.0322
1989 Biggio, Craig	1501	148	121	27	0.021	0.234	31.70	34.67	52.12	20.42	0.0347
1997 Widger, Chris	1044	116	100	16	0.039	0.245	40.21	28.42	52.19	11.98	0.0500
1988 Carter, Gary	1254	144	118	26	0.028	0.246	34.97	35.47	58.52	23.55	0.0467
1986 Virgil, Ozzie	1414	167	117	50	0.037	0.168	51.85	28.02	60.55	8.71	0.0428
2002 Piazza, Mike	1438	134	111	23	0.033	0.235	47.08	31.54	60.65	13.57	0.0422
1999 Varitek, Jason	1677	150	109	41	0.035	0.157	58.38	23.49	61.82	3.44	0.0369
2001 Hatteberg, Scott	872	106	98	8	0.061	0.377	52.77	39.97	74.77	21.99	0.0857

Career Results

And, of course, the career results. With a minimum of 4,000 SB opportunities, only 150 or so catchers qualified between 1972 and 2003. Tables 7 and 8 show the 15 best and worst by XSBR and XSB for that period. Tables 7 and 8 show the 15 best and worst by XSB and XSBR.

TABLE 7. BEST AND WORST 15 CATCHERS BY XSB (MIN 4,000 SB_PA CAREER)

Year Name	SB_PA	SBA	SB	CS	ATTDIFF	SBDIFF	NETATT	NETSB	XSB	ADDOUTS	XSBR
					Best						
Rodriguez, Ivan	20183	840	430	410	−0.021	−0.050	−428.77	−41.89	−287.96	140.82	−0.0143
Santiago, Benito	21932	1288	844	444	−0.017	0.085	−377.93	109.70	−106.01	271.92	−0.0048
Bench, Johnny	12882	712	426	286	−0.020	0.043	−257.39	30.45	−104.00	153.39	−0.0081
Johnson, Charles	13640	663	399	264	−0.014	0.031	−188.29	20.54	−86.99	101.30	−0.0064
Karkovice, Ron	10637	578	349	229	−0.013	0.054	−136.41	31.08	−42.39	94.02	−0.0040
Wilson, Dan	14203	712	468	244	−0.010	0.057	−141.88	40.70	−37.69	104.18	−0.0027
Lake, Steve	4132	294	162	132	−0.016	−0.001	−66.53	−0.22	−36.93	29.60	−0.0089
Lieberthal, Mike	10134	503	341	162	−0.014	0.104	−145.17	52.26	−29.13	116.04	−0.0029
Munson, Thurman	12179	760	442	318	−0.011	0.050	−131.78	37.89	−28.97	102.82	−0.0024
Ausmus, Brad	15778	866	542	324	−0.009	0.062	−139.86	53.34	−25.42	114.44	−0.0016
LaRue, Jason	4630	200	120	80	0.010	0.023	−45.03	4.81	−20.87	24.15	−0.0045

Year Name	SB_PA	SBA	SB	CS	ATTDIFF	SBDIFF	NETATT	NETSB	XSB	ADDOUTS	XSBR
Best											
Pierzynski, A. J.	4508	194	135	59	−0.017	0.125	−75.45	24.28	−18.03	57.41	−0.0040
Yeager, Steve	12866	875	548	327	−0.014	0.096	−179.53	84.24	−14.78	164.74	−0.0011
Boone, Bob	26007	1655	1013	642	−0.011	0.084	−284.91	138.55	−13.99	270.92	−0.0005
Valle, Dave	10423	612	383	229	−0.010	0.068	−102.34	41.34	−12.90	89.44	−0.0012
Worst											
Slaught, Don	13941	1034	721	313	0.001	0.151	8.08	156.60	162.08	154.00	0.0116
Kennedy, Terry	15649	1386	960	426	−0.003	0.138	−47.77	190.76	163.90	211.67	0.0105
Reed, Jeff	11255	881	629	252	0.007	0.137	74.63	120.30	168.08	93.45	0.0149
Virgil, Ozzie	8111	763	572	191	0.004	0.191	30.54	145.78	171.72	141.18	0.0212
Varitek, Jason	7201	536	384	152	0.021	0.150	148.81	80.48	179.83	31.02	0.0250
Hatteberg, Scott	4233	400	318	82	0.032	0.233	137.42	93.00	182.63	45.21	0.0431
Fletcher, Darrin	12521	988	748	240	0.007	0.158	81.74	155.84	198.40	116.65	0.0158
Carter, Gary	23448	2080	1364	716	−0.001	0.101	−27.19	209.23	205.12	232.31	0.0087
Benedict, Bruce	10961	1026	711	315	0.006	0.154	69.36	158.00	209.92	140.56	0.0192
Hundley, Todd	12088	920	688	232	0.005	0.203	55.13	186.63	212.97	157.83	0.0176
Ashby, Alan	14885	1405	1022	383	0.003	0.168	42.65	235.62	250.78	208.12	0.0168
Fisk, Carlton	25934	1754	1187	567	0.000	0.145	−7.11	253.60	257.80	264.92	0.0099
Fitzgerald, Mike	7722	824	649	175	0.020	0.212	153.09	174.37	264.62	111.53	0.0343
Simmons, Ted	18794	1490	999	491	0.008	0.141	147.90	209.48	290.66	142.75	0.0155
Piazza, Mike	16141	1364	1023	341	0.014	0.184	230.65	250.63	385.63	154.98	0.0239

TABLE 8. BEST AND WORST 15 CATCHERS BY XSBR (MIN 4,000 SB_PA CAREER)

Year Name	SB_PA	SBA	SB	CS	ATTDIFF	SBDIFF	NETATT	NETSB	XSB	ADDOUTS	XSBR
Best											
Rodriguez, Ivan	20183	840	430	410	−0.021	−0.050	−428.77	−41.89	−287.96	140.82	−0.0143
Lake, Steve	4132	294	162	132	−0.016	−0.001	−66.53	−0.22	−36.93	29.60	−0.0089
Bench, Johnny	12882	712	426	286	−0.020	0.043	−257.39	30.45	−104.00	153.39	−0.0081
Johnson, Charles	13640	663	399	264	−0.014	0.031	−188.29	20.54	−86.99	101.30	−0.0064
Santiago, Benito	21932	1288	844	444	−0.017	0.085	−377.93	109.70	−106.01	271.92	−0.0048
LaRue, Jason	4630	206	120	86	−0.010	0.023	−45.03	4.81	−20.87	24.15	−0.0045
Karkovice, Ron	10637	578	349	229	−0.013	0.054	−136.41	31.08	−42.39	94.02	−0.0040
Pierzynski, A. J.	4508	194	135	59	−0.017	0.125	−75.45	24.28	−18.03	57.41	−0.0040
Lieberthal, Mike	10134	503	341	162	−0.014	0.104	−145.17	52.26	−29.13	116.04	−0.0029
Wilson, Dan	14203	712	468	244	−0.010	0.057	−141.88	40.70	−37.69	104.18	−0.0027
Munson, Thurman	12179	760	442	318	−0.011	0.050	−131.78	37.89	−28.97	102.82	−0.0024
Ausmus, Brad	15778	866	542	324	−0.009	0.062	−139.86	53.34	−25.42	114.44	−0.0016
Valle, Dave	10423	612	383	229	−0.010	0.068	−102.34	41.34	−12.90	89.44	−0.0012
Yeager, Steve	12866	875	548	327	−0.014	0.096	−179.53	84.24	−14.78	164.74	−0.0011
Boone, Bob	26007	1655	1013	642	−0.011	0.084	−284.91	138.55	−13.99	270.92	−0.0005
Worst											
Benedict, Bruce	10961	1026	711	315	0.006	0.154	69.36	158.00	209.92	140.56	0.0192
Virgil, Ozzie	8111	763	572	191	0.004	0.191	30.54	145.78	171.72	141.18	0.0212
Webster, Lenny	5118	415	312	103	0.012	0.177	61.00	73.38	109.64	48.64	0.0214
Hodges, Ron	4687	428	297	131	0.008	0.194	37.54	83.07	104.93	67.39	0.0224
Biggio, Craig	4935	492	379	113	0.012	0.161	58.41	79.09	111.51	53.10	0.0226
Humphrey, Terry	4174	387	241	146	0.020	0.136	84.74	52.51	96.29	11.55	0.0231
Correll, Vic	4316	358	270	88	0.009	0.217	36.95	77.73	100.61	63.66	0.0233
Freehan, Bill	5497	435	287	148	0.018	0.159	99.99	69.22	128.43	28.44	0.0234
Blackwell, Tim	4380	436	307	129	0.011	0.174	49.35	75.71	103.49	54.14	0.0236
Piazza, Mike	16141	1364	1023	341	0.014	0.184	230.65	250.63	385.63	154.98	0.0239
Varitek, Jason	7201	536	384	152	0.021	0.150	148.81	80.48	179.83	31.02	0.0250
Nolan, Joe	4706	436	348	88	0.011	0.270	51.25	117.65	147.12	95.87	0.0313
Pocoroba, Biff	4675	470	348	122	0.022	0.198	101.58	92.98	157.20	55.62	0.0336
Fitzgerald, Mike	7722	824	649	175	0.020	0.212	153.09	174.37	264.62	111.53	0.0343
Hatteberg, Scott	4233	400	318	82	0.032	0.233	137.42	93.00	182.63	45.21	0.0431

Thoughts, Observations, and Conclusions

Looking at that career chart, Ivan Rodriguez stands out as nearly a freak of nature. He has about as many stolen bases prevented as the #2, #3, and #4 catchers on the list (Santiago, Bench, and Charles Johnson), and his rate of prevention is almost double the closest catcher. He is to controlling the running game what Nolan Ryan was to no-hitters, or Babe Ruth was to home runs.

That catcher with the second-best career rate of SB prevention is Steve Lake , a backup catcher from the late 1980s who never amassed more than 179 AB in a season, but posted better rates of prevention than Johnny Bench

Though intuition should generally not be relied upon when evidence is available, it is heartening to see some semblance of similarity between reputation and results. Ivan Rodriguez's presence atop the list surprises no one, nor would many quibble with Johnny Bench or Benito Santiago, Charles Johnson, Thurman Munson, or Bob Boone. Jason LaRue, winner of Baseball Prospectus' 2002 Golden Gun award (http://www.baseballprospectus.com/news/2002 0102wolverton.html), ranks highly as well. On the bottom end of the scale, Mike Piazza, Scott Hatteberg, Ted Simmons, and Todd Hundley all apparently deserve their poor reputations.

Piazza, in particular, is interesting because he holds six of the bottom 11 seasons of the past 30 years in total SB prevention. His combination of poor prevention and tenure behind the plate earn him the dubious title of worst-throwing catcher of the past 30 years, with only Simmons seriously challenging him for the title. Maybe a move to first base isn't such a bad idea.

What's the value of all this stolen base prevention? As noted earlier, it's difficult to assign meaningful run values, since the stolen base is a situation-specific strategic weapon that can have significant value beyond its expected run value. And even if you're doing to do so it's not quite right to ignore the extra outs produced. But with that caveat, a conservative estimate would be to credit about a fifth of a run (0.21 runs) for each stolen base prevented, as that's the weighted average difference between the SB outcome and the No Attempt outcome for the different out-situation decision trees presented earlier.

Dealing with the additional outs generated (ADDOUTS column) particularly by poor defensive catchers is also problematic. Taking the run value of the extra outs and adding them to the SB prevention figures gives a lot of extra credit to catchers who were run against often, regardless of their success rates. Part of the way to treat this might be to recognize that one of the strategic advantages of the stolen base with less than 2 outs is to avoid a double-play situation. Recognizing that a fraction of the runners caught stealing would have been routinely put out on a batter's play later in the inning, and crediting the catcher only with the extra

FIGURE 11. RUNNER'S DECISION TREE, 0 OUTS, DOUBLE PLAY EXPLICITLY FACTORED IN

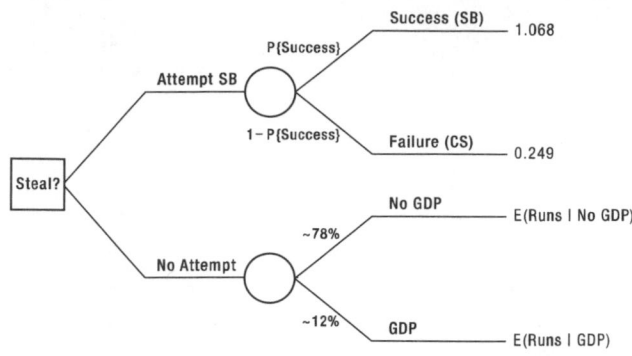

out value beyond that may be a more rational way to award credit in this situation. The decision diagram in figure 11 makes this clearer.

Another problem left unresolved with this analysis is the interaction between the catcher, the pitcher, and the battery's combined effectiveness versus the running game. Catchers who work disproportionately with lefties, or pitchers with exceptional pickoff moves (either due to the composition of the staff, or being the personal catcher of a lefty) may skew the results somewhat.

Also, pickoffs were left out of this analysis, as the focus of the article was on catchers' ability to prevent steals through reducing attempt rates, and with a pickoff it is often unclear what the runner's intent was. He could have been trying to steal, or perhaps he got caught sleeping, or between steps, or was otherwise fooled while simply taking a lead.

However, despite these areas for future research to elaborate, it is clear that catchers show significant differences in their ability to dissuade the opposition from using one of the tools in their arsenal—the stolen base. This takes the form of both the commonly recognized "percentage of runners thrown out" statistic, and the less-commonly quantified "intimidation" factor, where runners don't even try to steal in the first place.

The two premiere catchers of this generation also happen to be polar opposites in this ability. Ivan Rodriguez dominates the running game like no other catcher of the past 30 years, whereas Mike Piazza is arguably the worst catcher in controlling the running game over the same span. With the value of SB prevention between them totaling a 140+ run gap, it is enough to make up for Piazza's vastly better offense? Through 2003, Piazza's career VORP (Value Over Replacement Player) is about 190 runs greater than I-Rod's, so the SB prevention gap effectively closes most of the distance, and probably closes it completely when we recall that our ⅕th run per SB prevented was a conservative estimate. Both are clearly Hall of Famers, and perhaps the top two catchers in overall value ever.

Top 50 Prospects

by Rany Jazayerli

In each of the five previous editions of our Top Prospects chapter, we've led off with a discussion on the value of prospects and the importance of developing them. Frankly, that discussion has been beaten to death. Some truths in baseball should be self-evident.

If you need convincing that a strong farm system is still a necessary ingredient for building a successful major league team, we're not going to sway you with a 1,000-word essay on the subject. But you might be persuaded by a quick look at the Florida Marlins' roster. In a nutshell, the Marlins might never have reached the playoffs without Dontrelle Willis. They might not have won a single post-season series without Miguel Cabrera.

Miracle teams like the Marlins, teams that give theoretical hope and faith to fans of every franchise that a quantum leap in a single season really is possible, are almost never the result of a talent infusion from outside the organization. Free agency remains a proven method to of improving a franchise's *existing* foundation of talent. Even with the rise of the non-tender market and the accelerated player turnover of the last few years, the most reliable way to build that foundation of talent remains from within. Even the Yankees, the supposed exception all of baseball's rules, prove the point: Where would they be without Jeter, Bernie, Posada, Rivera, and Soriano, not to mention now-departed homegrown stars like Andy Pettitte?

The problem is that prospects are like tornadoes: Everyone agrees that they're important, but no one has come up with a reliable way of forecasting either one of them. Cabrera, our #31 prospect a year ago, looked like a promising third baseman and a potential star, but we had no way of knowing that, a year later, he would be one of the 10 most valuable commodities in the game. And Willis, who in retrospect was blessed with a baffling and effortless delivery that would allow him to dominate major league hitters from the very start, spent most of 2002 toiling in Low-A ball, and was the last player cut from this chapter last year.

The Marlins' two prized prospects set the tone for what was an even more unpredictable year for prospects than usual. The actual best rookie pitcher in the National League was Brandon Webb, who started his major league career with a phenomenal run of 13 consecutive quality starts. Webb was not even considered for our Top Prospects chapter last winter. And the runner-up for NL rookie honors, Scott Podsednik, had just been cast off by the Mariners' organization the year before, and no one even expected him to stick on a major league roster all season.

Angel Berroa, who had hit .215 in Triple-A in 2002 after battling through knee surgery, beat out established Japanese superstar Hideki Matsui for Rookie of the Year honors. In fourth place was Jody Gerut, who led all rookies in slugging average after missing all of 2001 with an injury and being let go by the Rockies. Consider that neither Podsednik nor Gerut, two of the ten best rookies in baseball last year, were listed in Baseball America's comprehensive *Prospect Handbook* listing the top 30 prospects in *each* organization.

The bottom line is that while we, as an industry, have made considerable progress in establishing the value of a top prospect, we have made precious little progress in determining the identity of those top prospects.

Not that our failures should stop us, any more than meteorologists should stop trying to predict the weather. Every failed prospect has a lesson to teach us; every gem that slips under the prospect radar until hitting it big in the majors has a story behind his unexpected success. Learning from our past will help us turn our failures into successes.

(One of the things we've learned is that a list of the top 40 prospects simply doesn't cast a wide enough net to ensnare all the potential impact players a year later, which is why we've adjusted the chapter's title this year.)

But the most important lesson is one we learn every year: the more information we have, the better. Just as weather forecasts have improved over the years as meteorologists have collected ever more information on current weather conditions at ever more points on the map, predicting the future of a baseball player improves when the foundation of our judgment—performance analysis—is augmented with information about his health, his scouting reports, his physical traits, his work ethic, and anything and everything else that might have the slightest impact on his future.

(However, we don't claim to be infallible. Scouting reports can be inaccurate; reports about a player's work ethic can be misinformed; a player's listed date of birth can be pure fiction. Any careful evaluation of a player needs to take the possibility of error into account.)

Long-time readers will note one significant change from previous editions of our Top Prospect list. Along with a **translation** of each prospect's statistics from the last two seasons, we have included a five-year forecast trend of WARP (Wins Above Replacement Player), for the 2004 through 2008 seasons, based on Nate Silver's PECOTA algorithm. The beauty of the PECOTA system is that it can be used to project as far into the future as needed. While the accuracy of the system goes down over time, naturally, even a blurry glimpse of a young player's distant future can yield considerable insight.

Thanks to our use of PECOTA this year, we are proud to say that our information base is the strongest it's ever been, and we are optimistic that, as a result, our Top Prospect list will prove to be the most accurate one we've ever done.

But no amount of new information can change one inescapable conclusion: The *2004 BP* Prospect of the Year is . . .

1. Joe Mauer   C   Minnesota Twins   Age 21

	AVG	OBP	SLG	Defense
2002	.227	.299	.300	C: 12
2003	.290	.342	.380	C: 14

5-Year WARP Trend: 0.1, 0.5, 0.7, 1.1, 1.5

The first pick of the strongest draft of the new century is now the top prospect in baseball. Mauer is, to put it bluntly, something of an anomaly in the recent annals of prospectdom, because his offensive and defensive skills are so jarringly different that they defy stereotypes; he's best thought of as two different players. On offense, he's a left-handed frozen rope machine who should contend for multiple batting titles while hitting a couple dozen homers a year in his prime. Defensively, he's a frozen rope machine from behind the plate, one who's thrown out nearly half the runners who have tried to steal on him.

If that combination doesn't strike you as strange, consider that no catcher has won a batting title since Ernie Lombardi led the NL in hitting in 1942. Mauer could be Wade Boggs at the plate; he could be Johnny Bench behind it. His profile is so unique in recent baseball history that I would hesitate to put any limits on what he can achieve in his career.

As with a stock prospectus, we should note a possible risk factor: There's a fair amount of anecdotal evidence that warns us against tall catchers, and Mauer's 6′ 4″. BP is working on a study measuring the health risks of tall catchers; with no definitive study already done that proves those risks, Mauer's talent keeps him at #1.

2. Jeremy Reed   OF   Chicago White Sox   Age 23

	AVG	OBP	SLG	Defense
2002	.257	.298	.379	OF: −2
2003	.299	.369	.446	OF: −1

5-Year WARP Trend: 1.4, 1.6, 1.9, 2.1, 2.1

Sometimes, a prospect comes along that puts up such ridiculous numbers, with no history of more pedestrian numbers to help us keep perspective, that it becomes difficult to fairly evaluate him. Jeremy Reed is such a prospect. Since he was drafted in the third round in 2002 out of Long Beach State, he has done nothing but hit—and at a level that would seem to be unsustainable for as long as he has. After hitting .333 in high A-ball last season, he was promoted to Double-A and hit .409, becoming the first player to hit .400 or better at that level or higher (min: 200 AB) since Erubiel Durazo in 1999. His translated numbers and PECOTA projections—two of his five closest comps are Tony Gwynn and Don Mattingly—suggest that he's the most promising hitter in the game, even more so than Mauer. There's some concern that his freakish ability to hit in the upper .300s will turn out to be a fluke, but even if it is, his offensive game is well-rounded enough that he'll be an All-Star in the majors if he hits just .300. And if it isn't a fluke?

3. Andy Marte   3B   Atlanta Braves   Age 20

	AVG	OBP	SLG	Defense
2002	.215	.263	.387	3B: −2
2003	.229	.303	.390	3B: −18

5-Year WARP Trend: −0.3, 0.0, 0.7, 1.0, 2.3

A year ago, a young Latin third baseman named Miguel Cabrera excelled in his first season at high-A ball, and despite modest power numbers served notice that he had the ability to arrive quickly as an impact player—an arrival that occurred more quickly than anyone anticipated. A year later, Marte fits that same profile. Just 20 years old, he followed up on his promising season in 2002 by hitting 16 homers in the Florida State League (seven more than Cabrera hit in 2002), while improving on his already solid plate discipline and (numbers above aside) defense. A player with Marte's diversity of skills, and at such a young age, has so many ways to develop into a true superstar player. As a bonus, he plays for an organization whose can't-miss prospects almost never, in fact, miss. Marte is as safe a bet as a prospect can be without ever playing a game in the high minors.

4. Prince Fielder   1B   Milwaukee Brewers   Age 20

	AVG	OBP	SLG	Defense
2002	.199	.283	.341	1B: −17
2003	.229	.305	.400	1B: −15

5-Year WARP Trend: −0.7, −0.3, 0.7, 1.0, 2.1

We all had an inkling that Cecil's son was something special when he was launching upper-deck homers at Tiger Stadium during batting practice . . . when he was 12 years old. That man-child has grown into a man, and that hitting precocity has turned into performance. Prince is a different type of hitter than his father: He bats left-handed, for one, and shows the potential to hit for a better average than his dad ever did. Like Cecil, Prince is always going to have to watch his weight, though like dad he's a good athlete for someone his size. Few teenagers have ever shown his combination of power and plate discipline; comparisons to a left-handed Frank Thomas aren't out of line if he keeps the pounds off.

5. David Wright **3B** **New York Mets** **Age 21**

	AVG	OBP	SLG	Defense
2002	.197	.274	.308	3B: −7
2003	.216	.297	.385	3B: 1

5-Year WARP Trend: −0.3, 0.3, 0.9, 1.0, 1.6

Generally speaking, it's dangerous to call any prospect "the next Joe Smith," where Joe Smith is an established major league star. It places unfair expectations on the prospect while simultaneously selling short his own unique talents. But if anyone on this list is worthy of such a direct comparison, it's David Wright, the next Scott Rolen. Like Rolen, Wright is a right-handed-hitting third baseman with a wide array of talents, including the ability to hit for average and power, plate discipline, above-average speed, and Gold Glove defensive potential. He has shown these talents over two consecutive seasons, and last year excelled in the difficult Florida State League. He trails Marte in these rankings primarily because Marte's a year younger. But much like Rolen shone in a late-season call-up before winning Rookie of the Year honors in 1997, Wright could be up by August and a Rookie of the Year candidate by April '05.

6. Edwin Jackson **RHP** **Los Angeles Dodgers** **Age 20**

	H/9	BB/9	K/9	HR/9	ERA	PERA
2002	7.9	3.8	4.7	0.4	4.36	3.60
2003	7.7	3.7	7.2	1.0	4.76	4.04

5-Year WARP Trend: 2.9, 1.3, 2.0, 2.8, 2.8

For years, the Dodgers have had one of the weakest farm systems around. Those days are over. Jackson was more highly regarded as an outfielder than as a pitcher when he was drafted in 2001, and in fact was used as a DH when he wasn't pitching his first season. He was told to put the bat away as his fastball continued to pick up velocity, and last year broke through with a terrific Double-A season, culminated by winning his major league debut, against Randy Johnson, on his 20th birthday. (The last pitcher to win his major league debut at a younger age was Dwight Gooden.) Jackson throws one of the best fastballs in the minor leagues—in the upper 90s with movement—his arm

hasn't been abused, and he'll be working in one of the best pitcher's parks in the game. That's a recipe for success if I've ever seen one.

7. Zack Greinke **RHP** **Kansas City Royals** **Age 20**

	H/9	BB/9	K/9	HR/9	ERA	PERA
2003	8.2	1.5	5.6	1.2	3.82	3.94

5-Year WARP Trend: 2.2, 2.0, 2.3, 2.4, 3.0

To all those people who want to compare Greinke to a young Bret Saberhagen, or a young Greg Maddux, there's only one problem: Greinke is actually a more advanced pitcher than they were at the same age. Maddux walked 52 men in 186 innings at age 19; Saberhagen walked 48 in 187 innings. Greinke walked 18 in 140. He throws four pitches with movement and command, he has excellent mechanics, and as someone who didn't start pitching full-time until his senior year of high school, he's got a fresh arm for someone from a warm-weather state. Jackson has better stuff and a higher upside, but Greinke's better command makes him the less risky of the two. Frankly, you can't go wrong with either one. There Is No Such Thing As A Pitching Prospect, but if there were, he'd be Zack Greinke.

8. B. J. Upton **SS** **Tampa Bay Devil Rays** **Age: 19**

	AVG	OBP	SLG	Defense
2003	.228	.302	.345	SS: −35

5-Year WARP Trend: −0.2, −0.1, 0.2, 0.4, 0.8

The Pirates, with the first pick in the 2002 draft, were undecided whether to take Upton or Ball State right-hander Brian Bullington. In the end, the Bucs decided to take the safe route; their aversion to risk was the Devil Rays' gain. Upton is a potential five-tool/Seven Skill shortstop who needs only to add power and cut down on his errors (he made 56 last year) to fulfill that potential. Most shortstops with his tools get undermined by poor plate discipline, but Upton shows good patience. He was young for his high school class and became the first shortstop to reach Double-A before his 19th birthday since Alex Rodriguez. The Devil Rays are going to be the ugly stepsisters of the AL Beast for the foreseeable future, but they have some of the best young talent in the division, at least until Chuck LaMar finds a way to screw things up.

9. Rickie Weeks **2B** **Milwaukee Brewers** **Age: 21**

	AVG	OBP	SLG	Defense
2003	.228	.348	.380	2B: −4

5-Year WARP Trend: 1.0, 1.6, 2.0, 2.0, 2.4

If you want a good example of the uncertainties surrounding high school players, consider that Weeks—who might turn out to be the best player of the high school class of 2000—went completely undrafted that year. He then spent three years at Southern University compiling numbers so absurd that not even the Division I-AA competition could dampen their impact. He signed late as the #2 draft pick last summer, but showed enough five-tool talent after he signed to merit a top-10 ranking. Opinions are divided over whether he'll stay at second base or move to the outfield, but he should have the bat to succeed wherever he plays.

10. Kazuo Matsui   SS   New York Mets   Age 28

	AVG	OBP	SLG	Defense
2002	.319	.370	.518	SS: N/A
2003	.282	.336	.478	SS: N/A

5-Year WARP Trend: 3.7, 3.4, 2.6, 2.6, 1.9

"Little Matsui," as Kazuo hates to be called, may wind up being the better Matsui on this side of the Atlantic. Like his namesake Hideki, Kazuo was a legitimate superstar in Japan. Hideki's rookie season wasn't quite as stellar as anticipated, but Clay Davenport's most recent statistical analysis shows that power seems to be the one trait that does not carry over well from Japan to the major leagues. Kazuo's game, relying less on power than Hideki and more on defense and speed, should translate more easily to the American game. Since new teammate Jose Reyes has been booted across the keystone to make room for him, not only is KazMat the frontrunner for NL Rookie of the Year honors, he's neck-and-neck with Rafael Furcal as the second-best shortstop in the league behind Edgar Renteria.

11. Justin Morneau   1B   Minnesota Twins   Age 23

	AVG	OBP	SLG	Defense
2002	.255	.304	.409	1B: −10
2003	.245	.315	.462	1B: −1

5-Year WARP Trend: 1.2, 1.2, 1.9, 2.7, 2.9

Most of the players on this list are hitting prospects. Morneau's already a hitter. It He'd fit perfectly as the Twins' #3 hitter on Opening Day if Ron Gardenhire gives him the chance. The product of a British Columbia high school program which has become the newest hotbed of talent in North America, Morneau has a beautiful swing and numbers which are only slightly less attractive, despite being hampered by nagging injuries over the years. He showed flashes of his power during a mid-season promotion to Minnesota last summer, and despite the Twins' ridiculous logjam of OF/1B/DH types on their roster, should be an everyday cog in their lineup at some point this year. He should eventually settle in as a .300/25-homer hitter for years to come.

12. Scott Kazmir   LHP   New York Mets   Age 20

	H/9	BB/9	K/9	HR/9	ERA	PERA
2002	5.3	5.3	10.6	0.0	1.76	2.50 (15 IP)
2003	9.2	4.8	8.2	1.4	4.78	5.50

5-Year WARP Trend: 1.4, 0.7, 0.9, 2.1, 2.7

Good things come in small packages, and sometimes so does lightning. Kazmir is listed at six feet even (and that's almost certainly an exaggeration), but like Billy Wagner a decade before him, that doesn't stop his left arm from touching 100 miles an hour, or from striking out 179 batters in 127 professional innings to date. Like any pitcher his size, there may always be questions that his body won't be able to stand up to the rigors of starting. (Wagner was a successful starter in the minors, but was converted to relief anyway because of concerns he would break down.) The Mets are cognizant of this in the post-Dallas Green era, and have kept Kazmir on a ridiculously low pitch count since he was drafted—it's taken him 30 starts to throw those 127 innings. So long as he stays healthy—and there have been no significant concerns with his arm so far—he's going to keep striking out hitters at an astonishing rate for many years to come.

13. Bobby Crosby   SS   Oakland Athletics   Age 24

	AVG	OBP	SLG	Defense
2002	.238	.297	.349	SS: −2
2003	.268	.352	.480	SS: −1

5-Year WARP Trend: 1.8, 1.8, 2.0, 2.0, 1.9

How do you keep finishing in first place on a $40 million payroll? By being so proactive in filling holes on your roster that you draft your star shortstop's eventual replacement more than two years before he's eligible for free agency. Such foresight is par for the course in Oakland, where the A's grabbed Crosby in the 2001 draft with an eye to 2004. Sure enough, Tejada is an Oriole, Crosby is ready to take his place . . . and the A's nabbed two extra picks in this year's draft, allowing them to repeat the cycle at another position. Crosby has consistently put up numbers that would make him a good prospect in left field, and with a full year at Triple-A is in little danger of being overwhelmed in Oakland this year. The only caveat with him—and the only reason he's not in our Top 10—is that the he's played in a great hitter's environment at every minor league level, and the adjustment to the cavernous dimensions of Network Associates Coliseum can be difficult.

14. Casey Kotchman   1B   Anaheim Angels   Age 21

	AVG	OBP	SLG	Defense
2002	.211	.297	.343	1B: 0
2003	.256	.335	.396	1B: 0

5-Year WARP Trend: −0.1, 0.5, 1.1, 1.3, 1.8

Sometimes, there's nothing wrong with nepotism. The Angels were thrilled to grab Kotchman with the 13th overall pick in 2000, and not just because his dad worked as a scout for the team. Despite being slowed by wrist injuries in his first two pro seasons and a torn hamstring last year, Kotchman has a lifetime .326 average as a pro, befitting a player with arguably the prettiest-looking swing in the minors. He also plays a nifty first base, making the comparisons to Mark Grace—or to Will Clark if he develops power as expected—not only inevitable but warranted. Kotchman has only to find a way to stay healthy to emerge as one of the best first basemen in the game.

15. Alexis Rios CF Toronto Blue Jays Age 23

	AVG	OBP	SLG	Defense
2002	.254	.286	.346	OF: −7
2003	.301	.346	.463	OF: −12

5-Year WARP Trend: 0.4, 0.5, 1.1, 0.8, 1.1

This is a good example of why teams draft raw talent in the first round: because sometimes, that talent can be refined. Rios was widely derided as a signability pick when the Blue Jays selected him in 1999, and indeed, the Puerto Rican got the lowest draft bonus of any first-rounder that year. After a couple of disappointing seasons to start his career, Rios started to show signs he might not be a wasted pick after all in 2002, when he hit .305 in the Florida State League despite battling through various injuries. But nothing prepared us for his 2003 season, when he dominated the Southern League, hitting .352 with 11 homers (his previous career high was three). He then followed up his summer season with a monster winter campaign in Puerto Rico, hitting 12 homers by the time we went to press. His plate discipline has only improved from bad to merely inadequate, but he's in one of the best organizations in baseball to keep that flaw from becoming fatal. He's not far from joining the Blue Jays' outfield alongside another former high school pick who was laughed at as a reach in the first round: Vernon Wells.

16. Ryan Wagner RHP Cincinnati Reds Age 21

	H/9	BB/9	K/9	HR/9	ERA	PERA
2003	5.8	3.7	8.5	0.6	2.42	2.81

5-Year WARP Trend: 1.9, 1.5, 1.0, 1.5, 1.4

The all-time NCAA record holder for strikeouts per nine innings in a season made yet another compelling case that college results do translate to the pros. It's a little strange to call Wagner a prospect, when you consider that he's thrown more innings in the majors than in the minor leagues. Aided by a slider that was probably major league caliber when he was still a sophomore, Wagner needed less than a month of minor league refinement before making a spectacular debut in the Reds' bullpen. He's a safe bet to be one of the best relievers in the game this year, unless the Reds follow through on their threat to move him to the rotation. Chad Cordero, the Expos' first-round pick, was also an elite college closer who was pitching successfully in the majors just months after he was drafted. It's too soon to say whether Wagner and Cordero represent a one-year phenomenon or the start of a new trend of teams drafting college closers with the expectation that they can make an immediate major league impact.

17. Guillermo Quiroz C Toronto Blue Jays Age 22

	AVG	OBP	SLG	Defense
2002	.202	.254	.343	C: −1
2003	.240	.317	.453	C: 2

5-Year WARP Trend: 0.2, 0.4, 1.0, 1.3, 1.7

Quiroz was inked by the Blue Jays for a $1.2 million signing bonus, and three years later he was well on his way to being deemed a bust. That's an easy label to earn when you've hit .162 and .199 in the South Atlantic League the previous two years. But over the last two seasons Quiroz has justified his bonus and then some. He swatted 46 extra-base hits in 2002, then repeated the trick with 47 last season in just 108 games last year, while trading in 10 of his doubles for more homers. Quiroz may never win a batting title, but then Joe Mauer may never hit 35 homers, a mark which Quiroz should challenge at his peak. Toss in catch-and-throw skills that got him his signing bonus in the first place, and you've got the new Lance Parrish.

18. Jeff Mathis C Anaheim Angels Age 21

	AVG	OBP	SLG	Defense
2002	.230	.277	.366	C: 2
2003	.240	.297	.388	C: −2

5-Year WARP Trend: −0.1, 0.2, 0.8, 1.1, 2.4

As teams have become more selective when it comes to drafting high-risk players, the players they do select have become better gambles. Historically, high school catchers have been among the worst players to draft in the first round, but the Angels used a supplemental first rounder on Mathis in the same draft that Mauer went #1. Mathis is a terrific defensive catcher for someone who didn't even play the position full-time in high school, and he's hit 80 doubles over the past two seasons, including 11 two-baggers in just 24 games in Double-A last year. If those doubles turn into homers, he could surpass Quiroz as a two-way threat; even if they don't, he'll be Brian Harper with better defense, which is still a hell of a player.

19. Dallas McPherson 3B Anaheim Angels Age 23

	AVG	OBP	SLG	Defense
2002	.208	.288	.331	3B: −10
2003	.229	.314	.445	3B: −2

5-Year WARP Trend: 0.5, 1.1, 1.4, 1.6, 2.3

The Angels selected Kotchman, Mathis, and McPherson with their first three picks in the 2001 draft, which is the sort of draft that fills scouts' dreams while they're on the road 300 days a year. McPherson is a secondary skills demon, mashing 23 homers and drawing 60 walks in just 105 games last year. (He also hit over .300 in both A-ball and Double-A.) His future defensive position is still up in the air; his defensive abilities at third base are probably unsustainable at the position, and he was rumored as headed to right field to be Tim Salmon's long-term successor before the Angels signed Vladimir Guerrero. Like Salmon, McPherson is capable of hitting 30 homers and drawing 90 walks every year, making him an All-Star candidate at any position.

20. J. J. Hardy — SS — Milwaukee Brewers — Age 21

	AVG	OBP	SLG	Defense
2002	.219	.247	.306	SS: 17
2003	.240	.316	.380	SS: 9

5-Year WARP Trend: −0.5, 0.0, 0.4, 0.3, 0.5

If you're looking for another Sign of the Apocalypse, look no further: The Milwaukee Brewers have three of the top 20 prospects in the game. Hardy improved offensively last season as much as anyone on this list. A year after hitting a limp .228 in a late-season call-up to Double-A, he returned to the level last year and hit .279 with 12 homers and more walks than strikeouts. His defense has always been considered as ahead of his offense, and in fact his defensive numbers are the most impressive of any player on this list other than Joe Mauer's. Hardy may take his lumps in Milwaukee this season if, as expected, he's rushed to the majors. But by 2006, he and Weeks could be teaming up to form one of the finest double play combinations in baseball.

21. Cole Hamels — LHP — Philadelphia Phillies — Age 20

	H/9	BB/9	K/9	HR/9	ERA	PERA
2003	7.8	4.6	8.9	0.3	3.02	3.66

5-Year WARP Trend: 2.2, 1.4, 1.4, 3.0, 3.5

There must have been something in the water—Hamels is the third high school pitcher selected in the first round of the 2002 draft alone to make this list. (Of course, the first high school pitcher selected that year, Chris Gruler, has already undergone rotator cuff surgery.) Like Kazmir, Hamels is a left-handed pitcher with great strikeout rate, but while Kazmir relies on heat, Hamels relies on composure, and arguably the best change-up in the minor leagues. In addition to his strikeouts, you have to be impressed by the fact that the next home run he surrenders will be the first of his pro career. A freak fracture of his humerus in high school—he ran into a car mirror while playing street football with some friends—shows no signs of being reinjured so far, although the possibility of a Tom Browning/Tony Saunders repeat of that fracture drops him down a few notches on our list.

22. Franklin Gutierrez — OF — Los Angeles Dodgers — Age 21

	AVG	OBP	SLG	Defense
2002	.222	.268	.370	OF: −3
2003	.231	.284	.441	OF: −5

5-Year WARP Trend: −0.2, −0.1, 0.7, 1.2, 3.3

What offensive skill correlates most closely with run scoring? Our constant hammering of the importance of walks notwithstanding, it isn't plate discipline. It's power, which is why Gutierrez is one of the best hitting prospects in the game despite only intermittent command of the strike zone. His raw power finally manifested itself on the field last season, as he hit 20 homers in the pitcher-friendly Florida State League, then slugged nearly .600 in a late-season promotion to Double-A. The comparisons to Juan Gonzalez are a little overblown, but only a little. Gutierrez has a better chance at a 500-homer career than any other player on this list.

23. Dustin McGowan — RHP — Toronto Blue Jays — Age 22

	H/9	BB/9	K/9	HR/9	ERA	PERA
2002	12.0	5.1	6.1	1.6	6.63	7.12
2003	9.2	3.2	6.1	0.3	4.67	3.96

5-Year WARP Trend: 0.4, 0.2, 0.7, 0.9, 0.9

Over the past 15 years, the Blue Jays have nailed more of their first-round picks than any other team in the game. Every one of their top picks from 1987 to 1998 reached the majors, including Shawn Green, Shannon Stewart, and Vernon Wells. Alexis Rios was their first-rounder in 1999. McGowan was actually the second of the Jays' first-round picks in 2000, but he looks like he won't let being drafted as a high school pitcher keep him from continuing the tradition. (Of course, as high school pitchers go, he has a long way to go to reach the levels of their 1995 first-rounder—Roy Halladay.) McGowan relies on a classic fastball-curveball combination with exceptional command of both. He stormed through A-ball, didn't miss a beat after a mid-season promotion to Double-A, and could be in the Blue Jays' rotation by Labor Day. Given the Jays' strength on offense and their playoff aspirations, McGowan is the most likely pitcher on this list to play the part of Dontrelle Willis this season.

24. Grady Sizemore — CF — Cleveland Indians — Age 21

	AVG	OBP	SLG	Defense
2002	.232	.311	.328	OF: −14
2003	.257	.316	.418	OF: −17

5-Year WARP Trend: −0.6, 0.0, 0.5, 0.9, 1.1

Two-sport stars like Drew Henson and Joe Borchard didn't focus solely on their baseball careers until their 20s, and by then it might have been too late. In contrast, Sizemore, who was given a $2 million bonus by the Expos (yes, the Expos) to give up a football scholarship to the University of Washington, is already beginning to fulfill his potential. He was the third player the Expos gave up in the Bartolo Colon trade, but may soon surpass Brandon Phillips and Cliff Lee as the best prospect in the deal. His power is coming (he hit 13 homers last year after hitting just six in his first three pro seasons), and would complete the package that already contains speed, defense, and plate discipline. He'll be an important cog in the Indians' lineup by 2006.

25. James Loney   **1B**   **Los Angeles Dodgers**   **Age 20**

	AVG	OBP	SLG	Defense
2002	.230	.289	.377	1B: −4
2003	.226	.275	.345	1B: 0

5-Year WARP Trend: −0.9, −0.6, −0.0, 0.4, 1.5

For years, the Dodgers were infamous for making some of the strangest—and worst—first-round picks in baseball. So it looked like business as usual two summers ago when the Dodgers used their first pick on Loney—who was scouted by most teams as a pitcher—and announced they were moving him to first base. Only Loney justified the move by blasting his way through rookie ball and holding his own in the Florida State League in his first pro summer. He returned to Vero Beach last season and, recovering from off-season wrist surgery, hit just .222 in his first 45 games. From that point on, he hit .301/.369/.436 as one of the youngest players in the league, then held his own in the Arizona Fall League, where most of the players are culled from the high minors. Loney is an excellent athlete with a nifty glove; there's very little difference between him and Casey Kotchman a year ago. If his wrist problem proves to be an anomaly and not an omen, he's as good a bet to make a quantum leap this season as anyone on this list.

26. David DeJesus   **CF**   **Kansas City Royals**   **Age 24**

	AVG	OBP	SLG	Defense
2002	.228	.315	.364	OF: −6
2003	.267	.365	.419	OF: −7

5-Year WARP Trend: 1.1, 1.1, 1.2, 1.2, 1.2

We're not sure that there's such a thing as an ideal #2 hitter, but DeJesus comes awfully close. He gets on base (career .405 OBP in the minors), hits line drives, has enough power to keep pitchers honest, and has enough speed to beat out grounders and foil the double play. He also plays a fine center field, and is the heir apparent to Carlos Beltran after Beltran chases the money next winter. In the meantime, DeJesus would make a great supersub fourth outfielder, though the Royals may start him in the minors in '04 with the signing of Juan Gonzalez. That'd be a shame; for someone who has yet to get through a full season in the minors without an injury of some sort, a season of part-time play adding up to 350 or so at-bats could be just the tonic his body needs. DeJesus hasn't let his injuries keep him from improving every season, so if can find a way to stay healthy, before long he might start looking like an ideal leadoff man.

27. Chin-Hui Tsao   **RHP**   **Colorado Rockies**   **Age 23**

	H/9	BB/9	K/9	HR/9	ERA	PERA
2002	8.6	3.0	6.3	1.2	3.68	4.56
2003	8.6	2.9	6.8	1.4	4.12	4.76

5-Year WARP Trend: 1.1, 1.2, 1.2, 1.0, 1.0

The Rockies finally have a pitching prospect up to the challenge of Coors Field, which is why Tsao is the first Rockies pitcher ever to make our Top Prospect list. Tsao almost made the list after his first pro season in 2000 (and before blowing out his elbow). He returned from Tommy John surgery in 2002 and was throwing as hard as ever last season, with even better numbers than before his injury. In almost any other organization, he would be a Top 20 prospect, but, historically, teams playing in hitter's parks have had difficulty developing pitchers, above and beyond what you would expect from park effects alone. Jason Jennings showed that Coors Field could at least be battled to a draw; it's up to Tsao, along with fellow farmhand Jeff Francis, to prove that it can be beaten.

28. Khalil Greene   **SS**   **San Diego Padres**   **Age 24**

	AVG	OBP	SLG	Defense
2002	.250	.294	.397	SS: −3
2003	.253	.303	.403	SS: −7

5-Year WARP Trend: 1.2, 1.3, 1.3, 1.1, 1.2

The 2002 Golden Spikes Award winner—and first-round draft pick—breezed through the minors and was playing in San Diego by the end of his first full pro season. There are warning signs here; he was drafted as a college senior and is already 24, so he lacks the upside of some of the players on this list, and his strike zone judgment (just 36 walks in 548 minor league AB) could use a lot of work. But he's already penciled in as the Padres' starting shortstop this year, and his impressive defensive instincts—he's an above-average shortstop despite below-average speed and arm strength for the position—give hope that he'll eventually figure things out on offense as well. Expect a somewhat disappointing rookie season, then an improved sophomore campaign once everything clicks into place.

29. Matt Riley   **LHP**   **Baltimore Orioles**   **Age 24**

	H/9	BB/9	K/9	HR/9	ERA	PERA
2002	12.3	4.6	6.4	1.7	7.37	7.24
2003	8.9	4.0	7.7	0.9	4.21	4.51

5-Year WARP Trend: 0.7, 0.6, 0.9, 0.4, 0.4

In recent years, it's become fashionable to say of a pitcher that undergoes Tommy John surgery, "it might be the best thing for him in the long run." Perhaps no pitcher in history has benefited from blowing out his elbow more than Riley did. Four years ago, Riley was a phenom, a lefty with a lightning arm who jumped into the Orioles' rotation only weeks after his 20th birthday. He was also headstrong and stubborn, with a reputation of being uncoachable. He underwent Tommy John the following spring and didn't return to the mound until 2002. He returned with his old stuff, but also as a new man, with newfound maturity and a calmer demeanor on the mound. His comeback was completed last season, when he struck out 150 batters in

143 innings between Double-A and Triple-A, then made two excellent starts for the Orioles in September. After all he's been through, Riley is still only 24, and he's a much better bet for long-term success today then ever before. All pitchers are at risk for a career-threatening injury, so why not bet on one that's already suffered one and emerged better than ever?

30. Dioner Navarro   C   New York Yankees   Age 20

	AVG	OBP	SLG	Defense
2002	.182	.246	.285	C: 1
2003	.272	.322	.413	C: −3

5-Year WARP Trend: −0.3, 0.1, 0.5, 0.9, 1.4

Everyone's heard of Joe Mauer. Few have heard of Dioner Navarro. Which is most peculiar, because the difference between the two is smaller than you'd expect. (It's especially peculiar because Navarro is a Yankee.) Some compare Navarro to Ivan Rodriguez—particularly with regard to his small stature (5′10″)—and some laugh at the comparison, which is fair given that Rodriguez was an everyday catcher in the major leagues at age 19. But Navarro isn't far off the I-Rod track. He hit for a terrific average, showed decent power for a teenager in Double-A, and while his walk rate was below average, it was at least partially offset by the fact that he makes such excellent contact, striking out just 53 times all year. His defensive skills, while not in the Mauer class, are still outstanding for a converted infielder. Mauer may be the best catching prospect in baseball, but Navarro has a case for being called the most underrated.

31. Delmon Young   OF   Tampa Bay Devil Rays   Age: 18

Here's a hint for teams wondering how to snag two of the top prospects in baseball: field a really, really bad team year after year. Courtesy of having the worst record in the AL in 2001 and 2002, the Devil Rays had the #2 and #1 picks in back-to-back years, and were able to select the best high school hitter in each draft. Young becomes the first high school player ever to make our top prospect list the winter after he was drafted, but really, it was an easy choice. He's been one of the most-touted players in his age group since he turned 13, and is one of the most polished hitters to come out of high school since Alex Rodriguez. (He only turned 18 last September, as he was also one of the youngest high school players in the draft.) Young didn't make his pro debut until the Arizona Fall League, then schooled pitchers five years older than him (though a bunch diluted by teams' reluctance to send top arms to the AFL), hitting .417 in 47 at-bats. He's got the bloodlines (he's Dmitri's brother), the confidence, and most important, the bat to make it big.

32. Josh Barfield   2B   San Diego Padres   Age 21

	AVG	OBP	SLG	Defense
2002	.253	.279	.342	2B: −3
2003	.255	.305	.412	2B: 1

5-Year WARP Trend: 0.1, 0.5, 0.9, 1.0, 1.8

Cecil Fielder isn't the only member of the 1987 Toronto Blue Jays to field a legacy on this list. Jesse's son exploded onto the scene in his third pro season, putting up the best numbers of any second baseman in the minors by hitting .337 with 68 extra-base hits. Like most top second base prospects, his offense is ahead of his defense at this point—you don't become a top prospect at second base by flashing the leather—although the Padres swear he won't need to change positions in the future. He did have minor wrist surgery to correct a nagging problem after the season, which may slow him down in the first half this year. The Pads will also wait to see how Barfield adjusts after leaving the hitter's paradise that is the California League. He's got a shot to replace Mark Loretta when the incumbent's contract expires after the '05 season.

33. Greg Miller   LHP   Los Angeles Dodgers   Age 19

	H/9	BB/9	K/9	HR/9	ERA	PERA
2002	7.9	4.2	4.7	0.5	4.46	3.86
2003	8.6	3.7	7.5	0.9	4.39	4.42

5-Year WARP Trend: N/A

If you've read *Baseball Prospectus* for very long, you know that one of our dictums is that high school pitchers are generally poor draft choices, and that a first-round pick spent on a high school pitcher might as well have been used to select the owner's daughter.

That dictum is being put to its sternest test in a while. Of the top 11 pitchers on this list, one was drafted as a college reliever, two were international signings...and the other eight were all drafted out of high school. Four of them—Greinke, Kazmir, Hamels, and Miller—were selected in the first round of the 2002 draft alone. There are many reasons for this: (1) a greater emphasis on college talent in the draft has started to create some high school bargains; (2) teams are doing a better job of keeping their pitchers healthy; (3) natural selection bias, which means that the best college pitchers are so polished (think Mark Prior) that they hardly spend enough time in the minors to ever land on a prospect list.

Veering back on topic...Miller had scouts comparing him to Sandy Koufax as he buzzed through the Florida State League with a tremendous fastball and curveball, then got promoted to Double-A while still 18 and proceeded to strike out 40 batters in 27 innings. (His combination of youth and performance are so rare that PECOTA could not find enough comparable players to generate an accurate forecast.) So why does he rank this low? Because he developed shoulder bursitis at the end of the season, and while it's considered minor, there's no such thing as a minor shoulder problem in a teenage pitcher. If he stays healthy, he could join Edwin Jackson to give the Dodgers two of the best young starters in baseball by 2006.

34. Edwin Encarnacion   3B   Cincinnati Reds   Age 21

	AVG	OBP	SLG	Defense
2002	.220	.265	.369	3B: −11
2003	.241	.296	.371	3B: −20

5-Year WARP Trend: −0.1, 0.2, 0.8, 1.0, 1.8

There's always a romance to the story of a throw-in player who ends up being the best player in a deal, dating at least back to the time a minor leaguer named Ryne Sandberg was thrown in to even out a trade of Larry Bowa for Ivan DeJesus. (Twenty-one years after he cost the Phillies a Hall of Fame second baseman, Bowa cost them a playoff spot with his borderline-psychotic approach to managing. Would somebody stop this man, please?) Two years ago, Encarnacion was that throw-in when the Reds and Rangers came together on their Rob Bell-for-Ruben Mateo blockbuster. Now, after two years of consistent progress at the plate and on the field, he's one of the most complete third base prospects in the game. He has enough range that the Reds have dabbled with him at shortstop, and he has shown a lot of pop (60 doubles and 30 homers the last two seasons) for a player in his early 20s. He hit much better in his second crack at Double-A pitching late last year. All his indicators are positive; a berth in our Top 10 next season isn't out of the question.

35. Chris Snelling   OF   Seattle Mariners   Age 22

	AVG	OBP	SLG	Defense
2002	.261	.338	.420	OF: 0
2003	.283	.325	.420	OF: 0

5-Year WARP Trend: 0.7, 1.1, 1.2, 1.6, 1.7

Our favorite Australian player had what might charitably be described as a consolidation year, as he spent the first half of the season rehabbing a torn ACL. He picked up right where he left off, hitting .333 in a tough Double-A park before a late promotion to Triple-A. We admit to having a soft spot for Snelling; in addition to his hitting talent, he's an intelligent, charismatic player—he's nearly as prolific a quote machine as he is a hit machine. What he doesn't have is the willingness to give 95% when giving 100% can get him hurt, which is why he has yet to get through a season without an injury. He's smart enough to figure out the math one day, and the sooner the better, before his injuries leave a lasting mark. The signing of Raul Ibanez blocks his most obvious path to a major league job, but if the early moves of the Bavasi Administration are any indication, Snelling will probably be pilfered away shortly by an organization that actually knows what it's doing.

36. Jason Bay   OF   Pittsburgh Pirates   Age 25

	AVG	OBP	SLG	Defense
2002	.234	.311	.395	OF: −9
2003	.274	.383	.497	OF: −3

5-Year WARP Trend: 1.3, 1.3, 1.4, 1.3, 1.1

The classic overachieving late bloomer, Bay was a 22nd-round pick who didn't even reach Double-A until he was nearly 24. Since then he has done nothing but hit: .290 in Binghamton, .309 in Mobile, .303 in Portland, and .287 in the majors last year, with excellent power and plate discipline, highlighted by his 19 walks and 12 extra-base hits in just 87 major league at-bats last season. He doesn't have blinding speed, but somehow he still managed to swipe 65 bases over the last two years, and has a career 84% stolen base percentage. If we were scouts, we'd say he plays above his tools, which is one of the best compliments you can pay a player. If you're looking for an exciting talent that looks good in uniform, look elsewhere. If you're looking for someone who can play baseball, you've found your man.

37. Clint Nageotte   RHP   Seattle Mariners   Age 23

	H/9	BB/9	K/9	HR/9	ERA	PERA
2002	11.2	4.6	6.8	0.9	6.19	5.89
2003	9.3	5.1	7.0	0.7	5.03	4.90

5-Year WARP Trend: 0.6, 0.4, 0.5, 0.5, 0.4

The minor league strikeout leader for 2002, Nageotte was promoted to Double-A last season and again struck out over a man an inning, courtesy of one of the best sliders in the minors. His combination of ability, performance, a favorable home ballpark in Seattle and an organization which has proven its ability to develop pitchers is tough to beat. There are concerns about his mechanics, as well as about his inability to develop a changeup, which have led to suggestions that his long-term destination is the bullpen. The Mariners have done a great job in recent years when it comes to slowly ratcheting up the responsibilities entrusted to young pitchers like Joel Pineiro and Rafael Soriano. Expect Nageotte to join the Mariners' bullpen by the end of the season, and expect him to get a shot at the rotation some time in 2005.

38. Ervin Santana   RHP   Anaheim Angels   Age 21

	H/9	BB/9	K/9	HR/9	ERA	PERA
2002	11.1	4.1	5.9	1.7	6.80	6.53
2003	8.4	3.8	6.3	1.4	4.10	4.89

5-Year WARP Trend: 0.9, 0.2, 0.6, 1.7, 1.0

Santana, who used to go by "Johan," was forced to change his name under MLB's new policy that pro players, like racehorses and members of the Screen Actors Guild, must possess a unique name. OK, not really, but it would be nice if they did. Santana, unlike his former namesake in Minnesota, is a right-hander, but he possesses similarly electric stuff. He deserves a Congressional Medal of Honor for posting a 2.53 ERA in Rancho Cucamonga last year. He's skinnier than Paris Hilton and has thrown over 300 innings between his 19th and 21st birthday, so he's certainly an injury risk. But he's in an organization whose new ownership is particularly eager to give opportunities to Hispanic players, and could easily follow Bartolo Colon in the Angels' 2006 rotation.

39. David Bush RHP **Toronto Blue Jays** **Age 24**

	H/9	BB/9	K/9	HR/9	ERA	PERA
2002	9.9	3.3	7.5	1.5	4.20	5.49
2003	9.9	2.0	6.3	1.6	4.37	5.32

5-Year WARP Trend: 1.1, 0.9, 0.8, 0.7, 0.7

Bush's career is marked by his ability to make adjustments. A catcher in high school, he moved to the mound at Wake Forest University and became a dominant reliever. Then, after Bush was selected in the second round in 2002 and had a strong first summer in the bullpen, the Blue Jays made the gutsy—and historically imprudent—decision to make him a starting pitcher. Amazingly, Bush made the transition look so easy that it makes you wonder why he never started before. Like his teammate McGowan, he was dominant in both A-ball and Double-A, and finished with just 28 walks in 158 innings. His emergence was so surprising and ahead of schedule that caution is the watchword, but at the moment he's the best college-trained starter in the minor leagues.

40. Gabe Gross OF **Toronto Blue Jays** **Age 24**

	AVG	OBP	SLG	Defense
2002	.213	.282	.354	OF: −1
2003	.253	.350	.416	OF: −2

5-Year WARP Trend: 0.5, 0.9, 1.0, 1.1, 1.1

A two-sport star at Auburn who wisely gave up quarterbacking to focus on baseball, Gross was a first-round pick in 2001, then got off to a horrible start in Double-A in 2002. He rebounded to hit much better in the second half, then hit .319 with a .423 OBP in his second stint there last season before a late promotion to Triple-A. He lacks any one outstanding tool, but does everything well, and is still getting better. His all-around talents make him a good comp for Bobby Kielty, whose job he'll be trying to take before long. Given his age advantage, Gross will probably be the better player in the long run.

41. Joe Blanton RHP **Oakland Athletics** **Age 23**

	H/9	BB/9	K/9	HR/9	ERA	PERA
2002	11.5	4.5	5.0	1.0	6.48	5.98 (18 IP)
2003	9.5	1.9	6.4	1.2	4.14	4.66

5-Year WARP Trend: 1.3, 1.4, 1.4, 1.4, 1.0

All the hype and hysteria surrounding Oakland's "Moneyball" draft of 2002 obscures one slightly relevant point: taken as a whole, it wasn't an exceptional draft for the A's. While players like Nick Swisher and Jeremy Brown look like they'll be decent major league players, at the moment Blanton is the only draftee who stands out as a potential All-Star. He's a collegiate right-hander out of Kentucky with exceptional command of both a major league fastball and curveball. He destroyed the Midwest League last season, striking out 144 batters against just 19 walks, and was so fazed by a two-level promotion to Double-A in August that he reeled off a 1.26 ERA in 36 innings, allowing just 28 baserunners. He still needs to develop a quality third pitch, but with a major league rotation that features Rich Harden as a #5 starter, the A's can afford to let him spend the whole year in Triple-A doing just that.

42. Russ Adams SS **Toronto Blue Jays** **Age 23**

	AVG	OBP	SLG	Defense
2002	.205	.285	.280	SS: −3
2003	.240	.310	.345	SS: −19

5-Year WARP Trend: 0.3, 0.6, 0.8, 0.9, 1.2

The Blue Jays had their hearts set on Khalil Greene in the first round of the 2002 draft, but when Greene was nabbed by the Padres, one pick ahead of Toronto, the Jays settled for Adams. Eighteen months later, it's not clear that the Padres got the better player. Like Greene, Adams was a very polished draftee as a college senior who lacks the speed of a classic shortstop but makes up for it with good positioning and first-step quickness. Adams lacks Greene's power but has much better plate discipline, which is to say he fits the Jays' profile better anyway. He lacks the star potential of many of the players on this list, but between his defensive versatility and polished approach at the plate, he's a good bet to have a long and occasionally distinguished major league career. Think Mark Loretta.

43. Adam Wainwright RHP **St. Louis Cardinals** **Age 22**

	H/9	BB/9	K/9	HR/9	ERA	PERA
2002	10.1	5.0	6.7	0.9	5.94	5.47
2003	9.2	2.5	5.5	1.1	4.64	4.60

5-Year WARP Trend: 0.7, 0.6, 0.9, 0.8, 0.5

The best pitching prospect in the Braves' organization is now, courtesy of his inclusion as the key to the J. D. Drew trade, the lonely jewel in a Cardinals' farm system that is otherwise barren of talent. Wainwright is a testament to what the Braves do so well: draft high school pitchers in the early rounds of the draft, then find a way to develop them and keep them healthy. Wainwright showed exceptional command and an ability to keep the ball down in his first taste of Double-A, so not even his borderline strikeout rate could keep him off this list. He'll be given every opportunity to win a job in the Cardinals' rotation as soon as he's ready, but losing the benefit of the Mazzone Pitching Clinic has to be seen as an overall negative.

44. Scott Hairston   2B   Arizona Diamondbacks   Age 24

	AVG	OBP	SLG	Defense
2002	.247	.315	.439	2B: −12
2003	.219	.280	.383	2B: −5

5-Year WARP Trend: 0.9, 1.0, 1.3, 1.3, 1.6

Even after a disappointing season at the plate—Hairston tried to play through a muscle strain in his back, with predictable results—he quieted many critics who were unconvinced by his bat even after his stellar season in 2002. Unfortunately, he only raised more doubts about his defense, and now even his supporters suspect he'll have to move to the outfield eventually. His numbers last season aside, Hairston can rake, and his bat can carry him to left field if it has to.

45. Bobby Jenks   RHP   Anaheim Angels   Age 23

	H/9	BB/9	K/9	HR/9	ERA	PERA
2002	8.3	6.9	6.5	0.7	4.80	4.90
2003	7.7	7.2	8.5	0.5	3.28	4.49

5-Year WARP Trend: 0.3, 0.9, −0.1, 1.0, 0.4

If the survival of the human race depended on the ability of one man to throw a baseball as hard as possible, who would you pick? My money would be on Jenks, which is why he's made this list two years running despite only a rudimentary understanding of how to actually pitch. Jenks is our generation's Steve Dalkowski, a man blessed with a supernatural ability to generate velocity, but cursed to forever battle his mechanics, his control, and alcohol. Dalkowski never pitched in the majors, and Jenks may still burn out before he makes it too. But starting with the Arizona Fall League in 2002, Jenks has made significant strides in harnessing his control. He posted a 2.17 ERA in Double-A last summer, and was last seen scaring the bejezus out of hitters in the Puerto Rican winter league, where he had surrendered just 33 hits in 52 innings as we went to press. A move to the bullpen may not only be the best thing for Jenks, but for the game as a whole—freed from the need to pace himself, Jenks may start registering numbers never before seen on a radar gun.

46. Jeremy Hermida   OF   Florida Marlins   Age 20

	AVG	OBP	SLG	Defense
2002	.204	.278	.265	OF: −2
2003	.210	.288	.299	OF: −15

5-Year WARP Trend: −1.6, −1.2, −0.7, −0.5, 0.2

Of any hitter on this list, Hermida has the farthest to go to become a major league hitter. We're willing to bet he makes it there. He was considered the best high school hitter in the 2002 draft, and while we're not normally impressed by scouting reports, when you combine them with his command of the strike zone (he led the South Atlantic League with 80 walks), it means we can discount his lack of power (.393 slugging average) for now. A player who can hit for average and knows the strike zone at age 19 has a good chance of picking up homers along the way. Hermida may still be on this list three years from now, but his talent makes him worthy of our patience.

47. Sean Burnett   LHP   Pittsburgh Pirates   Age 21

	H/9	BB/9	K/9	HR/9	ERA	PERA
2002	7.3	2.5	4.1	0.5	3.70	3.12
2003	8.5	1.9	4.1	0.2	4.49	3.17

5-Year WARP Trend: 1.4, 1.4, 1.0, 1.5, 2.2

The Anti-Jenks. Over the last two years, Burnett has struck out a total of 182 batters in 315 innings, a ratio significantly below the league average both years. So what's he doing on this list? Those of you who are familiar with DIPS theory know that a pitcher primarily has control over three things: strikeouts, walks, and homers. While Burnett is distinctly below average at the first, he's without peer at the other two. In those same 315 innings, he's walked just 62 batters—and allowed only six home runs. So what's the gimmick: Burnett's a former first-round pick with a tremendous change-up and a good sinking fastball for a left-hander. Tommy John is still the patron saint of left-handers with low strikeout rates, and even if Burnett has to settle for being Kirk Rueter, that's not a bad outcome as downsides go.

48. J. J. Davis   OF   Pittsburgh Pirates   Age 25

	AVG	OBP	SLG	Defense
2002	.240	.295	.435	OF: −8
2003	.257	.315	.502	OF: −5

5-Year WARP Trend: 0.8, 1.1, 0.9, 1.0, 1.3

After being picked in the first round in 1997, Davis took five years to reach Double-A, showing inconsistent power and huge strikeouts rates. So pardon us for reserving our judgment when, after letting go of his dream to move back to the mound (he was a top pitcher in high school), he finally had a breakout season in 2002. But after showing even more improvement in his first taste of Triple-A last season, Davis has a chance to be the rare high school project-turned-suspect that actually made it good. He set career highs in homers (26) and steals (23), and while he still doesn't walk much, he struck out only 85 times in 122 games—this from the same player who whiffed 171 times just three years earlier. He also has the prototypical right fielder's arm you would expect from a former pitcher. Between Davis and Bay, the Pirates should have little problem replacing Reggie Sanders and Kenny Lofton from last year's Opening Day outfield. Now about that Brian Giles guy...

49. Gavin Floyd   RHP   Philadelphia Phillies   Age 21

	H/9	BB/9	K/9	HR/9	ERA	PERA
2002	9.0	4.9	4.9	1.9	5.51	6.05
2003	10.4	3.8	5.5	1.8	5.84	6.21

5-Year WARP Trend: 0.5, 0.1, 0.4, 1.2, −0.4

The top five picks in the 2001 draft should go down in history as one of the strongest top-fives ever: Mauer, Mark Prior, Dewon Brazelton (cough), Floyd, and Mark Teixeira (who, coincidentally, attended the same high school as Floyd). Floyd has done nothing since he was drafted to cast doubts on his draft status, methodically working his way up the Phillies' system with good numbers at every level. The Phillies have done an admirable job of keeping his pitch counts down, allowing him to throw only 138 innings in a full minor league season last year. His strikeout rates are a little low for a pitcher with his reputation, especially one whose curveball is purported to be a devastating out pitch. Expect Floyd to get a full season in Double-A this year as the Phillies give him the time he needs to learn how to put hitters away, then contend for a rotation spot in 2005. Sometimes slow and steady really does win the race.

50. Charlie Zink   RHP   Boston Red Sox   Age 24

	H/9	BB/9	K/9	HR/9	ERA	PERA
2002	9.0	3.9	5.7	0.3	4.26	4.16
2003	9.7	5.3	4.1	1.8	5.62	6.44

5-Year WARP Trend: −0.4, 0.1, −0.1, 0.1, 0.2

Our choice for this year's Mr. Irrelevant is a knuckleball pitcher, which is appropriate enough when you consider how knuckleball pitchers have been consistently overlooked, despite their success, for more than a century. Skeptics will point out Zink's unimpressive 3.90 ERA in high-A ball last year, along with a strikeout-to-walk ratio of just 112 to 78. And if Zink were a traditional pitcher with those numbers, he wouldn't so much as sniff this list. But knuckleball pitchers are a different breed. Compare Zink's raw numbers last year with another 23-year-old pitcher throwing the knuckleball for the first time, Tim Wakefield:

Zink,   2003: 175 IP, 144 H, 78 BB, 112 K, 14 HR, 3.80 ERA
Wakefield, 1990: 190 IP, 187 H, 85 BB, 127 K, 24 HR, 4.73 ERA

Wakefield spent that entire season in low-A ball; Zink started last season in high-A ball and finished it in Double-A.

Zink is only the second pitcher in the last 20 years to successfully rely on the knuckler over a full minor league season before his 25th birthday. And like Wakefield, Zink

has the perseverance required of any great knuckleballer; he parlayed a collegiate career at some place called the Savannah College of Art & Design into a pro contract, and had a 1.41 ERA working with a conventional repertoire in his pro debut in 2002.

As for his pedestrian numbers, keep in mind that since major league players are not selected for their ability to hit the knuckleball, most knuckleball pitchers, from Tim Wakefield to Steve Sparks to Jared Fernandez, pitch better in the majors than their minor league numbers would suggest. And not only do the Red Sox already understand the value of having a knuckler on staff, they're an organization that, when it comes to performance, is more interested in the destination than the journey. There are likely to be some potholes along the way, but when you consider that Zink may be 10 years away from his peak, he could still be pitching in the majors when most of the others on this list have retired.

Honorable Mention

Chad Gaudin, RHP, Tampa Bay Devil Rays: Has any starting pitcher reached the majors before his 21st birthday with as little fanfare as Gaudin? Maybe it's because he was a 29th-round draft pick, maybe it's because he's listed at only 5′11″, and maybe it's because he's a Devil Ray, but Gaudin has gotten almost no attention for a performance record that includes a career 2.06 ERA and a K:BB ratio of better than 3:1 in the minors. It's true that he was promoted to Tampa Bay out of desperation more than anything else, but it's also true that he managed a 3.60 ERA in 40 innings with the Rays last year.

Adrian Gonzalez, 1B, Texas Rangers: The #1 overall pick in the 2000 draft spent most of last season recovering from a wrist injury, and it showed: He hit just five homers all year, and the Marlins happily traded him away as partial payment for Ugueth Urbina. He's a better hitter than he showed last year, and could easily be back on our list as a Top 25 prospect next season.

Angel Guzman, RHP, Chicago Cubs: One of the most promising pitching prospects in baseball before suffering a torn labrum at the end of June, and until he takes the mound again there's simply no way to know whether Guzman is going to fulfill his immense potential or end up as yet another data point for TINSTAAPP.

Brendan Harris, 3B/2B, Chicago Cubs: While our Albert Pujols comparison last year was just a wee bit off, Harris remains one of the more underrated prospects in the game, a player with both the glove and the bat to play regularly in the majors at either second base or third base. If he develops power, he's got a good chance to be a late-blooming offense-minded infielder in the Jeff Kent mold.

Justin Huber, C, New York Mets: A Top 40 player a year ago, Huber continued to develop offensively and wasn't fazed at all by a promotion to Double-A. His ranking has slipped because of the decreasing likelihood that he'll ever be a solid catcher defensively, and his bat isn't so strong that he's likely to ever be a solid first baseman offensively. If he can outstrip his projected growth in either direction, he could have a solid career at either position, but right now he's looking a lot like Craig Wilson Lite.

Adam LaRoche, 1B, Atlanta Braves: Like a lot of guys on the HM list, LaRoche didn't make the Top 50 list because of a limited upside, but he's perfectly capable of hitting .280 with 20 homers as the Braves' first baseman this season and being a dark horse candidate for Rookie of the Year honors. But it's hard to get too excited about the long-term prospects of a first baseman without one dominant offensive skill.

Akinori Otsuka, LHP, San Diego Padres: While Kazuo Matsui got all the press as this year's trendy Japanese import, the Padres' acquisition of Otsuka got all the publicity of a Corey Feldman film festival. This is a serious oversight. Yes, Otsuka is 32, and yes, he's been signed to be a middle reliever. But inning for inning, Otsuka was as successful a closer in Japan as Kazuhiro Sasaki, and over his final two seasons, he posted a 2.16 ERA in 96 innings, walking just 11 batters—and striking out 132. There's no reason he can't be the best left-handed set-up man in baseball this year.

Kelly Shoppach, C, Boston Red Sox: If we were to rank prospects based on the length of their expected careers, Shoppach would be Top 50 material, because if nothing else he should be able to carve out a lengthy career as a backup catcher in the Kelly Stinnett mold. He has the secondary skills to be better than that, and will probably have at least one season where he's one of the better catchers in his league.

Terrmel Sledge, OF, Montreal Expos: Bud Selig needs to be brought before a tribunal at the Hague for denying the Expos the right to bring up Sledge last September. At 27, he doesn't have much upside left in him, but Sledge is already a league-average left fielder and should give his team a lot of bang for the league-minimum buck for the next few years. Could form a great value platoon with Juan Rivera in '04.

Jason Stokes, 1B, Florida Marlins: Stokes and Adrian Gonzalez have been connected ever since the Marlins used their first two selections on them in 2000, and that connection continued a year ago when both of them needed off-season wrist surgery. Even with a weakened wrist, Stokes hit 17 homers in the Florida State League following a near-Triple Crown campaign in the Midwest League in 2002. He'll only go as far as his bat will carry him, so he needs to show that his 30-homer power has returned this season.

Merkin Valdez, RHP, San Francisco Giants: Over the years, the Braves have done an excellent job of knowing which of their pitching prospects to keep and which to trade away. But they may have made a mistake with Valdez, who was included in the Russ Ortiz trade, then dominated the South Atlantic League last season with nearly as many strikeouts (166) as baserunners allowed (168). It's a long way from the SAL to the NL, but the Giants are hinting that he could be apprenticing in their bullpen by the end of this season.

Kevin Youkilis, 3B, Boston Red Sox: Henceforth to be remembered for eternity as The Greek God of Walks, Youkilis continued to parlay his undeniable talent for drawing walks into a ridiculous on-base percentage...at least until he reached Triple-A. After posting a .487 OBP in Double-A, Youkilis struggled in a short stretch at Triple-A, hitting just .165 at that level over the season's final month. He's capable of drawing walks at any level, but whether he can show additional skills will determine whether he's the new Dave Magadan or just Lance Blankenship with worse defense.

Marginal Payroll/Marginal Wins, 1995–2003

by Doug Pappas

The oft-recited assertion that "small markets can't compete" in Major League Baseball is usually supported by a table showing that "winners" like the Yankees, Dodgers, and Red Sox spend far more on players than "losers" like the Devil Rays, Pirates, and Brewers. This argument is misleading in at least three respects.

First, "small market" is often mistakenly used as a synonym for "low revenue." A team's revenue, and the size of the payroll it can support, is far more dependent on its recent success (and the terms of its stadium lease) than on the size of its market. According to MLB's official revenue figures for 2001, the Seattle Mariners took in more money than any other club except the Yankees—over three times as much as the Florida Marlins, who play in a larger market. Playing in a 35-year-old stadium, the Cardinals outgrossed Baltimore, Philadelphia and Detroit, all of which occupy markets at least twice the size of St. Louis. Cleveland and Minneapolis-St. Paul are almost exactly the same size, but the Indians grossed $100 million more than the Twins.

Second, a snapshot of one season's "winners" and "losers" ignores the ebb and flow of team fortunes. If Major League Baseball had proposed contraction 10 years earlier, the Indians and Mariners would have been among the leading candidates for extermination. The Oakland Athletics, heroes of *Moneyball* for doing more with less, had the majors' highest Opening Day payroll in 1991, the same year the Pirates won their third division title in a row. Over the past 20 years, the Padres and Twins have played in more World Series than the Dodgers or Red Sox. Most tellingly of all, the original list of eight clubs considered for contraction, prepared in December 2000, included *all three of the clubs* which have won the World Series since then.

Third, and most importantly, some teams are better run than others. In 2003 only two of the five teams with Opening Day payrolls of more than $100 million made the playoffs. Two others finished last. The world champion Marlins started the season with a payroll of $49 million; that's less than the Reds or Pirates spent, and even less than the Tigers paid for their 119-loss disaster. If the Marlins can win the World Series with a $49 million payroll, these clubs can't blame their failure on a lack of resources.

Player contracts are investments. In baseball as in the business world, some investments are better than others. MLB's three-tiered salary structure makes a strong farm system the best investment of all, because the reserve system and limits on eligibility for salary arbitration ensure that young players are systematically underpaid. The St. Louis Cardinals have paid Albert Pujols just $1.7 million for three seasons in which he finished fourth, second and second in the MVP voting—$100,000 less than they paid Steve Kline to pitch middle relief in 2003. Smart clubs realize that the worst investment of all is an aging or mediocre player, signed as a free agent for top dollar, who performs no better than a prospect or waiver claim can be expected to play.

The easiest way to measure front office efficiency is simply to divide a club's payroll by its wins to come up with "dollars per win." However, neither side of this equation reflects reality. The worst team a club can field won't go 0–162, and despite some owners' best efforts, it's impossible to spend $0 on a major league roster. It's necessary to look at *marginal* wins and *marginal* payroll.

The Marginal Payroll/Marginal Wins (MP/MW) system evaluates the efficiency of a club's front office by comparing its payroll and record to the performance it could expect to attain by fielding a roster of replacement-level players, all of whom are paid the major league minimum salary. The formula is:

$$[(\text{winning percentage} - .300) \times 162] \Big/ [\text{club payroll} - (28 \times \text{major league minimum})]$$

The left side of this formula assumes that a replacement-level club would play .300 ball. That translates to 48.6 wins in a 162-game season, which before the 2003 Tigers was worse than any actual major league club since the institution of the amateur draft. The previous low was the 52–110 (.321) record of the NL's two 1969 expansion clubs, the Expos and Padres, who began play with no minor league system, no way to sign free agents, and no players any other NL club really wanted to keep. After subtracting the replacement-level .300 winning percentage from the club's actual winning percentage, the resulting number is multiplied by 162 to calculate the number of marginal wins over a full 162-game season. This adjusts the formula for strike-shortened seasons and clubs which fail to make up a postponed game or two.

The right side of the formula assumes a 25-man active roster and three-man disabled list. It uses Opening Day payroll numbers where available, because these are the best measure of a team's expectations entering the season. Once the season begins, payrolls vary with the club's performance: Bad teams trade away their higher-salaried players, while contenders add payroll for the stretch drive. Opening Day payrolls are available for most seasons since 1986; for the others, I've used payroll figures reflecting rosters as of August 31. Either way, the formula multiplies the major league minimum by 28, then subtracts this number from the club's actual payroll to yield its marginal payroll.

Finally, the MP/MW formula divides a club's marginal payroll by its marginal wins. The resulting figure reflects how much money a club has spent, per win above the theoretical minimum. The lower the number, the more efficiently the club spent its cash. Comparing this number to the club's actual winning percentage provides another way to evaluate teams:

- Low MP/MW, good record: Efficient ballclub (2003 Marlins, Athletics)
- Low MP/MW, bad record: Not spending enough to compete (2003 Devil Rays)
- High MP/MW, good record: Spending its way to the top (2003 Yankees)
- High MP/MW, bad record: Poorly-run club (2003 Mets, Rangers)

The following pages present MP/MW results for every team since 1995, together with commentary on each season. In the coming weeks, we'll be running a series on teams' MP/MW for the years 1977–1994 at BP's Web site, www.baseballprospectus.com.

TABLE 1. MARGINAL PAYROLL/MARGINAL WIN, 1995

Team	W	L	Pct	Marginal Wins	Opening Payroll	Marginal Payroll	Marginal $/ Marginal Win
Baltimore	71	73	0.493	31.3	$40,835,519	$37,783,519	$1,208,106
Boston	86	58	0.597	48.2	$28,363,250	$25,311,250	$525,675
Detroit	60	84	0.417	18.9	$35,862,501	$32,810,501	$1,736,005
NY Yankees	79	65	0.549	40.3	$46,547,016	$43,495,016	$1,079,951
Toronto	56	88	0.389	14.4	$49,791,500	$46,739,500	$3,245,799
Chicago White Sox	68	76	0.472	27.9	$39,632,834	$36,580,834	$1,311,141
Cleveland	100	44	0.694	63.9	$35,185,500	$32,133,500	$502,872
Kansas City	70	74	0.486	30.2	$27,608,830	$24,556,830	$814,489
Milwaukee	65	79	0.451	24.5	$16,189,600	$13,137,600	$535,682
Minnesota	56	88	0.389	14.4	$24,527,500	$21,475,500	$1,491,354
California	78	67	0.538	38.5	$28,974,167	$25,922,167	$672,520
Oakland	67	77	0.465	26.8	$35,961,500	$32,909,500	$1,229,113
Seattle	79	66	0.545	39.7	$34,241,540	$31,189,540	$786,382
Texas	74	70	0.514	34.7	$32,367,266	$29,315,266	$846,039
Atlanta	90	54	0.625	52.7	$45,199,000	$42,147,000	$800,513
Florida	67	76	0.469	27.3	$23,670,000	$20,618,000	$755,180
Montreal	66	78	0.458	25.7	$12,031,000	$8,979,000	$350,058
NY Mets	69	75	0.479	29.0	$24,301,440	$21,249,440	$732,108
Philadelphia	69	75	0.479	29.0	$28,615,000	$25,563,000	$880,724
Chicago Cubs	73	71	0.507	33.5	$35,410,834	$32,358,834	$965,215
Cincinnati	85	59	0.590	47.0	$34,394,667	$31,342,667	$666,511
Houston	76	68	0.528	36.9	$31,624,000	$28,572,000	$774,309
Pittsburgh	58	86	0.403	16.7	$17,043,000	$13,991,000	$840,300
St. Louis	62	81	0.434	21.6	$30,956,000	$27,904,000	$1,289,597
Colorado	77	67	0.535	38.0	$31,144,138	$28,092,138	$738,781
Los Angeles	78	66	0.542	39.2	$30,350,001	$27,298,001	$697,267
San Diego	70	74	0.486	30.2	$25,923,334	$22,871,334	$758,585
San Francisco	67	77	0.465	26.8	$34,712,849	$31,660,849	$1,182,478

The 1995 season started three weeks late, after the players went back to work without a labor agreement following a federal court order that effectively barred MLB from opening the season with replacement players. Once play began, the Cleveland Indians showed Bill James, the makers of *Major League* and others how badly they had been misjudged.

The 100–44 Indians debuted a new model for success: Trade off all your high-salaried veterans to collect a roster full of top young talent, then lock them all up with long-term contracts as early in their careers as possible, ideally with the aid of additional money from a new ballpark. Albert Belle, Kenny Lofton, Jim Thome, and Carlos Baerga all began the year with multi-year deals signed long before they were eligible for free agency; Manny Ramirez, and Omar Vizquel would get theirs before the 1996 season.

Toronto proved the majors' least efficient team, as the core of its championship club aged and declined while retaining its high salaries. The Blue Jays traded ace David Cone to the New York Yankees in mid-season, vaulting the Yankees to the top of the final payroll standings. Across town the Mets' trades of Bret Saberhagen and Bobby Bonilla left them with the majors' lowest payroll at year's end. Strategic salary dumps like these are the reason why a club's Opening Day payroll is a better measure of its ability to compete than its final payroll.

TABLE 2. MARGINAL PAYROLL/MARGINAL WIN, 1996

Team	W	L	Pct	Marginal Wins	Opening Payroll	Marginal Payroll	Marginal $/ Marginal Win
Baltimore	88	74	0.543	39.4	$48,726,832	$45,674,832	$1,159,260
Boston	85	77	0.525	36.4	$39,676,000	$36,624,000	$1,006,154
Detroit	53	109	0.327	4.4	$21,941,000	$18,889,000	$4,292,955
NY Yankees	92	70	0.568	43.4	$52,189,370	$49,137,370	$1,132,197
Toronto	74	88	0.457	25.4	$28,486,708	$25,434,708	$1,001,366
Chicago White Sox	85	77	0.525	36.4	$41,940,000	$38,888,000	$1,068,352
Cleveland	99	62	0.615	51.0	$45,317,914	$42,265,914	$828,501
Kansas City	75	86	0.466	26.9	$18,480,750	$15,428,750	$574,289
Milwaukee	80	82	0.494	31.4	$20,482,000	$17,430,000	$555,096
Minnesota	78	84	0.481	29.4	$21,961,500	$18,909,500	$643,180
California	70	91	0.435	21.8	$26,892,500	$23,840,500	$1,091,859
Oakland	78	84	0.481	29.4	$19,404,500	$16,352,500	$556,207
Seattle	85	76	0.528	36.9	$39,221,501	$36,169,501	$979,461
Texas	90	72	0.556	41.4	$35,862,028	$32,810,028	$792,513
Atlanta	96	66	0.593	47.4	$47,930,000	$44,878,000	$946,793
Florida	80	82	0.494	31.4	$30,079,500	$27,027,500	$860,748
Montreal	88	74	0.543	39.4	$15,410,500	$12,358,500	$313,668
NY Mets	71	91	0.438	22.4	$23,456,500	$20,404,500	$910,915
Philadelphia	67	95	0.414	18.4	$29,473,500	$26,421,500	$1,435,951
Chicago Cubs	76	86	0.469	27.4	$30,954,000	$27,902,000	$1,018,321
Cincinnati	81	81	0.500	32.4	$40,719,334	$37,667,334	$1,162,572
Houston	82	80	0.506	33.4	$26,894,000	$23,842,000	$713,832
Pittsburgh	73	89	0.451	24.4	$21,253,500	$18,201,500	$745,963
St. Louis	88	74	0.543	39.4	$38,741,666	$35,689,666	$905,829
Colorado	83	79	0.512	34.4	$37,858,490	$34,806,490	$1,011,817
Los Angeles	90	72	0.556	41.4	$34,647,000	$31,595,000	$763,164
San Diego	91	71	0.562	42.4	$27,133,026	$24,081,026	$567,949
San Francisco	68	94	0.420	19.4	$34,605,225	$31,553,225	$1,626,455

A recurrent theme through the first 25 years of free agency was the owners' systematic underestimation of their own future revenue. MLB's revenue doubled from 1996 to 2001, the period of the last collective bargaining agreement. With more money to spend, the owners spent more on players, so salaries kept pace with revenue. The owners' warnings of impending bankruptcy were no more credible in 1996 than they had been a generation before.

The Yankees went to their first World Series in 15 years, spending heavily but relatively efficiently. Their mirror image, the Montreal Expos, spent wisely but too lightly, missing the Wild Card by two games despite the majors' lowest payroll. Cleveland and Texas provided more ammunition for supporters of new stadiums in other cities, winning their divisions while playing in the AL's newest parks, while Detroit management deluded itself into believing that a new ballpark would solve the Tigers' problems.

The Atlanta Braves finished with the NL's best record and highest payroll. The second-highest payroll belonged to Cincinnati. Marge Schott may have been cheap in other respects, but throughout her tenure with the Reds her clubs paid higher salaries than most of their larger-market rivals. San Diego won without paying high salaries—in fact, while being outspent by every other club in its division.

TABLE 3. MARGINAL PAYROLL/MARGINAL WIN, 1997

Team	W	L	Pct	Marginal Wins	Opening Payroll	Marginal Payroll	Marginal $/ Marginal Win
Baltimore	98	64	0.605	49.4	$55,085,778	$50,885,778	$1,030,076
Boston	78	84	0.481	29.4	$43,138,750	$38,938,750	$1,324,447
Detroit	79	83	0.488	30.4	$16,454,500	$12,254,500	$403,109
NY Yankees	96	66	0.593	47.4	$58,499,544	$54,299,544	$1,145,560
Toronto	76	86	0.469	27.4	$45,894,833	$41,694,833	$1,521,709
Chicago White Sox	80	81	0.497	31.9	$54,205,000	$50,005,000	$1,567,707
Cleveland	86	75	0.534	37.9	$54,122,460	$49,922,460	$1,316,029
Kansas City	67	94	0.416	18.8	$31,225,000	$27,025,000	$1,436,266
Milwaukee	78	83	0.484	29.9	$21,420,333	$17,220,333	$576,230
Minnesota	68	94	0.420	19.4	$32,947,500	$28,747,500	$1,481,830
Anaheim	84	78	0.519	35.4	$29,196,579	$24,996,579	$706,118
Oakland	65	97	0.401	16.4	$21,911,000	$17,711,000	$1,079,939
Seattle	90	72	0.556	41.4	$39,421,395	$35,221,395	$850,758
Texas	77	85	0.475	28.4	$50,112,268	$45,912,268	$1,616,629
Atlanta	101	61	0.623	52.4	$50,488,500	$46,288,500	$883,368
Florida	92	70	0.568	43.4	$47,738,000	$43,538,000	$1,003,180
Montreal	78	84	0.481	29.4	$18,485,500	$14,285,500	$485,901
NY Mets	88	74	0.543	39.4	$38,432,900	$34,232,900	$868,855
Philadelphia	68	94	0.420	19.4	$35,503,500	$31,303,500	$1,613,582
Chicago Cubs	68	94	0.420	19.4	$39,829,333	$35,629,333	$1,836,564
Cincinnati	76	86	0.469	27.4	$46,237,000	$42,037,000	$1,534,197
Houston	84	78	0.519	35.4	$32,930,000	$28,730,000	$811,582
Pittsburgh	79	83	0.488	30.4	$9,071,667	$4,871,667	$160,252
St. Louis	73	89	0.451	24.4	$44,129,167	$39,929,167	$1,636,441
Colorado	83	79	0.512	34.4	$42,851,500	$38,651,500	$1,123,590
Los Angeles	88	74	0.543	39.4	$43,400,000	$39,200,000	$994,924
San Diego	76	86	0.469	27.4	$34,692,579	$30,492,579	$1,112,868
San Francisco	90	72	0.556	41.4	$33,464,780	$29,264,780	$706,879

The 1997 season opened with labor peace for the first time in four seasons. It closed with the worst championship team MLB had ever known.

The Florida Marlins were the first Wild Card team to win a World Series, but that wasn't their problem; owner Wayne Huizenga was. Huizenga personified a generation of greedy, grasping owners who lied about their finances and treated their fans with contempt. He bought himself a title by increasing the Marlins' payroll from $25 million in late 1996 to $53 million by mid-1997, adding a passel of free agents to a core of good young players. When ungrateful South Florida taxpayers refused to reward him with a free ballpark, Huizenga responded by slashing the club's payroll to $15 million by late 1998. A year after their championship, the Marlins had alienated their entire fan base en route to a 54–108 record.

Other clubs skipped the championship stage on their way to the bargain bin. Detroit, Montreal, and Pittsburgh topped the list of efficient spenders by fielding mediocre, but dirt-cheap, rosters. The new CBA encouraged this practice. By increasing the percentage of shared local revenue and diverting a disproportionate share of revenue-sharing money to the very lowest-revenue clubs, it effectively subsidized clubs that weren't even trying to compete.

TABLE 4. MARGINAL PAYROLL/MARGINAL WIN, 1998

Team	W	L	Pct	Marginal Wins	Opening Payroll	Marginal Payroll	Marginal $/ Marginal Win
Baltimore	79	83	0.488	30.4	$68,988,134	$64,228,134	$2,112,768
Boston	92	70	0.568	43.4	$51,547,000	$46,787,000	$1,078,041
NY Yankees	114	48	0.704	65.4	$63,460,567	$58,700,567	$897,562
Tampa Bay	63	99	0.389	14.4	$25,317,500	$20,557,500	$1,427,604
Toronto	88	74	0.543	39.4	$48,666,000	$43,906,000	$1,114,365
Chicago White Sox	80	82	0.494	31.4	$36,840,000	$32,080,000	$1,021,656
Cleveland	89	73	0.549	40.4	$59,583,500	$54,823,500	$1,357,017
Detroit	65	97	0.401	16.4	$22,725,000	$17,965,000	$1,095,427
Kansas City	72	89	0.447	23.8	$32,962,500	$28,202,500	$1,182,633
Minnesota	70	92	0.432	21.4	$26,182,500	$21,422,500	$1,001,051
Anaheim	85	77	0.525	36.4	$38,702,000	$33,942,000	$932,473
Oakland	74	88	0.457	25.4	$20,063,000	$15,303,000	$602,480
Seattle	76	85	0.472	27.9	$52,027,136	$47,267,136	$1,695,862
Texas	88	74	0.543	39.4	$55,304,595	$50,544,595	$1,282,858
Atlanta	106	56	0.654	57.4	$59,536,000	$54,776,000	$954,286
Florida	54	108	0.333	5.4	$33,434,000	$28,674,000	$5,310,000
Montreal	65	97	0.401	16.4	$9,162,000	$4,402,000	$268,415
NY Mets	88	74	0.543	39.4	$49,517,999	$44,757,999	$1,135,990
Philadelphia	75	87	0.463	26.4	$34,370,000	$29,610,000	$1,121,591
Chicago Cubs	90	73	0.552	40.8	$49,433,000	$44,673,000	$1,093,644
Cincinnati	77	85	0.475	28.4	$21,995,000	$17,235,000	$606,866
Houston	102	60	0.630	53.4	$40,629,000	$35,869,000	$671,704
Milwaukee	74	88	0.457	25.4	$32,393,012	$27,633,012	$1,087,914
Pittsburgh	69	93	0.426	20.4	$13,352,000	$8,592,000	$421,176
St. Louis	83	79	0.512	34.4	$52,575,000	$47,815,000	$1,389,971
Arizona	65	97	0.401	16.4	$30,571,500	$25,811,500	$1,573,872
Colorado	77	85	0.475	28.4	$47,434,648	$42,674,648	$1,502,628
Los Angeles	83	79	0.512	34.4	$47,970,000	$43,210,000	$1,256,105
San Diego	98	64	0.605	49.4	$45,368,000	$40,608,000	$822,024
San Francisco	89	74	0.546	39.9	$40,570,833	$35,810,833	$898,551

The 1998 season was the Year of the Yankees, whose dominance (125–50, including the postseason) brought back memories of the Gehrig-DiMaggio juggernaut of the late 1930s. Yet this Yankee team spent less than the sub-.500 Orioles. They owed much of their success, and all of their efficiency, to George Steinbrenner's three-year suspension.

Steinbrenner was out of baseball from 1990 to 1993, banished for his dealings with Howard Spira. In his absence, the Yankees kept their top prospects instead of trading them for aging veterans. The homegrown core of Bernie Williams, Derek Jeter, Jorge Posada, Andy Pettitte, and Mariano Rivera remained in The Bronx through 2003,

winning four World Series and qualifying for the playoffs in nine consecutive seasons.

The differing paths the two expansion clubs would take became apparent. Arizona signed free agents Jay Bell and Andy Benes, traded for Matt Williams, and has posted one losing season in franchise history; Tampa Bay blew its free agent money on closer Roberto Hernandez and 40-year-old Wade Boggs—both as useful to an expansion franchise as a 12-pack of condoms at a Dungeons & Dragons convention—and has yet to win more than 69 games in a season.

TABLE 5. MARGINAL PAYROLL/MARGINAL WIN, 1999

Team	W	L	Pct	Marginal Wins	Opening Payroll	Marginal Payroll	Marginal $/ Marginal Win
Baltimore	78	84	0.481	29.4	$78,902,282	$78,302,282	$2,493,275
Boston	94	68	0.580	45.4	$59,553,500	$53,953,500	$1,188,403
NY Yankees	98	64	0.605	49.4	$85,034,692	$79,434,692	$1,607,990
Tampa Bay	69	93	0.426	20.4	$33,952,500	$28,352,500	$1,389,828
Toronto	84	78	0.519	35.4	$44,509,333	$38,909,333	$1,099,134
Chicago White Sox	75	86	0.466	25.9	$24,560,000	$18,960,000	$705,729
Cleveland	97	65	0.598	48.4	$68,061,627	$62,461,627	$1,290,529
Detroit	69	92	0.429	20.8	$34,104,666	$28,504,666	$1,368,537
Kansas City	64	97	0.398	15.8	$23,706,000	$18,106,000	$1,146,130
Minnesota	64	98	0.394	15.2	$19,242,500	$13,642,500	$898,272
Anaheim	70	92	0.432	21.4	$51,830,166	$46,230,166	$2,160,288
Oakland	87	75	0.537	38.4	$23,234,333	$17,634,333	$459,227
Seattle	79	83	0.488	30.4	$49,963,503	$44,363,503	$1,459,326
Texas	95	67	0.586	46.4	$74,834,931	$69,234,931	$1,492,132
Atlanta	103	59	0.636	54.4	$73,585,000	$67,985,000	$1,249,724
Florida	64	98	0.395	15.4	$18,876,000	$13,276,000	$862,078
Montreal	68	94	0.420	19.4	$16,175,500	$10,575,500	$545,129
NY Mets	97	66	0.595	47.8	$62,450,427	$56,850,427	$1,189,217
Philadelphia	77	85	0.475	28.4	$30,297,500	$24,697,500	$869,630
Chicago Cubs	67	95	0.414	18.4	$60,191,500	$54,591,500	$2,966,929
Cincinnati	96	67	0.589	46.8	$33,162,761	$27,562,761	$588,809
Houston	97	65	0.599	48.4	$51,629,000	$46,029,000	$951,012
Milwaukee	74	87	0.460	25.9	$41,395,762	$35,395,762	$1,384,233
Pittsburgh	78	83	0.484	29.9	$22,197,666	$16,597,666	$555,394
St. Louis	75	86	0.466	26.9	$45,698,333	$40,098,333	$1,492,540
Arizona	100	62	0.617	51.4	$66,078,999	$60,478,999	$1,176,634
Colorado	72	90	0.444	23.4	$55,864,837	$50,264,837	$2,148,070
Los Angeles	77	85	0.475	28.4	$79,265,953	$73,665,953	$2,593,872
San Diego	74	88	0.457	25.4	$47,828,346	$42,228,346	$1,662,533
San Francisco	86	76	0.531	37.4	$44,943,557	$39,343,557	$1,051,967

As the season opened, Sandy Grady of the *Philadelphia Daily News* opined in the April 5, 1999 *USA Today:* "It's almost a fraud—a mockery of expectations—if you live in Montreal, Oakland, Kansas City, Pittsburgh, Minnesota, Florida, or Milwaukee. The chances of teams from those places still playing in October are zilch." Over the next five seasons one of these seven clubs would win the World Series, two more would combine for six postseason appearances, and two more would make serious runs at the playoffs. The only two true failures, the Pirates and Brewers, were also the only two to move into the new ballparks MLB insisted were necessary for clubs like these to compete.

In 1999, the clubs which spent less than $1 million/win fell into three camps. Oakland and Cincinnati had good, cheap teams; Houston fielded a very good team on a moderate payroll; the White Sox, Twins, Pirates, and three-fifths of the NL East were both bad and cheap.

Four AL clubs spent far more than the others. Three of the four qualified for the postseason; the fourth, the Orioles, qualified for Social Security. None of the five clubs spending more than $2 million/win won more than 78 games, with the last-place Cubs coming close to breaking the $3 million/win barrier.

TABLE 6. MARGINAL PAYROLL/MARGINAL WIN, 2000

Team	W	L	Pct	Marginal Wins	Opening Payroll	Marginal Payroll	Marginal $/ Marginal Win
Baltimore	74	88	0.457	25.4	$81,447,435	$75,847,435	$2,986,119
Boston	85	77	0.525	36.4	$77,940,333	$72,340,333	$1,987,372
NY Yankees	87	74	0.540	38.9	$92,538,260	$86,938,260	$2,232,600
Tampa Bay	69	92	0.429	20.8	$62,765,129	$57,165,129	$2,744,554
Toronto	83	79	0.512	34.4	$46,238,333	$40,638,333	$1,181,347
Chicago White Sox	95	67	0.586	46.4	$31,133,500	$25,533,500	$550,291
Cleveland	90	72	0.556	41.4	$75,880,971	$70,280,971	$1,697,608
Detroit	79	83	0.488	30.4	$58,265,167	$52,665,167	$1,732,407
Kansas City	77	85	0.475	28.4	$23,433,000	$17,833,000	$627,923
Minnesota	69	93	0.426	20.4	$16,519,500	$10,919,500	$535,270
Anaheim	82	80	0.506	33.4	$51,464,167	$45,864,167	$1,373,179
Oakland	91	70	0.565	43.0	$31,971,333	$26,371,333	$613,783
Seattle	91	71	0.562	42.4	$58,915,000	$53,315,000	$1,257,429
Texas	71	91	0.438	22.4	$70,795,921	$65,195,921	$2,910,532
Atlanta	95	67	0.586	46.4	$84,537,836	$78,937,836	$1,701,246
Florida	79	82	0.491	30.9	$20,072,000	$14,472,000	$468,491
Montreal	67	95	0.414	18.4	$34,807,333	$29,207,333	$1,587,355
NY Mets	94	68	0.580	45.4	$79,509,776	$73,909,776	$1,627,969
Philadelphia	65	97	0.401	16.4	$47,308,000	$41,708,000	$2,543,171
Chicago Cubs	65	97	0.401	16.4	$60,539,333	$54,939,333	$3,349,959
Cincinnati	85	77	0.525	36.4	$46,867,200	$41,267,200	$1,133,714
Houston	72	90	0.444	23.4	$51,289,111	$45,689,111	$1,952,526
Milwaukee	73	89	0.451	24.4	$36,505,333	$30,905,333	$1,266,612
Pittsburgh	69	93	0.426	20.4	$28,928,333	$23,328,333	$1,143,546
St. Louis	95	67	0.586	46.4	$61,453,863	$55,853,863	$1,203,747
Arizona	85	77	0.525	36.4	$81,027,333	$75,427,333	$2,072,179
Colorado	82	80	0.506	33.4	$61,111,190	$55,511,190	$1,662,012
Los Angeles	86	76	0.531	37.4	$88,124,286	$82,524,286	$2,206,532
San Diego	76	86	0.469	27.4	$54,821,000	$49,221,000	$1,796,387
San Francisco	97	65	0.599	48.4	$53,737,826	$48,137,826	$994,583

Notwithstanding the Commissioner's increasingly shrill laments about "competitive balance," MLB in 2000 was as balanced as it has ever been. No club finished with a winning percentage above .599 or below .401. At the extremes—the 97–65 Giants and 65–97 Cubs—the Cubs outspent the Giants by almost $7 million, as San Francisco won with the division's lowest payroll.

Two of the AL's three most cost-effective teams, the White Sox and Athletics, qualified for the playoffs. The 2000 Yankees, who lost 15 of their final 18 regular-season games before awakening in time for the postseason, became the first playoff qualifier to spend more than $2 million/ marginal win. This figure would have been much higher if computed based on end-of-season payrolls: The Yankees added almost $21 million in salaries over the course of the season, while the Orioles shed $22 million as they fell out of contention.

Minnesota and Florida showed that even a bad team can be efficient if it cuts payroll deeply enough, and would soon demonstrate that when those deep slashes in payroll make room for good, young, cheap players, a team can contend within two or three seasons. The NL's biggest disappointments included the Diamondbacks and Dodgers, who missed the playoffs with two of the league's three highest payrolls.

TABLE 7. MARGINAL PAYROLL/MARGINAL WIN, 2001

Team	W	L	Pct	Marginal Wins	Opening Payroll	Marginal Payroll	Marginal $/ Marginal Win
Baltimore	63	98	0.391	14.8	$72,426,328	$66,826,328	$4,517,947
Boston	82	79	0.509	33.9	$109,558,908	$103,958,908	$3,065,792
NY Yankees	95	65	0.594	47.6	$109,791,893	$104,191,893	$2,189,480
Tampa Bay	62	100	0.383	13.4	$54,951,602	$49,351,602	$3,682,955
Toronto	80	82	0.494	31.4	$75,798,500	$70,198,500	$2,235,621
Chicago White Sox	83	79	0.512	34.4	$62,363,000	$56,763,000	$1,650,087
Cleveland	91	71	0.562	42.4	$91,974,979	$86,374,979	$2,037,146
Detroit	66	96	0.407	17.4	$49,831,167	$44,231,167	$2,542,021
Kansas City	65	97	0.401	16.4	$35,643,000	$30,043,000	$1,831,890
Minnesota	85	77	0.525	36.4	$24,350,000	$18,750,000	$515,110
Anaheim	75	87	0.463	26.4	$46,568,180	$40,968,180	$1,551,825
Oakland	102	60	0.630	53.4	$33,810,750	$28,210,750	$528,291
Seattle	116	46	0.716	67.4	$75,652,500	$70,052,500	$1,039,355
Texas	73	89	0.451	24.4	$88,504,421	$82,904,421	$3,397,722
Atlanta	88	74	0.543	39.4	$91,851,587	$86,251,587	$2,189,127
Florida	76	86	0.469	27.4	$35,504,167	$29,904,167	$1,091,393
Montreal	68	94	0.420	19.4	$34,774,500	$29,174,500	$1,503,840
NY Mets	82	80	0.506	33.4	$93,174,428	$87,574,428	$2,621,989
Philadelphia	86	76	0.531	37.4	$41,664,167	$36,064,167	$964,283
Chicago Cubs	88	74	0.543	39.4	$64,015,833	$58,415,833	$1,482,635
Cincinnati	66	96	0.407	17.4	$45,227,882	$39,627,882	$2,277,464
Houston	93	69	0.574	44.4	$60,382,667	$54,782,667	$1,233,844
Milwaukee	68	94	0.420	19.4	$43,089,333	$37,489,333	$1,932,440
Pittsburgh	62	100	0.383	13.4	$52,698,333	$47,098,333	$3,514,801
St. Louis	93	69	0.574	44.4	$77,270,855	$71,670,855	$1,614,208
Arizona	92	70	0.568	43.4	$81,206,513	$75,606,513	$1,742,086
Colorado	73	89	0.451	24.4	$71,068,000	$65,468,000	$2,683,115
Los Angeles	86	76	0.531	37.4	$108,980,952	$103,380,952	$2,764,197
San Diego	79	83	0.488	30.4	$38,333,117	$32,733,117	$1,076,747
San Francisco	90	72	0.556	41.4	$63,332,667	$57,732,667	$1,394,509

After the 2001 season, MLB released financial information showing that player compensation had risen 113% between 1995 and 2001. MLB used this information to argue that salaries were out of control and small markets could no longer compete. These same disclosures showed, however, that MLB's total revenue rose 134% over this time. There was plenty of money to go around, so long as it was spent wisely.

The wise spenders are easy to spot. Oakland won 102 games with the majors' second-lowest payroll; Minnesota contended all season with the lowest. Seattle won 116 games with a payroll lower than Toronto's. On the other hand, the Phillies showed the limits of efficiency, missing the division title by two games while being outspent by $50 million.

At the other end of the spectrum, the five members of the $3 million/win club practiced five different types of inefficiency. The Orioles paid top dollar to hold onto the remnants of a 1993 All-Star team; the Devil Rays wasted money on free agents instead of developing a farm system; the Rangers bid against themselves for Alex Rodriguez and bought poor pitchers for the money; the Pirates overpaid third-tier free agents; and Boston's bench earned more than the entire Twins team.

TABLE 8. MARGINAL PAYROLL/MARGINAL WIN, 2002

Team	W	L	Pct	Marginal Wins	Opening Payroll	Marginal Payroll	Marginal $/ Marginal Win
Baltimore	67	95	0.414	18.4	$60,493,487	$54,893,487	$2,983,342
Boston	93	69	0.574	44.4	$108,366,060	$102,766,060	$2,314,551
NY Yankees	103	58	0.640	55.0	$125,928,583	$120,328,583	$2,186,212
Tampa Bay	55	106	0.342	6.7	$34,380,000	$28,780,000	$4,269,007
Toronto	78	84	0.481	29.4	$76,864,333	$71,264,333	$2,423,957
Chicago White Sox	81	81	0.500	32.4	$57,052,833	$51,452,833	$1,588,050
Cleveland	74	88	0.457	25.4	$78,909,448	$73,309,448	$2,886,199
Detroit	55	106	0.342	6.7	$55,048,000	$49,448,000	$7,334,741
Kansas City	62	100	0.383	13.4	$47,257,000	$41,657,000	$3,108,731
Minnesota	94	67	0.584	46.0	$40,225,000	$34,625,000	$752,982
Anaheim	99	63	0.611	50.4	$61,721,667	$56,121,667	$1,113,525
Oakland	103	59	0.636	54.4	$39,679,746	$34,079,746	$626,466
Seattle	93	69	0.574	44.4	$80,282,668	$74,682,668	$1,682,042
Texas	72	90	0.444	23.4	$105,302,124	$99,702,124	$4,260,775
Atlanta	101	59	0.631	53.7	$93,470,367	$87,870,367	$1,637,463
Florida	79	83	0.488	30.4	$41,979,917	$36,379,917	$1,196,708
Montreal	83	79	0.512	34.4	$38,670,500	$33,070,500	$961,352
NY Mets	75	86	0.466	26.9	$94,633,593	$89,033,593	$3,314,008
Philadelphia	80	81	0.497	31.9	$57,955,000	$52,355,000	$1,641,382
Chicago Cubs	97	65	0.599	48.4	$75,690,833	$70,090,833	$1,448,158
Cincinnati	78	84	0.481	29.4	$45,050,390	$39,450,390	$1,341,850
Houston	84	78	0.519	35.4	$63,448,417	$57,848,417	$1,634,136
Milwaukee	56	106	0.346	7.4	$50,287,333	$44,687,333	$6,038,829
Pittsburgh	72	89	0.447	23.8	$42,323,598	$36,723,598	$1,539,954
St. Louis	97	65	0.599	48.4	$74,098,267	$68,498,267	$1,415,253
Arizona	98	64	0.605	49.4	$102,820,000	$97,220,000	$1,968,016
Colorado	73	89	0.451	24.4	$56,851,043	$51,251,043	$2,100,453
Los Angeles	92	70	0.568	43.4	$94,850,952	$89,250,952	$2,056,474
San Diego	66	96	0.407	17.4	$41,425,000	$35,825,000	$2,058,908
San Francisco	95	66	0.590	47.0	$78,299,835	$72,699,835	$1,547,132

The big news of the 2001–02 off-season was MLB's plan to contract the Twins and Expos. In announcing the planned contraction on November 6, 2002, Commissioner Selig declared: "The teams to be contracted have a long record of failing to generate enough revenues to operate a viable major league franchise." The Twins responded by winning their division by 13 games, then repeating in 2003. As noted earlier, the last three World Series have all been won by clubs on the original list of eight candidates for contraction.

If MLB really wanted to contract "on the merits," the clubs facing the axe would have been the Tigers and the Brewers, neither of which made the list. Between them, Detroit and Milwaukee used the increased revenue from their new ballparks to pay $5 million or more to Damion Easley, Jeffrey Hammonds, Jose Lima, Mark Loretta, and

Dmitri Young, thereby doing more than the Yankees to inflate player salaries. Milwaukee spent $6 million per marginal win, Detroit an incredible $7.3 million. Even the Mets and Rangers, who finished last with division-high payrolls, spent far more wisely than the Terrible Two.

Oakland and Minnesota remained MLB's most efficient spenders, but only the Athletics inspired a best-selling book. Although the Athletics and Twins took different approaches to player development, both clubs were built around a nucleus of young, low-salaried players produced by their own farm systems, with free agents and pricier veterans brought in only to fill specific needs. The AL West finished in reverse order of team payroll, with the World Champion Angels winning 99 games with a roster only slightly more expensive than Baltimore's.

TABLE 9. MARGINAL PAYROLL/MARGINAL WIN, 2003

Team	W	L	Pct	Marginal Wins	Opening Payroll	Marginal Payroll	Marginal $/ Marginal Win
Baltimore	71	91	0.438	22.4	$73,877,500	$65,477,500	$2,923,103
Boston	95	67	0.586	46.4	$99,946,500	$91,546,500	$1,972,985
NY Yankees	101	61	0.623	52.4	$152,749,814	$144,349,814	$2,754,767
Tampa Bay	63	99	0.389	14.4	$19,630,000	$11,230,000	$779,861
Toronto	86	76	0.531	37.4	$51,269,000	$42,869,000	$1,146,230
Chicago White Sox	86	76	0.531	37.4	$51,010,000	$42,610,000	$1,139,305
Cleveland	68	94	0.420	19.4	$48,584,834	$40,184,834	$2,071,383
Detroit	43	119	0.265	-5.6	$49,168,000	$40,768,000	($7,280,000)
Kansas City	83	79	0.512	34.4	$40,518,000	$32,118,000	$933,663
Minnesota	90	72	0.556	41.4	$55,505,000	$47,105,000	$1,137,802
Anaheim	77	85	0.475	28.4	$79,031,667	$70,631,667	$2,487,031
Oakland	96	66	0.593	47.4	$50,260,834	$41,860,834	$883,140
Seattle	93	69	0.574	44.4	$86,959,167	$78,559,167	$1,769,351
Texas	71	91	0.438	22.4	$103,491,667	$95,091,667	$4,245,164
Atlanta	101	61	0.623	52.4	$106,243,667	$97,843,667	$1,867,246
Florida	91	71	0.562	42.4	$49,050,000	$40,650,000	$958,726
Montreal	83	79	0.512	34.4	$51,948,500	$43,548,500	$1,265,945
NY Mets	66	95	0.410	17.8	$117,176,429	$108,776,429	$6,107,625
Philadelphia	86	76	0.531	37.4	$70,780,000	$62,380,000	$1,667,914
Chicago Cubs	88	74	0.543	39.4	$79,868,333	$71,468,333	$1,813,917
Cincinnati	69	93	0.426	20.4	$59,355,667	$50,955,667	$2,497,827
Houston	87	75	0.537	38.4	$71,040,000	$62,640,000	$1,631,250
Milwaukee	68	94	0.420	19.4	$40,627,000	$32,227,000	$1,661,186
Pittsburgh	75	87	0.463	26.4	$54,812,429	$46,412,429	$1,758,047
St. Louis	85	77	0.525	36.4	$83,486,666	$75,086,666	$2,062,820
Arizona	84	78	0.519	35.4	$80,640,333	$72,240,333	$2,040,687
Colorado	74	88	0.457	25.4	$67,179,667	$58,779,667	$2,314,160
Los Angeles	85	77	0.525	36.4	$105,872,620	$97,472,620	$2,677,819
San Diego	64	98	0.395	15.4	$47,928,000	$39,528,000	$2,566,753
San Francisco	100	61	0.621	52.0	$82,852,167	$74,452,167	$1,431,191

The 2003 season was the season played under the current CBA, with its luxury tax and increased revenue sharing. The target of these changes, the New York Yankees, responded by boosting their payroll by another $26 million. The money was not well spent: The Yankees, who were the AL East's most efficient spenders in 2002, threatened Baltimore's perennial position as the division's least efficient club. New York's Opening Day payroll included seven players earning more than $10 million and seven more earning $5 to $8 million.

Elsewhere in the AL, the Twins and Athletics used their revenue-sharing money for its intended purpose, increasing their Opening Day payrolls by more than $10 mil-lion to retain their talent base. Despite outspending the World Champion Marlins, Detroit won fewer games than the MP/MW formula thought possible.

The New York Mets started the 2003 season with MLB's second-highest payroll and finished it with the fourth-worst record, easily the worst non-Detroit performance. By contrast, the Braves got the quality they paid for, tying with the Yankees for the majors' best record despite spending $45 million less. Except for injury-riddled Cincinnati, NL Central clubs largely got what they paid for, while as usual during the Barry Bonds/Brian Sabean era, San Francisco was the most efficient club in the NL West.

Over There! A Second Review of Translating Japanese Statistics, and Translating the Mexican League

by Clay Davenport

O K, let's just jump right into this and lead off with Godzilla, then work through the difficulties involved with translating Japanese player performance from there.

Table 1 was the translation I set up for Matsui at the end of 2002, based on the work I had done trying to adjust Japanese statistics to an American baseball environment. This suggested that Matsui would be an outstanding player here, just as he was in Japan. Not as good, mind you; in 2002's real world, he hit .334/.458/.692, so the numbers above do make a substantial downward adjustment. When the 2003 season played itself out, however, we wound up with a translation that looked like this 2.

(Yes, I know those aren't Matsui's actual statistics. The translation scheme converts everything, including major league statistics, to a league with a .270 batting average, .340 on-base percentage, .440 slugging average, and a .260 Equivalent Average (EqA).)

That's not a bad player by any means, but it is considerably less than what we expected. The walk loss I understand—a lot of his walks in Japan were intentional, and since he didn't inspire the same fear here he lost those—but the power shortage was disturbing. It was especially disturbing because Japan's other prominent non-pitching import, Ichiro Suzuki, also came up short in the power department, while hitting for a higher average than expected (see table 3).

TABLE 1. BP 2002 HIDEKI MATSUI STATS

HIDEKI MATSUI — Bats L — Throws R — Born 12-Jun-74 — Age 30

YEAR	TEAM	LG	AB	H	DB	TP	HR	BB	SO	R	RBI	SB	CS	AVG	OBP	SLG	EQA	EQR
1998	Yomiuri	JpC	492	126	28	5	29	91	112	98	92	3	4	.256	.379	.510	.291	85
1999	Yomiuri	JpC	468	121	31	5	31	82	109	90	81	0	3	.259	.371	.545	.294	82
2000	Yomiuri	JpC	479	130	39	4	32	97	114	107	97	4	2	.271	.396	.570	.312	95
2001	Yomiuri	JpC	492	145	30	8	29	108	97	104	97	3	1	.295	.422	.565	.321	102
2002	Yomiuri	JpC	535	161	38	8	41	117	99	118	111	3	1	.301	.431	.632	.337	124
Total per 650PA			541	150	36	7	36	109	117	113	105	3	2	.277	.401	.566	.312	107

TABLE 2. BP 2003 HIDEKI MATSUI STATS

YEAR	TEAM	LG	AB	H	DB	TP	HR	BB	SO	R	RBI	SB	CS	AVG	OBP	SLG	EQA	EQR
2003	NYYanks	AL	626	191	37	2	20	66	77	87	114	2	2	.305	.374	.466	.280	91

TABLE 3. ICHIRO SUZUKI STATS

ICHIRO SUZUKI — Bats L — Throws L — Born 22-Oct-73 — Age 30

TEAM/YEARS	LG	AB	H	DB	TP	HR	BB	SO	R	RBI	SB	CS	AVG	OBP	SLG	EQA	EQR
Japan, 1998–2000	599	206	44	4	19	51	52	99	86	17	3	.344	.403	.525	.309	105
US, 2001–2003	607	218	29	7	10	43	48	114	59	38	13	.359	.410	.483	.300	99

The methods used to create the adjustments last year looked at every player who had played in both the United States and Japan since 1993. I compared how each player hit, relative to his league, in the U.S. and Japan, and noted the differences—particularly how his Equivalent Average (EqA) changed. EqA measures the player's total offense (at least his ability to hit for average, hit for power, draw walks, and steal bases) and corrects for park and league offensive levels, creating as level a playing field as possible. If the total EqA for the group was higher in Japan than it was in the U.S., that meant the Japanese leagues were easier than the U.S. leagues. This is what I found. I concluded that the Japanese leagues had a difficulty level slightly higher than the American Triple-A leagues; moreover, that the level of play was on the edge of what, historically, has been considered "major league" over here. You can read those initial studies on the web at: http://www.baseballprospectus.com/news/20020129davenport.html and http://www.baseballprospectus.com/news/20020221davenport.html.

There were a couple of problems with that study which this one will try to correct.

The first problem, which is still an issue, is that the overwhelming majority of the player comparisons were made for Western players who went from the U.S. to Japan. The majority of the comparisons going from Japan to the U.S. are for Western players coming back. Only a few—Suzuki, So Taguchi, Tsuyoshi Shinjo, and now Matsui—came from native Asian players. Something like 40% of the players who go to Japan play far below their established skill level and leave quickly. It's not clear whether that's because they can't adjust to the cultural differences, or if they were in Japan because they were washed up, and everyone here knew it, but they got past the Japanese scouts. These homesick (or washed up) players drag the statistics of the transfers down substantially, more than I made allowance for, and make the Japanese leagues look tougher than I think they really are. This time around, I've limited myself to those players who spent at least two years in Japan, figuring that the culturally stressed either wouldn't return or wouldn't be invited back by their teams. This does, of course, create the possibility that I am now adjusting the league down too far.

Problem #2 was more disturbing, at least to me. One of the basic assumptions made by the Translation programs is that the difficulty adjustments between leagues are proportional to the skills involved—meaning that average and power, for instance, will both go down if you move to a league that is tougher overall. I only need to establish the difficulty level in terms of runs in order to make good estimates for how batting average, power, walks, and steals will change. It also means that a player with the higher EqA in League One will still have a higher EqA when translated to League Two. This works well for the American minors; the only real problems come from park-specific effects (like doubles on the Metrodome turf).

It does not work for Japan. The relationship between hitting for average and power in Japan is clearly different; in particular, it appears that power comes cheap. The best approach I found was to make a second pass through the program—one to translate the statistics in the normal way, and the second one to do nothing except cut the power back even further. It also means that players whose chief offensive tool is power will see their EqAs reduced more than other players.

So how well does this "new" approach work? There were 37 players in the study who had spent at least two consecutive years in both the U.S. and Japan, plus Matsui, who had more plate appearances in one year than many of the players included had in two. I looked only at the three seasons prior to moving from one continent to the other, and only at the first three years after moving (unless, of course, they didn't stay three years). The aggregate results of that trial are shown in table 4.

Keep in mind that all of the above stats have been translated to eliminate park and league effects. The old DT for the group was four points short in batting average but eight points over in OBP, while going over by 20 points in slugging and seven in EqA. In the revision, the bias in batting average is cut in half, the biases in on-base and slugging are cut by 75%, and the EqA bias is reduced by 86%. Even more impressive are the reductions in the root-mean-square errors, calculated for each individual's statistics (that's what the dAVG, dOBP, etc., are; lower numbers = better). The average error in batting average actually went up, albeit by a trivial (1%) amount. That's an easy sacrifice to

TABLE 4. ALTERNATE TRANSLATION METHOD

Translations	AVG	OBP	SLG	EqA	dAVG	dOBP	dSLG	dEqA
Playing in US:	.270	.332	.464	.263				
Old Translation, in Japan:	.266	.340	.484	.270	24.6	30.0	54.5	22.5
New Translation, in Japan:	.268	.334	.459	.262	24.9	25.5	40.2	16.7

make when the other errors are reduced so dramatically: on-base average by 15%, slugging and EqA by 26%.

Let's look at some specific cases. The dates indicate the years being used in the translation.

Hideki Matsui (Japan 2000–02, US 2003)

Translation	AVG	OBP	SLG	EqA
US	.305	.374	.466	.280
Old Japan	.290	.417	.590	.324
New Japan	.297	.392	.495	.295

OK, so he still didn't hit for as much power as expected, but it is now a modest 29-point shortfall instead of a 124-point mega-error. This would have been a much better forecast than the one I actually made, as 226 points of error (the sum of the absolute errors for each of the four categories) get cut to 70.

Ichiro Suzuki (Japan 1998–2000, US 2001–03)

Translation	AVG	OBP	SLG	EqA
US	.363	.413	.488	.303
Old Japan	.344	.403	.525	.309
New Japan	.348	.393	.484	.296

There is no more mystery of missing power, and we go from 72 error points to 46.

Roberto Petagine (US 1996–98, Japan 1999–2001)

Translation	AVG	OBP	SLG	EqA
US	.280	.384	.507	.294
Old Japan	.281	.410	.564	.317
New Japan	.288	.385	.484	.290

An old stathead favorite, the new power reduction technique takes him back to his American levels of play, that of a good, but not great, first baseman; note that most of the American translation was from Triple-A, not the majors. The old error was 107 points; now it is 36.

Leo Gomez (US 1994–96, Japan 1997–99)

Translation	AVG	OBP	SLG	EqA
US	.260	.359	.470	.272
Old Japan	.271	.359	.506	.283
New Japan	.274	.349	.469	.271

Gomez went straight from the Cubs to a six-year run with the Chunichi Dragons. His translation was very good before (error, 58), but is even better now (26).

Karl (Tuffy) Rhodes (US 1993–95, Japan 1996–98)

Translation	AVG	OBP	SLG	EqA
US	.255	.333	.462	.266
Old Japan	.276	.360	.484	.278
New Japan	.278	.351	.458	.269

Old "Three Home Runs on Opening Day" Rhodes tied the Japanese home run record in 2001, but the numbers here only reflect his first three years in Japan. Once more, a big reduction in the slugging error drives the overall total down from 82 to 48.

Tsuyoshi Shinjo (Japan 1998–2000, US 2001–03)

Translation	AVG	OBP	SLG	EqA
US	.261	.320	.396	.238
Old Japan	.234	.280	.397	.226
New Japan	.234	.280	.397	.226

No change. The new adjustments are not the same for every player, but kick in around league average and increase from there. Shinjo was below the line where the new adjustment made any difference at all, even though his value does in fact turn on his slugging ability. I recognize that is theoretically inconsistent, but it does work better this way, and I'm one of those who will choose the practical over the theory every chance I get.

Alex Cabrera (US 1997, 1998, 2000 for US line, Japan 2001–03)

Translation	AVG	OBP	SLG	EqA
US	.252	.290	.516	.259
Old Japan	.296	.397	.638	.332
New Japan	.296	.372	.524	.292

Cabrera, who tied the Japanese home run record in 2002, has an odd U.S. line: four partial seasons with EqAs between .241 and .253 (1997 and 1998 in Mexico, 2000 in Tucson and Arizona; he spent 1999 in Taiwan, and I haven't been able to acquire those statistics) and a monstrous partial season in El Paso in 2000 with an EqA of .320. With either the old or the new version of the Japanese translation, his North American translation is obliterated, but the new one is much closer to his "old" self, with the error dropping from a staggering 346 to "only" 167.

Derrick May (US 1998–2000, Japan 2001–03)

Translation	AVG	OBP	SLG	EqA
US	.262	.318	.416	.245
Old Japan	.275	.336	.497	.271
New Japan	.268	.326	.468	.259

May spent his last couple of years in the U.S. playing for Rochester. When you can't break into the recent Oriole outfields, you need to look abroad. The old forecast produced 138 points of error; the new version neatly slices that down to a more reasonable 80.

Alex Ramirez (US 1998–2000, Japan 2001–03)

Translation	AVG	OBP	SLG	EqA
US	.268	.294	.479	.250
Old Japan	.294	.338	.522	.278
New Japan	.282	.323	.495	.265

The former Indian and Pirate outfielder has found a new home as a Yakult Swallow, and had a big year in 2003, leading the Central League in home runs, slugging, total bases, hits, and RBI, while coming up second in batting average and runs scored. The error in the stats did run to 141 points, but the revision cuts that to only 74.

Kazuo Matsui (Japan 2001–03)

Translation	AVG	OBP	SLG	EqA
Old Japan	.314	.370	.552	.298
New Japan	.300	.348	.486	.275

Formerly a shortstop for the Seibu Lions but now headed to the Mets, Kazuo Matsui has been frequently compared to his new cross-town rival, Derek Jeter. Compared to Jeter's translations for the same age range (.354/.436/.539, .322), Matsui has similar power and speed numbers, but is expected to walk less and hit for a much lower batting average; the older translation was more favorable across the board. I'd expect him to be a good shortstop here, not an elite one, unless he turns out to be as great a fielder as his reputation.

Enough with the old and new translations already. We're going to skip through a number of players who, so far, have only played in Japan, and who you should probably know about.

Kyosuke Fukudome

	AVG	OBP	SLG	EqA
Translation	.290	.364	.478	.279

A former shortstop turned right fielder for the Chunichi Dragons, Fukudome was the Central League's batting champ in 2002 and slipped to seventh last year, albeit with increased power. He's 27, and won't be eligible for U.S. play until 2008 at the earliest.

Akinori Iwamura

	AVG	OBP	SLG	EqA
Translation	.276	.333	.463	.262

A Gold Glove third baseman for Yakult, Iwamura is still only 25 and at least four or five years away from posting. He suffered a wrist injury in 2003, so his numbers were off across the board.

Tadahito Iguchi

	AVG	OBP	SLG	EqA
Translation	.269	.337	.446	.262

A second baseman for the Japan Series champion Hawks, the translated line above doesn't tell you that his 2003 was his best season ever (.307/.385/.464, .286), that he steals 30–40 bases a year, and that he's a Gold Glove winner. Supposedly, the Hawks had promised to post him after the 2003 season, but it didn't happen, keeping Iguchi in Japan for at least another year.

Kenji Jojima

	AVG	OBP	SLG	EqA
Translation	.280	.329	.477	.264

Another Gold Glover, this time a catcher, who also led the Pacific League in total bases. That's right, a catcher who led the league in TB and played in every game. He was the league's MVP last year, leading the Hawks to the pennant, and would be eligible for posting after the 2005 season.

Michihiro Ogasawara

	AVG	OBP	SLG	EqA
Translation	.315	.381	.490	.289

I think Ogasawara is the best Japanese hitter in the league right now, in terms of performance and consistency from one year to the next. A third baseman for the Fighters, who now play in the hinterlands of Sapporo, he's an underrated player within his own league but apparently content with that status. He is signed through 2006, when he would be 33, and doesn't appear likely to be a U.S. player.

Norihiro Nakamura

	AVG	OBP	SLG	EqA
Translation	.269	.358	.473	.275

Nakamura was very close to coming to the Mets last year, where he would have been their starting third baseman. In 200102 he produced a translated line of .290/.370/.496, .285, but a knee injury last year really sapped his production and kept him out of Olympic qualifiers.

And what about the top Japanese pitchers? The revision to pitchers isn't as large as it is for hitters; I tweaked the difficulty level up a little to take care of the power difference, but past pitchers coming to America have held up well. The top Japanese pitchers right now, from our perspective, are:

Kazumi Saito

	ERA	H/9	BB/9	SO/9
Translation	3.93	8.5	3.3	6.1

Twenty-six years old in 2004, Saito broke through in a big way in 2003, going 20–3 to lead his Hawks to the Japanese championship. It was the first time he had thrown more than 90 innings in a season, and he was the co-winner of Sawamura Award, Japan's version of the Cy Young. Twenty wins is a bigger deal in Japan than here, largely because they play a shorter season; it was the first time in four years that anybody had won 20, and the first time in 18 years that a Pacific League pitcher did it.

Kei Igawa

	ERA	H/9	BB/9	SO/9
Translation	4.08	8.7	3.7	6.4

Saito's co-winner of the Sawamura Award was this man, who led his Hanshin Tigers to the championship of the Central League, going 20–5 while also winning the Central League MVP. This was Igawa's third consecutive season working at more or less this level, although it was the first time he's had any support from his team. He's only 25 this season.

Daisuke Matsuzaka

	ERA	H/9	BB/9	SO/9
Translation	3.93	8.0	3.4	7.5

Despite not being an award winner in 2003, and despite missing most of 2002 to an injury, Matsuzaka looks like the best pitcher in Japan. No other starting pitcher in the league can match his fastball, and his performance record is already strong at a young age; he's even younger than Saito and Igawa, and won't turn 24 until September.

Koji Uehara	ERA	H/9	BB/9	SO/9
Translation	4.17	8.6	1.5	6.0

Twenty-nine-year-old Uehara is the ace of the Yomiuri Giants, and has been a star ever since he went 20–4 as a rookie in 1999. The Giants are often referred to as the Yankees of Japan, complete with a Steinbrenneresque owner who will outspend the rest of the league in his desire to win. Uehara has benefited from the support (72–28 lifetime record), and made a splash by using an agent (albeit unofficially) during his most recent contract negotiations.

Akinori Otsuka	ERA	H/9	BB/9	SO/9
Translation	3.28	7.0	1.5	9.9

Signed by the Padres this off-season, it is hard to figure out how he wasn't considered the top relief pitcher in Japan. His translated numbers are almost as good as Sasaki's, yet when he was posted after the 2002 season he didn't receive a single offer. A closer in Japan, he'll set up for San Diego and should be very good right away.

South of the Border

While we're looking at Japanese statistics, let's also look closer to home, at the Mexican League.

Our vision of Mexican League statistics has also undergone a big change, although in this case it has nothing to do with a new way to translate the numbers. The upheaval in the Mexican League has come from being able to apply an old technique for the first time, as we were finally able to secure a full game-by-game report of the 2003 Mexican League season . . . and that means park factors.

Park factors are some of the more difficult data to get for a league, since you have to have full game logs in order to do it properly. Not having park data has never stopped us from analyzing a league as far as possible; in almost every American league, for instance, you can just assume a neutral park and it will barely affect your results, since inter-league differences are much larger than intra-league park effects. In Mexico, however, it is different. Only three of 16 teams in Mexico play in a park within five points of average; the rest are either way above or way below average.

As it happens, most of the players who have made the jump from the Mexican leagues to the American minor leagues (or majors, in Julio Franco's case) have come from the high-offense parks. This makes sense, as those are the places where a hitter can more easily run up a .380 average or hit 30 home runs, eye-catching numbers in any environment. The trouble is that since all of the hitters in

the study came from high-offense parks—parks whose hitting bias wasn't sufficiently recognized—our analyses of league difficulty were distorted. I have been under-rating the strength of the league for years. Previously I'd rated the quality of the league as being similar to the Carolina and other High-A leagues. With good park estimates in hand, I'll have to raise that to Double-A level.

For championship purposes, the Mexican summer league is divided into two divisions, the Northern and Southern. The natural geography of the teams, however, suggests three divisions: the lowland, the highland, and the north. Two years ago, the league actually was split up exactly this way.

Five of the league's teams are located in the lowlands around the Bay of Campeche, the shallow body of water between mainland Mexico and the Yucatan peninsula. The climate is fully tropical, hot and humid; this is the part of the country with the Mayan ruins, the jungle, and regular visits from hurricanes. This is not a wealthy area, and the attendance is poor even by Mexican standards, with three of the four smallest crowds in the league. Between the lack of money and the wet climate, these cities are unattractive to outside players. The combination of playing at sea level and playing in high humidity means that these five teams all play as extreme pitcher's parks within the league. (About the humidity: Baseball yarn is hydrophilic, meaning that it will absorb water from the air in humid conditions; the yarn loses resiliency when wet, making for a deader ball.). Starting from about 8 o'clock on the Bay and following the coast eastward, they are:

- Veracruz Red Eagles, 14 meters elevation, .915 park factor
- Tabasco Olmecs (play in Villahermosa, Tabasco state), 10 meters elevation, .830 park
- Campeche Pirates, 5 meters elevation, .912 park
- Yucatan Lions (play in Merida, Yucatan state), 10 meters, .879 park
- Cancun Lobstermen, around the top of the Yucatan Peninsula, and facing the Caribbean, 10 meters elevation, .940 park

Five teams are also located in the highlands in and near Mexico City. Central Mexico is a very high plateau cut by valleys, and I do mean high—Mexico City is half again as high as Denver (which is 5,280 ft, or 1,609 meters). On the plateau, the climate is milder and drier. This is the heartland of Mexico, politically, culturally, and financially. It's heavily populated, cosmopolitan, relatively rich (especially Mexico City and Puebla), and has the means to attract foreign players. All, not surprisingly, play as strong hitter's parks.

- Cordoba Coffeegrowers, 900 meters, 1.089 park factor. Cordoba is on the border of the highlands and the lowlands, on the road between Mexico and Veracruz.

- Oaxaca Warriors, 1,550 meters, 1.078 park factor.

- Puebla Parrots, 2,179 meters, 1.103 park factor.

- Angelopolis Tigers, 2,179 meters, 1.132 park factor. The Tigers used to play in Mexico, but spent 2003 sharing Puebla's stadium. League champions of 2003.

- Mexico City Red Devils, 2,303 meters, 1.190 park factor.

The remaining six teams in the league are located in the country's north, in three states that border Texas. The six are a microcosm of the Mexican league's geography: The two with the lowest park factors lie along the Rio Grande, the two with the highest factors are high in the Mesa del Norte, and the two in the middle, park factor-wise, are in foothill regions. All three more-or-less neutral parks are located here, along with two pitcher's parks and one hitter's park. Baseball is more popular here, close to the U.S., than it is in the rest of the country, and the area has four of the top five teams in attendance. The teams are:

- Reynosa Broncos, 40 meters elevation, .937 park.

- Two Laredos Owls, 150 meters elevation, .926 park. The Owls play their home games in both Nuevo Laredo, Mexico, and across the river in Laredo, Texas, making them the only binational professional team in the world. Their name probably loses more in translation than any other; Tecolotes de los Dos Laredos has a beautiful rhythm that English can't match.

- Monterrey Sultans, 512 meters, .976 park.

- Monclova Steelers, 615 meters, .980 park.

- Vaqueros Laguna, who play in Torreon, 1,124 meters, 1.149 park.

- Saltillo Serapemakers, 1,599 meters, 1.024 park.

None of the large cities of western Mexico, like Guadalajara, Aguascalientes, Hermosillo, Culiacan, and Mazatlan, have teams in the Mexican League. What appears to be an oversight is actually easy to explain—May through August is the rainy season, and scheduling would be virtually impossible. The Mexican Pacific League, a winter league which plays from October through December, fills some of that gap, operating along the country's northwest between Mazatlan and the U.S. border. Generally speaking, too, the farther south you go in Mexico, the less popular baseball becomes, and it just isn't part of the Guadalajara (mariachis!) culture.

TOP 2003 MEXICAN LEAGUE HITTERS, BY RUNS ABOVE A REPLACEMENT PLAYER AT THE SAME POSITION

Name	Team	Pos	RAR	EqBA	EqOBP	EqSLG
1. Noe Munoz	Saltillo	C	10	.249	.320	.417
2. Felix Jose	Devils	DH	8	.252	.346	.441
3. Carlos Villalobos	Puebla	3B	5	.270	.342	.449
4. Roberto Mejia	Oaxaca	2B	4	.267	.310	.460
5. Darryl Brinkley	Yucatan	OF	3	.288	.334	.416
6. Corey Paul	Saltillo	OF	3	.249	.341	.391
7. Sergio Guerrero	Campeche	2B	3	.268	.313	.412
8. Oswaldo Morejon	Yucatan	2B	2	.259	.326	.369
9. Dionys Cesar	Veracruz	SS	2	.272	.324	.371
10. Jayson Bass	Saltillo	OF	2	.227	.321	.396

TOP 2003 MEXICAN LEAGUE PITCHERS, BY VORP

Name	Team	VORP	IP	EqERA	PERA	Stuff
1. Pablo Ortega	Puebla	34	161	3.60	3.98	5
2. Ravelo Manzanillo	Salt/Yuc	27	118	3.37	3.49	14
3. Jorge Campillo	Tigers	25	119	3.55	4.19	4
4. Dan Serafini	Monterrey	25	96	3.10	3.69	20
5. Angel Moreno	Veracruz	23	127	3.84	3.83	23
6. Felipe Lira	Oaxaca	23	169	4.36	4.28	4
7. Isabel Giron	Vaqueros	22	148	4.15	5.28	−8
8. Obed Vega	Cancun	22	141	4.11	4.36	−3
9. Bronswell Patrick	Devils	21	134	4.11	4.28	0
10. Danny Magee	Campeche	20	170	4.43	5.01	−4

Team Name Key and Park Factors

by Clay Davenport

These "park factors" are actually factors for the teams, and represent the park factor faced by this team (meaning it does include road games and recognizes unbalanced schedules). They are based only on runs scored and allowed by the teams and their opponents. Factors for 2001 are an average of the 1999–2003 single-year factors; for 2002 they use the average of 2000–2003 single-season factors; for 2003 they use the average of the 2001–2003 factors. Averages are only computed for years the team is in the same park. Japanese park factors are only available for 2001–2003. Mexican park factors are only from 2003.

Code	Team	League	Organization (2003)	2001	2002	2003
ABE	Aberdeen Ironbirds	New York-Penn (A-)	Orioles	—	948	948
ABQ	Albuquerque Isotopes	Pacific Coast (AAA)	Marlins	—	—	1167
AKR	Akron Aeros	Eastern (AA)	Indians	990	994	1000
ALT	Altoona Curve	Eastern (AA)	Pirates	943	956	945
ANA	Anaheim Angels	American (Major)	Angels	995	994	987
ARI	Arizona Diamondbacks	National (Major)	Diamondbacks	1028	1044	1060
ARK	Arkansas Travelers	Texas (AA)	Angels	1010	1020	1030
ASH	Asheville Tourists	South Atlantic (A)	Rockies	1148	1161	1175
ATL	Atlanta Braves	National (Major)	Braves	975	986	986
AUB	Auburn Doubledays	New York-Penn (A-)	Blue Jays	1005	996	988
AUG	Augusta Greenjackets	South Atlantic (A)	Red Sox	984	993	1006
BAK	Bakersfield Blaze	California (A+)	Devil Rays	989	991	970
BAL	Baltimore Orioles	American (Major)	Orioles	965	959	959
BAT	Batavia Muckdogs	New York-Penn (A-)	Phillies	1034	1053	1069
BCR	Battle Creek Yankees	Midwest (A)	Yankees	—	—	1001
BIL	Billings Mustangs	Pioneer (Rookie)	Reds	972	973	954
BIN	Binghamton Mets	Eastern (AA)	Mets	1073	1067	1060
BIR	Birmingham Barons	Southern (AA)	White Sox	959	956	975
BLT	Beloit Snappers	Midwest (A)	Brewers	1023	1026	1034
BLU	Bluefield Orioles	Appalachian (Rookie)	Orioles	1101	1096	1103
BNC	Burlington (NC) Indians	Appalachian (Rookie)	Indians	958	960	969
BOI	Boise Hawks	Northwest (A-)	Cubs	1044	1050	1053
BOS	Boston Red Sox	American (Major)	Red Sox	1016	1010	1010
BOW	Bowie Baysox	Eastern (AA)	Orioles	982	980	982
BRI	Bristol White Sox	Appalachian (Rookie)	White Sox	979	967	950
BRO	Brooklyn Cyclones	New York-Penn (A-)	Mets	1004	1004	1004
BRV	Brevard County Manatees	Florida State (A+)	Expos	950	954	948
BUF	Buffalo Bisons	International (AAA)	Indians	997	997	1004
BUR	Burlington Bees	Midwest (A)	Royals	1021	1000	998
CAR	Carolina Mudcats	Southern (AA)	Marlins	1006	1017	1009
CAS	Casper Rockies	Pioneer (Rookie)	Rockies	1043	1043	1043
CCN	Cancun Langosteros	Mexican		—	—	940
CDB	Cordoba Cafeteros	Mexican		—	—	1089
CDR	Cedar Rapids Kernels	Midwest (A)	Angels	987	989	981
CGA	Columbus (GA) Redstixx	South Atlantic (A)		—	1029	1018	—
CHB	Chiba Lotte Marines	Japanese Pacific		—	1001	1001	1001
CHC	Chicago Cubs	National (Major)	Cubs	977	961	976
CHR	Charlotte Knights	International (AAA)	White Sox	1024	1010	977
CHT	Chattanooga Lookouts	Southern (AA)	Reds	1015	1011	1012

591

Code	Team	League	Organization (2003)	2001	2002	2003
CHU	Chunichi Dragons (Nagoya)	Japanese Central	—	933	933	933
CIN	Cincinnati Reds	National (Major)	Reds	1022	1035	998
CLE	Cleveland Indians	American (Major)	Indians	1008	1003	997
CLG	Calgary	Pacific Coast (AAA)	—	1130	1135	—
CLN	Clinton LumberKings	Midwest (A)	Rangers	1031	1022	1049
CLR	Clearwater Phillies	Florida State (A+)	Phillies	1036	1019	1012
CMB	Capitol City (Columbia) Bombers	South Atlantic (A)	Mets	998	993	989
CMP	Campeche Piratas	Mexican	—	—	—	912
COH	Columbus Clippers	International (AAA)	Yankees	990	1003	1001
COL	Colorado Rockies	National (Major)	Rockies	1148	1141	1126
CSC	Charleston (SC) RiverDogs	South Atlantic (A)	Devil Rays	987	984	974
CSP	Colorado Springs Sky Sox	Pacific Coast (AAA)	Rockies	1107	1111	1124
CWS	Chicago White Sox	American (Major)	White Sox	1017	1026	1018
CWV	Charleston (WV) Alley Cats	South Atlantic (A)	Blue Jays	988	990	993
DAY	Daytona Cubs	Florida State (A+)	Cubs	1024	1025	1020
DEL	Delmarva Shorebirds	South Atlantic (A)	Orioles	938	923	929
DET	Detroit Tigers	American (Major)	Tigers	966	966	966
DNV	Danville Braves	Appalachian (Rookie)	Braves	966	961	949
DOS	Dos Laredo Tecolotes	Mexican	—	—	—	926
DUN	Dunedin Blue Jays	Florida State (A+)	Blue Jays	1063	1085	940
DUR	Durham Bulls	International (AAA)	Devil Rays	1005	1006	1017
DYT	Dayton Dragons	Midwest (A)	Reds	1037	1037	1030
EDM	Edmonton Trappers	Pacific Coast (AAA)	Expos	994	988	961
ELP	El Paso Diablos	Texas (AA)	Diamondbacks	1118	1117	1129
ELZ	Elizabethton Twins	Appalachian (Rookie)	Twins	959	958	965
ERI	Erie SeaWolves	Eastern (AA)	Tigers	1063	1068	1043
EUG	Eugene Emeralds	Northwest (A-)	Padres	999	995	988
EVE	Everett AquaSox	Northwest (A-)	Mariners	1068	1093	1058
FKU	Fukuoka Daiei Hawks	Japanese Pacific	—	966	966	966
FLA	Florida Marlins	National (Major)	Marlins	950	957	955
FRD	Frederick Keys	Carolina (A+)	Orioles	1000	1007	1012
FRE	Fresno Grizzlies	Pacific Coast (AAA)	Giants	1040	1033	1011
FRI	Frisco RoughRiders	Texas (AA)	Giants	—	—	953
FTM	Ft. Myers Miracle	Florida State (A+)	Twins	952	958	947
FTW	Ft. Wayne Wizards	Midwest (A)	Padres	970	956	958
GRB	Greensboro Bats	South Atlantic (A)	Marlins	1010	1018	1021
GRF	Great Falls White Sox	Pioneer (Rookie)	White Sox	962	946	968
GRN	Greenville Braves	Southern (AA)	Braves	1052	1015	1005
HAG	Hagerstown Suns	South Atlantic (A)	Giants	1042	1041	1015
HAR	Harrisburg Senators	Eastern (AA)	Expos	1038	1026	1012
HDS	High Desert Mavericks	California (A+)	Brewers	1146	1134	1147
HEL	Helena Brewers	Pioneer (Rookie)	Brewers	—	—	942
HIC	Hickory Crawdads	South Atlantic (A)	Pirates	1043	1053	1050
HNS	Hanshin Tigers (Nishinomiya)	Japanese Central	—	979	979	979
HOU	Houston Astros	National (Major)	Astros	1041	1041	1038
HRO	Hiroshima Carp	Japanese Central	—	1055	1055	1055
HUD	Hudson Valley Renegades	New York-Penn (A-)	Devil Rays	997	989	983
HUN	Huntsville Stars	Southern (AA)	Brewers	1002	998	998
IDA	Idaho Falls Padres	Pioneer (Rookie)	Padres	1008	1017	1033
IND	Indianapolis Indians	International (AAA)	Brewers	1015	1034	1027
IOW	Iowa Cubs	Pacific Coast (AAA)	Cubs	962	966	984
JAM	Jamestown Jammers	New York-Penn (A-)	Marlins	1048	1048	1031
JAX	Jacksonville Suns	Southern (AA)	Dodgers	977	980	960
JCY	Johnsn City Cardinals	Appalachian (Rookie)	Cardinals	1040	1022	1002
JUP	Jupiter Hammerheads	Florida State (A+)	Marlins	956	949	963
KAN	Kannapolis Intimidators	South Atlantic (A)	White Sox	985	981	976
KCR	Kansas City Royals	American (Major)	Royals	1071	1085	1100
KIN	Kinston Indians	Carolina (A+)	Indians	982	974	969
KNE	Kane County Cougars	Midwest (A)	As	971	962	940
KNG	Kingsport Mets	Appalachian (Rookie)	Mets	985	984	970
LAD	Los Angeles Dodgers	National (Major)	Dodgers	926	917	917
LAK	Lakeland Tigers	Florida State (A+)	Tigers	1036	1022	1029
LEL	Lake Elsinore Storm	California (A+)	Padres	955	964	964
LEX	Lexington Legends	South Atlantic (A)	Astros	1021	1021	1021

Code	Team	League	Organization (2003)	2001	2002	2003
LKC	Lake County Captains	South Atlantic (A)	Indians	—	—	947
LNC	Lancaster Jethawks	California (A+)	Diamondbacks	1135	1137	1118
LNS	Lansing Lugnuts	Midwest (A)	Cubs	1045	1035	1008
LOU	Louisville Bats	International (AAA)	Reds	1024	1024	997
LOW	Lowell Spinners	New York-Penn (A-)	Red Sox	996	1010	1028
LVG	Las Vegas 51s	Pacific Coast (AAA)	Dodgers	1055	1053	1053
LWD	Lakewood BlueClaws	South Atlantic (A)	Phillies	924	924	924
LYN	Lynchburg Hillcats	Carolina (A+)	Pirates	1056	1060	1058
MAR	Martinsville Astros	Appalachian (Rookie)	Astros	958	973	971
MCD	Mexico Diablos Rojos	Mexican	—	—	—	1190
MCL	Monclova Acereros	Mexican	—	—	—	980
MCN	Macon Braves	South Atlantic (A)	—	1003	1004	—
MCT	Tigres de Mexico	Mexican	—	—	—	1132
MED	Medicine Hat	Pioneer (Rookie)	—	995	992	—
MEM	Memphis Redbirds	Pacific Coast (AAA)	Cardinals	939	920	919
MHV	Mahoning Valley Scrappers	New York-Penn (A-)	Indians	1057	1085	1121
MIC	Michigan	Midwest (A)	(Battle Creek)	1030	1017	—
MID	Midland Rockhounds	Texas (AA)	A's	1064	1058	1053
MIL	Milwaukee Brewers	National (Major)	Brewers	995	995	995
MIN	Minnesota Twins	American (Major)	Twins	1031	1026	1009
MOB	Mobile Bay Bears	Southern (AA)	Padres	1010	1016	1031
MOD	Modesto A's	California (A+)	A's	976	971	945
MON	Montreal Expos	National (Major)	Expos	1009	1003	1067
MSO	Missoula Ospreys	Pioneer (Rookie)	Diamondbacks	980	988	988
MTR	Monterrey Sultanes	Mexican	—	—	—	976
MUD	Mudville Nine	California (A+)	Same as Stockton	921	—	—
MYR	Myrtle Beach Pelicans	Carolina (A+)	Braves	915	922	925
NAS	Nashville Sounds	Pacific Coast (AAA)	Pirates	916	911	895
NBR	New Britain Rock Cats	Eastern (AA)	Twins	991	991	990
NHV	New Haven Ravens	Eastern (AA)	Blue Jays	964	948	956
NIP	Nippon Ham Fighters (Tokyo)	Japanese Pacific	—	1034	1034	1034
NOR	Norfolk Tides	International (AAA)	Mets	966	962	958
NRW	Norwich Navigators	Eastern (AA)	Giants	965	964	966
NWJ	New Jersey Cardinals	New York-Penn (A-)	Cardinals	959	958	975
NWO	New Orleans Zephyrs	Pacific Coast (AAA)	Astros	886	877	874
NYM	New York Mets	National (Major)	Mets	946	945	950
NYY	New York Yankees	American (Major)	Yankees	975	990	976
OAK	Oakland A's	American (Major)	A's	991	993	1003
OAX	Oaxaca Guerreros	Mexican	—	—	—	1078
OGD	Ogden Raptors	Pioneer (Rookie)	Dodgers	1030	1036	1031
OKL	Oklahoma Redhawks	Pacific Coast (AAA)	Rangers	939	934	932
OMA	Omaha Royals	Pacific Coast (AAA)	Royals	970	974	979
ONE	Oneonta Tigers	New York-Penn (A-)	Tigers	1019	1036	1037
ORL	Orlando Rays	Southern (AA)	Devil Rays	985	983	988
ORX	Orix Blue Wave (Kobe)	Japanese Pacific	—	1028	1028	1028
OSA	Kintetsu Buffaloes (Osaka)	Japanese Pacific	—	980	980	980
OTT	Ottawa Lynx	International (AAA)	Orioles	994	972	986
PAW	Pawtucket Red Sox	International (AAA)	Red Sox	993	979	993
PCH	Charlotte	Florida State (A+)	(formerly Port Charlotte)	998	1001	—
PEO	Peoria Chiefs	Midwest (A)	Cardinals	963	974	976
PHI	Philadelphia Phillies	National (Major)	Phillies	966	956	939
PIE	Piedmont	South Atlantic (A)	—	1010	—	—
PIT	Pittsburgh Pirates	National (Major)	Pirates	1009	1009	1009
PMB	Palm Beach Cardinals	Florida State (A+)	Cardinals	—	—	995
PME	Portland Sea Dogs	Eastern (AA)	Red Sox	1046	1036	1048
POR	Portland Beavers	Pacific Coast (AAA)	Padres	936	923	929
POT	Potomac Cannons	Carolina (A+)	Reds	1058	1050	1069
PRI	Princeton Devil Rays	Appalachian (Rookie)	Devil Rays	1030	1032	1057
PRO	Provo Angels	Pioneer (Rookie)	Angels	995	995	995
PTS	Pittsfield	New York-Penn (A-)	—	942	—	—
PUE	Puebla Pericos	Mexican	—	—	—	1103
PUL	Pulaski Blue Jays	Appalachian (Rookie)	Blue Jays	1010	1018	1011
QUD	Quad City River Bandits	Midwest (A)	Twins	1012	1033	1044
RCU	Rancho Cucamonga Quakes	California (A+)	Angels	974	976	979

Code	Team	League	Organization (2003)	2001	2002	2003
REA	Reading Phillies	Eastern (AA)	Phillies	1011	1017	1005
REY	Reynosa Broncos	Mexican	—	—	—	937
RIC	Richmond Braves	International (AAA)	Braves	995	998	981
ROC	Rochester Red Wings	International (AAA)	Twins	1004	1009	1037
ROM	Rome Braves	South Atlantic (A)	Braves	—	—	956
ROU	Round Rock Express	Texas (AA)	Astros	972	972	979
SAC	Sacramento RiverCats	Pacific Coast (AAA)	A's	968	968	974
SAN	San Antonio Missions	Texas (AA)	Mariners	907	910	908
SAR	Sarasota Red Sox	Florida State (A+)	Red Sox	1008	1021	1016
SAV	Savannah Sand Gnats	South Atlantic (A)	Expos	971	974	992
SBN	South Bend SilverHawks	Midwest (A)	Diamondbacks	992	1004	988
SBR	Inland Empire 66ers	California (A+)	Mariners	945	942	935
SDP	San Diego Padres	National (Major)	Padres	923	915	918
SEA	Seattle Mariners	American (Major)	Mariners	961	942	949
SEI	Seibu Lions (Tokorozawa)	Japanese Pacific	—	1007	1007	1007
SFG	San Francisco Giants	National (Major)	Giants	935	935	942
SGA	South Georgia Waves	South Atlantic (A)	Dodgers	—	981	981
SHV	Shreveport	Texas (AA)	—	967	967	—
SJO	San Jose Giants	California (A+)	Giants	946	944	938
SLC	Salt Lake Stingers	Pacific Coast (AAA)	Angels	1085	1078	1088
SLM	Salem (VA) Avalanche	Carolina (A+)	Astros	1008	998	990
SLO	Salem-Keizer Volcanoes	Northwest (A-)	Giants	1043	1036	1050
SLT	Saltillo Seraperos	Mexican	—	—	—	1024
SLU	St. Lucie Mets	Florida State (A+)	Mets	999	1009	1019
SPO	Spokane Indians	Northwest (A-)	Indians	997	1013	1010
STA	Staten Island Yankees	New York-Penn (A-)	Yankees	1014	999	948
STL	St. Louis Cardinals	National (Major)	Cardinals	981	980	974
STO	Stockton Ports	California (A+)	Rangers	—	907	924
SWB	Scranton/Wilkes-Barre Red Barons	International (AAA)	Phillies	992	995	1000
SYR	Syracuse SkyChiefs	International (AAA)	Blue Jays	1035	1036	1013
TAB	Tabasco Olmecas	Mexican	—	—	—	830
TAC	Tacoma Rainiers	Pacific Coast (AAA)	Mariners	921	932	928
TAM	Tampa Yankees	Florida State (A+)	Yankees	965	955	962
TBY	Tampa Bay Devil Rays	American (Major)	Devil Rays	999	998	997
TCV	Tri-City Valley Cats	New York-Penn (A-)	Astros	—	994	994
TEN	Tennessee Smokies	Southern (AA)	Cardinals	1061	1061	1050
TEX	Texas Rangers	American (Major)	Rangers	1048	1052	1053
TOL	Toledo Mud Hens	International (AAA)	Tigers	1006	1013	1011
TOR	Toronto Blue Jays	American (Major)	Blue Jays	1028	1030	1034
TRI	Tri-City Dust Devils	Northwest (A-)	Rockies	895	895	895
TRN	Trenton Thunder	Eastern (AA)	Yankees	993	994	1011
TUC	Tucson Sidewinders	Pacific Coast (AAA)	Diamondbacks	1089	1080	1104
TUL	Tulsa Drillers	Texas (AA)	Rockies	987	988	981
UTI	Utica	New York-Penn (A-)	—	1017	—	—
VAN	Vancouver Canadians	Northwest (A-)	A's	925	940	948
VAQ	Vaqueros Laguna	Mexican	—	—	—	1149
VER	Vermont Expos	New York-Penn (A-)	Expos	999	971	970
VIS	Visalia Oaks	California (A+)	Rockies	993	999	1008
VRC	Veracruz Rojos del Aguila	Mexican	—	—	—	915
VRO	Vero Beach Dodgers	Florida State (A+)	Dodgers	1072	1069	1075
WIC	Wichita Wranglers	Texas (AA)	Royals	990	981	969
WIL	Wilmington Blue Rocks	Carolina (A+)	Royals	982	989	996
WIS	Wisconsin Timber Rattlers	Midwest (A)	Mariners	1003	1006	1026
WMI	West Michigan Whitecaps	Midwest (A)	Tigers	941	946	962
WNC	Wilmington (NC)	South Atlantic (A)	—	922	—	—
WNS	Winston-Salem Warthogs	Carolina (A+)	White Sox	1013	1005	995
WPT	Williamsport Crosscutters	New York-Penn (A-)	Pirates	964	943	917
WTN	West Tennessee Diamond Jaxx	Southern (AA)	Cubs	964	970	972
YAK	Yakima Bears	Northwest (A-)	Diamondbacks	985	989	995
YKL	Yakult Swallows (Tokyo)	Japanese Central	—	977	977	977
YKO	Yokohama Bay Stars	Japanese Central	—	1032	1032	1032
YOM	Yomiuri Giants (Tokyo)	Japanese Central	—	1005	1005	1005
YUO	Yucatan Leones	Mexican	—	—	—	879

Index

The following is an alphabetical index of the players in *Baseball Prospectus 2004*. Players not listed here can be found at http://www.baseballprospectus.com.

Biographies

Mark Armour is the husband of Jane, the father of Maya and Drew, a co-author of the brilliant baseball treatise *Paths to Glory*, the director of SABR's Baseball Biography Project, a beer and wine drinker, and a scholar of early punk rock. In his spare time, he writes software for an Internet company.

David Cameron resides in High Point, North Carolina. He spends his days working as a cost accountant, which is even less exciting than it sounds. At night, he can usually be found at one of the multitude of minor league ballparks in the area.

Will Carroll writes "Under The Knife" and hosts Baseball Prospectus Radio. That's pretty much all he wants to do in life, and on certain days, things work out that way. Will would like to thank everyone that makes his work possible, but he doesn't want to reveal any sources. His work this year is dedicated to his two favorite women, Lois and Barbara.

Clay Davenport is a metereologist living in Bowie, Maryland, with his wife, Susan. Outside of the day job and baseball, he picks up a ridiculous amount of trivial knowledge from God knows where and tosses it back out in bars. Or at least he used to.

Gary Huckabay doesn't regret making the calls to the likes of Rany, Clay, Chris, and Joe in 1995, and is pretty much awe-struck by his good fortune in life. He lives on Mount Diablo in Northern California with creatures named Kathy, Odin, Annie, and Simmon. Gary earned his MBA from the UC Davis Graduate School of Management, and has done his time wearing suits at places like KPMG Peat Marwick, and divisions of General Electric and Vivendi Universal. His greatest achievement is marrying way over his head. His first child is due on Opening Day, 2004, and he's already disowned a friend over the gift of an extremely tiny Los Angeles Dodgers uniform.

Rany Jazayerli has finally completed an arduous odyssey through medical school and residency, one that began when Baseball Prospectus was still a figment in Gary Huckabay's imagination. He now pops pimples, pushes aloe, and occasionally saves lives as one of the youngest board-certified dermatologists in the country. He lives in suburban Chicago with his wife of seven years, Belsam, and his daughter of one year, Cedra.

Chris Kahrl is one of the original BP team and its first University of Chicago grad (we're now at three and counting), tempted away from the serfdom of academia by that Huckabay character, and now fully invested in a career in sports publishing. Having settled down outside the nation's capital, Chris has discovered that life is a little more complicated and a little more wonderful than dares or dreams suggest.

Jonah Keri is a Los Angeles–based journalist, covering the stock market for a major daily newspaper. His BP duties consist of editing the Web site (www.baseballprospectus.com), turning up interesting subjects to interview for his series of Baseball Prospectus Q&As, and pouring heart and soul into this book. Jonah's perpetual smile stems from the warmth, brilliance, and good humor of his wife, Angèle Fauchier. In his spare time (ha!) he enjoys early tee times, hoops, and lolling by the Pont Alexandre.

Doug Pappas is chairman of SABR's Business of Baseball Committee. He practices law during the week, haunts the New York Public Library's microfilm on Saturdays, and writes about what he has found on Sundays. He hopes to finish his web site before the new CBA expires.

Dave Pease lives in San Diego with his girlfriend Debbie and works for a wireless communications company. A recent SDSU graduate, he has been recently re-introduced to the concept of "leisure time" and has come to enjoy working on the house, playing Battlefield 1942, and reviewing the average ages of NL West rosters.

Dayn Perry is a Mississippi native now living in Austin, Texas with his dog Sandy. He works as a writer for Fox-Sports.com and relishes the ridiculously accommodating work hours afforded by toiling for a West Coast employer while dwelling in the central time zone. He works patiently and earnestly to disabuse people of the notion that Elvis is originally from Memphis, and he desperately hopes baseball never adds another team with a nickname not ending in "s." A lifelong Cardinals fan, he finds the Cubs neither charming nor amusing on any level.

Joe Sheehan is one of the Internet's most popular baseball columnists and a founding member of Baseball Prospectus. He lives in Rosemead, California with his wife, Sophia, and her enormous reserves of patience. When not writing, he enjoys playing golf poorly, playing poker well, and cooking far too much food for a two-person home.

Nate Silver attended the University of Chicago, home of the atomic bomb and the first Heisman Trophy winner, and has been stuck in the Second City ever since. He holds a B.A. in Economics and sunlights as a financial consultant in addition to his work for BP. A lifelong Tigers fan, Nate consoles himself by playing poker, watching *Law & Order* reruns, and visiting the city's innumerable watering holes.

Ryan Wilkins is the youngest, most idealistic, and best-looking member of Baseball Prospectus. When not playing Igor to Jonah Keri's Dr. Frankenstein as Assistant Editor of BP Online, Ryan can often be found on the streets of Berkeley, California, eating Zachary's Chicago Style Pizza and watching pretentious foreign films with his girlfriend, Sandy. In his free time, he enjoys going to concerts and helping Gary Huckabay remodel his home.

Michael Wolverton has been doing statistical performance analysis for over a decade, the last seven of those years with Baseball Prospectus. His 2003 was spent reveling in the success of his alma maters Rice University (College World Series champion) and Stanford University (College World Series runner-up), and his favorite team, the Texas Rangers (Major League Baseball, uh, participant). He lives in the San Francisco Bay Area with his wife, Cindy, and sons Scott, 7, and Mark, 4.

Keith Woolner currently works as a software product manager in North Carolina. He holds degrees in mathematics, computer science, and management from M.I.T., and a Master's degree in Decision Analysis from Stanford University. During Game 7 of the 2003 ALCS, Keith's mother, who doesn't follow baseball and was only watching the game because neither Christopher Lowell nor "Trading Spaces" were on, called to ask him why Grady Little sent Pedro Martinez out to start the 8th inning, when he was obviously tired. He still doesn't have a good answer for her.

Derek Zumsteg lives, writes, and drinks on Seattle's East side with his lovely, talented, and tolerant wife, Jill. He has run out of clever things to write in his short-form biographies, which is kind of silly, considering he's a writer and all.

Author Dedications

Jonah Keri: To my father George Keri, for nurturing a future stathead by giving me *Abstracts* when I was too young to be reading Bill James. Thanks also to two members of the BP group that I'm proud to call friends and colleagues: Joe Sheehan, for recruiting and mentoring a hyperactive Canuck; and Chris Kahrl, a person of tremendous character and the best editing partner this side of Ryan Wilkins.

Gary Huckabay: My efforts on this book are dedicated to my wife, Kathy Schofield, who has tolerated me for 12 years and makes me a better man.

Chris Kahrl: To Jonah Keri, my relentlessly upbeat editorial partner, particularly for his patience with me; and to the interns of Baseball Prospectus, Chaim Bloom, Susan Graham, Austin Johnson, Adam Katz, Steve Lin, Sean Passanisi, Cliff Roscow, and Zack Wolf, and James Click and Jason Grady in BP's technical support staff. It's going to be a lot of fun for the old gang to watch all of you surpass us in all things in the months and years to come.

Dayn Perry: To my parents and my dog—three of the most loyal and abiding mammals you could ever hope to have in your life.

Ryan Wilkins: To my wonderful girlfriend, Sandy, who tolerates my obsession with the greatest game in the world with the patience of a saint. To Gary Huckabay, who was crazy enough to bring me into BP for reasons I still don't understand, and has served as a fantastic mentor. To Ben Matasar, who's always there to chat. To Jonah Keri, for helping make me a better editor. And finally to my parents, Tim and Lisa, who still think BP is a big, fat waste of my time.

Keith Woolner: To my wife, Kathy, as always. I'd also like to thank Joe Hardy, Morris Buttermaker, Bingo Long, Ray Kinsella, Billy Chapel, Dottie Hinson, Billy Heywood, Rick Vaughn, Jack Elliot, Roy Hobbs, Henry Rowengartner, Scotty Smalls, Steve Nebraska, Billy Wyatt, Ryan Dunne, Sam Craig, and, of course, Joe Schlabotnik.